3

Australian Constitutional Law

Materials and Commentary

Seventh Edition

This is the seventh edition of the work previously published under the following titles:

Australian Constitutional Law; Cases, Materials and Text
F I Fajgenbaum and P J Hanks, 1972

Fajgenbaum and Hanks' Australian Constitutional Law
P J Hanks, 1980

Australian Constitutional Law
P J Hanks, 1985

Australian Constitutional Law: Materials and Commentary
P J Hanks, 1990

Australian Constitutional Law: Materials and Commentary
P J Hanks, 1993

Australian Constitutional Law: Materials and Commentary
P J Hanks and D Z Cass, 1999

Australian Constitutional Law

Materials and Commentary

Seventh Edition

Peter Hanks QC

LLB (Syd), LLM (Penn) of the Victorian and New South Wales Bars
Barrister and Solicitor of the Supreme Court of Western Australia

Patrick Keyzer

BA (Hons), LLB (Hons), GradDipLegPrac, LLM (Syd)
Associate Professor of Law, University of Technology, Sydney
Barrister of the High Court of Australia and Supreme Court of
New South Wales, the Northern Territory and Queensland

Jennifer Clarke

B Juris, LLB (Monash)
Senior Lecturer, Faculty of Law, Australian National University
Legal Practitioner of the Supreme Court of the
Australian Capital Territory and the Northern Territory

LexisNexis Butterworths

Australia

2004

LexisNexis

AUSTRALIA	LexisNexis Butterworths
	PeopleSoft House, 475–495 Victoria Avenue, CHATSWOOD NSW 2067
	On the internet at: www.lexisnexis.com.au
ARGENTINA	LexisNexis Juris Prudencia, BUENOS AIRES
AUSTRIA	LexisNexis ARD Orac GmbH & Co KG, VIENNA
BRAZIL	LexisNexis, SAO PAULO
CANADA	LexisNexis Butterworths, LexisNexis Quick Law, MARKHAM, Ontario
CHILE	LexisNexis Ltd, SANTIAGO
CZECH REPUBLIC	Nakladatelství Orac sro, PRAGUE
FRANCE	Juris-Classeur Groupe LexisNexis, PARIS
GERMANY	LexisNexis, FRANKFURT
HONG KONG GREATER CHINA	LexisNexis Butterworths, HONG KONG
HUNGARY	HVG-Orac Publishing Ltd, BUDAPEST
INDIA	LexisNexis, NEW DELHI
ITALY	Dott Giuffrè Editore SpA, MILAN
IRELAND	Butterworths (Ireland) Ltd, DUBLIN
JAPAN	LexisNexis, TOKYO
KOREA	LexisNexis, SEOUL
MALAYSIA	Malayan Law Journal Sdn Bhd, KUALA LUMPUR
NEW ZEALAND	LexisNexis Butterworths, WELLINGTON
POLAND	Wydawnictwo Prawnicze LexisNexis, WARSAW
SINGAPORE	LexisNexis Butterworths, SINGAPORE
SOUTH AFRICA	Butterworths Publishers (Pty) Ltd, DURBAN
SWITZERLAND	Staempfli Verlag AG, BERNE
TAIWAN	LexisNexis, TAIWAN
UNITED KINGDOM	LexisNexis Butterworths Tolley, LONDON, EDINBURGH
USA	LexisNexis Group, NEW YORK, New York
	LexisNexis, MIAMISBURG, Ohio

National Library of Australia Cataloguing-in-Publication entry

Hanks, Peter, 1941–.
Australian Constitutional law: materials and commentary.
7th ed.
Includes index.
ISBN 0 409 31946 5 (pbk.).
1. Constitutional law — Australia. I. Keyzer, Patrick, 1966–. II. Clarke, Jennifer, LLB. III. Title.
342.94

Desktop published in Century Gothic and Sabon. Printed in Australia by Ligare Pty Ltd.

Visit LexisNexis Butterworths at www.lexisnexis.com.au

Contents

Contents

Detailed Contents

Preface to the Seventh Edition

This is the seventh edition of *Australian Constitutional Law: Materials and Commentary*, first published, under the joint authorship of Jack Fajgenbaum and Peter Hanks, in 1972.

Peter Hanks was responsible for the next four editions (from 1980–1994). The seventh edition, as with the sixth edition (1999), is the product of joint thinking and writing.

Who did what?

Peter Hanks and Patrick Keyzer shared responsibility for the structure and writing of most of the seventh edition. The two exceptions are Chapter 2, '"Indigenous People" in Australian Constitutional Law' and Chapter 12, 'Territories', both written by Jennifer Clarke (with Chapter 12 including input from Patrick Keyzer).

The responsibility for reworking and updating (in many cases, significantly rewriting) the bulk of the material for this edition was shared between Patrick Keyzer and Peter Hanks. Jennifer Clarke reworked Chapter 2, and carried writing responsibility for Chapter 12. Patrick Keyzer reviewed and edited Chapter 12; Peter Hanks reviewed and edited the text of all chapters. Patrick Keyzer also supervised the final production of the book, and contributed to the preparation of the tables.

What is in this book?

Although there have been many changes in the organisation and content of this book over the past 32 years, its basic objective has remained: namely, to examine the institutional and federal aspects of Australian constitutional law.

The preface to the sixth edition identified significant recent changes in the constitutional agenda. In the 1990s, major political issues such as native title and free speech were placed on that agenda, and the High Court became much more self-conscious in its work in relation to the outcome of particular cases and the court's methods of interpretation and reasoning. Public criticism of the High Court's work increased, as did public consciousness of the court's work.

The five-and-a-half years since completion of the sixth edition has seen important changes in the composition of the High Court. Those changes have inevitably generated new uncertainties about the shape and direction of constitutional law. Although the uncertainty surrounding the implied freedom to discuss political and governmental affairs was apparently resolved by the court's unanimous judgment in *Lange v Australian Broadcasting Corporation* (1997) 189 CLR 520, changes on the bench have generated new uncertainty as the new justices openly questioned that judgment and the judicial style that gave rise to it.

It seems that the court has become more openly divided over methods of constitutional interpretation and reasoning. The 'outbreak of calm' that many expected to follow the appointment of justices popularly regarded as judicial conservatives has not eventuated: rather, the divisions between justices have become more marked than they were in the 1990s, and uncertainty about the future path of constitutional law has been accentuated. Plainly, the High Court continues to play an important (if less predicatble) role in defining the limits within which governments exercise political power and in defining the relationship between the exercise of that power and the rights of citizens.

This year (2004) the High Court will grapple with a number of challenges arising from its approach to Ch III of the Constitution. In the last edition, we noted the significance of the High Court's judgment in *Kable v Director of Public Prosecutions (NSW)* (1996) 189 CLR 51; but that case is assuming even greater significance today. New questions have emerged in recently heard cases that will provide vital clues about the approach of the new justices.

Domestic and international pressures continue to contribute to the sense of change. The debate within Australia about republicanism has heightened awareness of the actual constitutional document, as well as the system of government it represents. Indigenous peoples' claims for land and a control over decisions affecting their lives have continued, and contributed to adjustments in the constitutional framework. The globalisation of modern life has continued to affect constitutional law no less than other aspects of Australian society.

Despite the changes in the constitutional law agenda, the underlying issues and dilemmas remain. These issues focus on the proper role of constitutional law and judges in a democratic polity. This edition continues the tradition of analysing the major ongoing constitutional issues facing the High Court and exploring the tensions between the principles of parliamentary democracy and judicial law-making, while confronting the challenges represented by the expanding agenda.

Chapter 12 is entirely new to this edition. It reviews the place of the territories in the Australian constitutional setting, the relationship between territory governments and the Commonwealth and limitations on territory powers. These are questions that have come to occupy more of the High Court's attention; and we concluded that the time had come for the development of a sustained treatment of the constitutional position of the territories.

Other chapters have been revised and expanded, largely to reflect five years' development of the law. Chapter 3 has been substantially rewritten, and contains additional material describing the ways in which international and comparative law influence the development of Australian constitutional law. Chapters 4 and 5 have been updated to take into account recent constitutional developments in Queensland, Victoria and Western Australia. The discussion of intergovernmental immunities in Chapter 8 has accommodated the decision in *Austin v Commonwealth* (2004) 195 ALR 321; the discussion of legislative procedures includes the substantial recent decision in *Attorney-General (WA) v Marquet* (2003) 202 ALR 233. Chapter 11 includes a more detailed treatment of implied rights arising from the separation of judicial power, and the aftermath of the court's decision in *Kable v DPP (NSW)* (1996) 189 CLR 51. A significant new judgment, *Roberts v Bass* (2002) 194 ALR 161, has been included in that chapter, as are several cases on aspects of the guarantee of jury trial — including *Katsuno v Queen* (1999) 199 CLR 40 *Brownlee v Queen* (2001) 207 CLR 278, and *Cheung v Queen* (2001) 209 CLR 1.

These additions, and the new Chapter 12, have required us to make some compromises elsewhere. Although this edition is longer than the sixth edition, we have found it necessary to treat some areas in less detail than is desirable; and to omit altogether discussion of other areas. Our objective is not to present a comprehensive encyclopaedia of Australian constitutional law, but to explore its principal themes and examine some basic issues which affect the location and the exercise of public power in Australia. The topics we have chosen for that examination raise fundamental questions about the organisation and functioning of our system of government, and illuminate the process of constitutional adjudication.

Thanks to ...

Our work on this edition has been assisted by a number of people.

Peter Hanks acknowledges the continuing support of his secretary, Ann Parker, and the very substantial contributions of Patrick Keyzer and Jennifer Clarke. Life as a barrister leaves less time (or energy) for reflective thinking and writing than Peter ever anticipated. It is a tribute to the other two authors' patience, hard work, sharp thinking and constant encouragement that this seventh edition is about to be launched. Peter also thanks his partner, Professor Jenny Morgan, for her support, ideas and friendship.

Patrick Keyzer thanks Peter Hanks QC for the opportunity to participate in this project, and Jennifer Clarke for being such an accommodating co-author. Patrick also thanks Sir Gerard Brennan for the opportunity to work at the High Court; Professor Gerard Carney for advice; Professor Terry Carney for mentoring and inspiration; Geoff James for setting the standard in preparing counsel (special thanks to Geoff for referring me to the book by Douglas Lockwood about Darwin's colourful history); Michael Jones for his courage in the face of overwhelming odds; and some other amazing lawyers for teaching me so much: Peter O'Brien, Stephen Gageler SC, Professor Cheryl Saunders, Stephen Southwood QC and Bret Walker SC. Patrick also thanks James Stellios and Fiona Wheeler for looking over some of the chapters, and Geoff Holland and Sue Chrysanthou for excellent research assistance and diligent proof-reading. Most importantly of all, Patrick thanks Suzie O'Toole and Gemma for their love and support throughout this (and all other concurrently operating) projects. My work on this book is dedicated to all of these people and to my families, the Keyzers and the O'Tooles.

Jennifer Clarke thanks the indefatigable and unflappable Angeline Baker for research assistance, and her constitutional law colleagues James Stellios, John Williams, Leslie Zines and Fiona Wheeler for many conversations about Chapter 12. Special thanks to Fiona for reading the long penultimate draft. Thanks also to the ANU Law Faculty's Head of School, Phillipa Weeks, for creating a climate in which someone on a fractional appointment could do this much writing. Besides the people thanked in the preface to the sixth edition for help in answering questions, Jennifer thanks others who answered more this time around, including Donald Denoon, Robert Orr, JP Fonteyne, Pene Mathew and Bryan Fair. Thanks also to Sita Jones for help in locating references and other details. Finally, Jennifer thanks her co-authors for their patience and encouragement, the grandparents and neighbours who provided extra childcare, and her family, Ken, Vivien and Jessie, for tolerating her spending far too many non-working hours at the screen.

LexisNexis Butterworths have been very supportive and understanding throughout this project, which took far longer than any of us had intended. We particularly thank Diana Piper and Robert Wilson, who have encouraged, persuaded and guided us through the creative process. We also thank Andrew Wright for his invaluable assistance and patient commitment in guiding this edition through the editorial process.

Currency

The law is stated as at 30 April 2004.

Peter Hanks, Patrick Keyzer & Jennifer Clarke
May 2004

Acknowledgments

The authors and publisher are grateful to the holders of copyright in material from which extracts appear in this work, particularly the following:

- Australian Government Publishing Service
- Australian Historical Studies, University of Melbourne
- Australian National University Law School
- Division of Law, Macquarie University
- Harper Collins Publishers (Aust) Pty Limited
- Hutchinson Education Limited
- Longman Group, UK, Limited
- Macmillan Press Limited, England
- Macmillan Publishers Australia Pty Limited
- Melbourne University Law Review
- Melbourne University Press
- Memorial University of Newfoundland, Canada
- Monash University Law Review
- Nelson ITP
- Quadrant Magazine Co
- Queensland University Press
- Sweet & Maxwell Limited
- University of Chicago Law Review
- UNSW Press

While every effort have been taken to establish and acknowledge copyright, the publshers tender their apologies for any accidental infringement. They would be pleased to come to a suitable arrangement with the rightful owners in each case.

Table of Cases

References are to paragraphs; bold entries are case extracts

References are to paragraphs; bold entries are case extracts

References are to paragraphs; bold entries are case extracts

References are to paragraphs; bold entries are case extracts

References are to paragraphs; bold entries are case extracts

References are to paragraphs; bold entries are case extracts

References are to paragraphs; bold entries are case extracts

References are to paragraphs; bold entries are case extracts

References are to paragraphs; bold entries are case extracts

References are to paragraphs; bold entries are case extracts

Table of Statutes

References are to paragraphs

Commonwealth

Aboriginal and Torres Strait Islander Heritage Protection Act 1984 .... 2.4.42, 2.4.45, 2.4.47, 6.4.22, 6.4.34

Aboriginal and Torres Strait Islanders (Queensland Discriminatory Laws) Act 1975 .... 2.4.41

Aboriginal and Torres Strait Islanders (Queensland Reserves and Communities Self-Management) Act 1978 .... 2.4.41

Aboriginal Land Rights (Northern Territory) Act 1976 .... 2.4.59, 2.4.60, 2.4.65
s 67 .... 2.4.59
s 67A 2.4.59
s 71 .... 2.4.59
s 73 .... 2.4.59
s 73(1)(a) 2.4.59
s 73(1)(b) 2.4.59
s 73(1)(d) 2.4.59
s 74 .... 2.4.59

Aboriginal Land Rights (Northern Territory) Act 1978 .... 12.6.32

Acts Interpretation Act 1901 .... 6.4.36C, 12.2.5
s 15 .... 5.2.25E
s 15A 6.5.5C, 8.2.74, 10.2.26C
s 16A 4.2.21, 12.6.37
s 17 .... 12.6.18
s 27 .... 12.6.37
s 29(2) 12.6.37
s 30(2) 8.1.29, 8.1.31
s 48(4) 7.4.22
s 74(a)(i) 12.6.37
Pt IVA Div 1 .... 8.2.74

Acts Interpretation Act 1904 .... 6.4.36C

Air Force Act 1923 .... 8.2.82C, 8.2.83

Air Navigation Act 1920 .... 10.2.15, 10.2.20C
s 4 .... 3.3.9, 3.3.10
s 26 .... 3.3.11

Air Navigation Regulations
reg 6(1) 10.2.20C
reg 198 .... 8.1.37, 10.2.20C
reg 199 .... 8.1.37, 10.2.20C
reg 199(4) 8.1.37, 10.2.20C
reg 200B 3.3.11, 10.2.20C, 10.2.24, 10.2.25

Appropriation Act (No 1) 1974 .... 9.7.9, 9.7.14
s 3 .... 9.7.12C
s 7 .... 9.7.12C
Sch 2 .... 9.7.12C
Sch 2 Div 530 .... 9.7.12C
Sch 2 Div 530 item 4 .... 9.7.12C

Ashmore and Cartier Islands Acceptance Act 1933 .... 12.2.2, 12.2.5

Ashmore and Cartier Islands Acceptance Amendment Act 1978 .... 12.2.5

Ashmore and Cartier Islands Acceptance Amendment Act 1985 .... 12.2.5

Atomic Energy Act 1953
s 34 .... 12.3.17
s 35 .... 2.4.61, 12.3.17

Audit Act 1901 .... 8.2.9

Auditor-General Act 1997 .... 12.6.50

Australia Act 1986 .... 1.2.4, 1.4.1, 1.4.3, 1.4.17, 1.4.21, 1.4.25, 1.4.26, 1.4.27, 1.6.8, 2.3.17, 3.3.47, 3.3.48, 4.2.2, 4.2.19, 5.4.44C, 5.4.49, 6.2.2, 6.2.4, 6.2.6, 6.2.7E, 6.2.8, 6.2.9, 6.2.17, 7.2.5E
s 1 .... 3.3.48, 6.2.7E, 6.2.10, 6.2.18, 7.1.4
s 2 .... 1.4.16, 5.4.23E, 5.4.47, 6.1.1, 6.2.7E
s 2(1) 6.3.22C, 6.2.7E
s 3 .... 1.4.26, 3.3.48, 5.3.5, 5.4.23E, 5.4.44C, 6.1.1, 6.2.7E, 6.2.11
s 3(2) 6.2.7E
s 4 .... 1.4.26, 6.2.7E
s 5 .... 1.4.26, 6.2.7E
s 5(a) 6.3.22C
s 6 .... 1.6.10, 5.3.5, 5.4.11, 5.4.23E, 5.4.26, 5.4.44C
s 7 .... 1.4.26, 4.2.15, 7.1.7, 7.2.3E, 7.2.9
s 7(5) 7.3.10
s 8 .... 1.4.26, 5.1.9, 5.1.12, 6.2.7E
s 9 .... 1.4.26, 6.2.7E
s 10 .... 1.4.26, 7.2.3E
s 11 .... 6.1.1, 6.2.7E, 6.4.48C
s 12 .... 1.4.26, 6.2.7E
s 14 .... 7.2.8
s 15 .... 1.4.27

Australia (Request and Consent) Act 1985 .... 1.4.25
s 3 .... 6.2.8

References are to paragraphs

References are to paragraphs

References are to paragraphs

References are to paragraphs

References are to paragraphs

References are to paragraphs

References are to paragraphs

References are to paragraphs

References are to paragraphs

References are to paragraphs

References are to paragraphs

Canada

Ceylon

References are to paragraphs

Chapter

1

What is Australian Constitutional Law?

1   Introduction

[1.1.1]   This is a book about the theory and practice of Australian constitutional law. The distinctive organising principle of the book is its integration of theoretical perspectives and doctrinal analysis. It does this not merely by signalling that a certain case is an example of a particular theory, but by focusing the commentary on a number of themes that recur throughout constitutional law. These include:

- the nature of public power;
- the role of the judiciary in reviewing acts of the legislature;
- the interpretive method of the judiciary, principally in the High Court;
- the role that comparative law and international law play in the court's jurisprudence;
- the distinction between law and politics;
- the role of history in constitutional decision-making.

By drawing attention to these recurring themes, we will show that constitutional legal theory is not a separate or esoteric topic; rather, it is an integral part, the skeleton as it were, which structures the body of knowledge known as constitutional law doctrine.

But first we need briefly to consider some important preliminary questions, such as:

- What is a constitution?
- Where does it come from?
- What is sovereignty?

1

- Who made the Constitution?
- What does it contain?
- What are its important features?
- How is it interpreted?

These questions are the focus of this chapter.

2   Preliminary questions

What is a constitution?

[1.2.1]   Broadly speaking, a constitution is the basic law of a state. A constitution contains the *fundamental* or *organic* rules of law which *constitute* the state and its institutions. It defines the entities that have state power. For example, s 51 of the Commonwealth Constitution says that the Commonwealth Parliament has power to make laws over certain matters. The Constitution states the type of power that those entities have. For example, s 51 provides that the power of the Commonwealth Parliament is to 'make laws', so it is legislative power. The Constitution defines the limits of the exercise of that power. To continue the example, s 51 lists the topics on which the Commonwealth is empowered to make laws, and says this power is 'subject to this Constitution', which indicates that other parts of the Constitution may restrict the manner and content of that exercise of power.

In setting out the basic law of a state, a constitution will ordinarily outline the main institutions of the state, or 'branches of government'. The Commonwealth Constitution establishes three branches of government:

- the *legislature* (s 1);
- the *executive* (s 61); and
- the *judiciary* (s 71).

The legislature is the Commonwealth Parliament; the executive the Commonwealth Government (headed by the Governor-General, 'advised' by an executive council comprised of the Prime Minister and Ministers) and the departments and other agencies of government; and the judiciary is the system of federal courts, including the High Court.

As well as establishing the three branches of government, the Constitution vests each of them with appropriate power. So the legislature is vested with legislative power (s 51), the executive is vested with executive power (s 61), and the judiciary with judicial power (s 71). Generally speaking, the Commonwealth's executive power includes those accorded by common law (prerogative powers), as well as powers derived from legislation. Legislative power enables parliament to make laws, and judicial power enables the judiciary to resolve disputes about rights and liabilities and, in the course of so doing, to decide what is the law.

In addition to establishing the machinery of the Commonwealth Government and defining its powers, the Constitution establishes a *federal* system, a system in which legislative power is divided between two levels of government, state and Commonwealth, with the further provision for establishment of territory governments.

Where does a constitution come from?

[1.2.2] A constitution is sometimes formulated after a revolution, in which a formerly dependent entity breaks its formal links with a former imperial power. In this case, the constitution will usually be the first law passed by the newly independent assembly. For instance, after the American Revolution (marked by the Declaration of Independence in 1776), the American colonies passed their own state constitutions. The sovereignty of such a constitution is said to reside with the delegates of the people who made the fundamental law setting up the new institutions of state and vesting them with power, or in the new assembly itself.

In Australia, the Commonwealth Constitution was born, not out of a revolution against the British Empire, but out of a negotiated agreement conducted by selected members of the colonies' political elite for limited autonomy at the very end of the 19th century. The Commonwealth Constitution was enacted by the United Kingdom Parliament as s 9 of the Commonwealth of Australia Constitution Act 1900 (UK).

What were the foundations of Australian constitutional law?

[1.2.3] Australian constitutional law was built upon a number of historical foundations, apart from the 19th century negotiations. These include:

- Australia's status as a penal colony;
- the almost complete absence of white women in the early years of that society and their later exclusion from political power; and
- the dispossession of the indigenous people of Australia from their land and their political subjugation.

The ramifications of these elements in our history are still being investigated and understood, both in relation to constitutional law and to Australian society in general. However, one point is clear, namely that the Constitution that emerged was not designed to advance the interests of people who did not participate in its development, and was not concerned with the advancement of civil rights that might predicate their involvement in national policy and affairs: see further Irving (1996) and Chesterman and Galligan (1997).

What is sovereignty?

[1.2.4] Sovereignty in constitutional law refers to the source of legitimacy that supports the constitutional arrangements of the state. For example, in late medieval England, the constitution would have been described as deriving its force from the monarch. In the United States, the people are said to be the sovereign force behind the US Constitution. The first words of the US Constitution declare:

> We the people of the United States ... do establish this Constitution for the United States of America.

The sovereignty of the Commonwealth Constitution, by contrast, derived from an Act of the United Kingdom Parliament. In recent times, at least since the passage of the Australia Acts in 1985 and 1986 by the Commonwealth and United Kingdom Parliaments, some judges and commentators have suggested that sovereignty of the Commonwealth Constitution resides within the Australian people: see for example *Australian Capital Television Pty Ltd v Commonwealth* (1992) 177 CLR 106 **[11.3.7C]** at 138 per Mason CJ; Lindell (1986). Certainly the presence of s 128 in the Constitution, and the power it gives to the people to change the Constitution, suggests that the Constitution's continued force derives from our acquiescence in its terms, especially in view of the termination of the vestigial remnants of the United Kingdom's powers in Australia by the Australia Acts (see further **[1.4.26]**).

Constitutional monarchy or independent republic?

[1.2.5] Linked to the question of sovereignty is the issue of Australia's transition to a republic. Although Australia has attained political independence, (see **[1.4.3]** and **[1.4.28]**) it remains technically a constitutional monarchy, in which the Governor-General represents the Queen who is the formal Head of State. National debate over the position of the monarchy in Australia's constitutional arrangements now centres on whether Australians should cut the last formal ties with the British monarchy and become a fully independent republic: Mason (1995). In February 1998, the Australian Government convened a constitutional convention of elected and appointed delegates to consider whether Australia should become a republic. The Convention resolved to support a system for the appointment of a new head of state, with formal ratification by two-thirds of the Commonwealth Parliament in conjunction with community consultation. In November 1999, a referendum was held on the question whether Australia should become a republic with the Queen and Governor-General being replaced by a president appointed by a two-thirds majority of the members of the Commonwealth Parliament. The referendum failed nationally and in each State (it passed in the Australian Capital Territory, though not in the Northern Territory): for further analysis see Galligan, 1999 and Kirby, 2000.

Who made the Constitution?

[1.2.6] The Australian Constitution was drafted by a select group of delegates to a series of constitutional conventions held in Australia during the late 1890s, and then endorsed by the voters at referenda. Although representative of a class of Australian, rather than United Kingdom residents, the Convention delegates were not representative of the wider Australian community. They did not, for example, include men other than professionals or landed gentry. They included one representative of the new Labor Party, but no working men. They did not include any women. They included none of the original inhabitants of Australia, the Aboriginal peoples and Torres Strait Islanders. These exclusions were, of course, totally in keeping with the social, political and legal expectations of the period. Nevertheless, it is important to remember the narrow base of the Constitution when thinking about the legitimacy of the document, the system of government that resulted, the way the Constitution has been interpreted, and contemporary initiatives to alter it.

In fact, as noted above (see **[1.2.3]**), the society out of which the Commonwealth Constitution was born exhibited important features that inform Australian constitutional law and its subjects. Australia was a former penal colony, it was situated in Asia, and it was a white colonial power that virtually destroyed the legal, social and political structures of the indigenous inhabitants. Although these features are not historically unusual, they are part of the background to Australian constitutionalism and they explain some aspects of the Constitution. For example, the genesis of s 117 of the Constitution, which prohibits state discrimination against residents of other states, emerged from a wish not to impinge on state laws that restricted the rights of immigrants from Asia. Similarly, the old s 127, removed by referendum in 1967, eliminated Aboriginal people from counting for the census and denied them citizenship rights and entitlements: **[2.4.3]–[2.4.8]**; Chesterman and Galligan (1997) pp 58–83. Racism also characterised the Commonwealth's government of territories: see further Chapter 12.

Who and what are its subjects?

[1.2.7] The subjects of constitutional law are many and include governments, such as the Commonwealth, the states and the territories; the people who are citizens of these various entities; other persons such as aliens and corporations; things such as currency; activities such as trade and commerce; and purposes such as defence.

Not all subjects necessarily receive equal treatment under the Constitution. In recent times a number of contentious issues have arisen concerning the status of territory citizens and territory governments, as distinct from state citizens and state governments. For example, it has been suggested that citizens of a territory do not share the same constitutional protections, as do citizens of a state. In *Newcrest Mining Ltd (WA) v Commonwealth* (1997) 190 CLR 513 **[11.2.14C]**, McHugh J said (in *obiter*) that, as territory residents are not 'people of the Commonwealth' within s 24 of the Constitution, they have no constitutional right to participate in elections for the House of Representatives: 190 CLR at 585. The failure of euthanasia legislation in the Northern Territory and of a heroin trial in the Australian Capital Territory reinforces the different and weaker nature of territory legislative autonomy. The constitutional position of the territories is considered in Chapter 12.

The status of Aboriginal Australians as subjects of Australian constitutional law is considered in detail in Chapter 2.

What does it contain? Text, structures of government, history and interpretation

[1.2.8] The Commonwealth Constitution is a written document. Its text is divided into a number of parts:

■ a preamble and the covering clauses of the United Kingdom Act; and

■ eight chapters comprising the actual body of the Constitution which commence in s 9 of the covering clauses.

The preamble to the Act records that the people have agreed to unite in one indissoluble Federal Commonwealth under the Crown. It incorporates the concepts of popular supremacy, federalism and constitutional monarchy. The first eight covering clauses of the Act deal with formal matters and the ninth covering clause sets out the 128 sections (arranged in eight chapters) of the Constitution itself. The eight chapters deal with the Parliament, the Executive, the Judicature, Finance and

Trade, the States, New States, 'Miscellaneous' matters and the Alteration of the Constitution.

[1.2.9] The Constitution also denotes *principles* that have been held to arise from the text, the structures of government described in that text and the purposes to which the text is directed. The most important of these are the principles of representative government, responsible government, federalism, and the separation of powers. These principles are reflected, although not explicitly stated, in the text. So, for example, s 64 of the Constitution, which establishes that each head of a department of state (called a minister) shall be a member of the Federal Executive Council and shall not hold office unless he or she is or becomes a Member of Parliament, embodies the principle of responsible government; namely, that the executive shall be drawn from the elected legislature. Section 7, which requires that the Senate be composed of the same number of senators of each original state represents the federal principle of state representation in the upper house. The requirement in s 24 that the Members of Parliament be directly chosen by the people indicates that Australia is a system of representative government. The vesting of legislative, executive and judicial power in three separate branches of government suggests the principle of the separation of governmental powers.

[1.2.10] A constitution is applied within a changing social context. It was written and is interpreted as part of the legal history of a nation. So as well as text and principle, a constitution embodies a *history*. That history might be explicit or implicit. An example of the explicit history of the Constitution is found in Covering cl 6 which records that, at the time of drafting, New Zealand was considered as one of the colonies that might federate in the Commonwealth of Australia. Sometimes the history of the Constitution means looking beyond the text of the instrument to the Convention debates. The High Court's interpretation of s 92 since 1988 has recorded the historical fact that the free trade movement that precipitated federation was concerned only to prohibit colonial discriminatory measures of a protectionist kind. The constitutional guarantee of 'trial by jury' in s 80 of the Constitution includes the requirement that a jury verdict be unanimous, since this was an essential feature of that institution at the time of federation. However, social mores change, and other features of that institution at 1901 — the exclusion of women, Aboriginal people or men without property from juries — are now understood not to be essential to that institution: see *Cheatle v The Queen* (1993) 177 CLR 541 at 560 **[11.2.34]**.

[1.2.11] Finally, and importantly, a constitution must be *interpreted*. The methods of constitutional interpretation are not dictated by the text yet they form an intrinsic part of it. Michael Coper has argued that '[t]he task of interpretation will always be with us and we need to integrate it into our concept of the Constitution': Coper (1996). Common to all systems of interpretation is a level of uncertainty caused by contending interpretations. A striking example is the High Court's conflicting views on the position of the territories within the Commonwealth. One stream of authority suggests that the territories are not part of the Commonwealth, and are therefore not protected by any constitutional guarantees flowing from, say, s 51(xxxi) or Ch III of the Constitution. A different stream of authority rejected that view. This has produced decisions that reflect the differences of opinion in our contemporary law: see, for example, *Newcrest Mining NL v Commonwealth* (1997) 190 CLR 513 **[11.2.14C]**.

Is the Constitution law or politics?

[1.2.12] The existence of opposing interpretations of the Constitution inevitably raises questions about the motivations of judges who arrive at different views. The insights of the legal realist and critical legal studies movements demonstrate that the development of the law by judges is a discretionary exercise that involves leeways of choice. Judgment is both a public and a personal exercise and judges make choices that reflect their public and personal views. The Constitution is a political document (in the sense that it divides power among polities and creates the structures within which political behaviour takes place) and its interpretation today is a political exercise ('political' in the sense of subjective and discretionary decision-making behaviour). The answer to the question is 'both' — the Constitution is about law *and* about politics.

Some of the important elements in the Constitution

[1.2.13] The Constitution originally contained 128 sections and cannot be summarised in a single paragraph, but a brief overview of some of its more important features follows.

First, and most importantly, the Constitution contemplates different types of power — legislative, executive and judicial power — and creates different structures for the exercise of those powers.

Second, the Constitution in s 51 gives to the Commonwealth a long list of *concurrent legislative powers*. These are powers that, for the most part, the Commonwealth shares with the states. They include the power with respect to trade and commerce, banking, marriage, and external affairs. These powers are *enumerated*, and they are *express*. Attached to each of these powers and to the executive and judicial powers in s 61 and s 71 respectively are implied powers that enable the Commonwealth to do what is necessary or convenient for the effective exercise of these express powers (except what is otherwise prohibited).

Third, the Constitution gives the Commonwealth some *express*, *exclusive legislative powers*. For instance, s 52 gives the Commonwealth exclusive power over the seat of government of the Commonwealth, Commonwealth places and transferred public service departments. Again, s 90 gives the Commonwealth exclusive power over customs and excise duties.

Fourth, the Constitution restricts the exercise of Commonwealth and state power. Some restrictions, prohibitions or limitations are *express*. For example, the Constitution prohibits the Commonwealth from making any law establishing any religion (s 116) or from compulsorily acquiring property without compensation: s 51(xxxi). It prevents the states imposing customs or excise duties (s 90) or discriminating against residents of other states: s 117. Other limitations are *implied*. For example, the principle of federalism on which the Constitution is constructed protects each level of government from the reach of at least some laws made at another level of government. The principle of representative democracy derived from ss 7 and 24 is the basis of an implied freedom of communication on political matters. The separation of judicial power effected by Ch III of the Constitution, imposes limits upon the exercise of Commonwealth and state legislative and executive powers.

Fifth, the Constitution enshrines the principle of *inconsistency*. Any state law that is inconsistent with a Commonwealth law will be invalid (meaning inoperative) to the extent of that inconsistency: s 109.

Sixth, because the Constitution establishes a federal system of government in which two levels of government operate, ss 106–108 preserve *state constitutions, law-making powers, and laws* respectively, so that those elements are not extinguished by the creation of the Commonwealth, except to the extent that the Constitution expressly restricts them. (For this reason, state powers are frequently described as 'residual' in that they consist of the residue that remains after the powers of the Commonwealth are defined.)

Finally a formal mechanism for *constitutional change* is contained in s 128 which requires that a referendum be passed by a majority of voters throughout Australia, as well as a majority of voters in a majority of states.

How is a constitution interpreted?

[1.2.14] Constitutional law is contained in a combination of the text of the Constitution and the interpretations given to that text by the judiciary, principally the High Court. As Michael Coper suggests, there is no single meaning 'just "out there", revelling in its detached objectivity' because language is 'intrinsically rich in multiple meanings': Coper (1996). Because judicial opinion is so critical to the substance of constitutional law, the way in which judges interpret the instrument is critical. The issues raised are discussed in more depth below at **[1.4.39]–[1.4.49]**. Briefly, it is clear that there are many ways of categorising the various approaches to constitutional interpretation. So, while Sir Anthony Mason has suggested a classification based upon the categories of originalism, intentionalism, literalism and progressive interpretation (Mason (1996)). Sampford and Preston identify 12 'external elements of selected theory' (Sampford and Preston (1996)) and Goldsworthy distinguishes only two categories, originalism and non-originalism: Goldsworthy (1997).

Broadly speaking there are three approaches to constitutional interpretation that we will develop in this chapter and at different parts of the book:

- *textualism* (or literalism or legalism);

- *intentionalism* (or originalism or sometimes called legalism); and

- *progressivism* (or dynamism or organicism).

The textualists emphasise the importance of referring to the text of the Constitution itself to deduce the meaning of a constitutional term: see, for example, *McGinty v Western Australia* (1996) 186 CLR 140 at 235. Textualism is closely related to intentionalism. The intentionalist school calls for judges to decide questions of constitutional law according to the intentions of the framers: see, for example, the High Court's unanimous judgment in *Cole v Whitfield* (1988) 165 CLR 360 **[10.4.27C]**. Finally there are those who ascribe to a progressive or dynamic interpretation of the text, according to which the Constitution ought to be interpreted in the light of changes in historical standards: see, for example, *Theophanous v Herald & Weekly Times Ltd* (1994) 182 CLR 104 **[11.3.2C]** at 173–4 (Deane J).

The textualist–intentionalist–progressivist divide is overlaid with a distinction between the claim that judges *declare* the law and the acknowledgment that they *make* the law. Hence, those adopting the declaratory approach tend to rely on a combination of textualism and intentionalism, and those who acknowledge that there is judicial law-making are more likely to be progressivists.

[1.2.15] The effect of the different approaches is that different sources of law and techniques of reasoning are relied upon in interpreting the instrument. So, for example, the textualist emphasises the significance of the words of the provision itself; the intentionalist draws on historical evidence to determine the meaning of a provision (which may or may not conflict with a 'textual' or 'literal' reading); and the progressivist refers to contemporary policy on the significance of the provision.

[1.2.16] No judge is totally committed to one method of interpretation over another (although some judges are explicit about their preferences). In fact, most judges, most of the time, rely on a combination of techniques: they consider the natural or ordinary meaning of the words; they examine historical evidence; they consider previous interpretations of the courts; and they discuss the practical effect of an interpretation. So text, history, intention, precedent and contemporary mores are all relevant to the task of interpretation.

For example, when the High Court found that the Constitution contained an implication of freedom of political speech, the court relied on the words in the Constitution which state that our political representatives are to be 'directly chosen by the people', and found that the concept of direct choice suggests that the Constitution creates a representative democracy: *Australian Capital Television Pty Ltd v Commonwealth* (1992) 177 CLR 106 **[11.3.7C]**. It was then only a matter of inference that this system of government requires a measure of freedom to discuss political and governmental affairs. The judges considered historical materials, interpretations in earlier cases and the meaning of the phrase, 'directly chosen by the people', in the contemporary context of mass communication and complex government. They concluded that, although the precise content of representative democracy reflected in that phrase was not set in stone, it did include some key ideas. One of those ideas was that representative democracy protected the communication between elected representatives and the electorate, and amongst voters to communicate themselves. The freedom to discuss political and governmental affairs arising from the structure of representative government reflected in the text of the Constitution, was recognised.

[1.2.17] Each of the three broad methods of constitutional interpretation described above has its limitations. Intentionalism or textualism raises the difficulty of identifying the founders' intention(s). The main evidence of that intention is the debates of Constitutional Conventions held in the 1890s, but these debates are incomplete and inconclusive. They do not include the records of the drafting committees, nor do they tell us anything about the lobbying and negotiation that accompanied the debates. More importantly, they do not describe the assumptions made by the founders about the common law context within which the new system of government ought to operate. And sometimes those assumptions may be outdated and outmoded, as *Cheatle v The Queen* (1993) 177 CLR 541 demonstrated: see **[1.2.10]**. In any event, the text of the debates must itself be interpreted. Even using the debates, it took the High Court more than 80 years to agree on the meaning of s 92's deceptively simple requirement that 'trade, commerce and intercourse between the States shall be absolutely free'.

Similarly, the reader's assumptions about what was intended can alter over time. In a detailed historical survey, Wheeler argued that, contrary to previously accepted views, the framers did not intend to incorporate a doctrine of the separation of powers into the Constitution: Wheeler (1996) pp 99–102. And yet one of the striking features of the High Court's jurisprudence over the last 10 years has been the application of the doctrine of the separation of judicial power as a brake on the exercise of legislative and executive power — a trend that appears to have gathered steam: see, for example, *Kable v Director of Public Prosecutions (NSW)* (1996) 189 CLR 51 **[6.4.48C]**, **[11.3.30]**. A progressive approach might be favoured in this context since it recognises the significance of the role of the High Court in protecting the citizen from over-zealous legislation. On the other hand, it may be open to the criticism that, if judges are to rely on contemporary standards, they may make decisions based on shifting and uncertain values that have a questionable grounding in history.

Ultimately, finding the intention behind the text of the Constitution and interpreting the Constitution are part of the same complex process. There may be only a limited number of plausible interpretations that are possible, but the adversarial dynamic of constitutional law-making ensures that there will always be more than one.

[1.2.18] The choice of interpretive method is not an esoteric question of academic theory. The principles of constitutional interpretation discussed in this book overlap with the principles and approaches adopted in all statutory interpretation, one of the fundamental skills of legal practice. Choice of interpretive method has broad-ranging practical effects because it signals, especially to the wider community, the nature of the role the High Court plays in legal and political affairs.

---

3   The nature of constitutional law

[1.3.1] The focus of constitutional law is public power. It is concerned with the ways in which the power of the state is organised and applied, with the relationships between the different institutions which exercise the power of the state and with the relationships between those institutions and other individual and social interests.

Although constitutional law employs the language of public rights rather than private rights, it will transcend the distinction between the public and private arenas. For example, the decision made in *University of Wollongong v Metwally* (1984) 158 CLR 447 **[8.1.57C]**, that the Commonwealth Parliament could not retrospectively revive Pt II of the Anti-Discrimination Act 1977 (NSW), had an immediate impact on the rights which individuals could pursue against other individuals who discriminated on the ground of race in the provision of employment, education, accommodation and other services. Again, the decision in *Gazzo v Comptroller of Stamps (Vic)* (1981) 149 CLR 227 **[8.2.88]**, that the Commonwealth's power over marriage and matrimonial causes did not allow it to grant immunity from state taxes to transfers of property made pursuant to Family Court orders, had an immediate effect on the financial and property relationships between separating spouses (largely to the disadvantage of women). The decision of the High Court in *Australian Capital Television v Commonwealth* (1992) 177 CLR 106 **[11.3.7C]** that the Commonwealth could not use its power over broadcasting to compel commercial television stations to provide free-time to political parties during election campaigns protected a significant source of revenue for media organisations but also recognised and protected an implied freedom to discuss political and governmental affairs that could be used by individuals to protect their free speech activities. (However, contrast *Langer v Commonwealth* (1996) 186 CLR 302 **[4.6.15C]**, **[11.3.15]**.)

[1.3.2]   The terms in which the discourse of constitutional law is conducted are those of public power: the contending ideas have been developed to explain or rationalise claims for that power. In this way, because it reflects basic ideas about the way in which public power should be organised and exercised, it has a heavily political character. Another indication of its political character lies in its constitutive function; in the fact that it sets the outer limits, the ground rules, for the political process. For instance, the decision of the High Court in *Commonwealth v Tasmania* (the *Tasmanian Dam* case) (1983) 158 CLR 1 recognised the constitutional power of the Commonwealth to implement the Convention for the Protection of the World Cultural and Natural Heritage. That decision opened the way for the Commonwealth to develop a national policy for the protection of environmentally sensitive areas and to impose that policy on state governments and private entrepreneurs. But the decision did not ensure that the Commonwealth would do that; rather, it ensured that only the Commonwealth now had an expanded range of political choices. So it remained open to the Commonwealth to choose not to intervene to protect a particular area, a choice that might be influenced by such considerations as the need to encourage economic development or the desire to avoid antagonistic reactions from state governments.

Again, the High Court decided in 1988 that s 92 of the Commonwealth Constitution permitted government controls on interstate trade, so long as those controls did not discriminate in a protectionist way against interstate traders: *Cole v Whitfield* (1988) 165 CLR 360. But this constitutional proposition says nothing about the desirability of such controls or whether they should be introduced by governments. Those questions remain a matter for political choice; the constitutional rule does no more than clear the way for the exercise of that choice. In *Mabo v Queensland (No 2)* (1992) 175 CLR 1, when it recognised the existence of native title, the High Court did not determine that the government should maintain native title; rather, the decision said that native title existed and left to the government the decision whether to maintain or extinguish it. Following that decision, the Keating Government decided to give statutory recognition of native title (1993) and the Howard Government took steps to limit native title (1998).

[1.3.3]   Even if one accepts that constitutional law has a political aspect, it also has a distinctly *legal* character. It can be described (with reasonable accuracy) as a set of rules that define the institutions of government, assign to them areas of operation, set limits to their functions, establish their interrelationships and prescribe the relative rights and obligations of other, non-governmental, interests.

This dual character, political and legal, is not unique to constitutional law. As indicated above, the realist approach to law (see Llewellyn (1931)), and more recently the critical legal studies approach (see Kairys (1982)), have both been based on the claim that all legal rules have a heavily political character. Indeed, even the most technical and apparently abstract legal rules perform both functions of reflecting and moulding the distribution of power in society. But constitutional law's combination of those elements is more overt, more conscious and more central. Indeed, it can be said to be symbiotic, in that the very reason for the development and existence of constitutional rules is to define, organise, contain and enhance the exercise of political power; and the content of these rules responds to historical, social, economic and political developments.

[1.3.4]   This dynamic and responsive character of constitutional law was expressed by Isaacs J in *Commonwealth v Kreglinger and Furnau Ltd* (1926) 37 CLR 393, when he described constitutions as 'made, not for a single occasion, but for the continued life and progress of the community', whose meaning must be affected by 'the silent operation of constitutional principles': 37 CLR at 413. In *Victoria v Commonwealth* (the *Payroll Tax* case) (1971) 122 CLR 353 at 396, Windeyer J offered this explanation of the High Court's landmark decision in the *Engineers'* case (1920) 28 CLR 129 **[8.2.31C]**:

> As I see it the *Engineers'* case, looked at as an event in legal and constitutional history, was a consequence of developments that had occurred outside the law courts as well as a cause of further developments there. That is not surprising for the Constitution is not an ordinary statute: it is a fundamental law. In any country where the spirit of the common law holds sway the enunciation by courts of constitutional principles based on the interpretation of a written constitution may vary and develop in response to changing circumstances.

[1.3.5]   More recently, in *Commonwealth v Tasmania* (the *Tasmanian Dam* case) (1983) 158 CLR 1 **[3.3.21C]**, Brennan J referred to the need to interpret constitutional provisions broadly. The question before the court was whether the Commonwealth Parliament could rely on its power to legislate with respect to external affairs to prevent the construction by Tasmania of a hydro-electric dam on land owned by Tasmania but entered on an international register of world heritage properties. The majority of the court concluded that the external affairs power would support this legislation. Brennan J stressed the need for a broad approach to the Commonwealth's legislative powers at 221:

> [Such an approach] gives the Constitution a dynamic force which is incompatible with a static constitutional balance. The complexity of modern commercial, economic, social and political activities increases the connexions between particular aspects of those activities and the heads of Commonwealth power and carries an expanding range of those activities into the sphere of Commonwealth legislative competence.

[1.3.6]   However, constitutional law retains many of the characteristics traditionally associated with 'law'. It is not so flexible or infinitely adaptable as to lack definition; and it is largely (but not exclusively) based on legal reasoning and lawyers' concepts. (The need to look beyond that reasoning and those concepts is discussed at **[1.4.42]**– **[1.4.49]** below.) Sir Owen Dixon's call for 'close adherence to legal reasoning [as] the only way to maintain the confidence of all parties in federal conflicts', made on his appointment as Chief Justice of the High Court of Australia ((1952) 85 CLR at xiv) is not a complete description of contemporary judicial attitudes. Be that as it may, it still represents an important aspect of constitutional adjudication. The dynamic, flexible and responsive conception of constitutional law is in a constant state of tension with the desire for 'stability in constitutional law', expressed by Barwick CJ in *Attorney-General (Cth) (Ex rel McKinlay) v Commonwealth* (1975) 135 CLR 1 at 17 **[4.6.9C]**.

Stability is, of course, a characteristic that is functional. Constitutional law must have a degree of certainty, clarity and predictability if it is to perform its function of defining the parameters within which the political process is to operate. 'Continuity and coherence in the law demand that in this court the principle of *stare decisis* should ordinarily be applied', said six members of the High Court in *Jones v Commonwealth* (1987) 71 ALR 497 at 498. However, because the social, economic and physical environment within which the political process operates is itself fluid and quite unpredictable, stability cannot be an absolute value. Change may be needed. As Isaacs J said in *Australian Agricultural Co v Federated Engine-Drivers and Fireman's Association of Australasia* (1913) 17 CLR 261 at 278, '[I]t is not, in my opinion, better that the Court should be persistently wrong than that it should be ultimately right': see further Keyzer (1999).

[1.3.7] The priority that judges place on stability and on change is linked to the interpretive method they adopt, whether it reflects the tenets of textualism, intentionalism or progressivism: see **[1.2.11]–[1.2.18]** above. It is also linked to the theoretical approach that underlies their method of judicial interpretation: see **[1.4.38]–[1.4.49]** below. For example, a textual approach to interpretation places a higher value on stability than on change, and so eschews the use of sources other than the original text itself in interpretation. McHugh J's view in *Theophanous v Herald and Weekly Times Ltd* (1994) 182 CLR 104 **[11.3.11]** at 198 best exemplifies this approach:

> Since the decision in the *Engineers'* case, however, this court has consistently held that it is not legitimate to construe the Constitution by reference to political principles or theories that find no support in the text of the Constitution. The theory of constitutional interpretation that has prevailed since the *Engineers'* case is that one starts with the text and not with some theory of federalism, politics or political economy.

In *McGinty v Western Australia* (1996) 186 CLR 140 **[11.3.17C]** McHugh J spelt out the strict textual approach when he portrayed other methods as adding words to the text. He said that the Constitution does not contain any 'hypothetical s 129': 186 CLR at 235. To assert otherwise would amount to inserting into the text a free-standing principle of representative democracy: 186 CLR at 232.

The intentionalist school calls for judges to decide questions of law according to the intentions of the framers. It generally also prizes stability over change. So in *R v Pearson; Ex parte Sipka* (1983) 152 CLR 254, a majority decided that the meaning of s 41 of the Constitution should be interpreted 'from its terms and context and by reference to the circumstances in which the section was to operate immediately after Federation': 152 CLR at 276.

By contrast, progressive or dynamic interpretation of the text holds that the Constitution ought to be interpreted in the light of changes in historical standards. Deane J in *Theophanous v Herald and Weekly Times Ltd* (1994) 182 CLR 104 **[11.3.11]** said that the Constitution should be interpreted as 'a living force': 182 CLR at 173–4.

[1.3.8] Although stability is often a hallmark of textualism and intentionalism, and progressivism represents change, as discussed above **[1.2.11]–[1.2.18]** there is no strict correlation between the method of interpretation and a preference for stability or for change. An intentionalist interpretation can be 'activist' in its orientation, and a progressivist interpretation can rely on the founders' intentions, which are normally associated with a more 'conservative' role for the High Court. For example, the phenomenon of intentionalism leading to change is illustrated by the decision in *Cole v Whitfield* (1988) 165 CLR 360 **[10.4.27C]**, where, after years of ascribing a range of meanings to s 92, a unanimous court decided the meaning of the words 'interstate commerce shall be absolutely free' by reference to the intentions of those who drafted the document, as evidenced in the Convention debates and in the process discarded the established meanings.

Alternatively, research into intent may reveal an error in the orthodox understandings of a provision, so that an interpretation which has been assumed to be conservative may, in fact, be subsequently revealed as a radical departure from the founders' intentions, requiring justification in sources other than in the intent as represented in the text: see the discussion of the doctrine of separation of powers in Wheeler (1996).

[1.3.9] Sometimes, paradoxically perhaps, progressivists can rely on intentions of the drafters. This is illustrated by the reasoning of Deane J in *Theophanous v Herald and Weekly Times Ltd* (1994) 182 CLR 104 **[11.3.2C]** and **[11.3.11]** at 171–2, where he referred to the writings of one of the framers of the Constitution, Andrew Inglis Clark, although his Honour did not cite the intentions to indicate a preference for the status quo. Inglis Clark had said:

> The Constitution was not made to serve a temporary and restricted purpose, but was framed and adopted as a permanent and comprehensive code of law, by which the exercise of the governmental powers conferred by it should be regulated as long as the institutions which it created to exercise the powers should exist. But the social conditions and the political exigencies of the succeeding generations of every civilised and progressive community will inevitably produce new governmental problems to which the language of the Constitution must be applied, and hence it must be read and construed, not as containing a declaration of the will and intentions of men long since dead, and who cannot have anticipated the problems that would arise for solution by future generations, but as declaring the will and intentions of the present inheritors and possessors of sovereign power, who maintain the constitution and have the power to alter it, and who are in the immediate presence of the problems to be solved. It is they who enforce the provisions of the Constitution and make a living force of that which would otherwise be a silent and lifeless document. Every community of men is governed by present possessors of sovereignty and not by the commands of men who have ceased to exist … (Inglis Clark, 1901).

[1.3.10] The other factor that suggests that there is no strict correlation between the method of interpretation and notions of stability and change is that no judge ever holds entirely to one view of interpretation. Brennan J's opinion in *Theophanous v Herald and Weekly Times Ltd* (1994) 182 CLR 104 **[11.3.2C]** and **[11.3.11]** illustrates the difficulties. He began by adhering to a strictly textual approach, but then indicated the numerous exceptions to it, at 143–4:

> The Court, owing its existence and its jurisdiction ultimately to the Constitution, can do no more than interpret and apply its text, uncovering implications where they exist. The Court has no jurisdiction to fill in what might be thought to be lacunae left by the Constitution. If there be a lacuna in the text, it can be filled, if at all, only by the common law or by another law which binds the courts and people of the Commonwealth and applies in all parts of Australia. Under the Constitution, this Court does not have nor can it be given nor, *a fortiori*, can it assume a power to attribute to the Constitution an operation which is not required by its text construed in the light of its history [*Cole v Whitfield* (1988) 165 CLR 360 at 385], the common

law and the circumstances or subject matter to which the text applies. The notion of 'developing' the law of the Constitution is inconsistent with the judicial power it confers. Clearly the Court cannot change the Constitution, nor can it convert constitutional silence into a legal rule with constitutional force. I do not mean that, in changing conditions, the Constitution does not have a changing effect [*Commonwealth v Tasmania* (the *Tasmanian Dam* case) (1983) 158 CLR 1 at 221], that the denotation of its terms does not change [*R v Brislan; Ex parte Williams* (1935) 54 CLR 262; *Jones v Commonwealth (No 2)* (1965) 112 CLR 206], that the course of judicial interpretation does not reveal that a past constitutional doctrine is untenable [*Amalgamated Society of Engineers v Adelaide Steamship Co Ltd* ('the *Engineers*' case') (1920) 28 CLR 129; *Cole v Whitfield* (1988) 165 CLR 360] or that new situations do not reveal new doctrines inherent in the constitutional text [*Nationwide News Pty Ltd v Wills* (1992) 177 CLR 1]. The Constitution speaks continually to the present and it operates in and upon contemporary conditions [*Fishwick v Cleland* (1960) 106 CLR 186 at 197; *Spratt v Hermes* (1965) 114 CLR 226 at 272].

Goldsworthy made a similar point when he argued that the High Court's orthodox method of interpretation is 'moderate originalism' but that there are 'legitimate methods of constitutional evolution' including discernment of the enactment (as opposed to application), intention, extensions in the denotation of a term and the adoption of a non-literal purposive interpretation: Goldsworthy (1997) pp 28–35. Do Goldsworthy's exceptions, like Brennan J's, amount to a case of 'exceptions swallowing the rule'?

The interpretation of the Constitution represents a relationship between stability and flexibility, between originalism and dynamism, between text and context, between history and change.

[1.3.11] Underlying the choice of interpretive method, and judges' preference for stability or change, is a deeper issue: What is the underlying jurisprudential theory behind the preference? This is a more difficult question that raises complex issues of law and philosophy. Certain judgments can be seen to represent a particular theoretical approach, and can be critiqued or analysed accordingly.

For example, McHugh J's comments in *Theophanous v Herald & Weekly Times Ltd* (1994) 182 CLR 104 **[11.3.10]** at 198 and in *McGinty v Western Australia* (1996) 186 CLR 140 **[11.3.2C]** at 235, that political principles and theories have no role in constitutional interpretation, corresponds to a positivist view of law which holds that law consists only in those rules made by the superior law-making authority, and identified by the accepted rule of recognition: see Hart (1994). A reader who did not accept this view of law might be sceptical of McHugh J's reasoning.

Alternatively, Mason J's view in *Capital Duplicators Pty Ltd v Australian Capital Territory (No 2)* (1993) 178 CLR 561 is more characteristic of a liberal view of law, which suggests that policies and principles as well as the text have a role in constitutional interpretation: see Dworkin (1986). If one's view of what is law excluded those policies and principles, then Mason J's view could be questioned.

Finally, in *McGinty v Western Australia* (1996) 186 CLR 140 **[11.3.17C]** at 201, Toohey J said that although 'the essence of representative democracy remains unchanged' it is 'the current perception which is embodied in the Australian Constitution'. That view represents the idea that legal interpretation is structured by the 'community of beliefs' shared by those who interpret the law, including the judges, practitioners and the public: see Fish (1982).

[1.3.12] The point about the need to balance stability and flexibility in constitutional law, is reflected in judicial attitudes to stare decisis, the authority of earlier judicial decisions. These are treated both as authoritative and as amenable to change. In *Queensland v Commonwealth* (1977) 139 CLR 585, two members of the High Court, Gibbs and Stephen JJ, who had dissented in *Western Australia v Commonwealth* (the *Territorial Senators* case) (1975) 134 CLR 201 **[4.2.32C]**, declined to depart from the earlier decision, although a third justice, Barwick CJ, would have overruled that decision.

A similar deference to an earlier decision was shown in *HC Sleigh Ltd v South Australia* (1977) 136 CLR 475 **[9.4.34]**, where the court refused to depart from the decision in *Dennis Hotels Pty Ltd v Victoria* (1960) 104 CLR 529 **[9.4.12C]**, which had involved a highly artificial and much criticised analysis of state taxes. Mason J expressed his attitude as follows:

> Generally speaking, the court should be slow to depart from its previous decisions, especially in constitutional cases where the overturning of past decisions may well disturb the justifiable assumptions on which legislative powers have been exercised by the Commonwealth and the States and on which financial appropriations, budget plans and administrative arrangements have been made by governments (136 CLR at 501).

This deference was referred to in *Ha v New South Wales* (1997) 189 CLR 465 **[9.4.60C]** at 491, and in a joint judgment, the majority, Brennan CJ, McHugh, Gummow and Kirby JJ, said:

> To support the overturning of such a long and consistent line of authority, the defendant's submissions needed to show a clear departure from the text of the Constitution.

Nevertheless, the court did overturn that long and consistent line of authority in *Ha v New South Wales*.

[1.3.13] The court has shown itself quite prepared to overturn previously accepted dogma in many significant areas. The *Engineers'* case (1920) 28 CLR 129 **[8.2.31C]**, *Commonwealth v Cigamatic Pty Ltd (in liq)* (1962) 108 CLR 372 **[8.2.98C]**, *Strickland v Rocla Concrete Pipes Ltd* (1971) 124 CLR 468 **[10.3.4C]** and *Cole v Whitfield* (1988) 165 CLR 360 **[10.4.27C]** are illustrations of the court's willingness to discard established propositions. In *Cole v Whitfield*, the court noted (in its unanimous judgment) that, '[i]n the interests of certainty', it did 'not readily discard or depart from settled principle': 165 CLR at 400. Nevertheless, the court felt free, even obliged, to abandon the reading of the s 92 guarantee of free interstate trade and commerce that had represented orthodoxy for some 40 years.

[1.3.14] The ambivalence of judges towards the doctrine of stare decisis is an example of what some legal commentators describe as the indeterminacy of law. Following Derrida, Scott has argued that this ambivalence is inherent in law because legal decision-making is caught in a system of binary oppositions: Scott (1988) p 43. Similarly, in relation to international law, Koskenniemi has argued that international judges are forced by the structure of legal decision-making to justify their decisions according to two mutually dependent but inconsistent justifications: Koskenniemi (1989) pp 40–2. The High Court has been forced to confront similar issues when faced with two competing lines of authority in Australian constitutional law. The decision in *Capital Duplicators Pty Ltd v Australian Capital Territory (No 2)* (1993) 178 CLR 561 **[9.4.53C]** invalidated a territory tax imposed on the sale of X-rated videos on the basis that the tax amounted to an excise duty, the imposition of which was exclusive to the Commonwealth. The decision relied upon ascribing a wide meaning to the term *excise*. In the course of the decision, Mason CJ, Brennan, Deane, and McHugh JJ rejected an argument that the wide view should be reconsidered at 591:

> [The] argument *against* reconsideration would not prevail if it were clear that the [narrow] interpretation ... is correct.

This comment illustrates the logical difficulties posed for the High Court by the existence of two persuasive lines of authority. Moreover, it illustrates the fundamental contradiction that arises from the court's need to decide, as a preliminary question, whether or not to reconsider the wide line of authority. In order to decide the procedural question of whether or not to reconsider, the court is forced to make some preliminary assessment of the correctness of one of the views, although that is the very issue which cannot yet be determined because it can only be dealt with on the merits.

[1.3.15] The equivocal nature of the High Court's attitude to earlier constitutional decisions emerges from the comments of Windeyer J, in *Damjanovic and Sons Pty Ltd v Commonwealth* (1968) 117 CLR 390, a case which had also centred on the extent of the protection offered to trading and commercial activities by s 92 of the Commonwealth Constitution, the least stable aspect of Australia's constitutional law. Conceding that the court's responsibility was to interpret and apply the text of the Constitution, he cautioned that the court was not free to disregard 'authoritative expositions in earlier cases' (at 407–8):

> This restrains the predilections and idiosyncrasies of an individual judge from dominating his interpretation of the Constitution. It thus makes for a stable law and a stable economy. Speaking in a general sense, I therefore hold myself guided, if not strictly governed, by the earlier decisions of this court on this topic.

[1.3.16] In some cases the court may be prepared to depart from the previous decision where it does not feel bound by it. In *Lange v Australian Broadcasting Corporation* (1997) 189 CLR 520 **[11.3.13C]** the Full Court said at 554:

> This Court is not bound by its previous decisions [*Baker v Campbell* (1983) 153 CLR 52 at 102; *Damjanovic & Sons Pty Ltd v Commonwealth* (1968) 117 CLR 390 at 395–6; *Queensland v Commonwealth* (1977) 139 CLR 585 at 610]. Nor has it laid down any particular rule or rules or set of factors for re-opening the correctness of its decisions. Nevertheless, the Court should reconsider a previous decision only with great caution and for strong reasons [*Hughes and Vale Pty Ltd v State of New South Wales* (1953) 87 CLR 49 at 102; *Queensland v Commonwealth* (1977) 139 CLR 585 at 602, 620]. In *Hughes and Vale Pty Ltd v New South Wales* [(1953) 87 CLR 49 at 102. See also *H C Sleigh Ltd v South Australia* (1977) 136 CLR 475 at 501; *Commonwealth v Hospital Contribution Fund* (1982) 150 CLR 49 at 56], Kitto J said that in constitutional cases 'it is obviously undesirable that a question decided by the Court after full consideration should be re-opened without grave reason'. However, it cannot be doubted that the Court will re-examine a decision if it involves a question of 'vital constitutional importance' [*Queensland v Commonwealth* (1977) 139 CLR 585 at 630. See also *Commonwealth v Cigamatic Pty Ltd (in liq)* (1962) 108 CLR 372 at 377] and is 'manifestly wrong' [*Australian Agricultural Co v Federated Engine-Drivers and Firemen's Association of Australasia* (1913) 17 CLR 261 at 278–278; *The Tramways Case [No 1]* (1914) 18 CLR 54 at 58, 69, 83; but cf *Queensland v Commonwealth* (1977) 139 CLR 585 at 621]. Errors in constitutional interpretation are not remediable by the legislature [*Queensland v The Commonwealth* (1977) 139 CLR 585 at 630; *Street v Queensland Bar Association* (1989) 168 CLR 461 at 588],

and the Court's approach to constitutional matters is not necessarily the same as in matters concerning the common law or statutes. But these general statements concerning the occasions when the Court will reconsider one of its previous decisions give little guidance in this case when the judgments and orders in *Theophanous* and *Stephens* are examined.

However, the High Court went on to state that neither of the earlier implied freedom of political communication cases, *Theophanous v Herald & Weekly Times Ltd* (1994) 182 CLR 104 **[11.3.2C]** and *Stephens v West Australian Newspapers Ltd* (1994) 182 CLR 211 **[11.3.12]**, established such a 'binding statement of constitutional principle' (189 CLR at 554) because the court had been evenly divided on whether the particular defence was good in law and because the crucial judgment of Deane J had taken a different view of the freedom to that taken by the other members of the majority ('the reasoning which gave rise to the answers in *Theophanous* had the direct support of only three of the seven justices') and so 'the appropriate course is to examine the correctness of the defences pleaded in the present case as a matter of principle and not of authority': 189 CLR at 556. For further consideration of the High Court's decisions on the topic of constitutional precedent and the at times conflicting approaches taken in those cases, see Keyzer (1999).

4   The sources of constitutional law

[1.4.1]   The study of constitutional law does not focus on a single comprehensive instrument and its judicial interpretation. Although the Commonwealth Constitution provides a relatively detailed account of the definition and location of public power in Australia, it is by no means comprehensive or exhaustive. First, it is necessary to refer to other formal instruments, such as the various state Constitution Acts, the Australia Act 1986 (UK and Cth) **[6.2.7E]** and instruments such as the Letters Patent establishing the office of Governor-General **[7.2.19]**. Second, we need to isolate and analyse the rules observed by the participants in the governmental process, even though these rules are neither expressed in statute nor enforced by the courts. These rules, referred to as constitutional conventions, play an important part in organising and regulating public power. They may regulate activities that are left uncontrolled by the formal rules, or they may qualify the practical operation of the formal rules laid down in legislation or by the courts.

Conventions play a particularly important role in constructing and regulating the relationship between parliament and the executive, and the relationships between different elements in the executive: see **[7.3.7]**, **[7.4.2]**, **[7.4.24]**. In the debate over whether Australia ought to become a republic (and, if so, what type of republic), the question has been raised as to whether the constitutional conventions associated with the powers of the Head of State ought to be codified, either in the Constitution itself or in another legal instrument.

Jennings' work on constitutional conventions raises interesting questions about the uncertain but important nature of constitutional conventions: Are they non-legal rules that are similar to custom and therefore unenforceable? From what basis do they derive their binding force? Why are they not simply better labelled as 'politics' not law? See Jennings (1972).

Commonwealth Constitution

[1.4.2] Nevertheless, the primary sources of Australian constitutional law lie in formal documents, of which the pre-eminent document is the Commonwealth Constitution. Drafted by a restricted group of Australian colonial politicians and lawyers at a series of Constitutional Conventions in the 1890s (see **[1.2.6]**) and given formal legal status by an Act of the United Kingdom Parliament, the Commonwealth of Australia Constitution Act 1900 (UK) s 9, the Commonwealth Constitution created a new political and legal entity, the Commonwealth of Australia, while preserving the former colonies as theoretically autonomous provinces, called states of the new nation. The Commonwealth Constitution, enacted for Australia in this way, has always been regarded as an 'organic' document, in the sense that it is seen as superior to legislation passed by the Commonwealth or state parliaments.

[1.4.3] Geoffrey Lindell has made the point that, in 1901, the legal paramountcy of the Commonwealth Constitution was seen as an inevitable consequence of its enactment by the United Kingdom Parliament: Lindell (1986) pp 32–3. In Dixon's words, the Constitution did not claim to be binding because of 'the direct expression of a people's inherent authority to constitute a government' but because it was 'a statute of the British Parliament enacted in the exercise of its legal sovereignty over the law everywhere in the King's Dominions': Dixon (1935) p 597. Lindell argued that the attainment of Australian constitutional independence was an evolutionary process, which was certainly completed with the passage of the Australia Act 1986. That view attracted judicial support in *Australian Capital Television Pty Ltd v Commonwealth* (1992) 177 CLR 106 at 138 **[11.3.7C]**, where Mason CJ said that the Australia Act 1986 (UK) 'marked the end of the legal sovereignty of the Imperial Parliament and recognised that ultimate sovereignty resided in the Australian people'. That independence need not affect the original rationalisation for the paramountcy of the Commonwealth Constitution: 'nothing has happened to change the pre-existing inability of the [Australian] Parliaments ... to legislate inconsistently with the Constitution': Lindell (1986) p 37. But Lindell acknowledged that a reference to the authoritative source discounted by Dixon would conform more closely to social and political reality (p 37):

> In short, that explanation can be found in the words in the preamble to the Constitution Act namely, the agreement of the people to federate, supported by the role given to them in approving proposals for constitutional alteration under s 128 of the Constitution, as well as their acquiescence in the continued operation of the Constitution as a fundamental law. According to this approach the Constitution now enjoys its character as a higher law because of the will and authority of the people.

[1.4.4] Whatever the juridical and political bases for the fundamental or organic character of the Commonwealth Constitution, it has proved to be a remarkably immutable document. The procedure which it specifies in s 128 for its alteration (passage of a bill through at least one House of Parliament and endorsement of the bill at a referendum (with majorities in at least four of the six states as well as an overall majority)), has been a real barrier to constitutional reform. Forty-four proposals for alteration have been passed through parliament and put to a referendum. Of these, only eight have been approved by a majority of electors nationally and a majority of electors in a majority of the states: see further Bennett and Brennan (1999). 'Constitutionally speaking,' Geoffrey Sawer observed in 1967, 'Australia is the frozen continent': Sawer (1967) p 208 (see also Lee (1988)).

The 'double majority' requirement is responsible for only a small part of this stability. Of the 36 rejected proposals, only five were supported by a majority of electors throughout Australia, and only three of these attracted majority support in half the states: Constitutional Commission (1988) p 873.

[1.4.5] However, as Leslie Zines pointed out in 1976, the textual rigidity of the Commonwealth Constitution can be complemented by a substantial flexibility in its application. An adventurous Commonwealth Government could extend its reach by relying on formerly unexplored aspects of the Constitution and by pressing for new judicial interpretations of those aspects that had been given a narrow reading:

> Assertions as to the law that were confidently made by judges, lawyers and academics only a few years ago have become matters of argument and debate as a result of a government with firm ends in view encouraging further thought and examination of means and methods of achieving those objects (Zines (1976) p 82).

A similar point was made in Crommelin and Evans (1977), and by 1988 judicial interpretation had adjusted some of the pivotal concepts in the Commonwealth Constitution, opening the way to new forms of legislative and executive action: see, for example, *Commonwealth v Tasmania* (the *Tasmanian Dam* case) (1983) 158 CLR 1 **[3.3.21C]**; *Mabo v Queensland (No 2)* (1992) 175 CLR 1 **[2.2.30]**; Chapter 2. One effect of the High Court's bout of activism in the early- to mid-1990s was to engender a debate within the Australian community concerning the proper limits of judicial activism, or law-making: see **[1.2.12]** above. (For earlier examples, see *Commonwealth v Bank of New South Wales* (1949) 79 CLR 497 **[10.4.10C]**; *Amalgamated Society of Engineers v Adelaide Steamship Co Ltd* (the *Engineers'* case) (1920) 28 CLR 129 **[8.2.31C]**.)

[1.4.6] The Commonwealth Constitution divided legislative authority between the new Commonwealth and the states by conferring on the new Commonwealth Parliament power to legislate 'with respect to' a list of topics (the bulk of which appear in s 51), and declaring that state parliaments should continue to have the legislative powers of their colonial predecessors, except to the extent that the new Constitution 'exclusively vested' a power in the Commonwealth Parliament or withdrew a power from state parliaments: s 107. This type of division of powers is not the only one possible in a federal state. The Canadian Constitution lists the powers of the provinces and leaves the residue to the central government: see Hogg (1992).

Implicit in this system is the idea that the Commonwealth's legislative power is specific, while that of the states is general (sometimes, but inaccurately, described as 'residual'). However, the course of history and judicial interpretation have demonstrated that this division does not necessarily restrict or limit the Commonwealth Parliament. The listed topics have been shown to be sufficiently elastic to allow some expansion of Commonwealth power: see, for example, the *Engineers'* case (1920) 28 CLR 129 **[8.2.31C]**; *Strickland v Rocla Concrete Pipes Ltd* (1971) 124 CLR 468 **[10.3.4C]**; *Commonwealth v Tasmania* (the *Tasmanian Dam* case) (1983) 158 CLR 1 **[3.3.21C]**.

Also implicit in the division of legislative power is the prospect of conflict between Commonwealth and state legislation. The Commonwealth Constitution anticipated this problem and provides that, in the event of 'inconsistency', the Commonwealth legislation prevails and the state legislation is 'invalid': s 109. The inconsistency or supremacy principle is common to any legal regime in which power is divided between the centre and the constituent parts. For example, in European Community law, the European Court of Justice has recognised the existence of the principle, although it does not appear in any of the legal instruments establishing the EC: see *Costa v Ente Nazionale Electricity Board* [1964] ECR 585; [1964] CMLR 425. The judicial reading of s 109 and the further expansion of Commonwealth power at the expense of the states that has resulted from that reading are explored in **[8.1.1]–[8.1.79]**.

[1.4.7] The Commonwealth Constitution created a new executive government, formally headed by the Queen (in 1901 Victoria; today, Elizabeth II) who is represented by the Governor-General (s 61), to be 'advised' (according to convention, controlled) by an Executive Council (s 62) composed of Ministers appointed by the Governor-General (who, according to convention, are drawn exclusively from the political group or party which controls the House of Representatives). Although the Commonwealth Constitution was cryptic on this point, it was implicit in s 106 that the former colonies' executive governments would continue, as state executive governments, retaining the same status and powers as held by them prior to federation. The structure of these executive governments and the formal rules and conventions that regulate their functions are discussed in Chapter 5. The nature of the executive arrangements at both Commonwealth and state level is still a topic of national debate, even after the failure of the 1999 republic referendum: see **[1.2.5]** above.

[1.4.8] The Commonwealth Constitution established the High Court of Australia (s 71), giving it appellate jurisdiction over decisions of state Supreme Courts and any other federal court created by the Commonwealth Parliament, and original jurisdiction in the matters specified in ss 75 and, contingently, 76. The Commonwealth Parliament was also authorised to create other federal courts: s 71. Sections 71 and 77 allowed the Commonwealth Parliament to confer 'federal jurisdiction' on state courts, whose structure and status would continue to be controlled by state legislation: s 106. However, the exercise of judicial power by state courts may be controlled by implications arising from the Commonwealth Constitution: *Kable v DPP (NSW)* (1996) 189 CLR 51 **[6.4.48C]**. The highly complex relationships between federal and state courts and federal and state jurisdictions are analysed by Cowen and Zines (1978).

The Constitution also retained appeals to the Privy Council (an imperial institution), subject to an exception in some constitutional cases. However, it gave the Commonwealth Parliament power to limit those appeals: s 74. Subsequent interpretation of these provisions has led to the development of the constitutional doctrine of the separation of federal judicial power: see **[6.4.3]–[6.4.51]**.

[1.4.9] The High Court's constitutional work, its adjudication on the validity of Commonwealth and state legislation and governmental action, has been undertaken primarily as an exercise of its original jurisdiction, although some constitutional matters also come to the court on appeal from state Supreme Courts and the Federal Court. A former Chief Justice of the High Court noted that, although 'the Constitution makes no specific provision for judicial review for constitutional validity ... the framers plainly intended that the Court undertake this function':

Mason (1986) p 3. For example, one of the delegates to the 1898 Convention, Isaac Isaacs (who later became Chief Justice of the High Court and Governor-General of Australia), observed that, despite the 'infinite trouble' being taken in the drafting of the Commonwealth Constitution, 'the makers of the Constitution' would include the judges who interpreted it and applied it to the resolution of real problems: Convention Debates (Melbourne, 1898) p 283. The point was expressed unequivocally by another framer, Alfred Deakin, when speaking as Commonwealth Attorney-General on the 1902 Judiciary Bill:

> The Constitution is to be the supreme law, but it is the High Court which is to determine how far and between what boundaries it is supreme. The federation is constituted by distribution of powers, and it is this court which decides the orbit and boundary of every power (House of Representatives, Debates (1902) p 10,967).

The question whether, and in what manner, the judiciary may review acts of the legislature is a continuing controversy in any political democracy controlled by the rule of law: see Ely (1980) (an account of the principle in the American context). The Supreme Court of the United States established the legitimacy of judicial review early in its existence, in the landmark decision *Marbury v Madison* 1 Cranch 137; 5 US 137 (1803). The principle was endorsed in Australian jurisprudence in *Australian Communist Party v Commonwealth* (the *Communist Party* case) (1951) 83 CLR 1; and more recently in *Plaintiff S157/2002 v Commonwealth* (2003) 211 CLR 476 at 492 and 513.

The legal and political evolution of the High Court's judicial review role is reviewed in Galligan (1987) pp 42–117. The technical legal question as to whether the jurisdiction of the High Court (appellate or original) extends to ruling on the constitutional validity of Acts of Parliament is discussed by Lane (1966). Since *Lange v Australian Broadcasting Corporation* (1997) 189 CLR 520 **[11.3.3C]**, **[11.3.13C]**, there is no doubt as to the High Court's position on its function in this context:

> The Constitution displaced, or rendered inapplicable, the English common law doctrine of the general competence and unqualified supremacy of the legislature. It placed upon the federal judicature the responsibility of deciding the limits of the respective powers of State and Commonwealth governments (189 CLR at 564).

[1.4.10] The Constitution included a series of provisions dealing with financial and trade matters. These were intended to provide some integration of commercial activities (in this context, ss 90, 92 and 99 were particularly important: see **[9.4.2E]**, **[9.3.1E]**, **[10.4.1E]**) and to ensure that the new Commonwealth had access to the revenue needed to finance its operations while the states retained substantial financial independence. For a variety of reasons, some of those intentions have miscarried. Only in 1988 did s 92 receive a reading from the High Court which returned to its 'common market' purpose: *Cole v Whitfield* (1988) 165 CLR 360 **[10.4.27C]**.

The current judicial reading of s 90 has denied the states access to a significant tax base, thereby enlarging the Commonwealth's control over fiscal policy. At the same time, this interpretation allowed the states to use artificial legislative drafting in order to dilute that control and to frustrate the historical purpose of s 90: see, for example, *Hematite Petroleum Pty Ltd v Victoria* (1983) 151 CLR 599 **[9.4.37C]**; *Dennis Hotels Pty Ltd v Victoria* (1960) 104 CLR 529 **[9.4.12C]**. With the High Court's decision in *Ha v New South Wales* (1997) 189 CLR 465 **[9.4.60C]** and the subsequent development of the Commonwealth's Goods and Services Tax, this latter possibility has now been virtually eliminated. Further, the High Court's consistent approach to s 99 has reduced the constraints of that provision to a mere drafting formula: see *Elliott v Commonwealth* (1936) 54 CLR 657 **[9.3.13C]**.

To a significant extent these cases turn upon the issue of the level of economic integration which is mandated by the Constitution. This question is highly contested, as indicated by the strong dissent of Dawson J in *Capital Duplicators Pty Ltd v Australian Capital Territory (No 2)* (1993) 178 CLR 561, where he drew on the experience of comparative jurisdictions to show that other federations countenance state taxes on goods without any apparent harm to centralised economic planning. This area is a prime example of the influence of constitutional law on the economic structure of the Australian political system, illustrated by the apparent loss of $5 billion in revenue to the states following the decision in *Ha v New South Wales* (1997) 189 CLR 465 **[9.4.60C]**.

Historically, state financial independence foundered on the twin rocks of the 1929 Great Depression and the Second World War. In the first of these national crises, the states were persuaded to sign the Financial Agreement, subsequently endorsed by an alteration to the Commonwealth Constitution (s 105A), under which they effectively surrendered their capacity to borrow on the international capital market: see **[9.5.1]**– **[9.5.8]**. In the second crisis, the Commonwealth moved decisively to centralise the imposition and collection of income taxation, thus denying the states access to this most significant tax base. This manoeuvre was promptly endorsed by the High Court in *South Australia v Commonwealth* (the *First Uniform Tax* case) (1942) 65 CLR 373 **[9.6.3C]** to accommodate the Commonwealth's stated need for increased revenue during World War II. Later, the High Court decided, in *Melbourne Corporation v Commonwealth* (1947) 74 CLR 31 **[8.2.45C]** that the Commonwealth may not legislate to impair the autonomy and integrity of the states. Emboldened by this decision, the states later applied to the High Court to have the *First Uniform Tax* case reconsidered and overruled; but it was then upheld as 'precedent' in *Victoria v Commonwealth* (1957) 99 CLR 575 **[9.6.8C]**. Later, the High Court's reading of s 90 in *Hematite Petroleum Pty Ltd v Victoria* (1983) 151 CLR 599 **[9.4.37C]** and in *Ha v New South Wales* (1997) 189 CLR 465 **[9.4.60C]** reinforced the dependence of the states on Commonwealth grants to fund their budgets: see **[9.6.1]**.

[1.4.11] One stark omission from the Commonwealth Constitution is any systematic statement of fundamental political and individual values. Whereas the United States Constitution carries a comprehensive Bill of Rights and the Canadian Constitution, by 1982 referendum, includes a Charter of Rights and Freedoms, our Constitution includes only a few scattered and limited guarantees:

- a basic, but very limited, right to vote appears to be guaranteed by s 41 **[4.5.7C]**;

- property is protected against compulsory acquisition by the Commonwealth (but not by the states) by s 51(xxxi) **[11.2.1E]**;

- trials of indictable Commonwealth offences (but not state offences) must be by jury under s 80 **[11.2.24E]**;

- traders and travellers are guaranteed the freedom to cross state borders under s 92 **[10.4.1E]**;

- freedom of religion is protected against Commonwealth (but not state) interference, and the Commonwealth (but not the states) may not establish any religion under s 116 **[11.2.41E]**;

- and discrimination against any 'subject of the Queen' on the basis of state residence is prohibited by s 117 **[11.2.57E]**.

For further discussion see Wilcox (1993).

It may be a reflection of the sensibilities of Australian lawyers and judges that, until recently, the trend of judicial decision has been to read down most of these guarantees: *R v Pearson; Ex parte Sipka* (1983) 152 CLR 254 (s 41) **[4.5.7C]**; *R v Archdall* (1928) 41 CLR 128 (s 80) **[11.2.28]**; *Adelaide Company of Jehovah's Witnesses Inc v Commonwealth* (1943) 67 CLR 116 (s 116) **[11.2.48C]**; *Henry v Boehm* (1973) 128 CLR 482 (s 117) **[11.2.60]**. During the 1990s, the High Court began to take a more expansive view of constitutional rights. It has taken a more assertive approach to the reading and application of s 117 (*Street v Queensland Bar Association* (1989) 168 CLR 461 **[11.2.61C]**) and has developed an implied freedom to discuss political and governmental affairs: *Australian Capital Television Pty Ltd v Commonwealth* (1992) 177 CLR 106 **[11.3.7C]**; *Nationwide News Pty Ltd v Wills* (1992) 177 CLR 1 **[11.3.9]**.

The increased sensitivity to individual rights and freedoms reflected in these more recent decisions has obliged the court to embark on the difficult tasks of policy evaluation and interest balancing, tasks for which earlier generations of justices showed a marked distaste. It also ignited a debate within the High Court and the community about the proper role of judges in constitutional cases. One justice, McHugh J, stated his view that the majority in the implied freedom of communication cases had inserted a new provision relating to representative democracy into the Constitution (*McGinty v Western Australia* (1996) 186 CLR 140 **[11.3.17C]** at 232) and one state Premier claimed that the High Court had invented rights: see also **[11.1.5]**. Also implicated in the debate is the method of interpretation used by the judges in finding implied rights: see **[1.2.14]–[1.2.18]**.

These sentiments indicate that although the present generation of High Court justices appears to have taken up the task politicians and the electorate have failed to perform (the development of individual constitutional guarantees for Australia) uncertainty exists as to how far or how quickly they are prepared to develop those rights. In *Lange v Australian Broadcasting Corporation* (1997) 189 CLR 520 **[11.3.13C]**, the court appeared to retreat somewhat from an expansion of implied rights, indicating that those rights must be anchored firmly in the text and structure of the Constitution.

The Constitutional Commission in its 1988 report recommended that a new chapter be inserted in the Commonwealth Constitution, guaranteeing a substantial catalogue of rights and freedoms against government action: Constitutional Commission (1988) Ch 9. However, in September 1988 the people rejected a more modest proposal to create a guarantee of democratic elections, and to strengthen and extend the presently lop-sided guarantees of private property, jury trial and freedom of religion: see Lee (1988) pp 538–40, 541–5.

State Constitution Acts

[1.4.12] Each of the states has its own formal constitutional document, entitled a Constitution Act, whose origins lie in United Kingdom legislation (the inescapable mark of colonial status). However, these original imperial documents have been replaced by local legislation and, in general, they are subject to amendment or repeal by state parliaments in the same way as other, more mundane, legislation. In

McCawley v R [1920] AC 691 **[5.4.2]**, the Privy Council held that the Constitution Act 1867 (Qld) would be amended by any inconsistent legislation subsequently passed by the Queensland Parliament, even where the later legislation made no express reference to the Constitution Act. In the Privy Council's view, the Constitution Acts of the Australian states were uncontrolled and, subject to one qualification, 'occupied precisely the same position as a Dog Act or any other Act, however humble its subject matter': [1920] AC at 704.

[1.4.13] The one qualification made by the Privy Council in *McCawley v R* related to any special procedural restrictions on amending legislation which might have been specified in a Constitution Act: [1920] AC 691 at 712, 714 **[5.4.2]**. Restrictions of this type have been placed, for example, in ss 7A and 7B of the Constitution Act 1902 (NSW). These sections require approval by referendum of legislation to amend those parts of the Constitution Act which establish the Legislative Council, fix the maximum life of the Legislative Assembly, prescribe compulsory voting for parliamentary elections, deal with the distribution of Assembly electorates and the conduct of Assembly elections. The efficacy of these restrictive procedures was affirmed by the High Court and the Privy Council in *Attorney-General (NSW) v Trethowan* (1931) 44 CLR 394 **[5.4.17C]** (High Court); (1932) 47 CLR 97 **[5.4.18]** Privy Council). These restrictive procedures are sometimes referred to as 'manner and form' provisions. A similar procedural restriction protects certain aspects of the Queensland, South Australian and Western Australian Constitution Acts: see **[1.6.9]**. Less restrictive procedural requirements appear in the Tasmanian and Victorian Constitution Acts: see **[5.4.12E]–[5.4.16]**.

In each case, the restriction applies only to isolated aspects of the system of government established by the constitutional document, so that the bulk of the provisions in the document remain amenable to alteration or repeal in the same way as other state legislation. A tentative challenge to this idea was made by some members of the New South Wales Court of Appeal in *Building & Construction Employees' and Builders Labourers' Federation of NSW v Minister for Industrial Relations* (1986) 7 NSWLR 372 **[5.4.8]**.

[1.4.14] The mixture of restrictive and flexible procedures for amending state Constitution Acts is acknowledged in s 106 of the Commonwealth Constitution, which declares that '[t]he Constitution of each State of the Commonwealth shall, subject to this Constitution, continue as at the establishment of the Commonwealth until altered in accordance with the Constitution of the State'. (On the significance of s 106 for the enforcement of restrictive procedures, see *Western Australia v Wilsmore* [1981] WAR 179; (1981) 33 ALR 13 **[5.4.33]** and also **[1.6.10]**.)

This reference to s 106 should also serve to remind us of a proposition which may be so obvious that there is a risk of its being overlooked; namely, the institutions and processes of government established by state Constitution Acts are subject to the Commonwealth Constitution. This document does not merely define and control our national institutions of government. That may be its principal focus, but several of its provisions are directly relevant to the states. Moreover, it may be that the implications drawn from the Commonwealth Constitution will extend to and constrain state institutions of government, although this will depend upon the nature of the implication under discussion: see *Kable v DPP (NSW)* (1996) 189 CLR 51 **[6.4.48C]**; *Stephens v West Australian Newspapers Ltd* (1994) 182 CLR 211 **[11.3.12]**; *McGinty v Western Australia* (1996) 186 CLR 140 **[11.3.17C]**.

[1.4.15] Despite the general flexibility of state constitutions, until recently few fundamental changes had been made to the governmental structures established by the original colonial Constitution Acts. Apart from the abolition of the Queensland Legislative Council in 1922, the only significant changes were the gradual introduction of universal adult suffrage for parliamentary elections (**[4.5.4]**), the general extension to four years of the maximum lives of the Houses of Parliament in all states except Queensland (**[4.3.1]**–**[4.3.7]**) and the reform of the system for choosing members of the New South Wales Legislative Council.

[1.4.16] The state Constitution Acts define the basic formal institutions of government: the parliaments, the executive governments and, in some cases, the state Supreme Courts. The legislative authority of the parliaments is defined in broad terms, not by reference to specific topics, as in the case of the Commonwealth Parliament (**[1.2.13]**), but by reference to the territory of the state. For example, the New South Wales Parliament is empowered to 'make laws for the peace, welfare and good government of New South Wales in all cases whatsoever': Constitution Act 1902 (NSW) s 5. The broad terms of the states' legislative powers have recently been confirmed by s 2 of the Australia Act 1986 **[6.2.7E]**, **[6.3.17E]**. In *Union Steamship Co Ltd v King* (1988) 166 CLR 1 **[6.3.22C]** at 10, the court said that these phrases denote 'plenary power'.

[1.4.17] For many years, the form of words quoted in **[1.4.16]** above was read by courts as restricting state parliaments so that they could only legislate for persons, events or other phenomena connected to the territory of the state: see, for example, *Welker v Hewett* (1969) 120 CLR 503 **[6.3.8C]**. That reading must be reassessed in the light of the passage of the Australia Acts 1986 **[1.4.1]**, a reassessment which has begun with the High Court's decision in *Union Steamship Co of Australia Pty Ltd v King* (1988) 166 CLR 1 **[6.3.22C]**.

   The form of words has also been treated by some judges as importing some fundamental principles of human rights into the definition of the legislative power of state parliaments: *Building & Construction Employees' and Builders Labourers' Federation (NSW) v Minister for Industrial Relations* (1986) 7 NSWLR 372 **[5.4.8]**. The question having been left open in *Union Steamship Co of Australia Pty Ltd v King* (1988) 166 CLR 1 **[5.4.9]**, the proposition was rejected by several of the majority judges and both the minority judges in *Kable v DPP (NSW)* (1996) 189 CLR 51 **[5.4.9]**.

[1.4.18] The state Constitution Acts also define the location of executive power, in the Governor, representing the Crown, and the Executive Council of each state, with the latter body consisting of the current ministers, who are appointed to their offices by the Governor. The constitutional powers of the executive government (the summoning and dissolving of parliament, the appointment and dismissal of ministers and assent, in the name of the Crown, to legislation passed by the Houses of Parliament) are defined in the Constitution Acts. However, for a clear understanding of the structure and function of executive governments we need to look beyond the formal rules to constitutional conventions that have evolved from political practice. These questions are discussed in **[7.3.7]**, **[7.4.2]**, **[7.4.24]**.

[1.4.19] In most of the Australian colonies, superior courts of record were established prior to the introduction of representative institutions of government. Their structure and function as Supreme Courts of the several states, is now defined in local state legislation; in some cases, as in Victoria and South Australia, in the Constitution Act itself; in others, as in New South Wales, in a Supreme Court Act. The jurisdiction of each Supreme Court is defined in very wide terms, and is subject to reduction and augmentation by the Commonwealth Parliament under s 77(ii) and (iii) of the Commonwealth Constitution. In contrast to the equivalent provisions in the Commonwealth Constitution, the state Constitution Acts are not regarded as requiring a separation of judicial power from the other functions of government: see **[6.4.43]–[6.4.47]**. However, in exercising federal judicial power conferred on them under s 77(iii) of the Constitution, state Supreme Courts are required to conform to the basic tenets of federal judicial power, including the separation of powers and any implications that arise from the nature of judicial power and judicial process. That requirement may impact on the way in which state courts exercise their functions: see *Kable v DPP (NSW)* (1996) 189 CLR 51 **[6.4.48C]**.

[1.4.20] Because the state Constitution Acts are not required to address the structural and functional issues of the federal system, nor to accommodate the range of economic and political interests which the federal system brings into conflict, the state documents have a narrower focus than the Commonwealth Constitution. They make no attempt to construct a framework for economic activity or to spell out the location of fiscal power. Apart from an isolated, and probably ineffective, provision guaranteeing freedom of conscience and religion in the Tasmanian Constitution Act 1934 (Tas) s 46, the state Constitutions make no reference to fundamental values or freedoms. They are very much concerned with the mechanics of the institutions of government.

Statute of Westminster

[1.4.21] The Statute of Westminster 1931 (UK) marked an important stage in Australia's transition from a British colony to independence. It was only a stage. The final substantial step came with the passage of the Australia Acts 1986 **[1.4.1]**. The last symbolic step, the creation of an Australian Head of State, was placed on the constitutional agenda in 1997. The Constitutional Convention (Election) Act 1997 (Cth) provided for the establishment of a partly elected, partly appointed, convention to investigate the question whether Australia should become a republic. The Convention answered the question in the affirmative and the matter was put to the voters at a referendum. That referendum failed, but the issue has recently been revived. However, regardless of these final, important, symbolic changes to Australia's constitutional structure, we should not underestimate the historical and continuing significance of the Statute of Westminster.

[1.4.22] In 1926, a conference of the prime ministers of the United Kingdom, Canada, Australia, New Zealand, Newfoundland and South Africa declared that all of the participants were 'autonomous communities within the British Empire, equal in status, in no way subordinate one to another in any aspect of their domestic or external affairs': Report of Imperial Conference (1926) Cmd 2768. This conference had been called on the request of Canadian Prime Minister Mackenzie King, concerned over what he saw as British interference in a Canadian political crisis, and over the Privy Council's decision in *Nadan v R* [1926] AC 482 which declared invalid Canadian legislation passed almost 40 years earlier to abolish certain appeals to the Privy Council. In 1930, legislation was drafted to express this idea and it was enacted as the Statute of Westminster 1931 (UK).

By s 10(1), the substantive provisions of the statute were not to apply to Australia until adopted by the Commonwealth Parliament. It was not until 1942 that the necessary legislation, the Statute of Westminster Adoption Act 1942 (Cth), was passed, under which the Statute of Westminster was held to have been adopted as from 3 September 1939 (the day on which Australia went to war with Germany as a consequence of the United Kingdom's declaration of war).

[1.4.23] The Statute of Westminster removed several constitutional disabilities under which the Commonwealth Parliament had operated. Section 2 removed the inability of the Commonwealth (because of its former 'colonial' status) to amend or repeal United Kingdom legislation intended to apply to Australia (as exemplified by *Union Steamship Co of New Zealand Ltd v Commonwealth* (1925) 36 CLR 130): see **[6.2.13]**. Section 3 removed the inability to legislate extra-territorially (as exemplified by *Merchant Service Guild of Australasia v Commonwealth Steamship Owners' Association (No 3)* (1920) 28 CLR 495): see **[6.3.36]**. Section 4 terminated the legal power of the United Kingdom to legislate for Australia: see **[6.2.18]**.

The abolition of these disabilities was a belated legal recognition of the political reality of Australia's autonomy and its emergence as a de facto independent member of the international community. For an account of this emergence, see Zines (1977) pp 22–35, 38–43. Some commentators also argue that removal of the Queen as Australia's Head of State will be a belated legal recognition of the political fact of Australia's independence from the Crown: see, for example, Craven (1992).

Australia Acts of 1986

[1.4.24] The Statute of Westminster said nothing about the Australian states, so that, despite the unqualified fact of Australia's political autonomy, state parliaments remained subject to the constitutional disabilities which flowed from their former colonial status. They could not legislate to repeal or amend United Kingdom legislation extending to the states, such as the legislation providing for appeals to the Privy Council, the Judicial Committee Acts of 1833 and 1844 (UK). Australian residents continued to be subject to sometimes obscure provisions of United Kingdom legislation which had long since been repealed in that country: see, for example, *Ukley v Ukley* [1977] VR 121 **[6.2.4]**. Some state legislation was required to be 'reserved' for assent by the Crown, acting on the advice of the United Kingdom: Australian States Constitution Act 1907 (UK) s 1(1). And the conventional judicial view limited state parliaments' capacity to legislate for persons and events outside the state: see, for example, *Welker v Hewett* (1969) 120 CLR 503 **[6.3.8C]**; *Robinson v Western Australian Museum* (1977) 138 CLR 283 **[6.3.15]**. In addition, the United Kingdom, rather than the relevant local state government, was the Crown's source of advice on the appointment of state Governors: see **[7.2.10]**.

[1.4.25] By 1984, the Commonwealth and state governments had agreed that legislation should be enacted to end these relics of the states' colonial past. Following further negotiations with the United Kingdom, a series of Acts was passed by the state, Commonwealth and United Kingdom Parliaments. Each state parliament legislated to request the Commonwealth Parliament to enact the two Acts: see, for example, the Australia Acts (Request) Act 1985 (Vic). The Commonwealth Parliament then passed the two Acts at the end of 1985. The first and substantive Act was entitled the Australia Act 1986 (Cth). The second Act, the Australia (Request and Consent) Act 1985 (Cth), was a legislative request, directed to the United Kingdom

Parliament, designed to remove the technical barrier to United Kingdom legislation operating in Australia as a whole: s 4 of the Statute of Westminster. It requested of the United Kingdom Parliament that it complement the Commonwealth Parliament's Australia Act by enacting a United Kingdom Australia Act. The United Kingdom Parliament responded to that request by passing the Australia Act 1986 (UK).

So, at the end of this series of enactments, there were two substantially identical versions of the Australia Act, each one declared to come into operation on 3 March 1986, one passed by the Commonwealth Parliament under s 51 (xxxviii) of the Commonwealth Constitution, the other passed by the United Kingdom Parliament in the exercise of its surviving imperial authority, invoked by the Commonwealth Parliament's request and consent.

[1.4.26] The Australia Act 1986 marks a complete break between Australian and United Kingdom institutions (unless the Queen of Australia is regarded as a United Kingdom institution). Section 1 terminates the power of the United Kingdom Parliament to legislate for Australia (replacing, for this purpose, s 4 of the Statute of Westminster, which is repealed in its application to Australia by s 12 of the Australia Act). Section 3 gives state parliaments the power to repeal or amend the remnants of United Kingdom legislation extending to the states, other than the Commonwealth of Australia Constitution Act (UK) or the Statute of Westminster (exempted by s 5) or the Australia Act (exempted by s 11). Section 9 terminated the obligation to reserve some state legislation for the Crown's assent. Section 2 gave state parliaments extraterritorial legislative power.

So far as the executive government is concerned, s 10 declared that the United Kingdom 'shall have no responsibility for the government of any State'. The powers of the Crown in relation to a state, apart from the power of appointing and removing a Governor, are exercisable only by the state's Governor, except when the Crown is personally present in the state. The Crown is to act on the advice of the Premier of the state: s 7.

Section 11 of the Australia Act abolishes appeals to the Privy Council from Australian courts, other than the High Court, from which such appeals are effectively impossible, because they now require a certificate from the High Court, a certificate which the court has indicated it will never issue: *Kirmani v Captain Cook Cruises Pty Ltd (No 1)* (1985) 159 CLR 351.

[1.4.27] The Australia Acts are given constitutional status, as well as performing a constitutional function, by s 15, which provides that the Statute of Westminster and the Australia Act are not to be repealed or amended except in accordance with the alteration procedure in s 128 of the Commonwealth Constitution or by legislation passed under s 51(xxxviii) of the Constitution (that is, at the request or with the concurrence of all the state parliaments). The prospect of any parliament seeking deliberately to legislate inconsistently with the Australia Act is more than remote, as Zines points out ((1992) p 264):

> The Act is a statute which liberates the States from their former colonial restrictions and brings to an end United Kingdom legislative and governmental responsibility. It is not in the field of practical politics to suggest that the Commonwealth or the States would attempt to have restored the earlier limitations on power, appeals to the Privy Council or the supremacy of the British Parliament.

The practical point of s 15 is to ensure that, in the case of inadvertent conflict between any of the provisions of the Australia Act and later Australian legislation passed through the normal legislative process, the Australia Act will be seen as of fundamental or 'organic' status and will prevail over that legislation.

[1.4.28] Despite the de facto legal and political independence of the Commonwealth and the states, Australia remains a constitutional monarchy, or, as it is expressed in the preamble to the Constitution, 'an indissoluble federal Commonwealth *under the Crown*'. From the end of the century and the centenary of Australia's federation, the debate as to whether Australia should remain a constitutional monarchy or become a republic has re-emerged.

Republicanism as a theory of political democracy originated in classical times, and was revived in various forms in other political systems: England in the 17th century; France and the United States of America in the 18th century; and several European countries in the 20th century.

The question raises issues of both substance (what to include in a republican constitution, and what kind of republican values are to be adopted) and procedure (how to achieve that goal). On the question of substance, commentators have proposed that Australia should become a republic simply by replacing any references in the Constitution to the Queen with references to a President. This is the so-called 'minimalist' position: Winterton (1995). Others propose more widespread change, perhaps including in the Constitution a Bill of Rights, or a statement regarding Aboriginal and non-Aboriginal reconciliation.

In 1993, the Commonwealth established the Republic Advisory Committee that recommended pursuing the minimalist position.

On the question of procedure, in 1997 the Commonwealth Parliament enacted the Constitutional Convention (Election) Act 1997 (Cth) and announced the establishment of a People's Convention consisting of both nominated and elected (on a non-compulsory vote) delegates. The role of the Convention was to determine whether or not Australia should become a republic.

In February 1988, the Australian Government held a Constitutional Convention that comprised of elected and appointed delegates to resolve the question whether Australia should become a republic. The Convention resolved to support a method of appointment of a new head of state that consisted of formal ratification by two-thirds of the Commonwealth Parliament in conjunction with community consultation. In November 1999, a referendum was held on the question of whether Australia should become a republic with the Queen and Governor-General being replaced by a President appointed by a two-thirds majority of the members of the Commonwealth Parliament. The referendum failed nationally and failed in each state (it passed in the Australian Capital Territory, though not in the Northern Territory): for further analysis, see Galligan, 1999 and Kirby, 2000.

Other legislation

[1.4.29] Several aspects of the structure and process of government are defined by ordinary legislation that carries no special status. Although this legislation cannot be described as 'organic', in that it is liable to be changed by ordinary parliamentary legislation, it is fundamental in the sense that it defines basic elements of the system of Australian government or establishes aspects of their relationships.

[1.4.30] This legislation includes the Commonwealth Electoral Act 1918 (Cth), prescribing qualifications for membership of the Commonwealth Parliament (**[4.4.3]**), voting rights ([**4.5.2**]) and the system for distributing electorates: see [**4.6.3**]–[**4.6.5**]. The equivalent state provisions appear in state Constitution Acts and other legislation, such as the Parliamentary Electorates and Elections Act 1912 (NSW), the Electoral Act 1992 (Qld), the Constitution Act Amendment Act 1958 (Vic) and the Electoral Boundaries Commission Act 1982 (Vic): see [**4.4.5**], [**4.5.3**], [**4.6.6**].

[**1.4.31**] Aspects of federalism are structured by s 64 of the Judiciary Act 1903 (Cth), which effectively removes the Commonwealth Government's assumed immunity from state legislation (*Maguire v Simpson* (1977) 139 CLR 362 [**8.2.107**]; *Commonwealth v Evans Deakin Industries Ltd* (1986) 166 CLR 254 [**8.2.108**]; *Re Residential Tenancies Tribunal of New South Wales; Ex parte Defence Housing Authority* (1997) 190 CLR 410 [**8.2.112C**]) and by the Commonwealth Places (Application of Laws) Act 1970 (Cth) (which adopts state legislation as the applicable law for places owned by the Commonwealth, where otherwise state laws could not run): see [**8.2.120**].

Prerogative instruments

[**1.4.32**] Australia's recent political history (that is, its last 200-odd years of political history) has been that of transition from imperial British colony through self-governing British dependency to independent autonomy. Aspects of Australia's colonial past are still reflected in such prerogative instruments as the Letters Patent Relating to the Office of Governor of Victoria [**7.2.5E**], and the Letters Patent Relating to the Office of Governor-General of the Commonwealth of Australia.

[**1.4.33**] These instruments deal with procedural formalities. Unlike the previous instruments, which they replaced in 1986 and 1984 respectively, they do not purport to confer any legal powers or authorities on the local vice-regal representatives: see [**7.3.2E**] (Victorian Letters Patent), [**7.2.19**] (Commonwealth Letters Patent). The deletion of those matters of substance from the current Letters Patent reflects the now widely accepted view that Australian institutions of government, including the local representatives of the Crown, are autonomous and self-sufficient. The Letters Patent do no more than illustrate the point that, legally, state Governors and the Governor-General are representatives of the monarch, a position which would alter if Australia were to become a republic.

Constitutional conventions

[**1.4.34**] Important aspects of the Australian system of government are not stated in formal written rules. In particular, the relationship between the legal head of each executive government (state and Commonwealth) and the political head of that government is only alluded to in the formal rules, as in ss 62, 63 and 64 of the Commonwealth Constitution. That relationship, which is commonly labelled as 'responsible government', depends for its definition on constitutional conventions, rules which are not enforced by the courts but which depend on a variety of political and financial considerations for their legitimacy and authority. For a discussion of the impact of constitutional conventions, see Jennings (1972).

[**1.4.35**] The most basic of these conventional rules is that a state Governor, or the Commonwealth Governor-General, will exercise the significant legal powers vested in that office on the advice of the parliamentary leader of the political party which controls the lower House of Parliament (or, in the case of Queensland, the only House of Parliament). So, when making appointments to public offices or dissolving parliament, the Governor acts in accordance with the advice given by the Premier, and the Governor-General acts in accordance with the advice given by the Prime Minister. The political leaders are thus 'responsible' for the acts formally taken by the Governor or Governor-General.

This convention depends for its strength on the fact that the business of government cannot be carried on without access to finance, access which is legally controlled by parliament (taxes cannot be imposed, and government funds cannot be spent, without express parliamentary authorisation). In dealing with financial legislation, the lower house is dominant: see **[5.2.5]**, **[5.2.10]**. The party which politically controls the lower house will control the government's access to essential finance, hence, the leader of that party can control the exercise of the government's legal powers.

[1.4.36]   A second convention, which is the corollary of the first, is that the political situation in the lower House of Parliament determines the choice of the leader of the government (state Premier or Prime Minister) and the composition of the ministry. Although the Governor-General, for example, is given the power to appoint ministers to administer the 'Departments of State' by s 64 of the Commonwealth Constitution, it has never been supposed that this choice was in any sense free. Similarly, it has always been accepted that the right of the current ministry to control the exercise of the Governor's or Governor-General's powers would evaporate as soon as that ministry lost the support of the lower House of Parliament: see **[7.3.6]**.

[1.4.37]   These propositions about the links between the formal head of government, the political head of government and parliament depend for their enforcement on political and financial sanctions. They are not enforced by the courts, except indirectly through the courts' insistence that taxation revenues cannot be collected and government funds cannot be expended without parliamentary authorisation: *Commonwealth v Colonial Combing, Spinning and Weaving Co Ltd* (1922) 31 CLR 421; *Commonwealth v Burns* [1971] VR 825. However, the proposition that state Governors and the Governor-General act on ministerial advice has been recognised and endorsed in many judicial decisions. The nature and justification of constitutional conventions is explored in **[7.3.7]**, **[7.3.13]**, **[7.4.2]**, **[7.4.24]**. Becoming a republic raises important questions about the status and location of constitutional conventions:

■ Should the same convention continue to apply as between an Australian Head of State and the leader of the lower House of Parliament?

■ Should this and other conventions be codified?

■ Should they be enacted into legislation; or should they be inserted into the Constitution?

Judicial decisions

[1.4.38]   In recent years an increasing awareness of similarities between the constitutional systems of Australia and Canada, Europe or the United States, has led to a corresponding increase in the use of comparative jurisprudence in the development of Australian doctrine, although this influence is mitigated by judicial awareness of relevant difference as well. For example, compare the influence of *New York Times Co v Sullivan* 376 US 254 (1964) on *Theophanous v Herald & Weekly Times Ltd* (1994) 182 CLR 104, with the rejection of the European principle of proportionality in *Leask v Commonwealth* (1996) 187 CLR 579 at 600–1 per Dawson J. For a further discussion of the influence of international law and comparative law upon Australian constitutional law, see Chapter 3.

[1.4.39] The most fertile source of constitutional law in Australia lies in the work of the High Court of Australia. From its establishment in 1903, the assumption has been that this court is the interpreter of the Commonwealth Constitution and the arbiter of the constitutional validity of state and Commonwealth legislation and executive action. There is no specific reference to this adjudicative role in the Constitution. However, such a role was foreshadowed by colonial history, where local courts and the Privy Council ruled on the validity of colonial legislation, and by the United States model, where the Supreme Court had first asserted that it could determine the validity of governmental action in *Marbury v Madison* 1 Cranch 137; 5 US 137 (1803). The drafters of the Constitution were well aware that the judges would play a central and creative role. In 1898, Isaac Isaacs told his fellow delegates to the Sydney Constitutional Convention:

> We are taking infinite trouble to express what we mean in this Constitution; but as in America so it will be here, that the makers of the Constitution were not merely the Conventions who sat, but the judges of the Supreme Court (Convention Debates (1898) p 283).

That attitude should be compared to the orthodox view in the United Kingdom, where the judiciary do not decide on the constitutional validity of government action. That role is now being undertaken for the United Kingdom by the European Court of Justice. For a discussion of the role of the European Court and comparisons with Australia, see Bronitt, Burns and Kinley (1995).

[1.4.40] The role which the members of the High Court have played in developing Australian constitutional law has been described as essential to its survival. In the face of the conservatism of the formal alteration process (see **[1.2.12]**) it has been judicial interpretation and re-interpretation which has managed to keep the structure of government, as expressed in the Constitution, in touch with the demands of a changing society and developing economy.

[1.4.41] The political role of the High Court is plain. If the Commonwealth Constitution defines the distribution of political power within Australia, by establishing spheres of activity for the central and regional governments and asserting a balance between public and private interests, then the process of attributing a functional meaning to that distribution and enforcing that distribution in particular cases will have a distinctly political significance. Brian Galligan makes this (probably uncontroversial) point in his stimulating study of the High Court:

> In its adjudicative role, the court is involved in resolving high-level disputes that are thrown up by the on-going business of federal government ... By interpreting the constitution which sets up the machinery of government and controls the political process, the Court is itself, to a significant extent, shaping the political system and process ((1987) pp 2–3).

[1.4.42] That the High Court's role is political, a claim first associated with the realist approach to law (see Llewellyn (1931)) and later revived by critical legal studies (Kairys (1982)), was conceded by Dixon J in *Melbourne Corporation v Commonwealth* (the *State Banking* case) (1947) 74 CLR 31 **[8.2.45C]**. However, he resisted the claim that the court decided constitutional issues according to political considerations. Dixon J considered that 'political rather than legal considerations' established the inability of the Commonwealth to destroy the independence of the states (at 82):

> The Constitution is a political instrument. It deals with government and governmental powers. The statement is, therefore, easy to make though it has a specious plausibility. But it is really meaningless. It is not a question whether the considerations are political, for nearly every consideration arising from the Constitution can be so described, but whether they are compelling.

As Leslie Zines points out, Dixon's final proposition, about 'compelling' considerations, added little to the debate: Zines (1992) p 345.

[1.4.43] Dixon J's assertion was supported by former Prime Minister Robert Menzies in 1967, when he said that the constitutional judgments of the High Court of Australia lacked the 'political flavour' which characterised the work of the United States Supreme Court: Menzies (1967) p 55. The High Court had developed, he said, 'politically neutral conceptions of constitutional law': Menzies (1967) p 30. Making the same plea for value-free adjudication, Sir Owen Dixon, on the occasion of his assuming the office of Chief Justice of the High Court, referred to 'close adherence to legal reasoning [as] the only way to maintain the confidence of all parties in Federal conflicts', and insisted that there was 'no other safe guide to judicial decisions in great conflicts than a strict and complete legalism': 85 CLR at xiii.

[1.4.44] In his review of the High Court's constitutional work, Brian Galligan argues that this claimed technique of value-free legalism is a mask for an intensely political process. After noting that the Australian political climate is inherently hostile to active judicial review because of the value of parliamentary supremacy inherited from British political tradition and the polarisation of Australian politics between labour and capital, Galligan points to the dominant liberal consensus of American political culture, which supports the policy-oriented approach of the United States Supreme Court. He then argued ((1987) p 39):

> In the more difficult environment of Australian politics, legalism has been championed by the Court because it is an effective political strategy for exercising judicial review. By actively cultivating an impartial image and professing an apolitical method, the High Court has been able to carry out its delicate political function with ease.

[1.4.45] Just as the observations of Sir Owen Dixon noted above (**[1.4.42]**, **[1.4.43]**) do not do complete justice to the reasoning of the High Court over the past 90-odd years, Galligan's thesis has been criticised for adopting Dixon's label, 'legalism', to describe the High Court's preferred technique, and for failing adequately to acknowledge the complexities of constitutional adjudication. Jeffrey Goldsworthy argues for a distinction between 'literalism' and 'interpretivism' in the approach to constitutional problems, and criticises much of Galligan's analysis of individual High Court decisions: Goldsworthy (1989) (for Galligan's response to these criticisms, see Galligan (1989)).

The complexity of the judicial task is explored by Zines: (1997) pp 483–4. Zines also expresses a more complicated view of the techniques used by the High Court (p 433):

> [I]t seems that many judges who emphasise the importance of legalism do not regard that method of approach as denying resort to broad social and political values they perceive

in the Constitution. On many occasions they consider the practical consequences of a law in determining validity and, at any rate sometimes, concern themselves with what they regard as the purpose of the particular constitutional provision.

The purpose-oriented approach is illustrated by the landmark decisions in *Cole v Whitfield* (1988) 165 CLR 360 **[10.4.27C]** (where the seven members of the court managed to agree on the purpose of s 92's guarantee of the 'absolute freedom' of interstate trade), *Street v Queensland Bar Association* (1989) 168 CLR 461 **[11.2.61C]** (where the court emphasised the national purpose of s 117's prohibition of discrimination against residents of other states), and *Australian Capital Television Pty Ltd v Commonwealth* (1992) 177 CLR 106 **[11.3.7C]** (where a majority of the court held that the Commonwealth Constitution contained an implied guarantee of freedom of communication). The tensions inherent in such an approach are illustrated by the judgments of Gibbs CJ and Mason J in *Hematite Petroleum Pty Ltd v Victoria* (1983) 151 CLR 599 **[9.4.37C]**, where the court split on the purpose of s 90's exclusive grant to the Commonwealth of authority over 'excise duties'.

[1.4.46] Our view is that the function of assigning a meaning to the text of the Commonwealth Constitution and using that meaning to resolve disputes about the legitimacy of governmental action cannot be value-free. This point has been argued strongly by Stephen Gageler. '[L]egalism', he wrote, 'is incapable of fulfilling its own agenda', because 'a neutrally based *a priori* approach to constitutional line drawing is in its own terms impossible', and because the High Court's 'choice between any number of reasonable alternative positions assumes an air of arbitrariness': Gageler (1987) p 178.

[1.4.47] The words used in s 92, for example, have no inevitable, single or natural meaning. They will take their meaning from a wide variety of contexts: history, economics, political theory and, perhaps, the dictionary. The choice between competing meanings will be made by the interpreters (the justices of the High Court) and their sensitivity to history or to contemporary economic ideas will profoundly influence the meaning attributed to the words of the section.

The meaning attributed to s 92 has shifted several times over the past eight decades: from the anti-protectionist reading given in *Fox v Robbins* (1909) 8 CLR 115 **[10.4.8]**, through the laissez faire reading endorsed in *Commonwealth v Bank of New South Wales* (1949) 79 CLR 497 **[10.4.10C]**, to the return of the anti-protectionist reading in *Cole v Whitfield* (1988) 165 CLR 360 **[10.4.27C]**. Further, the judicial resort to political and economic considerations to support a particular reading has been overt. To take a few examples from relatively recent decisions: Barwick CJ referred to '[t]he protection of the individual' as central to s 92: *North Eastern Dairy Co Ltd v Dairy Industry Authority of New South Wales* (1975) 134 CLR 559 **[10.4.23]** at 582; Gibbs and Wilson JJ in *Uebergang v Australian Wheat Board* (1980) 145 CLR 266 **[10.4.25]** at 300 claimed that the section required the court 'to preserve a balance between competing interests, a balance which favours freedom for the individual citizen in the absence of compelling considerations to the contrary'; whilst Mason J in *North Eastern Dairy Co Ltd v Dairy Industry Authority of New South Wales* (1975) 134 CLR 559 **[10.4.23]** at 615 referred to the 'predominant public character' of the section and declared that its meaning was not 'to be ascertained by reference to the doctrines of political economy which prevailed in 1900'.

[1.4.48] To take another example, s 7 and s 122 of the Commonwealth Constitution appear to express contradictory propositions. The former strongly implies that the Senate is the political institution which represents the interests of the states, while the latter permits Commonwealth territories to be represented in the Senate. How can that textual conflict be resolved without resort to some basic values or presuppositions about the character of the institutions of government created by the Constitution? In *Western Australia v Commonwealth* (the *Territorial Senators* case) (1975) 134 CLR 201 **[4.2.32C]**, the High Court was obliged to resort to those values to determine the validity of Commonwealth legislation providing for the representation of the Northern Territory and the Australian Capital Territory in the Senate. Four members of the court saw democratic values as dominant, while the minority justices preferred federal (states' rights) values. For a valuable analysis of this decision, see Zines (1997) pp 467–9.

[1.4.49] The role which broad political considerations play in the constitutional work of the High Court is further developed in Hanks (1987). To return to the point that we made in **[1.4.41]** and **[1.4.44]**, we believe that these considerations are inescapable. The reading of the constitutional text must reflect judicial choices about the way in which public authority should be organised and contained, because there is no other useful guide to those choices. For a discussion of the relationship between judicial choice and democracy, in the context of implied rights, see Winterton, and Patapan and Wood in Sampford and Preston (1996). To deny the existence of these political values, to assert that constitutional decisions are dictated by the text of the Constitution (to insist on 'strict and complete legalism', as Dixon J claimed to in **[1.4.43]**) is to shield those values from the scrutiny and criticism which is crucial to the legitimacy of the High Court's constitutional function. The comments of a former Chief Justice of Australia, Sir Anthony Mason, are directly on point ((1986) p 5):

> When judges fail to discuss the underlying values influencing a judgment, it is difficult to debate the appropriateness of those values. As judges who are unaware of the original underlying values, subsequently apply that precedent in accordance with the doctrine of *stare decisis*, those hidden values are reproduced in the new judgment — even though community values may have changed.

5   Characterisation: a summary

What is characterisation?

[1.5.1] The major function of the High Court in interpreting the Constitution is to decide whether a particular law is within Commonwealth power. This process is known as 'characterisation'. Characterisation relies on a number of principles which are summarised here. However, this summary is no more than a 'snapshot' of a much larger picture, the contours of which can only be fully understood by a comprehensive reading of the materials in this book. Moreover, like all processes of interpretation, characterisation is not an exact science, and therefore the principles summarised below should be seen as general guidelines, not rigid prescriptions.

'With respect to'

[1.5.2] The main heads of Commonwealth legislative power are contained in s 51. The section begins with the words '[t]he Parliament shall ... have power to make laws ... with respect to ...' and continues to list specific topics such as trade and commerce, banking, defence, marriage and external affairs.

The characterisation process begins by asking whether the law is one which can be described as a law 'with respect to' a topic enumerated in s 51. As Leslie Zines states, 'logically', this involves answering two basic questions (Zines (1997) p 17):

- What is the scope or definition of the subject matter of the head of power?

- Is the law one which can be described as a law on that particular subject matter so defined?

[1.5.3] Three preliminary points should be made. First, the heads of power in s 51 are sometimes divided into two categories: purposive powers and non-purposive (or subject matter) powers. Purposive powers are those dealing with purposes such as defence. Non-purposive or subject matter powers deal with subject matter in the form of particular activities, persons or things, such as trade and commerce, banking, insurance, corporations or aliens. The importance of this distinction is that some aspects of the principles of characterisation (such as the role played by the 'purpose' of the law) may vary according to the category into which the power falls.

The second preliminary point is that, in relation to subject matter heads of power, a distinction is sometimes drawn between laws which fall within the 'core', 'central area' or 'heart' of the power, and those which fall within its 'incidental' or 'peripheral' range. For example, a law placing conditions on the import or export of goods is a law within the core of the international trade and commerce power (*Murphyores Inc Pty Ltd v Commonwealth* (1976) 136 CLR 1 **[10.2.33C]** at 19–20 per Mason J) whereas a law regulating production for export is within the incidental range of that power. Again the principles of characterisation vary in their application according to these distinctions.

The third preliminary point is that characterisation and interpretive method are closely linked, and we shall see, therefore suffer from similar inconsistencies. See the discussion above at **[1.2.14]–[1.2.18]**.

General principles of characterisation

Plenary Commonwealth legislative power

[1.5.4] A general principle of interpretation and of characterisation is that Commonwealth legislative power is to be interpreted broadly. In *Jumbunna Coal Mine NL v Victorian Coal Miners' Association* (1908) 6 CLR 309, O'Connor J said that in construing Commonwealth power it must be remembered that 'we are interpreting a Constitution broad and general in its terms, intended to apply to ... varying conditions': 6 CLR at 367–8, These words were later invoked by Dixon J in *Australian National Airways Pty Ltd v Commonwealth* (1945) 71 CLR 29 at 81:

> It is a Constitution we are interpreting, an instrument of government meant to endure and conferring powers expressed in general propositions wide enough to be capable of flexible application to changing circumstances.

As well as expressing a preference for a broad reading of Commonwealth legislative power, this approach reflects a dynamic or progressive method of interpretation, as noted above at **[1.2.14]**. The principle that Commonwealth legislative power should be interpreted broadly was adopted and affirmed by Dixon J in *Bank of New South Wales v Commonwealth* (the *Bank Nationalisation* case) (1948) 76 CLR 1 at 334, when he said the word 'banking' in s 51(xiii) should have ascribed to it 'the wide meaning and flexible application of a general expression designating, as a subject of legislative power, a matter forming part of the commercial, economic and social organisation of the community'. This process of characterisation, in which a power is given a broad general meaning, is often said to recognise that the power is *plenary* in nature.

Context and text

[1.5.5]   Operating in tandem with the plenary principle is the principle of contextual interpretation. In *Jumbunna Coal Mine NL v Victorian Coal Miners' Association* (1908) 6 CLR 309, O'Connor J qualified the broad principle with a textual note that 'the Court should ... always lean to the broader *interpretation unless there is something in the context or in the rest of the Constitution* to indicate that the narrower interpretation will best carry out its object and purpose': 6 CLR at 368 (emphasis added). While *Jumbunna* is often cited as authority for the proposition that Commonwealth legislative power should be interpreted broadly, it also suggests that there are limits on that breadth derived from the text of the Constitution and from its surrounding context. (The importance of context in ordinary statutory interpretation is discussed in *CIC Insurance Ltd v Bankstown Football Club Ltd* (1997) 187 CLR 384 at 408.)

Implications

[1.5.6]   A related principle is that, as the Constitution is to be interpreted in a broad and flexible manner, its interpretation should include making necessary implications where they are suggested by either the text or the structure of the Constitution: *Lange v Australian Broadcasting Corporation* (1997) 189 CLR 520 **[11.3.13C]**. This is the approach adopted by Dixon J in *Australian National Airways Pty Ltd v Commonwealth* (1945) 71 CLR 29 at 85, where he said:

> We should avoid pedantic and narrow constructions in dealing with an instrument of government and I do not see why we should be fearful about making implications.

In that case, the implication made was one which enabled Commonwealth legislative power in relation to the territories to be interpreted so that the Commonwealth could legislate for communications with its territories. Other examples of the implications principle include the implication drawn from federalism that the Commonwealth cannot legislate so as to discriminate against the states or burden their capacity to function (*Melbourne Corporation v Commonwealth* (1947) 74 CLR 31) and the implication of freedom of political communication drawn from the structure of representative government created by the Constitution: *Australian Capital Television Pty Ltd v Commonwealth* (1992) 177 CLR 106.

Plain and natural meaning

[1.5.7] The implications principle enunciated by Dixon J in *Australian National Airways Pty Ltd v Commonwealth* (1945) 71 CLR 29 **[1.5.6]** runs up against another of the major principles of characterisation, the principle from the *Engineers'* case (1920) 28 CLR 129 **[8.2.31C]**, which, until recent times, was regarded as expressing the fundamental principles of interpretation in Australian constitutional law. *Engineers'* rejected the method of characterisation used in the first 20 years of federation, a method which had constructed constitutional implications in order to protect state legislative power.

These implications were known as the 'reserved powers' doctrine, according to which certain powers were impliedly reserved to the states (*R v Barger* (1908) 6 CLR 41) **[9.2.15C]** and the 'implied immunities' doctrine, according to which the states were immune from Commonwealth legislative power: *Federated Amalgamated Government Railway and Tramway Service Association v New South Wales Railway Traffic Employees Association* (the *Railway Servants'* case) (1906) 4 CLR 488. *Engineers'* exploded both of these doctrines and stated that each Commonwealth legislative power ought to be characterised according to its plain and natural meaning, without resort to any implications.

[1.5.8] The *Engineers'* case also illustrates the way in which characterisation principles are linked to interpretive method. In finding these new principles of characterisation, three underlying features of interpretive method were emphasised in *Engineers'*. First, the majority relied on the text (in order to ascertain intention):

> It is ... the manifest duty of this Court to turn its earnest attention to the provisions of the Constitution itself. ... [I]t is the ... special duty of this Court faithfully to expound and give effect to it according to its own terms, finding the intention from the words of the compact and upholding it throughout precisely as framed (28 CLR at 141).

Second, the majority rejected the use of 'necessity' as a basis for implications in constitutional interpretation because that would involve an assessment of what the joint judgment (Knox CJ, Isaacs, Rich, and Starke JJ) refers to as 'political sense' of what was 'necessary' (28 CLR at 151) or 'personal opinion' of judges (28 CLR at 141) or 'fact' rather than on 'law or constitutional practice': 28 CLR at 145. So the principle of necessary implications was 'indefensible' as a means of interpretation: 28 CLR at 152.

The third interpretive technique was a strict deference to parliament by the judiciary based upon the proposition of parliamentary supremacy (28 CLR at 151):

> The extravagant use of the granted powers in the actual working of the Constitution is a matter to be guarded against by the constituencies and not by the courts.

Hence, the characterisation process in *Engineers* exhibits features associated with textualism, legalism and a strict separation of law and politics.

This does not mean that implications may never be made, however. As Dixon J noted in *West v Commissioner of Taxation* (1937) 56 CLR 657 at 681–2:

> Since the *Engineer's* case a notion seems to have gained currency that in interpreting the Constitution no implications can be made. Such a method of construction would defeat the intention of any instrument, but of all instruments a written constitution seems the last to which it could be applied. I do not think that the judgment of the majority of the court in the *Engineer's* case meant to propound such a doctrine.

Implied limits and heads of power

[1.5.9]   As well as containing heads or sources of power for the Commonwealth, the Constitution contains limits on power, whether express or implied. These are variously referred to as limits, restrictions, prohibitions, immunities or guarantees. A further issue then concerns the order in which the process of characterisation should occur when it involves balancing the scope of the head of power against an implied limitation on that head of power. Since *Re Australian Education Union; Ex parte Victoria* (1995) 184 CLR 188, it is clear that interpretation of the head of power and interpretation of the effect of the implied limit upon the head of power must occur simultaneously as part of the same process, rather than sequentially. In that case, the majority (Mason CJ, Brennan, Deane, Toohey, Gaudron and McHugh JJ) adopted Brennan J's proposition in *Re State Public Services Federation; Ex parte Attorney-General (WA)* (the *SPSF* case) (1993) 178 CLR 249 at 275, where he said that 'construction of a head of legislative power is itself ascertained by reference to the entire context of the Constitution and that its scope may be limited by implication'.

Specific principles of characterisation

[1.5.10]   In addition to the general principles just mentioned, characterisation raises a number of more specific principles.

Sufficient connection

[1.5.11]   In order for a law to be characterised as a law on a subject or power, there must be 'a relevance to or connection with the subject assigned to the Commonwealth Parliament' (*Grannall v Marrickville Margarine Pty Ltd* (1955) 93 CLR 55 at 77) or, as the current test states, a 'sufficient connection' between the law and the power: in *Re Dingjan; Ex parte Wagner* (1995) 183 CLR 323 at 353 per Toohey J; *Cunliffe v Commonwealth* (1994) 182 CLR 272 at 314 per Brennan J; *In Re The Maritime Union of Australia; Ex parte CSL Pacific Shipping Inc* (2003) 200 ALR 39 at [35] per Gleeson CJ, McHugh, Gummow, Hayne, Kirby, Callinan and Heydon JJ. The sufficiency of the connection will be assessed by looking at the operation or effect of the law and the subject matter of the power: *Bank of New South Wales v Commonwealth* (1948) 76 CLR 1 at 187. It is the law's 'actual operation' or 'direct legal operation' in 'creating changing, regulating or abolishing rights, duties, powers or privileges' which establishes that the law is within power (*Bank of New South Wales v Commonwealth* (1948) 76 CLR 1 at 187 per Dixon J), although Zines notes that the practical effect of the law is often referred to as well: Zines (1997) p 26.

Denotation and connotation

[1.5.12]   In order to decide whether a law has an operation or effect upon a listed subject matter it will, of course, be necessary to define the meaning of the subject matter: see [1.5.2], [1.5.3]. This will not always be easy, particularly as s 51 was drafted almost a century ago. One principle of characterisation which allows the court to resolve the gap between the meaning as it stood in 1901 and the meaning as it might be interpreted today is the notion of denotation and connotation. According to this somewhat idiosyncratic notion, the connotation of a term is its essential character in 1900, which does not change over time, and its denotation is anything which exhibits these characteristics. So over time, although the connotation remains the same, the denotation can extend to include things which were unforeseen at the time, but which nevertheless exhibit the same essential features. The classic example often made is that the connotation (or essential nature) of the word 'vehicle' at the turn of the century was that it was a conveyance, and it therefore denoted wagons, carriages, bicycles and trains. However, at a later point in time, aircraft fall within the denotation of 'vehicle' because they exhibit the essential characteristic of 'vehicle', namely they are also a conveyance.

Two cases are ordinarily referred to as illustrations of the distinction. In *R v Brislan; Ex parte Williams* (1935) 54 CLR 262, three members of the majority (Rich, Starke and Evatt JJ) said the connotation of 'postal, telegraphic, telephonic and other like services' in s 51(v) was that they were all methods of communication, and thus the denotation could extend to include radio, a means of communication not known in 1901. By contrast, in *Attorney-General (NSW) v Brewery Employees Union of New South Wales* (the *Union Label* case) (1908) 6 CLR 469, a majority said that the connotation of 'trade marks' in s 51(xviii) was that a business connection existed between the product and the manufacturer, and hence a trade mark indicating the use of union labour in production of the goods was not within the denotation of the term.

Regulate, prohibit absolutely or conditionally, participate, protect

[1.5.13] Once a law is characterised as a law with respect to a particular subject matter in s 51, the Commonwealth has a number of regulatory options open to it. It may prohibit the activity altogether or it may place conditions upon it. In *Murphyores Inc Pty Ltd v Commonwealth* (1976) 136 CLR 1 **[10.2.33C]**, the court held that if the Commonwealth had the power under the interstate trade and commerce power (s 51(i)) to prohibit the export of minerals absolutely, then the Commonwealth could prohibit their export conditionally by requiring the consent of the relevant Minister prior to export.

When a law has an operation or effect upon a matter within power, the Commonwealth also may participate in the activity. In *Australian National Airways Pty Ltd v Commonwealth* (1945) 71 CLR 29 **[10.2.5]**, the court held that it was permissible under the interstate trade and commerce power (s 51(i)) for the Commonwealth to engage in interstate trade and commerce by operating an interstate airline.

Finally, characterisation of a law within power allows the Commonwealth to protect persons or things who are the subject of the power by regulating the actions of third parties where the actions of the latter may harm those subjects of the power. In *Actors And Announcers Equity Association of Australia v Fontana Films Pty Ltd* (1982) 150 CLR 169 **[10.3.18C]**, the court said it was within the corporations power (s 51(xx)) for the Commonwealth to ban secondary boycotts of corporations by unions because that union activity could cause harm to the corporation.

Dual (or multiple) characterisation

[1.5.14] A law may be characterised as one with respect to a particular subject matter notwithstanding that it is also a law with respect to another head of power, or a law on a subject not within Commonwealth power: *Actors And Announcers Equity Association of Australia v Fontana Films Pty Ltd* (1982) 150 CLR 169 **[10.3.18C]** at 191, 192 per Stephen J. This is known as the principle of dual characterisation.

The principle is illustrated by the decision in *Murphyores Inc Pty Ltd v Commonwealth* (1976) 136 CLR 1 **[10.2.33C]**, in which a customs regulation which required a mining company to obtain the consent of the Minister for the Environment before a mineral could be exported from an environmentally sensitive area was recognised as a law with an environmental goal, but was nevertheless also a law dealing with export and was therefore a law with respect to trade and commerce with other countries within s 51(i). Mason J said that it is 'no objection to the validity of a law otherwise in power that it touches or affects a topic on which the Commonwealth has no power to legislate': 136 CLR at 22.

Relationship between Commonwealth powers

[1.5.15]   Generally, the interpretation of one head of power so as to exclude certain matters does not exclude those same matters from coming within another head of power. For example, although the Commonwealth cannot (subject to the principle of implied incidental power) use the interstate trade and commerce power (s 51(i)) to legislate with respect to intrastate trade and commerce, it may reach matters of intrastate trade by relying on another head of power, such as the corporations power (s 51(xx)): *Strickland v Rocla Concrete Pipes Ltd* (1971) 124 CLR 468.

However, there is an exception to this principle which arises when one head of power *expressly* excludes from its range certain matters, and those matters could nevertheless fall within another head of power. For example, the terms of the banking power in s 51(xiii) expressly exclude the intrastate activities of state banks, so that the Commonwealth cannot avoid this restriction by regulating state banks using the corporations power in s 51(xx): *Bank of New South Wales v Commonwealth* (1948) 76 CLR 1.

Core and incidental range of each power

[1.5.16]   Each head of power includes the power to authorise acts, matters or things which are reasonably necessary to effectuate the purpose of the power: *Grannall v Marrickville Margarine Pty Ltd* (1955) 93 CLR 55 **[10.2.8]**; *Burton v Honan* (1952) 86 CLR 167. The source of this incidental power is either express, being derived from s 51(xxxix), or implied. (Zines notes that, although the language specifies necessity, in fact the principle includes anything that is 'appropriate' to fulfil the object of the power: Zines (1997) p 39.) This is the doctrine of implied incidental power. So, for example, even though ordinarily production is not within the trade and commerce power, it may be that, in certain circumstances where it is necessary for the Commonwealth to effectuate the purpose of trade and commerce, it could regulate production: *Grannall v Marrickville Margarine Pty Ltd* (1955) 93 CLR 55.

Although the court has recognised that each power consists notionally of two elements, it is important to recognise that the core and the incidental range of the power are both parts of the same unified power: *Cunliffe v Commonwealth* (1994) 182 CLR 272 at 318 per Brennan J. This qualification is important when considering the role of 'purpose' in characterising a law.

Relevance of purpose

[1.5.17]   What is the role of 'purpose' in the characterisation process? Can the court have regard to the purpose of the law in deciding whether or not the law is on a subject matter within Commonwealth legislative power? The relevance of purpose varies according to whether the power is purposive or non-purposive; and in the case of non-purposive powers, whether the law is within the core or the incidental range of the power. In addition, where purpose is relevant, a further principle of proportionality may also have a role to play.

Dual characterisation and purpose

[1.5.18]   As noted in relation to dual characterisation **[1.5.14]**, if the law falls within the core area of the power, the purpose of the law, even if it is beyond power, will not invalidate the law. Mason J said in *Murphyores Inc Pty Ltd v Commonwealth* (1976) 136 CLR 1 at 19 **[10.2.33C]** that a law dealing with import and export was a matter clearly within the subject matter of trade and commerce and it was not to the point to say that it also dealt with extraneous matters such as the environment. He continued, noting that it was 'far too late in the day to say that a law should be characterised by reference to the motives which inspire it': 136 CLR at 20. The result of this approach is that the Commonwealth may use a power such as international or interstate trade and commerce to indirectly control other matters, such as the environment.

The court's reluctance to look at motive stems, in part, from the view that purpose or motive is a political consideration, which is in a separate sphere from law: see **[1.2.12]**, **[1.2.14]–[1.2.18]**, **[1.3.1]–[1.3.16]** above. In *Australian National Airways Pty Ltd v Commonwealth* (1945) 71 CLR 29 at 70, Rich J commented that 'this Court is not in the smallest degree concerned to consider whether ... a project is politically, economically, or socially desirable or undesirable'. Compare this with decisions on s 90 in which two justices explicitly referred to the need to maintain a particular view of the section because of the reliance of states upon the financial arrangements which that interpretation had encouraged: *Philip Morris Ltd v Commissioner of Business Franchises (Vic)* (1989) 167 CLR 399 **[9.4.47]** at 438 per Mason CJ and Deane J. Although the justices would have denied they were making a decision based, in part, upon political factors, it is clear that those factors exerted some influence on the decision.

The same could be said of the court's current commitment to the 'practical effect' or 'substance' rather than 'form' in characterising legislation: *Hematite Petroleum Pty Ltd v Victoria* (1983) 151 CLR 599 **[9.4.37C]**; *Cole v Whitfield* (1988) 165 CLR 360 **[10.4.27C]**. In a carefully crafted assessment, Booker, Glass and Watt argue that the High Court's form of legalism 'is a legalism which takes some account of policy considerations': Booker, Glass and Watt (1994) p 58; see also Zines (1996).

Non-purposive or subject matter powers

[1.5.19]   When the validity of law depends upon it falling within the incidental range of a non-purposive or subject matter power, then the closer one moves to the periphery of the power, the more relevant the purpose of the law becomes in determining whether or not the law has an operation or effect upon a matter within power: *Cunliffe v Commonwealth* (1994) 182 CLR 272 at 319 per Brennan J.

For example, slaughtering is production and therefore antecedent to trade and commerce. It follows that the licensing of slaughtering works will not ordinarily be a matter within the Commonwealth's power over trade and commerce with other countries: s 51(i). However, in *O'Sullivan v Noarlunga Meat Ltd* (1954) 92 CLR 565 **[10.2.11C]**, the purpose of the law was found to be to facilitate the export of the meat. The purpose of the law thus had the potential to affect, beneficially or adversely, export, a matter squarely within the definition of trade and commerce. A licensing system to establish sanitary conditions to enable meat to be exported was a law within the incidental range of the trade and commerce power, and thus the regulation was necessary for the Commonwealth to effectuate a purpose within power, namely the safe export of meat.

Similarly, in order for the Commonwealth to regulate interstate airline services under the interstate trade and commerce power (s 51(i)) it could, using the incidental range of the power, do everything reasonably necessary to fulfil the object of the power. It could, for example, regulate intrastate airlines services, at least where the Commonwealth's purpose was to regulate matters necessary to make effectual interstate trade and commerce, by promoting airline safety, efficiency and regularity: *Airlines of New South Wales Pty Ltd v New South Wales (No 2)* (1965) 113 CLR 54 **[10.2.20C]**.

By contrast, the court has said that other matters, economic in nature, such as efficiency and profitability of interstate services, cannot be regulated on the basis that they are necessary to make effectual the Commonwealth's power over trade and commerce: *Attorney-General (WA); Ex rel Ansett Transport v Australian National Airlines Commission* (1976) 138 CLR 492 **[10.2.26C]**. These matters were not within the incidental range of the power.

[1.5.20] Although purpose may be relevant when deciding whether a law comes within the incidental range of power, it is important to note that the overriding test is that of sufficiency of connection: *Leask v Commonwealth* (1996) 187 CLR 579 at 600–2 per Dawson J. Purpose is important only because purpose may help establish the connection between the operation or effect of the law and the power: *Leask v Commonwealth* (1996) 187 CLR 579 at 591 per Brennan CJ.

Purposive powers and 'purpose'

[1.5.21] Clearly the purpose of a law will be relevant in the characterisation of a law within a purposive power. In order for a law to be 'with respect to' the defence of the Commonwealth, the law must be for the purpose of defence, or reasonably conducive to that purpose. As Dawson J pointed out, '[t]o determine the validity of a law said to be supported by a purposive power, a court must ask whether it is a law for the specified purpose': *Leask v Commonwealth* (1996) 187 CLR 579 at 606.

Some other powers may be a mix of purposive and non-purposive power and will require this purposive analysis also. For example, under the external affairs power (s 51(xxix)) the Commonwealth may regulate a number of matters including the implementation of international treaties. This aspect of the external affairs power is clearly purposive in nature, although other aspects of the power, such as the regulation of acts, matters or things outside Australia, are not. In order to characterise a law as being within the treaty implementation aspect of the external affairs power, the court must decide whether the purpose of the law conforms with the purpose of the treaty: *R v Burgess; Ex parte Henry* (1936) 55 CLR 608 **[3.3.9]**;

Deane J in *Commonwealth v Tasmania* (the *Tasmanian Dams* case) (1983) 158 CLR 1 at 260 **[3.3.21C]**.

'Proportionality' and purposive powers

[1.5.22]   One of the methods the court uses to determine whether the law is a law for a purpose within s 51 is the 'reasonable proportionality' test, or whether the law is 'appropriate and adapted' or 'reasonably appropriate': *Leask v Commonwealth* (1996) 187 CLR 579 at 591 per Brennan CJ. All formulations require the court to assess the relationship or 'fit' between the legislative means expressed in the legislation and the legitimate object of the legislative power. The test of proportionality may require the court to consider whether 'the law goes further than is necessary to achieve that purpose' (Dawson J in *Leask v Commonwealth* (1996) 187 CLR 579 at 606) or whether there is a less restrictive means for achieving the same end.

'Proportionality' and non-purposive or subject matter powers

[1.5.23]   When considering non-purposive or subject matter powers, the principle is long established that once the matter, act or thing falls within power, it does not matter whether the legislative means chosen to achieve an aim within power go beyond what is necessary or desirable to achieve that aim (*Burton v Honan* (1952) 86 CLR 169 at 179 per Dixon CJ; *Leask v Commonwealth* (1996) 187 CLR 579 at 602 per Dawson J), or that the law also pursues a purpose or goal not within power.

However, the role that proportionality plays in the characterisation of non-purposive powers is not entirely clear. In *Leask v Commonwealth* (1996) 187 CLR 579 at 606 per Dawson J and at 624 per Gummow J, it was stated clearly that proportionality is not relevant to the characterisation of non-purposive powers, except where the court is balancing a head of power against a constitutional limitation on power: see **[1.5.26]** below. Toohey J (187 CLR at 614) seemed to agree with Dawson J and Gummow J when he said that 'reasonable proportionality' is 'most likely to arise' in the latter context only. Brennan CJ did not discard proportionality altogether. His Honour said that, where there is a challenge to a non-purposive law on the ground that its operation and effect do not reveal a sufficient connection to the subject of a head of power, 'proportionality is a concept used to ascertain whether an Act achieves an effect or purpose within power'. However, Brennan CJ was careful to limit its meaning by saying that it does not mean 'necessity or desirability' when used in this context: 187 CLR at 593. McHugh J was equivocal, stating that, where a sufficient connection is established, proportionality is irrelevant, but where a law is passed for a purpose beyond power, the concept 'may sometimes prove helpful in determining whether the subject matter of the impugned law is sufficiently connected to the subject of federal power': 187 CLR at 616. Kirby J was disposed to a more liberal use of the concept although he was still guarded in his language. His Honour referred to 'a growing acceptance of the notion as a useful test of general application' that 'may be useful in the task of constitutional characterisation': 187 CLR at 635.

Political versus judicial considerations; desirability and necessity

[1.5.24] The reluctance of some members of the court to use the terminology of proportionality can be attributed to its association with questions of desirability of legislation, which could lead the court into questions of politics rather than law. The characterisation of purposive powers (and some aspects of non-purposive power such as treaty implementation) raises fine questions of degree and judgment for the court in a more explicit fashion than characterisation of non-purposive powers. In *Leask v Commonwealth* (1996) 187 CLR 579 at 600, Dawson J said that the concept of proportionality, which originated in Europe, is 'inappropriate' to the Australian Constitution 'where legislative power is with few exceptions conferred by reference to subject matter rather than aims or objectives'. By contrast, in European Union law legislative power is conferred in terms of aims and the European Court of Justice therefore necessarily delves into 'essentially political rather than judicial considerations': 187 CLR at 601.

[1.5.25] So, to this point in our discussion, proportionality is relevant:

- where the court needs to assess whether the legislative means fit a legitimate end within power;

- in characterisation of a purposive power; and

- possibly in characterisation of a non-purposive power where the law is within the incidental range of the power, but only in order to determine whether there is a sufficient connection between the law and the power.

Proportionality has one other role to fulfil, and that is in relation to constitutional limits.

Proportionality and constitutional limits

[1.5.26] The concept of reasonable proportionality has one other important application, and that is where a law is challenged on the ground that it infringes a constitutional limitation or immunity. In cases where the limitation or immunity is not absolute but must be balanced against some other legitimate objective, the court will ask whether the law is reasonably proportionate to the other legitimate end: *Leask v Commonwealth* (1996) 187 CLR at 593 per Brennan CJ; at 606 per Dawson J; at 614 per Toohey J.

For example, where a state defamation law was claimed to infringe a constitutional limitation by burdening freedom of communication (a freedom protected by the constitutional requirement of representative democracy), the High Court invoked the proportionality test in order to ask whether the defamation law was 'reasonably appropriate and adapted to serve a legitimate end': *Lange v Australian Broadcasting Corporation* (1997) 189 CLR 520 at 567 **[11.3.13C]**. The court decided that the common law of extended qualified privilege and its statutory counterparts were proportionate to a legitimate goal, namely the protection of reputation of people in government and political life.

Another example involves s 92 cases. The question being whether the law infringes the constitutional guarantee that interstate trade, commerce and intercourse be 'absolutely free', the court will assess whether the law is proportionate to some legitimate end: *Castlemaine Tooheys Ltd v South Australia* (1990) 169 CLR 436 at 473–4 per Mason CJ, Brennan, Deane, Dawson and Toohey JJ **[10.4.38C]**. In that case, the court had to determine the validity of South Australian legislation which imposed a higher deposit on non-refillable bottles than on refillable bottles used by manufacturers of beverages in circumstances where out-of-state manufacturers mostly used non-refillable bottles so that the out-of-state product had to be sold at a higher price than local beverages. Although the court agreed that the South Australian legislation was designed to achieve legitimate goals, namely litter control and energy conservation, it held that the legislation failed the proportionality test. The legislative means were disproportionate to those ends for various reasons including the discrepancy between the refund for non-refillable and refillable bottles, and the fact that other means were available to South Australia to conserve its energy resources such as prohibiting the use of natural gas in the manufacture of non-refillable bottles.

[1.5.27] Earlier, we saw that interpretive method will reflect a number of contending principles **[1.2.14]–[1.2.18]**. So too does characterisation. There is no clear method of characterisation, nor is there any established order as to the way in which the principles should be applied. For example, a broad reading of a head of power in s 51 may suggest a broad interpretation of its subject matter, whereas reading the Constitution as a flexible instrument may justify an implication such as federalism, which in turn would suggest a more narrow interpretation of the same subject matter. Similarly the proportionality test leaves open to the court a number of possibilities.

Just as with interpretive method, the outcomes of characterisation are not entirely predictable and may be read differently according to the philosophical perspective of the audience. A critical legal studies view of characterisation might suggest that the range of possible applicable principles and lack of clear method is such that judges can choose any outcome they wish. A liberal view might argue that ultimately a good judge has to justify her or his decisions according to reasoned argument, text, history, practice and precedent and this will only be possible if those decisions are coherent. Although the range of principles expand the interpretive possibilities, they do not necessarily make the decision indeterminate.

6   Constitutional alteration

Commonwealth Constitution

[1.6.1] Section 128 of the Commonwealth Constitution provides that the Constitution may be altered only by a law passed by the parliament and approved by:

- a majority of the electors throughout the Commonwealth; and
- a majority of the electors in a majority of the states.

[1.6.2] The proposed law for the alteration of the Constitution must be passed by an absolute majority in each house of the Commonwealth Parliament and be submitted to the electors not less than two months and not more than six months after its passage through both houses. Alternatively, the Governor-General may submit a proposed law to the electors where the law has been passed by only one house, *if* the originating house has passed the proposed law twice, each time by an absolute majority, *and if* the second passage of the proposed law has taken place at least three months after the other house has rejected or failed to pass the proposed law or passed the proposed law with any amendment unacceptable to the originating house.

As a practical matter, the alternative procedure allows a proposed law to be submitted to a referendum when only the House of Representatives has passed it. The Governor-General will not exercise the power conferred by s 128 except on the advice of responsible ministers, whose advice will reflect the political position adopted by the House of Representatives: Sawer (1956) pp 124–5; Constitutional Commission (1988) pp 18–23.

[1.6.3] Section 128 further constrains the power of alteration by insisting that an alteration of the Constitution which diminishes the proportionate representation of any state in either House of Parliament, or the minimum number of representatives of a state in the House of Representatives, or increases, diminishes or otherwise alters the limits of any state must be approved by the majority of electors in that state.

[1.6.4] The procedure established by s 128 has proven to be difficult to negotiate. Of the 44 proposals to alter the Constitution which have been submitted to the electors to date, only eight have been approved in accordance with s 128 and taken effect. A list of the 44 proposed alterations appears in Bennett and Brennan (1999). The proposals which have been passed are:

- Constitution Alteration (Senate Elections) 1906.

- Constitution Alteration (State Debts) 1909.

- Constitution Alteration (State Debts) 1928.

- Constitution Alteration (Social Services) 1946.

- Constitution Alteration (Aboriginals) 1967.

- Constitution Alteration (Senate Casual Vacancies) 1977.

- Constitution Alteration (Retirement of Judges) 1977.

- Constitution Alteration (Referendums) 1977.

[1.6.5] The conduct of a referendum under s 128 is prescribed by Commonwealth legislation: Referendum (Machinery Provisions) Act 1984 (Cth). The legislation obliges the Electoral Commissioner to distribute, no later than 14 days before the voting day for a referendum, a pamphlet containing an argument in favour of the proposed law and an argument against the proposed law, where those arguments have been authorised by a majority of the members of the parliament who voted for the proposed law and by a majority of the members of the parliament who voted against the proposed law and forwarded to the Electoral Commissioner: s 11(1), (2). The Commonwealth is otherwise prohibited from expending money in respect of the presentation of the argument for and the argument against the proposed law: s 11(4). See *Reith v Morling* (1988) 83 ALR 667.

[1.6.6] It appears that none of the provisions of the Constitution, including s 128, is beyond the reach of s 128: see Thomson (1983) pp 335–40; Lane (1986) p 643. Certain alterations to the text of the Constitution will require the approval of the electors in the particular state affected by the alteration: see **[1.6.3]**.

[1.6.7] Some commentators have proposed that the covering clauses of the Commonwealth Constitution (that is, the sections of the Commonwealth of Australia Constitution Act 1900 (UK)) cannot be altered or contradicted by a law passed under s 128 (Lane (1986) p 1) so that the power to amend or repeal the covering clauses lies exclusively with the United Kingdom Parliament. It has also been proposed that s 128 cannot be used to provide for the secession of a state from the Commonwealth: Craven (1986) p 2. These views have been contested: Latham (1953–55) p 18; Cannaway (1938) p 109. The Constitutional Commission has argued that the power to effect such an amendment or repeal is to be found in s 128 of the Commonwealth Constitution: Constitutional Commission (1988) pp 120–3.

[1.6.8] It appears that some changes to Australia's constitutional structures may be effected by processes outside s 128. The parliament of a state may refer to the Commonwealth any matter which lies within the legislative power of the state and the Commonwealth thereupon acquires the power to legislate with respect to that matter within the referring state: Commonwealth Constitution s 51(xxxvii).

The Commonwealth Parliament may, at the request or with the concurrence of the parliaments of all the states directly concerned, exercise any legislative power which, at the establishment of the Constitution, could be exercised only by the United Kingdom Parliament: Commonwealth Constitution, s 51(xxxviii). Pursuant to this power, the Commonwealth Parliament has legislated, at the request of all the Australian states, to confer on the state parliaments power to legislate with respect to the territorial sea and to terminate the residual colonial status of the states: Coastal Waters (State Powers) Act 1980 (Cth); Australia Act 1986 (Cth).

However, the powers conferred by these provisions are expressed to be 'subject to this Constitution', and any legislation enacted under s 51(xxxvii) or s 51(xxxviii) must give way to any inconsistent provisions in the Commonwealth Constitution, and would be subject to amendment in the same way as other legislation passed by the Commonwealth: Crawford (1992) pp 189–90.

The states

[1.6.9] The constitutional structures of each of the Australian states are defined primarily by an Act of the relevant state parliament. According to s 107 of the Commonwealth Constitution, the constitution of each state is to continue 'until altered in accordance with the Constitution of the State'. For the most part, the several state Constitution Acts are subject to amendment or repeal by the state parliaments in the same way as other legislation: *McCawley v R* [1920] AC 691 at 704 **[5.4.2]**. However, certain aspects of some of the Constitution Acts are 'entrenched', so that a particular legislative procedure must be followed to amend or repeal the provisions dealing with those aspects.

In New South Wales, a bill to abolish or alter the constitution or powers of the Legislative Council must not be presented to the Governor for the royal assent until the bill has been approved at a referendum of the electors qualified to vote for the Legislative Assembly: Constitution Act 1902 (NSW) s 7A(2). A similar procedure is prescribed for a bill which would extend the life of the Assembly beyond four years, or affect the system of compulsory voting, the distribution of Legislative Assembly electorates and the conduct of Legislative Assembly elections: s 7B.

In Queensland, a bill to re-establish the Legislative Council, a bill to extend the life of the Assembly beyond three years and a bill which would affect the office of Governor, or the Governor's powers, cannot be presented to the Governor for the royal assent until it has been approved by the electors voting at a referendum: Constitution Act Amendment Act 1934 (Qld) ss 3, 4; Constitution Act 1867 (Qld) s 53.

In South Australia, a bill to abolish the House of Assembly or Legislative Council, to alter the powers of the Council or to change the established procedures for altering the Constitution Act or resolving deadlocks, and a bill which would affect the system for distributing seats in the Legislative Assembly cannot be presented to the Governor for the royal assent until it has been approved by the electors voting at a referendum: Constitution Act 1934 (SA), ss 10a, 88. A bill which would alter the constitution of the Legislative Council or the House of Assembly cannot be presented to the Governor for the royal assent until it has been approved by absolute majorities in each house of the parliament: s 8.

In Tasmania, a bill which would affect the maximum life of the House of Assembly (fixed at four years) must be approved by no less than two-thirds of the members of the house: Constitution Act 1934 (Tas) s 41A.

In Victoria, a bill which would alter the constitution of the parliament, the Council or the Assembly, and a bill which would alter those parts of the Constitution Act dealing with the Crown, the Supreme Court and the expenses of the Executive Council, the Legislative Council and the Legislative Assembly must not be presented to the Governor for the royal assent until it has been approved by absolute majorities in each House of Parliament: Constitution Act 1975 (Vic) s 18(2).

In Western Australia, a bill which would affect the office of Governor, abolish the Legislative Council or Assembly, provide for other than direct election to the Council or Assembly or reduce the size of the Council or Assembly cannot be presented to the Governor for the royal assent until it has been approved by the electors voting at a referendum: Constitution Act 1889 (WA) s 73. A bill which would amend the system for redistributing electorates in the Legislative Assembly and Legislative Council cannot be presented to the Governor for the royal assent until it has been approved by absolute majorities in each House of Parliament: Electoral Distribution Act 1947 (WA) s 13.

[1.6.10] The requirement that special procedures be followed when a state parliament legislates respecting its own constitution, powers or procedure is supported by s 6 of the Australia Act 1986 (Cth) (see [5.4.22]) and s 106 of the Commonwealth Constitution: see *Western Australia v Wilsmore* [1981] WAR 179; (1981) 33 ALR 13 [5.4.33].

7 References

[1.7.1] *Articles*

Campbell, 'Changing the Constitution — Past and Future' (1989) 17 *Melbourne Uni LR* 1.

Cannaway, 'The Safety Valve of the Constitution' (1938) 12 *ALJ* 108.

Craven, 'The Constitutional Minefield of Australian Republicanism' [1992] *Policy* 33.

Dixon, 'The Law and the Constitution' (1935) 51 *LQR* 590.

Fish, 'Working on the Chain Gang: Interpretation in the Law and in Literary Criticism' (1982) 9 *Critical Inquiry* 201.

Gageler, 'Foundations of Australian Federalism and the Role of Judicial Review' (1987) 17 *Federal LR* 162.

Galligan, 'Realistic "Realism" and the High Court's Political Role' (1989) 18 *Federal LR* 40.

Galligan, 'The Republic Referendum', (1999) *Quadrant* (October) 46.

Goldsworthy, 'Realism about the High Court' (1989) 18 *Federal LR* 27.

Goldsworthy, 'Originalism in Constitutional Interpretation' (1997) 25 *Federal LR* 1.

Hanks, 'The Political Dimension of Constitutional Adjudication' (1987) 10 *UNSWLJ* 141.

Inglis Clark, *Studies in Australian Constitutional Law*, Charles F Maxwell, Melbourne, 1901.

Keyzer, 'When is an Issue of "Vital Constitutional Importance"? Principles which Guide the Reconsideration of Constitutional Decisions in the High Court of Australia', (1999) 2 *Constitutional Law and Policy Review* 13.

Kirby, 'The Australian Referendum on a Republic — Ten Lessons' (2000) 46(4) *Australian Journal of Politics and History* 510.

Lane, 'Judicial Review or Government by the High Court' (1966) 5 *Sydney LR* 203.

Latham, 'Changing the Constitution' (1953–55) 1 *Sydney Uni LR* 14.

Lee, 'Reforming the Australian Constitution: The Frozen Continent Refuses to Thaw' [1988] *Public Law* 535.

Lindell, 'Why is Australia's Constitution Binding? The Reasons in 1900 and Now, and the Effect of Independence' (1986) 16 *Federal LR* 29.

Llewellyn, 'Some Realism about Realism' (1931) 44 *Harvard LR* 1222.

Mason, 'The Role of a Constitutional Court in a Federation: A Comparison of the Australian and the United States Experience' (1986) 16 *Federal LR* 1.

Mason, 'Towards 2001 — Minimalism, Monarchism or Metamorphism?' (1995) 21 *Monash Uni LR* 1.

Scott, 'Deconstructing Equality-versus-Difference: or, The Uses of Poststructuralist Theory for Feminism' (1988) 14 *Feminist Studies* 33.

Thomson, 'Altering the Constitution: Some Aspects of Section 128' (1983) 13 *Federal LR* 323.

Winterton, 'An Australian Republic' (1988) 16 *Melbourne Uni LR* 467.

Winterton, 'The States and the Republic: A Constitutional Accord' (1995) 6 *Public LR* 107.

Wheeler, 'Original Intent and the Doctrine of the Separation of Powers in Australia' (1996) 7 *Public LR* 96.

Zines, 'Social Conflict and Constitutional Interpretation' (1996) 22 *Monash LR* 195.

[1.7.2] *Papers and reports*

Bennett and Brennan, 'Constitutional Referenda in Australia', Research Paper No 2 1999–2000, Department of the Parliamentary Library, Canberra, 1999.

Constitutional Commission, *Final Report*, AGPS, Canberra, 1988.

Constitutional Convention (2–13 February 1998), *Transcript of Proceedings*, Proof Hansard, AGPS, Canberra, 1998.

Coper, 'Thinking about Constitutional Change', paper presented to Australian Society of Labor Lawyers 18th National Conference, Canberra, 4–6 October 1996.

[1.7.3] *Texts*

Booker, Glass and Watt, *Federal Constitutional Law*, 2nd ed, Butterworths, Sydney, 1998.

Bronitt, Burns and Kinley, *Principles of European Community Law*, Lawbook Co, Sydney, 1995.

Chesterman and Galligan, *Citizens Without Rights: Aborigines and Australian Citizenship*, Cambridge University Press, Melbourne, 1997.

Coper, *Encounters with the Australian Constitution*, CCH Australia Ltd, Sydney, 1987.

Cowen and Zines, *Federal Jurisdiction in Australia*, 2nd ed, Oxford University Press, Melbourne, 1978.

Craven, *Secession: The Ultimate States' Right*, Melbourne University Press, Melbourne, 1986.

Crawford, 'Amendment of the Constitution' in *Australian Federation*, (ed Craven), Melbourne University Press, Melbourne, 1992, p 177.

Crommelin and Evans, 'Explorations and Adventures with Commonwealth Powers' in *Labor and the Constitution 1972–1975*, (ed Evans), Heineman Educational, Melbourne, 1977, pp 24–66.

Dworkin, *Law's Empire*, Harvard University Press, Cambridge MA, 1986.

Ely, *Democracy and Distrust*, Harvard University Press, Cambridge MA, 1980.

Evans, 'The Most Dangerous Branch? The High Court and the Constitution in a Changing Society', in *Australian Lawyers and Social Change*, (eds Hambly and Goldring), Law Book Co, Sydney, 1974, pp 13–76.

Galligan, *The Politics of the High Court*, Queensland University Press, St Lucia, Queensland, 1987.

Hogg, *Constitutional Law of Canada*, 3rd ed, Carswell, Ontario, 1992.

Hart, *The Concept of Law*, 2nd ed, Clarendon Press, Oxford, 1994.

Irving, ed, *A Woman's Constitution?: Gender & History in the Australian Commonwealth*, Hale & Iremonger, 1996.

Jennings, *The Law and the Constitution*, 5th ed, University of London Press, London, 1972.

Koskenniemi, *From Apology to Utopia: The Structure of International Legal Argument*, Finnish Lawyers Publishing Co, Helsinki, 1989.

Kairys, *The Politics of Law: A Progressive Critique*, Pantheon Books, New York, 1982.

Lane, *Commentary on the Australian Constitution*, Law Book Co, Sydney, 1986.

Lane, *Commentary on the Australian Constitution*, 2nd ed, LBC Information Services, Sydney, 1997.

Mason, 'The Interpretation of a Constitution in a Modern Liberal Democracy' in *Interpreting Constitutions*, (eds Sampford and Preston), Federation Press, Sydney, 1996.

Menzies, *Central Power in the Australian Commonwealth*, Cassell, London, 1967.

Neal, *The Rule of Law in a Penal Colony: Law and Power in Early New South Wales*, Cambridge University Press, Melbourne, 1991.

O'Donovan, *Sexual Divisions in Law*, Weidenfeld & Nicolson, 1985.

Parkinson, *Tradition and Change in Australian Law*, Law Book Co, Sydney, 1994.

Sawer, *Australian Federal Politics and Law 1901–1929*, Melbourne University Press, Melbourne, 1956.

Sawer, *Australian Federalism in the Courts*, Melbourne University Press, Melbourne, 1967.

Summers, *Damned Whores and God's Police: The Colonisation of Women in Australia*, 2nd ed, Penguin, Melbourne, 1994.

Wilcox, *An Australian Charter of Rights*, Law Book Co, Sydney, 1993.

Zines, 'Commentary' in *Australian Lawyers and Social Change*, (eds D Hambly and J Goldring), Law Book Co, Sydney, 1976, pp 81–95.

Zines, 'The Growth of Australian Nationhood and its Effect on the Powers of the Commonwealth' in *Commentaries on the Australian Constitution*, (ed Zines), Butterworths, Sydney, 1977, pp 1–49.

Zines, *The High Court and the Constitution*, 4th ed, Butterworths, Sydney, 1997.

Chapter

2

'Indigenous' People and Constitutional Law

1 What defines 'indigenous' identity? Why should (constitutional) law respond?

Construction of 'indigenous' identity by law

[2.1.1] In Australia, theories of 'indigenous' identity have long been underpinned, and given expression, by law, including the Constitution. When law employs social terms like 'Aboriginal', 'indigenous' or 'race', it creates more bounded legal categories, assuming that their members can be ascertained with certainty because they have something in common. This raises two important questions: first, whether there is a universal 'indigenous' identity or experience to which law can attach; and second, what (if any) justifications underpin laws specifically targeting 'indigenous' people? Law's binding force (its enforcement by police, its licences to allocate state resources or to take private ones) means legal categories can also change social identity: by changing how people defined as 'indigenous' behave, or how those not so defined behave towards them: Weaver (1984). Constitutional law has profoundly changed 'indigenous' identity in Australia: by helping to create 'Aborigines' and 'Torres Strait Islanders' out of the members of hundreds of pre-colonial language groups, by denying the relevance of their consent to colonisation, land deprivation and federation, by defining their identity in the racist language of the late 19th century, and by failing to protect them against racial discrimination. Constitutional interpretation has marched in step with government policy and legislation relating to 'indigenous' Australians, rather than offering a critique of it.

54

What is different about 'indigenous' Australians?

[2.1.2] There are at least five grounds on which law has treated, or might treat, 'indigenous' Australians as different from other Australians: descent from Australia's prior occupants, 'racial' difference, cultural difference, experience of discrimination (including historically) and contemporary socio-economic disadvantage. Some of these grounds (for example, 'race') have formed the basis of laws, including constitutional provisions, discriminating against Aboriginal people and Torres Strait Islanders; others (for example, culture or socio-economic disadvantage) have founded more recent pluralistic or remedial legislation. The exact basis of laws addressed to 'indigenous' people is not always clear, and there are risks that emphasised differences are seen as conclusive of 'indigenous' identity or as uniformly shared by all 'indigenous' people. This is evident in recent reform proposals for constitutional protection of 'indigenous rights' or 'treaties' between 'indigenous' and 'non-indigenous' Australians to advance 'reconciliation' (for example, Council for Aboriginal Reconciliation (2000), Behrendt (2003) Ch 6). Such proposals also sometimes fail to distinguish clearly between the bases for distinctively 'indigenous' rights and universal human rights still denied to Aboriginal people or Torres Strait Islanders. Constitutional change seems unlikely to address 'indigenous' difference adequately, offering mainly symbolic value (see below **[2.4.57]**), or barriers to obvious discrimination: see **[2.1.12]** and **[2.4.18]**. As discussed below, it is also increasingly difficult to distinguish parts of the 'indigenous' from the 'non-indigenous' population.

Descent from prior occupants

[2.1.3] 'Indigenous' Australians are descended from the 'first possessors' of the Australian continent and islands. Perhaps this fact alone justifies their different legal treatment? As the discussion of native title at **[2.2.34]–[2.2.43]** indicates, this title, built partly on the pre-colonial origins of contemporary indigenous land traditions, has translated into a property right which only 'indigenous' Australians may hold, but one which is inferior to Crown-granted titles. Lokan has argued that Australian courts could never fashion 'indigenous' rights based solely on first possession because 'a claim based on simple priority in time contains a strong element of windfall': Lokan (1999) at 72; the courts will always be influenced by their desire to distribute resources more broadly among the population as a whole. Unfortunately, in Australia, this desire (accompanied by racism), has led to misallocation of resources largely to people descended from later migrants: see **[2.2.42]** and **[2.4.33]**. However, countries which have experimented with privileging constitutionally the rights of those descended from prior inhabitants over those whose ancestors came later (for example, Fiji between 1990 and 1997) are also not free of inequality.

'Race'

[2.1.4] This term is found in the Constitution: see **[2.4.1]** and **[2.4.36]–[2.4.52]**. The Constitution was adopted at an historical high-point for racism. In 1901, 'white' superiority was accepted in Australian public culture, which held (under the influence of social Darwinism) that the identity and fate of the 'aboriginal race' could be explained biologically. Thus, although in 1901 Aboriginal poverty, illness and premature death stemmed from loss of the means of subsistence (land), untreated diseases, displacement from the workforce during the 1890s depression (in the east) and rapid colonisation and associated violence (in the west and north), public culture tended to regard Aboriginal people's predicament as genetically inherited and therefore unchangeable. It was anticipated that 'indigenous' Australians would die out under pressure from later migrants. Purportedly to 'protect' these populations while they remained alive, during the late 19th and early 20th centuries most Australian jurisdictions introduced 'Aboriginal Protection' Acts limiting the civil rights (freedom of movement, the right to work, the right to education) of people of predominantly Aboriginal or Torres Strait Islander descent (and sometimes their children).

[2.1.5]   At the turn of the 20th century, the term 'aboriginal native' was used in laws (including s 127 of the Constitution — see **[2.4.41]**) to refer to Aboriginal people with few 'non-indigenous' ancestors; there was some later doubt as to whether it referred to Torres Strait Islanders, whom the invaders periodically regarded as more 'civilised' than Aboriginal people. In the first decades of the 20th century, more refined racial classifications emerged as, particularly in the west and north, the population of 'mixed race' people began to increase. Sex (voluntary or involuntary) across the colour bar had been a fact of life in colonial Australia, where men vastly outnumbered women, particularly in rural areas and Western Australia. While violence, disease and malnutrition had kept the numbers of children of 'white' men and Aboriginal women relatively small during the 19th century, when confined in 20th century reserves under 'protection' laws these 'mixed race' people began to have more 'mixed race' children. The term 'half-caste', offensive in modern usage, acquired general currency, including in legislation, to describe people of 'mixed' descent. To control this population, 'protection' laws began to authorise removal from their mothers of 'half-caste' children and to prohibit inter-racial sex outside officially-sanctioned marriage.

[2.1.6]   By the 1930s, statutory definitions of 'Aboriginality' began to expand. Terms like 'quarter-caste' ('quadroon') and 'one-eighth-caste' ('octoroon') were adapted from United States usage (where slaves had borne slave owners' children). The expansion was partly due to a desire to stop anyone of Aboriginal descent taking 'white' jobs during the 1930s depression, and partly due to the rise of eugenics, which theorised that 'racial' identity, like other socially undesirable characteristics, could be 'bred out' if the sexuality of *all* women of Aboriginal descent was controlled (controlling the women had greater official appeal than controlling the men with sexual access to them). After World War II, discrediting of eugenics by the Nazi experiment changed racial thinking again, leading to the idea that 'race' could not be explained on purely biological grounds. (Many people were also liberated from 'protection' laws post-War, reflecting in part Aboriginal and Torres Strait Islander contributions to the defence forces and wartime rural economy.)

[2.1.7]   It has been accepted since the mid-20th century that all 'racial' identity, including the privileged social status known as 'white' identity, is socially constructed:

> [In science, g]eographic variability, not race, is self-evident. No one can deny that *Homo sapiens* is a strongly differentiated species; few will quarrel with the observation that differences in skin colour are the most striking outward sign of this variability. But the fact of variability does not require the designation of races. There are better ways to study human differences (Gould (1977) pp 231–2).

In any event, Australia's history of inter-racial sex meant that, by the 20th century, significant numbers of Australians had both 'indigenous' and 'non-indigenous' ancestors. In the past, legal and social discrimination provided people aware of their 'indigenous' ancestry with an incentive to try 'to pass' as 'white', but there were others for whom this effort was unnecessary because that identity had been suppressed in past generations. With the removal of some discrimination since the 1970s, increasing numbers of Australians have been prepared to identify as 'indigenous'. Births of 'indigenous' children to 'non-indigenous' mothers have also begun to increase; now only members of small remote populations report no 'non-indigenous' ancestry: Australian Bureau of Statistics (2003). While people identifying as Aboriginal or Torres Strait Islanders are likely to have an ancestor from one of these ethnic groups, there remain other Australians of similar ancestry who do not so identify. Factors besides biology must play a role in constructing these identities.

Culture

[2.1.8] The post-World War II notion of 'race' has referred as much to shared cultural differences as to genetic variability in human populations. 'Culture' comprehends a wide range of (communal) human behaviour, including world-view, self-identification and sense of history. Cultural difference, like genetic variability, can stem from geographic isolation of human populations (although much longer periods of isolation are required to produce genetic variation).

It is no more possible to identify a single set of 'indigenous' cultural characteristics than it is to identify uniform 'Australian' cultural characteristics. We can say that the norms underpinning Australian public culture and law are primarily derived from Anglo-Australian culture (even if, as some have argued, they manifest Aboriginal influences — for example, egalitarianism). We know that there was considerable cultural diversity in pre-colonial Australia, some of which remains, and that post-1788 experiences of government policies and social discrimination have generated commonalities and differences in 'indigenous' experience. Nonetheless, persistent cultural tendencies which originate in pre-colonial Aboriginal cultures include distinctive patterns of communication, views about personal responsibility, attitudes to family, child-rearing, authority and resources, and conceptions of the relationship between people and ancestral land. Similarly distinctive cultural tendencies are observable in Torres Strait Islander culture. Historical experience has also produced distinctive cultural attitudes to public institutions (particularly criminal justice institutions, in which 'indigenous' Australians continue to experience discrimination), and some distinctive cultural attributes which stem from the segregation or institutionalisation of the past (for example, mistrust of the police). Finally, Pearson and others have argued that the late-20th century lifting of alcohol prohibition on Queensland reserves, accompanied by economic change and indigenous Australians' full admission to the welfare state, have produced in some places a 'new dysfunctional culture: to drink is to be Aboriginal': Pearson (2001); see also McKnight (2002).

[2.1.9] In the 21st century the 'indigenous' population is probably more culturally diverse than ever, not least because it includes people who have recently identified themselves as such, and others with 'non-indigenous' family members living in largely 'non-indigenous' settings. Paradoxically, Australian law 'recognised' recently for the first time 'indigenous' rights based on traditions founded in pre-colonial legal systems: *Mabo v Queensland (No 2)* (1975) 175 CLR 1; *Members of the Yorta Yorta Community v Victoria* (2002) 194 ALR 538.

In 'recognising' native title, the High Court has decided that the common law will allocate land to only those 'indigenous' people who, despite Australia's long history of attempting to suppress 'indigenous' cultural norms, have somehow managed to continue subscribing to them. This shows that cultural pluralism fluctuates according to dynamics in the dominant culture itself, not according to whether or not 'indigenous' conditions justify it. Despite often remarkable consistency in ethnographic accounts of indigenous cultural difference over time, Australian public culture's moral evaluation of those differences has changed often. For example, Captain James Cook evaluated Aboriginal people's 'state of nature' more favourably than those who followed him to found the colony of New South Wales. Similarly, a major aim of the 'assimilation' policy of many goverments from the mid-20th century was socialisation of Aboriginal people and Torres Strait Islanders *away from* 'indigenous' cultural values.

[2.1.10] During the assimilation era, the idea that indigenous disadvantages were *biologically inherited* was replaced by the idea that they resulted from *divergent cultural practices*. But achieving cultural assimilation and its concomitants, economic and social integration of 'indigenous' Australians into the 'wider community', required significant public spending, particularly in education, health, welfare and housing. It has been argued that Australian governments abandoned 'assimilation' in the 1970s for a new policy, 'self-determination', in order to avoid this spending: Beckett (1988) 12. 'Self-determination' was justified by 'indigenous' Australians' cultural distinctiveness; it posited a 'special, collective relationship with the state' under which Australians made 'their own' decisions about their future. 'Self-determination' has been criticised on numerous grounds (including lack of responsiveness to local 'indigenous' social organisation, and for turning 'indigenous' groups into agents for delivering government services determined elsewhere (for example, Cowlishaw (1999)); it has also functioned as 'a charter for Aborigines to live at a lower material level than other Australians: their poverty [was] rendered exotic and so no longer comparable to other forms of poverty': ibid.

[2.1.11] Consistently with *Mabo (No 2)*, in the 21st century, the expression of selected 'indigenous' cultural norms (for example, language, land traditions and associated art) is accepted, even insisted on, as a marker of authentic 'indigenous' identity. However, contemporary Australian public culture is at best ambivalent about other 'indigenous' cultural claims — for example, that 'indigenous' culture is more tolerant of physical violence than Anglo-Australian culture, or that publicly funded 'indigenous' organisations should operate according to their own standards of decision-making or resource allocation, not those of the public sector or corporations law. The Queensland government only recently responded to claims about 'grog culture' of some former reserves by allowing promulgation of local drinking controls — for years such controls were seen as an inappropriate intrusion on Aboriginal people's civil rights; some have met strong local opposition. More general claims for statutory 'recognition' of 'indigenous customary law' have been largely rejected (see Australian Law Reform Commission (1986)); the common law also refuses to extend native title principles to provide such 'recognition': see below **[2.2.32]**.

Historical experience of discrimination

[2.1.12] Perhaps law should treat 'indigenous' Australians differently because law (or other elements of Australian society) has discriminated against them (in the past)? There are two possible reasons for doing this: to compensate for the discrimination itself, or to compensate for its contemporary legacies.

Since the 1970s, Commonwealth, state and territory legislation has outlawed racial discrimination and provided remedies for those who experience it. However, these Acts focus on the formal equality of individual victims, not social equality, and are not always effective to address persistent but subtle discrimination, for example, by employers or public housing providers against multiple members of a racial group: Hunyor (2003), Rosales-Castaneda (2003), De Plevitz (2003), Thornton (1990). Further, racial discrimination legislation is always open to repeal, even when founded on international human rights obligations.

This was demonstrated in 1998, when the Commonwealth Parliament amended the Native Title Act 1993 to allow discriminatory treatment of native title compared with Crown-granted titles, and to ensure that the Racial Discrimination Act 1975 (Cth) — which implements the United Nations Convention on the Elimination of All Forms of Racial Discrimination — did not operate to undermine this discrimination. This episode, and 1990s experiments by the Western Australia and the Northern Territory governments with mandatory sentencing laws which impacted more severely on Aboriginal people than on others, led to calls for a constitutional amendment enshrining either the principle of racial equality or a limitation on racially discriminatory laws. Such a limitation was first proposed in the 1960s, when parliament considered the bill for the 'Aborigines and the political census' and 'race power' amendments: see below **[2.4.40]** and **[2.4.41]**. However, such a constitutional limitation would need to be carefully drafted to avoid the same interpretative pitfalls as racial discrimination legislation. This issue is taken up at **[2.4.15]–[2.4.29C]**.

[2.1.13] Many older 'indigenous' Australians lived most of their lives in the shadow of racial discrimination: see, for example, the discussion of the removal of Northern Territory Aboriginal children from their families in *Kruger v Commonwealth* (1997) 190 CLR 1 **[11.3.21C]**, **[11.3.32C]**. Perhaps that experience alone justifies remedial laws? Such arguments typically meet three objections: first, that past events are difficult to evaluate from this temporal distance; second, that contemporary Australians should not be held responsible for discrimination which they themselves did not engage in; and third, that many other Australians (notably other members of the social underclass and some women) experienced similar discrimination. While the second argument overlooks the *indirect advantages* to the ancestors of other Australians of past discrimination — for example, (as 'white' employers) greater availability of cheap but controlled rural labour, (as 'white' workers) greater availability of properly paid work, (as new settlers) greater availability of land — the first and third arguments highlight significant political obstacles to proper redress for past discrimination.

Even if all past discrimination could be reconstructed accurately, nobody is prepared to compensate for it. This is demonstrated by recent negotiations between the Queensland Government and 'indigenous' organisations over appropriate compensation for alleged historical misappropriation of wages of residents of Queensland reserves. The government's offer of an apology and $55 million ($2000–$4000 per individual, depending on age, not years in the workforce) is considered to fall well short of the $1 billion (in today's terms) misappropriated: Kidd (1997), 2000. While Queensland makes its offer 'in a spirit of reconciliation', it is not prepared to meet the true costs of the historical injustice alleged. As in other states founded on colonialism, the fact that 'this state has got rich on Aboriginal poverty' is not considered an appropriate basis for redress: Kidd, quoted in O'Brien (2002).

[2.1.14] Many 'indigenous' Australians' historical experiences have played a significant role in their contemporary material poverty, educational disadvantage and poor health — and those of their children. 'Aboriginal affairs' has been seriously under-funded for most of Australia's history; some governments relied for most of the 20th century on private charitable organisations to supplement (with the labour of 'missionaries' and other volunteers) their spending on public social services taken for granted by other Australians. Queensland reserve dwellers and members of other incarcerated populations were unable to accumulate wealth by working in free labour markets for proper remuneration, and were therefore unable to transmit wealth to their children. Poor education and social discrimination made them unable to take advantage of 'equal pay' as technology overtook unskilled employment in the late 20th century. A number of older 'indigenous' Australians also struggle with psychological problems stemming from their removal from their families as small children by governments under 'protection' or 'welfare' legislation, and their own children suffer from the consequences of inadequate parenting: see generally, HREOC (1997). This raises the question of whether the law might better attend to the contemporary state of 'indigenous' Australians, whether or not that condition has strong historical causes.

Contemporary socio-economic disadvantage

[2.1.15]   Whether or not Australian law should respond to 'indigenousness' as socio-economic disadvantage is a highly politicised issue. The present Commonwealth Government claims to pursue 'practical reconciliation' — advancement of 'indigenous' Australians through what it argues is increased spending on health, housing, education and employment equality — yet research indicates that the socio-economic gap between 'indigenous' and 'non-indigenous' Australians is widening: Altman and Hunter (2003). 'Practical reconciliation' is rhetorically opposed to historical explanations for contemporary disadvantage. While that opposition is maintained, it seems unlikely that 'practical reconciliation' can address adequately all causes of contemporary disadvantage.

It is nonetheless arguable that the most important differences between 'indigenous' and 'non-indigenous' Australians, and increasingly within Australia's 'indigenous' populations, are socio-economic. For example, poor health and low life expectancy characterise the 'indigenous' experience: men die on average at age 56, the life expectancy for other Australian men a century ago; rates for women match those for other Australians in the 1920s: Australian Bureau of Statistics (2003). The geographical distribution of the 'indigenous' population — about 27 per cent lives in remote Australia and 43 per cent in regional towns, whereas 67 per cent of the wider population lives in cities — means it has experienced disproportionately recent economic changes causing rural decline (job losses and withdrawal of services). In 2001, unemployment rates for 'indigenous' Australians were more than double and (given the masking effect of a 'work for the dole' scheme) often more like five times the rate for other Australians; adult income was $150 less per week and home ownership half the Australian average. The Aboriginal and Torres Strait Islander population also needs particular investments because it contains many large households headed by women and a huge number of children: almost 40 per cent are aged under 15; the 'indigenous' fertility rate is twice the national average. Yet one-third of 'indigenous' people still leave school before age 15, and take-up of university places occurs at only one-quarter of the rate which might be expected given the size of the 'indigenous' population: see generally Altman and Hunter (2003).

[2.1.16] Paradoxically, the period (late 20th century) during which 'indigenous' people achieved formal advancement of their legal rights was also one in which some remote 'communities' experienced significant social deterioriation, including dramatic increases in rates of homicide, suicide and inter-personal violence: Pearson (2001). 'Self-determination' appears to have masked these increased social problems. While their causes (which range from economic change to increased substance abuse) are complex, many Aboriginal people now argue strongly that Australian law and public policy should respond to this particular form of indigenous difference.

[2.1.17] Finally, 2001 census figures indicate that moving to the city and finding a 'non-indigenous' partner increasingly allows 'indigenous' people to escape poverty and disadvantage in favour of living standards comparable to those of their 'non-indigenous' neighbours: Gardiner-Garden (2003). For this reason, it is increasingly argued that 'indigenousness' is an inappropriate surrogate term for 'socio-economic disadvantage', and that laws aimed at this form of 'indigenous' difference ought to abandon it in favour of criteria which address the disadvantage itself: Gardiner-Garden (2003). However, this perspective typically does not inform the 'treaty' or 'indigenous rights' debates.

Demonstrating 'indigenousness' for legal purposes

[2.1.18] Twentieth-century changes in racial theories and policies brought about corresponding changes in how 'indigenous' identity is proven legally. Early 20th century Australian public culture and law accepted that 'race' could be ascertained 'objectively' (on the basis of skin colour) by outsiders; similarly, in the 1950s, people who didn't appear to outsiders to act like Aboriginal people could sometimes escape such classification. By the 1970s it was accepted that 'racial' identification was largely a matter for the individuals and 'communities' concerned.

[2.1.19] Brennan J grappled with the concept of 'race' in *Commonwealth v Tasmania* (the *Tasmanian Dam* case) (1983) 158 CLR 1 at 243–4:

> 'Race' ... is not a precise concept ... There is, of course, a biological element in the concept ...
>
> A need to identify the biological element ... followed the enactment of a Race Relations Act in New Zealand and in England. In ... *King-Ansell v Police* [(1979) 2 NZLR 531], Richardson J said:
>
>> ... all four expressions 'race', 'colour', 'national origins' and 'ethnic origins' are concerned with antecedent rather than acquired characteristics.
>
> It does not follow that the identifying characteristics must be genetically determined at birth. The ultimate genetic ancestry of any New Zealander is not susceptible to legal proof. Race is clearly used in its popular meaning.

His Honour discounted the importance of, if not the necessity for, scientific proof of the biological element:

> The real test is whether the individuals or the group regard themselves and are regarded by others in the community as having a particular historical identity in terms of their colour or their racial, national or ethnic origins
>
> ... Membership of a race imports a biological history or origin which is common to other members of the race, but Richardson J is surely right in denying the possibility of proving ultimate genetic ancestry. However ... I do not think his Honour was propounding his 'real test' of common regard as ... conclusive or exhaustive. Actual proof of descent from ancestors who were acknowledged members of the race or actual proof of descent from ancestors none of whom were members of the race is admissible to prove or to contradict ... an assertion of membership of the race. Though the biological element is ... an essential element of membership of a race, it does not ordinarily exhaust the characteristics of a racial group. Physical similarities, and a common history, a common religion or spiritual beliefs and a common culture are factors that tend to create a sense of identity among members of a race and to which others have regard in identifying people as members of a race ...

[2.1.20] While some Aboriginal or Torres Strait Islander descent remains an ingredient of the definition of 'indigenous' identity in Commonwealth Acts and for the purposes of s 51(xxvi) Constitution, that definition also requires self-identification and 'community' recognition: *Shaw v Wolf* (1998) 83 FCR 113 at 120–2 per Merkel J; *Commonwealth v Tasmania* (the *Tasmanian Dam* case) (1983) 158 CLR 1 at 274 per Deane J. In *Shaw*, Merkel J remarked at 137:

> It is unfortunate that the determination of a person's Aboriginal identity, a highly personal matter, has been left by a Parliament that is not representative of Aboriginal people to be determined by a Court which is also not representative of Aboriginal people ... It is to be hoped that one day ... that determination might be made by independently constituted bodies or tribunals which are representative of Aboriginal people.

[2.1.21] Judicial policing of 'indigenous' identity occurs because Australia has no doctrine of (limited) 'indigenous' self-government, as exists in the United States (see **[2.2.22]**), where 'tribes' determine their membership. *Shaw v Woolf* involved a dispute about eligibility for election of candidates for the Aboriginal and Torres Strait Islander Commission (ATSIC), a Commonwealth statutory authority. Merkel J found some candidates were not Aboriginal because they did not meet the descent requirement. However, he held those contesting their identity to a high standard of proof (*Briginshaw v Briginshaw* (1938) 60 CLR 336), and did not disqualify others whose claims to 'community' recognition were founded on acknowledgment by only a limited section of the state's 'indigenous' population. *Shaw* has been criticised by Tasmanian Aboriginal groups as opening up 'Aboriginality' to spurious identity claims, and has led to the establishment of an ATSIC electoral roll overseen by a nominated 'indigenous' body: see *Patmore v Independent Indigenous Advisory Committee* (2002) 122 FCR 559; *Clements v Independent Indigenous Advisory Committee* [2003] FCAFC 143; compare *In the Matter of The Aboriginal Lands Act 1995* [2001] TASSC 81 and [2001] TASSC 105. See generally De Plevitz and Croft (2003).

2   Colonisation and sovereignty

Sovereignty

[2.2.1]   In the colonial era, 'international' law (the law governing the relations between European states) permitted 'sovereign' European states to take over territory outside their borders, establishing 'sovereign' governments there. Non-Europeans were not treated as enjoying sovereignty over their territories. The takeover of territory by one European power from another involved a change in sovereignty, but the takeover of territory from non-Europeans was treated as involving establishment of a sovereign government for the first time.

International law governing Australia's acquisition

[2.2.2]   Normative attempts to justify European colonialism began long before 1788. European violence and territorial acquisition in the Holy Land from the 11th century was justified by reference to the sacredness of the territory and the universality of Christ's Church. Papal authority was relied on for territorial acquisition in Ireland and the Americas. After Columbus' 'discovery', the pope conferred on Spain 'power, authority and jurisdiction' over most of the 'New World' for 'the expansion of the Christian rule': Williams (1992).

Legal discourse on colonisation changed over time, reflecting changes in European thought and methods and purposes of colonial acquisition. The 16th century theologian Franciscus de Victoria articulated a theory for the treatment of 'Indians' in his 1557 'Law of Nations'. In his view, the only just cause for dispossessing the Americans was a lack of 'reason' on their part. Spain had not established title to the Americas simply by 'discovering' them. Thus, while the Americans were not subject to papal authority, they were subject to the 'Law of Nations' (what we now call public international law). This law encoded European ideas of appropriate behaviour by 'civilised' states. It required the Americans to accept the Spanish, to trade with them and to allow them access to 'common' resources, including 'common' property. Spanish dominion over the Americans could be established for their benefit (including their Christian conversion), 'just as if the natives were infants'; the 'Law of Nations' thus required the Americans to accept missionaries. If the Americans defied the 'Law of Nations', the Spanish were justified in making war on them: Williams (1992) Ch 2.

[2.2.3]   After centuries of attempting to consolidate control over the ethnically and culturally different Irish and Welsh, England became involved in 'New World' colonialism after the Reformation. English imperialism was fuelled by the commercial ambitions of its emerging merchant class and domestic overpopulation. It was justified by accounts of Spanish colonial 'cruelties' and chauvinistic ideas about land use. The 'savages' would welcome 'civilised' Protestants 'planted' among them, teaching them how to behave and use land productively: Williams (1992) Chs 4 and 5.

For 17th century philosopher John Locke (also a British colonial official), property in land depended on investment of labour in it. Many native Americans were cultivators, but for Locke they were in a 'pre-political' and 'pre-propertied' stage of development, so that their territories could be appropriated by Europeans. See *Report of the Royal Commission on Aboriginal Peoples* (1996) pp 44–5; Dorsett (1995) pp 228–35.

[2.2.4] The 'Law of Nations' of the time reflected these ideas. It allowed European states to acquire *inhabited* territory from one another:

- by 'conquest', including by force (a method not permitted today); or

- by surrender, including under a treaty (sometimes referred to as 'cession').

It also permitted acquisition of 'uninhabited territory' (*terra nullius*) by discovery and occupation. Britain's American colonies were established by this method, despite prior indigenous occupation.

[2.2.5] By the late 18th century, these ideas had hardened in 'international' law. When 'New South Wales' was established, the concept of *terra nullius* included territory occupied by 'backward populations' lacking European forms of government and 'failing' to cultivate their territories. The international lawyer Emer de Vattel, influential in Britain, wrote in his 1758 *Law of Nations*:

> Every nation is ... obliged by the law of nature to cultivate the land that has fallen to its share; and it has no right to enlarge its boundaries ... but in proportion as the land in its possession is incapable of furnishing it with necessaries ...
>
> It is asked whether a nation may lawfully take possession of some part of a vast country, in which there are none but erratic nations whose scanty population is incapable of occupying the whole! ... Their ... habitation ... cannot be accounted a true and legal possession; and the people of Europe, too closely pent up at home, finding land of which the savages stood in no particular need, and of which they made no actual and constant use, were lawfully entitled to take possession of it ... We do not ... deviate from the views of nature, in confining the Indians within narrower limits ... (Extracted in McRae et al (1991) pp 76–8).

[2.2.6] Indigenous Australians were not treated as enjoying original sovereignty over Australia. There was no official military conquest of any of them, although there were many military and police offensives against them after British sovereignty was established: see **[2.2.24]**. There was no official attempt to procure surrender of territory by them, although there was at least one private attempt to procure a surrender of Aboriginal land: see **[2.2.45]** below.

Cook's *Instructions* seemed to reflect Vattel's concern with 'confining the Indians within narrower limits':

> You are also with consent of the natives to take possession of convenient situations in the country in the name of the King of Great Britain, or, if you find the country uninhabited take possession for His Majesty by setting up proper marks and inscriptions as first discoverers and possessors (quoted in Bennett and Castles (1979) pp 253–4).

However, Cook claimed possession of the whole continent and islands without consent in a ceremony on Possession Island, off Cape York, on 22 August 1770. According to Castles, he did so '[a]lmost of necessity in the circumstances', there being 'no real possibility of acquiring territory with the consent of the Aborigines', given the expedition's fleeting contact with people who apparently lacked 'possession' of their lands: Castles (1982) p 22.

[2.2.7] Did Britain follow Cook's discovery with 'occupation' in the sense required by international law? Deane and Gaudron JJ observed in *Mabo v Queensland (No 2)* (1992) 175 CLR 1 at 78 that:

> ... contemporary international law would seem to have required a degree of actual occupation of a 'discovered' territory over which sovereignty was claimed by settlement and it is scarcely arguable that the establishment by Phillip in 1788 of a penal camp at Sydney Cove constituted occupation of the vast areas of the hinterland of eastern Australia ...

Initial colonisation did not involve 'confinement within narrower limits' of the indigenous population. Aboriginal people were dispossessed of their traditional lands. The Van Diemen's Land population was exported to Flinders Island. Small 'reserves' were first set aside for Aboriginal people in the 1840s. The only serious attempt to protect Aboriginal occupation, the South Australian Letters Patent **[2.3.15]**, was undermined by local insistence that Aboriginal people did not truly possess land: Reynolds (1992) Ch 5.

[2.2.8] International law rules about the acquisition of territory continued to change in the 19th century, as European powers made a 'grab for Africa'. In its *Advisory Opinion on Western Sahara* [1975] ICJR 12, the International Court of Justice determined that 'the State practice of [1884] indicates that territories inhabited by tribes or peoples having a social and political organisation [like Western Sahara] were not regarded as *terrae nullius*'. In such cases, 'acquisition of sovereignty was not generally considered as effected unilaterally through "occupation" ... but through agreements concluded with the local rulers': [1975] ICJR at 39.

[2.2.9] This raises important questions about the role of (ill-informed) European perceptions of indigenous populations in the formulation of legal norms. Two persistent problems for Aboriginal people (if not for Torres Strait Islanders) have been the perception of Aboriginal occupation of Tasmania and the mainland as 'erratic', not ordered, and the perception that Aboriginal societies were not organised polities. The former view inaccurately represented traditional land use, which ranged from sedentariness to territorially- and seasonally-confined nomadism. The latter view may have reflected Aboriginal values of secular egalitarianism (no 'head men') and 'localism' (politics focused locally, not pan-Aboriginally), but such values neither indicate an absence of laws nor justify those laws' displacement.

Can the lawfulness of Australian sovereignty be questioned?

[2.2.10] 'Indigenous' claims for improved human rights, increased autonomy, greater legal pluralism, recognition of and compensation for past injustices and even improved material conditions are sometimes framed as claims to 'sovereignty': Behrendt (2003) Ch 4. While these claims reflect a desire for change in sovereign institutions, they are separate from the question of Australia's sovereignty under international law: *ibid*.

[2.2.11] The legality of Britain's acquisition of Australia has not been determined by an international tribunal but would be difficult to agitate today. Such questions must be resolved under the law of the relevant period. Indigenous Australians do not have standing before the International Court of Justice — only states have standing. Disputes may only be brought to the court with the consent of the parties, and it is unlikely that the Australian Government would agree to the court adjudicating its sovereignty. Indigenous Australians could try to seek an advisory opinion from the court, but such an opinion can only be requested by the United Nations General Assembly or Security Council. The court is unlikely to entertain such a request in the absence of a challenge to Australian sovereignty by another state: see Balkin (1988) p 34.

[2.2.12] Nor will the High Court entertain challenges to Australian sovereignty, as Brennan J explained in *Mabo v Queensland (No 2)* (1992) 175 CLR 1 at 31:

> The acquisition of a territory by a sovereign state for the first time is an act of state which cannot be challenged, controlled or interfered with by the courts of that state.
>
> This principle, stated by Gibbs J in the *Seas and Submerged Lands* case, *New South Wales v Commonwealth* (1975) 135 CLR at 388, precludes any contest between the executive and the judicial branches of government as to whether a territory is or is not within the Crown's Dominions.

British 'imperial law', 'municipal law' and indigenous people: the law applicable to colonies and the status of their populations

[2.2.13] British 'imperial common law' governed the method and consequences of acquisition of colonial territory: Walters (1996). These principles developed out of the Norman conquest of England (1066), the conquest (1171) and reconquest (1603) of Ireland (*The Case of Tanistry* (1608) Davis 28; 80 ER 516), consolidation of control over Wales between 1277 and 1536 (*Witrong v Blany* (1674) 3 Keb 401; 84 ER 789) and the relationship between England and Scotland before union in 1707.

[2.2.14] British imperial law permitted the Crown to annex territory under its prerogative powers (powers given to the Crown by the common law) as an 'act of state'. Although legislation could be used, it was not necessary. Australian colonies were constituted when the Crown proclaimed sovereignty over them, not when they were 'discovered'. The dates on which sovereignty was asserted are discussed at **[2.3.1]–[2.3.3]**. These dates are critical in native title claims, as discussed at **[2.3.9]–[2.3.10]**.

[2.2.15] What law applied in newly colonised territory? There were at least five possibilities: the law of the colonised, the law of England (English 'municipal' law, including the common law), some combination of the two, different ('personal') laws for colonised people and English settlers, or different laws for different parts of the colony (ethnic enclaves).

What was the legal status of colonised people? Were they aliens (that is, like other Europeans), 'subjects' of the English monarch, or something else? Did the answer depend on how they were colonised, or where they lived? Practical considerations (for example, the relative sizes of the invaded and invading populations, the capacity of the English to enforce their law) could influence the answers to these questions, as could English legal chauvinism — the belief that the best protection that could be extended to Englishmen (and some 'civilised' others) was that of English law.

These factors can be seen at work in England's first colonial experiment, Ireland. Before 1603, despite attempts to introduce English law, the 'wild Irish' were largely subject to brehon law, except in English enclaves ('the Pale', to which statute applied English law). They were aliens whose segregation meant they must buy charters of denization before they could exercise rights in 'the Pale': Dorsett (2002). The reconquest of Ireland involved statutory application to Ireland of English 'municipal' law, and conversion of the Irish into subjects: Dorsett (2002), Walters (1996). There was less tolerance of local 'customs' under this English 'municipal' common law than under British 'imperial' common law, which had governed the pre-1603 England–Ireland relationship: Walters (1996) at 797. Principles governing the relationship between the common law and other legal orders had a different history: they emerged out of the 'common law's struggle for dominance over local legal orders (for example, manorial land tenure law during the decline of the feudal system): Dorsett (2002). A legacy of this struggle was a set of narrow common law principles controlling the terms on which it would 'recognise' other orders as 'customs': Dorsett (2002).

[2.2.16E] Walters, 'Mohegan Indians v Connecticut (1705–73) and the legal status of Aboriginal customary laws and government in British North America'

(1996) 33(4) Osgoode Hall Law Journal 785

[790] By the late seventeenth century, British imperial common law began to distinguish between two types of colonies: those acquired by conquest and/or cession from foreign peoples and those acquired by the discovery and occupation — or settlement — of uninhabited territories. In settled territories, British settlers were considered to have carried with them relevant parts of English municipal law which formed the basis of the colonial law by which they would be governed. The Crown (or Parliament) then established the necessary local common-law courts and representative legislatures to give that colonial legal system an institutional framework. Aside from this constitutive function, however, the Crown had no right to legislate for the colony; settlers were protected from the royal prerogative by principles of English law as their 'birthright'. In conquered/ceded territories, the Crown did have the right to legislate without Parliament; it could therefore establish new laws for the conquered nation through an instrument of prerogative [791] legislation. However, until such prerogative legislation was enacted, British courts presumed that the existing laws and institutions of the local people continued in force at common law insofar as they had not already been abrogated by act of state, were not inconsistent with subjection to British sovereignty (thus, local law remained in force 'excepting in point of soveraignty'), and were not contrary to British conceptions of justice and humanity (local law could not be *malum in se*). By this common-law 'principle of continuity', previously foreign legal systems were incorporated within the imperial constitutional order: the existing local legal system became one of the municipal legal systems of the empire parallel to the internal systems of England and England's other imperial possessions but subject to and deriving legitimacy from the over-arching imperial constitution.

Where English colonies were established in conquered/ceded territories where local laws were unsuitable for English settlers, a degree of legal pluralism in the newly acquired territory was often acknowledged. Relevant parts of English law were usually introduced as the colonial municipal law of the settlers but, with respect to local laws and peoples, three general results were possible: local law might be abrogated and local peoples subjected to the same colonial law as settlers; elements of local law might remain in force as part of the local colonial system (much as particular customs were recognized by the English municipal common law in England); or, finally, local law together with its institutions might remain in force as a distinct system under imperial law independent from the local colonial legal system introduced for settlers.

~~~

Notes

[2.2.17]   The principles referred to by Walters were established by a string of 17th and 18th century decisions, including *Calvin's* case (1608) 7 Co Rep 2a; 77 ER 377, *Blankard v Galdy* (1693) Holt KB 341 at 342; 90 ER 1089 and *Campbell v Hall* (1774), Lofft 655, and reiterated by the textbook writer Blackstone in his Commentaries.

Calvin's case established that those born within the dominions of the Crown were subjects, not aliens. The Chief Justice of the Court of Common Pleas, Lord Coke, explained:

> [T]hey that are born under the obedience, power, faith, ligealty, or ligeance of the King, are natural subjects, and no aliens ...
>
> There is found in the law four kinds of ligeances; the first is ... originally ... due by nature and birth-right ... The second is ... not by nature but by acquisition or deniza- tion ... The third is ... wrought by the law; and that is when an alien that is in amity cometh into England ... [and] within the King's protection ... The fourth is a legal obe- dience ... because the municipal laws of this realm have prescribed the order and form of it; and this is to be done upon oath ...
>
> [D]enization of an alien may be effected ... by conquest, as if the King and his subjects should conquer another kingdom or dominion, as well *antenati* as *postnati*, as well they which fought in the field, as they which remained at home, for defence of their country, or employed elsewhere, are all denizens of the kingdom or dominion con- quered ...
>
> [T]he protection and government of the King is general over all his dominions and kingdoms, as well in time of peace by justice, as in time of war by the sword, and ... all be at his command, and under his obedience ... [S]eeing the King's power, com- mand, and protection extendeth out of England, that ligeance cannot be local ... (7 Co rep 2a at 5b–9b; 77 ER at 383–8).

[2.2.18E]   Blackstone's Commentaries on the Laws of England
Tucker's Blackstone's commentaries (1803)

SECTION THE FOURTH

OF THE COUNTRIES SUBJECT TO THE LAWS OF ENGLAND

... Plantations or colonies, in distant countries, are either such where the lands are claimed by right of occupancy only, by finding them desart [*sic*] and uncultivated, and peopling them from the mother country; or where, when already cultivated, they have either gained, by conquest, or ceded to us by treaties. And both these rights are founded upon the law of nature, or at least upon that of nations. But there is a difference between these two species of colonies, with respect to the laws by which they are bound. For it hath been held, that if an uninhabited country be discovered and planted by English subjects, all the English laws then in being, which are the birthright of every subject, are immediately there in force. But this must be understood with very many and very great restrictions. *Such colonists carry with them only so much of the English law, as is applicable to their own situation and the condition of an infant colony*; such, for instance, as the general rules of inheritance, and of protection from personal injuries ... The artificial refinements and distinctions incident to the property of a great and commercial people, the laws of police and revenue, (such especially as are inforced by penalties) the mode of maintenance for the established clergy, the jurisdiction of spiritual courts, and a multitude of other provisions, are neither necessary nor convenient for them, and therefore are not in force. What shall be admitted and what rejected, at what times, and under what restrictions, must, in case of dispute, be decided in the first instance by their own provincial judicature, subject to the revision and control of the king in council: the whole of their constitution being also liable to be new-modelled and reformed by the general superintending power of the legislature in the mother country. But in conquered or ceded countries, that have already laws of their own, the king may indeed alter and change those laws; but, till he does actually change them, the antient laws of the country remain, unless such as are against the law of God, as in the case of an infidel country ... Our American plantations are principally of this latter sort, being obtained in the last century either by right of conquest and driving out the natives (with what natural justice I shall not at present enquire) or by treaties. And therefore the common law of England, as such, has no allowance or authority there; they being no part of the mother country, but distinct (though dependent) dominions. They are subject however to the control of the parliament, though (like Ireland, Man, and the rest) not bound by any acts of parliament, unless particularly named. [emphasis added]

~~~

Notes

[2.2.19] Blackstone considered that 'only so much of the English law, as is applicable ... to the condition of an infant colony' was carried by British settlers to 'desart and uncultivated' lands. Note also Blacktone's qualification of the 'conquered colony' principle: even in those possessions, the British would not tolerate the continuity of 'infidel' laws (those which Walters describes as 'contrary to British conceptions of justice and humanity' or *malum in se*). Note also Blackstone's confusion on the legal basis for the British possessions in the Americas; territories like western Canada were obtained by 'settlement'.

[2.2.20] Blackstone's last point about the colonies being 'not bound by any acts of parliament, unless particularly named' applied to all British colonies. The legal inheritance of 'settlers' in a previously 'desart and uncultivated' colony included not only the English common law but also all British statutes in force on the date of settlement (at least those 'applicable to an infant colony'). However, settler colonies did not inherit British amendments to that legislative inheritance unless these were specifically addressed to the colony. 'Municipal' British legislation was designed only for application in Britain; in ordinary settler colonies it was anticipated that local legislatures would amend or replace it.

[2.2.21] In the Australian colonies, these principles in theory meant that English common law and British statutes in force in 1788 (to the extent that these suited local conditions) applied to eastern Aboriginal people from the date at which sovereignty was asserted, and that at least those Aboriginal people born after sovereignty was asserted became British subjects. However, imperial policy was ambivalent on these questions for some time. For the first 50 years after 1788, confusion reigned in New South Wales as to how the colonies were obtained (by conquest or settlement?), whether Aboriginal people were 'subjects' or aliens, and whether English law applied to them: Bayne (1988) pp 213–4; Kercher (1998b) at 411 and **[2.2.29]**. Even Phillip's *Instructions* **[2.3.14]** distinguished between 'our subjects' and 'the natives'.

[2.2.22] United States 'federal Indian law' developed in a different direction. In 1776, there were some 'Indian tribes' within the 13 federating states, and many others in territory belonging to other European powers to the west and south, political outsiders to the new federation. The US Constitution conferred on Congress power 'To regulate Commerce ... with the Indian Tribes' (art I, s 8), prohibited states from entering treaties (art I, s 10, cl 1) and provided that 'all

Treaties made... under the Authority of the United States shall [along with the Constitution and laws of Congress] be the supreme Law of the Land...' (Art VI, cl 2).

Despite Congress' express power to legislate with respect to 'Indian tribes', the early US Supreme Court also began to develop doctrines governing them based on the inherent powers of the United States as a sovereign nation under the 'law of nations', the tribes' non-membership of the federal union, and the court's recognition of their territorial base as 'Indian title' (the more robust ancestor of Australian native title). The court characterised tribes as 'domestic dependent nations' with power to regulate their internal affairs under the 'pupillage' or 'wardship' of Congress, immune from state jurisdiction: *Cherokee Nation v Georgia* (1831) 5 Peters 1; *Worcester v Georgia* (1831) 6 Peters 515; *Ex parte Crow Dog* 109 US 556 (1883); *United States v Kagama* 118 US 373 (1886). They were political entities with which the federal government could enter 'treaties' in the constitutional sense; Congress adopted a policy of (unequal and typically unjust) treaty-making until 1871.

These principles form the basis of US 'federal Indian law'. Because of the absence of comparable constitutional arrangements and decisions, such principles are unknown in Australia.

[2.2.23] *Calvin's* case **[2.2.17]** was not applied to members of 'Indian tribes'. Despite an 1868 constitutional amendment guaranteeing United States citizenship to 'all persons born ... in the United States, and subject to the jurisdiction thereof', the Supreme Court denied members of 'Indian tribes' citizenship until it was extended to them by statute: see Citizenship Act 1924; Getches, Wilkinson and Williams (1993) pp 738–9.

Were the Australian colonies conquered? Did indigenous law or sovereignty survive colonisation?

[2.2.24] Early New South Wales and Van Diemen's Land were penal colonies for which the Governor often made laws: Evatt (1938) pp 420–1; Neal (1991). As Brennan J pointed out in *Mabo v Queensland (No 2)* (1975) 175 CLR 1 at 37, there are doubts about the validity of some such exercises of legislative power by the executive — at least those contrary to the laws of England: see Campbell (1964). The fact that these colonies were under largely executive administration has sometimes been taken to suggest that they were conquered, not settled, with the result that principles of British 'imperial' law recognised their pre-existing legal systems.

This hypothesis derives some support from the fact that considerable direct violence was perpetrated against Aboriginal people by the state during the first 150 years, most of it land-related. Many Aboriginal people resisted in a manner which could be characterised as guerilla warfare. Martial law was declared around Bathurst in the 1820s and in Tasmania in the 1830s following violence between Aboriginal people and settlers or governments. However, important legal material to support a theory that Australia was conquered is lacking. There was never an official declaration of war against Aboriginal people. Rather, the violence perpetrated against them occurred after they became British subjects under the rule in *Calvin's* case (1608) 7 Co Rep 2a; 77 ER 377 **[2.2.17]**. That violence was often carried out by the arm of government charged with protecting British subjects, the police, and not by the army.

[2.2.25]   In the 19th century, a few Aboriginal people and lawyers sought to persuade colonial courts that Aboriginal people should be governed by their own laws, in part because they were a 'conquered' people. In its first year of operation, 1824, the Supreme Court of New South Wales ruled that the British were subject to English law for offences against Aboriginal people: *R v Johnston*, per Forbes CJ. In 1827, the Supreme Court made explicit its view that Aboriginal people were also subject to English law for offences against the invaders: *R v Lowe*, per Forbes CJ. However, the court initially disavowed jurisdiction over offences by Aboriginal people against one another, a year after the Australian Courts Act 1828 (Imp) declared that the law of England applied to the colony and explicitly directed colonial courts to exercise English criminal jurisdiction: see **[2.2.33]**. In 1829 (*R v Ballard or Barrett*), Forbes CJ and Dowling J ruled that Aboriginal people were not subject to English law for offences *inter se*. The text of *Ballard* and other cases is reproduced in Kercher, *Decisions of the Superior Courts of New South Wales, 1788–1899*.

[2.2.26C]   R v Ballard or Barrett

Supreme Court of New South Wales, 13 June 1829
Dowling, Proceedings of the Supreme Court, Vol 22,
Archives Office of New South Wales, 2/3205

Forbes CJ: [99] Certainly this is a case *sui generis*, and the Court must deal with it upon general principles, in the absence of any fixed known rule upon the subject. … [T]he Court is of opinion that the prisoner ought to be discharged for want of jurisdiction … [100] … The prisoner is accused of the murder of one of his own tribe — one of the original natives of this Country, in the same state as himself — wandering about the country, and living in the uncontrolled freedom of nature … I believe it has been the practice of the Courts of this country, since the Colony was settled, never to interfere with or enter into the quarrels that have taken place between or amongst the natives themselves … [101] It has been the policy of the Judges, & I assume of the Government, in like manner with other Colonies, not to enter into or interfere with any cause of dispute or quarrel between the aboriginal natives.

His Honour referred to the application of British law to offences across racial lines.

[B]ut I am not aware that British laws have been applied to the aboriginal natives in transactions solely between themselves, whether of contract, tort, or crime. Indeed it appears to me that it is a wise principle to abstain in this Colony, [102] as has been done in the North American British Colonies, with the institutions of the natives which, upon experience will be found to rest upon principles of natural justice. There is one most important distinction between the savage & civilized state of man, namely that amongst savages there are no magistrates. The savages decide their differences upon a principle of retaliation. They give up no natural rights. This is not merely matter of theory but practice. In the civilized state, man gives up certain natural rights, in exchange for the advantage of social security, & other benefit arising from the institutions of civilized life. It may be a question admitting of doubt, whether any advantages could be gained, without previous preparation, by ingrafting the institutions of our country, upon the natural system which savages have adopted for their own government. It is known as matter of experience [103] that the savages of this part of the globe, have a mode of dressing wrongs committed amongst themselves, which is perfectly agreeable to their own natures & dispositions, and is productive, amongst themselves, of as much good, as any novel or strange institution which might be imparted to them. In the absence of a magistracy which is an institution peculiar to an advanced state of refinement, the savage is governed by the laws of his tribe — & with these he is content. In point of practice, how could the laws of England be applied to this state of society? By the law of England the party accused is entitled to his full defence. Then how could this beneficent principle be acted upon, where the parties are wholly unacquainted with our language, laws & customs? I am not prepared to say, that the mode of administering justice or repairing a wrong amongst a wild savage people, is not best left to themselves. If their institutions, however barbarous or abhorrent [104] from our notions of religion and civilization, become matured into a system and produced all the effects upon their intercourse, that a less objectionable course of proceeding (in our judgment) could produce, then I know not upon what principle of municipal jurisdiction it would be right to interfere with them. The most important object of all human associations is to procure protection & security from internal as well as external aggression. This principle will be found to influence the associations of some of the wildest savage tribes. They make laws for themselves, which are preserved inviolate, & are rigidly acted upon. However, shocking some of their institutions may be to our notions of humanity & justice, yet I am at loss to know how, or upon what principle this court could take cognizance of offences committed by a barbarous people amongst themselves. They cannot be supposed to be acquainted [105] with our laws, & nature prompts them to disdain the interposition of a race of people whom they find fixed in a country to which they did not originally belong. There is reason & good sense in the principle that in all transactions between the natives & British subjects, the laws of the latter shall prevail, because they afford equal protection to all men whether actually or by fiction of law brought within their cognizance. But I know no principle of municipal or national law, which shall subject the inhabitants of a newly found country, to the operation of the laws of the finders, in matters of dispute, injury, or aggression between themselves. If part of our system is to be introduced amongst them, why not the whole? Where will you draw the line: the intervention of our courts of justice, even if practicable, must lead to other interferences, as incompatible as impolitic, in the affairs of [106] harmless inoffensive savages ...

~~~

Notes

[2.2.27] Forbes CJ maintained this view early in *R v Murrell* and *Bummaree* (1836) Legge 73: see Kercher (*Decisions of the Superior Courts of New South Wales, 1788–1899*). However, in the final decision in that case (delivered just before he left the colony in poor health), Forbes CJ and Dowling J concurred with Burton J that the court did enjoy jurisdiction over intra-Aboriginal offences. Burton J referred to both the common law and the Australian Courts Act 1828 (UK), but appeared to regard Aboriginal people as aliens, not subjects. The text of *Ballard* and other cases (above) and *Murrell* (below) is reproduced in Kercher, *Decisions of the Superior Courts of New South Wales, 1788–1899*.

[2.2.28C]   **R v Murrell and Bummaree**

Supreme Court of New South Wales, 11 April 1836
Supreme Court, Miscellaneous Correspondence relating to Aborigines,
State Records of New South Wales, 5/1161, pp 210–216

Burton J (with whom Forbes CJ and Dowling J agreed): [210] ...[T]he grounds of my opinion ...are these:

[211] 1st although it be granted that the aboriginal natives of New Holland are entitled to be regarded by Civilized nations as a free and independent people, and are entitled to the possession of those rights which as such are valuable to them, yet the various tribes had not attained at the first settlement of the English people amongst them to such a position in point of numbers and civilization, and to such a form of Government and laws, as to be entitled to be recognized as so many sovereign states governed by laws of their own.

2ndly, That a tract of country before unappropriated by any one has been taken into actual possession by the King of England under the sanction of Parliament comprehended within the following limits.

His Honour set out the 1825 proclamation extending New South Wales to the 129th parallel of longitude: see **[2.3.1]**.

[212] 3rdly, That the English nation has obtained and exercised for many years the rights of Domain and Empire over the country thus possessed and particularly it is designated by [the Australian Courts Act 1828] as His Majesty's Settlement and Colony of New South Wales; and Courts of Judicature have been established and the laws of England are declared to be those which shall be administered within it and a local legislature is given to it.

4thly, An offence is stated upon the Record to have been committed by the prisoner within this Colony, [213] a place where by the Common Law and by the [Australian Courts Act] the law of England is the law of the land, which if committed by him at Westminster in England, would render him amenable to the Jurisdiction of His Majesty's Court of Kings Bench; and by [the Australian Courts Act] it is enacted that this Court 'shall have cognizance of all pleas civil, criminal, or mixed, in all cases whatsoever as fully and amply to all intents and purposes in New South Wales and all and every the Islands and territories which nor are, or hereafter may be subject to or dependent upon the Government thereof as His Majesty's Courts of Kings Bench, Common Pleas, and Exchequer at Westminster or either of them lawfully have or hath in England', and that this Court 'shall be at all times a Court of Oyer and Terminer and gaol delivery in and for New South Wales and the Dependencies thereof' and that 'the Judges shall have and exercise such and the like Jurisdiction and authority in New South Wales and the dependencies thereof as the Judges of the Courts of Kings Bench, Common Pleas, and [214] Exchequer in England or any of them lawfully have & exercise, and as shall be necessary for carrying in effect the several Jurisdictions, powers and authorities committed to it'.

5thly, This Court has repeatedly tried and even executed aboriginal natives of this Colony, for offences committed by them upon subjects of the King, ... and there is no distinction in law in respect to the protection due to his person between a subject living in this Colony under the Kings Peace and an alien living therein under the Kings Peace ...

[215] Respecting those difficulties and inconveniences and hardships ... referred to as likely to arise from this decision ... Some ... as for example the probability of multiplied business to Magistrates and others concerned in the administration of Justice, I look upon as little likely to occur, but if occurring certain to produce the best results as to the, Natives themselves: difficulties, it is the business of the local legislature to remove and hardships I doubt not that His Majesty, or those vested with the exercise of His Royal Prerogative of Mercy, will be ready in every case which may justly call it forth, to extend it to people so circumstanced as they. But I am of opinion that the greatest possible inconvenience and scandal to this community would be consequent if it were to be holden by this Court that it has no Jurisdiction in such a case as the present — to be holden in fact that crimes of murder [216] and others of almost equal enormity may be committed by those people in our Streets without restraint so they be committed only upon one another! & that our laws are no sanctuary to them.

~~~

Notes

[2.2.29] In 1841 in *R v Bonjon*, a Port Phillip judge, Willis J, expressed the view that Aboriginal crimes *inter se* were a matter for the 'tribes' under their own law on the United States model: see above **[2.2.22]**. This view was overruled by the Colonial Office with Dowling CJ's support: see Hookey (1984), Kercher (1998a). A parallel debate over the jurisdiction of courts over Aboriginal people occurred in Western Australia: Hunter (2003).

Murrell was based partly on *terra nullius* reasoning: Kercher (1998b). By the late 19th century, it was firmly established that the common law had applied to the Australian colonies because they were 'tract[s] of territory *practically unoccupied,* without settled inhabitants or settled law, at the time when ... peacefully [sic] annexed to the British dominions': *Cooper v Stuart* (1889) 14 App Cas 286 at 291.

This reasoning was affirmed as late as 1971 in *Milirrpum v Nabalco* (the *Gove Land Rights* case) (1971) 17 FLR 141. However, as Deane and Gaudron JJ pointed out in *Mabo v Queensland (No 2)* (1992) 175 CLR 1, judicial reasoning supporting the proposition that Australia was previously uninhabited consisted of 'little more than bare assertion': 175 CLR at 103–4 **[2.2.30]**.

In the 1970s, some Aboriginal people sought to persuade the High Court that the Australian colonies were obtained by conquest of 'indigenous' sovereigns. At that time, the Australian courts denied the existence of a common law doctrine of native title. The conquest theory was advanced in the hope that prior Aboriginal land laws continued to operate because they had not been abrogated by the invading sovereign or parliament.

In *Coe v Commonwealth* (1979) 24 ALR 118, Jacobs and Murphy JJ expressed willingness to reopen the question of how the Australian colonies were acquired. However, the two other justices, Gibbs and Aickin JJ, proclaimed it 'fundamental to our legal system [that] the Australian colonies became British possessions by settlement and not by conquest': 24 ALR at 129. For them, the question was one of law, not fact (at 129):

> [A] distinction was drawn between a colony acquired by conquest or cession, in which there was an established system of law of European type, and [one] acquired by settlement in a territory which, by European standards had no civilised inhabitants or settled law. Australia has always been regarded as belonging to the latter class.

[2.2.30]   In *Mabo v Queensland (No 2)* (1992) 175 CLR 1, the High Court affirmed that the Australian colonies were acquired by settlement, not conquest, but rejected the idea that they were unoccupied when acquired: Simpson (1993). As discussed at **[2.2.12]** above, it was not open to the court to decide this question for international law purposes. However, it decided the question for the purposes of Australian real property law; namely, the law of native title, discussed at **[2.2.32]–[2.2.43]** below. Brennan J outlined the basis on which the English common law became the law of the Australian colonies (at 37–8):

> In a settled colony in inhabited territory, the law of England was not merely the personal law of the English colonists; it became the law of the land, protecting and binding colonists and indigenous inhabitants alike and equally ... [A]s the indigenous inhabitants were regarded as barbarous or unsettled and without a settled law, the law of England including the common law became the law of the Colony (so far as it was locally applicable) as though New South Wales were 'an uninhabited country ... discovered and planted by English subjects' [*Cooper v Stuart*] ... Its introduction to New South Wales was confirmed by s 24 of the Australian Courts Act 1828 (UK) ...

[2.2.31]   Of course, the protection of the common law (for example, the rights to life, liberty, property and jury trial enshrined in Magna Carta) was of little assistance to Aboriginal people in the colonial period. Besides the violence of the 'frontier', there was widespread official and private kidnapping of Aboriginal people which was not treated as false imprisonment: Bayne (1988) p 214. As noted below at **[2.2.33]**, in the case of Aboriginal suspects, the punitive expedition often substituted for the jury trial. Further, as discussed at **[2.2.39]–[2.2.40]**, before 1992 the common law justified the dispossession of Aboriginal people and Torres Strait Islanders.

[2.2.32]   Since 1992, the doctrine of native title has accorded limited recognition to indigenous land traditions: see **[2.2.34]–[2.2.37]**. However, the possibility that other 'indigenous' traditions might be recognised by the common law has been rejected, as has the 'notion that the application of Commonwealth or state laws to Aboriginal people is in any way subject to their acceptance, adoption, request or consent': *Walker v New South Wales* (1994) 82 CLR 45 at 47. According to Mason CJ in that case, '[s]uch notions amount to the contention that a new source of sovereignty resides in the Aboriginal people'. In *Coe v Commonwealth (No 2)* (1993) 118 ALR 193, Mason CJ said at 200:

> *Mabo (No 2)* is entirely at odds with the notion[s] that sovereignty adverse to the Crown resides in the Aboriginal people ... [and] ... that there resides in the Aboriginal people a limited kind of sovereignty embraced in the notion that they are a 'domestic dependent nation' entitled to self-government and full rights ... or that as a free and independent people they are entitled to any rights and interests other than those created or recognised by the laws of the Commonwealth, the State of New South Wales and the common law.

[2.2.33]   In light of the confusion over applicability to a penal colony of English law, the Australian Courts Act 1828 (UK), s 24, fixed a date from which imperial legislation, enacted before their establishment, was to be treated as operating in the colonies. It stated:

> ... that all Laws and Statutes in force within the Realm of England at the time of the passing of this Act (not being inconsistent herewith ...) shall be applied in the Administration of Justice in the courts of New South Wales and Van Diemen's Land respectively, so far as the same can be applied within the said colonies.

Section 24 also conferred on the Governors and Legislative Councils power to clear up 'doubts' about the application of English law via local ordinances. Imperial statutes applied to Western Australia from 1829: *Western Australia v Commonwealth* (the *Native Title Act* case) (1995) 183 CLR 373 at 425. In theory, therefore, indigenous Australians became entitled after 1828 to the protection of imperial legislation, including the immunities from cruel and unusual punishment or executive suspension of laws in the Bill of Rights 1688. However, whether or not the 'suitability for local conditions' exception allowed for the non-application of these protections in Australia, many Aboriginal people were denied these protections. In the eighteenth and nineteenth (and in some places in the twentieth) centuries, Aboriginal criminality was often met with official punitive expeditions against entire Aboriginal populations. Some expeditions were led or formally sanctioned by Governors or 'protectors' of Aboriginal people. 'Successful' expeditions killed Aboriginal people indiscriminately, without regard to individual responsibility. Aboriginal people were not tried by their peers and were disadvantaged by the common law rule that only Christians could give evidence on oath: Reynolds (1987); Bayne (1988) p 214.

[2.2.34]   The doctrine of native title accords limited 'recognition' to 'indigenous' land traditions. 'Indigenous' claimants must prove traditional connections to land grounded in legal systems which existed at the date when sovereignty was asserted over the relevant land and which have 'had a continuous existence and vitality since': *Members of the Yorta Yorta Aboriginal Community v Victoria* (2002) 194 ALR 538 at [43]–[47]. The relevant date is the date of assertion of *sovereignty*, not when the state or territory was established as a separate colony. The date of sovereignty is critical because, according to Gleeson CJ, Gummow and Hayne JJ in *Yorta Yorta* at [43]–[44]:

> Upon the Crown acquiring sovereignty, the [indigenous] normative or law-making system which existed could not thereafter validly create new rights, duties or interests.

Rights or interests in land created after sovereignty and which owed their origin and continued existence *only* to a normative system other than that of the new sovereign power, would not and will not be given effect by the legal order of the new sovereign ... [T]he assertion of sovereignty by the British Crown necessarily entailed ... that there could thereafter be no parallel law-making system in the territory ...

See also Callinan J, 194 ALR 538 at [186].

[2.2.35]   That is, Australian law does not recognise the 'continuous existence and vitality' of indigenous legal systems as legal systems, but only as sources of norms shaping property rights which Australian law 'recognises' on its own terms. For example, although the judges genuflect to the 'essentially spiritual' connection of 'indigenous' people to 'country' and state that '[i]t is wrong to see Aboriginal connection with land as reflected only in concepts of control of access to it' (*Ward v Western Australia* (2002) 191 ALR 1 at [14], [90]); the common law will not recognise 'indigenous' traditions which are inconsistent with it: *Commonwealth v Yarmirr* (2001) 208 CLR 1 at [47]–[49]. Australian law also perceives indigenous land traditions as conferring limited sets of identifiable rights, rather than establishing more fundamental people–land relationships: *Ward v Western Australia* (2002) 191 ALR 1 at [94]–[95]. And the courts have refused to give effect to land-related traditions which generate rights diverging widely from those familiar to Anglo-Australian property law (for example, rights to control expression of land-related motifs: *Ward v Western Australia* (2002) 191 ALR 1 at [59]–[60]; *Bulun Bulun v R & T Textiles Pty Ltd* (1998) 86 FCR 244 at 256; and *Western Australia v Ward* (2000) 99 FCR 316 at [100]–[108]). While the High Court blames some of these outcomes on the definition of 'native title' in the Native Title Act 1993 (Cth), it seems unlikely that judicial development of the common law would have proceeded in a different direction: Clarke (2002).

[2.2.36]   The High Court characterises its 'recognition' of 'indigenous' land traditions as an 'intersection' of traditional norms and introduced law: *Fejo v Northern Territory* (1998) 195 CLR 96 at 128; *Yanner v Eaton* (1999) 201 CLR 351 at 384; *Commonwealth v Yarmirr* (2001) 208 CLR 1 at 37–38; *Ward v Western Australia* (2002) 191 ALR 1 at [85]; although others characterise it as a 'fatal collision': Boge (2001); or 'road train crash': Pearson (2002).

Dorsett has argued that the Australian approach to 'recognition' reflects old limitations in the common law's approach to 'custom':

> [Sir Matthew] Hale [in *The History of the Common Law of England* 1713 said]:
>
> > *First*, The Common Law does determine what of these Customs are good and reasonable, and what are unreasonable and void. *Secondly*, The Common Law gives to those Customs, that it adjudges reasonable, the Force and Efficacy of their Obligation. *Thirdly*, The Common Law determines what is that Continuance of Time that is sufficient to make such a Custom. *Fourthly*, The Common Law does interpose and authoritatively decide the Exposition, Limits and Extension of such Customs.
>
> Thus, as Hale makes plain, the common law not only appropriates to itself the right to determine which customs are enforceable [eg, typically those practised 'from time immemorial'], but the parameters of those customs ... [T]he common law determines both the circumstances under which it will recognise custom, and the shape that that interest will take within the common law (Dorsett (2002)).

[2.2.37]   However, the High Court resists this classification of its approach. In *Fejo v Northern Territory* (1998) 195 CLR 96, Gleeson CJ, Gaudron, McHugh, Gummow, Hayne and Callinan JJ said at 130:

[In this case] it was sought to draw some analogy [between native title and] rights recognised in English land law like rights of common or customary rights. But reference to those rights in the present context is misplaced. They are creatures of the common law finding their origins in grant or presumed grant. And the rights that are now in issue — native title rights — are not creatures of the common law. That a right owing its existence to one system of law (a right of freehold tenure) may be subject to other rights created by that same legal system (such as customary rights or rights of common) is not surprising. But very different considerations arise when there is an intersection between rights created by statute and rights that owe their origin to a different body of law and traditions.

As in the pre-*Mabo* era, it seems that the Australian courts prefer to take an isolationist, ahistorical approach to the question of 'recognition' of 'indigenous' rights to land.

Sovereignty and land

[2.2.38]   The introduced common law included the doctrine of tenure, as Deane and Gaudron JJ explained in *Mabo v Queensland (No 2)* (1992) 175 CLR 1 at 80–1:

> The English common law ... relating to real property developed as the product of concepts shaped by the feudal system of mediaeval times. The basic tenet was that, consequent upon the Norman Conquest, the Crown was the owner of all land in the kingdom. A subject could hold land only as a tenant ... of the Crown ... The primary estate of a subject, the estate in fee simple, became, for almost all practical purposes, equivalent to full ownership of the land itself. Nonetheless, the underlying thesis of the English law of real property remained that the radical title to (or ultimate ownership of) all land was in the Crown ...
>
> It has ... long been accepted ... that ... the common law which became applicable upon the establishment ... of New South Wales included that general system of land law ... [U]pon the establishment of the Colony, the radical title to all land vested in the Crown.

Brennan J described radical title as 'a postulate of the doctrine of tenure and a concomitant of sovereignty' (175 CLR at 48) and the doctrine of tenure as one 'which could not be overturned without fracturing the skeleton which gives our land law its shape and consistency': 175 CLR at 45. He explained at 48:

> By attributing to the Crown a radical title to all land within a territory over which the Crown has assumed sovereignty, the common law enabled the Crown, in exercise of its sovereign power, to grant an interest in land to be held of the Crown or to acquire land for the Crown's royal demesne [that is, its own estate]. The notion of radical title enabled the Crown to become Paramount Lord of all who hold a tenure granted by the Crown and to become absolute beneficial owner of unalienated land required for the Crown's purposes.

[2.2.39]   Before 1992, Australian courts maintained that assertion of sovereignty gave the Crown 'full beneficial ownership' of all land in a colony. However, as Brennan J explained in *Mabo v Queensland (No 2)* (1992) 175 CLR 1, that proposition was based on an unwarranted conflation of the concepts of sovereignty and property, and on acceptance of the historically inaccurate idea that the colonies were 'unoccupied' when acquired (at 43–5):

> There is a distinction between the Crown's title to a colony and the Crown's ownership of land in the colony ...

The general rule of the common law was that ownership could not be acquired by occupying land that was already occupied by another ...

It was only by fastening on the notion that a settled colony was *terra nullius* that it was possible to predicate of the Crown the acquisition of ownership of land in a colony already occupied by indigenous inhabitants. It was only on the hypothesis that there was nobody in occupation that it could be said that the Crown was the owner because there was no other. If that hypothesis be rejected, the notion that sovereignty carried ownership in its wake must be rejected too.

[2.2.40]   The pre-*Mabo (No 2)* view, that the Crown obtained 'ownership' of all land in an Australian colony, explains why governments saw no need for land cession treaties in Australia: see **[2.2.45]**. By contrast, in the United States and New Zealand, common law native title was recognised in the early 19th century. In eastern Canada, indigenous land rights were given official protection by the Royal Proclamation of 1763. In those jurisdictions, historical land cession treaties were based on an understanding that the title obtained by the sovereign was burdened by a title of the land's prior occupiers. Land cession treaties were used to extinguish these indigenous titles before the Crown exercised 'radical title' powers to grant land to third parties.

[2.2.41]   Australian law also now accepts that the Crown's 'radical title' was burdened by the 'native titles' of 'indigenous' occupants: *Mabo v Queensland (No 2)* (1992) 175 CLR 1. This happened in Western Australia as well as in the east of the continent: *Western Australia v Commonwealth* (the *Native Title Act* case) (1995) 183 CLR 373 at 421–34.

Native title is an 'allodial' (non-tenurial) real property right. Unlike other titles, it does not owe its existence to a prior Crown grant. When a court 'declares' the existence of a common law property right, as it did in *Mabo (No 2)*, that right is treated as capable of existing before the date of judgment. In this case, native title was capable of existing at any time after sovereignty was asserted over a particular colony.

[2.2.42]   In *Mabo (No 2)*, the High Court crafted legal principle to accommodate 204 years of unilateral Crown grants of native title land. According to the court, these grants were a lawful exercise of the Crown's radical title powers. Their effect was to 'extinguish' native title rights to the extent of any inconsistency between those rights and rights conferred by the Crown-granted titles: see also *Wik Peoples v Queensland* (1996) 187 CLR 1; *Fejo v Northern Territory* (1998) 195 CLR 96, *Ward v Western Australia* (2002) 191 ALR 1. This approach to extinguishment is harsher than the approach adopted by North American courts, which have allowed indigenous titles to survive some grants: McNeil (1997). Despite extensive use of overseas precedents in *Mabo (No 2)*, the present court regards them as of little assistance: *Fejo v Northern Territory* (1998) 195 CLR 96 at 130 per Gleeson CJ, Gaudron, McHugh, Gummow and Hayne JJ; at 148–150, 154 per Kirby J.

The common law rule that the Crown may extinguish native title by granting an inconsistent title to the same land has been characterised as racially discriminatory because it differs from the common law rule applicable to Crown-granted land titles. That rule states that the Crown may not renege on, or interfere with, a granted title unless parliament 'clearly and plainly' authorises it to do so: *Stead v Carey* (1845) 1 CB 496 at 523; 135 ER 634 at 645. '[A Crown] grant cannot be superseded by a subsequent inconsistent [Crown] grant made to another person': *Western Australia v Commonwealth* (the *Native Title Act* case) (1995) 183 CLR 373, citing *Earl of Rutland's* case (1608) 8 Co Rep 55a at 55b, 56a; 77 ER 555 at 446–7.

[2.2.43] According to a majority of justices (Mason CJ, Brennan, McHugh and Dawson JJ), at common law extinguishment of native title by an inconsistent Crown grant does not give rise to a claim for compensatory damages: *Mabo v Queensland (No 2)* (1992) 175 CLR 1 at 15. This rule appears to be the same as the rule applied to Crown-granted titles. However, it is common for legislation which authorises interference with Crown-granted titles to provide compensation. This has occurred in relation to native title only for the period since the commencement of the Racial Discrimination Act 1975 (Cth), or where there is a risk that otherwise interference with native title has involved an 'acquisition of property' otherwise than on just terms as required by s 51(xxxi) of the Constitution: see **[2.4.34]–[2.4.35]**.

Use of land cession treaties in other jurisdictions meant that payment of compensation for extinguishment of 'indigenous' title became established governmental practice, even if not always required by the common law. (United States law, for example, requires payment of compensation for extinguishment of 'Indian title' 'recognised' by the federal government, but not 'unrecognised' 'Indian title': Dorsett and Godden (1998) Ch 7.)

The possibility that governmental dealings with native title give rise to a Crown fiduciary duty to indigenous people is discussed further at **[2.5.1]–[2.5.12]**ff.

Sovereignty and the offshore

[2.2.44] When Australia was colonised the common law treated the 'realm' as ending at the low-water mark. The Crown did not enjoy 'sovereignty' over the offshore in the same sense as over a land mass. However, parliament could legislate in relation to the offshore, including by incorporating it into the Crown's territory. The Crown could also annex offshore areas under the royal prerogative, just as it could annex land, although it was required by the common law and later international law to preserve recognised rights to fish and navigate: *New South Wales v Commonwealth* (the *Seas and Submerged Lands* case) (1975) 135 CLR 337; *Commonwealth v Yarmirr* (2001) 208 CLR 1 at 55.

For Torres Strait Islanders and many coastal Aboriginal groups, the near offshore is a continuation of their traditional land estates. In *Commonwealth v Yarmirr* (2001) 208 CLR 1, the High Court allowed a native title claim to the near offshore because native title legislation extended offshore: 208 CLR 1 at 60. In doing so, the majority justices rejected an argument that offshore native title could not be recognised by the common law because the common law did not run below the low-water mark.

'Treaty' now?

[2.2.45] No constitutional treaties were entered into with indigenous Australians — as noted above (**[2.2.6]**), acquisition of sovereignty over the Australian colonies was based on 'settlement'. An 1835 treaty between John Batman and Aboriginal people from Melbourne purported to cede land — half a million acres — in exchange for an initial payment, plus a 'yearly rent or tribute', of blankets, tomahawks, knives, scissors, looking glasses, handkerchiefs, flour and clothing. This 'treaty' was almost certainly a fraud: see Campbell (1987). Governor Bourke proclaimed all such treaties void, adopting the North American rule that only the Crown could enter such treaties: *Mabo v Queensland (No 2)* (1992) 175 CLR 1 at 108 per Deane and

Gaudron JJ. For the treaty and Bourke's proclamation, see Bennett and Castles (1979) pp 258–60.

[2.2.46] Recent bouts of advocacy for a 'treaty' between 'indigenous' Australians and the Commonwealth Government have occurred in the late 1970s–early 1980s (Rowse (2002); *Two Hundred Years Later* (1983); Harris (1979)) and again in the late 1990s (for example, treatynow.org), especially under the auspices of the former statutory Council for Aboriginal Reconciliation, whose mandate included considering whether 'reconciliation' between 'indigenous' and non-'indigenous' Australians would be advanced by 'a formal document or … documents of reconciliation': Council for Aboriginal Reconciliation Act 1991 (Cth) s 6(1)(g). In 2000, the *Final Report* of the expiring Council recommended that:

> **5. Each government and parliament:**
>
> — recognise that this land and its waters were settled as colonies without treaty or consent and that *to advance reconciliation it would be most desirable if there were agreements or treaties*; and
>
> — negotiate a process through which this might be achieved that protects the political, legal, cultural and economic position of Aboriginal and Torres Strait Islander peoples (Council for Aboriginal Reconciliation: 2000, ch 10 Recommendations, emphasis added).

It is sometimes suggested that treaties might be constitutionally enabled or entrenched by an amendment similar to s 105A of the Commonwealth Constitution, which underpins the 1927 Financial Agreement between the Commonwealth and the states.

[2.2.47] However, there is no consensus on the proper subject matter of 'treaties', or what they would achieve which could not already be achieved by existing legal means given the necessary political will. A treaty is not necessary to provide constitutional legitimacy for the introduced legal system, which is founded on the assertions of sovereignty discussed at **[2.3.1]**–**[2.3.3]**; nor is it necessary to facilitate extinguishment of native title: see **[2.2.42]**, **[2.3.9]**, **[2.4.33]**. A treaty is not necessary to increase government spending on 'indigenous' poverty, or even to amend the Constitution to insert a non-discrimination guarantee. In the 1970s–80s, governments sought to avoid using the term 'treaty', lest it 'imply an internationally recognised agreement between two nations' or the possibility that Aboriginal people retain an aspect of prior sovereignty: *Two Hundred Years Later* (1983) p 21. Even this anxiety seems to have abated in the vaguer 1990s 'treaty debate'.

[2.2.48] de Costa (2003) criticises the view that a 'treaty' might emerge from sustained moral and political campaigning for increased 'indigenous' rights, rather than from an exercise of existing political power by 'indigenous' people, or because governments seek to take something from them:

> This approach assumes that Australian society as a whole is open to — or at least is neutral towards — the principles at stake. This view requires some belief that the status quo is not permanently embedded in the Australian legal landscape, in the history and the present of its prosperity, in its national imagination and psychology. Moreover, it relies on an assumption that a new status quo is possible if you bring together Australians in all their diversity and educate them towards a new moral consensus. This strikes me as wildly optimistic, if not actually contradictory. It is certainly paradoxical that a process designed to lead to the exchange of consent between peoples would begin with the harmonisation of the 'nation' as a whole. This was the fate of

reconciliation ... [under the Council for Aboriginal Reconciliation] it called for a national harmony that logically undercut the rationale for consent-exchange ...

... [W]e should not think for a moment that Indigenous peoples in treaty countries such as Canada, New Zealand or the United States see their acts of consent-exchange as having fundamentally placed them on the same basic path to recognition and justice. Grievances are the norm. Indigenous peoples understand that treaty-making has always been an instrumental exercise for the settler state: treaties are acts and calculations about power, not collective expressions of principle. In the genesis of treaties, in the means by which they were negotiated, in their partial implementations, but mostly in their neglect, treaties are well understood (de Costa (2003) at 16, 19).

3   The Australian colonies and states

Establishment of the Australian colonies

[2.3.1]   Queensland, Victoria, Tasmania and the eastern parts of South Australia and the Northern Territory were carved out of the original colony of New South Wales. New South Wales was originally proclaimed as extending westward to the 135th parallel of longitude; a line running through Ramingining in central Arnhem Land and South Australia's Eyre Peninsula. This boundary was extended westwards to the 129th parallel (the present Western Australian border) by an 1825 proclamation.

Thus, Aboriginal people in Gove, eastern Arnhem Land, making native title claims must prove traditional connections to land dating back to 1788, but for western Arnhem Landers the relevant date is 37 years later. These dates are rendered even more arbitrary by the different periods between official assertions of sovereignty over, and arrival of white people in, each area. Missions were established in eastern Arnhem Land in the early 20th century, about 30 years after the first push into the west by pastoralists, and 80 years after establishment of a settlement off the western Arnhem Land coast.

In 1829, Fremantle took possession of 'the whole of the West Coast of New Holland' in the King's name. The Swan River Act 1829 (UK) (10 Geo IV c 22) excluded from its operation land within New South Wales or Van Diemen's Land, but did not define the colony's eastern boundary. Stirling was appointed Governor on 4 March 1831. His Letters Patent and Commission fixed the eastern boundary at the 129th parallel: *Western Australia v Commonwealth* (the *Native Title Act* case) (1995) 183 CLR 373 at 423–9.

[2.3.2]   Mason J discussed the establishment of the various colonies in *New South Wales v Commonwealth* (the *Seas and Submerged Lands* case) (1975) 135 CLR 337, where the High Court held that 'sovereignty' over areas beyond the low-water mark (excluding bays historically included in the states) was exercisable by the Commonwealth under international law, not by the states under constitutional law: see **[6.3.40C]**.

(a) *New South Wales*

The territorial limits of ... New South Wales were defined in two commissions issued to Governor Phillip. The second ... constituted by letters patent dated 2nd April 1787, described the Colony as 'extending from the Northern Cape or extremity of the coast called Cape York ... to the southern extremity of the said territory of New South Wales or South Cape [of what is now Tasmania] ... including all the islands adjacent in the Pacific Ocean within the latitudes aforesaid ...'

The specific inclusion of islands ... is inconsistent with the notion that the Colony includes the sea ...

(b) *Tasmania*

The extent of the Colony ... was set out in the commission issued by letters patent dated 16th July 1825 which described the Governor's jurisdiction as extending to 'our Island of Van Diemen's Land, and all Islands and Territories lying to the Southward of Wilson Promontory ...' Here again there is nothing in the description which includes within the Colony the sea or its solum.

(c) *Western Australia*

The territorial limits ... were defined in the commission issued by letters patent dated 4th March 1831 to Governor Stirling. It referred to the Colony as 'extending from Cape Londonderry ... to West Cape Howe ... and from the Hertogs Island on the western coast ... to [129] degrees of east longitude ... including all the islands adjacent in the Indian and Southern Oceans' within a defined area. The northern limits ... were extended by a commission issued by letters patent dated 10th July 1873 to Governor Weld but not so as to alter the seaward boundary ... [T]hat ... followed the line of the coast in a fashion similar to the seaward boundary of New South Wales.

(d) *South Australia*

The seaward boundary of South Australia was described in letters patent dated 19th February 1836 issued pursuant to s 1 of the ... [South Australian Colonisation Act 1834] as 'On the South the Southern Ocean, including all and every the Bays and Gulfs thereof together with ... Kangaroo Island and all and every the Islands adjacent ...' By including 'Bays and Gulfs' the description departed from the approach taken in the case of the earlier Colonies ...

(e) *Victoria*

The first description of boundaries is ... in s 1 of the Australian Constitutions Act 1850...in which the Colony was described as including 'the Territories ... comprised within the District of *Port Phillip*, including the Town of *Melbourne*' ...

The boundaries were redefined by the commission issued to Governor Darling by letters patent dated 23rd June 1863 in which it was stated that the Colony consisted 'of the Territories bounded ... on the South by the Sea'.

(f) *Queensland*

The first definition of boundaries is contained in letters patent dated 6th June 1859 issued under s 7 of the New South Wales Constitution Act, 1855 [Imp]. It excised from [New South Wales] certain territory which lay to the north of a designated line ... set as the southern boundary of the new Colony. Specifically included were 'all and every the adjacent islands their members and appurtenances in the Pacific Ocean'.

[B]y letters patent dated 13th March 1862 issued under s 2 of the Australian Colonies Act 1861 there was annexed to the Colony so much of New South Wales [between the 26th parallel south and the 141st and 138th meridians east — a strip of land running south from Mornington Island]. By deed poll dated 22nd August 1872 the Governor ... pursuant to ... letters patent ... transferred to the Colony 'all the Islands lying and being within sixty miles of the coasts of the said Colony'. Certain islands in the Torres Strait were subsequently included within the Colony by proclamation dated 18th July 1879 (135 CLR at 459–61).

The letters patent establishing South Australia are discussed further at **[2.3.15]**.

[2.3.3]   In *Wacando v Commonwealth* (1981) 148 CLR 1, the High Court held that Darnley Island (along with other eastern Torres Strait islands, including the Meriam Islands considered in *Mabo v Queensland (No 2)* (1992) 175 CLR 1) had been validly annexed to Queensland in 1879 under Imperial Letters Patent of 1878 and the Queensland Coast Islands Act 1879 (Qld). The Colonial Boundaries Act 1895 (UK) was also subsequently enacted to ensure the validity of the annexation.

The Northern Territory was separated from New South Wales by Letters Patent under the Australian Colonies Act 1861 (UK) on 6 July 1863, and placed under control of South Australia. The Letters Patent, like those establishing South Australia, included some 'bays and gulfs': *Commonwealth v Yarmirr* (2001) 208 CLR 1 at 70. After the Commonwealth was established, the territory was transferred to the Commonwealth under s 111 of the Constitution: *Kruger v Commonwealth* (1997) 190 CLR 1 at 49–50 (see Chapter 12). Commonwealth administration of the Northern Territory has had important consequences for its Aboriginal population: see **[2.4.58]–[2.4.61]**.

Land policy, colonial self-government and the fate of Imperial Aboriginal 'protection' measures

[2.3.4]   In early Australia, Governors exercised the Crown's 'radical title' powers on London's advice. However, after 1842, the exercise of these powers was constrained by imperial legislation, which allocated revenues raised from sales of 'waste lands' (unalienated or unreserved Crown lands) to fund further British migration to Australia. As Brennan J said in *Mabo v Queensland (No 2)* (1992) 175 CLR 1 at 52, 'the nation obtained its patrimony by sales and dedications of land which dispossessed its indigenous citizens'. Lack of local control over land policy and revenue created pressure for colonial self-government.

[2.3.5C]   **Wik Peoples v Queensland**

(1996) 134 ALR 637

The Wik Peoples claimed native title to land covered by two pastoral leases: one granted under the Land Act 1910 (Qld); the other under the Land Act 1962 (Qld). The Queensland Government and pastoralists argued that native title to the land had been extinguished by the lease grants.

 In the Federal Court, Drummond J held (because he regarded himself as bound by an earlier Full Federal Court decision in *North Ganalanja Aboriginal Corp v Queensland* (1995) 132 ALR 565) that the lease grants extinguished the Wik native title. In the process, his Honour explained how the Crown's *prerogative* (radical title) power to alienate land had been curtailed in early Australia.

Drummond J: [645] Until 1831, full power of disposal of [New South Wales's] waste lands was vested in the Governor ... [including] power to negotiate and make promises for ... grants ...

[Before] 1832, the practice prevailed of issuing, not grants, but only [646] promises of grants, — or more correctly speaking permissions to select land, to be afterwards confirmed by grants ... on the performance of certain conditions by the person receiving the promise ...

After 1826, selection was permitted within 'Limits of Location'.

In 1831, the Secretary of State, Lord Ripon, implemented a new system for the disposal of all Crown lands by sale at public auction price ... [Regulations for this system] made under the prerogative power of the Crown were published in ... 1831. By the early 1830s ... squatting was widespread in [New South Wales]. Large tracts of Crown lands, situate outside the boundaries of settlement and usually suitable only for grazing, were being used by pastoralists to run their cattle and sheep without either the authority or sanction of the Crown. Recognising the reality of the situation, the [New South Wales] Government further extended the limits of location; these, by 1835, in direct response to Batman's treaty with the Aborigines of Port Phillip Bay ... included that district. In 1836, by ... local [647] Act the [New South Wales] authorities implemented a system of annual pasturing licences in respect of grazing lands outside the new limits ...

By this time, the situation of the Aboriginal inhabitants of the Colony was the subject of much concern to the Imperial and colonial authorities ...

His Honour referred to Bourke's response to Batman's treaty, and to legislation introduced by Governor Gipps to overturn a similar deal relating to the New Zealand south island.

[648] As the boundaries of white settlement encroached ... on ... native lands, conflict between the settlers and Aborigines increased ...

In 1842, the principles ... in Lord Ripon's regulations received statutory recognition [in] the [Australian] Land Sales Act 1842 (UK) ... It was the first Imperial statute regulating the mode of disposal of Crown lands in [New South Wales] (and the other Australian colonies that then existed) ... [Section] 2 ... provided that the waste lands of the Crown ... were not to be alienated by the Crown either in fee simple or for any less estate or interest otherwise than by way of sale conducted in accordance with the regulations ... Section 5 authorised the Governor to make such conveyances and alienations. Section 3 [allowed establishment of Aboriginal reserves] ... Section 19 ... provided that half of the gross proceeds of such sales was to be applied to meet the costs of assisting emigrants not possessing the means to do so, of moving to the Colony; the balance was to be appropriated to the colonial public service. The [649] effect of the statute was to curtail the Royal prerogative [that is, radical title] with respect to the waste lands of the Crown. Thereafter, only dispositions of such lands made in accordance with its provisions were permissible ... Section 20 ... provided:

> ... nothing herein contained shall affect or be construed to affect any Contract, or to prevent the Fulfilment of any Promise or Engagement, made by or on the Behalf of her Majesty with respect to any Lands situate in any of the said Colonies in Cases where such Contracts, Promises or Engagements shall have been lawfully made before the time at which this Act shall take effect in any such Colony ...

[652] ... [T]he [Australian] Land Sales Act Amendment Act 1846 (UK) ... [followed] agitation by the pastoralists for greater security of tenure than that provided ... by ... local Acts ... [It] made express provision for the grant of leases and occupation licences of Crown lands ...

~~~

Notes

[2.3.6] When the case reached the High Court, Gummow J summarised later developments associated with colonial self-government in *Wik Peoples v Queensland* (1996) 187 CLR 1 at 173–4:

> An element of representative government was provided by the Australian Constitutions Act 1842 (UK) ... but s 29 excluded from the competence of the [New South Wales] Legislative Council any law which interfered ... with the sale of Crown lands in the colony or with the revenue arising therefrom ...
>
> [Section] 2 of the New South Wales Constitution Act 1855 (UK) ... vested in the New South Wales legislature the entire management and control of the waste lands belonging

to the Crown in New South Wales and the power of appropriation of the gross proceeds of the sales of any such lands. Then s 30 of the Constitution Act 1867 (Q) ... provided that it was to be lawful for the legislature of that colony to make laws for regulating the sale, letting, disposal and occupation of waste lands of the Crown within Queensland ... s 40 stated:

> The entire management and control of the waste lands belonging to the Crown in the said Colony of Queensland and also the appropriation of the gross proceeds of the sales of such lands and of all other proceeds and revenues of the same from whatever source arising within the said colony including all royalties mines and minerals shall be vested in the Legislature of the said colony ...

> The result was to withdraw from the Crown ... significant elements of the prerogative. The management and control of waste lands in Queensland was vested in the legislature and any authority of the Crown in that respect had to be derived from statute.

[2.3.7] The Victoria Constitution Act 1855 (UK) also contained a 'statutory control of the disposition of waste lands' provision. The Australian Waste Lands Act 1855 (UK) provided similarly in the case of Van Diemen's Land and South Australia, as did the Western Australia Constitution Act 1890 (UK) for that colony: see, in the latter case, *Ward v Western Australia* (2002) 191 ALR 1 at [165]–[167] and generally *Cudgen Rutile (No 2) v Chalk* [1975] AC 520 at 533. After South Australia's acquisition of the Northern Territory in 1863, the South Australian Parliament enacted the Northern Territory Lands Act 1872, which provided that lands in that jurisdiction should be alienated pursuant to statute and not otherwise: *Fejo v Northern Territory* (1998) 195 CLR 96 at [10]. Similar statutes have applied in the Northern Territory since.

Federation did not disturb these arrangements: land policy and alienation has remained mainly a matter for the states. This is very different from the position in the United States and Canada, where authority to extinguish native title has been reposed exclusively in federal governments and not at the state or provincial level: see **[2.3.11]–[2.3.13]**.

[2.3.8] Under the principles discussed by Drummond J in *Wik Peoples v Queensland* (1996) 134 ALR 637 **[2.3.5C]** at 245–52; and by Gummow J on appeal (1996) 187 CLR 1 **[2.3.6]** at 173–4, the Crown, exercising radical title, may grant only those titles which parliament (legislation) permits it to grant. The grantee, in turn, enjoys only those rights which the statute permits the Crown to grant. Colonial and state parliaments authorised Governors to grant titles known to the common law (for example, freehold). But like the Imperial Parliament before them, they also began to create new statutory titles. Among these were pastoral leases, devised as a legal response to squatting.

[2.3.9] In determining whether statutory title grants have extinguished native title at common law, the courts consider the degree of inconsistency between the rights conferred on the grantee and those conferred on Aboriginal people by native title: *Wik Peoples v Queensland* (1996) 187 CLR 1; *Ward v Western Australia* (2002) 191 ALR 1. To determine the rights conferred on a grantee, courts look to the statutory provisions authorising the grant. It is not open to the Crown to vary the terms of statutory titles inconsistently with statute, or for grantees to exceed the rights conferred on them by statute: *Cudgen Rutile (No 2) v Chalk* [1975] AC 520. This constitutional principle explains the 1997 political fall-out from *Wik Peoples v Queensland*. In *Wik*, a narrow High Court majority confirmed that pastoral lessees' rights were limited to those conferred by statute, and that these did not necessarily extinguish native title completely. Many lessees, however, had believed that they enjoyed greater rights to land than those conferred by the relevant legislation.

[2.3.10]   After legislative controls were imposed on land alienation, native title could be extinguished only where a parliament authorised the Crown to deal with land inconsistently with native title. These developments are sometimes treated as having neutralised the discriminatory common law vulnerability of native title to extinguishment by the Crown: see **[2.2.42]** above. For example, in *Wik Peoples v Queensland* (1996) 187 CLR 1, Kirby J described the principles applicable to native title as 'species of a general proposition applied by the courts in the construction of legislation' that 'to deprive a person of pre-existing property interests ... legislation ... must clearly do so, either by express enactment or by necessary implication': 187 CLR at 247–9.

However, the courts require a lower standard of 'necessary implication' for native title than for Crown-granted titles. Legislation which appears to authorise uncompensated interference with Crown-granted titles will not be treated as doing so unless parliament expresses such an intention clearly: *Commonwealth v Hazeldell* [1921] 2 AC 373. But an intention to allow interference with native title has been discerned where Crown lands legislation which does not even mention native title authorises inconsistent dealings with native title land: *Wik Peoples v Queensland* (1996) 187 CLR 1; *Ward v Western Australia* (2002) 191 ALR 1; *Wilson v Anderson* (2002) 190 ALR 313.

[2.3.11]   Before the Australian colonies achieved self-government, imperial authorities imposed several 'Aboriginal protection' measures. These were overtaken by imperial legislation establishing colonial constitutions, or by changes to the constitutions themselves. However, it is sometimes argued that pre-self-government controls remain legally relevant. Such arguments are sometimes based on analogies with an imperial constraint on Britain's former North American colonies: the Royal Proclamation of 1763.

That proclamation, promulgated by George III after the defeat of the French, reserved for 'Indians' lands not included in Britain's accumulated colonies (a strip on the eastern seaboard) or granted to the Hudson's Bay Company (in the far north). The proclamation outlawed private purchases of 'Indian' lands, stating that land could only be obtained from 'Indians' by 'treaty' on behalf of the Imperial Crown.

Imperial intervention on behalf of the Australian 'natives' was much less forceful. London took a 'hands off' attitude, especially after self-government, despite the fact that their control of 'waste lands' (see **[2.3.4]–[2.3.7]**) placed colonial parliaments in a strong position to interfere with Aboriginal rights.

[2.3.12]   The Royal Proclamation's protection of 'Indian lands' ensured that, in North America, even before courts developed doctrines of 'Indian title', indigenous dispossession proceeded by 'treaties' with 'compensation'. In the shadow of United States legislation based on the 1763 Proclamation, the United States Supreme Court recognised 'Indian title' in the 1820s: *Johnson v M'Intosh* 8 Wheat 543 (1823). 'Indian title' in the 'Indian territory' was subject to extinguishment by the federal government, not by the states, because the court treated 'Indian tribes' as 'domestic dependent nations' over which Congress alone enjoyed constitutional power.

[2.3.13] The Canadian Supreme Court did not develop a common law doctrine of 'aboriginal title' until *Calder v Attorney-General (British Columbia)* [1973] SCR 313 [1973]; (1973) 34 DLR (3d) 145. However, Canadian courts had long recognised the Royal Proclamation of 1763 as protecting 'Indian title' in areas covered by it (it probably did not extend to British Columbia): *St Catherine's Milling and Lumber Co v R* (1888) 14 AC 46. The British North America Act 1867 (UK) allowed the provinces to make land laws (s 92), but conferred exclusive power over 'Indians, and Lands reserved for the Indians' on the Dominion: s 91(24). Thus, only the federal government could extinguish 'Indian title'. It did so under the Indian Act 1876 (Can), which authorised treaty-making.

[2.3.14] Imperial constraints on colonial Governors in Australia included their instructions. Phillip was required 'to endeavour, by every possible means, to open an intercourse with the natives, and to conciliate their affections, enjoining all our subjects to live in amity and kindness with them' and to punish any destruction, or interruption of the 'several occupations', of Aboriginal people by 'our subjects': McRae et al (2003) p 19. However, the instructions also empowered Phillip to grant land to former convicts, a power which quickly destroyed 'amity and kindness' between Aboriginal people and settlers.

[2.3.15] The South Australia Colonisation Act 1834 (UK) allowed the Crown to establish one or more provinces in 'waste lands', empowering Commissioners to make orders for sale of public lands. The Colonial Office included in the Letters Patent establishing the province this proviso:

> PROVIDED ALWAYS that nothing in those our Letters Patent contained shall affect or be construed to affect the rights of any Aboriginal Natives of the said Province to the actual occupation or enjoyment in their own Persons or in the Persons of their Descendants of any Lands therein now actually occupied or enjoyed by such Natives ... (See Heatley and Nicholson (1989) pp 25, 355).

However, the proviso was overtaken by constitutional change. The South Australia Act 1842 (UK) repealed the Colonisation Act, but preserved 'laws' and 'ordinances' made under it: *Milirrpum v Nabalco* (1971) 17 FLR 141 at 274–83. The Australian Waste Lands Act 1855 (UK) vested control over Crown lands in the colonial legislature: see **[2.3.7]**. The Constitution Act (1855) (SA) contained no provisions protecting Aboriginal rights.

[2.3.16] In the Federal Court decision in *Wik Peoples v Queensland* (1996) 134 ALR 637, the Wik argued that their native title had been preserved by a combination of an 1849 Order-in-Council under the Australian Land Sales Act 1842 (UK) (as amended in 1846) and the proviso originally contained in s 20 of that Act (reproduced in 134 ALR at 649: see **[2.3.5C]**). The proviso preserved pre-existing 'Contracts, Promises or Engagements' of grants against the new rule that grants must be made pursuant to statute only. Like the rule from which it derogated, the proviso was carried over into the Queensland Constitution, where it remains today. The 1849 Order-in-Council applied to leases granted after 1850. It provided:

> And whereas it is expedient that all such pastoral leases should contain such conditions, clauses of forfeiture, exceptions, and reservations, as may be necessary for securing the peaceable and effectual occupation of the lands comprised in such leases, and for preventing the abuses and inconveniences incident thereto: it is hereby ordered ... that it should be lawful for the Governor for the time being ... to insert in any pastoral lease hereafter to be made, such conditions and clauses of forfeiture,

exceptions or reservations, as to him shall seem requisite for the purposes last aforesaid. [Extracted in (1996) 134 ALR 637 at 656]

The Wik argued that the Order-in-Council and some Colonial Office despatches to Governor FitzRoy were 'promises or engagements' within the proviso. They said those 'promises or engagements' limited the legislative power of Queensland to the making of laws authorising grants of pastoral leases only where the leases contained reservations protecting Aboriginal rights to use pastoral land.

Drummond J rejected this argument, following the view of Wilson and Dawson JJ in *Mabo v Queensland (No 1)* (1988) 166 CLR 186 that 'promises or engagements' meant pre-1842 arrangements or undertakings for the grant of Crown lands made by colonial Governors, not 'promises' to Aboriginal people. The despatches were not undertakings on behalf of the Crown to Aboriginal people. Rather, they were merely evidence of imperial concern that Aboriginal people not be denied access to pastoral lands. It was left to colonial Governors to decide whether or not to give effect to that concern by exercising powers conferred by the Order-in-Council. In any event, imperial policy of protecting Aboriginal rights to pastoral leasehold was overtaken by the New South Wales Constitution Act 1855 (UK), transferring control over Crown lands to the colonial legislature: see **[2.3.4]–[2.3.7]**. (The Australian Waste Lands Act 1855 (UK) repealed the 1842 Act on which the Order-in-Council was based.)

[2.3.17] Imperial concern for Aboriginal people led to insertion of a unique provision, s 70, in the Constitution Act 1889 (WA), which established responsible government in Western Australia:

> There shall be payable to Her Majesty, in every year, out of the Consolidated Revenue Fund the sum of five thousand pounds ... to be appropriated to the welfare of the Aboriginal Natives ... The ... sum shall be issued to the Aborigines Protection Board by the Treasurer ... and may be expended by the said Board at their discretion, under the sole control of the Governor, anything in 'The Aborigines Protection Act, 1886', to the contrary notwithstanding. Provided always, that if and when the gross revenue of the Colony shall exceed Five hundred thousand pounds in any financial year, an amount equal to one per centum of such gross revenue shall ... be substituted for the said sum of Five thousand pounds in and for the financial year next ensuing ...

Section 70 envisaged the continued existence of the Aborigines Protection Board established by the Aborigines Protection Act 1886 (WA). The Board 'was remarkable in that it was not directly responsible ... to either the executive government of the Colony or its legislature. Rather it was directly responsible to the Governor': Johnston (1989) p 320.

[2.3.18] Although s 70 was initiated by Governor Broome, to the new Western Australian legislature it was an insult. The colonial parliament tried twice to repeal it, in 1894 and 1897, but imperial authorities advised that these attempts had failed for want of compliance with 'manner and form' provisions in s 33 of the Australian Constitutions Act 1842 (UK), applied to Western Australia by the Australian Constitutions Act 1850 (UK) and in force until 1907. (The manner and form requirements related to reservation of bills for assent by the Queen on the advice of the United Kingdom Government. Section 73 of the Constitution Act 1899 (WA) required bills to amend it to be so reserved. Section 33 of the Australian Constitutions Act 1850 (UK) stated that assent to bills so reserved must occur within two years of their presentation and then be proclaimed by the Governor. The 1894 bill did not obtain assent within two years; assent to the 1897 bill was not proclaimed in Perth.)

A third, retrospective (to 1897) repeal, by the Aborigines Act 1905 (WA), met these manner and form requirements. It substituted a state department for the Board, and replaced the constitutional expenditure guarantee with a statutory requirement to spend at least £10,000: see Johnston (1989) and *Yougarla v Western Australia* (2001) 207 CLR 344 at 350–4. This was the same amount as that guaranteed by s 3 of the Commonwealth Constitution for the Governor-General's salary, and less than one-fifth of the amount spent on federation celebrations in Sydney in 1901: Irving (1997) at 19.

[2.3.19] In *Yougarla v Western Australia* (2001) 207 CLR 344, the High Court rejected an argument that the 1905 repeal was ineffective for failure to comply with yet another 'manner and form' requirement — s 32 of the Australian Constitutions Act 1850. The court held that this requirement — that reserved colonial legislation be placed before the Imperial Parliament for 30 days before the monarch assented to it — had applied only to constitutional changes relating to the election, constitution and powers of the Western Australian legislature. Further, it had been repealed by the 1890 Imperial Act annexing the Constitution Act 1899 (WA) because it was 'repugnant' with the new constitutional arrangements. Western Australian self-government (like self-government elsewhere in Australia) expressly preserved the (otherwise 'repugnant') oversight of colonial legislation by the imperial *executive* through reservation of Bills, but did not preserve the imperial *legislature's* scrutiny of that legislation: 207 CLR 344 at 354–6.

Exclusion of 'indigenous' people from state franchises

[2.3.20] As noted at **[2.1.4]–[2.1.6]**, many Aboriginal people and Torres Strait Islanders were under discriminatory 'protection' laws from the early 20th century: such laws were in force in Victoria, Queensland and Western Australia at federation. Indigenous Australians were at this time excluded from the electoral franchise by the laws of two colonies. The Constitution Acts Amendment Act 1899 (WA) and the Elections Act 1885 (Qld) prevented the name of an 'aboriginal native of Australia' being entered on the electoral roll unless that person held freehold title to land. The freehold qualification appears to have been one which no 'aboriginal native' could meet. It was subsequently removed. Other colonies (for example, New South Wales and Victoria) excluded from the franchise people in receipt of 'charitable aid'. 'Protection' laws and policies in those colonies involved distribution of rations to Aboriginal mission and reserve residents: Chesterman and Galligan (1997) pp 15, 66; McCorquodale (1986) **[2.3.21]**. The exclusion of Aboriginal people and Torres Strait Islanders from state franchises was eroded over time. However, some Aboriginal people remained disenfranchised in Western Australia until the enactment of the Electoral Act Amendment Act 1962 (WA), and some indigenous Queenslanders only obtained the state franchise upon enactment of the Election Acts Amendment Act 1965 (Qld).

[2.3.21] Low levels of 'indigenous' political participation in Australian political parties and parliaments have led some state parliaments to explore the question of whether they should contain seats designated for 'indigenous' voters only. In New South Wales, where just over 2 per cent of the population is 'indigenous', '[t]here has never been an Aboriginal person elected to ... Parliament': New South Wales Parliament (1998). A recent New South Wales parliamentary inquiry entertained the idea of both designated seats and an interim Aboriginal Assembly: ibid. By contrast, a Queensland parliamentary committee recently rejected both ideas for the present, despite the state's poor record on 'indigenous' political participation: it has a 3.5 per cent 'indigenous' population but has only ever returned one 'indigenous' member of parliament: Queensland Parliament (2003) at 7, 53–6.

New Zealand has had designated seats for Maori voters since 1867. Maori were not obliged to vote until 1956, when they were forced to choose between the general electoral roll and the Maori roll according to their level of Maori descent. From 1975, Maori could choose whether to vote on the general roll or the Maori roll. However, the position of Maori as a minority (about 10 per cent of the population) and the small number of seats allocated them (four out of 99) meant Maori concerns were rarely given effective voice until a 1993 change to the country's electoral system increased Maori representation in parliament. This suggests that 'the electoral system is more relevant to self determination than reserved seats': see generally McGill (1997); Iorns-Magallanes (2003).

The Northern Territory is presently the only jurisdiction in which Aboriginal people (Mr John Ah Kit and Ms Marion Scrymgour) hold Ministerial portfolios. Mr Ernie Bridge (the Member for Kimberley) was a Minister in the WA Labor Burke, Dowding and Lawrence Cabinets from 1986–1996 before resigning to become an independent member of the state parliament.

4   Citizenship rights and entitlements

[2.4.1] As adopted in 1901, the Commonwealth Constitution contained three provisions which marked out indigenous people for special treatment: s 25, s 51(xxvi) and s 127.

Sections 25 and 127 qualified section 24, which provided that the House of Representatives was to be 'chosen in the several States ... in proportion to the respective numbers of their people' [4.2.27E].

Section 25 (which remains in the Constitution) provides as follows:

> For the purposes of the last section, if by a law of any State all persons of any race are disqualified from voting at elections for the more numerous House of Parliament of the State, then, in reckoning the number of the people of the State or of the Commonwealth, persons of that race resident in that State shall not be counted.

Section 127, deleted by the fifth of Australia's eight successful constitutional referenda, provided:

> In reckoning the numbers of the people of the Commonwealth, or of a State or other part of the Commonwealth, aboriginal natives shall not be counted.

Section 51(xxvi) originally gave the Commonwealth Parliament power to make laws with respect to:

> The people of any race, other than the aboriginal race in any state, for whom it is deemed necessary to make special laws ...

In 1967, after the same referendum, the words 'other than the aboriginal race in any state' were deleted.

People of the Commonwealth? Indigenous Australians, federation and the political census

[2.4.2] At federation, Australia's Aboriginal and Torres Strait Islander population was (under)estimated at 66,950. The 2001 census counted around 410,000: ABS (2003). The 1901 figures included 521 people in Victoria, 26,670 in Queensland, 8065 in New South Wales, 3070 in South Australia, 23,363 in South Australia's Northern Territory and none in Tasmania (it being widely believed that Tasmanians became 'extinct' with the death of Truganini in 1876, despite the existence of a community of 'half caste' people on eastern Bass Strait islands): Chesterman and Galligan (1997) p 63; *Shaw v Wolf* (1998) 83 FCR 113 at 125–6; Ryan (1996) Ch 15.

Like Cook and the colonial Governors, proponents of federation saw no need to obtain the consent of Aboriginal people or Torres Strait Islanders to their inclusion in the new federation. Most Aboriginal people and Torres Strait Islanders were excluded from voting in referenda which 'approved' the new Constitution because they did not have the state franchise: see **[2.3.20]**.

[2.4.3] The delegates to the 1890s Constitutional Conventions were not interested in indigenous Australians, as Sawer observed:

> ... It is not merely that the Founders treated aboriginal questions as a matter for the States. The Commonwealth was not initially given any independent territory on the mainland and its ultimate acquisition of such territory, though likely, was by no means certain; general questions of land settlement, industrial development, employment relations and education were also left to the States, and few of the powers given to the Commonwealth had any obvious or direct relevance to aboriginal policy, so that a decision to leave aboriginal questions to the states was rationally defensible. What is surprising is that the position of the aborigines was not even mentioned .... [R]eferences in the Convention Debates to [s 51(xxvi) and former s 127] are of the scantiest. In those concerning section 51(xxvi) the exclusion of the aborigines was never mentioned at all — it was simply taken for granted ...; in those concerning section 127, the aborigines were mentioned, barely ...

> [G]iving evidence ... before the 1927–9 Royal Commission on the Constitution, the Chief Protector of Aborigines, Western Australia [Mr AO Neville, the subject of the 2002 feature film, *Rabbit Proof Fence*], suggested that the indifference of the Founders ... was due to two main reasons; firstly, there were no reliable counts of the aboriginal population then available and contemporary guesses grossly underestimated their probable numbers, and secondly it was widely thought that the aborigines were a dying race whose future was unimportant. To this it should be added that the debates on section 51(xxvi) ... did reveal ... a widespread attitude of white superiority to all coloured peoples ... (Sawer (1966) pp 16–17).

[2.4.4] As British subjects resident in the various colonies, indigenous Australians were included in the new Constitution's reference to 'the people' of the colonies having 'agreed to unite in one indissoluble Federal Commonwealth': *Mabo v Queensland (No 2)* (1992) 175 CLR 1 at 106 per Deane and Gaudron JJ. Even Northern Territory Aboriginal people seem to have been included, since the territory was then part of South Australia. Covering cl 5, which stated that Commonwealth laws bind the 'people of every State and of every part of the Commonwealth' also seems always to have applied to indigenous Australians.

The prohibition in former s 127, on counting of 'aboriginal natives' in the numbers of 'the people of the Commonwealth', did not necessarily mean that Aboriginal people or Torres Strait Islanders were not 'people of the Commonwealth', only that they were not counted as such for political purposes: Sawer (1966) p 25. They were ignored in the 'reckoning' of these numbers in the allocation of House of Representatives seats.

[2.4.5] Constitution Alteration (Aboriginals) 1967 (Cth), which removed s 127, also removed the words 'other than the aboriginal race in any State' from s 51(xxvi). The 'yes' vote authorising these amendments was the largest in Australian history, around 90 per cent: Attwood and Markus (1997) p 55; Bennett (1985). This referendum is discussed further at **[2.4.39]–[2.4.41]**. For a discussion of the procedure for constitutional amendment, see Chapter 1.

[2.4.6] Who were the 'aboriginal natives' contemplated by s 127? In 1901, Alfred Deakin, the first Attorney-General, gave a two-paragraph opinion that 'aboriginal natives' did not include so-called 'half-castes'. According to Sawer, the task of not counting them was left to the Bureau of Census:

> [T]he Commonwealth ... took the view that section 127 was also a qualification on the census and statistics power — section 51(xi) — and that ... when taking censuses and publishing population figures, the Bureau must not include full-blooded [sic] aborigines ...
>
> The Constitution does not provide any definition of 'aboriginal natives'. Bureau of Census interpretation, based upon [Deakin's opinion], restricts the expression to full-bloods [*sic*] ... Yet the Bureau has presumed to treat the Torres Strait Islanders as *not* being "aboriginal natives" within s 127 ... (Sawer (1966) pp 26–7).

[2.4.7] The referendum deleting s 127 was widely perceived as conferring 'citizenship' on Aboriginal people and Torres Strait Islanders: Attwood and Markus (1997). However, as discussion of s 41 and the Commonwealth franchise at **[2.4.10]**–**[2.4.13]** indicates, s 127 did not prevent Aboriginal people from voting. The Convention Debates made clear that it was concerned with the political census for the purposes of s 24 and other constitutional provisions which were transitional (ss 89 and 93 on distribution of customs duties) or had been overtaken by constitutional amendment (s 105, on Commonwealth takeover of state debts, superseded by s 105A): Sawer (1966) p 28.

[2.4.8] Former s 127 overlapped with s 25, which remains in the Constitution today as a disincentive to exclusion of racial groups from state electoral franchises. (There is some doubt, however, as to whether the states remain capable of imposing such racial restrictions: see *McGinty v Western Australia* (1996) 186 CLR 140 **[4.5.14]** per Brennan CJ, Gaudron and Toohey JJ.)

Both s 25 and former s 127 are based on Amendment XIV, §2 of the United States Constitution, which excludes 'Indians not taxed' (that is, members of self-governing 'tribes') from the federal political census, and denies states which interfere with African-Americans' federal voting rights Congressional representation based on their black populations. Amendment XIV, §2, ratified in 1868, overtook art I, §2, cl 3, which originally allowed southern states to count slaves as 'three-fifths of other persons' for Congressional representation purposes.

If s 127 had not been in the Constitution before 1962 (when some Aboriginal people were still disenfranchised in Western Australia and Queensland: see **[2.3.20]**), s 25 would have operated to prevent these people being counted in the numbers of the people of those states for the purposes of allocating House of Representatives seats. However, s 127 was a more blanket provision: it prevented the counting of all 'aboriginal natives' in the political census, whether they were enfranchised at the state level or not. Thus, before 1967, the Constitution provided no incentive for Western Australia or Queensland to enfranchise their disenfranchised Aboriginal populations. Even if they did so, these states would not obtain increased proportions of House of Representative seats: see Sawer (1966) pp 29–30.

[2.4.9] In its *Final Report*, the Council for Aboriginal Reconciliation recommended that a referendum be conducted to repeal s 25, replacing it with a 'new section making it unlawful to adversely discriminate against any people on the grounds of race': Council for Aboriginal Reconcilation (2000). In 1988, the Constitutional Commission recommended repeal of s 25 because 'it is no longer appropriate to include in the Constitution a provision which contemplates the disqualification of members of a race from voting'. However, the Commission rejected the view of its Rights Committee that 'section 25 presents a chilling analogy with the [apartheid] electoral system in South Africa'. On the contrary, s 25 was designed to encourage racial enfranchisement: Constitutional Commission (1988) pp 156–7.

Indigenous Australians and the Commonwealth franchise

[2.4.10] One of the first Acts of the new Commonwealth excluded Aboriginal people and Torres Strait Islanders from its franchise. Section 4 of the Commonwealth Franchise Act 1902 (Cth) provided:

> No aboriginal native of Australia Asia Africa or the Islands of the Pacific except New Zealand shall be entitled to have his name placed on an Electoral Roll unless so entitled under section forty-one of the Constitution.

As in s 127 **[2.4.1]**, 'aboriginal native' was undefined. Its meaning became a matter of impressionistic perception by non-Aboriginal electoral officials. Robert Garran, Secretary of the Attorney-General's Department, applied Deakin's interpretation of s 127 to this Act. That meant that so-called 'half-castes' could vote. They were to be distinguished from 'aboriginal natives' by applying, said Garran, a 'preponderance of blood' (sic) test. 'Blood' meant 'ancestry' which, in the Australian political tradition discussed at **[2.1.4]–[2.1.6]**, meant skin colour: see Chesterman and Galligan (1997) Ch 4; Stretton and Finnimore (1993) p 530; Commonwealth of Australia (1961) p 4.

[2.4.11] Electoral exclusion of 'aboriginal natives' was not constitutionally required. As its text suggested, s 4 of the Commonwealth Franchise Act was subject to s 41 of the Constitution. Section 41 gave to an adult person, with a right to vote for the lower house in a state parliament, protection against being denied the vote in Commonwealth elections: see **[4.5.1E]**; *R v Pearson; Ex parte Sipka* (1983) 152 CLR 254 **[4.5.7C]**. Section 41 was inserted to entrench the right to vote of South Australian women (enfranchised at the state level before federation) in Commonwealth elections. It also operated to preserve the right to vote of the small number of Aboriginal people entitled to a state franchise at federation. These may have included some South Australian 'aboriginal native' women.

However, s 41 did not allow 'aboriginal native' descendants of these people to vote in Commonwealth elections. In *R v Pearson; Ex parte Sipka* (1983) 152 CLR 254 **[4.5.7C]**, the High Court held that s 41 was a transitional provision only. The words 'or acquires' did not catch people who obtained the state franchise after federation.

Section 41 was subject to the Commonwealth Parliament's power to control its own franchise under ss 30 and 51(xxvi); a power exercised to enact the Commonwealth Franchise Act 1902.

[2.4.12]   While this narrow application of s 41 was resolved legally in the 1980s, it had affected Aboriginal people since 1912, when Robert Garran amended the Electoral Handbook to the same effect: Brazil and Mitchell (1981), vol 1, p 480. Some Aboriginal people entitled to vote under s 41 were denied the vote by unconstitutional administrative practice, as evidenced by a study of voting patterns at Point McLeay, South Australia, by Stretton and Finnimore:

> ... Aborigines were enrolled for both the State and the Commonwealth without any apparent hindrance until 1922. In 1921 South Australia adopted a joint electoral roll as did other States during the 1920s. The ... new enrolment form implied that *no* Aborigines ... could vote for the Commonwealth. On the new, joint roll a small circle beside any name indicated 'not entitled to vote for the Commonwealth'. These marks began to disfigure the pages of the roll. Between 1922 and 1946 seventeen Aborigines at Point McLeay, who had been on the Commonwealth roll until 1921, lost their Commonwealth vote. Seven of them had been on the roll since 1905 or probably earlier. There is no way to check before 1905 because the State rolls have been lost.
>
> Individual bureaucratic whim rather than legal consistency seems to have determined who was barred ... Exclusions multiplied in the 1930s. Eleven long-enrolled Aboriginal voters were disenfranchised at Point McLeay in 1933 ...
>
> Electoral officers also had to decide whether people were 'preponderantly' of Aboriginal descent since 'half castes' were permitted to vote. They were often inconsistent. Some States defined Aborigines differently for different purposes [under 'protection' laws] ... A former electoral officer whom we interviewed confirmed that in South Australia in the 1930s officers used appearance, rather than knowledge of peoples' parentage, to decide whether or not an Aborigine was an 'octoroon', 'quadroon', or 'half-caste' and therefore entitled to vote in federal elections.
>
> In these activities many electoral officers went further than Garran had advised ... In 1945, the Chief Electoral Officer told Professor AP Elkin ... that an Aborigine must not only have obtained State enrolment before the Franchise Act of 1902 ... but must have 'retained that enrolment continuously since' ... [I]n 1961, giving evidence to a Commonwealth Select Committee, the Chief Electoral officer for Victoria had the embarrassing task of explaining why Aboriginal voters had been excluded ... He replied that he was 'under the impression that the Commonwealth had only recently granted that right to all aborigines ...'
>
> South Australian electoral officers in 1936 had no doubts. When the Chief Protector of Aboriginals asked the Electoral Office for clarification of Aboriginal voting rights he was told, falsely, that the Commonwealth Electoral Act barred all Aborigines ... (Stretton and Finnimore (1993) pp 530–3).

[2.4.13]   Australian citizenship was invented in 1948, although Australians still remained 'British subjects'. However, the right to enrol to vote was retained by resident British subjects who did not become Australian citizens. This right was not extended to 'Aboriginal natives' until the following year. In 1949, the Commonwealth Electoral Act 1918 (which replaced the Franchise Act) was amended to confer the franchise on an 'Aboriginal native of Australia' who was entitled to vote at the state level, or who had been a member of the defence forces. However, about 30,000 indigenous adults in Western Australia, Queensland and the Commonwealth-administered Northern Territory were denied the Commonwealth franchise until the race-based exclusion was completely removed by the Commonwealth Electoral Act 1962.

Most of these people were so-called 'full bloods', but about 4000 were West Australians and Queenslanders of less than 'full' but 'preponderantly' Aboriginal descent. These figures did not include 'thousands' of 'mixed-descent' West Australians and Queenslanders who had been entitled to vote in Commonwealth elections before 1962, but did not know that they were entitled: Commonwealth of Australia (1961) pp 2, 4; Chesterman and Galligan (1997) Ch 4. Resident non-citizen British subjects could still acquire the right to vote until 1984, the year in which 'Aboriginal natives' were first *required* to enrol to vote. See Australian Citizenship Act 1948 (Cth) s 7; Commonwealth Electoral Act 1918 (Cth) ss 39 and 42 as amended by Commonwealth Electoral Legislation Amendment Act 1983.

[2.4.14] Only two 'indigenous' people have ever been elected to the Commonwealth Parliament, both to the Senate: Neville Bonner (a Liberal from Queensland between 1971 and 1983) and Aden Ridgeway (a Democrat from New South Wales who took up his seat in 1998). In 1995, a Council for Aboriginal Reconciliation submission relating to the proposed 'social justice package' attached to the Native Title Act 1993 proposed that the question of designated seats for Aboriginal people and Torres Strait Islanders, first raised with Prime Minister Lyons by Aboriginal protesters on the New South Wales sesquicentenary in 1938, be explored: Council for Aboriginal Reconciliation (1995), 22. This 'package' never eventuated.

Native title, the states and the Racial Discrimination Act, and the push for a constitutional limitation on racially discriminatory laws

[2.4.15] At the turn of the 20th century, 'race' was accepted as a legitimate ground for official discrimination. As Williams has pointed out, the constitutional framers were concerned not to interfere with the 'right' of the states to discriminate against their residents (including British subjects) on racial grounds. Section 117 of the Constitution, the 'non-discrimination against state residents' provision, was framed narrowly so that it would not interfere with state 'Factory Acts', which discriminated against non-white labour: Williams (1997).

[2.4.16] The 'right' to discriminate on racial grounds is now outlawed at international law by the Convention on the Elimination of All Forms of Racial Discrimination and domestically by legislation (including the Racial Discrimination Act 1975 (Cth) based on the Convention).

Key provisions of the Racial Discrimination Act are found in Part II:

8 (1) This Part does not apply to, or in relation to the application of, special measures to which paragraph 4 of Article 1 of the Convention applies ...

9 (1) It is unlawful for a person to do any act involving a distinction, exclusion, restriction or preference based on race, colour, descent or national or ethnic origin which has the purpose or effect of nullifying or impairing the recognition, enjoyment or exercise, on an equal footing, of any human right or fundamental freedom in the political, economic, social, cultural or any other field of public life...

(2) A reference in this section to a human right or fundamental freedom in the political, economic, social, cultural or any other field of public life includes any right of a kind referred to in Article 5 of the Convention.

10 (1) If, by reason of, or of a provision of, a law of the Commonwealth or of a State or Territory, persons of a particular race, colour or national or ethnic origin do not enjoy a right that is enjoyed by persons of another race, colour or national or ethnic origin, or enjoy a right to a more limited extent than persons of another race, colour or national or ethnic origin, then, notwithstanding anything in that law, persons of the first-mentioned race, colour or national or ethnic origin shall, by force of this section, enjoy that right to the same extent as persons of that other race, colour or national or ethnic origin.

(2) A reference in subsection (1) to a right includes a reference to a right of a kind referred to in Article 5 of the Convention.

As pointed out by Brennan, Toohey and Gaudron JJ in *Mabo v Queensland (No 1)* (1988) 166 CLR 166 at 216–17, the rights referred to in art 5 of the Convention include the civil rights to own property, alone as well as in association with others, and the right to inherit: art 5(d)(v) and (vi).

[2.4.17]   Although it is written in the lofty language of the International Convention, the Racial Discrimination Act is not a constitutional standard. It can be repealed or amended (expressly or impliedly) as easily as any other Commonwealth Act. Although the language of s 10 of the Racial Discrimination Act suggests that it limits Commonwealth laws, it cannot prevent subsequent enactment of a discriminatory Commonwealth law. Parliament may not fetter its legislative power in this way: *Pareroultja v Tickner* (1993) 42 FCR 32. The fact that the Racial Discrimination Act can be repealed has led to calls for the constitutional entrenchment of a racial non-discrimination clause (Council for Aboriginal Reconciliation (1995) 17 and (2000) Ch 10), although achievement of such a constitutional amendment may be difficult, given the low success rates of Australian constitutional referenda: see **[1.6.4]**.

[2.4.18]   However, the RDA has operated as if it *were* a constitutional constraint on the states and territories, because of the possibility that its equality and non-discrimination standards might invoke s 109 constitutional inconsistency (or the equivalent territorial doctrine) so as to invalidate unequal or discriminatory state or territory laws. This effect, and its importance for native title, emerged out of six cases, all but one of which dealt with racial discrimination against Aboriginal people or Torres Strait Islanders — *Gerhardy v Brown* (1935) 159 CLR 70; *Koowarta v Bjelke-Petersen* (1982) 153 CLR 168; *Viskauskas v Niland* (1983) 153 CLR 280; *University of Wollongong v Metwally* (1984) 158 CLR 447; *Mabo v Queensland (No 1)* (1988) 166 CLR 186; and *Western Australia v Commonwealth* (the *Native Title Act* case) (1995) 183 CLR 373 — and has been recently confirmed in a native title case, *Ward v Western Australia* (2002) 191 ALR 1.

The following discussion should be read together with the discussion of s 109 in Chapter 8 (especially **[8.1.74C]**) and the discussion of the 'external affairs power' in Chapter 3 (especially *Koowarta v Bjelke-Petersen* (1982) 153 CLR 168 **[3.3.15C]**). The semi-constitutional operation of the Racial Discrimination Act on the states gives us an insight into one possible set of ways in which a constitutional guarantee of equality or a limitation on discriminatory laws might operate in Australia. It highlights the complexity of the judicial task of measuring these rather abstract concepts against the detail of legislation or government behaviour, and the role played by constitutional method in such decisions. The Racial Discrimination Act cases and the legislative developments associated with them also highlight starkly the politics of attempts to protect 'indigenous' rights when other's rights are at stake, or appear to be at stake.

[2.4.19] In 1985, the High Court decided *Gerhardy v Brown* (1985) 159 CLR 70, on the constitutional relationship between the Racial Discrimination Act and state legislation conferring a specially designed land rights title to traditional territory on an Aboriginal group, the Pitjantjatjara Land Rights Act 1981 (SA).

In *Gerhardy*, the court treated ss 9 and 10 of the RDA as requiring identical treatment of people of different races, regardless of any differences between them. This would have meant that the South Australian legislation was constitutionally inconsistent with the RDA provisions because it treated the Pitjantjatjara people differently from others (it took away the federally granted rights of non-Pitjantjatjaras to racial equality and non-discrimination — the second test of s 109 inconsistency: see **[8.1.21]**). However, the court upheld the Pitjantjatjara Land Rights Act as a 'special measure' consistent with s 8 of the RDA, making s 109 of the Constitution inapplicable. The High Court's approach to the interpretation of ss 9 and 10 has been criticised for failing to appreciate that appropriately different treatment of genuine difference does not constitute discrimination under the Convention, and need not be excused as a 'special measure'. Rather, 'special measures' are designed to eliminate difference by improving disadvantaged human rights: see Sadurski (1986); Pritchard (1995); Clarke (1997b).

Note that the court in *Gerhardy* concluded that the South Australian legislation could have been invalidated by s 10 of the RDA despite the language of s 10, which purports to cure inequality by 'topping up' the rights of a disadvantaged group rather than striking down the discriminatory measure. Mason J said that s 10 might operate as drafted where there was no inconsistency between the two laws, but that s 109 of the Constitution would always invalidate the state law where the two were inconsistent. In his view, inconsistency was present where a state law *prohibited* the members of a racial group from enjoying rights enjoyed by others (as was the case here), but might not be present where the state law merely omitted to confer the same rights on all racial groups. In the latter case, s 10's wording would produce the omitted rights to achieve racial equality: at 98–9.

[2.4.20] The potential significance for native title of the s 109 argument from *Gerhardy* was as follows. Since, before 1992, native title was not recognised by the Australian courts, state governments exercised their legislatively confined radical title powers to grant land (see **[2.3.4]–[2.3.7]**) without regard to the possible existence of native title in the land. Indeed, the state Crown Lands Acts which supported the grants also took no account of native title. On the discriminatory common law native title principles discussed at **[2.2.42]–[2.2.43]**, this was lawful, the resulting grants were valid, and native title was correspondingly extinguished. But the holders of other property rights were not treated so summarily: holders of Crown-granted titles were protected against extinguishment of their titles by common law principle except where a parliament 'clearly and plainly' authorised their dispossession (see **[2.2.42]**); in the 20th century, most Australian parliaments enacted legislation which controlled the circumstances in which such dispossession could occur (typically, for public purposes, with notice and for compensation). Before 1992, the protections of this state compulsory acquisition legislation did not extend to native title — again, because it was not known to exist. Thus, after the RDA commenced in 1975, it was possible that state governments which granted native title land to other people (including private individuals), typically without notice or compensation, were acting under laws rendered invalid for constitutional inconsistency with the RDA. If the legislation authorising the Crown in right of a state to grant land was valid, the

Crown had no power to make those grants, and the grants themselves would also be invalid. (It might be argued that registration under the Torrens system cured this invalidity, but not all types of rights and interests in land are so registrable (for example, mining tenements are not), and 'old system' land remained unregistered.)

[2.4.21] After *Gerhardy*, the High Court decided *Koowarta v Bjelke-Petersen* (1982) 153 CLR 168: see **[3.3.15C]**. *Koowarta* established that the RDA was a valid exercise of the Commonwealth's 'external affairs' power (s 51(xxix) Constitution), and that a 'person' under s 9 included a state Minister. However, because Koowarta sought damages and not a declaration that the Minister's refusal to grant land was invalid, the court did not consider the impact on the Minister's decision of Commonwealth Constitution s 109. Nonetheless, this decision confirmed that the actions of the Crown in right of a state in granting land were vulnerable to challenge under the RDA.

[2.4.22] Next, the High Court decided two 'covering the field' cases about the s 109 relationship between the RDA and state anti-discrimination legislation. *Viskauskas v Niland* (1983) 153 CLR 280 **[8.1.53]** established the invalidity of state racial discrimination legislation because the RDA at the time 'covered the field'. *University of Wollongong v Metwally* (1984) 158 CLR 447 **[8.1.57C]** held (by a narrow majority) that a subsequent Commonwealth amendment declaring that the RDA 'shall be deemed never to have been intended' to cover the field was constitutionally invalid because parliament was incapable of *deeming* that a s 109 inconsistency had never existed. Thus, where (as discussed below, see **[2.4.26]–[2.4.27]**) state land laws have been inconsistent with the RDA, the Commonwealth Parliament cannot simply deem them valid retrospectively (and nor can a state parliament). However, the High Court seems prepared to allow a co-operative 'solution' to this kind of inconsistency which involves *both* a change in Commonwealth law and a new state Act reviving the previously invalid state legislation: see *Western Australia v Commonwealth* (the *Native Title Act* case) (1995) 183 CLR at 454–5.

[2.4.23] *Mabo v Queensland (No 1)* (1988) 166 CLR 186, discussed in **[8.1.72]**, confirmed that at least some state land dealings could be invalidated under s 109 Constitution by the RDA if they involved racially discriminatory treatment of potential holders of native title. The High Court was prepared to accord RDA protection to 'property rights' which had not yet been 'recognised' by Australian law. *Mabo (No 1)* concerned the common law native title claim ultimately upheld in *Mabo v Queensland (No 2)* (1992) 175 CLR 1. The majority held that the Queensland Parliament's extinguishment of native title was inconsistent with RDA s 10, because the Queensland Coast Islands Declaratory Act 1985 (Qld) treated property rights stemming from indigenous tradition differently from those stemming from a Crown grant. The former were removed so that the latter could be confirmed. Thus (to apply Mason J's *Gerhardy* reasoning), the state Act was overtly discriminatory in that it *prohibited* the Meriam from enjoying rights enjoyed by others, which it bolstered; it did not merely *omit to confer* on the Meriam human rights protections conferred on other people's rights. Because it removed the equality conferred by s 10 RDA, it was completely inconsistent with s 10 and therefore completely invalid.

[2.4.24] The *Mabo (No 1)* majority were unsympathetic to an argument (upheld by Wilson J) that the Queensland Act merely brought about the 'formal equality' required by the RDA by removing property rights (native title) which could only be enjoyed by indigenous Australians, and confirming property rights (those granted by the Crown) which could in theory be enjoyed by all Australians. Brennan, Toohey and Gaudron JJ rejected this argument as one which confused the source of the rights with their existence: 166 CLR at 218. In determining how the RDA and the Convention protect property rights, these justices (and Deane J) were unafraid to refer to another human rights standard, art 17 of the Universal Declaration of Human Rights 1948. This article states that '[n]o one shall be arbitrarily deprived of his property'. '[A]rbitrarily' in international law means 'not only "illegally" but also "unjustly"': 166 CLR at 217. The Queensland Act infringed the immunity from arbitrary deprivation of Meriam property rights while leaving the corresponding immunity of other property rights intact: 166 CLR at 217–19; see also 166 CLR at 230 per Deane J.

[2.4.25] *Mabo v Queensland (No 1)* (1988) 166 CLR 186 was not particularly controversial at the time. However, it became controversial after the High Court 'discovered' native title four years later in *Mabo v Queensland (No 2)* (1992) 175 CLR 1. As discussed at **[2.2.34]**, under the common law, native title can exist without being proven in a court or other forum, and its existence can date back to as early as 1788. 'Discovery' of native title in 1992 highlighted the possibility that some state land titles granted since 1975 were invalid for discrimination against the holders of native title to that land.

State governments reacted sharply, as did mining and other rural industries. There were calls for amendment or repeal of the RDA, since state laws are invalid only *to the extent* of any inconsistency with the RDA, and only while the RDA is on the statute books: see **[8.1.6]**. However, there was a risk that discriminatory amendment of the RDA might render it *ultra vires* the Commonwealth's external affairs power.

[2.4.26] Uncertainty over the validity of titles granted after the commencement of the RDA motivated enactment of the Native Title Act 1993 (Cth). In *Western Australia v Commonwealth* (the *Native Title Act* case) (1995) 183 CLR 373 at 451, the High Court declined to say whether it thought general post-1975 state land grants had been invalidated where they were racially discriminatory.

In this case, the court applied the *Mabo (No 1)* approach to a more complex state law, the Land (Titles and Traditional Usage) Act 1993 (WA). The Western Australian Act amended state land and resource laws. It was enacted on 2 December 1993, a month before the Native Title Act 1993 (Cth) (NTA 1993) commenced. Section 7 of the state Act purported to extinguish prospectively all native title in Western Australia, substituting inferior statutory rights. The substituted rights were more vulnerable to interference than native title (as protected by the RDA); to put it another way, more vulnerable to interference (for a wider range of purposes) than Crown-granted property rights under Western Australian law.

The High Court held s 7 and associated provisions in the state Act invalid for inconsistency with RDA s 10. It made clear that s 10 is inconsistent with 'a State law which purports to authorise expropriation of property characteristically held by the "persons of a particular race" for purposes additional to those generally justifying expropriation or on less stringent conditions (including lesser compensation)' than those imposed on the acquisition of other people's titles: 183 CLR at 437.

The court also considered another provision of the Land (Titles and Traditional Usage) Act (s 5), which purported unilaterally to overcome invalidity of state land title grants brought about by the RDA and Constitution s 109: see **[2.4.18]–[2.4.25]** above. It held that any such invalidity could not be overcome by Western Australian legislation alone: 183 CLR at 451.

[2.4.27] What, if anything, could or should be done about Crown-granted titles which were possibly invalidated by the RDA? Consistently with Australia's historical denial of native title, there was no real suggestion after *Mabo (No 2)* that the land should be given back to any rightful native title holders. Rather, the Commonwealth responded to the claims for 'certainty' of the holders of Crown-granted titles.

The compromise struck by the Native Title Act 1993 (Cth) (NTA 1993) involved the non-application of RDA standards to native title in the period 1975–94. This permitted the enactment, after the commencement on 1 January 1994 of the Native Title Act 1993 ('NTA 1993'), of state legislation 'validating' any invalid title grants made between 31 October 1975 and that date. State 'validation' legislation of this kind would otherwise have been inconsistent with the RDA, because it validates titles granted in a racially discriminatory manner. The original NTA 1993 otherwise generally preserved the operation of the RDA (an earlier law of the same parliament), but made an exception in the case of these 'title validation' laws. According to the judges in *Western Australia v Commonwealth* (the *Native Title Act* case) (1995) 183 CLR 373 at 454–5, this mechanism was constitutionally effective.

A clear benefit of a constitutionally entrenched guarantee of equality may be to remove the temptation for governments to compromise minority human rights with schemes of this kind. However, the cynical political culture which produces Australian reluctance to amend the Constitution may be equally capable of producing a desire to scale back constitutional guarantees where it is perceived that they give Aboriginal people or Torres Strait Islanders 'too much' or deny important members of the political majority 'certainty'. Such developments are evident overseas. A 2002 referendum in the Canadian province of British Columbia produced an 80 per cent 'yes' response to a series of eight questions on government negotiation of 'indigenous' rights in the province's stalled 'treaty process'. The questions were framed so as to produce support for government policies to reduce existing rights (for example, tax exemptions) and limit potential future rights (for example, to self-government): see de Costa (2002) and CBC News (2002).

[2.4.28] In applying the Western Australian 'validation' provisions (referred to in **[2.4.27]**), the High Court in *Ward v Western Australia* (2002) 191 ALR 1, confirmed that Mason J's approach to the RDA in *Gerhardy* was the correct one. This means that the RDA only ever invalidated those Crown-granted titles which *were granted over native title land but could not have been granted over other titles* (for example, freehold grants), not those Crown-granted titles which *were equally able to be granted over native title and other privately owned land* (for example, in many jurisdictions, mining tenements). Only the former category of *previously invalid* Crown-granted titles have been *validated* by the NTA 1993 and associated state validation legislation. Holders of other titles granted after 1975 did not need to have their titles validated, although under s 10 RDA, the Crown in right of a state may need to pay native title holders compensation if they were left out of the original compensation scheme.

[2.4.29C]   **Ward v Western Australia**

(2002) 191 ALR 1

(footnotes omitted)

Gleeson, Gummow, Gaudron and Hayne JJ:

... 3. Section 9(1) of the RDA

[101] [Their Honours set it out]...

The issue arises as to whether s 9(1) operates in respect of an act authorised by a State or Territory statute, the act having a discriminatory effect upon the enjoyment of native title rights and interests...

Because legislative sanction is now necessary before anything can be done with Crown land which would extinguish or affect native title [their Honours referred to the West Australian constitutional provision giving control over Crown lands allocation to the legislature — see **[2.3.7]**], s 9(1) does not operate to invalidate discriminatory acts of that kind. The appropriate provision is that in s 10(1).

4. Section 10(1) of the RDA

[Their Honours set it out] ... A number of points may be made at once. First, the sub-section does not use the word 'discriminatory' or cognate expressions. Yet these terms are used throughout the authorities in which s 10(1) has been considered. That to which the sub-section in terms is directed is the *enjoyment* of rights by some but not by others or to a more limited extent by others; there is an unequal enjoyment of rights that are or should be conferred irrespective of race, colour or national or ethnic origin. 'Enjoyment' of rights directs attention to much more than what might be thought to be the purpose of the law in question ... It is therefore wrong to confine the relevant operation of the RDA to laws whose purpose can be identified as discriminatory.

Secondly, at first sight, neither the grant of an interest in land nor the vesting of land in another appears to be a discriminatory act. Thirdly, on its face, s 10(1) operates by force of federal law to extend the enjoyment of rights enjoyed under another federal law or a Territory or State law. Fourthly, as Mason J pointed out in *Gerhardy*, different considerations arise in two kinds of case. His Honour said:

> If racial discrimination arises under or by virtue of State law because the relevant State law merely omits to make enjoyment of the right universal, ie by failing to confer it on persons of a particular race, then s 10 operates to confer that right on persons of that particular race. In this situation the section proceeds on the footing that the right which it confers is complementary to the right created by the State law. Because it exhibits no intention to occupy the field occupied by the positive provisions of State law to the exclusion of that law the provisions of the State law remain unaffected.

This may be contrasted with the case where the State law in question imposes a discriminatory burden or prohibition. As Mason J said in *Gerhardy*:

> When racial discrimination proceeds from a prohibition in a State law directed to persons of a particular race, forbidding them from enjoying a human right or fundamental freedom enjoyed by persons of another race, by virtue of that State law, s 10 confers a right on the persons prohibited by State law to enjoy the human right or fundamental freedom enjoyed by persons of that other race. This necessarily results in an inconsistency between s 10 and the prohibition contained in the State law.

The same is true of a State law that deprives persons of a particular race of a right or freedom previously enjoyed by all regardless of race.

Three situations may be considered: (i) a State law expressed in general terms forbids the enjoyment of a human right or fundamental freedom and, because the burden falls upon all racial groups, there is no discrimination upon which s 10(1) may operate; (ii) a State law, for example, provides for the extinguishment of land titles but provides for compensation only in respect of non-native title; on the above analysis, this falls in the first category identified by Mason J for the operation of s 10(1) and, whilst the extinguishment remains valid, there is ...

a right to compensation provided to native title holders; (iii) a State law, for example, extinguishes only native title and leaves other titles intact; the situation falls in the second category identified by Mason J and the discriminatory burden of extinguishment is removed because the operation of the State law is rendered invalid by s 109 of the Constitution.

Gerhardy, Mabo v Queensland [No 1] and the *Native Title Act Case* all concerned State laws in this second category. In *Gerhardy*, however, the Court held that the legislation was a 'special measure' ... In both *Mabo [No 1]* and the *Native Title Act Case*, s 109 of the Constitution was held to operate upon the relevant State legislation. It is this result that has been said to confer upon native title holders the same 'immunity from legislative interference' with the relevant human right as that of other members of the community...

... [I]n *Mabo [No 1]* ... [s]ix members of the Court held that s 3 of the 1985 State Act had the effect of extinguishing land rights claimed under traditional law and custom by the Miriam people. Four members of the Court (Brennan, Deane, Toohey and Gaudron JJ) concluded that on that construction of the 1985 State Act, it was inconsistent with s 10(1) of the RDA. A critical step in the reasoning of the majority was that the 1985 State Act operated to deprive only Torres Strait Islanders of whatever may have been their traditional rights to the land and had no operation on the rights of others. So much followed from the 1985 State Act deeming that at an earlier date (when the islands were annexed to and became part of Queensland) the islands were vested in the Crown in right of Queensland freed of all other rights, interests and claims. At that earlier date there were no rights, interests or claims to the islands except under traditional law ...

It was upon this basis that the majority concluded that s 109 of the Constitution applied ... The majority concluded that the human rights of the Miriam people to own and inherit property, and not to be deprived arbitrarily of their property, were denied or diminished. Section 10(1) of the RDA was read by the majority as saying that all members of the community shall enjoy those rights. Accordingly, a State statute which took them away or diminished them was, to that extent, inconsistent with s 10(1) and invalid. This, so Deane J said, was 'the only way' that s 10 could operate 'to procure the result which the section is designed to guarantee'.

Focusing attention upon procuring the result guaranteed by s 10 of the RDA should not, however, be understood as enlarging accepted principles about the operation of s 109 any more than it should be permitted to obscure the fact that s 10(1) may have relevant operation in two ways.

The operation of s 10(1) was considered further in the *Native Title Act Case*. It was said in the joint reasons of six members of the Court that:

> Where, under the general law, the indigenous 'persons of a particular race' uniquely have a right to own or to inherit property within Australia arising from indigenous law and custom but the security of enjoyment of that property is more limited than the security enjoyed by others who have a right to own or to inherit other property, *the persons of the particular race are given, by s 10(1), security in the enjoyment of their property* 'to the same extent' as persons generally have security in the enjoyment of their property. Security in the right to own property carries immunity from arbitrary deprivation of the property[103]. Section 10(1) thus protects the enjoyment of traditional interests in land recognised by the common law. (emphasis added)

Of the operation of s 109 of the Constitution in relation to s 10(1) of the RDA, it was said in the joint judgment in the *Native Title Act* case that:

> If a law of a State provides that property held by members of the community generally may not be expropriated except for prescribed purposes or on prescribed conditions (including the payment of compensation), a State law which purports to authorise expropriation of property characteristically held by the 'persons of a particular race' for purposes additional to those generally justifying expropriation or on less stringent conditions (including lesser compensation) is inconsistent with s 10(1) of the [RDA].

Again it will be seen that the conclusion that the State law provided for differential treatment of land holding according to race, colour, or national or ethnic origin was critical. This was because it is that understanding of the legal operation of the State law which underpins the conclusion that there is direct inconsistency between that law and the relevant federal law, the RDA.

If s 10(1) does not operate to invalidate the relevant State legislation, the ... [validation] provisions of the NTA, and equivalent State provisions, are not engaged. It is therefore of the first importance to ascertain the precise operation and effect of any potentially discriminatory legislation affecting or authorising acts affecting native title rather than assuming that the NTA is to apply ...

In determining whether a law is in breach of s 10(1), it is necessary to bear in mind that the sub-section is directed at the enjoyment of a right; it does not require that the relevant law, or an act authorised by that law, be 'aimed at' native title, nor does it require that the law, in terms, makes a distinction based on race. Section 10(1) is directed at 'the practical operation and effect' of the impugned legislation and is 'concerned not merely with matters of form but with matters of substance' ...

Some care is required in identifying and making the comparison between the respective 'rights' involved. In *Mabo [No 1]* the 'right' referred to was 'the human right to own and inherit property (including a human right to be immune from arbitrary deprivation of property)'. 'Property' in this context includes land and chattels as well as interests therein and extends to native title rights and interests.

It is because native title characteristically is held by members of a particular race that interference with the enjoyment of native title is capable of amounting to discrimination on the basis of race, colour, or national or ethnic origin. In *Mabo [No 1]* the Court, by majority, rejected the argument that, as native title has different characteristics from other forms of title and derives from a different source, it can legitimately be treated differently from those other forms of title ...

In the joint judgment in the *Native Title Act Case*, it was said, to the same effect, that:

> [t]he [RDA] does not alter the characteristics of native title, but it confers on protected persons rights or immunities which, being recognised by 'the tribunals and all other organs administering justice', allow protected persons security in the enjoyment of their title to property to the same extent as the holders of titles granted by the Crown are secure in the enjoyment of their titles.

[I]t may be thought that if native title has different characteristics to other forms of title and it is those very characteristics which provide elements of strength but which also render native title vulnerable to extinguishment (i) that the RDA should not operate in the manner suggested by the joint judgment in the *Native Title Act Case* or (ii) that, if it does so, it does, in fact, alter the characteristics of native title.

The rights upon which s 10 of the RDA operates are defined in s 10(2) to include 'a right of a kind referred to in Article 5 of the [International] Convention [on the Elimination of all Forms of Racial Discrimination]'. Relevant to the decision in *Mabo [No 1]*, art 5 includes '[t]he right to own property alone as well as in association with others' and '[t]he right to inherit' — rights which are identified in terms of complete generality.

Only if there were some basis for distinguishing between different types of ownership of property or different types of inheritance might it be correct to say, in the context of s 10(1) of the RDA, that to deprive the people of a particular race of a particular species of property or a particular form of inheritance not enjoyed by persons of another race is not to deprive them of a right enjoyed by persons of that other race. No basis for such a distinction is apparent in the text of the Convention. Nor is any suggested by the provisions of the RDA.

... [T]he RDA must be taken to proceed on the basis that different characteristics attaching to the ownership or inheritance of property by persons of a particular race are irrelevant to the question whether the right of persons of that race to own or inherit property is a right of the same kind as the right to own or inherit property enjoyed by persons of another race. In this respect the RDA operates in a manner not unlike most other anti-discrimination legislation which proceeds by reference to an unexpressed declaration that a particular characteristic is irrelevant for the purposes of that legislation.

... [T]he Court has rejected the argument that native title can be treated differently from other forms of title because native title has different characteristics from those other forms of title and derives from a different source. This conclusion about the operation of the RDA should not now be revisited.

... [D]iscrimination can occur in a variety of circumstances. In addition to the operations of s 10(1) to which reference has been made, the sub-section may also be engaged by legislation which regulates or impairs the enjoyment of native title without effecting extinguishment ...

Finally, the legislation may attract s 10(1) of the RDA because it purports on its face to extinguish native title without compensation or on less stringent conditions (including lesser compensation) than those which govern the expropriation of the property of the people of another race. *Mabo [No 1]* and the *Native Title Act Case* were concerned with legislative extinguishment that resulted in the 'arbitrary deprivation of property'; the force of the adjective 'arbitrary' appears to have been to emphasise the absence of (and need for) compensation. In such cases, it is appropriate to compare that lack of compensation in respect of native title with what it appears are rights of compensation generally afforded to holders of other forms of title ...

In the joint judgment in the *Native Title Act* case, a similar approach was taken. However, it should be noted that that case concerned State legislation purporting on its face to extinguish native title and to replace it with rights derived from that very legislation. This provided that those (statutory) rights could be extinguished, suspended or impaired by action taken under the general laws of the State ...

This approach was thus dependent upon the terms of the legislation under consideration in that case.

In other cases, involving different legislation, it will be appropriate to compare the effect of that legislation upon native title holders with the effect on other title holders. This will not necessarily involve any analysis of the general laws of the State or Territory. If, under the relevant legislative scheme, no provision is made respecting compensation for interference with, or abrogation of, any rights and interests in land, then the failure to compensate in respect of native title would not be sufficient to engage s 10(1). However, it may be that the power conferred by the legislation is exercised in a manner that, as a matter of fact, is discriminatory and thereby engages s 10(1) ...

~~~

[2.4.30] The RDA's future application to native title was also largely overtaken by the NTA 1993. For discussion of the NTA 1993, see: *Western Australia v Commonwealth* (the *Native Title Act* case) (1995) 183 CLR 373; *North Ganalanja Aboriginal Corp v Queensland* (the *Waanyi* case) (1996) 185 CLR 595; *Fejo v Northern Territory* (1998) 195 CLR 96.

The NTA 1993 did four things. First, as discussed at **[2.4.26]–[2.4.27]**, it allowed 'validation' of land dealings which might have been invalid because of the RDA. Second, it established a statutory regime for the making of native title claims. Third, it established an Aboriginal and Torres Strait Islander Land Fund (into which the Commonwealth paid $200 million initially, and the equivalent of $121 million in 1994 terms per year, over a 10-year period). The fund was envisaged as compensating people whose native title has been extinguished.

Fourth, the NTA 1993 introduced new principles for future (post-1994) use of native title land ('future acts'). These differed from the common law of native title in two respects. They provided that native title could survive the grant of an inconsistent interest in the same land; rather than being extinguished by such a grant, native title would simply be suppressed by it. More importantly, they introduced a 'same treatment as freehold' standard for dealings with native title land. With exceptions, that meant that governments and state parliaments could only do to native title what they could do to freehold. On top of this, when granting mining titles, state governments were required to negotiate with native title holders (the 'right to negotiate').

'Indigenous leaders' agreed to enactment of the NTA, including its discriminatory 'validation' provisions. One reason why they did this was because the Commonwealth proposed introducing a 'social justice package' by way of compensation. That package has never materialised.

[2.4.31]   A later Act which is inconsistent with an earlier Act of the same parliament will impliedly repeal it: see **[5.4.3]** and **[2.4.17]**. However, in *Western Australia v Commonwealth* (the *Native Title Act* case) (1995) 183 CLR 383, the High Court suggested that the NTA 1993 and the RDA were consistent (at 483–4):

> [T]he Native Title Act can be regarded either as a special measure under s 8 of the Racial Discrimination Act or as a law which, though it makes racial distinctions, is not racially discriminatory so as to offend the Racial Discrimination Act or the International Convention on the Elimination of All Forms of Discrimination [sic] ...

[2.4.32]   The NTA 1993 was unravelled after the decision in *Wik Peoples v Queensland* (1996) 187 CLR 1 **[2.3.6]**, where a majority of the High Court decided that native title was capable of coexisting with the grant of a pastoral lease to the same land. This meant that the NTA 1993 had always been capable of applying to pastoral leasehold land.

However, before *Wik*, several state governments insisted that native title was extinguished by pastoral lease grants, and that the NTA 1993 could not apply to pastoral leasehold or former pastoral leasehold. Refusing to wait for the court to decide the issue, and ignoring dicta describing the opposite point of view as 'fairly arguable' (*North Ganalanja Aboriginal Corp v Queensland* (1996) 185 CLR 595), the states granted mining tenements over pastoral leasehold land in defiance of the 'right to negotiate' regime for such grants in the NTA 1993. This action again placed state governments in the position of granting titles under legislation constitutionally inconsistent with Commonwealth legislation, in this case, the NTA 1993. This time, the inconsistency was clear. Unlike the 'rubbery and elusive' RDA standards, the mandatory NTA 1993 procedures were clearly spelt out.

[2.4.33]   The states were not penalised for contravening the NTA 1993. Rather, they were saved by 1998 amendments (implementing the Commonwealth Government's 'Ten Point Plan'). The amendments allowed the states to enact further 'validation' legislation to overcome the invalidity of pre-*Wik* mining tenements granted without observing the 'right to negotiate'.

The Native Title Amendment Act 1998 (Cth) (NTAA 1998) radically reshaped the NTA 1993. In many respects, it is inconsistent with RDA standards; this was the view of the UN Committee on the Elimination of All Forms of Racial Discrimination in 1999 (CERD Decision 2(54) on Australia A/54/18, para 21(2), 18 March 1999; Decision 2(55) on Australia A/54/18, para 23(2), 16 August 1999) and 2000 (CERD/ C/304/Add 101, 19 April 2000). The NTAA 1998 'confirmed' the common law extinguishment of a small number of unextinguished native titles. It established a new 'future acts' regime which allowed the grant or exercise of many other property rights over native title land. It allowed governments to interfere with native title more easily than with other property rights. Because these amendments were inconsistent with the RDA, they operated to repeal its protection of native title: see Clarke (1997b). Now that Commonwealth legislation has established these discriminatory standards, discriminatory state laws will be consistent with it, and therefore not invalid under s 109 of the Constitution. Indeed, the NTAA 1998, like the NTA 1993, encourages the states and territories to adopt legislation with a similar impact.

Acquisition of property and native title

[2.4.34] This section should be read with the discussion of s 51(xxxi) of the Constitution in **[11.2.1E]–[11.2.23]** and the discussion of territories in Ch XX.

The Native Title Amendment Act 1998 (Cth), which interferes with and sometimes extinguishes native title (see **[2.4.33]**), provides 'just terms' compensation. Compensation is provided on the assumption that native title is 'property' within s 51(xxxi) of the Constitution, and that it is 'acquired' when extinguished by Commonwealth legislation. Deane and Gaudron JJ expressed this view in *Mabo v Queensland (No 2)* (1992) 175 CLR 1 at 111:

> Our conclusion that rights under ... native title are true legal rights ... would ... have the consequence that any legislative extinguishment of those rights would constitute an expropriation of property, to the benefit of the underlying estate, for the purposes of s 51(xxxi).

Gummow J agreed with this view in *Newcrest Mining (WA) Ltd v Commonwealth* (1997) 190 CLR 513 at 613. Section 51(xxxi) applies not only where the Commonwealth acquires 'property' for itself, but where it allows 'acquisition' of 'property' by other persons. If native title is extinguished, the 'underlying estate' benefited would usually be that of the Crown in right of a state. On common law principles, where native title is extinguished, the Crown's radical title interest expands to full beneficial ownership of land.

[2.4.35] However, there is *dicta* suggesting that a s 51(xxxi) 'acquisition' does not occur where the Crown in right of the Commonwealth extinguishes native title in exercise of radical title powers. There are not many places where this could occur, as the Commonwealth enjoys radical title over very little land. However, in the past it could have occurred in Commonwealth territories. In *Newcrest v Commonwealth* (1997) 190 CLR 513, it was argued that to apply s 51(xxxi) to the Northern Territory 'would potentially invalidate every grant ... of title ... by the Commonwealth ... since 1911 to the extent to which ... such grant may be inconsistent with ... native title' because 'just terms' compensation was never paid for interference with native title rights: at 613. Gummow J (with whom Kirby J agreed: at 651) responded at 613:

> Such apprehensions are not well founded. The characteristics of native title as recognised at common law include an inherent susceptibility to extinguishment or defeasance by *the grant* of freehold or of some lesser estate which is inconsistent with native title rights; this is so whether the grant be supported by the prerogative or by legislation.

This statement seems to suggest that the extinguishment of native title does not attract 'just terms' compensation.

Constitutional power with respect to 'the people of any race'

[2.4.36] The Commonwealth Parliament created in 1901 enjoyed no specific legislative power over 'indigenous' Australians. The original s 51(xxvi) gave parliament power to make laws with respect to '[t]he people of any race, other than the aboriginal race in any State, for whom it is deemed necessary to make special laws'. The words 'other than the aboriginal race in any state' were deleted by constitutional amendment in 1967: see **[2.4.1]**. After 1967, the power extended to people of 'the 'Aboriginal race' and Torres Strait Islanders. However, this power remained one shared with the states. By contrast, the powers of the Dominion of Canada, and most of those of the United States Congress, in relation to indigenous people are exclusive powers.

[2.4.37] Samuel Griffith proposed an exclusive Commonwealth 'race' power against a background of extensive use of 'coloured' (Polynesian and Melanesian) labour in Queensland maritime and agricultural industries. Imperial and Queensland legislation had controlled this labour since the 1870s: Polynesian Labourers' Act 1868 (Qld); Pearl-Shell and Beche-de-Mer Fishery Act 1881 (Qld); Queensland Pearl-Shell and Beche-de-Mer Fisheries (Extra-Territorial) Act 1888 (Qld); Pacific Islanders Protection Act 1872 (UK) (which outlawed 'blackbirding'). The Federal Council of Australasia also legislated on the subject. Griffith proposed that the Commonwealth be able to deal with 'alien races' *in Australia*. The power would extend to British subjects. It was intended to authorise racial discrimination of a kind prohibited (at the state level) by the United States Constitution's 'equal protection' clause (Amendment XIV, §1). Sawer explained:

> [S]econdary sources ... make it clear that (xxvi) was intended to enable the Commonwealth to pass ... laws which before 1900 had been passed by many States, concerning 'the Indian, Afghan and Syrian hawkers; the Chinese miners, laundrymen, market gardeners and furniture manufacturers; the Japanese settlers and Kanaka plantation labourers of Queensland, and the various coloured races employed in the pearl fisheries of Queensland and Western Australia' [quoting Harrison Moore]. Such laws were designed 'to localize them within defined areas, to restrict their migration, to confine them to certain occupations, or to give them special protection and secure their return after a certain period to the country whence they came' [quoting Quick and Garran: *Yick Wo v Hopkins* (118 US 356 (1886))], in which the Supreme Court of the USA held invalid a San Francisco bylaw which conferred on officials an arbitrary power to license laundries ... exercised so as to refuse licences to Chinese while issuing them to other applicants. The ground of the decision was denial of equal protection of the laws ... [They] observe that no such guarantee is contained in the Australian Constitution ...
>
> Griffith ... said: '... I have ... in ... mind ... the immigration of coolies from British India, or any eastern people subject to civilised powers. The Dutch and English governments in the east do not allow their people to emigrate to serve in any foreign country unless there is a special law ... of that country protecting them, and affording special facilities for their coming and going ... [N]o state should be allowed, because the federal parliament did not choose to make a law on the subject, to allow the state to be flooded by such people...' ... Everything Griffith was concerned about could have been achieved under the immigration, aliens and external affairs powers ... The discussion ... tended to be in terms of 'aliens', but Barton showed clearly that ... the persons coming under it might well be British subjects. Nor need they be migrants; they could be born in Australia. Nor need they be coloured, nor from uncivilised [sic] countries ... [N]o-one suggested that laws discriminating against racial minorities were ... undesirable (Sawer (1966) pp 20–2).

[2.4.38] The lack of a specific Commonwealth power over indigenous Australians did not affect the Commonwealth's ability to give the Commonwealth vote to Aboriginal people and Torres Strait Islanders under its power to control its own franchise (s 51(xxxvi) and s 30) in 1962. That power was not limited by implications based on the omission, before 1967, of 'the aboriginal race in any state' from s 51(xxvi). Similarly, the Commonwealth was able to regulate the departure from Australia of Aboriginal people and Torres Strait Islanders under s 51(xxvii), the immigration power.

[2.4.39]   The suggestion that s 51(xxvi) be amended to cover 'the aboriginal race' was raised before the 1929 Royal Commission on the Constitution. The Commission's response reflected 1920s 'Aboriginal protection' standards:

> We recognise that the effect of the treatment of aborigines on the reputation of Australia furnishes a powerful argument for a transference of control to the Commonwealth. But we think that on the whole the States are better equipped for *controlling* aborigines than the Commonwealth. *The States control the police and the lands*, and they to a large extent control the conditions of industry (quoted in Williams and Bradsen (1997) p 119, emphasis added).

[2.4.40]   The 1967 referendum was not the first attempt to change s 51(xxvi), as Kirby J pointed out in *Kartinyeri v Commonwealth* (1998) 195 CLR 337. Proposals to expand Commonwealth power were raised in 1944 (by the Labor Government), 1959 (by a Parliamentary Committee), 1964 (by the opposition) and 1966 (by a backbencher). The proposal to alter the Constitution in the form eventually passed by the 1967 referendum was introduced by Prime Minister Holt in March 1967 and supported by Opposition Leader Whitlam. See: Hanks (1984); Attwood and Markus (1997); Williams and Bradsen (1997).

[2.4.41]   The large 'yes' vote in the referendum on 'the Aborigines question' (the two questions about s 51(xxvi) and s 127) was attributable to a remarkable political campaign conducted by the Federal Council for the Advancement of Aborigines and Torres Strait Islanders (FCAATSI): see Attwood and Markus (1997); Bandler (1989).

FCAATSI's campaign centred on the idea that the Constitution denied Aboriginal people 'citizenship'. It sought to bring the Commonwealth's considerable financial resources to bear on the poor material conditions of indigenous Australians in the states. However, the 'citizenship' plank of the campaign ignored the fact that indigenous Australians had been enfranchised everywhere since 1965. The 'financial' plank ignored the Commonwealth's similar record in the exercise of its existing power over Aboriginal people in the territories (under s 122, discussed in Chapter 12) and its 'State grants' power under s 96 **[9.6.2E]**, which could be used to fund improvements in Aboriginal living conditions.

The best reason for constitutional change lay in the continued existence of state 'protection' laws (see **[2.1.4]–[2.1.6]**) in Queensland and Western Australia. An amended s 51(xxvi) would allow Commonwealth legislation to override these laws. This eventually occurred with the Aboriginal and Torres Strait Islanders (Queensland Discriminatory Laws) Act 1975 (Cth) and Aboriginal and Torres Strait Islanders (Queensland Reserves and Communities Self-Management) Act 1978 (Cth), although the Commonwealth was reluctant to implement these laws' full effect.

[2.4.42]   There are only a few cases on the 'race' power, s 51(xxvi). In the 1990s, two Commonwealth Acts excited debate about its scope. The Hindmarsh Island Bridge Act 1997 (Cth) (which ousted the application of the Aboriginal and Torres Strait Islander Heritage Protection Act 1984 (Cth) to an area of land in South Australia) and the Native Title Amendment Act 1998 (Cth) (see **[2.4.33]**) raised questions about whether the amended power allowed laws which discriminate *against*, as well as for the benefit of, indigenous Australians, contrary to the political sentiments of the 1967 referendum. There is no decision which resolves this debate, although it was canvassed by several judges in *Kartinyeri v Commonwealth* (1998) 195 CLR 337: see **[2.4.45]**.

There is earlier *dicta* suggesting that the power is limited to laws benefiting indigenous Australians. Murphy J expressed this view in *Koowarta v Bjelke-Petersen* (1982) 153 CLR 168 at 242 and *Commonwealth v Tasmania* (the *Tasmanian Dam* case) (1983) 158 CLR 1 at 80. In the latter case, Brennan J suggested that the Constitution Alteration (Aboriginals) 1967 (Cth) amounted to 'an affirmation of the will of the Australian people that the odious policies of oppression and neglect of Aboriginal citizens were to be at an end, and that the primary object of the power is beneficial'. And the Racial Discrimination Act 'manifested the Parliament's intention that the power will hereafter be used only for the purpose of discriminatorily conferring benefits upon the people of a race for whom it is deemed necessary to make special laws': 158 CLR at 242. Deane J suggested that the referendum indicated that the discriminatory 'race' power was amended to allow parliament to make 'laws benefiting the people of the Aboriginal race': 158 CLR at 273.

However, there is no textual foundation for such an implication. And the view that the power allows adversely discriminatory laws is also supported by dicta: see, for example, *Koowarta v Bjelke-Petersen* (1982) 153 CLR at 186 per Gibbs CJ; *Western Australia v Commonwealth* (the *Native Title Act* case) (1995) 183 CLR 373 at 461.

[2.4.43]   Two cases on the amended s 51(xxvi), *Koowarta v Bjelke-Petersen* (1982) 153 CLR 168 and *Commonwealth v Tasmania* (the *Tasmanian Dam* case) (1983) 158 CLR 1, concentrated on other issues, in particular parliament's implementation of international conventions via the external affairs power (see Chapter 3 and the discussion of racial non-discrimination standards at **[2.4.16]–[2.4.28]**). In *Koowarta*, five judges (Gibbs CJ, Aickin, Stephen, Wilson and Brennan JJ (Mason J not deciding; Murphy J not deciding but inclined to dissent)) held that the 'race' power did not support the Racial Discrimination Act 1975 (Cth). In the *Tasmanian Dam* case, a majority of the court (Mason, Murphy, Brennan and Deane JJ) held that provisions of the World Heritage Properties Conservation Act 1983 (Cth) which protected Aboriginal cultural heritage were supported by s 51(xxvi).

Because of their facts, these cases did not raise the question of whether the 'race' power supports laws discriminating against indigenous Australians.

[2.4.44]   The third case, *Western Australia v Commonwealth* (the *Native Title Act* case) (1995) 183 CLR 383, was concerned with the 'race' power, although it turned on constitutional inconsistency between a discriminatory Western Australian law and the Racial Discrimination Act 1975 (Cth): see **[8.1.74C]** and **[2.4.26]**. Nonetheless, the Western Australian government sought to challenge the Native Title Act 1993 (Cth) on the ground that it was not supported by s 51(xxvi) because it was really a law interfering with the states' powers over land.

As discussed at **[2.4.31]**, the Native Title Act 1993 was consistent with the non-discrimination standards laid down by the Racial Discrimination Act 1975 (Cth). However, for the purposes of assessing the Native Title Act's constitutional character, the justices considered those standards irrelevant. Rather, the court assessed the Act's operation by reference to *the background common law*. The Act, they said, substantially improved the position of most native title holders by comparison with their position at common law. The use of the common law as a base against which to measure a law's operation is orthodox constitutional interpretation. However, as discussed at **[2.2.42]–[2.2.43]**, the common law of native title is racially discriminatory. It is thus a very low standard from which to measure any 'improvement' in the position of native title holders. Further, the judges' assessment of the Native Title Act's operation was made globally, not provision-by-provision. This approach allowed the court to gloss the negative impact of the discriminatory 'title validation' provisions (see **[2.4.26]–[2.4.27]**) on some native titles, emphasising instead the 'entire package', which benefited most native title holders: see generally Clarke (1997b).

Because of the court's 'beneficial' characterisation of the Native Title Act, this case also did not raise the question of whether the amended s 51(xxvi) allows laws which discriminate against indigenous Australians.

The case of *Kartinyeri v Commonwealth*

[2.4.45] This case ((1998) 195 CLR 337) was the legal climax of a long political controversy. The South Australian Government had approved a proposal to develop tourist facilities on Hindmarsh Island in South Australia, and to build a bridge from the mainland to the island. The plaintiffs applied to the Commonwealth Minister for Aboriginal and Torres Strait Islander Affairs for a declaration under the Aboriginal and Torres Strait Islander Heritage Protection Act 1984 (Cth) that the area affected by the proposed bridge and development constituted a significant Aboriginal area under threat of injury or desecration. The Minister received a report from an independent reporter and made a declaration under the Act preventing the bridge's construction. The declaration was quashed by the Federal Court in *Chapman v Tickner* (1995) 55 FCR 316, which was upheld by the Full Court in *Tickner v Chapman* (1995) 57 FCR 451.

The Minister appointed a new reporter, but her appointment was challenged and held to be invalid in *Wilson v Minister for Aboriginal and Torres Strait Islander Affairs* (1996) 189 CLR 1 **[6.4.34]**. The state appointed a Royal Commissioner to inquire into the legitimacy of the plaintiffs' claims. The Commissioner reported adversely to the plaintiffs. Following a change in the Commonwealth government, the Commonwealth Parliament passed the Hindmarsh Island Bridge Act 1997, which declared that the Minister for Aboriginal and Torres Strait Islander Affairs should not exercise functions conferred on him by the Heritage Protection Act in relation to the area where the bridge was to be built.

The plaintiffs challenged the validity of the Hindmarsh Island Bridge Act on the basis that it discriminated against Ngarrindjeri people and was therefore not authorised by s 51(xxvi). Five of the six judges who sat in *Kartinyeri* analysed the Act simply as a partial repeal of the Heritage Protection Act. They concluded, as Brennan CJ and McHugh J put it, that '[t]he power to make laws includes a power to unmake them': 195 CLR at 355–6. For these two justices, that was the end of the matter. Since there was no dispute that s 51(xxvi) empowered parliament to enact the Heritage Protection Act, and since the Act did not 'so [change] the character of [the Heritage Protection Act] as to deprive that Act of its constitutional support' (195 CLR at 356–7, s 51(xxvi)) also authorised the Act. There was no need to consider whether the power was limited to laws which 'benefited' indigenous Australians.

However, Gaudron, Gummow and Hayne JJ (who characterised the Hindmarsh Island Bridge Act in the same way as Brennan CJ and McHugh J) also considered the scope of the power generally, as did Kirby J in dissent.

Two justices (Gummow and Hayne JJ) expressed the view that s 51(xxvi) was not limited by a requirement that the power be used to enact only laws which benefit Aboriginal people or Torres Strait Islanders:

> The text is not limited by any implication such as that contended for by the plaintiffs. This is so whether one has regard alone to the terms of the Constitution after the 1967 [Constitutional Alteration] Act took effect or also to that statute. The circumstances surrounding the enactment of the 1967 Act, assuming regard may properly be had to them, may indicate an aspiration of the legislature and the electors to provide federal legislative powers to advance the situation of persons of the Aboriginal race. But it does not follow that this was implemented by a change to the constitutional text which was hedged by limitations unexpressed therein (195 CLR at 382).

Although Gummow and Hayne JJ referred to the possibility of the power not supporting 'a law enacted in "manifest abuse" of [parliament's] power of judgment [as to what is "deemed necessary"]', in their view '[t]here is no "manifest abuse" of … legislative judgment for the Parliament to accelerate matters [under the Heritage Protection Act] by determining that, in respect of particular areas, the Ministerial power of declaration was withdrawn': 195 CLR at 378–9. The issue of 'necessity' in relation to s 51(xxvi) laws is discussed further at **[2.4.46]–[2.4.51]**.

Gaudron J, however, took a different approach:

> [T]he bare deletion of an exception or limitation on power is not … capable of effecting a curtailment of power … [T]he consequence of an amendment of that kind is to augment power. Accordingly, if, prior to 1967, s 51(xxvi) authorised special laws which were not for the benefit of the people of a particular race, the referendum did not…alter that position …

> The criterion for the exercise of power under s 51(xxvi) is that it be deemed *necessary* — not expedient or appropriate — to make a law which provides differently for the people of a particular race … Clearly, it is for the Parliament to deem it necessary to make a law of that kind. To form a view as to that necessity, however, there must be some difference pertaining to the people of the race involved or their circumstances or, at least, some material upon which the Parliament might reasonably form a political judgment that there is a difference of that kind. Were it otherwise, the words 'for whom it is deemed necessary to make special laws' would have no operation and s 51(xxvi) would simply be a power to make laws for the people of any race.

> [T]wo things follow. The first is that s 51(xxvi) does not authorise special laws affecting rights and obligations in areas where there is no relevant difference between the people of the race to whom the law is directed and the people of other races … [Her Honour gave as an example the irrelevance of race to citizenship laws.]

> The second … is that the law must be reasonably capable of being viewed as appropriate and adapted to the difference asserted … Unless [that is the case] … it could not be concluded that the Parliament formed the view that there was such a difference …

> Because the power … [is limited in this way] its scope necessarily varies according to circumstances as they exist from time to time. In this respect the power … is not unlike the power conferred by s 51(vi) … with respect to defence …

> [I]t is difficult to conceive of circumstances in which a law presently operating to the disadvantage of a racial minority would be valid. It is even more difficult to conceive of a present circumstance pertaining to Aboriginal Australians which could support a law operating to their disadvantage … [P]rima facie, at least, the circumstances which presently pertain to Aboriginal Australians are circumstances of serious disadvantage,

[including] their material circumstances and the vulnerability of their culture ... [P]rima facie, at least, only laws directed to remedying their disadvantage could reasonably be viewed as appropriate and adapted to their different circumstances. ...

[T]he test of constitutional validity is not whether it is a beneficial law. Rather, the test is whether the law ... is reasonably capable of being viewed as appropriate and adapted to a real and relevant difference which the Parliament might reasonably judge to exist. It is the application of that test to today's circumstances ... that leads to the conclusion that ... s 51(xxvi) presently only authorises laws which operate to the benefit of Aboriginal Australians (195 CLR at 363–8).

Gaudron J's 'proportionality' approach to 'necessity' would invalidate some provisions of the Native Title Amendment Act 1998 (Cth) (see **[2.4.33]**); namely, those which extinguish a small number of native titles which existed before its commencement.

Gaudron J's approach was rejected by Gummow and Hayne JJ: 195 CLR at 378–9. Their Honours also rejected the approach taken by Kirby J, who interpreted s 51(xxvi) in the light of the power's history, 20th century racist laws, and international law standards. Kirby J rejected as 'unstable' the 'manifest abuse' test referred to by Gummow and Hayne JJ:

First, the power is not simply to make laws with respect to '[t]he people of any race' ... [P]ar (xxvi) is to be contrasted with par (xix) which affords such a plenary power ... with respect to 'aliens'. In par (xxvi), words have been added which must have work to do ...

Secondly, the words of qualification in par (xxvi) must be read as a composite idea ... The word 'for' is ambiguous. It could mean 'for the benefit of'. Or it could mean 'in respect of'. The history of the power in its original form tends to favour the latter meaning. However ... where the framers ... intended that idea, it was so expressed ... in pars (xxxi), (xxxvi) ('in respect'); in par (xxii) ('in relation thereto'); and par (xxxii) ('with respect to). The test of necessity in par (xxvi) is a strong one. It is to be distinguished from advisability, expedience or advantage ... It ... indicates that a particular need might enliven the necessity to make a special law ...

Thirdly, a crucial element in the history of the constitutional text is the amendment of par (xxvi) in 1967. Because there have been so few amendments to the Australian Constitution, it has not hitherto been necessary to develop a theory of the approach to be taken to the meaning of the text where a provision is altered ... [C]onventional rules of statutory construction permit a court to take into account the legislative change. But this is much more important in elucidating a constitutional text ... especially ... because of the necessity ... to involve the electors ... in the law-making process ... [T]his Court, to understand the amendment, should appreciate, and give weight to, the purpose of the change. The stated purpose here was to remove two provisions in the Constitution which ... discriminated against Australian Aboriginals. Whatever the initial object of the original exception to par (xxvi), by the time that the words were removed, the amendment did not simply lump the Aboriginal people of Australia in with other races as potential targets for detrimental or adversely discriminatory laws ... To construe the resulting power in par (xxvi) as authorising the making of laws detrimental to, and discriminatory against, people on the ground of race, and specifically Aboriginal race, would be a complete denial of the clear and unanimous object of the Parliament in proposing the amendment.

The criterion of 'manifest abuse' is inherently unstable. The experience of racist laws in Germany ... and South Africa ... was that of gradually escalating discrimination ... By the time a stage of 'manifest abuse' ... is reached, courts have generally lost the capacity to influence or check such laws ... (195 CLR at 411, 413 and 416).

Not being convinced by the argument that the Hindmarsh Island Bridge Act was a simple repeal of the Heritage Protection Act, Kirby J held the Hindmarsh Island Bridge Act invalid under s 51(xxvi), on the basis that the power did not authorise laws having an adverse effect on Aboriginal people.

[2.4.46] *Koowarta v Bjelke-Petersen* (1982) 153 CLR 168 and *Commonwealth v Tasmania* (the *Tasmanian Dam* case) (1983) 158 CLR 1 and *Western Australia v Commonwealth* (the *Native Title Act* case) (1995) 183 CLR 383 establish three important limits to s 51(xxvi). The first is that laws made in reliance on it must relate to *particular 'races'*, or things of significance to them, not to 'races' in general. The second is that the law must be 'special', in the sense that it singles out the people of a particular 'race' for treatment different from the treatment given other people. A s 51(xxvi) law may apply to other people or subject matter, so long as it applies *differentially* to the people of a particular 'race'. As the discussion below indicates, there is some overlap between these two requirements.

Third, as the discussion of the views of Gaudron and Kirby JJ in *Kartinyeri* in **[2.4.45]** indicated, the law must be one which parliament 'deems necessary' for the people of a race. The principle in *Australian Communist Party v Commonwealth* (1951) 83 CLR 1 will prevent parliament 'reciting itself into power' by determining that a group of people who are not members of a 'race' are to be treated as such. (However, as noted at **[2.1.5]–[2.1.7]** and **[2.1.19]–[2.1.21]**, 'racial' boundaries are not bright lines.) However, the text of s 51(xxvi) allows parliament considerable discretion as to the *necessity* for the law. This requirement means that parliament must direct its 'mind' to the question of whether the law *is* necessary. It is not enough that parliament simply adopts a standard set by someone else. Whether or not 'the Court retains some supervisory jurisdiction to examine the question of necessity against the possibility of a manifest abuse of the races power' (*Western Australia v Commonwealth* (the *Native Title Act* case) (1995) 183 CLR 383 at 460) remains an open question, even after *Kartinyeri v Commonwealth* (1998) 195 CLR 337.

[2.4.47] The first limit was explained by Gibbs CJ in *Koowarta v Bjelke-Petersen* (1982) 153 CLR 168 at 186–7:

> [I]t is clear that under s 51(xxvi), in its present form, the Parliament has power to make laws prohibiting discrimination against people of the Aboriginal race by reason of their race.
>
> However ss 9 and 12 [of the Racial Discrimination Act] ... prohibit discrimination generally on the ground of race; that is, they protect the persons of any race from discriminatory action by reason of their race. On behalf of the Commonwealth it was submitted that the Act is a special law within par (xxvi) because it selects as its subject the people of any race against whom discrimination on racial grounds is, or may be, practised. This argument cannot be accepted, for it gives insufficient weight to the words 'for whom it is deemed necessary to make special laws'. It is true that ... 'any' can be understood as having the effect of 'all', but it would be self-contradictory to say that a law which applies to the people of all races is a special law. It is not possible to construe par (xxvi) as if it read simply 'The people of all races'. In the context provided by par (xxvi), the word 'any' is used in the sense of 'no matter which'. The Parliament may deem it necessary to make special laws for the people of a particular race, no matter what the race. If the Parliament does deem that necessary, but not otherwise, it can make laws with respect to the people of that race.

[2.4.48] A law will apply to a particular 'race' if it applies to a 'sub-group' of members of that 'race'. Deane J remarked in *Commonwealth v Tasmania* (the

Tasmanian Dam case) (1983) 158 CLR 1 at 274 that the words 'people of any race' in s 51(xxvi) were to be given 'a wide and non-technical meaning':

> The phrase is ... apposite to refer to all Australian Aboriginals collectively ... [It] is also apposite to refer to any identifiable racial sub-group among Australian Aboriginals.

See also Murphy J: 158 CLR at 180.

In *Kartinyeri v Commonwealth* (1998) 195 CLR 337, the plaintiffs argued that 'people of any race' in s 51(xxvi) referred to Aboriginal people in general, and not to a 'sub-group'. This submission was rejected by all judges who found it necessary to consider it: Gaudron J at 368; Gummow and Hayne JJ at 377–8; Kirby J at 394–5.

[2.4.49] A s 51(xxvi) law may apply to things of unique significance to the people of a race, as Mason J explained in the *Tasmanian Dam* case (1983) 158 CLR 1 at 58:

> The ... cultural heritage of a people is so much of a characteristic or property of the people to whom it belongs that it is inseparably connected with them, so that a legislative power with respect to the people of a race, which confers power to make laws to protect them, necessarily extends to the making of laws protecting their cultural heritage.
>
> A law which protects the cultural heritage of the people of the aboriginal race constitutes a special law for the purpose of par. (xxvi) because the protection of that cultural heritage meets a special need of that people ... [S]omething which is of significance to mankind may have a special and deeper significance to a particular people because it forms part of their cultural heritage ... If it be found on the facts that the [archaeological] sites do have a particular significance for [Aborigines] because the sites are part of their cultural heritage, there is a special need to protect the sites for them, a need which differs from, and in one sense transcends, the need to protect it for mankind.

See also: Murphy J at 181; Brennan J at 245–6; Deane J at 274–5; compare Gibbs CJ at 110–1.

[2.4.50] The court confirmed this approach in the context of characterising the Native Title Act for constitutional purposes in *Western Australia v Commonwealth* (the *Native Title Act* case) (1995) 183 CLR 383 at 452–3, 459:

> The constitutional character of the Native Title Act is determined by its operation. Its operation must be ascertained not only from its terms but from the circumstances in and upon which the Act takes effect and the change it makes in the law. Under the common law, as stated in *Mabo [No 2]*, Aboriginal people and Torres Strait Islanders who are living in a traditional society possess, subject to the conditions stated in that case, native title to land that has not been alienated or appropriated by the Crown. The ... enjoyment of the title is precarious under the common law; it is defeasible by legislation or by the exercise of the Crown's (or a statutory authority's) power to grant inconsistent interests in the land or to appropriate the land and use it inconsistently with enjoyment of the native title ...
>
> The Act removes the common law defeasibility of native title, and secures the Aboriginal people and Torres Strait Islanders in the enjoyment of their native title subject to ... prescribed exceptions ... The Act confers its protection upon native title holders who, ex hypothesi, are members of a particular race. As '[t]he relationship between the Aboriginal people and the land which they occupy lies at the heart of traditional Aboriginal culture and traditional Aboriginal life' [quoting Deane J in *Tasmanian Dam* case], the significance of security in the enjoyment of native title by the Aboriginal people who hold native title is undoubted.

[2.4.51] The difference between the second and third requirements, that a law be 'special' and that it be 'deemed necessary', was explained in the joint judgment (with which Dawson J agreed) in *Western Australia v Commonwealth* (the *Native Title Act* case) (1995) 183 CLR 383. The judges rejected the approach to 'special' and 'necessary' taken by Stephen J. Stephen J had stated in *Koowarta v Bjelke-Petersen* (1982) 153 CLR 168 at 210 that:

> I regard the reference to special laws as confining what may be enacted under this paragraph to laws which are of their nature special to the people of a particular race. It must be because of their special needs or because of the special threat or problem which they present that the necessity of the law arises; without this particular necessity as the occasion for the law, it will not be a special law such as s 51(xxvi) speaks of.

In *Western Australia v Commonwealth* (the *Native Title Act* case) (1995) 183 CLR 373 at 460–2, the justices responded:

> If, as this passage suggests, the requirement that a law enacted under s 51(xxvi) be special were held to evoke a judicial evaluation of the needs of the people of a race or of the threats or problems that confronted them in order to determine whether the law was, or could be deemed to be, 'necessary', the Court would be required to form a political value judgment. Yet it is clear that that judgment is for the Parliament, not for the Court. If the Court retains some supervisory jurisdiction to examine the question of necessity against the possibility of a manifest abuse of the races power, this case is not the occasion for an examination of that jurisdiction. The removal of the common law general defeasibility of native title by the Native Title Act is sufficient to demonstrate that the Parliament could properly have deemed that Act to be 'necessary'.
>
> 'Special' qualifies 'law'; it does not relate to necessity. Therefore the special quality of a law must be ascertained by reference to its differential operation upon the people of a particular race, not by reference to the circumstances which led the Parliament to deem it necessary to enact the law. A special quality appears when the law confers a right or benefit or imposes an obligation or disadvantage especially on the people of a particular race. The law may be special even when it confers a benefit generally, provided the benefit is of special significance or importance to the people of a particular race. That was the view of the majority in the *Tasmanian Dam Case* ... [T]he Native Title Act is 'special' in that it confers uniquely on the Aboriginal and Torres Strait Islander holders of native title (the 'people of any race') a benefit protective of their native title. Perhaps the Act confers a benefit on all the people of those races. The special quality of the law thus appears. Whether it was 'necessary' to enact that law was a matter for the Parliament to decide and, in the light of *Mabo [No 2]*, there are no grounds on which this Court could review the Parliament's decision, assuming it had power to do so.

[2.4.52] The Native Title Act was a 'special law', although it imposed significant restrictions on the behaviour of state governments and other land users. Although the court granted parliament considerable discretion in 'deeming' whether such a law was 'necessary', it held one provision unconstitutional on both s 51(xxvi) 'necessity' grounds and separation of powers grounds. The provision was s 12, which declared that the common law of Australia in respect of native title was to have the force of a law of the Commonwealth. The majority of the court (Mason CJ, Brennan, Deane, Toohey, Gaudron and McHugh JJ) said:

> Section 12 does not in terms make a law in the sense of creating rights or imposing obligations. It takes the common law as an entirety and purports to invest it with the force of a law of the Commonwealth. If s 12 be construed as an attempt to make the common law a law of the Commonwealth, the attempt encounters some constitutional obstacles. There can be no objections to the Commonwealth making a law by adopting as a law of the Commonwealth a text which emanates from a source other than the Parliament. In such a case, the text becomes by adoption, a law of the Commonwealth

and operates as such. But the common law is not found in a text; its content is evidenced by judicial reasons for decision ...

In construing s 12, the 'common law' must be understood either as a body of law created and defined by the courts or as a body of law which, having been declared by the courts at a particular time, may in truth be — and be subsequently declared to be — different. Whether the common law be understood by reference to its source in judicial reasons for decision or by reference to its content as developing from time to time, there are objections to its being treated as a law of the Commonwealth.

If the 'common law' in s 12 is understood to be the body of law which the courts create and define, s 12 attempts to confer legislative power upon the judicial branch of government. That attempt must fail ...

... If one construes s 12 as importing the common law as an organic, developing but unwritten body of law, a further objection arises ... It is common ground that s 51(xxvi) can support a law only if that law is one which the Parliament has deemed necessary for the people of a race. The content of any such law is one which the Parliament must itself consider although a delegation to the Executive Government to make a law of a regulatory kind to implement an Act of the Parliament can find support in that paragraph. The common law relating to native title is not regulatory; it is substantive law the content of which is declared from time to time by the courts. *Mabo [No 2]* is a dramatic example of how the declaration of the common law relating to native title can change when a new judicial examination is made of the basic legal principles which underlie a proposition earlier accepted. Ex hypothesi, when a court declares a change in the common law, the Parliament has not considered whether it is necessary to make that change as a special law for the people of any race (183 CLR at 484–6).

A new constitutional preamble?

[2.4.53] In its final report, the Council for Aboriginal Reconciliation recommended that 'the Commonwealth Parliament prepare legislation for a referendum which seeks to ... recognise Aboriginal and Torres Strait Islander peoples as the first peoples of Australia in a new preamble to the Constitution': Council For Aboriginal Reconciliation (2000).

The 1998 Constitutional Convention determined that a new republican Constitution should include a preamble, but that '[c]are should be taken to draft the Preamble in such a way that it does not have implications for the interpretation of the Constitution'. Amongst the elements to be included in the preamble were '[a]cknowledgment of the original occupancy and custodianship of Australia by Aboriginal peoples and Torres Strait Islanders', and, possibly, '[a]ffirmation of the equality of all people before the law' and '[r]ecognition that Aboriginal people and Torres Strait Islanders have continuing rights by virtue of their status as Australia's indigenous peoples': Commonwealth of Australia (1998) pp 3–4. Earlier proposals to incorporate a reference to Aboriginal people and Torres Strait Islanders in a new preamble had been raised by the Rights Committee of the 1988 Constitutional Commission and the Aboriginal and Torres Strait Islander Commission: Winterton (1997) n 9.

[2.4.54] In 1999, a referendum proposing the insertion of a preamble into the Constitution was rejected by 60 per cent of voting Australians. The text of the preamble put to the electorate was as follows:

[2.4.55E]   **Constitutional Alteration (Preamble) 1999**

3 Insertion of preamble The Constitution is altered by inserting after the Title the preamble set out in the Schedule to this Act.

4 Effect of preamble

The Constitution is altered by inserting after section 125 the following section:

125A Effect of preamble

The preamble to this Constitution has no legal force and shall not be considered in interpreting this Constitution or the law in force in the Commonwealth or any part of the Commonwealth.

Schedule — Preamble to the Constitution

Preamble

With hope in God, the Commonwealth of Australia is constituted as a democracy with a federal system of government to serve the common good.

We the Australian people commit ourselves to this Constitution:

- proud that our national unity has been forged by Australians from many ancestries;

- never forgetting the sacrifices of all who defended our country and our liberty in time of war;

- upholding freedom, tolerance, individual dignity and the rule of law;

- honouring Aborigines and Torres Strait Islanders, the nation's first people, for their deep kinship with their lands and for their ancient and continuing cultures which enrich the life of our country;

- recognising the nation-building contribution of generations of immigrants;

- mindful of our responsibility to protect our unique natural environment;

- supportive of achievement as well as equality of opportunity for all;

- and valuing independence as dearly as the national spirit which binds us together in both adversity and success.

<div align="center">~~~</div>

[2.4.56] What is the point of a preamble with no implications for constitutional interpretation? Presumably it would also have no implications for interpretation of Commonwealth legislation, even legislation such as the Native Title Amendment Act 1998 (Cth), which removes the rights of 'the nation's first people' based on 'their deep kinship with their lands' and 'their ancient and continuing [and enriching] cultures'.

[2.4.57] While constitutional preambles often invoke symbolic values or narrate a history of the political institutions to which they apply, these symbols and that history are never uncontested. Indeed, processes like constitutional reform tend to obscure uncomfortable truths about 'national' beginnings, generating powerful alternative 'myths of origin'.

The justifications for referring to Australia's pre-colonial occupation suggested by Winterton provide an insight into the way in which 'recognition' of Aboriginal people and Torres Strait Islanders is pursued for nation-building purposes.

> First, Australia's soul will never be at rest until reconciliation is achieved with her indigenous peoples. No greater recognition can be accorded than express mention in our fundamental national compact, the Constitution.

Secondly, and perhaps more important, is the consideration that the present constitutional preamble could be seen as impliedly perpetuating the myth of terra nullius since it fails to acknowledge an Australian presence prior to the Australian colonies mentioned in the preamble. Just as the advent of a republic requires the narration of the events in the preamble to be brought forward, so the demise of terra nullius may be seen to require that the origins of Australia prior to European settlement be recorded (Winterton (1997) p 187).

Two criticisms might be made of these views. First, 'the myth of *terra nullius'* is arguably already 'perpetuated' in a concrete, not merely symbolic, way by Commonwealth legislation which treats native title as an inferior property right. The symbolism of a constitutional preamble, particularly an unenforceable one, will not alter this.

Second, Winterton proposes that the preamble commence '[w]hereas the original, indigenous Australians held in trust this continent of which all Australians are now trustees': Winterton (1997) p 189. However, because it makes no reference to the *process* by which 'trusteeship' was transferred, such wording masks the violence and dispossession of Australia's foundation. Since 'it is through the narration of Aboriginal subjects by predominantly non-Aboriginal institutions that the central anxiety of a prior, and more authentic Aboriginal claim to power is effaced' (Chandra-Shekeran (1998) p 107), the process of 'inclusion' of indigenous Australians in a new Constitution may really be a process of denying them access to political power on more meaningful grounds, for example, by reference to the unfairness of historical dispossession or to the injustice of present economic disadvantage.

Northern Territory self-government and Aboriginal people

[2.4.58]   The Commonwealth granted self-government to the Northern Territory in 1978: see Chapter 12. The Northern Territory (Self-Government) Act 1978 (Cth) is not the only instrument defining Northern Territory legislative power.

[2.4.59]   Before self-government, the Commonwealth enacted the Aboriginal Land Rights (Northern Territory) Act 1976, which remains in force. That Act established a regime for the grant of titles to land in the territory by the Commonwealth. The grantees are Aboriginal land trusts. Trusts hold title for the benefit of Aboriginal people traditionally entitled to it (s 71) under the administration of land councils. A land grant is usually made after a successful land claim to Crown land or an Aboriginal-owned pastoral lease by its traditional Aboriginal owners. The Northern Territory Government is unable to grant valid titles to land under claim (s 67A), and 'Aboriginal land' is immune from compulsory acquisition under Northern Territory law: s 67. Approximately 50 per cent of the Northern Territory's land mass is now Aboriginal land. The Land Rights Act provides that Northern Territory laws may apply to Aboriginal land to the extent that they are capable of operating concurrently with the Land Rights Act: s 74. Valid territory laws might be rendered inoperative under this provision: *Attorney-General (NT) v Hand* (1989) 25 FCR 345. However, the Land Rights Act imposes a more fundamental constraint on Northern Territory laws. Section 73 provides:

(1) The power of the Legislative Assembly of the Northern Territory under the Northern Territory (Self-Government) Act 1978 in relation to the making of laws extends to the making of:

(a) laws providing for the protection of, and the prevention of the desecration of, sacred sites in the Northern Territory, including sacred sites on Aboriginal land, and in particular, laws regulating or authorizing the entry of persons on those sites, but so that any such laws shall provide for the right of Aboriginals to have access to those sites in accordance with Aboriginal tradition and shall take into account the wishes of Aboriginals relating to the extent to which those sites should be protected;

(b) laws regulating or authorizing the entry of persons on Aboriginal land, but so that any such laws shall provide for the right of Aboriginals to enter such land in accordance with Aboriginal tradition;

(c) laws providing for the protection or conservation of, or making other provision with respect to, wildlife in the Northern Territory, including wildlife on Aboriginal land, and, in particular, laws providing for schemes of management of wildlife on Aboriginal land, being schemes that are to be formulated in consultation with the Aboriginals using the land to which the scheme applies, but so that any such laws shall provide for the right of Aboriginals to utilise wildlife resources; and

(d) laws regulating or prohibiting the entry of persons into, or controlling fishing or other activities in, waters of the sea, including waters of the territorial sea of Australia, adjoining, and within 2 kilometres of, Aboriginal land, but so that any such laws shall provide for the right of Aboriginals to enter, and use the resources of, those waters in accordance with Aboriginal tradition;

but any such law has effect to the extent only that it is capable of operating concurrently with the laws of the Commonwealth, and in particular with this Act, the National Parks and Wildlife Conservation Act 1975 ...

This section 'both confirms and circumscribes the legislative power' of the Northern Territory: Renwick (1990). Northern Territory laws about sacred sites will exceed the power defined by s 73(1)(a) if those laws authorise the *desecration* of sacred sites. Similarly, laws regulating entry to Aboriginal land or territorial waters which restrict traditional Aboriginal rights to enter those areas will exceed the power defined by s 73(1)(b) or (d).

[2.4.60] The executive authority of Northern Territory Ministers is set out in the Northern Territory Self-Government Regulations (promulgated under s 35 of the Act): see Chapter 12. The regulations contain a list of subjects over which Ministers have authority. These do not include Aboriginal land and uranium. However, the regulations state that Northern Territory Ministers may exercise authority under other Commonwealth Acts (for example, the Aboriginal Land Rights Act) or Commonwealth–territory agreements (for example, the agreement for administration of the Jabiluka uranium mine: see *Margarula v Minister for Resources* (1998) 157 ALR 160).

[2.4.61] A further aspect of the Self-Government Act affects Aboriginal rights. As discussed in Chapter 12, the Self-Government Act allowed the Commonwealth to retain for itself some land which would otherwise have been transferred to the Northern Territory. Land retained included areas (like Kakadu) which became Commonwealth national parks under the National Parks and Wildlife Conservation Act 1975 (Cth). While some of this land is now Aboriginal land under the Land Rights Act, it continues to be administered by a Commonwealth authority. Under the National Parks and Wildlife Conservation Act, this authority is directed by park boards of management on which Aboriginal people have majority membership.

5   Is the Crown a fiduciary for indigenous people?

[2.5.1] It is sometimes suggested that indigenous claims would benefit from characterising the relationship between indigenous people and governments as fiduciary. In Australia, it would be difficult to suggest that legislatures are constrained by fiduciary principles, given the strength of the parliamentary sovereignty principle and the courts' reluctance to imply constitutional limitations which are not textually based: see *Lange v Australian Broadcasting Corporation* (1997) 189 CLR 520 **[11.3.13C]**; *Wik Peoples v Queensland* (1996) 187 CLR 1 at 255–6 per Kirby J. It is likely that any such principles only constrain the conduct of the Crown.

[2.5.2] Fiduciary law is one of several equitable doctrines concerned with power imbalances. The word 'fiduciary' simply means 'trust-like'. Fiduciary law can apply whether or not there is a formal transaction between the parties. Thus, while the relationship between trustee and beneficiary under a trust deed is fiduciary in nature, so is the relationship between a guardian and his ward and a lawyer and her client. Some fiduciary relationships arise out of the courts' recognition of the trust and confidence placed by a vulnerable party in a more powerful party.

If a fiduciary relationship exists, the more powerful party (the fiduciary) is subject to identifiable obligations, which may require that:

- the fiduciary not misuse its position, or opportunities arising from it, to its own (or another's) advantage; and

- the fiduciary not have a personal or inconsistent interest in matters to which the obligation relates, unless the weaker party (the beneficiary) consents or the law requires it.

Fiduciary obligations appear attractive because, like other equitable obligations, their enforcement is not subject to Statutes of Limitation. Rather, enforcement is governed by the more flexible doctrine of laches. It is thus possible that fiduciary claims could be used to address historical grievances which cannot be addressed by actions in tort.

[2.5.3] United States and Canadian jurisprudence characterises the relationship between indigenous people and governments as fiduciary. However, the United States Government's 'trust' relationship with 'Indians' is considered 'self-imposed' (by treaty practice) or imposed by Congress under legislation (for example, the Trade and Intercourse Acts): see *Seminole Nation v United States* 316 US 286 (1942).

Parallel practices and instruments are difficult to identify in Australia; and it is not clear that Australian courts would characterise any 'duties' imposed by such practices and instruments as fiduciary: see **[2.5.8]–[2.5.9]** and **[2.5.11]**. As noted in **[2.2.22]**, the 'wardship' relationship between Congress and 'Indian tribes' is unique and cannot be adapted for use in Australia.

[2.5.4] Fiduciary reasoning was used by the Canadian Supreme Court in *Guerin v R* (1984) 13 DLR (4th) 321, where fiduciary obligations were said to arise out of a surrender of native title to the Crown. It is not clear whether such obligations (and the relationship which founds them) arose out of the uniqueness of 'aboriginal title' or from provisions of the Federal Indian Act allowing its surrender. One of the Act's provisions substitutes for the Australian common law rule that native title may only be surrendered to the Crown; another allows the Crown to determine how to use surrendered land in the best interests of 'Indians'. In *Guerin*, the duty was breached because the Crown leased land on terms contrary to those in a surrender agreement.

In *Mabo v Queensland (No 2)* (1992) 175 CLR 1, Brennan J suggested that '[i]f native title were surrendered to the Crown in expectation of a grant of tenure to the indigenous title holders, there may be a fiduciary duty on the Crown to exercise its discretionary power to grant a tenure in land so as to satisfy the expectation': 175 CLR at 60. However, Toohey J subsumed *Guerin* into a broader analysis under which '[t]he fiduciary relationship arises ... out of the *power* of the Crown to extinguish traditional title by alienating the land or otherwise; it does not depend on an exercise of that power': 175 CLR at 203. The limitations of Toohey J's analysis are discussed in **[2.5.6]** below.

[2.5.5] The Supreme Court of Canada has also utilised fiduciary reasoning in interpreting the limitations on executive and legislative power expressed in s 35(1) of the Constitution 1982. Section 35(1) protects unextinguished 'aboriginal and treaty rights' from extinguishment and unjustified infringement. The court's assessment of whether a legislative infringement is justified involves considering the 'special trust relationship' between the Crown and indigenous peoples: *R v Sparrow* (1990) 70 DLR (4th) 385; 70 DLR (4th) 385; *Delgamuukw v British Columbia* (1998) 153 DLR (4th) 195.

In this context, the court has not employed the 'fiduciary relationship' to found enforceable duties but as an interpretive tool to determine whether a law which prima facie infringes s 35(1) is valid: Elliott (1996) pp 152–3, 163. It does this by requiring that a valid legislative objective (for example, conservation) is being pursued, that 'aboriginal rights' are given priority after pursuit of that objective and infringed as little as possible, that Aboriginal people are consulted, and that compensation is paid.

[2.5.6] Parkinson explored obstacles to adaptation of Canadian fiduciary law to Australia in a comment on the New South Wales Court of Appeal's decisions in *Breen v Williams* (1994) 35 NSWLR 522 (a case about patient access to medical records) and *Williams v Minister, Aboriginal Land Rights Act 1983* (1994) 35 NSWLR 497. In *Williams v Minister, Aboriginal Land Rights Act 1983*, the Court of Appeal decided that the Statute of Limitations did not prevent Williams from seeking compensation for harm done to her in childhood as a result of a decision made by the Aborigines Welfare Board in 1947 to remove her from a home for Aboriginal children to a home for white children because she was 'fair-skinned'. Kirby P said that there was an arguable case that the Board had breached its fiduciary duty to Williams, the relationship of guardian and ward being one of the established fiduciary categories. He said it was 'distinctly arguable that a person who suffers as a result of a want of proper care on the part of a fiduciary, may recover equitable compensation from the fiduciary for the losses occasioned by the want of proper care': 35 NSWLR at 511.

Parkinson criticised this proposed use of fiduciary law, and Toohey J's invocation of Canadian authority in *Mabo v Queensland (No 2)* (1992) 175 CLR 1 (see **[2.5.4]**), as lacking 'an appreciation … of the vast differences between Australia and Canada in understanding of the nature of fiduciary obligations': Parkinson (1995) pp 339–40. Parkinson noted:

> [First, c]entral to Australian fiduciary law is the notion that a fiduciary is one who has either undertaken to act in the interests of another, creates an expectation that he or she will act in the interests of the other, or is under a legal duty to do so from some other source such as statute … [T]he Supreme Court of Canada has adopted a much more expansive definition in which it is far from essential … that the person has given an undertaking or is subject to a legal obligation to act in the interests of another. In *LAC Minerals Ltd v International Corona Resources Ltd* [(1989) 61 DLR (4th) 14] [the majority] … approved a definition of fiduciary obligations … as arising where:
>
> (1) The fiduciary has scope for the exercise of some discretion or power.
>
> (2) The fiduciary can unilaterally exercise that power or discretion so as to affect the beneficiary's legal or practical interests.
>
> (3) The beneficiary is particularly vulnerable to, or at the mercy of the fiduciary holding the discretion or power.
>
> Thus Canadian fiduciary law is as much about the abuse of power and discretion as it is about the abuse of trust …
>
> Second, the Canadian courts have sometimes spoken of the fiduciary duty as a positive obligation to act in the best interests of another when traditionally, the relevant obligation has been to avoid a conflict between one's duty and personal interest … Traditionally … fiduciary obligations arise *because* the person is under an obligation to act in the interests of another, and equitable remedies are available where the person places interest in conflict with duty or gains an unauthorised profit from the position. The Canadian courts are in danger of standing this reasoning on its head: because the law deems someone to be a fiduciary, therefore, they have a legal duty to act in the interests of another, and failure to fulfil that positive obligation represents a breach of fiduciary duty giving rise to a claim for equitable compensation. A similar problem arises from [Toohey J's reasoning] … in *Mabo* … On this view, fiduciary obligations may be imposed whenever someone is in a position of power and the other is in a position of vulnerability …
>
> Third, [there are the s 35(1) Constitution 1982 cases, which have] … little to do with the traditional law of fiduciary obligations.
>
> Fourth, the Canadian courts have exploited the potential … from equity's power to award compensation for breach of fiduciary duty to create new forms of civil wrong … [for example, for a parent's sexual abuse of his or her child]
>
> This usage of fiduciary law to supplement the law of tort … is alien to Australian law. However … [t]here are strong arguments in favour of extending the Australian law of fiduciary obligations to allow for compensation in cases where trust has been violated and influence abused in a way which does not overlap with the existing law of tort … ((1995) pp 440–2).

[2.5.7] The differences between Canada and Australia seem to have these implications for Aboriginal and Torres Strait Islander claims:

- First, Australian courts may regard the trust placed by indigenous people when surrendering native title as generating a fiduciary relationship.

- However, the courts are unlikely to recognise a general fiduciary relationship arising, as Toohey J would have it in *Mabo v Queensland (No 2)* (1992) 175 CLR 1, from the mere vulnerability of native title to extinguishment by the Crown. Vulnerability alone is not enough to found such relationships; the reposing of trust or confidence in another is required. This has not occurred where the

Crown has exercised radical title powers unilaterally: see *Bodney v Westralia Airports Corporation* (2000) 109 FCR 178.

■ Whether or not fiduciary principles extend to situations of governmental institutionalisation of indigenous children removed from their families depends on whether the Australian courts develop the flexible 'compensation jurisdiction' referred to by Parkinson. Otherwise, those claims must be made in tort, subject to limitation principles.

[2.5.8] Even where governments give 'undertakings' to indigenous people, these may not found enforceable obligations. Perhaps the most compelling objection to characterising the Crown–Aboriginal relationship as fiduciary lies in the nature of government itself. Governments govern 'for the good of the wider community'; their duty to do so should not be limited by narrower duties to a section of it. At most, the obligation may be political; a political trust, not a fiduciary obligation recognised by the law.

Tito v Waddell (No 2) [1977] 1 Ch 106 concerned the government of the United Kingdom and British Phosphate Commissioners' treatment of the indigenous inhabitants of Ocean Island in the former Gilbert Islands (now Kiribati), the Banabans.

The Banabans sued the Commissioners (representing New Zealand, Australia and the United Kingdom) and the Attorney-General of the United Kingdom to enforce the benefits of several transactions authorising phosphate mining. These included a 1913 agreement between the Banabans and the former Pacific Phosphate Company (over which a colonial official presided), which required that specified royalties be collected in a special Banaban Fund; a 1928 compulsory acquisition Ordinance providing for royalties to be held 'in trust' for Banabans; a 1931 acquisition under that Ordinance which fixed a royalty rate but ignored the 'trust' requirement; and a 1937 amendment which abolished the 'trust' in favour of a general direction that the money be spent for the 'natives'. In 1942, after the island was virtually destroyed by mining, a Fijian island was bought for the Banabans out of 'their' money. They moved there after the Japanese destroyed Ocean Island in World War II. In 1947, they accepted, without independent advice, the Commissioners' offer for acquisition of their remaining Ocean Island land. In *Tito v Waddell (No 2)* [1977] 1 Ch 106, they argued that the government's failure to advise them adequately in 1947 breached fiduciary obligations imposed by the earlier transactions.

Although Megarry VC criticised official actions towards the Banabans, he refused to treat these as breaches of fiduciary obligation (at 211, 216):

> ... When it is alleged that the Crown is a trustee, ... the governmental powers and obligations of the Crown ... readily provide an explanation which is an alternative to a trust. If money or other property is vested in the Crown and is used for the benefit of others, one explanation can be that the Crown holds on a true trust for those others. Another explanation can be that ... the Crown is ... administering that property in the exercise of the Crown's governmental functions ...

> First, the use of a phrase such as 'in trust for', even in a formal document ... does not necessarily create a trust enforceable by the courts ... Second, the term 'trust' is one which may properly be used to describe not only relationships ... enforceable by the courts in their equitable jurisdiction, but also other relationships such as the discharge, under the direction of the Crown, of the duties or functions belonging to the prerogative and the authority of the Crown. Trusts of the former kind ... are ... 'trusts in the lower sense'; trusts of the latter kind ... 'trusts in the higher sense' ...

[T]hird ... whether an instrument has created a true trust or a trust in the higher sense is a matter of construction, looking at the whole of the instrument in question, its nature and effect, and ... its context. Fourth, a material factor may be ... the description ... of the person alleged to be the trustee. An impersonal description ... in the form of a reference to the holder of a particular office for the time being, may give some indication that what is intended is not a true trust ...

Megarry VC treated the Ocean Island dealings as consistent with governmental, not 'true trust', obligations. Trustees might segregate out trust funds, but so do governments: at 219. The Banaban Fund appeared to be established in perpetuity, whereas the law of trusts would require that its capital be distributed after a certain time (the so-called 'perpetuity period'). The fact that the Crown did not sign the 1913 agreement and surrounding documents indicated that the money was 'to be devoted to the general benefit of the natives'. The language of the Ordinance suggested a 'higher' trust.

[2.5.9] In *Guerin v R* (1984) 13 DLR (4th) 321, the Supreme Court of Canada treated the surrendered native title rights as 'private' rights existing independently of government. This probably allowed the court to avoid the 'political trust' doctrine: Elliott (1996). However, the Banabans had agreed in 1913 to give up their rights to some land. Whatever the doctrine's exact application, *Tito v Waddell (No 2)* [1977] 1 Ch 106 indicates that even governmental transactions with indigenous land which appear to involve 'trust' may not be legally enforceable.

[2.5.10] Of course, legislation may found obligations to indigenous people which are not fiduciary; for example, obligations in tort. In *Tito v Waddell (No 2)* [1977] 1 Ch 106 at 230, Megarry VC rejected an argument that the Ordinance founded fiduciary obligations:

I cannot see why the imposition of a statutory duty to perform certain functions, or the assumption of such a duty, should as a general rule impose fiduciary obligations ... Of course, the duty may be of such a nature as to carry with it fiduciary obligations: impose a fiduciary duty and you impose fiduciary obligations.

This approach raises doubts about arguments that institutionalisation of Aboriginal children and adults under 'protection' legislation (see **[2.1.4]** and **[2.1.6]**) amounted to a breach of the Crown's fiduciary duty (as guardian) to those children (as wards). There is little doubt that many Aboriginal people suffered irreparable emotional, even physical, harm in such settings: *Bringing Them Home* (1997). Some of that harm may found actions in tort. Nonetheless, many such actions are now time-barred: *Kruger v Commonwealth* (1997) 190 CLR 1 at 140–1 per Gaudron J. However, the fact that they are time-barred does not mean that tortious obligations can be treated as fiduciary instead.

'Protection' laws did impose on officials and governments duties to care for, and to act for the welfare of, their 'wards': *Bringing Them Home* (1997) p 261. Toohey J referred to this legislation and other Acts as possible bases for fiduciary obligations in *Mabo v Queensland (No 2)* (1992) 175 CLR 1 at 203:

[I]f ... the relationship between the Crown and the Meriam people with respect to [native] title alone were insufficient to give rise to a fiduciary obligation, both the course of dealings by the Queensland Government with respect to the Islands since annexation — for example the creation of reserves in 1882 and 1912 and the appointment of trustees in 1939 — and the exercise of control over or regulation of the Islanders themselves by welfare legislation — such as the Native Labourers' Protection Act 1884 (Q), the Torres Strait Islanders Act 1939 (Q) under which an Island Court was established and a form of 'local government' instituted, and the Community Services (Aborigines) Act 1984 (Q) — would certainly create such an obligation.

[2.5.11] It is difficult enough to establish that statutes imposing duties on public officials create privately enforceable obligations in tort. (The tort of breach of statutory duty may be established where a plaintiff proves that parliament intended to create private rights in him or her and the statutory standards are not met. A duty of care may be superimposed on statutory functions where its imposition does not intefere with 'delicate' or 'policy' decisions.)

If tortious remedies are available, or if there are good 'policy' reasons why they are not, it appears fiduciary obligations will not be lightly imposed on statutory relationships between indigenous people and the Crown. In *Director of Aboriginal and Islanders Advancement v Peinkinna* (1978) 17 ALR 129, the Privy Council decided that a state 'protection' Act, the Aborigines Act 1971 (Qld), allowing the Director to authorise mining on an Aboriginal reserve, did not make the Director a trustee for the reserve's Aboriginal residents. The Director's power was an *administrative* power only. For more recent decisions rejecting arguments that governments and officials stood in fiduciary relationships to children in their care under 'protection' legislation, see *Cubillo v Commonwealth* (2000) 174 ALR 97 and *Williams v Minister, Aboriginal Land Rights* [2000] Aust Torts Reports 81-578. This conclusion was reached in *Cubillo* despite the existence of an official guardianship provision in the relevant 'protection' legislation.

[2.5.12] Finally, if any fiduciary duty owed by the Crown to indigenous people is not constitutionally entrenched, it can be overridden by inconsistent legislation, as Brennan CJ indicated in *Wik Peoples v Queensland* (1996) 187 CLR 1 at 82–3:

> To compare the relative positions of the Crown and the holders of native title is not to show the existence of any ... fiduciary duty. Even if there were some fiduciary relationship, it could not affect the interpretation to be placed on the [Land Act 1910 (Qld)]. Indeed, the proposition that the Crown is under a fiduciary duty to the holders of native title to advance, protect or safeguard their interests while alienating their land is self-contradictory. The sovereign power of alienation was antipathetic to the safeguarding of the holders of native title. In conferring the power of alienation, Parliament imposed no guidelines to be observed in its exercise ...

See also *Director of Aboriginal and Islanders Advancement v Peinkinna* (1978) 17 ALR 129.

6   References

[2.6.1]   *Articles*

Beckett, 'Aboriginality, citizenship and nation state' (1988) 24 *Social Analysis* 3.

Bennett, 'The 1967 Referendum' (1985) 2 *Australian Aboriginal Studies* 30.

Campbell, 'Prerogative Rule in New South Wales, 1788–1823', (1964) 50 *Royal Australian Historical Society* 161.

Chandra-Shekeran, 'Challenging the Fiction of the Nation in the "Reconciliation" Texts of Mabo and Bringing Them Home' (1998) 11 *Australian Feminist LJ* 107.

Clarke, 'Should Parliament Enact the Hindmarsh Island Bill 1996?' (1997a) 3 *ALB* 15.

de Costa, 'Treaty how?' (2003) 4(1) *The Drawing Board: an Australian Review of Public Affairs* 1 <http://www.econ.usyd.edu.au/drawingboard/journal/0307/decosta.pdf>.

De Plevitz (2003), 'The *Briginshaw* "standard of proof" in anti-discrimination legislation: "pointing with a wavering finger" (2003) 27 *MULR* 308.

De Plevitz and Croft, 'Aboriginality under the microscope: the biological descent test in Australian law' (2003) 7 *QUTLJJ*.

Dorsett, 'Civilisation and Cultivation: Colonial Policy and Indigenous Peoples in Canada and Australia' (1995) 4 *Griffith LR* 214.

Dorsett, 'Since time immemorial: a story of common law' (2002) 26 *MULR* 15.

Elliott, 'Aboriginal Peoples in Canada and the United States and the Scope of the Special Fiduciary Relationship' (1996) 24 *ManLJ* 137.

Evatt, 'The Legal Foundations of New South Wales' (1938) 11 *ALJ* 409.

Hunyor, 'Skin deep: proof and inferences of racial discrimination in employment' (2003) 25(4) *Sydney Law Review* 535.

Iorns Magallanes, 'Dedicated parliamentary seats for indigenous peoples: political representation as an element of indigenous self-determination' (2003) 10(4) *E-Law* <http://www.murdoch.edu.au/elaw/issues/v10n4/iorns104_text.html#Notes_C>.

Johnston, 'The Repeals of Section 70 of the Western Australian Constitution Act 1889: Aborigines and Governmental Breach of Trust' (1989) 19 *WALR* 318.

Kercher (1998a), 'Recognition of indigenous legal autonomy in 19th century New South Wales' (1998) 4(13) *Indigenous Law Bulletin* 7.

Kercher (1998b), '*R v Ballard, R v Murrell* and *R v Bonjon*' (1998) 3(3) *Australian Indigenous Law Reporter* 410.

Lokan, 'From recognition to reconciliation: the functions of Aboriginal rights law' (1999) 23 *MULR* 65.

McNeil, 'Extinguishment of Native Title: the High Court and American Law' (1997) 2 *AILR* 365.

McCorquodale, 'The Legal Classification of Race in Australia' (1986) 10 *Aboriginal History* 7.

Parkinson, 'Fiduciary Law and Access to Medical Records: Breen v Williams' (1995) 17 *Syd LR* 433.

Renwick, 'Protection of Aboriginal Sacred Sites in the Northern Territory' (1990) 19 *FLR* 378 at 413.

Rosales-Castaneda, 'Flogging a moribund horse while the emperor is naked: issues in proving institutional racial discrimination in state housing in Western Australia (2003) 10(4) *E-Law* <www.murdoch.edu.au/elaw/issues/v10n4/rosales104_text.html>.

Sadurski, '*Gerhardy v Brown* v The Concept of Discrimination: Reflections on the Landmark Case That Wasn't' (1986) 11 *Sydney LR* 5.

Sawer, 'The Australian Constitution and the Australian Aborigine' (1966–67) 2 *FLR* 17.

Simpson, 'Mabo, International Law, Terra Nullius and the Stories of Settlement: an Unresolved Jurisprudence' (1993) 19 *Melbourne Uni LR* 195.

Stretton and Finnimore, 'Black Fellow Citizens: Aborigines and the Commonwealth Franchise' (1992–3) 98–101 *Aust Historical Studies* 521.

Walters, '*Mohegan Indians v Connecticut* (1705–1773) and the legal status of Aboriginal customary laws and government in British North America' (1996) 33(4) *Osgoode Hall Law Journal* 785.

Williams, 'Race, Citizenship and the Formation of the Australian Constitution: Andrew Inglis Clark and the 14th Amendment' (1996) 42 *Australian J of Politics and History* 10.

Williams and Bradsen, 'The Perils of Inclusion: the Constitution and the Race Power' (1997) 19 *Adelaide LR* 95.

Winterton, 'A New Constitutional Preamble' (1997) 8 *Public LR* 186.

[2.6.2] *Papers, reports and online resources*

Altman and Hunter, *Monitoring 'practical reconciliation': evidence from the reconciliation decade 1991–2001*, Centre for Aboriginal Economic Policy Research discussion paper 254/2003, ANU, 2003 <http://www.anu.edu.au/caepr/Publications/DP/2003_DP254.pdf>.

Australian Bureau of Statistics, *Population characteristics: Aboriginal and Torres Strait Islander Australians 2001*, Canberra, 2003.

Australian Law Reform Commission, *The recognition of Aboriginal customary laws*, Report no 31, 1986 <http://www.austlii.edu.au/au/other/alrc/publications/reports/31>.

Brazil and Mitchell, *Opinions of the Attorneys-General of the Commonwealth of Australia*, AGPS, 1981, vol 1.

CBC News, 'BC treaty vote results favour government' <http://www.cbc.ca/stories/2002/07/03/treaty020703> 4 July 2002.

Clarke, *The Native Title Amendment Bill 1997: A Different Order of Uncertainty?*, Centre for Aboriginal Economic Policy Research discussion paper 144/97, ANU, 1997b.

Clarke, *The Yorta Yorta case: next time someone tells you native title has not lived up to expectations, tell them about its 'foster' family*, ANU Centre for Public and International Law Occasional Paper, 2002 <http://law.anu.edu.au/cipl>.

Commonwealth of Australia, Constitutional Commission, *Final Report of the Constitutional Commission*, AGPS, 1988.

Commonwealth of Australia, Constitutional Convention, 'Communique', *Final Report of the Constitutional Convention*, Vol 1, Ch 7 <http://www.dpmc.gov.au/convention/report1/7comm3.htm> January 1999.

Commonwealth of Australia, House of Representatives, *Report from the Select Committee on Voting Rights of Aborigines*, Pt 1, Commonwealth Government Printer, 1961.

Commonwealth of Australia, Human Rights and Equal Opportunity Commission, *Bringing Them Home*, AGPS, 1997.

Commonwealth of Australia, Senate *Two Hundred Years Later*, AGPS, 1983.

Council for Aboriginal Reconciliation, *Reconciliation: Australia's challenge* (Final report to Parliament) 2000 <http://www.austlii.edu.au/au/other/IndigLRes/car/2000/16>.

de Costa, 'The treaty process in British Columbia: some thoughts for Australian treaties', Murdoch University Treaty Conference papers 2002 <http://www.treaty.murdoch.edu.au/Conference%20Papers/Ravi%20de%20Costa.htm>.

Gardiner-Garden (2003) *Defining Aboriginality in Australia*, Commonwealth of Australia Department of the Parliamentary Library, Current Issues Brief 10/2002–3.

Hunter, 'The boundaries of colonial criminal law in relation to inter-Aboriginal conflict (*inter se* offences) in Western Australia in the 1830s–40s', paper presented to the Australia and New Zealand Legal History Association Conference, 2003.

Kercher, *Decisions of the Superior Courts of New South Wales, 1788–1899*, Division of Law, Macquarie University, available online <http://www.law.mq.edu.au/scnsw/>. Notes to the text of *R v Johnston* et al, *R v Lowe*, *R v Ballard* and *R v Murrell* appear at <http://www.law.mq.edu.au/scnsw/html/subject_index_a–c.htm>.

McGill, *Reserved seats in Parliament for Indigenous Peoples — the Maori example*, Research note 51, Australia, Department of the Parliamentary Library, 1997 <http://www.aph.gov.au/library/pubs/rn/1996–97/97rn51.htm>.

New South Wales Parliament, Legislative Council, Standing Committee on Social Issues, *Enhancing Aboriginal political representation: inquiry into designated seats in the New South Wales Parliament* (1998).

O'Brien, 'Aborigines "insulted" by lost wages compensation plan' <http://www.abc.net.au/7.30/s581249.htm> 13 June 2002.

Pearson, 'The light on the hill: Ben Chifley Memorial Lecture' (2000) <http://www.capeyorkpartnerships.com/noelpearson/lightonhill-12-8-00.htm>.

Pearson, 'On the human right to misery, mass incarceration and early death' (2001) <http://www.koori.usyd.edu.au/centre/oration/2001.html>.

Pearson, 'Native title's days in the sun are over' (2002) <http://www.capeyorkpartnerships.com/media/articles/age-28-8-00.htm>.

Pritchard, 'Special Measures' in Racial Discrimination Act: A Review, (ed) Race Discrimination Commissioner, AGPS, 1995.

Queensland Parliament, Legal, Constitutional and Administrative Review Committee, *Hands on Parliament: a parliamentary committee inquiry into Aboriginal and Torres Strait Islander people's participation in Queensland's democratic processes*, 2003, <www.parliament.qld.gov.au/Committees/Comdocs/LegalRev/LCARCR043.pdf>.

Report of the Royal Commission on Aboriginal Peoples, Vol 1, Canada Communications Group, 1996.

Rowse, 'Some contemporary resonances of the treaty debate 1979–83' <http:www.treaty.murdoch.edu.au/Conference%20Papers/Tim%20Rowse.doc> 2002.

[2.6.3] *Texts*

Attwood and Markus, *The 1967 Referendum, or When Aborigines Didn't Get the Vote*, Aboriginal Studies Press, Canberra, 1997.

Balkin, 'Sovereign Rights of Indigenous Peoples' in *International Law and Aboriginal Human Rights*, (ed) Hocking, Lawbook Co, Sydney, 1988.

Bandler, *Turning the Tide*, Aboriginal Studies Press, Canberra, 1989.

Bayne, 'Politics, the Law and Aborigines' in *The Australian People*, (ed) Jupp, Angus and Robertson, Sydney, 1988.

Beckett, *Torres Strait Islanders: Custom and Colonialism*, CUP, Sydney, 1987.

Behrendt, *Achieving social justice: Indigenous rights and Australia's future*, Federation Press, Sydney, 2003.

Bennett and Castles, *A Source Book of Australian Legal History*, Lawbook Co, Sydney, 1979.

Boge, 'Fatal collision at the intersection? The Australian common law and traditional Aboriginal land rights' in Boge (ed), *Justice for all? Native title in the Australian legal system*, Lawyers Books Publications, Brisbane, 2001.

Brennan, *Securing a Bountiful Place for Aborigines and Torres Strait Islanders in a Modern, Free and Tolerant Australia*, Constitutional Centenary Foundation, Melbourne, 1994.

Campbell, *John Batman and the Aborigines*, Kibble Books, Melbourne, 1987.

Chesterman and Galligan, *Citizens Without Rights*, CUP, Melbourne, 1997.

Coates, *Canada's Colonies*, James Lorimer and Co, Toronto, 1985.

Council for Aboriginal Reconciliation, *Going forward: social justice for the first Australians* <http://www.austlii.edu.au/au/other/IndigLRes/car/1995/2/>.

Council for Aboriginal Reconciliation, *Final report*, 2000 <http://www.austlii.edu.au/au/other/IndigLRes/car/2000/16/>.

Cowlishaw, *Rednecks, Eggheads and Blackfellas: a study of racial power and intimacy in Australia*, Allen and Unwin, 1999.

Dickason, *Canada's First Nations*, Oxford University Press, 1992.

Dorsett and Godden, *A Guide to Overseas Precedents of Relevance to Native Title*, Australian Institute of Aboriginal and Torres Strait Islander Studies, 1998.

Getches, Wilkinson and Williams, *Federal Indian Law*, 3rd ed, West Publishing, St Paul, Minnesota, 1993.

Gould, *Ever Since Darwin: Reflections in Natural History*, WW Norton and Co, New York, 1977.

Gumbert, *Neither Justice nor Reason*, University of Queensland Press, Brisbane, 1984.

Hanks, 'Aborigines and Government' in *Aborigines and the Law*, (eds) Hanks and Keon-Cohen, George Allen and Unwin, Sydney, 1984.

Harris, *It's Coming Yet: An Aboriginal Treaty Within Australia Between Australians*, Aboriginal Treaty Committee, Canberra, 1979.

Heatley and Nicholson, *Selected Constitutional Documents on the Northern Territory*, Northern Territory Department of Law, Darwin, 1989.

Hookey, 'Settlement and Sovereignty' in *Aborigines and the Law*, (eds) Hanks and Keon-Cohen, George Allen and Unwin, Sydney, 1984.

Irving, *To constitute a nation: a cultural history of Australia's Constitution*, Cambridge University Press, 1997.

Kidd, *The way we civilise: Aboriginal affairs: the untold story*, University of Queensland Press, 1997.

Kidd, *Black lives, government lies*, UNSW Press, Sydney, 2000.

McKnight, *From hunting to drinking: the devastating effects of alcohol on an Australian Aboriginal community*, Routledge, London, 2002.

Madden and Fieldhouse (eds), *The Empire of the Bretaignes, 1175–1688*, Greenwood Press, Westport, Connecticut, 1985.

Neal, *The Rule of Law in a Penal Colony*, CUP, 1991.

Palmer, *Kidnapping in the South Seas: Being a Narrative of a Three Months Cruise of HM Ship Rosario*, Penguin, Melbourne, 1973 (original 1871).

Reynolds, *The Law of the Land*, 2nd ed, Penguin, Melbourne, 1992.

Reynolds, *Fate of a Free People*, Penguin, Melbourne, 1995.

Rowse, 'A Spear in the Thigh for Senator Evans' in *Quicksands: Foundational Histories in Australia and Aotearoa New Zealand*, (eds) Neumann and Thomas, UNSW Press, Sydney, 1999.

Ryan, *The Aboriginal Tasmanians*, 2nd ed, Allen and Unwin, Sydney, 1996.

Thornton, *The Liberal Promise: Anti-Discrimination Legislation in Australia*, 1990.

Weaver, 'Struggles of the Nation-state to Define Aboriginal Ethnicity: Canada and Australia' in *Minorities and Mother Country Imagery*, (ed) Gold, St John's Newfoundland Memorial University, Newfoundland, 1984.

Webber, 'Beyond Regret: Mabo's Implications For Australian Constitutionalism' in D Ivison, P Patton, W Sanders, *Political Theory and the Rights of Indigenous Peoples*, Cambridge University Press, 2000.

Williams, *The American Indian in Western Legal Thought: The Discourses of Conquest*, Oxford University Press, New York, 1992.

Chapter

3

The International Dimension

1 Introduction

[3.1.1] It is commonplace to suggest that we live in an increasingly globalised world. National boundaries are gradually diminishing in importance as Australia negotiates international treaties that remove national restrictions on the movement of goods and services, capital and labour. The information revolution and the advent of the Internet have greatly expanded opportunities for the exchange of information and for international trade. Law has adapted to accommodate and facilitate these changes. This chapter considers the extent to which international developments impact upon Australian constitutional law.

[3.1.2] In this chapter, we consider three aspects of the international dimension of Australian constitutional law.

The first section examines the historical development of Australia's international legal personality and considers the treaty-making process, the roles of the different branches of the Commonwealth Government in international affairs, and the increasing role of the states and territories at an intergovernmental level in treaty-making.

The chapter's second section considers the scope of the power to make laws with respect to external affairs, and is divided into three parts. In the first part, we consider the Commonwealth's power to regulate things *geographically* 'external to' Australia. In the second part, we consider the Commonwealth's power to introduce international obligations, including treaty obligations, into domestic law. A particular focus here is the impact of Commonwealth laws supported by the external affairs power on the powers of the states and territories and the various tests that have been devised by the High Court to ensure that the domestic implementation of international obligations conforms to those international obligations. Finally, in this section we examine the scope of the external affairs power to regulate matters that are not otherwise the subject of international treaty (what we call, broadly, 'international affairs').

The third and final section of the chapter examines the many additional ways in which international law can influence Australian constitutional law. This section examines the use of international legal principles in the interpretation of statutes, in the development of the common law (which in turn informs the construction of the Constitution, as the High Court noted in *Lange v Australian Broadcasting Corporation* (1997) 189 CLR 520 at 566) and, in particular, the question whether international legal principles can be applied directly to the interpretation of the Constitution. We also consider how the High Court uses comparative law to enrich its understanding of the Constitution.

[3.1.3]   At the outset, we should say something about the nature of international law and the relationship between international law and municipal law.

The two sources relevant for our purposes are treaty or convention law, and custom.

Treaty or convention law can take one of two forms: it can be codified; or it can be the subject of progressive development. It can represent the state of law recognised by a majority of the international community, or it can signal the direction that law may take. *Customary law* is the second main source of international law, and exists when the dual requirements are met of sufficient, uniform state practice and belief in the obligatory nature of that practice: Greig (1976).

The dynamic nature of international law gives rise to one of the problems faced by judges in constitutional cases in this area — namely, whether an international agreement contains an 'obligation' requiring Australia to introduce implementing legislation: *Airlines of New South Wales Pty Ltd v New South Wales (No 2)* (1965) 133 CLR 54 **[3.3.11]**; *Victoria v Commonwealth* (the *Industrial Relations Act* case) (1996) 187 CLR 416 **[3.3.40C]**. However, as Deane J noted in *Commonwealth v Tasmania* (the *Tasmanian Dam* case) (1983) 158 CLR 1 at 261–2 **[3.3.21C]**:

> [A]bsence of precision does not, however, mean any absence of international obligation. In that regard, it would be contrary to both the theory and practice of international law to adopt the approach which was advocated by Tasmania and deny the existence of international obligations unless they can be defined with the degree of precision necessary to establish a legally enforceable agreement under the common law.

The identification, development and implementation of international obligations is considered in the following section of this chapter.

2   Australia's international personality

[3.2.1]   Australia is an active member of the international community, a role which, it has been said, was anticipated when the Commonwealth Constitution was being drafted but which only emerged as a reality over the first 40 years of the twentieth century: see Zines (1977) pp 22–35, 38–43.

The assumptions made by the drafters of the Constitution were emphasised by Deane J in *Commonwealth v Tasmania* (the *Tasmanian Dam* case) (1983) 158 CLR 1 at 255 (**[3.3.21C]**):

> As early as the 1891 Convention, Sir Henry Parkes identified, as a basic object of the proposed Federation, the creation of 'one great union government which shall act for the whole'. 'That government [he continued] must, of course, be sufficiently strong to act with effect, to act successfully, and it must be sufficiently strong to carry the name and the fame of Australia with unspotted beauty and with uncrippled power throughout the world. One great end, to my mind, of a federated Australia is that it must of necessity secure for Australia a place in the family of nations, which it can never attain while it is split up into separate colonies ...' (xxiii *A Record of the Debates of the National Australasia Convention* (1891), p 14, and see, also, the comments of Mr Alfred Deakin made at the Imperial Conference of 1907 and quoted by Evatt and McTiernan JJ in *Burgess' case*, at 685).

The subject matter of the external affairs power is continually expanding, as Australia's international personality expands. As Brennan CJ, Toohey, Gaudron, McHugh and Gummow JJ explained in *Victoria v Commonwealth* (the *Industrial Relations Act* case) (1996) 187 CLR 416 at 482 **[3.3.40C]**:

> ... the Commonwealth of Australia was established at a time of evolving law and practice in the external relations between sovereign powers and between the self-governing units of the Empire. It would be a serious error to construe par (xxix) as though the subject-matter of those relations to which it applied in 1900 were not continually expanding. Rather, the external relations of the Australian colonies were in a condition of continuing evolution and, at that time, were regarded as such. Accordingly, it is difficult to see any justification for treating the content of the phrase 'external affairs' as crystallised at the commencement of federation, or as denying it a particular application on the ground that the application was not foreseen or could not have been foreseen a century ago.

[3.2.2] In *New South Wales v Commonwealth* (the *Seas and Submerged Lands* case) (1975) 135 CLR 337 at 373 **[3.3.3]**, Barwick CJ outlined Australia's progress towards full international status in the following passage:

> Whilst the new Commonwealth was upon its creation the Australian colony within the Empire, the grant of the power with respect to external affairs was a clear recognition, not merely that, by uniting, the people of Australia were moving towards nationhood, but that it was the Commonwealth which would in due course become the nation state, internationally recognised as such and independent. The progression from colony to independent nation was an inevitable progression, clearly adumbrated by the grant of such powers as the power with respect to defence and external affairs. Section 61, in enabling the Governor-General as in truth a Viceroy to exercise the executive power of the Commonwealth, underlines the prospect of independent nationhood which the enactment of the Constitution provided. That prospect in due course matured, aided in that behalf by the Balfour Declaration and the Statute of Westminster and its adoption.

[3.2.3] These passages reflect two concerns that permeate the law in this area. One is the separation of power, particularly between the legislature and the executive, and the other is federalism, the division of power between the Commonwealth and the states.

The first concern is raised by the fact that the Commonwealth possesses two types of constitutional power in relation to international law: the executive power in s 61 (which enables the executive to negotiate and make international treaties) *and* legislative power over external affairs in s 51(xxix) (which enables the Commonwealth to implement treaties into Australian domestic law): *Victoria v Commonwealth* (the *Industrial Relations Act* case) (1996) 187 CLR 416 **[3.3.40C]**. The role of the legislative and executive branches of government — and the role of the judicial branch in checking the lawfulness of the exercise of power by each — is a key theme in the material that follows.

The second concern, federalism, is also a central theme of the cases, particularly in the decisions of the High Court during the 1980s. The Commonwealth's external affairs power, as with every other power listed in s 51, is expressed to be 'subject to this Constitution', including the implied limitations on Commonwealth power over the states recognised in the *Melbourne Corporation* case. The extent and nature of state power in light of the expanding Commonwealth external affairs power will also be considered in the material that follows.

The different roles and functions of the legislature, the executive and the judicature

The steps involved in executive treaty-making

[3.2.4] Under international law, the adoption by the executive government of the Commonwealth of treaty obligations may involve several stages. The first stage will be negotiation between the potential parties to a proposed treaty. The negotiation may, of course, be bilateral or multilateral, depending on the nature of the intended treaty. Although the terms 'treaty' and 'convention' are often used interchangeably, strictly speaking a treaty is a bilateral agreement between Australia and another state, while a convention is a multilateral agreement made with the international community at large. In the Australian system, the negotiation of treaties is a function of the executive government and, typically, the Minister for Foreign Affairs.

Once the negotiation process has been concluded, representatives of the parties may initial the text of the treaty to indicate approval of the text for subsequent signature. The text of the treaty will then be signed by Heads of State or their authorised delegates. In the case of Australia, the authorised delegate will be the Minister for Foreign Affairs, authorised by the federal Executive Council: Campbell (1984) p 64.

This signature may be sufficient to attach the international obligations expressed in the treaty to the signatory parties. However, in the case of some treaties, the further stage of ratification may be necessary before obligations arise. Ratification consists of two acts (*Trick or Treaty* (1995) p 33):

- first, the domestic act of decision by the Governor-General-in-Council; and

- second, the international act of depositing an instrument of ratification by the Department of Foreign Affairs and Trade, expressing acceptance of the terms of the treaty and including any *reservations*.

Because Australia has a federal system of government, the executive government will typically enter treaties subject to a 'federal reservation' (sometimes called a 'federal clause'). A federal reservation, annexed to Australia's ratification of a treaty or convention, signals that the Commonwealth is accepting an obligation within the international community that it may not have the power to implement nationally.

(However, note the effect of the *Tasmanian Dam* case on such considerations: see **[3.3.21C]** and **[3.3.23]**.)

Whether ratification will be necessary will depend on the intentions of the parties to the treaty, as expressed or implied in the documents that create the relevant obligation. So far as Australia is concerned, ratification of *bilateral* treaties is the exception rather than the rule. Signature alone is generally sufficient, with ratification being used only in the case of treaties that are politically sensitive or that call for implementing legislation: Campbell (1984) p 66.

It is more common for *multilateral* treaties (or conventions) to include a clause requiring the parties to ratify the treaty before the treaty comes into force. This is because the constitutional law of some countries prevents the executive government from assuming a treaty obligation without the approval of the legislature. This is the case in the United States, for example, although not in Australia. Where ratification is constitutionally necessary for one of the parties to a treaty, it is usual to require all parties to ratify the treaty after signature. In the case of Australia, the process of ratification may involve asking the Houses of the Commonwealth Parliament to 'approve' the treaty. This is the common practice. However, because the executive government has traditionally been regarded as constitutionally autonomous in treaty-making, it has always been assumed that this parliamentary approval has no domestic legal significance, and the practice of tabling is done for the information of the parliament only. In Australia, ratification is an executive act and, where it is required, it is performed by the Minister for Foreign Affairs, after formal approval by the Federal Executive Council: Campbell (1984) pp 54, 66; O'Connell (1965) pp 230–50.

[3.2.5] The most visible product of Australia's participation in the international community has been Australia's participation in the negotiation of, and accession to, over 900 international treaties: see *Minister for Immigration and Ethnic Affairs v Teoh* (1995) 183 CLR 273 at 316. These treaties deal with an extraordinarily wide range of matters, containing broad aspirational provisions as well as detailed rules to be observed in formal relations between the signatory nations.

However, under Australian law, signature and ratification of a treaty have no effect on the domestic law of Australia. This was the common law position at the time of federation (see *Walker v Baird* [1892] AC 491 at 497), and remains the case today: *Victoria v Commonwealth* (the *Industrial Relations Act* case) (1996) 187 CLR 416. In *Attorney-General for Canada v Attorney-General for Ontario* [1937] AC 326 at 347, the Privy Council remarked:

> Within the British Empire there is a well-established rule that the making of a treaty is an executive act, while the performance of its obligations, if they entail alteration of the existing domestic law, requires legislative action. Unlike some other countries, the stipulations of a treaty duly ratified do not within the Empire, by virtue of the treaty alone, have the force of law.

[3.2.6] In *Koowarta v Bjelke-Petersen* (1982) 153 CLR 168 at 211–12 **[3.3.15C]**, Stephen J noted that, during the drafting of the Commonwealth Constitution, it had been contemplated that treaties made by the Commonwealth 'should become the law of the land ... but the Constitution as finally adopted attempted no such departure from settled common law doctrine; the exercise of treaty-making power was not to create municipal law'. This principle has been regularly confirmed including most recently in: *Dietrich v R* (1992) 177 CLR 292 at 305; *Minister for Immigration and*

Ethnic Affairs v Teoh (1995) 183 CLR 273 **[3.2.8C]**; *Victoria v Commonwealth* (the *Industrial Relations Act* case) (1996) 187 CLR 416 **[3.3.40C]**. But does that mean that administrative officials of the executive government can have *no* regard to international obligations when they exercise their discretionary power?

[3.2.7]   In *Minister for Immigration and Ethnic Affairs v Teoh* (1995) 183 CLR 273 **[3.2.8C]**, the High Court decided that ratification of an international treaty by the executive can create a 'legitimate expectation' in domestic administrative law that the executive and its agencies will act in accordance with the terms of the ratified treaty, even where those terms have not been incorporated by legislation into Australian law.

[3.2.8C]   Minister for Immigration and Ethnic Affairs v Teoh
(1995) 183 CLR 273

The respondent, Teoh, entered Australia from Malaysia in 1988, was granted a temporary residence permit and married an Australian citizen. Three children of the marriage and another four children of Teoh's wife lived with Teoh and his wife. Following Teoh's conviction for drug offences, the Minister for Immigration decided to refuse Teoh's application for permanent residence in Australia. An Immigration Review Panel recommended that the Minister's decision not be reconsidered, notwithstanding the compassionate claims of Teoh's children to have their father (or step-father) continue residence in Australia and support them. A single judge of the Federal Court dismissed Teoh's application for review of the Panel's decision.

  The Full Court of the Federal Court allowed an appeal, holding that the Minister had failed to pay regard to the legitimate expectation of Teoh's children that Teoh's application for permanent residence would be treated in a manner consistent with Australia's obligations under the United Nations Convention on the Rights of the Child, ratified by the Commonwealth on 17 December 1990 although not implemented by any Act of the Commonwealth. Article 3(1) of the Convention declared that, in all actions concerning children, including those undertaken by administrative bodies, 'the best interests of the child shall be the primary consideration'.

  The Minister appealed, by special leave, to the High Court of Australia.

Mason CJ and Deane J: [286] It is well established that the provisions of an international treaty to which Australia is a party do not form part of Australian law unless [287] those provisions have been validly incorporated into our municipal law by statute. [(32) *Chow Hung Ching v The King* (1948) 77 CLR 449 at 478; *Bradley v The Commonwealth* (1973) 128 CLR 557 at 582; *Simsek v Macphee* (1982) 148 CLR 636 at 641–2; *Koowarta v Bjelke-Petersen* (1982) 153 CLR 168 at 211–12, 224–5; *Kioa v West* (1985) 159 CLR 550 at 570; *Dietrich v The Queen* (1992) 177 CLR 292 at 305; *J H Rayner (Mincing Lane) Ltd v Department of Trade and Industry* [1990] 2 AC 418 at 500.] This principle has its foundations in the proposition that in our constitutional system the making and ratification of treaties fall within the province of the Executive in the exercise of its prerogative power whereas the making and the alteration of the law fall within the province of Parliament, not the Executive. [(33) *Simsek v Macphee* (1982) 148 CLR 636 at 641–2] So, a treaty which has not been incorporated into our municipal law cannot operate as a direct source of individual rights and obligations under that law. In this case, it is common ground that the provisions of the Convention have not been incorporated in this way. ...

  But the fact that the Convention has not been incorporated into Australian law does not mean that its ratification holds no significance for Australian law. Where a statute or subordinate legislation is ambiguous, the courts should favour that construction which accords with Australia's obligations under a treaty or international convention to which Australia is a party, [(34) *Chu Kheng Lim v Minister for Immigration* (1992) 176 CLR 1 at

38] at least in those cases in which the legislation is enacted after, or in contemplation of, entry into, or ratification of, the relevant international instrument. That is because Parliament, prima facie, intends to give effect to Australia's obligations under international law. ...

[288] Apart from influencing the construction of a statute or subordinate legislation, an international convention may play a part in the development by the courts of the common law. ...

But the courts should act in this fashion with due circumspection when the Parliament itself has not seen fit to incorporate the provisions of a convention into our domestic law. Judicial development of the common law must not be seen as a backdoor means of importing an unincorporated convention into Australian law. A cautious approach to the development of the common law by reference to international conventions would be consistent with the approach which the courts have hitherto adopted to the development of the common law by reference to statutory policy and statutory materials. [(38) *Lamb v Cotogno* (1987) 164 CLR 1 at 11–12.] ...

[290] Junior counsel for the appellant contended that a convention ratified by Australia but not incorporated into our law could never give rise to [291] a legitimate expectation. No persuasive reason was offered to support this far-reaching proposition. The fact that the provisions of the Convention do not form part of our law are a less than compelling reason — legitimate expectations are not equated to rules or principles of law. Moreover, ratification by Australia of an international convention is not to be dismissed as a merely platitudinous or ineffectual act, [(45) see *Minister for Foreign Affairs and Trade v Magno* (1992) 37 FCR 298 at 343; *Tavita v Minister of Immigration* [1994] 2 NZLR 257 at 266] particularly when the instrument evidences internationally accepted standards to be applied by courts and administrative authorities in dealing with basic human rights affecting the family and children. Rather, ratification of a convention is a positive statement by the executive government of this country to the world and to the Australian people that the executive government and its agencies will act in accordance with the Convention. That positive statement is an adequate foundation for a legitimate expectation, absent statutory or executive indications to the contrary, that administrative decision-makers will act in conformity with the Convention [(46) cf *Simsek v Macphee* (1982) 148 CLR 636 at 644.] ...

[I]f a decision-maker proposes to make a decision inconsistent with a legitimate expectation, procedural fairness requires that the persons affected should be given notice and an adequate opportunity of [292] presenting a case against the taking of such a course. So, here, if the delegate proposed to give a decision which did not accord with the principle that the best interests of the child were to be a primary consideration, procedural fairness called for the delegate to take the steps just indicated.

Toohey J delivered a separate judgment to the same effect. Gaudron J held that, because the Convention gave expression to an important right valued by the Australian community, there was an expectation that the Convention would be given effect. Procedural fairness required the Minister's delegate, if she was considering the possibility of proceeding on some other basis, to inform the person who would be affected and give that person an opportunity to persuade the delegate to follow the Convention; and, because the delegate had not adopted that procedure, there had been a lack of procedural fairness.

McHugh J dissented.

[305] **Mc Hugh J**: In my opinion, no legitimate expectation arose in this case because: (1) the doctrine of legitimate expectations is concerned with procedural fairness and imposes no obligation on a decision-maker to give substantive protection to any right, benefit, privilege or matter [306] that is the subject of a legitimate expectation; (2) the doctrine of legitimate expectations does not require a decision-maker to inform a person affected by a decision that he or she will not apply a rule when the decision-maker is not bound and has given no undertaking to apply that rule; (3) the ratification of the Convention did not give rise to any

legitimate expectation that an application for resident status would be decided in accordance with Art.3 ...

[315] *The terms of the Convention did not give rise to a legitimate expectation in this case*

However, if, contrary to my opinion, the doctrine of legitimate expectations is to be extended to cases where a person has no actual expectation that a particular course will be followed or a state of affairs continued, the terms of the Convention did not give rise to any legitimate expectation that the Minister or his delegate would exercise their powers under the Act in accordance with Australia's obligations under the Convention.

Conventions entered into by the federal government do not form part of Australia's domestic law unless they have been incorporated by way of statute. They may, of course, affect the interpretation or development of the law of Australia. Thus, in interpreting statutory provisions that are ambiguous, the courts will 'favour a construction of a Commonwealth statute which accords with the obligations of Australia under an international treaty'. In that respect, conventions are in the same position as the rules of customary international law. International conventions may also play a part in the development of the common law. The question in this case, however, is not concerned with the interpretation of a statute or with the development of the common law. It is whether the ratification of the Convention on the Rights of the Child gave rise to a legitimate expectation that its terms would be implemented by the decision-maker in this case.

In exercising the discretion under the Migration Act in circumstances such as the present case, the terms of the Convention were matters which the Minister or his delegate could take into account. Nothing in the Act indicates that the terms of the Convention were outside the range of matters that a decision-maker could properly take into account. Furthermore, the Minister conceded that, in the circumstances of this case, the break up of the family unit was a matter of major significance. But that does not mean that the residents of Australia had a legitimate expectation that, upon the [316] ratification of the Convention, federal officials and statutory office holders would act in accordance with the Convention.

In international law, conventions are agreements between States. Australia's ratification of the Convention is a positive statement to other signatory nations that it intends to fulfil its obligations under that convention. If it does not do so, it is required to disclose its failure in its reports to the Committee on the Rights of the Child. I am unable to agree with the view expressed by Lee J in the Full Court that the 'ratification of the Convention by the Executive was a statement to the *national* and international community that the Commonwealth recognised and accepted the principles of the Convention' (my emphasis). The ratification of a treaty is not a statement to the national community. It is, by its very nature, a statement to the international community. The people of Australia may note the commitments of Australia in international law, but, by ratifying the Convention, the Executive government does not give undertakings to its citizens or residents. The undertakings in the Convention are given to the other parties to the Convention. How, when or where those undertakings will be given force in Australia is a matter for the federal Parliament. This is a basic consequence of the fact that conventions do not have the force of law within Australia.

McHugh J went on to record his concern for the 'enormous' effect on administrative decision-making that would take place if officials were required to take into account the 900 or so treaties to which Australia is a party: 183 CLR at 316–17.

~~~

[3.2.9] The Commonwealth Government responded to the *Teoh* decision by releasing a joint executive statement by the Minister for Foreign Affairs and the Attorney-General, which said that the government remained 'fully committed to observing its treaty obligations' but that to alleviate any 'uncertainty' following the High Court's decision in *Teoh*, the Ministers stated that 'entering into an international treaty is not reason for raising any expectation that government decision-makers will act in accordance with the treaty if the relevant provisions of that treaty have not been enacted into domestic Australian law': Joint Press Release on *Teoh* by Minister for Foreign Affairs, Senator Gareth Evans, and the Attorney-General, Michael Lavarch (10 May 1995). The government subsequently introduced the Administrative Decisions (Effect of International Instruments) Bill 1995 into the House of Representatives on 28 June 1995. The bill was referred to the Senate Legal and Constitutional Legislation Committee on 28 August 1995 and, by majority, was recommended for enactment, but lapsed with the calling of an election in March 1996.

[3.2.10] In November 1995, the Senate Legal and Constitutional References Committee reported on its original reference concerning the treaty-making power and the external affairs power. It made 11 recommendations, including:

- that a complete audit be made of treaties to which Australia was a party;

- annual reporting by the executive to the parliament;

- establishment of a treaties database;

- increased consultation with interest groups;

- establishment of a Heads of Government Treaties Council;

- establishment of a joint parliamentary committee with the function of inquiring into the effects of entry into treaties; and

- tabling of treaties in parliament prior to entry.

The Committee left open the question whether parliament should have the power to approve treaties. See *Trick or Treaty? Commonwealth Power to Make and Implement Treaties* (1995) pp 301–4.

[3.2.11] In May 1996, the Minister for Foreign Affairs and the Attorney-General in the newly elected Liberal–National Coalition Government responded to *Trick or Treaty?* by announcing reforms to the treaty-making process aimed at alleviating what the Minister for Foreign Affairs referred to in the joint statement as a 'democratic deficit' in Australian treaty-making. The reforms required by the Joint Statement of 2 May 1996 by the Minister for Foreign Affairs and the Attorney-General included:

- treaties to be tabled in parliament at least 15 days before the government took binding action under international law;

- tabling was to include a 'national interest analysis' which discussed the economic, environmental, social and cultural effects of the treaty, as well as its financial cost, the manner of its implementation, and what further consultation might be required before implementation;

- the establishment of a Joint Parliamentary Committee on Treaties to consider the tabled treaties and the analyses;

- the creation of an advisory Treaties Council as an adjunct to the Council of Australian Governments; and

- the establishment of a treaties database accessible on the Internet.

[3.2.12] The government accepted most of the recommendations of the Committee, including the establishment of a Joint Standing Committee on Treaties, the establishment of a Treaties Council, the tabling requirements, and the national interest analyses. However, although the government accepted the need to provide more accessible information about treaties, it rejected the need for a full-scale audit.

It also declined to provide a list of departments responsible for each treaty, referring instead to the shared departmental responsibilities for treaties and biannual lists of treaties under negotiation that included agency contacts. In relation to implementation, it agreed to table annual lists of Commonwealth implementing legislation, indicating that it was already obliged to make periodic reports on implementation under a range of multilateral treaties, and said it was not feasible to report on all action at the Commonwealth and state levels. It rejected the recommendation that a joint project on the meaning of treaties be established. It promised to review the treaty-making process, including consideration of the process of parliamentary approval. See *Australia and International Treaty Making*, Department of Foreign Affairs and Trade, June 1997, pp 59–71.

[3.2.13] In February 1997, responding to the decision in *Minister for Immigration and Ethnic Affairs v Teoh* (1995) 183 CLR 273 **[3.2.8C]**, the Commonwealth Government released a joint statement on behalf of the Minister for Foreign Affairs, the Attorney-General and the Minister for Justice on the effect of treaties in administrative decision-making. The statement said that the High Court in *Teoh* had affirmed the principle that provisions of a treaty to which Australia is a party do not form part of Australian law unless those provisions have been validly incorporated into domestic law by statute, but that the case 'at the same time gave treaties an effect in Australian law ... which they [treaties] did not previously have'. The result was 'not consistent' with the proper role of the legislature under the Constitution, because, although the executive had the power to make treaties, parliament retained the power 'to change Australian law to implement treaty obligations'. The ministerial statement said that the act of entering into a treaty did *not* give rise to legitimate expectations in administrative law, and indicated that legislation would be introduced to give effect to this view: *Australia and International Treaty Making*, Department of Foreign Affairs and Trade, June 1997, pp 91–2.

[3.2.14] The Administrative Decisions (Effect of International Instruments) Bill 1997 was introduced into parliament on 18 June 1997. Clause 5 of the bill provided that the fact that Australia was bound by, or party to, a particular international instrument did not give rise to a legitimate expectation that might provide a basis at law for invalidating the effect of an administrative decision. The bill was referred to a parliamentary committee.

In October 1997, the Senate Legal and Constitutional Legislation Committee reported that the bill restored the roles of the executive and parliament to a pre-*Teoh* position, confirmed the fundamental role of parliament to implement treaty obligations, and ensured administrative certainty and complemented changes to the treaty-making process. It recommended that the bill be passed by the Senate without amendment: Senate Legal and Constitutional Legislation Committee, *Administrative Decisions (Effect of International Instruments) Bill 1997*, AGPS, Canberra, 1997. This bill had not been enacted at the time of writing.

[3.2.15] In summary, the parameters of the relationship between international law and domestic law, including constitutional law, have been altered by a process consisting of reports of the Senate, and the use of executive statements and legislation. First, there is no longer a clear division of responsibilities between the executive in making treaties and the legislature in implementing treaties. The new picture is much more complex as various legislative committees (including the Joint Parliamentary Committee on Treaties) are taking a much more active role in determining the nature of Australia's international treaty commitments, and due to the additional oversight that treaties be tabled in parliament prior to ratification. In addition, by a combination of executive statement and legislative action, these two branches of government have asserted their dominance over judicial pronouncement of new common law rules regulating the relationship between international and domestic law such as that which occurred in *Teoh*. (However, as noted above, legislative action to confirm this has not yet been taken.)

Further, as these reforms to treaty-implementation practices were taking place, the states and territories have asserted a more prominent role. We now turn to the federal dimension of treaty-making and implementation.

Accommodating the interests of the states in treaty implementation

[3.2.16] It is clear beyond dispute that, in international affairs, Australia is and can only be represented by the Commonwealth. 'The states did not develop international personality': Zines (1992) pp 235–6. As Barwick CJ put it in *New South Wales v Commonwealth* (the *Seas and Submerged Lands* case) (1975) 135 CLR 337 at 373 **[3.3.3]**:

> Whilst the power with respect to external affairs is not expressed to be a power exclusively vested in the Commonwealth, it must necessarily of its nature be so as to international relations and affairs. Only the Commonwealth has international status. The colonies never were and the States are not international persons.

The Commonwealth's essentially exclusive power with respect to international relations is buttressed by a number of other constitutional powers, including s 51(xxx): the Commonwealth's power to legislate with respect to 'the relations of the Commonwealth with the islands of the Pacific' and also the defence power, s 51(vi) (which may be rendered exclusive by an expression of intention to that effect pursuant to s 114 of the Constitution).

[3.2.17] However, in the mid-1990s, after a number of major decisions in which Commonwealth legislation supported by the external affairs power rendered state laws invalid to the extent of their inconsistency (see, for example, *Koowarta v Bjelke Petersen* (1982) 153 CLR 168 **[3.3.15C]**; *Commonwealth v Tasmania* (the *Tasmanian Dam* case) (1983) 158 CLR 1 **[3.3.21C]** below), the topic of treaty implementation aroused the sustained interest of the states and territories.

In 1995, the state and territory governments, unhappy with the expanded reach of the external affairs power reflected in such cases as *Commonwealth v Tasmania* (1983) 158 CLR 1 **[3.3.21C]** and *Victoria v Commonwealth* (the *Industrial Relations Act* case) (1996) 187 CLR 416 **[3.3.40C]**, proposed a series of reforms to the treaty-making process, including the establishment of a Treaties Council consisting of the Commonwealth, the state premiers and chief ministers of the territories, to consult on the matters which affected the polities: see *Position Paper on Reform of the Treaties Process* (1995).

[3.2.18]   In June 1996, the Council of Australian Governments (COAG) agreed to the establishment of a Treaties Council and adopted revised Principles and Procedures for Commonwealth–State Consultation on Treaties. These stated that the Commonwealth should 'wherever practicable', take into account the views of the states and territories in formulating Australian negotiating policy and before becoming a party to an international instrument. The Commonwealth should inform states and territories of any treaty discussions in which Australia was considering participation. It should maintain the Standing Committee on Treaties consisting of senior Commonwealth, state and territory officials, as well as other existing Commonwealth, state and territory Ministerial Councils which deal with specific issues. In appropriate cases, a state or territory representative may be included in delegations to international conferences that deal with matters within state–territory power. Before the Commonwealth becomes party to any treaty, it should consult with the states and territories to secure agreement on the manner in which obligations incurred should be implemented. The Commonwealth did not support the use of 'federal reservations' (see **[3.2.4]**), but did not object to the inclusion in treaties of a short 'federal statement' which would not affect Australia's obligations under the treaty.

[3.2.19]   Is the undoubted capacity of the Commonwealth Government to enter into an international treaty matched by a capacity on the part of the Commonwealth Parliament to legislate so as to give effect within Australia to the terms of that treaty? Or may the Commonwealth Parliament only legislate so as to implement the terms of those treaties which relate to matters otherwise within its legislative competence (as spelt out in s 51 of the Constitution), leaving implementation of other international agreements to state parliaments? If the Commonwealth signs and ratifies a treaty and thereby accepts an international obligation in relation to some other matter which, according to the division of legislative responsibilities effected by the Constitution, is 'reserved' for the states — must the Commonwealth remain in default of that obligation until the state parliaments legislate to implement the terms of the treaty?

This question has been raised directly before the High Court in several cases, and it caused, as Leslie Zines wrote in 1992, 'acute differences among the judges of the High Court': Zines (1992) p 237. However, cases such as *Commonwealth v Tasmania* (the *Tasmanian Dam* case) (1983) 158 CLR 1 **[3.3.21C]**; *Richardson v Forestry Commission* (1988) 164 CLR 261 **[3.3.34C]**; and *Victoria v Commonwealth* (the *Industrial Relations Act* case) (1996) 187 CLR 416 **[3.3.40C]**, have resolved most of the uncertainties about fundamental propositions and have largely removed the need for the Commonwealth (as Zines put it) to act 'cautiously before ratifying agreements related to subjects normally within state exclusive power': Zines (1992) p 237.

[3.2.20]   One of the uncertainties relating to the relative ambit of the executive and legislative powers with respect to treaties, with implications for the ambit of the Commonwealth's power over the states, has now been resolved in a way that expands the Commonwealth's power to realise Australia's international personality.

In *Commonwealth v Tasmania* (the *Tasmanian Dam* case) (1983) 158 CLR 1 **[3.3.21C]**, Dawson J had commented that '[i]t has not been questioned in recent years that the treaty-making power of this country is unlimited', although his Honour saw it as 'axiomatic that any expansion in the treaty-making power has not produced a corresponding expansion in the external affairs power': 158 CLR at 303.

Other members of the court sharply disputed Dawson J's axiom: see, for example, Mason, Murphy and Deane JJ in the *Tasmanian Dam* case. But no member of the court has ever suggested a constraint on the Commonwealth Government's power to negotiate and enter into international agreements, although some commentators have suggested that this power should be subject to limitations drawn from the Constitution: see, for example, Sawer (1984) p 200; Crommelin (1984) p 210. Those commentators appear to have in mind that the source of the treaty-making power is s 61 of the Constitution, which declares that '[t]he executive power of the Commonwealth ... extends to the execution and maintenance of this Constitution, and of the laws of the Commonwealth'. The extent of this power is then to be defined by reference to the Commonwealth's legislative powers.

To employ this argument as a means of confining the Commonwealth's treaty-making power could be criticised on two grounds. First, the process of reasoning begs the question as to the extent of the Commonwealth's legislative power (which, according to the dominant judicial view, is itself dependent on the existence of an international obligation that binds Australia). Second, and more substantially, a restricted Commonwealth capacity to enter into international agreements would leave Australia with a diminished capacity to participate in the international community, imposing limitations that, ultimately, could work to Australia's disadvantage. Mason J made substantially the same point (in the context of arguing against divided legislative power to implement treaties) in *Koowarta v Bjelke-Petersen* (1982) 153 CLR 168 at 225 **[3.3.15C]**:

> The ramifications of such a fragmentation of the decision making process as it affects the assumption and implementation by Australia of its international obligations are altogether too disturbing to contemplate. Such a division of responsibility between the Commonwealth and each of the States would have been a certain recipe for indecision and confusion, weakening Australia's stance and standing in international affairs.

[3.2.21]   The recent changes to the treaty-making process discussed above (**[3.2.18]**–**[3.2.19]**) may, at an earlier stage, overcome some of the difficulties associated with concern over usurpation of state power by the Commonwealth, and dominance of the legislature by the executive.

3   The external affairs power

[3.3.1]   The primary, direct means by which international law enters into the domestic legal system is through the external affairs power: Commonwealth Constitution s 51(xxix) **[3.3.2E]]**. The power enables the Commonwealth to legislate with respect to four matters:

- matters external to Australia;
- the implementation of international obligations, including treaty obligations;

- matters of international concern that are not otherwise the subject of international treaty obligations; and

- relations with other countries.

[3.3.2E]   **Commonwealth Constitution**

51 The Parliament shall, subject to this Constitution, have power to make laws for the peace, order and good government of the Commonwealth with respect to: ...

    (**xxix**) External affairs: ...

~~~

Matters geographically external to Australia

[3.3.3] In *New South Wales v Commonwealth* (the *Seas and Submerged Lands* case) (1975) 135 CLR 337, several members of the court confirmed that s 51(xxix) enabled the regulation of 'external affairs' in the geographical sense, that is, affairs external to Australia.

The case concerned the constitutional validity of the Seas and Submerged Lands Act 1973 (Cth). Australia was a party to the Convention on the Territorial Sea and the Contiguous Zone and the Convention on the Continental Shelf. These conventions declared that rights (essentially the same as those covered by ss 6 and 11 of the Act) over the territorial sea and the continental shelf were vested in coastal states. However, each of the conventions subjected these rights to qualifications and obligations which were not covered by the Act. (For instance, art 14 of the Convention on the Territorial Sea and the Contiguous Zone qualified a state's sovereignty over the territorial sea by granting 'the right of innocent passage through the territorial sea' to the ships of all states.)

The Act declared, in s 6, that 'the sovereignty in respect of the territorial sea' was vested in the Commonwealth and, in s 11, that the 'sovereign rights of Australia ... in respect of the continental shelf of Australia, for the purpose of exploring it and exploiting its natural resources' were vested in the Commonwealth.

A majority of the court held that the Act was supported by s 51(xxix). Barwick CJ, McTiernan, Mason, Jacobs and Murphy JJ held that the Act was valid because it gave effect to the two conventions. Three (perhaps four) members of the majority reasoned that another aspect of the s 51(xxix) power could support the Seas and Submerged Lands Act. Barwick CJ said (135 CLR at 360):

> [the legislative power] ... is not limited, in my opinion, to the making of arrangements with other nations or the implementation of such international arrangements as may properly be made in Australia's interest with other nations, though doubtless these may be the most frequent manifestations of the exercise of the power. The power extends, in my opinion, to any affair which in nature is external to the continent of Australia and the island of Tasmania subject always to the Constitution as a whole. For this purpose, the continent of Australia and the island of Tasmania are, in my opinion, bounded by the low-water mark on the coast.

Mason J made a similar point, saying '[t]he power conferred by s 51(xxix) extends to matters or things geographically situated outside Australia': 135 CLR at 471.

Jacobs J said that the external affairs power gave the Commonwealth 'the power to make laws in respect of any person or place outside and any matter or thing done or to be done or prohibited to be done outside the boundaries of the Commonwealth':

135 CLR at 497. Jacobs J referred to the territorial limitation on the powers of the states and concluded (135 CLR at 498):

> The words of s 51 of the Constitution do not import any similar territorial limitation and there now is none in the case of the Australian legislature. The words 'external affairs' can now be given an operation unaffected by any concept of territorial limitation. The result is that the Commonwealth, outside the boundaries of the States and subject to any particular constitutional injunctions, may make laws on all subject matters in exercise of its sovereignty.

Murphy J was not so explicit but he said that the Seas and Submerged Lands Act would be a law with respect to external affairs, even if there were no conventions: 135 CLR at 503–4.

[3.3.4] The proposition that s 51(xxix) will support legislation dealing with persons, activities or things outside Australia was unequivocally endorsed by five members of the High Court (Mason CJ, Deane, Dawson, Gaudron, and McHugh JJ) in *Polyukhovich v Commonwealth* (1991) 172 CLR 501. The justices concluded that 1988 amendments to the War Crimes Act 1942 (Cth), which provided that certain acts of violence committed in Europe between 1 September 1939 and 8 May 1945 were punishable as crimes in Australia, were laws with respect to external affairs.

After referring to the judgment of Jacobs J in the *Seas and Submerged Lands* case (1975) 135 CLR 337 **[3.3.4]**, Mason CJ expressed his conclusion in the following terms (172 CLR at 530–1):

> The legislation makes conduct outside Australia unlawful, thereby visiting that conduct with legal consequences under Australian law ... [T]o the extent that s 9 operates upon conduct which took place outside Australia and makes that conduct a criminal offence, the section is properly characterised as a law with respect to external affairs and is a valid exercise of power ... I arrive at this conclusion on the footing that it is not necessary that the Court should be satisfied that Australia has an interest or concern in the subject matter of the legislation in order that its validity be sustained. It is enough that Parliament's judgment is that Australia has an interest or concern. It is inconceivable that the Court could overrule Parliament's decision on that question.

Deane J said that, whatever may have been the position before Australia emerged as a fully independent sovereign state (at 602):

> ... it should now be accepted that any law which can properly be characterised as a law with respect to any matter, thing or person occurring or situate outside Australia is a law with respect to 'External affairs' for the purposes of s 51(xxix). In referring to 'a law with respect to any matter ... occurring ... outside Australia', I intend to include, among other things, what Jacobs J described [in the *Seas and Submerged Lands* case, 135 CLR at 497] as 'any matter or thing done or to be done or prohibited to be done outside the boundaries of the Commonwealth'.

Dawson J said that s 51(xxix) provided 'the authority for Commonwealth legislation extending to circumstances which are geographically external to Australia, without reference to the other legislative powers conferred by s 51 of the Constitution': 172 CLR at 634.

Gaudron J said that the decision in the *Seas and Submerged Lands* case (1975) 135 CLR 337 **[3.3.4]** gave 'considerable support' to the proposition that any law enacted by the Commonwealth Parliament 'is necessarily a law with respect to external affairs to the extent that it operates upon acts matters and things external to Australia'; and, 'more fundamentally, it is a view which proceeds from the ordinary meaning of the words "[e]xternal affairs" in s 51(xxix)': 172 CLR at 696.

McHugh J said that s 51(xxix) was not confined to the making of laws authorising or implementing arrangements with other nations, to affairs concerning Australia's relations with other countries, which affected Australia's standing in the international community or to matters connected with Australia. The term 'external affairs' in s 51(xxix) 'should be interpreted to include any matter, thing, event or relationship existing or arising or which might exist or arise outside Australia': 172 CLR at 714.

On the other hand, Brennan and Toohey JJ would have given s 51(xxix) a more narrow operation. Brennan J said that, before the Commonwealth Parliament could legislate with respect to some matter outside Australia, there must be some genuine connection between the external matter and Australia. While parliament must decide in the first instance whether there was any connection between Australia and the external matter, 'if the legislative judgment cannot reasonably be supported, the law will be held to be outside the power conferred by s 51(xxix)': 172 CLR at 552. Brennan J concluded that the amendments to the War Crimes Act were invalid because they attached legal sanctions to conduct whose perpetrators and victims may have had, at the time of the conduct, no connection with Australia.

Toohey J also held that s 51(xxix) required that there be some connection between Australia and the external matter so that the matter was one 'in which Australia has an interest': 172 CLR at 653. Although Toohey J said that it was for the parliament to determine whether Australia had such an interest, he proceeded to hold that, in view of Australia's involvement in World War II, Australia had an interest in the subject matter of the 1988 amendments to the War Crimes Act: see 172 CLR at 655.

[3.3.5] In *Victoria v The Commonwealth* (the *Industrial Relations Act* case) (1996) 187 CLR 416 at 485 **[3.3.40C]**, Brennan CJ, Toohey, Gaudron, McHugh and Gummow JJ approved the following proposition of Dawson J in *Polyhukovich* (172 CLR at 632) about the scope of the external affairs power:

> [T]he power extends to places, persons, matters or things physically external to Australia. The word 'affairs' is imprecise, but it is wide enough to cover places, persons, matters or things. The word 'external' is precise and unqualified. If a place, person, matter or thing lies outside the geographical limits of the country, then it is external to it and falls within the meaning of the phrase 'external affairs'.

Brennan CJ, Toohey, Gaudron, McHugh and Gummow JJ said that this view 'must now be taken as representing the view of the Court'.

[3.3.6] However, the question whether some type of connection (between the subject matter of the legislation and Australia) might be required, as Brennan and Toohey JJ indicated in their separate judgments in *Polyukhovich*, was apparently left open in *Horta v Commonwealth* (1994) 181 CLR 183 (and more recently in *R v Hughes* (2000) 202 CLR 535). *Horta* concerned federal legislation implementing a bilateral maritime boundary treaty between Australia and Indonesia relating to petroleum exploration and mining in the Timor Gap, an area of continental shelf between the coast of East Timor and mainland Australia, over which both countries claimed rights under international law.

Horta, a leader in the East Timorese pre-Independence resistance movement, challenged the constitutional validity of the domestic legislation authorising the Commonwealth to issue exploration and mining permits in the area, arguing that the treaty between Australia and Indonesia was a sham because Indonesia's annexation of East Timor in 1975 was invalid under international law. The High

Court side-stepped this delicate question by upholding the legislation on the simple ground that it dealt with a place that was geographically external to Australia, the Timor Gap. On the question of the need for a connection between the legislation's subject matter and Australian concerns, the court was equivocal. While the court acknowledged that five of its members had required no such connection, the connection was in any event established on these facts (181 CLR at 194):

> Regardless of whether the mere fact that a matter or thing is territorially outside Australia is of itself sufficient to bring a matter or thing within the phrase 'External affairs' for the purposes of s 51(xxix) or whether one or other of those additional factors is necessary, it is clear that the area of the Timor Gap and the exploration of ... petroleum resources ... is geographically external to Australia. [T]here is an obvious and substantial nexus between each of them and Australia.

It does seem difficult to reconcile the narrow approach to characterisation taken by Brennan and Toohey JJ in *Polyukhovich* **[3.3.4]** with a construction of the word 'external' as 'unqualified'. However, in *R v Hughes* (2000) 202 CLR 535 at 556, Gleeson CJ, Gaudron, McHugh, Gummow, Hayne and Callinan JJ applied *Horta*, saying that the offences with which the accused was charged related to making of investments in the United States and therefore 'relate to matters territorially outside Australia, but touching and concerning Australia, and so would attract s 51(xxix)'.

Implementation of international obligations

[3.3.7]   It is now recognised that s 51(xxix) will support Commonwealth legislation that implements an international agreement to which Australia is a party (or introduces the substance of the obligations assumed by Australia under that agreement into Australian law). A key theme of the cases in this area is the effect of a Commonwealth law implementing an international obligation on the residual powers of the states.

A preliminary question to be considered is whether the obligation on which the exercise of the Commonwealth's power claims to be based is indeed an international obligation. To enliven this aspect of s 51(xxix), it is necessary for an obligation to exist as a matter of fact. While the executive branch selects and enters into treaties, and the legislature retains power to implement those treaties to the extent that the legislature sees fit, the judiciary enjoys the power to determine whether an international obligation actually exists: *Queensland v Commonwealth* (the *Daintree Rainforest* case) (1989) 167 CLR 232.

In that case, s 6(3) of the World Heritage Properties Conservation Act 1983 authorised the Governor-General to declare certain property to be property to which s 9 of the Act would apply. Once the property was so proclaimed, certain acts in relation to that property would be prohibited by s 9. According to s 6(2), the property that could be made the subject of a s 6(3) proclamation included property that had been nominated by the Commonwealth for inclusion on the World Heritage List (maintained under an international convention) where protection of that property by Australia was a matter of international obligation.

Relying on this power, the Governor-General made a proclamation bringing the Daintree Rainforest in Queensland (an area that the Commonwealth had nominated for inclusion on the World Heritage List) within the protection of s 9. Queensland challenged the validity of the provision authorising the proclamation on a number of grounds, including that the legislation left the Commonwealth with the power to define the subject matter of its international obligations.

Mason CJ, Brennan, Deane, Toohey, Gaudron and McHugh JJ noted this aspect of the legislation, but concluded that, in the absence of any suggestion of 'bad faith' either in the nomination or the listing of the relevant property, the inclusion of the property in the List was 'conclusive of its status in the eyes of the international community' and 'conclusive of Australia's international duty to protect and conserve it': at 242. The existence of an obligation was ultimately a question of fact for the court to determine in the circumstances of the case: 167 CLR at 239.

[3.3.8] One argument for concluding that the international obligation asserted by the Commonwealth ought not be allowed to justify domestic legislation would be in cases where the Commonwealth acts in 'bad faith' (or, to adopt the Latin phrase, lacks *bona fides*). This possible limitation, adverted to by the court in the *Daintree Rainforest* case (1989) 167 CLR 23 **[3.3.7]**, is considered further in **[3.3.20]** below.

[3.3.9] Placing that limitation to one side, the foundation case on treaty implementation is *R v Burgess; Ex parte Henry* (1936) 55 CLR 608, where members of the High Court considered the breadth of the power to implement treaties, and the requirement of conformity between the treaty and the enactment which purported to rely on the treaty. The issue raised before the High Court was the validity of Air Navigation Act 1920 (Cth), s 4. The section authorised the Governor-General to make regulations to give effect to the Convention for the Regulation of Aerial Navigation (the Paris Convention).

All members of the court, Latham CJ, Starke, Dixon, Evatt and McTiernan JJ, held that the section was valid and that the Commonwealth Parliament could legislate to implement the provisions of the Convention, even though some of those provisions dealt with matters otherwise within the competence of the states. However, the reasons offered by the justices differed. Evatt and McTiernan JJ, in a joint judgment, said at 687 that the power conferred by s 51(xxix):

> ... certainly includes the power to execute within the Commonwealth treaties and conventions entered into with foreign powers. The legislative power in s 51 is granted 'subject to this Constitution' so that such treaties and conventions could not be used to enable the Parliament to set at nought constitutional guarantees elsewhere contained such for instance, as ss 6, 28, 41, 80, 92, 99, 100, 116, or 117. But it is not to be assumed that the legislative power over 'external affairs' is limited to the execution of treaties or conventions; and ... the Parliament may well be deemed competent to legislate for the carrying out of 'recommendations' as well as the 'draft international conventions' resolved upon by the International Labour Organisation or of other international recommendations or requests upon other subject matters of concern to Australia as a member of the family of nations.

Earlier, Evatt and McTiernan JJ had said that it was 'no longer possible to assert that there is any subject matter which must necessarily be excluded from the list of possible subjects of international negotiation, international dispute or international agreement' (55 CLR at 681), concluding at 681–2:

> In truth, the King's power to enter into international conventions cannot be limited in advance of the international situations which may from time to time arise. And in our view the fact of an international convention having been duly made about a subject brings that subject within the field of international relations so far as such subject is dealt with by the agreement.

They implied that, in order to provide the basis for legislation under s 51(xxix), a treaty must not be 'merely a device to procure for the Commonwealth an additional domestic jurisdiction': 55 CLR at 687.

Latham CJ adopted a similarly broad view of the power in s 51(xxix), although he did not comment on Evatt and McTiernan JJ's proposition that the power extended to implementing recommendations of international agencies. His Honour rejected the argument that a distinction should be drawn between international and domestic affairs (55 CLR at 640) and said that it was 'impossible to say a priori that any subject is necessarily such that it could never properly be dealt with by international agreement': 55 CLR at 641. He said, as had Evatt and McTiernan JJ, that the only relevant limits on the power were that it could not be used so as indirectly to amend the Constitution and that it was subject to prohibitions contained in the Constitution (55 CLR at 642), but concluded at 644:

> The Commonwealth Parliament was given power to legislate to give effect to international obligations binding the Commonwealth or to protect national rights internationally obtained by the Commonwealth whenever legislation was necessary or deemed to be desirable for this purpose.

Starke J was more equivocal on the scope of s 51(xxix). While not committing himself to any definite view, his Honour said (foreshadowing the approach taken by Stephen J in *Koowarta v Bjelke-Petersen* (1982) 153 CLR 168 **[3.3.15C]**) at 658:

> It may be ... that the laws will be within power only if the matter is 'of sufficient international significance to make it a legitimate subject for international co-operation and agreement' (Willoughby on *The Constitutional Law of the United States*, 2nd ed (1929), p 519).

Dixon J also appeared to take a narrower view of s 51(xxix) than had Latham CJ, Evatt and McTiernan JJ. His Honour said (also foreshadowing Stephen J's views in *Koowarta's* case **[3.3.15C]**) at 669:

> If a treaty were made which bound the Commonwealth in reference to some matter indisputably international in character, a law might be made to secure observance of its obligations if they were of a nature affecting the conduct of Australian citizens. On the other hand, it seems an extreme view that merely because the Executive Government undertakes with some other country that the conduct of persons in Australia shall be regulated in a particular way, the legislature thereby obtains a power to enact that regulation although it relates to a matter of internal concern which, apart from the obligation undertaken by the Executive, could not be considered as a matter of external affairs.

Dixon J did not commit himself to what he had described as the 'extreme view', which was essentially the view put forward by Latham CJ, Evatt and McTiernan JJ. He concluded (as did Starke J) that the Paris Convention dealt with matters which were 'indisputably international in character' (that is, 'the international recognition of sovereignty over the air and the relations of governments to the aircraft of other governments') and, accordingly, the Commonwealth Parliament could legislate so as to implement its terms even on the relatively narrow view of s 51(xxix).

All members of the court agreed that, when the Commonwealth Parliament claimed to implement an international treaty, 'the particular laws or regulations which are passed by the Commonwealth should be in conformity with the [treaty] which they profess to be executing': 55 CLR at 688. Apart from Starke J, the justices held that the regulations made under s 4 of the Air Navigation Act 1920 were, in several ways, inconsistent with the requirements of the Paris Convention and therefore fell outside s 4 of the Act and were invalid. However, the court suggested that the Commonwealth had some latitude in implementing a treaty. For instance, Dixon J said at 674–5:

It is apparent that the nature of this power necessitates a faithful pursuit of the purpose, namely, a carrying out of the external obligation, before it can support the imposition upon citizens of duties and disabilities which otherwise would be outside the power of the Commonwealth. No doubt the power includes the doing of anything reasonably incidental to the execution of the purpose. But wide departure from the purpose is not permissible, because under colour of carrying out an external obligation the Commonwealth cannot undertake the general regulation of the subject matter to which it relates.

[3.3.10]   Following the decision in *R v Burgess; Ex parte Henry* (1936) 55 CLR 608 **[3.3.9]**, the Commonwealth Government drafted new regulations which were formally made by the Governor-General under s 4 of the Air Navigation Act 1920 (Cth). Although there were some differences between the regulations and the provisions of the Paris Convention, the High Court held the regulations to be valid in *R v Poole; Ex parte Henry (No 2)* (1939) 61 CLR 634. Rich J said that a law for carrying out and giving effect to the Convention need not 'be a reproduction of the rules contained in the Convention': 61 CLR at 644. Starke J declared, at 648, that:

> ... within reason it is or at least should be for the discretion of the rule-making authority to determine, in the particular case, what are the appropriate and effective means of carrying out and giving effect to the Convention.

[3.3.11]   The High Court returned to the treaty implementation aspect of s 51(xxix) in *Airlines of New South Wales Pty Ltd v New South Wales (No 2)* (1965) 113 CLR 54, where the court again considered the breadth of the treaty implementation power and the conformity required between the treaty provisions and the enacting law. At issue was the validity of the Air Navigation Regulations 1920–47 made under s 26 of the Air Navigation Act 1920. The validity of the regulations, it was argued, depended on s 51(i) and s 51(xxix) of the Constitution. It was argued that the regulations implemented the Chicago Convention on Air Navigation, to which Australia was a party. The court was unanimous in holding that the Commonwealth Parliament could legislate to implement the Convention (or to authorise regulations for implementing the Convention). However, Barwick CJ took the opportunity (not presented by the issues before the court) to reject the broader view of s 51(xxix) developed by Latham CJ, Evatt and McTiernan JJ in *Burgess'* case (1936) 55 CLR 608 **[3.3.9]**. He said that the Chicago Convention (which had replaced the Paris Convention considered in *Burgess'* case) brought into existence an external affair, 'having regard to its subject matter, the manner of its formation, the extent of international participation in it and the obligations which it imposed'. While all those features were not essential in order for a treaty to attract the power in s 51(xxix), Barwick CJ said at 85:

> ... [T]he mere fact that the Commonwealth has subscribed to some international document does not necessarily attract any power to the Commonwealth Parliament. What treaties, conventions, or other international documents can attract the power given by s 51(xxix) can best be worked out as occasion arises.

The majority of the court (Barwick CJ, McTiernan, Menzies and Owen JJ) held that the regulations (apart from reg 200B) were directed towards implementing the treaty and were therefore valid. Barwick CJ indicated the delicate balance between the judgments of parliament and of the court in the following passage, at 86:

> Whilst choice of the legislative means by which the Treaty or convention shall be implemented is for the legislative authority, it is for this Court to determine whether particular provisions, when challenged, are appropriate and adapted to that end. The

Courts will closely scrutinise the challenged provisions to ensure that what is proposed to be done substantially falls within the power.

The minority (Kitto, Windeyer and Taylor JJ) decided that the regulations did not 'carry the Commonwealth any distance at all towards discharging obligations incumbent upon it under the Convention' (113 CLR at 118 per Kitto J) and were therefore invalid. This disagreement (over the validity of the regulations) reflected a difference over the question whether the Convention imposed clear obligations on Australia, the minority concluding that it did not. In so far as the minority proceeded on the premise that Commonwealth legislation made under s 51(xxix) must implement a treaty obligation, see now: *Commonwealth v Tasmania* (the *Tasmanian Dam* case) (1983) 158 CLR 1 **[3.3.21C]**; *Victoria v Commonwealth* (the *Industrial Relations Act* case) (1996) 187 CLR 416 **[3.3.40C]**.

[3.3.12] Until the 1970s, judicial inquiry into, and debate over, the treaty implementation aspect of the external affairs power was largely avoided through the adoption, by successive Commonwealth governments, of the cautious practice of leaving implementation of many international treaties to state parliaments (and delaying Australian ratification of those treaties until the Commonwealth governments were assured each state parliament would legislate so as to bring state laws into conformity with the treaties' provisions). Evatt and McTiernan JJ remarked on this practice in *Burgess'* case (1936) 55 CLR 608 **[3.3.9]** in the context of International Labour Organisation conventions: 55 CLR at 682. This practice may decline with the introduction of greater state involvement in the treaty-making process.

[3.3.13]   The pursuit of this practice by successive Commonwealth governments and the retarding effect which it had on Australia's ratification of international treaties is described by Crock ((1983) pp 345–8). She points out that by 1957 Australia had ratified only 20 of 107 ILO conventions, and she notes two ILO conventions which took 34 years to be ratified.

The practice of leaving implementation of international treaties to state parliaments may be reflected in a 'reservation' annexed to Australia's ratification of a treaty or convention (this practice was noted above at **[3.2.4]** and **[3.3.12]**). For example, when Australia ratified the International Covenant on Civil and Political Rights, it advised that implementation of the various aspects of the Covenant would be a matter for the 'constitutionally appropriate authority' within the Australian federal system. Crock explains:

> The function of the reservation has been to allow ratification in spite of dissent among the States and lack of conformity in state laws to the Treaty's mandatory provisions. While Australia accepts Art 50 of the Covenant [which extends the Covenant's provisions to 'all parts of federal States'], the primary obligation it creates to ensure implementation of the Covenant throughout a federation is therefore interpreted as being spread between the Commonwealth and state governments (Crock (1983) p 248).

[3.3.14] The Whitlam Labor Government (1972–75) was not committed to this non-assertive policy: Crommelin and Evans (1977) p 47. The Hawke Labor Government, elected in 1983, also exhibited (through its enactment of legislation to prevent construction of a dam on the Gordon River, which led to the litigation in *Commonwealth v Tasmania* (the *Tasmanian Dam* case) (1983) 158 CLR 1 **[3.3.21C]**) an enthusiasm for direct Commonwealth implementation of treaties. Three major

High Court decisions on the Commonwealth's treaty implementation power centred on implementing legislation passed during the Whitlam Labor Government (*Koowarta v Bjelke-Petersen* (1982) 153 CLR 168 **[3.3.15C]**) and the Hawke Labor Government: the *Tasmanian Dam* case (1983) 158 CLR 1 **[3.3.21C]**; *Richardson v Forestry Commission* (1988) 164 CLR 261 **[3.3.34C]**).

[3.3.15C]   Koowarta v Bjelke-Petersen

(1982) 153 CLR 168

On 30 September 1975, Australia ratified the International Convention on the Elimination of All Forms of Racial Discrimination. Among the provisions of the Convention were the following articles:

2(1) States Parties condemn racial discrimination and undertake to pursue by all appropriate means and without delay a policy of eliminating racial discrimination in all its forms and promoting understanding among all races, and, to this end:

...

(d) Each State Party shall prohibit and bring to an end, by all appropriate means, including legislation as required by circumstances, racial discrimination by any persons, group or organisation;

...

5 In compliance with the fundamental obligations laid down in article 2 of this Convention, States Parties undertake to prohibit and to eliminate racial discrimination in all its forms and to guarantee the right to everyone, without distinction as to race, colour, or national or ethnic origin, to equity before the law, notably in the enjoyment of the following rights:

...

(d) Other civil rights, in particular:

  ...

  (v) The right to own property alone as well as in association with others;

  ...

  (ix) The right to freedom of peaceful assembly and association; ...

(e) Economic, social and cultural rights, in particular:

  (i) The rights to work, to free choice of employment, to just and favourable conditions of work, to protection against unemployment, to equal pay for equal work, to just and favourable remuneration;

  ...

  (iii) The right to housing; ...

On 11 June 1975, the Commonwealth enacted the Racial Discrimination Act 1975 (Cth) ss 9 and 12 of which provided as follows:

9(1) It is unlawful for a person to do any act involving a distinction, exclusion, restriction or preference based on race, colour, descent or national or ethnic origin which has the purpose or effect of nullifying or impairing the recognition, enjoyment or exercise, on an equal footing, of any human right or fundamental freedom in the political, economic, social, cultural or any other field of public life.

(2) The reference in sub-section (1) to a human right or fundamental freedom in the political, economic, social, cultural or any other field of public life includes a reference to any right of a kind referred to in Article 5 of the Convention.

...

(4) The succeeding provisions of this Part do not limit the generality of sub-section (1).

...

12(1) It is unlawful for a person, whether as a principal or agent —

(a) to refuse or fail to dispose of any estate or interest in land, or any residential or business accommodation, to a second person;

(b) to dispose of such an estate or interest or such accommodation to a second person on less favourable terms and conditions than those which are or would otherwise be offered;

(c) to treat a second person who is seeking to acquire or has acquired such an estate or interest or such accommodation less favourably than other persons in the same circumstances;

(d) to refuse to permit a second person to occupy any land or any residential or business accommodation; or

(e) to terminate any estate or interest in land of a second person or the right of a second person to occupy any land or any residential or business accommodation,

by reason of the race, colour or national or ethnic origin of that second person or of any relative or associate of that second person.

In 1976, the Aboriginal Development Commission contracted with the lessees of Crown land in Queensland to purchase that leasehold on behalf of a group of Aboriginal people: the Winychanam people. The agreement was expressed to be subject to the approval of the Minister for Lands in Queensland as required by the Land Act 1962 (Qld).

In June 1976, the Minister for Lands refused to approve the transfer of the lease and on 8 December 1976 the Minister explained that this refusal was based on 'declared Government policy' which was opposed to 'proposals to acquire large areas of additional freehold or leasehold land for development by Aborigines or Aboriginal groups in isolation'.

Koowarta, a member of the Winychanam group, began proceedings in the Supreme Court of Queensland against the Premier of Queensland and others (after obtaining the approval of the Commissioner for Community Relations) under the Racial Discrimination Act. Koowarta claimed a declaration that the defendants had acted contrary to that Act, an injunction to restrain them from continuing to breach that Act and damages. The defendants in their defence alleged that the Racial Discrimination Act was invalid, and that Koowarta had no standing.

At about the same time, Queensland began proceedings in the High Court of Australia against the Commonwealth claiming a declaration that the Racial Discrimination Act was invalid. The High Court then ordered the removal into the High Court of parts of the proceedings in *Koowarta v Bjelke-Petersen*, to enable determination of the questions of law raised by the defence.

Gibbs CJ: [189] It has never been doubted that the words of s 51(xxix) are wide enough to empower the Parliament, in some circumstances at least, to pass a law which carries into effect within Australia the provisions of an international agreement to which Australia is a party.

Gibbs CJ referred to *R v Burgess; Ex parte Henry* (1936) 55 CLR 608 **[3.3.9]**; *R v Poole; Ex parte Henry (No 2)* (1939) 61 CLR 634 **[3.3.10]**; *Airlines of New South Wales Pty Ltd v New South Wales (No 2)* (1965) 113 CLR 54 **[3.3.11]** and *New South Wales v Commonwealth* (the *Seas and Submerged Lands* case) (1975) 135 CLR 337 **[3.3.3]**. It was established, he said, that s 51(xxix) was not limited to laws dealing with matters and things occurring outside Australia: '[E]ven on the narrowest view of the power, laws which regulate conduct within Australia by Australians may be laws with respect to external affairs': 153 CLR at 191. He also noted that s 51(xxix) was a distinct and independent power but was subject to limitations expressed or implied in the Constitution. He continued:

[192] The crucial question in the case is whether under the power given by s 51(xxix) the Parliament can enact laws for the execution of any treaty to which it is a party, whatever its subject matter, and in particular for the execution of a treaty which deals with matters that are purely domestic and in themselves involve no relationship with other countries or their inhabitants. ...

[193] It should be made clear that no question arises as to the power of Australia to enter into the Convention. The Governor-General, exercising the prerogative power of the Crown, can make treaties on subjects which are not within the legislative power of the Commonwealth. However, the treaties when made are not self-executing; they do not give rights to or impose duties on members of the Australian community unless their provisions are given effect by statute. The power of the Parliament to carry treaties into effect is not necessarily as wide as the executive power to make them. ...

[198] There are strong arguments which support the conclusion that s 51(xxix) does not empower the Parliament to give effect in Australia to every international agreement, whatever its character, to which Australia is a party. If the Parliament is empowered to make laws to carry into effect within Australia any treaty which the Governor-General may make, the result will be that the executive can, by its own act, determine the scope of Commonwealth power. Moreover, the power might be attracted not only by a formal agreement, such as a treaty, but also by an informal agreement: see *R v Burgess; Ex parte Henry* (55 CLR at 687). If the view of Evatt and McTiernan JJ is correct, the executive could, by making an agreement, formal or informal, with another country, arrogate to the Parliament power to make laws on any subject whatsoever ... In other words, if s 51(xxix) empowers the Parliament to legislate to give effect to every international agreement which the executive may choose to make, the Commonwealth would be able to acquire unlimited legislative power. The distribution of powers made by the Constitution could in time be completely obliterated; there would be no field of power which the Commonwealth could not invade, and the federal balance achieved by the Constitution could be entirely destroyed. ...

Gibbs CJ said that the court was unlikely to find that the Commonwealth had entered into any treaty as a mere device or in bad faith: 'The doctrine of bona fide would at best be a frail shield and available in rare cases': 153 CLR at 200. His Honour continued:

[200] It is apparent that a narrower interpretation of para (xxix) would at once be more consistent with the federal principle upon which the Constitution is based, and more calculated to carry out the true object and purpose of the power which, after all, is expressed to relate, not to internal or domestic affairs, but to external affairs. I conclude, therefore, that the view of Evatt and McTiernan JJ must be rejected, and that a law which gives effect within Australia to an international agreement will only be a valid law under s 51(xxix) if the agreement is with respect to a matter which itself can be described as an external affair. ...

[201] It seems to me immaterial that the agreement resulted from much international discussion and negotiation, that many nations are parties to it, and that there is international interest in it. Since the law whose validity is to be tested is one that gives legal effect within Australia to the provisions of the agreement, the test must be whether the provisions given effect have themselves the character of an external affair, for some reason other than that the executive has entered into an undertaking with some other country with regard to them. ... What I have said is not intended to suggest that there is a limited class of matter which, by their nature, constitute external affairs, and that only such matters are subject to the power conferred by s 51(xxix). Any subject matter may constitute an external affair, provided that the manner in which it is treated in some way involves a relationship with other countries or with persons or things outside Australia. A law which regulates transactions between Australia and other countries, or between residents of Australia and residents of other countries, would be a law with respect to external affairs, whatever its subject matter. ...

[202] The fact that many nations are concerned that other nations should eliminate racial discrimination within their own boundaries does not mean that the domestic or internal affairs of any one country thereby become converted into international affairs. There may be legitimate international concern as to the domestic affairs of a nation. An Australian law which is designed to forbid racial discrimination by Australians against Australians within the territory of Australia does not become international in character, or a law with respect to external affairs, simply because other nations are interested in Australia's policies and practices with regard to racial discrimination. ...

[203] For these reasons ss 9 and 12 of the Act were not within the legislative power conferred by s 51(xxix) and are invalid ...

Gibbs CJ concluded that, even if there was in international law a legal principle of non-discrimination on the grounds of race, an obligation imposed by that legal principle could 'only be given effect within Australia in the manner for which the Constitution provides, ie if the subject matter is not within Commonwealth power, by a law of a State': 153 CLR at 206.

Stephen J: [212] ... [T]he natural contextual meaning of para (xxix) includes, although it extends rather further than, what may be called the highest common factor to be deduced from the judgments in this court concerning the meaning of the paragraph: namely, a power to implement by legislation within Australia such treaties, on matters international in character and hence legitimately the subject of agreement between nations, as Australia may become party to. This minimal meaning, upon which all would agree, may be deduced from the following passages from four of the leading authorities in this court: *R v Burgess; Ex parte Henry* (1936) 55 CLR 608 at 644, 658, 669 and 687; *Frost v Stevenson* (1937) 58 CLR 528 at 596–7; *Airlines of New South Wales Pty Ltd v New South Wales (No 2)* (1965) 113 CLR 54 at 85, 126, 136 and 152; *New South Wales v Commonwealth* (1975) 135 CLR 337 and 360 337–8, 390, 450, 470, 503.

Stephen J said that the few express restrictions upon the Commonwealth's legislative power restricted the ambit of s 51(xxix), and that the grant in s 51(xxix) was not to be restricted by reference to the limited powers contained in other paragraphs of s 51. The difficult question was the extent to which the federal nature of the Constitution limited the broad power seemingly conferred by s 51(xxix). Stephen J observed that two limits on the power conferred by s 51(xxix) had been suggested:

[216] ... that to fall within power, treaties must be bona fide agreements between States and not instances of a foreign government lending itself as an accommodation party so as to bring a particular subject matter within the other party's treaty power; and that to fall within power a treaty must deal with a matter of international rather than merely domestic concern. ... It will not be enough that the challenged law gives effect to treaty obligations. A treaty with another country, whether or not the result of a collusive arrangement, which is on a topic neither of especial concern to the relationship between Australia and that other [217] country nor of general international concern will not be likely to survive that scrutiny.

The great post-war expansion of the areas properly the subject matter of international agreement has ... made it difficult indeed to identify subject matters which are of their nature not of international but of only domestic concern ... But this does no more than reflect the increasing awareness of the nations of the world that the state of society in other countries is very relevant to the state of their own society. Thus areas of what are of purely domestic concern are steadily contracting and those of international concern are ever expanding. Nevertheless the quality of being of international concern remains, no less than ever, a valid criterion of whether a particular subject matter forms part of a nation's 'external affairs' ...

[218] That prohibition of racial discrimination, the subject matter of the Racial Discrimination Act, now falls squarely within that concept I regard as undoubted. That a consequence would seem to be an intrusion by the Commonwealth into areas previously the exclusive concern of the States does not mean that there has been some alteration of the original federal pattern of distribution of legislative powers. What has occurred is, rather, a growth in the content of 'external affairs'. This growth reflects the new global concern for human rights and the international acknowledgment of the need for universally recognised norms of conduct, particularly in relation to the suppression of racial discrimination.

Stephen J referred to the Charter of the United Nations, to the writings of commentators on international law, to the Universal Declaration of Human Rights and to the International Convention on the Elimination of All Forms of Racial Discrimination. The pursuit of human rights had, more than any other idea, dominated international affairs after World War II, he said.

[220] This brief account of the international post-war developments in the area of racial discrimination is enough to show that the topic has become for Australia, in common with other nations, very much a part of its external affairs and hence a matter within the scope of s 51(xxix).

Even were Australia not a party to the Convention, this would not necessarily exclude the topic as a part of its external affairs. It was contended on behalf of the Commonwealth that, quite apart from the Convention, Australia has an international obligation to suppress all forms of racial discrimination because respect for human dignity and fundamental rights, and thus the norm of non-discrimination on the grounds of race, is now part of customary international law, as both created and evidenced by state practice and as expounded by jurists and eminent publicists. There is, in my view, much to be said for this submission and for the conclusion that, the Convention apart, the subject of racial discrimination should be regarded as an important aspect of Australia's external affairs, so that legislation much in the present form of the Racial Discrimination Act would be supported by power conferred by s 51(xxix). As with slavery and genocide, the failure of a nation to take steps to suppress racial discrimination has become of immediate relevance to its relations within the international community ...

Mason J: [224] The [external affairs] power applies to a treaty to which Australia is a party, for it is not in question that such a treaty is an external affair or a matter of external affairs, subject only to the qualification, if it be a qualification, that the treaty is a genuine treaty — a matter to be mentioned later. It would seem to follow inevitably from the plenary nature of the power that it would enable the Parliament to legislate not only for the ratification of a treaty but also for its implementation by carrying out any obligation to enact a law that Australia assumed by the treaty. It is very difficult to see why such a law would not be a law with respect to an external affair, once it is accepted that the treaty is an external affair. ...

It is a well settled principle of the common law that a treaty not terminating a state of war has no legal effect upon the rights and duties of Australian citizens and is not incorporated into Australian law on its ratification by Australia (*Chow Hung Ching v R* (1948) 77 CLR 449 at 478; *Bradley v Commonwealth* (1973) 128 CLR 557 at 582). In this respect Australian law differs from that of the United States where treaties are self-executing and create rights and liabilities without the need for legislation by Congress (*Foster v Neilson* (1829) 2 Pet 253 at 314 [27 US 164 at 202; 7 Law Ed 415 at 436]). ... To achieve this result the provisions have to be enacted as part of our domestic law, whether by Commonwealth or state statute. Section 51(xxix) arms [225] the Commonwealth Parliament with a necessary power to bring this about. So much was unanimously decided by this Court in *R v Burgess; Ex parte Henry* (1936) 55 CLR 608 ...

Burgess has been regarded as a landmark decision, notwithstanding that the outcome seems to have been so inevitable. Any other result would have been plainly unacceptable, not only because it would have entailed a failure to acknowledge the plenary nature of the power and the important purpose which it served, but also because the consequence of the failure would have been to leave the decision on whether Australia should comply with its international obligations in the hands of the individual States as well as the Commonwealth, for the Commonwealth would then lack sufficient legislative power to fully implement the treaty. The ramifications of such a fragmentation of the decision-making process as it affects the assumption and implementation by Australia of its international obligations are altogether too disturbing to contemplate. Such a division of responsibility between the Commonwealth and each of the States would have been a certain recipe for indecision and confusion, seriously weakening Australia's stance and standing in international affairs.

The exercise of the power is of course subject to the express and to the implied prohibitions to be found in the Constitution. The Commonwealth could not, in legislating to give effect to a treaty, evade the constitutional prohibitions contained in ss 92, 113 and 116. Nor, to take an example posed in argument, could it amend the Constitution otherwise than by the means provided for in s 128; it certainly could not do so by the expedient of assuming a treaty obligation to amend the Constitution and then attempting to legislate directly without resort to s 128 so as to give effect to that treaty obligation. Likewise the exercise of the power is subject to the implied general limitation affecting all the legislative powers conferred by s 51 that the Commonwealth cannot legislate so as to discriminate against the States or inhibit or impair their continued [226] existence or their capacity to function (*Victoria v Commonwealth*, the *Payroll Tax* case (1971) 122 CLR 353 at 372, 374–5, 388–91, 403, 411–12, 424).

Mason J noted that the states claimed that the Constitution distinguished between internal and external affairs, and continued:

The Constitution does not draw any distinction between external affairs and internal affairs so as to give power over the former but deny all power over the latter. The true position, in accordance with received doctrine, is that a law, which according to its correct characterisation is on a permitted topic, does not cease to be valid because it also happens to operate on a topic which stands outside power. The critical question is whether in the present case the law is with respect to external affairs, not whether it is with respect to internal affairs.

The fallacy in the argument is compounded by the assumption on which it proceeds — that affairs are either internal or external in the sense that the two categories are mutually exclusive. The assumption is false. An affair will very often have characteristics which endow it with both internal and external qualities. *Burgess* provides us with an instructive example. Australia's entry into the Paris Convention, an act affecting our relationships with other countries, was an external affair. But the question whether Australia should enter the Convention, a matter of domestic concern and consequence, was also an external affair. Likewise, the implemen[227]tation of the Convention by legislation was both an external and an internal affair — external because it related to the treaty and carried it into effect, internal because the legislation was domestic, operating substantially, though not entirely, within Australia. So it was that the law was with respect to external affairs, even though the operation of many of its provisions was inside, rather than outside, Australia ...

Mason J then referred to the argument that a wide reading of s 51(xxix) would enable the Commonwealth by negotiating treaties with other countries to legislate on any topic, no matter that it stood outside the specific powers conferred on the Commonwealth by the Constitution, noted that the doctrine of reserved powers was decisively rejected in the *Engineers'* case (1920) 28 CLR 129 **[8.2.31C]**, and continued:

The rejection of the doctrine was a fundamental and decisive event in the evolution of this Court's interpretation of the Constitution and in the later cases the correctness of the rejection has never been doubted. The consequence is that it is quite illegitimate to approach any question of interpretation of Commonwealth power on the footing that an expansive construction should be rejected because it will effectively deprive the States of a power which has hitherto been exercised or could be exercised by them. ...

[228] Doubtless the framers of the Constitution did not foresee accurately the extent of the expansion in international and regional cooperation which has occurred since 1900. Extradition and the repatriation of fugitive offenders and customs and tariff agreements probably represented the type of treaties which were then thought to call for domestic legislation by way of implementation. It is that expansion, rather than any change in the meaning of 'external affairs' as a concept, that promises to give the Commonwealth an entree into new legislative fields ...

[229] As the object of conferring the power was to equip the Commonwealth with comprehensive capacity to legislate with respect to external affairs, it is not to the point to say that such is the scope of external affairs in today's world that the content of the power given to the Commonwealth is greater than it was thought to be in 1900.

The consequence of the expansion in external affairs is that in some instances the Commonwealth now legislates on matters not formerly within the scope of its specific powers, to the detriment of the exercise of state powers. But in the light of current experience there is little, if anything, to indicate that there is a likelihood of a substantial disturbance of the balance of powers as distributed by the Constitution. To the extent that there is such a disturbance, then it is a necessary disturbance, one essential to Australia's participation in world affairs. ...

Mason J rejected the proposed restriction on s 51(xxix); namely, that the treaty in question must relate to a matter which is international in character or of international concern. His Honour continued:

... It is difficult to perceive why a genuine treaty, especially when it is multi-lateral and brought into existence under the auspices of the United Nations or an international agency, does not in itself relate to a matter of international concern and is not in itself an external affair. It is scarcely sensible to say that when Australia and other nations enter [230] into a treaty the subject matter of the treaty is not a matter of international concern — obviously it is a matter of concern to all the parties ...

[231] Agreement by nations to take common action in pursuit of a common objective evidences the existence of international concern and gives the subject matter of the treaty a character which is international. I speak of course of a treaty which is genuine and not of a colourable treaty, if that can be imagined into which Australia has entered solely for the purpose of attracting to the Commonwealth Parliament the exercise of a legislative power over a subject matter not specifically committed to it by the Constitution.

Mason J concluded that s 51(xxix) extended to the implementation of the Convention because it was an international treaty binding Australia to enact domestic legislation to eliminate racial discrimination: 153 CLR at 234.

Brennan J: [258] When a particular subject affects or is likely to affect Australia's relations with other international persons, a law with respect to that subject is a law with respect to external affairs ... Today it cannot reasonably be asserted that all aspects of the internal legal order of a nation are incapable of affecting relations between that nation and other nations. ...

Where a particular aspect of the internal legal order of a nation is made the subject of a treaty obligation, there is a powerful indication that the subject does affect the parties to the treaty and their relations one with another. They select that aspect as an element of their relationship, the obligee nations expecting and being entitled in international law to action by the obligor nation in [259] performance of the treaty. And therefore to subject an aspect of the internal legal order to treaty obligations stamps the subject of the obligation with the character if an external affair ...

It follows that to search for some further quality in the subject, an 'indisputably international' quality, is a work of supererogation. The international quality of the subject is established by its effect or [260] likely effect upon Australia's external relations and that effect or likely effect is sufficiently established by the acceptance of a treaty obligation with respect to that subject.

I would agree, however, that a law with respect to a particular subject would not necessarily attract the support of para (xxix) if a treaty obligation had been accepted with respect to that subject *merely* as a means of conferring legislative power upon the Commonwealth Parliament. Such a colourable attempt to convert a matter of internal concern into an external affair would fail because the subject of the treaty obligation would not in truth affect or be likely to affect Australia's relations with other nations ...

Brennan J held that the Racial Discrimination Act had been enacted to implement the International Convention on the Elimination of All Forms of Racial Discrimination and ss 9 and 12 of the Act were enacted in performance of Australia's obligation under the Convention. They were therefore valid.

Murphy J held that the Racial Discrimination Act was a law with respect to external affairs because it implemented the Convention. His Honour held that the power in s 51(xxix) extended to the implementation of any treaty to which Australia was a party, whether or not the subject matter of the treaty could be described as 'of international concern'. Murphy J also said that the power in s 51(xxix) extended to the enactment of legislation on a matter of international concern, independent of the existence of any treaty obligation.

Aickin and Wilson JJ agreed with the reasons and conclusions of Gibbs CJ. Wilson J also offered supplementary reasons in support of those conclusions.

In the result, the demurrer to Koowarta's action was overruled and the action remitted to the Supreme Court of Queensland for trial. Queensland's action was dismissed.

~~~

Notes

[3.3.16] If *R v Burgess; Ex parte Henry* (1936) 55 CLR 608 **[3.3.9]** tended to support a broad reading for the treaty implementation aspect of s 51(xxix), *Koowarta v Bjelke-Petersen* (1982) 153 CLR 168 **[3.3.15C]** may *appear* to have narrowed the reading. In *Koowarta*, a majority of the court upheld the validity of the Racial Discrimination Act 1975, but a differently constituted majority said that the Commonwealth could legislate to implement only those treaties which dealt with particular topics although the majority did not interpret the power as requiring evidence of the 'international' nature of the topic over and above its appearance in a treaty.

Hence, it is difficult to accept that the decision in *Koowarta's* case *established* a narrow reading for s 51(xxix). The view expressed by Gibbs CJ, Wilson and Dawson JJ, that the Commonwealth could only implement those treaties which dealt with a subject matter 'international in character' was rejected by the majority which upheld the validity of the Racial Discrimination Act. The view, expressed by Stephen J, that the Commonwealth could only implement those treaties which dealt with a subject matter of 'international concern', was rejected by the other six members of the court.

[3.3.17] It may be that the decision provides no clear guidance on the extent of the treaty implementation power. Rather, it offers a range of alternatives as to the general principles against which that power might be measured. At least one of those alternatives (that proposed by Gibbs CJ, Wilson and Dawson JJ) is precluded by the actual result of the case, which was that the Racial Discrimination Act was valid. The exclusion of that option was recognised in the *Tasmanian Dam* case (1983) 158 CLR 1 **[3.3.21C]** when Gibbs CJ and Wilson J abandoned the limitation for which they had argued in *Koowarta's* case in favour of the limitation proposed by Stephen J, which had two attractions. In theoretical terms, it could have been described as the 'lowest common denominator'; that is, the narrowest view of s 51(xxix) consistent with the result of the case. Pragmatically, it would have had the effect (as applied by those justices in the *Tasmanian Dam* case) of precluding the Commonwealth from legislating to impose its conservation policies on Tasmania.

[3.3.18] In *Koowarta v Bjelke-Petersen* (1982) 153 CLR 168 **[3.3.15C]**, three of the justices, Stephen, Mason and Murphy JJ, argued for a reading of s 51(xxix) which would allow the Commonwealth Parliament to legislate on matters of international concern even where those matters were not included in a treaty to which Australia was a party. This view, which is consistent with the High Court's decision in *R v Sharkey* (1949) 79 CLR 121 **[3.3.46]**, was not supported by a majority in *Koowarta's* case. However, can such a principle be drawn out of the reasoning of those justices who upheld the validity of the Racial Discrimination Act? Could it be argued that, for Mason, Murphy and Brennan JJ, the negotiation of the International Convention on the Elimination of All Forms of Racial Discrimination was a sufficient, but not an essential, indication of the international nature of the subject matter of racial discrimination?

[3.3.19] Members of the court raised several specific limits on the treaty implementation power. As with other heads of power, it is subject to the express limitations on Commonwealth legislative power in such provisions as ss 92 and 116, and to those implied limits on Commonwealth legislative power which can be extracted from *Melbourne Corporation v Commonwealth* (the *State Banking* case) (1947) 74 CLR 31 **[8.2.45C]**, *Victoria v Commonwealth* (the *Payroll Tax* case) (1971) 122 CLR 353 **[8.2.50C]** and *Queensland Electricity Commission v Commonwealth* (1985) 159 CLR 192 **[8.2.59C]**. (The second of these limits is explored in *Commonwealth v Tasmania* (the *Tasmanian Dam* case) (1983) 158 CLR 1: see **[3.3.21C]**.)

A 'bona fides' rule?

[3.3.20]   We touched on the concept of a 'bad faith' rule in our discussion of *Horta v Commonwealth* (1994) 181 CLR 183 **[3.3.6]**. In *Koowarta v Bjelke-Petersen* (1982) 153 CLR 168 **[3.3.15C]**, some justices proposed this limitation on the treaty implementation power, one which could be described as unique to s 51(xxix) and which reflects judicial unease with the prospect of Commonwealth exploitation of a broadly construed treaty implementation power. Stephen J indicated that one 'safeguard against improper exercise of the "external affairs" power' was the requirement that the implemented treaty have been entered into in good faith: 153 CLR at 216. Brennan J developed this point, speaking of a treaty obligation undertaken 'merely as a means of conferring legislative power upon the Commonwealth Parliament' as a 'colourable attempt [which] would fail': 153 CLR at 260.

That caveat had previously been expressed in *Burgess'* case (1936) 55 CLR 608 **[3.3.9]** by Latham CJ (55 CLR at 642), Starke J (55 CLR at 658), Dixon J (55 CLR at 669) and Evatt and McTiernan JJ (55 CLR at 687) and in *Airlines of New South Wales Pty Ltd v New South Wales (No 2)* (1965) 113 CLR 54 **[3.3.11]** by Barwick CJ: 113 CLR at 85.

In *Koowarta v Bjelke-Petersen* (1982) 153 CLR 168 **[3.3.15C]** Gibbs CJ was sceptical of the value of any such restriction, describing it as 'at best ... a frail shield' (153 CLR at 200), and Mason J was equivocal, saying that he was not speaking of 'a colourable treaty, if that can be imagined': 153 CLR at 231.

There are substantial difficulties in applying any such restriction to the treaty-making power of the Commonwealth Executive and to the treaty implementation power of the Commonwealth Parliament. As Gibbs CJ recognised, the nature of the restriction is difficult to grasp: it surely could not be invoked whenever the executive had entered into a treaty in the full knowledge that parliament had no power, outside s 51(xxix), to legislate on the subject matter of the treaty: 153 CLR at 200. If the restriction is meant to prevent the executive from entering into a treaty where the parties have no interest in setting international standards but are motivated only by the desire to expand Commonwealth legislative power, there are two difficulties. At the theoretical level, we must remember that the accession to a treaty is an executive act, undertaken formally by the Crown's representative, the Governor-General. How do we overcome the view expressed by, for example, Fullagar J in *Australian Communist Party v Commonwealth* (1951) 83 CLR 1? His Honour said that, where the Governor-General was authorised to take action, which in his opinion was necessary for the defence of the Commonwealth, that opinion could not be examined by the courts, 'for it is not open to impute *mala fides* with respect to an act of the King by himself of his representative': 83 CLR at 257–8. While the High Court's decisions in *R v Toohey; Ex parte Northern Land Council* (1981) 151 CLR 170 and *FAI Insurances Ltd v Winneke* (1982) 151 CLR 342 have made some breaches in the wall that protects vice-regal actions from judicial review, do those decisions have any impact on the prerogative function of negotiating and signing international agreements?

At the practical level, if judicial review of the motives of the executive were permissible, by what evidence would those motives be established? Further, how would that evidence be collected? In this context, the willingness of the court to set aside a claim of Crown privilege could be crucial. See *Sankey v Whitlam* (1978) 142 CLR 1.

[3.3.21C]   Commonwealth v Tasmania
(The *Tasmanian Dam* case)
(1983) 158 CLR 1

In November 1972 the United Nations Educational, Scientific and Cultural Organisation (UNESCO) adopted the Convention for the Protection of the World Cultural and Natural Heritage. Australia ratified the Convention in August 1974 and by June 1983 there were 74 parties to the Convention. Amongst the provisions of the Convention were the following:

Article 4

Each State Party to this Convention recognises that the duty of ensuring the identification, protection, conservation, presentation and transmission to future generations of the cultural and natural heritage referred to in Articles 1 and 2 and situated on its territory, belongs primarily to that State ...

Article 5 provided that the parties were to ensure that effective measures were taken for the protection, conservation and presentation of cultural and natural heritage situated on their property. These measures included: the adoption of policies which gave the heritage a function in the life of the community; the establishment of services for its protection; the development of research methods to counteract dangers to it; the taking of appropriate legal, scientific, technical, administrative and financial measures necessary for its identification, protection, conservation, presentation and rehabilitation; and the development of training centres for its protection.

Article 6

1 Whilst fully respecting the sovereignty of the States on whose territory the cultural and natural heritage mentioned in Articles 1 and 2 is situated, and without prejudice to property rights provided by national legislation, the States Parties to this Convention recognise that such heritage constitutes a world heritage for whose protection it is the duty of the international community as a whole to co-operate.

Article 6 also required parties to help in identifying, protecting, conserving and preserving such heritage (cl 2), and to undertake not to take any deliberate measures to damage it (cl 3).

Article 12 of the Convention provided for the nomination by a state party of property forming part of its cultural and national heritage and the listing, by the World Heritage Committee, of those nominated properties which were regarded 'as having outstanding universal value' on the World Heritage List.

Article 34 of the Convention was a 'federal clause'. It provided that, where implementation of provisions of the Convention came 'under the legal jurisdiction of the federal or central legislative power, the obligations of the federal or central Government shall be the same as for those States Parties which are not federal States', but where implementation of provisions of the Convention came 'under the legal jurisdiction of individual constituent States ... the federal Government shall inform the competent authorities of such States ... of the said provisions, with its recommendation for their adoption'.

In September 1981, the Premier of the state of Tasmania requested the Commonwealth Government to nominate three national parks in the south-west of that state for listing on the World Heritage List. In December 1982, the World Heritage Committee entered the three national parks in the World Heritage List.

In the meantime, however, the Tasmanian Parliament had enacted the Gordon River Hydro-Electric Power Development Act 1982, which authorised the Hydro-Electric Commission of Tasmania to construct a dam (the Franklin Dam) on the Gordon River within the national parks nominated for listing in the World Heritage List. Construction of the dam commenced in July 1982.

On 31 March 1983, the Governor-General made the World Heritage (Western Tasmania Wilderness) Regulations under s 69 of the National Parks and Wildlife Conservation Act 1975 (Cth). The regulations prohibited 'the construction of a dam or associated works' and a wide variety of other activities (including the carrying out of 'any other works') in the area covered by the Tasmanian legislation, 'except with the consent of the Minister'.

On 22 May 1983, the Commonwealth Parliament enacted the World Heritage Properties Conservation Act 1983, s 9 of which provided as follows:

9(1) Except with the consent in writing of the Minister, it is unlawful for a person, whether himself or by his servant or agent —

  (a) to carry out any excavation works on any property to which this section applies;

  (b) to carry out operations for, or exploratory drilling in connection with, the recovery of minerals on any property to which this section applies;

  (c) to erect a building or other substantial structure on any property to which this section applies or to do any act in the course of, or for the purpose of, the erection of a building or other substantial structure on any property to which this section applies;

  (d) to damage or destroy a building or other substantial structure on any property to which this section applies;

  (e) to kill, cut down or damage any tree on any property to which this section applies;

  (f) to construct or establish any road or vehicular track on any property to which this section applies;

  (g) to use explosives on any property to which this section applies; or

  (h) if an act is prescribed for the purposes of this paragraph in relation to particular property to which this section applies, to do that act in relation to that property.

Section 6 identified the property to which s 9 applied:

6(1) A Proclamation may be made under sub-section (3) in relation to identified property that is not in any State.

(2) A Proclamation may also be made under sub-section (3) in relation to identified property that is in a State and is property to which one or more of the following paragraphs applies or apply:

  (a) the Commonwealth has, pursuant to a request by the State, submitted to the World Heritage Committee under Article 11 of the Convention that the property is suitable for inclusion in the World Heritage List provided for in paragraph 2 of the Article, whether the request by the State was made before or after the commencement of this Act and whether or not the property was identified property at the time when the request was made;

  (b) the protection or conservation of the property by Australia is a matter of international obligation, whether by reason of the Convention of otherwise;

  (c) the protection or conservation of the property by Australia is necessary or desirable for the purpose of giving effect to a treaty (including the Convention) or for the purpose of obtaining for Australia any advantage or benefit under a treaty (including the Convention);

  (d) the protection or conservation of the property by Australia is a matter of international concern (whether or not it is also a matter of domestic concern) whether by reason that a failure by Australia to take proper measures for the protection or conservation of the property would, or would be likely to, prejudice Australia's relations with other countries or for any other reason; ...

(3) Where the Governor-General is satisfied that any property in respect of which a Proclamation may be made under this sub-section is being or is likely to be damaged or destroyed, he may, by Proclamation, declare that property to be property to which section 9 applies.

Other sections of the Act prohibited trading corporations from carrying out any of the activities covered by s 9, and any person from damaging a site of particular significance to the people of the Aboriginal race; and provided for the assessment and payment of compensation by the Commonwealth to any person whose property might be acquired under the Act.

On 26 May 1983 the Governor-General issued proclamations under s 6(3) of the Act, declaring that the Act applied to the area covered by the Gordon River Hydro-Electric Power Development Act 1982 (Tas).

The Commonwealth began proceedings in the High Court of Australia against Tasmania, seeking declarations that construction of the Franklin Dam was unlawful. Tasmania began proceedings in the High Court against the Commonwealth, seeking declarations that the Commonwealth legislation was invalid. A series of questions was stated for the opinion of the Full Court, including the question whether the World Heritage (Western Tasmania Wilderness) Regulations were valid and whether s 9 of the World Heritage Properties Conservation Act 1983 was valid.

The Chief Justice reviewed the provisions of the Convention for the Protection of the World Cultural and Natural Heritage and concluded that, 'although the Convention imposes on the States Parties to the Convention certain obligations, Arts 4, 5 and 6 do not impose on any State Party an obligation to take any specific action, and there is no other provision of the Convention which imposes any legal obligation in Australia to take action to protect the Parks from possible or actual damage'. After referring to the views of s 51(xxix) expressed in *Koowarta v Bjelke-Petersen* (1982) 153 CLR 168 **[3.3.15C]**, Gibbs CJ referred to the principle in *Jumbunna Coal Mine NL v Victoria Coal Miners' Association* (1908) 6 CLR 309 (see **[1.5.4]**) that federal powers be interpreted broadly unless the context indicated otherwise, and said that '[t]he federal nature of the Constitution requires that some limits be imposed on the power to implement international obligations conferred by para (xxix) ...'. His Honour said that to interpret the provision broadly would lend support for its 'unlimited expansion' because, unlike other powers there was 'almost no aspect of life which under modern conditions may not be the subject of an international agreement, and therefore the possible subject of Commonwealth legislative power': 158 CLR at 100. After referring to Stephen J's judgment in *Koowarta* **[3.3.15C]**, Gibbs CJ continued:

Gibbs CJ: [100] It is not altogether clear what Stephen J meant when he insisted that the subject of a treaty must be of international concern if legislation with regard to it is to come within the power conferred by [101] s 51 (xxix). He clearly did not mean that it was necessary that the subject of the agreement must itself be an external affair, for it was on that question that he differed from the minority. However, he cannot have meant that the mere fact that a matter has become the subject of an international agreement means that it is a matter of international concern, because he expressly said that it is not enough that the challenged legislation gives effect to treaty obligations. ... Whether a matter is of international concern depends on the extent to which it is regarded by the nations of the world as a proper subject for international action, and on the extent to which it will affect Australia's relations with other countries. For myself, I should have preferred a more precise test. However, the result is that unlike some other powers, but like the defence power, the application of the external affairs power 'depends upon facts, and as those facts change so may its actual operation as a power enabling the legislature to make a particular law': *Andrews v Howell* (1941) 65 CLR 255 at 278.

The Convention, and the Recommendation, in their relevant aspects, and as applicable to Australia, deal with matters entirely domestic — matters which contemplate action within Australia, which involve no reciprocity of relationship with other nations (as a convention regarding the protection of historic memorials from bombardment might do) and which do not directly affect the interests of other nations, for example, by protecting them from actual or potential risks (as a convention relating to the eradication of diseases or the prohibition of the illegal export of cultural property might do). The protection of the environment and the cultural heritage has [102] been of increasing interest in recent times, but it cannot be said to have become such a burning international issue that a failure by one nation to take protective measures is likely adversely to affect its relations with other nations, unless of course damage or pollution extends beyond the borders. ... It cannot be said that the rules of customary international law cast any obligation on a nation to preserve the heritage within its own boundaries. Although it appears that the subject has been regarded as fit for international action, that action has fallen short of creating definite and binding national obligations. The question whether the subject matter on the Convention is one of international concern within the test propounded by Stephen J is one of some difficulty, because, since the external affairs power, like the defence power, 'applies to authorise measures only to meet facts' (cf *Australian Textiles Pty Ltd v Commonwealth* (1945) 71 CLR 161 at 181), the court must form its own impression of the facts, in part on the basis of judicial notice. In the present case I regard as decisive the fact that the Convention does not impose any obligation on the Commonwealth to enact legislation for the protection of any part of the national heritage within Australia; and of course the Recommendation does not purport to do so. I also take into account my opinion that relations with other countries are not likely to be significantly affected by whatever action Australia takes in relation to the protection of the Parks. These considerations, and the nature of the matters with which the Convention and the Recommendation deal, lead me to the conclusion that the external affairs power has not been attracted in the present case.

Gibbs CJ referred to the decision in *R v Burgess; Ex parte Henry* (1936) 55 CLR 608 **[3.3.4]** and *Airlines of New South Wales Pty Ltd v New South Wales (No 2)* 113 CLR 54 **[3.3.6]**, and continued:

[106] These cases recognise, as one might expect, that if an international convention imposes obligations on the Commonwealth, the Parliament has a discretion as to the manner in which those obligations are carried out. However, they strongly suggest that if an international convention imposes no obligations on the Commonwealth, the power given by s 51(xxix) is not available. (The case in which a convention gives a benefit may be put aside, for the enactments in the present case do not secure any benefit given by the Convention.) In other words, the external affairs power does not enable the Parliament to make laws with respect to any matter which is dealt with by an international convention to which Australia is a party, even if the matter is one of international concern, when the laws do not give effect to the convention ...

In the present case, as I have endeavoured to show, the Convention imposed no relevant obligations on the Commonwealth. The Act does not give effect to any international obligation and is for that reason not a valid exercise of the external affairs power. Further, it fails to afford any protection to property, notwithstanding Art 6.1 of the Convention, and for that reason also cannot be said to implement the terms of the Convention.

[107] For these reasons I hold that the World Heritage (Western Tasmania Wilderness) Regulations and ss 6(2)(a)–(d) and 9 of the Act are invalid in the present circumstances. The position might be different (at least as to ss 6(2)(d) and 9) if Australia came under an international obligation to protect or conserve the property by taking the measures mentioned in s 9.

Mason J referred to the different approaches to s 51(xxix) taken by the justices in *Koowarta v Bjelke-Petersen* (1982) 153 CLR 168 **[3.3.15C]** and continued:

Mason J: [122] If we take the decision as turning on Stephen J's view of the power, because it reflects the narrowest expression of it by the justices who constituted the majority, the case is authority for the proposition that the power authorises a law which gives effect to an obligation imposed on Australia by a bona fide international convention or treaty to which Australia is a party, at any rate so long as the subject matter of the convention or treaty is one of international concern, or of concern to the relationship between Australia and the other party or parties. ...

Mason J referred to the three tests of international concern put forward by Tasmania: whether the law implements an obligation under the Convention; whether the subject matter falls within relations with other countries (whether or not it is also a domestic activity); or whether it involves persons or things outside Australia.

Mason J: [123] The first of the three tests seeks to express the idea that it is the implementation of an obligation imposed on Australia by a treaty that attracts the external affairs power, that it is the treaty obligation and its implementation that constitutes the relevant subject or matter of external affairs. To my mind this is too narrow a view. As I pointed out in *Koowarta* 153 CLR at 224–7, the treaty itself is a matter of external affairs, as is its implementation by domestic legislation. The insistence in *Burgess* that the legislation carry into effect provisions of the Convention in accordance with the obligation which that Convention imposed on Australia is not inconsistent with what I have said, though it does raise a question as to the scope of the legislative power in its application to a treaty, a matter to be discussed later. At this point it is sufficient to say that there is no persuasive reason for thinking that the international character of the subject matter or the existence of international concern is confined to that part of a treaty which imposes an obligation on Australia. A provision in a treaty which is designed to [124] secure to Australia a benefit may be just as much a matter of international concern, possessing an international character, with a potential to affect Australia's relationships with other countries, as a provision in a treaty which imposes an obligation upon Australia.

Mason J referred to the problem of determining when a subject matter affected Australia's relations and when it did not. His Honour said '[n]o doubt this problem might have been more readily answered in 1900' when 'international discussion, negotiation, cooperation and agreement took place on a very limited scale in relation to limited subjects'; but today when we 'are accustomed to discuss, negotiate, cooperate and agree on an ever-widening range of topics, it is impossible to enunciate a criterion by which potential for international action can be identified from topics which lack this quality': 158 CLR at 124. Mason J referred to 'many instances of the common pursuit' including international conventions on economic, social and cultural rights; racial discrimination; the political rights of women; education; freedom of association; employment discrimination; equal remuneration for men and women; and concluded that there 'are virtually no limits to the topics which may hereafter become the subject of international cooperation and international treaties or conventions': 158 CLR at 124. Mason J continued:

[124] It is submitted that the suggested requirement that the subject matter must be 'of international concern' means that it must be international in character in the sense that there is a mutuality of interest or benefit in the observance of the provisions of the convention. Thus, we are invited to say that a convention by which the contracting parties agree to enact domestic laws requiring [125] persons in motor vehicles to wear seat belts does not deal with a matter of international concern because no nation can derive a benefit from the wearing of seat belts in another country. This is by no means self-evident. Drivers and passengers cross international boundaries. They are likely to observe in other countries the practices which they observe at home. International cooperation resulting in a convention insisting on compliance with uniform safety standards may well benefit all countries. The illustration is instructive because it demonstrates how difficult it is to say with accuracy of any treaty or convention that observance of its provisions will not benefit a contracting party.

The point is that, if a topic becomes the subject of international cooperation or an international convention it is necessarily international in character — the existence of cooperation and the making of a convention establish that the subject matter is an appropriate vehicle for the creation of international relationships or, in the case of a bilateral treaty, a relationship between the parties to it. And participation in a convention indicates a judgment on the part of participating nations that they will derive a benefit from it. All this indicates an absence of any acceptable criteria or guidelines by which the court can determine the 'international character' of the subject matter of a treaty or convention. The existence of international character or international concern is established by entry by Australia into the convention or treaty.

In any event, as I observed in *Koowarta* (153 CLR at 229), the court would undertake an invidious task if it were to decide whether the subject matter of a convention is of international character or concern. On a question of this kind the court cannot substitute its judgment for that of the executive government and Parliament. The fact of entry into, and of ratification of, an international convention, evidences the judgment of the executive and of Parliament that the subject matter of the convention is of international character and concern and that its implementation will be a benefit to Australia. Whether the subject matter as dealt with by the convention is of international concern, whether it will yield, or is capable of yielding, a benefit to Australia, whether non-observance by Australia is likely to lead to adverse international action or reaction, are not questions on which the court can readily arrive at an informed opinion. Essentially they are issues involving nice questions of sensitive judgment which should be left to the executive government for determination. The court should accept and act upon the decision of the executive [126] government and upon the expression of the will of Parliament in giving legislative ratification to the treaty or convention.

Mason J dismissed arguments based on federalism by saying that they had been decisively rejected in *Koowarta v Bjelke-Petersen* (1982) 153 CLR 168.

It is, of course, possible that the framers of the Constitution thought or assumed that the external affairs power would have a less extensive operation than this development has brought about and that Commonwealth legislation by way of implementation of treaty obligations would be infrequent and limited in scope. The framers of the Constitution would not have foreseen with any degree of precision, if at all, the expansion in international and regional affairs that has occurred since the turn of the century, in particular the cooperation between nations that has resulted in the formation of international and regional conventions. But it is not, and could not be, suggested that by reason of this circumstance the power should now be given an operation which conforms to expectations held in 1900. For one thing it is impossible to ascertain what those expectations may have been. For another the difference between those expectations and subsequent events as they have fallen out seems to have been a difference in the frequency and volume of external affairs rather than a difference in kind. Only if there was a difference in kind could we begin to construct an argument that the expression 'external affairs' should [127] receive a construction which differs from the meaning that it would receive according to ordinary principles and interpretation. Even then mere expectations held in 1900 could not form a satisfactory basis for departing from the natural interpretation of words used in the Constitution. ...

Accordingly, it conforms to established principle to say that s 51(xxix) was framed as an enduring power in broad and general terms enabling the Parliament to legislate with respect to all aspects of Australia's participation in international affairs and of its relationship with other countries in a changing and developing world and in circumstances and situations that could not be easily foreseen in 1900 ...

Mason J referred to the rejection of the reserved powers doctrine in the *Engineers' case* (1920) 28 CLR 129 at 150–1 **[8.2.31C]**; and said that the federal implication that the Commonwealth may not discriminate against a state was one implication upon which Tasmania could rely: 158 CLR at 128–9. His Honour replied:

[129] If the carrying out of, or the giving effect to, a treaty or convention to which Australia is a party is a matter of external [130] affairs, and so much is now accepted, it is very difficult to see why a law made under s 51(xxix), that is, a law with respect to the matter of external affairs, should be limited to the implementation of an obligation. To say this is to import an arbitrary limitation into the exercise of the power, one which might deprive Australia of the benefits which a treaty or convention seeks to secure. Take, for example, a treaty by which another country undertakes to provide technological and other benefits in connection with a

joint enterprise to be undertaken in this country between Australia and the other party to the treaty. Why would the power not extend to Commonwealth legislation facilitating the enjoyment by Australia of the benefits promised by the treaty and to facilitating the carrying on of the activities for which it makes provision? ...

[131] The extent of the Parliament's power to legislate so as to carry into effect a treaty will, of course, depend on the nature of the particular treaty, whether its provisions are declaratory of international law, whether they impose obligations or provide benefits and, if so, what the nature of these obligations are, and whether they are specific or general or involve significant elements of discretion and value judgment on the part of the contracting parties. I reject the notion that once Australia enters into a treaty Parliament may legislate with respect to the subject matter of the treaty as if that subject matter were a new and independent head of Commonwealth legislative power. The law must conform to the treaty and carry its provisions into effect. The fact that the power may extend to the subject matter of the treaty before it is made or adopted by Australia, because the subject matter has become a matter of international concern to Australia, does not mean that [132] Parliament may depart from the provisions of the treaty after it has been entered into by Australia and enact legislation which goes beyond the treaty or is inconsistent with it.

Turning to the Convention for the Protection of the World Cultural and Natural Heritage, Mason J said that arts 4, 5 and 6 imposed binding obligations on Australia. The qualifications in art 6 gave some discretion as to how the obligation was to be performed and were not inconsistent with a binding obligation. Article 34, the federal clause, assumed that the Convention imposed obligations. Mason J concluded that the World Heritage (Western Tasmania Wilderness) Regulations were 'appropriate and adapted to the desired end ... the protection and conservation of property which has been entered in the World Heritage List': 153 CLR at 138–9. So, too, were the relevant provisions of the World Heritage Properties Conservation Act 1983. Neither the regulations nor the Act placed a special disability on a state or inhibited or impaired a state's continued existence or capacity to function: 153 CLR at 139–41, 143. Finally, neither the regulations nor the Act involved an acquisition of property: 'neither the Commonwealth nor anyone else acquires by virtue of the legislation a proprietary interest of any kind in the property. The power of the Minister to refuse consent ... is merely a power of veto. He cannot positively authorise the doing of acts on the property. As the State remains in all respects the owner, the consent of the Minister does not overcome or override an absence of consent by the State in its capacity as owner': 153 CLR at 146. Accordingly, the regulations and s 9 of the Act were valid laws with respect to external affairs.

Brennan J: [218] For my part, I would adhere to the view that I expressed in *Koowarta* (1982) 153 CLR at 259–60: a treaty obligation stamps the subject of the [219] obligation with the character of an external affair unless there is some reason to think that the treaty had been entered into merely to give colour to an attempt to confer legislative power upon the Commonwealth Parliament. Only in such a case is it necessary to look at the subject matter of the treaty, the manner of its formation, the extent of international participation in it and the nature of the obligations it imposes in order to ascertain whether there is an international obligation truly binding on Australia. Applying the test which I hold to be appropriate to the circumstances of the present case, the acceptance by Australia of an obligation under the Convention suffices to establish the power of the Commonwealth to make a law to fulfil the obligation. But even if one applies a stricter test — a test that satisfies the qualification expressed by Stephen J — the subject of an obligation accepted by Australia under the Convention is a matter of international concern. The qualification expressed by Stephen J is not difficult to satisfy. ...

It is difficult to imagine a case where a failure by Australia to fulfil an express obligation owed to other countries to deal with the subject matter of a treaty in accordance with the terms of the treaty would not be a matter of international concern, a matter capable of affecting Australia's external relations ... [220] ... Applying the test proposed by Stephen J [in

Koowarta v Bjelke-Petersen], the subject of an obligation binding upon Australia under the Convention enlivens the Commonwealth power.

The more fundamental question is whether the Convention imposes an obligation upon Australia. If the Convention does not impose an obligation, it would be necessary to consider whether the subject with which it deals is nevertheless a matter of international concern. In such a case (and I venture to recall what I said in *Koowarta* (1982) 153 CLR at 258), it would be necessary to determine whether the subject affects or is likely to affect Australia's relations with other international persons, an inquiry of some difficulty.

Brennan J said that the balance to be struck between federal and state powers must not be construed as at federation, and that the Constitution must be interpreted broadly in accordance with varying conditions over time: 158 CLR at 220.

[221] For that reason, where the question is whether the Constitution has used an expression in the wider or in the narrower sense, the Court should, in my opinion, always lean to the broader interpretation unless there is something in the context or in the rest of the Constitution to indicate that the narrower interpretation will best carry out its object and purpose.

That canon of construction ensures that the Parliament is enabled to fulfil the object for which the power was designed. The application of that canon of construction to the affirmative grants of paramount legislative powers gives the Constitution a dynamic force which is incompatible with a static constitutional balance. The complexity of modern commercial, economic, social and political activities increases the connexions between particular aspects of those activities and the heads of Commonwealth power and carries an expanding range of those activities into the sphere of Commonwealth legislative competence. This phenomenon is nowhere more manifest than in the field of external affairs. ...

[222] In the present case, the scope of the external affairs power invoked by the Commonwealth cannot depend upon the undoubted power of a State to legislate for and to control the use of its waste lands; the scope of the external affairs power here depends upon the existence and content of an obligation owed by Australia to other countries by virtue of the operation of international law upon the provisions of the Convention.

I should wish to guard against the suggestion that it is necessary to find such an obligation before one can find an external affair which enlivens the power under s 51(xxix), but in the circumstances of the present case no other foundation for the power appears.

Brennan J concluded that the Convention imposed 'a clear obligation upon Australia to act under arts 4 and 5' because Australia's failure to protect and conserve listed property would 'affect Australia's relations with other nations and communities': 158 CLR at 226. He held that the Wilderness Regulations were valid as 'reasonably conducive to the performance of the obligation imposed by the Convention' (158 CLR at 232–5), that s 9(1)(a)(g) and s 9(2) of the Act were too wide to be described as an implementation of the Convention (158 CLR at 236–7) and that s 9(1)(h) and the regulations prescribing acts in relation to particular property under s 9(1)(h) were valid: 158 CLR at 238–9.

Deane J referred to *R v Burgess; Ex parte Henry* (1936) 55 CLR 608 **[3.3.4]** and *Koowarta v Bjelke-Petersen* (1982) 153 CLR 168 **[3.3.15C]**. He accepted and agreed with 'the views expressed by a majority of the court in *Burgess'* case' — 'that the "substantial subject matter of external affairs" includes "the carrying out", within or outside Australia, of an agreement binding the Commonwealth in relation to other countries whatever the subject matter of the agreement may be': 158 CLR at 258. His Honour continued:

Deane J: [258] It is ... relevant for present purposes to note that the responsible conduct of external affairs in today's world will, on occasion, require observance of the spirit as well as the letter of international agreements, compliance with recommendations of international agencies and pursuit of international objectives which [259] cannot be measured in terms of binding obligation ...

On the other hand, a law cannot properly be characterised as a law with respect to external affairs if its direct operation is upon a domestic subject matter which is not in itself within the ambit of external affairs and if it lacks the particular operation which is said to justify such characterisation. Thus, a law would not properly be characterised as a law with respect to external affairs if it failed to carry into effect or to comply with the particular provisions of a treaty which it was said to execute (see *Burgess'* case and *Airlines of NSW (No 2)*) or if the treaty which the law was said to carry into effect was demonstrated to be no more than a device to attract domestic legislative power: *Burgess'* case (55 CLR at 687, 642 and 669); *Koowarta* (153 CLR at 231, 260). More importantly, while the question of what is the appropriate method of achieving a desired result is a matter for the Parliament and not for the court (see *Poole (No 2)*, at 644, 647–8 and 655; *Airlines of NSW (No 2)*, at 136), the law must be capable of being reasonably considered to be appropriate and adapted to achieving what is said to impress it with the character of a law with respect to external affairs ...

Deane J then referred to the principle of proportionality as a means of satisfying the appropriate and adapted test. But see now *Victoria v Commonwealth* (the *Industrial Relations Act* case) (1996) 187 CLR 416 **[3.3.40C]**:

[260] Implicit in the requirement that a law be capable of being reasonably considered to be appropriate and adapted to achieving what is said to provide it with the character of a law with respect to external affairs is a need for there to be a reasonable proportionality between the designated purpose or object and the means which the law embodies for achieving or procuring it. Thus, to take an extravagant example, a law requiring that all sheep in Australia be slaughtered would not be sustainable as a law with respect to external affairs merely because Australia was a party to some international convention which required the taking of steps to safeguard against the spread of some obscure sheep disease which had been detected in sheep in a foreign country and which had not reached these shores. The absence of any reasonable proportionality between the law and the purpose of discharging the obligation under the convention would preclude characterization as a law with respect to external affairs notwithstanding that Tweedledee might, 'contrariwise', perceive logic in the proposition that the most effective way of preventing the spread of any disease among sheep would be the elimination of all sheep. The law must be seen, with 'reasonable clearness', upon consideration of its operation, to be 'really, and not fancifully, colourably, or ostensibly, referable' to and explicable by the purpose or object which is said to provide its character; cf, as [261] regards the defence power, *Rex v Foster* ((1949) 79 CLR 43 at 84); *Shrimpton v The Commonwealth* ((1945) 69 CLR 613 at 623–4); *Marcus Clarke & Co Ltd v The Commonwealth* ((1952) 87 CLR 177 at 215–16 and 256). In that regard, the 'peculiar' or 'drastic' nature of what the law provides or the fact that it pursues 'an extreme course' is relevant to characterization; cf *Rex v Foster* (79 CLR at 96–7).

Later, Deane J dealt with the topic of specificity of international obligations:

[261] International agreements are commonly 'not expressed with the precision of formal domestic documents as in English law' ... That absence of precision does not, however, mean any absence of international obligation. In that regard, it would be contrary to both the theory and practice of international law to adopt the approach which was advocated by Tasmania and deny the existence of international obligations unless [262] they be defined with the degree of precision necessary to establish a legally enforceable agreement under the common law ...

However loosely such obligations may be defined, it is apparent that Australia, by depositing its instrument of ratification, bound itself to observe the terms of the Convention and assumed real and substantive obligations under them ... Those obligations include the primary 'duty of ensuring', among other things, the protection, conservation and presentation of the relevant property (art 4) and an express undertaking to 'endeavour, in so far as possible, and as appropriate for each country', to 'take the appropriate legal, scientific, technical, administrative and financial measures necessary for the identification, protection, conservation, presentation and rehabilitation' thereof (art 5(d)) ...

Deane J referred to the federal clause in the Convention:

[263] It was submitted on behalf of Tasmania that the effect of the provisions of art 34 is to absolve the Commonwealth of the obligation to carry the Convention into effect in so far as the protection or conservation of properties situated within a State is concerned. In my view, there is a plain answer to that submission. Article 34 acts on the distribution of powers under the Constitution. As I have indicated, I consider that, under that distribution of powers, the carrying into effect of the Convention is within the paramount legal jurisdiction of the Commonwealth Parliament by virtue of the express grant of legislative power contained in s 51(xxix). It follows that, far from absolving the Commonwealth of the obligation to implement the provisions of the Convention, art 34 underlines, in express terms, the 'obligations' of the Commonwealth in that regard. I would add that, even if I had been [264] persuaded that the Commonwealth could avoid the obligation to carry the Convention into effect by relying upon the provisions of art 34, I would have been of the view that the decision whether or not reliance should, in fact, be placed on the provisions of that article would be a matter for decision by the Commonwealth in the conduct of Australia's external affairs.

~~~

[3.3.22] Deane J concluded that the World Heritage (Western Tasmania Wilderness) Regulations were valid because they were capable of being considered as an implementation of the Convention (principally because the 'extremely wide' restrictions which they imposed applied only in that area of the national parks where the Hydro-Electric Commission was constructing a dam): 158 CLR at 278–9. However, Deane J held that paras (a)–(g) of s 9(1) of the Act could not be supported by s 51(xxix) of the Constitution and were invalid. This was because 'all of the prohibitions contained in paras (a) to (g) ... are automatically imposed in respect of any property which is proclaimed by the Governor-General pursuant to s 6(3), regardless of their appropriateness for the purpose of protecting or conserving the property and regardless of whether any relationship at all exists between all or any of the prohibited acts and the nature and source of likely damage to the property': 158 CLR at 266. There was a lack of 'reasonable proportionality' between those provisions and the purpose of protecting and conserving the relevant property and thereby complying with the obligations under the Convention: 158 CLR at 266–7.

Deane J concluded that, because the regulations prohibited a wide variety of specific activities and 'any other works', they effectively excluded the Hydro-Electric Commission from putting the land to any use at all. Although the Commonwealth gained no material benefit from this exclusion, the exclusion was imposed to enable the Commonwealth to fulfil its international obligations and should be regarded as an acquisition of property within s 51(xxxi) of the Constitution. In his view, the Act (which established a system of assessing compensation for any acquisition effected by the regulations) did not provide 'just terms' to Tasmania or the Hydro-Electric Commission for this acquisition and so the regulations were invalid. However, s 9(1)(h) of the Act did not involve an acquisition of property because the only prohibited acts were those involving damage to or destruction of the relevant property and the construction of a dam.

Accordingly s 9 of the Act, other than paras (1)(a) to (1)(g), was a valid law with respect to external affairs.

Murphy J delivered a separate judgment to substantially the same effect as Mason and Deane JJ on the scope of the external affairs power. Murphy J said that s 51(xxix) 'extended to the execution of treaties by discharging obligations or obtaining benefits, but it is not restricted to treaty implementation': 158 CLR at 170.

The Commonwealth could, he said, legislate on any matter of international concern which might be demonstrated by 'the other nation States generally [or] by the world's scientific community or a significant part of it': 158 CLR at 171. He agreed with Mason J that the regulations and the Act implemented the obligations imposed on Australia by the Convention and were valid.

Wilson J delivered a separate judgment to the same effect as Gibbs CJ. Dawson J held (as had Gibbs CJ and Wilson J) that the Commonwealth could not legislate so as to implement the Convention because the subject matter of the Convention was not of sufficient 'international concern' to make it part of Australia's external affairs: 158 CLR at 311. He did not decide whether the Convention imposed obligations on Australia.

In the result, the court decided that the World Heritage (Western Tasmania Wilderness) Regulations were invalid, as were s 9(1)(a) to (g) of the World Heritage Properties Conservation Act. But s 9(1)(h) of the Act was held to be valid and, as a result, it was unlawful for any person (except with the Commonwealth Minister's consent) to carry out any works associated with the construction of the Franklin Dam. The court also upheld the validity of s 10(4) of the Act, and held that s 11 of the Act was invalid. The majority of the court held that s 11 was a special law with respect to the people of the Aboriginal race and, accordingly, supported by s 51(xxvi), though one member of that majority, Deane J, held that s 11 infringed s 51(xxxi) because it acquired property otherwise than on just terms. That conclusion, when combined with the votes of the minority that s 11 was not supported by s 51(xxvi), rendered s 11 invalid.

Notes

Expansive reading of Commonwealth power

[3.3.23] The decision in the *Tasmanian Dam* case (1983) 158 CLR 1 **[3.3.21C]** generated a strongly critical reaction from the defenders of the states' political autonomy. That reaction was expressed in the written submission of the Queensland Premier to the Constitutional Commission's Advisory Committee on the Distribution of Powers. He called for:

> ... urgent action to halt the misuse of the external affairs power that has occurred in recent years as a result of the expanded interpretation given to it by the High Court ... [Y]our Committee will recognise that the traditional balance of power between the Commonwealth and the States is being destroyed by the expansionary interpretation given to s 51(xxix) (*Advisory Committee on Distribution of Powers* (1987) p 82).

A similar point was to be made by Dawson J in *Richardson v Forestry Commission* (1988) 164 CLR 261 **[3.3.34C]**. As there was 'no practical limit to the scope of the external affairs power', his Honour said that s 51(xxix) 'has the potential to obliterate the division of legislative power otherwise effected by s 51': 164 CLR at 321. Concern for the position of the states permeated Justice Dawson's jurisprudence on the external affairs power. See also Dawson (1984).

'Obligation' and 'international concern'

[3.3.24] When compared to *Koowarta v Bjelke-Petersen* (1982) 153 CLR 168 **[3.3.15C]**, the court's decision and reasons in *Commonwealth v Tasmania* (the *Tasmanian Dam* case) (1983) 158 CLR 1 **[3.3.21C]** certainly involve an expansion of the scope of s 51(xxix). A majority of the court now concluded that the Commonwealth Parliament could legislate to implement, for Australia, any international obligation which the Commonwealth Government had assumed under a bona fide international treaty, and that the subject matter of the obligation, which might otherwise lie outside the powers conferred on the Commonwealth, was not relevant to this proposition.

[3.3.25] Although that conclusion cleared the way for a significant expansion of the Commonwealth's legislative authority, the decision did not represent an unequivocal endorsement of Commonwealth legislative hegemony. In particular, Brennan J saw the presence of an obligation as integral to the treaty implementation aspect of s 51(xxix). In the absence of a relevant obligation in the treaty, the Commonwealth Parliament could only legislate under the external affairs power to implement the treaty where its subject matter was of international concern. The question would be 'whether the subject affects or is likely to affect Australia's relations with other international persons', which posed, Brennan J conceded, 'an inquiry of some difficulty': 158 CLR at 220.

[3.3.26] How much of a restriction on the expansionist use of s 51(xxix) was Brennan J suggesting? Although he stressed the need to locate an obligation in the treaty (unless the treaty could be shown to deal with a matter of international concern), he demonstrated a relatively liberal approach to the location of such an obligation in the Convention. This was not, he said, an exercise in 'jurisprudential analysis of the terms of the Convention'; rather, the question was whether failure to observe the terms of the World Heritage Convention would affect Australia's relations with other nations and communities; and, unless the international community were hypocritical and cynical, 'only an affirmative answer is possible': 158 CLR at 226. This approach was broadly similar to that of Mason J (158 CLR at 132–4) and Deane J: 158 CLR at 261–2. It was adopted in *Richardson v Forestry Commission* (1988) 164 CLR 261 **[3.3.34C]** by, for example, Wilson J: 164 CLR at 300. Commenting on this aspect of the decision in *Commonwealth v Tasmania* (the *Tasmanian Dam* case) (1983) 158 CLR 1, Geoffrey Sawer suggested that there would be 'few occasions upon which the approach of Brennan J leads him to differ in the result from the rest of the ... majority': Sawer (1984) p 213.

[3.3.27] In the absence of an obligation, would Brennan J's insistence that the treaty must, to be part of 'external affairs', deal with a matter of international concern represent a significant constraint on the expansionist use of s 51(xxix)? On the one hand, Mason J insisted that this concept raised no real barrier to the implementation of international agreements, his Honour considering that '[t]he existence of international character or international concern is established by entry by Australia into the convention or treaty': 158 CLR at 125.

On the other hand, Brennan J indicated that he did not see the World Heritage Convention as dealing with a matter of international concern when he observed that 'no other foundation for the power [apart from an obligation] appears': 158 CLR at 222. And the minority justices concluded that the Convention did not deal with a matter of international concern. Gibbs CJ, for example, said that interest in the protection of the environment and cultural heritage had increased, but this interest had not 'become such a burning international issue' that Australia's failure to take protective measures would affect its relations with other nations: 158 CLR at 101–2.

[3.3.28] In *Victoria v Commonwealth* (the *Industrial Relations Act* case) (1996) 187 CLR 416 **[3.3.40C]**, all judges, including Dawson J who disagreed with the broad approach taken by the majority, rejected the view that for a treaty to fall within the power it must be on a matter of international concern: 187 CLR at 485 per Brennan CJ, Toohey, Gaudron, McHugh and Gummow JJ; 187 CLR at 570–1 per Dawson J. However, the majority did not reject 'matters of international concern' as an *alternative* basis to enliven the power.

[3.3.29] Underlying the different evaluations of the subject matter of the Convention adopted, for example, by Gibbs CJ and Mason J in the *Tasmanian Dam* case (1983) 158 CLR 1 **[3.3.21C]**, were contrasting views of the court's capacity to determine the question of 'international concern'.

Mason J said there were no 'acceptable criteria or guidelines by which the Court can determine the "international character" of the subject matter of a treaty or convention', and that the court should not undertake the 'invidious task' of substituting 'its judgment for that of the executive government and Parliament ... that the subject matter of the convention is of international character and concern and that its implementation will be a benefit to Australia'. These were not questions on which the court could 'readily arrive at an informed opinion': 158 CLR at 125.

While Gibbs CJ would 'have preferred a more precise test', and acknowledged that the question was 'one of some difficulty', he said 'the court must form its own impression of the facts, in part on the basis of judicial notice': 158 CLR at 101–2.

Given that a majority of the court saw the notion of 'international concern' as providing an alternative basis for invoking s 51(xxix), the view expressed by Mason J may be impossible to sustain. Mason J acknowledged that s 51(xxix) included subject matters of international concern not yet incorporated in a treaty (158 CLR at 131–2), as did Murphy J (148 CLR at 172), Deane J (158 CLR at 258–9), and, more equivocally, Brennan J: 158 CLR at 222. If an international concern, independent of a formal agreement to which Australia is a party, was indeed an alternative 'external affair' within s 51(xxix), it is clear that some standards and processes will have to be adopted for determining whether that concern exists.

Federal concerns

[3.3.30] As indicated above (at **[3.2.3]**), a key theme in these cases was concern for the relative power of the states. As in *Koowarta v Bjelke-Petersen* (1982) 153 CLR 168 (1982) at 198 **[3.3.15C]**, Gibbs CJ stressed the need in the *Tasmanian Dam* case (1983) 158 CLR 1 **[3.3.21C]** to take account of the federal character of the Constitution, which divided legislative authority between the Commonwealth and the states. To accept that s 51(xxix) included the power to implement any treaty obligation on matters of domestic concern, he said, would enlarge the Commonwealth's authority to embrace 'literally all fields of activity' and ensure that '[t]he division of power between the Commonwealth and the states which the Constitution effects could be rendered quite meaningless': 158 CLR at 100. This approach was criticised by Mason J as one of the 'ritual invocations of "the federal balance"': 158 CLR at 129. He implied that it was based on an assumption of state 'reserved powers' (158 CLR at 128), as did Deane J: 158 CLR at 254. Gibbs CJ sought to anticipate and avoid this criticism. He denied that he was suggesting 'that by the Constitution any powers are reserved to the states'. Rather, he was asserting that no single legislative power should be interpreted so as to give the Commonwealth Parliament 'a universal power of legislation': 158 CLR at 100.

However, the majority in the *Tasmanian Dam* case must be taken to have rejected this attempt to confine s 51(xxix). It was their view that the topics which might be brought within s 51(xxix) depended upon the evolving international order and its current agenda, not upon the conception of federalism in the minds of the nineteenth century drafters of the Commonwealth Constitution. For example, Brennan J said that the Commonwealth's legislative powers should be read broadly so as to give 'the Constitution a dynamic force which is incompatible with the static constitutional balance', acknowledging that 'the complexity of modern commercial, economic, social and political activities ... carries an expanding range of those activities into the sphere of Commonwealth legislative competence': 158 CLR at 221.

Furthermore, the notion of a 'federal balance' is not an apt description of the Australian federal model. Section 109 of the Constitution clearly indicates that the Commonwealth has legislative supremacy. There is no 'balance' then, but rather an environment of what may be described as 'controlled dominance'. The degree of dominance is controlled by those express constitutional provisions that evoke federal divisions of power (such as s 114), and the doctrine of the implied autonomy and integrity of the states recognised in *Melbourne Corporation v Commonwealth* (the *State Banking* case) (1947) 74 CLR 31 **[8.2.45C]**. The majority justices' view of the World Heritage Convention's 'federal clause', art 34, is broadly reflective of their attitude to the minority's references to the federal character of the Commonwealth Constitution.

Brennan J referred to the hypothesis underpinning art 34; namely, that entering into the Convention would not affect the distribution of powers within a federal state party. That hypothesis, he said, was not consistent with the constitutional law of Australia. Entering into the Convention brought the power to implement it to the Commonwealth: 158 CLR at 228.

Article 34, Deane J said, 'acts on the distribution of powers under the Constitution', which gave to the Commonwealth Parliament the power to carry the Convention into effect. Far from denying the obligatory nature of the Commonwealth's commitments under the Convention, art 34 underlined, in express terms, the Commonwealth's obligations: 158 CLR at 263. See also Mason J (158 CLR at 136) and Murphy J: 158 CLR at 178.

Of the minority justices, Gibbs CJ was non-committal on this point (158 CLR at 106–7), but Wilson and Dawson JJ said art 34 was significant, as it operated to confine the Commonwealth's obligation under the Convention to informing the competent authorities in the states (in this case, Tasmania) of the substantive provisions of the Convention and recommending to those authorities that they take action to implement the Convention: 158 CLR at 195, 313.

Bona fides

[3.3.31]   Again, as in *Koowarta v Bjelke-Petersen* (1982) 153 CLR 168 **[3.3.15C]**, the majority justices in the *Tasmanian Dam* case (1983) 158 CLR 1 **[3.3.21C]** indicated one judicially enforced control on the expansionist use of s 51(xxix): in the words of Brennan J, a treaty obligation was an 'external affair' within s 51(xxix) 'unless there is some reason to think that the treaty had been entered into merely to give colour to an attempt to confer legislative power upon the Commonwealth Parliament' (158 CLR at

219); see also Deane J's reference to 'a device to attract legislative power': 158 CLR at 259. The justices seemed to favour 'an initial presumption of "genuineness"': Sawer (1984) p 202. The critical question focuses on the process by which this presumption might be displaced: What would be the elements of a 'colourable treaty'; and through what evidence would those elements be established?

On the first point, no member of the court has yet attempted to answer Gibbs CJ's objection, in *Koowarta's* case (1982) 153 CLR 168 **[3.3.15C]**, that this constraint on the use of s 51(xxix) was 'at best a frail shield': 153 CLR at 200. Gibbs CJ said that 'bad faith' could not be established by showing that the government, when it entered into a treaty, knew that the Commonwealth lacked the legislative power, apart from the contingent power, under s 51(xxix), to legislate on the treaty's subject matter.

On the second point, Sawer suggested that 'the trend of decision seems to favour rather than discourage judicial investigation of the ministerial purposes which provide the substance of "Crown" decisions', and referred to *R v Toohey; Ex parte Northern Land Council* (1981) 151 CLR 170 and *FAI Insurance Ltd v Winneke* (1982) 151 CLR 342: Sawer (1984) p 204. However, the position adopted in the *Tasmanian Dam* case (1983) 158 CLR 1 by Mason J on the capacity of the court to assess the international character or concern of a treaty's subject matter, suggests that this is an area where 'the trend of decision' may not venture further. Mason J said that these were questions in which 'the court cannot substitute its judgment for that of the executive government and Parliament' because they were 'issues involving nice questions of sensitive judgment which should be left to the executive government for determination': 158 CLR at 125.

The conformity test

[3.3.32]   The one clearly viable limitation on the treaty implementation power which emerged from the *Tasmanian Dam* case (1983) 158 CLR 1 **[3.3.21C]** is the requirement that legislation which implements a treaty must conform to that treaty. For Brennan and Deane JJ, the legislation enacted under the Convention was that which could 'reasonably be considered conducive to the performance' of the obligation imposed by the Convention (Brennan J, 158 CLR at 232) or that which was capable of being reasonably seen 'to be "really, and not fancifully, colourably, or ostensibly, referable" to ... the purpose' of the Convention: 158 CLR at 260 per Deane J. Applying that approach, those justices found the parts of s 9(1) (other than para (h)) to go beyond what was required to implement the Convention and, accordingly, joined Gibbs CJ, Dawson and Wilson JJ in holding those parts invalid.

It is not immediately clear that Mason and Murphy JJ had a different view of the necessary degree of conformity with the Convention. Murphy J wrote of legislation which 'may reasonably be regarded as appropriate for implementation of provisions of the treaty' (158 CLR at 172) and Mason J wrote that the 'legislative provisions [must be] appropriate and adapted to the desired end': 158 CLR at 138. It may be, given the relatively imprecise nature of these various formulations of the necessary 'conformity', that the differences of judicial opinion over the validity of the bulk of s (9)(1) of the Act merely reflected different assessments of the requirements of the Convention and of the terms of the Act.

[3.3.33]   The High Court's decision in *Richardson v Forestry Commission* (1988) 164 CLR 261 **[3.3.34C]** expanded upon a number of issues raised by the *Tasmanian*

Dam case (1983) 158 CLR 1 **[3.3.21C]**. Besides confirming the broad approach to the treaty implementation aspect of the power, the court considered:

- the issue of when a law can be said to conform to the terms of the treaty;

- the extent of the Commonwealth's power to enact a law in the absence of a treaty obligation;

- the concept of a treaty obligation; and

- the extent of Commonwealth power to enact laws based on non-obligatory aspects of an international agreement.

[3.3.34C]   **Richardson v Forestry Commission**
(1988) 164 CLR 261

The Lemonthyme and Southern Forests (Commission of Inquiry) Act 1987 (Cth) provided for the establishment of a Commission of Inquiry into two areas in Tasmania for the purpose of ascertaining whether any part of the area was, or contributed to, a world heritage area within the Convention for the Protection of the World Cultural and Natural Heritage (the Convention). (The central parts of the Convention are set out in the *Tasmanian Dam* case (1983) 158 CLR 1 **[3.3.21C]**.)

Section 16(1) of the Act declared that it was unlawful for any person to do any of the following acts, except with the written consent of the Minister, until 42 days after the end of the period of one year from 8 May 1987 or after the Minister's receipt of the Commission's final report:

(a) for the purposes of, or in the course of carrying out, forestry operations, to kill, cut down or damage a tree in, or remove a tree or a part of a tree from, the protected area;

(b) to construct or establish a road or vehicular track within the protected area:

(c) to carry out an excavation works within the protected area;

(d) to do any other act prescribed for the purposes of this paragraph, being an act capable of adversely affecting the protected area.

According to s 19(1), the Minister was to 'have regard only to Australia's obligations under the convention' when determining whether or not to give consent under s 16.

The two areas consisted of some 283,300 hectares (about 4.5 per cent of Tasmania's land surface). They were adjacent to the world heritage area in the south-west of Tasmania which was at the centre of the dispute in the *Tasmanian Dam* case **[3.3.21C]**. The two areas were largely wilderness areas owned by the state of Tasmania and used for forestry operations. About 235 hectares of land were privately owned and used for grazing operations.

The Commonwealth Minister for the Environment and the Arts began proceedings in the High Court of Australia for an injunction to restrain the Forestry Commission of Tasmania, a statutory authority with control and management of state forest timber, and a private company which harvested and milled timber in Tasmania, from acting in contravention of s 16 of the Lemonthyme and Southern Forests (Commission of Inquiry) Act.

Mason CJ granted interlocutory injunctions and reserved a series of questions for the consideration of the Full Court, including the question whether the Lemonthyme and Southern Forests (Commission of Inquiry) Act was invalid.

After referring to the decision in the *Tasmanian Dam* case (1983) 158 CLR 1 **[3.3.21C]**, Mason CJ and Brennan J held that the Convention imposed an obligation on each party to identify, protect, conserve and present the world heritage situated on its territory, and that in the matter of identification, this obligation rested exclusively, not primarily, with the relevant party. They said that the obligation to identify property which may become the subject of protection was 'an element in the duty to ensure protection'. Therefore 'the

Convention does not sustain the view that the duty to ensure protection does not arise or attach to land until the State identifies and delineates that land as part of the heritage' (164 CLR at 290):

Mason CJ and Brennan J: [290] It is for each State to determine what it will do by way of protecting a particular property pending resolution of its status as part of the heritage. But the taking of action by a State to protect or conserve a particular property in its territory pending resolution of the status of that property as part of the heritage is to carry out and give effect to the Convention because the taking of the action is incidental to the State's duty to ensure protection of the heritage and to the attainment of the object of the Convention. Granted ultimate identification of the property as part of the heritage, the absence of such action by way of interim protection in the meantime would expose the property to the possibility of irreparable damage.

The taking of action by way of interim protection pursuant to the external affairs power, eg, by the enactment of legislation [291] prohibiting destruction of, or damage to, particular property, pending a determination of its status as a property to be nominated for inclusion in the World Heritage List may be supported as action which can reasonably be considered appropriate and adapted to the attainment of the object of the Convention, namely the protection of the heritage.

Mason CJ and Brennan J rejected the defendants' argument that the prohibitions imposed by the Lemonthyme and Southern Forests (Commission of Inquiry) Act went beyond Australia's obligations under the Convention:

[292] No doubt some of the acts prohibited by s 16(1)(a), (b) and (c) may be so trivial that they do not present a significant risk of real impairment to the world heritage characteristics of the land in question. None the less the class of acts prohibited, namely tree-felling and removal in the course of forestry operation, road and track construction and excavation, are generally speaking acts involving a potential risk of injury to any qualifying areas which may be in the Lemonthyme and Southern Forests areas. It is therefore appropriate to single them out as objects of prohibition unless the plaintiff consents in writing to them. We should have thought that only by such a means of regulation is it possible to ensure protection of the land in conformity with the Convention. But it is not necessary to go so far. It is enough to say that, subject to the question which we have reserved for later consideration, the provisions are a means for effectuating a desired end which is within power, namely ensuring protection of land which may be identified as part of the world heritage.

Nor, Mason CJ and Brennan J held, did the Lemonthyme and Southern Forests (Commission of Inquiry) Act violate the implied prohibition upon discrimination against a state, by singling out Tasmania:

[293] ... The short answer to this submission is that the defendants have not established any foundation for a case of invalid discrimination in the sense of a differential treatment of [294] Tasmania which is not occasioned by the subject to which the law relates. The obligation of protection necessarily falls to be discharged with respect to particular properties and a law which is calculated merely to discharge Australia's treaty obligations with respect to a particular property does not invalidly discriminate against the State in whose territory the property is situated. In any event, there is no evidence to suggest that there are areas in other States which have equal or stronger claims to protection under the Convention.

Finally, Mason CJ and Brennan J rejected the defendants' argument that there was no reasonable basis for concluding that the area of land covered by the Lemonthyme and Southern Forests (Commission of Inquiry) Act had potential world heritage characteristics and for subjecting the entirety of the protected area to the regime of protection during the interim protection period:

Broadly speaking, that evidence indicates that there are particular stands of rare timber, aboriginal cave dwellings and archaeological sites. It also indicates that the area, especially the Southern Forests area, which is less well known, may possess important world heritage

characteristics, particularly cave dwellings [295] and archaeological sites, as yet unidentified.
...

The matters to which we have referred provide a basis for a legislative judgment that substantial parts of the area, the location of which cannot be identified at this time with any certainty, may conceivably possess world heritage characteristics which should be protected. If part of an area might possess world heritage characteristics and if that part might be damaged unless the area is protected by legislative measures appropriate to preserve that part, a failure to take those measures involves a risk that the Convention obligation will not be discharged. It is only by taking those measures that the risk of failing to discharge the Convention obligation can be avoided. As the external affairs power is a plenary power, it extends to support a law calculated to discharge not only Australia's known obligations but also Australia's reasonably apprehended obligations. The power extends to support a law required to discharge a treaty obligation which is known to exist and also a law which is required to ensure the discharge of a treaty obligation which is reasonably apprehended to exist. In making provision for the establishment of the Commission of Inquiry and for the regime of interim protection [296] of the protected area, Parliament has made a legislative judgment about the situation and the Convention obligation that may be proved to exist. It is not for us to impugn the bona fides of that judgment. It is enough that the legislative judgment could reasonably be made or that there is a reasonable basis for making it. Particularly is this so when the ultimate decision to be made by the Executive Government, whether the area, or parts of it, should be proposed for inclusion in the World Heritage List, involves a calculus of factors, including factors which are cultural, economic and political. Of course, if the legislative judgment cannot reasonably be supported, the Court will not hesitate to declare that it is invalid as an excess or abuse of power: see *Gerhardy v Brown* (1985) 159 CLR 70 at 139.

Consequently we would answer the first question by declaring that the Act is valid in its entirety.

Deane J said that in characterising a law to see if it fell within a purposive head of power such as external affairs or the defence power, the purpose or object of a law would be relevant: 164 CLR at 307. His Honour said: 'The primary purpose or object of the [external affairs power] is the conduct of the nation's international affairs, including the advancement of its international relations and interests and the discharge of its international obligations, and the power extends to authorise the enactment of some purely domestic measures for the pursuit of that purpose or object': 164 CLR at 308. However, see now *Victoria v Commonwealth* (the *Industrial Relations Act* case) (1996) 187 CLR 416 **[3.3.40C]** for a discussion of the question whether external affairs power is purposive in nature. Deane J then quoted a passage from Latham CJ's judgment in *R v Burgess; Ex parte Henry* (1939) 61 CLR 634 at 644:

Deane J: [308] The Commonwealth Parliament was given power to legislate to give effect to international obligations binding the Commonwealth or to protect national rights internationally obtained by [309] the Commonwealth whenever legislation was necessary or deemed to be desirable for this purpose.

Thus, the external affairs power encompasses the purposive power to carry out treaties by domestic legislation: 'all powers necessary or proper for performing ... obligations ... towards foreign countries, arising under treaties': cf *British North America Act* 1867, s 132 and per Latham CJ, *Burgess* (1936) 55 CLR at 637–43. It authorises not only domestic laws enacted for the purpose of 'a carrying out' of the external obligation but also laws providing for 'anything reasonably incidental to the execution of [that] purpose' per Dixon J (1936) 55 CLR at 674. ...

Deane J said there was 'inevitably a degree of tension between the legislative function of the Parliament and the judicial function of the court' in characterising purposive powers.

[310] In the context of the scope of contemporary international relations and of the nature of modern warfare, there are few domestic laws which could not arguably be seen as capable

of affecting or bearing upon the country's external affairs or defence. It would, however, be to ignore the constitutional context of the specific grants of legislative power contained in paras (xxix) and (vi) of s 51 to hold that the fact that the economic, social and moral well-being of the Commonwealth and its citizens is conducive to international standing and prestige, to the domestic observance of fundamental human rights and other standards or objectives enshrined in international conventions and to an adequate defence establishment or capacity, means that the combined effect of those two subsections is effectively to confer general legislative powers on the Parliament with respect to the economic, social and moral well-being of the Commonwealth and its citizens, subject only to the proviso that it must be possible to identify, in the case of an impugned law, a relevant purpose of advancing or serving the nation's external affairs or defence ...

[313] The provisions of the Act, read in the context of the material before the Court, disclose that a purpose or object which the Act as a whole is designed to serve is the identification, delineation and protection of actual and potential world heritage areas and the procurement of information and advice with respect to that identification and delineation and with respect to related questions, such as the relationship between world heritage areas and adjoining areas and the availability of alternative resources. Those are all matters involved in, or conducive to, the identification, discharge and pursuit of the international obligations, aspirations and objectives which Australia undertook or to which it subscribed by becoming a party to the Convention. That being so an underlying purpose or object which the Act manifests is a legitimate subject of external affairs, namely, the discharge and pursuit of obligations, aspirations and objectives imposed or recognised and accepted by an international treaty to which Australia is a party. It will, on occasion, be convenient to refer to that purpose or object as 'the international purpose or object'.

Deane J held that the provisions of Pt II of the Act, establishing the Commission of Inquiry into the Lemonthyme and Southern Forests areas, were plainly within the legislative competence of the parliament to make laws with respect to external affairs. His Honour continued:

[314] Once one passes from the provisions of the Act concerned with the actual establishment and conduct of the Commission (ie Pt II) to the provisions of the Act concerned with the interim preservation and protection of the protected areas (ie Pt III), one passes from provisions aimed at obtaining information and advice to provisions establishing a legislative regime which, to a significant degree, prevents or freezes the development and inhibits the use of the lands to which it applies. As has been said, the protection of actual and potential world heritage areas is a purpose or object to which Australia has subscribed by becoming a party to the Convention. It is, however, far from self-evident that a law establishing a conservation regime of direct Commonwealth control, in relation to domestic matters which are not of themselves subjects of Commonwealth legislative or administrative powers, over a large area of State territory containing no listed or nominated world heritage areas, can properly be characterised, for the purposes of s 51(xxix), as a law with respect to external affairs simply because the affected territory is adjacent to World Heritage areas or is said to include some parts which could be considered as natural or cultural heritage appropriate for nomination for World Heritage listing. Even if it be accepted that the international purpose or object underlies the provisions of the Act imposing the restrictive Commonwealth regime, those provisions will, as has been seen, bear the character of a law with respect to external affairs for the purposes of s 51(xxix) only if it appears that their domestic operation to impose and provide for the enforcement of restrictions and restraints in relation to the protected areas is reasonably capable of being seen as appropriate and adapted to the genuine pursuit of that purpose or object ...

Deane J referred to the existence within the protected areas of 'freehold land owned by individuals': 164 CLR at 316.

[317] [T]he material before the Court leads inevitably to the conclusion that there has been no real effort made to confine the prohibitions of the overall protective regime, with the overriding of the ordinary rights of citizens and the ordinary jurisdiction of the State of

Tasmania which it would involve, to activities which it might reasonably be thought represented some real actual or potential threat to what might properly be seen, for the purposes of the Convention, as natural or cultural heritage ... On the material before the Court, it is impossible to say that it appears that there is reasonable proportionality between the provisions of Pt III of the Act, when they are viewed as a whole, imposing that overall restrictive regime and the designated intention, purpose or object. That being so, those provisions are not, when so viewed, capable of being reasonably considered to be appropriate and adapted to achieve the purpose or object which is said to provide them with the character of a law with respect to external affairs. Accordingly, the provisions of Pt III of the Act cannot, taken collectively, be sustained by s 51(xxix) of the Constitution. The question arises whether those provisions of Pt III are all invalid or whether some of them are severable and either valid, when viewed independently, or susceptible of being read down to validity.

Deane J concluded that s 16(1)(b), (c) and (d) were wholly invalid but that only part of s 16(1)(a) was invalid; namely, its prohibition on the removal of a tree or part of a tree.

Dawson J indicated that he continued to regard the decision in *Commonwealth v Tasmania* (the *Tasmanian Dam* case) (1983) 158 CLR 1 **[3.3.21C]** as inconsistent with the Constitution. However, as the parties had not questioned that decision, he was prepared to assume its authority: 164 CLR at 321–3. He referred to *Koowarta v Bjelke-Petersen* (1982) 153 CLR 168 **[3.3.15C]** and *R v Burgess; Ex parte Henry* (1936) 55 CLR 608 **[3.3.9]** and continued:

Dawson J: [325] It has been said more than once that where legislation implements a treaty, it is the implementation of the treaty which is the subject matter falling within the external affairs power rather than the subject matter of the treaty. Thus Mason J in the *Tasmanian Dam* case rejected the notion that once Australia enters into a treaty Parliament may legislate with respect to the subject matter of the treaty as if that subject matter were a new and independent head of Commonwealth legislative power. He continued (1983) 158 CLR at 131–2:

> The law must conform to the treaty and carry its provisions into effect. The fact that the power may extend to the subject matter of the treaty before it is made or adopted by Australia, because the subject matter has become a matter of international concern to Australia, does not mean that Parliament may depart from the provisions of the treaty after it has been entered into by Australia and enact legislation which goes beyond the treaty or is inconsistent with it.

I must confess that I have some difficulty with those remarks. I cannot see why, if it is international concern which gives a subject matter the character to bring it within the description of external affairs, the conclusion of a limited treaty upon that subject matter should place outside the external affairs power that part of the subject matter which is beyond the limits of the treaty. Nor can I see why legislation passed with respect to a matter of international concern should no longer be legislation with respect to external affairs simply because Australia becomes a party to a treaty upon a more limited basis than is reflected by the legislation.

I suspect that the tendency to bring the focus back to the treaty stems from a desire to find practical limits to the ambit of the external affairs power lest the Court be seen to have relinquished in all but a theoretical sense the capacity to determine for itself the constitutional validity of legislation passed pursuant to that head of power. I think that a similar inclination lies behind the view that the external affairs power, like the defence power, is purposive in nature: see the *Tasmanian Dam* case, per Deane J (1983) 158 CLR at 260–1.

Dawson J said that the Convention gave to each signatory an absolute discretion to determine the measures appropriate for the identification and protection of the cultural and natural heritage within its territory:

[327] The only possible question is whether the measures contained in the legislation are reasonably capable of being considered appropriate by the legislature for the identification and preservation of the nation's heritage and to answer that question in the negative would be tantamount to an imputation of mala fides. No such imputation has been made in this case.

The Convention does not require proportionality between its aims and the measures taken to achieve them. That is a matter which is expressly left to the discretion of the parties. If the power thereby bestowed upon the legislature seems somewhat open-ended, it is not the result of any abdication by the Court of its role as an arbiter of constitutional [328] validity but stems from the far-reaching view that a law which fulfils the provisions of a bona fide treaty, whatever they might be, is a law with respect to external affairs.

For these reasons and upon the assumptions which I have made I think that the answer to the first question is that the Lemonthyme and Southern Forests (Commission of Inquiry) Act 1987 (Cth) is wholly valid.

~~~

[3.3.35] Wilson J said he was obliged to accept the authority of the decision in the *Tasmanian Dam* case (1983) 158 CLR 1 **[3.3.21C]**, to the effect that the Convention imposed obligations on Australia, for the observance of which the Commonwealth could legislate. He dealt with the defendants' first submission, that the Convention did not oblige Australia to protect property which had not been identified as part of the world heritage. He said that, although the Convention did not contain an express obligation to that effect, Australia was obliged to identify world heritage areas in its territory. Accordingly, parliament must be conceded the right to take appropriate measures to protect a world heritage area during the process of identification. He also held at 304:

> The protective provisions [of the Act] fall within the range of discretion conceded to the Parliament in carrying out the obligation which the Convention imposes on it.

Toohey J delivered judgment in substantially the same terms as Mason CJ and Brennan J. He also held that the Lemonthyme and Southern Forests (Commission of Inquiry) Act did not discriminate against Tasmania as a member of the federation, nor did it hinder or impair the continued existence of Tasmania or its capacity to function.

Gaudron J delivered judgment in terms similar to those adopted by Deane J, holding that s 16(1)(d) was invalid and, on the material before the court, s 16(1)(a), (b) and (c) must be held to be invalid. She explained her view in the following passage at 347–8:

> Because s 16 must be viewed as affording general environmental protection rather than protection of the qualities and features which may be of outstanding universal value, it is not on the material before the court reasonably capable of being viewed as appropriate or adapted to the circumstances that the areas may be or contain areas constituting part of the world heritage. It cannot on the available material be characterised as a law with respect to external affairs. Nor, in my view, is that conclusion altered by the possibility that the proscription may be relaxed with the consent of the Minister.

Notes

Conformity and characterisation

[3.3.36] The majority's decision in *Richardson v Forestry Commission* (1988) 164 CLR 261 **[3.3.34C]** that the protective provisions of the Act amounted to an implementation of the Convention's obligation indicates a degree of judicial deference to the judgment of parliament on the measures appropriate for the purpose of implementing such an obligation.

For example, Mason CJ and Brennan J clearly regarded it as sufficient to support the legislation that there was 'a basis for a legislative judgment that substantial parts of the area … may conceivably possess world heritage characteristics' and that a failure to protect those parts 'involves a risk that the Convention obligation will not be discharged'. It was 'enough that the legislative judgment could reasonably be made or that there is a reasonable basis for making it': 164 CLR at 295–6. Wilson J referred to 'the range of discretion conceded to the Parliament in carrying out the obligation which the Convention imposes upon it': 164 CLR at 304. Dawson J saw that discretion as extremely wide; '[t]he only possible question', he said, was whether the legislation was 'reasonably capable of being considered appropriate by the legislature' for the discharge of the Convention's obligation, and a negative answer 'would be tantamount to an imputation of mala fides': 164 CLR at 327.

It seems that Toohey J had in mind a more rigorous, objective assessment of the legislation. Thus, 'viewed objectively', the present legislation was capable of being reasonably considered as appropriate and adapted to the implementation of the Convention: 164 CLR at 336. Gaudron J adopted a similar approach, although her conclusion differed from that of Toohey J: 164 CLR at 345–8.

Deane J certainly employed a more rigorous standard. Although he insisted that it was for parliament to select the appropriate means of implementing the Convention (164 CLR at 310, 311) he said that there must be 'reasonable proportionality' between the legislation (here, the restrictions imposed by s 16 on the use of the land in question) and the purpose of protecting potential world heritage areas, a test which the legislation failed: 164 CLR at 317. Earlier, he had indicated that this approach was a means towards ensuring that s 51(xxix) was not expanded into a general power to legislate on 'the economic, social and moral wellbeing of the Commonwealth and its citizens' (164 CLR at 310) giving particular point to the comments of Dawson J on the court appearing to have relinquished its capacity to determine the validity of legislation passed under s 51(xxix): 164 CLR at 325.

Obligation

[3.3.37]   The willingness of the court in *Richardson v Forestry Commission* (1988) 164 CLR 261 **[3.3.34C]** to find in the Convention an obligation on Australia to identify property of world heritage value and to protect property with such a potential pending its identification and recognition, indicates an expansive view of the basis on which the s 51(xxix) power depends. That is, this decision continues 'the relaxed concept of "obligation" derived from the views of the majority in the *Tasmanian Dam* case', as Wilson J put it: 164 CLR at 300.

Absence of a treaty obligation

[3.3.38]   Equally, the decision in *Richardson v Forestry Commission* (1988) 164 CLR 261 **[3.3.34C]** was a clear endorsement of the central proposition in *Commonwealth v Tasmania* (the *Tasmanian Dam* case) (1983) 158 CLR 1 **[3.3.21C]**; namely, that s 51(xxix) will support Commonwealth legislation which discharges an obligation imposed on Australia by an international treaty, whatever the subject matter of that obligation. However, the decision does not resolve the question left open in the *Tasmanian Dam* case; that is, the precise extent of s 51(xxix) in the absence of a treaty obligation. Gaudron J clearly favoured the widest possible view of s 51(xxix), as expressed by Mason, Murphy and Deane JJ in the *Tasmanian Dam* case (164 CLR at 342), whereas Toohey J was more equivocal, describing the treaty obligation as 'sufficient, though not necessary', to invoke s 51(xxix) (164 CLR at 332), as was the joint judgment of Mason CJ and Brennan J: 164 CLR at 289. However, the last two justices were prepared to extend the power to the discharge of 'Australia's reasonably apprehended obligations': 164 CLR at 295.

[3.3.39]   In any event, the decision in *Queensland v Commonwealth* (the *Daintree Rainforests* case) (1989) 167 CLR 232 **[3.3.7]** demonstrates that, in identifying an international obligation, the High Court will not adopt a narrow or restrictive approach but will defer to the attitude of the international community. In that case, Mason CJ, Brennan, Deane, Toohey, Gaudron and McHugh JJ said, at 241–2:

> From the viewpoint of the international community, the submission by a State Party of a property for inclusion in the World Heritage List and inclusion of the property in the List by the Committee are the means by which the status of a property is ascertained and the duties attaching to that status are established. The State Party's submission of a property is some evidence of its status but the Committee's listing of a property is conclusive, for the benefits of listing are available only to properties having the status of being part of the cultural heritage or natural heritage ... In the international community a decision by a municipal court that a property does not have that status cannot prevail over an evaluation made by the Committee which results in the property's inclusion in the World Heritage List. So long as a property is included in that list, the State Party on whose territory the property is situated and who submitted an inventory including the property as part of the cultural heritage or natural heritage is under an international duty to protect and conserve it. ...

> As the inclusion of the property in the List is conclusive of its status in the eyes of the international community, it is conclusive of Australia's international duty to protect and conserve it. Its inclusion is therefore conclusive of the constitutional support for the proclamation of 15 December 1988 ...

Dawson J adopted an even less restrictive approach to the identification of Australia's obligation under the Convention, at 248:

> Once property has been identified by the Commonwealth as part of the cultural or natural heritage of Australia it is under an international obligation to protect it. That obligation exists regardless of any further assessment of the status of the property.

Dawson J observed that, if it was 'startling' that the court could not examine a bona fide decision by the Commonwealth that a property was part of Australia's cultural or natural heritage, he could 'only comment' at 249:

> ... that the way in which the Convention is framed lays the foundation for legislation leading to that result. The validity of the legislation is a consequence of the expansive view of the external affairs power taken in the *Tasmanian Dam* case.

[3.3.40C]   **Victoria v Commonwealth**

(The *Industrial Relations Act* case)
(1996) 187 CLR 416

The Industrial Relations Act 1988 (Cth) was amended by the Industrial Relations Reform Act 1993 (Cth) and the Industrial Relations Amendment Act (No 2) 1994 (Cth). The amendments imposed obligations upon employers in relation to minimum wages, equal pay, termination of employment, discrimination in employment and family leave, and provided for collective bargaining and the right to strike.

Victoria, South Australia and Western Australia each brought proceedings against the Commonwealth seeking declarations that certain provisions of the Act were invalid. The three matters were, by consent, heard together and a case stated by Dawson J for consideration by the Full Court.

The Commonwealth argued that many of the provisions contained in the amending Acts were enacted pursuant to its power with respect to external affairs. A number of the provisions reflected matters the subject of international conventions and recommendations made by the International Labour Organisation; while others, such as freedom of association and the right to strike, were claimed to reflect rights under customary international law.

The states challenged the legislation on a number of grounds, including that it was beyond the external affairs power. This aspect of the challenge rested upon three main premises:

- first, that to fall within the treaty implementation aspect of the external affairs power, the matter must also be one of 'international concern';

- second, that the relevant ILO conventions and recommendations did not impose any obligation on the Commonwealth which was sufficient to fall within the external affairs power; and

- third, that there was no conformity between the international instruments and the domestic law.

In addition, the states proposed arguments based upon the scope of the conciliation and arbitration power in s 51(xxxv) and the corporations power in s 51(xx), the implied prohibition against discrimination against the states, and the just terms guarantee in s 51(xxxi).

After referring to the fact that the Imperial government consulted with the colonies in relation to the making of international agreements prior to federation and with the Commonwealth after that date, Brennan CJ, Toohey, Gaudron, McHugh and Gummow JJ noted that the Commonwealth assumed international personality by about 1919. Their Honours continued:

Brennan CJ, Toohey, Gaudron, McHugh and Gummow JJ: [478] As things stood in 1900, the subjects of treaties were various. This is significant for the present case, because it indicates that the limited view of the scope of federal legislative power, urged by the plaintiff States, does not proceed from an accurate understanding of the range of subject matter to which s 51(xxix) applied as it stood as long ago as federation.

The justices said there had been 'continual expansion in the range of the subject-matter of treaties entered into between Great Britain and other states': 187 CLR at 478. They referred to a range of international agreements and institutions which existed prior to federation, including: the International Telegraph Union (1865), the Universal Postal Union (1874), the International Convention for the Protection of Industrial Property (1883), the Hague Convention for the Pacific Settlement of International Disputes (1899), and other agreements in the fields of 'what now would be called international human rights, world health and environmental protection': 187 CLR at 479. Their Honours continued:

[482] It would be a serious error to construe par (xxix) as though the subject-matter of those relations to which it applied in 1900 were not continually expanding. Rather, the external relations of the Australian colonies were in a condition of continuing evolution and, at that time, were regarded as such. Accordingly, it is difficult to see any justification for treating the content of the phrase 'external affairs' as crystallised at the commencement of federation, or as denying it a particular application on the ground that the application was not foreseen or could not have been foreseen a century ago. ...

[483] There was some suggestion in the submissions of the plaintiff States in the present case that what has come to pass with the legislation they seek to impugn is something beyond contemplation at the time of the adoption of the Constitution. Any such proposition is, as we have endeavoured shortly to illustrate, too widely stated. The treaties which were part of the subject matter of foreign relations in 1900, and the treaties that have since been made, embrace an ever-expanding range of topics.

The content of the relevant executive power of the Commonwealth under s 61, and the legislative power of the Parliament under s 51(xxix), are to be understood accordingly. Thus, as long ago as 1936, Evatt and McTiernan JJ said (*R v Burgess* 55 CLR at 687):

> But it is not to be assumed that the legislative power over 'external affairs' is limited to the execution of treaties or conventions; and ... the Parliament may well be deemed competent to legislate for the carrying out of 'recommendations' as well as the 'draft international conventions' resolved upon by the International Labour Organisation or of other international recommendations or requests upon other subject matters of concern to Australia as a member of the family of nations.

Their Honours also said in that case (55 CLR at 680–1):

> [A] consequence of the closer connection between the nations of the world (which has been partly brought about by the modern revolutions in communication) and of the recognition by the nations [484] of a common interest in many matters affecting the social welfare of their peoples and of the necessity of co-operation among them in dealing with such matters, that it is no longer possible to assert that there is any subject matter which must necessarily be excluded from the list of possible subjects of international negotiation, international dispute or international agreement.

The justices referred to the states' argument for a return to the narrow view of the treaty implementation aspect of the external affairs power consistent with Stephen J's view in *Koowarta v Bjelke-Petersen* (1982) 153 CLR 168 **[3.3.15C]**:

> ... the Solicitor-General for Victoria contended for a criterion of validity which resembled that adopted by Stephen J or alternatively that of the minority judges in *Koowarta*. He submitted that, even upon this limited footing, the result in The *Tasmanian Dam* Case (158 CLR 1) would have been the same. Therefore, the submission proceeded, there was no occasion to seek leave to reopen the correctness of The *Tasmanian Dam* Case.

> The difficulty in the path of these submissions is that subsequently the majority in The *Tasmanian Dam* Case adopted the broader view. It is not to the point that the same result might have been achieved by application of the view previously taken by Stephen J. It is to seek to distort the principles of *stare decisis* and of *ratio decidendi* ... to contend that a decision lacks authority because it might have been reached upon a different path of legal reasoning to that which was actually followed. That would be to replace what was decided by that [485] which might have been decided. According to basic constitutional principle, and with qualifications not presently relevant, the intrusion of Commonwealth law into a field that has hitherto been the preserve of State law is not a reason to deny validity to the Commonwealth law provided it is, in truth, a law with respect to external affairs. ...

[486] *(iii) The legislative implementation of a treaty*

There may be some treaties which do not enliven the legislative power conferred by s 51(xxix) even though their subject matter is of international concern. For example, Professor Zines has suggested that a treaty expressed in terms of aspiration (for example 'to promote full employment') cannot support a law which adopts one of a variety of possibly contradictory ways that might be selected to fulfil the aspiration. He writes (Zines (1992) p 250):

> Accepting ... that the agreement by nations to take common action in pursuit of a common objective amounts to a matter of external affairs, the objective must, nonetheless, be one in relation to which *common* action can be taken. Admittedly, this raises questions of degree; but a broad objective with little precise content and permitting widely divergent policies by parties does not meet the description.

When a treaty is relied on under s 51(xxix) to support a law, it is not sufficient that the law prescribes one of a variety of means that might be thought appropriate and adapted to the achievement of an ideal. The law must prescribe a regime that the treaty has itself defined with sufficient specificity to direct the general course to be taken by the signatory states. But, as Judge Dillard observed in his opinion in the *Appeal Relating to the Jurisdiction of the ICAO Council,* ((1972) ICJ Rep 46 at 107n) the point at which ideals merge into legal obligations 'constitutes one of the most delicate and difficult problems of law and especially so in the international arena where generally accepted objective criteria for determining the meaning of language in light of aroused expectations are more difficult to ascertain and apply than in domestic jurisdictions'. However, Deane J has pointed out in the *Tasmanian Dam* case (158 CLR at 261–2):

> [A]bsence of precision does not, however, mean any absence of international obligation. In that regard, it would be contrary to both the theory and practice of international law to adopt the approach which was advocated by Tasmania and deny the existence of international obligations unless they be defined with the degree of precision necessary to establish a legally enforceable agreement under the common law.

Where the legislative power is said to be enlivened by a treaty binding on the Commonwealth of Australia, and the law prescribes a regime affecting a domestic subject matter, a question arises as to the **[487]** connection which must exist between the law and the treaty. To be a law with respect to 'external affairs', the law must be reasonably capable of being considered appropriate and adapted to implementing the treaty. Thus, it is for the legislature to choose the means by which it carries into or gives effect to the treaty provided that the means chosen are reasonably capable of being considered appropriate and adapted to that end (*Airlines of NSW* 113 CLR at 136; *Tasmanian Dam* case 158 CLR at 130–1, 172, 232, 259; *Richardson v Forestry Commission* 164 CLR 261 at 288–9, 303, 311–12, 336, 342). But that is not to say that an obligation imposed by treaty provides the outer limits of a law enacted to implement it. [See the statements collected by Gaudron J in *Richardson v Forestry Commission* (164 CLR at 341–2).] The term 'purpose' has been used to identify the object for the advancement or attainment of which a law was enacted. Hence, the statement by Brennan J in *Cunliffe v Commonwealth* (182 CLR at 322) that the external affairs power has 'a purposive aspect'. As this phrase indicates, care is required in relevant analysis. Where a treaty relating to a domestic subject matter is relied on to enliven the legislative power conferred by s 51(xxix) the validity of the law depends on whether its purpose or object is to implement the treaty. This was explained, in a passage with which we respectfully agree, by Dawson J in *Richardson v Forestry Commission* (164 CLR at 326):

> The power to make laws with respect to external affairs contains no expression of purpose and in that respect it is like most of the other powers contained in s 51 of the Constitution. It is not a power to make laws for the purpose of cementing international relations or achieving international goodwill or even for implementing international treaties. The implementation of treaties falls within the power because it is a subject matter covered by the expression 'external affairs'. And the purpose of legislation which purports to implement a treaty is considered not to see whether it answers a requirement of purpose to be found in the head of power itself, but to see whether the legislation operates in fulfilment of the treaty and thus upon a subject which is an aspect of external affairs.
>
> In this context, purpose is not something found in the head of power. Rather, it is a test for determining whether the law in question is reasonably capable of being considered as giving effect to the treaty and therefore as being a law upon a subject which is an aspect of external affairs.

It has been said that a law will not be capable of being seen as appropriate and adapted in the necessary sense unless it appears that there is 'reasonable proportionality' between that purpose or object **[488]** and the means adapted by the law to pursue it (*Richardson v Forestry Commission* 164 CLR at 311–12). The notion of 'reasonable proportionality' will not always be particularly helpful. The notion of proportion suggests a comparative relation of one thing to another as respects magnitude, quantity or degree; to ask of the legislation whether it may reasonably be seen as bearing a relationship of reasonable proportionality to the provisions of the treaty in question appears to restate the basic question. This is where the law selects means which are reasonably capable of being considered appropriate and adapted to achieving the purpose or object of giving effect to the treaty, so that the law is one upon a subject which is an aspect of external affairs.

In the *Tasmanian Dam* case, the Wilderness Regulations that were under attack implemented only in part the supporting Convention. They were nevertheless upheld. A criterion of validity expressed in *R v Burgess; Ex parte Henry* namely, whether the regulations could fairly be regarded as 'sufficiently stamped with the purpose of carrying out the terms of the convention' (*Ex parte Henry* 55 CLR at 688) was applied by Brennan J (*Tasmanian Dam* case 158 CLR at 234). Deane J dealt as follows with 'partial' legislative implementation (*Tasmanian Dam* case 158 CLR at 268):

> It is competent for the Parliament, in a law under s 51(xxix), partly to carry a treaty into effect or partly to discharge treaty obligations leaving it to the States or to other Commonwealth legislative or executive action to carry into effect or discharge the outstanding provisions or obligations or leaving the outstanding provisions or obligations unimplemented or unperformed. On the other hand, if the relevant law 'partially' implements the treaty in the sense that it contains provisions which are consistent with the terms of the treaty and also contains significant provisions which are inconsistent with those terms, it would be extremely unlikely that the law could properly be characterised as a law with respect to external affairs on the basis that it was capable of being reasonably considered to be appropriate and adapted to giving effect to the treaty.

[489] Deficiency in implementation of a supporting Convention is not necessarily fatal to the validity of a law; but a law will be held invalid if the deficiency is so substantial as to deny the law the character of a measure implementing the Convention or it is a deficiency which, when coupled with other provisions of the law, make it substantially inconsistent with the Convention.

Applying the test of conformity stated above, Brennan CJ, Toohey, Gaudron, McHugh and Gummow JJ concluded that the provisions dealing with minimum wages, equal remuneration for work of equal value, and parental leave were valid because they gave effect to the terms of the international instruments they purported to implement. The justices considered the provisions concerning equal remuneration for work of equal value which gave effect to international conventions and to international recommendations:

[508] The power of the Commission in s 170BC(3) to make an order is conditional upon the requirement that the order 'can reasonably be regarded as appropriate and adapted to giving effect to' one of the Conventions or Recommendations referred to. That wording plainly reflects the criterion for validity of a law enacted in reliance on s 51(xxix) to implement a treaty. It was supported by a number of [509] members of this Court in the *Tasmanian Dam* case (158 CLR at 130–1, 172, 232, 259–60). If the broad provisions of the Division had the effect that they allowed the Commission to make orders that were not so limited, arguably the section would be beyond power. The limitation has the effect that the general nature of the provision is confined in effect by the constitutional limit on the power of the Parliament to enact such legislation. It is not the case that the Commission is given the power to determine the constitutionality of its own order as might be the case if the words of par (b) were preceded by the words that appear in par (a), 'the Commission is satisfied that'. Rather, the test is an objective one, and is subject to judicial review by this Court or the Industrial Relations Court of Australia (the Industrial Relations Court).

The section refers separately to a measure being reasonably regarded as appropriate and adapted for giving effect to Recommendation No 90 or Recommendation No 111. That provision can be supported under s 51(xxix) if, but only if, the terms of these Recommendations themselves can reasonably be regarded as appropriate and adapted to giving effect to the terms of the Conventions to which they relate. In our view, they can be so regarded. Hence measures that fall within the terms of s 170BC(1) and implement the terms of the Recommendations will fall within the terms of s 170BC(3)(b)(i). On this line of reasoning, the words 'can reasonably be regarded as appropriate and adapted to' in s 170BC(3)(b) may be superfluous in relation to the Recommendations but are obviously designed to cover the situation where the Recommendations are relied upon of themselves to support an exercise of the external affairs power. This is a point which, at this stage, it is not necessary to decide.

Although the Family Responsibilities Convention did not specify maternity, paternity or parental leave, their Honours said that the legislation implementing the Convention was valid.

[522] The Family Responsibilities Convention itself does not refer to maternity, paternity or parental leave. It rises no higher than Arts 1, 3 and 4 which relevantly provide:

Article 1

1 This Convention applies to men and women workers with responsibilities in relation to their dependent children, where such responsibilities restrict their possibilities of preparing for, entering, participating in or advancing in economic activity ...

[523] **Article 3**

1 With a view to creating effective equality of opportunity and treatment for men and women workers, each Member shall make it an aim of national policy to enable persons with family responsibilities who are engaged or wish to engage in employment to exercise their right to do so without being subject to discrimination and, to the extent possible, without conflict between their employment and family responsibilities.

2 For the purposes of paragraph 1 of this Article, the term 'discrimination' means discrimination in employment and occupation as defined in Articles 1 and 5 of the Discrimination (Employment and Occupation) Convention, 1958.

Article 4

With a view to creating effective equality of opportunity and treatment for men and women workers, all measures compatible with national conditions and possibilities shall be taken:

(a) to enable workers with family responsibilities to exercise their right to free choice of employment; and

(b) to take account of their needs in terms and conditions of employment and in social security.

Further, Art 7 provides:

All measures compatible with national conditions and possibilities, including measures in the field of vocational guidance and training, shall be taken to enable workers with family responsibilities to become and remain integrated in the labour force, as well as to re-enter the labour force after an absence due to those responsibilities.

Also relevant are the terms of the Family Responsibilities Recommendation referred to in s 170KA(1)(b). Paragraph 22 of that Recommendation provides:

(1) Either parent should have the possibility, within a period immediately following maternity leave, of obtaining leave of absence (parental leave), without relinquishing employment and with rights resulting from employment being safeguarded.

(2) The length of the period following maternity leave and the duration and conditions of the leave of absence referred to in subparagraph (1) of this Paragraph should be determined in each country by one of the means referred to in Paragraph 3 of this Recommendation.

(3) The leave of absence referred to in subparagraph (1) of this Paragraph may be introduced gradually.

Paragraph 3 of the Recommendation refers to applying the provisions of the Recommendation by 'laws or regulations, collective agreements, work rules, arbitration awards, court decisions or a [524] combination of these methods, or in any other manner consistent with national practice'.

The quoted Articles of the Family Responsibilities Convention impose obligations on Australia and, whilst they are expressed in more than terms of aspiration, they are set forth in general terms. There is no specific provision relating to parental leave. Nevertheless, in the conditions of society and industrial organisation in this country, an obvious means of discharging the obligations imposed by Arts 3, 4 and 7 is to provide for parental leave.

Thus, the challenged provisions are reasonably capable of being considered appropriate and adapted to fulfilling one element of Australia's obligations under the Family Responsibilities Convention. That is because the law falls within the terms of the obligation imposed by Arts 4(b) and 7. These specify that 'all measures ... shall be taken ... to take account of their needs in terms and conditions of employment' (Art 4(b)) and to enable them to 'become and remain integrated in the labour force' (Art 7). Division 5 can reasonably be seen as an attempt to do this. That is reinforced by the reference to parental leave in the Family Responsibilities Recommendation. This confirms the appropriateness of a law relating to parental leave to fulfilling Australia's obligations under the Family Responsibilities Convention. As we have explained earlier in these reasons, the circumstance that only part of the broad obligations imposed on Australia by the Family Responsibilities Convention is implemented in the Division of itself is no objection to its validity. [(292) See the authorities in fn 249.]

Brennan CJ, Toohey, Gaudron, McHugh and Gummow JJ held that provisions dealing with termination went 'beyond the terms of the Convention to a constitutionally impermissible degree': 187 CLR at 518. Although Article 4 of the Convention prohibited termination of employment unless there was a valid reason, and Article 5 set out reasons which would not be considered 'valid', the criterion in the Convention was the need for a valid reason. By contrast the legislation, by referring to 'harsh, unjust and unreasonable' termination, included in s 170EDA(1)(b) an 'additional ground of unlawful termination that goes beyond the requirement for the reason for termination to be valid': 187 CLR at 517.

The justices held that the provisions giving a former employee a remedy for unfair dismissal, where he or she was dismissed on the ground of age, sexual preference or physical disability, were a valid exercise of the external affairs power because the provisions discharged an obligation assumed by Australia under International Labour Convention 111, the Discrimination (Employment and Occupation) Convention.

Articles 2 and 3 of the Convention obliged each party to enact legislation for the purpose of eliminating discrimination in employment. Article 1 defined discrimination to mean any distinction made on the basis of certain specified characteristics (such as race and sex) and any other distinction determined by a party to the Convention after consultation with representative organisations of employers and employees. The Commonwealth had nominated, as additional grounds of discrimination in employment for the purposes of the Convention, age, sexual preference, physical disability and mental disability. The Commonwealth had carried out the required consultation in relation to the first three grounds; but could not demonstrate that it had carried out that consultation in relation to the ground of mental disability. In their joint judgment, Brennan CJ, Toohey, Gaudron, McHugh and Gummow JJ said that, because it appeared that there had been the consultation required by the Convention prior to the determination by Australia to discharge its Convention obligations by adding the grounds of 'age', 'physical disability' and 'sexual preference', the provisions of the Industrial Relations Act 1993 (Cth) dealing with discrimination on those grounds were supported by s 51(xxix) of the Constitution. However, because it appeared that the nomination of 'mental disability' as a ground of discrimination had not been preceded by the required consultation, inclusion of that ground in the Act was unsupported by s 51(xxix): 187 CLR at 532.

Dawson J said that he supported the view he had put in previous cases, including most recently in *Richardson v Forestry Commission* (1988) 164 CLR 261 **[3.3.34C]** that 'the mere fact that a treaty is international in character does not mean that the matters with which it deals cease to be of a domestic nature and become part of a country's external affairs.' His Honour continued:

Dawson J: [567] A law with respect to treaties or the implementation of treaties would operate on treaties as a subject matter. Thus it might deal with the nature of the obligations which could be undertaken by treaty or the manner in which they were to be implemented — for example, whether by regulation or statute. Such a law would be a law with respect to external affairs because it would operate upon a matter which is external to Australia, namely, treaties with other countries. But a law actually implementing a treaty is a law with respect to the subject matter of the treaty and the nature of that subject matter is to be found 'by reference to the nature of the rights, duties, powers and privileges which it changes, regulates or abolishes' (*Fairfax v Federal Commissioner of Taxation* 114 CLR at 7 per Kitto J). It may or may not be with respect to matters external to Australia. And, of course, such a law may deal with matters both internal and external to Australia, and be a law with respect to external affairs. The view of the external affairs power which I favour is not based on the incorrect assumption that 'affairs are either internal or external in the sense that the two categories are mutually exclusive' (*Koowarta v Bjelke-Petersen* 153 CLR at 226 per Mason J). Indeed, in my opinion, it is the prevailing view which involves a characterisation fallacy. That fallacy is to characterise a law which implements a treaty as a law with respect to treaties even though such a law does not operate upon treaties as a subject matter. ...

Dawson J said that this conclusion followed not from implications concerning the federal nature of the Constitution but from 'a distinction which is expressly made by the language used in s 51(xxix) and is not dependent upon implication': 187 CLR at 568. He disputed Mason J's view in *Koowarta v Bjelke-Petersen* (1982) 153 CLR 168 that to adopt any other view would lead to fragmentation of the decision-making process, and a weakening of Australia's international standing. He said that Australia is a federation and a 'fragmentation' of the decision-making process is 'part and parcel of a federal system': 187 CLR at 568; and referred to the Canadian experience of regularly using federal state clauses in treaties to accommodate its federal requirements. 'No doubt there have been times when Canada has been inconvenienced by the "watertight compartments which are an essential part of her original structure" ... but convenience is hardly to be weighed against the basic principle of federalism': 187 CLR at 569.

Dawson J rejected the test of 'international concern' proposing instead that the correct test was one of 'externality':

[569] The external affairs power is a broad power but for a law to fall within its terms, it must, in my view, operate upon something which is external to Australia. That is to give the power no narrow construction. A glance at the many treaties entered into by Australia in recent years shows that laws implementing the vast majority of them would deal with matters having an external aspect sufficient to satisfy such a test. (Eg, to name but a few subjects, Australia is a party to treaties dealing with extradition, the law of the sea, marine pollution, the exploration for and exploitation of petroleum resources in areas of the continental shelf, air navigation, atmospheric pollution, diplomatic representation, international telecommunications, international child abduction, drug trafficking, conservation of migratory animals, smuggling of endangered species, and international trade.) But a law which has an entirely domestic operation cannot, in my view, be a law with respect to external affairs merely because it implements a treaty or is upon a subject matter which is of international concern.

Dawson J referred to the view that the external affairs power was purposive, and continued:

[572] The external affairs power is not purposive. As I pointed out in *Richardson* (164 CLR 261 at 325–6), it is not a power to make laws for the purpose of cementing international relations or achieving international goodwill or even for implementing treaties. It is a power to make laws with respect to particular matters, namely, external affairs, and the subject matter of a law either answers that description or it does not. A purposive power is different. Taking the defence power, which is truly purposive, it is possible to ask whether a law is for the purpose of defence and to take the view that the disproportion of the law to the achievement of that purpose suggests that it is not a law for that purpose. It is not possible to ask whether a law is for the purpose of external affairs. Either it falls within that description or it does not and whether it does or does not is to be determined by reference to the acts, facts, matters or things upon which it operates. The question to be asked is not, as in the case of a purposive power, what the law is for, but what it operates upon. The concept of proportionality has no useful part to play in answering that question.

Dawson J concluded that, although he disagreed with the reasoning of the majority, and as the parties did not challenge the authority of the *Tasmanian Dam* case, he would, on the basis of precedent, agree with the orders proposed by the majority.

~~~

Notes

[3.3.41] In *Victoria v Commonwealth* (the *Industrial Relations Act* case) (1996) 187 CLR 416 **[3.3.40C]** the court clarified a number of apparent contradictions in its external affairs jurisprudence. The narrow view of s 51(xxix) taken by Stephen J in *Koowarta v Bjelke-Petersen* (1982) 153 CLR 168 at 216–17 **[3.3.15C]**, that a law implementing a treaty must be on a topic 'of especial concern to the relationship between Australia and that other country' or 'of general international concern' was rejected. The court noted that, in the *Tasmanian Dam* case (1983) 158 CLR 1 **[3.3.21C]**, it had adopted a broader view: that the presence of a treaty obligation provided a conclusive indication that a matter was of international concern.

[3.3.42] The *Industrial Relations Act* case **[3.3.40C]** also clarified the way in which the concept of 'proportionality' is to be used in the context of the external affairs power. In the *Tasmanian Dam* case (1983) 158 CLR 1 at 260–1 **[3.3.21C]**, Deane J had suggested that it was proper for the court to consider whether the domestic legislation was a proportionate response to the treaty. If it was not, then s 51 (xxix) might not be available to support it. As Brennan CJ, Toohey, Gaudron, McHugh and Gummow JJ noted in the *Industrial Relations Act* case:

> It has been said that a law will not be capable of being seen as appropriate and adapted in the necessary sense unless it appears that there is 'reasonable proportionality' between that purpose or object and the means adapted by the law to pursue it (164 CLR 261 at 311–12). The notion of 'reasonable proportionality' will not always be particularly helpful. The notion of proportion suggests a comparative relation of one thing to another as respects magnitude, quantity or degree; to ask of the legislation whether it may reasonably be seen as bearing a relationship of reasonable proportionality to the provisions of the treaty in question appears to restate the basic question. This is whether the law selects means which are reasonably capable of being considered appropriate and adapted to achieving the purpose or object of giving effect to the treaty, so that the law is one upon a subject which is an aspect of external affairs (187 CLR at 487–8).

The difference is between the court asking whether the legislation is reasonably appropriate and adapted or is reasonably capable of being considered appropriate and adapted. The latter approach shows more deference to the legislature and is also easier to reconcile with the proposition that partial implementation of a treaty is permissible.

[3.3.43] Finally, Dawson J, who had dissented in the earlier cases on the external affairs power, joined in the order made by Brennan, Toohey, Gaudron, McHugh and Gummow JJ, ending a long period of division within the court over the issue. There is no requirement in this context for 'federal balance', and the controlling doctrine in the external affairs area, as with the other paragraphs of s 51, is that of implied autonomy and integrity recognised by the court in *Melbourne Corporation v Commonwealth* (the *State Banking* case) (1947) 74 CLR 31 **[8.2.45C]**. In fact, the *Industrial Relations Act* case was the first decision since the *State Banking* case in which the general aspect of that doctrine, preventing the Commonwealth from legislating in a way that interferes with the states' capacity to function independently, was applied by the High Court.

Matters of 'international concern'

[3.3.44]   In *Commonwealth v Tasmania* (the *Tasmanian Dam* case) (1983) 158 CLR
1 **[3.3.21C]** a majority of the court said that 'international concern' might provide an
alternative basis for the Commonwealth to invoke s 51(xxix). That possibility
received qualified confirmation in *Polyukhovich v Commonwealth* (1991) 172 CLR
501, where the High Court held that a series of amendments made in 1988 to the
War Crimes Act 1942 (Cth) were valid. The amendments provided that certain acts
of violence committed in Europe between 1 September 1939 and 8 May 1945 were
punishable as crimes in Australia. These amendments were laws with respect to
external affairs, the majority held, because the amendments dealt with events or
occurrences which had occurred outside Australia: see **[3.3.3]**. Two members of the
court also considered whether the 1988 amendments could be supported by other
aspects of s 51(xxix).

Brennan J, who dissented on the s 51(xxix) aspect of the case (because he required
a connection between Australia and the subject matter of legislation enacted under
the external affairs power), found that the amendments did not discharge any
international obligation imposed on Australia, whether by express treaty or
customary international law, to prosecute war criminals: 172 CLR at 558–9. After
acknowledging that the external affairs power was not restricted to supporting laws
to discharge international treaty obligations, Brennan J then asked whether there
was an 'international concern' in the punishment of war criminals which could
support the 1988 amendments. Brennan J explained his view of this term as follows,
at 561–2:

> One purpose of the external affairs power is to furnish the Commonwealth with
> legislative authority to ensure that Australia acts in accordance with standards
> expected of and by the community of nations, even though those standards are not, or
> have not yet achieved the status of, obligations in international law. The observation
> of those standards may rightly be regarded as a matter of international concern.
> However, unless standards are broadly adhered to or are likely to be broadly adhered
> to in international practice and unless those standards are expressed in terms which
> clearly state the expectation of the community of nations, the subject of those
> standards cannot be described as a true matter of international concern. It may be that
> there are few occasions when the external affairs power is enlivened by the existence
> of a matter of international concern without a corresponding obligation in
> international law, but whether the enlivening factor be an obligation or a concern it is
> necessary to define it with some precision in order to ascertain the scope of the power
> ... It would be erroneous to attribute a scope to the external affairs power which
> depended on the broadest meaning which could be given to the imprecise phrase
> 'international concern'; that phrase is not a constitutional text and is used to indicate
> that the power relates to matters affecting Australia's external relations even if those
> matters are not obligations under international law.

Brennan J concluded that it had not been shown that the apprehension and trial
of war criminals in countries other than those in which the crimes were committed
were ever matters of international concern: at 562.

Toohey J agreed with Brennan J that the 1988 amendments to the War Crimes Act
did not discharge an international obligation of Australia and did not deal with a
matter which had been shown to be of 'international concern', a term which he
regarded as extending to 'a matter touching the public business of Australia in
relation to an event outside Australia': at 657.

[3.3.45] It is likely that Brennan J's conclusion that the apprehension and trial of war criminals did not constitute a matter of international concern calls for re-consideration in the light of recent developments, including:

- the establishment of the International Criminal Tribunal for Rwanda and the International Criminal Tribunal for the Former Yugoslavia;

- the enactment of the International War Crimes Tribunals Act 1995 (Cth) (and similar legislation by the United States, Sweden and the United Kingdom); and

- the international community's renewed enthusiasm for the establishment of an International Criminal Court: see McCormack and Simpson (1997).

Relations with other countries

[3.3.46] Another aspect of the legislative power conferred by s 51(xxix), the power to legislate with respect to relations with other countries, was explored in *R v Sharkey* (1949) 79 CLR 121. Sharkey had been convicted of sedition under s 24D(1) of the Crimes Act 1914 (Cth). The offence consisted, according to s 24B(2), of publishing any matter with a 'seditious intention' which was defined, in s 24A(1), to include an intention:

> (b) to excite disaffection against the Sovereign or the Government or Constitution of the United Kingdom or against either House of the Parliament of the United Kingdom;

> (c) to excite disaffection against the Government or Constitution of any of the King's Dominions.

When Sharkey challenged the validity of those provisions, the High Court held that s 24A(1)(c) was valid under the external affairs power because it was concerned with the relations of the Commonwealth with other countries. Latham CJ expressed this view in the following terms, at 136–7:

> The relations of the Commonwealth with all countries outside Australia, including other Dominions of the Crown, are matters which fall directly within the subject of external affairs, a subject with respect to which the Commonwealth Parliament has power to pass laws — Constitution, s 51(xxix). The preservation of friendly relations with other Dominions is an important part of the management of the external affairs of the Commonwealth.

See also: 79 CLR at 149 per Dixon J; 79 CLR at 157 per McTiernan J; 79 CLR at 163 per Webb J.

[3.3.47] In *Kirmani v Captain Cook Cruises Pty Ltd (No 1)* (1985) 159 CLR 351, some members of the High Court adopted a similar approach in reaching the conclusion that the Commonwealth Parliament could legislate, under s 51(xxix), so as to repeal provisions of the Merchant Shipping Act 1894 (UK), which extended to Australia.

The provisions of the Merchant Shipping Act limited the liability of a shipowner to damages for personal injury to £15 for each ton of the ship's tonnage. The owners of a ship used exclusively within New South Wales, displacing some 283 tons, sought to invoke the limitation of liability contained in the Merchant Shipping Act when sued for damages by a person who had been injured while travelling on the ship. The question then arose whether s 104(3) of the Navigation Amendment Act 1979 (Cth), which purported to repeal the provisions of the Merchant Shipping Act in Australia, was a valid law.

Until the passage of the Australia Act 1986 (UK and Cth), state parliaments were not regarded as competent to repeal those provisions: Colonial Law Validity Act 1865 (UK) s 2.

But the enactment of the Navigation Amendment Act raised the question whether the Commonwealth had any constitutional foundation on which it could construct its repealing legislation, particularly in relation to activities which did not form part of overseas or interstate trade and commerce.

Mason, Murphy and Deane JJ decided that s 104(3) of the Navigation Amendment Act was supported by s 51(xxix) of the Constitution. Mason J noted 'that the expression "external affairs" was adopted in preference to "foreign affairs" [in s 51(xxix)], so as to make it clear that the relationships between the Commonwealth and other parts of the British Empire, especially the United Kingdom, were comprehended': 159 CLR at 379.

A central feature of the relationship with the United Kingdom, he said, was the continued operation, of their own force, of certain statutes of the United Kingdom Parliament in Australia (at 380):

> The consequence is that repeal or amendment of such a statute is an important element in our relationship with the United Kingdom.

Deane J also saw the question of the direct operation of United Kingdom legislation in Australia as lying at the heart of relations between the two countries. Once that conclusion was reached, he said at 439:

> ... it follows that a law repealing such a local operation of a United Kingdom Act is a law for the peace, order and good government of Australia with respect to 'external affairs' since, as has been seen, the 'relations of the Commonwealth with all countries outside Australia, including other Dominions of the Crown, are matters which fall directly within the subject of external affairs': per Latham CJ, *R v Sharkey* 79 CLR at 136.

On the other hand, Gibbs CJ, Wilson and Dawson JJ concluded that the repeal of the Merchant Shipping Act provisions was not supported by the external affairs power. Gibbs CJ said that s 104(3) of the Navigation Amendment Act did not deal with the relations between Australia and the United Kingdom but dealt with the law of an Australian state.

[3.3.48] Since the decision in *Kirmani v Captain Cook Cruises Pty Ltd (No 1)* (1985) 159 CLR 351 **[3.3.47]**, the Australia Act 1986 has removed the residual authority of the United Kingdom Parliament to legislate for Australia (s 1) and empowered state parliaments to repeal United Kingdom statutes extending to the states: s 3.

The first of these changes may serve to expand the Commonwealth's 'external affairs' power. The power would, for example, now authorise the Commonwealth to legislate so as to forbid Australian citizens from complying in Australia with United Kingdom legislation purporting to apply in Australia.

According to Gibbs CJ in *Kirmani's* case, an Act of the Commonwealth 'which denies recognition to a foreign law which purports to affect things done in Australia, but which is not part of the law of Australia, is a law with respect to external affairs': 159 CLR 371.

4   International law as a 'legitimate influence' on Australian law

[3.4.1] In addition to the impact of international law on the institutions of the constitutional system, and its direct introduction through the external affairs power, international law influences Australian law in several ways. International law (both conventional and customary) may be used as an aid in interpreting the common law and statute law; or, according to one view, as an aid in interpreting constitutional provisions. Comparative law principles are used in constitutional interpretation; and international legal institutions affect the Australian legal system, both in respect of particular legal doctrines, and in the federal division of powers.

International treaties, the common law and statute law, including administrative discretions

[3.4.2] It is now well established that entry into a treaty does not, of itself, create any domestic legal obligations: *Dietrich v R* (1992) 177 CLR 293 at 306, 321 and 360; *Minister for Immigration and Ethnic Affairs v Teoh* (1995) 183 CLR 273 at 286–7, 298; *Koowarta v Bjelke-Petersen* (1982) 153 CLR 168 at 212 **[3.3.15C]**; *Re East; Ex parte Nguyen* (1998) 196 CLR 354 at 362. However, although international treaties and conventions do not form part of Australian law until they are implemented by legislation, it is a standard rule of statutory construction that unimplemented international agreements can be referred to by judges in aid of interpretation of legislation, at least in order to resolve an uncertainty or ambiguity (*Dietrich v R* (1992) 177 CLR 292); and possibly also to assist in determining community standards relevant to development of the common law: *Minister for Immigration and Ethnic Affairs v Teoh* (1995) 183 CLR 273 **[3.2.8C]**. In *Teoh*, Mason CJ and Deane J said at 287:

> Where a statute or subordinate legislation is ambiguous, the courts should favour that construction which accords with Australia's obligations under a treaty or international convention to which Australia is a party, at least in those cases in which the legislation is enacted after, or in contemplation of, the relevant international instrument.

[3.4.3] In *Mabo v Queensland (No 2)* (1992) 175 CLR 1 **[2.2.12]**, having referred to an international agreement, Brennan J said at 42:

> The common law does not necessarily conform with international law, but international law is a legitimate and important influence on the development of the common law, especially when international law declares the existence of universal human rights.

The influence of international law extends to the development of the common law in constitutional cases: see *Western Australia v Commonwealth* (the *Native Title Act* case) (1995) 183 CLR 373 **[8.1.74C]** at 436 (Mason CJ, Brennan, Deane, Toohey, Gaudron and McHugh JJ). For example, in *Malika Holdings v Stretton* (2001) 204 CLR 328, Kirby J made the point that 'the *International Covenant on Civil and Political Rights*, art 14.1 treats as an entitlement, in the determination of rights and obligations in a suit at law, access to a competent, independent and impartial tribunal': 204 CLR at [328]. Australian constitutional law rests on a bed of common law principle: *Lange v Australian Broadcasting Corporation* (1997) 189 CLR 520 **[11.3.3C]** at 566; and to the extent that international principles influence the development of the common law, they may inform the context within which constitutional law is developed.

[3.4.4] A difficulty arises in the field of judicial review of administrative action, in particular where the statute does not refer to an international convention, and the decision-maker is exercising a discretionary power under an Act of parliament.

In *Teoh's* case (1995) 183 CLR 273 **[3.2.8C]**, a majority of the High Court, Mason CJ, Deane, Toohey and Gaudron JJ, said that ratification of an international treaty can give rise to a legitimate expectation that the decision-maker will act in conformity with the convention. So, if the decision-maker proposes to make a decision inconsistent with a legitimate expectation, procedural fairness requires that the persons affected should be given notice and an adequate opportunity of presenting a case against the taking of such a course: Mason CJ and Deane J, 183 CLR at 365. See also Toohey J, 183 CLR at 371–2; and Gaudron J, 183 CLR at 375–6.

[3.4.5] Extensive criticism of the *Teoh* decision led to a range of responses from government, including the making of an executive statement by two successive governments to the effect that entering into an international treaty did not give rise to any expectation that government decisions would be made in accordance with the treaty, where its provisions had not been enacted into Australian law. See **[3.2.13]**.

International law and the Constitution

[3.4.6] It has also been suggested that international custom may exert an influence upon constitutional interpretation. In *Newcrest Mining (WA) Ltd v Commonwealth* (1997) 190 CLR 513, Kirby J said at 657:

> Where the Constitution is ambiguous, this court should adopt that meaning which conforms to the principles of fundamental rights rather than an interpretation which would involve a departure from such rights.

His Honour said that, although the court should not adopt an interpretive principle which introduced, by the back door, treaties not yet incorporated into Australian law, the relationship between the two systems was 'undergoing evolution': 190 CLR at 657. Kirby J continued at 657–8:

> To the full extent that its text permits, Australia's Constitution, as the fundamental law of government in this country, accommodates itself to international law, including insofar as that law expresses basic rights. The reason for this is that the Constitution not only speaks to the people of Australia who made it and accept it for their governance. It also speaks to the international community as the basic law of the Australian nation which is a member of that community.

Kirby J referred to provisions of foreign constitutions which protected the right to just terms in the event of compulsory acquisition of property by government and continued at 660–1:

> In effect, the foregoing constitutional provisions do no more than reflect universal and fundamental rights by now recognised by customary international law ... When the foregoing principles, of virtually universal application, are remembered, it becomes even more astonishing to suggest that the Australian Constitution, which in 1901 expressly and exceptionally recognised and gave effect to the applicable universal principle, should be construed today in such a way as to limit the operation of that express requirement in respect of some laws made by its Federal Parliament but not

others. Where there is an ambiguity in the meaning of the Constitution, as there is here, it should be resolved in favour of upholding such fundamental and universal rights ... The Australian Constitution should not be interpreted so as to condone an unnecessary withdrawal of the protection of such rights. At least it should not be so interpreted unless the text is intractable and the deprivation of such rights is completely clear. Neither of these conditions applies here. Nor should arbitrary deprivation of property be lightly attributed to a constitution, such as the Australian Constitution, given the history of its origins and its purpose. That purpose is to be the basic law for the government of a free people in a nation which relates to the rest of the world in a context in which the growing influence of international law is of ever increasing importance.

The influence of comparative law

[3.4.7] Comparative law has long been a rich source of jurisprudential influence on Australian law, including constitutional law. The recognition, in *Australian Communist Party v Commonwealth* (1951) 83 CLR 1, of the principle of judicial review under which legislative power is limited by a written Constitution interpreted and applied by an independent judiciary was based in part upon the foundational US Supreme Court decision, *Marbury v Madison* (1803) 1 Cranch 137. Similarly, *McCulloch v Maryland* 17 US 159 (1819), another watershed US Supreme Court decision, is frequently cited in Australian constitutional law as authority for the propositions that Commonwealth legislative power be read broadly (*O'Sullivan v Noarlunga Meat Ltd* (1954) 92 CLR 565 at 597); but that the legislative means adopted by the parliament should be appropriate and adapted to a legitimate objective within power: *Jumbunna Coal Mine NL v Victorian Coal Miners' Association* (1908) 6 CLR 309 at 357–8.

[3.4.8] Recent indications suggest that the High Court will continue with this trend, although sometimes the influence is seen in the adoption of comparative law principles, and other times in their rejection. As Justice Heydon remarked before his elevation to the High Court, US 'authority ... can usually be found to support any proposition': Heydon (2003). In the implied freedom of political communication cases, the court has relied upon United States, Canadian, English and European authorities in a number of contexts, including:

- the question whether defamation law inhibits freedom of communication: *Theophanous v Herald and Weekly Times* (1994) 182 CLR 104 **[11.3.2C]** at 129–32 (Mason CJ, Toohey and Gaudron JJ); at 157–63 (Brennan J); at 177 (Deane J); at 189 (Dawson J); and at 195 (McHugh J);

- the distinction between categories of public property and the degree of protection afforded to speech on different categories of public property: *Levy v Victoria* (1997) 189 CLR 579 **[11.3.14]** at 638–9 (Kirby J); and

- the recognition that activity constitutes political communication: *Levy v Victoria* (1997) 189 CLR 579 **[11.3.14]** at 594 (Brennan J); at 613 (Toohey and Gummow JJ); at 622–3 (McHugh J); at 637–8 (Kirby J).

Each of those issues was resolved by reference to comparative principles.

[3.4.9] In other contexts, the court has moulded the shape of Australian constitutional law by rejecting principles from other jurisdictions, by defining Australian law against the contrast provided by the laws of other systems. In discussing the characterisation process, Dawson J suggested in *Leask v Commonwealth* (1996) 187 CLR 579 that proportionality, the origins of which are European, is an inappropriate concept 'in Australian constitutional law where legislative power is with few exceptions conferred by reference to subject matter rather than aims or objectives': 187 CLR at 600.

In *Lange v Australian Broadcasting Corporation* (1997) 189 CLR 520 **[11.3.3C]** and in *Kruger v Commonwealth* (1997) 190 CLR 1 **[11.3.5]**, the court confirmed that a breach of an implied constitutional right did not give rise to a cause of action in damages apart from any cause of action arising under the general law of contract or tort: *Lange*, 189 CLR at 562–6 (Brennan CJ, Dawson, Toohey, Gaudron, McHugh, Gummow and Kirby JJ); *Kruger*, 190 CLR at 46–7 (Brennan CJ); at 124–6 (Gaudron J). Whether the court adopts or rejects comparative law, it has an influence upon Australian constitutional law, and is another instance of the increasing effect of globalisation.

International institutions

[3.4.10]   The final example of the influence of international law on Australian law occurs through international institutions. In 1980, after wide consultation with the states (see Charlesworth (1994)), Australia ratified the International Covenant on Civil and Political Rights. In 1991, Australia acceded to the First Optional Protocol to the Covenant, which allowed the Human Rights Committee of the United Nations to receive communications from people who believed their rights under the Covenant had been violated. On the same day, a Tasmanian man, Toonen, lodged a communication with the United Nations Human Rights Committee under the Optional Protocol, alleging that ss 122 and 123 of the Tasmanian Criminal Code, which prohibited consensual sexual acts between men in private, breached arts ss 17(1) (privacy) and 26(1) (equality before the law) and of the Covenant.

In April 1994, the Committee found that the Tasmanian Code breached art 17 in the Covenant, and that therefore Australia was in breach of its obligations. Eight months later, Tasmania not having repealed the relevant provisions, the Commonwealth enacted the Human Rights (Sexual Conduct) Act 1994 (Cth), s 4 of which provided that sexual conduct involving consenting adults in private was not to be subject to any arbitrary interference with privacy within the meaning of art 17 of the Covenant.

Toonen and another Tasmanian, Croome, then commenced an action in the High Court challenging the validity of ss 122 and 123 of the Code, on the ground that those sections were inconsistent with the Commonwealth law. The state of Tasmania objected that the action did not give rise to a 'matter' within s 76 of the Constitution because there was no prospect that either of the plaintiffs would be prosecuted under the Code. In February 1997, the High Court decided that the plaintiffs' action raised a controversy which could properly be resolved by the court and that the case should proceed to a hearing on its merits: *Croome v Tasmania* (1997) 191 CLR 119. Tasmania then withdrew its defence, and its parliament repealed the relevant provisions on 1 May 1997.

[3.4.11]   The significance of these examples is twofold. First, they demonstrate that an international institution can directly influence the Commonwealth to enact a law that, by invoking s 109 of the Constitution, could render state law inoperative. The international institution became implicated in the development of Australian law.

Second, the intervention of the international institution is significant because it triggered movement in the federal relationship. Australian constitutional law is not impervious to the reach of international institutions, or of international treaties. Charlesworth notes that some saw this as a 'common sense application of international human rights standards to an unjust ... Tasmanian law' while others viewed it as a 'usurpation by the United Nations of Australian and Tasmanian sovereignty': Charlesworth (1994) p 462. Mason has argued that Australia is 'abrogating its sovereignty' by failing to provide a mechanism for the 'Australian legal system to adjudicate such issues before an international body does so': Mason (1996) p 28.

5   References

[3.5.1]   *Articles*

Allars, 'One Small Step for Legal Doctrine, One Giant Leap Towards Integrity in Government: *Teoh's* Case and the Internationalisation of Administrative Law' (1995) 17 *Sydney LR* 204.

Charlesworth, 'Protecting Human Rights' (1994) 68 *Law Institute J* 462.

Crock, 'Federalism and the external affairs power' (1983) 14 *Melbourne Uni LR* 238.

Crommelin, 'Comment on the External Affairs Power' (1984) 14 *Federal LR* 208.

Dawson, 'The Constitution — Major Overhaul or Simple Tune-Up?' (1984) 14 *Melbourne University Law Review* 353.

Derkley, 'Gay Law Reform — a Long and Hard-fought Battle' (1997) 32 *Australian Lawyer* 20, June.

Donaghue, 'Balancing Sovereignty and International Law: The Domestic Impact of International Law in Australia' (1995) 17 *Adelaide LR* 213.

Fisher, 'External Affairs and Federalism in the *Tasmanian Dam* Case' (1989) 5 *Queensland Uni of Technology LJ* 157.

Heydon, 'Judicial Activism and the Death of the Rule of Law' (2003) *Quadrant* (January–February) 9.

Mason, 'The Influence of International Transnational Law on Australian Municipal Law' (1996) 7 *Public LR* 20.

Opeskin, 'Constitutional Modelling: The Domestic Effect of International Law in Commonwealth Countries — Part I and Part II' [2000] *Public Law* 607 and [2001] *Public Law* 97.

Rothwell, 'The High Court and the external affairs power: a consideration of its outer and inner limits' (1993) 15 *Adel L Rev* 209.

Sawer, 'The External Affairs Power' (1984) 14 *Federal LR* 199.

Thomson, 'Is it a Mess? The High Court and the War Crimes Case: External Affairs, Defence, Judicial Power and the Australian Constitution' (1992) 22 *Uni of Western Australia LR* 197.

[3.5.2]   *Papers and reports*

Australia, Senate Legal and Constitutional References Committee, *Trick or Treaty? Commonwealth power to make and implement treaties*, Canberra, 1995

Advisory Committee on Distribution of Powers, *Report to the Constitutional Commission*, AGPS, Canberra, 1987.

Charlesworth, *Dangerous Liaisons: Globalisation and Australian Public Law*, paper delivered for the Public Law Weekend, ANU, 7 November 1997.

Department of Foreign Affairs and Trade, *Australia and International Treaty Making*, AGPS, Canberra, 1997.

Senate Legal and Constitutional Legislation Committee, *Administrative Decisions (Effect of International Instruments) Bill 1997*, AGPS, Canberra, 1997.

[3.5.3] *Texts*

Allars, *Australian Administrative Law*, Butterworths, Sydney, 1997.

Alston and Chiam, *Treaty-Making and Australia: Globalisation versus Sovereignty?*, Federation Press, Sydney, 1995.

Campbell, 'Australian Treaty Practice and Procedure' in *International Law in Australia*, (ed Ryan), 2nd ed, Law Book Co, Sydney, 1984, p 53.

Coper, *The Franklin Dam Case*, Butterworths, Sydney, 1983.

Crommelin and Evans, 'Explorations and adventures with Commonwealth powers' in *Labor and the Constitution 1972–1975*, (ed Evans), Heinemann Educational, Sydney, 1977, p 24.

Howard, *Australian Federal Constitutional Law*, 3rd ed, Lawbook Co, Sydney, 1985.

Lane, *The Australian Federal System*, 2nd ed, Law Book Co, Sydney, 1979.

Lumb, *The Constitution of the Commonwealth of Australia Annotated*, 4th ed, Butterworths, Sydney, 1986.

McCormack and Simpson (eds), *The Law of War Crimes: National and International Approaches*, Kluwer Law International, The Hague, 1997.

O'Connell, *International Law*, Stevens, London, 1965.

Opeskin and Rothwell, *International Law and Australian Federalism*, Melbourne University Press, Melbourne, 1997.

Walker, 'Treaties and the Internationalisation of Australian Law' in *Courts of Final Jurisdiction: The Mason Court in Australia*, (ed Saunders), Federation Press, Sydney, 1996.

Wynes, *Legislative, Executive and Judicial Powers in Australia*, 5th ed, Law Book Co, Sydney, 1976.

Zines, *The High Court and the Constitution*, Butterworths, 3rd ed, Sydney, 1992.

Zines, 'The Growth of Australian Nationhood and its Effect on the Powers of the Commonwealth' in *Commentaries on the Australian Constitution*, (ed Zines), Butterworths, Sydney, 1977, pp 1–49.

Chapter

4

Parliament

---

1 Introduction

What is parliament?

[4.1.1] There are several answers to the question, 'What is parliament?'. The answers depend upon one's perspective and experiences. From one perspective, parliament is the linchpin of an ordered, democratic society; the embodiment of the principles of responsible and representative government which are reflected in the Constitution. From another perspective, parliament is a facade, behind which political parties manipulate society in order to serve sectional interests. Other observers regard parliament as a marionette, manipulated by the bureaucracy; and there are other (more idealistic, realistic or cynical) perspectives.

There are also a number of ways in which we might describe parliament. We could describe the way in which individual members relate to other institutions or groups (political parties, the electorate, pressure groups) or the way in which parliament as an institution relates to those groups. We could analyse the business of parliament (as recorded in *Hansard* and its votes and proceedings). But, for the lawyer, the starting point will almost certainly be the legal rules that define parliament, establish its structure, determine its life, specify its membership and prescribe the procedures by which those members are elected.

The legal rules form the framework within which a more complete picture of parliament can be constructed, using the skills and insights of sociologists, political scientists and economists. This chapter is not intended to provide that complete picture, although parts of it will come into focus as we construct the framework. The framework should not be regarded as a concrete, finished product with fixed dimensions and shape for the rules that define parliament are not themselves fixed and certain. Legislation is subject to amendment, judicial pronouncements may be ambiguous, or disregarded by later judges, and many of the more definite rules only make sense when modified or supplemented by other, less certain or more debatable, rules (sometimes called *conventions*, and discussed further at **[5.2.17]**).

2   The structure of parliament

Background

[4.2.1]   There are nine institutions in Australia that have some claim to the title, 'parliament'. They are: the Commonwealth Parliament; the six state parliaments; and the legislative assemblies of the Northern Territory and the Australian Capital Territory. The institutions share legislative power, in a system that is labelled 'federalism'.

The six state parliaments and the Commonwealth Parliament are legally autonomous: none of them is answerable to any other. Constitutional rules define and limit the respective powers of each parliament. The two territory legislatures stand in a special category because they were created by and remain under the direct legal control of the Commonwealth Parliament. They are completely subject to the Commonwealth Parliament and may be altered or abolished by the Commonwealth Parliament at any time: *Berwick Ltd v Gray* (1976) 133 CLR 603; *Northern Land Council v Commonwealth* (1986) 161 CLR 1.

Before the creation of the Commonwealth Parliament and the establishment of our federal system on 1 January 1901, each of the six Australian colonies had its own parliament, and the structure of those parliaments was left largely unregulated by the new Commonwealth Constitution. To find the legal rules which define the state parliaments we must look to state legislation, or to pre-1901 colonial legislation, and to imperial statutes passed by the United Kingdom Parliament.

[4.2.2]   The establishment of the colonial (later, state) and Commonwealth parliaments was sanctioned by the United Kingdom Parliament. In 1901 that was regarded as of prime legal importance, for the parliament at Westminster was seen as the ultimate source of government power; it was sovereign and its legislative pronouncements were seen by Australian judges, lawyers and most politicians as superior to local (colonial) legislation. As recently as 28 years ago, that superiority was assumed by Australian courts, as the judgments in *Bistricic v Rokov* (1976) 135 CLR 552 and *Ukley v Ukley* [1977] VR 121 **[6.2.4]** demonstrate. In each case, the judges (with the exception of Murphy J in the former case) assumed that the United Kingdom Parliament could legislate for New South Wales or Victoria and override state legislative authority, 'although it may seem to many to be anachronistic': *Bistricic v Rokov* (1976) 135 CLR 552 at 651. It was only with the passage of the Australia Act 1986 (Cth and UK) **[6.2.7E]** that Australian parliaments were fully liberated from this subservient status.

State and territory parliaments

History

[4.2.3] The first representative legislature established in Australia was the New South Wales Legislative Council, set up by the Australian Constitutions Act (No 1) 1842 (UK) 5 & 6 Vict c 76. That Act authorised the Governor of the colony with the advice and consent of the Legislative Council to 'make laws for the peace, welfare and good government of the colony'. Eight years later, other Legislative Councils with similar powers were set up in Victoria, Van Diemen's Land, South Australia and Western Australia by the Australian Constitution Act 1850 (UK) 13 & 14 Vict c 59. This Act invited each of the Legislative Councils (including that of New South Wales) to draft and pass its own Constitution Act.

[4.2.4] Tasmania (as Van Diemen's Land was renamed) and South Australia accepted the invitation and the limitations imposed by the 1850 Act: Constitution Act 1856 (SA) 19 & 20 Vict No 2; Constitution Act 1855 (Tas) 18 Vict No 17. Colonial legislation established bicameral legislatures that, with the Governor, had the power to legislate for the peace, welfare and good government of the colonies.

[4.2.5] The New South Wales and Victorian bills went further than the 1850 Act had permitted and further imperial legislation was passed in 1855 to authorise the Queen to assent to the bills passed in the two colonies: New South Wales Constitution Act 1855 (UK) 18 & 19 Vict c 54 with Constitution Act 1855 (NSW) 17 Vict No 4; Victorian Constitution Act 1855 (UK) 18 & 19 Vict c 55 with Constitution Act 1855 (Vic). That 1855 legislation also authorised the Queen-in-Council to establish the northern part of New South Wales as a separate colony, and this was effected in 1859 when an Order-in-Council established the colony of Queensland with a system of government substantially the same as that of New South Wales: Order in Council Empowering the Governor of Queensland to Make Laws of 6 June 1859.

[4.2.6] In each of those five colonies (New South Wales, Queensland, South Australia, Tasmania and Victoria), a bicameral legislature was set up with general legislative power. Members of the upper houses (called the Legislative Council) were elected on a property franchise (South Australia, Tasmania and Victoria) or nominated for life by the Governor (New South Wales and Queensland). Members of the lower houses (called the Legislative Assembly or, in South Australia and Tasmania, the House of Assembly) were elected on a less restricted property or educational franchise.

[4.2.7] In 1890, Western Australia was allowed a similar form of parliamentary government: Western Australia Constitution Act 1890 (UK) 53 & 54 Vic c 26 with Constitution Act 1889 (WA) 52 Vict No 23. As in New South Wales and Queensland, positions in the Legislative Council were filled by nominees of the Governor (although this was converted in 1893 to election on a restricted property franchise). The Legislative Assembly was elected on a property-based franchise, and the legislature was given broad powers to 'make laws for the peace, order and good government of the colony'.

[4.2.8] In 1947, the Commonwealth Parliament established a Legislative Council for the Northern Territory, with a minority of elected members: Northern Territory (Administration) Act 1910 (Cth), s 4. In 1974, the Legislative Council was replaced by a fully elected Legislative Assembly: Northern Territory (Administration) Act 1910 (Cth), s 6. The Legislative Assembly continued after the grant of self-government to the Northern Territory in 1978: Northern Territory (Self-Government) Act 1978 (Cth), s 13(1). A person who is qualified to vote at an election for a member of the Commonwealth House of Representatives for the Northern Territory under the Commonwealth Electoral Act 1918 (Cth) is qualified to vote in elections for the Northern Territory Legislative Assembly: s 14.

[4.2.9] In 1988, the Commonwealth Parliament established the Australian Capital Territory Legislative Assembly at the time of the grant of self-government: Australian Capital Territory Self-Government Act 1988 (Cth), s 8(1). A person is qualified to vote for the Assembly if he or she is entitled to vote at an election for a member of the House of Representatives for the territory and is on the electoral roll: s 67; see also Electoral Act 1992 (ACT), Pt V.

The current structures

[4.2.10] At the time of its establishment, each of the new colonial parliaments was authorised 'to make laws altering all or any of the provisions' of its Constitution Act and, for the most part, the provisions dealing with the structure of each state parliament are to be found in relatively modern replacements of the colonial legislation.

New South Wales

[4.2.11] 'The Legislature' of New South Wales is defined to mean 'the King with the advice and consent of the Legislative Council and Legislative Assembly'. The Assembly consists of 109 members, elected to represent single member electorates. The Council consists of 45 members, one-third of whom are elected at a time, on the basis of a state-wide constituency: Constitution Act 1902 (NSW) ss 3, 21, 34, 35(1), 6th Sch Pt 1.

Until 1933, the members of the New South Wales Legislative Council were appointed by the Governor for life. The transition of the Legislative Council from an appointed body through an indirectly elected body to a body elected by the state's electors is described by Kirby P in *Bignold v Dickson* (1991) 23 NSWLR 683 at 687–9.

Queensland

[4.2.12] The Constitution Act 1867 (Qld) vests legislative power in 'Her Majesty ... by and with the advice and consent of the Assembly to make laws for the peace welfare and good government of the colony in all cases whatsoever' (s 2), defines the parliament as consisting of the Crown and the Legislative Assembly (s 2A(1)), and affirms that the Assembly is an elected body: s 28.

Until 1922, the Queensland Parliament consisted of an elected Legislative Assembly and a Legislative Council, whose members were appointed for life. In that year, the parliament enacted the Constitution Act Amendment Act 1922, which abolished the Council. The Council had been swamped by recently appointed members pledged to vote for its abolition; the 'suicide squad', as Morrison described them: Morrison (1960) p 269.

South Australia

[4.2.13]   In South Australia, the parliament is defined as the Legislative Council and the House of Assembly, with each house elected on a broad franchise. Although the Crown is not included in the formal definition of the parliament, it is implicit in several provisions of the Constitution Act that the Crown is an essential participant in the enactment of legislation: Constitution Act 1934 (SA) ss 4, 8, 11, 14, 19, 20A, 27, 32, 56, 64, 88.

Tasmania

[4.2.14]   The Tasmanian Parliament consists of the Governor, representing the Crown, the Legislative Council and the House of Assembly. The Council consists of 19 members, each of whom is elected to represent a single member electorate. The Assembly consists of 35 members, representing five electorates (each returning seven members): Constitution Act 1934 (Tas) ss 18, 22.

Victoria

[4.2.15]   In Victoria, legislative power is vested in a parliament consisting of the Crown, the Legislative Council and the Legislative Assembly, with the members of each house elected on a wide franchise. The 88 members of the Assembly represent single member electorates. From the next general election after the enactment of the Constitution (Parliamentary Reform) Act 2003 (Vic), the 40 members of the Council will represent eight regions, each returning five members: Constitution Act 1975 (Vic) ss 15, 26, 27, 35.

Western Australia

[4.2.16]   The Western Australian constitution defines the parliament as consisting of the Governor, representing the Queen, the Legislative Council and the Legislative Assembly: Constitution Act 1889 (WA) ss 2, 12, 46; Constitution Acts Amendment Act 1899 (WA) ss 5, 6, 18, 19.

Northern Territory

[4.2.17]   The Northern Territory Self-Government Act 1978 (Cth) describes the Legislative Assembly as having 25 members representing electorates whose size is calculated by dividing the whole number of electors in the territory, as nearly as can be ascertained, by the number of members to be elected. Each electoral division must contain a number of electors not exceeding, or falling short of, the quota calculated under that subsection by more than one-fifth of the quota: ss 4(1), 6, 13.

Australian Capital Territory

[4.2.18]   The Australian Capital Territory Self-Government Act 1988 (Cth) describes the Legislative Assembly as having 17 members: s 8(2). This number can be changed by regulations made by the Governor-General and in accordance with a resolution by the Legislative Assembly: ss 8(3), 74(a)(i). Electorate size is calculated by a quota: the number of territory electors is divided by the number of members to be elected to the Assembly. No electoral redistribution can result in any electorate having more electors than 110 per cent of the quota or less than 90 per cent of the quota: s 67D.

The role of the monarch

[4.2.19] The references in the various definitions of state parliaments to 'the King' or 'the Queen' underline the fact that Australia is, formally at least, a constitutional monarchy, but those references do not mean that the Queen participates in the business of state parliaments. She does not summon or dissolve parliament nor does she assent to bills passed by the Houses of Parliament. Those functions are performed by state Governors in whom state legislation expressly vests certain powers; see, for example: Constitution Act 1902 (NSW) ss 23, 24; Constitution Act 1975 (Vic) ss 20, 38; Constitution Act 1889 (WA) ss 2(3), 3, 12, 13. The representative status of the Governor is expressly recognised in: Australia Act 1986 (Cth) s 7; Constitution Act 1867 (Qld) s 11A; Constitution Act 1975 (Vic) s 6; Constitution Act 1889 (WA) s 50(1).

[4.2.20] In the Northern Territory, those functions are performed by an Administrator. Laws passed by the Legislative Assembly require either the assent of the Administrator or the Commonwealth Governor-General to be effective: Northern Territory Self-Government Act 1978 (Cth), s 6. The Administrator's assent is required for laws dealing with matters transferred to the territory under the self-government legislation: ss 7(2)(a), 35. In relation to non-transferred matters, the Administrator has the option of reserving a proposed law for the assent of the Governor-General: s 7(2)(b)(iii). The Governor-General's assent to the proposed law is then required for the law to take effect: s 8(1).

[4.2.21] The Australian Capital Territory is a body politic established 'under the Crown': Australian Capital Territory (Self-Government) Act 1988 (Cth), s 7. In the ACT, the Governor-General is vested with power to dissolve the Legislative Assembly (s 16), and to appoint a Commissioner to exercise the powers of the ACT Executive (ss 36–38) in accordance with his or her instructions: s 16(2) and (4). The Governor-General may disallow ACT enactments within six months after their making: s 35. The powers of the Governor-General are exercisable on the advice of Commonwealth Ministers: see Acts Interpretation Act 1901 (Cth), s 16A. See further Lindell, 1992.

Restructuring parliaments

[4.2.22] The flexibility of the structure of state legislatures has been affirmed by the High Court on a number of occasions. In *Taylor v Attorney-General (Qld)* (1917) 23 CLR 457 **[5.3.13]**, the High Court held that the Queensland Parliament could legislate to abolish the Legislative Council. The basis for this legislative power was s 5 of the Colonial Laws Validity Act 1865 (UK) which declared that 'every representative legislature shall ... have ... full power to make laws respecting the constitution powers and procedures of such legislature'. However, some limits on this power to restructure state parliaments were suggested. Isaacs J declared that 'the Crown is not included in the ambit of such a power' and that 'probably the "representative" character of the legislature is a basic condition of the power relied on': 23 CLR at 474.

[4.2.23] In *Clayton v Heffron* (1960) 105 CLR 214 **[5.3.16C]**, the High Court came to a similar general conclusion; namely, that the New South Wales Parliament could legislate to abolish the Council. A majority of the court proposed that the basis for such legislation lay in the general legislative power of the parliament to make laws for the peace, welfare and good government of the state: Constitution Act 1902 (NSW) s 5. Again, some reservations were expressed. Dixon CJ, McTiernan, Taylor and Windeyer JJ declared that 'there are many reasons for assuming that the assent of the Crown must always remain necessary': 105 CLR at 251.

[4.2.24] On its commencement in 1901, the Commonwealth Constitution left the structure of the former colonial, now state, parliaments undisturbed. Section 106 of the Commonwealth Constitution continued the constitution of each state as it was at the establishment of the Commonwealth, until altered in accordance with the constitution of the state. Section 107 declares that state parliaments are to retain all their legislative powers except for those powers expressly withdrawn from the state parliaments by the new Commonwealth Constitution. The territory legislatures, being creatures of Commonwealth statute, can be altered or abolished by valid legislation authorised by s 122 of the Constitution.

Commonwealth Parliament

The federal movement

[4.2.25] When, during the last quarter of the 19th century, Australians began to talk seriously about a single national government, a number of pressures pushed them towards a federal system; that is, a system which would graft new, national, political institutions onto the existing and separate colonial structures. Few people believed that a single, central government was practicable because Australia was vast, her population was thinly distributed, and communication systems were not well developed. There were other strong pressures for a federal system. The residents of small colonies distrusted the large urban centres of Sydney and Melbourne. The larger, more industrialised colonies were reluctant to submit all aspects of their economies and societies to a central, perhaps more conservative, administration. The adoption of a federal system was naturally suggested by the models of the United States of America, Canada and Switzerland, although the first of those was the most persuasive model.

[4.2.26] Federal preoccupations were reflected in the structure proposed for the new Commonwealth Parliament. Sir Samuel Griffiths' 1891 draft set the pattern, proposing a parliament of the Queen, a Senate with equal membership (eight) for each state and elected by each state's parliament, and a House of Representatives consisting of members directly elected in each state according to the state's population (with a minimum of four per state).

By the time the draft had been through the conventions of 1897 and 1898, approved by the voters in the various colonies and finally enacted by the United Kingdom Parliament, some changes had been effected. Senators, for instance, were to be directly elected, but the essential features remained: a three-part legislature consisting of the Crown, Senate and House of Representatives, the last intended to reflect the popular will throughout Australia, the second to reflect the concerns of the states as separate entities and to advance or protect their separate interests in the parliament. Some of the implications of this federal role for the Senate are discussed in *Western Australia v Commonwealth* (1975) 134 CLR 201 **[4.2.32C]**.

[4.2.27E]   Commonwealth Constitution

1   The legislative power of the Commonwealth shall be vested in a Federal Parliament, which shall consist of the Queen, a Senate and a House of Representatives, and which is hereinafter called 'The Parliament', or 'The Parliament of the Commonwealth' ...

7   The Senate shall be composed of senators for each State, directly chosen by the people of the State, voting, until the Parliament otherwise provides, as one electorate.

But until the Parliament of the Commonwealth otherwise provides, the Parliament of the State of Queensland, if that State be an Original State, may make laws dividing the State into divisions and determining the number of senators to be chosen for each division, and in the absence of such provision the State shall be one electorate.

Until the Parliament otherwise provides there shall be six senators of each Original State. The Parliament may make laws increasing or diminishing the number of senators for each State, but so that equal representation of the several Original States shall be maintained and that no Original State shall have less than six senators.

The senators shall be chosen for a term of six years, and the names of the senators chosen for each State shall be certified by the Governor to the Governor-General ...

24   The House of Representatives shall be composed of members directly chosen by the people of the Commonwealth, and the number of such members shall be, as nearly as practicable, twice the number of the senators.

The number of members chosen in the several States shall be in proportion to the respective numbers of their people, and shall, until the Parliament otherwise provides, be determined whenever necessary, in the following manner:

(i)   A quota shall be ascertained by dividing the number of the people of the Commonwealth as shown by the latest statistics of the Commonwealth, by twice the number of the senators;

(ii)   The number of members to be chosen in each State shall be determined by dividing the number of the people of the State, as shown by the latest statistics of the Commonwealth, by the quota; and if on such division there is a remainder greater than one-half of the quota, one more member shall be chosen in the State.

But notwithstanding anything in this section, five members at least shall be chosen in each Original State.

~~~

Notes

[4.2.28] For all practical purposes, the powers of the Queen under the Commonwealth Constitution are exercised by a Governor-General. That person is described in s 2 of the Constitution as 'Her Majesty's representative in the Commonwealth', capable of exercising those powers which the 'Queen may be pleased to assign to him'. The need for any such assignment is doubtful, as many powers are expressly vested in the Governor-General by the Commonwealth Constitution; see, for example: ss 5 (summoning, proroguing and dissolving parliament), 56 (recommending money bills to parliament), 57 (dissolving both houses in a deadlock situation), 58 (assenting to legislation). Additionally, s 61 declares, in very general terms, that 'the executive power of the Commonwealth ... is exercisable by the Governor-General as the Queen's representative'.

There are some functions which only the Queen may exercise, such as the formal appointment of the Governor-General (s 2) the 'disallowance' of legislation passed by the Commonwealth Parliament (s 59) and the giving of assent to legislation which must, under the Constitution, be 'reserved for the Queen's pleasure': s 60. The last category covers a very small class of legislation: see **[5.1.11]**.

Apart from those exceptions (and they have very little practical significance for, in each case, the Queen would only act on the advice of her Australian ministers), it is the Governor-General who discharges the important functions of the Crown under the Commonwealth Constitution. This point was succinctly stated by the Queen's official secretary in 1975 when he indicated that the Queen would not intervene in the constitutional crisis immediately after 11 November 1975:

> As we understand the situation here, the Australian Constitution firmly places the prerogative powers of the Crown in the hands of the Governor-General as the representative of the Queen in Australia (Sawer (1977) p 211).

[4.2.29] The Commonwealth Constitution fixed the size of both the Senate and the House of Representatives. The former was to consist of 36 senators: s 7; the latter to have, as nearly as practicable, twice as many members: s 24. The limits imposed by this ratio were explored in *Attorney-General (NSW) (Ex rel McKellar) v Commonwealth* (1977) 139 CLR 527 **[4.6.18]**.

Parliament was authorised to alter the number of senators for each state, so long as the House of Representatives continued to have, as nearly as practicable, twice as many members as the Senate and each original state retained equality of representation (s 7) and to alter the size of the House of Representatives (s 27) so long as each original state retained at least five members: s 24. Such an alteration was effected by the Representation Act 1948 (Cth) s 4, which increased to 10 the number of senators for each state, and by the Representation Act 1983 (Cth) s 4, which increased to 12 the number of senators for each state.

[4.2.30] The system for determining the size of the House of Representatives is spelt out in the Commonwealth Electoral Act 1918 (Cth) ss 45–48. Earlier versions of this system were examined by the High Court in *Attorney-General (Cth) (Ex rel McKinlay) v Commonwealth* (1975) 135 CLR 1 **[4.6.9C]** and *Attorney-General (NSW) (Ex rel McKellar) v Commonwealth* (1977) 139 CLR 527 **[4.6.18]**. For the moment, we should note that the system is subject to the following constitutional restraints:

- the House of Representatives shall 'as nearly as practicable' be twice the size of the Senate;

- members of the house are chosen in each state (members cannot be shared between two or more states);

- the number of members allocated to each state shall be in proportion to their respective numbers of people; but

- each original state must have at least five members in the house.

[4.2.31] Sections 7 and 24 of the Commonwealth Constitution (and a number of associated provisions) appear to assume that senators and members of the house represent the states or the people of the states. However, in 1922 legislation gave to the Northern Territory a non-voting member of the House of Representatives. That member was given a limited vote in 1936, and a similar representation was allowed to the Australian Capital Territory in 1948. The two members' voting rights were enlarged in 1959 and extended to full voting rights in 1966 (for the Australian Capital Territory) and 1968 (for the Northern Territory). In 1973 the Australian Capital Territory was given a second member and, in 1974, legislation was passed through the double dissolution procedure (that is, despite the opposition of the Senate) giving each territory two senators with full voting rights. This legislation is now consolidated in the Commonwealth Electoral Act 1918 (Cth) ss 40–44 (representation of territories in the Senate) and ss 51–54 (representation of territories in the House of Representatives).

[4.2.32C] Western Australia v Commonwealth

(The *Territorial Senators* case)
(1975) 134 CLR 201

The Senate (Representation of Territories) Act 1973 (Cth) was enacted at a joint sitting of the Commonwealth Parliament and received the royal assent on 7 August 1974. The Act provided that the Australian Capital Territory and the Northern Territory should each be represented in the Senate by two senators (s 4), that each senator was to have all the powers, immunities and privileges of a state senator, in particular, the senator could vote on all questions arising in the Senate (s 5), and that each senator was to serve only until the next general election of Members for the House of Representatives: s 7(2).

The states of Western Australia and New South Wales brought actions in the High Court, seeking declarations that the Act had not been properly enacted. The state of Queensland also brought an action, seeking a declaration that the Act was invalid because the substance of the Act was inconsistent with the Commonwealth Constitution. These actions were heard and decided together. The court's decision on the first ground of challenge is discussed in [5.3.33].

Stephen J: [256] By s 7, the first section of Pt II Ch I of the Constitution, the Senate is to be 'composed of senators for each State, directly chosen by the people of the State, voting ... as one electorate' and each original State is initially to have an irreducible minimum of six senators, that equal representation to be maintained should the number of senators for each State subsequently be altered. Every successive section of Pt II serves only to confirm the effect of s 7, that the Senate is to be a chamber composed of senators for each State. These senators are to be elected by qualified electors in each State: s 8; they are to be chosen according to the laws of each State by a Commonwealth law providing for a method uniform for all the States: ss 9 and 10; the failure of a State to provide its representation in the Senate is not to delay [257] the despatch of business by the Senate: s 11; it is the Governor of the State who issues writs for the election of senators for the State (s 12) and he must be notified of a casual vacancy in the representation of his State: s 21 ... Sections 15 and 23 are especially notable; the former confers upon the Parliament or executive government 'of the State for which he was chosen' the function of filling the place of a senator which becomes vacant before the expiration of his term of service; the latter gives one vote to each senator including the President, thus maintaining the policy of equal representation enunciated in s 7.

The effect of this brief survey of Pt II may be summarised by the description given to the Senate by Quick and Garran when they said, at 414 of their *Annotated Constitution of the Australian Commonwealth*: 'It is the chamber in which the States, considered as separate entities, and corporate parts of the Commonwealth, are represented'.

The framers of the Constitution had to make provision for the possibility of new States and the sections comprised in Ch VI, other than s 122, are devoted to that subject; by s 121 Parliament is empowered to determine the extent of representation of such a new State in either House of the Parliament. Once admitted or established as a State that new polity becomes a 'State' as defined in covering cl 6 of the Constitution Act and the sections of Pt II will then, without more, apply to it, other than those parts of s 7 which confer special rights upon the original States. Thus the admission of new States will leave undisturbed the character of the Senate as a States' house.

Such then being the constitutional structure of the Senate it is, to my mind, apparent that 'representation' in s 122 must bear a meaning which accords with that structure. Such a meaning cannot extend to the creation of senators of Territories, taking their places in the Senate on an equal footing with senators of States nor indeed to the creation of any office carrying with it the power to affect by vote the deliberations of the Senate. To give to 'representation' any such meaning is wholly to distort the intended character of the Senate as a chamber 'composed of senators for each State'. It is this very type of distortion which the Senate (Representation of Territories) Act 1973 would, if [258] valid, effect. I accordingly regard the Act as invalid; it is not authorized by the power conferred upon Parliament by s 122 ...

That there is nothing inappropriate in using the word 'representation' to describe the function of a person having in a legislative chamber no voting power is apparent from a reading of the original Northern Territory Representation Act 1922. It provided for the representation of that Territory in the Parliament of the Commonwealth by means of a member of the House of Representatives elected by Northern Territory electors but having no vote on any question and who was not to be taken into account for quorum or special majority purposes, although he otherwise had all the powers, immunities and privileges of a member ...

Such a concept can hardly be supposed to have been unfamiliar to some at least of those responsible for the framing of our Constitution; Lord Bryce's *American Commonwealth*, 2nd ed (revsd) (1889) was at that time a standard guide to that great federal Constitution upon which so much of our own Constitution is based and in a chapter devoted to the Territories of the United States the learned author discusses the system whereby, although denied representation by elected senators or representatives, the citizens of a Territory might send delegates to sit and speak, but not to vote, in Congress: vol I p 555, and see vol II p 414 ...

[260] When s 122 refers to the allowance of representation 'to the extent and on the terms' which Parliament thinks fit, it contemplates not only the imposition of terms, for instance perhaps a term that the representative be elected by residents of the Territory qualified in such manner as Parliament may specify, but also the possible limitation of the subject matter of representation as, for instance, by restriction to matters directly affecting the Territory, the representatives' right to speak in debate being limited accordingly.

I have, in what I have said above, treated 'composed' in s 7 of the Constitution as meaning 'exclusively comprised of'. This accords, I think, with the primary meaning of 'compose' as describing the act of putting together from parts or elements, the whole being constituted by the collection of those parts ...

Mason J summarised the provisions of the Senate (Representation of Territories) Act 1973 and continued:

Mason J: [268] A senator for the Territory is then in all important respects equal to a senator for a State. Therein lies the principal objection to the validity of this Act. The question is whether s 122 does allow the Parliament to provide for the election of senators for a Territory having full voting rights in the House ...

With respect to representation of a Territory in either House of the Commonwealth Parliament the Parliament has, by virtue of s 122, power to determine (a) the extent of the representation and (b) the terms of that representation ... The inclusion in s 122 of a specific power to allow representation upon any terms which the Parliament thinks fit makes it plain that the Parliament may confer on representatives of a Territory rights and privileges identical or inferior to those enjoyed by a member of either House ...

It has not been suggested that s 122, viewed in isolation, is an insufficient source of legislative power to sustain the law now in question. But it has been asserted in accordance with received doctrine that s 122 cannot be read as though it was a segregated head of power disconnected from the rest of the provisions of the [269] Constitution. One must 'treat the

Constitution as one coherent instrument for the government of the federation, and not as two constitutions, one for the federation and the other for its territories': see per Kitto J in *Lamshed v Lake* (1958) 99 CLR 132 at 154. It was then submitted that when s 122 is read in the light of Ch I of the Constitution the conclusion is inescapable that s 122 does not confer power upon the Parliament to allow the representation of the Territories in the Senate by members having the right to vote, at least on matters not directly affecting the Territories.

It was urged that s 7 of the Constitution exhaustively defines the composition of the Senate in providing that it 'shall be composed of senators for each State, directly chosen by the people of the State', each of whom shall have one vote (s 23) and serve for a term of six years. Attention was drawn to other provisions in Pt II of Ch I of the Constitution which were said to conflict with, or to be incapable of application to, a senator representing a Territory, thereby reinforcing the notion that the Senate is a States' house and that a senator is necessarily a senator from a State.

But for the presence of s 122 these arguments would have overwhelming force — not only is the composition of the Senate limited by s 7 to senators from the States but the conception of a senator as the representative of a State pervades the provisions of Pt II of Ch 1. Thus s 11 provides that the Senate may proceed to the despatch of business notwithstanding the failure of any State to provide for its representation. Section 15 provides for the filling of a casual vacancy by the Parliament of a State or the Governor of a State, and s 21 provides that notification of a vacancy shall be given to the Governor of the State in the representation of which the vacancy has occurred.

A similar problem arises in relation to representation of the Territories in the House of Representatives. Section 24 of the Constitution provides that the House 'shall be composed of members directly chosen by the people of the Commonwealth'. If the expression 'people of the Commonwealth' signifies the people of the federated States, then in terms the section excludes from the composition of the House the elected representatives of the Territories save perhaps the Australian Capital Territory, and so there arises once again an apparent conflict between the provisions of Ch I and s 122.

Just as s 122 requires to be read with Ch I so also account must be taken of s 122 in the interpretation of ss 7 and 24. If [270] they are to be read as limiting the composition of each House for all time to representatives of the States, it follows that the power given to Parliament by s 122 to 'allow the representation of such Territory in either House of Parliament to the extent and on the terms which it thinks fit' must be confined to a power to provide for the appointment of representatives of the Territories who are voteless, if not voiceless. To so construe the power is to deprive it of significant content, notwithstanding the wide and general words by which it is conferred. The section would then admit only of representation by a person who was not a member of the House and who did not enjoy the rights of a member to vote. The attribution of such a restricted concept of 'representation' to s 122 would stand in stark contrast with the concept of 'representation' in the complete sense of membership which is evident in s 121.

The apparent opposition which arises from the reference to representation of the Territories in s 122 and the absence of any such reference in ss 7 and 24 is irreconcilable only if it be assumed that Ch I in making provision for the composition of the Senate and the House is necessarily speaking for all time. To my mind this assumption is misconceived. Sections 7 and 24 should be regarded as making provision for the composition of each House which nevertheless, in the shape of s 122, takes account of the prospective possibility that Parliament might deem it expedient, having regard to the stage which a Territory might reach in the course of its future development, to give it representation in either House by allowing it to elect members of that House. To the framers of the Constitution in 1900 the existing condition of the Territories was not such as to suggest the immediate likelihood of their securing representation in either House, but the possibility of such a development occurring in the future was undeniable. The prospect of its occurrence was foreseen and in my view it found expression in s 122.

Understood in this light, ss 7 and 24 make exhaustive provision for the composition of each House until such time as Parliament might see fit to allow representation to a Territory under s 122. This interpretation not only gives full scope to the language of that section but it supports and gives authority to the course of constitutional development by which in recent years Parliament might see fit to allow representation to a Territory in the House of Representatives, first by a member without voting rights, then by a member with qualified voting rights and finally by a member with unqualified voting rights, see the Northern Territory Representation Act 1922, the Northern [271] Territory Representation Act 1959, the Northern Territory Representation Act 1968 ...

Two matters remain to be mentioned. The first is the grim spectre conjured up by the plaintiffs of a Parliament swamping the Senate with senators from the Territories, thereby reducing the representation of the States disproportionately to that of an ineffective minority in the chamber. This exercise in imagination assumes the willing participation of the senators representing the States in such an enterprise, notwithstanding that it would hasten their journey into political oblivion. It disregards the assumption which the framers of the Constitution made, and which we should now make, that Parliament will act responsibly in the exercise of its powers.

Furthermore, such significance as the plaintiff's argument may have is diminished when it is appreciated that the Constitution provides no safeguard against the pursuit by Parliament of a similar course at the expense of the original States in allowing for the representation of new States in the Senate. Although s 7 provides that equal representation of the original States shall be maintained in that chamber, neither the section nor the remaining provisions of Pt II of Ch I place any restriction on the number of senators which Parliament may accord to a new State as its representation in the Senate. Here, again, the assumption is that Parliament will act responsibly.

~~~

Notes

[4.2.33] McTiernan J adopted the reasons of Mason J. In separate judgments Jacobs and Murphy JJ held that the Senate (Representation of Territories) Act 1973 (Cth) was adequately supported by s 122 of the Constitution. The judgments of Barwick CJ and Gibbs J were to substantially the same effect as that of Stephen J.

[4.2.34] Writing of this aspect of the decision in *Western Australia v Commonwealth* (1975) 134 CLR 201 **[4.2.32C]**, Geoffrey Sawer remarked that the 4:3 split on the court was 'surprising having regard to the weakness of the case against the majority decision': Sawer (1977) p 54. What was that case? That the conflict between ss 7 and 122 was to be resolved by allowing a proposition implicit in s 7 of the Constitution to dominate s 122; namely, that 'the central and dominant purpose of the Constitution [was to create] an indissoluble federal Commonwealth': 134 CLR at 226 per Barwick CJ. The Senate was to be and remain a states' house.

There is no doubt that those who debated and drafted the Constitution at the Conventions of 1891, 1897 and 1898 meant to establish a chamber which would represent and protect the interests of each state. The 1891 draft provided that senators were to be appointed by the state parliaments. At the 1897–98 Conventions this system was replaced by direct election, but casual vacancies were still to be filled by a joint sitting of the relevant state Houses of Parliament.

But one, at least, of the convention delegates made the point that the Senate could not function as a states' house. Speaking at the Sydney Convention, Alfred Deakin said:

The men returned as radicals would vote as radicals; the men returned as conservatives would vote as conservatives. The contest will not be, never has been, and cannot be, between States and States. It must be and will be between the representatives of the States according to the different political principles upon which they are returned (Convention Debates, Sydney (1897) p 584).

Events justified that prediction. Geoffrey Sawer observed that the Senate 'is in fact, and hopelessly, made up mainly of representatives from the major political parties whose chief loyalty is to their respective party organisations': Sawer (1977) p 128.

[4.2.35] Given that reality, the decision in *Western Australia v Commonwealth* (1975) 134 CLR 201 **[4.2.32C]** did not sanction any fundamental change in the nature of the Senate. The decision allowed the Senate to grow from 60 to 64 senators at the elections of 13 December 1975; of the four newly created places, two were won by the new government and two by the opposition. Since 1975, the territory Senators have been evenly divided between the two major political groups, Labor and conservative.

[4.2.36] Nonetheless, there may be long-term implications in the decision. Might a future parliament enact legislation enlarging the representation of one or both territories so as to distort the character and political complexion of the Senate? Is there anything in the Constitution, as interpreted in this case, which would prevent parliament adding to the Senate 100 senators from the Australian Capital Territory? Is it consistent with this decision, as Stephen J argued in *Attorney-General (NSW) (Ex rel McKellar) v Commonwealth* (1977) 139 CLR 527 at 561–2 **[4.6.18]**, that parliament could provide that the territory senators be appointed by the Executive Council?

[4.2.37] The judgments in the *Territorial Senators'* case **[4.2.32C]** provide a clear illustration of the creative, value-dominated nature of the judicial process, and of the inadequacy of Gibbs J's claim that the function of the court 'is to consider not what the Constitution might best provide but what, upon its proper construction, it does provide': 134 CLR at 249.

Michael Coper made the point, writing of this decision, 'that linguistic or textual considerations were quite inconclusive; for each argument which led to one conclusion, a respectable principle of interpretation could be invoked to point to the opposite conclusion': Coper (1977) p 209. The minority, for example, said that s 7 of the Constitution provided that the Senate should be composed of (not merely include) senators from each state. That positive statement had a negative corollary: the Senate representation allowed to the territories by s 122 should not include voting rights. But the majority said that the word 'representation' should have the same meaning in s 122 as it did in other sections, and its meaning in other provisions clearly included voting rights.

Similarly, both the majority and the minority made use of arguments based on the historical purposes of the provisions, on the possible abuse of constitutional power and on the state of the United States Constitution in 1900. Their use of these same tools of interpretation led to diametrically opposed results. The case illustrated, as Leslie Zines observed, that textual and other considerations can produce 'competing arguments that are all rational', so that the justices' decisions were controlled by their preference between 'the federal principle [or] the principle of representation': Zines (1997) p 469.

[4.2.38] In 1977 the states of Queensland and Western Australia sought to reopen the decision in the *Territorial Senators'* case **[4.2.32C]**. The two states, in actions for declarations in the High Court, challenged the validity of the legislation providing for territory representation in both the Senate and the House of Representatives. The challenge was rejected by a majority of the court in *Queensland v Commonwealth* (1977) 139 CLR 585.

Mason, Jacobs and Murphy JJ adhered to their opinion as expressed in the *Territorial Senators'* case; namely, s 122 was unlimited in its terms and prevailed over any narrow implications drawn from ss 7 and 24.

Gibbs and Stephen JJ repeated their opinion that the Senate (Representation of Territories) Act 1973 was invalid, but felt obliged to follow the decision in the *Territorial Senators'* case. Stephen J recognised that the reconciliation of ss 7 and 122 of the Constitution was complex and an issue on 'which different minds might reach different conclusions, no one view being inherently entitled to any pre-eminence', and said that to describe the decision in that case as 'plainly wrong' was 'merely pejorative': 139 CLR at 603. He accepted that the extent of the territories' representation in the Senate was now 'a matter for the Parliament': 139 CLR at 604. Gibbs J said that the change in the composition of the High Court since the decision in the *Territorial Senators'* case could not 'justify the review of an earlier decision': 139 CLR at 600. However, his Honour indicated that he would not support an extension of the current territorial representation, '[h]aving regard to the very great importance, in preserving the federal balance of the Constitution, which attaches to Part II of Ch I of the Constitution': 139 CLR at 600–1.

Barwick CJ and Aickin J dissented, declaring that s 122 should not be read as justifying voting membership in the Houses of Parliament for territory representatives. They saw no compelling reason for following the *Territorial Senators'* case, which was, in their opinion, wrongly decided and inconsistent with the fundamental federal structure of the Constitution.

---

3   Duration of parliament

[4.3.1] Each of the Australian parliaments has a limited life. That is, the period during which it may legitimately function without facing the electorate is fixed by legislation and, in the case of some parliaments, there are built-in guarantees of regular elections, guarantees which cannot be overridden by ordinary legislation.

As a general rule, constitutional provisions distinguish between upper and lower houses. The members of the latter are obliged to face the electors together once the house is 'dissolved', while the members of the former usually retire in rotation, only one-half or one-third facing the electors at each election. In the normal course of events, the upper houses are not 'dissolved'. In addition, most of the lower houses have no minimum duration. They are liable to dissolution, and their members to face a consequential general election, at any time before their maximum time span has passed, but members of most upper houses are guaranteed a minimum term.

State parliaments

New South Wales

[4.3.2] The New South Wales Legislative Assembly is given a maximum duration of four years, measured from the return of the election writs from the last general election, subject to its earlier dissolution by the Governor. That period may only be extended by legislation approved by a majority of voters at a referendum: Constitution Act 1902 (NSW) ss 7B(1)(b), 24.

The New South Wales Legislative Council is a perpetual institution, one-half of whose members retire on each expiry or dissolution of the Assembly. This means that each member of the Council holds her or his seat until the second general election of the Assembly after her or his election to the Council, when she or he will be eligible to stand for re-election: Constitution Act 1902 (NSW) s 22B(2).

Queensland

[4.3.3] In Queensland, where the Council was abolished by legislation in 1922, the duration of the Assembly is limited to three years from the return of the writs after a general election, subject to earlier dissolution by the Governor. The extension of this period can only be effected by legislation which has been approved by a majority of voters at a referendum: Constitution Act Amendment Act 1890 (Qld) ss 2, 4.

South Australia

[4.3.4] The South Australian House of Assembly has a maximum duration of four years, measured from its first meeting after a general election. The Governor may dissolve the Assembly but only if (Constitution Act 1934 (SA) ss 28, 28a(1)):

- three years have expired since the Assembly's first meeting after the general election; or

- the government has been defeated on a vote of confidence in the Assembly; or

- 'a Bill of special importance passed by the House of Assembly is rejected by the Legislative Council'; or

- the Governor simultaneously dissolves the two houses under s 41(1)(i) of the Constitution Act 1934 (SA), where the houses are deadlocked over proposed legislation.

Apart from the exceptional power of the Governor to dissolve both houses under the Constitution Act 1934 (SA) s 41 **[5.3.11]**, the state's Legislative Council is a perpetual institution, with members holding their seats for a minimum of six years, and half the members retiring at each general election for the House of Assembly, provided that at least six years have elapsed since those members were elected: Constitution Act 1934 (SA) s 14.

Tasmania

[4.3.5] The Tasmanian House of Assembly has a maximum duration of four years, measured from the return of the writs at the last general election, subject to earlier dissolution by the Governor: Constitution Act 1934 (Tas) s 23(2). The Legislative

Council is a perpetual institution, with members holding their seats for six years and one-sixth of the members retiring (and being eligible for re-election) each year: Constitution Act 1934 (Tas) s 19.

Victoria

[4.3.6] Following the enactment of the Constitution (Parliamentary Reform) Act 2003 (Vic), the Victorian Legislative Assembly has a fixed term of four years (subject to earlier dissolution only as permitted by s 8(3) of the Constitution Act 1975), expiring on the Tuesday which is 25 days before the last Saturday in November nearest to the fourth anniversary of the day on which it was elected: Constitution Act 1975 (Vic), s 38(2).

According to s 8(3) of the Constitution Act 1975, the Victorian Governor may only dissolve the Assembly in accordance with s 8A or s 65E(2) of the Constitution Act.

Section 8A(1) authorises the dissolution of the Legislative Assembly if a motion of no confidence in the premier and other ministers (of which three clear days' notice has been given) is passed by the Assembly and the Assembly does not pass a motion of confidence in the then premier and ministers within eight clear days.

Section 65E(2) authorises the premier to advise the Governor to dissolve the Assembly where the Assembly and the Council are deadlocked (as defined in ss 65C(3) or 65D(1) of the Constitution Act) over a bill that originated in the Assembly.

As a result of passage of the Constitution (Parliamentary Reform) Act 2003 (Vic) the duration of the Victorian Legislative Council is tied directly to the Legislative Assembly. The Council in existence immediately before that Act received royal assent (on 8 April 2003) is to continue until the dissolution or other lawful termination of the Legislative Assembly last elected before that date: Constitution Act 1975, s 28(1). It follows that the terms of all members of the Legislative Council, whether elected in October 1999 or November 2002, will expire on the dissolution or termination of the Legislative Assembly elected in November 2002.

Once a new Legislative Council is elected after the dissolution or termination of that Legislative Assembly, the duration of the Legislative Council is tied to the life of the Legislative Assembly: Constitution Act 1975, s 28(2).

Western Australia

[4.3.7] The Western Australian Legislative Assembly is given a maximum duration of four years from the Assembly's first meeting following the last general election; subject to earlier dissolution by the Governor: Constitution Acts Amendment Act 1899 (WA) s 21(1).

The state's Legislative Council is a perpetual institution, whose members hold their seats for four years: the seats of all members become vacant 'at the expiration of four years beginning on 22 May next following' the general election for the Council. Writs for the general election for the Council are to be issued at any time in the period commencing one year before the vacancies and ending before the 10 April preceding the vacancies: Constitution Acts Amendment Act 1899 (WA) s 8.

Territory parliaments

Northern Territory

[4.3.8] The Legislative Assembly of the Northern Territory has a maximum duration of four years, beginning from the date of the first meeting of the Legislative Assembly after a general election: Northern Territory (Self-Government) Act 1978 (Cth), s 17(2).

Australian Capital Territory

[4.3.9] The Australian Capital Territory (Self-Government) Act 1988 (Cth), s 67B provides that the times of elections are to be provided by enactment. The timing of elections is dealt with in Pt VIII of the Electoral Act 1992 (ACT). General elections are held on the third Saturday in October in the third year after the year in which the last ordinary election was held. If any federal election is called for the same day then the election is held on the first Saturday in December in the year in which it would ordinarily be held: Electoral Act 1992, s 100.

Commonwealth Parliament

[4.3.10E]   Commonwealth Constitution

13   As soon as may be after the Senate first meets, and after each first meeting of the Senate following a dissolution thereof, the Senate shall divide the senators chosen for each State into two classes, as nearly equal in number as practicable; and the places of the senators of the first class shall become vacant at the expiration of *three years,* and the places of those of the second class at the expiration of *six years,* from the beginning of their term of service; and afterwards the places of senators shall become vacant at the expiration of six years from the beginning of their term of service.

The election to fill vacant places shall be made *within one year before* the places are to become vacant.

For the purposes of this section the terms of service of a senator shall be taken to begin on the first day of *July* following the day of his election, except in the cases of the first election and of the election next after any dissolution of the Senate, when it shall be taken to begin on the first day of *July* preceding the day of his election. ...

28   Every House of Representatives shall continue for three years from the first meeting of the House, and no longer, but may be sooner dissolved by the Governor-General.

~~~

Notes

[4.3.11] Section 57 of the Commonwealth Constitution allows for the dissolution of the Senate where a deadlock has persisted between the two houses for at least three months. There have been six such double dissolutions (for the House of Representatives is dissolved at the same time): 1914, 1951, 1974, 1975, 1983 and 1987. Accordingly, the Senate has been obliged on seven occasions (including its first meeting in 1901) to 'divide the senators chosen for each State into two classes', the short-term (three year) and the long-term (six year) senators. On each occasion that division has been made on the basis of the votes polled by each senator at his or her election: the first three senators (1901 and 1914), the first five senators (1951, 1974,

1975 and 1983) or the first six senators (1987) elected in each state were declared to be the long-term senators. This practice rests upon a formal resolution of the Senate adopted at its first meeting in 1901, a resolution which can be revoked by the Senate.

Adjournment, prorogation and dissolution

[4.3.12] The Houses of Parliament, once elected, meet in formal session to transact their business. From the lawyer's perspective that business consists of making legislation, that is, the enactment of bills. There is a wide range of business transacted in parliament: questions to government ministers, debates on issues of policy and administration, tabling of official reports, and motions of no confidence in the government. All of these are reported in *Hansard* and their more formal aspects recorded in the journals of the houses. How are the houses brought together? Who decides how long parliament shall sit, or when it should face a general election? The constitutional legislation provides a broad framework for the answers to these questions, and the provisions of the Commonwealth Constitution are typical.

[4.3.13E]   **Commonwealth Constitution**

5   The Governor-General may appoint such times for holding the sessions of the Parliament as he thinks fit, and may also from time to time, by Proclamation or otherwise, prorogue the Parliament, and may in like manner dissolve the House of Representatives.

      After any general election the Parliament shall be summoned to meet not later than thirty days after the day appointed for the return of the writs.

      The Parliament shall be summoned to meet not later than six months after the establishment of the Commonwealth.

6   There shall be a session of the Parliament once at least in every year, so that twelve months shall not intervene between the last sitting of the Parliament in one session and its first sitting in the next session.

~~~

Notes

[4.3.14] There are equivalent provisions in the state constitutions, though most states do not have provisions similar to s 5 (second paragraph) of the Commonwealth Constitution, for example, see:

- Constitution Act 1902 (NSW) ss 10, 11;

- Constitution of Queensland 2001 ss 18, 19;

- Constitution Act 1934 (SA) ss 6, 7;

- Constitution Act 1934 (Tas) ss 11, 12;

- Constitution Act 1975 (Vic) ss 20, 38, 41;

- Constitution Act 1889 (WA) ss 3, 4.

    For the territories, see:

- Northern Territory Self-Government Act 1978 (Cth) s 22;

- Australian Capital Territory Self-Government Act 1988 (Cth) s 17.

[4.3.15] The power to call parliament together ('fixing the time and place for holding the sessions of Parliament') and to send the lower house to a general election ('dissolving the lower House') is vested in the Governor-General (for the Commonwealth and for the ACT), the Governors of the states, and the Administrator of the Northern Territory. The degree of their independent discretion is discussed at **[7.4.1]–[7.4.26]**. The Governor-General and Governors also have the power to 'prorogue' parliament, that is, to terminate a session of parliament.

Each of these functions (summoning, proroguing and dissolving) is an Australian remnant of prerogative powers of the Crown in relation to the United Kingdom Parliament and each of them has a distinct purpose and function, distinctions which are still clearly drawn:

- The summoning of parliament is the means of convening a sitting of a newly elected parliament or a parliament, perhaps several years old, which has been prorogued by the Crown.

- The proroguing of parliament is the means by which a parliament is dismissed from further sitting, pending its reconvening, without going so far as to dissolve that parliament. This process must be distinguished from that of adjournment, a less formal procedure in the hands of each house of parliament, by which its deliberations are suspended for a relatively short period.

- The dissolution of parliament is the formal step by which a parliament is irrevocably destroyed, and a new parliament can only be formed after a general election.

[4.3.16] Prorogation is a little-used procedure in Australia. Rather, the practice has been adopted of allowing the one session of parliament to continue from its first meeting after one general election to its dissolution before the next general election. Generally, when the parliament is not sitting, this will be because each house has adjourned and not because the Governor-General has prorogued it. It could be argued that the adoption of this practice is inconsistent with s 6 of the Commonwealth Constitution. That point was raised in the Senate in 1919, and the answer given then seems to be generally accepted; namely, that s 6 does not require a distinct session (terminated by prorogation) in every year but requires that 12 months should not pass without a sitting of parliament: Sawer (1956) p 179; Odgers (1976) pp 619–20; Lumb (1986) p 42.

4 Members of parliament: qualifications and disqualifications

[4.4.1] At both state and Commonwealth level, legislation specifies:

- those people who may seek election to parliament;
- those who are not eligible;

- those who (even though eligible when elected) may lose their seats through some misconduct; and

- the procedures for settling disputes on such issues.

The legislative provisions specifying qualifications and disqualifications for election to the Commonwealth Parliament are typical (although simpler than some of their state and territory counterparts).

[4.4.2E]   Commonwealth Constitution

16   The qualifications of a senator shall be the same as those of a member of the House of Representatives ...

34   Until the Parliament otherwise provides, the qualifications of a member of the House of Representatives shall be as follows:

    (i)   He must be of the full age of twenty-one years, and must be an elector entitled to vote at the election of members of the House of Representatives, or a person qualified to become such elector, and must have been for three years at the least a resident within the limits of the Commonwealth as existing at the time when he is chosen:

    (ii)   He must be a subject of the Queen, either natural-born or for at least five years naturalized under the law of the United Kingdom, or of a Colony which has become or becomes a State, or of the Commonwealth, or of a State ...

42   Every senator and every member of the House of Representatives shall before taking his seat make and subscribe before the Governor-General, or some person authorised by him, an oath or affirmation of allegiance in the form set forth in the schedule to this Constitution.

43   A member of either House of the Parliament shall be incapable of being chosen or of sitting as a member of the other House.

44   Any person who —

    (i)   Is under any acknowledgment of allegiance, obedience, or adherence to a foreign power, or is a subject or a citizen or entitled to the rights or privileges of a subject or a citizen of a foreign power: or

    (ii)   Is attainted of treason, or has been convicted and is under sentence, or subject to be sentenced, for any offence punishable under the law of the Commonwealth or of a State by imprisonment for one year or longer: or

    (iii)   Is an undischarged bankrupt or insolvent: or

    (iv)   Holds any office of profit under the Crown, or any pension payable during the pleasure of the Crown out of any of the revenue of the Commonwealth: or

    (v)   Has any direct or indirect pecuniary interest in any agreement with the Public Service of the Commonwealth otherwise than as a member and in common with the other members of an incorporated company consisting of more than twenty-five persons:

shall be incapable of being chosen or of sitting as a senator or a member of the House of Representatives.

But sub-section (iv) does not apply to the office of any of the Queen's Ministers of State for the Commonwealth, or any of the Queen's Ministers for a State, or to the receipt of pay, half-pay, or a pension by any person as an officer or member of the Queen's navy or army, or to the receipt of pay as an officer or member of the naval or military forces of the Commonwealth by any person whose services are not wholly employed by the Commonwealth.

45   If a senator or member of the House of Representatives —

      (i)   Becomes subject to any of the disabilities mentioned in the last preceding section: or

      (ii)   Takes the benefit, whether by assignment, composition, or otherwise, of any law relating to bankrupt or insolvent debtors: or

      (iii) Directly or indirectly takes or agrees to take any fee or honorarium for services rendered to the Commonwealth, or for services rendered in the Parliament to any person or State:

      his place shall thereupon become vacant.

46   Until the Parliament otherwise provides, any person declared by this Constitution to be incapable of sitting as a senator or as a member of the House of Representatives shall, for every day on which he so sits, be liable to pay the sum of one hundred pounds to any person who sues for it in any court of competent jurisdiction.

47   Until the Parliament otherwise provides, any question respecting the qualification of a senator or of a member of the House of Representatives, or respecting a vacancy in either House of Parliament, and any question of a disputed election to either House, shall be determined by the House in which the question arises.

~~~

Notes

[4.4.3] The Commonwealth has, by statute, modified the effect of some of these constitutional provisions, in particular ss 34, 46 and 47. The power to alter these provisions of the Constitution comes from s 51(xxxvi), which gives the parliament the power to make laws with respect to 'Matters in respect of which this Constitution makes provision until the Parliament otherwise provides'.

Section 163 of the Commonwealth Electoral Act 1918 (Cth) fixes the qualifications of a Member of the House of Representatives or the Senate. To qualify, a person must be of the full age of 18 years, an Australian citizen and either an elector entitled to vote at a House of Representatives election or a person qualified to become such an elector.

Section 353 provides that 'the validity of any election or return may be disputed by petition addressed to the Court of Disputed Returns and not otherwise'. Section 354(1) declares that 'the High Court shall be the Court of Disputed Returns'.

Section 376 provides that either House of Parliament may refer to the Court of Disputed Returns 'any question respecting the qualifications of a Senator or of a Member of the House of Representatives or respecting a vacancy in either House of Parliament'.

[4.4.4] The Common Informer (Parliamentary Disqualifications) Act 1975 (Cth) effectively replaced the common informer provisions in s 46 of the Constitution. The Act limits the amount that a person is liable to pay when sued by a common informer, where that person has sat as a senator or as a Member of the House of Representatives while declared by the Constitution to be a person incapable of so sitting. The Act fixes the amount at $200 for the whole of the period before being served with the original process in the suit and $200 for each day after service of that process (if the person is proved to have been incapable of sitting). Section 3(2) of the Act prescribes a 12-month limitation period. The suit must be brought in the High Court (s 5), which is given a discretion under s 3(3) to refuse to make an order if an order would lead to a person being penalised more than once.

[4.4.5] In each of the states and territories, legislation in broadly similar terms specifies the qualifications for membership of parliament, the factors that can disqualify a person from membership and the procedure for settling disputes on these matters. The principal qualifications are a minimum age, a minimum period of residence in the state, and nationality. Disqualifications extend to those who are public servants, Members of Commonwealth Parliament, bankrupts, Crown contractors, those convicted of serious criminal offences (the extent of these disqualifications varies between the various states and territories), and for failing to attend the parliament without excuse. Jurisdiction to resolve disputes over qualifications is vested in the respective Houses of Parliament or in the state Supreme Courts sitting as Courts of Disputed Returns:

- Constitution Act 1902 (NSW) ss 12, 13, 13A, 13B, 13C, 14; Parliamentary Electorates and Elections Act 1912 (NSW) ss 155, 156, 175B;

- Constitution of Queensland 2001 (Qld), ss 6, 7, 21, 22, 24, 43; Parliament of Queensland Act 2001 (Qld), ss 64, 72–74; Electoral and Other Acts Amendment Act 2002 (Qld), s 7;

- Constitution Act 1934 (SA) ss 31, 42, 43, 44, 45, 46, 47, 48a, 49, 50, 51, 53, 54, 54a; Electoral Act 1985 (SA) ss 52, 102, 103, 107, 132;

- Constitution Act 1934 (Tas) ss 14, 30, 31, 32, 33, 34, 35; Electoral Act 1985 (Tas) ss 85, 87, 96, 98, 214, 220, 222, 224;

- Constitution Act 1975 (Vic) ss 23, 29, 36, 44, 45, 46, 47, 48, 49, 50, 54, 55, 56, 57, 58, 59, 60, 61, 61A; Electoral Act 2002 (Vic) ss 22, 70;

- Constitution Acts Amendment Act 1899 (WA) ss 7, 20, 31, 32, 33, 34, 35, 36, 37, 38, 39; Electoral Act 1907 (WA) ss 157, 162, 164, 174;

- Northern Territory Self-Government Act 1978 (Cth), Pt III, Div 2; Northern Territory Electoral Act 2004 (NT), Div 3;

- Australian Capital Territory Self-Government Act 1988 (Cth), ss 14, 67; Electoral Act 1992 (ACT), ss 252, 256–60.

[4.4.6] The positive qualifications for membership of parliament have received relatively little attention from the courts. One such instance was the High Court's unanimous decision *Re Wood* (1988) 167 CLR 145. Three questions were referred to the High Court by resolution of the Senate under s 376 of the Commonwealth Electoral Act 1918 (Cth) **[4.4.3]**. The questions asked whether there was a vacancy in the Senate for the place for which Senator Wood had been returned and, if so, how that vacancy was to be filled. Wood, who had been elected to the Senate as a candidate for the Nuclear Disarmament Party in New South Wales, was a British subject who had not taken out Australian citizenship before his election. The court found that Wood was not entitled to be nominated for election as a senator, nor could he meet the constitutional requirement for a senator referred to in s 16 of the Commonwealth Constitution. Although Wood had become an Australian citizen after his election, his election was void because '[t]he election and return of such an unqualified candidate is wholly ineffective to fill a vacant Senate place': 167 CLR at 164.

A subsidiary issue raised in *Re Wood* related to the effect which s 44(i) of the Commonwealth Constitution might have on the election of persons with dual citizenship, including Australian and United Kingdom citizenship. The court left this issue unexplored. That issue was raised for decision in the following case, which focused on two disqualification provisions, s 44(i) and s 44(iv).

[4.4.7C]   **Sykes v Cleary (No 2)**
                                   (1992) 176 CLR 77

A by-election was held for the House of Representatives seat of Wills on 11 April 1992. There were 22 candidates. Philip Cleary was declared elected on 22 April 1922. At the time of his nomination as a candidate, and at the time of the taking of the poll on 11 April 1992, Cleary held a permanent appointment as a teacher under the Teaching Service Act 1981 (Vic), although he was on leave without pay from that position. Immediately before the declaration of the poll, Cleary resigned his appointment.

Following Cleary's election, another candidate, Ian Sykes, petitioned the High Court, sitting as the Court of Disputed Returns, to declare the result of the election void. Sykes claimed that Cleary was disqualified from being chosen as a Member of Parliament by s 44(iv) of the Constitution, in that he had held an office of profit under the Crown at the time of being chosen. Sykes also claimed that two other candidates, John Delacretaz and Bill Kardamitsis (who had filled third and second places in the poll), were disqualified from being chosen as a Member of Parliament by s 44(i), because they were entitled to the rights or privileges of subjects or citizens of foreign powers.

Mason CJ, Toohey and McHugh JJ:

[95] *Interpretation of s 44(iv)*

The disqualification of a person who holds an office of profit under the Crown has its origins in the law which developed in England in relation to disqualification of the members of the House of Commons. Section 44(iv) is modelled on a provision of the Act of Settlement 1701, which was repealed and replaced by provisions of the Succession to the Crown Act 1707. It has been said that the English provisions give effect to three main considerations or policies. They are: (1) the incompatibility of certain non-ministerial offices under the Crown with membership in the House of Commons (here, membership must be taken to cover questions of a member's relations with, and duties to, his or her constituents); (2) the need to limit the control or influence of the executive government over the House by means of an undue proportion of office-holders being members of the House; and (3) the essential condition of a certain number of ministers being members of the House for the purpose of ensuring control of the executive by Parliament ...

[96] The exclusion of permanent officers of the executive government from the House was a recognition of the incompatibility of a person at the one time holding such an office and being a member of the House. There are three factors that give rise to that incompatibility. First, performance by a public servant of his or her public service duties would impair his or her capacity to attend to the duties of a member of the House. Secondly, there is a very considerable risk that a public servant would share the political opinions of the minister of his or her department and would not bring to bear as a member of the House a free and independent judgment. Thirdly, membership of the House would detract from the performance of the relevant public service duty ...

[97] Although a teacher is not an instance of the archetypical public servant at whom the disqualification was primarily aimed, a permanent public servant who is a teacher falls within the categories of public servants whose public service duties are incompatible, on the three grounds mentioned previously, with the duties of a member of the House of Representatives or of a senator ...

The taking of leave without pay by a person who holds an office of profit under the Crown does not alter the character of the office which he or she holds. The person remains the holder of an office, notwithstanding that he or she is not in receipt of pay during the period of leave.

Mason CJ, Toohey and McHugh JJ held that s 44(iv)'s reference to 'any office of profit under the Crown' included an office of profit under the Crown in right of a state:

[98] [T]he long-standing reasons for disqualifying Commonwealth public servants from membership of the Houses of Parliament have similar force in relation to State public servants. The risk of a conflict between their obligations to their State and their duties as members of the House to which they belong is a further incident of the incompatibility of being, at the same time, a State public servant and a member of the Parliament.

It follows that the first respondent, as the holder of an office of profit under the Crown, fell within s 44(iv) until he resigned that office on 16 April 1992.

Mason CJ, Toohey and McHugh JJ held that the disqualification expressed in s 44(iv) operated at each stage of the process of being chosen as a Member of Parliament, including nomination as a candidate: 176 CLR at 99–100. Mason CJ, Toohey and McHugh JJ decided that the election should be declared void. They then turned to the question whether the second and third respondents (Delacretaz and Kardamitis) had been qualified to be chosen at the by-election. They found the following facts:

Delacretaz was born in Switzerland in 1923 and was, from the time of his birth, a Swiss citizen. He migrated to Australia in 1951 and became an Australian citizen in 1960, renouncing allegiance to any state of which he was a citizen. Under the law of Switzerland, a person will be released from citizenship upon his or her demand if he or she has no residence in Switzerland and has acquired another nationality. Delacretaz had made no application to the government of Switzerland to renounce or terminate his Swiss citizenship. Kardamitis was born in Greece in 1952 and was, from the time of his birth, a Greek citizen. He migrated to Australia in 1969 and became an Australian citizen in 1975, renouncing all other allegiance. Since then, he had been active in public affairs in Australia. Under the law of Greece, a Greek national may have his or her nationality discharged if he or she has acquired another nationality and then obtains the approval of the appropriate Greek Minister.

[105] *Interpretation of s 44(i)* ...

The common law recognises the concept of dual nationality, so that, for example, it may regard a person as being at the same time a citizen or national of both Australia and Germany. At common law, the question of whether a person is a citizen or national of a particular foreign State is determined according to the [106] law of that foreign State. This latter principle is, in part, a recognition of the principle of international law, restated in the *Nottebohm* Case [*Liechtenstein v Guatemala* [1955] ICJ 4 at 20], that:

> ... it is for every sovereign State ... to settle by its own legislation the rules relating to the acquisition of its nationality, and to confer that nationality by naturalization granted by its own organs in accordance with that legislation.

[107] ... But, there is no reason why s 44(i) should be read as if it were intended to give unqualified effect to that rule of international law. To do so might well result in the disqualification of Australian citizens on whom there was imposed involuntarily by operation of foreign law a continuing foreign nationality, notwithstanding that they had taken reasonable steps to renounce that foreign nationality. It would be wrong to interpret the constitutional provision in such a way as to disbar an Australian citizen who had taken all reasonable steps to divest himself or herself of any conflicting allegiance. It has been said that the provision was designed to ensure: 'that members of Parliament did not have a split allegiance and were not, as far as possible, subject to any improper influence from foreign governments.' What is more, s 44(i) finds its place in a Constitution which was enacted at a time, like the present, when a high proportion of Australians, though born overseas, had adopted this country as their home. In that setting, it could scarcely have been intended to disqualify an Australian citizen for election to Parliament on account of his or her continuing to possess a foreign nationality, notwithstanding that he or she had taken reasonable steps to renounce that nationality. In this respect it is significant that s 42 of the Constitution requires

a member of Parliament to take [108] an oath or affirmation of allegiance in the form set out in the schedule to the Constitution.

What amounts to the taking of reasonable steps to renounce foreign nationality must depend upon the circumstances of the particular case. What is reasonable will turn on the situation of the individual, the requirements of the foreign law and the extent of the connection between the individual and the foreign State of which he or she is alleged to be a subject or citizen. And it is relevant to bear in mind that a person who has participated in an Australian naturalisation ceremony in which he or she has expressly renounced his or her foreign allegiance may well believe that, by becoming an Australian citizen, he or she has effectively renounced any foreign nationality.

Mason CJ, Toohey and McHugh JJ found that, although Delacratz and Kardamitsis were Australian citizens, Delacratz had not demanded release from Swiss citizenship and Kardamitsis had not sought the approval of the appropriate Greek Minister for discharge of his Greek nationality. It could not be said that either of them had taken reasonable steps to divest himself of foreign citizenship and the rights and privileges of such a citizen. Thus, that they were disqualified by s 44(i) of the Constitution.

~~~

[4.4.8] Brennan J agreed with Mason CJ, Toohey and McHugh JJ that s 44(iv) rendered Cleary incapable of being chosen as a Member of the House of Representatives. He held that, because neither Delacretaz nor Kardamitsis had taken 'steps reasonably open under the relevant laws of his native country — Switzerland in one case, Greece in the other — to renounce his status as a citizen of that country and to obtain his release from the duties of allegiance and obedience imposed on citizens by the laws of that country', neither of them was capable of being chosen as a Member of the House of Representatives: 176 CLR at 114.

Deane J held that Cleary's appointment as a teacher in the Victorian teaching service was an office of profit under the Crown, but that the disqualification effected by s 44(iv) did not operate until the declaration of the poll; so that Cleary was not disqualified by s 44(iv). Deane J held that both Delacretaz and Kardimitsis had done all that could reasonably be expected of them to extinguish any relationship with their former countries, and, accordingly, were not disqualified by s 44(i).

Dawson J agreed with Mason CJ, Toohey and McHugh JJ. Gaudron J agreed with Mason CJ, Toohey and McHugh JJ that s 44(iv) rendered Cleary incapable of being chosen as a Member of the House of Representatives. However, Gaudron J held that both Delacretaz and Kardimitsis had, upon taking out Australian citizenship, effectively renounced their former nationalities, and, so that they were not disqualified by s 44(i).

Notes

[4.4.9] In *Sue v Hill* (1999) 199 CLR 462 the High Court considered the validity of the election of the Queensland 'One Nation' Senate candidate, Heather Hill, who was born in the United Kingdom in 1960 and migrated to Australia in 1971. She applied for and was granted Australian citizenship in 1998. Gaudron J observed (at 505):

At the time Mrs Hill was granted Australian citizenship, the Australian Citizenship Act 1948 (Cth) contained no requirement for the renunciation of foreign citizenship. Nor, apparently, was there any practice whereby citizenship was renounced, the recipient of Australian citizenship being required only to pledge his or her 'loyalty to Australia and its people, whose democratic beliefs I share, whose rights and liberties I respect, and whose laws I will uphold and obey'.

The High Court concluded that the denial of efficacy to the statutes of the United Kingdom Parliament effected by the Australia Acts (see further **[6.2.7E]**) provided a conclusive answer to the question raised — the United Kingdom was a foreign power and Hill was a subject of a foreign power for the purposes of s 44(i) of the Constitution: 199 CLR 462 at 492 (Gleeson CJ, Gummow and Hayne JJ), 528 (Gaudron J).

In *Re Webster* (1975) 132 CLR 270 the High Court (constituted by Barwick CJ) considered two questions referred to it by the Senate. The questions were, first, whether Senator Webster was incapable of being chosen or of sitting as a senator; and, second, whether Senator Webster had become incapable of sitting as a senator. Webster was managing director, secretary, manager and one of nine shareholders of a company that regularly sold goods to a Commonwealth Government department.

Barwick CJ said the historical background to s 44(v) indicated that it was intended to protect the independence of parliament against undue influence exerted by the Crown, not to avoid possible conflicts of interest on the part of Members of Parliament. It followed, Barwick CJ said, that s 44(v) was confined to those contracts which gave the Crown an opportunity to influence the contractor; that is, a continuing contract under which something remained to be done. The contract, he said, must hold out 'the possibility of financial gain by the existence or the performance of the agreement [so] that the person could conceivably be influenced by the Crown in relation to parliamentary affairs': 132 CLR at 280.

In the present case, according to Barwick CJ, there was no continuing agreement, merely a series of separate agreements between the company and the department. In any event, he said, Senator Webster, as a shareholder of the company, had no pecuniary interest in the transactions of the company 'under the general law [and] there is good reason to conclude that the same is true in relation to s 44(v)': 132 CLR at 287. The Chief Justice accordingly concluded that Senator Webster was not disqualified from election to or membership of the Senate.

For a different view of the question whether a shareholder would be caught by s 44(v), see Evans (1975) p 469. For a criticism of the approach adopted by Barwick CJ to the purpose of s 44(v), see Hanks (1977) pp 196–7.

[4.4.10]   In 1998, it was claimed that the Parliamentary Secretary to the Minister for Defence, Warren Entsch MP, was a director of a company that supplied concrete to the Defence Department. The government used its control of the House of Representatives to exonerate Entsch, by determining (pursuant to s 47 of the Constitution) that Entsch was not disqualified by s 44(v) of the Constitution. The house did not refer the question to the High Court, as the Senate had done in the *Webster* case.

[4.4.11]   At the state level, disqualifying provisions can be altered by legislation. Indeed, it could be said that disqualifications are unlikely to be applied against any Member of Parliament who can invoke the support of the government.

Under s 61A of the Constitution Act 1975 (Vic), each of the houses of the Victorian Parliament has the power to exempt any person from the effect of the disqualifying provisions where the house is satisfied that the matter leading to the disqualification:

(a) has ceased to have effect;

(b) was in all the circumstances of a trifling nature; and

(c) occurred or arose without the actual knowledge or consent of the person or was accidental or due to inadvertence.

This exemption is to be effected by a resolution of the relevant house: Constitution Act 1975 (Vic) s 61A. The operation of this provision was demonstrated in 1984:

> The session commenced on an embarrassing note for the government. It appeared that the Labour MLA for Morwell, Val Callister, had breached s 44(d) of the Constitution Act 1975, by virtue of her acceptance, as an MP, of an 'office or profit under the Crown', namely membership of the Environment Council. Her seat had technically become vacant, but the Speaker had deferred the issue of a writ, pending consideration of the case by the House. The government moved that Callister's acceptance 'had ceased to have effect, was in all the circumstances of a trifling nature and was accidental or due to inadvertence'. The government further moved that, in accordance with s 61A of the Constitution Act 1975, 'the said appointment be deemed never to have occurred' (VPD (A), 4 September 1984). The opposition, while not opposing Callister's reinstatement, sought to amend the motion to express 'deep concern' at the government's handling of the situation. The amendment was defeated, the motion was carried, and the electorate of Morwell regained its (technically lost) representation ((1984) 31 Australian J of Politics and History at 319).

5 Voting for parliament: the franchise

[4.5.1E]   **Commonwealth Constitution**

8   The qualification of electors of senators shall be in each State that which is prescribed by this Constitution, or by the Parliament, as the qualification for electors of members of the House of Representatives; but in the choosing of senators each selector shall vote only once ...

30   Until the Parliament otherwise provides, the qualification of electors of members of the House of Representatives shall be in each State that which is prescribed by the law of the State as the qualification of electors of the more numerous House of Parliament of the State, but in the choosing of members each elector shall vote only once ...

41   No adult person who has or acquires a right to vote at elections for the more numerous House of Parliament of a State shall, while the right continues, be prevented by any law of the Commonwealth from voting at elections for either House of the Parliament of the Commonwealth ...

~~~

[4.5.2] Sections 8 and 30 of the Constitution contemplate that the Commonwealth Parliament can adjust the franchise subject to the constraint expressed in the Constitution s 41. That power has been exercised in the Commonwealth Electoral Act 1918 (Cth).

Section 93(1) provides that, to be qualified to vote, a person must have attained 18 years of age, and be an Australian citizen or a British subject who was enrolled to vote immediately before 26 January 1984. Section 93(6) provides that, to be entitled to vote, an elector must have 'his real place of living ... at some time within the three months immediately preceding polling day for that election, within [the relevant electorate]'.

Several categories of persons are precluded from voting by s 93(7) and (8), including:

- holders of temporary entry permits;

- prohibited non-citizens;

- persons of unsound mind;

- persons convicted and under sentence for an offence punishable by imprisonment for five years or longer; and

- persons convicted of treason or treachery.

[4.5.3] In each of the states and territories, legislation defines the franchise for elections to both Assembly and Council in substantially identical terms. The common requirements are three:

- that the voter is an Australian citizen (or a British subject already enrolled to vote on a nominated date);

- has reached 18 years of age; and

- has resided in the state for a minimum period (which varies from three to six months).

In each state some classes of people are disqualified from voting. These disqualifications are considerably narrower than those for membership of parliament and are likely to become even narrower. South Australia removed (in 1976) the disqualification, common to all Australian electoral systems, of persons attainted of treason or serving a sentence of imprisonment. Victoria removed (in 1980) the disqualification of persons serving a sentence of imprisonment but retained conviction of treason as a disqualification. The relevant provisions can be found in the following legislation:

- Constitution Act 1902 (NSW) s 22; Parliamentary Electorates and Elections Act 1912 (NSW) ss 20–21;

- Electoral Act 1992 (Qld) ss 64, 101;

- Constitution Act 1934 (SA) s 48; Electoral Act 1985 (SA) ss 29, 52;

- Constitution Act 1934 (Tas) ss 28, 29; Electoral Act 1985 (Tas) s 22;

- Constitution Act 1975 (Vic) s 48;

- Electoral Act 1907 (WA) ss 17, 18.

Each of the self-governing territories incorporate the voter qualifications adopted by the Commonwealth under the Commonwealth Electoral Act (1918):

- Electoral Act 1992 (ACT), s 100;

- Northern Territory (Self-Government) Act 1978 (Cth), ss 20 and 21.

[4.5.4] The achievement of a relatively uniform and non-discriminatory franchise throughout Australia is recent. From 1908, when women were given the right to vote in Victoria, it might have been said that Australian parliaments were elected on the basis of adult suffrage. However, state upper houses continued to be elected on a property franchise until 1950 (Victoria), 1963 (Western Australia), 1968 (Tasmania), and 1973 (South Australia).

The New South Wales Legislative Council was until 1933 a nominated chamber. Between 1933 and 1978 it was elected on a rotation system by the Members of the Legislative Assembly and the non-retiring Members of the Council, an electorate of about 140 voters. From 1978, the Council has been elected by adult suffrage.

Another defect in the universality of Australia's adult suffrage was the denial of voting rights to Aboriginal people until the 1960s (see further Galligan & Chesterman, 1997). The Queensland and Western Australian legislation disqualified different categories of Aboriginal people (Elections Act 1915 (Qld) ss 11, 11A; Electoral Act 1907 (WA) s 19(e)), and, because of s 39(5) of the Commonwealth Electoral Act 1918 (Cth), Aboriginal people resident in those states could not vote in Commonwealth elections, unless they had been members of the defence forces.

In 1962, the Commonwealth and Western Australian disqualifications were removed: Commonwealth Electoral Act 1962 (Cth) ss 2, 3; Electoral Act Amendment Act 1962 (WA) s 3. Queensland followed suit in 1965: Elections Acts Amendment Act 1965 (Qld) ss 3, 4. However, enrolment was not rendered compulsory for Aboriginal people (as it is for all other persons qualified to vote) until 1971 in Queensland, and 1983 in Western Australia, when their enrolment was also made compulsory for the Commonwealth electoral roll.

The reduction of the minimum voting age was achieved with more speed and uniformity than the democratisation of Council elections. New South Wales and Western Australia led the way in 1970, followed by South Australia in 1971 and Queensland, Victoria, Tasmania and the Commonwealth in 1973:

- Commonwealth Electoral Act 1973 (Cth) s 3;

- Parliamentary Electorates and Elections (Amendment) Act 1970 (NSW) s 2;

- Elections Act and The Criminal Code Amendment Act 1973 (Qld) s 9;

- Electoral Act Amendment Act 1972 (SA) s 8;

- Electoral Act 1973 (Tas) s 6;

- Constitution Act Amendment Act 1973 (Vic) s 4;

- Electoral Act Amendment Act 1970 (WA).

[4.5.5] Is there a minimum franchise established by the Commonwealth Constitution? The United States Supreme Court has held that the express provisions of the 14th, 15th, 19th and 24th amendments to the United States Constitution protect the right to vote in federal, state and local elections. For example, state legislation requiring voters to satisfy election registrars of their ability to 'understand and give a reasonable interpretation of any section' of the federal or state constitutions was struck down by the Supreme Court because the statute had been enacted and was being applied for a discriminatory purpose: *Louisiana v United States* 380 US 145 (1965). Again, a state statute which conditioned the right to vote upon payment of a poll tax was declared invalid: it denied 'the equal protection of the law' guaranteed by the 14th Amendment. Wealth bears no relation to voter qualification, the court said: *Harper v Virginia Board of Election* 383 US 663 (1966).

There are, in the Commonwealth Constitution, no equivalents to these clauses in the United States Constitution. However, we might infer some constitutional protection from the requirement of s 24 that the Members of the House of Representatives shall be 'directly chosen by the people of the Commonwealth'. Would a literacy test, or a property test, or the denial of the vote to people under the age of 25 be consistent with that requirement? This issue was discussed in *Attorney-General (Commonwealth) (Ex rel McKinlay) v Commonwealth* (1975) 135 CLR 1 **[4.5.12]**, and *McGinty v Western Australia* (1996) 186 CLR 140 **[4.5.14]**.

[4.5.6] In 1972, the Commonwealth Electoral Act 1918 (Cth) fixed the age of 21 years as the minimum voting age for Commonwealth elections. A 1971 amendment to the Constitution Act 1934 (SA) fixed the age of 18 years as the minimum voting age for South Australian elections. The Age of Majority (Reduction) Act 1970–1971 (SA), passed at the same time, declared that every 'person of and above the age of eighteen years shall be sui juris and of full age or capacity'.

Susan King, who had attained the age of 18 but had not yet turned 21, was refused enrolment on the Commonwealth electoral register. She applied to the Magistrate's Court in Adelaide, under s 58 of the Commonwealth Electoral Act, for an order directing that she be enrolled; the matter was removed to the High Court under s 40 of the Judiciary Act 1903 (Cth). King's argument, that she was entitled to enrol for and vote at Commonwealth elections, was based on s 41 of the Commonwealth Constitution **[4.5.1E]**. In *King v Jones* (1972) 128 CLR 221, that argument was rejected by the High Court on the basis that, whatever might be the nature of the right conferred by s 41 of the Constitution, it extended only to an 'adult person', a term which carried the meaning which it had in 1900; namely a person who had attained the age of 21 years.

Another possible restriction of s 41 was raised by most justices but not resolved. This was the view, expressed by John Quick and Robert Garran, that s 41 guaranteed the right to vote at Commonwealth elections only to those persons who had acquired a state franchise before the Commonwealth Parliament enacted the federal franchise (which it did in 1902): Quick and Garran (1901), p 487. Barwick CJ, Windeyer and Stephen JJ found it unnecessary to decide whether that view was correct: 128 CLR at 229, 251, 267. Menzies J explicitly rejected it. Section 41, he said, was 'not a provision to make temporary arrangements for the period between the establishment of the Constitution and the making of Commonwealth laws': 128 CLR at 246. Gibbs J was equivocal. While he said it was unnecessary to express a final opinion, he described the Quick and Garran argument as 'far from clearly correct': 128 CLR at 259.

The High Court was obliged to confront this issue in the following case.

[4.5.7C]   **R v Pearson; Ex parte Sipka**

(1983) 152 CLR 254

On 4 February 1983, both Houses of the Commonwealth Parliament were dissolved by the Governor-General under s 57 of the Constitution, and an election for both houses announced. On the same day, writs were issued for the election, nominating 5 March 1983 as the polling day. Section 43 of the Commonwealth Electoral Act 1918 (Cth) had the effect of closing the electoral roll from 6 pm on 4 February 1984:

43 Notwithstanding anything contained in either of the last two preceding sections —

(a) claims for enrolment or transfer of enrolment which are received by the Registrar after six o'clock in the afternoon of the day of issue of the writ for an election shall not be registered until after the close of the polling at the election ...

Four persons, who were otherwise entitled to be enrolled under the Commonwealth Electoral Act and who were entitled to be enrolled as electors for the New South Wales Parliament, lodged forms claiming both Commonwealth and state enrolments with Divisional Returning Officers. (These officers administered both the Commonwealth and the state electoral rolls, by arrangement between the Commonwealth and New South Wales.) The four were placed on the roll of electors for New South Wales but their claims for enrolment on the roll of Commonwealth electors were deferred until after 5 March 1983.

The four then applied to the High Court of Australia for a writ of mandamus, requiring the Chief Australian Electoral Officer and other officials to add their names to the Commonwealth roll of electors and to permit them to vote at the forthcoming election. The High Court's decision was handed down on 24 February 1983.

Murphy J: [268] ... Section 41 is one of the few guarantees of the rights of persons in the Australian Constitution. It should be given the purposive interpretation which accords with its plain words, with its context of other provisions of unlimited duration, and its contrast with transitional provisions. Constitutions are to [be] read broadly and not pedantically. Guarantees of personal rights should not be read narrowly. A right to vote is so precious that it should not read out of the Constitution by implication. Rather every reasonable presumption and interpretation should be adopted which favours the right of people to participate in the elections of those who represent them.

Plain meaning. The purpose conveyed by its plain words is a constitutional guarantee that every adult person who has a right to vote at State elections shall not be prevented by any Commonwealth law from voting at Federal elections. The only sensible meaning is that the persons described are entitled to vote in Federal elections. The respondents contend that s 41 does not confer any right to vote at Federal elections; it merely says that no Commonwealth laws shall prevent the persons described from voting in Federal elections and that the right to vote must be found elsewhere. This ridicules the constitutional guarantee. Such a pedantic interpretation should not be adopted to nullify this important personal right. Further, like other constitutional statutory provisions s 41 is presumed to be prospective, ambulatory and constantly speaking. Its words are not transitional.

Murphy J referred to the context of s 41 (none of its associated provisions was of limited duration) and contrasted it with various transitional provisions. He noted that, before 1901, the immediate concern was that without s 41, women in South Australia might be denied the vote in federal elections and that Aborigines entitled to vote in some states might also be disenfranchised. He noted that a Parliamentary Select Committee on the Voting Rights of Aboriginals had received advice in 1961, from the Solicitor-General, Kenneth Bailey, and from Professor Geoffrey Sawer that s 41 should be read as having a prospective operation and was not limited to voters who were qualified at the date when the first Commonwealth Franchise Act came into operation. He continued:

[270] Following the Report of the Select Committee the disqualification of Australian Aborigines was removed in 1962 by amendment of the Commonwealth Electoral Act No 31 of 1962 (s 2). Until then, the only right of Australian Aboriginals to vote in Federal elections was derived from the guarantee in s 41 ... The history of discrimination against Aboriginal voting rights repudiates the argument that giving the [271] s 41 guarantee the full scope of its plain meaning would be an undesirable departure from the allegedly 'Uniform Federal Franchise' introduced in 1902.

If the respondents' view of s 41 is adopted, it has been, and is open to the Federal Parliament to restrict the Federal franchise in other ways so as to deprive persons with a State franchise from voting at Federal elections ... Parliament [could] disqualify persons in receipt of unemployment benefits or other social services. Section 41 protects those with a right to vote in State elections from any such disfranchisement ...

Brennan, Deane and Dawson JJ: [278] ... Though it is right to see s 41 as a constitutional guarantee of the right to vote, the means by which that guarantee is secured is itself definitive of the extent of the guarantee. Voting, that is, the exercise of an existing right to vote, at elections of the Commonwealth Parliament cannot 'be prevented by any law of the Commonwealth'. But s 41 does not in terms confer a right to vote. If a right to vote is claimed by an elector in reliance upon the statutory franchise now prescribed by the laws of the Commonwealth, those laws are definitive of the right and s 41 has no work to do. But if [279] and so long as a right to vote was claimed by an elector in reliance upon the constitutional franchise — whether existing at the establishment of the Commonwealth or the result of a later modification before the prescription of a statutory franchise by the Commonwealth Parliament — s 41 precluded any law of the Commonwealth from preventing the exercise of that voting right. In other words, those who, by State laws, were able to acquire a right to vote at elections of the more numerous House of the State and who, by reason of ss 30 and 8, thereby acquired the right to vote at elections of the Parliament of the Commonwealth, were entitled to continue voting at the latter elections so long as they continued to be entitled to vote at elections of the more numerous House of the State Parliament. They could not be prevented by any law of the Commonwealth from doing so.

The applicants seek to extend the operation of s 41 beyond this point by converting the prohibition against preventing a person from voting at a Federal election into a source of a right to vote at such an election. If s 41 were given this operation, the power conferred upon the Parliament to legislate for a uniform franchise would be destroyed. A Parliament of a State would be empowered to give the Federal franchise to those whom the Commonwealth Parliament has excluded or disqualified; for example, property owners who do not live in the State, aliens, prohibited immigrants or convicts under sentence for more serious offences.

If that operation were accorded to s 41, the Parliament of a State would be empowered to increase the number of its electors for the purposes of s 128 beyond the number entitled under the uniform franchise ... But that operation is wholly unsupported by the terms of s 41 ... The right to vote to which s 41 relates is the constitutional franchise conferred by ss 30 and 8. The purpose of s 41 is clear from its constitutional context: it was to ensure that those who enjoyed the constitutional franchise should not lose it when the statutory franchise was enacted. The statute was to govern the subsequent acquisition of the right to vote at Federal elections. The persons to whom s 41 applies are the persons who acquired the right to vote pursuant to ss 30 and 8. After the Parliament enacted the Commonwealth Franchise Act 1902, which was entitled 'An Act to provide for a Uniform Federal Franchise', no person could acquire the right to vote at Federal elections save in accordance with its terms.

[280] It follows, of course, that the practical effect of s 41 is spent. Most of the electors who acquired a right to vote at Federal elections under ss 30 and 8 of the Constitution would have died. Since 12 June 1902, when the Commonwealth Franchise Act came into force, no person has acquired a right to vote the exercise of which is protected by s 41. None of the present applicants is a person to whom s 41 applies. None of them is therefore entitled to enrol or to vote by reason of s 39B of the Act.

The applications must be dismissed with costs.

Gibbs CJ, Mason and Wilson JJ delivered a joint judgment in similar terms to the judgment of Brennan, Deane and Dawson JJ.

~~~

Notes

[4.5.8]   The different perspectives on s 41 offered by the majority justices and by Murphy J provide another illustration of the equivocal and inconclusive indications which textual analysis offers to constitutional adjudication. The majority claimed that 's 41 does not in terms confer a right to vote' (152 CLR at 260 per Gibbs CJ, Mason and Wilson JJ; 152 CLR at 278 per Brennan, Deane and Dawson JJ) but only 'prevents the Commonwealth Parliament from taking away a right to vote' (152 CLR at 260, per Gibbs CJ, Mason and Wilson JJ). But the reading of s 41 preferred by Murphy J, that every adult person entitled to vote at state elections was entitled to vote in Commonwealth elections, is not obviously a misinterpretation of the words of the section. John Quick and Robert Garran, whose opinion on the reading of s 41 was cited by the majority (152 CLR at 262 per Gibbs CJ, Mason and Wilson JJ) made the point that this reading required words such as 'acquires' and 'prevented' to be read in quite a narrow way: Quick and Garran (1901) p 487.

Moreover, as Murphy J pointed out (152 CLR at 271–2), the history of s 41 is inconsistent with this reading. A proposal to alter the draft of s 41 so as to confine its protection to those persons with a state franchise, acquired before the introduction of the Commonwealth franchise, was not adopted during the drafting process. In addition, Murphy J's reading had the support of such eminent constitutional scholars as Bailey, Lane and Sawer: 152 CLR at 270, 273.

[4.5.9] The most substantial justification for the majority's reading of s 41 lies in their references to the historical context in which the section was drafted and to the policy implications of allowing the section to function as a continuing guarantee of the right to vote. For the majority, it was those historical and policy considerations that justified their narrow interpretation of the text of s 41.

The history to which they referred was the marked variation in voting rights between the various colonies in 1901. The most substantial difference was that women had equal voting rights in South Australia and Western Australia, but in no other part of Australia. This history indicated, they said, that s 41 was intended to ensure that the more liberal voting rights of South Australian and Western Australian women, which were transferred into the Commonwealth sphere by ss 8 and 30 of the Commonwealth Constitution, would not be denied when a uniform federal franchise was introduced, as foreshadowed by s 30.

There were two policy considerations, according to the majority. First, to read s 41 as a continuing guarantee would allow state parliaments to undermine the uniformity of the federal franchise. Second, a state parliament could manipulate the federal franchise so as to increase the number of electors in that state who could vote in a constitutional referendum under s 128.

For each of these considerations there are counterarguments, many of which were developed in Murphy J's judgment.

[4.5.10] Even if the reading of s 41 favoured by Murphy J had been adopted, it does not follow that the applicants would have succeeded in obtaining mandamus. Their success would have been contingent on the court deciding that s 43(a) of the Commonwealth Electoral Act was a law of the Commonwealth which prevented the applicants from voting at elections for the Commonwealth Parliament. However, s 43(a) might better be described as a law which regulated the procedural aspects of the Commonwealth franchise. There is an obvious, practical need to have some system of voter registration so that, as a minimum, electoral rolls can be consolidated, corrected, copied and distributed to polling places; indeed, it might be seen as reasonable also to require some investigation and verification of claims for enrolment. These processes require time, and s 43(a) might be seen as doing no more than allowing the Australian Electoral Commission a reasonable time in which to carry out those processes.

[4.5.11] In 1988 the Constitutional Commission observed of this decision that 'for practical purposes section 41 is now a dead letter and the Constitution does not effectively guarantee anyone a right to vote': Constitutional Commission (1988) p 129. The Commission's concluding assertion paid no regard to the possibility that s 24 of the Commonwealth Constitution guarantees a minimum franchise: see **[4.5.12]–[4.5.14]**.

If s 41 were a constitutional guarantee of the right to vote (as Murphy J argued), it would be a rather unbalanced and elastic guarantee. Any person's constitutionally protected right to vote in Commonwealth elections would depend upon that person retaining the right to vote for the lower house of state parliament in his or her state of residence. If the right to vote in state elections were withdrawn by a state parliament, that protection would disappear, and the way would be opened for the Commonwealth Parliament to remove the federal franchise. Territory residents would, of course, have no constitutional protection.

The Constitutional Commission expressed the view that '[t]he right to vote in elections of legislatures is … a basic democratic right and one which merits constitutional protection': Constitutional Commission (1988) p 140. The Commission proposed that the Commonwealth Constitution should be altered to ensure that the right to vote in Commonwealth, territory and state elections was available to all Australian citizens who had attained the age of 18 years, subject to compliance with reasonable conditions, prescribed by legislation, relating to residence and enrolment, and subject to possible legislative disqualification on two grounds: current imprisonment for an offence, and incapacity to understand the nature and significance of enrolment and voting because of unsoundness of mind: Constitutional Commission (1988) pp 128–9.

In June 1988, the House of Representatives and the Senate passed the Constitution Alteration Fair Elections 1988, which would have, inter alia, given effect to the Commission's recommendation by inserting a s 124G into the Commonwealth Constitution. At a referendum held on 3 September 1988, this proposal was rejected by the voters.

[4.5.12]   The question whether a right to vote might be guaranteed by ss 7 and 24 of the Commonwealth Constitution was considered by several members of the High Court in *Attorney-General (Cth) (Ex rel McKinlay) v Commonwealth* (1975) 135 CLR 1. The central issue in that case turned on the requirements for the distribution of House of Representatives seats contained in s 24; in particular, on whether that provision required that electorates contain the same number of voters, so that their votes could be said to have the same value: see **[4.6.9C]**.

On the negative side, Gibbs J said that s 24 was irrelevant to the content of the franchise and asserted that 'people might constitutionally be denied the franchise on the ground of race, sex or lack of property': 135 CLR at 44. Mason J said that 'the Constitution does not guarantee or insist upon universal adult suffrage': 135 CLR at 62. Stephen J also asserted that the parliament could restrict the franchise 'to male British subjects over 21, maybe with a superadded property qualification', because 'representative democracy is descriptive of a whole spectrum of political institutions', but cautioned that '[t]he spectrum has finite limits' and that some quality might be regarded as so essential that a voting system lacking that quality would be inconsistent with s 24: 135 CLR at 57, 58.

On the positive side, McTiernan and Jacobs JJ said that s 24 did not leave the Commonwealth Parliament free to select any qualifications for the franchise and said that 'the long established universal adult suffrage' meant that it was 'doubtful' whether 'anything less … could now be described as a choice by the people': 135 CLR at 36. Murphy J rejected the argument that s 24 imposed no constraints on the

Commonwealth Parliament's power to prescribe the franchise, and treated the section as demanding that House of Representatives elections be democratic and as preventing the parliament 'depriving women of a vote, [or] imposing ... property qualifications on voters': 135 CLR at 70.

[4.5.13] The proposition that ss 7 and 24 require a broadly based franchise for the election of the Commonwealth Parliament derived further support from the High Court's decisions in *Nationwide News Pty Ltd v Wills* (1992) 177 CLR 1 **[11.3.9]** and *Australian Capital Television Pty Ltd v Commonwealth (No 2)* (1992) 177 CLR 106 **[11.3.7C]**, where the court recognised that the system of representative government gave rise to an implied freedom of communication on political and government matters.

In *Nationwide News*, Deane and Toohey JJ said that, in implementing representative government, the Constitution reserved to the people 'the ultimate power of governmental control', so that 'all citizens of the Commonwealth who are not under some special disability are entitled to share equally in the exercise of those ultimate powers of governmental control' involved in voting: 177 CLR at 71–2.

In *Australian Capital Television*, Gaudron J described 'representative parliamentary democracy' as 'a fundamental part of the Constitution': 177 CLR at 210. Although Mason CJ apparently conceded that the parliament could set the qualifications for electors, he also said that Australia's system of representative government required that 'elected representatives exercise power on behalf of the Australian people': 177 CLR at 138, 139. Even the more cautious statements are difficult to reconcile with a flexible franchise, his Honour went on to say: 177 CLR at 139. McHugh J said that the Constitution gives effect to a system of representative government (177 CLR at 229), and Dawson J said that the choice of Members of Parliament for which ss 7 and 24 provided 'must be a true choice': 177 CLR at 187.

[4.5.14] In *McGinty v Western Australia* (1996) 186 CLR 140, the High Court revisited the issue that was central to *McKinlay's* case (1975) 135 CLR 1 **[4.6.9C]**, namely whether s 24 of the Constitution and the principle of representative democracy required that electoral divisions have equal numbers of electors. In the course of resolving that question, some members of the High Court commented upon the content of the franchise.

Brennan CJ noted that, during the 20th century, the age of majority had been reduced from 21 to 18 and the legal incapacity of women to vote removed. Aboriginal people, once disqualified from the franchise, were no longer so disqualified. He observed at 166–7:

> In view of the fact that the franchise has historically expanded in scope, it is at least arguable that the qualifications of age, sex, race and property which limited the franchise in earlier times could not now be reimposed so as to deprive a citizen of the right to vote.

Dawson J said, at 183, that the Constitution left to parliament to provide the particular form of representative government:

> For example, the qualifications of electors are to be provided for by parliament under ss 8 and 30 and may amount to less than universal suffrage, however politically unacceptable that may be today.

Gaudron J said that, notwithstanding the limited nature of the franchise in 1901, ss 7 and 24 would not allow 'the franchise ... to be denied to women or to members of a racial minority or to be made subject to a property or educational qualification':

186 CLR at 221–2. Toohey J also noted that, in 1900, the perception of what representative democracy involved was different to current perceptions. But, he said, 'today's standards' would not allow a system which denied universal adult franchise: 186 CLR at 201.

[4.5.15] The High Court's reasoning in *Cheatle v The Queen* (1993) 177 CLR 541, that the institution of trial by jury in s 80 of the Constitution no longer contemplates the exclusion of females or property qualifications for jurors (as s 80 had done in 1900), provides some analogous support for the approach of McTiernan and Jacobs JJ in *McKinlay's* case **[4.6.9C]**. The court (Mason CJ, Brennan, Deane, Dawson, Toohey, Gaudron and McHugh JJ) observed that 'a liberalisation of the qualifications of jurors involves no more than an adjustment of the institution to confirm with contemporary standards and to bring about a situation which is more truly representative of the community': 177 CLR at 560.

6   The distribution of seats

[4.6.1] With the exception of the Tasmanian House of Assembly, where each of the five electorates returns seven members on the basis of proportional representation, the lower houses of the Commonwealth and state parliaments are elected on the basis of single member electorates. So, too, are the Legislative Councils in Tasmania and Western Australia; the last two are based on two member electorates or provinces, but at each election only one seat falls vacant. In the Tasmanian Legislative Assembly (the lower house), in the Victorian Legislative Council (the upper house) and in the Australian Capital Territory the 'Hare-Clark' method of proportional representation is adopted: see Electoral Act 1985 (Tas) s 188(1)(d), Sch 4; Electoral Act 2002 (Vic), s 114A; Proportional Representation (Hare-Clark) Entrenchment Act 1994 (ACT), s 4; Electoral Act 1992 (ACT), sch 2 and 4.

The division of the total electorate into separate constituencies is a vital element in the electoral process and the constitution of parliament. This is effected by quite elaborate legislation, the common features of which are periodic reviews of and changes to electoral boundaries by independent commissioners. In several of the states, and at the Commonwealth level, these procedures have recently been modified so as to make the work of the commissioners 'self-executing' and thereby reduce the prospect of political interference.

The legislation which provides a distribution system for the House of Representatives is more elaborate than the legislation of the several states because of the need to divide or allocate seats between the six states before distributing seats within each state.

[4.6.2E]   **Commonwealth Constitution**

24   [The terms of this provision are set out in **[4.2.27E]**.]

29   Until the Parliament of the Commonwealth otherwise provides, the Parliament of any State may make laws for determining the divisions in each State for which members of

the House of Representatives may be chosen, and the number of members to be chosen for each division. A division shall not be formed out of parts of different States.

~~~

[4.6.3] As amended by the Commonwealth Electoral Legislation Amendment Act 1983 (Cth), the Commonwealth Electoral Act 1918 (Cth) establishes detailed procedures for the regular and independent review of House of Representatives electorates, and prescribes a flexible standard of one vote one value for those electorates. The flexibility lies in the permitted deviation of ±10 per cent from equality, and in the direction that, as far as practicable the number of voters in each electorate in a state or territory will be equal three years and six months after the redistribution: s 66(3).

Two distinct processes are prescribed by the Commonwealth Electoral Act:

- the allocation of House of Representative seats between the states; and

- distribution of allocated seats within each state.

[4.6.4] The *allocation process* is dealt with in Pt III (representation in the parliament), Div 3 (representation of the states in the House of Representatives) of the Act. These provisions replaced the Representation Act 1905, parts of which had been challenged and found to be invalid in *Attorney-General (Cth) (Ex rel McKinlay) v Commonwealth* (1975) 135 CLR 1 **[4.6.9C]** and *Attorney-General (NSW) (Ex rel McKellar) v Commonwealth* (1977) 139 CLR 527 **[4.6.17]**.

Section 46 of the Act obliges the Electoral Commissioner to begin a reassessment of the allocation of seats between the states between 11 and 12 months after the first meeting of the House of Representatives following a general election, adopting the suggestion of Gibbs J in *McKinlay's* case that the allocation process 'be set in train at a fixed time after the first meeting of any Parliament, so that the determination would be available for use at the next election': 135 CLR at 51.

The Electoral Commissioner is directed to rely on the latest population statistics, supplied by the Australian Statistician (ss 23, 24); that is, the process of allocating seats is not tied to the last official census, a link which the High Court had criticised in *McKinlay's* case: see, for example, 135 CLR at 53 per Gibbs J.

Section 48 obliges the Electoral Commissioner to allocate the House of Representatives seats amongst the states in direct proportion to their populations. The section prescribes a formula for giving effect to this allocation, identical to the formula prescribed, 'until the Parliament otherwise provides', by paras (i) and (ii) of s 24 of the Constitution. Its adoption in the Commonwealth Electoral Act follows the High Court's decision in *McKellar's* case **[4.6.17]** invalidating a different formula which allowed each state an extra seat if, on dividing its population by the quota, there was a remainder of any size.

Section 50 of the Act provides that the Electoral Commissioner's reallocation (certified to the Minister, published in the *Gazette* and tabled in parliament under s 49) will take effect for the next general election of the House of Representatives. (Section 76 makes special provision to accommodate any increase or reduction in a state's allocation of seats where the general election is called on before a redistribution, made necessary by the reallocation, can be effected in that state.) Section 50, in providing that the reallocation is immediately effective, goes further than the High Court's decision in *McKinlay* required: see the comments of Gibbs J on the validity of a general election based on an out-dated allocation: 135 CLR at 53.

[4.6.5] The *distribution process* is dealt with in Pt III (electoral divisions) of the Commonwealth Electoral Act, the opening sections of which provide that each state and the Australian Capital Territory shall be distributed into electorates, each represented by one member in the House of Representatives: ss 56, 57.

The Electoral Commissioner is obliged to keep enrolments in the electorates under monthly review (s 58) and to commence the redistribution process for any state if:

- there has been a change in the number of seats allocated to the state;

- if more than one-third of the state's electorates are, and have been for two months, 'malapportioned Divisions' (that is, more than 10 per cent above or below the state's average electorate enrolment (s 59(10)); or

- if seven years has passed since the last distribution in the state (s 59(2)).

The obligation to commence the redistribution process is qualified by s 59(3) and (4), so as to prevent the commencement of that process in the last year of the life of the House of Representatives.

The timing of redistributions of the Australian Capital Territory (which has two seats in the House of Representatives (s 51)) is covered by s 59(7), (8) and (9).

Section 60 requires the Electoral Commission to appoint a Redistribution Committee for the purpose of each redistribution of a state. A similar requirement for the Australian Capital Territory is stated in s 61. The Committee is required to 'make a proposed distribution of the State or Territory': s 66(1). The criteria for this 'proposed distribution', as specified in s 66(3), are identical to those specified in s 73(4) for the final distribution (see below).

After publication of the 'proposed distribution' (s 68) and an opportunity for objections (s 69), the Redistribution Committee together with the Chairperson and other members of the Electoral Commission, constituting 'an augmented Electoral Commission' (s 70), are to consider the objections to the proposed distribution (s 72) and make a determination distributing the electorates in the relevant state or the Australian Capital Territory: s 73(1).

Sections 73(3) and 73(4) lay down the criteria for this distribution. Section 73(3) directs that each state or territory is to be distributed into electoral divisions equal in number to the number of members of the House of Representatives to be chosen in the state or territory at a general election. Section 73(4) directs the augmented Electoral Commission to endeavour to ensure, as far as practicable, the number of electors in each electoral division will remain within two per cent of the average enrolment in that state or territory three years and six months after the making of the determination. In addition, the Commission is to give due consideration to a number of factors, including:

- community of interests;

- means of communication and travel;

- the trend of population changes;

- physical features and area of the electoral division; and

- the boundaries of existing divisions in the state or territory.

According to s 73(6), the redistribution made under s 73(1) comes into operation at the next general election and is not to be used for any by-election to fill a casual vacancy before that general election.

Having made its determination under s 73, the augmented Electoral Commission must state the reasons for the determination in writing: s 74. Details of the redistribution and the reasons are to be forwarded to the Minister and laid before each House of Parliament: s 75. However, the houses are not given the power, which they had under the previous version of the Commonwealth Electoral Act to disallow a redistribution: *McKinlay's* case (1975) 135 CLR 1 **[4.6.9C]**.

Section 76 prescribes a quick procedure for a 'mini-redistribution' of a state where:

▪ the number of electorates ('Divisions') in the state differs from the number of members to be chosen in the state (following a new determination under s 48(1)); and

▪ the Governor-General has issued writs for a general election.

The procedure involves either consolidating adjoining electorates into one new electorate (where the number of electorates is too large) or dividing pairs of adjoining electorates into three new electorates (where the number of electorates is too small). This 'mini-redistribution' accommodates the mandate of s 50 of the Act, that a re-allocation between the states take effect from the next general election.

Section 77 provides some protection against judicial review for the Commission's determinations, in terms similar to the protection provided to the Commissioner's allocation decisions by s 48(3). The extent of that protection is still to be tested.

[4.6.6] In most states, legislation establishes a permanent Electoral Commissioner or Electoral Commissioners who are charged with the responsibility of redistributing electorates. In Tasmania, the five House of Assembly electorates are identical to those for the Commonwealth House of Representatives. This identity is maintained by ad hoc legislation whenever the boundaries are altered at a federal redistribution.

The degree of political control over the distribution process varies from state to state. Under the Western Australian legislation, the initiation of a redistribution does not require any political decision. Further, while adoption of a redistribution proposal needs action by the government, that action should automatically follow the Distribution Commissioners' report. In *Tonkin v Brand* [1962] WAR 2, the Western Australian Supreme Court declared that the government had a legal duty to set in train the machinery for electoral redistribution.

The New South Wales and South Australian legislation goes further by guaranteeing the independence of the Electoral Commissioners and the democratic basis of electoral distribution, not only against executive pressure, but also against amending or repealing legislation passed through the normal parliamentary process: see **[5.4.14]**.

The relevant provisions can be found in the following legislation:

▪ Constitution Act 1902 (NSW) ss 7B, 25–28A; Parliamentary Electorates and Elections Act 1912 (NSW) Pt II;

▪ Electoral Act 1992 (Qld) ss 35–57;

▪ Constitution Act 1934 (SA) Pt V;

▪ Constitution Act 1934 (Tas) ss 26, 27, Schedules 3, 4;

- Constitution Act 1975 (Vic), ss 94F, 94G; Electoral Boundaries Commission Act 1982 (Vic);

- Electoral Distribution Act 1947 (WA).

[4.6.7] Even where legislation establishes the independence of Electoral Commissioners and of the redistribution process (by providing that the Commissioners' decision shall not be vetoed or frustrated), there is substantial scope for political interference. Amending legislation can prescribe new criteria, demanding that special weight be given to, for example, rural votes or that a wide variation from the quota be allowed.

[4.6.8] In Victoria, amendments to the Constitution Act 1975 made by the Constitution (Parliamentary Reform) Act 2003 seek to entrench the independence of the Electoral Commissioner and the integrity of the processes established by the Electoral Act 2002: see Constitution Act 1975, ss 94F, 94G.

The redistribution systems established in South Australia and New South Wales include a genuinely independent Commission whose decisions are implemented automatically, a basic criterion of one vote, one value and, most significantly, protection of the systems against legislative interference. A challenge to the constitutional validity of the South Australian system was dismissed by the Privy Council in *Gilbertson v Attorney-General (SA)* [1978] AC 772 **[6.4.44]**.

[4.6.9C] **Attorney-General (Cth) (Ex rel McKinlay) v Commonwealth**

(1975) 135 CLR 1

In three separate suits, three voters sought declarations that various sections of the Commonwealth Electoral Act 1918 (Cth) were invalid because they were inconsistent with the first paragraph of s 24 of the Constitution, and that the boundaries of several House of Representatives electorates in Victoria, Queensland and South Australia were not fixed according to law.

The Commonwealth Electoral Act provided for the distribution and redistribution of House of Representatives electorates within each state. The Act provided, in s 18, that the number of electors in a state should be divided by the number of members to be returned for the state, thus establishing a quota. Section 19 directed the Distribution Commissioners to give due consideration to a range of factors, and not to depart from the 'quota' (the average number of voters in each Division) 'to a greater extent than one-tenth more or one-tenth less'.

Sections 24 and 25 of the Commonwealth Electoral Act provided that any proposed distribution required the approval of both Houses of Parliament and a proclamation by the Governor-General to be effective. Until such approval and proclamation, the old distribution remained in force.

House of Representatives seats for all states other than Western Australia had last been redistributed during 1968. According to evidence before the High Court, the ratios between the current enrolments in the largest and smallest electorates were 2:1 (Queensland), 1.8:1 (Victoria) and 1.7:1 (South Australia). The evidence on this disparity was obscure; it is not clear whether the evidence was drawn from voting figures from the election of 18 May 1974 or from more recent electoral office returns: 135 CLR at 39 per McTiernan and Jacobs JJ; 135 CLR at 63–4 per Murphy J.

During the hearing of these challenges, two of the plaintiffs amended their statements of claim to seek declarations that parts of the Representation Act 1905 (Cth) were invalid, because of inconsistency with the second paragraph of s 24 of the Constitution. These provisions of the Representation Act dealt with the allocation and reallocation of House of Representatives seats between the six states, a process which is essentially preliminary to the distribution process laid down in the Commonwealth Electoral Act.

According to s 2 of the Representation Act, the Chief Electoral Officer was to 'ascertain the numbers of the people of the Commonwealth, and ... of the several States'. He was to rely on the latest Commonwealth census (ss 3(1) and 4(1)); a census was to be held every 10th year 'or at such other time as is prescribed': Census and Statistics Act 1905 (Cth) s 8. The Chief Electoral Officer was then to divide the number of people of the Commonwealth by twice the number of senators, thus producing a 'quota'. The population of each state was then to be divided by the quota to produce the allocation of members for that state, allowing an extra member for any remainder: Representation Act ss 9, 10.

However, any alteration in the number of members to be chosen from a state was not to take effect until the government, the Distribution Commissioners and the Houses of Parliament had initiated, conducted and endorsed a redistribution of electorates for that state: Representation Act s 12(a), with Commonwealth Electoral Act ss 24, 25. The last such reallocation had been made in 1974, giving Western Australia an extra seat, based on the 1971 census.

McTiernan and Jacobs JJ held that the relevant sections of the Representation Act were valid, but said that s 12(a) could not validly operate so as to defeat the requirement of s 24 of the Constitution that the number of members chosen in the respective states should be in proportion to the respective numbers of their people. On the validity of the system of electoral redistribution in the Commonwealth Electoral Act, they said that the words 'chosen by the people' in s 24 expressed a constitutional requirement but were not words which could be rewritten or paraphrased in an exact manner:

McTiernan and Jacobs JJ: [35] The words embrace the notion of equality of numbers in so far as the choice of members must be by the people of the Commonwealth. Inequality of distribution of numbers between districts or divisions in respect of which members are chosen is one factor which may lead to a choice on the basis of such an unequal distribution being unable to be described as a choice by the people of the Commonwealth ...

[36] The words 'chosen by the people of the Commonwealth' fall to be applied to different circumstances at different times and at any particular time the facts and circumstances may show that some or all members are not, or would not in the event of an election, be chosen by the people within the meaning of these words in s 24. At some point choice by electors could cease to be able to be described as a choice by the people of the Commonwealth. It is a question of degree. It cannot be determined in the abstract ... For instance, the long established universal adult suffrage may now be recognized as a fact and as a result it is doubtful whether, subject to the particular provision in s 30, anything less than this could now be described as a choice by the people.

But there is nothing in our history and our development as a nation which would require that before a member be described as chosen by the people of the Commonwealth absolute or as [37] nearly as practicable absolute equality of numbers of the people exist in every constituted electoral district in a State. Even though the notion of equality is present the matter remains one of degree.

McTiernan and Jacobs JJ said that there was no inconsistency between some inequality in electorates and the constitutional requirement in s 24: 'A margin of one-tenth is not one which in these circumstances takes away the quality of choice which s 24 of the Constitution enjoins': 135 CLR at 37. However, McTiernan and Jacobs JJ said no provision in the Commonwealth Electoral Act 'can validly operate in so far as by such an operation members of the House of Representatives would not on a general election be chosen by the people of the Commonwealth': 135 CLR at 38. They then considered the 'substantial inequalities' that had developed in three states, South Australia, Victoria and

Queensland. They noted that, in Queensland, the division largest in number of electors in May 1974 had almost twice the number of electors as the division with the smallest number and had 38.5 per cent more electors than the quota under s 19 of the Commonwealth Electoral Act. That variation from equality was not 'such that a choosing of members by those divisions is not a choosing of members by the people within the meaning of s 24 of the Constitution': 135 CLR at 39. McTiernan and Jacobs JJ then turned to the United States authorities:

[39] On the words of Art I s 2 of the Constitution of the United States of America the Supreme Court has determined that 'chosen … by the people of the several States' requires that as nearly as practicable one man's vote in a congressional election must be worth as much as another's: *Wesberry v Sanders* 376 US 1 (1964). The facts were that Georgia's Fifth Congressional District, one of ten, had a population of 832,680. The average population of the ten districts was 394,312 and one district had a population of only 272,154. The district was thus 'grossly out of balance' with other congressional districts of Georgia (per Clark J 376 US 19 (1964)).

Although the actual result in *Wesberry v Sanders* may well be the result which would follow from the application to those facts of the principle which we have earlier suggested, the requirement in the reasoning of the majority that there be 'as near as practicable' equality postulates a degree of equality which goes beyond what we would accept as applicable to our Constitution.

Gibbs J: [43] If the words of s 24 are read in their natural sense, without seeking for implications or hidden meanings, they appear to have nothing whatever to do with the determination of electoral divisions within a State. The plaintiffs rest their submission on the opening words of the section. Those words require the House of Representatives to be 'composed of members directly chosen by the people of the Commonwealth'. It is said that the members must be chosen by, or perhaps more precisely by electors representing, all the people, and that it must be implied or inferred that all people are to be placed on the same footing, so that each member will represent the same number of people or at least of electors. Further, it is said that the section is intended to ensure that the House of Representatives is elected on democratic prin[44]ciples and that such principles require that electoral divisions should contain equal numbers of people or of electors. We have to decide whether s 24, properly interpreted, does have this effect. If it does not, we are not justified in importing new requirements into it simply because, as a matter of policy, they may seem to be desirable. Our duty is to declare the law as enacted in the Constitution and not to add to its provisions new doctrines which may happen to conform to our own prepossessions.

The obvious purpose of the opening words of s 24 is to ensure that members of the House of Representatives are chosen directly by popular vote, and not by some indirect means, such as by the Parliament or Executive Government of a State, or by an electoral college. When the section says that members shall be chosen 'by the people' it cannot mean by all the people of the Commonwealth — obviously it means by those people who are qualified to vote … It clearly appears from other sections of the Constitution — ss 25, 30, 41 and 128 — that it was recognised that people might constitutionally be denied the franchise on the ground of race, sex or lack of property — the Constitution goes no further than to ensure that an adult who has the right to vote at elections for the more numerous House of the Parliament of a State shall not be prevented by a law of the Commonwealth from voting at elections for either House of the Parliament of the Commonwealth: s 41 … [E]ven if, contrary to what I have said, 'people' in s 24 did mean all people, the further construction that the plaintiffs seek to put on the section could not be justified. The section says nothing in terms as to the weight to be given to the votes of those people who cast them. It [45] does not mention equality. Moreover, the concluding words of s 24, by providing a minimum number of members for each original State, create an exception to the rule that the number of members chosen in the several States shall be in proportion to the respective numbers of their people, and have the result that so long as the population of any State is so small that its representation, if fixed proportionately,

Parliament ... header

would be less than five, it will be impossible to achieve equality in the number of people or of electors in electoral divisions throughout Australia.

... Neither in 1901 nor subsequently has there been a universal recognition of the so-called principle that electorates should be numerically equal.

Gibbs CJ referred to the historical disparities in the size of House of Commons electorates, as well as those of colonial and state parliaments.

[46] No doubt most people would agree that for the healthy functioning of a democratic system of government it is desirable that the electorate should be fairly apportioned into electoral districts whose boundaries are not gerrymandered, that the ballots should be secretly and honestly conducted, that the vote should be fairly counted and that corrupt electoral practices should be suppressed, but opinions may well differ as to how these ideals should be attained. The Constitution does not lay down particular guidance on these matters; the framers of the Constitution trusted the Parliament to legislate with respect to them if necessary, no doubt remembering that in England, from which our system of representative government is derived, democracy did not need the support of a written constitution ...

Gibbs J referred to several decisions of the United States Supreme Court, to the effect that art 1, s 2 of the United States Constitution (expressed in terms similar to s 24) required an equality of voters in electorates for the Federal House of Representatives: *Wesberry v Sanders* 376 US 1 (1964); *Kirkpatrick v Preisler* 394 US 526 (1969); *Wells v Rockefeller* 394 US 542 (1969); *White v Weiser* 412 US 783 (1973). He said that the United States decisions had 'provoked strong differences of opinion between eminent judges in the Supreme Court of that nation'; but 'they cannot assist us in the construction of our Constitution': 135 CLR at 47. He concluded that the attack on ss 19, 24 and 25 of the Commonwealth Electoral Act failed. His Honour turned to the question whether ss 2, 3, 4 and 12 of the Representation Act were invalid because they contravened the second paragraph of s 24 of the Constitution.

[49] The second paragraph of s 24 of the Constitution commences by laying down what appears to be an unqualified rule, namely, [50] 'The number of members chosen in the several States shall be in proportion to the respective numbers of their people' ... Although those words are on their face absolute, there are other constitutional requirements, equally absolute and no less important, that must also be observed. 'Every House of Representatives shall continue for three years from the first meeting of the House, and no longer, but may be sooner dissolved by the Governor-General': s 28. Writs for general elections of members of the House of Representatives 'shall be issued within ten days from the expiry of a House of Representatives or from the proclamation of a dissolution thereof': s 32. These requirements lie at the very heart of our system of government, and in the event of a conflict would necessarily prevail over s 24. For example, an election could not be postponed, when otherwise necessary, simply because the number of members to be chosen in the several States had not been determined on the basis of the most recent reliable figures. The apparently absolute words of s 24 may therefore need some qualification to enable them to work in harmony with the rest of the Constitution.

When the Parliament exercises its power to provide for the manner in which a determination of the number of members to be chosen in the several States is made under s 24, there are a number of practical questions to which it must direct its attention ...

[51] Two ... questions that will arise for the consideration of the Parliament are how frequently the determination is to be made, and how the respective numbers of the people of the States are to be ascertained. The Representation Act, in its present form, answers these questions by relating both the making of the determination and the ascertainment of the numbers to the census ... Under legislation now in force it is provided that the census is to be taken 'in the year One thousand nine hundred and eleven and in every tenth year thereafter or at such other time as is prescribed': s 8 of the Census and Statistics Act 1905–1973 (Cth). Although the regulation-making power has in recent years been used to bring about a census every five, instead of every ten, years, it would of course be lawful to prescribe that the census

should be taken much less frequently. The relevant words of s 24 of the Constitution require that the 'number of members chosen in the several States shall be' in the requisite proportion. These words naturally suggest that the proportion is to exist on each occasion when the members are chosen, ie each time an election is held. To ensure that this requirement is observed, it appears necessary that a new determination should be made within a reasonably short time before every election … This would present no difficulty if the House of Representatives continued for its normal term of about three years. The making of a determination could be set in train at a fixed time after the first meeting of any Parliament, so that the determination would be available for use [52] at the next election. This would mean that the census would not always provide the latest reliable statistics from which to ascertain the numbers of the people of the States. However, the Constitution requires that the number of members chosen should be in the correct proportion, and it does not require that census figures should be used. The constitutional requirement must be given effect, notwithstanding that on some occasions statistics other than those provided by the census may have to be used in ascertaining the numbers. It appears to me that laws made by the Parliament to provide the manner in which the number of members chosen in the several States shall be determined cannot validly permit of any evasion of the requirement that a determination must be made within a reasonable time before each election. That means that when the House continues for its normal term, a determination must be made during the period of three years or less for which it continues …

[53] Consistently with the opinions I have expressed it must be held that ss 3 and 4 of the Representation Act are invalid because their effect is to require a determination to be made only when a census is taken and not before every regular election. The provisions of s 12(b) are, however, in my opinion, valid. When a vacancy arises in the House and a by-election has to be held there is no occasion to choose members in the several States. The by-election merely restores to the State in which it is held the representation to which it was previously entitled. It maintains the status quo. There is no need to apply to such an election a determination altering the number of members to be chosen in the various States.

The provisions of s 12(a) would in my opinion be valid if the section went on to provide a procedure, or if it operated in a context, which ensured that redistribution would take place with all due diligence should the need for it become manifest as a result of the furnishing of a certificate under s 6 of the Representation Act and of the determination under s 9 that follows from it. However, the combined effect of s 12(a) of the Representation Act and ss 24 and 25 of the Commonwealth Electoral Act is that no redistribution need ever be made and that the determination might never take effect. For this reason, in my opinion, s 12(a) is invalid.

Although it is obvious, it should be remarked that it does not follow from the fact that the Representation Act is in part invalid that the numbers chosen in the several States in the past have not been in their correct proportion. Even if it were established that the numbers were not or are not in their correct proportion (and there is no evidence to that effect), that would not mean that elections conducted in the past have been invalidly conducted, or that an election conducted in future on the basis of the existing determination as to the number of members to be chosen in the several States would be invalid. As I have already pointed out, there is an overriding constitutional duty to hold elections in certain circumstances. There is also a constitutional duty to ensure that each State is proportionately represented in the House of Representatives, but a failure to perform that duty does not invalidate an election held otherwise in compliance with the Constitution. Since, no doubt, the Parliament will act to give effect to the requirements of s 24 now that they have been pointed out, it is unnecessary to consider what remedies might be available if it did not.

Barwick CJ, Stephen and Mason JJ delivered separate judgments to the same effect as Gibbs J. On the validity of the Representation Act, Stephen and Mason JJ adopted the reasons of Gibbs J. However, on the validity of the Commonwealth Electoral Act, Stephen and Mason JJ qualified their rejection of the plaintiff's argument.

Stephen J: [56] Three great principles, representative democracy (by which I mean that the legislators are chosen by the people), direct popular election, and the national character of the lower House, may each be discerned in the opening words of s 24 ...

The principle of representative democracy does indeed predicate the enfranchisement of electors, the existence of an electoral system capable of giving effect to their selection of representatives and the bestowal of legislative functions upon the representatives thus selected. However, the particular quality and character of the content of each one of these three ingredients of representative democracy, and there may well be others, is not fixed and precise. I take each in turn. The extent of the franchise; whether it extends to all residents or to all residents over a given age or is restricted, perhaps, to male British subjects over twenty-one, maybe with a superadded property qualification and whether more or less replete with disqualifications on grounds of incapacity or criminality or the like, it will none the less constitute an enfranchisement of electors. The electoral system, with its innumerable details including numbers and qualifications of representatives, single or multi-member electorates, voting methods and the various methods, including varieties of proportional representation, whereby the significance and outcome of the votes cast may be determined; in each there is scope for variety and no one formula can pre-empt the field as alone consistent with representative democracy. Again the [57] wide range of legislative functions which a legislature thus elected may possess is so clear in our federal polity, with its history of a variety of colonial legislatures, that it requires no elaboration.

It is, then, quite apparent that representative democracy is descriptive of a whole spectrum of political institutions, each differing in countless respects yet answering to that generic description. The spectrum has finite limits and in a particular instance there may be absent some quality which is regarded as so essential to representative democracy as to place that instance outside those limits altogether; but at no one point within the range of the spectrum does there exist any single requirement so essential as to be determinative of the existence of representative democracy.

Mason J: [61] All that the paragraph in s 24 requires is that there should be a direct choice of the members by the people—a prescription which does not cease to be satisfied because there is some, or even a marked, variation in the number of persons or electors in the electoral divisions within a State. The existence of such variations does not detract from the accuracy of the description of our existing electoral system as one in which the members of the House are directly chosen by the people of the Commonwealth.

It is perhaps conceivable that variations in the numbers of electors or people in single member electorates could become so grossly disproportionate as to raise a question whether an election held on boundaries so drawn would produce a House of Representatives composed of members directly chosen by the people of the Commonwealth, but this is a matter quite removed from the proposition that s 24 insists upon a practical equality of people or electors in single member electorates.

Murphy J held that s 12(a) of the Representation Act was invalid. His Honour did not consider the validity of ss 3 and 4. On the Commonwealth Electoral Act he said that the words 'chosen by the people' in s 24 'should be construed in the same way as it was by the United States Supreme Court but having as the standard of equality the alternatives of equal numbers of people and equal numbers of electors': 135 CLR at 70–1. He cited seven factors that led him to this conclusion:

Murphy J: [71] (a) The obvious importance placed on the phrase by its positioning in the opening sentence of that part of the Constitution devoted to the House of Representatives, and the fact that it is expressed in the language of command.

(b) The democratic theme of equal sharing of political power which pervades the Constitution. In 1902, the authority on the Constitution, Professor W Harrison Moore wrote:

> The predominant feature of the Australian Constitution is the prevalence of the democratic principle, in its most modern guise. (*Constitution of the Commonwealth of Australia*, 1st ed (1902), p 327).

and

> The great underlying principle, is, that the rights of individuals are sufficiently secured by ensuring, as far as possible, to each a share, and *an equal share,* in political power. (My emphasis.) (Ibid, p 329.)

(c) The reference is to the 'people of the Commonwealth', which emphasises the intention of sharing of political power.

(d) The absence of any other means of redress for those deprived of an equal share of representation, even where it is grossly unequal ... History here and elsewhere [72] reveals that with few exceptions, legislators who hold office because of an unbalanced electoral system will not act to change the system. The more unbalanced it becomes, the more severe are the consequences of correction and the more reluctant are the legislators to change it.

(e) The fact that the phrase was taken directly from the United States Constitution. The construction placed upon it by the United States Supreme Court that it commands electoral equality is compelling in its reasoning and applicable to our Constitution ...

[73] (f) The automatic result of equal representation for equal numbers of people and of electors follows when representatives are chosen on the basis provided by s 29: 'In the absence of other provision, each State shall be one electorate.' (In the election for the first Parliament, two of the States were single electorates.) As the United States Supreme Court has observed, it would be extraordinary and unacceptable to suggest that in such a State-wide election, the votes cast in some parts could be weighted at two or three times the value of votes cast by those living in more populous parts of the State:

> We do not believe that the Framers of the Constitution intended to permit the same vote diluting discrimination to be accomplished through the device of districts containing widely varied numbers of inhabitants. *Wesberry v Sanders* 376 US 8 (1964) [11 Law Ed 2d 487].

(g) The fact that the laws made by the Parliament pursuant to ss 29 and 30 are subject to the Constitution, and therefore subject to the commands in s 24.

Murphy J then turned to the question whether equality was to be measured in people or electors:

[75] In my opinion, the standard of equality is to be measured in each State in numbers of electors rather than numbers of people. The emphasis in 'chosen by the people' in s 24 is on a choosing by all the people capable of choosing, that is, the electors. The number of members in each State is to be proportionate (subject to the minimum) to the population of each State. But in the choosing in each State, the electors share the voting power equally, whether the State is one electorate or in divisions. This view is supported by the reasoning in the United States cases which refer repeatedly to equality of voting power and similar expressions as the principle underlying the command. It is reinforced by the 'one person, one vote' mandate in s 30 of the Constitution.

~~~

Notes

[4.6.10]   The presentation of the issues in this case to the High Court had some curious features. Apart from the fact that some of the information on electoral enrolments was based on the voting figures from the election of 18 May 1974 and other information came from the more up to date electoral rolls, there was an inherent, and critical, ambiguity in the plaintiff's attack on the Commonwealth Electoral Act. The statements of claim asserted that s 24 of the Constitution demanded that electorates within any one state be composed of equal numbers of people or of equal numbers of voters. Those two demands cannot be reconciled.

A similar contradiction can be found in the United States Supreme Court decisions on which the plaintiffs relied. The judgment of the court in *Wesberry v Sanders* 376 US 1 (1964) asserts the constitutional principle that 'one man's vote in a congressional election is to be worth as much as another's': 376 US at 7, and refers to the intention of the framers that 'population ... was to be the basis of the House of Representatives': 376 US at 9.

Individual members of the High Court made some attempt to resolve this ambiguity: see, in particular, McTiernan and Jacobs JJ, 135 CLR at 35–6; Murphy J, 135 CLR at 75.

Do you agree with Murphy J's observation that there is no great practical difference between measuring in people or in electors?

Bearing in mind that the Commonwealth Parliament has the power to prescribe the qualifications for electors (s 51(xxxvi) read with s 30), is there any enduring value in a constitutional guarantee based on the number of electors? Or would such a guarantee assume that the Commonwealth Parliament's power to prescribe qualifications for electors is limited by some democratic principle? See **[4.5.12]–[4.5.15]**.

[4.6.11] The electoral distribution struck down by the United States Supreme Court in *Wesberry v Sanders* 376 US 1 (1964) was that of the electorates within the state of Georgia for the federal House of Representatives. The largest congressional district had a population of 823,680; the smallest had a population of 272,254; and the average population for districts within the state was 394,312. Compare these disparities with those which, according to the plaintiff's evidence, existed in Queensland in 1975:

	Georgia	Queensland
ratio of largest to smallest electorate	3:1	2:1
largest deviation from quota or average	108.9%	91.5%

In *McKinlay's* case, McTiernan and Jacobs JJ observed that the principle which they favoured 'may well' have achieved the result arrived at in *Wesberry v Sanders,* that is, it could have struck down the Georgia distribution: 135 CLR at 39. But, clearly, the principle could not strike down the Queensland distribution. What is the substantial distinction between the two situations?

McTiernan and Jacobs JJ, in their joint judgment, found that s 24(1) of the Commonwealth Electoral Act and s 12(a) of the Representation Act had the potential to frustrate the mandates contained in s 24 of the Constitution, that the House of Representatives should be chosen by the people of the Commonwealth and that the number of members chosen in the several states should be in proportion to the respective numbers of their people. However, they did not declare those sections to be invalid; rather, they declared that the two provisions could not validly operate so as to frustrate the requirements of s 24 of the Constitution. What is the difference between that approach and the approach adopted by, say, Gibbs J, who held that s 12(a) of the Representation Act was invalid? What would be the practical effect of a declaration such as that proposed by McTiernan and Jacobs JJ? Could it be said that it sacrifices certainty in the interests of flexibility? See 'Constitutional Validity of Legislation According to the Circumstances' (1976) 50 *ALJ* 205 at 205–6.

[4.6.12] How might the requirement, accepted by all members of the High Court, that the members chosen for the several states should be in proportion to the population of the states, be enforced? Is it a requirement that the court is equipped to enforce? Note that Gibbs J discounted the possibility of invalidating any election based on an unconstitutional allocation of seats and said that it was 'unnecessary to consider what remedies might be available if [parliament] did not … act to give effect to the requirements of s 24 now that they have been pointed out': 135 CLR at 53.

[4.6.13]   In 1988, the Constitutional Commission expressed the view that 'one vote one value is a fundamental principle of democracy', but conceded that a tolerance of ±10 per cent 'represents a reasonable application of that principle': Constitutional Commission (1988) p 154.

The Commission recommended that the Commonwealth Constitution should be amended to 'require that electoral divisions be determined at such times as are necessary to ensure that the principle of one vote one value with ±10% tolerance is maintained' for Commonwealth, state and territory electorates. '[F]or reasons of practicality', the Commission said, 'any provision to entrench the principle of one vote one value in the Constitution should refer to the number of electors and not persons in an electorate': Constitutional Commission (1988) p 155. The Commission concluded (p 155):

> We accept that a ± 10 per cent tolerance will not of itself ensure the realisation of the principle of equal suffrage. It does not, for example, address the problem of gerrymanders. However, it will correct the gross discrepancies that exist now. Very importantly, the ± 10 per cent tolerance is the best practical formulation of a general principle. It avoids the interpretational problems associated with the phrase 'as nearly as practicable, the same'. Perhaps absolute equality is not achievable. Our aim is to entrench a reasonable standard of political equality in the Constitution. Although some of us would prefer to set a ± 5 per cent tolerance, we agree that the ± 10 per cent tolerance is an acceptable guarantee at this time.

In June 1988, the House of Representatives and the Senate passed the Constitution Alteration (Fair Elections) Act 1988 (Cth) which would have, inter alia, given effect to the Commission's recommendation by inserting ss 124A–124F into the Commonwealth Constitution. At a referendum held on 3 September 1988, this proposal was rejected by the voters.

[4.6.14]   The High Court's recognition of the constitutional principle of representative democracy in *Nationwide News Ltd v Wills* (1992) 177 CLR 1 **[11.3.9]** and *Australian Capital Television Pty Ltd v Commonwealth (No 2)* (1992) 177 CLR 176 **[11.3.7C]** appeared to open the possibility that the court would find in s 24 of the Constitution a guarantee of electoral equality. If, in the words of Deane and Toohey JJ in *Nationwide News Pty Ltd v Wills*, the Constitution required that 'all citizens of the Commonwealth who are not under some special disability are entitled to share equally in the exercise of those ultimate powers of governmental control' (177 CLR at 71–2), then equality of voting power might be thought to be constitutionally required.

However, the High Court's decision in *McGinty v Western Australia* (1996) 186 CLR 140 **[4.5.14]**, **[11.3.17C]** cast doubt on that prospect. A majority of the court (Brennan CJ, Dawson, McHugh and Gummow JJ; Toohey and Gaudron JJ dissenting) held that there was no constitutional requirement, whether derived from s 24 of the Commonwealth Constitution or from the Constitution Act 1889 (WA), that demanded that electorates for the Western Australian Parliament have equal numbers of voters. Three members of the majority (Dawson, McHugh and Gummow JJ) said that neither the principle of representative democracy nor the language of s 24 required equality of value for House of Representatives votes.

McHugh J said that ss 29 and 30 of the Commonwealth Constitution, electoral practices in Australia and Great Britain at the time of federation and various constitutional provisions which authorised unequal voting power made it 'impossible to hold that the Constitution requires equality of electoral districts': 186 CLR at 245. Brennan CJ assumed, without deciding, that there was such a principle, but held that it did not extend to the state parliaments: 186 CLR at 175–6.

The High Court returned to the requirements of s 24, and the principle of representative democracy, in *Langer v Commonwealth* (1996) 186 CLR 302 **[4.6.15C]**.

[4.6.15C]   Langer v Commonwealth
(1996) 186 CLR 302

Langer had published material advocating that voters complete ballot papers for the House of Representatives by not recording a preference for the candidates of the major parties. Section 329A of the Commonwealth Electoral Act 1918 (Cth) prohibited the publication or distribution of any material encouraging voters to vote otherwise than in compliance with s 240 of the Act, which required voters in an electorate to indicate a preference for each and every candidate in that electorate.

Sections 268(1)(c) and s 270(2) saved certain votes cast otherwise than in compliance with s 240: if the relevant voting paper contained only one blank square, or contained completed squares but repeated numbers in the squares. In the latter situation, the voting paper would be treated as 'exhausted' as soon as the repeated number was first entered on the ballot paper, and the relevant vote would not be distributed (on the distribution of preferences) to any candidate against whose name a repeated number was entered. The material published by Langer drew attention to the savings provisions and urged voters to vote by placing repeated numbers in the squares opposite the candidates of the principal parties. Langer was prosecuted under s 329A.

In his defence, Langer argued that s 329A interfered with the requirement contained in s 24 of the Constitution that candidates be 'directly chosen by the people' because it effectively limited a person's ability to choose *not* to vote for a particular candidate. A second argument, raised but not pursued by the plaintiff, was that s 329A constituted an interference with the implied freedom of communication concerning political matters: see **[11.3.15]**.

A majority of the court (Dawson J dissenting) rejected the plaintiff's arguments and held that the Commonwealth's power with respect to elections, expressed in ss 31 and 51(xxxvi) of the Commonwealth Constitution, extended to the regulation of conduct of persons. Section 24 of the Constitution only required the parliament to prescribe a method of voting in which electors could choose their candidates, in the sense of choosing between candidates nominated, but did not give voters the constitutional right not to indicate their preference for all candidates. The compulsory preferential voting system established by the Commonwealth Electoral Act satisfied the s 24 requirement and any provisions that sought to protect that system were valid.

Brennan CJ: [315] The method of choosing members of the House of Representatives is governed by the Act. The Parliament is empowered to prescribe that method by ss 31 and 51(xxxvi) of the Constitution ...

[316] What the Constitution requires is that the law prescribe a method of voting which leaves the voter free to make a choice, not that the law leave the voter free to choose the method of voting by which a voter's choice is to be made. A method which requires full preferential voting satisfies the constitutional requirement ...

[317] The legislative power over elections for the House of Representatives conferred by ss 31 and 51(xxxvi) is a plenary power ... Provided the prescribed method of voting permits

a free choice among the candidates for election, it is within the legislative power of the Parliament. Section 24 of the Constitution does not limit the Parliament's selection of the method of voting by which a voter's choice is made known so long as the method allows a free choice. Section 240 permits a voter to make a discriminating choice among the candidates for election to the House of Representatives. An election in which members of the House of Representatives are elected pursuant to such a method of voting achieves what s 24 requires, namely, a House of Representatives composed of members directly chosen by the people.

It follows that the Parliament is empowered to prescribe a method of voting in an election for the House of Representatives that requires a voter to fill in a ballot paper in accordance with s 240, although that method requires a voter to choose by allocating preferences among candidates for whom the voter does not wish to vote. It is not to the point that, if a ballot paper were filled in otherwise than in accordance with s 240, the vote would better express the voter's political opinion.

Since s 240 can reasonably be regarded as prescribing a method of freely choosing members of the House of Representatives, a law which is appropriate and adapted to prevent the subversion of that method is within power. Section 329A is such a law. The saving provisions do not affect its validity. They are designed to minimise the exclusion of ballot papers from the scrutiny provided the voter's intention clearly appears from the voter's partial compliance with the method prescribed by s 240. But the saving provisions do not detract from the power to enact s 329A in order to protect what the Parliament intends to be the primary method of choosing members of the House of Representatives.

Once the generality of the power to enact laws relating to elections is appreciated and the validity of s 240 is accepted, s 329A can be seen to be a provision appropriate and adapted to the protection of the method of electing members of the House of Representatives.

Dawson J: [323] The Constitution does not require the provision of any particular electoral system. [*McGinty v Western Australia* (1996) 186 CLR 140] Thus, the provision in s 240 for a preferential voting system is clearly within power notwithstanding that it requires a choice to be made in a specified manner and, standing alone, requires a [324] preference to be expressed in respect of each candidate. [*Judd v McKeon* (1926) 38 CLR 380 at 383, 385–386.]

... The Constitution having established in s 24 that the House of Representatives shall be composed of members directly chosen by the people of the Commonwealth, the elections with respect to which parliament is given power to make laws by ss 31 and 51(xxxvi) must necessarily be elections fulfilling the requirements of s 24. That is to [325] say, the legislative power conferred by those provisions is a purposive power: a power to make laws for the purpose of implementing s 24.

Since, as I have said, the choice which is required by s 24 must be a genuine choice, [see *Australian Capital Television Pty Ltd v The Commonwealth* (1992) 177 CLR 106 at 187; *Theophanous v Herald and Weekly Times Ltd* (1994) 182 CLR 104 at 189–190] those eligible to vote must have available to them the information necessary to exercise such a choice ... [F]or the reasons which I have given, the power conferred by ss 31 and 51(xxxvi) may properly be regarded as a purposive power and it is therefore open to test the validity of a law enacted in the purported exercise of that power by asking whether the law is reasonably and appropriately adapted to the achievement of an end which lies within power. To my mind, s 329A (or, more accurately, the law inserting it in the Act) is not such a law. It is a law which is designed to keep from voters information which is required by them to enable them to exercise an informed choice. It can hardly be said that a choice is an informed choice if it is made in ignorance of a means of making the choice which is available and which a voter, if he or she knows of it, may wish to use in order to achieve a particular result.

If s 240 stood alone, s 329A would be supportable as a protection of the preferential system of voting provided by the Act. Upon any view, some limitations upon freedom of communication are necessary to ensure the proper working of any electoral system. However ... ss 268 and 270 qualify the method of voting prescribed by s 240 and s 270 makes available optional or selective preferential voting as opposed to full preferential voting ... the Act permits voters intentionally to record a preference for only one or some of the candidates standing for election by completing their ballot-paper in the manner which I have described above. To prohibit communication of this fact (or at any rate communication in the form of encouragement) is to restrict the access of voters to information essential to the formation of the choice required by s 24 of the [326] Constitution. Thus, s 329A has the intended effect of keeping from voters an alternative method of casting a formal vote which they are entitled to choose under the Act.

... To impart information which can be used (and information about the availability of an optional or selective preferential vote is of that kind) is necessarily to encourage its use if the recipient of the information is so inclined ... To put the matter shortly, to make available useful information is ordinarily to encourage its use. This is particularly so in the context of an election. The effect of s 329A in any practical sense must, in my view, be to discourage, if not prevent, persons from imparting to eligible voters knowledge that the electoral system permits optional or selective preferential voting. It cannot, therefore, be a law which is reasonably and appropriately adapted to the achievement of an end which lies within the ambit of the relevant legislative power.

~~~

[4.6.16] Toohey and Gaudron JJ held that the words 'directly chosen by the people' in s 24 of the Constitution were consistent with election of Members of Parliament according to either a 'full preferential voting system, or the modified preferential voting system effected by ss 249, 268 and 270 of the Act' (186 CLR at 333) and that the legislation was reasonably capable of being viewed as appropriate and adapted to a legitimate purpose, that purpose being 'full, equal and effective participation in the electoral process': 186 CLR at 334.

McHugh J said that as the efficacy of the system was 'dependent upon the directions [in s 240] being obeyed' (186 CLR at 337) and parliament could validly enact this voting system, it could also 'prohibit people from encouraging voters to disregard the system': 186 CLR at 340. He said that the words of s 24 did not 'confer individual rights on electors'; and that the rights conferred by s 24 were given to 'the people of the Commonwealth', not individuals: 186 CLR at 343.

Gummow J said that s 329A was valid because s 24 of the Constitution did not prescribe a particular form of the franchise, and that it was not in the form of a personal right: 186 CLR at 349. He agreed with Brennan CJ that optional preferential voting was not the method of voting provided for in the legislation.

Notes

[4.6.17] In *McGinty v Western Australia* (1996) 186 CLR 140 **[4.5.14]**, **[11.3.17C]**, a majority of the High Court rejected a challenge to the validity of the distribution of electorates for the Legislative Assembly and the Legislative Council of Western Australia. An argument that s 24 of the Commonwealth Constitution required equality of voters in electorates for the House of Representatives was rejected by several members of the court.

Dawson J said that, beyond requiring direct choice, the Constitution left the matter of electoral systems to the Commonwealth Parliament: 186 CLR at 184.

McHugh J described the Constitution as making 'the federal Parliament the final arbiter of [the question of the relative size of electorates] just as it makes federal Parliament the final arbiter on whether there should be universal suffrage, secret ballot, preferential or proportional voting or first past the post voting': 186 CLR at 244.

Gummow J said that the reference in s 24 to 'directly chosen by the people of the Commonwealth' was a broad expression requiring a popular vote; other provisions in the Constitution (ss 24 to 30) left the matter at large to be resolved by the parliament; and *McKinlay* stood for the proposition that s 24 did not require equality in electoral divisions: 186 CLR at 279; and he observed that 'the Constitution did not entrench the secret ballot, compulsory voting, preferential or proportional voting, nor any universal adult suffrage': 186 CLR at 283.

[4.6.18] *Attorney-General (NSW) (Ex rel McKellar) v Commonwealth* (1977) 139 CLR 527 raised the validity of sections of the Representation Act 1905 (Cth) which had not been questioned in *McKinlay's* case (1975) 135 CLR 1 **[4.6.9C]**. The plaintiff sought a declaration that ss 1A and 10 of the Representation Act were invalid:

1A In this Act, 'the people of the Commonwealth' does not include the people of any Territory.

...

10 For the purpose of determining the number of members of the House of Representatives to be chosen in the several States, the following procedure shall be followed:

   (a) A quota shall be ascertained by dividing the number of people of the Commonwealth, as shown by the certificate (for the time being in force) of the Chief Electoral Officer, by twice the number of Senators for the States.

   (b) The number of Members to be chosen in each State shall, subject to the Constitution, be determined by dividing the number of people of the State, as shown by the certificate (for the time being in force) of the Chief Electoral Officer, by the quota; and if on such division there is a remainder, one more Member shall be chosen in the State.

The court (Barwick CJ, Gibbs, Stephen, Mason, Murphy and Aickin JJ) unanimously held that s 1A was valid. Gibbs, Stephen, Mason, Jacobs and Murphy JJ held that s 10(a) was valid. When determining the number of seats available to be divided between the six states, and when making that division, s 24 of the Constitution required the population of the territories and any representation of the territories in the parliament to be excluded from the calculations. Stephen J explained at 553:

In such a process, concerned exclusively with the States, the population figures of entities other than the States would seem to have no part to play, any more than would the number of representatives of those populations. Each appears to be wholly irrelevant to the subject matter of the second paragraph of s 24, the ensuring of proportionality of representation for each State. The subject matter of the second paragraph, 'the number of members to be chosen in the several States', being devoted exclusively to a subject matter of concern only to the States, one would expect that in any formula devised for the ascertainment of those numbers its components would comprise matters exclusively relevant to the States. On this view the 'people of the Commonwealth' referred to in sub-para (i) would be confined to people of the States and the reference to senators would be similarly restricted.

However, the whole court concluded that s 10(b), as it then read, was invalid. Two reasons were offered for this conclusion:

■ Section 24 of the Constitution required that the number of Members of the House of Representatives should be, as nearly as practicable, twice the number of the senators. All the justices agreed that the addition of an extra Member to the number of members allocated to any state, if there was 'a remainder' after its population had been divided by the quota, was likely to defeat that 'nexus' requirement of s 24.

■ Section 24 of the Constitution also required that the number of Members of the House of Representatives allocated to each state should be in proportion to its population. Stephen, Mason, Jacobs and Aickin JJ held that the addition of an extra member to the number of members allocated to any state if there was 'a remainder' after its population had been divided by the quota, was also likely to defeat that 'proportionality' requirement of s 24. Barwick CJ, Gibbs and Murphy JJ did not commit themselves on this point.

Until 1964, s 10(b) had adopted the method of dealing with 'remainders' used (pending the parliament 'otherwise providing') in s 24 of the Constitution; that is, an extra member was only to be allocated to a state if, after dividing its population by the quota, there was a remainder greater than one-half of the quota. The court decided that the Representation Act 1964 (Cth), by which s 10(b) was amended to its current form, was invalid. Consequently, s 10(b) stayed as it had read before the 1964 amendment. In that form, it was fully consistent with s 24 of the Constitution and was therefore valid.

[4.6.19] One consequence of the decision in *McKellar's* case **[4.6.17]** was that, since 1964, the House of Representatives had been constituted in a way inconsistent with s 24 of the Constitution; that is, it had too many members. Could such a conclusion be used to attack the validity of any of the proceedings in parliament or legislation produced by parliament in that period? As one might expect, the courts have always been reluctant to allow arguments of this type to be pressed to their logical conclusions.

For instance, in *Victoria v Commonwealth* (the *PMA* case) (1975) 134 CLR 81 **[5.3.26C]**, the High Court held that the joint sitting procedure of s 57 of the Constitution could not be used to enact legislation unless there had been strict compliance with all the preliminary processes. But the judges who came to this conclusion would not agree that the election of parliament following a defective double dissolution could be impugned on the basis of failure to comply with those preliminary processes. Gibbs J said that, assuming an invalid dissolution (purportedly under s 57) of both houses and a consequential election, he could 'see no difficulty in holding that the new Parliament would have validly assembled': 134 CLR at 157. Similar observations were made by Barwick CJ (134 CLR at 120), Stephen J (134 CLR at 178) and, more equivocally, Mason J: 134 CLR at 183–4. For a similar approach, see: *Clayton v Heffron* (1960) 105 CLR 214 at 247 **[5.3.16C]**; *Simpson v Attorney-General* [1955] NZLR 271.

7   Parliamentary privileges

[4.7.1] The houses of the several Australian parliaments, their committees and their members are recognised as possessing certain legal powers, privileges and immunities, which are generally described as parliamentary privileges. For the most part, the privileges are derived from specific legislative grants, such as the Commonwealth Constitution s 49 or the Constitution Act 1975 (Vic) s 19(1).

The terms in which most of the legislative grants have been expressed refer to the privileges of the House of Commons in the United Kingdom Parliament. The privileges of that house developed over many centuries of confrontation, negotiation and compromise between that house, on the one hand, and the Crown, the law courts and the House of Lords, on the other. In the United Kingdom, parliamentary privilege is described as part of the law and custom of parliament, whose existence and validity are recognised by the courts but which is, in general, enforced by the Houses of Parliament and not by the courts: see de Smith (1981) p 315.

[4.7.2] On the establishment of colonial legislatures in Australia in the mid-19th century, it was argued by some colonial parliamentarians that the privileges of the House of Commons had passed to their institutions. The courts consistently expressed the view that there was no wholesale transfer to the colonial legislatures of the privileges of the House of Commons: *Kielley v Carson* (1842) 4 Moo PC 63; 113 ER 225; *Fenton v Hampton* (1858) 11 Moo PC 347; 14 ER 727; *Doyle v Falconer* (1866) LR 1 PC 328 at 339; *Barton v Taylor* (1886) 11 App Cas 197 at 203; *Norton v Crick* (1894) 15 LR (NSW) 172. However, the courts accepted that the colonial (now state) legislatures inherited those privileges of the House of Commons which were reasonably necessary to their existence and the proper exercise of their functions and duties: *Kielley v Carson* (1842) 4 Moo PC 63 at 88, 92; 113 ER 225 at 234, 236; *Armstrong v Budd* (1969) 71 SR (NSW) 386. This relatively restrictive view of the privileges of colonial legislatures prompted most of the Australian parliaments to legislate so as to declare their privileges in expansive terms.

Commonwealth Parliament

[4.7.3E]   Commonwealth Constitution

49   The powers, privileges, and immunities of the Senate and of the House of Representatives, and of the members and the committees of each House, shall be such as are declared by the Parliament, and until declared shall be those of the Commons House of Parliament of the United Kingdom, and of its members and committees, at the establishment of the Commonwealth.

~~~

Notes

[4.7.4] The Commonwealth Parliament has exercised the power to declare certain aspects of the parliament's powers, privileges and immunities, in the Parliamentary Privileges Act 1987 [4.7.6]–[4.7.8]. That Act declares that it is not intended to displace the powers, privileges and immunities of each house, and of the members and committees of each house, as in force before the commencement of the Act, except to the extent that the Act expressly provides otherwise: s 5.

In addition, specific powers to administer oaths and affirmations to witnesses have been conferred on two joint committees of the Commonwealth Parliament: Public Works Committee Act 1913 s 20(1); Public Accounts Committee Act 1951 s 10(1). The Parliamentary Papers Act 1908 provides for the publication of parliamentary papers and protects the printer and publisher of those papers from any liability arising out of the publication. And the Parliamentary Proceedings Broadcasting Act

1946 authorises the broadcast of parliamentary proceedings and gives immunity from civil or criminal liability for the broadcasting of any part of those proceedings.

Accordingly, the parliament's powers, privileges and immunities derive from three sources:

- the powers, privileges and immunities held by the House of Commons on 1 January 1901;

- the Parliamentary Privileges Act 1987; and

- legislation conferring particular powers, privileges or immunities.

[4.7.5C]   R v Richards; Ex parte Fitzpatrick and Browne
(1955) 92 CLR 157

Fitzpatrick and Browne had been taken into custody by Richards, the Chief Commissioner of Police at Canberra, who was acting on warrants issued by the Speaker of the House of Representatives. The warrants asserted that the House of Representatives had, on 10 June 1955, resolved that Fitzpatrick (in the case of one warrant) and Browne (in the case of the second warrant) 'being guilty of a serious breach of privilege, be for his offence committed to the custody of the ... Chief Commissioner of Police ... and that he be kept in custody until the tenth day of September, 1955, or until earlier prorogation or dissolution', and directed Richards to execute the warrants by taking Fitzpatrick and Browne into custody and keeping them in custody until 10 September 1955 or until the earlier prorogation or dissolution of the parliament. Fitzpatrick and Browne applied to the High Court for writs of habeas corpus.

Dixon CJ, McTiernan, Williams, Webb, Fullagar, Kitto and Taylor JJ: [161] The Speaker's warrants were, as they say on their face, issued pursuant to resolutions of the House. The basis upon which the House appears to have proceeded and upon which the warrants were issued is that the Parliament has not declared so far the powers, privileges, and immunities of the Senate and of the House [162] of Representatives, and that the latter part of s 49 is in operation, with the consequence that the powers of the House of Representatives are those of the Commons House of Parliament of the United Kingdom and of its members and committees at the establishment of the Commonwealth.

The question, what are the powers, privileges and immunities of the Commons House of Parliament at the establishment of the Commonwealth, is one which the courts of law in England have treated as a matter for their decision. But the courts in England arrived at that position after a long course of judicial decision not unaccompanied by political controversy. The law in England was finally settled about 1840.

... Stated shortly, it is this: it is for the courts to judge of the existence in either House of Parliament of a privilege, but, given an undoubted privilege, it is for the House to judge of the occasion and of the manner of its exercise. The judgment of the House is expressed by its resolution and by the warrant of the Speaker. If the warrant specifies the ground of the commitment the court may, it would seem, determine whether it is sufficient in law as a ground to amount to a breach of privilege, but if the warrant is upon its face consistent with a breach of an acknowledged privilege it is conclusive and it is no objection that the breach of privilege is stated in general terms. This statement of law appears to be in accordance with cases by which it was finally established, namely, the *Case of the Sheriff of Middlesex* (1840) 11 Ad&E 273 [113 ER 419].

So far as this country is concerned, it is established authoritatively by the decisions of the Privy Council in *Dill v Murphy* (1864) 1 Moo PC (NS) 487 [15 ER 784] and in *Speaker of the Legislative Assembly of Victoria v Glass* (1871) LR 3 PC App 560.

[164] In the present case the warrant would clearly be sufficient if it had been issued by the Speaker of the House of Commons in pursuance of the resolution of that House. Indeed, the

contrary is not urged. It would be sufficient because it recites in each case that the person concerned has been guilty of a serious breach of privilege and it recites a resolution to that effect, and the resolution proceeds that for his offence he be committed to the custody of the person for the time being performing the duties of Chief Commissioner of Police at Canberra, or to the custody of the Keeper of the Gaol at such place as Mr Speaker from time to time directs. The operative words of the warrant directed to Mr Richards are these:— 'These are therefore to command you the said Edward Richards to receive the said Raymond Edward Fitzpatrick' (in one case) 'and Frank Courtney Browne' (in the other) 'into your custody and with such assistance as you may require to keep him in your custody subject to any direction given by me in pursuance of the said resolution until' the dates and the events which are mentioned.

Now, if, under the law which we have attempted to describe, that warrant were produced to a court sitting in London, as we are here, as a warrant of the House of Commons, it would be regarded by the court as conclusive of what it states, namely, that a breach of privilege had been committed and that the House, acting upon that view, had directed that the two persons concerned should be committed and the Speaker, accordingly, had issued his warrant. In the ordinary phrase current in the law courts, it would not be possible to go behind that warrant. It states a contempt or breach of privilege in general terms, and not in particular terms, but it is completely consistent with a breach having occurred and it states that one did occur.

The question in the case is whether that state of the law applies under s 49 of the Constitution to the House of Representatives. If you take the language of the latter part of s 49 and read it apart from any other considerations, it is difficult in the extreme to see how any other answer could be given to the question than that that law is applicable in Australia to the House of Representatives. For s 49 says that, until the powers, privileges and immunities of the House are declared by Act of Parliament, the powers, privileges and immunities of the House shall be those of the Commons House of Parliament of the United Kingdom at the establishment of the Commonwealth. The language is such as to be apt to transfer to the House the full powers, privileges and immunities of the House of Commons. As Lord Cairns has said, an essential ingredient, not a [165] mere accident, in those powers, is the protection from the examination of the conclusion of the House expressed by the warrant ...

The justices referred to an argument that, under the Commonwealth Constitution, it was the duty of the courts to consider whether any act was beyond the power which the Constitution assigns to that body. 'As a general proposition', they said, 'the truth of that consideration admits of no denial.'

The answer, in our opinion, lies in the very plain words of s 49 itself. The words are incapable of a restricted meaning, unless that restricted meaning be imperatively demanded as something to be placed artificially upon them by the more general considerations which the Constitution supplies. Added to that simple reason are the facts of the history of this particular branch of the law. Students of English constitutional history are well aware of the controversy which attended the establishment of the powers, privileges and immunities of the House of Commons. Students of English constitutional law are made aware at a very early stage of their tuition of the judicial declarations terminating that controversy, and it may be said that there is no more conspicuous chapter in the constitutional law of Great Britain than the particular matter with which we are dealing. It is quite incredible that the framers of s 49 were not completely aware of the state of the law in Great Britain and, [166] when they adopted the language of s 49, were not quite conscious of the consequences which followed from it. We are therefore of opinion that the general structure of this Constitution, meaning by that the fact that it is an instrument creating a constitution of a kind commonly described as rigid in which an excess of power means invalidity does not provide a sufficient ground for placing upon the express words of s 49 an artificial limitation ...

Then it was argued that this is a constitution which adopts the theory of the separation of powers and places the judicial power exclusively in the judicature as established under the Constitution, the executive power in the executive, and restricts the legislature to legislative powers. It is said that the power exercised by resolving upon the imprisonment of two men and issuing a warrant to carry it into effect belonged to the judicial power and ought therefore not to be conceded under the words of s 49 to either House of the Parliament. It is correct that the Constitution is based in its structure upon the separation of powers. It is true that the judicial power of the Commonwealth is reposed exclusively in the courts contemplated by Chap III. It is further correct that it is a general principle of construction that the legislative powers should not be interpreted as allowing of the creation of judicial powers or authorities in any body except the courts which are described by Chap III of the Constitution ...

[167] The consideration we have already mentioned is of necessity an answer to this contention, namely, that in unequivocal terms the powers of the House of Commons have been bestowed upon the House of Representatives. It should be added to that very simple statement that throughout the course of English history there has been a tendency to regard those powers as not strictly judicial but as belonging to the legislature, rather as something essential or, at any rate, proper for its protection. This is not the occasion to discuss the historical grounds upon which these powers and privileges attached to the House of Commons. It is sufficient to say that they were regarded by many authorities as proper incidents of the legislative function, notwithstanding the fact that considered more theoretically — perhaps one might even say, scientifically — they belong to the judicial sphere. But our decision is based upon the ground that a general view of the Constitution and the separation of powers is not a sufficient reason for giving to these words, which appear to us to be so clear, a restrictive or secondary meaning which they do not properly bear.

Dixon CJ, McTiernan, Williams, Webb, Fullagar, Kitto and Taylor JJ rejected an argument that s 49 was spent because the parliament had exercised its power to legislate so as to define the privileges of the houses. They rejected as 'ill-founded' a further argument that, because no rules or orders had been made under s 50 of the Commonwealth Constitution, the House of Representatives could not exercise its powers and privileges.

~~~

[4.7.6] The Parliamentary Privileges Act 1987 (Cth) s 5 declares that the powers, privileges and immunities of each House of Parliament, their members and committees, as in force under s 49 of the Constitution immediately before the commencement of the Act, continue in force. Notwithstanding the preservation effected by s 5, the Act limits the powers, privileges and immunities of the Houses of the Commonwealth Parliament in several ways:

- Section 4 limits the conduct which can amount to an offence against a house, including a contempt of parliament: s 3(3). It appears that the conduct in question must be seen to have an effect, intention or likely effect to interfere with the house's (or a parliamentary committee's) authority or function or with a member's free performance of parliamentary duties.

- Section 6 removes the threat which critics of parliament and members formerly faced, of being punished for contempt of parliament by reason of defaming or criticising the parliament, a house, a committee or a member.

- Section 9 reinforces that removal, and enhances the power of the courts to review and control the exercise of punitive powers by the houses. A general warrant, in the terms issued by the Speaker of the House of Representatives in the case of Fitzpatrick and Browne and upheld by the High Court in *R v Richards; Ex parte Fitzpatrick and Browne* (1955) 92 CLR 157 **[4.7.5C]** can no longer be issued. The warrant committing the person to custody must particularise the alleged offence. On the authority of *Stockdale v Hansard* (1839) 9 Ad & E 1; 112 ER 1112, courts could then determine whether the matters set out in the warrant could in law amount to a contempt of parliament.

■   Section 7 both limits and expands the punitive powers of the parliament. Whereas a house could formerly imprison a person adjudged guilty of contempt for the duration of the current session of parliament, imprisonment is now limited to six months but is not affected by the end of the session of parliament. Previously, a house could not impose a fine in punishment of a contempt (*R v Pitt* (1762) 97 ER 861) but the Act permits the imposition of a fine.

[4.7.7]   Sections 12 and 13 of the Parliamentary Privileges Act introduce criminal offences that may be tried in the courts. The conduct that constitutes these offences may also be regarded as a contempt of parliament, because in 1901 the House of Commons would have claimed, and been conceded by the courts, the power to punish intimidation of witnesses and the unauthorised disclosure of evidence: May (1989) pp 131–2.

Neither s 12 nor s 13 removes the power which the Houses of Parliament would have, by virtue of s 49 of the Commonwealth Constitution, of imposing a penalty, consistent with s 7 of the Act, for a contempt of parliament. Could a person who has been dealt with by one of the houses in the exercise of its power to punish for contempt be prosecuted under either of these sections? Or, could such a person plead *autrefois acquit* or *autrefois convict*?

[4.7.8]   Section 16 of the Parliamentary Privileges Act underlines the legal immunity of proceedings in parliament, declared by the Bill of Rights 1688 (Eng) art 9. In practical terms, the immunity means that Members of Parliament are protected against any criminal or civil liability that might otherwise arise out of statements made in the course of debates or proceedings in parliament. Members of the Parliament cannot be compelled to give evidence before a court or royal commission relating to anything said in the course of debates or proceedings in parliament. Further, persons who give evidence before a parliamentary committee are similarly protected.

A Member of Parliament is competent, although not compellable, to give evidence that a particular document has been tabled in parliament (*Sankey v Whitlam* (1978) 142 CLR 1 at 35–7 per Gibbs ACJ) or that a particular Member of Parliament was present in the house on a particular day: *Amman Aviation Pty Ltd v Commonwealth* (1988) 19 FCR 223 at 230 per Beaumont J. But no court or tribunal can receive evidence of proceedings in parliament which involves any question as to the substance of those proceedings.

[4.7.9]   So, in *Amman Aviation Pty Ltd v Commonwealth* (1988) 19 FCR 223 at 231, Beaumont J refused to admit into evidence an extract from *Hansard*, which the applicant claimed would have established that a Minister had been improperly influenced by the applicant's commercial competitor when deciding to cancel the applicant's contract, saying:

> Such an examination, in a contentious area, cannot be reconciled with the complete freedom of speech envisaged in the Bill of Rights and the Act. It would be otherwise if the tender were for a non-contentious purpose, for instance, to prove that certain documents were tabled in Parliament, without disclosing who tabled them ... or ... to prove the time of proceedings. If what is involved in a tender of evidence from *Hansard* is simply not capable of being contentious, it is difficult to see how the right of free speech could be affected.
>
> But what is sought here is to use *Hansard* to justify an inference that Senator Evans was influenced by Sir Peter Abeles in the context of the respondent's decision to terminate

the applicant's contract. This is a highly contentious matter. In my view, the present tender is by way of or for the purpose of questioning the motive, intention or good faith of the senator and is thus proscribed by s 16(3)(b). Also, in my opinion, the tender is by way of, or for the purpose of, inviting the drawing of inferences or conclusions from what was said in the Senate and is thus made unlawful by s 16(3)(c). The tender must be rejected accordingly.

[4.7.10] In *Hamsher v Swift* (1992) 33 FCR 545, French J refused to allow the introduction into evidence of a statement made by the Minister for Immigration in the Senate. The applicants claimed that the statement showed that the minister had made particular decisions under the Migration Act 1958 (Cth) or that it provided the basis on which the applicants could construct an estoppel against the minister. The minister had raised no objection to the evidence in question, but French J said that the prohibition expressed in s 16 of the Parliamentary Privileges Act did not depend upon an objection being raised (at 564):

> [Section] 16(3) is expressed in terms of an absolute prohibition. Whether that prohibition can be overcome by any permission of the House of Parliament concerned may be doubtful and need not be decided here. But it is apparent under the legislation as it now stands that the prohibition contained in s 16(3) cannot be waived by an individual Member or be taken to have been waived in the absence of objection.

French J concluded that s 16(3)(b) and (c) prohibited the use of the minister's statement for the purposes sought by the applicant.

State parliaments

New South Wales

[4.7.11] The New South Wales Parliament depends for most of its privileges upon the rather uncertain principle of necessity. In *Armstrong v Budd* (1969) 71 SR (NSW) 386, the New South Wales Court of Appeal held that the Legislative Council in that state had an implied power to expel a member of the Council if the Council adjudged the member to have been guilty of conduct unworthy of a member. Wallace P noted that in *Kielley v Carson* (1842) 4 Moo PC 63; 13 ER 225, the Privy Council had acknowledged that colonial legislatures possessed those powers and privileges which were reasonably necessary to the proper exercise of their functions. He continued at 71 SR (NSW) 402:

> [T]he critical question is to decide what is 'reasonable' under present-day conditions and modern habits of thought to preserve the existence and proper exercise of the functions of the Legislative Council as it now exists. It would be unthinkable to 'peg' [the concept of what is reasonable] to the conditions in New South Wales when it had just emerged from convict days. Indeed, when *Kielley v Carson* was decided convicts were still being sent to western portions of Australia and had only ceased to be sent out to New South Wales one year earlier. This is not to say that the implied power as enunciated by the Privy Council can be enlarged by the passage of time, but the word 'reasonable' in this context must have an ambulatory meaning to enable it to have sense and sensibility when applied to the conditions obtaining in 1969.

There have been several specific conferrals of powers and privileges on the New South Wales Parliament. Either house of the parliament, or one of its committees, may summon witnesses to give evidence (Parliamentary Evidence Act 1901 (NSW) s 4) and administer an oath or 'solemn declaration' to those witnesses: s 10. A failure or refusal to answer lawful questions constitutes a contempt of parliament punishable, by order of either house, by imprisonment for a maximum of one month under warrant of the President of the Council or the Speaker of the Assembly: s 11. Any witness who wilfully make a false statement is liable, on prosecution, to five years' penal servitude: s 13.

The Parliamentary Standing Committee on Public Works is authorised to summon witnesses and compel the production of documents (Public Works Act 1912 (NSW) s 21) and its chairman may commit recalcitrant witnesses to gaol for a maximum of one month or fine them a maximum of $100: s 22(1).

Absolute privilege against liability for defamation is extended to witnesses attending before either house or a committee: Parliamentary Evidence Act 1901 (NSW) s 12; and to the publication of documents by order or under the authority of either House and the publication of the debates of either house: Defamation Act 1974 (NSW) s 17.

[4.7.12]   Can a member's statements made in parliament be questioned outside of parliament if the member waives his or her parliamentary privilege? This issue was considered in *Arena v Nader* (1997) 42 NSWLR 427.

In September 1997, a member of the New South Wales Legislative Council, Mrs Franca Arena, stated in the Council that prominent people would be exposed in a police royal commission as paedophiles. Arena claimed that the Premier and Opposition Leader had held a private meeting to discuss the royal commission and that 'an agreement was reached to ensure that people in high places would not be named as it would have been too traumatic for the community to realise how many of its so-called upstanding citizens were involved in criminal activities': Legislative Council, *Debates*, 17 September 1997, p 64.

On 24 September 1997, the parliament enacted the Special Commissions of Inquiry Amendment Act 1997 (NSW), which, among other things, gave each house of parliament the power to authorise the Governor to issue a commission to a judge or queen's counsel to inquire into and report to the Governor and the house on any matter relating to parliamentary proceedings. The house passing such a resolution could also waive parliamentary privilege in connection with any special commission. The member could retain parliamentary privilege in respect of anything said or done by the member in parliamentary proceedings but could give evidence to a special commission if the member chose to waive privilege.

The Legislative Council then resolved to establish a special commission of inquiry, and appointed John Nader QC to report into the matters that Arena had raised in the Council. Arena challenged the validity of the relevant provisions of the Special Commissions of Inquiry Amendment Act 1997.

The NSW Court of Appeal (Priestley, Handley and Meagher JJA) held that the privileges, immunities and powers conferred by Article 9 of the Bill of Rights were conferred upon the institution of parliament as a whole; and while those privileges could be invoked by individual members of parliament they are an attribute of office and not a personal privilege; a house of parliament could take steps to waive a member's privilege and permit an external inquiry into statements made inside the House while at the same time the relevant statute operated not to waive a member's privilege: see 42 NSWLR at 437.

In refusing an application for special leave to appeal from the judgment of the Court of Appeal, (1997) 71 ALJR 1604, the High Court (Brennan CJ, Gummow and Hayne JJ) said, at 1605:

A House of Parliament in which allegations are made has a legitimate interest in knowing, and perhaps a duty to ascertain, whether there is substance in allegations made by a member on a matter of public interest. It is within the power of the Parliament to authorise that House to engage, or to authorise the engagement, of a Commissioner to inquire into such allegations and to report to the House ... The Act does not alter the powers of the House: rather it affects the privileges which govern the manner in which the House transacts its business.

[4.7.13] In *Egan v Willis* (1998) 195 CLR 424, the High Court considered the extent of the New South Wales Parliament's power to punish contempt and the scope of judicial power to review the existence of parliamentary privilege.

In May 1996 the Legislative Council called on the Leader of the Government in that house, Egan, to table certain documents in the Council or deliver them to the Clerk of the Council. Following Egan's failure to comply, the Council passed a resolution judging Egan guilty of contempt and suspending him from the Council for the remainder of the day's sitting. After refusing to leave the house, Egan was taken out of the chamber and the building by the Usher of the Black Rod.

A majority of the High Court (494, 511) applied the principle expressed by Dixon CJ, on behalf of the court, in *R v Richards; Ex parte Fitzpatrick and Browne* (1955) 92 CLR 157 **[4.7.5C]** at 162 that 'it is for the courts to judge of the existence in either House of Parliament of a privilege, but, given an undoubted privilege, it is for the House to judge of the occasion and of the manner of its exercise'. Gaudron, Gummow and Hayne JJ described that proposition as having 'equal application to the present case', and as ensuring 'that intervention by the courts is only "at the initial jurisdictional level" ...': 195 CLR 424 at 446; see also 195 CLR 424 at 460 (McHugh J), 490 (Kirby J), 509 (Callinan J).

The court upheld the doctrine of reasonable necessity (see **[4.7.11]**): see. in particular, 195 CLR 424 at 495–6 (Kirby J), 514 (Callinan J). A house of the New South Wales Parliament may suspend a member for a limited period when that member is called upon to produce a non-privileged document in the house and the member refuses to do so.

Queensland

[4.7.14] The Queensland Legislative Assembly, its members and committees enjoy the powers, rights, privileges and immunities defined by legislation and until defined by legislation those powers, rights or immunities that by custom, statute or otherwise are enjoyed by the House of Commons in the United Kingdom, parliament and its members and committees at the establishment of the Commonwealth in 1 January 1901: Constitution of Queensland 2001, s 9. These privileges would include the power to order the attendance of witnesses and the production of documents, and the power to punish, by fine (or, failing payment of the fine, imprisonment), contempt of parliament. They would also protect members of parliament from criminal or civil liability in respect of anything said or published by them during proceedings in parliament.

South Australia

[4.7.15] The South Australian Legislative Council, House of Assembly, their committees and their members have been granted the privileges, immunities and powers of the House of Commons in the United Kingdom Parliament, its committees and members as at 24 October 1856: Constitution Act 1934 (SA) s 38.

However, no member of either house of the South Australian Parliament can claim a privilege against any process issued by a court of law, other than an immunity from the writ of *capias ad satisfaciendum* during a session of parliament or within 10 days prior to the meeting of parliament, and an excuse for non-attendance as a witness in any court when attending parliament: s 39.

Tasmania

[4.7.16] The Tasmanian Legislative Council, House of Assembly and their committees are authorised to order the attendance of witnesses and the production of documents: Parliamentary Privileges Act 1858 (Tas) s 1. The Council and the Assembly are authorised to punish, by fine (or, failing payment of the fine, imprisonment) certain contempts, enumerated in the same terms as in Queensland: s 4. The President of the Council or the Speaker of the Assembly may issue a warrant for imprisonment in pursuance of a resolution of the relevant house (ss 5, 7), and may order the detention of a person creating or joining in a disturbance in the house during its sitting, pending consideration by the house: s 6.

Members of the Tasmanian Parliament are protected against criminal and civil liability for anything said or published by them during proceedings in parliament: Criminal Code 1924 (Tas) s 202; Defamation Act 1957 (Tas) s 10(1).

Victoria

[4.7.17] There has been a complete transfer of the powers and privileges of the House of Commons to the Victorian Parliament. Section 19(1) of the Constitution Act 1975 (Vic) confers on the Legislative Council, Legislative Assembly, their committees and their members the privileges, immunities and powers of the House of Commons in the United Kingdom Parliament, its committees and members as at 21 July 1855.

In addition, each House of the Victorian Parliament and any committee of the parliament is authorised to administer an oath or affirmation to a witness appearing before the house or the committee: Constitution Act 1975 (Vic), ss 19A(2), (3), (6). The necessity for this additional grant arises from the fact that the equivalent power was only conferred on the House of Commons and its committees by the Parliamentary Witnesses Oaths Act 1871 (UK), 16 years after the date by reference to which the powers and privileges of the Victorian Parliament were defined. Evidence given by a witness before a committee of a House of the Victorian Parliament is absolutely privileged against an action for defamation and who can be charged with perjury for wilfully giving false evidence: Constitution Act 1975 (Vic) ss 19A(7), (8).

Because of the general conferral of the powers and privileges of the House of Commons effected by s 19, either house of the Victorian Parliament may impose the punishment of imprisonment for a contempt of the house and, by declining to include particulars of the contempt in the warrant for imprisonment, effectively exclude judicial review of its action: *Dill v Murphy* (1864) 1 Moo PC, NS, 487; 15 ER 784; *Speaker of the Legislative Assembly v Glass* (1871) LR 3 PC 560.

Western Australia

[4.7.18] The Western Australian Legislative Council, Legislative Assembly, their committees and their members have been granted the privileges, immunities and powers of the House of Commons in the United Kingdom Parliament, its committees and members as they stand 'for the time being': Parliamentary Privileges Act 1891 (WA) s 1.

However, each house's power to punish for contempt is limited to seven categories of contempt, defined in substantially the same terms as those used in the Queensland legislation: s 8. The President of the Council or the Speaker of the Assembly may issue a warrant for imprisonment in pursuance of a resolution of the relevant house (ss 9, 10) and may order the detention of a person creating or joining in a disturbance in the house during its sitting, pending consideration by the house: s 11.

The Western Australian Legislative Council, the Legislative Assembly and their committees are authorised to order the attendance of witnesses and the production of documents: s 4. Members of the Western Australian Parliament are protected against criminal and civil liability for anything said or published by them during proceedings in parliament: Criminal Code Act 1913 (WA) ss 5, 351(1).

8   References

[4.8.1] *Articles*

Galligan and Chesterman, 'Aborigines, Citizenship and the Australian Constitution: Did the Constitution Exclude Aboriginal People from Citizenship?' (1997) 8 *Public Law Review* 45.

Evans, 'Pecuniary Interests of Members of Parliament under the Australian Constitution' (1975) 49 *ALJ* 464.

Hanks, 'Vice-Regal Initiative and Discretion' [1975] *ACLD DT* 294.

Lindell, 'Judicial Review and the Composition of the House of Representatives' (1974) 6 *Federal LR* 84.

Lane, 'Commonwealth Electors' Voting Rights' (1968) 42 *ALJ* 127.

Lindell, 'The Arrangements for Self-government for the Australian Capital Territory: A Partial Road to Republicanism in the Seat of Government?' (1992) 3 *Public Law Review* 5.

Paterson, 'Federal Electorates and Proportionate Distribution' (1968) 42 *ALJ* 139.

Sexton, 'The Role of Judicial Review in Federal Electoral Law' (1978) 52 *ALJ* 28.

[4.8.2] *Papers and reports*

Commonwealth Parliament, *Report of the Joint Committee on Pecuniary Interests of Members of Parliament*, Parliamentary Paper no 182 of 1975.

Constitutional Commission, *Final Report*, AGPS, 1988.

[4.8.3] *Texts*

Beasley, 'The Parliament of the Commonwealth' in *Essays on the Australian Constitution*, (ed Else-Mitchell), 2nd ed, Law Book Co, Sydney, 1961.

Brazil, 'Commentary' in *Labor and the Constitution 1972–1975*, (ed Evans), Heinemann Educational, Melbourne, 1977.

Campell, *Parliamentary Privilege in Australia*, Melbourne University Press, Melbourne, 1966.

Carney, *Members of Parliament: Law and Ethics*, Prospect, Sydney, 2000.

Coper, 'Commentary' in *Labor and the Constitution 1972–1975*, (ed Evans), Heinemann Educational, Melbourne, 1977.

Davis (ed), *The Government of the Australian States*, Longman, London, 1960.

de Smith, *Constitutional and Administrative Law*, Penguin, Ringwood, Victoria, 1981.

Emy, *The Politics of Australian Democracy*, 2nd ed, Macmillan, Melbourne, 1978.

Evans (ed), *Labor and the Constitution 1972–1975*, Heinemann Educational, 1977.

Greig, *International Law*, Butterworths, 2nd ed, London, 1976

Hanks, 'Aborigines and Government: The Developing Framework' in *Aborigines and the Law*, (eds Hanks and Keon-Cohen), George Allen and Unwin, Sydney, 1984.

Hanks, 'Parliamentarians and the Electorate' in *Labor and the Constitution 1972–1975*, (ed Evans), Heinemann Educational, Melbourne, 1977.

Holmes, *The Government of Victoria*, University of Queensland Press, Brisbane, 1976.

Jaensch, *The Government of South Australia*, University of Queensland Press, Brisbane, 1977.

Lumb, *Constitutions of the Australian States*, 4th ed, University of Queensland Press, Brisbane, 1977.

Lumb, *The Constitution of the Commonwealth of Australia Annotated*, 4th ed, Butterworths, Sydney, 1986.

Morrison, 'The Government of Queensland' in *The Government of the Australian States*, (ed Davis), Longmans, London, 1960, pp 249–332.

May, *Treatise on the Law, Privileges, Proceedings and Usages of Parliament*, 21st ed, Butterworths, London, 1989.

Odgers, *Australian Senate Practice*, 5th ed, AGPS, Canberra, 1976.

Parker, *The Government of New South Wales*, University of Queensland Press, Brisbane, 1978.

Quick and Garran, *The Annotated Constitution of the Australian Commonwealth*, Angus & Robertson, Sydney, 1901.

Sawer, *Australian Federal Politics and Law 1901–1929*, Melbourne University Press, Melbourne, 1956.

Sawer, *Australian Federalism in the Courts*, Melbourne University Press, Melbourne, 1967.

Sawer, *Federation Under Strain*, Melbourne University Press, Melbourne, 1977.

Townsley, *The Government of Tasmania*, University of Queensland Press, Brisbane, 1976.

Zines, *The High Court and the Constitution*, 4th ed, Butterworths, Sydney, 1997.

Chapter

5

Legislative Procedures

1 Standard procedure

Introduction

[5.1.1]   Among parliament's functions is the making of law through the enactment of legislation: its pre-eminent function from a lawyer's perspective. How do the individuals who constitute parliament join together and, as a parliament, produce a statute? There are rules of law which define the necessary process of enactment. In order to identify an Act of Parliament, we need to check to see whether it has complied with that process. However, identifying the relevant rules may raise complex issues, because the rules defining the process of enactment may vary from one type of legislation to another, or may be subject to alteration by an Act of Parliament, or may be non-justiciable.

[5.1.2]   The standard definitions of parliament are those found in such legislation as s 1 of the Commonwealth Constitution, s 3 of the Constitution Act 1902 (NSW) or s 15 of the Constitution Act 1975 (Vic). Parliament consists of two houses and the Crown, represented by the Governor-General or the Governor: see **[4.2.8]–[4.2.14], [4.2.21E]–[4.2.25]**. The Queensland legislation, of course, refers to only one house and the Governor: see Constitution Act 1867 (Qld) s 2. The notion, that each of these three institutions (in Queensland, two institutions) is an essential ingredient in parliament and that legislation can only be enacted when each of the component institutions approves it, is not stated explicitly in the legislation, but such provisions as ss 1, 53, 57 and 58 of the Commonwealth Constitution leave room for no other inference.

The legislation

[5.1.3E]   **Commonwealth Constitution**

1   The legislative power of the Commonwealth shall be vested in a Federal Parliament, which shall consist of the Queen, a Senate, and a House of Representatives, and which is hereinafter called 'The Parliament', or 'The Parliament of the Commonwealth'. ...

22   Until the Parliament otherwise provides, the presence of at least one-third of the whole number of the senators shall be necessary to constitute a meeting of the Senate for the exercise of its powers. ...

23   Questions arising in the Senate shall be determined by a majority of votes, and each senator shall have one vote. The President shall in all cases be entitled to vote; and when the votes are equal the question shall pass in the negative. ...

39   Until the Parliament otherwise provides, the presence of at least one-third of the whole number of the members of the House of Representatives shall be necessary to constitute a meeting of the House of the exercise of its powers. ...

40   Questions arising in the House of Representatives shall be determined by a majority of votes other than that of the Speaker. The Speaker shall not vote unless the numbers are equal, and then he shall have a casting vote. ...

50   Each House of the Parliament may make rules and orders with respect to —

   (i)   The mode in which its powers, privileges, and immunities may be exercised and upheld:

   (ii)   The order and conduct of its business and proceedings either separately or jointly with the other House. ...

58   When a proposed law passed by both Houses of the Parliament is presented to the Governor-General for the Queen's assent, he shall declare, according to his discretion, but subject to this Constitution, that he assents in the Queen's name, or that he withholds assent, or that he reserves the law for the Queen's pleasure.

The Governor-General may return to the House in which it originated any proposed law so presented to him, and may transmit therewith any amendments which he may recommend, and the Houses may deal with the recommendation.

~~~

Notes

[5.1.4]   The equivalent legislation in each of the states is rather less detailed, except in Victoria (see s 18 of the Constitution Act 1975 (Vic), as amended by s 17 of the Constitution (Parliamentary Reform) Act 2003 (Vic)), which prescribes the majorities required to pass specific types of legislation. In the remainder of cases the inevitable inference is that most questions are resolved by a simple majority. (A simple majority is one more than half the number of members voting; an absolute majority is one more than half of the total number of members eligible to vote, no matter how many members vote.) But, in so far as any of the state parliaments is defined as consisting of two houses and the Crown, and the power to make laws is vested in that institution (see the legislation referred to in [4.2.8]–[4.2.14]), it must follow that approval by each of those components is necessary before parliament can be said to have legislated. That inference is reinforced by the presence of such provisions as s 5B of the Constitution Act 1902 (NSW), ss 66 and 67 of the Constitution Act 1975 (Vic) and s 41 of the Constitution Act 1934 (SA), which provide for elaborate alternative procedures where the two houses of parliament cannot agree on proposed legislation: see [5.3.9], [5.3.10].

[5.1.5] The courts have consistently acted on the assumption that, to produce an Act of Parliament, a bill must be approved by each of the houses and by the Crown. In *Stockdale v Hansard* (1839) 9 Ad & E 1; 112 ER 1112, the Queen's Bench dismissed a plea that the House of Commons could, by resolution, protect a printer who had published libellous material from being sued for libel. Patteson J said at 9 Ad & E 190:

> The proposition is certainly very startling, that any man, or body of men, however exalted, except those branches of the legislature concurring, should by passing a resolution that they have the power to do an act illegal in itself, be able to bind all persons whatsoever, and preclude them from enquiring into the existence of that power and the legality of that act.

In *Stevenson v R* (1865) 2 WW & A'B 143, the Victorian Supreme Court held that the approval by the Legislative Assembly of a bill imposing customs duties could not authorise the collection of those duties. Stawell CJ declared that resolutions by the Assembly were not equal to an Act of Parliament and the claim that one house might authorise a tax was 'in direct violation of the established principle that no tax can be imposed save with the full assent of the three estates of the realm': 2 WW & A'B at 159.

The standing orders

[5.1.6] Each of the 15 houses of parliament (Commonwealth, state and territory) has adopted its own standing orders regulating the procedure within the house on any bill. These standing orders are based upon those of the House of Commons in the United Kingdom Parliament and specify the stages through which bills should pass as they are considered by the house and, ultimately, approved and passed on to the next stage (to the other house or to the Crown's representative for the royal assent). The typical stages through which a bill passes are:

- *first reading*: a formality which gives the bill a place in the house's agenda;

- *second reading*: the occasion when the policy underlying the bill is debated; the House will either approve the motion for a second reading, or reject it by amending the motion;

- *committee stage*: when the bill 'goes into committee', the house considers it, clause by clause, and debates detailed amendments; and

- *third reading*: once the detailed consideration is concluded, the bill is reported back to the house. Immediately, as a general rule, the sponsor of the bill moves that the bill be read a third time, and that motion will be treated as a formality. The clerk to the house will read the long title of the bill as he or she did at the first and second reading stages. The bill has then passed the house.

[5.1.7] These procedures are prescribed by the internal rules of the houses. They may be altered or suspended by a resolution of the relevant house. But, are they justiciable?

In *Edinburgh and Dalkeith Railway Co v Wauchope* (1842) 8 Cl & F 710; 8 ER 279, the House of Lords rejected the argument that a private Act of Parliament could be impugned on the ground that, in passing it, the House of Commons had not observed its own standing orders. Lord Campbell declared that 'no court of justice can inquire into ... what passed in Parliament during [a bill's] progress in its various stages through both houses': 8 Cl & F at 725; 8 ER at 285.

More recently, in *British Railways Board v Pickin* [1974] AC 765, the House of Lords rejected an attack on a private Act of Parliament, grounded on an alleged defect in the enacting procedure; namely, the fraud of the respondents, who had promoted the private Act. Lord Morris was unequivocal, at 790:

> It must surely be for Parliament to lay down the procedures which are to be followed before a Bill can become an Act. It must be for Parliament to decide whether its decreed procedures have in fact been followed. It must be for Parliament to lay down and to construe its standing orders and further to decide whether they have been obeyed: it must be for Parliament to decide whether in any particular case to dispense with compliance with such orders.

It is at least doubtful whether, in view of the High Court's decision in *Victoria v Commonwealth* (the *PMA* case) (1975) 135 CLR 81 **[5.3.26C]**, Australian courts would take such a deferential attitude. Certainly the High Court would not endorse Lord Morris's proposition that '[i]n the courts there may be argument as to the correct interpretation of the enactment: there must be none as to whether it should be on the statute book at all': [1974] AC at 787. See the *PMA* case (1975) 134 CLR 81 at 164; Conklin (1975); Lindell (1977) p 168.

Royal assent

[5.1.8]   Assent to or approval of legislation by the Crown is an integral part of the legislative process. But the Crown (whether in the person of the Queen or a Governor-General or Governor) has a very limited role. Even the formal constitutional documents recognise no power in the Crown to amend bills passed by the houses of parliament. The Governor-General may return bills to one of the Commonwealth Houses of Parliament with a recommendation for amendment: Commonwealth Constitution s 58. But the power was intended to have a very limited operation; namely, to enable 'inaccuracies or discrepancies [which] have crept into' legislation to be corrected with a minimum of formality: Quick and Garran (1901) p 692; Lumb (1986) p 229.

[5.1.9]   The first paragraph of s 58 makes clear the limited discretion of the Crown. The Governor-General has three options: to assent, to withhold assent or to reserve the bill 'for the Queen's pleasure'. This limited discretion is now an integral part of the parliamentary system, as the Queensland Supreme Court held in *R v Commissioner for Transport; Ex parte Cobb & Co Ltd* [1963] Qd R 547. An Act passed by the Queensland Parliament and assented to by the Governor was attacked on the ground that part of the Act regulated coastal shipping and the Governor was obliged by the Merchant Shipping Act 1889 (UK) to reserve legislation dealing with that topic for the Queen's assent, that is, he could not assent to such legislation. (The requirement that such legislation be reserved was removed by s 9 of the Australia Act 1986: see **[5.2.3]**.) In support of the Act, it was argued that the part to which the Governor could not assent should be separated from the rest, which would then be valid. The Queensland Full Supreme Court rejected that argument, because such a separation (or 'severance') would recognise that the Governor could give his assent to part of a bill. Stanley J said at 568:

> The Queen does not legislate by her own power, nor does the Legislative Assembly by its own power. The combined powers of both are required to convert a Bill into an Act.

Therefore in my opinion the problem of severance cannot arise in this matter. The Queen cannot assent to part of a Bill; nor can the Governor assent on her behalf to part of a Bill. If any part of the Bill be not acceptable, the whole Bill is sent back to the Assembly. If part only could be assented to, that part by itself might achieve something radically different from what the Assembly intended. The Sovereign no longer originates legislation.

[5.1.10] The function of the Crown in assenting to legislation could not be described as an independent one. Legislation is given the royal assent because the ministry advises the Governor-General or Governor to assent. Assent is a formal act, an automatic and inevitable response to the prompting of the government of the day. The rationale for this is succinctly stated by Sawer (1977) pp 184–5. The refusal to give assent, when advised by the ministry, would lead either to the dismissal of the Governor-General or Governor, or to the resignation of the ministry and an election in which the former ministry would confront the Governor-General or Governor.

Reservation

[5.1.11] Section 74 of the Commonwealth Constitution denies to the Governor-General the power to assent to any legislation that would limit appeals from the High Court to the Privy Council. Bills for this purpose must be reserved for the assent of the Queen. This limitation was designed to give the United Kingdom Government a veto over any reduction in the appellate jurisdiction of the Privy Council. It was intended that the Privy Council should impose British ideas of law and justice on Australia, and thereby protect British interests here: La Nauze (1972) p 261.

However, the limitation ceased to have any practical significance in 1975, when the Privy Council (Appeals from the High Court) Act 1975 (Cth) removed the last category of High Court decisions in which an appeal might be taken to the Privy Council without a certificate from the High Court.

Until 1986, state Governors were required to reserve certain types of legislation for assent by the Queen: Hanks (1985) p 68. By s 9 of the Australia Act 1986, those requirements are declared to have no force or effect.

Disallowance

[5.1.12] Section 59 of the Commonwealth Constitution authorises the Queen to 'disallow any law within one year from the Governor-General's assent', and thereby 'annul the law'. Seventy years ago, the power was described as one that 'can no longer be exercised in relation to dominion legislation': Conference on Operation of Dominion Legislation, Cmd 2479, 1929, para 23. More recently, it was described as 'now a dead letter': Lumb and Moens (1995) p 333. A similar theoretical possibility of disallowance of state legislation, conferred by s 32 of the Australian Constitutions Act 1842 (UK), was formally removed by s 8 of the Australia Act 1986.

2   Special procedures (financial legislation)

[5.2.1]   Within a parliamentary system, the enactment of financial legislation is of particular importance. Without access to finance, no government can function. The business of government is not only to keep the peace but also to regulate a wide range of economic and technological activity and, more importantly when it comes to finance, to provide a large number of services for the community, such as, education, health, transport and social security. In order to provide directly the range of services which we now expect of our governments, government must also disburse thousands of millions of dollars in salaries, subsidies, grants and benefits.

[5.2.2]   Given the constraints of our economic system, the bulk of this money must be raised through taxation. In order to collect that revenue, legislation entitling the government to demand payment must be enacted by parliament: *Attorney-General v Wilts United Dairies Ltd* (1920) 37 TLR 884; *Commonwealth v Colonial Combing Spinning and Weaving Co Ltd* (1922) 31 CLR 421; *Congreve v Home Office* [1976] QB 629.

Once the money is raised through taxation, it is not available for government expenditure until parliament has enacted further legislation authorising the government to spend the money. The need for legislative 'appropriation' of the money required to support the Commonwealth Government's expenditure is stated in s 83 of the Commonwealth Constitution. It has been regarded as a fundamental rule of public law in the United Kingdom since the late 17th century. It has been endorsed by such decisions as: *Alcock v Fergie* (1867) 4 WW & A'B 285; *New South Wales v Bardolph* (1934) 52 CLR 455; *Commonwealth v Burns* [1971] VR 825; *Brown v West* (1990) 169 CLR 195.

[5.2.3]   So, unless a government can have taxation and appropriation legislation passed by parliament, it has no prospect of carrying on the business of government. Given a bicameral parliamentary system, in which the two houses represent different political communities (because they are, for example, elected at different times, or by different voters, or for different terms, or by different voting systems]), there is always a risk that a government will be unable to obtain passage of financial legislation through both houses of parliament. Indeed, the critical importance of finance to a government may be a sufficient temptation for one of the houses of parliament to refuse to pass the necessary legislation, in the hope of coercing the government into changing policy.

The constitutional documents at both state and Commonwealth level make some attempt to regulate this problem, to spell out the relative rights of the two houses of parliament, and of the government (this, of course, is not a problem in the polities (Queensland, the Australian Capital Territory and the Northern Territory) with a single house of parliament). However, the efficacy of these provisions is doubtful.

State parliaments

[5.2.4E]   **Constitution Act 1975 (Vic)**

62 (1) A Bill for appropriating any part of the Consolidated Fund or for imposing any duty, rate, tax, rent, return or impost must originate in the Assembly.

(2) Subject to section 65, a Bill for appropriating any part of the Consolidated Fund or for imposing any duty, rate, tax, rent, return or impost may be rejected but not altered by the Council.

63 The Assembly may not originate or pass any vote resolution or Bill for appropriating any part of the Consolidated Fund or of any duty rate tax rent return or impost for any purpose which has not been first recommended by a message of the Governor to the Assembly during the session in which such vote resolution or Bill is passed.

64 (1) A Bill shall not be taken to be a Bill for appropriating any part of the Consolidated Fund or for imposing any duty rate tax rent return or impost by reason only of its containing provisions for the imposition of appropriation of fines or other pecuniary penalties or for the demand or payment or appropriation of fees for licences or fees for services under such Bill.

(2) The Council may once at each of the undermentioned stages of a Bill which the Council cannot alter return such Bill to the Assembly suggesting by message the omission or amendment of any terms or provisions therein, and the Assembly may if it thinks fit make any such omissions or amendments with or without modifications:

Provided that the Council may not suggest any omission or amendment the effect of which will be to increase any proposed charge or burden on the people.

(3) The stages of a Bill at which the Council may return the Bill with a message as aforesaid shall be —

(a) the consideration of the Bill in Committee;

(b) the consideration of the report of the Committee; and

(c) the consideration of the question that the Bill be read a third time.

65 (1) In this section '**Annual Appropriation Bill**' means a Bill which deals only with the annual appropriation of the Consolidated Fund for the ordinary annual services of the Government for a particular year only but does not include a Bill to appropriate money for appropriations for or relating to the Parliament.

(2) For the purposes of sub-section (1), '**ordinary annual services**' includes —

(a) the construction or acquisition of public works, land or buildings; and

(b) the construction or acquisition of plant or equipment which normally would be regarded as involving an expenditure of capital; and

(c) services proposed to be provided by the Government which have not formerly been provided by the Government.

(3) An Annual Appropriation Bill must deal only with appropriation.

(4) Sub-section (5) applies if an Annual Appropriation Bill is passed by the Assembly and within 1 month of its passing by the Assembly —

(a) the Council rejects or fails to pass it; or

(b) the Council returns it to the Assembly with a message suggesting any amendment to which the Assembly does not agree.

(5) If this sub-section applies, the Annual Appropriation Bill, with any amendments suggested by the Council and made by the Assembly, must be presented to the

Governor for Her Majesty's Assent and becomes an Act of Parliament on the Royal Assent being signified notwithstanding that the Council has not passed the Bill.

(6) The words of enactment for an Annual Appropriation Bill that is to be presented to the Governor for Her Majesty's Assent under sub-section (5) are to be altered to 'Her Majesty and the Legislative Assembly in accordance with section 65(5) of the Constitution Act 1975 enact as follows:'.

(7) There is to be endorsed on the Annual Appropriation Bill when it is presented to the Governor for Her Majesty's Assent under sub-section (5), the certificate of the Speaker signed by the Speaker that the Bill is a Bill to which section 65(5) of the Constitution Act 1975 applies and has been passed in accordance with that section.

(8) The certificate of the Speaker under this section is conclusive evidence for all purposes and cannot be questioned in any court.

(9) The alteration of an Annual Appropriation Bill to give effect to sub-section (6) is not to be taken to be an amendment of the Bill.

~~~

Notes

[5.2.5] The constitutional legislation of three other states (South Australia, Tasmania and Western Australia) follow a common system for money bills: both taxation and appropriation bills must originate in the Assembly. However, before an appropriation bill can originate there, a message recommending the appropriation must be received from the Governor. A taxation bill or appropriation bill, once passed by the Assembly, cannot be amended by the Council, although the Council may reject such bills. Proposals for the resolution of deadlocks over financial legislation were made by royal commissions in Tasmania (1982) and Western Australia (1985), but those proposals have not been implemented: Constitutional Commission (1988) pp 228–9.

[5.2.6] It is from legislative provisions such as ss 62–5 of the Constitution Act 1975 (Vic), along with other provisions dealing with the links between ministers of the Crown and parliament, that we can construct the legal foundation of the system of responsible government. A government must have the confidence of the Assembly. This is because money bills, whether for taxation or appropriation, originate from the Assembly. Only the government, not the opposition or a backbencher, can propose any taxation or expenditure measure to the Assembly, because a recommending message from the Governor is a prerequisite. Further, the Council is denied the important power of amending taxation or appropriation bills; it can only pass them or reject them, and rejection of the government's annual appropriation bill would be a cumbersome weapon. To protect the Council against exploitation by the Assembly and the government, each of the Constitution Acts prohibits 'tacking': that is, the annual appropriation bill is not to contain any provision dealing with matters other than appropriation, provisions which the Council cannot amend because of its inability to amend money bills.

See also: Constitution Act 1934 (SA) ss 59–64; Constitution Act 1934 (Tas) ss 37–41, 42–5; Constitution Acts Amendment Act 1899 (WA) s 46.

[5.2.7] All of these provisions work towards establishing the financial supremacy of the Assembly. But how close to that supremacy do the constitutional provisions in South Australia, Tasmania and Western Australia approach? They allow the Council to reject a money bill, or to delay its passage indefinitely or to request amendments, so that, while no money bill can be introduced without the initiative of the government, and will make little progress without the approval of the Assembly, no money bill can complete the legislative process without the approval of the Council.

Until 2003, when the Constitution (Parliamentary Reform) Act 2003 (Vic) was passed, the Victorian provisions relating to the enactment of financial legislation also left the upper house, the Legislative Council, with substantial power to prevent the enactment of taxation and appropriation bills. The Council's power had been demonstrated several times. It rejected or delayed annual appropriation bills in 1865, 1867, 1877, 1947 and 1952: Cowen (1957) pp 35, 37–9. However, the 2003 amendments (reflected in **[5.2.4E]** above) deal with this problem by providing the Premier with the power to advise the Governor to give assent to an annual appropriation bill. Further, a new Division 9A of the Constitution Act 1975 (Vic) deals with disputes relating to deadlocked bills: see **[5.3.9E]** below.

[5.2.8]   The Constitution Act 1902 (NSW) s 5A provides a relatively simple solution to the problem of blocked appropriation bills, as follows:

5A

(1) If the Legislative Assembly passes any Bill appropriating revenue or moneys for the ordinary annual services of the Government and the Legislative Council rejects or fails to pass it or returns the Bill to the Legislative Assembly with a message suggesting any amendment to which the Legislative Assembly does not agree, the Legislative Assembly may direct that the Bill with or without any amendment suggested by the Legislative Council, be presented to the Governor for the signification of His Majesty's pleasure thereon, and shall become an Act of the Legislature upon the Royal Assent being signified thereto, notwithstanding that the Legislative Council has not consented to the Bill.

(2) The Legislative Council shall be taken to have failed to pass any such Bill, if the Bill is not returned to the Legislative Assembly within one month after its transmission to the Legislative Council and the Session continues during such period.

(3) If a Bill which appropriates revenue or moneys for the ordinary services of the Government becomes an Act under the provisions of this section, any provision in such Act dealing with any matter other than such appropriation shall be of no effect.

The concept of legislation appropriating money for 'the ordinary annual services of the government' was borrowed from ss 53 and 54 of the Commonwealth Constitution: see **[5.2.23]** below. The interpretation of this 'virtually meaningless expression' (as Pearce describes it: Pearce (1977) p 134) has been a subject for debate. One view is that the term refers to recurrent expenditure, salaries, administrative expenses and maintenance of established government programs, but excludes capital expenditure on new plant and equipment. Another view is that the term refers to all government expenditure, whether recurrent or capital, on any government service which the government might reasonably be expected to provide: Pearce (1977) pp 130–4. The issue is discussed in more detail in **[5.2.23]**.

Other provisions in the Constitution Act 1902 (NSW) provide that all appropriation and taxation bills shall originate in the Assembly (s 5) and that a message from the Governor is an essential precondition to the Assembly considering these bills: s 46. While there is no statutory prohibition on the Council amending financial legislation, s 5A(1) clearly contemplates that the Council will not amend, but may request the Assembly to amend, appropriation bills.

Commonwealth Parliament

[5.2.9E]   **Commonwealth Constitution**

53   Proposed laws appropriating revenue or moneys, or imposing taxation, shall not originate in the Senate. But a proposed law shall not be taken to appropriate revenue or moneys, or to impose taxation, by reason only of its containing provisions for the imposition or appropriation of fines or other pecuniary penalties, or for the demand or payment or appropriation of fees for licences, or fees for services under the proposed law.

The Senate may not amend proposed laws imposing taxation, or proposed laws appropriating revenue or moneys for the ordinary annual services of the Government.

The Senate may not amend any proposed law so as to increase any proposed charge or burden on the people.

The Senate may at any stage return to the House of Representatives any proposed law which the Senate may not amend, requesting, by message, the omission or amendment of any items or provisions therein. And the House of Representatives may, if it thinks fit, make any of such omissions or amendments, with or without modifications.

Except as provided in this section, the Senate shall have equal power with the House of Representatives in respect of all proposed laws.

54   The proposed law which appropriates revenue or moneys for the ordinary annual services of the Government shall deal only with such appropriation.

55   Laws imposing taxation shall deal only with the imposition of taxation, and any provision therein dealing with any other matter shall be of no effect.

Laws imposing taxation, except laws imposing duties of customs or of excise, shall deal with one subject of taxation only; but laws imposing duties of customs shall deal with duties of customs only, and laws imposing duties of excise shall deal with duties of excise only.

56   A vote, resolution, or proposed law for the appropriation of revenue or moneys shall not be passed unless the purpose of the appropriation has in the same session been recommended by message of the Governor-General to the House in which the proposal originated.

~~~

Notes

[5.2.10]   As with the state legislation, these provisions reflect the superiority of the Lower House of Parliament in financial legislation. But the superiority is, as with all state parliaments except that of New South Wales, qualified. The only functions denied to the Senate are (a) the origination of all appropriation and taxation bills and (b) the amendment of all taxation bills, of certain appropriation bills and of any bill where the amendment would increase any proposed charge or burden on the people. There is no specific denial of the Senate's power to reject or delay indefinitely any money bill. The right of the Senate to reject or defer consideration of appropriation legislation was a critical issue in October and November 1975, to which we shall shortly turn: **[5.2.17]**.

[5.2.11]   Why does s 53 deny to the Senate the power to amend most financial legislation yet allow it to suggest amendments, perhaps repeatedly, and to reject financial legislation? Why is the House of Representatives' superiority in financial matters incomplete?

Section 53 was drafted to reflect a hard-fought compromise between the delegates to the Constitutional Conventions, particularly the 1897 Convention in Adelaide. Delegates from the smaller colonies, South Australia, Tasmania and Western Australia (Queensland did not attend), pressed for equal voting rights on all matters for the Senate and the House of Representatives. They wanted to protect the interests of the smaller states, each of which would have the same representation in the Senate as did each of the two larger states. On the other hand, delegates from the larger colonies of New South Wales and Victoria were anxious that the powers of the Senate over money bills should be clearly subordinate to the power of the House of Representatives (where the two larger colonies must have a majority).

Some delegates from the smaller colonies were prepared to concede a degree of Senate inferiority in order to preserve the federal movement, and the present s 53 represents the concessions which those few delegates were prepared to make. An integral part of the compromise was s 57 of the Constitution: La Nauze (1972) pp 138–46, 187–91.

Today, we might describe that compromise as unsatisfactory, as leaving too many ambiguities and contradictions, and as failing to provide an effective means of resolving conflicts over financial legislation. Writing of s 57 as a means of resolving deadlocks over appropriation, Castles said ((1975) p 287):

> Today, when government funds loom much more largely in the life of society, compared to the second half of the nineteenth century, the delay of three months or more before those deadlock provisions might operate in money matters might seem inordinate. Before the turn of the century however, before the birth of the modern welfare State, and the more limited role accepted then for government activity, this means of resolving even conflicts on supply does not seem to have been regarded with great concern.

[5.2.12] The point, that the compromises expressed in ss 53 and 57 did not produce a durable solution, is expressed clearly in the following passage by Howard and Saunders ((1977) p 259):

> The three-month interval which is required in addition to the time-consuming processes of the normal parliamentary passage of legislation, plus dissolution and re-election, made s 57 an unsuitable provision for the resolution of a deadlock caused by the failure of the Senate to pass an Appropriation Bill (as speedily became apparent in the weeks after the Senate deferred supply in 1975). The historical explanation for this seems to depend upon a mixture of expediency, assumptions about contemporary constitutional practice and expectations of future constitutional development.
>
> The patent inconsistency between ss 53 and 57 is symptomatic of the generally unsatisfactory nature of the provisions relating to the powers and composition of the Senate if read literally and in isolation from the rest of the Constitution. To a considerable extent this is owing to the fact that with the exception of the (equally unsatisfactory) financial clauses, the provisions relating to the Senate were the most contentious at the conventions. They are the direct result of a contemporary political compromise.

The Senate's deferral of supply: 1975

[5.2.13] In October 1975, the Senate resolved that the Commonwealth Government's loan bill and appropriation bills (which had been passed by the House of Representatives) 'be not further proceeded with until the Government agrees to submit itself to the judgment of the people': Senate, *Debates*, vol s 63, 15 and 16

October 1975, pp 1156, 1221, 1241. Despite repeated calls from the government and the House of Representatives that the bills should be passed, the Senate persisted in its attitude.

[5.2.14]   On 10 November 1975 the Governor-General consulted with the Chief Justice of Australia, Sir Garfield Barwick, seeking Barwick's advice on the legal dimensions of dismissing the Prime Minister. The Chief Justice's advice (see **[7.4.15E]**) included the following passage:

> The Constitution of Australia is a federal constitution which embodies the principle of ministerial responsibility. The Parliament consists of two houses, the House of Representatives and the Senate, each popu.larly elected, and each with the same legislative power, with the one exception that the Senate may not originate nor amend a money Bill.
>
> Two relevant constitutional consequences flow from this structure of the Parliament. First the Senate has constitutional power to refuse to pass a money Bill; it has power to refuse supply to the government of the day. Secondly, a Prime Minister who cannot ensure supply to the Crown, including funds for carrying on the ordinary services of government, must either advise a general election (of a kind which the constitutional situation may then allow) or resign. If, being unable to secure supply, he refuses to take either course, Your Excellency has constitutional authority to withdraw his commission as Prime Minister.

[5.2.15]   On 11 November 1975 the Governor-General terminated Prime Minister Gough Whitlam's commission and commissioned the then Opposition Leader Malcolm Fraser as Prime Minister on condition that the appropriation bills were passed and that the Prime Minister should advise the Governor-General to proclaim a double dissolution under s 57 of the Constitution. The Senate immediately passed the appropriation bills, the motion for their immediate passage being moved by the Labor leader in the Senate who did not know of Whitlam's dismissal: Sawer (1977) p 165. At all stages throughout the crisis, the Labor Government and the House of Representatives had rejected the Senate's claim to a right to refuse or defer supply. The Governor-General issued a formal statement explaining his action. The Governor-General's statement (see **[7.4.14E]**) included the following passage:

> The Constitution combines the two elements of responsible government and federalism. The Senate is, like the House, a popularly elected chamber. It was designed to provide representation by States, not by electorates, and was given by s 53, equal powers with the House with respect to proposed laws, except in the respects mentioned in the section. It was denied power to originate or amend Appropriation Bills but was left with power to reject them or defer consideration of them. The Senate accordingly has the power and has exercised the power to refuse to grant supply to the Government. The Government stands in the position that it has been denied supply by the Parliament with all the consequences which flow from that fact.
>
> There have been public discussions about whether there is a convention deriving from the principles of responsible government that the Senate must never under any circumstances exercise the power to reject an Appropriation Bill. The Constitution must prevail over any convention because, in determining the question how far the conventions of responsible government have been grafted on to the federal compact, the Constitution itself must in the end control the situation.

[5.2.16]   So far as the question of legal power is concerned, the majority of the High Court had already expressed its opinion. In *Victoria v Commonwealth* (the *PMA* case) (1975) 135 CLR 81 **[5.3.26C]** at 121, Barwick CJ said:

> The Senate is a part of the Parliament and, except as to laws appropriating revenue or money for the ordinary annual services of the Government or imposing taxation, is

co-equal with the House of Representatives. Bills may originate and do originate in the Senate. Section 53 of the Constitution makes it abundantly clear that the Senate is to have equal power with the House of Representatives in respect of all laws other than those specifically expected. The only limitations as to the equality of the powers of the Senate with those of the House of Representatives are those imposed by the first three paragraphs of that section, to the terms of which the limitations must be confined.

See also the comments of Gibbs J (135 CLR at 143), Stephen J (135 CLR at 168) and Mason J: 135 CLR at 185.

[5.2.17] The Senate's action in October and November 1975 has been attacked on the ground that, while s 53 allowed to the Senate power to reject financial legislation, that power was not intended to be used to bring down a government supported by the House of Representatives. Rather, it was intended as a final protection for the smaller states, which they might invoke against any *specific* financial legislation which threatened their interests. This argument relies, initially, on statements made by delegates to the Constitutional Conventions of the 1890s. As Howard and Saunders put it ((1977) p 256):

> [T]he exercise of the Senate's power of veto of a financial Bill was usually contemplated in the context either of a Bill appropriating revenue for a particular project or of a Bill imposing taxation, for it was possible to imagine a dispute over the policy expressed in such Bills.

The argument is that the system of responsible government (under which governments are formed from the party which controls the House of Representatives) requires the Senate to use its legal powers with restraint. To ensure that the governmental system functions effectively, the literal terms of the Constitution are modified by a rule of political practice (a constitutional convention), which by regulating the use of discretionary powers 'keeps the legal constitution in touch with the growth of ideas': Jennings (1959) p 23; see also Marshall and Moodie (1967) pp 26–35; de Smith and Brazier (1989) pp 28–47. The argument in support of such a convention is set out at length in Hall and Iremonger ((1976) pp 91–107) and in Howard and Saunders ((1977) pp 252–67); it is also discussed in Castles ((1975) pp 287–90) and in Sawer ((1975) pp 121–8).

[5.2.18] As a practical matter, the argument was settled by the Governor-General when he dismissed Prime Minister Whitlam on 11 November 1975: 'The Constitution,' he said, 'must prevail over any convention because, in determining how far the conventions of responsible government have been grafted onto the federal compact, the Constitution itself must in the end control the situation': see **[7.4.14E]**. For an elaboration of this approach and a refutation of the argument that convention prevented the Senate rejecting an appropriation bill, see Richardson (1976) and Howard and Saunders (1977) pp 288–92.

Non-compliance with procedures and forms: ss 53, 54 and 56

[5.2.19] Sections 53, 54 and 56 lay down the procedures to be followed for the enactment and the form of certain 'proposed laws'. What would be the effect of a failure to follow those procedures or to comply with that form? For example, could the annual Appropriation Act be attacked on the ground that the Act originated in the Senate (s 53), or that it was not recommended by a message of the Governor-General (s 56), or that it did not deal only with appropriation (s 54)? Could an Act imposing taxation be attacked on the ground that it had originated in the Senate, or had been amended in the Senate (s 53)?

[5.2.20] In *Osborne v Commonwealth* (1911) 12 CLR 321, two members of the High Court remarked on the distinction between ss 53 and 54 (which refer to a 'proposed law' or 'proposed laws') and s 55 (which refers to 'laws'). In the course of considering whether a failure to comply with the form prescribed by s 55 would be fatal to the validity of the Act, Griffith CJ said at 336:

> Sections 53 and 54 deal with 'proposed laws', that is, Bills or projects of law still under consideration and not assented to — and they lay down rules to be observed with respect to proposed laws at that stage. Whatever obligations are imposed by these sections are directed to the houses of Parliament whose conduct of their internal affairs is not subject to review by a court of law.

Barton J accepted that ss 53 and 54 'relate ... only to the order of business between the two houses in dealing with the progress of Bills, and are, therefore, and from the necessity of the thing, merely directory': 12 CLR at 352.

[5.2.21] It seems that the enforcement of these procedures and forms is left to the two houses of parliament. If the Senate originates a money bill, the House of Representatives can decline to consider the bill; and if the Senate amends a taxation bill or a bill appropriating money for the ordinary annual services of the government, the House of Representatives can refuse to consider the amendments. If the House of Representatives does proceed to consider the bill, as transmitted from the Senate, it could be said to have waived its privileges, and so to have sanctioned the Senate's action. Similarly, if the Senate passes an appropriation bill which does not comply with s 54, it could be said to have waived the protection which s 54 offered it: see Pearce (1977) pp 121–2; Lumb and Moens (1995) pp 304, 314.

Edmund Barton (who chaired the drafting committee for the Constitution) expressed this view at the Adelaide Constitutional Convention in 1897:

> Where the words 'proposed laws' have been used, those sections deal with the position which would arise where, as between the two houses, a house as a matter of procedure originated, or otherwise dealt with or amended a Bill which by this Constitution it is desired that the house should not originate or amend. These are questions that must be settled between the houses, because no court in the world has ever yet dealt with the question whether as between the two houses in their own relations, one or other house has exceeded its powers in originating or amending Bills (Convention Debates, Adelaide (1897), pp 576–7).

[5.2.22] In *Northern Suburbs General Cemetery Reserve Fund v Commonwealth* (1993) 176 CLR 555, a majority of the High Court agreed that s 54 of the Constitution does not impose justiciable restraints on the passage of Commonwealth legislation. Mason CJ, Deane, Toohey and Gaudron JJ referred to the 'traditional view' that failure on the part of the parliament to comply with procedural provisions such as s 54 (which referred to 'a proposed law') 'is not contemporaneously justiciable and does not give rise to the invalidity of the resulting Act when it has been passed by the two Houses of the Parliament and received the royal assent': 176 CLR at 578. Brennan J observed that s 54 related 'to the passage of a Bill, not to the validity or effect of the Act when passed and assented to': 176 CLR at 585.

[5.2.23] The terms of ss 53, 54 and 56 raise some difficult questions. For example, what is meant by appropriation 'for the ordinary annual services of the Government'?

It is clear that this refers to a species of appropriation legislation (it was not intended to cover *all* appropriations) but what is the species? The purpose of the distinction between appropriation for the ordinary annual services of the government and other appropriation is also clear. The Senate can amend the latter legislation but not the former. But does that understanding bring us any closer to defining the distinction?

Apparently, the delegates to the Constitutional Conventions of the 1890s accepted that appropriation for the ordinary annual services of the government involved authorising the government to spend money on matters of settled policy where no new development or capital expenditure was involved. The first appropriation bills observed this distinction so that, in each year, one bill appropriated money for salaries of government employees, maintenance of plant and equipment and general recurrent expenses while another bill appropriated money for capital expenditure on works and buildings.

However, in 1952 Solicitor-General Bailey advised the government that expenditure on capital items could be regarded as expenditure on the ordinary annual services of the government. Indeed, the only expenditure not in that class was that of grants to the states. Bailey repeated his advice, on this occasion to the Joint Public Accounts Committee of the Parliament in 1961. The nub of his opinion was contained in one passage:

> '[T]he ordinary annual services of the Government' may be described as those services provided or maintained within any year which the Government may, in the light of its powers and authority, reasonably be expected to provide or maintain as the occasion requires through the departments of the public service and other Commonwealth agencies and instrumentalities. Accordingly, if the expenditure is to be incurred for an item which is itself such a service, it may be regarded, without more, as proper for inclusion in an ordinary Appropriation Bill (Parliamentary Paper No 79 of 1961, para 11).

In 1964, the government redrafted its supply bills (the interim appropriation bills which, when enacted, give the government sufficient money to carry out its functions until the Appropriation Acts are passed) along the lines suggested by Bailey. The Senate put considerable pressure on the government to abandon the new procedure and 12 months later the government reverted to the old distinction, which has been maintained ever since. Expenditure is divided into two bills, with the second covering expenditure of a capital nature, grants to the states and new policies, and being open to amendment by the Senate.

Non-compliance with form: s 55

[5.2.24] There is no doubt that failure to comply with the form demanded by s 55 is fatal to the validity of legislation (or at least that part of the legislation which offends against s 55).

It is rather curious that s 55 should have been drafted in a fashion so different from s 54, for the purpose of both sections was clearly the same; namely, to protect the Senate against exploitation by a government and the House of Representatives of the Senate's inability to amend most financial legislation. Speaking of s 55, Barton ACJ in *Buchanan v Commonwealth* (1913) 16 CLR 315 at 328 explained this purpose in the following passage:

> The paragraph is clearly to protect the House representing the States from being faced with the alternative of rejecting a tax Bill necessary for the adjustment of finances, or

passing it with the addition of some matter of policy independent of taxation, to which they might be emphatically opposed.

The questions thrown up by s 55 are questions of detail: What is a 'law imposing taxation'? When does a law 'deal only with the imposition of taxation'? What is 'one subject of taxation'? The meaning of these phrases, and the implications of s 55 for the drafting of Commonwealth legislation, are explored in the following cases.

[5.2.25C]   **Air Caledonie v Commonwealth**

(1988) 165 CLR 462

Section 1 of the Migration Amendment Act 1987 (Cth) added s 34A to the Migration Act 1958 (Cth), which provided as follows:

> 34A(1)   Where a passenger, other than a prescribed passenger, travels to Australia on an overseas flight, the passenger shall pay the prescribed fee for immigration clearance of that passenger by an officer at the airport at which the passenger intends to enter Australia.
>
> (2)   The fee shall be collected by the international air operator operating the flight.
>
> (3)   The international air operator shall pay to the Commonwealth the amount of the fee payable by a passenger, whether or not the operator has collected that amount from the passenger.
>
> (4)   An amount payable to the Commonwealth by an international air operator under subsection (3) is a debt due to the Commonwealth and may be recovered in a court of competent jurisdiction.

Regulations prescribed the fee as $5, and declared that a person under 12 years of age was a 'prescribed passenger'.

The plaintiffs, who were international air operators within s 34A, began proceedings against the Commonwealth in the High Court seeking a declaration that s 34A was invalid. The Commonwealth demurred, and this demurrer was heard by the Full Court.

Mason CJ, Wilson, Brennan, Deane, Dawson, Toohey and Gaudron JJ concluded that 'the fee which s 34A purported to exact was, at least in so far as it related to passengers who were Australian citizens, a tax and the provisions of the section were, for relevant purposes, a law "imposing taxation"': 165 CLR at 470–1. On this aspect of the case, see **[9.2.6]**. The justices continued:

Mason CJ, Wilson, Brennan, Deane, Dawson, Toohey and Gaudron JJ: [471] We turn to consider the effect on the validity of the amending Act of that conclusion.

The first paragraph of s 55 of the Constitution contains two distinct limbs. The first limb consists of the mandatory injunction that laws imposing taxation deal only with the imposition of taxation. The second limb is the specification of the consequences of breach of the first limb, namely, that any provision in such laws dealing with any matter other than the imposition of taxation shall be of no effect. In a case where a law, as enacted, purports both to impose taxation and to deal with other matters, the application of the two limbs of the paragraph to confine validity to so much of the law as deals with the imposition of taxation will ordinarily be straightforward. The position is, however, more complicated in a case such as the present where the impugned law is a provision imposing taxation which an amending Act seeks to insert in an existing Act which deals only with matters other than the imposition of taxation and the validity of which is not in issue.

An obvious purpose of the constitutional requirement that a law imposing taxation deal only with the imposition of taxation was to confine the impact of the limitations upon the Senate's powers with respect to proposed taxing laws to provisions actually dealing with the imposition of taxation, that is to say, to prevent 'tacking'. That being so, there is something to be said for the view that, in a case where an amending Act inserts a taxing provision in an existing Act, all that s 55 requires is that the amending Act itself deal only with the imposition of taxation. On balance, however, it seems to us that the requirement of s 55 should be construed as extending to laws in the form in which they stand from time to time after enactment, that is to say, as extending to Acts of the Parliament on the statute book. That construction gives full effect to the ordinary meaning of the words of this section. It is also supported both by the contrast between the reference to 'laws' in s 55 and the references to 'proposed laws' and a 'proposed law' in ss 53 and 54 and by considerations relating to the nature of an amending Act which is ordinarily to be construed as part of the principal Act (see, eg, Acts Interpretation Act 1901 (Cth), s 15) and is commonly treated as 'exhausted' upon commencement and incorporation of the amendments which it effects in the principal Act. Indeed, no submission disputing that construction was advanced on behalf of the Commonwealth. On that construction, s 55 requires that both an amending [472] Act imposing taxation and the amended principal Act deal only with the imposition of taxation.

If an amending Act purports to insert a provision imposing taxation in an existing valid Act which contains provisions dealing only with other matters, it seeks to bring about something which the Constitution directly and in terms forbids and which is not within the competence of the Parliament to achieve (cf *Attorney-General (NSW); Ex rel McKellar v Commonwealth* (1977) 12 ALR 129; 139 CLR 527 at 550 per Gibbs J, at 560 per Stephen J with whom Mason J agreed). In such a case, one cannot disregard the barrier of the constitutional injunction against a law dealing both with the imposition of taxation and other matters on the basis that, once the result which that injunction forbids has been achieved, the second limb will rectify the breach by invalidating all the other provisions of the principal Act. The injunction of the first limb constitutes a restriction on legislative power. Its effect in the present case is to invalidate the relevant provisions of the amending Act and one never reaches the situation where the second limb operates to strike down all of the provisions of the principal Act dealing with matters other than the imposition of taxation.

It follows that the effect of the conclusion that s 34A was a law imposing taxation is that s 7 of the Migration Amendment Act 1987 was ineffective to amend the Migration Act by adding s 34A to its provisions ...

The Commonwealth's demurrer to the plaintiffs' statement of claim must be overruled and it should be declared that s 34A was invalid ...

~~~

Notes

[5.2.26] The High Court's conclusion, that s 34A of the Migration Act 1958 (Cth) was invalid, was a creative invocation of s 55 of the Constitution. That provision declares that, in the event of the Commonwealth law imposing taxation and dealing with other matters, those parts of the law which deal with other matters 'shall be of no effect'. Yet the High Court held that it was s 34A, the law imposing taxation, which was invalid.

If the 'obvious purpose' of s 55, as described by the court, was to protect the Senate against exploitation, at the hands of the House of Representatives and the government, of its inability to amend laws imposing taxation (an inhibition set out in s 53 of the Constitution), surely the focus must be on the legislation as presented to the Senate. To achieve that purpose, s 55 should be read as insisting that the Senate, when presented with a bill for the imposition of taxation, not be presented with additional material in the same bill.

[5.2.27] With that argument in mind, we can ask how the purpose of s 55 was advanced by the decision in this case. How did the enactment of s 34A, as an amendment passed 29 years after the principal Act, threaten to exploit the Senate's inability to amend laws imposing taxation?

[5.2.28] The need for care in the drafting of Commonwealth taxing laws was emphasised in *Re Dymond* (1959) 101 CLR 11. The High Court was asked whether most of the provisions in the Sales Tax Assessment Act (No 2) 1930 (Cth) were invalid because the Act included a provision imposing taxation, while the bulk of the Act dealt with matters other than the imposition of taxation.

Fullagar J, with whom Dixon CJ, Kitto and Windeyer JJ agreed, held that the Act was valid because the provision in question imposed a penalty, not a tax. However, Fullagar J went on to express his opinion (necessarily *obiter*) that, if the provision had imposed taxation, the bulk of the Act would have fallen foul of s 55 of the Constitution. The other parts of the Act dealt with the collection of tax, assessments, objections and appeals, and offences and penalties. Fullagar J endorsed some observations of Isaacs J in *Federal Commissioner of Taxation v Munro* (1926) 38 CLR 153 at 187–92, to the effect that s 55 was intended to protect the position of the Senate: 101 CLR at 20. He then outlined what he saw as the drafting requirements of s 55, at 20–1:

> It may very well be that an Act imposing an income tax could, without offending against s 55, contain all or most of the provisions in fact contained in Pt III of the Income Tax and Social Services Contribution Assessment Act, which is headed 'Liability to Taxation'. Such provisions do not impose taxation, but they deal with the imposition of taxation, because the specification of the persons who are to be liable to taxation and the definition of their liability is part of the denotation of the term 'imposition of taxation'. But provisions for administration and machinery, the appointment and powers and duties of a commissioner of taxation, the making of returns and assessments, the determination of questions of law and fact relating to liability, the collection and recovery of tax, the punishment of offences, stand on a different footing. They 'deal with' matters which must be dealt with if the imposition of the tax is to be effective. But they cannot be said to deal with the imposition of taxation, because their subject matter is not comprehended within the meaning of the term 'imposition of taxation'.

On the other hand, three justices of the court, McTiernan, Taylor and Menzies JJ, took a broader view of the class of provisions that could be described as 'dealing with the imposition of taxation' and therefore included in a law imposing taxation.

Taylor J pointed out that a number of justices had consistently held that provisions for the assessment, collection and recovery of tax are provisions which deal with the imposition of taxation; and endorsed the proposition that a provision 'fairly relevant or incidental to the imposition of a tax on one subject of taxation': 101 CLR at 24.

Menzies J (with whom McTiernan J agreed) noted that Isaacs J had been in the minority in *Federal Commissioner of Taxation v Munro* (1926) 38 CLR 153, where Starke J had held that it was 'not unlawful to include in a taxing Act provisions incidental and auxiliary to the assessment and collection of tax' (38 CLR at 216); and that a similar view was part of the decision of the High Court in *Moore v Commonwealth* (1951) 82 CLR 547: see 101 CLR at 26–7. Menzies J noted that British parliamentary convention, on which ss 53, 54 and 55 of the Constitution were based, prevented the Lords from altering taxation bills so as to change a tax's duration, mode of assessment, levy, collection, appropriation or management; the persons who pay, receive, manage or control the tax; or the limits within which the tax was leviable: 101 CLR at 27–8.

On 4 March 2004, the High Court reserved its judgment in *Permanent Trustee Australia Ltd v Commissioner for State Revenue (Vic)* M277 of 2003. The appellant argued that the Commonwealth Places (Mirror Taxes) Act 1998 (Cth) contravened the first paragraph of s 55 of the Constitution, by including provisions dealing with assessment, objections, appeals and collection in a law imposing taxation; and the respondent argued that, if the Act was subject to s 55, those provisions dealt with the imposition of taxation, and the *obiter* views of the majority in *Re Dymond* should be rejected. The resolution of the appeal will require the court to resolve the differences of opinion in *Re Dymond*.

[5.2.29C] **Mutual Pools & Staff Pty Ltd**
v Commissioner of Taxation
(1992) 173 CLR 450

The Sales Tax Act (No 1) 1930 (Cth) imposed sales tax upon the sale value of goods manufactured in Australia where those goods were sold by the taxpayer, treated as stock for sale by retail or applied by the taxpayer to her or his own use. Section 3(1)(c) of the Sales Tax Assessment Act (No 1) 1930 (Cth) deemed a swimming pool that was constructed on site to be manufactured goods.

The first plaintiff (Mutual Pools) carried on the business of constructing swimming pools on site. From September 1986 to August 1990, the first plaintiff paid sales tax upon the sale value of the swimming pools constructed on site by it. Together with another swimming pool manufacturer, the first plaintiff brought an action in the High Court of Australia seeking declarations that the Sales Tax Act (No 1) did not lawfully impose tax upon that part of the value of a swimming pool that was constructed on site; and that, to the extent that the Sales Tax Act (No 1) and the Sales Tax Assessment Act (No 1) purported to impose such a tax, they were invalid by reason of the second paragraph of s 55 of the Constitution. The Commissioner for Taxation demurred to the statement of claim. That demurrer came on for hearing before the Full Court of the High Court.

Dawson, Toohey and Gaudron JJ: **[467]** For the purposes of this case it is enough to recognise that an excise duty is 'a tax imposed "upon" or "in respect of" or "in relation to" goods': *Browns Transport Pty Ltd v Kropp* (1958) 100 CLR 117 at 129. 'Goods' is not a word of precise meaning but, in the context of excise duties, it signifies articles of commerce or things which, even if not saleable or without any discernible sale value (*Federal Commissioner of Taxation v TAB (Qld)* (1990) 170 CLR 508 at 511), may be the subject of trading or commercial transactions: see *Matthews v Chicory Marketing Board (Vict)* (1938) 60 CLR 263 at 300 ... Under s 3(1) of the Sales Tax Assessment Act (No 1) 'goods' includes commodities.

Quite clearly, while the materials which are used in the construction of a swimming pool constructed in situ may be goods, the finished product is not. On the contrary, a swimming pool constructed in situ forms part of the land and is denied the character of goods. Indeed, the Commissioner of Taxation concedes that a swimming pool constructed in situ is a fixture although 'fixture' is, perhaps, not an appropriate term because an in-ground swimming pool constructed in situ never has any separate existence as a chattel apart from the land. That is why the legislature found it **[468]** necessary to deem a swimming pool constructed in situ to be manufactured goods. In doing so it recognised that it was not that. As Cave J observed in *R v County Council of Norfolk* (1891) 60 LJQB 379 at 380–1:

> ... generally speaking, when you talk of a thing being deemed to be something, you do not mean to say that it is that which it is to be deemed to be. It is rather an admission that it is not what it is to be deemed to be, and that, notwithstanding it is not that particular thing, nevertheless, for the purposes of the Act, it is to be deemed to be that thing.

It is true that a deeming provision does not always create what has been called a 'statutory fiction'. It may be used for the purpose of definition or for expressing a conclusion: *Hunter Douglas Australia Pty Ltd v Perma Blinds* (1970) 122 CLR 49 at 65–6. But in this case there can be no doubt that, in deeming a swimming pool constructed in situ to be manufactured goods, the legislature was deeming it to be something which it is not and never has been ...

It may be, and it is unnecessary to decide the point in this case, that there are things not ordinarily within the concept of goods which may be brought within that concept by a deeming provision which widens the definition of goods in such a way that the imposition of a tax upon those things may nevertheless remain a duty of excise. If that is so it will be because the tax is in the nature of a tax upon goods even though imposed upon things not ordinarily within the concept of goods.

The justices referred to *Waterhouse v Deputy Commissioner of Land Tax* (1914) 17 CLR 665, where the High Court held invalid a provision that deemed a person to be the owner of land and therefore liable to land tax in circumstances where the person was not the owner of the land.

[469] That case is a difficult one but it illustrates the point that the parliament cannot bring legislation within power by deeming facts to be as they are not or by deeming things to have a character which they do not bear. No more, in our view, can a restriction imposed by the Constitution — as by s 55 — be avoided by deeming facts to be as they are not. And if the application of the second paragraph of s 55 could be avoided by the use of a deeming provision to bring things within the description of an excise duty which otherwise fall quite outside that description, it is difficult to see why a state could not in legislation deem goods not to constitute goods so as to avoid the consequence that a tax upon those goods is a duty of excise in contravention of the exclusive power of the Commonwealth to impose duties of excise under s 90 of the Constitution. But as Starke J observed in *Resch v Federal Commissioner of Taxation* (1942) 66 CLR 198 at 213: 'Parliament cannot by any definition or provision that it may adopt contravene the provisions of the Constitution.' ...

[470] The first paragraph of s 55 of the Constitution provides that laws imposing taxation shall deal only with taxation and any other provision therein dealing with any other matter shall be of no effect. That paragraph thus prescribes the effect of a failure to comply with its requirement — a provision dealing with any other matter shall be of no effect.

The second paragraph of s 55 provides that laws imposing taxation, except laws imposing duties of customs or excise, shall deal with one subject of taxation only, but does not specify what is to happen if a law offends against that requirement. However, the better view is that contravention will lead to the entire law being invalid. In *Osborne v Commonwealth* (1911) 12 CLR 321 at 353, Barton J expressed that view saying:

> Where the tax bill deals with more subjects than one, there is ordinarily no means, as there is in respect of bills within the first paragraph, of casting out that which offends against the [471] Constitution, as there is no means of knowing which subject of taxation represents more than the other or others the will of parliament.

That passage was approved by the court in the *Second Fringe Benefits Tax Case, State Chamber of Commerce and Industry v Commonwealth* (1987) 163 CLR 329 at 342–4.

The second paragraph likewise does not spell out the consequence where a law which imposes duties of excise deals with something other than duties of excise. But that situation is closer to that dealt with by the first paragraph and, although the words 'and any provision therein dealing with any other matter shall be of no effect' do not appear at the end of the second paragraph, we think that it should be read in an appropriate case as if they do. The second paragraph of s 55 proceeds upon the assumption that duties of customs or of excise may involve more than one subject of taxation. Thus, where duties of excise are imposed by a law, the law may deal with more than one subject of taxation provided the law is confined to duties of excise. Any other subject is impermissible. The situation, at all events in a case such as the present one, is unlike that referred to by Barton J in *Osborne v Commonwealth*, where a law imposing taxation deals with more than one subject and there is no means of saying that it was the inclusion of one subject as opposed to another which led to the contravention of s 55. When a law imposing excise duties also deals with something other than excise duties, it may be possible to say that it is that other subject which offends against the Constitution. This is the case here.

The justices held that the provisions of the Sales Tax Assessment Act (No 1) which produced the result that the Sales Tax Act (No 1) dealt not only with duties of excise but also with something other than duties of excise should be treated as of no effect. Mason CJ,

Brennan and McHugh JJ delivered a separate judgment in which they endorsed the reasons of Dawson, Toohey and Gaudron JJ. Deane J dissented.

~~~

Notes

[5.2.30] In *Resch v Federal Commissioner of Taxation* (1942) 66 CLR 198, the High Court rejected a challenge to the Income Tax Assessment Act 1922 (Cth). Section 16B of the Act provided that, where a company was wound up and its assets distributed to its shareholders, that part of the assets which represented undistributed profits should be included in the shareholders' taxable income. It was objected that the Act dealt with more than one subject of taxation, contrary to the second paragraph of s 55 of the Constitution; namely, the taxation of income and the taxation of capital receipts. The court rejected this argument. Dixon J observed at 225:

> The distinction between profits of a capital nature and profits in the nature of income in the strict sense is not one which the Act maintains. Nor is it a discrimination which the legislature is bound to regard.

[5.2.31] In *State Chamber of Commerce and Industry v Commonwealth* (1987) 163 CLR 329, the High Court rejected a challenge to the validity of the Fringe Benefits Tax Act 1986 (Cth). That Act, when read with its associated Assessment Act, imposed a tax on employers, including state governments, where those employers provided fringe benefits (such as motor vehicles, school fees or credit card accounts) to their employees, or to other persons who held state offices. One of the arguments raised against the validity of the Fringe Benefits Tax Act was that the Act, when read with the Assessment Act, dealt with several categories of fringe benefits as if each category was a different subject of taxation. In particular, it was argued that the principal subject of the tax imposed by the Act was fringe benefits provided by private employers to their employees, and the imposition of a tax by reference to benefits otherwise provided introduced a further subject or subjects of taxation.

In their joint judgment, Mason CJ, Wilson, Dawson, Toohey and Gaudron JJ endorsed the opinion of Barton J, expressed in *Osborne v Commonwealth* (1911) 12 CLR 321 at 352–3, that non-compliance with the second paragraph of s 55 would result in total invalidity:

> As Barton J noted, at 353, the purpose of the second paragraph was to prevent 'the tacking together of tax Bills of different kinds and unlimited number in one measure', just as the first paragraph was to prevent tacking of extraneous matter to a tax Bill. The point of insisting on a law imposing taxation dealing with one subject of taxation only was to ensure separate consideration by each House of particular kinds of taxation, so that each would be considered on its merits and not just as an element in an overall package of taxes. And, as Barton J also pointed out (at 353), partial invalidity confined to the offending provision was not an available option in the case of the second paragraph for there is no means of identifying an offending subject of taxation. His Honour ascribed to the second paragraph an important role in enabling the Senate to protect the people of the States from financial aggression on the part of the Commonwealth (163 CLR at 342–3).

The justices noted that in *Resch v Federal Commissioner of Taxation* (1942) 66 CLR 198 at 223, Dixon J had said that s 55 was not directed to the categories of taxes referred to by economists and lawyers; rather, was 'concerned with political relations, and must be taken as contemplating broad distinctions between possible subjects of taxation based on common understanding and general conceptions, rather than on any analytical or logical classification'.

Although the court was bound to insist on compliance with the requirements of s 55, the justices said, the court would 'naturally give weight to the Parliament's understanding that its Tax Act deals with one subject of taxation only' because the application of the test outlined by Dixon J involved a question of fact or value judgment. The court should not resolve such a question against the parliament's understanding with the consequence that the statute was constitutionally invalid, unless the answer was clear: 163 CLR at 344.

Mason CJ, Wilson, Dawson, Toohey and Gaudron JJ noted that the common understanding of the expression 'fringe benefits' was not confined to benefits provided by an employer to the employer's employee and that it extended to benefits which were related to employment whether or not they were provided by the employer. After summarising the provisions of the Fringe Benefits Tax Act and the Assessment Act, the justices said (at 349) that the legislation:

> ... has been framed on the footing that there is but a single subject of taxation, formulated according to a broad conception of what constitutes fringe benefits. That conception embraces benefits, not being salary or wages, referable to the employment relationship, whether provided by the employer or not and whether received by the employee or not. So understood the legislation presented for the consideration of each House of the Parliament a 'unity of subject matter' rather than distinct and separate subjects of taxation.

Mason CJ, Wilson, Dawson, Toohey and Gaudron JJ acknowledged the possibility that the legislation used definitions so far-reaching that they were arbitrary and oppressive because an employer could be taxed in circumstances beyond the employer's control. However, it did not follow that the tax was imposed on more than one subject of taxation, at 350:

> It was open to the Parliament, in seeking to impose an effective and comprehensive fringe benefits tax, to select the employer as the person liable to pay the tax. The employer is the person who ordinarily provides the benefit and stands to gain from its provision to his employee. In the ultimate analysis, the fact that the employer is liable in some situations to pay tax on benefits provided by others to persons who are not his employees, without his having any right of recoupment, does not affect the characterisation of the subject of taxation.

It was not to the point, Mason CJ, Wilson, Dawson, Toohey and Gaudron JJ said, that legal analysis could demonstrate a distinction between the operation of the tax in one situation from its operation in another situation. In selecting a single subject of taxation the parliament may prefer substance to form, they said: 163 CLR at 350. Nor did the extension of the tax to the states as employers breach the second paragraph of s 55. Further, the extension of the term 'employee' to include a state Member of Parliament, who did not stand in an employee–employer relationship with the state, did not introduce an additional subject of taxation, at 353:

> As a matter of common understanding the tax imposed on a State in respect of benefits provided to such persons should not be regarded otherwise than as an aspect of a comprehensive fringe benefits tax.

Mason CJ, Wilson, Dawson, Toohey and Gaudron JJ also dismissed an argument that the Fringe Benefits Tax Act discriminated against the states: see **[8.2.65]**. Brennan J agreed with the judgment of the majority on the s 55 issue. Deane J delivered a separate judgment to the same effect as the majority on the s 55 issue.

3   Alternative procedures

State parliaments

[5.3.1]   The common motivation in establishing an alternative process for legislation has been to find a means of resolving disputes or deadlocks between two houses of parliament. The efficiency of the various procedures, such as s 5B of the Constitution Act 1902 (NSW) or s 57 of the Commonwealth Constitution, and their utility in achieving this end is a matter of debate. However, it seems clear that these procedures were promoted for that purpose, even if, in their final form, they are so cumbersome and accident-prone as to discourage their use.

[5.3.2]   The potential for conflict between the two houses in a bicameral parliament is inherent in their constitutions, for they represent different electorates and are likely to reflect quite distinct political values. We need go back no further than the beginning of this century to observe the conflict, although it had been endemic since the 1850s when bicameral parliaments were established in most of the Australian colonies. By 1908 each of the states' lower houses was elected on the basis of adult suffrage. There were no property, educational or sexual restrictions although there were some racial restrictions (see **[4.5.4]**), though four of the Legislative Councils (those of South Australia, Tasmania, Victoria and Western Australia) were elected on a narrow property franchise, while those of New South Wales and Queensland consisted of members appointed for life by the Governors. These distinct constituencies brought the houses into frequent conflict. However, in none of the colonies were there any established procedures to resolve disputes or deadlocks between the houses.

[5.3.3]   In the first 70-odd years of responsible government, a New South Wales or Queensland government frustrated by its upper house could advise the Governor to appoint extra members sympathetic to the government. That tactic worked in Queensland in 1921 when the Labor Government advised the Governor to appoint additional, and compliant, legislative councillors so that a bill abolishing the Council would be enacted: Morrison (1960) p 269. A similar gambit was frustrated in New South Wales in 1926, when JT Lang advised the Governor to appoint 25 legislative councillors all pledged to vote for the abolition of the Council and, following their appointment, some of the new members voted against the Council's abolition. Lang advised the Governor to appoint extra, and presumably more reliable, councillors but the Governor baulked at a second swamping operation: Evatt (1967) p XIV.

[5.3.4]   The abolition of the Queensland Upper House (1921) and the conversion of the New South Wales Upper House to an indirectly elected body (1933) removed the problem of inter-house conflicts in the former state and also removed a relatively straightforward method of resolving those conflicts in the latter state. The conflicts, of course, did not go away with the disappearance of appointed upper houses. Because upper and lower houses are elected in different ways, they will always represent different electorates. Even though the franchise for each house may be identical **[4.5.3]**, a variety of factors ensures that the two houses represent different electorates. Generally, members of the upper house are elected for a longer period, or on the basis of a different voting system (in Tasmania, legislative councillors represent single member constituencies and House of Assembly members are elected by proportional representation, while in South Australia the systems are reversed) or on the basis of a different distribution of electoral boundaries: in Western Australia, the Legislative Council distribution gives rural voters a 3:1 advantage over metropolitan voters while the Legislative Assembly only allows rural voters a 2:1 advantage: see Constitutional Commission (1988) p 148.

[5.3.5]   Section 5 of the Colonial Laws Validity Act 1865 (UK) confirmed that the colonial legislatures and their successors, the state parliaments, could introduce new procedures for passing legislation, procedures which could allow for the enactment of legislation on which the two houses of a legislature or parliament were in dispute:

> 5   Every Colonial Legislature shall have, and be deemed at all Times to have had, full Power within its Jurisdiction to establish Courts of Judicature, and to abolish and reconstitute the same, and to alter the Constitution thereof, and to make Provision for the Administration of Justice therein; and every Representative Legislature shall, in respect to the Colony under its Jurisdiction, have, and be deemed at all Times to have had, full Power to make Laws respecting the Constitution, Powers, and Procedure of such Legislature; provided that such laws shall have been passed in such Manner and Form as may from Time to Time be required by any Act of Parliament, Letters Patent, Order in Council, or Colonial Law for the Time being in force in the said Colony.

The significance of s 5, as emphasising the flexibility of state constitutions, was considered in *Taylor v Attorney-General (Qld)* (1917) 23 CLR 457 **[5.3.13]**, and in *McCawley v R* [1920] AC 691 **[5.3.14]**. Its potential for supporting a reduction of flexibility in state constitutions was considered in *Attorney-General (NSW) v Trethowan* (1931) 44 CLR 394 **[5.4.17C]**.

The Colonial Laws Validity Act was repealed, in its application to state parliaments by s 3(1) of the Australia Act 1986. The potentially restrictive aspect of s 5 of the Colonial Laws Validity Act is continued by s 6 of the Australia Act **[5.4.23E]**, though the enabling aspect of that provision has not been re-enacted. Accordingly, the power of each state parliament to legislate so as to vary its own constitution, powers and procedure will now depend on that parliament's general law-making power, as expressed (for example) in s 5 of the Constitution Act 1902 (NSW) or s 16 of the Constitution Act 1975 (Vic): see *Clayton v Heffron* (1960) 105 CLR 214 **[5.3.16C]** at 250.

The legislation

[5.3.6]   Three of the states have established formal legislative procedures for the resolution of deadlocks between the houses. (Proposals for constitutional amendments in Tasmania and Western Australia, made by royal commissions in 1982 and 1985, have not been implemented: see Constitutional Commission (1988) pp 254–5.) The least cumbersome of these is that of New South Wales.

[5.3.7E]   **Constitution Act 1902 (NSW)**

5B(1) If the Legislative Assembly passes any Bill other than a Bill to which section 5A of this Act applies, and the Legislative Council rejects or fails to pass it or passes it with any amendment to which the Legislative Assembly does not agree, and if after an interval of three months the Legislative Assembly in the same Session or in the next Session again passes the Bill with or without any amendment which has been made or agreed to by the

Legislative Council, and the Legislative Council rejects or fails to pass it or passes it with any amendment to which the Legislative Assembly does not agree, and if after a free conference between managers there is not agreement between the Legislative Council and the Legislative Assembly, the Governor may convene a joint sitting of the Members of the Legislative Council and the members of the Legislative Assembly.

The Members present at the joint sitting may deliberate upon the Bill as last proposed by the Legislative Assembly and upon any amendments made by the Legislative Council with which the Legislative Assembly does not agree.

No vote shall be taken at the joint sitting.

(2) After the joint sitting and either after any further communication with the Legislative Council in order to bring about agreement, if possible, between the Legislative Council and the Legislative Assembly, or without any such communication the Legislative Assembly may by resolution direct that the Bill as last proposed by the Legislative Assembly and either with or without any amendment subsequently agreed to by the Legislative Council and the Legislative Assembly, shall, at any time during the life of the Parliament or at the next general election of Members of the Legislative Assembly, be submitted by way of referendum to the electors qualified to vote for the election of Members of the Legislative Assembly.

The referendum shall be held and conducted as may be provided by law, and if, at any time no such law exists, the law for the time being in force relating to the holding and conduct of a general election of Members of the Legislative Assembly shall, mutatis mutandis, apply to and in respect of the holding and conduct of the referendum, with such modifications, omissions, and additions as the Governor may by notification published in the Gazette declare to be necessary or convenient for the purposes of such application.

(3) If at the referendum a majority of the electors voting approve the Bill it shall be presented to the Governor for the signification of His Majesty's pleasure thereon and become an Act of the Legislature upon the Royal Assent being signified thereto, notwithstanding that the Legislative Council has not consented to the Bill.

(4) For the purposes of this section the Legislative Council shall be taken to have failed to pass a Bill if the Bill is not returned to the Legislative Assembly within two months after its transmission to the Legislative Council and the Session continues during such period.

~~~

[5.3.8] Subsection 5 declares that a bill to which s 7A of the Constitution Act applies may be enacted in accordance with the procedure laid down in s 5B. The approval of such a bill by the electors under s 5B shall be regarded as approval by the electors for the purpose of s 7A. Subsection 6 lays down the formal procedure for the summoning of a joint sitting, and for the conduct of such a sitting.

[5.3.9E]   **Constitution Act 1975 (Vic)**

Division 9A — Provisions Relating to Disputes concerning Bills

65A(1) In this Division —

'**Deadlocked Bill**' means a Disputed Bill to which section 65C(3) or 65D(1) applies;

'**Dispute Resolution**' means a resolution reached by the Dispute Resolution Committee recommending to the Assembly and the Council that the Disputed Bill specified in the resolution —

(a) be passed as transmitted by the Assembly to the Council without amendment; or

(b) be passed with the amendment or amendments specified in the resolution; or

(c) not be passed;

'**Dispute Resolution Committee**' means the Committee established under section 65B;

'**Disputed Bill**' means a Bill which has passed the Assembly and having been transmitted to and received by the Council not less than 2 months before the end of the session has not been passed by the Council within 2 months after the Bill is so transmitted, either without amendment or with such amendments only as may be agreed to by both the Assembly and the Council.

(2)   For the purposes of this Division, any omission or amendment suggested by the Council in accordance with section 64 is deemed to be an amendment made by the Council.

(3)   This Division does not apply to an Annual Appropriation Bill within the meaning of section 65.

Section 65B provides for the establishment of a Dispute Resolution Committee 'as soon as conveniently practicable after the commencement of each Parliament', with seven members appointed by the Legislative Assembly and five members appointed by the Council.

Section 65C directs the Dispute Resolution Committee to reach a Dispute Resolution on a Disputed Bill within 30 days after a Disputed Bill is referred to the Committee by the Assembly; any Dispute Resolution reached by the Committee is to be tabled in the Assembly and the Council; but, if the Committee does not reach a Dispute Resolution, the Disputed Bill becomes a Deadlocked Bill.

65D(1) If either the Assembly or the Council fails to give effect to the Dispute Resolution within the period of 30 days or the period of 10 sitting days (whichever period is longer) after the tabling of the Dispute Resolution in that House, the Disputed Bill becomes a Deadlocked Bill.

(2)   For the purposes of sub-section (1), the Assembly or the Council fails to give effect to the Dispute Resolution —

(a)   if the Dispute Resolution provided that the Disputed Bill be passed by the Council as transmitted by the Assembly to the Council without amendment, and the Council does not pass the Bill without amendment;

(b)   if the Dispute Resolution provided that the Disputed Bill be passed with the amendment or amendments specified in the Dispute Resolution, and the Assembly or the Council does not pass the Bill with the specified amendment or amendments;

(c)   if the Dispute Resolution provided that the Disputed Bill not be passed, and the Assembly or the Council resolves not to accept the Dispute Resolution.

(3)   If the Assembly or the Council has, in relation to a Bill to which section 18(1B) applies, given effect to a Dispute Resolution, it is only lawful to present the Bill to the Governor for Her Majesty's assent if the Bill has been approved by the majority of electors voting at a referendum.

(4)   If the Assembly or the Council has, in relation to a Bill to which section 18(2) or 18(2AA) applies, given effect to a Dispute Resolution, it is only lawful to present the Bill to the Governor for Her Majesty's assent if the third reading of the Bill was passed by a special majority or an absolute majority, as the case may be.

65E(1) This section applies in the case of a Deadlocked Bill.

(2)   The Premier may advise the Governor in writing that the Assembly be dissolved as a result of this section applying to the Deadlocked Bill specified in the advice.

(3)   There is to be attached to the advice under sub-section (2) a copy of the Deadlocked Bill endorsed with the certificate of the Speaker signed by the Speaker that the Bill is a Bill to which section 65E of the **Constitution Act 1975** applies.

(4)   The certificate of the Speaker under this section is conclusive evidence for all purposes and cannot be questioned in any court. (5) If the Premier does not give advice under

sub-section (2), the Deadlocked Bill may be re-introduced in the Assembly in accordance with section 65F.

65F(1) This section applies if during the existence of the Assembly first elected after the previous Assembly has been dissolved under section 65E(2) or otherwise dissolved or lawfully determined, a Deadlocked Bill from the previous Assembly is again introduced in the Assembly.

(2)   For the purposes of this section, a Deadlocked Bill may be introduced in the Assembly in the form in which —

(a)   it was introduced in the previous Assembly; or

(b)   it was passed by the previous Assembly and transmitted to the previous Council; or

(c)   it is consistent with the Dispute Resolution reached in respect of the Deadlocked Bill.

(3)   If a Bill introduced in accordance with this section again becomes a Disputed Bill, the Premier may advise the Governor in writing to convene a joint sitting of the Assembly and the Council.

(4)   There is to be attached to the advice under sub-section (3) a copy of the Disputed Bill endorsed with the certificate of the Speaker signed by the Speaker that the Bill is a Bill to which section 65F(3) of the **Constitution Act 1975** applies. (5) The certificate of the Speaker under this section is conclusive evidence for all purposes and cannot be questioned in any court.

...

(6)   A joint sitting of the Assembly and the Council convened in accordance with this section may consider all the Bills that are Disputed Bills in accordance with this section.

65G(1) A joint sitting of the Assembly and the Council convened in accordance with section 65F must consider a Disputed Bill to which that section applies in the form in which it was last passed by the Assembly and transmitted to the Council.

(2)   Subject to sub-section (3), the joint sitting of the Assembly and the Council is to be conducted in accordance with the rules adopted by the members present at the joint sitting.

(3)   At the joint sitting of the Assembly and the Council —

(a)   the members have the same privileges and immunities as the members of the Assembly in relation to proceedings before that House;

(b)   subject to sub-section (4), a question is to be decided by a majority of the votes cast by the members present at the joint sitting;

(c)   in the event of an equality of votes on a question, the question is to be taken to have been determined in the negative.

(4)   If an absolute majority of the total number of the members of the Assembly and the Council passes the third reading of the Disputed Bill with or without any amendments at the joint sitting of the Assembly and the Council, the Bill so passed is to be taken to have been duly passed by both Houses of the Parliament, whether or not it is a Bill to which section 18(2) or 18(2AA) applies.

(5)   Subject to sub-sections (6) and (7), a Bill passed in accordance with this section must be presented to the Governor for Her Majesty's Assent and becomes an Act of Parliament on the Royal Assent being signified.

(6)   If a Bill to which section 18(1B) applies is passed in accordance with this section, it must be submitted to a referendum.

(7)   A Bill that is referred to in sub-section (6) and that is approved by the majority of electors voting at a referendum must be presented to the Governor for Her Majesty's assent and becomes an Act of Parliament on the Royal Assent being signified.

(8) There is to be endorsed on the Bill when it is presented to the Governor for Her Majesty's Assent under sub-section (5) or (7), the certificate of the Speaker signed by the Speaker that the Bill is a Bill to which section 65G of the **Constitution Act 1975** applies and has been passed in accordance with that section.

(9) The certificate of the Speaker under this section is conclusive evidence for all purposes and cannot be questioned in any court.

(10) If a Bill is passed in accordance with this section, the Bill is deemed for all purposes to be a Bill that has been passed by the Assembly and the Council.

~~~

Notes

[5.3.10] The procedure established by Division 9A of the Constitution Act 1975 (Vic) prescribes a series of steps for overcoming the resistance of the Legislative Council to a proposed law that is supported by the Council: deliberation by the Dispute Resolution Committee; consideration of any proposal to resolve the dispute by the Assembly and the Council; early dissolution of the Assembly; a general election for the Assembly and the Council (a general election for the Council being tied to the dissolution of the Assembly: s 28 of the Constitution Act 1975 **[4.3.6]**); approval of the proposed law again by the Assembly; the revival of the dispute between the Assembly and the Council over the proposed law; a joint sitting of the Assembly and Council; and approval of the proposed law (with or without further amendment) by an absolute majority of the members of the Assembly and the Council.

At that point, the proposed law is treated as if it has been approved by the Assembly and the Council and, unless it is a proposed law to which s 18(1B) applies, it becomes an Act of Parliament upon the royal assent being signified. (Section 18(1B) of the Constitution Act prohibits the presentation to the Governor for royal assent of bills amending or repealing certain provisions in the Constitution Act unless the bill has been passed by the Assembly and the Council and approved by the majority of the electors voting at a referendum: see also **[5.4.15]**.)

[5.3.11] A cumbersome but incomplete procedure for resolving disputes between the Assembly and the Council is specified in s 41 of the Constitution Act 1934 (SA). Like the Victorian procedure, it assumes a dispute between the Assembly and the Council over a bill passed by the Assembly. It then provides for the following steps:

- dissolution of the Assembly (s 41);

- approval of the bill by an absolute majority in the new Assembly (s 41(b), (d));

- rejection of the bill by the Council (s 41(e));

- dissolution of the Council and the Assembly (s 41(1)(i)) or the election of two extra members of the Council (s 41(1)(ii)).

No further stages are specified. The South Australian system does not provide for any means of resolving a deadlock which persists after dissolution of the Council (which must be accompanied by a second dissolution of the Assembly). The whole procedure is fraught with expense and political risk for any government, and is likely to produce no positive gain.

However, amendments to the Constitution Act 1934 made in 1985 provide a more streamlined process by which some steps may be taken towards resolving a dispute between the two houses of parliament (although those steps may not actually produce a resolution). Where the House of Assembly passes 'a Bill of special importance' (so certified by the Speaker under s 28a(3)) and the Council rejects the bill (or is deemed to have rejected the bill under s 28a(4)), the Governor may dissolve the Assembly: s 28a(1). This has the effect of bringing on an election for the whole of the Assembly and may bring on an election for half the Council: s 14(2), (3).

[5.3.12] The machinery established by s 5B of the Constitution Act 1902 (NSW) has been used only once, and then unsuccessfully. In 1959, the Labor Government attempted to use the procedure for the enactment of a bill to abolish the Legislative Council. Some members of the Council sought an injunction restraining the referendum referred to in s 5B(2), which was refused (*Clayton v Heffron* (1960) 105 CLR 214 **[5.3.16C]**) and, at the referendum which followed, the voters rejected the bill.

[5.3.13] Section 5B of the Constitution Act 1902 (NSW) is closely modelled on the Parliamentary Bills Referendum Act 1908 (Qld), the validity of which was challenged in *Taylor v Attorney-General (Qld)* (1917) 23 CLR 457. (At that time, the Queensland Parliament consisted of two houses — the Assembly, with members elected on a popular franchise, and the Council, with members appointed for life. The Council was abolished in 1922: see **[4.2.12]**.)

The Parliamentary Bills Referendum Act 1908 (Qld) provided that when a bill had been passed by the Legislative Assembly in two successive sessions and on each occasion had been rejected by the Legislative Council, it might be submitted to the electors at a referendum. If approved by them, the bill could then be presented to the Governor for royal assent and would become an Act of Parliament in the same manner as if it had been passed by both houses of parliament.

In 1915 and 1916 the Legislative Assembly passed, in two successive sessions, a bill to abolish the Legislative Council. The Legislative Council twice rejected the bill and in April 1917 the Governor issued a proclamation directing that the bill be submitted to a referendum of electors. The plaintiffs, who were members of the Legislative Council, began proceedings in the Supreme Court of Queensland claiming declarations that the Act of 1908 was invalid, and that the Legislative Council could not be abolished. They also claimed an injunction to restrain the holding of the referendum. The Supreme Court granted an interlocutory injunction to restrain the referendum. The defendants appealed to the High Court which ordered the case removed to the court's original jurisdiction, and dissolved the interlocutory injunction after the Attorney-General of Queensland undertook that no action would be taken to present the abolition bill to the Governor for royal assent if approved at the referendum. The referendum was held on 5 May 1917 and the voters rejected the bill. Notwithstanding that the issue was now moot, the case was argued before the High Court in August 1917, and the court's decision handed down on 6 September 1917.

Central to the High Court's reasoning was the second clause of s 5 of the Colonial Laws Validity Act 1865 (UK) **[5.3.5]**. Barton J (with whom Gavan Duffy and Rich JJ agreed) held that s 5 of the Colonial Laws Validity Act established the validity of the Parliamentary Bills Referendum Act 1908. As a 'representative legislature', the Queensland Parliament had full power to legislate on its constitution, powers and procedure (at 23 CLR 468):

> I take the constitution of a legislature, as the term is here used, to mean the composition, form or nature of the House of legislature where there is only one House,

or of either House if the legislative body consists of two Houses. Probably the power does not extend to authorise the elimination of the representative character of the legislature within the meaning of the Act.

Barton J concluded that the Act of 1908 was 'a law "respecting the powers" of the legislature in certain cases ... It ... provides for the substitution of the popular vote as often as the circumstances indicated may occur': 23 CLR at 469. Moreover, the bill to abolish the Council would be, if passed, a law 'respecting the constitution' of the legislature, supported by s 5 of the Colonial Laws Validity Act.

Isaacs J (with whom Powers J agreed) held that the Act of 1908 was fully supported by s 5 of the Colonial Laws Validity Act and by cl 22 of the Order in Council of 6 June 1859, which had established the Queensland Parliament. That clause had authorised the parliament to make laws altering or repealing all or any of the provisions of this Order-in-Council in the same manner as any other laws 'for the good government of the colony'.

Isaacs J agreed that the Queensland legislature could use the referendum procedure to legislate for the abolition of the Legislative Council. In the course of his judgment, he suggested some limits to the power to reconstruct the legislature, at 474:

> When power is given to a colonial legislature to alter the constitution of the legislature, that must be read subject to the fundamental conception that, consistently with the very nature of our constitution as an Empire, the Crown is not included in the ambit of such a power.
>
> I read the words 'constitution of such legislature' as including the change from a uni-cameral to a bicameral system, or the reverse. Probably the 'representative' character of the legislature is a basic condition of the power relied on, and is preserved by the word 'such', but, that being maintained, I can see no reason for cutting down the plain natural meaning of the words in question so as to exclude the power of a self-governing community to say that for State purposes one House is sufficient as its organ of legislation.

[5.3.14]   The essentially flexible character of state Constitution Acts was confirmed by the Privy Council in *McCawley v R* [1920] AC 691. In the course of deciding that the Queensland Parliament could enact legislation inconsistent with certain provisions of the Constitution Act 1867 (Qld) without first expressly repealing those provisions, the Privy Council distinguished, at 703:

> ... between constitutions the terms of which may be modified or repealed with no other formality than is necessary in the case of other legislation, and constitutions which can only be altered with some special formality, and in some cases by a specially convened assembly ... Some communities, and notably Great Britain, have not in the framing of constitutions felt it necessary, or thought it useful, to shackle the complete independence of their successors. They have shrunk from the assumption that a degree of wisdom and foresight has been conceded to their generation which will be, or may be, wanting to their successors, in spite of the fact that those successors will possess more experience of the circumstances and necessities amid which their lives are lived. Those constitution framers who have adopted the other view must be supposed to have believed that certainty and stability were in such a matter the supreme desiderata. Giving effect to this belief, they have created obstacles of varying difficulty in the path of those who would lay rash hands upon the ark of the constitution.

The Privy Council said that the Constitution Acts of the Australian states were, in the sense outlined above, uncontrolled (at 706):

[W]hat was given was given completely, and unequivocally, in the belief fully justified by the event, that these young communities would successfully work out their own constitutional salvation.

The Queensland Parliament's power to legislate on constitutional topics in the same manner as it might legislate on other topics (the Privy Council drew an analogy between the Constitution Act and 'a Dog Act or any other Act': [1920] AC at 704) was confirmed by s 5 of the Colonial Laws Validity Act, by cl 22 of the Order-in-Council and by s 2 of the Constitution Act 1867 (Qld), which authorised the Queensland Parliament 'to make laws for the peace welfare and good government of the colony in all cases whatsoever'. The Privy Council said of this last provision that '[i]t would be almost impossible to use wider or less restrictive language': [1920] AC at 712.

The Privy Council made one qualification to their general description of the Queensland Constitution Act as uncontrolled: where the Act had indicated that a special legislative procedure should be followed when legislating on a particular topic, this could introduce some rigidity into the Constitution Act: [1920] AC at 712, 714. See **[5.4.2]**.

[5.3.15]   The second basis for the Queensland Parliament's power to introduce new legislative procedures, proposed by Isaacs J in *Taylor v Attorney-General (Qld)* (1917) 23 CLR 457 **[5.3.13]**, was cl 22 of the Order-in-Council of 6 June 1859. Each of the original state (or colonial) constitutions contained an equivalent of this clause:

- New South Wales Constitution Act 1855 (UK) s 4;

- Constitution Act 1856 (SA) s 34;

- For Tasmania: Australian Constitutions Act (No 2) 1850 (UK) s 32;

- Victorian Constitution Act 1855 (UK) s 4;

- Constitution Act 1855 (Vic) s 60;

- Constitution Act 1889 (WA) s 73.

In the following decision, the High Court of Australia examined a third basis which could support state legislation reconstructing legislative procedures, a basis which had been suggested by the Privy Council in *McCawley's* case [1920] AC 691 at 712 **[5.3.14]**.

[5.3.16C]   **Clayton v Heffron**

                                       (1960) 105 CLR 214

In 1933, s 5B was added to the Constitution Act 1902 (NSW): see **[5.3.7E]**. In 1959 and again in 1960, the New South Wales Legislative Assembly passed a bill for the abolition of the Legislative Council. The bill was, on each occasion, sent to the Council which declined to consider the bill and returned it to the Assembly. The Assembly then requested a free conference of managers but the Council refused the request. The Governor then sent messages to both houses convening a joint sitting but the Council resolved that its members should not attend. In fact, 23 legislative councillors did attend a joint sitting with the Legislative Assembly. The Legislative Assembly then resolved that the bill to abolish the Council should be submitted to a referendum.

Five members of the Council, one member of the Assembly and one member of the Commonwealth House of Representatives then brought a suit in the New South Wales Supreme Court against the Premier, other ministers and the Electoral Commissioner seeking declarations that s 5B was valid, or that the bill to abolish the Council had not complied with s 5B, and injunctions to restrain the holding of the referendum. An interlocutory injunction was granted by McLelland CJ in Equity, but on the hearing of the suits before the full bench of five judges, the relief sought was denied. The plaintiffs appealed to the High Court of Australia.

Dixon CJ, McTiernan, Taylor and Windeyer JJ dismissed three arguments: that the Abolition Bill had failed to comply with s 7A of the Constitution Act 1902 (NSW); that there had been a breach of the privileges of the Legislative Council; and that the Council had not rejected the Abolition Bill. They then turned to the argument that, because there had been no free conference between the two houses and no joint sitting of the members of the Houses, there was a fatal defect in the procedure.

Dixon CJ, McTiernan, Taylor and Windeyer JJ: [246] There is no doubt that the words 'after a free conference between managers' contain an implied direction that such a conference shall take place. In the same way the words relating to the joint sitting of members of the houses import an intention that the Governor shall then exercise the authority to convene a joint sitting of members. But it is an entirely different thing to find in the direction an intention that a departure from the procedure shall spell invalidity in the statute when it is passed approved and assented to ... The power here is to enact a public general statute and the power to do this extends to a statute altering the constitution of the legislature so that if the statute is to be void every future piece of legislation passed by the legislature of the State so constituted will have no force or effect. The matter of procedure prescribed is a matter affecting the process in Parliament of legislating, a matter at once outside the ordinary scope of inquiry by the courts and also one not necessarily of public notoriety. The point of procedure concerns a step preliminary to the calling by the Governor of a joint sitting of the members of the two houses. Such a meeting was convened in point of fact and a meeting of certain members of the two houses took place at the time and place appointed. The point that in itself it could not amount to a joint meeting of members because the Council had resolved that its members should not attend is untenable. The preliminary step of appointing managers freely to confer rested on the cooperation of both houses in a conflict. It would rest with either house to neglect the duty and so bring the [247] proceedings to nought ... Before one reaches the conclusion that the failure to fulfil the requirement of holding a free conference will result in the invalidity of the law if adopted, it is natural to treat the fact that the Legislative Council may decline a conference of managers as a reason to be added to the other considerations for holding that it is not a matter going to validity. Lawyers speak of statutory provisions as imperative when any want of strict compliance with them means that the resulting act, be it a statute, a contract or what you will, is null and void. They speak of them as directory when they mean that although they are legal requirements which it is unlawful to disregard, yet failure to fulfil them does not mean that the resulting act is wholly ineffective, is null and void. It is almost unnecessary to say that the decided cases illustrating the distinction relate to much humbler matters than the validity or invalidity of the constitution of the legislature of a State. But in them all the performance of a public duty or the fulfilment of a public function by a body of persons to whom the task is confided is regarded as something to be contrasted with the acquisition or exercise of private rights or privileges and the fact that to treat deviation in the former case from the conditions or directions laid down as meaning complete invalidity would work inconvenience or worse on a section of the public, is treated as a powerful consideration against doing so. Is it possible to imagine a stronger case of inconvenience than the invalidation perhaps at some future time of a constitutional provision possessing all the outward appearance of a valid law on the ground than when it was made managers of the Council had not met managers of the Assembly before the members of the two houses were required by the Governor to meet?

Dixon CJ, McTiernan, Taylor and Windeyer JJ held that a free conference of managers of the two houses was not an essential condition for the ultimate validity of legislation passed through s 5B. They then turned to the question whether s 5B was valid.

[249] There are two sources of possible constitutional power enabling the legislature to adopt s 5B: one is s 5 of the Constitution Act, 1902–1956 (NSW), the other is s 5 of the Colonial Laws Validity Act 1865 (28 & 29 Vict c 63) ...

[250] [Section] 5 of the Constitution Act 1902–1956 appears on consideration to contain a sufficient power not only to change the bicameral system into a unicameral system but also to enable the resolution of disagreements between the two houses by submitting an Act passed by the Assembly for the approval of the electors in substitution for the assent of the Council and, moreover, to include in the application of that legislative process Bills for the abolition of the Legislative Council and Bills otherwise falling within the description dealt with by s 7A. The reasoning supporting this conclusion is indeed simple. It rests on the plain if very general words of s 5 of the Constitution Act. The first paragraph of the section is as follows: 'The Legislature shall, subject to the provisions of the Commonwealth of Australia Constitution Act have power to make laws for the peace, welfare and good government of New South Wales in all cases whatsoever'. The expression 'legislature' is defined in s 3 to mean the Sovereign with the consent of the Legislative Council and Legislative Assembly ... The first paragraph confers a complete and unrestricted power to make laws with reference to New South Wales. There is doubtless a territorial limitation implied in the reference to New South Wales but there is no limitation of subject matter. The laws may be constitutional or at the other extreme they may deal with subjects of little significance. Clearly the power extends to laws altering the Constitution Act itself: cf *McCawley v R* [1920] AC 691, 703–6, 709; (1926) 28 CLR 106, 114–17, 120 ... There are many reasons for assuming that the assent of the Crown must always remain necessary but what ground is there for supposing that the legislature must always remain defined in terms of two houses? The purpose of the provision is to express the full legislative power of a State the authority of which is continued under ss 106 and 107 of the Constitution of the Commonwealth. The Legislature was endowed with constituent as well as ordinary legislative power ...

[252] It seems obvious that the combined effect of s 4 of the Constitution Statute and s 1 of the Constitution Act was to confer upon the legislature of New South Wales a full constituent power ... The authority thus conferred is that exercised in adopting s 5 of the Constitution Act 1902 and it formed an ample foundation for that enactment. It must be remembered that the negative restrictions which s 7A imposes under the operation of s 5 of the Colonial Laws Validity Act were complied with when s 5B was enacted. That being so, once it is seen that s 5 gives the legislature a full constituent power the question why should the power of the legislature not extend to the enactment of s 5B almost answers itself. What it means is that the power to legislate, including the power to legislate for the abolition of the Council, may be exercised by the Crown with the consent of the Assembly provided the proposed law is approved by the majority of the electors voting at a referendum. That is a law falling within the authority described by s 5 of the Constitution Act 1902. That being so it is valid.

~~~

[5.3.17] Fullagar J held that the validity of s 5B was settled by *Taylor v Attorney-General (Qld)* **[5.3.13]**, that the procedure specified by s 5B was mandatory, and that, as there had been neither a free conference not a joint sitting, 'the submission of the [Abolition] Bill to a referendum and the subsequent assent by the Governor cannot produce a valid Act of the legislature of New South Wales': 105 CLR at 262.

Kitto J shared the view of the majority on the validity of s 5B: 105 CLR at 265. His Honour regarded the requirements of s 5B as mandatory but said that the section implied that the Council must be prepared to participate in the proceedings (at 268):

> The words in which a condition is stated ... surely cannot mean that the very chamber whose opposition to the Bill is to be prevented from proving a final obstacle to its enactment may, by refusing co-operation, make its opposition successful.

Menzies J held s 5B to be valid, for substantially the same reasons as the majority. His view of the procedures specified in s 5B was the same as that of Kitto J.

~~~

Notes

[5.3.18] The distinction between mandatory and directory procedures, although central to the reasoning of the justices in *Clayton v Heffron*, has been somewhat discredited over the past 30 years. In *Tasker v Fulwood* [1978] 1 NSWLR 20 at 23, the New South Wales Court of Appeal said that the use of the labels 'mandatory' and 'directory' tended to conceal the real issue when legislation prescribed a procedure to be followed when public power is exercised; namely, did the legislature intend that a failure to comply with the stipulated procedure or requirement would invalidate the act done or that the validity of the act would be preserved notwithstanding non-compliance? That approach was also endorsed by the Full Court of the Federal Court in *Yappeen Holdings Pty Ltd v Calardu Pty Ltd* (1992) 36 FCR 478 at 494.

In answering that question in *Clayton v Heffron*, Fullagar J relied on the *form* of s 5B, which made the referendum conditional upon completing the earlier steps. On the other hand, the majority pointed to the 'powerful consideration' of the possible 'inconvenience or worse on the section of the public' which would follow if the steps were regarded as essential to validity.

Commonwealth Parliament

[5.3.19] The first draft of the Commonwealth Constitution, prepared by Sir Samuel Griffith and adopted at the 1891 Convention, made no provision for resolving deadlocks between the two Houses of the Commonwealth Parliament. The pressure for the inclusion of some procedure to deal with inter-house disputes came from the two largest colonies, New South Wales and Victoria, whose populations would ensure them the domination of the House of Representatives, but who would be outnumbered by the four smaller states in the Senate. An attempt to insert a deadlock provision was defeated at the Adelaide Convention in 1897, although most observers saw that defeat as anything but final, for without such a provision the voters in New South Wales and Victoria were unlikely to vote for federation. At the Sydney Convention in 1897, after the Convention's largest and most intricate debate, the delegates agreed in principle to the insertion of a provision for resolving deadlocks and went on to agree on the outlines of the procedure specified in the present s 57. The delegates who voted for a deadlock provision were drawn, by and large, from New South Wales, South Australia and Victoria; those who opposed it were from Tasmania and Western Australia. (Queensland did not participate in these Conventions.) La Nauze tells us of the political considerations that lay behind the adoption of the deadlock provision:

> Although equal representation in the Senate had been so decisively confirmed [by the convention], the support of the large States had not been given without implied conditions. To defend it in the coming [referenda] campaigns without some safeguard against an indefinite blocking of the popular will would be difficult in New South Wales and impossible in Victoria ... The representatives of Victoria and New South Wales seemed to feel that they must have some machinery, any machinery, for ending deadlocks to justify publicly their concession of equal representation in the Senate. The South Australians, almost to a man, seemed to be anxious to meet these fears of

political embarrassment, provided a method could be found which would not put them at the mercy of a simple majority of Australian electors ((1972) pp 188, 190).

[5.3.20]   At the Melbourne Convention of 1898, the delegates settled, or assumed they were settling, the procedure. 'Deadlocks would be finally resolved by a three-fifths majority in a joint sitting of both houses after the election following a dissolution [of both houses]': La Nauze (1972) p 217. This settlement was thrown into some confusion when the voters of New South Wales approved the draft Commonwealth Constitution by a small majority (71,595 to 66,228): the relevant New South Wales legislation required an affirmative vote of 80,000. The New South Wales Premier, G Reid, proposed a series of alterations to the 1898 draft of the Constitution and a Premiers' conference (at which Queensland and the five colonies which had participated in the Conventions were represented) agreed on eight changes, among them the substitution of an absolute majority (instead of a three-fifths majority) at the joint sitting specified in s 57: La Nauze (1972) pp 242–3. The new draft was then approved by the necessary majorities in referenda in New South Wales, Queensland, South Australia, Tasmania and Victoria. Western Australia waited until 1900 before putting the draft to a referendum, which approved the draft.

[5.3.21E]   **Commonwealth Constitution**

57 If the House of Representatives passes any proposed law, and the Senate rejects or fails to pass it, or passes it with amendments to which the House of Representatives will not agree and if after an interval of three months the House of Representatives, in the same or the next session, again passes the proposed law with or without any amendments which have been made, suggested, or agreed to by the Senate, and the Senate rejects or fails to pass it, or passes it with amendments to which the House of Representatives will not agree, the Governor-General may dissolve the Senate and the House of Representatives simultaneously. But such dissolution shall not take place within six months before the date of the expiry of the House of Representatives by effluxion of time.

If after such dissolution the House of Representatives again passes the proposed law, with or without any amendments which have been made, suggested, or agreed to by the Senate and the Senate rejects or fails to pass it, or passes it with amendments to which the House of Representatives will not agree, the Governor-General may convene a joint sitting of the members of the Senate and of the House of Representatives.

The members present at a joint sitting may deliberate and shall vote together upon the proposed law as last proposed by the House of Representatives, and upon amendments, if any, which have been made therein by one House and not agreed by the other, and any such amendments which are affirmed by an absolute majority of the total number of the members of the Senate and House of Representatives shall be taken to have been carried, and if the proposed law, with the amendments, if any, so carried is affirmed by an absolute majority of the total number of the members of the Senate and House of Representatives, it shall be taken to have been duly passed by both Houses of the Parliament, and shall be presented to the Governor-General for the Queen's assent.

~~~

Notes

[5.3.22]   Writing in 1972, La Nauze remarked of the Convention Debates on s 57 that there was 'a certain retrospective unreality about the debate, for it is humanly impossible not to reflect that the apprehensions on both sides were illusory': (1972) p 183. In so far as the delegates were obsessed with potential conflict between the smaller and larger states, no doubt La Nauze's observation is sound, as Deakin so acutely observed:

> The contest will not be, never has been, and cannot be, between States and States. It must be and will be between the representatives of the States according to the different political principles upon which they are returned (Convention Debates, Sydney, 1897, p 584).

However, the delegates' concern to provide some means of resolving deadlocks was not out of touch with political reality, for the different bases on which the two federal houses are elected ensures that the political composition of the houses will often differ. The combination of unequal constituencies (both Tasmania and New South Wales return 10 senators, but the former returns five and the latter 51 representatives), different terms (senators hold their seats for six years, representatives for a maximum of three years), different voting systems (proportional representation for senators, single member constituencies for the house) and elections at different times (there is no legal requirement that the elections be synchronised) means that the Senate is likely to reflect a different political community from that reflected by the House of Representatives.

Before the introduction of proportional representation for the Senate, disparities between political strengths in each house were often absurd. After the general election of May 1913, the Liberal Party had 38 of 75 seats in the House of Representatives, but only seven of the 36 Senate places. When proportional representation replaced the cruder voting systems in 1949, the probability of extreme imbalance in the Senate disappeared. Even so, the composition of the Senate was likely to be quite different from that in the house. The later Menzies Governments, and the Holt, Gorton, McMahon, Whitlam, Fraser, Hawke, Keating and Howard Governments all had to contend with a Senate in which their parties were in the minority.

[5.3.23] The s 57 procedure has now been exploited six times, although only once (in 1974) has it been pushed through to its final stages with a joint sitting passing the disputed legislation. In 1987, the Hawke Labor Government abandoned plans to convene a joint sitting following the double dissolution and election of that year, when a flaw was discovered in the bill which was to go to the joint sitting: see *Australian Journal of Politics and History* (1988) at 218.

[5.3.24] The fourth use of the s 57 procedure (November 1975) was also characterised by some observers as an abuse of that procedure. When the Governor-General, Sir John Kerr, dismissed Prime Minister Whitlam, he commissioned a new Prime Minister, J M Fraser, on condition that he undertook to obtain supply and that he advised a double dissolution. The double dissolution could only be based (and was based according to the Governor-General's proclamation of 11 November 1975) on 21 bills, each of which had been sponsored by the Whitlam Government, opposed by the Fraser-led Opposition and had been through the essential preliminary procedures specified in s 57.

Referring to a passage in Stephen J's judgment in *Western Australia v Commonwealth* (1975) 134 CLR 201 at 262 **[5.3.33]**, Katz argued that the proper purpose of the double dissolution power is to resolve a deadlock over a bill or bills which have complied with the s 57 procedure; that the purpose of the 1975 double dissolution was different (to resolve a deadlock over the appropriation bills); and that, therefore, the double dissolution was invalid: Katz (1976) pp 396–9. This argument is discussed in detail (and rejected) in Howard and Saunders (1977) pp 236–7 and Sawer (1977) pp 57–63.

[5.3.25] The double dissolution of 1974 was challenged before the High Court in three separate proceedings. In the first of these proceedings, injunctions were sought to prevent the holding of the joint sitting specified in s 57. The injunctions were sought after the results of the general election of 18 May 1974 made it clear that the government could command an absolute majority at the joint sitting. The court refused to grant the injunctions, and most of the judges indicated that the proper remedy for any defect in the s 57 procedure would be to challenge the validity of any legislation after its passage through the joint sitting: *Cormack v Cope* (1974) 131 CLR 432 **[5.5.3C]**. The second challenge was brought in the following case, *Victoria v Commonwealth* (the *PMA* case) (1975) 134 CLR 81 **[5.3.26C]**. The third challenge was brought in *Western Australia v Commonwealth* (the *Territorial Senators* case) (1975) 134 CLR 201 **[5.3.33]**.

[5.3.26C] **Victoria v Commonwealth**

(The *PMA* case)
(1975) 134 CLR 81

The Petroleum and Minerals Authority Bill (the PMA Bill) was first passed by the House of Representatives on 12 December 1973. It was introduced in the Senate on 13 December 1973 where, on the motion of the Opposition, debate was adjourned. The Senate then rose for the Christmas adjournment. On 14 February 1974 the Governor-General prorogued parliament to 28 February. The Senate resumed debate on the PMA Bill on 19 March 1974 and, on 2 April 1974, rejected the motion that it be read a second time. The House of Representatives passed the PMA Bill a second time on 8 April 1974. On 10 April 1974, the Senate resolved to defer consideration of the PMA Bill for six months.

The Governor-General dissolved both houses on 11 April 1974. After the subsequent general election, the PMA Bill was again passed by the Representatives and rejected by the Senate. The Governor-General convened a joint sitting of the houses and the PMA Bill was approved by that sitting on 6 August 1974. It then received the royal assent as the Petroleum and Minerals Authority Act 1973.

The plaintiffs (the states of Victoria, Queensland, Western Australia, New South Wales) began proceedings in the High Court of Australia, seeking declarations that the PMA Act 1973 was not a valid law of the Commonwealth. The defendant filed a defence to the effect that the PMA Bill had complied with the s 57 procedure and that the questions raised by the plaintiffs were not justiciable. The state of Victoria sought to have the defence struck out and the summons seeking this result was referred by Stephen J to the Full Court of the High Court.

Barwick CJ: [117] The submission of the defendants are:

(A) That the resolutions and orders of the Senate on 13 December 1973 without more may amount to a rejection or failure by it to pass the proposed law.

(B) That in determining whether the Senate rejected or failed to pass any proposed law regard may be had not only to any relevant resolutions of the Senate but to all relevant facts. Speeches of senators within the Senate may be such. Statements whether by senators or others outside the Senate may also be relevant. All the sub-paragraphs of para 6 of the defence contain relevant facts.

(C) That the interval of three months referred to in s 57 is from the first passing of the proposed law by the House of Representatives.

(D) That the words of condition in the first paragraph of s 57 are used in a directory sense.

(E) Statement of claim raises non-justiciable issues.

The Commonwealth in the last submission advanced an argument of great significance. The submission was that this court has no power to declare that a law which had not been passed in accordance with the lawmaking requirement of s 57 of the Constitution was invalid, a submission somewhat akin to, though not identical with, but of like consequence to, a submission which had been made by the Commonwealth in *Cormack v Cope* (1974) 131 CLR 432.

[118] [T]he undeniable assertion [made in *Cormack v Cope*] that this court is the guardian of the Constitution, and the authorities there cited, are fully relevant to the resolution of the submissions made in this case. Part of that Constitution provides for lawmaking processes. Section 57 is a notable example of that prescription. The court, in my opinion, not only has the power but, when approached by a litigant with a proper interest to do so, has the duty to examine whether or not the lawmaking process prescribed by the Constitution has been followed and, if it has not, to declare that that which has emerged with the appearance of an Act, though having received the royal assent, is not a valid law of the Commonwealth ...

Barwick CJ said that he completely disagreed with the argument 'that the Governor-General had the power unexaminably to decide whether or not the condition of s 57 had been satisfied'.

[119] The powers given to the Governor-General by s 57 are statutory powers — the statute being an organic instrument — conditioned on the existence of facts ... I can see no basis on which the Constitution can be read as giving the Governor-General a power to decide the facts on which the legality of his own actions or the validity of an Act may depend. Of course, the Governor-General must form a view for himself as to whether the circumstances of the proposed law satisfy the requirements of the first paragraph of s 57. But his power is contingent on the existence in fact of the conditions which that paragraph expresses: in my opinion, the power to decide the fact is reposed in this court and in this court alone. That is a facet of the undoubted position of the court as the guardian of the Constitution.

Barwick CJ also rejected an argument that the terms of s 57 were merely directory, so that failure to conform to its requirements would not affect the validity of what was done. It was 'quite inappropriate' to apply the distinction between a directory and a mandatory statutory provision to s 57: 134 CLR at 119–20. He then turned to the possible consequence of the exercise by the Governor-General of the double dissolution power in circumstances where the preconditions to the exercise of that power were later found not to exist.

[120] The dissolution itself is a fact which can neither be void nor be undone. If, without having power to do so, the Governor-General did dissolve both houses, there would be no basis for setting aside the dissolution or for treating it as not having occurred. None the less, the double dissolution would not have been authorised, and therefore it would not satisfy the second paragraph of s 57 and provide a warrant for a joint sitting. The joint sitting, pursuant to the third paragraph of that section, which was dependent upon such a dissolution, which, though not void, was not lawful, would not have power to affirm any law. It is not necessary, in my opinion, to regard any part of s 57 as directory in order to conclude that, though the proclamation be unlawful, the sequential dissolution in fact occurred and was incapable of being disregarded, reversed or undone.

Turning to the question whether the Senate had 'failed to pass' the bill on 13 December, Barwick CJ noted that the Commonwealth's argument was based on the premise that s 57's purpose was to enable the will of the House of Representatives to prevail.

[121] It seems to me that this submission is untenable. The Senate is a part of the Parliament and, except as to laws appropriating revenue or money for the ordinary annual services of the government or imposing taxation, is co-equal with the House of Representatives. Bills may originate and do originate in the Senate. Section 53 of the Constitution makes it abundantly clear that the Senate is to have equal powers with the House of Representatives in respect of all laws other than those specifically excepted. The only limitations as to the equality of the

powers of the Senate with those of the House of Representatives are those imposed by the first three paragraphs of that section, to the terms of which the limitations must be confined.

It is evident from the terms of the Constitution that the Senate was intended to represent the States, parts of the Commonwealth, as distinct from the House of Representatives which represents the electors throughout Australia. It is often said that [122] the Senate has, in this respect, failed of its purpose. This may be so, due partly to the party system and to the nature of the electoral system: but even if that assertion be true it does not detract from the constitutional position that it was intended that proposed laws could be considered by the Senate from a point of view different from that which the House of Representatives may take. The Senate is not a mere house of review: rather it is a house which may examine a proposed law from a stand-point different from that which the House of Representatives may have taken.

That a Bill needs consideration and debate is beyond question, though one cannot but observe that due to the dominance of the executive in the House of Representatives and perhaps, at times, in the Senate, opportunity for debate may be very attenuated. But, whatever exigencies of party policies, the Constitution cannot be read as if laws ought to be passed by the Senate without debate, or as if the House of Representatives may in any respect command the Senate in relation to a Bill. Thus, in approaching the meaning of the word 'fails' in s 57, it must be borne in mind that the Senate is both entitled and bound to consider a proposed law and to have a proper opportunity for debate and that its concurrence, apart from the provisions of s 57, is indispensable to a valid Act of the Parliament.

It seems that the word 'fails' in s 57 involves the notion that a time has arrived when, even allowing for the deliberate processes of the Senate, the Senate ought to answer whether or not it will pass the Bill or make amendments to it for the consideration of the House: that the time has arrived for the Senate to take a stand with respect to the Bill. If that time has arrived and the Senate rather than take a stand merely prevaricates, it can properly be said at that time to have failed to pass the Bill. In considering whether such a time has arrived, it may be that antecedent conduct of the Senate, particularly in relation to the proposed law, may be relevant. But it will be the conduct of the Senate itself and not the conduct or opinions or anticipatory statements of individual senators, whatever may be their party standing or party authority, which can have any relevance to the question whether, the situation having been reached where the Senate is called upon to give an answer on the Bill, it has failed to pass it ...

[123] In order to deny that the Senate has failed to pass the Bill, it may be enough to say that all the processes available to the Senate in the consideration of a Bill have not been exhausted. It may be that even before those processes are exhausted the Senate may fail to pass within the meaning of s 57. In 1951 the reference of the Commonwealth Banking Bill to a select committee did not prevent the conclusion that the Senate had failed to pass, having regard to its entire conduct in regard to the Bill. It was said that the reference to the select committee in the particular circumstances was no more than prevarication. On other occasions and in different circumstances, the same conclusion perhaps may not be drawn from a reference of a Bill to a select committee.

However, I have no doubt that it cannot properly be said that when the Senate resolved on 13 December 1973 to adjourn the debate on the motion for a second reading until in effect the next sitting day, it had failed to pass the Bill. In my opinion, it could not be said that the time had arrived that day when the Senate was in any sense obliged to express itself definitively on the Bill. The concept of failure to pass must, it seems to me, mean more than 'not pass'. Failure in this sense imports, as I have said, the notion of the presence of an obligation as a house to take a definitive stand.

My conclusion therefore is that the Senate did not fail to pass [124] the proposed law on 13 December 1973 within the meaning and operation of s 57 of the Constitution. The adjournment by the Senate of the debate until what was in effect the next day of sitting cannot be said, in my opinion, to have been a mere prevarication. Indeed, the suspension of standing orders to allow of the making of the motion for a second reading, scarce portends an intention to prevaricate.

The next question is whether or not the period of three months in the first paragraph of s 57 is to run from the date of the Senate's relevant treatment of the Bill, or whether it runs from the first passage of the Bill by the House of Representatives. Reading s 57 as a piece of English, I am unable to see any basis upon which the words 'if after an interval of three months' could be referable other than to the action of the Senate ...

But, apart from reading the section as a piece of English, the purpose behind the section, it seems to me, is to fix a period of time after the Senate has considered the law and taken up a definitive position with respect to it, during which the House of Representatives should have time to consider, no doubt in the light of what has been said in debate in the Senate, whether the law should go forward again. Also, the decision of the Senate whether it should maintain its former attitude to the Bill may well be affected by the lapse of time. I cannot see any policy which would be satisfied by annexing the interval of three months to the first passage of the proposed law by the House of Representatives ...

[125] There is no question that the first paragraph of s 57 gives the House of Representatives the initiative both in the formulation of the proposed law and in its re-enactment after an interval of three months, but the purpose of a double dissolution is not to ensure that the will of the House prevails. Rather it is a means by which the electorate can express itself and perhaps thus resolve the 'deadlock' which has been demonstrated to exist between the House and the Senate ... Further, the purpose of the joint sitting if the 'deadlock' continues is not [126] to secure the will of the House of Representatives. It is to secure the view of the absolute majority of the total number of the members of both houses, which may or may not represent the will of the House of Representatives. It is little to the point that it may generally be expected that the members of the more numerous House will carry the day in a joint sitting. But that is not a necessary consequence. This argument on the construction of s 57 which the Crown put forward is, in my opinion, untenable.

In my opinion, the requirements of the first paragraph of s 57 were not satisfied in relation to the Bill. The Senate had not failed to pass it on 13 December 1973, and the interval of three months from the date of the Senate's rejection of the Bill which should have elapsed before the House of Representatives again passed the proposed law did not elapse. A consequence is that, had there been no other proposed laws which satisfied the provisions of s 57, the Governor-General would not have had authority to dissolve the Senate and the House of Representatives simultaneously merely because of what occurred in the Senate on 13 December 1973 in relation to the Bill.

I therefore conclude that the Bill, though assented to by the Governor-General, is not a valid law of the Commonwealth.

Gibbs, Stephen and Mason JJ agreed that the issues were justiciable. McTiernan J asserted that the case presented a 'political question ... not within the judicial power of the Commonwealth, vested by s 71 of the Constitution in the court, to decide': 134 CLR at 135. Jacobs J expressed no opinion on this issue. Gibbs and Mason JJ also agreed that the provisions of s 57 were mandatory. Gibbs, Stephen and Mason JJ agreed that the three month interval was to be measured from the Senate's rejection or failure to pass and that the Senate had neither rejected nor failed to pass the PMA Bill on 13 December 1973. McTiernan J expressed no opinion on these issues. On the effect of a procedural flaw on the election of a new parliament, Gibbs, Stephen and Mason JJ offered the following comments:

Gibbs J: [157] One consequence of ... an invalid dissolution would clearly be that a proposed law affirmed by an absolute majority at any subsequent joint sitting of members of the Senate and House of Representatives would not be valid for it would not have satisfied the conditions of law making laid down by s 57. But the conditions which s 57 attaches to the exercise of the powers which it confers do not also attach to the powers given by ss 12 and 32 of the Constitution to cause writs to be used for the election of members of the Senate and of the

House of Representatives. If the Senate were in fact dissolved, and if thereafter writs for an election were issued, the election was held and a new Parliament was summoned to meet, I can see no difficulty in holding that the new Parliament would have validly assembled. This of course is not to suggest that this court could not intervene to uphold the Constitution and prevent an invalid proclamation for the dissolution of the Senate from being given effect.

Stephen J: [178] In the case of s 57 no such consequences would, in my view, ensue; once the Governor-General has in fact dissolved both chambers, whether or not he is justified in doing so in terms of s 57, the existing Parliament will have been brought effectively to an end and the new Parliament which results from the issue of writs and the holding of an election following such dissolution will be quite unaffected by whatever may or may not have preceded that dissolution.

Mason J: [183] It does not follow, despite the suggestion to the contrary made by the Solicitor-General, that the court could intervene to declare invalid a dissolution of the Parliament and an ensuing election. The jurisdiction of the court is engaged because there is at issue the validity of a statute enacted by the Parliament, a question [184] which it will decide in a suit for a declaration as to validity. Intervention by the court at any other stage of the parliamentary process involves different considerations of a complex character, jurisdictional and discretionary, some of which were discussed in *Clayton v Heffron* (1960) 105 CLR 214, *Cormack v Cope* (1974) 131 CLR 432, and the decisions there referred to. Even if it be thought that a logical consequence of granting relief to the plaintiffs now would be to expose a prospective dissolution of Parliament under s 57 to judicial scrutiny, this does not demonstrate that relief cannot be granted in the present cases.

~~~

[5.3.27] Jacobs J dissented on the substantive issues before the court. He held that s 57 allowed the Senate three months in which to pass a bill passed by the House of Representatives. That is, the Senate 'fails to pass' a proposed law if it does not pass the proposed law as soon as it is transmitted to the Senate from the House of Representatives, and the Senate continues in a state or condition of failing to pass the proposed law for so long as it does not pass the proposed law. This interpretation, according to Jacobs J, was justified by the ordinary meaning of the phrase, by the need to avoid uncertainty in the application of s 57 and by the purpose of s 57, to achieve the passage of legislation in a form acceptable to the House of Representatives. He also concluded that, in the present case, the Senate had positively 'failed to pass' the PMA Bill on 13 December or during the immediately following days, if s 57 required the phrase 'fails to pass' to be read in that sense. It had not been 'reasonable for the Senate to adjourn leaving this business undone': 134 CLR at 199.

~~~

Notes

[5.3.28] In *Cormack v Cope* (1974) 131 CLR 432 **[5.5.3C]**, the High Court had foreshadowed this decision. While refusing to enjoin the joint sitting, the majority of the court had held that the procedures specified in s 57 were justiciable and Barwick CJ had indicated that the PMA Act had not satisfied those procedures. An argument that the phrase 'any proposed law' in s 57 was confined to a single bill was rejected. The court held that a double dissolution could be proclaimed and a joint sitting convened in respect of any number of bills which had been through the necessary s 57 procedures.

The majority also expressed the opinion that it was not part of the Governor-General's function to specify the business which might be discussed at the joint sitting which he convened. Accordingly, that part of his proclamation which invited the members of both houses to 'deliberate and vote together on' six named bills was of no legal effect. Rather, it was 'surplusage' or 'unnecessary material', but only Barwick CJ thought that its presence in the proclamation could invalidate the proclamation.

[5.3.29] It is clear that the majority in the *PMA* case saw the phrase 'fails to pass' as implying some definite action, or some clear default, on the part of the Senate. Barwick CJ, Gibbs J and Mason J spoke of the failure to pass a bill after a reasonable time had been allowed for consideration: 134 CLR at 122, 148, 186 (respectively). Stephen J talked of the Senate taking advantage of its normal processes 'for ulterior purposes, for delaying rather than considering and then passing or rejecting, a proposed law': 134 CLR at 171. At the same time, the majority refused to regard statements made by senators during the Senate debates as going to the proof of this issue. Surely, this creates a fundamental dilemma: how is it possible to determine whether the normal processes are being used 'for ulterior purposes', or whether the Senate has 'had a reasonable opportunity to pass' a bill, unless one examines the actions and attitudes of those people who constitute the Senate? No doubt there are real dangers in treating parliamentary debates as an authoritative source on such issues, but how else might the question (as posed by the majority) be sensibly answered?

[5.3.30] Geoffrey Sawer made the point that, if the majority view of 'fails to pass' is 'applied to the circumstances of 1951 without any reference to what was said in debates, the result is inconclusive'. On that occasion, the Prime Minister R G Menzies advised the Governor-General to dissolve both houses after the Senate had agreed to a second reading motion on the Commonwealth Bank Bill and then resolved to refer the bill to a select committee for consideration and report. Menzies advised the Governor-General that this amounted to a failure to pass and that, as the bill had earlier been passed by the Representatives, amended by the Senate and passed again by the Representatives after the necessary three months' delay, he should proclaim a double dissolution. The Governor-General acted on this advice. Sawer goes on to observe that 'only the tone of debate can tip the scale' when the Senate has done no more than use its ordinary procedures, as it did in 1951. Indeed, he remarks that a judicial examination of the 1951 events (which ignored the Parliamentary Debates) may well have found that the s 57 procedures had not been followed: Sawer (1977) pp 50–1.

[5.3.31] Is there any way, given the majority's approach to the phrase 'fails to pass', that the court can avoid making a political assessment of proceedings in parliament? Might this inevitability support the argument that s 57 is not justiciable? Consider the point made by Sawer: 'Judicial supervision is not necessary in this matter, because the necessary consequence of the operation of s 57 is to leave ultimate judgment on a predominantly political question to the electors, *both* the Representatives electors *and* the Senate electors': Sawer (1977) p 54; see also the judgment of Jacobs J in *Western Australia v Commonwealth* (1975) 134 CLR 201 **[5.3.33]** at 275–6.

[5.3.32] The majority judgments in the *PMA* case asserted that the High Court could, in appropriate proceedings, review a double dissolution and joint sitting under s 57 and decide that these were ineffective because the legislation on which they were founded, and in whose enactment they purported to form distinct stages, had not complied with the earlier procedural steps specified in s 57. But the majority justices denied that a failure to adhere to the procedural steps would invalidate the double dissolution and the subsequent general election: 134 CLR at 120 per Barwick CJ; 134 CLR at 156 per Gibbs J; 134 CLR at 178 per Stephen J; 134 CLR at 183 per Mason J. Their views have been described by Sawer as 'logically unsatisfying' (Sawer (1977) p 52), and by Zines as 'unconvincing': Zines (1977) p 231. Zines suggested that 'policy considerations, involving political and social consequences' could justify the judges' view that the validity of legislation may be tested but not the validity of a dissolution or election: Zines (1977) p 232. On the other hand, Sawer argued that these considerations are not 'particularly pressing, since most of the Members of the Houses held to have been invalidly dissolved would be available for re-summoning, unless the proceedings have been delayed unreasonably, in which case it is likely that the dissolved House of Representatives would have expired by effluxion of time': Sawer (1977) pp 53–4. However, it must be doubted whether the re-summoning of the members of the unlawfully dissolved houses would be sufficient to overcome the problems created by a ruling that the dissolution had been unlawful.

[5.3.33] The third challenge to the 1974 double dissolution came in *Western Australia v Commonwealth* (the *Territorial Senators* case) (1975) 134 CLR 201, where the High Court was asked to declare invalid the Senate (Representation of Territories) Act 1973 (Cth). The grounds of attack were, first, that there had not been full compliance with the s 57 procedures (which had been used to enact the Act) and, second, that the provisions of the Act were in conflict with s 7 of the Constitution. (That second issue is dealt with in **[4.2.32C]**.)

The Senate (Representation of Territories) Bill 1973 was first passed by the House of Representatives on 30 May 1973 and was rejected by the Senate on 7 June 1973. It was passed a second time by the House of Representatives on 27 September 1973 and again rejected by the Senate on 14 November 1973. Following the double dissolution of 11 April 1974, a general election and further disagreement between the houses over the bill, a joint sitting passed the bill and it received the royal assent on 7 August 1974 as the Senate (Representation of Territories) Act 1973.

The High Court (Barwick CJ, McTiernan, Gibbs, Stephen, Mason, Jacobs and Murphy JJ) was unanimous in rejecting the first ground of the plaintiffs' attack. There had, the justices said, been a sufficient compliance with the requirements of s 57 of the Constitution. The principal argument raised by the plaintiffs, in support of their claim that the legislation had not complied with s 57, was based on the delay between the Senate's second rejection of the bill (14 November 1973) and the Governor-General's dissolution of the two houses (11 April 1974). The plaintiffs argued that the Governor-General could only exercise his power under s 57 if he did so without undue delay: unless the deadlock between the houses was exploited (within a limited period), the basis for a double dissolution would disappear.

In support of this argument, the plaintiffs said that the parliament's bicameral character would be impaired if the government and the House of Representatives were able 'to store up over a period a great number of measures which, following one double dissolution, might then be enacted at a joint sitting of both chambers', as Stephen J put it: 134 CLR at 251.

Stephen J pointed out that s 57 imposed no time limit on the Governor-General's double dissolution power, although other time limits were expressed in the section. There was no basis for reading into s 57 a requirement that the power be exercised immediately after a deadlock had occurred. If the power was only to be exercised without undue delay or within a reasonable time, how was that period to be measured? It would, Stephen J said, be 'quite inappropriate that [the court] should conjecture as to when delay by His Excellency exceeds the limits of reasonableness and becomes undue delay': 134 CLR at 252.

Mason J said, at 265–6:

> The notion on which the suggestion is based, that the disagreement comes to an end if the power is not exercised forthwith, is not only artificial but in many circumstances would be entirely at variance with the facts ...
>
> The plaintiffs' argument either requires the introduction into the first paragraph of the section of some words such as 'thereupon', 'forthwith' or 'immediately thereafter' which, if inserted, would need to be strictly applied, or alternatively leaves the power subject to some restriction which is vague and imprecise and is therefore unacceptable. The first alternative would, if it were accepted, destroy the possibility of further nego-tiation between the Houses after a second rejection by the Senate — any negotiation would produce a delay fatal to the exercise of the power.

The other members of the court, apart from Barwick CJ, agreed that s 57 did not require the Governor-General to use the power to dissolve both houses within any limited time. Barwick CJ said that the action of the Governor-General in dissolving both houses under s 57 must be (at 221):

> ... proximate to the time that the difference [between the Houses] emerged. It would be quite incongruous that at a considerable remove of time and after the business of the Parliament had been proceeding for many months, it should be dissolved to enable the electorate to pass upon a question which could appear to have been shelved: to vote in relation to a Bill or a difference between the houses which had in truth become stale.

In particular, Barwick CJ said, bills twice rejected by the Senate could not be 'stockpiled'; they could not be laid aside against the possibility of some remote double dissolution. However, he concluded that there had not been such a delay in the present case as to make the dispute over the Senate (Representation of Territories) Bill no longer current on 11 April 1974.

[5.3.34]   In the *Territorial Senators* case, Jacobs J, who held that s 57 did not impose any time limits on the Governor-General's double dissolution power, also addressed the question whether compliance with the s 57 procedures was justiciable. He accepted that this question had been resolved in the *PMA* case **[5.3.26C]**. But he said that, apart from that decision, he would have decided that there was no place for adjudication by the court in questions of procedure arising under s 57:

> The procedure prescribed leads to the expression by the people of their preference in the choice of their elected representatives, a preference expressed with the knowledge that a joint sitting of those representatives may need to take place, and no court in the absence of a clearly conferred power has the right to thwart or interfere with the people's expression of their choice. The people's expression cures any formal defects which may have previously existed. That is democratic government within the terms of the Constitution by which the people elected to be governed (134 CLR at 275–6).

Murphy J (who had not participated in the decision in the *PMA* case) also held that the issue of compliance with s 57 was not justiciable.

[5.3.35]   In the course of his judgment in the *Territorial Senators* case **[5.3.33]**, Stephen J suggested that a double dissolution could only be proclaimed for the purpose of resolving a deadlock over legislation (at 261):

> [T]he power may ... only be exercised in reliance upon the fact of [the] twice repeated rejection and not in purported reliance upon some quite different event. If it should

appear, perhaps from some recital in the dissolution proclamation, that His Excellency had purported to dissolve both chambers for some other reason, not itself involving satisfaction of the necessary condition precedent called for by s 57, the fact that there did also exist circumstances which would have provided a proper ground for dissolution will not make the dissolution one authorised by s 57.

On the other hand, Mason J noted at 265:

> [T]he power to dissolve can be exercised even in circumstances in which the Government and the House of Representatives lose their enthusiasm for the proposed law and desire a double dissolution for other reasons having no connexion with the Senate's rejection of the proposed law.

Given that Stephen J appears to have been contemplating an 'ulterior motive' obvious on the face of the Governor-General's proclamation, there may be little practical difference between him and Mason J.

[5.3.36] The observations of two members of the court in the *Territorial Senators* case **[5.3.33]** raise an important issue: To what extent is the Governor-General's power under s 57 an independent one which is to be exercised at his or her own discretion? Jacobs J said at 278:

> Neither the Queen nor the Governor-General acts personally. This is true of the powers of the Governor-General under s 57. He in all respects exercises his powers under the section on the advice of an Australian minister.

Murphy J said, in support of his view that compliance with the procedures of s 57 was not justiciable (at 293):

> The decision whether the procedures in s 57 for a double dissolution had been observed is a political decision, confided by the Constitution, not to the judiciary, but to the Governor-General on the advice of the Executive Council (Constitution s 62).

Similarly, Mason J spoke of the power to dissolve at a time and for reasons chosen by 'the Government and the House of Representatives': at 265.

[5.3.37] In the *Territorial Senators* case **[5.3.33]**, Stephen J said that a joint sitting (summoned by the Governor-General as the penultimate stage in the s 57 legislative procedure) 'may not consider a measure other than that for the consideration of which it has been convened'; that is, specified in the Governor-General's proclamation summoning the joint sitting: at 262.

However, in *Cormack v Cope* (1974) 131 CLR 432 **[5.5.3C]** Stephen J had said that the terms of the Governor-General's proclamation could not affect the business of the joint sitting 'one way or another' by omitting to specify or by specifying the bills to be considered: 131 CLR at 471. This view was adopted by Gibbs and Mason JJ in the *Territorial Senators* case: 134 CLR at 242, 267 (respectively).

At the other end of the spectrum, Barwick CJ had said in *Cormack v Cope* that the Governor-General had, when summoning the joint sitting of August 1974 'exceeded his function in specifying the business of the joint sitting': 131 CLR at 458.

It is sobering to reflect that, from this wide range of judicial opinions, a government's legal advisers may be obliged to draft practicable and legally sound instruments (proclaiming a double dissolution or summoning a joint sitting) should that government wish to use the s 57 procedures for the enactment of legislation.

[5.3.38] The Constitutional Commission described the s 57 procedure, as developed through political practice and interpreted by judicial decision, as 'unsatisfactory [and] open to abuse'. A government could 'obtain a double dissolution by the device of passing a bill known to be totally unacceptable to the non-government party or parties', as had happened in 1914 and 1951. Or a government could store up a twice rejected bill and use it as the basis for a double dissolution 'at a time considered opportune for its own political success': Constitutional Commission (1988) pp 256–7. The Commission recommended that s 57 be amended so as to allow a double dissolution only during the last year of the term of the House of Representatives, and to clarify that the Governor-General acts on the advice of Ministers. The Commission also proposed clarification of the concepts of failure to pass and passage with unacceptable amendments, and a requirement that, at the joint sitting, a specified minimum number of senators vote in favour of the bill: Constitutional Commission (1988) pp 247–8.

4   Restrictive procedures

[5.4.1] Restrictive procedures for the enactment of certain types of legislation were inserted in the first Constitution Acts of the Australian colonies. Section 60 of the Constitution Act 1855 (Vic) declared that it 'shall not be lawful to present to the Governor of the said Colony for Her Majesty's assent any Bill by which an alteration in the constitution of the ... Legislative Council and Legislative Assembly ... may be made unless on its second and third readings it shall have been approved by' absolute majorities in each chamber.

The clear purpose of this, and other similar provisions in the Constitution Acts of the colonies, was to protect specified aspects of the constitutional structure against interference through the normal legislative process. These provisions reflect a judgment on the part of those who enacted them that certain elements in the structure of government were so fundamental or so highly valued that they should be preserved against any future interference. The provisions were, of course, a conservative device intended to frustrate any radical (or indeed minor) reforms sponsored by a mere majority of the legislators. Yet, paradoxically, these provisions demanding special majorities or special legislative procedures were themselves enacted by the normal procedures, that is, by the simple majorities which the provisions purported to disenfranchise.

[5.4.2] While such special legislative procedures have long been prescribed in Australian constitutional instruments, it was not until 1931 (in *Trethowan's* case (1931) 44 CLR 394 **[5.4.17C]**) that the efficacy of such provisions was tested. In 1920, the Privy Council suggested in *McCawley v R* [1920] AC 691 **[5.3.14]** that such provisions could be effective, that a parliament which ignored such procedural restrictions might be held to have failed to legislate.

The basic point decided in *McCawley* was that the Queensland Parliament could enact legislation, the terms of which were inconsistent with the terms of the Constitution Act 1867 (Qld), without first expressly repealing the latter Act. Rather, the enactment of inconsistent legislation would impliedly repeal so much of the earlier Constitution Act as conflicted with it.

In the course of their opinion, their Lordships referred to s 9 of the Constitution Act 1867 which required a two-thirds majority in both houses for legislation altering the constitution of the Legislative Council and observed that 'the legislature in this isolated section carefully [selected] one special and individual case in which limitations are imposed upon the power of the Parliament of Queensland to express and carry out its purpose in the ordinary way, by a bare majority': [1920] AC at 712. And later they commented that '[t]he legislature of Queensland is the master of its own household, except in so far as its powers have in special cases been restricted': [1920] AC at 714.

These observations were not part of the decision in *McCawley's* case, and there was some reason for supposing that, if a government which controlled parliament (that is, with simple majorities in each house) put its mind to it, that government could legislate in disregard of such procedural restrictions as s 60 of the Constitution Act (Vic) or s 9 of the Constitution Act 1867 (Qld).

State parliaments

Background: parliamentary sovereignty

[5.4.3] The parliaments of the states are given, under their several Constitution Acts, wide legislative powers. To what extent do those powers authorise the state legislatures to alter their respective structures and procedures so as to restrict or tighten up the process of legislation? How much does the English doctrine of parliamentary sovereignty affect the answer to that question?

The sovereignty of parliament is said to be 'the most fundamental rule' of English constitutional law: de Smith (1981) p 73. The rule is expressed by de Smith in the following terms (p 73):

> The Queen in Parliament is competent, according to United Kingdom law, to make or unmake any law whatsoever or any matter whatsoever; and no United Kingdom court is competent to question the validity of an Act of Parliament.

So, it is said, no Act of Parliament (consisting of Crown, Lords and Commons) can be invalid since parliament has the right to make or unmake any law whatever; and, as a corollary, no person or body of persons has the right to override or derogate from an Act of Parliament. So stated, the rule of parliamentary sovereignty is a rule about the legal authority of English Parliament. It is a rule about its legislative supreme power, that no law enacted by parliament can be invalidated by reason of conflict with any other law, including laws of its own making.

[5.4.4] This rule of parliamentary sovereignty is a rule of common law; that is, it expresses the attitude adopted by the courts towards parliamentary legislation, an attitude of deference to the will of parliament. There is, however, no decision of any English court that is based squarely on the rule. The most explicit judicial support comes from such cases as *British Railways Board v Pickin* [1974] AC 765, where the House of Lords rejected an attack on legislation passed by the United Kingdom Parliament, an attack supported by the claim that parliament had not followed its internally established procedures when enacting the legislation. One can certainly find, scattered through the speeches in the case, unequivocal assertions that the courts could not inquire into the validity of an Act of Parliament, such as that of Lord Morris ([1974] AC at 789):

In the courts there may be argument as to the correct interpretation of the enactment: there must be none as to whether it should be on the statute books at all.

And, Lord Wilberforce (at 793):

The remedy for a parliamentary wrong, if one has been committed, must be sought from Parliament, and cannot be gained from the courts.

And, Lord Simon (at 798):

[Parliamentary democracy's] peculiar feature in constitutional law is the sovereignty of parliament. This involves that, contrary to what was sometimes asserted before the eighteenth century; and in contradiction to some other democratic systems, the courts in this country have no power to declare enacted law to be invalid.

While that case did not raise the issue of parliamentary sovereignty in the same way as *Trethowan's* case (1931) 44 CLR 394 **[5.4.17C]**, it clearly provides solid support for the rule. More support is provided by the text writers, for example Dicey (1959) Ch 1, 'The Nature of Parliamentary Sovereignty'.

[5.4.5]   If the rule of parliamentary sovereignty is a common law rule, why cannot parliament alter it by statute? Ivor Jennings argued that the rule means only that any law made by parliament is a valid law, and that this includes a law altering this basic rule: Jennings (1959) Ch IV. Parliament could, according to Jennings, alter this basic rule by enacting a statute that transfers legislative authority in respect of any number of matters to a different legislative body of its own creation. Such a law would mean that parliament, consisting of the Crown, Lords and Commons would no longer have the legislative power to enact statutes on those matters.

Jennings' basic argument may be put another way. The rule of parliamentary sovereignty makes parliament all-powerful, but parliament itself is a creature of law. Logically prior to a proposition about the power of parliament must be the rules that identify and define parliament. Therefore, it is possible for parliament to enact a statute altering the laws identifying and defining the legislative body; and it can alter this law in relation to all legislation or in relation to legislation with respect to particular subject matters.

[5.4.6]   On the other hand, it has been argued that the rule of parliamentary sovereignty cannot be altered by statute. For example, H W R Wade argued that the rule of parliamentary sovereignty is an ultimate rule of the legal system and so beyond the reach of statute: Wade (1955). It is itself the source of the authority of statute and, just as no statute can establish it, no statute can alter it. Ultimate rules of a legal system are accepted, not derived.

Implicit in Wade's argument is the proposition that the law identifying and defining parliament is also an ultimate rule which cannot be altered by statute. Wade argued that the legal system does not authorise parliament to fetter its future legislative action. On the arguments about parliamentary sovereignty see also Gray (1953); Marshall (1957); Dicey (1959) xxxiv–xcvi; Heuston (1964); de Smith (1981) pp 73–101; Allan (1985).

[5.4.7]   The legislatures of the Australian states, in contrast to the English Parliament and its successor, the United Kingdom Parliament, are established by statute and have their legislative powers defined by statute. There is thus no controversy as to the source of legislative authority, and absolute legislative power is denied. However, the English rule about parliamentary sovereignty is not without influence, for the interpretation of those provisions of the state Constitution Acts conferring legislative power has been influenced by principles that operate in England as part of the law of parliamentary sovereignty. For example, in *R v Burah* (1878) 3 App Cas 889, the Privy Council said of the Indian legislature (and the same was regarded as true of the Australian legislatures: *Powell v Appollo Candle Co* (1885) 10 App Cas 282) that, when acting within the limits which circumscribe its powers, it had plenary powers of legislation as large, and of the same nature, as those of the Imperial Parliament itself: 3 App Cas at 905.

The same point was made by the Privy Council in *McCawley v R* [1920] AC 619 **[5.3.14]**, where it was said that state Constitution Acts were uncontrolled, and that 'it would be almost impossible to use wider or less restrictive language' than the terms used to define the states' legislative powers: [1920] AC at 712.

[5.4.8] In *Building Construction Employees and Builders' Labourers Federation v Minister for Industrial Relations (NSW)* (1986) 7 NSWLR 372, two members of the New South Wales Court of Appeal suggested that there might be substantive limits to the sovereignty of the New South Wales Parliament. Street CJ declined to accept as authoritative an observation by the Privy Council in *Ibralebbe v R* [1964] AC 900 at 923 that the words 'peace order and government' referred to 'the widest lawmaking powers appropriate to a Sovereign': 7 NSWLR at 385. His Honour said that the equivalent phrase in s 5 of the Constitution Act 1902 (NSW), 'peace, welfare and good government', could be seen (at 387):

> … as the source of power in the courts to exercise an ultimate authority to protect our parliamentary democracy, not only against tyrannous excesses on the part of a legislature that may have fallen under extremist control, but also in a general sense as limiting the power of Parliament. … [L]aws inimical to, or which do not serve, the peace, welfare and good government of our parliamentary democracy … will be struck down by the courts as unconstitutional.

This view was supported by Priestley JA (7 NSWLR at 421–2), and disputed by Mahoney JA: 7 NSWLR at 413. Kirby P also disputed Street CJ's view as inconsistent with *British Railways Board v Pickin* [1974] AC 765 **[5.4.4]** and with:

> … years of unbroken constitutional law and tradition in Australia and, beforehand, in the United Kingdom [which] has repeatedly reinforced and ultimately respected the democratic will of the people as expressed in Parliament (7 NSWLR at 405).

[5.4.9] In *Union Steamship Co of Australia Pty Ltd v King* (1988) 166 CLR 1, the High Court took the opportunity, in a unanimous judgment, of refuting the views of Street CJ in the *BLF* case (1986) 7 NSWLR 372 **[5.4.8]**, which Mason CJ, Wilson, Brennan, Deane, Dawson, Toohey and Gaudron JJ described as 'somewhat surprising': 166 CLR at 9. The justices referred to several decisions of the Privy Council and said (at 10):

> These decisions and statements of high authority demonstrate that, within the limits of the grant, a power to make laws for the peace, order and good government of a territory is as ample and plenary as the power possessed by the Imperial Parliament itself. That is, the words 'for the peace, order and good government' are not words of limitation. They did not confer on the courts of a colony, just as they do not confer on the courts of a State, jurisdiction to strike down legislation on the ground that, in the opinion of a court, the legislation does not promote or secure the peace, order and good government of the colony. Just as the courts of the United Kingdom cannot invalidate laws made by the Parliament of the United Kingdom on the ground that they do not secure the welfare and the public interest, so the exercise of its legislative power by the Parliament of New South Wales is not susceptible to judicial review on that

score. Whether the exercise of that legislative power is subject to some restraints by reference to rights deeply rooted in our democratic system of government and the common law ... a view which Lord Reid firmly rejected in *British Railways Board v Pickin* [1974] AC 765 at 782, is another question which we need not explore.

The concluding reservation might have been thought to provide scope for further arguments attacking the concept of parliamentary sovereignty in Australia. However, the substance of the High Court's observations are discouraging to those arguments. Moreover, in *Kable v Director of Public Prosecutions (NSW)* (1996) 189 CLR 51, several members of the court scotched the possibility. Dawson J, with whom Brennan CJ and McHugh J agreed on this point, said (at 75–6):

> ... in *Union Steamship Co of Australia Pty Ltd v King* this Court reserved the question whether the exercise of that legislative power is subject to restraints to be found in fundamental principle. This case throws up the question reserved ... and it should now be answered by saying that no non-territorial restraints upon parliamentary supremacy arise from the nature of a power to make laws for peace, order (or welfare), and good government or from the notion that there are fundamental rights which must prevail against the will of the legislature. The doctrine of parliamentary supremacy is a doctrine as deeply rooted as any in the common law. It is of its essence that a court, once it has ascertained the true scope and effect of an Act of Parliament, should give unquestioned effect to it accordingly.

[5.4.10] This does not mean, of course, that state parliamentary supremacy may not be limited by federal constitutional limitations on power. So, in *Kable v Director of Public Prosecutions (NSW)* (1996) 189 CLR 51 **[6.4.48C]**, a majority of the High Court (Toohey, Gaudron, McHugh and Gummow JJ; Brennan CJ and Dawson J dissenting) recognised that the state parliaments could not abolish state courts, and could not vest powers in state courts that were repugnant to their character as courts in which Ch III jurisdiction could be vested pursuant to s 77 of the Constitution. See further **[6.4.47]–[6.4.51]**.

[5.4.11] If the powers conferred by imperial law on the Australian state parliaments are as plenary and of the same nature as those of the Imperial Parliament, are they disabled from reconstituting themselves or from fettering their own legislative action? Can they deprive themselves and their successors of the power to legislate on any particular topic or to repeal any statute they may enact? Can they transfer or surrender some or all of their power to new legislative bodies of their own creation? The answers to these questions are controlled by considering the various constituent statutes, not by considering the English rules of parliamentary sovereignty. However, those constituent statutes may be interpreted in light of principles that form part of the rules of parliamentary sovereignty.

Until 1986, the answers to these questions were considered to depend largely on s 5 of the Colonial Laws Validity Act 1865 (UK) **[5.3.5]**. However, that provision has now been replaced by s 6 of the Australia Act 1986 (see **[5.4.23E]**), which probably has substantially the same effect.

The legislation

[5.4.12E]   **Constitution Act 1902 (NSW)**

7A(1) The Legislative Council shall not be abolished nor, subject to the provisions of subsection six of this section, shall its constitution or powers be altered except in the manner provided in this section.

(2) A Bill for any purpose within subsection (1) shall not be presented to the Governor for His Majesty's assent until the Bill has been approved by the electors in accordance with this section.

(3) On a day not sooner than two months after the passage of the Bill through both Houses of the Legislature the Bill shall be submitted to the electors qualified to vote for the election of Members of the Legislative Assembly.

Such day shall be appointed by the Legislature.

(4) When the Bill is submitted to the electors the vote shall be taken in such manner as the Legislature prescribes.

(5) If a majority of the electors voting approve the Bill, it shall be presented to the Governor for His Majesty's assent.

(6) The provisions of this section shall extend to any Bill for the repeal or amendment of this section, but shall not apply to any Bill for

(a) the repeal; or

(b) the amendment from time to time; or

(c) the re-enactment from time to time with or without modifications

of any of the following sections of this Act, namely, sections thirteen, fourteen, fifteen, 17B, 17C, eighteen, nineteen, twenty, twenty-one, twenty-two and 38A, or of any provision for the time being in force so far as it relates to the subject-matter dealt with in any of those sections.

(7) *[repealed]*

(8) In this section a reference to the Legislative Council shall be construed as a reference to the Legislative Council as reconstituted in accordance with this Act.

~~~

Notes

[5.4.13] Section 7A was enacted by the New South Wales Parliament in 1929 at a time when both houses were controlled by the conservative political parties. The Council had survived, through the defection of Labor appointees, an attack by J T Lang's Labor Government in 1925. However, the Labor Party was determined to follow Queensland's example and abolish the New South Wales Legislative Council. The politicians who saw the Council as essential to their interests came up with this 'entrenching' provision as a protection against the probable return of the Labor Party to a majority in the Assembly, from which position the Labor Party could use the Governor's appointing power to obtain a majority in the Council. In 1930, following its return to power, the Lang Labor Government again moved to abolish the Council, and the protection extended by s 7A was tested: see *Attorney-General (NSW) v Trethowan* (1931) 44 CLR 394 **[5.4.17C]**.

[5.4.14] The pattern set by s 7A has been followed in several other constitutional provisions which demand a referendum of electors as part of the legislative process:

■ Constitution Act 1902 (NSW) s 7B: any bill to extend the life of the Assembly beyond four years; and any bill to amend or repeal ss 11B (compulsory voting), 26, 27, 28 (distribution of Assembly electorates) or 29 and the Seventh Schedule (conduct of Assembly elections).

- Constitution (Fixed Term Parliaments) Special Provisions Act 1991 (NSW) s 9: any bill to repeal or amend the Act (which prescribes a fixed term for the parliament which first met on 2 July 1991).

- Constitution Act Amendment Act 1934 (Qld) s 3: any bill to re-establish the Council (s 4); any bill to extend the life of the Assembly beyond three years.

- Constitution Act 1934 (SA) s 10a: any bill to abolish the Assembly or the Council, to alter the powers of the Council, or to affect the established procedures for altering the Constitution Act or resolving deadlocks (s 88); any bill which would alter the system for distributing seats in the Legislative Assembly.

- Constitution Act 1975 (Vic) s 18(1B): any bill to repeal, alter or vary the provisions listed in paragraphs (a) to (p).

- Constitution Act 1889 (WA) s 73: any bill which affects the office of Governor, abolishes the Legislative Council or Assembly, provides for other than direct election to the Council or Assembly, or reduces the size of the Council or Assembly.

Each of the above provisions also demands that any bill to amend or repeal that provision shall be approved by the electors at a referendum before being submitted to the Governor for royal assent.

[5.4.15]   Section 18(2) of the Constitution Act 1975 (Vic) prohibits the presentation to the Governor of certain bills (including a bill to amend s 18(2)) unless those bills have been passed by a 'special majority' — defined in s 18(1A) to mean '3/5ths of the whole number of the members of the Assembly and of the Council respectively'.

A less restrictive legislative procedure is prescribed by s 18(2AA) of the Constitution Act 1975 (Vic), which prohibits the presentation to the Governor of certain bills unless those bills have been passed by an absolute majority in each house. (An absolute majority is a majority of those eligible to vote — whether voting or not.) Section 18(2) also demands that any bill to amend or repeal it be passed by the same special procedure.

Section 18(2A) requires absolute majorities in the Assembly and the Council for a bill by which s 85 of the Constitution Act (dealing with the jurisdiction of the Supreme Court) may be repealed, altered or varied.

A similar procedure (approval by absolute majorities) is prescribed by s 8 of the Constitution Act 1934 (SA) for bills altering the constitution of the Council or the Assembly. Section 10a(2)(d) demands that a bill to amend or repeal s 8 be passed through the referendum procedure.

[5.4.16]   Section 41A of the Constitution Act 1934 (Tas) is another example of a restrictive procedure. It provides:

> The Assembly may not pass any Bill to amend s 23 unless no less than two-thirds of its Members vote for passing the Bill or for a motion on the passing of which the Bill will be deemed to have passed.

Section 23 fixes the maximum life of the Assembly at four years. There is no special procedure prescribed for the amendment or repeal of s 41A. Accordingly, the restriction imposed by s 41A is of doubtful efficacy.

[5.4.17C]   **Attorney-General (NSW) v Trethowan**

(1931) 44 CLR 394

In 1930, the Labor Government of New South Wales announced that it intended to press for the passage of legislation abolishing the Legislative Council. The Legislative Council then passed two government bills: one to repeal s 7A of the Constitution Act 1902; the other to abolish the Council. It seems that the Council did this because it recognised that the government could have sufficient new councillors appointed to ensure passage of the bills and it believed that the bills would be the subject of a referendum, as required by s 7A. The bills were then passed by the Legislative Assembly and the government announced that it would not submit them to a referendum but would advise the Governor to give the bills the royal assent.

Immediately, two members of the Council began a suit in the Supreme Court against the President of the Legislative Council and the Ministers in the government seeking a declaration that compliance with the provisions of s 7A was essential and injunctions to restrain the presentation to the Governor of the two bills until they had been approved by the electors in accordance with s 7A.

Long Innes J at first instance granted an interim injunction and referred the suit to the Full Court of the Supreme Court. The Full Court issued the declaration and the injunctions sought by the plaintiffs. The defendants appealed to the High Court of Australia.

Rich J referred to an argument that the New South Wales Parliament retained full power to amend its Constitution Act:

Rich J: [417] The argument leaves out of account an occurrence of great constitutional importance to the dominions. It ignores the passing of the Colonial Laws Validity Act 1865. Section 5 of that Act confers upon representative legislatures in the dominions full power to make laws respecting the constitution, powers and procedure of such legislatures, provided that such laws shall have been passed in such manner and form as may from time to time be required by any Act of Parliament, letters patent, Order-in-council, or colonial law for the time being in force therein. This is a parallel power, but it is not alternative. It is the final and authoritative expression of every colonial representative legislature's power to make laws respecting its own constitution, powers and procedure ...

[418] Two methods of controlling the operations of the legislature appear to be allowed by the express terms of [s 5 of the Colonial Laws Validity Act]. The constitution of the legislative body may be altered; that is to say, the power of legislation may be reposed in an authority differently constituted. Again, laws may be passed imposing legal requirements as to manner and form in which constitutional amendments must be passed. In my opinion the efficacy of s 7A depends upon the answer to the questions — does it fall within the proviso as to a requirement of manner and form? and does it introduce into the legislative body a new element? If the true answer to either of these questions is yes, then the Legislative Council cannot be abolished without a referendum unless and until s 7A is repealed, and s 7A cannot be repealed except by a Bill approved at a referendum before it is presented for the royal assent ... The first question is whether sub-s 6, which is a colonial law for the time being in force, requires a manner and form in which a law repealing s 7A must be passed. In my opinion it does ...

[419] In my opinion the proviso to s 5 relates to the entire process of turning a proposed law into a legislative enactment, and was intended to enjoin fulfilment of every condition and compliance with every requirement which existing legislation imposed upon the process of law-making. This view is enough to dispose of the case; but if what is done under sub-s 6 did not fall under the proviso, the question would still remain whether for the purpose of abolishing the Legislative Council and the purpose of repealing s 7A a new element is not introduced into the legislative authority. It was conceded that under s 5 it was competent to the legislature to establish a third chamber whose assent would be required to complete any legislative act. It could not be denied that, if a third chamber could be introduced, a body of

persons of another character might also be created a constituent element of the legislature ... If the legislative body consists of different elements for the purpose of legislation upon different [420] subjects, the natural method of applying the definition would be to consider what was the subject upon which the particular exercise of power was proposed, and to treat s 5 as conferring upon the body constituted to deal with that subject authority to pass the law although it related to the powers of the legislature. An examination of s 7A shows that a legislative body has been created for the purpose of passing or co-operating in passing a particular law. There is no reason why this authority need extend to all laws ...

McCawley's case [1920] AC 691; 28 CLR 106 reaffirms the full power of such a legislature as that of New South Wales, which passed s 7A, to regulate its own constitution. Such a power naturally extends to the enactment of safeguards aimed at restraining improvident or hasty action. There is no reason why a parliament representing the people should be powerless to determine whether the constitutional salvation of the State is to be reached by cautious and well considered steps rather than by rash and ill considered measures ...

[421] I am, therefore, of opinion that neither of the Bills in question may be lawfully presented to the Governor for the royal assent, and be validly assented to, until it is approved by a majority of the electors.

Dixon J: [425] [T]he case depends upon the question whether the Bill for the repeal of s 7A may be presented for the royal assent and become a valid law without compliance with the condition which that section itself prescribes requiring that a Bill for its repeal shall first be approved by a majority of the electors. This question must be answered upon a consideration of the true meaning and effect of the written instrument from which the Parliament of New South Wales derives its legislative power. It is not to be determined by the direct application of the doctrine of parliamentary sovereignty ... The incapacity of the British legislature to limit its own power otherwise than by transferring a portion or abdicating the whole of its sovereignty has been accounted for by [426] the history of the High Court of Parliament, and has been explained as a necessary consequence of a true conception of sovereignty. But in any case it depends upon considerations which have no application to the legislature of New South Wales, which is not a sovereign body and has a purely statutory origin. Because of the supremacy of the Imperial Parliament over the law, the courts merely apply its legislative enactments and do not examine their validity, but because the law over which the Imperial Parliament is supreme determines the powers of a legislature in a dominion, the courts must decide upon the validity as well as the application of the statutes of that legislature. It must not be supposed, however, that all difficulties would vanish if the full doctrine of parliamentary supremacy could be invoked. An Act of the British Parliament which contained a provision that no Bill repealing any part of the Act including the part so restraining its own repeal should be presented for the royal assent unless the Bill were first approved by the electors, would have the force of law until the Sovereign actually did assent to a Bill for its repeal. In strictness it would be an unlawful proceeding to present such a Bill for the royal assent before it had been approved by the electors. If, before the Bill received the assent of the Crown, it was found possible, as appears to have been done in this appeal, to raise for judicial decision the question whether it was lawful to present the Bill for that assent, the courts would be bound to pronounce it unlawful to do so. Moreover, if it happened that, notwithstanding the statutory inhibition, the Bill did receive the royal assent although it was not submitted to the electors, the courts might be called upon to consider whether the supreme legislative power in respect of the matter had in truth been exercised in the manner required for its authentic expression and by the elements in which it had come to reside. But the answer to this question, whether evident or obscure, would be deduced from the principle of parliamentary supremacy over the law. This principle, from its very nature, cannot determine the character or the operation of the constituent powers of the legislature of New South Wales which are the result of statute ... [427] The difficulty of the supreme legislature lessening its own powers does not arise from the flexibility of the constitution. On the contrary, it may be said that is precisely the point at which the flexibility of the British constitution ceases to be absolute. Because it rests upon the supremacy over the law, some changes which detract from that supremacy cannot be made effectively. The necessary limitations upon the flexibility of the constitution of New South Wales result from a consideration of exactly an opposite character. They arise directly or indirectly from the sovereignty of the Imperial Parliament. But in virtue of its sovereignty it was open to the Imperial Parliament itself to give, or to empower the legislature of New South Wales to give to the constitution of that State as much or as little rigidity as might be proper.

Dixon J referred to the original constitution statute, 18 and 19 Vict c 54, s 4 of which authorised the New South Wales Parliament to amend or repeal its original Constitution Act 1855, and to the Constitution Act 1902 which involved an exercise of that power. His Honour referred to the Colonial Laws Validity Act 1865, and continued:

[429] [I]t was a declared object of that Act to remove doubts respecting the powers of colonial legislatures and these questions depend upon considerations out of which such doubts arose. Upon the subjects with which it deals, the statement of the law contained in the Colonial Laws Validity Act was meant to be definitive, and a subject with which it deals is the constituent power of such legislatures and the manner in which that power shall be exercised … This provision both confers power and describes the conditions to be observed in its exercise. It authorises a representative legislature to make laws respecting its own constitution, its own powers and its own procedure … it is plenary save in so far as it may be qualified by a law which falls within the description of the proviso. The power to make laws respecting its own constitution enables the legislature to deal with its own nature and composition. The power to make laws respecting its own procedure enables it to prescribe rules which have the force of law [430] for its own conduct. Laws which relate to its own constitution and procedure must govern the legislature in the exercise of its powers including the exercise of its powers to repeal those very laws. The power to make laws respecting its own powers would naturally be understood to mean that it might deal with its own legislative authority. Under such a power a legislature, whose authority was limited in respect of subject matter or restrained by constitutional checks or safeguards, might enlarge the limits or diminish or remove the restraints. Conversely, the power might be expected to enable a legislature to impose constitutional restraints upon its own authority or to limit its power in respect of subject matter. But such restraints and limitations, if they are to be real and effective and achieve their end, must bind the legislature. If the legislature, nevertheless, continues to retain unaffected and unimpaired by its own laws the power given by this provision to legislate respecting its own power, it is evident that it may always repeal the limitations and restraints which those laws purport to impose. Moreover, this means, as *McCawley's* case [1920] AC 691, 28 CLR 106 establishes, that no formal repeal is necessary to resume the power and the legislature remains competent to make laws inconsistent with the restraints or limitations which its former statutes have sought to create. If and in so far, therefore, as s 5 confers a superior and indestructible power to make laws with respect to the legislature's own powers, it cannot enable it to impose upon those powers any effective restraints or restrictions …

Considered apart from the proviso, the language in which this provision is expressed could not reasonably be understood to authorise any regulation, control or impairment of the power it describes … [431] But the proviso recognises that the exercise of the power may to some extent be qualified or controlled by law … Such a law … cannot do more than prescribe the mode in which laws respecting these matters must be made. To be valid, a law respecting the powers of the legislature must 'have been passed in such manner and form as may from time to time be required by any … colonial law' (sc, a law of that legislature) 'for the time being in force'. Its validity cannot otherwise be affected by a prior law of that legislature. In other words no degree of rigidity greater than this can be given by the legislature to the constitution.

The law proposed by the Bill to repeal s 7A of the Constitution Act 1902 to 1929 answers the description 'a law respecting the powers of the legislature' just as the provisions of s 7A itself constitute a law with respect to those powers. But the proposal cannot be put into effect save by a law which 'shall have been passed in such manner and form as may be required by any' prior law of the New South Wales legislature. Unless it be void, s 7A is undeniably a prior law of the New South Wales legislature. It is no less a law of that legislature because it requires the approval of the electors as a condition of its repeal. But it is not void unless this requirement is repugnant to s 5 of the Colonial Laws Validity Act. No requirement is repugnant to that section if it is within the contemplation of its proviso, which concedes the efficacy of enactments requiring a manner or form in which laws shall be passed. If, therefore, a provision that a particular law respecting the powers of the legislature may not be made unless it is approved by the electors, requires a manner or form in which such a law [432] shall be passed, then s 7A is a valid law and cannot be repealed without the approval of the electorate.

I have arrived at the conclusion that such a provision is properly described as requiring a manner in which the law shall be passed and falls within the category allowed by the proviso ...

[433] For these reasons I think s 7A is valid and effective, and the appeal should be dismissed.

Starke J delivered a concurring judgment. Gavan Duffy CJ and McTiernan J dissented on the ground that s 7A(6) did not prescribe a 'manner and form' for legislating, but purported to 'destroy or permanently diminish the authority' of the New South Wales Parliament to legislate on the subject of its own constitution: 44 CLR at 443.

~~~

Notes

[5.4.18] On appeal, the Privy Council affirmed the decision of the High Court: *Attorney-General (NSW) v Trethowan* (1931) 47 CLR 97; [1932] AC 526. Its decision was that s 7A of the Constitution Act was within the power conferred by s 5 of the Colonial Laws Validity Act and that, because of the proviso to s 5, it could not be repealed except in the manner provided in subs (6). Of the decision, RTE Latham wrote: '*Trethowan's* case ... is an instance where the diffidence of the Privy Council amounted to timidity. The board avoided a fundamental issue, squarely raised, by a decision "on the words of the statute"': Latham (1949) p 525.

To what extent did the High Court avoid that criticism and come to grips with the fundamental issue?

[5.4.19] If we assume that subs (6) had not been included in s 7A, the bicameral parliament would have retained the power to abolish the Legislative Council. It could have repealed s 7A through its normal legislative process and, once s 7A was repealed, it could then have abolished the Council through its normal legislative process.

However, while s 7A remained on the statute books, the New South Wales Parliament could not have abolished the Council through its normal legislative process. While s 7A survived, it laid down a binding manner and form that conditioned the validity of legislation abolishing the Council, and s 7A would survive until repealed. It might, of course, be repealed by implication as well as expressly but the enactment or *purported* enactment by the bicameral parliament of a bill to abolish the Council would not have repealed, impliedly or expressly, the assumed s 7A.

[5.4.20] A later Act impliedly repeals an earlier Act when, and to the extent that, the provisions or terms of the later Act are inconsistent with those of the earlier Act (see, for example, *Kartinyeri v Commonwealth* (1998) 195 CLR 337). But an earlier Act is not repealed because the procedure adopted for the enactment of a later Act is inconsistent with that prescribed by the terms of the earlier Act. There is no inconsistency of provisions or terms between an Act (or so-called Act) enacted, or purportedly enacted, by the bicameral parliament, and an earlier Act which prescribes a different manner and form for the later Act's enactment, a manner which has not been observed.

[5.4.21] Assuming still that s 7A did not contain subs (6), would a single Act of the bicameral parliament which contained provisions repealing s 7A and abolishing the Legislative Council be a valid Act abolishing the Council, if it had not been submitted to a referendum? At the time the Act received the royal assent, can its provisions abolishing the Legislative Council be said to have been passed in the manner and form required by law? At the time it was presented for the royal assent, did not the law require that it be first approved at a referendum?

[5.4.22] Would the decision in *Trethowan's* case have been reached without the proviso to s 5 of the Colonial Laws Validity Act? Could it have been reached in the absence of the whole of s 5? Did s 5 add anything to the power given to the New South Wales Parliament by the Constitution Act 1855 (NSW) and the Constitution Act 1902 (NSW)? Could not the New South Wales Parliament find sufficient power to enact s 7A in the following provisions: New South Wales Constitution Act 1855 (UK) ss 4, 9; Constitution Act 1902 (NSW) s 5? See *Clayton v Heffron* (1960) 105 CLR 214 at 250–2 **[5.3.16C]**.

[5.4.23E] Australia Act 1986

The Australia Act 1986 contains the following provisions:

3(1) The Act of the Parliament of the United Kingdom known as the Colonial Laws Validity Act 1865 shall not apply to any law made after the commencement of this Act by the Parliament of a State.

...

6   Notwithstanding sections 2 and 3(2) above, a law made after the commencement of this Act by the Parliament of a State respecting the constitution, powers or procedure of the Parliament of the State shall be of no force or effect unless it is made in such manner and form as may from time to time be required by a law made by that Parliament, whether made before or after the commencement of this Act.

~~~

The significance of the replacement of s 5 of the Colonial Laws Validity Act with s 6 of the Australia Act was explored by the High Court in *Attorney-General (WA) v Marquet* (2003) 202 ALR 233 **[5.4.44C]**; see also Lee (1988) pp 309–11 and Goldsworthy (1987) pp 410–12.

[5.4.24] *Trethowan's* case could have been resolved without any discussion of sovereignty, legislative powers and procedures and manner and form. The plaintiffs sought an injunction to enforce a clear prohibition set down in s 7A of the Constitution Act; namely, s 7A(2) provided that a bill to abolish the Council 'shall not be presented to the Governor' until approved at a referendum. That prohibition was unequivocal and the judges needed to decide one thing only: would they enforce it?

However, the case was argued and decided at all levels as if that was not the issue; rather, the issue was assumed to be: Can legislation passed in defiance of s 7A(2) and s 7A(6) have the effect of abolishing the Council and repealing s 7A? The assumption was made (and, indeed, the High Court insisted on this before giving leave to appeal) that the bills in question had been approved by the Assembly, the Council *and* the Governor, and the question asked was: 'are the resulting (hypothetical) Acts valid?'.

Taylor v Attorney-General (Qld) (1917) 23 CLR 457 **[5.3.13]** and *Clayton v Heffron* (1960) 105 CLR 214 **[5.3.16C]** were argued on similar hypothetical bases.

[5.4.25] The majority clearly rejected McTiernan J's argument that s 7A was, in substance, a law depriving the New South Wales Parliament of legislative power. Would the majority's decision have been different if s 7A had required that bills to repeal it or abolish the Legislative Council be approved by 60 per cent of the electors? 80 per cent? 100 per cent? Would such a provision be characterised as an abdication of legislative power and so invalid?

[5.4.26] Writing of the successor to s 5 of the Colonial Laws Validity Act, s 6 of the Australia Act, Goldsworthy has said that 'a distinction must be drawn between manner and form requirements and attempts to restrict Parliament's substantive powers', and he referred to King CJ's discussion of this problem in *West Lakes Ltd v South Australia* (1980) 25 SASR 389 **[5.4.37C]** at 397: Goldsworthy (1987) p 419. Goldsworthy applied this distinction to a variety of possible restrictive procedures, including veto rights given to outside bodies; the requirement that legislation adopt a specified form of words; special majority requirements; and referendum requirements: see Goldsworthy (1987) pp 417–23.

[5.4.27] In *South Eastern Drainage Board v Savings Bank of South Australia* (1939) 62 CLR 603, the High Court rejected a challenge to s 14 of the South Eastern Drainage Amendment Act 1900 (SA), which was inconsistent with certain provisions of the Real Property Act 1886 (SA). Section 6 of the 1886 Act declared that 'no law, so far as inconsistent with this Act, shall apply to land subject to the provisions of this Act, nor shall any future law, so far as inconsistent with this Act, so apply unless it shall be expressly enacted that it shall so apply notwithstanding the provisions of the Real Property Act 1886'. The 1900 Act did not contain an express declaration of the type specified in s 6 of the 1886 Act.

Dixon J rejected an argument that s 5 of the Colonial Laws Validity Act 1865 rendered s 14 of the 1900 Act invalid because of its failure to contain the declaration specified in s 6 of the 1886 Act (at 625):

> Section 6 of the Real Property Act is, in my opinion, not a law respecting the constitution, powers or procedure of the South Australian legislature ... The section is a declaration as to what meaning and operation are to be given to future enactments, not a definition or restriction of the powers of the legislature.

Evatt J said that the legislature of South Australia had 'plenary power to couch its enactments in such literary form as it may choose' and could not 'be effectively commanded by a prior legislature to express its intention in a particular way': 62 CLR at 633. He said that *Trethowan's* case **[5.4.17C]** had nothing to do with the matter. Although s 6 of the 1886 Act was not a mere interpretation section and purported to lay down a rigid rule binding upon all future parliaments, its command was 'quite ineffective and inoperative': 62 CLR at 633–4.

[5.4.28] The reason offered by Dixon J for concluding that s 5 of the Colonial Laws Validity Act was irrelevant to the issues in the *South Eastern Drainage Board* case is difficult to reconcile with the terms of s 5. The question was not, as Dixon J proposed, whether s 6 of the earlier Act, the Real Property Act 1886, was a law respecting the constitution, powers and procedure of the legislature. Rather, the question was whether the later Act, s 14 of the South Eastern Drainage Amendment

Act 1900 answered that description; and, if so, whether s 6 of the earlier Act prescribed a manner and form for enacting the later Act.

Even if s 5 of the Colonial Laws Validity Act was irrelevant to the problem in the *South Eastern Drainage* case, it might be argued that compliance with the form laid down by s 6 of the Real Property Act 1886 was essential in order to produce legislation on the topic specified in that section. It might be said that, unless s 14 of the South Eastern Drainage Amendment Act 1900 contained the formula specified by the Act of 1886, 'the supreme legislative power in respect to the matter had [not] been exercised in the manner required for its authentic expression': see Dixon J in *Attorney-General (NSW) v Trethowan* (1931) 44 CLR 394 at 426 **[5.4.17C]**.

[5.4.29C]　　　**Bribery Commissioner v Ranasinghe**
[1965] AC 172

The Ceylon (Constitution) Order-in-Council 1946 contained the following clauses:

18　Save as otherwise provided in sub-s (4) of s 29, any question proposed for decision by either chamber shall be determined by a majority of votes of the Senators or Members, as the case may be, present and voting ...

29　(1)　Subject to the provisions of this Order, Parliament shall have power to make laws for the peace, order and good government of the Island ...

　　(4)　In the exercise of its powers under this section, Parliament may amend or repeal any of the provisions of this Order or any other Order of Her Majesty in Council in its application to the Island:

Provided that no Bill for the amendment or repeal of any of the provisions of this Order shall be presented for the Royal Assent unless it has endorsed on it a certificate under the hand of the Speaker that the number of votes cast in favour thereof in the House of Representatives amount to not less than two-thirds of the whole number of Members of the House (including those not present).

Every certificate of the Speaker under this subsection shall be conclusive for all purposes and shall not be questioned in any court of law.

Section 55 of the Order-in-Council provided that the appointment, transfer and disciplinary control of judicial officers was to be vested in a judicial service commission.

The Bribery Amendment Act 1958 (Ceylon) created bribery tribunals with jurisdiction to hear, try and determine prosecutions for bribery. The tribunal was to consist of three members chosen from a panel appointed by the Governor-General on the advice of the Minister for Justice. The members of the tribunals were clearly judicial officers within s 55 of the Order-in-Council, but there was nothing in the Bribery Amendment Act to show that it had been passed by the necessary two-thirds majority. Certainly the bill for the Act did not carry the Speaker's certificate required by s 29(4) of the Order-in-Council when presented for royal assent.

The respondent was prosecuted for bribery before a bribery tribunal. He was convicted but, on appeal to the Supreme Court of Ceylon, the conviction was declared null and inoperative because the members of the tribunal had not been lawfully appointed. The prosecutor appealed to the Privy Council, whose opinion was delivered by Lord Pearce.

Lord Pearce: [196] When a sovereign parliament has purported to enact a Bill and it has received the royal assent, is it a valid Act in the course of whose passing there was a procedural defect, or is it an invalid Act which parliament had no power to pass in that manner?

The strongest argument in favour of the appellant's contention is the fact that s 29(3) expressly makes void any Act passed in respect of the matters entrenched on and prohibited by s 29(2), whereas s 29(4) makes no such provision, but merely couches the prohibition in procedural terms.

The appellant's argument placed much reliance on the opinion of this Board in *McCawley v R* [1920] AC 691 ... Just as in that case the legislature of the colony of Queensland was held to have power by a mere majority vote to pass an Act that was inconsistent with the provisions of the existing Constitution of the colony as to the tenure of judicial office, so, it was said, the legislature of Ceylon had no less a power to depart from the requirements of a section such as s 55 of the Order-in-Council, notwithstanding the wording of s 18 and s 29(4). Their Lordships are satisfied that the attempted analogy between the two cases is delusive and that *McCawley's* case, so far as it is material, is in fact opposed to the appellant's reasoning. In view of the importance of the matter it is desirable to deal with this argument in some detail.

The Privy Council noted that *McCawley's* case concerned the Constitution Act 1867 (Qld), s 2 of which gave the legislature 'power to make laws for the peace, welfare and good government of the colony in all cases whatsoever', and continued:

[197] The only express restriction on this comprehensive power was contained in a later section, s 9, which required a two-thirds majority of the Council and of the Assembly as a condition precedent to the validity of legislation altering the constitution of the Council. As to this Lord Birkenhead LC, delivering the board's opinion, remarked [1920] AC 691 at 712: 'We observe, therefore, the legislature in this isolated instance carefully selecting one special and individual case in which limitations are imposed upon the power of the Parliament of Queensland to express and to carry out its purpose in the ordinary way, by a bare majority'. This observation was coupled with the summary statement at 714: 'The legislature of Queensland is the master of its own household, except in so far as its powers have in special cases been restricted. No such restriction has been established, and none in fact exists, in such a case as is raised in the issues now under appeal'.

These passages show clearly that the board in *McCawley's* case [1920] AC 691 took the view, which commends itself to the Board in the present case, that a legislature has no power to ignore the conditions of law-making that are imposed by the instrument which itself regulates its power to make law. This restriction exists independently of the question whether the legislature is sovereign, as is the legislature of Ceylon, or whether the Constitution is 'uncontrolled', as the board held the Constitution of [198] Queensland to be. Such a Constitution can, indeed, be altered or amended by the legislature, if the regulating instrument so provides and if the terms of those provisions are complied with: and the alteration or amendment may include the change or abolition of those very provisions. But the proposition which is not acceptable is that a legislature, once established, has some inherent power derived from the mere fact of its establishment to make a valid law by the resolution of a bare majority which its own constituent instrument has said shall not be a valid law unless made by a different type of majority or by a different legislative process. And this is the proposition which is in reality involved in the argument.

It is possible now to state summarily what is the essential difference between the *McCawley* case [1920] AC 691 and this case. There the legislature, having full power to make laws by a majority, except upon one subject that was not in question, passed a law which conflicted with one of the existing terms of its Constitution Act. It was held that this was valid legislation, since it must be treated as pro tanto an alteration of the Constitution, which was neither fundamental in the sense of being beyond change nor so constructed as to require any special legislative process to pass upon the topic dealt with. In the present case, on the other hand, the legislature has purported to pass a law which, being in conflict with s 55 of the Order-in-Council, must be treated, if it is to be valid, as an implied alteration of the constitutional provisions about the appointment of judicial officers. Since such alterations, even if express, can only be made by laws which comply with the special legislative procedure laid down in s 29(4), the Ceylon legislature has not got the general power to legislate so as to amend its Constitution by ordinary majority resolutions, such as the Queensland legislature was found to have under s 2 of its Constitution Act, but is rather in the position, for affecting such amendments, that that legislature was held to be in by virtue of its s 9, namely, compelled to operate a special procedure in order to achieve the desired result.

Lord Pearce referred to *Trethowan's* case **[5.4.17C]**, declaring that 'the effect of s 5 of the Colonial Laws Validity Act, which is framed in a manner somewhat similar to s 29(4) of the Ceylon Constitution was that where a legislative power is given subject to certain manner and form, that power does not exist unless and until the manner and form is complied with'. He continued:

[199] The legislative power of the Ceylon Parliament is derived from s 18 and s 29 of its Constitution. Section 18 expressly says 'save as otherwise ordered in sub-s (4) of s 29'. Section 29(1) is expressed to be 'subject to the provisions of this Order'. And any power under s 29(4) is expressly subject to its proviso. Therefore in the case of [200] amendment and repeal of the Constitution the Speaker's certificate is a necessary part of the legislative process and any Bill which does not comply with the condition precedent of the proviso, is and remains, even though it receives the royal assent, invalid and ultra vires.

No question of sovereignty arises. A parliament does not cease to be sovereign whenever its component members fail to produce among themselves a requisite majority, eg, when in the case of ordinary legislation the voting is evenly divided or when in the case of legislation to amend the Constitution there is only a bare majority if the Constitution requires something more. The minority are entitled under the Constitution of Ceylon to have no amendment of it which is not passed by a two-thirds majority. The limitation thus imposed on some lesser majority of members does not limit the sovereign powers of parliament itself which can always, whenever it chooses, pass the amendment with the requisite majority.

~~~

Notes

[5.4.30] In *Harris v Minister of the Interior* [1952] (2) SA 428, the Appellate Division of the South African Supreme Court held that the Separate Representation of Voters Act 1951 (Sth Africa), which provided for separate representation in parliament for Europeans and non-Europeans, was not an authentic Act of Parliament because it had been passed through the normal legislative processes, whereas s 152 of the South Africa Act 1909 (UK) required a two-thirds majority at a joint sitting of both houses. The South Africa Act 1909 had no special sanctity because of its imperial status; the Statute of Westminster 1931 (UK) authorised the South African Parliament to alter or repeal the South Africa Act as if it were an Act of the local legislature. In the course of his judgment, Centlivres CJ said that in South Africa 'legal sovereignty is or may be divided between Parliament as ordinarily constituted and Parliament as constituted under ... the proviso to s 152': [1952] (2) SA at 464. Later he said (at 468):

The Union is an autonomous State in no way subordinate to any other country in the world. To say that the Union is not a sovereign State, simply because its Parliament functioning bicamerally has not the power to amend certain sections of the South Africa Act, is to state a manifest absurdity. Those sections can be amended by Parliament sitting unicamerally. The Union is, therefore, through its legislature able to pass any laws it pleases.

[5.4.31] The proposition that a parliament could be compelled to follow special legislative procedures, even where the Colonial Laws Validity Act was not applicable, was suggested by Dixon J in *Attorney-General (NSW) v Trethowan* (1931) 44 CLR 394 **[5.4.17C]** at 426. The proposition, as expressed by Dixon J, depends on the argument that, if the courts are expected to concede supreme authority to an Act of Parliament, then the courts must have some method of recognising what is, and what is not, an Act of Parliament. There must be rules of recognition which the courts apply to determine whether an alleged Act of

Parliament is, in truth, such an Act. These rules of recognition are susceptible to change or alteration in the same way as other rules of law: by Act of Parliament. So the courts, when confronted with a purported statute, should test the legitimacy of the 'statute' by measuring it against the appropriate rules of recognition. If it measures up, it is a statute; if it does not comply, then it is not a statute and not entitled to any more respect from the courts than a scrap of paper would receive. As Dixon J said, the courts are 'called upon to consider whether the supreme legislative power in respect of the matter had in truth been exercised and by the elements in which it had come to reside': 44 CLR at 426.

It could be said that neither s 5 of the Colonial Laws Validity Act **[5.3.5]**, nor s 6 of the Australia Act **[5.4.23E]**, established any novel proposition; they simply declared the obvious rule that, in order to legislate, a parliament must follow the currently prescribed legislative procedure.

[5.4.32]   In *Victoria v Commonwealth* (the *PMA* case) (1975) 134 CLR 81 **[5.3.26C]**, Gibbs J considered and rejected a submission that the High Court had no jurisdiction to investigate the legislative process which might have led to the enactment of legislation. In the course of doing so, he discussed the general question raised in the preceding paragraph (at 163–4):

> The principle that the courts may not examine the way in which the law-making process has been performed has no application where a legislature is established under or governed by an instrument which prescribes that laws of a certain kind may only be passed if the legislature is constituted or exercises its functions in a particular manner, eg by the members of both Houses sitting together (as was required by the South Africa Act: *Harris v Minister of the Interior* 1952 (2) SALR 428; sub nom *Harris v Donges* [1952] 1 TLR 1245) or by a two-thirds majority (which was rendered necessary by the Ceylon (Constitution) Order in Council considered in *Bribery Commissioner v Ranasinghe* [1965] AC 172). These cases decide that when the law requires a legislature to enact legislation in a particular manner, the courts may investigate whether the legislature has exercised its powers in the manner required; this is recognised also in *McCawley v R* [1920] AC 691 at 703–4, 712, 714; (1920) 28 CLR 106, at 114–15, 123, 125 and *McDonald v Cain* [1953] VLR 411 at 419, 425–6, 433–5. In all of these cases it happens that the restrictions on the manner of the exercise of legislative power that had to be considered related to amendments to the Constitution, but the principle which has been evolved is not limited to constitutional amendments. Nor did the decision in these cases in any way depend upon the provisions of s 5 of the Colonial Laws Validity Act, 1865; that Act no longer applied to the laws of Ceylon or South Africa at the times when the decisions that respectively related to those countries were given. The principle that underlies these decisions was expressed succinctly by Lord Pearce in *Bribery Commissioner v Ranasinghe* [1965] AC at 197 in the following words: 'a legislature has no power to ignore the conditions of lawmaking that are imposed by the instrument which itself regulates its power to make law'. He distinguished the English authorities by saying that 'in the Constitution of the United Kingdom there is no governing instrument which prescribes the lawmaking powers and the forms which are essential to those powers' [1965] AC at 195. (If the Parliament Acts, 1911 and 1949 (UK) can properly be regarded as an instrument of that kind, questions such as those that now arise will nevertheless be unlikely to fall for decision under those Acts, because they provide, by ss 2(3) and 3, that when a Bill is presented for the Royal assent there shall be indorsed upon it the certificate of the Speaker of the House of Commons that the provisions of the section have been duly complied with, and that any such certificate shall be conclusive for all purposes.) The duty of the courts to inquire whether the conditions of law making have been fulfilled does not depend on whether or not a legislature is sovereign; the legislatures of Ceylon and of

South Africa were sovereign legislatures. Nor does it depend on whether the legislature forms part of a unitary or a federal system; Ceylon and South Africa were unitary constitutions. The remarks of their Lordships in *McCawley v R* [1920] AC at 703–4; (1920) 28 CLR at 114–15 support this view, and appear inconsistent with what was later suggested in *Clayton v Heffron* (1960) 105 CLR at 245. The distinction is between legislatures which are, and those which are not, governed by an instrument which imposes conditions on the power to make laws.

[5.4.33] In *Western Australia v Wilsmore* (1981) 33 ALR 13, the Supreme Court of Western Australia held that restrictive legislative procedures, at least as expressed in the Constitution Acts of the Australian states, were made effective by s 106 of the Commonwealth Constitution.

Wilsmore had sued the state of Western Australia for a declaration that the Electoral Act Amendment Act (No 2) 1979 (WA) was invalid because the legislation had not been passed by absolute majorities in the Assembly and the Council, as required by s 73 of the Constitution Act 1889 (WA). The declarations were refused by Brinsden J but, on appeal, they were granted by the Full Court: *Wilsmore v Western Australia* [1981] WAR 159. The state of Western Australia then applied to the Full Court for leave to appeal to the Privy Council.

The Full Court decided that such an appeal was excluded by s 39(2)(a) of the Judiciary Act 1903 (Cth), which prohibits appeals to the Privy Council from any decision of a state court exercising federal jurisdiction. According to s 30(2)(a) of the Judiciary Act, a state court dealing with a 'matter arising under the [Commonwealth] Constitution' is exercising federal jurisdiction. The Full Court said that, because the matter before the court from which leave to appeal was now sought raised questions about the alteration of the state constitution, it arose under s 106 of the Commonwealth Constitution:

> 106 The Constitution of each State of the Commonwealth shall, subject to this Constitution, continue as at the establishment of the Commonwealth, or as at the admission or establishment of the State, as the case may be, until altered in accordance with the Constitution of the State.

Burt CJ, with whom Lavan and Jones JJ agreed, said at 33 ALR 18:

> One can concede that s 73 of the State Constitution as a law is entirely dependent for its authority upon Imperial legislation and it would still remain true to say that to alter the State Constitution other than in accordance with that Constitution would offend against s 106 of the Commonwealth Constitution. By the force of that section it would be ineffective and, again, by the force of that section, the State Constitution prior to the purported amendment and in the instant case, the right which the respondent possessed under it would 'continue'.
>
> So the question in the case can be said to arise under both the State Constitution and the Commonwealth Constitution and to say that requires one to say that it is a matter 'arising under the Constitution' within the meaning of s 30(2)(a) of the Judiciary Act. That conclusion can be expressed by saying that s 106 of the Commonwealth Constitution by its own force and for its own purposes is a law which requires that such manner and form provisions as are to be found in the State Constitution conditioning the power to amend the Constitution be observed. And when the question arises as to whether this has or has not been done it is a matter 'arising under the Constitution' within the meaning of s 30(2)(a) of the Judiciary Act.

[5.4.34] Western Australia then appealed to the High Court of Australia, which allowed the appeal, holding that the procedure laid down in s 73 of the Constitution Act 1889 (WA) did not purport to lay down a restrictive procedure for amendments to the Electoral Act: *Western Australia v Wilsmore* (1982) 149 CLR 79. In the course of his judgment, Wilson J (with whom Gibbs CJ, Stephen and Mason JJ agreed) said that it was unnecessary to pursue 'the source of the legal efficacy of [the s 73 procedure]' (at 96):

> It matters not in the present contest whether the proviso [to s 73, laying down the procedure] is of binding force because of s 5 of the Colonial Laws Validity Act 1865 (UK), s 5 of the Western Australian Constitution Act 1890 (UK), s 106 of the Australian Constitution or simply because, on such authority as may be gleaned from *Ranasinghe*, it finds a place in the Constitution Act itself.

[5.4.35] In *Commonwealth Aluminium Corporation Ltd v Attorney-General (Qld)* (the *Comalco* case) [1976] Qd R 231 the plaintiff challenged the validity of the Mining Royalties Act 1974 (Qld) on the ground that the Act had not been passed in accordance with procedures prescribed by the Commonwealth Aluminium Corporation Pty Ltd Agreement Act 1957 (Qld).

The 1957 Act authorised the Queensland Government to enter into an agreement with the Commonwealth Aluminium Corporation Pty Ltd (Comalco) under which Comalco would pay the government specified royalties on bauxite mined in Queensland. The Act provided that the agreement should have the force of law as though enacted in the Act (s 3) and that the agreement should not be varied nor the rights of Comalco under the agreement 'derogated from' except pursuant to another agreement between the government and Comalco: s 4. However, the 1974 Act (which was not preceded by any agreement between the government and Comalco), gave to the Governor-in-Council the power to alter the royalties to be paid by Comalco.

A majority of the Full Court of the Queensland Supreme Court rejected the challenge to the Mining Royalties Act 1974. Wanstall J held that the proviso to s 5 of the Colonial Laws Validity Act did not oblige the Queensland Parliament to comply with any procedure laid down by s 4 of the 1957 Act because that Act did not prescribe a 'manner and form' for the enactment of legislation:

> On the contrary its only purpose and intention qua the legislature is to prohibit future *legislation* on that subject [variation of the agreement] *in any manner or form*. Such legislation is to be replaced by executive government action ... To be a 'manner and form' provision within s 5 it must be one operative on the legislative process at some point (*Trethowan's* case ... per Rich J at 419) ([1976] Qd R at 237).

After quoting from the judgment of Dixon J in *Attorney-General (NSW) v Trethowan* (1931) 44 CLR 394 **[5.4.17C]**, Wanstall J concluded:

> [T]o be effective, the qualification as to manner or form must be one which operates within the legislation process as such, albeit not necessarily within the legislative chamber. It is only such a qualification which avoids being repugnant to s 5, ie one which may be categorised as a *condition of the exercise of the legislative power*. In my respectful opinion it is unreal so to attempt to categorise a law which forbids that exercise, as does s 4 by conferring the exclusive right of variation on another body. Because it is not a manner or form provision it may be repealed or altered by the normal process of legislating inconsistently with its provisions ... ([1976] Qd R at 239).

Dunn J, who agreed that the challenge should be rejected, held that s 5 of the Colonial Laws Validity Act was irrelevant because neither the 1958 Act nor the 1974 Act was a law 'respecting the constitution, powers and procedure' of the Queensland Parliament.

Hoare J dissented, holding that s 4 of the 1957 Act prescribed a manner and form for producing legislation (and was valid because it was, at least, a law 'for the peace, welfare and good government of Queensland' within s 2 of the Constitution Act 1867). He also considered that the 1974 Act was obliged to follow that manner and form because it was a law with respect to the constitution powers and procedure of the legislature — '[for] the very reason that it conflicts with a law which provides for a manner and form': [1976] Qd R at 248.

[5.4.36] The *Comalco* case [1976] Qd R 231 **[5.4.35]** throws into sharp focus a basic policy issue which underlies the whole question of restrictive legislative procedures: how far should one parliament be permitted to impose on a future parliament restrictive procedures, procedures with which the first parliament was not obliged to comply? Should the courts accept that an elected parliament, facing a series of contemporary problems, may not deal with those problems in the way which seems appropriate to it, because an earlier parliament (not faced with those problems but claiming clairvoyance) had decreed that a special and restrictive legislative procedure must be followed by any future parliament? Are the courts to endorse what is, essentially, a denial by yesterday's legislators that today's legislators lack prudence and sound judgment?

[5.4.37C] ## West Lakes Ltd v South Australia
(1980) 25 SASR 389

An agreement between the Premier of South Australia and West Lakes Ltd provided for the development, by the company, of an area of waste land subject to a special town planning code set out in the agreement. The agreement provided that it might be varied by further agreement between the Premier and West Lakes Ltd. The West Lakes Development Act 1969 ratified the agreement and provided that the agreement should have effect as if its terms were 'expressly enacted in this Act': s 3. Section 16 authorised 'the Minister' to make regulations altering the planning code set out in the agreement. No such regulation was to be made except with the consent in writing of West Lakes Ltd: s 16(4). In 1980, the government introduced into parliament a bill to amend the 1969 Act by providing that the company's consent would be unnecessary for the making of a regulation to allow floodlights to be installed on a sports ground located in the development area.

West Lakes Ltd began proceedings in the South Australian Supreme Court for a declaration that the state was bound by the agreement to the extent that it could not support the passage of the bill and an injunction to restrain the state from furthering the bill.

King CJ said that one of the issues raised before the court was whether the parliament of South Australia had the power to pass the 1980 bill into law without the consent of West Lakes Ltd. The company had argued that parliament in 1969 had enacted that the terms of the agreement could not be amended by a subsequent Act of Parliament except with the company's consent.

King CJ: [393] The exercise by a parliament of its legislative powers requires some understood and recognised procedure for the declaration of the will of the parliament. Ordinarily, that procedure is established by the Standing Orders of the Houses of Parliament, and by the internal practices and usage of the parliament. Generally speaking, it is not within the function or competence of the Courts to inquire into the internal procedures of the parliament, nor into any questions as to whether they have been observed. The parliament may, however, choose to pass an Act giving the force of law to procedures as to the manner and form in which legislation, or legislation of a particular class, must be passed ...

King CJ quoted two passages from the judgment of Dixon J in *Trethowan's* case (1931) 44 CLR 394 at 425–6 and Gibbs J's exposition in the *PMA* case (1975) 135 CLR 81 at 163–4. His Honour continued:

[396] *Bribery Commissioner v Ranasinghe* [1965] AC 172, a decision of the Privy Council, is authority both for the proposition that a legislature, whose powers are derived from a written instrument, does not have inherent power derived from the mere fact of its establishment to pass laws by resolution of a bare majority in disregard of a legal requirement that they be passed in a specified manner or form, and for the further proposition that the Courts have jurisdiction to declare invalid a law passed in disregard of such a legal requirement. Reference may also be made to *McDonald v Cain* [1953] VLR 411 as authority for the latter proposition ...

The Parliament can only exercise the power to make laws respecting the constitution powers and procedure of the legislature by enacting legislation in the manner and form (if any) prescribed by its own legislation. This is expressly provided in s 5 of the Colonial Laws Validity Act. I think, however, that it is quite clear that the bill under consideration is not a proposed law respecting any of the topics enumerated in s 5 of the Colonial Laws Validity Act. The question of whether the Parliament can only exercise its powers to make laws respecting topics other than those enumerated in s 5 of the Colonial Laws Validity Act in the manner and form (if any) required by its own legislation or whether it may ignore any such requirement, is one of great constitutional importance. In view of the conclusions which I reached as to the other issues in the case, it is unnecessary for me to decide that question, and I think that it is undesirable therefore that I should express any view upon it. When it falls for decision, the question will involve a consideration of the way in which the constitutional principles discussed above are to be applied to a legislature which derives its authority from constitutional sources of the kind which are the foundation of the authority of the South Australian Parliament. It will, moreover, involve a consideration of the true effect of the decision of the High Court in *South-Eastern Drainage Board (South Australia) v Savings Bank of South Australia* (1939) 62 CLR 603.

A question might arise as to whether a particular statutory provision is truly a manner and form provision, which must be observed (at least as to legislation which falls within s 5 of the Colonial Laws Validity Act) as a condition of the validity of the Act, or whether it is a limitation or restraint of substance, which would not invalidate legislation inconsistent with the limitation or restraint. [397] ... The question whether the special majority provision related to manner and form did not arise in *Ranasinghe's* case, at 172. The Colonial Laws Validity Act did not apply and the case turned upon the provision being one of the 'the conditions of lawmaking that are imposed by the instrument which itself regulates the power to make law' (*Ranasinghe's* case, at 197). There must be a point at which a special majority provision would appear as an attempt to deprive the parliament of powers rather than as a measure to prescribe the manner or form of their exercise. This point might be reached more quickly where the legislative topic which is the subject of the requirement is not a fundamental constitutional provision. When one looks at extra-parliamentary requirements, the difficulty of treating them as relating to manner and form becomes greater. It is true that Dixon J in *Trethowan's* case (1931) 44 CLR 394 gave 'manner and form' a very wide meaning. At pp 432–3, referring to the use of the expression in the proviso to s 5 of the Colonial Laws Validity Act, he said:

> The more natural, the wider and the more generally accepted meaning includes within the proviso all the conditions which the Imperial Parliament or that of the self-governing State or Colony may see fit to prescribe as essential to the enactment of a valid law.

Trethowan's case, supra, however, concerned a requirement that an important constitutional alteration be approved by the electors at a referendum. Such a requirement, although extra-parliamentary in character, is easily seen to be a manner and form provision because it is confined to obtaining the direct approval of the people whom the 'representative legislature' represents. If, however, parliament purports to make the validity of legislation on a particular topic conditional upon the concurrence of an extra-parliamentary individual, group of individuals, organisation or corporation, a serious question must arise as to whether the provision is truly a law prescribing the manner or form of legislation, or whether it is not rather a law as to substance, being a renunciation of the power to legislate on that topic unless the condition exists. The problem of distinguishing between substance on the one hand and manner and form on the other is discussed in Professor Friedman's article on *Trethowan's Case, Parliamentary Sovereignty and the Limits of Legal Change* (1950) 24 *Australian Law Journal* 103, at pp 105–6 and by the learned author of Lumb on *The Constitutions of the Australian States* (1963) p 112; see also the judgment of McTiernan J in *Trethowan's* case (1931) 44 CLR 394 and *Commonwealth Aluminium Corporation Limited v Attorney-General* [1976] Qd R 231.

King CJ said that he could not treat the West Lakes Development Act 1969 as prescribing the manner or form of future legislation.

[398] A provision requiring the consent to legislation of a certain kind, of an entity not forming part of the legislative structure (including in that structure the people whom the members of the legislature represent), does not, to my mind, prescribe a manner or form of lawmaking, but rather amounts to a renunciation pro tanto of the lawmaking power. Such a provision relates to the substance of the lawmaking power, not to the manner or form of its exercise ... It follows, in my view, that even if the statute bears the meaning attributed to it, it does not prescribe a manner or form of legislation and Parliament may legislate inconsistently with it. Parliament may therefore validly enact the bill which is under attack.

King CJ went on to conclude that the 1969 Act did not purport to impose any restrictive legislative procedure on the South Australian Parliament. He held that there was no impediment to the enactment of the 1980 bill, and that the court had no jurisdiction to prevent any minister of the Crown proposing any bill for the consideration of parliament or furthering such a bill.

Zelling J said that the court had no jurisdiction to intervene at this stage of the legislative process; and he cited *Rediffusion (Hong Kong) Ltd v Attorney-General (Hong Kong)* [1970] AC 1936 and *Cormack v Cope* (1974) 131 CLR 433 **[5.5.3C]**. He also held that the West Lakes Development Act did not contain any manner and form provision so as to attract the application of s 5 of the Colonial Laws Validity Act.

Zelling J: [413] In the alternative Mr Williams argued that the statute provided a manner and form outside the Colonial Laws Validity Act. He relied for this argument principally on the advice of the Privy Council in *Bribery Commissioner v Ranasinghe* [1965] AC 172. It would appear from that case that it is possible to have a manner and form provision which is not one referring to the constitution powers and procedures of the legislature so as to attract the operation of s 5 of the Colonial Laws Validity Act. That conclusion would seem to follow also from the judgment of Gibbs J in *Victoria v The Commonwealth and Connor* (1974) 134 CLR 81 at 163. While I accept, without deciding, that it is possible to have a section entrenched by a manner and form provision which does not fall within s 5 of the Colonial Laws Validity Act, nevertheless, given the general rules that the Acts of one Parliament do not bind its successors, it would require very clear words before a court would find that that was what had happened. It is one thing to find manner and form provisions in a statute affecting the constitution, it is quite another to find Lord Birkenhead's proverbial Dog Act or a provision thereof elevated to constitutional status. No such clarity of provision exists in the statute at bar, with or without the indenture superadded.

[414] In my opinion, the short answer in the instant case is that there is no manner and form procedure provided by the West Lakes Development Act irrespective of whether the amending bill is a law respecting the constitution powers and procedures of the legislature of South Australia, or whether it is not.

However, there is an even simpler answer than the last two to the propositions put by Mr Williams. That is, that for an entrenchment statute to avoid being repealed by a subsequent Act of the same Parliament passed without any special manner and form, the entrenching clause must itself be entrenched. On the true construction of this Act I cannot see any entrenchment of the entrenching clause or clauses relied on by Mr Williams, even if all the other propositions put by him were in fact correct. The answer to the fourth question is therefore: No.

Matheson J held that s 5 of the Colonial Laws Validity Act was irrelevant because the proposed bill was not a law 'respecting the constitution powers and procedures' of the South Australian Parliament. He then turned to the argument based on *Ranasinghe's* case [1965] AC 172 **[5.4.29C]**. He could not see how the West Lakes Development Act 1969 could fall within the proposition in that case 'that a legislature has no power to ignore the conditions of lawmaking that are imposed by the instrument which itself regulates its power to make law' ([1965] AC at 197). The 1969 Act was not such an instrument.

Matheson J: [422] Counsel also relied on a passage in the judgment of Gibbs J in *Victoria v Commonwealth and Connor* (1975) 134 CLR 81 at 163, who, after referring to several decisions including *Ranasinghe's* case [1965] AC 172, said: 'In all of these cases it happens that the restrictions on the manner of the exercise of legislative power that had to be considered related to amendments to the Constitution, but the principle which has been invoked is not limited to constitutional amendments'. This statement was obiter and not expressed by any of the other Justices, but be that as it may, I do not think his Honour meant that all Acts of Parliament, no matter what their subject matter, can contain manner and form requirements which bind successive parliaments. I do not think his Honour extended the principle of these cases in such a way that the plaintiff can successfully invoke it here and I am certainly not prepared so to extend it. I stress that immediately after the passage which I have just quoted, his Honour went on to quote Lord Pearce's dictum in *Ranasinghe's* case, *supra*, 'The Legislature has no power to ignore the conditions of lawmaking that are imposed *by the instrument which itself regulates its power to make law.*' I have already expressed my view that the West Lakes Development Act 1969–1970, is not such an instrument. In my opinion the second argument fails, and, although this question does not arise here, I do not subscribe to the view that, where Parliament enacts a section providing for a different method of legislation for the particular type of legislation covered by it, it can bind a later Parliament by providing at the same time that the entrenching section itself can only be repealed by the same procedure.

Matheson J agreed that the court should not prevent any Minister of the Crown from proposing or taking steps to further any bill for the consideration of parliament.

~~~

Notes

[5.4.38] The argument developed by the plaintiff in this case lacked even the superficial plausibility of the plaintiff's argument in the *Comalco* case [1976] Qd R 231 **[5.4.35]**. The 1969 Act, on its face, did not purport to limit the capacity of the parliament to legislate, or insist that legislation be passed according to a particular procedure; whereas s 4 of the Commonwealth Aluminium Corporation Pty Ltd Agreement Act 1957 (Qld) could be read as purporting to do just that.

The real interest in this decision, therefore, does not lie in the failure of the plaintiff's attack on the 1980 bill but in the judges' discussion of the arguments, principally the argument which sought to exploit *Bribery Commissioner v Ranasinghe* [1965] AC 172 **[5.4.29C]**. Each of the judgments indicates substantial reluctance to permit the use of that decision (and its reasoning) to reduce the flexibility of parliament's legislative procedures.

[5.4.39] King CJ suggested two ways in which the effect of the *Ranasinghe* argument could be limited or avoided. First, 'a special majority provision' might be upheld where it controlled enactment of some fundamental constitutional provision (as in s 7A of the Constitution Act 1902 (NSW) **[5.4.12E]**) but not where it controlled enactment of ordinary legislation: 25 SASR at 397. And, second, a restrictive procedure which required the consent of some persons or body outside 'the representative legislative structure' would be a renunciation of the law-making power rather than the prescription of legislative procedures: 25 SASR at 398.

Matheson J did not develop his arguments to the same degree; but his unwillingness to accept the full implications of the *Ranasinghe* reasoning (as developed by Gibbs J in the *PMA* case) is clear from his assertion that one parliament could not bind a later parliament to follow a restrictive procedure when repealing a restrictive procedure: 25 SASR at 422. (This appears to be an attack on the effectiveness of a clause modelled on s 7A(6) of the Constitution Act 1902 (NSW).)

On the other hand, Zelling J accepted, at least for the purposes of argument, the implications of the reasoning in *Ranasinghe*. He would have limited its impact by insisting on 'very clear words before a court would find that' a restrictive legislative procedure had been effectively prescribed. Moreover, he said, such a restrictive procedure 'must itself be entrenched' (that is, protected by a restrictive legislative procedure) before it could be effective: 25 SASR at 413–14.

[5.4.40] There are indications, then, in *West Lakes Ltd v South Australia* (1980) 25 SASR 389 **[5.4.37C]** of a judicial reaction against the logical thrust of arguments based on *Ranasinghe's* case [1965] AC 172 **[5.4.29C]**. Underlying the judgments of King CJ and Matheson J, it seems, is an unwillingness to allow the law-making process to be rigidified any more than the High Court and Privy Council decisions in *Attorney-General (NSW) v Trethowan* (1931) 44 CLR 394 **[5.4.17C]**, (1931) 47 CLR 97 **[5.4.18]** compel. We may be seeing here a revival, in the Australian context, of the idea of the sovereignty of parliament as the basic norm or the ultimate legal rule of the Constitution (at least in the state context): see **[5.4.6]**.

[5.4.41] In *City of Collingwood v Victoria* [1993] 2 VR 66, Harper J held that the Victoria Park Act 1992 (Vic) could not, in law, accomplish any alteration or variation to s 85 of the Constitution Act 1975 (Vic), because the manner and form of the enactment of the Victoria Park Act did not meet the requirements of s 85 of the Constitution Act. Section 85(1) conferred unrestricted jurisdiction on the Supreme Court of Victoria. Section 85(5) declared that no Act was to be taken to repeal, alter or vary s 85 unless the Act did so directly or expressly referred to s 85, and unless the introduction of the bill for the Act was accompanied by a statement of the reasons for repealing, altering or amending s 85. Harper J concluded that the Victoria Park Act did contain provisions purporting to limit the jurisdiction of the Supreme Court. However, because that Act did not directly repeal, alter or vary s 85 and did not state an express intention to do so, the provisions in question did not limit the Supreme Court's jurisdiction, at 78:

> [T]he Victoria Park Act is one which the Parliament was competent to enact; but, because the manner and form of its enactment did not meet that which is required by s 85 of the Constitution Act before legislation may be taken to repeal, alter or vary that section, the Victoria Park Act (whatever its purpose may be) does not in law accomplish such alteration or variation.

Harper J did not refer to s 6 of the Australia Act, nor to any of the cases which had discussed procedural restrictions on state parliaments.

[5.4.42] No appeal was brought from the decision of Harper J in *City of Collingwood v Victoria* [1993] 2 VR 66 **[5.4.41]**. However, the Victorian Parliament enacted the Victoria Park Land Act 1992 (Vic), in substantially the same terms as the Victoria Park Act 1992, though this time following the procedure prescribed in s 85(5) of the Constitution Act 1975 (Vic). The City of Collingwood issued proceedings in the Supreme Court of Victoria, claiming a declaration that the Victoria Park Land Act was invalid. On the application of the state of Victoria, the question whether the Victoria Park Land Act was a statute that the parliament was competent to pass was referred to the Full Court of the Supreme Court.

The Full Court answered the question in the affirmative: *City of Collingwood v Victoria (No 2)* [1994] 1 VR 652. In a judgment with which Southwell and Teague JJ agreed, Brooking J held that the Victoria Park Land Act did not interfere with the jurisdiction of the Supreme Court. Brooking J then considered the effect of ss 18 and 85 of the Constitution Act. He noted that s 18 required that any bill to alter the constitution of the parliament, the Council or the Assembly, or which would repeal, alter or vary certain parts of the Constitution Act must be passed by absolute majorities in each house. He also noted that s 85 made special provision concerning the repeal, alteration or variation of that section, and continued at 670:

> Thus a large part of the Act of 1975 is protected against repeal, alteration or variation otherwise than in accordance with s 18 and so the present Constitution is a 'controlled' one in many respects. By the constitutional law of Victoria the Supreme Court has, ever since the giving of the Constitution of 1855, had and exercised the power of keeping Parliament and its houses within the limitations imposed upon them by the Constitution. Ever since its creation by the Supreme Court (Administration) Act 1852 (15 Vict No 10) the Supreme Court has been the superior court of Victoria. What happened in 1975 was that certain provisions concerning the constitution, position, powers and jurisdiction of the court and the position of the judges were plucked out of the Supreme Court Act 1958 and became Pt III of the new Constitution Act. As a result of this and of the provisions of ss 18 and 85 of the new Act, the constitutional provision of the court became entrenched in the sense of being protected against what might be called inadvertent legislative impairment and protected against legislative alteration without the assent of an absolute majority of each house.

[5.4.43] The issue of compliance with s 85(5) of the Constitution Act 1975 (Vic) returned to the Supreme Court in *Broken Hill Proprietary Co Ltd v Dagi* [1996] 2 VR 117. The Court of Appeal (constituted by five judges) allowed an appeal from Cummins J, who had found the appellant guilty of contempt of court because it had procured the passage by the Papua New Guinea Parliament of legislation intended to frustrate proceedings against the appellant in the Supreme Court of Victoria. In making that finding, Cummins J held that s 46 of the Public Prosecutions Act 1994 (Vic) was invalid, because it had not been passed in the manner and form required by s 85(5) of the Constitution Act. (Section 46 provided that no application could be made to the Supreme Court for punishment of any person for contempt of court except by the Attorney-General.)

On appeal, the Court of Appeal held that the manner and form prescribed by s 85(5) had been followed when s 46 was enacted. In particular, the requirement expressed in s 85(5)(b), that the Member of Parliament who introduced the relevant bill make a statement of the reasons for altering the jurisdiction of the Supreme Court, had been met. In a judgment with which Winneke P and Brooking JA agreed, Phillips JA noted that the reasons offered by the Attorney-General (who had introduced the relevant bill) were open to a number of criticisms. Nevertheless, they amounted to a statement of reasons for the purposes of s 85(5)(b), at 189:

This Court has the power, and indeed the duty, to inquire into the question of compliance with manner and form provisions which Parliament itself has enacted (*Victoria v Commonwealth* (1975) 134 CLR 81 at 117–8, 162–4, 180 and 181–2; see also *Collingwood v Victoria (No 2)* [1994] 1 VR 652 at 669–70) and in this case the question for the Court is whether the relevant member of Parliament did make a statement of the reasons for repealing, altering or varying s 85; for that alone can satisfy the requirement, enacted by the Parliament on an earlier occasion, in s 85(5)(b). Despite the criticisms that were levelled at what was said in Parliament in this instance, it is plain that there was included within the second reading speech what purported to be 'a statement ... of the reasons' for altering or varying s 85 in relation to the jurisdiction, powers or authorities of the Supreme Court. It may be that the declared reasons are now thought by one side or the other to have been insufficient, inadequate or even misconceived, but that does not mean that a statement of reasons was not given and in all the circumstances I think that this Court should regard s 85(5)(b) as having been complied with.

[5.4.44C]　　Attorney-General (WA) v Marquet

(2003) 202 ALR 233

In 2001, two bills were passed by the Legislative Assembly and the Legislative Council of Western Australia — the Electoral Distribution Repeal Bill 2001 and the Electoral Amendment Bill 2001. The first bill would have repealed the Electoral Distribution Act 1947 (WA), s 13 of which prohibited the presentation of a bill to amend the Act unless the bill was passed by absolute majorities in each of the Assembly and the Council. The second bill would have changed the number of members of the Legislative Council and the method of determining electoral districts. Neither bill was passed by an absolute majority in the Council.

Marquet, the Clerk of the Parliament of Western Australia, commenced proceedings in the Supreme Court of Western Australia seeking determination of the question whether the bills could be presented to the Governor for assent. A majority of the Supreme Court (Malcolm CJ, Anderson, Steytler and Parker JJ; Wheeler J dissenting) held that it was not lawful for Marquet to present the bills to the Governor. The Attorney-General applied to the High Court for special leave to appeal. The application was heard by six justices.

Gleeson CJ, Gummow, Hayne and Heydon JJ traced the history of the Electoral Distribution Act and s 13 of that Act from the original Constitution Act 1889 (WA). Taking into account that history and the fact that definition of electoral boundaries was legally essential to the election of the parliament, they held that the Repeal Bill and the Amendment Bill were properly characterised as bills to amend the Electoral Distribution Act 1947: 202 ALR 233 at 245. They then turned to the issue whether the Repeal Bill and the Amendment Bill could only be enacted by following the s 13 procedure.

Gleeson CJ, Gummow, Hayne and Heydon J:

[247] *Section 13 of the Electoral Distribution Act as a manner and form provision*

[63] Discussion of the application of manner and form provisions has provoked much debate about the theoretical underpinnings for their operation. Thus, to ask whether a Parliament has power to bind its successors by enacting a manner and form provision has, in the past, led into debates cast in the language of sovereignty or into philosophical debates about whether a generally expressed power includes power to relinquish part of it. Neither the language of sovereignty, nor examination in the philosophical terms described, assists the inquiry that must be made in this case. Sooner or later an analysis of either kind comes to depend upon the content that is given to words like 'sovereignty' or 'general power'. It is now nearly 50 years since HWR Wade convincingly demonstrated (HWR Wade, 'The Basis of Legal Sovereignty' [1955] *Cambridge Law Journal* 172) that the basal question presented in a case like the present, when it arises and must be considered in a British context, is about the relationship

between the judicial and legislative branches of government and, in particular, what rule of recognition the courts apply to determine what is or is not an act of the relevant legislature. When Diceyan theories about the role of the Parliament at Westminster held sway the answer which Wade identified as having been given in England to the question of what rule of recognition an English court would apply in relation to the Acts of that Parliament was: any Act enacted in the ordinary way by that Parliament regardless of any earlier provision about manner and form: *Vauxhall Estates Ltd v Liverpool Corporation* [1932] 1 KB 733 at 743 per Avory J; *Ellen Street Estates Ltd v Minister for Health* [1934] 1 KB 590 at 597 per Maugham LJ; *British Coal Corporation v The King* [1935] AC 500 at 520 per Viscount Sankey LC; *Manuel v Attorney-General* [1983] Ch 77 at 89 per Sir Robert Megarry VC.

[64] Sir Owen Dixon explained that such an analysis proceeded from an understanding of the relationship between the judicial and the legislative branches of government that was apt to a structure of government which did not depend ultimately upon the constitutional assignment of particular powers to the legislature or provide for a constitutional division of powers between polities: Dixon, 'The Law and the Constitution', (1935) 51 *Law Quarterly Review* 590 at 604. It was a structure of government in which the only relevant fundamental or constitutional rule engaged was the rule of recognition. This was 'the pivot of the legal system': Dixon, 'The Law and the Constitution', (1935) 51 *Law Quarterly Review* 590 at 593. There was no other fundamental or constitutional rule which applied. And that is why a different answer was to be given when considering the legislation of subordinate legislatures where a superior legislature (the Imperial Parliament) had provided for some manner and form provision. There was a higher, more fundamental, rule that was engaged. Given such constitutional developments in Britain as devolution, and the undertaking of treaty obligations in relation to Europe, analysis of the first kind described might now be thought (HWR Wade, Constitutional Fundamentals, (1989) at 40–47) to encounter difficulties today. It is, of course, neither necessary nor appropriate to explore those difficulties here.

[65] In an Australian context it was, at first, important to recognise that the colonial legislatures stood in the second category we have identified. They were subordinate legislatures, and manner and form provisions could be and were imposed upon them by Imperial legislation. Section 73 of the 1889 Constitution can be seen as one example of such a provision. (It must be recalled that the 1889 Constitution depended for its operation upon enabling Imperial legislation — the Western Australia Constitution Act 1890 (Imp).) In addition, the Colonial Laws Validity Act 1865 (Imp) gave effect to manner and form provisions found not only in Imperial law but also in colonial law. That too was seen as the imposition of manner and form provisions by superior law.

[66] Now, however, it is essential to begin by recognising that constitutional arrangements in this country have changed in fundamental respects from those that applied in 1889. It is not necessary to attempt to give a list of all of those changes. Their consequences find reflection in decisions like *Sue v Hill* (1999) 199 CLR 462. Two interrelated considerations are central to a proper understanding of the changes that have happened in constitutional structure. First, constitutional norms, whatever may be their historical origins, are now to be traced to Australian sources. Secondly, unlike Britain in the nineteenth century, the constitutional norms which apply in this country are more complex than an unadorned Diceyan precept of parliamentary sovereignty. Those constitutional norms accord an essential place to the obligation of the judicial branch to assess the validity of legislative and executive acts against relevant constitutional requirements ...

[67] For present purposes, two changes in constitutional arrangements are critically important: first, the fact of federation and creation of the States, and secondly, the enactment by the federal Parliament of the Australia Act. Section 106 of the Constitution provides that '[t]he Constitution of each State ... shall, subject to this Constitution, continue as at the establishment of the Commonwealth ... until altered in accordance with the Constitution of the State.' Then, in 1986, pursuant to a reference of power under s 51(xxxviii) of the Constitution, the federal Parliament enacted the Australia Act in order, as its long title said, 'to bring constitutional arrangements affecting the Commonwealth and the States into

conformity with the status of the Commonwealth of Australia as a sovereign, independent and federal nation'. The Australia Act, too, is to be traced to its Australian source — the Constitution of the Commonwealth. The Australia Act takes its force and effect from the reference of power to the federal Parliament, made under s 51(xxxviii), and the operation that the Act is to be given as a law of the Commonwealth in relation to State law by s 109 of the Constitution: *Sue v Hill* (1999) 199 CLR 462 at [61]–[62]. Although the phrase 'subject to this Constitution' appears both in s 51 and s 106, it was decided in *Port MacDonnell Professional Fishermen's* **[249]** *Assn Inc v South Australia* (1989) 168 CLR 340 at 381 that 'the dilemma ... must be resolved in favour of the grant of power in par (xxxviii)'.

[68] The Australia Act had two provisions of particular relevance to manner and form provisions. First, s 3(1) provided that the Colonial Laws Validity Act should not apply to any law made after the commencement of the Australia Act by the Parliament of a State and, second, the provisions of s 6 earlier set out were enacted. It is of particular importance to recognise that the Australia Act stands as a form of law to which the Parliament of Western Australia is relevantly subordinate. To the extent to which s 6 applies, the powers of the Parliament of Western Australia to legislate are confined. What has been seen as the conundrum of whether a body given general power to legislate can give up part of that power need not be resolved. By federal law, effect must be given to some manner and form provisions found in State legislation.

The Justices noted that no challenge was made to the validity of the Australia Act.

[70] That this should be so is not surprising when it is recalled that in *Port MacDonnell Professional Fishermen's Assn Inc v South Australia* all seven Justices constituting the Court concluded, (1989) 168 CLR 340 at 381, that 'the continuance of the Constitution of a State pursuant to s 106 is subject to any Commonwealth law enacted pursuant to the grant of legislative power in par (xxxviii)' of s 51. Section 6 of the Australia Act, therefore, is not to be seen as some attempt to alter s 106 or s 107 otherwise than in accordance with the procedures required by s 128. Section 6 was enacted in the valid exercise of power given to the federal Parliament by s 51(xxxviii).

Section 13 of the Electoral Distribution Act and s 6 of the Australia Act

[71] Was either the Repeal Bill or the Amendment Bill, if it became law, within s 6 of the Australia Act? That is, was it 'a law ... respecting the constitution, powers or procedure of the Parliament of the State'? If either Bill, on its becoming law, would meet that description, s 6 of the Australia Act would be engaged and the law would 'be of no force or effect unless it [was] made in such manner and form as ... required by a law' made by the Western Australian Parliament.

[72] The meaning to be given to the expression 'constitution, powers or procedure of the Parliament' must be ascertained taking proper account of the history that lay behind the enactment of the Australia Act. In particular, it is necessary to give due weight to the learning that evolved about the operation of the Colonial Laws Validity Act, s 5 of which also spoke of 'laws respecting the constitution, powers, and procedure' of the legislatures to which it applied.

[73] In s 5 of the Colonial Laws Validity Act the expression 'constitution, powers, and procedure' appeared in that part of the section which provided that [250] a representative legislature 'shall ... have, and be deemed at all times to have had, full power to make laws respecting' those subjects. The reference to manner and form requirements in the proviso to the section was treated (*Attorney-General (NSW) v Trethowan* (1932) 47 CLR 97) as a condition upon which the full power referred to in s 5 was exercisable. Section 6 of the Australia Act takes a different form. It provides directly for the requirement to observe manner and form. Nonetheless, the use of the expression 'constitution, powers or procedure' in the Australia Act is evidently intended to build on the provisions of the Colonial Laws Validity Act. (The use of the conjunction 'or' rather than 'and' in the collocation is readily explained by the drafting change from grant of power to requirement to obey manner and form.)

[74] On its face, the expression 'constitution, powers or procedure' of a legislature describes a field which is larger than that identified as 'the constitution' of a legislature. It is not necessary or appropriate to attempt to describe the boundaries of the areas within the field that the three separate integers of the expression 'constitution, powers or procedure' cover, let alone attempt to define the boundaries of the entire field ... It is enough to focus on the expression the 'constitution' of the Parliament.

[75] The 'constitution' of a State Parliament includes (perhaps it is confined to) its own 'nature and composition': *Attorney-General (NSW) v Trethowan* (1931) 44 CLR 394 at 429 per Dixon J ...

[76] For some purposes, the nature and composition of the Western Australian Parliament might be described sufficiently as 'bicameral and representative'. But the reference in s 6 of the Australia Act to the 'constitution' of a State Parliament should not be read as confined to those two descriptions if they are understood, as the submissions of the Attorneys-General for New South Wales and Queensland suggested, at a high level of abstraction. That is, s 6 is not to be read as confined to laws which abolish a House, or altogether take away the 'representative' character of a State Parliament or one of its Houses. At least to some extent the 'constitution' of the Parliament extends to features which go to give it, and its Houses, a representative character. Thus, s 6 may be engaged in cases in which the legislation deals with matters that are encompassed by the general description 'representative' and go to give that word its application in the particular case. So, for example, an upper House whose members are elected in a single State-wide electorate by proportional representation is differently constituted from an upper House whose members are separately elected in single member provinces by first past the post voting. Each may properly be described as a 'representative' chamber, but the parliament would be differently constituted if one form of election to the upper House were to be adopted in place of the other.

[251] [77] Not every matter which touches the election of members of a Parliament is a matter affecting the Parliament's constitution. In *Clydesdale v Hughes* (1934) 51 CLR 518 at 528, three members of the Court held that a law providing that the holding of a particular office did not disable or disqualify a person from sitting as a member of the Legislative Council of Western Australia was not a law which, for the purposes of s 73 of the 1889 Constitution, effected an alteration or change in the constitution of that House: see also *Western Australia v Wilsmore* (1982) 149 CLR 79 at 102. Again, however, it is neither necessary nor appropriate to attempt to trace the metes and bounds of the relevant field.

[78] ... The Repeal Bill did away with the scheme under which there were two Houses elected from 57 districts and six regions respectively, where the 57 districts were to be ascertained in accordance with the rules prescribed by s 6 of the Electoral Distribution Act. Those rules depended upon the division between the metropolitan and other areas and the application of a tolerance of 15 per cent more or less. Upon the Repeal Bill coming into force the manner of effecting representation in the Parliament would have been at large. Considered separately, then, the Repeal Bill was for a law respecting the constitution of the Parliament of Western Australia.

[79] The Amendment Bill, if it came into force, would have provided for 57 electoral districts and six electoral regions, but they would have been differently drawn from the way for which the Electoral Distribution Act provided. The criteria to be applied in drawing electoral boundaries under the Amendment Bill would have differed according to whether the electoral district had an area of less than 100,000 square kilometres. The tolerance in the smaller districts would have been reduced from 15 per cent to 10 per cent; in the larger districts the formula was more complicated, but again the tolerance was changed from 15 per cent. In addition, and no less significantly, under the Amendment Bill, the number of members of the Council would have been increased, from the 30 specified by s 5 of the Constitution Acts Amendment Act 1899, to 36. The Amendment Bill was for a law respecting the constitution of the Parliament of Western Australia.

Gleeson CJ, Gummow, Hayne and Heydon JJ said it was unnecessary to decide whether, apart from s 6 of the Australia Act, it was necessary to follow the procedure in s 13 of the Electoral Distribution Act. They rejected an argument that prorogation of the parliament after the bills' passage through the Assembly and the Council caused the bills to lapse and prevented their presentation to the Governor: 202 ALR 233 at [85].

The justices concluded that it would not be lawful to present the two bills to the Governor for the royal assent. They ordered that special leave to appeal be granted, the appeal being treated as instituted and heard instanter but dismissed: 202 ALR 233 at [252].

~~~

[5.4.45] Kirby J dissented, on the basis that s 13 of the Electoral Distribution Act 1947 was not entrenched and that Act could be repealed by the passage of the bills through the normal legislative processes; Callinan J agreed with Gleeson CJ, Gummow, Hayne and Heydon JJ that the application for special leave should be granted and the appeal dismissed.

Commonwealth Parliament

Background: an inflexible Constitution

[5.4.46] The Commonwealth Constitution establishes a restrictive legislative procedure for one class of legislation, that which alters the Constitution: s 128. It seems clear that compliance with this procedure is essential. The substantial number of cases in which Commonwealth legislation, passed by the normal legislative process, has been held invalid because of a conflict with the terms of the Commonwealth Constitution clearly supports that proposition.

The proposition can also be supported by reasoning. The Commonwealth Parliament is given, under the Constitution, power to legislate on specific topics, most of which are listed in ss 51, 52, 76 and 77, but principally in s 51. Amongst those topics we cannot find any reference to the alteration of the Constitution. The power to legislate on that topic comes only from s 128, and the power given by that section is given subject to strict procedural limits.

[5.4.47] The position of the Commonwealth Parliament is clearly different from that of the state parliaments. The latter have a general legislative power which authorises them to alter their Constitution Acts, a power confirmed by s 5 of the Colonial Laws Validity Act and by s 2(2) of the Australia Act 1986. The Commonwealth Parliament on the other hand has a series of narrowly defined legislative powers, over specified topics.

Again, the state Constitution Acts have no special status and can be amended and repealed by state parliaments in the same way as any piece of legislation: *McCawley v R* [1920] AC 691 **[5.3.14]**. The Commonwealth Constitution was enacted by the United Kingdom Parliament for Australia, and would override any inconsistent local legislation, state or Commonwealth. As part of an imperial enactment extending to Australia, the Commonwealth Constitution had a special status, confirmed by s 2 of the Colonial Laws Validity Act. Any colonial law (which included Commonwealth legislation) which was repugnant to an Imperial Act extending to the colony (which included Australia) was to be 'absolutely void and inoperative' **[6.2.2]**. Section 2 of the Colonial Laws Validity Act was repealed, in its application to the Commonwealth

Parliament, by the Statute of Westminster 1931 (UK) s 2 **[6.2.15E]**. However, s 8 preserved the special overriding status of the Commonwealth Constitution:

> 8 Nothing in this Act shall be deemed to confer any power to repeal or alter the Constitution Act of the Commonwealth of Australia or the Constitution Act of the Dominion of New Zealand otherwise than in accordance with the law existing before the commencement of this Act.

[5.4.48] There is a second clear distinction between the position of the Commonwealth Parliament and that of the state parliaments. While the latter have the power to establish special restrictive (or alternative) legislative procedures, the Commonwealth Parliament cannot, for its legislative procedures are defined by the Commonwealth Constitution (ss 1, 23, 40, 58) and those procedures may be altered only if the Constitution is altered. Accordingly, it would not be open to the Commonwealth Parliament to enact, say, an Act implementing the International Covenant on Civil and Political Rights and include in the Act a clause demanding that no repeal or amendment could take effect unless approved by a two-thirds majority in each house of parliament. Such an Act would involve an alteration of the Constitution and, unless passed in accordance with s 128, would be invalid. These issues are discussed in Winterton (1980).

[5.4.49] However, it may be open to the Commonwealth Parliament to use the power given to it by s 51(xxxviii) of the Commonwealth Constitution to introduce restrictive legislative procedures. That provision authorises the parliament to make laws with respect to:

> The exercise within the Commonwealth at the request or with the concurrence of the parliaments of all the States directly concerned, of any power which can at the establishment of this Constitution be exercised only by the parliament of the United Kingdom or by the Federal Council of Australasia.

This power was given a broad reading by the High Court in *Port Macdonnell Professional Fishermen's Association Inc v South Australia* (1989) 168 CLR 340. It provided the constitutional basis for the offshore settlement of 1980, and for the Australia Act 1986 (Cth), which achieved a significant enlargement of state powers: see **[6.2.8]**.

It could be argued that, in 1901, only the United Kingdom Parliament could legislate to require the Commonwealth Parliament to follow a restrictive procedure when legislating on, for example, human rights. It might then follow that, if the state parliaments requested the Commonwealth Parliament to legislate in those terms, s 51(xxxviii) would authorise the parliament to do so. However, the power conferred by s 51(xxxviii) is declared to be 'subject to this Constitution', and it could be argued that the clear purpose of s 51(xxxviii) is to permit legislation dealing with matters of concern to the states rather than to provide a method of, in effect, altering the Constitution. The possibility that s 51(xxxviii) could support legislation amending the Constitution is reviewed by Craven (1986) pp 176–90. See also Crawford (1992) pp 191ff.

[5.4.50E]   **Commonwealth Constitution**

128 This Constitution shall not be altered except in the following manner:

The proposed law for the alteration thereof must be passed by an absolute majority of each House of Parliament, and not less than two or more than six months after its passage through both Houses the proposed law shall be submitted in each State to the electors qualified to vote for the election of members of the House of Representatives.

But if either House passes any such proposed law by an absolute majority, and the other House rejects or fails to pass it or passes it with any amendment to which the first-mentioned House will not agree, and if after an interval of three months the first-mentioned House in the same or the next session again passes the proposed law by an absolute majority with or without any amendment which has been made or agreed to by the other House, and such other House rejects or fails to pass it or passes it with any amendment to which the first-mentioned House will not agree, the Governor-General may submit the proposed law as last proposed by the first-mentioned House, and either with or without any amendments subsequently agreed to by both Houses, to the electors in each State qualified to vote for the election of the House of Representatives.

When a proposed law is submitted to the electors the vote shall be taken in such manner as the Parliament prescribes. But until the qualifications of electors of members of the House of Representatives becomes uniform throughout the Commonwealth, only one-half the electors voting for and against the proposed law shall be counted in any State in which adult suffrage prevails.

And if in a majority of the States a majority of the electors voting approve the proposed law, and if a majority of all the electors voting also approve the proposed law, it shall be presented to the Governor-General for the Queen's assent.

No alteration diminishing the proportionate representation of any State in either House of the Parliament, or the minimum number or representatives of a Senate in the House of Representatives, or increasing, diminishing, or otherwise altering the limits of the State, or in any manner affecting the provisions of the Constitution in relation thereto, shall become law unless the majority of the electors voting in that State approve the proposed law.

~~~

Notes

[5.4.51]   The alteration procedure is a difficult one to negotiate. At the time of writing, 44 proposals for alteration had been put to the electorate, of which only eight were approved: MacMillan, Evans and Storey (1983) pp 22–35 (for an assessment of the attempts to alter the Constitution to 1983); Campbell (1989) (pp 7–10 for an account of the 1988 referenda); Kirby (2000). A table outlining the results in the 44 proposals appears in Bennett and Brennan (2000) pp 18–23. The May 1977 referenda considerably improved the average, for on that occasion the electorate voted to approve three of the four proposals; but, even then, the difficulty of the procedure was emphasised when the fourth proposal failed to obtain approval in the necessary four states, even though more than 62 per cent of the voters throughout Australia voted in its favour. (Note that, for some alterations to the Constitution, s 128 specifies approval by a majority of electors in the state affected, which, for certain alterations, could require approval by a majority of electors in *all* states: see Lumb (1986) p 386.)

[5.4.52]   It has been argued that the alteration process is not available for the passage of *any* change to the Constitution. For example, can the process be used to accomplish the following changes in our constitutional systems:

- conversion of the Commonwealth to a unitary form of government;

- conversion of the Commonwealth to a republican form of government; or

- secession of one or more states from the Commonwealth?

It could be said that the preamble to the Commonwealth of Australia Constitution Act 1900 (UK) (of which the Commonwealth Constitution forms s 9) entrenches certain aspects of our constitutional structure. The preamble recites that the people of five colonies (not including Western Australia) 'have agreed to unite in one indissoluble federal Commonwealth under the Crown of the United Kingdom'.

In 1933, the state of Western Australia petitioned the House of Commons in the United Kingdom Parliament, seeking the enactment of legislation to allow the state to withdraw from the Commonwealth. The law officers of the Crown gave as their opinion that the United Kingdom Parliament could amend or repeal the Commonwealth of Australia Constitution Act 1900. '[T]he provisions for the alteration of the Constitution which are contained in the Constitution itself (s 128) in no way affect the sovereign powers of the United Kingdom Parliament': O'Connell and Riordan (1971) p 416. The opinion said nothing about the power of the Commonwealth Parliament to effect this change through the s 128 procedure, but it is consistent with the general tone of the opinion and earlier correspondence that no such power existed. Indeed, Lumb asserts that the law officers believed that 'to enact secession legislation was within the power of the Imperial Parliament alone': Lumb (1986) p 388.

On the other hand, several writers have treated s 128 as a paramount provision which authorises radical changes to the Constitution: see Latham (1949) p 18; Canaway (1938) p 109; Sawer (1957) p 5; Encel, Horne and Thompson (1977) p 155. For a detailed discussion of the capacity of s 128 to support a dissolution of the Australian federation, see Craven (1986) pp 160–75.

5   Judicial review of the legislative process

[5.5.1]   The procedure for enacting legislation consists of a number of distinct stages. For most legislation, each of the houses of parliament and the Crown's representative must assent to a bill before it becomes a statute. For certain types of legislation, or in certain circumstances, a different procedure may be followed (see [5.3.1]), or must be followed: see [5.4.1].

The procedure to be followed may be prescribed by statute or by the standing orders of the various houses of parliament. In Australia, these standing orders are normally made in pursuance of statutory authority and failure to follow them will not affect the validity of enacted legislation, because their enforcement is regarded (by the courts) as a matter of parliamentary privilege: [5.1.7]. On the other hand, failure to observe the procedures laid down in statutes will affect the validity of enacted (or supposedly enacted) legislation, where the procedures are regarded as mandatory: *Victoria v Commonwealth* (the *PMA* case) (1975) 134 CLR 81 [5.3.26C]; *Attorney-General (NSW) v Trethowan* (1931) 44 CLR 394 [5.4.17C].

[5.5.2] It seems clear that the validity of an alleged Act of Parliament can be challenged, once the Act has gone through (or allegedly gone through) the legislative process. But is it possible to anticipate such a challenge? When it appears that a bill, not yet enacted, has not followed some prescribed step in the legislative process, or that some step is about to be ignored, can the courts be called on to intervene and restrain further parliamentary action? Or must the legislative process have run its course (however defective) before the courts may decide on the matter?

[5.5.3C] **Cormack v Cope**

(1974) 131 CLR 432

On 11 April 1974 the Governor-General proclaimed a double dissolution of the Commonwealth Parliament, reciting six bills (including the Petroleum and Minerals Authority Bill 1973) as grounds for the dissolution. After the subsequent general election and continued deadlock between the two houses, the Governor-General convened a joint sitting to deliberate and vote on the six bills.

Two senators commenced proceedings in the original jurisdiction of the High Court against the President of the Senate, the Speaker of the House of Representatives, the clerks of both Houses, the Prime Minister, the Attorney-General and the Commonwealth, claiming declarations that the convening of the joint sitting was invalid and injunctions to restrain the introduction into the joint sitting of any of the bills or their presentation to the Governor-General for royal assent. The state of Queensland issued a separate writ in the High Court against the members of the Commonwealth Executive Council seeking similar declarations and injunctions in respect of the Petroleum and Minerals Authority Bill.

The plaintiffs relied on two alleged defects in the s 57 procedure:

• the dissolution procedure had been used for six bills at once, whereas it was available for only one bill at a time; and

• the Petroleum and Minerals Authority Bill had not met the requirements of s 57, in that three months had not elapsed between the Senate's rejection or failure to pass and the second passing by the House of Representatives.

The plaintiffs applied for interlocutory injunctions, pending the hearing of their actions and Barwick CJ, before whom the application had been made, referred to the Full High Court the motion for injunctions and the question whether the declarations sought by the plaintiffs should be made. Argument was heard before the court the same day (2 August) and the court's judgment was delivered on 5 August. The judges dealt first with the action brought by the two senators.

Barwick CJ referred to a submission advanced on behalf of the Commonwealth, that the court could not inquire into the regularity of the actions of the Governor-General when the latter participated in the process of law-making. The submission was founded on the propositions that s 49 of the Constitution conferred on the Senate and the House of Representatives all the powers, privileges and immunities of the House of Commons and the courts in the United Kingdom traditionally refrained from any interference in the law-making activities of the parliament.

Barwick CJ: [452] But the submission, in my opinion, was basically misconceived. We are not here dealing with a parliament whose laws and activities have the paramountcy of the houses of Parliament in the United Kingdom. The lawmaking process of the Parliament in Australia is controlled by a written Constitution. This is particularly true of the special lawmaking process for which s 57 makes provision. It has been pointed out by the Privy Council in unequivocal language in the case of *Bribery Commissioner v Ranasinghe* [1965] AC 172 that where the lawmaking process of a legislature is laid down by its constating instrument, the courts have a right and duty to ensure that the lawmaking process is observed ...

[453] These words were written with respect to a Constitution which required a particular majority for the passage of an Act of a particular nature. The analogy in the case of s 57 is that the Constitution requires the various steps which I have outlined to be validly taken as a part of the lawmaking process. Speaking of the position of the court in relation to such lawmaking processes, laid down by the constating instrument, Lord Pearce said in that case (AC at 194): 'The court has a duty to see that the Constitution is not infringed and to preserve it inviolate', language which is singularly appropriate to the position of this court in relation to the Australian Constitution.

While it may be true the court will not interfere in what I would call the intra-mural deliberative activities of the Parliament, it has both a right and a duty to interfere if the constitutionally required process of lawmaking is not properly carried out ...

[454] Ordinarily, the court's interference to ensure a due observance of the Constitution in connexion with the making of laws is effected by declaring void what purports to be an Act of Parliament, after it has been passed by the Parliament and received the royal assent. In general, this is a sufficient means of ensuring that the processes of lawmaking which the Constitution requires are properly followed and in practice so far the court has confined itself to dealing with laws which have resulted from the parliamentary process. But nothing in that process has its precise analogy of or to that prescribed by s 57. In my opinion, the court in point of jurisdiction is not limited to that method of ensuring the observance of the constitutional processes of lawmaking. It seems to me that in any appropriate, though no doubt unusual, case when moved by parties who have an interest in the regularity of the steps of the lawmaking process at the time intervention is sought, the court is able, and indeed in a proper case bound, to interfere.

Barwick CJ held that the s 57 procedure could be used for more than one bill at a time. However, he indicated that the Governor-General's proclamation convening a joint sitting could be void because it purported to direct the joint sitting to vote on the six bills, and the Governor-General had no power to determine the agenda for the joint sitting. Barwick CJ also said that the Petroleum and Minerals Authority Bill had not satisfied the procedural requirements of s 57, because there had not been the necessary three months' delay, though he concluded:

[460] But having regard to the fact that if the joint sitting proves not to have been duly convened and affirms laws which do not satisfy s 57, those laws or some of them made in pursuance of its votes could be declared void at the instance of a proper plaintiff, I am of opinion that the court should not grant an interlocutory injunction. In so deciding, I have borne in mind the interests of the plaintiffs to seek the relief they have sought, but this consideration is not so great or compelling as to outweigh other considerations to which weight must be given. Not only is there difficulty in finding appropriate persons to enjoin, but having regard to the court's power to declare void Acts not passed in conformity with the provisions of s 57 the court, in my opinion, ought not now to intervene by way of interlocutory relief.

McTiernan J held the issue of compliance with s 57 was not justiciable. On the issues of judicial intervention through injunction, the other members of the court were divided.

Menzies J: [464] It is a firmly established principle that this court may declare or treat as invalid any law of the Parliament made without the authority of the Constitution. The exercise of this authority assumes the completion of the parliamentary process to turn a Bill into an Act. It is no part of the authority of this court, however, to restrain Parliament from making unconstitutional laws. It is of course convenient to speak of an unconstitutional law but the phrase means merely that [465] the purported law is not a law at all. This court does not consider in advance whether if Parliament were to pass a particular Bill it would result in a valid law. Another aspect of the same matter is that the introduction of a Bill does not affect rights; it is the making of a law that does that. Then a person who has the requisite interest may challenge the validity of the law.

Closely associated with these principles is another principle of great constitutional importance, namely that the court will not interfere with the proceedings of parliament or the houses of parliament. The validity of the law that follows from what parliament has done is one thing. The proceedings of parliament that lead to a valid or an invalid law are another. It is not for this court to prevent parliament from doing what, in the opinion of this court, will result in an invalid law.

Gibbs J: [466] I am disposed to think that this court has jurisdiction to interfere at any stage of the special lawmaking process permitted by s 57, in order to prevent a violation of the Constitution and that an assertion of the privileges of Parliament would not deprive the court of the jurisdiction with which the Constitution invests it. However, although I accept that such a jurisdiction exists, in my opinion it would be wrong to exercise it by granting the relief sought in the present case.

There can be no doubt that a proposed law, which has been affirmed by an absolute majority of the total members of both houses of Parliament at a joint sitting, will be invalid and void unless the requirements prescribed by s 57 have been satisfied. The only power to enact a law at a joint sitting is that given by s 57. The provisions of that section are not merely directory but attach conditions to the grant of the power and if those conditions have not been fulfilled, the power will not have been validly exercised. Once a proposed law had been affirmed at a joint sitting, this court would have undoubted jurisdiction to pronounce on its validity and it would be appropriate then to do so. In other words, after the proceedings of the joint sitting had been completed, this court would have jurisdiction to give, and could conveniently give, an adequate remedy if there had been a breach of the provisions of s 57, and it is not necessary, in order to prevent a violation of the Constitution, that the court should interfere in the legislative or administrative processes prescribed by s 57 before any proposed law has been passed.

These circumstances are relevant and important in deciding whether the discretionary remedies of declaration and injunction [467] should be granted in a case such as the present.

Stephen J: [472] … I am of the view that this court does not intervene in matters involving the lawmaking process … There may be exceptions to this rule in cases in which, if such cases there be, the product of any irregularity in legislative procedure is other than a statute which is capable of challenge in this court by those affected by its terms upon the ground that it is not a true product of the constitutionally appointed legislative process. It suffices to say that this not such a case; if the past legislative history of the measure now described as the Petroleum and Minerals Authority Bill is ultimately shown not to have involved compliance with s 57 and yet is affirmed by the requisite majority at a joint sitting and becomes an Act there will, no doubt, be opportunity for those affected by its terms to attack its validity.

I may add that in my view this limitation of intervention by the court depends not upon discretionary but jurisdictional grounds …

It is upon this jurisdictional ground that I would dismiss the plaintiffs' motion for injunctions and declarations and would answer in the negative the question referred to the court.

Mason J: [473] In my view, proceedings at a joint sitting, pursuant to s 57 are proceedings in Parliament under Ch 1 of the Constitution. Whether this court has jurisdiction to intervene in the parliamentary process by granting an injunction or making a declaration, the effect of which would be to prevent the parliamentary sitting convened by the Governor-General from taking place, is a question which I do not find it necessary to decide finally. It is sufficient for me to say that, assuming such a jurisdiction to exist, no case is here made out for its exercise.

My principal reason for coming to this conclusion is that the grounds upon which the plaintiffs rely in order to invalidate the joint sitting or to limit its deliberations, are all grounds upon which the validity of the Bills would be open to challenge in the event that they are passed by a majority at the joint sitting and are assented to …

[474] Intervention in the parliamentary process by the grant of interlocutory relief before a Bill is assented to and becomes law, is to be justified, if at all, as an exceptional measure essential to prevent a violation of the Constitution: see *Hughes & Vale Pty Ltd v Gair* (1954)

90 CLR 203. As the six Bills, if passed at the joint sitting and assented to are open to challenge in properly constituted proceedings seeking a declaration of invalidity on the grounds now argued, I can see no sufficient basis for the court in this case taking the exceptional step of granting relief by way of intervening in the parliamentary process.

Barwick CJ, McTiernan, Menzies and Stephen JJ went on to dismiss the application for an interlocutory injunction by the state of Queensland on the ground that it had 'no sufficient interest to maintain this suit': 131 CLR at 475 per Barwick CJ.

Gibbs and Mason JJ dismissed Queensland's application for the same reasons they dismissed the application of the two senators.

~~~

Notes

[5.5.4] The joint sitting proceeded, and duly passed the six bills which were then given royal assent. The Petroleum and Minerals Authority Act 1973 was challenged in *Victoria v Commonwealth* (the *PMA* case) (1975) 134 CLR 81 **[5.3.26C]** and the High Court held that there had not been the three-month delay required by s 57 and that the Act was, therefore, invalid. Three other Acts passed at the joint sitting were challenged in *Western Australia v Commonwealth* (the *Territorial Senators* case) (1975) 134 CLR 201 **[5.3.33]**. They were the Commonwealth Electoral Act (No 2) 1973, the Senate (Representation of Territories) Act 1973 and the Representation Act 1973. The challenge was unsuccessful.

In the *PMA* case, Gibbs J offered an example of the type of case where the court would grant an injunction to restrain some step in the legislative process. He rejected an argument that a parliament, elected after an improperly proclaimed double dissolution, would be invalidly assembled, and said that '[t]his of course is not to suggest that this court could not intervene to uphold the Constitution and prevent an invalid proclamation for the dissolution of the Senate from being given effect': 134 CLR at 157. Mason J, while dealing with a similar argument, suggested that it might be 'a logical consequence' of the court's decision in the *PMA* case that 'a prospective dissolution of Parliament under s 57 [would be exposed] to judicial scrutiny': 134 CLR at 184.

[5.5.5] The question whether the courts should intervene in the legislative process of parliament is raised only infrequently. On the occasions that the issue has been raised, quite divergent attitudes have been adopted by the judges. The decisions which favour judicial intervention are, for the most part, decisions of state courts.

[5.5.6] In *Taylor v Attorney-General (Qld)* [1917] St R Qd 208, the Queensland Supreme Court granted an interlocutory injunction to restrain the holding of a referendum on a bill which had been passed by the Legislative Assembly but blocked by the Legislative Council. The court concluded that the injunction was justified because the alternative procedure provided by the Parliamentary Bills Referendum Act 1908 (Qld) was not validly available for the passage of the proposed legislation. On appeal, the High Court decided that there was no defect in the legislative process. The appeal was heard after the interlocutory injunction had been dissolved and the Attorney-General had undertaken that the bill in question would not be presented to the Governor for the royal assent: see **[5.3.13]**.

[5.5.7] In *Trethowan v Peden* (1930) 31 SR (NSW) 183, the New South Wales Supreme Court was prepared to issue and continue an interim injunction to prevent officials of the state parliament and members of the state government from presenting two bills to the Governor for royal assent, a presentation which was prohibited by s 7A of the Constitution Act 1902 (NSW) **[5.4.12E]**. Street CJ said that the injunction did not involve an interference with the proceedings of the houses of parliament; rather, it would prevent 'a threatened violation of the statutory inhibition' in s 7A: 31 SR (NSW) at 205. On appeal to the High Court, the question of the propriety of issuing an injunction was excluded from the appeal: see **[5.4.17C]**.

[5.5.8] In *McDonald v Cain* [1953] VLR 411, an interim injunction was granted by a single judge of the Victorian Supreme Court to restrain the presentation of a bill to the Governor for royal assent, pending the court's determination whether the bill's presentation was prohibited by s 60 of the Constitution Act 1855 (Vic) (see now s 18(2) of the Constitution Act 1975). The Full Supreme Court dissolved the interim injunction, on the ground that the bill was not covered by s 60. Of the three members of the Full Court, O'Bryan J said that it would be proper for the court to grant the remedy of a declaration against officers of the state parliament. If it appeared responsible Ministers intended to contravene the law by advising the Governor to assent to a bill unlawfully presented to the Governor, the court would grant an injunction against the Ministers: [1953] VLR at 438. The other members of the court were more equivocal, though Martin J indicated that the grant of the non-coercive remedy of declaration did not interfere with the rights of parliament: [1953] VLR at 426.

[5.5.9] In *Clayton v Heffron* [1961] SR (NSW) 768, the New South Wales Supreme Court declined to issue an injunction to restrain the holding of a referendum on a bill, passed by the Legislative Assembly and blocked by the Legislative Council. The court's refusal was based on the substantial merits of the case, rather than on any reluctance to intervene in the legislative process. In the course of their joint judgment, Evatt CJ and Sugerman J suggested that, as a matter of discretion, the court might be unwilling to intervene in the legislative process. On the other hand, they suggested that the subject matter of the proposed legislation might justify intervention, at 768:

> The present case is concerned with a measure whose purpose is to alter the constitution of the legislative body itself — to replace a legislature of two houses by a legislature consisting of one only of such houses. A degree of convenience amounting virtually to necessity makes it proper to determine at an appropriately early stage whether such a measure, if ultimately enacted, will have been enacted with constitutional validity and in accordance with the forms required for its enactment; and the urgency in the public interest of an early determination of this question has been recognised by the entry into the agreement earlier referred to ...

[5.5.10] In *Eastgate v Rozzoli* (1990) 20 NSWLR 188, the New South Wales Court of Appeal refused to grant an interlocutory injunction which would have restrained the Speaker of the Legislative Assembly from presenting to the Governor for royal assent the Mental Health Bill 1990. (It appeared that the objection to the bill was that, if enacted, it would permit detention of persons whose conduct was not unlawful. No objection was raised to the procedure which the bill had followed in parliament.) In the course of his judgment, Kirby P said that Australian 'courts have asserted the power to issue an injunction to restrain the officers responsible for presenting [a] Bill to the Governor for the royal assent [and] a power to make a declaration as to the validity of the legislation at that stage', but it was 'now settled practice in Australia that such an injunction will virtually never be issued, or a declaration made, at that stage. It will be left to the applicant to seek relief after the royal assent has been given and the Bill has become law': 20 NSWLR at 199.

Priestly and Handley JJA said that it would be essential, before the court would begin to consider intervening in the processes of parliament, 'that the plaintiff's basis of legal challenge to the Bill would cease to be available once the law-making process had been completed by the Bill being enacted into law': 20 NSWLR at 204.

[5.5.11] In *Bignold v Dickson* (1991) 23 NSWLR 683, the New South Wales Court of Appeal refused to issue an injunction to prevent the submission to a referendum of a bill to reduce the size of the Legislative Council in that state. The plaintiff's argument that the date appointed for the referendum did not comply with the Constitution Act 1902 (NSW) s 7A(3) was rejected by the court.

Of the three members of the Court of Appeal (Kirby P, Samuels and Priestley JJA), only Kirby P referred to the issue of the court's jurisdiction and discretion to intervene in the legislative process. He said the present case was quite different from *Eastgate v Rozzoli* (1990) 20 NSWLR 188 **[5.5.10]** because the plaintiff's case was based on a negative stipulation in s 7A and involved an attack on an Act that had already been enacted as well as on the legislative process for the bill to reduce the size of the Council. Kirby P noted that *Trethowan v Peden* (1930) 31 SR (NSW) 183 **[5.5.7]** was authority for the proposition that the court could and should intervene to prevent a breach of s 7A; and, although that decision had been criticised in obiter dicta in the High Court, it had never been expressly overruled: 23 NSWLR at 704. It was unnecessary, Kirby P said, to resolve the issues of power and discretion because the plaintiff was not entitled to relief in any event.

[5.5.12] The High Court has taken a generally negative attitude towards the question of judicial intervention in the legislative process, apart from the appeals in *Taylor v Attorney-General (Qld)* (1917) 23 CLR 457 **[5.3.13]** and *Attorney-General (NSW) v Trethowan* (1931) 44 CLR 394 **[5.4.17C]**, where the question was excluded from the appeals.

[5.5.13] In *Hughes and Vale Pty Ltd v Gair* (1954) 90 CLR 203, the High Court refused to grant an injunction to restrain the presentation to the Governor of Queensland of a bill for an Act which would, the plaintiff argued, contravene s 92 of the Commonwealth Constitution by restricting the absolute freedom of interstate trade. Dixon CJ, with whom Webb, Fullagar, Kitto and Taylor JJ agreed, pointed out that the injunction granted by the New South Wales Supreme Court in *Trethowan v Peden* (1930) 31 SR (NSW) 183 **[5.5.7]** had been based on the 'express negative provision' in s 7A of the Constitution Act 1902 (NSW), prohibiting the course of action restrained by the injunction. Such was not the case here. But even in the case of a provision such as s 7A, it seemed Dixon CJ was unhappy about judicial intervention, at 204:

> For myself I have long entertained a doubt as to the correctness of the decision of the Full Court of New South Wales in that case even on the terms of that Act.

[5.5.14] In *Clayton v Heffron* (1960) 105 CLR 214, the High Court held that there had been no failure to comply with the mandatory procedures prescribed by s 5B of the Constitution Act 1902 (NSW): see **[5.3.16C]**. However, Dixon CJ, McTiernan, Taylor and Windeyer JJ also considered whether it would have been appropriate to issue an injunction, if there had been a deficiency in the mandatory procedures. They said that for the court to inquire into the parliamentary process before its completion was, at 235:

> ... an inquiry which according to the traditional view courts do not undertake. The process of law-making is one thing: the power to make the law as it has emerged from the process is another. It is the latter which the court must always have jurisdiction to examine and pronounce upon. Of course the framers of a constitution may make the validity of a law depend upon any fact, event or consideration they may choose, and if one is chosen which consists in a proceeding within parliament the courts must take it under their cognisance in order to determine whether the supposed law is a valid law; but even then one might suppose only after the law in question has been enacted and when its validity as law is impugned by someone affected by its operation.

[5.5.15] The questions of jurisdiction and discretion discussed in such cases as *Trethowan v Peden* (1930) 31 SR (NSW) 183 **[5.5.7]**, *Clayton v Heffron* (1960) 105 CLR 214 **[5.3.16C]** and *Cormack v Cope* (1974) 131 CLR 432 **[5.5.3C]** may be resolved by legislative provisions such as s 10a(7) of the Constitution Act 1934 (SA):

> **10a(7)** Any person entitled to vote at an election for a member or members of the House of Assembly or the Legislative Council shall have the right to bring an action in the Supreme Court for a declaration, injunction or other legal remedy to enforce any of the provisions of this section either before or after any bill referred to in this section is presented to the Governor for Her Majesty's assent.

Section 10a(2) prohibits the presentation to the Governor for royal assent of any bill to abolish the Assembly or Council, to alter the powers of the Council, to change the provisions for altering the Constitution Act or for resolving deadlocks or for repealing or amending s 10a until the bill has been approved by the electors at a referendum.

Similar provisions can be found in s 53(5) of the Constitution Act 1867 (Qld) and s 73(6) of the Constitution Act 1889 (WA).

[5.5.16] Section 10a(7) could be read as merely overcoming the problem of standing to bring proceedings; as liberalising the restrictive rules developed by the courts to determine who may be permitted to challenge the validity of government action. However, the reference to 'an action in the Supreme Court ... either before or after any Bill ... is presented to the Governor' suggests that the subsection was intended to deal with at least some of the questions of jurisdiction and discretion. That reading is supported by a comparison with s 88(5) of the Constitution Act 1934 (SA), which appears to be limited to overcoming the problem of standing:

> **88(5)** Any person entitled to vote at a general election of members of the House of Assembly shall have the right to bring an action in the Supreme Court for a declaration, injunction or other legal remedy to enforce any of the provisions of this section.

(Section 88 provides that a bill to alter the system for the distribution of Assembly electorates or to alter s 88 shall not be presented to the Governor for the royal assent unless the bill has been approved by the electors at a referendum.)

If s 10a(7) and its Queensland and Western Australian equivalents do go beyond the problem of standing, what impact do they have on the questions of jurisdiction and discretion? They almost certainly dispel the serious doubts over the courts' jurisdiction to intervene in the legislative process; doubts expressed in the joint judgment of Dixon CJ, McTiernan, Taylor and Windeyer JJ in *Clayton v Heffron* (1960) 105 CLR 214 **[5.5.14]** at 235 and by Menzies and Stephen JJ in *Cormack v Cope* (1974) 131 CLR 432 **[5.5.3C]** at 464–5, 472. But, if these provisions establish a jurisdiction to intervene, what effect do they have on those factors which, according to many judicial views, would persuade a court to exercise its discretion against intervention? See, for example, *Trethowan v Peden* (1930) 31 SR (NSW) 183 **[5.5.7]**, *McDonald v Cain* [1953] VLR 411 **[5.5.8]**, and Barwick CJ in *Cormack v Cope* (1974) 131 CLR 432 **[5.5.3C]** at 460.

6   References

[5.6.1]   *Articles*

Allan, 'The Limits of Parliamentary Sovereignty' [1985] *Public Law* 614.

Beinart, 'Parliament and the Courts' [1954] *South African LR* 134.

Campbell, 'Changing the Constitution — Past and Future' (1989) 17 *Melbourne Uni LR* 1.

Canaway, 'The Safety Valve of the Constitution' (1938) 12 *ALJ* 108.

Castles, 'Constitutional Conventions and the Senate' [1975] *ACLD* DT286.

Conklin, 'Pickin and its Applicability to Canada' (1975) 25 *Uni of Toronto LJ* 193.

Cowen, 'Legislature and Judiciary' (1953) 16 *Modern LR* 273.

Cowen, 'A Historical Survey of the Victorian Constitution 1856–1956' (1957) *Melbourne Uni LR* 9.

Goldsworthy, 'Manner and Form in the Australian States' (1987) 16 *Melbourne Uni LR* 403.

Gray, 'The Sovereignty of Parliament Today' (1953–4) 10 *Uni of Toronto LJ* 54.

Katz, 'Simultaneous Dissolution of Both Houses of the Australian Federal Parliament, 1975' (1976) 54 *Canadian Bar Rev* 392.

Latham, 'Changing the Constitution' (1949) 1 *Syd L Rev* 14.

Lee, 'The Australia Act 1986: Some Legislative Conundrums' (1988) 14 *Monash LR* 298.

O'Brien, 'The Power of the House of Representatives over Supply' (1976) 3 *Monash LR* 8.

Richardson, 'The Legislative Power of the Senate in Respect of Money Bills' (1976) 47 *ALJ* 285.

Sawer, 'Some Legal Assumptions of Constitutional Change' (1957) 4 *WA Annual LR* 1.

Wade, 'The Basis of Legal Sovereignty' [1955] *Cambridge LJ* 172.

Winterton, 'Can the Commonwealth Parliament enact manner and form legislation?' (1980) 11 *Federal LR* 167.

[5.6.2]   *Papers and reports*

Constitutional Commission, *Final Report*, AGPS, Canberra, 1988.

[5.6.3]   *Texts*

Campbell, Glasson, Lee and Sharpe, *Legal Research: Materials and Methods*, 3rd ed, Lawbook Co, Sydney, 1988.

Craven, *Secession: The Ultimate State Right*, Melbourne University Press, Melbourne, 1986.

Crawford, 'Amendment of the Constitution' in *Australian Federation Towards the Second Century: A Work to Mark the Centenary of the Australasian Federation Conference*, (ed Craven), Melbourne University Press, 1992, pp 177ff.

Crisp, *Australian National Government*, Longman Cheshire, 1965; 4th ed, Melbourne, 1978.

Davies, 'The Government of Victoria' in *The Government of the Australian States*, (ed Davis), Longmans, London, 1960, pp 73–247.

Davis (ed), *The Government of the Australian States*, Longmans, London, 1960.

de Smith, *Constitutional and Administrative Law*, 4th ed, Penguin, New York, 1981.

Dicey, *The Law of the Constitution*, 10th ed, Macmillan, London, 1959.

Encel, Horne and Thompson (eds), *Change the Rules!: Towards a Democratic Constitution*, Penguin, Melbourne, 1977.

Eggleston, 'Commentary' in *Labor and the Constitution 1972–1975*, (ed Evans), Heinemann Educational, Melbourne, 1977, pp 297–301.

Evans (ed), *Labor and the Constitution 1972–1975*, Heinemann Educational, Melbourne, 1977.

Evatt, *The King and His Dominion Governors*, 2nd ed, Cheshire, Melbourne, 1967.

Hall and Iremonger, *The Makers and the Breakers*, Wellington Lane Press, Sydney, 1976.

Hanks, *Australian Constitutional Law*, 2nd ed, Butterworths, Sydney, 1980; 3rd ed, Butterworths, Sydney, 1985.

Heuston, *Essays in Constitutional Law*, 2nd ed, Stevens, London, 1964.

Howard and Saunders, 'The Blocking of the Budget and the Dismissal of the Government' in *Labor and the Constitution 1972–1975*, (ed Evans), Heinemann Educational, Melbourne, 1977, pp 251–87.

Jennings, *The Law and the Constitution*, 5th ed, University of London Press, London, 1959.

La Nauze, *The Making of the Australian Constitution*, Melbourne University Press, Melbourne, 1972.

Lindell, 'Duty to Exercise Judicial Review' in *Commentaries on the Australian Constitution*, (ed Zines), Butterworths, Sydney, 1977, pp 150–90.

Lumb, *The Constitutions of the Australian States*, 4th ed, University of Queensland Press, St Lucia, 1977.

Lumb and Moens, *The Constitution of the Commonwealth of Australia Annotated*, 5th ed, Butterworths, Sydney, 1995. (4th ed, 1986)

MacMillan, Evans and Storey, *Australia's Constitution: Time for Change?*, Law Foundation of NSW and George Allen and Unwin, Sydney, 1983.

Marshall, *Parliamentary Sovereignty and the Commonwealth*, Clarendon Press, Oxford, 1957.

Marshall and Moodie, *Some Problems of the Constitution*, 4th ed, Hutchinson, London, 1967.

Morrison, 'The Government of Queensland' in *The Government of the Australian States*, (ed Davis), Longmans, London, 1960, pp 249–332.

O'Connell and Riordan, *Opinions on Imperial Constitutional Law*, Lawbook Co, Sydney, 1971.

Odgers, *Australian Senate Practice*, 5th ed, AGPS, Canberra, 1976.

Pearce, 'The Legislative Power of the Senate' in *Commentaries on the Australian Constitution*, (ed Zines), Butterworths, Sydney, 977, pp 119–37.

Quick and Garran, *Annotated Constitution of the Australian Commonwealth*, Angus & Robertson, Sydney, 1901.

Quinton (ed), *Political Philosophy*, Oxford University Press, London, 1967.

Sawer, *Federation Under Strain*, Melbourne University Press, Melbourne, 1977.

Wade and Phillips, *Constitutional Law: An Outline of the Law and the Practice of the Constitution, Including Central and Local Government and the Constitutional Relations of the British Commonwealth*, 7th ed, Longman, London, 1965.

Zines, 'The Double Dissolutions and The Joint Sitting' in *Labor and the Constitution 1972–1975*, (ed Evans), Heinemann Educational, Melbourne, 1977, pp 217–39.

Chapter

6

Limits to Legislative Power

1 Introduction

[6.1.1] Australia's recent history as a series of British colonies is reflected in her institutions of government, with legislatures constructed along the general lines of the Westminster model; executive power formally vested in a Governor-General and state Governors, who present many of the characteristics of agents of a distant monarch and who are advised by Ministers in a close facsimile of the Westminster system of responsible government; and judicial power vested in courts modelled on the English court system.

Australia's judicial institutions achieved autonomy as recently as 1986, when s 11 of the Australia Act 1986 (Cth) abolished appeals from state courts to the Privy Council, as almost all appeals from the High Court to the Privy Council had been abolished in 1975, by the Privy Council (Appeals from the High Court) Act 1975 (Cth). The 1975 and 1986 legislation left only the technical possibility of appeals from the High Court on 'inter se questions', with a certificate of that court, under s 74 of the Commonwealth Constitution, a possibility so remote as to be a practical impossibility: see *Kirmani v Captain Cook Cruises Pty Ltd (No 2)* (1985) 159 CLR 351.

At the same time, state legislatures were freed from several constraints on their legislative power, constraints which had been developed to serve Imperial interests. These constraints had included an inability to repeal or amend United Kingdom legislation extending to the Australian states (an inability removed by s 3 of the Australia Act 1986), and a territorial limit on state legislative competence (probably removed by s 2 of the Australia Act 1986). The Commonwealth Parliament had been freed from these constraints upon the adoption of the Statute of Westminster 1931 (UK), with effect from 3 September 1939, by the Statute of Westminster Adoption Act 1942 (Cth).

[6.1.2] The Australian constitutional system also reflects ideas about the appropriate organisation of institutions of government developed in England during the 17th and 18th centuries and adopted in the drafting and interpretation of the United States Constitution in the 18th and 19th centuries, ideas which were designed to prevent an accumulation or concentration of governmental power. These ideas focused on the separation of the institutions of government, typically divided into legislature, executive and judiciary.

The purpose of this chapter is to explore the extent to which Australian constitutional law continues to reflect the constraining and limiting concepts developed to protect Imperial interests and to check and balance governmental power. The extent to which implied rights arising from the separation of judicial power constrain and limit governmental power is explored further in Chapter 11.

2   Imperial legislation and local legislation

The states

Colonial background

[6.2.1] When the first Australian colony was founded as New South Wales in 1788, it was assumed that the colonists brought with them a substantial part of the laws of England (not, it will be observed, of Great Britain; the 18th and 19th century governments of Great Britain and the United Kingdom were certainly anglocentric). The accepted rule at that time was that when a colony was acquired by peaceful settlement rather than conquest, the colonists took with them so much of existing English law as was suitable to conditions in the colony. The view that Australia was not conquered but settled by British colonists was based on the racist assumption that the inhabitants were neither civilised nor organised under any settled system of law: see *Cooper v Stuart* (1889) 14 App Cas 286. One of the consequences of that assumption, that the land rights of the original inhabitants were extinguished on British occupation, was repudiated by the High Court in *Mabo v Queensland (No 2)* (1992) 175 CLR 1. However, the basic proposition, that the legal system of Australia is derived from those elements of English law imported into Australia by the first colonists, survived that decision. In the early 19th century, when the proposition was not as certain and settled as it had become by the end of that century, the United Kingdom Parliament enacted a statute to declare that the laws of England in force at that date should apply in the colony of New South Wales so far as they were applicable to conditions there: Australian Courts Act 1828 (UK) (9 Geo IV c 83) s 28; see Castles (1963–66) pp 5–11, 13–19.

[6.2.2] The inherited English law was subject to modifications in two ways. The United Kingdom Parliament might legislate for the colonies (that is, pass legislation intended to extend not only to the United Kingdom but also to the overseas territories of the Crown), and the local colonial legislatures might make some modifications to the inherited law. Be that as it may, the extent of this modifying power was a matter of considerable dispute and a number of colonial enactments were declared invalid because they had infringed some fundamental principle of English law: Campbell (1964–67); Castles (1963–66) pp 22–31.

The confusion generated by this approach to local legislation was largely clarified by ss 2 and 3 of the Colonial Laws Validity Act 1865 (UK). Section 2 declared 'absolutely void and inoperative' any colonial law which was repugnant to the provisions of any United Kingdom legislation extending to the colony: see **[6.2.5]**. Section 3 provided that, in the absence of such conflict, no colonial law could be impeached because of its 'Repugnancy to the Law of England'. However, the rules that the United Kingdom Parliament could still legislate for Australia and that the states could not legislate so as to repeal or amend United Kingdom legislation extending to Australia were not disturbed until the passage of the Australia Act 1986 **[6.2.7E]**.

[6.2.3]   The continuing power of the United Kingdom Parliament to legislate for the Australian states was discussed by the High Court in *China Ocean Shipping Co v South Australia* (1979) 145 CLR 172. In concluding that ss 503 and 504 of the Merchant Shipping Act 1894 (UK) remained part of the law of South Australia despite the evolution of Australian political autonomy, the court pointed to s 509 of the Act which declared that the relevant sections were to 'extend to the whole of Her Majesty's Dominions' and to the 19th century orthodoxy that the United Kingdom Parliament had the paramount power to legislate for Australia. Neither the Commonwealth of Australia Constitution Act 1900 (UK) nor the Statute of Westminster 1931 (UK) removed that power, although each of them marked a significant step towards Australian independence from the United Kingdom. Stephen J expressed the court's view on the continuing authority (in 1979) of the United Kingdom Parliament, at 212:

> The legislative power of the Parliament at Westminster albeit responsive only to prior Australian initiatives, remains, for Australia, a factor in present-day constitutional law, despite the undoubted changes in relationships which have occurred and which are reflected in the current realities of national political power and in Australia's own nationhood.

Stephen J conceded that the continuation of Imperial laws regulating merchant shipping in the Australian states had created an unsatisfactory situation, at 214:

> It is a situation which has remained substantially unaltered through the lives of many successive governments, Imperial law continuing to overlay what might be thought to be proper areas for the operation of Australian laws. It no doubt calls for radical reform but it is by legislative initiative, possible ever since the adoption of the Statute of Westminster, that it must be achieved and not, at least in my view, by the adoption of the defendant's present submission [that the Imperial legislation was no longer in force in Australia].

[6.2.4]   Until the passage of the Australia Act 1986 (Cth), the United Kingdom Parliament was regarded as technically competent to legislate for the Australian states. However, the evolution of Australian political autonomy generated increasing reluctance on the part of Australian courts to accept that the United Kingdom Parliament had actually exercised its residual legal power.

In *Ukley v Ukley* [1977] VR 121, the Full Court of the Victorian Supreme Court concluded that the Foreign Tribunals Evidence Act 1856 (UK), which applied in Victoria because the United Kingdom Parliament had extended it to Victoria, had not been repealed in Victoria by the Evidence (Proceedings in Other Jurisdictions)

Act 1975 (UK). The latter Act contained no express reference to Victoria, or to any of the Australian states, though it was argued that, because the 1975 Act repealed the whole of the 1856 Act, it had the effect of repealing that Act in Victoria.

The Full Court examined what it described as the 'gradual change over the last hundred years' in judicial and political attitudes towards United Kingdom legislation in overseas territories of the Crown. The judges referred to *Copyright Owners Reproduction Society Ltd v EMI (Aust) Pty Ltd* (1958) 100 CLR 597 **[6.2.20]** and to s 4 of the Statute of Westminster 1931 (UK) **[6.2.15E]**. Notwithstanding that the Statute of Westminster failed to exempt the states from the power of the United Kingdom Parliament, the court said:

> [I]t cannot be doubted that in these times the Parliament at Westminster would not legislate so as to affect the law in operation in an Australian State except at the request of and with the consent of the State concerned ([1977] VR at 130).

The court proceeded to reject an argument that a United Kingdom statute repealing an earlier Act which had applied to Victoria would automatically repeal the earlier Act in Victoria. 'The strong and unbending convention', that the Imperial Parliament would only legislate for a self-governing dominion with the consent of that dominion, told against such an argument: at 131.

[6.2.5]　The extension to the Australian states of legislation enacted by the United Kingdom Parliament was regarded, until 1986, as limiting the legislative power of state parliaments: they could not legislate to repeal or amend Imperial legislation which extended to the state (as distinct from having been received at the time of British settlement or occupation). Section 2 of the Colonial Laws Validity Act 1865 (UK) declared 'absolutely void and inoperative' any colonial law which was repugnant to the provisions of any United Kingdom legislation extending to the colony. Section 3 provided that, in the absence of such conflict, no colonial law could be impeached because of its 'Repugnancy to the Law of England'.

The Colonial Laws Validity Act was drafted in the Colonial Office, largely as a response to the efforts of Boothby J of the South Australian Supreme Court. From his appointment to the bench in 1853 until his removal in 1867, Boothby J pursued a consistent policy of protecting English law (both statute and common law) against local legislative innovations. He declared invalid the Constitution Act, the Real Property Act, two Electoral Acts, legislation establishing the Court of Appeal and the appointment of the Chief Justice of the South Australian Supreme Court, on the ground that the local legislation was inconsistent with 'fundamental' principles of English common law.

The prime purpose of the Act of 1865 was to free colonial legislatures from the restrictions which Boothby J's judgments had imposed. Consequently the critical section was s 3, a point emphasised in *Union Steamship Co of New Zealand Ltd v Commonwealth* (1925) 36 CLR 130 **[6.2.13]** by Higgins J at 155–6:

> The object of the Act of 1865 was not so much to preserve the rights of the British Parliament against encroaching colonial legislatures, as to make it clear that a colonial legislature, acting for the colony in pursuance of the powers of legislation conferred, might act freely and without constraint from London, excepting only so far as a British Act, applying or extending to the Colony, definitely contradicted the colonial legislation ... The colonial Act is to be valid except to the extent of any actual repugnancy or direct collision between the two sets of provisions. Such a concession on the part of the supreme Parliament marks a very high level of liberality, foresight, statesmanship.

[6.2.6] However, by 1986 the prime focus of attention was s 2 of the Colonial Laws Validity Act, which inhibited the legislative powers of state parliaments in a fashion which bore no relation to their contemporary political status. The Australia Act was, essentially, a legal endorsement of that contemporary status: see Goldring (1986) p 204.

Legal autonomy for the states

[6.2.7E] **Australia Act 1986 (Cth)**

WHEREAS the Prime Minister of the Commonwealth and the Premiers of the States at conferences held in Canberra on 24 and 25 June 1982 and 21 June 1984 agreed on the taking of certain measures to bring constitutional arrangements affecting the Commonwealth and the States into conformity with the status of the Commonwealth of Australia as a sovereign, independent and federal nation:

AND WHEREAS in pursuance of paragraph 51(xxxviii) of the Constitution the Parliaments of all the States have requested the Parliament of the Commonwealth to enact an Act in the terms of this Act:

BE IT THEREFORE ENACTED by the Queen, and the Senate and the House of Representatives of the Commonwealth of Australia, as follows:

Termination of power of Parliament of United Kingdom to legislate for Australia

1   No Act of the Parliament of the United Kingdom passed after the commencement of this Act shall extend, or be deemed to extend, to the Commonwealth, to a State or to a Territory as part of the law of the Commonwealth, of the State or of the Territory.

Legislative powers of Parliaments of States

2(1) It is hereby declared and enacted that the legislative powers of the Parliament of each State include full power to make laws for the peace, order and good government of that State that have extra-territorial operation.

(2)   It is hereby further declared and enacted that the legislative powers of the Parliament of each State include all legislative powers that the Parliament of the United Kingdom might have exercised before the commencement of this Act for the peace, order and good government of that State but nothing in this subsection confers on a State any capacity that the State did not have immediately before the commencement of this Act to engage in relations with countries outside Australia.

Termination of restrictions on legislative powers of Parliaments of States

3(1) The Act of the Parliament of the United Kingdom known as the Colonial Laws Validity Act 1865 shall not apply to any law made after the commencement of this Act by the Parliament of a State.

(2)   No law and no provision of any law made after the commencement of this Act by the Parliament of a State shall be void or inoperative on the ground that it is repugnant to the law of England, or to the provisions of any existing or future Act of the Parliament of the United Kingdom, or to any order, rule or regulation made under any such Act, and the powers of the Parliament of a State shall include the power to repeal or amend any such act, order, rule or regulation in so far as it is part of the law of the State.

Powers of State Parliaments in relation to merchant shipping

4   Sections 735 and 736 of the Act of the Parliament of the UK known as the Merchant Shipping Act 1894, insofar as they are part of the law of a State, are hereby repealed.

Commonwealth Constitution, Constitution Act and Statute of Westminster not affected

5   Sections 2 and 3(2) above —

(a)   are subject to the Commonwealth of Australia Constitution Act and to the Constitution of the Commonwealth; and

(b)   do not operate so as to give any force or effect to a provision of an Act of the Parliament of a State that would repeal, amend or be repugnant to this Act, the Commonwealth of Australia Constitution Act, the Constitution of the Commonwealth or the Statute of Westminster 1931 as amended and in force from time to time. ...

State laws not subject to disallowance or suspension of operation

8   An Act of the Parliament of a State that has been assented to by the Governor of the State shall not, after the commencement of this Act, be subject to disallowance by Her Majesty, nor shall its operation be suspended pending the signification of Her Majesty's pleasure thereon.

State laws not subject to withholding of assent or reservation

9(1)   No law or instrument shall be of any force or effect in so far as it purports to require the Governor of a State to withhold assent from any Bill for an Act of the State that has been passed in such manner and form as may from time to time be required by a law made by the Parliament of the State.

(2)   No law or instrument shall be of any force or effect in so far as it purports to require the reservation of any Bill for an Act of a State for the signification of Her Majesty's pleasure thereon. ...

Termination of appeals to Her Majesty in Council

11(1) Subject to subsection (4) below, no appeal to Her Majesty in Council lies or shall be brought, whether by leave or special leave of any court or of Her Majesty in Council or otherwise, and whether by virtue of any Act of the Parliament of the United Kingdom, the Royal Prerogative or otherwise, from or in respect of any decision of an Australian court. ...

(4)   Nothing in the foregoing provisions of this section —

(a)   affects an appeal instituted before the commencement of this Act to Her Majesty in Council from or in respect of a decision of an Australian court; or

(b)   precludes the institution after that commencement of an appeal to Her Majesty in Council from or in respect of such a decision where the appeal is instituted —

(i)   pursuant to leave granted by an Australian court on an application made before that commencement; or

(ii)   pursuant to special leave granted by Her Majesty in Council on a petition presented before that commencement,

but this subsection shall not be construed as permitting or enabling an appeal to Her Majesty in Council to be instituted or continued that could not have been instituted or continued if this section had not been enacted.

Amendment of Statute of Westminster

12   Sections 4, 9(2) and (3) and 10(2) of the Statute of Westminster 1931, in so far as they are part of the law of the Commonwealth, of a State or of a Territory, are hereby repealed.

~~~

Notes

[6.2.8] The Australia Act 1986 (Cth) was enacted by the Commonwealth Parliament as Act No 142 of 1985, relying on s 51(xxxviii) of the Commonwealth Constitution, and at the request of the parliaments of the Australian states: see, for example, the Australia Acts (Request) Act 1985 (Vic). At the same time, the Commonwealth Parliament enacted the Australia (Request and Consent) Act 1985, s 3 of which requested and consented to the enactment by the United Kingdom

Parliament of legislation substantially identical to the Australia Act 1986 (Cth) as United Kingdom legislation extending to Australia. (This formal request and consent by the Commonwealth Parliament was intended to clear the obstacle erected by s 4 of the Statute of Westminster: see **[6.2.15E]**.) The United Kingdom Parliament then enacted the Australia Act 1986 (UK). As Zines explains, this series of legislation at three levels was used 'to ensure that no argument could occur as to the validity of the arrangements': Zines (1992) p 263.

[6.2.9] The High Court's decision in *Port MacDonnell Professional Fishermen's Association Inc v South Australia* (1989) 168 CLR 340 has put at rest any doubts as to the validity of the Australia Act 1986 (Cth). In the unanimous opinion of the court, s 51(xxxviii) of the Constitution should be given a broad interpretation reflecting its 'national purpose of a fundamental kind', which is that of 'plugging gaps which might otherwise exist in the overall plenitude of the legislative powers exercisable by the Commonwealth and State parliaments under the Constitution': 168 CLR at 378, 379.

[6.2.10] Section 1 of the Australia Act is prospective. It terminates the capacity of the United Kingdom to extend its legislation to Australia 'after the commencement of this Act'; that is, 3 March 1986, the date fixed for its commencement in *Commonwealth Gazette* No S85, 2 March 1986. However, the section will not prevent United Kingdom legislation enacted prior to that date being found to extend to Australia, so that the problems posed for judicial solution in the *China Ocean Shipping* case (1979) 145 CLR 172 **[6.2.3]** and *Ukley v Ukley* [1977] VR 121 **[6.2.4]** have not been totally eliminated.

[6.2.11] Section 3 of the Australia Act is also prospective. It liberates state parliaments from the constraints of the Colonial Laws Validity Act 1865 (UK) and, to remove any possible doubts over the powers of state parliaments, authorises each state parliament to repeal or amend any United Kingdom legislation which extends to the state. These effects are limited to any state law made 'after the commencement of this Act'; that is, 3 March 1986. It follows that state legislation passed before that date is still at risk of being invalidated if found to be 'repugnant' to United Kingdom legislation.

The Commonwealth

Initial colonial status

[6.2.12] From its establishment in 1901, the Commonwealth of Australia was subject, just as the Australian colonies had been and the states were, to the legislative power of the United Kingdom Parliament. That parliament could legislate for, and extend its legislation to, the Commonwealth as a whole. An example of this was the enactment of the Copyright Act 1911 (UK), discussed in *Copyright Owners Reproduction Society Ltd v EMI (Aust) Pty Ltd* (1958) 100 CLR 597 **[6.2.20]** and the Naval Discipline (Dominion Naval Forces) Act 1911 (UK) considered by the High Court in *R v Bevan; Ex parte Elias and Gordon* (1942) 66 CLR 452.

[6.2.13] In the period from 1901 until the adoption of the Statute of Westminster by the Commonwealth Parliament in 1942, the legislative power of the Commonwealth Parliament was subject to the same Imperial restrictions as those imposed on the states: see **[6.2.5]**. That is, parliament was subject to s 2 of the Colonial Laws Validity Act 1865 (UK) and, therefore, incompetent to repeal or amend legislation of the United Kingdom Parliament extending to Australia.

This point was demonstrated in *Union Steamship Co of New Zealand Ltd v Commonwealth* (1925) 36 CLR 130. The High Court decided that provisions of the Navigation Act 1912 (Cth) were repugnant to the Merchant Shipping Acts 1894 and 1906 (UK), which extended to Australia. Isaacs J said that the Merchant Shipping Acts dealt with the subject of merchant shipping 'from the standpoint of what is now recognised as the British Commonwealth of Nations [while the Navigation Act] treats the subject-matter from an all-Australian standpoint': 36 CLR at 147. He likened repugnancy between United Kingdom and Commonwealth legislation under s 2 of the Colonial Laws Validity Act to inconsistency between Commonwealth and state legislation under s 109 of the Commonwealth Constitution. He said that the Commonwealth legislation was repugnant to the Merchant Shipping Acts because the two pieces of legislation could not 'stand together'. They could only do this, Isaacs J said, if they were 'identical; and not merely identical in terms but identical in obligation': 36 CLR at 150.

[6.2.14]   However, political developments were outpacing the law. In 1926, an Imperial Conference of Dominion Prime Ministers declared that the British Empire had:

> ... one most important element in it which, from a strictly constitutional point of view, has now, as regards all vital matters, reached its full development — we refer to the group of self-governing communities composed of Great Britain and the dominions. Their position and mutual relation may be readily defined. *They are autonomous communities within the British Empire, equal in status, in no way subordinate one to another in any aspect of their domestic or external affairs, though united by a common allegiance to the Crown, and freely associated as members of the British Commonwealth of Nations* (Report of Imperial Conference (1926) Cmd 2768).

The report recognised that existing administrative legislative and judicial forms were not in accord with the political position and recommended the appointment of a committee to review the legal relationship between the United Kingdom and the dominions. In 1929, an Imperial Conference on Dominion Legislation and Merchant Shipping Legislation recommended that the United Kingdom Parliament legislate to free the self-governing dominions from their position of legal subservience to United Kingdom legislation. This conference drafted, and recommended the enactment of, what are now ss 2, 3 and 4 of the Statute of Westminster 1931 (UK).

In 1930, a further Imperial Conference of Dominion Prime Ministers endorsed the 1929 recommendations and proposed that, after resolutions had been passed by the various dominion parliaments, the United Kingdom Parliament should enact the Statute of Westminster.

Legal autonomy for the Commonwealth

[6.2.15E]   **Statute of Westminster 1931 (UK)**

1   In this Act the expression 'Dominion' means any of the following Dominions, that is to say, the Dominion of Canada, the Commonwealth of Australia, the Dominion of New Zealand, the Union of South Africa, the Irish Free State and Newfoundland.

2(1)   The Colonial Laws Validity Act, 1865, shall not apply to any law made after the commencement of this Act by the Parliament of a Dominion.

(2) No law and no provision of any law made after the commencement of this Act by the Parliament of a Dominion shall be void or inoperative on the ground that it is repugnant to the law of England, or to the provisions of any existing or future Act of Parliament of the United Kingdom, or to any order, rule or regulation made under any such Act, and the powers of the Parliament of a Dominion shall include the power to repeal or amend any such Act, order, rule or regulation in so far as the same is part of the law of the Dominion.

3 It is hereby declared and enacted that the Parliament of a Dominion has full power to make laws having extra-territorial operation.

4 No Act of Parliament of the United Kingdom passed after the commencement of this Act shall extend, or be deemed to extend, to a Dominion as part of the law of that Dominion, unless it is expressly declared in that Act that that Dominion has requested, and consented to, the enactment thereof. ...

8 Nothing in this Act shall be deemed to confer any power to repeal or alter the Constitution or the Constitution Act of the Commonwealth of Australia or the Constitution Act of the Dominion of New Zealand otherwise than in accordance with the law existing before the commencement of this Act.

9(1) Nothing in this Act shall be deemed to authorize the Parliament of the Commonwealth of Australia to make laws on any matter within the authority of the States of Australia, not being a matter within the authority of the Parliament or Government of the Commonwealth of Australia.

(2) Nothing in this Act shall be deemed to require the concurrence of the Parliament or Government of the Commonwealth of Australia in any law made by the Parliament of the United Kingdom with respect to any matter within the authority of the States of Australia, not being a matter within the authority of the Parliament or Government of the Commonwealth of Australia, in any case where it would have been in accordance with the constitutional practice existing before the commencement of this Act that the Parliament of the United Kingdom should make that law without such concurrence.

(3) In the application of this Act to the Commonwealth of Australia the request and consent referred to in section four shall mean the request and consent of the Parliament and Government of the Commonwealth.

10(1) None of the following sections of this Act, that is to say, sections two, three, four, five and six, shall extend to a Dominion to which this section applies as part of the law of that Dominion unless that section is adopted by the Parliament of the Dominion, and any Act of that Parliament adopting any section of this Act may provide that the adoption shall have effect either from the commencement of this Act or from such later date as is specified in the adopting Act.

(2) The Parliament of any such Dominion as aforesaid may at any time revoke the adoption of any section referred to in subsection (1) of this section.

(3) The Dominions to which this section applies are the Commonwealth of Australia, the Dominion of New Zealand and Newfoundland.

11 Notwithstanding anything in the Interpretation Act, 1889, the expression 'Colony' shall not, in any Act of the Parliament of the United Kingdom passed after the commencement of this Act, include a Dominion or any Province or State forming part of a Dominion.

~~~

Notes

[6.2.16] The Commonwealth Parliament exercised the power given to it in s 10(1) of the Statute of Westminster by enacting the Statute of Westminster Adoption Act 1942 (Cth):

3 Sections two, three, four, five and six of the Imperial Act entitled the Statute of Westminster 1931 (which is set out in the Schedule to this Act) are adopted and the adoption shall have effect from the third day of September, One thousand nine hundred and thirty-nine.

[6.2.17] The substantive provisions of the Statute of Westminster did not extend to the Australian states. In 1972, the New South Wales Law Reform Commission published a *Working Paper on Legislative Powers* in which it recommended that the United Kingdom Parliament be asked to legislate for the Australian states in terms similar to those used in the Statute of Westminster. In 1982, a conference of Commonwealth and state political leaders agreed to proceed along those lines. That agreement was refined at a second conference in 1984, when the process which led to the enactment of the Australia Act 1986 (Cth) and the Australia Act 1986 (UK) was settled: see **[6.2.7E]**.

[6.2.18] Section 1 of the Australia Act 1986 **[6.2.7E]** appears to have put an end to the possibility, left open by s 4 of the Statute of Westminster, of the United Kingdom Parliament legislating for the Commonwealth of Australia. No doubt, as with the states **[6.2.10]** there remains the possibility of the United Kingdom legislation passed before 3 March 1986 being found to extend to Australia. However, the requirement, specified in s 4 of the Statute of Westminster, that such legislation declare that the Commonwealth has requested and consented to its enactment, must render that possibility remote: see *Copyright Owners Reproduction Society Ltd v EMI (Aust) Pty Ltd* (1958) 100 CLR **[6.2.20]**.

[6.2.19] It might also be said that there remains the possibility that the United Kingdom Parliament could repeal both the Statute of Westminster and the Australia Act. In *British Coal Corporation v R* [1935] AC 500, Lord Sankey LC said at 520:

> It is doubtless true that the power of the Imperial Parliament to pass on its own initiative any legislation that it thought fit extending to Canada remains unimpaired; indeed, the Imperial Parliament could, as a matter of abstract law, repeal or disregard s 4 of the Statute. But that is theory and has no relation to realities.

Even 'as a matter of abstract law', it is most unlikely that Australian courts would recognise such an unsolicited repeal as part of the law of Australia. The growth of Australian autonomy since the 1930s, and the more recent development of Australian nationalism, must be regarded as having entrenched both the Statute of Westminster and the Australia Act as elements in Australia's *grundnorm*. On this point, see Zines (1992) p 265.

[6.2.20] The absolute necessity for United Kingdom legislation, passed after the commencement of the Statute of Westminster and purporting to extend to the Commonwealth of Australia, to contain the declaration referred to in s 4 of the Statute was emphasised by the High Court in *Copyright Owners Reproduction Society Ltd v EMI (Aust) Pty Ltd* (1958) 100 CLR 597. The court decided that although the Copyright Act 1911 (UK) had extended to Australia because it contained an express provision to that effect, the repeal of the 1911 Act by the Copyright Act 1956 (UK) did not affect the former Act's operation in Australia. Dixon CJ said at 604:

> The Act of 1956 contains no declaration that the Commonwealth of Australia has requested or consented to the enactment thereof. The repeal, therefore, of the Act of 1911 which is effected by the Act of 1956, does not, because of s 4 of the Statute of Westminster 1931 (adopted by Act No 56 of 1942), extend to Australia.

Dixon CJ noted that the Copyright Act 1956 (UK) contained a provision to the effect that the Act of 1911 was to continue in operation in any other country where it was in force. He observed at 604:

> It may be remarked that perhaps in view of s 4 of the Statute of Westminster this provision does not operate in point of law in Australia, and what its operation in the United Kingdom can be in point of fact it is difficult to see.

The court also concluded that an amendment made to the Copyright Act 1911 (UK) by the Copyright (Mechanical Instruments: Royalties) Act 1928 (UK) did not operate in Australia because it contained no expression of the United Kingdom Parliament's intention that it should extend to Australia. Dixon CJ said at 612:

> It is true that in 1928 the Statute of Westminster had not yet been passed but the convention was strong and unbending which governed the exercise of the legislative power of the Parliament of the United Kingdom to affect the law in operation in a dominion. Every presumption of the construction was against such an intention. Further, the concurrence of the dominion was treated as an indispensable condition.

[6.2.21] The adoption of the Statute of Westminster 1931 (UK) **[6.2.15E]** put an end to the restraint on Commonwealth legislative power which had flowed from the extension of United Kingdom legislation to Australia and from the conventional view that the Commonwealth had the status of a British colony, subject to the continuing power of the United Kingdom Parliament: see **[6.2.12]**.

Section 2(1) terminated the application of the Colonial Laws Validity Act to laws made by the Commonwealth Parliament after the commencement of the Statute of Westminster; that is, in the case of the Commonwealth of Australia, from 3 September 1939: Statute of Westminster Adoption Act 1942 (Cth), s 3 **[6.2.16]**. Section 2(2) makes clear that this termination does not revive the common law limitation on 'colonial' legislatures which had been expressed in s 2 of the Colonial Laws Validity Act; namely, no law made by the Commonwealth Parliament after 3 September 1939 'shall be void or inoperative on the ground that it is repugnant to the law of England'.

[6.2.22] It is clear that s 2 of the Statute of Westminster removes the constraint on Commonwealth legislative power expressed in s 2 of the Colonial Laws Validity Act. However, the concluding clause of s 2(2) of the Statute may go further and confer additional legislative power on the Commonwealth Parliament; additional, that is, to the powers listed in the Commonwealth Constitution. Such a reading of s 2(2) of the Statute of Westminster is supported by some of the judgments in *Kirmani v Captain Cook Cruises Pty Ltd (No 1)* (1985) 159 CLR 351.

The central issue raised in that case was whether the Commonwealth Parliament had the power to legislate so as to repeal s 503(1) of the Merchant Shipping Act 1894 (UK), which was part of the law of New South Wales and which limited the liability of a shipowner to pay damages for personal injury suffered by a passenger on the ship. The Commonwealth Parliament had purported to repeal s 503(1), in so far as it was 'part of the law of the Commonwealth', by s 104(3) of the Navigation Amendment Act 1979 (Cth).

Mason, Murphy and Deane JJ decided that the Commonwealth's repeal of s 503(1) of the Merchant Shipping Act was supported by s 51(xxix), the 'external affairs' power. Brennan J decided that the repeal was supported by s 2(2) of the Statute of Westminster. Gibbs CJ, Wilson and Dawson JJ dissented from both of these propositions.

Brennan J referred to two decisions of the Privy Council, *Moore v Attorney-General (Irish Free State)* [1935] AC 484 and *British Coal Corporation v R* [1935] AC 500. In the former case, the Privy Council had said at 498:

> The effect of the Statute of Westminster was to remove the fetter which lay upon the Irish Free State Legislature by reason for the Colonial Laws Validity Act. That legislature can now pass Acts repugnant to an Imperial Act.

Brennan J noted (159 CLR at 408) that Owen Dixon had detected an ambiguity in this statement:

> It may mean that it can pass Acts because they are repugnant to an Imperial Act, or it may mean it can pass Acts notwithstanding that they are so repugnant.

> The first meaning makes the Statute of Westminster the source of a new legislative power depending on the existence of an Imperial statute, a power directed to the repeal and amendment of such Imperial statutes and independent of and additional to the existing legislative powers of the Dominion Parliament.

> The second meaning finds in the Statute of Westminster no new grant of power but only the removal of restraint on the exercise of power otherwise existing, the restraint arising from the existence of legislation covering the same field but proceeding from another source, namely the British Parliament (Dixon (1936) p 105).

Brennan J said that the first of the two meanings proposed by Dixon was the proper reading of s 2(2). This attributed 'to the Statute the effect of an organic law', giving to the Commonwealth Parliament the full power needed to make it wholly independent of the United Kingdom Parliament: 159 CLR at 409.

A similar broad reading of s 2(2) was endorsed by Mason and Deane JJ: 159 CLR at 377, 429–30.

However, each of the three justices acknowledged that the plenary nature of the power conferred by s 2(2) was limited by s 9(1) of the Statute of Westminster which was intended, according to Mason J, 'to ensure that the operation of the Statute did not result in an accretion of Commonwealth power to the detriment of the powers possessed by the States': 159 CLR at 378.

It was the view of Brennan J that the repeal of s 503(1) of the Merchant Shipping Act was not within the authority of the state parliaments and therefore s 9(1) of the Statute of Westminster did not affect the Commonwealth Parliament's power under s 2(2) of the Statute to repeal s 503(1): 159 CLR at 418–19.

[6.2.23] If s 9(1) was intended to preserve the federal distribution of powers (a point conceded by other members of the court in *Kirmani's* case), then the Commonwealth could use the power conferred by s 2(2) to repeal Imperial legislation dealing with a topic outside those allocated to the Commonwealth in the Constitution, only so long as the states lacked the capacity to repeal United Kingdom legislation extending to the states.

It would appear, therefore, that the enactment of s 3 of the Australia Act 1986 **[6.2.7E]** has put an end to the power said, by Mason, Brennan and Deane JJ, to have been given to the Commonwealth Parliament by s 2(2) of the Statute of Westminster.

3   Territorial limits on legislative power

[6.3.1] From the beginning of self-government in the Australian colonies, the legislative power of their parliaments was assumed to be subject to a territorial limit; they should not legislate so as to regulate, control, penalise or attach legal consequences to events or persons outside their territory. The origins of this principle were clearly Imperial. The United Kingdom kept a tight rein on colonial legislatures and ensured that its own international and Imperial interests would not be compromised by some impetuous or wayward legislative body in Mauritius, Jamaica or New South Wales: see O'Connell and Riordan (1971) pp 84–5, 89.

In Australia, the territorial restriction was taken up by the courts and articulated as a proposition that prevented the states legislating for persons or things that were not connected with their territory. In that form, the restriction survived until at least 1986, and possibly beyond. Even today, the legislative power of state parliaments may be regarded as limited in this way: see **[6.3.25]**. Whether the territorial limits continue to affect state legislatures depends on an evaluation of the effect of s 2 of the Australia Act 1986 **[6.2.7E]**.

The High Court's decision in *Union Steamship Co of Australia Pty Ltd v King* (1988) 166 CLR 1 **[6.3.22C]** indicates that the requirement for a territorial connection will be 'liberally applied'. The possibility of state legislation being held invalid because it lacks such a connection remains: see Gilbert (1987) p 43. However the court has persisted with the liberal approach: in *Mobil Oil Australia Pty Ltd v Victoria* (2002) 211 CLR 1, Gleeson CJ said at 26:

> There is nothing either uncommon, or antithetical to the federal structure, about legislation of one State that has legal consequences for persons or conduct in another State or Territory ... The idea that all transactions and relationships giving rise to legal consequences can be located 'in' one particular State or Territory is unrealistic. Furthermore, the concept of the relationship between a State and its residents requires a much narrower focus if it is to be of assistance in the resolution of a problem such as arises in the present case. For the claim of a resident of New South Wales against a Victorian company which has manufactured, in Victoria, a defective product that was later supplied in New South Wales to be brought into representative proceedings in a Victorian court does not impinge on the relationship between the New South Wales resident and the New South Wales Government. Different considerations might arise, for example, if the New South Wales Parliament, adopting a policy hostile to group proceedings, or class actions, set out to prevent residents of New South Wales from participating in litigation of that kind. But no such problem arises here.

See also Gaudron, Gummow and Hayne JJ: 211 CLR at 36 and 38.

[6.3.2] How is the Commonwealth Parliament affected by this restriction? Until the adoption of the Statute of Westminster 1931, it was regarded as subject to this colonial constraint, with some occasional relaxation. Since that adoption in 1942, the Commonwealth Parliament might be thought to have an unlimited territorial (or extra-territorial) competence. In fact, the confirmation of that unlimited power did not come until 1975, in *New South Wales v Commonwealth* (the *Seas and Submerged Lands* case) (1975) 135 CLR 337 **[6.3.40C]**.

State parliaments

[6.3.3] The judicial endorsement of the extra-territorial incompetence of colonial and state parliaments is generally traced to the Privy Council's decision in *Macleod v Attorney-General (NSW)* [1891] AC 455. The Privy Council held that it was not a crime, punishable in New South Wales under s 54 of the Criminal Law Amendment Act 1883 (NSW) for a resident of the colony to enter into a bigamous marriage in the United States of America. Section 54 was drafted in wide terms. It declared that a bigamous marriage was a crime, 'wheresoever such second marriage takes place'.

The Privy Council said that to read s 54 as it stood would make any person who committed bigamy 'anywhere in the habitable globe ... amenable to the criminal jurisdiction of New South Wales'. This was held to be 'an impossible construction' because it would be 'inconsistent with the powers committed to a colony, and, indeed, inconsistent with the most familiar principles of international law': [1891] AC at 457. Later, the Privy Council said that, if the section were read literally, 'it would follow as a necessary result that the statute was ultra vires of the colonial legislature to pass': [1891] AC at 459.

[6.3.4] In *Ashbury v Ellis* [1893] AC 339, the Privy Council explained that the territorial limitation on the power of the New Zealand legislature was implicit in the grant of power 'to make Laws for the Peace, Order and Good Government of New Zealand'. Thus, so long as New Zealand had some connection with the subject matter of the legislation, its legislation could reach persons outside the colony.

[6.3.5] The positive approach to the issue of territorial limits on state legislative competence was developed by the High Court in the course of dealing with two challenges to the validity of New South Wales taxing legislation. In the first of these, *Commissioner of Stamp Duties (NSW) v Millar* (1932) 48 CLR 618, the court decided that s 103(1)(b) of the Stamp Duties Act 1920 (NSW) was beyond the legislative competence of the New South Wales Parliament. Section 103(1)(b) provided that when a person, wherever domiciled, died holding shares in a company, wherever registered or incorporated, which at the time of death was carrying on any mining, agricultural or forestry business in New South Wales, the whole value of those shares should be liable to death duty. Millar had died domiciled in Victoria, holding shares in a Victorian company which carried on part of its business (mining operations) in New South Wales. The Commissioner of Stamp Duties demanded that Millar's estate pay death duty to New South Wales calculated on the full value of the deceased's shares in the Victorian company.

In a joint judgment, Rich, Dixon and McTiernan JJ noted that the business which a company conducted in New South Wales could be a small part of its undertaking and might contribute little to the value of the company's shares, or even reduce that value. But s 103(1)(b) did not tax the economic advantage derived from a company's connection with New South Wales. Rather, it taxed the whole value of the share (at 632–3):

> It assumes to tax the share as property out of the jurisdiction. In doing so, it adopts a connection which is too remote to entitle its enactment to the description a law "for the peace, welfare, and good government of New South Wales": s 5 of the Constitution Act 1902. Or, to state the matter in another way, although some connection between the shareholder and New South Wales may be discovered in the existence there or part of the company's undertaking, the enactment goes beyond legislating in respect of that connection.

[6.3.6] In the second case, *Broken Hill South Ltd v Cmr of Taxation (NSW)* (1937) 56 CLR 337, the High Court rejected a challenge to the validity of the Income Tax (Management) Acts 1912 and 1928 (NSW), which levied income tax on persons who received income 'derived from any source in the State' and provided that, where property in New South Wales was mortgaged as security for any loan, the interest paid on that loan was income 'derived from any source in the State'.

In the *Broken Hill South* case, the taxpayer was a Victorian company which had lent money to another Victorian company. The loan was made in Victoria, secured by a mortgage, to a trustee of several properties owned by the borrower. The mortgage secured payment of the loan and payment of interest. Some of the mortgaged property was located in New South Wales. The New South Wales Commissioner of Taxation had demanded that the taxpayer pay state income tax on the interest payments under the loan agreement. Latham CJ said at 358:

> [T]he real principle to be applied in determining the territorial competence of a dominion legislature is whether the particular law in question is really a law for the peace, welfare and good government of the territory in question and not merely whether the law operates by reference to some extraterritorial elements.

Latham CJ said that the New South Wales legislation taxed the interest because payment of the interest was secured by New South Wales property. This provided the connection with the state. The existence of the security, and the benefit of that security, depended on the law of New South Wales. Dixon J expressed the following general principle at 375:

> The power to make laws for peace, order and good government of a State does not enable the State Parliament to impose by reference to some act, matter or thing occurring outside the State a liability upon a person unconnected with the State whether by domicil, residence or otherwise. But it is within the competence of the State legislature to make any fact, circumstance, occurrence or thing in or connected with the territory the occasion of the imposition upon any person concerned therein of a liability to taxation or of any other liability. It is also within the competence of the legislature to base the imposition of liability on no more than the relation of the person to the territory. The relation may consist in presence within the territory, residence, domicil, carrying on business there, or even remoter connections. If a connection exists, it is for the legislature to decide how far it should go in the exercise of its powers. As in other matters of jurisdiction or authority courts must be exact in distinguishing between ascertaining that the circumstances over which the power extends exist and examining the mode in which the power has been exercised. No doubt there must be some relevance to the circumstances in the exercise of the power. But it is of no importance upon the question of validity that the liability imposed is, or may be, altogether disproportionate to the territorial connection or that it includes many cases that cannot have been foreseen.

Here, the connection between the subject matter of the legislation and the state lay in the fact that property in New South Wales was secured, under the law of New South Wales, to ensure the payment of money to the taxpayer. The liability to pay a tax was related to that payment.

[6.3.7] There are some tensions between the two decisions in *Commissioner of Stamp Duties (NSW) v Millar* (1932) 48 CLR 618 **[6.3.5]** and *Broken Hill South Ltd v Cmr of Taxation (NSW)* (1937) 56 CLR 337 **[6.3.6]**. The *Broken Hill South* case appeared to adopt a far more tolerant view of state legislative power than did *Millar's* case. In *Millar's* case the majority of the court appeared to stress the need for a close connection between the subject matter of state legislation and the state: the offending legislation failed because it had adopted a connection which was 'too remote'. In *Broken Hill South*, Dixon J said it was for the legislature to decide 'how far it should go' once a connection was established. The fact that legislation imposed a liability 'altogether disproportionate to the territorial connection' could not affect its validity.

Again, the results in the two cases appear divergent. The New South Wales Parliament could not impose a tax on the full value of shares in a foreign company which did part of its business in New South Wales (*Millar's* case) but it could tax the full value of interest payments on a foreign loan, partly secured by property in New South Wales: *Broken Hill South*. It may be possible to reconcile the two decisions, by focusing on the differences in the legal interests held by shareholders (the interest involved in *Millar's* case) and debenture-holders (the interest involved in *Broken Hill South*). Latham CJ adopted this form of analysis in *Broken Hill South* (1937) 56 CLR 337 **[6.3.6]** at 356, 358–9.

[6.3.8C] Welker v Hewett
(1969) 120 CLR 503

The Road Maintenance (Contribution) Act 1958 (NSW) provided for the payment of a tax by the owners of commercial goods vehicles using roads in the state. Section 10 of the Act made it an offence for a person not to keep a record, or not to make the monthly return or payment, or to make an incomplete, false or misleading return or payment. Section 10A of the Act provided that, where the owner of a commercial goods vehicle was a body corporate, each director, member of the governing body or manager of that body corporate should be personally liable to furnish the return and pay the charges.

Welker, a resident of South Australia, was one of two directors of Jupiter Transport Pty Ltd, a company incorporated in South Australia. He had not entered New South Wales. One of the company's vehicles made journeys on New South Wales roads. The company lodged monthly returns under the Act but did not pay the charge. Welker also failed to pay the charges. After being convicted of an offence against s 10A of the Act, Welker sought and was denied review by the New South Wales Court of Appeal. He then appealed to the High Court of Australia.

Kitto J held that, on its proper construction, s 10A only applied to a company's directors and other officers where those persons were physically in the State. However, his Honour proceeded to consider whether s 10A would have been valid if it applied to a director outside New South Wales at the time when the company failed to pay its road maintenance charge.

Kitto J: [512] The question that arises on this assumption is whether the Parliament of New South Wales has power to deal with a person who is not within its territory. It has the power, of course, if it so limits the application of the law as to base its operations upon some connexion that the absent director has with New South Wales, provided that the connexion is such as to make the enactment of the law relevant to the peace, welfare and good government of New South Wales, but otherwise it has not, for the Parliament has no general power to make strangers to its territory liable in its courts to judgments or sentences by way of enforcing contributions to the revenue of the State. If the operation of s 10A in respect of a director were limited to the case of one who had been actually concerned in the travelling of the company's vehicle on the streets of New South Wales on the journeys that gave rise to the company's liability to pay the statutory charges, or had been actually concerned in the company's failure to pay the charges (assuming them to be validly imposed on the company), it may well be that the limitation would suffice to restrain the section within the State's constitutional power. As was said in a well-known passage in the judgment of Dixon J in *Broken Hill South Ltd v Commissioner of Taxation* (NSW) (1937) 56 CLR at 375 which the Privy Council affirmed in *Johnson v Commissioner of Stamp Duties (NSW)* [1956] AC at 353 and recently reaffirmed in *Thompson v Commissioner of Stamp Duties (NSW)* [1969] 1 AC at 335, 'it is within the competence of the State legislature to make any fact, circumstance, occurrence or thing in or connected with the territory the occasion of the imposition upon any person concerned therein of a liability to taxation or of any other liability'. The words 'concerned [513] therein' are of the essence of this proposition, for what is being described is a connexion between the person upon whom the liability is imposed and the State — a connexion through the selected fact, circumstance, occurrence or thing and therefore a connexion one link of which is a concern, in the sense of a personal implication or involvement in that fact, circumstance, occurrence or thing.

But upon what connexion between the State and a director who is and always has been out of the State does s 10A base its attempt to impose a civil and criminal liability upon the director? Certainly not upon his having been a director at the time when the company incurred its liability for charges under the Act by reason of the travelling of the vehicle on the public streets of New South Wales. The service of the notice is within the authority of s 10A if the recipient is at that time a director ... The failure being a failure to pay money which the company owes to the State of New South Wales, anyone who is really concerned in the failure, in the sense that he has contributed by action or inaction to its coming about, might no doubt be validly penalized by New South Wales legislation which bases its penalising provisions upon the fact of his having so contributed. But s 10A does not base its provisions upon any relation of the director to the company's failure to pay the charges. The draftsman appears to have assumed what is simply not true, that if a company fails to pay its debt each of its directors must have been personally concerned in the failure ... In the case of a company such as Jupiter Transport Pty Ltd, where no one director has any power by himself to make a decision binding upon the company, it is impossible to infer from the bare fact that A is a director that he [514] was a participant in, or could have prevented, the company's failure to pay a debt which it should have paid but has not. He could not authorise the payment; he had no wider or other power with respect to the debt than to cast a vote at a board meeting in favour of its being paid, and he may have been prevented by illness or distance or some other compelling circumstance from doing even that. To say, therefore, that the company has failed to pay the debt and that he is a director is not to say that he is or has been concerned in the non-payment ...

Barwick CJ and Menzies J agreed with Kitto J's reasons for judgment. Windeyer J agreed that the appeal should be allowed, but gave no reasons. McTiernan J dissented.

~~~

Notes

[6.3.9] The validity of s 10 of the Road Maintenance (Contribution) Act had been upheld in two earlier decisions. In the first decision, *Ex parte Iskra* [1963] SR (NSW) 538, the Full Supreme Court of New South Wales decided that the New South Wales Parliament could impose the obligations in the Act on a Victorian resident, who had driven his Victorian registered semi-trailer on a journey from Melbourne to Sydney, thus he could be prosecuted for his failure to lodge a record of this journey with the Commissioner. Brereton J, with whose reasons Sugerman and Manning JJ agreed, said that the state parliament could validly make an act done outside the state a punishable offence, 'provided there is in the prohibited act an element sufficiently connected with the State': [1963] SR (NSW) at 552. In the present legislation, a fact or circumstance connected with New South Wales supported s 10 (at 559):

> The fact or circumstance here is the use of roads in the State for profit; the person charged is connected therewith by being the owner of the vehicle so using the roads. It is clearly for the peace, order and good government of the State that such persons should contribute to the maintenance of the roads to which in the course of winning their rewards they cause wear and tear.

[6.3.10]   The second decision, *O'Sullivan v Dejneko* (1964) 110 CLR 498, took this reasoning one step further. The High Court decided that the obligations in the Road Maintenance (Contribution) Act could validly apply to a resident of South Australia, who had permitted another person to drive the former's commercial goods vehicle in New South Wales. Taylor, Windeyer and Owen JJ said that the use of a motor vehicle on New South Wales roads was a matter with which the New South Wales Parliament could validly deal (at 509):

> Here it is the presence in New South Wales of the vehicle and the use of it upon the public streets of the State that attracts the constitutional authority of the State and enables its legislature to impose the obligation of contributing to the upkeep of its streets upon the person who owns it, no matter where he is domiciled or resides or carries on business.

[6.3.11]   The High Court's decision in *Welker v Hewett* (1969) 120 CLR 503 **[6.3.12]** was that the addition of an extra link to the chain (in the form of s 10A) removed the connection with New South Wales which was essential to the legislation's validity. In effect, the approach adopted by Kitto J converted the theories and concepts of company law into constitutionally-entrenched barriers to state legislation. The adoption, by road transport operators, of a corporate structure gave those operators the constitutional protection against state taxes which the decisions in *Ex parte Iskra* [1963] SR (NSW) 538 **[6.3.9]** and *O'Sullivan v Dejneko* (1964) 110 CLR 498 **[6.3.10]** had denied them. In effect, the state parliaments were found to be incapable of piercing the corporate veil of a company located outside the state.

[6.3.12]   *Welker v Hewett* was followed by the High Court in *Cox v Tomat* (1971) 126 CLR 105. A majority of that court held that s 15(2) of the Road Maintenance (Contribution) Act 1965 (WA) was invalid. This section extended all the obligations imposed by the Act on an owner of a commercial goods vehicle who was a corporation to every person who was a director of that corporation.

Barwick CJ said that it was the physical operation of a vehicle on the state's roads which formed the territorial basis for the power to impose liabilities on persons not otherwise connected with the state (at 111–12):

> The stretch of the State's legislative power, founded on that territorial event, does not reach, in my opinion, beyond those who are in a substantial sense participants in that event ...

> Neither the interest of the director in the result of the company's business nor his undoubted duty to exercise his power as a member of the board of directors of the company, in my opinion, necessarily involves the director in participation in the physical operation of such assets of the company as the commercial goods vehicle in this case.

[6.3.13C]   **Pearce v Florenca**
                               (1976) 135 CLR 507

The Seas and Submerged Lands Act 1973 (Cth) included the following provisions:

> 6 It is by this Act declared and enacted that the sovereignty in respect of the territorial sea, and in respect of the airspace over it and in respect of its bed and subsoil, is vested in and exercisable by the Crown in right of the Commonwealth. ...
>
> 16 ... The preceding provisions of this Part — ...
>
> (b) do not limit or exclude the operation of any law of a State in force at the date of commencement of this Act or coming into force after that date, except in so far as the law

is expressed to vest or make exercisable any sovereignty or sovereign rights otherwise than as provided by the preceding provisions of this Part.

In *New South Wales v Commonwealth* (the *Seas and Submerged Lands* case) (1975) 135 CLR 337 **[6.3.40C]** the High Court of Australia held that this Act was valid.

Florenca was a professional fisherman and a resident of Western Australia. He had been charged before a Western Australia magistrate with an offence under s 24(1)(a) of the Fisheries Act 1905 (WA). The section made it an offence for any person to have in his or her possession any undersized fish 'whether taken within Western Australian waters or elsewhere'. He was prosecuted for having undersized fish in his possession at a point within 1.5 miles of the Western Australian coast. The magistrate dismissed the charges against the respondent on the ground that the Seas and Submerged Lands Act 1973 (Cth) had rendered the Fisheries Act inoperative in any area below the low-water mark of the coast of Western Australia.

The prosecutor applied to the Supreme Court of Western Australia for an order to review the magistrate's decision. The matter was then removed to the High Court under s 40 of the Judiciary Act 1903 (Cth).

Gibbs J: [514] During the course of the nineteenth century the advisers to the Colonial Office formulated a principle that a colonial legislature has no power to enact laws having effect beyond the limits of the colony, and this view came to be accepted by the colonial courts (*Ray v M'Mackin* (1875) 1 VLR 274; *R v Barton* (1879) 1 QLJ (Supp) 16). In *Macleod v Attorney-General (NSW)* [1891] AC 455 the support of the Judicial Committee was given to the opinion that the jurisdiction of colonial legislatures is 'confined within their own territories', but the decision of that case turned on a question of construction, rather than a question of power, and the remarks on the latter question were obiter dicta ... **[515]** Of course, as was pointed out in *British Columbia Electric Railway Co Ltd v R* [1946] AC 527 at 542, a legislature which passes a law having extra-territorial operation may find that the legislation proves to be unenforceable but it does not follow that the legislation is invalid on that account. Another explanation of the principle that colonial legislatures are subject to limitations in respect of their power of enacting legislation which has an extra-territorial effect is that it derives from the fact that a colonial legislature is empowered only to legislate for the 'peace, order and good government' of the colony and that those words themselves import a territorial connexion ...

[516] The doctrine as to the limitation on the power of colonial legislatures to legislate with extra-territorial effect, as originally enunciated, proved to be too widely stated ... This Court, in *O'Sullivan v Dejneko* (1964) 110 CLR 498, upheld the validity of a New South Wales statute which imposed liabilities on a person resident in South Australia who had never been in New South Wales. In that case also the operation of the legislation held to be valid was clearly not confined within the territory of New South Wales. It is in my opinion now right to say, as Lord Uthwatt said in *Wallace Brothers and Co Ltd v Commissioner of Income Tax, Bombay* (1948) LR 75 Ind App 86 at 98: 'There is no rule of law that the territorial limits of a subordinate legislature define the possible scope of its legislative enactments or mark the field open to its vision.' ...

[517] [I]t is now often said that the test of validity of a State statute is simply whether it is legislation for the peace, order and good government of the State (*R v Foster; Ex parte Eastern and Australian Steamship Co Ltd* (at 307)), and that no additional restriction placed upon mere territorial considerations should be placed upon the constitutional powers of a State: *Australasian Scale Co Ltd v Commissioner of Taxes (Qld)* (1935) 53 CLR 534 at 561–2. However, the test whether a law is one for peace, order and good government of the State is, as so stated, exceedingly vague and imprecise, and a rather more specific test has been adopted; it has become settled that a law is valid if it is connected, not too remotely, with the State which enacted it, or, in other words, if it operates on some circumstance which really appertains to the State. The rule was expressed in that way in *Commissioner of Stamp Duties (NSW) v Millar* (1932) 48 CLR 618 at 632–3, and *Broken Hill South Ltd v Commissioner of Taxation (NSW)* (1937) 56 CLR 337 at 375, the judgments in which were approved by the

Judicial Committee in *Johnson v Commissioner of Stamp Duties (NSW)* [1956] AC 331 at 353
...

[518] Even in its modern form, the rule requiring a relevant connexion between the persons or circumstances on which the legislation operates and the State is still capable of giving rise to that practical inconvenience and uncertainty to which the report of the 1929 Conference on the Operation of Dominion Legislation alluded (see the passage cited by Evatt J in *Trustees Executors and Agency Co Ltd v Federal Commissioner of Taxation* (1933) 49 CLR 220 at 233–4). For that reason it is obviously in the public interest that the test should be liberally applied, and that legislation should be held valid if there is any real connexion — even a remote or general connexion — between the subject matter of the legislation and the State. And it has been established by a series of well-known decisions, which are collected in *Cobb & Co Ltd v Kropp* [1967] 1 AC 141 at 154–6, that within their limits the legislatures of the States have powers 'as plenary and as ample' as those of the Imperial Legislature itself. It would seem anomalous and unfitting that the enactments of such a legislature should be held invalid on narrow or technical grounds.

... I would, with respect, accept the view expressed by Mason J in the *Seas and Submerged Lands* case [*New South Wales v Commonwealth* (1975) 135 CLR 337] at 468–9, that the power to make laws for the peace, order and good government of the colony was [519] large enough to enable the colonial legislatures to enact legislation which applied to the off-shore waters. The same is true now of State legislatures. The very fact that the waters are the off-shore waters of the State provides the nexus necessary to render valid a law operating within those waters. There is an intimate connexion between the land territory of a State and its off-shore waters. Those waters have been popularly regarded as the waters of the State, and as vital to its trade. The people of the State have traditionally exploited the resources of the off-shore waters and used them for recreation. The enforcement of the laws of the State would be gravely impeded if a person could escape from the reach of the laws and the authority of the State by going below low-water mark...The principle that legislation enacted by a State and operating outside its territory must be connected in some relevant way with the State if it is to be valid may have been appropriate to the so-called dependent and inferior legislatures of colonial times, but its only modern justification is that it may avoid conflicts with other rules of law applicable to the area in which the legislation is intended to operate. In this way the principle may fulfil a useful purpose in providing a touch-stone for the validity of a law enacted by one State and intended to take effect within the territory of another. But no rational purpose is served by holding that a law of a State cannot validly operate within its off-shore waters. It has now been held that those waters form part of the territory of the Commonwealth, but the Constitution itself sufficiently provides for the resolution of any conflict that may arise between a law of the Commonwealth and a law of a State: by virtue of s 109 the former will prevail... [520]...from the point of view of the States, every consideration of practical convenience requires that the power of a State to legislate in respect of its offshore waters should be as ample as its power to legislate for its land territories. The history of the exercise of State powers in the past, the present public interest, and the reason on which the principle requiring a territorial nexus seems to rest all combine to lead to the conclusion that the fact that the persons, things or events to which the legislation of a State applies occur within the off-shore waters provides sufficient connexion with the State to render the legislation valid.

... A law to regulate fishing within off-shore waters has a close connexion with the State and can truly be described as a law for the peace, order and good government of the State. Such a law is within the competence of a State legislature.

Mason J: [522] The Parliament of a State may legislate extra-territorially. ... The decision in *New South Wales v Commonwealth* ... at 337 does not deny this proposition. In that case it was decided that the territorial boundaries of the States end at low-water mark but neither the decision nor the judgments qualify the rule that the Parliament of a State has a capacity to legislate extraterritorially. Indeed, the judgments of both the majority and the minority affirm this capacity, in particular the capacity of a State Parliament to enact legislation having effect in territorial waters surrounding the State, ante, especially at 370–1, 468–9, 475, 495–7. It had earlier been acknowledged in *Bonser v La Macchia*, supra, that a State had power to legislate with respect to fisheries located within and without territorial waters. It is against this background that the provisions of the Fisheries Act fall to be considered.

Mason J proceeded to hold that, on its proper construction, s 24(1)(a) penalised the possession of undersized fish, in Western Australia or Western Australian waters, wherever caught. His Honour continued:

[524] So construed s 24 is unquestionably valid. This is not to say that I am of the opinion that the section would have been invalid if it had, according to its terms, a more extensive operation. I do not find it necessary or desirable, in the absence of comprehensive argument, to discuss possible limitations on the power of the Parliament of a State to enact extra-territorial legislation in the exercise of its power to make laws for the peace, order and good government of the State, in particular the question whether in order to support the validity of a State statute having an application in territorial waters surrounding the State, there needs to be shown a nexus (other than that supplied by the mere application of the law in territorial waters) between the exercise of legislative power and the State. Whether this question is of more than theoretical importance is a question which may presently be put aside.

Barwick CJ and Stephen J delivered judgments to the same effect as Mason J. Murphy J agreed that the appeal should be allowed because the presumption of validity had not been disturbed.

~~~

Notes

[6.3.14] The judgment of Gibbs J in *Pearce v Florenca* (1976) 135 CLR 507 [6.3.13C] suggested that the High Court might be moving towards a substantial modification of the rule laid down in *Commissioner of Stamp Duties (NSW) v Millar* (1932) 48 CLR 618 [6.3.5]. For example, he said that the rule 'raises certain logical difficulties' because s 5 of the Colonial Laws Validity Act authorises state parliaments to increase their own powers. His Honour said that 'even in its modern form, the rule ... is still capable of giving rise to ... practical inconvenience and uncertainty'; he thus declared that 'even a remote connection' should be enough to validate legislation.

[6.3.15] The proposition put forward by Gibbs J in *Pearce v Florenca* that 'there is an intimate connection between the land territory of a State and its off-shore waters' (135 CLR at 519) would, if accepted by the High Court, make a significant judicial concession to the legislative powers of the states. However, *Robinson v Western Australian Museum* (1977) 138 CLR 283 placed that proposition in doubt. The court was asked, in that case, to determine the validity of the Western Australian legislation, vesting the title to certain historic wrecks in the government of Western Australia. These wrecks lay in waters off the coast of the state, and the wreck which was the subject of this litigation (a former Dutch ship, the *Gilt Dragon*, wrecked in 1656) lay 2.87 miles from the coast, about 50 miles north of Perth. The argument raised a number of issues, one of which was the competence of the Western Australian Parliament to legislate for wrecks and archaeological sites in coastal waters. Four judges considered that issue.

Barwick CJ and Murphy J held that the Western Australian Parliament had power to legislate for its territory, though waters within three nautical miles of its coast 'neither form part of the territory of the State nor are themselves the subject of legislative power of the State': 138 CLR at 294. However, a state law might operate in those waters if it satisfied 'the test of being a law for the government of the State':

138 CLR at 294. Both judges concluded that the control of historic wrecks and archaeological sites on the bed of the sea was not a matter within the state's legislative competence.

On the other hand, Gibbs and Mason JJ held that the legislation was within the power of the Western Australian Parliament. Gibbs J said that the legislation was valid because it operated 'in the off-shore waters within three miles from the coast of Western Australia' and that, if further support were needed, it could be found in the historical significance of this wreck for Western Australia: 138 CLR at 304–5. (Barwick CJ had rejected the argument that the wreck had any historical significance for Western Australia: 138 CLR at 295–6.) Mason J said at 331:

> State laws relating to fishing and fisheries in territorial waters and beyond are examples of laws having a valid extraterritorial operation, there being a sufficient connexion with the peace, order and good government of the State. Likewise, in my opinion, there is a sufficient connexion between legislation regulating the ownership or possession of historical wrecks on or near the coasts of Western Australia and the peace, order and good government of the State.

Stephen J disposed of the case without considering any of the substantive issues. Jacobs J held that the Western Australian legislation was invalid because it was inconsistent with the investiture in the Commonwealth of sovereignty in respect of the territorial sea by s 6 of the Seas and Submerged Lands Act 1973 (Cth).

Therefore, in the result, only one judge (Gibbs J) was prepared to concede an automatic nexus between the state and the adjacent territorial sea. For the present, however, this question has been settled by Commonwealth legislation: see **[6.3.27]–[6.3.34]**.

[6.3.16]   On the other hand, it could be that the control of fishing (the issue involved in *Pearce v Florenca*) is a special case and that the courts will more readily concede extra-territorial validity to state fishing laws, along the lines argued for by Gibbs J. In *Raptis & Son v South Australia* (1977) 138 CLR 346, the High Court considered the effect and validity of the Fisheries Act 1971 (SA), which purported to regulate fishing to a substantial distance off the South Australian coast. The specific issue before the court was whether a person who held a fishing licence under the Fisheries Act 1952 (Cth) and who had fished in Investigator Strait (between the mainland and Kangaroo Island) was subject to the South Australian legislation. The majority of the court (Barwick CJ, Gibbs, Stephen and Jacobs JJ) held that the South Australian Act could not control that person, because Investigator Strait lay outside the territory of South Australia; indeed, it lay more than three miles outside South Australia. But this decision was not based on any lack of legislative competence in the South Australian Parliament — rather, it was based on the inconsistency between the state law and the Commonwealth law and the consequential invalidity of the state law under s 109 of the Commonwealth Constitution. Gibbs J said that it was 'clear, and not I think controverted, that the provisions of the State Act will validly apply to waters as closely connected with South Australia as those of Investigator Strait, even if those waters do not lie within territorial limits': 138 CLR at 355.

Stephen J (with whose reasons Barwick CJ agreed) said that the South Australian legislation would 'apply within league [three nautical miles] seas around the coast of the State. That the necessary nexus with the government of the territory of the State will be present, so as to confer extra-territorial competence upon the legislature of the State, was not denied in the present case': 138 CLR at 379. He did not assert (as did Gibbs J) that the Act would validly operate beyond that area, but his decision that the state legislation was, in its operation in Investigator Strait, inconsistent with the Commonwealth legislation, assumes that the state Act was otherwise valid, that is, within the legislative competence of the South Australian Parliament. Jacobs J took much the same approach. The Fisheries Act 1971 (SA) was invalid in its application to Investigator Strait because it was inconsistent with the Fisheries Act 1952 (Cth), not because of any extra-territorial incapacity: 138 CLR at 394.

[6.3.17E]   **Australia Act 1986**

2(1) It is hereby declared and enacted that the legislative powers of the Parliament of each State include full power to make laws for the peace, order and good government of that State that have extra-territorial operation.

(2) It is hereby further declared and enacted that the legislative powers of the Parliament of each State include all legislative powers that the Parliament of the United Kingdom might have exercised before the commencement of this Act for the peace, order and good government of that State but nothing in this subsection confers on a State any capacity that the State did not have immediately before the commencement of this Act to engage in relations with countries outside Australia.

~~~

Notes

[6.3.18] There is debate as to the effect of this section. The use of the phrase 'declared and enacted' might be read as indicating that s 2(1) was not intended to achieve any enlargement of state legislative power. Such a reading would be reinforced by the inclusion in s 2(1) of the possibly limiting words 'for the peace, order and good government of that state'. (The analogy with the legislative powers of the United Kingdom Parliament, developed in s 2(2), could be said to be similarly limited.) This view of s 2 is developed, in a closely argued essay, by Gilbert, who concludes that 'State law-making powers are to be understood in the Dixonian or common-law sense that validity always requires a sufficient relationship between the law and the territorially-based interest of the enacting State': Gilbert (1987) p 42.

[6.3.19] The contrary view, that s 2 of the Australia Act has enlarged the legislative capacity of the Australian states, is developed in a strongly argued paper by Mark Moshinsky. He sees s 2 as extending an unfettered power to legislate extra-territorially to the Australian states. The previous requirement of a connection with the state no longer applies: Moshinsky (1987) p 785. It is part of this argument that the phrase 'peace, order and good government of the State' does not import a territorial limitation, but provides 'a safeguard against unjust and capricious law-making, which would be of no relevance to the peace, order and good government of the State': Moshinsky (1987) p 782.

[6.3.20] That last point is that the phrase limits both intra-territorial and extra-territorial legislative competence by focusing on the quality of the legislation. Some support for this radical view of that phrase could be derived from the judgments of Street CJ and Priestley JA in *Building Construction Employees' and Builders Labourers' Federation (NSW) v Minister for Industrial Relations* (1986) 7 NSWLR 372 **[6.4.43]**. In the course of rejecting a challenge to New South Wales legislation which purported to validate certain ministerial actions relating to the deregistration of a trade union, Street CJ said that '[l]aws inimical to, or which do not serve, the peace, welfare and good government of our parliamentary democracy ... will be struck down by the court as unconstitutional': 7 NSWLR at 384. Earlier, Street CJ had described a parliamentary democracy as involving a democratically elected parliament and an independent judiciary: 7 NSWLR at 382.

Priestley JA also raised the possibility that state legislation 'must in fact be for the peace, welfare and good government of the State in order to be valid'. It was at least arguable, Priestley JA said, that a statute declaring 'that all blue-eyed babies should be murdered' could be held to be 'so manifestly not for the peace, order and good government of the State as to be ultra vires the written authority of the Parliament to make laws': 7 NSWLR at 421.

[6.3.21]   This view, that the phrase 'peace, order and good government of the State' could be a substantive limitation on the power of state parliaments, is unorthodox (and was ultimately rejected by a majority of the High Court in *Kable v Director of Public Prosecutions (NSW)* (1996) 189 CLR 51 **[6.4.23]**, **[6.4.35]**, **[6.4.48C]**, **[11.3.30]**ff. It was criticised for that reason by the High Court in *Union Steamship Co of Australia Ltd v King* (1988) 166 CLR 1 **[6.3.22C]**, a case which largely focused on the question of the states' extra-territorial powers.

[6.3.22C]   Union Steamship Co of Australia Pty Ltd v King
(1988) 166 CLR 1

Section 7(1)(a) of the Workers' Compensation Act 1926 (NSW) provided that a worker injured in the course of his or her employment should receive compensation from his or her employer. Section 46 provided as follows:

46(1) This act applies in respect of an injury to a worker who is a seaman employed on a New South Wales ship or a ship whose first port of clearance and whose destination are in New South Wales.

(2) In this section the term 'New South Wales ship' means any ship which is —

(a) registered in this State; or ...

King had been employed by Union Steamship as a seaman on a ship registered in New South Wales. He claimed to have suffered injury while working on the ship outside New South Wales, and lodged a claim for compensation against his employer under the Workers' Compensation Act.

The Compensation Court awarded compensation to King. Union Steamship appealed to the New South Wales Court of Appeal on the ground that s 46 of the Workers' Compensation Act was invalid. When that appeal was dismissed, Union Steamship appealed to the High Court of Australia.

Mason CJ, Wilson, Brennan, Deane, Dawson, Toohey and **Gaudron JJ:** [8] The question then is whether s 46 is a valid exercise of the power of the Parliament of New South Wales to make laws for the peace, welfare and good government of the State. The appellant submits that it is not such a law on the ground that there is no sufficient nexus between the law and the territory of New South Wales. In [9] support of this submission the appellant says that registration may be a mere convenience for foreigners and that there may be many situations in which a ship registered in New South Wales is made the subject of contractual and other arrangements and put to uses which are entirely remote from New South Wales.

The scope and content of the power conferred by s 5 of the Constitution Act 1902 (NSW) to make laws 'for the peace, welfare, and good government of New South Wales' is still a topic of current debate: see *Australian Building Construction Employees' and Builders Labourers' Federation of New South Wales v Minister for Industrial Relations* (1986) 7 NSWLR 372. This may seem somewhat surprising. The explanation is historical and it is to be found in the evolving relationships between the United Kingdom and its colonies, especially the relationships with the Australian colonies and, after federation, with the Commonwealth of Australia and the Australian States.

The power to make laws 'for the peace, welfare and good government' of a territory is indistinguishable from the power to make laws 'for the peace, order and good government' of a territory. Such a power is a plenary power and it was so recognised, even in an era when emphasis was given to the character of colonial legislatures as subordinate law-making bodies. The plenary nature of the power was established in the series of historic Privy Council decisions at the close of the nineteenth century: *R v Burah* (1878) 3 App Cas 889; *Hodge v R* (1883) 9 App Cas 117; *Powell v Apollo Candle Co Ltd* (1885) 10 App Cas 282; *Riel v R* (1885) 10 App Cas 675. They decided that colonial legislatures were not mere agents or delegates of the Imperial Parliament.

Lord Selborne, speaking for the Judicial Committee in *Burah*, said (at 904) that the Indian legislature 'has, and was intended to have, plenary powers of legislation, as large, and of the same nature, as those of Parliament itself'. Later, Sir Barnes Peacock in *Hodge*, speaking for the Judicial Committee, stated (at 132) that the legislature of Ontario enjoyed by virtue of the British North America Act 1867 (Imp): 'authority as plenary and as ample within the limits prescribed by s 92 as the Imperial Parliament in the plenitude of its power possessed and could bestow. Within these limits of subjects and area the local legislature is supreme, and has the same authority as the Imperial Parliament ...'. In *Riel* Lord Halsbury LC, delivering the opinion of the Judicial Committee, rejected (at 678) the contention that a statute was invalid if a court concluded that it was not calculated as a matter of fact and policy to secure the peace, order and good government of the territory. His Lordship went on [10] to say (at 678) that such a power was 'apt to authorise the utmost discretion of enactment for the attainment of the objects pointed to'. In *Chernard and Co v Joachim Arissol* [1949] AC 127, Lord Reid, delivering the opinion of the Judicial Committee, cited (at 132) *Riel* and the comments of Lord Halsbury LC with evident approval. More recently Viscount Radcliffe, speaking for the Judicial Committee, described a power to make laws for the peace, order and good government of a territory as 'connot[ing], in British constitutional language, the widest law-making powers appropriate to a Sovereign': *Ibralebbe v R* [1964] AC 900 at 923.

These decisions and statements of high authority demonstrate that, within the limits of the grant, a power to make laws for the peace, order and good government of a territory is as ample and plenary as the power possessed by the Imperial Parliament itself. That is, the words 'for the peace, order and good government' are not words of limitation. They did not confer on the courts of a colony, just as they do not confer on the courts of a State, jurisdiction to strike down legislation on the ground that, in the opinion of a court, the legislation does not promote or secure the peace, order and good government of the colony. Just as the courts of the United Kingdom cannot invalidate laws made by the Parliament of the United Kingdom on the ground that they do not secure the welfare and the public interest so the exercise of its legislative power by the Parliament of New South Wales is not susceptible to judicial review on that score. Whether the exercise of that legislative power is subject to some restraints by reference to rights deeply rooted in our democratic system of government and the common law (see *New Zealand Drivers' Association v New Zealand Road Carriers* [1982] 1 NZLR 374 at 390; *Fraser v State Services Commission* [1984] 1 NZLR 116 at 121; *Taylor v New Zealand Poultry Board* [1984] 1 NZLR 394 at 398), a view which Lord Reid firmly rejected in *British Railways Board v Pickin* [1974] AC 765 at 782, is another question which we need not explore.

But when it came to legislation having an extraterritorial operation, it was thought that colonial legislatures were incompetent to enact such legislation. The passage already quoted from the opinion delivered by Sir Barnes Peacock in *Hodge* suggests that a power to make laws for the peace, order and good government of a territory [11] was limited to the area of the territory: see also *Kielley v Carson* (1842) 4 Moo PC 63 at 85; 13 ER 225 at 233; *Phillips v Eyre* (1870) LR 6 QB 1 at 20; *Ray v M'Mackin* (1875) 1 VLR 274 at 280; *Macleod v Attorney-General for New South Wales* [1891] AC 455; *Ashbury v Ellis* [1893] AC 339; *Peninsular and*

Oriental Steam Navigation Co v Kingston [1903] AC 471; *Attorney-General for Canada v Cain* [1906] AC 542.

In the context of a grant of legislative power to a legislature in a colony forming part of a far-flung empire, it was natural to conclude, as did the law officers in the nineteenth century, that laws made in the exercise of such a power were binding and valid only within the boundaries of the colony: O'Connell and Riordan, *Opinions on Imperial Constitutional Law* (1971), pp 84 et seq. The prevailing rule of construction applicable to Imperial statutes was that they had no force beyond the Sovereign's dominions, not even to bind subjects, unless that application was expressly mentioned or was necessarily implied: *Jeffreys v Boosey* (1854) 4 HLC 815 at 939; 10 ER 681 at 730. Furthermore, there were powerful policy considerations which combined to generate an absolute doctrine of colonial extraterritorial incompetence. The need to protect British maritime and commercial interests from colonial legislation operating outside colonial boundaries and the possibility that colonial laws or acts done under such laws might involve Great Britain in a breach of international law or of an international obligation were prominent factors which contributed to the development of the doctrine.

How far the doctrine went in inhibiting a colony from enacting a rule of conduct for its subjects or residents outside its boundaries was not altogether clear. In *Macleod* Lord Halsbury LC quoted (at 458) the remarks of Parke B in *Jeffreys v Boosey* (HLC at 926; ER at 725):

> The legislature has no power over any persons except its own subjects, that is, persons natural-born subjects, or resident, or whilst they are within the limits of the Kingdom. The legislature can impose no duties except on them; and when legislating for the benefit of persons, must, prima facie, be considered to mean the benefit of those who owe obedience to our laws, and whose interests the legislature is under a correlative obligation to protect.

In *Delaney v Great Western Milling Co Ltd* (1916) 22 CLR 150 at 161–2, Griffith CJ quoted and applied those remarks.

[12] However, in *Croft v Dunphy* [1933] AC 156 the Judicial Committee, in upholding Canadian hovering legislation which was designed to operate beyond territorial waters, observed (at 163) that there was 'no reason to restrict the permitted scope of such legislation by any other consideration than is applicable to the legislation of a fully Sovereign State'. The decision must be taken as rejecting the doctrine of extraterritorial incompetence as having an application to a dominion. The decision was not based on s 3 of the Statute of Westminster 1931 (Imp) which abolished the doctrine so far as the dominions were concerned. No doubt with *Croft v Dunphy* in mind, Viscount Sankey LC in *British Coal Corporation v R* [1935] AC 500 at 520 referred to the doctrine as 'a doctrine of somewhat obscure extent'.

It might have been possible to confine the authority of *Croft v Dunphy* to the legislatures of the dominions as distinct from those of the colonies and States, on the footing that, following the Balfour Declaration of 1929, self-governing dominions had achieved fully independent and sovereign status. But that is not how things have turned out. It is now accepted beyond any question that colonial legislatures had power to make laws which operate extraterritorially: *Bonser v La Macchia* (1969) 122 CLR 177 at 189, 224–5; *R v Bull* (1974) 131 CLR 203 at 263, 270–1, 280–2; *New South Wales v Commonwealth* (the *Seas and Submerged Lands* case) (1975) 135 CLR 337 at 468–9, 494–5; 8 ALR 1; *Pearce v Florenca* (1976) 135 CLR 507 at 514–20, 522; 9 ALR 289.

The same comment applies with equal force to the Parliaments of the Australian States. Immediately following *Croft v Dunphy*, Evatt J in *Trustees Executors & Agency Co Ltd v FCT* (1933) 49 CLR 220 stated (at 235) that the supposed territorial restrictions on State Parliaments were confined to 'a very small compass indeed'. It has been said that the words 'peace, order and good government' are now the source of whatever territorial limitations exist in relation to the Parliaments of the States: *R v Foster; Ex parte Eastern and Australian Steamship Co Ltd* (1959) 103 CLR 256 at 307; *Johnson v Commissioner of Stamp Duties* [1956] AC 331. As Windeyer J noted in *Foster* (at 308), the words simply express the fact that in 'a general and remote sense the purpose and design of every law is to promote the welfare of the community', to use the words [13] of Professor W Harrison Moore in *Commonwealth of Australia*, 2nd ed (1910), pp 274–5.

Earlier in *Broken Hill South Ltd v Commissioner of Taxation (NSW)* (1937) 56 CLR 337 Dixon J had given more precise expression to the limitations which arise from the terms of the grant of the power so far as those limitations might affect laws having an operation outside the territory. His Honour said (at 375):

> … it is within the competence of the State legislature to make any fact, circumstance, occurrence or thing in or connected with the territory the occasion of the imposition upon any person concerned therein of a liability to taxation or of any other liability. It is also within the competence of the legislature to base the imposition of liability on no more than the relation of the person to the territory. The relation may consist in presence within the territory, residence, domicil, carrying on business there, or even remoter connections. If a connection exists, it is for the legislature to decide how far it should go in the exercise of its powers. As in other matters of jurisdiction or authority courts must be exact in distinguishing between ascertaining that the circumstances over which the power extends exists and examining the mode in which the power has been exercised. No doubt there must be some relevance to the circumstances in the exercise of the power. But it is of no importance upon the question of validity that the liability imposed is, or may be, altogether disproportionate to the territorial connection or that it includes many cases that cannot have been foreseen.

See also *Johnson*, at 353; *Thompson v Commissioner of Stamp Duties* [1969] 1 AC 320 at 335–6.

The Solicitor-General for New South Wales, appearing for the Attorney-General for that State as intervener, submitted that even the statement of Dixon J is too restrictive an interpretation of the Parliament's legislative authority. The nineteenth century Privy Council decisions, he submitted, recognise that the grant of power is as large and ample as that enjoyed by the Imperial Parliament itself. As that Parliament is not subject to any territorial restraint, so the Parliament of New South Wales is likewise free from such a restraint. The short answer to this contention is that the nineteenth century decisions, in comparing the scope and extent of the grant of legislative power to colonial legislatures with the power of the Imperial Parliament, explicitly qualified that comparison by reference to the limits of the grant itself: see, for example, the passage already quoted from the opinion in *Hodge*, at 132. Accordingly, the nineteenth [14] century decisions do not deny that the words 'peace, order and good government' may be a source of territorial limitation, however slight that limitation may be. And, as each State Parliament in the Australian federation has power to enact laws for its State, it is appropriate to maintain the need for some territorial limitation in conformity with the terms of the grant, notwithstanding the recent recognition in the constitutional rearrangements for Australia made in 1986 that State Parliaments have power to enact laws having an extraterritorial operation: see Australia Act 1986 (Cth) s 2(1); Australia Act 1986 (UK) s 2(1). That new dispensation is, of course, subject to the provisions of the Constitution (see s 5(a) of each Act) and cannot affect territorial limitations of State legislative powers inter se which are expressed or implied in the Constitution. That being so, the new dispensation may do no more than recognise what has already been achieved in the course of judicial decisions. Be this as it may, it is sufficient for present purposes to express our agreement with the comments of Gibbs J in *Pearce* (CLR at 518) where his Honour stated that the requirement for a relevant connection between the circumstances on which the legislation operates and the State should be liberally applied and that even a remote and general connection between the subject matter of the legislation and the State will suffice.

Once this position is reached, the rejection of the appellant's submission that s 46 is ultra vires becomes inevitable. The fact that the ship is registered in New South Wales is a sufficient connection with the State to enable the Parliament to apply its laws to the ship and to justify the application to seamen employed on that ship of a statute entitling them as against their employer to workers' compensation benefits. As a matter of international law the country which offers its flag to a ship has authority to regulate the conditions upon which the ship may sail under it: see O'Connell, *The International Law of the Sea* (1984), vol 2, p 752. Generally speaking the law of the flag is the law of the place of registration, though this is not an absolute rule: O'Connell, p 753. As registration of the ship was a sufficient connection with the State, it was for the legislature to decide how far it would go, as Dixon J pointed out in *Broken Hill South*, at 375.

The justices concluded that the Workers' Compensation Act was not inconsistent with the Seaman's Compensation Act 1911 (Cth). They dismissed the appeal.

~~~

Notes

[6.3.23] The decision in the *Union Steamship Co of Australia v King* (1988) 166 CLR 1 **[6.3.22C]** appears to have left open the question whether s 2 of the Australia Act 1986 **[6.3.17E]** has effected a change in the powers of state parliaments or simply endorsed such decisions as the *Broken Hill South* case (1937) 56 CLR 337 **[6.3.6]** and *Pearce v Florenca* (1976) 135 CLR 507 **[6.3.13C]**: see the equivocal statement of the justices, 166 CLR at 14. Although the justices urged, as a minimum, that the requirement of a territorial connection should be 'liberally applied', so that 'even a remote and general connection' would be sufficient (166 CLR at 14), they indicated that some territorial limitation was appropriate for the maintenance of a balance between the states.

[6.3.24] Indeed, the justices suggested in the *Union Steamship* case **[6.3.22C]** that 'territorial limitations of State legislative powers *inter se*' could be 'implied in the [Commonwealth] Constitution': 166 CLR at 14. That is, the states, as members of the Australian federation, may be held to have a territorially restricted competence in order to serve the interests of that federation, rather than the Imperial interests which prompted the initial development of the concept of extra-territorial incompetence. The considerations which support a 'federal' territorial limit on state competence are developed by Gilbert: (1987) pp 35, 40, 41–2. The contrary view, that the federal system does not require such a limitation, is developed by Moshinsky: (1987) pp 783–4.

[6.3.25] If the rule of extra-territorial incompetence is to be supported on the ground that it serves a federal interest, it may be that the rule will require significant adjustment. The rule, as developed by the courts in the series of decisions which runs from *Millar's* case (1932) 48 CLR 618 **[6.3.5]** to *Robinson v Western Australian Museum* (1977) 138 CLR 283 **[6.3.15]**, may be inappropriately structured. Is the rule, with its insistence that any liability imposed on a person must be 'in respect of' or 'relevant to' some factor which connects that person to the legislating state, adequately framed to serve that purpose? Is the injection of complex legal concepts into this area of governmental power really calculated to serve that purpose?

[6.3.26] In *Port Macdonnell Professional Fishermen's Association Inc v South Australia* (1989) 168 CLR 340, the High Court, in a unanimous judgment, indicated the continuing vitality of the 'territorial connection' criterion of validity.

Section 13 of the Fisheries Act 1982 (SA) authorised South Australia to enter into an arrangement with the Commonwealth for the management by South Australia of fisheries outside South Australia. Section 14 of the Act provided that the regulatory provisions of the Act extended to any area in respect of which an arrangement had been made under s 13. An arrangement was then made between South Australia and the Commonwealth, under which South Australia was to control rock lobster fishing in an area extending up to 200 nautical miles from the state's coast. The validity of these provisions was challenged.

The court (Mason CJ, Brennan, Deane, Dawson, Toohey, Gaudron and McHugh JJ) noted that *Union Steamship Co of Australia Pty Ltd v King* (1988) 166 CLR 1 **[6.3.22C]** had given effect to a rule 'that what is essential to the extraterritorial operation of a State law is a connection between the enacting State and the extra-territorial persons, things or events on which the law operates': 168 CLR at 372. The court referred to the comments of Gibbs J in *Pearce v Florenca* (1976) 135 CLR 507 **[6.3.16]** at 518, that the requirement for a relevant connection 'should be liberally applied', and continued:

> It follows that the limitation on the extra-territorial operation of the State Fisheries Act depends not on the distance of the arrangement area from the sea boundary of the State's territory but on the existence and nature of a connexion between South Australia and the activities which constitute the fishery in the assigned area.
>
> The circumstances in this case ... demonstrate a real and substantial connexion. The fishery described in the arrangement is a finite resource available for exploitation and exploited by South Australian residents; it is a significant source of South Australian trade and employment. Since the area of water referred to in the second arrangement is to be construed as confined to waters on the South Australian side of lines of equi-distance, the land territory of South Australia is the closest land territory to the fishery. A law for the management of the fishery is a law for the peace, welfare and good gov-ernment of South Australia. Significantly, in the light of the federal considerations referred to in the *Union Steamship* case, the court noted that the South Australian leg-islation did not claim to extend into waters with which Victoria might have an equal or stronger connection (168 CLR at 372–3, 374).

The off-shore settlement, 1980

[6.3.27] In *New South Wales v Commonwealth* (the *Seas and Submerged Lands* case) (1975) 135 CLR 337 **[6.3.40C]** the High Court held, by a majority, that the sea boundaries of the former Australian colonies ended at the low-water mark, and that s 6 of the Seas and Submerged Lands Act 1973 (Cth) which vested 'sovereignty in respect of the territorial sea' in the Commonwealth was a valid law of the Commonwealth Parliament. Section 16 of the Seas and Submerged Lands Act provided that the Act did not limit or exclude the operation of any law of a state except to the extent that the state law dealt with sovereignty or sovereign rights over the territorial sea otherwise than as provided by the Act.

The effect of the Act and the High Court's decision was to place all off-shore areas, beyond the low-water mark, outside the territory of each state but to permit state legislation to apply in those areas on the same basis as it might apply, for example, in another state; that is, if there was a sufficient territorial connection: see *Pearce v Florenca* (1976) 135 CLR 507 **[6.3.13C]**. (Neither the Act nor the decision had any impact on those inland waters, bays, harbours and river estuaries, which were not part of the territorial sea. They remained part of the territory of each state.)

The Act and the decision indicated that a wider range of state legislation, dealing with the exploitation of off-shore mineral resources, would be invalid because that legislation assumed state ownership of (or sovereignty over) the off-shore sea-bed. See, for example, the Petroleum (Submerged Lands) Act 1967 (Vic) which applied Victorian law to off-shore areas and prohibited off-shore exploration for and recovery of petroleum without the consent of the Victorian Government.

[6.3.28] On 29 June 1979, a Premiers' conference reached agreement (described as the 'off-shore constitutional settlement') on the redistribution of constitutional responsibility for off-shore areas. The scheme was to be implemented by a series of complementary Acts, passed by the Commonwealth and state parliaments. The principal focus of the agreement, and of the legislative package, was the extension of state legislative power over the territorial sea (that is, a band of sea three nautical miles from the coastlines of the states) and the conferral on the states of title to the sea-bed under the territorial sea.

[6.3.29] In 1980, each state parliament formally requested the Commonwealth Parliament to enact a Coastal Waters (State Powers) Act: see, for example, the Constitutional Powers (Coastal Waters) Act 1980 (Vic). These formal requests were made in order to bring into operation the provisions of s 51(xxxviii) of the Commonwealth Constitution:

> **51** The Parliament shall, subject to this Constitution, have power to make laws for the peace, order and good government of the Commonwealth with respect to —
>
> …
>
> **(xxxviii)** The exercise within the Commonwealth, at the request or with the concurrence of the Parliaments of all the States directly concerned, of any power which can at the establishment of this Constitution be exercised only by the Parliament of the United Kingdom; …

[6.3.30] The Commonwealth Parliament then enacted the Coastal Waters (State Powers) Act 1980, s 5 of which extended the legislative powers of the states:

> **5** The legislative powers exercisable from time to time under the constitution of each State extend to the making of —
>
> (a) all such laws of the State as could be made by virtue of those powers if the coastal waters of the state, as extending from time to time, were within the limits of the State, including laws applying in or in relation to the sea-bed and subsoil beneath, and the airspace above, the coastal waters of the State;
>
> (b) laws of the State having effect in or in relation to waters within the adjacent area in respect of the State but beyond the outer limits of the coastal waters of the State, including laws applying in or in relation to the sea-bed and subsoil beneath, and the airspace above, the firstmentioned waters, being laws with respect to —
>
>> (i) subterranean mining from land within the limits of the State; or
>>
>> (ii) ports, harbours and other shipping facilities, including installations, and dredging and other works, relating thereto, and other coastal works; and
>
> (c) laws of the State with respect to fisheries in Australian waters beyond the outer limits of the coastal waters of the State, being laws applying to or in relation to those fisheries only to the extent to which those fisheries are, under an arrangement to which the Commonwealth and the State are parties, to be managed in accordance with the laws of the State.

Section 3(1) defined 'adjacent area in respect of the State' by reference to complex descriptions in sch 2 to the Petroleum (Submerged Lands) Act 1967 (Cth). Those descriptions use latitudinal and longitudinal references, and describe areas extending a substantial distance off the coast of each state. 'Coastal waters of the State' were defined to mean that part of the territorial sea of Australia (no wider than three nautical miles: s 4(2)) which is within each state's adjacent area.

[6.3.31] At the same time, the Commonwealth Parliament enacted the Coastal Waters (State Title) Act 1980, s 4 of which gave the states ownership (subject to some reservations) of the sea-bed:

4(1) By force of this Act, but subject to this Act, there are vested in each State, upon the date of commencement of this Act, the same right and title to the property in the sea-bed beneath the coastal waters of the State, as extending on that date, and the same rights in respect of the space (including space occupied by water) above that sea-bed, as would belong to the State if that sea-bed were the sea-bed beneath waters of the sea within the limits of the State.

(2) The rights and title vested in a State under sub-section (1) are vested subject to —

(a) any right or title to the property in the sea-bed beneath the coastal waters of the State of any other person (including the Commonwealth) subsisting immediately before the date of commencement of this Act, other than any such right or title of the Commonwealth that may have subsisted by reason only of the sovereignty referred to in the Seas and Submerged Lands Act 1973;

(b) a right of the Commonwealth, or an Authority of the Commonwealth authorized by the Commonwealth or by a law of the Commonwealth, to use the sea-bed and space referred to in sub-section (1) for the purposes in relation to communications, the safety of navigation, quarantine or defence, and to place, construct and maintain equipment and structures for the purposes of such use; and

(c) a right of the Commonwealth to authorize the construction and use of pipelines for the transport across the sea-bed referred to in sub-section (1) of the petroleum (including petroleum in gaseous form), recovered, in accordance with a law of the Commonwealth, from any area of the sea-bed beyond the coastal waters of the State.

Section 5(1) declared that the states were not to acquire title to any part of the sea-bed occupied by the Commonwealth or a Commonwealth authority until 'the Minister', by notice in the *Gazette*, declared that it should take effect over that part of the sea-bed.

[6.3.32] Simultaneously, the Commonwealth Parliament enacted other legislation to give effect to the remaining aspects of the 'off-shore constitutional settlement':

- the Petroleum (Submerged Lands) Amendment Act 1980 established joint Commonwealth–state authorities to regulate off-shore petroleum mining;

- the Fisheries Amendment Act 1980 and the Navigation Amendment Act 1980 authorised the establishment of joint Commonwealth–state authorities to administer off-shore fisheries; and

- the Historic Shipwrecks Amendment Act 1980 provided for the Historic Shipwrecks Act 1976 (Cth) (brought into operation after the decision in *Robinson v Western Australian Museum* (1977) 138 CLR 283 **[6.3.15]**) to continue to operate in the territorial sea until a state government requested that it cease to apply.

[6.3.33] The use of s 51(xxxviii) to support the Coastal Waters (State Powers) Act 1980 (Cth) raises two problems. The first of these is whether that provision is adequate to support legislation which effectively redistributes constitutional power within the Australian federal system. In *Port Macdonnell Professional Fishermen's Association Inc v South Australia* (1989) 168 CLR 340, the High Court concluded, in a unanimous judgment, that s 5(c) of the Coastal Waters (State Powers) Act 1980 (Cth) was valid, being supported by s 51(xxxviii) of the Commonwealth Constitution.

The court (Mason CJ, Brennan, Deane, Dawson, Toohey, Gaudron and McHugh JJ) described this aspect of the Commonwealth Parliament's power as expressing 'a national purpose of a fundamental kind' (168 CLR at 378); and as designed 'to ensure that a plenitude of residual legislative power is vested in and exercisable in co-operation by the parliaments of the Commonwealth and the States': 168 CLR at 381. The court said that s 51(xxxviii) had been addressed to (at 378):

> ... the perceived need to ensure that legislative powers necessary for the purposes of the new nation could be exercised locally notwithstanding that, prior to federation, they were beyond the competence of local legislatures ...
>
> Shortly stated, the effect of s 51 (xxxviii) is to empower the Commonwealth Parliament to make laws with respect to the local exercise of any legislative power which, before Federation, could not be exercised by the legislatures of the former Australian colonies. In the early days of the Constitution, there may well have been some inhibition against giving that grant of legislative power its full scope and effect in that it could have been seen as controlled by the then status of the Commonwealth within the British Empire. Today, any room for such inhibition has long been denied by "the silent operation of constitutional principles" in the context of complete independence and international sovereignty ... That being so, there is no extrinsic reason why s 51(xxxviii) should not be given the broad interpretation which befits it as a constitutional provision with a national purpose of a fundamental kind.

Section 51(xxxviii), the court said, represented 'both actual and potential enhancement of State legislative powers': actual because it presented the states with the opportunity to participate in the legislative process (through the state parliaments' request or concurrence); potential because the state parliaments were 'potential recipients of legislative power under a law made pursuant to the paragraph': 168 CLR at 379.

The court said that s 5(c) of the Coastal Waters (State Powers) Act 1980 was supported by s 51(xxxviii) because, at the establishment of the Commonwealth, only the United Kingdom Parliament had 'the power to control by external ... legislation the extent of the legislative powers of the States (then Colonies) under their respective Constitutions' (168 CLR at 380), so that s 5(c) was 'a law with respect to the exercise of that formerly exclusive legislative power of the United Kingdom Parliament': 168 CLR at 381.

[6.3.34] The second question raised by the use of s 51(xxxviii) to support the Coastal Waters (State Powers) Act 1980 (Cth) relates to the power of the Commonwealth Parliament to repeal that legislation and the other elements in the Off-Shore Settlement. Would a repeal require (as the enactment did) the request or concurrence of all the states directly concerned?

There may be principled objections to the idea that the Commonwealth Parliament should have its legislative power restricted (by the requirement to seek the concurrence of the states). Such a restriction appears inconsistent with s 1 of the Commonwealth Constitution, which vests the legislative power of the Commonwealth in the Commonwealth Parliament. But for every Commonwealth enactment, we must be able to locate a specific grant of legislative power: What (other than s 51(xxxviii)) would be the source of the Commonwealth Parliament's power to legislate so as to repeal the Coastal Waters (State Powers) Act 1980?

Commonwealth Parliament

[6.3.35] Because the Commonwealth Parliament is authorised 'to make laws ... with respect to ... trade and commerce with other countries' (s 51(i)) or 'external affairs' (s 51(xxix)) one would expect those specific grants of power to carry an authority to legislate extra-territorially. The necessary implication, in such provisions as these, of some extra-territorial competence was emphasised by the High Court in *Crowe v Commonwealth* (1935) 54 CLR 69, where s 51(i) was held to authorise the Commonwealth legislative control of the sale and distribution outside Australia of Australian dried fruits. Starke J said at 85–6:

> The power of self-governing dominions to make laws having extraterritorial operation was considered by the Judicial Committee in *Croft v Dunphy* [1933] AC 156. Once it is found, as I gather from that case, that the particular topic of legislation is with respect to one of its powers enumerated in s 51 of the Constitution upon which the Commonwealth Parliament may competently legislate for the peace, order and good government of the Commonwealth, then no reason exists for restricting the permitted scope of such legislation by any other consideration than is applicable to the legislation of a fully sovereign State. Export, transport and sale, are all parts of that class of relation which constitutes trade and commerce. The subjects of legislation in the present case are the control of the export of Australian dried fruits, and the sale and disposition of such fruits after export. But those subjects are part of the concept of trade and commerce with other countries. The restrictions imposed by the Act and Regulations are all connected with the exportation of dried fruits from Australia (Act s 15; reg No 30 of 1935, cl 9). The legislative authority of the Commonwealth is thus attracted, and the legislation falls within the power to make laws for the peace, order and good government of the Commonwealth with respect to trade and commerce among other countries.

[6.3.36] However, other legislative powers of the Commonwealth are not expressed in a form that implies extra-territorial power. The High Court was initially reluctant to concede extra-territorial power to the Commonwealth Parliament. In a series of cases, culminating in *Merchant Service Guild of Australasia v Commonwealth Steamship Owners' Association (No 3)* (1920) 28 CLR 495, the High Court insisted that s 51(xxxv) did not authorise the Commonwealth Parliament to make laws for the settlement of industrial disputes over conditions of employment outside Australia. Section 51(xxxv) gave the Commonwealth Parliament power to make laws with respect to 'conciliation and arbitration for the prevention and settlement of industrial disputes extending beyond the limits of any one State'. Knox CJ, Isaacs, Rich and Starke JJ said at 503:

> We think that sub-s xxxv of s 51, on its proper judicial construction, is intended to secure, so far as possible by conciliation and arbitration, uninterrupted industrial services to the people of the Commonwealth, and therefore the term 'industrial disputes' in that sub-s unextended by covering s V means disputes as to the terms and conditions of industrial operations in Australia only.

Perhaps this was a surprising result given that the power extends to disputes '*beyond the limits of* any one State'.

[6.3.37] In 1926 an Imperial conference of dominion Prime Ministers, meeting in London, formally recognised the equality in status of Great Britain and the self-governing dominions: see **[6.2.14]**. In 1929, an Imperial conference reported that the subject of territorial limitations on dominion legislation was 'full of obscurity' and that the dominions had been obliged to resort to indirect methods of reaching conduct which, because of the limitations, might lie beyond their direct power but which they regarded as essential to control as part of their self-government. The 1929 conference recommended that legislation should be passed by the United Kingdom Parliament making it clear that the limitation does not exist.

[6.3.38] In 1931, the United Kingdom Parliament passed the Statute of Westminster, the provisions of which were drafted at an Imperial Conference of 1930 which had confirmed the 1929 report quoted above. The immediately relevant provision was s 3:

> It is hereby declared and enacted that the Parliament of a Dominion has full power to make laws having extraterritorial operation.

Section 1 defined 'Dominion' to include the Commonwealth of Australia. Section 10 provided that s 3 should not extend to Australia until adopted by legislation of the Commonwealth Parliament. In 1942 the Commonwealth Parliament adopted s 3 (and other substantive provisions of the Statute of Westminster) by the Statute of Westminster Adoption Act 1942 (Cth). The adoption was declared to have effect from 3 September 1939: see **[6.2.15E]**. It was then inevitable that *Merchant Service Guild of Australasia v Commonwealth Steamship Owners' Association (No 3)* (1920) 28 CLR 495 **[6.3.35]** would be reopened.

[6.3.39] In *R v Foster; Ex parte Eastern and Australian Steamship Co Ltd* (1959) 103 CLR 256, the High Court held that s 72(a) and 72(b) of the Conciliation and Arbitration Act 1904 (Cth) authorised the Conciliation and Arbitration Commission to settle an industrial dispute extending outside Australia and that the section was within the power given to the Commonwealth Parliament by s 51(xxxv) of the Constitution. Responding to an argument that the parliament's power was territorially limited, Dixon CJ (with whose reasons Fullagar and Kitto JJ agreed) said at 267–8:

> It cannot be invalid for extra-territoriality; for s 3 of the Statute of Westminster declares and enacts that the Parliament of a Dominion has full power to make laws having an extraterritorial operation. Since the adoption of the Statute of Westminster by Act No 56 of 1942 it can be no objection to the validity of a law of the Commonwealth that it purports to operate outside Australia. The result may be an enlargement of federal power, but it is not an enlargement against which s 9(1) of the Statute of Westminster can have anything to say.

Windeyer J said at 308:

> So far as the Commonwealth is concerned, it is now for Parliament alone to judge whether a measure in respect of any topic on which it has power to legislate is in fact for the peace order and good government of the Commonwealth.

[6.3.40C]   **New South Wales v Commonwealth**
(The *Seas and Submerged Lands* case)
(1975) 135 CLR 337

The Seas and Submerged Lands Act 1973 (Cth) claimed to implement, as part of Australian law, two international conventions to which Australia was a party, the Convention of the Territorial Sea and the Contiguous Zone and the Convention on the Continental Shelf. The two substantive provisions of the Act were ss 6 and 11:

> 6 It is by this Act declared and enacted that the sovereignty in respect of the territorial sea and in respect of the airspace over it and in respect of its bed and subsoil, is vested in and exercisable by the Crown in right of the Commonwealth.

11 It is by this Act declared and enacted that the sovereign rights of Australia as a coastal State in respect of the continental shelf of Australia, for the purposes of exploring its natural resources, are vested in and exercisable by the Crown in right of the Commonwealth.

The six states began actions in the High Court of Australia, seeking declarations that the Act was invalid, in whole or in part. The legislation was held to be valid by five justices (Barwick CJ, McTiernan, Mason, Jacobs and Murphy JJ) with two dissentients (Gibbs and Stephen JJ), primarily because the Act gave effect to the international conventions and was, therefore, a law with respect to external affairs: s 51(xxix). Jacobs J held that the Act did not implement the treaties but was, nevertheless, valid under the external affairs power. During the course of their judgments, some members of the court discussed the scope of the Commonwealth Parliament's power to legislate extra-territorially.

Barwick CJ: [360] External affairs is a larger expression than foreign affairs, though the expressions are often used interchangeably. In my opinion, the description 'external affairs' covers a larger area of legislative power than would the description 'foreign affairs'. The description of the subject matter of the power and preference for external affairs rather than foreign affairs in the Constitution was doubtless designed to include within the subject matter inter-colonial matters which in Imperial days may not have been regarded as foreign affairs. But the motive of the choice of the description will not govern the content of the legislative power. That is not limited, in my opinion, to the making of arrangements with other nations or the implementation of such international arrangements as may properly be made in Australia's interest with other nations, though doubtless these may be the most frequent manifestations of the exercise of the power. The power extends, in my opinion, to any affair which in its nature is external to the continent of Australia and the island of Tasmania subject always to the Constitution as a whole. For this purpose, the continent of Australia and the island of Tasmania are, in my opinion, bounded by the low-water mark on the coasts ... I agree with the Supreme Court of the United States in thinking that, in this area of discourse, 'once the low-water mark is passed, the international domain is reached': *United States v Texas* 339 US 707 at 719 (1950) [94 Law Ed 1221 at p 1228].

Mason J: [470] Once it is accepted that the boundaries of the Colonies terminated at low-water mark there is in my opinion no reason why the Commonwealth's power to make laws with respect to 'external affairs' (s 51(xxix)) should not be regarded as conferring upon it a plenary power to legislate upon the topic of the territorial sea and its solum ...

The plaintiffs' argument proceeds on the footing that the power is no more than a power to make laws with respect to Australia's relationships with foreign countries. Why the power should be so confined is not readily apparent. The power is expressed in the widest terms; it relates to 'affairs' which are external to Australia. 'Affairs' include 'matters' and 'things' as well as 'relationships' and a constitutional grant of plenary legislative power 'should be construed with all the generality which the words used admit' (*R v Public Vehicles Licensing* [471] *Appeal Tribunal (Tas); Ex parte Australian National Airways Pty Ltd* (1964) 113 CLR 207 at 225).

Jacobs J referred to the term 'external affairs' in s 51(xxix) and to the States' argument that the Commonwealth's power was limited to legislating on the relationships between Australia and other countries.

Jacobs J: [497] In my opinion the Commonwealth has the power to make laws in respect of any person or place outside and any matter or thing done or to be done or prohibited to be done outside the boundaries of the Commonwealth.

The power to make laws in respect of any place outside and any matter or thing done or to be done outside the boundaries of the Commonwealth is clearly not vested in the States. It is in my view now vested in the Australian Crown by virtue of the external affairs power.

The words 'external affairs' must be given their ordinary meaning. It is true that the operation of the power may have been limited in 1900 by the concept that Australia, lacking sovereignty, could legislate only for its territory; but that limitation, if it existed, did not alter the meaning of the words. It is not a sufficient reason for reading down the meaning of these words that there are other provisions of the Constitution, for example, s 51(xxx), which expressly confer power to legislate with extra-territorial effect or which, for example, s 51(x), may place a particular limitation in favour of the States on the power to legislate extra-territorially.

The express power of the Australian Crown to make laws with respect to places outside, or matters or things done outside the boundaries of the Commonwealth is no more fettered by notions of extra-territoriality than is the power possessed by the British Crown ... [498] [N]o statute of [the British Parliament at Westminster] could be held invalid on any ground whatsoever, even if it invaded the rights of the Crown or of the subject under the common law, even if it operated extra-territorially and even if it violated international law.

Clearly the Crown in the Australian Executive Council and in the Australian Parliament has one bound which the British Parliament has not, for it cannot transgress the Constitution. But subject to that Constitution it in Council and in Parliament has that pre-eminence and excellence as a sovereign Crown which is possessed by the British Crown and Parliament. Exactly when it attained those qualities is a matter of the constitutional history of the British Commonwealth of Nations largely reflected in the Imperial Conferences following the Great War. Legal recognition came through the Statute of Westminster, 1931 and its later adoption by Australia. Now the Constitution is the only limitation. There is no gap in the constitutional framework. Every power right and authority of the British Crown is vested in and exercisable by the Crown in Australia subject only to the Constitution. The State legislatures do not have that sovereignty which the British legislature and now the Australian legislature possess. A State can only legislate in respect of persons acts matters and things which have a relevant territorial connexion with the State, a connexion not too remote to entitle the law to the description of a law for the peace, welfare and good government of the State. See *Johnson v Commissioner of Stamp Duties (NSW)* [1956] AC 331. The words of s 51 of the Constitution do not import any similar territorial limitation and there now is none in the case of the Australian legislature. The words 'external affairs' can now be given an operation unaffected by any concept of territorial limitation. The result is that the Commonwealth, outside the boundaries of the States and subject to any particular constitutional injunctions, may make laws on all subject matters in exercise of its sovereignty.

~~~

Notes

[6.3.41] The reasoning of Barwick CJ, Mason and Jacobs JJ in the *Seas and Submerged Lands* case **[6.3.40C]** indicates that factors which are generally regarded as limiting the legislative powers of the states are regarded as supporting the Commonwealth's legislative power. The fact that persons, things or events are located outside Australia will provide the basis on which the Commonwealth Parliament may construct a law under s 51(xxix).

[6.3.42] The proposition that the location of persons, things or events outside Australia is sufficient in itself to enliven the Commonwealth's legislative power was endorsed by five members of the High Court in *Polyukhovich v Commonwealth* (1991) 172 CLR 501. The court was asked to determine the validity of s 9 of the War Crimes Act 1942 (Cth), as amended in 1988. Section 9 declared that a person who committed a war crime in Europe between 1 September 1939 and 8 May 1945 was guilty of an indictable offence against the Act.

Mason CJ referred to the observations of Windeyer J in *R v Foster; Ex parte Eastern and Australian Steamship Co Ltd* (1959) 103 CLR 256 at 308 **[6.3.38]**, and of Jacobs J in *New South Wales v Commonwealth* (the *Seas and Submerged Lands* case) (1975) 135 CLR 337 at 498 **[6.3.40C]**, and concluded:

> The legislation makes conduct outside Australia unlawful, thereby visiting that conduct with legal consequences under Australian law. The conduct made unlawful

constitutes a criminal offence triable and punishable in the ordinary criminal courts in this country. But, to the extent that s 9 operates upon conduct which took place outside Australia and makes that conduct a criminal offence, the section is properly characterized as a law with respect to external affairs and is a valid exercise of power, subject to a consideration of the argument based on usurpation of judicial power ... [I]t is not necessary that the Court should be satisfied that Australia has an interest or concern in the subject matter of the legislation in order that its validity be sustained. It is enough that Parliament's judgment is that Australia has an interest or concern. It is inconceivable that the Court could overrule Parliament's decision on that question. That Australia had such an interest or concern in the subject-matter of the legislation here, stemming from Australia's participation in the Second World War, goes virtually without saying.

... I do not regard the circumstance that the law operates on the past conduct of persons who, at the time of the commission of that conduct, had no connexion with Australia as detracting in any way from the character of s 9 as a law with respect to external affairs. The externality of the conduct which the law prescribes as the foundation of the criminal offence is enough without more to constitute it as a law with respect to external affairs. In this respect it makes no difference whether the law creates a criminal liability by reference to past or future conduct, so long as the conduct is external to Australia (172 CLR at 530–1).

The 'argument based on usurpation of judicial power', referred to by Mason CJ, is considered in **[6.4.19]**. The same approach was adopted by Deane J (172 CLR at 599–604), Dawson J (172 CLR at 632–7), Gaudron J (172 CLR at 694–6), and McHugh J (172 CLR at 712–14).

Toohey J said that an 'external affair is a matter which is external in the sense that it lies outside Australia but it is a matter which is of concern to Australia ... a matter in which Australia has an interest': 172 CLR at 653. However, in his Honour's view, it was for the parliament to determine whether or not a matter qualified as something in which Australia has an interest: it 'must be a matter which the Parliament recognises as touching or concerning Australia in some way': 172 CLR at 654.

Brennan J dissented on this aspect of the case, holding that s 9 of the War Crimes Act was not supported by the external affairs power. He said that, to bring legislation dealing with a matter outside Australia within s 51(xxix), there must be some genuine connection between the external matter in question and Australia. Although parliament should determine in the first instance whether there was any connection between Australia and some matter outside Australia, 'if the legislative judgment cannot reasonably be supported, the law will be held to be outside the power conferred by s 51(xxix)': 172 CLR at 552. Brennan J concluded that s 9 of the War Crimes Act was invalid because it imposed liability on persons whether or not they, or their alleged victims, had any connection with Australia at the time of the events said to give rise to liability.

4   Separation of powers

[6.4.1] In his outstanding review of English constitutional law and its overseas progeny, de Smith referred to 'the doctrine of the separation of powers' as one which is usually regarded as desirable in a system of government, although enthusiasm for the doctrine's virtues is not unanimous: de Smith and Brazier (1989) p 19. The incomplete endorsement or adoption of the doctrine as part of Australian constitutional law supports de Smith's comment. Although one aspect of the doctrine has been treated as occupying a central place in the Commonwealth Constitution and limiting the Commonwealth Parliament's legislative powers, other aspects have not been accorded constitutional status. The doctrine was not regarded as relevant to the states until *Kable v Director of Public Prosecutions (NSW)* (1996) 189 CLR 51: see **[6.4.23]**, **[6.4.35]**, **[6.4.48C]**, **[11.3.30]**ff.

[6.4.2] As de Smith explains, the doctrine of the separation of powers asserts that governmental functions can be divided into three categories: legislative, executive and judicial; that the institutions of government should be similarly divided, and that each function of government should be exercised only by the relevant institution of government, so that the functions and institutions of government are kept strictly separate: see de Smith and Brazier (1989) pp 19–20.

Two immediate difficulties are presented by this doctrine, one theoretical or conceptual, the other practical. The conceptual difficulty lies in the assumption that the functions of government can be neatly divided into three categories. However, the business of contemporary government has such complex characteristics that this neat division is frequently impossible. This difficulty is amply demonstrated in the Australian context by the divisions of judicial opinion over the correct classification (judicial or executive? judicial or legislative?) of such functions as reviewing taxation assessments, cancelling the registration of trade unions and investigating restrictive trade practices. For a detailed account of the disagreements and of the complexities, see Zines (1992) pp 151–84.

From the practical perspective, a rigorous separation of governmental functions (assuming that the functions can be separately identified) could disrupt totally the affairs of government. Even in the United States of America, whose Constitution was drafted to incorporate the doctrine, a substantial exercise of legislative functions by the executive branch has been accepted as consistent with the Constitution. Certainly, the doctrine would be inconsistent with the system of responsible government which was developed in Britain in the 18th century, adopted in the Australian colonies in the mid-19th century and endorsed in the Commonwealth Constitution (see **[7.3.11E]**), a system which requires the executive branch to be directed by ministers who are members of, and politically supported by, the legislature.

The Commonwealth

[6.4.3] The drafting of the Commonwealth Constitution appears to reflect the separation of powers doctrine. Three chapters deal separately with three institutions of government:

- Ch I: parliament;
- Ch II: the executive; and
- Ch III: the judicature.

Three sections 'vest' each of the functions of government in one of these institutions:

1 The legislative power of the Commonwealth shall be vested in a Federal Parliament, which shall consist of the Queen, a Senate, and a House of Representatives, and which is herein-after called "The Parliament," or "The Parliament of the Commonwealth."
...

61 The executive power of the Commonwealth is vested in the Queen and is exercisable by the Governor-General as the Queen's representative, and extends to the execution and maintenance of this Constitution, and of the laws of the Commonwealth. ...

71 The judicial power of the Commonwealth shall be vested in a Federal Supreme Court, to be called the High Court of Australia, and in such other federal courts as the Parliament creates, and in such other courts as it invests with federal jurisdiction. The High Court shall consist of a Chief Justice, and so many other Justices, not less than two, as the Parliament prescribes.

[6.4.4] A consideration of the historical context in which the Commonwealth Constitution was drafted suggests that the arrangements referred to in **[6.4.3]** were not accidental and were intended as more than a convenient drafting device. The United States constitutional model was adopted in many ways by the drafters of the Commonwealth Constitution. Sawer made the observation that the drafters probably regarded the separation of powers 'to be in some degree connected with federal ideas': Sawer (1967) p 153. Their adoption of many important aspects of United States federalism is abundantly clear.

On the other hand, the Commonwealth Constitution incorporates responsible government, in which the legislature and the executive are effectively united. This incorporation is reflected in ss 44, 62 and 64 of the Constitution: see **[7.3.11E]**. Sawer has also pointed to some incomplete aspects of Ch III of the Constitution (the absence of any prescribed qualifications for membership of the High Court, of any prescribed duration for membership of the court or indeed of any obligation to make appointments to the court) and has observed that '[t]he historical probabilities are that only a very limited separation of powers was intended': Sawer (1967) p 154.

Judicial power

[6.4.5C] **New South Wales v Commonwealth**
(The *Wheat* case)
(1915) 20 CLR 54

Section 101 of the Commonwealth Constitution provides:

101 There shall be an Inter-State Commission, with such powers of adjudication and administration as the Parliament deems necessary for the execution and maintenance, within the Commonwealth, of the provisions of this Constitution relating to trade and commerce, and of all laws made thereunder.

Section 103 provides that members of the Commission 'shall hold office for seven years', subject to removal in the same way as justices of the High Court. The Commonwealth Parliament enacted the Interstate Commission Act 1912 (Cth). Part V of the Act (headed 'Judicial Powers of the Commission') designated the Commission as a court of record and gave the Commission power to award damages, and to issue injunctions and declarations. The Commission was authorised to fix penalties for disobedience to its orders, and was given all the powers, rights and privileges of the High Court necessary for the exercise of its jurisdiction.

The Commission investigated the New South Wales Government's seizure under the Wheat Acquisition Act 1914 (NSW), of wheat in the course of interstate trade. The Commission declared that the Act, and the actions of the New South Wales Government, infringed s 92 of the Commonwealth Constitution. It issued an injunction to restrain the New South Wales Government from interfering with the interstate movement of wheat. New South Wales appealed to the High Court, raising the question (inter alia) whether the Commission had jurisdiction to grant the injunction.

Griffith CJ: [61] Section 71 of the Constitution provides that the judicial power of the Commonwealth shall be vested in the High Court and in such other federal Courts as the Parliament creates and in such other Courts as it invests with federal jurisdiction. Section 72 provides that the Justices of the High Court and of the other Courts created by [62] Parliament (ie, federal Courts) shall hold office during good behaviour. It is plain from the provisions of s 103 as to the term of office of the Inter-State Commissioners that they were not to be a federal Court within the meaning of s 72. But it is contended that s 102 should be read as an exception from, or as a supplement to, the provisions of s 72. I am unable to accept this argument. In my judgment the provisions of s 71 are complete and exclusive, and there cannot be a third class of Courts which are neither federal Courts nor State Courts invested with federal jurisdiction ...

I pass to the independent argument founded, on both sides, on s 101. That section is contained in Ch IV, which is headed 'Finance and Trade,' and deals in substance with the powers of the Parliament and of the States with respect to matters of finance and trade, and not in Ch III which is headed 'The Judicature.'

It provides that the Inter-State Commission shall have 'such powers of adjudication and administration as the Parliament deems necessary for the execution and maintenance ... of the provisions [63] of this Constitution relating to trade and commerce, and of all laws made thereunder'...

It is contended that this power implicitly authorises the creation of a Court, because the primary, and, in one sense, the sole, function of a Court is to adjudicate. ...

[64] In my judgment, the functions of the Inter-State Commission contemplated by the Constitution are executive or administrative, and the powers of adjudication intended are such powers of determining questions of fact as may be necessary for the performance of its executive or administrative functions, that is, such powers of adjudication as are incidental and ancillary to those functions.

Isaacs J: [88] When the fundamental principle of the separation of powers as marked out in the Australian Constitution is observed and borne in mind, it relieves the question of much of its obscurity.

By the first Chapter the legislative power of the Commonwealth is vested in a Parliament consisting of the Sovereign and two Houses, and for this purpose the Governor-General is the Royal representative. By Ch II, headed 'The Executive Govern[89]ment', the executive power of the Commonwealth is vested in the Sovereign simply, the Governor-General again being the representative. There might be some ambiguity as to what is meant by executive power, arising from the fact that sometimes in relation to the British Constitution the Judiciary are classed among the executive officers of the Crown. See, for instance, *Halsbury's Laws of England*, vol vii, pp 19, 20 and 21. And in one sense Judges do execute laws. They execute laws relating to the Judiciary, by performing their judicial functions. But, in the contrasted sense, executive powers are distinct from judicial powers. ...

Chapter III is headed 'The Judicature', and vests the judicial power of the Commonwealth not in the Sovereign simply, or as he may in Parliament direct, but in specific organs, namely, Courts strictly so called. They are the High Court, such other federal Courts as Parliament creates, and such other Courts as it invests with federal jurisdiction. There is a mandate to create a High Court; there is a discretionary power to create other federal Courts; and there is a discretionary power to invest with federal jurisdiction such Courts as Parliament finds already in existence, that is, State Courts. But that exhausts the judicature. And as to federal

Courts, the Justices are to have a specific tenure. And the distinct [90] command of the Constitution is that whatever judicial power — that is, in the contrasted sense — is to be exerted in the name of the Commonwealth, must be exercised by these strictly so called judicial tribunals. This command is, as I have said, only emphasised by the manner in which the appeal from the Inter-State Commission is introduced. Section 77 enables Parliament to define the jurisdiction of any federal Court other than the High Court — which means, either original or appellate jurisdiction.

It would require, in view of the careful delimitation I have mentioned, in my opinion, very explicit and unmistakable words to undo the effect of the dominant principle of demarcation. And still more does that necessity press me when I remember how vast a portion of the constitutional field is covered by trade and commerce. So far from finding any such unambiguous words, the language appears to me to point in the opposite direction.

Isaacs J said that s 101 of the Constitution had established 'a novel administrative and consultative organ with quasi-judicial functions ... [with] a duty to actively watch the observance of those laws [relating to trade and commerce], to insist on obedience to their mandates, and to take steps to vindicate them if need be': 20 CLR at 92, 93. His Honour concluded:

[93] But a Court has no such active duty: its essential feature as an impartial tribunal would be gone, and the manifest aim and object of the constitutional separation of powers would be frustrated. A result so violently opposed to the fundamental structure and scheme of the Constitution requires, as I have before observed, extremely plain and unequivocal language.

Powers and Rich JJ delivered concurring judgments on this issue. Barton and Gavan Duffy JJ dissented.

~~~

[6.4.6] In *Waterside Workers' Federation of Australia v JW Alexander Ltd* (1918) 25 CLR 434, a majority of the High Court decided that the Commonwealth Court of Conciliation and Arbitration could not be given the power to make orders against a party to an industrial award, penalising any breach of the award, because the Arbitration Court was not constituted as a court in accordance with s 72 of the Constitution. According to s 12 of the Commonwealth Conciliation and Arbitration Act 1904 (Cth), the President of the Arbitration Court was to be appointed 'from among the Justices of the High Court', and was to hold that office for seven years, subject to reappointment for a similar term.

Barton, Isaacs, Starke and Rich JJ held that s 72 of the Constitution required that all appointments to a federal court must be for life, so that if the members of a body created by the Commonwealth Parliament were appointed for a different term (as with the Arbitration Court), that body was not a federal court for the purposes of Ch III of the Constitution. Isaacs and Rich JJ said that the judicial power was concerned with ascertaining, declaring and enforcing existing rights and liabilities. Their Honours offered the following justification for their reading of s 72 (as demanding that judges of federal courts, including justices of the High Court be appointed for life):

[Section] 72 is one of the strongest guarantees in the Constitution for the security of the States. The Constitution places by s 74 the whole fate of the State Constitutions, where they compete with the Federal Constitution, in the hands of the High Court. That Court's decision in such a question is final, unless in the exercise of its discretion it grants a certificate permitting an appeal to His Majesty in Council.

It is plain that the independence of the tribunal would be seriously weakened if the Commonwealth Parliament could fix any less permanent tenure than for life, subject to proved misbehaviour or incapacity. It is not like the case of unitary Parliament having one interest only to consider, namely, the one territory. It is the case of a Federation, where the central legislative and executive bodies are largely competitive with, and in a sense adverse to, the State authorities. On the whole, the suggested inconvenience sinks into insignificance when the greater considerations are borne in mind (25 CLR at 469–79).

The justices also held that the principal function of the Arbitration Court, the settlement or prevention of industrial disputes by conciliation or arbitration, was not a judicial function but was analogous to the making of legislation. It followed that the function could be vested in the Arbitration Court even though it did not qualify as a federal court.

[6.4.7] In 1977, s 72 of the Commonwealth Constitution was altered so as to ensure that appointments to the High Court and other federal courts (other than appointments made before the alteration) would terminate when the appointee attained the age of 70 years. The section now permits the Commonwealth Parliament to fix, prospectively, a retirement age of less than 70 years.

This alteration does not affect the central propositions about the exercise of judicial power made in *Waterside Workers' Federation of Australia v JW Alexander Ltd* (1918) 25 CLR 434 **[6.4.6]**, namely, that the judicial function of enforcing, through penalties for breach, industrial awards could only be given by the Commonwealth Parliament to courts, and that an institution could only be a federal court if its members were appointed and held their tenure under s 72 of the Constitution.

[6.4.8] In 1926 the Commonwealth Parliament passed the Commonwealth Conciliation and Arbitration Act 1926, which reconstituted the Commonwealth Court of Conciliation and Arbitration. It was to consist of three judges, each with life tenure (and the other protections prescribed by s 72). It was given the powers to make industrial awards and to enforce those awards, powers which the High Court decided in the *Waterside Workers'* case **[6.4.6]** were respectively non-judicial and judicial.

The court functioned in this reconstituted form, and with this mixture of functions, until 1956, when the High Court and the Privy Council found that its mixture of functions offended the separation of powers doctrine: *R v Kirby; Ex parte Boilermakers' Society of Australia* (1956) 94 CLR 254 **[6.4.12C]**; *Attorney-General (Cth) v R; Ex parte Boilermakers' Society of Australia* (1957) 95 CLR 529 **[6.4.13]**.

In *Victorian Stevedoring and General Contracting Co Pty Ltd v Dignan* (1931) 46 CLR 73 **[6.4.36C]**, Evatt J referred to this mixture of functions in the Commonwealth Conciliation and Arbitration Court as demonstrating that non-judicial functions could validly be given to a federal court: 46 CLR at 116–7. The same point was made by Latham CJ in *R v Federal Court of Bankruptcy; Ex parte Lowenstein* (1938) 59 CLR 556. After noting the mixture of functions in the Arbitration Court, he said at 566:

> Thus, in my opinion, it is not possible to rely upon any doctrine of absolute separation of powers for the purpose of establishing a universal proposition that no court or person who discharges Federal judicial functions can lawfully discharge any other function which has been entrusted to him by statute.

A similar point was made in the same case by Starke J: 59 CLR at 576–7.

[6.4.9] However, the High Court had already laid the foundation for a contrary proposition. In *Re Judiciary and Navigation Acts* (the *Advisory Opinions* case)

(1921) 29 CLR 257, the court decided that Pt XII of the Judiciary Act 1903 (Cth) was invalid. The Part authorised the Governor-General to refer to the High Court for its determination 'any question of law as to the validity of any Act or enactment of the Parliament'. The majority of the court (Knox CJ, Gavan Duffy, Powers, Rich and Starke JJ) held that this function was judicial, but that it could not be exercised by the High Court because it was not part of the judicial power of the Commonwealth. Their Honours referred to ss 75, 76 and 77 of the Commonwealth Constitution at 264–5:

> Section 75 confers original jurisdiction on the High Court in certain matters, and s 76 enables Parliament to confer original jurisdiction on it in other matters. Section 77 enables Parliament to define the jurisdiction of any other Federal Court with respect to any of the matters mentioned in ss 75 and 76, to invest any Court of the States with Federal jurisdiction in respect of any such matters, and to define the extent to which the jurisdiction of any Federal Court shall be exclusive of that which belongs to or is invested in the Courts of the States. This express statement of the matters in respect of which and the Courts by which the judicial power of the Commonwealth may be exercised is, we think, clearly intended as a delimitation of the whole of the original jurisdiction which may be exercised under the judicial power of the Commonwealth, and as a necessary exclusion of any other exercise of original jurisdiction.

Knox CJ, Gavan Duffy, Powers, Rich and Starke JJ said that the reference in s 76 to a 'matter' imported the idea that there must be a 'subject-matter for determination in a legal proceeding', and that this required 'some immediate right, duty or liability to be established by the determination of the Court': 29 CLR at 265. They concluded at 266–7:

> [A] matter under the judicature provisions of the Constitution must involve some right or privilege or protection given by law, or the prevention, redress or punishment of some act inhibited by law. The adjudication of the Court may be sought in proceedings inter partes or ex parte, or, if Courts had the requisite jurisdiction, even in those administrative proceedings with reference to the custody, residence and management of the affairs of infants or lunatics. But we can find nothing in Chapter III of the Constitution to lend colour to the view that Parliament can confer power or jurisdiction upon the High Court to determine abstract questions of law without the right or duty of any body or person being involved.

[6.4.10] Although the decision in the *Advisory Opinions* case (1921) 29 CLR 257 **[6.4.9]** could be expressed in quite narrow terms (that the judicial functions which could be given to courts by the Commonwealth Parliament were limited to those specified in ss 75 and 76), it might support a wider proposition. Dixon J cited the decision for a wider proposition, in *Victorian Stevedoring and General Contracting Co Pty Ltd v Dignan* (1931) 46 CLR 73 **[6.4.36C]**, when he said that 'the Parliament is restrained ... from reposing any other than [essentially] judicial power in [the] tribunals' described in the Constitution: 46 CLR at 97–8.

[6.4.11] The notion that there is a reciprocal aspect to the separation of powers doctrine (that judicial functions can be given only to courts, and that only judicial functions can be given to courts) gained further support from the High Court's decision in *Queen Victoria Memorial Hospital v Thornton* (1953) 87 CLR 144, that s 28 of the Re-establishment and Employment Act 1945 (Cth) was invalid. That section gave state courts the power to order an employer to hire ex-service personnel. The court concluded that, because the court was given a complete discretion under the section, the function was not judicial. As it was not judicial, the Commonwealth Parliament could not vest the function in a state court under s 77(iii) of the

Constitution. Dixon CJ, McTiernan, Williams, Webb, Fullagar, Kitto and Taylor JJ observed at 151:

> Many functions perhaps may be committed to a court which are not themselves exclusively judicial, that is to say which considered independently might belong to an administrator. But that is because they are not independent functions but form incidents in the exercise of strictly judicial powers. Here there is nothing but an authority which clearly is administrative.

The basic proposition, to which that possibility referred to in the immediately preceding paragraph forms an exception, was formulated in the following decision.

[6.4.12C] R v Kirby; Ex parte Boilermakers' Society of Australia

(The *Boilermakers'* case)
(1956) 94 CLR 254

The Commonwealth Court of Conciliation and Arbitration, as reconstituted in 1926, consisted of judges whose conditions of appointment and tenure conformed to s 72 of the Commonwealth Constitution as interpreted in *Waterside Workers' Federation of Australia v JW Alexander Pty Ltd* (1918) 25 CLR 434 **[6.4.6]**.

Section 25 of the 1926 Act gave the court power, for the purpose of preventing or settling industrial disputes, to make orders or awards altering the standard working hours in an industry, fixing or determining the principles for fixing the basic wage for adult males and females and making provisions for long service leave.

Section 29(1) of the Act empowered the court:
* to impose penalties for breach of an order or award;
* to order compliance with an order or award;
* to enjoin contravention of the Act or breaches of orders and awards; and
* to give interpretations of orders and awards.

Section 29A gave the court the same power to punish contempts of its power and authority whether in relation to its judicial power or otherwise as was possessed by the High Court in respect of contempts of the High Court.

In June 1955, the court, exercising the power conferred by s 29A, fined the Boilermakers' Society of Australia £500 for contempt of court. The contempt consisted of its disobedience to an earlier order of the court, made under s 29(1)(b) and (c), ordering the Society to comply with an award of the court and restraining further breaches by the Society of that award. The Society applied to the High Court for a writ of prohibition, which would prohibit the Court of Conciliation and Arbitration from further proceeding on the contempt judgment, on the ground that the vesting of judicial and non-judicial functions in the Arbitration Court was repugnant to Ch III of the Commonwealth Constitution.

Dixon CJ, McTiernan, Fullagar and Kitto JJ: [267] In a federal form of government a part is necessarily assigned to the judicature which places it in a position unknown in a unitary system or under a flexible constitution where Parliament is supreme. A federal constitution must be rigid. The government it establishes must be one of defined powers; within those powers it must be paramount, but it must be incompetent to go beyond them. The conception of independent governments existing in the one area and exercising powers in different fields of action carefully defined [268] by law could not be carried into practical effect unless the ultimate responsibility of deciding upon the limits of the respective powers of the governments were placed in the federal judicature. The demarcation of the powers of the judicature, the constitution of the courts of which it consists and the maintenance of its distinct functions become therefore a consideration of equal importance to the States and the Commonwealth. While the constitutional sphere of the judicature of the States must be secured from encroachment, it cannot be left to the judicial power of the States to determine either the ambit of federal power or the extent of the residuary power of the States. The powers of the federal judicature must therefore be at once paramount and limited. The organs to which federal judicial power may be entrusted must be defined, the manner in which they may be constituted must be prescribed and the content of their jurisdiction ascertained. These very general considerations explain the provisions of Ch III of the Constitution which is entitled 'The Judicature' and consists of 10 sections. It begins with s 71 which says that the judicial power of the Commonwealth shall be vested in a Federal Supreme Court to be called the High Court of Australia and in such other courts as the Parliament creates or it invests with federal jurisdiction. There is not in s 51, as there is in the enumeration of legislative powers in Art 1, s 8, of the American Constitution, an express power to constitute tribunals inferior to the Federal Supreme Court ...

[269] Had there been no Ch III in the Constitution it may be supposed that some at least of the legislative powers would have been construed as extending to the creation of courts with jurisdictions appropriate to the subject matter of the power. This could hardly have been otherwise with the powers in respect of bankruptcy and insolvency (s 51(xvii)) and with respect to divorce and matrimonial causes (s 51(xxii)). The legislature would then have been under no limitations as to the tribunals to be set up or the tenure of the judicial officers by whom they might be constituted. But the existence in the Constitution of Ch III and the nature of the provisions it contains make it clear that no resort can be made to judicial power except under or in conformity with ss 71–80. An exercise of a legislative power may be such that 'matters' fit for the judicial process may arise under the law that is made. In virtue of that character, that is to say because they are matters arising under a law of the Commonwealth, they belong to federal judicial power. But they can be dealt with in federal jurisdiction only as the result of a law made in the exercise of the power conferred on the Parliament by s 76(ii) or that provision considered with s 71 and s 77. Section 51(xxxix) extends to furnishing [270] courts with authorities incidental to the performance of the functions derived under or from Ch III and no doubt to dealing in other ways with matters incidental to the execution of the powers given by the Constitution to the federal judicature. But, except for this, when an exercise of legislative powers is directed to the judicial power of the Commonwealth it must operate through or in conformity with Ch III. For that reason it is beyond the competence of the Parliament to invest with any part of the judicial power any body or person except a court created pursuant to s 71 and constituted in accordance with s 72 or a court brought into existence by a State. It is a proposition which has been repeatedly affirmed and acted upon by this Court: see *New South Wales v Commonwealth* (1915) 20 CLR 54 at 62, 89, 90, 108, 109; *Waterside Workers' Federation of Australia v J W Alexander Ltd* (1918) 25 CLR 434; *British Imperial Oil Co Ltd v Federal Commissioner of Taxation* (1925) 35 CLR 422; *Silk Bros Pty Ltd v State Electricity Commission (Vict)* (1943) 67 CLR 1; *R v Davison* (1954) 90 CLR 353. Indeed to study Ch III is to see at once that it is an exhaustive statement of the manner in which the judicial power of the Commonwealth is or may be vested. It is true that it is expressed in the affirmative but its very nature puts out of question the possibility that the legislature may be at liberty to turn away from Ch III to any other source of power when it makes a law giving judicial power exercisable within the Federal Commonwealth of Australia. No part of the judicial power can be conferred in virtue of any other authority or otherwise than in accordance with the provisions of Ch III. The fact that affirmative words appointing or limiting an order or form of things may have also negative force and forbid the doing of the thing otherwise was noted very early in the development of the principles of interpretation: 1 Plow 113 [75 ER 176]. In Ch III we have a notable but very evident example.

[271] A number of considerations exist which point very definitely to the conclusion that the Constitution does not allow the use of courts established by or under Ch III for the discharge of functions which are not in themselves part of the judicial power and are not [272] auxiliary or incidental thereto. First among them stands the very text of the Constitution. If attention is confined to Ch III it would be difficult to believe that the careful provisions for the creation of a federal judicature as the institution of government to exercise judicial power and the precise specification of the content or subject matter of that power were compatible with the exercise by that institution of other powers. The absurdity is manifest of supposing that

the legislative powers conferred by s 51 or elsewhere enabled the Parliament to confer original jurisdiction not covered by ss 75 and 76. It is even less possible to believe that for the Federal Commonwealth of Australia an appellate power could be created or conferred that fell outside s 73 aided possibly by s 77(ii) and (iii) ...

To one instructed only by a reading of Ch III and an understanding of the reasons inspiring the careful limitations which exist upon the judicial authority exercisable in the Federal Commonwealth of Australia by the federal judicature brought into existence for the purpose, it must seem entirely incongruous if nevertheless there may be conferred or imposed upon the same judicature authorities or responsibilities of a description wholly unconnected with judicial power. It would seem a matter of course to treat the affirmative provisions stating the character and judicial powers of the federal judicature as exhaustive. What reason could there be in treating it as an exhaustive statement, not of the powers, but only of the judicial power that may be exercised by the judicature? It hardly seems a reasonable hypothesis that in respect of the very kind of power that the judicature was designed to exercise its functions were carefully limited but as to the exercise of functions foreign to the character and purpose of the judicature it was meant to leave the matter at large ...

[274] With reference to the federal judicature, the true contrast in federal powers is not between judicial power lying within Ch III and judicial power lying outside Ch III. That is tenuous and unreal. It is between judicial power within Ch III and [275] other powers. To turn to the provisions of the Constitution dealing with those other powers surely must be to find confirmation for the view that no functions but judicial may be reposed in the judicature. If you knew nothing of the history of the separation of powers, if you made no comparison of the American instrument of government with ours, if you were unaware of the interpretation it had received before our Constitution was framed according to the same plan, you would still feel the strength of the logical inferences from Chs I, II and III and the form and contents of ss 1, 61 and 71. It would be difficult to treat it as a mere draftsman's arrangement. Section 1 positively vests the legislative power of the Commonwealth in the Parliament of the Commonwealth. Then s 61, in exactly the same form, vests the executive power of the Commonwealth in the Crown. They are the counterparts of s 71 which in the same way vests the judicial power of the Commonwealth in this Court, the federal courts the Parliament may create and the State courts it may invest with federal jurisdiction. This cannot all be treated as meaningless and of no legal consequence.

Probably the most striking achievement of the framers of the Australian instrument of government was the successful combination of the British system of parliamentary government containing an executive responsible to the legislature with American federalism. This meant that the distinction was perceived between the essential federal conception of a legal distribution of governmental powers among the parts of the system and what was accidental to federalism, though essential to British political conceptions of our time, namely the structure or composition of the legislative and executive arms of government and their mutual relations. The fact that responsible government is the central feature of the Australian constitutional system makes it correct enough to say that we have not adopted the American theory of the separation of powers. For the American theory involves the Presidential and Congressional system in which the executive is independent of Congress and office in the former is inconsistent with membership of the latter. But that is a matter of the relation between the two organs of government and the political operation of the institution. It does not affect legal powers. It was open no doubt to the framers of the Commonwealth Constitution to decide that a distribution of powers between the executive and legislature could safely be dispensed with, once they rejected the system of the independence of the executive. But it is only too evident from the text of the Constitution that that was not their decision. In any case the separation of the [276] judicial powers from other powers is affected by different considerations. The position and constitution of the judicature could not be considered accidental to the institution of federalism: for upon the judicature rested the ultimate responsibility for the maintenance and enforcement of the boundaries within which governmental power might be exercised and upon that the whole system was constructed. This would be enough in itself, were there no other reasons, to account for the fact that the Australian Constitution was framed so as closely to correspond with its American model in the classical division of powers between the three organs of government, the legislature, the executive and the judicature. But, whether it was necessary or not, it could hardly be clearer on the face of the Constitution that it was done. The fundamental principle upon which federalism proceeds is the allocation of the powers of government. In the United States no doubts seem to have existed that the principle should be applied not only between the federal Government and the States but also among the organs of the national Government itself.

Dixon CJ, McTiernan, Fullagar and Kitto JJ noted that the Arbitration Court had functioned in its present form since 1936, and that there were dicta of several High Court justices supporting the validity of the Arbitration Court's mixture of functions. They concluded:

[296] Notwithstanding the presumptive force which has been given to these matters in the consideration of the present case, it has been found impossible to escape the conviction that Ch III does not allow the exercise of a jurisdiction which of its very nature belongs to the judicial power of the Commonwealth by a body established for purposes foreign to the judicial power, notwithstanding that it is organised as a court and in a manner which might otherwise satisfy ss 71 and 72, and that Ch III does not allow a combination with judicial power of functions which are not ancillary or incidental to its exercise but are foreign to it.

Williams, Webb and Taylor JJ dissented.

~~~

Notes

[6.4.13] On appeal, the Privy Council agreed with the majority of the High Court, and expressed its reasons in similar terms: *Attorney-General (Cth) v R; Ex parte Australian Boilermakers' Society* (1957) 95 CLR 529. The Judicial Committee referred to the drafting structure of the Commonwealth Constitution as embodying the separation of powers principle (at 538):

Section 1 which vests legislative power in a Federal Parliament at the same time, negatives such power being vested in any other body. In the same way, s 71 and the succeeding sections while affirmatively prescribing in what courts the judicial power of the Commonwealth may be vested and the limits of their jurisdiction negatives the possibility of vesting such power in other courts or extending their jurisdiction beyond those limits. It is to Ch III alone that the Parliament must have recourse if it wishes to legislate in regard to the judicial power ... There could not well be a clearer case for the application of the maxim *Expressio unius exclusio alterius*.

Later they referred to a broader, political, justification for their decision at 540–1:

[I]n a federal system the absolute independence of the judiciary is the bulwark of the constitution against encroachment whether by the legislature or by the executive. To vest in the same body executive as well as judicial power is to remove a vital constitutional safeguard.

[6.4.14] The Privy Council's reference to the maxim of interpretation *expressio unius exclusio alterius* is reflected in the statement of the majority of the High Court that Ch III was 'a notable but very evident example' of the fact that 'affirmative words' could have 'a negative force': 94 CLR at 270. However, this approach to interpretation is not inevitable. Amongst the alternative explanations for the drafting of s 71 is the simple point that it was convenient for the drafters of the Constitution to deal with what they conceived as the functions and institutions of government serially, rather than simultaneously.

[6.4.15] The Privy Council also appealed to the role of the courts as a 'bulwark of the Constitution', a function which demanded that executive and judicial power not be vested in the same body: 95 CLR at 540–1. It is not clear whether their Lordships had in mind the role of the courts as arbiters of the federal distribution of powers, or as protectors of the citizen against the executive government. In either event, it is unclear how the mixture of functions in the Arbitration Court would threaten the integrity of the 'bulwark'.

In the High Court, the majority referred less equivocally to the judiciary's role in the federal system, and said this would be enough to support the constitutional separation of powers: 94 CLR at 276. Again, the argument was not developed to the point where the mixed functions of the Arbitration Court could be seen to threaten the courts' role as arbiter of the federal system. The argument might relate to a reduction in public confidence in the impartiality of a judiciary which exercised non-judicial powers, or it might relate to the risk of the judiciary unconsciously absorbing the values and perspectives involved in its non-judicial functions and thereby distorting the performance of its judicial functions. A similar point had been made earlier by Isaacs and Rich JJ in *Waterside Workers' Federation of Australia v J W Alexander Pty Ltd* (1918) 25 CLR 434 at 469–70 **[6.4.6]**, and has been further developed in *Kable v DPP (NSW)* (1996) 189 CLR 51 **[11.3.30]**ff.

[6.4.16] The immediate consequence of the decision in the *Boilermakers'* case was a reconstitution of the body responsible for the implementation of the Conciliation and Arbitration Act 1904 (Cth). By the Conciliation and Arbitration Act 1956 (Cth), the Arbitration Court was abolished and replaced with two separate bodies: the Conciliation and Arbitration Commission, charged with the responsibility of settling interstate industrial disputes through conciliation and arbitration, with members appointed for limited terms (although protected against earlier removal, by s 14(1) of the principal Act, except on address from each House of the Commonwealth Parliament on the ground of proved misbehaviour or incapacity); and the Commonwealth Industrial Court, with jurisdiction to interpret and enforce, through penalties for breach, awards made by the Commission, consisting of judges with the tenure required by s 72 of the Constitution, as interpreted in *Waterside Workers' Federation of Australia v JW Alexander Pty Ltd* (1918) 25 CLR 434 **[6.4.6]**.

In 1976, the jurisdiction of the Australian Industrial Court (as it had been renamed) was transferred to the Industrial Division of the newly-established Federal Court of Australia: Conciliation and Arbitration Amendment Act (No 3) 1976 (Cth). In 1989, the Conciliation and Arbitration Commission was abolished. A new body, the Industrial Relations Commission, was established with similar responsibilities and with similar terms of appointment and tenure for its members as the Conciliation and Arbitration Commission: Industrial Relations Act 1988 (Cth).

[6.4.17] The proposition from *New South Wales v Commonwealth* (the *Wheat* case) (1915) 20 CLR 54 **[6.4.5C]**, that the judicial power of the Commonwealth should only be entrusted to courts, has never been seriously challenged. In 1988, the Constitutional Commission supported the proposition as consistent with '[t]he rule of law [which] requires that basic rights granted by the law should be determined by independent judges': Constitutional Commission (1988) p 392. They endorsed the following statement of Jacobs J in *R v Quinn; Ex parte Consolidated Foods Corporation* (1977) 138 CLR 1 at 11:

The historical approach to the question whether a power is exclusively a judicial power is based upon the recognition that we have inherited and were intended by our Constitution to live under a system of law and government which has traditionally protected the rights of persons by ensuring that those rights are determined by a judiciary independent of the parliament and the executive. But the rights referred to in such an enunciation are the basic rights which traditionally, and therefore historically, are judged by that independent judiciary which is the bulwark of freedom. The governance of a trial for the determination of criminal guilt is the classic example. But there are a multitude of such instances.

The proposition that the separation of judicial power and judicial functions effected by Chapter III of the Constitution serves the purpose of protecting individual liberty is explored further in **[6.4.18]–[6.4.23]**; see also **[11.3.23]–[11.3.37]**.

[6.4.18] The Builders Labourers' Federation was registered as an organisation of employees under the Conciliation and Arbitration Act 1904 (Cth). Sections 143(2) and 118A(1) gave the Federal Court jurisdiction to hear and determine an application for the cancellation of the registration of an organisation. The Commonwealth Parliament enacted the Building Industry Act 1985 (Cth), which authorised the Conciliation and Arbitration Commission to declare, after conducting a hearing, that the Federation had engaged in certain conduct, and authorised the Minister, after the Commission had made such a declaration, to direct the cancellation of the Federation's registration.

In September 1985, the Minister applied to the Commission for a declaration under the Building Industry Act. After conducting a hearing, the Commission made a declaration under that Act on 10 April 1986. The Minister then announced that he would introduce into the Commonwealth Parliament new legislation directly cancelling the Federation's registration. The Federation began proceedings in the High Court, challenging the validity of the Commission's declaration. On 14 April 1986, the Commonwealth Parliament enacted the Builders Labourers' Federation (Cancellation of Registration) Act 1986 (Cth), which cancelled the registration of the Federation.

The Federation then began proceedings in the High Court, challenging the validity of the Cancellation of Registration Act: *Australian Building Construction Employees' and Builders Labourers' Federation v Commonwealth* (1986) 161 CLR 88. One of the grounds of challenge was that the Act exercised or interfered with the judicial power of the Commonwealth. The challenge was rejected by the High Court. In a unanimous judgment, the court (Gibbs CJ, Mason, Brennan, Deane and Dawson JJ) said that, just as the parliament could select the organisations which were entitled to participate in the system of industrial conciliation and arbitration, so it was 'appropriate for the Parliament to decide whether an organization so selected should be subsequently excluded and, if need be, to exclude that organization by an exercise of legislative power': 161 CLR at 95.

The court said that 'the Parliament may legislate so as to affect and alter rights in issue in pending litigation without interfering with the exercise of judicial power in a way that is inconsistent with the Constitution'. Further, it was held that although the parliament could not interfere with the judicial process itself (*Liyanage v R* [1967] AC 259), it could interfere with the substantive rights which were at issue in the proceedings: 161 CLR at 96. They concluded at 96–7:

The Cancellation of Registration Act does not deal with any aspect of the judicial process. It simply deregisters the Federation, making redundant the legal proceedings which it commenced in this Court. It matters not that the motive or purpose of the Minister, the Government and the Parliament in enacting the statute was to circumvent the proceedings and forestall any decision which might be given in those proceedings.

The consequence is that the Cancellation of Registration Act is a valid law of the Commonwealth Parliament.

[6.4.19] Section 9 of the War Crimes Act 1945 (Cth) was amended in 1988 so as to provide that a person who, in Europe between 1 September 1939 and 8 May 1945, committed a war crime was guilty of an indictable offence against the Act. The validity of s 9 was challenged in *Polyukhovich v Commonwealth* (1991) 172 CLR 501. One of the grounds of challenge was that the retrospective character of the 1988 amendment amounted to a usurpation of judicial power because a retrospective criminal law in effect directed the courts to find that conduct amounted to a crime when, at the time when it was committed, it did not.

Mason CJ acknowledged that a Bill of Attainder (a law declaring that a named person was guilty of a crime and imposing a sanction on that person) would involve a breach of the separation of judicial power. (See also Dawson J (172 CLR at 648), and McHugh J: 172 CLR at 721.) However, Mason CJ said, a retrospective law did not offend that separation. He said that this proposition had been accepted by the High Court in *R v Kidman* (1915) 20 CLR 425. His Honour continued:

> Before the present case it had never occurred to anyone to suggest that an ex post facto law of the kind under consideration here, not being a bill of attainder, could amount to a usurpation of judicial power because such an ex post facto law simply does not amount to a trial by legislature. It leaves for determination by the court the issues which would arise for determination under a prospective law (172 CLR at 540).

McHugh J developed the same analysis:

> The Act in question in this case is not a Bill of Attainder or a Bill of Pains and Penalties. It differs from an ordinary criminal statute only in the fact that it operates retrospectively and not prospectively. It does not select a specifically designated person or group and impose a punishment on that person or group. It does not make any determination of fact. It does not adjudge any person or group to be guilty of any offence. There is not a scintilla of difference between the roles of the judge and jury in a trial under this Act and the roles of the judge and jury in a trial under a hypothetical law, in substantially identical terms to this Act, passed on 1 September 1939 and operating prospectively. The only difference between the present Act and that hypothetical law would be that the present Act makes it a legislative offence to do what was not a legislative offence at the time when it was done. That is to say, the difference is that the present Act retrospectively, and not prospectively, imposes penal sanctions on proscribed conduct. The imposition of penal sanctions on proscribed conduct, however, is an exercise of legislative, not judicial, power. Accordingly, the present Act does not interfere in any way with the judicial process or with the judicial power of the Commonwealth (172 CLR at 721–2).

The same approach was adopted by Dawson J: 172 CLR at 649–51.

On the other hand, Deane J concluded that s 9 involved a breach of the separation of judicial power. He expressed the conclusion of his analysis in the following terms at 631–2:

> The critical question upon the answer to which this judgment turns is ultimately one of abstract constitutional law. It is whether the Commonwealth Parliament possesses power to legislate that a 'person ... is guilty' of a crime against Commonwealth law if, in the past, he has done some specified thing which was not, when done, such a crime. That question must, in my view, be answered in the negative for the reason that a law

which declares that a person 'is guilty' of a crime against a law of the Commonwealth if he has done an act which did not, when done, in fact contravene any such law is inconsistent with Ch III of the Constitution. Both in substance and in form, the central operation of the Act is as such a legislative declaration of criminal guilt. It prohibits nothing, prescribes no rule of conduct and is incapable of being contravened since, by its terms, it is inapplicable to acts committed after its enactment. As I have endeavoured to explain, it is not to the point that the Act identifies a 'person' whom it declares to be 'guilty' of past crimes against the law of the Commonwealth not by name but, in the case of the plaintiff, by reference to whether, within a long past period and in another country, he did an alleged act which was not such a crime when done and which has never, if done where it was allegedly done, been prohibited by any applicable law of the Commonwealth, including the Act. Nor is it to the point that the operation of the Act to declare that such a person 'is guilty' of such a past crime is obscured by the requirement of a trial to determine whether a particular accused is such a person. What is to the point for the purposes of the present case is the combined effect of two propositions which are basic to the criminal jurisprudence of this country. The first of those propositions is almost a truism. It is that criminal guilt, under our system of law, means being guilty of a contravention of the requirements of a then existing and applicable penal law ... The second of those two propositions is that the function of determining whether a person is in fact guilty of a crime against a law of the Commonwealth is a function which appertains exclusively to, and which cannot be excluded from, the judicial power which our Constitution vests solely in the courts which it designates. That being so, it is beyond the competence of the Parliament to declare, as s 9(1) of the Act purports to do, that a 'person ... is guilty' of a crime against a law of the Commonwealth by reason of having committed a past act which did not, when done, contravene any applicable Commonwealth law and was therefore not in fact such a crime.

Brennan J did not discuss the issue of separation of judicial power, as he held s 9 to be invalid on other grounds.

Toohey J said that a retroactive criminal law would violate the separation of judicial power if it purported 'to operate in such a way as to require a court to act contrary to accepted notions of judicial power': 172 CLR at 689. Those accepted notions included the interest of individuals in knowing in advance what the law requires of them, so that they can control their fates, and the public interest in 'a climate of security and humanity' in which people do not live in fear of capricious state action: 172 CLR at 688–9. On the other hand, a retroactive criminal law would be valid if the considerations against retroactivity were outweighed by the public interest in punishing the transgressor; namely, where 'the alleged moral transgression is extremely grave' or where it 'is closely analogous to, but does not for some technical reason amount to, legal transgression': 172 CLR 689. Those considerations were sufficient to ensure that s 9 survived the challenge based on separation of judicial power.

Gaudron J also concluded that the retrospective character of s 9 involved a breach of the separation of judicial power: 172 CLR at 704–8.

[6.4.20C]   Chu Kheng Lim v Minister for Immigration, Local Government and Ethnic Affairs
(1992) 176 CLR 1

Two groups of Cambodian nationals (referred to as the plaintiffs in these proceedings) arrived in Australia in 1989 and 1990. None of them had a valid entry permit under the Migration Act 1958 (Cth), and they were all detained in custody by delegates of the Minister for Immigration, Local Government and Ethnic Affairs. Shortly after arrival, each of the plaintiffs applied for refugee status. Their applications were rejected by a delegate of the Minister at the beginning of April 1992. Upon applications made by each plaintiff, the Federal Court set aside the delegate's decisions and adjourned the plaintiffs' further applications for orders that they be released from custody to 7 May 1992.

On 5 May 1992, the Commonwealth Parliament added Pt 4B to the Migration Act 1958. Section 54L authorised the continued detention, after 6 May 1992, of a 'designated person' already in custody; further, s 54N authorised the detention, without warrant, of a 'designated person' who was not in custody on 6 May 1992. Section 54R read as follows:

> **54R** A court is not to order the release from custody of a designated person.

The term 'designated person' was defined in s 54K:

> **54K** 'Designated person' means a non-citizen who:
>
> (a) has been on a boat in the territorial sea of Australia after 19 November 1989 and before 1 December 1992; and
>
> (b) has not presented a visa; and
>
> (c) is in Australia; and
>
> (d) has not been granted an entry permit; and
>
> (e) is a person to whom the department has given a designation by:
>
> > (i)   determining and recording which boat he or she was on; and
> >
> > (ii) giving him or her an identifier that is not the same as an identifier given to another non-citizen who was on that boat;
>
> and includes a non-citizen born in Australia whose mother is a designated person ...

The plaintiffs then commenced proceedings in the High Court, seeking a declaration that s 54R and several other provisions of the Migration Act were invalid and injunctions against the Minister.

Brennan, Deane and Dawson JJ: [26] The Constitution is structured upon, and incorporates, the doctrine of the separation of judicial from executive and legislative powers. Chapter III gives effect to that doctrine in so far as the vesting of judicial power is concerned. Its provisions constitute 'an exhaustive statement of the manner in which the judicial power can be conferred in virtue of any other authority or otherwise than in accordance with the provisions of Ch III' [*R v Kirby; Ex parte Boilermakers' Society of Australia* (1956) 94 CLR 254, per Dixon CJ, McTiernan, Fullagar and Kitto JJ at 270]. Thus, it is [27] well settled that the grants of legislative power contained in s 51 of the Constitution, which are expressly 'subject to' the provisions of the Constitution as a whole, do not permit the conferral upon any organ of the Executive Government of any part of the judicial power of the Commonwealth. Nor do those grants of legislative power extend to the making of a law which requires or authorises the courts in which the judicial power of the Commonwealth is exclusively vested to exercise judicial power in a manner which is inconsistent with the essential character of a court or with the nature of judicial power. [See, eg, *Polyukhovich v Commonwealth* (1991) 172 CLR 501, at 607, 689, 703–4; 101 ALR 545.]

There are some functions which, by reason of their nature or because of historical considerations, have become established as essentially and exclusively judicial in character. The most important of them is the adjudgment and punishment of criminal guilt under a law of the Commonwealth. That function appertains exclusively to [*Waterside Workers' Federation of Australia v J W Alexander Ltd* (1918) 25 CLR 434, at 444] and 'could not be excluded from' [*R v Davison* (1954) 90 CLR 353, at 368, 383] the judicial power of the Commonwealth. [See, also, *Polyukhovich v Commonwealth* (1991) 172 CLR, at 536–9, 608–10, 613–14, 632, 647, 649, 685, 705–7, 721.] That being so, Ch III of the Constitution precludes the enactment, in purported pursuance of any of the subsections of s 51 of the Constitution, of any law purporting to vest any part of that function in the Commonwealth Executive.

In exclusively entrusting to the courts designated by Ch III the function of the adjudgment and punishment of criminal guilt under a law of the Commonwealth, the Constitution's concern is with substance and not mere form. It would, for example, be beyond the legislative power of the Parliament to invest the Executive with an arbitrary power to detain citizens in custody notwithstanding that the power was conferred in terms which sought to divorce such detention in custody from both punishment and criminal guilt. The reason why that is so is that, putting to one side the exceptional cases to which reference is made below, the involuntary detention of a citizen in custody by the State is penal or punitive in character and, under our system of government, exists only as an incident of the exclusively judicial function of adjudging and punishing criminal guilt. Every citizen is 'ruled by the law, and by the law alone' and 'may with us be punished for a breach of law, but he can be [28] punished for nothing else' [Dicey, *Introduction to the Study of the Law of the Constitution*, 10th ed (1959), p 202]. As Blackstone wrote [*Commentaries*, 17th ed (1830), Bk 1, paras 136–7], relying on the authority of Coke [*Institutes of the Laws of England*, (1809), Pt 2, p 589]:

> The confinement of the person, in any wise, is an imprisonment. So that the keeping [of] a man against his will ... is an imprisonment ... To make imprisonment lawful, it must either be by process from the courts of judicature, or by warrant from some legal officer having authority to commit to prison; which warrant must be in writing, under the hand and seal of the magistrate, and express the causes of the commitment, in order to be examined into (if necessary) upon a habeas corpus.

Brennan, Deane and Dawson JJ acknowledged that there were some exceptions to the general proposition that the power to order that a citizen be involuntarily confined in custody is part of the judicial power. These included the arrest and detention in custody, pursuant to executive warrant, of a person accused of a crime, and involuntary detention in cases of mental illness or infectious disease. Otherwise, and putting to one side parliament's power to punish for contempt and the power of military tribunals to punish for breach of military discipline, 'the citizens of this country enjoy, at least in times of peace, a constitutional immunity from being imprisoned by Commonwealth authority except pursuant to an order by a court in the exercise of the judicial power of the Commonwealth': 176 CLR at 28–9.

[29] If the first element — ie 'non-citizen' — of the definition of 'designated person' for the purposes of Div 4B had been omitted with the consequence that those provisions purported to apply to Australian citizens, Div 4B would be plainly beyond the legislative competence of the Parliament and invalid. The reason for that would not only be the absence of any relevant head of Commonwealth legislative power to found the application to citizens of this country of laws of the kind contained in Div 4B. It would also be that Div 4B, if not confined to non-citizens, would purport both to authorise involuntary imprisonment of citizens by executive designation and to deprive the courts of jurisdiction to order that a citizen, who had been so designated by the Executive, be released from custody if his or her detention in custody was found to be unlawful. Such a conferral upon the Executive of an essentially unexaminable power to imprison a citizen would, for the reasons given above, be inconsistent with the Constitution's doctrine of the separation of judicial from executive and legislative power and its exclusive vesting of judicial power in the courts. Ultimately, the critical question in the present case is whether the effect of the confinement of the application of the provisions of Div 4B to non-citizens or aliens is to avoid such conflict between the provisions of Div 4B and Ch III of the Constitution.

Brennan, Deane and Dawson JJ said that it was an accepted aspect of the parliament's power to legislate with respect to 'aliens' under s 51(xix) of the Constitution to authorise the detention of an alien in custody for the purposes of expulsion and deportation. 'Such limited authority to detain an alien in custody can be conferred on the Executive without infringement of Ch III's exclusive vesting of the judicial power of the Commonwealth in the courts which it designates': 176 CLR at 32. Their Honours decided that ss 54L and 54N of the Migration Act were valid, and then turned to s 54R. Their Honours construed s 54R as purporting to direct the courts, including the High Court, not to order the release from custody of a person who was a 'designated person', regardless of the circumstances.

[35] If it were apparent that there was no possibility that a 'designated person' might be unlawfully held in custody under Div 4B, it would be arguable that s 54R did no more than

spell out what would be the duty of a court of competent jurisdiction in any event. If that were so, s 54R would be devoid of significant content. In fact, of course, it is manifest that circumstances could exist in which a 'designated person' was unlawfully held in custody by a person purportedly acting in pursuance of Div 4B. The reason why that is so is that the status of a person as a 'designated person' does not automatically cease when detention in custody is no longer authorised by Div 4B. One example of such circumstances would be a case where a designated person continued to be held in involuntary custody notwithstanding that ss 54L and 54P had [36] become inapplicable by reason of the provisions of s 54Q(1) or (2). Another would be a case where a designated person continued to be held in custody in disregard of a request for removal duly made under s 54P(1). Yet another would be a case where a designated person who had elected not to make an entry application continued to be held in custody against his or her will notwithstanding that the maximum period of two months prescribed by s 54P(2) had well and truly expired. In all of those cases, the person concerned would remain a designated person for the purposes of Div 4B (including s 54R) but could no longer be lawfully held in involuntary custody in Australia pursuant to the provisions of the Division. It is unnecessary to seek further examples. Once it appears that a designated person may be unlawfully held in custody in purported pursuance to Div 4B, it necessarily follows that the provision of s 54R is invalid.

Ours is a Constitution 'which deals with the demarcation of powers, leaves to the courts of law the question of whether there has been any excess of power, and requires them to pronounce as void any act which is ultra vires' [*R v Richards; Ex parte Fitzpatrick & Browne* (1955) 92 CLR, per Dixon CJ, McTiernan, Williams, Webb, Fullagar, Kitto and Taylor JJ at 165]. All the powers conferred upon the Parliament by s 51 of the Constitution are, as has been said, subject to Ch III's vesting of that judicial power in the courts which it designates, including this court. That judicial power includes the jurisdiction which the Constitution directly vests in this court in all matters in which the Commonwealth or a person being sued on behalf of the Commonwealth is a party [Constitution, s 75(iii)] or in which mandamus, prohibition or an injunction is sought against an officer of the Commonwealth [s 75(v)]. A law of the Parliament which purports to direct, in unqualified terms, that no court, including this court, shall order the release from custody of a person whom the Executive of the Commonwealth has imprisoned purports to derogate from that direct vesting of judicial power and to remove ultra vires acts of the Executive from the control of this court. Such a law manifestly exceeds the legislative powers of the Commonwealth and is invalid. Moreover, even to the extent that s 54R is concerned with the exercise of jurisdiction other than this court's directly vested constitutional jurisdiction, it is inconsistent with Ch III. In terms, s 54R is a direction by the Parliament to the courts as to the manner in which they are to exercise their jurisdiction. It is one thing for the Parliament, within the limits of the legislative power conferred upon it by the Constitution, to grant [37] or withhold jurisdiction. It is a quite different thing for the Parliament to purport to direct the courts as to the manner and outcome of the exercise of their jurisdiction. The former falls within the legislative power which the Constitution, including Ch III itself, entrusts to the Parliament. The latter constitutes an impermissible intrusion into the judicial power which Ch III vests exclusively in the courts which it designates.

Gaudron J agreed with the reasons of Brennan, Deane and Dawson JJ on the invalidity of s 54R. Mason CJ, Toohey and McHugh JJ dissented on that issue, holding that s 54R was valid because it could be read down so that it only prevented a court ordering the release of a person lawfully held in custody, a 'construction which involves superfluity', as Mason CJ put it: 176 CLR at 13.

~~~

Notes

[6.4.21]   More than 80 years after the *Wheat* case (1915) 20 CLR 54 **[6.4.5C]**, the basic proposition that only courts can be entrusted with the judicial power of the

Commonwealth, is deeply entrenched. In 1995, all members of the High Court held that several provisions of the Racial Discrimination Act 1975 (Cth) were invalid because the sections conferred judicial power on the Human Rights and Equal Opportunity Commission, a body established to administer anti-discrimination laws: *Brandy v Human Rights and Equal Opportunity Commission* (1994) 183 CLR 245. The relevant sections provided that, where the Commission had resolved a complaint of discrimination and decided that an act of discrimination had been committed, the Commission's decision could be registered with the Federal Court. Upon registration, the Commission's decision would take effect as if it was an order of that court unless the court reviewed the decision. Any review by the court was not to be based on 'new evidence' unless the court gave leave for that new evidence to be admitted.

Mason CJ, Brennan and Toohey JJ said that the Racial Discrimination Act, in providing for registration of a determination of the Commission and its enforcement as if it were an order of the Federal Court, purported to give the Commission the judicial power of the Commonwealth. They added that the jurisdiction of the Federal Court to review a decision of the Commission was not an answer to that conclusion: 183 CLR at 264. Deane, Dawson, Gaudron and McHugh JJ said that, if it were not for the provisions dealing with the registration and enforcement of the Commission's determinations, it would be plain that the Commission did not exercise judicial power 'because its determination would not be binding or conclusive between any of the parties and would be unenforceable': 183 CLR at 269.

However, the registration provisions reversed that situation. The effect of registration was to make the determination enforceable as if it were a decision of the Federal Court, and to invest part of the judicial power of the Commonwealth in the Commission (at 270):

> The circumstances in which a determination may be made by the Commission are prescribed by the Act and, except upon a review, the Federal Court is precluded from any consideration of those circumstances either upon the registration of a determination or in relation to its enforcement. The determination remains the determination of the Commission and in no sense becomes the determination of the Federal Court.

Having concluded that registration of the determination did not amount to the commencement of proceedings in the original jurisdiction of the Federal Court, Deane, Dawson, Gaudron and McHugh JJ said that 'the existence of the review procedure does not bear upon the question whether the determination was made in the exercise of the judicial power ... The existence or exercise of a right of appeal from a decision made in the exercise of judicial power does not convert that decision into one of an administrative kind': 183 CLR at 270–1. See also *Attorney-General (Cth) v Breckler* (1999) 197 CLR 83 at 110.

[6.4.22]   The possibility of reversing the reciprocal *Boilermakers'* proposition (that federal courts may not be given non-judicial functions) was raised by Barwick CJ and Mason J in *R v Joske; Ex parte Australian Building Construction Employees and Builders' Labourers' Federation* (1974) 130 CLR 87 at 90 and 102. However, that possibility has not been realised. For example, the High Court's decision in *Wilson v Minister for Aboriginal and Torres Strait Islander Affairs* (1996) 189 CLR 1 **[6.4.34]** demonstrates the vitality of the proposition that the Commonwealth Parliament cannot confer non-judicial functions on courts. A majority of the High Court (Brennan CJ, Dawson, Toohey, Gaudron, McHugh and Gummow JJ; Kirby J dissenting) held that the appointment of a judge of the Federal Court as a reporter under the Aboriginal and Torres Strait Islander Heritage Protection Act 1984 (Cth), to report to the Minister on the question whether a bridge should be constructed at Hindmarsh Island in South Australia, breached the separation of judicial power required by Ch III of the Constitution.

The function conferred on a reporter, Brennan CJ, Dawson, Toohey, McHugh and Gummow JJ said, placed 'the judge firmly in the echelons of administration, liable to removal before the report is made and shorn of the usual judicial protections, in a position equivalent to that of a ministerial adviser': 189 CLR at 18–19. The function was essentially political and involved the reporter giving to the executive what amounted to an advisory opinion: 189 CLR at 19.

[6.4.23] Far from being abandoned, the *Boilermakers'* proposition is expanding and, in its expanded form, is being used by the High Court to limit the capacity of governments, Commonwealth and state, to confer controversial functions on the courts. For example, in *Kable v Director of Public Prosecutions (NSW)* (1996) 189 CLR 51 **[6.4.23]**, **[6.4.35]**, **[6.4.48C]**, a majority of the High Court (Toohey, Gaudron, McHugh and Gummow JJ; Brennan CJ and Dawson J dissenting) held that the New South Wales Parliament could not legislate to confer jurisdiction on the state's Supreme Court to order the preventive detention of a person identified in the relevant legislation. See also **[11.3.30]**ff.

Conferring that function on the Supreme Court, the majority held, offended the separation of judicial power required by Ch III, which was held to constrain the legislative power of the New South Wales Parliament in the present case. Although state parliaments were generally not constrained by the separation of judicial power (see **[6.4.43]** below), no state parliament could confer on a state court a non-judicial function that was fundamentally incompatible with the exercise of judicial power because state courts functioned as part of a national judicial system. The function of ordering the preventive detention of a nominated person compromised the integrity of that system, which (as Gaudron J put it) depended on the courts 'acting in accordance with the judicial process and, in no small measure, on the maintenance of public confidence in that process': 189 CLR at 107. Gummow J described the legislation (the Community Protection Act) as having serious ratifications for the judiciary in that the judiciary became involved in a political decision to incarcerate a citizen, giving the judiciary the appearance of being an arm of the executive which implemented the will of the legislature: 189 CLR at 134.

Exceptions to the separation rule

[6.4.24] Although the proposition in the *Boilermakers'* case (1956) 94 CLR 254 **[6.4.12C]** has not been abandoned and, indeed, has been expanded to provide the foundation for the significant decisions in *Wilson v Minister for Aboriginal and Torres Strait Islander Affairs* (1996) 189 CLR 1 **[6.4.22]** and *Kable v Director of Public Prosecutions (NSW)* (1996) 189 CLR 51 **[6.4.23]**, **[6.4.35]**, **[6.4.48C]**, the High Court has developed a series of qualifications and exceptions to the proposition.

For example, in *R v Joske; Ex parte Shop Distributive and Allied Employees' Association* (1976) 135 CLR 194, the High Court upheld the validity of the provisions in the Conciliation and Arbitration Act which gave the Industrial Court wide powers to rectify or validate actions of, or to approve schemes to reorganise, industrial trade unions following the court's decision to invalidate rules of the union.

The High Court said that this power was incidental to the clearly judicial function of adjudicating on the validity of the union's rules. Barwick CJ said at 201:

> [T]he relief which a court is authorised to give consequentially upon its judicial determination of some situation can rarely if ever be denied the quality of an exercise of judicial power.

[6.4.25] Other decisions have acknowledged particular breaches in the separation of judicial power. According to the unanimous decision of the High Court in *R v Richards; Ex parte Fitzpatrick and Browne* (1955) 92 CLR 157, s 49 of the Constitution gives the Senate or the House of Representatives the power to determine conclusively whether a contempt of parliament has been committed and to impose punishment. Dixon CJ, McTiernan, Williams, Webb, Fullagar, Kitto and Taylor JJ acknowledged that the Constitution was based on the separation of powers and that judicial power was vested exclusively in the courts referred to in Ch III. However, the justices said, the contempt power of the House of Commons (by reference to which the powers of the Senate and the House of Representatives are defined in s 49) had historically been regarded as not strictly judicial but 'as proper incidents of the legislative function', and concluded at 167:

> [A] general view of the Constitution and the separation of powers is not a sufficient reason for giving to these words [in s 49 of the Constitution], which appear to us to be so clear, a restrictive or secondary meaning which they do not properly bear.

[6.4.26] Courts-martial, established within the armed services and outside the confines of Ch III, may administer military justice. In *R v Bevan; Ex parte Elias and Gordon* (1942) 66 CLR 452, Starke J followed a decision of the United States Supreme Court, *Dynes v Hoover* 61 US 65 (1858), in which it was held that courts-martial established under the laws of the United States formed no part of the judicial system of the United States and that their proceedings could not be controlled by the civil courts. Thus, his Honour held that the Commonwealth's defence power, s 51(vi) of the Constitution, was sufficient to support legislation establishing a system of military justice independent of Ch III. According to Starke J, s 51(vi), s 51(xxxix) and s 69:

> … indicate legislative provisions special and peculiar to [the defence] forces in the way of discipline and otherwise, and indeed the Court should incline towards a construction that is necessary, not only from a practical, but also from an administrative point of view (66 CLR at 468).

A similar view was expressed by Williams J: 66 CLR at 481.

The court's decision in *R v Bevan* was cited by several members of the High Court in *R v Cox; Ex parte Smith* (1945) 71 CLR 1 as authority for the proposition that Ch III of the Constitution does not affect the establishment and the functions of courts-martial: see 71 CLR at 13 per Latham CJ; 71 CLR at 23 per Dixon J; 71 CLR at 27–8 per Williams J.

[6.4.27] In *Re Tracey; Ex parte Ryan* (1989) 166 CLR 518, Mason CJ, Wilson and Dawson JJ said at 541:

> [T]he defence power is different because the proper organization of the defence force requires a system of discipline which is administered judicially, not as part of the judicature erected under Ch III but as part of the organization of the force itself. Thus the power to make laws with respect to the defence of the Commonwealth contains within it the power to enact a disciplinary code standing outside Ch III and to impose upon those administering that code the duty to act judicially.

Mason CJ, Wilson and Dawson JJ went on to conclude that there was no practical limit to the kind of conduct of members of the armed services which can be regulated by such a disciplinary code and dealt with by service tribunals: at 545.

Brennan and Toohey JJ said at 573–4:

> History and necessity combine to show that courts martial and other service tribunals, though judicial in nature and though erected in modern times by statute, stand outside the requirements of Ch III of the Constitution ... [W]hen [the jurisdiction of service tribunals] falls to be exercised, the power which is exercised is not the judicial power of the Commonwealth; it is a power sui generis which is supported solely by s 51(vi) for the purpose of maintaining or enforcing service discipline.

However, the offences which could be created and punished under a code of service discipline were limited to those which served 'the purpose of maintaining or enforcing service discipline': 166 CLR at 170.

Deane and Gaudron JJ, in separate judgments, agreed that the judicial powers of military tribunals lay outside Ch III of the Constitution: 166 CLR at 582–3 per Deane J; 166 CLR at 598 per Gaudron J. But they held that the peacetime jurisdiction of military tribunals had to be confined to offences which were distinct from those penalised under the ordinary criminal law: 166 CLR at 591 per Deane J; 166 CLR at 603 per Gaudron J.

A similar range of views was expressed by the High Court in *Re Nolan; Ex parte Young* (1991) 172 CLR 460 and in *Re Tyler; Ex parte Foley* (1994) 181 CLR 153.

[6.4.28] In *R v White; Ex parte Byrnes* (1963) 109 CLR 665, the High Court held that public service disciplinary tribunals, established under the Public Service Act 1922 (Cth) with the power of imposing punishment for disciplinary offences, do not offend the separation of judicial power. In their joint judgment, Dixon CJ, Kitto, Taylor, Menzies and Windeyer JJ said that, by creating so-called 'offences', the Public Service Act did 'no more than define what is misconduct on the part of a public servant warranting disciplinary action on behalf of the Commonwealth and the disciplinary penalties that may be imposed or recommended for such misconduct'. Further, they held that the bodies given power to deal with such 'offences' did not 'sit as a court of law exercising judicial power': 109 CLR at 670–1.

[6.4.29] One qualification to the separation rule has been accepted on essentially pragmatic grounds: namely, it is permissible for the parliament to authorise a Ch III court to delegate aspects of its judicial functions to an officer of the court.

For example, in *Harris v Caladine* (1991) 172 CLR 84, a majority of the High Court held that s 37A of the Family Law Act 1975 (Cth), which authorised registrars of the Family Court to exercise certain judicial functions of the court (the making of consent orders for dissolution of a marriage and for custody, guardianship or welfare of, and access to, children), did not offend the separation of judicial power principle. The provision was valid even though the registrars were not appointed as judges of the court and lacked the tenure prescribed by s 72 of the Constitution.

Mason CJ and Deane J said that allowing the limited exercise of judicial functions by non-judicial officers was an inevitable consequence of the decision in *Commonwealth v Hospital Contribution Fund* (1982) 150 CLR 49, where it had been held that a state court could exercise the federal jurisdiction conferred on it by Commonwealth legislation through an officer of the court as well as through a judge.

Mason CJ and Deane J said:

> It makes little sense, either as a matter of logic or policy to require that the power be
> exercised solely by federal judges to the exclusion of officers of the court when, in the
> case of invested federal jurisdiction, the power may be exercised by officers of State
> courts. More importantly, as a matter of construction, it is not permissible to read s 71
> as speaking differently in its application to federal and State courts. ...
>
> It seems to us that, so long as two conditions are observed, the delegation of some
> part of the jurisdiction, powers and functions of the Family Court as a federal court to
> its officers is permissible and consistent with the control and supervision of the Family
> Court's jurisdiction by its judges. The first condition is that the delegation must not be
> to an extent where it can no longer properly be said that, as a practical as well as a
> theoretical matter, the judges constitute the court. This means that the judges must
> continue to bear the major responsibility for the exercise of judicial power at least in
> relation to the more important aspects of contested matters. The second condition is
> that the delegation must not be inconsistent with the obligation of a court to act judi-
> cially and that the decisions of the officers of the court in the exercise of their delegated
> jurisdiction, powers and functions must be subject to review or appeal by a judge or
> judges of the court. For present purposes it is sufficient for us to say that, if the exercise
> of delegated jurisdiction, powers and functions by a court officer is subject to review
> or appeal by a judge or judges of the court on questions of both fact and law, we con-
> sider that the delegation will be valid. Certainly, if the review is by way of hearing de
> novo, the delegation will be valid. The importance of insisting on the existence of
> review by a judge or an appeal to a judge is that this procedure guarantees that a liti-
> gant may have recourse to a hearing and a determination by a judge. In other words,
> a litigant can avail him or herself of the judicial independence which is the hallmark of
> the class of court presently under consideration (172 CLR at 93, 95).

As the rules made by the Family Court under s 37A of the Family Law Act
provided for a hearing de novo by a judge of the court on any appeal against an order
of a registrar, s 37A and the delegation were valid: 172 CLR at 96–7.

Dawson, Gaudron and McHugh JJ also stressed that effective supervision by the
judges of the court was an essential condition of valid delegation of judicial functions
to officers of a federal court: 172 CLR at 122 per Dawson J; at 151 per Gaudron J;
at 164 per McHugh J. So long as that supervision was preserved through a system
which allowed review by a judge or judges of any order made by an officer of the
court, a federal court could delegate or be authorised to delegate aspects of its
judicial functions to officers of the court: 172 CLR at 121 per Dawson J; at 150 per
Gaudron J; at 164 per McHugh J.

Brennan and Toohey JJ dissented. Brennan J said that the Constitution required
that the power of federal courts to hear and determine matters in the exercise of
federal jurisdiction must be exercised by Ch III judges; that is, persons appointed and
holding tenure in accordance with s 72 of the Constitution, at 111:

> ... the powers which can properly be exercised by persons who are not judges do not
> include the power of adjudication of a legal controversy pending in the court except
> for the exercise of powers 'truly ancillary to an adjudication by the court'.

(This phrase was taken by Brennan J from the judgment of Windeyer J in *Kotsis v
Kotsis* (1970) 122 CLR 69 at 92.)

The 'primary and manifest purpose' of the separation of judicial power, Brennan J
said, 'is to guarantee impartiality and independence in the hearing and determination
of legal controversies and that purpose would be frustrated if court officers, lacking
the protection which those provisions are intended to secure, were empowered to
hear and determine legal controversies': 172 CLR at 108–9.

Callinan J was likewise critical of *Harris v Caladine* (1991) 172 CLR 84 in *Luton v Lessels* (2002) 210 CLR 333, when he observed at 387:

> That some degree of delegation of judicial power does not impinge on Ch III but a greater (non-specific) helping of it might, does not, with respect, strike me as a very satisfactory basis for a determination of whether judicial power is, or is not, being exercised. Judges are not mere supervisors. Nor do they have the power of appointment of other judges conferred by Ch III upon the Executive. The fact that delegates may be bound to perform their duties in a judicial way provides no substitute for the performance of judicial duties by duly appointed judges.

[6.4.30]   The most significant qualification to the *Boilermakers'* proposition may be the *persona designata* rule endorsed by a majority of the High Court in *Hilton v Wells* (1985) 157 CLR 57. In that case, the High Court was asked to rule on the validity of s 20 of the Telecommunications (Interception) Act 1979 (Cth), which authorised 'a Judge of the Federal Court of Australia' to issue a warrant authorising the interception of telecommunications for the purpose of investigating a narcotics offence. All the members of the court accepted that this function was administrative rather than judicial, as decided in *Aston v Irvine* (1955) 92 CLR 353 at 363; *Baker v Campbell* (1983) 153 CLR 50 at 92; *Brewer v Castles (No 1)* (1984) 1 FCR 55.

The majority justices, Gibbs CJ, Wilson and Dawson JJ, acknowledged that, if s 20 conferred power on the Federal Court of Australia, it would be invalid. However, the majority endorsed the following statement from the judgment of Bowen CJ and Deane J in *Drake v Minister for Immigration and Ethnic Affairs* (1979) 24 ALR 577 at 583–4:

> There is nothing in the Constitution which precludes a justice of the High Court or a judge of this or any other court created by the Parliament under Ch III of the Constitution from, in his personal capacity, being appointed to an office involving the performance of administrative or executive functions including functions which are quasi judicial in their nature. Such an appointment does not involve any impermissible attempt to confer upon a Ch III court functions which are antithetical to the exercise of judicial power. Indeed, it does not involve the conferring of any functions at all on such a court (157 CLR at 69).

Gibbs CJ, Wilson and Dawson JJ analysed s 20 of the Telecommunications (Interception) Act and concluded that the power conferred on Federal Court judges by that section was conferred on them, not as members of the court, but as *persona designata*. They referred to the fact that the section provided for the conferral of the same power on selected judges of state and territory Supreme Courts: because s 20 referred to judges of those courts as designated persons, it should be understood as referring to Federal Court judges in the same way. Their Honours continued:

> Secondly, the nature of the power conferred is of importance in deciding whether the judge on whom it is conferred is intended to exercise it in his capacity as a judge or as a designated person. If the power is judicial, it is likely that it is intended to be exercisable by the judge by virtue of that character; if it is purely administrative, and not incidental to the exercise of judicial power, it is likely that it is intended to be exercised by the judge as a designated person (157 CLR at 57).

It followed, Gibbs CJ, Wilson and Dawson JJ held, that s 20 conferred no power on the Federal Court and did not infringe the rule laid down in the *Boilermakers'* case (1956) 94 CLR 254 **[6.4.12C]**.

In their dissenting judgment, Mason and Deane JJ noted that s 20 conferred the function of issuing warrants on 'a Judge', contemplated that the function would be undertaken by a judge as the holder of judicial office and imposed the administrative function of issuing warrants on a judge of the Federal Court as 'an unavoidable concomitant of his judicial office':

> In the case of a new appointment to office, it is a responsibility which he assumes with his office. Once assumed, it can be laid down only with his office. No special provision at all is made in respect of facilities for its discharge. In these circumstances it would be quite extraordinary if it was the legislative intent that the function should be conferred upon the judges of the Federal Court otherwise than as part of the duties to be performed by them in the course of their discharge of the functions of that Court ... (157 CLR at 85).

Mason and Deane JJ had earlier acknowledged that a judge might be invested with non-judicial functions in the judge's personal capacity. However, such a conclusion was possible only if the judge was intended to act personally, detached from the court of which the judge was a member: 157 CLR at 80. The *persona designata* exception should be strictly applied because 'it has the potential, if it is not kept within precise limits to undermine the doctrine in the *Boilermakers'* case': 157 CLR at 81.

Mason and Deane JJ offered the following pointed criticism of the majority's approach at 83–4:

> To the intelligent observer, unversed in what Dixon J accurately described — and emphatically rejected — as 'distinctions without differences' (*Meyer* (1937) 58 CLR at 97), it would come as a surprise to learn that a judge, who is appointed to carry out a function by reference to his judicial office and who carries it out in his court with the assistance of its staff, services and facilities, is not acting as a judge at all, but as a private individual. Such an observer might well think, with some degree of justification, that it is all an elaborate charade.

[6.4.31] In 1988, the Constitutional Commission observed of the decision in *Hilton v Wells* (1985) 157 CLR 57 **[6.4.30]**:

> Because of the flexible approach taken by the High Court to that principle, it has rarely resulted in any provision conferring jurisdiction on a court being invalid. Indeed if *Hilton v Wells* is followed, the principle that courts cannot exercise non-judicial power will become close to being a mere formal prescription ... (Constitutional Commission (1988) p 393).

A similar criticism of the decision was developed by Zines. If *Hilton v Wells* survived, he wrote, 'it is hard to see that any important issue is involved. The parliamentary draftsman need not even display any special skill in avoiding constitutional "traps" in this case': Zines (1992) p 183.

[6.4.32] The Constitutional Commission also observed that, because *Hilton v Wells* 1985) 157 CLR 57 **[6.4.30]** was 'decided on a bare majority of a five-judge court, reconsideration is not foreclosed': Constitutional Commission (1988) p 393. However, in *Jones v Commonwealth* (1987) 71 ALR 497, a majority of the High Court refused to allow *Hilton v Wells* to be reopened. 'Continuity and coherence in the law demand that in this court the principle of *stare decisis* should ordinarily be applied', said Mason CJ, Wilson, Brennan, Deane, Dawson and Toohey JJ: 71 ALR at 498. The justices also said that the difference between the majority and minority in *Hilton v Wells* was on the interpretation of s 20 of the Telecommunications (Interception) Act, rather than on any issue of constitutional principle (at 499):

> The minority considered that s 20 imposed an obligation on a judge to perform the function, that of dealing with an application for the issue of a warrant, thereby raising consequences having importance for the exercise of judicial power. On the other hand

the majority proceeded on the view that s 20 did not impose an obligation on a judge to perform the function, whether he consented to do so or not.

[6.4.33] In 1995, the High Court returned to the question whether the power to issue warrants for the interception of telecommunications could validly be conferred on Federal Court judges. In *Grollo v Palmer* (1995) 184 CLR 348, the High Court (Brennan CJ, Deane, Dawson, Toohey, McHugh and Gummow JJ) held that the power conferred by ss 45 and 46 of the Telecommunications (Interception) Act 1979 (Cth) on an 'eligible judge' to issue an interception warrant was not part of the judicial power of the Commonwealth. Further, a majority of the court (McHugh J dissenting) held that the conferral of that power on an 'eligible judge' was not incompatible with the judge's performance of his or her judicial functions or with the proper discharge by the judiciary of the responsibility of exercising judicial power.

Brennan CJ, Deane, Dawson and Toohey JJ adopted the principle laid down by the United States Supreme Court in *Mistretta v United States* 488 US 361 (1989) at 404 to the effect that validity depended on 'whether a particular extrajudicial assignment undermines the integrity of the judicial branch':

> The conditions ... on the power to confer non-judicial functions on judges as designated persons are twofold: first, no non-judicial function that is not incidental to a judicial function can be conferred without the judge's consent; and second, no function can be conferred that is incompatible either with the judge's performance of his or her judicial functions or with the proper discharge by the judiciary of its responsibilities as an institution exercising judicial power (the incompatibility condition). These conditions accord with the view of the Supreme Court of the United States in *Mistretta v United States* ... (184 CLR at 364–5).

Brennan CJ, Deane, Dawson and Toohey JJ explained the so-called 'incompatibility condition' in the following terms (at 365):

> The incompatibility condition may arise in a number of different ways. Incompatibility might consist in so permanent and complete a commitment to the performance of non-judicial functions by a judge that the further performance of substantial judicial functions by that judge is not practicable. It might consist in the performance of non-judicial functions of such a nature that the capacity of the judge to perform his or her judicial functions with integrity is compromised or impaired. Or it might consist in the performance of non-judicial functions of such a nature that public confidence in the integrity of the judiciary as an institution or in the capacity of the individual judge to perform his or her judicial functions with integrity is diminished. Judges appointed to exercise the judicial power of the Commonwealth cannot be authorised to engage in the performance of non-judicial functions so as to prejudice the capacity either of the individual judge or of the judiciary as an institution to discharge effectively the responsibilities of exercising the judicial power of the Commonwealth.

Brennan CJ, Deane, Dawson and Toohey JJ concluded that judges were eminently suited to the task of issuing interception warrants, and such a power was not incompatible with the exercise of their judicial function (at 367):

> Yet it is precisely because of the intrusive and clandestine nature of interception warrants and the necessity to use them in today's continuing battle against serious crime that some impartial authority, accustomed to the dispassionate assessment of evidence and sensitive to the common law's protection of privacy (see *Haisman v Smelcher* [1953] VLR 625 at 627) and property (both real and personal), be authorised to control the official interception of communications. In other words, the professional experience and cast of mind of a judge is a desirable guarantee that the appropriate balance will be kept between the law enforcement agencies on the one hand and

criminal suspects or suspected sources of information about crime on the other. It is an eligible judge's function of deciding independently of the applicant agency whether an interception warrant should issue that separates the eligible judge from the executive function of law enforcement. It is the recognition of that independent role that preserves public confidence in the judiciary as an institution.

The justices rejected the opinion of Mason and Deane JJ in *Hilton v Wells* that the judicial function of the preservation of individual liberty would be compromised by this type of extrajudicial work.

[6.4.34]   The issue of incompatibility was explored by the High Court in two cases decided in 1996. In the first of those cases, *Wilson v Minister for Aboriginal and Torres Strait Islander Affairs* (1996) 189 CLR 1, a majority of the court (Brennan CJ, Dawson, Toohey, Gaudron, McHugh and Gummow JJ; Kirby J dissenting) held that the appointment of a Federal Court judge as a reporter under the Aboriginal and Torres Strait Islander Heritage Protection Act 1984 (Cth) was incompatible with the Federal Court's responsibility to exercise the judicial power of the Commonwealth.

In their joint judgment, Brennan CJ, Dawson, Toohey, McHugh and Gummow JJ acknowledged (189 CLR at 13) that the separation of judicial functions from the political functions of government was not so rigid as to preclude the conferring on a judge (with the judge's consent) of certain non-judicial functions. However, the exercise of those non-judicial functions must be compatible with the performance of judicial functions. In particular, the non-judicial function must be one that is clearly independent of the executive government. Accordingly, it would be necessary to inquire whether the non-judicial function was closely connected with the functions of the legislature or the executive government; whether the function was required to be performed in accordance with any instruction, advice or wish of the legislature or the executive government; and whether any discretion given to the judge was required to be exercised on political grounds: see 189 CLR at 17.

In the present case, a reporter under the Aboriginal and Torres Strait Islander Heritage Protection Act was required to report to the Minister on the question whether a particular site should be protected under the Act. The report was an essential preliminary step to the making by the Minister of a declaration protecting the site because of its significance to indigenous people. Brennan CJ, Dawson, Toohey, McHugh and Gummow JJ observed that the reporter's function was (at 18–19):

> ... an integral part of the process of the Minister's exercise of power. The performance of such a function places the judge firmly in the echelons of administration, liable to removal before the report is made and shorn of the usual judicial protections, in a position equivalent to that of a ministerial adviser.

The justices noted that the reporter's function was essentially political, because it involved weighing the competing interests of Aboriginal applicants and of others whose pecuniary or proprietary interests might be affected by the making of a declaration under the Act and giving the executive of what amounted to an advisory opinion: 189 CLR at 19–20.

Kirby J published a vigorous dissent, accusing the majority of engaging in an 'illicit embrace' with the minority view expressed in *Hilton v Wells*, a decision that had not been challenged in the litigation. Kirby J expressed a preference for an historical approach to the question whether judges could engage in some types of executive tasks, noting that federal and state judges had undertaken many inquiries on behalf of the Commonwealth (as Royal Commissioners, statutory office-holders or otherwise) — with one of the earliest such inquiries undertaken by Griffith CJ in 1918: 189 CLR at 44. Kirby J observed at 38:

> ... the Act was written against the background of the constitutional separation of powers. But it was also enacted after a century of the use of judges in Australia, including federal judges, to conduct inquiries and to provide reports upon their enquiries. Far from envisaging a widely focussed inquiry, such as has been a feature of many investigations conducted by judges for the Executive government of the Commonwealth in the past, the functions of the reporter under the Act are quite narrow. True, they can be sensitive and important. But this makes it appropriate that a Minister should have available, for a particular case, the special qualities of experience, reputation and integrity that a judge can bring to the office ...

And further at 48:

> The actual duties of a reporter are considerably closer to those of the holder of a judicial office than, say, the duties of an 'eligible judge' in providing a warrant for telephonic interception which the authority of this Court has upheld. Justice Mathews is in no way involved in functions incompatible with those of a judge as, for example, involvement in criminal investigation and prosecutorial duties arguably is. On the contrary, the very reason for her appointment to provide a report in the instant case is clearly to utilise the particular qualities which are normal to a judge in Australia: accuracy in the application of the law; independence and disinterestedness in evaluating evidence and submissions; neutrality and detachment; and efficiency and skill in the provision of a conclusion. Whilst the principles stated in *Hilton* and *Grollo* stand ... I am unpersuaded that the appointment of a federal judge as a person to provide a report ... is inconsistent with the Constitution.

[6.4.35] In *Kable v Director of Public Prosecutions (NSW)* (1996) 189 CLR 51 **[6.4.48C]**, a majority of the High Court (Toohey, Gaudron, McHugh and Gummow JJ; Brennan CJ and Dawson J dissenting) held that the Community Protection Act 1994 (NSW), which conferred on the Supreme Court of New South Wales jurisdiction and power to order the preventive detention of one identified person (Kable) was invalid because the function was incompatible with the exercise by the Supreme Court of the judicial power of the Commonwealth. Toohey J described the function conferred on the Supreme Court as answering (at 98):

> ... that aspect of incompatibility which was identified in *Grollo v Palmer* as 'the performance of non-judicial functions of such a nature that public confidence in the integrity of the judiciary as an institution ... is diminished'. The function exercised by the Supreme Court under the Act offends Ch III which, as I said in *Harris v Caladine* (1991) 172 CLR 84 at 135, reflects an aspect of the doctrine of the separation of powers, serving to protect not only the role of the independent judiciary but also the personal interests of litigants in having those interests determined by judges independent of the legislature and the executive. The function offends that aspect because it requires the Supreme Court to participate in the making of a preventive detention order where no breach of the criminal law is alleged and where there has been no determination of guilt.

Gaudron J described the function given to the Supreme Court as compromising the integrity of the judicial system brought into existence by Ch III of the Constitution: 189 CLR at 107. McHugh J said that the New South Wales legislation compromised the institutional impartiality of the Supreme Court: 189 CLR at 121. Gummow J adopted some of the observations of the United States Supreme Court in *Mistretta v United States* 488 US 361 (1989) at 407, to the effect that the legitimacy of the courts depended on their reputation for impartiality and non-partisanship, which 'must not be borrowed by the political branches to cloak their work in the neutral colours of judicial action': 189 CLR at 133.

For further consideration of *Kable* and its significance in heralding recognition that rights may emerge from the separation of judicial power, see **[11.3.30]**ff.

Legislative and executive powers

[6.4.36C]   **Victorian Stevedoring and General**
                                  Contracting Co Pty Ltd v Dignan
                                  (1931) 46 CLR 73

Dixon J: [88] Section 3 of the Transport Workers Act 1928–29 provides that the Governor-General may make Regulations, not inconsistent with that Act, which, notwithstanding anything in any other Act but subject to the Acts Interpretation Act 1901–1918 and the Acts Interpretation Act 1904–1916, shall have the force of law, with respect to the employment of transport workers, and in particular for regulating the engagement, service and discharge of transport workers, and for regulating or prohibiting the employment of unlicensed persons as transport workers, and for the protection of transport workers ... Section 3 of the Transport [89] Workers Act assumes to commit to the executive government an extensive power to make regulations which, notwithstanding anything in any other Act of Parliament, shall have the force of law. The validity of this provision is now attacked upon the ground that it is an attempt to grant to the executive a portion of the legislative power vested by the Constitution in the Parliament, which is inconsistent with the distribution made by the Constitution of legislative, executive and judicial powers. Section 1 of the Constitution provides that the legislative power of the Commonwealth shall be vested in a Federal Parliament which shall consist of the Sovereign, a Senate, and a House of Representatives; s 61, that the executive power of the Commonwealth [90] is vested in the Sovereign and is exercisable by the Governor-General as the Sovereign's representative and extends to the execution and maintenance of the Constitution and of the laws of the Commonwealth; s 71, that the judicial power of the Commonwealth shall be vested in a Federal Supreme Court to be called the High Court of Australia and in such other Federal courts as the Parliament creates and in such other courts as it invests with Federal jurisdiction. These provisions, both in substance and in arrangement, closely follow the American model upon which they were framed. The Constitution of the United States provides — Art I s 1: 'All legislative powers herein granted shall be vested in a Congress of the United States which shall consist of a Senate and House of Representatives,' Art II s 1: 'The executive power shall be vested in a President of the United States'; s 3: 'he shall take care that the laws be faithfully executed.' Art III s 1: 'The judicial power of the United States shall be vested in one Supreme Court, and in such inferior courts as the Congress may from time to time ordain and establish.'

In adopting this division of the functions of government, the members of the Convention of 1787 meant that the theory of the separation of powers should be embodied in the fundamental law which they were framing ...

[92] [A]lthough it may be true that the formulation of enforceable rules of conduct for the subject or the citizen, because they are considered expedient, is the very characteristic of law-making, yet it has always been found difficult or impossible to deny to the executive, as a proper incident of its functions, authority to require the subject or the citizens to pursue a course of action which has been determined for him by the exercise of an administrative discretion. But in what does the distinction lie between a law of Congress requiring compliance with directions upon some specified subject which the administration thinks proper to give, and a law investing the administration with authority to legislate upon the same subject?

Dixon J referred to several decisions of the United States Supreme Court which had attempted, without success, to develop 'a precise formula to express the separation between legislative and executive powers.

His Honour continued:

[94] But in any case no decision of the Supreme Court of the United States, of which I am aware, allows Congress to empower the executive to make regulations or ordinances which may overreach existing statutes. ...

[96] When they adopted the distribution of powers which they found in the Constitution of the United States, the framers of the Constitution of the Commonwealth of Australia were, of course, by no means unaware of the significance given to the distribution and of the consequences flowing from it. But an independent consideration of the provisions of the Commonwealth Constitution unaided by any such knowledge cannot but suggest that it was intended to confine to each of the three departments of government the exercise of the power with which it is invested by the Constitution, the doing of that which can be done in virtue only of the possession of such a power. The arrangement of the Constitution and the emphatic words in which the three powers are vested by ss 1, 61 and 71 combine with the careful and elaborate provisions constituting or defining the repositories of the respective powers to provide evidence of the intention with which the powers were apportioned and the organs of government separated and described ...

Dixon J referred to the earlier decisions *New South Wales v Commonwealth* (the *Wheat case*) (1915) 20 CLR 54, *Waterside Workers' Federation of Australia v J W Alexander Ltd* (1918) 25 CLR 434, and *Re Judiciary and Navigation Acts* (1921) 29 CLR 257, in which Knox CJ, Gavan Duffy, Powers, Rich and Starke JJ said (29 CLR at 264): 'The Constitution of the Commonwealth is based upon a separation of the functions of government, and the powers which it confers are divided into three classes — legislative, executive and judicial: *New South Wales v Commonwealth* 20 CLR at 88. In each case the Constitution first grants the power and then delimits the scope of its operation'.

[97] From these authorities it appears that, because of the distribution of the functions of governments and of the manner in which the [98] Constitution describes the tribunals to be invested with the judicial power of the Commonwealth, and defines the judicial power to be invested in them, the Parliament is restrained both from reposing any power essentially judicial in any other organ or body and from reposing any other than that judicial power in such tribunals. The same or analogous considerations apply to the provisions which vest the legislative power of the Commonwealth in the Parliament, describe the constitution of the legislature and define the legislative power. Does it follow that in the exercise of that power the Parliament is restrained from reposing any power essentially legislative in another organ or body?

Dixon J noted that, in *Baxter v Ah Way* (1909) 8 CLR 626, legislation delegating to the executive authority to proclaim the inclusion of goods in the category of prohibited imports was upheld, rejecting an argument based on the maxim *delegatus non potest delegare*, and emphasising the plenary nature of the legislative power. The separation of powers was not expressly mentioned. He referred to *Roche v Kronheimer* (1921) 29 CLR 329, where the High Court upheld the validity of s 2 of the Treaty of Peace Act 1919, which empowered the executive to make such regulations as appeared to it to be necessary for carrying out or giving effect to the economic clauses of the Treaty of Versailles.

[100] When, at the beginning of this year, a regulation made under s 3 of the Transport Workers Act came before us in *Huddart Parker Ltd v Commonwealth* (1931) 44 CLR 492, the attack upon the validity of the section was based rather upon the scope of the commerce power, and but little reliance was placed upon the legislative character of the power conferred upon the executive. But in the judgments of Starke J and of Evatt J and in my own judgment, with which Rich J expressed his agreement, the question was stated whether it was within the power of the Parliament to make a law which, in the language of Starke J (44 CLR at 506) 'prescribes no rule in relation to such employment: it remits the whole matter to the regulation of the Governor-in-Council'; and the answer given by each of us was that *Roche v Kronheimer* decided that it is within the power of Parliament to do so. A reconsideration of the matter has confirmed by opinion that the judgment of the court in that case does so mean to decide ...

I think the judgment really meant that the time had passed for assigning to the constitutional distribution of powers among the separate organs of government, an operation which confined the legislative power to the Parliament [101] so as to restrain it from reposing in the executive an authority of an essentially legislative character. I, therefore, retain the opinion which I expressed in the earlier case that *Roche v Kronheimer* did decide that a statute conferring upon the executive a power to legislate upon some matter contained within one of the subjects of the legislative power of the Parliament is a law with respect to that subject, and that the distribution of legislative, executive and judicial powers in the Constitution does not operate to restrain the power of the Parliament to make such a law. This does not mean that a law confiding authority to the executive will be valid, however extensive or vague the subject matter may be, if it does not fall outside the boundaries of Federal power. There may be such a width or such an uncertainty of the subject matter to be handed over that the enactment attempting it is not a law with respect to any particular head or heads of legislative power. Nor does it mean that the distribution of powers can supply no considerations of weight affecting the validity of an Act creating a legislative authority. For instance, its relevance is undeniable to the particular problem suggested in *Re Initiative and Referendum Act* [1919] AC 935 at 945. The interpretation by this court of Chapter III of the Constitution and that of Chapters I and II which has now been adopted in view of *Roche v Kronheimer*, may appear to involve an inconsistency or, at least, an asymmetry, and there are not wanting those who think a course of judicial decision no sufficient warrant for anything so unsatisfactory. But the explanation should be sought not in a want of uniformity in the application to the different organs of government of the consequences of the division of powers among them, but in the ascertainment of the nature of the power which that division prevents the legislature from handing over. It may be acknowledged that the manner in which the Constitution accomplished the separation of powers does logically or theoretically make the Parliament the exclusive repository of the legislative power of the Commonwealth. The existence in Parliament of power to authorise subordinate legislation may be ascribed to a conception of that legislative power which depends less upon juristic analysis [102] and perhaps more upon the history and usages of British legislation and the theories of English law. In English law much weight has been given to the dependence of subordinate legislation for its efficacy, not only on the enactment, but upon the continuing operation of the statute by which it is so authorised. The statute is conceived to be the source of obligation and the expression of the continuing will of the legislature. Minor consequences of such a doctrine are found in the rule that offences against subordinate regulations are offences against the statute (*Willingale v Norris*) and the rule that upon the repeal of the statute, the regulation fails (*Watson v Winch*). Major consequences are suggested by the emphasis laid in *Powell's* case and in *Hodge's* case upon the retention by the legislature of the whole of its power of control and of its capacity to take the matter back into its own hands. After the long history of parliamentary delegation in Britain and the British colonies, it may be right to treat subordinate legislation which remains under parliamentary control as lacking the independent and unqualified authority which is an attribute of true legislative power, at any rate when there has been an attempt to confer any very general legislative capacity. But, whatever may be its rationale, we should now adhere to the interpretation which results from the decision in *Roche v Kronheimer* ...

Gavan Duffy CJ and Starke J concurred in a joint judgment. Rich and Evatt JJ concurred in separate judgments. Only Evatt J considered the separation of powers doctrine.

Evatt J: [117] It is very difficult to maintain the view that the Commonwealth Parliament has no power, in the exercise of its legislative power, to vest executive or other authorities with some power to pass regulations, statutory rules and by-laws which, when passed, shall have full force and effect. Unless the legislative power of the Parliament extends this far effective government would be impossible. ...

[118] In truth the full theory of 'Separation of Powers' cannot apply under our Constitution. Take the case of an enactment of the Commonwealth Parliament which gives to a subordinate authority other than the executive, a power to make by-laws. To such an instance the theory of a hard and fast division and sub-division of powers between and among the three

authorities of government cannot apply without absurd results. It is clear that the regulation making power conferred in such a case upon the subordinate authority is not judicial power. If it is a 'power' of the Commonwealth at all, it must, according to the theory, be either legislative or executive power. But, if the former, the statute granting power would be invalid because the legislature itself was not exercising the power; and if the latter, the statute would be bad because an authority other than the executive government of the Commonwealth was vested with executive power in defiance of s 61 of the Constitution. It is no longer disputed that if Parliament passes a law within its powers, it may, as part of its legislation, endow a subordinate body, not necessarily the executive government, with power to make [119] regulations for the carrying out of the scheme described in the statute. Does the Constitution impliedly prohibit Parliament from enlarging the extent of the powers to be conferred on subordinate authorities?

In my opinion every grant by the Commonwealth Parliament of authority to make rules and regulations, whether the grantee is the executive government or some other authority, is itself a grant of legislative power. The true nature and quality of the legislative power of the Commonwealth Parliament involves, as part of its content, power to confer law-making powers upon authorities other than Parliament itself. If such power to issue binding commands may lawfully be granted by Parliament to the executive or other agencies, an increase in the extent of such power cannot of itself invalidate the grant. It is true that the extent of the power granted will often be a very material circumstance in the examination of the validity of the legislation conferring the grant. But this is for a reason quite different and distinct from the absolute restriction upon parliamentary action which is supposed to result from the theory of separation of powers.

The matter may be illustrated by an example. Assume that the Commonwealth Parliament passes an enactment to the following effect: 'The executive government may make regulations having the force of law upon the subject of trade and commerce with other countries or among the States'. Such a law would confer part of the legislative power of the Commonwealth upon the executive government, and those who adhere to the strict doctrine of separation of powers, would contend that the law was ultra vires because of the implied prohibition contained in ss 1, 61 and 71 of the Constitution. For the reasons mentioned such a view cannot be accepted.

At the same time, I think that in ordinary circumstances a law in the terms described would be held to be beyond the competence of the Commonwealth Parliament. The nature of the legislative power of the Commonwealth authority is plenary, but it must be possible to predicate of every law passed by the Parliament that it is a law with respect to one or other of the specific subject matters mentioned in ss 51 and 52 of the Constitution. The only ground [120] upon which the validity of such a law as I have stated could be affirmed, is that it is a law with respect to trade and commerce with other countries or among the States. But it is, in substance and operation, not such a law, but a law with respect to the legislative power to deal with the subject of trade and commerce with other countries or among the States. Thus, s 51(i) of the Constitution operates as a grant of power to the Commonwealth Parliament to regulate the subject of inter-State trade and commerce, but the grant itself would not be truly described as being a law with respect to inter-State trade and commerce. Section 51(i) is, however, correctly described as a law with respect to the powers of Parliament, and it finds its proper and natural place in a Constitution Act. ...

[121] On final analysis therefore, the Parliament of the Commonwealth is not competent to 'abdicate' its powers of legislation. This is not because Parliament is bound to perform any or all of its legislative powers or functions, for it may elect not to do so; and not because the doctrine of separation of powers prevents Parliament from granting authority to other bodies to make laws or by-laws and thereby exercise legislative power, for it does so in almost every statute; but because each and every one of the laws passed by Parliament must answer the description of a law upon one or more of the subject matters stated in the Constitution. A law by which Parliament gave all its law-making authority to another body would be bad merely because it would fail to pass the test last mentioned.

~~~

Notes

[6.4.37] In *Dignan's* case (1931) 46 CLR 73 **[6.4.36C]**, Dixon J identified two theories of government underpinning the rule that the Congress of the United States cannot delegate legislative power. These theories are identified with Montesquieu and Locke, respectively. The theory of Montesquieu was that of the separation of power. This theory posited that abuse of governmental authority could be inhibited and restrained by distributing that authority among autonomous institutions of government, legislative, executive and judicial, which checked and balanced each other. The theory is not a theory about federal government, but one about government in general.

The second theory is derived from John Locke, published in his two *Treatises on Civil Government* in 1690. He argued that government rests on the consent of the governed and that the people in establishing institutions of government had entrusted them with certain powers, and that it would be a breach of that trust for any institution to delegate any power entrusted to it.

[6.4.38] Dixon J appears to have argued, in *Dignan's* case (1931) 46 CLR 73 **[6.4.36C]**, that neither of these two theories form part of the theory of Australian constitutional law. In *Wishart v Fraser* (1941) 64 CLR 470, he said at 484:

> Upon principle I have never understood how the theory, which is applied to the United States, that the legislature could not [delegate] at all any authority considered to be legislative could have any place in our Constitution.

Then he made a reference to *Dignan's* case.

This theoretical argument and Dixon J's holding that s 3 of the Transport Workers Act 1928 was valid suggest that Dixon J believed that the Commonwealth Constitution contains no doctrine about the separation of powers as between legislature and executive. However, Dixon J's judgment on this point is equivocal. He insisted that the Constitution demands that judicial power be exercised only by Ch III courts and that such courts exercise only judicial power. He also said that 'an independent consideration of the provisions of the Commonwealth Constitution ... cannot but suggest that it was intended to confine to each of the three departments of government the exercise of the power with which it is invested by the Constitution, the doing of that thing which can be done in virtue only of the possession of such a power': 46 CLR at 96. Finally, he offered a theoretical basis for his decision which, he thought, may have been consistent with the separation of powers. This was the theory of English law that subordinate legislation which remains under parliamentary control might lack the independent and unqualified authority which is an attribute of true legislative power: 46 CLR at 102. It appears that Dixon J confessed to, but avoided, an argument based upon the general doctrine of the separation of powers.

[6.4.39] In *Attorney-General (Cth) v R; Ex parte Australian Boilermakers' Society* (1957) 95 CLR 529 **[6.4.13]**, the Privy Council held that Ch III of the Constitution was an exclusive and exhaustive statement about the judicial power and judicial tribunals of the Commonwealth, with the result that that judicial power could be vested only in Ch III courts and that no non-judicial power could be vested by the Commonwealth Parliament in those courts. In its judgment, the Privy Council relied heavily on a threefold separation of powers as one that was demanded by a literal interpretation of the Constitution. 'But first and last, the question is one of construction and they doubt whether, had Locke and Montesquieu never lived nor the Constitution of the United States never been framed, a different interpretation of the Constitution could validly have been reached': 95 CLR at 540. Nevertheless, the Privy Council did affirm *Dignan's* case and said that it did not wish to be understood as casting doubt 'on the line of authorities where the union of legislative and executive power has been considered': 95 CLR at 545.

Sawer argued that the decision in the *Boilermakers'* case might require a reconsideration of *Dignan's* case: Sawer (1961) pp 183–7. He argued that, because the Privy Council emphasised the threefold separation of powers contained in the Commonwealth Constitution, because it said that the rules allowing delegation do not rest on a theoretical rejection of the doctrine of the separation of powers, and because it described subordinate legislative authority as 'a regulative power akin to legislative power', there may be restrictions on constitutionally permissible delegation which require the Commonwealth Parliament to provide more or less defined standards or policies controlling the exercise of the delegated rule-making power. The assumption is that the executive cannot determine legislative policies that ought to be determined by parliament. He argued that the system of responsible government may represent the full extent to which legislative and executive power may be mixed.

Perhaps Sawer made too much of the use by the Privy Council of the separation of powers theory and not enough of its affirmation of *Dignan's* case. If Professor Sawer's hypothesis is correct, how is permissible delegation distinguished from the impermissible delegation? By what criteria can it be determined whether a delegating statute fails to provide sufficient standards or policies controlling the subordinate authority?

[6.4.40]   Section 13 of the Dried Fruits Export Control Act 1924 (Cth) provided:

13 For the purpose of enabling the board effectively to control the export and the sale and distribution after export of Australian dried fruits, the Governor-General may by proclamation prohibit the export from the Commonwealth of any dried fruits except in accordance with a licence issued by the Minister subject to such conditions and restrictions as are prescribed after recommendations to the Minister by the board.

In *Crowe v Commonwealth* (1935) 54 CLR 69, it was argued that the section was invalid. The Commonwealth Law Reports summarised the argument as follows at 79–80:

Section 13 contains an improper delegation of the legislative power of the Commonwealth.

The limit of the power is that Parliament can transfer only such of its powers as are in respect of matters incidental to the execution of its own formulated legislative action — powers that are administrative and not legislative.

The argument was summarily dismissed by Rich, Starke and Dixon JJ. In a joint judgment, Evatt and McTiernan JJ said at 94:

An analysis of the section shows that Parliament has by no means surrendered its law-making authority over the subject-matter committed to it by s 51(i) of the Constitution. The Act confers very wide powers upon the Dried Fruits Control Board which is constituted by the Act. But this is done, not so much for the purpose of setting up a regulation or law-making body in substitution for Parliament as for the purpose of giving the board full and complete executive control in a business sense over every detail of the export trade in one particular commodity produced in Australia for export. The regulation-making powers of the Governor-General are intended to be exercised, not as legislative or quasi-legislative directions in relation to trade and commerce generally but as aids to the setting up of a machine for the marketing abroad of these Australian fruits.

Hence s 13 cannot be regarded as a law with respect only to the legislative power of trade and commerce with other countries. The principles applied in *Roche v Kronheimer*, and elaborated in *Victorian Stevedoring and General Contracting Co Pty Ltd* and *Meakes v Dignan*, negative the argument that in the present scheme of legislation the Commonwealth Parliament has parted with so much of its legislative authority over the subject-matter mentioned in s 51(i) of the Constitution that the scheme is not a law with respect to such subject-matter.

[6.4.41] In *Dignan's* case (1931) 46 CLR 73 **[6.4.36C]**, Dixon J indicated the difficulty faced by United States courts in enforcing the separation between legislative and executive power because of the difficulties in distinguishing between them. The Supreme Court of the United States has only twice held statutes of the Federal Congress invalid for improper delegation of legislative power: see *Panama Refining Co v Ryan* 293 US 388 (1934); *Schechter Poultry Corporation v United States* 295 US 495 (1934). However, it should be noted that in no case has the United States Congress attempted so broad a delegation as that considered in *Dignan's* case and that there have been cases in which the Supreme Court has narrowly construed a statute's delegating rule-making power so as to avoid the task of invalidating them for undue delegation: see, for example, *Kent v Dulles* 357 US 116 (1958).

An American scholar, K C Davis ((1969) p 713), has argued:

> [N]on-delegation doctrine is almost a complete failure. It has not prevented the delegation of legislative power. Nor has it accomplished its later purpose of assuring that delegated power will be guided by meaningful standards. More importantly, it has failed to provide needed protection against unnecessary and uncontrolled discretionary power. The time has come for the courts to acknowledge that the non-delegation doctrine is unsatisfactory and to invent better ways to protect against arbitrary administrative power.

He argued that in so far as the American doctrine insisted that delegating statutes provide standards controlling administrative agencies, the vaguest of standards has been held permissible, and that this is quite desirable because of the complexity of the undertakings of modern government. Standards which have been held permissible have failed to provide any indication of the kinds of policies subordinate rule-making authorities ought to fulfil, for example, power to make such regulations on particular topics as are 'just and reasonable', 'in the public interest' or 'demanded by public interest, convenience and necessity' (p 720):

> A modern regulatory agency would probably be an impossibility if power could not be delegated with vague standards. Typically, a regulatory agency must decide many major questions that could not have been anticipated at the time of the statutory enactment; typically, legislators are unable to write meaningful standards that will help in answering such major questions ...

[6.4.42] The point made by Evatt J in *Dignan's* case (1931) 46 CLR 73 at 119–20 **[6.4.36C]**, that a wholesale delegation of the Commonwealth's legislative power would amount to an invalid abdication by the parliament, was affirmed by some members of the High Court in *Giris Pty Ltd v Commissioner of Taxation* (1969) 119 CLR 365, when considering the validity of s 99A of the Income Tax Assessment Act 1936 (Cth).

Section 99A(4) provided for assessment of the amount of tax payable by the trustee of an estate. Section 99A(2) provided that the section was not to apply (with the result that a different method of assessing the tax payable, prescribed in s 99 would be used), where 'the Commissioner is of the opinion that it would be unreasonable that this section should apply in relation to that trust estate in relation to that year of income'. According to s 99A(3), the Commissioner was to take account of several specified matters and 'such other matters, if any, as he thinks fit'.

All members of the High Court decided that s 99A was valid, largely because the courts would import some limits on the Commissioner's discretion, and provide an opportunity for judicial review of excessive exercises of that discretion. (Windeyer J supported this reasoning with a 17th-century quotation from Chief Justice Coke: 'reasonableness in these cases belongeth to the knowledge of the law and therefore to be decided by the justices': 119 CLR at 384.) However, Barwick CJ observed that, 'whilst Parliament may delegate legislative power it may not abdicate it'. In the end, he saw s 99A as no more than a delegation of a legislative function: 119 CLR at 373–4.

Kitto J noted that the operation of a taxation law could validly be made to depend upon the formation of an administrative discretion as to some fact, at 379:

> But it may conceivably be that the position is different where a provision purports to authorise an administrative officer to exclude from the application of the law any case in which he disapproves of its application. If sub-s (2) had the effect of setting the Commissioner free, in choosing between s 99A and s 99, to do what he thought fit within the limits of the powers of the Parliament, possibly it should be held invalid as an attempt to invest an officer of the executive government with part of the legislative power of the Commonwealth.

Menzies J also acknowledged that 'at some point ... the shifting of responsibility from Parliament to the Commissioner would require consideration of the constitutionality of the delegation': 119 CLR at 381.

Windeyer said that, on the whole, s 99A was not beyond the bounds of constitutional validity, though was 'very close to the boundary, and ... would be questionable as a precedent for legislation of a similar character': 119 CLR at 385.

The states

Judicial power

New South Wales

[6.4.43] In *Building Construction Employees and Builders' Labourers Federation of New South Wales v Minister for Industrial Relations* (1986) 7 NSWLR 372, the New South Wales Court of Appeal held that the Constitution Act 1902 (NSW) did not entrench a separation of judicial power within the constitution of the state. It followed that the Builders Labourers Federation (Special Provisions) Act 1986 (NSW) could not be impugned on the ground that it interfered with the exercise of judicial power by the courts. The 1986 Act was passed at a time when proceedings were pending in the Supreme Court of New South Wales challenging the validity of a ministerial decision to cancel the registration of a trade union, the Builders' Labourers Federation. Section 3 of the 1986 Act declared that the cancellation of the registration must be accepted as valid, notwithstanding any proceedings then before the courts, and notwithstanding any decision in such proceedings.

Kirby P accepted that the 1986 Act was a legislative judgment and, if the separation of judicial power was entrenched in the New South Wales constitution, the Act would violate that entrenchment, a proposition established by the Privy Council in *Liyanage v R* [1967] 1 AC 259. However, there was no provision in the Constitution Act 1902 (NSW) that entrenched the separation of powers or inhibited the parliament from legislating in the terms of the 1986 Act. In that sense, the New South Wales Parliament was 'uncontrolled' as that expression was used in *McCawley v R* [1920] AC 691 **[5.3.13]**, **[5.4.2]**. Nor was there anything in the drafting or structure of the Constitution Act to support the argument that the separation of judicial power was constitutionally required. Finally, the history of judicial arrangements in New South Wales denied the suggestion of a constitutional separation. Section 49 of the Constitution Act 1855 (NSW), which established self-government in the colony and was endorsed by the United Kingdom Parliament in the Constitution Statute 1855 (UK), gave the parliament power to abolish, alter or vary all the courts in the colony, so that it was:

> ... specifically contemplated that, in respect of New South Wales, power would be held by the legislature not just to impinge upon courts and the judicial function but even to abolish, alter or vary such courts. Pursuant to that power, detailed provisions have been made by local legislation providing for the qualification and appointment of judges, their tenure of office, their independence and the conduct of business. All of these matters are dealt with by ordinary Acts of the New South Wales Parliament. Similarly, other courts have been created and abolished by such Acts. By virtue of the Constitution Statute and the Constitution Act, there is therefore no limitation on the power of the New South Wales Parliament similarly to abolish, alter or vary the constitution, organization and business of the Supreme Court. Any limitations in that regard must be derived from politics and convention, grounded in history. They are not based upon legal restrictions (7 NSWLR at 401).

Street CJ, Glass, Mahoney and Priestley JJA delivered judgments to the same effect on this issue.

The statements in this case about the power of states to abolish state courts must now be read in light of the decision of the High Court in *Kable v Director of Public Prosecutions (NSW)* (1996) 189 CLR 51 **[6.4.48C]** and **[11.3.30]**ff.

South Australia

[6.4.44] In *Gilbertson v South Australia* [1978] AC 772, the Privy Council rejected a challenge to the constitutional validity of s 86 of the Constitution Act 1934 (SA), which allowed for an appeal to the Supreme Court of South Australia from an order of the Electoral Districts Boundaries Commission, dividing the state into electoral districts for the purpose of House of Assembly elections. The ground of such an appeal would be 'that the order has not been duly made in accordance with this Act'. It was argued that s 86 purported to confer non-judicial power on the Supreme Court, which was inconsistent with the fundamental law of the state.

The Privy Council agreed with the majority of the Supreme Court of South Australia that the Ordinance of 1837 which had established the Supreme Court as a court of judicature was not part of the fundamental law of South Australia. It could be amended by the South Australian Parliament, which had 'plenary power to confer upon the Supreme Court ... whatever jurisdiction Parliament thought fit, notwithstanding that such jurisdiction might involve the exercise of powers which do not fall within the concept of judicial power as it has been applied to constitutions based on the separation of powers — which the State constitution *of* South Australia is not': [1978] AC at 783.

Victoria

[6.4.45]   In Victoria, some elements of the separation of judicial power appear to be recognised by provisions in the Constitution Act 1975 (Vic), requiring that a special procedure be followed by the parliament when legislating on the jurisdiction and structure of the Supreme Court. Section 18(2) of the Constitution Act prohibits the presentation to the Governor of certain bills unless those bills have been passed by absolute majorities in each house of parliament. The bills include those which alter various parts of the Constitution Act, including Pt III establishing the Supreme Court and defining its jurisdiction: see **[5.4.15]**. Section 85(1) of the Constitution Act confers unrestricted jurisdiction on the Supreme Court of Victoria. Section 85(5) declares that no Act is to be taken to repeal, alter or vary s 85 unless the Act did so directly or unless the Act expressly referred to s 85, and unless the introduction of the bill for the Act was accompanied by a statement of the reasons for repealing, altering or amending s 85.

However, in *City of Collingwood v Victoria (No 2)* [1994] 1 VR 652, the Appeal Division of the Victorian Supreme Court held that the Constitution Act 1975 (Vic) did not entrench the separation of judicial power as a constitutional doctrine. It was clear, Brooking J said at 663–4:

> ... that one cannot derive from the Constitution Act 1975 any intention that the judicial power of the State is to be exercised only by the courts of the State (however one might define courts for this purpose). Nor can one derive any intention that Parliament may not interfere with the judicial process of the courts of this State or (the more narrow view) the judicial process of the Supreme Court in the sense in which it is now accepted that the federal Parliament may not interfere with the judicial process of the federal judicature. The provisions of the [Constitution] Act differ most markedly from the provisions of the Constitution considered in the *Boilermakers' Case* and are quite insufficient to sustain any of the suggested implications. The plaintiff's argument faces the particular difficulty that Pt III of the Act is concerned not with the Victorian judicature but with a single court, quite apart from the additional difficulty created by s 85(8).

> Since Pt III of the Act deals not with the judicature but only with the Supreme Court, it cannot be suggested that the Act vests the judicial power of Victoria in the Victorian judicature as the Commonwealth Constitution vests the federal judicial power in the federal judicature. And of course it cannot be suggested that Pt III vests the judicial power of Victoria in the Supreme Court: the other courts are by s 2(2) of the Act to continue in existence except in so far as they may be abolished, altered or varied, and s 85(8) recognises that Parliament may already have conferred and may in the future confer on a court, tribunal, body or person jurisdiction which would otherwise be exercisable by the Supreme Court. All that can be said is that Pt III vests in the Supreme Court part of the judicial power of Victoria or preserves the effect of the previous investing. The Act recognises that the judicial power of the Supreme Court is not sacrosanct: it may be augmented or diminished by Parliament, subject to the observance of any applicable requirement of the Act. The whole of Pt III may be repealed if the requirements of ss 18 and 15 are observed. That the jurisdiction and powers of the Supreme Court are not immutable is shown by s 85(4), whereby Parliament may confer additional jurisdiction or powers on the Supreme Court. Section 85(6) shows that Parliament may trench upon the jurisdiction of the Supreme Court by excluding or restricting its judicial review of a decision of another court, tribunal, body or person. Section 85(8) makes it clear that Parliament may confer on a court, tribunal, body or

person jurisdiction which would otherwise be exercisable by the Supreme Court. Section 85(9) shows that Parliament may limit the jurisdiction of the Supreme Court by conferring exclusive jurisdiction on another court.

I should add that the express provisions of ss 18 and 85 of the Constitution Act 1975 seem to me to be intended to determine the extent to which the power of Parliament to legislate so as to affect the Supreme Court is to be limited and to be inconsistent with any notion that the Act by implication embodies some doctrine of separation of powers which prevents Parliament from interfering with the judicial process of the Supreme Court.

[6.4.46] In *Broken Hill Pty Co Ltd v Dagi* [1996] 2 VR 106, the Victorian Court of Appeal (constituted by five judges) rejected a challenge to the validity of s 46 of the Public Prosecutions Act 1994 (Vic). The section provided that any application to the Supreme Court for the punishment of a person for a contempt of court involving interference with the due administration of justice (apart from a contempt that involved a breach of a court order) could only be made by the Attorney-General. (The section preserved the power of the Supreme Court to deal with a contempt 'summarily of its own motion'.) The rejected challenge was based on the argument that s 46 affected the jurisdiction of the Supreme Court but had not been enacted as required by s 85(5) of the Constitution Act 1975 (Vic).

Although an argument based on the separation of judicial power was not raised before the Court of Appeal, two judges warned that legislative restrictions of the Supreme Court's jurisdiction could raise such an issue. Phillips JA said he was 'attracted by the suggestion' that parliament could not 'fetter this court in a way which went to its very core as an institution within the overall framework of government in the widest sense': [1996] 2 VR at 190. Hayne JA said there was 'a serious question whether Parliament may … so change the Constitution of this State as to remove as one element of its governance a superior court of record with the powers and jurisdiction inherent in such a court': [1996] 2 VR at 205. His Honour said that, although the point had not been argued, it was 'one that can no longer be answered by an unthinking reference to Dicey's precept that Parliament is sovereign': [1996] 2 VR at 205.

[6.4.47] The proposition that state parliaments are not constrained by a constitutional separation of judicial power when legislating must now be qualified in the light of the High Court's decision in *Kable v Director of Public Prosecutions (NSW)* (1996) 189 CLR 51 **[6.4.48C]** and **[11.3.30]**ff, which concluded that state legislation conferring a non-judicial function on a state court could be so incompatible with the inherent character of judicial power that it offended Ch III of the Commonwealth Constitution.

[6.4.48C]   Kable v Director of Public Prosecutions (NSW)
(1996) 189 CLR 51

The Community Protection Act 1994 (NSW) provided, so far as relevant, as follows:

3(1) The object of this Act is to protect the community by providing for the preventive detention (by order of the Supreme Court made on the application of the Director of Public Prosecutions) of Gregory Wayne Kable.

(2) In the construction of this Act, the need to protect the community is to be given paramount consideration.

(3) This Act authorises the making of a detention order against Gregory Wayne Kable and does not authorise the making of a detention order against any other person.

(4) For the purposes of this section, Gregory Wayne Kable is the person of that name who was convicted in New South Wales on 1 August 1990 of the manslaughter of his wife, Hilary Kable. ...

5(1) On an application made in accordance with this Act, the Court may order that a specified person be detained in prison for a specified period if it is satisfied, on reasonable grounds:

    (a) that the person is more likely than not to commit a serious act of violence; and

    (b) that it is appropriate, for the protection of a particular person or persons or the community generally, that the person be held in custody.

(2) The maximum period to be specified in an order under this section is 6 months.

(3) An order under this section may be made against a person:

    (a) whether or not the person is in lawful custody, as a detainee or otherwise; and

    (b) whether or not there are grounds on which the person may be held in lawful custody otherwise than as a detainee.

(4) More than one application under this section may be made in relation to the same person.

According to s 4 of the Act, 'the Court' was the Supreme Court of New South Wales; s 14 declared that detention proceedings were civil proceedings; s 15 provided that the proceedings were to be determined on the balance of probabilities; and s 8 provided that only the state's Director of Public Prosecutions could apply for an order under s 5.

Kable was serving a sentence of imprisonment for the manslaughter of his wife. Shortly before the end of his sentence, the Act was passed and the Director of Public Prosecutions applied to the Supreme Court for an order under s 5 of the Community Protection Act, relying on a number of threatening letters which Kable had sent to various people. A judge of the Supreme Court ordered that Kable be detained for six months under the Act. The New South Wales Court of Appeal rejected Kable's appeal against that order. By special leave of the High Court, Kable appealed to the High Court of Australia, raising the contention that the Community Protection Act was invalid.

Toohey J held that the Community Protection Act was a law 'for the peace, welfare and good government of New South Wales' within s 5 of the Constitution Act 1902 (NSW) and did not amount to an exercise of judicial power by the Parliament. His Honour turned to the argument that the Community Protection Act violated the separation of the judicial power of the Commonwealth required by Ch III of the Constitution.

Toohey J: [94] Section 71 of the Constitution vests the judicial power of the Commonwealth in the High Court 'and in such other federal courts as the Parliament creates, and in such other courts as it invests with federal jurisdiction'. Section 77(iii) empowers the parliament to make laws '[i]nvesting any court of a State with federal jurisdiction'. Effect is given to s 77(iii) by s 39(2) of the Judiciary Act 1903 (Cth) which invests the 'several Courts of the States' with 'federal jurisdiction' in all matters in which the High Court has original jurisdiction or in which original jurisdiction can be conferred upon it, subject to s 38 which identifies those matters in which the jurisdiction of the High Court is exclusive of those courts. To the extent that they are invested with federal jurisdiction, the federal courts and the courts of the States exercise a common jurisdiction. [*Breavington v Godleman* (1988) 169 CLR 41 at 166–7.] It follows that in the exercise of its federal jurisdiction a State court may not act in a manner which is incompatible with Ch III of the Commonwealth Constitution.

Toohey J said that in the present case the Supreme Court was exercising federal jurisdiction vested in it by s 39 of the Judiciary Act, because the appellant had invoked several arguments arising out of the Commonwealth Constitution before the Supreme Court, and continued:

[95] The Supreme Court of New South Wales was required, at first instance and on appeal, to determine questions arising under the Constitution. In those circumstances s 39(2) of the Judiciary Act, read with s 77(iii) of the Constitution, conferred jurisdiction on the Supreme Court to determine those questions. Section 71 of the Constitution ensured that the judicial power of the Commonwealth was engaged in those circumstances.

The argument advanced on behalf of the appellant was that the Act vests in the Supreme Court of New South Wales a non-judicial power which is offensive to Ch III of the Constitution. Hence any exercise of that power would be unconstitutional and the Act conferring the power would be invalid. Reliance was placed on what Dixon CJ, McTiernan, Fullagar and Kitto JJ said in *R v Kirby; Ex parte Boilermakers' Society of Australia* [(1956) 94 CLR 254 at 268]:

> The organs to which federal judicial power may be entrusted must be defined, the manner in which they may be constituted must be prescribed and the content of their jurisdiction ascertained. These very general considerations explain the provisions of Ch III of the Constitution.

The argument is not one which relies upon the alleged separation of legislative and judicial functions under the Constitution of New South Wales. Rather it is that the jurisdiction exercised under the Act is inconsistent with Ch III of the Commonwealth Constitution because the very nature of the jurisdiction is incompatible with the exercise of judicial power. ...

[96] In *Grollo v Palmer* [(1995) 184 CLR 348; 131 ALR 225] the court held that the vesting in designated judges of the Federal Court of the power to issue interception warrants was not incompatible either with the judge's performance of his or her judicial functions or with the proper discharge by the judiciary of its responsibilities as an institution exercising judicial power. Nevertheless the court emphasised that 'no function can be conferred that is incompatible ... with the proper discharge by the judiciary of its responsibilities as an institution exercising judicial power'. [(1995) 184 CLR 348 at 365] It is true that the proposition was enunciated in the context of the power to confer non-judicial functions on judges as designated persons but in my view it holds good whenever Ch III of the Constitution is operative. And *Mistretta v United States*, [488 US 361 (1989) at 404] to which the majority judgment refers with approval, is couched in terms of constitutional doctrine. The emphasis in the judgment of the Supreme Court of the United States is on 'the integrity of the Judicial Branch'.

The appellant's argument of incompatibility of function rests on several foundations. But fundamentally it relies upon the nature of the Act whereby the Supreme Court may order the imprisonment of a person although that person has not been adjudged guilty of any criminal offence. The Supreme Court is thereby required to participate [97] in a process designed to bring about the detention of a person by reason of the court's assessment of what that person might do, not what the person has done.

Toohey J referred to the extraordinary character of the legislation and of the functions it required the Supreme Court to perform and held that the functions were incompatible with the exercise of the judicial power of the Commonwealth because their performance would diminish public confidence in the integrity of the judiciary as an institution: 189 CLR at 98.

Gaudron J said that state courts were 'the creatures of the States' so that 'the Commonwealth must take the State courts as it finds them': 189 CLR at 102.

Gaudron J: [102] Neither the recognition in Ch III that State courts are the creatures of the States nor its consequence that, in the respects indicated, the Commonwealth must take State courts as it finds them detracts from what is, to my mind, one of the clearest features of our Constitution, namely, that it provides for an integrated Australian judicial system for the exercise of the judicial power of the Commonwealth. Moreover, neither that recognition nor that consequence directs the conclusion that State parliaments may enact whatever laws they choose with respect to State courts. If Ch III requires that State courts not exercise particular powers, the parliaments of the States cannot confer those powers upon them. That follows from covering cl 5, which provides that the Constitution is 'binding on the courts, judges, and people of every State and of every part of the Commonwealth, notwithstanding anything in the laws of any State', and from s 106, by which the Constitution of each State is made subject to the Australian Constitution. And so much was recognised in *Commonwealth v Queensland*

[(1975) 134 CLR 298 at 315; 7 ALR 351], where it was said that State legislation in violation of 'the principles that underlie Ch III' is invalid.

The question whether the Constitution requires that State courts not have particular powers conferred upon them depends, in my view, on a proper understanding of the integrated judicial system for which Ch III **[103]** provides — the 'autochthonous expedient' [*R v Kirby; Ex parte Boilermakers' Society of Australia* (1956) 94 CLR 254 at 268], as it has been called. One thing which clearly emerges is that, although it is for the States to determine the organisation and structure of their court systems, they must each maintain courts, or, at least, a court for the exercise of the judicial power of the Commonwealth. Were they free to abolish their courts, the autochthonous expedient, more precisely, the provisions of Ch III which postulate an integrated judicial system would be frustrated in their entirety. To this extent, at least, the States are not free to legislate as they please.

Two other matters of significance emerge from a consideration of the provisions of Ch III. The first is that State courts are neither less worthy recipients of federal jurisdiction than federal courts nor 'substitute tribunals' [See *Commonwealth v Limerick Steamship Co Ltd and Kidman* (1924) 35 CLR 69 at 116], as they have sometimes been called. To put the matter plainly, there is nothing anywhere in the Constitution to suggest that it permits of different grades or qualities of justice, depending on whether judicial power is exercised by State courts or federal courts created by the parliament.

The second and, perhaps, the more significant matter which emerges from a consideration of the provisions of Ch III is, as I pointed out in *Leeth v Commonwealth* [(1992) 174 CLR 455 at 498–9; 107 ALR 672], that State courts, when exercising federal jurisdiction 'are part of the Australian judicial system created by Ch III of the Constitution and, in that sense and on that account, they have a role and existence which transcends their status as courts of the States'. Once the notion that the Constitution permits of different grades or qualities of justice is rejected, the consideration that State courts have a role and existence transcending their status as State courts directs the conclusion that Ch III requires that the parliaments of the States not legislate to confer powers on State courts which are repugnant to or incompatible with their exercise of the judicial power of the Commonwealth. ...

The *Boilermakers'* doctrine, as it is sometimes called, prevents the Parliament of the Commonwealth from conferring judicial power on bodies other than courts and prevents it from conferring any power that is not judicial power or a power incidental thereto on the courts specified in s 71 of the Constitution. It also prevents the parliament from conferring functions on judges in their individual capacity if the functions are inconsistent with the exercise of judicial power in the sense explained in *Grollo v* **[104]** *Palmer* [(1995) 184 CLR 348; 131 ALR 225]. The limitation on State legislative power is more closely confined and relates to powers or functions imposed on a State court, rather than its judges in their capacity as individuals, and is concerned with powers or functions that are repugnant to or incompatible with the exercise of the judicial power of the Commonwealth.

Although the limitation is one relating to the conferral of powers on courts, rather than on judges in their capacity as individuals, it is, nevertheless, one that is closely related to the limitation on Commonwealth power to confer functions on judges of this and other federal courts in their capacity as individuals. In both cases the limitation derives from the necessity to ensure the integrity of the judicial process and the integrity of the courts specified in s 71 of the Constitution.

Gaudron J held that the function conferred on the Supreme Court by the Community Protection Act was incompatible with the exercise of the judicial power of the Commonwealth.

McHugh J: **[109]**

The States do not have unlimited power in respect of State courts

Subject to the operation of the Commonwealth of Australia Constitution Act 1900 (Imp) (the Constitution), the State of New South Wales is governed by the New South Wales

Constitution. The latter Act is not predicated on any separation of legislative, executive and judicial power [*Clyne v East* (1967) 68 SR(NSW) 385 at 395, 396–7, 400–1; *Kotsis v Kotsis* (1970) 122 CLR 69 at 76; *Gilbertson v South Australia* [1978] AC 772 at 783; *Building Construction Employees and Builders' Labourers Federation of New South Wales v Minister for Industrial Relations* (1986) 7 NSWLR 372 at 400–1, 418–19; *Mabo v Queensland* (1988) 166 CLR 186 at 202; 83 ALR 14] although no doubt it assumes that the legislative, executive and judicial power of the State will be exercised by institutions that are functionally separated. Despite that assumption, I can see nothing in the New South Wales Constitution nor the constitutional history of the State that would preclude the State legislature from vesting legislative or executive power in the New South Wales judiciary [*Gilbertson* [1978] AC 772 at 783] or judicial power in the legislature or the executive. Nor is the federal doctrine of the separation of powers — one of the fundamental doctrines of the Constitution — directly applicable to the State of New South Wales. Federal judicial power may be vested in a State court although that court exercises non-[110]judicial as well as judicial functions. Moreover, when the Parliament of the Commonwealth invests the judicial power of the Commonwealth in State courts pursuant to s 77(iii) of the Constitution, it must take the State court as it finds it. [*Federated Saw Mill, Timberyard and General Wood-workers' Employés' Association (Adelaide Branch) v Alexander* (1912) 15 CLR 308 at 313; *Le Mesurier v Connor* (1929) 42 CLR 481 at 495–7; *Peacock v Newtown Marrickville and General Co-operative Building Society No 4 Ltd* (1943) 67 CLR 25.] This is because the Constitution recognises that the jurisdiction, structure and organisation of State courts and the appointment, tenure and terms of remuneration of judges of State courts is not a matter within the legislative power of the Federal Parliament. But in my opinion none of the foregoing considerations means that the Constitution contains no implications concerning the powers of State legislatures to abolish or regulate State courts, to invest State courts or State judges with non-judicial powers or functions, or to regulate the exercise of judicial power by State courts and judges.

The working of the Constitution requires and implies the continued existence of a system of State courts with a Supreme Court at the head of the State judicial system ...

McHugh J referred to covering cl 5, s 118, s 51(xxiv), s 51(xxv) and s 77 of the Constitution.

One of the reasons for enacting s 77(iii) was that it was 'a very convenient means of avoiding the multiplicity and expense of legal tribunals'. [*Commonwealth v Limerick Steamship Co Ltd and Kidman* (1924) 35 CLR 69 at 90.] ... [111] If a State could abolish its court system, the powers conferred by s 77(ii) and (iii) would be rendered useless and the constitutional plan of a system of State courts invested with federal jurisdiction, as envisaged by Ch III, would be defeated ... It is hardly to be supposed that the Constitution intended that a State could defeat the exercise of the grants of power conferred on the Parliament of the Commonwealth by s 77 by the simple expedient of abolishing its courts and setting up a system of tribunals that were not courts.

State Supreme Courts cannot be abolished

Furthermore, s 73 of the Constitution implies the continued existence of the State Supreme Courts by giving a right of appeal from the Supreme Court of each State to the High Court, subject only to such exceptions as the Commonwealth Parliament enacts. Section 73(ii) gives this court jurisdiction to determine appeals from the decisions of any 'court exercising federal jurisdiction; or of the Supreme Court of any State, or any other court of any State from which at the establishment of the Commonwealth an appeal [lay] to the Queen in Council'. The right of appeal from a State Supreme Court to this court, conferred by that section, would be rendered nugatory if the Constitution permitted a State to abolish its Supreme Court.

It necessarily follows, therefore, that the Constitution has withdrawn from each State the power to abolish its Supreme Court or to leave its people without the protection of a judicial system. That does not mean that a State cannot abolish or amend the constitutions of its existing courts. Leaving aside the special position of the Supreme Courts of the States, the States can abolish or amend the structure of existing courts and create new ones. However, the Constitution requires a judicial system in and a Supreme Court for each State and, if there is a system of State courts in addition to the Supreme Court, the Supreme Court must be at the apex of the system. With the abolition of the right of appeal to the Privy Council, therefore, this court is now the apex of an Australian judicial system.

State courts are part of an Australian judicial system

At federation each Colony had courts. Each Colony had a Supreme Court from which an appeal could be taken to the Privy Council ... [112] The right of appeal from the State Supreme Courts to the Privy Council continued after federation ... However, s 74 also gave the parliament power to 'make laws limiting the matters' in which special leave to appeal from the High Court to the Privy Council could be asked. That power extended to abolishing all matters in respect of which leave could be sought. [*Attorney-General (Cth) v T & G Mutual Life Society Ltd* (1978) 144 CLR 161 19 ALR 385.] Nevertheless, until that power was exercised, the Constitution intended that, subject to the grant of a certificate by the High Court in respect of an inter se matter, Australia should have an integrated system of State and federal courts administering a single body of common law under the supervision of the Judicial Committee of the Privy Council which stood at the apex of the system.

McHugh J referred to Australia's unified common law system which applies in each state but is not itself the creature of any state. His Honour noted that Sir Own Dixon had referred, in an address to the American Bar Association, to 'the reasons which make it possible for an Australian to regard his country as governed by a single legal system. It is a system or corpus composed of the common law, modified by the enactments of various legislatures: Dixon, 'Sources of Legal Authority', *Jesting Pilate* (1965) 198 p 201'. McHugh J said that, once the last right of appeal to the Privy Council was abolished by s 11 of the Australia Acts 1986, the High Court became the ultimate appellate court of the nation, and now held 'the constitutional duty of supervising the nation's legal system and, subject to any relevant statutory or constitutional limitations, of maintaining a unified system of common law': 189 CLR at 113–14.

[114] It follows that State courts exercising State judicial power cannot be regarded as institutions that are independent of the administration of the law by this court or the federal courts created by the Parliament of the Commonwealth. In exercising federal jurisdiction, a court of a State administers the same law as the Federal Court of Australia when it exercises the identical federal jurisdiction. In exercising federal jurisdiction, a State court must deduce any relevant common law principle from the decisions of all the courts of the nation and not merely from the decisions of the higher courts of its State. A judge exercising the federal jurisdiction invested in a State court must see the common law in exactly the same way that a judge of a federal court created under s 71 of the Constitution sees it.

Furthermore, a State court when it exercises federal jurisdiction invested under s 77(iii) is not a court different from the court that exercises the judicial power of the State. The judges of a State court who exercise the judicial power of the State are the same judges who exercise the judicial power of the Commonwealth invested in their courts pursuant to s 77(iii) of the Constitution. Indeed, it is not uncommon for a judge of a State court to administer State legislation in the course of the exercise of federal jurisdiction. It is common ground, for example, that in this very case Levine J made his order in the exercise of federal jurisdiction because he became seized of federal jurisdiction when the appellant contended that the Act was in breach of the Constitution.

Under the Constitution, therefore, the State courts have a status and a role that extends beyond their status and role as part of the State judicial systems. They are part of an integrated system of State and federal courts and organs for the exercise of federal judicial power as [115] well as State judicial power. Moreover, the Constitution contemplates no distinction between the status of State courts invested with federal jurisdiction and those created as federal courts. There are not two grades of federal judicial power. The terms of s 71 of the Constitution equate the vesting of judicial power in the federal courts with the vesting of federal judicial power in the State courts ...

Legislatures cannot alter or undermine the constitutional scheme set up by Ch III

It is axiomatic that neither the Commonwealth nor a State can legislate in a way that might alter or undermine the constitutional scheme set up by Ch III of the Constitution ... In *Commonwealth v Queensland,* in a judgment with which Barwick CJ, Stephen and Mason JJ agreed, Gibbs J held that it is implicit in Ch III that a State cannot legislate in a way that has the effect of violating 'the principles that underlie Ch III'. [(1975) 134 CLR 298 at 314–15; 7 ALR 351.]

[116] Because the State courts are an integral and equal part of the judicial system set up by Ch III, it also follows that no State or federal parliament can legislate in a way that might undermine the role of those courts as repositories of federal judicial power. Thus, neither the Parliament of New South Wales nor the Parliament of the Commonwealth can invest functions in the Supreme Court of New South Wales that are incompatible with the exercise of federal judicial power. Neither parliament, for example, can legislate in a way that permits the Supreme Court while exercising federal judicial power to disregard the rules of natural justice or to exercise legislative or executive power. Such legislation is inconsistent with the exercise of federal judicial power. However, the Act does not seek to interfere with the invested federal jurisdiction of the Supreme Court. On its face it is directed to the exercise of State, not federal, jurisdiction. But for present purposes that is irrelevant. The compatibility of State legislation with federal judicial power does not depend on intention. It depends on effect. If, as Gibbs J pointed out in *Commonwealth v Queensland* [(1975) 134 CLR 298 at 314–15; 7 ALR 351], State legislation has the effect of violating the principles that underlie Ch III, it will be invalid.

Courts exercising federal jurisdiction must be perceived to be free from legislative or executive interference

One of the basic principles which underlie Ch III and to which it gives effect is that the judges of the federal courts must be, and must be perceived to be, independent of the legislature and the executive government. [*R v Quinn; Ex parte Consolidated Food Corporation* (1977) 138 CLR 1 at 11; 16 ALR 569; *Harris v Caladine* (1991) 172 CLR 84 at 135, 159; 99 ALR 193; *Grollo v Palmer* (1995) 184 CLR 348 at 365, 376–7, 392; 131 ALR 225; *Wilson v Minister for Aboriginal and Torres Strait Islander Affairs* (1996) 151 CLR 1; 138 ALR 220.] Given the central role and the status that Ch III gives to State courts invested with federal jurisdiction, it necessarily follows that those courts must also be, and be perceived to be, independent of the legislature and executive government in the exercise of federal jurisdiction. Public confidence in the impartial exercise of [623] federal judicial power would soon be lost if federal or State courts exercising federal jurisdiction were not, or were not perceived to be, independent of the legislature or the executive government.

In the case of State courts, this means they must be independent and appear to be independent of their own State's legislature and executive government as well as the federal legislature and government. Cases concerning the States, the extent of the legislative powers of the States and the actions of the executive governments of the States frequently attract the exercise of invested federal jurisdiction. The Commonwealth Government and the residents and governments of other States are among those who litigate issues in the courts of a State. Quite [117] often the government of the State concerned is the opposing party in actions brought by these litigants. Public confidence in the exercise of federal jurisdiction by the courts of a State could not be retained if litigants in those courts believed that the judges of those courts were sympathetic to the interests of their State or its executive government.

While nothing in Ch III prevents a State from conferring non-judicial functions on a State Supreme Court in respect of non-federal matters, those non-judicial functions cannot be of a nature that might lead an ordinary reasonable member of the public to conclude that the court was not independent of the executive government of the State. A State law which gave the Supreme Court powers to determine issues of a purely governmental nature — for example, how much of the State Budget should be spent on child welfare or what policies should be pursued by a particular government department — would be invalid. It would have the effect of so closely identifying the Supreme Court with the government of the State that it would give the appearance that the Supreme Court was part of the executive government of the State. The law would fail not because it breached any entrenched doctrine of separation powers in the State Constitution ... but because it gave the appearance that a court invested with federal jurisdiction was not independent of its State government.

In addition, in the case of the Supreme Court, although non-judicial functions may be vested in that court, they cannot be so extensive or of such a nature that the Supreme Court would lose its identity as a court ...

Furthermore, although nothing in Ch III prevents a State from conferring executive government functions on a State court judge as *persona designata*, if the appointment of a judge as *persona designata* gave the appearance that the court as an institution was not independent of the executive government of the State, it would be invalid ...

[118] It follows therefore that, although New South Wales has no entrenched doctrine of the separation of powers and although the Commonwealth doctrine of separation of powers cannot apply to the State, in some situations the effect of Ch III of the Constitution may lead to the same result as if the State had an enforceable doctrine of separation of powers. This is because it is a necessary implication of the Constitution's plan of an Australian judicial system with State courts invested with federal jurisdiction that no government can act in a way that might undermine public confidence in the impartial administration of the judicial functions of State courts. If it could, it would inevitably result in a lack of public confidence in the administration of invested federal jurisdiction in those courts. State governments therefore do not have unrestricted power to legislate for State courts or judges. A State may invest a State court with non-judicial functions and its judges with duties that, in the federal sphere, would be incompatible with the holding of judicial office. But under the Constitution the boundary of State legislative power is crossed when the vesting of those functions or duties might lead ordinary reasonable members of the public to conclude that the State court as an institution was not free of government influence in administering the judicial functions invested in the court.

McHugh J held that the Community Protection Act would inevitably impair public confidence in the impartial administration by the Supreme Court of its judicial functions, and was, accordingly, invalid as it infringed Ch III of the Constitution.

Gummow J held that the Supreme Court of each state was part of an integrated Australian legal system, that the meaning of the term 'Supreme Court' depended on the construction of the Commonwealth Constitution and not merely on the relevant state legislation. It was 'a constitutional expression': 189 CLR at 141. Because decisions of each Supreme Court were subject to appeal to the High Court under s 73(ii) of the Constitution, 'the functions of the Supreme Courts of the States, at least, are intertwined with the exercise of the judicial power of the Commonwealth ... By this means, the judicial power of the Commonwealth is engaged, at least prospectively, across the range of litigation pursued in the courts of the States': 189 CLR at 142. It followed that the constitutional principle against the conferral of incompatible functions on judges of federal courts also applied to the Supreme Courts of the states.

Brennan CJ and Dawson J dissented, holding that the concept of incompatibility of functions as applied to judges of federal courts had no counterpart in the context of possible limitations on the power of a state parliament to invest state courts with non-judicial powers.

~~~

[6.4.49]   Many attempts have been made to invoke the *Kable* principle in support of attacks on the validity of Commonwealth, state and territory legislation. However, almost all those attempts have failed: see, for example, *R v Wynbyne* (1997) 99 A Crim R 1; *R v Moffatt* [1998] 2 VR 229; *Nicholas v The Queen* (1998) 193 CLR

173; *H A Bachrach Pty Ltd v Queensland* (1998) 195 CLR 547; *Felman v Law Institute of Victoria* [1998] 4 VR 324; *John Fairfax Publications Pty Ltd v Attorney-General (NSW)* (2000) 181 ALR 694; *Schutt Flying Academy (Australia) Pty Ltd v Mobil Oil Australia Ltd* [2000] 1 VR 545; *Johnson v Esso* (2000) 104 FCR 564; *Silbert v Director of Public Prosecutions (WA)* [2004] HCA 9.

[6.4.50] For example, in *John Fairfax Publications Pty Ltd v Attorney-General (NSW)* (2000) 181 ALR 694, Spigelman CJ (with whom Meagher JA agreed) rejected an attack on the validity of s 101A(7), (8) and (9) of the Supreme Court Act 1970 (NSW), which provided that any appeal by the Attorney-General on a question of law from an order acquitting a person of contempt of court should be heard in camera and prohibited publication of submissions made on the appeal or of the identity of the respondent to the appeal.

Spigelman CJ concluded that the provisions under challenge did not offend the *Kable* principle, at [72]–[75]:

> Some forms of Parliamentary modification of the principle of open justice will be struck down by the constitutional principle identified in *Kable*. For example, a provision requiring the Court to sit in camera in all cases involving the State of New South Wales, either generally or in some specific respect in which the interests of the State were involved, would, in my opinion, be invalid.

> However, in the present case, the specific measure under consideration does not, in my opinion, represent an infringement which impinges on the 'integrity' of the Supreme Court as a repository of federal power. Nor does it impinge on the independence, or the appearance of independence, of the court. Nor does it constitute such a distortion of its predominant or essential characteristics as to involve the court determining the issues of law posed for its consideration, otherwise than by the exercise of the judicial power of the Commonwealth.

> The restrictions imposed on the presence of the public and on publicity by s 101A (7), (8) and (9), represents the implementation of a policy that an individual (or, as is often the case, a media company) has a right not to have an acquittal of a criminal charge called into question. This constitutes a limited and justifiable exception to the general principle, which the public is, in my opinion, likely to appreciate.

> The adoption of a policy that an appeal on a point of legal principle relating to contempt, which cannot affect the decision on the specific case, should not be the subject of public debate, is not, in my opinion, so significant a modification of the judicial process required by Chapter III of the Constitution as to be incompatible with the exercise of the judicial power of the Commonwealth.

[6.4.51] The decision of the Queensland Court of Appeal in *Re Criminal Proceeds Confiscation Act 2002 (Qld)* [2003] QCA 249 represents one of the few positive applications of the *Kable* principle. The court held invalid s 30 of the Criminal Proceeds Confiscation Act 2002, which requires the Supreme Court of Queensland to hear a state application for a restraining order in the absence of the person whose property is the subject of the application. In a judgment with which White and Wilson JJ agreed, Williams JA said at [58]:

> ... the direction or command to the judge hearing the application to proceed in the absence of any party affected by the order to be made is such an interference with the exercise of the judicial process as to be repugnant to or incompatible with the exercise of the judicial power of the Commonwealth. Then, because the Supreme Court of Queensland is part of an integrated Australian judicial system for the exercise of the judicial power of the Commonwealth, such a provision is constitutionally invalid.

On 2 March 2004 the High Court heard an appeal from the judgment of the Queensland Court of Appeal in *Fardon v Attorney-General (Qld)* [2003] QCA 416, in which the Court of Appeal had rejected a challenge to the Dangerous Prisoners Act 2003 (Qld), which authorises the Supreme Court of Queensland to incarcerate a person beyond the expiry of the person's term of imprisonment on the ground of predicted dangerousness. The appeal provides the High Court with the opportunity to develop (or confine) the *Kable* principle.

Legislative and executive powers

[6.4.52]   The delegation by parliament of substantial legislative powers had become commonplace in the United Kingdom by 1860. In that year the United Kingdom Parliament enacted 154 statutes, 33 of which delegated substantial rule-making powers. In 1887, Lord Thring, the then parliamentary counsel, wrote that delegation was 'probably the only mode in which parliamentary government can, as respects its legislative functions, be satisfactorily carried on': Allen (1965) p 35. However, the power of colonial legislatures to delegate legislative power was challenged in three cases between 1878 and 1885. The challenges were based on the argument that the colonial legislatures were delegates of the Imperial Parliament and therefore could not further delegate the powers given to them by that parliament: *delegatus non potest delegare*. In each of the cases, the challenge was rejected: *R v Burah* (1878) 3 App Cas 889; *Hodge v R* (1883) 9 App Cas 117; *Powell v Appollo Candle Co* (1885) 10 App Cas 282.

Implicit in all these cases, which upheld the power of delegation, was the notion that too much delegation would be invalid. In *Hodge v R* (1883) 9 App Cas 117, the Privy Council emphasised that the Ontario legislature had retained its powers and could abolish the delegate or withdraw its authority. In *R v Burah* (1878) 3 App Cas 889, the Privy Council declared that the legislature could not confer broad legislative power on a new legislative body.

[6.4.53]   The Manitoba legislature enacted the Initiative and Referendum Act in 1917. The Act provided that a proposed law could be submitted to the legislature, if supported by a petition signed by eight per cent of the voters. Unless the proposed law were enacted by the legislature, it was to be submitted to a referendum of all the voters in the Province. Once approved at such a referendum, the proposed law was to take effect as though it was an Act of the Provincial legislature. The Act also provided that five per cent of the voters could petition for the repeal of any Act of the legislature, or of any law enacted by the new procedure; if the legislature did not act on this petition, the proposal could be 'enacted' through a referendum. The Lieutenant-Governor-in-Council of Manitoba referred the question of the Act's validity to the Manitoba Supreme Court which decided that the Act was invalid.

On appeal, the Judicial Committee of the Privy Council confirmed that decision: *Re Initiative and Referendum Act* [1919] AC 935. It pointed out that the legislative power of the Canadian Provinces was defined in s 92 of the British North America Act 1867 (UK) as power to legislate with respect to specified topics. The only relevant topic was 'the amendment from time to time ... of the Constitution of the Province, excepting as regards the office of the Lieutenant-Governor'. Under the Provincial Constitution, the Privy Council said, the Lieutenant-Governor was part of the legislature. However, the Initiative and Referendum Act rendered the Lieutenant-Governor powerless to prevent a proposed law from becoming an actual law if approved by a majority of the voters. Thus, the Lieutenant-Governor was 'wholly excluded from the new legislative authority' and, accordingly, the Initiative and Referendum Act was beyond the power of the Manitoba legislature.

The Privy Council then referred to an argument that the Initiative and Referendum Act might also be invalid because it involved an abdication of legislative power. The Privy Council declined to deal finally with this argument, though it said at 945:

> Section 92 of the Act of 1867 entrusts the legislative power in a province to its legislature and to that legislature only. No doubt a body, with a power of legislation on the subjects entrusted to it so ample as that enjoyed by a provincial legislature in Canada, could, while preserving its own capacity intact, seek the assistance of subordinate agencies, as had been done when in *Hodge v R* (1883) 9 App Cas 117, the legislature of Ontario was held entitled to entrust to a board of commissioners authority to enact regulations relating to taverns; but it does not follow that it can create and endow with its own capacity a new legislative power not created by the Act to which it owes its own existence. Their Lordships do no more than draw attention to the gravity of the constitutional questions which thus arise.

[6.4.54] The application of the general proposition that a legislature is free to delegate law-making functions to an executive agency to the Australian states was confirmed by the Privy Council in *Cobb & Co Ltd v Kropp* [1967] 1 AC 141. At the same time, the Privy Council preserved the possibility, alluded to in *Re Initiative and Referendum Act* [1919] AC 935, that state legislation might be invalid if it abdicated legislative power.

The issue in *Cobb & Co Ltd v Kropp* concerned the validity of the state Transport Facilities Acts 1946 to 1955 and 1946 to 1959, which authorised the Commissioner for Transport to license services for the carriage of passengers and goods and to determine the amount of the licensing fee to be paid by each licensee. The appellant argued that the Acts were invalid because they set up the commissioner for transport as a new legislative power and abrogated to the Commissioner the Queensland Parliament's power to impose taxation.

On behalf of the Privy Council, Lord Morris noted that the Queensland Parliament was authorised to make laws for the 'peace, welfare and good government' of the state of Queensland, a phrase that was 'habitually employed to denote the plenitude of sovereign legislative power, even though that power be confined to certain subjects or within certain reservations': *McCawley v R* [1920] AC 691. Within certain limits, the power was full and plenary. For that reason, the attack on the State Transport Facilities Acts, Lord Morris said, 'wholly fails'. It could not 'rationally be said that there was any abandonment or abdication of power in favour of a newly created legislative authority': [1967] 1 AC at 154.

Lord Morris referred to *R v Burah* (1878) 3 App Cas 889; *Hodge v R* (1883) 9 App Cas 117; and *Powell v Appollo Candle Co* (1885) 10 App Cas 282, and said:

> [N]othing comparable with 'a new legislative power' armed with 'general legislative authority' has been created by the passing by the Queensland legislature of the various Transport Acts. The circumstance that the commissioner was endowed with certain powers of decision and measures of discretion does not in any realistic sense support the contention that the Queensland legislature exceeded its plenary and ample powers.
>
> [T]he Queensland legislature were fully warranted in legislating in the terms of the Transport Acts now being considered. They preserved their own capacity intact and they retained perfect control over the commissioner for transport inasmuch as they could at any time repeal the legislation and withdraw such authority and discretion as

they had vested in him. It cannot be asserted that there was a levying of money by pretence of prerogative without grant of Parliament or without parliamentary warrant.

The legislature were entitled to use any agent or any subordinate agency or any machinery that they considered appropriate for carrying out the objects and purposes that they had in mind and which they designated. They were entitled to use the commissioner for transport as their instrument to fix and recover the licence and permit fees. They were not abrogating their power to levy taxes and were not transferring that power to the commissioner. What they created by the passing of the Transport Acts could not reasonably be described as a new legislative power or separate legislative body armed with general legislative authority: see *R v Burah* 3 App Cas 889. Nor did the Queensland legislature 'create and endow with its own capacity a new legislative power not created by the Act to which it owes its own existence': see *Re The Initiative and Referendum Act* [1919] AC 935 at 945; 35 TLR 630 (PC). In no sense did the Queensland legislature assign or transfer or abrogate their powers or renounce or abdicate their responsibilities. They did not give away or relinquish their taxing powers. All that was done was done under and by reason of their authority. It was by virtue of their will that licence and permit fees became payable ([1967] 1 AC at 155–7).

[6.4.55]   In *Dean v Attorney-General (Qld)* [1971] St R Qd 391, the plaintiff sought a declaration that a state of emergency proclaimed under s 22 of the State Transport Facilities Act 1938 was void. One of the arguments raised was that s 22 was invalid because it provided for the establishment of another legislative body in addition to the Legislative Assembly. Section 22 provided that 'where at any time it appears to the Governor-in-Council that any circumstances exist ... whether by fire, flood, storm, tempest, act of God, or by reason of any other cause or circumstance whatsoever whereby the peace, welfare, order, good government, or the public safety of the State ... is imperilled, the Governor-in-Council may, by Proclamation ... declare that a state of emergency exists'. The same section provided that when any such proclamation of emergency was in force the Governor-in-Council might by Order in Council give such directions and prescribe such matters as he or she should deem necessary or desirable to secure the peace, welfare, order, good government, and/or public safety of the state. The argument was rejected by Stable J, who said at 402:

> [Section 22] is headed 'Emergency powers' and, with the very greatest respect to Parliament I say that it appears to me to have been passed in the realisation that from time to time sudden situations may arise with which a deliberative body is not geared immediately to deal. And it is noted that by s 26 of The State Transport Acts all proclamations and Orders-in-Council, which themselves are only temporary, must be laid before the Legislative Assembly within fourteen days after publication in the Gazette *if Parliament is in session*, and if not, then within fourteen days after the commencement of the next session. Parliament may thereafter pass a resolution disallowing the proclamation and Order-in-Council. Thus Parliament has in effect said to the Governor-in-Council, 'When an emergency within the meaning of s 22 arises you may act. We prescribe the manner in which you may act — by a proclamation of emergency followed by executive action to be set out in an Order-in-Council. Your orders and directions shall be obeyed. But we, the Parliament, require that what you proclaim and order to be laid before us when we are available to consider it, and we may disallow it'. On the face of it this is not the constitution of a second legislative body. It is a provision which realises that in the State situations may arise in the nature of an emergency which require swift and flexible action of an executive rather than of a deliberative character. I would dare say that the categories of emergency, like the categories of negligence, are never closed. Thus I regard s 22 as properly providing a framework within which the Governor-in-Council may act when it appears to him that

a situation within s 22 has arisen or is likely to arise. In my view such considerations as those to which I referred in *Cobb & Co Ltd v Kropp* [1965] Qd R 285 at 292, and which were accepted by the Privy Council in *Cobb & Co Ltd v Kropp* [1967] AC 141 at 157, have application in this case.

[6.4.56] Implicit in the argument and the judgment in *Cobb & Co Ltd v Kropp* [1967] AC 141 **[6.4.52]** was the general proposition: that the abdication by a legislature of its power is constitutionally objectionable. How can we distinguish abdication from delegation? And how can we reconcile such a proposition with *Trethowan's* case (1931) 44 CLR 394 **[5.4.17C]**?

5   The definition of judicial power

[6.5.1]   An enduring consequence of the *Boilermakers'* case has been the need, when drafting Commonwealth legislation, to draw a sharp distinction between judicial and non-judicial functions, so as to ensure that the former are not given to bodies which are not courts, and that the latter are not given to bodies which are courts. The most difficult aspect of this task is distinguishing between judicial and non-judicial power of the Commonwealth. Judicial power is a concept which cannot be defined with precision. Windeyer J expressed this imprecision in *R v Trade Practices Tribunal; Ex parte Tasmanian Breweries Pty Ltd* (1970) 123 CLR 361 **[6.5.12C]** at 394:

> The concept seems to me to defy, perhaps it were better to say transcend, purely abstract conceptual analysis. It inevitably attracts consideration of predominant characteristics and also invites comparison with the historic functions and processes of courts of law.

In attempting to define 'the judicial power of the Commonwealth', so as to distinguish it from other governmental powers, the High Court has isolated a number of characteristics which are taken as indicative, rather than decisive, of the character of a power. None of the characteristics is treated as conclusive by itself. They focus on the process of decision-making, the nature of the decision, the historical functions of courts and on the nature of the tribunal in which the power is vested. (In a marginal case, the power may take its colour from the body in which it is vested.)

[6.5.2]   The classic description of judicial power was offered in *Huddart Parker and Co Pty Ltd v Moorehead* (1909) 8 CLR 330, where the High Court concluded that the power given to the Comptroller-General of Customs under s 15B of the Australian Industries Preservation Act 1906 (Cth) was not judicial. That section authorised the Comptroller-General to require a person to answer questions and produce documents relating to what the Comptroller-General believed was an offence against the Act. Failure to comply with the Comptroller-General's requirement attracted a penalty. The court said that this power was analogous to that of an examining magistrate in deciding whether or not to commit for trial. Neither the magistrate nor the Comptroller-General determined guilt or innocence. Griffith CJ said at 357:

> I am of opinion that the words 'judicial power' as used in s 71 of the Constitution mean the power which every sovereign must of necessity have to decide controversies

between its subjects, or between itself and its subjects, whether the rights relate to life, liberty or property. The exercise of this power does not begin until some tribunal which has power to give a binding and authoritative decision (whether subject to appeal or not) is called upon to take action.

[6.5.3] The identification of governmental functions as judicial or non-judicial is a process which involves considerable uncertainty and ambiguity. In attempting to define 'the judicial power of the Commonwealth', so as to distinguish it from other governmental powers, the High Court has isolated a number of characteristics which are taken as indicative, rather than decisive, of the character of a power. None of the characteristics is treated as conclusive by itself. The characteristics include:

- the width of the discretion conferred on the decision-maker; the wider the discretion, the more likely it is that the function is non-judicial;

- the characteristics of the decision given by the decision-maker; a 'final and conclusive' decision is more likely to be judicial;

- the question whether the decision-maker is creating a new set of legal rights (non-judicial) or is authoritatively identifying and declaring existing rights (judicial);

- the history of the function in question; and

- the nature of the decision-maker's role; if it can be described as independent, as settling a dispute between parties, it is more likely to be described as judicial than if it appears to be partisan, intervening on its own motion to promote a particular policy objective.

The following decisions of the High Court demonstrate the application of these criteria.

Historical considerations

[6.5.4C] **R v Davison**
(1954) 90 CLR 353

The Bankruptcy Act 1924 (Cth) allowed a debtor to petition for the sequestration of her or his estate on the ground of inability to pay her or his debts. Such a petition for voluntary bankruptcy was heard, and an order of sequestration made, by a registrar or deputy registrar in bankruptcy.

Davison was made bankrupt on his own petition. When charged with committing certain offences as a bankrupt, Davison contended that he was not a bankrupt because there was no valid sequestration order. It was argued that the making of a sequestration order was an exercise of judicial power which could not be vested in non-judicial officers of the Bankruptcy Court.

Dixon CJ and McTiernan J: [366] Many attempts have been made to define judicial power, but it has never been found possible to frame a definition that is at once exclusive and exhaustive. In *Labour Relations Board of Saskatchewan v John East Iron Works Ltd*, [(1949) AC 134] Lord Simonds, LC, speaking for their Lordships of the Privy Council says, 'Without attempting to give a comprehensive definition of judicial power, they accept the view that its broad features are accurately stated in that part of the judgment of Griffith CJ in *Huddart, Parker & Co Pty Ltd v Moorehead* (1909) 8 CLR at 357, which was approved by this Board in *Shell Co of Australia Ltd v Federal Commissioner of Taxation* (1931) AC 275. Nor do they doubt, as was pointed out in the latter case, that there are many positive features which are essential to the existence of judicial power, yet by themselves are not conclusive of it, or that any combination of such features will fail to establish [367] a judicial power if, as is a common characteristic of so-called administrative tribunals, the ultimate decision may be determined not merely by the application of legal principles to ascertained facts but by considerations of policy also' (1949) AC at 149. The definition given by Griffith CJ to which Lord Simonds refers is as follows:— 'I am of opinion that the words 'judicial power' as used in s 71 of the Constitution mean the power which every sovereign authority must of necessity have to decide controversies between its subjects, or between itself and its subjects, whether the rights relate to life, liberty or property. The exercise of this power does not begin until some tribunal which has power to give a binding and authoritative decision (whether subject to appeal or not) is called upon to take action' (1909) 8 CLR at 357. Another well known definition is that given by Palles CB in *The Queen v Local Government Board* (1902) 2 IR 349, the learned Chief Baron said: 'I have always thought that to erect a tribunal into a 'Court' or 'jurisdiction', so as to make its determinations judicial, the essential element is that it should have power, by its determination within jurisdiction, to impose liability or affect rights. By this I mean that the liability is imposed, or the right affected by the determination only, and not by the fact determined, and so that the liability will exist, or the right will be affected, although the determination be wrong in law or in fact. It is otherwise of a ministerial power. If the existence of such a power depends upon a contingency, although it may be necessary for the officer to determine whether the contingency has happened, in order to know whether he shall exercise the power, his determination does not bind. The happening of the contingency may be questioned in an action brought to try the legality of the act done under the alleged exercise of the power. But where the determination binds, although it is based on an erroneous view of facts or law, then the *power* authorising it is judicial' (1902) 2 IR at 373.

In the United States some very brief definitions of judicial power have gained currency. For example, it has been described simply as that power vested in courts to enable them to administer justice according to law: Sutherland J, *Adkins v Children's Hospital* 261 US 525 (1923) at 544 [64 Law Ed 785, at 790, 791]. More widely quoted is the statement of Miller J that it is the power of a court to decide and pronounce a judgment and carry it into effect between persons and parties who bring a case before it for decision: see *Muskrat v United States* 219 US 346 (1911) at 356 [55 Law Ed 246 at 250].

It will be seen that the element which Sir Samuel Griffith emphasised is that a controversy should exist between subjects or [368] between the Crown and a subject, that which Palles CB emphasised is the determination of existing rights as distinguished from the creation of new ones, and those elements emphasised by Miller J are adjudication, the submission by parties of the case for adjudication and enforcement of the judgment. It may be said of each of these various elements that it is entirely lacking from many proceedings falling within the jurisdiction of various courts of justice in English law. In the administration of assets or of trusts the Court of Chancery made many orders involving no *lis inter partes*, no adjudication of rights and sometimes self-executing. Orders relating to the maintenance and guardianship of infants, the exercise of a power of sale by way of family arrangement and the consent to the marriage of a ward of court are all conceived as forming part of the exercise of judicial power as understood in the tradition of English law. Recently courts have been called upon to administer enemy property. In England declarations of legitimacy may be made. To wind up companies may involve many orders that have none of the elements upon which these definitions insist. Yet all these things have long fallen to the courts of justice. To grant probate of a will or letters of administration is a judicial function and could not be excluded from the judicial power of a country governed by English law. Again the enforcement of a judgment or judicial decree by the court itself cannot be a necessary attribute of a court exercising judicial power. The power to award execution might not belong to a tribunal, and yet its determinations might clearly amount to an exercise of the judicial power. Indeed it may be said that an order of a court of petty sessions for the payment of money is an example. For warrants for the execution of such an order are granted by a justice of the peace as an independent administrative act. But to say that a thing may be done in the course of the exercise of judicial power is not to say that it may not be done without the exercise of judicial power. The legislature may commit some functions to courts falling within Chapter III although much the same function might be performed administratively. In the judgment of this Court in *Queen*

Victoria Memorial Hospital v Thornton (1953) 87 CLR 144, the observation occurs:— 'Many functions perhaps may be committed to a court which are not themselves exclusively judicial, that is to say which considered independently might belong to an administrator. But that is because they are not independent functions but form incidents in the exercise of strictly judicial powers' (1953) 87 CLR at 151.

[369] It is this double aspect which some acts or functions may bear that makes it so difficult to define the judicial power. The appointment of a new trustee may be regarded as something to be done in the course of the judicial administration of trusts or assets. But there is no reason why it should not be treated from another point of view and regarded as an act to be done by an administrative body authorised to exercise some governmental control, for example over public charities. An extreme example of a function that may be given to courts as an incident of judicial power or dealt with directly as an exercise of legislative power is that of making procedural rules of court. The proper attribution of this power is a matter that has received much attention in the United States: cf *Wayman v Southard* (1825) 10 Wheat 1 [6 Law Ed 253]; *Bank of United States v Halstead* (1825) 10 Wheat 51 [6 Law Ed 264]; *United States v Union Pacific Railroad Co* 98 US 569 (1878) at 604 [25 Law Ed 143 at 151]; *Ex parte City Bank* (1845) 3 Howard 291 at 317 [11 Law Ed 603 at 614]; *Livingston v Story* (1835) 9 Peters 632 at 655 [9 Law Ed 255 at 263]; *Fidelity & Deposit Co of Maryland v United States* 187 US 315 (1902) [47 Law Ed 194], and *The Rule Making Power*, 12 American Bar Ass 599, by Dean Pound, whose thesis is that historically and even analytically it is the function of the courts to regulate their procedure. The learned writer places more reliance in all matters of judicial power upon history than upon juristic analysis: 'In doubtful cases, however, we employ a historical criterion. We ask whether, at the time our constitutions were adopted, the power in question was exercised by the Crown, by Parliament, or by the judges. Unless analysis compels us to say in a given case that there is a historical anomaly, we are guided chiefly by the historical criterion'. Nevertheless it is clear enough that making rules of procedure may in one point of view be regarded as a legislative function, though in another point of view it may be considered as an incident of judicial power. The truth is that the ascertainment of existing rights by the judicial determination of issues of fact or law falls exclusively within judicial power so that the Parliament cannot confide the function to any person or body but a court constituted under ss 71 and 72 of the Constitution and this may be true also of some duties or powers hitherto invariably discharged by courts under our system of jurisprudence but not exactly of the foregoing description. But there are many functions or duties that are not necessarily of a judicial character but may be performed judicially, whether because they are incidental [370] to the exercise of judicial power or because they are proper subjects of its exercise. How a particular act or thing of this kind is treated by legislation may determine its character. If the legislature prescribes a judicial process, it may mean that an exercise of the judicial power is indispensable. It is at that point that the character of the proceeding or of the thing to be done becomes all important. Where the difficulty is to distinguish between a legislative and a judicial proceeding, the end accomplished may be decisive. ...

In the present case the thing done is the making of an order characteristic of courts. The primary power to make the very order is entrusted to the court established under ss 71 and 72. The power of the registrar is secondary and in a sense derivative. Further by the definition of the expression 'the Court' the legislature has made it clear that for certain purposes he is to enjoy the very powers conferred upon the court and is to act exactly as the court ... It is clear that s 24(1)(a) of the Bankruptcy Act confers upon the registrar a power which is also exercisable by the court [371] and a power to be exercised by him in the same way and by the same form of instrument as would be used by the judge. He is, in other words, the substitute for the judge. Within the meaning of s 54 he is by definition 'the Court'. By definition also he is the court within the meaning of s 57. It is therefore his function to decide whether good and sufficient cause exists for refusing to make a sequestration order. Although no doubt it is exceptional for difficulties to arise under this heading, they are by no means unknown; see *Re Bachelor* (1855) 25 TL (OS) 248; *Re Betts; Ex parte Official Receiver* (1901) 2 KB 39; *Re Hancock* (1904) 1 KB 585. When s 24(1) is construed with the definition of 'the Court' and applied to ss 54 and 57, it becomes clear that the function of making an order of sequestration is treated as judicial and is confided to the registrar in the same character as it is confided to the court. In other words it is the intention of the legislature that the registrar should make an order operating as an order of the court. That is exactly what in fact he did in the present case. For upon its face the order is one which could not be made except by a court constituted as it is in conformity with s 71 and s 72 of the Constitution.

Dixon CJ and McTiernan J concluded that the Bankruptcy Act invalidly vested judicial power in the registrars, and that the sequestration order in question was void.

Kitto J: [380] It is well to remember that the framers of the Constitution, in distributing the functions of government amongst separate organs, [381] were giving effect to a doctrine which was not a product of abstract reasoning alone, and was not based upon precise definitions of the terms employed. As an assertion of the two propositions that government is in its nature divisible into law-making, executive action and judicial decision, and that it is necessary for the protection of the individual liberty of the citizen that these three functions should be to some extent dispersed rather than concentrated in one set of hands, the doctrine of the separation of powers as developed in political philosophy was based upon observation of the experience of democratic states, and particularly upon observation of the development and working of the system of government which had grown up in England. Even in England, however, there had never been a complete dissociation of the legislature, the executive and the judiciary from one another, and it is safe to say that neither in England nor elsewhere had any precise tests by which the respective functions of the three organs might be distinguished ever come to be generally accepted. The reason, I think, is not far to seek. In an article in *Chambers's Encyclopaedia* (1950 ed), vol XI, pp 153–55, Mr CH Wilson points out that the separation of powers doctrine is properly speaking a doctrine not so much about the separation of functions as about the separation of functionaries. He refers to the fact that legislation, administration and judicial decision are different stages of the same power or function, namely the making of rules which regulate the behaviour of citizens, in that broadly (though by no means exactly) the legislature makes the laws of most general application and with sovereign authority, the civil departments make laws of more concrete application and with a limited and derived authority, and the courts make laws of the most concrete kind of all, namely judicial rulings binding upon specific persons, within an authority still more strictly circumscribed. Then he goes on to say: 'If, then, the agents of this process are, in most forms of constitutional government, divided into three main classes the division must be, not a fundamental functional one, but one for either technical or precautionary purposes. For it still remains true firstly, that different skills and professional habits are needed at the different levels of law-making, and, secondly, that concern for individual liberty will always see one of its chief safeguards in the precautionary dispersal of law-making power.'

It may accordingly be said that when the Constitution of the Commonwealth prescribes as a safeguard of individual liberty a distribution of the functions of government amongst separate bodies, and does so by requiring a distinction to be maintained [382] between powers described as legislative, executive and judicial, it is using terms which refer, not to fundamental functional differences between powers, but to distinctions generally accepted at the time when the Constitution was framed between classes of powers requiring different 'skills and professional habits' in the authorities entrusted with their exercise.

For this reason it seems to me that where the Parliament makes a general law which needs specified action to be taken to bring about its application in particular cases, and the question arises whether the Constitution requires that the power to take that action shall be committed to the judiciary to the exclusion of the executive, or to the executive to the exclusion of the judiciary, the answer may often be found by considering how similar or comparable powers were in fact treated in this country at the time when the Constitution was prepared. Where the action to be taken is of a kind which had come by 1900 to be so consistently regarded as peculiarly appropriate for judicial performance that it then occupied an acknowledged place in the structure of the judicial system, the conclusion, it seems to me, is inevitable that the power to take that action is within the concept of judicial power as the framers of the Constitution must be taken to have understood it.

The subject of bankruptcy provides an illustration in point. As a matter of practical necessity, it is by means of a general law that the legislature provides for the acquisition of the status of bankruptcy and for the consequences of its acquisition. While it may be considered that in that status and those consequences, considered by themselves, there is nothing which imperatively requires a judicial act for the inception of the status, it is certain that in 1900, both in England and in the Australian Colonies, it was and had long been an established branch of judicial activity to subject debtors to the operation of the bankruptcy law, by the particular method of making sequestration orders upon the hearing of petitions presented to a court either by creditors or by debtors themselves. An essentially judicial procedure, a curial proceeding initiated by petition, had been prescribed from early times, and had always been dealt with in accordance with the basic principles by which courts of justice governed themselves in disposing of judicial business. ...

[383] [E]ven though in many cases there might be no controversy to be resolved, a decision to make a man bankrupt affects the relative positions of persons whose interests are opposed, and ... between those opposing interests there is as much reason for insisting upon an impartial adjudication according to law as there is in the case of litigation inter partes. If bankruptcy is decreed, the debtor gains the advantage of relief from most kinds of liabilities to his creditors, but he loses his property (with a few exceptions), and becomes subject to a number of disabilities and duties and liable to certain punitive proceedings. The unsecured creditors, on the other hand, gain the advantage of having the debtor's property fairly divided amongst them, including property of other persons which is to be treated as his for a variety of reasons, and they have the benefit of special methods of discovering what and where that property is and of securing its realisation; but each, broadly speaking, loses his antecedent rights against the person and property of the debtor.

[384] All this is true of voluntary sequestrations no less than of compulsory, and although issues seldom arise for decision on the hearing of debtors' petitions, questions calling for judicial solution can arise in an acute form ...

These considerations lead me to conclude that, while it may well not be correct to say of a power to bring into operation with respect to a debtor statutory provisions such as are contained in the Bankruptcy Act 1924–1950 (Cth) that it is necessarily judicial in character simply because it has that result, yet it is certainly true that the grant to a court of a power to produce that result by the particular process of receiving a debtor's petition for the sequestration of his estate, hearing the petition in conformity with the settled principles governing judicial proceedings, and granting the prayer of the petition by making a sequestration order, is a grant of judicial power within the meaning of s 71 of the Constitution.

Fullagar and Taylor JJ delivered concurring judgments. Webb J dissented.

~~~

Judicial standards and processes

[6.5.5C]   ## R v Spicer; Ex parte Australian Builders' Labourers Federation
(1957) 100 CLR 277

Following the High Court's decision in the *Boilermakers'* case (1956) 94 CLR 254 **[6.4.12C]**, the Federal Parliament enacted the Conciliation and Arbitration Act 1956, which amended the Conciliation and Arbitration Act 1904 to establish the Commonwealth Conciliation and Arbitration Commission and the Commonwealth Industrial Court. It was intended that the Commission would carry out the functions of conciliating and arbitrating interstate industrial disputes and the court would perform the judicial functions associated with industrial conciliation and arbitration.

Among the powers vested in the court was the power of disallowing a rule of an industrial organisation, conferred by s 140 of the Conciliation and Arbitration Act 1904:

> 140(1) The Court may, upon its own motion or upon application made under this section, disallow any rule of an organization which, in the opinion of the Court —
>
> (a) is contrary to law, or to an order or award;
>
> (b) is tyrannical or oppressive;
>
> (c) prevents or hinders members of the organization from observing the law or the provisions of an order or award; or
>
> (d) imposes unreasonable conditions upon the membership of any member or upon any applicant for membership,
>
> and any rule so disallowed shall be void.
>
> (2) Any member of an organization may apply to the Court for the disallowance of any rule of the organization on any of the grounds specified in the last preceding sub-section.
>
> (3) The Court may, in its discretion, instead of disallowing that rule, direct the organisation concerned to alter the rule within a specified time, so as to bring it into conformity with the requirements of this Act and, if, at the expiration of that time, the rule has not been so altered, the Court may then disallow the rule and the rule shall be void.

In *Consolidated Press Ltd v Australian Journalists' Association* (1947) 73 CLR 549, the High Court had held that an equivalent power, conferred on the Arbitration Court by s 58D of the Conciliation and Arbitration Act 1904, was not a judicial power, so that no appeal could be brought to the High Court, under s 73(ii) of the Constitution, from a decision made under s 58D.

In 1957, an application was made to the Industrial Court for an order under s 140 in relation to certain rules of the Australian Builders' Labourers Federation. The Federation applied to the High Court for an order of prohibition to restrain the Industrial Court from hearing the s 140 application.

After referring to the former s 58D of the Conciliation and Arbitration Act 1904 and the decision in *Consolidated Press Ltd v Australian Journalists' Association* (1947) 73 CLR 549, Dixon CJ continued:

Dixon CJ: [289] Bearing the stamp of this characterisation, without any change in the provisions delimiting and describing the power, the power has been transferred bodily to a court created under ss 71 and 72 of the Constitution and armed with judicial powers. Why this course was taken we cannot know. Perhaps the decision in the case of *Consolidated Press Ltd v Australian Journalists' Association* (1947) 73 CLR 549 escaped notice; and that may be true too of the decision in the *Shipping Board Case* (1925) 36 CLR 442 as to the power to cancel registration. If the characterisation was correct and it remains true of the power after the transfer, then the provision must be invalid. As to the correctness of the characterisation, it is proper to say that a close examination of the provision suggests additional reasons in support of it. In the first place the draftsman of s 140 has not approached his task as if he were giving jurisdiction over a 'matter' in accordance with s 76(ii) of the Constitution. Provided the necessary existence of a 'matter' can be extracted from the nature of the power or authority given or from the terms in which it is given or from the implications, that might not be fatal. The question was discussed in *R v Commonwealth Court of Conciliation and Arbitration; Ex parte Barrett; Barrett v Opitz* (1943) 70 CLR 141 at 164–169 and in *Hooper v Hooper* (1955) 91 CLR 529 at 535–538. But while, if the conditions stated are fulfilled, it is possible that the legislative power given by s 76 and by s 77(i) and (iii) may be validly exercised by an enactment expressed in terms of authorisation or empowering, it is more natural to treat a provision so expressed as an exercise of some other legislative power. In the next place the fact that the court is authorised to act of its own motion tells rather strongly against the view that it is intended to exercise part of the judicial power of the Commonwealth. Again, this is not necessarily decisive: for clearly there may be 'matters' for judicial decision where a court exercising judicial powers must act of its own motion, as for example in the case of certain contempts. But these are special cases. In the third place, you find the word 'may' employed in conferring the power and that is apt enough if it were intended to give a complete discretion based wholly on industrial or administrative considerations. Sub-section (3), though otherwise of little importance in [290] the question, does lead some support to this interpretation of the provision.

In the fourth place, the criteria set by pars (b), (c) and (d) are vague and general and give much more the impression of an attempt to afford some guidance in the exercise of what one may call an industrial discretion than to provide a legal standard governing a judicial decision. Parenthetically, it may be remarked that the meaning is by no means self-evident of the expression 'impose unreasonable conditions upon the membership of any member'.

Having regard to the foregoing considerations it is difficult to see any safe ground upon which we can now proceed to treat the transfer of the power described in s 140 to the new Commonwealth Court as involving an entire change in the meaning and effect of the provision so that the decision in *Consolidated Press Ltd v Australian Journalists' Association* (1947) 73 CLR 549 no longer holds and the provision takes on the character of a grant of portion of the judicial power of the Commonwealth. It is a great deal to spell out of the change in the definition of court. The words 'upon its own motion' are still there. It is hardly possible to treat those words as simply going beyond power and having no other effect and then with the aid of s 15A of the Acts Interpretation Act to disregard them altogether. If this could be done the path might be less impossible. For had it not been for those words it might conceivably have been considered a permissible course to treat the word 'may' as meaning no more than to grant a power or jurisdiction. If that had been possible, then perhaps its exercise would become obligatory upon the new court and not discretionary, once the jurisdiction was invoked and the requisite conditions were satisfied. But even so, an attempt to construe s 140 down so that it could assume the shape of a grant of portion of the judicial power of the Commonwealth would seem somewhat heroic.

Kitto J: [305] Section 140 seems to me an example of a provision which, though it empowers a court to do an act — the disallowing of a rule — which is not insusceptible of a judicial performance, nevertheless is found [306] to mean, on a clear preponderance of considerations, that the function for which it provides is to be performed as an administrative function, with a more elastic technique, and more of an eye to consequences and industrial policy generally, than could properly be expected of a court. The authority given is to act in pursuance of an opinion, formed either spontaneously or upon representations made by a person who may or may not be affected by the rule in question. The kinds of rules which may be disallowed are described as possessing any of several qualities which are indicated in terms so broad as to be more appropriate for conveying general conceptions to a person engaged administratively in performing a function conceived of as part of a system of industrial regulation than for stating, to a body acting judicially, grounds of jurisdiction which it is to interpret and apply with precision. The immediate context provided by ss 132, 133 and 139 strongly suggests a similarity of nature between the power of the registrar under those sections (see especially s 139(4)) and the power given by s 140. Moreover — and this is the most important consideration of all — s 140 belongs to a group of provisions, comprising all those which deal with the registration and regulation of industrial organisations, which as a group are characterised by the purpose of facilitating the prevention and settlement of inter-State industrial disputes by conciliation and arbitration under the Act. It is difficult to think that s 140 intends a consideration of an organisation's rules to be undertaken otherwise than with a view to the improvement of the organisation as an instrument for the representation of employees in everything connected with the maintenance and restoration of industrial harmony. To read the section as creating a jurisdiction to apply fixed standards to particular situations, and to make decrees with a judicial disregard of consequences, would be plainly incongruous with the scheme of the Act and the terms of the section. In particular, it seems to me to be required, as a matter of practical good sense, that in forming an opinion as to whether a rule of an organisation is 'tyrannical' or 'oppressive', or imposes 'unreasonable' conditions upon the membership of a member or upon an applicant for membership, the repository of the power should look to the effect which the existence or non-existence of the rule will be likely to have upon the working of the machinery of conciliation and arbitration under the Act; and this points unmistakably to an intention that the performance of the function provided for by the section is to be approached in a manner incompatible with the restraints peculiar to judicial power.

McTiernan and Taylor JJ delivered concurring judgments; Williams and Webb JJ dissented.

~~~

[6.5.6C] **R v Commonwealth Industrial Court;**
Ex parte Amalgamated Engineering Union
(1960) 103 CLR 368

Following the decision in *R v Spicer; Ex parte Australian Builders' Labourers Federation* (1957) 100 CLR 277 **[6.5.5C]**, the Federal Parliament repealed s 140 and enacted a new s 140:

140(1) A rule of an organization —

(a) shall not be contrary to a provision of this Act, the regulations or an award or otherwise be contrary to law or be such as to cause the rules of an organization to fail to comply with such a provision;

(b) shall not be such as to prevent or hinder the members of the organization from observing the law or the provisions of an award; and

(c) shall not impose upon applicants for membership, or members, of the organization, conditions, obligations or restrictions which, having regard to the objects of this Act and the purposes of the registration of organizations under this Act, are oppressive, unreasonable or unjust.

(2) A member of an organization may apply to the Court for an order declaring that the whole or a part of a rule of the organization contravenes the last preceding sub-section.

(3) Subject to the next succeeding sub-section, the Court has jurisdiction to hear and determine an application under the last preceding sub-section.

(4) An organization in respect of which an application is made under this section shall be given an opportunity of being heard by the Court.

(5) An order under this section may declare that the whole or a part of a rule contravenes sub-section (1) of this section and, where such an order is made, the rule, or that part of the rule, as the case may be, shall be deemed to be void from the date of the order.

An application was made to the Industrial Court for an order declaring that a rule of the Amalgamated Engineering Union contravened s 140(1). The Union applied to the High Court for an order of prohibition, to restrain the Industrial Court from hearing the s 140 application.

Fullagar J: [376] If we look only at sub-ss (1) to (4) inclusive, we must say at once, I think, that it is clear that the new power is entirely different in nature from the old power, that it is a judicial power in the strict sense, and that to exercise it is to exercise the judicial power of the Commonwealth. Under the new section the Court is not authorised to do anything of its own motion. An application may be made to it by a member of an organisation for an order declaring that a rule of the organisation has one or more of the qualities specified in sub-s (1) of the section. When such an application is made, a duty is cast upon the Court to determine, as a mixed question of law and fact, whether the challenged rule does or does not possess one of those qualities. If it answers this question in the negative, it must dismiss the application. If it answers it in the affirmative, it must make the declaration sought. It has no discretion in the matter. The function which it is called upon to perform is to hear and determine a matter in controversy, the issue depending on antecedently existing law and fact. The fundamental difference between the old s 140 and the new s 140 may be expressed by saying that under the old section the Court by its own act — the act of 'disallowance' — nullifies the rule, whereas under the new section it determines judicially whether the [377] rule is antecedently nullified by sub-s (1). And this difference is the difference between a judicial power and a non-judicial power.

Fullagar J noted that s 140(5), by its use of the word 'may', appeared to give a discretion to the court. The Union had argued that, as a consequence, the power conferred by the new s 140 was substantially the same as the former s 140. Fullagar J said that it was unlikely that s 140(5) had been intended radically to change the character of the function conferred by s 140: 'The whole purpose of the new s 140 was to avoid the rock on which the old section had been wrecked': 103 CLR at 378. His Honour continued:

[378] But there are more particular considerations which, as I think, compel the rejection of the argument. It is not possible, in my opinion, to attribute to the word 'may' in sub-s(5) the effect of making discretionary the exercise of the jurisdiction given by sub-s (3). It is true that, unless it has that effect, the first part of sub-s (5) seems merely repetitive. But sub-s (2) has given a right to a defined class of persons, members of an organisation, and the jurisdiction given by sub-s (3) is given to a court for the benefit of that class of persons. In such a case the well established general rule is that words which are merely permissive in form connote a duty, and that, if the conditions of jurisdiction exist, the jurisdiction must be exercised and the appropriate order made. To overcome this very important rule of construction, some much stronger and more direct provision would be required than anything that can be found in sub-s (5).

Again, I do not think it is right to regard the latter part of sub-s (5) as intended to qualify in any way anything that has gone before. It is a mistake, in my opinion, to treat sub-s (5) as limiting by reference to time the effect of a declaratory order. On the contrary its purpose is, I think, to enlarge the effect which, in the absence of sub-s (5), such an order would have. What I conceive to be the general effect of the new s 140 is this. Sub-section (1) forbids an organisation to have any rule which possesses one or more of certain specified characteristics. (Some of the rules prohibited would be unlawful without express enactment.) Rules which fall within the forbidden classes are void. This, as it seems to me, must be so: I cannot accept the view that such rules are treated by the section as valid until they are pronounced invalid. If they contravene sub-s (1), they are invalid and void. The question of the validity of such a rule may arise in a variety of ways before a variety of tribunals, including the Commonwealth Industrial Court itself. If it does so arise, it is for the tribunal before which it arises to determine whether it falls within the forbidden classes, and the decision can affect only the parties to the proceeding. This would be the position, if sub-s (1) stood alone. But sub-s (1) does not stand alone. It is followed by sub-ss (2) and (3), which give to the Commonwealth Industrial Court a special jurisdiction to determine, on the application of a member of an organisation and after hearing the organisation, the question whether a particular rule is among those prohibited and invalidated by sub-s (1). But, in the absence of any further provision, an order declaring that a rule contravenes sub-s (1) would still have binding effect only as between the applicant and the organisation. Then sub-s (5) comes in and gives a wider effect to the order by saying in effect that for all purposes and in all proceedings the rule is to be deemed to be void. But the order is to have that final and conclusive effect only as from the date of its making. It is not to affect anything done in the past, or any decision given by any tribunal in the past. The extension by sub-s (5) of the effect of a declaratory order does not affect the character of the process which leads to the making of the order, or the character of the order. The process is a judicial process and the order is a judicial order.

Kitto J said that s 140 did not provide that contravention of s 140(1) was per se a cause of invalidity.

Kitto J: [380] ... [T]he section considered as a whole appears to me to embody a coherent plan for which the whole function of sub-s (1) is to take an essential preliminary step. The step is to lay down propositions in relation to which the rest of the section is to operate, propositions in the form of prohibitions to be observed by every rule on pain of a liability to invalidation by the operation [381] of sub-s (5) upon the non-observance being judicially declared in proceedings brought for the purpose by a member, rather than to enact absolute prohibitions intended to have a separate and independent invalidating effect ...

Kitto J said that the fact that s 140(1) did not invalidate of its own force a rule offending against provisions established a significant similarity between the power which s 140 gave to the Industrial Court and the power conferred by the former s 140, held invalid in the *Australian Builders' Labourers'* case (1957) 100 CLR 277. His Honour continued:

But there the resemblance ends. The recasting which has resulted in the new provision has been sufficiently radical to remove one [382] major disadvantage under which the former section laboured when it was challenged in the *Australian Builders' Labourers'* Case (1957) 100 CLR 277: it was still in the very form which had led to its being characterised as conferring non-judicial power in the earlier case of *Consolidated Press Limited v Australian Journalists' Association.* [(1947) 73 CLR 549.] The present section is new in form and for the most part new in language, and it must be characterised now for the first time. The principal act which the section empowers the Court to do is differently described and is different in substance. The word 'disallow', which was the word used by the former section, was peculiarly appropriate to the exercise by the Court of a choice as to whether or not a rule should be left in force. Now the Court is given no power to do anything to a rule; its power is to hear an application for an order; to determine a question concerning an existing situation; and, if it determines that question adversely to the rule, to declare what is the situation that it finds. When one turns to the indications relevant to the question whether the section intends the Court to make its decision as a judicial tribunal adjudicating upon a justiciable issue or as an administrative body exercising a supervisory function in the interests of industrial peace, the differences between the two sections are striking. If they are placed side by side the fact becomes obvious that in the drafting of the new section the endeavour has been to eliminate all the features of the old section which were regarded in the *Australian Builders' Labourers'* Case (1957) 100 CLR 277 as indicating an intention to give a power of administrative disallowance. Foremost among these was a provision which made it inevitable that the word 'may' in the grant of power should be treated as merely permissive, so that the duty inherent in true jurisdiction should not attach. It was a provision enabling the Court to act of its own motion. There is no such provision now. A typically judicial procedure is laid down. An application must be made; it must be made by a member, that is to say a person who has an interest to procure the elimination of any legally objectionable provision from the rules of his organisation, whether the provision has a direct disadvantageous impact upon him or not. The Court's function is described as a jurisdiction. The process which it is to follow is described as hearing and determining an application. The organisation must be given an opportunity of being heard. And the process is confined to the ascertainment of a pre-existing state of affairs, the question for decision being only whether a rule is or is not contrary to provisions of the Act or regulations or of the law as found elsewhere, or whether its operation is or is not of [383] one of the described kinds. The order to be made is in terms merely declaratory, and does not purport to effect any change in the legal situation.

In my opinion it should be held, in view of these considerations, that the operation of sub-ss (3), (4) and (5) together is to define a 'jurisdiction' in the sense of s 77 of the Constitution, and that the jurisdiction is with respect to a 'matter' within the meaning of s 76(ii) of the Constitution. The 'matter' consists in a claim of right which the section enables a member to make and to have acceded to, that is to say a claim to a declaratory order under sub-s (5) in respect of any rule which contravenes sub-s (1) and as to which the organisation does not avail itself of any opportunity of alteration which it may be given under sub-s (6). Where the right is established, the Court must give effect to it. There is not the 'complete discretion based wholly on industrial or administrative considerations' [(1957) 100 CLR, at 289] which played so large a part in the bringing down of the old section.

Emphasis has been placed by the prosecutors upon the scope which there is in some of the provisions of sub-s (1) for uncertainty of opinion. It must be conceded that the words 'oppressive', 'unreasonable' and 'unjust', in relation to conditions, obligations or restrictions imposed by a rule upon applicants for membership or upon members, describe attributes which are not demonstrable with mathematical precision, and are to be recognised only by means of moral judgments according to generally acknowledged standards. There is a degree of vagueness about them which, in the context of the former section, assisted the conclusion that the intention was to confer on the Court a general administrative discretion for the amelioration of rules. But the notions which the words convey, more readily to be associated with administrative than with judicial decisions though they be, must be conceded, having regard to the nature of criteria with which courts are familiar in other fields, to be not so indefinite as to be insusceptible of strictly judicial application; and their employment in the present context is not sufficient to show, against the strong indications which there are to the contrary, that the Court is intended to exercise its power under the section otherwise than judicially. It must not be overlooked that the adjudication which the Court is required to make in regard to the indicated standards is to be made having regard to the objects of the Act and the purposes of the registration of organisations under it.

Dixon CJ agreed with the reasons of Kitto J. McTiernan, Taylor and Menzies JJ delivered separate judgments to the same effect as Fullagar J. Windeyer J also held s 140 valid, assuming that it had the effect ascribed to it by Kitto J.

~~~

Notes

[6.5.7]   The National Security (Contracts Adjustment) Regulations, made under the National Security Act 1939 (Cth), authorised a state or territory court to make 'such order as it thinks just varying the terms of [a] contract or agreement', where the court was satisfied, on the application of any person, that circumstances attributable to the war meant that:

> ... the performance or further performance of a contract or agreement to which the person is a party, in accordance with the terms thereof, has become or is likely to become inequitable or unduly onerous ...

In *Peacock v Newtown, Marrickville & General Co-Operative Building Society No 4 Ltd* (1943) 67 CLR 25, the High Court (Latham CJ, Rich, Starke, McTiernan and Williams JJ) held that the power conferred by the Contracts Adjustment Regulations was judicial. Latham CJ noted that the Regulations authorised courts to alter rights and not merely to declare and give effect to existing rights. However, the Chief Justice said at 35, that did not show that the powers conferred by the regulations were non-judicial:

> In some cases the powers are analogous to those exercised by a court when it declares that a contract is discharged by impossibility, breach, or frustration. The circumstances which control the exercise of the powers created by the Regulations are similar in their effect, as between the parties, to facts which affect the discretion of a court of equity when it declines to order specific performance of a contract on the ground that it is unconscientious or oppressive. Contracts may be varied by a court under Money Lenders Acts, Rent Restriction Acts and Moratorium Acts in the States of Australia and in Great Britain. Under these Acts courts exercise their powers in order to prevent performance of contracts becoming inequitable or unduly onerous. An outstanding example of a case where a court exercising judicial power is not limited to the declaration or enforcement of existing rights, but where it makes orders altering the rights of the parties, is to be found in the exercise of jurisdiction in matrimonial causes in relation to nullity of marriage, judicial separation, and divorce. In my opinion the objection that, for the reason stated, the powers conferred upon the courts by reg 4 are not judicial in character cannot be supported.

Latham CJ also rejected an argument that the width of the discretion given to courts under the Regulations was inconsistent with judicial power (at 36):

In the present case the tribunals specified in the Regulations are, it is true, directed to act according to equity, good conscience and the merits of the case. I should regret to be bound to hold that such a direction disqualified a tribunal from being a court. There is, however, no authority which supports such a proposition. Technicalities and legal forms and rules of evidence may be varied indefinitely without depriving a tribunal of a judicial character. If, however, it had been provided in the Regulations that the tribunals were to be exonerated from all rules of law and equity, the case would, I agree, be different. The Regulations, however, do not so provide.

[6.5.8] Section 27 of the Re-establishment and Employment Act 1945 (Cth) conferred on an ex-serviceman a conditional right to preference in employment, unless the employer had reasonable and substantial cause for not engaging the ex-serviceman. In determining as between two or more ex-servicemen who was entitled to preference, the employer was to take account of their comparative qualifications (s 27(4)) and the matters listed in s 27(3):

(a) the length, locality and nature of the service of that person;

(b) the comparative qualifications of that person and of the other applicants for engagement or employment in the position concerned;

(c) the qualifications required for the performance of the duties of the position;

(d) the procedure (if any) provided by law for engaging persons for employment in the position; and

(e) any other relevant matters.

Section 28 provided that any person who claimed to be entitled to preference under s 27 could, if that person had been refused employment, apply to a state court of summary jurisdiction. That court was directed to consider the matters specified in ss 27(3) and 37(4) and make 'such order as it thinks just and reasonable in the circumstances'. Section 28(3) directed the court not to make an order directing an employer to engage a person if the court was satisfied that the person would be unable, or was unfit, to perform the duties of the position, or had, since discharge from the armed services, been convicted of an offence of such a nature that the person was unsuitable for engagement in the employment.

In *Queen Victoria Hospital v Thornton* (1953) 87 CLR 144, the High Court held that s 28 conferred non-judicial power on a state court and was invalid. In a single judgment, the court (Dixon CJ, McTiernan, Williams, Webb, Fullagar, Kitto and Taylor JJ) said at 151:

> In relation to s 27(4) a court of summary jurisdiction constituted by a magistrate has a discretion which is complete except that he is to be under a duty to consider the matters referred to in sub-s (3)(a) to (e). So long as the court takes them into account it may do as it thinks fit in making the appointment. No antecedent rights exist in any of the persons concerned which the court of summary jurisdiction is called upon to ascertain, examine or enforce. There is no issue of fact submitted to it for decision. Its function appears to be entirely administrative and to differ in no respect from the function of the employer himself in considering applications for employment which are affected by s 27(4). Many functions perhaps may be committed to a court which are not themselves exclusively judicial, that is to say which considered independently might belong to an administrator. But that is because they are not independent functions but form incidents in the exercise of strictly judicial powers. Here there is nothing but an authority which clearly is administrative.

[6.5.9] Where a provision is challenged as conferring a degree of discretion that is incompatible with judicial power, the question is whether the provision confers an uncontrolled discretion such that it is not capable of strictly judicial application: *R v Commonwealth Industrial Court; Ex parte Amalgamated Engineering Union, Australian Section* (1960) 103 CLR 368 at 383. As Mason and Murphy JJ remarked in *R v Joske; Ex parte Shop Distributive and Allied Employees' Association*, there 'are countless instances of judicial discretion with no specification of the criteria by reference to which that are to be exercised — nevertheless they have been accepted as involving the exercise of judicial power': (1976) 135 CLR 194 at 215–16. See also *Sue v Hill* (1999) 199 CLR 462 at [45].

Kirby J recently reviewed this area of the law in *Attorney-General (Cth) v Breckler* (1999) 197 CLR 83, concluding that the 'questions of policy' approach is not determinative, but only provides an indicator that the power under review is 'judicial' at [83]–[84]:

> Arguments about provisions for initiating proceedings in a tribunal, the extent to which the tribunal is involved in questions of policy and the manner in which its decisions may be reviewed in a court, can be no more than factors which add weight to a conclusion derived from the application of more critical criteria. This is because particular procedures and functions are frequently found both in courts and in non-court tribunals. A function may be administrative or judicial, depending on the way in which it is to be exercised. Thus courts must frequently apply vague and indeterminate criteria which involve imprecise conclusions, moral judgments, evaluative assessments and discretionary considerations that are nonetheless proper to their functions as courts. In a particular context the familiar criteria of 'just and equitable' may pass muster for an adjudicative tribunal whilst a touchstone of 'contrary to the public interest' may be judged inapt to judicial adjudications and more apt to lawmaking.
>
> The characterisation of a power as judicial cannot therefore depend only on the use of particular verbal formulae. It must also be derived from: (1) a consideration of what the tribunal in question is authorised to do; (2) whether its functions purport to deprive those affected of access to the courts for the resolution of connected legal controversies; and (3) to what extent the tribunal's decisions, once made, are directly enforceable, as the orders of courts typically are.

Administrative decision-making

[6.5.10] In *British Imperial Oil Co Ltd v Federal Cmr of Taxation* (1925) 35 CLR 422, the High Court held that ss 44, 50 and 51 of the Income Tax Assessment Act 1922 (Cth) conferred judicial power on a Taxation Board of Appeal and were thus invalid. The Boards of Appeal were administrative bodies, whose members were appointed for renewable terms of seven years: s 41(4). Under s 50(4), a taxpayer who objected to an assessment by the Commissioner of Taxation could ask the Commissioner to forward the taxpayer's objection to the High Court or a state Supreme Court (where the objection raised questions of law only) or to one of those courts or a Board of Appeal (where the objection raised questions of fact).

Section 51(1) authorised the Board of Appeal hearing the taxpayer's appeal to make such order as it thought fit, including an order increasing or reducing the assessment. Section 51(2) provided that an order of a Board of Appeal on a question of fact was final and conclusive on all parties; s 51(6) directed a Board, if requested by a party, to state a case for the opinion of the High Court on a question of law arising in the appeal; and s 51(8) provided that an appeal lay to the High Court from any order made under s 51(1), except a decision of a Board on a question of fact.

780409319460

page 529 of 12322

Knox CJ expressed his conclusions on the validity of ss 44, 50 and 51 as follows, at 432:

> The power conferred on the Board of determining questions of law, the association of the Board as a tribunal of appeal with the High Court and the Supreme Court of a State, and the provision for an appeal to the High Court in its appellate jurisdiction from any order of the Board, except a decision on a question of facts ... establish that the expressed intention of Parliament was to confer on the Board portion of the judicial power of the Commonwealth, which at any rate includes the power to adjudicate between adverse parties as to legal claims rights and obligations, and to order right to be done in the matter.

[6.5.11] Following the decision in the *British Imperial Oil* case (1925) 35 CLR 422 **[6.5.9]**, the Federal Parliament amended the Income Tax Assessment Act 1922. A new s 41 established Boards of Review, whose members had the same tenure as the former Boards of Appeal. Section 44(1) authorised a Board of Review to review decisions of the Commissioner of Taxation and, for the purpose of those reviews, to exercise all the powers and functions of the Commissioner. Where a Board carried out such a review, its decision was to be deemed a decision of the Commissioner. Section 51(1) obliged the Commissioner to refer a taxpayer's objection to the Commissioner's assessment of tax to a Board of Review. On review, the Board was directed to confirm, reduce, increase or vary the assessment: s 51(4). Section 51(6) provided that either the taxpayer or the Commissioner could appeal to the High Court from a decision of a Board which involved a question of law. Section 51A provided that, if a taxpayer requested that the taxpayer's objection to an assessment be referred to the High Court or a state Supreme Court, the Commissioner should do so. The court could then hear the appeal and make such order as it thought fit: s 51A(5). Apart from an appeal to the High Court under s 51A(10), an order of the court under s 51A was declared to be 'final and conclusive on all parties': s 51A(6).

In *Shell Co of Australia Ltd v Federal Cmr of Taxation* (1930) 44 CLR 530, the Privy Council held that the new provisions did not confer judicial power on the Boards of Review and were valid. The Privy Council referred with approval to the judgment of Isaacs J in the High Court, from which the present appeal was brought: *British Imperial Oil Co Ltd v Federal Commissioner of Taxation (No 2)* (1926) 38 CLR 153. Isaacs J had referred to a number of significant differences between the new Boards of Review and the old Boards of Appeal, including the change in name and the assimilation of the powers and functions of the Boards of Review to those of the Commissioner, not of the courts (as had been the case with the Boards of Appeal).

The Privy Council then quoted Griffith CJ's definition of 'judicial power' in *Huddart Parker & Co Pty Ltd v Moorehead* (1909) 8 CLR 330 at 357 **[6.5.2]**, and continued:

> This definition of 'judicial power' suggests to their Lordships a further material difference in the status of the two Boards not alluded to by Isaacs J. It will have been noticed that under the new sec 51A the orders which the Court, under sub-sec 5, may make are by sub-sec 6 made final and conclusive on all parties except as provided by the section; and that by sub-sec 10 it is provided that the Commissioners or a taxpayer may appeal to the High Court in its appellate jurisdiction from any order made by the Court under sub-sec 5. But under the new sec 51, dealing with the orders of the Board of Review, there is no provision in any way corresponding to these sub-secs 6 and 10 of sec 51A. The orders of the Board of Review are not there stated to be conclusive for any purpose whatsoever. On the other hand, under sec 51(2) of the Act of 1922, the

orders of the Board of Appeal on questions of fact were expressly declared to be final and conclusive on all parties. The distinction is, their Lordships think, both striking and suggestive. The decisions of the Board of Review are under the amending Act made the equivalent of the decision of the Commissioner. No assessment of his, even when paid, is conclusive upon him. He retains under sec 37 the fullest power of subsequent alteration or addition, and it would appear that that power remains with him notwithstanding any decision in respect of the same assessment by the Board of Review. It is only the decision of the Court which, in respect of an assessment, is now made final and conclusive on all parties — a convincing distinction, as it seems to their Lordships, between a 'decision' of the Board and a 'decision' of the Court. The authorities are clear to show that there are tribunals with many of the trappings of a Court which, nevertheless, are not Courts in the strict sense of exercising judicial power. It is conceded in the present case that the Commissioner himself exercised no judicial power. The exercise of such power in connection with an assessment commenced, it was said, with the Board of Review, which was in truth a Court. In that connection it may be useful to enumerate some negative propositions on this subject: (1) A tribunal is not necessarily a Court in this strict sense because it gives a final decision; (2) nor because it hears witnesses on oath; (3) nor because two or more contending parties appear before it between whom it has to decide; (4) nor because it gives decisions which affect the rights of subjects; (5) nor because there is an appeal to a Court; (6) nor because it is a body to which a matter is referred by another body. (See *R v Electricity Commissioners* [1924] 1 KB 171.)

Their Lordships are of opinion that it is not impossible under the Australian Constitution for Parliament to provide that the fixing of assessments shall rest with an administrative officer, subject to review, if the taxpayer prefers, either by another administrative body, or by a Court strictly so called, or, to put it more briefly to say to the taxpayer 'If you want to have the assessment reviewed judicially, go to the Court; if you want to have it reviewed by businessmen, go to the Board of Review' ...

The Board of Review appears to be in the nature of administrative machinery to which the taxpayer can resort at his option in order to have his contentions reconsidered. An administrative tribunal may act judicially, but still remain an administrative tribunal as distinguished from a Court, strictly so-called. Mere externals do not make a direction to an administrative officer by an ad hoc tribunal an exercise by a Court of judicial power. Their Lordships find themselves in agreement with Isaacs J, where he says [(1926) 38 CLR, at 175]:— 'There are many functions which are either inconsistent with strict judicial action ... or are consistent with either strict judicial or executive action. ... If consistent with either strictly judicial or executive action, the matter must be examined further' [(1926) 38 CLR, at 178]. 'The decisions of the Board of Review may very appropriately be designated ... "administrative awards," but they are by no means of the character of decisions of the Judicature of the Commonwealth.' They agree with him also when he says that unless 'it becomes clear beyond reasonable doubt that the legislation in question transgresses the limits laid down by the organic law of the Constitution, it must be allowed to stand as the true expression of the national will'. [(1926) 38 CLR, at 180.]

In that view they have come to the conclusion that the legislation in this case does not transgress the limits laid down by the Constitution because the Board of Review is not exercising judicial powers, but is merely in the same position as the Commissioner himself; namely, it is another administrative tribunal which is reviewing the determination of the Commissioner, who admittedly is not judicial, but executive (44 CLR at 543–5).

R v Trade Practices Tribunal;
Ex parte Tasmanian Breweries Pty Ltd
(1970) 123 CLR 361

Part II of the Trade Practices Act 1965 established the Trade Practices Tribunal, whose members were appointed for renewable seven-year terms: s 11. (It was common ground in the case that the Tribunal was not a court within Ch III of the Constitution.) Part III of the Act provided for the appointment of a Commissioner of Trade Practices, with the responsibility of administering the Act. Part IV of the Act was headed 'Examinable Agreements and Practices'. An examinable agreement was defined in s 35 as an agreement between parties who carried on business in competition with each other, under which agreement the parties accepted certain restrictions on their businesses. An examinable practice, as defined in s 36, included engaging in monopolisation.

Part VI of the Act was headed 'Examination of Agreements and Practices by the Tribunal'. The Commissioner was authorised, under s 47(1), to apply to the Tribunal where the Commissioner had reason to believe that an agreement was examinable and was of the opinion that the agreement was contrary to the public interest. (A similar application could be made by the Commissioner under s 47(2) of the Act in relation to a practice.) Under s 49 of the Act, if the Tribunal was satisfied that an examinable agreement or practice existed, it was to make a determination to that effect and determine whether, in its opinion, the agreement or practice was contrary to the public interest. Section 50 set out the factors which the Tribunal was to take into account in determining whether an agreement or practice was contrary to the public interest:

> 50(1) In considering whether any restriction, or any practice other than a practice of monopolisation, is contrary to the public interest, the Tribunal shall take as the basis of its consideration the principle that the preservation and encouragement of competition are desirable in the public interest, but shall weigh against the detriment constituted by any proved restriction of, or tendency to restrict, competition any effect of the restriction or practice as regards any of the matters referred to in the next succeeding sub-section if that effect tends to establish that, on balance, the restriction or the practice is not contrary to the public interest.
>
> (2) The matters that are to be taken into account in accordance with the last preceding sub-section are —
>
> (a) the needs and interests of consumers, employees, producers, distributors, importers, exporters, proprietors and investors;
>
> (b) the needs and interests of small businesses;
>
> (c) the promotion of new enterprises;
>
> (d) the need to achieve the full and efficient use and distribution of labour, capital, materials, industrial capacity, industrial know-how and other resources;
>
> (e) the need to achieve the production, provision, treatment and distribution, by efficient and economical means, of goods and services of such quality, quantity and price as will best meet the requirements of domestic and overseas markets; and
>
> (f) the ability of Australian producers and exporters to compete in overseas markets.
>
> (3) In considering the public interest in relation to a practice of monopolisation, the Tribunal shall weigh against any detriment (including detriment constituted by any proved restriction of, or tendency to restrict, competition) that has resulted or can be expected to result, from the practice any effect of the practice as regards any of the matters referred to in paragraphs (a) to (f) of the last preceding sub-section if that effect tends to establish that, on balance, the practice is not contrary to the public interest.

Section 52 authorised the Tribunal to make orders restraining the parties from giving effect to an agreement or practice, and those orders were to have the force of law. Part VII of the Act was headed 'Enforcement of Orders of Tribunal'. Under s 67 of the Act, a person who did not comply with an order of the Tribunal was guilty of contempt of the Tribunal; and, under s 68, such a contempt could be punished by the Industrial Court as if it were a contempt of that court. Section 102 of the Act provided that the validity of a determination of the Tribunal could not be challenged, subject to the jurisdiction of the High Court to issue mandamus, prohibition or certiorari or grant an application.

The Commissioner applied to the Tribunal for a determination in relation to an agreement to which Tasmanian Breweries Pty Ltd was a party. Tasmanian Breweries Pty Ltd applied to the High Court for a writ of prohibition restraining the Tribunal from hearing the Commissioner's application.

Kitto J: [373] [I]t has not been found possible to frame an exhaustive definition of judicial power. But this is not to say that the expression is meaningless. The uncertainties that are met with arise, generally if not always, from the fact that there is a 'borderland in which judicial and administrative functions overlap' (*Labour Relations Board of Saskatchewan v John East Iron Works Ltd* [1949] AC 134 at 148), so that for reasons depending upon general reasoning, analogy or history, some powers which may appropriately be treated as administrative when conferred on an administrative functionary may just as appropriately be seen in a judicial aspect and be validly conferred upon a federal court. The judgments in *Reg v Davison* (1954) 90 CLR 353 provide illustrations of this.

But I do not think that any such difficulty confronts us here. There are no traditional concepts to be applied as there were in *Reg v Davison*, and two considerations, one negative and the other positive, appear to me when taken together to require the conclusion that the powers entrusted to the Tribunal are essentially non-judicial. The powers must, of course, be performed in a judicial manner, that is to say with judicial fairness and detachment, but the same is true of many administrative powers. Close examination of the relevant provisions of the Act shows, I think, that on the one hand no exercise of any of the Tribunal's powers is an adjudication (in the proper sense of the word), and that on [374] the other hand the result achieved by an exercise of any of the powers is a result foreign to the nature of judicial power.

In *Labour Relations Board of Saskatchewan v John East Iron Works Ltd* [1949] AC at 149, Lord Simonds for the Privy Council said:

> It is a truism that the conception of the judicial function is inseparably bound up with the idea of a suit between parties, whether between Crown and subject or between subject and subject.

This is not to say that some powers may not be held to be judicial though no adjudication in a lis inter partes is involved, for there may be sufficient justification for such a conclusion in an analogy with an admittedly judicial function, or in the fact that the power is ancillary to a judicial function, or in some such consideration: see *Reg v Davison* (1954) 90 CLR at 368. But in general the notion is there, even if in the background, of arbitrament upon a question as to whether a right or obligation in law exists. Griffith C J fastened upon it in the passage in his judgment in *Huddart, Parker & Co Pty Ltd v Moorehead* (1909) 8 CLR 330 at 357 which the Privy Council has repeatedly approved, not as a comprehensive definition but as a statement of the broad features of judicial power: see *Labour Relations Board of Saskatchewan v John East Iron Works Ltd* [1949] AC at 149. It will be remembered that to him the central idea was 'the power which every sovereign authority must of necessity have to decide controversies between its subjects, or between itself and its subjects, whether the rights relate to life, liberty or property'. See also the statements of Palles CB and Holmes J cited in *Reg v Davison* (1954) 90 CLR at 367, 370. Thus a judicial power involves, as a general rule, a decision settling for the future, as between defined persons or classes of persons, a question as to the existence of a right or obligation, so that an exercise of the power creates a new charter by reference to which that question is in future to be decided as between those persons or classes of persons. In other words, the process to be followed must generally be an inquiry concerning the law as it is and the facts as they are, followed by an application of the law as determined to the facts as determined; and the end to be reached must be an act which, so long as it stands, entitles and obliges the persons between whom it intervenes, to observance of the rights and obligations that the application of law to facts has shown to exist. It is right, I think, to conclude from the cases on the subject that a power which does not involve such a process [375] and lead to such an end needs to possess some special compelling feature if its inclusion in the category of judicial power is to be justified.

The powers of the Tribunal do not present any such feature, and they are not directed to any determination or order which resolves an actual or potential controversy as to existing rights or obligations. The Commissioner alone is authorised to institute proceedings before the Tribunal. He is of course a party to the proceedings (see eg s 71), but he does not come before the Tribunal asserting a right to relief in either a personal or a representative capacity. He makes allegations of fact relevant to the questions the Tribunal is required by the Act to consider, and the Tribunal, if it is satisfied that the agreement or practice is examinable, has then to form and give expression to its own opinion as to whether the relevant restriction or practice is 'contrary to the public interest'. Even where the Commissioner makes submissions on these questions in order to assist the Tribunal, he is not seeking the vindication of any right or obligation. In particular, if he submits that a particular restriction or practice is or is not contrary to the public interest he is not thereby contending that a decision should be made for or against the existence of any right or obligation so as to be binding as between the parties to the restriction or practice, or as between them and either the Crown or the public. The inquiry is not into the validity of the agreement or the legality of the practice, as s 51 shows most clearly. Even in relation to an agreement, the question is not whether it is contrary to public policy in the sense in which the term is used in the common law: cf *In re Chemists' Federation Agreement (No 2)* [1958] 1 WIR 1192 at 1212. The determination does not resolve any question as between opposed interests. It merely records whether the Tribunal has satisfied itself, first, that an agreement or practice has the characteristics which the Act comprehends in the word 'examinable', and, secondly, that the restriction or practice, if examinable, is contrary to the public interest. Such determinations as these have quite often to be made in the exercise of administrative power. The fact that an official is given a power conditionally upon being satisfied of a particular state of facts — and so is authorised to determine unexaminably 'the jurisdictional fact' upon which his power depends (if the expression be thought appropriate) — is no indication that in deciding whether he is so satisfied he is exercising judicial power. In the well-known judgment of Palles CB in *R v Local Government Board for Ireland* [1902] 2 IR 349 there is a passage which has been [376] repeatedly cited in this Court and has been relied upon in the present case as tending against this view. The learned Chief Baron observed that if the existence of a ministerial power depends upon a contingency, although it may be necessary for the officer to determine whether the contingency has happened, in order to know whether he shall exercise the power, his determination does not bind, for as his Lordship went on to say:

> The happening of the contingency may be questioned in an action brought to try the legality of the act done under the alleged exercise of the power. But where the determination binds, although it is based on an erroneous view of the facts or law, then the *power* authorising it is judicial. [[1902] 2 IR at 374.]

The reference is to a power which depends upon the happening of a contingency. We are here concerned with a power which depends upon nothing but the Tribunal's own satisfaction that certain conditions exist. The determination of the Tribunal that it is so satisfied — the making of its 'findings' (as s 49 calls them) — does not bind in the sense in which Palles CB used the expression; that is to say, it does not conclude for all purposes any question as to which the Tribunal declares itself satisfied. It answers only the question whether the Tribunal is in fact so satisfied — and does not answer even that question conclusively, for if the Tribunal were to record that it was so satisfied when in fact it was not, the next step, which the Tribunal is authorised to take only if it is so satisfied, could be set aside by this Court in exercise of the jurisdictions which s 102(2) acknowledges.

A determination that an agreement or a practice is examinable therefore has, in my opinion, no point of contact with the concept of judicial action unless it derives it from the nature of the power to which it is preliminary. But the power which the Tribunal may exercise if satisfied on the preliminary point is to determine 'in accordance with its opinion', a question that is essentially non-justiciable. I so describe it for the reason that it does not depend upon the application of any ascertainable criterion. The Act requires the Tribunal in considering the question of the public interest to make a basic assumption and to take certain matters into consideration (s 50), but the question upon which it has to pronounce is not as to whether the relevant restriction or practice satisfies an ascertained standard but as to whether it satisfies a description the content of which has no fixity — a description which refers the Tribunal ultimately to its own idiosyncratic conceptions and modes of thought. In words which I take from the joint [377] judgment in *Reg v Spicer; Ex parte Waterside Workers' Federation of Australia* (1957) 100 CLR 312 at 317, it may be said here that there is no 'claim of right depending on the ascertainment of facts and the application to the facts of some legal criterion provided by the legislature'. The judgment proceeded:

> The existence of some judicial discretion to apply or withhold the appointed legal remedy is not necessarily inconsistent with the determination of such a matter in the exercise of the judicial power of the Commonwealth. But it is perhaps necessary to add that the discretion must not be of an arbitrary kind and must be governed or bounded by some ascertainable tests or standards. [(1957) 100 CLR 312 at 317.]

Similarly, to confer a power of discretionary judgment as to whether a restriction or practice has a specified quality may be to confer judicial power, but only if the quality is so described that its existence is to be judged by applying an objective test or standard supplied by the legislature. When the Tribunal, in conformity with s 49(1)(b), 'determines, in accordance with its opinion, whether the relevant restrictions to which the proceedings relate are contrary to the public interest' it necessarily supplies for itself its own subjective criterion for deciding, as a matter of individual opinion, though on the assumption required by s 50(1) and taking into account all the matters specified in the Act, where the public interest appears to it to lie in the circumstances in which the restrictions or practice operate. Thus the work of the Tribunal is work which would be appropriate for the legislature itself to do if it had the time to consider individual cases. It would be obviously impracticable for the Parliament to apply its own ideas as to what is contrary to the public interest, either by passing a special Act for every individual case or by laying down a definition which in every case would be sure to produce a result satisfactory to it. There is probably no practicable alternative to setting up an authority which with some but incomplete guidance from the legislature will apply its own notions concerning the public interest. This course the Trade Practices Act adopts, contenting itself with prescribing the qualifications for membership of the Tribunal, giving a limited measure of guidance, and then relying upon the Executive's choice of members to ensure, so far as assurance is possible, that the notions applied will be such as the Parliament would approve.

None of the powers of the Tribunal, then, involves any adjudication upon a claim of right. This negative consideration, however, [378] does not stand by itself. The effect given by the Act to a determination under s 49 that a restriction or practice is contrary to the public interest is to render unenforceable for the future an agreement under which the restriction is accepted or the practice is provided for (s 51), and to enable the Tribunal to make such orders as it thinks proper for restraining future conduct which falls within certain descriptions (s 52). The determination itself has no operative effect: it constitutes the factum by reference to which the Act operates to alter the law in relation to the particular case. And an order under s 52 (or an interim restraining order under s 54) is in like case. It presents a direct contrast with an injunction granted by a court as a means of enforcing obligations that have been established by adjudication. The order restrains future conduct, not as being in breach of ascertained obligations, but as being in conformity with ascertained obligations or practices — not in order to ensure observance of them but to prevent observance of them, because it is considered that their observance would be against the public interest. The Act, particularly s 52(7), operates upon the order to give its provisions the force of law, and thus to alter the law for the future in relation to the particular case.

For these reasons the powers of the Tribunal seem to me to be of a nature foreign to the concept of judicial power.

McTiernan, Owen, Windeyer and Walsh JJ delivered separate judgments to the same effect. Menzies J dissented.

~~~

[6.5.13C]   **Precision Data Holdings Ltd v Wills**

(1991) 173 CLR 167

Section 171 of the Australian Securities Commission Act 1989 (Cth) established the Corporations and Securities Panel. The Panel was authorised to exercise certain powers under ss 733 and 734 of the Corporations Law 1990. The Corporations Law 1990 was, for the purpose of the present proceedings, a law of the Victorian Parliament. Section 733 authorised the Panel, on an application by the Australian Securities Commission, to declare that an acquisition of shares or conduct was 'unacceptable', where the Panel was satisfied that 'unacceptable circumstances' had occurred in the acquisition of shares and that the public interest made such a declaration desirable.

Section 734 authorised the Panel, where a s 733 declaration had been made, to make a range of orders on the application of the Australian Securities Commission, including orders prohibiting the exercise of rights attached to shares, directing the disposal of shares or cancelling an agreement. If a person contravened those orders, the Federal Court or the relevant state Supreme Court was empowered to make an order for the purpose of securing compliance with the Panel's orders.

In the present case, the Australian Securities Commission applied to the Panel for declarations under s 733, alleging that several companies and individuals had engaged in 'unacceptable conduct' in connection with a reverse takeover of Titan Hills Ltd in May 1991. The Australian Securities Commission included, in its application to the Panel, an application for orders under s 734.

The plaintiffs, who were respondents to the Australian Securities Commission's application to the Panel, began proceedings in the High Court, seeking a declaration that ss 733 and 734 of the Corporations Law were invalid because they vested judicial power in the Panel. It was contended that, because the Panel was established under Commonwealth law, it could not exercise powers which involved the adjudication of disputes about rights and obligations arising from the operation of the law upon past events or conduct, and that ss 733 and 734 purported to give the Panel such powers.

The court disposed of the challenge by deciding that ss 733 and 734 did not confer judicial power on the Panel. (Accordingly, the court did not need to deal with the complex questions raised by the fact that those provisions were contained in Victorian legislation, while the provision authorising the Panel to exercise those powers was contained in a Commonwealth law.)

Mason CJ, Brennan, Deane, Dawson, Toohey, Gaudron and **McHugh JJ:** [188]

Does the Panel exercise judicial power?

It is convenient to consider the plaintiffs' submission that ss 733 and 734 vest the exercise of judicial power in the Panel. Only in the event that this submission is accepted will it be necessary to consider the plaintiffs' second submission, namely, that the Panel, though it is not a federal court constituted as Ch III of the Constitution prescribes, is exercising the judicial power 'of the Commonwealth'. It was submitted that the Panel is empowered to hear and determine a dispute between parties, on the application of the ASC, by making a declaration as to past conduct, involving the making of findings of fact, and by making orders affecting the existing rights of parties. Thus, once the Panel declares under s 733(3) an acquisition of shares to have been an unacceptable acquisition, or conduct engaged in by a person in relation to shares in, or the affairs of, a company to have been unacceptable conduct, the Panel is authorised to make orders affecting such rights. By way of example, the panel may make an order prohibiting the exercise of voting rights or the acquisition or disposal of specified shares, or an interest in those shares, or an order that the exercise of the voting or other rights attached to specified shares be disregarded. In this setting, so the argument runs, the making of a declaration and the consequential orders amount to an authoritative and binding determination which is characteristic of the exercise of judicial power.

True it is that the making of binding declarations of right by way of adjudication of disputes about rights and obligations arising from the operation of the law upon past events or conduct is a classical instance of the exercise of judicial power. [*Re Cram; Ex parte Newcastle Wallsend Coal Co Pty Ltd* (1987) 163 CLR 140 at 148–149.] But the declarations for which s 733 provides are not binding declarations of right in the sense in which that term is used, more particularly in the context of the exercise of judicial power. That is because the adjudication which the Panel under s 733 is called upon to make is not an adjudication of a dispute about rights and obligations arising solely from the operation of the law on past events or conduct.

The acknowledged difficulty, if not impossibility, of framing a definition of judicial power that is at once exclusive and exhaustive arises from the circumstance that many positive features which are [**189**] essential to the exercise of the power are not by themselves conclusive of it. Thus, although the finding of facts and the making of value judgments, even the formation of an opinion as to the legal rights and obligations of parties, are common ingredients in the exercise of judicial power, they may also be elements in the exercise of administrative and legislative power. [*Re Ranger Uranium Mines Pty Ltd; Ex parte Federated Miscellaneous Workers' Union of Australia* (1987) 163 CLR 656 at 665–667; *Re Cram* (1987) 163 CLR at 149.] Again, functions which are ordinary ingredients in the exercise of administrative or legislative power can, in some circumstances, be elements in the exercise of what is truly judicial power.

It follows that functions may be classified as either judicial or administrative according to the way in which they are to be exercised. [*Reg v Hegarty; Ex parte City of Salisbury* (1981) 147 CLR 617 at 628; *Re Ranger Uranium Mines* (1987) 163 CLR at 665.] So, if the ultimate decision may be determined not merely by the application of legal principles to ascertained facts but by considerations of policy also, then the determination does not proceed from an exercise of judicial power. [*Reg v Davison* (1954) 90 CLR 353 at 366–367 per Dixon CJ and McTiernan J, citing the comments of Lord Simonds LC in *Labour Relations Board of Saskatchewan v John East Iron Works Ltd* [1949] AC 134 at 149.] That is not to suggest that considerations of policy do not play a role, sometimes a decisive role, in the shaping of legal principles.

Furthermore, if the object of the adjudication is not to resolve a dispute about the existing rights and obligations of the parties by determining what those rights and obligations are but to determine what legal rights and obligations should be created, then the function stands outside the realm of judicial power. In *Re Ranger Uranium Mines* (1987) 163 CLR at 666 the Court said:

> The power of inquiry and determination is a power which properly takes its legal character from the purpose for which it is undertaken. Thus inquiry into and determination of matters in issue is a judicial function if its object is the ascertainment of legal rights and obligations. But if its object is to ascertain what rights and obligations should exist, it is properly characterised as an arbitral function when performed by a body charged with the resolution of disputes by arbitration.

The Court was then speaking with reference to an arbitral function of the Conciliation and Arbitration Commission but, as the judgment shows, [(1987) 163 CLR, at 665–666; see also *Re Cram* (1987) 163 CLR at 149] the remarks apply with equal force to [**190**] determinations made for administrative, executive or legislative purposes.

When the function to be performed by the Panel under s 733 is examined in the light of the principles stated above, it becomes apparent that the decision to be made by the Panel is not an adjudication of a dispute about *existing* rights and obligations. The Commission alone can institute proceedings before the Panel and invoke an exercise of its authority. In applying for a declaration under s 733, the Commission is not seeking the vindication of any right or obligation; a declaration, when made, does not resolve an actual or potential controversy as to existing rights. Nor does the Panel, in granting or refusing a declaration, make its decision solely by reference to the application of the law to past events or conduct. Although the function entrusted to the Panel is that of making a declaration about past events or conduct, the function is one in which the Panel is bound to take account of the considerations of commercial policy mentioned in s 731 ['[T]he desirability of ensuring that the acquisition of shares in companies takes place in an efficient, competitive and informed market.'] and 'any other matters the Panel considers relevant' in arriving at the conclusion that it is in the public interest to make a declaration, as well as to apply the provisions of ss 732 and 733 to the facts which it finds. Furthermore, the object of the inquiry undertaken by the Panel and of the declaration which it makes under s 733 is to enable the Panel to make one or more of the orders set out in s 734. In other words, the object of the Panel's inquiry and determination is to create a new set of rights and obligations, that is, rights and obligations arising from such orders as the Panel may make in a particular case, being rights and obligations which did not exist antecedently and independently of the making of the orders. It follows from what has already been said that, in creating that new set of rights and obligations, considerations of policy, including commercial policy, as well as factors not specified by the legislature yet deemed relevant by the Panel, on which it may form a subjective judgment, must inevitably play a prominent part. The materiality of these considerations is reflected in the prescription in s 172 of the ASC Act of the qualifications for appointment as a Panel member, namely, that he or she have knowledge or experience in one or more of the fields of business, the administration of companies, the financial markets, law, economics and accounting. There is no necessity that any member has a legal qualification.

In some situations, the fact that the object of the determination is [191] to bring into existence by that determination a new set of rights and obligations is not an answer to the claim that the function is one which entails the exercise of judicial power. The Parliament can, if it chooses, legislate with respect to rights and obligations by vesting jurisdiction in courts to make orders creating those rights or imposing those liabilities. It is an expedient which is sometimes adopted when Parliament decides to confer upon a court or tribunal a discretionary authority to make orders which create rights or impose liabilities. This legislative technique and its consequences in terms of federal jurisdiction were discussed by Dixon J in *R v Commonwealth Court of Conciliation and Arbitration; Ex parte Barrett* (1945) 70 CLR 141 at 165 et seq. Leaving aside problems that might arise because of the subject-matter involved or because of some prescribed procedure not in keeping with the judicial process, where a discretionary authority is conferred upon a court and the discretionary authority is to be exercised according to legal principle or by reference to an objective standard or test prescribed by the legislature and not by reference to policy considerations or other matters not specified by the legislature, it will be possible to conclude that the determination by the court gives effect to rights and obligations for which the statute provides and that the determination constitutes an exercise of judicial power. [*Reg v Trade Practices Tribunal; Ex parte Tasmanian Breweries Pty Ltd* (1970) 123 CLR 361 at 377, per Kitto J.] However, where, as here, the function of making orders creating new rights and obligations is reposed in a tribunal which is not a court and considerations of policy have an important part to play in the determination to be made by the tribunal, there is no acceptable foundation for the contention that the tribunal, in this case the Panel, is entrusted with the exercise of judicial power.

The fact that the Panel is given a power to make orders conditionally upon its having declared the acquisition to have been an unacceptable acquisition or the conduct to have been unacceptable conduct does not indicate that the Panel is exercising judicial power in making the declaration or subsequently in making orders. As the making of a declaration necessarily proceeds in part, at least, from an assessment of considerations of commercial policy, not solely from an application of the law to the facts as found, neither the making of a declaration nor the making of orders is binding in the same sense that a judicial determination would be binding. Both are subject to judicial review. The consequence is that, for much the same reasons as the Trade Practices Tribunal was held not to exercise judicial power in discharging its functions [192] under ss 49, 50 and 52 of the Trade Practices Act 1965 (Cth) (16), the Panel does not exercise judicial power in making or refusing a declaration under s 733 or in making or refusing orders under s 734.

The availability of further judicial review was critical to the character of the decision-making process under challenge.

~~~

6   References

[6.6.1]   *Articles*

Campbell, 'Colonial Legislation and the Laws of England' (1964–7) 2 *Tasmanian Uni LR* 148.

Castles, 'Reception and Status of English Law in Australia' (1963–6) 2 *Adelaide LR* 1.

Castles, 'Limitations on the Autonomy of the Australian States' [1962] *Public Law* 175.

Davis, 'A New Approach to Delegation' (1969) 36 *University of Chicago LR* 713.

Dixon, 'The Statute of Westminster 1931' (1936) 10 *ALJ (Supplement)* 96.

Gilbert, 'Extraterritorial State Laws and the Australia Acts' (1987) 17 *Federal LR* 25.

Goldring, 'The Australia Act 1986' [1986] *Public Law* 192.

Goldsworthy, 'Ownership of the Territorial Sea and Continental Shelf of Australia' (1976) 50 *ALJ* 175.

Moshinsky, 'State Extraterritorial Legislation and the Australia Acts 1986' (1987) *ALJ* 779.

O'Connell, 'The Commonwealth Fisheries Power and *Bonser v La Macchia*' (1970) 3 *Adelaide LR* 501.

O'Connell, 'The Doctrine of Colonial Extra-Territorial Incompetence' (1959) 75 *LQR* 318.

Salmond, 'The Limitations of Colonial Legislative Power' (1917) 33 *LQR* 117.

Sawer, 'The Separation of Powers in Australian Federalism' (1961) 35 *ALJ* 177.

Swinfen, 'The Genesis of the Colonial Laws Validity Act' [1967] *Juridical Rev* 29.

Trindade, 'The Australian States and the Doctrine of Extra-Territorial Legislative Incompetence' (1971) 45 *ALJ* 233.

Willis, 'Delegatus Non Potest Delegare' (1943) *Canadian Bar Rev* 257.

[6.6.2]   *Papers and reports*

Constitutional Commission, *Final Report*, AGPS, Canberra, 1988.

Law Reform Commission (NSW), *Working Paper on Legislative Powers*, 1972.

[6.6.3]   *Texts*

Allen, *Law and Orders*, Clarendon Press, 3rd ed, London, 1965.

Castles, *Introduction to Australian Legal History*, Law Book Co, Sydney, 1971.

de Smith, *Constitutional and Administrative Law*, 4th ed, Penguin, London, 1981.

de Smith and Brazier, *Constitutional and Administrative Law*, 6th ed, Penguin Books, London, 1989.

Hookey, 'Settlement and Sovereignty', in *Aborigines and the Law*, (eds Hanks and Keon-Cohen), George Allen and Unwin, Sydney, 1984.

Howard, *Australian Federal Constitutional Law*, 3rd ed, Law Book Co, Sydney, 1985.

Lane, *Commentary on the Australian Constitution*, Law Book Co, Sydney, 1986.

Locke, *Second Treatise on Civil Government*, 1690 (reprinted, Blackwell, Oxford, 1946).

Lumb, *The Law of the Sea and Australian Off-Shore Areas*, 2nd ed, University of Queensland Press, St Lucia, 1978.

Lumb, *The Constitutions of the Australian States*, 4th ed, University of Queensland Press, St Lucia, 1986.

O'Connell and Riordan, *Opinions on Imperial Constitutional Law*, Law Book Co, Sydney, 1971.

Sawer, *Australian Federalism in the Courts*, Melbourne University Press, Melbourne, 1967.

Sawer, *Australian Federal Politics and Law 1929–49*, Melbourne University Press, Melbourne, 1963.

Zines, *The High Court and the Constitution*, 4th ed, Butterworths, Sydney, 1997 (3rd ed, 1992).

Chapter

7

The Executive

1 The Crown

[7.1.1] Australia is a constitutional monarchy. Our legal and governmental systems are based on that proposition. The Queen or her representative is an integral part of each of the Australian parliaments: see, for example, Commonwealth Constitution s 1 **[4.2.27E]**; Constitution Act 1975 (Vic) s 15 **[4.2.19]**. Statutes of state and the Commonwealth parliaments are described (in their opening words) as having been enacted by the Queen with the advice and consent of the houses of parliament. Justice is administered by the law courts in the name of the Queen. The Queen or her representative is the formal head of the executive governments of the Australian states and the Commonwealth of Australia.

The monarchical character of the Australian system of government is clearly stated in the Commonwealth Constitution. The executive power of the Commonwealth is formally vested in the Queen, although it is exercisable by the Governor-General (Commonwealth Constitution s 61), who is appointed by the Queen: Commonwealth Constitution: s 2. The persons appointed to administer federal departments are 'the Queen's Ministers of State for the Commonwealth' (Commonwealth Constitution s 64) and their salaries are payable out of the Consolidated Revenue Fund to the Queen, as is the salary of the Governor-General: Commonwealth Constitution ss 3, 66. The Commander-in-Chief of the naval and military forces of the Commonwealth is 'the Governor-General as the Queen's representative': Commonwealth Constitution s 68.

In 1999, a constitutional referendum rejected the Constitution Alteration (Establishment of Republic) 1999, which would have altered the Constitution so as to establish the Commonwealth of Australia as a republic with a President chosen by a two-thirds majority of the members of the Commonwealth Parliament.

[7.1.2] In 1988, the Constitutional Commission pointed out that it was proper to regard the Queen as Head of State of the Commonwealth because of the role in government which the Constitution assigns to her:

> She is a constituent part of the Federal Parliament (s 1) and the Governor-General assents to Bills passed by the two Houses of Parliament in her name (s 58). She appoints the Governor-General to be her representative in the Commonwealth and she alone may remove the Governor-General from office (s 2). The executive power of the Commonwealth is formally vested in the Queen, but is declared to be exercisable by the Governor-General (s 61). The persons appointed to administer federal departments are declared to be 'the Queen's Ministers of State for the Commonwealth' (s 64). The salaries payable from the Consolidated Revenue Fund to the Governor-General and the Ministers are formally payable to the Queen (ss 3 and 66) (Constitutional Commission (1988) p 311).

[7.1.3] In 1953, the Federal Parliament emphasised a central aspect of Australia's autonomy by declaring that the Queen should be referred to as the Queen of 'the United Kingdom, Australia and Her other Realms and Territories': Royal Style and Titles Act 1953 (Cth) s 4. The Queen's current title in relation to Australia is 'Queen of Australia and Her other Realms and Territories': Royal Style and Titles Act s 2.

The Queen of Australia is the Head of State of the Commonwealth of Australia and of each of the Australian states and of the Northern Territory. The Queen of Australia is represented, in different polities, by different persons: the Governor-General of the Commonwealth and the Governor of each Australian state. There is no Queen of Queensland or Victoria, notwithstanding the asserted existence of such a monarchy in the old Constitution Act 1867 (Qld) s 4 or in the Constitution Act 1975 (Vic) sch 2. See: Winterton (1992) p 274; Zines (1997) p 314.

[7.1.4] The succession to the Crown, as King or Queen of Australia, is presently determined by the common law and statutory rules which determine succession to the Crown of the United Kingdom of Great Britain and Northern Island. Title to the Crown is hereditary; lineal Protestant descendants of Sophia, Electress of Hanover at the end of the 17th century, alone are eligible: Act of Settlement 1701 (UK) s 1. Although those rules are presently part of the law of Australia, having been received at the time of European settlement, any changes to the law of succession effected by the United Kingdom Parliament cannot take effect in Australia: Australia Act 1986 (Cth) s 1 **[6.2.7E]**; Constitutional Commission (1988) p 81.

The Constitutional Commission proposed, in 1988, that the Federal Parliament has the power to alter the rules of succession to the Crown of Australia: Constitutional Commission (1988) p 81; Zines (1997) pp 314–15. An Australian alteration to the law of succession which departed from the law currently in force in the United Kingdom might be seen as conflicting with Covering Cl 2 of the Commonwealth Constitution, which declares that provisions of the Constitution 'referring to the Queen shall extend to her Majesty's heirs and successors in the sovereignty of the United Kingdom'. However, Zines has argued that the covering clause merely assumes the existence of the law currently in force in Australia relating to succession, rather than prescribing the law on succession: Zines (1997) pp 315–16.

[7.1.5] Although the legal structures appear to vest considerable powers in the Queen, almost all of the Queen's functions in relation to the government of Australia are exercised by her representatives, the Governor-General of the Commonwealth and the Governors of the Australian states. The only power which the Queen retains in relation to the functions of government is the power of appointment of these representatives, see for example: Winterton (1983) p 20; Howard (1985) p 111; Constitutional Commission (1988) pp 311–12.

[7.1.6] The term 'the Crown' is frequently used to refer to the executive governments in Australia, as it is in the United Kingdom. Each of these governments is treated by the law as a legal person, enjoying rights and affected by liabilities under the common law and legislation, capable of suing and being sued and bound by decisions of courts and tribunals. However, these rights, liabilities and susceptibilities are not identical to those of other legal persons, individuals or corporations. The law recognises a number of important distinctions between the legal status of the government and that of subjects.

This legal personality of the executive government is represented by the Crown, by the Queen; that is, the law regards the government as a legal person and that person is the Queen. However, in this context the terms 'the Crown' and 'the Queen' have become depersonalised. The terms refer, not to the Queen in her personal capacity, but to the office of monarch or the institution of the monarchy. When we talk of the Crown in the context of Australian government in the late 20th century, we refer to a complex system of which the formal head is the monarch. We do not refer to a replica of 16th century English government, where real power was vested in and exercised by the monarch personally. Rather, we mean that collection of individuals and institutions (Ministers, public servants, a Cabinet, the Executive Council, a Governor or Governor-General, and statutory agencies) which exercise the executive functions of government.

The law sees these individuals and institutions as agents of the Crown, and a whole range of executive functions as acts of the Crown. Indeed, many important decisions and actions of government are announced and performed as if they were decisions and actions of the Queen. The declaration of war or peace, the signing of international treaties, the appointment of judges and Cabinet Ministers, the summoning or dissolution of parliament and the promulgation of a host of regulations, rules and orders which direct and control many aspects of the community's affairs; all of these are carried out as if they reflected the personal wishes of the Queen. Further, many other vital governmental functions, while not performed in the name of the Queen, are entrusted to Ministers and public servants who act as *servants of the Crown*, not as private individuals when they perform the tasks committed to them.

[7.1.7] There are ways in which this relic of medieval monarchy fails to fit neatly into our contemporary political and governmental system. In particular, how does the idea of the Crown as the personification of the government square with our federal system in which there are many autonomous governments? And how can it be squared with the reality of Australia as a nation, politically independent of (indeed, engaged in international relations with) the United Kingdom? If the one person, the Queen, embodies the legal personality of the governments of all these entities, how can they maintain their autonomy? One should recognise that this rather abstract puzzle has been posed for us by history. The perception of the Crown as the executive government was adopted by Australian law at a time when the Australian colonies were not autonomous, and when the United Kingdom asserted very real control over Australian affairs. The evolution of Australian political independence has simply outstripped most of our legal theories. Some High Court justices have expressed dissatisfaction with the use of the phrase 'the Crown' on the basis that it is no longer consonant with Australia's true constitutional arrangements: see *Commonwealth v Western Australia* (1999) 196 CLR 392 at 410. Nevertheless, the terminology is still used.

The traditional approach has been adjusted at least to the extent of distinguishing one government from another by speaking of 'the Crown in right of the Commonwealth', 'the Crown in right of Victoria' etc, and 'the Crown in right of the United Kingdom'. It is as if there is a series of independent corporations, each representing for legal purposes the personality of an autonomous government, but with each corporation seen as the legal property of one person, namely the Queen. However, this simile is further complicated by the permanent delegation of control over each corporation to an agent or representative (the Governor-General of the Commonwealth of Australia or the Governor of Victoria, for example). The delegation is effected, in the case of the Commonwealth, by ss 2 and 61 of the Constitution (see **[7.2.18E]**); and, in the case of the states, by s 7 of the Australia Act 1986: see **[7.2.3E]**.

[7.1.8] We must, of course, remember that this notion of the Crown as the personification of the government is largely a facade, a relic of medieval reality, retained in this more populist age because it is a convenient facade. The supposed power of the Queen is tempered, indeed controlled, by her principal servants or Ministers who in turn rely for their positions upon the tolerance and support of their political colleagues within and outside of parliament. The formal legal rules, to which the courts, in their sentimental conservatism, have adhered, are very much qualified by conventions which determine how the legal powers are to be exercised. When executive decisions are made or executive actions carried out, whether by the Queen, Governor, by a Minister or a public servant, in reality these decisions or actions are almost always in furtherance of policies promoted by a political party or coalition and implemented by the current Minister, the Crown's principal advisers. The degree of independent initiative which may be retained by the Queen or her representative is a controversial question which we shall explore later: see **[7.4.1]**–**[7.4.26]**.

Facade though it may be, this notion of the Crown as the legal personification of the government is deeply embedded in the law. A significant number of legal powers and immunities are conceded to the government by the courts because those powers and immunities were traditionally associated with the Crown.

2 Governors

The states

[7.2.1] The Australian states had their origins as 19th (or, in the case of New South Wales, late 18th) century British colonies. The original structure of government in those colonies was established by prerogative instruments issued in the name of the Crown and by statutes passed by the United Kingdom Parliament. The principal authority in each colony was its Governor who, for several decades, exercised very wide legislative and executive powers. The office of Governor was established and largely regulated by prerogative instruments: Campbell (1964). That was an inevitable consequence of the Governor's role, which was to act as representative of the Crown (in fact, of the Secretary of State for the colonies) rather than of the United Kingdom Parliament. This representative role soon placed the Governors in a difficult position as political institutions developed in the colonies and attempted to assert control over the Governors.

[7.2.2]   Today the Crown is still 'represented' in each state by a Governor, whose office is created by Letters Patent issued under the authority of the Queen or by state legislation. The Governor exercises a broad range of powers, some vested in the office by the Letters Patent and some (indeed, the bulk) by legislation. These instruments also lay the basis for the system of responsible government.

[7.2.3E]   Australia Act 1986 (Cth)

Powers and functions of Her Majesty and Governors in respect of States

7(1) Her Majesty's representative in each State shall be the Governor.

(2) Subject to subsections (3) and (4) below, all powers and functions of Her Majesty in respect of a State are exercisable only by the Governor of the State.

(3) Subsection (2) above does not apply in relation to the power to appoint, and the power to terminate the appointment of, the Governor of a State.

(4) While Her Majesty is personally present in a State, Her Majesty is not precluded from exercising any of Her powers and functions in respect of the State that are the subject of subsection (2) above.

(5) The advice to Her Majesty in relation to the exercise of the powers and functions of Her Majesty in respect of a State shall be tendered by the Premier of the State. ...

Termination of responsibility of United Kingdom Government in relation to State matters

10 After the commencement of this Act Her Majesty's Government in the United Kingdom shall have no responsibility for the Government of any State.

~~~

[7.2.4E]   Constitution Act 1975 (Vic)

The Governor to be Queen's representative

6 The Governor appointed by Her Majesty shall be Her Majesty's representative in Victoria.

~~~

[7.2.5E]   Letters Patent Relating to the
Office of Governor of Victoria

LETTERS PATENT RELATING TO THE OFFICE OF GOVERNOR OF VICTORIA ISSUED BY HER MAJESTY THE QUEEN ON 14 FEBRUARY 1986

(Operative 3 March 1986)

Elizabeth the Second, by the Grace of God of the United Kingdom of Great Britain and Northern Ireland and of Our other Realms and Territories Queen, Head of the Commonwealth, Defender of the Faith.

To All to Whom these Presents shall come, Greeting!

Whereas by the Australia Act 1986 of the Commonwealth of Australia provision is made in relation to the office of the Governor of the State of Victoria and corresponding provision will also be made in the Act which is expected to result from the Australia Bill at present before Parliament in the United Kingdom (which Acts are hereinafter together referred to as "the Australia Acts"):

And whereas We desire to make new provisions relating to the office of Governor and for persons appointed to administer the government of the State.

Now know Ye that We do hereby declare Our Will and Pleasure, and direct and ordain as follows:

I There shall be a Governor of the State of Victoria.

II The Letters Patent dated the 29th October 1900, as amended by Letters Patent dated the 30th April 1913, relating to the office of Governor of the State of Victoria, and Our Instructions to the Governor dated the 29th October 1900, as amended by Our Instructions dated the 30th April 1913, are revoked.

III There shall be an Executive Council to advise the Governor on the occasions when the Governor is permitted or required by any statute or other instrument to act in Council. The Premier (or in his absence the Acting Premier) shall tender advice to the Governor in relation to the exercise of the other powers and functions of Governor.

IV No person shall act as Governor without first taking before the Chief Justice or another Judge of the Supreme Court the usual Oath or Affirmation of Allegiance and the usual Oath or Affirmation of Office.

V An Administrator shall act as Governor if and so long as there is a vacancy in the office of Governor or the Governor is administering the Government of the Commonwealth or is unable or unwilling to act as Governor or not having commissioned a Deputy Governor is on leave or is out of the State.

VI The Lieutenant-Governor shall be the Administrator but if there is no Lieutenant Governor or if he is unable or unwilling to act as Governor then the Chief Justice shall be the Administrator and if there is no Chief Justice or if he is unable or unwilling to act as Governor then the next most senior Judge of the Supreme Court able and willing to act as Governor shall be the Administrator.

VII A request in writing under the hand of the Premier (or in his absence the Acting Premier) that the person named therein (being one of the persons referred to in Clause VI) shall assume office as Administrator shall be sufficient authority for that person to do so.

VIII The Governor with consent of the Premier (or in his absence the Acting Premier) may commission a Deputy Governor to perform and exercise for not more than two months some or all of the powers and functions of the Governor.

IX The existing Commissions relating to the office of Governor, Lieutenant-Governor and Administrator and all existing appointments to the Executive Council shall continue in force until revoked.

X The Governor in Council by Letters Patent may from time to time make alter or revoke any Letters Patent relating to the office of Governor.

XI These Our Letters Patent shall come into operation at the same time as the Australia Acts come into force.

~~~

[7.2.6E] <h2 style="text-align:center">Constitution Act 1902 (NSW)</h2>

PART 2A — THE GOVERNOR

Appointment of Governor

9A(1) There shall continue to be a Governor of the State.

(2) The appointment of a person to the office of Governor shall be during Her Majesty's pleasure by Commission under Her Majesty's Sign Manual and the Public Seal of the State.

(3) Before assuming office, a person appointed to be Governor shall take the Oath or Affirmation of Allegiance and the Oath or Affirmation of Office in the presence of the Chief Justice or another Judge of the Supreme Court.

Section 9B provides for the appointment of a Lieutenant-Governor and an Administrator of the state. Section 9C deals with the administration of government by the Lieutenant-Governor or Administrator in certain circumstances: a vacancy in the office of Governor; the Governor's acting as Administrator of the Commonwealth; the Governor's absence from the state or the Governor's incapacity. Section 9D deals with the appointment of a deputy for the Governor during a temporary absence or illness. Section 9E provides that an Oath or Affirmation of Allegiance is 'an Oath or Affirmation swearing or affirming to be faithful and bear true allegiance to Her Majesty and her Majesty's heirs and successors according to law'; and an Oath or Affirmation of Office is 'an Oath or Affirmation swearing or affirming well and truly to serve Her Majesty and Her Majesty's heirs and successors in the particular office and to do right to all manner of people after the laws and usages of the state, without fear or favour, affection or ill-will'.

Letters Patent and Instructions cease to have effect

9F The Letters Patent dated 29 October 1900, as amended, relating to the office of Governor of the State and all Instructions to the Governor cease to have effect on the commencement of the Constitution (Amendment) Act 1987.

Section 9G provides for the continuation of existing appointments under the Letters Patent or pursuant to Instructions.

Public Seal of the State

9H(1) The Governor shall provide, keep and use the Public Seal of the State. ...

~~~

Notes

[7.2.7] Letters Patent, in substantially the same terms as those issued for Victoria were also issued for Queensland, South Australia, Tasmania and Western Australia.

[7.2.8] Other state Constitution Acts contain at least a recognition of the status and functions of the Governor:

- Constitution Act 1934 (SA) ss 6, 68, 69, 70, 71;

- Constitution Act 1934 (Tas) ss 6, 8, 10, 12, 38;

- Constitution Act 1889 (WA) ss 3, 12, 50, 51, 68, 73, 74;

- Constitution Act Amendment Act 1899 (WA) ss 3, 43, 45.

The Queensland Constitution Act (1867) is unique. Amendments inserted by the Constitution Act Amendment Act 1976 (Qld) declare the Governor to be 'the Queen's representative in Queensland' (s 11A); that in appointing and dismissing Ministers the Governor 'shall not be subject to direction by any person nor be limited as to his sources of advice' (s 14(2)) and that the office of Governor shall not be abolished or altered without the approval of Queensland electors, voting at a referendum: s 53. In Queensland, matters relating to the appointment, powers and functions of the Governor of Queensland are now located in Part 2 of Ch 3 of the Constitution of Queensland 2001.

[7.2.9] The Letters Patent issued in February 1986, in anticipation of the passage by the United Kingdom Parliament of the Australia Act 1986, recognise the local character of the office of Governor. This is particularly clear in cl X, which gives to the Governor in Council the power to make, revoke or alter Letters Patent relating to the Governor's office. The 1986 Letters Patent replaced earlier instruments, issued on 29 October 1900, cl XV of which had reserved to the Queen the power to revoke or amend the Letters Patent.

That same point is expressed in s 7 of the Australia Act 1986 and s 9A of the Constitution Act 1902 (NSW).

[7.2.10] To appreciate the significance of that point, we need only note that, prior to 1986, the legal forms treated the Governor as the agent of the United Kingdom Government and gave that government control over the choice and appointment of each Governor. For example, the state of Western Australia had no Governor for 14 years after 1933 because the United Kingdom Government would not recommend to the King the appointment of the person (an Australian) proposed by the Western Australian Government. However, a series of appointments of Australians as state Governors from 1946 onwards led one writer to observe in 1960 that 'we may assume ... there is no longer any official British objection to the appointment of Australians as Governors and that the wishes of the State Government are likely to be met by the British Government': Anderson (1960), p 14.

[7.2.11] However, in 1976 the United Kingdom Government refused to advise the Queen to reappoint the then Governor of Queensland, Colin Hannah, whose term was about to expire. Hannah had generated local controversy when he had publicly criticised the Commonwealth Government's economic policies in October 1975. The United Kingdom Government's refusal to advise Hannah's reappointment was clearly linked to that controversy. For the Queensland Government's reaction to this incident, see Qld Hansard, Legislative Assembly, 7 December 1976, p 2170.

[7.2.12] At one time the United Kingdom Government regarded its formal control of the Governors of the Australian states (or colonies) as authorising a direct intervention in local affairs: see Bailey (1933) pp 399–400, 405–6. The last such intervention was in 1916 when Governor Strickland of New South Wales was recalled by the United Kingdom Government because he had failed to act on his Ministers' advice. The Australian Labor Party, then in power in New South Wales, had split over the issue of conscription for armed service. Premier Holman and several other members of the ALP left the Party but stayed in government with the support of the former opposition. Holman then introduced legislation to extend the life of the Legislative Assembly so as to avoid the necessity of a general election in December 1916. When the Governor announced that he would not assent to this legislation, because Holman had originally been commissioned Premier as leader of the ALP, Holman appealed to the United Kingdom Government. The Governor's commission was then revoked by the King, but not before the Governor had assented to the controversial legislation.

[7.2.13] Nine years later, however, the United Kingdom Government refused to intervene in a dispute between New South Wales Premier Lang and Governor de Chair. The Governor had declined to act on Lang's advice to appoint additional members to the Legislative Council (a tactic designed to ensure the passage of legislation to abolish the Council). When the Governor sought instructions from

Colonial Secretary Amery, the latter said that 'established constitutional principles require that the question should be settled between the Governor and the ministry'. The Colonial Secretary repeated this non-interventionist stance when Lang appealed to him.

[7.2.14] The current Letters Patent (those of Tasmania, South Australia, Victoria and Western Australia) confer no substantial powers on the Governor: they are concerned with matters of machinery or process. This is another contrast with the former Letters Patent, which purported to authorise each Governor, for example, to appoint officials, pardon offenders, grant Crown lands and summon and dissolve parliament. The deletion of such conferrals of substantial power from the current Letters Patent reflects the view that the Australian states are, within the constraints of the Commonwealth Constitution's federal system, self-sufficient: that the source of each state's legal or constitutional powers lies in its Constitution Act and in the fact of its political autonomy.

This conception of the autonomy and self-sufficiency of state governments was expressed over 100 years ago in the dissenting judgment of Higinbotham CJ in *Toy v Musgrove* (1888) 14 VLR 349. The Victorian Supreme Court decided that the Governor of Victoria could not exclude an alien from Victoria because the power to do so had not been delegated to the Governor by the Queen, nor conferred by legislation. Higinbotham CJ dissented on the ground that Victoria was self-governing and therefore held all the legal powers necessary for self-government, including the power to exclude aliens (which was conceded to be part of the Queen's prerogative powers in relation to the United Kingdom). In a strongly reasoned dissenting judgment, Higinbotham CJ offered the following conclusion:

> The system of responsible government would be utterly unworkable without the discretionary prerogative powers vested in the Crown, and which are not provided for by any statute ... I would say that all the prerogatives necessary for the safety and protection of the people the administration of the law, and the conduct of public affairs in and for Victoria, under our system of responsible government, have passed as an incident to the grant of self-government (without which the grant itself would be of no effect), and may be exercised by the representative of the Crown, on the advice of responsible ministers (14 VLR at 397).

The drafting of the current Letters Patent appears to endorse Higinbotham's approach to the powers of the states, bearing out Bailey's observation: 'Statesman rather than lawyer, Higinbotham had the future with him': Bailey (1933) p 397. See also Lumb (1991) pp 67–8.

[7.2.15] The primary source for each Governor's powers in relation to the government of the state will be the state's Constitution Act. For example, the Constitution Act 1975 (Vic) confers the following powers on the Governor of Victoria:

- he or she is authorised to fix the time and place for any session of parliament (s 8(1)); may prorogue parliament (s 8(2)(a)); and may dissolve the Assembly (s 8(2)(b));

- he or she may summon parliament 'to meet for the despatch of ... business' (s 20);

- he or she may appoint a maximum of 18 'officers ... who shall be entitled to be elected members of either House of Parliament'. These officers are to be the 'responsible Ministers of the Crown and members of the Executive Council' (s 50(1), (2));

■ the Governor-in-Council may appoint persons to all public offices in Victoria, other than the offices of responsible Ministers, where the power of appointment is vested in the Governor alone (s 83);

■ no bill for the appropriation of government funds can be originated in parliament unless that bill has been recommended by a message from him or her (s 63);

■ judges of the Supreme Court are appointed by him or her with the advice of the Executive Council (s 75(5));

■ judges of the Supreme Court may be removed by him or her upon the address of the Legislative Council and the Legislative Assembly (s 77(1));

■ no part of government funds is to be expended unless he or she authorises that expenditure by a warrant directed to the Treasurer (s 93).

(Note that some of these powers are conferred on the Governor-in-Council or the Governor with the advice of the Executive Council, while other powers are conferred on the Governor alone. The significance of that distinction is discussed in **[7.4.2]**– **[7.4.10]**). According to cl III of the Letters Patent **[7.2.5E]**, the powers to be exercised by the Governor-in-Council are to be controlled by advice from the Executive Council; and the Governor's other powers are subject to advice from the Premier. The significance of these requirements is explored in **[7.4.1]**–**[7.4.26]**.

[7.2.16]   Other legislation confers specific authorities on the Governor. For example, the Electoral Act 2002 (Vic) gives the Governor certain powers directed towards the administration of elections for the Legislative Council and Assembly. The Governor-in-Council may:

■ appoint the Electoral Commissioner (s 12);

■ make arrangements with the Governor-General of the Commonwealth for a joint enrolment process for electors (s 20); and

■ issue writs for the holding of simultaneous elections for the Legislative Council and the Legislative Assembly (s 61(1)).

The Commonwealth

[7.2.17]   The Commonwealth of Australia was formally created by a statute of the United Kingdom Parliament, the Commonwealth of Australia Constitution Act 1900. The bulk of that statute was drafted at a series of conventions during the last decade of the 19th century, attended by representatives of the six Australian colonies and of New Zealand, and, as a proposed federal Constitution, approved by the voters of each of the Australian colonies at referenda in 1897, 1899 and 1900. Most of the members of the federal conventions who drafted and settled (apart from some minor alterations introduced at the stage of enactment) the federal Constitution were men experienced in colonial politics and government. It should not surprise us, therefore, that the Commonwealth Constitution establishes an executive government for the Commonwealth which is patterned on the executive governments of the states and of the United Kingdom.

There was, admittedly, some debate at the 1891 convention on the type of executive best suited to the central government of a federal system. Some delegates (including Griffith, to be the first Chief Justice of the High Court of Australia) argued that responsible government would give the Lower House (the House of Representatives) dominance over the Upper House (the Senate), and that the Senate's power was essential to preserve the balance of federation (each of the states was to have equal representation in the Senate). Some attempts were made to introduce ministries elected by parliament or, at least, sanctioned by the Senate. Those attempts failed: see La Nauze (1972) pp 53, 127, 152.

[7.2.18E]   Commonwealth Constitution

2 A Governor-General appointed by the Queen shall be Her Majesty's representative in the Commonwealth, and shall have and may exercise in the Commonwealth during the Queen's pleasure, but subject to this Constitution, such powers and functions of the Queen as Her Majesty may be pleased to assign to him. ...

61 The executive power of the Commonwealth is vested in the Queen and is exercisable by the Governor-General as the Queen's representative, and extends to the execution and maintenance of this Constitution, and of the laws of the Commonwealth.

~~~

[7.2.19] Letters Patent Relating to the Office of Governor-General were issued by the 'Queen of Australia' on 21 August 1984. They revoked the original Letters Patent, issued on 29 October 1900; and declared:

- that appointment of a person as Governor-General or as Administrator of the Commonwealth 'shall be during Our pleasure by Commission under Our Sign Manual and the Great Seal of Australia' (cll II(a), III(a));

- that a person appointed as Administrator was only to assume the administration of the Government of the Commonwealth at the request of the Governor-General or the Prime Minister (or next most senior Minister) of the Commonwealth (cl III(c)); and

- authorised the Governor-General, by instrument in writing, to appoint any person to be his or her deputy, to exercise such powers and functions of the Governor-General as he or she thinks fit to assign to him or her (cl IV(a)).

[7.2.20] Legal recognition of the Australian character of the office of Governor-General came much earlier than in the case of the state Governors, which were treated as agents of the United Kingdom Government until 1986: see [7.2.9]. The first formal recognition of the autonomy of the Commonwealth executive government, as represented in the office of the Governor-General, was in the Balfour Declaration of 1926, a formal statement issued by a conference of United Kingdom and dominion Prime Ministers. The Declaration asserted:

> Great Britain and the dominions ... are autonomous communities within the British Empire equal in status, in no way insubordinate one to another in any aspect of their domestic or external affairs, though united by a common allegiance to the Crown ...
>
> In our opinion it is an essential consequence of the equality of status existing among the members of the British Commonwealth of Nations that the Governor-General of a dominion is the representative of the Crown, holding in all essential respects the same position in relation to the administration of public affairs in the dominion as is held by His Majesty the King in Great Britain, and that he is not the representative or agent of

His Majesty's government in Great Britain or of any department of that government (Keith (1932) pp 154–5, 161).

[7.2.21] The practice of appointing the Governor-General on the advice of the Queen's Australian Ministers was firmly established in 1930 when the Scullin Labor Government prevailed upon George V to appoint Isaac Isaacs, then the Chief Justice of the High Court, as Governor-General: Encel (1974), pp 27–9. An Imperial conference in that year issued a formal statement declaring that the appointment of a dominion Governor-General was a matter to be settled between the monarch and the dominion government.

[7.2.22] Section 2 of the Commonwealth Constitution refers to the Governor-General having 'such powers and functions ... as Her Majesty may be pleased to assign to him' **[7.2.18E]**. Until the issue of the current Letters Patent **[7.2.19]** in 1984, the principal assignment of functions had been in the original Letters Patent of 1900. These had purported to assign the powers of appointing judges and other public officials, and of summoning, proroguing or dissolving parliament.

Further specific assignments were made in 1954 and 1973. Those specific assignments, to appoint Australian diplomats and to recognise foreign consular and diplomatic representatives in Australia, were revoked by the Queen, on the advice of Prime Minister Hawke, on 1 December 1987. As the Constitutional Commission explained, that revocation and the earlier replacement of the 1900 Letters Patent recognised that the powers assigned were already exercisable under s 61 of the Constitution: Constitutional Commission (1988) p 343.

[7.2.23] Section 61 of the Constitution rests 'the executive power of the Commonwealth' in the Queen and declares that this executive power 'is exercisable by the Governor-General'. The assignments of power in the 1900 Letters Patent and the specific assignments of 1954 and 1973 reflected a view that the 'executive power of the Commonwealth' extended no further than the powers which were expressly created by the Constitution or by Commonwealth legislation; that is, that the 'executive power of the Commonwealth' did not include those powers which had come to be regarded as inherent in the Crown under English law, the royal prerogatives, unless those powers were assigned to the Governor-General under s 2 of the Constitution.

Although that view was expressed by the majority of the High Court (Knox CJ, Gavan Duffy and Higgins JJ; Isaacs and Starke JJ dissenting) in *Commonwealth v Colonial Combing Spinning and Weaving Co Ltd* (1922) 31 CLR 421, contrary views were expressed (or were necessarily implicit) in *R v Burgess; Ex parte Henry* (1936) 55 CLR 608 **[3.3.9]** (Evatt and McTiernan JJ); *Official Liquidator of EO Farley Ltd v Federal Commissioner of Taxation* (1940) 63 CLR 278 **[8.2.43]** at 303 per Dixon J; at 322 per Evatt J; and *Australian Communist Party v Commonwealth* (1951) 83 CLR 1 at 230 per Williams J.

[7.2.24] The trend of judicial views away from the majority view in *Commonwealth v Colonial Combing Spinning and Weaving Co Ltd* (1922) 31 CLR 421 **[7.2.23]** culminated in the High Court's decision in *Barton v Commonwealth* (1974) 131 CLR 477. The plaintiffs sought a declaration from the High Court that a formal request by the Commonwealth Government to the Brazilian Government to detain and extradite the plaintiffs was invalid. The plaintiffs were Australian citizens against whom criminal charges had been laid in New South Wales and for whom arrest warrants were outstanding. The Extradition (Foreign States) Act 1966 (Cth) authorised the Commonwealth Government to request the extradition of persons from countries with which Australia had an extradition treaty. However, as there was no such treaty between Australia and Brazil, the Act did not cover extradition from Brazil to Australia. The plaintiffs argued that there was no prerogative power, independent of statute, in the Commonwealth Government to request extradition.

Mason J traced the history of extradition in the United Kingdom and concluded that, at the end of the 19th century, the Crown had the power to request the extradition of a fugitive offender from a country with which it had no extradition treaty. He then turned to the executive power of the Commonwealth:

> The Constitution established the Commonwealth of Australia as a political entity and brought it into existence as a member of the community of nations. The Constitution conferred upon the Commonwealth power with respect to external affairs and, subject perhaps to the Statute of Westminster 1931 and the Balfour Declaration, entrusted to it the responsibility for the conduct of the relationships between Australia and other members of the community of nations, including the conduct of diplomatic negotiations between Australia and other countries. By s 61 the executive power of the Commonwealth was vested in the Crown. It extends to the execution and maintenance of the Constitution and of the laws of the Commonwealth. It enables the Crown to undertake all executive action which is appropriate to the position of the Commonwealth under the Constitution and to the spheres of responsibility vested in it by the Constitution. It includes the prerogative powers of the Crown, that is, the powers accorded to the Crown by the Common law. ...
>
> I conclude, therefore, that, subject to a consideration of the effect of the Commonwealth Act, the making of a request to a foreign state for the surrender of a fugitive offender alleged to have committed an offence against the laws of Australia is an act which falls within the executive power of the Commonwealth. Likewise, I am of opinion that the making of a request for the detention of a fugitive offender as a preliminary to his extradition to Australia is an act that falls within the executive power of the Commonwealth (131 CLR at 498–9).

Mason J went on to conclude that the Extradition (Foreign States) Act 1966 (Cth) did not destroy this prerogative power. McTiernan and Menzies JJ agreed with Mason J on this point. Barwick CJ and Jacobs J delivered judgments to the same effect.

[7.2.25] *Barton v Commonwealth* (1974) 131 CLR 477 was recently considered in *Oates v Attorney-General (Cth)* (2003) 197 ALR 105. The Attorney-General of the Commonwealth requested that Poland extradite to Australia an Australian citizen, Oates, to face charges under the Companies (Western Australia) Code and Criminal Code of Western Australia. Oates applied to the Federal Court for a declaration that the request was invalid, and an order quashing the request, on the ground that the offences identified in the request were not recognised by the 1932 extradition treaty between Australia and Poland and that the executive's power to request his extradition from Poland was limited to the offences listed in the 1932 treaty.

Gleeson CJ, McHugh, Gummow, Kirby, Hayne and Heydon JJ rejected that argument, and considered and approved the approach taken by Mason J in *Barton v Commonwealth*, observing that a state (such as Australia) 'may invoke comity as well as obligation' and, if another state (such as Poland) chose to accede to a request although not bound to do so, that was a matter for the second state: 197 ALR at 113 [35]. Their Honours accepted that the decision in *Barton's* case was not determinative of the issue before the court, but it did make the result for which Oates contended a surprising one (at 114 [36]):

> It means that, if Australia had no treaty of extradition with Poland, the request under consideration would have been lawful, but, because there is a treaty, then the request would be unlawful if it related to offences not covered by the treaty.

The justices concluded that neither the Extradition (Foreign States) Act 1966 (Cth) considered in *Barton* nor the Extradition Act 1988 (Cth), which replaced the 1966 Act, restricted the executive's power to make a request: 197 ALR at 116 [45].

[7.2.26]　The reference, by Mason J in *Barton v Commonwealth* (1975) 131 CLR 477 **[7.2.24]** at 498 to 'executive action which is appropriate to the position of the Commonwealth under the Constitution and to the spheres of responsibility vested in it by the Constitution', raises a question of some complexity. How are the inherent aspects of the Crown's executive powers (the royal prerogatives) distributed between the Commonwealth and the states?

The federal nature of our Constitution must have some effect on the extent of the executive power of the Commonwealth Government, if only because the Constitution is built on a system of sharing or distributing power. As far as the prerogative powers were concerned, the effect of federalism was explored in some detail by Evatt J in *Federal Commissioner of Taxation v Official Liquidator of EO Farley Ltd* (1940) 63 CLR 278 and previously in his doctoral thesis, *The Royal Prerogative* (1924). He suggested that the executive prerogatives (for example, to declare war or make peace) would be powers under the Commonwealth Constitution; that proprietary prerogatives (for example, the right to excheats, royal metals and treasure trove) would vest in the executive governments of the states; and that prerogative preferences (for example, to be paid in priority to other creditors of an insolvent debtor) and immunities (for example, from court process) would be held by both Commonwealth and state governments. See further **[8.2.43]** and **[8.2.90C]–[8.2.93C]**.

The effect of federalism on the limits of the Commonwealth's executive power, was considered in the following case.

[7.2.27C]　　　　　　　　**Davis v Commonwealth**
　　　　　　　　　　　　　　(1988) 166 CLR 79

Section 22 of the Australian Bicentennial Authority Act 1980 (Cth) prohibited the use, without the consent of the Australian Bicentennial Authority, of prescribed symbols or expressions in connection with a business. Amongst the prescribed expressions was '200 years', when used in conjunction with '1788', '1988' or '88'.

The Australian Bicentennial Authority was a company limited by guarantee and registered under the Companies Ordinance 1962 (ACT).

The plaintiffs sought the consent of the Authority to sell T-shirts bearing the figures '1788' and '1988' and the words '200 years of suppression and depression'. The Authority refused its consent and the plaintiffs began proceedings in the High Court against the Commonwealth and the Authority for a declaration that the Australian Bicentennial Authority Act was invalid. The defendants demurred to the plaintiffs' statement of claim.

Mason CJ, Deane and Gaudron JJ: [92] The scope of the executive power of the Commonwealth has often been discussed but never defined. By s 61 of the Constitution [93] it extends to the execution and maintenance of the Constitution. As Mason J observed in *Barton v Commonwealth* (1974) 131 CLR 477 at 498, the power:

> ... extends to the execution and maintenance of the Constitution and of the laws of the Commonwealth. It enables the Crown to undertake all executive action which is appropriate to

the position of the Commonwealth under the Constitution and to the spheres of responsibility vested in it by the Constitution.

These responsibilities derived from the distribution of legislative powers effected by the Constitution itself and from the character and status of the Commonwealth as a national polity: *Victoria v Commonwealth & Hayden* (the *Australian Assistance Plan* case) (1975) 134 CLR 338 at 396–7. So it is that the legislative powers of the Commonwealth extend beyond the specific powers conferred upon the Parliament by the Constitution and include such powers as may be deduced from the establishment and nature of the Commonwealth as a polity: see the discussion by Dixon J in *Australian Communist Party v Commonwealth* (the *Communist Party* case) (1951) 83 CLR 1 at 187–8 ....

The Constitution distributes the plenitude of executive and legislative powers between the Commonwealth and the States: see *Colonial Sugar Refining Co Ltd v Attorney-General (Cth)* (1912) 15 CLR 182 at 214–5, per Isaacs J; *Smith v Oldham* (1912) 15 CLR 355 at 365, per Isaacs J. On this footing, as Isaacs J pointed out in *Commonwealth & Central Wool Committee v Colonial Combing, Spinning and Weaving Co Ltd* (the *Wooltops* case) (1922) 31 CLR 421 at 437–9, s 61 confers on the Commonwealth all the prerogative powers of the Crown except those that are necessarily exercisable by the States under the allocation of responsibilities made by the Constitution and those denied by the Constitution itself. Thus the existence of [94] Commonwealth executive power in areas beyond the express grants of legislative power will ordinarily be clearest where Commonwealth executive or legislative action involves no real competition with State executive or legislative competence.

If we ask the question whether the commemoration of the Bicentenary is a matter falling within the peculiar province of the Commonwealth in its capacity as the national and federal government, the answer must be in the affirmative. That is not to say that the States have no interest or no part to play in the commemoration. Clearly they have such an interest and such a part to play, whether as part of an exercise in cooperative federalism or otherwise. But the interests of the States in the commemoration of the Bicentenary is of a more limited character. It cannot be allowed to obscure the plain fact that the commemoration of the Bicentenary is pre-eminently the business and the concern of the Commonwealth as the national government and as such falls fairly and squarely within the federal executive power.

Implicit in what we have just said is a rejection of any notion that the character and status of the Commonwealth as the government of the nation is relevant only in the ascertainment of the scope of the executive power in the area of Australia's external relations. In the legislative sphere the nature and status of the Commonwealth as a polity has sustained legislation against subversive or seditious conduct: *Burns v Ransley* (1949) 79 CLR 101 at 116; *R v Sharkey* (1949) 79 CLR 121 at 148–9; see the *Communist Party* case, at 187–8. And there was no suggestion in the judgments in the *Australian Assistance Plan* case (134 CLR at 362, 375, 397 and 412–13) that the character and status of the Commonwealth as a national government was not relevant in ascertaining the scope of the executive power in its application domestically. Indeed, the judgments in that case contradict the suggestion, the Australian Assistance Plan being a domestic scheme.

Mason CJ, Deane and Gaudron JJ held that s 51 (xxxix) of the Constitution, together with s 61, authorised the parliament to legislate to confer protection on the Authority; and that the appropriation of funds for the purposes of the Authority was within s 81 of the Constitution. However, they concluded that s 22 of the Bicentennial Authority Act gave the Authority 'an extraordinary power to regulate the use of expressions in everyday use in this country, though the circumstances of that use in countless situations could not conceivably prejudice the commemoration of the Bicentenary'. The Act therefore provided 'for a regime of protection which is grossly disproportionate to the need to protect the commemoration and the Authority': 166 CLR at 99–100. They held s 22 invalid to the extent that it referred to the expression '200 years'.

Wilson and Dawson JJ agreed with the conclusion of Mason CJ, Deane and Gaudron JJ that the protection afforded by the Bicentennial Authority Act went beyond the power of the parliament. They also agreed that 'the character and status of the Commonwealth as a national government is an element to be considered in the construction of s 61 of the Constitution' (166 CLR at 103); and stressed that the division of executive power within the Commonwealth ought be guided by the recognition that the Commonwealth's powers are enumerated (see further [7.2.30]).

Brennan J: [110] This court has not settled the questions whether and to what extent it is within the executive power of the Commonwealth for the Executive Government of the Commonwealth to exercise its prerogative powers or to engage in lawful activities or enterprises calculated to advance the national interest. Though the Constitution gives no express answer to these questions, the answer may be derived from what the Constitution was intended to do and has done. With great respect to those who hold an opposing view, the Constitution did not create a mere aggregation of colonies, redistributing powers between the government of the Commonwealth and the governments of the States. The Constitution summoned the Australian nation into existence, thereby conferring a new identity on the people who agreed to unite "in one indissoluble Federal Commonwealth", melding their history, embracing their cultures, synthesising their aspirations and their destinies. The reality of the Australian nation is manifest, though the manifestations of its existence cannot be limited by definition. The end and purpose of the Constitution is to sustain the nation. If the executive power of the Commonwealth extends to the protection of the nation against forces which would weaken it, it extends to the advancement of the nation whereby its strength is fostered. There is no reason to restrict the executive power of the Commonwealth to matters within the heads of legislative power. So [111] cramped a construction of the power would deny to the Australian people many of the symbols of nationhood — a flag or anthem, for example — or the benefit of many national initiatives in science, literature and the arts. It does not follow that the Executive Government of the Commonwealth is the arbiter of its own power or that the executive power of the Commonwealth extends to whatever activity or enterprise the Executive Government deems to be in the national interest. But s 61 does confer on the Executive Government power 'to engage in enterprises and activities peculiarly adapted to the government of a nation and which cannot otherwise be carried on for the benefit of the nation', to repeat what Mason J said in the *AAP* case. In my respectful opinion, that is an appropriate formulation of a criterion to determine whether an enterprise or activity lies within the executive power of the Commonwealth. It invites consideration of the sufficiency of the powers of the States to engage effectively in the enterprise or activity in question and of the need for national action (whether unilateral or in cooperation with the States) to secure the contemplated benefit. The variety of enterprises or activities which might fall for consideration preclude the a priori development of detailed criteria but, as cases are decided, perhaps more precise tests will be developed.

Toohey J delivered a separate judgment to the same effect as Wilson and Dawson JJ.

~~~

Notes

[7.2.28] In *Victoria v Commonwealth* (the *AAP* case) (1975) 134 CLR 338, the High Court was asked to decide whether the Commonwealth Government could commit revenue to the promotion of the Australian Assistance Plan, which would coordinate the development of welfare services throughout Australia. Barwick CJ said: 'With exceptions that are not relevant to this matter and which need not be stated, the executive may only do that which has been or could be the subject of valid legislation': 134 CLR at 362. Gibbs J said that the language of s 61 of the Constitution limited the power of the executive and made 'it clear that the Executive cannot act in respect of a matter which falls entirely outside the legislative competence of the Commonwealth': 134 CLR at 379. Once it was concluded that the parliament could not legislate to establish the Plan, it followed that public moneys of the Commonwealth could not lawfully be expended for the purposes of the plan: 134 CLR at 379.

Mason J said that the ambit of the Commonwealth's executive power was limited and did 'not reach beyond the area of responsibilities allocated to the Commonwealth by the Constitution, responsibilities which are ascertainable from the distribution of powers, more particularly the distribution of legislative powers, effected by the Constitution itself and the character and status of the Commonwealth as a national government': 134 CLR at 396. However, several considerations, such as the scope of the incidental power in s 51(xxxix) and powers to be implied from 'the existence and character of the Commonwealth as a national government', gave the Commonwealth 'a capacity to engage in enterprises and activities peculiarly adapted to the government of a nation and which cannot otherwise be carried on for the benefit of the nation': 134 CLR at 397. He continued at 397–8:

> The functions appropriate and adapted to a national government will vary from time to time. As time unfolds, as circumstances and conditions alter, it will transpire that particular enterprises and activities will be undertaken if they are to be undertaken at all, by the national government.

[7.2.29]   In the *AAP* case (1975) 134 CLR 338, Jacobs J said that the area of the exercise of the Crown's prerogatives on the advice of the Commonwealth Government was limited by the terms of the Constitution:

> Primarily its exercise is limited to those areas which are expressly made the subject matters of Commonwealth legislative power. But it cannot be strictly limited to those subject matters. The prerogative is now exercisable by the Queen through the Governor-General acting on the advice of the Executive Council on all matters which are the concern of Australia as a nation. Within the words 'maintenance of this Constitution' appearing in s 61 lies the idea of Australia as a nation within itself and in its relationship with the external world, a nation governed by a system of law in which the powers of government are divided between a government representative of all the people of Australia and a number of governments each representative of the people of the various States (134 CLR at 405–6).

Jacobs J said that the 'growth of national identity' resulted in 'a corresponding growth in the area of activities which have an Australian rather than a local flavour':

> Thus, the complexity and values of a modern national society result in a need for coordination and integration of ways and means of planning for that complexity and reflecting those values. Inquiries on a national scale are necessary and likewise planning on a national scale must be carried out. Moreover, the complexity of society, with its various interrelated needs, requires coordination of services designed to meet those needs. Research and exploration likewise have a national, rather than a local, flavour (134 CLR at 412–13).

[7.2.30]   As noted at **[7.2.27C]**, Mason J's construction of the 'nationhood power' was approved by Mason CJ, Deane and Gaudron JJ, and by Brennan J in his separate judgment, in *Davis v Commonwealth* (1988) 166 CLR 79 at 92–4 and 111.

In *Davis v Commonwealth* (1988) 166 CLR 79 **[7.2.27C]**, Wilson and Dawson JJ expressed some reservations about the broader approach developed by Mason J in the *AAP* case. Wilson and Dawson JJ stressed that any conception of a 'nationhood power' was grounded in the express powers conferred on the Commonwealth making the development of an implied power unnecessary:

> We agree with the conclusion reached by Mason CJ, Deane and Gaudron JJ and wish only to add some comments about the extent to which power is vested in the

Commonwealth Parliament to make laws with respect to matters not specifically enumerated in s 51 or elsewhere in the Constitution.

If the specifically enumerated powers are taken to include par (xxxix) of s 51, then we consider that in the ultimate analysis the Commonwealth Parliament does not possess any legislative power which could not be assigned to a particular provision or combination of provisions. Section 51(xxxix), it will be recalled, confers power to make laws with respect to matters incidental to the execution of any power vested by the Constitution in the Parliament or in either House thereof, or in the government of the Commonwealth, or in the Federal Judicature, or in any department or officer of the Commonwealth. The subject has been considered in the context of the suppression of seditious or subversive activities. In *Australian Communist Party v The Commonwealth* ('*the Communist Party Case*') (1951) 83 CLR 1, at pp 187–188, Dixon J did not doubt that particular laws upon those matters might be supported under powers obtained by combining the appropriate part of the text of s 51(xxxix) with the text of some other power, including the executive power under s 61. However, he found such an exercise had an artificial aspect and preferred to find the source of the power to legislate against subversive conduct 'in principle that is deeper or wider than a series of combinations of the words of s 51(xxxix) with those of other constitutional powers'. The power was to be found, he said, in the very nature of the polity established by the Constitution and the capacity which it must of necessity have to protect its own existence.

But this view was a minority view. The majority of the members of the Court considered the validity of the impugned Act by reference to the question whether it was supported by s 51(xxxix) in association with either s 51(vi) or s 61 ... We are unable to conceive of an implication of the kind described that would not be sufficiently and accurately described in the terms of s 61 supported by s 51(xxxix). Indeed, the execution and maintenance of the Constitution and of the laws of the Commonwealth are concepts which seem to us to comprehend all that is to be implied 'from the existence and nature of the Constitution as the foundation of a body politic'.

Of course, subversion, sedition and the like are matters of a very special kind, striking, as they do, at the very foundation of the Constitution. See the *Communist Party Case*; *Burns v Ransley* (1949) 79 CLR 101, at p 116; *R v Sharkey* (1949) 79 CLR 121, at pp 148–149; *Ex parte Walsh and Johnson; In re Yates* (1925) 37 CLR 36, at pp 94–95. It would be dangerous to attempt to derive too much from the cases dealing with those matters. This is particularly so when the decision in each of these cases was referable to the incidental power conferred by s 51(xxxix). A fortiori, those cases do nothing to support the notion that the Commonwealth Parliament has power to legislate with respect to anything that it regards as of national interest and concern. As Gibbs J pointed out in *Victoria v The Commonwealth and Hayden* (1975) 134 CLR 338, at p 378, 'the growth of the Commonwealth to nationhood did not have the effect of destroying the distribution of powers carefully effected by the Constitution'.

[7.2.31] Professor Cheryl Saunders has also emphasised the importance of the controlling text, saying that 'it is a considerable leap from an implied nationhood power of the kind (developed by Mason J in the *AAP* case) to acceptance of the existence of an independent, substantive legislative power derived from the fact of nationhood': Saunders (1984) at 269. Was that leap made by Kirby J in his dissenting judgment in *Re Wakim; Ex parte McNally* (1998) 198 CLR 511? In *Wakim*, six justices of the High Court rejected an argument that the jurisdiction cross-vesting scheme, in particular that part of the scheme that contemplated the vesting of state jurisdiction in federal courts, was a valid exercise of the implied incidental power read with s 71 of the Constitution.

Kirby J, dissenting, remarked that:

An additional and connected source of constitutional authority arises from the implied nationhood power. That power has been repeatedly recognised in decisions of this Court as deriving from Australia's very existence and character as a sovereign nation. It extends not only to Australia's external activities, but also internally. ... It is a source of power reflective of the unique position occupied by the Commonwealth within Australia's federal polity. In the past that power has been elaborated in connexion with the Legislature and the Executive Government of the Commonwealth. But there is no reason of principle why it should not also apply in the case of the Judicature.

Justice Kirby then referred to the statements made by Mason and Jacobs JJ in the *AAP* case (see **[7.2.29]** above), and continued:

Federal legislation providing consent to the vesting of State jurisdiction in federal courts falls squarely within the purposes envisaged by the implied nationhood power as it relates to the Judicature. The legislation possesses an 'Australian rather than a local flavour'. It seeks to facilitate national cooperation and 'co-ordination' in response to the 'complexity ... of a modern national society' (*Victoria v The Commonwealth and Hayden* (1975) 134 CLR 338 at 412 per Jacobs J). The Commonwealth, in its relationship with the States and Territories, is in a unique position to respond to the issues arising under the establishment of a national system of jurisdiction-sharing. It has done so for high national purposes.

Obviously, the implied nationhood power is strictly limited in its scope. It would be inconsistent with the distribution of powers provided by the Constitution were the nationhood power to be given an ambit that trespassed impermissibly upon the powers of the States. That would effect a disturbance of the federal balance (cf *Victoria v The Commonwealth and Hayden* (1975) 134 CLR 338 at 364 per Barwick CJ, 378 per Gibbs J, 398 per Mason J). A characterisation of legislative purposes as 'national' is not sufficient to attract the support of the nationhood power if those purposes fall within areas of law-making belonging to the States (*Victoria v The Commonwealth and Hayden* (1975) 134 CLR 338 at 364 per Barwick CJ, 378 per Gibbs J, 398 per Mason J. In *The Commonwealth v Tasmania* (1983) 158 CLR 1 at 252, Deane J held that the implied nationhood power was limited in scope by reference to the federal nature of the Constitution and accordingly 'confined within areas in which there is no real competition with the States'). But the cross-vesting legislation of the Commonwealth, in so far as it gives consent to the vesting of State jurisdiction in federal courts, cannot be characterised in that way. It is legislation which every Australian State and Territory supported in this Court. In no way does it encroach impermissibly upon the legislative domain of the States or subvert the federal nature of the Constitution. On the contrary, it is clearly intended to support the legislative initiatives which the States have themselves taken. In the jurisprudence of this Court, the implied nationhood power is not limited to flags and symbols. It extends to cooperative national activities that are compatible with the Constitution and which reflect the modern needs of a dynamic and democratic federal polity. ...

This conclusion does not employ 'convenience' as a criterion of constitutional validity rather than legal analysis. Analysis does not become less legal because it is uncongenial. The incidental power under the Constitution affords the legal answer to the question concerning the legislative power to sustain the federal part of the cross-vesting scheme. The incidental power was fully argued in these proceedings. And one aspect of the incidental power is the implied nationhood power. What can be more conducive to the national society of Australia as envisaged by the Constitution than the provision of legislative consent to a scheme that ensures justice, efficiency and clarity in the nation's court system? This is something at the very heart of the nation's existence and of its identity as such. Provided no other impediment exists, the Parliament of the Commonwealth is empowered to act as it has.

[7.2.32] Although the 'implied nationhood power' was not invoked by any members of the majority in *Re Wakim; Ex parte McNally* (1999) 198 CLR 511 to support the state-to-federal aspect of the jurisdictional cross-vesting scheme, the balance of judicial opinion reflected in the court's decisions, *Barton v Commonwealth* (1974) 131 CLR 477 **[7.2.24]**, *Victoria v Commonwealth* (the *AAP* case) (1975) 134 CLR 338 **[7.2.28]** and *Davis v Commonwealth* (1988) 166 CLR 79 **[7.2.27C]**, clearly indicates that the 'executive power of the Commonwealth ... exercisable by the Governor-General' extends beyond those powers which are expressly conferred by the Constitution. The power includes those functions, powers and privileges which can be described as inherent in a national government.

For that reason, the 1984 replacement of the 1900 Letters Patent and the 1987 revocation of the 1954 and 1973 assignments **[7.2.22]** had not disarmed the Commonwealth Government but had removed sources of confusion. It is to s 61 of the Constitution that we must look for the full extent of the Commonwealth's executive powers. That section is seen as including 'all the common law prerogatives appropriate to the Commonwealth's responsibilities, subject to express provisions of the Constitution': Zines (1997) p 252.

Professor George Winterton has described s 61 as authorising 'the Commonwealth Government [to] exercise *all* the executive prerogatives extant in 1901'. He proceeded to list the 'important powers of the Commonwealth Government [which] derive, at least substantially, from the common law powers of the Crown'.

These included:

> ... the prerogatives of foreign affairs, such as making treaties, requesting extradition and appointing diplomats, the war prerogative, the power to declare peace, prerogatives relating to the stationing and control of the armed forces, and powers to build recreational facilities, to conduct inquiries, and to conclude contracts. Of course, the Commonwealth has also inherited the immunities, preferences and exceptions of the Crown, such as the priority of Crown debts and freedom from distress for rent (Winterton (1983) p 49).

See also Zines (1992), p 254.

[7.2.33] These decisions also highlight the federal complication, which will have the effect of limiting the scope of the Commonwealth's inherent powers in order to preserve areas of autonomous executive powers and privileges for the states.

Until *Davis v Commonwealth* (1988) 166 CLR 79 **[7.2.27C]**, the general view was that the Commonwealth's inherent executive powers are confined to matters in respect of which the Commonwealth can legislate; so that the federal distribution of executive power mirrors the federal distribution of legislative powers: see, for example, Winterton (1983) pp 29–30; Zines (1992) pp 255–6.

This was the approach favoured by Wilson and Dawson JJ in *Davis v Commonwealth* (1988) 166 CLR 79 at 101–3: see **[7.2.30]**.

3   Councils, Cabinets and Ministers

The states

[7.3.1E]   **Constitution Act 1975 (Vic)**

Salaried officers in Parliament

50(1) The Governor may from time to time appoint any number of officers so that the entire number shall not at any one time exceed eighteen who shall be entitled to be elected members of either House of the Parliament and to sit and vote therein.

(2) Such officers shall be responsible Ministers of the Crown and members of the Executive Council, and ten at least of such officers shall be members of the Council or the Assembly.

(3) Not more than six of such officers shall at any one time be members of the Council and not more than thirteen of such officers shall at any one time be members of the Assembly.

Ministers to be in Council or Assembly

51 A responsible Minister of the Crown shall not hold office for a longer period than three months unless he is or becomes a member of the Council or the Assembly.

Power of Ministers to speak in either House

52(1) Notwithstanding anything contained in any Act any responsible Minister of the Crown who is a member of the Council or of the Assembly may at any time with the consent of the House of the Parliament of which he is not a member sit in such House for the purpose only of explaining the provisions of any Bill relating to or connected with any department administered by him, and may take part in any debate or discussion therein on such Bill, but he shall not vote except in the House of which he is an elected member.

(2) It shall not be lawful at any one time for more than one responsible Minister under the authority of this section to sit in the House of which he is not a member.

Responsible Minister not required to vacate seat on appointment to office

53(1) Notwithstanding anything in this Act where a person is appointed by the Governor to be a responsible Minister of the Crown the acceptance by him of the appointment shall not prevent him from becoming a member of the Council or the Assembly or from sitting and voting as a member or if he is a member shall not vacate his seat.

Appointment to public offices

88 Subject to the express provisions of any other Act the appointment to public offices under the Government of Victoria hereafter to become vacant or to be created whether such offices be salaried or not shall be vested in the Governor in Council with the exception of the appointments of the officers liable to retire from office on political grounds which appointments shall be vested in the Governor alone.

Governor in Council may order that Ministers exercise duties etc concurrently

88A The Governor in Council may by Order published in the Government Gazette direct that all or any of the functions powers and duties of a Minister of the Crown shall be exercisable concurrently with another Minister of the Crown or shall cease to be so exercisable.

~~~

Letters Patent Relating to the Office of Governor of Victoria

III There shall be an Executive Council to advise the Governor on the occasions when the Governor is permitted or required by any statute or other instrument to act in Council. The Premier (or in his absence the Acting Premier) shall tender advice to the Governor in relation to the exercise of the other powers and functions of Governor.

~~~

Constitution Act 1902 (NSW)

PART 4 — THE EXECUTIVE

Continuation of Executive Council

35B There shall continue to be an Executive Council to advise the Governor in the government of the State.

Members of the Executive Council

35C(1) The Executive Council shall consist of such persons as may be appointed by the Governor, from time to time, as members of the Executive Council.

(2) The members of the Executive Council shall hold office during the Governor's pleasure.

(3) The Governor may appoint one of the members of the Executive Council as Vice President of the Executive Council.

Meetings of the Executive Council

35D(1) The Governor shall preside at meetings of the Executive Council.

(2) The Vice-President of the Executive Council or, in the absence of the Vice-President the senior member present shall preside at any meeting of the Executive Council from which the Governor is absent.

(3) The quorum for a meeting of the Executive Council is 2 members.

(4) For the purposes of this section, the seniority of members of the Executive Council shall be determined according to the order of their respective appointments as members of the Executive Council.

DIVISION 3 — APPOINTMENT OF MINISTERS OF THE CROWN

Appointment of Ministers

35E(1) The Premier and other Ministers of the Crown for the State shall be appointed by the Governor from among the members of the Executive Council.

(2) The Premier and other Ministers of the Crown shall hold office during the Governor's pleasure.

DIVISION 4 — FUNCTIONS OF MINISTERS OF THE CROWN

Authority for Minister of the Crown to act for and on behalf of another Minister of the Crown

36(1) The Governor may, from time to time, authorise a Minister of the Crown to act for and on behalf of another Minister of the Crown for any period specified or described by the Governor. ...

Unavailability of Minister of the Crown

37 A Minister of the Crown may exercise or perform for and on behalf of another Minister of the Crown a function appertaining or annexed to the office of that other Minister if the first-mentioned Minister is satisfied that the other Minister is unavailable and that any Minister of the Crown authorised under section 36 to exercise or perform that function is unavailable.

~~~

Notes

[7.3.4] In each of the states, there are statutory provisions equivalent to the provisions of the Victorian and New South Wales Constitution Acts set out above (**[7.3.1E]** and **[7.3.3E]**); although these provisions may differ in their detail. The relevant provisions are:

- Constitution Act 1867 (Qld) s 14;
- Constitution of Queensland 2001 Ch 3, Pts 3 and 4;
- Constitution Act 1934 (SA) ss 45, 65–71a;
- Constitution Act 1934 (Tas) ss 8A, 8S, 32;
- Constitution Act 1889 (WA) s 74;
- Constitution Act Amendment Act 1899 (WA) ss 37, 43.

[7.3.5] In every state we can confidently predict that ministers will be appointed from among the current members of parliament. Indeed, the South Australian and Victorian legislation provide that Ministers must be (or must become within three months) members of one of the houses of parliament. In those two states the legislation also guarantees minimum representation in the ministry for each house. The West Australian legislation merely provides that one minister shall be a member of the Legislative Council; it establishes no such membership requirement for the other ministers.

In none of the other states is there an insistence that ministers be members of parliament, merely a provision which exempts ministers of the Crown from the general rule which disqualifies 'holders of offices of profit under the Crown' from becoming members of parliament, an exemption which is also found in the South Australian, Victorian and Western Australian legislation. Although it is true that in New South Wales, Queensland and Tasmania, 'strictly speaking there is no legal necessity for a single Minister to be in Parliament' (Keith (1928) p 55), the exempting provisions just referred to contemplate the possibility. It might be argued that a provision such as s 47 of the Constitution Act 1902 (NSW) also contemplates that possibility. It refers to the appointment to public office of persons who are liable to retire from offices under the Crown 'on political grounds', a clear reference to ministers of the Crown who may feel obliged to abandon their portfolios if defeated at a general election or deprived of the confidence of parliament: see also Constitution of Queensland 2001 s 44; Constitution Acts Amendment Act 1899 (WA) ss 43, 44.

[7.3.6] Be that as it may, it would be too superficial a judgment to conclude that, in these three states, the necessary qualifications for appointment as a minister of the Crown does not include membership of parliament. It has been claimed that one member of the first ministry in Queensland was not a member of parliament: Encel (1962) pp 20–7. Beyond that one possibility, every person who has held a portfolio in every government formed in the Australian colonies and states since the granting of responsible government has been a member of parliament. Can that be ascribed to no more than habit, or to an unthinking imitation of the British model? Or is it in fact necessary for the Governor, when commissioning a ministry, to confine the choice to persons who are members of the legislature? Is there some sanction which demands that the selection be so confined, a sanction not explicitly stated in legislation, but nevertheless coercive? The fact that the parliament (and the lower house in particular) controls all public finances is certainly relevant. A government which could not work with (indeed, control) parliament must be short-lived; without a regular supply of finance the business of government must break down: see Lumb (1991) p 72. It is difficult to envisage how parliament could now be persuaded to continue to offer that necessary degree of cooperation if the political leaders of parliament were to be deprived of their normal expectations of public advancement (or 'patronage' as the 18th century British parliamentarians called it). It might be that a complete separation of legislature and executive could, in theory, be effected in (let us say) New South Wales. But now that those two institutions have been intertwined for more than 130 years, is it conceivable that the legislature would permit the separation?

[7.3.7] In each state the current ministers provide the functional membership for the Executive Council. In South Australia and Victoria the legislation provides that ministers shall *ex officio* be members of the Executive Council. In the other states, their right to membership depends on a deeply entrenched practice or convention. Again, according to convention, ministers in New South Wales, South Australia and Western Australia resign from the Executive Council when they leave the ministry; a minister who failed to resign could be dismissed from the Executive Council by the Governor. In Queensland, Tasmania and Victoria, ministers are appointed executive councillors for life, but are not summoned to attend meetings of the council once they leave the ministry.

The role of the Executive Council has been described as the formal or legal manifestation of the Cabinet:

> As a matter of formal law the chief executive authority is an Executive Council, and the chief executive officer is the Governor, who presides over the Executive Council. ...
>
> The Executive Council ... like the Privy Council in the United Kingdom, is, so far as the positive, formal law is concerned — the law which is administered by the courts — the body which exercises the chief executive authority in the State, not only by virtue of the Constitution Acts but also by virtue of other Acts of Parliament, many of which confer powers on the Governor-in-Council (which is another way of saying the Executive Council) (Anderson (1960) p 10).
>
> The Executive Council ... regularly meets once a week ... It makes formally a number of decisions, many of them of a trivial nature, and operates as the legal personality of the Cabinet when important decisions of Cabinet have to be clothed in the legal form of an Executive Council Minute (Townsley (1976) p 96).

[7.3.8] The Executive Council is a purely formal institution and its regular meetings serve no function other than the formal ratification of decisions already taken by Ministers, either individually or in Cabinet. It is the Cabinet which holds the substantial executive power yet it receives no recognition in any of the formal constitutional documents. The Cabinet is not mentioned in the Letters Patent nor in any of the Constitution Acts. Even in the United Kingdom, where the Cabinet was developed as the linchpin of the Constitution, that body 'has been virtually ostracised by the parliamentary draftsman': de Smith and Brazier (1989) p 160. But the reality has been recognised by the courts. In *FAI Insurances Ltd v Winneke* (1982) 151 CLR 342, Murphy J said: 'The Cabinet, which has no place in the formal Constitution, is a committee of Ministers of the ruling parliamentary party or parties': 151 CLR at 373.

The same point was made by Anderson in 1960:

> In the political, as distinct from the legal sense, then, the chief executive authority —
> and the authority chiefly responsible for legislative policy — is the Cabinet, consisting
> in each State of all the ministers of the Crown ... The Executive Council, then, is not
> normally a deliberate body and full meetings of it are rare: it exists to give legal form
> to decisions already taken elsewhere by, or with the approval of, the Cabinet
> (Anderson (1960) p 11).

Cabinets were formed in each of the Australian colonies as soon as responsible
self-government was granted. They were based on the British model developed in the
eighteenth and early 19th centuries.

Until the 1890s the lack of homogeneity and stability in colonial politics bedevilled
the functioning of Australian Cabinets. Changes of ministry were frequent and the
Governors found it difficult to choose the appropriate person to form a ministry;
between 1856 and 1900, South Australia had 42 ministries; New South Wales had
29 and Victoria 28: Encel (1974) p 36. As Sawer puts it, '[p]olitics were in fact more
a matter of faction and of personal intrigue than of distinct party opposition': Sawer
(1956) p 1. However inefficiently the early Cabinets may have functioned, it is clear
that they are now an ineradicably established institution; '"Cabinet Government"
[is] an accurate label for the formal structure and the functioning of executive
authority in Australia' (Encel (1962) pp 15–16), although it would be a serious error
to conclude that Australian Cabinets continue to follow the United Kingdom model
closely, or to function in the same way and according to the same rules.

[7.3.9] The orthodox legal view is that the Executive Council, rather than the
Cabinet, is the important and legally powerful institution within the executive
government. It was the Victorian Executive Council, according to Aickin J in *FAI
Insurances Ltd v Winneke* (1982) 151 CLR 342, which gave 'the force of law to, and
thus makes effective, decisions of the executive government, ie the Cabinet and
individual Ministers': 151 CLR at 382. Sawer made the following point in 1956
(1956, p 116):

> This submission that Cabinets are known to the law must not be carried too far. Many
> empowering statutes require in terms the making of a formal decision or instrument
> by a named authority — usually the Governor-in-Council, or a minister — and even
> if the policy question is first settled by Cabinet, the formal step must still be taken
> before the decision can be 'known to the law'. There are no recorded examples of laws
> which in express terms make Cabinet decision a formal authentication of the
> governmental will. Such provision could quite well be made so far as constitutional
> law is concerned, and with the development of Cabinet secretariats and proper records
> of Cabinet decisions, the practical difficulties would be less than might be assumed,
> but there are still sound practical reasons for avoiding such a course: a main purpose
> of ministerial conclave in cabinet is speed and informality of procedure, and this
> would be imperilled if the precise terms of a decision had to be worked out in order
> to constitute a legally effective formal record. But when a legal issue is substantially
> one of fact, in which acts of the government as a collective person with knowledge and
> intention become relevant, there seems no reason why Cabinet proceedings should not
> be proved in a relevant case; they would of course be the subject of qualified privilege
> for purposes of defamation, etc. Questions whether a minister had authority to
> negotiate or vary a contract binding the Crown, and had in fact done so, might
> provide examples as well as the waiver or estoppel type of problem illustrated by
> *Davenport's* case (cf *New South Wales v Bardolph* (1934) 52 CLR 455, especially the
> judgment of Evatt J on trial).

[7.3.10] The functional relations between the individuals and institutions who comprise the executive government, particularly between the Governor and the ministers (whether as individuals or collectively, as Cabinet or Executive Council), can be complex. The basic issue is whether the Governor must exercise the powers conferred on that office in accordance with the advice of ministers. An indication that there might be such a constraint is expressed in cl III of the Victorian Letters Patent **[7.2.5E]**. A similar indication appears in s 35B of the Constitution Act 1902 (NSW) **[7.3.3E]**. However, s 35A of that Act appears to counteract that indication. And there is a strong inference, in s 7(5) of the Australia Act 1986 **[7.2.3E]**, that the executive powers, formally vested in the Queen or the vice-regal representative, should be exercised on ministerial advice.

These functional relations are examined in more detail in **[7.4.1]–[7.4.26]**. For the present, we can say that the clue to these relationships lies in the term 'responsible government', which has been applied to the Australian state governmental systems for more than a century: the ministry is responsible, or answerable, to parliament for its running of the government, which implies that the Governor is directed by the ministry, and does not frustrate its responsibility.

The Commonwealth

[7.3.11E]   **Commonwealth Constitution**

62 There shall be a Federal Executive Council to advise the Governor-General in the government of the Commonwealth, and the members of the Council shall be chosen and summoned by the Governor-General and sworn as Executive Councillors, and shall hold office during his pleasure.

63 The provisions of this Constitution referring to the Governor-General in Council shall be construed as referring to the Governor-General acting with the advice of the Federal Executive Council.

64 The Governor-General may appoint officers to administer such departments of State of the Commonwealth as the Governor-General in Council may establish.

Such officers shall hold office during the pleasure of the Governor-General. They shall be members of the Federal Executive Council, and shall be the Queen's Ministers of State for the Commonwealth.

After the first general election no Minister of State shall hold office for a longer period than three months unless he is or becomes a senator or a member of the House of Representatives.

65 Until the Parliament otherwise provides, the Ministers of State shall not exceed seven in number, and shall hold such offices as the Parliament prescribes, or, in the absence of provision, as the Governor-General directs.

66 There shall be payable to the Queen, out of the Consolidated Revenue Fund of the Commonwealth, for the salaries of the Ministers of State, an annual sum which, until the Parliament otherwise provides, shall not exceed twelve thousand pounds a year.

67 Until the Parliament otherwise provides the appointment and removal of all other officers of the Executive Government of the Commonwealth shall be vested in the Governor-General in Council, unless the appointment is delegated by the Governor-General in Council or by a law of the Commonwealth to some other authority.

~~~

[7.3.12] Parliament has exercised the power granted in s 65 (and s 51(xxxvi)) of the Constitution, and increased the maximum number of ministers of state for the

Commonwealth to 30: Ministers of State Act 1952 (Cth) s 4. Until 1956 all ministers were members of Cabinet; but in that year, when the number of ministers was increased from 20 to 22, the ministry was divided into two groups: those who were Cabinet Ministers (numbering 12) and those who were merely members of the ministry.

When the Labor Party took government in 1972, it abandoned the distinction between the inner and outer ministry and operated with a Cabinet of 27 Ministers. When the Liberal–National–Country Party Government entered office in 1975, it reverted to the pre-1972 system of an inner and outer ministry. The ministry sworn in on 22 December 1975 had 24 members, a reduction of three. Of these, 12 were designated as 'members of the inner Cabinet': (1975) 1 *Aust Govt Weekly Digest* 1050–1. On its election in 1983, the Labor Government retained the system of an inner and outer ministry, as did the Liberal–National Party Government elected in 1996.

In 1980, the Commonwealth Parliament enacted the Parliamentary Secretaries Act 1980 (Cth), which provided for the appointment of parliamentary secretaries to assist ministers of state. In 1999, s 3 and Schedule 1 of the Ministers of State and Other Legsialtion Amendment Act 1999 (Cth) repealed the Parliamentary Secretaries Act and authorised parliamentary secretaries to be appointed under an amendment to s 4 of the Ministers of States Act 1952 (Cth). Today, 'parliamentary secretaries' are often appointed to assist Ministers of State. They are regarded to be ministers of state for the purposes of s 64 of the Constitution: *Re Patterson; Ex parte Taylor* (2001) 207 CLR 391 at 451–2 (Gummow and Hayne JJ).

[7.3.13]   As with the Australian states, the Cabinet is ignored in the Commonwealth Constitution: it 'is not in any formal legal sense the Executive', and it 'functions according to convention': *Minister for Arts, Heritage and Environment v Peko-Wallsend Ltd* (1987) 75 ALR 218 at 222, 225 per Bowen CJ.

In *Whitlam v Australian Consolidated Press* (1985) 60 ACTR 7, Blackburn J described the Federal Cabinet as 'a group of persons who have in common certain political aims [which] are necessarily broad', an institution which 'is part of the machinery of the government of the country': 60 ACTR at 14, 15.

In *Minister for Arts, Heritage and Environment v Peko Wallsend Ltd* (1987) 75 ALR 218, Bowen CJ stressed the central significance of the Cabinet in our governmental structure and functions at 225:

> It is to Cabinet that the highest decisions of policy affecting Australia are brought. Often the questions arising involve intense conflict of interests or of opinion in the community. In Cabinet these conflicts have to be resolved. Decisions have to be taken in the public interest ...

[7.3.14]   Despite (or, perhaps, because of) this significance, no legal powers or functions are conferred on Cabinet, either by the Constitution or by legislation: 75 ALR at 222 per Bowen CJ; at 226 per Sheppard J; at 244, 245 per Wilcox J. The invariable practice, in drafting legislation which confers legal powers and functions on the executive government, is to vest the power or function in the Governor-General, a minister or another officer of the Commonwealth (such as the permanent head of department): 75 ALR at 226 per Sheppard J. Nevertheless, the exercise of such legal powers and functions will frequently conform to decisions of the Cabinet (at 225):

After a decision of Cabinet is made it may require for its implementation an Act of Parliament or a decision of a particular Minister or of the Governor-General in Council.

The question whether the Cabinet should be subject, in the making of its decisions, to some form of legal accountability through the judicial review processes developed to control administrative decisions has only been raised relatively recently (see *Minister for Arts Heritage and Environment v Peko-Wallsend Ltd* (1987) 15 FCR 274; 75 ALR 218; *South Australia v O'Shea* (1987) 163 CLR 378).

[7.3.15] If the Cabinet is immune from judicial review in the performance of its functions, no such immunity attaches to the Executive Council: *R v Toohey, Ex parte Northern Land Council* (1981) 151 CLR 170; *Minister for Arts, Heritage and Environment v Peko-Wallsend Ltd* (1987) 75 ALR 218 at 223–4 per Bowen CJ; at 227 per Sheppard J. Although courts may not review Cabinet decisions, they are certainly not restricted in their power to review the decisions of the executive government officers that exercise power directed by Cabinet decisions. As Gibbs J noted in *R v Toohey; Ex parte Northern Land Council* (1981) 151 CLR 170 at 193:

> ... no convincing reason can be suggested for limiting the ordinary power of the courts to inquire whether there has been a proper exercise of a statutory power by giving to the Crown a special immunity from review. If a statutory power is granted to the Crown for one purpose, it is clear that it is not lawfully exercised if it is used for another. The courts have the power and duty to ensure that statutory powers are exercised only in accordance with law. They can in my opinion inquire whether the Crown has exercised a power granted to it by statute for a purpose which the statute does not authorize.

[7.3.16] The Executive Council has been described as the body whose decisions provide 'the formal legal act which gives effect to the advice tendered to the Crown by the Ministers of the Crown': *Australian Communist Party v Commonwealth* (1951) 83 CLR 1 at 179 per Dixon J. The persons eligible for appointment to the Executive Council are not restricted to Ministers of state; membership of Council is at the discretion of the Governor-General, though Ministers of state are *ex officio* members and it is a well-established practice to appoint only Ministers to the Council. They cease to be members only if they resign from the Council, for it is the practice to make appointments for an unlimited term. Only those members of the Executive Council who are currently Ministers of state for the Commonwealth are summoned to attend Council meetings. The functions of the Executive Council were described by the Constitutional Commission in 1988:

> **5.110** Meetings of the Council are formally convened either by the Governor-General or by a deputy appointed by the Governor-General under section 126 of the Constitution who has been authorised to summon meetings of the Council. The practice has been to appoint as deputy the Vice-President of the Council who is a Minister appointed to the position of Vice-President on the advice of the Prime Minister.

> **5.111** Although not, strictly speaking, a member of the Executive Council, the Governor-General presides over meetings of the Council. Meetings may also be presided over by any of his duly appointed and authorised deputies. At present the practice is for the Governor-General to appoint all Ministers to be deputies to preside over meetings of the Council at which the Governor-General is unable to be present, according to a prescribed order of precedence.

> **5.112** Neither the Constitution nor any Act of the Parliament specifies a quorum for meetings of the Council. At a meeting of the Executive Council on 12 January 1901 it

was decided that at least two members of the Executive Council, exclusive of the Governor-General, shall be necessary to constitute a meeting of the Executive Council for the exercise of its powers. Current practice requires the presence of either the Governor-General (or Vice-President of the Council) and two other Executive Councillors who are Ministers, or three Executive Councillors who are Ministers.

5.113 Meetings of the Council are arranged when there is business to transact. It meets frequently during the Autumn and Budget sessions of the Parliament. The business to be transacted is listed in a document, called the Schedule, and at the conclusion of a meeting this is signed by those present, including, if present, the Governor-General.

5.114 The business is of a purely formal nature. What is presented is a recommendation, known as a Minute, that something which is required, by the Constitution or by statute, to be done or made by the Governor-General in Council be so done or made. This Minute is signed by the responsible Minister and is accomplished by an explanatory memorandum. Once the recommendation is approved, the Governor-General marks the Minute 'Approved' and signs it. Some other instrument, for example, regulations may have to be executed to give legal effect to the decision.

5.115 If the Governor-General is not present at a meeting of the Executive Council, the Schedule and each approved Minute are subsequently submitted for the Governor-General's signature (Constitutional Commission (1988), pp 333–4).

For a detailed review of the structure and operations of the Commonwealth Executive Council, see Sawer (1977) pp 91–106.

4   The Crown and its Ministers

[7.4.1] The executive government of each of the states and of the Commonwealth reflects a tension between legal technicality and political reality. A substantial number of legal powers and discretions is formally vested in the Governor-General and Governors; yet the ministers (that is, the leaders of the dominant political party) have a strong interest in controlling the way in which those powers and discretions are exercised. The formal powers range from the politically sensitive (indeed crucial) power to dissolve parliament to the mundane power to appoint public servants and make regulations. Some of the formal powers are stated in constitutional instruments, but the great bulk appear in Acts of Parliament. We can say that, as a general (if not universal) rule, these powers are exercised in line with policy settled by the Crown's political advisers and at the initiative of those advisers. Generally speaking, the Governor-General and the Governors do not act except on the advice of ministers.

[7.4.2] This simple proposition reflects a complex political relationship called 'responsible government', developed over several centuries of experience in England, the United Kingdom and the overseas political progeny of the Westminster system of government. The relationship is not spelt out in any formal, justiciable rules. One can find allusions to it in the formal constitutional instruments, such as ss 62, 63 and 64 of the Commonwealth Constitution [7.3.11E], the state Letters Patent [7.3.2E] and s 35B of the Constitution Act 1902 (NSW) [7.3.3E]. But the rules of responsible government are essentially induced from political experience. The sanctions which attach to disobedience of these rules are administered, not by the courts, but by the various participants in the political process: the Crown, the ministers and the parliament. Because of their non-justiciable nature, these rules are frequently described as conventions. And because they are induced, rather than preordained, there can be doubt and disagreement about their content.

Be that as it may, these rules do have coercive force; their breach can have serious repercussions for the actor. And it would be wrong to say that they have no legitimacy or authority. The content of the rules is not haphazard, accidental or without rational basis; rather, the rules are based on an accommodation of the needs and demands of the participants in the processes of government.

[7.4.3] The amenability of the Crown to political control grew, through the 17th and 18th centuries, out of the Crown's need for, and parliament's control over, finance. And it is that central factor which even now, underpins the relationship. The business of government (the Crown's business) demands access to a steady supply of money. Public servants must be paid, buildings maintained, equipment purchased, public works undertaken, social and economic programmes implemented. Parliament controls that access because revenues cannot be raised without legislation and government money cannot be spent without legislation. Both taxation and appropriation require parliamentary approval.

The necessity for parliamentary authorisation of taxation is expressed in the Bill of Rights 1689 (Eng), and in such judicial pronouncements as: *Attorney-General v Wilts United Dairies Ltd* (1920) 37 TLR 884 at 886; *Commonwealth v Colonial Combing Spinning and Weaving Co Ltd* (1922) 31 CLR 421 at 444–5; *Brown v West* (1990) 169 CLR 195 at 205–6; *Bowles v Bank of England* [1913] 1 Ch 57 at 84–5. The rule that there can be no expenditure of government funds without parliamentary authorisation is expressed in s 83 of the Commonwealth Constitution, ss 39 and 45 of the Constitution Act 1902 (NSW), ss 34 and 39 of the Constitution Act 1867 (Qld), ss 89 and 93 of the Constitution Act 1975 (Vic), and ss 64 and 72 of the Constitution Act 1889 (WA). It has also been endorsed in such decisions as: *Alcock v Fergie* (1867) 4 WW & A'B (L) 285; *Australian Alliance Insurance Co v Goodwyn* [1916] St R Qd 255; *Auckland Harbour Board v R* [1924] AC 318; *Commonwealth v Burns* [1971] VR 825; *Attorney-General (NSW) v Gray* [1977] 1 NSWLR 406.

And within parliament, one of the houses has greater control than the other over that access: see **[5.2.10]–[5.2.11]** and **[5.2.15]**. The political party which controls that house controls the Crown's access to money. The price which the Crown must pay for continued access to that money is the acceptance of the leaders of the controlling political party as the Crown's advisers or manipulators. It is, at heart, a simple equation built on exchange: money for power.

[7.4.4] The formal instruments relating to the Governor-General's powers and functions do make occasional reference to an obligation to follow ministerial advice such as:

- the issue of writs for a general election of the House of Representatives (Constitution s 32);
- the issue of writs for a by-election in the absence of the Speaker of the House (s 33);

- the establishment of departments of state (s 64);
- the appointment of public servants (s 67);
- the appointment of federal judges and their removal (s 72); and
- the appointment of members of the Interstate Commission and their removal (s 103).

All of these functions are vested in the 'Governor-General-in-Council', meaning 'the Governor-General acting with the advice of the federal Executive Council'.

Nevertheless, there are a substantial number of functions vested in the Governor-General alone. For example, the Governor-General:

- 'may ... dissolve the House of Representatives' (s 5);
- 'may dissolve the Senate and the House of Representatives simultaneously' and 'may convene a joint sitting' of the two houses (s 57);
- may, 'according to his discretion' assent to legislation passed by both houses of parliament (s 58);
- 'may appoint ... the Queen's Ministers of State for the Commonwealth', who 'shall hold office during the pleasure of the Governor-General' (s 64);
- has 'the command in chief of the naval and military forces of the Commonwealth' (s 68); and
- may submit a proposal to alter the Constitution, passed by one house but not by the other, to a referendum for the approval of the voters (s 128).

[7.4.5] The Constitution Acts of the states reflect a similar dichotomy. Under the Constitution Act 1975 (Vic) the 'Governor-in-Council' may:

- in certain limited circumstances vary dates specified in Acts of Parliament (s 70);
- appoint judges of the Supreme Court (ss 75, 80 and 81);
- vary judges' pension rights (s 83(4)); and
- appoint to public offices, other than ministers of the Crown (s 88).

On the other hand, the more sensitive political functions are vested in the Governor alone. He or she may:

- summon and prorogue parliament and dissolve the Assembly (ss 8 and 20);
- appoint 'responsible Ministers of the Crown' (s 50);
- remove judges of the Supreme Court upon an address from both houses (s 77); and
- issue warrants for the expenditure of money in the Consolidated Fund (s 93).

The Constitution Act 1902 (NSW) confers one function on 'the Governor with the advice of the Executive Council', namely, 'the appointment of all public offices under the Government' other than Ministers of the Crown: s 47. Functions vested in the Governor alone include:

- convening a joint sitting of the houses where there is a deadlock (s 5B(1));
- summoning and proroguing parliament and dissolving the Assembly (ss 10, 23 and 24);
- approving the standing rules and orders of the houses (s 15(2));
- appointing a day for the reconstitution of the Council (s 17A(1));
- authorising one Executive Councillor to deputise for another (s 36);

- authorising disbursement of 'His Majesty's revenue' (s 44); and
- appointing '[o]fficers liable to retire from office on political grounds' (s 47).

[7.4.6] However, it seems clear that this dichotomy has no constitutional significance. It is clear that, when the Commonwealth Constitution was drafted, the delegates intended that all the functions given to the Governor-General should be exercised on the advice of Ministers. This relationship was spelt out for those functions which, by the 1890s, had become statutory functions of the Crown in the United Kingdom context; but it was not spelt out for those functions which were, at that time, still treated as prerogative (inherent) powers of the Crown in the United Kingdom. The drafting of the clauses dealing with the Governor-General's functions was criticised by George Reid (Premier of New South Wales) at the 1897 Adelaide Convention. He said:

> For a long time now I have been impressed with the view that since we are now expressing, in precise written characters, the various functions of the Governor, and conditions under which the power of the Commonwealth is to be exercised, it would be well in this clause [that is, clause 58, which became s 61 of the Commonwealth Constitution], whilst providing that the executive power and authority of the Commonwealth shall be vested in the Queen, and shall be exercised by the Governor-General as the Queen's representative, that we should add that which will in reality be the practice, that it is by and with the advice of the Executive Council (Convention Debates, Adelaide (1897), p 908).

Edmund Barton, chairman of the drafting committee, responded that there was:

> ... no necessity to add the words 'with the advice of the Governor-in-Council' because in a constitution of this kind it is no more possible than it is under the English Constitution for the prerogative to be exercised as a personal act of the Crown. The prerogative is never in these days exercised as a personal act of the Crown as we understand it, but there are certain acts which have become, either by the gradual march of statute law or in any other way, nothing but ordinary executive acts and these are expressed to be exercisable only with the advice of the Executive Council. There are others again which have not been expressly affected by legislation and while these remain nominally in the exercise of the Crown they are really held in trust for the people, although they are exercises of the prerogative ... [L]et us understand that the Imperial Parliament has in all its drafting of the colonial Constitutions drawn the distinction. Yet it is understood that the Crown exercises the prerogative only upon ministerial advice, and it is exercised not personally by the Crown, but only with, the advice of the ministry or a minister (Convention Debates, Adelaide (1897), p 910).

[7.4.7] The delegates proceeded to accept the drafting committee's recommendation, and so the apparent distinction between functions to be exercised on advice and 'independent' functions was retained. But commentators had no doubt that the distinction was 'historical and technical, rather than practical or substantial': Quick and Garran (1901) p 707. Nor did they have any doubt on the appropriate relationship between the Governor-General and the ministers of state ((1901) p 406):

> [A]ll those powers which involve the performance of executive acts, whether parts of the prerogative or the creatures of statute, will, in accordance with constitutional practice, as developed by the system known as responsible government, be performed by the Governor-General, by and with the advice of the federal Executive Council. (See note s 275.) If the section now under review had been made to read 'the Governor-General-in-Council may appoint such times for holding the sessions of the Parliament,' etc, the words 'in Council' would have been an invasion of the royal prerogative; because it is invariably recognised as a prerogative of the Crown to summon, prorogue

and dissolve Parliament. The words would moreover have been mere surplusage; nothing would have been gained, since parliamentary government has well established the principle that the Crown can perform no executive act, except on the advice of some minister responsible to Parliament. Hence the power nominally placed in the hands of the Governor-General is really granted to the people through their representatives in Parliament. Whilst, therefore, in this Constitution some executive powers are, in technical phraseology, and in accordance with venerable customs, vested in the Governor-General, and other in the Governor-General in Council, they are all substantially in *pari materia*, on the same footing, and, in the ultimate resort, can only be exercised according to the will of the people.

[7.4.8] The view put forward by Quick and Garran in 1901, that the Governor-General exercised his functions on the advice of his Ministers, was widely accepted over the succeeding years. In *New South Wales v Bardolph* (1934) 52 CLR 455, McTiernan J said that '[c]onstitutional rules would prevent the Governor ... from making the contract without ministerial advice': 52 CLR at 517. In *Western Australia v Commonwealth* (the *Territorial Senators* case) (1975) 134 CLR 201 **[4.2.32C]** Jacobs J said at 278:

> [The Governor-General] does not act as a persona designata in a curial or quasi-judicial role. He acts either on the advice of the Executive Council or as an officer under the instructions of the Queen, in all cases subject to the Constitution. No doubt it was envisaged in 1900 that the Queen would at times give instructions on the advice of her United Kingdom ministers but it may now be taken that not only the Governor-General as the medium through which the Queen exercises her executive and prerogative powers but also the Queen herself acts on the advice of her Australian ministers in all matters appertaining to the government of the Commonwealth. Neither the Queen nor the Governor-General acts personally. This is true of the powers of the Governor-General under s 57. He in all aspects exercises his powers under the section on the advice of an Australian minister.

Murphy J made the same point. 'The decision [under s 57]', he said, 'is to be made by the Governor-General on the advice of the Executive Council (Constitution s 62)': 134 CLR at 293. Substantially the same point was made by Gibbs J in *Victoria v Commonwealth* (the *PMA* case) (1975) 134 CLR 81 **[5.3.26C]** at 156.

[7.4.9] The proposition, that the Governor of Victoria must act on ministerial advice, formed the basis of the decision in *FAI Insurances Ltd v Winneke* (1982) 151 CLR 342. The High Court decided that, when the Governor exercised a legal power which could affect an individual (here, the cancellation of an insurer's registration under the Workers Compensation Act 1958 (Vic)), the Governor was just as much subject to the rules of natural justice as any Minister would be. This decision was supported by the argument that, when exercising the power in question, the Governor did 'not act personally [but] on the advice of his Ministers': 151 CLR at 349 per Gibbs CJ. Mason J, whose reasons were adopted by Stephen J, elaborated on the relationship between the Governor (or the Governor-General) and ministers, at 364–5:

> In passing I should observe that ministerial responsibility means (1) the individual responsibility of Ministers to Parliament for the administration of their departments, and (2) the collective responsibility of Cabinet to Parliament (and the public) for the whole conduct of administration (Emy, 'The Public Service and Political Control' in the appendix to the report of the Royal Commission on Australian Government Administration (1976) vol 1, p 16; Mackintosh, *The Government and Politics of Britain*, 4th ed (1977), p 17). The principle that in general the Governor defers to, or acts upon, the advice of his Ministers, though it forms a vital element in the concept of

responsible government, is not in itself an instance of the doctrine of ministerial responsibility. It is a convention, compliance with which enables the doctrine of ministerial responsibility to come into play so that a Minister or Ministers become responsible to Parliament for the decision made by the Governor in Council, thereby contributing to the concept of responsible government. 'The principal convention of the British constitution', says de Smith in his *Constitutional and Administrative Law*, 3rd ed (1977), p 113, 'is that the Queen shall exercise her formal legal powers only upon and in accordance with the advice of her Ministers, save in a few exceptional situations'. Conformably with this principle there is a convention that in general the Governor-General or the Governor of a State acts in accordance with the advice tendered to him by his Ministers and not otherwise (Sawer, *Federation under Strain* (1977), p 142; see also Keith, *Responsible Government in the Dominions*, 2nd ed (1928), pp 107–8). He does this by acting in conformity with the advice given by the Executive Council on consideration of the recommendation by the responsible Minister which may in some cases reflect Government policy as settled by Cabinet or determined by the Minister. The Royal Instructions to the Governor of Victoria expressly allow him to disregard advice (cl VI). This does not affect the convention that he will act on advice. But it is not to be thought that the Queen, the Governor-General or a Governor is bound to accept without question the advice proffered. History and practice provide many instances in which the Queen or her Australian representatives have called in question the advice which has been tendered, have suggested modifications to it and have asked the Ministry to reconsider it even though in the last resort the advice tendered must be accepted (see, for example, de Smith, *Constitutional and Administrative Law*, 3rd ed (1977), p 99).

When Parliament by statute confers a discretionary power on the Governor acting with the advice of the Executive Council it ordinarily assumes that the convention will apply and that the Governor will act in accordance with the advice tendered to him and not otherwise, ultimately, if not sooner. It may be too much to say that the effect of the statute is to replace the force of convention with the force of law.

[7.4.10] This view is generally borne out by experience. But there have been occasions when holders of those offices have acted against ministerial advice and have asserted a substantial independence of action.

[7.4.11] We can put to one side those occasions where the current ministry has, through its loss of control over the lower house of parliament, been deprived of the legitimacy which should entitle it to direct the affairs of government. Incidents such as the refusals of Governors-General to dissolve the House of Representatives in August 1904, July 1905 and May 1909, following the ministry's defeat in the house, and the refusals of Victorian Governors to dissolve the Legislative Assembly in 1924, 1943 and 1952 in similar circumstances (see Hanks (1980) pp 394–5), can be reconciled with the general proposition of responsible government. If the right of Ministers to control the Crown's actions depends on their ability to deliver parliamentary approval of finance for government (see **[7.4.3]**) then, once the Ministers have demonstrably lost that ability, they must be regarded as having also lost the right to control the Crown's actions.

However, the intervention by a state Governor in 1932 and the Governor-General in November 1975 challenged the legitimacy of a ministry which had retained control of the lower house of parliament.

Dismissal of the Lang Government (1935)

[7.4.12] At the height of the Great Depression, in 1931–32, the New South Wales Government, led by Premier Lang, confronted the Commonwealth Government over major issues of economic policy. The Lang Government suspended payment of interest owing by the state on overseas loans. Under the Financial Agreement 1927 (Cth) between the Commonwealth and the states (declared by s 105A(5) of the Commonwealth Constitution to be binding on the Commonwealth and states, notwithstanding any contrary laws), the interest was payable by the state to the Commonwealth for transmission to the state's creditors. The Commonwealth Parliament passed the Financial Agreement Enforcement Act 1932 (Cth) to authorise seizure of state revenues, and Commonwealth collection of taxes and other money owing to the state. The validity of that legislation was upheld by the High Court on 6 April 1932 in *New South Wales v Commonwealth (No 1)* (the *Garnishee* case) (1932) 46 CLR 155.

Premier Lang then instructed state public servants not to bank moneys collected in taxes and charges but to forward those moneys to the Treasurer. A month later, the state Governor, Philip Game, expressed concern that this instruction involved a breach of the Commonwealth law and requested Lang to establish its legality or withdraw it. Lang refused to withdraw the instruction and offered no comment on its disputed legality. On 13 May 1932, the Governor pressed Lang 'to abide by the law' or resign. When Lang refused to resign, the Governor immediately terminated Lang's commission, appointed the Leader of the Opposition, Stevens, as Premier and, on Stevens' advice, dissolved the Legislative Assembly. At the time of the dissolution, Lang had the support of 55 of the 90 members in the Assembly.

The electorate returned Stevens with a majority in the Assembly. No doubt the conflict between Lang's Government and the Commonwealth Government had placed the state Governor in a difficult position. However, it can be said that the Governor acted prematurely, if not improperly. The legal process was still available to test the legality of Lang's instruction of 12 April 1932.

A draft memorandum prepared in the United Kingdom Dominions Office, approved by the United Kingdom Attorney-General but not despatched to the state Governor before the dismissal, suggested another course which the Governor could have followed:

> So long as the courts have not settled the issue and the possibility of raising the issue in the courts still remains, it could not, I think, be said to be unconstitutional if a Governor refrained from taking the initiative in restraining his ministers from action alleged to be illegal. If the courts had pronounced against the legality of any particular action and the ministers still persisted in continuing to perform such action, the position would of course require further consideration (Morrison (1976) p 337).

The dismissal of the Whitlam Government (1975)

[7.4.13] On 15 October 1975, the Senate resolved not to proceed further with legislation to give effect to the Federal Labor Government's financial programme, including the appropriation Bills, until the government agreed to a general election for the House of Representatives: Cth Hansard, Senate, 15 October 1975, p 1156.

The government and the House of Representatives refused to accede to this demand and, on 11 November 1975, Prime Minister Whitlam called on Governor-General Kerr with the intention of advising the Governor-General to request state

Governors to issue writs for a half-Senate election. The Governor-General immediately informed the Prime Minister that he had terminated the latter's commission, by handing him the following letter:

> Dear Mr Whitlam,
>
> In accordance with s 64 of the Constitution I hereby determine your appointment as my chief adviser and head of the government. It follows that I also hereby determine the appointments of all the ministers in your government.
>
> You have previously told me that you would never resign or advise an election of the House of Representatives or a double dissolution and that the only way in which such an election could be obtained would be by my dismissal of you and your ministerial colleagues. As it appeared likely that you would today persist in this attitude I decided that, if you did, I would determine your commission and state my reasons for doing so. You have persisted in your attitude and I have accordingly acted as indicated. I attach a statement of my reasons which I intend to publish immediately.
>
> It is with a great deal of regret that I have taken this step both in respect of yourself and your colleagues.
>
> I propose to send for the leader of the opposition and to commission him to form a new caretaker government until an election can be held.
>
> Yours sincerely,
>
> *[signed John R Kerr]*

Attached to the letter was a statement of the Governor-General's reasons.

[7.4.14E] Statement by the Governor-General

I have given careful consideration to the constitutional crisis and have made some decisions which I wish to explain.

Summary

It has been necessary for me to find a democratic and constitutional solution to the current crisis which will permit the people of Australia to decide as soon as possible what should be the outcome of the deadlock which developed over supply between the two houses of Parliament and between the government and the opposition parties. The only solution consistent with the Constitution and with my oath of office and my responsibilities, authority and duty as Governor-General is to terminate the commission as Prime Minister of Mr Whitlam and to arrange for a caretaker government able to secure supply and willing to let the issue go to the people.

I shall summarise the elements of the problem and the reasons for my decision which places the matter before the people of Australia for prompt determination.

Because of the federal nature of our constitution and because of its provisions the Senate undoubtedly has constitutional power to refuse or defer supply to the government. Because of the principles of responsible government a Prime Minister who cannot obtain supply, including money for carrying on the ordinary services of government, must either advise a general election or resign. If he refuses to do this I have the authority and indeed the duty under the Constitution to withdraw his commission as Prime Minister. The position in Australia is quite different from the position in the United Kingdom. Here the confidence of both houses on supply is necessary to ensure its provision. In the United Kingdom the confidence of the House of Commons alone is necessary. But both here and in the United Kingdom the duty of the Prime Minister is the same in a most important respect — if he cannot get supply he must resign or advise an election.

If a Prime Minister refuses to resign or to advise an election, and this is the case with Mr Whitlam, my constitutional authority and duty require me to do what I have now done — to withdraw his commission — and to invite the Leader of the Opposition to form a caretaker government — that is one that makes no appointments or dismissals and initiates no policies, until a general election is held. It is most desirable that he should guarantee supply. Mr Fraser will be asked to give the necessary undertakings and advise whether he is prepared to recommend a double dissolution. He will also be asked to guarantee supply.

The decisions I have made were made after I was satisfied that Mr Whitlam could not obtain supply. No other decision open to me would enable the Australian people to decide for themselves what should be done.

Once I had made up my mind, for my own part, what I must do if Mr Whitlam persisted in his stated intentions I consulted the Chief Justice of Australia, Sir Garfield Barwick. I have his permission to say that I consulted him in this way.

The result is that there will be an early election for both houses and the people can do what, in a democracy such as ours, is their responsibility and duty and theirs alone. It is for the people now to decide the issue which the two leaders have failed to settle.

Detailed Statement of Decisions

On 16 October the Senate deferred consideration of Appropriation Bills (Nos 1 & 2) 1975–1976. In the time which elapsed since then events made it clear that the Senate was determined to refuse to grant supply to the government. In that time the Senate on no less than two occasions resolved to proceed no further with fresh Appropriation Bills, in identical terms, which had been passed by the House of Representatives. The determination of the Senate to maintain its refusal to grant supply was confirmed by the public statements made by the Leader of the Opposition, the opposition having control of the Senate.

By virtue of what has in fact happened there therefore came into existence a deadlock between the House of Representatives and the Senate on the central issue of supply without which the ordinary services of the government cannot be maintained. I had the benefit of discussions with the Prime Minister and, with his approval, with the Leader of the Opposition and with the Treasurer and the Attorney-General. As a result of those discussions and having regard to the public statements of the Prime Minister and the Leader of the Opposition I have come regretfully to the conclusion that there is no likelihood of a compromise between the House of Representatives and the Senate nor for that matter between the government and the opposition.

The deadlock which arose was one which, in the interests of the nation, had to be resolved as promptly as possible and by means which are appropriate in our democratic system. In all the circumstances which have occurred the appropriate means is a dissolution of the Parliament and an election of both houses. No other course offers a sufficient assurance of resolving the deadlock and resolving it promptly.

Parliamentary control of appropriation and accordingly of expenditure is a fundamental feature of our system of responsible government. In consequence it has been generally accepted that a government which has been denied supply by the Parliament cannot govern. So much at least is clear in cases where a ministry is refused supply by a popularly elected lower house. In other systems where an upper house is denied the right to reject a money Bill denial of supply can occur only at the instance of the lower house. When, however, an upper house possesses the power to reject a money Bill including an Appropriation Bill, and exercises the power by denying supply, the principle that a government which has been denied supply by the Parliament should resign or go to an election must still apply — it is a necessary consequence of parliamentary control of appropriation and expenditure and of the expectation that the ordinary and necessary services of government will continue to be provided.

The Constitution combines the two elements of responsible government and federalism. The Senate is, like the House, a popularly elected chamber. It was designed to provide representation by States, not by electorates, and was given by s 53, equal powers with the House with respect to proposed laws, except in the respects mentioned in the section. It was denied power to originate or amend Appropriation Bills but was left with power to reject them or defer consideration of them. The Senate accordingly has the power and has exercised the power to refuse to grant supply to the government. The government stands in the position that it has been denied supply by the Parliament with all the consequences which flow from that fact.

There have been public discussions about whether there is a convention deriving from the principles of responsible government that the Senate must never under any circumstances exercise the power to reject an Appropriation Bill. The Constitution must prevail over any convention because, in determining the question how far the conventions of responsible government have been grafted on to the federal compact, the Constitution itself must in the end control the situation.

Section 57 of the Constitution provides a means, perhaps the usual means, of resolving a disagreement between the houses with respect to a proposed law. But the machinery which it provides necessarily entails a considerable time lag which is quite inappropriate to a speedy resolution of the fundamental problems posed by the refusal of supply. Its presence in the Constitution does not cut down the reserve powers of the Governor-General.

I should be surprised if the law officers expressed the view that there is no reserve power in the Governor-General to dismiss a ministry which has been refused supply by the Parliament and to commission a ministry, as a caretaker ministry which will secure supply and recommend a dissolution, including where appropriate a double dissolution. This is a matter on which my own mind is quite clear and I am acting in accordance with my own clear view of the principles laid down by the Constitution and of the nature, powers and responsibility of my office.

There is one other point. There has been discussion of the possibility that a half-Senate election might be held under circumstances in which the government has not obtained supply. If such advice were given to me I should feel constrained to reject it because a half-Senate election held whilst supply continues to be denied does not guarantee a prompt or sufficiently clear prospect of the deadlock being resolved in accordance with proper principles. When I refer to rejection of such advice I mean that, as I would find it necessary in the circumstances I have envisaged to determine Mr Whitlam's commission and, as things have turned out have done so, he would not be Prime Minister and not able to give or persist with such advice.

The announced proposals about financing public servants, suppliers, contractors and others do not amount to a satisfactory alternative to supply.

Government House, Canberra 2600
11 November 1975

~~~

[7.4.15E] Memorandum of Advice from the Chief Justice

The Governor-General's statement of reasons referred to advice given to the Governor-General by Chief Justice Barwick on 10 November 1975. The terms of this advice were published on 18 November 1975.

In response to Your Excellency's invitation I attended this day at Admiralty House. In our conversations I indicated that I considered myself, as Chief Justice of Australia, free, on Your Excellency's request, to offer you legal advice as to Your Excellency's constitutional rights and duties in relation to an existing situation which, of its nature, was unlikely to come before the court. We both clearly understood that I was not in any way concerned with matters of a purely political kind, or with any political consequences of the advice I might give.

In response to Your Excellency's request for my legal advice as to whether a course on which you had determined was consistent with your constitutional authority and duty, I respectfully offer the following.

The Constitution of Australia is a federal constitution which embodies the principle of ministerial responsibility. The Parliament consists of two houses, the House of Representatives and the Senate, each popularly elected, and each with the same legislative power, with the one exception that the Senate may not originate nor amend a money Bill.

Two relevant constitutional consequences flow from this structure of the Parliament. First, the Senate has constitutional power to refuse to pass a money Bill; it has power to refuse supply to the Government of the day. Secondly, a Prime Minister who cannot ensure supply to the Crown, including funds for carrying on the ordinary services of government, must either advise a general election (of a kind which the constitutional situation may then allow) or resign. If, being unable to secure supply, he refuses to take either course, Your Excellency has constitutional authority to withdraw his commission as Prime Minister.

There is no analogy in respect of a Prime Minister's duty between the situation of the Parliament under the federal Constitution of Australia and the relationship between the House of Commons, a popularly elected body, and the House of Lords, a non-elected body, in the unitary form of government functioning in the United Kingdom. Under that system, a government having the confidence of the House of Commons can secure supply, despite a recalcitrant House of Lords. But it is otherwise under our federal Constitution. A government having the confidence of the House of Representatives but not that of the Senate, both elected houses, cannot secure supply to the Crown.

But there is an analogy between the situation of a Prime Minister who has lost the confidence of the House of Commons and a Prime Minister who does not have the confidence of the Parliament, ie of the House of Representatives and of the Senate. The duty and responsibility of the Prime Minister to the Crown in each case is the same: if unable to secure supply to the Crown, to resign or to advise an election.

In the event of that, conformably to this advice, the Prime Minister ceases to retain his commission. Your Excellency's constitutional authority and duty would be to invite the Leader of the Opposition, if he can undertake to secure supply, to form a caretaker government (ie one which makes no appointments or initiates any policies) pending a general election, whether of the House of Representatives, or of both houses of the Parliament, as that government may advise.

Accordingly, my opinion is that, if Your Excellency is satisfied in the current situation that the present government is unable to secure supply, the course upon which Your Excellency has determined is consistent with your constitutional authority and duty.

Garfield Barwick

~~~

Notes

[7.4.16] Immediately after terminating Whitlam's commission, Governor-General Kerr commissioned Opposition Leader Fraser as a caretaker Prime Minister on condition that Fraser obtain passage of the Supply Bills and advise the Governor-General to dissolve both the Senate and the House of Representatives. It was a further condition of this appointment that Fraser's government would act as a caretaker government, making no appointments or dismissals and initiating no policies before a general election was held.

Within one hour, the Supply Bills had been passed through the Senate and were on their way to the Governor-General for the royal assent. Prime Minister Fraser then announced his commission to the House of Representatives which, on the motion of Whitlam, resolved:

> That this House expresses its want of confidence in the Prime Minister and requests Mr Speaker forthwith to advise His Excellency the Governor-General to call the honourable member of Werriwa to form a government (Cth Hansard, House of Representatives, 11 November 1975, pp 2930–2).

The Speaker of the House attempted to arrange an appointment to call on the Governor-General, who asked the Speaker to call at 4.45 pm. By that time the Governor-General had signed a proclamation dissolving both the Senate and the House of Representatives under s 57 of the Constitution. That proclamation was made on the advice of Prime Minister Fraser, in whom the House of Representatives had so recently declared its lack of confidence.

The proclamation of the double dissolution cited 21 bills which had fulfilled the requirements of s 57. Essentially they were measures put forward by the former Labor Government, passed on two separate occasions by the Labor-controlled House of Representatives and rejected on two separate occasions by the Liberal–National-Country Party-controlled Senate. The double dissolution proclamation was countersigned by Prime Minister Fraser, the leader of the political forces which were (or had been) opposed to the passage of the 21 bills. The next day, 12 November 1975, the Prime Minister forwarded to the Governor-General an opinion of Solicitor-General Byers to the effect that each of the 21 bills had fulfilled the requirements of s 57.

[7.4.17] Governor-General Kerr's decisive intervention in the political dispute between government and opposition, between House of Representatives and Senate, threw much of the accepted thinking (the conventional wisdom) on our political system into confusion. It raised, for many people, serious doubts about the responsiveness of our system of government, and it has generated a considerable volume of written analysis, criticism and justification. The list of Kerr's critics and defenders is long. It includes, in the former group: Sawer (1977); Emy (1978); Hall and Iremonger (1976); Cooray (1978); Howard and Saunders (1977); Reid (1980); Crisp (1983) pp 412–14; and Howard (1985) pp 135–8. In the latter group are: O'Connell (1976); St John (1976); West (1976); and Ellicott (1977). In evaluating this affair, several points need to be kept in mind.

[7.4.18] First, the Governor-General was in October and November 1975 placed under considerable pressure. He believed himself to be at the centre (although a more realistic assessment might have placed him only close to the centre) of an intense political dispute. That dispute threatened to plunge Australia into a financial crisis and was without precedent in 20th century Australia.

The basis for this unprecedented crisis had been laid at the constitutional conventions of the 1890s. The delegates from the larger colonies (who sought a politically dominant position for the House of Representatives) and those from the smaller colonies (who had pressed for a significant role for the Senate) reached an uneasy compromise. They clearly indicated that a system of responsible government would be based on the House of Representatives: ss 28, 53, 56 and 57 of the Constitution point to the link between ministry and house. However, at the same time, they left the Senate with the power to withhold finance from a ministry formed from the House of Representatives: s 53. That compromise was perhaps inevitable; without it there may have been no federation of the six colonies. But it was a compromise which could only work if it were not taken seriously as the basis of government. The compromise did not threaten the stability of government for 75 years because the Senate did not presume to use its powers under s 53 and because Governors-General conceded full political supremacy to the House of Representatives.

[7.4.19] Second, the Governor-General could be said to have followed a devious course in moving to a resolution of that crisis. He listened to advice from his Prime

Minister, Treasurer, Attorney-General and Solicitor-General and did not indicate that he would act against that advice: see, for example, Emy (1978) pp 171–2, 174; Sawer (1977) pp 148–9, 170–1. He did not, until he dismissed the Labor Party ministry, indicate that the course which the ministry proposed to follow was one which he, the Governor-General, could not take. He secretly consulted Chief Justice Barwick, a person whose political career (he had been Attorney-General and External Affairs Minister in a Liberal–Country Party Government) was likely to make it difficult for observers to accept his impartiality in the current dispute.

It has been said, by Kerr's defenders, that it was necessary for the Governor-General to take such a secretive and deceptive course because, if he had expressed any reservations about the advice tendered to him, Prime Minister Whitlam would have procured his dismissal. However, that argument assumes that it is the Governor-General, not the ministry, which is responsible for government policy and actions. As Emy points out ((1978) p 173), in response to this defence:

> The Crown or its representative bears no direct responsibility for what is done in its name. If the Governor-General was indeed unable to countenance his ministers' policies he should have resigned. He was not entitled to invoke his own concept of the public interest against that of his ministers.

[7.4.20]   Third, the Chief Justice of the High Court should not have accepted Kerr's invitation to advise him. Not only could Barwick's political background be used to attack his impartiality, but his entry into such an intense political controversy could only damage the reputation of the court. And, despite Barwick's assertion to the contrary, matters relating to the dispute and its projected resolution could have been litigated before the court: Sawer (1977) p 158. Indeed, a case then currently awaiting the court's decision, *Attorney-General (Cth) (Ex rel McKinlay) v Commonwealth* (1975) CLR 1 **[4.6.9C]**, could have had serious consequences for the Governor-General's proposed course of action: Sawer (1977) pp 157–8.

A Governor-General had sought the advice of a Chief Justice, on the exercise of the former's powers, only once in the previous 75 years. That was in 1914, when Governor-General Munro-Ferguson consulted with Chief Justice Griffith on the request by Prime Minister Cook for the first double dissolution of parliament. That consultation was carried out with the express consent of the Prime Minister.

[7.4.21]   Fourth, the Governor-General failed to play the constructive role for which his office was suited. He did not attempt to negotiate any settlement between the government and the opposition; he did not place any pressure on the opposition or the government; he gave no one (and here we return to the second point) any indication of how he saw the dispute and its ultimate solution, and he certainly acted prematurely. There are good reasons to suppose that supply would have been passed by the Senate before the end of November (when the government's money would have run out). It is a notorious fact that some opposition senators were preparing to vote for supply when the Governor-General intervened: Crisp (1983) p 412. The Governor-General would have placed the government in no jeopardy had he delayed acting until then because supply would have been passed as soon as the dispute was resolved; whether through a settlement or through his intervention. Much the same point has been made by Reid ((1980) p 10):

> In brief, the Governor-General's action of November 11, 1975 was patently an Executive resolution of a party-political conflict. Our elected politicians, using the power of the respective Houses of Parliament, in an exhibition of political brinksmanship, were jeopardising the apparatus of State, the interests of the

'professional' Public Service and of the people in the community directly dependent upon both. Rather than allow the political conflict to take a course that the Constitution permitted (I believed the politicians were heading for a resolution of their own), we saw a manifestation of an intolerance of politics and of politicians in the orders of the Chief Executive. This entailed the dismissal of the Prime Minister and then the dismissal of all the elected politicians, sending them to the electorate at a stage when the struggle between the political leaders in Parliament had up to 20 days to run. It seems that considerations of Christmas took priority over allowing the parliamentary political conflict between our elected personnel to runs its course.

[7.4.22] However, all these objections go to the style of the Governor-General's actions. The fifth, and probably most critical issue, revolves around the substance of the Governor-General's intervention and the reasons offered in support of that intervention. By dismissing the Labor Party ministry in order to force a dissolution, the Governor-General discarded the ministry based on the popularly elected House of Representatives in favour of a ministry supported by the Senate with its heavy electoral bias. That action must be regarded as conceding substantial political influence to the Senate, an influence which Kerr's predecessors had generally denied. In 1914, for example, Governor-General Munro-Ferguson rejected the Senate's request for access to the reasons advanced by Prime Minister Cook in his advice on the double dissolution. The Governor-General said that he had been advised that:

> ... to accede to the request ... would imply a recognition of a right in the Senate to make ministers of state for the Commonwealth directly responsible to that chamber ... and that such recognition would not be in accordance with the accepted principles of responsible government (Crisp (1983) p 405).

In 1931, Governor-General Isaacs refused a request by the Senate that he not approve regulations under the Transport Workers Act 1928 (Cth), as advised by the ministry, because regulations in substantially identical terms had been disallowed by the Senate under s 48(4) of the Acts Interpretation Act 1901 (Cth). Isaacs stressed that he was bound to act on the advice of his Ministers, in accordance with 'the normal principle of responsible government'. He continued:

> If, as you request me to do, I should reject their advice, supported as it is by the considered opinion of the House of Representatives, and should act upon the equally considered contrary opinion of the Senate, my conduct would, I fear, even on ordinary constitutional grounds, amount to an open personal preference of one house against the other — in other words, an act of partisanship.

The full terms of Isaacs' response to the Senate's request are set out in Cth Hansard, Senate, 10 June 1931, pp 259–7.

[7.4.23] The Governor-General's intervention in 1975 was justified by the Governor-General and the Chief Justice in a series of unargued (and inconsistent) assertions. The basic assertion was that the Governor-General had the responsibility, under s 61 of the Constitution, to maintain the Constitution and the power, under s 64, to appoint and dismiss Ministers. No convention of responsible government, it was said, could modify or reduce those legal provisions. Such a legalistic assertion ignores the basic argument that a parliamentary democracy can only tolerate the trappings of autocracy when they are tempered by democracy. This point was made by Marshall and Moodie. Only by surrendering real power to elected Ministers has the monarchy 'survived into an age when hereditary status no longer carried with it authority to rule, and when powerful sections of the community insisted that the government be responsible to them': Marshall and Moodie (1967) p 42.

The difficulty is that the terms of the Constitution could not by themselves provide a basis for resolution of the crisis. As Emy said ((1978) p 182):

> [The Constitution] is not just a book of rules but an act of settlement. To pretend that the law, in political matters, possesses some unique decisiveness, is to take a doctrinal rather than a wholly literal interpretation. Ultimately, Sir John's action appeared dubious because he tried to answer the question of what was constitutional or unconstitutional solely in the language of law. He tried to identify the lawyer's concept of constitutionality with the concept of constitutionalism [discussed by Emy at p 13]. In so doing, he overlooked the fact that what is legal is not always politically legitimate, and that other people could rightfully distinguish between the legality and the legitimacy of what he did himself.

However, neither the Governor-General nor the Chief Justice was consistent. Neither emphasised legality to the complete exclusion of convention or legitimacy. They were prepared to take what they saw as a conventional view of the Constitution when that view supported their interventionist approach. Each of them asserted, without argument, that rejection of supply by the Senate *obliged* the ministry to advise a dissolution of the House of Representatives or resign, because under the Commonwealth Constitution the ministry was responsible to both Senate and house. Where, in the Constitution, are these rules stated? If they are not formal legal rules of the Constitution but conventions of responsible government, from what experience are they induced, and by what rational arguments can they be supported?

[7.4.24] The term 'conventions of the Constitution' is a familiar, if somewhat elusive, term to most students of government and politics. A V Dicey is generally credited with developing the notion of constitutional conventions. He observed that the rules which make up constitutional law are of two types. The first are those rules which are enforced by the courts; 'the other set of rules consist of conventions understandings, habits, or practices which, though they may regulate the conduct of ... officials, are not in reality laws at all since they are not enforced by the courts. This portion of constitutional law may, for the sake of distinction, be termed the "conventions of the constitution", or "constitutional morality"': Dicey (1908) p 24.

J S Mill had already referred to the 'unwritten maxims of the Constitution' (Mill (1971) p 148), and Anson had described these precepts as 'the custom of the Constitution': Anson (1886) p 23. Jennings later explained that these conventions 'provide the flesh which clothes the dry bones of the law; they make the legal Constitution work; they keep it in touch with the growth of ideas': Jennings (1959) pp 81–2. De Smith argued that the rules of strict law (the justiciable rules) can 'give a grotesquely misleading picture of the rules actually observed' by the participants in government. Accordingly, the conventions which those participants observe ought to be treated as part of constitutional law: de Smith and Brazier (1989) p 29.

Perhaps the clearest description of the function of these conventional rules was provided by Marshall and Moodie. They pointed out that these conventions will be found in all constitutions, even the recently established. No rule of law is self-applying and conventions are quickly developed to govern the application of the rules; to interpret the rules or to prescribe the circumstances of their application. No matter how detailed the formal rules may be, in a changing world it is rarely possible in advance to eliminate doubts by legislation ((1967) p 26):

> The result is often to leave a significant degree of discretion to those exercising the rights or wielding the powers legally conferred, defined, or permitted. As Dicey pointed out, it is to regulate the use of such discretionary power that conventions develop.

[7.4.25] It has been suggested that conventions play a larger role in the countries which, like Australia, have written constitutions as 'the greater the degree of constitutional rigidity, the greater is the need for the benefits of informal adaptation which conventions bring': Munro (1975) p 219. Recognising that constitutions are concerned with political power and its distribution and that their primary function is to fix or stabilise a particular, selected, distribution of power while allowing for gradual, evolutionary shifts in power, a critical function of the political rules or conventions is to express or describe the current distribution of power. And in a society which professes and practises (with some pragmatic modifications) democracy, the political rules or conventions have another critical function; namely, they connect or link the political system with the general view or consensus of what may or may not be done within the political process. An action that is likely to destroy public respect for the existing distribution of power could not be described (in a democratic society) as conforming to the political rules or conventions. Marshall and Moodie explain 'that the conventions describe the way in which certain legal powers must be exercised if the powers are to be tolerated by those affected': Marshall and Moodie (1967) p 35.

[7.4.26] There is nothing in the Australian experience to support the proposition asserted by Kerr and Barwick that the Commonwealth ministry is responsible to both the Senate and the House of Representatives. As Sawer wrote ((1977) pp 146, 227 n 11):

> [It has never] been suggested by constitutional writers that there is a rigid rule requiring advice to dissolve or action by the Crown to procure dissolution merely because of denial of supply by an upper house. Denial of supply by a *lower* house is one of many ways by which loss of confidence in the government may be expressed, and has always been considered in that context. Denial of supply by an upper house, like any other upper house expression of no confidence in a government with a lower house majority, has ever since the Reform Act of 1832 been regarded as irrelevant to principles governing responsible government ... (The circumstance that the Senate is elective makes no difference to this principle, because ... the Senate has never claimed authority to determine the composition of the ministry; this determination is the core of responsible government).

A careful analysis of the political relationship between house, ministry and senate also provides no support for the Barwick–Kerr assertion of responsibility to both houses (p 171):

> In this context ... 'responsible' is a word having no legal significance: its meaning is provided solely by the working rules of responsible government commonly called 'conventions', and under those rules it is not possible for a government to be 'responsible' to two houses so elected that they can have different political majorities.

Ultimately, the Governor-General's action in dismissing the Labor Government can be criticised because it involved the rejection of an established and defensible view of the relationship between parliament and executive, and the assertion of a novel (indeed, revolutionary) view of that relationship, a view which, if adhered to, would throw that relationship into confusion.

5 References

[7.5.1] *Articles*

Campbell, 'Commonwealth Contracts' (1970) 44 *ALJ* 14.

Hanks, 'Vice-Regal Initiative and Discretion' [1975] *ACLD* 194.

Kerr, 'The Governor-General in Australia' (1975) 17 *J Indian Law Institute* 1.

Morrison, 'Dominions Office Correspondence on New South Wales Constitutional Crises 1930–32' (1976) 61 *J Royal Australian Historical Society* 323.

Munro, 'Laws and Conventions Distinguished' (1975) 91 *LQR* 218.

O'Connell, 'The Dissolution of the Australian Parliament' (1976) 57 *Parliamentarian* 1.

Reid, 'The Changing Political Framework' (1980) 24 *Quadrant* 5.

Sawer, 'Cabinets Councils and Ministers in Australia' [1956] *Public Law* 110.

Sawer, 'The Governor Generalship of the Commonwealth of Australia' (1976) 52 *Current Affairs Bulletin* 20.

St John, 'The Dismissal of the Whitlam Government' (1976) 20 *Quadrant* 63.

West, 'Constitutional Crisis 1975 — An Historian's View' (1976) 48 *Australian Quarterly* 48.

[7.5.2] *Papers and reports*

Constitutional Commission, *Final Report*, Australian Government Publishing Service, Canberra, 1988.

Hasluck, 'The Office of the Governor General', 9th Queale Memorial Lecture, Australian Institute of Management, South Australian Division, 1972.

[7.5.3] *Texts*

Anderson, 'The Constitutional Framework' in *The Government of the Australian States*, (ed Davis), Longman, London, 1960, pp 1–53.

Anson, *Law and Custom of the Constitution*, Clarendon, Oxford, 1886.

Bailey, 'Self-Government in Australia, 1860–1900' in *Cambridge History of the British Empire*, vol 7, Cambridge University Press, Cambridge, 1933, pp 397–424.

Campbell, 'Ministers, Public Servants and the Executive Branch' in *Labor and the Constitution 1972–1975*, (ed Evans), Heinemann Educational, Melbourne, 1977, pp 136–56.

Cooray, *Conventions, the Australian Constitution and the Future*, Legal Books, Sydney, 1979.

Crisp, *Australian National Government*, 5th ed, Longman Cheshire, Melbourne, 1983.

de Smith and Brazier, *Constitutional and Administrative Law*, 6th ed, Penguin, Melbourne, 1989.

Dicey, *Law of the Constitution*, 7th ed, Macmillan, London, 1908.

Ellicott, 'Commentary' in *Labor and the Constitution 1972–1975*, (ed Evans), Heinemann Educational, Melbourne, 1977, pp 288–96.

Emy, *The Politics of Australian Democracy*, 2nd ed, Macmillan, Melbourne, 1978.

Encel, *Cabinet Government in Australia*, Melbourne University Press, Melbourne, 1962; 2nd ed, 1974.

Evans (ed), *Labor and the Constitution 1972–1975*, Heinemann Educational, Melbourne, 1977.

Evatt, *The King and His Dominion Governors*, Oxford University Press, London, 1936.

Evatt, *The Royal Prerogative*, Lawbook Co, Sydney, 1987 (1924).

Foott, *Dismissal of a Premier (The Philip Game Papers)*, Morgan, Sydney, 1968.

Hall and Iremonger, *The Makers and the Breakers*, Wellington Lane Press, Sydney, 1976.

Hanks, *Australian Constitutional Law*, 2nd ed, Butterworths, Sydney, 1980.

Howard and Saunders, in *Labor and the Constitution 1972–1975*, (ed Evans), Heinemann Educational, Melbourne, 1977, pp 251–87.

Howard, *Australian Federal Constitutional Law*, 3rd ed, Law Book Co, Sydney, 1985.

Jennings, *The Law and the Constitution*, 5th ed, University of London Press, London, 1959.

Keith, *Responsible Government in the Dominions*, 2nd ed, Clarendon Press, Oxford, 1928.

Keith, *Speeches and Documents on the British Dominions*, Oxford University Press, London, 1932.

Lumb, *Constitutions of the Australian States*, 5th ed, Queensland University Press, Brisbane, 1991.

Marshall and Moodie, *Some Problems of the Constitution*, 4th ed, Hutchinson, London, 1967.

Mill, *Considerations on Representative Government*, Oxford University Press, London, 1971.

Quick and Garran, *Annotated Constitution of the Australian Commonwealth*, Angus & Robertson, Sydney, 1901.

Richardson, 'Executive Power of the Commonwealth' in *Commentaries on the Constitution*, (ed Zines), Butterworths, Sydney, 1977, pp 50–87.

Saunders, 'The National Implied Power and Implied Restrictions on Commonwealth Power' (1984) 14 *Federal Law Review* 267 and 275.

Townsley, *The Government of Tasmania*, University of Queensland Press, Brisbane, 1976.

Winterton, *Parliament, the Executive and the Governor-General*, Melbourne University Press, 1983.

Winterton, 'The Constitutional Position of Australian State Governors', in *Australian Constitutional Perspectives*, (eds Lee and Winterton), Law Book Co, Sydney, 1992.

Zines, 'The Growth of Australian Nationhood and its effect on the Powers of the Commonwealth' in *Commentaries on the Constitution*, (ed Zines), Butterworths, Sydney, 1977.

Zines, *The High Court and the Constitution*, 4th ed, Butterworths, Sydney, 1997.

Chapter

8

Federalism: the Legal Relationships

1 Inconsistency of Commonwealth and state laws

Federal supremacy

[8.1.1] Where two or more legislative authorities share power to make laws which are to operate in a single territory and for its inhabitants, conflict between the laws of each authority is inevitable. Some of that conflict could be avoided by allocating to each authority exclusive power over specific topics or subject matters; for example, one legislature might be empowered to make laws for the regulation of shipping and the other legislature given authority to legislate on aircraft. Each of these assignments could be declared to be exclusive, that is, given to the designated legislature to the exclusion of the other legislature. However, even when that expedient is adopted (as it has been, for example, in the Indian and Canadian Constitutions), the possibility of conflict is not eliminated. For, in order to promote the safety of shipping, the first legislature might attempt to keep the area around the sea lanes free of any activity which could obstruct ships or interfere with their navigational aids, and such a law could come into direct conflict with a law made by the second legislature fixing the routes to be flown by commercial and other aircraft.

The reality is that once two bodies are given the power to control human activities in the one geographical area (even if we believe that these activities have been neatly categorised and divided between the controlling bodies) there must come a time when their edicts or regulations conflict. If disorder (and double jeopardy) is to be avoided a rule is needed to resolve that conflict. The rule that is applied in all federal systems is that the central law-maker prevails: Wheare (1963) p 74. In the United States, this result is said to be implicit in art VI, cl 2 of the United States Constitution, which declares that '[t]his Constitution, and the Laws of the United States which shall be made in Pursuance thereof ... shall be the supreme Law of the Land': *Gibbons v Ogden* (1824) 9 Wheat 1. In Canada, the rule of 'federal paramountcy' was a product of judicial creativity (outside the narrow areas of agriculture and immigration where federal supremacy is expressly conferred by s 95, British North America Act): *Huson v South Norwich* (1895) 24 SCR 143.

[8.1.2] In the case of the Australian federal system, the potential for this type of conflict is high, for the allocation of legislative powers between the Commonwealth Parliament and the state parliaments assumes a sharing of responsibilities, rather than an exclusive division. That is, the power of the Commonwealth Parliament to make laws with respect to interstate and overseas trade and commerce (s 51(i)), taxation (s 51(ii)), defence (s 51(vi)) and so on is not given to the Commonwealth alone. The power to legislate on these topics is not taken away from the states (with a few exceptions: for example, Commonwealth Constitution ss 90, 114, 115). There are some Commonwealth legislative powers which are expressed to be exclusive (for example, s 52 of the Commonwealth Constitution) or which are intrinsically exclusive (ss 51(iv), 51(xxix), 51(xxx) of the Commonwealth Constitution). However, the bulk of those powers are best described as concurrent, that is, shared with the state parliaments whose legislative powers are defined in very general terms in their own Constitution Acts.

The framers of the Commonwealth Constitution clearly recognised this potential for Commonwealth–state conflict and made express provision to deal with it.

[8.1.3E] <h3 style="text-align:center">Commonwealth of Australia
Constitution Act 1900 (UK)</h3>

5 This Act, and all laws made by the Parliament of the Commonwealth under the Constitution, shall be binding on the courts, judges, and people of every State and of every part of the Commonwealth, notwithstanding anything in the laws of any State; and the laws of the Commonwealth shall be in force on all British ships, the Queen's ships of war excepted, whose first port of clearance and whose port of destination are in the Commonwealth.

~~~

[8.1.4E] <h3 style="text-align:center">Commonwealth Constitution</h3>

109 When a law of a State is inconsistent with a law of the Commonwealth, the latter shall prevail, and the former shall, to the extent of the inconsistency, be invalid.

~~~

Notes

[8.1.5] Before s 109 of the Constitution can operate, it is necessary to demonstrate that there is a law of the Commonwealth Act and a law of a state in conflict. If one or both of the laws are invalid, there can be no s 109 inconsistency. In the event that the state law is invalid (otherwise than by the operation of s 109), the Commonwealth law will simply operate in the 'field' left vacant by the state law. Similarly, if the Commonwealth law is constitutionally invalid, the state law will operate in the open field. So, for example, in *Pirrie v McFarlane* (1925) 36 CLR 170

[8.2.82C], where Commonwealth power existed but no Commonwealth law had been made relying on that power, a valid state law operated in the relevant area.

Once analysis has been conducted to determine that the Commonwealth and state laws operating in the circumstances are valid and operative (see further **[8.1.76]**–**[8.1.79]**), the resolution of a s 109 problem can be approached by considering (1) what does 'law' mean for the purposes of s 109? (2) what does the word 'inconsistent' mean in s 109 (what is the test of inconsistency and how is it applied)?; and (3) what is involved when a state law is then 'invalid'? (Inconsistency or 'repugnancy' issues relating to Commonwealth and territory laws are also considered in this chapter: see **[8.1.78]**–**[8.1.80]**.)

'Law'

[8.1.6] The reference in s 109 to 'law' is generally assumed to be a reference to legislation. In *Amalgamated Society of Engineers v Adelaide Steamship Co Ltd* (the *Engineers'* case) (1920) 28 CLR 129 **[8.2.31C]**, Knox CJ, Isaacs, Rich and Starke JJ referred to s 109 as giving 'supremacy, not merely to any particular class of Commonwealth Acts but to every Commonwealth Act, over not merely State Acts passed under concurrent powers but all State Acts': 28 CLR at 155. In *Commonwealth v Colonial Combing, Spinning and Weaving Co Ltd* (1922) 31 CLR 421, Knox CJ and Gavan Duffy J said that 'the phrase "the laws of the Commonwealth" [wherever used in the Constitution] probably means Acts of the Parliament of the Commonwealth': 31 CLR at 431.

Common law

[8.1.7] Lane suggested that the term may extend to federal or state common law: Lane (1979) p 866; so that a right or power established by federal common law could override the provisions of a state Crimes Act. For example, the prerogative right of the Crown in right of the Commonwealth to be paid its debts in priority to private creditors could be 'a law of the Commonwealth'; it is a right conferred by federal common law, by the common law which defines the functions, powers and immunities of the Commonwealth Executive. And, as 'a law of the Commonwealth', that prerogative right would override any state legislation which purported to restrict its operation.

However, when the High Court was first faced with a conflict between that prerogative right and state legislation, none of the justices saw s 109 as resolving the conflict: *Uther v Federal Commissioner of Taxation* (1947) 74 CLR 508 **[8.2.90C]**. Latham CJ, who held that the state legislation overrode the Commonwealth prerogative, treated s 109 as concerned only with Commonwealth and state legislation: 74 CLR at 520. Dixon J, who held that the state legislation was invalid, reached this result without recourse to the effect of s 109; a question which, he said, it was 'unnecessary to pursue': 74 CLR at 532.

More recently, in *Lange v Australian Broadcasting Corporation* (1997) 189 CLR 520, the High Court adopted Sir Owen Dixon's account of the relationship between the common law and the Constitution (Dixon, 1957), and concluded that there is no separate federal and state common law in Australia (at 562–3):

> With the establishment of the Commonwealth of Australia, as with that of the United States of America, it became necessary to accommodate basic common law concepts and techniques to a federal system of government embodied in a written and rigid

constitution. The outcome in Australia differs from that in the United States. There is but one common law in Australia which is declared by this Court as the final court of appeal. In contrast to the position in the United States, the common law as it exists throughout the Australian States and Territories is not fragmented into different systems of jurisprudence, possessing different content and subject to different authoritative interpretations ...

[8.1.8]   In *Commonwealth v Cigamatic Pty Ltd* (1962) 108 CLR 372 **[8.2.98C]**, the High Court overruled *Uther's* case and held that state legislation could not displace or modify a Commonwealth prerogative (that is, a common law right traditionally enjoyed by the executive government). However, Dixon CJ, with whom Kitto and Windeyer JJ agreed, was even more dismissive of the relevance of s 109 than he had been in *Uther v Federal Commissioner of Taxation* (1947) 74 CLR 508 **[8.2.90C]**. In asserting the incompetence of state legislatures to affect the prerogative rights of the Commonwealth, Dixon CJ said:

> I do not speak of legal rights which are the immediate product of Federal statute and so protected by s 109 of the Constitution (108 CLR 378).

[8.1.9]   Perhaps the state legislatures' incompetence was a result of the 'prerogative' powers of the Crown forming part of the Commonwealth's executive power under s 61 of the Constitution (*Victoria v Commonwealth* (1996) 187 CLR 416); so that the conflict truly arose between the Commonwealth Constitution and a repugnant state law, rather than between a 'common law' right of the Commonwealth and a state law. This form of analysis was adopted in *Kable v DPP (NSW)* (1996) 189 CLR 51 **[6.4.24]**, **[6.4.35]**, **[6.4.48C]**, where a majority of the High Court struck down state legislation on the basis that it was inconsistent with the principles underpinning Chapter III of the Constitution: see, in particular, the judgment of Gummow J: 189 CLR at 132.

Industrial awards

[8.1.10]   If the term 'law' in s 109 is confined to legislation, it includes Acts of Parliament and subordinate legislation, such as regulations made under the authority of an Act of Parliament, but it does not include industrial awards made by the Industrial Relations Commission (or its predecessors) under the Workplace Relations Act 1996 (Cth) (and its predecessor legislation). However, those awards may be treated as adopted or endorsed by the Workplace Relations Act and so, in combination with that Act override inconsistent state laws: *Clyde Engineering Co Ltd v Cowburn* (1926) 37 CLR 466 **[8.1.20]**; *Ex parte McLean* (1930) 43 CLR 472.

In *Ex parte McLean* (1930) 43 CLR 472 **[8.1.27C]**, as in the judgment of Isaacs J in *Clyde Engineering Co v Cowburn* (1926) 37 CLR 466 **[8.1.20]**, the inconsistency was said to be, not between the Commonwealth industrial award and the state law, but between the Commonwealth legislation authorising the award and the state law. The practical consequences of this conception of industrial awards are limited. First, it affects the way in which an argument about s 109 inconsistency should be developed. Rather than arguing that the award and a state law are inconsistent, one should argue that the principal Act, which incorporates and gives effect to the award, is inconsistent with the state law. This means that an indication of intention to cover the field must be found in the principal Act, not merely in the award. Second, it is to the Act, rather than to the award, that the court will look in order to define the field with which the law of the Commonwealth deals.

Subordinate legislation generally

[8.1.11] These analytical complications do not extend to such subordinate legislation as Commonwealth regulations. These can be described as laws of the Commonwealth, and state laws will be invalid if inconsistent with Commonwealth regulations, as confirmed by the various judgments in the High Court and the Privy Council's opinion in *O'Sullivan v Noarlunga Meat Ltd* (1954) 92 CLR 565; (1956) 95 CLR 177 **[8.1.36]**, **[8.1.45]**, and in the High Court in *Airlines of New South Wales (No 1)* (1964) 113 CLR 1 and *Airlines of New South Wales (No 2)* (1965) 113 CLR 54 **[8.1.37]**. Rules of court are also classified as 'laws' for the purposes of s 109: *Flaherty v Girgis* (1987) 162 CLR 574 **[8.1.52]**.

[8.1.12] A law of the Commonwealth enacted in relation to a particular territory under s 122 of the Constitution is also a 'law' for the purposes of s 109 and can override a state law: *Lamshed v Lake* (1958) 99 CLR 132. The question whether a territory law is repugnant to a Commonwealth law is a separate question and is considered at **[8.1.80]**–**[8.1.82]** below, and in Chapter 12.

Administrative orders and directions

[8.1.13] On the other hand, administrative orders and directions will not be treated as laws of the Commonwealth for the purposes of s 109: *Airlines of New South Wales Pty Ltd v New South Wales (No 1)* (1964) 113 CLR 1 per Taylor J (with whom Kitto and Windeyer JJ agreed: 113 CLR at 31; see also Menzies J: 113 CLR at 46).

'Inconsistent'

The direct approaches to inconsistency

[8.1.14] Conflict between Commonwealth and state legislation is always argued and resolved in terms of s 109 of the Commonwealth Constitution. That provision is apparently direct and simple in its statement but it has, over the years, had a varying impact on state legislation. In the early years of this century, the section was given a relatively narrow reading by the High Court of Australia, so that a wide range of state legislation was allowed to co-exist with Commonwealth legislation. However, from the mid-1920s the High Court developed a more expansive reading of s 109, so that more state legislation came to be struck down because of some perceived inconsistency with Commonwealth legislation. The shift in the impact of s 109 came about through the High Court's expansion of the meaning of 'inconsistent' in s 109. Early decisions during the first 20 years of the court's work had insisted, rather narrowly, that two laws were inconsistent only when it was impossible for a person simultaneously to obey both laws, when obedience to one law automatically and inevitably involved disobedience to the other law. This is sometimes referred to as the 'impossibility of simultaneous obedience' test.

This test of inconsistency was initially developed by the High Court in the context of assessing the validity of federal industrial awards. The original members of the court, Griffith CJ, Barton and O'Connor JJ, had adopted the view that no federal industrial award could be made under the Conciliation and Arbitration Act 1904 (Cth) if that award was inconsistent with a state law. This inferiority, the converse of the supremacy conferred by s 109, flowed from the majority's view of the nature of 'conciliation and arbitration' in s 51(xxxv) of the Constitution; it was regularly attacked by Isaacs and Higgins JJ, appointed to the court three years after the original members: see, for example, *Federated Saw Mill etc Employee's Association v James Moore & Sons Pty Ltd* (1909) 8 CLR 465; and *Australian Boot Trade Employees Federation v Whybrow & Co* (1910) 10 CLR 266 **[8.1.15]**.

[8.1.15] In *Australian Boot Trade Employees Federation v Whybrow & Co* (1910) 10 CLR 266 the High Court was asked whether an award, proposed by the Commonwealth Court of Conciliation and Arbitration, would be inconsistent with a state law. The award would have fixed a 'minimum rate of wages to be paid to male employees on time-work' in the boot trade in New South Wales, Queensland, South Australia and Victoria of 1s 1½d per hour. In each of those states, a state law provided that employees in that industry should be paid a (lower) minimum wage of 1 s per hour.

Four members of the court, Griffith CJ, Barton, O'Connor and Higgins JJ, held that the inconsistency of the Commonwealth award and the state law depended on a negative answer to the question, 'could an employer simultaneously obey the award and the law?' Barton J said neither prescribed an inflexible rate. He continued at 299:

> The affirmative words of the [Commonwealth] award ... do not 'import a contradiction' between it and the determinations. It is impossible to say that the employer cannot obey the one without disobeying the other. Therefore, the former and the latter may stand together. Therefore, according to the proper test, they are not inconsistent.

Higgins J adopted the same approach (although his rejection of the majority's view of the inferiority of Commonwealth awards rendered hypothetical his discussion of the proposed award's inconsistency). He said at 339:

> [T]he enforcement of both laws does not expose a person to a conflict of duties. There is merely an additional duty, not an inconsistent duty.

On the other hand, Isaacs J (for whom the issue was also hypothetical) suggested a broader approach to the question of inconsistency. He was 'disposed to agree' that this question should be resolved by asking whether the superior law-maker had 'appropriated the ground' or had indicated, 'expressly or impliedly', that it wished its rule to be the only rule on that area, 'then the least entry upon that area by the Federal arbitrator, is an unwarranted intrusion and inconsistent with the "law of the land"': 10 CLR at 330.

[8.1.16] Despite Isaacs J's claim, in *Clyde Engineering Co Ltd v Cowburn* (1926) 37 CLR 466 at 489 **[8.1.20]**, that Griffith CJ had agreed with Isaacs J's broader view of inconsistency, the High Court continued to use the 'impossibility of simultaneous obedience' test; although (perhaps confusingly) judicial discussion of inconsistency rarely occurred in the context of s 109 problems: *Attorney-General (Qld) v Attorney-General (Cth)* (1915) 20 CLR 148; *Federated Seamen's Union v Commonwealth Steamship Owners' Association* (1922) 30 CLR 144; *Federated Engine Drivers' and Firemen's Association v Adelaide Chemical and Fertiliser Co Ltd* (1920) 28 CLR 1.

[8.1.17] One example of a s 109 case in this early period which appeared to rely on the impossibility of simultaneous obedience test was *R v Licensing Court of Brisbane; Ex parte Daniell* (1920) 28 CLR 23. Section 166 of the Liquor Act 1912

(Qld) provided that a local referendum (on liquor trading) 'shall be held at the Senate election in the year 1917'. But s 14 of the Commonwealth Electoral (Wartime) Act 1917 (Cth) declared that 'no referendum or vote of electors of any state or part of a state shall be taken under the law of a state' on a Senate polling day. The court held that the two laws were inconsistent. The majority (Knox CJ, Isaacs, Gavan Duffy, Powers, Rich and Starke JJ; Higgins J dissenting) went on to hold that a local referendum held in part of Brisbane on 5 May 1917 (the Senate polling day) had no legal effect and could not form the basis for administrative proceedings to declare that part of Brisbane 'dry'. In their joint judgment, the majority described the inconsistency as:

> [A] conflict, or inconsistency, between the State Act authorising and commanding the vote on that day and the Commonwealth Act ... forbidding the vote on that day. Then s 109 of the Constitution enacts that in such a case the State law, to the extent of the inconsistency, is invalid (28 CLR at 29).

[8.1.18]   The reasons behind this narrow view of inconsistency were not articulated by the early court. However, it may be more than a coincidence that it was developed and maintained by the three original members of the court, Griffith CJ, Barton and O'Connor JJ, who had also espoused the 'reserved powers' doctrine; the proposition that the Commonwealth Constitution should be interpreted in the way which did the least damage to the autonomy (the 'reserved power') of the states: *Peterswald v Bartley* (1904) 1 CLR 497 **[8.2.21]**; *R v Barger* (1908) 6 CLR 41 **[8.2.22]**; *Huddart Parker & Co Pty Ltd v Moorehead* (1909) 8 CLR 330 **[8.2.24]**. A narrow view of inconsistency would serve the same general purpose (preservation of state autonomy) as the 'reserved powers' approach to other parts of the Constitution. It may also be more than a coincidence that the most committed judicial opponent of the 'reserved powers' doctrine, Isaacs J, consistently argued for a broader view of inconsistency.

This explanation of the different views of inconsistency (as reflecting the justices' general ideas on the appropriate federal balance: states' rights or centralism?) suffers from one defect. Higgins J, who shared Isaacs J's distaste for the 'reserved powers' doctrine, was a persistent advocate of the narrow, 'impossibility of simultaneous obedience' approach to s 109: see, for example, his dissent in *Clyde Engineering Co Ltd v Cowburn* (1926) 37 CLR 466 **[8.1.20]**. But, despite that flaw in the pattern, the explanation gathers some support from the following observations of O'Connor J in *Woodstock Central Dairy Co Ltd v Commonwealth* (1912) 15 CLR 241, although it should be noted they were in relation to administrative law rather than s 109 (at 250):

> It is a well-known principle of interpretation that a Statute will not be taken as intended to abridge the liberty of the subject unless the legislature has used plain language to express that intention. The same principle must, I think, be applied in considering whether the Commonwealth legislature has expressed an intention to exercise a power which, when once exercised, will necessarily restrict the liberty of State legislatures in regard to the same subject matter.

[8.1.19]   If the narrow view of inconsistency was prompted by concern for states' rights, the pressures for the adoption of a broader approach were becoming irresistible. The court had begun to move towards a more centralist or nationalist interpretation of the Constitution during the 1914–18 war, impressed, no doubt, by the military and economic demands of total war. The last of the court's original members, Barton J died in January 1920, Griffith CJ had retired three months earlier, and Isaacs J was establishing his intellectual leadership of the new court.

Indeed, 1920 was the watershed, for in that year the court decided *Amalgamated Society of Engineers v Adelaide Steamship Co Ltd* (the *Engineers'* case) (1920) 28 CLR 129 **[8.2.31C]**, in which it threw out many of the concepts and approaches to constitutional interpretation which the court had developed and maintained over the first 15 years of its work. Among the discarded intellectual baggage was the 'reserved powers' doctrine. Once the court accepted that the legislative powers of the Commonwealth were to be read broadly and without regard to preserving the states' position, s 109 issues were likely to appear on the court's agenda more frequently. (In a sense, the 'reserved powers' doctrine had done the job of preempting s 109 problems.) And, once the issues were raised, the logic of the court's new approach to constitutional interpretation demanded a significant shift in its reading of s 109.

The indirect approach to inconsistency

[8.1.20] The shift came in *Clyde Engineering Co Ltd v Cowburn* (1926) 37 CLR 466, where a majority of the High Court held that the Forty-Four Hours Week Act 1925 (NSW) was inconsistent with the Conciliation and Arbitration Act 1904 (Cth), which supported an award for the engineering industry throughout Australia. The state legislation provided that a worker's ordinary working hours should not exceed 44 hours a week (s 6(1)(a)) and that any worker covered by a federal award fixing a longer working week should be paid the full award wages for working 44 hours: s 13. The award, made by the Commonwealth Court of Conciliation and Arbitration, provided that each worker covered by the award should be paid a fixed wage for a working week of 48 hours, and that any worker who did not attend for the full time 'should lose his pay for the actual time of such non-attendance'.

Knox CJ and Gavan Duffy J began to develop an alternative s 109 test when they described the test of inconsistency adopted in *Australian Boot Trade Employees Federation v Whybrow & Co* (1910) 10 CLR 266 **[8.1.15]** as:

> ... not sufficient or even appropriate in every case. Two enactments may be inconsistent although obedience to each of them may be possible without the other. Statutes may do more than impose duties; they may, for instance, confer rights; and one statute is inconsistent with another when it takes away a right conferred by that other even though the right be one which might be waived or abandoned without disobeying the statute which conferred it (37 CLR at 478).

This approach has become known as the 'conferral of rights' test of inconsistency.

Isaacs J began to articulate a third inconsistency test when he acknowledged that an employer could obey both the state legislation and the Commonwealth award by immediately returning to any worker, who worked a 44-hour week, the money withheld from the worker's wages. However, he maintained that inconsistency could exist even where simultaneous obedience was possible (at 489):

> If ... a competent legislature expressly or impliedly evinces its intention to cover the whole field, that is a conclusive test of inconsistency where another legislature assumes to enter to any extent upon the same field ... If such a position as I have postulated be in fact established, the inconsistency is demonstrated, not by comparison of detailed provisions, but by the mere existence of the two sets of provisions ...

This approach has become known as the 'cover the field' test of inconsistency.

Applying the cover the field test, Isaacs J explained that the Conciliation and Arbitration Act not only authorised the Commonwealth Arbitration Court to settle interstate industrial disputes but indicated that such a settlement (expressed in an award) was 'to end the dispute and thereby conclude the parties'. Whatever the

Arbitration Court decided in the award was a conclusive settlement 'both as to what is granted and what is refused' (at 491–2):

> As to the industrial conditions in dispute, an award by force of the Act covers the field, even where a wage is stated as the minimum or where hours are stated as the maximum, and establishes what on that field are to be the reciprocal rights and obligations of the parties bound. Any entry, therefore, of a State upon this field is an intrusion upon occupied federal territory and inconsistent with the award, regardless of the specific terms of the State legislation whether direct or indirect.

The same approach was taken by Starke J, who described the state law as undoing 'what the Commonwealth tribunal considered a right and just settlement of [the industrial] dispute taken as a whole. Such provisions are, in my opinion, inconsistent with the law of the Commonwealth and, therefore, invalid': 37 CLR at 527. Rich J adopted the same approach as Knox CJ and Gavan Duffy J (see 37 CLR at 522) while Higgins and Powers JJ dissented, on the ground that an employer could obey the state law without disobeying the Commonwealth award: 37 CLR at 503, 516.

The operation of the three tests

[8.1.21]   The judgments in *Clyde Engineering Co Ltd v Cowburn* (1926) 37 CLR 466 **[8.1.20]** suggest that inconsistency between Commonwealth and state laws can exist in any one of three situations:

- where simultaneous obedience is impossible;
- where one law takes away a right or privilege conferred by the other; and
- where the state law invades a field which the Commonwealth law was intended to cover.

Those alternatives were recently acknowledged by Gleeson CJ, Gaudron, McHugh, Gummow, Kirby, Hayne and Callinan JJ in *Telstra Corporation Ltd v Worthing* (1997) 197 CLR 61, where the court reversed a judgment of the New South Wales Court of Appeal to the effect that an employer whose workers compensation liabilities were prescribed by Commonwealth legislation (the Safety, Rehabilitation and Compensation Act 1988) was also subject to state workers compensation legislation. Their Honours said at 76–7:

> The applicable principles are well settled. Cases still arise where one law requires what the other forbids. It was held in *Wallis v Downard-Pickford (North Queensland) Pty Ltd* that a State law which incorporated into certain contracts a term which a law of the Commonwealth forbad was invalid. However, it is clearly established that there may be inconsistency within the meaning of s 109 although it is possible to obey both the Commonwealth law and the State law. Further, there will be what Barwick CJ identified as 'direct collision' where the State law, if allowed to operate, would impose an obligation greater than that for which the federal law has provided. Thus, in *Australian Mutual Provident Society v Goulden*, in a joint judgment, the Court determined the issue before it by stating that the provision of the State law in question 'would qualify, impair and, in a significant respect, negate the essential legislative scheme of the Commonwealth Life Insurance Act'. A different result obtains if the Commonwealth law operates within the setting of other laws so that it is supplementary to or cumulative upon the State law in question ...
>
> In *Victoria v Commonwealth*, Dixon J stated two propositions which are presently material. The first was: 'When a State law, if valid, would alter, impair or detract from the operation of a law of the Commonwealth Parliament, then to that extent it is invalid.' The second, which followed immediately in the same passage, was: 'Moreover,

if it appears from the terms, the nature or the subject matter of a Federal enactment that it was intended as a complete statement of the law governing a particular matter or set of rights and duties, then for a State law to regulate or apply to the same matter or relation is regarded as a detraction from the full operation of the Commonwealth law and so as inconsistent.' The second proposition may apply in a given case where the first does not, yet, contrary to the approach taken in the Court of Appeal, if the first proposition applies, then s 109 of the Constitution operates even if, and without the occasion to consider whether, the second proposition applies.

[8.1.22] Of the approaches to inconsistency listed above, the first two (impossibility of simultaneous obedience, and rights conferral) are relatively simple. They involve no more than a comparative analysis of the legal operation of two pieces of legislation: What are the legal rights and duties which are created or affected by each piece of legislation? How do those rights and duties compare? Can we say that the duties created by one law make impossible compliance with the duties created by the other law? If not, can we say that the duties created by one law make impossible enjoyment of the rights created by the other law? To confirm the legal analytical nature of these tests of inconsistency, Barwick CJ (with the concurrence of Stephen and Aickin JJ) has contrasted them with the 'cover the field' test and described them as 'textual collision between the provisions of the Australian Act and of the State Act': *Miller v Miller* (1978) 141 CLR 269 at 275.

In *Cowburn*, this analysis revealed (as in the earlier, and inverted, *Australian Boot Trade Employees Federation v Whybrow & Co* (1910) 10 CLR 266 **[8.1.15]**) that the duty imposed on employers by state law (the payment of a full award wage for 44 hours' work) did not make impossible compliance with the duty imposed by Commonwealth law (the payment of a full award wage for 48 hours' work). However, the duty imposed by that state law did make impossible enjoyment of the right conferred on the employer by Commonwealth law (to demand 48 hours of work from each employee who was paid a full award wage).

[8.1.23] *Colvin v Bradley Bros Pty Ltd* (1943) 68 CLR 151 provides another example of the type of conferral of rights inconsistency found, in *Clyde Engineering Co Ltd v Cowburn* (1926) 37 CLR 466 **[8.1.20]**, by Knox CJ, Gavan Duffy and Isaacs JJ. An order, made under the Factories and Shops Act 1912 (NSW), prohibited the employment of women on milling machines. Section 41 of the Act made this prohibited employment an offence on the part of the employer. However, an award made by the Arbitration Court under the Conciliation and Arbitration Act 1904 (Cth) declared that an employer who was party to the award 'may employ females on work in the industries and callings covered by this award'.

Bradley Bros Pty Ltd was covered by the award, but was prosecuted under s 41 of the state Act for employing women on milling machines. The prosecution was dismissed and, on appeal, the High Court confirmed that the state law was inconsistent with a law of the Commonwealth and therefore invalid. Latham CJ said:

> There is an express prohibition by the State authority which is permitted by the Commonwealth authority. A Commonwealth arbitration award prevails over a State statute creating an offence if the State statute is inconsistent with the award (*Ex parte McLean* (1930) 43 CLR 472). In this case there is, in my opinion, a clear inconsistency, and therefore the Commonwealth award prevails (68 CLR at 160).

Starke J referred to 'a direct collision between the two laws in the present case'; the state law which 'provides in effect that females shall not be employed' and the Commonwealth law which 'in effect permits employers parties to the award to employ females': 68 CLR at 161. Williams J also referred to a 'direct' inconsistency: 68 CLR at 163. A similar problem was resolved with identical reasoning in *Blackley v Devondale Cream (Vic) Pty Ltd* (1968) 117 CLR 253.

[8.1.24]   The relative simplicity of these approaches to inconsistency is recognised in the label frequently applied to them, 'direct' inconsistency, see (in addition to the passages cited in **[8.1.23]**) *R v Credit Tribunal; Ex parte General Motors Acceptance Corporation Australia* (1977) 137 CLR 545 **[8.1.56]** at 563, 565 per Mason J; *Ansett Transport Industries (Operations) Pty Ltd v Wardley* (1980) 142 CLR 237 **[8.1.63C]** at 253 per Stephen J. The label underlines the complexity of the third (or 'indirect') approach to inconsistency. The indirect approach can be found not only where two laws contradict one another, but where there is some overlap or duplication between two laws, although there will not always be inconsistency between overlapping laws. Rather, they might be regarded as complementary (as in *Airlines of New South Wales Pty Ltd v New South Wales (No 2)* (1965) 113 CLR **[8.1.37]**) or as reinforcing one another (as in *Victoria v Commonwealth* (the *Shipwrecks* case) (1937) 58 CLR 618 **[8.1.51]**).

Isaacs J in *Clyde Engineering Co Ltd v Cowburn* (1926) 37 CLR 466 **[8.1.20]** proposed a three-part test for deciding whether two laws might be inconsistent in this 'indirect' sense:

- What field or subject matter does the Commonwealth law deal with or regulate?

- Was the Commonwealth law intended to cover that field, to regulate that subject matter completely and exhaustively? Was the Commonwealth law intended as *the* law (and not merely a law) on that subject matter?

- Does the state law attempt to regulate some part of that subject matter or to enter on the field covered by the Commonwealth law?

The Commonwealth intention, to provide *the* law on the subject matter, is paramount: any state attempt to regulate a part of that subject matter will conflict with the Commonwealth intention and be rendered invalid by s 109.

[8.1.25]   The 'cover the field' approach to s 109 can have serious implications for the autonomy and effective power of the states. Could the Commonwealth Parliament exclude the operation of state legislation in all those 'fields' where, according to the Commonwealth Constitution, Commonwealth and state powers are to be concurrent? The Commonwealth cannot pass laws prohibiting a state parliament from passing a law in a given area: *Gerhardy v Brown* (1985) 159 CLR 70 at 81 (Gibbs CJ), 121 (Brennan J); nor may the Commonwealth pass a valid law preventing state courts from exercising jurisdiction in respect of civil offences: *Re Tracey; Ex parte Ryan* (1989) 166 CLR 518 at 547 (Mason CJ, Wilson and Dawson JJ), 575 (Brennan and Toohey JJ). In *Wenn v Attorney-General (Vic)* (1948) 77 CLR 84, Dixon J, with whom Rich J agreed, explained the interrelationship of state and federal legislative power in this context in the following way:

> To legislate upon a subject exhaustively ... is, I think, an exercise of legislative authority different in kind from a bare attempt to exclude State concurrent power from a subject the Federal legislature has not effectively dealt with (77 CLR at 120).

However, so long as the relevant Commonwealth law is constitutionally valid, no objection could be raised on the basis that that the law 'trenches on state functions' (77 CLR at 120) — unless, presumably, the law infringed the implied prohibition on Commonwealth power recognised in *Melbourne Corporation v Commonwealth* (the

State Banking case) (1947) 74 CLR 31 **[8.2.45C]**. Subject to the *Melbourne Corporation* doctrine, the Commonwealth may effectively exclude the states through the enactment of 'field-covering' Commonwealth legislation, legislation which the courts would read as intended to be an exhaustive and exclusive statement of the law on the topic it dealt with.

However, that dramatic impact on state legislative autonomy can be tempered by the open nature of this 'cover the field' test. The answers to the specific questions involved in that test depend on judicial evaluation or interpretation of abstract and often equivocal material, an issue which is discussed in Chapter 1. How, for example, does a court identify the field or the subject matter with which a Commonwealth (or state) law deals? See **[8.1.35]–[8.1.43]**. How does a court decide whether the Commonwealth law was intended by parliament to cover that field; to be the exhaustive and exclusive rule on that subject? What interpretive method will the court use to determine these questions? See **[1.2.11]–[1.3.16]**. Compare the majority and minority judgments in *Ansett Transport Industries (Operations) Pty Ltd v Wardley* (1980) 142 CLR 237 **[8.1.63C]**.

[8.1.26] In *Clyde Engineering Co Ltd v Cowburn* (1926) 37 CLR 466 **[8.1.20]**, Isaacs J sought to apply the three-part test by reviewing the terms of the Conciliation and Arbitration Act 1904 (Cth) which, he said, indicated the field dealt with and showed parliament's intention to cover that field: 37 CLR at 490–1. (The reliance on the terms of the Act, rather than the award, reflect a view that awards made under the Conciliation and Arbitration Act are not themselves laws of the Commonwealth: **[8.1.9]**.) Isaacs J referred to a series of sections which, he said, showed that parliament intended an industrial award made under the Conciliation and Arbitration Act to decide every part of an industrial dispute and thereby conclude the relations between the parties: to cover the field of the parties' industrial relations. However, later decisions of the court have suggested that it is necessary to go beyond the terms of the Conciliation and Arbitration Act to determine the field dealt with: see *TA Robinson & Sons Pty Ltd v Haylor* (1957) 97 CLR 177 **[8.1.46]** at 184. Be that as it may, the sections relied on by Isaacs J in *Cowburn* suggest that, in establishing the law-maker's intention to cover a field, the courts will often need to work with equivocal material, requiring the identification and application of techniques of judicial interpretation: see **[1.2.11]–[1.3.16]**. For example, the sections directed the Court of Conciliation and Arbitration to investigate all matters affecting an industrial dispute before it, to make an award 'determining the dispute', 'according to equity, good conscience, and the substantial merits of the case', which award was to be framed without unnecessary technicalities and to be binding on all parties to the dispute.

[8.1.27C]   **Ex parte McLean**
                                   (1930) 43 CLR 472

McLean was a shearer who was hired by a grazier to shear sheep, according to the terms of a written agreement signed by each of them. An award made by the Commonwealth Arbitration Court, which covered the shearing industry throughout Australia, provided that employers and workers in the shearing industry should observe the conditions of the award and of any agreement into which they entered. Section 44 of the Conciliation and Arbitration Act 1904 (Cth) made it an offence for any person to breach an award.

During the course of McLean's employment, a dispute arose between him and his employer. McLean stopped working and his employer prosecuted him under s 4 of the

Masters and Servants Act 1902 (NSW), which made it an offence for a 'servant', who contracted to perform work for another person, to neglect to fulfil the contract. McLean was convicted by a magistrate, but applied to the New South Wales Supreme Court for prohibition on the ground that any failure on his part to carry out his work was covered by the Commonwealth award. The matter was then removed to the High Court of Australia under s 40 of the Judiciary Act 1903 (Cth).

Dixon J: [483] Section 44 of the Commonwealth Conciliation and Arbitration Act 1904–1928 penalises any breach or non-observance of an award, and, inasmuch as the award in this case commanded performance of the applicant's contract, his neglect to fulfil it would constitute an offence under this provision. The same acts or omissions were therefore made subject to the penal sanctions of the Federal enactment and the somewhat different penal sanctions of the State enactment.

When the Parliament of the Commonwealth and the Parliament of the State each legislate upon the same subject and prescribe what the rule of conduct shall be, they make laws which are inconsistent, notwithstanding that the rule of conduct is identical which each prescribes and s 109 applies. That this is so is settled, at least when the sanctions they impose are diverse *Hume v Palmer* (1926) 38 CLR 441. But the reason is that, by prescribing the rule to be observed the Federal statute shows an intention to cover the subject matter and provide what the law upon it shall be. If it appeared that the Federal law was intended to be supplementary to or cumulative upon State law, then no inconsistency would be exhibited in imposing the same duties or in inflicting different penalties. The inconsistency does not lie in the mere coexistence of two laws which are susceptible of simultaneous obedience. It depends upon the intention of the paramount legislature to express by its enactment, completely, exhaustively, or exclusively, what shall be the law governing the particular conduct or matter to which its attention is directed. When a Federal statute discloses such an intention, it is inconsistent with it for the law of a State to govern the same conduct or matter. But in the present case, conduct which the State law prescribes, namely, the performance of contracts of service, is a matter with which the Commonwealth Parliament has not itself attempted to deal. Although neglect by a shearer to perform such a contract constitutes an offence against Federal law, this does not arise from any statement by the Federal legislature of what the law shall be upon that subject. The conduct which the Federal statute penalises is the breach of industrial awards. There is 'no collision between an intention to deal exclusively with disobedience of awards [the Commonwealth law] and [484] a law for the punishment of breach of contract [the State law]' … But the provisions of [the Conciliation and Arbitration] Act itself, which establish awards made under its authority, may have a meaning and effect consistently with which State law could not further affect a matter for which such an award completely provides. If the Act means not only to give the determinations of the arbitrator binding force between the disputants but to enable him to 'prescribe completely or exhaustively what upon any subject in dispute shall be their industrial relations', then s 109 would operate to give paramountcy to these provisions of the statute, unless they were ultra vires and they in turn would give to the award an exclusive operation which might appear equivalent almost to paramountcy.

Following the reasons given by Isaacs, Rich and Starke JJ in *Clyde Engineering Co Ltd v Cowburn* (1926) 37 CLR 466 and applied afterwards in *H V McKay Pty Ltd v Hunt* (1926) 38 CLR 308, Dixon J said that 'the Constitution empowered the Parliament to give and that Parliament had given the award this exclusive authority'.

[486] It may be assumed that provisions of State law which prohibit acts or omissions irrespective of the relation of employer and employed, and without regard to any other industrial relation or matter, are not superseded under s 109 merely because it happens that in their industrial aspect the same acts or omissions by parties to a dispute are forbidden by Federal award and by this means made punishable under the Federal statute. But, in this case, the State law, s 4 of the Masters and Servants Act 1902, deals directly with the relation of employer and employed, and in virtue of that industrial relation makes penal the very default which the Federal law punishes somewhat differently in the regulation of the same relation …

[T]he substance of what the Federal award did in this case was to command performance of the prescribed contracts as an industrial duty proper to be imposed and enforced by Federal law according to the sanctions [487] which it provides, while the State law required performance of the same contract as an industrial duty proper to be imposed and enforced by its authority and according to its sanctions. According to the doctrine deduced from the judgments of the majority of the court in the cases of *Clyde Engineering Co v Cowburn* (1926) 37 CLR 466 and *H V McKay Pty Ltd v Hunt* (1926) 38 CLR 308, the Commonwealth Conciliation and Arbitration Act gives full and complete efficacy and exclusive authority to this regulation of the Federal tribunal, and s 109 makes this statute prevail.

Dixon J concluded that no offence had been committed against state law by the applicant, and the order nisi for prohibition should be made absolute.

Isaacs CJ and Starke J delivered a joint judgment to the same effect. Rich J agreed with the judgment of Dixon J.

~~~

Notes

Overlapping laws

[8.1.28]   Both Dixon J in *Ex parte McLean* (1930) 43 CLR 472 **[8.1.27C]** at 483 and Isaacs J in *Cowburn's* case (1926) 37 CLR 466 **[8.1.20]** at 489 noticed the problem of overlapping state and Commonwealth criminal laws. Dixon J suggested as a general principle that if the Commonwealth prohibits certain conduct, any state law prohibiting the same conduct will be inconsistent, at least, where the state and Commonwealth penalties differ. More recent decisions have confused, rather than resolved, this problem.

In *R v Loewenthal; Ex parte Blacklock* (1974) 131 CLR 338 the High Court decided that a person who had allegedly damaged Commonwealth property could not be prosecuted for a breach of s 469 of the Criminal Code (Qld) because this section was, in the context of the facts of this case, inconsistent with s 29 of the Crimes Act 1914 (Cth). Section 469 of the Criminal Code provided that 'any person who wilfully and unlawfully destroys or damages any property is guilty of an offence' and liable to imprisonment with hard labour for two or three years. Section 29 of the Crimes Act provided that 'any person who wilfully and unlawfully destroys or damages any property ... belonging to the Commonwealth...shall be guilty of an offence' and liable to imprisonment for two years.

Menzies J said 'that s 29 of the Crimes Act should be regarded as exhaustive' because it provided 'a common rule [operating throughout Australia] to or from which the legislation of a State can neither add nor subtract': 131 CLR at 342. It seems he regarded the Commonwealth law as covering the field of protection of Commonwealth property. On the other hand, Mason J held that there was a direct inconsistency between s 469 of the Criminal Code and s 29 of the Crimes Act, and that it was unnecessary to consider whether the Commonwealth Parliament had intended to cover the field:

> Although the provisions are substantially identical in describing the conduct which gives rise to the offence, the penalties prescribed differ. A difference in the penalties prescribed for conduct which is prohibited or penalised by Commonwealth and State laws has been held to give rise to inconsistency between those laws (see *Hume v Palmer* (1926) 38 CLR 441; *Ex parte McLean* (1930) 43 CLR 472), at least when it appears that the Commonwealth statute by prescribing the rule to be observed evinces an intention to cover the subject matter to the exclusion of any other law ... [T]here is here

a direct conflict (in the matter of penalty) between the Commonwealth and the State law; in such a case it is impossible to see how the existence of inconsistency in the constitutional sense can be avoided by an argument which seeks to attribute to the Commonwealth law an intention not to cover the relevant field. [131 CLR at 346–7]

The judgments of Menzies and Mason JJ show a striking difference in approach to the problem of overlapping criminal laws (and highlight the ambiguity inherent in Dixon J's apparently qualified proposition in *Ex parte McLean* **[8.1.27C]**: see Rumble (1980) p 56). For Menzies J, the Commonwealth had covered the field because it had made wilful damage to Commonwealth property a federal offence: the inconsistency lay in the state attempting to penalise the same activity (indirect inconsistency). But for Mason J the inconsistency arose, not because the state had attempted to penalise that activity, but because it had attached a different penalty to that activity (direct inconsistency). The difficulty in extracting a common proposition from *R v Loewenthal; Ex parte Blacklock* (1974) 131 CLR 338 was not resolved by the other members of the court, who managed to adopt the reasons of both Menzies and Mason JJ: 131 CLR 338 at 340 (Barwick CJ); at 347–8 (Jacobs J).

The contradictions inherent in *R v Loewenthal; Ex parte Blacklock* would come into sharp focus if a court were faced with two laws, Commonwealth and state, which made the same activity a criminal offence and imposed identical penalties. How would a court decide whether the state law was inconsistent with the Commonwealth law? (On this constitutional question, see: Murray-Jones (1979) pp 45–52; Rumble (1980) pp 52–9, 70, 76.)

[8.1.29]   The High Court has emphasised the limits of the principle put forward by Dixon J in *Ex parte McLean* **[8.1.27C]**. In particular, the High Court has said that laws laying down different penalties for the same conduct can only be described as overlapping and therefore inconsistent when they deal with the same subject matter: *R v Winneke; Ex parte Gallagher* (1982) 152 CLR 211.

In *R v Winneke; Ex parte Gallagher* (1982) 152 CLR 211, Gallagher challenged his conviction for an offence under the Evidence Act 1958 (Vic) for failing to answer a question before a state Royal Commission, on the ground that the Evidence Act was inconsistent with the Royal Commission Act 1902 (Cth). The Royal Commissioner was conducting two inquiries simultaneously, one under the state Act and one under the Commonwealth Act, each of which provided a (different) penalty for failure to answer questions. The High Court rejected this challenge. Gibbs CJ said that the imposition of different penalties for the same conduct did not necessarily result in inconsistency. If they dealt with the same subject, inconsistency could probably result. But, where two laws dealt with different subject matters, 'each may validly apply in relation to the same set of facts': 152 CLR at 218. He explained at 218–19:

> In the present case the Commonwealth Act and the State Act deal with different subjects. The Commonwealth Act deals with inquiries conducted under Commonwealth authority and the State Act with inquiries conducted under State authority ... If the two inquiries were separately conducted, and one question was relevant to both inquiries, that question might have been asked at each inquiry, and a refusal on both occasions would clearly have constituted two separate offences, one against Commonwealth law and one against State law. When the inquiries are held together, and a question relevant to both is asked, a refusal to answer constitutes a contravention of both Acts, so that the offender might be prosecuted and convicted under either the State or the Commonwealth Act (see s 11 of the Crimes Act 1914 (Cth) as amended).

Gibbs CJ pointed out that 'the injustice of exposing the witness to double punishment for the one refusal' was avoided by s 30(2) of the Acts Interpretation Act 1901 (Cth) (see **[8.1.31]**) and concluded at 219:

> The different penalties provided by the two Acts are in respect of what are in truth independent offences which are created by law to serve different purposes. It is not right to say that the Acts provide different penalties for the one offence. There is no inconsistency between Acts which prescribe different penalties for offences which, albeit constituted by the same conduct, are in substance different from one another.

See also the judgment of Wilson J: 152 CLR 211 at 233.

The limits outlined in *R v Winneke; Ex parte Gallagher* (1982) 152 CLR 211 **[8.1.29]** were confirmed by the High Court in *McWaters v Day* (1989) 168 CLR 289 **[8.1.32]**.

[8.1.30] The contradictions inherent in *R v Loewenthal; Ex parte Blacklock* (1974) 131 CLR 338 were not resolved in the High Court in *Viskauskas v Niland* (1983) 153 CLR 280 **[8.1.53]**, although that case indicated that the principle put forward by Dixon J in *Ex parte McLean* extends beyond overlapping criminal laws. One of the bases on which the court, in its unanimous judgment, found part of the Anti-Discrimination Act 1977 (NSW) to be inconsistent with the Racial Discrimination Act 1975 (Cth) was that, although the state Act dealt with the subject of racial discrimination in terms substantially similar to those of the Commonwealth Act, it provided different consequences for breaches. In each case the Act provided for an award of damages in favour of a person discriminated against, but the bases for the calculation of those damages and the limit on those damages differed (at 292–3):

> Under the Commonwealth Act, the court may award damages in respect of inter alia, loss of dignity, humiliation and injury to feelings, and no limit is provided to the amount of damages that may be awarded. Under the State Act the damages that may be awarded are 'for any loss or damage suffered by reason of the respondent's conduct' and there is a pecuniary limit … [T]he test as stated in *Ex parte McLean* … applies exactly — the two legislatures have legislated upon the same subject, and have prescribed what the rules of conduct will be and (if it matters) the sanctions imposed are diverse. Clearly in respect of that subject matter there is inconsistency.

[8.1.31] The answer to the question raised by overlapping criminal laws might be provided by s 11 of the Crimes Act 1914 (Cth) and s 30(2) of the Acts Interpretation Act 1901 (Cth). The former section provides as follows:

> **11** (1) Where the act or omission of a person is an offence against a law of the Commonwealth and is also an offence against another law of the Commonwealth or some other law, the person may be prosecuted and convicted under either of those laws.
>
> (2) Nothing in this Act shall render any person liable to be punished twice in respect of the same offence.

The latter provides:

> 30 …
>
> (2) Where an act or omission constitutes an offence under both —
>
> > (a) an Act and a State Act; or
> >
> > (b) an Act and an Ordinance of a Territory, and the offender has been punished for that offence under the State Act or the Ordinance, as the case may be, he shall not be liable to be punished for the offence under the Act[.]

These two provisions at least contemplate the concurrent operation of Commonwealth and state laws penalising the same activity and could be read as a statement of legislative intention not to cover the field. As such, they would avoid the type of inconsistency which, it seems, Menzies J found in *R v Loewenthal; Ex parte Blacklock* (1974) 131 CLR 338 **[8.1.28]**. Menzies J made no reference to these two provisions. Mason J dismissed them as irrelevant to the question of inconsistency: 131 CLR at 347. The provisions may well be irrelevant where there is direct inconsistency, of the type which Mason J found in *R v Loewenthal; Ex parte Blacklock*, but it is difficult to accept that they are irrelevant to that type of inconsistency which depends upon the Commonwealth Parliament's intention. Indeed, Mason J later acknowledged this (limited) relevance in *R v Credit Tribunal; Ex parte General Motors Acceptance Corporation Australia* (1977) 137 CLR 545 **[8.1.56]** at 563.

For a detailed discussion of the questions raised by these two provisions, see Rumble (1980) pp 62–4, 68–70.

[8.1.32]   However, although inconsistent criminal laws may be resolved by the application of these several provisions, it appears that inconsistent penalties attaching to conduct that is prohibited under both Commonwealth and state laws will not necessarily result in s 109 inconsistency.

For example, in *McWaters v Day* (1989) 168 CLR 289, an inconsistency issue arose between Queensland law which made it an offence punishable by a fine of up to $1400 or imprisonment up to nine months to drive under the influence of alcohol. Federal defence force disciplinary legislation made it an offence punishable by up to 12 months' imprisonment for defence force members or defence civilians to drive under the influence of alcohol on defence land. McWaters had charged Day with driving under the influence under the Queensland law, and Day argued that his driving activities on service land were governed by the Commonwealth law only. In response, McWaters argued that the state law was not inconsistent with the Commonwealth law, but was intended to impose supplementary or cumulative obligations upon defence force members and defence civilians. The unanimous High Court agreed that the Commonwealth defence force disciplinary provisions were cumulative upon and not exclusive of the ordinary criminal law; and, on this basis, *R v Loewenthal; Ex parte Blacklock* (1974) 131 CLR 338 **[8.1.28]** was distinguished.

In the course of its judgment, the High Court said at 168 CLR 295–6:

> As evidence of the inconsistency contended for, the respondent points to the different penalties which the respective laws stipulate and to the fact that the Commonwealth offence differs in substance by containing a requirement that the person charged be incapable of having proper control of the vehicle concerned. It is true that a difference in penalties prescribed for conduct prohibited by Commonwealth and State laws has been held to give rise to inconsistency between those laws for the purposes of s 109 … Equally, a difference between the rules of conduct prescribed by Commonwealth and State laws might give rise to such inconsistency. But the mere fact that such differences exist is insufficient to establish an inconsistency in the relevant sense. It is necessary to inquire whether the Commonwealth statute, in prescribing the rule to be observed, evinces an intention to cover the subject-matter to the exclusion of any other law … In the words of Dixon J in *Ex parte McLean* at 483:
>
> > The inconsistency does not lie in the mere coexistence of two laws which are susceptible of simultaneous obedience. It depends upon the intention of the paramount Legislature to express by its enactment, completely, exhaustively, or exclusively, what shall be the law governing the particular conduct or matter to which its attention is directed.

Accordingly, a difference in penalties under federal and state laws attaching to substantially the same conduct does not necessarily result in a s 109 inconsistency. It also appears to be necessary to demonstrate that the federal law evinced an intention to cover the field and exclude any other law for an inconsistency to occur.

It seems difficult to reconcile this approach with general principles: surely inconsistent penalties manifest directly inconsistent laws, inconsistent policies and inconsistent intentions. In *McWaters v Day*, the court seemed to require *both* a direct inconsistency and an intention-based inconsistency. The balance of authority indicates that direct inconsistency is a sufficient criterion for s 109 inconsistency: see *Telstra Corporation Ltd v Worthing* (1999) 197 CLR 61 at 76 **[8.1.21]**.

[8.1.33] The preferable view was expressed by some members of the majority in *Hume v Palmer* (1926) 38 CLR 441. In that case Palmer laid an information that Hume had breached the New South Wales Navigation Act 1901 for a sea traffic offence which was alleged to have occurred in Port Jackson. At the hearing before a state stipendiary magistrate, Hume objected to the jurisdiction of the magistrate on the basis that proceedings should have been brought under the Commonwealth Navigation Act 1912 and regulations, as the events occurred in the course of an interstate trading journey. The High Court held that the laws were inconsistent, on a number of grounds. Knox CJ said at 448:

> The rules prescribed by the Commonwealth law and the State law respectively are for present purposes substantially identical, but the penalties imposed for their contravention differ … In these circumstances, it is, I think clear … that the provisions of the law of the state for the breach of which the appellant was convicted are inconsistent with the law of the Commonwealth within the meaning of sec 109 of the Constitution and are therefore invalid.

Isaacs J identified a number of features of the laws as being inconsistent, including the penalties imposed: 38 CLR at 450–1. Starke J said at 462:

> The federal law covers the whole subject matter of the State Regulations in relation to navigation and shipping in inter-State and foreign trade and commerce. It produces in its code of sea rules 'a uniform whole', and makes it the law for the regulation of navigation and shipping within the ambit of the Federal power. But, in addition, the Federal law has imposed somewhat different sanctions upon contraventions of its code, than are imposed under the State code for the same acts … It is not difficult to see that the Federal code would be 'disturbed or deranged' if the State code applied a different sanction in respect of the same act. Consequently the State regulations are, in my opinion, inconsistent with the law of the Commonwealth and rendered invalid by force of sec 109 of the Constitution.

Identification of the field (characterisation)

[8.1.34] A critical part of the 'cover the field' test of inconsistency should be the identification of the field which the Commonwealth law deals with; critical because a state law will be inconsistent with the Commonwealth law, on this test, only if the Commonwealth law covers that field and the state law enters that field. In this context, identification of the field is basically identical to the characterisation process described in brief in Chapter 1: see **[1.5.1]–[1.5.27]**.

In identifying the field of the Commonwealth law in *Ex parte McLean* (1930) 43 CLR 472 **[8.1.27C]**, Dixon J looked to the terms of the Conciliation and Arbitration Act: this law of the Commonwealth indicated clearly the field or subject matter to be regulated, 'industrial relations which are in dispute', and, consequently, any state law which dealt with another field or subject matter (for example, the protection of animals) could not be said to invade the field covered by that law of the Commonwealth: 43 CLR at 485–6.

[8.1.35] However, in relation to direct inconsistency, Latham CJ apparently supported the view that 'characterisation' was not important for s 109 purposes: see *Colvin v Bradley Bros Pty Ltd* (1943) 68 CLR 151 **[8.1.23]**. One of the arguments proposed in support of the state law forbidding employment of women on milling machines was that it was 'directed to community welfare' and could not, therefore, be inconsistent with a Commonwealth law (permitting that employment in a particular industry) 'directed only to relations between particular employers and employees'. He rejected that argument and explained at 157–8:

> [I]n my opinion, it cannot be said that where there is actual inconsistency between a State law and a Federal law or, as alleged in this case, between an order made under State law and an award made under Federal law, the fact that one law may from one point of view be placed within a particular legislative category (for example, health or social conditions) and the other law may from another point of view be placed within another legislative category (for example, industrial arbitration) prevents the application of s 109 of the Constitution. The application of s 109 does not depend upon any assignment of legislation to specific categories which are to be assumed on an a priori basis to be mutually exclusive.

Later, he said that 'classification of statutes according to their true nature is, in my opinion, a matter that is irrelevant to the application of s 109': 68 CLR at 159.

Latham CJ was not speaking in the context of the 'cover the field' type of inconsistency. He and the other members of the court found a direct conflict between the state law's prohibition and the Commonwealth law's permission: see **[8.1.23]**. Moreover, Latham CJ's insistence that Commonwealth legislation always had a single, predominant or paramount characterisation (that a Commonwealth law could not be a law with respect to more than one subject matter (see, for example, his judgment in *Melbourne Corporation v Commonwealth* (the *State Banking* case) (1947) 74 CLR 31 **[8.2.45C]**)) is no longer current: see **[1.5.18]**. We should also note that Latham CJ's approach to characterisation is not typical: see, for example, *Actors and Announcers Equity Association v Fontana Films Pty Ltd* (1982) 150 CLR 169 at 192 **[10.3.18C]**.

[8.1.36] It is difficult to see how the 'cover the field' test of inconsistency can be applied without classifying or characterising the contending statutes. Indeed, this process has formed the basis of many s 109 decisions. In *O'Sullivan v Noarlunga Meat Ltd* (1954) 92 CLR 565, Fullagar J (with whom Dixon CJ and Kitto J agreed) pointed out that the Commerce (Meat Export) Regulations (Cth) and the Metropolitan and Export Abattoirs Act 1936 (SA) had the same subject matter; namely, the use of premises for slaughtering stock for export. It was therefore unnecessary to consider whether Latham CJ's statement in *Colvin v Bradley Bros Pty Ltd* (1943) 68 CLR 151 **[8.1.35]** was 'not expressed somewhat too widely': 92 CLR at 593. Fullagar J went on to hold that the Commonwealth law covered the field and that the state law was inconsistent because it attempted to enter that field.

On appeal, the Privy Council confirmed Fullagar J's view that the Commonwealth regulations and state Act were inconsistent because the Act dealt with 'precisely the field which in their Lordship's opinion the regulations evince an intention exhaustively to cover': (1955) 95 CLR 177 at 187. The Privy Council indicated that there would still be room for the valid operation of those state laws not directed to the control of slaughter for export, such as state town planning laws which 'would normally be irrelevant to the regulation of the export trade': 95 CLR at 187.

[8.1.37] The relationship between characterisation and identification of the field was also canvassed in *Airlines of New South Wales Pty Ltd v New South Wales (No 2)* (1965) 113 CLR 54. In this case the High Court rejected a challenge to the Air Transport Act 1964 (NSW) which, it was claimed, was inconsistent with the Air Navigation Regulations (Cth).

The Commonwealth Regulations prohibited (regs 198 and 199) commercial air operations, including operations within any state, unless licensed by the Director General of Civil Aviation, who was directed to consider only 'safety, regularity and efficiency of air navigation' when deciding an application for a licence. The state Act prohibited commercial air operations inside New South Wales, unless licensed by the Commissioner of Motor Transport, who was directed to consider public transport needs, the encouragement of competition and the suitability of the applicant, when deciding an application for a licence.

Kitto J dealt with the argument that the Air Navigation Regulations covered the field of the licensing of commercial air operations in the following way (at 121–2):

> The topic and the only topic to which regs 198 and 199 direct their attention, so far as they apply to intra-State operations, is the safety, regularity and efficiency of air navigation. Regulation 199(4) makes that clear. The State Act, on the other hand, does not concern itself with that topic in any way. The fact that each piece of legislation sets up a licensing system operating independently of the licensing system established by the other may from time to time lead to a situation in which A, though holding a licence under the State Act for a proposed service, may be unable to obtain a licence for that service under reg 199, while B, though holding a licence for the service under reg 199, may be unable to obtain a licence for it under the State Act. But any ground for suggesting inconsistency disappears if the situation is more fully described, as by saying that consideration of matters concerning the safety, regularity and efficiency of air navigation has led the Federal Director-General of Civil Aviation to conclude that A, though not B, should be debarred from conducting the service, while consideration of matters concerning public needs in relation to air transport services or concerning other topics mentioned in s 6(3) of the State Act has led the State Commissioner for Motor Transport to conclude that B, though not A, should be debarred from conducting the service. The Federal Regulations and the State Act each employ a licensing system to serve a particular end; but the ends are different, and that means that the two sets of provisions are directed to different subjects of legislative attention. In my opinion there is no mutual inconsistency in any relevant sense.

The characterisation of Commonwealth and state laws, or the identification of their fields, forms the basis of the following decision. (On this aspect of inconsistency see also: Stephen J in *Ansett Transport Industries (Operations) Pty Ltd v Wardley* (1980) 142 CLR 237 **[8.1.63C]**; the unanimous judgment of the court in *Viskauskas v Niland* (1983) 153 CLR 280 **[8.1.53]**; and *Commercial Radio Coffs Harbour Ltd v Fuller* (1986) 161 CLR 47 **[8.1.41]**.)

[8.1.38C]   **New South Wales v Commonwealth**

(The *Hospital Benefits* case)
(1983) 151 CLR 302

The National Health Act 1953 (Cth) provided for a health insurance scheme, under which hospital benefits organisations, formed under state or territory law and which complied with detailed rules imposed under the Act, could be registered under the Act and so achieve substantial tax advantages under the Income Tax Assessment Act 1936 (Cth). These detailed rules dealt with the relationship between a registered hospital benefits organisation and its members. Membership was to be open to the public; and a 'basic table' of benefits was to be provided by each organisation in return for specified contributions. Section 68(2) of the Act directed that an organisation's rules:

- establish a fund;
- to which all its income should be credited; and
- from which the payments out were strictly limited to: benefits for contributions; the costs of providing health services for contributors; and 'costs incurred by the organisation wholly and exclusively in the carrying on in that State of business as a registered hospital benefits organisation ...'.

Section 73B(1)(b) authorised the Minister to impose further conditions on registered hospital benefits organisations.

The Hospital Benefits (Levy) Act 1982 (Vic) came into operation on 1 August 1982. It provided that an organisation carrying on the business of hospital benefits in Victoria should pay a levy each month to the Comptroller of Stamps: s 3. The levy was to be calculated on the basis of the number of its members and the amount of its income from contributors: s 2(1). The amount of the levy was to be paid into the Consolidated Revenue Fund: and an equivalent amount transferred from that fund to the Hospitals and Charities Fund: s 9. Finally, the Act declared that any member of an organisation covered by the Act was not obliged to pay for outpatient services at a public hospital in Victoria.

The Health Insurance Levies Act 1982 (NSW) came into operation on 1 January 1983. It was in substantially the same terms as the Victorian Act; but it exempted members of organisations covered by the Act from payment for ambulance services as well as out-patient hospital services.

On 30 or 31 December 1982 the Minister administering the Commonwealth Act imposed on each registered hospital benefits organisation operating in Victoria an additional condition:

> That the organisation will not pay the monthly levy imposed and required to be paid to the Comptroller of Stamps under the Victorian Hospital Benefits (Levy) Act 1982 or under that Act as it may be amended from time to time.

At the same time, a corresponding condition was imposed on each registered hospital benefits organisation operating in New South Wales. In separate proceedings in the High Court of Australia, the states of New South Wales and Victoria and one hospital benefits organisation sought declarations that the conditions imposed by the Minister were invalid. At the same time, another hospital benefits organisation sought a declaration that the Health Insurance Levies Act 1982 (NSW) was invalid. The actions were consolidated and a case stated for the opinion of the Full Court of the High Court. Among the questions asked in the case stated were whether the two state Acts were 'inconsistent with the National Health Act 1953 and to the extent of that inconsistency, invalid', and whether s 73B(1) of the National Health Act 1953 authorised the Minister to impose the condition imposed on 30 or 31 December 1982.

Gibbs CJ, Murphy and Wilson JJ: [316] It is argued that the State Acts are invalid by reason of the application of s 109 of the Constitution. The argument takes a number of forms. In the first place, it is said that the State legislation intrudes into a field which is exhaustively and exclusively covered by the National Health Act. In the second place, it is said that the State Acts are in direct conflict with the Commonwealth Act. Further, it is argued that the discriminatory character of the tax is such as to render the legislation inconsistent with the law of the Commonwealth.

The first of these submissions requires that the field said to be exhaustively covered by the Commonwealth law be clearly identified and that the State laws be shown to enter upon that field ...

Gibbs CJ, Murphy and Wilson JJ said that the field of Commonwealth regulation, (or the character of the Commonwealth law) was 'the relationship between the organisation and the contributor, particularly the nature and amount of the benefits to be provided to contributors and the purposes for which moneys in the fund may be applied': 151 CLR at 317. However, they said that the Act did not evince an intention 'to exclude all operation of State laws on registered organisations' and that 'it expressly recognises the continued operation of such laws and their capacity to make an impact on the fund', referring to the provision of the Commonwealth Act which recognised that costs incurred by the organisation in the carrying on of business in the state could be paid out of the fund. Similarly, they said, the continued operation of state laws imposing 'land tax, rates, payroll tax and so on' would not be inconsistent with the Commonwealth Act: 151 CLR 317. They rejected the Commonwealth's argument that 'the imposition of the tax is a clear case of inconsistency because its necessary effect is to intrude into the financial situation which the Act regulates a charge in favour of the Crown in right of a State. With respect, if that is so, then why does not every impost incurred under the authority of a State law merit the same condemnation?': 151 CLR at 318. They continued:

[319] On any view the levy in each case is a tax. It is levied on organisations which carry on within the State concerned the business of providing hospital benefits to contributors. The amount of the tax is calculated by a formula in which the number of contributors is a major factor. When received the proceeds of the tax are paid into the Consolidated Fund and form part of the ordinary revenues of the State. What happens thereafter, so far as the financial resources derived from the tax are concerned, is immaterial to the character of the tax ...

From what we have said it follows that the State Acts do not deal with a subject matter which the Commonwealth Act intends to regulate completely and exclusively. If the State Acts did deal with the question of the benefits registered organisations should or might provide to their contributors, they would enter upon a field from which the Commonwealth Act displaces State law. But they do not either require or authorise an organisation to pay any benefit, or affect the basis on which benefits are payable. If a contributor is required to pay charges for out-patient hospital treatment, he will still be entitled to benefits in exactly the same amount as if the State Acts had not been passed ... [320] ... The State Acts impose a tax, and since, for the reasons given, the amount of the tax is a cost within s 68(2)(c)(ii), it may be debited to the fund. The authority for the debit is, however, the Commonwealth Act. For these reasons we reject the contentions that the State Acts are legislation on a subject which is dealt with exhaustively and exclusively by the Commonwealth Act, and that there is a direct inconsistency between the provisions of the State Acts on the one hand and the Commonwealth Act on the other. From a practical point of view the State Acts may affect the finances of registered organisations, but so would any other cost incurred in carrying on their business.

~~~

[8.1.39] Gibbs CJ, Murphy and Wilson JJ held that the state legislation did not contradict any specific protection which the Commonwealth legislation might have given to registered organisations. They proceeded to hold that s 73B(1)(b) was limited to authorising further conditions relevant to the relationship between a registered hospital benefits organisation and its members. It did not authorise the Minister to impose the condition imposed on 30 or 31 December 1982. Mason J delivered judgment to the same effect.

Deane J dissented. He agreed that the state Acts could not be 'invalid merely for the reason that they may impinge upon the general subject of either hospital benefits organisations or registered hospital benefits organisations', because the

Commonwealth Act did not deal with either of those subjects: 151 CLR at 334. But the Commonwealth Act did deal 'exhaustively and preclusively' with a more closely defined subject matter: in particular, 'it exhaustively states what benefits may be included in a basic table and expressly provides that a basic table may incorporate "no other benefits" without losing its character as such': 151 CLR at 335. However, reading the state legislation as a whole, it was plain that the entitlement of contributors to free out-patient (and ambulance) services was a benefit provided at the indirect cost of the hospital benefits organisations:

In the result, the New South Wales and Victorian Acts trespass in a field which the Commonwealth Act has exhaustively and preclusively covered, namely, the field dealing with the subject of what benefits may and may not be provided by, or at the direct or indirect cost of a registered hospital benefits organisation to contributors for benefits under the organisation's basic hospital benefits table: 151 CLR at 338.

Accordingly, the court answered, by a majority of four justices to one, the questions raised in the case stated as follows:

- Neither the Hospital Benefits (Levy) Act 1982 (Vic) nor the Health Insurance Levies Act 1982 (NSW) was inconsistent with the National Health Act 1953 (Cth).

- Section 73B(1) of the National Health Act 1953 (Cth) did not authorise the Minister to impose the conditions which he purported to impose on 30 or 31 December 1982.

Notes

[8.1.40] In *New South Wales v Commonwealth* (the *Hospital Benefits* case) (1983) 151 CLR 302 [8.1.38C], there was no disagreement over the proposition that the Commonwealth and state laws could only be inconsistent, on the 'cover the field' test of inconsistency, if they could be characterised as dealing with the same subject matter. Nor was there any disagreement over the subject matter or characterisation of the National Health Act 1953 (Cth). It dealt with the relationship between registered health benefits organisations and their contributors, including the standard benefits which those organisations could provide to their contributors. On this subject matter, the justices were agreed, the Commonwealth law was intended to be exhaustive and exclusive; it was intended to cover this field.

Disagreement arose over the appropriate characterisation of the two state Acts. For the majority, they were laws which imposed taxes. While the practical result of the legislation might be that the organisations' funds were depleted (through the payment of the tax) by an amount equivalent to the cost of providing extra services to the organisations' contributors (see 151 CLR at 320 at Gibbs CJ, Murphy and Wilson JJ; and 151 CLR at 328 per Mason J), the legal operation of the state Acts did not affect the legal relationship between the organisations and their contributors; neither was given any rights or duties in relation to the other, over and above the rights and duties conferred and imposed by the National Health Act. The dissenting justice, Deane J, on the other hand, characterised the state laws by looking at their practical effect. Money was collected by each state from the health benefits organisations, funnelled through government accounts and applied to paying the costs of extra services which were then supplied to the organisations' contributors: see 151 CLR at 337–8.

[8.1.41] In *Commercial Radio Coffs Harbour Ltd v Fuller* (1986) 161 CLR 47 the High Court held that no inconsistency existed between state and Commonwealth laws because the laws were characterised as dealing with distinct subject matters. Section 81 of the Broadcasting and Television Act 1942 (Cth) authorised the Australian Broadcasting Tribunal to grant a licence for the operation of a radio transmitter. In July 1985, the tribunal granted a licence to Commercial Radio Coffs Harbour Ltd (the company) to operate a transmitter in the Coffs Harbour area. Among the conditions of the licence were specifications as to the location and height of the transmission antenna. The Environmental Planning and Assessment Act 1979 (NSW) authorised local councils to control the use of land, subject to a right of appeal to the Land and Environment Court. The relevant council approved the company's proposal to use the specified land for a transmission antenna. A local resident appealed to the Land and Environment Court, where the company objected that the Environmental Planning and Assessment Act was inconsistent with the Broadcasting and Television Act. The latter Act, it was argued, was intended to cover the field of the provision of radio broadcasting services throughout Australia.

The High Court (after the matter was removed there under s 40 of the Judiciary Act 1903) rejected this argument. Wilson, Deane and Dawson JJ said that the Broadcasting and Television Act concentrated 'on the technical efficiency and quality of broadcasting services, [leaving] room for the operation of laws, both State and Commonwealth, dealing with other matters relevant to the operation of such services': 161 CLR at 56–7. State land use planning law was, therefore, in the context of the facts of this case, not inconsistent with the Commonwealth law on broadcasting.

[8.1.42] A similar approach was adopted by the High Court in *Love v Attorney-General (NSW)* (1990) 169 CLR 307, to support the court's decision that s 16 of the Listening Devices Act 1984 (NSW) was not inconsistent with s 219B(1) of the Customs Act 1901 (Cth). In a unanimous judgment, the court (Mason CJ, Brennan, Dawson, Toohey and Gaudron JJ) decided the Acts were not inconsistent in either a direct or indirect sense. The Customs Act only regulated the use of listening devices in federal narcotics inquiries. The Listening Devices Act did not authorise an act rendered unlawful by the Customs Act, but provided that the use of a listening device, as authorised by the Supreme Court, would not be a breach of the general prohibition against the use of listening devices in New South Wales. Similarly, there was no indirect inconsistency (at 318):

> The conclusion that the State Act does not purport to permit breaches of federal law compels the further conclusion that the Customs Act is not inconsistent with that Act by virtue of an intention to cover the field in relation to the use of listening devices by members of the Australian Federal Police and persons acting by arrangement with them in the course of federal narcotics inquiries. The fact that the State Act recognises the grant of a federal warrant and exempts the use of a listening device pursuant to a federal warrant from the prohibition in s 5(1) indicates that the field covered by Div 1A of Pt XII of the Customs Act is one into which the State Act does not purport to intrude.

[8.1.43] The question whether legislation should be characterised for constitutional purposes, by looking only at its direct legal operation or by considering its practical effect, is a recurring one. In general, in the past the High Court has preferred the former course: *Fairfax v Federal Commissioner of Taxation* (1965) 114 CLR 1 **[9.2.22C]**; *Murphyores Inc Pty Ltd v Commonwealth* (1976) 136 CLR 1 **[10.2.33C]**; *Wragg v New South Wales* (1953) 88 CLR 353 **[10.4.13]**. However, the court has recently shown a sensitivity to arguments based on practical effects, at least in the context of claims that state legislation has invaded the Commonwealth's monopoly of excise duties (s 90) (see, for example, *Ha v New South Wales* (1977) 189 CLR 465 at 498 **[9.2.11]** and **[9.4.60]**) and in the context of claims that legislation has denied the absolute freedom of interstate trade protected by s 92: *SOS (Mowbray) Pty Ltd v Mead* (1972) 124 CLR 529; *Finemores Transport Pty Ltd v New South Wales* (1978) 139 CLR 338; *Cole v Whitfield* (1988) 165 CLR 360 **[10.4.27C]**. It may be that this trend towards characterisation of legislation by reference to its practical effect, rather than its direct legal operation, will affect s 109 decisions as well.

Commonwealth intention to cover the field

[8.1.44] Once the field is identified, the court must decide whether the Commonwealth law-maker intended to 'cover' that field, although the separation of the two questions may often seem artificial. In *Ex parte McLean* (1930) 43 CLR 472 **[8.1.27C]**, Dixon J did no more than refer to Isaacs J's judgment in *Clyde Engineering Co v Cowburn* (1926) 37 CLR 466 **[8.1.20]** where 'the view ... was substantially that the Constitution empowered the Parliament to give and that Parliament had given the award this exclusive authority': 43 CLR at 484.

[8.1.45] Unless the Commonwealth legislation indicates that it intends, or does not intend, to cover the field, there is room for dispute as to its intention.

For example, in *O'Sullivan v Noarlunga Meat Ltd* (1954) 92 CLR 565, a statutory majority of the High Court (Dixon CJ, Fullagar and Kitto JJ) held that the Commerce (Meat Export) Regulations (Cth) were intended to cover the field of the use of premises for the slaughter of stock for export. After summarising the terms of the legislation (92 CLR at 588–91), Fullagar J described them as 'extremely elaborate and detailed', compelling the conclusion that 'the regulations evince an intention to express completely and exhaustively the requirements of the law with respect to the use of premises for the slaughter of stock for export': 92 CLR at 591–2. On the other hand, McTiernan, Webb and Taylor JJ held that the regulations were not intended to provide an exhaustive code on the regulation of premises for the slaughter of stock for export. Taylor J, with whom Webb J agreed, said that the Regulations did not prescribe rules of conduct but laid down requirements upon which the grant of an export permit was conditional. He continued at 603:

> If this be the correct view of the effect of the regulations then it is clear that their provisions were not intended to supersede, *pro tanto*, all other existing requirements for the establishment of slaughter houses.

On appeal, the Privy Council adopted Fullagar J's analysis of the regulations: *O'Sullivan v Noarlunga Meat Ltd* (1956) 95 CLR 177. The comprehensive nature of the Regulations showed an intention exhaustively to cover the field of slaughtering for export.

[8.1.46] The equivocal nature of the inferences to be drawn from the coverage or comprehensiveness of a Commonwealth law is well illustrated by a comparison of two High Court decisions. In the first decision, *TA Robinson & Sons Pty Ltd v Haylor* (1957) 97 CLR 177, the court rejected a challenge to the validity of the Long Service Leave Act 1955 (NSW), which gave employees a right to paid leave after ten years' service with an employer. The employer argued that this Act was inconsistent with the Conciliation and Arbitration Act 1904 (Cth) and an award made under that

Act fixing the rights and obligations of the employer and its employees. The award in question made no mention of long service leave but the employer argued that this silence reflected an intention that there should be no right to long service leave so that 'the ground is covered to the exclusion of the State Act': 97 CLR at 183. The court (Dixon CJ, McTiernan, Williams, Webb, Kitto and Taylor JJ) rejected this argument stating that, if the conciliation commissioner who made the award 'had entertained any such intention he should have expressed it in his award': 97 CLR at 184.

[8.1.47] By contrast, in the second decision, *Australian Broadcasting Commission v Industrial Court (SA)* (1977) 138 CLR 399, the court upheld a challenge to the validity of s 15(1)(e) of the Industrial Conciliation and Arbitration Act 1972 (SA), which gave to the Industrial Court of South Australia power to order reemployment of an employee whose dismissal was 'harsh, unjust or unreasonable'. This provision was, the court held, inconsistent with the provisions of the Broadcasting and Television Act 1942 (Cth) dealing with the employment of employees by the Australian Broadcasting Commission.

Mason J, with whom Barwick CJ and Gibbs J agreed, pointed out that the Commonwealth Act distinguished between permanent and temporary employees of the Commission. In dealing with the employment of permanent employees, the Act set out 'a comprehensive and exclusive code regulating the appointment, termination of appointment, promotion, transfer, retirement and dismissal of officers in the service of the Commission': 138 CLR at 415. It showed an intention to cover the field of employment of permanent employees. Turning to temporary employees, Mason J acknowledged that the provisions of the Act were 'very much less detailed and less comprehensive than those which apply to [permanent employees]': 138 CLR 416. Nevertheless, he inferred a Commonwealth intention to cover the field of the Commission's employment of temporary employees from two provisions of the Broadcasting and Television Act from ss 42 and 43(6).

> 42 Nothing in this Division shall affect the operation of any award made by the Commonwealth Court of Conciliation and Arbitration, or of any determination made by the Public Service Arbitrator, prior to the commencement of this section and applicable to the Commission and any of its officers or temporary employees.
>
> 43 ...
>
> (6) Subject to this Division, the terms and conditions of employment of officers and temporary employees appointed in pursuance of this section are such as are determined by the Commission with the approval of the Public Service Board.

Mason J explained why the Act managed to 'cover the field' of employment of temporary employees in such a cryptic fashion (at 417):

> The absence of detailed provisions applying to them is not an indication that it is contemplated that other laws will apply to them, but rather that the employer has an unqualified authority to make decisions affecting their employment and the termination of their services.

[8.1.48] The approach taken in *Australian Broadcasting Commission v Industrial Court (SA)* (1977) 138 CLR 399 [8.1.47] was adopted in *Metal Trades Industry Association v Amalgamated Metal Workers' and Shipwrights' Union* (1983) 152 CLR 632. The High Court decided that the Employment Protection Act 1982 (NSW), giving dismissed employees certain enforceable rights against their former employers, was inconsistent with the provisions of awards made under the Conciliation and Arbitration Act 1904 (Cth). The awards dealt with termination of employment and specified the rights of former employees against employers. Gibbs CJ, Wilson and Dawson JJ said at 644:

> On their proper construction, the awards do not leave any room for a State law to attach additional obligations on an employer in consequence of a termination of employment under the awards. In attempting to do so the State Act is inconsistent with the awards.

[8.1.49]   In *Dao v Australian Postal Commission* (1987) 162 CLR 317 **[8.1.67]** the High Court expressly adopted Mason J's analysis from *Australian Broadcasting Commission v Industrial Court (SA)* (1977) 138 CLR 399 **[8.1.47]**. The court concluded that provisions of the Anti-Discrimination Act 1977 (NSW) prohibiting sex discrimination in employment were invalid in their application to the Australian Postal Commission because they were inconsistent with ss 42 and 51 of the Postal Services Act 1975 (Cth). Those sections authorised the Commission to specify requirements, qualifications and conditions for employment by the Commission. Mason CJ, Wilson, Deane, Dawson and Toohey JJ described the observations of Mason J in *Australian Broadcasting Commission v Industrial Court (SA)* (1977) 138 CLR 399 **[8.1.47]**, quoted above, as 'relevant and applicable in their entirety' to the present case: 162 CLR at 339.

On the problem of spelling out the Commonwealth law-maker's intention from the degree of coverage or detail in the Commonwealth law, compare the majority and minority judgments in *Ansett Transport Industries (Operations) Pty Ltd v Wardley* (1980) 142 CLR 237 **[8.1.63C]**. See also *Re Residential Tenancies Tribunal of New South Wales and Henderson; Ex parte Defence Housing Authority* (1997) 190 CLR 410 **[8.2.112C]** where Kirby J (in dissent) said the issue was often 'controversial' (190 CLR at 497) and continued (at 497):

> There are indications here which point in opposing directions. There is not in this case, as often now appears in federal legislation, an express preservation of State laws of general application. On the other hand, there are no detailed federal provisions which would make absolutely clear the expulsion of State laws. Behind constitutional evaluations of this character there doubtless lie different judicial conceptions as to the role of federal legislation and the function of s 109 in securing the Commonwealth's legislative supremacy under the Constitution.

[8.1.50]   To take another approach, the court might infer from the subject matter of the legislation that the Commonwealth Parliament must have intended to lay down an exclusive code. Some subjects, over which the Commonwealth Parliament has power, are such that uniform control or regulation is the only practicable system: for example, weights and measures (s 51(xv)), copyrights, patents and trade marks (s 51(xviii)), currency (s 51(xii)) and quarantine (s 51(ix)); so that, when the Commonwealth Parliament legislates on these matters, one could reasonably infer that the parliament meant its legislation to apply to the exclusion of any state legislation. Topics which have been judicially nominated as requiring uniform regulation include: the prevention of collisions at sea (*Hume v Palmer* (1926) 38 CLR 441 at 462 **[8.1.33]**; *Victoria v Commonwealth* (the *Shipwrecks* case) (1937) 58 CLR 618 at 628 **[8.1.51]**); preference in employment for former members of the armed forces (*Wenn v Attorney-General (Vic)* (1948) 77 CLR 84 at 112 **[8.1.55]**); bankruptcy, patents and trade marks (*Victoria v Commonwealth* (the *Shipwrecks* case) (1937) 58 CLR 618 at 638); the protection of Commonwealth property (*R v Loewenthal; Ex parte Blacklock* (1974) 131 CLR 338 at 342–3 **[8.1.28]**); and the fulfilment of international treaty obligations: *Viskauskas v Niland* (1983) 153 CLR 280 **[8.1.53]**.

[8.1.51] On the other hand, in *Victoria v Commonwealth* (the *Shipwrecks* case) (1937) 58 CLR 618, the High Court inferred from the legislation's subject matter a Commonwealth intention not to cover the field. The court was asked to decide whether s 13 of the Marine Act 1928 (Vic) was inconsistent with s 329 of the Navigation Act 1912 (Cth). The state law authorised state officials to order the removal of any ship sunk in any port within Victoria. The Commonwealth law authorised the (Commonwealth) Minister to order the removal, or to arrange for the removal, of any ship wrecked or abandoned on or near the coast of Australia, if, inter alia, the ship was in waters used for international or interstate trade.

The court decided that the Commonwealth Parliament had not intended in s 329 to cover the field of removal of wrecks. Starke J described concurrent Commonwealth and state authority as 'both useful and necessary': 58 CLR at 628. Dixon J said at 630–1:

> There is nothing in the language of s 329 [of the Commonwealth Act] and certainly nothing in its nature or subject matter suggesting that, if a wreck fell within the description to which the section relates, the Commonwealth authority should have the exclusive power of determining whether or not the owner ought to remove it. Such a wreck might seriously affect the movement of craft engaged in domestic trade and yet be thought unimportant for the purposes of overseas and inter-State trade, although not so completely outside the waters used by vessels in that trade as to be beyond the Commonwealth power. There is no reason for treating s 329 as intending to do more than confer a concurrent or parallel power to enforce the removing of wrecks.

[8.1.52] A similar form of analysis was applied by the High Court in *Flaherty v Girgis* (1987) 162 CLR 574, where the court decided that Pt 10 r 1 of the Supreme Court Rules 1970 (NSW) was not inconsistent with Pt II of the Service and Execution of Process Act 1901 (Cth). Each authorised the service, outside New South Wales, of originating process in litigation in the state's Supreme Court. However, they specified different circumstances in which out-of-state service would be permitted and different procedures to be followed.

Mason ACJ, Wilson and Dawson JJ noted that the Commonwealth legislation dealt with the subject of extra-territorial service of process within the Commonwealth, and that there was (at 595):

> ... no actual conflict in the co-existence of the laws of the States and the federal provisions dealing with that subject-matter nor does the nature of the subject-matter preclude concurrent or parallel powers. Indeed, the apparent aim of the federal legislation is to overcome the jurisdictional impediment of State boundaries in the service of process and the execution of judgments within the Commonwealth and this would not suggest any intention of preventing proper efforts on the part of the States towards the same end.

It followed that the Commonwealth legislation could not be read as intended to cover the field with which it dealt. Brennan and Deane JJ, in separate judgments, agreed that there was no general inconsistency between the state and Commonwealth legislation.

[8.1.53] In *Viskauskas v Niland* (1983) 153 CLR 280, the High Court used a combination of the factors discussed above (subject matter of the legislation and comprehensiveness of the legislation's detail) to infer an intention to cover the field.

The court had been asked to declare that sections of the Anti-Discrimination Act 1977 (NSW) were inconsistent with the Racial Discrimination Act 1975 (Cth). The relevant sections of the state Act prohibited discrimination on grounds of race in a wide variety of situations, including the provision of goods and services: s 19. Enforcement of these prohibitions involved investigation and conciliation by a state official, followed by inquiry and orders (damages or injunctions) by a state tribunal: Pt IX. The Commonwealth Act, enacted to give effect in Australia to an international convention, prohibited racial discrimination in, amongst a wide variety of situations, the provision of goods and services (s 13) and provided for inquiry and conciliation by a Commonwealth Commission, and enforcement through civil action in a court of competent jurisdiction: Pt III.

The High Court (Gibbs CJ, Mason, Murphy, Wilson and Brennan JJ), in a unanimous judgment, conceded that it was possible to obey both laws but held that the state Act was inconsistent with the Commonwealth's intention to 'cover the field'. They discovered this intention in the following way (at 292):

> The Commonwealth Parliament has chosen the course of itself legislating to prohibit racial discrimination, and having done so it can only fulfil the obligation cast upon it by the convention if its enactment operates equally and without discrimination in all the States of the Commonwealth. It could not, for example, admit the possibility that a State law might allow exceptions to the prohibition of racial discrimination or might otherwise detract from the efficacy of the Commonwealth law. The subject matter of the Commonwealth Act suggests that it is intended to be exhaustive and exclusive, and this conclusion is supported by the fact that the provisions of Pt II (and especially those of s 9) are expressed with complete generality, and by the further fact that s 6 reveals an intention to bind the Crown in right of each State as well as the Crown in right of the Commonwealth. It appears from both the terms and the subject matter of the Commonwealth Act that it is intended as a complete statement of the law for Australia relating to racial discrimination.

[8.1.54]   However, as with so many issues in constitutional law, the identification of a subject matter as requiring centralised regulation is not necessarily an automatic process, free from ambiguity and subjective values. The proposition that some topics demand a single central code, while others allow diversity, is a reflection of political and of personal experience in such areas as business or public administration. Why, for example, should we accept the view of Evatt J (expressed in *Victoria v Commonwealth* (the *Shipwrecks* case) (1937) 58 CLR 618 at 638 **[8.1.51]**) that the topic of bankruptcy requires central control while the topic of aliens does not?

Express intention to cover the field

[8.1.55]   A more certain guide to the intention of the Commonwealth law-maker may be provided by the inclusion, in its legislation, of a clause expressly excluding the operation of state legislation, although this may lead to the problem sometimes described as the Commonwealth 'manufacturing' inconsistency. In *Victoria v Commonwealth* (the *Shipwrecks* case) (1937) 58 CLR 618 **[8.1.51]**, Evatt J suggested that such a clause could invalidate the Commonwealth law, as the Commonwealth's specific legislative powers did not include the 'power to define or limit the legislative or executive powers of a State': 58 CLR at 638. See the discussion of *Gerhardy v Brown* (1985) 159 CLR 70 at **[8.1.25]** above.

However, it is now settled that the Commonwealth may legislate in those terms. In *Wenn v Attorney-General (Vic)* (1948) 77 CLR 84, the High Court held that the

Re-establishment and Employment Act 1945 (Cth) covered the field of employment preferences for ex-members of the armed forces, although the Act made provision for preference only in hiring and not in promotion. Accordingly, the Discharged Servicemen's Preference Act 1943 (Vic), which provided for preference in hiring and promotion, was inconsistent with the Commonwealth law. A Commonwealth intention to cover the field was found in the following provision of the Re-establishment and Employment Act:

> 24 ... (2) The provisions of this Division shall apply to the exclusion of any provisions, providing for preference in any matter relating to the employment of discharged members of the forces, of any law of a State.

Latham CJ observed that the Commonwealth's intention to cover the field could therefore be inferred 'from the nature and scope' of the legislation (at 110):

> Where such an inference can properly be drawn the Commonwealth legislation prevails over any State law by virtue of s 109 of the Constitution. In the Commonwealth Act now under consideration, however, the Commonwealth Parliament has not left this matter to be determined by an inference (possibly disputable) from the nature and scope of the statute. The Parliament has most expressly stated an intention which in the other cases mentioned was discovered only by a process of inference. If such a parliamentary intention is effective when it is ascertained by inference only, there can be no reason why it should not be equally effective when the intention is expressly stated.

Dixon J described s 24(2) as showing that the Commonwealth Parliament 'intended to provide ... what would be the only rule upon the subject and so would operate uniformly and without differentiation based on locality or other conditions': 77 CLR at 119. In response to the argument that s 24(2) was beyond the constitutional power of the Commonwealth Parliament, he said at 120:

> There is no doubt great difficulty in satisfactorily defining the limits of the power to legislate upon a subject exhaustively so that s 109 will of its own force make inoperative State legislation which otherwise would add liabilities, duties, immunities, liberties, powers or rights to those which the Federal law had decided to be sufficient. But within such limits an enactment does not seem to me to be open to the objection that it is not legislation with respect to the Federal subject matter but with respect to the exercise of State legislative powers or that it trenches upon State functions. Beyond those limits no doubt there lies a debatable area where Federal laws may be found that seem to be aimed rather at preventing State legislative action than dealing with a subject matter assigned to the Commonwealth Parliament.

(On the analogous question of the limits of the Commonwealth's constitutional power to confer an immunity from state laws, see *Australian Coastal Shipping Commission v O'Reilly* (1962) 107 CLR 46 **[8.2.87]**; *Gazzo v Comptroller of Stamps (Vic)* (1981) 149 CLR 227 **[8.2.88]**; *Botany Municipal Council v Federal Airports Corporation* (1992) 175 CLR 453 **[8.1.73]**.)

Express intention to avoid inconsistency

[8.1.56] What if parliament indicates, through an express provision, that it does not intend to cover the field? Would that be equally effective? In *R v Credit Tribunal; Ex parte General Motors Acceptance Corporation Australia* (1977) 137 CLR 545, the High Court decided that s 40 of the Consumer Credit Act 1972 (SA) was not inconsistent with Pt V of the Trade Practices Act 1974 (Cth). Both the state and Commonwealth legislation implied in consumer sale detailed conditions to protect consumers though there were differences of detail between the state and

Commonwealth conditions. Section 75 of the Trade Practices Act provided that, apart from preventing conviction under both the Act and any state or territory legislation, Pt V was 'not intended to exclude or limit the concurrent operation of any law of a State or Territory'.

Mason J (with whose reasons Barwick CJ, Gibbs and Stephen JJ agreed) referred to *Wenn v Attorney-General (Vic)* (1948) 77 CLR 84 **[8.1.55]**, that a Commonwealth law could expressly indicate an intention to cover the field with which it dealt:

> Equally a Commonwealth law may provide that it is not intended to make exhaustive or exclusive provision with respect to the subject with which it deals, thereby enabling State laws, not inconsistent with Commonwealth law, to have an operation. Here again the Commonwealth law does not of its own force give State law a valid operation. All that it does is to make it clear that the Commonwealth law is not intended to cover the field, thereby leaving room for the operation of such State laws as do not conflict with Commonwealth law (137 CLR at 563).

Mason J expanded on this last point. An express indication of intention not to cover the field could not avoid direct inconsistency, where, for example, it was impossible to obey both laws: 137 CLR at 563–4. The distinction drawn by Mason J between direct and indirect inconsistency in *R v Credit Tribunal; Ex parte General Motors Acceptance Corporation Australia* (1977) 137 CLR 545 was confirmed in *Palmdale AGCI Ltd v Workers Compensation Commission (NSW)* (1978) 140 CLR 236.

Can the Commonwealth express an intention to avoid s 109 inconsistency *retrospectively*?

[8.1.57C]   University of Wollongong v Metwally
(1984) 158 CLR 447

Following the High Court's decision in *Viskauskas v Niland* (1983) 153 CLR 280 **[8.1.53]**, that Pt II of the Anti-Discrimination Act 1977 (NSW) which dealt with racial discrimination was inconsistent with the Racial Discrimination Act 1975 (Cth) and therefore invalid, the Commonwealth Parliament enacted the Racial Discrimination Amendment Act 1983 (Cth), which came into operation on 19 June 1983, one month after the decision in *Viskauskas v Niland*. This Act inserted s 6A in the 1975 Act:

6A(1) This Act is not intended, and shall be deemed never to have been intended, to exclude or limit the operation of a law of a State or Territory that furthers the objects of the Convention and is capable of operating concurrently with this Act.

Metwally had made a complaint of racial discrimination against the University of Wollongong under the Anti-Discrimination Act 1977 (NSW) in February 1982. The High Court handed down its decision in *Viskauskas v Niland* in May 1983 and the Commonwealth Parliament inserted s 6A into the Racial Discrimination Act 1975 (Cth) in June 1983. The New South Wales Anti-Discrimination Tribunal then heard Metwally's complaint, found it to be established, and ordered the University of Wollongong to pay Metwally damages of $46,500.

The university appealed against this decision to the Court of Appeal of New South Wales. One of the grounds of appeal was that s 6A of the Racial Discrimination Act 1983 (Cth) was invalid. That question was removed to the High Court of Australia under s 40(1) of the Judiciary Act 1903 (Cth).

Gibbs CJ: [455] When a law of a State is inconsistent with a law of the Commonwealth and becomes, to the extent of the inconsistency, invalid, the invalidity is brought about by s 109 of the Constitution and not directly by the law of the Commonwealth: see *Federated Saw Mill &c Employees of Australasia v James Moore & Son Pty Ltd* (1909) 8 CLR 465 at 536; *Wenn v Attorney-General (Vic)* (1948) 77 CLR 84 at 120; *R v Railways Appeals Board (NSW);*

Ex parte Davis (1957) 96 CLR 429 at 439. The Commonwealth Parliament cannot enact a law which would affect the operation of s 109 either by declaring that a State law, although not inconsistent with any Commonwealth law shall be invalid, or that a State law which is inconsistent with a Commonwealth law shall be valid. If there were a direct conflict between a Commonwealth law and a State law as, for example, where one law forbids what the other [456] commands, or one takes away a right which the other confers, an assertion in the Commonwealth law that it was not intended to be inconsistent with the State law would be meaningless and ineffective. However, when there is no direct inconsistency between the two laws, the question is whether the State law is inconsistent with the Commonwealth law because the latter intends to cover the subject matter with which the State law deals, and an indication in the Commonwealth law of the intention of the Parliament in that regard would be material and in most cases decisive: see the discussion by Mason J in *R v Credit Tribunal; Ex parte General Motors Acceptance Corporation* (1977) 137 CLR 545 at 562–4 and *Palmdale-AGCI Ltd v Workers' Compensation Commission* (NSW) (1977) 140 CLR 236 at 243–4. It is perhaps possible to imagine a case in which a Commonwealth Act did in truth fully cover the whole field with which it dealt, notwithstanding that it said that it was not intended to do so, but such a case may be left for consideration until it arises.

It is said in *Butler v Attorney-General (Vic)* (1961) 106 CLR 268 that 'invalid' in s 109 of the Constitution means, not void, but 'inoperative' ... It follows that if a Commonwealth statute which, on its proper construction, had revealed an intention to cover exclusively and exhaustively the subject-matter with which it dealt, so that in consequence a State statute dealing with the same subject-matter was rendered inoperative, were subsequently amended in such a way as to manifest an intention that it was not intended to exclude the operation of the State law, the operation of the State statute would thereupon revive ... It was submitted that since the Commonwealth Parliament has power to make its enactments retrospective, it could retrospectively amend the Commonwealth Act, so as to indicate an intention not to [457] exclude the operation of the State law, and thereby cause the Anti-Discrimination Act to have a valid operation from its inception, notwithstanding that in truth it was inconsistent with the Commonwealth Act at all times before the Amendment Act was passed. The acceptance of this argument would mean that the Commonwealth Parliament could enact a law which would retrospectively deprive s 109 of the Constitution of its operation ... If the respondents' argument were correct, the Commonwealth Parliament could retrospectively reveal that the Commonwealth law had an intention, which it lacked at the earlier time, either to cover, or not to cover, the whole field, with the result that the State law would be retrospectively invalidated or validated ... But Commonwealth statutes cannot prevail over the Constitution ... Before the Amendment Act came into effect, the Commonwealth Act, on its proper construction, was intended to be a complete and exclusive statement of the law of Australia with regard to racial discrimination, and Pt 11 of the Anti-Discrimination Act was inconsistent with that law and therefore invalid by force of s 109. What the Amendment Act in effect provides is that the Commonwealth Act should now be understood as though it did not have that intention and that Pt II of the Anti-Discrimination Act was therefore not inconsistent with it. In other words, the Parliament has attempted to exclude the operation of s 109 by means of a fiction. The short answer to the submissions of the respondents is that the Parliament cannot exclude the operation of s 109 by providing that the intention of the Parliament shall be deemed to have been different from what it actually was and that what was in truth an inconsistency shall be deemed to have not existed ... [458] [Section 109] is of great importance for the ordinary citizen, who is entitled to know which of two inconsistent laws he is required to observe. With all respect, I do not agree with the remark of Evatt J in *Victoria v Commonwealth* (1937) 58 CLR 618 at 634, that the section does 'no more than declare a rule of last resort'. For these reasons I hold that Pt II of the Anti-Discrimination Act was inoperative at the time when the alleged discrimination against Mr Metwally occurred.

Mason J: [460] It is not in issue, for the purposes of determining the questions before us, that s 6A is valid and effective to achieve the concurrent operation of both Acts. What the University denies is that s 6A is valid and effective to bring about a retrospective concurrent operation.

... The Parliament could not ... either prospectively or retrospectively provide that a State law which was inconsistent with a Commonwealth law should have, or have had, full force and effect, notwithstanding that inconsistency. This is because the invalidity of the inconsistent State law is brought about by the operation of s 109; the Commonwealth law does not operate of its own inherent force to invalidate the State enactment: *Wenn v Attorney-General (Vic)* (1948) 77 CLR 84 at 119–20; *R v Railways Appeals Board (NSW); Ex parte Davis* (1957) 96 CLR 429 at 439; *R v Credit Tribunal; Ex parte General Motors Acceptance Corporation* (1977) 137 CLR 545 at 563.

But there is no objection to the enactment of Commonwealth legislation whose effect is not to contradict s 109 of the Constitution but to remove the inconsistency which attracts the operation of that section. So, where inconsistency between Commonwealth and State laws arises, as it did in *Viskauskas*, because the Commonwealth law, according to its true construction, is intended to regulate the subject-matter exhaustively or exclusively, the Commonwealth [461] Parliament may legislate to remove that inconsistency by providing that the Commonwealth law is not intended to regulate the subject-matter exhaustively or exclusively, thereby opening the way to the concurrent operation of a State law on the subject matter. It is, of course, well settled that: 'a Commonwealth statute may provide that it is not intended to make exhaustive or exclusive provision with respect to the subject with which it deals thereby enabling State laws, not in direct conflict with a Commonwealth law, to have an operation': *Palmdale-AGCI Ltd v Workers' Compensation Commission* (NSW) (1977) 140 CLR 236 at 243.

What the Parliament can enact prospectively in the exercise of its legislative powers it can also enact retrospectively: *R v Kidman* (1915) 20 CLR 425. Just as a Commonwealth law can validly provide that it is not intended to operate as an exhaustive or exclusive regulation of the subject-matter so it may validly provide that it never was intended to so operate: *Strickland v Rocla Concrete Pipes Ltd* (1971) 124 CLR 468 at 492. Indeed, as I understand the argument, this is not disputed.

The point of departure is reached when and only when the retrospective operation of the Commonwealth statute displaces an inconsistency or cause of inconsistency with a State law which has previously arisen. According to the argument, this is because the Commonwealth statute is attempting to give a valid operation to a State statute which was rendered inoperative by s 109. This analysis mis-states the legal operation of s 6A. It says nothing about the State Act; it amends the Commonwealth Act by altering its prospective and retrospective operation. In so doing, as we have seen, it removes the inconsistency with the State Act. And in removing the inconsistency, s 6A does not attempt to contradict the operation of s 109. What the statutory provision does is to eliminate the basis on which s 109 can operate.

The argument attributes to s 109 the character of a constitutional fetter on Commonwealth legislative power, inhibiting the Parliament from retrospectively amending a Commonwealth statute which is inconsistent with a State statute so as to remove the inconsistency. The argument misconceives the nature and effect of the section. In conjunction with covering cl 5 of the Constitution, the object of the section is to secure paramountcy of Commonwealth laws over conflicting State laws. It achieves this object by rendering the State law invalid 'to the extent of the inconsistency' and no further. It is, of course, well settled that when the section [462] renders a State law 'invalid' the State law is inoperative. The State law is not repealed by the Commonwealth law; nor is it void ab initio: *Carter v Egg and Egg Pulp Marketing Board (Vic)* (1942) 66 CLR 557 at 573, 599.

Mason J noted that this had been made clear by *Butler v Attorney-General (Vic)* (1961)106 CLR 268 **[8.1.79]**.

The consequence is that if the federal Act is repealed with retrospective effect then the basis of invalidity of the State law is eliminated.

The foregoing discussion supports the fundamental proposition which I have already stated: that the object of s 109, no more and no less, is to establish the supremacy of Commonwealth law where [463] there is a conflict between a Commonwealth law and State law. Where no such conflict arises or such a conflict is removed by subsequent retrospective Commonwealth legislation s 109 has no role to play — there is no problem which requires to be solved by an insistence on the supremacy of Commonwealth law.

The section is not a source of individual rights and immunities except in so far as individual rights and immunities are necessarily affected because the section renders inoperative a State law which is inconsistent with a Commonwealth law. Nor is the section a source of protection to the individual against the unfairness and injustice of a retrospective law. That is a matter which lies quite outside the focus of the provision. In these circumstances to distil from s 109 an unexpressed fetter upon Commonwealth legislative power is to twist the section from its true meaning and stand it upon its head.

Mason J held that, upon the insertion of s 6A in the Racial Discrimination Act 1975 (Cth), Pt II of the Anti-Discrimination Act 1977 (NSW) revived, and that revival was retrospective.

Murphy J said that neither federal nor state parliament could render valid what s 109 had made invalid. Section 6A could have a prospective operation and both the federal parliament and the state parliament 'could legislate retrospectively so that a fresh State law would come into existence giving present legal force to the procedures which have been followed and the remedies which have been obtained by Mr Metwally'. However, the federal parliament could not, through the enactment of retrospective legislation, achieve the retrospective revival of a state law rendered invalid, in respect of a past period, by the operation of s 109: 'This would elevate legislation above the Constitution': 158 CLR at 469.

Brennan J said that section 109 had a 'temporal aspect': 158 CLR at 473. He said that the 'period during which the State law was inconsistent with the Commonwealth law is a matter of history, not of legislative intention': 158 CLR 474. Therefore '[w]here the condition governing s 109 is in truth satisfied, it is not within the power of the Parliament to deem it not to be satisfied. The Parliament can remove an inconsistency, it cannot deem an inconsistency to be removed', he said, referring to Mason J in *R v Credit Tribunal; Ex parte General Motors Acceptance Corporation Australia* (1977) 137 CLR at 563 **[8.1.56]**.

Deane J: [476] The proposition for which Mr Metwally, with the support of the respondent Attorney-Generals for the Commonwealth and New South Wales and the intervening Attorney-Generals for South Australia and Western Australia, contends is a timely one in that it is readily adaptable to Orwellian notions of doublethink. It is that, under s 109 of the Constitution, the Commonwealth Parliament can, by retrospective legislation, produce the consequences in any field in which it possesses legislative power that a State law which was invalid at a particular time was valid at that time or that a State law which was valid at a particular time was invalid at that time and that an act which was not unlawful under State law at the time when it was done was unlawful, or even criminal, under that law at that time or that an act which was unlawful, or even criminal, under State law at the time when it was done was not unlawful under that law at that time.

[T]he submission [that it would be 'anomalous' to interpret s 109 in such a way so as to detract from Commonwealth supremacy and parliamentary sovereignty] fails adequately to acknowledge that ... [477] the provisions of the Constitution should properly be viewed as ultimately concerned with the governance and protection of the people from whom the artificial entities called Commonwealth and States derive their authority. So viewed, s 109 is not concerned merely to resolve disputes between the Commonwealth and a State as to the validity of their competing claims to govern the conduct of individuals in a particular area of legislative power. It serves the equally important function of protecting the individual from the injustice of being subjected to the requirements of valid and inconsistent laws of Commonwealth and State Parliaments on the same subject ...

[478] A parliament may legislate that, for the purposes of the law which it controls, past facts or past laws are to be deemed and treated as having been different to what they were. It cannot, however objectively, expunge the past or 'alter the facts of history': cf *Akar v*

Attorney-General (Sierra Leone) [1970] AC 853 at 870 ... For the purposes of an organic law, such as the Constitution, which lies above the law which such a parliament may make, it may be a relevant fact that that parliament has enacted that some fact or law which in truth existed is to be deemed never to have been. If, however, that organic law is framed so as to act upon the reality, the retrospective fictions of the subordinate law will be unavailing ...

Section 109 of the Constitution is not concerned with legal fictions. It is concerned with the reality of contemporaneous inconsistency between a valid law of the Commonwealth and an otherwise valid law of a State. According to its terms, its operation is immediate. Its terms are unqualified and self-executing. If there is inconsistency between an otherwise valid law of a State and a valid law of the Commonwealth the State law *shall* be, to the extent of the inconsistency, invalid. It is not the Commonwealth law which operates to make the State law invalid, it is the Constitution itself: see *Federated Saw Mill &c Employees of Australasia v James Moore & Son Pty Ltd* (1909) 8 CLR 465 at 536; *Wenn v Attorney-General (Vic)* (1948) 77 CLR 84 at 120. It is the Constitution and not the Commonwealth Parliament which tells the citizen faced with the dilemma of inconsistent Common[479]wealth and State laws which both, according to their terms, apply to him or her that the State law is invalid and can be disregarded. If, at some subsequent time, the Commonwealth repeals or amends its law to remove the inconsistency, the State law will then become again valid or operative not from some prior date but from the time when there was, in fact, no longer inconsistency. The fact that the Commonwealth Parliament legislates retrospectively to introduce the fiction that, for the purposes of its law, its inconsistent law never existed or had a different operation to that which it in fact had cannot alter the objective fact that at the previous time when s 109 operated that inconsistency did exist. Nor can it alter the fact that the immediate and self-executing provisions of s 109 have already operated upon that inconsistency to invalidate the State law not for the period in which the Commonwealth Parliament, by the introduction of a fiction for its purposes, has subsequently said that its law had a different operation to that which it in fact had but for the period in which the fact of that inconsistency existed. So to say is not to construe s 109 of the Constitution as imposing a restriction on Commonwealth legislative power. It is simply to recognise that while the Commonwealth can retrospectively legislate for itself it cannot retrospectively impose *as State law* the provisions of a law which the Constitution has said was invalid because of contemporaneous inconsistency which has subsequently been removed. That is something which, if it is to be done, must be done retrospectively by the relevant State.

It follows that the Commonwealth Parliament, being subordinate to the Constitution, could not, by its 1983 Amending Act, reverse the past operation of s 109 of the Constitution which had rendered invalid or inoperative the relevant provisions of the New South Wales Act. The Commonwealth Parliament possessed no power unilaterally to override that operation of the Constitution either by amending the terms of s 109 or by creating a legally effective illusion that the section had never operated at all by the introduction of a retrospective fiction into its law. That being so, the position remains that the relevant provisions of the New South Wales Act were not operative at the time the acts complained of in the present case were committed and the conduct for which the appellant has been held responsible was not unlawful under the provisions of the New South Wales Act.

~~~

[8.1.58] Wilson and Dawson JJ delivered judgments in substantially the same terms as Mason J. In the result, a majority of the court (Gibbs CJ, Murphy, Brennan and Deane JJ) decided that Pt II of the Anti-Discrimination Act 1977 (NSW) did not have a valid operation before the commencement of the Racial Discrimination Amendment Act 1983 (Cth).

Notes

[8.1.59] While the four majority justices were agreed in *University of Wollongong v Metwally* (1984) 158 CLR 447 **[8.1.57C]** that the Commonwealth Parliament could not achieve the retrospective revival of a state law rendered invalid by s 109 of the Constitution, there was significant disagreement among them over the broader question of the Commonwealth's capacity to manipulate its legislative supremacy.

Murphy J said that, while the Commonwealth Parliament could not 'undo the previous invalidating effect of s 109, it [could] clear the way for the state Parliament to make a fresh state Act to apply retrospectively in the same terms': 158 CLR at 469; see also Deane J: 158 CLR at 480.

Brennan J appeared to concede that s 6A could be read as a retrospective vacating of the field formerly covered by the Racial Discrimination Act, thereby providing the opportunity for the states to enter that field through the enactment of fresh retrospective legislation. For Brennan J, apparently, the incapacity of the Commonwealth Parliament to deny an established incapacity meant only that retrospective Commonwealth legislation could not revive invalid state legislation: 158 CLR at 475.

If the Commonwealth Parliament could clear the way for state legislation retrospectively to enter a field, it would seem that the Commonwealth Parliament could also retrospectively cover a field so as to exclude state legislation already present in that field. That point was recognised by Murphy J (158 CLR at 468); and conceded as a possibility by Deane J: 158 CLR at 480. However, Gibbs CJ rejected the proposition that the Commonwealth Parliament could retrospectively indicate its intention to cover a field so as retrospectively to invalidate pre-existing state law, because 'Commonwealth statutes cannot prevail over the Constitution': 158 CLR at 457.

[8.1.60] The minority views in *University of Wollongong v Metwally* (1984) 158 CLR 447 **[8.1.57C]**, on the other hand, were consistent and simple; namely, the Commonwealth Parliament could legislate retrospectively to create or remove inconsistency with state legislation where that inconsistency depended on the Commonwealth Parliament's intention to cover the field, although it was beyond the power of the Commonwealth Parliament to revive a state law which remained directly inconsistent with a Commonwealth law: 158 CLR at 460 per Mason J; 158 CLR at 483 Dawson J.

[8.1.61] Much of the disagreement between the majority and minority in *Metwally's* case (1984) 158 CLR 447 **[8.1.57C]** can be attributed to their different perceptions of the purpose of s 109. Both Gibbs CJ and Deane J, amongst the majority, described s 109 as concerned with 'protecting the individual from the injustice of being subjected to the requirements of valid and inconsistent laws of Commonwealth and State Parliaments on the same subject': 158 CLR at 477 per Deane J; see also 158 CLR at 458 per Gibbs CJ. On the other hand, Mason and Dawson JJ, amongst the minority, rejected this view of s 109. As Zines has observed, the conversion of a provision affirming Commonwealth supremacy into a partial limitation on Commonwealth power was 'somewhat ironical', particularly when it was applied to prevent the Commonwealth from ensuring the operation of state law: Zines (1997) p 413.

[8.1.62] It would appear that this view of s 109, as protecting the individual citizen against dual regulation or control, would advance the centralising effect of s 109. If, as Gibbs CJ and Deane J assert, one of the objectives of s 109 is to free the individual from the 'injustice of being subjected to the requirements of valid and inconsistent laws of Commonwealth and State Parliaments on the same subject' (158 CLR at 477 per Deane J) then the court should be much less willing to tolerate the concurrent existence of Commonwealth and state legislation such as that which was allowed to survive in *Airlines of New South Wales Pty Ltd v New South Wales (No 2)* (1965) 113 CLR 54 **[8.1.37]**, or *New South Wales v Commonwealth* (the *Hospital Benefits* case) (1983) 151 CLR 302 **[8.1.38C]**.

[8.1.63C]   Ansett Transport Industries (Operations) Pty Ltd v Wardley

(1980) 142 CLR 237

Section 18 of the Equal Opportunity Act 1977 (Vic) prohibited an employer from discriminating against a person on the ground of sex when determining who should be offered employment; or discriminating against an employee on the ground of sex or marital status by dismissing the employee. Section 37 of the Act authorised the Equal Opportunity Board to inquire into a complaint of discrimination and to order any person to comply with the Act.

The Airline Pilots Agreement 1978 had been certified by the Flight Crew Officers' Industrial Tribunal, and therefore had the same force as an award of the Commonwealth Conciliation and Arbitration Commission: Conciliation and Arbitration Act 1904 (Cth) s 28(3). Clause 6A authorised an employer to employ pilots 'subject to the provisions of this Agreement. Clause 6B authorised an employer' to dismiss a pilot 'by seven days' notice in writing' (during the first six months of employment) or 'by one month's notice in writing' (after the completion of six months of service). A dismissed pilot was entitled to have the dismissal reviewed by a Grievance Board unless dismissal occurred during the first 12 months of the pilot's employment.

Ansett had been ordered by the Equal Opportunity Board to employ Wardley, a woman, as a pilot. Ansett began proceedings in the Supreme Court, seeking declarations that the Equal Opportunity Act did not apply to Ansett in its employment or dismissal of pilots. These proceedings were removed to the High Court under s 40 of the Judiciary Act 1903 (Cth).

Stephen J referred to Ansett's argument that the Airline Pilots Agreement gave it an unqualified right to dismiss its pilots on any ground, while the State Act purported to limit the grounds for dismissal, thus producing direct collision.] **[246]** In my view there is in this case no inconsistency within the meaning of s 109 of the Constitution. I regard the right of termination of the contract of employment which cl 6 of the Agreement confers as no absolute right, such as that for which Ansett contends. The right which it confers is not one which is capable of exercise regardless of the unlawfulness under State law of the ground for its exercise. On the contrary it is a right the nature of which is to be understood against the background to its operation which general laws of the land, whether State or federal in origin, provide ...

Stephen J: [247] When the power of termination which cl 6B confers upon the parties to the contract of employment comes to be construed it can be seen to contain nothing in its quite unexceptional wording to suggest that it should stand inviolate, unresponsive to a general law applicable to the community at large and directed to the prevention of some evil practice which, of its nature, may manifest itself in a variety of ways, including the exercise by an employer of his power of dismissal. The concern of the Agreement is, after all, entirely unremarkable, being exclusively devoted to the settlement of an industrial dispute. This is an inherently improbable source in which to discover, in the form of a simple power to bring their contract to an end conferred upon both parties to a contract of employment, a right on the employer's part to practise discrimination upon the grounds of sex, contrary to, and immune from the prohibition of, State law...

[248] The question as a whole resolves itself, in the end, into a search for legislative intent. While the Agreement and the Act each deals with aspects of the engagement and dismissal of employees, they are essentially dissimilar both in character and in general content. The Act gives legislative effect throughout the Victorian community to a broad social policy concerned with the status of women in that community. It forbids certain acts of discrimination against them on the grounds of sex or marital status and promotes equality of opportunity between the sexes. It applies to widespread areas of human activity: to education, the provision of accommodation and the supply of a great variety of services, as well as to employment. Within these areas it confines itself to the matter of discrimination on the [249] grounds of sex or marital status ...

Stephen J distinguished between Acts on different subject matters which nevertheless contained inconsistent provisions, and two measures which were concerned with different subjects: 142 CLR at 249–50.

[250] The Victorian legislature has concerned itself quite generally with the social problem of discrimination based upon sex or marital status and occurring in a variety of areas of human activity. It has declared various manifestations of such discrimination to be unlawful. This is a subject matter upon which the Commonwealth's Conciliation and Arbitration Act is understandably silent, silent because of its general irrelevance to the subject matter of that Act. That silence will necessarily extend to the factum through which it operates, the present Agreement. The disputes with which the Conciliation and Arbitration Act are concerned are disputes as to industrial matters, pertaining to the relationship of employer and employee; they have nothing inherently to do with questions of discrimination on the grounds of sex. No doubt it may happen that in a particular dispute, apparently of an industrial character, some question of discrimination of this sort may appear to be involved. The precise nature of its involvement may then determine whether or not the dispute is indeed an industrial dispute. However, in the present case the Agreement gives not the slightest indication of any such involvement and has all the hallmarks of being made in settlement of an entirely [251] orthodox industrial dispute. In the context of this Agreement it may be said of the topic of discrimination that, in the words of this Court in *Collins v Charles Marshall Pty Ltd* (1955) 92 CLR 529 at 533, it 'simply is not a subject within the purview of the award' ...

[253] Concluding, as I have, that there is here no question of direct collision between Agreement and Act, there is, a fortiori, no such inconsistency arising under the doctrine of 'covering the field', and this very much for the reasons which I have stated in dealing with direct collision. Whatever field the Agreement may cover, the question of dismissal upon the discriminatory ground that the pilot is a woman is in my view no part of it.

Stephen J concluded that he would refuse the declarations sought.

Mason J: [259] [T]he major thrust of Ansett's case is to establish the existence of what has been called 'direct inconsistency', that is, the disconformity which is created by the presence of an absolute right to dismiss for any reason whatsoever, which Ansett finds in the Agreement, and the presence in the State Act of a prohibition against dismissal for the prescribed reasons ... [260] As the various tests which have been applied by the Court are all designed to elucidate the issue of inconsistency it is not surprising that they are interrelated and that in a given case more than one test is capable of being applied so as to establish inconsistency. Especially is this so when it is the giving of a permission or the grant of a right by Commonwealth law that is the foundation of a claim of inconsistency. If, according to the true construction of the Commonwealth law, the right is absolute, then it inevitably follows that the right is intended to prevail to the exclusion of any other law. A State law which takes away the right is inconsistent because it is in conflict with the absolute right and because the Commonwealth law relevantly occupies the field. So also with a Commonwealth law that grants a permission by way of positive authority. The Commonwealth legislative intention which sustains the conclusion that the permission is granted by way of positive authority also sustains the conclusion that the positive authority was to take effect to the exclusion of any other law. Again it produces inconsistency on both grounds: cf *Airlines of New South Wales Pty Ltd v New South Wales* (1965) 113 CLR 54, where the permission for which Commonwealth law provided was neither absolute nor comprehensive.

Inconsistency between a Commonwealth award or an agreement having the force of an award and a State law involves special considerations. They were discussed in *Robinson (TA) and Sons Pty Ltd v Haylor* (1957) 97 CLR 177 at 182–3, and they explain the presence of s 65 in the Act. In truth the case which Ansett makes is one of inconsistency between the Act and the State Act, s 109 giving **[261]** paramountcy to the Act with the result that the State Act cannot operate if, pursuant to the Act, the Commission has exercised its power to the exclusion of the provisions made by State law on the topic. The issue therefore turns upon the interpretation of the Agreement and, despite the emphasis given to the claim of direct inconsistency, the question is whether the provisions of the Agreement were intended to operate, subject to, or in disregard of, the general law ...

[262] From my examination of the Agreement as a whole, I conclude that it should not be viewed as a general industry award which seeks to determine exhaustively the respective rights of employer and employee. Although the Agreement does deal with many of the matters usually found in an award, such as pay, hours of work and leave, its emphasis is on setting out in exact detail the manner and procedure governing the advancement of a pilot in terms of seniority and rights dependent thereon. Clause 6B does not deal with the substantive right of dismissal. Instead, its opening words assume the right of the employer under the general law to terminate the employment of a pilot and the import of the clause as laid down in paras 1, 2, 3 and 4 is to prescribe the procedure and regulate the means whereby the right to terminate may be effected ...

[263] Consequently, I do not find any direct inconsistency between cl 6B and the State Act. The Agreement does not confer on Ansett a substantive right of dismissal; it merely assumes the right of dismissal for which the general law provides. The right of an employer under the general law to dismiss an employee has **[264]** been altered in Victoria by the State Act in that an employer may not discriminate against an employee on the ground of sex in offering employment, refusing to offer employment or in the terms on which employment is offered (s 18(1)) or by dismissing an employee by reason of sex (s 18(2)(b)). The Agreement is to be read in the light of this alteration in the general law. The grounds on which I have reached the conclusion that there is no direct inconsistency also require the conclusion that cl 6B of the Agreement does not seek to cover the field of the employer's substantive right to dismiss ...

Mason J refused to make the declarations sought.

Aickin J: **[274]** The argument in this case was primarily directed to the question whether the Agreement was intended to cover the field of the terms of employment of airline pilots by Ansett ... regarded as an example of 'direct conflict' in that the Agreement appears to permit the dismissal without review of a pilot during his first six months of service on either the giving of notice of seven days, or upon payment of seven days' salary, upon any ground whatever, whereas the State Act prohibits dismissal on specified grounds. It is therefore convenient to consider first the question of direct conflict.

I turn now to a consideration of the Agreement in so far as it applies to a pilot who has been employed for a period of less than twelve months ... If it were the fact that the termination involved discrimination on the basis of sex or race the State Act would on its face enable a complaint to be made which could be followed by an order from the Board directing a reinstatement or a re-employment of the pilot so dismissed. This appears to me to involve 'direct conflict' in the sense of making unlawful that which the Agreement permits.

The Agreement makes an express provision for dismissal of such a pilot, or termination of his employment without restricting **[276]** in any way the grounds upon which such termination may be given. The State Act would enable such a decision to be set at nought by the Board ordering reinstatement or re-employment, and apparently payment in respect of any period between the termination and the reinstatement. This appears to me to involve inconsistency in the sense that the State Act would if valid 'impair alter or detract from the operation of' the Agreement. I take that phrase from the reasons for judgment of Dixon J in *Victoria v Commonwealth* (1937) 58 CLR 618 at 630 ...

[280] The two different aspects of inconsistency are no more than a reflection of different ways in which the Parliament may manifest its intention that the federal law, whether wide or narrow in its operation, should be the exclusive regulation of the relevant conduct. Whether it be right or not to say that there are two kinds of inconsistency, the central question is the intention of a particular federal law. The field of its operation may be regarded as wide or narrow and produce inconsistency because of the intention to cover a particular field exclusively or because of an intention to regulate specific conduct so that any other regulation of that conduct is inconsistent because the attempt to regulate the identical conduct in a different manner, or perhaps at all, necessarily impairs the operation of the federal regulation of that conduct.

Aickin J said that he would declare that the Equal Opportunity Act would not apply to Wardley's dismissal if that dismissal was in accordance with the Airline Pilots Agreement. Barwick CJ agreed with the conclusions and reasons of Aickin J. Murphy J said the declarations sought by Ansett should be refused. The agreement was not exhaustive and did not give an unqualified right to terminate employment. Wilson J also held that the declarations sought by Ansett should be refused because the agreement was not concerned with the grounds for dismissal, but left those to be defined by the general law.

~~~

Notes

[8.1.64] There is, in some of the judgments in *Ansett Transport Industries (Operations) Pty Ltd v Wardley* (1980) 142 CLR 237 **[8.1.63C]**, a suggestion of confusion over the nature of the inconsistency argued by Ansett: Mason J identified 'the major thrust of Ansett's case' as intended to establish 'direct inconsistency' (142 CLR at 259), while Aickin J said the argument 'was primarily directed to the question whether the agreement was intended to cover the field': 142 CLR at 274. This may be not so much a product of confusion as an indication that, in many situations, the separate tests of inconsistency depend upon substantially the same considerations: when we ask 'What field was the Commonwealth law intended to cover?', we are also asking 'What right or immunity did the Commonwealth law intend to confer?'

Aickin J asserted that, 'whether ... or not ... there are two kinds of inconsistency', the central question was the intention of the federal law: 142 CLR at 280. A similar point was made by Stephen J (142 CLR at 248) and Mason J (142 CLR at 260, 261).

[8.1.65] In *Ansett Transport Industries (Operations) Pty Ltd v Wardley* (1980) 142 CLR 237 **[8.1.63C]**, the difference between the minority (Barwick CJ and Aickin J) and three of the majority justices (Mason, Murphy and Wilson JJ) seemed to lie in their perceptions of the intention of the Commonwealth law-maker. For the majority, the Commonwealth law was not intended to cover the field of dismissal, or was not intended to give the employer an unqualified right to dismiss: rather, it was intended to deal with the procedure to be followed when the employer exercised its right to dismiss, a right which flowed from and could be modified by other law. That intention was inferred from the agreement's silence in the face of such restrictions on dismissal as existed in 1978, for example, the Equal Opportunity Act 1977 (Vic) and s 5 of the Conciliation and Arbitration Act 1904 (Cth).

However, the minority maintained that the agreement was intended to deal with all aspects of dismissal, grounds and procedure: that it was intended to prescribe completely and exhaustively the rights of employer and employees on, among other matters, Ansett's right to dismiss pilots, the procedure to be followed and the pilots' rights to seek review. That intention was discovered, not so much in the terms of the agreement, as in the essential nature of the process (industrial dispute followed by agreement) which produced that agreement: see 142 CLR at 279.

[8.1.66]   On the other hand, the difference between the fourth majority justice in *Ansett Transport Industries (Operations) Pty Ltd v Wardley* (1980) 142 CLR 237 **[8.1.63C]**, Stephen J, and Barwick CJ and Aickin J lay in the former's view that the Equal Opportunity Act and the agreement dealt with entirely different subject matters. Stephen J rejected the views of the other majority judges that the agreement dealt only with the procedures to be followed on dismissal: 142 CLR at 253–4. The agreement did confer on Ansett a right of dismissal; but this should be understood as a part of the 'employment relationships as between Ansett and its pilots'. The agreement was 'concerned with industrial matters' and the right to dismiss must be read in that context; it was not intended as a right to dismiss on grounds far removed from industrial considerations. Or, to employ the language appropriate to the 'cover the field' test, the agreement dealt with the field of the industrial relations between employer and employees (and covered that field); the Equal Opportunity Act dealt with another field, the elimination of sexual discrimination, in that it implemented a 'broad social policy concerned with the status of women'.

In emphasising the different subject matters or fields of the Commonwealth and state laws, Stephen J was anticipating the High Court's approach in *New South Wales v Commonwealth* (the *Hospital Benefits* case) (1983) 151 CLR 302 **[8.1.38C]**.

[8.1.67]   In *Dao v Australian Postal Commission* (1987) 162 CLR 317, the High Court decided that ss 25 and 113 of the Anti-Discrimination Act 1977 (NSW), which made it unlawful for an employer to discriminate against a person on the ground of the person's sex in determining who should be offered employment, were inconsistent with ss 42 and 51 of the Postal Services Act 1975 (Cth), which authorised the Australian Postal Commission to appoint officers only when the Commission was satisfied that the appointee met such requirements as were determined by the Commission.

In a unanimous judgment, Mason CJ, Wilson, Deane, Dawson and Toohey JJ rejected the appellants' argument that the refusal of the Commission to appoint them as officers, on the basis that their body weights were below the minimum required by the Commission, constituted discrimination on the ground of their sex. They said there was a collision or direct inconsistency between ss 25 and 113 of the Anti-Discrimination Act and s 42. They said that the relevant principle had been discussed by Mason J in *Ansett Transport Industries (Operations) Pty Ltd v Wardley* (1980) 142 CLR 237 **[8.1.63C]** at 260: when the Commonwealth law gave an absolute right, 'then it inevitably follows that the right is intended to prevail to the exclusion of any other law'. The same result followed where the 'Commonwealth law ... grants a permission by way of positive authority'. In either case, it could be said that a state law's qualification of that right or permission produced both direct and indirect inconsistency.

[8.1.68]   In *Dobinson v Crabb* (1990) 170 CLR 218, a majority of the High Court (Dawson, Toohey and McHugh JJ; Brennan and Gaudron JJ dissenting) held that there was no inconsistency between s 143(6) of the Conciliation and Arbitration Act 1904 (Cth), which provided that, upon cancellation of the Australian Building Construction Employees' and Builders Labourers' Federation's (the BLF), registration its property was, subject to any order made by the Federal Court, to be held and applied for the purposes of the BLF in accordance with its constitution and rules, and, s 7(1) of the BLF (De-recognition) Act 1985 (Vic), authorised the Governor-in-Council to make an order vesting the BLF's funds and property in a state custodian. BLF officials argued that there was an inconsistency between the Commonwealth and state laws of both a direct and indirect (cover the field) type. In their joint judgment, Dawson and McHugh JJ said that there was no direct conflict. When the state custodian took possession of the BLF's property, he took it subject to any order which the Federal Court might make to meet the BLF's debts and obligations: 170 CLR at 229. Nor was there any direct conflict between the Victorian legislation and that part of s 143(6) which vested the property of the former registered organisation in the association after de-registration. The situation, Dawson and McHugh JJ said (170 CLR at 231), was analogous to that identified by Stephen J in *Ansett Transport Industries (Operations) Pty Ltd v Wardley* (1980) 142 CLR 237 **[8.1.63C]**. Stephen J had described the power of an employer, under a Commonwealth industrial agreement, to terminate a contract of employment as 'a right the nature of which is to be understood against the background to its operation which general laws of the land, whether state or federal in origin, provide': 142 CLR at 246.

A similar comparison to *Ansett Transport Industries (Operations) Pty Ltd v Wardley* was made by Gaudron J: 170 CLR at 246. Because s 143(6) of the Conciliation and Arbitration Act was silent on a number of machinery matters, it was inappropriate to read it as intended to be exhaustive and exclusive; otherwise, it would have the effect, in the words of Stephen J in *Ansett Transport Industries (Operations) Pty Ltd v Wardley*, of 'creating a partial vacuum': 170 CLR at 246.

[8.1.69] In *Re Residential Tenancies Tribunal of New South Wales and Henderson; Ex parte Defence Housing Authority* (1997) 190 CLR 410 **[8.2.112C]**, a majority of the High Court (Dawson, Toohey and Gaudron JJ; Brennan CJ, McHugh and Gummow JJ agreeing; Kirby J dissenting) held that the Defence Housing Authority 1987 (Cth) and the Residential Tenancies Act 1987 (NSW) were not inconsistent.

The Residential Tenancies Act 1987 (NSW) provided that the Residential Tenancies Tribunal (the RTT) constituted under s 80 of the Act had the power, on the making of an application by a landlord under a residential tenancy agreement, to make an order authorising the landlord or any other person to enter the premises. The Defence Housing Authority Act 1987 (Cth) empowered the Defence Housing Authority (the DHA) to provide adequate housing for members of the Australian Defence Force, and officers and employees of the Commonwealth Department of Defence. Section 7 provided that the DHA had the power 'to do all things necessary or convenient to be done for, or in connection with, the performance of its functions' and listed these as including: purchase of land and houses; development of land; building, demolishing, converting, renting and general management of houses; determination and collection of rents; eviction; provision and improvement of amenities for persons living in houses rented out by it; entering into contracts; and anything incidental to any of its powers: s 7(1)(a)–(h), (p), (x).

The owner of residential premises leased to the DHA filed an application with the RTT for orders that the DHA allow the owner to inspect the premises and that the

DHA give the owner a key to the premises. The DHA disputed the RTT's jurisdiction on four grounds, including inconsistency under s 109. The majority (Kirby J dissenting) rejected the s 109 argument. Dawson, Toohey and Gaudron JJ (with whom Brennan CJ agreed and McHugh and Gummow JJ concurred in separate judgments) said that the Commonwealth legislation was 'neither comprehensive nor exclusive, for in conferring the powers which it does upon the DHA it assumes an existing legal system within which and by means of which those powers might be exercised'; it was, they said, 'meaningless to speak of the power to rent out houses and land or evict tenants in the absence of any law relating to landlord and tenant': 190 CLR at 432. The justices continued at 433:

> The Defence Housing Authority Act makes no provision for the creation and enforcement of those rights and obligations which are necessary for the performance of its function and it is obvious that it was intended to operate within a legal framework provided by the common law and State law and, for that matter, federal law should any federal law have a relevant application.

[8.1.70]   The apparent blurring of the approaches to inconsistency in *Ansett Transport Industries (Operations) Pty Ltd v Wardley* (1980) 142 CLR 237 **[8.1.63C]** may have reflected the way in which the case was argued before the court, or it may have reflected the terms of the relevant Commonwealth and state laws which meant that no purpose would have been served by drawing a sharp distinction between those approaches: a conclusion, that the Victorian legislation did not undermine a right or privilege conferred by the agreement, could not be reached without also concluding that the state law did not enter a field covered by the Commonwealth law. But neither the decision nor the reasoning of the justices suggests that, in every case of alleged inconsistency, the two approaches will produce identical answers. That is, the distinction between these approaches, asserted by Isaacs J in *Clyde Engineering Co Ltd v Cowburn* (1926) 37 CLR 466 **[8.1.20]** at 490–1, and endorsed by Mason J in *R v Credit Tribunal; Ex parte General Motors Acceptance Corporation Australia* (1977) 137 CLR 545 **[8.1.56]** at 563–4 and by several members of the court in *University of Wollongong v Metwally* (1984) 158 CLR 447 **[8.1.57C]** (at 455–6 per Gibbs CJ; at 460 per Mason J; at 474–5 per Brennan J; and at 483 per Dawson J) must be regarded as firmly established. The 'cover the field' approach should be recognised as expanding the impact of s 109 beyond the somewhat limited range which it would have if inconsistency were limited to what some justices have described as 'direct' inconsistency.

[8.1.71]   The development of this 'indirect' approach to identifying inconsistent Commonwealth and state laws has significant implications for the political autonomy of the Australian states. The development has invited (to adapt Rumble's observation) 'one of the federal partners, the Commonwealth, to deny to a State, another federal partner, part of its law making power': Rumble (1980) p 79. It is implicit in this concept of inconsistency that the Commonwealth Parliament may occupy some field of social or economic regulation to the exclusion of state legislatures; and that s 109 provides the foundation for centralised (rather than shared) legislative control of a wide range of social and economic activities.

   Of course, the High Court could qualify this invitation and apply some weight to the states' side of the federal balance. The court might assert some implicit constitutional restraint on an overreaching Commonwealth Parliament. Dixon CJ was able to employ such a restraint, the 'federal character of the Constitution', to support his proposition that Commonwealth legislation could not cover the field of taxation so as to prevent the states legislating to raise their own revenues: *Victoria v Commonwealth* (the *Second Uniform Tax* case) (1957) 99 CLR 575 at 614 **[9.6.8C]**. The court has also developed 'federal assumptions' to give the state executive governments a degree of immunity from some Commonwealth legislation: *Melbourne Corporation v Commonwealth* (1947) 74 CLR 31 **[8.2.45C]**; *Queensland Electricity Commission v Commonwealth* (1985) 159 CLR 192 **[8.2.59C]**. Or the court might develop judicial protection for state legislative autonomy by exploiting the ambiguities inherent in the 'cover the field' test of inconsistency.

For a review of these possible qualifications, see Hanks (1986) pp 132–4.

[8.1.72] The High Court's decision in *Mabo v Queensland (No 1)* (1988) 166 CLR 186 illustrates the potential for expansion of Commonwealth authority which s 109 offers. A majority of the court (Brennan, Deane, Toohey and Gaudron JJ) held that the Queensland Coast Islands Declaratory Act 1985 (Qld) was invalid because it was inconsistent with s 10 of the Racial Discrimination Act 1975 (Cth).

The Queensland legislation purported to extinguish any traditional land rights of the descendants of the original inhabitants of the Torres Strait Islands which might have survived the annexation of those islands by Queensland in 1879. If the legislation was valid, it would have provided the state of Queensland with a defence to an action brought in the High Court against the state, some three years before the passage of the Act, by the Meriam people (traditional occupiers of Murray Island in Torres Strait) seeking a declaration that they retained traditional and legally enforceable rights to Murray Island. Section 10(1) of the Racial Discrimination Act provided that, where a state law conferred a narrower right on persons of a particular race, colour or national or ethnic origin than the right of other persons, the first-mentioned group of persons should, 'notwithstanding anything in that law … enjoy that right to the same extent' as the other persons. Among the rights covered by s 10(1) were the right to own property and the right not to be arbitrarily deprived of property: the International Convention on the Elimination of All Forms of Racial Discrimination art 5.

The court approached the validity of the Queensland legislation on the assumption (later established in *Mabo v Queensland (No 2)* (1992) 175 CLR 1) that the plaintiffs' traditional title was still in existence when the Racial Discrimination Act 1975 came into force. On that assumption and leaving aside the 1985 Queensland Act, Brennan, Toohey and Gaudron JJ said, the general law of Queensland would recognise two categories of legal rights over Murray Island: traditional rights and rights granted under Queensland Crown lands legislation. The former rights were held by the Meriam people, the latter by people of other races, and national or ethnic origins etc:

> By extinguishing the traditional legal rights characteristically vested in the Miriam [*sic*] people, the 1985 Act abrogated the immunity of the Miriam people from arbitrary deprivation of their legal rights in and over the Murray Islands. The Act thus impaired their human rights while leaving unimpaired the corresponding human rights of those whose rights in and over the Murray Islands did not take their origin from the laws and customs of the Miriam people. If we accord to the traditional rights of the Miriam people the status of recognised legal rights under Queensland law (as we must in conformity with the assumption made earlier), the 1985 Act has the effect of precluding the Miriam people from enjoying some, if not all, of their legal rights in and over the Murray Islands while leaving all other persons unaffected in the enjoyment of their legal rights in and over the Murray Islands. Accordingly, the Miriam people enjoy

their human right of the ownership and inheritance of property to a 'more limited' extent than others who enjoy the same human right.

In practical terms, this means that if traditional native title was not extinguished before the Racial Discrimination Act came into force, a state law which seeks to extinguish it now will fail. It will fail because s 10(1) of the Racial Discrimination Act clothes the holders of traditional native title who are of the native ethnic group with the same immunity from legislative interference with their enjoyment of their human right to own and inherit property as it clothes other persons in the community. A state law which, by purporting to extinguish native title, would limit that immunity in the case of the native group cannot prevail over s 10(1) of the Racial Discrimination Act which restores the immunity to the extent enjoyed by the general community. The attempt by the 1985 Act to extinguish the traditional legal rights of the Miriam people therefore fails (166 CLR at 218–19).

Deane J delivered a separate judgment to the same effect. Mason CJ and Dawson J declined to decide the s 109 issue pending thorough investigation of the existence and nature of the traditional rights claimed by the plaintiff. Wilson J dissented on the ground that the Queensland legislation did not discriminate in the way proscribed by s 10(1) of the Racial Discrimination Act; namely, it did not create an inequality between the Miriam people and persons of another race but removed a source of inequality: 166 CLR at 206.

[8.1.73] The Commonwealth can use its legislative supremacy to protect Commonwealth agencies from state laws: *O'Reilly v Australian Coastal Shipping Commission* (1962) 107 CLR 46 **[8.2.87]**. The Commonwealth can also use that supremacy to protect private individuals from state laws where those individuals are involved in an activity that falls within one of the subjects on which the Commonwealth can make laws.

That second point is established by *Botany Municipal Council v Federal Airports Corporation* (1992) 175 CLR 453, where the High Court held that the Commonwealth could legislate so as to authorise a contractor, engaged in the construction of the third runway for the Sydney airport, to carry out the works 'in spite of a law, or a provision of a law, of the State of New South Wales that ... relates to ... environmental assessment': reg 9(2) of the Federal Airports Corporation Act.

Mason CJ, Brennan, Deane, Dawson, Toohey, Gaudron and McHugh JJ said that the regulation was designed to ensure that the works were carried out in accordance with Commonwealth standards and was 'neither prevented nor hindered by state law'; this was achieved by conferring an immunity from liability under state law for the contractor's actions. The justices rejected an argument that the regulation was an invalid attempt to interfere with state legislative power (at 464–5):

> Legislation which attains those objects and confers that immunity is necessarily inconsistent with state law and therefore becomes inoperative by operation of s 109 of the Constitution. Viewed in this way, reg 9(2) is plainly valid. This is not a case in which the Commonwealth law is aimed at preventing or controlling state legislative action rather than dealing with a subject-matter assigned to the Commonwealth Parliament [*Wenn v Attorney-General (Vic)* (1948) 77 CLR 84, per Dixon J at p 120]. Nor is it a case in which the Commonwealth law invalidly seeks to displace or expand the operation of s 109.
>
> There can be no objection to a Commonwealth law on a subject which falls within a head of Commonwealth legislative power providing that a person is authorized to undertake an activity despite a state law prohibiting, restricting, qualifying or regulating that activity. Indeed, unless the law expresses itself directly in that way, there is the

possibility that it may not be understood as manifesting an intention to occupy the relevant field to the exclusion of State law.

[8.1.74C]   **Western Australia v Commonwealth**
(The *Native Title Act* case)
(1995) 183 CLR 373

Section 7(1)(a) of the Land (Titles and Traditional Usage) Act 1993 (WA) extinguished any native title to land that existed immediately before the commencement of the Act; and s 7(1)(b) created a new entitlement in members of an Aboriginal group that had held native title to land immediately before the commencement 'to exercise rights of traditional usage in relation to that land under and subject to this Act'. Section 11(1) of the Native Title Act 1993 (Cth) provided that native title could not be extinguished contrary to that Act; and s 7(1) provided that nothing in the Act affected the operation of the Racial Discrimination· Act 1975. Section 10(1) of the Racial Discrimination Act provided that, where a state law conferred a narrower right on persons of a particular race, colour or national or ethnic origin than the right of other persons, the first-mentioned group of persons should, 'notwithstanding anything in that law ... enjoy that right to the same extent' as the other persons. Among the rights covered by s 10(1) were the right to own property and the right not to be arbitrarily deprived of property.

The Wororra Peoples and the Yawuru Peoples sued the state of Western Australia in the High Court for a declaration that the Land (Titles and Traditional Usage) Act was inconsistent with the Racial Discrimination Act and therefore inoperative and invalid. In a separate proceeding, the state of Western Australia sued the Commonwealth for a declaration that the Native Title Act 1993 (Cth) was invalid. Mason CJ reserved several questions for consideration by the Full Court.

Mason CJ, Brennan, Deane, Toohey, Gaudron and **McHugh JJ:** [437] By the operation of s 10(1) of the Racial Discrimination Act, equality of enjoyment of the human rights to own and inherit property is conferred on the 'persons of a particular race'. The Racial Discrimination Act does not alter the characteristics of native title, but it confers on protected persons rights or immunities which, being recognised by 'the tribunals and all other organs administering justice', allow protected persons security in the enjoyment of their title to property to the same extent as the holders of titles granted by the Crown are secure in the enjoyment of their titles ... Where, under the general law, the indigenous 'persons of a particular race' uniquely have a right to own or to inherit property within Australia arising from indigenous law and custom but the security of enjoyment of that property is more limited than the security enjoyed by others who have a right to own or to inherit other property, the persons of the particular race are given, by s 10(1), security in the enjoyment of their property 'to the same extent' as persons generally have security in the enjoyment of their property. Security in the right to own property carries immunity from arbitrary deprivation of the property. Section 10(1) thus protects the enjoyment of traditional interests in land recognised by the common law. However, it has a further operation.

If a law of a State provides that property held by members of the community generally may not be expropriated except for prescribed purposes or on prescribed conditions (including the payment of compensation), a State law which purports to authorise expropriation of property characteristically held by the 'persons of a particular race' for purposes additional to those generally justifying expropriation or on less stringent conditions (including lesser compensation) is inconsistent with s 10(1) of the Racial Discrimination Act.

[438] The two-fold operation of s 10(1) ensures that Aborigines who are holders of native title have the same security of enjoyment of their traditional rights over or in respect of land as others who are holders of title granted by the Crown and that a State law which purports to diminish that security of enjoyment is, by virtue of s 109 of the Constitution, inoperative. The security of enjoyment of what the WA Act includes in 'title' by the holders thereof is the benchmark by which to determine whether, for the purposes of the Racial Discrimination Act,

the Aborigines who hold native title enjoy their human rights in relation to land to a more limited extent than do persons of other races. To determine whether the prospective provisions of the WA Act are inconsistent with s 10(1) of the Racial Discrimination Act, it is necessary to compare the position of the Aborigines who hold s 7 rights with the position of the holders of forms of title other than native title. Or, as s 10(1) of the Racial Discrimination Act confers on the Aborigines who hold native title security of enjoyment to the same extent as the holders of other forms of title have security of enjoyment, it is equally valid to compare the position of the Aborigines who hold s 7 rights with the position in which those Aborigines would be if the WA Act had not purported to extinguish their native title and substitute s 7 rights in its place: *Mabo (No 1)* (1988) 166 CLR at 218, 231. If, by virtue of the WA Act, Aborigines on whom s 7 rights are conferred do not enjoy the same security of enjoyment of those rights as do the holders of 'title', there is an inconsistency between the WA Act and s 10(1) of the Racial Discrimination Act: *Gerhardy v Brown* (1985) 159 CLR 70 at 98–99. And, if there be such an inconsistency, the WA Act is invalid to the extent of the inconsistency: *Gerhardy v Brown* (1985) 159 CLR 70 at 121, 146. On the other hand, if the WA Act were to ensure to Aborigines the same security of possession and enjoyment of s 7 rights as the Racial Discrimination Act confers on the Aboriginal holders of native title, there would be no inconsistency in respect of security of title between the WA Act and the Racial Discrimination Act.

Mason CJ, Brennan, Deane, Toohey, Gaudron and McHugh JJ held that the effect of s 7 of the Land (Titles and Traditional Usage) Act was to reduce the rights of the holders of native title in a way that was inconsistent with s 10 of the Racial Discrimination Act: 183 CLR at 442. The justices then turned to Western Australia's attack on the Native Title Act 1993 (Cth), an attack which raised the issue as to whether Commonwealth legislative power could be used to create an exclusive statutory regime:

[464] It is beyond the power of the Parliament of the Commonwealth to enact a law that is inconsistent with s 107. It is therefore beyond the legislative power of the Commonwealth Parliament to withdraw from any State Parliament a legislative power that is conferred on or confirmed to that Parliament by s 107. Nor does the Parliament of the Commonwealth have power directly to control the content of a State law. By virtue of s 107 of the Constitution, a valid law of a State operates according to its tenor except to the extent, if any, that s 109 of the Constitution renders the State law 'invalid'. In *Gerhardy v Brown* (1985) 159 CLR 70 at 121, Brennan J said:

> It is ... outside the powers of the Commonwealth Parliament to prohibit the parliament of a State from exercising that parliament's powers to enact laws, whether discriminatory or not, with respect to a topic within its competence. It is not to the point that a law, if enacted by the State parliament, will be invalid by reason of its inconsistency with a Commonwealth law. A Commonwealth law purporting to prohibit a State parliament from enacting a law finds no support in s 109 of the Constitution; rather, s 109 operates on a law that a State parliament has lawfully enacted.

If, by reason of inconsistency with a law of the Commonwealth, a State law is to the extent of the inconsistency 'invalid' — that is 'suspended, inoperative and ineffective', *Butler v Attorney-General (Vic)* (1961) 106 CLR 268 at 268 per Windeyer J — the effect on the State law is not produced directly by operation of the Commonwealth law but by s 109 of the Constitution, the operation of which is [465] attracted by the inconsistency ... It was an inevitable consequence of the constitutional distribution of specific legislative powers to the Commonwealth and residual legislative powers to the States that there would be cases of inconsistency between the legislative provisions governing the same act, matter or thing. Section 109 of the Constitution prescribes which law should prevail and which should be 'invalid'. But the effect of s 109 on a State law that is inconsistent with a law of the Commonwealth is not to impose an absolute invalidity. On the contrary, the State law remains valid though it is rendered inoperative to the extent of the inconsistency, but only for so long as the inconsistency remains ... The extent of the inconsistency depends on the text and operation of the respective laws.

Neither the operation of s 109 nor the existence of a State law inconsistent with a proposed law of the Commonwealth affects the extent of a legislative power of the Commonwealth. Given power to make laws with respect to prescribed subjects, the Commonwealth may, if it chooses, make a law with respect to a prescribed subject that is exclusive and exhaustive. Then if any State law has been or is enacted to apply to that subject, an inconsistency arises and the State law becomes inoperative so long as both laws are on the statute book ...

[466] If the Commonwealth intends to make a law the exclusive and exhaustive law upon a subject within its legislative power, the intention may appear from the text or from the operation of the law. The text may reveal the intention either by implication or by express declaration. And if it be within the legislative power of the Commonwealth to declare that the regime prescribed by the Commonwealth law shall be exclusive and exhaustive, it is equally within the legislative power of the Commonwealth to prescribe that an area be left for regulation by State law ...

If the application of State law to a particular subject matter be expressly excluded by a valid law of the Commonwealth, a State law which is expressed to apply to the subject matter is inconsistent with the Commonwealth law and s 109 of the Constitution is thereby enlivened. Such a State law is rendered inoperative not because the Commonwealth law directly invalidates the State law but by force of s 109 of the Constitution ...

[467] The critical question is the scope of Commonwealth legislative power. Provided the power supports a Commonwealth law making its regime exclusive and exhaustive, the law may validly exclude in terms the application of State law to the subject matter. In *Botany Municipal Council v Federal Airports Authority* (1992) 175 CLR 453 at 465, this Court adopted the remarks of Dixon CJ in *Australian Coastal Shipping Commission v O'Reilly* (1962) 107 CLR 46 at 56–57:

> The argument that under a legislative power of the Commonwealth the operation of State laws cannot be directly and expressly excluded has been used without effect in a succession of cases beginning with *The Commonwealth v Queensland* (1920) 29 CLR 1. It may be worth remarking that the interpretation, long since adopted by this Court, of s 109 is hardly consistent in thought with such an argument. The Court has interpreted s 109 as operating to exclude State law not only when there is a more direct collision between federal and State law but also when there is found in federal law the manifestation of an intention on the part of the federal Parliament to 'occupy the field': see *Hume v Palmer* (1926) 38 CLR 441; *Ex parte Nelson (No 2)* (1929) 42 CLR 258; *Ex parte McLean* (1930) 43 CLR 472. Surely, consistency with that doctrine demands that a legislative power, such as that given by s 51(i) together with s 98, must extend to a direct enactment which expressly excludes the operation of State law provided the enactment is within the subject matter of the federal power. Indeed there can really be no other way of expressing the intention and accomplishing the federal legislative purpose.

Where it is within the legislative competence of the Commonwealth Parliament to prescribe an exclusive statutory regime, a Commonwealth law which merely expresses an exclusion of the operation of a State law is not construed as an attempt to invalidate the State law directly: *Collins v Charles Marshall Pty Ltd* (1955) 92 CLR 529 at 548–549; *Metal Trades Industry Association v Amalgamated Metal Workers' and Shipwrights' Union* (1983) 152 CLR 632 at 641–643, 648–649. It is construed as an expression of intention that the Commonwealth law should have exclusive operation. Being construed as a declaration of intention that the Commonwealth law should operate exclusively of State law on the topic, the Commonwealth law is within power. Unless the Commonwealth law were expressed in terms which precluded that construction, the form of expression does not take the law outside Commonwealth power.

Mason CJ, Brennan, Deane, Toohey, Gaudron and McHugh JJ proceeded to hold that s 11(1) of the Native Title Act 1993 (Cth) was a valid law.

~~~

[8.1.75]   The reasoning in *Western Australia v Commonwealth* (the *Native Title Act* case) (1995) 183 CLR 373 **[8.1.74C]** also indicates that the High Court may be reluctant to constrain the expansion of Commonwealth power brought about by a generous reading of s 109 by the use of any implications: see **[8.1.71]**. The majority said at 478 that s 51(xxvi), the races power:

> ... must extend to the support of a law which excludes, wholly or in part, State or Territory law from operating to affect native title. The power cannot be limited by an implication which exempts the States from the application of such a law without denying what is at the heart of s 51(xxvi).

'Invalid'

[8.1.76]   A decision that a state law is inconsistent with a Commonwealth law means, so s 109 says, that the state law is 'invalid to the extent of the inconsistency'. The state law is not, however, destroyed. It might be more accurate to say that those aspects of the state law which are inconsistent with the Commonwealth law become inoperative; other aspects of the state law continue to operate. In *Clyde Engineering Co Ltd v Cowburn* (1926) 37 CLR 466 **[8.1.20]**, the decision that the Forty-Four Hours Week Act 1925 (NSW) was inconsistent with the Conciliation and Arbitration Act 1904 (Cth) and an award made under the Act only prevented the state Act applying to employers and employees covered by the federal award. The Act would still have validly applied to other employers and employees.

[8.1.77]   It may be, of course, that a state law is not drafted in such a way that its provisions can have a separate or independent operation. In *Wenn v Attorney-General (Vic)* (1948) 77 CLR 84 **[8.1.55]**, Dixon and Rich JJ concluded that a state Act, which provided preference in promotion for ex-members of the armed forces, was, in its application to private employers, inconsistent with a Commonwealth Act. They said that the 'burden of establishing interdependence' had been discharged. The state Act had been intended to provide a single code on employment of ex-service personnel, applicable to all employers.

[8.1.78]   However, apart from that problem, the state law will continue to have some legal operation, as explained by Evatt CJ, Sugerman and Wallace JJ in *Lamb v Cockatoo Docks & Engineering Co Pty Ltd* [1961] SR (NSW) 459 at 468: 'the "law of a State" comes into existence and remains in existence even though, for the time being, or from time to time, its operative force may be suspended'.

[8.1.79]   One consequence of the view that 'invalid' means 'inoperative' is that the state law will revive if the Commonwealth law is repealed or otherwise disappears. This point is firmly established in *Butler v Attorney-General (Vic)* (1961) 106 CLR 268, where the High Court was asked whether the state Act, held invalid because of inconsistency with a Commonwealth Act in *Wenn v Attorney-General (Vic)* (1948) 77 CLR 84 **[8.1.55]**, had revived once that Commonwealth Act had been declared no longer a valid law of the Commonwealth in *Illawarra District County Council v Wickham* (1959) 101 CLR 467. The court (Fullagar, Kitto, Windeyer, Taylor and Menzies JJ) was unanimous that the state Act revived. Taylor J explained the decision in the following way:

> [T]he words 'to the extent of the inconsistency' must be taken to have a temporal as well as a substantive connotation ... The Federal Act can 'prevail' only whilst it

remains in force and invalidity of the State Act is produced only as the counterpart of the 'supremacy' of the Federal Act (106 CLR at 283).

Repugnancy of laws in the self-governing territories

[8.1.80] Section 109 does not, in its terms, apply to territory laws. The High Court has confirmed that the common law doctrine of 'repugnancy of laws', developed to rationalise inconsistent statutes, operates to resolve inconsistencies between Commonwealth statutes and the laws of the self-governing territories in a way that is similar (although not identical) to the approaches developed in the context of s 109 of the Constitution.

Territory legislation derives its legal authority from the relevant Act of the Commonwealth Parliament that authorises the territory legislature to make laws. For that reason, it is plain that the Commonwealth Parliament can displace any territory legislation. The question whether Commonwealth legislation has that displacing effect, because the relevant territory law is repugnant to a Commonwealth law, involves different forms of analysis depending on whether the relevant Commonwealth law was made before or after the Commonwealth's grant of legislative power to the territory legislature.

In *Northern Territory v GPAO* (1999) 196 CLR 553, the High Court considered whether the Family Law Reform Act 1995 (Cth) limited the continued operation of the Community Welfare Act 1983 (NT), enacted pursuant to the authority given to the Northern Territory legislature by the Northern Territory (Self-Government) Act 1979. Gleeson CJ and Gummow J (with whom Hayne J agreed at 650) said that, where a Commonwealth Act does not expressly provide that it is to override (or not override) territory law, the question will be whether the Commonwealth law, by necessary implication, has an overriding effect: 196 CLR 553 at 581. That implicit overriding effect will be found when the Commonwealth law makes exhaustive or exclusive provision on the subject with which it deals. If such an intention is not apparent, the court will consider whether the two laws are 'directly inconsistent' in the sense outlined in **[8.1.21]–[8.1.24]** above: 196 CLR 553 at 582. In the same case, Kirby J said that, '[i]f the federal law is clearly applicable, gives effect to rules having national application or results in legislative commands inconsistent with, or repugnant to, the territory law, the latter must give way. Federal law must be obeyed': 196 CLR 553 at 630; see also 196 CLR 553 at 636–638.

[8.1.81] In *Western Australia v Ward* (2002) 191 ALR 1, a different sequence of legislation produced a different result. One issue for the court involved the interaction between the Racial Discrimination Act 1975 (Cth) and Northern Territory legislation. Gleeson CJ, Gaudron, Gummow and Hayne JJ noted that the power of the Northern Territory Legislative Assembly to make laws for the government of the territory (conferred by s 6 of the Northern Territory (Self-Government) Act 1979) was expressed to be 'subject to' that Act. Section 57 of that Act excludes, from the power of alteration or repeal given to the Legislative Assembly, any Act of the Commonwealth Parliament in force in the territory immediately before the commencement of the Self-Government Act. Accordingly, the Racial Discrimination Act 1975 operated in the Northern Territory according to its terms: see 191 ALR 1 at [127]–[133].

[8.1.82] In *Northern Territory v GPAO* (1998) 196 CLR 553, Gleeson CJ and Gummow J (with whom Hayne J agreed) took the opportunity to consider the different situations of the Australian Capital Territory and the Northern Territory in this context. Within the Australian Capital Territory, s 28 of the Australian Capital Territory (Self-Government) Act 1988 (Cth) supplies a specific test of inconsistency: a law of the territory's Legislative Assembly has no effect if it is inconsistent with a Commonwealth law, 'but such a provision shall be taken to be consistent with such a [Commonwealth] law to the extent that it is capable of operating concurrently with that [Commonwealth] law'. Gleeson CJ and Gummow J noted that this criterion of inconsistency is narrower than that which applies under s 109: 196 CLR 553 at 582. In other words, if the territory law and the Commonwealth law are capable of operating concurrently, the other tests of inconsistency discussed earlier in this chapter will not apply. There is no equivalent provision in the Northern Territory Self-Government Act 1978. For further analysis of these decisions see Chapter 12.

2　Intergovernmental immunities

[8.2.1] The structure of our federal system presents a second problem concerned with the legal or juristic relationship between Commonwealth and states. The system establishes legislatures at both the central (Commonwealth) and the regional (state) levels and it establishes executive governments at both levels. The legislatures are given law-making powers that overlap; and the governments are charged with a wide range of policy development, executive and administrative functions. The Australian federal system presents the potential, not only for conflicts between Commonwealth and state legislation, but also for tension between laws made by one legislature and the activities of another executive government. In a federal system where there was only one (central) legislature, or where executive governments existed only at the provincial level, this problem could not arise; but, given the institutions of government and the distribution of powers in the Commonwealth Constitution, conflicts of law are inevitable.

The resolution of the problem will be fundamental to our federal system for, if we concede that a state parliament may direct the Commonwealth Government on such matters as the location of defence establishments, post offices and airports or may demand that the Commonwealth Government pay state taxes (land tax or stamp duty, for example) on its operations, then the political autonomy of the Commonwealth is substantially reduced. Similarly, if the Commonwealth were to be allowed complete immunity from state laws, we would have a federal system in which the balance of power leant towards the central government. Whatever answer we give to the question: 'Are the units within the federation subject to each other's laws?'; that answer will affect the fundamental structure of the federal system.

[8.2.2] The text of the Commonwealth Constitution does not provide direct guidance. The Constitution deals only with specific aspects of the broad problem. For example, a series of provisions confers on the states and the Commonwealth specific exemptions from Commonwealth and state legislation:

- s 51(xiii) gives the Commonwealth Parliament power to make laws with respect to 'banking, other than State banking';

- s 51(xiv) gives the Commonwealth Parliament power to make laws with respect to 'insurance, other than State insurance'; and

- s 114 prevents the states from taxing 'property of any kind belonging to the Commonwealth', and prevents the Commonwealth from taxing 'property of any kind belonging to a State'.

One might argue that the presence of these specific limitations on power preclude the implication of other limitations on power so that, as a general rule, both states and Commonwealth are subject to each other's laws. But another series of provisions appears to proceed on the assumption that both states and Commonwealth enjoy a general immunity, to which it is necessary to create specific exceptions:

- s 51(xxxi) gives the Commonwealth Parliament power to make laws with respect to 'the acquisition of property on just terms from any State or person'; and

- s 98 extends the Commonwealth Parliament's power over trade and commerce 'to railways the property of any State'.

[8.2.3] Once we place these and similar exceptions to one side, s 109 of the Constitution provides the mechanism for resolving conflicts between Commonwealth and state laws. We could assume from that provision that, whenever the Commonwealth Parliament legislates, its legislation should be given full effect and should bind state governments and regulate their activities (subject of course to any specific constitutional prohibitions on Commonwealth power to regulate the states). Then, in the absence of conflicting Commonwealth legislation, state laws should have full effect and so bind the Commonwealth Government. Taking this approach, s 109 might be read as an invitation to the Commonwealth Parliament to legislate so as to regulate state authorities and to legislate so as to free the Commonwealth Government from the effect of state legislation. However, that assumption has rarely been made by the courts. The judges have preferred to seek the answer to this fundamental question by drawing implications from the whole Constitution, by resorting to their own conceptions of the type of federalism most appropriate to Australia, or by exploiting some of the traditional methods of 'interpreting' the Constitution. See [1.2.14]–[1.3.16].

The Crown's presumptive immunity

[8.2.4] Before considering the ways in which the High Court has addressed the problem of clashing laws it is necessary to consider the complicating factor of 'Crown immunity'. The answer to the general question posed in [8.2.1] above is complicated by the legal proposition that the executive government is a legal person and that person is the monarch. When lawyers and judges speak of the executive government they often refer to it as 'the Crown'; government ministers are 'Ministers of the Crown'; and the legal rights and liabilities of the government are affected by such legal concepts as Crown immunity or the prerogative priority of the Crown. These concepts were developed by English courts, as English law adjusted to the transition from a feudal monarchy to a parliamentary democracy. Some cynics might observe that the law's adjustment to that transition has been rather half-hearted; certainly the executive government is often spoken of as if it were merely an extension of the monarchy and its legal position, vis-à-vis the individual, is still very much affected by one-sided rules which accord the government many privileges more appropriate to a medieval monarch.

Nevertheless, the notion of the Crown as the personification of the executive government has not only survived and developed in English law, but has been transferred to Australian law. In the Australian context the notion has, of necessity, become more complex for our federal system assumes seven autonomous executive governments; that is, seven autonomous Crowns. That assumption has been confused by what Sawer describes as 'the shibboleth that the Crown is one and indivisible': Sawer (1967) p 124. The 'indivisibility of the Crown' was a major, if unconvincing, plank in the High Court's reasoning in the *Engineers'* case (1920) 28 CLR 129 **[8.2.31C]**: see the comments in **[8.2.36]**. Gibbs ACJ's description of this 'doctrine' as 'remote from practical realities' and 'of little practical assistance' is a good indication of its contemporary significance: *Bradken Consolidated Ltd v Broken Hill Proprietary Co Ltd* (1979) 145 CLR 107 at 122 **[8.2.7]**. In Sawer's words, 'the courts merely act as if the rule [of indivisibility] did not exist': Sawer (1967) p 124. So, lawyers and judges speak of 'the Crown in right of the Commonwealth', or 'the Crown in right of South Australia', and this is despite the fact that 'the Crown' in these legal concepts is vested in the one person: Queen Elizabeth II. In truth, when we talk of 'the Crown in right of the Commonwealth' or 'the Crown in right of a State', we are talking about an institution, a legal corporation, with a series of rights and liabilities, an institution which exists in law quite independent of the physical existence of the monarch, but which traces its origins, and much of its rights and liabilities, back to the institution of the English monarchy.

[8.2.5] An important right of the English monarchy, relevant to our present discussion, is the Crown's presumptive immunity from parliamentary legislation. That is, while the United Kingdom Parliament may make its laws applicable to the Crown (or government), there is a general presumption that parliament when it legislates does not intend to bind the Crown. To overcome that general presumption, parliament should include a clear statement in its legislation; for example, an Act dealing with the protection of residential tenancies would normally be treated by the courts as not affecting the rights of the Crown as landlord unless it carried a provision declaring 'This Act shall bind the Crown'. The presumption of immunity might also be rebutted, even where there is no such express provision, if a court finds that, as a matter of 'necessary implication', parliament must have intended to bind the Crown.

[8.2.6] The rule that legislation does not bind the Crown except by express words or necessary implication has been transferred to Australian law, although it has undergone a reassessment. The rule now appears to have lost much of its rigidity, so as to increase the prospect of a finding of a 'necessary implication' of intention to bind the Crown. In *Bropho v Western Australia* (1990) 171 CLR 1, the High Court decided that s 17 of the Aboriginal Heritage Act 1982 (WA) applied to employees and agents of the West Australian Government, notwithstanding that the Act did not expressly declare an intention to bind the Crown. Section 17 made it an offence for a person to interfere with a site of cultural, spiritual or historical significance to Aboriginal people, except with the authorisation of the trustees of the Western Australian Museum or the consent of the Minister.

In an action brought against the Western Australian Development Corporation (an agency declared by Western Australian Development Corporation Act 1983 (WA) to enjoy the status, immunities and privileges of the Crown), Bropho had sought a declaration and injunction to restrain the corporation from redeveloping the Swan Brewery site, which included two areas of cultural and spiritual significance within the Aboriginal Heritage Act. The West Australian Supreme Court struck out Bropho's statement of claim on the ground that the corporation had a presumptive immunity from legislation, which immunity was not displaced by the Aboriginal Heritage Act. The Supreme Court applied the established view that, in the absence of an express reference to the Crown, legislation does not bind the Crown unless an intention that it should do so can be discerned by way of necessary implication.

In their joint judgment, Mason CJ, Deane, Dawson, Toohey, Gaudron and McHugh JJ described this approach to the Crown's presumptive immunity as tending 'to discount the significance of its character as an aid to statutory construction and to treat it as if it were an inflexible principle': 171 CLR at 16. The justices observed that 'there may well have been convincing reasons' for such an approach when the Crown encompassed only the sovereign, her personal representatives and the basic organs of government: 171 CLR at 18. However, those reasons had little relevance in the contemporary Australian context (at 19):

> [T]he historical considerations which gave rise to a presumption that the legislature would not have intended that a statute bind the Crown are largely inapplicable to conditions in this country where the activities of the executive government reach into almost all aspects of commercial, industrial and developmental endeavour and where it is commonplace for governmental commercial, industrial and developmental instrumentalities and their servants or agents, which are covered by the shield of the Crown either by reason of their character as such or by reason of specific statutory provision to that effect, to compete and have commercial dealings on the same basis as private enterprise.

It was in that contemporary context, the justices said, that it was necessary to decide whether to preserve in Australian law an inflexible rule which required general words in legislation to be read as excluding the Crown unless an intention to bind the Crown was expressed or manifest from the terms of the statute.

After making the point that there had been a number of situations in which the rigidity of the presumption had not controlled the interpretation of legislation (particularly in the case of the various Criminal Codes and general criminal law statutes), the justices said that 'a stringent and rigid test for determining whether the general words of a statute should not be read down so as to exclude the Crown is unacceptable': 171 CLR at 22. A more flexible approach should be adopted. Where the question was, for example, whether the sovereign or her personal representative was liable to prosecution for a statutory offence, the presumption against such a legislative intention 'would be extraordinarily strong'. But where the question was, as in the present appeal, whether the employees of a government corporation were bound by legislation of 'vital significance to a particular section of the community', the presumption of immunity would be 'little more than a starting point', and the question of immunity or amenability should be decided on the basis of the context and purpose of the legislation.

Turning to s 17 of the Aboriginal Heritage Act, the justices noted that the Act obliged the Minister to ensure that 'all places in Western Australia' of Aboriginal significance were recorded; that the Act was declared to apply to all objects (of Aboriginal significance) 'irrespective of where found or situated in the State'; and that 93 per cent of Western Australia was Crown land and approximately 50 per cent of Western Australia was vacant Crown land (that is, not subject to Crown leases or licences). In this context, the justices said, 'the Act would be extraordinarily ineffective to achieve its stated purpose of preserving Western Australia's Aboriginal sites and objects' if it did not apply to Crown land: 171 CLR at 24. The conclusion that it had been the legislative intention that s 17 apply indifferently to natural persons, including government employees, was, the justices said at 25, 'all but inevitable':

> [C]onsideration of the subject matter and disclosed policy and purpose of the Act seems to us to make it apparent that it was not the legislative intent that the activities of government employees, be they bulldozer drivers, demolition workers or dynamiters, acting in the course of their duties, should be excluded from s 17's prohibition of destroying or damaging Aboriginal sites and objects without the authorisation of the Trustees or the consent of the Minister. Construed in context, the general words of s 17 disclose a clear legislative intent that they not be read down so as to be inapplicable to government employees in the course of their duties as such.

[8.2.7] Notwithstanding the dilution of the presumptive immunity in *Bropho v Western Australia* (1990) 171 CLR 1 **[8.2.6]**, that immunity still plays a role in Australian law. In that context, the operation of the rule is subject to the federal complexities referred to in **[8.2.4]**. In *Bradken Consolidated Ltd v Broken Hill Proprietary Co Ltd* (1979) 145 CLR 107, the High Court was asked whether the Trade Practices Act 1974 (Cth) applied to the Queensland Commissioner for Railways, who was, the court agreed, entitled to all the rights and privileges of the Crown in right of the state of Queensland. Gibbs ACJ said that, according to the rule of construction, the Act clearly bound the Crown in right of the Commonwealth: 145 CLR at 116. He posed the problem before the court in the following terms at 116:

> The Act is, however, silent on the question whether it is intended to bind the Crown in right of a State. The question thus arises whether the rule to which I have referred means that a statute of the Commonwealth will not be construed as binding the Crown in right of a State unless it appears by express words or necessary implication that it was intended to do so. In other words, does the rule apply to the Crown in all its capacities, or only to the Crown in right of the community whose legislation is under consideration? When construing a Commonwealth statute does 'the Crown', for the purpose of this rule, mean only the Crown in right of the Commonwealth or does it include the Crown in right of a State?

Gibbs ACJ thought that the balance of Australian authorities favoured what he described as the 'wider rule of construction'; namely, that Commonwealth legislation would be read as not intended to bind the Crown in right of a state unless that intention appeared expressly or by necessary implication. Gibbs ACJ said he did not wish to decide whether the rule was based upon the 'indivisibility of the Crown' (145 CLR at 122) and emphasised another justification at 123:

> It is a consequence of our federal system that 'two governments of the Crown are established within the same territory, neither superior to the other' (*Federal Commissioner of Taxation v Official Liquidator of E O Farley Ltd*) (1940) 63 CLR 278 at 312, per Dixon J). Legislation of the Commonwealth may have a very different effect when applied to the government of a state from that which it has in its application to ordinary citizens. It seems only prudent to require that laws of the parliament should not be held to bind the states when the parliament itself has not directed its attention to the question whether they should do so. And, of course, as was said in *Province of Bombay v Municipal Corporation of Bombay* [1947] AC at 63: 'it

must always be remembered that, if it be the intention of the legislation that the Crown shall be bound, nothing is easier than to say so in plain words'.

Gibbs ACJ concluded that there was no indication, by express words or necessary implication, that the Trade Practices Act was intended to bind the Crown in right of a state. Accordingly, it did not bind the Queensland Commissioner for Railways. Stephen, Mason and Jacobs JJ delivered judgments to the same effect.

[8.2.8] How is the presumptive immunity enjoyed by one government (or Crown) within the federal system to be removed at the instance of another component of the system? To put the question more precisely, what form of words would the courts treat as clearly expressing a legislative intention to bind the Crown in right of another component of the federal system? If the immunity of the Crown is available to the Crown at both levels of the Australian federation, as *Bradken's* case **[8.2.7]** establishes, it would seem to follow that the immunity could be removed by any of the legislatures within that federation. However, judicial dicta suggest that a clause declaring simply that 'this Act shall bind the Crown' would be inadequate.

These *dicta* include observations of Dixon J in *Essendon Corporation v Criterion Theatres Ltd* (1947) 74 CLR 1 **[8.2.93C]**. In that case, his Honour concluded that a reference to the Crown in s 265(b) of the Local Government Act 1928 (Vic) was a reference only to the Crown in right of the state of Victoria. That reading was largely dictated by the context. But he went on to say that 'the presumption' was against 'expanding the meaning of references to the Crown ... to cover the Commonwealth', and he cited several earlier decisions where similar references had been read as confined to the Crown in right of the relevant state and quoted, approvingly, the following statement from Anglin CJ of the Canadian Supreme Court in *Cauthier v R* (1918) 56 Can SCR 176 at 194:

> It may be accepted as a safe rule of construction that a reference to the Crown in a provincial statute shall be taken to be the Crown in right of the province only, unless the statute in express terms or by necessary intendment makes it clear that the reference is to the Crown in some other sense.

In *Commonwealth v Bogle* (1953) 89 CLR 229 **[8.2.96]–[8.2.97]**, Fullagar J, with whom Dixon, Webb and Kitto JJ agreed, said that the question whether the Prices Regulation Act 1948 (Vic) applied to the Commonwealth raised 'a question of construction ... on the threshold [of any constitutional question]. In considering that question we are, or should be, assisted by a presumption that references to the Crown are references to the Crown in right of the State only': 89 CLR at 259.

On the basis of those statements, then, the full presumption of Crown immunity would be displaced only by a clause in a state Act declaring that 'this Act shall bind the Crown in right of the state and the Crown in right of the Commonwealth'; or by a clause in a Commonwealth Act declaring that 'this Act shall bind the Crown in right of the Commonwealth and in right of the several States'. Such a clause would take care of the presumptive or interpretive immunity; however, it would not resolve, indeed it would merely lead to, the fundamental constitutional issue. Is such a clause valid?

Foundation of intergovernmental immunities

[8.2.9] From 1904, the very first year of its operation, until 1920 the High Court maintained that the Commonwealth and the states were, in general, immune from each other's legislation. In *D'Emden v Pedder* (1904) 1 CLR 91, the court held that the Stamp Duties Amendment Act 1902 (Tas) could not oblige a Commonwealth public servant to pay a state tax on his salary. The tax was a stamp duty on the written receipt which the Audit Act 1901 (Cth) obliged him to give when paid his salary. The court (Griffith CJ, Barton and O'Connor JJ) developed the following statement of principle (at 111):

> When a State attempts to give to its legislative or executive authority an operation which, if valid, would fetter, control, or interfere with the free exercise of the legislative or executive power of the Commonwealth, the attempt, unless expressly authorised by the Constitution, is to that extent invalid and inoperative.

[8.2.10] In *Deakin v Webb* (1904) 1 CLR 585, the court held that a state could not impose an income tax on the salary paid to Commonwealth Cabinet Ministers. The court described the imposition of the income tax as diminishing the recompense allotted by the Commonwealth to its officers, thereby interfering with the Commonwealth's agencies; and as inhibiting the freedom of the Commonwealth to transfer its officers from state to state: 1 CLR at 616.

[8.2.11] In *Commonwealth v New South Wales* (1906) 3 CLR 807, the court held that the Commonwealth, as the transferee of land in New South Wales, was not liable to pay to the state the stamp duty on transfer of land imposed by state legislation: first, because the state legislation did not indicate an intention to apply to the Crown; and, second, because the imposition of a tax on the Commonwealth's dealings with land would amount to the attachment by the state of a 'condition to the discharge of a Federal duty [which] is an act of interference or control': 3 CLR at 815.

[8.2.12] In *Federated Amalgamated Government Railway & Tramway Service Association v New South Wales Railway Traffic Employees Association* (the *Railway Servants'* case) (1906) 4 CLR 488, the court held that a New South Wales Government instrumentality could not be subjected, as an employer, to the Conciliation and Arbitration Act 1904 (Cth). Griffith CJ, Barton and O'Connor JJ said that to subject the state railways to Commonwealth legislation regulating the rights of employers and employees would interfere with the control of those railways. Such an interference they considered to be inconsistent with the principle of intergovernmental immunity, which was reciprocal and not limited to taxation. Nor, in the court's view, was the state's immunity confined to those functions which could be described as governmental, because no activity undertaken by a state could be regarded as anything other than governmental: 4 CLR at 538–9.

[8.2.13] In *Baxter v Commissioner of Taxation (NSW)* (1907) 4 CLR 1087 **[8.2.14]**, the court confirmed the principle of intergovernmental immunities and the result in *Deakin v Webb* (1904) 1 CLR 585 **[8.2.10]**, despite the Privy Council's contrary decision in *Webb v Outrim* [1907] AC 81. In a joint judgment, Griffith CJ, Barton and O'Connor JJ refused to follow *Webb v Outrim* on the basis that the Privy Council's decision had dealt with a matter directly concerned with the reciprocal rights and obligations of the Commonwealth and the states; an 'inter se matter' within s 74 of the Constitution. According to the justices, s 74 clearly indicated that the High Court was to have exclusive judicial authority on such questions, so that, if the Privy Council delivered judgment on any such question, the High Court could decline to follow that judgment: 4 CLR at 1118. (Section 74 of the Constitution declares that no appeal shall be taken to the Privy Council from the High Court on any question as to the limits inter se of the constitutional powers of the Commonwealth and those of any state or states, or as to the limits inter se of the constitutional powers of any two or more states, except with a certificate of the High Court.)

Having disposed of the Privy Council's contrary view, Griffith CJ, Barton and O'Connor JJ affirmed their support for the principle of intergovernmental immunity and held that New South Wales could not impose an income tax on the salary paid by the Commonwealth to a customs official. Isaacs J dissented on this point: although a state could not fetter, control or interfere with the free exercise by the Commonwealth of its powers, the state income tax did not offend that principle because it did not affect the Commonwealth officer in his capacity as an agent of the Commonwealth, nor did it single out the officer for adverse discriminatory treatment. Rather, the state Act simply required the officer to bear his share of the burden imposed on all citizens in return for the benefits provided by the state: 4 CLR at 1161.

[8.2.14] The rule laid down in *D'Emden v Pedder* (1904) 1 CLR 91 **[8.2.9]** was supported by two lines of argument, the first historical and the second conceptual. The High Court first accepted and applied the doctrine of intergovernmental immunities as developed by the United States Supreme Court. In *Baxter v Commissioners of Taxation (NSW)* (1907) 4 CLR 1087 **[8.2.13]**, Griffith CJ, Barton and O'Connor JJ described the distribution of legislative powers between the Commonwealth and state parliaments and reasoned at 1122:

> [A]s the scheme of the Australian Constitution was in this respect practically identical with that of the Constitution of the United States of America, which had been interpreted by the Supreme Court of that republic in a long series of cases familiar to the Australian publicists by whom the Australian Constitution was framed, it ought to be inferred that the intention of the framers was that like provisions should receive a like interpretation.

The conceptual argument was stated as follows in the same case (at 1121):

> The purpose of the Constitution was the creation of a new state, the Commonwealth, intended to take its place amongst the free nations, with all such attributes of sovereignty as were consistent with its being still 'under the Crown'. It is essential to the attribute of sovereignty of any government that it shall not be interfered with by any external power. The only interference, therefore, to be permitted is that prescribed by the Constitution itself. A similar consequence follows with respect to the constituent States. In their case, however, the Commonwealth is empowered to interfere in certain prescribed cases. But under the scheme of the Constitution there is a large number of subjects upon which the legislative powers of both the Commonwealth and the States may be exercised. In such a state of things it is not only probable but as shown by the experience of the United States under a similar distribution of powers certain, that questions will constantly arise as to the operation of laws which, although unobjectionable in form, and prima facie within the competence of the legislature which enacted them, would, if literal effect were given to them, interfere with the exercise of the sovereign powers of the other two of the sovereign authorities concerned. Applying then the doctrine *quando lex aliquid concedit concedere videtur et illud sine quo res ipsa valere non potest*, which is a maxim applied to the construction of all grants of power ... it follows that a grant of sovereign powers includes a grant of a right to disregard and treat as inoperative any attempt by any other authority to control their exercise.

(The Latin proposition quoted above means: 'When the law gives something, it also gives that without which the thing given would be valueless'.)

[8.2.15] The doctrine reflected the original court's view of Commonwealth–state relations under the new Constitution, and particularly the view that the new federal system of government involved an equal partnership of Commonwealth and states. In *Webb v Outrim* [1907] AC 81, the Privy Council (to which an appeal had been brought direct from the Victorian Supreme Court) rejected the doctrine; but, as noted in **[8.2.13]**, the High Court reaffirmed the doctrine and denied the validity of the Privy Council's decision in *Webb v Outrim* at the next available opportunity in *Baxter v Commissioners of Taxation* (1907) 4 CLR 1087. The court said that questions of intergovernmental immunity were *inter se* matters within s 74 of the Constitution, and that this section clearly intended to make the High Court the final arbiter of such matters. (The Commonwealth Parliament shortly afterwards amended the Judiciary Act to prevent appeals on *inter se* matters from state courts direct to the Privy Council: see now Judiciary Act 1903 (Cth) s 39(2)(a).)

[8.2.16] However, the High Court did modify the doctrine in four distinct ways. First, the court held, in *Chaplin v Commissioner of Taxes (SA)* (1911) 12 CLR 375, that the Commonwealth Parliament could legislate so as to expose the salaries paid to Commonwealth employees to non-discriminatory state taxation. The court rejected an argument that the Commonwealth Parliament could not allow what the Constitution prohibited; it said that the Commonwealth could relinquish a constitutional privilege granted to it. In coming to this conclusion, the court adhered to a suggestion outlined by Griffith CJ, Barton and O'Connor JJ in *Baxter v Commissioners of Taxation* (1907) 4 CLR 1087 **[8.2.13]**, that the 'Federal Parliament can, if it pleases, make its grants to its servants subject to the right of the States to tax them': 4 CLR at 1187.

[8.2.17] Second, in *R v Sutton* (the *Wire Netting* case) (1908) 5 CLR 789, the court held that the states, when importing goods, were subject to Commonwealth customs control. In *Attorney-General (NSW) v Collector of Customs* (the *Steel Rails* case) (1908) 5 CLR 818, the court held that the states were subject to Commonwealth customs duty on the goods which they imported. In that case, Griffith CJ and O'Connor J said that the customs power was exclusive to the Commonwealth (Constitution s 90) and the power was such that it would be frustrated if the states were immune from its operation (at 833):

> If a power conferred upon the Commonwealth in express terms is of such a nature that its effective exercise manifestly involves a control of some operation of a State Government the doctrine [of implied immunity] has no application to that operation.

An argument that s 114 of the Constitution prevented the imposition of customs duties was rejected on the ground that these duties were taxes on the process of importation, not on property.

[8.2.18] Third, in *Federated Engine Drivers' and Firemen's Association of Australia v Broken Hill Proprietary Co Ltd* (the *Federated Engine Drivers'* case) (1911) 12 CLR 398, the High Court held that the doctrine of state immunity from the Conciliation and Arbitration Act 1904 (Cth), established in *Federated Amalgamated Government Railway & Tramway Service Association v New South Wales Railway Traffic Employees Association* (the *Railway Servants'* case) **[8.2.12]**, did not extend to protect a municipal corporation, established under state legislation, from Commonwealth legislation when the corporation was carrying out non-governmental functions. The Melbourne Corporation was held to be subject to the Conciliation and Arbitration

Act in its capacity as employer of operators of industrial machines used for the supply and sale of electricity to consumers.

[8.2.19]   Fourth, in *Federated Municipal and Shire Council Employees' Union of Australia v Melbourne Corporation* (1919) 26 CLR 508, a majority of the High Court (Isaacs, Higgins, Rich, Gavan Duffy and Powers JJ; Griffith CJ and Barton J dissenting) held that local government bodies established under state laws and responsible for the construction and maintenance of public roads were not state government agencies and were not immune from the Conciliation and Arbitration Act 1904 (Cth) in their capacity as employers of labour for that construction and maintenance. In their joint judgment, Isaacs and Rich JJ explained *D'Emden v Pedder* (1904) 1 CLR 91 **[8.2.9]** as based on inconsistency between Commonwealth and state laws (26 CLR at 532–3) and made no reference to *Federated Amalgamated Government Railway & Tramway Service Association v New South Wales Railway Traffic Employees Association* (the *Railway Servants'* case) (1906) 4 CLR 488 **[8.2.12]**.

The 'reserved powers' doctrine

[8.2.20]   Simultaneously with the development of the implied immunities doctrine, the original justices of the High Court adopted a narrow, restrictive approach to the interpretation of the Commonwealth's legislative powers, an approach variously described as the 'reserved powers' doctrine or the 'implied prohibitions' doctrine. Here the concern was not to protect the constituent governments of the federation against direct regulation or control by other legislatures, but to ensure that the residual legislative powers of the states (acknowledged in s 107 of the Commonwealth Constitution) were not diminished through an expansive reading of the Commonwealth's legislative powers.

[8.2.21]   In *Peterswald v Bartley* (1904) 1 CLR 497 **[9.4.7]** the High Court decided that a licence fee imposed by New South Wales on brewers was not an excise duty within s 90 of the Commonwealth Constitution, and was not, therefore, within the exclusive competence of the Commonwealth Parliament. In adopting a relatively narrow view of the term 'excise duty', the court was influenced by what it described as the 'general provision', the 'whole purview' and 'the spirit' of the Constitution at 507:

> The Constitution contains no provisions for enabling the Commonwealth Parliament to interfere with the private or internal affairs of the States, or to restrict the power of the States to regulate the carrying on of any business or trades within their boundaries, or even, if they think fit, to prohibit them altogether. That is a very important matter to be borne in mind in considering whether this particular provision [s 90] ought to be construed so as to interfere with the States' powers in that respect.

[8.2.22]   In *R v Barger* (1908) 6 CLR 41 **[9.2.15C]** a majority of the court held that the Excise Tariff Act 1906 (Cth) was outside the powers of the Commonwealth Parliament. The Act, which imposed a tax on the manufacturers of agricultural machinery with an exemption for those manufacturers who paid their employees 'fair and reasonable' wages, was not a law with respect to taxation within s 51(ii). The taxation power, the majority of the court said, had to be read in the light of the prohibition, implicit in the Constitution, against Commonwealth 'control of the internal affairs of the States': 6 CLR at 72.

[8.2.23] In *Attorney-General (NSW) v Brewery Employees' Union of New South Wales* (1908) 6 CLR 469, the court held (again by a majority) that Pt VII of the Trade Marks Act 1905 (Cth), which authorised manufacturers to affix a workers' trade mark to their goods if manufactured by trade union labour, was outside the powers of the Commonwealth Parliament. In particular, it was not a law with respect to trade marks within s 51(xviii) of the Commonwealth Constitution. Griffith CJ started from the proposition that ss 51(i) and 107 left (or reserved) the control of 'internal trade and commerce' to the states. Other grants of power to the Commonwealth Parliament must be read in the light of that reservation (at 503):

> In my opinion it should be regarded as a fundamental rule in the construction of the Constitution that when the intention to reserve any subject matter to the States to the exclusion of the Commonwealth clearly appears, no exception from that reservation can be admitted which is not expressed in clear and unequivocal words. Otherwise the Constitution will be made to contradict itself, which upon a proper construction must be impossible.

A strict reading of s 51(xviii) confined 'trade marks' to marks indicating an industrial property rather than any 'kind of mark which might be used in trade': 6 CLR at 512.

[8.2.24] Similar considerations prompted a majority of the court to hold, in *Huddart Parker & Co Pty Ltd v Moorehead* (1909) 8 CLR 330 **[10.3.3]**, that ss 5 and 8 of the Australian Industries Preservation Act 1906 (Cth) were invalid. These sections prohibited combinations in restraint of trade and trade monopolies by foreign, trading and financial corporations. However, said the majority, the sections were not supported by s 51(xx), the corporations power. While 'the words of pl xx, if they stood alone, might be capable of' supporting the legislation, s 51(xx) 'ought not to be construed as authorising the Commonwealth to invade the field of State law as to domestic trade'. The provision gave the Commonwealth limited powers to control the interstate recognition of corporations but not their corporate activities, 'the control of which is exclusively reserved to the States': 8 CLR at 354 per Griffith CJ.

Erosion of the two doctrines

[8.2.25] The appointment to the High Court in 1906 of two additional justices, Isaacs and Higgins JJ, broke the unanimity of the court on both the implied immunities and implied prohibitions (or reserve powers) doctrines. While Isaacs J initially accepted the implied immunities doctrine (see, for example, *Federated Engine Drivers' and Firemen's Association of Australia v Broken Hill Proprietary Co Ltd* (the *Federated Engine Drivers'* case) (1911) 12 CLR 398 **[8.2.18]** at 451–3), he argued for a relatively narrow application of the doctrine. In *Baxter v Commissioners of Taxation (NSW)* (1907) 4 CLR 1087 **[8.2.13]**, Isaacs J accepted the authority of *D'Emden v Pedder* 1904) 1 CLR 91 **[8.2.9]** but dissented from the court's decision that a Commonwealth public servant's salary was immune from state income tax because he held that the tax did not interfere with Commonwealth Government activities: 4 CLR at 1160–1.

[8.2.26] In *Attorney-General (Qld) v Attorney-General (Cth)* (1915) 20 CLR 148, Isaacs J joined with the rest of the court in rejecting a claim that tenants of Queensland Crown lands were immune from Commonwealth land tax. His argument was that the Commonwealth's power of taxation should 'be given its full natural meaning' and not restricted by 'an implied prohibition, somewhere in the structure of the Constitution, not contained in any word or phrase and not deducible by means of any principle of construction': 20 CLR at 171–2.

[8.2.27] A similar concentration on the language of the grant of Commonwealth legislative power is apparent in the joint judgment of Isaacs and Rich JJ in *Federated Municipal and Shire Council Employees' Union of Australia v Melbourne Corporation* (1919) 26 CLR 508 **[8.2.19]**. They argued that *D'Emden v Pedder* (1904) 1 CLR 91 **[8.2.9]** was founded on s 109 of the Constitution, 'and nothing else': 26 CLR at 532. Manifestly, therefore, there could be no reciprocity. The Commonwealth or its agents might be immune from state legislation because of the existence of overriding Commonwealth legislation, but local councils set up under state law could not claim an immunity from Commonwealth laws made under s 51(xxxv), the industrial arbitration power: 26 CLR at 532. While Isaacs and Rich JJ refrained from describing *Federated Amalgamated Government Railway & Tramway Service Association v New South Wales Railway Traffic Employees Association* (the *Railway Servants'* case) (1906) 4 CLR 488 **[8.2.12]** as wrong, their analysis of the claim of immunity is impossible to reconcile with that decision.

[8.2.28] Higgins J, on the other hand, was outspoken in his criticism of the implied immunities doctrine. In *Baxter v Commissioners of Taxation (NSW)* (1907) 4 CLR 1087 **[8.2.13]** and **[8.2.25]**, he joined Isaacs J in dissenting from the court's decision that New South Wales could not tax the salary of a Commonwealth public servant. In concluding that a state could tax a Commonwealth payment, Higgins J rejected the American cases on which *Deakin v Webb* (1904) 1 CLR 585 **[8.2.10]** had been based (4 CLR at 1164) and accepted as authoritative the view of the Privy Council in *Webb v Outrim* [1907] AC 81 that there was no constitutional immunity for Commonwealth payments. (See also his judgment in *Federated Engine Drivers' and Firemen's Association of Australia v Broken Hill Proprietary Co Ltd* (the *Federated Engine Drivers'* case) (1911) 12 CLR 398 **[8.2.19]** at 459–60.)

[8.2.29] Isaacs and Higgins JJ were less equivocal in their condemnation of the implied prohibitions (or reserved powers) doctrine. For Isaacs J, it was 'contrary to reason to shorten the expressly granted powers [of the Commonwealth] by the undefined residuum [of the States]' and the Commonwealth's power of taxation was subject to 'no limitation … but those expressly enacted': *R v Barger* (1908) 6 CLR 41 **[8.2.23]** at 84–5. In the same case, Higgins J said at 113:

> To say that the Federal Parliament cannot make a law because legislation on the subject belongs to the State is rather to invert the true position. The Commonwealth has certain powers, and as to those powers it is supreme; the State has the rest. We must find what the Commonwealth powers are before we can say what the State powers are. The Federal Parliament has certain specific gifts; the States have the residue. We have to find out the extent of the specific gifts before we make assertions as to the residue.

[8.2.30] The appointment to the High Court of new justices, Gavan Duffy, Powers and Rich JJ in 1913 and Starke J in 1920, and the death and retirement of the founding justices (O'Connor J died in 1912, Barton J in 1920; Griffith CJ retired in 1919) shifted the balance of opinion on the bench: Sawer (1967) p 128. Finally, in 1920 the court seized the opportunity presented by a challenge to the jurisdiction of the Commonwealth Conciliation and Arbitration Court to review all the earlier cases which had laid down the implied immunities and implied prohibitions (or reserved powers) doctrines.

Commonwealth laws and state governments

[8.2.31C]　　**Amalgamated Society of Engineers v
Adelaide Steamship Co Ltd**

(The *Engineers'* case)
(1920) 28 CLR 129

The Amalgamated Society of Engineers, a trade union with members throughout Australia, served a log of claims on 844 employers throughout Australia, claiming from them improved wages and conditions of employment for the union's members. When the employers did not concede the claims, the union began proceedings in the Commonwealth Arbitration Court against the 844 employers seeking a resolution of the industrial dispute between the union and the employers. The court's jurisdiction was defined in the Conciliation and Arbitration Act 1904 (Cth):

> 18 The Court shall have jurisdiction to prevent and settle, pursuant to this Act, all industrial disputes.

Section 4 of the Act defined 'industrial disputes':

> 'Industrial dispute' means an industrial dispute extending beyond the limits of any one State and includes —
>
> (i) any dispute as to industrial matters, and
>
> (ii) any dispute in relation to employment in an industry carried on by or under the control of the Commonwealth or a State, or any public authority constituted under the Commonwealth or a State, and
>
> (iii) any threatened or impending or probable industrial dispute.

Among the employers who were made parties to these proceedings were the West Australian Minister for Trading Concerns, the West Australian State Implement and Engineering Works and the West Australian State Sawmills. These respondents objected that the Commonwealth Conciliation and Arbitration Act could not apply to them as employers. The president of the court, Higgins J, stated a case for the opinion of the Full High Court under s 18 of the Judiciary Act 1903 (Cth). The critical question posed for a decision by the High Court was: 'Has the Parliament of the Commonwealth power to make laws binding on the States with respect to conciliation and arbitration for the prevention and settlement of industrial disputes extending beyond the limits of one State?'

Knox CJ, Isaacs, Rich and Starke JJ (delivered by Isaacs J): [141] The more the decisions are examined, and compared with each other and with the Constitution itself, the more evident it becomes that no clear principle can account for them. They are sometimes at variance **[142]** with the natural meaning of the text of the Constitution; some are irreconcilable with others, and some are individually rested on reasons not founded on the words of the Constitution or on any recognised principle of the common law underlying the expressed terms of the Constitution, but on implication drawn from what is called the principle of 'necessity', that being itself referable to no more definite standard than the personal opinion of the judge who declares it. The attempt to deduce any consistent rule from them has not only failed, but has disclosed an increasing entanglement and uncertainty, and a conflict both with the text of the Constitution and with distinct and clear declarations of law by the Privy Council.

It is therefore, in the circumstances, the manifest duty of this court to turn its earnest attention to the provisions of the Constitution itself. That instrument is the political compact of the whole of the people of Australia, enacted into binding law by the Imperial Parliament, and it is the chief and special duty of this court faithfully to expound and give effect to it according to its own terms, finding the intention from the words of the compact, and upholding it throughout precisely as framed ... In doing this, to use the language of Lord Macnaghten in *Vacher & Sons Ltd v London Society of Compositors* [1913] AC 107 at 118, 'a judicial tribunal has nothing to do with the policy of any Act which it may be called upon to interpret. That may be a matter for private judgment. The duty of the [143] court, and its only duty, is to expound the language of the Act in accordance with the settled rules of construction'.

It is proper, at the outset, to observe that this case does not involve any prerogative 'in the sense of the word', to use the phrase employed by the Privy Council in *Theodore v Duncan* [1919] AC 696 at 706; 26 CLR 276 at 282, 'in which it signifies the power of the Crown apart from statutory authority'. Though much of the argument addressed to us on behalf of the States rested on the prerogative, this distinction was not observed, but it exists, and so far as concerns prerogative in the sense indicated, it is unnecessary to consider it ... In this case we have to consider the effect of certain statutory authority of the States, but in relation to pl xxxv only, and it is necessary to insert a word of caution. If in any future case concerning the prerogative in the broader sense, or arising under some other Commonwealth power — for instance, taxation — the extent of that power should come under consideration ... [144] the special nature of the power may have to be taken into account. That this must be so is patent from the circumstance that the legislative powers given to the Commonwealth Parliament are all prefaced with one general express limitation, namely, 'subject to this Constitution', and consequently those words, which have to be applied *seriatim* to each *placitum*, require the court to consider with respect to each separate *placitum*, over and beyond the general fundamental considerations applying to all the *placita*, whether there is anything in the Constitution which falls within the express limitation referred to in the governing words of s 51. That inquiry, however, must proceed consistently with the principles upon which we determine this case, for they apply generally to all powers contained in that section.

The justices referred to the argument that neither the Commonwealth nor the states could legislate so as to control the other, and to Griffith CJ's view in *Attorney-General (Qld) v Attorney-General (Cth)* (1915) 20 CLR 148 at 163 that 'the implication of mutual non-interference [arose] prima facie from necessity', and continued:

[145] It is an interpretation of the Constitution depending on an implication which is formed on a vague, individual conception of the spirit of the compact, which is not the result of interpreting any specific language to be quoted, nor referable to any recognised principle of the common law of the Constitution, and which, when started, is rebuttable by an intention of exclusion equally not referable to any language of the instrument or acknowledged common law constitutional principle, but arrived at by the court on the opinions of judges as to hopes and expectations respecting vague external conditions. This method of interpretation cannot, we think, provide any secure foundation for Commonwealth or State action, and must inevitably lead — and in fact has already led — to divergencies and inconsistencies more and more pronounced as the decisions accumulate.

The justices referred to some inconsistencies in decisions of the United States Supreme Court. They said decisions of the United States Supreme Court were not a 'secure basis' to determine Australian constitutional law (28 CLR at 146), especially since the Australian political system contained two features which distinguished the Australian Constitution from its United States counterpart, namely indivisible sovereignty of the Crown and responsible government: 28 CLR at 146.

[148] It is plain that, in view of the two features of common and indivisible sovereignty and responsible government, no more profound error could be made than to endeavour to find our way through our own Constitution by the borrowed light of the decisions, and sometimes the dicta, that American institutions and circumstances have drawn from the distinguished tribunals of that country ... We therefore look to the judicial authorities which are part of our own development, which have grown up beside our political system, have guided, it, have been influenced by it and are consistent with it, and which, so far as they existed in 1900, we must regard as in the contemplation of those who, whether in the convention or in the Imperial Parliament, brought our Constitution into being, and which, so far as they are of later date, we are bound to look to as authoritative for us ...

What, then, are the settled rules of construction? The first, and 'golden rule' or 'universal rule' as it has been variously termed, has been settled in *Grey v Pearson* 6 HLC 61 at 106 and the *Sussex Peerage* case 11 Cl & Fin 85 at 143, in well-known passages which are quoted by Lord Macnaghten in *Vacher's* case [1913] AC at 117–18. Lord Haldane LC, in the same case (at 113) made some observations very pertinent to the present occasion. His Lordship, after stating that speculation on the motives of the legislature was a topic which judges cannot profitably or properly **[149]** enter upon, said: 'Their province is the very different one of construing the language in which the legislature has finally expressed its conclusions, and if they undertake the other province which belongs to those who, in making the laws, have to endeavour to interpret the desire of the country, they are in danger of going astray in a labyrinth to the character of which they have no sufficient guide. In endeavouring to place the proper interpretation on the sections of the statute before this house sitting in its judicial capacity, I propose, therefore, to exclude consideration of everything excepting the state of the law as it was when the statute was passed, and the light to be got by reading it as a whole, before attempting to construe any particular section. Subject to this consideration, I think that the only safe course is to read the language of the statute in what seems to be its natural sense' ...

The justices noted that the Privy Council had used a similar approach when interpreting written constitutions, including the Commonwealth Constitution.

[150] Before approaching, for this purpose, the consideration of the provisions of the Constitution itself, we should state explicitly that the doctrine of 'implied prohibition' against the exercise of a power once ascertained in accordance with ordinary rules of construction, was definitely rejected by the Privy Council in *Webb v Outrim* [1907] AC 81; 4 CLR 356. Though subsequently reaffirmed by three members of this court, it has as often been rejected by two other members of the court, and has never been unreservedly accepted and applied. From its nature, it is incapable of consistent application, because **[151]** 'necessity' in the sense employed — a political sense — must vary in relation to various powers and various states, and, indeed, various periods and circumstances. Not only is the judicial branch of the government inappropriate to determine political necessities, but experience, both in Australia and America, evidenced by discordant decisions, has proved both the elusiveness and the inaccuracy of the doctrine as a legal standard. Its inaccuracy is perhaps the more thoroughly perceived when it is considered what the doctrine of 'necessity' in a political sense means. It means the necessity of protection against the aggression of some outside and possibly hostile body. It is based on distrust, lest powers, if once conceded to the least degree, might be abused to the point of destruction. But possible abuse of powers is no reason in British law for limiting the natural force of the language creating them. It may be taken into account by the parties when creating the powers, and they, by omission of suggested powers or by safeguards introduced by them into the compact, may delimit the powers created. But, once the parties have by the terms they employ defined the permitted limits, no court has any right to narrow those limits by reason of any fear that the powers as actually circumscribed by the language naturally understood may be abused ... If it be conceivable that the representatives of the people of Australia as a whole would ever proceed **[152]** to use their national powers to injure the people of Australia considered sectionally, it is certainly within the power of the people themselves to resent and reverse what may be done. No protection of this court in such a case is necessary or proper. Therefore, the doctrine of political necessity, as a means of interpretation, is indefensible on any ground. The one clear line of judicial inquiry as to the meaning of the Constitution must be to read it naturally in the light of the circumstances in which it was made, with knowledge of the combined fabric of the common law, and the statute law which preceded it, and then *lucet ipsa per se*.

The Constitution was established by the Imperial Act 63 & 64 Vict c 12. The Act recited the agreement of the people of the various colonies, as they then were, 'to unite in one indissoluble Federal Commonwealth under the Crown of the United Kingdom of Great Britain and Ireland, and under the Constitution hereby established'. 'The Crown', as that recital recognises, is one and indivisible throughout the Empire. Elementary as that statement appears, it is essential to recall it, because its truth and its force have been overlooked, not merely during the argument of this case, but also on previous occasions. Distinctions have been relied on between the 'Imperial King', the 'Commonwealth King' and the 'State King'. It has been said that the Commonwealth King has no power to bind the first and the last, and, reciprocally, the last cannot bind either of the others. The first step in the examination of the Constitution is to emphasise the primary legal axiom that the Crown is ubiquitous and indivisible in the King's dominions. Though the Crown is one and indivisible throughout the Empire, its legislative, executive and judicial power is exercisable by different agents in different localities, or in respect of different purposes in the same locality, in accordance with the common law, or the statute law binding the Crown: *Williams v Howarth* [1905] AC 551: *Municipalities'* case 26 CLR 553; *Theodore v Duncan* [1919] AC 706, and *Commonwealth v Zachariassen and Blom* 27 CLR 552. The Act 63 & 64 Vict c 12, establishing the federal Constitution of Australia, being passed by the Imperial Parliament for the express purpose of regulating [153] the royal exercise of legislative, executive and judicial power throughout Australia, is by its own inherent force binding on the Crown to the extent of its operation. It may be that even if s V of the Act 63 & 64 Vict c 12 had not been enacted, the force of s 51 of the Constitution itself would have bound the Crown in right of a State so far as any law validly made under it purported to affect the Crown in that right; but, however that may be, it is clear to us that in presence of both s V of the Act and s 51 of the Constitution that result must follow. The Commonwealth Constitution as it exists for the time being, dealing expressly with sovereign functions of the Crown in its relation to Commonwealth and to States, necessarily so far binds the Crown, and laws validly made by authority of the Constitution, bind, so far as they purport to do so, the people of every State considered as individuals or as political organisms called States — in other words, bind both Crown and subjects.

The grant of legislative power to the Commonwealth is, under the doctrine of *Hodge v R* 9 App Cas at 132 and within the prescribed limits of area and subject matter, the grant of an 'authority as plenary and as ample ... as the Imperial Parliament in the plenitude of its power possessed and could bestow', a doctrine affirmed and applied in a remarkable degree in *Attorney-General for Canada v Cain and Gilhula* [1906] AC at 547 ... [154] It is undoubted that those who maintain the authority of the Commonwealth Parliament to pass a certain law should be able to point to some enumerated power containing the requisite authority. But we also hold that, where the affirmative terms of a stated power would justify an enactment, it rests upon those who rely on some limitation or restriction upon the power, to indicate it in the Constitution.

Applying these principles to the present case, the matter stands thus: Section 51(xxxv) is in terms so general that it extends to all industrial disputes in fact extending beyond the limits of any one State, no exception being expressed as to industrial disputes in which States are concerned; but subject to any special provision to the contrary elsewhere in the Constitution ... But it is a fundamental and fatal error to read s 107 as reserving any power from the Commonwealth that falls fairly within the explicit terms of an express grant in s 51, as that grant is reasonably construed, unless that reservation is as explicitly stated. The effect of State legislation, though fully within the powers preserved by s 107, may in a given case depend on s 109. However valid and binding on the people of the State where no relevant Commonwealth legislation exists, the moment it encounters repugnant Commonwealth legislation operating on the same field the State legislation must give way. This is the true foundation of the doctrine stated in *D'Emden v Pedder* 1 CLR 91 in the so-called rule quoted, which is after all only a paraphrase of s 109 of the Constitution. The supremacy thus established by express [155] words of the Constitution has been recognised by the Privy Council without express provision in the case of the Canadian Constitution (see, for example, *La Compagnie Hydraulique v Continental Heat and Light Co* [1909] AC at 198). The doctrine of 'implied prohibition' finds no place where the ordinary principles of construction are applied so as to discover in the actual terms of the instrument their expressed or necessarily implied meaning. The principle we apply to the Commonwealth we apply also to the States, leaving their respective acts of legislation full operation within their respective areas and subject matters, but, in case of conflict, giving to valid Commonwealth legislation the supremacy expressly declared by the Constitution, measuring that supremacy according to the very words of s 109 ... We therefore hold that States, and persons natural or artificial representing States, when parties to industrial disputes in fact, are subject to Commonwealth legislation under pl xxxv of s 51 of the Constitution, if such legislation on its true construction applies to them.

The justices proceeded to rationalise the earlier decisions of the court: *'D'Emden v Pedder* (1904) 1 CLR 91 was a case of conflict between Commonwealth law and State law', and had been settled by s 109; the decision was sound. *Deakin v Webb* 1904) 1 CLR 585 and *Baxter v Commissioners of Taxation* (NSW) (1907) 4 CLR 1087 could also be explained in this way and, therefore, survived. However, the *Railway Servants'* case (1906) 4 CLR 488 (where *'D'Emden v Pedder* was applied *e converso'*) was wrong and could no longer be regarded as law.

[160] We have anxiously endeavoured to remove the inconsistencies fast accumulating and obscuring the comparatively clear terms of the national compact of the Australian people; we have striven to fulfil the duty the Constitution places upon this court of loyally permitting that great instrument of government to speak with its own voice, clear of any qualifications which the people of the Commonwealth or, at their request, the Imperial Parliament have not thought fit to express, and clear of any questions of expediency or political exigency which this court is neither intended to consider nor equipped with the means of determining.

Higgins J delivered a concurring judgment. Gavan Duffy J dissented.

~~~

Notes

[8.2.32]   Writing of the *Engineers'* case in 1937, RTE Latham (the son of Latham CJ) criticised the majority judgment for cutting off 'Australian constitutional law from American precedents, a copious source of thoroughly relevant learning, in favour of the crabbed English rules of statutory interpretation, which are one of the sorriest features of English law'. Latham continued at 564:

> The fundamental criticism of the decision is that its real ground is nowhere stated in the majority judgment. This real ground was the view held by the majority that the Constitution had been intended to create a nation, and that it had succeeded; that in the Great War the nation had in fact advanced in status while the States stood still, and (as was a patent fact) that the peace had not brought a relapse into the *status quo ante bellum*; that a merely contractual view of the Constitution was therefore out of date, and its persistence in the law was stultifying the Commonwealth industrial power, which they believed to be a real and vital power; and finally, that the words of the Constitution permitted the view of the federal relationship which the times demanded. A judgment on these lines would have made the *Engineers'* case frankly a quasi-political decision, based on a far-sighted view of ultimate constitutional policy, of the type with which the Supreme Court of the United States in its greatest periods has made us familiar. It would have been no more political than several of Sir Isaac Isaacs' most notable judgments.

[8.2.33]   A more generous appraisal of the *Engineers'* decision, and one which attempted to place it in its historical context, was made by Windeyer J in *Victoria v Commonwealth* (the *Payroll Tax* case) (1971) 122 CLR 353 **[8.2.50C]** at 395–6:

> The colonies which in 1901 became States in the new Commonwealth were not before then sovereign bodies in any strict legal sense; and certainly the Constitution did not make them so. They were self-governing colonies which, when the Commonwealth came into existence as a new dominion of the Crown, lost some of their former powers and gained no new powers They became components of a federation, the Commonwealth of Australia. It became a nation. Its nationhood was in the course of

time to be consolidated in war, by economic and commercial integration, by the unifying influence of Federal law, by the decline of dependence upon British naval and military power and by a recognition and acceptance of external interests and obligations. With these developments the position of the Commonwealth, the Federal Government, has waxed; and that of the States has waned. In law that is a result of the paramount position of the Commonwealth Parliament in matters of concurrent power. And this legal supremacy has been reinforced in fact by financial dominance. That the Commonwealth would, as time went on, enter progressively, directly or indirectly, into fields that had formerly been occupied by the States, was from an early date seen as likely to occur. This was greatly aided after the decision in the *Engineers'* case (1902) 28 CLR 129, which diverted the flow of constitutional law into new channels. I have never thought it right to regard the discarding of the doctrine of the implied immunity of the States and other results of the *Engineers'* case as the correction of antecedent errors or as the uprooting of heresy. To return today to the discarded theories would indeed be an error and the adoption of a heresy. But that is because in 1920 the Constitution was read in a new light, a light reflected from events that had, over 20 years, led to a growing realisation that Australians were now one people and Australia one country and that national laws might meet national needs. For lawyers, the abandonment of old interpretations of the limits of constitutional powers was readily acceptable. It meant only insistence on rules of statutory interpretation to which they were well accustomed. But reading the instrument in this light does not to my mind mean that the original judges of the High Court were wrong in their understanding of what at the time of federation was believed to be the effect of the constitution and in reading it accordingly. As I see it the *Engineers'* case, looked at as an event in legal and constitutional history, was a consequence of developments that had occurred outside the law courts as well as a cause of further developments there. That is not surprising for the Constitution is not an ordinary statute: it is a fundamental law. In any country where the spirit of the common law holds sway the enunciation by courts of constitutional principles based on the interpretation of a written Constitution may vary and develop in response to changing circumstances. This does not mean that the courts have transgressed lawful boundaries: or that they may do so.

[8.2.34] There are many aspects to the reasoning of the majority in the *Engineers'* case which are unconvincing. (See, in addition to the discussion here, Sawer (1967) pp 130–2 and Zines (1997) pp 10–12.) For example, how useful a guide to judicial decision-making is the proposition that the court must find the intention of the drafter of the Constitution 'from the words of the compact … upholding it throughout precisely as framed'?: 28 CLR at 142. Do the words of the Constitution (or of any instrument) convey a single unequivocal meaning in all circumstances and to all readers? Indeed, are words any more than ambiguous symbols, the precise meaning of which can only be grasped with the aid of various preconceptions, prejudices and insights which the reader brings to the task of interpretation? The words in legislation do not speak and act for themselves; they express ideas, the nature and significance of which will be appreciated in different ways by different readers and at different times. See the discussion at **[1.2.14]–[1.3.16]**.

[8.2.35] The majority offered two reasons for rejecting American precedents on the legal relationship between Commonwealth and states: the 'common sovereignty' or 'the indivisibility of the Crown' and the system of responsible government. How is either of these concepts relevant to the question of the capacity of the Commonwealth Parliament to legislate so as to bind or control state governments?

The 'indivisibility of the Crown' is an artificial concept. It asserts that, as the executive government of each political unit in the British Commonwealth (as we once called it) is legally vested in the one monarch, those executive governments are, legally, the same institution. But such an assertion is quite misleading. The United Kingdom, Canada and the Commonwealth of Australia do not have the same legal personality; they are autonomous, each with its own legal identity capable of negotiating and contracting with the others. It might be more accurate to account for their common Head of State by saying that the government of each of those nations is vested in a separate corporation, and these corporations are currently treated by the several legal systems of each nation as being owned by the same person, but those corporations (the Crown in right of the United Kingdom, the Crown in right of Canada, the Crown in right of the Commonwealth of Australia) are not identical or indivisible.

Presumably, the argument about the indivisibility of the Crown is an argument that the Constitution binds the Crown which means (as the Crown is indivisible) that both Commonwealth and state government are subject to the Constitution and can be made subject to Commonwealth and state legislation. However, the abstract and misleading theory of indivisibility gives very little help in resolving problems about the legal relationships between the units in a federal system: see the discussion in **[8.2.4]**.

What of the second distinction referred to by the majority? It is true that the relationship between executive government and legislature is radically different in Australia from that in the United States. In Australia the several executive governments are responsible to and may (in theory) be controlled by the legislature (see **[7.3.5]–[7.3.6]**); in the United States the executive governments are elected separately from the legislatures and (short of removal through impeachment) are not subject to the legislatures' control. However, where does that distinction (admittedly not trivial) take us? How does it affect the problem of the capacity or incapacity of the Commonwealth Parliament to legislate so as to affect the legal position of state governments?

We might conclude that, of the two distinctions offered by the majority, the first had some basis in abstract logic but was an unrealistic appraisal of our federal system; and the second, while expressing a real difference between the Australian and the American systems of government, was logically irrelevant to the problem under consideration.

[8.2.36]   The globalisation of law is now seen as a fact of life and judges increasingly refer to comparative and international decisions in their opinions: see **[3.4.1]–[3.4.11]** generally. How does this factor affect the *Engineers'* decision, which was based, in part, upon a rejection of the explicit use of decisions of the United States Supreme Court: 28 CLR at 148?

[8.2.37]   In the course of their rather lengthy and disjointed judgment, the majority justices suggested some exceptions to any general rule on intergovernmental amenability. For example, they emphasised that the present case involved no state prerogative powers, and reserved their right to reconsider the problem 'when such a question is involved in a decision': 28 CLR 143. What did they mean by 'prerogative'? Is it possible that the state governments might be immune from Commonwealth legislation when exercising those powers which the courts have traditionally regarded as inherent in the monarch, but not immune when exercising statutory powers? Why should the prerogative powers of the Crown attract any such immunity? The possible immunity of prerogative powers was to be considered in

Federal Commissioner of Taxation v Official Liquidator of EO Farley Ltd (1940) 63 CLR 271 **[8.2.43]**.

A second possible exception mentioned by the majority was Commonwealth taxing legislation. A cryptic reference to the Commonwealth's taxation power appears in 28 CLR at 143–4. Its meaning is obscure. Were the judges referring to Commonwealth taxation of the states, or Commonwealth taxation of state prerogative functions? This possible limitation was to be explored in *Victoria v Commonwealth* (the *Payroll Tax* case) (1971) 122 CLR 353 **[8.2.50C]**.

A third exception, which has been developed since the *Engineers'* case, limits the Commonwealth from legislating so as to discriminate against the states: *Melbourne Corporation v Commonwealth* (1947) 74 CLR 31 **[8.2.45C]** per Dixon J. Finally, a fourth possible exception would limit the Commonwealth from legislating so as to interfere with or curtail the essential functioning of the state: *Melbourne Corporation v Commonwealth* (1947) 74 CLR 31 **[8.2.45C]** per Rich and Starke JJ. See **[8.2.45C]**–**[8.2.66]** and **[8.2.70]**–**[8.2.78]**.

[8.2.38] An important aspect of the majority judgment was its formal denunciation of 'the doctrine of "implied prohibition"': 28 CLR at 150, 155. The majority insisted that powers granted to the Commonwealth Parliament were not to be reduced by applying some limitation not expressly stated in the Constitution. This assertion was to have an important effect on the development of constitutional law in Australia. The attitude which had been strongly expressed in early High Court decisions, that the powers of the Commonwealth Parliament should be read narrowly so as to preserve the maximum area for unimpeded state regulation, was undermined by this assertion. Decisions such as *R v Barger* (1908) 6 CLR 41 **[8.2.22]**, and *Huddart Parker & Co Pty Ltd v Moorehead* (1909) 8 CLR 330 **[8.2.24]** had held that the taxation power (s 51(ii)) and the corporations power (s 51(xx)) should be construed narrowly in order to prevent the Commonwealth Parliament extending its legislation into areas presumed to have been preserved for state regulation and, through the impact of s 109, ousting the states from those areas.

Once the *Engineers'* case was decided, and the doctrine of implied prohibitions rejected, the way was laid for an expansive reading and exploitation of the Commonwealth's powers: see, for example, *Fairfax v Commissioner of Taxation* (1965) 114 CLR 1 **[9.2.22C]** and *Strickland v Rocla Concrete Pipes Ltd* (1971) 124 CLR 468 **[10.3.4C]**, where the narrow interpretations of s 51(ii) and s 51(xx) respectively were discarded by the High Court. However, the view that the Commonwealth's powers should be read so as to avoid a wholesale 'takeover' of state responsibilities has still been held by some members of the High Court: *Attorney-General (WA) v Australian National Airlines Commission* (1976) 138 CLR 492 **[10.2.26C]**; *Commonwealth v Tasmania* (the *Tasmanian Dam* case) (1983) 158 CLR 1 **[3.3.21C]**, **[10.3.26C]**.

[8.2.39] It might have been thought that an immediate consequence of the *Engineers'* case would be the subjection to the jurisdiction of the Commonwealth Arbitration Court, of disputes between the states as employers and their public servants, so long as the disputes had the necessary interstate element required by s 51(xxxv) of the Constitution. The case had been argued and decided on the basis that the distinction between trading and governmental functions of state governments (the former amenable to, the latter immune from, Commonwealth legislation) should be abandoned.

However, a separate and simultaneous development was to limit the impact of the *Engineers'* decision in the area of industrial relations. This development was the High Court's move to a restrictive reading of the term 'industrial dispute' in s 51(xxxv). Earlier decisions, for example, *Jumbunna Coal Mine NL v Victorian Coal Miners Association* (1908) 6 CLR 309, had said that an 'industrial dispute' should be given its popular meaning — a dispute between employer and employees over conditions of employment. Support for a narrower reading of the term emerged in *Federated Municipal and Shire Council Employees Union of Australia v Melbourne Corporation* (1919) 26 CLR 508 at 554, 555, 584. That narrower view was endorsed by a majority of the court in *Australian Insurance Staffs Federation v Accident Underwriters Association* (1923) 33 CLR 517 and *Federated State School Teachers Association of Australia v Victoria* (1929) 41 CLR 569. The narrower view was that an industrial dispute was a dispute in an industry and that industry was confined to the 'world of productive industry and organised business', to use Dixon CJ's later summary of the ideas in *Ex parte Professional Engineers Association* (1959) 107 CLR 208 at 234.

The view was that the Commonwealth Parliament's power to legislate for the settlement, through conciliation and arbitration of interstate industrial disputes was limited to disputes in those industries which could be described as productive; that is, concerned in the production, distribution or maintenance of physical things; or in those industries which could be described as businesses organised for profit. This definition was seen as excluding disputes between the states and their administrative staff (most public servants) or between the states and public school teachers or between the states and fire officers.

In 1983, this narrow reading of 'industrial dispute' was overturned in *R v Coldham; Ex parte Australian Social Welfare Union* (1983) 153 CLR 297 **[8.2.58]**. However, while this decision opened the way for full implementation of the principles in the *Engineers'* case, and hence a broad reading of 'industrial dispute', the court indicated that it might reassess those principles.

[8.2.40]   In *Re Australian Education Union; Ex parte Victoria* (1995) 184 CLR 188 **[8.2.72C]**, the court referred to the broad view of 'industrial dispute' taken in *R v Coldham; Ex parte Australian Social Welfare Union* (1983) 153 CLR 297 **[8.2.58]**. It discussed, without deciding, the nature of the relationship between the broad view, which allowed the Commonwealth to include within its ambit state sector employees, and the maintenance of an 'administrative services exception' which might preclude the inclusion of some state sector employees. The majority said that the broader view taken in *R v Coldham; Ex parte Australian Social Welfare Union* 'eroded the basis on which the administrative services exception had been maintained', but that the exception was not 'contradicted' by the authorities: 184 CLR at 222.

Despite the equivocal nature of these statements, the outcome of the case was to extend the application of the Commonwealth industrial relations system to Victorian public sector employees, except in relation to their dismissal on the basis of redundancy. Neither could Commonwealth legislation intrude upon state decisions regarding conditions of employment or termination of high level employees of the state: see **[8.2.72C]**. Both of these results were based upon the fourth exception to *Engineer's* noted above at **[8.2.37]**. The case marked the first application by the court of the exception which limits the Commonwealth's ability to legislate in such a way as to interfere with or curtail the essential functioning of the state, since its articulation in 1947 in *Melbourne Corporation v Commonwealth* (the *State Banking* case) (1947) 74 CLR 31 **[8.2.45C]**.

[8.2.41] In *Australian Railways Union v Victorian Railways Commissioners* (1930) 44 CLR 319 the High Court accepted a limit to the general principle in the *Engineers'* case. The Victorian Government Railways argued that an award made by the Commonwealth Arbitration Court under the Conciliation and Arbitration Act 1904 (Cth) could not bind the railways because payment of the wages covered by the award would be dependent on the state parliament appropriating the necessary money from the state treasury, and the Commonwealth Parliament had no power to compel that appropriation. The High Court admitted that the Commonwealth lacked legislative power to compel appropriation of the money (in effect, to enforce the award) but held that this did not affect the Commonwealth's capacity to make an award binding on the state. The court's acceptance of the argument that the Commonwealth could not enforce a financial liability lawfully imposed on a state by Commonwealth law was a significant qualification to the rule in the *Engineers'* case.

[8.2.42] However, in *New South Wales v Commonwealth* (the *Garnishee* case) (1932) 46 CLR 155, the High Court held that the Commonwealth Parliament could legislate to enforce the payment of interest by garnisheeing (seizing) moneys, such as taxes and bank credits, owing to the state, in order to enforce the state's obligations under the Financial Agreement. The Financial Agreement had been made between the Commonwealth and the states under s 105A of the Commonwealth Constitution. Under the agreement, the Commonwealth took over the substantial public debts of the states, and the states undertook to make regular interest payments to the Commonwealth on the debts. Rich and Dixon JJ said that Commonwealth legislation to enforce performance of a state's obligations was authorised by ss 51(xxxix), 75 (iii), 78 and 105A(3) of the Constitution, combined with s 105A(5). They regarded the negative implications of *Australian Railways Union v Victorian Railways Commissioner* (1930) 44 CLR 319 **[8.2.41]** as overcome by s 105A(5):

> In our opinion the effect of this provision is to make any agreement of the required description obligatory upon the Commonwealth and the states to place its operation and efficacy beyond the control of any law of any of the seven parliaments, and to prevent any constitutional principle or provision operating to defeat or diminish or condition the obligatory force of the agreement. In the case of the states there is no constitutional qualification of the binding force of such an agreement to which the words 'notwithstanding anything contained in ... the Constitution of the several States' could more appropriately relate than that which requires parliamentary appropriation of funds to satisfy the condition upon which the liabilities of the states are incurred (46 CLR at 177).

Dixon and Rich JJ also referred to, and were impressed by, the magnitude of the financial liabilities of the states taken over by the Commonwealth under the Financial Agreement and 'the plain dependence of the Commonwealth upon the performance by the States of their obligations under the agreement to enable it to meet those liabilities': 46 CLR at 177.

[8.2.43] In *Federal Commissioner of Taxation v Official Liquidator of EO Farley Ltd* (1940) 63 CLR 278, some members of the High Court discussed the nature and extent of one of the possible exceptions to the *Engineers'* rule: that relating to the prerogative.

EO Farley Ltd was being wound up under the Companies Act 1899 (NSW), which did *not* bind the Crown, neither in right of the state nor in right of the Commonwealth. The company owed money to both the state and Commonwealth governments and there were insufficient assets to pay these debts. It was accepted that each class of debt was to be satisfied before debts of equal degree owed to private creditors; this was the prerogative right of priority for Crown debts: see **[8.2.90C]–[8.2.92]**. It was also accepted that, apart from legislation, the Crown in right of the Commonwealth and the Crown in right of the state would share the money available in proportion to their debts. The High Court held that no Commonwealth legislation purported to alter that position by claiming priority for debts due to the Commonwealth over debts due to the state. Only Dixon and Evatt JJ discussed the constitutional question of the Commonwealth's legislative power to claim that priority.

Dixon J argued that a state parliament could not impair or destroy the Commonwealth's prerogative priority and its right to stand equally with the state when competing for the payment of debts due to each of them. He then considered the power of the Commonwealth Parliament to adjust this equality of ranking:

> The right of the State to receive payment of its debts before the subject springs from a prerogative of government; and the State's claim to stand on an equality with the Commonwealth in respect of demands upon the same fund is the consequence of the federal system by which two governments of the Crown are established within the same territory, neither superior to the other.
>
> They are not rights conferred by the federal Constitution, but they do depend on the existence of the state as a separate government. The federal Constitution does not imply as a matter of meaning or intention that debts due to the Crown in right of the state shall, in a distribution of assets, stand on an equality with debts due to the Commonwealth. If it did so, there would, of course, be an end of the matter. But it does mean to establish two governments, state and federal, side by side, neither subordinate to the other, and it is this that gives rise to their equality in a competition of claims to be satisfied out of assets in a course of administration. The right of the state to rank equally with the Commonwealth is not a thing that falls exactly under s 106 of the Constitution. Even if it be treated as forming part of the 'constitution' of the state, it is not easy to regard it as existing as at the establishment of the Commonwealth. But to destroy the equality does spell an interference with an existing governmental right of the state flowing from the constitutional relations of the two polities. The *Engineers'* case (1920) 28 CLR 129 shows that this consideration may not be enough to protect the right of the state from the exercise of a specific legislative power of the Commonwealth. The claim that debts of equal degree due to the Crown in right of the state and in right of the Commonwealth rank equally in a distribution of assets, unlike the claim that the Crown is to be preferred to the subject, does not depend upon the prerogative and is therefore not within the reservation made in the *Engineers'* case (1920) 28 CLR at 143 in favour of the 'prerogative in the broader sense,' whatever that reservation may mean. On two previous occasions I have attempted to reduce to a brief legal statement the doctrine which I understand that case to establish: See *Australian Railways Union v Victorian Railways Commissioner* (1930) 44 CLR at 390 and *West v Commissioner of Taxation* (NSW) (1937) 56 CLR at 682. It is a rule of construction of the legislative powers expressly conferred by the Constitution upon the parliament of the Commonwealth. For present purposes it is enough to repeat the general proposition. 'The principle is that whenever the Constitution confers a power to make laws in respect of a specific subject matter, prima facie it is to be understood as enabling the parliament to make laws affecting the operations of the states and their agencies. The prima facie meaning may be displaced by considerations based on the nature or the subject matter of the power or the language in which it is conferred or on some other

provisions in the Constitution. But, unless the contrary thus appears, then, subject to' certain 'reservations, the power must be construed as extending to the States' (1937) 56 CLR at 682.

The power given by s 51(xvii) to make laws with respect to bankruptcy and insolvency is an example of a legislative power which, as a result of this principle, might be interpreted as enabling the parliament of the Commonwealth to destroy or vary the ranking of debts due to the state and Commonwealth in any administration of assets falling under the description of bankruptcy or insolvency. For it is a specific power, and priority in the distribution of assets among a bankrupt's creditors is a matter to be governed by bankruptcy legislation. It is a subject to be dealt with as a coherent whole, and prima facie no reason appears why the position of the Crown in right of the state and of the Commonwealth as a creditor should not be governed by laws made in the exercise of the power, alike with the position of ordinary creditors (63 CLR at 312–14).

However, Dixon J went on to add that the power to make laws with respect to taxation did not include a power to subordinate a state's claim for payment of a debt to the Commonwealth's claim for payment of a taxation debt at 316–17:

Neither in the nature nor in the form of the taxation power is there anything to suggest that the relations of the two governments inter se or any rights of the States are involved. Indeed, in the *Engineers'* case (1920) 28 CLR 143 the taxation power was singled out as an instance of a legislative power the extent of which in relation to the States might in the future come up for special consideration. It is not like powers over specific fields of law or activity or conduct, such as bankruptcy and insolvency, bills of exchange and promissory notes, copyright, patents and trade marks, currency, coinage and legal tender, weights and measures, etc. The specific subject matter in powers of that character could not be effectually regulated if, when the State in the course of its operations entered on the field, it was immune from the Federal law. Such reasoning, however, has no application when the question is whether, as an incident of or for the better effectuation of a power of raising revenue by taxing the citizen, Commonwealth legislation may destroy the equality upon which the claims of the two governments stand by reason of the coordinate position of the State and Commonwealth under the Constitution.

Incidental powers are not stretched to cover such important consequences as interferences with the fiscal and governmental rights of the States or the relations between the States and the Commonwealth.

Evatt J, on the other hand, believed that by legislation enacted under the taxation power of the Commonwealth could require a taxpayer to pay his or her taxation debt to the Commonwealth ahead of debts owing to a state.

[8.2.44] In *South Australia v Commonwealth* (the *First Uniform Tax* case) (1942) 65 CLR 373 **[9.6.3C]**, a majority of the High Court upheld the validity of s 221(1) of the Income Tax and Social Service Contribution Assessment Act 1936 (Cth). This provision required a taxpayer to discharge his or her liability for Commonwealth income tax for any year before paying state income tax for that year (s 221(1)(a)) and it required trustees in bankruptcy and liquidators of companies to pay Commonwealth tax in priority to state taxes owed by insolvent individuals and companies: s 221(1)(b). Dixon J did not participate in that decision.

However, in *Victoria v Commonwealth* (the *Second Uniform Tax* case) (1957) 99 CLR 575 **[9.6.8C]**, Dixon CJ persuaded a majority of the High Court to hold s 221(1)(a) invalid — because it was not incidental to the power to legislate with respect to taxation to forbid taxpayers to discharge other debts before they paid their tax debts. Speaking of Commonwealth power over taxation, Dixon CJ said, in a judgment with which Kitto J concurred at 614:

Here we are dealing with powers of taxation in a federal system of government. Further, you must look at the purpose disclosed by the law said to be incidental to the main power. Here the purpose is to make it more difficult for the States to impose an income tax ... To support s 221(1)(a) it must be said to be incidental to the Federal power of taxation to forbid the subjects of a State to pay the tax imposed by the State until that imposed by the Commonwealth is paid and, moreover, to do that as a measure assisting to exclude the States from the same field of taxation. This appears to me to be beyond any true conception of what is incidental to a legislative power and, under colour of recourse to the incidents of a power expressly granted, to attempt to advance or extend the substantive power actually granted to the Commonwealth, until it reaches into the exercise of the constitutional powers of the States.

Section 221(1)(b) was held to be a valid exercise of the bankruptcy and insolvency power in s 51 (xvii). That is, the Commonwealth Parliament could demand priority for the payment of Commonwealth taxes in the context of bankruptcy or insolvency, but not otherwise.

[8.2.45C]   **Melbourne Corporation v Commonwealth**

(The *State Banking* case)
(1947) 74 CLR 31

The Banking Act 1945 (Cth) provided:

48(1) Except with the consent in writing of the Treasurer, a bank shall not conduct any banking business for a State or for any authority of a State, including a local government authority.

Penalty: One thousand pounds.

(2) Any consent of the Treasurer under this section may apply to all such business conducted by any particular bank or at a particular office of a bank, or to the business of any particular State or authority conducted by any particular bank or at any particular office of a bank.

(3) Until a date fixed by the Treasurer by notice published in the Gazette, this section shall apply only in relation to banking business conducted for a State or for an authority of a State including a local government authority, specified by the Treasurer by notice in writing, and if an office of a bank is specified in the notice, at the office so specified.

Section 4 defined 'bank' to mean 'a body corporate authorised under Pt II of this Act to carry on banking business in Australia'. These bodies corporate were listed in the first schedule of the Act and were all the private banks then operating in Australia. Section 5(1) declared that nothing in s 48 'shall apply with respect to State banking'.

In May 1947, the Treasurer of the Commonwealth wrote to the Melbourne City Council ('The Melbourne Corporation'), and advised it that, as from 1 August 1947, it would be 'specified' in accordance with s 48(3): 'In effect this will mean that as from the date on which this specification was made a private bank will not be able legally to conduct business on behalf of any local governing authority specified in the notice'. The Treasurer also indicated that he was satisfied that the Commonwealth Bank was 'in a position to provide full banking facilities to' the council.

The Commonwealth Bank had been set up as a statutory agency by the Commonwealth Bank Act 1911 (Cth). It operated, in 1947, under the Commonwealth Bank Act 1945 (Cth), s 9 of which declared that the bank should give effect to a monetary and banking policy determined by the Commonwealth Government.

The Melbourne City Council began an action in the High Court of Australia against the Commonwealth, seeking a declaration that s 48 of the Banking Act was beyond the legislative powers of the Commonwealth, contrary to the terms of the Constitution and void. The Commonwealth demurred to the statement of claim and the demurrer was argued before the Full Court. The states of South Australia and Western Australia were given leave to intervene in support of the plaintiff. The state of Victoria, by leave, intervened to support the Commonwealth.

Latham CJ: [55] In the *Engineers'* case (1920) 28 CLR 129 it was decided that 'laws validly made by authority of the Constitution bind, so far as they purport to do so, the people of every State considered as individuals or as political organisms called States in other words, both bind Crown and subjects' (1920) 28 CLR at 153. Thus the validity of a Commonwealth law is to be determined by reference to the terms of the Constitution, without applying any presumption that there are certain powers reserved to the States which must not be impaired or interfered with by Federal laws.

But this principle does not mean that the States are in the position of subjects of the Commonwealth. The Constitution is based upon and provides for the continued co-existence of Commonwealth and States as separate governments, each dependent of the other within its own sphere. The *Engineers'* case recognises, in the case of State legislation, a difference between 'provisions which apply generally to the whole community without discrimination' and 'an act of the State legislature discriminating against Commonwealth officers.' ... [56] In *West's* case (1937) 56 CLR 687 Evatt J referred to the distinction between general laws and laws 'discriminating against' Commonwealth or State officials and said: 'A different angle of approach to the question of discriminatory legislation is this, that it must at least be implied in the Constitution, as an instrument of federal government, that neither the Commonwealth nor a State legislature is at liberty to direct its legislation toward the destruction of the normal activities of the Commonwealth or States'.

The Chief Justice referred to a number of decisions of the United States Supreme Court which expressed the same proposition, 'that Federal laws expressed in general terms may apply to the States ... but the Federal laws which "discriminate" against the States are not laws authorised by the Constitution': 74 CLR at 60. His Honour continued:

[61] ... The Commonwealth Parliament has no power to make laws with respect to State government functions as such, and the State parliaments have no power to make laws with respect to Commonwealth governmental functions as such. It is upon this ground, in my opinion, that what is called 'discriminatory' legislation may properly be held to be invalid ... Similarly, Federal legislation which, though referring to a subject of Federal power, is really legislation about what is clearly a State governmental function, may be said to 'interfere unduly' with that function and therefore to be invalid. 'Undue' interference is a rather vague conception, and an attempt to apply it as a standard [62] for determining the validity of legislation would invite and would certainly produce differences of opinion which would often be due to other than objective considerations. In my opinion the invalidity of a Federal law which seeks to control a State governmental function is brought about by the fact that it is in substance a law with respect to a subject as to which the Commonwealth Parliament has no power to make laws. Though there will sometimes be difficulties in applying such a criterion, this is a more satisfactory ground of decision than an opinion that a particular Federal 'interference' with a State function reaches a degree which is 'undue'.

The application of these principles in the present case brings about the conclusion that s 48 of the Banking Act is invalid. The section requires the consent of the Treasurer to the conduct of banking business by a bank only in the case of States and State authorities, including local governing authorities. It singles out States and State agencies and creates a rule for them and for no others. It is in substance legislation about States and State authorities. It can fairly be described as being aimed at or directed against States and it none the less falls within this disqualifying category because it is also aimed at and directed against what are called 'private banks'. On this ground, in my opinion, s 48 is invalid.

Rich J: [64] I may say at once that I agree with the submissions that the section relates to banking, and that it does not relate to State banking in the sense in which that phrase is used in the placitum, namely the carrying on by the State of the business of banking ...

[65] The question then is, whether the provision being prima facie within power, it is obnoxious to the Constitution. The first point to be kept in mind is that the Constitution expressly provides for a federal form of government ...

Rich J referred to the overthrow of the reserved powers doctrine in the *Engineers'* case and continued:

[66] There is no general implication in the framework of the Commonwealth Constitution that the Commonwealth is restricted from exercising its defined constitutional powers to their fullest extent by a supposed reservation to the States of an undefined field of reserved powers beyond the scope of Commonwealth interference. But this is always subject to the provisions of the Commonwealth Constitution itself. That Constitution expressly provides for the continued existence of the States. Any action on the part of the Commonwealth, in purported exercise of its constitutional powers, which would prevent a state from continuing to exist and function as such is necessarily invalid because inconsistent with the express provisions of the Constitution, and it is to be noted that all the powers conferred by s 51 are conferred 'subject to this Constitution'. Such action on the part of the Commonwealth may be invalid in two classes of case, one, where the Commonwealth singles out the States or agencies to which they have delegated some of the normal and essential functions of government, and imposes on them restrictions which prevent them from performing those functions or impede them in doing so; another, where, although the States or their essential agencies are not singled out, they are subjected to some provision of general application, which, in its application to them, would so prevent or impede them. Action of the former type would be invalid because there is nothing in the Commonwealth Constitution to authorise such action by the Commonwealth. A general income tax Act which purported to include within its scope the general revenues of the States derived from State taxation would be an instance of the latter …

Rich J concluded that the free use of banking facilities by government was 'regarded as essential to the efficient working of the business of government' and accordingly s 48 was invalid: 74 CLR at 67.

After reviewing a number of United States and Australian decisions, Starke J continued:

Starke J: [74] So we may start from the proposition that neither Federal nor State governments may destroy the other nor curtail in any substantial manner the exercise of its powers or 'obviously interfere with one another's operations': see *Graves v New York; Ex rel O'Keefe* 306 US 466 (1939). The American authorities are not controlling nor in many cases safe guides to the interpretation of the Australian Constitution. But I do agree that a distinction between 'governmental' or 'the primary and inalienable functions of a constitutional government' (see *Coomber v Justices of Berks* (1883) 9 App Cas 74) and the '"trading" activities of a State' is 'too shifting a basis for determining constitutional power and too entangled in expediency to serve as a dependable legal criterion': *New York v United States* 326 US at 580 (1946). When a government acts under its constitutional power then its activities are governmental functions: see *Graves v New York; Ex rel O'Keefe* 306 US 477 (1939); *Helvering v Gerhardt* 304 US at 926–7 (1938), per Black J; *New York v United States* 326 US at 590 (1946), Douglas J, Part 1, in his dissenting opinion. And I cannot [75] agree that the presence or absence of discrimination affords a decisive test or legal criterion of constitutional power. As was pointed out in *New York v United States* 326 US at 587 (1946) by Stone CJ, Reed, Murphy and Burton JJ, a tax which is not discriminatory 'may nevertheless so affect the State, merely because it is a State that is being taxed, as to interfere unduly with the State's performance of its sovereign functions of government'. It is a practical question, whether legislation or executive action thereunder on the part of a Commonwealth or of a State destroys, curtails or interferes with the operations of the other, depending upon the character and operation of the legislation and executive action thereunder. No doubt the nature and extent of the activity affected must be considered and also whether the interference is or is not discriminatory but in the end the question must be whether the legislation or the executive action curtails or interferes in a substantial manner with the exercise of constitutional power by the other. The management and control by the States and by local governing authorities of their revenues and funds is a constitutional power of vital importance to them. Their operations depend upon the control of those revenues and funds. And to curtail or interfere with the management of them interferes with their constitutional power. Yet the Commonwealth by its legislation prescribes that, except with the consent in writing of the

Treasurer, no bank shall conduct any banking business for a State, including any local governing authority. It operates to prevent the States and local governing authorities from dealing with their old and tried bankers except with the consent in writing of the Treasurer. The object is, of course, to compel the States and the local governing authorities to bank with the Commonwealth Bank, which is a central bank. And it was said that the handling of public funds is the appropriate function of a central bank. But that does not establish any constitutional power of the Commonwealth to compel the States so to bank. The States and the local governing authorities, and not the Commonwealth, have the power and the duty of administering, controlling and banking their revenues and funds.

Dixon J: [78] The prima facie rule is that a power to legislate with respect to a given subject enables the Parliament to make laws which, upon the subject, affect the operations of the States and their agencies. That, as I have pointed out more than once, is the effect of the *Engineers'* case (1920) 28 CLR 129 stripped of embellishment and reduced to the form of a legal proposition. It is subject, however, to certain reservations and this also I have repeatedly said. Two reservations, that relating to the prerogative and that relating to the taxation power, do not enter into the determination of this case and nothing need be said about them.

It is, however, upon the third that, in my opinion, this case turns. The reservation relates to the use of [79] Federal legislative power to make, not a general law which governs all alike who come within the area of its operation whether they are subjects of the Crown or the agents of the Crown in right of a State, but a law which discriminates against States, or a law which places a particular disability or burden upon an operation or activity of a State, and more especially upon the execution of its constitutional powers. In support of such a use of power the *Engineers'* case (1920) 28 CLR 129 has nothing to say. Legislation of that nature discloses an immediate object of controlling the State in the course which otherwise the executive government of the State might adopt, if that government were left free to exercise its authority. The control may be attempted in connection with a matter falling within the enumerated subjects of Federal legislative power. But it does not follow that the connection with the matter brings a law aimed at controlling in some particular the State's exercise of its executive power within the true ambit of the Commonwealth legislative power. Such a law wears two aspects. In one aspect the matter with respect to which it is enacted is the restriction of State action, the prescribing of the course which the executive government of the State must take or the limiting of the courses available to it. As the operation of such a law is to place a particular burden or disability upon the State in that aspect it may correctly be described as a law for the restriction of State action in the field chosen. That is a direct operation of the law.

In the other aspect, the law is connected with a subject of Commonwealth power ... [I]f in its second aspect the law operates directly upon a matter forming an actual part of a subject enumerated among the Federal legislative powers, its validity could hardly be denied on the simple ground of irrelevance to a head of power. Speaking generally, once it appears that a Federal law has an actual and immediate operation within a field assigned to the Commonwealth as a subject of legislative power, that is enough. It will be held to fall within the power unless some further reason appears for excluding it. That it discloses another purpose and that the purpose lies outside the area of Federal power are considerations which will not in such a case suffice to invalidate the law ... [80] But it is one thing to say that a Federal law may be valid notwithstanding a purpose of achieving some result which lies directly within the undefined area of power reserved to the States. It is altogether another thing to apply the same doctrine to a use of Federal power for a purpose of restricting or burdening the State in the exercise of its constitutional powers. The one involves no more than a distinction between the subject of a power and the policy which causes its exercise. The other brings into question the independence from Federal control of the State in the discharge of its functions.

[T]o attempt to burden the exercise of State functions by means of the power to tax needs no ingenuity, and that, no doubt, is why that power occupies such a conspicuous place in the long history in the United States and here of the question how far Federal power may be used to interfere with the States in the exercise of their powers.

Dixon J referred to decisions of the United States Supreme Court which established 'that a taxing law discriminating against a State is unconstitutional and void': 74 CLR at 81.

[81] What is important is the firm adherence to the principle that the Federal power of taxation will not support a law which places a special burden upon the States. They cannot be singled out and taxed as States in respect of some exercise of their functions. Such a tax is aimed at the States and is an attempt to use Federal power to burden or, maybe, to control State action. The objection to the use of Federal power to single out States and place upon them special burdens or disabilities does not spring from the nature of the power of taxation. The character of the power lends point to the objection but it does not give rise to it. The federal system itself is the foundation of the restraint upon the use of the power to control the States. The same constitutional objection applies to other powers, if under them the States are made the objects of special burdens or disabilities. Not of course all powers, for some of them are concerned with the States specially or contemplate some measure in particular relation to a State. Examples can be seen in paras (xxxi), (xxxii), (xxxiii), and (xxxiv) of s 51.

The meaning and nature of the power cannot be left out of account. Of this the defence power is a conspicuous example. But plainly the greater number of powers contemplate legislation of general application.

I do not think that either under the Constitution of the United States or the British North America Act or the Commonwealth Constitution has countenance been given to the notion that the legislative powers of one government in the system can be used in order directly to deprive another government of powers or authority committed to it or restrict that government in their exercise, notwithstanding the complete overthrow of the general doctrine of reciprocal immunity of government agencies and the discrediting of the reasoning used in its justification. For that reason the distinction has been constantly drawn between a law of general application and a provision singling out governments and placing special burdens [82] upon the exercise or the fulfilment of functions constitutionally belonging to them. It is but a consequence of the conception upon which the Constitution is framed. The foundation of the Constitution is the conception of a central government and a number of State governments separately organised. The Constitution predicates their continued existence as independent entities. Among them it distributes powers of governing the country. The framers of the Constitution do not appear to have considered that power itself forms part of the conception of a government. They appear rather to have conceived the States as bodies politic whose existence and nature are independent of the powers allocated to them. The Constitution on this footing proceeds to distribute the power between State and Commonwealth and to provide for their interrelation, tasks performed with reference to the legislative powers chiefly by ss 51, 52, 107, 108 and 109.

In the many years of debate over the restraints to be implied against any exercise of power by Commonwealth against State and State against Commonwealth calculated to destroy or detract from the independent exercise of the functions of the one or the other, it has often been said that political rather than legal considerations provide the ground of which the restraint is the consequence. The Constitution is a political instrument. It deals with government and governmental powers. The statement is, therefore, easy to make though it has a specious plausibility. But it is really meaningless. It is not a question whether the considerations are political, for nearly every consideration arising from the Constitution can be so described, but whether they are compelling …

The considerations I have just mentioned have been used in relation to the question what the Federal Government may do with reference to the States and the question of what a State may do with reference to the Federal Government. But these are two quite different questions and they are affected by considerations that are not the same. The position of the Federal Government is necessarily [83] stronger than that of the States. The Commonwealth is a government to which enumerated powers have been affirmatively granted. The grant carries all that is proper for its full effectuation. Then supremacy is given to the legislative powers of the Commonwealth.

These two considerations add great strength to the implication protecting the Commonwealth from the operation of State laws affecting the exercise of Federal power. But they also amplify the field protected. Further, they limit the claim of the States to protection from the exercise of Commonwealth power. For the attempt to read s 107 as the equivalent of a specific grant or reservation of power lacked a foundation in logic. Accordingly, the considerations upon which the States' title to protection from Commonwealth control depends arise not from the character of the powers retained by the States but from their position as separate governments in the system exercising independent functions. But, to my mind, the efficacy of the system logically demands that, unless a given legislative power appears from its content, context or subject matter so to intend, it should not be understood as authorising the Commonwealth to make a law aimed at the restriction or control of a State in the exercise of its executive authority. In whatever way it may be expressed an intention of this sort is, in my opinion, to be plainly seen in the very frame of the Constitution ...

[84] [Section] 48 forbids the banks to do the business of the States unless the Treasurer of the Commonwealth consents. Section 5 of the Crimes Act 1914–41 operates to make the Treasurer and any subordinate officer of the State guilty of the same offence as the bank if they should procure the bank to disregard the prohibition.

There is thus a law directly operating to deny to the States banking facilities open to others, and so to discriminate against the States or to impose a disability upon them. The circumstance that the primary prohibition is laid upon the banks and not upon the States does not appear to be a material distinction. It is just as effectual to deny to the States the use of the banks and that is its object. This, I think, is not justified by the power to make laws with respect to banking.

I cannot see that it is to the point to argue that under s 51(xiii) the Commonwealth might give the Commonwealth Bank a monopoly complete, except for State banks, and that what s 48 does is to give a monopoly restricted to State business. That is only to say that instead of establishing a monopoly with all its advantages and disadvantages shared by the whole community, States have been singled out and deprived of the freedom of choice which the existing system afforded.

At bottom the principle upon which the States become subject to Commonwealth laws is that when a State avails itself of any part of the established organisation of the Australian community it must take it as it finds it. Except in so far as under its legislative power it may be able to alter the legal system, a State must accept the general legal system as it is established. If there be a monopoly in banking lawfully established by the Commonwealth, the State must put up with it.

But it is the contrary of this principle to attempt to isolate that State from the general system, deny it the choice of the machinery the system provides and so place it under a particular disability. Whether the right to exercise such a choice is of great or of small importance to the States is not a material matter for inquiry. It is enough that it forms part of the functions of the executive government of the States in administering the finances of the States.

It may be conceded that the Financial Agreement under s 105A of the Constitution and the adoption of the system of uniform taxation of incomes place the finances of the States in a very different [85] position from that which they occupied when the Commonwealth was first established. Further, these measures may well be supposed to lend such a provision as s 48 the appearance of a corollary, at all events from the point of view of a central bank. But these are considerations that cannot affect the interpretation of s 51(xiii). Section 105A cuts across the Constitution and, as it has been construed in this court, imposes upon the States absolute liabilities to the Commonwealth enforceable against the revenues of the States. Extensions of constitutional power or supremacy may explain, but they do not justify further extensions.

In my opinion s 48 of the Banking Act is void because an inseverable part of it is directed to control or restrict the executive government of the States in the use of banks for the conduct of their banking business.

Williams J delivered a concurring judgment in which he appeared to adopt the views both of Latham CJ and of Rich and Starke JJ. McTiernan J dissented. He referred to writings on the function of central banks and central banking and said that s 48 had, as its object, the proper division of business between the central bank of a country and its trading banks. It was 'in substance a law with respect to the subject of banking' and so within s 51(xiii): 74 CLR at 94.

~~~

Notes

[8.2.46] This decision marked a significant move away from the *Engineers'* case: (1920) 28 CLR 129 **[8.2.31C]**. It established a clear exception, prohibiting discriminatory legislation, to the general *Engineers'* rule that the Commonwealth could legislate so as to bind the states (an exception not foreshadowed in the *Engineers'* case). Three of the five justices in the majority based this exception on implications drawn from their understanding of the federal system. Furthermore, the reasoning of Rich and Starke JJ suggested an even broader, more general exception which would invalidate non-discriminatory Commonwealth legislation which had the effect of interfering with 'normal and essential' state functions.

[8.2.47] One immediate result of the decision in *Melbourne Corporation v Commonwealth* (the *State Banking* case) (1947) 74 CLR 31 **[8.2.45C]** was the enactment of the Banking Act 1947 (Cth) which nationalised the private banks. A principal object of this nationalisation was to achieve the central control over state government banking business which the *State Banking* case had denied to the Commonwealth. It is possible that this nationalising legislation was prompted by some remarks of Dixon J in the *State Banking* case: 74 CLR at 84. No doubt these remarks were equivocal, for in *Bank of New South Wales v Commonwealth* (the *Bank Nationalisation* case) (1948) 76 CLR 1 the High Court invalidated the nationalisation scheme. The reasons for the court's decision and its confirmation by the Privy Council are presently irrelevant: see **[10.4.10C]**. However, one of the plaintiffs' arguments in the *Bank Nationalisation* case was that the Banking Act 1947 was invalid since its effect in relation to the state governments was identical to that achieved by s 48 of the Banking Act 1945. The justices (the same bench as that which decided the *State Banking* case) either rejected or ignored this argument. Latham CJ and McTiernan J rejected the argument on the ground that the 1947 Act did not discriminate against the states: 76 CLR at 243, 397. Rich and Williams JJ in their joint judgment ignored the argument. Starke J rejected it, saying at 325–6:

> If the Parliament of the Commonwealth has power to enact the Banking Act 1947, no constitutional power or function of a State is curtailed or impeded. The States can through their own banks, provide their own financial facilities or resort to the general banking system otherwise established. The *Melbourne Corporation* case is distinguished because there the States were subject to a particular direction.

Dixon J rejected the argument at 337:

> The State would be bound to take the banking system as any general law, made in exercise of Federal power, left it. Just as when the Federal Government desires to use or take advantage of anything the nature or character of which is determined by an exercise of the exclusive power of the State, it must take as it finds it, so the States when they avail themselves of services or facilities regulated or determined by Federal law, must accept it as part of the system enjoyed by the whole community. Such things are a consequence of the distribution of powers and stand apart altogether from some

exercise of legislative power which singles out the States or which operates specially to impede them in their functions.

The general principle supported by Rich, Starke and, apparently, Williams JJ in the *Bank of New South Wales v Commonwealth* (the *Bank Nationalisation* case) (1948) 76 CLR 1 did receive substantial support in: *Victoria v Commonwealth* (the *Payroll Tax* case) (1971) 122 CLR 353 **[8.2.50C]**; *Commonwealth v Tasmania* (the *Tasmanian Dam* case) (1983) 158 CLR 1 **[8.2.57]**; *Queensland Electricity Commission v Commonwealth* (1985) 159 CLR 192 **[8.2.59C]**; *Richardson v Forestry Commission* (1988) 164 CLR 261 **[8.2.68]**. However, the reluctance or refusal of the High Court to commit itself to that principle for some years when it was of more than speculative interest must have diminished its credibility. However, in the later case of *Re Australian Education Union; Ex parte Victoria* (1995) 184 CLR 188 **[8.2.72C]** the High Court specifically endorsed the existence of the principle when it said it would 'proceed on the footing that the limitation has two elements, the non-discriminatory element having particular relevance' to the argument in that case: 184 CLR 227. See also *Victoria v Commonwealth* (1996) 187 CLR 416.

[8.2.48] Latham CJ rejected the argument that the Commonwealth legislation could be invalid because of any implication from the federal nature of the Constitution. To him, s 48 was invalid because it was not a law with respect to banking, but a law with respect to the states. But why is it not possible to classify the law as one with respect to states and with respect to banking? The contrary view, that a Commonwealth law may have 'two aspects', was expressed by Dixon J: 74 CLR at 79; and has been generally endorsed by the High Court.

[8.2.49] As suggested in **[8.2.46]**, the decision *Melbourne Corporation v Commonwealth* (the *State Banking* case) (1947) 74 CLR 31 **[8.2.45C]** marked a significant move away from the *Engineers'* principle, but the extent of that move was difficult to assess because of the sharp differences in approach adopted by the majority justices. Latham CJ said that a law could only have a single characterisation and a Commonwealth law would be invalid if it was a law 'aimed at or directed against States' (74 CLR 62) rather than a law with respect to a matter in s 51. Dixon J said that the states could claim immunity from a Commonwealth law 'which discriminates against States, or ... places a particular disability or burden' upon them: 74 CLR 79. Rich and Starke JJ said that there was a limit against general, non-discriminatory Commonwealth legislation which threatened 'the continued existence of the States' (74 CLR at 66 per Rich J) or 'curtail[ed] or interfere[d] in a substantial manner with the exercise of constitutional power by the other': 74 CLR at 74 per Starke J.

The three approaches were also to be reflected in *Victoria v Commonwealth* (the *Payroll Tax* case) (1971) 122 CLR 353 **[8.2.50C]**. Over the succeeding years, the approach of Latham CJ was to be abandoned and Dixon J's approach endorsed (and invoked to strike down Commonwealth legislation in 1985). The broader approach of Rich and Starke JJ was also to attract judicial support, although for some years that support was best described as hypothetical for, until 1995, no Commonwealth legislation was declared invalid on the ground that it threatened the continued existence of the states or interfered with the exercise of state constitutional functions: *Commonwealth v Tasmania* (the *Tasmanian Dam* case) (1983) 158 CLR 1 **[8.2.57]**; *Queensland Electricity Commission v Commonwealth* (1985) 159 CLR 192 **[8.2.59C]**; *State Chamber of Commerce v Commonwealth* (1987) 163 CLR 329

[8.2.66]; *Richardson v Forestry Commission* (1988) 164 CLR 261 **[8.2.68]**. In 1995, in *Re Australian Education Union; Ex parte Victoria* (1995) 184 CLR 188 **[8.2.72C]**, the broader, more general principle was applied.

Another area of uncertainty, the use by the Commonwealth of its taxation power so as to impose taxation on the states, a question which had been left open in the *Engineers'* case (1920) 28 CLR 129 **[8.2.31C]** at 143–4, was clarified in the following decision.

[8.2.50C]   Victoria v Commonwealth
(The *Payroll Tax* case)
(1971) 122 CLR 353

The Payroll Tax Act 1941 (Cth) imposed a tax of 2.5 per cent on all wages paid or payable by an employer. The tax was to be paid to the Commonwealth by the employer. The Payroll Tax Assessment Act 1941 (Cth) defined 'employer' to include the Crown in right of a state: s 3.

The state of Victoria began an action in the High Court of Australia, seeking a declaration that it was beyond the power of the Commonwealth Parliament to levy a tax on wages paid or payable by the state to its employees in certain government departments, or to enact that the state should pay the tax to the Commonwealth on those wages, and a declaration that the legislation imposing this tax on the state was invalid. The government departments referred to in the plaintiff's statement of claim (that is, the departments whose payroll, according to the plaintiff, could not be taxed) included the Premier's Department, the Education Department, the Crown Law Department and the Treasury.

The Commonwealth demurred to the statement of claim, asserting that the legislation was within the power of the Commonwealth Parliament to make laws with respect to taxation. The demurrer was heard before the Full Court.

Barwick CJ referred to the plaintiff's argument that the Act was invalid because it 'so trenches upon the governmental functions of the State as to burden, impair and threaten the independent exercise of those functions': 122 CLR at 365. Barwick CJ quoted two passages from the *Engineers'* case: the first, 28 CLR at 152–3, to the effect that 'the indivisibility of the Crown' meant that the Commonwealth Constitution and legislation enacted under the Constitution bind, if so intended, individuals and the 'political organisms called States'; the second, 28 CLR at 153–4, that the Commonwealth's legislative powers were not subject to an implied qualification granting immunity to the states.

Barwick CJ: [367] These principles were not only stated in universal terms but, in my opinion, are by their very nature of universal validity. According to these principles, the grant to the Parliament of legislative power with respect to each subject matter enumerated in the Constitution enables laws to be made within the ambit of the subject matter which, if so intended, will bind the Crown in right of a State in like manner that they bind individuals and corporations.

[368] It may be, of course, that the description of the subject matter properly construed excludes the Crown in right of a State either completely or to a defined extent from the ambit of the subject matter. Section 51(xiii) is an obvious example of such an express limitation of subject matter. But if there be no such express limitation, the legislative power to bind the Crown in right of a State by a valid law with respect to a subject matter within s 51(ii) is, in my opinion unqualified ...

Barwick CJ referred to s 114 of the Constitution and said that the 'tax rated to the amount of wages paid is not a tax upon property' (122 CLR at 369). He denied that the

Federalism: the Legal Relationships

Commonwealth Constitution should be read as incorporating 'some unexpressed contractual term of a fundamental nature': 122 CLR at 372. His Honour continued:

[372] That the Government cannot 'aim' its legislation against a State, its powers or functions of government is both true and fundamental to our constitutional arrangements. But, in my opinion, this does not derive from any implied limitation upon any legislative power granted to the Commonwealth. It is true simply because the topics of legislation allotted to the Commonwealth by the Constitution do not include the States themselves nor their governmental powers or functions as a subject matter of legislative power. As will appear from my understanding of the judgments in *Melbourne Corporation v Commonwealth* (1947) 74 CLR 31, a law of the Commonwealth which in substance takes a State or its power or functions of government as its subject matter is invalid because it cannot be supported upon any granted legislative power. If the subject matter of the law is in substance the States or their powers or functions of government, there is no room, in my opinion, for holding it to be at the same time and in the same respects a law upon one of the enumerated topics in s 51 ... Of course, a law may be at the same time thought to be a law with respect to either of two of the topics enumerated in s 51 and it may be satisfactory in such a case not to say with respect to which of the two subject matters the law should preferably be referred. But when a law may possibly be regarded as having either of two [373] subjects as its substance, one of which is within Commonwealth power and the other is not, a decision must be made as to that which is in truth the subject matter of the law.... In other words, it seems to me to follow necessarily from the decision of the court in the *Engineers'* case (1920) 28 CLR 129, and from the reasons given for that decision, that the validity of a Commonwealth law will be determined by its relation to a granted subject matter of legislative power construed as a provision of an Act of the Imperial Parliament, 'read naturally in the light of the circumstances in which it was made'. By that direct approach no warrant will, in my opinion, be found in the Constitution for a law of which the powers or functions of a State is or are in truth the subject matter. It is for lack of an appropriate subject matter rather than the presence of an implied limitation upon some granted power that such a law, in my opinion, would fail. That, in my opinion, is the real ground of and, in any case, the only acceptable ground for the decision in *Melbourne Corporation v Commonwealth* (1947) 74 CLR 31.

The reason for the inability of a State to make a law binding on the Commonwealth is a completely unrelated circumstance. It derives from the fact that the Crown has not by the Constitution submitted itself to the legislatures of the States. The endeavour to found the inability of a State to bind the Commonwealth upon a doctrine of mutual immunity derived from necessity was clearly and convincingly exploded by the court in the *Engineers'* case ...

[376] I should now deal with the submission that the subject matter of taxation, because of the extensive effect a law on that topic may have, has an inherent limitation which excludes a State from its ambit. I am unable to accept such a submission. The argument offered in support of it seems to me little, if anything, more than an attempt to construct a legal safeguard against an apprehended abuse of a power to make a law of taxation binding the Crown in right of a State. But the fallacy of attempting to erect such a limitation is clearly disposed of by the court in the *Engineers'* case. The language of s 51(ii) and its ascertained meaning by construction, in my opinion, gives no warrant for any limitation upon the legislative topic of taxation beyond those expressly made in s 51(ii) itself and by s 114 of the Constitution.

From a passage in the judgment of the majority justices in the *Engineers'* case the plaintiff sought to get some support for the proposition that there was something so special about the power to tax that of necessity there was within the grant of the legislative power a limitation excepting the Crown in right of the State from the ambit of the power. So much weight was put upon this passage and such comments have been made upon it in subsequent dicta that I think it worthwhile to set out the passage in full: ...

Barwick CJ quoted that paragraph from the *Engineers'* case, beginning with the words 'It is proper, at the outset' (28 CLR at 143–4), then referred to observations of Dixon J in *Australian Railways Union v Victorian Railways Commissioners* (1930) 44 CLR at 490 and *West v Commissioner of Taxation (NSW)* (1937) 56 CLR at 682, and continued:

[378] What is sought to be said by the plaintiff is that the court in the passage quoted from the *Engineers'* case excepted the legislative power with respect to taxation from the generality of its judgment as expressed in the other passages which I have already quoted from that case. But, in my opinion, the submission is founded on a misconception of what the court there said ...

In considering the passage from the *Engineers'* case which I have set out, the first observation that should be made is that in truth the justices did not single out the power with respect to taxation as an exception but merely used it as an instance of those legislative powers whose exercise might be thought likely to give [379] rise to a conflict between the prerogative of the Crown and legislation based on a granted power. Secondly, it is of paramount importance to understand what was the reservation which their Honours were minded to make.

[380] [T]he most it seems to me that can be taken from their Honours' reservation is that the question whether a Commonwealth law made under a granted power can affect an exercise of the Crown's prerogative might need some time to be examined. In my opinion, however, on such examination it will be found that the possibility against which their Honours thought fit to enter a caveat is really not one that can occur under the Australian Constitution ...

I turn now to *Melbourne Corporation v Commonwealth* (1947) 74 CLR 31 ...

[382] [F]requent reference is to be found in the reasons of the participating justices to the undoubted truth that the Constitution contemplates the continued existence of the States. This is expressed by saying that the Commonwealth may not 'aim' its legislation against the States; or, that the States cannot be singled out and taxed as States in respect of some exercise of their functions. But these in my respectful opinion are merely forms of expressing the legal principle that legislation of the kind described is in substance legislation upon or with respect to the States themselves and their functions as such. Such a law is 'not justified by the power to make laws with respect to banking'. There is however no ratio decidendi common to those justices who formed the majority of the participating justices in *Melbourne Corporation v Commonwealth* (1947) 74 CLR 31. It is not permissible to construct such a ratio by the aggregation of various elements from separate reasons given by their Honours (see *Great Western Railway Company v Owners of SS Mostyn* per Viscount Dunedin [1928] AC 57 at 73–4). But, in my opinion, the real ground of the decision and, in any case, the only acceptable ground, is that s 48 of the Banking Act lacked an appropriate subject matter.

Any other view must, in my opinion, involve concepts incapable of exact expression and certainly of practical application. For example, the concept of an 'undue' interference with State functions attracting invalidity provides but a question begging formula. And to attempt to use a distinction between governmental and other functions of a State in the modern world as a [383] legal criterion of validity is, in my opinion, without promise ...

In my opinion, the power of the Parliament with respect to taxation is not in any wise excepted from the basic principle that a valid law made by the Parliament may bind the Crown in right of a State according to its terms.

Gibbs J said that the decisions in *R v Sutton* (1908) 5 CLR 789 and *Attorney-General (NSW) v Collector of Customs (NSW) (Steel Rails case)* (1908) 5 CLR 818 established that the Commonwealth Parliament could legislate under s 51(ii) to impose taxes on the States, and that the inclusion in the Constitution of s 114, expressly forbidding the Commonwealth to tax the property of a State, would not have been necessary had the Commonwealth lacked power to impose any tax upon the States. Nor was there any implication from the federal nature of the Constitution that no general law imposing taxation may validly be extended to the States: 122 CLR at 423. Gibbs J then turned to the question whether there was a limitation which applied generally to protect the States from Commonwealth laws.

Gibbs J: [424] In my respectful opinion, the view of Sir Owen Dixon, that a Commonwealth law is bad if it discriminates against States, in the sense that it imposes some special burden or disability upon them, so that it may be described as a law aimed at their restriction or control, should be accepted. With all respect, however, I am not disposed to agree that a law which is not discriminatory in this sense is necessarily valid if made within one of the enumerated powers of the Commonwealth. A general law of the Commonwealth which would prevent a State from continuing to exist and function as such would in my opinion be invalid. It is true that in many cases a law which offended in this way would prove to be discriminatory, and I am conscious of the imprecision of the test so far as it applies to general and non-discriminatory laws. The further formulations of the test by Rich and Starke JJ in the *Melbourne Corporation* case (1947) 71 CLR 31 are not free from difficulty. To say that what the Constitution impliedly forbids is a law which would prevent the States from performing the normal and essential functions of government or impede them in doing so is to draw a distinction between essential and inessential functions of government which is inappropriate to modern conditions and has probably never been valid (cf per Windeyer J in *Ex parte Professional Engineers' Association* (1959) 107 CLR at 274–6). To inquire whether a law curtails or interferes in a substantial manner with the exercise of constitutional power by the States leads only to the further question what is the constitutional power of the States that is protected. For the purposes of the present case it is, however, unnecessary to attempt to resolve these difficulties because the pay-roll tax in its present form would not be invalid on any [425] view of the question. Although in some cases it may be possible to show that the nature of a tax on a particular activity, such as the employment of servants, renders the continuance of that activity practically impossible, it has not been shown that the tax in the present case prevents the States from employing civil servants or operates as a substantial impediment to their employment. The tax has now been imposed upon and paid by the States for nearly thirty years, and it has not been shown to have prevented the States from discharging their functions or to have impeded them in so doing. They may have less money available for public purposes because they have to pay the tax, but that could be said in every case in which a tax is imposed on the States, and in itself it cannot amount to an impediment against State activity sufficient to invalidate the tax.

~~~

[8.2.51] Gibbs J concluded that the Payroll Tax Assessment Act, which exempted private schools from payment of the tax, did not discriminate against the states. McTiernan J delivered judgment to the same effect as Barwick CJ, with whose reasons Owen J agreed. Menzies and Walsh JJ delivered separate judgments to the same effect as Gibbs J. Windeyer J held that the Payroll Tax Act could validly impose a tax on the states as employers. He said that 'implications arising from the existence of the states as parts of the Commonwealth and as constituents of the federation may restrict the manner in which the Parliament can lawfully exercise its power to make laws with respect to a particular subject matter': 122 CLR at 403; and that a Commonwealth Act that levied a tax upon the states alone would be invalid, not because it was not a law with respect to taxation but 'because of the principles and limitations, call them implications or what you will, recognised in the *Melbourne Corporation* case (1947) 74 CLR 31' (122 CLR at 404).

Notes

[8.2.52] Barwick CJ argued, as Latham CJ had in *Melbourne Corporation v Commonwealth* (the *State Banking* case) (1947) 74 CLR 31 **[8.2.45C]**, that a Commonwealth law which was aimed at a state would be invalid because it was not a law with respect to one of the heads of Commonwealth legislative power. He also criticised the judgment of Dixon CJ in the *State Banking* case on the ground that it was logically inconsistent to hold that s 48 of the Banking Act 1945 was a law with respect to banking, within s 51(xiii), *and* a law with respect to states. But is the latter description inconsistent with the former? Why should it be impossible to describe a law as dealing with two subject matters? The possibility of dual characterisation was acknowledged by Barwick CJ (122 CLR at 372–3) but said to be inappropriate where one of those characters lay outside Commonwealth power: 122 CLR at 373. The contrary view was argued by Windeyer J (122 CLR at 403–4) and must now be regarded as the orthodox view: see, for example, *Queensland Electricity Commission v Commonwealth* (1985) 159 CLR 192 **[8.2.59C]**; and the discussion in **[1.5.18]**.

[8.2.53] Barwick CJ rejected the argument that there were any implied limitations on the legislative power of the Commonwealth. He suggested (122 CLR at 370–1) that this argument proceeded on the assumption that the Commonwealth Constitution was a compact or contractual union between independent states. He rejected that assumption and said the states derived their existence from the Constitution itself, and that the Constitution adopted the constitutional arrangements of the colonies as the constitutional arrangements of the states under the new federal system. Therefore, in so far as the Constitution was not a treaty of union between states, there was no room for implying some immunity or protection from Commonwealth legislation.

On the other hand, Barwick CJ accepted the proposition that state parliaments cannot enact laws binding on the Commonwealth because 'the Crown has not by the Constitution submitted itself to the legislatures of the States': 122 CLR at 373. This proposition is similar to an idea put forward by Fullagar J in *Commonwealth v Bogle* (1953) 89 CLR 229 **[8.2.96]**, **[8.2.97]**.

[8.2.54] Menzies, Windeyer, Walsh and Gibbs JJ accepted the argument that the federal nature of the Constitution implied some limitations on the Commonwealth's legislative power. Windeyer J adopted the approach of Dixon J in *Melbourne Corporation v Commonwealth* (the *State Banking* case) (1947) 74 CLR 31 **[8.2.45C]** that the Commonwealth Parliament could not use its legislative power to discriminate against the states. Menzies, Walsh and Gibbs JJ went further and supported the Rich–Starke proposition (from the *State Banking* case) that general, non-discriminatory Commonwealth laws might be invalid if they interfered with the performance by the states of their constitutional functions. Their acceptance of this proposition was not affected by its apparent rejection in *Bank of New South Wales v Commonwealth* (the *Bank Nationalisation* case) (1948) 76 CLR 1 **[8.2.47]**. In that case it had been argued that the Banking Act 1947 (Cth) was invalid because, even though it did not single out the states as had s 48 of the Banking Act 1945 (Cth), its *effect* in relation to the states was the same as that of s 48. The argument was rejected.

[8.2.55] The general principle that non-discriminatory laws of the Commonwealth may be invalid in so far as they interfere with the performance by the states of their constitutional functions does not rest on any reservation made in the *Engineers'* case to the general principle it advanced. Neither Menzies, Walsh nor Gibbs JJ were prepared to formulate the proposition in precise and comprehensive terms. They were clearly alive to the great difficulties involved in that formulation.

Is the principle capable of formulation? The observations of the majority in the *Engineers'* case might be relevant to the general statements of principle found in the judgments of Menzies, Walsh and Gibbs JJ:

[I]t is an interpretation of the Constitution depending on an implication which is formed on a vague, individual conception of the spirit of the compact (28 CLR at 145).

Are judicially manageable criteria available by which the proposed general principle might be applied? Is it possible to anticipate from their judgments what kind of legislative action by the Commonwealth will be invalid because of the application of this principle? Menzies J, for example, suggested that a Commonwealth tax on state tax revenues would be invalid: 122 CLR at 393. Why would it be invalid? What would distinguish it from the payroll tax? Would not the state remain as free to receive the taxed revenues as it remains free to employ labour when it pays payroll tax?

[8.2.56] In *Victoria v Australian Building Construction Employees' and Builders Labourers' Federation* (1982) 152 CLR 25, the High Court rejected a challenge to an order of the Federal Court of Australia restraining a Royal Commissioner, who held Letters Patent issued by the Governor of Victoria, from proceeding with an inquiry into the affairs of a trade union while legal proceedings against that union were pending in the Federal Court. The court's power to issue this order came from ss 23 and 31 of the Federal Court of Australia Act 1976 (Cth), which empowered the court to make orders in relation to matters within its jurisdiction and to publish contempts of court. It had been argued on behalf of the Victorian Government that the Federal Court's order involved an interference with the state prerogative which was, according to the reservations made in the *Engineers'* case (1920) 28 CLR 129 **[8.2.31C]** at 143–4, beyond the reach of Commonwealth legislative power.

Mason J said there was nothing in the Commonwealth Constitution:

> ... which subordinates the exercise of [Commonwealth legislative] powers to the prerogatives of the Crown in right of the States. Elsewhere [that is, apart from s 51] the emphasis, as in s 109, is on the supremacy throughout the Commonwealth of all laws validly made under the Constitution. There is no secure foundation for an implication that the exercise of the Parliament's legislative powers cannot affect the prerogative in right of the States and the weight of judicial opinion, based on the thrust of the reasoning in the *Engineers'* case, is against it (152 CLR at 93).

Mason J said that, if it was necessary to make any implication to protect the states from the Commonwealth, that implication should prevent the Commonwealth discriminating against the states and impairing their continued existence or their capacity to function. The conferral on the Federal Court of its power to restrain a contempt of court by a state Royal Commissioner did not offend those implications. The power was in general and non-discriminatory terms and its exercise did not impair the state's existence or capacity to function: 152 CLR at 93–4.

Stephen, Murphy and Aickin JJ agreed, in separate judgments, that no special immunity attached to state prerogative functions. The other members of the court, Gibbs CJ, Wilson and Brennan JJ, did not decide the point.

[8.2.57] The general principle supported by Menzies, Walsh and Gibbs JJ was raised by the state of Tasmania in *Commonwealth v Tasmania* (the *Tasmanian Dam* case) (1983) 158 CLR 1 **[3.3.21C]**, **[10.3.26C]**. Tasmania argued that Commonwealth legislation, which prohibited the construction of a hydro-electric dam upon Tasmanian Crown lands, was invalid because it impaired a governmental function of the state: the management of Crown lands.

The dissenting justices, Gibbs CJ, Wilson and Dawson JJ, did not consider the argument as they held the Commonwealth legislation invalid on the other grounds.

Of the majority justices, Mason and Brennan JJ supported the view that Commonwealth legislation was subject to some broad constraint along the lines developed by Menzies, Walsh and Gibbs JJ in *Victoria v Commonwealth* (the *Payroll Tax* case) (1971) 122 CLR 353 **[8.2.50C]**. Mason J said that a non-discriminatory Commonwealth law, which 'inhibits or impairs the continued existence of a State or its capacity to function', would be invalid. There must be, Mason J said, 'a substantial interference with the State's capacity to govern, an interference which will threaten or endanger the continued functioning of the State as an essential constituent element in the federal system': 158 CLR at 139.

Although the present legislation restricted the state in the exercise of its powers, it did not impair the state's continued existence or its capacity to function, Mason J said. He acknowledged the possibility that Commonwealth control over state government activities in a large area of the state might impair its capacity to function, but the present controls affected only 14,125 hectares, a relatively small area. (The possibility was tested in *Richardson v Forestry Commission* (1988) 164 CLR 261 **[8.2.68]**.)

Brennan J indicated that the constraint on Commonwealth legislation was limited to protecting the functioning of the organs of state government. The present legislation did not overstep that constraint because it did not purport 'to restrict the use by the central department of government or by Parliament or by the Supreme Court of the buildings appointed for their use in performing their respective functions': 158 CLR at 214. Brennan J returned to this constraint in *State Chamber of Commerce v Commonwealth* (1987) 163 CLR 329 **[8.2.66]** at 362–5.

Murphy and Deane JJ did not commit themselves on the principle supported by Mason and Brennan JJ, concluding that the present Commonwealth legislation did not breach that principle, assuming it was a constitutional principle: 158 CLR at 169, 281.

[8.2.58] A concrete example of a situation in which the general principle gave states immunity from Commonwealth legislation that interfered with their constitutional functions can be found in *R v Coldham; Ex parte Australian Social Welfare Union* (the *Social Welfare Union* case) (1983) 153 CLR 297. The High Court overturned a series of High Court decisions, stretching back 60 years, in which the Commonwealth's conciliation and arbitration power, s 51(xxxv), had been confined to the settlement of disputes in 'industries' meaning a productive industry or organised business carried on for the purpose of making profits: see, for example, *Federated State School Teachers' Association of Australia v Victoria* (1929) 41 CLR 569 **[8.2.39]**. In the *Social Welfare Union* case, the court held that the s 51(xxxv) phrase 'industrial dispute' (to the settlement of which Commonwealth legislative power was directed and, therefore, limited) should be given its popular meaning; namely, a dispute between employer and employee about the terms and conditions of employment. It followed that a dispute between social workers and their employers (a number of government-funded local community organisations) over the conditions of employment was an industrial dispute and, since it involved employees and employers in more than one state, the dispute was subject to Commonwealth legislative power.

The court was clearly alive to the implications this decision could have for the state governments as employers. The narrow view of an 'industrial dispute' had meant that such a dispute could only arise in the quasi-commercial or trading services of a state, not in a state's administrative services (despite the *Engineers'* case): *R v*

Commonwealth Conciliation and Arbitration Commission; Ex parte Professional Engineers' Association (1959) 107 CLR 208 at 233–4. Of this limited state immunity from the Commonwealth's arbitration power, the High Court (Gibbs CJ, Mason, Murphy, Wilson, Brennan, Deane and Dawson JJ) said:

> If the reasons hitherto given for reaching that conclusion are no longer fully acceptable, it may be that the conclusion itself finds support in the prefatory words of s 51 where the power is made 'subject to this Constitution' ... The implications which are necessarily drawn from the federal structure of the Constitution itself impose certain limitations on the legislative power of the Commonwealth to enact laws which affect the States (and vice versa). The nature of those limitations was discussed in *Melbourne Corporation v Commonwealth* (1947) 74 CLR 31, especially at 55–60, 66, 70–5, 82–3; *Victoria v Commonwealth* (the *Pay-roll Tax* case) (1971) 122 CLR 353, especially at 385–93, 402–3, 406–11, 417–24, and the other cases there cited. If at least some of the views expressed in those cases are accepted, a Commonwealth law which permitted an instrumentality of the Commonwealth to control the pay, hours of work and conditions of employment of all State public servants could not be sustained as valid, but as Walsh J pointed out in the *Pay-roll Tax* case (at 410) the limitations have not been completely and precisely formulated and for present purposes the question need not be further examined (153 CLR at 313).

Does that statement suggest, despite its equivocation, a return to the limited view of Commonwealth legislative power regarded as authoritative before the *Engineers'* case? Does the statement suggest a reinstatement of *Federated Engine Drivers' and Firemen's Association of Australia v Broken Hill Proprietary Co Ltd* (the *Federated Engine Drivers'* case) (1911) 12 CLR 398 **[8.2.18]**, and the distinction which that decision asserted between governmental functions and non-governmental, trading functions? Could that reinstatement, and the immunity or protection suggested in the passage from *R v Coldham; Ex parte Australian Social Welfare Union* (the *Social Welfare Union* case), quoted above, be reconciled with the holding in the *Engineers'* case 'that States ... when parties to industrial disputes in fact, are subject to Commonwealth legislation under pl xxxv of s 51 of the Constitution, if such legislation on its true construction applies to them'?: 28 CLR at 155.

The notion that state governments could claim constitutional immunity from Commonwealth laws affecting their relations with state employees was tested (and rejected by the majority of the High Court) in *State Chamber of Commerce v Commonwealth* (1987) 163 CLR 329 **[8.2.59C]**. See also *Richardson v Forestry Commission* (1988) 164 CLR 261 **[8.2.68]**. However, in *Australian Education Union and Australian Nursing Federation; Ex parte Victoria* (1995) 184 CLR 188 **[8.2.72C]** at 228–33, the court relied on the general principle in deciding that the state of Victoria was immune from those provisions of Commonwealth industrial legislation which purported to regulate the terms and conditions of employment of 'high level' state employees, and the dismissal of other employees on the ground of redundancy. The precise nature of the rule which prevents Commonwealth legislation from singling out the states for special burdens, the 'discrimination' rule, must now be regarded as settled by the following decision of the High Court.

[8.2.59C]   **Queensland Electricity Commission v Commonwealth**

(1985) 159 CLR 192

The Queensland Electricity Commission was constituted by s 9 of the Electricity Act 1976 (Qld) and declared to represent the Crown in right of the state of Queensland. The function of the Commission was to generate electrical power and to distribute that power through Electricity Boards, constituted under ss 101–103 of the Electricity Act 1976. Although the Boards did not represent the Crown, they functioned under the control of the state government.

During 1984, the Commission, the Boards and some of their employees became involved in an industrial dispute. The terms of the employees' employment were controlled by state legislation and industrial awards. During the course of the dispute, the Queensland Parliament passed further legislation, varying the conditions of employment by the Commission and the Boards. On 18 April 1985 a Commissioner of the Commonwealth Conciliation and Arbitration Commission found that there existed an industrial dispute, within the Conciliation and Arbitration Act 1904 (Cth), between the employees' union, the Electrical Trades Union of Australia, and the Queensland Electricity Commission.

The Commonwealth Parliament then enacted the Conciliation and Arbitration (Electricity Industry) Act 1985, which came into operation on 31 May 1985. The Act was declared, by s 6(1), to apply 'to the industrial dispute between the Electrical Trades Union of Australia and certain authorities that was found to exist by a Commissioner on 18 April 1985'.

According to s 6(2), the Act was also to apply to any industrial dispute found to exist between a specified union of employees and one or more electricity authorities 'if the industrial dispute could result in the making of an award that would be binding on an electricity authority of Queensland and would establish terms or conditions of employment of employees of that authority'. No union of employees had been specified for the purpose of s 6(2).

Section 7 of the Act directed the Arbitration Commission 'to settle the industrial dispute as expeditiously as is appropriate having regard to all the circumstances'. Section 8(1) removed the power, which the Arbitration Commission would otherwise have had under s 41(1)(d) of the Conciliation and Arbitration Act 1904, to dismiss or refrain from hearing a matter which had been, was being or could be dealt with by a state Industrial Authority of Queensland or in which further proceedings were unnecessary or undesirable in the public interest.

Section 9(1) provided that the powers of the Arbitration Commission in relation to the industrial dispute 'shall ... be exercised by the Full Bench'. However, s 9(6) authorised the Full Bench to separate that part of the industrial dispute which involved employers other than electricity authorities of Queensland, so that the separated part would be dealt with in accordance with the standard procedures under the Conciliation and Arbitration Act 1904.

The Queensland Electricity Commission and nine Electricity Boards began proceedings against the Commonwealth in the High Court of Australia, seeking a declaration that the Conciliation and Arbitration (Electricity Industry) Act 1985 (Cth) was not a valid law of the Commonwealth Parliament. A similar action was brought by the state of Queensland. The Commonwealth demurred to the statement of claim and these demurrers were heard by the Full Court.

Mason J: [211] The plaintiffs attack the validity of the legislation on two grounds: (1) that the Parliament's legislative powers are subject to an implied prohibition against discriminating against States (or their agencies) or the residents of States; and (2) that the presence of the words 'of [212] any one State' in the description 'extending beyond the limits of any one State' in s 51(xxxv) of the Constitution is inconsistent with the notion that laws made in exercise of the power may differ depending on the identity of the States in which the interstate dispute arose.

The first ground taken by the plaintiffs invokes the principle which was applied in *Melbourne Corporation v Commonwealth* (1947) 74 CLR 31 to invalidate s 48 of the Banking Act 1945 (Cth) ...

Mason J reviewed the development of the law relating to the Commonwealth's ability to apply its legislation to the states, from the *Engineers'* case (1920) 28 CLR 129 **[8.2.31C]**. He noted that *Melbourne Corporation v Commonwealth* (the *State Banking* case) (1947) 74 CLR 31 **[8.2.45C]** had reinforced a reservation to the *Engineers'* rule. He reviewed the judgments in the *State Banking* case, observing that Dixon J's approach to characterisation had since been accepted as correct, so that the view of Latham CJ must be rejected: 159 CLR at 215. He considered *Victoria v Commonwealth* (the *Payroll Tax* case) (1971) 122 CLR 353 **[8.2.50C]**; *Commonwealth v Tasmania* (the *Tasmanian Dam* case) (1983) 158 CLR 1 **[8.2.57]**; and *Koowarta v Bjelke-Petersen* (1982) 153 CLR 168. His Honour continued:

[217] This review of the authorities shows that the principle is now well established and that it consists of two elements: (1) the prohibition against discrimination which involves the placing on the States of special burdens or disabilities; and (2) the prohibition against laws of general application which operate to destroy or curtail the continued existence of the States or their capacity to function as governments: *Victoria v Australian Building Construction Employees' and Builders Labourers' Federation* (1982) 152 CLR 25 at 93. The second element of the prohibition is necessarily less precise than the first; it protects the States against laws which, complying with the first element because they have a general application, may nevertheless produce the effect which it is the object of the principle to prevent.

Three comments should be made in relation to the prohibition as it has been expressed. First, the principle prohibits discrimination against a particular State as well as against the States generally. Discrimination against a particular State, at least so long as it involves the imposition of a special burden or disability on that State, by isolating it from the general law applicable to others, including other States, falls squarely within the principle. Secondly, notwithstanding its basis in a constitutional conception of a relationship between a central government and separate State governments and the emphasis given to its application to the exercise of executive power by the States, the principle, as Stephen J indicated in *Koowarta*, protects legislatures as well as executive governments. Thirdly, it does not follow that every law which deprives a State of a right, privilege or benefit which it enjoys will amount to discrimination in the sense already discussed. A law which deprives a State of a right, privilege or benefit not enjoyed by others, so as to place the State on an equal footing with others, is not a law which isolates the State from the general law. So, in *Federal Commissioner of Taxation v Official Liquidator of E O Farley Ltd* (1940) 63 CLR at 313–14 Dixon J suggested that a Commonwealth law enacted under s 51(xvii) might regulate the Crown's priority in [218] payment of debts in bankruptcy and insolvency, both in respect of the Commonwealth and the States: see also *Re Foreman & Sons Pty Ltd*; *Uther v Federal Commissioner of Taxation* (1947) 74 CLR 508 at 529; *Victoria v Commonwealth* ('the *Second Uniform Tax* case') (1957) 99 CLR 575 at 611–12. And this leads to the more general proposition that the Commonwealth Parliament may by an exercise of its legislative powers abrogate a prerogative of the States without necessarily offending the prohibition against discrimination.

The prohibition against discrimination operates to strike down laws which apply to agencies of a State as well as to a State itself: see, eg, *Melbourne Corporation* (1947) 74 CLR at 78–9 ... The foundation for the implication is not the special character and privileges of the Crown in right of the States, but the constitutional conception of the Commonwealth and the States as constituent entities of the federal compact having a continuing existence reflected in a central government and separately organised State governments. To restrict the prohibition to a State and such of its agencies as represent the Crown in right of that State would significantly limit the protection given to the States which, as governments, are free to choose whether a function should be carried out by a department of government or by an authority brought into existence for that purpose. The object of the implied prohibition is to protect the State in the exercise of its functions from the operation of discriminatory laws whether the functions are discharged by the executive government or by an authority brought into existence by the State to carry out public functions even if the authority acts independently and is not subject to government direction and even if its assets and income are not property of the State ...

[219] There can be no objection to an exercise of the conciliation and arbitration power which establishes a particular tribunal or a particular procedure for the settlement of disputes in one industry, say the electricity industry. In relation to that industry Parliament might, if it saw fit, require that, in the interests of expedition, the jurisdiction of the Commission be exercised by a Full Bench. It might even provide that disputes in that industry be not referred to a State industrial authority but be determined by the Commission itself. Such a law would apply to all without differentiation. But when the Parliament singles out disputes in the electricity industry to which agencies of the State of Queensland are parties and subjects them to special procedures which differ from those applying under the principal Act to the prevention and settlement of industrial disputes generally, and of industrial disputes in the electricity industry in particular, it discriminates against the agencies of the State by subjecting them to a special disability in isolating them from the general law contained in the principal Act.

The limitation in the power of the Commission provided for in s 8(1), the restriction of the exercise of the Commission's jurisdiction to the Full Bench (s 9(1)) and the power given to the Commission by s 9(6) to hear the Queensland element of the dispute separately and then to declare that s 9 does not apply to the remainder of the dispute, are three patent illustrations of the differential treatment for which the Act provides ...

It has been acknowledged that some federal legislative powers are concerned with the States specially or contemplate some measure in particular relation to a State or are of such a nature that they may require to be exercised in relation to a particular State, eg, defence power: *Melbourne Corporation* (1947) 74 CLR at 81. Conciliation and arbitration is not such a power ...

Mason J referred to the argument that the Conciliation and Arbitration (Electricity Industry) Act 1985 could not be treated as discriminating against Queensland because it applied to some private employers as well as to Queensland statutory authorities. His Honour continued:

A law may discriminate against a State even if it subjects some others (eg, private employers) as well as agencies of [221] the State to a special burden or disability. In such a situation the true effect of the law may be to isolate the State agency and the private employers from the general law. This, on the assumption that I am presently making, is the effect of the Act. It discriminates against the State of Queensland by singling out disputes to which employers in that State are parties, those employers being for the most part authorities brought into existence by the State to carry out public functions, and then subjecting those disputes to a regime of differential treatment ...

What I have already said leads to the conclusion that ss 8 and 9 of the Act are invalid. As these sections are the principal operative provisions, in each action I would overrule the demurrer and declare that the entire Act is invalid as being beyond power.

Deane J said that, since the decision in *Melbourne Corporation v Commonwealth* (the *State Banking* case) (1947) 74 CLR 31 **[8.2.45C]**, the conclusions of Dixon J about the foundation, rationale and content of the restriction on Commonwealth legislative power had attracted substantial support. Deane J described that restriction, referred to as 'the third reservation', in the following terms:

Deane J: [247] Its central operation is to preclude the exercise of Commonwealth legislative or executive powers 'to control the States' or in a manner which would be inconsistent with the continued existence of the States as independent entities and their capacity to function as such. It is not suggested that that central operation of the reservation applies here. What is relevant to the present case is that the reservation also extends to preclude discriminatory treatment of the States in the sense of the use or exercise by the Commonwealth of such powers to single out the States to place upon them 'special burdens or disabilities' ...

[248] The implication precluding discrimination in the relevant sense against the States or a particular State extends to preclude such discrimination against the agencies through which the States discharge particular governmental functions ...

... To be caught by the reservation, the law must, as has been indicated above, discriminate in the sense that its operation involves a singling out of the States to make them 'the objects of special burdens or disabilities': cf *Melbourne Corporation* (1947) 74 CLR at 81. That is not to say that a law cannot discriminate against the States in the relevant sense if it is cast in general terms and is of apparently general application. Quite apart from the case where such a general law applies to the States in a way which would prevent them from performing their essential functions or which would impede them in so doing (cf per Rich J, *Melbourne Corporation* (1947) 74 CLR at 66; per Walsh J, the *Pay-roll Tax* case (1971) 122 CLR at 411), a general law may operate in the context of particular [249] circumstances to single out the States for discriminatory treatment ... The point may be conveniently illustrated by reference to the *Pay-roll Tax* case. The decision in that case was that Commonwealth legislation imposing a general pay-roll tax to be paid by employers on wages paid to their employees validly applied to the States and their agencies. The fact that the States' pay-rolls were particularly large no doubt meant that the effect of the legislation was particularly onerous in its application to them in the sense that they paid more tax than all or most other employers. That did not, however, mean that the legislation was discriminatory against the States in the sense that it singled them out to be made objects of special burdens or disabilities. On the other hand, if the legislation had been confined to the imposition upon all employers other than the Crown in right of the Commonwealth of liability to pay-roll tax upon wages paid to 'public servants', it might still properly have been seen, as a matter of form, as a law of general application. Such confined legislation would, nonetheless, have discriminated against the States in the relevant sense for the reason that, as a matter of substance, its operation would have been, in circumstances where the States and State instrumentalities were the only non-Commonwealth employers of 'public servants', to single out the States for the imposition of a special burden.

... The fact that the formal operation of a law is to impose a burden or disability upon the States or State instrumentalities by reference to their character as such will ordinarily suffice to establish that, as a matter of substance, the law relevantly discriminates against the States. The failure of a law to operate by reference to such a formal criterion of liability will not, however, preclude a conclusion that, as a matter of substance, the law relevantly so discriminates. That question of substance must ultimately be resolved by reference to the actual operation of the law in the circumstances. If, as a matter of substance, the actual operation of the law is to discriminate against [250] the States or a particular State in the relevant sense, it will be within the scope of the reservation regardless of how disguised the substance may be by ingenious expression or outward form: see per Rich J, *Melbourne Corporation* (1947) 74 CLR at 67; and, generally, *Hematite Petroleum Pty Ltd v Victoria* (1983) 151 CLR 599 at 662–3.

The nature of the reservation as a general implication of the words of the Constitution makes it subject to being overridden by the express words or plain intendment of a specific provision of the Constitution ... It is clear that the nature or subject-matter of a specific grant of legislative power can, in appropriate circumstances, countervail against that operation of the reservation.

Deane J referred to some Commonwealth powers which, because of their 'content, context or subject-matter', would authorise legislation that singled out the states or their instrumentalities to place upon them special burdens or disabilities: acquisition of property on just terms from a particular state (s 51(xxxi)), defence (s 51(vi)), quarantine (s 51(ix)) and medical services such as immunisation (s 51(xxiiiA)). As to the power conferred by s 51(xxxv), 'a singling out of a State or a State instrumentality for discriminatory treatment would ... only be within the intended scope of the legislative power with respect to conciliation and arbitration if it can be seen to be justified as an integral part of a coherent legislative provision with respect to conciliation and arbitration for the prevention or settlement of the particular dispute': 159 CLR at 251–2.

[253] The discriminatory operation of s 6(2) of the Act cannot be justified as itself coming within the intended scope of the grant of legislative power contained in s 51(xxxv). The disputes mentioned in s 6(2) are not existing disputes. They could relate to a wide diversity of matters. The involvement of the electricity authorities in them could be central or peripheral. They could be centred or have their origins in Queensland or in some other State. There is nothing in their designated character which could warrant the conclusion that the discriminatory treatment of the electricity authorities in relation to them was a necessary or integral part of a coherent scheme of conciliation and arbitration for their settlement. There is nothing in the nature of that discriminatory treatment which could properly be seen as bringing it itself within what can be seen, from the content, context or subject-matter of s 51(xxxv), to be the intended scope of that grant of legislative power.

Section 6(1) of the Act stands in contrast of s 6(2). It applies the provisions of the Act to a particular identified interstate industrial dispute: see *R v Ludeke; Ex parte Queensland Electricity Commission* (1985)159 CLR 178. Of itself, s 6(1) makes no distinction between the parties to the dispute. The electricity authorities are not affected by s 6(1) by reason of their being singled out for the imposition of special burdens or disabilities. They are affected by s 6(1) by reason of the fact that they are parties to the particular industrial dispute to which the legislation applies.

~~~

[8.2.60]   Deane J held that ss 6(2), (3), (4) and (5), 8 and 9 of the Act were invalid, and that ss 6(1) and 7, while left with little real function to perform, were valid. Gibbs CJ, Wilson and Dawson JJ held, in separate judgments, that the entire Act was invalid, for substantially the same reasons as Mason J. Brennan J analysed the problem before the court in substantially the same terms as Deane J. He held that, although the Act discriminated against the Queensland electricity authorities, ss 6(1), 7, 8 and 9 were supported by s 51(xxxv) of the Constitution. The Commonwealth Parliament had been 'entitled to make a political assessment that there were distinguishing features of the dispute mentioned in s 6(1) which made the dispute one which required speedy settlement': 159 CLR at 243. However, s 6(2) revealed '[n]o purpose of recurring industrial peace', and its 'imposition of such a discriminatory burden on the electricity authorities of Queensland cannot find support in s 51(xxxv) of the Constitution': 159 CLR at 243. Accordingly, the Act was invalid in its application to disputes mentioned in s 6(2).

The court overruled the demurrer and declared the Conciliation and Arbitration (Electricity Industry) Act 1985 (Cth) invalid.

Notes

[8.2.61]   The court's approach to the validity of the Conciliation and Arbitration (Electricity Industry) Act resolved the explicit ambiguity in both *Melbourne Corporation v Commonwealth* (the *State Banking* case) (1947) 74 CLR 31 **[8.2.45C]** and *Victoria v Commonwealth* (the *Payroll Tax* case) (1971) 122 CLR 353 **[8.2.50C]**. In each of those cases, some members of the court had insisted that Commonwealth legislation which imposed special burdens on the states would be invalid because the legislation could not be characterised as a law with respect to one of the subjects assigned to the Commonwealth Parliament, not because there was any constitutional principle which prevented the Commonwealth from using its legislative powers to discriminate against the states. Implicit in this argument was the proposition that the

Commonwealth legislation could, indeed should, be characterised as dealing with one subject matter and that this characterisation concluded the question of the legislation's validity. See, for example, Latham CJ in the *State Banking* case (74 CLR at 61) and Barwick CJ in the *Payroll Tax* case: 122 CLR at 372–3.

The contrary view in those cases was that Commonwealth legislation could have several aspects: that it could simultaneously be characterised as a law with respect to several subject matters; but that a law otherwise within the power of the Commonwealth Parliament would be invalid if the law singled out the states for special burdens because there was a constitutional rule against such discriminatory legislation. See, for example, Dixon J in the *State Banking* case (74 CLR at 79–80) and Windeyer J in the *Payroll Tax* case: 122 CLR at 403–4.

As Mason and Dawson JJ observed in the *Queensland Electricity Commission* case, the second approach to the characterisation of Commonwealth legislation (recognising that it may relate to several topics) has been endorsed by the broad trend of constitutional decisions: 159 CLR at 215 per Mason J; at 261 per Dawson J.

[8.2.62] At one level, this conflict of approach appeared to be unimportant: the two approaches led to the same result; namely, that Commonwealth legislation aimed at the states would be invalid. However, the conflict has important implications which go beyond the legal relationships between the Commonwealth and the states. In the context of defining the Commonwealth's powers to regulate aspects of the Australian economy and Australian society, putting aside the states' amenability to or immunity from that regulation, the concept of single characterisation supported a relatively narrow approach to the Commonwealth's legislative powers: see, for example, *R v Barger* (1908) 6 CLR 42 **[9.2.15C]**. However, the alternative approach, which accepts that Commonwealth legislation may be characterised as dealing with several subjects, has been used to support a broad reading of the Commonwealth's powers: see, for example, *Fairfax v Commissioner of Taxation* (1965) 114 CLR 1 **[9.2.22C]**; *Actors and Announcers Equity Association v Fontana Films Pty Ltd* (1982) 150 CLR 169 **[10.3.18C]**. This has been done by conceding the validity of Commonwealth legislation so long as at least one of the subjects with which it deals has been designated by the Constitution as a Commonwealth responsibility.

[8.2.63] Returning to the intergovernmental issue at the heart of *Queensland Electricity Commission v Queensland* (1985) 159 CLR 192 **[8.2.59C]**, it should be noted that members of the court conceded that some of the Commonwealth's legislative powers might allow the Commonwealth to aim its restrictive legislation at the states: 159 CLR at 208 per Gibbs CJ; 159 CLR at 219 per Mason J; 159 CLR at 233 per Brennan J; 159 CLR at 250 per Deane J. Indeed, Brennan and Deane JJ invoked this point to uphold the validity of parts of the Conciliation and Arbitration (Electricity Industry) Act. Brennan J referred to s 51(xxxv) of the Constitution as authorising special legislative treatment of a particular industrial dispute, to which a state might be a party, provided that special treatment was afforded because of the character of the dispute, not because the employers were state authorities: 159 CLR at 239. Deane J said that state authorities could be singled out for discriminatory treatment by legislation under s 51(xxxv) if that treatment was part of a coherent legislative provision for the prevention or settlement of a particular industrial dispute: 159 CLR at 251–2.

[8.2.64] Most members of the court in *Queensland Electricity Commission v Queensland* (1985) 159 CLR 192 **[8.2.59C]** made explicit the point which had been implicit in *Melbourne Corporation v Commonwealth* (the *State Banking* case) (1947) 74 CLR 31 **[8.2.45C]**; namely, that the constitutional immunity from discriminatory Commonwealth legislation protected not only the central governmental institutions of the states ('agencies which represent the Crown or the State': 159 CLR at 207 per Gibbs CJ), but all 'agencies of the State, brought into existence for a public purpose': 159 CLR at 218 per Mason J. See also: 159 CLR at 238 per Brennan J; 159 CLR at 225 per Wilson J; 159 CLR at 248 per Deane J.

[8.2.65] Although the *Queensland Electricity Commission* case (1985) 159 CLR 192 **[8.2.59C]** was decided and the Conciliation and Arbitration (Electricity Industry) Act held invalid on the basis of the specific principle, concerning discriminatory Commonwealth laws, enunciated by Dixon J in the *State Banking* case (1947) 74 CLR 31 **[8.2.45C]**, all members of the court expressed support for a more general principle, approximating to the principle proposed by Rich and Starke JJ in the *State Banking* case, concerning general, non-discriminatory Commonwealth legislation.

Gibbs CJ declared that a general law, within the enumerated powers of the Commonwealth, would be invalid 'if it would prevent a State from continuing to exist and function as such': 159 CLR at 206. Mason J, after noting that the Commonwealth could not discriminate against the states, said that there was a second, 'less precise', prohibition on the Commonwealth legislating so that laws of general application operated 'to destroy or curtail the continued existence of the States or their capacity to function as governments': 159 CLR at 217. Wilson J said that, if a Commonwealth law resulted in a threat to the structural integrity of the states, it would 'offend the constitutional implications whether it be a discriminatory law or a law of general application': 159 CLR at 226. Brennan J said that s 106 of the Commonwealth Constitution 'necessarily implied' a prohibition against Commonwealth legislation 'which operate to destroy or curtail the continued existence of the States or their capacity to function as a government, ie their capacity to exercise their powers': 159 CLR at 231.

Deane J referred to a constitutional restraint on the exercise or use of the Commonwealth's powers which precluded the Commonwealth from controlling the states or exercising those powers 'in a matter which would be inconsistent with the continued existence of the States as independent entities and their capacity to function as such': 159 CLR at 247. Dawson J, while recognising that there were 'difficulties inherent in any attempt to formalise the doctrine', said there was a general proposition implicit in the Constitution's federal structure 'that the Commonwealth Parliament cannot impair the capacity of the States to exercise for themselves their constitutional functions': 159 CLR at 260.

[8.2.66] The state of Queensland attempted to invoke this general constraint on Commonwealth legislative power in its second challenge to the validity of several Commonwealth Acts which established the fringe benefits tax. Having failed in an earlier challenge based on s 114 of the Constitution (*Queensland v Commonwealth* (1987) 162 CLR 74 **[8.2.78]**), the state government was given leave to intervene in a later challenge to the legislation: *State Chamber of Commerce and Industry v Commonwealth* (1987) 163 CLR 329. The legislation in question imposed a tax on all employers who provided fringe benefits, other than salary, wages and other financial benefits such as superannuation, to employees. The legislation applied to the states in their capacity as employers, and expressly required the states to pay the tax on benefits provided to state government Ministers, members of state parliaments and judges of state courts, as well as state employees.

The majority of the court, Mason CJ, Wilson, Dawson, Toohey and Gaudron JJ delivered a joint judgment in which they rejected an argument that the legislation discriminated against, or singled out, the states, an argument based on the extension of the state's tax liability to benefits provided to such non-employees as members of parliament, which had no counterpart in the tax imposed on private employers. 'Far from isolating the States for special treatment in the form of a special burden', they said, 'the legislation subjects them, in common with others who pay salary or wages, to liability to pay tax on fringe benefits as part of a comprehensive fringe benefits tax': 163 CLR at 356.

They also rejected an argument based on the following more general principle at 356:

> The alternative contention that the legislation interferes with, impairs or curtails the States in the exercise of their functions of government rests on the view that anything which inhibits a State in establishing the terms and conditions upon which the persons who constitute the organs of government shall be remunerated is an interference with the capacity of the State to govern. The short answer is that the States are subject to the Commonwealth Parliament's exercise of the taxation power; they have no immunity from Commonwealth taxation: the *Pay-roll Tax* case. And, as it is accepted that the imposition of income tax on the salaries of State Ministers, members of parliament and judges is not an infringement of any implied prohibition under the Constitution, it must follow that the imposition of a tax on the States in respect of fringe benefits provided by the States to such persons as part of a general fringe benefits tax on those who pay salaries and wages is not an infringement of the implied prohibition.

Brennan and Deane JJ dissented. Deane J held that the extension of the states' tax liability to fringe benefits paid to persons who were members of parliament imposed a discriminatory burden on the states. Brennan J applied the broader principle. The Governor, the parliament, the ministry and the Supreme Court of a state were 'essential organs of government ... on which the "existence and nature" of the body politic depends': 163 CLR at 362. The rewards paid to the officers of those organs ensured that they could function. A tax on the value of these rewards was 'a tax on what is done to secure the continued existence and functioning of the government of the State': 163 CLR at 363. The state could invoke an 'immunity from a non-discriminatory federal tax ... in protection of the State's freedom to benefit the officers of the essential organs of government and thereby to ensure or facilitate the performance by those organs of their respective functions': 163 CLR at 364.

All members of the court dismissed a challenge to the legislation based on s 55 of the Constitution: see [5.2.31].

[8.2.67] In *South Australia v Commonwealth* (1992) 174 CLR 235, a majority of the High Court (Mason CJ, Deane, Dawson, Toohey and Gaudron JJ; Brennan and McHugh JJ dissenting) held that a Commonwealth income tax levied on the interest derived from the investments of a state instrumentality was not a tax on property within s 114. However, the court was unanimous in holding that an income tax levied by the Commonwealth upon capital gains derived by a state upon the sale of its property was a tax on property belonging to the state within s 114 of the Commonwealth Constitution and, therefore, invalid.

In their joint judgment, Mason CJ, Deane, Toohey and Gaudron JJ said that the immunity from taxation conferred by s 114 was expressed in wide terms; that there were no doubt policy reasons for a broad interpretation of s 114; but that the 'course of judicial decisions' had confined the operation of the section so as to protect the states (and the Commonwealth) against a tax imposed by reason of the ownership or holding of property:

> Accordingly, a tax is properly characterised, for the purposes of s 114, as a 'tax on property' if, and only if, it is imposed upon a taxpayer by reference to a relationship between the taxpayer and the relevant property and the relationship is such that the tax represents a tax on the ownership or holding of the property in question (174 CLR at 248).

Dealing with the income tax imposed by the Commonwealth on interest derived by the State Bank from moneys lent, Mason CJ, Deane, Toohey and Gaudron JJ said at 253:

> In the ultimate analysis the tax is imposed not upon the ownership or holding of property belonging to the taxpayer but upon gains of a revenue kind in the form of interest on money lent derived by the taxpayer in the relevant period, the derivation being ascertained by reference to the conceptions, principles and practices already mentioned. Granted that the taxpayer comes under a liability because he or she derives income which can be identified with a chose in action of which he or she is the owner or holder, nevertheless the true character of the tax is, as the name implies, that of income tax rather than a tax on the ownership or holding of property. The derivation of income by a taxpayer is a subject relevantly different from the ownership or holding of property.

However, a capital gains tax, Mason CJ, Deane, Toohey and Gaudron JJ said, was a tax at 254–5:

> ... imposed on the disposal or deemed disposal of an asset owned by a taxpayer, the tax being effectively imposed upon the net capital gain which accrues to the taxpayer ... [T]he reason for the imposition of the tax is the exercise by the taxpayer of the right of disposition, a right central to the concept of ownership of property. Furthermore, the capital gains tax imposed by the Act has the additional element already mentioned, namely, that the amount of the capital gain is computed by reference to the length of time during which the taxpayer has been the owner of the asset. Viewed in this light, the tax is a tax on the ownership or holding of property belonging to the taxpayer.

[8.2.68] A further attempt to invoke the general principle, which was said to protect the states from certain non-discriminatory Commonwealth laws, was made in *Richardson v Forestry Commission* (1988) 164 CLR 261. The case involved an attack on the validity of the Lemonthyme and Southern Forests (Commission of Inquiry) Act 1987 (Cth), which prohibited a wide range of activities in two areas of Tasmania pending the completion of an inquiry to determine whether the areas constituted, or contributed to, a world heritage area within the Convention for the Protection of the World Cultural and Natural Heritage. (The question whether s 51(xxix), the external affairs power, supported the Act is considered at **[3.3.34C]**.) The areas in question covered 283,300 hectares, about 4.5 per cent of Tasmania's land surface. Almost all the land was owned by the state of Tasmania. The state argued that the legislation should be seen as discriminating against the state; and that, even if it was not discriminatory, it impaired the legislative and executive functions of the state and its prerogatives in relation to Crown lands.

The court dealt first with the discrimination argument. It said that the legislation could not be said to single out Tasmania in the sense proscribed by such decisions as

Melbourne Corporation v Commonwealth (the *State Banking* case) (1947) 74 CLR 31 **[8.2.45C]** and *Queensland Electricity Commission v Queensland* (1985) 159 CLR 192 **[8.2.59C]**. The obligation created by the Convention to protect areas of world heritage significance 'necessarily falls to be discharged with respect to particular properties'; and to protect those properties did 'not invalidly discriminate against the State in whose territory the property is situated': 164 CLR at 294 per Mason CJ and Brennan J; see also 164 CLR at 305 per Wilson J; 164 CLR at 337 per Toohey J.

The alternative argument, that the legislation impaired the state's legislative and executive functions was also rejected by those members of the court who considered it. Wilson J said that, despite the size of the affected area, there was 'no warrant for invoking an implied limitation' on the Commonwealth's express legislative powers, bearing in mind the limited duration of Commonwealth control and the scope which was left for the exercise of ordinary governmental functions on the part of Tasmania: 164 CLR at 305. Toohey J said the Act did not impair the state's existence or capacity to function. The most which could be said was that it prohibited certain conduct on the land in question for a limited time: 164 CLR at 337.

[8.2.69] In *Australian Capital Television Pty Ltd v Commonwealth* (1992) 177 CLR 106 **[11.3.7C]**, it was contended that s 95D(3) and (4) of the Broadcasting Act 1942 (Cth) were invalid because they interfered with the essential governmental functions of the states, again relying on the general principle. The provisions imposed a regime of controls on the use of electronic media for political advertising during, and for the purposes of, state and local government elections.

McHugh J upheld the challenge, and held that s 95D(3) and (4) constituted 'an interference with the functions of the state as an independent body politic': 177 CLR at 244. His Honour said at 242:

> [T]he powers of the Commonwealth do not extend to interfering in the constitutional and electoral processes of the States. It is for the people of the State, and not for the people of the Commonwealth, to determine what modifications, if any, should be made to the Constitution of the State and to the electoral processes which determine what government the State is to have. The use of a Commonwealth power to make a law which 'discloses an immediate object of controlling' the processes by which the people of the States elect their governments in accordance with their Constitutions should be seen as not 'within the true ambit of the Commonwealth legislative power'.

Brennan J also held these provisions to be invalid. In his Honour's view, they offended against the implication which protected the functioning of the states from the burden of control by Commonwealth law at 163–4:

> The functions of a State include both the machinery which leads to the exercise of the State's powers and privileges and the machinery by which those powers and privileges are exercised. Some functions are performed by the electors, some by the officials of the State. Among the functions of the State I would include the discussion of political matters by electors, the formation of political judgments and the casting of votes for the election of a parliament or local authority. Laws which affect the freedom of political discussion in matters relating to the government of a State, whether by enhancement or restriction of the freedom, are laws which burden the functioning of the political branches of the government of the State with statutory constraints and restrictions.

Dawson J held that the restrictions on political advertising did not threaten or endanger the continued functioning of the states, or unduly impair their capacity to perform their constitutional functions: 177 CLR at 202. The remaining members of the court (Mason CJ, Deane, Toohey and Gaudron JJ) expressed no opinions on the question, holding the legislation invalid for other reasons: see **[11.3.7C]**.

[8.2.70] The stated purpose of this general principle is to protect the continued existence and independence of the states. In so far as the concern is to protect the independence of the state so that, as Gibbs J said in *Victoria v Commonwealth* (the *Payroll Tax* case) (1971) 122 CLR 353 at 424 **[8.2.50C]**, the capacity of the states to function as independent units will not depend upon the manner in which the Commonwealth exercises its powers, is that concern consistent with the decisions in the *Uniform Tax* cases? In those cases the High Court held that the Commonwealth's grants power, in s 96 of the Constitution, authorised the making of grants by the Commonwealth to the states on any condition including the condition that the states refrain from exercising their powers in a manner specified by the Commonwealth: *South Australia v Commonwealth* (1942) 65 CLR 373 (see **[9.6.3C]**); *Victoria v Commonwealth* (1975) 99 CLR 575: see **[9.6.8C]**. Have not the *Uniform Tax* cases made the general principle otiose and irrelevant? How are the states independent when their legislative and governmental action can be controlled by conditions attached to Commonwealth grants of money on which the states are now dependent?

It is difficult to formulate a reasonably precise and judicially manageable formula stating the conditions in which states will be protected from general non-discriminatory Commonwealth legislation. This difficulty might be taken to indicate that the process of limiting the use of Commonwealth legislative power over the states ought to be a political rather than a judicial process. In the *Engineers'* case (1920) 28 CLR 129 **[8.2.31C]**, the majority said at 151:

> But the extravagant use of the granted powers in the actual working of the Constitution is a matter to be guarded against by the constituencies and not by the courts. When the people of Australia, to use the words of the Constitution itself united in a federal Commonwealth they took power to control by ordinary constitutional means any attempt on the part of the national Parliament to misuse its powers.

[8.2.71] The difficulty in formulating a precise and judicially manageable formula for the conditions in which states are protected from general, non-discriminatory Commonwealth legislation is illustrated by the High Court's decision in *Australian Education Union and Australian Nursing Federation; Ex parte Victoria* (1995) 184 CLR 188 **[8.2.72C]**, where the general principle articulated by Rich and Starke JJ in *Melbourne Corporation v Commonwealth* (the *State Banking* case) **[8.2.45C]** was again invoked, but this time with some success.

[8.2.72C]   **Re Australian Education Union and Australian Nursing Federation; Ex parte Victoria**

(1995) 184 CLR 188

Following a general election in October 1992 in Victoria, the newly-elected government introduced radical changes to the state's industrial relations system. At the same time, the government made offers of voluntary redundancy payments to a large number of public sector employees, whose employment was then covered by state industrial awards. Several trade unions, representing public sector employees, in response filed logs of claims against the state of Victoria and other states in the Commonwealth Industrial Relations Commission, with the objective of obtaining federal awards to govern the employment of their members. The Commission found that there were industrial disputes between the trade unions and the states, extending beyond the limits of one state.

The state of Victoria applied to the High Court for orders of prohibition and certiorari to prevent the Commission from deciding the disputes. The Commonwealth and the states of Tasmania, South Australia, New South Wales and Queensland intervened. The principal argument advanced by the states was that the Commonwealth, through the Commission, could not direct the states as to whom they should employ or cease to employ and could not set the terms and conditions of employment of state employees engaged in carrying out the functions of government. McHugh J referred the applications for orders of prohibition and certiorari to the Full Court of the High Court.

Mason CJ, Brennan, Deane, Toohey, Gaudron and McHugh J affirmed the proposition that s 51(xxxv) could extend to the states (184 CLR at 222); and referred to the existence of the 'administrative services exception' and said that it might be based upon the general implied limitation on Commonwealth legislative power: 184 CLR at 224.

Mason CJ, Brennan, Deane, Toohey, Gaudron and McHugh J: [224] It is convenient to examine first the relationship between the limitation and the power conferred by s 51(xxxv) of the Constitution, leaving the scope and content of the limitation for later consideration. In *Re Lee; Ex parte Harper*, Mason, Brennan and Deane JJ stated ((1986) 160 CLR 430 at 453):

> Although the purpose of the implied limitations is to impose some limit on the exercise of Commonwealth power in the interest of preserving the existence of the states as constituent elements in the federation, the implied limitations must be read subject to the express provisions of the Constitution. Where a head of Commonwealth power, on its true construction, authorizes legislation the effect of which is to interfere with the exercise by the states of their [225] powers to regulate a particular subject-matter, there can be no room for the application of the implied limitations.

In the *SPSF* case, the relationship between the implied limitation and the power was expressed in slightly different terms. Mason CJ, Deane and Gaudron JJ said (1993) 178 CLR 249 at 271–2:

> [W]e should point out that the statement made in *Re Lee; Ex parte Harper* (1986) 160 CLR 430 at 453, per Mason, Brennan and Deane JJ, that the implied limitations must be read subject to the express provisions of the Constitution, should not be understood as excluding consideration of implications derived from the Constitution until the scope of s 51(xxxv) is ascertained by reference to its terms alone. Rather, the scope of that provision must be ascertained by reference not only to its text but also to its subject-matter and the entire context of the Constitution, including any implications to be derived from its general structure.

Mason CJ, Brennan, Deane, Toohey, Gaudron and McHugh JJ quoted observations by Brennan J in the *State Public Service Federation* case (1993) 178 CLR 249 at 274–5, to the effect that 'implications derived from the general structure of the Constitution may qualify express provisions conferring legislative power'; and 'the construction of a head of legislative power is itself ascertained by reference to the entire context of the Constitution and ... its scope may be limited by implication'. The justices continued:

> The correct approach to the question is that stated in the passages just quoted ...

Although the comments of Dixon J [in *Melbourne Corporation v Commonwealth* (the *State Banking* case) (1947) 74 CLR 31 **[8.2.45C]** at 79–80] were couched principally in terms of discrimination against states and the imposition of a particular disability or burden upon an operation or activity of a state or the execution of its constitutional powers, his Honour clearly had in mind, as did Latham CJ, Rich and Starke JJ, that the legislative powers of the Commonwealth cannot be exercised to destroy or curtail the existence of the states or their continuing to function as such. Whether this means that there are two implied limitations, two elements or branches of one limitation, or simply one limitation is a question which does not need to be decided in this case. However, for convenience, we shall proceed on the footing that the limitation has two elements, the non-discriminatory element having a particular relevance to the argument now being considered ...

[228] The prosecutor submitted that the statements in the *Tasmanian Dam* case, when they refer to impairment of a state's capacity 'to function as a government', extend to any impairment of capacity to exercise government functions. The prosecutor's submission is not

in accordance with the natural meaning of the words used. Nor does it accord with the substance of the views expressed in a number of judgments in which the implied limitation has been discussed …

Mason CJ, Brennan, Deane, Toohey, Gaudron and McHugh JJ discussed the view of Latham CJ in the *State Banking* case (1947) 74 CLR 31 **[8.2.45C]**, which referred to 'functions or activities essential to the existence of government' as including the raising of money by taxation and provision for the custody, management and disposition of public revenue moneys; the power of borrowing money, of providing for the custody and expenditure of loan moneys and making provision for the custody and expenditure of public moneys by using a bank. They referred to *Re Tracey; Ex parte Ryan* (1989) 166 CLR 518 and the view that state courts are an essential branch of the government. Finally they noted that in *Victoria v Commonwealth* (the *Payroll Tax* case) (1971) 122 CLR 353 **[8.2.50C]**, Menzies J had used a 'narrower expression', namely the 'constitutional functions of government'.

In our view, the prosecutor's submission on this point is against the weight of modern authority and draws a distinction which is unsatisfactory. To say that the limitation protects the existence of the states and their capacity to function as a government is to give effect more accurately to the constitutional foundation for the implied limitation identified by Dixon J in the passages earlier quoted from *Australian Railways Union*, including s 106 of the Constitution. To press the limitation as far as the prosecutor seeks to take it would travel beyond the language of s 106 and would confer protection on [230] the exercise of powers by the states to an extent which is inconsistent with the subordination of those powers to the powers of the Commonwealth through the operation of s 109 of the Constitution. And the argument, if successful, would protect a substantial part of a state's workforce from the impact of federal awards, notwithstanding that the operation of those awards in relation to school teachers, health workers and other categories of employees would not destroy or curtail the existence of the state or its capacity to function as a government.

The fact is that the existence of the states and their Constitutions and their capacity to function as governments would not be impaired by the operation of federal awards made in respect of the vast majority of the employees sought to be covered by the logs of claims, at any rate if the award provisions were confined to minimum wages and working conditions which take appropriate account of any special functions or responsibilities which attach to them. The freedom of state governments to determine terms and conditions of employment of employees would be restricted but that is a consequence of the application of the arbitration power to states. Whether the making of a comprehensive award would result in a relevant impairment is another question which we leave for later discussion.

We are unable to accept the distinction which the prosecutor drew between 'governmental functions' and trading functions. The argument was that states function as a government when carrying out public functions for a public purpose. On this view, health, education and police functions are governmental functions. Indeed, it is difficult to see why, on this view, trading functions are not governmental, if they are undertaken by government in the public interest. The distinction is unsatisfactory for that reason.

Mason CJ, Brennan, Deane, Toohey, Gaudron and McHugh JJ rejected the argument advanced by the states that their 'administrative services' were protected against Commonwealth regulation: the exception, the justices said, was based on a concept that was 'difficult to define or describe': 184 CLR at 230–1.

The justices then described an argument, advanced by the Solicitor-General for South Australia, as having 'some force'. The argument was 'that the implied limitation protects the integrity or autonomy of a state' by protecting 'internal services [such as] policy formulation, reporting to Parliament, the collection and administration of government revenue and the provision of services to Parliament and the judiciary', but did not protect 'external services': 184 CLR at 231.

[231] *(g) Conclusion with respect to the scope and content of the implied limitation*

Our rejection of the particular submissions made by the prosecutor and supporting interveners other than that advanced by South Australia as to the scope and content of the implied limitation leads us, subject to consideration of one gloss put forward by the prosecutor, to express the scope and content of the limitation in this way. The limitation consists of two elements: (1) the prohibition against discrimination which involves the placing on the states of special burdens or disabilities ('the limitation against discrimination') and (2) the prohibition against laws of general application which operate to destroy or curtail the continued existence of the states or their capacity to function as governments [*Queensland Electricity Commission* (1985) 159 CLR 192 at 217, per Mason J] ...

[232] At this point it is convenient to consider South Australia's argument based on impairment of a state's 'integrity' or autonomy'. Although these concepts as applied to a state are by no means precise, they direct attention to aspects of a state's functions which are critical to its capacity to function as a government. It seems to us that critical to that capacity of a state is the government's right to determine the number and identity of the persons whom it wishes to employ, the term of appointment of such persons and, as well, the number and identity of the persons whom it wishes to dismiss with or without notice from its employment on redundancy grounds. An impairment of a state's rights in these respects would, in our view, constitute an infringement of the implied limitation. On this view, the prescription by a federal award of minimum wages and working conditions would not infringe the implied limitation, at least if it takes appropriate account of any special functions or responsibilities which attach to the employees in question. There may be a question, in some areas of **[233]** employment, whether an award regulating promotion and transfer would amount to an infringement. That is a question which need not be considered. As with other provisions in a comprehensive award, the answer would turn on matters of degree, including the character and responsibilities of the employee.

In our view, also critical to a state's capacity to function as a government is its ability, not only to determine the number and identity of those whom it wishes to engage at the higher levels of government, but also to determine the terms and conditions on which those persons shall be engaged. Hence, Ministers, ministerial assistants and advisers, heads of departments and high level statutory office holders, parliamentary officers and judges would clearly fall within this group. The implied limitation would protect the states from the exercise by the Commission of power to fix minimum wages and working conditions in respect of such persons and possibly others as well. And, in any event, Ministers and judges are not employees of a state ...

However, the rejection of the arguments put forward by the prosecutor and the intervening states — arguments which would have given the implied limitation a wide-ranging operation — means that the Commission has power to make awards binding the states and their agencies in relation to minimum wages and working conditions which take account of the special functions and responsibilities, if any, of a broad range of public servants and employees, including many **[234]** members of the SPSF. On the other hand, as we have indicated, the operation of the implied limitation would preclude the Commission from making an award binding the states in relation to qualifications and eligibility for employment, term of appointment and termination of employment, at least on the ground of redundancy. It would also preclude the Commission from making an award binding the states in relation to the terms and conditions of employment or engagement of persons such as Ministers, ministerial assistants and advisers, heads of department and senior office holders — as well as parliamentary officers and judges ...

Mason CJ, Brennan, Deane, Toohey, Gaudron and McHugh JJ found that the requirement that the relevant industrial dispute extended beyond the limits of one state was satisfied: 184 CLR at 235–8. They then considered whether s 111(1A) of the legislation was discriminatory under *Queensland Electricity Commission* (1985) 159 CLR 192 **[8.2.59C]**. The effect of s 111(1A) was to preclude the Commonwealth Conciliation and Arbitration Commission from exercising its powers in s 111(1)(g) to dismiss or refrain from hearing matters when proceedings were not necessary or desirable in the public interest. The new subsection was inserted after a system of individual employment agreements had been introduced in Victoria to replace the old system of compulsory arbitration.

[239] The prosecutor submitted that s 111(1A) discriminates against Victoria and employers and employees in that state by denying them recourse to s 111(1)(g). The new provision is said to discriminate against Victoria and any other state that enacts similar legislation; alternatively, it is said that the legislation is aimed at Victoria.

No doubt the events which had recently taken place in Victoria, particularly the enactment of the Victorian legislation, were the occasion for the introduction of s 111(1A) but that is not enough to justify characterization of the provision as one which is aimed at Victoria. The provision is framed in general terms and is capable of applying to any state which introduces a system similar to the Victorian system. The fact that Victoria is the only state presently affected by s 111(1A) is not a compelling consideration, though it could conceivably be so in the absence of a rational and relevant connection between the basis on which that provision denies access, the application of s 111(1)(g) and the exercise of the powers conferred by the last-mentioned provision ...

[240] ... If the view be taken, as it has been taken by the Commonwealth Parliament that, in the public interest, industrial disputes should be resolved by means of compulsory arbitration, it is logical for the Parliament to conclude that a power given to the Commission to refrain from proceeding where it is in the public interest to do so should only be exercisable when an alternative system of compulsory arbitration is available. Further, the introduction of s 111(1A) can be supported on the ground that it eliminated or alleviated problems that would arise once state compulsory arbitration was no longer available. Applications under s 111(1)(g) would involve delay, even if the Commission decided to proceed due to the absence of compulsory arbitration. And, if the Commission were to decline to proceed and leave the dispute to voluntary arbitration, interstate industrial disputes might not be resolved satisfactorily.

~~~

[8.2.73] Dawson J dissented for two reasons. First, he found that the disputes under consideration did not extend beyond the limits of one state because they were disputes between a state government and its employees: 184 CLR at 249. Secondly, Dawson J rejected two distinctions which were critical to the judgment of the majority: he rejected the coherence of any distinction between the number and identity of employees, and their terms and conditions of employment and therefore did not accept, as did the majority, that the latter could be regulated and the former could not; and he rejected as 'artificial' any distinction between higher level and lower level employees: 184 CLR at 249–50.

[8.2.74] In *Victoria v Commonwealth* (the *Industrial Relations* case) (1996) 187 CLR 416 **[3.3.40C]**, the court relied on the discrimination aspect of *Melbourne Corporation v Commonwealth* (the *State Banking* case) (1947) 74 CLR 31 **[8.2.45C]**, when upholding Commonwealth legislation which introduced numerous changes to the industrial relations system, including: a minimum wage 'safety net' for employees not covered by an award (state or Commonwealth) or by an agreement which prevailed over an award; protection against unfair dismissal; parental leave; and equal pay provisions.

In a joint judgment, the majority (Brennan CJ, Toohey, Gaudron, McHugh and Gummow JJ), relied on s 15A of the Acts Interpretation Act 1901 (Cth) to read down provisions in the Industrial Relations Act 1988 (Cth) which purported to regulate the terms and conditions of high level employees, so that they did not regulate those employees. In relation to those provisions in Div 1 or Pt VIA of the Act which established a minimum wage for employees who were not protected by an award or an agreement which prevailed over an award, the justices said they were not discriminatory. The criteria upon which persons were to be subject to a minimum wage order 'bear a real and rational relationship with the general system of wage fixation as it has developed in this country' and the provisions did not 'necessarily operate with a different impact' on Western Australia: 187 CLR at 500.

[8.2.75C]   **Austin v Commonwealth**
(2003) 195 ALR 321

In August 1996, the Commonwealth Government announced its intention to impose a 15% surcharge on superannuation contributions made by or on behalf of members of superannuation funds. Legislation to give effect to that policy was enacted early in 1997, imposing a tax liability, not on the recipient of superannuation, but on the superannuation provider. That legislation (referred to here as the Surcharge Legislation) was expressed not to apply so as to impose a tax on property of any kind belonging to a state within s 114 of the Constitution. (As to s 114, see **[8.2.78]–[8.2.79]**.) Towards the end of 1997, legislation to extend the superannuation surcharge to 'members of constitutionally protected superannuation funds' was enacted: the Superannuation Contributions Tax (Members of Constitutionally Protected Superannuation Funds) Imposition Act 1997 (Cth) and the Superannuation Contributions Tax (Members of Constitutionally Protected Superannuation Funds) Assessment and Collection Act 1997 (Cth) (referred to here as the Protected Funds Surcharge Legislation).

The members of the constitutionally protected superannuation funds included state judicial officers. In New South Wales and Victoria, retirement benefits were provided out of public funds, in the form of a non-contributory pension, equal to 60% of the current judicial salary, for which a judge qualified after 10 years' service and after attaining a specified age (60 in NSW, 65 in Victoria).

Whereas the Surcharge Legislation imposed liability to pay the annual surcharge on superannuation providers and calculated the surcharge by reference to the amount of annual superannuation contributions, the Protected Funds Surcharge Legislation imposed liability to pay the surcharge upon members of the constitutionally protected superannuation funds — relevantly, on state judicial officers. The Surcharge Legislation set the amount of the annual surcharge for each judicial officer by reference to a figure calculated by an actuary to reflect the value of the pension to which the judicial officer was entitled on retirement. Payment of the surcharge was deferred until the judicial officer retired but its quantum continued to increase each year, so that, as Gaudron, Gummow and Hayne JJ observed, the amount of the surcharge would continue to grow while the judicial officer remained in service after the time that her or his right to retire with a full pension had accrued, and the increase in the total amount of the surcharge would continue even though the worth of the pension was diminishing because the pension would be payable for a shorter period of time: 195 ALR 321 at [90].

Judicial office-holders in New South Wales (Justice Austin of that state's Supreme Court) and Victoria (Master Kings of that state's Supreme Court) commenced proceedings in the High Court challenging the validity of the Protected Funds Surcharge Legislation.

Gleeson J agreed with Gaudron, Gummow and Hayne JJ that the first plaintiff (Justice Austin) was liable to pay the superannuation surcharge, but the second plaintiff (Master Kings) was not. He said that the feature of the Acts of greatest significance to a judge in the position of the first plaintiff was the incurring and accumulation of a liability to pay a substantial capital sum, on retirement, in discharge of an accrued superannuation contributions surcharge debt, at a time when payment of his pension commenced. Federal judges faced a reduction in the amount of their periodical pension payments, other high income earners incurred no personal liability; 'the difference', Gleeson CJ said 'is obvious': 195 CLR 321 at [14]. His Honour then observed that one of the most striking differences between *Melbourne Corporation v Commonwealth* (1947) 74 CLR 31 **[8.2.45C]** and the *Engineers* case (1920) 28 CLR 129 **[8.2.31C]**, was the approach to United States authority.

Gleeson CJ: [19] ... In the joint judgment of Knox CJ, Isaacs, Rich and Starke JJ in the *Engineers' Case* there was an emphatic and, it might be thought, extravagant rejection of the possibility of guidance from that source: (1920) 28 CLR 129 at 147. Yet in *Melbourne Corporation* all the judgments paid careful attention to United States authority. Both nations have what Latham CJ described as 'a constitution establishing not only a federal Government with specified and limited powers, but also state governments which, in respect of such powers as they possess under the Constitution, are not subordinate to the federal Parliament or Government': (1947) 74 CLR 31 at 50. Such a constitution necessarily gives rise to a problem as to whether, and to what extent, a federal law, which on its face is a law with respect to a subject of federal legislative power, may burden or affect a state government.

After referring in detail to Dixon J's judgment in *Melbourne Corporation* and the judgments of Brennan and Deane JJ in *Queensland Electricity Commission v Commonwealth* (1985) 159 CLR 192 **[8.2.59C]**, Gleeson CJ continued:

[24] Discrimination is an aspect of a wider principle; and what constitutes relevant and impermissible discrimination is determined by that wider principle. In *Queensland Electricity Commission* (1947) 74 CLR 31 at 218, Mason J, in the course of explaining why the implied limitation on Commonwealth powers applies in relation to state agencies as well as states, said that the foundation for the implication is 'the constitutional conception of the Commonwealth and the states as constituent entities of the federal compact having a continuing existence reflected in a central government and separately organized state governments'. Federal legislation that would be inconsistent with that conception includes, but is not limited to, legislation aimed at the destruction of the states or state agencies, or of one or more of their governmental attributes or capacity. Dawson J expressed the general proposition that arises by implication from the federal structure of the Constitution as being that 'the Commonwealth Parliament cannot impair the capacity of the states ... to function effectually as independent units': (1985) 159 CLR 192 at 260. He regarded discrimination, and the placing of a special burden on the states by a law of general application, as two examples of potential contravention of that limitation on power. A law which singles out a state or state agency may have as its object to restrict, burden or control state activity: (1985) 159 CLR 192 at 207 per Gibbs CJ. Or a law of general application may so interfere with or impede state activity as to impose an impermissible burden on the exercise of its functions. It is not possible to state exhaustively every form of exercise of Commonwealth legislative power that might be contrary to the general proposition stated above. Just as the concept of discrimination needs to be understood in the light of the general principle, so also does the concept of burden. The adverse financial impact on the states of the pay-roll tax, or the fringe benefits tax, both of which were held valid, far exceeded the financial consequences of the laws held invalid in *Melbourne Corporation* or *Queensland Electricity Commission*. It was the disabling effect on state authority that was the essence of the invalidity in those cases. It is the impairment of constitutional status, and interference with capacity to function as a government, rather than the imposition of a financial burden, that is at the heart of the matter, although there may be cases where the imposition of a financial burden has a broader significance.

Gleeson CJ said that *Re Australian Education Union; Ex parte Victoria* provided 'an illustration of a Commonwealth law of general application which operated to impair the capacity of the states to function as governments' (195 ALR 321 at [25]); and noted that the same principle formed the ground of Starke J's judgment in *Melbourne Corporation*: 195 ALR 321 at [26]. Gleeson CJ continued:

[28] It is plain, and was accepted in the *Australian Education Union Case*, that quite apart from the consideration that they are not employees, the conciliation and arbitration power does not extend to enable the Parliament directly or indirectly to dictate to the states the terms and conditions of engagement of judges. An attempt to do so would be an impermissible

interference with the capacity of states to function as governments. For the same reason, the Parliament's power to make laws with respect to taxation does not extend to enable it to legislate to single out state judges for the imposition of a special fiscal burden. Judges, like other citizens, are subject to general, non-discriminatory taxation, and the mere fact that the incidence of taxation has a bearing upon the amount and form of remuneration they receive does not mean that federal taxation of state judges is an interference with state governmental functions. It is otherwise when, as here, a federal law with respect to taxation treats state judges differently from the general run of high income earners and federal judges, and to their practical disadvantage. That differential treatment is constitutionally impermissible, not because of any financial burden it imposes upon the states, but because of its interference with arrangements made by states for the remuneration of their judges. The practical manifestation of that interference is in its capacity to affect recruitment and retention of judges to perform an essential constitutional function of the state. Evidence of that capacity is to be found in the legislative response which the state of New South Wales was, in effect, forced to make. The Parliament could never have compelled the state of New South Wales to alter the design of its judicial pension scheme. Indeed, at the time of the Acts, the state judicial pension scheme was not materially different from the federal judicial pension scheme. But the state scheme was substantially altered as a result of the practical necessity that followed from the subjection of state judges to a discriminatory federal tax.

[29] The validity of the Acts is to be determined as at the time of their enactment. They were not rendered valid by subsequent state legislative action. However, the Commonwealth argues that any burden on the state of New South Wales, in consequence of the fiscal imposition on its judges, could be, and was, ameliorated by legislation of the kind that was subsequently enacted by the state. For the reasons already given, it is not a question of any financial burden on the states. Judges are relatively few in number, and the arrangements made for their remuneration are not of major significance in any government budget. The issue is one of interference; of impairment of the constitutional integrity of a state government. Such interference is not denied by pointing out that a state could and did make a substantial alteration to the design of its judicial pension scheme; on the contrary, the need to make such alteration demonstrates the interference.

Responding to the Commonwealth's argument that it was necessary to impose the surcharge directly on state judges because s 114 of the Constitution prevented the Commonwealth taxing the states in their capacity of provider of superannuation benefits to judges, Gleeson CJ said:

[30] ... Section 114 is a particular instance, covered by express prohibition, of federal taxation inconsistent with the federal nature of the Constitution. What would otherwise be covered by the implied prohibition recognised in Melbourne Corporation and other cases cannot be justified on the ground that it is an indirect means of achieving that which is prohibited by s 114.

Gaudron, Gummow and Hayne JJ held that the Protected Funds Surcharge Legislation made the first plaintiff (Justice Austin) liable to pay the surcharge; and turned to challenge to the validity of that Legislation based upon principles said to be derived from Melbourne Corporation v Commonwealth (1947) 74 CLR 31 [8.2.45C].

Gaudron, Gummow and Hayne JJ: [123] At some stages in the argument in the present case it was suggested to be sufficient to render the legislation invalid in its application to the first plaintiff and other state judicial officers that the legislation treated them differently to beneficiaries under the unfunded private sector schemes ... and differently from Ch III judges, by imposing the taxation liability upon them rather than the provider of the benefits. This differential treatment was said, without more, to attract the Melbourne Corporation doctrine; the like was treated as the unlike and thereby the states were burdened in a 'special way'. That would appear to give 'discrimination' a standing on its own which in this field of discourse it does not have.

[124] There is, in our view, but one limitation, though the apparent expression of it varies with the form of the legislation under consideration. The question presented by the doctrine in any given case requires assessment of the impact of particular laws by such criteria as 'special burden' and 'curtailment' of 'capacity' of the states 'to function as governments'. These criteria are to be applied by consideration not only of the form but also 'the substance and actual operation' of the federal law: *Re Australian Education Union; Ex parte Victoria* (1995) 184 CLR 188 at 240; *Queensland Electricity Commission v Commonwealth* (1985) 159 CLR 192 at 249–50; *Industrial Relations Act Case* (1996) 187 CLR 416 at 500. Further, this inquiry inevitably turns upon matters of evaluation and degree and of 'constitutional facts' which are not readily established by objective methods in curial proceedings ...

The scope of the doctrine

[125] In *Queensland Electricity* (1985) 159 CLR 192 at 260, in a passage with which we respectfully agree, Dawson J referred to these difficulties as inherent in any attempt to formalise the *Melbourne Corporation* doctrine and added:

> These difficulties explain why there has been a preference to speak in terms of those aspects of legislation which may evidence breach of the doctrine rather than to generalize in terms of the doctrine itself. Discrimination against the states or their agencies may point to breach as may a special burden placed upon the states by a law of general application.

The reasoning in the foundation decisions, and that in the contemporary United States cases, bears out the view later taken by Dawson J in this passage.

Gaudron, Gummow and Hayne JJ referred to *Essendon Corporation v Criterion Theatres Ltd* (1947) 74 CLR 1 **[8.2.90C]**; *Melbourne Corporation v Commonwealth* (the *State Banking* case) (1947) 74 CLR 31 **[8.2.45C]**; and continued:

[130] Thereafter, in *Bank of NSW v Commonwealth* (the *Banking Case*) [(1948) 76 CLR 1], Dixon J distinguished between (a) a federal law of general application which the states must take as they find it as part of a system enjoyed by the whole community, if they wish to avail themselves of the services or facilities regulated or determined by that federal law; [Later, in *Commonwealth v Cigamatic Pty (in liq)* (1962) 108 CLR 372 at 378, Dixon CJ made the corresponding point respecting the choice by the executive arm of the Commonwealth to enter into sale of goods transactions, a field where the states had enacted laws of general application.] (b) a law which discriminates against the states and in that way singles them out in order to curtail their freedom in the execution of their constitutional powers; and (c) laws which, without discriminating against the states and singling them out, nevertheless operate against them in such a way as to be beyond federal power. The *Banking Case* fell into category (a); *Melbourne Corporation* fell into category (b); and, with respect to category (c), Dixon J referred to the discussion in *New York v United States* 326 US 572 (1946).

Gaudron, Gummow and Hayne JJ referred to *Helvering v Gerhardt* 304 US 405 (1938); *Graves v New York; Ex rel O'Keefe* 306 US 466 (1930); *New York v United States* 326 US 572 (1946); returned to the judgments of Starke J, Rich J, Latham CJ and Dixon J in *Melbourne Corporation*; and continued:

[139] It follows from the reasoning in these judgments in *Melbourne Corporation* that invalidity does not necessarily attend any federal law which requires a state in the performance of its functions to bear a burden or to suffer a disability to which others are not subject. That was the conclusion reached by Brennan J in *Queensland Electricity* (1985) 159 CLR 192 at 233 after consideration of what had been said, not only by Sir Owen Dixon in *Melbourne Corporation* and in *Victoria v Commonwealth* (1957) 99 CLR 575 at 609, but by Williams J in the latter case: (1957) 99 CLR 575 at 609; and by Barwick CJ and Gibbs J in the *Pay-roll Tax Case*, *Victoria v Commonwealth* (1971) 122 CLR 353 at 375, 426 respectively.

Taxation

[140] Special considerations arise where it is the reach of the federal legislative power with respect to taxation that is in question ...

[141] ... following the *Pay-roll Tax Case* and *The Second Fringe Benefits Tax Case, State Chamber of Commerce and Industry v Commonwealth* (1987) 163 CLR 329, it cannot be said that the imposition upon the states of a tax of general application necessarily imposes some special burden or disability upon them so that the law may be described as one aimed at the restriction or control of the states. In the *Pay-roll Tax Case*, the point was explained as follows by Gibbs J (1971) 122 CLR 353 at 425:

> Although in some cases it may be possible to show that the nature of a tax on a particular activity, such as the employment of servants, renders the continuance of that activity practically impossible, it has not been shown that the tax in the present case prevents the states from employing civil servants or operates as a substantial impediment to their employment. The tax has now been imposed upon and paid by the states for nearly thirty years, and it has not been shown to have prevented the states from discharging their functions or to have impeded them in so doing. They may have less money available for public purposes because they have to pay the tax, but that could be said in every case in which a tax is imposed on the states, and in itself it cannot amount to an impediment against state activity sufficient to invalidate the tax.

[142] It might have been thought that the constitutional text itself, particularly in s 114, dealt exhaustively with that measure of immunity conferred with respect to federal taxation. Indeed, in some respects, s 114 would protect the states against imposts in circumstances which attract the operation of the *Melbourne Corporation* doctrine: *SGH Ltd v Commissioner of Taxation* (2002) 76 ALJR 780 at 789–791 [45]–[55]; 188 ALR 241 at 253–256, fn168. Nevertheless, the emphasis by Dixon J in *Melbourne Corporation* (1947) 74 CLR 31 at 80 respecting the lack of ingenuity needed to burden the exercise of state functions by use of the taxation power has led to a general acceptance that, while the states enjoy no general immunity from the exercise of that power, federal laws which do not fall within the prohibition in s 114 nevertheless may fall foul of the *Melbourne Corporation* doctrine.

Queensland Electricity

[143] To fix separately upon laws addressed to one or more of the states and upon laws of so-called 'general application', and to present the inquiry as differing in nature dependent upon the form taken by laws enacted under the one head of power, tends to favour form over substance. The substance is provided by considerations which arise from the constitutional text and structure pertaining to the continued existence and operation of the states. Further, to treat as the decisive criterion of validity the form of an impugned law with respect to taxation is to distract attention from the generality of the terms in which in s 51(ii) the power is expressed (save for the specific reference to discrimination). It is to attend insufficiently to what in this realm of discourse is the essential question in all cases. This is whether the law restricts or burdens one or more of the states in the exercise of their constitutional powers. The form taken by a particular law may, as Dawson J explained in the passage from *Queensland Electricity* set out at [125], assist more readily in answering that question, but in all cases the question must be addressed.

Gaudron, Gummow and Hayne JJ quoted two passages from the judgment of Mason J in *Queensland Electricity*, including the following passage, to the effect that the principle applied in *Melbourne Corporation* consisted of two elements:

> (1) the prohibition against discrimination which involves the placing on the states of special burdens or disabilities; and (2) the prohibition against laws of general application which operate to destroy or curtail the continued existence of the states or their capacity to function as governments: *Victoria v Australian Building Construction Employees' and Builders Labourers' Federation* (1982) 152 CLR 25 at 93. The second element of the prohibition is necessarily less precise than the first; it protects the states against laws which, complying with the first element because they have a general application, may nevertheless produce the effect which it is the object of the principle to prevent: 159 CLR at 216.

However, that is to be read with an earlier passage in that judgment. Mason J, with reference to what had been said by Dixon J in the *Banking Case* (1948) 76 CLR 1 at 338 concerning laws of general application, there said (1982) 159 CLR 192 at 216:

Plainly, his Honour was speaking of a law which, though referable to a head of legislative power, is, by reason of its impact on the states and their functions, inconsistent with the fundamental constitutional conception which underlies the prohibition against discrimination.

[145] That 'fundamental constitutional conception' has proved insusceptible of precise formulation. Nevertheless, an understanding of it is essential lest propositions such as those expressed by Mason J in *Queensland Electricity* take on, by further judicial exegesis, a life of their own which is removed from the constitutional fundamentals which must sustain them.

The later decisions

[146] Some guidance as to the content of the limited state immunity is provided by the later decisions in this Court. In *The Tasmanian Dam Case*, (1983) 158 CLR 1 at 140, 213–15, Mason J and Brennan J pointed out that the concern was with the capacity of a state to function as a government rather than interference with or impairment of any function which a state government may happen to undertake. Later, in the *Native Title Act Case*, (1995) 183 CLR 373 at 480, it was said in the joint judgment of six members of the Court that the relevant question for the application of the *Melbourne Corporation* doctrine was not whether Commonwealth law effectively restricted state powers or made their exercise more complex or subjected them to delaying procedures. Their Honours continued, (1995) 183 CLR 373 at 480:

> The relevant question is whether the Commonwealth law affects what Dixon J called the 'existence and nature' of the state body politic. As the *Melbourne Corporation Case* illustrates, this conception relates to the machinery of government and to the capacity of its respective organs to exercise such powers as are conferred upon them by the general law which includes the Constitution and the laws of the Commonwealth: Constitution, Covering Clause V. A Commonwealth law cannot deprive the state of the personnel, property, goods and services which the state requires to exercise its powers and cannot impede or burden the state in the acquisition of what it so requires.

Later in that judgment, (1995) 183 CLR 373 at 481, their Honours distinguished between a federal law which impaired capacity to exercise constitutional functions and one which merely affected 'the ease with which those functions are exercised'.

[147] In *Melbourne Corporation*, (1947) 74 CLR 31 at 80, 99–100 respectively, Dixon J spoke of the 'restriction or control of the state ... in respect of the working of the judiciary', and Williams J of laws seeking to direct the states as to the manner of exercise of judicial governmental functions. Later, in *Australian Education Union*, (1995) 184 CLR 188 at 229, the joint judgment identified the state courts as an essential branch of the government of the state.

[148] In the present case, the question thus becomes whether the two laws with respect to taxation, the Protected Funds Imposition Act and the Protected Funds Assessment Act, restrict or control the states, in particular New South Wales and Victoria, in respect of the working of the judicial branch of the state government.

[149] Unlike the situation in the *Pay-roll Tax Case* and *The Second Fringe Benefits Tax Case*, these laws do not impose a taxation liability upon the states themselves. It is the plaintiffs who are taxed ...

[150] Similar considerations, where the tax is imposed not upon the state itself but upon officers or employees thereof, were considered in the United States in the period when *Melbourne Corporation* was decided. In *Helvering*, 304 US 405 at 419–20 (1938) ... , the Supreme Court spoke of a state function which was important enough to demand immunity from a tax upon the state itself but which did not extend to a tax which might well be substantially entirely absorbed by private persons; there, the burden on the state was 'so speculative and uncertain' as not to warrant restriction upon the federal taxing power.

[151] However, as Dixon CJ pointed out in the *Second Uniform Tax Case*, *Victoria v Commonwealth* (1957) 99 CLR 575 at 610, *Melbourne Corporation* itself was an instance where a restriction was imposed not on the state or its servants but on others, yet the federal law impermissibly interfered with the governmental functions of a state. Section 48 of the Banking Act imposed a prohibition upon banks but was effectual to deny to the states the

use of the banks and that was the object of the law: (1947) 74 CLR 31 at 62, 66–67, 75, 84, 100–101.

[152] The joint judgment of six members of the Court in *Australian Education Union* (1995) 184 CLR 188 at 233 (see also the *Industrial Relations Act Case* (1996) 187 CLR 416 at 498) is of central importance for the present case, in particular for two propositions. They are that (a) it is 'critical to a state's capacity to function as a government' that it retain ability to determine 'the terms and conditions' on which it engages employees and officers 'at the higher levels of government', and (b) 'Ministers, ministerial assistants and advisers, heads of departments and high level statutory office holders, parliamentary officers and judges would clearly fall within this group'. One result, with which *Australian Education Union* was immediately concerned, would protect the states to some degree from the exercise by the Commonwealth Industrial Relations Commission of power under federal law to fix minimum wages and working conditions in respect of [367] persons to whom the federal law otherwise would extend. Another result is to support the foundation for the case made by the first plaintiff.

Conclusion respecting Melbourne Corporation *doctrine*

[153] The Protected Funds Imposition Act and the Protected Funds Assessment Act are invalid in their application to the first plaintiff ...

[155] As a general proposition, it is for the state of New South Wales, as for the other states, to determine the terms and conditions upon which it appoints and remunerates the judges of its courts. The concept of remuneration includes provision of retirement and like benefits to judges, spouses and other dependants ... The state of New South Wales chose to discharge its responsibilities for the establishment and maintenance of its judicial branch by providing the unfunded and non-contributory scheme in the NSW Pensions Act ...

[157] Other methods for the provision of such remuneration might have been chosen by the New South Wales legislature ... New South Wales might have chosen a funded scheme which would generate state property on which the Commonwealth was forbidden by s 114 of the Constitution to impose any tax. Rather than pursue that or some other course, the legislature made provision for a non-contributory scheme with payment of benefits out of the Consolidated Fund of the state. The method so selected by the state legislature affected the terms and conditions for the engagement by the executive branch of judges and the organisation and working of the third branch of government of the state ...

[159] The provision of secure judicial remuneration at significant levels serves to advantage and protect the interest of the body politic in several ways. Secure judicial remuneration at significant levels assists, as the United States Supreme Court has emphasised, *United States v Hatter* 532 US 557 at 568 (2001), to encourage persons learned in the law, in the words of Chancellor Kent written in 1826, *Commentaries on American Law*, (1826), vol 1, Lecture XIV at 276, 'to quit the lucrative pursuits of private business, for the duties of that important station'.

[160] It also, as the Victorian Attorney-General indicated when introducing legislation, Judicial and Other Pensions Legislation (Amendment) Act 2001 (Vic), to provide some relief against the effects of the surcharge legislation, assists the attraction to office of persons without independent wealth and those who have practised in less well paid areas: Victoria, Legislative Assembly, *Parliamentary Debates*, 3 May 2001 at 1021. Further, the Supreme Court of the United States has stressed, *United States v Hatter* 532 US 557 at 568 (2001), that such provision helps 'to secure an independence of mind and spirit necessary if judges are "to maintain that nice adjustment between individual rights and governmental powers which constitutes political liberty": Wilson, *Constitutional Government in the United States*, (1911) at 143'. The Supreme Court went on, *United States v Hatter* 532 US 557 at 569 (2001), to refer to the statement by Chief Justice John Marshall that an ignorant or dependent judiciary would be the 'greatest scourge ... ever inflicted'.

[161] Views may vary from time to time as to the relevant importance of these considerations and the measures to give effect to them. But in the constitutional framework in

this country these are matters, respecting state judges, for determination by state legislatures. That constitutional framework also constrains those legislatures, in particular, by requiring them to take as they find federal laws of 'general application' as part of the system enjoyed by the whole community *Bank of NSW v Commonwealth* (1948) 76 CLR 1 at 337. Hence the statement by Frankfurter J in *O'Malley v Woodrough*, 307 US 277 at 282 (1939):

> To subject them to a general tax is merely to recognize that judges are also citizens, and that their particular function in government does not generate an immunity from sharing with their fellow citizens the material burden of the government whose Constitution and laws they are charged with administering.

[162] However, that is not the present case. Section 5 of the Protected Funds Assessment Act speaks of 'high-income members of constitutionally protected superannuation funds'. They are taxed in a fashion which differs from that required by the Surcharge Imposition Act and the Surcharge Assessment Act. A law taxing them is not in the sense of the authorities a law of 'general application' which, with reference to the classification by Dixon J, falls into category (a) identified at [130] ...

Gaudron, Gummow and Hayne JJ rejected the Commonwealth's argument that differential treatment of members of constitutionally protected superannuation funds was justified by the operation of s 114 of the Constitution. It was, the justices said, 'no answer to a case of alleged invalidity to assert that the federal law in question takes its form from a perceived need to escape the peril of invalidity presented by another constitutional restraint upon federal legislative power': 195 ALR 321 at [164]. The justices noted that question 2(a) of the case stated asked whether the Protected Funds Surcharge Legislation was invalid because it discriminated against New South Wales or imposed a particular burden or disability on the operations and activity of that state; and continued:

[165] ... That issue may be narrowed by asking whether that result comes about by a sufficiently significant impairment of the exercise by the state of its freedom to select the manner and method for discharge of its constitutional functions respecting the remuneration of the judges of the courts of the state. That requires consideration of the significance for the government of the state of its legislative choice for the making of provision for judicial remuneration. Having regard to what is said earlier in these reasons ... that significance is to be taken as considerable.

[166] In *The Second Fringe Benefits Tax Case*, in a passage which is no less significant for its presence in a dissenting judgment, given the later statement in *Australian Education Union* referred to at [152], Brennan J observed:

> The essential organs of government — the Governor, the Parliament, the Ministry and the Supreme Court — are the organs on which the 'existence and nature' of the body politic depends. (I mention only the Supreme Court, for that is the court of general jurisdiction in which, subject to the jurisdiction of this Court, the laws of the state are finally interpreted and the constitutional and administrative law of the state is applied.) The existence and nature of the body politic depends on the attendance to their duties of the officers of the essential organs of government and their capacity to exercise their functions. The emoluments which a state provides to the officers of the essential organs of government ensure or facilitate the performance by those organs of their respective functions.

[167] The circumstances that judicial pensions do not require contributions but are fixed as a proportion of the remuneration of a serving judge and are to be paid at the full rate only upon a substantial period of service as well as attainment of a minimum age, indicates the importance attached by legislatures to such schemes in the remuneration of the judicial branch.

[168] There then is posed the 'practical question' identified by Starke J in *Melbourne Corporation*. This, in the end, is whether, looking to the substance and operation of the federal laws, there has been, in a significant manner, a curtailment or interference with the exercise of state constitutional power.

Gaudron, Gummow and Hayne JJ noted that the first plaintiff had been assessed on the basis that the surchargeable contributions amounted to more than 61 per cent of his annual remuneration; if he were to meet the surcharge year by year during the tenure of his office, 'he would be chancing fortune' and 'the interest of the state in providing an adequate level of remuneration would have been denied'. Further, the provisions in the Protected Funds Surcharge Legislation for the accumulation of indebtedness supplied 'a disincentive to the first plaintiff to meet the public interest of the state in retaining his judicial services for the maximum possible term', because interest on that amount would continue to accumulate if he stayed in office after qualifying for the maximum judicial pension. 'If the first plaintiff does serve the public interest in this way by remaining in office until final retirement age, then the interest of the state in providing remuneration at what it regards as an appropriate level is again undermined, here by the imposition of a very large lump sum debt': 195 ALR 321 at [169]. The justices continued:

[170] The Commonwealth, in its submissions, urges against speculation upon what it says are the indirect effects of its laws upon the government of the state. However, one tendency of the federal laws readily apparent from their legal operation is to induce the state to vary the method of its judicial remuneration. The liberty of action of the state in these matters, that being an element of the working of its governmental structure, thereby is impaired. No doubt there is no direct legal obligation imposed by the federal laws requiring such action by the state. But those laws are effectual to do so, as was the Banking Act ...

[172] Earlier in these reasons at [141], there is set out a passage from the judgment of Gibbs J in the *Pay-roll Tax Case*. His Honour referred to the absence over many years of indications that the states had been impeded by the pay-roll tax in the discharge of their functions. The present case stands differently. It discloses a state of affairs well beyond the speculative and the uncertain. In New South Wales there is now the *Judges' Pensions Amendment Act 1998* (NSW) ('the 1998 Act'). As the long title to that statute discloses, it was enacted to amend the NSW Pensions Act so as to provide for the commutation of pensions under that statute for a particular purpose. That purpose was the payment of the superannuation contributions surcharge.

Gaudron, Gummow and Hayne JJ quoted, in [173] of their reasons, the Second Reading Speech on the bill for the 1998 Act, including the following passages:

> The bill will enable a retired judge or other person entitled to be paid a pension to elect to have part of the pension commuted for the purpose of payment of the superannuation contributions surcharge ...
>
> The amendments proposed are essential to provide judges and other persons entitled to a pension or reversionary pension under the Act with a mechanism to pay the superannuation contributions surcharge from the benefit they are entitled to receive.

The occasion for the provision of that mechanism thus was supplied solely by the operation of the federal legislation; the provision of the mechanism was a response which changed what had been the legislative scheme respecting the terms and conditions for the remuneration of state judges, in particular as indicated in the NSW Pensions Act ...

[174] The conclusion reached is that, in its application to the first plaintiff, the [Protected Funds Surcharge Legislation is] invalid on the ground of the particular disability or burden placed upon the operations and activities of New South Wales. The reasoning for that conclusion would apply also to the application of the legislation to the judges of other state courts as members of unfunded non-contributory pension schemes resembling that provided by the NSW Pensions Act ...

~~~

[8.2.76] McHugh J held that the Protected Surcharge Legislation was invalid because it 'discriminates against State judicial officers in a way that interferes in a significant respect with the states' relationships with their judges'. The legislation interfered with the financial arrangements that govern the terms of judges' offices, 'not as an incidence of a general tax applicable to all but as a special measure designed to single them out and place a financial burden on them that no one else in the community incurs': 195 ALR 321 at [229].

Earlier, McHugh J quoted a passage from the judgment of Mason J in *Queensland Electricity Commission v Commonwealth* (1985) 159 CLR 192 at 217, to the effect that the principle derived from *Melbourne Corporation* consists of two elements:

> (1) the prohibition against discrimination which involves the placing on the states of special burdens or disabilities; and (2) the prohibition against laws of general application which operate to destroy or curtail the continued existence of the states or their capacity to function as governments.

After referring to similar views expressed in *Queensland Electricity Commission* by Gibbs CJ, Wilson, Deane and Dawson JJ, and to the recognition by Brennan CJ, Toohey, Gaudron, McHugh and Gummow JJ in the *Industrial Relations Act* case, (1996) 187 CLR 416 at 500, 541–2, that the *Melbourne Corporation* principle had two elements, McHugh J said:

> Given this long line of judicial exposition of the principle, I am unable to agree with that part of the reasons of the joint judgment, at [124], that the *Melbourne Corporation* principle involves only 'one limitation, though the apparent expression of it varies with the form of the legislation under consideration'. With respect, since *Queensland Electricity Commission* it has been settled doctrine that there are two rules arising from the necessary constitutional implication (195 ALR 321 at [223]).

[8.2.77]   Kirby J (who dissented from the court's judgment that the Protected Funds Surcharge Legislation was invalid) disagreed with McHugh J and agreed with Gaudron, Gummow and Hayne JJ that:

> ... the two aspects of the implied limitation upon federal legislative power, noted in past decisions, are essentially manifestations of the one constitutional implication. Both are referable to the underlying conception concerning the nature of the Australian federation ... [E]ach identified defect is to be determined by reference to the effect of the impugned legislation on the continuing existence of the states, and whether there is an impermissible degree of impairment of the state's constitutional functions. The presence of discrimination against a State may be an indication of an attempted impairment of its functions as the Constitution envisaged them. But any discrimination against states must be measured against that underlying criterion. It affords the touchstone of the implied limitation explained in the Court's decision in *Melbourne Corporation* (195 ALR 321 [281]).

However, not any impairment would be sufficient to establish invalidity of a federal statute at 321 [282]–[284]:

> ... the mere encroachment of legislation, fiscal or otherwise, upon a state, does not amount to an impermissible impairment sufficient to render the federal legislation invalid ... The language of 'control' ... and 'impact' are unhelpful. It is the capacity of a state to function, rather than the mere ease with which its constitutional functions can be exercised, that is determinative ... In order to come to a conclusion on this issue, it is the operation and effect of the federal legislation that must be analysed ... [A] substantial impairment of the functions of the Supreme Court or the ability of the state to determine its composition would certainly constitute an impermissible encroachment by the Federal Parliament upon an essential component part of the government of a state. Such an impairment would render invalid any such federal legislation.

Kirby J found that the Protected Funds Surcharge Legislation did not contravene that principle, because it did not 'affect the selection and retention of state judicial officers to such a degree that the State judiciary is placed in jeopardy of not fulfilling its constitutional functions' so as to impair 'the essential governmental activities of a State' and threaten 'the continued existence and integrity of a State': 195 ALR 321 at [316].

[8.2.78] A form of limited protection for the states against Commonwealth legislation is expressed in s 114 of the Constitution, which provides that the Commonwealth cannot impose a tax on property of any kind belonging to a state. In *Queensland v Commonwealth* (1987) 162 CLR 74, the High Court held that the imposition of fringe benefits tax on the states, calculated on the value of state-owned cars and houses provided to some of its employees, was not a tax on property belonging to a state. Mason, Brennan and Deane JJ described s 114 as protecting a state at 98:

> ... from a tax on the ownership or holding of property but ... not ... from a tax or transactions which affect its property ... This ... gives a powerful measure of protection to the financial integrity of a state without preventing the Commonwealth from taxing every form of transaction to which a state is a party.

Mason, Brennan and Deane JJ said that taxes on the possession, use or the proceeds of sale of state-owned property would offend s 114. However, in their view the fringe benefits tax was none of those, because it was not imposed on the state's ownership or use of the property concerned but because the state provided employees with benefits in connection with their employment.

Wilson and Dawson JJ agreed with Mason, Brennan and Deane JJ. Gibbs CJ dissented, classifying the fringe benefits tax on the provision of state-owned cars and housing as a tax on the use of the state's property: 162 CLR at 93.

[8.2.79] In *Deputy Commissioner of Taxation v State Bank of New South Wales* (1992) 174 CLR 219, the High Court held that a Commonwealth sales tax imposed upon the sale value of goods manufactured by the State Bank of New South Wales for its own use was a tax on property belonging to a state and therefore invalid. In its joint judgment, the court (Mason CJ, Brennan, Deane, Dawson, Toohey, Gaudron and McHugh JJ) said that, in *Queensland v Commonwealth* (1987) 162 CLR 74 **[8.2.78]**, 'a tax on the use of state property or a tax on the use of property for state purposes was instanced as an illustration of a tax which fell within the prohibition contained in s 114': 174 CLR at 227. They said, of the Commonwealth's sales tax under challenge in the present case at 228:

> The plaintiff says that the tax imposed by s 17(1) is not imposed on the use of property as such but is imposed on application to use. According to the argument, the distinction is important because application to use is a transitory or momentary event which stands in high contrast with ownership or use of property over a long period. The short answer to this submission is that a tax on application to use of property is not the less a tax on the use of property because it attaches to a momentary activity rather than to use or ownership over a period. The tax attaches to use, that being the exercise of a right central to the concept of ownership, and that is enough to bring the tax within the ambit of the constitutional prohibition.

The court proceeded to reject the Commonwealth's argument that the State Bank of New South Wales, a statutory corporation established by the State Bank Act 1981 (NSW), was not the state for the purpose of s 114 (at 230–1):

> Once it is accepted that the Constitution refers to the Commonwealth and the states as organisations or institutions of government in accordance with the conceptions of ordinary life, it must follow that these references are wide enough to denote a corporation which is an agency or instrumentality of the Commonwealth or a state as

the case may be. The activities of government are carried on not only through the departments of government but also through corporations which are agencies or instrumentalities of government. Such activities have, since the nineteenth century, included the supply on commercial terms of certain types of goods and services by government owned instrumentalities with independent corporate personalities.

The court referred to the distinction, current at the beginning of the 20th century, between traditional and inalienable functions of government on the one hand and business, commercial and trading functions undertaken by government on the other hand, and continued at 231–2:

> That distinction has since been discarded. And it can have no place in the interpretation of s 114, which must take account of the historical circumstance that colonial governments in Australia carried on a wide range of governmental functions which were not traditional and inalienable.

State laws and the Commonwealth

[8.2.80] In the *Engineers'* case (1920) 28 CLR 129 **[8.2.31C]**, the majority said in their joint judgment at 155:

> The principle we apply to the Commonwealth we apply also to the states, leaving their respective acts of legislation full operation within their respective areas and subject matters but, in case of conflict, giving to valid Commonwealth legislation the supremacy expressly declared by the Constitution, measuring that supremacy according to the very words of s 109.

The principle referred to was that Commonwealth legislative powers should be read as authorising the Commonwealth Parliament to legislate so as to bind the states.

Later, the majority explained such decisions as *D'Emden v Pedder* (1904) 1 CLR 91 **[8.2.9]** and *Deakin v Webb* (1904) 1 CLR 585 **[8.2.10]** as depending on s 109 of the Commonwealth Constitution. State legislation taxing salaries paid by the Commonwealth was inconsistent with the Commonwealth legislation fixing the rate of salary and therefore invalid. In so far as those cases declared that state taxation of Commonwealth salaries was an invalid interference with the Commonwealth's constitutional functions, the cases were 'erroneous': 28 CLR at 156–7.

[8.2.81] The *Engineers'* case (1920) 28 CLR 129 **[8.2.31C]**, therefore, appeared to lay down a general reciprocal rule: state legislation would bind the Commonwealth just as Commonwealth legislation binds the states, although the Commonwealth might protect itself against state legislation by enacting an inconsistent law.

However, that reciprocal proposition has not survived. While the High Court did at an early stage affirm the dual nature of the *Engineers'* rule (*Pirrie v McFarlane* (1925) 36 CLR 170 **[8.2.82C]**), the subsequent development of this area of constitutional law has seen a steady and continual reduction in the capacity of states to bind the Commonwealth. Indeed, this reduction has persisted to the point where the states are denied any power to legislate so as to diminish or affect the legal rights of the Commonwealth: *Commonwealth v Cigamatic Pty Ltd* (1962) 108 CLR 372 **[8.2.98C]**.

This denial poses some very real practical problems. For example, if the Commonwealth Government decides to construct in Melbourne a regional office building for the Department of Social Security, it will be free from any restrictions and regulations laid down in state town planning, health and safety legislation.

Further, according to this notion of Commonwealth exemption from state legislation, when the Commonwealth enters into some commercial transaction (such as the sale of government publications or the purchase of office equipment) its rights and liabilities arising out of the transaction would not depend on, or be affected by, state legislation.

The High Court has recognised the real difficulties posed by such a result (if the Commonwealth's rights or liabilities do not depend on state law, then in which legal system are those rights to be found?) and has developed a number of ill-defined exceptions to the general exemption (see **[8.2.103]–[8.2.109]**) and has recognised wide, although not universal, waiver of the exemption in s 64 of the Judiciary Act 1903 (Cth): *Maguire v Simpson* (1977) 139 CLR 362 **[8.2.107]**; *Commonwealth v Evans Deakin Industries Ltd* (1986) 161 CLR 254 **[8.2.108]**.

[8.2.82C]   **Pirrie v McFarlane**
                                      (1925) 36 CLR 170

McFarlane was a member of the Royal Australian Air Force. In November 1924 he was instructed by his superior officer to drive an RAAF motor car on public roads in Melbourne. While driving the car, he was stopped by Pirrie, a member of the Victoria Police, who asked to see his driver's licence. McFarlane held no driver's licence under the Motor Traffic Act 1915 (Vic). Pirrie then lodged an information in the Melbourne Magistrates' Court and McFarlane was charged with a breach of s 6 of the Motor Traffic Act. That section reads:

> 6(1) No person shall drive a motor car upon any public highway without being licensed for that purpose and no person shall employ to drive a motor car any person who is not so licensed ...
>
> (4) Any person driving a motor car as aforesaid shall on demand by any member of the police force produce his licence and if he fails so to do shall be guilty of an offence against this Act ...

At the hearing of the charge the magistrate dismissed the information on the ground that the Motor Car Act could not validly apply to members of the defence forces. Pirrie obtained an order nisi to review the decision from the Victorian Supreme Court. When the order nisi came on for argument before the Supreme Court, the matter was removed to the High Court under s 40A of the Judiciary Act 1903 (Cth).

Starke J: [226] The argument denying the power of the states to affect Commonwealth officers based upon some prohibition expressed or implied [227] in the Constitution can no longer be sustained (*Engineers'* case (1920) 28 CLR 129, adopting the view of the Judicial Committee in *Webb v Outrim* [1907] AC 81, 4 CLR 356; *Caron v R* [1924] AC 999, and overruling such cases as *Deakin v Webb* (1904) I CLR 585; *Baxter v Commissioners of Taxation* (1907) 4 CLR 1087 and the *Railway Servants'* case (1906) 4 CLR 488). So the immunity claimed in this case must rest upon some law enacted by the Parliament: *Engineers'* case; *D'Emden v Pedder* (1904) 1 CLR 91; coupled with s 109 of the Constitution which provides that 'when a law of a state is inconsistent with a law of the Commonwealth, the latter shall prevail, and the former shall, to the extent of the inconsistency, be invalid'. How, then, is the Motor Car Act 1915, and particularly s 6 thereof, inconsistent with any law of the Commonwealth? ...

[228] An Air Force is organised under the Defence and Air Force Acts with all necessary arms and equipment for training in peace and service in war. And its government, discipline, and military duty are provided for on much the same lines as in Great Britain. These Acts restrict to some extent the civil rights and duties of soldiers, but nowhere do they exempt them from obedience to the civil law. If the Imperial Parliament had prescribed that no person should drive a motor car upon any public highway in Great Britain without being licensed for that purpose and declared that the law should apply to persons in the public service of the Crown as well as to other persons, the duty of soldiers to obey that law would be clear: see Motor Car Act 1903 (3 Edw VII c 36; cf *Cooper v Hawkins* [1904] 2 KB 164). This duty would be superimposed upon their military obligations and in no wise inconsistent with them.

What difference does it make that in Australia the Constitution has distributed legislative power between the Commonwealth and the states? Unless there be some limitation upon the states, expressed or implied in the Constitution, with respect to interference with persons who are federal officers, then the case must be founded upon some inconsistency between the law of the state and the law of the Commonwealth. There is no express limitation in the Constitution, and the *Engineers'* case (1920) 28 CLR 129 denies any such implied limitation. When a power exists in the states, then 'they are entitled to the same complete independence in its exercise as is the national government in wielding its own authority,' subject only to the provisions of s 109 of the Constitution (cf *Cooley's Principles of Constitutional Law*, 3rd ed p 35). The Motor Car Act, it is said, will paralyse the Defence Forces of the Commonwealth and impair the efficiency of their service: they cannot, in Victoria, be trained in peace nor used in war without the sanction of the state. Extravagant arguments such as this may well be considered when the state passes legislation calculated to lead to such dangerous consequences (cf *Caron v R* [1924] AC 999). All the state has done in this case is to regulate [**229**] the use of motor cars and to require all citizens to observe provisions for the preservation of public safety and security. The Act is directed to acts of a purely local character, and its object is peculiarly within the authority of the state. It is not aimed particularly at the Defence Forces of the Commonwealth, nor is it in opposition to any express provision of the laws of the Commonwealth. A civil duty is, no doubt, established for all citizens using the public highways of Victoria, reasonable in itself and in no wise interfering with or infringing the military duties and obligations of the Defence Forces of the Commonwealth. Again, we were urged to consider the possible consequences of s 4 of the Act relating to the registration of motor cars. Must the Commonwealth, it was said, register all its motor vehicles required for defence purposes? It will be time enough to answer that question when it arises. It may be found that s 4 does not require either the Commonwealth or the state governments to register any motor vehicle. But, however that may be, the Commonwealth has ample legislative power to maintain its Forces free from any inconvenient legislation of the states.

The magistrate, in my opinion, was wrong in his decision, and the defendant should have been convicted of the offence charged against him.

~~~

[8.2.83] Knox CJ and Higgins J delivered judgments to the same effect. Isaacs and Rich JJ dissented. In a judgment with which Rich JJ agreed, Isaacs J held that the Victorian Act was not intended to bind the Crown, and that if it had been so intended it would be invalid for two reasons. First:

> [A]n enactment expressly or by necessary implication purporting to bind the Crown in right of the Commonwealth in respect of 'primary and inalienable functions of the constitutional government' of the Commonwealth — that is, of the King in right of the Commonwealth (see *Coomber v Justices of Berks*) — is entirely outside the range of the state Constitution. Those functions were expressly taken from the states and vested exclusively in the Commonwealth by the Constitution itself (36 CLR at 199).

The second reason was the inconsistency between any such state law and Commonwealth legislation, the Air Force Act 1923 (Cth), which authorised the RAAF to choose its own drivers for the purpose of public defence: 36 CLR at 200–12.

Notes

[8.2.84] Isaacs and Rich JJ, who dissented in *Pirrie v McFarlane* (1925) 36 CLR 170 **[8.2.82C]**, had subscribed to the joint judgment in the *Engineers'* case (1920) 28 CLR 128 **[8.2.31C]**, which appeared to demolish the notion of intergovernmental immunity. But in this case they made two points about the capacity of the states to legislate so as to control the Commonwealth and its agents. State legislation would have to give way to inconsistent Commonwealth legislation because of s 109 of the Commonwealth Constitution, and state legislation would be invalid if it interfered with any matter which, by the Constitution, was reserved for the exclusive control of the Commonwealth. Neither Rich J nor Isaacs J referred to the provision of the Constitution which gave this exclusive control to the Commonwealth. They were probably referring to s 52(ii) which gives the Commonwealth Parliament the 'exclusive power to make laws ... with respect to ... matters relating to any department of the public service the control of which is by this Constitution transferred to the executive government of the Commonwealth'. (Section 69 transferred, inter alia, the naval and military defence departments in each state to the Commonwealth.)

It is clear that there can be no reciprocal rule on the power of the Commonwealth and states to regulate each other's activities. Not only does the Constitution give supremacy to Commonwealth legislation where there is a conflict, but it places certain matters within the exclusive control of the Commonwealth Parliament. A state law, otherwise valid, would be invalid to the extent that it touched those 'exclusive' matters. These are restrictions to which the Commonwealth Parliament is not subject. In particular, once a Commonwealth law is found to be within one of the parliament's enumerated powers, it will not be struck down as invalid because it touches on some matter reserved exclusively for the states. That was the very point decided by the High Court in the *Engineers'* case. So the structure of the Constitution, the division of legislative powers between Commonwealth and states and the notion of legislative supremacy for Commonwealth law, clearly work against an even-handed reciprocal rule in this area. We might accept that, generally, states can legislate so as to control the Commonwealth Government but we are obliged, by the terms of the Commonwealth Constitution, to make some substantial exceptions to that proposition.

[8.2.85]   Howard has attempted to explain the decision in *Pirrie v McFarlane* (1925) 36 CLR 170 **[8.2.82C]** and to reconcile the decision with such later cases as *Commonwealth v Cigamatic Ltd* (1962) 108 CLR 372 **[8.2.98C]**, which, he said, laid down a doctrine of total Commonwealth immunity from state law. He said that *Pirrie v McFarlane* 'is not in fact inconsistent with the total immunity doctrine because that doctrine applies only where it is the Commonwealth itself as a juristic entity which is impleaded and not where state law is sought to be enforced against individual persons employed by the Commonwealth': Howard (1985) p 224.

Evans observed of this argument that the distinction between the Commonwealth and its servants was 'perfectly intelligible' but, in practical terms, it could lead to substantial problems ((1972) pp 530–1):

> ... state law could hamstring Commonwealth activities equally efficiently (at least until inconsistent legislation is passed) by operating on the Commonwealth's servants or on the Commonwealth itself ... In practice the activities of the Commonwealth and the activities of its servants are inextricably intertwined.

Zines does not share Evans' appreciation of the theoretical attractions of the distinction. '[I]t is hard to see how', he wrote, 'for present purposes any distinction could be made between the Crown and the servants of the Crown carrying out their duties to the Crown': Zines (1997) pp 360–1.

[8.2.86]   In *West v Commissioner of Taxation (NSW)* (1937) 56 CLR 657, the High Court held that the Special Income and Wages Tax (Management) Act 1933 (NSW) validly imposed a state income tax on a Commonwealth superannuation pension received by a New South Wales resident formerly employed by the Commonwealth. Latham CJ looked for the answer to the validity of state legislation in specific constitutional provisions. He found that the Commonwealth legislation authorising payment of the pension had not protected the pension from state taxation, although the Commonwealth Parliament had the power to legislate to confer such a protection. This excluded the possibility of s 109 inconsistency between the Commonwealth legislation and the state taxing law, which did not discriminate against incomes from Commonwealth sources. If the state tax had discriminated, or purported 'to deal specifically with Federal salaries or pensions', it could be in conflict with s 52(ii) of the Constitution which gave exclusive power to the Commonwealth Parliament over the departments of the public service transferred to the Commonwealth, 'including the salaries and pensions of Commonwealth officers': 56 CLR at 668. Or such legislation might be seen as lying outside the state parliament's power to make laws for the peace, welfare and good government of the state, because it dealt with the government of the Commonwealth: 56 CLR at 669.

Starke and Evatt JJ adopted a similar approach, although Evatt J denied that the Commonwealth Parliament could legislate to grant Commonwealth salaries and pensions an immunity from state taxation.

On the other hand, Rich, Dixon and McTiernan JJ apparently assumed that the states were generally incompetent to tax Commonwealth salaries and pensions, because they stressed the importance of a provision in the relevant Commonwealth legislation which, in Dixon J's words, 'treats [the pension] as potentially subject to taxation by a state': 56 CLR at 678. That consideration and the non-discriminatory character of the state tax combined to destroy the foundation of the claimed immunity from state taxation: 56 CLR at 679. Dixon J went on to consider why a state tax which discriminated against Commonwealth pensions, salaries or other payments would be invalid. One reason would be inconsistency, under s 109, between the state tax and the Commonwealth law which authorised the payment at 681–2:

Surely it is implicit in the power given to the executive government of the Commonwealth that the incidents and consequences of its exercise shall not be made the subject of special liabilities or burdens under state law. The principles which have been adopted for determining for the purposes of s 109 whether a state law is consistent with a Federal statute are no less applicable when the question is whether the state law is consistent with the Federal Constitution. Since the *Engineers'* case a notion seems to have gained currency that in interpreting the Constitution no implications can be made. Such a method of construction would defeat the intention of any instrument, but of all instruments a written constitution seems the last to which it could be applied. I do not think that the judgment of the majority of the court in the *Engineers'* case meant to propound such a doctrine. It is inconsistent with many of the reasons afterwards advanced by Isaacs J himself for his dissent in *Pirrie v McFarlane* (1925) 36 CLR at 191.

[8.2.87] The view expressed by Latham CJ in *West v Commissioner of Taxation (NSW)* (1937) 56 CLR 657 **[8.2.86]**, that the Commonwealth Parliament could legislate to grant immunity from state taxation to Commonwealth pensioners must be regarded as vindicated by the High Court's decision in *Australian Coastal Shipping Commission v O'Reilly* (1962) 107 CLR 46. In that case, the question before the High Court was whether the Australian Coastal Shipping Commission was liable to pay stamp duty on receipts issued by it in Victoria. The Stamps Act

1946 (Vic) imposed such a liability. The commission was set up as a statutory corporation by the Australian Coastal Shipping Commission Act 1956 (Cth), to establish, maintain and operate shipping services for the carriage of passengers, goods and mails in interstate, overseas and territorial trade. It was conceded that the commission was not an instrumentality of the Crown, so it had no special immunity from the state legislation. However, s 36(1) of the Commonwealth legislation provided that the commission was not subject to taxation under a law of a state or territory to which the Commonwealth was not subject.

The court (Dixon CJ, McTiernan, Kitto, Taylor, Menzies, Windeyer and Owen JJ) held that s 36(1) was valid. In his judgment (with which Kitto, Taylor and Owen JJ agreed) Dixon CJ referred to a series of decisions of the United States Supreme Court:

> An analogy is to be found in the cases where the United States employs contractors for its government purposes. The question has repeatedly arisen whether an immunity claimed from state taxes exists. Of this a majority of the Supreme Court speaking through Black J has said recently: 'Today the United States does business with a vast number of private parties. In this court the trend has been to reject immunising these private parties from non-discriminatory state taxes as a matter of constitutional law. Cf *Penn Dairies v Milk Control Commission* (1943) 318 US 270. Of course this is not to say that Congress, acting within the proper scope of its power, cannot confer immunity by statute where it does not exist constitutionally. Wise and flexible adjustment of inter-governmental tax immunity calls for political and economic considerations of the greatest difficulty and delicacy. Such complex problems are ones which Congress is best qualified to resolve. As the Government points out Congress has already extensively legislated in this area by permitting states to tax what would have otherwise been immune'. The doctrine propounded in the foregoing passage applies to federalism in Australia. Given the power in reference to a subject matter of legislation to set up a Federal governmental corporation, the power of the Parliament extends to excluding the imposition of state taxes on its operations and the exclusion of liability on the part of the corporation to state taxes upon its activities. The fact that a government agency is set up at all brings under consideration the question whether its operations should or should not be exposed to state taxes. How that question should be decided is a matter of policy. But the legislative power under which, *ex hypothesi*, the agency is validly set up must surely be enough to enable the legislature to decide it (107 CLR at 55–6).

[8.2.88] The High Court's decision in *Gazzo v Comptroller of Stamps (Vic)* (1981) 149 CLR 227 should be contrasted with *Australian Coastal Shipping Commission v O'Reilly* (1962) 107 CLR 46 **[8.2.87]**. A majority (Gibbs CJ, Stephen and Aickin JJ, with Mason and Murphy JJ dissenting) decided that s 90 of the Family Law Act 1975 (Cth) was invalid. The section exempted from state taxes transfers of property under maintenance agreements between husband and wife approved by the Family Court. This exemption was not, the majority said, a law with respect to marriage (s 51(xxi)), or divorce and matrimonial causes: s 51(xxii). Gibbs J conceded that, if s 90 'render[ed] effective orders made by a court under the … Family Law Act … and is therefore incidental to the subject matter of the power given by paras (xxi) and (xxii)', it would be valid. But he thought that the purpose of an order approving the transfer of property between husband and wife could be fully achieved whether or not state tax was payable on the transfer. He regarded *Australian Coastal Shipping Commission v O'Reilly* (1962) 107 CLR 46 **[8.2.87]** as 'quite distinguishable from the present case' (149 CLR at 238) and went on to explain the basis of exemption from state legislation at 238:

The question whether a [Commonwealth] law is reasonably incidental to the subject matter of the power is always one of degree, and it depends to some extent on the nature of the power. Thus the Parliament might, under the defence power, exempt soldiers travelling on duty from the necessity of complying with the traffic regulations of a state, but it could not validly grant a similar exemption in favour of a married person travelling to avail himself or herself of an order for access made under the Family Law Act.

Another majority justice, Stephen J, purported to follow Menzies J's judgment in *O'Reilly's* case (1962) 107 CLR 46 **[8.2.87]**: 149 CLR at 243–4. However, this appears to have been based on a confusion as to the basis of Menzies J's reasoning: see Zines (1997) p 344.

Zines has described the majority judgments in *Gazzo v Comptroller of Stamps (Vic)* (1981) 149 CLR 227 as 'unsatisfactory in their reasoning' and observed that, because 'the decision was a two to three majority, it is a very weak precedent': Zines (1997) p 346.

The status of *Gazzo* must now be regarded as significantly weakened by the unanimous judgment of the High Court in *Botany Municipal Council v Federal Airports Authority* (1992) 175 CLR 453 **[8.2.73]**, to the effect that the Commonwealth could legislate so as to authorise a contractor to carry out work on a Commonwealth-owned airport in spite of the provisions of any state law relating to environmental assessment.

[8.2.89]   An important feature of the judgments in *West v Commissioner of Taxation (NSW)* (1937) 56 CLR 657 **[8.2.86]** is the sharp distinction in approach adopted by Latham CJ and Dixon J. The former appealed to the express provisions of the Commonwealth Constitution and state Constitution Acts to resolve the issues before the court. The latter appealed in his judgment to a proposition which he said was 'implicit in the power given to the executive government of Commonwealth' that it should not be subjected to special burdens under state law: 56 CLR 681. Dixon J also asserted that a written constitution should be the last instrument to be interpreted literally and without resort to implications. This sharp distinction in approach (the one relying on a legislative reading of the text of the Constitution, the other appealing to broad political propositions implied in the Constitution) was to be repeated in a number of other decisions in this area: see, for example, *Uther v Federal Commissioner of Taxation* (1947) 74 CLR 509 **[8.2.90C]**; *Melbourne Corporation v Commonwealth* (1947) 74 CLR 31 **[8.2.45C]**; *Essendon Corporation v Criterion Theatres Ltd* (1947) 74 CLR 1 **[8.2.93C]**.

[8.2.90C]   ## Uther v Federal Commissioner of Taxation
(1947) 74 CLR 509

Richard Foreman and Sons Pty Ltd was a company in voluntary liquidation under the Companies Act 1936 (NSW). The liquidator of the company, Uther, had paid a dividend of 4s in the pound to various creditors of the company, and there remained £1459 of the company's assets for distribution. The Federal Commissioner of Taxation then lodged a claim for £594 sales tax and £172 payroll tax owing by the company.

It was common ground that, apart from ss 282 and 297 of the Companies Act, the Commonwealth would be entitled to a degree of priority in the payment of these debts over other creditors. The common law had developed a hierarchy of debts for the payment of the creditors of 'insolvent estates'. Debts were classified in an order of degrees. For example, a judgment debt ranked higher than a debt due under statute, which was of a higher degree than a debt due under a contract made under seal, which ranked above a debt arising out of a simple contract. Creditors of each degree were entitled to be paid out of the assets of the debtor before any creditor of the next degree. When there were insufficient assets to meet the debts due to creditors of a particular degree, those creditors shared the assets in proportion to their debts. However, the Crown had a prerogative right of priority to be paid before private individuals or corporations who were creditors of the same degree.

Section 297 of the Companies Act 1936 (NSW) listed the sequence in which certain debts were to be paid, but the only priority given to the Commonwealth was for money owing to it as unpaid income tax. In respect of all other debts owing to it, the Commonwealth was to rank equally with private creditors. Section 282 affirmed that, apart from preferred creditors, the assets of an insolvent company were to be applied to satisfying its liabilities.

The liquidator applied to the Supreme Court of New South Wales under s 286 of the Companies Act to determine whether the Commissioner of Taxation was entitled to be paid the sales and payroll tax owing by the company in priority to all other unsecured creditors. The Supreme Court (Roper J) believed the matter raised a question as to the limits inter se of the powers of the Commonwealth and the states and, because of s 40A of the Judiciary Act 1903 (Cth), proceeded no further with the case. The High Court then made an order under s 40 of the Judiciary Act, removing the case into the High Court.

Latham CJ: [520] The principle enunciated and applied in [*Melbourne Corporation*] cannot, in my opinion, be applied in favour of the Commonwealth in the same way as it may properly be applied in favour of a state. A state has no means of protecting itself against Commonwealth legislation if that legislation is valid. The position in the case of the Commonwealth, however, is very different. The Commonwealth Constitution, s 109, provides that when a law of a state is inconsistent with a law of the Commonwealth the latter shall prevail and the former shall to the extent of the inconsistency, be invalid. This provision, as has often been pointed out, relates only to state laws which, apart from s 109, would be valid. A valid Commonwealth law prevails over an otherwise valid state law where the latter is inconsistent with the former. Accordingly, the Commonwealth Parliament is in a position to protect the Commonwealth against state legislation which, in the opinion of the Parliament, impairs or interferes with the performance of Commonwealth functions or the exercise of Commonwealth rights ...

Latham CJ noted that, in the *First Uniform Tax* case, *South Australia v Commonwealth* (1942) 65 CLR 373, it was held that the Commonwealth Parliament could legislate to provide for priority for Commonwealth taxes over debts due to creditors other than state governments.

[521] Accordingly, there is no need to invoke any principle of non-interference with governmental functions ... The Commonwealth Parliament has the means of protection in its own hands, and by suitable legislation can prevent the application of inconsistent state legislation ...

Latham CJ accepted that there were some subjects beyond state legislative power, such as the functions of the Governor-General in relation to the summoning and the dissolution of the Commonwealth Parliament because laws on those subjects were not laws 'for the peace, welfare and good government of New South Wales in all cases whatsoever' within s 5 of the Constitution Act 1902 (NSW). Was the Commonwealth prerogative right of priority in respect of debts owed to the Commonwealth one of those matters?

The Commonwealth of Australia was not born into a vacuum. It came into existence within a system of law already established. To much of that law the Commonwealth is necessarily subject; for example, the Commonwealth has no general power to legislate with respect to the law of property, the law of contract, the law of tort. In relation to those subjects speaking generally, it lives and moves and has its being within a system of law which consists of the common law (in the widest sense) and the statute law of the various states. The question of the application of general law to the Commonwealth came before this court in *Pirrie v McFarlane* (1925) 36 CLR 170. It was there held [522] that general provisions in a Traffic Act relating to motor cars applied to the Commonwealth when there was no Commonwealth law with which the state law was inconsistent: see the report (1925) 36 CLR at 182–3, 213–14, 228–9. Provision for the ranking of debts inter se in the liquidation of companies in the forum of a state is a common feature of ordinary company law. It is as much a part of the general law of the community as a traffic law. It usually involves distinction between classes of creditors. It is a general law which can be applied to the Commonwealth where the Commonwealth is a creditor in the same way as to other creditors. If the state legislation abolishes or reduces the priority in payment to which the Commonwealth is entitled at common law the Commonwealth may, by Commonwealth legislation, prevent that state law from operating. But, in my opinion, until the Commonwealth Parliament passes such legislation, the state law is applicable according to its terms.

Rich, Starke and Williams JJ delivered judgments to the same effect. Dixon and McTiernan JJ dissented, the latter on the ground that the Sales Tax Assessment Act and the Pay-roll Tax Assessment Act conferred a statutory right of priority on the Commissioner of Taxation.

Dixon J: [528] We are here concerned with nothing but the relation between the Crown in right of the Commonwealth as a creditor for public moneys and the subjects of the Crown as creditors for private moneys. There are no conflicting claims between state and Commonwealth. The conflict is between the Commonwealth and its own subjects. What title can the state have to legislate as to the rights which the Commonwealth shall have as against its own subjects?

The fact that the priority claimed by the Commonwealth springs from one of the prerogatives of the Crown is an added reason, a reason perhaps conclusive in itself, for saying that it is a matter lying completely outside state power. But there is the antecedent consideration that to define or regulate the rights or privileges, duties or disabilities, of the Commonwealth in relation to the subjects of the Crown is not a matter for the states. General laws made by a state may affix legal consequences to given descriptions of transaction and the Commonwealth, if it enters into such a transaction, may be bound by the rule laid down. For instance, if the Commonwealth contracts with a company the form of the contract will be governed by s 348 of the Companies Act. Further, state law is made applicable to matters in which the Commonwealth is a party by s 79 of the Judiciary Act. But these applications of state law, though they may perhaps be a source of confusion, stand altogether apart from the regulation of the legal situation which the Commonwealth, as a government, shall occupy with reference to private rights ...

[529] A federal system is necessarily a dual system. In a dual political system you do not expect to find either government legislating for the other. But supremacy, where it exists, belongs to the Commonwealth, not to the states. The affirmative grant of legislative power to the Parliament over the subjects of bankruptcy and insolvency may authorise the enactment of laws excluding or reducing the priority of the Crown in right of the states in bankruptcy and it has been held that the taxation power extends to giving the Commonwealth a right to be paid taxes before the states are paid: *South Australia v Commonwealth* (1942) 65 CLR 373. But these are the results of express grants of specific powers, plenary within their ambit, to the Federal legislature, whose laws, if within power, are made paramount. Because of their content or nature, the [530] express powers in question are considered to extend to defining the priority of debts owing to the states or postponing state claims to taxes. The legislative power of the states is in every material respect of an opposite description. It is not paramount but, in case of a conflict with a valid Federal law, subordinate. It is not granted by the Constitution. It is not specific, but consists in the undefined residue of legislative power which remains after full effect is given to the provisions of the Constitution establishing the Commonwealth and arming it with the authority of a central government of enumerated powers. That means, after giving full effect not only to the grants of specific legislature powers

but to all other provisions of the Constitution and the necessary consequences which flow from them.

It is a fundamental constitutional error to regard the question of the efficacy of s 282 of the Companies Act 1936 of New South Wales as if it were an exercise of an express grant, contained in the Constitution, to the states of a power to make laws with respect to the specific subject of the winding up of insolvent companies. It is a provision enacted in intended pursuance of a general legislative power to make laws for the peace, welfare and good government of New South Wales in all cases whatsoever. The content and strength of this power are diminished and controlled by the Commonwealth Constitution. It is of course a fallacy, in considering what a state may or may not do under this undefined residuary power to reason from some general conception of the subjects which fall within it as if they were granted or reserved to the states as specific heads of power. But no fallacy in constitutional reasoning is so persistent or recurs in so many and such varied applications. In the present case the fallacious process of reasoning could not begin from s 107 as the error has so commonly done in the past. For it is not a question whether the power of the parliament of a colony becoming a state continues as at the establishment of the Commonwealth. The colony of New South Wales could not be said at the establishment of the Commonwealth to have any power at all with reference to the Commonwealth. Like the goddess of wisdom the Commonwealth uno ictu sprang from the brain of its begetters armed and of full stature. At the same instant the colonies became states; but whence did the states obtain the power to regulate the legal relations of this new polity with its subjects? It formed no part of the old colonial power. The federal Constitution does not give it. Surely it is for the peace, order and good government of the Commonwealth, not for the peace, welfare and good government of New South Wales, [531] to say what shall be the relative situation of private rights and the public rights of the Crown representing the Commonwealth, where they come into conflict. It is a question of the fiscal and governmental rights of the Commonwealth and, as such, is one over which the state has no power.

~~~

Notes

[8.2.91] In *Commonwealth v Cigamatic Pty Ltd* (1962) 108 CLR 372 **[8.2.98C]** the majority of the High Court (Dixon CJ, Kitto, Windeyer, Menzies and Owen JJ) overruled the decision in *Uther's* case, endorsing Dixon J's dissenting judgment in that case.

[8.2.92] In his judgment in *Uther's* case (1947) 74 CLR 509 **[8.2.90C]**, Dixon J recognised one of the real problems associated with a general immunity for the Commonwealth Government from state legislation. He said that when the Commonwealth enters into a transaction, it may be bound by state laws which affix legal consequences to that type of transaction. He also said that s 79 of the Judiciary Act 1903 (Cth) could subject the Commonwealth as a litigant to state law.

This was a recognition of the fact that, without a system of law by which the Commonwealth's rights and liabilities are defined, the Commonwealth can have no rights or liabilities. Yet the Commonwealth daily enters into a variety of arrangements, transactions and relationships which are clearly intended to have some legal consequences. It buys and sells commodities, contracts for the provision of services, and leases property (real and personal). If the various state laws which regulate such transactions do not affect the Commonwealth's rights and liabilities, where are those rights and liabilities to be found?

Presumably, Dixon J's proposal that state laws would affect the Commonwealth in such situations was meant to resolve the difficulties created by a general exemption. But that proposal may create as many problems as it attempts to eradicate. For instance, how do we distinguish between those situations where the Commonwealth's legal relations with its subjects are immune from state legislation and those situations where the Commonwealth's transactions with its subjects are subject to state legislation? The recent case *Re Residential Tenancies Tribunal of New South Wales and Henderson; Ex parte Defence Housing Authority* (1997) 190 CLR 410 **[8.2.112C]** attempted to resolve this problem by creating a distinction between state laws which purport to affect the executive capacities of the Commonwealth and state laws which merely regulate the exercise of those capacities. This distinction has also been subject to criticism: see **[8.2.115]**, **[8.2.116]**.

It might be argued that Latham CJ's approach to this issue both avoids these difficult distinctions and achieves a workable result. He said that the Commonwealth was not born into a vacuum, and that 'it lives and moves and has its being within a system of law which consists of the common law ... and the statute law of the various states': 74 CLR at 521. He went on to point out that 'the Commonwealth may, by Commonwealth legislation, prevent that state law from operating': 74 CLR at 522.

See now *Maguire v Simpson* (1977) 139 CLR 362 **[8.2.107]** and *Commonwealth v Evans Deakin Industries Ltd* (1986) 161 CLR 254 **[8.2.108]**.

[8.2.93C]   Essendon Corporation v Criterion Theatres Ltd
(1947) 74 CLR 1

Criterion Theatres Ltd was the owner of land in the city of Essendon. From 30 September 1942 to 11 September 1944 the land was occupied by the Commonwealth Government.

The Council of the City of Essendon levied rates on both the owner and the occupier of the land, under the Local Government Act 1928 (Vic):

> **264**(1) The council of every municipality shall once at least in every year, and may from time to time as it sees fit in manner hereinafter mentioned, make and levy rates to be called 'General rates' equally in respect of all rateable property within the municipal district ...

> **265** Every general rate which the council of any municipality is by this Act authorised to make or levy shall be made and levied by it ...

> (b) upon every person who occupies, or if there is no occupier or if the occupier is the Crown ... then upon the owner of any rateable property whatsoever within the municipal district.

Criterion Theatres Ltd and the Commonwealth failed to pay the rates, and the council brought an action in the High Court for the recovery of the rates. Criterion Theatres Ltd lodged a defence in which it denied its liability to pay rates. The Commonwealth lodged a demurrer to the statement of claim, claiming that the Local Government Act did not render the Commonwealth liable to pay rates. The demurrer and the question of Criterion Theatres Ltd's liability were argued before the Full High Court.

The majority of the court (Latham CJ, Dixon, McTiernan and Williams JJ) held that the reference to 'the Crown' in s 265(b) of the Local Government Act meant the Crown in right of the state of Victoria; therefore, where land was occupied by the Commonwealth, the section imposed no liability on the owner of the land. Rich J dissented on this point.

All members of the court held that the reference to 'every person who occupies' in s 265(b) of the Local Government Act did not render the Commonwealth liable to pay the rates. Rich, McTiernan and Williams JJ reached that conclusion by interpreting the phrase as not extending to the Crown in right of the Commonwealth. Latham CJ held that it did extend to the Commonwealth but that it was in conflict with s 114 of the Commonwealth Constitution, by imposing a tax on 'a kind of property' belonging to the Commonwealth: 74 CLR 13–14. Dixon J assumed that the phrase did refer to the Commonwealth but that, as so construed, the Local Government Act would be invalid.

Dixon J: [17] For my part, I cannot see how the Commonwealth can be made liable for rates in respect of the Army's use or occupation of land for military purposes during the war ...

The first step in the reasoning upon which I rely is a simple proposition about the nature of the rates. The rates are not a charge for services. They go into the general funds of the municipality to be applied to any objects within its powers. The municipality levies the rates as a subordinate authority of the state and they are a tax: *Municipal Council of Sydney v Commonwealth* (1904) 1 CLR 208. The second step is a proposition no less simple but one concerning the law of the Constitution. It is that the state may not levy a tax directly upon the Commonwealth in respect of the execution of its duties or the exercise of its functions. That proposition I shall proceed to justify.

Dixon J said that he did not base his decision on s 114 of the Constitution because the Commonwealth's occupation of the land was 'not that of passive ownership but of the actual carrying on of measures of defence', and continued:

[18] ... I ... prefer to base my decision upon the ground that the Constitution does not permit the state to tax that kind of action of the Commonwealth ... Clearly enough the Commonwealth took and retained possession of the land in executing a function of government. Let it be added, should there still be those who think it matters, one of 'the primary and inalienable functions of a constitutional government': *Coomber v Justices of Berks* (1883) 9 App Cas 74. The imposition of the tax that is attempted is directly upon the Commonwealth itself and to make it [19] worse the occasion of the imposition is the act of the Commonwealth in so taking and retaining possession of the land. I believe that I am on sound ground in saying that the Constitution does not allow this. I say sound ground because I do not think it is a proposition involved in the general overthrow of the discredited doctrine by which a wide immunity from state legislation was given to agents and instruments employed by the Federal Government. There is a world of difference between, on the one hand, a denial to the states of a power to tax the Commonwealth in respect of the execution of its duties or the exercise of its authority and, on the other hand, the earlier doctrine protecting so-called instrumentalities of government, Federal or state, from the exercise of some legislative power of the other government on the ground that to concede that they fell within the operation of the power at all would concede to the second government a means, an indirect means, of burdening, or interfering with, the first. But even when the earlier doctrine was abandoned by this court an express reservation was made covering, among other things, the power of taxation. The reservation is expressed in a somewhat indefinite manner, perhaps designedly, but it appears at least certain that, because of the special nature of the power to tax, it was considered that there might be implied restraints upon its use to which the legislative powers of neither government were generally subject: *Amalgamated Society of Engineers v Adelaide Steamship Co Ltd* (1920) 28 CLR 143.

The retreat from the earlier doctrine began in the United States later, I think, and its abandonment was effected by progressive steps and not, as here, *uno ictu.*

Dixon J referred to a series of decisions of the United States Supreme Court, which had moved away from the proposition that the governments within the federal union were immune from each other's legislation. Yet these decisions had indicated that tax laws raised special problems and suggested that 'an attempt by means of the tax power on the part of one member of the federal system to interfere with the other' would be invalid. His Honour continued:

[21] I have said so much about the way the old doctrine has been dealt with in the United States because, as it appears to me, the development leaves untouched the proposition upon which my decision depends. That proposition is expressed in the judgment of the court in the *Allegheny County* case (1944) 322 US 174 thus: 'Unshaken, rarely questioned, and indeed not questioned in this case, is the principle that possessions, institutions, and activities of the Federal Government itself in the absence of express Congressional consent are not subject to any form of state taxation' (at 177) ...

[22] Indeed in the majority opinion it is claimed that, from the basic doctrine that properties, functions and instrumentalities of the Federal Government are immune from taxation by its constituent parts, the court has never departed or wavered in its application. The justification for this claim lies in the distinction between the basic doctrine of the Federal Government's immunity from state taxation and the doctrine now renounced giving extensive inter-governmental immunity. Thus in *SRA (Inc) v Minnesota* (1946) 327 US 558 the court says: 'The supremacy of the Federal Government in our union forbids the acknowledgment of the power of any state to tax property of the United States against its will. Under an implied constitutional immunity, its property and operations must be exempt from state control in tax, as in other matters' (at 561).

To my mind the incapacity of the states directly to tax the Commonwealth in respect of something done in the exercise of its powers or functions is a necessary consequence of the system of government established by the Constitution. It is hardly necessary at this stage of our constitutional development to go over the considerations which make it impossible to suppose that the Constitution intended that the states should levy taxes upon the Commonwealth — the nature of the Federal Government, its supremacy, the exclusiveness or paramountcy of its legislative powers, the independence of its fiscal system and the elaborate provisions of the Constitution governing the financial relations of the central Government to the constituent states. To describe the establishment of the Commonwealth as the birth of a nation has been a commonplace. It was anything but the birth of a taxpayer.

The idea that a tax liability might be directly imposed upon the Commonwealth by state law would not, I think, have been entertained, if it had not been for misapprehensions which obtain concerning the effect of the *Engineers'* case (1920) 28 CLR 129. One such misapprehension is that the decision meant that the Constitution implies nothing; that it means nothing that it does not say in express words. I shall repeat two statements upon this subject which I thought it necessary to make in *West v Commissioner of Taxation (NSW)* (1937) 56 CLR at 681–2. One deals with what the *Engineers'* case actually did [23] decide: the other with implications that are to be made in the Constitution: 'There is little justification for seeking to find in the *Engineers'* case authority for more than was decided. The importance alike of the principle there applied and of the application given to it is sufficiently great and far reaching. It is a principle adopted for the interpretation of the legislative powers of the Parliament. The principle is that whenever the Constitution confers a power to make laws in respect of a specific subject-matter, prima facie it is to be understood as enabling the Parliament to make laws affecting the operations of the states and their agencies. The prima facie meaning may be displaced by considerations based on the nature or the subject matter of the power or the language in which it is conferred or on some other provision in the Constitution. But, unless the contrary thus appears, then, subject to two reservations, the power must be construed as extending to the states. The first reservation is that in the *Engineers'* case the question was left open whether the principle would warrant legislation affecting the exercise of a prerogative of the Crown in right of the states. The second is that the decision does not appear to deal with or affect the question whether the Parliament is authorized to enact legislation discriminating against the states or their agencies' (1937) 56 CLR at 682. To this should be added a third reservation, namely, that to which I have already referred concerning the taxation powers of the governments. The second passage contains almost all that I have to say about the need of implying some restraints on state action with reference to the Commonwealth. 'Surely it is implicit in the power given to the executive government of the Commonwealth that the incidents and consequences of its exercise shall not be made the subject of special liabilities or burdens under state law. The principles which have been adopted for determining for the purposes of s 109 whether a state law is consistent with a Federal statute are no less applicable when the question is whether the state law is consistent with the federal Constitution. Since the *Engineers'* case a notion seems to have gained currency that in interpreting the Constitution no implications can be made. Such a method of construction would defeat the intention of any instrument, but of all instruments a written constitution seems to be the last to which it could be applied. I do not think that the judgment of the majority of the court in the *Engineers'* case meant to propound such a doctrine'.

[24] The expression 'special liabilities or burdens under state law' relates to 'the incidents and consequences' of the exercise of Commonwealth power. But a tax directly upon the Commonwealth is subject to the same objection.

It is, perhaps, desirable to add that this case cannot be considered as one in which the Commonwealth comes in to avail itself of privileges, facilities or a course of business established by or under state law to which a charge or even a tax is incident ...

For the foregoing reasons, I am of the opinion that the Commonwealth is not liable to the municipality for the rates it seeks to recover.

~~~

Notes

[8.2.94] In the *Engineers'* case (1920) 28 CLR 129 **[8.2.31C]**, the majority of the High Court expressed some reservation about taxing legislation, but that reservation was equivocal and did no more than leave open the question of the application of the *Engineers'* rule to taxing legislation. This reservation was made in the context of the Commonwealth taxing the states and was expressed in rather complex terms which brought in state prerogative functions: 28 CLR at 143. It might, therefore, be difficult to appeal to the 'reservation' in the *Engineers'* case to support the proposition that the states cannot tax the Commonwealth.

[8.2.95] The assertion that the establishment of the Commonwealth was the birth of a nation, and not of a taxpayer, seems little more than rhetoric. But, if it is to be taken as a constitutional proposition, should it not form the basis for a general Commonwealth immunity from state laws? How would Dixon J justify drawing a distinction between a state taxation law and a state motor car licensing law of the type considered in *Pirrie v McFarlane* (1926) 36 CLR 170 **[8.2.82C]**?

Indeed, there are signs in the judgment of Dixon J that he was developing a general Commonwealth immunity. In particular he cited, with apparent approval, the opinion of the Supreme Court of the United States in *SRA (Inc) v Minnesota* 327 US 558 (1946), where the court had said that the property and operations of the Federal Government 'must be exempt from state control in tax, *as in other matters*': 74 CLR at 22 (emphasis added). Certainly, if we look at Dixon J's judgment in this case in the context of his dissent in *Uther v Federal Commissioner of Taxation* **[8.2.90C]** and of his agreement with Fullagar J in *Commonwealth v Bogle* (1953) 89 CLR 229 **[8.2.96]**, then it is clear that Dixon J was developing such a general immunity.

[8.2.96] In 1949, the Commonwealth established migrant hostels, managed by a Commonwealth Department. In January 1952, the Commonwealth arranged for a company, Commonwealth Hostels Ltd, to be incorporated under the Companies Act 1938 (Vic), with the shares held by Commonwealth public servants; the directors of the company were appointed (and could be removed) by the responsible Commonwealth Minister. The company took over the management of several migrant hostels, including Brooklyn hostel in Victoria. In April 1952, Commonwealth Hostels Ltd announced that it was increasing the charges for accommodation at the Brooklyn hostel. Bogle, a resident of the hostel since July 1951, refused to pay the increased charges, claiming that the company was prevented from increasing those charges by the Victorian Prices Regulation Order No 436 made under the Prices Regulation Act 1948 (Vic), which limited the charges which could be made for the provision of board and lodging.

The Commonwealth and Commonwealth Hostels Ltd sued Bogle in the High Court to recover the unpaid accommodation charges. Kitto J stated several questions for the opinion of the Full Court, which decided that the company was not an agency or instrumentality of the Commonwealth Crown and that the Prices Regulation Act 1948 (Vic) and the order made under that Act applied to the company: *Commonwealth v Bogle* (1953) 89 CLR 229.

The decision that the company was not an instrumentality of the Commonwealth Crown was crucial, as revealed by the following passage from Fullagar J's judgment (with whom Dixon CJ, Webb and Kitto JJ agreed) at 259:

> In the view which I have ultimately taken of this case it is not necessary to decide whether the Commonwealth is bound by the Prices Regulation Act (Vic) ... however, ... in my opinion, the Commonwealth is not bound by that Act ... To say that a state can enact legislation which is binding upon the Commonwealth in the same sense in which it is binding upon a subject of the state appears to me to give effect to a fundamental misconception. The question whether a particular state Act binds the Crown in right of a state is a pure question of construction. The Crown in right of the state has assented to the statute, and no constitutional question arises. If we ask whether the same statute binds the Crown in right of the Commonwealth, a question of construction may arise on the threshold. In considering that question we are, or should be, assisted by a presumption that references to the Crown are references to the Crown in right of the state only. If the answer to the question of construction be that the statute in question does purport to bind the Crown in right of the Commonwealth, then a constitutional question arises. The Crown in right of the state has assented to the statute, but the Crown in right of the Commonwealth has not, and the constitutional question, to my mind, is susceptible of only one answer, and that is that the state Parliament has no power over the Commonwealth. The Commonwealth — or the Crown in right of the Commonwealth, or whatever you choose to call it — is, to all intents and purposes, a juristic person, but it is not a juristic person which is subjected either by any state Constitution or by the Commonwealth Constitution to the legislative power of any state Parliament.

Fullagar J observed that the Commonwealth might 'become affected by state laws', for example, by making a contract in Victoria — in which case, the terms and effect of that contract might have to be sought in the Goods Act 1928 (Vic). However, he said:

> ... I should think it impossible to hold that the Parliament of Victoria could lawfully prescribe the uses which might be made by the Commonwealth of its own property, the terms upon which that property might be let to tenants, or the terms upon which the Commonwealth might provide accommodation for immigrants introduced into Australia. [89 CLR at 260]

[8.2.97] The exception to Fullagar J's general proposition of Commonwealth immunity referred to the Commonwealth becoming 'affected by state laws'. This recognition that the Commonwealth regularly enters into transactions which must have some legal dimension, was also mentioned by Dixon J in *Uther v Federal Commissioner of Taxation* (1947) 74 CLR 509 **[8.2.90C]**: see, in particular, **[8.2.92]**. Such an exception will inevitably create serious problems. It assumes that we can distinguish between those situations where the Commonwealth 'makes use of its own property' (when there will be immunity from state law), and those situations when the Commonwealth 'makes a contract' (where it will be subject to state law). How can we make that distinction? What guidance is offered by *Maguire v Simpson* (1977) 139 CLR 362 **[8.2.107]** and *Commonwealth v Evans Deakin Industries Ltd* (1986) 161 CLR 254 **[8.2.108]**?

[8.2.98C] ## Commonwealth v Cigamatic Pty Ltd

(1962) 108 CLR 372

The Supreme Court of New South Wales ordered that Cigamatic Pty Ltd be wound up under the Companies Act 1936 (NSW) and that its assets be distributed among its creditors according to the order of priority specified in s 297 of the Act. The Commonwealth claimed to be a creditor of Cigamatic Pty Ltd. In particular, it claimed that the company owed the government £17,013 under the Sales Tax Assessment Act 1930 (Cth) and £126 under the Post and Telegraph Act 1901 (Cth).

As in *Uther v Federal Commissioner of Taxation* (1947) 74 CLR 509 **[8.2.90C]**, it was common ground that, apart from ss 282 and 297 of the Companies Act 1936 (NSW), the Commonwealth would be entitled to a degree of priority over other creditors. The nature of this priority and the provisions of ss 282 and 297, are described in the introduction to *Uther v Federal Commissioner of Taxation* **[8.2.90C]**.

The Commonwealth began an action in the High Court of Australia, seeking a declaration that it was entitled to be paid its debts in priority to other creditors and an injunction to restrain the liquidator of the company from satisfying any other debts until the Commonwealth's debts had been satisfied. The company and the liquidator (the defendants in the action) demurred to the plaintiff's statement of claim, saying that the Commonwealth was bound by the provisions of the Companies Act 1936 (NSW). The demurrer was heard before the Full Court.

Dixon CJ: [376] In the first instance the Commonwealth rests its claim on the right at common law of the Crown to priority of payment when in any administration of assets debts of equal degree due to the Crown and due to subjects of the Crown come into competition. This right arose from the sovereignty of the Crown and was [377] accordingly expressed in terms of prerogative but it is today one of the fiscal rights of government and of course it clearly attaches to the Commonwealth. The claim of the Commonwealth in the present case resting on its rights is, however, denied on the ground that by force of the state Companies Act it is excluded. This conclusion is doubtless supported, if not completely at all events to no inconsiderable degree, by the judgments of the majority in *Uther v Federal Commissioner of Taxation* (1947) 74 CLR 508, but it seems to me now as it seemed to me then to imply a fundamental proposition about the power of legislatures of the state which ought not to be entertained. The proposition that is implied is that an exercise of state legislative power may directly derogate from the rights of the Commonwealth with respect to its people. It is a proposition which must go deep in the nature and operation of the federal system. There can be no doubt as to the nature or the source of the right of the Commonwealth in an administration of assets to be paid in preference to subjects of the Crown if there is a competition among debts of equal degree. It springs from the nature of the Commonwealth as a government of the Queen. Therefore to treat those rights as subject to destruction or modification or qualification by the legislature of a state must mean that under the Constitution there resides in a state or states a legislative power to control legal rights and duties between the Commonwealth and its people. Indeed in *Uther's* case Rich J actually says: 'In so far as the right of the Crown in the right of the Commonwealth to rank as a preferential creditor is based merely on the prerogative of the Crown as such, I see no reason why the state legislature cannot validly abridge or abolish it just as it could any other Crown prerogative of this sort' (at 523). Except by adopting such a doctrine I cannot see how it could be thought that state legislative power could directly deprive the Commonwealth of the priority to which it is entitled under the law derived from the prerogative. Believing, as I do, that the doctrine thus involved is a fundamental error in a constitutional principle that spreads far beyond the mere preference of debts owing to the Commonwealth, I do not think we should treat *Uther's* case as a decisive authority upon that question which we should regard as binding. It is not a question, as it appears to me, of interpreting some positive power of the state over a given subject matter. It is not a question of making some implication in favour of the Commonwealth restraining some acknowledged legislative power of the state. If you express the priority belonging to the [378] Commonwealth as a prerogative of the Crown in right of the Commonwealth, the question is whether the legislative powers of the states could extend over one of the prerogatives of the Crown in right of the Commonwealth. If, as in modern times I think it is more correct to do, you describe it as a fiscal right belonging to the Commonwealth as a government and affecting its Treasury, it is a question of state legislative power affecting to control or abolish a federal fiscal right. It is not a question of the authority of the power of a state to make some general law governing the rights and duties of those who enter into some description of transaction, such as the sale of goods, and of the Commonwealth in its executive arm choosing to enter into a transaction of that description. It is not a question of the exercise of some specific grant of power which according to the very meaning of the terms in which it is defined embraces the subject matter itself: for it is not the plan of the Constitution to grant specific powers to the states over defined subjects. It is, I think, a question which cannot be regarded as simply governed by the applicability of the principles upon which *Melbourne Corporation v Commonwealth* (1947) 74 CLR 31 depended. In truth it imports a principle which if true would apply generally with respect to the legal rights of the Commonwealth in relation to its subjects. I do not speak of legal rights which are the immediate product of federal statute and so protected by s 109 of the Constitution. But because it imports such a principle I think we ought not to give effect to the view taken in *Uther's* case that s 297 of the Companies Act, 1936 of New South Wales operated directly to nullify the priority to which the Commonwealth might have been entitled. I shall not recapitulate the reasons against this conclusion which I gave in *Uther's* case.

Kitto and Windeyer JJ concurred with Dixon CJ. Menzies J delivered a separate judgment in which he adopted the dissenting judgment of Dixon J in *Uther v Federal Commissioner of Taxation* (1947) 74 CLR 509 **[8.2.90C]**. Owen J concurred with Menzies J. McTiernan and Taylor JJ dissented, following the decision in *Uther's* case.

~~~

Notes

[8.2.99] In a series of cases, culminating in *Victoria v Commonwealth* (the *Second Uniform Tax* case) (1956) 99 CLR 575, the High Court considered the reciprocal issue: Could the Commonwealth Parliament legislate so as to interfere with the prerogative right of the states to priority in the payment of their debts, by giving absolute priority to Commonwealth debts? Ultimately, the majority of the court was prepared to uphold such legislation when it operated in the context of bankruptcy and insolvency, but would not concede that the Commonwealth Parliament could give priority to Commonwealth debts outside that context: see **[8.2.43]**, **[8.2.44]**. Of course, when one is considering the issue of priority for the payment of debts, the context of bankruptcy and insolvency is the critical context; and, in so far as the Commonwealth has power to rearrange priorities in that context (including the priority of the Crown in right of the states), it has a significant power which, according to *Commonwealth v Cigamatic Ltd* (1962) 108 CLR 372 **[8.2.98C]**, the states do not have.

[8.2.100] The proposition established by the High Court in *Commonwealth v Cigamatic Ltd* (1962) 108 CLR 372 **[8.2.98C]** goes very far; indeed, it probably overruled that part of the *Engineers'* case (1920) 28 CLR 129 **[8.2.31C]** which implied that state parliaments have the power to legislate so as to bind the Commonwealth: 28 CLR at 155. The proposition established by the *Cigamatic* case was that state parliaments have no power to enact legislation binding on the Commonwealth which defines or regulates its rights and duties towards its subjects, or that regulates or controls the governmental rights, including fiscal and prerogative rights, of the Commonwealth.

The *Cigamatic* proposition was a general one. It was not a specific exception (limited to the Commonwealth's prerogative rights) to a general rule that state parliaments could legislate so as to bind the Crown. The proposition did not depend on any exercise of Commonwealth legislative power which, by virtue of s 109, would invalidate inconsistent state legislation. Such a proposition makes *Pirrie v McFarlane* (1925) 36 CLR 170 **[8.2.82C]** a decision of doubtful authority.

The extent of Commonwealth immunity from state law is uncertain because, as we shall consider later, Dixon CJ put forward the idea that the Commonwealth may in some situations be affected by state law (as he had in *Uther v Federal Commissioner of Taxation* (1947) 74 CLR 509 **[8.2.90C]**, **[8.2.92]** and as Fullagar J had in *Commonwealth v Bogle* (1953) 89 CLR 229 **[8.2.96]**, **[8.2.97]**). However, it is arguable that all activity of the Commonwealth is governmental activity and that all state statutes which purport to bind the Commonwealth involve an attempt to regulate its governmental rights and are therefore invalid.

[8.2.101]   The argument of Dixon CJ in support of the proposition established in *Commonwealth v Cigamatic Ltd* (1962) 108 CLR 372 **[8.2.98C]** is to be found in *Uther v Federal Commissioner of Taxation* (1947) 74 CLR 509 **[8.2.90C]**, and is quite simple. The steps are:

- before federation and the establishment of the Commonwealth, the colonies that became states had no legislative power with reference to the Commonwealth;

- the legislative power of the states after federation was that of the colonies before federation, subject to the Commonwealth Constitution; and

- the Commonwealth Constitution did not give the states legislative power with reference to the Commonwealth.

Therefore, the conclusion is, the states have no legislative power over the Commonwealth.

The first two steps in the argument are unassailable; the third is, however, dubious. The state parliaments were not expressly given power to legislate with reference to the Commonwealth or to bind the Crown in right of the Commonwealth, but may have such an implicit power. Individuals become subject to state legislative power by their involvement in situations which are within the legislative jurisdiction of the state parliaments, that is, by their involvement in situations which can be described as 'in and for Victoria' or related to the 'peace, welfare and good government of New South Wales'. The assumption of the *Engineers'* case (1920) 28 CLR 129 **[8.2.31C]** was that there was no general constitutional barrier preventing the state parliaments enacting laws, otherwise valid, which bind the Commonwealth.

> The Commonwealth Constitution as it exists for the time being, dealing expressly with sovereign functions of the Crown in relation to Commonwealth and to states, necessarily so far binds the Crown, and laws validly made by authority of the Constitution bind, so far as they purport to do so, the people of every state considered as individuals or as political organisms called states — in other words, bind both Crown and subjects (28 CLR at 153).

The general propositions of the *Engineers'* case (1920) 28 CLR 129 **[8.2.31C]** applied equally to Commonwealth and states.

Why should it be assumed that the Commonwealth is different from other persons and institutions that become subject to state legislative power by entering into situations within the legislative power of the states? Dixon J implied it from the federal system which he described as a dual system, in which one does not expect to find either government legislating for the other. But why does one not expect to find either government legislating for the other? In a federal system where legislative power in relation to the same territory is allocated between state and Commonwealth parliaments and where executive power is likewise distributed between state and Commonwealth governments, is it not legitimate to expect that, since the Crown is no longer beyond the reach of legislative power (as it claimed to be in the 17th century), that the Crown in all its Australian guises is within the reach of otherwise valid exercises of the legislative power of all the Australian parliaments?

[8.2.102] The proposition advanced by Dixon CJ in *Commonwealth v Cigamatic Ltd* (1962) 108 CLR 372 **[8.2.98C]** and *Uther v Federal Commissioner of Taxation* (1947) 74 CLR 509 **[8.2.90C]** is not reciprocal: it does not in any way limit Commonwealth power over the states. The implication made from the dual federal system, that the Commonwealth, as a government, is different from other persons and institutions within the legislative power of the states so that it is not within the ambit of state legislative jurisdiction, is not applied to protect the states from Commonwealth legislative power. The dual federal system does not create an equality or reciprocal relationship between governments. Dixon J, in *Uther's* case, explained this on a number of grounds.

First, he said that the Commonwealth has, under the Constitution, been granted supremacy. However, the supremacy conferred on the Commonwealth is only a supremacy of Commonwealth law over inconsistent state law pursuant to s 109 of the Constitution.

Secondly, Dixon J said that the legislative powers of the Commonwealth Parliament are specifically defined and are plenary within their ambit. But is not the undefined residue of state power also plenary within its ambit? See *Cobb & Co v Kropp* [1967] 1 AC 141 **[6.4.53]** at 154.

The grant of specific legislative power to the Commonwealth and residual legislative power to the states can be explained by the fact that the Commonwealth was set up on the foundation of existing colonial governments with established powers. A new institution of central government was created with limited, but defined, governmental powers. Why should the grant of specific powers to the Commonwealth Parliament carry a power to bind the Crown in right of the states, and the grant of residual power to the states carry no reciprocal power?

[8.2.103] Dixon CJ did not propose a complete immunity of the Crown in right of the Commonwealth from state law. In *Federal Commissioner of Taxation v Official Liquidator of EO Farley Ltd* (1943) 63 CLR 278 **[8.2.43]**, Dixon J said at 308:

> In many respects the executive government of the Commonwealth is affected by the condition of the general law. For instance, the general law of contract may regulate the formation, performance and discharge of the contracts which the Commonwealth finds it necessary to make in the course of the ordinary administration of government. Where there is no Federal statute affecting the matter, an exercise of the legislative power of the state over the general law of contract might incidentally apply in the case of the Commonwealth alike with the citizen. In the practical administration of the law, the decision of questions of that sort depends less upon constitutional analysis than on s 80 and perhaps s 79 of the Judiciary Act 1903–1939. There is, however, a clear distinction between the general law, the content or condition of which, though a matter for the legislatures of the states, may incidentally affect Commonwealth administrative

action, and, on the other hand, governmental rights and powers belonging to the Federal executive as such.

[8.2.104E]   **Judiciary Act 1903 (Cth)**

79 The laws of each State or Territory, including the laws relating to procedure, evidence, and the competency of witnesses, shall, except as otherwise provided by the Constitution or the laws of the Commonwealth, be binding on all Courts exercising federal jurisdiction in that State or Territory in all cases to which they are applicable.

80 So far as the laws of the Commonwealth are not applicable or so far as their provisions are insufficient to carry them into effect, or to provide adequate remedies or punishment, the common law of England as modified by the Constitution and by the statute law in force in the State or Territory in which the Court in which the jurisdiction is exercised is held shall, so far as it is applicable and not inconsistent with the Constitution and the laws of the Commonwealth, govern all Courts exercising federal jurisdiction in the exercise of their jurisdiction in civil and criminal matters.

~~~

[8.2.105]   These two difficult sections are concerned with choice of law questions in courts exercising federal jurisdiction. They make certain laws of a state binding on courts exercising federal jurisdiction within that state, but only in so far as they are applicable. They come into operation only when litigation is commenced, for they are directives to courts, not the parties in advance of their commencing litigation. However, the two provisions do 'not purport to do more than pick up state laws with their meaning unchanged': *Pedersen v Young* 1964 (110) CLR 162 at 165 per Kitto J. That is, it could be argued that they do not resolve the immunities argument. It seems that, in order fully to resolve that difficulty, ss 79 and 80 must be read with s 64 of the Judiciary Act:

64 In any suit to which the Commonwealth or a State is a party, the rights of the parties shall, as nearly as possible, be the same, and judgment may be given and costs awarded on either side, as in a suit between subject and subject.

[8.2.106]   This group of sections (that is, ss 64, 79 and 80) might be seen as a legislative submission, by the Commonwealth Parliament, of the Commonwealth to state law. Or they could be treated as assimilative provisions which enact, as Commonwealth law, the applicable state law. Kitto J expressed this argument in *Asiatic Steam Navigation Co Ltd v Commonwealth* (1956) 96 CLR 397 at 427:

[T]he rights referred to in s 64 include the substantive rights to be given effect to in the suit. If that be so, it follows that s 64 must be interpreted as taking up and enacting, as the law to be applied in every suit to which the Commonwealth or a state is a party, the whole body of the law, statutory or not, by which the rights of the parties would be governed if the Commonwealth or state were a subject instead of being the Crown. The portion of that law which is taken by s 64 from statutes, whether Imperial, Commonwealth or state, is then to be applied in such suits by the independent force of that section; and if, in its original setting any provision of that law was so expressed as not to apply to the Crown, s 64 nevertheless explicitly makes it applicable, as completely as possible, to the determination of the rights of the Commonwealth or state against its opponents and of their rights against the Commonwealth or state.

[8.2.107]   Although judicial views on the meaning of s 64 differed over the years and there were some views which were considerably narrower than those of Kitto J (see Pryles and Hanks (1974) pp 203–7), his reading of that section was endorsed by a majority of the High Court in *Maguire v Simpson* (1977) 139 CLR 362. In that case, the Commonwealth Trading Bank initiated proceedings in the Supreme Court of New South Wales to recover a debt (an overdraft on a current account) of $5325.17 from a fund which represented the debtor's assets. Other creditors of the debtor objected that ss 14 and 63 of the Limitations Act 1969 (NSW) barred the bank's claim. When the Commonwealth Bank said it was immune from the Limitations Act, the matter was removed to the High Court under s 40A of the Judiciary Act 1903 (Cth).

The court decided that the Commonwealth Bank was an agent of the Crown in right of the Commonwealth and so entitled to the immunities of the Crown in right of the Commonwealth. The court assumed that amongst those immunities was immunity from state legislation. However, the court pointed out that the provisions of s 64 of the Judiciary Act were directly relevant to the Commonwealth Bank's attempt to recover the debt because the proceedings where the recovery was sought were a 'suit to which the Commonwealth ... [was] a party'. Stephen J found it unnecessary to go further than to decide that s 64 made state procedural laws applicable: s 14 was procedural and barred the action to recover the debt.

The other members of the court, Barwick CJ, Gibbs, Mason, Jacobs and Murphy JJ, committed themselves to the position that s 64 referred to substantive law as well as procedural law and ensured that, whenever the Commonwealth was a party to a suit, its substantive rights were to be settled, as nearly as possible, as if it were a private litigant. In the present case, this meant that, not only was its action barred by s 14 (a procedural restriction), but its cause of action was destroyed by s 63 of the Limitation Act (a substantive alteration of its rights). Mason J referred to *Commonwealth v Cigamatic Ltd* (1962) 108 CLR 372 **[8.2.98C]** and said that he had not considered the doctrine enunciated in that case:

> However, I should point out that no mention was made of s 64 in that case, although there seems to be no reason why it should not have had an application if it extended to substantive rights. Nonetheless, as the section was not argued I do not regard the decision as constituting authority for the proposition that the section does not apply to substantive rights (139 CLR at 402).

Jacobs J referred to at 404:

> ... the somewhat curious situation that the effect of the Judiciary Act was not discussed in the reasons for judgment of any member of the Court in *Cigamatic* and yet it would appear to me that, at least in respect of the money owing to the Commonwealth under the Post and Telegraph Act 1901 and the Telephone Regulations and the Telegraph Regulations, the provisions of the Judiciary Act were as relevant there to be considered as they are in the present case. Nevertheless it appears to me that the question whether the reasoning in *Cigamatic* involves a revival of the doctrine of implied immunity of instrumentalities and whether it is essentially inconsistent with the *Engineers'* case should not be pursued unless the determination is essential to the present decision.

[8.2.108] In *Commonwealth v Evans Deakin Industries Ltd* (1986) 161 CLR 254, the High Court endorsed the view of s 64 outlined in *Maguire v Simpson* (1977) 139 CLR 362 **[8.2.107]**. In *Evans Deakin*, a company had entered into a contract with the Commonwealth to construct a building at Brisbane airport. Evans Deakin then agreed with the company to supply and erect steel components for the building, as a subcontractor. After the work was completed, but before the Commonwealth had paid the company or the company had paid Evans Deakin, the company went into liquidation. Evans Deakin then exercised its rights under the Subcontractors' Charges Act 1974 (Qld) and gave notice to the Commonwealth that the

Commonwealth should pay Evans Deakin directly the money owing under the subcontract. When the Commonwealth did not comply, Evans Deakin began proceedings in the Queensland Supreme Court for an order, under the Subcontractors' Charges Act, that the Commonwealth should pay Evans Deakin the money owing. The Queensland Supreme Court overruled a demurrer lodged by the Commonwealth which asserted that the Commonwealth was not bound by the Act.

On appeal, the majority of the High Court (Gibbs CJ, Mason, Wilson, Deane and Dawson JJ) confirmed the reading of s 64 given in *Maguire v Simpson* (1977) 139 CLR 362 **[8.2.107]**:

> [I]n every suit to which the Commonwealth is a party s 64 requires the rights of the parties to be ascertained, as nearly as possible, by the same rules of law, substantive and procedural, statutory and otherwise, as would apply if the Commonwealth were a subject instead of being the Crown (161 CLR at 262–3).

The five justices conceded 'that there must be a suit to which the Commonwealth is a party before s 64 commences to operate': 161 CLR at 263. However, this did not mean that the cause of action against the Commonwealth must arise under some other law of the Commonwealth before s 64 could apply. The commencement of a suit against the Commonwealth, the precondition for s 64, required no more than the bringing of an action against the Commonwealth in a court of competent jurisdiction at 264:

> Once the suit is commenced the substantive rights of the parties shall be, as nearly as possible as in a suit between subject and subject. If the Commonwealth were a subject, Evans Deakin, as subcontractor, would, on the facts alleged in the statement of claim, be entitled to enforce the charge given by the Subcontractors' Charges Act.

The justices said it was unnecessary to consider whether in some cases the special position of the Crown should be taken into account. Here the Commonwealth had made 'a contract of a kind commonly entered into by ordinary members of the public'; it had not been 'performing a function peculiar to government'; and determining its rights and liabilities under the Subcontractors' Charges Act 'would not be incompatible with the position of the Commonwealth as detrimental to the public welfare': 161 CLR at 265.

The justices made the important point that the impact of s 64 extended beyond the context of litigation (at 265–6):

> If it is possible to say that once a suit is commenced the Commonwealth will be held liable, it follows that it can also be said, before the suit is commenced, that the events which have happened have created a liability which will be recognised and enforced in legal proceedings. A payment in satisfaction of such a liability will not be unlawful.
>
> It is therefore only a half-truth to say that s 64 has the effect that upon the commencement of a suit the Commonwealth becomes subject to obligations which did not exist beforehand. The section does not have a retrospective operation. At all times before a suit is commenced, it can be known what the rights of the parties will be once the suit is commenced.

In other words, the subjection of the Commonwealth to state legislation, once a suit is commenced, is a central factor to be taken into account in determining the legal rights and obligations of the Commonwealth before that suit has been commenced.

The majority justices concluded by noting that the correctness of the decision in *Commonwealth v Cigamatic Pty Ltd* (1962) 108 CLR 372 **[8.2.98C]** had not been raised in argument, 'and we do not need to consider it': 161 CLR at 267.

[8.2.109] Writing in the light of *Maguire v Simpson*, Zines observed that 'the decision in *Cigamatic* seems wrong unless some justification can be eked out of the words 'as nearly as possible', and that the reasoning in *Maguire v Simpson* 'also seems to be inconsistent with the dicta of Fullagar J in *Bogle's* case': Zines (1997) p 369. (The problems posed by the phrase 'as nearly as possible' are discussed in Pryles and Hanks (1974) pp 206–7 and Zines (1997) pp 370–1.)

Zines also makes the point that s 64 cannot be relevant to the problem considered in *Pirrie v McFarlane* (1925) 36 CLR 170 **[8.2.82C]** which was concerned with a prosecution rather than a 'suit', that is, a civil proceeding. (That point was implicitly acknowledged in *Commonwealth v Evans Deakin Industries Ltd* (1986) 161 CLR 254 **[8.2.108]** at 265.)

[8.2.110] A further restriction on the reach of s 64 was adopted by the High Court in *Deputy Commissioner of Taxation v Moorebank* (1988) 165 CLR 55. The court (Mason CJ, Brennan, Deane, Dawson and Gaudron JJ) decided that the Deputy Commissioner could sue in the Queensland Supreme Court to recover taxes payable under the Income Tax Assessment Act 1936 (Cth), notwithstanding that the limitation period set by the Limitation of Actions Act 1974 (Qld) had expired. The court said that the provisions of the Income Tax Assessment Act dealing with the collection and recovery of tax 'relevantly cover the field', and that the state limitation period would 'undermine ... the coherent scheme which the Assessment Act embodies': 165 CLR at 67. The Assessment Act was intended, the court said, to give the Commissioner for Taxation wide powers relating to the recovery of taxes.

In concluding that s 64 could not apply state law to a situation where its application would be inconsistent with a law of the Commonwealth (in the s 109 sense), the court said at 64:

> [W]here the Commonwealth legislative scheme is complete on its face, s 64 will not operate to insert into it some provision of state law for whose operation the Commonwealth provisions can, when properly understood, be seen to have left no room.

[8.2.111] For many years, the question of the correctness of *Commonwealth v Cigamatic Pty Ltd* (1962) 108 CLR 372 **[8.2.98C]** was largely a theoretical one. As Zines noted, the principle was never applied by the High Court (although it was applied by other courts) and the broad reading given to s 64 of the Judiciary Act 1903 (Cth) meant that the consequences of *Cigamatic* could be 'avoided': Zines (1998) p 88. This did not stop it being a regular topic for academic debate: Zines (1998) p 89. The principle was reconsidered by the High Court in the following case.

[8.2.112C]   **Re Residential Tenancies Tribunal of New South Wales and Henderson; Ex parte Defence Housing Authority**
(1997) 190 CLR 410

The Defence Housing Authority ('the DHA') was established under s 4 of the Defence Housing Authority Act 1987 (Cth). Under s 5(1) of that Act, the function of the DHA was to provide adequate and suitable housing for members of the Australian Defence Force. Section 5(2) required the DHA to provide such housing as the Minister directed was necessary to meet the operational needs of the Defence Force. Section 31(2) stated that, where the Minister was satisfied that it was desirable in the public interest to do so, the Minister could give directions to the DHA with respect to the performance of its function and the exercise of its powers.

The Residential Tenancies Act 1987 (NSW) conferred functions on the Residential Tenancies Tribunal of New South Wales with respect to landlords and tenants. With one 'immaterial exception' (Dawson Toohey and Gaudron JJ, 190 CLR at 430), s 4 was expressed to bind the Crown 'not only in right of New South Wales but also, so far as the legislative power of Parliament permits, the Crown in all its other capacities'.

The owner of premises leased to the DHA brought an application in the Residential Tenancies Tribunal, under s 24 of the NSW Act, for an order allowing inspection of the premises. The DHA obtained an order nisi for prohibition in the High Court which would have prevented the Tribunal from hearing the application. Amongst the arguments advanced by the DHA were an argument based on s 109 of the Constitution (see **[8.1.69]**); an argument based on s 52(ii) of the Constitution; and an argument that the principle in *Commonwealth v Cigamatic Ltd* (1962) 108 CLR 372 **[8.2.98C]** applied to prevent the state law from binding the Commonwealth.

The court discharged the *order nisi* and the majority (Dawson Toohey and Gaudron JJ; Brennan CJ, McHugh and Gummow JJ agreeing; Kirby J dissenting) decided that the state legislation did apply to the DHA.

Brennan J agreed with Dawson, Toohey and Gaudron JJ that there was no inconsistency under s 109 and that s 52(ii) had no application. He also agreed that a distinction should be drawn between the capacities and functions of the Crown in right of the Commonwealth and the transactions in which that Crown may choose to engage in exercise of its capacities and functions.

Brennan CJ: [424] By 'capacities and functions' I mean the rights, powers, privileges and immunities which are collectively described as the 'executive power of the Commonwealth' in s 61 of the Constitution. The executive power of the Commonwealth, being vested in the Queen and exercisable by the Governor-General, derives its content mediately or immediately from the Constitution. Executive power may be conferred by a law of the Commonwealth or it may be the power which, at least in earlier times, was seen as part of the Royal prerogative. The executive power of the Commonwealth may be modified by valid laws of the Commonwealth: *Brown v West* (1990) 169 CLR 195 at 205; but it is beyond the legislative reach of the states. The states have no legislative power that can modify a grant of power to the Crown in right of the Commonwealth by a law of the Commonwealth nor any legislative power that can modify a prerogative power conferred by the [425] Constitution. In *Cigamatic* (1962) 108 CLR 372 at 378, Dixon CJ clearly distinguished between the prerogatives of the Crown in right of the Commonwealth and transactions into which the Crown may choose to enter ...

[426] A state law which purports on its face to impose a burden on the Crown in right of the Commonwealth fails for one of two reasons. If the burden falls on the enjoyment of the Commonwealth prerogative, the law would be offensive to s 61 of the Constitution; if it falls on the enjoyment of a statutory power, it would be inconsistent with the Commonwealth law conferring the power and would be invalid by reason of s 109 ...

[427] However, there is no reason why the Crown in right of the Commonwealth should not be bound by a state law of general application which governs transactions into which the Crown in right of the Commonwealth may choose to enter. The executive power of the Commonwealth, exercised by its choice to enter the transaction, is not affected merely because the incidents of the transaction are prescribed by a state law. That, I understand, was the view which Dixon CJ was expressing in the passage cited from his Honour's judgment in *Cigamatic*.

Dawson, Toohey and Gaudron JJ held that the Defence Housing Authority Act was not inconsistent with the Residential Tenancies Tribunal Act: 190 CLR at 432. The justices said that the matters dealt with by the Residential Tenancies Act did not fall within the exclusive power of the Commonwealth under s 52(ii): 190 CLR at 438.

Dawson, Toohey and **Gaudron JJ:** [438] It was submitted by the DHA and by the Attorney-General for the Commonwealth intervening that state laws cannot by their own force bind the Crown in right of the Commonwealth. That submission was said to be supported by the decision of this Court in *Commonwealth v Cigamatic Pty Ltd (In Liquidation)* (1962) 108 CLR 372, but in truth it represents a basic misconception of what was decided in that case.

In the present context, the Crown in right of the Commonwealth means the government of the Commonwealth exercising the executive power vested in it by s 61 of the Constitution. That power includes the prerogatives of the Crown because the setting in which the Crown is invested with executive power is that of the common law and the prerogatives of the Crown are those rights, powers, privileges and immunities which it possesses at common law. Of course, those prerogatives are not immutable but, being derived from the common law, are susceptible to statutory alteration or abolition where the necessary legislative power exists. Under s 61 the executive power vested in the Crown is exercisable by the Governor-General as the Crown's representative. The activities of the Commonwealth government are conducted formally on behalf of the Crown through the Governor-General acting on the advice of the Federal Executive Council. The Federal Executive Council consists of the Crown's Ministers of State drawn, subject to a minor qualification, from the House of Representatives and the Senate. In reality, the Crown acts in its day to day activities through the agency of its public service and through other institutions or instrumentalities created for the purpose. The Crown's functions nowadays extend beyond the traditional, or clearly regal, functions of government to activities of an entrepreneurial or commercial kind which, in general, were previously engaged in only by subjects of the Crown.

It is necessary at the outset to observe a distinction between the capacities of the Crown on the one hand, by which we mean its rights, powers, privileges and immunities, and the exercise of those capacities on the other. In referring to the capacities of the Crown so defined, we [439] are speaking of the same thing of which Dixon J spoke when he used the words 'capacity or functions' in *West v Commissioner of Taxation (NSW)* (1937) 56 CLR 657 at 682 in quoting from the dissenting judgment of Isaacs J in *Pirrie v McFarlane* (1925) 36 CLR 170 at 191. Elsewhere he used other expressions to convey essentially the same meaning, such as the 'governmental rights and powers belonging to the Federal executive as such' or 'the rights or privileges, duties or disabilities, of the Commonwealth in relation to the subjects of the Crown'. In *Cigamatic* (1962) 108 CLR 372 at 378, Dixon CJ also spoke of the 'legal rights of the Commonwealth in relation to its subjects' and that expression is, as shall appear, of some use in applying the principle which he expounded.

The purpose in drawing a distinction between the capacities of the Crown and the exercise of them is to draw a further distinction between legislation which purports to modify the nature of the executive power vested in the Crown — its capacities — and legislation which assumes those capacities and merely seeks to regulate activities in which the Crown may choose to engage in the exercise of those capacities.

In *Cigamatic* (1962) 108 CLR 372, it was held that a state legislature had no power to impair the capacities of the Commonwealth executive, but at the same time it was recognised that the Commonwealth might be regulated by state laws of general application in those activities which it carried on in common with other citizens. Dixon J had earlier drawn the same distinction in *Federal Commissioner of Taxation v Official Liquidator of EO Farley Ltd* (1940) 63 CLR 278 at 308, where he said:

> In many respects the executive government of the Commonwealth is affected by the condition of the general law. For instance, the general law of contract may regulate the formation, performance and discharge of the contracts which the Commonwealth finds it necessary to make in the course of the ordinary administration of government. Where there is no Federal statute affecting the matter, an exercise of the legislative power of the state over the general law of contract might incidentally apply in the case of the Commonwealth alike with the citizen ... There is, however, a clear distinction between the general law, the content or condition of which, though a matter for the legislatures of the states, may [440] incidentally affect Commonwealth administrative action, and, on the other hand, governmental rights and powers belonging to the Federal executive as such.

The fundamental principle which lies behind those observations is that which was recognised in *Melbourne Corporation v Commonwealth* (1947) 74 CLR 31, namely, that the Constitution is predicated upon the continued separate existence of the Commonwealth and the states, not only in name, but as bodies politic to which the Constitution proceeds to distribute powers of government. In the application of the principle, however, it is necessary to differentiate between the Commonwealth on the one hand and the states on the other.

Dawson, Toohey and Gaudron JJ noted that the Commonwealth was given enumerated legislative powers which might authorise the Commonwealth to affect the executive capacities of a state; that the Commonwealth's laws would prevail over state laws under s 109 of the Constitution; but the states were protected against Commonwealth laws that imposed a special burden on them or inhibited or impaired the continued existence of the states or their capacity to function. On the other hand, the states lacked specific legislative powers that might be construed as authorising them to restrict or modify the executive capacities of the Commonwealth:

No implication limiting an otherwise given power is needed; the character of the Commonwealth as a body politic, armed with executive capacities by the Constitution, by its very nature places those capacities outside the legislative power of another body politic, namely a state, without specific powers in that respect. Having regard to the fundamental principle recognised in *Melbourne Corporation v Commonwealth*, only an express provision in the Constitution could authorise a state to affect the capacities of the Commonwealth executive and there is no such authorisation.

[441] ... Dixon J in *Uther* (1947) 74 CLR 508 at 529 suggested that the bankruptcy and insolvency power granted to the Commonwealth Parliament by s 51(xvii) might extend as a matter of construction to laws excluding or reducing the priority of the Crown in right of a state in the payment of debts due to it ... But the fundamental point made in *Cigamatic* (1962) 108 CLR 372 is that in the absence of a like power being conferred upon the states, the priority of the Crown in right of the Commonwealth in the payment of debts is not something over which the states have legislative power.

In *Cigamatic* this Court adopted the view which Dixon J had expressed in dissent in *Uther*. Both cases were concerned with the power of a state legislature to restrict or abolish a particular capacity enjoyed by the Crown in right of the Commonwealth — its prerogative right to the payment of all debts due to it in priority to all other debts of equal degree. The view which was adopted treats that prerogative as part of the definition of Commonwealth executive power going, as it does, to the rights or privileges of the Crown in right of the Commonwealth ... [T]he important consideration is whether a suggested capacity is enjoyed by the Commonwealth executive, not its character [442] as a prerogative or otherwise. The principle that a state law cannot affect the capacities of the Commonwealth executive clearly extends beyond those rights, powers, privileges or immunities which might be described as having their origin in the prerogative.

Both in *Uther* and *Cigamatic* a distinction is drawn between state laws affecting Commonwealth executive capacities and state laws of general application regulating activities carried on by the Crown in the exercise of those capacities in the same manner as its subjects. Thus in *Uther* (1947) 74 CLR 508 at 528, Dixon J said:

The fact that the priority claimed by the Commonwealth springs from one of the prerogatives of the Crown is an added reason, a reason perhaps conclusive in itself, for saying that it is a matter lying completely outside state power. But there is the antecedent consideration that to define or regulate the rights or privileges, duties or disabilities, of the Commonwealth in relation to the subjects of the Crown is not a matter for the states. General laws made by a state may affix legal consequences to given descriptions of transaction and the Commonwealth, if it enters into such a transaction, may be bound by the rule laid down.

In that passage Dixon CJ spoke of the legal rights of the Commonwealth in relation to its subjects. Sometimes that relationship [443] will be one of equality: for example, the capacity of the Crown to enter into contracts is no more or less than that of its subjects. Sometimes the relationship will be one of privilege or immunity on the part of the Crown alone: for example, the right to the payment of debts in priority to others. Where the relationship is one of privilege or immunity it is immediately apparent that any diminution of the privilege or immunity will alter the relationship of the Crown with its subjects. But it is equally so when the relationship is one of equality and the Crown is singled out and treated differently, for the relationship then ceases to be one of equality.

When Dixon CJ spoke of general laws he meant laws of general application which bind the Crown and its subjects alike. Such laws are laws which do not have an impact upon any relationship of equality. But a state law which discriminates against the Commonwealth government and imposes a disability upon it will have an impact upon such a relationship and will constitute an interference with its executive capacities. In the same way, a Commonwealth law which discriminates against a state and imposes a disability upon it will constitute an interference with state executive capacities.

Dawson, Toohey and Gaudron JJ referred to *Queensland Electricity Commission v Commonwealth* (1985) 159 CLR 192; and *Melbourne Corporation v Commonwealth* (1947) 74 CLR 31.

There is nothing in the principles recognised in *Melbourne Corporation v Commonwealth* or in any extrapolation of those principles to be found in the judgment of Dixon J in *Uther* or in the reasons of the majority in *Cigamatic* which would suggest that the Crown or its agents enjoy any special immunity from the operation of laws of general application, state or federal. Indeed, the contrary is [444] affirmed. The rule of law requires such a result. In *A v Hayden* (1984) 156 CLR 532 at 562, Murphy J described as elementary the principle that:

> The executive power of the Commonwealth must be exercised in accordance with the Constitution and the laws of the Commonwealth. The Governor-General, the federal Executive Council and every officer of the Commonwealth are bound to observe the laws of the land.

Of course, the laws of the land are not confined to the laws of the Commonwealth but include the common law and the statute law in force in each of the states. Thus in *Pirrie v McFarlane* (1925) 36 CLR 170, a person acting in the execution of his duties as a member of the Royal Australian Air Force was held to be bound by the provisions of a Victorian Act requiring him to hold a driver's licence when driving a vehicle on a public highway in the course of those duties ...

Whilst the principle that executive power must be exercised in accordance with the law applies to both Commonwealth and state governments, the Commonwealth enjoys a paramount position within its area of legislative competence because of s 109 of the Constitution. A valid Commonwealth law will prevail over any inconsistent state law. Thus, if there had been a law validly enacted under the defence power relieving servicemen of the obligation to hold drivers' licences when acting in the execution of their duties, the result in *Pirrie v McFarlane* would have been different ...

[445] Yet in *Commonwealth of Australia v Bogle* (1953) 89 CLR 229, Fullagar J, with whom Dixon CJ and Webb and Kitto JJ agreed, denied that a state statute might bind the Commonwealth. He was speaking generally, and not of a state statute purporting to interfere with the executive capacities of the Commonwealth. Indeed, in direct contrast with observations made in the authorities discussed above, he said (1953) 89 CLR 229 at 259:

> To say that a state can enact legislation which is binding upon the Commonwealth in the same sense in which it is binding upon a subject of the state appears to me to give effect to a fundamental misconception.

Those words are obiter and are, in any event, contrary to the later decision of this Court in *Cigamatic*. They form no part of the reasoning leading to the actual conclusion in *Bogle* and in the light of *Cigamatic* it can hardly be said that Dixon CJ and Kitto J, in agreeing to the reasoning and conclusion of Fullagar J in *Bogle*, were assenting to that proposition.

In any event, and with the greatest of respect, the proposition is [446] insupportable. Of course, as a matter of construction and aided by the presumption which we have discussed, a court may conclude that a statute was not intended to bind the Crown, but that is not to say that a state parliament lacks the power to bind the Crown in right of the Commonwealth and its agencies. It cannot do so where the result would affect the executive capacities of the Commonwealth for the reasons already given. But the Commonwealth executive is not above the law and where a state statute is applicable it forms part of the law.

The reason given by Fullagar J for the view which he expressed is that the Crown in right of a state is bound by a state statute (provided it extends to the Crown as a matter of construction) because the Crown has assented to the statute whereas the Crown in right of the Commonwealth has not assented to the state statute and is thus not bound. However, the Crown, whether in right of a state or the Commonwealth, acts as part of the legislature when it assents to legislation. Once a statute is validly passed by the legislature (for which purpose the assent of the Crown is necessary) it passes into law and its binding force upon the Crown, whether in right of the Commonwealth or a state, cannot be dependent upon the assent of the executive government. The reason why a Commonwealth statute extending to the Crown binds the Commonwealth executive is to be found in the supremacy of parliament over the executive, such supremacy being exercised by legislation passed pursuant to power conferred on the Parliament by the Constitution, not the assent of the Crown as part of the parliamentary process. Within the scope of its grant of legislative power, the parliament of a state is no less supreme than the Parliament of the Commonwealth, although state legislation which is inconsistent with Commonwealth legislation is inoperative under s 109 of the Constitution to the extent, and during the continuance, of the inconsistency. It was to s 109 that Dixon J was referring in *Uther* (1947) 74 CLR 508 at 529, when he said that 'supremacy, where it exists, belongs to the Commonwealth'. And, of course, by exercising the legislative power granted to it by the Constitution the Commonwealth Parliament can legislate to exclude the operation of a state law with respect to the Commonwealth executive or its agencies. But that is a very different thing from saying, as Fullagar J did, that a state legislature cannot enact legislation which is binding on the Commonwealth in the same way as it is binding upon a 'subject of the state'.

Fullagar J in *Bogle* sought to support his view by observing, (1953) 89 CLR 229 at 260, [447] that 'it is surely unthinkable that the Victorian Parliament could have made a law rendering the Commonwealth liable for torts committed in Victoria'. That, however, is to disregard the distinction, which is fundamental to the decision in *Cigamatic*, between the capacities of the executive government and the exercise of them. The immunity of the Crown from liability in tort, however dubious its origins, is a prerogative of the Crown operating at common law to define the relationship between the Crown and its subjects in a manner analogous to the Crown entitlement to priority in the payment of debts. In that way it involves the capacities of the Crown. It is for that reason that, supposing it not to have been abrogated by statute, the immunity of the Crown in right of the Commonwealth from liability in tort would lie outside the power of a state legislature and not for the reason that a state legislature cannot bind the Crown in right of the Commonwealth.

In an effort to recognise practical realities in a situation in which the Commonwealth executive increasingly engages in transactions upon the same basis as ordinary citizens in a state, Fullagar J acknowledged that the Commonwealth may be 'affected by state laws' in, for example, entering into a contract in a state. But it is impossible to say what is meant by 'affected by state laws' if it does not mean that the Crown in right of the Commonwealth is bound by them. As we have said, it is not a matter of choice for the Commonwealth executive whether or not it is bound by the law of the land. If in regulating activities engaged in by the Crown and its subjects alike a state statute extends as a matter of construction to the Crown in right of the Commonwealth, then that Crown is bound by the statute in the same way as the subject is bound, subject always to any inconsistency with a valid Commonwealth law.

Nothing has emerged in this case to indicate any purported alteration or denial of the executive capacity of the Crown in right of the Commonwealth by the provisions of the Residential Tenancies Act. The DHA is the creature of the Defence Housing Authority Act and that Act is predicated upon the existence of a legal system of which the Residential Tenancies Act forms a part. The latter Act does nothing to alter or deny the function of the DHA, notwithstanding that it regulates activities carried out in the exercise of that function in the same way as it regulates the same activities on the part of others. If, and to the extent that, the DHA in carrying out its functions is acting in the exercise of the executive capacity of the Commonwealth, the Residential Tenancies Act neither alters nor denies that capacity notwithstanding that it regulates its exercise.

McHugh J agreed with the reasons of Dawson, Toohey and Gaudron JJ that there was no s 109 inconsistency, nor did s 52(ii) apply.

McHugh J: [451] It is settled doctrine that the states have no constitutional power to bind the Commonwealth ... In the absence of a grant of power, express or implied, no polity within a federation has the power to bind another polity within that federation. Within their respective domains, the polities that make up a federation are regarded as sovereign. Because that is so, it is a necessary implication of the document that creates the federation that no polity in that federation can legislate for another. Federalism is concerned with the allocation of legislative power, and it is a natural and, to my mind, necessary implication of a federation that no polity can legislate in a way that destroys or weakens the legislative authority of another polity within that federation ...

Before the *Engineers' Case* ... this rule was regarded as a fundamental rule of constitutional law in this country, as applicable to the Commonwealth as it was to the states. But it is a rule that arises by implication from the nature of a federation. In the event of inconsistency with an express term of the document that creates the federation, it must give way. That was all that the *Engineers' Case* decided. This Court held in that case that, having regard to the affirmative grants of power to the Commonwealth which are contained [452] in the Constitution, the states could not rely on the implication to resist the application of federal laws. Nevertheless, as *Melbourne Corporation v Commonwealth* ... demonstrated, the states are not wholly unprotected by the implication, for the Commonwealth cannot 'make a law aimed at the restriction or control of a state in the exercise of its executive authority'.

... However, the fact that legislation of the states cannot of its own force bind the Commonwealth does not mean that state legislation may not attach legal consequences to the activities of the Commonwealth Executive.

If the Parliament of the Commonwealth authorises the Executive Government to carry out an activity, its legislation, in the absence of an indication to the contrary, will be read as indicating that the Executive is to be bound by the common law rules and statutes applying in the states. The Constitution is framed on 'the unexpressed assumption that the one common law surrounds us and applies where it has not been superseded by statute': Dixon, 'The Common Law as an Ultimate Constitutional Foundation', *Australian Law Journal*, vol 31 (1957) 240 at 241 ...

[453] That being so, it is axiomatic that, subject to a contrary legislative intention, the common law is binding on the executive activities of the Commonwealth government. If federal legislation authorises a Commonwealth instrumentality to buy land, sell goods or enter into contracts, the common law rules concerning those matters are taken as binding the Commonwealth unless the legislation indicates to the contrary. Similarly, federal legislation will be construed as indicating that Commonwealth executive activity is to be carried out in accordance with the existing statute law of the state unless the legislation indicates to the contrary. In such cases, state law may apply to the Commonwealth even when it takes the form of imposing affirmative duties on the Commonwealth government.

Moreover in some cases, quite apart from the operation of s 64 of the Judiciary Act, the terms of federal legislation may indicate that state law is to apply during the continuance as well as the creation of a relationship between the Commonwealth and a citizen. In such cases, if a question arises as to whether a particular state provision applies to the Commonwealth, the matter is resolved by recourse to s 109 of the Constitution.

A different area is reached, however, when state laws purport to alter rights acquired by the Commonwealth as the result of executive activity or to fetter an executive capacity or power of the Commonwealth where the source of authority for that activity, capacity or power is s 61 of the Constitution rather than federal legislation. These cases fall outside s 109 and are determined by the fundamental constitutional principle expounded in *Cigamatic*. That case decided that the states cannot legislate so as to abolish the Commonwealth's prerogative right to priority of payment 'when in any administration of assets debts of equal degree due to the Crown and due to subjects of the Crown come into competition' (1962) 108 CLR 372 at 376. Dixon CJ said, (1962) 108 CLR 372 at 377, that 'to treat those rights as subject to destruction or modification or qualification by the legislature of a state must mean that under the Constitution there resides in a state or states a legislative power to control legal rights and duties between the Commonwealth and its people' ...

[454] In my view, there can be no doubt that ... the states have no power to alter legal rights or obligations existing between the Commonwealth and its subjects even though they are not the immediate product of a federal statute. Just as the states cannot alter the common law right of the Commonwealth to priority in the payment of its debts, so they cannot alter the existing contractual or proprietary rights and obligations of the Commonwealth in relation to its subjects that arise from the exercise of the executive power conferred by s 61 of the Constitution. It would be absurd to suppose that Dixon CJ, while denying that the states could alter the Commonwealth's common law priority in payment of the debt, accepted that the states could alter the common law rights of the Commonwealth that gave rise to the debt.

... [L]ogically it is impossible to see any ground for distinguishing between the common law prerogative rights of the Crown and the rights conferred by s 61 of the Constitution ...

It follows from *Cigamatic* that, once the executive power of the Commonwealth arising from s 61 of the Constitution has authorised a relationship creating rights and duties, a state has no power to alter that relationship even by a law that operates generally within the state. I do not think that the validity of this proposition turns on any distinction between the capacities of the Commonwealth and the exercise of them. It is not a distinction which I find illuminating in this constitutional context. Nor can I see anything in the judgment of Dixon CJ in *Cigamatic* which supports such a distinction.

The executive capacity of the Commonwealth can only mean its legal right or power to do or refrain from doing something. I cannot see any constitutional rationale for a doctrine that would hold, for example, that the states cannot prevent the Commonwealth from entering into a specific class of contract but can alter the legal rights and obligations of the Commonwealth and the subject once they have [455] entered into a contract of that class. Moreover, the distinction between a capacity of the Commonwealth and its exercise is not easily drawn. If a state law prevents the Commonwealth from using its contractual right to forfeit a lease or terminate an employment, is the state law fettering a Commonwealth capacity or only the exercise of it?

In most cases, state law including the common law will govern the creation of a relationship between the Commonwealth and a subject even when the creation of the relationship arises from the Constitution's grant of executive power. If the Commonwealth chooses to enter into the relationship without negating the consequences of relevant state law, it necessarily submits to the state law governing the incidents of the relationship. But, for the reasons given by Dixon CJ in *Cigamatic*, once the Commonwealth has entered into such a relationship and created legal rights and duties in accordance with that state law, it is not open to the state to change their nature or effect. If the Commonwealth enters into a contract relying on the grant of executive power conferred by s 61 of the Constitution, a state has no power to change the consequences of that contract even by a law of general application.

Many activities of the Commonwealth government, however, do not result in relationships with the ordinary subjects of the Commonwealth. In some cases, these activities may concern only the Commonwealth and its servants and agents. In other cases, they may have no more than indirect or potential consequences for the subjects of the Commonwealth. If the activity falls within the terms of s 52 of the Constitution, the states plainly have no power over the activity. But many activities occur within the territorial boundaries of the states and outside the protection that s 52 gives to Commonwealth activities.

If the activity is authorised by a federal enactment, the case will be governed by s 109 of the Constitution. But much Commonwealth activity does not depend on statutory authorisation. In the ordinary course of administering the government of the Commonwealth, authority is frequently given to Commonwealth servants and agents to carry out activities in the exercise of the general powers conferred by the Constitution. Section 61 of the Constitution 'enables the Crown to undertake all executive action which is appropriate to the position of the Commonwealth under the Constitution and to the spheres of responsibility vested in it by the Constitution': *Barton v Commonwealth* (1974) 131 CLR 477 at 498. The provision of transport for officers of the Commonwealth and the carrying of Commonwealth property, for example, may depend upon no more than a combination of the powers conferred by ss 61, 81, 82 and 83 of the Constitution. Can a general state law validly regulate the Commonwealth transport system? Can it insist upon compulsory insurance for and periodic maintenance inspections of Commonwealth vehicles? Can [456] it require the Commonwealth to use only drivers licensed by state law?

The judgment of Fullagar J in *Commonwealth v Bogle* (1953) 89 CLR 229 at 259–60, a judgment with which Dixon CJ, Webb, Kitto and Taylor JJ agreed, denies that the states have any power to control the Commonwealth.

McHugh J quoted two passages from Fullagar J's judgment in *Bogle* (1953) 89 CLR 229 at 259, including the statement that '[t]he Commonwealth is not a juristic person which is subjected either by any state Constitution or by the Commonwealth Constitution to the legislative power of any state Parliament'.

I do not think that there is any warrant for concluding that this passage is contrary to what Dixon CJ said in *Cigamatic*. To the contrary, I think that the judgment of Dixon CJ in *Cigamatic* is entirely in accord with what he had agreed to in *Bogle* and with what he had been saying ever since *Uther* (1947) 74 CLR 508 at 528–30.

Moreover, properly understood, I think that the above passages are a correct statement of the law. I do not think that Fullagar J was saying that every act or omission of a Commonwealth servant or agent executed in the course of carrying out an activity on behalf of the Commonwealth is outside the law of the states. His Honour's statement was not directed to the aggregate of the legal and personal capacities enjoyed by the Commonwealth and its individual servants and agents. Rather, Fullagar J was directing himself to those extraordinary executive powers and capacities which the Constitution gives to the Commonwealth itself to carry out as a political sovereign in the federation. He was saying that the states cannot control or restrain the Commonwealth in the discharge of its powers or capacities [457] arising under the Constitution. The states could not, for example, control or regulate the Commonwealth's capacity or power to engage in diplomatic relations with another country. In so far as a general state law purported to have that effect on a diplomat's work, it would be invalid. But that does not mean that a diplomat engaged on Commonwealth business can ignore state traffic laws.

Whether or not a general law of the state validly applies to a Commonwealth servant or agent acting in the course of his or her duties depends on a number of considerations, the chief of which are the nature of the Commonwealth activity upon which the servant or agent is engaged and the act or omission which the state law purports to regulate. In my opinion, however, the answer to the question whether a servant or agent of the Commonwealth Crown must obey a state law does not depend on any general proposition that the Commonwealth cannot authorise its servants or agents to perform their duties contrary to the penal laws of a state.

In determining whether a Commonwealth authorisation of executive activity is outside the law of a state, one naturally begins with the proposition that the Constitution is superimposed on a background of common law rules and principles: *Uther* (1947) 74 CLR 508 at 521. Except where those rules and principles are inconsistent with the grant of executive power under the Constitution or a federal statute made pursuant to the Constitution, the carrying out of Commonwealth executive activity must conform with those rules. By the Bill of Rights 1688 and probably by the common law, the Crown had no power to authorise its servants to ignore the law. But in a federation that does not mean that the Executive Government of one polity of the federation is bound to obey the law of another polity in that federation. The rule that the Crown cannot give its agents any dispensation to ignore a statute was formulated for a unitary system of government. Just as the common law rule of the supremacy of Parliament had to be modified to accord with the Constitution, so must the rule that the Crown cannot authorise a breach of a law be modified to accord with the division of legal power between the Commonwealth and the states. In a federation, an anterior question must be answered before that rule has any operation. That question is, is there a law that the servants and agents of the relevant Sovereign must obey? It follows therefore that, in determining whether the Commonwealth Crown has power to authorise its servants or agents to disobey a state law, the first question is, is the state law binding on the Commonwealth Crown? Only when that question is answered can one determine whether the Commonwealth Crown can authorise its servants to ignore the law of a state.

If a state law attempted to discriminate against the exercise of an executive activity arising from the operation of s 61 of the Constitution, it would be plainly invalid for the reasons given by [458] Dixon J in *West v Commissioner of Taxation (NSW)* (1937) 56 CLR 657 at 681–2. On the other hand, a general law that merely regulates the manner or mode of performing an activity which a servant or agent of the Commonwealth carries out in the course of executing functions and duties arising from the operation of s 61 of the Constitution is unlikely to constitute an infringement of those extraordinary capacities or powers of the Commonwealth to which I have referred. Such laws are to be contrasted with state laws that purport to bind the Commonwealth itself in exercising the capacities and powers conferred by s 61 of the Constitution alone or in conjunction with other powers of the Commonwealth. State laws purporting to have that effect can only operate as interpretation clauses. They show that the state law is intended to apply to the Commonwealth. However, they can do so only to the extent that the Commonwealth submits to the law by express words or conduct or by inference from its silence. But that is all.

McHugh J said that the *Cigamatic* doctrine did not apply to the Authority, because the doctrine only protected those rights of the Commonwealth the source of which was the executive power (including but not limited to the prerogatives): 190 CLR at 458–9. It did not apply to rights of the Commonwealth created by Commonwealth legislation; for these the Commonwealth could rely on the protection accorded to it by s 109: 190 CLR at 459. McHugh J agreed with Dawson, Toohey and Gaudron JJ that s 109 had no application: 190 CLR at 460. Gummow J, like McHugh J, did not find the distinction relied upon by the majority 'illuminating' (190 CLR at 472); but he nevertheless agreed with Dawson, Toohey and Gaudron JJ that the *Cigamatic* principle did not apply because the type of statutory corporation represented by DHA did not enjoy 'the preferences, immunities and exceptions, including that zone of immunity conferred by the *Cigamatic* doctrine, which are enjoyed by the Executive Government and denied to citizens and corporations in their dealings inter se': 190 CLR at 472.

Quoting Dixon J in *Commonwealth v Cigamatic Ltd* (1962) 108 CLR 372, Kirby J said the issues raised 'go deep in the nature and operation of the federal system'.

Kirby J: [479] [T]he provision of housing to the naval and military defence forces of the Commonwealth was a responsibility which passed to the Commonwealth soon after its establishment. Ample general power to provide for such housing by federal legislation was afforded by the Constitution. Provision for serving and former officers of the defence forces became the subject of early federal legislation. Responsibility for administering such legislation was shared by a number of departments.

Kirby J said that the operation of the state law was excluded by s 52(ii) of the Constitution. As s 52(ii) was not a transitional provision (190 CLR at 487) and defence housing was a 'matter relating to a department of the public service' (190 CLR at 491) the state law intruded upon that matter and therefore did not apply to the DHA: 190 CLR at 493. Kirby J said the two laws were inconsistent under s 109: 190 CLR at 495. Kirby J said that 'for the purpose of considering the suggested implied immunity, [the] DHA was relevantly the Commonwealth' (190 CLR at 502) and that the immunity had an 'unsatisfactory character' as it came in a variety of formulations: 190 CLR at 502.

[503] I disagree with the constitutional immunity urged by DHA in these proceedings based on *Bogle* and *Cigamatic*. No such doctrine is expressly stated in the Constitution. Although implications may arise from the text and structure of the Constitution, to be viable, they must be 'logically or practically necessary' to the operation of the Constitution: *Australian Capital Television Pty Ltd v Commonwealth* (1992) 177 CLR 106. Given the relative inflexibility of the Constitution, and its resistance to formal amendment, the derivation of implications, not expressly stated and thus approved and impliedly accepted by the people of Australia, must be kept to cases where the implication is [504] obvious, necessary and can be precisely defined. An immunity of the scope urged in these proceedings by DHA meets none of these criteria.

Kirby J rejected the proposition that the states have no legitimate power, because not expressly given such power, to regulate the legal relations of the Commonwealth with its subjects. He also rejected the view that the immunity derived from 'the necessities of federal government': 190 CLR at 505. He referred to ss 109, 52(ii) and 114 and said the Commonwealth had 'ample means' to protect itself from the reach of state law: 190 CLR at 505. The immunity, expressed as broadly as it was in *Commonwealth v Bogle* was an 'unconscious revival' of the pre-*Engineer's* position which was not challenged here: 190 CLR at 505. He said any supposed 'want of separate assent' from the Commonwealth to be bound was not a 'satisfactory explanation' for the immunity in the light of the notion of the indivisibility of the Crown and historical acceptance that legislation might validly bind the Crown: 190 CLR at 506.

Kirby J said the ability of the state to bind the Commonwealth 'in defined circumstances' was only an aspect of an 'integrated federal system': 190 CLR at 507. It was part of the 'rule of law' whereby all those present in a state are bound by valid legislation and in any case s 109 was 'ample means to protect [the] national character' of the Executive government of the Commonwealth: 190 CLR at 507.

[508] The development of a constitutional doctrine of mutuality, co-operation and inter-relationship is much more in keeping with the nature of the federal polity established by the Australian Constitution. The supposed constitutional doctrine of implied immunity of the Commonwealth from state laws, so broadly expressed in *Bogle* and even in *Cigamatic*, should, in my view, be reverently laid to rest.

Kirby J said s 64 of the Judiciary Act did not apply: 190 CLR at 511.

~~~

Notes

[8.2.113]   How far does *Re Residential Tenancies Tribunal of New South Wales and Henderson; Ex parte Defence Housing Authority* (1997) 190 CLR 410 **[8.2.112C]** go towards clarifying the application of *Commonwealth v Cigamatic Ltd* (1962) 108 CLR 372 **[8.2.98C]**? The majority in *Re Residential Tenancies Tribunal* claimed simply to uphold the principle in *Cigamatic*: 190 CLR at 438–48 per Dawson, Toohey and Gaudron JJ; 190 CLR at 451, 453 per McHugh J; and 190 CLR at 473, 474 per Gummow J. But, according to Dawson, Toohey and Gaudron JJ, some may have been operating under a 'misconception' that *Cigamatic* stood for the proposition that the Commonwealth was immune from the reach of state law: 190 CLR at 438.

Rather, according to the majority in *Re Residential Tenancies Tribunal*, the decision in *Cigamatic* was based on a distinction between state laws which purported to modify the Commonwealth's executive 'capacities' and 'legislation which assumes those capacities and merely seeks to regulate activities in which the Crown may choose to engage in the exercise of those capacities': 190 CLR at 439. According to the majority in *Re Residential Tenancies Tribunal*, in *Cigamatic* the latter were valid but the former were not. Zines says that the distinction made by the joint judgment in *Re Residential Tenancies Tribunal*, and agreed to by Brennan J (190 CLR at 424) 'does nothing to remove uncertainty in this area': Zines (1998) at 91. In the result, it may be that the real effect of the case is to shift the onus to the Commonwealth to show that the activities which a state law seeks to regulate are an inherent part of the Commonwealth's executive 'capacities' and therefore are beyond the reach of state legislative power.

[8.2.114]   A state cannot alter or deny a capacity of the Commonwealth, but it can regulate the exercise of a Commonwealth capacity. In the words of Brennan CJ, in *Re Residential Tenancies Tribunal of New South Wales and Henderson; Ex parte Defence Housing Authority* (1997) 190 CLR 410 **[8.2.112C]**, when the Commonwealth choses to enter a transaction, the incidents of that transaction can be prescribed by state law: 190 CLR at 427. McHugh J rejected the distinction saying that he did not find it 'illuminating': 190 CLR at 454. His Honour said the distinction was 'not easily drawn' and that there was no 'constitutional rationale' for distinguishing, for example, between a state law which would 'prevent the Commonwealth from entering into a specific class of contract, and one which would alter the legal rights and obligations of the Commonwealth and subject once they [had] entered into a contract of that class': 190 CLR at 454–5.

How tenable is the distinction? Zines says it enters into 'slippery ground', which recalls the now discarded distinction in s 92 case law between laws which regulated interstate trade (and were therefore valid) and those which burdened it (which were not): Zines (1998) at 92. He points out that this uncertainty may affect town planning laws, landlord and tenant legislation, health and safety rules, building codes and hire car legislation.

[8.2.115]   In *Re Residential Tenancies Tribunal of New South Wales and Henderson; Ex parte Defence Housing Authority* (1997) 190 CLR 410 **[8.2.112C]**, Dawson, Toohey and Gaudron JJ said that laws of general application which affect the Commonwealth in its activities in common with other citizens may be valid under *Commonwealth v Cigamatic Ltd* (1962) 108 CLR 372 **[8.2.98C]**: 190 CLR at 439. But this proposition seems to leave a number of cases unanswered. States may not bind the Commonwealth in relation to its prerogatives because these are part of its executive capacities: 190 CLR at 441. States may not discriminate against the Commonwealth because this would 'constitute an interference with its executive capacities': 190 CLR at 443. States may not diminish a 'privilege or immunity' which the Crown alone enjoys over its subjects, because this would 'alter the relationship of the Crown with its subjects': 190 CLR at 443. But what of a state law of general application which nevertheless impairs or denies the executive capacity of the Commonwealth? Here we are thrown back on the distinction between general laws in relation to those capacities and the general laws in relation to exercise of those capacities.

[8.2.116]   One justification given by the majority in *Re Residential Tenancies Tribunal of New South Wales and Henderson; Ex parte Defence Housing Authority* (1997) 190 CLR 410 **[8.2.112C]** for the difference between state and Commonwealth legislative power is related to the structure of Australian federalism. Dawson,

Toohey and Gaudron JJ said that, in a federal system where Commonwealth power is enumerated in the Constitution, and state power exists merely in an 'undefined residue', the states lack any specific express authorisation to legislate with respect to Commonwealth executive power: 190 CLR at 440. This is a view which harks back to Sir Owen Dixon in *Uther v Federal Commissioner of Taxation* (1947) 74 CLR 509 **[8.2.90C]** at 529 and also in *Commonwealth v Cigamatic Ltd* (1962) 108 CLR 372 **[8.2.98C]** at 377. The justices put it this way:

> [T]he character of the Commonwealth as a body politic, armed with executive capacities by the Constitution, by its very nature places those capacities outside the legislative power of another body politic, namely a state, without specific powers in that respect (190 CLR at 440).

Why does the state, within the areas in which it has power, and, subject to s 109 and other federal implications, necessarily lack the power to alter the capacities of the Crown in right of the Commonwealth?

The contrary view was put in *Re Residential Tenancies Tribunal of New South Wales and Henderson; Ex parte Defence Housing Authority* (1997) 190 CLR 410 **[8.2.112C]** by Kirby J, who also referred to federal principles in justification. He said that 'the states are themselves creations of the Constitution' and that '[e]very power of the parliament of a colony which became a state was "continued[d] as at the establishment of the Commonwealth"': 190 CLR at 504. Is the difference between Commonwealth and state legislative power based simply on the fact that the Commonwealth has been granted specific express heads of power and the state has not? Why should state power, within its confines, be any less 'plenary' than Commonwealth legislative power, which, it is conceded, can alter Commonwealth and state executive power?: see 190 CLR at 441. Recall that *Engineer's* was meant to operate in relation to both levels of power; the principle that legislative power be interpreted in its plain natural meaning applied also to state legislative power.

[8.2.117] How tenable is the opinion of Dawson, Toohey and Gaudron JJ in *Re Residential Tenancies Tribunal of New South Wales and Henderson; Ex parte Defence Housing Authority* (1997) 190 CLR 410 **[8.2.112C]** at 445, that Dixon CJ and Kitto J did not agree with Fullagar J's view in *Commonwealth v Bogle* (1953) 89 CLR 229 **[8.2.96]** that state laws can bind the Commonwealth? The opinion was not shared by McHugh J: 190 CLR at 456.

In *Re Residential Tenancies Tribunal*, Gummow J said that the *Cigamatic* doctrine did not apply to the DHA because it has not had 'imparted to it' the 'zone of immunity conferred by the *Cigamatic* doctrine': 190 CLR at 472. He noted that this was consistent with a trend in Australian law towards the use of statutory corporations 'to conduct what in other hands could have been seen as no more than ordinary commercial transactions': 190 CLR at 471. The aim of this trend had been to 'assist rather than to detract from the position of those dealing with such bodies': 190 CLR at 471. In the light of increasing privatisation and corporatisation of government activities, how would the adoption of this view affect the doctrine in *Commonwealth v Cigamatic Ltd* (1962) 108 CLR 372 **[8.2.98C]** as reinterpreted in *Re Residential Tenancies Tribunal*?

[8.2.118] Where the Commonwealth carries out activities within a place, in a state, being a place that the Commonwealth has acquired for public purposes, then the Commonwealth will have an additional basis for claiming immunity from state laws. Section 52(i) of the Commonwealth Constitution gives the Commonwealth

Parliament 'exclusive power to make laws for peace, order and good government of the Commonwealth with respect to ... [t]he seat of government of the Commonwealth and all places acquired by the Commonwealth for public purposes'.

In *Worthing v Rowell and Muston Pty Ltd* (1970) 123 CLR 89, the High Court elaborated, for the first time, on the meaning and effect of s 52(i). A majority of the court (Barwick CJ, Menzies, Windeyer and Walsh JJ; McTiernan, Kitto and Owen JJ dissenting) held that s 52 gave the Commonwealth sole legislative authority in Commonwealth places, excluding the legislative authority of the states in those places: 123 CLR at 103, 120, 131 and 139. It followed that state occupational health and safety legislation did not apply to a private employer whose worksite was located on a Royal Australian Air Force base, because the base was a place acquired by the Commonwealth for public purposes.

This means that a state law attaching legal consequences to activities in the state (and *not* directed at any Commonwealth place) has no force or effect in a place that is acquired by the Commonwealth: *R v Phillips* (1971) 125 CLR 93. The measure of exclusivity is emphasised by the proposition that, in the event that the Commonwealth gives up its ownership of a Commonwealth place, state laws may not automatically revive and operate in that place: see *Attorney-General (NSW) v Stocks and Holdings (Constructors) Pty Ltd* (1970) 124 CLR 262. (However, contrast *Paliflex Pty Limited v Chief Commissioner of State Revenue* (2003) 202 ALR 376, where the High Court held that state land tax legislation enacted in 1956 validly imposed a land tax in respect of land that had been acquired by the Commonwealth for public purposes in 1922 and had been transferred to the appellant, a private company, in January 1998.)

[8.2.119] The principle underpinning the exclusion of state laws from Commonwealth places was explained by Brennan CJ in *Allders International Pty Ltd v Commissioner of State Revenue (Victoria)* (1996) 186 CLR 630 at 638:

> The denial of power to the parliaments of the states does not depend upon the enactment of a law in exercise of a power conferred on the Commonwealth Parliament by s 52. Section 52, unlike s 109, does not suspend the operation of a valid state law that is inconsistent with a valid Commonwealth law; it denies the validity of a measure enacted by the state Parliament to the extent that s 52 confers on the Parliament of the Commonwealth power to enact a measure having the same operation.

So, in *Allders* a majority of the court (Brennan CJ, Gaudron, McHugh, Gummow and Kirby JJ; Dawson and Toohey JJ dissenting) held that state stamp duty legislation, imposing a tax on all leases of premises in the state, could not validly apply to a lease of land in a Commonwealth place (Tullamarine airport). See further Keyzer and Manion (1996).

[8.2.120] After the High Court's judgment in *Worthing v Rowell and Muston Pty Ltd* (1970) 123 CLR 89 **[8.2.118]**, the Commonwealth Parliament enacted the Commonwealth Places (Application of Laws) Act 1970 (Cth). Subject to some exceptions (including state laws imposing taxes), s 4(1) of the Act declares that state laws from time to time in force shall apply to each place in that state that is or was a Commonwealth place at that time. The exceptions include state laws imposing any tax, state laws conferring judicial power, state laws which, if enacted by the Commonwealth, would be beyond the power of the Commonwealth Parliament and any state law which would, apart from s 52(i), be invalid in its operation in or to Commonwealth places: ss 4(5), 4(2)(a). It follows that a state law that is invalid because it purports to modify the Commonwealth's executive capacities (see *Residential Tenancies Tribunal of New South Wales and Henderson; Ex parte Defence Housing Authority* (1997) 190 CLR 410 **[8.2.112C]**) or because it is inconsistent with a law of the Commonwealth, cannot operate in, or in relation to, a Commonwealth place.

The purpose of the Act was to ensure that ordinary laws of the states, such as the general criminal law, town planning laws and motor traffic regulations, continue to apply in Commonwealth places in the states; however, those laws now apply as laws of the Commonwealth — they have been picked up and re-enacted by the Commonwealth Parliament through s 4(1) of the Act.

[8.2.121] After the High Court's judgment in *Allders International Pty Ltd v Commissioner of State Revenue (Victoria)* (1996) 186 CLR 630 **[8.2.119]**, the Commonwealth Parliament enacted the Commonwealth Places (Mirror Taxes) Act 1998 (Cth). Section 6(2) of the Mirror Taxes Act declares that, subject to the Act:

> ... the excluded provisions of a State taxing law, as in force at any time before or after the commencement of this Act, apply, or are taken to have applied, according to their tenor, at that time, in relation to each place in the State that is or was a Commonwealth place at that time.

Section 6(1) of the Mirror Taxes Act defines 'excluded provisions' as meaning the provisions of a state taxing law that are excluded by s 52(i) of the Constitution. A 'state taxing law', according to s 3 of the Mirror Taxes Act is a state law listed in the Schedule to the Act or a state law imposing taxation that is prescribed by regulations.

According to s 6(6) of the Mirror Taxes Act, s 6 does not have effect in relation to a state unless an arrangement between the Commonwealth and that state is in operation. Such an arrangement is made under s 9 of the Act, and will provide for the state to administer the applied taxing law. Section 23(1) of the Mirror Taxes Act provides for the amounts received under the applied law to be credited to the Consolidated Revenue Fund; but s 23(2) provides for those amounts to be paid out to the collecting state:

> The Commonwealth is liable to pay to a State amounts equal to amounts that are credited to the Consolidated Revenue Fund as mentioned in subsection (1) in relation to an applied law of the State.

That is, the system established by the Mirror Taxes Act is that a state's taxing laws apply as laws of the Commonwealth in and in relation to Commonwealth places in that state, but are administered by the state with the proceeds of any taxes going (through the Commonwealth's Consolidated Revenue Fund) to that state.

The effect of the reference, in s 6(2) of the Mirror Taxes Act, to a state taxing law 'as in force' is sufficient to ensure that a state taxing law that is invalid because it purports to modify the Commonwealth's executive capacities (see *Residential Tenancies Tribunal of New South Wales and Henderson; Ex parte Defence Housing Authority* (1997) 190 CLR 410 **[8.2.112C]**) or because it is inconsistent with a law of the Commonwealth, will not be picked up and applied in or in relation to a Commonwealth place.

It should also be noted that the Mirror Taxes Act provides, in s 6(3), that the Act does not pick up a state taxing law if it would not be within the authority of the Commonwealth Parliament to make that law applicable in relation to a Commonwealth place.

The problems presented by s 52(i) and the Commonwealth Places (Application of Laws) Act 1970 (Cth) are reviewed in: Ryan and Hiller (1971); Rose (1971); Hanks (1996) pp 255–8.

3   References

[8.3.1]   *Articles*

Cowen, 'Alsatias for Jack Sheppards? The Law in Federal Enclaves in Australia' (1960) 2 *Melb Uni L Rev* 454.

Dixon, 'The Common Law as an Ultimate Constitutional Foundation' (1957) 31 *Aust L Jo* 240.

Donaldson, 'Commonwealth Liability to State Law' (1985) 16 *Uni WA L Rev* 135.

Evans, 'Rethinking Commonwealth Immunity' (1972) 5 *Fed L Rev* 521.

Hanks, '"Inconsistent" Commonwealth and State Laws: Centralising Government Power in the Australian Federation' (1986) 16 *Fed L Rev* 107.

Howard, 'Some Problems of Commonwealth Immunity and Exclusive Legislative Powers' (1972) 5 *Fed L Rev* 31.

Keyzer and Manion, 'Commonwealth Places Acquired for Public Purposes and State Taxes on Commonwealth Property' (1996) 19 *UNSWLJ* 33.

Lane, 'The Law in Commonwealth Places' (1970) 44 *ALJ* 403.

Lane, 'The Law in Commonwealth Places — A Sequel' (1971) 45 *ALJ* 616.

Lee, 'Commonwealth Liability to State Law — The Enigmatic Case of Pirrie v McFarlane' (1987) 17 *Fed L Rev* 132.

Murray-Jones, 'The Tests for Inconsistency Under Section 109 of the Constitution' (1979) 10 *Fed L Rev* 25.

O'Connell, 'The Crown in the British Commonwealth' (1957) 6 *Int & Comp LQ* 103.

Rose, 'The Commonwealth Places (Application of Laws) Act 1970' (1971) 4 *Fed L Rev* 263.

Rumble, 'Nature of inconsistency under section 109 of the Constitution' (1980) 11 *Fed L Rev* 40.

Ryan and Hiller, 'Recent Litigation and Legislation on Commonwealth Places' (1971) 2 *ACL Rev* 163.

Sackville, 'The Doctrine of Immunity of Instrumentalities in the United States and Australia' (1969) 7 *Melb Uni L Rev* 15.

Sawer, 'Implications and the Constitution' (1948–9) 4 *Res Judicatae* 15.

Sawer, 'State Statutes and the Commonwealth' (1961) 1 *Tas Uni L Rev* 580.

Zines, 'Sir Owen Dixon's Theory of Federalism' (1965) 1 *Fed L Rev* 221.

Zines, 'Mr Justice Evatt and the Constitution' (1968–69) 3 *Fed L Rev* 153.

Zines, 'Nature of the Commonwealth' (1998) 20 *Adel L Rev* 83.

[8.3.2]   *Texts*

Dixon, 'Marshall and the Australian Constitution' in Dixon, *Jesting Pilate*, Law Book Co, Sydney, 1965, pp 166–79.

Hanks, *Constitutional Law in Australia*, Butterworths, 2nd ed, Sydney, 1996.

Hogg, *Liability of the Crown*, Law Book Co, Sydney, 1971, Ch 7 ('Statutes').

Howard, *Australian Federal Constitutional Law*, Law Book Co, 3rd ed, Sydney, 1985, pp 57–60 ('Inconsistency'); pp 143–229 ('Balance of Power'); pp 546–64 ('Commonwealth Places').

Lane, *Australian Federal System*, Law Book Co, 2nd ed, Sydney, 1979, pp 357–87 ('Commonwealth Acquired Places'); pp 863–98 ('Inconsistency of Laws'); pp 955–1009 ('Commonwealth–State Relations').

Latham JG, 'Interpretation of the Constitution' in Else-Mitchell (ed), *Essays on the Australian Constitution*, Law Book Co, Sydney, 1961, pp 1–48.

Latham RTE, *The Law and the Commonwealth*, Oxford University Press, London, 1949.

Lumb and Moens, *Constitution of the Commonwealth of Australia Annotated*, Butterworths, 5th ed, Sydney, 1995, pp 299–301 (s 52(i)); pp 513–24 (s 109).

McNairn, *Governmental and Inter-governmental Immunity in Australia and Canada*, University of Toronto Press, Toronto, 1977, Ch 2 ('Governmental and Intergovernmental Immunity in a Federal System').

Menzies, *Central Power in the Australian Commonwealth*, Cassell, London, 1968, Ch 3 ('Growth by Judicial Interpretation of Commonwealth Powers — The Engineers' Case').

Pryles and Hanks, *Federal Conflicts of Laws*, Butterworths, Sydney, 1974.

Sawer, *Australian Federalism in the Courts*, Melbourne University Press, Melbourne, 1967, Ch 8 ('Federalism as a Legal Principle').

Wheare, *Federal Government*, 4th ed, Oxford University Press, London, 1963.

Zines, *The High Court and the Constitution*, 4th ed, Butterworths, Sydney, 1997.

Chapter

9

Federalism: Distribution of Fiscal Powers

1 Introduction

[9.1.1] Finance is crucial for government. At the basic level, governments need money with which to establish and maintain public facilities (roads, schools, transport and hospitals) and with which to employ the human resources that do the government's work: public servants, police officers, magistrates, judges and ministers. In order to accumulate the money for this basic expenditure, governments resort to taxation and to borrowing (although of these two sources of revenue, taxation makes by far the greater contribution).

So one objective of government's fiscal policies is to accumulate, largely through taxation, sufficient money to provide those facilities and services which the community demands of government. But that is only *one* objective, for government taxing and spending programs may have a wide variety of purposes and effects.

[9.1.2] For example, taxing legislation may be constructed so as to stimulate or protect local manufacturing industry. Heavy import duties on foreign motor vehicles are imposed, not so much to raise extra revenue as to make those vehicles less competitive as against Australian-made motor vehicles; that is, to stimulate consumer demand for the local product, to increase the market share of local manufacturers, to protect the investment of capital in local manufacturing plants and to guarantee employment for local labour in those plants. An emerging issue, given the increasing effect of international standards (such as international trade law) on Australian law, is the extent to which local, constitutional power can control these outcomes in the face of those standards: see Chapter 3.

Again, income tax may be imposed on people at rates which vary according to their net incomes. Low income earners are taxed at a rate of (say) 20 per cent, while people with high net incomes pay tax at a rate of (say) 60 per cent. These varying rates of taxation have the effect of reducing (but not eliminating) income inequalities; they tend to redistribute income from the well paid to the poorly paid and that effect is not accidental. Or, income tax legislation may offer special exemptions to those taxpayers who invest in and receive part of their income from mining and exploration companies. The clear purpose and effect of such exemptions is to encourage public investment in those companies and thus to stimulate the activities of those companies. Similar indirect stimuli can be seen in the provisions of income tax legislation which offer taxation rebates to those taxpayers who invest in life assurance and superannuation policies (thus encouraging the accumulation by insurers and by superannuation funds of large capital investment funds).

[9.1.3]   On the other hand, governments may spend money to achieve a wide variety of policy objectives. People who are unable to enter the paid workforce (because of some incapacity, or family commitment, or because job opportunities have contracted) are provided with basic income support: aged, invalid and sole parent's pensions, and unemployment and sickness benefits. That expenditure (a very high proportion of the national budget) is intended to cushion the impact of personal and social change on individuals in our society.

Other government expenditure may go to subsidising the operations of a copper mine in Tasmania. The purpose of this expenditure is to protect the capital and labour invested in the mine during a period when the world market for copper is in an acute depression. Or the government may offer subsidies to home buyers. This expenditure could have a variety of objectives; to stimulate the home-building industry, to take some pressure off the demand for rental accommodation, and to help a politically significant group (young adults) achieve its major personal objective: home ownership.

In short, government taxing and spending measures are a very important means by which government can implement a wide range of policies. Activity can be regulated, protected, stimulated, discouraged or redirected through fiscal policies.

[9.1.4]   Given the importance of fiscal powers and fiscal policies to contemporary governments, the sharing of that power and the distribution of the capacity to implement those policies is crucial to any federal system. What is the extent of the fiscal power assigned to the Commonwealth under our Constitution? And what powers to tax and to spend are allotted to the states? By answering these questions we can construct a substantially accurate picture of the distribution of power within the Australian federation.

Our Constitution makes an attempt to divide various aspects of fiscal power between the Commonwealth and states. The states are, for example, denied the power to levy customs and excise duties: s 90. The Commonwealth may not, when it legislates with respect to taxation, discriminate between states or parts of states (s 51(ii)); nor give preference to states or parts of states in any revenue law: s 99. The Commonwealth's power to raise capital funds through public borrowings is controlled under s 105A; and its power to spend money may be restricted to expenditure either on certain topics or through the agency of the state governments: ss 81, 96. These provisions, laying the basis for a distribution of fiscal power, have been exploited and manipulated by various governments, and interpreted and developed by the High Court, over the past 80-odd years. That manipulation and interpretation has brought us to the point where fiscal power is effectively centralised. The Commonwealth Parliament may use its taxing power to achieve a wide range of objectives; it may evade the prohibitions against regional discrimination or preference; the states are excluded from the two significant areas of growth taxes, taxes on income and on commodities; the Commonwealth can control the borrowing programs of the states. Further, the Commonwealth has been conceded the right to spend money on whatever projects it chooses.

2   Commonwealth taxing power

Background

[9.2.1E]   **Commonwealth Constitution**

51   The Parliament shall subject to this Constitution have power to make laws for the peace, order and good government of the Commonwealth with respect to ...

  (ii)   Taxation; but so as not to discriminate between States or parts of States: ...

~~~

[9.2.2]   Most of the cases in which the definition of a tax (as distinct from other financial contributions to government revenue) has been explored are cases involving s 90 of the Constitution, the central issue in those cases being whether a payment of money to a state was a tax upon goods and thus an excise duty. As we will see below, different approaches to characterisation may be taken depending on whether the question is whether a Commonwealth law is supported by s 51(ii) or whether a state law ought be struck down by s 90. However, there is common ground in the jurisprudence of s 51(ii) and s 90: each provision is concerned with taxation, so a first step in determining the ambit of each provision is to identify the meaning of that term. What is regarded as the classic definition of a tax was given in one such case, *Matthews v Chicory Marketing Board* (1938) 60 CLR 263 at 270 per Latham CJ: 'a tax ... is a compulsory exaction of money by a public authority for public purposes, enforceable by law, and is not a payment for services rendered'.

In that case, the High Court held that Victorian legislation, which authorised an agency to make a levy on the producers of chicory and to use the money so raised in payment of expenses, repayment of borrowings, effecting insurance and improving the quality of chicory, imposed taxation upon chicory and was an excise duty.

[9.2.3]   In *Air Caledonie International v Commonwealth* (1988) 165 CLR 462 **[9.2.6]**, the High Court cautioned at 467, in its unanimous judgment, that Latham CJ's statement:

> ... should not be seen as providing an exhaustive definition of tax. Thus, there is no reason in principle a tax should not take a form other than the exaction of money or why the compulsory exaction of money under statutory powers could not be properly

seen as taxation notwithstanding that it was by a non-public authority or for purposes which could not properly be described as public.

So, if it is no longer necessary for a tax to be collected by a public authority or to be directed to 'public purposes', then a tax may now be defined as: a compulsory but not arbitrary charge enforceable by statute, which does not lie within the class of charges not properly characterised as a tax (including, but not limited to, fees for services rendered, charges for the acquisition of property, or fines and penalties). The elements of this definition of a 'tax', including the elements of the *Matthews* test and its subsequent development, will now be considered in more detail.

A compulsory exaction or charge

[9.2.4]   A critical element of a tax is compulsion — if a person has no choice but to pay the charge, this will be sufficient to meet that requirement: *Victoria v Commonwealth* (the *Pay-Roll Tax* case) (1971) 122 CLR 353 **[9.6.8C]** at 416.

However, the charge will be regarded as compulsory even if the statutory scheme offers an alternative to payment — if the alternative to payment is a burden which the taxpayer would naturally seek to avoid. This realistic approach to the requirement of compulsion was taken by Dixon J in *Attorney-General (NSW) v Homebush Flour Mills Ltd* (1937) 56 CLR 390, a case that involved a compulsory acquisition scheme under which the state expropriated flour from millers, who were then given compensation and a first option to buy their flour back at a higher price. The millers were required to store the flour until it was sold by the state. Homebush Flour Mills challenged the validity of the scheme on the basis that it was an excise duty, a tax which can only be levied by the Commonwealth Parliament under s 90 of the Constitution. Dixon J emphasised at 413 that it was the effect of the law which must be taken into account:

> When the desired contributions are obtained not by direct command but by exposing the intended contributor if he does not pay, to worse burdens or consequences which he will naturally seek to avoid the payment becomes an exaction. The fact that no legal obligation to pay is imposed or enforced by direct legal remedies, civil or criminal, will not, in my opinion, prevent the exaction fulfilling the description of a tax; because in truth it is exacted by means of sanctions designed to that end, sanctions consisting in the detriments arising from the adoption by the taxpayer of the alternative left open by the legislation.

In *Air Caledonie International v Commonwealth* (1988) 165 CLR 462 **[9.2.6]**, an 'immigration clearance' charge was considered to be a compulsory exaction because it would be unrealistic to suggest that immigrants or returning citizens had a choice whether to pay the charge on arriving in Australia.

The compulsory nature of the charge need not impact on the taxpayer directly — if one person is practically compelled to pay a tax imposed on another person, that will be sufficient to satisfy the 'compulsion' element of the test: *MacCormick v Federal Commissioner of Taxation* (1984) 158 CLR 622 **[9.2.25]** at 636, 653.

While compulsion is a necessary component of a tax, it is not sufficient of itself to mark a fee as a tax. Compulsory fees are common in statutory licensing schemes, yet those fees are not classified as taxes.

Fee for services rendered

[9.2.5] The exclusion from the notion of a tax of charges for services rendered is demonstrated by *Harper v Victoria* (1966) 114 CLR 361, where the High Court held that Victorian legislation did not impose a tax when it required all eggs to be graded, tested and marked by a government agency and imposed a fee on the owners of the eggs 'to defray the expenses incurred therefor'. McTiernan J said it was a fee for 'services rendered', the purpose of which was to 'defray the costs of those services': 114 CLR at 377.

However, the line between a charge for services rendered and a tax can be a narrow one. In *Parton v Milk Board (Vic)* (1949) 80 CLR 229, the High Court held that Victorian legislation imposed a tax when it required dairy distributors to contribute money to a fund administered by a government agency. The agency was to apply the fund to the cost of promoting milk consumption, to compensating dairy distributors whose activities were restricted by the agency and to administrative expenses. In supporting his conclusion that the legislation imposed a tax, Dixon J said at 258:

> It is a compulsory exaction. It is an exaction for the purposes of expenditure out of a Treasury fund. The expenditure is by a government agency and the objects are governmental. It is not a charge for services. No doubt the administration of the Board is regarded as beneficial to what may loosely be described as the milk industry. But the Board performs no particular service for the dairyman or the owner of a milk depot for which his contribution may be considered as a fee or recompense.

[9.2.6] A similar point was made by the High Court in *Air Caledonie International v Commonwealth* (1988) 165 CLR 462. In their unanimous judgment, Mason CJ, Wilson, Brennan, Deane, Dawson, Toohey and Gaudron JJ held that s 34A of the Migration Act 1958 imposed a tax and, because it appeared in an Act that dealt with other matters, offended s 55 of the Constitution: see **[5.2.25C]**. The section required any passenger travelling to Australia on an overseas flight to pay a 'prescribed fee for immigration clearance of that passenger by an officer at the airport at which the passenger intends to enter Australia'. The court said at 468 that the s 34A 'fee' had:

> ... all the positive attributes which have been accepted in this court as prima facie sufficient to stamp an exaction of money with the character of tax: it was compulsory; it was exacted by a public authority (the Commonwealth itself) for public purposes (consolidated revenue: see Constitution, s 81); it (or its 'amount') was enforceable by law.

The court then considered whether the 'fee' was a 'payment for services rendered'. To fit into that category, the justices said at 470, it would need to be:

> ... a fee or charge exacted for particular identified services provided or rendered individually to, or at the request or direction of, the particular person required to make the payment.

They noted that Australian citizens had a legal right to re-enter Australia without 'clearance' by the executive government. While it might be necessary to subject citizens to administrative procedures when re-entering Australia in order to control the entry of non-citizens, requiring the returning citizen to submit to that inconvenience could not 'properly be seen as the provision or rendering of "services" to, or at the request or direction of, the citizen concerned': 165 CLR at 470. Moreover, the justices said, the second reading speech of the responsible Minister, made at the time when s 34A was added to the Migration Act, showed that the moneys to be raised under the section were not related to particular services but were intended to cover the administrative costs of the relevant government department associated with issuing visas to non-citizens and screening entrants to Australia.

[9.2.7] In *Northern Suburbs General Cemetery Reserve Trust v Commonwealth* (1993) 176 CLR 555, the High Court rejected an argument that a levy imposed on employers by the Training Guarantee Act 1990 (Cth) was not a tax but a fee for services. Under the Training Guarantee (Administration) Act 1990 (Cth) the moneys raised through the levy were paid into a fund, from which payments could be made to those states and territories which entered into an agreement with the Commonwealth. Under the agreement, the states and territories were to apply the payments to providing training programs for those employers who had paid the levy.

In their joint judgment, Mason CJ, Deane, Toohey and Gaudron JJ said that the legislation fell a long way short of requiring that the money raised through the levy be expended in training programs for eligible employers. The Administration Act did not 'establish any sufficient relationship between the liability to pay the charge and the provision of employment related training by the ultimate expenditure of the money collected to regard the liability to pay the charge as a fee for services or as something akin to a fee for services': 176 CLR at 568.

Fees for privileges or statutory licences

[9.2.8] In *Harper v Minister for Sea Fisheries* (1989) 168 CLR 314, the High Court held that a licence fee demanded by Tasmania for the right to take abalone in state fishing waters was not a tax. The fee charged for the privilege of exploiting that limited natural resources was 'a charge for the acquisition of a right akin to property': 168 CLR at 335 per Brennan J. Although Dawson, Toohey and McHugh JJ agreed with Brennan J, they cautioned that the conclusion in the present case did not carry the consequence that an exaction of money could never be a tax if it was demanded for the purpose of conserving a public natural resource; such an exaction would be seen as a tax if it had no discernible relationship with the value of what was acquired: 168 CLR at 336–7.

[9.2.9] Statutory licence fees are common, and are not regarded to be taxes so long as the fee is 'reasonably related' to the value the privilege provided or the actual costs of providing the privilege — if it is not 'reasonably related' to that value, the size of the fee can point to it being a tax. If a fee or charge is 'devoted to building up consolidated revenue', this will point to it being a tax. So in *Hematite Petroleum Pty Ltd v Victoria* (1983) 151 CLR 599 **[9.4.37C]**, a fee for a licence to operate an oil pipeline was held to be a tax because it was an 'enormous impost' on the production of oil: 151 CLR at 647.

The question is whether the charge is reasonably related to the expenses incurred in providing the relevant privilege. It is not necessary to demonstrate the charges directly correspond to the value to the user of the privilege or to the actual cost of providing the privilege: *Airservices Australia v Canadian Airlines* (1999) 202 CLR 133 at 176 per Gleeson CJ and Kirby J, 188–9 per Gaudron J, 241 per McHugh J, 261 per Gummow J and 302 per Hayne J. This will often be the case when a statutory corporation has been set up with a power to provide services on a user-pays basis: 202 CLR at 238–9 (McHugh J).

However, as Gummow J pointed out in *Airservices*, the validity of a law is determined by reference to its operation, not by reference to parliamentary objectives: 202 CLR at 261. For that reason, the volume of the revenue derived from state tobacco franchise licence fees, when compared with the amounts spent on regulating the tobacco industry, persuaded the High Court that the licence fees challenged in *Ha v New South Wales* (1997) 189 CLR 465 **[9.4.60C]** were taxes. After a fivefold increase in the total amount of revenue derived, the majority justices concluded that 'the States have far overreached their entitlement to exact what might properly be characterised as fees for licences to carry on businesses': 189 CLR at 503 (Brennan CJ, McHugh, Gummow and Kirby JJ). In *Ha*, the charges were not reasonably appropriate and adapted to a permissible regulatory purpose.

Fines and penalties

[9.2.10] Finally, taxes are said to be distinguished from financial penalties and arbitrary exactions. A tax is a payment 'demanded as a contribution to revenue irrespective of any legality or illegality in the circumstances upon which the liability depends', while a penalty is a payment 'claimed as solely a penalty for an unlawful act or omission rather than non-payment of or incidental to a tax': *R v Barger* (1908) 6 CLR 40 **[9.2.15C]** at 99 per Isaacs J.

Or, as the court said in *MacCormick v Federal Commissioner of Taxation* (1984) 158 CLR 622 **[9.2.27]** at 639 and *Northern Suburbs General Cemetery Reserve Trust v Commonwealth* (1993) 176 CLR 555 **[9.2.26]** at 571, penalties included in tax legislation are distinguished from taxing provisions because the penalties operate only where there had been a 'failure to discharge antecedent obligations on the part of the person on whom the exaction falls'.

[9.2.11] For example, in *Re Dymond* (1959) 101 CLR 11 **[5.2.28]**, Fullagar J, with whom Dixon CJ, Kitto and Windeyer JJ agreed, held that s 46 of the Sales Tax Assessment Act (No 1) 1930 (Cth) imposed a penalty, not a tax. The section provided that any person who failed to furnish a proper sales tax return should 'be liable to pay additional tax at [a specified rate] or the sum of one pound, whichever is the greater'. Fullagar J explained at 22:

> The liability is imposed by the Act not as a consequence of a sale of goods but as a consequence of an attempt to evade payment of a tax on a sale of goods. The exaction is directly punitive, and only indirectly fiscal. It is imposed for the protection of revenue, but as a sanction and not for the sake of revenue as such.

Consequently, the Assessment Act was not caught by s 55 of the Constitution.

While taxes are, formally at least, distinguished from financial penalties, it is clear that a tax can be used to regulate or control behaviour in the same way as penal laws are reinforced by the threat of a fine. Is it within the Commonwealth Parliament's power under s 51(ii) to attempt the control of individual behaviour through the imposition of heavy taxes on conduct which the Commonwealth wishes to curtail?

Taxes must not be arbitrary

[9.2.12] In *Deputy Federal Commissioner of Taxation v Truhold Benefit Pty Ltd* (1985) 158 CLR 678 **[9.2.28]**, Gibbs CJ, Mason, Wilson, Deane and Dawson JJ explained at 684 the distinction between a tax and an arbitrary exaction:

[L]iability can only be imposed by reference to ascertainable criteria with a sufficiently general application and ... the tax cannot lawfully be imposed as a result of some administrative decision based upon individual preference unrelated to any test laid down by the legislation.

Characterisation according to substantive effect, not form

[9.2.13] Earlier decisions tended to suggest that the form of the imposition or exaction is critical. In *Vacuum Oil Co Pty Ltd v Queensland* (1934) 51 CLR 108, the High Court held that the Motor Spirit Vendors Act 1933 (Qld) did not impose a tax. The Act prohibited any person from selling petrol in Queensland without a licence and required that every licensee should purchase and pay for locally produced power alcohol equivalent to 2.1 per cent of the volume of the licensee's sales of petrol. Dixon J conceded that this legislation achieved the same result as would legislation which taxed petrol vendors and paid the proceeds of the tax to power alcohol manufacturers. But, Dixon J said at 125:

> [T]he compulsory payment required of the suppliers of petrol does not answer the description of taxation. It is not a liability to the State, or to any public authority, or to any definite body or person authorised by law to demand or receive it. The liability to make the payment is not imposed by the enactment itself, but arises only when the suppliers of petrol proceed to fulfil the requirements of the enactment and purchase power alcohol; and then liability arises exclusively out of the contract of sale ...

[9.2.14] Some early decisions involved an examination of the substance, rather than the form, of the legislation. In *Attorney-General (NSW) v Homebush Flour Mills Ltd* (1937) 56 CLR 390, the High Court was faced with a challenge to the Flour Acquisition Act 1931 (NSW) which expropriated all flour milled in New South Wales, vested it in the state government and gave the miller of the flour two rights: first, a right to compensation at £8.10s a ton; and, second, a right to buy back the acquired flour at £10 a ton. Until the flour was sold by the government, the miller (who now had first option to buy) was required by the Act to store the flour at his own expense and risk.

The court held that this legislation imposed a tax (and hence a duty of excise within s 90 of the Constitution) upon the millers of flour, the amount of the tax being the difference between the compensation and the resale price. The argument that the Act involved no compulsion to pay (an essential ingredient in the standard definition of a tax) was not accepted by the court, which said that any flour miller who did not repurchase the acquired flour would go out of business. Dixon J said at 413:

> When the desired contributions are obtained not by direct command but by exposing the intended contributor if he does not pay, to worse burdens or consequences which he will naturally seek to avoid the payment becomes an exaction ...

(On governmental attempts to disguise taxation as a form of consensual arrangement, see also *Commonwealth v Colonial Combing Spinning and Weaving Co Ltd* (1922) 31 CLR 421 at 444–5.)

In *Ha v New South Wales* (1997) 189 CLR 465 **[9.4.60C]**, Brennan CJ, McHugh, Gummow and Kirby JJ made the point that, where the issue relates to a constitutional limitation on power, substance rather than form provides the key to characterisation:

When a constitutional limitation or restriction on power is relied on to invalidate a law, the effect of the law in and upon the facts and circumstances to which it relates — its practical operation — must be examined as well as its terms in order to ensure that the limitation or restriction is not circumvented by mere drafting devices. In recent cases, this Court has insisted on an examination of the practical operation (or substance) of a law impugned for contravention of a constitutional limitation or restriction on power. [189 CLR at 498] One of the earliest judgments on characterisation for the purposes of s 51(ii) of the Constitution, *R v Barger* (1908) 6 CLR 41 **[9.2.15C]**, emphasised the role of the substantive effect of legislation in deciding whether a law was 'with respect to ... taxation' so as to fall within the power granted by s 51(ii).

[9.2.15C]	**R v Barger**	
	(1908) 6 CLR 41	

The Excise Tariff Act 1906 (Cth) imposed a tax on the manufacturers of agricultural machinery with an exemption for those manufacturers who paid their employees 'fair and reasonable' wages. The Commonwealth Government brought proceedings in the High Court against two manufacturers of agricultural machines. In each case, the Commonwealth sought to recover excise duties on machinery which, it alleged, had not been manufactured under any of the conditions of employment specified in the Act.

The defendants' demurrers (in which they claimed that the Act was invalid) were heard before the Full Court, where argument was confined to the question whether the Excise Tariff Act 1906 was valid.

Griffith CJ, Barton and O'Connor JJ: [66] The Attorney-General claimed that the Commonwealth should have this power, and very properly pointed out that in many cases the result of the exercise of the power of taxation is to bring about indirect consequences which are designed by the legislature, and which could not practically, or could not so easily, be brought about by other means. The policy of protective tariffs rests upon this basis. The effect of a protective tariff may be to raise or lower prices, or to raise or lower rates of wages. In a federal State it may not be within the competence of the taxing authority to interfere directly with prices or wages, but the circumstance that a tax affects those matters indirectly is irrelevant to the question of competence to impose the tax. In other words, [67] the circumstance that an indirect effect may be produced by the exercise of admitted power is irrelevant to the question whether the legislature is competent to prescribe the same result by a direct law ...

Again, the motive which actuates the legislature, and the ultimate end desired to be attained, are equally irrelevant. A statute is only a means to an end, and its validity depends upon whether the legislature is or is not authorised to enact the particular provisions in question, entirely without regard to their ultimate indirect consequences ...

The scheme of the Australian Constitution ... is to confer certain definite powers upon the Commonwealth, and to reserve to the States, whose powers before the establishment of the Commonwealth were plenary, all powers not expressly conferred upon the Commonwealth ...

[69] The grant of the power of taxation is a separate and independent grant ... In interpreting the grant it must be considered not only with reference to other separate and independent grants, such as the power to regulate external and interstate trade and commerce, but also with reference to the powers reserved to the States.

It was not contested in argument that regulation of the conditions of labour is a matter relating to the internal affairs of the States, and is therefore reserved to the States and denied to the Commonwealth, except so far as it can be brought within one of the 39 powers enumerated in s 51.

We are thus led to the conclusion that the power of taxation, whatever it may include, was intended to be something entirely distinct from a power to directly regulate the domestic affairs of the States, which was denied to the Parliament ...

[72] The Constitution must be considered as a whole, and so as to give effect, as far as possible, to all its provisions. If two provisions are in apparent conflict, a construction which will reconcile the conflict is to be preferred. If, then, it is found that to give a particular meaning to a word of indefinite, and possibly large, significance would be inconsistent with some definite and distinct prohibition to be found elsewhere, either in express words or by necessary implication, that meaning must be rejected. It follows that if the control of the internal affairs of the States is in any particular forbidden, either expressly or by necessary implication, the power of taxation cannot be exercised so as to operate as a direct interference. Prima facie, the selection of a particular class of goods for taxation by a method which makes the liability to taxation dependent upon conditions to be observed in the industry in which they are produced is as [73] much an attempt to regulate those conditions as if the regulations were made by direct enactment.

The distinction has already been pointed out between the indirect effect of the imposition of taxes upon the importation or production of particular goods which may, in effect, be prohibitive, and the direct regulation of the conditions of the production of goods.

... It is clear that the power to pass such an Act must be vested either in the Parliament or in the State legislatures. If the tax is an excise duty within the meaning of s 90, the power of the Parliament is exclusive, and the State could not impose it.

Griffith CJ, Barton and O'Connor JJ said that a state legislature could regulate conditions of labour by prescribing those conditions, subject to a penalty; by imposing a licence fee; or by following the model of the present Commonwealth legislation.

[75] In any of the cases supposed the purpose of the Act, apparent on its face, whatever attempt might be made to disguise it in the title, would be, not to raise money for the purposes of government, but to regulate the conditions of labour. From this point of view an inquiry into the purpose of an Act is not an inquiry into the motives of the legislature, but into the substance of the legislation. And for the purpose of determining whether an attempted exercise of legislative power is warranted by the Constitution regard must be had to substance — to things, not to mere words. ...

[76] In our opinion the exclusive power of the Parliament to impose duties of excise cannot be construed as depriving the States of the exclusive power to make such enactments as we have suggested above ...

The justices went on to hold that, even if the Excise Tariff Act 1906 were a law with respect to taxation, it would be invalid because it authorised discrimination between states or parts of states, and authorised preference to a state or part thereof over another state or part thereof, contrary to ss 51(ii) and 99 of the Constitution. This issue is discussed in **[9.3.12]** below.

Isaacs J: [94] The unlimited nature of the taxing power ... is incontestable. Its exercise upon all persons, things and circumstances in Australia is, in my opinion, unchallengeable by the courts, [95] unless ... a judicial tribunal finds it repugnant to some express limitation or restriction ...

[97] [S]uch a conclusion, as my learned brethren preceding me have reached, necessarily gives determinative force to the purpose and effect of the Act, and the assumed object and motive of the legislature in passing it, and this is not permissible in such a case.

The Act is by this process taken to be equivalent to an enactment containing no reference to a tax, and consisting merely of regulative provisions; the words of the Commonwealth Parliament are rejected, and others it has not used are constructively substituted. No similar case can be found. It would be perfectly easy to destroy every Excise Act in a similar manner. All that is necessary is to apply the doctrine of equivalence. The Commonwealth imposes, say, a gun tax or a dog tax of £1 a year. That might be regarded as a penalty on keeping a gun or a dog; such a tax is very frequently said colloquially to be a penalty. A motor car tax might, in like manner, be held equivalent to a penalty on the possession of motor cars. The State might penalise the possession of opium by a £100 fine for every ounce. If the Commonwealth, for the purpose of suppressing the evil, imposes a tax of £100 an ounce could it be said it was only a penalty for regulation, and not a tax? But I do not see how such an Act could stand, if this Excise Tariff 1906 is bad. Let us get even closer to the present Act. Take the case of cigarettes. A differential excise tax of, say, six pence per pound is placed on cigarettes if made by machine. Is that a penalty on using machinery and unlawful? ... [98] What difference of principle is there between any of the cases suggested? In all of them the tax is on the goods, but for various reasons, motives, objects, or purposes which seem to the legislature appropriate to actuate it in the exercise of the granted power ... It must not be forgotten that, always apart from express restrictions — there being no more limit on the power of Commonwealth taxation than on that of a State — persons may be taxed in any class, at any rate, for any reason. Manufacturers may be taxed at one rate, for one reason, at another for another, or exempted for a third. How can a court step in and say the employment of labour at low rates is not a reason which the legislature may select, and adjudge that such a reason converts the Act into one of penal regulation.

[99] We are therefore thrown back on the fundamental distinction between taxation and regulation.

The true test as to whether an Act is a taxing Act, and so within the Federal power, or an Act merely regulating the rates of wages in internal trade, and so within the exclusive power of the State, is this: Is the money demanded as a contribution to revenue irrespective of any legality or illegality in the circumstances upon which the liability depends, or is it claimed as solely a penalty for an unlawful act or omission, other than non-payment of or incidental to a tax?

It is not sufficient to say the effect is the same. It may even be the very purpose of the Federal taxing authority to drive the taxed object out of existence; but as the power to tax includes the power 'to embarrass or to destroy', neither the purpose nor the effect is an objection to the exercise of the power.

Isaacs J went on to hold that the Act did not discriminate or give preference within the meaning of those terms in s 51(ii) and s 99. Higgins J delivered a separate judgment to the same effect as Isaacs J.

~~~

Notes

[9.2.16] The majority judgment in *R v Barger* (1908) 6 CLR 41 **[9.2.15C]** was influenced by the doctrine, since discarded, of state reserved powers: the rule that the specific legislative powers of the Commonwealth Parliament were to be interpreted so as to reserve for the states the maximum possible area of autonomous legislative power. Isaacs J said that this approach was akin to determining the extent of a specific gift in a will by first determining the extent of the residue: 6 CLR at 84.

It is true that the adherents of the doctrine tended to interpret the meaning of the specific powers granted to the Commonwealth by first working out the extent of powers 'reserved' to the states. That approach to the interpretation of the Commonwealth Constitution was decisively rejected by the High Court in *Amalgamated Society of Engineers v Adelaide Steamship Co Ltd* (the *Engineers'* case) (1920) 28 CLR 129 (see **[8.2.31C]**), although *Barger's* case itself was not overruled in the *Engineers'* case.

The judgments of two members of the High Court in *Fairfax v Federal Commissioner of Taxation* (1965) 114 CLR 1 **[9.2.22C]** clearly regarded *Barger's* case as wrong: see Kitto and Taylor JJ, 114 CLR at 12, 14. Similarly, the High Court's reasoning in *Northern Suburbs General Cemetery Reserve Trust v Commonwealth* (1993) 176 CLR 555 **[9.2.26]** cannot be reconciled with *Barger's* case. In *Murphyores Inc Pty Ltd v Commonwealth* (1976) 136 CLR 1 **[10.2.31C]**,

Mason J, with whom Gibbs and Jacobs JJ agreed, described *Barger's* case as 'no longer ... having authority': 136 CLR at 23.

[9.2.17] The majority in *R v Barger* (1908) 6 CLR 41 **[9.2.15C]** recognised that it was permissible in some circumstances to exercise the taxation power so as to affect commodity prices or wages. One clear example was that of protective tariffs: 6 CLR at 66–7. The majority referred to these as indirect effects and said that they were, because of their indirect nature, 'irrelevant to the question of competence to impose the tax': 6 CLR at 66. But why were these effects described as indirect? Was it because in 1908 it was generally assumed that the Commonwealth's taxing power could be used to create a protective tariff so as to affect local commodity prices and wages? Or was it because these effects are speculative, depending for their identification on economic analysis?

It is clear that a court cannot assess the effects of a protective tariff on commodity prices and wages without examining the economic environment within which the tariff operates. There may be very real controversy as to the nature of that environment (for different economists have quite different perspectives). Further, the environment may be subject to frequent change. Therefore, to test the validity of Commonwealth legislation by its economic effect would involve the judges in weighing evidence and opinions outside their normal range of competence and experience.

[9.2.18] Despite that general reluctance to look at the economic effects of taxing legislation, the majority in *R v Barger* (1908) 6 CLR 41 **[9.2.15C]** held that the Excise Tariff Act 1906 was not a law with respect to taxation, but a law with respect to conditions of labour. How could the majority have reached that conclusion without considering the economic effect of the legislation? Surely the majority assumed that employers would seek to avoid paying the tax by improving the conditions of their employees. That assumption could only be justified if it was clear that the payment of the tax would impose a heavier burden on employers than would the improvement of their employees' conditions. This could only become clear after a detailed evaluation of labour and material costs, overheads, and productivity in the relevant industry, again matters beyond the normal competence and experience of the judiciary.

[9.2.19] In *R v Barger* (1908) 6 CLR 41 **[9.2.15C]**, the majority said that the Excise Tariff Act 1906 was not a law with respect to taxation because its purpose was not to raise money for the government. This involved making a speculative assumption, without any examination of the evidence, that the taxpayers who were subject to the Act would seek to satisfy the conditions in the proviso exempting them from the tax liability. This purpose was not evident as a legal operation of the statute.

The proposition also involved the assumption that taxing legislation is legislation for the single purpose of raising revenue for government. However, many activities are taxed in order to discourage them, so that the revenue which the measure produces may be small. Generally taxes are levied not merely to raise revenue but also to control the allocation of a community's resources amongst various objects of investment and consumption, to regulate the level of economic activity and to redistribute income and capital: see **[9.1.2]–[9.1.3]**. We know, for example, that an anti-inflationary increase in income tax rates may produce a smaller tax revenue. However, most frequently, these effects are not apparent as purposes on the face of Acts, for their observation depends on an investigation of the general environment in which the Acts have been enacted and a consideration of their effect on that environment.

[9.2.20] In *Osborne v Commonwealth* (1911) 12 CLR 321, a landowner challenged the validity of the Land Tax Act 1910 (Cth) which imposed a tax on the owners of land at rates which increased as the value of the land owned increased. It was argued that the purpose of the Act was not so much to raise revenue as to prevent the holding of a large quantity of land by a single person. The contention was rejected by the High Court (Griffith CJ, Barton, O'Connor, Isaacs and Higgins JJ). Barton J said at 344:

> Now, this legislation has nothing in its terms which dictates who shall hold land and who shall not, or how much land any person shall hold. Assuming that the taxation which it imposes is drastic, as it is alleged to be, it is not the function of the court to say that drastic taxation on landed interests will prevent residents from owning large areas, or prevent landholders from residing out of Australia, or prevent absentees from holding land within the Commonwealth. Nor is it our function to say what degree of inducement to abstain from doing these things amounts to a prevention of the doing of them ... Questions of the abuse of power are for the people and Parliament. We can only determine whether the power exists, and if so, whether Parliament has in fact and in substance acted within it. It is of the essence of the taxing power that when exercised to the full it may destroy the interest or the industry taxed. But even so, interference would involve the court in the political function of deciding in what degree Parliament is justified in using a power on the exercise of which the Constitution itself places no limit.

Was this case decided consistently with *R v Barger* (1908) 6 CLR 41 **[9.2.15C]**? Zines has suggested that the distinction between *Barger's* case and *Osborne v Commonwealth* (1911) 12 CLR 321 'lay in the fact that in the former the object to be achieved — namely, the control of labour conditions, rather than the collection of revenue — was regarded as being apparent on its face': Zines (1997) p 30.

[9.2.21] Three interrelated Commonwealth Acts required a wool producer to pay to the Federal Commissioner of Taxation a prescribed proportion of the sale value of his or her wool. The amount so paid was to be credited against the producer's liability for tax and provisional tax in respect of the year in which the wool was sold, provisional tax for the following year and any income tax already due and unpaid. Any unapplied residue was to be returned to the producer. The High Court, in *Moore v Commonwealth* (1951) 82 CLR 547, held that these Acts were laws with respect to taxation, rejecting the argument that they were laws to combat inflation by freezing some of the extraordinary income wool producers were making on a booming market. Fullagar J said at 578:

> It cannot matter whether the ultimate purpose of the Act was to meet some exigency of the Treasury by collecting income tax in advance, or to 'freeze' certain moneys which, if left in circulation, might injuriously affect the financial stability of the country. These things are matters of policy, with which the courts cannot concern themselves, and which indeed they have no satisfactory means of ascertaining. What matters in cases of this kind is what the Act does, not the ultimate purpose which it was intended to serve. What an Act does is to be ascertained by an examination of its terms.

Can this proposition be reconciled with the majority judgment in *R v Barger* (1908) 6 CLR 41 **[9.2.15C]**?

[9.2.22C]   Fairfax v Federal Commissioner of Taxation

(1965) 114 CLR 1

Under ss 23(j) and (ja) of the Income Tax and Social Services Contribution Assessment Act 1936 (Cth) the income of a superannuation fund had been exempt from income tax. In 1961, the Act was amended so that, according to s 121C of the Act, the income of a superannuation fund would not be exempt under s 23(j) and (ja) unless the Commissioner of Taxation was satisfied that 30 per cent of the fund's assets were invested in 'public securities' including a 20 per cent investment in 'Commonwealth securities'. (Both types of securities were defined in s 6 of the Act.)

 Fairfax, Henderson and Palmer were the trustees of The Sydney Morning Herald Centenary Fund, a superannuation fund established for employees of John Fairfax and Sons Ltd. The Commissioner of Taxation assessed income tax on the income of the fund for the year ended 30 June 1962, on the basis that the fund's investments did not meet the standards in s 121C of the Act.

The trustees appealed to the High Court against that assessment as provided for in s 187 of the Act. Kitto J stated a case under s 198 of the Act for the opinion of the Full Court on the question whether the 1961 amendments made by s 11 of the Income Tax and Social Services Contribution Assessment Act 1961 were valid.

Kitto J: [6] The contention of the appellant trustees is that no head of Federal legislative power will support the enactment of s 11. It is, they say, a law with respect to the investment of the moneys of superannuation funds, a subject which is not one upon which the Parliament has any power to make laws. The commissioner's answer is that s 11 is a law with respect to taxation, whatever else it is, and is therefore to be upheld as an exercise of the power conferred on the Parliament by s 51(ii) of the Constitution.

The argument for invalidity not unnaturally began with the proposition that the question to be decided is a question of substance and not of mere form, but the danger quickly became evident that the proposition may be misunderstood as inviting a speculative inquiry as to which of the topics touched by the [7] legislation seems most likely to have been the main preoccupation of those who enacted it. Such an inquiry has nothing to do with the question of constitutional validity under s 51 of the Constitution. Under that section the question is always one of subject matter, to be determined by reference solely to the operation which the enactment has if it be valid, that is to say by reference to the nature of the rights, duties, powers and privileges which it changes, regulates or abolishes; it is a question as to the true nature and character of the legislation: is it in its real substance a law upon, 'with respect to', one or more of the enumerated subjects, or is there no more in it in relation to any of those subjects than an interference so incidental as not in truth to affect its character? See per Latham CJ in *Bank of New South Wales v Commonwealth* (1948) 76 CLR 1 at 185–7, and per Higgins J in *Huddart Parker & Co Pty Ltd v Moorehead* (1909) 8 CLR 33 at 409–11.

The need to distinguish between form and substance appears from what has just been said. The possibility has to be recognised, as it was in the United States as long ago as *McCulloch v Maryland* (1819) 4 Wheat 316 at 423, that under the guise of exercising one or more of the powers of the Parliament legislation may in truth endeavour only to accomplish objects beyond those powers: *Bank of New South Wales v Commonwealth* (1948) 76 CLR I at 187; see, for example, *Waterhouse v Deputy Federal Commissioner of Land Tax (SA)* (1914) 17 CLR 665. Accordingly the task of characterising laws according to subject matter must be performed with care lest mere words mislead. The court, as Higgins J said in *R v Barger* (1908) 6 CLR 41 'is not to be bound by the name which Parliament has chosen to give the Act' — one may add, or has chosen to give anything else — 'but is to consider what the Act is in substance — what it does, what it commands or prescribes' (1908) 6 CLR at 118. The appellant's argument in its final form accepted this as its real starting point and proceeded to say that s 11, though it is couched in terms of taxation and wears the badge of a tax law prominently upon it, really operates to expose trustees of superannuation funds to a liability which it miscalls a tax, a liability which in truth is a penalty or sanction for a failure to pursue a prescribed course of conduct by such trustees with respect to the investment of moneys.

Kitto J referred to the United States Supreme Court decision in *Child Labor Tax* case, *Bailey v Drexel Furniture Co* 259 US 20 (1922) in which legislation which imposed a tax on profits received on sales of products made with the use of child labour was invalid. His Honour said that the Supreme Court had 'emphasised that the Act imposed its heavy exaction upon a departure from a detailed and specified course of conduct in business' and thus its 'prohibitory and regulatory effect and purpose are palpable': 114 CLR at 9. After describing the effect of ss 121C and 121D, Kitto J continued:

> The words of the Supreme Court of the United States may be adapted, not unfairly, to the case: in the light of these features of the enactment, a court must be blind not to see that the 'tax' is imposed to stop trustees of superannuation funds from failing to invest sufficiently in Commonwealth and other public securities.

> But is this enough to justify the conclusion that what purports to be a set of provisions for imposing a tax upon the investment income of superannuation funds is in reality not a law with respect to taxation at all, but only a law with respect to the investment [10] of such funds? ...

> [12] In my opinion the judgment of the majority in *Barger's* case provides no satisfactory guide in the case before us, partly because the doctrine of the reserved powers of the States in the wide form in which it was held by their Honours, has long since been exploded (see *Amalgamated Society of Engineers v Adelaide Steamship Co* (1920) 28 CLR 129 at 154), but more fundamentally, because we ought to maintain the principle which may be stated in words taken from the judgment of Clark J in *United States v Sanchez* 340 US 42 (1950): 'It is beyond serious question that a tax does not cease to be valid merely because it regulates discourages, or even definitely deters the activities taxed. *Sonzinsky v United States* 300 US 506 at 513–14 (1937). The principle applies even though the revenue obtained is obviously negligible, *Sonzinsky v United States* or the revenue purpose of the tax may be secondary, *J W Hampton & Co v United States* 276 US 394 (1928). Nor does a tax statute necessarily fall because it touches on activities which Congress might not otherwise regulate' 340 US at 44 (1950).

Kitto J referred to the position adopted by the minority in *R v Barger* (1908) 6 CLR 41 **[9.2.15C]**, which was that the Commonwealth's taxation power was:

> ... 'plenary and absolute; unlimited as to amount, as to subjects, as to objects, as to conditions, as to machinery' (1908) 6 CLR at 114, so that 'the Parliament has prima facie, power to tax whom it chooses, [13] power to exempt whom it chooses, power to impose such conditions as to liability or as to exemption as it chooses': per Higgins J (1908) 6 CLR at 114. It may be that the power is subject to some implied as well as express limitations; but with that reservation the soundness of the propositions thus stated is not now, I think, open to doubt.

> In the result I think that this case should be decided against the appellants upon the broad principle which Sir Owen Dixon stated in *Melbourne Corporation v Commonwealth* (1947) 74 CLR 31: 'Speaking generally, once it appears that a federal law has an actual and immediate operation within a field assigned to the Commonwealth as a subject of legislative power, that is enough. It will be held to fall within the power unless some further reason appears for excluding it. That it discloses another purpose and that the purpose lies outside the area of federal power are considerations which will not in such a case suffice to invalidate the law' (1947) 74 CLR 79. The operation of s 11 is to replace a total exemption from all income tax with a conditional special liability to income tax on 'investment income'. The legislative policy is obvious and may be freely acknowledged: it is to provide trustees of superannuation funds with strong inducement to invest sufficiently in Commonwealth and other public securities. The raising of revenue may be of secondary concern. But the enactment does not prescribe or forbid conduct. Its character is neither fully or fairly described by saying that it makes trustees of superannuation funds liable to pay for failing to do what the legislature wishes. To adapt the language of Higgins J in *R v Barger* (1908) 6 CLR 41 at 119, the substance of the enactment is the obligation which it imposes, and the only obligation

imposed is to pay income tax. In substance as in form, therefore, the section is a law with respect to taxation.

I would answer the question in the case stated: Yes.

Taylor J delivered a judgment to the same effect as Kitto J. Menzies J delivered a concurring judgment.

Menzies J: [17] Whether or not a law is one with respect to taxation cannot be determined by looking at its economic consequences, however apparent they must have been at the time of its enactment; nor is an inquiry into the motives of the legislature permissible. There may be laws ostensibly imposing tax, which, nevertheless, are not laws with respect to taxation. For example, a special prohibitive tax upon income derived from the sale of heroin or from the growing or treatment of poppies for the production of heroin may not be a law with respect to taxation but rather a law made for the suppression of the trade in that drug by imposing penalties described as taxes for participation in it. The reason for denying to such a law the character of a law with respect to taxation would not be either its economic consequences or the motive behind its enactment. It would simply be that its true character is not a law with respect to taxation. The problem in every case is, therefore, to ascertain from the terms of the law impugned its true nature and character.

In this case, there is no reason — apart from the likely consequences upon the investing of the assets of superannuation funds and the motives imputed to the legislature — for denying to s 11, which relates to exemption from income tax, the character of a law with respect to taxation. Those consequences and imputed motives, for the reason which I have given, to not deprive the law of its character as such a law.

Barwick CJ agreed. Windeyer J delivered a concurring judgment.

~~~

Notes

[9.2.23]   None of the judges in *Fairfax v Federal Commissioner of Taxation* (1965) 114 CLR 1 **[9.2.22C]** overruled the decision in *R v Barger* (1908) 6 CLR 41 **[9.2.15C]**, although it is difficult to imagine how that decision could survive in the light of the reasons for judgment given by Kitto J. In *Murphyores Inc Pty Ltd v Commonwealth* (1976) 136 CLR 1, Mason J said that the decision in *Fairfax's* case 'swept away the last vestigial remnants of *Barger's* case': 136 CLR at 28. See the discussion at **[1.5.14]** and **[1.5.17]**–**[1.5.18]**.

[9.2.24]   Why, in the view of Menzies J in *Fairfax's* case (114 CLR at 17), might a special prohibitive tax upon income derived from the sale of heroin not be law with respect to taxation? Is it a question of the rate of a tax? Ought the rate of a tax govern its validity under s 51(ii)? Can a prohibitive tax imposed on an activity, or the fruits of that activity, become a penalty notwithstanding that the activity is in no way made unlawful?

In examining the legal operation of a statute imposing a prohibitive tax on income derived from the sale of heroin, what discloses its true nature as not being a law with respect to taxation? In *R v Barger* (1908) 6 CLR 41 **[9.2.15C]** Isaacs J offered a similar hypothetical problem, a tax of £100 an ounce on the possession of opium; though he indicated that he thought such a tax would be *within* s 51(ii): 6 CLR at 97.

[9.2.25]   The proposition that a Commonwealth taxation law may be invalid because it has an operation in an area that is regarded as beyond Commonwealth control and thus, on balance, cannot be characterised as a law with respect to taxation is supported by Latham CJ's argument in *Melbourne Corporation v Commonwealth* (the *State Banking* case) (1947) 74 CLR 31 **[8.2.45C]** that s 48 of the Banking Act was invalid, and by the argument of Barwick CJ in *Victoria v Commonwealth* (the *Payroll Tax* case) (1971) 122 CLR 353 **[8.2.50C]** that laws imposing discriminatory taxes upon states may be invalid. Latham CJ and Barwick CJ each assumed that there are certain matters which are beyond the range of Commonwealth legislative power to effect because of the distribution of power in the Australian federal system. However, that approach to characterisation does not represent the current orthodoxy: see **[1.5.14]** and **[1.5.17]–[1.5.18]** and the following case.

[9.2.26]   In *Northern Suburbs General Cemetery Reserve Trust v Commonwealth* (1993) 176 CLR 555, the High Court rejected a challenge to the validity of the Training Guarantee Act 1990 (Cth), which imposed a levy on those employers who did not expend a minimum proportion of their payroll on training their employees. One of the arguments raised against the validity of the Act was that its purpose was not to raise revenue but to control the training activities of employers through a penalty imposed on those employers who did not train their employees in the way required by the Act and the Training Guarantee (Administration) Act 1990 (Cth).

In their joint judgment, Mason CJ, Deane, Toohey and Gaudron JJ (with whose reasons on this issue Brennan J agreed) conceded that the imposition of the levy on employers was a secondary object of the scheme established by the Act and, indeed, was not listed among the Act's stated objects (at 569):

> But the fact that the revenue-raising burden is merely secondary to the attainment of some other object or objects is not a reason for treating the charge otherwise than as a tax: *Fairfax v Federal Commissioner of Taxation* (1965) 114 CLR 1 at 12 per Kitto J. One might as well suggest that a protective customs duty is not tax because its primary object is the protection of a particular local manufacturing industry from overseas competition.
>
> If a law, on its face, is one with respect to taxation, the law does not cease to have that character simply because Parliament seeks to achieve, by its enactment, a purpose not within Commonwealth legislative power.

After referring to *Osborne v Commonwealth* (1911) 12 CLR 321 **[9.2.20]**, *Radio Corporation Pty Ltd v Commonwealth* (1938) 59 CLR 170, *Fairfax v Federal Commissioner of Taxation* (1965) 114 CLR 1 **[9.2.22C]** and *Moore v Commonwealth* (1951) 82 CLR 547 **[9.2.21]**, Mason CJ, Deane, Toohey and Gaudron JJ continued:

> [I]n the ultimate analysis, the considerations pointing to a tax rather than a penalty are decisive. Neither the Act nor the Administration Act mandates or proscribes conduct of any kind. The legislative provisions do not make it an offence to fail to spend the minimum training requirement; nor do they provide for the recovery of civil penalties for such a failure. Consequently, the charge is not a penalty because the liability to pay does not arise from any failure to discharge antecedent obligations on the part of the person on whom the exaction falls: *MacCormick v Federal Commissioner of Taxation* (1984) 158 CLR 622 at 639 ... The fact that the legislature has singled out those who do not spend the minimum training requirement as the class to bear the burden of the charge and to quantify the amount of the liability by reference to the shortfall does not deprive the charge of the character of a tax.
>
> The law 'fairly answers the description of a law "with respect to one given subject-matter appearing in s 51" regardless of whether it is, at the same time, more obviously or equally a law with respect to some other subject-matter': *Re F; Ex parte F* (1986) 161 CLR at 387–8, citing with approval *Actors and Announcers Equity Association v Fontana Films Pty Ltd* (1982) 150 CLR 169 at 194. Accordingly, the conclusion that the Act and the Administration Act are laws with respect to taxation is unaffected by

the omission of the purpose of raising revenue from the statement of legislative objects (176 CLR at 571–2).

Dawson J (with whose reasons on this issue McHugh J agreed) said:

> [T]o say that the legislation is not designed to raise money is somewhat elliptical. In so far as it operates to impose the charge, the clear intent of the legislation is to raise revenue and to do so for the purpose of expenditure under training guarantee agreements. The fact that the wider object of the legislation is to encourage employers to pay for training programs themselves and so avoid the charge does not alter the true nature or character of the impost. After all, any protective tariff ultimately aims to eliminate the activity which gives rise to its incidence, yet a protective tariff is clearly a tax. There is more than a hint of *Barger's* case in this aspect of the plaintiff's argument, but that case, if it survived *Osborne v Commonwealth*, was laid to rest in *Fairfax v Commissioner of Taxation* (176 CLR at 589).

[9.2.27]   In *MacCormick v Federal Commissioner of Taxation* (1984) 158 CLR 622, Brennan J acknowledged at 655 the plenary character of the power in s 51(ii):

> As the taxation power extends to 'any form of tax which ingenuity may devise', the Parliament may select such criteria as it chooses, subject to any express or implied limitations prescribed by the Constitution, irrespective of any connexion between them.

Brennan J was responding to an attack on the validity of the Taxation (Unpaid Company Tax — Vendors) Act 1982 (Cth) and the Taxation (Unpaid Company Tax — Promoters) Act 1982 (Cth), legislation designed to recoup taxation revenue lost through some of the more blatant tax avoidance (or evasion) schemes which flourished during the late 1970s, colloquially referred to as 'asset-stripping' and 'bottom of the harbour' schemes.

Under these schemes, the shares in a company with an unpaid company tax liability were sold, through the promoters of the schemes, to purchasers of little (if any) substance, at a price which represented around 90 per cent of the gross value of the company's assets. The assets were then stripped from the company by the new shareholders, the company's records destroyed, the new shareholders evaporated, and the Commissioner for Taxation left with the empty and insolvent shell of the company.

The legislation imposed a tax upon the vendors of shares in any company, and upon the promoters of the sale of such shares, where the company had an undischarged company tax liability and the sale was followed by a stripping the company's assets which left the company incapable of discharging its tax liability. According to the Taxation (Unpaid Company Tax) Assessment Act 1982, the amount of the tax, referred to as recoupment tax, was calculated by reference to the unpaid company tax. Provisions in the Taxation (Unpaid Company Tax — Vendors) Act and the Taxation (Unpaid Company Tax — Promoters) Act ensured that the recoupment tax would be collected only once, from either the vendor or the promoter; but payment of the recoupment tax by either the vendor or the promoter did not extinguish the company's original liability for company tax.

The legislation was attacked on the ground that s 51(ii) of the Constitution demanded a connection between the objects of taxation (that is, the person on whom liability to pay a tax was imposed) and the subject of taxation (that is, the criteria according to which the tax liability was created; namely, the event or thing which gave rise to the liability). This argument was also expressed as a constitutional objection to any legislation which required one person to discharge another person's tax liability. It was said that an Act which required a person to pay a tax imposed upon another could not be a law with respect to taxation within s 51(ii). This argument was doubted, although not explicitly rejected, by Gibbs CJ, Wilson, Deane and Dawson JJ: 158 CLR at 636. In any event, these justices said, there was a connection between the taxpayers and the subject of the recoupment tax, which was the transaction that resulted in the stripping of the company's assets.

The argument against the legislation's validity was subjected to extensive criticism by Brennan J as involving a confusion between s 51(ii) and s 55 of the Constitution. The latter section was 'calculated to safeguard the powers of the Senate'. The concept of 'subject of taxation' did not affect the scope of the s 51(ii) power, but only the means by which that power was exercised: 158 CLR at 653.

However, the court did decide that s 23(1) of the Taxation (Unpaid Company Tax) Assessment Act was invalid because, in the language adopted by the plaintiffs in this case, it created 'an incontestable tax'. This provision provided that a certificate signed by the Commissioner of Taxation, stating that company tax was due and payable and remained unpaid, was 'conclusive evidence of the matter stated in the certificate' for the purpose of the assessment of the recoupment tax imposed on vendors and promoters involved in the sale of the asset-stripped company. Murphy and Brennan JJ referred to the integrity of federal judicial power; that is, the general proposition that the conclusive determination of rights and liabilities is a judicial function which could not be committed to a non-judicial arm of the Commonwealth Government: 158 CLR at 645–6, 658–9. Gibbs CJ, Wilson, Deane and Dawson JJ adopted (158 CLR at 640) Dixon CJ's proposition from *Deputy Federal Commissioner of Taxation v Brown* (1958) 100 CLR 32 at 40:

> [U]nder the Constitution liability for tax cannot be imposed upon the subject without leaving open to him some judicial process by which he may show that in truth he was not taxable or not taxable in the sum assessed, that is to say that an administrative assessment could not be made absolutely conclusive upon him if no recourse to the judicial power were allowed.

[9.2.28] A further challenge to the Taxation (Unpaid Company Tax) Assessment Act 1982 (Cth) was made in *Deputy Federal Commissioner of Taxation v Truhold Benefit Pty Ltd* (1985) 158 CLR 678. The case focused on s 6(2) of the Act, which dealt with the situation where the vendor of shares in an 'asset-stripped' company was itself a company. If the Commissioner of Taxation formed the opinion that the vendor company was unlikely to pay the recoupment tax owing by it as vendor under the Taxation (Unpaid Company Tax —Vendors) Act, a secondary tax liability fell on any person entitled to participate in the capital distribution of the vendor company.

Section 6(2) was attacked on the ground that it provided for the imposition of an arbitrary tax because the persons on whom the secondary tax liability could be imposed need have no connection with the original company, whose assets had been stripped and whose unpaid company tax gave rise to the primary liability for recoupment tax.

In their joint judgment, Gibbs CJ, Mason, Wilson, Deane and Dawson JJ noted that in *MacCormick v Federal Commissioner of Taxation* (1984) 158 CLR 622 **[9.2.27]**, 'the proposition that a law is not a law with respect to taxation unless there is a real connexion between the objects of the tax and its subject-matter was doubted': 158 CLR at 685. However, assuming that the proposition was well-founded, they said there was a connection between the persons who might be made liable under s 6(2) and the subject matter of the tax. Those persons formed 'links in a chain' which commenced with the sale by a company of its shares in a company with an unpaid company tax liability. They acknowledged that the tax might operate harshly on those who received no or little benefit from the transaction, and that the ultimate taxpayer might be remotely connected to the transaction. Nevertheless, there would always be some connection.

The justices also rejected an argument that the process by which the secondary tax liability could be imposed was arbitrary because it depended on the opinion of the Commissioner of Taxation (at 687–8):

> The Commissioner is to be guided and controlled by the policy and purpose of the enactment and, whatever the width of his discretion, it is not unexaminable should he exceed the limits which may be discerned from its provisions: *Giris Pty Ltd v Federal Commissioner of Taxation*. The legislation does not contemplate the formation of an opinion by the Commissioner in an arbitrary manner and any attack upon it on that ground cannot, in our view, succeed.

[9.2.29] The references, in *MacCormick v Federal Commissioner of Taxation* (1984) 158 CLR 622 **[9.2.27]** and *Deputy Federal Commissioner of Taxation v Truhold Benefit Pty Ltd* (1985) 158 CLR 678 **[9.2.28]**, to an 'arbitrary exaction' lying outside the s 51(ii) power, raise some difficult questions. It appears that legislation imposing a liability to pay money to public funds must have two characteristics to avoid being classed as an arbitrary exaction. First, it seems that a person's taxation liability must 'be imposed by reference to ascertainable criteria with a sufficiently general application' (158 CLR at 684); that is, the liability cannot be imposed by *ad hominem* legislation directed at specified individuals.

Second, the person upon whom the liability is imposed must have the opportunity to challenge the liability through some judicial process by showing that his or her circumstances do not attract the liability. This characteristic has some resonance with a doctrine which is expressed in the maxim: 'the stream cannot rise higher than its source'. In *Australian Communist Party v Commonwealth* (1951) 83 CLR 1, Fullagar J said that 'the validity of a law or of an administrative act done under a law cannot be made to depend on the opinion of the law-maker, or the person who is to do the act, that the law or the consequence of the act is within the constitutional power upon which the law in question itself depends for its validity': 83 CLR at 258.

These two aspects of the concept of an arbitrary exaction overlap, as the following passage, from the judgment of Gibbs CJ, Wilson, Deane and Dawson JJ in *MacCormick v Federal Commissioner of Taxation* (1984) 158 CLR 622 **[9.2.27]** at 640–1, illustrates:

> For an impost to satisfy the description of a tax it must be possible to differentiate it from an arbitrary exaction and this can only be done by reference to the criteria by which liability to pay the tax is imposed. Not only must it be possible to point to the criteria themselves, but it must be possible to show that the way in which they are applied does not involve the imposition of liability in an arbitrary or capricious manner. In *Giris Pty Ltd v Federal Commissioner of Taxation* (1969) 119 CLR 365 at 378–9, Kitto J pointed out that the expression 'incontestable tax' in the sense in which it is used in *Hankin* and *Brown* 'refers to a tax provided for by a law which, while making the taxpayer's liability depend upon specified criteria, purports to deny him all right to resist an assessment by proving in the courts that the criteria of liability were not satisfied in his case'. The purported tax is thereby converted to an impost which is made regardless of whether the circumstances of the case satisfy the criteria relied upon for characterisation of the impost as a tax and for characterisation of the law which

imposes it as a law with respect to taxation. Such an incontestable impost is not a tax in the constitutional sense and a law imposing such an impost is not a law with respect to taxation within s 51(ii). It is in this sense that an incontestable tax is invalid.

3   Discrimination and preference

[9.3.1E]   **Commonwealth Constitution**

51   The Parliament shall, subject to this Constitution, have power to make laws for the peace, order, and good government of the Commonwealth with respect to: ...

   (ii)   Taxation; but so as not to discriminate between States or parts of States: ...

99   The Commonwealth shall not, by any law or regulation of trade, commerce, or revenue, give preference to one State or any part thereof over another State or any part thereof.

~~~

Notes

[9.3.2]   The proviso to ss 51(ii) and 99 are two elements in a complex series of sections, which appear to be designed to promote integration of the national economy: see also s 90 **[9.4.2E]** and s 92 **[10.4.1E]**. Among that series of sections are:

- s 51(iii), which insists that Commonwealth bounties on the production of goods shall be uniform throughout the Commonwealth;

- s 88, which obliged the Commonwealth to impose 'uniform duties of customs' within two years of federation;

- s 90, which precludes the states from imposing customs and excise duties and paying bounties on production;

- s 92, which declares that interstate trade is to be 'absolutely free'; and

- s 102, which gives the Commonwealth Parliament a limited power to forbid preferential or discriminatory operations by state railways.

[9.3.3]   Our immediate concern is with the impact of the proviso to ss 51(ii) and 99 on the taxation power of the Commonwealth. The effect of s 90 on the taxation powers of the states is reviewed in **[9.4.1]–[9.4.68]**, and the potential difficulties posed by s 92 for taxation and other laws is examined in **[10.4.1E]–[10.4.41]**.

[9.3.4]   The restrictions laid down by the proviso to ss 51(ii) and 99 are similar but not identical. The former prohibits discrimination, the latter preference; but there is, in the context of taxation law, little practical difference between the prohibitions. It is difficult to see how a Commonwealth taxation law which gave preference to taxpayers in (say) Tasmania could avoid discriminating against taxpayers in other states.

In *Elliott v Commonwealth* (1936) 54 CLR 657 **[9.3.13C]**, Latham CJ recognised at 668 the basic similarity of the impacts of s 51(ii) and s 99:

The sections operate independently, but they overlap to some extent. Laws of taxation, including laws with respect to customs duties, fall under s 51(ii) and as laws of revenue they fall under s 99. Laws with respect to bounties on the export of goods fall under s 51(iii) and also, as laws of trade and commerce, under s 99. A preference in relation to any of these subjects which infringed s 99 would also be a prohibited discrimination or a prohibited lack of uniformity under one of the other sections. Preference necessarily involves discrimination or lack of uniformity, but discrimination or lack of uniformity does not necessarily involve preference.

Latham CJ's final point, that discrimination did not necessarily involve preference, should be read in the context of the issue before the court in *Elliott's* case: a claim that a Commonwealth trade and commerce law gave preference to some states over others. The court accepted that, in relation to trade and commerce, a preference must involve a 'tangible commercial advantage'. It can be argued that, in the context of revenue laws, preference is no more than the converse of discrimination. However, in assessing the scope of, and restrictions on, the Commonwealth's taxation power, these semantic distinctions are unimportant. The power is subject to both restrictions and the possibility that one restriction is more far-reaching than the other cannot have any liberating effect on that power.

[9.3.5]   Similarly, the different form of words used in ss 51(ii) and 99 to identify the areas or localities, which must not be treated in a discriminatory fashion or preferentially, is of no practical significance. Even if it is true that s 51(ii) would strike down a taxation law which discriminated between parts of the same state while s 99 does not prohibit a revenue law preferring part of one state over another part of the same state (Lane (1987) p 73; Rose (1977) pp 202–3), the Commonwealth's taxation power is subject to both the narrower restriction against preference and the broader restriction against discrimination. (Close attention to the language in the two provisions suggests that this distinction is illusory: to give preference to one part of (say) Victoria over another part of Victoria will inevitably involve a preference to part of one state over another, or vice versa.)

[9.3.6]   The two provisions, s 51(ii) and s 99, raise two common issues in the context of taxation laws: When can a law be said to discriminate or give preference? When is that discrimination or preference between states or parts of states?

The meaning of discrimination and preference

[9.3.7]   On the first issue (What is discrimination or preference?) the view has been consistently taken that a law will only discriminate or give preference when the law provides a different rule for different parts of Australia. On the other hand, a law which contains a uniform rule whose operation and effect differ throughout Australia is treated as neither discriminating nor giving preference. In discrimination law this would be described as the difference, respectively, between formal (or direct) discrimination and substantive (or indirect) discrimination, with only the former being invalid under the Constitution. Higgins J expressed this approach in *James v Commonwealth* (1928) 41 CLR 442 at 462:

> Where the rule laid down is general, applicable to all States alike, but is found to operate unequally in the several States not from anything done by the Commonwealth Parliament but from the inequality of the conditions existing in, or the law imposed by, the States themselves, the Commonwealth has not been guilty of discrimination or preference between States.

In that case, the High Court considered a challenge to the Dried Fruits Act 1928 (Cth), which set up a licensing system for the interstate trade in dried fruits. This was part of an attempt to rationalise the dried fruits industry, in which the supply considerably exceeded demand. A grower was forbidden to deliver his or her dried fruit for interstate carriage except under a licence issued by a prescribed authority in the grower's state. Licensing authorities were prescribed for the states of New South Wales, South Australia, Victoria and Western Australia, the only states where dried fruits were produced in commercial quantities for the interstate trade. The court held that the legislation ('a law ... of trade, commerce') gave a preference to the four states because a grower in Queensland and Tasmania could not obtain a licence. It did not matter that there were no growers in either of those states who required licences. What was critical was the legal form of the legislation. On its face the legislation gave preference to one state over another; and, of course, the facts might change.

[9.3.8] Similarly, in *Cameron v Federal Commissioner of Taxation* (1923) 32 CLR 68, the High Court held invalid Commonwealth income tax regulations which prescribed the value to be assigned to livestock in different states of Australia when calculating the profit made on the sale of that stock. The values assigned differed between the states. An argument that the prescribed values represented the fair value of each type in each state was rejected as irrelevant. Isaacs J said at 76–7:

> It does not matter whether those standards are arbitrary or measured, whether dictated by a desire to benefit or to injure, the simple fact is they are 'different', and those different legal standards being applied simply because the subject of taxation finds itself in one State or the other there arises the discrimination by law between States which is forbidden by the Constitution.

[9.3.9] On the other hand, in *Colonial Sugar Refining Co Ltd v Irving* [1906] AC 360, the Privy Council held valid a provision of the Excise Tariff Act 1902 (Cth) which exempted from duties of excise goods on which customs or excise duties had been paid under state legislation before 8 October 1901. Lord Davey said at 367–8:

> The rule laid down by the Act is a general one, applicable to all States alike, and the fact that it operates unequally in the several States arises not from anything done by the Parliament, but from the inequality of the duties imposed by the States themselves. The exemption from the excise duties on the ground of the previous payment of customs duties seems justifiable and right in establishing a system based on the absolute freedom of trade among the States and the substitution of a uniform excise for all interstate duties on goods as well as what are strictly called excise duties.

[9.3.10] The formal approach to the identification of discrimination (or preference) endorsed in this series of decisions, may require reassessment in the light of the High Court's decision in *Street v Queensland Bar Association* (1989) 168 CLR 461 **[11.2.61C]**. The question before the court was whether Rules of the Supreme Court of Queensland restricting admission to practice as a barrister to residents of that state offended s 117 of the Commonwealth Constitution. That section declares that a resident of one state shall not be subject to any disability or discrimination which would not be equally applicable to that person if he or she were resident in any other state. The members of the court said that the presence of discrimination was to be discovered by considering the practical operation and individual effect of the challenged law: 168 CLR at 487 per Mason J; at 507–8 per Brennan J; at 527 per Deane J; at 548 per Dawson J; at 569 per Gaudron J; at 581 per McHugh J. McHugh J observed at 581:

> Discrimination can arise just as readily from a law which treats as equals those who are different as it can from a law which treats differently those whose circumstances are not materially different.

[9.3.11] The apparent unanimity in the context of ss 51(ii) and 99 on the meaning of discrimination (unequal treatment rather than unequal operation) has still left room for judicial difference of opinion (or confusion) when it comes to identifying discrimination or preference. In *Conroy v Carter* (1968) 118 CLR 90, the High Court divided over the question whether the Poultry Industry Levy Collection Act 1965 (Cth) offended s 51(ii) by discriminating between states. The Act established processes for the collection of a special tax from poultry farmers. Section 5(1) provided that the Commonwealth might make an arrangement with a state for that state's Egg Board to collect the levy in that state on behalf of the Commonwealth. Section 6(1) provided that, where such an arrangement was made, the state authority could deduct the amount of the levy from any money which the state authority owed to a poultry farmer.

Menzies J (with whom Barwick CJ and McTiernan J agreed) described s 6(1) as exposing poultry farmers in a state where an arrangement had been made 'to a particular disadvantage at law to which a person in respect of hens kept in a State which has made no arrangement with the Commonwealth under s 5, is not exposed, namely the retention of the levy out of moneys owing by a State Egg Board to the taxpayer': 118 at CLR at 103–4. His Honour thought 'that this differentiation amounts to an unlawful discrimination': 118 at CLR at 104. On the other hand, Taylor J (with whom Kitto and Windeyer JJ agreed) said that any difference between taxpayers in one state and another arose from the fact that arrangements may not have been made with all states, so that s 6(1) would be incapable of application in some states: but this would not involve 'discrimination in the constitutional sense': 118 CLR at 102.

The difference of opinion over the validity of s 6(1)(b) was essentially a difference in analysis of the issue before the court. There appeared to be agreement that s 6(1)(b) would offend s 51(ii) of the Constitution if the 'disadvantage' suffered by Carter was the product of a different rule or tax liability imposed by the provision in Victoria; and that s 6(1)(b) would not offend s 51(ii) if Carter's 'disadvantage' was the product of the application of an identical or uniform rule to different circumstances in Victoria. One group of judges saw the 'disadvantage' as a product of a different rule, another group saw it as a product of different circumstances.

For further discussion of *Conroy v Carter*, see Lane (1968) pp 316–17 and Rose (1977) pp 206–8.

'Between states' etc

[9.3.12] The second issue involved in understanding ss 51(ii) and 99 has not attracted the degree of judicial solidarity which (so far) has attended discussion of the meaning of 'discrimination' and 'preference'. This issue involves identifying the types of discrimination or preference which are proscribed by the sections. It is discrimination or preference between states or parts of states, not between activities or between different classes of taxpayers, which is prohibited. So the issues here are: When can we say that a law which clearly discriminates or gives preference, discriminates or prefers *between states*? When can we say that such a law discriminates or prefers on some basis other than that of state locality?

This problem is highlighted by the contrast between the majority and the minority in *R v Barger* (1908) 6 CLR 41. The majority decided that the Excise Tariff Act 1906 (Cth) was not a law with respect to taxation: **[9.2.15C]**. That Act taxed the producers of farm machinery but gave an exemption to those producers who employed their workers on reasonable employment conditions. However, the majority went on to say that, if the Act was a law with respect to taxation, it infringed the proviso to ss 51(ii) and 99. Griffith CJ, Barton and O'Connor JJ held that the Act authorised a discriminatory tax. They proceeded to reject an argument that, if there was any discrimination, it operated by reference to the employment and economic characteristics of different localities, not their state characteristics (at 78):

> The words 'States or parts of States' must be read as synonymous with 'parts of the Commonwealth' or 'different localities within the Commonwealth'. The existing limits of the States are arbitrary and it would be a strange thing if the Commonwealth Parliament could discriminate in a taxing Act between one locality and another, merely because such localities were not coterminous with States or parts of States.

Isaacs and Higgins JJ dissented, for substantially identical reasons on this point. Referring to both ss 51(ii) and 99, Isaacs J said at 107–8:

> [The] treatment that is forbidden is in relation to the localities considered as parts of States, and not as mere Australian localities, or parts of the Commonwealth considered as a single country ...
>
> It does not include a differentiation based on other considerations which are dependent on natural or business circumstances, and may operate with more or less force in different localities; and there is nothing, in my opinion, to prevent the Australian Parliament, charged with the welfare of the people as a whole, from doing what every State in the Commonwealth has power to do for its own citizens, that is to say, from basing its taxation measures on considerations of fairness and justice, always observing the constitutional injunction not to prefer States or parts of States.

[9.3.13C]   Elliott v Commonwealth
(1935) 54 CLR 657

The Transport Workers (Seamen) Regulations 1935 (Cth) were part of a scheme for regulating interstate and overseas commerce. They established a system for licensing seamen and provided that unlicensed persons should not be engaged as seamen at 'prescribed ports'. Regulation 5 authorised the Minister to specify the 'prescribed ports ... in respect of which licensing officers shall be appointed for the purposes of those Regulations'. The Minister specified the ports of Sydney, Melbourne, Brisbane, Newcastle and Port Adelaide as the 'prescribed ports'.

Elliott was a seaman who lived in Sydney. He brought an action in the High Court of Australia against the Commonwealth claiming a declaration that the regulations were invalid in their application to seamen and an injunction to restrain the Commonwealth from enforcing the regulations against the plaintiff and other seamen. Elliott's application for an interlocutory injunction to restrain the Commonwealth from enforcing the licensing system pending the decision of the case was heard by the Full Court of the High Court and treated, by consent, as the trial of the action.

Latham CJ said that, before a law could be described as giving preference within s 99 the court would have to be satisfied that the law gave a tangible commercial advantage. This could not be said of the licensing system. The Chief Justice went on to consider whether the regulations, if they had involved a preference, would have infringed s 99:

Latham CJ: [672] If it had been intended to provide by s 99 that there should be no preference in laws of trade, commerce or revenue based upon locality it would have been very easy to say so. This has been done very definitely in the case of bounties (s 51(iii)). The words there used are 'uniform throughout the Commonwealth'. There is no reference to 'States or parts of States'. The difference between this provision and those contained in s 51(ii) and s 99 is a striking and conspicuous distinction, and it is emphasised by the close association of s 51(ii) and s 51(iii). Prima facie, words which relate to a similar subject matter and which are so different should receive a different interpretation ...

[673] *Any* absence of 'geographical uniformity' (which includes the presence of any discrimination or preference based upon locality) would constitute a breach of s 51(iii). The marked difference in language between the words of this section and those used in s 99 cannot, in my opinion, be ignored. In the case of s 51 (iii) it is sufficient, in order to invalidate, to find any differentiation based upon locality in the widest sense. In the case of s 99 it is necessary to show that a preference is to one State or part of a State over another State or part of a State.

Latham CJ referred to two decisions which, he said, supported Isaacs J's view of the treatment forbidden by s 51(ii) and s 99: see **[9.3.12]**. These were *Cameron v Deputy Federal Commissioner of Taxation* (1923) 32 CLR 68 and *James v Commonwealth* (1928) 41 CLR 442. His Honour continued:

[675] These authorities make it, in my opinion, proper to hold that the discrimen which s 99 forbids the Commonwealth to select is not merely locality as such, but localities which for the purpose of applying the *discrimen* are taken as States or parts of States. In the regulations in question the application of the regulations depends upon the selection of ports as ports and not of States or parts of States as such. In my opinion, s 99 does not prohibit such differentiation.

Section 99 expressly distinguishes between preferences to States and preferences to parts of States. It may be that a preference to Sydney and Newcastle in relation to trade and commerce may have a large effect in giving preference to the State of New South Wales as a whole, but I think that a law giving such preference must nevertheless be construed, according to its terms, as giving a preference to Sydney and Newcastle and not to the whole State. As a matter of construction this seems to me to be proper, and, if it is allowable to look at the actual facts, it is a matter of common knowledge that some trade to and from southern New South Wales passes through Melbourne, and that some trade from the north of New South Wales passes through Brisbane. I do not agree that, for the purposes of s 99, which so definitely distinguishes between States and parts of States, a State can be regarded as identified with its capital city or its principal port or ports.

Dixon J: [682] The case does not, in my view, depend upon the expression 'part of a State'. For even if, in prescribing a port in one State, the Minister cannot be considered to have adopted 'part of a State' within the sense of s 99 as the basis of his differentiation, I think that in specifying the chief ports in each of four States a course was taken which must be considered as affecting each of those States as a whole. We are concerned only with sea-borne trade of each State with other States and countries. For the most part that trade is done from the ports prescribed, namely, from the ports of the capital cities of each of these four States, and, in the case of New South Wales, the port second in importance, Newcastle. Whatever relates to carriage by sea from those ports relates to the international and interstate sea commerce of the States themselves.

Dixon J proceeded to hold that the regulations gave a commercial advantage to those states where the prescribed ports were located and that this was a preference contrary to s 99.

Evatt J reviewed *R v Barger* (1908) 6 CLR 41 **[9.2.15C]**, *Cameron v Deputy Federal Commissioner of Taxation* (1923) 32 CLR 68 **[9.3.8]** and *James v Commonwealth* (1928) 41 CLR 442 **[9.3.7]**. He could find no support, in the last two cases, for the approach of Isaacs J to 'States or parts of States' in s 51(ii) or s 99. His Honour continued:

Evatt J: [690] [T]here was a very solid foundation for the conclusion reached in *Barger's* case (1908) 6 CLR 41 by the majority of the Court — that s 99 forbids all preferences which arise solely as a legal consequence of association with or reference to any locality in 'Australia', ie, 'one or more of the States of Australia'. The opposing view of Isaacs J (105–11) — that the only preference forbidden by s 99 is preference to a State or a part of a State 'considered as' such — involves the proposition that s 99 is not infringed if (say) a Commonwealth enactment exempts from taxation 'all persons carrying on business or resident at Brisbane.' On Isaacs J's view, presumably, such an enactment would not give a preference to a part of Queensland 'considered as' a part of Queensland. But it is indisputable that such an enactment would give a preference to Brisbane, and, as Brisbane is part of the State of Queensland, the enactment would give a preference to a part of a State over the five remaining States of the Commonwealth ...

In his able argument, Mr Paterson gave a further illustration of a law of revenue which offends against s 99. He supposed that a Commonwealth law provided that persons resident in, and carrying on business at, Sydney, Newcastle, Melbourne, Brisbane, Port [691] Adelaide and Townsville (the six places specified in the present regulations) should be exempt from taxation if their incomes exceeded £500. In such a case, he said, first, that there would be an infringement of s 51(ii) because the law of taxation would 'discriminate between States or parts of States'. This view is obviously sound, because it is preposterous to suggest that, before the prohibitions of s 51(ii) or s 99 of the Constitution can apply, the name of one or more States must be branded upon the face of the offending legislation ...

The illustration given by counsel should be followed a little further. Does such an Act as he envisaged confer a preference contrary to s 99 as well as to s 51(ii)? He contended, and his contention has not, and I think cannot, be answered, that such a law would give preference to those residing or carrying on business in any of the six localities specified over all persons residing or carrying on business in any locality within Western Australia and Tasmania, as well as over all such persons in all localities in the four States except the localities preferred ...

[692] The logical result of the above discussion of principle and authority is that ... [693] ... [s] 99 may apply although the legislation or regulations contain no mention of a State *eo nomine*, for example, the section may be infringed if preference is given to part of a State (for example, that part of New South Wales which is represented by the port of Sydney) over another State (for example, Western Australia) or any part of another State (for example, Fremantle or Brisbane).

~~~

[9.3.14] Evatt J proceeded to hold that the regulations conferred a material advantage on employers in the prescribed ports and so infringed s 99. Rich J held that the regulations did not give a preference within s 99, there was 'no discrimination against individuals as denizens of States'. The licensing system was based on the need for 'action in particular localities. No account of state boundaries is taken': 54 CLR at 678. His Honour also concluded that the regulations conferred no 'benefit or advantage' and, therefore, no preference.

Starke J held that the regulations did not involve a preference; that is, an 'advantage or impediment in connection with commercial dealings'. He also held that 'the preference prohibited [by s 99] is preference to localities': 54 CLR at 680. McTiernan J said that, while the regulations could be said to discriminate, they did not confer a 'preference'. Moreover, the prescribed ports had been 'specified, not as cities or parts of New South Wales or Victoria, but as ports of the Commonwealth': 54 CLR 705.

In the result, the court gave judgment for the Commonwealth.

Notes

[9.3.15] Latham CJ relied, to a considerable extent, upon the difference between ss 51(ii) and 99, on the one hand, and s 51(iii) on the other. The last provision demanded uniformity 'throughout the Commonwealth' while the first two forbade discrimination or preference 'between states' etc. These different formulae should be regarded as significant, Latham CJ said:

> But an examination of the drafting history of these provisions suggests that there is no significance in their different forms of expression. Section 51(ii), and its predecessor in the 1897 draft constitution, cl 52(ii), had originally demanded that Commonwealth taxation be 'uniform throughout the Commonwealth'. However, it was feared that a decision of the United States Supreme Court, *Pollock v Farmers' Loan and Trust Co* 157 US 429 (1894), had construed a similar provision as demanding equality of tax burdens as between individuals. Accordingly, the clause was amended on the motion of the chairman of the drafting committee, Edmund Barton, at the 1898 Melbourne Convention, to put 'the matter into a form which would express the intention of the Convention, whilst avoiding a difficulty'. He said that the intention was that taxes should be 'one in form' throughout the Commonwealth ... to prevent a discrimination between citizens of the Commonwealth in the same circumstances (Convention Debates, Melbourne (1898), vol II, p 2397).

Section 99 had a more complex history. In the 1897 draft it forbade Commonwealth and state laws (of commerce or revenue) which gave preference to a state or a state's *ports* over another state or its *ports*. The change of one word ('what almost looked like a mere change of one letter of the alphabet': La Nauze (1972) p 216) was proposed by Barton at the 1898 Melbourne Convention, merely to clarify the provision. The proposal led to a long and complex debate in which the principal antagonists were New South Wales and Victorian politicians each anxious to prevent adoption of any provision which could advantage the other in the struggle for Riverina railway freight (see generally La Nauze (1972) pp 155–6, 215–17). Eventually, Barton's proposed change was adopted but the clause was further amended to exempt the states from its prohibition, and a new provision was added (now s 102) giving the Commonwealth Parliament power to prohibit preferential (state) railway rates if those rates were condemned by the Interstate Commission. At no stage in the debate was it suggested that s 99's prohibition on preference to named areas or localities (a natural way of expressing its original intended operation) required anything other than uniformity in the commerce and revenue laws covered by the provision.

[9.3.16] The view put forward by Isaacs and Higgins JJ in *R v Barger* (1908) 6 CLR 41 **[9.2.15C]** and supported by Latham CJ, McTiernan and (probably) Rich JJ in *Elliott v Commonwealth* (1935) 54 CLR 657 **[9.3.13C]** has some attractions. Let us assume that the policy behind ss 51(ii) and 99 (and ss 51(iii), 90 and 92) is the promotion of a national economy by preventing the Commonwealth playing fiscal and commercial favouritism with certain states at the expense of other states and so retarding the development of an integrated national economy. Even on that assumption, fiscal and commercial policies which involve regional differentiation may assist in developing a national economy. For example, tax concessions to individuals or businesses in arid or remote areas of Australia may be quite consistent with the development of a national economy. The Isaacs–Higgins approach would uphold such concessions if the localities to which they extended were identified or defined by reference to their climatic characteristics rather than by reference to the fact that they were states or parts of states.

On the other hand, the approach of Isaacs and Higgins JJ is subject to two criticisms. The approach is inexact and involves some complex and essentially vague judgments. How does a court distinguish between a law discriminating between Australian localities by reason of such characteristics as climate or isolation and a law discriminating between Australian localities by reason of their identity as states or parts of states? Secondly, does not the Isaacs–Higgins approach permit the Commonwealth to avoid, through careful drafting of legislation, the impact of ss 51(ii) and 99?

Further, the approach adopted by Dixon J does not preclude differentiation designed to promote a national economy. What it precludes is differentiation which uses locality as its criterion. If, for example, a Commonwealth law allowed taxpayers an income tax rebate for their expenditure on petrol if purchased at an above-average price, the law could not be attacked as contravening s 51(ii) or s 99 simply because the benefit of the rebate went to those people who purchased petrol outside capital cities. The differentiation between localities would flow from the application of a uniform rule to different facts, not from the specification of different rules for different localities: *James v Commonwealth* (1928) 41 CLR 442 at 462 **[9.3.7]**.

[9.3.17] In *Commissioner of Taxation v Clyne* (1958) 100 CLR 246, the validity of the Income Tax and Social Services Contribution Assessment Act (1936) (Cth) was challenged by a taxpayer against whom the Commissioner of Taxation was seeking to recover unpaid provisional income tax. The taxpayer argued that s 79A (inserted in the Act in 1945) discriminated between states or parts of states contrary to s 51(ii) and gave preference to a state or part thereof contrary to s 99, and that, as a consequence of the invalidity of s 79A, the whole Act was invalid. The section allowed residents of prescribed areas to deduct from their taxable income certain allowances. A resident of Zone A was allowed a deduction of £30 per year. Zone A covered the northern area of Australia, including parts of Western Australia, the Northern Territory and Queensland; Zone B included parts of all states except Victoria, as well as parts of the Northern Territory. The taxpayer lived in neither of these zones.

Dixon CJ, with whose reasons Williams, Kitto and Taylor JJ agreed, said that *Elliott v Commonwealth* **[9.3.13C]** had been the decision 'most discussed during the argument' and continued at 265–6:

> In that case the majority of the court gave to the words 'one State or any part thereof over another State or any part thereof' a restricted meaning. If legislation is attacked as violating that portion of s 99 it would appear that according to that interpretation the legislation will be good unless in some way the parts of the State are selected in virtue of their character as parts of a State. This view seems to accord with that expressed by Isaacs J in relation to s 51(ii) in *R v Barger*, a view, however, contrary to that taken by the majority of the court in that case. See further *WR Moran Pty Ltd v Deputy Federal Commissioner of Taxation* (NSW) [1940] AC at 849, 854. It is a view that was attacked by Evatt J in his dissenting judgment in *Moran's* case. For myself I have the greatest difficulty in grasping what exactly is the requirement that the selection of an area shall be as part of the State. No doubt it may be expressed in various ways, for example, 'in virtue of its character as part of the State' or 'qua part of the State' or 'because it is part of a State' or 'as such'. However it may be expressed, I find myself unable to appreciate the distinction between the selection by an enactment

of an area in fact forming part of a State for the bestowal of a preference upon the area and the selection of the same area for the same purpose 'as part of the State'.

Dixon CJ then proceeded to avoid the issue raised by the taxpayer's challenge to the zone allowances. The Chief Justice said that, even if s 79A was invalid, this would mean that the 1945 amending Act (which purported to insert s 79A in the principal Act) was invalid and that s 79A had never been inserted in the principal Act. Therefore, the validity of the principal Act would not be affected if s 79A were invalid.

[9.3.18] Some of the barriers presented to the Commonwealth by ss 51(ii) and 99 may be overcome through the use of the grants power contained in s 96. In *W R Moran Pty Ltd v Deputy Federal Commissioner of Taxation* (1940) 63 CLR 338, the Privy Council upheld a decision of the High Court in which challenges to several Commonwealth Acts had been rejected. One of the Acts imposed a tax on flour millers throughout Australia, and another provided for a payment to the Tasmanian Government of a sum equivalent to the money raised from Tasmanian taxpayers. It was understood that the Tasmanian Government would transfer this money to the Tasmanian taxpayers. An argument that, viewed together, the Acts gave preference to Tasmania, or discriminated between states, contrary to ss 51(ii) and 99, was rejected by both the High Court and the Privy Council, on the ground that Commonwealth grants to states under s 96 were not subject to the rule against discrimination or preference: see **[9.6.37]**.

---

4   Excise duties

[9.4.1] Up to this point we have been looking at the scope of the Commonwealth's taxing power. That is, we have been considering the distribution of revenue-raising power in the Commonwealth Constitution from the perspective of the Commonwealth Parliament: What is the nature of its power? What are the constitutional restraints on that power?

The Commonwealth Constitution also has an impact on the revenue-raising power of the states. Generally, the states have broad powers to levy taxation. The Constitution assumes that the states will continue to raise revenue through taxation, for the Commonwealth's power under s 51(ii) is not exclusive, and s 107 declares that state parliaments shall inherit all those powers of the former colonial parliaments which are not exclusively vested in the Commonwealth Parliament. However, the Constitution makes a specific exception to the general taxing power of the states.

[9.4.2E]   **Commonwealth Constitution**

90   On the imposition of uniform duties of customs the power of the Parliament to impose duties of customs and of excise, and to grant bounties on the production or export of goods, shall become exclusive.

On the imposition of uniform duties of customs all laws of the several States imposing duties of customs or of excise, or offering bounties on the production or export of goods, shall cease to have effect, but any grant of or agreement for any such bounty lawfully made by or under the authority of the Government of any State shall be taken to be good if made before the thirtieth day of June, one thousand eight hundred and ninety-eight, and not otherwise.

~~~

Notes

[9.4.3] The enduring difficulty posed by s 90 has been the problem of identifying the types of taxes which the states are excluded from imposing. The background to the framing of the Commonwealth Constitution and the context in which s 90 appears suggest that this was intended to be a relatively narrow group of taxes; that is, the states were not to impose taxes which could undermine the Commonwealth's absolute control over tariff policy. However, the current judicial orthodoxy is to the contrary: *Ha v New South Wales* (1997) 189 CLR 465 **[9.4.60C]** at 491–8 per Brennan CJ, McHugh, Gummow, Kirby JJ (joint judgment).

Those who argue that s 90 was concerned only with tariff policy point to the historical evidence. One of the most substantial political issues throughout the Australian colonies in the years leading up to federation was the free trade/protection debate: see McMinn (1979) pp 98–9, 113; *Cole v Whitfield* (1988) 165 CLR 360 **[10.4.27C]** at 385–92. There was strong support from both capital and labour, particularly in Victoria, for high import or customs duties on goods brought into Australia. These duties raised the prices at which imported goods could be sold in the Australian colonies and so allowed Australian-produced goods (for which production costs were relatively high) to compete with the imported goods. On the other hand, rural interests generally supported the concept of free trade (that is, of low or no import duties), partly because this kept down the prices of agricultural machinery and partly because rural interests were hoping for free access to overseas markets for their products: wheat, wool and other primary produce. The free trade movement was especially strong in New South Wales where it was, paradoxically, associated with urban, radical politics and where rural interests favoured protection: see Sawer (1956) p 14.

At the Constitutional Conventions of the 1890s, the decision was taken that the resolution of the argument over the tariff policy should be left to the new national government and parliament: see McMinn (1979) p 106; La Nauze (1972) pp 39, 41; *Cole v Whitfield* (1988) 165 CLR 360 **[10.4.27C]** at 385–92. Section 88 of the Commonwealth Constitution embodies that decision:

> 88 Uniform duties of customs shall be imposed within two years after the establishment of the Commonwealth.

Indeed, during the first years of the Commonwealth, party politics were conducted as a struggle between free trade supporters and protectionists, with the Australian Labor Party forming the third political force and attempting to hold the balance between the other two: see, for example, Sawer (1956) pp 15–19, 24, 34–7.

[9.4.4] Given this background, the purpose of s 90 seemed clear to some commentators. The Commonwealth was given exclusive power over customs duties to ensure that it, and not the states, should determine the level of protective tariffs which might, from time to time, be imposed on imported goods. The Commonwealth was given exclusive control of excise duties and bounties on the production of goods to ensure that no state should frustrate or undermine the former's tariff policy decisions. For example, a decision by the Commonwealth that the local motor vehicle manufacturing industry should not be protected against imports, and that customs duties on imported vehicles should therefore be reduced, would be frustrated if a state were permitted to pay a bounty on the production of motor vehicles to local manufacturers. Conversely, a decision by the Commonwealth to increase customs duties on imported motor vehicles (to give greater protection to local vehicle manufacturers) would be frustrated if a state were permitted to impose an excise tax on the local manufacture of vehicles.

[9.4.5] The argument that s 90 is concerned to ensure Commonwealth control of tariff policy is reinforced by the context in which it appears; namely, s 88, requiring uniform customs duties; the juxtaposition in s 90 of 'bounties on the production or export of goods' with 'duties of customs and of excise'; and the spelling out in s 93 that 'duties of customs' are paid on goods imported into a state and 'duties of excise' are 'paid on goods produced or manufactured in a State'. It is this context and the background to s 90 which, in combination, make a very strong case for the argument that the taxes forbidden to the states by that section were taxes which, because of their application to imported or locally produced goods, would interfere with the Commonwealth's tariff policies; that is, taxes which in their application discriminated between imported and locally produced goods. This view of the purpose of s 90 is spelt out in: *Parton v Milk Board (Vic)* (1949) 80 CLR 229 **[9.4.10]** at 264–7 per McTiernan J; *Dennis Hotels Pty Ltd v Victoria* (1960) 104 CLR 529 **[9.4.12C]** at 555–6 per Fullagar J; *Hematite Petroleum Pty Ltd v Victoria* (1983) 151 CLR 599 **[9.4.37C]** at 616, 638, 661–2 per Gibbs CJ, Murphy and Deane JJ; *Philip Morris Ltd v Commissioner for Business Franchises* (1989) 167 CLR 399 **[9.4.47]** per Toohey and Gaudron JJ; *Capital Duplicators Pty Ltd v Australian Capital Territory (No 2)* (1993) 178 CLR 561 **[9.4.53C]** per Brennan, Deane and Toohey JJ. This view has led some justices to the logical conclusion that s 90 only strikes down discriminatory state taxes.

[9.4.6] However, the trend of judicial decisions on s 90, including the restatement in *Ha v New South Wales* (1997) 189 CLR 465 **[9.4.60C]**, has been towards a wider definition of 'duties of excise' and seeing that section as serving a wider purpose than guaranteeing the Commonwealth's control of tariff policy. There are, in judgments delivered by the High Court, consistent references to s 90 giving the Commonwealth real control over the taxation of commodities, see, for example: *Parton v Milk Board (Vic)* (1949) 80 CLR 229 **[9.4.10]** at 260 per Dixon J; *Western Australia v Chamberlain Industries Pty Ltd* (1970) 121 CLR 1 **[9.4.25]** at 17 per Barwick CJ; *Hematite Petroleum Pty Ltd v Victoria* (1983) 151 CLR 599 **[9.4.37C]** at 631 per Mason J. As a statement of purpose, this proposition is ambiguous. It might better be described as a statement of a means towards an unstated end: see **[9.4.18]**. However, it seems likely that the purpose these justices saw s 90 as serving was the concentration, in the hands of the Commonwealth, of all power to implement tariff, revenue, social and economic policies through commodity taxes: see the discussion of Mason J's statement in *Hematite Petroleum Pty Ltd v Victoria* (1983) 151 CLR 599 in **[9.4.37C]**. To some commentators, such a broad-ranging objective is implausible, if our concern is the intentions of the politicians who drafted the Commonwealth Constitution. But, if our concern is to construct a rational or efficient distribution of fiscal power for contemporary economic and political needs (rather than those of the 1890s), it may be that this objective, and the consequentially wide definition of excise duties, can be justified. In the most recent statement on s 90, the joint judgment of Brennan CJ, McHugh, Gummow, and Kirby JJ stated that although the 'original purpose' of s 90 was the protection of Commonwealth tariff policy, the 1897 amendments ensured that the section 'conferred on the parliament ... a free-standing power': *Ha v New South Wales* 189 CLR 465 at 496 **[9.4.60C]**.

[9.4.7] The early reading of s 90 confirmed that its intention was to secure the Commonwealth's control of tariff policy and that it only prevented the states from imposing taxes on the importation of goods (customs duties) and taxes on the local production of goods (excise duties) and from subsidising the local production of goods (bounties). That reading of s 90 was spelt out in Quick and Garran (1901) p 837 and in one of the first decisions of the High Court of Australia. In *Peterswald v Bartley* (1904) 1 CLR 497, the court held that a flat-rate licence fee imposed on brewers of beer as the price of state permission to brew beer was not an excise duty. That term, said Griffith CJ, Barton and O'Connor JJ at 509:

> ... is intended to mean a duty analogous to a customs duty imposed upon goods either in relation to quantity or value when produced or manufactured and not in the sense of a direct tax or personal tax.

The court pointed out that the tax (or licence fee) was not calculated by quantity or value of the thing produced (1 CLR at 511) and repeated that excise duties were 'limited to taxes imposed upon goods in process of manufacture': 1 CLR at 512.

This relatively narrow view of s 90 was partly influenced by the early justices' belief that the Constitution should be construed so as to preserve intact the states' capacity to regulate their internal affairs (see 1 CLR at 507), the 'reserved powers' or 'implied prohibition' doctrine: see **[8.2.20]–[8.2.24]**. The narrow view was expressed in several ways: that the excise duty must be a tax upon locally produced goods, that it must be imposed at the point of production and that it must be a tax which is in proportion to quantity or value.

Even though the 'reserved powers' doctrine was unequivocally rejected in the *Engineers'* case (1920) 26 CLR 129 **[8.2.31C]**, the process of expanding the scope of s 90 and discarding the various strands of the *Peterswald v Bartley* reading of excise duty was not completed until 1949 and the decision in *Parton v Milk Board (Vic)* (1949) 80 CLR 229 **[9.4.10]**.

[9.4.8] In *Commonwealth v South Australia* (the *Petrol* case) (1926) 38 CLR 408, the High Court considered the validity of South Australian legislation which taxed the first sale in the state of petrol: Taxation (Motor Spirit Vendors) Act 1925 (SA). The Act was expressed to apply to the first sale of both locally-produced and imported petrol: s 2(1). The majority of the court adhered to the analysis of excise duties given in *Peterswald v Bartley* (1904) 1 CLR 497 **[9.4.7]**. Isaacs J said:

> Licences to sell liquor or other articles may well come within an excise duty law, if they are so connected with the production of the article sold or are otherwise so imposed as in effect to be a method of taxing the production of the article. But if, in fact, unconnected with production and imposed merely with respect to the sale of the goods as existing articles of trade and commerce, independently of the fact of their local production, a licence or tax on the sale appears to me to fall into a classification of governmental power outside the true context of the words 'excise duties' as used in the Constitution (38 CLR at 426).

However, Isaacs J concluded that to tax the first sale of locally-produced petrol was to impose an excise duty, because it was 'essentially a burden and a tax on the production of the goods', and the tax on the first sale of imported petrol was 'substantially a tax on imports — in other words, a customs duty': 38 CLR at 430.

Higgins, Powers and Starke JJ also held that the legislation imposed both an excise duty and a customs duty, while Knox CJ held that, in its application to the first sale of locally produced petrol, the legislation imposed an excise duty: 38 CLR at 419–20.

Rich J adopted a wider view of excise duties at 437:

> In my opinion, the Constitution gives exclusive power to the Commonwealth over all indirect taxation imposed immediately upon or in respect of goods, and does so by compressing every variety thereof under the term 'customs and excise'. If the expression 'duties of excise' be restricted to duties upon or in respect of goods locally produced the fiscal policy of the Commonwealth may be hampered. One authority should exercise the complementary powers of customs, excise and bounties without hindrance, limitation, conflict or danger of overlapping from the exercise of a concurrent power by another authority vested in the States.

[9.4.9] In *Matthews v Chicory Marketing Board* (1938) 60 CLR 263, a majority of the High Court (Rich, Starke and Dixon JJ) held that a Victorian tax upon the producers of chicory of £1 for every half acre planted with chicory was an excise duty, notwithstanding that the tax was unrelated to the quantity or value of chicory produced. Dixon J, after an extensive review of the historical usage of the term 'excise', said that it described 'a tax on or connected with commodities'. To confine it to taxes which had an arithmetical relation to quantity or value (at 304):

> ... would expose the constitutional provision made by s 90 to evasion by easy subterfuge and the adoption of unreal distinctions. To be an excise the tax must be levied 'upon goods', but those apparently simple words permit of much flexibility in application. The tax must bear a close relation to the production or manufacture, the sale or the consumption of goods and must be of such a nature as to affect them as the subjects of manufacture or production or as articles of commerce. But if the substantial effect is to impose a levy in respect of the commodity the fact that the basis of assessment is not strictly that of quantity or value will not prevent the tax falling within the description, duties of excise.

[9.4.10] The erosion of the *Peterswald v Bartley* (1904) 1 CLR 497 **[9.4.7]** conception of 'excise duties' continued (and might be said to have reached its climax) with *Parton v Milk Board (Vic)* (1949) 80 CLR 229. The High Court held that Victorian legislation imposing a tax on dairy distributors of one-eighth of a penny a gallon of milk sold or distributed in Melbourne was an excise duty. The majority, Rich, Dixon and Williams JJ, clearly saw s 90 as preventing the states from taxing any dealing in a commodity (other than consumption of that commodity). They apparently rejected the view that excise duties were confined to taxes on locally-produced goods and unequivocally asserted that a tax on distribution or sale of a commodity would be struck down by the section. Dixon J said at 260:

> In making the power of the Parliament of the Commonwealth to impose duties of customs and of excise exclusive it may be assumed that it was intended to give the Parliament a real control of the taxation of commodities and to ensure that the execution of whatever policy is adopted should not be hampered or defeated by State action. A tax upon a commodity at any point in the course of distribution before it reaches the consumer produces the same effect as a tax upon its manufacture or production. If the exclusive power of the Commonwealth with respect to excise did not go past manufacture and production it would with respect to many commodities have only a formal significance.

Rich and Williams JJ said at 252, that to be an excise duty, a tax:

> ... must be imposed so as to be a method of taxing the production or manufacture of goods, but the production or manufacture of an article will be taxed whenever a tax is

imposed in respect of some dealing with the article by way of sale or distribution at any stage of its existence, provided that it is expected and intended that the taxpayer will not bear the ultimate incidence of the tax himself but will indemnify himself by passing it on to the purchaser or consumer.

(The exclusion, by all three justices, of taxes on consumption was prompted by a Privy Council decision of dubious relevance: *Atlantic Smoke Shops v Conlon* [1943] AC 550: see **[9.4.32]**.)

The extent to which the judgments of the majority in *Parton's* case expanded the concept of 'excise duties' (and, consequently, contracted the taxing power of the states) was thrown into sharp focus by the two dissenting judgments: those of Latham CJ and McTiernan J.

Latham CJ maintained that *Peterswald v Bartley* (1904) 1 CLR 497 **[9.4.7]**, which had limited excise duties to taxes 'upon goods in the process of manufacture' (1 CLR at 512), should be followed. While a tax on the first sale by the manufacturer could be treated as a tax on manufacture or production (as in *Commonwealth v South Australia* (the *Petrol* case) (1926) 38 CLR 408 **[9.4.8]**), a tax upon any later sale or dealing in the commodity was not a tax upon production and, therefore, not an excise duty: 80 CLR at 245–6.

McTiernan J went back to a proposition of Isaacs J in the *Petrol* case, that taxes on the sale of 'goods as existing articles of trade and commerce, independently of the fact of local production' were not excise duties: 38 CLR at 430–1. McTiernan J said that to limit s 90 in this way, so that it only withdrew from the states the power to tax local manufacture or production, would conform to the object of s 90; that being 'a uniform fiscal policy for the Commonwealth'. Further, his Honour made it clear, through an example about customs and excise duties in the United Kingdom, that he meant a uniform *tariff* policy. See 80 CLR at 264–7.

[9.4.11] McTiernan J was in a minority in *Parton v Milk Board (Vic)* (1949) 80 CLR 229 **[9.4.10]** and his view of s 90's purpose was eclipsed by Dixon J's view that the section 'was intended to give the Parliament a real control of the taxation of commodities' (80 CLR at 260); a substantially broader objective. Sharp differences of judicial opinion over the objective of s 90 and over the inroads which the section would make on the states' taxing power were to persist (the most recent examples can be found in the judgment of Gibbs CJ compared to Mason J in *Hematite Petroleum Pty Ltd v Victoria* (1983) 151 CLR 599 **[9.4.37C]** and in the joint majority judgment of Brennan CJ, McHugh, Gummow and Kirby JJ; compared to the dissenting joint opinion of Dawson, Toohey and Gaudron JJ in *Ha v New South Wales* (1997) 189 CLR 465 **[9.4.60C]**); but, from *Parton v Milk Board (Vic)* on, the view argued for by Dixon J was to dominate the court's approach to s 90 issues.

The dominant view, that the purpose of s 90 is to place commodity taxes beyond the reach of the states' legislative power was, for a time, modified in two ways. First, some judges insisted, when deciding whether a state tax is a tax 'upon goods' and therefore an excise duty, that it is the form of the tax rather than its substance which is critical. This legalistic approach played a pivotal part in the majority's decision in *Dennis Hotels Pty Ltd v Victoria* (1960) 104 CLR 529 **[9.4.12C]**, a decision which drove a substantial wedge through any protection, broad or narrow, which s 90 might be thought to offer to the Commonwealth and its fiscal policies. In that case a licence fee was said to be a fee for the privilege of carrying on a business (a business franchise fee) rather than a tax upon goods caught by s 90 because the amount of the fee was calculated upon sales of liquor in a period before the licence period. While the majority of the court has not always taken that legalistic approach (see, for example, *Hematite Petroleum Pty Ltd v Victoria* (1983) 151 CLR 599 **[9.4.37C]**), the decision in *Dennis Hotels Pty Ltd v Victoria* (1960) 104 CLR 529 **[9.4.12C]** has (narrowly) survived and, until *Ha v New South Wales* (1997) 189 CLR 465 **[9.4.60C]**), formed the basis for very substantial state taxes on goods. For example, by following the *Dennis Hotels* formula, the state of New South Wales collected $852 million in 1995–96 from tobacco licence fees alone: see *Ha v New South Wales* (1997) 189 CLR 465 at 502 **[9.4.60C]**.

The second way in which the court modified the impact which its view of s 90 would otherwise have on state taxing powers was by developing the proposition that s 90 does not prevent the states taxing the consumption of goods. This modification has not been exploited by the states to the extent that they have exploited *Dennis Hotels Pty Ltd v Victoria* (1960) 104 CLR 529 **[9.4.12C]**, largely because of the difficulty of devising cost-effective systems for collecting consumption taxes: see *Dickenson's Arcade Pty Ltd v Tasmania* (1974) 130 CLR 177 **[9.4.29C]**.

[9.4.12C]   **Dennis Hotels Pty Ltd v Victoria**

(1960) 104 CLR 529

The Licensing Act 1958 (Vic) prohibited the selling of liquor except by a person licensed under the Act. Vignerons, brewers, spirit merchants, grocers, hotelkeepers and clubs were obliged to hold licences on which they paid annual licence fees. According to s 19(1)(a) of the Act, the fee for a victualler's licence (that is, the licence required for the sale of liquor in an hotel) was 6 per cent of the amount paid or payable for all liquor purchased by the licensee during a 12 month period ending on 1 June preceding the date of the application for the licence. According to s 19(1)(b) of the Act, the fee for a temporary licence was £1 for each day the licence was in force, plus 6 per cent of the amount paid or payable for all liquor purchased by the licensee for sale under the licence. Other provisions of the Act fixed licence fees for vignerons, brewers, spirit merchants, grocers, wine bars and clubs. In every case, except that of vignerons, the fee was equivalent to 6 per cent of turnover during the preceding year.

Dennis Hotels Pty Ltd was the licensee of an hotel in Victoria and had held a number of temporary licences. It began an action in the High Court of Australia against the state of Victoria, seeking to recover (as money had and received) £12,703 paid by the company to Victoria for renewal of its victualler's licence for the period 1 January to 31 December 1958, and £68 paid for temporary licences during the period 21 January to 5 July 1958. The company claimed that this money had been demanded from it under invalid provisions of the Licensing Act and had been paid by the company involuntarily. The state of Victoria demurred to the statement of claim, asserting that the Licensing Act was valid. The demurrer came on for hearing before the Full Court.

Dixon CJ: [539] A careful consideration of the Victorian licensing law, which is now embodied in the Licensing Act 1958 (No 6293), has made it clear to me that a connected series of provisions ensures that, subject to exceptions that are of no importance either because they are theoretical and not real or because they are too trivial to matter, all liquor sold in Victoria must bear a tax of six per cent of its wholesale price or value before it reaches the consumer. ...

It is, I believe, an undeniable proposition that, subject to the unimportant exceptions I have mentioned, because of the provisions of the Licensing Act no liquor can be bought by retail in Victoria unless in respect of it someone has paid, has become liable to pay or will be placed in a situation which will from the necessity of the case involve him in paying to the Victorian Treasury an amount equal to six per cent of the wholesale selling price of the liquor.

That proposition means to me that the provisions impose an excise duty within the meaning of s 90. It is a tax [540] 'upon' the goods. It is the kind of tax which tends to be recovered by the person paying it in the price he charges for the goods which bear the imposition. Only in two respects does the case appear to me to involve any question as to the connotation of the word 'excise' in s 90 — a connotation that has been discussed in past cases very fully in this court. The first of the two matters to which I refer is the fact that the proposition as I have framed it embraces liquors independently of their place of origin. The tax is an inland tax and not an import tax, but as I have described it, it falls without distinction upon liquors whether they originated in Victoria, in Australia but outside Victoria or outside Australia altogether. The tax is undoubtedly an inland tax but it does not distinguish between the goods upon which it falls in respect of their origin: it is indifferent to the possibility of their being domestically produced or imported. Certain licences such as an Australian wine licence and to some extent perhaps a brewer's licence, are restricted to Australian production but we need not enter upon that distinction between licenses; it is a side issue. For so far as I am concerned I think an inland tax upon goods of a class manufactured in Australia and abroad imposed without regard to their place of origin, is an excise. It may be that it is an excise because it includes goods of home manufacture and as to imported goods is not. That seems to be the way it was regarded in *Commonwealth and Commonwealth Oil Refineries v South Australia* (1926) 38 CLR 408. But it would be ridiculous to say that a State inland tax upon goods of a description manufactured here as well as imported here was not met by s 90, excluding as that section does both duties of customs and duties of excise, because the duty was not confined to goods imported and so was not a duty of customs and was not confined to goods manufactured at home and so was not a duty of excise. The brief statement in *Matthews v Chicory Marketing Board (Vic)* (1938) 60 CLR 263 that 'The basal conception of an excise in the primary sense which the framers of the Constitution are regarded as having adopted is a tax directly affecting commodities' (1938) 60 CLR at 303 may need elaborating but it expresses my view of the substance of the provision. The second matter which perhaps arises as to the connotation of 'excise' is closely connected with the first. It is whether the tax in order to be an excise must be imposed on the production of the goods or may be imposed upon the goods in the hands of any of the various persons through whom they pass in the course of distribution. Upon this I have expressed my view in *Matthews'* case (1938) 60 CLR at 291–303 and [541] in *Parton's* case (1949) 80 CLR at 260, 261, where there is a qualification with respect to consumption.

Dixon CJ noted that the Licensing Act imposed the licence fee on the renewal of a licence; that it made no provision for payment of the fee where a licence was not renewed; but that this omission was of no practical significance. His Honour then discussed the detailed provisions of the Licensing Act and the different situations in which licence fees were to be paid by people dealing in alcoholic liquor, and continued:

[547] It will be seen that under the system which operates as a result of the provisions that have been examined the tax of six per cent on wholesale prices covers the whole supply of liquor to the consumers in Victoria. The disappearance of this or that old licence, or the grant of this or that new licence has no effect on the liability to tax of the total amount of liquor obtained by the consumers.

Nothing has been said so far as to the relative proportions of the liquor passing under the system which respectively is imported and is produced in Australia or more particularly in Victoria. But it is common knowledge that the proportion imported is very small and the great proportion, particularly of beer, is produced in Victoria.

The fact that the licensing of a licensed victualler and for that matter the registration of a club forms part of the method of controlling the sale of liquor, the conduct of hotels and so on appears to me quite immaterial, as does the question whether the licence in the hands of the licensee is a valuable privilege for which the payment of the tax may be regarded as part of the consideration. Section 90 is quite unconcerned with the position of the individual. It is concerned wholly with the demarcation of authority between Commonwealth and State to tax commodities. Duties of excise and of customs are denied to the States simply because of their effect on commodities. Whether a tax is a duty of excise must be considered by reference to its relation to the commodity as an article of commerce. The six per cent upon the wholesale selling price of liquor appears to me simply to be a tax upon liquor, a tax imposed on liquor on its way to the consumer by whatever [548] channel it may proceed: it is in other words an addition to the excises the Commonwealth Parliament has chosen to impose on liquor. It is a tax which goes into the licensing fund kept in the Treasury under Pt XV. From that certain annual subventions are payable to municipalities and to the police superannuation fund and the costs are paid for administering the Act: see s 290. But the balance forming the greater bulk of the fund goes to the Consolidated Revenue of Victoria.

The tax is in my opinion an excise on liquor.

Fullagar J: [553] When it has been decided that the particular exaction in question is a tax, the question is then sometimes asked whether it is a 'direct' tax or an 'indirect' tax. As to this, I would say, that with the greatest respect, I think it a pity that this distinction was ever raised or mentioned in relation to s 90. I do not think it is capable of throwing any light on s 90. Attention to it may be thought to have been invited by the concluding words of the 'definition' of Griffith CJ in *Peterswald v Bartley* (1904) 1 CLR at 509. His Honour's words were 'and not in the sense of a direct tax or personal tax'.

Fullagar J noted that the distinction between direct and indirect taxes was no longer favoured by economists, and that, in any event, the distinction referred to in *Peterswald* was based upon the Canadian Supreme Court's reliance upon the writings of John Stuart Mill. His Honour continued:

There can be no such justification for 'the use of Mill's analysis', or for the use of Canadian precedents, when we come to interpret our own s 90, which was adopted in a quite different setting and employs much more specific terminology.

When we have found that an exaction which is in question is a tax, and when we have put aside the Canadian Constitution and the decisions on it as irrelevant, we come to the critical questions. These may be stated as being three in number — (1) Must it be a tax 'upon goods'? — (2) Must it be imposed upon the production or manufacture of goods? — (3) Must it be imposed by reference to quantity or value of the goods? The questions so stated raise for consideration, though not in the same order, the three elements regarded by the court in *Peterswald v Bartley* (1904) CLR 497 as essential.

Probably no one would dissent from the broad proposition that it is an essential element in the character of a duty of excise that it should be a tax 'upon goods'. But the whole weight of that expression is carried by, and ambiguity lurks in, the humble preposition, for which is sometimes substituted a prepositional phrase such as 'in respect of', or 'in relation to'. Taxes may be charged upon property, real or personal, in the sense that there is a direct remedy against the property for recovery of the tax. But nothing of that kind is meant when we speak, in the present universe of discourse, of a tax 'upon goods'. Goods as such cannot pay taxes: there must be a person to pay them. And what is meant by saying that a tax is a tax upon goods is that the person by whom the tax is payable is charged by reason of, and by reference to, some specific relation subsisting between him and particular goods. A tax will be rightly regarded as a tax upon goods if the person upon whom it is imposed is charged by reason of and by reference of the fact that he is the owner, importer, exporter, manufacturer, producer, processor, seller, purchaser, hirer or consumer of particular goods. This list may not be exhaustive.

Duties of customs and duties of excise are particular classes of taxes 'upon goods'. The relation of taxpayer to goods which characterises a duty of customs is found in the importation or exportation of goods. The taxpayer is taxed by reason of, and by reference to, his importation or exportation of goods. The relation is implicit in the terms itself, which has acquired an established meaning, so that difficulty is seldom felt as to whether a particular [555] exaction is or is not a duty of customs. It has often been observed that the meaning of the term 'duty of excise' is not so well established, and the crucial question in the present case, as I see it, is: What is the relation of taxpayer to goods which characterises a 'duty of excise' as that term is used in the Constitution and particularly in s 90?

The answer to this question given by the court in *Peterswald v Bartley* (1904) 1 CLR 497 was that the necessary relation is to be found in the manufacture or production of goods — that what characterises a duty of excise is that the taxpayer is taxed by reason of, and by reference to, his production or manufacture of goods. The relation is treated as implicit in the term itself. As to the scope of the terms 'manufacture' and 'production' see *Parton v Milk Board (Vic)* (1949) 80 CLR 229 per Latham CJ at 245, 246. After full consideration, and necessarily with the greatest respect for the contrary view, I am of opinion that the answer given in *Peterswald v Bartley* at 245, 246 was right and should be applied in the present case.

The reasons which support this conclusion are stated in *Peterswald v Bartley* itself and in later cases. They appear to me to be convincing. I will state them briefly as they appear to me. In the first place, there is the reference in s 93 to 'duties of excise paid on goods produced or manufactured in a State'. The words 'produced or manufactured' seem clearly to refer to the occasion of the imposition of the duty, and to be intended to cover all duties of excise and not merely a particular class of duties of excise. Then there is the repeated collocation in the Constitution of the term 'duties of customs' with the term 'duties of excise'. The collocation occurs in ss 55, 86, 87, 90 and 93. This seems amply to warrant the view of Griffith CJ that the duty intended by the term 'duty of excise' is a duty 'analogous to a custom duty', and this view fits in with what one would suppose to be the policy behind the relevant provisions of the Constitution. I would myself respectfully agree with the observations of McTiernan J in *Parton v Milk Board (Vic)* (1949) 80 CLR 229. His Honour said: 'Duties of customs on imported goods have a relationship to the price paid by the user or consumer of the goods similar to that which duties of excise imposed upon goods produced or manufactured in the country have to the price paid by the user or consumer of those goods. There is an important relationship between duties of customs and duties of excise levied upon production or manufacture ... It may be inferred from the event mentioned in s 90 and the inclusion of [556] customs, excise and bounties in the section that the duties of excise to which it refers have this relationship to duties of customs and that the object of the section is a uniform fiscal policy for the Commonwealth'.

Again, importance attaches, I think, to the nature of the duties of excise in force in most of the States under that name before the enactment of the Constitution Act. That nature is illustrated by the Customs and Excise Act 1890 of the colony of Victoria. The duties of customs and duties of excise contemplated by the Constitution are, I think, alike duties which are imposed as a condition of the entry of particular goods into general circulation in the community — of their introduction into the mass of vendible commodities in a State. When once they have passed into the general mass, they cease, I think, to be proper subject-matter for either duties of customs or duties of excise.

Fullagar J said that he was 'not satisfied that it was an essential element of a duty of excise that it should be measured by quantity or value of goods': 104 CLR at 556. He concluded that the licence fees were not excise duties because they did 'not fall upon any producer or manufacturer'; they did 'not affect production or manufacture'; and the tax was calculated on all purchases of liquor 'whether produced or manufactured in Victoria or imported from abroad or from another State': 104 CLR at 558.

Kitto J: [558] By a line of decisions beginning with *Peterswald v Bartley* (1904) 1 CLR 497, it is established that although in the United Kingdom the word 'excise' has come to be used as a convenient label for a mass of [559] heterogeneous taxes collected by the excise administration, in the Australian Constitution the expression has a more precise meaning. The court had occasion to consider this line of decisions in the recent case of *Browns Transport Pty Ltd v Kropp* (1958) 100 CLR 117, in which, after saying that the essential distinguishing feature of a duty of excise (in the relevant sense) is that it is a tax imposed 'upon', or 'in respect of' or 'in relation to goods', a reference was given to a passage in the judgment of Dixon J (as he then was) in *Matthews v Chicory Marketing Board (Vic)* (1938) 60 CLR 263. His Honour there stated more fully what such expressions as the foregoing attempt to convey. He said that to be an excise, 'The tax must bear a close relation to the production or manufacture, the sale or the consumption of goods and must be of such a nature as to affect them as the subjects of manufacture or production or as articles of commerce' (1938) 60 CLR at 304. The reference to consumption must be considered as omitted now, in view of what His Honour said later in *Parton v Milk Board (Vic)* (1949) 80 CLR at 261; but with that qualification the correctness of the proposition seems to me to be demonstrated by His Honour's examination of the subject ...

The contrast which these citations bring out is simply between a tax which is and a tax which is not imposed by reference to commodities, or even by reference to a specified mass of commodities. What is insisted upon may, I think, be expressed by saying that a tax is not a duty of excise unless the criterion of liability is the taking of a step in a process of bringing goods into existence or to a consumable state, or passing them down the line which reaches from the earliest stage in production to the point of receipt by the consumer. Indeed, the fact which in general justifies the description of an excise duty as an indirect tax, in the sense of John Stuart Mill's dichotomy, is that when, in the ordinary case, excise duty [560] becomes payable, it amounts to a statutory addition to the cost of a particular act or operation in the process of producing or distributing goods, so that in the costing of the goods in relation to which the act or operation is done, for the purpose of arriving at a selling price to be charged to the next recipient in the chain that leads to the ultimate consumer, the duty paid in respect of those goods may enter — and therefore, according to the natural course of business affairs, will enter — as a charge relating to those goods specifically. This, I apprehend, is what is meant by saying that an indirect tax 'enters at *once*' (the italics are mine) 'into the price of the taxed commodity' (1926) 38 CLR at 435, as the Privy Council said of a customs duty in *Bank of Toronto v Lambe* (1887) 12 App Cas 575 at 583, and by saying that such a tax is 'intended' or 'desired' or 'expected' to be passed on (Mill's own words, adopted by the Privy Council in *Bank of Toronto v Lambe* (1887)12 App Cas at 582), or has 'a general tendency' to be passed on (per Lord Warrington of Clyffe in *R v Caledonian Collieries* [1928] AC at 362) ...

To say so much is to exclude a tax which has no closer connexion with production or distribution than that it is exacted for the privilege of engaging in the process at all. The cases decided in this court have been marked by much diversity of opinion on some points, but I think it may be taken as settled that a tax is not a duty of excise unless the criterion of liability is such as I have mentioned.

Kitto J then reviewed the provisions of the Licensing Act and the various licence fees imposed by s 19, examined the factors by which the victualler's licence fee was calculated, and continued:

[564] No part of such a fee becomes payable at the time of a purchase of liquor for the victualler's premises, and no purchase of liquor for the premises necessarily results in any liability under the section on the part of the person making the purchase. If a particular licensed victualler buys liquor for his premises he does not, by doing so, make himself liable to pay one penny to the Crown. If he renews his licence after the ensuing 30 June, his doing so will involve him in a liability under the section, and past purchases, (which in the case supposed happen to have been his purchase) will be taken into account in working out the amount of his liability according to the statutory formula. But if he does not renew it, he will pay nothing under the section in respect of the purchases; and neither will anyone else who does not take a grant or renewal of a licence for the premises. If someone else does renew the licence, or gets a new licence for the premises, that person will pay the fee, and the fact that he had nothing to do with the purchases on which it is based will not matter.

In these circumstances it seems to me very difficult indeed to say that the fee is, in the relevant sense, a tax on each purchase of a quantity of liquor, and therefore a tax on the liquor. Even taking one circumstance alone, the difficulty is, to my mind, insuperable; I mean the circumstance — and under paras (c), (d), (e) and (g) it is [565] the only relevant circumstance — that the person making each individual purchase does not by doing so become liable for the fee or any part of it. ...

[T]he fact that the person who becomes liable to pay the fee may have had nothing to do with the purchases by reference to which it is calculated, does not mean that the fee is concerned with the liquor purchased rather than with the person who has to pay. It means rather that the fee is concerned with the taking out or renewing of the licence, and therefore with the person [566] who takes it out or renews it rather than with the person who made the purchases ... [567] In other words, the fees are taxes imposed not 'in respect of commercial dealings' [1934] AC at 59, but in respect of the acquisition of a right to engage in commercial dealings. They are imposed, not on goods, but on licences. Accordingly I would hold that the victuallers' licence fees are not duties of excise ...

[568] I turn to the temporary victualler's licence fee — or rather, since the fixed fee of (star)1 is obviously not a duty of excise, to the 'further fee' of six per cent on the gross amount of liquor purchased for sale or disposal under the licence. The reasons above given in reference to the victualler's licence fee appear to me to apply in substance here also. Had the purchasing of the liquor been made [569] the criterion of the liability, the right conclusion might no doubt have been that this fee was different in character from each of the others. But para (b) does not tax the purchasing of liquor. It measures the fee by reference to purchases some or all of which may already have been made when the licence is granted. What attracts the liability is the acceptance of the licence. The tax is not on the liquor; it is on the licence — on the obtaining of authority to sell and dispose of liquor generally at the relevant function. In my opinion it is not a duty of excise.

Menzies J: [582] The guidance of the Constitution itself is ... that a duty of customs is a duty charged at the point of importation and a duty of excise is one paid on the production or manufacture of goods, and that a tax upon some dealing with goods which is neither upon importation into Australia nor upon the production or manufacture of goods in Australia, is neither a duty of customs nor a duty of excise. I cannot find in the Constitution any indication that duties of customs and of excise were grouped together as a comprehensive description of any taxation in respect of goods so as to exclude the States altogether from that field. The import, [583] export, and the production of goods seem to me to constitute such a cohesive subject matter that considerations of policy as well as of revenue might well be thought to warrant a grant of exclusive taxing power to the Commonwealth with regard thereto without going further to extend that grant to cover taxation in respect of all dealings in goods ...

There is one other matter to be noticed. I find nothing in the language of the Constitution which would exclude from the categories of duties of customs or duties of excise, duties to be borne as well as paid by the importer or manufacturer. In other words, unless it be by the use of the words 'customs' and 'excise' themselves, the Constitution does not adopt the distinction between direct and indirect taxes so that, unless the usage of the words otherwise requires, an import duty on goods imported for use or consumption by the importer would be a customs duty, and a duty upon the production of goods for the producer's own use or consumption would be an excise duty, and both would be beyond the power of the Parliament of a State.

Menzies J then reviewed the High Court's decisions on s 90 and continued:

[589] This survey of the Australian cases shows that the position has now been reached that although an excise duty is a tax on the [590] production or manufacture of goods, a tax upon the sale or purchase of goods manufactured in Australia at any point before sale for consumption is to be regarded as a tax on production or manufacture; and furthermore, that a tax may be an excise notwithstanding that quantity or value of goods is not the basis of the duty. This position I feel bound to accept notwithstanding the reservations I would otherwise have about the glosses upon the main proposition ...

[591] Coming back now to the victualler's licence fee, I am disposed to regard it as an indirect tax in that not only are consumers likely to pay more for liquor than would be the case if licence fees were not charged, but, further, notwithstanding s 19(3), licensed victuallers probably endeavour to pass on to consumers the full amount of what they pay as licence fees; it is not, however, a sales or a purchase tax because, as I have already stated, a dealing with the goods does not expose the licensed victualler to liability for tax; the tax is upon the person seeking a licence to sell liquor upon particular premises in the future, not upon the liquor already purchased for sale at those premises although it is calculated upon such purchases; it

is a tax upon persons, like that considered in *Browns Transport Pty Ltd v Kropp* (1958) 100 CLR 117, namely, a tax upon a licensed victualler as the price for his franchise to carry on a business, the most important element of which is to sell liquor from the licensed premises independently of whether the liquor is produced in Australia or abroad, or partly in Australia and partly abroad. It is not in truth a tax on the production or manufacture of liquor, and none of the decided cases require that it should be treated as such a tax. For these reasons, I have come to the conclusion that the licensed victualler's fee is not a duty of excise. In reaching this conclusion, I am fortified by the views expressed in *Parton v Milk Board (Vic)* (1949) 80 CLR 229, by Latham CJ (at 248) and Dixon J (at 263). This was also the view of Isaacs J as appears from his statement in *Commonwealth and Commonwealth Oil Refineries Ltd v South Australia* (1926) 38 CLR at 426.

I find greater difficulty about the character of the fee for a temporary licence. It seems to me that once a temporary licence is granted, every purchase of liquor for sale under the licence, whether it be of local or overseas production, does attract tax at the rate of six per cent of the purchase price. In these circumstances I feel constrained by *Parton v Milk Board (Vic)* (1949) 80 CLR 229 to treat such fees to the extent that they are upon purchases of liquor produced in Australia, as duties of excise. As s 19(1)(b) is not susceptible to the application of what is now s 3 of the Acts Interpretation Act 1958 (Vic), I think the provision therein for a percentage fee is wholly invalid.

I would allow the demurrer to so much of the statement of claim as relates to licensed victuallers' fees, and overrule it so far as it relates to temporary licence fees.

~~~

[9.4.13]   McTiernan and Windeyer JJ delivered separate judgments to substantially the same effect as that of Dixon CJ, although McTiernan J found it unnecessary to decide whether a tax on goods imported into Australia could be an excise duty. Taylor J gave judgment for substantially the same reasons as Kitto J. In the result, Victoria's demurrer was allowed in part; that is, the plaintiff's claim that the Licensing Act was invalid was held to show no cause of action except in relation to s 19(1)(b), the temporary licence.

Notes

[9.4.14]   The decision in *Dennis Hotels Pty Ltd v Victoria* (1960) 104 CLR 529 **[9.4.12C]** provides a good illustration of the diffusion of judicial approach to s 90 problems, typical of most High Court decisions on the section; a diffusion which has, to some extent, been resolved by *Ha v New South Wales* (1997) 189 CLR 465 **[9.4.60C]**.

In *Dennis Hotels Pty Ltd v Victoria*, there is, first, a fundamental disagreement over the meaning of 'excise duties'. Dixon CJ, Kitto and Menzies JJ adopted the broad view put forward by Dixon J in *Parton v Milk Board (Vic)* (1949) 80 CLR 229 **[9.4.10]**, while Fullagar J adopted the narrow view endorsed by the court in *Peterswald v Bartley* (1904) 1 CLR 497 **[9.4.7]** and by McTiernan J in *Parton's* case. Even amongst those justices who appeared to agree on a broad definition of excise duties, there were differences of emphasis which could, in some cases, prove significant. Menzies J apparently rejected (through his dismissive reference to Rich J's proposition in *Commonwealth v South Australia* (the *Petrol* case) (1926) 38 CLR 408 **[9.4.8]**: 104 CLR at 590) what Dixon CJ clearly accepted; namely, that 'an inland tax upon goods ... imposed without regard to their place of origin, is an excise duty': 104 CLR at 540.

Second, the members of the court who were in basic agreement over the definition of excise duties adopted radically different approaches in applying that definition to the legislation before the court: contrast Dixon CJ's emphasis on the practical effect of the licence fee system with Kitto and Menzies JJ's concentration on the criterion of liability; namely, the circumstance upon which, according to their analysis of the Victorian legislation, the liability to pay the tax depended.

Third, those members of the court who adopted the same broad definition of 'excise duties' and the same approach to applying that definition differed in their perception of the legislation before the court: contrast Kitto J's assessment of s 19(1)(b) (the temporary licence fee system) with Menzies J's assessment of the same provision. For a discussion of the asymmetry between the categories of definition, purpose and interpretive method in s 90, see Cass (1997) pp 19–30.

[9.4.15] Some of the judgments in *Dennis Hotels Pty Ltd v Victoria* (1960) 104 CLR 529 **[9.4.12C]** also suggest a degree of judicial uncertainty and inconsistency. For example, Menzies J cited a passage from Dixon J's judgment in *Parton v Milk Board (Vic)* (1949) 80 CLR 229 **[9.4.10]** at 263, as supporting his conclusion that the licensed victualler's fee was not an excise duty: 104 CLR at 591. Indeed, Dixon J had unequivocally declared that he would not regard as an excise 'the licence fee of a licensed victualler calculated on the amount expended by him in the previous year in purchasing liquor': 80 CLR at 263. However, in *Dennis Hotels* Dixon CJ said he was now 'convinced … that the illustration [in *Parton v Milk Board (Vic)*] was entirely wrong': 104 CLR at 539.

Again, Fullagar J quoted from the judgment of McTiernan J in *Parton v Milk Board (Vic)* (1949) 80 CLR 229 at 267, to support his narrow view of 'excise duties': 104 CLR at 595–6. However, in *Dennis Hotels*, McTiernan J abandoned that narrow view because it was contrary to the decision of the majority in *Parton's* case: 104 CLR at 549. Further, Windeyer J confessed to having abandoned the narrow view of 'excise duties' after hearing the argument in the case: 104 CLR at 598. Finally, Menzies J felt constrained by the course of High Court decisions to abandon the narrow view of excise duties which, he said, was 'derived from the words of the Constitution itself': 104 CLR at 581.

[9.4.16] For all the diffusion of approach and lack of certainty among the judges in *Dennis Hotels Pty Ltd v Victoria* (1960) 104 CLR 529 **[9.4.12C]**, the decision confirmed the erosion of the conception of excise duties from *Peterswald v Bartley* (1904) 1 CLR 497 **[9.4.7]**. After *Dennis Hotels*, a tax on a commodity would be treated as an excise duty if it was imposed on some dealing in the commodity between production and final sale before consumption. Excise duties were not to be limited to taxes at the point of production nor to taxes imposed on locally produced goods. This broad view formed the foundation for all subsequent judicial discussion of s 90.

The contrary view, that excise duties were taxes that applied only to locally-produced goods, was to be revived by Murphy J (for example, in *Logan Downs Pty Ltd v Queensland* (1977) 137 CLR 59 **[9.4.27]** at 84–5) and followed in: *Philip Morris Ltd v Commissioner of Business Franchises (Vic)* (1989) 167 CLR 399 **[9.4.47]** at 463 per Dawson J; at 479 per Toohey and Gaudron JJ; *Capital Duplicators Pty Ltd v Australian Capital Territory (No 2)* (1993) 178 CLR 561 **[9.4.53C]** at 615 per Dawson J; at 627, 629–31 per Toohey and Gaudron JJ; *Ha v*

New South Wales (1997) 189 CLR 465 **[9.4.60C]** at 513–15 per Dawson, Toohey and Gaudron JJ.

[9.4.17] In *Dennis Hotels Pty Ltd v Victoria* (1960) 104 CLR 529 **[9.4.12C]**, Fullagar J justified his reversion to the narrow definition of excise duties by stressing the historical background to, and purpose, of s 90; namely, 'a uniform fiscal policy for the Commonwealth'. For Fullagar J, an excise duty was a tax on locally-produced goods imposed as a condition of its entry into general circulation in the community; that is, imposed at the point of production or imposed because of that production. A tax which applied generally to locally produced and imported commodities, which did not discriminate according to a commodity's source of origin, would not be an excise duty nor a customs duty.

[9.4.18] The majority in *Dennis Hotels Pty Ltd v Victoria* (1960) 104 CLR 529 **[9.4.12C]** did not share Fullagar J's view of the purpose of s 90. Dixon CJ referred to 'the basal conception of an excise in the primary sense which the framers of the Constitution are regarded as having adopted is a tax directly affecting commodities' (104 CLR at 540), a clear echo of his assertion in *Parton v Milk Board (Vic)* (1949) 80 CLR 229 **[9.4.10]** that s 90 'was intended to give the Parliament a real control of the taxation of commodities': 80 CLR at 260.

However, there are two ways of reading that assertion. One is that Dixon J (as he was in 1949) saw Commonwealth control of commodity taxes as the end or objective towards which s 90 was aimed (because the taxation of commodities is an important tool of economic management, apart altogether from the implementation of tariff policy). The other interpretation of Dixon CJ's assertion is that he saw s 90 as directed towards a narrow objective (the same one which Fullagar J identified) (Commonwealth control of tariff policy) but regarded a Commonwealth monopoly of commodity taxes as the appropriate means of achieving that control.

[9.4.19] The most striking contrast in *Dennis Hotels Pty Ltd v Victoria* (1960) 104 CLR 529 **[9.4.12C]** is between the formal, legalistic approach of Kitto, Taylor and Menzies JJ and the more pragmatic approach of Dixon CJ, McTiernan and Windeyer JJ in the application of the broad definition of 'excise duties' to the legislation under challenge. This tension, between an emphasis on the technical, legal form of legislation and a willingness to look at the legislation's practical effect, was to be a recurring feature of High Court decisions on s 90 for the next 25 years, see, for example: *Western Australia v Hamersley Iron Pty Ltd* (1969) 120 CLR 42 **[9.4.24]**; *Western Australia v Chamberlain Industries Pty Ltd* (1970) 121 CLR 1 **[9.4.25]**; *Logan Downs Pty Ltd v Queensland* (1977) 130 CLR 59 **[9.4.26]**; *Dickenson's Arcade Pty Ltd v Tasmania* (1974) 130 CLR 177 **[9.4.29C]**; *Hematite Petroleum Pty Ltd v Victoria* (1983) 151 CLR 599 **[9.4.37C]**.

[9.4.20] In *Dennis Hotels Pty Ltd v Victoria* (1960) 104 CLR 529 **[9.4.12C]** there was an even division of opinion on the question whether the court should consider the practical effect of the tax (Did it amount, in practice, to a burden on liquor on its way to the consumer?), or should only look at the criterion of liability of the tax: Was the circumstance which created the liability to pay the tax a dealing in the commodity? (Fullagar J found it unnecessary to consider this question.) It is, therefore, difficult to accept that *Dennis Hotels* established *anything* apart from the validity of s 19(1)(a) and the invalidity of s 19(1)(b) of the Licensing Act 1958 (Vic) (if we put on one side the strong support which the case established for a broad definition of 'excise duties'): see *Philip Morris Ltd v Commissioner of Business Franchises* (1989) 167 CLR 399 at 438, 481 **[9.4.47]**.

Yet, in later decisions, some justices of the High Court were to treat *Dennis Hotels* as establishing that a tax, imposed as a licence fee for the privilege of conducting a business and calculated on the basis of goods purchased in an earlier period, could not be an excise duty; see, for example: *Dickenson's Arcade Pty Ltd v Tasmania* (1974) 130 CLR 177 **[9.4.29C]** at 266, 236 per Gibbs and Stephen JJ; and in *MG Kailis (1962) Pty Ltd v Western Australia* (1974) 130 CLR 245 **[9.4.33]** at 259, 263 Gibbs and Stephen JJ; *Gosford Meats Pty Ltd v New South Wales* (1985) 155 CLR 368 **[9.4.45]** at 380, 399, 420 per Gibbs CJ, Wilson and Dawson JJ. In *Ha v New South Wales* (1997) 189 CLR 465 **[9.4.60C]**, the majority (Brennan CJ, McHugh, Gummow and Kirby JJ) said that states which acted upon this theory had clearly 'misunderstood' the *Dennis Hotels* position: 189 CLR at 502.

[9.4.21]   On the other hand, other members of the court have seized upon the division of opinion in *Dennis Hotels Pty Ltd v Victoria* (1960) 104 CLR 529 **[9.4.12C]** as a sufficient reason for restricting its authority: see, for example, Barwick CJ in *Dickenson's Arcade Pty Ltd v Tasmania* (1974) 130 CLR 177 **[9.4.29C]** at 188; *MG Kailis (1962) Pty Ltd v Western Australia* (1974) 130 CLR 245 **[9.4.33]** at 265 per Mason J; *Gosford Meats Pty Ltd v New South Wales* (1985) 155 CLR 368 **[9.4.45]** at 384–5 per Mason and Deane JJ.

Nevertheless, the device used in s 19(1)(a) of the Licensing Act 1928 (Vic) and which, according to three members of the court in *Dennis Hotels*, removed that tax from the category of excise duties has been widely used in the drafting of state taxing laws. Until *Ha v New South Wales* (1997) 189 CLR 465 **[9.4.60C]**, a series of judicial decisions accepted the device as a loophole through which the states could pass their commodity taxes (regardless, it seemed, of any effect which such disguised commodity taxes had in frustrating the purpose of s 90): see *Dickenson's Arcade Pty Ltd v Tasmania* (1974) 130 CLR 177 **[9.4.29C]**; *HC Sleigh Ltd v South Australia* (1977) 130 CLR 475 **[9.4.34]**; but contrast, *MG Kailis (1962) Pty Ltd v Western Australia* (1974) 130 CLR 245 **[9.4.33]** and *Evda Nominees Pty Ltd v Victoria* (1984) 154 CLR 311 **[9.4.44]**.

[9.4.22]   More recently, some members of the High Court have developed limits on *Dennis Hotels Pty Ltd v Victoria* (1960) 104 CLR 529 **[9.4.12C]**. In *Philip Morris Ltd v Commissioner of Business Franchises* (1989) 167 CLR 399 at 438 **[9.4.47]**, whilst upholding the validity of a tobacco licence fee which was modelled upon the *Dennis Hotels* formula, Mason CJ and Deane J limited the authority of *Dennis Hotels* to licensing regimes for the sale of alcohol and tobacco because the nature of these commodities placed them in a 'special category': 167 CLR at 440. In dissent, Brennan and McHugh JJ limited the authority of *Dennis Hotels* to 'legislation operating in indistinguishable terms': 167 CLR at 460. Toohey and Gaudron JJ adopted a reading of *Dennis Hotels* which owed more to the judgment of Fullagar J than to the reasons of the other majority justices: 167 CLR at 486.

In *Capital Duplicators Pty Ltd v Australian Capital Territory (No 2)* (1993) 178 CLR 561 **[9.4.53C]**, Mason CJ, Brennan, Deane and McHugh JJ said that the diversity of opinions in *Dennis Hotels* was 'not an adequate ground for now disregarding the significance of the court's repeated refusal to depart' from the franchise fee cases: 178 CLR at 592.

In *Ha v New South Wales* (1997) 189 CLR 465, a majority of the High Court:

- rejected the special category approach of Mason and Deane JJ in *Philip Morris Ltd v Commissioner of Business Franchises* (1989) 167 CLR 399 **[9.4.47]**;

- said that *Philip Morris* had been wrongly decided (189 CLR at 504); and

- confined *Dennis Hotels* to its facts.

[9.4.23]   Within three years of *Dennis Hotels Pty Ltd v Victoria* (1960) 104 CLR 529 **[9.4.12C]**, the High Court resolved the sharp differences of opinion by endorsing the broad conception of excise duties and (as a counterbalance) applying that conception in a technical fashion. In *Bolton v Madsen* (1963) 110 CLR 264, the court (Dixon CJ, Kitto, Taylor, Menzies, Windeyer and Owen JJ) said, in a unanimous judgment, that 'excise duties' were 'taxes directly related to goods imposed at some step in their production or distribution before they reach the hands of consumers': 110 CLR at 271. However, the justices went on to say that the question whether a tax was related to goods in that way was to be answered by asking whether the criterion of liability of the tax was a step in the production or distribution of the goods. It was not enough that the tax added to the cost of production or distribution: 110 CLR at 271.

[9.4.24]   The unanimity of approach demonstrated in *Bolton v Madsen* (1963) 110 CLR 264 **[9.4.23]** disappeared in *Anderson's Pty Ltd v Victoria* (1964) 111 CLR 353, when the new Chief Justice, Barwick CJ, stressed that the question whether a tax fell upon the step in the production or distribution of goods was a question of substance, not form: 111 CLR at 366. The debate was carried forward in *Western Australia v Hamersley Iron Pty Ltd* (1969) 120 CLR 42, which showed that the 'practical effect' approach, for which Barwick CJ had argued in *Anderson's Pty Ltd v Victoria*, could still attract significant support in the High Court, despite the unanimous proposition in *Bolton v Madsen* (1963) 110 CLR 264 **[9.4.23]**.

In *Western Australia v Hamersley Iron Pty Ltd*, the Stamp Act 1921 (WA) obliged a person who received money outside the state, as payment for goods and services supplied in the state, to issue a written receipt acknowledging the payment: s 101A. The Act then obliged any person who issued a receipt to pay a stamp duty on the receipt, calculated at 0.1 per cent of the amount of money received: s 16. Three members of the court held that the legislation did not impose an excise duty. For example, Kitto J (with whom McTiernan J agreed) said it was essential 'to identify the criterion of liability under s 101A'. This criterion was, he said, not anything to do with goods, the supply of goods or doing anything to goods. The criterion of liability was 'the event of someone's receiving payment for the goods outside the State, and not ... the manufacture or production or distribution of the goods': 120 CLR at 63.

On the other hand, three justices held that the legislation did impose an excise duty and, as they included the Chief Justice, their opinion prevailed: Judiciary Act 1903 (Cth) s 23(2)(b). For example, Barwick CJ emphasised that a person receiving money for goods supplied was obliged to issue a formal receipt, upon which tax was payable. The statute, he said, imposed a tax upon the receiving of money and not upon the issuing of a written receipt. It was a tax 'upon' goods if the money received was a payment for goods sold:

> [T]o say that a tax upon the act by which a purchaser discharges his obligations to a vendor under a contract for the sale of goods is not a tax upon the sale itself is, in my view, to play with words. ...

[A]lthough the duty imposed by the Act in respect of the receipt of money will have a much wider incidence than an excise duty, it is plain enough that it will assume the character of a duty of excise where the tax is payable, in effect, upon the sale price received upon the first sale and any subsequent sales in the course of distribution of goods produced in Western Australia or elsewhere in the Commonwealth (120 CLR at 55–6).

[9.4.25] *Western Australia v Hamersley Iron Pty Ltd* (1969) 120 CLR 42 **[9.4.24]** raised obliquely yet another problem in the application of the agreed definition of 'excise duties': namely, where a tax is levied on a range of transactions, only some of which involve a dealing in goods, is the tax nevertheless a tax upon goods and therefore an excise? This issue was considered in more detail in *Western Australia v Chamberlain Industries Pty Ltd* (1970) 121 CLR 1. The Stamp Act 1921 (WA) required a person who was paid any money to provide a receipt and pay stamp duty on the receipt at the rate of one cent for every $10 received. The question arose as to whether that obligation amounted to the imposition of a tax on goods where the payment of money was part of a transaction involving the distribution of goods.

The majority of the High Court (Barwick CJ, Menzies, Windeyer and Owen JJ) rejected the argument adopted by the minority (McTiernan, Kitto and Walsh JJ), that the tax on receipts of money could not be an excise duty because it fell generally on a wide range of transactions, whether or not those transactions involved goods. Barwick CJ said at 15:

> The plaintiffs, as I follow them, really say that unless a tax by an Act is in all the circumstances to which the Act is intended to apply a duty of excise, it cannot be a duty of excise in any of those circumstances. Quite apart from authority, that proposition, in my opinion, is evidently fallacious.

Barwick CJ identified the purpose s 90 was meant to serve as 'the control of the national economy as a unity which knows no State boundaries, by a legislature [the Commonwealth Parliament] without direct legislative power over that economy as such': 121 CLR at 17. His Honour said that this was what Dixon J had in mind when, in *Parton v Milk Board (Vic)* (1949) 80 CLR 229 **[9.4.10]**, he described s 90 as intended to give the Commonwealth 'a real control of the taxation of commodities': 80 CLR at 260. However, is it clear that Dixon J had in mind such a wider ranging purpose for s 90? See the alternative interpretations offered in **[9.4.18]** and the more developed, and competing arguments on the purposes of s 90 offered by Gibbs CJ and Mason J in *Hematite Petroleum Pty Ltd v Victoria* (1983) 151 CLR 599 at 617, 631–2 **[9.4.37C]**.

Controversy continues to the present day over the two opposing interpretations of the purpose of s 90, each of which is supported by appeals to history, context, constitutional intention, practice and precedent: compare Brennan CJ, McHugh, Gummow and Kirby JJ in *Ha v New South Wales* (1997) 189 CLR 465 **[9.4.60C]** at 491–498; with Dawson, Toohey and Gaudron JJ in the same case at 506–12 and 514. What does this uncertainty indicate about the process of constitutional interpretation? See Chapter 1 at **[1.2.11]**, **[1.2.14]–[1.2.18]**, **[1.3.4]–[1.3.16]**.

[9.4.26] The question whether a general state tax on a wide range of transactions fell within s 90 if the tax applied to a transaction in goods was raised again in *Logan Downs Pty Ltd v Queensland* (1977) 137 CLR 59 and, as in *Western Australia v Chamberlain Industries Pty Ltd* (1970) 121 CLR 1 **[9.4.25]**, it sharply divided the High Court. The court was asked to declare invalid s 7 of the Stock Act 1915 (Qld). The section authorised 'the Minister' to levy an annual tax, 'at rates to be fixed by

him', on each head of stock (horses, cattle, sheep and swine) owned by a person who
had at least eleven head of stock. Taxes totalling $4315 had been imposed on the
plaintiff for the three years 1972–74. The plaintiff owned sheep, kept for their wool
and sale for meat, cattle for breeding and sale for meat, pigs for breeding and sale for
meat, and horses for working the plaintiff's properties.

The court held, by a statutory majority under s 23(2)(b) of the Judiciary Act 1903
(Cth), that the section invalidly imposed an excise duty to the extent that it imposed
a tax on stock kept for production. Mason J said that to tax livestock used for their
product was 'a tax on production and it has a natural, though not a necessary,
relation to the quantity or value of what is produced'. He dismissed the objection
that the tax could not be an excise duty because it fell on the owners of all livestock
regardless of the purpose for which the stock was kept:

> The fact that the statutory definition of 'stock' in s 5A includes some animals, for
> example horses and foals, which are not usually used or kept for production, is of no
> relevance. If the tax otherwise has the character of an excise in its application to stock
> used for production, it does not lose this character merely because in its application to
> other animals it may not constitute an excise (137 CLR at 78).

Stephen J, with whom Barwick CJ agreed, pointed out what was implicit in all the
judgments in this case; that the tax on the horses could not be an excise duty because
they were not kept or used for their produce. To tax them was to tax, not the
production of a commodity, but its consumption. A tax on consumption or
ownership of goods after their production and distribution was not an excise duty:
137 CLR at 69–70. However, the fact that the tax was not in every instance a duty
of excise did not lead to the conclusion that it was not in any instance a duty of
excise: 137 CLR at 71.

Gibbs J dissented, maintaining that a tax on the ownership of stock, irrespective
of the purpose for which it was owned, was not an excise. The criterion of liability
under the Act was not any step in the production or distribution of a commodity, nor
was its practical effect to impose a tax at some point in its production or distribution:
137 CLR at 67.

Jacobs J said that it was necessary to look at the Act's criterion of liability. A tax
imposed on the owner of goods, not because of the 'course of the goods between
their production or manufacture and their ultimate consumption', would not be an
excise duty merely because the owner's 'goods may be on that course': particularly
is this so when the tax is imposed indifferently upon goods which are and goods
which are not, or are not in the course of becoming, commodities: 137 CLR at 83.

[9.4.27]   Murphy J also dissented in *Logan Downs Pty Ltd v Queensland* (1977)
137 CLR 59 **[9.4.26]**, but for radically different reasons. His Honour argued that the
definition of excise duties should be returned to that of a tax on local manufacture
or production, and referred to the judgments of McTiernan J in *Parton v Milk Board
(Vic)* (1949) 80 CLR 229 **[9.4.10]** at 263 and Fullagar J in *Dennis Hotels Pty Ltd v
Victoria* (1960) 104 CLR 529 **[9.4.12C]** at 552. Murphy J said:

> In general, taxes imposed without regard to the place of production or manufacture
> are neither duties of customs nor duties of excise. The essence of each duty is the
> tendency to discriminate between goods locally produced and other goods ... The
> extension of the constitutional concept in cases such as *Dennis Hotels* seems to me to
> be unjustified by the constitutional context or the assumed purpose of s 90. The
> meaning of excise may be elastic but it has stretched too far (137 CLR at 84–5).

Earlier he had described s 90 and associated provisions, such as ss 51(i), 92 and 99, as 'directed towards a national economy in the production and manufacture of goods': 137 CLR at 84.

[9.4.28] It was implicit in the judgments in *Logan Downs Pty Ltd v Queensland* (1977) 137 CLR 59 **[9.4.26]** (as Stephen J pointed out: 137 CLR at 69–70) that the tax, as it fell on the plaintiff's horses, could not be an excise duty because those animals, unlike the cattle, sheep and pigs were not being used as units of production. The taxpayer's relationship to the horses was that of consumer rather than producer. The assumption was that a tax on the consumption of a commodity lay outside the definition of an 'excise duty'. That assumption had been tested directly only once: in 1974, in *Dickenson's Arcade Pty Ltd v Tasmania* (1974) 130 CLR 177 **[9.4.29C]**.

[9.4.29C]   **Dickenson's Arcade Pty Ltd v Tasmania**
(1974) 130 CLR 177

Part II of the Tobacco Act 1972 (Tas) was headed 'Tax on the consumption of tobacco'. Section 3 imposed a tax on the consumption of tobacco, calculated at 7.5 per cent of the retail value of the tobacco. 'Consumption' was defined by s 2(2) as 'the smoking or chewing of tobacco by any person'. Section 6(1) authorised the Governor to make regulations providing for any convenient method for the collection of the tax. The Governor made the Tobacco Regulations 1972. These regulations required every person who sold tobacco by retail to arrange with the Commissioner of Taxes for the retailer to collect the consumption tax: reg 4. Payment of the tax was to be made to the retailer at the time of purchase (reg 2(1)) or to the Commissioner after consumption: reg 2(2).

Part III of the Tobacco Act 1972 (Tas) was headed 'Licensing of retailers of tobacco'. Section 9 prohibited any person from carrying on a retail tobacco business without a licence. According to s 11, the licence fee was a varying percentage (around 2.5 per cent) of the value of the tobacco handled by a retailer during 'the relevant assessment period'. That period was 'the period of twelve months ending six months before the commencement of the annual period in respect of which the licence is granted': s 11(3)(b).

Dickenson's Arcade Pty Ltd carried on the business of a tobacco retailer in Tasmania. The company brought an action against Tasmania in the High Court, claiming a declaration that the Act and regulations were invalid. The defendant demurred to the statement of claim and the demurrer was heard by the Full Court of the High Court.

Barwick CJ: [185] A duty of excise for the purposes of the Australian Constitution, to use the formulation substantially as approved in *Bolton v Madsen* (1963) 110 CLR 264 at 273, in its essence, is a tax upon 'the taking of a step in a process of bringing goods into existence or to a consumable state or of passing them down the line which reaches from the earliest stage in production to the point of receipt by the consumer', including the step which puts the goods into consumption. There was no logical reason, in my opinion, for ending at the point of entry into consumption the area which might yield a duty of excise. But seemingly under what was considered to be the constraint of the opinion of the Privy Council in *Atlantic Smoke Shops Ltd v Conlon* [1943] AC 550, the area has been so limited ... [A] tax upon the act of consuming goods, completely divorced from the manner or time of their acquisition by purchase, must now be regarded as outside the scope of s 90 and within the competence of a State legislature.

Barwick CJ said that the question whether a statute imposed a duty of excise was 'a matter of substance in which its intended operation as well as its form is of importance'. He referred, as he had in *Western Australia v Chamberlain Industries* (1970) 121 CLR 1 at 14 **[9.4.25]**, to a statement of Isaacs J in *Commonwealth v South Australia* (the *Petrol case*) (1926) 38 CLR 408 **[9.4.8]**, and continued:

Unless those views are applied, and the substance of the operation of the statute, rather than merely its form, is treated as definitive of the relevant nature of the tax it imposes or exacts, a premium will be placed on verbal sleight of hand and, in the end, the Constitution mocked.

The question in this case, in my opinion, is whether the intended operation of the Act is confined to the imposition of a tax on consumption of tobacco or whether that operation extends to impose a tax on its entry into consumption.

[187] Before going further in the matter, it is necessary, in my opinion, to clarify the concept of a tax on consumption, as consumption is made a point of reference in defining the area within which a duty of excise may be found to be operating. In relation to foodstuffs and the like, consumption implies their destruction by use. Though an appropriation of goods for use may be regarded by the economist as an act of consumption, I do not regard it as such in relation to the description of a duty of excise. I intended to indicate so much when I emphasised in my reasons for judgment in *Anderson's Pty Ltd v Victoria* (1964) 111 CLR 353 that the act of placing the goods in the possession of the purchaser was within the area in which a duty of excise could be found to exist. Thus the act of a vendor in making delivery of goods sold or of the purchaser in receiving the goods and reducing them into his possession are not in my opinion acts of consumption in the relevant sense. In relation to goods generally, consumption for present purposes involves, in my opinion, the act of the person in possession of the goods in using them or in destroying them by use, irrespective of the manner or means by which that possession was obtained ...

Barwick CJ said that, on the authority of *Dennis Hotels Pty Ltd v Victoria* (1960) 104 CLR 529 **[9.4.12C]**, the licensing provisions in Pt II of the Act were valid, although he said: 'I cannot confess to any great satisfaction in taking that course': 130 CLR at 189. His Honour then turned to the tax imposed by s 3, the consumption tax:

[191] Each act of smoking is said to attract an amount of tax equal to seven and one half per cent of the value of the amount of tobacco smoked at that time less, of course, the value of any 'dregs', ie unsmoked residues or butts, if the smoker within due time makes an appropriate application for a refund, see s 3(5). Nothing is said expressly in the Act about the consumption of tobacco given to the smoker though s 4(1) exempts from tax tobacco brought into the State by a traveller for disposal by gift provided it is consumed within 28 days of its being brought into the State.

The donee of tobacco, for example, a cigarette, may but does not necessarily identify its brand and, perhaps, in many situations, does not care. Whether or not the donor, or for that matter his donor, has paid an appropriate amount of tax in respect of the cigarette can scarcely be known. All this may equally be true of the friend or acquaintance who is given a 'fill' of his pipe. Thus, a person who has been given tobacco may not have the means of knowing the value for the purpose of the Act of what he smokes. Bearing in mind the habits of mankind in offering cigarettes and tobacco not merely to friends but to the merest acquaintance on social occasions, the idea that the agreeable recipient of the convivial cigarette or pipe fill should come under an obligation to make a return or give a notification of having smoked the gift and within seven days of that event — no doubt rarely remembered at the end of an evening of stimulating social intercourse — to pay a tax of seven and a half per cent of the value of that cigarette or pipe fill upon pain of a criminal prosecution, is so ludicrous that it is to my mind inconceivable that the legislature should so intend ... I cannot believe, however, that any such operation of the Act is intended. My incredulity of such a fanciful operation being intended by a legislature leads me to conclude in the absence of clear and unambiguous words that it was not intended to tax the consumption of tobacco in all circumstances, including the case of tobacco given to the smoker or chewer. That means, in my opinion, that it was intended only to tax the consumption of tobacco by or at the instance of a purchaser of tobacco purchased by or for him ...

Regulations, [193] Statutory Rules No 286 of 1972, made a week after the assent to the Bill and operative with the commencement of the Act, provide that tax be paid to a collector or authorised person where it is paid at the time of purchase: otherwise to the Commissioner (reg 2). Applicants for a retail tobacco licence must make an arrangement with the Commissioner for the appointment of a collector to receive on the premises to which the licence relates the 'tax payable in respect of the consumption of tobacco that is sold on those premises' (reg 4). The licensee may be the collector. Thus, the licensee is required either to be or to have on the premises an appointed collector authorised to collect the tax …

Thus, it is to my mind clear to demonstration that the intention of the Act is that what amounts of tax will be collected under the Act will be obtained by the addition by the retailer of tobacco to the purchase price of the tobacco sold of an amount which will be at least the amount of tax payable on consumption of the whole amount of tobacco purchased. In the unlikely event that the purchaser of the tobacco desires and chooses to pay later, the chances of recovery of the tax would appear to be nil …

[194] The intended operation of the Act is that the tax is payable only by the purchaser of the tobacco and it is intended to be collected at the point of purchase. Such a tax is not, in my opinion, a tax upon consumption in the sense of the decisions of this court. It is not a tax, as I construe the Act, unconnected with the purchase of tobacco; indeed, it is essentially connected with such purchase. In my opinion, it constitutes a tax upon a step in the movement of the tobacco into consumption. In the relevant sense it is a tax upon the tobacco. It is a duty of excise.

Gibbs J: [221] Since *Parton v Milk Board (Vic)* (1949) 80 CLR 229 no member of the court has dissented from, and almost every member who has had occasion to discuss the matter has expressly affirmed, the proposition that a tax imposed on consumption is not a duty of excise. …

[222] To say that the control by the Commonwealth Parliament of the taxation of goods will not be complete, or that its fiscal policy may be hampered, if the States can impose a tax at the point of consumption, is in my opinion not decisive against this view. The question cannot be answered by having regard to the position of the Commonwealth alone. The Constitution is a federal constitution, and s 90 is intended to effect a distribution of the power to impose taxation between the Commonwealth and the States. Of course, the section confers no power on the Commonwealth, which derives its power to impose taxation from s 51(ii), but it denies power to the States. The extent of the denial must be found in the words of the section themselves rather in economic, social or political theory. Section 90 does not refer to taxes on goods but to duties of customs and excise. Upon its proper construction s 90 stops short of denying power to the States to impose taxes on consumption.

Gibbs J said that, in order to decide 'whether a tax was a duty of excise the Court must identify the criterion of liability under the statute which imposes the tax.' He then examined the tax imposed by Pt II of the Act:

[224] The label given to it — 'Tax on the consumption of tobacco' — is not of importance. However, in my opinion Pt II on its proper construction does impose a tax which is correctly described by that label, that is, a tax on consumption It is true that the retailer can only lawfully carry on business if he makes arrangements to collect the tax and that for practical reasons a purchaser is likely to pay the tax to the retailer or his agent at the time when he buys his tobacco. However, the purchaser is not bound to make payment until he has in fact consumed the tobacco and the retailer is not liable for any tax which he does not collect. It is, in my opinion, impossible to say that Pt II, when properly construed, imposes a tax on the last retail sale of tobacco. It is immaterial, if in fact it is true, that the tax has substantially the same practical effect as a tax imposed on the last retail sale. The criterion of liability is consumption. The tax is not an excise.

~~~

[9.4.30]   Gibbs J then considered the licence fee imposed by Pt III of the Act and held that, on the authority of *Dennis Hotels Pty Ltd v Victoria* (1960) 104 CLR 529 [9.4.12C], it was not an excise duty. He said that *Dennis Hotels* was 'authority for what was decided, namely, that a licence fee quantified by reference to the amount paid or payable for goods purchased during a period preceding that in respect of which the licence was granted was not a duty of excise': 130 CLR at 226. McTiernan J held that the consumption tax was an excise duty because 's 90 does extend to a tax on the consumption of goods'. His Honour also held the licence fee to be an excise duty, as *Dennis Hotels* was not 'a precedent governing the present case': 130 CLR at 206. Menzies and Stephen JJ delivered separate judgments to the same effect as Gibbs J.

Mason J held that the regulations, providing for the collection of the consumption tax at the point of retail sale, levied the tax imposed by the Act before the tobacco passed into the hands of the consumer. Although the Act, viewed alone, imposed a tax on the consumption of goods which was not an excise, once the provisions of the regulations were taken into account, the effect of the tax was that of a sales tax paid by the purchaser (who was not necessarily the consumer) and it was therefore an excise. Accordingly, the regulations were invalid. Mason J held that the validity of the licence fee was determined by *Dennis Hotels*, but that case was not authority for any broad proposition. Accordingly the court held, by a statutory majority, under s 23(2)(b) of the Judiciary Act 1903 (Cth), that the consumption tax amounted to an excise duty and, by a majority of five justices to one, that the licence fee was not an excise duty.

Notes

[9.4.31]   The court's decision on the consumption tax in *Dickenson's Arcade Pty Ltd v Tasmania* (1974) 130 CLR 177 **[9.4.29C]** demonstrates the confusion so often generated in this area of constitutional law. Two justices (Barwick CJ and McTiernan J) held Pt II of the Act and the regulations invalid, but for different reasons. One judge (Mason J) held Pt II of the Act valid but the regulations invalid for reasons similar to those adopted by Barwick CJ, and three judges (Menzies, Gibbs and Stephen JJ) concluded that the Act and regulations were valid. The result, because of the Chief Justice's 'casting vote' under s 23(2)(b) of the Judiciary Act 1903, was that only the regulations, providing for a method of collecting the consumption tax, were held to be invalid. Yet the reasoning of one member of the majority, McTiernan J, was consistent with only one result, that the Act was invalid, and his finding that the regulations were also invalid was simply consequential on the invalidity of the Act.

[9.4.32]   Is there any sound reason why a tax upon the consumption of goods should be excluded from the definition of excise duties? There can be no doubt that the accepted wisdom on s 90 does exclude consumption taxes, or has done so since *Parton v Milk Board (Vic)* (1949) 80 CLR 229 **[9.4.10]**. Nor can there be any doubt that this exclusion was originally adopted by the Australian justices because of some remarks made by the Privy Council on an appeal from the Canadian Supreme Court, where the issue was the distinction between direct and indirect taxes drawn in the British North America Act: *Atlantic Smoke Shops v Conlon* [1943] AC 550 at 564–5.

If the purpose of s 90 is to preserve to the Commonwealth, unimpeded by state interference, control over tariff policy, why should a state be prevented from taxing the retail sale of a commodity but allowed to tax its consumption? Consider this example:

The Commonwealth decides to increase the level of protection offered to Australian motor vehicle manufacturers by raising import duties on foreign produced vehicles.

Overseas manufacturers lobby the Victorian Government, seeking some countervailing assistance. That government's advisers devise two schemes for protecting the local industry:

(a) By imposing a sales tax on locally manufactured motor vehicles sold in Victoria;

(b) By imposing differential registration fees on motor vehicles owned in Victoria. The fees, payable annually, would be higher for locally manufactured motor vehicles.

Clearly, the sales tax would be invalid as an excise duty; but the differential registration fees would be a tax upon consumption and, despite their potential for frustrating the Commonwealth's tariff policy, would be held by the High Court to be valid.

In *Dickenson's Arcade Pty Ltd v Tasmania* (1974) 130 CLR 177 **[9.4.29C]**, Gibbs J acknowledged this weakness in the exclusion of consumption taxes from excise duties when he said: '[I]f it is permissible to consider the economic effect of the tax, it is impossible, in my opinion, to draw a line between the last retail sale and the act of consumption': 130 CLR at 219. However, Gibbs J went on to adhere to the distinction between a sales tax and a consumption tax. Mason J also recognised the weakening effect which the exclusion of consumption taxes had on s 90. The purpose of that section was to give the Commonwealth 'a real power to control the taxation of commodities'; to exempt consumption taxes might be seen as an 'unacceptable limitation' on the Commonwealth's power. However, his Honour suggested that this was not a substantial limitation because 'a tax on consumption which is not also a tax on sale of goods is a phenomenon infrequently encountered': 130 CLR at 239.

How, apart from the accidents of legal reasoning, can this distinction be justified? Perhaps, one could find a pragmatic justification in that it compensates the states for the threat to their revenues posed by the expansion of the definition of excise duties since *Commonwealth v South Australia* (the *Petrol* case) (1926) 38 CLR 408 **[9.4.8]**. That is, having eroded the states' capacity to impose commodity taxes by establishing a broad definition of excise duties (a tax levied upon goods), the court offered, and has persisted in offering, a consolation to the states (a tax levied upon goods in the hands of the consumer). Whatever the justification for the exclusion of consumption taxes from the definition of excise, the distinction remains: *Ha v New South Wales* (1997) 189 CLR 465 at 499 **[9.4.60C]**.

[9.4.33] In *M G Kailis (1962) Pty Ltd v Western Australia* (1974) 130 CLR 245, the plaintiff sought a declaration that s 35G of the Fisheries Act 1905 (WA) was invalid. The section imposed a licence fee on fish processors in Western Australia. Although the Act was drafted in a confusing manner, four of the five justices in the case treated s 35G(2) as requiring a processor to pay an annual licence fee which was calculated as a percentage of the value of the fish acquired for processing during a 12-month period which ended six months before the commencement of the licence: an obvious attempt to copy s 19(1)(a) of the Licensing Act 1958 (Vic), which the High Court had upheld in *Dennis Hotels Pty Ltd v Victoria* (1960) 104 CLR 529 **[9.4.12C]**. However, the court held, by a majority of three justices to two, that s 35G imposed an excise duty. McTiernan J referred to a series of judicial statements to the effect that the substantial effect of state taxing laws should be considered in order to ensure that s 90 was not flouted. He described the licence fee as an excise duty but did not mention *Dennis Hotels*.

Mason J repeated what he had said in *Dickenson's Arcade Pty Ltd v Tasmania* (1974) 130 CLR 177 **[9.4.29C]** at 240, that *Dennis Hotels* 'should not be treated as authoritative in relation to the prescription of fees for licences to manufacture or produce goods'. To do that 'would ... give the constitutional prohibition contained in s 90 a formal operation, having little substantial importance' and would frustrate the purpose of s 90 (to give the Commonwealth a real control of the taxation of commodities): 130 CLR at 265. Here the licence fee was a tax which directly affected the price of fish processed in the state and had an impact on the goods' consumption and the consequent demand for production of those goods. It was, therefore, an excise duty.

The third member of the majority, Menzies J, read the Fisheries Act as demanding that the licence fee be paid on the basis of the current year's processing activities (rather than the activities of a preceding period). He said that, therefore, the Act did not fall within the authority of *Dennis Hotels*. (Although he could have said that it was covered by the decision in that case that the temporary licence fee, imposed by s 19(1)(b), was an excise duty.) He described the licence fee as a tax on the processing of fish, not merely the price of a licence to carry on business, and therefore an excise duty.

The two dissenting justices, Gibbs and Stephen JJ, regarded *Dennis Hotels* as relevant and authoritative.

[9.4.34] However, the court declined, when next presented with the opportunity, to overrule *Dennis Hotels Pty Ltd v Victoria* (1960) 104 CLR 529 **[9.4.12C]**. In *H C Sleigh Ltd v South Australia* (1977) 136 CLR 475, the plaintiff sought a declaration that the Business Franchise (Petroleum) Act 1974 (SA) imposed an invalid excise duty. The Act provided that no person should sell petroleum products without a licence. The licence fee, payable annually, was calculated on the basis of the licensee's turnover of petroleum products during a period of 12 months preceding the commencement of the licence. The court held, by a majority of five to one, that the licence fee was not an excise duty.

Mason J, with whose reasons Barwick CJ agreed, said that *Dennis Hotels* was decisive of the issues before the court. The submission that *MG Kailis (1962) Pty Ltd v Western Australia* (1974) 130 CLR 245 **[9.4.33]** had overruled *Dennis Hotels* was 'plainly misconceived ... The fact is that the three members of the majority in *Kailis'* case each had different reasons for subscribing to the conclusion that the licence fee was an excise': 136 CLR at 400. Mason J said that the court's decision in *Dickenson's Arcade Pty Ltd v Tasmania* (1974) 130 CLR 177 **[9.4.29C]** made it impossible to overrule *Dennis Hotels* and continued:

> Since *Dennis Hotels* it has been accepted that liquor licensing fees calculated by reference to past sales are not an excise and the States have continued to rely on liquor licensing fees as an important source of revenue. Likewise, since *Dickenson's Arcade* States have relied on tobacco licensing fees, similarly calculated, as an additional source of government revenue. It would, I think, lead to great uncertainty in government and commerce if the court were now to hold that *Dennis Hotels* or *Dickenson's Arcade* was wrongly decided. Such a course would disturb legislative and financial arrangements made on the faith of the existing decisions of this court.
>
> A departure from these decisions can be justified only in the event that the court is convinced that they are wrong. Yet the inherent difficulty of determining what is an excise in the constitutional sense, a difficulty reflected in the shifts of opinion that have taken place in the judicial exposition of s 90, makes it extremely hard to say that a particular decision IS wrong, notwithstanding that the reasoning on which it is based may not appear to be persuasive. So far as the present problem is concerned, nothing has occurred since *Dickenson's Arcade*, which was decided only two years ago, to suggest that it was wrongly decided. Nor, indeed, did the plaintiff's counsel so suggest, apart

from submitting that it had been overruled by *Kailis'* case, a submission which, as I have said, was misconceived. There is therefore, no basis for our refusing to follow *Dickenson's Arcade* if it transpires that the present case cannot be distinguished (136 CLR at 501–2).

Gibbs and Stephen JJ said that the validity of the Business Franchises (Petroleum) Act was established by *Dennis Hotels Pty Ltd v Victoria* and *Dickenson's Arcade*. In the words of Gibbs J:

> The Act in the present case does not impose a tax on goods, because the fee for a licence to carry on the business of selling petroleum products is quantified by reference to the value of the quantity of petroleum products sold during a period preceding that in respect of which the licence is granted. The decisions in *Dennis Hotels Pty Ltd v Victoria* and *Dickenson's Arcade Pty Ltd v Tasmania* established that such a fee is not a tax on goods and is therefore not a duty of excise (136 CLR at 491–2).

Murphy J, consistently with his judgment in *Logan Downs Pty Ltd v Queensland* (1977) 137 CLR 59 **[9.4.27]**, said that 'a non-discriminatory tax on sales or distribution or consumption is neither a duty of customs nor of excise'. He did 'not regard the test in *Dennis Hotels* ... and *Dickenson's Arcade* ... as satisfactory for determining whether s 90 of the Constitution applies': 136 CLR at 527.

Jacobs J dissented, observing that the licensing system, sanctioned by *Dennis Hotels*, could be exploited to allow the states to overcome s 90. That exploitation 'must be curbed now before the court is faced either with the virtual supersession of s 90 or a need at some later time to cry halt': 136 CLR at 526. He described *Dennis Hotels* as authority for the proposition that a licence fee for the sale of alcohol was not an excise duty where the fee was calculated as a percentage of purchases over a preceding period: 136 CLR at 518. He described *Dickenson's Arcade Pty Ltd v Tasmania* (1974) 130 CLR 177 **[9.4.29C]** as holding that a fee for a licence to sell tobacco (or 'a product containing a drug') was not an excise duty where the fee was calculated as a percentage of tobacco (or 'product') sold over a preceding period: 136 CLR at 520, 522. Those decisions should be confined to their specific facts.

[9.4.35]   The problem of reconciling the decision in *Dennis Hotels Pty Ltd v Victoria* (1960) 104 CLR 529 **[9.4.12C]** with the emerging revisionist view of s 90 caused even more acute confusion in *Philip Morris Ltd v Commissioner of Business Franchises* (1989) 167 CLR 399 **[9.4.47]**. The petrol franchise fee was particularly vulnerable to this uncertainty. In *Capital Duplicators Pty Ltd v Australian Capital Territory (No 2)* (1993) 178 CLR 561 **[9.4.53C]**, a majority (Mason CJ, Brennan, Deane and McHugh JJ) acknowledged that the reasons given in *Philip Morris* for not disturbing the earlier decisions did not support *H C Sleigh* 'with the same cogency' that they supported *Dennis Hotels* and *Dickenson's Arcade Pty Ltd v Tasmania* (1974) 130 CLR 177 **[9.4.29C]**: 178 CLR at 592. However, continued the majority, this only meant that where a licence fee were of 'sufficient magnitude', it might lack the regulatory character which the *Philip Morris* case had said was one of the features necessary for its validity: 178 CLR at 592.

In *Ha v New South Wales* (1997) 189 CLR 465 **[9.4.60C]**, the fragility of the franchise fee on petrol was confirmed. Brennan CJ, McHugh, Gummow and Kirby JJ said that, although it was not necessary to consider *HC Sleigh Ltd v South Australia* (1977) 130 CLR 475 **[9.4.34]**, 'the reservation expressed as to that case in *Capital Duplicators (No 2)* will not have passed unnoticed': 189 CLR at 504.

[9.4.36]   The series of cases decided by the Barwick court (*Western Australia v Hamersley Iron Pty Ltd* (1969) 120 CLR 42 **[9.4.24]**; *Western Australia v Chamberlain Industries Pty Ltd* (1970) 121 CLR 1 **[9.4.25]**; *Logan Downs Pty Ltd v Queensland* (1977) 137 CLR 59 **[9.4.26]**; *Dickenson's Arcade Pty Ltd v Tasmania* (1974) 130 CLR 177 **[9.4.29C]**; *MG Kailis (1962) Pty Ltd v Western Australia* (1974) 130 CLR 245 **[9.4.33]**; *HC Sleigh Ltd v South Australia* (1977) 130 CLR 475 **[9.4.34]**) suggested a real tension in the court. Those justices who would give a broad reading to s 90 and use it to diminish (perhaps eliminate) the states' commodity-taxing powers appeared to have dominated the court; yet they felt constrained to follow *Dennis Hotels Pty Ltd v Victoria* (1960) 104 CLR 529 **[9.4.12C]**, and were unwilling to withdraw the invitation, which that decision had extended to the states, to use the device of licence fees to levy commodity taxes. However, this group of justices had no secure control of the court, and often managed to influence decisions only through the extra weight given to the Chief Justice's vote by s 23(2)(b) of the Judiciary Act (as in *Western Australia v Hamersley Iron Pty Ltd* (1969) 120 CLR 42 **[9.4.24]**, *Dickenson's Arcade Pty Ltd v Tasmania* (1974) 130 CLR 177 **[9.4.29C]** and *Logan Downs Pty Ltd v Queensland* (1977) 137 CLR 59 **[9.4.26]**).

The retirement of Sir Garfield Barwick in 1981 offered the prospect of a shift in the balance of opinion on the court towards a view more tolerant of state commodity taxes. That balance was tested in the following case, which also gave four members of the court the opportunity to debate a fundamental question: What is the purpose of s 90?

[9.4.37C]   **Hematite Petroleum Pty Ltd v Victoria**

(1983) 151 CLR 599

The Pipelines Act 1967 (Vic) provided that no person should construct or operate a pipeline unless that person held a licence issued by 'the Minister': s 25(1). A licensee was prohibited from operating a pipeline unless the current annual pipeline operation fee had been paid: s 35(1). Until 1981, this fee was fixed at $35 a kilometre of pipeline. By the Pipelines Fees Act 1981 (Vic), new subsections were added to s 35:

35...

(2)   The pipeline operation fee shall be in the financial year 1981–1982:

(a)   in the case of a trunk pipeline, the amount of $10,000,000;

(b)   in the case of any other pipeline, an amount equal to $40 for every complete kilometre of pipeline operated under the licence.

Section 35(3) provided for annual adjustment of the fees by reference to the consumer price index. Section 35(8) defined 'trunk pipeline' to mean the pipelines to which specific licences had been issued. These were two pipelines, owned and operated by the plaintiffs, and a pipeline owned and operated by the Gas and Fuel Corporation of Victoria.

The plaintiffs had, since 1968, been recovering oil and gas from wells in Bass Strait off the Victorian coast. The oil and gas were carried to Longford, on the east coast of Victoria, where they were separated into crude oil, liquefied petroleum gas and natural gas. The first two products were then transported, through the two pipelines owned and operated by the plaintiffs, to a processing plant on Westernport, 184 km away on the south coast of Victoria. After further processing at that plant, the end products (propane, butane, ethane and crude oil) were either shipped or transported by road to the plaintiffs' customers. (The third product, natural gas, was sold and delivered by the plaintiffs to the Gas and Fuel Corporation at Longford. The corporation then transported the natural gas to Melbourne through the third pipeline.)

The plaintiffs began an action against Victoria in the High Court of Australia, in which they sought a declaration that the subsections added in 1981 to s 35 of the Pipelines Act 1967 were invalid, and an order that Victoria repay to the plaintiffs $19,992,920 licence fees paid by them under protest. The defendant demurred and the demurrer came on for hearing before the Full Court of the High Court.

Gibbs CJ: [616] The association in the Constitution of duties of excise with duties of customs suggests that the two forms of taxation were intended to perform related purposes. The reason for giving the Commonwealth exclusive power to impose duties of customs was clear enough. It was intended by the framers of the Constitution that there should be no interstate tariffs and that the taxation of imports into the Commonwealth should be exclusively within the province of the Commonwealth. Although the Commonwealth was given exclusive power to impose tariffs, it might still have been possible for the States, by imposing duties of excise, to prevent the accomplishment of a policy which the Parliament wished to effect by means of its tariff. For example, if the Commonwealth wished to protect local manufacturers, and accordingly imposed duty on certain imported goods, a State which believed in free trade might have imposed a corresponding excise duty on local manufactures of the same kind. Whether such action would have been likely is another question. Similarly, if the Commonwealth had adopted a policy of free trade, a State might have obstructed that policy by giving bounties to local manufacturers. Section 90 of the Constitution, however, made exclusive the power of the Parliament to impose duties of customs and of excise, and to grant bounties on the production and export of goods. This conjunction of customs, excise and bounties suggests that it was intended by s 90 to give the Commonwealth a real control of its tariff policy, but it is by no means evident from anything that appears in the Constitution that it was intended to go further, and 'to give the Parliament a real control of the taxation of commodities', to use the words of Dixon J in *Parton v Milk Board* [617] *(Vic)* (1949) 80 CLR 229 at 260, and still less clear that it was intended to give the Parliament 'the control of the national economy as a unity which knows no State boundaries' — *Western Australia v Chamberlain Industries Pty Ltd* (1970) 121 CLR 1 at 17.

On any possible view of its effect, s 90 itself confers on the Parliament only a very limited power to control the economy. There are many taxes which have a tendency to enter into the price of commodities but which are not excises, and which are accordingly within the power of the States to impose. Payroll tax is an obvious example. There are many other legislative measures which a State can take either to discourage or to encourage production and manufacture. On the one hand it can fix quotas on production or manufacture, or indeed forbid production or manufacture altogether; on the other hand it can, for example, favour producers and manufacturers by reducing their taxes and the charges made to them for power and freight, and by building ports and railways for their use and providing them with other assistance. Thus s 90 does not go very far towards giving the Commonwealth exclusive control of or influence over the production or manufacture of goods. Moreover, s 109 of the Constitution, which invalidates State laws to the extent to which they are inconsistent with laws of the Commonwealth, plays a major part in preventing any State law from frustrating Commonwealth legislative policy. The presence of s 109 may well have rendered it unnecessary to include in s 90 a reference to duties of excise for the purpose of invalidating a State excise duty which counteracted the effect of a Commonwealth tariff.

The power conferred on the Commonwealth by s 51(ii) to make laws with respect to taxation is unaffected by s 90. The Parliament may impose a tax whether it is an excise or not. On the other hand, s 90 seriously restricts the taxing power of the States; it narrows, artificially, the field of taxation open to them. The inability of the States to impose duties of excise has created greater difficulties for the States since the uniform tax arrangements have virtually prevented them from imposing income taxes. One view of experts in the field of public finance is that the wide extension made by this court to the definition of 'excise' is 'one of the greatest impediments preventing the achievement of a rational and lasting division of financial powers in the Australian federal system': Matthews and Jay: *Federal Finance*, 1972, p 318. One result must surely tend to be that the States will impose some forms of taxation which, although constitutionally permissible, are less economically desirable than taxes now categorised as duties of excise.

[618] The conclusion that the grant to the Commonwealth of the exclusive power to impose duties of excise gravely hampers the States in the conduct of their financial affairs without conferring any corresponding benefit on the Commonwealth does not mean that the prohibition which s 90 contains must be disregarded. It does, however, suggest that there is no good reason for giving a wide and loose construction to its provisions. It supports the view that there is no justification for deciding the question whether a tax is a duty of excise by considering whether the real or practical effect of the legislation is the same as that which would be produced by a duty of excise ... The question whether a State law infringes s 90 can be answered only by determining whether it imposes that sort of tax. One must first define 'excise', and then ask whether the tax imposed by the State statute comes within that definition. It is irrelevant that the State statute brings about the same practical result as a duty of excise, for s 90 does not forbid the States to achieve any particular economic result; it forbids them to enact a particular form of taxation. The decision in *Vacuum Oil Pty Ltd v Queensland* (1934) 51 CLR 108 strongly supports this approach. In that case it was accepted that the scheme of the Act there challenged did bring about the same result as levying an excise on petrol, but that did not result in its invalidation: see at 118, 124–5.

[619] If one were to have regard to practicalities, the decisions of this court would not inspire one with any firm conviction that the invalidation of State taxes on the ground that they are duties of excise has always either contributed to the effectuation of the policies of the Commonwealth Parliament or has had any other beneficial result of a practical kind. It is difficult to see what practical benefit (except to the taxpayer) ensued from the invalidation of a charge made by a marketing board to meet the expenses of its administration (*Parton v Milk Board (Vic)*), or a stamp duty on receipts of payments on sales (*Western Australia v Chamberlain Industries Pty Ltd*) or a levy on stock imposed to provide a fund to be used in providing husbandry services (*Logan Downs Pty Ltd v Queensland*).

Gibbs CJ referred to a series of cases in which licence fees had been held not to be excise duties: *Peterswald v Bartley* (1904) 1 CLR 497 **[9.4.7]**, where the fee was unrelated to the quantity of beer manufactured; *Hughes & Vale Pty Ltd v New South Wales* (1953) 87 CLR 49, where the fee was based on the weight and carrying capacity of and distance travelled by a vehicle and did not directly affect any goods carried; *Browns Transport Pty Ltd v Kropp* (1958) 100 CLR at 117, where the fee was a percentage of the gross revenue derived from carrying goods or persons by road and was imposed without regard to any commodity; and *Bolton v Madsen* (1963) 110 CLR 264 **[9.4.23]**, where the fee was based on the carrying capacity of and distance travelled by a vehicle and also did not affect the goods carried. His Honour said that *Brown's Transport Pty Ltd v Kropp* and *Bolton v Madsen* established that the question whether a tax was directly related to goods depended on the provisions of the legislation imposing the tax, rather than on the practical effect of the tax. The Chief Justice continued:

[622] In the present case, as I have already said, the pipeline operation fee imposed by s 35(2) in respect of the crude oil pipeline and the gas liquids pipeline is a tax paid for the right to use those pipelines for the conveyance of the liquid hydrocarbons from Longford to Long Island Point ... The conveyance of the liquid hydrocarbons to Long Island Point is an integral step in the production of the products sold by the plaintiffs. It does not appear that the same is true of the conveyance of the natural gas to Melbourne ... There is nothing in the Pipelines Act to suggest that any distinction is intended to be drawn between the fees payable in respect of the three trunk pipelines or that liability to the tax in any way depends on whether the things conveyed by the pipeline are to be subject to further processing. If for some reason production ceased at Long Island Point, and the plaintiffs sold the hydrocarbons on their arrival there, that would not affect the plaintiffs' liability for the fee. However, in the case of all three trunk pipelines, if the tax directly affects the goods conveyed it is imposed at a point in their production or distribution before they reach the hands of consumers. The question then is whether the tax directly affects the goods, or in other words whether the plaintiffs are

taxed by reason of the fact that they transport the hydrocarbons and by reference to the transportation.

... Clearly the payment of the fee is a condition of the right to use the pipeline. The amount of the fee does not depend on the extent to which the pipeline is used ... **[623]** However, for the purposes of the Pipelines Act it is immaterial whether the pipelines carry any particular quantity of, or indeed any, hydrocarbons ... If it appeared that in a particular year the plaintiffs would carry a greater (or lesser) amount of liquid hydrocarbons than in the previous licence period, that would be quite irrelevant to the amount of fee payable.

The conclusion appears to me inescapable that the fee is not imposed because the hydrocarbons are carried; it is imposed as a condition of the right to carry them.

The very size of the impost, the fact that it is exacted in respect of pipelines carrying the products of the Bass Strait Oil wells and the comparison with the pipeline operation fee charged in respect of other pipelines naturally give rise to the suspicion that the fees charged for the licences for the trunk pipelines are designed to avoid the limitation which s 90 imposes on the taxing power of the States. However, a tax is not an excise simply because it is large and discriminatory and aimed at companies which carry on a business thought to be lucrative enough to enable them to pay it. None of these circumstances show that there is any relationship between the **[624]** fee and any step taken by the plaintiffs in respect of the goods. And, for the reasons I have given, a tax is not an excise because its practical effect appears to be similar to that of an excise. The pipeline operation fee is, in my opinion, not a tax upon or directly affecting goods; it is what it purports to be, a fee for a licence to use the pipeline. It is not a duty of excise.

Mason J: **[628]** [T]he court has rejected the narrow view of excise — that it is confined to taxes upon production and manufacture. Instead it has adopted the broader view that it extends to taxes upon commodities to the point of receipt by the consumer. However, the apparent breadth of this approach is somewhat illusory because the court has from time to time insisted that there must be a strict relationship between the tax and the goods in order to constitute a tax upon goods. The continuing problem has been to define or describe that relationship accurately and instructively, especially with a view to distinguishing those taxes imposed at the point of sale or distribution which are an excise from those which are not. ...

[629] The *Bolton v Madsen* formula has not emerged unscathed from the more recent decisions on s 90. It no longer commands the acceptance of the court as a whole, or even of a majority, as a conclusive guide as to what is an excise. In *Anderson's* Barwick CJ expressed the broad view of an excise, that a tax is a duty of excise if it is upon or in respect of goods at any point, including the point of manufacture or production, as they pass to consumption, saying (at 365): '... in arriving at the conclusion that the tax is a tax upon the relevant step, consideration of many factors is necessary, factors which may not be present in every case and which may have different weight or emphasis in different cases. The "indirectness" of the tax, its immediate entry into the cost of the goods, the proximity of the transaction it taxes to the manufacture or production of the movement of the goods into consumption, the form and content of the legislation imposing the tax — all these are included in the relevant considerations'. In *Dickenson's Arcade Pty Ltd v Tasmania* (1974) 130 CLR 177 at 241, I agreed with his **[630]** Honour's comments. ...

The *Bolton v Madsen* formula has one advantage. Its application will lead to certainty and predictability in the determination of what is an excise. Unfortunately, the formula has a number of countervailing disadvantages. The criterion of liability which it expresses is very much a matter of form, not of substance. This would not matter if the constitutional conception of an excise was itself a matter of form. But there are powerful reasons for thinking that the grant of exclusive power to the Commonwealth to impose excise duties was not intended to be a mere matter of form.

Applied literally, as the decision in *Dennis Hotels Pty Ltd v Victoria* (1960) 104 CLR 529 convincingly demonstrates, the criterion of liability leads to the result that a licence fee charged on a step in production or distribution, calculated by reference to the quantity or value of goods produced or sold in the period for which the licence is held, is an excise, but not if the fee is calculated by reference to the quantity or value of the goods produced or sold in the previous licensing period. The distinction between the two licence fees just mentioned is a mere matter of form. It leaves the State free to levy licence fees and other duties in respect of the production, manufacture, sale or distribution of goods in any form except that which is caught by the *Bolton v Madsen* strict criterion of liability.

What, one might ask, was the high constitutional purpose intended to be served by prohibiting the States from imposing a tax in this very limited form? To prohibit the States from imposing a tax having an arithmetical relationship with goods produced or sold during a licence period, while leaving the States free to impose any other form of tax in respect of goods produced or sold, achieves [631] nothing. If this be the effect of s 90 it certainly adds nothing to the Commonwealth's economic and financial powers.

Yet it has been generally accepted that the grant of exclusive power to impose duties of excise in conjunction with a like power to impose customs duties, in a Constitution which frequently refers to the two duties — ss 86, 87, 90 and 93 '… was intended to give the Parliament a real control of the taxation of commodities and to ensure that the execution of whatever policy it adopted should not be hampered or defeated by State action' (*Parton v Milk Board (Vic)* (1949) 80 CLR 229 at 260, per Dixon J; see also 264–5, per McTiernan J; *Commonwealth and Commonwealth Oil Refineries Ltd v South Australia* (1926) 38 CLR 408 at 437, per Rich J; *Whitehouse v Queensland* (1960) 104 CLR 609 at 618, per Dixon CJ; *Western Australia v Chamberlain Industries Pty Ltd* (1970) 121 CLR 1 at 17, per Barwick CJ; *Dickenson's Arcade* (1974) 130 CLR at 238, per Mason J). Excise duties, like customs duties, are significant instruments for raising revenue. What is more important is that Parliament, possessing exclusive power to impose both forms of duties, can protect and stimulate home production by fixing appropriate levels of customs and excise duties. And it can lower the level of domestic prices by lowering customs and excise duties. By lowering customs duties alone it can put pressure on Australian producers and manufacturers to become more competitive.

If the States had power to impose excise duties then the Commonwealth Parliament's power to protect and stimulate home production and influence domestic price levels might be compromised. It is possible that by an exercise of the taxation power the Commonwealth could effectively prevent the States from imposing excise duties. A law enacted under s 51(ii) providing that no excise duties should be payable on designated goods would, by virtue of s 109, prevail over any inconsistent State law. This is not a reason for denying that the object of granting exclusive power to the Commonwealth was as I have expressed it to be. The Commonwealth's control is stronger if it possesses exclusive power, then there is no potential for conflict between Commonwealth and State legislation. The possibility of the imposition of taxes on goods by the States in the period prior to the enactment of inconsistent legislation by the Commonwealth undermines the Commonwealth's real control of the taxation of commodities and provides a further reason for rejecting the existence of s 109 as a basis for narrowing the ambit of [632] the Commonwealth's exclusive power under s 90. In any case to make the power exclusive is to free its exercise from some of the political controversies and constraints which would inevitably surround any attempt by the Commonwealth Parliament to pass inconsistent legislation designed solely to override a State law.

That s 90 confers on the Commonwealth Parliament an exclusive power to grant bounties on the production or export of goods reinforces the proposition that the grant of an exclusive power to impose duties of customs and excise was intended to give the Parliament a real control over the taxation of commodities. It could not have been intended that the States should have the power to burden home production by imposing taxes upon goods, when the Commonwealth was given exclusive power to stimulate production by granting bounties.

That the object of the power was to secure a real control over the taxation of commodities provides strong support for a broad view of what is an excise, one which embraces all taxes upon or in respect of a step in the production, manufacture, sale or distribution of goods for any such tax places a burden on production. A tax on goods sold, like a tax on goods produced, is a burden on production, though less immediate and direct in its impact. It is a burden on production because it enters into the price of the goods — the person who is liable to pay it naturally seeks to recoup it from the next purchaser. As the tax increases the price of the goods to the ultimate consumer, and thereby diminishes or tends to diminish demand for the goods, it is a burden on production.

To justify the conclusion that the tax is upon or in respect of the goods it is enough that the tax is such that it enters into the cost of the goods and is therefore reflected in the prices at which the goods are subsequently sold. It is not necessary that there should be an arithmetical relationship between the tax and the quantity or value of the goods produced or sold (*Matthews v Chicory Marketing Board (Vic)* (1938) 60 CLR 263 at 304), still less that such a relationship should exist in a specific period during which the tax is imposed. This is because there are many cases where an examination of the relevant circumstances will disclose that a tax is a duty of excise, notwithstanding that it is not expressed to be in relation to the quantity or value of the goods. As Dixon J said in *Matthews* (at 304):

> But if the substantial effect is to impose a levy in respect of the commodity the fact that the basis of assessment is not strictly [633] that of quantity or value will not prevent the tax failing within the description, duties of excise.

The contrary approach, that suggested by the defendant, is to ascertain the character of the tax 'solely by considering whether the taxing legislation picks out goods to be the subject of the imposition': *Chamberlain*, at 20. This approach ignores the fact that, in determining whether a tax is a duty of excise, the inquiry is a constitutional question. To strictly confine the inquiry to the terms of the statute levying the impost is to 'expose the constitutional provision made by s 90 to evasion by easy subterfuges and the adoption of unreal distinctions' (see *Matthews* at 304 per Dixon J; see also *Chamberlain*, at 14; *Logan Downs*, at 76).

... The philosophy which underlies the [*Bolton v Madsen* strict criterion of liability] is that in applying constitutional prohibitions or guarantees the court should not look beyond the direct legal operation of the impugned law according to its terms. It is a philosophy with which I profoundly disagree. It is necessary to examine the practical operation of a law as well as its terms in order to ascertain whether it imposes an excise ... Otherwise the constitutional prohibition is reduced to a formula which lends itself to evasion ... The criteria enunciated by Barwick CJ in *Anderson* (at 365) are a more reliable guide to what constitutes an excise. ...

[634] Here the significant features of the pipeline operation fee are: (1) that it is levied only upon a trunk pipeline, ie the Gas and Fuel Corporation pipeline, the gas liquids pipeline and the crude oil pipeline, through which flow the entirety of the hydrocarbons recovered from the Bass Strait fields; (2) that it is a fee payable for permission to operate a pipeline for which the plaintiffs otherwise hold a permit to own and use; (3) that the fee is a special fee which is extraordinarily large in amount, having no relationship at all to the amount of the fees payable for other pipeline operation licences — the fee payable for a trunk pipeline is $10,000,000 whereas the fee payable for any other pipeline is $40 per kilometre; and (4) that the fee is payable before an essential step in the production of refined spirit can take place — the transportation of the hydrocarbons from Longford to Long Island Point where the refinery is situated.

The co-existence of these features indicates that the pipeline operation fee payable by the plaintiffs is not a mere fee for the privilege of carrying on an activity; it is a tax imposed on a step in the production of refined petroleum products which is so large that it will inevitably increase the price of the products in the course of distribution to the consumer. The fee is not an exaction imposed in respect of the plaintiffs' business generally; it is an exaction of such magnitude imposed in respect of a step in production in such circumstances that it is explicable only on the footing that it is imposed in virtue of the quantity and value of the hydrocarbons produced from the Bass Strait fields. To levy a tax on the operation [635] of the pipelines is a convenient means of taxing what they convey for they are the only practicable method of conveying the hydrocarbons to the next processing point.

~~~

[9.4.38] Murphy J said that s 90 'should be read narrowly, to avoid adverse consequences to the States': 151 CLR at 638. He said that s 90 prohibited state taxation which discriminated between goods produced in the state and those produced outside the state, and prohibits state bounties on production (or export): 151 CLR at 638. Wilson J held that the licence fee was not an excise duty, for substantially the same reasons as Gibbs CJ.

Brennan J described the movement of crude oil and liquefied petroleum gas through the plaintiff's pipelines as 'an integral part of the process of converting the petroleum brought ashore from the Bass Strait field into the products sold from the Long Island Point Plant': 151 CLR at 655. Even adopting the approach of Kitto J in *Anderson's Pty Ltd v Victoria* (1964) 111 CLR 353 at 374, the licence fee was an excise duty because its criterion of liability was the operation of the pipelines: 'a step in the production, manufacture and distribution of the products sold by the plaintiffs': 151 CLR at 659. 'However', he said, 'for the reasons expressed by Mason J, I prefer the broader approach', that is, the approach spelt out by Barwick CJ in *Anderson's* case (111 CLR at 365–6): 151 CLR at 659. That approach led, Brennan J said, to the same conclusion: the taxes imposed on the plaintiff's operation of their pipelines were excise duties.

Deane J concluded, for substantially the same reasons as Mason J, that the licence fee imposed by s 35(2) was an excise duty.

Notes

[9.4.39] The decision in *Hematite Petroleum Pty Ltd v Victoria* (1983) 151 CLR 599 **[9.4.37C]** illustrates the tension, or the shifting balance, which is involved in the competing definitions of 'excise duties', and in the different approaches to applying that definition. The broad view of excise duty, adopted by four of the six justices, threatens the tax-raising capacity of the states; the narrow view adopted by Murphy J (and left open by Deane J) avoids, as Murphy J recognised, 'adverse consequences to the States': 151 CLR at 638. On the other hand, approaching the validity of legislation by concentrating on its criterion of liability limits (as both Gibbs CJ and Wilson J recognised: 151 CLR at 618, 650 (respectively)) the reduction of the states' taxation powers. To assess the validity of state legislation by considering its practical effect, however, further diminishes the range of taxes which the states may impose, if only because that approach cuts through state attempts to avoid, through the adoption of indirect means, the prohibition in s 90. The point is that, while the adoption of a broad definition of excise duties places the states' taxing powers at risk, the real threat to those powers materialises only when that definition is applied to legislation in a way which takes account of the legislation's practical effect.

In *Ha v New South Wales* (1997) 189 CLR 465 **[9.4.60C]**, that threat was finally realised. The majority (Brennan CJ, McHugh, Gummow and Kirby J) said that *Philip Morris Ltd v Commissioner of Business Franchises* (1989) 167 CLR 399 **[9.4.47]** 'clearly established' the proposition that 'the character of a tax required a consideration of the substantive operation as well as the text of the statute imposing the tax': 189 CLR at 491. The result was a loss in state revenues in the order of $5 billion a year.

[9.4.40] The insistence that the question whether legislation imposed a tax upon goods should be judged by looking at the legislation's criterion of liability could therefore be justified as an attempt to preserve the taxing powers of the states, to minimise the devastation which s 90 would otherwise work, rather than as an unthinking adoption of Dixon CJ's admonition that the only safe guide in constitutional issues was 'a strict and complete legalism': 85 CLR at xiv.

This concern for preserving some taxing capacity for the states was the silent theme underlying the analyses of, for example, Kitto J in *Dennis Hotels Pty Ltd v Victoria* (1960) 104 CLR 529 **[9.4.12C]** at 565–7 and Gibbs J in *Dickenson's Arcade Pty Ltd v Tasmania* (1974) 130 CLR 177 **[9.4.29C]** at 224. In *Hematite Petroleum Pty Ltd v Victoria* (1983) 151 CLR 599 **[9.4.37C]**, this theme was openly articulated by Gibbs CJ, Murphy and Wilson JJ, supported by a detailed argument on the part of Gibbs CJ and Murphy J as to the constitutional purpose of s 90.

Indeed, Gibbs CJ expressly supported the adoption of this legalistic approach in the context of s 90 as a means of minimising that section's impact on state taxing powers. He referred to the current interpretation and application of s 90 which narrowed the field of taxation open to the states, which had (combined with the uniform tax arrangements) created great difficulties for the states and, perhaps, pushed the states into imposing economically undesirable taxes: 151 CLR at 617. It is clear that, by insisting on a strict 'criterion of liability' application of the definition of excise duties, Gibbs CJ was seeking to avoid those consequences and to ensure that the impact of s 90 did not go beyond the achievement of its purpose. He identified that purpose as being 'to give the Commonwealth a real control of its tariff policy' and dismissed the broader purposes proposed by Dixon J in *Parton v Milk Board (Vic)* **[9.4.10]** and by Barwick CJ in *Western Australia v Chamberlain Industries Pty Ltd* (1970) 121 CLR 1 **[9.4.25]**.

Gibbs CJ's judgment involved some contradictory elements, presumably a reflection of his recognition of the limited purpose of s 90, on the one hand, and his unwillingness to depart from the conventional judicial reading of that section, established since *Parton v Milk Board (Vic)* (1949) 80 CLR 229 **[9.4.10]** on the other. The reconciliation of these two opposing ideas was achieved by insisting that the broad, potentially destructive, reading of s 90 be applied in a narrow, legalistic fashion which eschewed economic analysis. This paradoxical approach (serving the economic objectives of s 90 by excluding economic considerations from the consideration of a particular law's validity) is examined in Hanks (1986) pp 368–9.

[9.4.41] If we accept that s 90 had the limited purpose of reserving to the Commonwealth control over tariff policy, is not the approach adopted by Murphy J in *Hematite Petroleum Pty Ltd v Victoria* (1983) 151 CLR 599 **[9.4.37C]** more likely to achieve that result, and less likely to trespass unnecessarily on the state's taxing powers than the approach adopted by Gibbs CJ? It may be true that large parts of the state's taxing powers can be saved by a legalistic application of the broad definition of excise duties (consider the judgments of Kitto J in *Dennis Hotels Pty Ltd v Victoria* (1960) 104 CLR 529 **[9.4.12C]** and *Western Australia v Chamberlain Industries Pty Ltd* (1970) 121 CLR 1 **[9.4.25]**, and of Gibbs J in *Dickenson's Arcade Pty Ltd v Tasmania* (1974) 130 CLR 177 **[9.4.29C]**). However, that could be at the cost of permitting interference with the Commonwealth's tariff policies. A licence fee to be paid by the vendors of locally-produced goods but calculated on last year's turnover; a receipts duty on receipts issued in acknowledgment of payment for locally produced goods; and a tax on the consumption of locally produced goods: each of these would threaten to undermine the Commonwealth's tariff policy but would not, on the 'criterion of liability' approach, be an excise.

[9.4.42] The judgments in *Hematite Petroleum Pty Ltd v Victoria* (1983) 151 CLR 599 **[9.4.37C]** bring into sharp conflict the differences of judicial opinion over the purposes of s 90. Mason J did not accept, it seems, that s 90 was confined to giving the Commonwealth real control over tariff policy. His Honour adopted Dixon J's claim (in *Parton v Milk Board (Vic)* (1949) 80 CLR 229 **[9.4.10]**) that s 90 was intended to give the Commonwealth 'real control of the taxation of commodities'. However, that proposition did not advance the search for s 90's objective: it is essentially a statement of the means by which an unstated, or assumed, objective is to be achieved. It seems that Mason J regarded the real control of commodity taxation as intended to give the Commonwealth more than control over tariff policy; rather, it was intended to achieve the substantial centralisation of commodity taxes.

Among the ends towards which commodity taxes might be directed, Mason J mentioned the raising of revenue, implementing a policy of protection or free trade, and the lowering of domestic prices: 151 CLR at 631. While the second of these objectives could be served by adopting the limited definition of excise duties proposed by Murphy J, the first and third objectives require a much broader definition, such as the one proposed by Mason J; namely, a tax which enters into the price of the goods and diminishes or tends to diminish demand for the goods: 151 CLR at 632. (That definition might serve other objectives implicit in the 'real control of the taxation of commodities': the implementation of social policy through the adjustment of the balance between direct (potentially progressive) taxation and indirect (potentially regressive) taxation; and manipulation of consumption through selective taxes.)

The recent decision of *Ha v New South Wales* (1997) 189 CLR 465 **[9.4.60C]** makes explicit that the revenue-raising objective and free trade objective are behind the broad conception of excise duties. In relation to revenue-raising, Brennan CJ, McHugh, Gummow and Kirby JJ justified the broad purpose by saying that the states' 'principal source of revenue' was withdrawn at federation: 189 CLR at 493–494. They also said at 491:

> While taxes can and do affect trade, their immediate effect is to raise revenue. While the intended effect of s 90 on trade has often been invoked to illuminate the meaning of the term 'duties of excise' in s 90, it should not be forgotten that one of the chief purposes of Ch IV was to provide for the financial transition of the Colonies into the States of the Commonwealth and for the revenues required by the Commonwealth.

Indeed, the 'revenue to be derived from inland taxes on goods was ceded by the States to the Commonwealth': 189 CLR at 502.

In respect of free trade, the majority again emphasised its importance. They said the objective of 'inter-colonial free trade on the basis of a uniform tariff' (*Cole v Whitfield* (1988) 165 CLR 360 at 386) 'could not have been achieved if the States had retained the power to place a tax on goods within their borders': 189 CLR at 494. For the contrary view see Dawson, Toohey and Gaudron JJ: 189 CLR at 512.

[9.4.43] The point that the court's construction of s 90 had implications for the state's fiscal autonomy was made by Dawson J in *Gosford Meats Pty Ltd v New South Wales* (1985) 155 CLR 368 **[9.4.45]**, in the course of explaining (unconvincingly, so far as the majority of the court was concerned) why the court should follow the answers to the questions given in *Dennis Hotels Pty Ltd v Victoria* (1960) 104 CLR 529 **[9.4.12C]** and *Dickenson's Arcade Pty Ltd v Tasmania* (1974) 130 CLR 177 **[9.4.29C]**:

[I]t is important to recognise that those questions involve the financial relationship between the Commonwealth and the States and that the methods which the States may employ in raising revenue, particularly since the advent of uniform taxation, have been to a large extent dictated by the course of decision in this court. Legislation, with vital fiscal and budgetary consequences, has been carefully framed to conform to the principles laid down by authority and serious disruption is caused by any significant departure from those principles (155 CLR at 411).

[9.4.44] The High Court's concern with maintaining some tax base for the states was expressed in *Evda Nominees Pty Ltd v Victoria* (1984) 154 CLR 311. The court unanimously rejected a taxpayer's challenge to the Business Franchise (Tobacco) Act 1974 (Vic), which imposed a tax on tobacco retailers and wholesalers, in the form of a licence fee modelled precisely on the fee upheld in *Dennis Hotels Pty Ltd v Victoria* (1960) 104 CLR 529 **[9.4.12C]**. The court pointed out that taxes of this type had been upheld in *Dennis Hotels*, *Dickenson's Arcade Pty Ltd v Tasmania* (1974) 130 CLR 177 **[9.4.12C]** and *HC Sleigh Ltd v South Australia* (1977) 130 CLR 475 **[9.4.34]**. Because the states had 'organised their financial affairs in reliance on' those decisions it would not be appropriate to reconsider their correctness: 154 CLR at 316.

In *Ha v New South Wales* (1997) 189 CLR 465 **[9.4.60C]**, Brennan CJ, McHugh, Gummow and Kirby JJ decided to reconsider the franchise decisions on the basis that the states and territories had themselves called those decisions into question by inviting the court to reconsider the broad interpretation. They said at 499:

> In the present case ... the States, fully appreciating that the attack on the doctrine based on *Parton*, if successful, would destroy the reasoning in the franchise cases ... chose to invite the court to re-examine the *Parton* doctrine which has been accepted for nearly half a century.

[9.4.45] In *Gosford Meats Pty Ltd v New South Wales* (1985) 155 CLR 368, the majority of the High Court reiterated the point, made by Mason J in *MG Kailis (1962) Pty Ltd v Western Australia* (1974) 130 CLR 245 **[9.4.33]**, that the licence fee device should not be extended beyond the range of transactions covered by the decisions in *Dennis Hotels Pty Ltd v Victoria* (1960) 104 CLR 529 **[9.4.12C]**, *Dickenson's Arcade Pty Ltd v Tasmania* (1974) 130 CLR 177 **[9.4.29C]** and *HC Sleigh Ltd v South Australia* (1977) 130 CLR 475 **[9.4.34]**.

Mason, Murphy, Brennan and Deane JJ held (with Gibbs CJ, Wilson and Dawson JJ dissenting) that the Meat Industry Act 1978 (NSW) invalidly imposed an excise duty. Section 10 of the Act prohibited any person operating premises for slaughtering animals without a licence for those premises. Section 11C provided that the annual fee for such a licence was calculated by reference to the number of animals slaughtered on the premises during the 12-month period which ended on the 30 June preceding the licence period.

Mason and Deane JJ, in their joint judgment, described an excise duty as 'a tax upon internally produced or manufactured goods', whose 'constitutional conception ... is a matter of substance and not of form': 144 CLR at 383. They said that *Dennis Hotels* could not be decisive of the case then before them. That decision had:

> ... been allowed to stand as an authoritative decision on its own facts [but] it would fly in the face of both principle and authority to accept it as establishing a general proposition that can be applied to a tax made payable, in the form of a licence fee, by a manufacturer or producer of goods (155 CLR at 385).

Murphy J adhered to his view that s 90 prohibited state taxes which discriminated against goods produced or manufactured outside the state (customs duties) or inside the state (excise duties): 155 CLR at 387. The present tax discriminated against production of goods in New South Wales and was therefore an excise.

Brennan J noted, as had Mason and Deane JJ, that Fullagar J had been a crucial member of the majority in *Dennis Hotels*. Yet his approach in that case had been radically different from that of other members of the majority and he would have treated a similar licence fee tax on a producer as an excise duty:

> Although the authority of *Dennis Hotels* and *Dickenson's Arcade* is to be maintained in respect of legislation imposing fees for licences to sell goods calculated by reference to purchases or sales in preceding periods, those cases do not require the conclusion that a tax payable by a producer of goods and calculated by reference to steps in the production of goods taken in a preceding period is not a duty of excise (155 CLR at 410).

The minority justices regarded the validity of the licensing system as settled by *Dennis Hotels*, *Dickenson's Arcade*, *HC Sleigh* and *Evda Nominees Pty Ltd v Victoria* (1984) 154 CLR 311 **[9.4.44]**. Gibbs CJ, for example, said there was 'no logical ground' on which a licence fee based on past sales and purchases could be distinguished from a licence fee based on past production or manufacture: 155 CLR at 379.

Dawson J observed that there was 'no ultimate truth which lies at the end of any search for the meaning of the phrase "duty of excise" and that it was, therefore, all the more important to follow and not undermine 'doctrine which has been accepted in this court upon the subject': 155 CLR at 411. Moreover, the states had shaped their taxation policies 'to conform to the principles laid down by authority', and those policies would be disrupted by serious departure from those principles: 155 CLR at 411.

[9.4.46]   In *Hematite Petroleum Pty Ltd v Victoria* (1983) 151 CLR 599 **[9.4.37C]**, Gibbs CJ, Mason and Murphy JJ suggested that Commonwealth control of commodity taxes could be secured without the court giving s 90 an expansive reading. The Commonwealth Parliament could prevent state taxation of particular commodities by enacting legislation which precludes that taxation. This Commonwealth legislation would prevail and any state taxation laws would be invalid through the operation of s 109 of the Constitution: 151 CLR at 616 per Gibbs CJ; 151 CLR at 631 per Mason J; 151 CLR at 639 per Murphy J.

However, the orthodox view is that the Commonwealth Parliament cannot legislate so as to prevent the exercise of state taxing power: see Latham CJ in *South Australia v Commonwealth* (the *First Uniform Tax* case) (1942) 65 CLR 373 at 413 **[9.6.3C]** and Dixon CJ and Fullagar J in *Victoria v Commonwealth* (the *Second Uniform Tax* case) (1957) 99 CLR 575 at 614, 657 **[9.6.8C]**. While the grant of immunity from state taxes may be regarded as incidental to some of the Commonwealth Parliament's legislative powers (see *Australian Coastal Shipping Commission v O'Reilly* (1962) 107 CLR 46 **[8.2.82]**); the support offered by this incidental power is not unshakeable, as demonstrated by the High Court's decision in *Gazzo v Comptroller of Stamps (Vic)* (1981) 149 CLR 227 **[8.2.83]**.

The *Uniform Tax* cases and *Gazzo's* case raise substantial problems for the course suggested by Gibbs CJ, Mason and Murphy JJ. The Commonwealth Parliament cannot forbid the states to levy taxes on a nominated commodity; that, according to the *Uniform Tax* cases, is beyond the Commonwealth's power. And the Commonwealth Parliament can only confer immunity from state taxes on a nominated commodity if that immunity is judged by the High Court to be incidental to one of the Commonwealth's legislative powers: see *Gazzo's* case. Consider, for example, an immunity from state taxes conferred by the Commonwealth on all motor vehicles with engine capacities below 2000cc: To which of the Commonwealth's legislative powers would that be incidental? It might be incidental to the Commonwealth's own taxation power in s 51(ii) but only if it can be argued that this power would be frustrated if the commodities in question were amenable to state taxes. How can that argument be developed? This question is discussed in Constitutional Commission (1988) p 827.

[9.4.47] The coherence of the franchise fee cases was again called into question in *Philip Morris Ltd v Commissioner of Business Franchises* (1989) 167 CLR 399. Section 6 of the Business Franchise (Tobacco) Act 1974 (Vic) provided that a person could not carry on tobacco wholesaling or retailing unless the person was a holder of a licence under the Act. The fee to be paid for a licence was $50 plus 25 per cent of the value of tobacco sold by the applicant in 'the relevant period'. The 'relevant period' was the last preceding month but one before the month in respect of which a licence was granted. In a series of divergent, and often conflicting, opinions a majority of the High Court (Mason CJ, Deane, Dawson, Toohey and Gaudron JJ; Brennan and McHugh JJ dissenting) upheld the validity of the Act.

Mason CJ and Deane J reiterated the broad purpose of s 90, saying that ss 51(ii), 51(iii), 88, 90, and 92 ensured 'equality of opportunity both for interstate trade and commerce and for local manufacture and goods and ordain[ed] that the Commonwealth be an economic union, not an association of states each with its own domestic economy': 167 CLR at 426. They said that the 'point of dissension' in recent cases including *Western Australia v Chamberlain Industries Pty Ltd* (1970) 121 CLR 1 **[9.4.25]**, *Logan Downs Pty Ltd v Queensland* (1977) 137 CLR 59 **[9.4.26]** and *Hematite Petroleum Pty Ltd v Victoria* (1983) 151 CLR 599 **[9.4.37C]**, was not about whether a tax upon the taking of a step in the distribution of goods was an excise, but about whether, in characterising a tax, the court should look to its practical or substantial operation as well as the legal operation of the statute: 167 CLR at 432.

Mason CJ and Deane J said that 'the characterisation of a law by reference exclusively to its strict legal operation, without regard to its practical or substantial operation, is bound to yield, ... highly artificial results': 167 CLR at 433. *Dennis Hotels Pty Ltd v Victoria* (1960) 104 CLR 529 **[9.4.12C]** was authority only for 'the proposition that the presence or absence of the formula is a relevant [rather than 'critical'] consideration' in determining whether a licence fee is or is not an excise: 146 CLR at 437. Although it might have been 'attractive' to confine the franchise cases to their facts, especially in view of the fact that they disagreed with the decisions in those cases, the 'preferable approach' was to view alcohol and tobacco as belonging to a special category of cases. Liquor licensing had a 'unique history'; tobacco invited 'regulatory control'; and in neither case was the tax likely to be passed on 'as a significant component' of the cost: 167 CLR at 440. Mason CJ and Deane J held that the tobacco licence fees were valid.

Toohey and Gaudron JJ revived the narrow definition of excise and narrow purpose of s 90. They said that s 90 was designed to 'secure to the Commonwealth the power to effectuate economic policy with respect to Australian imports and exports': 167 CLR at 479. Although it may be a 'power over commodities' it was 'a power with a purpose'. They continued at 479:

> All that is necessary to secure that purpose and to perfect the power is to deny to each
> State the power to levy duties of customs on goods entering that State from overseas,

the power to levy duties of excise on goods produced or manufactured in that State and the power to grant bounties on goods produced or manufactured in that State.

Toohey and Gaudron JJ approached the case on the basis that the prohibition in s 90 referred to goods produced or manufactured in Australia: 167 CLR at 480. If the section was designed to give the Commonwealth control over commodity taxation it was 'difficult to see any basis for distinction' between taxes on sale and distribution, and taxes on consumption: 167 CLR at 480. They said that the franchise cases could be viewed either as an 'anomalous exception' to the broad view, or as a 'denial of [its] correctness', and said there was 'much to be said' for the former: 167 CLR at 481. Their Honours concluded that the tobacco licence fees were not excise duties because they affected goods in their character as articles of commerce rather than in their character as goods manufactured in Australia: 167 CLR at 485.

Dawson J also held that the tobacco licence fees were not excise duties, but on the basis that the earlier cases, *Dennis Hotels*, *Dickenson's Arcade Pty Ltd v Tasmania* (1973) 130 CLR 177 **[9.4.29C]** and *HC Sleigh Ltd v South Australia* (1977) 130 CLR 475 **[9.4.34]**, were authority for a wide legal proposition; namely, that a licence fee imposed on the vendor of goods would not be an excise duty where it was calculated by reference to past sales or purchases: 167 CLR at 472. In the course of his judgment, Dawson J made the following observations on the course of decisions on s 90 (at 473–4):

> Perhaps the basic error was to depart from the limited conception of excise duty which the court laid down in *Peterswald v Bartley*. To have regard, as the court did there, to the constitutional purpose which the context of s 90 reveals and to the restricted objectives to which s 90 gives expression would make it possible to speak sensibly of duties of excise as a matter of substance. But as the authorities stand at the moment it is not possible to do so and the application of the test laid down in *Bolton v Madsen* represents the only available method of imposing some practical limit on the reach of the section.

Brennan and McHugh JJ dissented. In separate judgments, they adopted narrow readings of *Dennis Hotels Pty Ltd v Victoria* (1960) 104 CLR 529 **[9.4.12C]**. Its authority should be confined, they said, to 'legislation operating in indistinguishable terms': 167 CLR at 460 per Brennan J. They saw a series of distinctions between the present licence fee and the fee upheld in *Dennis Hotels*: these included the relative brevity of the licence period (one month), the proximity of the past period (the second last month) and the relatively high rate of the tax: 167 CLR at 463–4 per Brennan J; at 500–1 per McHugh J. Brennan J also said that this licence fee was distinguishable from *Dennis Hotels* because it was not 'regulatory' (167 CLR at 461) and that it was a 'matter of indifference' who paid it in the chain of steps from production to final distribution: 167 CLR at 461. The 'once-only' nature of the tax meant that it was a tax on any step in the distribution of a commodity rather than a fee for the privilege of engaging in a business: 167 CLR at 462.

[9.4.48]   The reasons for judgment in *Philip Morris Ltd v Commissioner of Business Franchises* (1989) 167 CLR 399 **[9.4.47]** appear to have been driven by two contending pressures: a resistance to reopening the decisions in *Dennis Hotels Pty Ltd v Victoria* (1960) 104 CLR 529 **[9.4.12C]** and *Dickenson's Arcade Pty Ltd v Tasmania* (1974) 130 CLR 177 **[9.4.29C]**; and the need to reconcile those two cases with the general trend of decisions on s 90. The result was an untidy collection of qualifications and compromises; a result which suggests that the preferable course would have been to discard the two earlier decisions. (Brennan J remarked, perhaps regretfully, that the court's commitment, made during argument, 'to resolve the instant case in the light of existing authority ... has proved to be more difficult than it then appeared': 167 CLR at 443.)

Of the seven justices, only Dawson J accepted that the earlier cases were authority for the wide proposition that a licence fee imposed on the vendor of goods would not be an excise duty where it was calculated by reference to past sales or purchases. Mason CJ and Deane J limited the proposition from those two decisions to licensing regimes for the sale of alcohol and tobacco. Brennan and McHugh JJ did not accept the limitation proposed by Mason CJ and Deane J, but confined the authority of *Dennis Hotels* to 'legislation operating in indistinguishable terms'. Toohey and Gaudron JJ saw *Dennis Hotels* as standing for a proposition which owed more to the judgment of Fullagar J than to the judgments of the other six justices in that case.

[9.4.49] The judgment of Toohey and Gaudron JJ in *Philip Morris Ltd v Commissioner of Business Franchises* (1989) 167 CLR 399 **[9.4.47]** was an attack on the foundation on which *Dennis Hotels Pty Ltd v Victoria* (1960) 104 CLR 529 **[9.4.12C]** and every later decision was constructed; namely, the expanded definition of excise duties articulated by Rich and Williams JJ and by Dixon J in *Parton v Milk Board (Vic)* (1949) 80 CLR 229 **[9.4.10]**. Toohey and Gaudron JJ supported the narrow definition of excise duties, endorsed by the High Court in *Peterswald v Bartley* (1904) 1 CLR 497 **[9.4.7]**, by McTiernan J in *Parton v Milk Board (Vic)*, and by Fullagar J in *Dennis Hotels*: excise duties were taxes imposed on goods because of their local (Australian) production. An even narrower form of this definition had been advanced by Murphy J in *Hematite Petroleum Pty Ltd v Victoria* (1983) 151 CLR 599 **[9.4.37C]**. Murphy J had described excise duties as 'limited to taxes on production within the State': 151 CLR at 638.

In *Philip Morris Ltd v Commissioner of Business Franchises* (1989) 167 CLR 399 **[9.4.47]**, Toohey and Gaudron JJ acknowledged that there was much to be said for Murphy J's view of excise duties; but claimed that 'the overwhelming weight of authority favours the identification of the relevant goods caught up in [s 90's] prohibition as goods produced or manufactured in Australia': 167 CLR at 480. The claim that this definition is supported by 'the overwhelming weight of authority' may owe more to optimism than to accuracy. Acceptance of the definition would require rejection of almost all decisions since *Parton v Milk Board (Vic)* (1949) 80 CLR 229 **[9.4.10]**. But there were, in *Philip Morris*, signs that other members of the court could join with Toohey and Gaudron JJ in returning to the limited conception of an excise duty laid down in *Peterswald v Bartley* (1904) 1 CLR 497 **[9.4.7]**. Dawson J suggested that the High Court's departure from *Peterswald v Bartley* may have been 'the basic error': 167 CLR at 473. Brennan J speculated as to whether the time had arrived for a review of the cases under s 90 of the type undertaken by the court, in the context of s 92 of the Constitution in *Cole v Whitfield* (1988) 165 CLR 360 **[10.4.27C]**.

[9.4.50] One of the difficulties of s 90 is that any attempt to isolate its purpose and then to give to the section an operation which will achieve that purpose must eventually lead to frustration. If, for example, we see the purpose of s 90 as ensuring effective Commonwealth control of tariff policy, it is not enough to apply the section so as to prevent those state taxes on commodities which would undermine that tariff policy. State policies on the pricing of fuel, payroll tax, government credit for expanding industries, purchases for government consumption could all work against the Commonwealth's tariff policies. For example, the Commonwealth Government might decide to reduce the protection enjoyed by Australian motor vehicle manufacturers by lowering import duties on overseas motor vehicles. A state could counteract the effect of that decision by giving a local manufacturer the benefit of reduced electricity tariffs and a special exemption from payroll tax, by extending low-interest credit to the manufacturer to finance a new plant, and by making all its purchases of motor vehicles from the local manufacturer. Despite the capacity of these actions to frustrate the Commonwealth's tariff policies, s 90 would be powerless against them (as Gibbs CJ observed in *Hematite Petroleum Pty Ltd v Victoria* (1983) 151 CLR 599 **[9.4.37C]** at 617).

[9.4.51] By contrast, if we see s 90 as directed to a wider objective (concentrating, in the hands of the Commonwealth, the implementation of economic and social policies through commodity taxes) the states do retain the capacity to interfere with those policies. For example, a Commonwealth decision that tax on motor vehicles should be lowered so as to stimulate consumer spending could be counteracted by a state decision to tighten the terms of consumer credit. Again, a Commonwealth decision to lower sales taxes on all commodities so as to shift the balance between regressive and progressive taxes could be counteracted by a state decision to raise gas and electricity tariffs.

It is difficult to deny the point that, whatever purpose s 90 was intended to achieve, it will be inadequate for that purpose while control of economically significant policies remains divided between Commonwealth and states. This is not to suggest that the division should be terminated, that control of all economic policies should be centralised; it is intended only to emphasise the relative crudity of the Commonwealth Constitution (the failure of those responsible for its drafting to think through the difficult problems for which they were attempting to find a solution).

[9.4.52] The High Court reviewed the purpose of s 90 and its conferral of exclusive power over customs and excise duties in *Capital Duplicators Pty Ltd v Australian Capital Territory (No 1)* (1992) 177 CLR 248. A majority of the court (Brennan, Deane, Toohey and Gaudron JJ; Mason CJ, Dawson and McHugh JJ dissenting) held that the exclusive power of the Commonwealth to levy duties of excise prevented a territory legislature, as well as a state parliament, from imposing excise duties.

In their joint judgment, Brennan, Deane and Toohey JJ located the purpose of ss 88, 90, 92 and 99 of the Constitution as the creation of a free trade area embracing the whole of Australia. The collection and control of duties of customs and excise and the control of payment of bounties was central to the fulfilment of that purpose. Accordingly, on the establishment of the Commonwealth, s 86 transferred the powers of collection and payment to the Commonwealth and s 69 transferred the relevant colonial departments to the Commonwealth (at 276):

> It would frustrate the manifest purpose of s 86 if, after uniform duties of customs were imposed, part of the functions of collecting and controlling duties of excise or controlling the payment of bounties were to pass *from* the Executive Government of the Commonwealth to the Executive of a Territory Government whose legislature might be empowered to impose its own duties of excise or to grant its own bounties on the production or export of goods.

Later, Brennan, Deane and Toohey JJ said at 278:

> If s 90 is to play its part in achieving the 'essential objective' of abolishing internal customs barriers and in guaranteeing equality as regards the customs and excise duties which the people of the Commonwealth are to bear, it must be construed as restricting to the Parliament the sole legislative power to impose duties of customs and excise and to grant bounties on the production of goods ... If s 122 authorised the creation of a legislature for an internal territory with the powers referred to in s 90, it would be a Trojan horse available to destroy a central objective of the federal compact ...

[9.4.53C]   Capital Duplicators Pty Ltd v Australian Capital Territory (No 2)
(1993) 178 CLR 561

The Business Franchise ('X' Videos) Act 1990 (ACT) established a licensing scheme in the ACT for the sale of 'X' rated videos. Wholesale and retail sellers of 'X' rated videos were required to obtain a licence, which was renewable on a monthly basis. The fee system had three components: a 'basic fee' payable at the establishment of the licence; an 'advance fee' payable at the time of the first grant of the licence; and a 'franchise fee' payable with each subsequent licence renewal. The advance fee and the franchise fee were both calculated according to the value of sales during a particular month, although the relevant monthly period for the purposes of calculation differed. The advance fee was calculated by reference to the month for which the licence was granted or renewed. The franchise fee was determined according to the month which was two months prior to the month for which the renewal was sought.

The licensing system aimed to avoid imposing the fee twice in relation to the same videos. Hence the wholesalers' licence fees were calculated according to the wholesale value of the videos supplied during the relevant month. The retail fees were calculated according to the value of videos the retailer offered for sale in the relevant month, and which it manufactured or were supplied to it, otherwise than in accordance with the wholesale licence. The fee was calculated at a rate of 40 per cent of the wholesale value of the videos. In order to obtain a licence, the licensee was required to be a fit and proper person, determined according to various factors including: bankruptcy or liquidation; past convictions; and past contraventions of this Act and of the Publications Control Act 1989 (Cth) and the Taxation (Administration) Act 1987 (Cth).

A vendor of 'X' rated videos challenged the legislation on the basis that the fee structure it imposed amounted to a duty of excise, power over which was exclusive to the Commonwealth. Having decided in *Capital Duplicators Pty Ltd v Australian Capital Territory (No 1)* (1992) 177 CLR 248 that s 90 applied to the territories, the court proceeded to consider the substantive issues. Questions were referred to the court pursuant to s 18 of the Judiciary Act 1903 (Cth), the first of which was whether the licence fees imposed by the Act were invalid as duties of excise under s 90.

Mason CJ, Brennan, Deane and McHugh JJ: [584] The variety of views which have been expounded about the meaning of 'duties of excise' since *Peterswald* and the shifts in judicial opinion with respect to s 90 reflect the fact that the critical words of the section had no clearly established meaning when the Constitution was brought into existence.

[587] [S]ince *Parton*, there has been little support for the view that an excise is confined to a tax on, or by reference to, the local production or manufacture of goods. In *Dennis Hotels*, Fullagar J was alone in expressing that opinion. [(1960) 104 CLR at 555–6] Murphy J again was alone in stating a similar view in *Logan Downs Pty Ltd v Queensland*. [(1977) 137 CLR at 84–5] And, more recently, Toohey and Gaudron JJ expressed the same opinion in *Philip Morris*. [(1989) 167 CLR at 478–80] But that is the only support for the narrow view of 'duties of excise' that has been expressed in all the cases since *Parton*.

[588] Ranged against these expressions favouring a return to a narrow definition of excise is the very substantial weight of judicial opinion since *Parton*. ...

[589] The submissions advanced by the defendants and South Australia deny the proposition that 'duties of customs and of excise' in s 90 exhaust the categories of taxes on goods. Those submissions accept that a tax which, in form or even in substance, imposes a duty on the importation of goods or on the local production or manufacture of goods would be within the scope of s 90. But a tax which does not fall within either of those categories but which imposes a duty indifferently on all goods (whether imported or locally produced or [590] manufactured) is said to be outside the scope of s 90. These propositions were rejected expressly and, in our respectful opinion, rightly by Dixon CJ and Windeyer J in *Dennis Hotels*. [(1960) 104 CLR at 540, 600–1] Moreover, they are inconsistent with the purpose which Dixon J attributed to s 90 in *Parton* and which has been attributed to s 90 by subsequent judgments in this court. Adhering to that view of the purpose of s 90, the term 'duties of customs and of excise' in s 90 must be construed as exhausting the categories of taxes on goods. That leaves the question whether a tax on goods should be classified as a duty of customs to the extent to which it applies to imported goods and a duty of excise to the extent to which it applies to goods of local production or manufacture. Some support can be found for this distinction. However, once it is accepted that duties of excise are not limited to duties on production or manufacture, we think that it should be accepted that the preferable view is to regard the distinction between duties of customs and duties of excise as dependent on the step which attracts the tax: importation or exportation in the case of customs duties; production, manufacture, sale or distribution — inland taxes — in the case of excise duties. It is unnecessary in this case to consider taxes on the consumption of goods.

The very limited support manifested since *Parton* and, more particularly, since *Bolton v Madsen*, for a return to the narrow concept of excise is a telling argument against reconsideration of the broader interpretation which has prevailed since *Parton*. What is more, the case for reconsideration invites a return to a narrow concept of excise similar to the *Peterswald* definition which, for reasons already discussed, was discarded over forty years ago.

In that time, federal financial arrangements have been designed and implemented on the basis of the interpretation given by this court to s 90. To desert that interpretation now would have [591] widespread practical ramifications and generate extraordinary confusion. That argument against reconsideration would not prevail if it were clear that the interpretation for which the Territory and South Australia contend is correct. However, that is certainly not the case. Indeed, as we have indicated, we consider that that interpretation is fundamentally mistaken and involves a denial of what has, since Dixon J's judgment in *Parton*, been generally and (in our view) correctly accepted as the essential nature of a duty of excise for the purposes of our Constitution. In that regard, it must be stressed that, putting to one side the judgments of Murphy J and Toohey and Gaudron JJ to which we have referred, recent disagreement within the court about duties of excise has not been about whether the nature of a duty of excise was correctly identified by Dixon J in *Parton*. It has been about whether, in determining whether a particular statutory impost is a duty of excise for the purposes of s 90, one should have regard to 'the substance of the operation of the statute, rather than merely its form'. [*Dickenson's Arcade* (1974) 130 CLR 177]

Reconsideration of Dennis Hotels and Dickenson's Arcade

Rejection of the case for a return to a narrow concept of excise entails a rejection of the argument that *Dennis Hotels* and *Dickenson's Arcade* should be reconsidered in order to define more narrowly the nature of a duty of excise and thereby cut back the operation of s 90 of the Constitution. It should be apparent from what has been said above that we see more theoretical force in an argument that *Dennis Hotels* and *Dickenson's Arcade* should be reopened for the purpose of enabling reconsideration of the question whether, as a matter of the substance of the operation of the relevant statutory provisions rather than of mere form, the challenged licence fees in those cases should be characterised as duties of excise. However, it was not argued on behalf of any party or intervener in the present case that, even if the court was not prepared to adopt a narrower view of the nature of a duty of excise, *Dennis Hotels* and *Dickenson's Arcade* should nonetheless be reopened and overruled. Nor, on balance, do we think that they should be. For one thing, there are some grounds for treating tobacco and alcohol products as constituting a special category of goods for the purpose of considering whether what purports to be a licensing fee under a regulatory regime should be characterised as a duty of excise. For another, there are very strong practical [592] reasons why the rule of *stare decisis* should be observed in relation to those decisions. Not only was the authority of *Dennis Hotels* acknowledged in *Bolton v Madsen*, but also that decision was itself followed in the unanimous decision in *Anderson's Pty Ltd v Victoria*. Later, in *Dickenson's Arcade*, the court refused to depart from *Dennis Hotels* and, subsequently, in *H C Sleigh*, the court followed and applied the two earlier decisions. Since then, the court has twice refused to reconsider the correctness of *Dennis Hotels* and *Dickenson's Arcade*.

In *Philip Morris*, the most recent instance in which there was a refusal to reconsider the two decisions, the court refused to do so by a majority of six Justices to one. After refusing to reconsider the correctness of the earlier decisions, the court heard other arguments as to the effect of those decisions. In disposing of those arguments, the members of the court gave different reasons for supporting the two earlier decisions ... The diversity in the reasons given for not disturbing the earlier decisions is not an adequate ground for now disregarding the significance of the court's repeated refusal to depart from *Dennis Hotels* and *Dickenson's Arcade*. It is true that those reasons do not support *H C Sleigh* with the same cogency as they support *Dennis Hotels* and *Dickenson's Arcade*. All that means, however, is that, if a fee imposed in purported conformity with *H C Sleigh* were of sufficient magnitude to deny a regulatory character to the law which imposes it, the validity of the fee would require close consideration.

In refusing to reconsider the franchise decisions relating to liquor and tobacco, the court has recognized the fact that the States (and the Territories) have relied upon the decisions in imposing licence fees upon vendors of liquor and tobacco in order to finance the operations of government. Financial arrangements of great importance to the governments of the States have been made for a long time on the faith of these decisions. [*Evda Nominees*; *Philip Morris* (1989) 167 CLR at 438, 443, 489–90] If the decisions were to be overruled, the States and the Territories would be confronted with claims by the vendors of liquor and tobacco for the recoupment of licence fees already paid. That would certainly be the case if the court were to hold that such licence fees could not properly be characterized as no more than the imposition of a licence fee for the privilege of engaging in the relevant activity. Hence, considerations of certainty and the ability of legislatures and governments to make arrangements on the faith of the court's interpretation of the Constitution are formidable arguments against a reconsideration of *Dennis Hotels* and *Dickenson's Arcade*.

For the reasons stated, the case for a reconsideration of those decisions has not been made out.

Mason CJ, Brennan, Deane and McHugh JJ outlined the licensing regime established by the legislation and continued:

[596] *Validity of the Act*

The foregoing summary of the provisions of the Act reveals that the legislation cannot be described merely as a regulatory scheme in which the licensing fees are simply an element in an overall regime of controlling the distribution of 'X' videos to the public. The principal elements of the legislation are directed to the raising of revenue rather than to the creation of a regulatory scheme designed to protect the public.

There is no restriction whatsoever in the Act on the class of videos which can be sold; any video, no matter how violent or pornographic, may be sold. Nor is there any restriction on the class of purchasers; the Act does not preclude the sale of any video to children. Likewise, there is no restriction on advertising or display. And the conditions to be satisfied by an applicant for a licence under s 5 relate more obviously to the capacity of the applicant to pay the fees than to the protection of the public in connection with the distribution of violent and pornographic videos. Accordingly, the Act falls outside the category of regulatory schemes affecting liquor and tobacco which Mason CJ and Deane J held in *Philip Morris* could support the exaction of a licence fee on the footing that it is not an excise.

Furthermore, the size of the fee (40 per cent) is larger than the fee exacted in the other franchise cases and clearly exceeds the cost of implementing the scheme. No endeavour was made to justify the size of the fee on that score. Indeed, the true nature of the exaction is to be discerned from s 21 which refers to the fee being 'payable in relation to the supply or offer for retail sale' of the videos. [597] Hence, the purpose of exacting the licensing fees is not simply regulatory but has a very substantial revenue purpose.

In the view of Brennan J in *Philip Morris*, the fact that the legislative scheme is not regulatory and the substantial size of the fee are factors which are relevant in the characterization of the licence fee as an excise. In addition, the advance fee, being calculated by reference to sales made under the licence, plainly is an exaction made on a step in the process of distribution under the licence. And, though the franchise fee is calculated by reference to sales made in a past period, that period is no more than two months earlier than the licence period, each being for one month only. The proximity of the prior period to the period of the licence is a factor pointing in the direction of an excise because the transactions in the past period may well provide a reliable forecast of the transactions which will occur during the currency of the licence. [*Philip Morris* (1989) 167 CLR 399] Thus, the exaction is imposed not merely on the taxpayer's past dealings with the goods but in circumstances in which the magnitude of the past dealings with the goods is a likely indicator of the measure of the taxpayer's dealings with the goods during the term of the licence. With the exception of the non-regulatory character of the licensing scheme, the same factors would, on the view of McHugh J in *Philip Morris*, [(1989) 167 CLR 399] lead to the view that the exactions in the present case are excise duties.

In the result, in the light of the reasoning of the members of the court in *Philip Morris*, the conclusion is inevitable that certain licence fees imposed by the Act are an excise.

Dawson J : [599] The exercise which the defendants seek to have the court undertake is similar to that undertaken in *Cole v Whitfield* in relation to s 92 of the Constitution ...

Dawson J decided that leave ought to be granted to reconsider the definition of excise duties. He said that the narrow view in *Peterswald v Bartley* **[9.4.7]** was not based upon the (now discredited) reserved powers doctrine (178 CLR at 600); and that, to be consistent, the broad approach should include consumption taxes and business franchise fees because they, like distribution taxes which were included, had the same effect as production or manufacturing taxes: 178 CLR at 601. Moreover, the broad approach, without the addition of a strict criterion of liability test, made it difficult to distinguish an excise duty from other taxes: 178 CLR at 601. Dawson J said the narrow view was well supported in the authorities and by commentators: 178 CLR at 602–5. His Honour continued:

[605] The divergence of opinion upon the scope of an excise duty for constitutional purposes would, I think, in itself justify a review of the authorities. But, having regard to the preparedness of the court in *Cole v Whitfield* to undertake such a review in order to settle a far from unrelated issue, it seems to me that it cannot now reject the call for it to do so in relation to s 90. Not only is the issue a vexed one, but it is of high consequence to the States ... The effect of the decision in *Parton v Milk Board (Vic)* was to establish a conception of an excise duty which has the capacity to encompass all taxes on commodities. This potential for expansion was checked for a time by the application of the criterion of liability test. But that test no longer offers any practical constraint and even the franchise cases have been held by a majority to be artificially based and, on the view of some, to be at best justified as an historical anomaly. ...

[606] It is now trite that in general usage the word 'excise' has never had any certain connotation. Even in 1901 the word was used in England to describe a miscellany of heterogeneous taxes, not necessarily taxes upon goods, from which inland revenue was

derived. It is obvious, however, that the term 'duties of excise' was used in a restricted sense in the Constitution and upon the assumption that it could and would be given a precise meaning. ...

The Convention Debates were held in an Australian setting in which duties of excise were confined in the various colonies to taxes on the manufacture and production of spirits, beer and tobacco, the amount of the tax being determined by the quantity or value [607] manufactured or produced. See Mills, *Taxation in Australia*, (1925), pp 54, 81–2, 108–11, 138, 156–7, 182–3. ...

It has been accepted in other judgments that the term 'duties of excise' had in 1901 a special meaning in Australia.

It is against this background that the Convention Debates must be read. Although hardly conclusive, I think that they support the view that 'duties of excise' were understood to be duties chargeable upon the local manufacture and production of commodities. ...

[608] The view expressed by Griffith CJ in *Peterswald v Bartley* is also confirmed by contemporary commentators, notably, Quick and Garran ...

[609] Nor was it a matter of accident that the term 'duties of excise' was chosen as an expression bearing a confined meaning. The particular problem confronting those responsible for the drafting of the relevant provisions arose from the desire to create a common external tariff which would bind the States together in a customs union while at the same time creating a free trade area amongst the States by the elimination of internal customs duties and other restrictions. The protectionist effect of a common external tariff, which was the necessary feature of a customs union, could be undermined by the imposition, State by State, of differing duties of excise upon locally produced goods. The imposition of excise duties would diminish or extinguish the protection which customs duties were intended to confer upon locally produced goods. Although there was no consensus at federation on the desirable level of protection, there was consensus that setting a level should be a federal matter. For similar reasons, with certain limited exceptions, it was necessary to place within the exclusive province of the Commonwealth bounties on the production or export of goods. Thus, what I have called elsewhere [*Philip Morris Ltd v Commissioner of Business Franchises (Vic)* (1989) 167 CLR at 466] the twin objectives of a common tariff and interstate freedom of trade were to be served by ss 90 and 92 operating in conjunction.

The difference between excise duties and other taxes within the context of s 90 is to be seen in the purpose served by that section. That purpose is to secure the customs union to which the States agreed in the Constitution by ensuring a uniform policy with respect to external tariffs, whether free trade or protectionist. A tax should be characterized as an excise duty if it imposes a different level of tax on goods produced overseas and home-produced goods. It is this difference which determines the extent of protection (if any) for local production and manufacture.

In *Dickenson's Arcade Pty Ltd v Tasmania* [(1974) 130 CLR at 218–20; 2 ALR at 491–3] Gibbs J identified three different lines of thought which led to the conclusion finally reached in *Parton v Milk Board (Vic)* that the description of 'excise duties' given in *Peterswald v Bartley* was too narrow [610] and that a tax imposed upon the distribution of a commodity by a person who was not its producer or manufacturer could be an excise.

First, there was the theory, to which I have already referred, that a tax on the sale of goods can be regarded as a method of taxing their production or manufacture ...

In truth, every tax paid by a producer or distributor of goods has a tendency to be passed on to the extent that market forces allow and to increase the price of the goods ... That may be said of taxes such as land tax, payroll tax and even income tax levied upon the producers or distributors of goods. The tendency of a tax to be passed on and to increase the price of goods does not, therefore, serve to differentiate between excise duties and other taxes.

A different emphasis was placed on the matter by Dixon J in *Parton v Milk Board (Vic)* and represents the second line of thought identified by Gibbs J in *Dickenson's Arcade Pty Ltd v Tasmania*. [(1974) 130 CLR at 218–20]

Dawson J referred to the notion that the purpose of the section was to give parliament control over the taxation of commodities.

[611] It may be observed, with the greatest of respect, that his Honour's assumption is not warranted by anything which appears in Ch IV of the Constitution nor, for that matter, in any contemporary discussion of the subject ... If those framing the Constitution had wished to place in the hands of the Commonwealth the exclusive power to control the taxation of commodities they could have done so, but they did not and it was unnecessary to do so for the achievement of the objectives which they had in mind ...

[612] In *Hematite Petroleum Pty Ltd v Victoria* [(1983) 151 CLR at 616–17] Gibbs CJ pointed out that upon any view s 90 confers upon the Commonwealth Parliament only a very limited power to control the economy. Clearly within the province of the States are various taxes, such as payroll tax, or controls, such as quotas on production, which can affect the production or manufacture of goods. Moreover, there are measures available to the States, such as tax concessions, reduced freight charges or assistance in the provision of infrastructure, to encourage production ...

[I]t does not appear that the Commonwealth was intended to have exclusive power over domestic production and manufacture of goods and the supply of goods to the domestic market, any more than it has exclusive control over taxes which affect the production and manufacture of goods. Not only is production affected by the matters I have just described, but the supply of goods may be affected by the regulation of transport, health and safety, and a number of other matters within the province of State legislatures, some of which are beyond Commonwealth legislative power.

I might add that it has never been suggested, nor could it be, that the aim of federation was to create economic unity within the [613] Commonwealth ... State policies which legitimately affect resource allocation inevitably give rise to economic distortions. An economic distortion may be defined as 'any policy which interferes with the resource allocation functions of the market'. That means that it is not possible to eliminate all economic distortions in a federation. Necessarily, there is a tension between the advantages of complete economic integration and the political values which led the people of Australia to seek a federal rather than a unitary system of government. The problem in interpreting s 90, as with s 92, is to identify those distortions which the section proscribes and those which it does not. ...

[614] The third reason for departing from *Peterswald v Bartley* was said to be that the expression 'duties of excise' could not be confined to taxes on production and manufacture [*Dickenson's Arcade Pty Ltd v Tasmania* (1974) 130 CLR at 219] ... Since *Parton v Milk Board (Vic)* it has been accepted that an excise duty does not extend to a tax upon consumption ... Once it is accepted that s 90 must be confined, the only safe guide to its true meaning is the purpose which lies behind s 90. That purpose is indicated by the history of the section, its context and even by the express words of s 93 which, in speaking of duties of excise, restrict them to 'duties of excise paid on goods produced or manufactured in a State'.

I have already referred briefly to the view expressed by Murphy J but it is necessary to return to it in more detail because, although it departs from authority, it reflects, in my opinion, a correct interpretation of s 90. In *Hematite Petroleum Pty Ltd v Victoria* he said: [(1983) 151 CLR at 638]

> In the Australian Constitution an excise is a tax on production (including manufacture). State excise is a tax on production within the State. State customs duty is a tax on goods produced outside and (then) imported into the State. Section 90 prohibits State taxation which discriminates between goods produced in the State and those produced outside the State, and prohibits State bounties on production (or export). The constitutional concept of excise forbidden to the States is limited to taxes on production within the State; it does not extend to taxes on distribution or consumption unless these are in substance taxes on production within the State. In general, a tax on wholesale or retail sale which does not discriminate between goods on the

basis of their production within or without the State, is neither customs nor excise. In general a sales tax applied indiscriminately on all goods or on a class or classes of goods, wherever produced, would not contravene s 90 as an excise or a customs duty. I say in general, because a tax may in reality be a tax on production, even if expressed to be a sales tax. For example, a sales tax restricted to a particular commodity produced only or substantially only in the State, [616] might be in substance, though not in form, a tax on the production of that commodity in the State.

... I would, however, query whether an excise duty is confined to a tax upon production within the relevant State. [617] ... I can see no reason, questions of power and the application of s 92 aside, why a State tax upon the local production of goods, albeit production outside the State, should not constitute a duty of excise. Such a tax may interfere with the intended effect of an external tariff on goods of the same kind no less than a tax upon goods produced within the State and so be within the aim of s 90. But it is a question which is not, practically speaking, likely to arise and may be left for another day.

For constitutional purposes an excise duty is a tax which falls selectively upon the local production or manufacture of goods. Where the tax is imposed by reference to a step taken in the production or manufacture of goods, its character as an excise duty will ordinarily be clear even if the duty is not payable until after the step has been taken. But a tax may be expressed to be imposed upon a step subsequent to production or manufacture and yet in substance be a tax upon production or manufacture and so be an excise duty. For example, a tax upon sale by a producer or upon the first sale after production may be an excise duty if it selects only sales by the local producer or sales which are linked to local production so that the basis of the selection is local production. On the other hand, a tax upon all sales does not tax production or manufacture and for that reason is not an excise duty ...

Applying the narrow view of excise to the facts of the case Dawson J concluded that the imposts were not an excise: 134 CLR at 619.

[619] [T]hey are taxes upon sale or hire (both wholesale and retail include hiring by definition) and apply whether the goods sold or hired are locally manufactured or produced or imported. For that reason, the tax is a tax upon 'the sale of the goods as existing articles of trade and commerce, independently of the fact of their local production' and is not an excise duty. In fact, it does not appear whether the 'X' videos sold or hired in the Australian Capital Territory are wholly produced or manufactured locally or whether they include imported items. However, that is of no consequence because the legislation does not impose the tax, either in substance or in form, upon local manufacture or production.

~~~

[9.4.54] Toohey and Gaudron JJ delivered a joint judgment in which they endorsed the narrow view of excise duties; namely, that they were taxes that discriminated between commodities locally produced and other commodities. That view of excise duties served the purpose of s 90. They expressly endorsed (178 CLR at 629) the approach of Murphy J in *Logan Downs Pty Ltd v Queensland* (1977) 137 CLR 59 at 84 [9.4.27]:

In general, taxes imposed without regard to the place of production or manufacture are neither duties of customs nor duties of excise. The essence of each duty is the tendency to discriminate between goods locally produced and other goods.

Toohey and Gaudron JJ said that their approach to s 90 was:

... consistent with the approach taken in *Cole v Whitfield*, namely, to identify the purpose of the section which, in the case of s 92, is to strike down laws which impose discrimination of a protectionist nature. Likewise, s 90 strikes down such laws in relation to Australian exports and imports, that is, State taxation measures which discriminate against goods manufactured or produced in Australia (178 CLR at 631).

They said that the licence fees imposed by the Act were taxes upon commodities; but, because they were imposed whether the videos sold or hired were manufactured locally or imported, there was no discrimination and the tax was not a duty of excise: 178 CLR at 631–2.

Notes

[9.4.55] In *Philip Morris Ltd v Commissioner of Business Franchises* (1989) 167 CLR 399 **[9.4.47]**, Toohey and Gaudron JJ had said that the 'overwhelming weight of authority' favoured the narrow definition of excise: 167 CLR at 480. This assertion was explicitly denied in *Capital Duplicators Pty Ltd v Australian Capital Territory (No 2)* (1993) 178 CLR 561 **[9.4.53C]** by Mason CJ, Brennan, Deane and McHugh JJ who said that there had been 'little support for the view that an excise is confined to a tax on, or by reference to, the local production or manufacture of goods': 178 CLR at 584. Dawson J said the narrow view was well supported in the authorities and by commentators: 178 CLR at 602–5. Which statement is correct? Does it matter? How great should the weight of authority be in order for the court to uphold a particular precedent, or to reverse its previous positions? Compare the approach of the court in the excise cases with its approach to precedent in the implied freedom of communication matters: see *Lange v Australian Broadcasting Corporation* (1997) 189 CLR 520 **[11.3.3C]**, **[11.3.13C]**. What other factors weigh in the consideration of constitutional interpretation?

[9.4.56] In *Capital Duplicators Pty Ltd v Australian Capital Territory (No 2)* (1993) 178 CLR 561 **[9.4.53C]**, Mason CJ, Brennan, Deane and McHugh JJ referred to the need to maintain the *Parton* doctrine because 'federal financial arrangements have been designed and implemented on the basis of' it. To do otherwise would 'generate extraordinary confusion'. How tenable is this as a justification, in view of the fact that it is the states and territories themselves which would benefit from a reinterpretation of *Parton v Milk Board (Vic)* (1949) 80 CLR 229 **[9.4.10]** which reversed that decision and reverted to the position in *Peterswald v Bartley* (1904) 1 CLR 497 **[9.4.7]**? Lindell has pointed out that any expansion of state and territory revenues could only cause confusion to the states in a positive sense: Lindell (1997) p 36.

Federal financial arrangements were substantially altered after the decision in *Ha v New South Wales* (1997) 189 CLR 465 **[9.4.60C]**, in which the High Court maintained the *Parton* doctrine and limited the scope of *Dennis Hotels Pty Ltd v Victoria* (1960) 104 CLR 529 **[9.4.12C]**: see **[9.4.67]**.

[9.4.57] The majority in *Capital Duplicators Pty Ltd v Australian Capital Territory (No 2)* (1993) 178 CLR 561 **[9.4.53C]** said that the 'diversity in the reasons' given in *Philip Morris Ltd v Commissioner of Business Franchises* (1989) 167 CLR 399 **[9.4.47]** for 'not disturbing' the franchise decisions was not adequate ground for now disregarding the significance of the court's repeated refusal to depart from *Dennis Hotels Pty Ltd v Victoria* (1960) 104 CLR 529 **[9.4.12C]** and *Dickenson's Arcade Pty Ltd v Tasmania* (1974) 130 CLR 177 **[9.4.29C]**: 178 CLR at 592. Is there any point at which a constitutional doctrine becomes so diluted or weakened by the lack of judicial consensus as to its basis, that its authority is undermined? Why, apart from the reasons given in the cases regarding precedent, and apart from any federal financial stability, was the High Court so reluctant to overrule those decisions?

[9.4.58] In a continuation of the narrowing of the franchise cases, the majority in *Capital Duplicators Pty Ltd v Australian Capital Territory (No 2)* (1993) 178 CLR

561 **[9.4.53C]** drew upon the majority opinions in *Philip Morris Ltd v Commissioner of Business Franchises* (1989) 167 CLR 399 **[9.4.47]** to construct criteria which would determine when a tax, modelled upon the *Dennis Hotels Pty Ltd v Victoria* formula, would constitute an excise. These included: alcohol and tobacco being in a 'special category' of goods; the regulatory or revenue-raising nature of the legislation; the size of the licence fee; and the proximity of the past period used to calculate the licence fee: 178 CLR at 592, 596–7.

[9.4.59]   In *Capital Duplicators Pty Ltd v Australian Capital Territory (No 2)* (1993) 178 CLR 561 **[9.4.53C]**, Dawson J argued that the historical evidence, as well as constitutional context and economic considerations, supported the view that the purpose of s 90 was only to give the Commonwealth the power to protect its tariff policy. He said the Convention Debates 'were held in an Australian setting in which … excise was confined … to taxes on the manufacture and production of spirits, beer and tobacco' (178 CLR at 606), and that the purpose of the section was to ensure a customs union. In this context the only requirement was that tariff policy be uniform, not that it be necessarily free trade or protectionist: 178 CLR at 609. He said that the assumption that the purpose of s 90 was to give the Commonwealth control over commodity taxation was 'not warranted by anything which appears in Ch IV of the Constitution, nor for that matter, in any contemporary discussion of the subject': 178 CLR at 611. His Honour also took issue with the broad purpose approach to s 90 because, in his view, it ignored the effect which other taxes, such as land, payroll and even income tax upon producers or distributors of goods, could have.

[9.4.60C]   **Ha v New South Wales**
                          (1997) 189 CLR 465

Sections 28–30 of the Business Franchise Licences (Tobacco) Act 1987 (NSW) prohibited the sale of tobacco, by wholesale or retail, without a licence. Licences were issued on application under s 35 of the Act. Section 41(1)(a) and (c) provided a formula, similar to that considered in *Dennis Hotels Pty Ltd v Victoria* (1960) 104 CLR 529 **[9.4.12C]**, for calculating the amount payable for a retail or wholesale licence. The fee consisted of $10 plus a specified percentage of the value of tobacco sold in the 'relevant period', which was defined to mean 'the month commencing 2 months before the commencement of the month in which the licence expires'. The specified percentage payable as part of the licence fee was increased from 30 per cent in 1989 to 100 per cent in 1995. Section 47 of the Act required sellers of tobacco without a licence to pay an amount equal to the fee that would have been payable for the licence if the person had held one, and a penalty equal to twice that amount. Section 46 provided for reassessment of fees which had been assessed incorrectly.

The plaintiffs in the first proceeding did not hold a retail licence under the Act at the time that they conducted a duty-free store in Sydney selling tobacco. A delegate of the Chief Commissioner for Business Franchise Licences (Tobacco) issued a notice of assessment to the plaintiffs under s 47 of the Act. The plaintiffs in the second proceeding held a wholesale licence. The Chief Commissioner's delegate issued a notice of assessment under s 46 of the Act reassessing the fees. The plaintiffs refused to pay the fees and commenced proceedings in the High Court claiming that sections 46 and 47 of the Act were invalid because they imposed a duty of excise and were thus exclusive to the Commonwealth under the Constitution. A case was stated reserving this question for the opinion of the Full Court.

The Attorneys-General of the other states and the Northern Territory and the Australian Capital Territory joined with New South Wales to argue for a reconsideration of the broad view of excise, and, in the alternative, to argue that these imposts were merely fees for a licence to carry on the business of selling tobacco.

Brennan CJ, McHugh, Gummow and Kirby JJ: [490] The principle that an inland tax on a step in production, manufacture, sale or distribution of goods is a duty of excise has been long established. As a criterion of a duty of excise, it was expressed by Kitto J in *Dennis Hotels* [(1970) 104 CLR 529 at 559] and adopted by a unanimous Court in *Bolton v Madsen.* [(1963) 110 CLR 264 at 273] It can be traced back to the judgments in *Parton* [(1949) 80 CLR 229 at 252–253, 260, 261] and, before that, to the judgment of Dixon J in *Matthews v Chicory Marketing Board (Vict)* [(1938) 60 CLR 263 at 291–304]. As Brennan J said in *Philip Morris Ltd v Commissioner of Business Franchises (Vict)*: [(1989) 167 CLR 399 at 445]

> If there be any rock in the sea of uncertain principle, it is that a tax on a step in the production or distribution of goods to the point of receipt by the consumer is a duty of excise.

[491] The proposition that was not clearly established before *Philip Morris* was that the character of a tax required a consideration of the substantive operation as well as the text of the statute imposing the tax.

To support the overturning of such a long and consistent line of authority, the defendant's submissions needed to show a clear departure from the text of the Constitution. They submitted that *Parton* had departed without warrant from what they identified as the narrow view of 'duties of excise' expressed by Griffith CJ, speaking for the Court in *Peterswald v Bartley.* [(1904) 1 CLR 497 at 509] The defendants sought to show that departure by reference to the words of s 90 which identify 'production or export of goods' as the only subjects of bounties, to s 55 which draws a sharp distinction between laws imposing duties of customs and laws imposing duties of excise, and to s 93 which specifically applies duties of customs to 'goods imported into a State' and duties of excise to 'goods produced or manufactured in a State'.

To assess the validity of these arguments, it is necessary to see the provisions of ss 90 and 93 in the context of Ch IV of the Constitution and to understand the operation which Ch IV was designed to have at the time of Federation. Chapter IV deals with 'Finance and Trade'. While taxes can and do affect trade, their immediate effect is to raise revenue. While the intended effect of s 90 on trade has often been invoked to illuminate the meaning of the term 'duties of excise' in s 90, it should not be forgotten that one of the chief purposes of Ch IV was to provide for the financial transition of the Colonies into the States of the Commonwealth and for the revenues required by the Commonwealth. Prior to Federation, colonial revenues were derived chiefly from duties of customs and (except in Western Australia and the Northern Territory of South Australia) duties of excise. On the imposition of uniform duties of customs by the Commonwealth at 4.00 pm on 8 October 1901, the power to impose such duties passed exclusively to the Commonwealth except in the case of Western Australia which, by s 95 of the Constitution, was permitted to levy customs duty on a reducing scale over a period of five years 'on goods passing into that State and not originally imported from beyond the limits of the Commonwealth'.

Brennan CJ, McHugh, Gummow and Kirby JJ referred to the 'transitional scheme of finance' contained in ss 88, 86 87 and 93 of the Constitution, as explained by Mills in *Taxation in Australia*, (1925), pp 200–1. The justices continued:

[492] In the economic sphere, the paramount object of Federation was inter-State free trade with a uniform Tariff in the importation of goods from overseas, and so the preparation of a Tariff became the most urgent task of the new Commonwealth Government.

Section 93 prescribed the basis of accounting to the respective States for the duties which were collected by the Commonwealth. Consumption of goods within a State was prescribed to be the event which entitled that State to a credit for the amount of customs and excise duty collected on those goods by the Commonwealth. Goods to which s 93 applied that were consumed in a State were either imported into [493] another State or locally produced or manufactured in another State. That dichotomy served, for practical purposes, as the basis for identifying the revenues for which the Commonwealth was required to account to the State in which those goods were consumed. Section 93 was not concerned with duties of excise imposed otherwise than on production or manufacture in another State since, in practice, the agreed allocation of revenue was in respect only of customs duties or duties of excise on production or manufacture collected in the other State. It may be that there were no other inland taxes on goods that were of any significance at that time. However that may be, s 93 throws no light on the connotation of the term 'duties of excise' in s 90. In particular, s 93 does not imply that to be a duty of excise, an impost must be a tax on goods the discrimen of liability to which is their production or manufacture in Australia.

Although duties of excise were in practice levied on goods of local production or manufacture in the Australian Colonies, the review of the history of the word 'excise' by Dixon J in *Matthews v Chicory Marketing Board (Vict)* [(1938) 60 CLR 263 at 299] 'does not disclose any very solid ground for saying that, according to any established English meaning, an essential part of its connotation is, or at any time was, that the duty called by that name should be confined to goods of domestic manufacture or production'. His Honour noted that in Tasmania in 1829 duties of excise were levied indifferently on spirits of Tasmanian origin and on spirits imported from New South Wales. Blackstone identified an excise duty as:

> an inland imposition, paid sometimes upon the consumption of the commodity, or frequently upon the retail sale, which is the last stage before the consumption.

... There is no common use of the term 'excise' in the Convention Debates which might illuminate its meaning, save that it does not include the fees for a licence to carry on a business which, in England, were sometimes called excise licences. What is apparent, with respect to the financial position of the Colonies, is that it was understood at the time that in [494] becoming States what had been their principal sources of revenue would be withdrawn. ...

It is clear that an objective of the movement to Federation was 'inter-colonial free trade on the basis of a uniform tariff' as this Court pointed out in *Cole v Whitfield* [(1988) 165 CLR 360 at 386]. That objective could not have been achieved if the States had retained the power to place a tax on goods within their borders. If goods that attracted a State tax were imported into the State from outside the Commonwealth, Commonwealth tariff policy would have been compromised by the imposition of a State tax. The second paragraph of s 92 and the third paragraph of s 95 (by limiting the period of its operation) show [495] that such a tax was alien to the scheme of Ch IV. If a State tax were imposed on goods brought into the State having been produced or manufactured elsewhere in the Commonwealth, the tax would affect the freedom of trade in those goods [*Bath v Alston Holdings Pty Ltd* (1988) 165 CLR 411] and might be a duty of customs on the entry of the goods into the taxing State. If a State tax were imposed on goods of local production or manufacture within the State, it would be a duty of excise on any view of the term. As State power to tax goods whatever their place of production or manufacture was given up to the Commonwealth, Dixon J was surely right to say in *Parton*: [(1949) 80 CLR 229 at 260]

> In making the power of the Parliament of the Commonwealth to impose duties of customs and of excise exclusive it may be assumed that it was intended to give the Parliament a real control of the taxation of commodities and to ensure that the execution of whatever policy it adopted should not be hampered or defeated by State action.

The defendants' submission is that the exclusivity of the Commonwealth power to impose duties of excise has a more modest purpose and is designed merely to protect the integrity of the tariff policy of the Commonwealth. The history of s 90 denies that hypothesis although that was the original purpose in mind during the 1891 Convention. The level of protection given to local production or manufacture depended at the time of Federation — and, indeed, before and since that time — on the disparity between duties of customs on imported goods and duties of excise on goods of local production or manufacture. When the matter was debated at the 1891 Convention, the resolution tied duties of excise to goods of the same kind as those subject to duties of customs. The resolution agreed to at that Convention read as follows:

> That in order to establish and secure an enduring foundation for the structure of a federal government, the principles embodied in the resolutions following be agreed to:

(3) That the trade and intercourse between the federated colonies, whether by means of land carriage or coastal navigation, shall be absolutely free.

(4) That the power and authority to impose customs duties and duties of excise upon goods the subject of customs duties and [496] to offer bounties shall be exclusively lodged in the federal government and parliament, subject to such disposal of the revenues thence derived as shall be agreed upon.

So long as the objective of the Convention was limited to prescribing the powers needed to create a disparity between the tax on imported goods and the tax on goods of local production or manufacture, the insertion of the words 'upon goods the subject of customs duties' was appropriate. But at the Adelaide Convention in 1897, Sir George Turner moved an amendment to omit the qualifying phrase in order to enlarge the power of the Commonwealth Parliament. Although Mr McMillan had advocated the retention of the phrase in 1891, in 1897 he accepted that 'it would be as well not to do anything that would restrict the power of the Federal Parliament'. The amendment was agreed so that, both by intention and by expression, the exclusive power to impose duties of excise was conferred on the Parliament as a free-standing power. It was capable of exercise in conjunction with the exclusive power to impose customs duties in order to further either protectionism or external free trade but the exercise of the power was not to be confined to the fulfilment of either purpose. The history of s 90 denies any necessary linkage between the exclusivity of the power to impose duties of excise and Commonwealth tariff policy. ...

The dichotomy between laws imposing duties of customs and laws imposing duties of excise in s 55 of the Constitution is satisfied by the dichotomy between laws imposing a tax on the importation of goods and laws imposing an inland tax on some dealing with goods ...

[497] So far as it goes, it can be accepted that a purpose of s 90 is to give the Commonwealth fiscal control over imports, domestic production and exports. But free trade within the Commonwealth would not have been ensured by exclusive federal fiscal control of imports, domestic production and exports. As earlier noted, the imposition of State taxes upon other inland dealings with goods as integers of commerce, even if those taxes were not protectionist, would have created impediments to free trade throughout the Commonwealth. Why should s 90 be construed so as to subvert an objective which Federation was designed to achieve? [*Capital Duplicators Pty Ltd v Australian Capital Territory* (1992) 177 CLR 248 at 276, 279] It is immaterial that the States retain taxing and other powers the exercise of which might affect the overall costs of production, sale or distribution of goods and ultimately be shared by consumers; [*Browns Transport Pty Ltd v Kropp* (1958) 100 CLR 117 at 129] what is material is that the States yielded up and the Commonwealth acquired to the exclusion of the States the powers to impose taxes upon goods which, if applied differentially from State to State, would necessarily impair the free trade in those goods throughout the Commonwealth. [*Capital Duplicators (No 2)* (1993) 178 CLR 561 at 585] Section 51(ii) ensured that such taxes when imposed by the Parliament would be imposed uniformly throughout the Commonwealth.

The defendants' submissions now seek to reclaim the taxing powers ceded to the Commonwealth by a simple device in legislative drafting. So long as a State taxing statute taxes the sale or distribution of imported goods and goods of local production or manufacture indifferently and equally, the statute, it is said, cannot be characterised as a law imposing duties of excise. This submission proceeds on the footing that a criterion of liability must be local production or manufacture and that a statute which imposes a tax indifferently on goods irrespective of their origin does not impose a duty of excise. If this submission were accepted, the State power of taxation would extend in effect to the taxation of any commodity provided the taxing statute is not expressed to tax solely goods of local production or manufacture. The importation of an insignificant quantity of the [498] commodity would permit State taxation of the commodity provided it applied indifferently to the imported quantity and the quantity that is locally produced. In the present case, for example, even if the substantive effect of the tax were found to burden Australian production or manufacture of tobacco, the importation of a small percentage of the tobacco sold in Australia would permit the imposition of the tax under a State law. If accepted, the submission would frustrate whatever purpose might be attributed to s 90. That approach to the characterisation of laws impugned for contravention of s 90 was rejected as far back as *Peterswald v Bartley* [(1904) 1 CLR 497 at 511] itself.

In considering the validity of laws of this kind we must look at the substance and not the form. ...

When a constitutional limitation or restriction on power is relied on to invalidate a law, the effect of the law in and upon the facts and circumstances to which it relates — its practical operation — must be examined as well as its terms in order to ensure that the limitation or restriction is not circumvented by mere drafting devices. In recent cases, this Court has insisted on an examination of the practical operation (or substance) of a law impugned for contravention of a constitutional limitation or restriction on power. On that approach, even if the narrower view of 'duties of excise' were accepted, the question whether the imposts on the sellers of tobacco under the Act burden Australian-produced tobacco products would **[499]** have to be answered. However, for reasons stated above, the question is whether the imposts are an inland tax on a step in the distribution of tobacco products.

If it were not for the factors to which reference will be made in considering what have been known as the franchise cases, the defendants' submissions could and would have been dismissed by reference simply to the line of authority following *Parton* and culminating in *Capital Duplicators [No 2]*. No further analysis of the arguments supporting those submissions would have been called for. The repetition on this occasion does nothing to enhance their cogency, despite the care and vigour with which they were presented. *Evda Nominees Pty Ltd v Victoria* [(1984) 154 CLR 311] and *Capital Duplicators [No 2]* [(1993) 178 CLR 561 at 590–593] show that mere repetition of arguments does not require the Court to reopen settled authority to reconsider the arguments, at least where 'the States have organized their financial affairs in reliance on them'. [*Evda Nominees Pty Ltd v Victoria* (1984) 154 CLR 311 at 316] In the present case, however, the States, fully appreciating that the attack on the doctrine based on *Parton*, if successful, would destroy the reasoning in the franchise cases and conscious of the factors on which the plaintiffs rely to limit the protection which the franchise cases give to the States' tax base, chose to invite the Court to re-examine the *Parton* doctrine which has been accepted for nearly half a century.

Perhaps the States and Territories were conscious of the risk that the taxes in question in this case might be held to fall outside the protection offered by the franchise cases. However that might be, as the present case requires a declaration of the limits of the protection offered by the franchise cases so as to accord with the *Parton* doctrine, it seems right to accede to the defendants' application to reopen the *Parton* line of cases. But the correctness of the doctrine they establish must now be affirmed. Therefore we reaffirm that duties of excise are taxes on the production, manufacture, sale or distribution of goods, whether of foreign or domestic origin. Duties of excise are inland taxes in contradistinction from duties of customs which are taxes on the importation of goods. Both are taxes on goods, that is to say, they are taxes on some step taken in dealing with goods. In this case, as in *Capital Duplicators [No 2]* [(1993) 178 CLR 561 at 590], it is unnecessary to consider whether a tax on the consumption of goods would be classified as a **[500]** duty of excise. In the light of this doctrine, the second major proposition in the defendants' submissions falls for consideration.

2 Are the licence fees or the amounts payable under ss 46 and 47 of the Act merely fees for a licence to carry on a business?

This is substantially the same question as that which arose in *Coastace Pty Ltd v New South Wales*, [(1989) 167 CLR 503] in which imposts under the legislation as it stood between 28 January and 27 July 1987 were held to be valid. Since 1987, as we have seen, the variable component of licence fees calculated under s 41 of the Act have been increased by increasing the specified rate from 30 per cent of the value of tobacco sold in a relevant period to 100 per cent.

The imposts in *Coastace* were held to be valid by a majority whose opinions were markedly dissimilar. In particular, Mason CJ and Deane J upheld the imposts for reasons which their

Honours had stated more extensively in their judgment in *Philip Morris*. In that case, their Honours expressed the view that liquor and tobacco were commodities that invite regulatory control and, that being so, they were prepared to accept the correctness of *Dennis Hotels* and *Dickenson's Arcade* on a special basis ...

In *Philip Morris*, Brennan J in dissent declined to accept that approach, saying: [(1989) 167 CLR 399 at 459]

> The point is whether licence fees for dealing in liquor or tobacco are to be sequestered from the operation of general principles by which the character of fees for licences to deal in other commodities is ascertained. There are, in my opinion, three reasons why a negative answer must be given to that question. First, the Constitution makes no distinction among commodities for excise purposes. Second, if the nature of the commodity were relevant to the character of a tax related to dealings in it, liquor and tobacco are historically the prime excisable commodities. Third, if liquor and tobacco had been thought to be commodities to which special principles applied, the decisions in *Dennis Hotels* and *Dickenson's* [501] *Arcade* would have been distinguished on that ground in *H C Sleigh*. Thus, respectfully, I am in agreement with Stephen J in *H C Sleigh* [(1977) 136 CLR 475 at 496] on this point and in disagreement with the contrary view expressed by Mason CJ and Deane J. I would hold that liquor or tobacco are in no special category which denies to a tax on any step in their production or distribution the character of a duty of excise. However, the nature of these commodities is such that licensing schemes which affect them may be truly regulatory (as Taylor J held in *Dennis Hotels*) and that feature of a licensing scheme is relevant to the character of a fee exacted for a licence.

We are respectfully unable to accept the basis on which Mason CJ and Deane J accepted *Dennis Hotels* and *Dickenson's Arcade*. Were it not for that basis, Mason CJ and Deane J would have joined Brennan and McHugh JJ in holding the imposts in *Philip Morris* and *Coastace* to be duties of excise and, on that account, invalid. The concordance in their Honours' views was manifested in their joint judgment in *Capital Duplicators (No 2)*.

It is therefore unnecessary to canvass again the question whether the decisions in the franchise cases can be reconciled with the doctrine based on *Parton*. That exercise was undertaken by Brennan J in *Philip Morris* [(1989) 167 CLR 399 at 451–464] and we agree with the analysis and conclusions in his Honour's judgment. In *Philip Morris*, McHugh J was also in dissent. His Honour rejected the authority of the earlier franchise cases as support for any proposition save the validity of the imposts upheld in those cases. [(1989) 167 CLR 399 at 496, 497–498, 499] We do not apprehend that, in the result, there is any dissimilarity in the approach taken by the two Justices in dissent. Both Brennan J [(1989) 167 CLR 339 at 463] and McHugh J [(1989) 167 CLR 399 at 501] pointed to the proximity of the relevant period to the licence period, the shortness of the licence period, the size of the tax imposed *ad valorem* and the fact that it is to be borne only once in the course of distribution as indicia that were inconsistent with the tax being merely a licence fee having — to use the test stated by Kitto J in *Dennis Hotels* [(1960) 104 CLR 529 at 560] — 'no closer connexion with production or distribution than that it is exacted for the privilege of engaging in the process at all'. Brennan J added a reference [(1989) 167 CLR 399 at 463] to 'the revenue raising and non-regulatory purpose of the scheme'.

Those factors are present and relevant to the character of the licence [502] fees and the amounts payable under the Act in this case. Moreover, an amount equal to 75 or 100 per cent of the value of tobacco sold during a relevant period is levied by the Act. That amount could not conceivably be regarded as a mere fee for a licence required as an element in a scheme for regulatory control of businesses selling tobacco. The Act contains minimal provisions controlling businesses selling tobacco, chiefly those contained in s 36(2) which authorises the refusal of a licence to a person who has been convicted of an offence under s 59 of the Public Health Act 1991 (NSW) or, pursuant to s 36(2AA), if the Chief Commissioner is satisfied that 'the issue of a licence would be contrary to the public interest'. Subject to these provisions, renewal of a licence requires merely the due payment of the fees exacted. The licence fee is manifestly a revenue-raising tax imposed on the sale of tobacco during the relevant period. The licensing system is but 'an adjunct to a revenue statute'. [*Dennis Hotels* (1960) 104 CLR 529 at 576 per Taylor J]

Brennan CJ, McHugh, Gummow and Kirby JJ referred to the revenues raised under the Act between 1986 and 1996, concluding with $852 million in 1996: 189 CLR at 502.

The revenue to be derived from inland taxes on goods was ceded by the States to the Commonwealth under the Constitution. Although the early franchise cases admitted that *ad valorem* imposts of small amounts might properly be classified merely as licence fees having 'no closer connexion' with duties of excise, the States and latterly the Territories have sought to re-establish the pre-Federation tax bases of the Colonies by once more placing taxes on goods under a formula known as the *Dennis Hotels* formula.

If the theory on which the States and Territories acted was that a 'fee for a licence to carry on the business ... quantified by reference to the value of the quantity of [the commodity] sold during a period preceding that in respect of which the licence is granted' [*HC Sleigh* (1977) 136 CLR 475 at 491 per Gibbs J] (the *Dennis Hotels* formula) denied any impost the character of a duty of excise, the theory was misunderstood. Such a proposition fails to take account of the important qualification which Kitto J himself expressed [503] in *Dennis Hotels*, [(1960) 104 CLR 529 at 563] namely, that the exaction is 'not in respect of any particular act done in the course of the business'. The proposition that a tax imposed in accordance with the *Dennis Hotels* formula was necessarily cloaked with immunity from an attack under s 90 was rejected in *Philip Morris* [(1989) 167 CLR 399] by six members of the Court. It cannot be prayed in aid to support the imposts challenged in this case.

The maintenance of constitutional principle evokes a declaration that the *Dennis Hotels* formula cannot support what is, on any realistic view of form and of 'substantial result' [*Attorney-General (NSW) v Homebush Flour Mills Ltd* (1937) 56 CLR 390 at 412], a revenue-raising inland tax on goods. The States and Territories have far overreached their entitlement to exact what might properly be characterised as fees for licences to carry on businesses. The imposts which the Act purports to levy are manifestly duties of excise on the tobacco sold during the relevant periods. The challenged provisions of the Act are beyond power.

We are conscious that this judgment has the most serious implications for the revenues of the States and Territories. But, in the light of the significantly increasing tax rates imposed by State and Territory laws under the insubstantial cloak of the *Dennis Hotels* formula, the Court is faced with stark alternatives: either to uphold the validity of a State tax on the sale of goods provided it is imposed in the form of licence fees or to hold invalid any such tax which, in operation and effect, is not merely a fee for the privilege of selling the goods. Section 90 of the Constitution, by prescribing the exclusivity of the Commonwealth's power to impose duties of excise, resolves the question. So long as a State tax, albeit calculated on the value or quantity of goods sold, was properly to be characterised as a mere licence fee this Court upheld the legislative power of the States to impose it. [*Evda Nominees Pty Ltd v Victoria* (1984) 154 CLR 311] But once a State tax imposed on the seller of goods and calculated on the value or quantity of goods sold cannot be characterised as a mere licence fee, the application of s 90 must result in a declaration of its invalidity.

Brennan CJ, McHugh, Gummow and Kirby JJ said that it was contrary to the judicial process to prospectively overrule the franchise cases (if they had come to that conclusion): 189 CLR at 503, 504.

[504] In any event, the decision of this Court is not to overrule *Dennis Hotels* or *Dickenson's Arcade*. They may stand as authorities for the validity of the imposts therein considered. Properly understood, the test of 'no closer connexion' as stated by Kitto J in *Dennis Hotels* and explained by Brennan J in *Philip Morris* [(1989) 167 CLR 399 at 445–446] is maintained. It is not necessary now to reconsider *H C Sleigh*, though the reservation expressed as to that case in *Capital Duplicators (No 2)* [(1993) 178 CLR 561 at 593] will not have passed unnoticed. However, the consequence of rejecting the view that alcohol and tobacco are commodities that are in a special category for s 90 purposes means that *Philip Morris* and *Coastace* were wrongly decided.

Brennan CJ, McHugh, Gummow and Kirby JJ said that provisions of ss 36(1), 41(1), 41(3), 43, 45 and 47(1) of the Business Franchise Licences (Tobacco) Act 1987 (NSW) were invalid because they imposed duties of excise within s 90 of the Constitution.

Dawson, Toohey and Gaudron JJ referred to s 93 of the Constitution, a transitional provision providing that duties of excise collected in one state upon goods passing into another state for consumption shall be taken to have been collected not in the former but in the latter state. They said the words, are 'duties of excise paid on goods produced or manufactured in a State and afterwards passing into another State for consumption', were plainly intended to be descriptive of what is meant by the term 'duties of excise' as it is used in the Constitution: 189 CLR at 505–506. Their Honours continued:

Dawson, Toohey and Gaudron JJ: Not only does s 93 give the clearest indication that duties of excise are restricted to duties upon goods produced or manufactured in a State, but there is a compelling explanation for that restriction which is to be found in the circumstances which gave birth to s 90 itself. Two of the principal objectives of federation were, on the one hand, the creation of a common external tariff which would bind the States together in a customs union and, on the other, the creation of a free trade area internally by the elimination of customs duties at State borders and other restrictions upon the freedom of interstate trade. The degree, if any, to which the common external tariff would be protectionist was not a matter of consensus but it was agreed that it should be a matter for the Commonwealth Parliament. To the extent that it might be protectionist it would be undermined by the imposition, State by State, of excise duties on locally produced goods. The imposition of excise duties would diminish or extinguish the protection which customs duties were intended to confer upon locally produced goods. For similar reasons, subject to s 91, it was necessary to exclude the States from the granting of bounties upon the production or export of goods. Section 90 was central to the achievement of a common external tariff. Section 92 was the chief means by which an internal free trade area was to be achieved.

The correlation between customs duties and excise duties is made manifest by s 90. It was only upon the imposition by the Commonwealth of uniform customs duties that the power of the Parliament to impose customs and excise duties and to grant bounties became exclusive. It was only then that State laws imposing customs or excise duties or offering bounties ceased to have effect. The same correlation is to be seen throughout the Constitution — nowhere is excise mentioned in the text without an adjacent reference to customs.

Once it is accepted, as it is, that the term 'duties of excise' is used in s 90 in a confined sense, the confines must be found in the purpose of that section. The purpose was not to confer power to impose duties of customs and excise. The power to make laws with respect to taxation was already given to the Commonwealth Parliament by s 51(ii). The purpose was to confer exclusivity in the exercise of the power. Exclusivity was necessary lest the policies lying behind the [507] common external tariff be impaired. So far as excise duties were concerned, it was unnecessary to extend the exclusivity beyond duties imposed upon goods when produced or manufactured, because a tax imposed upon some later step in the distribution of the goods, for example — would not operate to impair any policy of protection to be found in an external tariff in respect of those goods.

Nevertheless, in *Parton v Milk Board (Vict)* [(1949) 80 CLR 229] this Court, by a majority, extended the meaning of 'duties of excise' in s 90 to include not only a tax upon the production or manufacture of goods, but also a tax upon any step in the distribution of goods before they reach the hands of the ultimate consumer. This was to widen the exclusivity of the Commonwealth's power to impose a tax upon goods beyond the purpose of s 90 and it is therefore not surprising that the justification for the extension was not sought in that section. The justification advanced involved two strands of reasoning. ...

The two propositions ... are, first, that s 90 was intended to give the Commonwealth Parliament control of the taxation of goods and, secondly, that a tax upon a step in the distribution of goods produces the same effect as a tax upon its manufacture or production.

Both of those propositions have been questioned in subsequent cases (not to mention academic commentary) with such force that they cannot now, in our view, be accepted.

In the first place, there is no basis for the assumption that s 90 was intended to confer an exclusive power to impose duties of customs and [508] excise for the purpose of giving the Commonwealth real control of the taxation of commodities and thereby power to effectuate its economic policies. If it had been intended to confer upon the Commonwealth exclusive power to tax commodities it would not have been difficult to frame a provision to that effect. But s 90 is not such a provision and in confining the exclusivity for which it provides to the imposition of duties of customs and excise it is apparent that it is part of a constitutional framework designed to achieve the objectives of a customs union. So much is suggested by the Convention Debates and by colonial legislation as it stood in the lead up to federation. Thus, a number of judgments have accepted that the term 'duties of excise' had a special meaning in Australia at 1901.

Moreover, even taking the wider view of s 90, it could afford the Commonwealth only a limited power to implement economic policy with respect to the production and manufacture of goods. The States retain substantial power to affect the production and manufacture of goods within their borders by various means including taxation (other than customs or excise duties but including the taxation of services), the regulation of such matters as transport, health and safety or even the imposition of quotas. In so far as the Commonwealth has power to intrude upon those areas to the exclusion of the States, it is to be found principally in s 51(i), (ii) and (iii) of the Constitution, coupled with the operation of s 109, not in the exclusivity conferred by s 90.

Secondly, it is plainly incorrect to assert that a tax upon a commodity at any point in the course of distribution before it reaches the consumer has the same effect as a tax upon its manufacture or production. Not only is it an incorrect assertion but it fails to comprehend that the purpose of making the power to impose excise duties exclusive to the Commonwealth was to prevent impairment by the States of the common external tariff. A tax upon the manufacture or production of goods increases the cost of those goods without effecting a corresponding increase in the cost of imported goods of the same kind. Any protection afforded by customs duties imposed upon the imported goods is thereby reduced. But a tax imposed upon a step [509] in the distribution of goods which falls indiscriminately upon locally produced and imported goods does not have that effect.

No doubt in saying that a tax imposed on production or manufacture and a tax imposed upon a step in the distribution of goods had the same effect, Dixon J had in mind the early classification of duties of excise as indirect taxes. An indirect tax was said to be one that has a tendency to be passed on in the price of goods whereas a direct tax was said to be one that tends to be borne by the person upon whom it is imposed. The distinction between indirect and direct taxes is now recognised as being economically unsound because market forces determine whether a tax will be passed on or not and there is nothing inherent in a particular tax which enables it to be classified as direct or indirect. Thus all taxes, even income tax, will be passed on to a greater or lesser extent depending upon market forces and the dichotomy between direct and indirect taxes is no longer seen as a satisfactory means of distinguishing between excise duties and other taxes. Nevertheless, the distinction lingers in the notion to be seen in the cases that an excise duty is at bottom a tax upon the production or manufacture of goods because the price to the consumer has an ultimate effect upon the demand for the goods and hence upon their production or manufacture. However, just as it is not possible to draw any practical distinction between direct and indirect taxes, so it is not possible to discern any direct or necessary connection between the ultimate price of goods and their cost of production or manufacture. Again, market forces will determine the effect of price upon demand and hence upon production or manufacture. For that reason it is not possible to say that a tax upon a step in the distribution of goods is in effect a tax upon their production or manufacture. And, of course, a tax which falls upon a step in the distribution of imported and locally produced goods alike can hardly be regarded as a tax upon the production of the imported goods.

Once the reasons given in *Parton* [(1949) 80 CLR 229] for extending the meaning of duties of excise are recognised as unsound, the extension is without any justification in economic or constitutional terms. In particular, it disregards the correlation between duties of customs and duties of excise which reveals the true purpose of s 90 and which identifies the limits placed by the Constitution upon the term 'duties of excise'.

The expansion of the concept of 'duties of excise' in *Parton* made it difficult to distinguish excise duties from other taxes. This is exemplified by the franchise cases which, speaking broadly, [510] established that a licence or franchise fee, exacted for the privilege of carrying on a business of selling goods, did not, even though a tax, constitute an excise duty where it was calculated by reference to the value of sales during a period preceding the period of the licence. The licence or franchise fee was, of course, not a tax upon the manufacture or production of the goods but that had been abandoned as the test of an excise duty. Instead, what emerged as supporting the franchise cases was a test known as the 'criterion of liability' test ...

This was thought for a time to be sufficient to support the franchise cases, because the legislation imposing the tax chose as the criterion of liability, not the taking of a step in the distribution of goods, but the carrying on of a business. However, the criterion of liability test came to be criticised upon the basis that it seized upon the statutory form of the tax and ignored substance. Eventually, the test was abandoned as the exclusive determinant of an excise duty, although the later cases have failed to reveal the nature of the substance which was sought. Excise duties were no longer confined to taxes upon local manufacture or production. They no longer needed to be calculated by reference to the quantity or value of the goods involved. The distinction between direct and indirect taxes was recognised as unsustainable, but the notion persisted that duties of excise must somehow affect production or manufacture and the exception of a tax upon consumption was, somewhat illogically, continued. What remained was that an excise duty must be a tax upon goods but that provided no distinguishing feature because not all taxes upon goods — a tax upon ownership, for example — would, even on the broadest view of the term, constitute excise duties.

Whilst the notion lingered that excise duties are at bottom taxes upon local manufacture or production, it became increasingly difficult to apply. Not only was the distinction between direct and indirect taxes discredited, but the expansion of the meaning of excise duties to encompass a tax upon the sale or distribution of goods removed any distinction between locally manufactured goods and imported goods. [511] A tax imposed upon locally manufactured goods and imported goods alike did not operate to discriminate against locally manufactured goods and rendered irrelevant the distinction between local manufacture and importation for the purpose of determining whether a tax constituted a duty of excise. As a result, increasing emphasis came to be placed upon the assumption of Dixon J in *Parton* [(1949) 80 CLR 229 at 260] that s 90 'was intended to give the Parliament a real control of the taxation of commodities and to ensure that the execution of whatever policy it adopted should not be hampered or defeated by State action.' Of course, were that assumption correct, then the search for the meaning of the term 'duties of excise' in s 90 would cease, for the exclusivity of Commonwealth power to impose duties of customs and excise would extend to all taxes upon goods and all taxes upon goods which were not customs duties would be excise duties. But, as we have said, no justification for the assumption is to be found either in s 90 or elsewhere in the Constitution, or in history, and it has not gained in force by its conversion from an assumption to an assertion.

Nevertheless, the assertion has been taken up and built upon in recent judgments. For example, in *Capital Duplicators Pty Ltd v Australian Capital Territory (No 2)*, [(1993) 178 CLR 561 at 585] Mason CJ, Brennan, Deane and McHugh JJ expressed the view that 'ss 90 and 92, taken together with the safeguards against Commonwealth discrimination in s 51(ii) and (iii) and s 88, created a Commonwealth economic union, not an association of States each with its own separate economy'. However, the union which s 90 was designed to achieve was a customs union, not an economic union if what is meant by that term is a single economy. Clearly the States were to retain considerable power to influence the economy within their boundaries. It is a feature of the federation that State policies may legitimately affect resource allocation. The purpose of a customs union is to ensure a uniform policy with respect to external tariffs, whether free trade or protectionist. That was the purpose of s 90. Freedom of trade internally was to be achieved, not by common external tariffs, but by ensuring the free movement of people, goods and communications across State boundaries. That was the purpose of s 92. As was recognised in *Cole v Whitfield*, [(1988) 165 CLR 360 at 391] the enemies of internal free trade are border taxes, discrimination and preferences. Neither s 92 nor s 51(ii) and (iii) nor s 88 sought to achieve an integration of the Australian economy such that conditions of trading were uniform throughout the country ...

[512] The States could not engage in discrimination of a protectionist kind against interstate goods, but otherwise they were left free to encourage or discourage trade within their boundaries, including trade in commodities, by such means as they saw fit provided that they did not do so by infringing the Commonwealth's exclusive power to impose duties of customs and excise and to grant bounties on the production or export of goods. That exclusivity was conferred to protect the common external tariff, not as part of a plan to create a single economy. Plainly it was inadequate for that purpose, either on its own or in combination with other sections of the Constitution, and could not have been intended to perform that function.

A State tax which fell selectively upon imported goods would, of course, be a customs duty and be prohibited by s 90. A State tax which fell selectively upon goods manufactured or produced in that State would be an excise duty and be prohibited by s 90. A State tax which discriminated against interstate goods in a protectionist way would offend s 92 and be invalid. But those three instances do not exhaust the categories of taxes upon goods and do not support, as a legal conclusion, the proposition that the Commonwealth was intended to have an exclusive power to tax commodities. That is a suggestion which appears to be made in this case, but clearly a State tax — a tax upon sale, for example — which does not fall selectively upon imported goods or locally produced or manufactured goods and does not discriminate against interstate goods, offends against none of the prohibitions imposed by the Constitution. In particular, such a tax would not affect freedom of interstate trade because all goods would compete in the State on the same footing: there would be no discrimination of a protectionist kind.

Dawson, Toohey and Gaudron JJ referred to Fullagar J in *Dennis Hotels Pty Ltd v Victoria* (1960) 104 CLR 529 at 556; Murphy J in *HC Sleigh Ltd v South Australia* (1977) 136 CLR 475 at 526–527, *Logan Downs Pty Ltd v Queensland* (1977) 137 CLR 59 at 84 and *Hematite Petroleum Pty Ltd v Victoria* (1983) 151 CLR 599 at 638; Toohey and Gaudron JJ in *Philip Morris Ltd v Commissioner of Business Franchises (Vict)* (1989) 167 CLR 399 at 479–480 and *Capital Duplicators Pty Ltd v Australian Capital Territory (No 2)* (1993) 178 CLR 561 at 630–631; and Dawson J in *Capital Duplicators Pty Ltd v Australian Capital Territory (No 2)* (1993) 178 CLR 561 at 609.

[514] Whether a tax which falls upon locally produced goods discriminates against those goods in favour of imported goods is a question of substance, not form. It is the answer to that question which, upon the correct view of duties of excise, determines whether the tax is an excise duty. The clearest case is, of course, where a customs duty exists so as to afford a measure of protection to the home product and a selective tax upon a product of that kind extinguishes or substantially diminishes the protection. But there would be discrimination with a selective tax even where there was no relevant customs duty. The tariff policy in that case must be that imported goods of the relevant kind compete with locally produced goods upon an equal footing in the home market and a tax imposed selectively upon the local production of those goods would burden them in relation to imported goods and so impair the policy.

Moreover, it is not of significance that a non-selective tax falls upon locally produced goods or substantially upon locally produced goods because there are no imported goods or substantially no imported goods of the relevant kind. In that situation there would be no impairment of the tariff policy. The tax would remain a non-selective tax and the mere absence of imported goods would not render it discriminatory in relation to the home product. ...

In these cases the defendants invite the Court to re-examine the decision in *Parton* with a view to establishing that the validity of the fees imposed in the franchise cases is to be supported upon the basis [515] that an excise duty is a tax which falls selectively upon the local production or manufacture of goods. In our view that contention is correct and we would accede to the re-opening of *Parton* ...

[I]n our opinion, *Parton* cannot be allowed to stand. No question arises whether the overruling of that decision should be merely prospective, but in view of the submission made by the defendants that any overruling of the franchise cases should be prospective only, we should express our agreement with Brennan CJ, McHugh, Gummow and Kirby JJ that this Court has no power to adopt such a course. ...

Dawson, Toohey and Gaudron JJ held that, because the licence fees, regarded as taxes upon goods, fell indiscriminately upon tobacco products regardless of whether they were locally manufactured or produced or were imported, and did not interfere with the Commonwealth's tariff policy, they were not duties of excise.

~~~

Notes

[9.4.61] In *Ha v New South Wales* (1997) 189 CLR 465 **[9.4.60C]**, the majority took up the invitation offered by the states to reassess the correctness of the *Parton* doctrine and firmly rejected the argument that s 90 was confined only to prohibiting to the states the power to impose taxes upon production and manufacture. They reaffirmed the broad view of excise that 'duties of excise are taxes on the production, manufacture, sale or distribution of goods, whether of foreign or domestic origin. Duties of excise are inland taxes in contradistinction from duties of customs which are taxes on the importation of goods. Both are taxes on goods, that is to say, they are taxes on some step taken in dealing with goods': 189 CLR at 499.

[9.4.62] As well as affirming the broad view of what constitutes an excise duty, the majority in *Ha v New South Wales* (1997) 189 CLR 465 **[9.4.60C]** severely limited the scope of the franchise cases, and effectively put an end to the states' and territories' reliance on those devices for revenue collection. The majority overruled *Philip Morris Ltd v Commissioner of Business Franchises* (1989) 167 CLR 399 **[9.4.47]** (189 CLR at 504) and (following the dissent of Brennan and McHugh JJ in *Philip Morris*) said that *Dennis Hotels Pty Ltd v Victoria* (1960) 104 CLR 529 **[9.4.12C]** and *Dickenson's Arcade Pty Ltd v Tasmania* (1974) 130 CLR 177 **[9.4.29C]** 'stood as authorities for the validity of the imposts therein considered': 189 CLR at 504. They were not authority for the proposition, put forward by Mason CJ and Deane J in *Philip Morris* that alcohol and tobacco constituted a special category of goods: 189 CLR at 500–501. Instead, the majority adopted the view of Brennan J in *Philip Morris* when he explained the test of 'no closer connection' stated by Kitto J in *Dennis Hotels*: 189 CLR at 504. The decisions in *Dennis Hotels* and *Dickenson's Arcade* could be reconciled with *Parton* only on the basis of the factors identified by Brennan CJ in *Philip Morris* as relevant to the question whether a tax was imposed in respect of a step in the production or distribution of goods (and hence an excise) or had no closer connection with production or distribution than that it was exacted for the privilege of engaging in either process.

[9.4.63] The majority in *Ha v New South Wales* (1997) 189 CLR 465 **[9.4.60C]** said that s 90 had a revenue-preserving function for the Commonwealth. Brennan CJ, McHugh, Gummow and Kirby JJ said that at federation 'the principal source of revenue would be withdrawn' from the states (189 CLR at 494) and 'one of the chief purposes of Ch IV was to provide ... for the revenues required by the Commonwealth': 189 CLR at 491. The minority disagreed. Dawson, Toohey and Gaudron JJ said the purpose of s 90 'was not to secure to the Commonwealth a revenue base; that is the function of s 51(ii)': 189 CLR at 517. How convincing is the majority's position in light of the existence of a separate head of power vesting the Commonwealth with the ability to raise revenue?

[9.4.64] Similar differences in opinion were evident between the majority and the minority in *Ha v New South Wales* (1997) 189 CLR 465 **[9.4.60C]** on a number of other issues, including:

■ the meaning of s 93 (compare Brennan CJ, McHugh, Gummow and Kirby JJ: 189 CLR at 492–493; with Dawson, Toohey and Gaudron JJ: 189 CLR at 506);

■ the significance of the 1897 amendment (compare Brennan CJ, McHugh, Gummow and Kirby JJ: 189 CLR at 496; with Dawson, Toohey and Gaudron JJ: 189 CLR at 514); and

■ the meaning of 'free trade' (compare Brennan CJ, McHugh, Gummow and Kirby JJ: 189 CLR at 494; with Dawson, Toohey and Gaudron JJ: 510–511).

Does the existence of opposing views on a number of issues critical to the reasoning process undermine the weight given to the decision ultimately reached? Or is this controversy simply the ordinary function of constitutional (and more generally, legal) techniques of argumentation?

[9.4.65] The major point of disagreement in *Ha v New South Wales* (1997) 189 CLR 465 **[9.4.60C]** (indeed, in all the s 90 cases) seems to be about the content of the concept of free trade. Both the majority and the minority share the view that federation was designed to encourage free trade within the Commonwealth: Brennan CJ, McHugh, Gummow and Kirby JJ: 189 CLR at 494; and Dawson, Toohey and Gaudron JJ: 189 CLR at 510–11. However, while the majority said that taxes imposed by states on production and manufacture would necessarily have 'created impediments to free trade throughout the Commonwealth' (189 CLR at 497), the minority said they would not. The difference between the two positions seems to lie in their differing conceptions as to the degree of freedom required for free trade.

Dawson, Toohey and Gaudron JJ identified the union which s 90 was designed to achieve as 'a customs union, not an economic union if what is meant by that term is a single economy'. They said that the Commonwealth's exclusivity in relation to customs and excise duties 'was conferred to protect the common external tariff, not as part of a plan to create a single economy': 189 CLR at 511–12.

The disagreement highlights that the meaning of the term 'free trade' is contested amongst lawyers (as well as amongst economists). One legal commentator has suggested that, of the five commonly-accepted levels of economic integration (from a customs union to a fully unified economic system), the High Court has, in relation to s 92, already chosen a low level of economic integration: Mellors (1991) p 58. On this view, the current interpretation lacks 'symmetry' with its s 92 interpretation: Coper (1992).

[9.4.66] The decision in *Ha v New South Wales* (1997) 189 CLR 465 **[9.4.60C]** was a failure for the states. They could have adopted the safe course of simply arguing that the tobacco licence fee fell within the *Dennis Hotels Pty Ltd v Victoria* (1960) 104 CLR 529 **[9.4.12C]** qualification to the *Parton v Milk Board (Vic)* (1949)

80 CLR 229 **[9.4.10]** doctrine. This would have preserved their limited, but accepted, power to levy the business franchise fee form of tax. Instead they chose to argue a position which, if accepted, would have extended their power to levy taxes by upholding their ability to tax the sale, distribution and possibly consumption of goods. But, as the court itself acknowledged, the option of arguing for a reconsideration of the broad *Parton* view was a high risk strategy:

> In the present case ... the States, fully appreciating that the attack on the doctrine based on *Parton*, if successful, would destroy the reasoning in the franchise cases and conscious of the factors on which the plaintiffs rely to limit the protection which the franchise cases give to the States' tax base, chose to invite the Court to re-examine the *Parton* doctrine which has been accepted for nearly half a century.

In the event the High Court narrowed *Dennis* to its specific facts, and indicated that, were it to hear a challenge to the petrol licence fees, it might not be disposed to find that it fell within *Dennis*: 186 CLR at 504.

[9.4.67] The day after the decision was handed down in *Ha v New South Wales* (1997) 189 CLR 465 **[9.4.60C]** the Commonwealth announced that, '[i]n response to a unanimous request from the States and Territories', it had 'agreed to introduce measures to protect State and Territory revenue': Treasurer, *Press Release,* 6 August 1997. The measures consisted of a complex set of temporary 'safety net' arrangements which provided for an increase in the rate of Commonwealth customs and excise duty on tobacco and petrol, and in the rate of wholesales sales tax on alcohol. The revenue collected by the Commonwealth was to be returned to the states (less administrative costs) as revenue replacement payments: see **[9.6.14]**. Because s 51(ii) of the Constitution requires that any Commonwealth tax must be uniform and cannot discriminate between states **[9.3.1E]–[9.3.18]**, the states and territories agreed to refund any excess revenues (above their respective losses of business franchise fee revenue) to manufacturers, wholesalers and retailers. In addition the package provided for a 100 per cent windfall gains tax to protect the states from claims for refunds of past business franchise fee payments.

A series of legislative changes implemented the rescue package. In relation to tobacco and petrol, the Commonwealth gazetted appropriate increases in tariff rates under the Tariff Act 1925 (Cth). The increased rates were subsequently translated into legislative form in the Customs Tariff Amendment Act (No 3) 1997 (Cth) and the Excise Tariff Amendment Act (No 3) 1997 (Cth). Changes to the method of calculating the tariff on tobacco were introduced in the Customs Tariff Amendment Act (No 5) 1997 (Cth), and Excise Tariff Amendment Act (No 5) 1997 (Cth). The increase in the rate of sales tax on alcohol was provided for in the Sales Tax (Customs) Alcoholic Beverages Act 1997 (Cth). The windfall tax was instituted in three Acts: the Franchise Fees Windfall Tax (Collection) Act 1997 (Cth); the Franchise Fees Windfall Tax (Imposition) Act 1997 (Cth); and the Franchise Fees Windfall Tax (Consequential Amendments) Act 1997. At the same time the Commonwealth introduced the States Grants (General Purposes) Amendment Act 1997 (Cth) to provide for revenue replacement repayments to the states and territories.

[9.4.68] The court has now repeatedly split, over many decades, on the issue of the constitutional meaning of the term 'excise'. After *Ha v New South Wales* (1997) 189 CLR 465 **[9.4.60C]** was decided, one member of the majority (Brennan CJ) and every member of the minority, Dawson, Toohey and Gaudron JJ, retired; and they have been replaced by new justices: Gleeson CJ, Hayne, Callinan and Heydon JJ. If the new appointees were all to take the view of excise held by Gaudron J, then the narrow view could be in the ascendancy again. However, following the decision in *Ha v New South Wales*, the Commonwealth introduced new taxation arrangements **[9.4.67]** on the basis of the broad view. What is the relationship between the constitutional decisions of the court and the political developments embodied in the new taxation arrangements? See **[1.3.1]–[1.3.16]**.

In view of the long history of judicial disagreement, its eventual attempted resolution in *Ha*, and the Commonwealth's legislative response to the case, any court considering the issue in the future would surely be reluctant to disturb the new status quo. This was evident in decisions such as *Evda Nominee Pty Ltd v Victoria* (1984) 154 CLR 311 **[9.4.44]**. What does this indicate about the nature of constitutional decision-making and constitutional precedent? For further discussion of the operation of the doctrine of precedent in the Australian constitutional context see Keyzer (1999).

5 Government loans

[9.5.1] Government borrowing has consistently played an important part in public finance, particularly where substantial capital funds are required for such projects as the purchase of expensive equipment or the construction of a public facility. In Australia, both the Commonwealth and state governments have relied on loans to fund the construction of dams, the upgrading of defence equipment or the expansion of energy resources. The extent of that reliance has diminished in recent years, as a series of surplus Commonwealth budgets have allowed most capital intensive projects to be funded out of revenue.

Nevertheless, the scale of Australian Government borrowings is very substantial. This may be demonstrated by reference to an example. At 30 June 1988, Commonwealth and state borrowings had accumulated a total debt of $50,644 million: 'Government Securities on Issue at 30 June 1988', *Budget Paper No 1*, Table 9. (This represented a reduction in total public debt of $2206 million during the 1987–88 year.) Loans raised during 1987–88 totalled $3568 million, all from Australian sources. Almost all payments out of the Commonwealth's Loan Fund went to the redemption of existing loans: $2661m was paid out to redeem loans in Australia; and $840 to redeem overseas loans: 'The Commonwealth Public Account 1988–89', *Budget Paper No 2*, Table 6.

Ten years later, at 30 June 1998, the total face value of net Commonwealth Government securities on issue stood at $91.8 billion: *Commonwealth Debt Management 1997–98*, p 7. This represented a reduction in debt from $107.3 billion in June 1997: *Commonwealth Debt Management 1997–98*, p 7. Loans raised during 1997–98, again all from Australia, totalled $6,278,670,000. Redemptions of $4,812,200 were made in respect of Australian loans, and $223,000,000 in respect of overseas loans: *1998–99 Budget Paper No 4*, Table 8, 236.

[9.5.2] There was a dramatic reduction in governmental reliance on borrowings over the five years between 1982–83 and 1987–88. In 1982–83, the Commonwealth raised $11,558 million through domestic and overseas loans, of which $2510 million was allocated to state works programs and $2595m to the Commonwealth's defence procurements. When placed in the context of Commonwealth taxation revenues of $40,586 million in 1982–83, the loan revenues can be seen as playing a minor but significant role in government finance: see Hanks (1985) p 189.

However, by 1987–88, Commonwealth taxation revenue was $74,897 million: 'The Commonwealth Public Account 1988–89', *Budget Paper No 2*, Table 1. In that context, net loan revenue (that is, the surplus of borrowings above redemptions) of some $67 million appeared insignificant. This reduction in reliance on borrowings was explained in the context of the Commonwealth's 1988–89 budget, as follows:

> Since 1980–81 and in many years before that, the Commonwealth and State Governments' borrowing requirements have led to annual increases in securities on issue. In 1987–88 the move of the Commonwealth Government budget into surplus and the use of surplus cash balances enabled substantial net redemptions of overseas and domestic debt (*Government Securities on Issue at 30 June 1988, Budget Paper No 1*, p 5).

This reduction in reliance on borrowings has continued over the years. In 1997–98 Commonwealth taxation revenue stood at $133,765,857 (*1998–98 Budget Papers No 4*, Table 4, p 21) while net loan revenue (excluding foreign loans) amounted to $1,243,479,000: *1998–99 Budget Paper No 4*, Table 8, p 236. In 1998, the Commonwealth referred to its negative net funding requirement of $15.2 billion in 1997–98 and commented:

> [T]he Commonwealth had no budget funding need in 1997–98 for a new debt issue program. The maintenance of a modest new issuance program of $2.2 billion ... in 1997–98 reflected broader debt management objectives and was directed at maintaining the liquidity and efficiency of the Commonwealth Government securities market (Treasury, *Commonwealth Debt Management 1997–98*, p 3).

(It should be noted that the Commonwealth's taxation revenue included at estimate for revenues received under safety net arrangements introduced to protect state and territory revenue.)

[9.5.3]   Despite the presently diminished significance of government borrowings as a source of revenue, it is clear that they can play an important role in public finance; not only by meeting a government's immediate needs for capital but also as a tool for influencing interest rates and other aspects of the money market. In the Australian federation, control over government borrowings has been centralised in the hands of the Loan Council, a body set up under the Financial Agreement 1927 (see **[9.5.5E]**) and largely controlled by the Commonwealth.

[9.5.4E]   **Commonwealth Constitution**

105A(1) The Commonwealth may make agreements with the States with respect to the public debts of the States, including —

(a)   the taking over of such debts by the Commonwealth;

(b)   the management of such debts;

(c)   the payment of interest and the provision and management of sinking funds in respect of such debts;

(d)   the consolidation, renewal, conversion, and redemption of such debts;

(e)   the indemnification of the Commonwealth by the States in respect of debts taken over by the Commonwealth; and

(f)   the borrowing of money by the States or by the Commonwealth, or by the Commonwealth for the States.

(2)   The Parliament may make laws for validating any such agreement made before the commencement of this section.

(3)   The Parliament may make laws for the carrying out by the parties thereto of any such agreement.

(4)   Any such agreement may be varied or rescinded by the parties thereto.

(5)   Every such agreement and any such variation thereof shall be binding upon the Commonwealth and the States parties thereto notwithstanding anything contained in this Constitution or the Constitution of the several States or in any law of the Parliament of the Commonwealth or of any State.

(6)   The powers conferred by this section shall not be construed as being limited in any way by the provisions of section one hundred and five of this Constitution.

~~~

[9.5.5E]   **Financial Agreement Act 1927**

This agreement was given legislative approval by the Commonwealth Parliament in the Financial Agreement Act 1928 (Cth) and the Financial Agreement Validation Act 1929 (Cth). It was amended in 1931, 1934 and 1944. A consolidated version of the agreement appears in the schedule to the schedule [sic] to the Financial Agreement Act 1944 (Cth). The following extracts are taken from that version.

Australian Loan Council

3(1)(a) There shall be an Australian Loan Council which shall consist of one representative of the Commonwealth who shall be —

(i)   The Prime Minister of the Commonwealth; or

(ii)   in the absence of the Prime Minister at any time from a meeting of the Council — a Minister nominated in writing by the Prime Minister,

and one representative of each State who shall be —

(iii)   the Premier of that State; or

(iv)   in the absence of the Premier at any time from a meeting of the Council — a Minister nominated in writing by the Premier of that State.

Provided that if, in the opinion of the Prime Minister or of any Premier of a State, special circumstances exist at any time which make it desirable so to do, the Prime Minister or the Premier, as the case may be, may nominate some other person to represent the Commonwealth or the State (as the case may be) as a member of the Loan Council. ...

(3)   The member representing the Commonwealth shall be the Chairman of the Loan Council. ...

(5)   A meeting of the Loan Council may at any time be convened by the member representing the Commonwealth and shall be so convened upon the request of at least three members representing States. ...

(8)   The Commonwealth and each State will from time to time, while Part III of this Agreement is in force, submit to the Loan Council a program setting forth the amount it desires to raise by loans during each financial year for purposes other than the conversion, renewal or redemption of existing loans or temporary purposes. Each program shall state the estimated total amount of such loan expenditure during the year, and the estimated amount of repayments which will be available towards meeting that expenditure. Any revenue deficit to be funded shall be included in such loan program, and the amount of such deficit shall be set out. Loans for Defence purposes approved by

the Parliament of the Commonwealth shall not be included in the Commonwealth's loan program or be otherwise subject to this Agreement.

(9)   If the Loan Council decides that the total amount of the loan program for the year cannot be borrowed at reasonable rates and conditions it shall decide the amount to be borrowed during the year, and may by unanimous decision allocate such amount between the Commonwealth and the States.

Clause 3(10) provides a formula for the distribution of loan funds between the Commonwealth and the states, should the members of the Council fail to arrive at a unanimous decision under cl 3(9).

(14) (a)   If the members of the Loan Council fail to arrive at a unanimous decision on any matter other than the matters in respect of which unanimous decision is required by subclauses (9), (10) and (11) of this clause and sub-clause (2) of Clause 4 of this Agreement, the matter shall be determined by a majority of votes of the members.

      (b)   On every question for decision by the Loan Council the member representing the Commonwealth shall have two votes and a casting vote, and each member representing a State shall have one vote.

(15) A decision of the Loan Council in respect of a matter which the Loan Council is by this Agreement empowered to decide shall be final and binding on all parties to this Agreement.

Future Borrowings of Commonwealth and States

4(1) Except in cases where the Loan Council has decided under sub-clause (2) of this clause that moneys can be borrowed by a State, the Commonwealth, while Part III of this Agreement is in force, shall, subject to the decisions of the Loan Council and subject also to Clauses 5 and 6 of this Agreement, arrange for all borrowings for or on behalf of the Commonwealth or any State, and for all conversions, renewals, redemptions, and consolidations of the Public Debts of the Commonwealth and of the States.

(2)   If at any time the Loan Council by unanimous decision so decides, a State may in accordance with the terms of the decision borrow moneys outside Australia in the name of the State, and issue securities for the moneys so borrowed. The Commonwealth shall guarantee that the State will perform all its obligations to bond holders in respect of the moneys so borrowed. For all the purposes of this Agreement, including the making of sinking fund contributions, the moneys so borrowed shall be deemed to be moneys borrowed by the Commonwealth for and on behalf of that State.

(3)   If any State after the 30th June, 1927, and before this Agreement has been approved by the Parliaments of the Commonwealth and of the States, has borrowed moneys in the name of the State and issued securities for the moneys so borrowed, such moneys shall for all the purposes of this Agreement, including the making of sinking fund contributions, be deemed to be moneys borrowed by the Commonwealth for and on behalf of that State.

(4)   While Part III of this Agreement is in force, moneys shall not be borrowed by the Commonwealth or any State otherwise than in accordance with this Agreement.

Borrowing by States

5(1) For any purpose (including the redemption of securities given or issued at any time for moneys previously borrowed or used in manner stated in this Clause) a State may, while Part III of this Agreement is in force —

      (a)   Subject to any maximum limits decided upon by the Loan Council from time to time for interest, brokerage, discount and other charges, borrow moneys within the State from authorities, bodies, funds or institutions (including Savings Banks) constituted or established under Commonwealth or State law or practice and from the public by counter sales of securities, and

      (b)   use any public moneys of the State which are available under the laws of the State.

(2) Any securities that are issued for moneys so borrowed or used shall be Commonwealth securities, to be provided by the Commonwealth upon terms approved by the Loan Council.

(3) Where any such borrowing or use is solely for temporary purposes, the provisions of this Agreement, other than this clause, shall not apply.

(4) Where any such borrowing or use is not solely for temporary purposes, and Commonwealth securities are issued in respect thereof, the moneys borrowed or used shall be deemed to be moneys borrowed by the Commonwealth for and on behalf of the State, and may be retained by the State. A State may convert securities given or issued at any time by that State for moneys previously borrowed or used in manner stated in this clause. New securities issued on any such conversion shall be Commonwealth securities to be provided by the Commonwealth upon terms approved by the Loan Council. The amount for which such new securities are issued shall be deemed to be moneys borrowed by the Commonwealth for and on behalf of the State.

(5) If the moneys deemed under this clause to be moneys borrowed by the Commonwealth on behalf of a State, together with the amounts raised by the Commonwealth for and on behalf of the State exceed the total amount of loan moneys decided upon by the Loan Council as the moneys to be raised for and on behalf of the State during the financial year in which the money is deemed to be borrowed, the excess shall, unless the Loan Council otherwise decides, be deemed to be moneys received by the State in the following year on account of its loan program for that year.

(6) For the purposes of this clause counter sales of securities shall be deemed to mean sales of securities made at the offices of the State Treasury, and at such other places as may be decided upon by the Loan Council.

(7) The Commonwealth shall not be under any obligation to make sinking fund contributions in respect of moneys borrowed or used pursuant to this clause to meet a revenue deficit of a State, but the provisions of sub-clause (10) of Clause 12 of this Agreement shall apply respectively to all moneys borrowed or used for that purpose. This sub-clause shall not apply to or in respect of any of the loans referred to in sub-clause (11) of Clause 12 of this Agreement.

(8) Except in cases where the Loan Council has otherwise decided under sub-clause (2) of Clause 4 of this Agreement a State shall not have the right to invite loan subscriptions by the issue of a public prospectus.

(9) Notwithstanding anything contained in this Agreement, any State may use for temporary purposes any public moneys of the State which are available under the laws of the State, or may, subject to maximum limits (if any) decided upon by the Loan Council from time to time for interest, brokerage, discount and other charges, borrow money for temporary purposes by way of overdraft or fixed, special or other deposit, and the provisions of this Agreement other than this sub-clause shall not apply to such moneys.

Borrowing by Commonwealth

6(1) For any purpose (including the redemption of securities given or issued at any time for moneys previously borrowed or used in manner stated in this clause) the Commonwealth may, while Part Ill of this Agreement is in force —

    (a) Subject to any maximum limits decided upon by the Loan Council from time to time for interest, brokerage, discount and other charges, borrow moneys within the Commonwealth for authorities, bodies, funds or institutions (including Savings Banks) constituted or established under Commonwealth or State law or practice and from the public by counter sales of securities, and

    (b) use any public moneys of the Commonwealth which are available under the laws of the Commonwealth.

(2)   Any securities that are issued for moneys so borrowed or used shall be Commonwealth securities, to be provided by the Commonwealth upon terms approved by the Loan Council.

(3)   Where any such borrowing or use is solely for temporary purposes, the provisions of this Agreement, other than this clause, shall not apply.

(4)   Where any such borrowing or use is not solely for temporary purposes, and Commonwealth securities are issued in respect thereof, the moneys borrowed or used may be retained by the Commonwealth. The Commonwealth may convert securities given or issued at any time by the Commonwealth for moneys previously borrowed or used in manner stated in this clause. New securities issued on any such conversion shall be Commonwealth securities to be provided by the Commonwealth upon terms approved by the Loan Council.

(5)   If the moneys so borrowed or used are not borrowed or used solely for temporary purposes and Commonwealth securities are issued in respect thereof, and such moneys, together with other moneys borrowed by the Commonwealth for and on behalf of the Commonwealth as part of the total amount of loan moneys decided upon by the Loan Council as the moneys to be raised for and on behalf of the Commonwealth during the financial year in which the securities are issued, exceed such total amount the excess shall unless the Loan Council otherwise decides be deemed to be moneys received by the Commonwealth in the following year on account of its loan program for that year.

(6)   For the purposes of this clause counter sales of securities shall be deemed to mean sales of securities made at the offices of the Commonwealth Treasury, and at such other places as may be decided upon by the Loan Council.

(7)   Notwithstanding anything contained in this Agreement, the Commonwealth may use for temporary purposes any public moneys of the Commonwealth which are available under the laws of the Commonwealth or may, subject to maximum limits (if any) decided upon by the Loan Council from time to time for interest, brokerage, discount and other charges, borrow money for temporary purposes by way of overdraft or fixed, special or other deposit, and the provisions of this Agreement other than this sub-clause shall not apply to such moneys.

~~~

Notes

[9.5.6] The Commonwealth's effective control of public borrowings by all Australian governments depends on its chairing of the Loan Council (cl 3(3)); its inflated voting rights (cl 3(14)(b)); and its control over the arrangement of all borrowings on behalf of the Commonwealth and the states: cl 4(1). The Commonwealth can also raise public loans within Australia, for defence purposes approved by the Commonwealth Parliament or for temporary purposes, without seeking Loan Council approval: cll 3(8), 6(1)(a), 6(7).

The states' ability to borrow money outside the Loan Council procedures is more circumscribed, being limited to borrowings within the relevant state or for temporary purposes: cll 5(1)(a), 5(9). A potential loophole for the states is the fact that the Financial Agreement does not cover borrowings by statutory authorities. However, a series of arrangements between the Commonwealth and states has provided for Loan Council approval of the annual borrowing programs of statutory authorities and local bodies: *1988–89 Budget Paper No 4*, pp 9, 43–4.

[9.5.7] In 1993–94, new Loan Council arrangements were introduced which aimed for a high degree of transparency in public sector finances rather than adherence to strict borrowing limits. The arrangements were 'designed to enhance the role of financial market scrutiny as a discipline on borrowings by the public sector': *1998–99 Budget Papers No 3*, 43.

[9.5.8] In *Bank of New South Wales v Commonwealth* (1948) 76 CLR 1, the High Court considered an argument that the Banking Act 1947 (Cth) was inconsistent with cl 5(9) of the Financial Agreement because, by nationalising the private trading banks, it destroyed the states' right to borrow money on overdraft. Only Rich and Williams JJ accepted that argument; Latham CJ, Starke, Dixon and McTiernan JJ did not (although the first three held the Act invalid on other grounds). Discussing the effect of the Financial Agreement, Rich and Williams JJ adopted Starke J's dictum in *New South Wales v Commonwealth (No 1)* (1932) 46 CLR 155 at 186 that the agreement was:

> ... part of the organic law of the Commonwealth. It can only be varied or rescinded by the parties thereto. Nothing in the Constitution or the Constitutions of the states can affect it or prevent its operation. It creates rights and duties as between the Commonwealth and the States upon and in respect of which the judicial power of the Commonwealth can be exerted (76 CLR at 279–80).

Rich and Williams JJ reviewed the clauses of the agreement and continued at 281:

> It was contended that cll 5(9) and 6(7) were not intended to create contractual rights and obligations, but were in the nature of saving clauses inserted in the agreement to make it clear that it was intended to except from its operation the practice of the States and of the Commonwealth of using for temporary purposes any public moneys which were available and of borrowing money by way of overdraft or fixed, special or other deposit. We accept the opinion already expressed by the Chief Justice and Williams J in *Melbourne Corporation v Commonwealth* (1947) 74 CLR 3 that cl 5(9) (and it necessarily follows cl 6(7)) create positive rights and obligations flowing from the agreement. It necessarily follows from cl 4(4) that the whole of the rights of the Commonwealth and of the States to borrow are included in the agreement and that no such rights exist outside the agreement. There would be a clear breach of cl 4(4) if the States or the Commonwealth borrowed moneys by way of overdraft in excess of the maximum limits decided upon by the Loan Council for interest and other charges. Clauses 5(9) and 6(7) create rights to borrow for temporary purposes by way of overdraft or fixed, special or other deposit and impose obligations on the exercise of these rights. The introductory words 'notwithstanding anything contained in this agreement' cannot have been intended to except cll 5(9) and 6(7) from the agreement altogether, because the subclauses conclude by providing that 'the provisions of this agreement other than this subclause shall not apply to such moneys'. The function of the introductory and concluding words is to make it clear that the rights and obligations of the States and Commonwealth with respect to the kinds of borrowings for temporary purposes described in the subclauses are wholly contained in these subclauses.

6 Commonwealth grants

[9.6.1] The picture which begins to emerge from the material in the preceding four sections is of some degree of Commonwealth dominance of revenue-raising in Australia. The taxation power is now interpreted broadly, and the prohibitions against discrimination or preference are read narrowly. Moreover, the states are excluded, through a broad interpretation of s 90, reaffirmed in *Ha v New South Wales* (1997) 189 CLR 465 **[9.4.60C]**, from imposing a wide variety of commodity taxes. But the picture, constructed as it is out of constitutional decisions, is unfinished. To complete it we need to examine the effect produced by the Commonwealth's use of its grants power, s 96 of the Constitution. That effect has been threefold: first, the Commonwealth used its grants power (and other sources of Commonwealth power) to take over, in 1942, from the states their income tax revenues; second, the Commonwealth used its grants power over some 30 years to discourage the states from resuming the taxation of incomes; and third, the Commonwealth now uses the grants power to support, on a massive scale, state finances. In 1997–98, Commonwealth grants to the states made up 42 per cent of state revenues: Commonwealth Grants Commission, *Annual Report 1997–98*, p 6. That level of support naturally gives to the Commonwealth very substantial power to influence, even to direct, state spending programs. To give the picture more detail, we need to take account of the effective Commonwealth control over public borrowing under the Financial Agreement: see **[9.5.1]–[9.5.8]**; and the apparent breadth of the Commonwealth's spending power: **[9.7.1]–[9.7.15]**.

The overall picture is often described as one of 'vertical fiscal imbalance', under which the Commonwealth raises more revenue than it is required to outlay and the opposite obtains for the states. For example, in 1997–98, the Commonwealth collected 72 per cent of total revenue collected in Australia and yet was responsible for only 57 per cent of outlays. By contrast the states collected 24 per cent of revenue and had outlays of 38 per cent: *1998–99 Budget Paper No 3*, p 13. (The remainder was taken up by local government.)

[9.6.2E]   Commonwealth Constitution

96   During a period of ten years after the establishment of the Commonwealth and thereafter until the Parliament otherwise provides, the Parliament may grant financial assistance to any State on such terms and conditions as the Parliament thinks fit.

~~~

[9.6.3C]   South Australia v Commonwealth
(The *First Uniform Tax* case)
(1942) 65 CLR 373

From the establishment of the Commonwealth in 1901, each of the six Australian states levied income taxes. The Commonwealth first levied an income tax in 1915 and, from that year until 1942, most incomes in Australia were subject to at least two forms of income tax: Commonwealth and state. In the financial year 1940–41, the six states raised £35.5 million and the Commonwealth raised £43.3 million from income taxes.

In June 1941 and in May 1942, the Commonwealth Government requested the states to vacate the field of income tax for the duration of the current war, and to accept compensation by way of financial assistance from the Commonwealth. On each occasion, all six states refused. Accordingly, on 7 June 1942 the Commonwealth Parliament enacted four Acts:

• The Income Tax Act 1942 (Cth) imposed a tax upon incomes at rates rising to 18s in the pound upon annual incomes in excess of £4000. (It was conceded that the revenue which would be raised from this Act would be approximately equal to the total of the revenues raised over the previous year through Commonwealth and state income taxes.)

- Section 31 of the Income Tax Assessment Act 1942 (Cth) inserted a new section, s 221, in the Income Tax Assessment Act 1936 (Cth). This new section forbade a taxpayer from paying state income tax for any year until that taxpayer had paid the Commonwealth income tax owing for the year.
- The States Grants (Income Tax Reimbursement) Act 1942 (Cth) authorised the annual payment, by way of financial assistance to each state, of a grant, upon condition that 'the Treasurer is satisfied that [the] State has not imposed a tax upon incomes' for that year. Each grant was to be equal to the average income tax revenues of that state in two preceding financial years, 1939–40 and 1940–41.
- The Income Tax (War-time Arrangements) Act 1942 (Cth) empowered the Commonwealth Treasurer to serve notices on the Treasurer of each state, requiring the transfer to the Commonwealth of all staff, office accommodation, furniture, equipment and records used by the states for the assessment and collection of income taxes.

Four states, South Australia, Victoria, Queensland and Western Australia, brought actions in the High Court of Australia against the Commonwealth, for a declaration that the Acts were invalid and for an injunction to restrain the Commonwealth from putting the Acts into operation. The plaintiffs' applications for interlocutory injunctions were heard by the Full Court and, by consent, treated as the trial of the actions.

Latham CJ: [409] [T]he controversy before the Court is a legal controversy, not a political controversy. It is not for this or any court to prescribe policy or to seek to give effect to any views or opinions upon policy. We have nothing to do with the wisdom or expediency of legislation. Such questions are for Parliaments and the people. It has been argued that the Acts now in question discriminate, in breach of s 51(ii) of the Constitution, between States. The Court must consider and deal with such a legal contention. But the Court is not authorised to consider whether the Acts are fair and just as between States — whether some States are being forced, by a political combination against them, to pay an undue share of Commonwealth expenditure or to provide money which other States ought fairly to provide. These are arguments to be used in Parliament and before the people. They raise questions of policy which it is not for the Court to determine or even to consider …

Latham CJ said that the Commonwealth Treasurer's second reading speeches on the bills for the four Acts and the Report of a Committee on Uniform Taxation could not be admitted as evidence of the intentions of the Commonwealth Parliament. Only the words of the statutes could express that intention.

[411] *The Acts as a Scheme* — In the first place it is contended by the plaintiffs that the Acts together constitute a 'scheme' directed towards an unlawful object, namely, the exclusion of State Parliaments from the sphere of legislation upon income tax. Reference is made to *Attorney-General for Alberta v Attorney-General for Canada* [1939] AC 117, and to *Deputy Commissioner of Taxation v Moran* [1940] AC 838 at 849; 63 CLR 338 at 341. The contention that an Act which does not refer to or incorporate any other Act, and which when considered by itself is not invalid, may be held to be invalid by reason of the enactment of other Acts, whether valid or invalid, meets many difficulties. Parliament, when it passes an Act, either has power to pass that Act or has not power to pass that Act. In the former case it is plain that the enactment of other valid legislation cannot affect the validity of the first-mentioned Act if that Act is left unchanged. The enactment of other legislation which is shown to be invalid equally cannot have any effect upon the first-mentioned valid Act, because the other legislative action is completely nugatory and the valid Act simply remains valid.

Latham CJ said it was not necessary to examine those questions in the present case because 'the intention to get rid of State income tax and of State income tax departments' was clear in the case of the Tax Act, the Grants Act and the War-time Arrangements Act. He said: 'The legislation which is attacked is not colourable — it admits its character upon its face': 65 CLR at 412.

[412] *The Tax Act* — The Income Tax Act is in its terms an ordinary tax Act, except that it imposes a very high rate of tax. It may be assumed, in favour of the plaintiffs, that the rates of tax which are imposed make it politically impossible for the States to impose further income tax. But it is not possible for the Court to impose limitations upon the Parliament as to the rate of tax which it proposes to impose upon the people. There is no legal principle according to which a tax of 10s in the pound should be held to be valid, but a tax of 11s or 15s or 18s or 20s should be held to be invalid. Indeed, it was not disputed by the plaintiffs that, if the Tax Act had been passed without the Grants Act, it would have been unchallengeable, whatever the result might have been in making it possible for a State to impose or collect income tax ...

The Tax Act is a law with respect to taxation. It simply exacts from citizens a contribution to the public revenue. It contains no provisions relating to any other matter. The argument which was successful in *Barger's* case (1908) 6 CLR 41 (that what professed to be a Tax Act was shown by its own terms not really to be such an Act) is not available here. The Act is merely and simply an Act imposing taxation upon incomes. The Commonwealth power to legislate is subject to certain limitations. There must be no discrimination between States or parts of States (Constitution, s 51(ii)), the [413] requirements of s 55 must be satisfied: See also ss 92, 99, 114 and 117. It is clear that the Tax Act does not infringe any of these provisions. It is argued that the Commonwealth cannot use its taxing power so as to prevent the States exercising their taxing power. It may be conceded that the Commonwealth Parliament has no power to prohibit a State exercising its taxing power. But there is no such prohibition in this Tax Act. As already stated, there is no sure foothold for an argument that the Commonwealth Parliament cannot impose so high a tax in relation to a particular subject matter that there is no room for any additional State impost. This argument was not put by the plaintiffs. ...

[415] *The Grants Act* — It is now necessary to deal with the far-reaching and fundamental general objection which is made to the Tax Act considered in association with the other Acts, but which is particularly directed against the Grants Act.

This objection is based upon the following principle which, it is argued, applies to all Commonwealth legislative powers, namely — the Commonwealth cannot direct its legislative powers towards destroying or weakening the constitutional functions or capacities of a State. (A corresponding rule should, it is said, be applied in favour of the Commonwealth as against the States.) In another form the principle is said to be that the Commonwealth cannot use its legislative powers to destroy either 'the essential governmental functions' or 'the normal activities' of a State.

Latham CJ said that 'the following preliminary comments' could be made on the condition expressed in the Grants Act:

[416] (a) The Act does not purport to repeal State income-tax legislation. The Commonwealth Parliament cannot do this ...

(b) The Grants Act does not require, in order that a State should qualify for a grant, that the State — or rather the State Parliament — should abdicate, or purport to abdicate, its power to impose taxes upon incomes. A State Parliament could not bind itself or its successors not to legislate upon a particular subject matter, not even, I should think, by referring a matter to the Commonwealth Parliament under s 51(xxxvii) of the Constitution ...

(c) The Act does not purport to deprive the State Parliament of the power to impose an income tax. The Commonwealth Parliament cannot deprive any State of that power: see Constitution, ss 106, 107 ...

[417] (d) The Grants Act offers an inducement to the State Parliaments not to exercise a power the continued existence of which is recognised — the power to impose income tax. The States may or may not yield to this inducement, but there is no legal compulsion to yield.

The Commonwealth may properly induce a State to exercise its powers (for example, the power to make roads: see *Victoria v Commonwealth* (1926) 38 CLR 399) by offering a money grant. So also the Commonwealth may properly induce a State by the same means to abstain from exercising its powers ...

But the position is radically different, it is urged, if the so-called inducement practically amounts to coercion ...

This identification of a very attractive inducement with legal compulsion is not convincing. Action may be brought about by temptation — by offering a reward — or by compulsion. But temptation is not compulsion ...

[418] The Grants Act does not compel the States to abandon their legislative power to impose a tax upon incomes. States which do not abstain from imposing [419] income tax cannot be said to be acting unlawfully. There is no command that they shall not impose such a tax.

State Functions and Capacities — It is clear, however, that the Grants Act is intended to bring about the result that the State shall not impose such a tax. The Act therefore must meet the challenge of the plaintiffs that the Commonwealth cannot direct its legislative powers against the constitutional functions or capacities — against the essential functions or the normal activities — of a State.

This statement reminds one who has followed the development of Australian constitutional law of 'the rule in *D'Emden v Pedder* (1904) 1 CLR 91' ...

It is argued for the plaintiffs that the authorities as they now stand leave it open to the Court to hold that, while there is no general principle of exemption of State instrumentalities from the [420] exercise of Federal power, the Federal nature of the Constitution, involving as it does the continued existence of the States, does involve the principle that the Constitution cannot use its legislative powers to destroy or weaken the constitutional functions or capacities or to control the normal activities of the States. It will be convenient to quote certain passages from cases upon which the plaintiffs rely which will show the plaintiffs' contention in its full strength ...

[422] In this case the plaintiffs do not rely on any express provision in the Commonwealth Constitution for the purpose of showing that the Tax Act and the Grants Act, as well as the other Acts considered together with them, are invalid. They rely upon the alleged implied prohibition as to non-interference by the Commonwealth with State Constitutional functions, capacities or activities ...

[423] The *Engineers'* case (1920) 28 CLR 129 did not deny the existence of implied powers or prohibitions (see the report at 155). Should then the particular implication for which the plaintiffs contend be made upon some ground other than the express terms of ss 106 and 107 of the Constitution?

In the first place it may be admitted that revenue is essential to the existence of any organised State, and that there cannot be either reliable or sufficient revenue without power of taxation. The power of taxation may fairly be said to be an essential function of a State.

But this admission states a universal opinion. There is no universal or even general opinion as to what are the essential functions, capacities, powers, or activities of a State. Some would limit them to the administration of justice and police and necessary associated activities. There are those who object to State action in relation to health, education, and the development of natural resources. On the other hand, many would regard the provision of social services as an essential function of government ... It is not for a court to impose upon any parliament any political doctrine as to what are and what are not functions of government, or to attempt the impossible task of distinguishing, within functions of government, between essential and non-essential or between normal or abnormal. There is no such basis for such a distinction. Only the firm establishment of some political doctrine as an obligatory dogma could bring about certainty in such a sphere, and Australia has not come to that.

Thus the principle for which the plaintiffs contend must be applied, if at all, in protection of all that a State chooses to do, and it must mean that Commonwealth legislation cannot be directed to weaken or destroy any State function or activity whatsoever.

But it cannot be denied that Commonwealth legislation may be valid though it does in fact weaken or destroy, and even is intended [424] to weaken or destroy, some State activity. Section 109 shows that this must be so in many cases. Commonwealth laws have in fact put an end to the existence of State Courts of Bankruptcy and State Patent, Trade Mark and Copyright Departments. The Commonwealth laws are not invalid on that account. They have produced the results stated just because they are valid.

It is true that the Commonwealth Parliament has no power to make laws with respect to the capacity and functions of a State Parliament. It has already been stated that the Commonwealth Parliament could not pass a law to prohibit a State Parliament from legislating in general or from legislating upon some particular subject matter. But this limit upon the power of the Commonwealth Parliament does not arise from any prohibition or limitation to be implied from the Constitution. It is simply the result of the absence of power in the Commonwealth Parliament to pass laws with respect to the functions or powers of State Parliaments. The Commonwealth Parliament cannot legislate with respect to any subject whatever unless a power to do so is conferred on it by the Constitution. No power such as that mentioned is given by the Constitution to the Parliament.

But the Acts in question are not laws with respect to State functions. They do not command or prohibit any action by the State or by the State Parliament.

Indirect Effects of Laws — A law may produce an effect in relation to a subject matter without being a law with respect to that subject matter. Questions of motive and object are irrelevant to the question of the true nature of a law. The nature (or 'substance' if that word is preferred) of a law is to be determined by what it does, not by the effect in relation to other matters of what the law does. A prohibition of import or a very high duty in a customs tariff may bring about the closing of business enterprises in a State. But the tariff is not a law with respect to those enterprises. Similarly a State law may prohibit the carrying on of occupations with the result that they are necessarily abandoned, with perhaps great consequential loss to the Commonwealth in customs duties or income-tax receipts. But the State law does not for this reason become a law with respect to customs duties or income tax. The true nature of a law is to be ascertained by examining its terms and, speaking generally, ascertaining what it does in relation to duties, rights or powers which it creates, abolishes or regulates. The question may be put in these terms: 'What does the law do in the way of changing or creating or destroying duties or rights or powers?' The consequential effects are irrelevant for this purpose. Even though an indirect [425] consequence of an Act, which consequence could not be directly achieved by the legislature, is contemplated and desired by Parliament, that fact is not relevant to the validity of the Act. (*R v Barger* (1908) 6 CLR 41 at 66, 67; *Osborne v Commonwealth* (1911) 12 CLR 321 at 335; *Attorney-General for Queensland v Attorney-General for the Commonwealth* (1915) 20 CLR 148 at 173, 174; *Sonzinsky v United States* 300 US 506 (1937) [81 Law Ed 772], and see note in the Lawyers' Edition (1937) 81 Law Ed 776 et seq) …

[427] Thus, although the Commonwealth Parliament cannot validly pass laws limiting the functions of State Parliaments — and vice versa — the Tax Act and the Grants Act are not invalid on that ground. They do not give any command or impose any prohibition with respect to the exercise of any State power, legislative or other. The Tax Act simply imposes Commonwealth taxation, and is authorised by s 51(ii) of the Constitution. The Grants Act authorises payments to States which choose to abstain from imposing income tax, and is valid by reason of s 96 of the Constitution, unless it is bad as involving some prohibited discrimination or preference. It is now necessary to deal specifically with that objection.

Discrimination — Section 96 provides that: 'During a period of ten years after the establishment of the Commonwealth and thereafter until the Parliament otherwise provides, the Parliament may grant financial assistance to any State on such terms and conditions as the Parliament thinks fit'. Plainly under this provision financial assistance could be given to a single State only. Thus variation in amounts given to different States is permissible. The section contains no express or implied prohibition against any kind of discrimination …

[428] It is true that in *Moran v Deputy Commissioner of Taxation* [1940] AC 838 at 858; 63 CLR 338 at 350 the Privy Council pronounced a warning that possibly (no decision was given on the question) a grant under s 96 might be used for the purpose of effecting discrimination in regard to taxation — 'under the guise of pretence of assisting a State with money'. It may be that, with a very misguided Parliament, such a case is perhaps conceivable. If the proceeds of a tax could be earmarked and if such proceeds were then distributed in whole or in part among the States upon a discriminatory basis the case apparently contemplated by the Privy Council would arise ... If the proceeds of a Commonwealth tax were as such devoted to some unlawful purpose, the case contemplated by the Privy Council might arise ... But it will not be easy to find a case where it can properly be held that an *appropriation* Act making grants to States is invalid because it involves an infringement of the provision that *Acts with respect to taxation* shall not discriminate between States or parts of States.

[429] The Tax Act now under consideration does not so discriminate. It imposes the same tax at the same rates upon all persons in all States throughout Australia. It does not make any discrimination whatever between States — it does not even refer to any State. The Act is also a law of revenue, and therefore must not give preference to any State (s 99). The Act does not give preference to any State. The Grants Act is an Act dealing with expenditure — an appropriation Act. It does draw distinctions between States. There is no constitutional reason why it should not do so. There never has been and there cannot be uniformity in payments made by the Commonwealth in or to States or persons in States. Discrimination in expenditure between States is found in every Commonwealth budget and in many appropriation Acts. It has never been argued either that such differentiation should be avoided or that it could be avoided.

Conclusion as to Tax Act and Grants Act — Thus the objections to the Tax Act and the Grants Act fail, whether those Acts are considered separately or as part of a scheme to bring about the abandonment by the States of the raising of revenue by taxation of incomes.

It is perhaps not out of place to point out that the scheme which the Commonwealth has applied to income tax of imposing rates so high as practically to exclude State taxation could be applied to other taxes so as to make the States almost completely dependent, financially and therefore generally, upon the Commonwealth. If the Commonwealth Parliament, in a Grants Act, simply provided for the payment of moneys to States, without attaching any conditions whatever, none of the legislation could be challenged by any of the arguments submitted to the Court in these cases. The amount of the grants could be determined in fact by the satisfaction of the Commonwealth with the policies, legislative or other, of the respective States, no reference being made to such matters in any Commonwealth statute. Thus, if the Commonwealth Parliament were prepared to pass such legislation, all State powers would be controlled by the Commonwealth — a result which would mean the end of the political independence of the States. Such a result cannot be prevented by any legal decision. The determination of the propriety of any such policy must rest with the Commonwealth Parliament and ultimately with the people. The remedy for alleged abuse of power or for the use of power to promote what are thought to be improper objects is to be found in the political arena and not in the Courts.

~~~

[9.6.4] Latham CJ went on to conclude that the Income Tax (War-time Arrangements) Act was invalid, rejecting an argument that it was supported by the defence power. He held that s 221 of the Income Tax Assessment Act 1936 (giving priority to the Commonwealth over the states in the payment of income tax) was a valid law with respect to taxation. Rich J held that each of the four pieces of legislation was valid, adopting the reasons of Latham CJ on the Tax Act, the Grants Act and the Assessment Act.

The limited grant of powers to the Commonwealth cannot be exercised for ends inconsistent with the separate existence and self-government of the states, nor for ends inconsistent with its limited grants (65 CLR at 443):

> The argument that the States Grants Act leaves a free choice to the States, offers them an inducement but deprives them of and interferes with no constitutional power, is specious but unreal … The real object of the provision is that already stated, and it is in my opinion neither contemplated by nor sanctioned by the Constitution, and in particular by s 96 thereof. As I have said, all State legislation and functions might ultimately be so controlled and supervised. The possibility of the abuse of a power is not, however, an argument against the existence of a power. But if the extent of the power claimed by the Commonwealth leads to 'results which it is impossible to believe … the statute contemplated … there is … good reason for believing that the construction which leads to such results cannot be the true construction of the statute' (*R v Clarence* (1888) 2 QBD 23 at 65).

Notes

[9.6.5] The four Acts challenged in *South Australia v Commonwealth* (the *First Uniform Tax* case) (1942) 65 CLR 373 **[9.6.3]** were assented to on 7 June 1942, the day after the battle of Midway Island (as Dixon CJ pointed out in *Victoria v Commonwealth* (the *Second Uniform Tax* case) (1956) 99 CLR 575 **[9.6.8C]** at 599). That battle can now be seen as marking the limit of Japanese military advances in the Pacific region and as the turning point in that theatre of the Second World War. This strategic analysis was by no means obvious on 7 June 1942, nor on 23 July 1942, when the court's decision in the *First Uniform Tax* case was handed down. The acute crisis which, it was thought, Australia faced and the need to marshal the country's resources in order to meet that crisis, could hardly be ignored by the justices who decided the case. Indeed, that necessity was cited by the Commonwealth Parliament in both the Assessment Act (as justifying the Commonwealth's priority) and the Arrangements Act (as the basis for transfer of state income tax personnel and other resources to the Commonwealth).

[9.6.6] The decision in *South Australia v Commonwealth* (the *First Uniform Tax* case) (1942) 65 CLR 373 **[9.6.3C]** can be regarded as the high-water mark of the doctrine from the *Engineers'* case (1920) 28 CLR 129 **[8.4.31C]**. Not only did it affirm, as the earlier decision had, the effective superiority of the Commonwealth within the federal system, but the majority justices insisted that the problems before the court should be approached as strictly legal questions. If s 96 said 'on such terms and conditions as the Parliament thinks fit', then that was what it meant and its plain meaning was not to be modified by the invocation of any unstated (or implied) propositions. It was not the court's concern that this reading of s 96 could be exploited by the Commonwealth Parliament so as to reduce the states to total economic (and policy) subservience. That was a political question to be resolved politically.

[9.6.7] In January 1946 the Commonwealth informed the states that it proposed to continue uniform income tax indefinitely. A Premiers' conference agreed on total tax reimbursement grants for the next two financial years, and on a formula for increasing the grants in subsequent years. In 1950 and 1951, Premiers' conferences discussed the resumption of state income tax. In July 1952, the Commonwealth informed the states that it was willing to discuss with them the question of the resumption of state income tax. Commonwealth and state treasury officials prepared a series of technical reports, but no agreement was reached between the Commonwealth and the states. In 1955 the states of Victoria and New South Wales began proceedings in the High Court to challenge the validity of the continuing uniform tax scheme.

[9.6.8C] <h2 align="center">Victoria v Commonwealth</h2>

(The Second Uniform Tax case)
(1957) 99 CLR 575

The States Grants (Tax Reimbursement) Act 1946 (Cth) authorised the annual payment of money to a state as financial assistance, on condition that the Commonwealth Treasurer was satisfied that the state had not, in that year, imposed a tax on incomes: s 5. The Act provided that £40m should be available for distribution in 1947 and 1948, thereafter to be adjusted in line with population changes and any increase in average wages: s 6. This sum was to be divided between states in proportion to their 'adjusted' populations: (see **[9.6.22]** for a description of this term). Section 12 provided that payments under the Act should be made out of the Consolidated Revenue Fund which was appropriated accordingly.

The Income Tax Assessment Act 1936 (Cth) provided:

221(1) For the better securing to the Commonwealth of the revenue required for the purposes of the Commonwealth

    (a) a taxpayer shall not pay any tax imposed by or under any State Act on the income of any year of income in respect of which tax is imposed by or under any Act with which this Act is incorporated until he has paid that last-mentioned tax or has received from the Commissioner a certificate notifying him that the tax is no longer payable.

The states of Victoria and New South Wales began actions in the High Court of Australia against the Commonwealth, in which they sought declarations that the State Grants (Tax Reimbursement) Act 1946 and s 221(1)(a) of the Income Tax Assessment Act 1936 were invalid. The Commonwealth demurred to the plaintiffs' statements of claim and the demurrers were heard by the Full Court of the High Court.

Dixon CJ summarised the terms of the four pieces of legislation challenged in *South Australia v Commonwealth* (the *First Uniform Tax* case) (1942) 65 CLR 373 **[9.6.3C]**; noted that there had been no state income taxes for 15 years; and continued:

Dixon CJ: [601] The whole plan of uniform taxation has thus become very much a recognised part of the Australian fiscal system. How far it really rests on the validity of the condition which forms an integral part of the Tax Reimbursement Acts and of s 221(1)(a) of the Income Tax and Social Services Contribution Assessment Act is, I think, open to question. But on the footing that it does so, the Court is now invited to depart from the decision in *South Australia v Commonwealth*, supra, either by treating it as wrongly decided or by distinguishing it as a decision resting in an essential degree on the scope of the defence power in time of war. Having regard to the lapse of time in which no State has taken proceedings seeking judicial relief against the statutes, to overrule the decision or even so to distinguish it must involve a grave judicial responsibility.

Dixon CJ summarised the terms of the Grants Act of 1946 and continued:

[603] The constitutional basis for this enactment is s 96. Section 96 forms part of the financial clauses of the Constitution which we know as a matter of history were the final outcome of the prolonged attempts to reconcile the conflicting views and interests of the colonies on that most difficult of matters.

Dixon CJ noted that the drafting of s 96 suggested an interim provision.

[604] The conclusion reached in Quick and Garran: *The Annotated Constitution of the Australian Commonwealth* (1901) p 870 was that the section might be considered for all practical purposes as a permanent part of the Constitution; and the Constitutional

Commission of 1927–1929, after hearing the meaning discussed of the limitation to 'a period of ten years after the establishment of the Commonwealth and thereafter until the Parliament otherwise provides', reported that they considered the words to be ineffective and recommended that they be repealed. In the cases in this Court in which s 96 has been considered, except [605] in the passage to which a reference has already been in the judgment of Evatt J in *Moran's* case, supra, it seems to have been taken for granted that the scope and purpose of the power conferred by s 96 was to be ascertained on the footing that it was not transitional but stood with the permanent provisions of the Constitution.

On this basis it is apparent that the power to grant financial assistance to any State upon such terms and conditions as the Parliament thinks fit is susceptible of a very wide construction in which few if any restrictions can be implied. For the restrictions could only be implied from some conception of the purpose for which the particular power was conferred upon the Parliament or from some general constitutional limitations upon the powers of the Parliament which otherwise an exercise of the power given by s 96 might transcend. In the case of what may briefly be described as coercive powers it may not be difficult to perceive that limitations of such a kind must be intended. But in s 96 there is nothing coercive. It is but a power to make grants of money and to impose conditions on the grant, there being no power of course to compel acceptance of the grant and with it the accompanying term or condition.

There has been what amounts to a course of decisions upon s 96 all amplifying the power and tending to a denial of any restriction upon the purpose of the appropriation of the character of the condition. The first case decided under s 96 was *Victoria v Commonwealth* (1926) 38 CLR 399. The enactment there in question, the Federal Aid Roads Act 1926 (No 46), did not express its reliance on s 96 either in terms or by reference to the grant of financial assistance. It authorised the execution by or on behalf of the Commonwealth of an agreement in a scheduled form with each of the States. It established a trust account in the books of the Treasury to be known as the Federal Aid Roads Trust Account and appropriated for payment into the fund such amount as was necessary for each agreement so executed. The schedule form of agreement set out in detail a plan or scheme for the construction of roads at the combined expense of State and Commonwealth. The roads, called Federal Aid Roads fell into three classes, (1) main roads opening up and developing new country; (2) trunk roads between important towns; and (3) arterial roads carrying concentrated traffic from developmental main trunk and other roads. Very specific provisions were made by which what the State did in pursuance of the plan was made subject to the control or approval of the Commonwealth. The amounts contributed by a State were to be about three-fourths [606] of those contributed by the Commonwealth. The contributions of the Commonwealth were to extend over ten years. It was provided that payments would be made to the State out of the moneys for the time being in the trust account in such amounts and at such times and subject to such conditions as the Commonwealth Minister might determine. The form of agreement should perhaps be studied in detail to appreciate how much is implied by the decision of the Court, but for present purposes the foregoing outline may be enough. The validity of the legislation was upheld by this Court as authorised by s 96. This means that the power conferred by that provision is well exercised although (1) the State is bound to apply the money specifically to an object that has been defined, (2) the object is outside the powers of the Commonwealth, (3) the payments are left to the discretion of the Commonwealth Minister, (4) the money is provided as the Commonwealth's contribution to an object for which the State is also to contribute to funds. Road-making no doubt may have been conceived as a function of the State so that to provide money for its performance must amount to financial assistance to the State. But only in this way was there 'assistance'.

In *Deputy Federal Commissioner of Taxation (NSW) v W R Moran Pty Ltd* (1939) 61 CLR 735, one of the matters decided was the validity of s 6 of the Wheat Industry Assistance Act 1938 (No 53). It is unnecessary to describe the legislative plan or scheme of which that section formed a part or to discuss the constitutional question from which I have isolated the question whether s 6 was valid. The provision was upheld (Evatt J dissenting) on the ground that it amounted to an exercise of the power contained in s 96.

Section 5 of the Wheat Industry Assistance Act established a fund fed from Consolidated Revenue to be called the Wheat Industry Stabilization Fund. Subsection (1) of s 6 provided that subject to the Act the moneys standing to the credit of the fund should be applied in accordance with the Act in making payments to the States as financial assistance; sub-s (6) provided that after certain deductions the amount paid in to the fund in any year should be applied in making payments to the States in effect in proportion to the quantities of wheat produced. Subsection (7) then made the following provision — 'Any amount granted and paid to a State in pursuance of the last preceding subsection shall be paid to that State upon condition that is distributed to the wheat growers in that State in proportion to the quantity of wheat sold or delivered for sale by each wheat grower during the year in respect of which the payment is made to the State'. Now it might have been thought [607] that these provisions were outside s 96 because they gave no assistance to the State as a body politic but used it only as a conduit or agency by which the moneys would be distributed among the wheat growers of the State. In that light the provision could not presumably have been upheld as an exercise of the power conferred by s 51(iii) to make laws with respect to bounties on the production or export of goods but so as not to discriminate between States or parts of States. The reason why apparently it could not be justified under that power was because the basis of the distribution of the moneys was not the production but the sale of wheat. In fact, however, the provision was considered to amount to financial assistance to the State notwithstanding that the State was bound to distribute the money it received to the wheat grower.

The decision, which was affirmed in the Privy Council (1940) AC 838; (1940) 63 CLR 338, without express reference to this use of s 96, must mean that s 96 is satisfied if the money is placed in the hands of the State notwithstanding that in the exercise of the power to impose terms and conditions the State is required to pay over the money to a class of persons in or connected with the State in order to fulfil some purpose pursued by the Commonwealth and one outside its power to effect directly. I should myself find it difficult to accept this doctrine in full and carry it into logical effect, but the decision shows that the Court placed no limitation upon the terms or conditions it was competent to the Commonwealth to impose under s 96 and regarded the conception of assistance to a State as going beyond and outside subventions to or the actual supplementing of the financial resources of the Treasury of a State.

From the reasons given in the Privy Council it clearly appears that their Lordships considered that it is no objection to a purported grant of financial assistance under s 96 that it discriminates as between States or that it is for the purpose of a distribution to a class of the people of a State; but what was said did not necessarily include such an imperative requirement as s 6(7) imposes: for that provision was not mentioned: [1940] AC at 857–9; (1940) 63 CLR at 349–50.

In *South Australia v Commonwealth* (1942) 65 CLR 373 the dissent of Starke J was on the ground that the Income Tax Reimbursement Act of 1942 included the object of 'making the Commonwealth the sole effective taxing authority in respect of incomes and compensating the States for the resulting loss in income tax' (at 443). 'No doubt', said [608] his Honour, 'means can be found to give the States financial assistance without crippling them in the exercise of their powers of self-government if the Commonwealth taxation creates economic difficulties for them. But I cannot agree that the provisions of s 96 enable the Commonwealth to condition that assistance upon the States abdicating their powers of taxation or, which in substance is the same thing, not imposing taxes upon income' (at 443, 444). Unless this view involves a departure from what was decided in the two cases with which I have dealt, Starke J said nothing in derogation of the interpretation of s 96 which those decisions involve. The judgments of the members of the Court forming the majority place positive reliance upon the decisions as affording definite support to the conclusion that the Income Tax Reimbursement Act was a valid exercise of the power conferred by s 96. Those judgments pronounce specifically against the view that that Act was invalid as attempting an interference with the exercise by the States of their constitutional functions ...

[609] In the present attack upon the validity of the Tax Reimbursement Act 1946–1948 the two States that are plaintiffs naturally rest heavily upon the argument that the Act is a law for the restriction or control of the States in the exercise of their taxing powers, that on its face the purpose appears of compelling the States to abstain from imposing taxes upon income. If s 96 came before us for the first time for interpretation, the contention might be supported on the ground that the true scope and purpose of the power which s 96 confers upon the Parliament of granting money and imposing terms and conditions did not admit of any attempt to influence the direction of the exercise by the State of its legislative or executive powers. It may well be that s 96 was conceived by the framers as (1) a transitional power, (2) confined to supplementing the resources of the Treasury of a State by particular subventions when some special or particular need or occasion arose, and (3) imposing terms or conditions relevant to the situation which called for special relief of assistance from the Commonwealth. It seems a not improbable supposition that the framers had some such conception of the purpose of the power. But the course of judicial decision has put any such limited interpretation of s 96 out of consideration. In any case it must be borne in mind that the power conferred by s 96 is confined to granting money and moreover to granting money to governments. It is not a power to make laws with respect to a general subject matter, which for reasons such as I gave in *Melbourne Corporation v Commonwealth* (1947) 74 CLR 31, may be taken to fall short of authorising a special attempt to control the exercise of the constitutional powers of the States where there is a connexion with some part of the subject matter of the federal [610] power. The very matter with which the power conferred by s 96 is concerned relates to State finance. Further there is nothing which would enable the making of a coercive law. By coercive law is meant one that demands obedience. As is illustrated by *Melbourne Corporation v Commonwealth*, supra, the duty may be imposed, not on the State or its servants, but on others and yet its intended operation may interfere unconstitutionally with the governmental functions of the State in such a way as to take the law outside federal power. But nothing of this sort could be done by a law which in other respects might amount to an exercise of the power conferred by s 96. For the essence of an exercise of that power must be a grant of money or its equivalent and beyond that the legislature can go no further than attaching conditions to the grant. Once it is certain that a law which is either valid under s 96 or not at all does contain a grant of financial assistance to the States, the further inquiry into its validity could not go beyond the admissibility of the terms and conditions that the law may have sought to impose. The grant of money may supply the inducement to comply with the term or condition. But beyond that no law passed under s 96 can go.

Once the interpretation is accepted in full which the decisions in *Victoria v Commonwealth* (1926) 38 CLR 399, and in *Moran's* case (1939) 61 CLR 735; [1940] AC 838; (1940) 63 CLR 338 combine to place upon the section it becomes difficult indeed to find safe ground for saying that the condition of the grant of financial assistance may not be that a particular form of tax shall not be imposed by the State. The interpretation flowing from these two decisions is not consistent with the view that there must be a need for relief or a reason for giving assistance which is not itself created by the Commonwealth legislation connected with the grant. It is inconsistent with the view that the terms or conditions cannot require the exercise of governmental powers of the State and require the State to conform with the desires of the Commonwealth in the exercise of such powers. It seems a short step from this to saying that the condition may stipulate for the exercise or non-exercise of the State's general legislative power in some particular or specific respect. Once this step is taken it becomes easier to ask than to answer the question — 'Why then does this not apply to the legislative power of imposing this or that form of taxation?'.

In short the result of my consideration of the two prior decisions upon s 96 has been to convince me that the decision of the majority [611] of the Court with respect to the Tax Reimbursement Act in *South Australia v Commonwealth* (1942) 65 CLR 373 was but an extension of the interpretation already placed upon s 96 of the Constitution. The three decisions certainly harmonise and they combine to give s 96 a consistent and coherent interpretation and they each involve the entire exclusion of the limited operation which might have been assigned to the power as an alternative.

Before the meaning of s 96 and the scope of the power it gives had been the subject of judicial decision no one seems to have been prepared to speak with any confidence as to its place in the constitutional plan and its intended operation. It may be said perhaps that while others asked where the limits of what could be done in virtue of the power the section conferred were to be drawn, the Court has said that none are drawn; that any enactment is valid if it can be brought within the literal meaning of the words of the section and as to the words 'financial assistance' even that is unnecessary. For it may be said that a very extended meaning has been given to the words 'grant financial assistance to any State' and that they have received an application beyond that suggested by a literal interpretation.

But even if the meaning of s 96 had seemed more certain, it would, in my opinion, be impossible to disregard the cumulative authority of the three cases I have discussed and conclude that ss 5 and 11 of the Tax Reimbursement Act are invalid. I therefore think that the validity of that Act must be upheld.

~~~

[9.6.9] Dixon CJ went on to hold that s 221(1)(a) of the Income Tax Assessment Act was not a valid law of the Commonwealth.

McTiernan J said that s 96 permitted conditional grants, such as that in the Grants Act. The power given by s 96 was 'a very general one and the terms and conditions on which Parliament may grant financial assistance to any State are within its discretion': 99 CLR at 623. He regarded the validity of the Grants Act as settled by *South Australia v Commonwealth* (the *First Uniform Tax* case) (1942) 65 CLR 373 **[9.6.3C]** which he refused to overrule. He agreed that s 221(1)(a) of the Assessment Act was no longer valid.

Williams J held that the Grants Act was supported by s 96:

> Nothing could be wider than the words 'on such terms and conditions as the Parliament thinks fit' and they must include at the very least any terms or conditions with which a State may lawfully comply. [99 CLR at 630]

> Indeed I would say that, if ever there was a case for the application of the rule of stare decisis, this is that case. [99 CLR at 655]

Notes

[9.6.10] Owen Dixon had been absent from the High Court when the *First Uniform Tax* case (1942) 65 CLR 373 **[9.6.3C]** was argued and decided. He was then Australian Minister in Washington. Some commentators have suggested that he might have persuaded the court to condemn the Grants Act of 1942 had he participated in that case; see, for example, Sawer (1967) p 134. His decision in *Victoria v Commonwealth* (the *Second Uniform Tax* case) (1957) 99 CLR 575 **[9.6.8C]** that the Grants Act of 1946 was supported by s 96 did appear to be based more on precedent than on principle. Consider, for example, his observations on the approach to s 96 which the court could have adopted 'if s 96 came before us for the first time for interpretation': 99 CLR at 609.

[9.6.11] However, it is by no means clear that a successful challenge to the Grants Act of 1946 would have put an end to the concentration in Commonwealth hands of the imposition and collection of income tax. 'No satisfactory legal reason could be advanced', said Dixon CJ, to support the prophecy that the uniform tax system would collapse without the Grants Act: 99 CLR at 597. In fact, Commonwealth monopoly of the field of income taxation has been demonstrated not to depend on the attachment of any express condition to s 96 grants: see **[9.6.17]**.

[9.6.12] Perhaps a decision that the Grants Act of 1946 went beyond s 96 might have advanced the interests of the states in some other way. If s 96 had been limited, along the lines which Dixon CJ suggested was its original conception, to allowing the Commonwealth to provide financial assistance to meet 'some special or particular need or occasion' (99 CLR at 609), the uniform tax system may not have unravelled, but the power of the Commonwealth to employ the states as its agents for the execution of a wide range of social policies (otherwise outside Commonwealth control) could have been undermined. That is, there would have been no constitutional basis for the entry, through 'specific purpose grants', of the Commonwealth into the financing (and, therefore, the regulation) of education, public housing and transport and other 'State responsibilities', which was initiated by the Menzies Federal Liberal–Country Party Government in 1964 and expanded over succeeding years, gradually at first and rapidly during the three years of the Whitlam Federal Labor Government, 1972–75: see **[9.6.29]**.

[9.6.13] However, as Dixon CJ pointed out in *Victoria v Commonwealth* (the *Second Uniform Tax* case) (1957) 99 CLR 575 **[9.6.8C]** at 610, the High Court's decisions in *Victoria v Commonwealth* (the *Federal Roads* case) (1926) 38 CLR 399 **[9.6.31]** and *Deputy Federal Commissioner of Taxation v WR Moran Pty Ltd* (1939) 61 CLR 735 **[9.6.36]** and the Privy Council's decision in *WR Moran Pty Ltd v Deputy Federal Commissioner of Taxation* (1940) 63 CLR 338 **[9.6.37]** are inconsistent with a reading of s 96 which would prevent the Commonwealth using 'specific purpose' grants so as to implement programs outside its listed legislative powers. These decisions must be regarded as entrenched by the *First* and *Second Uniform Tax* cases. A recent attempt to limit this use of s 96 was rejected by the High Court in *Attorney-General for Victoria (Ex rel Black) v Commonwealth* (1981) 146 CLR 559 **[9.6.42]**. These decisions and the use which the Commonwealth has made of 'specific purpose' grants are discussed below: see **[9.6.29]–[9.6.43]**.

[9.6.14] Commonwealth grants to states can be divided into three broad groups: general revenue grants, special assistance grants and specific purpose grants. The first of these are, broadly, compensation for lost income tax revenues and are provided to the states for their general budgets. They are not tied to any purpose. The second are now of little practical significance but were introduced in 1910 (and formalised through the establishment of a Commonwealth Grants Commission in 1933) to adjust financial inequalities between the states. The third are the mechanism by which the Commonwealth has implemented most of those spending programs which it was thought were outside its direct legislative powers.

[9.6.15] In addition to these three categories of grant, the Commonwealth makes other payments to the states and territories. The revenue replacement payments, introduced in 1997 following the High Court's decision in *Ha v New South Wales* (1997) 189 CLR 465 **[9.4.60C]**, are an example of the broad scope of s 96, and the profound effect of constitutional decisions upon federal financial arrangements. In *Ha*, a majority of the High Court decided that state business franchise fees levied on alcohol and tobacco, and possibly petrol, exceeded the revenue-raising power of the states anticipated under s 90 of the Constitution and threatened a 're-establish[ment of] the pre-Federation tax bases of the Colonies': 189 CLR at 502. The day after the High Court decision, which cast doubt upon the constitutional validity of business franchise fees collected by the states totalling $5 billion annually (*1998–99 Budget Paper No 3*, p 32), the Commonwealth announced its intention to institute a temporary 'safety net' for the loss of state and territory revenues: Treasurer, *Press Release*, 6 August 1997. The safety net comprised a package of legislative measures designed to increase the rates of Commonwealth customs and excise on tobacco and petrol and wholesale sales tax on alcohol, which the Commonwealth would collect: see **[9.4.67]**. At the same time, the Commonwealth introduced the States Grants (General Purposes) Amendment Act 1997 (Cth) which provided for the return of the moneys collected by the Commonwealth (less administrative costs) to the states and territories by way of revenue replacement repayments.

In addition, the agreement had to account for the effect of s 51(ii) of the Constitution which requires the Commonwealth to exercise its taxing power in a non-discriminatory manner, and the fact that the states and territories had in place differing regimes of excise duties. To overcome the discrepancy between the amount collected by the Commonwealth and the amount needed by the states and territories to replace their lost revenue, the states agreed to repay any amount in excess of its projected business franchise fee collections to manufacturers and wholesalers. Finally, the package provided for the introduction of a 100 per cent windfall gains tax to protect the states and territories from claims for refunds of past business franchise fee payments.

[9.6.16] In 1997 the Commonwealth signalled its intention to abolish financial assistance grants altogether (see **[9.6.25]**) and replace them with a goods and services tax, all of the revenue from which would go to the states.

General revenue grants

[9.6.17] The States Grants (Tax Reimbursement) Act 1946 (Cth) was replaced by the States Grants Act 1959 (Cth). Under this legislation, specified grants were made to each state for the year 1959–60, and a formula was prescribed for adjusting the grants in each succeeding year. These grants were not declared to be conditional upon the states refraining from the imposition of income taxes.

The deletion of that condition did not diminish the Commonwealth's power to penalise, if it so chose, a state's resumption of income taxation, a point made by Latham CJ in *South Australia v Commonwealth* (the *First Uniform Tax* case) (1942) 65 CLR 373 **[9.6.3C]** at 429, and referred to elliptically by Dixon CJ in *Victoria v Commonwealth* (the *Second Uniform Tax* case) (1957) 99 CLR 575 **[9.6.8C]** at 597: see **[9.6.11]**. Apart from the natural reluctance of state politicians to reintroduce such taxes (there are both political and economic risks here), the Commonwealth had, until 1976, made it clear that it would react against any such reintroduction. Take, for example, the following account of a confrontation between the Commonwealth and two states between 1968 and 1970:

> The Australian Government made it clear at the Premiers' Conference in June 1968 that it regarded State receipt duties on wages and salaries and comparable payments such as superannuation and pensions as an income tax and, as such, in breach of the financial assistance grants arrangements. (Payments of the type mentioned had been made liable to a new form of receipts duty introduced in Western Australia and Victoria in 1966–67 and 1967–68 respectively.) The Australian Government stated that it adhered firmly to the principle of uniform income taxation and was convinced of the desirability of avoiding multiplication of income taxes. If receipts duty on wages and salaries continued in existence when the grants arrangements were being reviewed in 1970, the Australian Government would regard that as a decisive factor in determining its attitude on the allocation to a State imposing that form of taxation. In

the meantime, should a State that continued the impost on wages and salaries impose it at a higher rate, the Australian Government would move forthwith to amend its legislation and seek to reduce that State's grant. (The duty as it applied to wages and salaries was subsequently removed by Victoria as from July 1970 and by Western Australia as from January 1971. Receipts duties generally ceased to apply on receipts after the end of September 1970.) (*1975–76 Budget Paper No 7*, Appendix II.)

Even after 1976, it was clear that the Commonwealth's promised tolerance of state income taxation would be limited: see **[9.6.24]**.

[9.6.18] In 1970, the six state Premiers put a series of joint proposals to the Commonwealth, seeking immediate increases in tax reimbursement grants and eventual re-entry of the states into the field of income taxation. The Commonwealth opposed the resumption of state income taxation, but agreed to review the formula for calculating grants to the states. A new formula was then introduced to apply for the five years from 1970–71 to 1974–75.

A further adjustment to the formula was made at the June 1975 Premiers' Conference. The Commonwealth rejected a proposal that the grants should be based on reimbursement for the income tax which the states refrained from imposing; rather it should 'be based on the States' financial needs [not] on movements in one of the revenue sources from which the financial assistance grants are financed'. The new formula was to apply for the five years from 1975–76 to 1979–80.

[9.6.19] However, in 1976, the new Commonwealth Government announced the replacement of the 'tax reimbursement' arrangement (and the recently-settled formula) with a new tax sharing scheme. The basis for this scheme was the proposition which the previous Commonwealth Government had rejected in June 1975; namely, that the level of grants to the states should vary with movements in the returns from Commonwealth income tax. (The tax sharing arrangements were only one part of a broad-ranging 'new federalism' policy which involved some retreat from the increasing use by the Commonwealth of specific purpose grants, the transfer of some government programs from the Commonwealth to the states and encouragement for the states to take some degree of control over levels of, and returns from, income tax: see **[9.6.24]**.)

[9.6.20] The States (Personal Income Tax Sharing) Act 1976 (Cth) provided for the states to share a proportion of 'net personal income tax collections' excluding special surcharges and special rebates. The proportion to be shared among the states was to rise from 33.6 per cent in 1976–77 to 36.87 per cent in 1978–79 and each succeeding year: ss 6, 7. The Act guaranteed that the states would not, for the first four years, receive less than they would have under the 1975 formula, and that no state would, in any year, receive less than in the preceding year. Despite these 'guarantees', the scheme had some real dangers for state revenues:

> The ability of the Commonwealth effectively to determine the size of the States' revenue base has also been indicated by its unilateral decisions to introduce personal tax indexation in 1976–77 and drastically to reform the rate structure in 1977–78. Although the Government's federalism policy was based on the premise that the States would be consulted about major changes in taxation arrangements affecting their entitlements, no such consultation seems to have occurred. The difficulties of reconciling the principle of consultation with budget security are, of course, not unimportant. The significance of the new arrangements is that, although Commonwealth income tax changes obviously continue to affect the Commonwealth's own revenue yields, they now reduce the Commonwealth's expenditure commitments

(in the form of tax sharing entitlements) as well, whereas under the financial assistance grants arrangements Commonwealth payments were independent of revenue yields. The States may well ponder on the fact that they entered into the tax sharing arrangements (and their percentage share was determined) at the time, when, after a period of very rapid growth in tax yields, the growth in revenue base was checked. (Mathews (1978) p 112).

Between 1976–77 and 1980–81, general revenue assistance to the states under the 1976 Act rose from $3696 million to $6018 million, an increase of 38.6 per cent. Over the same period, the Commonwealth's revenue from all taxation rose from $19,498 million to $32,280 million, an increase of 39.6 per cent.

[9.6.21]   Currently, Commonwealth financial assistance is distributed on the basis of each state's population and 'relativities' between states as recommended by the Commonwealth Grants Commission. The relativities are assessed according to the principle of 'horizontal fiscal equalisation' which provides that:

> ... each State should be given the capacity to provide the average standard of State-type public services, assuming it does so at an average level of operational efficiency and makes an average effort to raise revenue from its own sources (Commonwealth Grants Commission, *Annual Report 1997–98*, p 8).

The Grants Commission emphasises, however, that equalisation 'is designed to achieve equal capacity not equal results' because the general revenue grants are untied and 'each State is free', in relation to this particular revenue, 'to decide its own priorities': Commonwealth Grants Commission, *Annual Report 1997–98*, p 8. Since 1993–94, the Australian Capital Territory has been included in the general revenue-sharing arrangements which apply to the states: Commonwealth Grants Commission, *Annual Report 1997–98*, p 7.

[9.6.22]   At a Premiers' conference in May 1981, Commonwealth–state financial relations were reviewed and the Commonwealth Government agreed to adopt total tax receipts as the basis for calculating its tax sharing grants to the states. The States (Tax Sharing and Health Grants) Act 1981 (Cth) implemented the agreement. A complex formula in s 9 provided for an amount equal to 20.72 per cent of the Commonwealth's total tax receipts in the preceding year to be granted to the states. (The Treasurer was authorised, under s 7 of the Act, to nominate 'special surcharges' or 'special rebates' which were not taken into account in calculation of total tax receipts.)

According to the 1981 Act, the tax sharing grants were to be divided between the states in proportion to their 'adjusted' populations: for example, Tasmania's population was to be multiplied by 2.00188, New South Wales' by 1.02740 and South Australia's by 1.52676 before the grants were allocated. These relativities were reviewed by the Commonwealth Grants Commission (which recommended radical changes) and, by agreement between the Commonwealth and the states, were modified slightly in 1982: *1983–84 Budget Paper No 7*, pp 14–18.

In 1988, new per capita relativities were recommended by the Commonwealth Grants Commission and adopted by the Commonwealth and states, which would see a shift in grants from the less to the more populous states, subject to the former states receiving special revenue assistance to ease the adjustment. For example, in the 1988–89 financial year, Tasmania's population was to be multiplied by 1.528, New South Wales' by 1.026 and South Australia's by 1.381 before the general pool of financial assistance grants was allocated between the states: *1988–89 Budget Paper No 4*, Table 17.

Although the same trend has continued over the years, the outcomes are often mixed. In 1993, the tendency to reduce the shares of the more populous states and increase those of the less populous states was reversed for both New South Wales and Victoria. For these two states this position continued to hold in the following two years and for Victoria it continued for a further two years. Then from 1994–97 Tasmania's share of revenue was increased and Western Australia's was decreased: Commonwealth Grants Commission, *Annual Report 1997–98*, p 20. In 1998 the equalisation relativities redistributed funds away from Victoria, Queensland, Western Australia and the Northern Territory to the other states: *1998–99 Budget Paper No 3*, p 28. (In each of the relativities described here, Victoria was taken as the benchmark. Its population was to be multiplied by 1.000.)

In addition to annual updating of the relativities, the Grants Commission conducts a comprehensive review every five years of its method of calculation. In 1998, this review led to relativity adjustments for Medicare and health funding.

[9.6.23]   The 1981 Act also provided for the payment to the states of 'health grants': Pt III. These grants replaced a range of specific purpose grants (see **[9.6.33]–[9.6.34]**) which were formerly tied to expenditure on public hospitals and community health and school dental programs. They were now described as 'identified health grants' and were part of the retreat, referred to in **[9.6.33]**, from Commonwealth reliance on specific purpose grants:

> The identified health grants, which are for general purposes but are identifiable as Commonwealth contribution towards the cost of health programs, were to be an interim step towards full absorption of health grants into tax sharing grants (*1983–84 Budget Paper No 7*, p 22).

However, from 1 July 1988, identified health grants were withdrawn from the pool of general revenue grants, to be combined with Medicare compensation grants and paid as single specific purpose grants, designated as hospital funding grants (estimated to total $3025 million in 1988–89). This accounted for most of an estimated 12.6 per cent reduction in general revenue grants and an increase of 150.9 per cent in specific purpose health grants: *1988–89 Budget Paper No 4*, pp 32, 58, Table 30.

In 1993, the Commonwealth and the states signed the Medicare Agreement which led to a further adjustment. Under this Agreement, specific purpose payments for health were made to the states. As a result, the Commonwealth Grants Commission produced Medicare adjusted relativities between 1993 and 1998. In 1998–99, the health funding arrangements were again altered. The Commonwealth introduced general revenue grants, distributed in accordance with the relativities, which included the Medicare Bonus Pools and Guarantee payments previously paid as specific purpose payments under the 1993 Medicare Agreements: Commonwealth Grants Commission, *Annual Report 1997–98*, pp 13–15. General revenue grants declined further in 1989 and 1990, as the states' independent tax revenues increased (largely as a result of the booming property market, which generated substantial growth in revenue from stamp duties). The significant deterioration in the states' revenue position which accompanied the recession led to the Commonwealth guaranteeing to maintain the real value of its general revenue grants: *1992–93 Budget Paper No 1*, p 3.253. In 1992–93, general revenue assistance to the states was budgeted at $13,585.6m: *1992–93 Budget Paper No 1*, p 3.254.

[9.6.24] A second stage of the 1976 tax sharing scheme **[9.6.19]** was to be the re-entry by the states onto the field of income tax. The Tax (Arrangements with the States) Act 1978 (Cth) in effect invited the states to enact income tax legislation. However, the Act made it clear that this legislation must comply with stringent guidelines, including the adoption of the Commonwealth system for assessing and collecting income tax. The scheme, for which the Act provided the foundation, was summarised by the Commonwealth Treasury as follows:

(22) Under Stage 2 each State will be able to legislate to impose a surcharge on personal income tax in the State (but not company taxation or withholding tax on dividends and interest) additional to that imposed by the Commonwealth, or to give (at cost to the State) a rebate on personal income tax payable under Commonwealth law and to authorise the Commonwealth to collect the surcharge or grant the rebate as its agent.

(23) Any State surcharges or rebates will be expressed in percentage terms.

(24) Assessment provisions, and the basic income tax rate structure, will continue to be uniform throughout Australia, these being matters for the Commonwealth to determine.

(25) The Commonwealth will at all times remain the sole collecting and administrative agency in the income tax field.

(26) The level of any State surcharges or rebates will be a matter for consideration by each State; relevant decisions will be taken within an appropriate framework of consultation with the Commonwealth and, as considered appropriate by the surcharging or rebating State, with other States, but ultimately the level of surcharge or rebate will be a decision for each individual State. In exercising these powers the States will accept responsibility to work in parallel with and not in negation of the overall economic management policies of the Commonwealth. [1978–79 Budget Paper No 7, p 14]

By 1989, no state had taken up the invitation expressed in the Income Tax (Arrangements with the States) Act. In March of that year the Commonwealth Treasurer announced that the Hawke Federal Labor Government would introduce a bill for the repeal of the Act.

[9.6.25] In 1997, in response to a proposal by the states and territories to introduce a personal income tax surcharge, the Commonwealth reiterated its rejection of any division of income tax responsibility. Instead, it announced its intention to abolish all financial assistance grants to the states, including the revenue replacement repayments introduced after *Ha v New South Wales* (1997) 189 CLR 465 **[9.4.60C]** and introduce a goods and services tax (GST), the total revenue from which would go to the states: *Tax Reform — Not a Tax a New Tax System* (1997), Fact Sheets 270, 271. The GST was introduced on 1 July 2000 as a tax of 10 per cent on the sale or supply of most goods and services in Australia, collected by businesses and suppliers registered under the system on behalf of the Australian Taxation Office. Section 1.3 of the implementing legislation, A New Tax System (Goods and Services Tax) Act 1999 (Cth), is headed 'Commonwealth–State financial relations' and reads:

The Parliament acknowledges that the Commonwealth:

(a) will introduce legislation to provide that the revenue from the GST will be granted to the States, the Australian Capital Territory and the Northern Territory; and

(b) will maintain the rate and base of the GST in accordance with the Agreement on Principles for the Reform of Commonwealth-State Financial Relations endorsed at the Special Premiers' Conference in Canberra on 13 November 1998.

Under the Agreement referred to in s 1.3(b), the Commonwealth abolished (from 1 July 2000) wholesale sales tax and taxes collected on behalf of the states **[9.4.67]** after the constitutional validity of state taxes on tobacco was called in question in *Ha v New South Wales* (1997) 189 CLR 465 **[9.4.60C]**. At the same time, the state and territory governments abolished bed taxes, financial institutions duties, and stamp duties on marketable securities and adjusted their gambling taxes to take account of the impact of the GST on gambling operators. Provision was made for the progressive review and removal of other state taxes including debit taxes and stamp duties on financial instruments and leases will also be reviewed in 2005.

GST revenue replaces Commonwealth financial assistance grants currently paid to the states and territories by the Commonwealth which make up more than 95 per cent of their Commonwealth-provided revenue. The Commonwealth may still provide specific purpose grants (or special purpose payments): see **[9.6.29]–[9.6.43]**. GST revenue amounts are determined on the basis of population share, adjusted by recommendation of the Commonwealth Grants Commission after consultation with the states and territories: see ABS (2000), Appendix 1.

[9.6.26] Occasionally, other payments are added to general revenue assistance. For example, in 1998 the Commonwealth indicated that it intended to provide National Competition Payments to the states of up to $217.2 million in 1998–99 which would be conditional upon the states 'achieving satisfactory progress in the implementation of National Competition Policy reforms': *1998–99 Budget Paper No 3*, p 4. These were to be part of general revenue assistance and not therefore 'tied': see **[9.6.22]**.

Also in 1998–99, special revenue assistance of $25 million was provided to the Australian Capital Territory: *1998–99 Budget Paper No 3*, p 5. This was in the form of transitional allowances which were 'designed to assist the Territory in its transition to "State-like" funding from the generous levels of Commonwealth funding which existed before self-government'; and special needs: *1998–99 Budget Paper No 3*, p 30.

Special assistance grants

[9.6.27] Special assistance grants were first made in 1910 to Western Australia and in 1912 to Tasmania as compensation for their peculiar financial problems. A Commonwealth Grants Commission was established in 1933. It now functions under the Commonwealth Grants Commission Act 1973 (Cth), s 16 of which instructs it to inquire into any state application for a special assistance grant under s 96 of the Constitution. The Commission is also responsible for reviewing the formula under which the tax sharing pool is divided between the states: the relativities referred to in **[9.6.22]**. The Commission has no power to implement any decision which it might reach on an application for special assistance or on tax sharing relativities. It has only the power to 'inquire into and report to the Minister upon' matters within its responsibilities: Commonwealth Grants Commission Act 1973, ss 16, 17(1); States (Personal Income Tax Sharing) Act 1976 s 13(3). Implementation of any of the Commission's recommendations is then a matter for political decision.

[9.6.28] The principle upon which the Commission recommends special assistance was established in 1936:

> Special grants are justified when a State through financial stress from any cause is unable efficiently to discharge its functions as a member of the federation and should

be determined by the amount of help found necessary to make it possible for that State by reasonable effort to function at a standard not appreciably below that of other States (Commonwealth Grants Commission, *Third Annual Report*, 1936).

Since 1933, four states have applied to the Commission for, and ultimately received, special assistance grants. Western Australia received a grant in each year from 1934–35 to 1967–68. South Australia received grants between 1934–35 and 1958–59 and between 1970–71 and 1975–76. Tasmania received grants between 1934–35 and 1973–74. Queensland first applied for a special assistance grant in 1971 and received grants between 1971–72 and 1980–81. These grants were relatively small: $22.7 million in 1978–79, $44.5 million in 1979–80 and $5.4 million in 1980–81.

It seems that, over the years, the 'mendicant' states' claims for special assistance grants were pre-empted through adjustment of the relativities, which define each state's share of general revenue (tax sharing) grants: see **[9.6.22]**. At a Premiers' Conference in 1982, all the states agreed, as part of a 'package deal' on the introduction of new relativities that no state should claim a special assistance grant before the financial year 1985–86: see *1982–83 Budget Paper No 7*, pp 17–18, 24–5.

With significant changes in relativities for general revenue grants in 1988–89, special assistance grants were paid to the three smaller states in that financial year, '[t]o ease adjustment to the $650 million reduction in general revenue assistance [described as "savings"] and the implementation of the new relativities'. Western Australia was to receive $2.8 million, South Australia $10.2 million and Tasmania $16.3 million: *1988–89 Budget Paper No 4*, p 36, Table 18.

In 1992–93, special assistance grants were paid to the Northern Territory ($40 million) and Victoria ($139 million); the latter to compensate for Victoria's loss of revenue from the Bass Strait oil fields following a Commonwealth decision not to share its revenue from petroleum resource rental tax: *1992–93 Budget Paper No 1*, p 3.255.

Specific purpose grants

[9.6.29] Specific purpose grants have since the early 1950s become a major vehicle for the implementation of Commonwealth Government policies. A substantial proportion of Commonwealth grants to the states is now tied to expenditure on specific purposes, such as education, housing and roads, so that the Commonwealth can, through the agency of the states, undertake public expenditure programs (according to its own priorities) in areas which the Commonwealth Constitution appears to regard as state responsibilities.

The role of these grants is explained by the Commonwealth Treasury as follows:

> Specific purpose payments are made where the Commonwealth wishes to have some involvement in the direction of State–local sector expenditure. The extent of such involvement varies significantly from program to program. At one end there are programs, such as assistance for higher education, where the Commonwealth determines all aspects of expenditure and the States effectively act as agents for the Commonwealth in the dispersal of funds. At the other there are programs, such as hospital grants, where the Commonwealth imposes specific conditions on the expenditure of only a small part of the funds (although in this case it also requires that State hospitals not impose fees on Medicare patients). In most cases, however, the States administer specific purpose assistance under broad guidelines agreed with the Commonwealth.

While there is a large number of specific purpose payments, the bulk of this assistance is accounted for by a few major programs. In 1988–89, for example, it is estimated that payments for education, hospitals, housing and roads will account for over 80 per cent of total payments (*1988–89 Budget Paper No 4*, p 57).

[9.6.30] This possibility was confirmed by the High Court in *Victoria v Commonwealth* (the *Federal Roads* case) (1926) 38 CLR 399 (although it was 30 years before the Commonwealth began fully to exploit that possibility). It was argued in that case that the Commonwealth Parliament could not use s 96 to grant money to the states on condition that the money be used to construct 'Federal aid roads' nominated by the Commonwealth. Counsel for the state of Victoria, Robert Menzies (a nice irony, in view of his later resort to s 96 as the means of implementing Commonwealth education programs: see **[9.6.31]**), argued at 405:

Under that section [that is, s 96] the Parliament cannot attach as conditions to its grant any conditions which amount in substance to the exercise of any legislative power which is not within s 51 of the Constitution.

The High Court rejected this argument in one of its shortest judgments. The Act authorising the grants was valid because it was 'plainly warranted by the provisions of s 96 of the Constitution': 38 CLR at 406.

[9.6.31] For many years after *Victoria v Commonwealth* (the *Federal Roads* case) (1926) 38 CLR 399 **[9.6.30]**, the Commonwealth made only modest use of s 96. That changed in the early 1950s as the Commonwealth began to provide some financial support for tertiary education through conditional grants to the states. In the early 1960s the Commonwealth became involved in the funding of private primary and secondary education. Writing from the perspective of 1971, Gates said ((1974) p 170):

Although road grants are still the biggest item, the growth in the relative size of specific purpose grants is largely a consequence of the development of Commonwealth support for the State education systems. Nevertheless, there has been a remarkable extension of the grant system into other fields of public investment and into health and welfare services. Criticism of the heavy reliance of the State governments on Federal grants has usually centred on much rehearsed arguments about the weakening of their responsibility to their own electorates.

These arguments have gained strength with the increasing disposition of the Commonwealth Government to provide funds for specific purposes that fall within the constitutional province of the States. There seems little doubt that, in the last two decades, the States have lost a good deal of their former freedom to determine their own priorities in the composition of their expenditure, just as they had earlier lost most of their freedom to determine the overall level of their expenditure and the associated pattern of tax burdens.

[9.6.32] At the time when Gates was writing (that is, the financial year 1971–72) specific purpose grants amounted to $707 million (32 per cent of all Commonwealth grants, excluding loan fund allocations). From the 1973 budget (the first of the Whitlam Federal Labor Government) specific purpose grants rose steeply until they peaked in 1975–76 at $4152 million (which was 57 per cent of all Commonwealth grants, excluding loan fund allocations). That government's attitude to specific purpose grants was spelt out by Prime Minister Whitlam at a Premiers' Conference in June 1973:

From now on, we will expect to be involved in the planning of the function in which we are financially involved. We believe that it would be irresponsible for the national

Government to content itself with simply providing funds without being involved in the process by which priorities are set and by which expenditures are planned and by which standards are set (1976–77 *Budget Paper No 7*, p 31).

[9.6.33] The election of the Fraser Federal Liberal–Country Party Government at the end of 1975 led to a steady decline in the real value of specific purpose grants, and in the proportion which they constituted of all Commonwealth grants. Prime Minister Fraser committed his government to reducing the proportion of specific purpose grants at a Premiers' Conference in February 1976:

> Specific purpose assistance has been an area of very rapid growth in recent years. It would accordingly be surprising if, given the overriding need for expenditure restraint, it were not found that there are programs which are not a justifiable charge on the taxpayer — if they ever were — or in respect of which some savings are possible either in the short or longer term. We have been, and will continue to be, examining this area carefully in close consultation with the States.
>
> Secondly, there are some programs — or part of programs — which represent areas of expenditure which clearly deserve continuing Commonwealth support but in which there is no obvious need that my Government can see for the Commonwealth to be involved in a *specific* way. These are matters in respect of which priorities should appropriately be left to the States and their authorities to determine.
>
> In such cases, some form of *absorption* of specific purpose funds into general purpose funds would be appropriate (1975–76 *Budget Paper No 7*, p 31).

By 1980–81 specific purpose grants amounted to $5335 million (42 per cent of all Commonwealth grants, excluding loan fund allocations). The following financial year, 1981–82, saw a sharp drop in specific purpose grants when a series of grants, formerly tied to expenditure on public hospitals and health programs, were made as 'identified health grants', with no restriction on the states' use of the money: see **[9.6.19]**. Consequently, specific purpose grants in that year amounted to $4530 million (33 per cent of all Commonwealth grants, excluding loan fund allocations).

[9.6.34] However, recent years have seen an increase in specific purpose grants, as a result, first, of the Fraser Government's pre-election budget of 1982–83 and, second, of the election of the Hawke Federal Labor Government in March 1983. In 1982–83 (the last Fraser budget), specific purpose grants of $5783 million were 36 per cent of all Commonwealth grants, excluding loan fund allocations. In 1983–84 (the first Hawke Labor budget) they were estimated to amount to $6674 million, 37 per cent of all Commonwealth grants, excluding loan fund allocations.

By 1988–89, they were estimated to total $11,280 million, 46.3 per cent of all Commonwealth grants. The increase in specific purpose grants has been attributed to the shift, commencing July 1988, of the identified health grants from general revenue to specific purpose grants and to 'growth in Commonwealth assistance for roads ... and for public housing': *1988 Budget Paper No 4*, pp 57–9.

In 1992–93, specific purpose grants were divided into two groups: those that went 'to' the states, to be spent by them on designated programs, and those that went 'through' the states to such sources as higher education institutions, private schools and local governments. The first group was budgeted at $11,210.1 million, and the second group at 5,964.4 million: a total of $17,174.5 million. In the same period, total general purpose grants to the states and territories were budgeted at $14,701.7 million (*1992–93 Budget Paper No 1*, pp 3.262–3), so that specific purpose grants constituted 53.4 per cent of all Commonwealth grants, excluding loan fund allocations.

By 1998–99, reliance on specific purpose grants had declined from the 1992–93 levels. In 1998–99 specific purpose grants to the states amounted to $11.3 billion or 35 per cent of total financial assistance; specific purpose grants through the states came to $3.7 billion or 11.3 per cent of total financial assistance. Overall, in 1998–99, states received financial assistance (general revenue and specific purpose) of $31.7 billion. Approximately 53 per cent of this was in general revenue assistance and 47 per cent in special purpose payments: *1998–99 Budget Paper No. 3*, p 21. (The figure of $31.7 billion takes account of $313.4 million the states paid to the Commonwealth as a fiscal contribution in 1998–99.)

However, the overall trend is one of an increase in the proportion of specific purpose payments in the total financial assistance. In the last 20 years, from 1978 to 1998, as a percentage of total Commonwealth payments to the states, specific purpose payments have increased by 11 per cent: *1998–99 Budget Paper No. 3*, 39.

[9.6.35] The High Court has confirmed the capacity of s 96 to support a wide range of specific purpose grants. In *Attorney-General (Vic) (Ex rel Black) v Commonwealth* (1981) 146 CLR 559, the relators sought declarations that several Commonwealth Grants Acts were invalid. The Acts provided for the payment of financial assistance to each state on condition that the state, 'without undue delay', pay out the money to non-government schools nominated by the Commonwealth, at rates of payment nominated by the Commonwealth.

The relators' first argument, that the Grants Act infringed s 116 of the Commonwealth Constitution, was rejected: see **[9.6.42]**. Their second argument was that the Grants Act did not comply with s 96 of the Constitution because those Acts gave no financial assistance to the states but used them merely as agencies for the distribution of Commonwealth moneys. All the members of the court who considered this argument (Barwick CJ, Gibbs, Stephen, Mason, Aickin and Wilson JJ) rejected it. The relators had not asked the court to overrule any earlier decisions and each of the justices saw those decisions (*Victoria v Commonwealth* (the *Federal Roads* case) (1926) 38 CLR 399 **[9.6.30]**; *Deputy Federal Commissioner of Taxation v WR Moran Pty Ltd* (1939) 61 CLR 735 **[9.6.36]**; (1940) 63 CLR 338 **[9.6.37]** and the *First* and *Second Uniform Tax* cases (1942) 65 CLR 373 **[9.6.3C]**; (1957) 99 CLR 575 **[9.6.8C]** as decisive.

The judgment of Wilson J was typical of the court's reaction to the relators' argument. He noted that the Grants Act gave the states no discretion in the administration of the grants for non-government schools (there was only 'the barest acknowledgment of the formalities required by s 96'). This lack of discretion was 'all the more remarkable in the context of a Constitution which' gave the Commonwealth Parliament no power over education: 146 CLR at 659. However, these features of the scheme in the Grants Act raised only questions of policy, not of law:

> In the present state of the authorities, the legislation satisfies the requirements of s 96 for a valid law. It is a non-coercive law which in terms grants money to each of the States 'by way of financial assistance to the State'. The freedom of each State to decide whether to accept or reject the grant, however restricted it may be in a political sense, is legally fundamental to the validity of the scheme, and its existence as a matter of law cannot be denied. The conditions attaching to the grant are those to be determined by the Commonwealth, but this has always been so. It is not necessary that the grant should benefit the State Treasury directly, or that the purpose of the grant should be within the express legislative power of the Commonwealth, or that the State should be the instigator or even a party to the initiation of the scheme.

In addition to the significance of the State's decision to accept the grant, the necessity for it then to enter into an agreement with the eventual recipient of a grant is also significant. The State enters into that agreement, not as an agent for the Commonwealth, but as a principal.

In any event, the plaintiffs have no answer, in my opinion, to the defendants' contention that the legislation does extend financial assistance to the States. It satisfies the most stringent tests that can be applied to that criterion. The States have assumed a governmental responsibility for all primary and secondary education within their bounds. If there were no other contributors, the total financial responsibility would fall on the State, as until recently it always has done in the case of government schools. In such a situation, the initiative and sacrifice assumed by those responsible for the existence of a non-government school system affords relief directly to the State Treasury, without relieving the State of the general responsibility of oversight that it has assumed. The participation of the Commonwealth is a further source of help. In my opinion, there can be no doubt that Commonwealth grants to non-government schools within a State must have the effect of easing the claim that such schools would otherwise make upon State financial resources. It must not be forgotten that these schools are already receiving substantial financial assistance from State governments, and the level of this assistance must be affected by the existence of the Commonwealth scheme (146 CLR at 659–60).

[9.6.36] The question whether s 96 might be used to circumvent specific prohibitions in the Commonwealth Constitution, rather than merely to overcome an absence of specific power, was raised in *Deputy Federal Commissioner of Taxation v WR Moran Pty Ltd* (1939) 61 CLR 735. The Commonwealth had passed several tax Acts, imposing a tax on flour in the hands of the millers. The Wheat Industry Assistance Act 1938 (Cth) provided for payment to the states, in proportion to their wheat production, of moneys equivalent to the proceeds of the tax. The grants were made on condition that each recipient state distribute the money amongst local wheat growers. Section 14 made special provision for Tasmania, which had a flour milling industry but practically no wheat growers. A specific sum was to be granted to Tasmania without any specified conditions. However, it was understood between the Commonwealth and the states that Tasmania would pass the money on to local flour millers. The Tasmanian Parliament enacted the Flour Tax Relief Act 1938 to implement that understanding.

A New South Wales flour miller, WR Moran Pty Ltd, challenged the validity of the Commonwealth taxing legislation on the ground that, in combination with the grants legislation, it discriminated between states contrary to the proviso to s 51(ii). The High Court rejected the challenge. Latham CJ said that the taxation legislation did not discriminate between the states; the Constitution did not prevent a Grants Act from discriminating between the states; and the several pieces of legislation should be considered individually, not as parts of a 'scheme'. He made these comments about s 96:

Section 96 is a means provided by the Constitution which enables the Commonwealth Parliament, when it thinks proper, to adjust inequalities between States which may arise from the application of uniform non-discriminating Federal laws to States which vary in development and wealth. A uniform law may confer benefits upon some States, but it may so operate as to amount to what is called 'a Federal disability' in other States. Section 96 provides means for adjusting such inequalities in accordance with the judgment of Parliament. That section is not limited by any prohibition of discrimination. There is no general prohibition in the Constitution of some vague thing called 'discrimination'. There are the specific prohibitions or restrictions to which I have referred. The word 'discrimination' is sometimes so used as to imply an element of injustice. But discrimination may be just or unjust. A wise differentiation based upon relevant circumstances is a necessary element in national policy. The remedy for any abuse of the power conferred by s 96 is political and not legal in character (61 CLR at 763–4).

Evatt J dissented, treating the Assistance Act as part of a scheme to discriminate between states in taxation. He said that s 96 could not be used for the 'purpose of nullifying constitutional guarantees contained elsewhere in the Constitution': 61 CLR at 802.

[9.6.37] WR Moran Pty Ltd appealed to the Privy Council, which dismissed the appeal: *WR Moran Pty Ltd v Deputy Federal Commissioner of Taxation (NSW)* (1940) 63 CLR 338. In the course of its opinion, the Privy Council made a number of propositions:

- In assessing the validity of the pieces of legislation involved in the case, it was appropriate 'to treat them together and see how they interact ... [I]t is necessary to examine the scheme and to have regard to its ultimate effect or its function as shown in the various Acts': 63 CLR at 341.

- In assessing whether a taxation Act discriminated contrary to s 51(ii), it was necessary to consider the terms of any appropriation Act which might authorise refunds of tax to some taxpayers: 63 CLR at 345–6.

- Section 96 was not expressed to be 'subject to this Constitution' and must be regarded as superior to s 51, which was so expressed: 63 CLR at 346–7.

- Section 96 did not prohibit discrimination; and a use of that power to prevent 'unfairness or injustice to the state of Tasmania or indirectly to some or all of its population' was unobjectionable: 63 CLR at 349.

- However, s 96 could not be used by the Commonwealth Parliament 'with a complete disregard to nullify that constitutional safeguard' (at 350):

  Cases may be imagined in which a purported exercise of power to grant financial assistance under s 96 would be merely colourable. Under the guise or pretence of assisting a State with money, the real substance and purpose of the Act might simply be to effect discrimination in regard to taxation. Such an Act might well be ultra vires the Commonwealth Parliament. Their Lordships are using the language of caution because such a case may never arise, and also because it is their usual practice in a case dealing with constitutional matters to decide no more than their duty requires. They will add only that, in the view they take of the matter some of the legislative expedients objected to as ultra vires by Mr Justice Evatt in his forcible dissenting judgment may well be colourable, and such Acts are not receiving the approval of their Lordships. In the present case there seems to be no valid ground for suggesting that the sums payable to the Government of Tasmania pursuant to s 14 of the Wheat Industry Assistance Act 1938 (No 53) are not in the nature of genuine financial assistance to the State, paid for the purpose of equalising the burden on the inhabitants of Tasmania of taxation which was being imposed on all the millers throughout the Commonwealth for an end which might reasonably be considered to be both just and expedient.

[9.6.38] The Privy Council's approach to the issues raises several problems. First, the proposition that the separate pieces of legislation should be treated as a 'scheme' and their validity judged by their interaction cannot be reconciled with the High Court's decisions and statements of principle in the *First* and *Second Uniform Tax* cases (1942) 65 CLR 373 **[9.6.3C]**; (1957) 99 CLR 575 **[9.6.8C]**. (This illustrates one of the paradoxes of Australian constitutional law: the insignificant contribution made to its development by the Privy Council, for more than 60 years the ultimate appellate tribunal on many (although not all) constitutional issues.)

Second, the Privy Council apparently had in mind that a Grants Act could be revealed as a colourable device for effecting discrimination in taxation by studying the motives which prompted the passage of the Act. Yet legislative motive has been regularly and consistently dismissed as irrelevant for constitutional purposes: see, for example, *R v Barger* (1908) 6 CLR 41 **[9.2.15C]**; *South Australia v Commonwealth* (the *First Uniform Tax* case) (1942) 65 CLR 373 **[9.6.3C]**; *Fairfax v Federal Commissioner of Taxation* (1965) 114 CLR 1 **[9.2.22C]**; *Northern Suburbs General Cemetery Reserve Trust v Commonwealth* (1993) 112 ALR 87 **[9.2.26]**. That the investigation would be into motive is evidenced by the Privy Council's own attitude to the scheme in *Moran's* case; namely, it was legitimate because the Assistance Act was designed to correct an injustice caused by the operation of the non-discriminatory taxation laws. That is, the Privy Council approved parliament's motive in enacting a Grants Act which equalised the 'unfair' distribution between the states of the burden of the taxation laws.

An additional difficulty with this approach is that it demands that a court examine the fairness of the distribution of the tax burden and that the court determine whether the Grants Act goes no further than correcting any unfairness brought about by the taxation legislation. However, the Commonwealth Constitution contains no criteria for measuring the fairness of the distribution of tax burdens, other than that they must not discriminate between states (s 51(ii)) and no criteria for measuring the fairness of the corrective measure contained in a Grants Act. What criteria of fairness did the Privy Council use? Was its analysis (of the 'fairness' of the taxation burden and the Grants Act) convincing?

[9.6.39] On the other hand, the view adopted by the majority of the High Court, that s 96 was not subject to the constraints imposed by ss 51(ii) and 99, rather, that the limits on its exploitation were political rather than legal, does open up the real prospect of Commonwealth evasion of express restrictions on its legislative powers, at least when it can secure the cooperation of a state. Sawer's description of the legislation in *Moran's* case is apt: 'a Commonwealth–State conspiracy ... to evade constitutional restrictions': Sawer (1967) p 77.

[9.6.40] A pair of High Court decisions further illustrate the potential of s 96 for circumventing constitutional restrictions. In the first case, *PJ Magennis Pty Ltd v Commonwealth* (1949) 80 CLR 382, the court struck down the War Service Land Settlement Agreements Act 1945 (Cth). The Act authorised the Commonwealth to make an agreement with the state of New South Wales, under which agreement the state would compulsorily acquire land (at below market value) for farms for returned soldiers. The court said that this Act was a law 'with respect to ... the acquisition of property' and, as such, it must provide 'just terms' for the person whose property was acquired: Commonwealth Constitution s 51(xxxi). Payment of compensation at less than market value was not 'just terms', so the Act was invalid even though, under the Commonwealth–state agreement, the acquisition was to be effected by the state government, which was not subject to the constitutional requirement of 'just terms'.

[9.6.41] However, in the second case, *Pye v Renshaw* (1951) 84 CLR 58, the High Court rejected a challenge to the compulsory acquisition by the state of New South

Wales of land on the same 'unjust terms'. One basis for this challenge was that the state would not have acquired the land had it not been for a Commonwealth grant under s 96. This grant was expressed to be subject to the condition that the state use the money to acquire land at a price below its real value for the settlement of returned soldiers. The challenge might have failed for several reasons (one being that the validity of the state's compulsory acquisition would not depend on the validity of the Commonwealth's Grants Act), but the court (Dixon, Williams, Webb, Fullagar and Kitto JJ) rejected the proposition that the grants power was limited by s 51(xxxi) (at 83):

> The argument really comes to this. The Commonwealth cannot itself acquire land except upon just terms. A State can resume land on any terms, just or unjust, authorised by its Parliament. But the Commonwealth is not authorised by s 96 or any other provision of the Constitution to provide money for a State in order that the State may resume land otherwise than on just terms. This is the very argument which was rejected in [the *Federal Roads* case]: see also [the *First Uniform Tax* case], where Latham CJ said: 'The Commonwealth may properly induce a State to exercise its powers ... by offering a money grant'.

[9.6.42]   More recently, however, the High Court has suggested that s 96 grants may be subject to some of the specific restrictions on Commonwealth legislative power. In *Attorney-General (Vic) (Ex rel Black) v Commonwealth* (1981) 146 CLR 559, the court considered a challenge to several Grants Acts, authorising payments to the states on condition that the states pass on those payments to nominated non-government schools. One of the relators' arguments was that the payment, through the states, of money to church-controlled schools was equivalent to 'establishing any religion' and that each of the Grants Act was, therefore, a 'law for establishing any religion' which the Commonwealth was forbidden to make: Commonwealth Constitution s 116.

A majority of the court (Barwick CJ, Gibbs, Stephen, Mason, Aickin and Wilson JJ, Murphy J dissenting) held that the provision of government funds to church-owned schools could not be described as 'establishing any religion'. However, all members of the court, other than Stephen J (who said nothing on this point), indicated that laws made under s 96 were subject to the restrictions imposed by s 116. Gibbs J expressed this view at some length:

> It is plain, as *DFC of T (NSW) v W R Moran Pty Ltd* shows, that a condition may be imposed under s 96 for the purpose of persuading a State to do something which the Commonwealth itself could not do: *Pye v Renshaw* (1951) 84 CLR 58 provides another example. The cases show that the Parliament has wide power to fix the terms and conditions of a grant made under s 96. In *Victoria v Commonwealth* (the *Roads* case — 38 CLR at 406), it was said that the Federal Aid Roads Act 1926 was 'plainly warranted by the provisions of s 96 of the Constitution, and not affected by those of s 99 or any other provision of the Constitution', and the statement that grants made under s 96 are not affected by any other provision of the Constitution was repeated in *DFC of T (NSW) v WR Moran Pty Ltd* (61 CLR at 763, 771). On the other hand, in *Adelaide Company of Jehovah's Witnesses Inc v Commonwealth* (1943) 67 CLR 116 at 123, Latham CJ said that s 116 'prevails over and limits all provisions [of the Constitution] which give power to make laws', and McTiernan J said, at 156, that the section 'imposes a restriction on all the legislative powers of Parliament'. I consider that the ordinary rules of statutory construction should be applied, and that ss 96 and 116 should be read together, the result being that the Commonwealth has power to grant financial assistance to any State on such terms and conditions as the Parliament thinks fit, provided that a law passed for that purpose does not contravene s 116. It is

one thing to say that the Parliament, by a condition imposed under s 96, could achieve a result which it lacks power to bring about by direct legislation, but quite another to say that the Parliament can frame a condition for the purpose of evading an express prohibition contained in the Constitution. As the Judicial Committee pointed out in *W R Moran Pty Ltd v DFC of T (NSW)* (63 CLR at 346–7), the powers given by s 51 of the Constitution are expressly made 'subject to this Constitution' which includes s 96. On the other hand, s 116 is not expressed to be subject to the Constitution. Of course the same is true of s 99, but that section speaks of 'any law or regulation of trade, commerce or revenue' and a law under s 96 cannot properly be regarded as such a law: see *DFC of T (NSW) v WR Moran Pty Ltd*, at 775. However, whether or not the provisions of s 51 can be 'completely disregarded' in deciding upon the validity of a law made under s 96 (as to which see *WR Moran Pty Ltd v DFC of T (NSW)* at 349–50), I consider that the Parliament, acting under s 96, cannot pass a law which conflicts with s 116. To take an unlikely example, an Act which granted money to a State on condition that the State would prohibit entirely the exercise of a particular religion would, in my opinion, be a law for prohibiting the free exercise of that religion, and would be invalid (146 CLR at 592–3).

The other judgments contained only brief assertions that s 96 laws were subject to s 116, although Mason and Wilson JJ agreed that a grant to a state as part of a scheme to establish a church as a national church would be struck down by s 116: 146 CLR at 618, 651 (see also 146 CLR at 576 per Barwick CJ; at 621 per Murphy J.)

[9.6.43] *Attorney-General (Vic) (Ex rel Black) v Commonwealth* (1981) 146 CLR 559 **[9.6.42]** contained a brief discussion of a recurring problem in constitutional litigation: that of the plaintiffs' standing to challenge the validity of legislation. The plaintiffs included the Attorney-General of Victoria and several Australian taxpayers, some of whose children attended government schools. Barwick CJ, Stephen, Aickin and Wilson JJ made no comment on the plaintiffs' standing: they dismissed the actions because no substantial grounds of challenge had, they held, been established.

However, Gibbs and Murphy JJ did discuss the issue. His Honour rejected the Commonwealth's argument that, because the various Grants Acts had no legal operation in Victoria, the Victorian Attorney-General had no standing to challenge their validity; but he was sceptical about the other plaintiffs (at 589–90):

> In my opinion even where no question arises as to the limits *inter se* of the powers of the Commonwealth and the State, the Attorney-General of a State may sue to compel the Commonwealth to observe the fundamental law of the Constitution, which the citizens of any State have an interest to maintain, although it may not be such a special interest as would enable them as individuals to bring the suit. On the other hand, as at present advised, I gravely doubt whether the other plaintiffs have standing to sue; I hardly think that the fact that they are taxpayers, and in some cases parents of children at government schools, gives them a special interest in the subject matter of the action within the principles stated in *Australian Conservation Foundation Inc v Commonwealth* (1980) 28 ALR 257 at 267–8. However, in Canada an exception to the general principle appears to have been recognised in constitutional cases (*Thorson v Attorney-General of Canada (No 2)* (1974) 43 DLR (3d) 1) and since ... it is unnecessary to decide whether these individual plaintiffs have standing, I would express no concluded opinion on the question.

Murphy J held that not only the Attorney-General but also the individual plaintiffs had sufficient standing (at 634):

> To require a person who is not and will not be affected by the coercive operation of an Act to obtain the fiat of the Attorney-General of Australia or of a State would put

enforcement of constitutional guarantees at the mercy of political pressures exercisable through Parliaments, although the purpose of the constitutional guarantees was to provide certain protections, even against Parliaments. A citizen's right to invoke the judicial power to vindicate constitutional guarantees should not, and, in my opinion, does not, depend upon obtaining an Attorney-General's consent. Any one of the people of the Commonwealth has the standing to proceed in the courts to secure the observance of Constitutional guarantees. Objections to wide standing have no merit. Experience in other countries, especially the United States, has shown that the 'floodgates' argument is baseless, and that procedures are available to deal with frivolous challenges.

The balance of judicial opinion almost certainly lies against Murphy J on this point. However, given the decision of the Canadian Supreme Court referred to by Gibbs J, and the recommendations of the Australian Law Reform Commission in its report *Standing in Public Interest Litigation*, Report No 27, a shift in judicial opinion or legislative change cannot be ruled out.

7   Commonwealth spending power

[9.7.1] While the states have shown some resentment at the use by the Commonwealth of specific purpose grants, they expressed even greater alarm when the Whitlam Federal Labor Government proposed to abandon those grants as an instrument of Commonwealth policy and replace them with direct expenditure. Crommelin and Evans described this innovation in the following terms:

> The Whitlam Government did embark upon a genuine adventure with the Constitution in relation to its so-called 'spending' power, founded upon ss 81 and 61 of the Constitution. Given the financial dominance of the Commonwealth in the Australian federal system, it was obvious that the establishment of an unlimited power to appropriate and disburse Federal funds would signify a vital shift in the balance of power, relieving the Commonwealth of the necessity to involve the States in non-regulatory programs (Crommelin and Evans (1977) p 41).

[9.7.2] Why should the Commonwealth want to by-pass the states, given the unlimited scope of s 96 grants and the economic pressures on the states to accept specific purpose grants? There are political and administrative reasons behind such a move. The Commonwealth Government may be anxious to claim for itself, rather than share with state governments, the political credit for a particular spending program, and may believe that state government machinery is inefficient or obstructive; that is either not geared to the running of an innovative program or that it will resist the introduction and impede the operation of such a program. This type of consideration was expressed by former Prime Minister Whitlam in 1976:

> For a number of reasons the making of grants through State governments unnecessarily complicates the machinery of government. In the case of the Australian Assistance Plan and the Australian Legal Aid Office, for example, several States had shown either their unwillingness or their inability to provide urgently needed services. In both cases my Government made direct grants of funds under s 81 (Whitlam (1977) p 308).

[9.7.3]   Naturally, the state governments were not happy about this attempt to cut them out of spending programs. The then Victorian Solicitor-General, Dawson, put this resentment in relatively moderate terms in 1976:

> Allied with this tendency of the Labor Government to treat limitations upon its power somewhat off-handedly was a tendency in some areas not to want to do anything unless it could be seen to be being done from Canberra. I am thinking here particularly of the use of spending power. Much of what the Commonwealth attempted to do during Labor's years of office could without question have been achieved by means of grants to the States under s 96 of the Constitution. The provision of welfare services such as legal aid, unemployment benefits or the scheme envisaged in the Australian Assistance Plan was constitutionally feasible by means of grants, conditional grants, under s 96 of the Constitution. I make this point simply because a great deal of the exploration which took place in these areas tended to be unnecessary and counter-productive. May I take as my example the Regional Employment Development (RED) Scheme. This was a scheme by which the Commonwealth Government sought to provide unemployment relief by providing funds to local bodies, including local government bodies, to enable them to hire labour for approved works. The scheme was, so the State of Victoria contended, beyond the legislative competence of the Commonwealth and, that being so, it was outside the spending power. But the point I wish to make here is that in 1972 a similar scheme had operated simply and efficiently by channelling Commonwealth funds through the State Treasury for disbursement to State departments and instrumentalities and local government bodies. In 1974, this would not do and a cumbersome, inefficient and expensive machinery was set up (or so it seemed to the state) merely to assert Commonwealth powers (Dawson (1977) p 73).

What, then, is the nature and scope of the Commonwealth's direct spending power? May it undertake expenditure on any project, even in areas which lie outside its capacity to regulate or control through legislation passed under s 51 of the Constitution?

[9.7.4E]   Commonwealth Constitution

81   All revenues or moneys raised or received by the Executive Government of the Commonwealth shall form one Consolidated Revenue Fund, to be appropriated for the purposes of the Commonwealth in the manner and subject to the charges and liabilities imposed by this Constitution.

82   The costs, charges, and expenses incident to the collection, management, and receipt of the Consolidated Revenue Fund shall form the first charge thereon; and the revenue of the Commonwealth shall in the first instance be applied to the payment of the expenditure of the Commonwealth.

~~~

[9.7.5]   The debate over the extent of the Commonwealth's spending power has centred on s 81 of the Constitution. A variety of divergent views on that section have been expressed:

■   That it merely reaffirms that the Commonwealth Parliament may allocate funds to projects for which it has legislated, or can legislate, under s 51 of the Constitution.

■   That it gives to the Commonwealth Parliament the power to allocate funds to a somewhat wider range of projects which can be described as 'of national concern'.

■   That it gives to the Commonwealth Parliament the power to allocate funds to any project which it chooses. These divergent views have been complicated by a parallel dispute over whether the Commonwealth Government can establish administrative machinery to supervise the expenditure of money appropriated under s 81.

[9.7.6] As early as 1912, the Commonwealth Government adopted an optimistic view of its power under s 81. The Maternity Allowance Act 1912 (Cth) provided for the payment of five pounds to each woman (apart from some racist exceptions) giving birth to a live child in Australia. Strong doubts were expressed in the parliament about the power of the Commonwealth to enact the legislation, but the government claimed that s 81 gave the parliament a general spending power. However, even the protagonists of this generous view of s 81 conceded that the section would not support the establishment of the administrative system needed to implement the program. Despite the doubts, the Act was passed and the program implemented; and the validity of the legislation was not challenged in the courts. See Sackville (1973) pp 249–50; Saunders (1978) p 381.

[9.7.7] In 1928, a Royal Commission appointed to examine a proposal for Commonwealth child endowment concluded that it was, at best, doubtful whether the Commonwealth Parliament could use s 81 to support the payment of child endowment. The Commission therefore recommended against the introduction of a child endowment program. It would, the Commission said, be 'calamitous' to introduce the scheme, 'unless the validity of the necessary legislation was beyond dispute': Saunders (1978) p 397.

This pessimistic view appears to have dampened direct Commonwealth spending initiatives for many years. Perhaps the Commonwealth's refusal to initiate direct spending programs owed much to the economic depression of the 1930s and to the strong fascination of pre-Keynesian economic theory. Certainly, the realisation that spending channelled through state governments under s 96 would survive constitutional challenge (*Victoria v Commonwealth* (the *Federal Roads* case) (1926) 38 CLR 399 **[9.6.31]**) was a good reason for using that process rather than direct expenditure.

[9.7.8] However, the election of the Curtin Federal Labor Government in 1941 led to a spate of legislation based on the broad reading of s 81: Child Endowment Act 1941 (Cth); Widow's Pensions Act 1942 (Cth); Unemployment and Sickness Benefits Act 1944 (Cth); Pharmaceutical Benefits Act 1944 (Cth). All of these Acts introduced direct Commonwealth spending programs, with their necessary administrative machinery, in areas clearly outside the Commonwealth's direct legislative powers as defined in s 51 of the Constitution.

[9.7.9] The last of these programs was challenged by the Medical Society of Victoria, with the fiat of the Victorian Attorney-General, in *Attorney-General (Vic) (Ex rel Dale) v Commonwealth* (the *Pharmaceutical Benefits* case) (1945) 71 CLR 237. The court held by a majority (Latham CJ, Rich, Starke, Dixon and Williams JJ, McTiernan J dissenting) that the Pharmaceutical Benefits Act was invalid but their reasons differed.

Three members of the court (Latham CJ, Rich and Dixon JJ) held that the Act was invalid because of those aspects of the Act which went beyond appropriation or authorising expenditure. The Act imposed a series of controls on medical practitioners and pharmacists; thus, it purported to regulate conduct, these justices said, in areas outside the Commonwealth's legislative power. However, each of these justices made some observations on the extent of the Commonwealth's power to appropriate moneys.

Latham CJ said that s 81 of the Constitution was the constitutional basis for appropriation legislation and that the parliament could appropriate money for any purpose which it nominated (at 254):

> [T]he Commonwealth Parliament has a general, and not a limited, power of appropriation of public moneys. It is general in the sense that it is for Parliament to determine whether or not a particular purpose shall be adopted as a purpose of the Commonwealth.

Latham CJ expressly rejected the argument that the Commonwealth's appropriation power should be confined to those purposes for which it might otherwise legislate or to the governmental purposes of the Commonwealth: 71 CLR at 253, 256.

Dixon J (with whom Rich J concurred) took a narrower view. He regarded the Commonwealth's power of appropriation as based on the parliament's specific legislative powers rather than on s 81. However, he indicated that these legislative powers could support a relatively broad range of appropriations (at 269, 271–2):

> Even upon the footing that the power of expenditure is limited to matters to which the Federal legislative power may be addressed, it necessarily includes whatever is incidental to the existence of the Commonwealth as a state and to the exercise of the functions of a national government. These are things which, whether in reference to the external or internal concerns of government, should be interpreted widely and applied according to no narrow conceptions of the functions of the central government of a country in the world today ... In deciding what appropriation laws may validly be enacted it would be necessary to remember what position a national government occupies and, as I have already said, to take no narrow view, but the basal consideration would be found in the distribution of powers and functions between the Commonwealth and the States.

Starke and Williams JJ held the Pharmaceutical Benefits Act invalid because it appropriated money for a purpose which was not a purpose of the Commonwealth. Of s 81, his Honour said at 266:

> The purposes of the Commonwealth are those of an organised political body, with legislative, executive and judicial functions, whatever is incidental thereto, and the status of the Commonwealth as a Federal Government. And where else but from the Constitution and other Acts conferring authority upon the Commonwealth can its purposes or functions be discovered? Those purposes include matters in respect of which it can make laws by virtue of the Constitution or any other Act, and they also include the exercise of executive and judicial functions vested in the Commonwealth by the Constitution or by any other Act. Among other purposes of the Commonwealth must also be included, I think, matter arising from the existence of the Commonwealth and its status as a Federal Government. Thus, I should think that moneys appropriated for payment etc of members of Parliament, exploration and so forth, would be within the authority of the Commonwealth.
>
> But the Pharmaceutical Benefits Act 1944 is beyond any purpose of the Commonwealth. No legislative, executive or judicial function or purpose of the Commonwealth can be found which supports it, and it cannot be justified because of the existence of the Commonwealth or its status as a Federal Government.

Williams J said that the phrase 'purposes of the Commonwealth' in s 81 limited the purposes for which the Commonwealth Parliament could appropriate money (at 282):

> The object of the Constitution was to superimpose on the existing body politics consisting of the States a wider overriding body politic for certain specific purposes. It

was for these particular purposes and these alone that the body politics consisting of the States agreed to create the body politic known as the Commonwealth of Australia. These purposes must all be found within the four corners of the Constitution.

McTiernan J dissented, holding that the Act was no more than an Appropriation Act, which was within the power conferred by s 81 of the Constitution. He said that the Constitution should be seen as an instrument of government, adaptable to new needs and conditions. 'The purposes of the Commonwealth are not fixed or immutable. They expand and change with the growth and development of the nation'. It was for the parliament, not the courts, to select the purposes for which money could be appropriated: 71 CLR at 274.

[9.7.10] Following *Attorney-General (Vic) (Ex rel Dale) v Commonwealth* (the *Pharmaceutical Benefits* case) (1945) 71 CLR 237 **[9.7.9]**, the Commonwealth Government received legal advice that the Maternity Allowance Act 1912, Child Endowment Act 1941, Widow's Pensions Act 1942 and the Unemployment and Sickness Benefits Act 1944 were invalid: see Sackville (1973) p 256. The government then revived an earlier proposal to alter the Commonwealth Constitution by giving the parliament power to legislate with respect to a series of specific income security and welfare issues. In 1946, a referendum approved the insertion of pl (xxiiA) in s 51 of the Constitution. The Commonwealth Parliament now had clear power to make laws with respect to:

(xxiiiA)   The provision of maternity allowances, widow's pensions, child endowment, unemployment, pharmaceutical, sickness and hospital benefits, medical and dental services (but not so as to authorise any form of civil conscription), benefits to students and family allowances.

[9.7.11] While that Constitution alteration overcame the immediate problems created by *Attorney-General (Vic) (Ex rel Dale) v Commonwealth* (the *Pharmaceutical Benefits* case) (1945) 71 CLR 237 **[9.7.9]**, there is no doubt that the decision had a severe dampening effect on direct Commonwealth expenditure. When the Commonwealth did move into the funding of tertiary education in the early 1950s, it employed the safer mechanism of s 96 grants: see **[9.6.31]**. However, as noted above **[9.7.1]**, the Whitlam Federal Labor Government revived the use of direct expenditure shortly after its election in 1972, a revival which produced strong objections from the states (see **[9.7.10]**) and the following litigation.

[9.7.12C]   **Victoria v Commonwealth**
(The *AAP* case)
(1975) 134 CLR 338

The Appropriation Act (No 1) 1974–75 (Cth) appropriated substantial sums of money for expenditure by the Commonwealth Government. This appropriation was effected by the following provision.

3   The Treasurer may issue out of the Consolidated Revenue Fund and apply for the services specified in Schedule 2, in respect of the year ending on 30th June 1975, the sum of $2,863,510,000.

The second Schedule to the Act allocated a total of $141,637,000 to the Department of Social Security and this sum was divided, according to the schedule, between a range of programs. Among the specific expenditure projects was the following (found in Div 530 of the schedule):

4 *Australian Assistance Plan*

01 Grants to Regional Councils for Social Development $5,620,000

| 02 Development and evaluation expenses | 350,000 |
| Total | $5,970,000 |

This expenditure was not authorised by any other legislation, nor was the Australian Assistance Plan established or regulated by legislation. However, it was conceded by the parties to this action that the plan involved the expenditure, through Regional Councils for Social Development, of the appropriated money on investigating the need for community welfare services and fostering the development of services. These regional councils were to be established throughout Australia in areas or regions with substantial economic, social and political unity, and were intended to be independent, non-political, community-based bodies. The community welfare services included within the scope of the plan extended beyond the matters on which s 51 of the Constitution authorised the Commonwealth Parliament to legislate. They included, according to a discussion paper issued by the Social Welfare Commission, a statutory body set up by the Social Welfare Commission Act 1973 (Cth):

4.1 Child development services including:

Family day care programs.

Counselling services for 'at risk' families.

Day care services not included in the Child Care Act 1972, including before and after-school programs, and school holiday programs (which do not attract other Federal grants).

Parental education programs.

Fostering programs on a permanent or temporary basis.

4.2 Services to assist families including:

Professional counselling services

(i)   Social casework or group work; family casework services including marriage guidance;

(ii) Budget advisory services;

(iii) Home management advice;

(iv) Legal advice.

Domiciliary services

(i)   Home help, housekeeper, home management available to population generally;

(ii) Meals-on-wheels (Commonwealth assistance available under Delivered Meals Subsidy Act);

(iii) Allied services such as friendly visiting, home maintenance, laundry, shopping and other ancillary services designed to assist people to remain independent of institutional care.

The state of Victoria and its Attorney-General began an action in the High Court against the Commonwealth and the Minister for Social Security, seeking a declaration that the appropriation of $5.9 million was invalid, and an injunction to restrain the Commonwealth and the Minister for Social Security from spending any of that money for the purposes of the Australian Assistance Plan. The defendants lodged a defence claiming that the Appropriation Act and the Australian Assistance Plan were valid and denying the standing of state of Victoria and its Attorney-General to bring the action. The plaintiffs demurred to the statement of defence and the demurrer was heard before the Full Court of the High Court. The states of New South Wales and Western Australia were given leave to intervene in the argument of the demurrer.

Barwick CJ said that, before federation, the colonies' principal revenues came from customs and excise duties, which were taken over by the Commonwealth.

Barwick CJ: [355] It is apparent from the history of the proposals for federation that the plan of federation involved, and essentially involved, the sharing or distribution of the revenues of the Commonwealth. The then major source of colonial revenue had to be collected by the Commonwealth: that and other revenues of the Commonwealth gathered from the people of the states by non-discriminatory laws might well be beyond the needs of the administration by the Commonwealth of the powers allocated to it by the Constitution. The precise manner in which the States after federation should secure their share of the revenue so received by the Commonwealth had been the subject of much discussion but only of incomplete agreement.

Some matters, however, were finally resolved. It was provided that all revenue should form one Consolidated Revenue Fund. Section 87, though certainly only for a limited period, specified that part of the revenue from customs and excise which could be applied annually by the Commonwealth 'towards its expenditures'; s 94 provided for the payment to the States of 'all surplus revenue of the Commonwealth'. Section 96 gave power to make grants to any States upon terms determined by the Parliament. It was evidently necessary to make such an express provision if such grants were to be deductible from the Commonwealth revenues in the process of determining the surplus revenue. Quite clearly, the making of such grants, but for the existence of s 96, would not have been a purpose of the Commonwealth.

Just as legislative power was distributed, with specific topics assigned to the Commonwealth and the residue falling to the States, so, it seems to me, the surplus of the Commonwealth revenues, [356] the residue, after the servicing of the exercise of Commonwealth powers, was to come to the States, though in a manner left to be determined by the Parliament. This distribution of the revenue was effected, in my opinion, by the stipulation that the Consolidated Revenue Fund could only be appropriated and disbursed by constitutional or statutory authority, and that the Commonwealth could only expend the fund for Commonwealth purposes. Thus if the revenues in fact exceeded Commonwealth purpose requirements, there would be surplus revenue intended to be available for the States. The fact, if that be the right conclusion, that the payment of the surplus revenue was left in the control of the Parliament does not detract, in my opinion, from the basic concept of limiting the power of the Commonwealth, itself a legislative power, to appropriate and spend the Consolidated Revenue Fund as part of the distribution of legislative power by which the federation was effected. The failure to agree upon a permanent formula for distributing the revenue does not deny the essentially federal nature of the financial provisions of the Constitution. In my opinion, the words of s 81 do involve a restraint of the Commonwealth's power of appropriation and expenditure of the Consolidated Revenue Fund and ss 81 and 83 were part of what I may call the distribution of the available governmental revenue of the federation as between Commonwealth and States.

[357] It is as necessary now, with the uniform tax and reimbursement grant legislation in operation, that the claim of the States on the Consolidated Revenue Fund through s 94 be recognised and respected as it was when the principles of federation were in negotiation. The purpose of the restraint on the Parliament's legislative power to appropriate and authorise the expenditure of the Consolidated Revenue Fund is presently the same as it was in 1900, namely, the ensuring of surplus revenue so that there can be State participation in that Fund.

The Commonwealth's access to the Consolidated Revenue Fund by means of the use of s 96 has been aided by the decisions of the court in *Victoria v Commonwealth* (1926) 38 CLR 399 and *Osborne v Commonwealth* (1911)12 CLR 321. But these decisions lend no colour to the proposition that an appropriation of the Consolidated Revenue Fund may be without purpose or that the purpose of the appropriation may be to service some activity of the Commonwealth which it is not authorised by the Constitution to undertake. Section 96, included in the Constitution to enable moneys expended in grants to States to be debited to the Consolidated Revenue Fund as money appropriated for a purpose of the Commonwealth, as interpreted by this court, has enabled the Commonwealth to intrude in point of policy and perhaps of administration into areas outside Commonwealth legislative competence. No doubt, in a real sense, the basis on which grants to the claimant States have been quantified by the Grants Commission has further expanded the effect of the use of s 96. But a grant under s 96 with its attached conditions cannot be forced upon a State: the State must accept it with its conditions. Thus, although in point of economic fact, a State on occasions may have little option, these intrusions by the Commonwealth into areas of State power which action under s 96 enables, wear consensual aspect. Commonwealth expenditure of the Consolidated Revenue Fund to service a purpose which it is not constitutionally lawful for the [358] Commonwealth to pursue, is quite a different matter. If allowed, it not only alters what may be called the financial federalism of the Constitution but it permits the Commonwealth effectively to interfere, without the consent of the State, in matters covered by the residue of governmental power assigned by the Constitution of the State.

It is perhaps worth remarking at this point that the doctrine of the court established in the *Amalgamated Society of Engineers v Adelaide Steamship Co Ltd* (1920) 28 CLR 129 has supported the exercise to the full of Commonwealth legislative power. But however large and generous the interpretation of those powers, the Constitution requires that the powers of the States with respect to the residue, not embraced in Commonwealth power as thus construed, should not be trespassed upon by the Commonwealth without the concurrence of the State. Participation by the Commonwealth in policy-making or of administration in connexion with matters of State concern, matters within the residue left to the States by ss 106 and 107, must, in my opinion, be confined to the use by the Commonwealth of s 96 which, as I have said, involves the consent of a State. The Commonwealth, in my opinion, activity under s 96 apart, cannot enter that residual area left by the Constitution to the States, either by legislative or executive act.

Barwick CJ said that the assumption, made in the Constitution, that the states would share in the Commonwealth's surplus revenue, provided 'a clear reason in the formulation of the Australian Constitution to impose limits on the [spending] capacity of the Commonwealth': 134 CLR at 359. He rejected, as irrelevant to Australia, rulings of the United States Supreme Court on Congress' spending power.

[360] In my opinion, the words 'for the purposes of the Commonwealth' were intended to and do limit the legislative power of the Commonwealth to appropriate and authorise the expenditure of the Consolidated Revenue Fund. They must be construed and applied in the light of the circumstances and constitutional provisions to which I have referred. It follows inevitably, in my opinion, that they cannot be writ out of the Constitution by deciding that any purpose which the Parliament considers to be a Commonwealth purpose is an authorised purpose. That is but an example of 'words meaning what I says they mean', a notion more likely to be found in fantasy than in constitutional law. ...

[361] What then are purposes of the Commonwealth within s 81? The Commonwealth is a polity of limited powers, its legislative power principally found in the topics granted by ss 51 and 52: its executive power is described as extending to the execution and maintenance of the Constitution and of the laws of the Commonwealth. [362] No doubt some powers, legislative and executive, may come from the very formation of the Commonwealth as a polity and its emergence as an international state. Thus it may be granted that in considering what are Commonwealth purposes, attention will not be confined to ss 51 and 52. The extent of powers which are inherent in the fact of nationhood and of international personality has not been fully explored. Some of them may readily be recognised: and in furtherance of such powers money may properly be spent. One such power, for example, is the power to explore, whether it be of foreign lands or seas or in areas of scientific knowledge or technology. Again, there is power to create Departments of State, for the servicing of which, as distinct from the activities in which the Departments seek to engage, money may be withdrawn from the Consolidated Revenue Fund.

But, to anticipate a submission with which I must later deal, to say that a matter or situation is of national interest or concern does not, in my opinion, attract any power to the Commonwealth. Indeed, any student of the Constitution must be acutely aware of the many topics which are now of considerable concern to Australia as a whole which have not been assigned to the Commonwealth. Perhaps the most notable instance is in relation to the national economy itself. There is but one economy of the country, not six: it could not be denied that the economy of the nation is of national concern. But no specific power over the economy is given to the Commonwealth. Such control as it exercises on that behalf must be effected by indirection through taxation, including customs and excise, banking, including the activities of the Reserve Bank and the budget, whether it be in surplus or in deficit. The national nature of the subject matter, the national economy, cannot bring it as a subject matter within Commonwealth power.

However, to whatever source it be referred, any act or activity of the Commonwealth must fall within the confines of some power, legislative or executive, derived from or through the Constitution. In this connexion, I have not included any reference to the judicial power because, in my view, such a reference would be irrelevant to the matter in hand. In the long run, whether the attempt is made to refer the appropriation and expenditure to legislative or to executive power, it will be the capacity of the Parliament to make a law to govern the activities for which the money is to be spent, which will determine whether or not the appropriation is valid. With exceptions that are not relevant to this matter and which need not be stated, the executive may only do that which has been or could be the subject of valid legislation. Consequently, [363] to describe a Commonwealth purpose as a purpose for or in relation to which the Parliament may make a valid law, is both sufficient and accurate. In my opinion, the expression in s 51(xxxi) of the Constitution 'for any purpose in respect of which the Parliament has power to make laws'; is a reasonable synonym for the expression 'the purposes of the Commonwealth' in s 81.

Is the Australian Assistance Plan ... a purpose of the Commonwealth? Is it something the Commonwealth may lawfully implement? I have no doubt it is not. There is no granted power which either alone, or in combination with other powers, could support a scheme for the rearrangement of the Australian community into regions for deriving financial support directly from the Commonwealth or for integration of social welfare schemes or welfare planning as such. Nor is there power to grant money to or through the regional councils. An Act of the Parliament which sought to authorise the carrying out of the plan, including its financial provisions, would, in my opinion, be beyond the power of the Parliament. ...

It was then suggested that, because social welfare itself and, in particular, the co-ordination of the efforts of a large number of [364] diverse agencies was a national problem, there was power in the national Parliament to deal with it, by appropriation of funds as well as by particular legislation. But, as I have already pointed out, to describe a problem as national, does not attract power. Though some power of a special and limited kind may be attracted to the Commonwealth by the very setting up and existence of the Commonwealth as a polity, no power to deal with matters because they may conveniently and best be dealt with on a national basis is similarly derived. However desirable the exercise by the Commonwealth of power in affairs truly national in nature, the federal distribution of power for which the Constitution provides must be maintained.

In my opinion, no power resides in the Commonwealth to implement and carry out a social welfare plan such as the Australian Assistance Plan. It follows, in my opinion, that that plan is not a purpose of the Commonwealth within the meaning of the language of s 81. Accordingly, in my opinion, there is no power in the Parliament to appropriate and authorise the expenditure of money for that plan and its purposes. Item 4 in div 530 of the second schedule to the Act is, in my opinion, void and in respect of the plan and its purposes, the Act is ineffective to authorise the withdrawal from the Treasury of any money for the support and implementation of the plan.

Barwick CJ said the states had an interest in the Commonwealth's surplus revenue sufficient to give them standing in this suit:

[365] By confining the Commonwealth's expenditure of the Consolidated Revenue Fund within the proper constitutional bounds, the State takes a step towards the 'creation' of surplus revenue: it is endeavouring to ensure the observance of the Constitution in a respect that vitally affects it: it is asking that the federal distribution of the use of the Consolidated Revenue Fund be observed: it is claiming the invalidity of a statute as being beyond the competence of the Parliament, a statute which if acted upon would affect its interest in the existence and extent of surplus revenue.

I have no doubt that the State has an interest to maintain this suit ...

Stephen J said that the present proceedings were concerned with a 'special type of Act of Parliament':

Stephen J: [386] It is an Act which, while a necessary precondition to lawful disbursement of money by the Treasury, is not in any way directed to the citizens of the Commonwealth, [387] it does not speak in the language of regulation, it neither confers rights or privileges nor imposes duties or obligations. It only permits of moneys held in the Treasury being paid out, upon the Governor-General's warrant, to Departments of the government. Its importance is essentially confined to the polity in question, here the Federal polity; the control which, by its means, is exercised by the legislature over proposed government expenditure is of significance within the framework of that polity but has no direct effect upon the powers or interests of the other component parts of the federation, the States.

How then can the present plaintiffs, the State of Victoria and its Attorney-General, have any standing to complain of this legislative authorisation of proposed Federal expenditure? The answer is, in my view, that they cannot. The State itself has no concern with the mode of expenditure of Federal revenue unless it be associated with some claim to surplus revenue of the Commonwealth under s 94 of the Constitution but the present proceedings are no more appropriate to raise any such claim than were those in *Attorney-General (Vic) (Ex rel Dale) v Commonwealth* ('the *Pharmaceutical Benefits* case') (1945) 71 CLR 237. I would adopt what Latham CJ there said (at 247). The plaintiffs did not seek to support standing by reference to surplus revenue, no doubt both because of the Commonwealth's use of trust funds, sanctioned in *New South Wales v Commonwealth* (1908) 7 CLR 179 and exemplified, in refined form, in s 7 of the present Appropriation Act and because, in any event, the very large deficit budgeted for effectively eliminates it from consideration. ...

[390] I conclude that where the Federal legislation which is impugned is no more than an Appropriation Act whose provisions not only do not extend to and operate within any State and do not affect, still less interfere with, public rights but have no ordinary law-making function at all, not purporting to govern the conduct of the citizens of any State or of the Commonwealth and having no injurious effect upon their trading activities or other rights, the Attorney-General of a State has no standing to sue.

Mason J said that there had been some dispute over the source of the Commonwealth's power to appropriate moneys, and continued:

Mason J: [392] The weight of opinion in the *Pharmaceutical Benefits* case was that s 81 defined the scope and extent of that power, a view confirmed by the observation of the court in *Australian Woollen Mills Pty Ltd v Commonwealth* (1954) 92 CLR 424 at 454, where Dixon CJ, Williams, Webb, Fullagar and Kitto JJ said that the section 'authorises the appropriation of the revenues and moneys of the Commonwealth for the purposes of the Commonwealth'. See also *Attorney-General for Victoria v Commonwealth* (1935) 52 CLR 533 at 567–8; the *Second Uniform Tax* case (1957) 99 CLR 575 at 655.

In ascertaining the meaning of 'for the purposes of the Commonwealth', which is the critical expression in s 81, it is necessary to keep in mind the function and purpose of an Appropriation Act. Section 83 in providing that 'No money should be drawn from the Treasury of the Commonwealth except under appropriation made by law', gives expression to the established principle of English constitutional law enunciated by Viscount Haldane in *Auckland Harbour Board v R* [1924] AC 318 at 326: 'no money can be taken out of the consolidated fund into which the revenues of the State have been paid, excepting under a distinct authorisation from Parliament itself'. An Appropriation Act has a twofold purpose. It has a negative as well as a positive effect. Not only does it authorise the Crown to withdraw moneys from the Treasury, it 'restrict(s) the expenditure to the particular purpose', as Isaacs and Rich JJ observed in *Commonwealth v Colonial Ammunition Co Ltd* (1924) 34 CLR 198 at 224.

Their Honours, after noting that an Appropriation Act is 'financial, not regulative', continued at 224–5: 'It ... neither betters nor worsens transactions in which the executive engages within its constitutional domain, except so far as the declared willingness [393] of

Parliament that public moneys should be applied and that specified funds should be appropriated for such a purpose is a necessary legal condition of the transaction.' An Appropriation Act therefore is something of a *rara avis* in the world of statutes; its effect is limited in the senses already explained; apart from this effect it does not create rights, nor does it impose duties.

Mason J said that a limited spending would be consistent with the Commonwealth's limited legislative power, and would increase the states' chances of receiving 'surplus revenue'.

[394] However, the support which these considerations give to the plaintiffs' case are, I think, outweighed by other factors which point to an opposite conclusion.

The annual appropriations are a central feature of the financial arrangements made for the government of the country. It is not lightly to be supposed that the framers of the Constitution intended to circumscribe the process of parliamentary appropriation by the constraints of constitutional power and thereby to expose the items in an Appropriation Act to judicial scrutiny and declarations of invalidity. Consequences more detrimental and prejudicial to the process of Parliament would be difficult to conceive. Any item in the Act would be subject to a declaration of invalidity after the Act is passed, even after the moneys in question are withdrawn from Consolidated Revenue and perhaps even after the moneys are expended, for an appropriation, if it be unlawful and subject to a declaration of invalidity, does not cease to have that character because acts have taken place on the faith of it.

The adverse consequences of a narrow view of s 81 do not stop at this point. It has been the practice, born of practical necessity, in this country and in the United Kingdom, to give but a short description of the particular items dealt with in an Appropriation Act. No other course is feasible because in many respects the items of expenditure have not been thought through and elaborated in detail. How is the short description of an item contained in the schedule to the Act to serve as the fulcrum of constitutionality? If it fails to throw sufficient illumination on the area of doubt, is the court to have regard to supplementary material, as it has been invited to do in this case, and if so to what material will it have recourse? These questions, which to my mind admit of no satisfactory solution, illustrate the problems inherent in the narrow construction offered by the plaintiffs and the hazards attending the processes of Parliament if that construction is accepted.

Another consequence of the plaintiffs' view of s 81 is that it would deprive the Commonwealth of the power to make grants for purposes thought to be deserving of financial support by government, yet standing outside the area of Commonwealth power, and not involving any exercise of the Commonwealth's executive power. Over the years there have been many instances of appropriations made by the Parliament to persons and bodies and for purposes [395] which appear to have little, if any, connexion with the functions and powers of the Commonwealth under the Constitution. On the plaintiffs' argument these appropriations are invalid. The consequence would be that public money has been illegally withdrawn from the Treasury and paid away. And for the future the Commonwealth, subject to the authority which s 122 provides, could make such grants only through the agency of the States under s 96.

Although some have discovered in s 96 of the Constitution a power to make grants to the States which would not otherwise exist, the section should in my view be seen as a provision which puts beyond question the power of Parliament to attach conditions to grants made to the States, as to which doubts would certainly have existed had explicit provision not been made. But it could scarcely be doubted that in the absence of s 96 the Parliament would have enjoyed the power to make unconditional grants to the States. So much at least would be implied from the relationship subsisting between the Commonwealth and the States as constituent elements in the federation and the possession by the Commonwealth of its taxation and other financial powers. The presence of s 96 is therefore not a reason for confining s 81 as the plaintiffs would suggest.

[396] It follows, then, that I would give to the words 'for the purposes of the Commonwealth' in s 81 the meaning ascribed to them by Latham CJ in the *Pharmaceutical Benefits* case (1945) 71 CLR at 256, that is, for such purposes as Parliament may determine.

Mason J went on to conclude that the executive power of the Commonwealth Government did not extend to implementing the Australian Assistance Plan. The government could undertake those executive activities which were consistent with the responsibilities allocated to the Commonwealth by the Constitution. These included, not only the matters listed in s 51 (as within the Commonwealth's legislative power), but also 'enterprises and activities peculiarly adapted to the government of a nation and which cannot otherwise be carried on for the benefit of the nation', such as scientific and public health research. However, the executive power of the Commonwealth was not without limits and it did not extend to the activities included in the Australian Assistance Plan. 'The carrying into execution of that Plan', he said, 'should be restrained by injunction ...': 134 CLR at 401. He also held that the states had sufficient standing to challenge the Commonwealth's expenditure: this was based on their interest in maintaining the 'division of powers and ... consequential allocation of responsibilities between the Commonwealth and the States': 134 CLR at 401.

Jacobs J: [410] In my opinion the appropriation by the Commonwealth Parliament of moneys of the Commonwealth to the purposes stated in the Appropriation Act cannot by itself be the subject of legal challenge. The appropriation is a matter internal to the government of the Commonwealth. It may not make valid anything which cannot be validated. That depends on the breadth of the Commonwealth power of appropriation and expenditure expressed in s 81 and on the meaning of the words therein 'for the purposes of the Commonwealth'. However, even when those words are given a limited meaning it does not follow that the Appropriation Act or any part thereof can be declared invalid. [411] The appropriation is no more than an earmarking of the money, which remains the property of the Commonwealth. All it does is to disclose that the Parliament assents to the expenditure of moneys appropriated for the purposes stated in the appropriation. The Crown may then within the law governing appropriation of its money expend those moneys. It is given 'the authority and the opportunity' so to do: *Commonwealth v Colonial Ammunition Co Ltd* (1924) 34 CLR 198 at 222.

[412] For these reasons alone the plaintiffs have made out no case for relief even on the assumption that some part of the proposed expenditure may be beyond Commonwealth power. That assumption, however, does not appear to me to be correct. Moneys may be appropriated and therefore expended pursuant to that appropriation 'for the purposes of the Commonwealth'. It appears to me that the view of the majority of the court in *Attorney-General for Victoria v Commonwealth* (1945) 71 CLR 237 was that the power of appropriation was limited by the nature and purposes of the government of the Commonwealth but that, on the other hand, the purposes of the Commonwealth may not only fall within a subject matter of general or particular power prescribed in the Constitution but may also be other purposes which now adhere fully to Australia as a nation externally and internally sovereign: cf per Starke J at 266. The growth of national identity results in a corresponding growth in the area of activities which have an Australian rather than a local flavour. Thus, the complexity and values of a modern national society result in a need for co-ordination and integration of ways and means of planning for that complexity and reflecting those values. Inquiries on a national scale are necessary and likewise planning on a national scale must be carried out. Moreover, the complexity of society, with its various interrelated needs, requires co-ordination of services designed to [413] meet those needs. Research and exploration likewise have a national, rather than a local, flavour.

In two ways the Australian Assistance Plan is in substance within the powers of the Commonwealth. First, it is an expenditure of money in the exercise by the Commonwealth of its executive power to formulate and coordinate plans and purposes which require national rather than local planning and of its legislative powers to appropriate its funds accordingly. Secondly, in so far as the proposed expenditure does not fall directly within a specific power of the Commonwealth it is an expenditure of money which is incidental to the execution by the Commonwealth of its wide powers respecting social welfare. A considerable part of the proposed expenditure falls or may fall directly within Commonwealth power either in respect of specific subject matter or in respect of particular classes of persons but in so far as some expenditure may be outside Commonwealth powers in respect of specific subject matters or in respect of particular classes of persons it seems to me that the expenditure falls within the incidental power in s 51(xxxix). The purposes of the Commonwealth certainly include all the purposes comprehended within the subject matter of s 51 in respect of which the Commonwealth may legislate, including the subject matter comprised in s 51(xxxix). The purposes of the Commonwealth include purposes comprehended within the Commonwealth power in respect of matters incidental to the execution of the legislative power to appropriate and the executive power to expend moneys for the purposes of the Commonwealth. Moneys may therefore be appropriated and expended for that purpose as well as for purposes wholly comprehended within the other subject matters of Commonwealth power ...

Earlier, Jacobs J had said the prerogative powers of the Crown extended to the expenditure of money appropriated by parliament. As those prerogatives were part of the executive power of the Commonwealth, the Commonwealth Government could legitimately spend the moneys appropriated for the Australian Assistance Plan.

~~~

[9.7.13] McTiernan and Murphy JJ held, in separate judgments, that the Commonwealth Parliament could appropriate money for those purposes determined by parliament and that the act of spending appropriated moneys on the Australian Assistance Plan was within the executive power of the Commonwealth. They did not decide whether the plaintiff had standing to challenge an appropriation, although Murphy J was 'inclined to agree with what has been said by Stephen J': 134 CLR at 424. Gibbs J held, for reasons substantially the same as those of Barwick CJ, that the appropriation was outside the purposes of the Commonwealth, and that the expenditure by the Commonwealth Government was outside its executive power. In the result, the plaintiffs' demurrer was overruled and the action dismissed with costs.

Notes

[9.7.14] For all the diversity of approach and opinion shown by the justices in *Victoria v Commonwealth* (the *Australian Assistance Plan* case) (1975) 134 CLR 338 **[9.7.12C]**, five of the seven justices seemed to consider that the validity of a Commonwealth Appropriation Act was not an issue upon which the High Court could adjudicate.

McTiernan, Mason and Murphy JJ said that this was because s 81 of the Constitution left it to parliament to select the purposes for which it appropriated money. Stephen J said that the unique character of an Appropriation Act (it was an internal financial ear-marking of money) meant that no state or Attorney-General had sufficient standing to bring proceedings challenging its validity. (It is difficult to see how a private citizen, even if a taxpayer, would be in any better position, despite Stephen J's refusal to resolve that question.) Jacobs J also emphasised the peculiar character of an Appropriation Act: because it was 'internal to the government of the Commonwealth', it could not by itself be the subject of legal challenge. Even if 'purposes of the Commonwealth' were to be read narrowly, no justiciable issue would be raised by an Act which appropriated money for other purposes because the Act would not create rights, obligations or duties.

Saunders has suggested that, for Stephen, Mason and Jacobs JJ, the non-justiciability of an appropriation Act was based on its peculiar character as a 'measure internal to the processes of government': Saunders (1982) p 33. She argues that this view 'is wrong in history, in law and in principle'; and that, in view of some observations on the interaction between s 116 and s 96 made in *Attorney-General (Vic) (Ex rel Black) v Commonwealth* (1981) 146 CLR 559 **[9.6.42]**, the view 'will also be hard to sustain': Saunders (1982) pp 34–5.

Nevertheless, it is difficult to avoid the conclusion that, for the present at least, the decision in the *AAP* case reverses the narrowing effect of *Attorney-General (Vic) (Ex rel Dale) v Commonwealth* (the *Pharmaceutical Benefits* case) (1945) 71 CLR 237 **[9.7.9]** and opens the way for significant expansion of direct Commonwealth expenditure programs. The implementation of such programs will be (at least until the *Australian Assistance Plan* case is overruled) a political rather than a legal question; a political question in which the political and economic balance of the Australian federation will be at stake.

[9.7.15] In *Davis v Commonwealth* (1988) 166 CLR 79 the High Court rejected a challenge to the validity of s 10 of the Australian Bicentennial Authority Act 1980 (Cth), which appropriated \$17.95 million for the purposes of the Authority. Those purposes included the celebration of the bicentenary in 1988 of the first European settlement in Australia. The court concluded that this celebration was within the executive power of the Commonwealth: see **[7.2.26C]**; and Mason CJ, Deane and Gaudron JJ observed that '[a]n appropriation for a valid exercise of the executive power of the Commonwealth is necessarily an appropriation for a purpose of the Commonwealth within the meaning of s 81 of the Constitution', even on the narrow view of that section: 166 CLR at 95. The three justices noted at 96 that the *Australian Assistance Plan* case:

> ... stands as an authority for the proposition that the validity of an Appropriation Act is not ordinarily susceptible to effective legal challenge. It is unnecessary to consider whether there are extraordinary circumstances in which an appropriation of money by the Parliament may be susceptible to such challenge. It suffices to say that, if there be such cases, the present is not one of them.

8 References

[9.8.1] *Articles*
Arndt, 'Judicial Review under Section 90 of the Constitution: An Economist's View' (1952) 25 *ALJ* 667.

Bennett, 'Does an ACT Ordinance Constitute an Invalid Excise under s 90 of the Constitution?' (1994) 68 *ALJ* 913.

Campbell, 'The Commonwealth Grants Power' (1969) 3 *FLR* 221.

Campbell, 'Federal Spending Power: Constitutional Limitations' (1968) *Uni of Western Australia LR* 443.

Coper, 'The High Court and Section 90 of the Constitution' (1976) 7 *FLR* 1.

Cremean, 'Consumption Taxes, Licence Fees and Excise Duties' (1974) 9 *Melbourne Uni LR* 735.

Else-Mitchell, 'The Australian Grants Commission' (1974) *J Constitutional and Parliamentary Studies* (New Delhi) 560.

Else-Mitchell, 'The Rise and Demise of Coercive Federalism' (1977) 36 *Australian J Public Administration* 109.

Hanks, 'Section 90 of the Commonwealth Constitution: Fiscal Federalism or Economic Unity?' (1986) 10 *Adelaide LR* 365.

Keyzer, 'When Is An Issue Of "Vital Constitutional Importance"? Principles Which Guide the Reconsideration of Constitutional Decisions in the High Court of Australia' (1999) 2 *Constitutional Law and Policy Review* 13.

Jackson, 'The Law-making Role of the High Court' (1994) 11 *Aust Bar Rev* 197.

Lane, WR, 'Financial Relationships and Section 96' (1975) 34 *Public Administration* 45.

McLeod, 'State Taxation: Unrequited Revenue and the Shadow of Section 90' (1994) 22 *FLR* 476.

Sackville, 'Social Welfare in Australia: The Constitutional Framework' (1973) 5 *FLR* 248.

Saunders, 'Government Borrowing in Australia' (1990) 17 *Melbourne Uni Law Rev* 187.

Saunders, 'The Development of the Commonwealth Spending Power' (1978) 11 *Melbourne Uni LR* 369.

[9.8.2] *Papers and reports*

Australian Bureau of Statistics, 'Information Paper: Accruals-based Government Finance Statistics', Canberra, 2000.

Brotherton, *Capital Duplicators v Australian Capital Territory: Discrimination and Preference in the Commonwealth Constitution*, Commonwealth Law Forum (Session 2), 1993, p 25.

Constitutional Commission, *Final Report*, AGPS, Canberra, 1988.

[9.8.3] *Texts*

Barnes and Else-Mitchell, *Aspects of the New Federalism Policy*, Centre for Research on Federal Financial Regulations, ANU, Canberra, 1977.

Burns, *Intergovernmental Fiscal Transfers: Canadian and Australian Experiences*, Centre for Research on Federal Financial Relations, ANU, Canberra, 1977.

Cass, 'Lionel Murphy and Section 90 of the Constitution' in *Justice Lionel Murphy: Influential or Merely Prescient?*, (eds Coper and Williams), Federation Press, Sydney, 1997.

Coper, 'The Economic Framework of the Australian Federation: A Question of Balance' in *Australian Federation: Towards the Second Century*, (ed Craven), Melbourne University Press, Melbourne, 1992, pp 131–150.

Crommelin and Evans, 'Explorations and Adventures with Commonwealth Powers' in *Labor and the Constitution 1972–1975*, (ed Evans), Heinemann Educational, Melbourne, 1977, pp 24–66.

Dawson, 'Commentary' in *Labor and the Constitution 1972–1975*, (ed Evans), Heinemann Educational, Melbourne, 1977, pp 71–5.

Evans (ed), *Labor and the Constitution 1972–1975*, Heinemann Educational, Melbourne, 1977.

Gates, 'The Search for a State Growth Tax' in *Intergovernmental Relations in Australia*, (ed Mathews), Angus & Roberston, Sydney, 1974, p 985.

Hannan, 'Finance and Taxation' in *Essays on the Australian Constitution*, (ed Else-Mitchell), 2nd ed, Law Book Co, Sydney, 1961, pp 247–73.

Howard, *Australian Federal Constitutional Law*, 3rd ed, Law Book Co, Sydney, 1985, pp 409–41 ('Taxation').

James, *Intergovernmental Financial Relations in Australia*, Australian Tax Research Foundation, 1992.

La Nauze, *The Making of the Australian Constitution*, Melbourne University Press, Melbourne, 1972.

Lane PH, *A Manual of Australian Constitutional Law*, Law Book Co, Sydney, 1987, pp 61–79 (s 51(ii)); 355–74 (s 90); 411–18 (s 96).

Lane WR, 'Direct Taxes in Relation to the Division of Fiscal Powers' in *Intergovernmental Relations in Australia*, (ed Mathews), Angus & Roberston, Sydney, 1974, pp 132–58.

Lindell G, 'Excise' in *The Cauldron of Constitutional Change*, (ed Coper and Williams), Centre for International and Public Law, ANU, Canberra, 1997, pp 33–7.

McMinn, *A Constitutional History of Australia*, Oxford University Press, Melbourne, 1979.

Mathews, 'Fiscal Adjustment in the Australian Federation: Vertical Balance' in *Intergovernmental Relations in Australia*, (ed Mathews), Angus & Roberston, Sydney, 1974.

Mathews (ed), *Intergovernmental Relations in Australia*, Angus & Roberston, Sydney, 1974.

Mathews, *Australian Federalism 1977*, Centre for Research on Federal Financial Relations, ANU, Canberra, 1978.

Mathews and Jay, *Federal Finance*, Nelson, Melbourne, 1972.

Maxwell, *Commonwealth–State Financial Relations in Australia*, Melbourne University Press, 1967.

May, *Federalism and Fiscal Adjustment*, Clarendon, Oxford, 1969.

Mellors, *Economic Union and Product Taxation by the States*, Centre for Comparative Constitutional Studies, Uni. of Melbourne, Parkville, 1991.

Prest, 'Fiscal Adjustments in the Australian Federation: Vertical Balance' in *Intergovernmental Relations in Australia*, (ed Mathews), Angus & Roberston, Sydney, 1974, pp 184–201.

Quick and Garran, *Annotated Constitution of the Australian Commonwealth*, Angus & Roberston, Sydney, 1901.

Richardson, *Patterns of Australian Federalism*, Centre for Research on Federal Financial Relations, Canberra, ANU, 1973, Ch 4 ('Commonwealth–State Finances: Taxation'), Ch 5 ('Commonwealth–State Co-operation: The Grants Power').

Saunders, 'Parliamentary Appropriation' in *Current Constitutional Problems in Australia*, Centre for Research on Federal Financial Relations, ANU, Canberra, 1982.

Sawer, *Australian Federalism in the Courts*, Melbourne University Press, Melbourne, 1967.

Sawer, *Australian Federal Politics and Law 1901–1929*, Melbourne University Press, Melbourne, 1956.

Sawer, 'The States and Indirect Taxation' in *Intergovernmental Relations in Australia*, (ed Mathews), Angus & Roberston, Sydney, 1974, pp 178–83.

Sawer, 'The Future of State Taxes: Constitutional Issues' in *Fiscal Federalism: Retrospect and Prospect*, (ed Mathews), Centre for Research on Federal Financial Relations, ANU, 1974, pp 193–207.

Whitlam, 'The Labor Government and the Constitution' in in *Labor and the Constitution 1972–1975*, (ed Evans), Heinemann Educational, Melbourne, 1977, pp 305–29.

Zines, *The High Court and the Constitution*, 4th ed, Butterworths, Sydney, 1997.

Chapter

10

Control of Economic and Commercial Activity

---

1   Introduction

[10.1.1] Management of public finances (through taxation policy, revenue collection, public borrowing and public expenditure programmes) is a vital and sensitive aspect of contemporary government. A wide range of politically sensitive issues (such as inflation, unemployment, the productivity of labour and capital investment) is bound up with this management. Political debate, for example, frequently focuses on the extent of public expenditure programs. On the one side, it may be said that these programs should be held to a minimum because they are unproductive of wealth, they divert capital and other resources from the private (productive) sector and they fuel inflation; on the other side, it may be argued that public expenditure should be expanded in order to reduce unemployment, to stimulate a vital sector of the economy ignored by the private sector, or to ensure some equity in the provision of essential services (such as health care or housing).

[10.1.2] Whatever the merits of that debate, our purpose in Chapter 9 was to explore a rather narrow question. Where, in the Australian federal system, does authority lie to make and implement any decision which emerges from that debate? That is — is the management of public finances committed, in our federal system, to the Commonwealth — or is it shared between the Commonwealth and the states?

[10.1.3] In addition to those issues of broad fiscal policy, governments will frequently need to consider whether to intervene, in a more direct fashion, in the economy. That intervention most frequently takes the form of government regulation of private commercial activity, although it may also involve a government setting up its own business in competition with private enterprise: see, for example, the challenge to the establishment of a government-owned airline, implementing a 'two airline policy' considered in *Australian National Airways Ltd v Commonwealth* (1945) 71 CLR 29 **[10.2.5]**. The Australian economy provides a wide range of regulatory regimes and government enterprises. To take a few examples:

- The Trade Practices Act 1974 (Cth) prohibits a series of business practices, including market monopolisation (s 46), exclusive dealing (s 47), resale price maintenance (s 48, Pt VIII) and price discrimination. The Act also regulates company takeovers (s 50) and lays down a code of 'consumer protection', guaranteeing consumers specific rights against manufacturers and suppliers (Pt V).

- The Banking Act 1959 (Cth) insists that only those corporations licensed by the Commonwealth Treasurer may operate as banks (s 8), and gives to the Reserve Bank of Australia power to control vital aspects of each bank's business, including the power to insist that each bank deposit, with the Reserve Bank, part of its current deposits (s 20) and the power to fix the banks' lending policy (s 36). (This second power allows the Reserve Bank to ensure that funds are made available, at below market rates, for home finance; that is, to meet a demand which is a matter of great sensitivity in Australian politics.)

- The Travel Agents Act 1986 (NSW) prohibits any person from operating as a travel agent unless licensed by the Commissioner for Consumer Affairs (s 6) who is given detailed powers of supervision over the business activities of travel agents (see ss 20, 21).

- Complementary legislation passed by the Commonwealth and each of the states (the Wheat Marketing Act 1984) maintained the 'wheat industry stabilisation scheme', which fixed a quota of wheat for every wheat producer in Australia, and compelled each producer to sell his or her wheat to the Wheat Board in return for a guaranteed share of the Wheat Board's profits.

[10.1.4] Government decisions to implement regulatory systems or to set up public enterprises will reflect a variety of influences or pressures: commodity producers, for example, may press for a collective marketing system (such as the wheat stabilisation scheme) because they see competition as damaging to their interests; consumer organisations may demand product standards of the general type reflected in Pt V of the Trade Practices Act 1974 (Cth) or of the specific type set out in s 41D of the Marketing of Primary Products Act 1958 (Vic); or a government's political supporters may advocate the establishment of a public enterprise as a redistributive exercise.

On the other hand, these government decisions will rarely be universally welcomed. Collective marketing schemes will be attacked by some, relatively adventurous or enterprising, producers or by consumers; consumer protection standards will be criticised as unrealistic by producers; and public enterprises are rarely welcomed by their established competitors. Moreover, some economists will attack these government interventions as inefficient or counterproductive. In 1978, for example, the Industries Assistance Commission recommended that the wheat stabilisation scheme be substantially modified, and that producers be allowed to trade, without restriction, in the domestic wheat market. Again, in 1981, the Campbell Committee recommended that the Australian banking industry be deregulated; that Reserve Bank controls over banking activities be lifted, a recommendation which was largely adopted by the Hawke Federal Labor Government in 1985.

[10.1.5] It is not our concern to pursue the policy debate about 'deregulation' and 'privatisation' of economic activity. Rather, we want to examine the constitutional dimension of government regulatory policies. This is hardly a trivial or ephemeral question. Government controls of, and direct competition with, business activity are a well-established feature of Australian life and, even now that the elimination of government controls over, or competition with, business has become part of the common vocabulary of Australian politics, it will be some time before those controls and competitive enterprises are dismantled.

The point that debate about the appropriate location of power to implement policies says nothing about the content of those policies was acknowledged by the Constitutional Commission in 1988. In the course of recommending that the Commonwealth Constitution be amended to give the Commonwealth Parliament extensive powers over economic activity, the Commission said:

> We are not, of course, suggesting that if our recommendations are accepted the Commonwealth should legislate with respect to all aspects of trade and commerce. Nor do we believe that that would occur. It has not occurred in relation to interstate trade or the trade of trading corporations. It has not occurred in the United States where the federal legislature has full power to deal with all business, commerce and industry (Constitutional Commission (1988), para 11.60).

[10.1.6] In the Australian federal system, a decision by government to regulate some aspect of business or commercial activity, or a decision to participate in that activity, raises two fundamental questions. First, does the Commonwealth Constitution assign power over that activity to that government, or is the power assigned to another government within the federal system? And, second, does the regulation, or government participation, infringe any of the prohibitions in the Constitution?

The first question can be restated in terms of the Commonwealth's legislative power: What is the extent of the Commonwealth Parliament's power to legislate for the regulation of, or participation in, commercial activity? Once that question is answered, the federal division of governmental power between Commonwealth and states becomes more clear. This is not because the concession of a power to the Commonwealth automatically denies a similar power to the states. Almost without exception, the Commonwealth's powers over commercial activity are concurrent (or shared) with, not exclusive of, state power; rather, it is because the expansion or contraction of the activities which the Commonwealth may regulate leads to a consequential contraction or expansion of the activities which the states can control free from overriding Commonwealth legislation. Looming behind any decision that the Commonwealth can control some activity is s 109, which allows the Commonwealth's legislation to override or exclude state controls.

[10.1.7] The Commonwealth Parliament has a number of specific powers over selected commercial activities.

- The power in s 51(v) over 'postal, telegraphic, telephonic and other like services' gives it power to regulate radio and television broadcasting: *Herald & Weekly Times Ltd v Commonwealth* (1966) 115 CLR 418.

- The s 51(xiii) banking and s 51(xiv) insurance powers support wide-ranging systems of regulation: see, for example, the Banking Act 1959 (Cth) and the Life Assurance Act 1945 (Cth).

Again, the Commonwealth has other powers over a number of commercial activities: 'bills of exchange and promissory notes' (s 51(xvi)); 'weights and measures' (s 51(xv)); 'bankruptcy and insolvency' (s 51(xvii)); and 'copyrights, patents of inventions and designs, and trade marks': s 51(xviii). Relatively detailed codes dealing with these aspects of commercial activity have been enacted by the Commonwealth Parliament: Bills of Exchange Act 1909 (Cth); Weights and Measures (National Standards) Act 1960 (Cth); Copyright Act 1968 (Cth); Patents Act 1903 (Cth); Trade Marks Act 1905 (Cth); Bankruptcy Act 1966 (Cth).

[10.1.8] There are two other provisions in the Commonwealth Constitution which give, or could be read as giving, broad power over commercial activity to the Commonwealth Parliament. These are the trade and commerce power in s 51(i) and the corporations power in s 51(xx).

The first of these was regarded, for many years, as expressing all the Commonwealth's broad regulatory power over commercial activities, for the High Court had read the corporations power very narrowly in *Huddart Parker & Co Pty Ltd v Moorehead* (1909) 8 CLR 330 **[10.2.30]**. That narrow approach also affected the reading of the trade and commerce power, which was (and still is) seen as having limited potential to support wide-ranging regulation of commercial activity.

Partly because of the justices' resistance to economic argument and partly because of the continuing influence of the 'reserved powers' approach to constitutional interpretation (see **[10.2.28]**), the High Court has, by and large, maintained that the distinction said to be implicit in s 51(i) must be strictly observed. The distinction is said to be between international and interstate trade and commerce, on the one hand, and intrastate trade and commerce on the other. The maintenance of the distinction has meant that, despite the economic interdependence of local and national commercial activity and the emergence of a national Australian economy, the trade and commerce power offers to the Commonwealth a narrow base on which to build its regulatory and public enterprise programmes. The narrowness of that base is well illustrated by *Attorney-General (WA) v Australian National Airlines Commission* (1976) 138 CLR 492 **[10.2.26C]**.

The debate on the proper extent of s 51(i) seems to have gone into recess because of the revolutionary (although not entirely unexpected) High Court decision in *Strickland v Rocla Concrete Pipes Ltd* (1971) 124 CLR 468 **[10.3.4C]**, which rejected the restrictive *Huddart Parker* reading of the corporations power. Section 51(xx) is now seen as the major source of the Commonwealth's regulatory power over commercial activity; indeed, decisions such as *Actors & Announcers Equity v Fontana Films Pty Ltd* (1982) 150 CLR 169 **[10.3.18C]** and *Commonwealth v Tasmania* (the *Tasmanian Dam* case) (1983) 158 CLR 1 **[10.3.26C]** suggest that the Commonwealth can bring the activities (commercial or otherwise) of most Australian corporations under its direct control.

[10.1.9] The second of the questions posed in **[10.1.6]** brings us face to face with s 92 of the Constitution. This section guarantees that 'trade, commerce and intercourse among the States ... shall be absolutely free'. Section 92 is a restraint upon both Commonwealth and states. Any legislation which applies to interstate trade (and this includes legislation on a very wide range of subject matters, not only legislation on the subject of interstate trade) must run the gauntlet of s 92. The legislation's survival has historically depended on complex tests developed in intensive litigation. That litigation has produced more High Court decisions than any other aspect of the Constitution. The impact of this guarantee on the powers of the Commonwealth and the states is explored in **[10.4.1E]–[10.4.41]**.

[10.1.10] Regulation of commercial activity can face other constitutional difficulties. Two, in particular, affect only Commonwealth regulatory schemes. First, such a regulation could be treated, by the High Court, as involving an 'acquisition of property' and so require the provision of 'just terms' (appropriate compensation) to the person or business which is regulated: s 51(xxxi). Legislation based on the corporations power and used to control the practice of 'exclusive dealing' by breweries ran into this difficulty, although it survived: *Trade Practices Commission v Tooth & Co Ltd* (1979) 142 CLR 397 **[11.2.11C]**. So, too, did legislation designed to prevent the Tasmanian Hydro-Electric Commission constructing the Franklin Dam (*Commonwealth v Tasmania* (the *Tasmanian Dam* case) (1983) 158 CLR 1 **[3.3.21C]**); as did legislation imposing liens on aircraft in lieu of unpaid aviation service charges (*Airservices Australia v Canadian Airlines International Ltd* (1999) 202 CLR 133 **[10.2.22]**). The second difficulty is that posed by s 99 of the Constitution for a relatively narrow group of Commonwealth laws. This provision insists that no Commonwealth 'trade, commerce or revenue' law can 'give preference to one State or any part thereof over another State or any part thereof'.

---

2   Trade and commerce power

[10.2.1E]   **Commonwealth Constitution**

51 The Parliament shall, subject to this Constitution, have power to make laws for the peace, order, and good government of the Commonwealth with respect to:

(i)   Trade and commerce with other countries, and among the States: ...

...

98 The power of the Parliament to make laws with respect to trade and commerce extends to navigation and shipping, and to railways the property of any State.

~~~

Notes

[10.2.2] The basic problem with s 51(i), as with most of the Commonwealth's legislative powers, is to identify the activities which fall within it and those which fall outside it. The High Court has resolved this problem by focusing on a distinction implicit in the paragraph. That is, the court has adopted a relatively open view of the concept of trade and commerce but has insisted on a sharp distinction between interstate and international trade on the one hand and intrastate trade on the other.

[10.2.3] In *W & A McArthur Ltd v Queensland* (1920) 28 CLR 530, Knox CJ, Isaacs and Starke JJ observed that 'trade and commerce' were 'not terms of art. They are expressions of fact, they are terms of common knowledge, as well known to laymen as to lawyers, and better understood in detail by traders and commercial men than by judges': 28 CLR at 546. They went on to say that the activities which might be included in the phrase would depend on the growth of and changes in commercial activity (at 546–7):

> 'Trade and commerce' between different countries ... has never been confined to the mere act of transportation of merchandise over the frontier. That the words include that act is, of course, a truism. But that they go far beyond it is a fact quite as undoubted. All the commercial arrangements of which transportation is the direct and necessary result form part of 'trade and commerce'. The mutual communings, the negotiations, verbal and by correspondence, the bargain, the transport and the delivery are all, but not exclusively, parts of that class of relations between mankind which the world calls 'trade and commerce'.

[10.2.4] As with other heads of power, the trade and commerce power is treated as allowing the Commonwealth to regulate ancillary or incidental matters. In *Huddart Parker Ltd v Commonwealth* (1931) 44 CLR 492, the High Court held that the Commonwealth Parliament could legislate to give preference to union members for employment in loading or unloading ships involved in interstate and international trade. In the words of Dixon J, the legislation was valid because 'it directly regulates the choice of persons to perform the work which forms part of or is an incident in interstate and external commerce. It does so in spite of the fact that it affects employers in the selection of their servants and in spite of the industrial aspect which the provision undeniably presents': 44 CLR at 515–16.

This view was applied in *R v Wright; Ex parte Waterside Workers Federation of Australia* (1955) 93 CLR 528, where the High Court confirmed the validity of parts of the Stevedoring Industry Act 1949 (Cth), giving the Court of Conciliation and Arbitration authority to prescribe conditions of employment in the stevedoring industry. The trade and commerce power supported this legislation.

In *R v Foster; Ex parte Eastern and Australian Steamship Co Ltd* (1959) 103 CLR 256, Windeyer J observed that, under the trade and commerce power, the Commonwealth Parliament could regulate the conditions of work of persons working on board ships engaged in Australian interstate or overseas trade and commerce, a proposition which appears to be a natural extension of the *Huddart Parker* decision.

[10.2.5] In *Australian National Airways Pty Ltd v Commonwealth* (1945) 71 CLR 29 **[10.4.9]**, the plaintiff challenged the validity of the Australian National Airlines Act 1945 (Cth), which established a statutory commission with power to operate airline services between the states, and to and from and within the territories. The plaintiff argued that s 51(i) 'contemplates the legislative regulation of overseas and interstate trade and commerce and not the entry of the Government itself into that field of activity': 71 CLR at 80. Dixon J dealt with that argument as follows (at 81):

> I am of opinion that this argument ought not to be accepted. It plainly ignores the fact that it is a Constitution we are interpreting, an instrument of government meant to endure and conferring powers expressed in general propositions wide enough to be capable of flexible application to changing circumstances. It confuses the unexpressed assumptions upon which the framers of the instrument supposedly proceeded with the expressed meaning of the power. A law authorising the Government to conduct a transport service for interstate trade, whether as a monopoly or not, appears to me to answer the description, a law with respect to trade and commerce amongst the States.

It is only by importing a limitation into the descriptive words of the power that such a law can be excluded.

Dixon J also rejected an argument that the trade and commerce power only covered the interstate carriage or transport of persons who were themselves engaged in commerce, that it could not authorise the establishment of a government airline carrying people whose journeys were social or recreational. He said at 83:

> I shall act upon the opinion that, if not all interstate transportation, at all events all carriage for reward of goods or persons between States is within the legislative power, whatever may be the reason or purpose for which the goods or persons are in transit.

[10.2.6] Although interstate trade is not confined to the act of transportation and includes interstate financial transactions (*Commonwealth v Bank of New South Wales* (1949) 79 CLR 497 **[10.4.10C]** at 632–3) the High Court has emphasised that the concept of interstate trade has its limits. (These limits have been drawn in the context of defining the freedom conferred by s 92 and their application to the Commonwealth's powers under s 51(i) is considerably modified by the notion that each of the Commonwealth's legislative powers carries with it power over incidental or ancillary matters: see **[10.2.5]**, **[10.2.8]**.)

A Victorian health insurance organisation, which had contracted to pay benefits to its subscribers if those subscribers incurred medical expenses, was not engaged in interstate trade, even though some of its subscribers lived in other states: *Hospital Provident Fund Pty Ltd v Victoria* (1953) 87 CLR. No interstate trade was involved, because the contract of insurance did not expressly require payment to be made across state borders (either by the contributors or by the insurer).

Similarly, an agreement between petroleum refiners and distributors, under which one company supplied petroleum in state A to another company in return for that other company supplying petroleum in state B to the first company (known as the 'refinery exchange scheme') did not involve interstate trade: *HC Sleigh Ltd v South Australia* (1977) 136 CLR 475. This was because the agreement did 'not call for the sale or delivery of any product across State boundaries': 136 CLR at 506.

[10.2.7] The court has consistently held that production, even when earmarked for interstate trade, is not part of interstate trade and commerce: *Beal v Marrickville Margarine Pty Ltd* (1966) 114 CLR 283 and *Bartter's Farms v Todd* (1978) 139 CLR 499. Interstate trade in manufactured products only begins, the court has said, with the interstate movement of the products; the production is 'a mere intrastate preparation for a proposed act of interstate trade in manufactured goods, and [is] not itself a part of interstate trade': 114 CLR at 304–5. (The application, to s 51(i), of these last two decisions has been moderated as a result of the High Court's emphasis on the incidental aspects of s 51(i): see *O'Sullivan v Noarlunga Meat Ltd* (1954) 92 CLR 565 **[10.2.11C]**.)

For some years, it was thought that the first sale, within a state, of goods imported from another state was not part of interstate trade: *Wragg v New South Wales* (1953) 88 CLR 353 **[10.4.13]**. That assumption has been reversed (*Permewan Wright Consolidated Pty Ltd v Trewhitt* (1979) 145 CLR 1 **[10.4.24]**) but it would seem that second and subsequent sales of interstate products still lie outside the judicial concept of interstate trade. This does not mean that they lie beyond the protection afforded by s 92 because the High Court's decision in *Cole v Whitfield* (1988) 165 CLR 360 **[10.4.27C]** prescribes a 'practical' approach to s 92 issues. However, it would mean that subsequent dealings in out-of-state commodities are not subject to Commonwealth regulation as an integral part of interstate trade and commerce.

[10.2.8] Even though it has a relatively narrow view of what is interstate (or international) trade and commerce, the High Court's view of the range of activities which can be controlled under s 51(i) has been expanded through the standard technique of allowing the power to be exercised in relation to activities which are incidental or ancillary to trade and commerce. This extension has been justified partly by reference to the text of s 51 and partly by appeal to general principle. For example, in *Grannall v Marrickville Margarine Pty Ltd* (1955) 93 CLR 55 **[10.4.15]**, Dixon CJ explained why the Commonwealth might be able to control production or manufacture under s 51(i), even though those activities were not themselves part of trade and commerce (at 77):

> In the first place, the power is to legislate with *respect to* trade and commerce. The words 'with respect to' ought never to be neglected in considering the extent of a legislative power conferred by s 51 or s 52. For what they require is a relevance to or connection with the subject assigned to the Commonwealth Parliament ... In the next place, every legislative power carries with it authority to legislate in relation to acts, matters and things the control of which is found necessary to effectuate its main purpose, and thus carries with it power to make laws governing or affecting many matters that are incidental or ancillary to the subject matter.

[10.2.9] However, a paradox has developed in the application of these principles of interpretation to s 51(i). Despite occasional concessions to those who have pressed for a broad reading of s 51(i), the court has insisted that the range of activities open to Commonwealth control is sharply restricted by the phrase, in s 51(i), 'with other countries and among the States'. Dixon CJ highlighted the court's view of this phrase's significance in *Wragg v New South Wales* (1953) 88 CLR 353 **[10.4.13]** when he said, after conceding that ancillary or incidental matters might be regulated by the Commonwealth (at 386):

> But even in the application of this principle to the grant of legislative power made by s 51(i) the distinction which the Constitution makes between the two branches of trade and commerce must be maintained. Its existence makes impossible any operation of the incidental power which would obliterate the distinction.

[10.2.10] The 'two branches of trade and commerce' which Dixon CJ referred to were interstate (and international) trade, on the one hand, and intrastate trade, on the other. Running through High Court decisions on the scope of s 51(i) (and on the extent of the freedom guaranteed by s 92) is the assumption that trade and commercial activity in Australia can be divided into those 'two branches' one of which lies outside the scope of s 51(i) (and beyond the protection given by s 92). The court has, on occasion, been urged to soften the distinction or to concede that some intrastate trade and commerce is so integrated with interstate or international trade and commerce that its regulation should be seen as a Commonwealth, rather than a state, responsibility.

In response, the court has made some concessions and refused others. The decisions of the court which follow review those concessions and refusals and suggest a pattern of acceptance, by the court, of arguments based on the physical integration of commercial activities and rejection of arguments based on economic integration. That is, the court has been willing to accept the 'incidental' nature of activities which are physically connected to interstate or international trade and commerce, but has refused to accept the 'incidental' nature of activities whose links with interstate or international trade and commerce are economic.

[10.2.11C]   **O'Sullivan v Noarlunga Meat Ltd**
(1954) 92 CLR 565

The Commerce (Meat Export) Regulations were made under the Customs Act 1901 (Cth). The regulations provided that the export of meat was prohibited unless the treatment and storage of the meat had been carried out in an establishment registered under the regulations, and the provisions of the regulations had been complied with: reg 4S(1)(a), (b). The regulations also provided that all premises used for the slaughter of meat for export should be registered under the regulations: reg 5. Other provisions set down detailed standards for the construction of buildings, drainage and the location of buildings and yards used in the treatment and storage of meat.

Noarlunga Meat Ltd operated a slaughter house and abattoirs at Noarlunga in South Australia. The company's premises were registered under the Commerce (Meat Export) Regulations. (The company also held a licence under the Meat Export Control (Licences) Regulations, made under the Meat Export Control Act 1935 (Cth), which was a licence to export meat processed in its Noarlunga premises.)

The Metropolitan and Export Abattoirs Act 1936 (SA) provided that no person should use any premises for the purpose of slaughtering stock for export unless that person held a licence from the state Minister of Agriculture: s 52A(i). The company did not hold such a licence.

On 27 November 1953 the company slaughtered and froze 152 lambs for export. All of these carcasses were sold and delivered to the Australian Meat Board (an agency of the Commonwealth Government) and exported to the United Kingdom on 13 December 1953. The company was charged (on a complaint made by an inspector of the South Australian Agriculture Department) with using premises on 27 November 1953 to slaughter meat for export, contrary to s 52A of the Metropolitan and Export Abattoirs Act 1936 (SA). The company pleaded that the state legislation was inconsistent with the Commonwealth regulations and therefore invalid. The magistrate stated a case for the opinion of the Supreme Court. The South Australian Attorney-General moved before the High Court that the special case be removed into that court under s 40 of the Judiciary Act 1903 (Cth). The High Court so ordered.

Fullagar J held that, assuming the Commonwealth Regulations to be valid, they showed an intention 'to express completely and exhaustively the requirements of the law with respect to the use of premises for the slaughter of stock for export': 92 CLR at 592. That is, the Commonwealth law covered that field and, in so far as state law entered into that field, or attempted to regulate slaughter of stock for export, it would be invalid because of inconsistency: see **[8.1.36]**, **[8.1.45]**. His Honour then turned to the validity of the Commonwealth regulations.

Fullagar J: [596] The question which emerges is whether the Commonwealth power with respect to trade and commerce with other countries extends to authorising legislation regulating and controlling the slaughter of meat for export. In my opinion it does so extend.

... [T]he expression 'slaughter for export' is used in the relevant legislation as a composite expression which would be understood objectively in the trade. Whether 'slaughter for export' is taking place is not, from the point of view of the legislator, a question which depends entirely on some intention in the mind of the owner or slaughterer of a beast — an intention which may change from time to time as operations proceed. The whole process from killing to packing [597] will be conditioned in certain respects by the predetermined destination of the meat, and 'slaughter for export' is, in the mind of the legislator, a definite objective conception distinct from slaughter for home consumption. It does not, of course, follow that any corresponding position exists with regard to any commodity other than meat. It may very well be, for example, that such an expression as 'mining metals for export' or 'sowing wheat for export' is meaningless except by reference to some subjective element.

... [E]ven if counsel for the State of South Australia be right in saying that the course of commerce with other countries does not begin until a later stage, I am of opinion that the regulations must be held valid on the broad general principle of constitutional interpretation adopted in the earliest days of this court. In *D'Emden v Pedder* (1904) 1 CLR 91, the court accepted the famous enunciation of the principle by Marshall CJ in *M'Culloch v Maryland* (1819) 4 Wheat 316 at 321–3, as 'most welcome aid and assistance' and said: 'Where any power to control is expressly granted, there is included in the grant, to the full extent of the capacity of the grantor and without special mention, every power and every [598] control the denial of which would render the grant itself ineffective' (1904) 1 CLR at 110.

It is true that the Commonwealth possesses no specific power with respect to slaughterhouses. But it is undeniable that the power with respect to trade and commerce with other countries includes a power to make provision for the condition and quality of meat or of any other commodity to be exported. Nor can the power, in my opinion, be held to stop there. By virtue of that power all matters which may affect beneficially or adversely the export trade of Australia in any commodity produced or manufactured in Australia must be the legitimate concern of the Commonwealth. Such matters include not only grade and quality of goods but packing, getup, description, labelling, handling, and anything at all that may reasonably be considered likely to affect an export market by developing it or impairing it. It seems clear enough that the objectives for which the power is conferred may be impossible of achievement by the means of a mere prescription of standards for export and the institution of a system of inspection at the point of export. It may very reasonably be thought necessary to go further back, and even to enter the factory or the field or the mine. How far back the Commonwealth may constitutionally go is a question which need not now be considered, and which must in any case depend on the particular circumstances attending the production or manufacture of particular commodities. But I would think it safe to say that the power of the Commonwealth extended to the supervision and control of all acts or processes which can be identified as being done or carried out for export. The 'slaughter for export' of stock is such an act or process, and, in my opinion, the Commerce (Meat Export) Regulations are within the legislative power conferred upon the Commonwealth by s 51(i).

Dixon CJ and Kitto J agreed with the judgment of Fullagar J. McTiernan, Webb and Taylor JJ held that there was no inconsistency between the state and Commonwealth law. McTiernan J held that the Commonwealth law was valid under s 51(i) of the Constitution. Webb and Taylor JJ did not decide that issue. As the court was evenly divided on the issue of inconsistency, the opinion of the Chief Justice prevailed: Judiciary Act 1903 (Cth) s 23(2)(b).

~~~

Notes

[10.2.12]　At one level, the decision in *O'Sullivan v Noarlunga Meat Ltd* (1954) 92 CLR 565 **[10.2.11C]** is a straightforward decision. Production or preparation for international (or interstate) trade is so connected with that trade that it may be regulated under the trade and commerce power. This approach assumes a direct, physical and causal link between the production and the international or interstate trade.

In *Crowe v Commonwealth* (1935) 54 CLR 69, the High Court took a similar approach to the validity of the Dried Fruits Export Control Act 1924 (Cth) and regulations made under the Act. The Act and regulations regulated the manner in which an exporter of dried fruit could sell or dispose of that dried fruit *after* its export to the United Kingdom. It was argued, in the words of Dixon J, 'that the limits of the commerce power are exceeded because an attempt is made to control transactions occurring after the goods have ceased to be in the course of trade and commerce with other countries'. That objection was rejected by Dixon J who said that the Commonwealth's 'authority over exportation is complete, and what it may forbid unconditionally, it may allow conditionally': 54 CLR at 90. Evatt and McTiernan JJ said that 'the sale and marketing of the goods abroad constitutes a typical and essential part of [international] trade' in goods: 54 CLR at 94.

[10.2.13]   The reasons of Fullagar J in *O'Sullivan v Noarlunga Meat Ltd* (1954) 92 CLR 565 **[10.2.11C]** raise some difficult questions. The Commonwealth Regulations were valid because they dealt with production or preparation for export. They dealt with an activity which was clearly identifiable as part of the chain of activities which made up the export trade in meat. It was identifiable as part of that chain because of some clear objective features of the activity in which the processor or producer was engaged, not because of the subjective intention of the processor or producer.

What are the criteria by which the export-directed (or interstate trade-directed) character of a production or process is to be identified? Does meat (with rigorous and unusual standards set by such overseas customers as the United States and Iran) pose a simple problem to solve? Fullagar J said that 'slaughter for export' was 'a composite expression which would be understood objectively in the trade': 92 CLR at 596. But in other industries, production for export or interstate trade will not be distinctive. For example, the techniques used for mining bauxite will not vary if the bauxite is intended for export rather than domestic sale. In these cases, a range of factors might need to be considered in order to decide whether the production is for those purposes or for intrastate trade: the existence of contracts of sale, committing the product to interstate trade (as in *Beal v Marrickville Margarine Pty Ltd* (1966) 114 CLR 283); or the usual course of trade, showing that as a rule the product entered international trade (implicit, according to Zines, in *Swift Australian Co Pty Ltd v Boyd-Parkinson* (1962) 108 CLR 189 **[10.2.16]**: Zines (1997) p 67); or some other evidence of the producer's intention. All of these will be relevant.

In *United States v Darby* 312 US 100 (1941), for example, the United States Supreme Court held that Congress could, under its power to regulate commerce among the several states, control labour conditions in a furniture factory (at 117):

> … where an employer engaged … in the manufacture and shipment of goods in filling orders of extrastate customers, manufactures this product with the intent or expectation that according to the normal course of his business all or some part of it will be selected for shipment to those customers.

[10.2.14]   The decisions in *O'Sullivan v Noarlunga Meat Ltd* (1954) 92 CLR 565 **[10.2.11C]** and *Crowe v Commonwealth* (1935) 54 CLR 69 **[10.2.12]** recognise that international (or interstate) trade and commerce are *vertically* integrated with a series of local (intrastate) transactions. Production, manufacture, processing, transport, distribution and sale; each of these may not be central to, or even part of, international or interstate trade and commerce. However, even if not central to the concept, those transactions may, as a matter of practical reality, be so identified with international or interstate trade and commerce that the Commonwealth can control them. They are links in the chain which connect the international or interstate trade and commerce in a commodity, at one end, to the commodity's origins and, at the other end, to the commodity's destination.

[10.2.15]   A more difficult issue than the vertical integration of trade and commerce is the issue of its *horizontal* integration; that is, the question whether transactions directed towards intrastate trade and commerce so affect other transactions directed towards international or interstate trade and commerce that the transactions should be regarded as integrated and open to control under s 51(i). The High Court has not denied the possibility of this integration; rather, it has adopted a very cautious approach.

In *R v Burgess; Ex parte Henry* (1936) 55 CLR 608, the High Court considered the validity of part of the Air Navigation Act 1920 (Cth) which authorised the Governor-General to make regulations for the purpose of controlling air navigation. The Commonwealth said that uniform control of all air navigation (including intrastate air traffic) was necessary if it was to preserve the safety of international and interstate air traffic, and argued that the Act was therefore supported by s 51(i).

The court rejected this submission. 'Considerations of wisdom or expediency', said Latham CJ, could not 'control the natural construction of' s 51(i), which divided responsibility over international and interstate trade and intrastate trade, 'although these subjects are obviously in many respects very difficult to separate from each other': 55 CLR at 628. Dixon J said that s 51(i) compelled the distinction (between international and interstate trade and intrastate trade) however artificial and no matter what interdependence might be discovered: 55 CLR at 672. Evatt and McTiernan JJ denied that the 'possible "commingling" in air routes and airports', of intrastate and interstate air traffic justified Commonwealth control of all air traffic: 55 CLR at 677.

However, each of the justices left the way open for possible Commonwealth control of intrastate air traffic. This would depend, Latham CJ said, upon proving that foreign and interstate trade and intrastate trade were so intermingled that the Commonwealth could not regulate the former without regulating the latter: 55 CLR at 629. Evatt and McTiernan JJ made the same point. Commonwealth control of interstate trade must not 'be entirely frustrated and nullified': 55 CLR at 677. Dixon J said that intrastate trade could only be controlled 'to the extent necessary to make effectual [the] exercise' of the power over interstate commerce: 55 CLR at 671.

[10.2.16] Some members of the court addressed this issue in *Swift Australian Co Pty Ltd v Boyd-Parkinson* (1962) 108 CLR 189. Swift operated a poultry killing and processing plant in Queensland. About five per cent of the plant's output was exported from Australia, the balance being sold in Queensland or interstate. Swift's plant was registered under the Commerce (Meat Export) Regulations (Cth), which laid down detailed standards for the processing of meat for export, but not under the Poultry Industry Acts 1946–1959 (Qld), which prohibited the slaughter of poultry for human consumption on premises not licensed under the Queensland Acts.

Swift was prosecuted for a breach of the Poultry Industry Acts and argued, in its defence, that the Queensland legislation was invalid because it was inconsistent with the Commerce (Meat Export) Regulations. This argument depended on the conclusions, first, that the Commonwealth had intended, in the Regulations, to regulate all meat processing in plants where only a part of the processed meat was to be exported and, secondly, that the trade and commerce power would support such an intention.

A majority of the High Court, Dixon CJ, McTiernan, Kitto, Taylor, Windeyer and Menzies JJ, held that the regulations were only intended to regulate the processing of that poultry which was intended for export. They left the control of the other processing to state legislation. Of the majority justices, Dixon CJ, Kitto and

Windeyer JJ did not refer to the constitutional issue. McTiernan, Taylor, Menzies and Owen JJ did.

The basis of the argument for Commonwealth power was that the organisation of Swift's plant made necessary Commonwealth control over all the processing at the plant. At the time of slaughter, treatment, packing or storage, no one could predict which birds would be exported and which would be sold on the domestic market. If export standards were to be maintained, the argument went, the whole of the processing had to be conducted according to those standards. McTiernan J rejected this submission, citing the assertion of Latham CJ (in *R v Burgess; Ex parte Henry* (1936) 55 CLR 608 at 628 **[10.2.15]**) that the constitutional distinction between intrastate and other trade and commerce 'must be fully recognised': 108 CLR at 203. On the other hand, Menzies J said at 220 that it was:

> ... within the power of the Commonwealth to prohibit slaughtering for home consumption in premises registered for slaughtering for *export ... or to* regulate, in an establishment where slaughtering for export is carried on in the interests of overseas trade, operations not directly concerned with preparing goods for that trade.

Taylor J made a similar (though more equivocal) concession: 108 CLR at 213. Owen J, who dissented, found a Commonwealth intention and competence to regulate all meat processing on premises where animals were killed and prepared for export. He said at 226:

> I think it is undeniable that the trade and commerce power is wide enough to enable this to be done. To begin with it is difficult to imagine a state of affairs in which slaughter, treatment, storage and packing of meat for export is carried on in an establishment and the whole of the meat products resulting from those operations is ultimately exported. There must inevitably be some meat which, for a diversity of reasons, may be rejected for export yet be entirely suitable for home consumption. Again, as the facts in the present case show, it may be impossible to predicate at the time of slaughter, treatment, storage or packing whether any particular carcass or any particular part of a carcass will ultimately be exported or whether it will go into home consumption. Finally if the slaughter, treatment, storage or packing of meat for export is carried on in the same establishment as the slaughter of meat for home consumption, it may well be necessary that the whole of the operations carried on in the establishment should be governed by the set of regulations which are directed to the preparation of meat for export lest the condition or quality of meat which finally goes into export be prejudicially affected by the conditions under which the slaughter of meat for the home market takes place.

[10.2.17] This view, that the physical integration of the domestic and export processes justified Commonwealth control of all processes, was not radical. It had been foreshadowed in *R v Burgess; Ex parte Henry* (1936) 55 CLR 608 **[10.2.15]** at 629 per Latham CJ; at 671 per Dixon J; at 677 per Evatt and McTiernan JJ. The view did not involve the broad, expansionist reading of the Commonwealth's trade and commerce power which the United States Supreme Court had given to the commerce clause in the United States Constitution. In a series of decisions dating from 1937, that court had accepted that 'a close and substantial relation to interstate commerce' would justify congressional control of intrastate activities: *National Labour Relations Board v Jones & Laughlin Steel Corporation* 301 US 1 (1937) at 37. Relation was 'a matter of practical judgment, not to be determined by abstract notions' and the court would, by and large, defer to the judgment of Congress: *Polish National Alliance v National Labour Relations Board* 322 US 643 (1944) at 650. In particular, the court accepted that intrastate activities could be regulated if they had some economic effect on interstate commerce: *Wickard v Filburn* 317 US 111 (1942) **[10.2.29]**. However, at times there has been strong judicial resistance in Australia to arguments based on American cases. While some regulation of intrastate activities has been permitted by the High Court, the majority of justices have sharply distinguished between physical connections and economic connections.

[10.2.18] In *Redfern v Dunlop Rubber Australian Ltd* (1964) 110 CLR 194, the High Court held that the Commonwealth could, under s 51(i), regulate an activity which combined interstate and intrastate trade. Several retailers of motor vehicle tyres sued five tyre manufacturers for damages under the Australian Industries Preservation Act 1906 (Cth), which prohibited any contract or combination 'in relation to trade and commerce with other countries or among the States' in restraint of trade: s 4(1). (This early legislative attempt to proscribe anti-competitive business practices was based on s 51(i), rather than s 51(xx), which supports the present Trade Practices Act 1974: see **[10.3.18C]**.)

The plaintiffs, whose businesses were located in Victoria, alleged that the tyre manufacturers had agreed among themselves not to supply the plaintiffs with tyres at wholesale prices because the plaintiffs were retailing tyres at discount. (At the time, the practice of resale price maintenance was not proscribed: see now the Trade Practices Act 1974 (Cth) s 48.) The tyre manufacturers' factories were located in three states; but two manufacturers, Dunlop and Olympic, had one of their factories in Victoria; and one manufacturer, BF Goodrich, had its only factory in Victoria. They demurred to the plaintiffs' statement of claim on the ground, inter alia, that the contract or combination alleged by the plaintiffs was in relation to intrastate as well as interstate trade and commerce. (Given the location of the Dunlop, Olympic and Goodrich factories and of the plaintiffs' retail businesses, the factual basis for the demurrer was undeniable.) It followed, argued the manufacturers, that s 4(1) of the Australian Industries Preservation Act was invalid if it purported to prohibit the manufacturers' alleged contract or combination.

The High Court, Dixon CJ, McTiernan, Kitto, Taylor, Menzies, Windeyer and Owen JJ, rejected that argument. Taylor J said that legislation would not exceed the power in s 51(i) merely because it dealt with activities which combined interstate and intrastate trade. It was not a sound objection to a Commonwealth law that some of the interstate trade activities (here contracts or combinations in restraint of trade) 'may be found to relate also to other matters': 115 CLR at 213. Menzies J conceded that s 51(i) 'has never been regarded as having the scope which the Supreme Court of the United States has attributed to the trade and commerce power in the United States Constitution' because the High Court had always insisted on observing the distinction between intrastate and other trade. But:

> ... if a contract or combination is 'in relation to trade or commerce with other countries or among the States', the subsection can validly apply to participation in it, notwithstanding that it is in relation to other matters as well. Thus, participation in one combination in restraint of overseas, interstate and intrastate trade is validly within the scope of the section ... It is, of course, clear that Commonwealth power over trade and commerce can only extend to such intrastate trade and commerce as is inseparably connected with interstate trade and commerce, but full acceptance of this limitation is quite consistent with according to the Commonwealth power to prohibit or regulate acts which relate to intrastate trade and commerce if they relate to interstate or overseas trade and commerce as well (110 CLR at 221-1).

[10.2.19]   *Redfern v Dunlop Rubber Australian Ltd* (1964) 110 CLR 194 **[10.2.18]** involved the recognition that some commercial activities have a composite character and cannot easily be segregated into their intrastate, interstate and international aspects. This integrated character may be a result of the way in which a trader chooses to conduct business. In *Redfern*, it was alleged that the manufacturers had elected to make a single agreement, with effects on interstate and intrastate trade. If they had made two distinct agreements: (a) not to supply the Victorian retailers from their interstate factories; and (b) not to supply those retailers from their Victorian factories; the Commonwealth could have regulated the former agreement under s 51(i) but not the latter. This is essentially the reasoning which lies behind Owen J's approach in *Swift Australian Co Pty Ltd v Boyd-Parkinson* (1962) 108 CLR 189 at 226 **[10.2.16]**. The organisation of Swift's processing plant inextricably mixed its export and domestic trade processes. To regulate the former, the Commonwealth was justified in regulating the whole. In other situations, the composite or integrated character of a trading activity may come from some inherent feature of that activity rather than from the trader's chosen method of operations. The following decision illustrates that possibility.

[10.2.20C]   Airlines of New South Wales Pty Ltd v New South Wales (No 2)

(1965) 113 CLR 54

The Air Navigation Regulations (Cth) were made under the Air Navigation Act 1920 (Cth). They provided for a system of licensing, to be controlled by the Commonwealth Director-General of Civil Aviation, or aircraft used for public transport. Until 10 October 1964 the regulations were limited, by reg 6(1), to: (a) international air navigation within Australia; (b) air navigation in relation to international and interstate trade and commerce; (c) air navigation within the territories; (d) air navigation to or from the territories; and (e) air navigation which affected the safety of air navigation specified in (a), (b) or (d). A new paragraph was added to reg 6(1) to take effect from 10 October 1964. It extended the regulations to all air navigation within Australia.

The regulations included the following provisions:

- reg 198, which prohibited the use of aircraft in regular public transport operations unless licensed by the Director-General of Civil Aviation;

- reg 199, which provided that the Director-General, when deciding whether to issue a licence for an intrastate service, should consider matters relating to 'safety regularity and efficiency of air navigation and … no other matters'; and

- reg 200B, which provided that a licence issued under reg 198 gave the licensee complete authority to conduct aircraft public transport operations, irrespective of state law.

The State Transport (Co-ordination) Act 1931 (NSW) and the Air Transport Act 1964 (NSW) provided that a person should not carry by aircraft between places in New South Wales any passengers or goods unless the person, the aircraft and the route were licensed by the New South Wales Commissioner for Transport. In issuing a licence the Commissioner was to take account of the needs of the state and particular areas of the state for air transport services and the encouragement of competition in air transport.

Airlines of New South Wales Pty Ltd had held a licence under the State Transport (Coordination) Act to carry passengers and goods between Dubbo and Sydney. On 12 October 1964, the New South Wales Commissioner for Transport cancelled that licence and later refused to issue a licence to the company under the Air Transport Act. The company applied to the Commonwealth Director-General of Civil Aviation who granted it a licence under reg 198 of the Air Navigation Regulations covering the Dubbo–Sydney route.

The company then commenced a suit in the High Court against the state of New South Wales, seeking a declaration that the State Transport (Co-ordination) Act and the Air Transport Act were invalid because of their inconsistency with the Air Navigation Regulations; a declaration that the company, while it complied with the Air Navigation Regulations, was entitled to carry passengers and goods between Dubbo and Sydney; and an injunction to prevent the state from interfering with the plaintiff's air transport operations on that route. Taylor J referred two questions to the Full High Court: Were the Air Navigation Regulations valid? Were the regulations inconsistent with the state legislation?

Kitto J: [112] Because neither intrastate air navigation nor air navigation generally is per se a subject of Federal legislative power, a Federal law cannot operate to affect any activity of intrastate air navigation unless, in so operating, it possesses the character of a law not only with respect to intrastate air navigation but also with respect to some topic or collection of topics in respect of which the Constitution gives the Parliament power to make laws. This is not because of any doctrine of reserved powers, but simply because of the limited nature of the positive grants of power made by the Constitution to the Federal Parliament.

Kitto J described the licensing system established by regs 198 and 199, and continued:

[113] Thus the licensing system in its application to wholly intrastate air services is limited so as to serve only the purpose of aiding and protecting the safety, regularity and efficiency of air navigation generally. It is at this point that the crucial question arises. In so far as regs 198 and 199 aid and protect the safety, regularity and efficiency of intrastate air navigation, have they the character of a law with respect to any subject or subjects of Federal legislative power?

Kitto J said that decisions of the United States Supreme Court had held that the commerce clause in the United States Constitution would support legislation regulating intrastate activities which, upon consideration of economic effects, interfere with interstate commerce. His Honour referred to *United States v Wrightwood Dairy Co* 315 US 110 (1942) and *Wickard v Filburn* 317 US 111 (1942). Kitto J observed that, within the United States, these decisions had been criticised as 'less than unwavering bright lines' (*Baker v Carr* 369 US 186 at 283 (1962) per Frankfurter J), and as demonstrating that 'the American system is clearly no longer one of dual federalism': Schwartz, *American Constitutional Law* (1955) p 170. Kitto J continued:

[115] The Australian union is one of dual federalism, and until the Parliament and the people see fit to change it, a true federation it must remain. This court is entrusted with the preservation of constitutional distinctions, and it both fails in its task and exceeds its authority if it discards them, however out of touch with practical conceptions or with modern conditions they may appear to be in some or all of their applications. To import the doctrine of the American cases into the law of the Australian Constitution would in my opinion be an error. The Constitution supplies its own criteria of legislative power. To ask, as we are bound to, whether a given Federal law having an operation upon intrastate commerce is, in that operation, a law 'with respect to' commerce with other countries or among the States (or is within some other head of Federal power) is of course to ask a question which is not so precise that different answers may not appeal to different minds. But at least it is a legal question, a question of ascertaining the true character of the law by a consideration of what it does 'in the way of changing or creating or destroying duties or rights or powers': *South Australia v Commonwealth* (1942) 65 CLR at 424. It is the question the Constitution in terms presents.

It must, of course, be considered in the light of the nature of the particular form of commerce to which the law relates. It is, I think, a question as to whether, when the factual situations in which the law operations is understood, the law by its operation upon the intrastate section of the relevant form of commerce is seen to operate also upon the actual conduct of an activity or collection of activities in respect of which Federal power exists, for example, the actual carrying on of activities forming part of the overseas and interstate sections of that form of commerce. Where the intrastate activities, if the law were not to extend to them, would or might have a prejudicial effect upon matters merely consequential upon the conduct of an activity within Federal power, for example, where the profit or loss likely to result from interstate commercial air navigation would or might be affected, that mere fact would not suffice, in my judgment, to make the law a law 'with respect to' that activity itself. But, by contrast, where the law, by what it does in relation to intrastate activities, protects against danger of physical interference the very activity itself which is within Federal power, the conclusion does seem to me to be correct that in that application the law is a law within the grant of Federal power.

[116] We must therefore answer the question before us in the light of the nature of air navigation as it exists as a phenomenon of life in Australia and its Territories at the present time. In respects which hardly need to be emphasised it is sui generis among methods of transport, and indeed among all forms of trade and commerce. The speed at which modern aircraft move through the skies; their constant liability to sudden and wide deviation in flight by reason of mechanical or human deficiencies, the vagaries of the weather, the behaviour of other aircraft and other causes; the multiplicity of flights required to satisfy the demands of modern life; the multiplicity and inter-relation of the routes to be served; all these matters and more combine to make air navigation in this country a complex of activities of such a kind that what happens at any given time and place in the course of an air operation may substantially, even dramatically, affect other air operations close or distant in time or space. The significance of distances, of geographical relationships, is necessarily different for a problem concerning air navigation than for a problem concerning any other form of transport ... With all this in mind, it is impossible to assume in advance that any impairment of the safety, regularity or efficiency of intrastate air navigation will leave unimpaired the safety, regularity and efficiency of the other departments into which air navigation may be divided for constitutional purposes. It follows from these considerations, in my opinion, that a Federal law which provides a method of controlling regular public transport services by air with regard only to the safety, regularity and efficiency of air navigation [117] is a law which operates to protect against real possibilities of physical interference the actual carrying on of air navigation, and therefore is, in every application that it has, a law 'with respect to' such air navigation as is within Federal power, and none the less so because it is also legislation with respect to that intrastate air navigation which is not within the power.

In my opinion regs 198 and 199 are for these reasons valid laws of the Commonwealth, even in their application to regular public transport operations conducted wholly within the borders of a single State.

Kitto J discussed the external affairs power (s 51(xxix)) and rejected the argument that regs 198 and 199 gave effect to the Chicago Convention on international civil aviation: they were not, therefore, supported by the external affairs power. He then referred to reg 200B, whose operation he described as follows:

[119] I can see no escape from recognising that the operation which reg 200B purports to have is, not to protect from State interference a 'right' acquired under Federal law, but to supplement the grant of an exemption from a particular prohibition under Federal law by conferring in addition an immunity from any prohibition which State law may impose. The character of the regulation in its application to intrastate operation is therefore not that of a law with respect to a matter within Federal power, but is that of a law with respect to the application of State laws — a matter not within Federal legislative competence. By no line of reasoning that I have found it possible to accept can reg 200B be supported as valid Federal legislation.

Kitto J then considered whether the state legislation was inconsistent with the Commonwealth regulations:

[121] The topic and the only topic to which regs 198 and 199 direct their attention, so far as they apply to intrastate operations, is the safety, regularity and efficiency of air navigation. Regulation 199(4) makes that clear. The State Act, upon the other hand, does not concern

itself with that topic in any way. The fact that each piece of legislation sets up a licensing system operating independently of the licensing system established by the other may from time to time lead to a situation in which A, though holding a licence under the State Act for a proposed service, may be unable to obtain a licence for that service under reg 199, while B, though holding a licence for the service under reg 199, may be unable to obtain a licence for it under the State Act. But any ground for suggesting inconsistency disappears if the situation is more fully described, as by saying that consideration of matters concerning the safety, regularity and efficiency of air navigation has led the Federal Director-General for Civil Aviation to conclude that A, though not B, should be debarred from conducting the service, while consideration of matters concerning public needs in relation to air transport services or concerning other topics mentioned in s 6(3) of the State Act has led the State Commissioner for Motor Transport to conclude that B, though not A, should be debarred from conducting the service. The Federal Regulations and the State Act each employ a licensing system to serve a particular end; but the ends are different, and that means that the two sets of provisions are directed to different subjects [122] of legislative attention. In my opinion there is no mutual inconsistency in any relevant sense.

Barwick CJ, Menzies, Windeyer and Owen JJ agreed that regs 198 and 199 were supported by the trade and commerce power, McTiernan J dissented on that point, but held that regs 198 and 199 were supported by the external affairs power (as did Barwick CJ, Menzies and Owen JJ). Taylor J held that the two regulations were supported by neither the trade and commerce power nor the external affairs power. All the members of the court agreed that reg 200B was invalid in its application to intrastate trade. All the members of the court, other than Barwick CJ, held that the state legislation was not inconsistent with the Air Navigation Regulations: see **[8.1.37]**. On reg 200B Barwick CJ and Windeyer J made the following observations.

Barwick CJ: [88] It is one thing to say that the safety of interstate and international commercial air transport cannot be secured without including intrastate commercial air activities within the operation of the safety measures: it is quite another to say that the stimulation or authorisation of intrastate commercial air services is in any sense a safety measure. The non-existence of a commercial air transport service does not endanger the air operations of those who do operate commercial air transport services. Nor does the fact that interstate air navigation profits by or to a significant extent depends upon the existence of intrastate air navigation warrant the conclusion that in fostering interstate and foreign trade, the Commonwealth may stimulate and encourage intrastate trade. Consequently, reg 200B in its operation upon intrastate air navigation derives no support from ss 51(i) or 51(xxix). In my opinion in its purported operation in respect of intrastate commercial air transport it is invalid.

Windeyer J: [155] But saying that regs 198 and 199 are valid to the extent that they prohibit carrying on of regular transport operations without a Commonwealth airline licence and prescribe the conditions on which a licence may be had is one thing. It is another thing to say that Commonwealth law may make the grant of such a licence equivalent to the grant of a franchise or privilege to carry on such operations within a State with an immunity from the requirements of the State law and notwithstanding any prohibitions of the State law. That is what reg 200B purports to do to give what counsel called a 'positive authority', meaning a right in the licensee to conduct a regular air transport service within a State notwithstanding any State law to the contrary. But, as applied to a purely intrastate activity, this is obviously not a law with respect to interstate or overseas commerce. The safety of air navigation, commerce by air, with other countries and among the States could not be imperilled by the absence of any regular air transport service between Sydney and Dubbo. Regulation 200B is thus beyond Commonwealth power and invalid so far as it relates to activities wholly within a State.

~~~

Notes

[10.2.21] It is clear that in *Airlines of New South Wales Pty Ltd v New South Wales (No 2)* (1965) 113 CLR 54 **[10.2.20C]** the court was prepared to accept the *physical* integration of interstate, international and intrastate trade and commerce. It was the danger to the physical safety of interstate and international aircraft posed by intrastate aircraft using the same air space which justified the Commonwealth in regulating those intrastate aircraft. Given the complexity and speed of commercial air traffic, the operations of some of that traffic could only be controlled, regulated and protected by controlling *all* of the air traffic.

[10.2.22] In *Airservices Australia v Canadian Airlines International Ltd* (1999) 202 CLR 133, Gleeson CJ and Kirby J endorsed Barwick CJ's observation in *Airlines (No 2)* **[10.2.20C]** that 'the clear conclusion must be drawn that the safety of air operations in Australia does not admit of any distinction being drawn between aircraft engaged in intra-State and those in interstate or international air operations in connection with all those matters which go to make up what I can compendiously call safety precautions and procedures': 202 CLR at 174. See also McHugh J: 202 CLR at 253; and Gummow J: 202 CLR at 301. In *Airservices* Gleeson CJ, McHugh, Gummow, Kirby and Hayne JJ (Gaudron and Callinan JJ dissenting) upheld the validity of Commonwealth legislation that imposed a statutory lien on aircraft for unpaid aviation service charges as a law incidental to the regulation of a matter within s 51(i): 202 CLR at 174, 253, 301 and 305–6.

[10.2.23] Compare the analysis in *Airlines of New South Wales (No 2)* **[10.2.20C]** to the approach taken in *Redfern v Dunlop Rubber Australian Ltd* (1964) 110 CLR 194 **[10.2.18]**. In *Redfern*, the way in which the tyre manufacturers had chosen to integrate their restrictive practices, by making a single agreement or combination for both interstate and intrastate sales, justified Commonwealth control of that agreement or combination. In *Airlines of New South Wales (No 2)*, the physical integration which justified Commonwealth control was not the result of any conscious act by the entrepreneurs but was seen by the court as inherent in the nature of civil aviation.

[10.2.24] There are several points in *Airlines of New South Wales Pty Ltd v New South Wales (No 2)* (1965) 113 CLR 54 **[10.2.20C]** at which the court emphasised the physical nature of this integration. Take, for example, the observations of Kitto J on the relevance of an economic, as opposed to a physical, interference with interstate commerce. That interference 'would not suffice' to entitle the Commonwealth to regulate the activity which posed an economic threat, because such a threat or interference would be 'upon matters merely consequential upon' the interstate commerce: 113 CLR at 115.

Another example is the unequivocal rejection, by the court, of the argument that reg 200B was a valid law with respect to international and interstate commerce. It could not be such a law because it did nothing to advance the physical safety of that commerce. The Commonwealth had argued that, under s 51(i) of the Constitution, it could legislate to promote the economic well-being of international and interstate trade and commerce; that is, the Commonwealth said it could sponsor or promote intrastate air services, ensuring that adequate feeder services were developed, maintained and integrated with national and international services. But the court rejected this argument. The most that the Commonwealth could do was to exercise a veto over intrastate air services in the interests of safety, regularity and efficiency; it could not insist that there be any intrastate service. The economic effect of intrastate air services in feeding passengers to, and stimulating business for, interstate and international air services was not relevant. For example, Barwick CJ dismissed as irrelevant 'the fact that interstate air navigation profits by or to a significant extent depends upon the existence of intrastate air navigation': 113 CLR at 88.

The High Court was to return to this issue (the capacity of the Commonwealth to protect the economic health of interstate trade) in *Attorney-General (WA) v Australian National Airlines Commission* (1976) 138 CLR 492 **[10.2.26C]**.

[10.2.25] In practical terms, the decision in *Airlines of New South Wales Pty Ltd v New South Wales (No 2)* (1965) 113 CLR 54 **[10.2.20C]** resulted in a stalemate. The Commonwealth regulations, prohibiting intrastate air services without a Commonwealth licence (issued on the basis of 'safety, regularity and efficiency'), were valid. So, too, was the state legislation prohibiting intrastate air services without a state licence (issued on the basis of encouraging competition and filling state and local needs for air transport). Accordingly, no person could operate an air service from one part of New South Wales to another without two licences. Only Barwick CJ, who managed to invalidate reg 200B and still find inconsistency between the regulations and the state law, and Taylor J, who found all of the regulations invalid, avoided this inconvenient result. Some of the majority judges recognised the awkward results of their decision. Menzies J said at 114:

> It was argued that the decision of this court leaving intrastate air transport services to the veto of both Commonwealth and State would create a situation of stalemate or deadlock. This argument is irrelevant. A constitutional division of legislative power which is not exclusive may sometimes mean that those who are subject to both Commonwealth and State control have two sets of restrictions to surmount before they can do that which they want to do. This possibility was recognised by the Privy Council in *O'Sullivan v Noarlunga Meat Ltd*. The answer to stalemate or deadlock in such circumstances is cooperation.

Windeyer J said at 156–7:

> Unless the Commonwealth and the State can agree upon a person whom each will permit to carry on an air transport service between Sydney and Dubbo there can be no direct air service between those places. This is an inconvenience for members of the public who wish to travel by air. But the deadlock, as it has been called, does not demonstrate that the law of the State is inconsistent in the constitutional sense with the law of the Commonwealth. It demonstrates only differing policies of the Commonwealth and State governments.

This point, that the constitutional distinction between intrastate and other trade would leave some commercial activities without effective regulation in the absence of cooperation, had been made by Latham CJ in *R v Burgess; Ex parte Henry* (1936) 55 CLR 608 **[10.2.15]** at 629.

[10.2.26C]   **Attorney-General (WA) (Ex rel Ansett Transport Industries (Operations) Pty Ltd) v Australian National Airlines Commission**
(1976) 138 CLR 492

The Australian National Airlines Act 1945 (Cth) created the Australian National Airlines Commission. According to s 19 of the Act, the functions of the Commission were to transport passengers and goods for reward by air between the states, between a state and a territory and within a territory. The validity of s 19 had been upheld in *Australian National Airways Pty Ltd v Commonwealth* (1945) 71 CLR 29 **[10.2.5]**.

In 1973 the Act was amended by adding the following section:

> 19B(1) The Commission may, to the extent provided by sub-section (2), transport passengers or goods for reward by air or by land, or partly by air and partly by land, between places in the one State.
>
> (2) The powers of the Commission under sub-section (1) may be exercised for the purposes of the efficient, competitive and profitable conduct of the business of the Commission in respect of its function under paragraph (a) of sub-section (1) of section 19 or otherwise as incidental to the carrying on of that business.

The Commission operated an airline under the name of Trans-Australia Airlines (TAA). It proposed to commence a regular airline service between Perth and Darwin, with an intermediate stop at Port Hedland, Western Australia. Passengers and cargo from Perth and Darwin would be discharged at Port Hedland, where passengers and cargo for Perth and Darwin would be loaded. In the words of Mason J:

> Its proposal to commence such a service with an intermediate stopping place at Port Hedland is dictated by economic reasons, for it seems that a direct service between Perth and Darwin would be uneconomic, whereas a service with an intermediate stopping place at Port Hedland may well prove profitable by reason of the traffic available at Port Hedland for Perth and Darwin respectively (138 CLR at 518).

Ansett Transport Industries (Operations) Pty Ltd had for some time operated a regular airline service between Perth and Darwin with intermediate stopping places in the north of Western Australia, including a stopping place at Port Hedland.

The Attorney-General of Western Australia, at the relation of Ansett, began an action in the High Court against the Commission and the Commonwealth, seeking a declaration that s 19B of the Australian National Airlines Act 1945 (Cth) was invalid. Stephen J referred a number of questions for the decision of the Full Court, on which he sat.

Stephen J: [508] Does s 51(i), by its grant of legislative power over interstate trade and commerce, incidentally include a grant of power to legislate for intrastate trade and commerce when its only relationship to interstate trade and commerce lies in the fact that the purpose of engagement in such intrastate activity is to conduce to the efficiency, competitiveness and profitability of the interstate activity? ...

[509] It is notable that in considering the extent of the incidental power in the case of s 51(i) particular emphasis has always been placed upon distinction drawn by the Constitution between those aspects of trade and commerce assigned to Commonwealth legislative competence and that which is left to the States. In *R v Burgess; Ex parte Henry*, Dixon J said (1936) 55 CLR 608 at 672 that 'the express limitation of the subject matter of the power to commerce with other countries and among the States compels a distinction however artificial and whatever interdependence may be discovered between the branches into which the Constitution divides trade and commerce'. In *Wragg v New South Wales* (1953) 88 CLR 353 at 386 Dixon J again referred to that distinction which, he said, must be observed and maintained in the application, to s 51(i), of the doctrine of implied incidental power, that distinction made 'impossible any operation of the incidental power which would obliterate the distinction'. In *Redfern v Dunlop Rubber Australia Ltd* (1964) 110 CLR 194 at 220 Menzies J referred to the distinction as having always been insisted upon and in *Airlines of New South Wales Pty Ltd v New South Wales (No 2)* (1965) 113 CLR at 76–79 Barwick CJ affirmed this view, citing at length from the judgment of Dixon CJ in *Wragg's* case (1953) 88 CLR at 385–386.

The effect of this constitutional division of power over trade and commerce between the Commonwealth and the States has led to a quite narrowly confined ambit being given to the incidental power in the case of s 51(i), at least where what is in question is possible intrusion into the field of intrastate trade and commerce.

Stephen J referred to various judicial observations on the extent of the Commonwealth's power over interstate trade, including the observations made in *Airlines of New South Wales Pty Ltd v New South Wales (No 2)* to the effect that the Commonwealth could regulate intrastate trade and commerce if that were necessary for the Commonwealth law to be 'effective' as to interstate trade, but could not rely on the fact that international or interstate carriage by air may profit by, or to a significant degree depend upon, the level of intrastate carriage by air. Stephen J continued:

[510] In the light of the foregoing it is apparent that the permitted exercise of the power conferred by s 19B, and which is described in [511] sub-s (2) as 'incidental', extends beyond the ambit of that incidental power which s 51(i) carries with it. It follows that the validity of s 19B cannot gain any support by reliance upon s 51(i) ...

Stephen J went on to consider whether s 19B could be read down, through the application of s 15A of the Acts Interpretation Act 1901 (Cth). He concluded that s 19B could be confined to intrastate air transport which promoted the efficiency, competitiveness and profitability of territory air services and air services between a territory and other parts of Australia; and that, if read in that narrower way, s 19B would be valid because it would be a law 'for the government of any Territory' and so within the power conferred by s 122 of the Constitution: 138 CLR at 511. After pointing out that the power granted by s 122 was 'as large and universal a power of legislation as can be granted' (quoting Barwick CJ in *Spratt v Hermes* (1965) 114 CLR 226 at 242), Stephen J conceded that a law enacted under s 122 might have to observe some constitutional constraints:

[513] [T]he only such constitutional requirement which it has been suggested that s 19B infringes is its failure to observe the division of trade and commerce into two parts and to restrict itself to that part, interstate, territorial and overseas trade and commerce, which the Constitution alone allocates to Federal competence. When [514] the power under s 122, as distinct from that under s 51(i), is in question I would regard it as impermissible to seek to qualify it by reference to this constitutional division of the power over trade and commerce; the power conferred by s 122 is not, I think, to be limited by reference to an implication drawn from the terms of s 51(i) or s 92 ...

In considering the permissible scope of laws enacted under s 122 there is, I think, no reason for the exclusion of laws whose connexion with 'the government of a Territory' is confined to the production of desirable qualities in functions of government; thus a law which has as its object the reduction in cost of or the improvement in the efficiency of some governmental activity related to a Territory is, I think, a law with respect to the government of that Territory. In this respect the position is in marked contrast to that governing the scope of incidental powers to be implied in s 51(i) and which I have already noticed ...

Murphy J held that s 19B was supported by both the trade and commerce power, s 51(i), and the Territories power, s 122. He criticised the narrow reading of s 51(i) as 'the persistence of the doctrine that the national legislative powers are to be limited so that the reserved power of the States is not invaded': 138 CLR at 529. That narrow reading, he said, 'keeps the *pre-Engineers* ghosts walking': 138 CLR at 530.

Murphy J: [530] The sections in question authorise intrastate transport for the purposes of efficient competitive and profitable conduct of the interstate transport of the Commission. These criteria adopted by Parliament are well within the scope of the commerce power. It is permissible for Parliament to take account of commercial effects in legislating under the commerce power. It would be as illogical to exclude commercial considerations from [531] the construction of the commerce power as it would be to exclude defence considerations from the defence power (s 51(vi)) or industrial considerations from the industrial power (s 51(xxxv)). I find no basis in the Constitution for the distinction that Kitto J drew between physical and economic effects upon 'interstate commercial air navigation' in *Airlines of New South Wales v New South Wales (No 2)* (1965) 113 CLR 54 at 115.

This Court should not replace Parliament's judgment with its own unless the relation of the disputed sections to trade and commerce among the States (or other legislative power) clearly does not exist (*Stafford v Wallace* 258 US 495 (1922) [66 Law Ed 735]).

~~~

[10.2.27] Barwick CJ and Gibbs J agreed with Stephen J that s 19B could not be supported by s 51(i), whose distinction between intrastate and interstate trade 'must be maintained however much interdependence may now exist between those two divisions of trade and however artificial the distinction may be thought to be': 138 CLR at 502 per Gibbs J. Each of them emphasised that economic or commercial considerations could not be used to justify the Commonwealth regulating intrastate trading activities: 138 CLR at 499 per Barwick CJ; 138 CLR at 503 per Gibbs J. However, both Barwick CJ and Gibbs J disagreed with Stephen J on the capacity of the territories power (s 122) to support s 19B. They saw economic considerations as equally irrelevant to the scope of s 122 as they were to the scope of s 51(i).

Mason J found it unnecessary to decide whether s 51(i) supported s 19B because, like Stephen J, he held that the territories power (s 122) would support s 19B if that section were read down so as to authorise those intrastate air transport activities which promoted the efficient, competitive and profitable conduct of territory air services and air services between a territory and other parts of Australia. Mason J pointed out that considerations which might be relevant to the trade and commerce power, s 51(i), or to the guarantee of freedom of interstate trade, s 92, had little place in discussion of the scope of the territories power, s 122: 138 CLR at 525–6. He supported the relevance of economic considerations in the application of s 122.

Notes

[10.2.28] Zines points out that the decision in *Attorney-General (WA) v Australian National Airlines Commission* (1976) 138 CLR 492 **[10.2.26C]** can hardly be seen as concluding the issues raised 'even for the near future', for only five justices participated and, of them, only Stephen J's reasons conformed to the court's order. Nevertheless, the case raises important issues, not only for the trade and commerce power but for the general range of Commonwealth legislative power, 'the ultimate resolution of which will have a great effect on the nature and operation of Australian federalism': Zines (1997) p 73.

[10.2.29] The broad significance of *Attorney-General (WA) v Australian National Airlines Commission* (1976) 138 CLR 492 **[10.2.26C]** can be grasped if we reflect on the immediate practical implications of the decision. Trans-Australian Airlines, the Commonwealth-owned airline, was permitted to use economic considerations to integrate intrastate air transport with its territory activities, but could not use those considerations to integrate intrastate air transport with its interstate activities.

For example, Trans-Australian Airlines could carry passengers between Wodonga and Melbourne, even though both places are in Victoria, if the operation of that service contributed to the profitability of its passenger service between Canberra, in the Australian Capital Territory, and Melbourne. That is, Trans-Australian Airlines could break its flight between Canberra and Melbourne in Wodonga, pick up passengers there and fly them to Melbourne in order to increase seat occupancy rates and lower the unit cost of transporting passengers on the Canberra–Melbourne journey. However, Australian Airlines could not use similar considerations to justify breaking its Wagga–Melbourne flights in Wodonga, picking up passengers there and flying them to Melbourne. The contribution that intrastate trade might make to the profitability of the airline's interstate service would not be sufficient justification for undertaking that intrastate trade.

These immediate practical implications reveal a curious distinction in the High Court's approach to the powers of the Commonwealth: one of those powers (s 122) will be read sufficiently broadly to allow the Commonwealth to regulate activities which have some economic connection with matters central to the power; but another power (s 51(i)) will not be read in that way; more than economic connections must be shown before the Commonwealth will be permitted to regulate matters incidental to the power.

To say that the case establishes this distinction is of course, misleading. The decision reflects that distinction but only one of the five judgments, that of Stephen J, is built upon it. Barwick CJ and Gibbs J appear to regard economic and commercial considerations as constitutionally irrelevant; they can *never* be used to expand the range of activities subject to Commonwealth legislative power. Murphy J also denied the distinction, but for him economic factors were relevant to the scope of all Commonwealth powers. Mason J was equivocal. While he expressly refrained from dealing with s 51(i), his discussion of the relevance of economic factors for the territories power was in such strong terms that its application to the trade and commerce power would be relatively straightforward. (See, for example, his reference to 'the economic and technical factors which influence the establishment and organisation of commercial airline operations': 138 CLR at 524.)

[10.2.30] This disagreement is partly over the relevance of economic factors to constitutional decision-making (compare the differences of opinion within the court in such cases as *SOS (Mowbray) Pty Ltd v Mead* (1972) 124 CLR 529 and *Clark King & Co Pty Ltd v Australian Wheat Board* (1978) 140 CLR 120 over the significance of commercial and economic factors in assessing the impact of government controls on the freedom of interstate trade guaranteed by s 92). The disagreement is also over the appropriate federal balance for Australia. There is a strong current, running through most of the judgments in *R v Burgess; Ex parte Henry* (1936) 55 CLR 608 **[10.2.15]**, *Airlines of New South Wales Pty Ltd v New South Wales (No 2)* (1965) 113 CLR 54 **[10.2.20C]** and *Attorney-General (WA) v Australian National Airlines Commission* (1976) 138 CLR 492 **[10.2.26C]**, of concern for the powers of the states. The Commonwealth's power over international and interstate trade and commerce must not be permitted to reach across the sharp dividing line (drawn by s 51(i)) into intrastate trade and commerce) because the crossing of that line would reduce the powers of the states. In the words of Murphy J in *Attorney-General (WA) v Australian National Airlines Commission*, this restrictive view of s 51(i) 'keeps the pre-*Engineers* ghosts walking': 138 CLR at 530.

However, for all the justices' concern for the remnants of state powers and for ensuring that the states retain substantial areas over which they have exclusive control, the High Court has permitted some Commonwealth control of intrastate activities. *Airlines of New South Wales Pty Ltd v New South Wales (No 2)* (1965) 113 CLR 54 **[10.2.20C]** allowed Commonwealth control of intrastate air services where this was necessary for the physical safety of interstate air services and the court justified this expansion of Commonwealth controls by its assessment of practical considerations, such as the nature and complexity of contemporary air transport (an approach recently endorsed in *Airservices Australia v Canadian*

Airlines International Limited (1999) 202 CLR 133 **[10.2.22]** at 174, 253, 301, 305–6). Has the court worked out a compromise between the pressures to recognise the interdependence of so-called intrastate and other trade and commerce, on the one hand, and the pressures to maintain the 'dual federalism', which Kitto J said (113 CLR at 115) was embodied in 'the Australian union'? Can any compromise which takes account of physical effects but discounts economic effects be regarded as convincing, or as likely to endure?

For a stimulating critique of the High Court's approach to s 51(i) and its reluctance to consider economic factors, see Zines (1997) pp 75–9.

[10.2.31] One factor which seems to have discouraged the court (or most members of the court) from allowing economic considerations to influence their approach to s 51(i) has been their understanding of the United States Supreme Court's approach to the commerce clause of the United States Constitution. In *Airlines of New South Wales Pty Ltd v New South Wales (No 2)* (1965) 113 CLR 54 **[10.2.20C]**, Kitto J referred to the American cases and to some trenchant criticisms of those cases and said that the adoption of the American approach 'would … be an error': 113 CLR at 115.

The United States Constitution, art 1, s 8, cl 3, gives to Congress the power 'to regulate commerce with foreign nations and among the several States and with the Indian tribes'. The United States Supreme Court, in a long series of decisions from 1895 to 1936, took a narrow view of Congress's power under this clause.

In *United States v EC Knight Co* 156 US 1 (1895), the court held that Congress could not prevent the acquisition by a company of monopoly control over American sugar production. Any effect which the monopoly of production would have on interstate trade would be indirect and did not justify Congressional control of that production, which was a matter for the states. State powers were 'essential to the preservation of the autonomy of the States as required by our dual form of government': 156 US at 13.

In *United States v ALA Schechter Poultry Corporation* 295 US 495 (1935), the court struck down part of the National Industrial Recovery Act 1933 (US) which controlled working conditions in New York. To the argument that the plant's operations affected interstate trade (and so could be regulated under the commerce clause), the court responded by distinguishing between direct and indirect effects. Only the former would justify Congressional intervention (at 546):

> If the commerce clause were construed to reach all enterprises and transactions which could be said to have an indirect effect upon interstate commerce, the Federal authority would embrace practically all the activities of the people, and authority of the State over its domestic concerns would exist only by sufferance of the Federal Government.

The turning point was *National Labour Relations Board v Jones & Laughlin Steel Corporation* 298 US 1 (1937). The court upheld provisions of the National Labour Relations Act 1935 (US), which penalised unfair labour practices where those practices injured interstate commerce, and held that the steel manufacturing activities of the respondent corporation, the fourth largest steel producer in the United States, were subject to the Act. While manufacture was not itself part of commerce, Congress's power could be extended to control it (at 37):

> Although activities may be intrastate in character when separately considered, if they have such a close and substantial relation to interstate commerce that their control is essential or appropriate to protect that commerce from burdens or obstructions, Congress cannot be denied the power to exercise that control.

(The Supreme Court's change of approach followed closely upon the re-election, by an overwhelming majority, of President Roosevelt in November 1936 and the announcement on 7 February 1937, by the President in a message to Congress, of a proposal to 'reorganise the judicial branch', part of which would have involved a temporary but substantial increase in the size of the Supreme Court.)

From 1937, the court proceeded to concede to Congress extremely broad powers under the commerce clause. Its breadth is illustrated by the decision in *Wickard v Filburn* 317 US 111 (1942), where the court was asked to decide whether Congress could limit a farmer's production of wheat intended, not for interstate commerce, but for consumption on the farm. Evidence before the court established that the consumption of home-grown wheat had an effect on the market price of wheat in interstate trade (by reducing local demand for interstate wheat, or reducing local competition for interstate wheat, for example).

The court held that the commerce clause authorised Congressional control of the farmer's domestic wheat production. It conceded that there had been (until then) no decision of the court that production or manufacture could be regulated where none of the production was 'intended for interstate commerce or intermingled with the subjects thereof'. But it was important to consider the actual effects of the activity in question on interstate trade when deciding the extent of Congress's power: 317 US at 120. The court declared at 124–5:

> Once an economic measure of the reach of the power granted to Congress in the Commerce Clause is accepted, questions of Federal power cannot be decided simply by finding the activity in question to be 'production' nor can consideration of its economic effects be foreclosed by calling them 'indirect'. The present Chief Justice has said in summary of the present state of the law: 'The commerce power is not confined in its exercise to the regulation of commerce among the states. It extends to those activities intrastate which so affect interstate commerce, or the exertion of the power of Congress over it, as to make regulation of them appropriate means to the attainment of a legitimate end, the effective execution of the granted power to regulate interstate commerce ... The power of Congress over interstate commerce is plenary and complete in itself, may be exercised to its utmost extent, and acknowledges no limitations other than are prescribed in the Constitution ... It follows that no form of State activity can constitutionally thwart the regulatory power granted by the commerce clause to Congress. Hence the reach of that power extends to those intrastate activities which in a substantial way interfere with or obstruct the exercise of the granted power.' *United States v Wrightwood Dairy Co* 315 US 110, 119 (Law Ed 86 at 726, 62 s Ct 523).
>
> Whether the subject of the regulation in question was 'production', 'consumption', or 'marketing' is, therefore, not material for purposes of deciding the question of Federal power before us. That an activity is of local character may help in a doubtful case to determine whether Congress intended to reach it. The same consideration might help in determining whether in the absence of congressional action it would be permissible for the State to exert its power on the subject matter, even though in so doing it to some degree affected interstate commerce. But even if the appellee's activity be local and though it may not be regarded as commerce, it may still, whatever its nature, be reached by Congress if it exerts a substantial economic effect on interstate commerce, and this irrespective of whether such effect is what might at some earlier time have been defined as 'direct' or 'indirect'.

[10.2.32] There are, of course, ways in which the Commonwealth can use its relatively more narrow power under s 51(i) as a lever so as to exercise control, however indirect, over other associated activities. The following case illustrates this 'leverage' approach.

[10.2.33C]   # Murphyores Inc Pty Ltd v Commonwealth

(1976) 136 CLR 1

Murphyores Inc Pty Ltd and Dillingham Constructions Pty Ltd held mining leases on Fraser Island in Queensland, granted by the Governor of Queensland under the Mining Act 1968 (Qld). The companies were engaged in extracting zircon and rutile concentrates from their mining leases and they intended to export these concentrates.

The Customs (Prohibited Exports) Regulations made by the Governor-General under the Customs Act 1901 (Cth) prohibited the export of zircon and rutile concentrates from Australia, except with the written approval of the Minister for Minerals and Energy: reg 9. That prohibition came into force in 1973. In 1974 Murphyores and Dillingham Constructions sought the approval of the Minister for the export of the concentrates to be produced from their mining operations on Fraser Island.

On 17 December 1974 the Environmental Protection (Impact of Proposals) Act 1974 (Cth) was assented to. This Act provided for the appointment of commissions of inquiry to investigate the environmental aspects of any Commonwealth Government proposals, works, projects, agreements, recommendations and decisions. In July 1975, the Minister administering that Act appointed Commissioners to inquire into 'all or any part of the environmental aspects of the making of decisions by or on behalf of the Australian Government in relation to the exportation from Australia of minerals (including minerals that have been subjected to processing or treatment) extracted or which may hereafter be extracted from Fraser Island in the State of Queensland'. The Minister for Minerals and Energy then indicated that he would await the report of the Commissioners before deciding the application for export approval.

Murphyores and Dillingham Constructions began an action in the High Court in which they sought injunctions to restrain the Commissioners from holding the inquiry and from presenting their report. They also sought a declaration that the Minister for Minerals and Energy was not entitled to take into account, when considering the question of export approval, any report on the environmental aspects of the mining operations. The Commonwealth demurred to the statement of claim, and this demurrer was argued before the Full Court.

Mason J: [19] The power to legislate with respect to trade and commerce with other countries, including as it does power to prohibit and regulate the exportation of goods from Australia, necessarily comprehends the power to select and identify the persons who engage in, and the goods which may become the subject of, that activity: see *Huddart Parker Ltd v Commonwealth* (1931) 44 CLR 492; *Australian National Airways Pty Ltd v Commonwealth* (1945) 71 CLR 29. It is then for Parliament in its wisdom or for the person to whom Parliament delegates the power to decide who may export and what goods may be exported. The means and the criteria by which this choice is to be made are for Parliament to decide. There is nothing in the subject matter of the constitutional power which justifies the implication of any limitation on Parliament's power of selection. It does not follow, for example, that because the subject of the power is trade and commerce, selection of the exporter or of the goods to be exported must be made by reference to considerations of trading policy.

It is enough that the law operates on the topic of trade and commerce with other countries. A law which absolutely or conditionally prohibits exportation of goods is a law that operates on that topic. It is not a law which ceases to deal with that topic because it confers a discretion, unlimited in scope, to permit exportation of particular goods. In this respect it differs from a law whose connexion with the subject matter of power is more remote, when the limits of a statutory discretion may become important in characterising the law. See, for example, the cases on the defence power dealing with the National Security (Economic Organization) Regulations: *Shrimpton v Commonwealth* (1945) 69 CLR 613, *Dawson v Commonwealth* (1946) 73 CLR 157.

The point here is that by imposing a conditional prohibition on exportation, a prohibition which may be relaxed according to the [20] exercise of a discretion, the law is dealing with exportation of goods, a matter at the heart of trade and commerce with other countries. It is not to the point that the selection may be made by reference to criteria having little or no apparent relevance to trade and commerce; it is enough that the law deals with the permitted topic and it does not cease to deal with that topic because factors extraneous to the topic may be taken into account in the relaxation of the prohibition imposed by the law. It is now far too late in the day to say that a law should be characterised by reference to the motives which inspire it or the consequences which flow from it.

Mason J referred to a number of decisions which supported this approach, concluding with *O'Sullivan v Noarlunga Meat Ltd* (1954) 92 CLR 565 **[10.2.11C]** and continued:

[22] It is one thing to say that the trade and commerce power does not enable the Commonwealth to regulate and control directly matters standing outside the subject matter of power, such as the environmental aspects of mining in Queensland, it is quite another thing to say that the Commonwealth cannot in the exercise of that power make laws which have a consequential and indirect effect on matters standing outside the power, even by means of prohibiting conditionally engagement in trade and commerce with other countries. It is no objection to the validity of a law otherwise within power that it touches or affects a topic on which the Commonwealth has no power to legislate.

These principles have been applied more recently outside the field of trade and commerce, the most notable example being in *Herald and Weekly Times v Commonwealth* (1966) 115 CLR at 433–4, where Kitto J said with reference to the power conferred by s 51(v): ... [23] ... 'A law which qualifies an existing statutory power to relax a prohibition is necessarily a law with respect to the subject of the prohibition. Even if the qualification gives it the additional character of a law upon some other topic — even, indeed, if that other topic be not a subject of Federal legislative power — it is still a law with respect to the subject of the prohibition, and is valid if that subject be within Federal power.'

R v Barger (1908) 6 CLR 41, which might have been thought to assist the plaintiffs, can no longer be regarded as having authority. It depended on the now discredited doctrine of reserved powers. The minority who rejected this doctrine had no difficulty in holding the legislation to be valid. The decision of this court in *Fairfax v Federal Commissioner of Taxation* (1965) 114 CLR 1, it should now be acknowledged, swept away the last vestigial remnants of *Barger's* case.

So much for the constitutional argument. On principle and authority there is no reason deriving from the limits of constitutional power with respect to trade and commerce which requires that the discretion to issue a written approval should be confined, as the plaintiffs would suggest.

Mason J went on to hold that, on its proper construction, reg 9 of the Customs (Prohibited Exports) Regulations entitled the Minister for Minerals and Energy to take account of environmental factors when deciding an application for export approval.

McTiernan, Stephen and Murphy JJ delivered separate judgments to the same effect. Barwick CJ agreed with Stephen J. Gibbs and Jacobs JJ agreed with both Stephen and Mason JJ.

~~~

Notes

[10.2.34] *Murphyores Inc Pty Ltd v Commonwealth* (1976) 136 CLR 1 **[10.2.33C]** brings us back to the problem of characterisation discussed in *R v Barger* (1908) 6 CLR 412 **[9.2.15C]** and *Fairfax v Federal Commissioner of Taxation* (1965) 114 CLR 1 **[9.2.22C]**. It confirms the decision in the latter case that, so long as a law of the Commonwealth operates directly upon some activity which is central to the power granted to the Commonwealth, neither the indirect effect of the law nor the motives or purpose of the Commonwealth in making that law can detract from the law's validity.

Here, the direct operation of the law was to prohibit the export of a commodity from Australia; that is, to prohibit an activity central to trade and commerce with other countries (as in *Fairfax v Federal Commissioner of Taxation* (1965) 114 CLR 1 **[9.2.22C]**, the direct operation of a law was determined by looking at the legal rights and duties created or modified by the law). The court treated as irrelevant the assertion that the prohibition of the export of mineral sands would result in the abandonment of sand-mining on Fraser Island: that was an indirect effect of the law, which imposed no legal obligation to abandon sand-mining. Equally irrelevant were the claims that the Commonwealth wished to achieve that result and the fact that the export prohibition might be waived if the Commonwealth were satisfied that the sand-mining would not damage the environment on Fraser Island. The prohibition on export remained a law with respect to trade and commerce with other countries: it was not a law with respect to sand-mining or environmental protection.

[10.2.35] It is implicit in this analysis that the Commonwealth law would have exceeded the powers of the Commonwealth if it had prohibited sand-mining on Fraser Island, or if it had attempted to impose standards of environmental protection on the sand-mining there. Indeed, this proposition was made explicitly by Mason J:

> [T]he trade and commerce powers does not enable the Commonwealth to regulate and control directly matters standing outside the subject matter of the power, such as the environmental aspects of mining in Queensland ... (136 CLR at 22).

How is that proposition to be reconciled with the decision in *O'Sullivan v Noarlunga Meat Ltd* (1954) 92 CLR 565 **[10.2.11C]**, where the court held that reg 5 of the Commerce (Meat Export) Regulations (Cth) was valid? That regulation prohibited the use of any premises for the slaughter of meat for export unless registered; other regulations made registration contingent on adherence to detailed standards. Why is direct control of meat processing for export within the trade and commerce power, and direct control of mining for export outside that power?

The resolution of this apparent contradiction could lie in a more precise framing of the opposing propositions. In *O'Sullivan's* case, the court held that the Commonwealth could control directly those aspects of export production which might 'affect beneficially or adversely the export trade of Australia in any commodity', quality, labelling and packaging, for example: 92 CLR at 598. In the *Murphyores* case, the court assumed that the Commonwealth could not control directly those aspects of export production which could not affect the export trade, in particular, the local environmental impact of that production.

If we understand that the decision in *O'Sullivan's* case depended upon the incidental scope of s 51(i) (production for export can be controlled under s 51(i) where that control is incidental to the control of the export trade), then we can see why, in 1973, the Commonwealth was obliged to adopt an indirect approach when it sought to regulate the environmental impacts of sand-mining for export.

[10.2.36] The current judicial reading of s 51(i) is committed to a distinction recognised as long ago as 1953 as 'artificial and unsuitable to modern times': Dixon CJ in *Wragg v New South Wales* (1953) 88 CLR 353 **[10.4.13]** at 385–6. Despite the emergence of 'a most complex fabric of trade and business', in which superficially independent activities are closely interdependent (as a Commonwealth

Parliament committee described the Australian economy in 1959: *Joint Committee on Constitutional Review* (1959) para 1028), the High Court's insistence that intrastate trade and commerce be strictly segregated from other forms of trade and commerce emphasises a constitutional distinction which from the economic point of view is 'often irrelevant': see Constitutional Commission (1988) para 11.41. That distinction also burdens Australian economic and business activity with multiple systems of regulation (para 11.420):

> From the point of view of business, the market is national (or even international), but the law is regional, and therefore varied. Where the Commonwealth lays down standards for export and the States have different standards for domestic trade, this can result in two different production processes being required, unless the producer forgoes the opportunity to trade in one or more of those markets.

While the High Court's adherence to the distinction has largely ruled out s 51(i) as the foundation for national policies on economic and business activity, a more expansive judicial reading of another Commonwealth power holds out more promise. The decision of the High Court in *Commonwealth v Tasmania* (the *Tasmanian Dam* case) (1983) 158 CLR 1 **[10.3.26C]** opens the way for direct Commonwealth control of a wide range of manufacturing and production activities free of the distinctions and qualifications inherent in cases such as *O'Sullivan v Noarlunga Meat Ltd* (1954) 92 CLR 565 **[10.2.11C]** and *Murphyores Inc Pty Ltd v Commonwealth* (1976) 136 CLR 1 **[10.2.33C]**. That case suggests a broad potential for the corporations power, s 51(xx), as the basis for direct Commonwealth controls over the activities of foreign, trading and financial corporations; the power was sufficient, according to the majority in *Commonwealth v Tasmania* (the *Tasmanian Dam* case), to enable the Commonwealth to legislate to prevent the Tasmanian Hydro-Electric Commission carrying out environmentally damaging construction work in south-west Tasmania.

One of the curious aspects of the expansive reading of s 51(xx) is that it was developed over a 12-year period, from 1971 to 1983, while the High Court continued to maintain the distinction which inhibited any significant use, by the Commonwealth, of s 51(i). Zines points out this paradox with the comment that, if the restrictive reading of s 51(i) was intended to maintain a significant area of exclusive state regulatory power, the decisions on s 51(xx) 'undid a great deal of that work': Zines (1997) p 79. The High Court may have chosen to yield to the pressure to allow Commonwealth regulation of economic activity by opening the s 51(xx) door, while keeping the s 51(i) door closed, because this allowed the court to open the way to the development of national regulatory policies while avoiding the type of economic argument and analysis which invocation of s 51(i) would involve. This point is developed, implicitly, in Zines (1997) p 79.

3   Corporations power

[10.3.1E]   **Commonwealth Constitution**

51 The Parliament shall, subject to this Constitution, have power to make laws for the peace, order, and good government of the Commonwealth with respect to:

(xx) Foreign corporations and trading or financial corporations formed within the limits of the Commonwealth: ...

~~~

Notes

[10.3.2] Section 51(xx) is the second source of the Commonwealth's power to regulate economic activity; in 1994, it was the principal source of that power. It is framed in general terms, apparently permitting Commonwealth regulation of a wide variety of commercial entities. For many years, until the decision in *Strickland v Rocla Concrete Pipes Ltd* (1971) 124 CLR 468 **[10.3.4C]**, it had been thought that the provision authorised only a narrow range of Commonwealth legislation. Even after that decision, the range of corporate activities which are subject to Commonwealth control has not been settled. There are two fundamental questions: Over what types of corporation does the Commonwealth Parliament have control? What aspects of these corporations' affairs are subject to Commonwealth control? Considerable progress has been made towards resolving these questions; but neither can be described as a closed question. However, one thing is clear. In its use of the corporations power, the Commonwealth Parliament should not be frustrated by the distinctions which have afflicted the trade and commerce power.

[10.3.3] But it was not always thus. In *Huddart Parker & Co Pty Ltd v Moorehead* (1909) 8 CLR 330 the High Court adopted, under the influence of the reserved powers doctrine, a restrictive interpretation of s 51(xx). The court was asked to rule on the validity of ss 5 and 8 of the Australian Industries Preservation Act 1906 (Cth). These sections prohibited combinations in restraint of trade and trade monopolies in relation to all trade and commerce within Australia by foreign corporations and trading and financial corporations formed within the Commonwealth.

The court held by a majority (Griffith CJ, Barton, O'Connor and Higgins JJ, with Isaacs J dissenting) that the sections were invalid. Griffith CJ said that the words of s 51(xx) might, on their own, be capable of a wide construction. But the context of the Constitution, and in particular the reservation to the states of the power to enact domestic trade and commerce law and domestic criminal law, was critical. He held that s 51(xx) allowed the Commonwealth to legislate so as to control the legal capacity of corporations, but not so as to control those corporate activities which were within a corporation's capacity (at 354):

> [Section 51(xx)] ought not to be construed as authorising the Commonwealth to invade the field of State law as to domestic trade, the carrying on of which is within the capacity of trading and financial corporations formed under the laws of the State. In other words, I think that pl xx empowers the Commonwealth to prohibit a trading or financial corporation formed within the Commonwealth from entering into any field of operation, but does not empower the Commonwealth to control the operations of a corporation which lawfully enters upon a field of operation, the control of which is exclusively reserved to the States.

Barton J agreed. O'Connor J held that the power conferred by s 51(xx) was limited to supporting laws which provided for the recognition as legal entities of interstate or foreign corporations throughout the Commonwealth. Higgins J gave s 51(xx) a broader meaning. The Commonwealth Parliament could regulate the status and capacity of corporations and the conditions on which they might be permitted to carry on business but it could not regulate the contracts into which corporations might enter.

Isaacs J, in a strong dissent, said that s 51(xx) empowered the Commonwealth Parliament to regulate 'the conduct of the corporations in their transactions with or as affecting the public': 8 CLR at 395. He did offer some reservations. The power did not extend to regulating the formation or the internal affairs of companies, nor to providing for their liquidation. The Commonwealth could not prescribe the wages to be paid by corporations to their workers, nor the qualifications of directors: 8 CLR at 393–6. Despite those reservations, the power conceded by Isaacs J would have given the Commonwealth very substantial capacity to regulate economic activity throughout Australia, for a large part of that activity is conducted through corporations of the types listed in s 51(xx).

No doubt the commercial activities of individuals, of non-corporate business, could only be regulated under s 51(i) or the specific powers such as s 51(xiii) (banking) or s 51(xiv) (insurance), but the non-corporate sector does not make a significant contribution to economic activity in Australia. The mining, production and manufacture of such basic commodities as iron, steel, bauxite, aluminium, copper, coal, oil, uranium, natural gas and rubber is dominated by corporations. Corporations, not individual traders, dominate the petrochemical industry. The ownership of major communications media, the manufacture of consumer durables and the distribution and sale to the public of commodities; in every sphere of industrial and commercial activity, corporations are the major, if not the only, participants. In some cases the corporations represent hundreds of thousands of shareholders. In other cases they represent small partnerships or family businesses. Corporate structure is the overwhelming feature of Australian commercial activity. If we concede to the Commonwealth the power to regulate the 'external' functions of corporations, their relations with persons (including other corporations) outside those corporations, we are conceding a substantial power to regulate commercial activity.

Isaacs J's view was, of course, a minority view in 1909. However, the High Court's emphatic rejection of the reserved power (or implied prohibitions) doctrine in 1920 clearly opened the way for a reversal of *Huddart Parker & Co Pty Ltd v Moorehead* (1909) 8 CLR 330: *Engineers'* case (1920) 28 CLR 129 **[8.2.31C]** discussed in **[8.2.38]**. However, it was not until 1971 that the court was invited to reconsider *Huddart Parker*.

[10.3.4C] Strickland v Rocla Concrete Pipes Ltd
(1971) 124 CLR 468

Section 35 of the Trade Practices Act 1965 (Cth) declared that certain agreements were 'examinable'. Agreements made between business competitors where one of the parties to the agreement was 'a foreign corporation, or a trading or financial corporation formed within the limits of the Commonwealth': s 7(2). Other subsections of s 7 extended the operation of s 35 to agreements connected with interstate trade, Commonwealth instrumentalities and territories. Section 7(4) provided that these subsections should not limit the operation of the Act. Section 42 obliged the parties to examinable agreements to furnish particulars of the agreements to the Commissioner of Trade Practices. Failure to provide this information constituted an offence: s 43.

The defendant company, a trading corporation, was a party to an agreement which related exclusively to trade within Queensland. The agreement was allegedly designed to reduce competition between the manufacturers of concrete pipes and therefore examinable under the Trade Practices Act. The defendant company was charged under s 43 with having failed to provide particulars of an examinable agreement. The

Commonwealth Industrial Court dismissed the charge on the basis that *Huddart Parker & Co Pty Ltd v Moorehead* (1909) 8 CLR 330 **[10.3.3]** rendered invalid that part of the Trade Practices Act dealing with the intrastate activities of corporations. The informant appealed to the High Court.

Barwick CJ: [484] I address myself to the first question namely — should this court now accept its decision in *Huddart, Parker & Co Ltd v Moorehead* (1909) 8 CLR 330 as a correct construction of s 51(xx) of the Constitution. I am clearly of opinion that it should not. However, out of respect for those justices who formed the majority in deciding that case and having regard to the time which has elapsed since the decision was given, I should offer some analysis of the decision and state my reasons as concisely as possible for thinking that it was erroneous ...

[485] The case was decided in the year 1909 at a time when the current doctrine of this court was that the construction of the words of the Constitution by which legislative power is granted to the Parliament should be approached on the footing that there were certain legislative areas reserved by the Constitution to the States and that the Constitution should not be read as authorising the Parliament to invade those areas unless as a necessary incident to the exercise of some granted power. This was the so-called reserved powers doctrine which was exploded and unambiguously rejected by this court in the year 1920 in the decision of the *Amalgamated Society of Engineers v Adelaide Steamship Co Ltd* ('the *Engineers'* case') (1920) 28 CLR 129 ...

[488] It is plain enough from a reading of the reasons given by the majority in *Huddart, Parker & Co Pty Ltd v Moorehead* (1909) 8 CLR 330 that the influence of the then current reserved powers doctrine was so strong that the court was driven to emasculate the legislative power given by s 51(xx) and to confine it in substance to the statutory recognition of corporations falling within the terms of the paragraph and the fixing of the conditions upon which they might enter trade in Australia: for the rest, their trading activities in intrastate trade was a matter for the State legislation exclusively ...

... Section 107 of the Constitution so far from reserving anything to the States leaves them the then residue of power after full effect is given to the powers granted to the Commonwealth: and then subject to s 109. Section 51(i) contains no explicit or implicit prohibition and does not reserve the subject of intrastate trade to the States. It can thus be [489] seen that the earlier doctrine virtually reversed the Constitution. The question in relation to the validity of a Commonwealth Act is whether it fairly falls within the scope of the subject matter granted to the Commonwealth by the Constitution. That subject matter will be determined by construing the words of the Constitution by which legislative power is given to the Commonwealth irrespective of what effect the construction may have upon the residue of power which the States may enjoy.

I therefore conclude that the reasoning of this court in *Huddart, Parker & Co Pty Ltd v Moorehead* was in error and that it ought not be accepted now by this court. The question then remains whether the court's decision that s 5(1) and s 8(1) were invalid ought to be overruled.

I have set out s 5(1) and s 8(1) of the Australian Industries Preservation Act. They were clearly laws regulating and controlling amongst other things the trading activities of foreign corporations and trading and financial corporations formed within the limits of the Commonwealth. In my opinion such laws were laws with respect to such corporations. They dealt with the very heart of the purpose for which the corporation was formed, for whether a trading or financial corporation, by assumption, its purpose is to trade, trade for constitutional purposes not being limited to dealings in goods: cf *Bank of New South Wales v Commonwealth* (*Bank Nationalization* case) (1948) 76 CLR 1. If the corporation is exercising its powers it will be carrying out trade operations and in that pursuit making agreements with others in matters of trade. Agreements to restrict trade or endeavouring to monopolise it are activities in trade with which the law has been familiar for centuries. Sections 5(1) and 8(1) in controlling such activities are, in my opinion, clearly laws with respect to the topic of s 51(xx). I would conclude therefore that s 5(1) and s 8(1) were valid and that the court's decision to the contrary in *Huddart, Parker & Co Pty Ltd v Moorehead* (1909) 8 CLR 330 should be overruled.

However, having regard to Sir Samuel Griffith's remark in *Huddart, Parker & Co Pty Ltd v Moorehead* (at 345) and what was said in argument in these appeals I ought to observe that it does not follow either as a logical proposition, or, if in this instance there be a difference, as a legal proposition, from the validity of those sections, that any law which in the range of its command or prohibition includes foreign corporations or trading or financial corporations formed within the limits of the Commonwealth is [490] necessarily a law with respect to the subject matter of s 51(xx). Nor does it follow that any law which is addressed specifically to such corporations or some of them is such a law. Sections 5(1) and 8(1), in my opinion, were valid because they were regulating and controlling the trading activities of trading corporations and thus within the scope of s 51(xx). But the decision as to the validity of particular laws yet to be enacted must remain for the court when called upon to pass upon them. No doubt, laws which may be validly made under s 51(xx) will cover a wide range of activities of foreign corporations and trading and financial corporations: perhaps in the case of foreign corporations even a wider range than that in the case of other corporations: but in any case, not necessarily limited to trading activities. I must not be taken as suggesting that the question whether a particular law is a law within the scope of this power should be approached in any narrow or pedantic manner.

We were invited in the argument of these appeals to set as it were the outer limits of the reach of the power under this paragraph of s 51. This for my part I am not prepared to do: and indeed I do not regard the court as justified in doing so. The method of constitutional interpretation is the same as that with which we have been long familiar in the common law. The law develops case by case, the court in each case deciding so much as is necessary to dispose of the case before it.

The limits of the power can only be ascertained authoritatively by a course of decision in which the application of general statements is illustrated by example: *R v Burgess; Ex parte Henry* (1936) 55 CLR 608 at 669.

~~~

[10.3.5] Barwick CJ went on to conclude that s 7(4) purported to extend the operation of Pts V and VI of the Act beyond those areas which were within the Commonwealth's legislative power, and that s 7(4) could not be read down or severed from those Parts. Therefore, Pts V and VI, under which these proceedings had been brought, were invalid.

The other members of the court, McTiernan, Menzies, Windeyer, Owen, Walsh and Gibbs JJ, held that *Huddart Parker & Co Pty Ltd v Moorehead* (1909) 8 CLR 330 was wrongly decided and should be overruled. Menzies, Windeyer, Owen and Walsh JJ agreed that, while the Commonwealth could legislate to control the anti-competitive activities of those corporations listed in s 51(xx), the Trade Practices Act 1974 (Cth) purported, in Pts V and VI, to go beyond the Commonwealth's power and was, to that extent, invalid. McTiernan and Gibbs JJ dissented on this point, holding that s 7 could be read down so as to confine the operation of the Act to those activities over which the Commonwealth Parliament clearly had power.

Notes

[10.3.6] The Commonwealth Parliament reacted quickly to the High Court's decision in *Strickland v Rocla Concrete Pipes Ltd* (1971) 124 CLR 468 **[10.3.4C]** that Pts V and VI of the Trade Practices Act 1965 were invalid. Within three months of the decision, it passed the Restrictive Trade Practices Act 1971 in substantially identical terms to the 1965 Act but expressly limited in its application to agreements and practices in which corporations, of the types listed in s 51(xx), were involved.

[10.3.7] The election of a Federal Labor Government in December 1972 led to a more assertive approach by the Commonwealth to the High Court's expanded interpretation of s 51(xx). The Prices Justification Act 1973 (Cth) obliged companies (defined in terms similar to s 51(xx), with an annual turnover of at least $20 million) to delay price increases until these were investigated by the Prices Justification Tribunal. The Tribunal was not given power to prevent price increases; but, if the provisions of the Act restraining increases pending the Tribunal's investigation were valid, it clearly could have been given this power.

The Trade Practices Act 1974 (Cth) replaced the Restrictive Trade Practices Act 1971, and considerably expanded the range of controls over the trading activities of corporations. New provisions dealing with mergers of corporations were added to strengthened provisions outlawing restrictive agreements and practices. And a code for consumer protection, Pt V of the Act, proscribed unfair marketing practices and gave consumers the protection of implied warranties.

Two other pieces of legislation, based on the government's reading of s 51(xx), were drafted but not enacted. These were the Corporations and Securities Bill dealing with the financial aspects of corporate activities, especially share transactions, and the National Companies Bill, to control the formation and administration of corporations. The former was stalled by the Senate; the latter was to have been introduced into parliament on 11 November 1975. The proposition that s 51(xx) should be used to support comprehensive national regulation of the securities industry and company law was not revived until 1988: see **[10.3.34]**.

[10.3.8] While the High Court rejected the narrow *Huddart Parker* (1909) 8 CLR 330 **[10.3.3]** view of s 51(xx) in *Strickland v Rocla Concrete Pipes Ltd* (1971) 124 CLR 468 **[10.3.4C]**, the members of the court expressly refrained from defining the scope of the power. As Barwick CJ said, 'The law develops case by case': 124 CLR at 490. The judges were, however, prepared to indicate that a law dealing with agreements or practices restrictive of a s 51(xx) corporation's trading activity was within s 51(xx).

Barwick CJ went a little further and indicated that 'a law regulating corporations' would be valid: 124 CLR at 491. On the other hand, he cautioned that it did not follow 'that any law which in the range of its command or prohibition includes foreign corporations or trading or financial corporations formed within the limits of the Commonwealth is necessarily a law with respect to the subject matter of s 51(xx). Nor does it follow that any law which is addressed specifically to such corporations or some of them is such a law': 124 CLR 489–90. (On this point, contrast the approach of Mason, Murphy and Deane JJ in *Commonwealth v Tasmania* (the *Tasmanian Dam* case) (1983) 158 CLR 1 at 149, 179, 269–70 **[10.3.26C]**.) Barwick CJ went on to counter these cautionary observations. Commonwealth power was 'not necessarily limited to trading activities'; and the scope of the power should not 'be approached in any narrow or pedantic manner': 124 CLR at 490.

McTiernan and Walsh JJ agreed with Barwick CJ's observations. The other members of the court were not prepared to commit themselves beyond saying that s 51(xx) would support the Commonwealth regulation of corporate activities which were anti-competitive.

[10.3.9] We might look back to the dissenting judgment of Isaacs J in *Huddart Parker & Co Pty Ltd v Moorehead* (1909) 8 CLR 330 **[10.3.3]** for some guidance on the scope of permissible Commonwealth laws under s 51(xx). Indeed, the decision in *New South Wales v Commonwealth* (the *Incorporation* case) (1990) 169 CLR 482 **[10.3.35C]** has effectively endorsed one limitation on the corporations power proposed by Isaacs J; namely, that the power will not support legislation regulating the formation of corporations: 8 CLR at 393–4. Isaacs J also said that the Commonwealth could not regulate, under that provision, the liquidation of corporations, the internal administration of corporations, or wages and other conditions of employment provided by corporations for their employees: 8 CLR at 395, 396. It remains to be seen whether those observations are supported by the High Court: see Zines (1997) pp 104–7.

[10.3.10] Following the decision in *Strickland v Rocla Concrete Pipes Ltd* (1971) 124 CLR 468 **[10.3.4C]**, litigation involving s 51(xx) tended to focus on the issue of identifying the corporations which were subject to Commonwealth control, rather than on the issue of the legitimate extent of those controls. In *Mikasa (NSW) Pty Ltd v Festival Stores* (1972) 127 CLR 617 a challenge to Commonwealth legislation prohibiting resale price maintenance by trading corporations was confined to, and decided on, s 92 grounds. The High Court assumed that the legislation was within the Commonwealth's legislative powers.

Again, in *R v Australian Industrial Court; Ex parte CLM Holdings Pty Ltd* (1977) 136 CLR 235, the court assumed, in the absence of argument, that the consumer protection provisions of the Trade Practices Act 1974 (Cth), which gave consumers of goods and services rights against foreign, trading and financial corporations, were supported by s 51(xx).

It was not until the decision in *Actors and Announcers Equity v Fontana Films Pty Ltd* (1982) 150 CLR 169 **[10.3.18C]** and *Commonwealth v Tasmania* (the *Tasmanian Dam* case) (1983) 158 CLR 1 **[10.3.26C]** that the High Court was obliged to review the extent of the Commonwealth's powers under s 51(xx); but, even then, some members of the court managed to avoid commitment to any general principles.

[10.3.11] Until *Actors & Announcers Equity v Fontana Films Pty Ltd* (1982) 150 CLR 169 **[10.3.18C]** and *Tasmanian Dam* (1983) 158 CLR 1 **[10.3.26C]** were decided, the focus of judicial debate on s 51(xx) was on the identification of those corporations which were subject to Commonwealth control. In *R v Trade Practices Tribunal; Ex parte St George County Council* (1974) 130 CLR 533 the High Court was asked to restrain proceedings before the Trade Practices Tribunal under the Restrictive Trade Practices Act 1971 (Cth) against the St George County Council. The Act authorised proceedings against 'a foreign corporation, a trading corporation formed within the limits of the Commonwealth or a financial corporation so formed', if it had attempted to monopolise the trade in any commodity. The St George County Council claimed it was not a 'trading corporation' (there was no suggestion that it fell into either of the other two categories) because it had been established under the Local Government Act 1919 (NSW), as a public utility, to supply electricity and electrical appliances at the lowest feasible price to consumers. The council was, it claimed, a local government corporation, not a trading corporation.

A majority of the High Court (McTiernan, Menzies and Gibbs JJ; Barwick CJ and Stephen J dissenting) held that the council was not a 'trading corporation' and accordingly restrained the proceedings before the Trade Practices Tribunal. McTiernan J did not discuss the scope of the term as used in s 51(xx). He decided that, as used in the Restrictive Trade Practices Act, 'trading corporation' referred to 'a private enterprise company': 130 CLR at 547. However, Menzies and Gibbs JJ proceeded on the basis that 'trading corporation', as used in the Act, had the same meaning as the term in s 51(xx). They rejected the argument that a trading corporation was to be recognised by its activities, that a trading corporation was a corporation which traded. Rather, they said, it was to be recognised from its basic charter. Thus, a trading corporation was one which had been incorporated for the purpose of trading. Gibbs J expressed this approach as follows (at 562):

> It is necessary to determine the true character of the corporation upon a consideration of all the circumstances that throw light on the purpose for which it was formed.

Here, the Local Government Act 1919 (NSW), which authorised the establishment of the council and defined its powers and structure, showed that the Council was established for the purpose of fulfilling a function of local government. Therefore, it was a local government corporation, not a trading corporation.

Barwick CJ and Stephen J also approached the meaning of 'trading corporation' in the Act as if it was co-extensive with the same term in s 51(xx). For them, the activities of a corporation were of critical importance:

> [A] corporation whose predominant and characteristic activity is trading whether in goods or services will, in my opinion, satisfy the description (130 CLR at 543 per Barwick CJ).

> [T]he use of the participle 'trading' necessarily involves reference to function, either to the activities which a corporation is intended to undertake or to those which it in fact does undertake (130 CLR at 568 per Stephen J).

A careful reading of the judgments of Barwick CJ and Stephen J shows that, while each of them regarded the current activities of a corporation as an important element in its identification, Stephen J gave rather less emphasis to that factor than did Barwick CJ. Immediately before the passage quoted above, Stephen J had referred to the St George County Council as 'especially created to perform [a trading] function and none other', and that was a sufficient reason 'to describe it as a trading corporation': 130 CLR at 568. The ambiguity inherent in his judgment surfaced in *R v Federal Court of Australia; Ex parte WA National Football League (Inc)* (*Adamson's* case) (1979) 143 CLR 190 **[10.3.12]**.

[10.3.12]　In *R v Federal Court of Australia; Ex parte WA National Football League (Inc)* (*Adamson's* case) (1979) 143 CLR 190, a majority of the High Court (Barwick CJ, Mason, Jacobs and Murphy JJ; Gibbs, Stephen and Aickin JJ dissenting) decided that the Western Australian Football League, the South Australian National Football League and the West Perth Football Club were trading corporations. Accordingly, they were subject to the Trade Practices Act 1974 (Cth), s 45 of which forbade any trading or financial corporation to make or give effect to contracts, arrangements or understandings which restrict the supply of services or substantially lessen competition.

The Western Australian League and the West Perth Club were incorporated under the Associations Incorporation Act 1895 (WA) s 2 of which defined an 'Association' as excluding 'associations for the purpose of trading or securing pecuniary profit to the members from the transactions thereof'. The South Australian League was incorporated under the Associations Incorporation Act 1965 (SA), which was in substantially the same terms as the Western Australian legislation.

Mason J said that he preferred the minority view expressed by Barwick CJ in *R v Trade Practices Tribunal; Ex parte St George County Council* (1974) 130 CLR 533 **[10.3.11]**, and continued:

> 'Trading corporation' is not and never has been a term of art or one having a special legal meaning. Nor, as the Chief Justice pointed out, was there a generally accepted definition of the expression in the nineteenth century. Essentially, it is a description or label given to a corporation when its trading activities form a sufficiently significant proportion of its overall activities as to merit its description as a trading corporation.
>
> ... Not every corporation which is engaged in trading activity is a trading corporation. The trading activity of a corporation may be so slight and so incidental to some other principal activity, viz religion or education in the case of a church or school, that it could not be described as a trading corporation. Whether the trading activities of a particular corporation are sufficient to warrant its being characterised as a trading corporation is very much a question of fact and degree ... (143 CLR at 233–4).

Mason J reviewed the activities of the two leagues and the club, and concluded:

> The financial revenue of the Leagues is so great and the commercial means by which it is achieved so varied that I have no hesitation in concluding that trading constitutes their principal activity. In saying this I treat all their activities which I have listed and which produce revenue as trading activities. I do not limit the concept of trading to buying and selling at a profit; it extends to business activities carried on with a view to earning revenue.
>
> Likewise, in my opinion West Perth is a trading corporation, though it stands in a somewhat different category ... The fact that no part of the club's revenue or profit can be distributed to the members is a circumstance to be taken into account in deciding whether it is a trading corporation, though in my judgment it is outweighed by other considerations which point to the conclusion that West Perth is a trading corporation.
>
> The principal activity of the Club is its participation as a member club of the WA League in the competitions which it runs. Indeed, that is West Perth's major source of income. The comment which Fletcher Moulton LJ made of the Crystal Palace Club in *Walker v Crystal Palace Football Club Ltd* [1910] 1 KB 87 applies with equal force to West Perth. His Lordship said (at 92): 'Here is a company that carries on the game of football as a trade, getting up and taking part in football matches'. The only qualification to be made is that West Perth does not arrange or manage the competition matches (143 CLR at 235–6).

In his dissenting judgment, Stephen J said that the trading activities of the leagues and the club were incidental to their principal activities of promoting sport. They were not trading corporations because their predominant or characteristic activity was not trading.

[10.3.13] In *State Superannuation Board v Trade Practices Commission* (1982) 150 CLR 282, a majority of the High Court (Mason, Murphy and Deane JJ; Gibbs CJ and Wilson J dissenting) held that the State Superannuation Board was a financial corporation and so was subject to s 47(1) of the Trade Practices Act 1974 (Cth). The subsection prohibited a trading or financial corporation from engaging 'in the practice of exclusive dealing'. The State Superannuation Board was a body corporate established by the Superannuation Act 1925 (Vic) and continued in existence by the Superannuation Act 1958 (Vic). It was responsible for the administration of a superannuation fund for the purpose of providing pensions for Victorian government employees and for the investment of that fund.

In their joint judgment, Mason, Murphy and Deane JJ said that 'the court's approach to the ascertainment of what constitutes a "financial corporation" should be the same as its approach to what constitutes a "trading corporation", subject to making due allowance for the difference between "trading" and "financial"': 150 CLR at 303. They said that *R v Federal Court of Australia; Ex parte WA National Football League (Inc) (Adamson's* case) (1979) 143 CLR 190 **[10.3.12]** had 'concluded that the relevant character of the football leagues and the football club was to be ascertained by reference to their established activities' (150 CLR at 303), and continued:

> [I]t was essential to the majority's approach and to its rejection of *St George* that a corporation whose trading activities take place so that it may carry on its primary or dominant undertaking, for example, as a sporting club, may nevertheless be a trading corporation. The point is that the corporation engages in trading activities and these activities do not cease to be trading activities because they are entered into in the course of, or for the purpose of, carrying on a primary or dominant undertaking not described by reference to trade. As the carrying on of that undertaking requires or involves engagement in trading activities, there is no difficulty in categorising the corporation as a trading corporation when it engages in the activities (150 CLR at 304).

After noting that the purpose for which an inactive corporation had been formed might well be relevant, Mason, Murphy and Deane JJ said that the term 'financial corporation' was not a term of art. It did 'no more than describe a corporation which engages in financial activities or perhaps is intended to do so': 150 CLR at 305. They reviewed the activities of the State Superannuation Board, which included the investment of substantial sums of money in semi-government loans, commercial loans and housing loans, and concluded:

> The facts as we have recited them demonstrate beyond any question that the appellant engages in financial activities on a very substantial scale. Even if we confine our attention to such aspects of the appellant's investment activities as involve the making of commercial and housing loans, its business in this respect is very substantial and forms a significant part of its overall activities. No doubt these activities are all entered into for the end purpose of providing superannuation benefits to contributors, but, as we have seen, this circumstance constitutes no obstacle to the conclusion that the appellant is a financial corporation (150 CLR at 306).

In their dissenting judgment, Gibbs CJ and Wilson J held that the board was not a financial corporation within s 51(xx) because '[t]he predominant and characteristic activity of the Board is not to be described in terms of financial dealings but by reference to the service it provides to government in Victoria by way of a superannuation scheme': 150 CLR at 298.

[10.3.14] The decision in *State Superannuation Board v Trade Practices Commission* (1982) 150 CLR 282 **[10.3.13]** was a decision of a majority of only a five-member bench. As such, it might not have been followed by a later court, just as Mason J had felt free, in *R v Federal Court of Australia; Ex parte WA National Football League (Inc)* (1979) 143 CLR 190 **[10.3.12]**, to disregard *R v Trade Practices Tribunal; Ex parte St George County Council* (1974) 130 CLR 533 **[10.3.11]**: 143 CLR at 233. Any doubts about the authority of the majority's view on the reach of s 51(xx), as expressed in *State Superannuation Board v Trade Practices Commission*, were settled by the decision in *Commonwealth v Tasmania* (the *Tasmanian Dam* case) (1983) 158 CLR 1 **[10.3.26C]**.

[10.3.15] In *Fencott v Muller* (1983) 152 CLR 570, the High Court adopted a flexible and expansive approach to the reach of s 51(xx). One of the questions before the court was the proper description of a company, Oakland Nominees Pty Ltd. Was it a trading or financial corporation and so subject to the provisions of s 52(1) of the Trade Practices Act 1974 (Cth) (which prohibits those corporations from engaging in misleading or deceptive conduct)?

Oakland had been a 'shelf company', that is, an inactive company, for about three months after its formation. (Its objects were 'widely drawn, encompassing trading and financial activities': 152 CLR at 595.) It then accepted appointment as trustee of a unit trust, replacing another company in that position, for the purpose of recovering some outstanding money owing the unit trust and paying off the trust's creditors. After its appointment, Oakland began legal proceedings to recover the outstanding debt (due under a contract between Muller and the former trustee) and began negotiations with the creditors. In these proceedings (*Fencott v Muller*), Muller and the former trustee claimed that Oakland had breached s 52(1) of the Trade Practices Act during its negotiations with the creditors of the trust. Oakland objected that it was neither a trading nor a financial corporation and so was immune from the Trade Practices Act.

In a joint judgment, Mason, Murphy, Brennan and Deane JJ rejected Oakland's argument that, under the activities test adopted in *R v Federal Court of Australia; Ex parte WA National Football League (Inc)* (1979) 143 CLR 190 **[10.3.12]**, it could not be a trading or financial corporation. After conceding that Oakland had engaged in neither trading nor financial activities, they said:

> And so the question arises whether a corporation with objects and powers appropriate for a trading or financial corporation can bear that character before it engages in any trading or financial activity. That question did not arise for consideration in *Adamson's* case. The majority judgments in that case which held that the established activities of the football league concluded its character as a trading corporation did not suggest that trading activities are the sole criterion of character. Absent those activities, the character of a corporation must be found in other indicia. While its constitution will never be completely irrelevant, it is in a case such as the present where a corporation has not begun, or has barely begun, to carry on business that its constitution, including its objects, assumes particular significance as a guide (see *State Superannuation Board v Trade Practices Commission* (1982) 150 CLR at 304). Oakland's memorandum and articles of association reveal that the objects for which it was established include engaging in financial activities and carrying on a large variety of businesses, though it lay dormant — 'on the shelf' — after its corporation. In the circumstances of the present case, there is no better guide to its character than its constitution and its constitution establishes its character as a trading or financial corporation. It is immaterial whether it is a trading corporation or a financial corporation or which of those characters its future activities may give it (152 CLR at 601–2).

[10.3.16] The majority in *State Superannuation Board v Trade Practices Commission* (1982) 150 CLR 282 **[10.3.13]** had foreshadowed this approach when they had observed: 'It might well be necessary to look to the purpose for which such a corporation [ie a corporation which had not begun, or had barely begun, to carry on business] was formed in order to ascertain whether it is a corporation of the kind described': 150 CLR at 304–5.

Gibbs CJ, Wilson and Dawson JJ dissented in *Fencott v Muller* (1983) 152 CLR 570 **[10.3.15]**: while the corporation's purposes would be relevant where it has not yet begun activities, those purposes were not to be discovered only from the corporation's stated objects, but from '[t]he whole of the evidence as to the intended operations of the corporation': Gibbs CJ, 152 CLR at 590. The evidence here showed that Oakland had not been intended to engage in trading or financial activities.

[10.3.17]   The different views put forward in *R v Trade Practices Tribunal; Ex parte St George County Council* (1974) 130 CLR 533 **[10.3.11]**, *R v Federal Court of Australia; Ex parte WA National Football League (Inc)* (1979) 143 CLR 190 **[10.3.12]** and *State Superannuation Board v Trade Practices Commission* (1982) 150 CLR 282 **[10.3.13]** on the meaning of 'trading corporation' and 'financial corporation' would lead to an expansion or contraction of the Commonwealth's power under s 51(xx). But none of the judgments suggested that the interpretation of those phrases was influenced by the type of consideration put forward by Kitto J in *Airlines of New South Wales Pty Ltd v New South Wales (No 2)* (1965) 113 CLR 54 **[10.2.20C]**. He had said that 'the Australian union is one of dual federalism', that the distinction between intrastate and other commerce must be maintained: the clear implication being that the Commonwealth should not be permitted to expand its powers under s 51(i) at the expense of the autonomous powers of the states (113 CLR at 115).

Those considerations, if they were present in the minds of the justices who pressed for the narrower view of 'trading' or 'financial' corporations, were not articulated in any of the three cases where the court considered the reach of s 51(xx). However, those broad political considerations were articulated when the court began, in 1982, to come to grips with the issue which had lain dormant since *Strickland v Rocla Concrete Pipes Ltd* (1971) 124 CLR 468 **[10.3.4C]**: What type of controls can the Commonwealth impose under s 51(xx)?

[10.3.18C]   **Actors & Announcers Equity Association of Australia v Fontana Films Pty Ltd**

(1982) 150 CLR 169

Section 45D(1)(b)(i) of the Trade Practices Act 1974 (Cth) prohibited a person engaging in conduct in concert with another person that hindered or prevented the supply of goods or services by a third person to a fourth person where the fourth person was a corporation and the conduct was engaged in for the purpose, and would have or be likely to have the effect, of causing substantial loss or damage to the business of the fourth person or a related body corporate. Section 45D(5) provided that, where two or more persons engaged in conduct in concert with one another and were members or officers of a trade union, the trade union was to be liable for that conduct unless the trade union established that it took all reasonable steps to prevent the participants from engaging in that conduct. Section 45D(6) made the trade union responsible for any loss caused to a person as a result of that conduct. According to s 4(1), a 'corporation' included a foreign corporation, a trading or financial corporation formed within the limits of Australia, a corporation incorporated in a territory and a holding company of any such corporation. Section 4A(5) provided that a body corporate was to be deemed to be related to its holding company, its subsidiary bodies corporate and any subsidiary bodies corporate of its holding company.

 Fontana Films Pty Ltd was a producer of motion picture films and, from time to time, employed actors. Officers of Actors Equity, a trade union, demanded that Fontana Films agree to employ only those actors who were members of the union. When Fontana Films refused to agree, the union declared that no member of the union would work for Fontana Films and exerted pressure on theatrical agents not to supply actors to Fontana

Films. The company then ceased all production of films because it could not obtain the services of actors.

 Fontana Films applied to the Federal Court of Australia for an injunction, under s 45D of the Trade Practices Act, against Actors Equity, its officers and certain other persons to restrain them from acting in concert with any person to hinder or prevent the supply of actors to Fontana Films by theatrical agents. On an application for an interim restraining order, McGregor J found that the evidence prima facie established that Actors Equity, in concert with its officers, had engaged in conduct which was in breach of s 45D(1) of the Trade Practices Act. In reaching this finding, McGregor J (in the words of Gibbs CJ in the High Court) 'relied not only on the evidence, but also on the deeming provisions of s 45D(5)': 150 CLR at 176. McGregor J made an interim restraining order against Actors Equity, its officers and the other persons named in the proceedings. They appealed to the Full Court of the Federal Court, asserting that s 45D of the Trade Practices Act was invalid, and the matter was removed to the High Court under s 40 of the Judiciary Act for resolution of the constitutional question.

Gibbs CJ: [181] The limits of the power granted by s 51(xx) have not yet been defined. That paragraph of the Constitution presents considerable difficulties of interpretation. In the first place, the power is conferred by reference to persons. Paragraph (xix), in so far as it refers to aliens, and para (xxvi) are the only other paragraphs of s 51 which confer power in that way. Paragraph (xxvi) stands in a special position, for it proceeds on the assumption that special laws may be deemed necessary for the people of a particular race. However, having regard to the federal nature of the Constitution, it is difficult to suppose that the powers conferred by paras (xix) and (xx) were intended to extend to the enactment of a complete code of laws, on all subjects, applicable to the persons named in those paragraphs. It is unlikely, for example, that it was intended that the Parliament might provide that the rights and duties [182] of aliens should be determined by a special law, different from that which applies to Australian citizens, in relation to such matters as contracts, torts, succession and criminal responsibility. Similarly, in the case of the corporation described in s 51(xx), extraordinary consequences would result if the Parliament had power to make any kind of law on any subject affecting such corporations ... Other difficulties in relation to s 51(xx) are caused by the need to construe the Constitution as a whole, and thus to reconcile para (xx) with other parts of s 51: see *Bank of New South Wales v Commonwealth* (1948) 76 CLR 1 at 203–4, 356, 304 and 330 and *Strickland v Rocla Concrete Pipes Ltd* (1971) 124 CLR 468 at 507–8, per Menzies J. However, it is unnecessary, and undesirable, to attempt in the present case to define the outer limits of the power conferred by s 51(xx). The method which the courts have followed in the past, of approaching the solution of the difficult problems presented by such a provision as s 51(xx) gradually and with caution, proceeding no further at any time than the needs of the particular case require, is the most likely, in the end, to achieve the proper reconciliation between the apparent width of s 51(xx) and the maintenance of the federal balance which the Constitution requires. The authorities in which s 51(xx) has been considered are opposed to the view that a law comes within the power simply because it happens to apply to corporations of the kind described in that paragraph. The descriptive adjectives, 'foreign', 'trading' and 'financial' are important. In *Huddart Parker & Co Pty Ltd v Moorehead* (at 397) Isaacs J said: 'Just as their *incorporation* distinguishes them from natural individuals, so their trading or financial capacities distinguish them from other corporations, and it is as necessary to give effect to the words 'trading' and 'financial' as to the word 'corporation''.

 The words of para (xx) suggest that the nature of the corporation to which the laws relate must be significant as an element in the nature or character of the laws, if they are to be valid: cf per Walsh J in *Strickland v Rocla Concrete Pipes Ltd* (at 519). In other words, in the case of trading and financial corporations, laws which relate to their trading and financial activities will be within the power. This does not mean that a law under s 51(xx) may apply only to the foreign [183] activities of a foreign corporation for ex hypothesi the law will be one for the peace, order and good government of the Commonwealth. It means that the fact that the corporation is a foreign corporation should be significant in the way in which the law relates to it. For present purposes, however, it is enough that it is established by *Strickland v Rocla Concrete Pipes Ltd* that a law which governs the trading activities of trading corporations formed within the limits of the Commonwealth is within the scope of s 51(xx) (see especially at 490, 508, 525). Of course, the law in the present case does not regulate or govern the activities of trading corporations; it regulates the conduct of others. But the conduct to which the law is directed is conduct designed to cause, and likely to cause, substantial loss or damage to the business of a trading corporation formed within the limits of the Commonwealth. I can see no reason in principle why such a law should necessarily fall outside the scope of s 51(xx). A law may be one with respect to a trading corporation, although it casts obligations upon a person other than a trading corporation. An example is provided by s 5 of the Crimes Act 1914 (Cth) as amended, considered in *R v Australian Industrial Court; ex parte CLM Holdings Pty Ltd* (1977) 136 CLR 235 at 246–7. A law will fall within the power if the conduct to which it is directed is so relevant to the subject of the power that a law rendering such conduct unlawful can be described as a law with respect to that subject.

Gibbs CJ went on to conclude that s 45D(5) was 'reasonably incidental to the power conferred by s 51(xx)' because it required 'an organisation to take all reasonable steps to prevent its members from engaging in conduct intended and likely to cause' the damage at which s 45D(1) was aimed: 150 CLR at 187, 188.

Stephen J: [190] The law contained in s 45D(1)(b)(i) is composed of three elements: the existence of conduct by persons in concert which impedes a dealing in goods or services; the fact that that dealing is a dealing to which those persons are not themselves parties; and the presence of resultant and intended actual or likely detriment to one of the parties to the dealing, it being a corporation. It would no doubt be possible to describe the law by reference to any one of these elements, the conduct, the dealing or the detriment suffered by a corporation, ignoring in each instance the two other elements. The law could thus be described as one about concerted action affecting dealings, about dealings in goods or services or about detriments to corporations. But each such description would suffer from excessive width since it is only certain forms of concerted action, only dealings between those not parties to such actions and only detriments of a particular kind, suffered by a corporation, that the law affects. Its true character can only be conveyed by a description which picks up each of the elements, as does the description of it as a law prohibiting concerted action directed against a corporation's dealings in goods and services. Any attempt further to refine the description, while it may succeed in confining the subject matter of the law to one only of its elements, will necessarily lead to a departure from accuracy.

What I have said touches upon one of the major difficulties involved in the process of characterisation. An accurate description of any at all complex law will necessarily be relatively detailed if it is to encompass the several elements which together go to make up the impugned law. However, constitutional grants of power such as those in s 51 are customarily expressed quite differently — succinctly and in terms of wide generality. Thus, when an accurate, and hence relatively detailed, description of a law is sought to be matched against one or other of the tersely expressed grants of [191] legislative power contained in s 51 of the Constitution, it will not infrequently be found that different parts of the description of the law fall within different paragraphs of s 51; still other parts may be found to fall within none of those enumerated grants of power, because they concern elements of the law which are the subject only of State legislative power.

The pattern of distribution of legislative power in Australia is not based on a concept of mutual exclusiveness. It differs from that found in Canada's British North America Act of 1867, with its two lists of mutually exclusive matters, granted by ss 91 and 92, to the Canadian and provincial legislatures respectively — as to which see Hogg: *Constitutional Law of Canada* (1977), pp 80–7 and 95–6. Because the powers granted by s 51 are not exclusive, but instead remain available, so far at least as their subject matter permits, for exercise by the States, subject only to the terms of s 109 in the event of inconsistency, there is not, in Australia, the same need to seek for one sole or dominant character of each law. True it is that the Commonwealth's legislative power is confined to enumerated subject matters, to be found in s 51 and elsewhere in the Constitution. But because the States, unlike Canadian provinces, retain wide concurrent legislative powers, the according of validity to a particular law of the Commonwealth will not, in our non-exclusive system of allocation of legislative power, deprive the States of legislative capacity concerning the general subject matter of that law; only by the operation of s 109 may the effective operation of a State law be jeopardised.

Unaffected by restraints imposed by the existence of mutually exclusive grants of legislative power, this court's process of characterisation is free to recognise that laws may in truth possess a number of characters. Effect may thus be given to the reality to which Isaacs J referred in *Osborne v Commonwealth* (1911) 12 CLR 321 at 361, when he spoke of those lines of human affairs which 'from their inherent complexity cross each other at innumerable points' and make it 'impossible to frame an arbitrary classification, such as that contained in s 51 of the Constitution, which will completely segregate the transactions of life'. ...

[192] To recognise that a law may possess a number of quite disparate characters is, then, to accept reality. Few laws will involve only one element. Even the simplest form of law will commonly contain two elements when it forbids, regulates or mandates particular conduct on the part of a particular class of person. The conduct and the class will form distinct elements and if each happens to bear a relationship to different grants of legislative power the law may often be equally appropriately described by reference to either. If a law also includes reference to another class of persons, those affected by the conduct in question, a third element will thereby be introduced. Many laws will, because of the relatively complex concepts to which they give effect, involve still further elements. These elements may, of course, all bear one and the same character. However, where they do not, any search for a single character by which to describe the law is likely to prove fruitless.

Were constitutional dogma to require such a search to be pursued, the difficulty in choosing between competing elements might readily lead different minds, perhaps influenced by quite subjective considerations, to varying conclusions as to the dominant character of a law. But to accept as constitutionally permissible the fact that a law may bear several characters, each as valid as the other because each is reasonably capable of fairly describing the law as a whole, disposes of the need to rely upon what may prove to be quite subjective reasons for selecting one particular description only. With the disappearance of subjective criteria, the process of characterisation then becomes less uncertain and more a matter of logic than of idiosyncratic assertion.

Once it is recognised that a law may possess several distinct characters, it follows that the fact that only some elements in the description of a law fall within one or more of the grants of power in s 51 or elsewhere in the Constitution will be in no way fatal to its validity. So long as the remaining elements, which do not fall within any such grant of power, are not of such significance that the law cannot fairly be described as one with respect to one or more of such grants of power then, however else it may also be described, the law will be valid. If a law enacted by the Federal legislature can be fairly described both as a law with respect to a grant of power to it and as a law with respect to a matter or matters left to the States, that will suffice to support its validity as a law of the Commonwealth.

In characterising the law represented by s 45D(1)(b)(i) I have not had recourse to the context provided by the Act as a whole, and this [193] not only because the law speaks for itself, bearing on its face its several characters, but also because those who attack its validity do not assert the existence of some covert character, not apparent on its face. The attack is rather designed to establish as the law's sole character one only of its overt concerns, that of secondary boycotts. Accordingly, this is not a case where form and substance are to be distinguished; in this law they are at one.

That characterisation does not require a search for one sole or predominant character where the law in question can be seen to possess several characters is now well established in Australian constitutional law.

Stephen J referred to several decisions of the High Court, including: *Melbourne Corporation v Commonwealth* (1947) 74 CLR 31 at 79; *Strickland v Rocla Concrete Pipes*

Ltd (1971) 124 CLR 468 at 510; *Victoria v Commonwealth* (1971) 122 CLR at 400, 403–4; *Seaman's Union of Australia v Utah Development Co* (1978) 144 CLR 120 at 154; *Re Linehan; Ex parte Northwest Exports Pty Ltd* (1981) 147 CLR 259 at 264–5, 266–7 and 273–4.

[194] It follows that in testing validity the task is not to single out one predominant character of a law which, because it can be said to prevail over all others, leads to the attaching to the law of one description only as truly apt. It will be enough if the law fairly answers the description of a law 'with respect to' one given subject matter appearing in s 51, regardless of whether it may equally be described as a law with respect to other subject matters. This will be so whether or not those other subject matters appear in the enumeration of heads of legislative power in s 51.

If the task of characterisation be approached in this fashion, s 45D(1)(b)(i) may be seen clearly enough to possess the character of law with respect to trading corporations, whatever other characters it may also possess. What it does is to forbid conduct which has for its purpose, and which in addition would have or be likely to have the effect, of causing substantial loss or damage to a corporation. To that may be added the fact that the forbidden conduct is described, in the opening words of s 45D(1), in terms directly relating it to the trading activities of corporations. Whatever other descriptions might also be assigned to it, to fail to include as one characterisation of it that of a law about corporations would seem to me to be to ignore the obvious. To describe it as a law with respect to trading corporations seems entirely apt; it does no more than recognise what is the manifest purpose and direct effect of the law. The connexion with corporations forms a crucial component of the law, making wholly inappropriate any description of that connexion as being merely 'so incidental as not in truth to affect its [195] character': per Kitto J in *Fairfax v FC of T* (1965) 114 CLR 1 at 7.

The centrality of that connexion is emphasised rather than diminished, by the fact that the prohibition which the law imposes is not addressed to corporations but rather to those who act with a purpose of harming them. That the law takes this form is dictated by its aim of protecting corporations from a particular harm; in such a prohibitory law the focus will necessarily be upon the acts of those who intend harm. A law forbidding certain acts of third parties for the reasons that they were both intended, and also likely, to harm aliens would surely be as central to the grant of power with respect to aliens as a law which required aliens to do or refrain from particular conduct: the intended object of another's conduct is no less central, no less significant, in bestowing a character upon a law than is the actor to whom that law directly speaks.

Stephen J said that the extension of the definition of 'corporation' to holding corporations in s 4(1) and the reference to a related body corporate in s 45D(1)(b)(i) were in excess of power, but they could be severed without affecting the operation of s 45D(1)(b)(i) in the present proceedings: 150 CLR at 195.

He adopted the views of Mason J on the validity of s 45D(5) and (6).

Mason J: [204] The judgments in *Strickland* and in *R v Trade Practices Tribunal; Ex parte St George County Council* (1974) 130 CLR 533, especially at 542–3, and more recently in *R v Federal Court of Australia; Ex parte WA National Football League* (1979) 143 CLR 190, do not attempt to define the limits of the corporations power. They proceed upon the footing that the power extends to the regulation of the trading activities of foreign corporations and trading and financial corporations formed within the limits of the Commonwealth, without deciding whether it travels further.

Mason J referred to the argument by the Solicitor-General for the Commonwealth, to the effect that the power to prohibit trading activities of trading corporations was matched by a power to protect those activities:

The Solicitor-General's submission is correct so long as it is understood that by a law which protects the trading activities of trading corporations he means a law which has a direct legal operation on the subject of the power. Such a law is within power and valid. ...

[207] I should not wish it to be thought from what I have said that the corporations power is confined in its application to trading corporations to laws that deal with their trading activities. The subject of the power is corporations — of the kind described; the power is not expressed as one with respect to the activities of corporations, let alone activities of a particular kind or kinds. A constitutional grant of legislative power should be construed liberally and not in any narrow or pedantic fashion ...

Nowhere in the Constitution is there to be found a secure footing for an implication that the power is to be read down so that it relates to 'the trading activities of trading corporations' and, I would suppose, correspondingly to the financial activities of financial corporations and perhaps to the foreign aspects of foreign corporations. Even if it be thought that it was concern as to the trading activities of trading corporations and financial activities of financial corporations that led to the singling out in s 51(xx) of these domestic corporations from other domestic corporations it would be mere speculation to say that it was intended to confine the legislative power so given to these activities. The competing hypothesis, which conforms to the accepted approach to the construction of a legislative power in the Constitution is that it was intended to confer comprehensive power with respect to the subject matter so as to ensure that all conceivable matters of national concern would be [208] comprehended. The power should, therefore, in accordance with that approach, be construed as a plenary power with respect to the subjects mentioned free from the unexpressed qualifications which have been suggested.

It sufficiently appears from what has already been said that, even if s 51(xx) be relevantly restricted to legislation which affects trading corporations in their trading activities, s 45D(1)(b)(i) is within power, subject to qualifications shortly to be mentioned.

Mason J went on to observe that the extension of the definition of 'corporation' to holding corporations in s 4(1) and the reference to a related body corporate in s 45D(I)(b)(i) were ultra vires. His Honour said, as Stephen J had said, that these terms could be severed: 150 CLR at 209–10. Mason J then turned to s 45D(5):

[210] The effect of sub-s (5) is that when two or more persons who are members or officers of a trade union engaged in conduct in concert with one another the trade union is deemed to engage in that conduct in concert with the participants and to engage in that conduct for the purpose or purposes for which that conduct is engaged in by the participants, unless the organisation establishes that it took all reasonable steps to prevent the participants from engaging in that conduct.

The subsection is not an onus of proof provision. To escape the deeming operation it will avail the trade union nothing to prove that it did not act in concert with the officers or that it did not act in concert for the relevant purpose. To escape it must go further and show that it took all reasonable steps to prevent the participants from engaging in that conduct. Consequently the operation of the [211] subsection is very different from that of the provisions considered in *Williamson v Ah On* (1926) 39 CLR 95 and *Milicevic v Campbell* (1975) 132 CLR 307.

In substance s 45D(5) is a law which makes a trade union responsible for a boycott affecting a corporation when that boycott is imposed by members or officers of the trade union, a responsibility which the trade union can only avoid if it demonstrates it has taken the action mentioned in the subsection. As such it is a law about trade unions; to me it has a very remote connexion with corporations, a connexion so remote that the provision cannot be characterised as a law with respect to corporations of the relevant class. In my opinion it is beyond power. The result is that sub-s (6), at least to the extent to which it has an operation consequential upon sub-s (5) by reason of the words 'or is deemed by sub-section (5) to engage', is also beyond power.

~~~

[10.3.19] Murphy J held that s 45D, apart from s 45C(5) and (6), was within the corporations power, which was plenary and 'enables Parliament to make comprehensive laws covering all internal and external relations of foreign trading and financial corporations', enabling 'Parliament to protect trading, financial and foreign corporations from others and to protect others from such corporations': 150 CLR at 212. His Honour concluded that s 45D(5) was invalid. In his view, it was not supported by the corporations power and was inconsistent with the exercise of the judicial power conferred on federal courts by Ch III of the Constitution because it required the courts 'to make findings contrary to fact': 150 CLR at 214.

Brennan J said that it was not necessary to go beyond the decision in *Strickland v Rocla Concrete Pipes* (1971) 124 CLR 468, to conclude that s 45D(1) was supported by the corporations power. He said that a law which protected the business of a trading corporation necessarily dealt with its trading activity, and *Strickland v Rocla Concrete Pipes Ltd* had held that s 51(xx) of the Constitution would support laws dealing with the trading activities of a trading corporation. Accordingly, it was 'not necessary to determine whether any law which discriminates between corporations mentioned in para (xx) and the public at large is a law falling within the ambit of the corporations power': 150 CLR at 218.

Notwithstanding Brennan J's declaration that it was unnecessary to go beyond *Strickland v Rocla Concrete Pipes Ltd*, he made the following observations:

A law which, discriminating between one or more of the corporations mentioned in para (xx) and the public at large, protects both the trading and the non-trading business of trading corporations, wears the appearance of a law with respect to those corporations. It is of the nature of the power that it is a power to make law with respect to corporate persons, not with respect to functions, activities or relationships. The subject matter of activities or relationships which the law affects may be relevant to the question whether the law is truly to be described as a law with respect to corporations mentioned in para (xx), but the validity of the law cannot be determined as though the power were expressed as a power to make laws with respect to the trading or some other activity of or relationship with corporations mentioned in para (xx) (150 CLR at 222).

Brennan J concluded that s 45D(5) was invalid because it was not a law with respect to corporations:

The corporations power does not support a law which makes an organisation liable for conduct in which it has not engaged and which it has not counselled, aided or abetted (150 CLR at 223).

Aickin J agreed with Mason J. Wilson J agreed with Gibbs CJ.

In the result, the court declared s 45D(1)(b)(i) valid in its application to trading corporations, and s 45D(5) and the references to that subsection in s 45D(6) invalid.

Notes

[10.3.20] The judgments in *Actors & Announcers Equity v Fontana Films Pty Ltd* (1982) 150 CLR 169 **[10.3.18C]** showed a court split over the type of legislation which could be enacted under s 51(xx) and over the appropriate approach to the definition of Commonwealth powers. While not absolutely committed to the position, Gibbs CJ (and Wilson J) showed a strong inclination to limit the Commonwealth's power to regulating or protecting specified activities of the listed corporations. The limitation suggested does not find any direct support in the language of s 51(xx), for the word 'trading' in the paragraph qualifies the type of corporation subject to Commonwealth control rather than the type of control which the Commonwealth might impose. Rather, the suggested limit on s 51(xx) was suggested by 'the federal nature of the Constitution' and the 'extraordinary consequences' which would follow from a broad reading: 150 CLR at 181, 182. To adopt the words of Murphy J in *Attorney-General (WA) v Australian National Airlines Commission* (1976) 138 CLR 492 **[10.2.26C]**, this approach 'keeps the pre-*Engineers* ghosts walking'.

On the other hand, Mason, Murphy and Aickin JJ asserted that s 51(xx) was a power to legislate with respect to the named corporations, not with respect to specified activities. It should be 'construed liberally', and 'without making implications' (150 CLR at 207), giving the Commonwealth Parliament power over the corporations.

Standing in the middle were (or appeared to be) Stephen and Brennan JJ. They indicated that the validity of s 45D(1)(b)(i) could be settled by applying the proposition in *Strickland v Rocla Concrete Pipes Ltd* (1971) 124 CLR 468 **[10.3.4C]**; namely, that s 51(xx) at least allowed the Commonwealth to legislate with respect to trading activities of trading corporations. Their Honours reserved, for a future case where the issue needed to be resolved, the question whether s 51(xx) would authorise wider-ranging legislation.

[10.3.21]   However, Brennan J's analysis of s 45D(1)(b)(i) in *Actors & Announcers Equity v Fontana Films Pty Ltd* (1982) 150 CLR 169 **[10.3.18C]** and his application to that section of the proposition from *Strickland v Rocla Concrete Pipes Ltd* (as he read that case) suggested that he was far closer to Mason J than to Gibbs CJ in his view of the extent of permissible Commonwealth laws under s 51(xx); even though he did not adopt Mason J's direct, expansive view of that paragraph.

Brennan J's argument was set out in two paragraphs in 150 CLR at 221–2. Parts of that reasoning suggest that he was very close to adopting Mason J's view of s 51(xx): 'the power ... is a power to make law with respect to corporate persons not with respect to functions, activities or relationships': 150 CLR at 222. But other parts of the reasoning concentrated on the type of corporate activities which a law regulates or protects. According to his Honour's view, the Commonwealth can legislate with respect to the general business of a trading corporation because *one* of the activities regulated or protected by that legislation must, of necessity, be the corporation's trading activities (by which, according to Mason J in *R v Federal Court of Australia; Ex parte WA National Football League (Inc)* (1979) 143 CLR 190 **[10.3.12]**, the corporation is identified as a trading corporation); the legislation will legitimately regulate or protect all the business, including the other activities of the corporation. Even this second view was considerably broader than that of Gibbs CJ: see *Commonwealth v Tasmania* (the *Tasmanian Dam* case) (1983) 158 CLR 1 **[10.3.26C]** at 117–18 per Gibbs CJ.

[10.3.22]   Is it significant that in *Actors & Announcers Equity v Fontana Films Pty Ltd* (1982) 150 CLR 169 **[10.3.18C]** the broadest view of the Commonwealth's power under s 51(xx) was articulated by those judges (Mason and Murphy JJ) who had in *R v Federal Court of Australia; Ex parte WA National Football League (Inc)* (1979) 143 CLR 190 **[10.3.12]** taken the broadest view of the reach of s 51(xx); and that the narrowest view of the Commonwealth's power was suggested by that judge (Gibbs CJ) who had consistently taken the narrowest view of the power's reach?

[10.3.23]   Why did the judges who articulated the broadest view of the Commonwealth's power under s 51(xx) in *Actors & Announcers Equity v Fontana*

Films Pty Ltd (1982) 150 CLR 169 **[10.3.18C]** hold that s 45D(5) exceeded that power, while the judges who suggested the narrowest reading of that power hold that s 45D(5) was valid?

The opinion of the minority, that s 45D(5) was within s 51(xx) of the Constitution, was based on the incidental power inherent in s 51(xx). In the words of Gibbs CJ, s 45D(5) was 'reasonably incidental to the power conferred by s 51(xx)': 150 CLR at 187. The Chief Justice was here referring to the well-established proposition, as Dixon CJ put it in *Grannall v Marrickville Margarine Pty Ltd* (1955) 93 CLR 55, that:

> ... every legislative power carries with it authority to legislate in relation to acts, matters and things the control of which is found necessary to effectuate its main purpose, and thus carries with it power to make laws governing or affecting many matters that are incidental or ancillary to the subject matter (93 CLR at 77).

Earlier, Dixon CJ had conceded that '[t]hese matters of incidental powers are largely questions of degree': *Burton v Honan* (1952) 86 CLR 169 at 179. Given the use (in judicial discussion of questions of incidental power) of terms such as 'purpose', 'appropriate', 'remote' and 'reasonable', it is not difficult to see the force of Dixon CJ's concession.

Despite the failure, as Sawer says, of the High Court to develop a comprehensive theory of characterisation and incidental powers (Sawer (1967) p 101), it is possible to provide an outline of this approach to characterisation. It is essentially a judicial device employed to expand the range of matters for which the Commonwealth may legislate. When the standard approach to characterisation (Does the law have direct legal operation on some matter within the power granted to parliament?) suggests that a law is invalid, the court may save the law by establishing a 'reasonable connection' between the law's direct legal operation and some matter within Commonwealth power. In *Airlines of New South Wales Pty Ltd v New South Wales (No 2)* (1965) 113 CLR 54 **[10.2.20C]**, for example, the reasonable connection was the contribution to the physical safety of international and interstate air traffic which resulted from the regulation of intrastate air traffic.

Sometimes that connection will lie in the 'purpose' of the law (as perceived by the court); sometimes it will be established by evidence about the law's practical operation; and sometimes, it seems, the presence or absence of the connection is a matter of (judicial) common sense. (Dixon CJ had said that it would 'strike the mind as absurd' if a law demanding priority for payment of telephone accounts was treated as incidental to s 51(v), the postal, telegraphic and telephonic power: *Victoria v Commonwealth* (the *Second Uniform Tax* case) (1957) 99 CLR 575 at 625 **[9.6.8C]**.) For a thorough discussion of the difficulties inherent in the 'incidental' approach to characterisation, see Zines (1997) pp 37–54.

[10.3.24]   Resort to the incidental nature of the Commonwealth's powers need not generate the sharp difference of opinion seen in *Actors & Announcers Equity v Fontana Films Pty Ltd* (1982) 150 CLR 169 **[10.3.18C]**. In *Fencott v Muller* (1983) 152 CLR 570 **[10.3.15]** all seven justices agreed that s 82(1) of the Trade Practices Act 1974 (Cth) was a valid law, supported by s 51(xx). This provision enabled any person who had suffered loss because of a corporation's misleading or deceptive conduct (contrary to s 52(1) of the Act) to recover that loss from 'any person involved in the contravention'. To the argument that s 82(1) was not a law with respect to corporations because it did not affect a corporation's rights and duties, Mason, Murphy, Brennan and Deane JJ responded at 598–9:

The argument is too narrow. Once it is accepted, as it now is, that the corporations power extends to the regulation of the trading activities of trading corporations, it necessarily follows that, in some circumstances at least, the power must extend to the imposition of duties on natural persons. Two considerations combine to sustain this conclusion. The first is that corporations act through natural persons. The second — and it is a consequence of the first — is that, in order to be effective, a regulation of the activities of corporations calls for the imposition of duties on those natural persons who would, or might, in the ordinary course of events, participate in the corporate activities, the subject of the intended regulations. Accordingly, when in the legitimate exercise of the corporations power duties are imposed on corporations in relation to their trading activities, breach of which creates a civil liability, the power extends to the imposition of duties on natural persons, breach of which also creates a civil liability, not to engage in conduct which assists or facilitates a contravention by a corporation of duties thus imposed upon it. Then the imposition of duties on natural persons is seen to be an element or incident in the regulation of the corporate trading activities.

Another way of expressing this approach is to say that where a law prescribing the way in which corporations shall conduct their trading activities is supported by the corporations power, an ancillary provision reasonably adapted to deter other persons from facilitating a contravention of the law by a corporation is supported by the same power. It is within the competence of the Parliament to enact such a provision to secure compliance with a valid statutory command. A valid statutory command directed to a particular class may be strengthened by a provision imposing a liability upon other persons who are involved in a contravention by a person to whom the command is directed, provided that the ancillary provision is reasonably adapted to securing obedience to the command.

Gibbs CJ, Wilson and Dawson JJ held s 82(1) valid for the same reasons: see 152 CLR at 583–4, 611, 620.

[10.3.25] An immediate consequence of the decision in *Actors & Announcers Equity v Fontana Films Pty Ltd* (1982) 150 CLR 169 **[10.3.18C]** was to increase the difficulty of enforcing s 45D(1). Section 45D(5) had been enacted on the assumption that secondary boycotts served the collective industrial interests of trade unions and that those boycotts would only be stopped if trade unions, rather than individual officers or members, were made to answer for the boycotts (either through injunctions or damages awards). The strategy behind the drafting of s 45D(5) was obviously one of striking at the centre of a perceived problem rather than nibbling at its edges. Section 45D(5) made that central attack relatively easy to mount, because it made the union vicariously liable for actions of its officers or members, thus overcoming the often difficult problem facing a litigant of actually proving that a trade union knew of and endorsed the actions of particular officers or members. Indeed, the difficulty of actually marshalling that evidence would be enough, in the absence of s 45D(5), to frustrate enforcement of s 45D(1).

[10.3.26C] **Commonwealth v Tasmania**
(The *Tasmanian Dam* case)
(1983) 158 CLR 1

The Gordon River Hydro-Electric Power Development Act 1982 (Tas) authorised the Hydro-Electric Commission of Tasmania (the HEC) to construct a dam on the Gordon River in south-west Tasmania (the 'Gordon below Franklin Dam'). The HEC was a corporation established by the Hydro-Electric Commission Act 1944 (Tas) with responsibility for generating and distributing electricity in Tasmania. Construction of the dam commenced in July 1982.

The World Heritage Properties Conservation Act 1983 (Cth) provided as follows:

> 7 Where the Governor-General is satisfied that an identified property is being or is likely to be damaged or destroyed, he may, by Proclamation, declare that property to be property to which section 10 applies. ...
>
> 10(1) In this section —
>
> 'foreign corporation' means a foreign corporation within the meaning of paragraph 51(xx) of the Constitution;
>
> 'trading corporation' means a trading corporation within the meaning of paragraph 51(xx) of the Constitution;
>
> 'trading corporation' means a foreign corporation within the meaning of paragraph 51(xx) of the Constitution.
>
> (2) Except with the consent in writing of the Minister, it is unlawful for a body corporate that —
>
> (a) is a foreign corporation;
>
> (b) is incorporated in a Territory; or
>
> (c) not being incorporated in a Territory, is a trading corporation formed within the limits of the Commonwealth,
>
> whether itself or by its servant or agent —
>
> (d) to carry out any excavation works on any property to which this section applies;
>
> (e) to carry out operations for, or exploratory drilling in connection with, the recovery of minerals on any property to which this section applies;
>
> (f) to erect a building or other substantial structure on any property to which this section applies or to do any act in the course of, or for the purpose of, the erection of a building or other substantial structure on any property to which this section applies;
>
> (g) to damage or destroy a building or other substantial structure on any property to which this section applies;
>
> (h) to kill, cut down or damage any tree on any property to which this section applies;
>
> (j) to construct or establish any road or vehicular track on any property to which this section applies;
>
> (k) to use explosives on any property to which this section applies; or
>
> (m) if any act is prescribed for the purpose of this paragraph in relation to particular property to which this section applies, to do that act in relation to that property.
>
> (3) Except with the consent in writing of the Minister, it is unlawful for a body corporate of a kind referred to in sub-section (2), whether itself or by its servant or agent, to do any act, not being an act the doing of which is unlawful by virtue of that sub-section, that damages or destroys any property to which this section applies.
>
> (4) Without prejudice to the effect of sub-sections (2) and (3), except with the consent in writing of the Minister, it is unlawful for a body corporate of the kind referred to in paragraph (2)(c), whether itself or by its servant or agent, to do, for the purposes of its trading activities, an act referred to in any of paragraphs (2)(d) to (m) (inclusive) or an act referred to in sub-section (3).

Section 17 of the Act established a complex procedure for determining whether the Commonwealth should pay compensation to any person where the operation of the Act on that person amounted to an acquisition of that person's property. Other provisions of the Act prohibited any work on a site whose protection was an international obligation for Australia (ss 6, 9) or on a site of particular significance to people of the Aboriginal race: ss 8, 11. Sections 6 and 9 are set out, and their validity considered, at **[3.3.21C]**.

On 26 May 1983, the Governor-General declared, by proclamation, that s 10 applied to three areas in the south-west of Tasmania including the area where the HEC was constructing the Gordon below Franklin Dam. At the same time, the Governor-General made regulations under the Act prescribing certain acts for the purposes of s 10(2)(m). These were carrying out works in the course of constructing, or preparatory to constructing, or associated with construction of, a dam which would flood any part of the areas specified in the proclamations.

The Commonwealth began proceedings in the High Court of Australia, seeking a declaration that it would be unlawful for the HEC to continue to construct the Gordon below Franklin Dam. At the same time, the state of Tasmania initiated an action for a declaration that the World Heritage Properties Conservation Act 1983 (Cth) was invalid. These actions were heard and decided together. We are here concerned with only that part of the case which discusses the validity of ss 7 and 10 of the Commonwealth Act.

Gibbs CJ held that the Commission was not a 'trading corporation' because its 'true character', as revealed by its activities as well as the purposes of its formation, was 'a corporation sui generis', discharging a public function of vital importance to the State. Its trading activities, although significant, did not indicate its true character: 158 CLR at 116–17.

Gibbs CJ: [117] I further consider that, even if the Commission were a trading corporation, the provisions of ss 7 and 10 of the Act, if valid, could apply to the Commission only in relation to such of its activities as are properly regarded as trading activities. I adhere to the view [118] which I expressed in *Actors and Announcers Equity Association of Australia v Fontana Films Pty Ltd* (1982) 56 ALJR 366 at 370: 'The authorities in which s 51(xx) has been considered are opposed to the view that a law comes within the power simply because it happens to apply to corporations of the kind described in that paragraph ... The words of para (xx) suggest that the nature of the corporation to which the laws relate must be significant as an element in the nature or character of the laws, if they are to be valid'. In view of the conclusions which I reach on other aspects of the case, I need not elaborate this matter further. It is clear, however, that the activities of the Commission to which s 10, if valid, would apply, are not trading activities. The trade of the Commission is in respect of the supply of electricity; the acts prohibited by s 10 are anterior even to the generation of the electricity which is to be supplied. They may be regarded as acts preparatory to the trade; they certainly do not form part of it.

It follows that, in my opinion, the provisions of s 10 of the Act, if valid, would have no application to the Commission. Lest that view be not accepted, I should turn to consider the validity of the section. In my opinion, with the exception of one subsection, it is not a law with respect to trading corporations. This is made clear by the provisions of s 7, and by the scheme of the Act as a whole. As s 7 shows, s 10 applies only where the Governor-General is satisfied that any identified property is being or is likely to be damaged or destroyed. The object of ss 7 and 10, as appears from their own terms, is the protection of the heritage from damage or destruction. That conclusion is supported by a consideration of ss 9 and 11, which show that the same prohibitions as s 10 seeks to apply to corporations are made applicable by those other sections to cases which in no way involve corporations. In other words, for the purposes of the statute the character of the person who performs the forbidden acts is immaterial. Further, the prohibited acts are not such as might naturally be performed by a corporation in the course of trading.

Gibbs CJ referred to Kitto J's proposition, in *Fairfax v Federal Commissioner of Taxation* (1965) 114 CLR 1 at 7, that the question of constitutional validity under s 51 'is always one of subject matter, to be determined by reference solely to the operation which the enactment has if it be valid, that is to say by reference to the nature of the rights, duties, powers and privileges which it changes, regulates or abolishes'.

[119] ... Apart from s 10(4), the connection between ss 7 and 10 and the topic of trading corporations is not direct and substantial — it is exiguous and unreal. It is apparent that the relationship between trading corporations and the operative provisions of s 10 is merely incidental — the section is applied to trading corporations only in an attempt to use s 51(xx) as a source of power which would not otherwise exist. The true character of the section is not that of a law with respect to trading corporations.

However, s 10(4) applies only where the forbidden acts are done by a body corporate of the kind described in the section 'for the purposes of its trading activity'. Notwithstanding some doubts as to whether the connection made by s 10(4) with trading corporations by the use of those words is merely contrived, I consider that the subsection does have a sufficient connection with the topic of power granted by s 51(xx). I would therefore hold s 10(4) to be valid.

On this branch of the case I hold that s 10(4) is valid, but that the remainder of s 10 is invalid; that the Commission is not a trading corporation and that, in any case, such of its activities as would fall within the scope of s 10 if it were a trading corporation are not trading activities.

Mason J said that it had been established that the corporations power extended to the regulation and the protection of the trading activities of trading corporations, and continued:

Mason J: [148] Whether the power goes further remains to be decided. Barwick CJ, Murphy, Brennan JJ and I have indicated that it does ... It would be unduly restrictive to confine the power to the regulation and protection of the trading activities of trading corporations. After all, the subject matter of the power is persons, not activities. The suggested restriction might possibly deny to Parliament power to regulate borrowing by trading corporations, notwithstanding that there is much to be said for the view that one of the objects of s 51(xx) was to enable Parliament to regulate transactions between the categories of corporation mentioned and the public, indeed to enable Parliament to protect the public, should the need arise, in relation to the operations of such corporations.

There is, certainly, no sound reason for denying that the power should extend to the regulation of acts undertaken by trading corporations for the purpose of engaging in their trading activities. I do not understand Mr Merralls QC to deny that in some instances at least the power extends that far. ...

However, it seems to me that there are three powerful objections to the adoption of this limited construction. The first is that this [149] approach to the scope of the power in its application to the classes of corporations mentioned, though it has some plausibility in the case of trading corporations, has none at all in the case of financial and foreign corporations. It can scarcely have been intended that the scope of the power was to be limited by reference to the foreign aspects of foreign corporations and the financial aspects of financial corporations. And it would be irrational to conclude that the power is plenary in the case of those corporations, but limited in the case of trading corporations.

The second objection is that the interpretation fails to give effect to the principle that a legislative power conferred by the Constitution should be liberally construed. And the final objection is that a power to make laws with respect to corporations (of designated categories), as in the case of a power with respect to natural persons, would seem naturally to extend to their acts and activities. In *Koowarta* (1982) 153 CLR at 209, Stephen J, when referring to the power conferred by s 51(xxxvi) with respect to the people of any race, said that 'The content of the laws which may be made under it are left very much at large' and that 'they may be directed to any aspect of human activity'.

There is nothing in the context of s 51(xx) which compels the conclusion that the language in which the power is expressed should be given a restricted interpretation. In this respect I mention, without repeating, what I said in *Fontana* ... In the result we should recognise that the power confers a plenary power with respect to the categories of corporation mentioned.

It is of some interest to note that Griffith CJ in *Huddart Parker* made it clear that, but for the doctrine of reserved powers, this is the interpretation of s 51(xx) to which he would have been compelled ...

[150] Barwick CJ in *Rocla Pipes* (at 489–90), when referring to Griffith CJ's comments, said: '... that it does not follow either as a logical proposition, or, if in this instance there be a difference, as a legal proposition, from the validity of those sections, that any law which in the range of its command or prohibition includes foreign corporations or trading or financial corporations ... is necessarily a law with respect to the subject matter of s 51(xx)'. In substance these remarks amounted to a counsel of caution. However, when analysed in the light of

Barwick CJ's view of characterisation of a law as expressed in the *Pay-roll Tax* case, which I do not accept and which I shall discuss shortly, they suggest that his Honour was accepting that the potential reach of a law under s 51 (xx) would extend to the non-trading acts and activities of a trading corporation, subject only to its being characterised as a law with respect to the subject matter. Although it may be that his Honour entertained some doubt as to the universality of the illustrations given by Griffith CJ, the doubt appears to have stemmed from Barwick CJ's view of characterisation.

The argument presented in the present case tends to obscure the difference between two distinct and separate questions: (1) what is the scope of the power; and (2) is the law in truth a law with respect to the subject matter of the power, once its scope has been ascertained. Characterisation, the name given to the process of arriving at an answer to the second question, cannot begin until the first question is answered.

The Commission then argues that s 10 is not a law about trading and foreign corporations; rather it is a law about the activities which are prohibited by the section or, alternatively, about the Western Tasmania Wilderness area. There is no need to recall all that has been said on the topic of characterisation of a law. It is sufficient to mention the discussion in *Fontana* by Stephen J (1982) 150 CLR at 189–93; Brennan J (at 221–2); and myself (at 201–4). But it is necessary to reject the invitation proffered by Mr Merrals QC to accept what Barwick CJ [151] expressed in *Pay-roll Tax* case (122 CLR at 372–3), as constituting a correct approach to characterisation. There his Honour said: '... a law may be at the same time thought to be a law with respect to either of two of the topics enumerated in s 51 and it may be satisfactory in such a case not to trouble to say with respect to which of the two subject matters the law should preferably be referred. But when a law may possibly be regarded as having either of two subjects as its substance, one of which is within Commonwealth power and the other is not, a decision must be made as to that which is in truth the subject matter of the law'. His Honour then likened the manner in which the choice is to be made to the manner in which the validity of a law claimed to be within one of the two mutually exclusive lists in the Canadian Constitution is determined. He went on to say (at 373): 'The law must be upon one or other of the subjects. It cannot be on both'.

His Honour's statement reflects an approach similar to that which had been adopted by Latham CJ in *West v Commissioner of Taxation (NSW)* (1937) 56 CLR 657 at 668–9 and in *Melbourne Corporation* (at 50–1). But it does not accord with the approach that has been consistently taken by the court in modern times. It is now well settled (a) that a law upon a subject matter within Commonwealth power does not cease to be valid because it touches or affects a topic outside Commonwealth power or because it can be characterised as a law upon a topic outside power; and (b) that it is not necessary to characterise a law upon one topic to the exclusion of the other ... No doubt, as Stephen J suggested in *Fontana Films* (150 CLR at 194), the statement was made with reference to the argument that the character of the law in that case was with respect to the functions of a State. Be this as it may, his Honour's remarks cannot be accepted as a correct approach to characterisation in general.

The true principle is that the character of the law is to be ascertained from its legal operation, that is by reference to the rights, duties, obligations, powers and privileges which it creates. This is not to deny the validity of a law which exhibits in its practical operation a 'substantial connection' with a relevant head of power. Taking the practical effect of the relevant law into account led the court to uphold its validity in *Herald and Weekly Times*. So much appears from the judgments of Kitto and Menzies JJ. Kitto J said (115 CLR at 436): 'Undoubtedly it is right to scrutinise minutely the effect of a challenged law in all the variety of cases to which it applies according to its terms; but when that has been done the broader inquiry remains: what, then, is the law really doing by operation which the scrutiny reveals that it has?' And Menzies J said (at 440): 'A law governing a particular relationship may, however, be supported by a legislative power with respect to a subject matter notwithstanding that the connection between the legal relationship and the subject matter of legislative power is of practical rather than of legal significance'.

The requirement that there should be a substantial connection between the exercise of the power and its subject matter does not mean that the connection must be 'close'. It means only that the connection must not be 'so insubstantial, tenuous or distant' that it cannot be regarded as a law with respect to the head of power (*Melbourne Corporation* (74 CLR) at 79).

In this respect the Commission submits that s 7 is invalid because it selects damage to or destruction of property as the basis of the power to make a proclamation and not an act or prohibited act of a foreign or trading corporation. An event having no necessary connection with trading or foreign corporations is made the occasion for prohibiting them from damaging property. This demonstrates something that is evident from other provisions of the Act, namely that the object of s 10 is to protect the Western Tasmania Wilderness area. The Parliament has exercised the corporations power to achieve this end, not for some overriding purpose having a connection with trading and foreign corporations. But the point is [153] that the legislative power with respect to trading and foreign corporations is not, on the view which I have expressed, in any sense purposive. It is enough that the law has a real relationship with the subjects of the power; it matters not, when the power is not purposive, that the object of the exercise is to attain some goal in a field that lies outside the scope of the Commonwealth power. A law which prohibits trading and foreign corporations from doing an act is a law about trading and foreign corporations, notwithstanding that it is also a law about the act which is prohibited. It is a law which imposes obligations on such corporations, enforceable by injunctions. Consequently, it is simply impossible to say that the law has no substantial connection with trading and foreign corporations.

In the result then, subject to consideration of the argument based on s 100 of the Constitution, ss 7 and 10 are valid. The validity of s 10(4) is a necessary consequence of the validity of s 10(2) and (3).

Mason J rejected the argument that laws made under s 51(xx) were subject to the restriction imposed by s 100: 'the significance of the expression "law or regulation of trade and commerce" used in ss 99 and 100' he said, 'confines the prohibition to laws made, or capable of being made, under ss 51(i) and 98': 158 CLR at 154–5.

[155] *Is the Commission a Trading Corporation Within the Meaning of Section 10?*

This question must be answered in the affirmative for reasons which may be shortly stated in this way:

1.   The decision in *R v Trade Practices Tribunal; Ex parte St George County Council* (1974) 130 CLR 533, is no longer to be regarded as correct. A majority of the court in *R v Federal Court of Australia; Ex parte WA National Football League* (1979) 143 CLR 190, considered it to have been wrongly decided: see also *State Superannuation Board v Trade Practices Commission* (1982) 150 CLR 282 at 304.

2.   As Barwick CJ observed in his dissenting judgment in *St George County Council* (130 CLR at 541), the connection of the corporation with the government of a State will not take it outside s 51(xx). In making this statement his Honour referred to certain features of the County Council in that case and stated that they did not take the County Council outside the category of 'trading corporations'. The features were (1) that it was incorporated under the Local Government Act 1919 (NSW); (2) that it had power to levy a loan rate; (3) that there was a limitation on profit-making to ensure that the council performed a public service for the county district; and (4) that in reticulating electricity to the district it was performing a public service.

3.   The Commission's connection with the government of Tasmania is certainly closer than the connection of St George County Council with the Government of New South Wales. And the Commission's position in the structure of Government is certainly more important than that of the County Council. The Commission is the State authority responsible for generating and distributing electrical power in the State. It constructs and manages the relevant dams, generating plants and other works and makes the policy decisions and recommendations to the Minister in connection with its functions. But in *Launceston Corporation v Hydro-Electric Commission* (1959) 100 CLR 654, it was

decided that the Commission was an [156] independent statutory corporation and it was not a servant or agent of the Crown. Since then the Commission's Act has been amended, notably by the inclusion of ss 15A and 15B. Section 15A enables the Minister to notify the Commission of the policy objectives of the government with respect to any matter relating to generation, distribution, etc of electrical energy. Section 15B enables the Minister to give a direction to the Commission with respect to the performance of its functions, subject to certain limitations and qualifications. The Commission may object to the direction. If the Minister does not withdraw the direction or qualify it in a manner acceptable to the Commission, the matter is then submitted to the Governor for decision (s 5B(4) and (5)). The Commission is bound to comply with the direction, subject to any withdrawal or modification and subject to a decision of the Governor. However, it is specifically provided that the Minister's power to give a direction does not make the Commission a servant or agent of the Crown or confer on the Commission any status, privilege or immunity of the Crown (s 15B(9)). Accordingly it is not suggested that the decision in *Launceston Corporation* has been eroded by legislative developments.

4. The trading activities of the Commission therefore form a much less prominent feature of its overall activities than was the case with *St George County Council*. The Commission has an important policy-making role. It is the generator of electrical power for Tasmania for distribution to the public and for this purpose it engages on a large scale in the construction of dams and generating plants. In this respect its operations are largely conducted in the public interest.

5. However, *WA National Football League* demonstrates that these considerations do not exclude the Commission from the category of 'trading corporations'. The majority judgment in *State Superannuation Board* (1982) 150 CLR at 304 pointed out that the case decided that a trading corporation whose trading activities take place so that it may carry on some other primary or dominant undertaking (which is not trading) may nevertheless be a trading corporation.

6. The agreed facts show that the Commission sells electrical power in bulk and by retail on a very large scale. This activity in itself designates the Commission as a trading corporation.

7. The final question, one raised on behalf of the Commission, is whether it is possible to treat, for the purposes of s 51(xx), a corporation as a trading corporation in relation to its trading activities and as a non-trading corporation in relation to its non-[157]trading activities. My earlier conclusion that the legislative power is not confined to the trading activities of trading corporations is in one sense an answer to this submission. The other answer is that s 51(xx) designates as the subject of the power the corporate persona itself, that is the artificial person created by *incorporation*. There is no suggestion in the paragraph that it is looking to some hypothetical or notional *incorporation* which covers only the trading activities of a trading corporation.

I therefore conclude that the Commission is a trading corporation within the meaning of s 10 of the Commonwealth Act. And in my opinion the Commission is constructing the dam and associated works for the purposes of its trading activities. The dam will provide additional electrical energy for supply and sale by the Commission.

Mason J also rejected the claim made by Tasmania that s 10 involved an 'acquisition of property' within s 51(xxxi) of the Constitution. His reasoning was substantially the same as that of Brennan J on this issue.

Brennan J: [239] *The corporations power and ss 7 and 10 of the Act*

After noting that the HEC sold power, in bulk and by retail, to the value of more than $158m in 1981–82, Brennan J concluded that, on the basis of *R v Federal Court of Australia; Ex parte WA National Football League (Inc) (Adamson's case)* (1979) 143 CLR 190 **[10.3.12]** and *State Superannuation Board v Trade Practices Commission* (1982) 150 CLR 282 **[10.3.13]**, the HEC was a trading corporation. Brennan J continued:

[240] The constitutional issue thus arises: are the prohibitions contained in s 10 laws with respect to trading corporations? Laws with respect to trading corporations are laws with respect to artificial persons. To be such a law, the law must discriminate: that is to say, it must be a law which operates to confer a benefit or impose a burden upon those persons when its operation does not confer a like benefit or impose a like burden on others (*Fontana Films* (56 ALJR) at 385). Section 10 of the Act is discriminatory. It imposes a restriction upon the use of property by the several categories of corporations mentioned in paras (a), (b) and (c) of s 10(2), which include trading corporations formed within the limits of the Commonwealth, but it does not impose a like restriction on other persons. Section 10(2) and (3) direct their commands to trading corporations without any relevant qualification; s 10(4) directs its commands to trading corporations where the corporation does the relevant act in contravention of a command 'for the purposes of its trading activities'. Subsections (2) and (3) give rise to the question whether a law which merely prohibits trading corporations from doing an act that may be unconnected with its trade is a law with respect to trading corporations. That question has not hitherto been decided by this court. In *Strickland v Rocla Concrete Pipes Ltd* (1971) 124 CLR 468, Barwick CJ expressed the opinion that a law addressed specifically to trading [241] corporations is not, without more, sufficient to attract the corporations power (see at 489–90). Menzies J left that question open (124 CLR at 508). It was unnecessary to decide it in *Fontana Films*. If sub-s (4) of s 10 applies to the HEC's construction of the dam the question need not be decided now. For the reasons which I stated in *Fontana Films* (150 CLR at 218–9), I should not wish to decide a question wider than the circumstances of the case require. The acts prohibited by sub-s (4) are the acts referred to in sub-ss (2) and (3), and the qualification 'for the purposes of its trading activities' results in the affection of the trading activities of trading corporations. It is clearly a law with respect to trading corporations, but can its validity be sustained without deciding the validity of sub-ss (2) and (3)?

Brennan J held that subs (4) had an operation independent of subss (2) and (3) and that it was therefore unnecessary to decide the validity of subss (2) and (3).

Does sub-s (4) apply to the HEC's activities in constructing the dam? The agreed facts show that the HEC land has been vested in the HEC for the purpose of carrying out the Gordon below Franklin Scheme in order to produce electrical energy, the commodity in which the HEC trades. The dominant, if not exclusive, purpose of constructing the dam is to provide additional generating capacity for the HEC system, an element in the HEC's co-ordinated activity of generation, distribution and sale of electrical energy. The carrying out of the Gordon below Franklin Scheme is thus for the purpose of the HEC's trading activities. Upon the agreed facts, the construction activities of the HEC fall within s 10(4) ...

Brennan J rejected Tasmania's argument that the Commonwealth legislation was invalid because it effected an acquisition of property on other than just terms, contrary to s 51(xxxi) of the Constitution.

~~~

[10.3.27] Deane J declined to accept the Commission's argument that s 51(xx) should be confined to laws with respect to the trading activities of trading corporations:

The trading activities and the non-trading activities are likely to be conducted in the context of overall corporate strategy and financial planning and restraints. Their viability and financial stability are likely to be interdependent. Power and success on one side are likely to contribute to power and success on the other. Failure on one side is likely to involve failure of the whole. In my view, the legislative power conferred by s 51(xx) is not restricted to laws with respect to trading corporations in relation to their trading activities. It is a general power to make laws with respect to trading corporations (158 CLR at 270).

Deane J proceeded to hold that although s 10 did not effect an acquisition of property, the controls imposed by regulations made under the National Parks and Wildlife Conservation Act 1975 (Cth) did involve such an acquisition; and, as that acquisition was not 'on just terms', the regulations were invalid under s 51(xxxi) of the Constitution.

Murphy J delivered a separate judgment in which he held that ss 7 and 10 were within s 51(xx) for substantially the same reasons as Mason J.

Wilson J held that ss 7 and 10 were invalid. He said it was possible for a law to bear a dual character and that it did not matter that a law may properly be characterised as a law with respect to a subject outside Commonwealth power if it is nevertheless at the same time properly characterised as a law with respect to a subject within Commonwealth power: 158 CLR at 200. However, ss 7 and 10 were not laws concerned with regulating or controlling the Commission's trade in electricity, they were concerned with the protection of identified property from damage and destruction whether by a trading or foreign corporation or by anyone else: 158 CLR at 201. His Honour continued at 202:

> To be a law with respect to trading corporations the substance of the law must bear a sufficient relation to those characteristics of such corporations which distinguish them from corporations which cannot be so described: *Huddart Parker & Co Pty Ltd v Moorehead* (1909) 8 CLR 330, per Isaacs J at 397; *Actors and Announcers Equity Association of Australia v Fontana Films Pty Ltd* (1982) 150 CLR 169 at 182–3, per Gibbs CJ. In other words, the law must be about trading corporations.

> In the result, I am unable to ascribe to ss 7 and 10 the character necessary to their validity. In my opinion, the law is in truth what the long title of the Act describes it as being, namely, an Act relating to the protection and conservation of certain property, and for related purposes. Sections 7 and 10 are not laws with respect to trading corporations.

Dawson J held that s 10 was not within s 51(xx) for substantially the same reasons as Wilson J. His said it was unnecessary to decide whether the HEC was a trading corporation but, had it been necessary, he would have agreed with Gibbs CJ on this issue.

In the result, the court declared that s 7 and s 10(1) and (4) were valid. It was, the court declared, 'unnecessary to determine the validity of sub-ss (2) and (3) of s 10'. The court also declared that the facts as placed before the court established that the HEC was a trading corporation.

Notes

[10.3.28]   The issues before the court in *Commonwealth v Tasmania* (the *Tasmanian Dam* case) (1983) 158 CLR 1 **[10.3.26C]** extended beyond the validity of ss 7 and 10 of the Act and the scope of s 51(xx) of the Constitution:

- The case raised the validity of ss 6 and 9 of the Act, which prohibited a wide range of activities on identified property whose protection was a matter of international obligation for Australia. A majority of the court held that the UNESCO Convention for the Protection of the World Cultural and Natural Heritage obliged the Commonwealth to protect specific areas of south-west Tasmania (the identified property); that this was sufficient to give the Commonwealth Parliament power to legislate, to implement the Convention, under s 51(xxix), the external affairs power; and that a critical part of s 9 (subs (1)(h)) could be described as implementing the Convention. However, a different majority of the court held other parts of s 9 to be invalid. This aspect of the case was explored in **[3.3.21C]**.

■ A further issue was the validity of regulations made under s 69 of the National Parks and Wildlife Conservation Act 1975 (Cth). A narrow majority held that s 69 and the regulations were also supported by s 51(xxix), the external affairs power. However, one of the majority justices, Deane J, found that the regulations so limited the use of the land to which they applied that they amounted to an 'acquisition of property' within s 51(xxxi), and, as the regulations did not provide 'just terms', they infringed that provision of the Constitution. Accordingly, the regulations were held, by a different narrow majority, to be invalid.

■ Tasmania also challenged the validity of ss 8 and 11 of the World Heritage Properties Conservation Act 1983 (Cth), which prohibited a wide range of activities on identified property of particular significance to people of the Aboriginal race. A narrow majority held that these sections were supported by s 51(xxvi), the race power, which would support special legislation, not only conferring rights or protection or imposing duties on the people of any race, but also protecting the cultural heritage of the Aboriginal people. (The history and scope of s 51(xxvi) are discussed in Hanks (1984) pp 20–37.) However, Deane J found in s 11 the same defect as he had detected in the regulations under the National Parks and Wildlife Conservation Act 1975; namely, that they acquired property on other than just terms. Accordingly, a different narrow majority held s 11 to be invalid.

[10.3.29] Despite the complexity of the issues in *Commonwealth v Tasmania* (the *Tasmanian Dam* case) (1983) 158 CLR 1 **[10.3.26C]** and the intricate nature of the court's decision on those issues, we should not underestimate the decision's significance in the development of Australian constitutional law. Perhaps, most importantly, it asserted a broad reading of the external affairs power, s 51(xxix) unequivocally resolving the doubts which *Koowarta v Bjelke-Petersen* (1982) 153 CLR 168 **[3.3.15C]** had raised, and laying the foundations for Commonwealth entry into areas of regulation previously regarded as outside its competence, such as sexual discrimination, narcotic drug trafficking and industrial safety. It also gave a broad reading to the race power (s 51(xxvi)) so providing the Commonwealth with the basis on which it could, given the political will, build comprehensive Aboriginal land rights legislation.

But what does the decision tell us about the potential of the corporations power (s 51(xx))? Do the judgments on the validity of ss 7 and 10 of the Act take us any further than *Actors & Announcers Equity v Fontana Films Pty Ltd* (1982) 150 CLR 169 **[10.3.18C]** had in resolving the uncertainty over the type of legislation which s 51(xx) will support? As in *Actors & Announcers Equity v Fontana Films Pty Ltd*, *Commonwealth v Tasmania* (the *Tasmanian Dam* case) presented two opposing views on the scope of the corporations power: the narrow view supported by Gibbs CJ, Wilson and Dawson JJ, the broad view supported by Mason, Murphy and Deane JJ.

And, as in *Actors & Announcers Equity v Fontana Films Pty Ltd*, Brennan J expressly declined to commit himself to one view or the other; that is, he managed to decide what he saw as the issue before the court (could the Commonwealth legislate so as to stop the HEC building a dam on the Gordon River below the

Franklin River?) without going beyond the narrower view of s 51(xx). The complexities of his reasoning in *Actors & Announcers Equity v Fontana Films Pty Ltd* might have suggested that he would, if pressed, take the broader view of s 51(xx); or that his application of the narrower view left very little distance between him and, say, Mason J when it came to dealing with a concrete case: see **[10.3.21]**. But there is little, if any, room for such suggestions in his judgment in *Commonwealth v Tasmania* (the *Tasmanian Dam* case) (1983) 158 CLR 1 **[10.3.26C]**. The scope of s 51(xx) must, it seems, be left an open question for the time being. The resolution of that question will, of course, have critical implications for the distribution of governmental power within the Australian federal system.

[10.3.30]   Of equal, though more subtle, significance will be the resolution of a conflict of judicial method, or approach, revealed in *Commonwealth v Tasmania* (the *Tasmanian Dam* case) (1983) 158 CLR 1 **[10.3.26C]**. The conflict is, to oversimplify perhaps, between those justices who maintain that a piece of legislation will have a dominant, 'true character' or 'real substance' (from which its validity may be judged) and those justices who maintain that a piece of legislation may be characterised in several alternative ways (from any of which its validity may be judged).

The state of Tasmania had argued that the 'real substance' of ss 8 and 10 of the World Heritage Properties Conservation Act 1983 (Cth) was that of a law with respect to the protection of property, rather than that of a law with respect to trading corporations. This argument was based on the approaches of, for example, Latham CJ and Barwick CJ to issues of characterisation: see *Melbourne Corporation v Commonwealth* (the *State Banking* case) (1974) 74 CLR 31 **[8.2.45C]** and *Victoria v Commonwealth* (the *Payroll Tax* case) (1971) 122 CLR 353 **[8.2.50C]**. It was unequivocally rejected by Mason, Murphy and Deane JJ: 158 CLR at 151–2, 179–80 and 270–1. On the other hand, Gibbs CJ, Wilson and Dawson JJ adopted the approach argued by Tasmania: 158 CLR at 119, 201, 316–17; although they did not commit themselves to the extreme position taken up, for example, by Barwick CJ in the *Payroll Tax* case (1971) 122 CLR 353 **[8.2.45C]**; indeed, Wilson J conceded that a law could 'bear a dual character': 158 CLR at 200.

It is important to understand that this difference in approach to the characterisation of laws is not merely one of style, nor was it a coincidence that the justices who rejected the 'paramount' or 'true character' approach to characterisation upheld the validity of ss 7 and 10. Implicit in the approach adopted by Gibbs CJ, Wilson and Dawson JJ is a perception of the permissible range of Commonwealth laws narrower than that upon which the approaches of Mason, Murphy and Deane JJ were constructed. (The relative liberality of the multiple characterisation approach is brought out clearly in the judgment of Stephen J in *Actors & Announcers Equity v Fontana Films Pty Ltd* (1982) 150 CLR 169 at 190–5 **[10.3.18C]**.)

Where does Brennan J stand on this question? His judgment in *Tasmanian Dam* (1983) 158 CLR 1 **[10.3.26C]** is cryptic; but, is rejection of the approach argued for by Tasmania implicit in his decision that s 10(4) was valid?

[10.3.31]   Amidst the ambiguities and unresolved questions in *Commonwealth v Tasmania* (the *Tasmanian Dam* case) (1983) 158 CLR 1 **[10.3.26C]**, one unequivocal proposition stands out: the Hydro-Electric Commission was a trading corporation because trading was 'a substantial part of its overall activities, if not the predominant part' (158 CLR at 240 per Brennan J); even though it had 'wide semi-governmental powers and functions', and might 'be described as a "public utility" corporation, nevertheless its substantial sales of electricity made it a trading corporation for the purposes of s 51(xx)': 158 CLR at 293 per Deane J (see also: 158 CLR at 156 per Mason J; 158 CLR at 179 per Murphy J).

So a clear majority of the court has unequivocally endorsed the view taken by Mason, Murphy and Deane JJ in *State Superannuation Board v Trade Practices Commission* (1982) 150 CLR 282 **[10.3.13]**, that a trading corporation was to be identified primarily by reference to its activities; not its predominant or characteristic activities but any of its significant or substantial activities.

[10.3.32] The differences in judicial approach to the range of conduct that can be regulated under s 51(xx) remain unresolved, as the reasoning of the members of the court in *Re Dingjan; Ex parte Wagner* (1995) 183 CLR 323 demonstrates. Sections 127A and 127B of the Industrial Relations Act 1988 (Cth) authorised the Australian Industrial Relations Commission to review and set aside or vary a contract for services where the Commission was satisfied that the contract was unfair, unjust or against the public interest. Section 127C(1) provided that ss 127A and 127B applied only in relation to certain contracts:

- a contract to which a constitutional corporation was a party;
- a contract relating to the business of a constitutional corporation; and
- a contract entered into by a constitutional corporation for the purpose of its business.

The Commission varied contracts made between Tasmanian Pulp and Forest Holdings Ltd and a number of individuals, who had agreed to harvest and transport timber from areas leased by the company. The individuals then applied to the High Court for orders of prohibition to restrain the enforcement of the Commission's orders and certiorari to quash those orders, on the ground that ss 127A and 127B were invalid. The majority of the High Court (Brennan, Dawson, Toohey and McHugh JJ; Mason CJ, Deane and Gaudron JJ dissenting) held that the provisions were invalid because they were not supported by s 51(xx). Several different approaches to the scope of s 51(xx) and to the characterisation of legislation emerged.

Brennan J said that s 51(xx) is expressed as a power with respect to persons. To attract the support of s 51(xx), it is not enough that the law applies to constitutional corporations and to other persons indifferently (at 336):

> To attract that support, the law must discriminate between constitutional corporations and other persons, either by reference to the persons on whom it confers rights or privileges or imposes duties or liabilities or by reference to the persons whom it affects by its operation.

A law conferring power to vary or set aside an unfair or harsh contract (or contrary to the public interest) between a constitutional corporation and an independent contractor for work to be done for the purposes of the corporation's business would be a law supported by s 51(xx). A contract of that kind would be of a kind amenable to control by a law enacted under s 51(xx) because such a law would limit the corporation's freedom to contract and qualify its contractual rights to have the work done for the purposes of its business. But the provision at issue might apply to contracts (such as one between the Wagners and Dingjans) that had no direct effect on constitutional corporations (such as Tasmanian Pulp) or on their businesses, and consequently the provision was invalid. The connection between law and power was fortuitous and adventitious, and therefore insufficient. As applied by s 127C(1)(b), the provisions were too wide; they did not affect constitutional corporations in a discriminatory manner and were therefore invalid: 183 CLR at 339. This approach was not taken by any other member of the majority.

Dawson J, the second member of the majority, said the phrase 'trading or financial corporation' should be understood as a composite expression embracing both the corporate nature of the entity as well as its trading or financial character. Dawson J repeated the narrow view of the scope of s 51(xx) which his Honour, Gibbs CJ and Wilson J had adopted in *Commonwealth v Tasmania* (the *Tasmanian Dam* case) (1983) 158 CLR 1 **[10.3.26C]**. Dawson J said that a law directed at trading or financial corporations or foreign corporations either exclusively or along with others was not necessarily a law upon the subject matter of those corporations: 183 CLR at 345. It was necessary, for a law to be a valid law with respect to a trading or financial corporation, that the fact that the corporations affected by the law were trading or financial corporations 'should be significant in the way in which the law relates to it': 183 CLR at 346.

Dawson J adopted Barwick CJ's observation in *Strickland v Rocla Concrete Pipes*, that it is not the case that any law which in the range of its command or prohibition includes foreign corporations or trading or financial corporations formed within the limits of the Commonwealth is necessarily a law with respect to the subject matter of s 51(xx). For Dawson J, the reference to contracts involving s 51(xx) corporations seemed to be adopted by the Commonwealth merely as a means of introducing those corporations 'as a peg upon which to hang legislation, not upon the subject of constitutional corporations, but upon an entirely different subject'. On this basis, the Commonwealth provisions at issue were invalid because they regulated contracts, including contracts that may not be connected to s 51(xx) corporations in any way relevant to their character. Neither the nature nor the existence of the corporation was significant as an element in the conduct which the Industrial Relations Act, as applied by s 127C(1)(b), sought to regulate; and the reference to 'constitutional corporations' in that provision was used 'merely ... as a peg upon which to hang legislation, not upon the subject of constitutional corporations, but upon an entirely different subject': 183 CLR at 347.

Toohey J, the third member of the majority, held that s 51(xx) is a plenary power, to be 'construed with all the generality which the words used admit'. The test of characterisation was simply whether there is a sufficient connection between the law and the subject matter to be able to say that the law is one with respect to that subject matter. The connection must be substantial, not merely tenuous. The law must operate on the rights, duties, powers or privileges of corporations in such a way as to evidence a sufficient connection between the law and the corporations. Toohey J agreed with Dawson J that it would not be enough to identify corporations as a reference point so as to affect the activities of others, but regarded Dawson J's approach to characterisation as too narrow. On the facts of the case before the court, Toohey J concluded that there might be no connection other than that the contract sought to be reviewed relates in some unidentified way to the business of such a corporation. This would be a connection that was no more than remote and tenuous: 183 CLR at 354. The contract might have only the most indirect effect on the corporation or none at all. For these reasons, the relevant provisions were invalid.

McHugh J, the final member of the majority, like Toohey J, said that s 51(xx) is plenary, and should be construed with all the generality that its words will admit. Although laws that regulate the activities, functions, relationships or business of corporations are clearly laws with respect to corporations, the power conferred by s 51(xx) extends to any subject that affects the corporation. Disagreeing with Dawson J, McHugh J pointed out that, as long as the law in question can be characterised as a law with respect to trading, financial or foreign corporations, the Parliament of the Commonwealth may regulate many subject matters that are otherwise outside the scope of Commonwealth legislative power. That does not mean, however, that any law that refers to s 51(xx) corporations will be valid. For a law to be characterised as a law with respect to a head of power in s 51, the law must do more than simply refer to the subject matter of the power. McHugh J provided a lucid description of the applicable principles:

> In determining whether a law is 'with respect to' a head of power in s 51 of the Constitution, two steps must be taken. First, the character of the law must be determined. That is done by reference to the rights, powers, liabilities, duties and privileges which it creates. Secondly, a judgment must be made as to whether the law as so characterised so operates that it can be said to be connected to a head of power conferred by s 51. In determining whether the connection exists, the practical, as well as the legal, operation of the law must be examined. If a connection exists between the law and a s 51 head of power, the law will be 'with respect to' that head of power unless the connection is, in the words of Dixon J, 'so insubstantial, tenuous or distant' that it cannot sensibly be described as a law 'with respect to' the head of power.

> Where a law purports to be 'with respect to' a s 51(xx) corporation, it is difficult to see how it can have any connection with such a corporation unless, in its legal or practical operation, it has significance for the corporation. That means that it must have some significance for the activities, functions, relationships or business of the corporation. If a law regulates the activities, functions, relationships or business of a s 51(xx) corporation, no more is needed to bring the law within s 51(xx). That is because the law, by regulating the activities, etc, is regulating the conduct of the corporation or those who deal with it. Further, if, by reference to the activities or functions of s 51(xx) corporations, a law regulates the conduct of those who control, work for, or hold shares or office in those corporations, it is unlikely that any further fact will be needed to bring the law within the reach of s 51(xx).

> It is not enough, however, to attract the operation of s 51(xx) that the law merely refers to or operates upon the existence of a corporate function or relationship or a category of corporate behaviour. The activities, functions, relationships and business of s 51(xx) corporations are not the constitutional switches that throw open the stream of power conferred by s 51(xx). In *Actors and Announcers Equity Association v Fontana Films Pty Ltd*, Brennan J said: 'It is of the nature of the power that it is a power to make laws with respect to corporate persons, not with respect to functions, activities or relationships.'

> So, where a law seeks to regulate the conduct of persons other than s 51(xx) corporations or the employees, officers or shareholders of those corporations, the law will generally not be authorised by s 51(xx) unless it does more than operate by reference to the activities, functions, relationships or business of such corporations. A law operating on the conduct of outsiders will not be within the power conferred by s 51(xx) unless that conduct has significance for trading, financial or foreign corporations. In most cases, that will mean that the conduct must have some beneficial or detrimental effect on trading, financial or foreign corporations or their officers, employees or shareholders. Thus, laws that regulate conduct that promotes or protects the functions, activities, relationships or business of such corporations or laws that regulate conduct

conferring benefits on those corporations are laws with respect to s 51(xx) corporations even though they are also laws with respect to that conduct.

But a law that does no more than make some activity of a s 51(xx) corporation the condition for regulating the conduct of an outsider will ordinarily not be a law with respect to those corporations. If a law regulates conduct that has no significance for s 51(xx) corporations, it is not a law with respect to those corporations even if that conduct is connected to or even based on what a corporation does. Thus, a law that sought to regulate the remuneration of employment contracts made by financial analysts would not be a law with respect to s 51(xx) corporations even if the work of the analysts was entirely based upon the business activities of corporations. Laws that seek to regulate such contracts are laws with respect to employment contracts, but they are not laws with respect to corporations (183 CLR at 368–70).

The minority judgments were delivered by Mason CJ, Deane and Gaudron JJ. Gaudron J (with whom Mason CJ and Deane J agreed) said that, when s 51(xx) was approached in that way, it was clear that, 'at the very least, a law which is expressed to operate on or by reference to the business functions, activities or relationships of constitutional corporations is a law with respect to those corporations': 183 CLR at 364. Gaudron J continued at 365:

> As their business activities signify whether or not corporations are trading or financial corporations and the main purpose of the power to legislate with respect to foreign corporations must be directed to their business activities in Australia, it follows that the power conferred by s 51(xx) extends, at the very least, to the business functions and activities of constitutional corporations and to their business relationships. And those functions, activities and relationships will, in the ordinary course, involve individuals, and not merely individuals through whom the corporation acts, as in *Fencott v Muller*, or the control of whose conduct is directly connected with the regulation or protection of the corporation, as in *Actors and Announcers Equity Association*.

It followed, according to Gaudron J, that s 51(xx) extended to the persons by or through whom trading, financial or foreign corporations carried out their functions and activities and with whom they entered into relationships. Sections 127A and 127B of the Industrial Relationships Act 1988 (Cth), as applied by s 127C(1)(b), answered that description.

[10.3.33] One difficulty posed by *Re Dingjan* **[10.3.32]** is that a majority of the court (including three justices who dissented in the result) adopted a broad view of the scope of s 51(xx), describing it as 'plenary' (Mason CJ, Deane, Toohey, Gaudron and McHugh JJ), but one of the members of the majority in the result, Dawson J, developed a test of characterisation that narrowed the plenary ambit of the power. The proposition that s 51(xx) is a plenary power with respect to the types of corporation listed in that provision is plainly correct. Where there is conflict about the extent of constitutional power, the High Court has indicated a preference for the wider interpretation of the language used. This approach to constitutional interpretation was endorsed by O'Connor J in *Jumbunna Coal Mine NL v Victorian Coal Miners' Association* (1908) 6 CLR 309 at 367–8:

> ... it must always be remembered that we are interpreting a Constitution broad and general in its terms, intended to apply to the varying conditions which the development of our community must involve.

> For that reason, where the question is whether the Constitution has used an expression in the wider or in the narrower sense, the Court should, in my opinion, always lead to the broader interpretation unless there is something in the context or in the rest

of the Constitution to indicate that the narrower interpretation will best carry out its object and purpose.

In addition, it is a well-established principle that the words of a power are to be construed with all the generality the words admit. The conclusion is irresistible when one considers the questionable results produced by a narrow approach, as Mason J pointed out in *Commonwealth v Tasmania* (the *Tasmanian Dam* case) (1983) 158 CLR 1 at 158–9 **[10.3.26C]**:

> It can scarcely have been intended that the scope of the power was to be limited by reference to the foreign aspects of foreign corporations and the financial aspects of financial corporations. And it would be irrational to conclude that the power is plenary in the case of those corporations, but limited in the case of trading corporations.

In *Amalgamated Society of Engineers v Adelaide Steamship Co Ltd* (1920) 28 CLR 129 **[8.2.31C]** at 154, Knox CJ, Isaacs, Rich and Starke JJ rejected 'the doctrine of "implied prohibition" against the exercise of a power once ascertained in accordance with ordinary rules of construction' (28 CLR at 150); and said that, 'where the affirmative terms of a stated power would justify an enactment, it rests upon those who rely on some limitation or restriction upon the power, to indicate it in the Constitution': 28 CLR at 154. It would follow that, once a corporation has been defined, by reference to its actual or intended activities (and noting that trading or financial activities need not form a predominant part of a corporation's activities), then s 51(xx) is a plenary power with respect to those corporations.

[10.3.34] But what about characterisation? Again, the judgments in *Re Dingjan* (1995) 183 CLR 323 **[10.3.32]** expose a diversity of approaches. The judgments forming the majority (in support of the court's order) were those of Brennan, Dawson, Toohey and McHugh JJ. Brennan J developed a discrimination test that was not taken up by any other member of the court, except in passing. Dawson J endorsed Barwick CJ's view in *Strickland v Rocla Concrete Pipes Ltd* (1971) 124 CLR 468 **[10.3.4C]** that not every law referring to a s 51(xx) corporation will involve a valid exercise of that power; but Dawson J then proposed that, 'for a law to be a valid law with respect to a trading or financial corporation, the fact that it is a trading or financial corporation should be significant in the way in which the law relates to it'.

The problem with Dawson J's approach, besides its circularity, is that it can narrow the plenary ambit of the power over the types of corporations listed in s 51(xx). If s 51(xx) enables the regulation of non-trading activities that are preparatory to the trading activities of a trading corporation (as in the *Tasmanian Dam* case (1983) 158 CLR 1 **[10.3.26C]**) then the test of significance propounded by Dawson J must have been superseded in that case. Since a numerical majority of the court has concluded that s 51(xx) is not limited to the foreign, trading or financial activities of foreign, trading or financial corporations, but extends to enable the regulation of any matter that is sufficiently connected to a s 51(xx) corporation, Toohey J was right to observe that Dawson J's test of characterisation is too narrow.

In addition, Dawson J's comment that the Commonwealth was merely using s 51(xx) 'as a peg upon which to hang legislation, not upon the subject of constitutional corporations, but upon an entirely different subject' may reflect a misconception of the way in which the Commonwealth's powers under s 51 can and have been used. It is now well established that the Commonwealth can use its powers so as to regulate, indirectly, activities and things that fall outside the strict subject matter of a power. Consider, for example, *Murphyores Inc Pty Ltd v*

Commonwealth (1976) 136 CLR 1 **[10.2.33C]** (where the s 51(i) power over trade and commerce with other countries was used to effect environmental policy of preventing sand-mining on Fraser Island by preventing export of the mineral sands extracted from the Island, thereby rendering mining economically non-viable); or *Fairfax v Federal Commissioner of Taxation* (1965) 114 CLR 1 **[9.2.22C]** (where the s 51(ii) power over taxation was used to encourage investment in government bonds by burdening other forms of investment).

The better view is that s 51(xx) is a plenary power over the types of corporations listed in s 51(xx), and the test of characterisation is simply whether the law in question is sufficiently connected to one of the listed corporations. This approach, adopted in *Re Dingjan* (1995) 183 CLR 323 **[10.3.32]** by Mason CJ, Deane, Toohey, Gaudron and McHugh JJ (though with varying degrees of emphasis on the two elements in the analysis) relieves the matter of much difficulty and is consistent with the orthodox principles of construction considered above.

[10.3.35C]   **New South Wales v Commonwealth**

(The *Incorporation* case)
(1990) 169 CLR 482

The Corporations Act 1989 (Cth) provided for the incorporation of companies by the Australian Securities Commission, an agency established by the Australian Securities Commission Act 1989 (Cth). Incorporation was available only where the subscribers to the proposed company had lodged an activities statement, stating that trading activities (defined to include financial activities) would be the whole or a substantial part of the company's activities; that the company would carry on as its sole or principal business the business of banking; or that persons other than the subscribers would take control of the company: s 153.

A company incorporated under the Corporations Act was required to lodge annual activities statements (s 156), and any company which ceased to be either a trading corporation or a banking corporation was to be wound up: s 158. Section 112 of the Corporations Act prohibited the formation, otherwise than under the Act, of a partnership or association of more than 20 persons formed for gain and capable of being incorporated under the Corporations Act. Section 113 prohibited the *incorporation*, under state or territory law, of a body that would, on its *incorporation*, be a trading corporation. Section 9 defined trading corporation to include a financial corporation.

The states of New South Wales, Western Australia and South Australia began proceedings in the High Court for declarations that the Corporations Act, the Australian Securities Commission Act and a third piece of legislation, the Close Corporations Act 1989 (Cth), were invalid. Mason CJ reserved two questions for the consideration of the Full Court. The two questions asked whether the provisions of the Corporations Act dealing with the *incorporation* of trading and financial corporations and prohibiting their *incorporation* under state or territory law were valid.

Mason CJ, Brennan, Dawson, Toohey, Gaudron and McHugh JJ: [497] The power conferred by s 51(xx) is not expressed as a power with respect to a function of government, a field of activity or a class of relationships but as a power with respect to persons, namely, corporations of the classes therein specified: *Actors and Announcers Equity Association v Fontana Films Pty Ltd* (1982) 150 CLR 169 at 181, 216 and *The Commonwealth v Tasmania* (the *Tasmanian Dam* case) (1983) 158 CLR 1 at 157, 202, 240, 269, 314. The Commonwealth contention is that the words 'formed within the limits of the Commonwealth' serve merely to distinguish local trading or financial corporations from foreign corporations. No doubt the words do serve that function but their plain meaning goes beyond the mere drawing of that distinction. The expressions 'trading or financial' and 'formed within the limits of the

Commonwealth' serve to restrict the classes of domestic corporation which can be the subject of Commonwealth power. To fall within one limb of the power, a corporation must satisfy two conditions: it must be formed within the limits of the Commonwealth and it must be a trading or financial corporation. To fall [498] within the other limb, a corporation must be a foreign corporation, that is, a corporation formed outside the limits of the Commonwealth. The distinction based on the place of formation is obvious, but the basis of the distinction is formation. The word 'formed' is a past participle used adjectivally, and the participial phrase 'formed within the limits of the Commonwealth' is used to describe corporations which have been or shall have been created in Australia. (Clearly enough, the phrase is used to describe corporations formed after as well as those formed before federation.) The subject of a valid law is restricted by that phrase to corporations which have undergone or shall have undergone the process of formation in the past, present or future. That is to say, the power is one with respect to 'formed corporations'. That being so, the words 'formed within the limits of the Commonwealth' exclude the process of *incorporation* itself. Such corporations are distinguished from corporations which have been or shall have been created outside the limits of Australia.

No doubt, as the Commonwealth submitted, the words 'with respect to' in s 51 of the Constitution are words of wide import and par (xx), being a grant of legislative power, 'should be construed with all the generality which the words used admit': *Reg v Public Vehicles Licensing Appeal Tribunal (Tas); Ex parte Australian National Airways Pty Ltd* (1964) 113 CLR 207 at 225. But the generality imported by the words 'with respect to' cannot expand a power over existing ('formed') corporations into a power to form corporations. The power conferred by s 51(xx) to make laws with respect to artificial legal persons is not a power to bring into existence the artificial legal persons upon which laws made under the power can operate.

Both precedent and history support this construction of the text of s 51(xx). In *Huddart, Parker & Co Pty Ltd v Moorehead* (1909) 8 CLR 330 the five members of the court were unanimously of the opinion that the subject matter of s 51(xx) is confined to corporations already in existence and does not extend to the creation of corporations. That, they said, is the plain meaning of the words 'formed within the limits of the Commonwealth'. Obviously the legislative power of the Commonwealth could not embrace the creation of foreign corporations and, it was pointed out, if a distinction was intended between the power to legislate with respect to foreign corporations and the power to legislate with respect to trading or financial corporations, express words were to be [499] expected. The words 'formed within the limits of the Commonwealth' were, it was observed, inappropriate for this purpose. Such express words were to be found in s 51(xiii) which confers power to make laws with respect to 'Banking ... also ... the *incorporation* of banks' and their absence in s 51(xx) indicated the limited scope of that paragraph. The Court resolved in unambiguous terms the meaning of the words in the paragraph, thereby removing any doubt on the matter which might have arisen from the earlier comments of Griffith CJ and O'Connor J in *Jumbunna Coal Mine NL v Victorian Coal Miners' Association* (1908) 6 CLR 309 at 334–5, 355.

In contesting the construction placed upon the words 'formed within the limits of the Commonwealth' in *Huddart Parker*, the Commonwealth submitted that the judgments in that case were permeated by the reserved powers doctrine under which the legislative powers of the Commonwealth were interpreted restrictively upon the footing that certain powers were reserved by the Constitution to the States. This approach, which involved the interpretation of Commonwealth legislative power by reference to preconceptions of the extent of the residue of legislative power retained by the States, was categorically rejected in the *Engineers'* Case: *Amalgamated Society of Engineers v Adelaide Steamship Co Ltd* (1920) 28 CLR 129.

Huddart Parker was concerned with the validity of ss 5 and 8 of the Australian Industries Preservation Act 1906 (Cth). Those sections prohibited certain restrictive or monopolistic practices on the part of foreign, trading or financial corporations. In concluding that the relevant provisions were beyond power, a majority (Griffith CJ, Barton and O'Connor JJ) placed reliance upon the doctrine of reserved powers. But the question of the power to legislate for the creation of corporations was determined by all the members of the Court by reference to purely textual considerations, quite apart from the now discarded doctrine. Indeed, it was the view of the remaining members of the Court, Isaacs and Higgins JJ, concerning the doctrine of reserved powers which was to prevail in the *Engineers'* Case. However, in *Huddart Parker* they reached the same conclusion upon the meaning of the words 'formed within the limits of the Commonwealth' as the other members of the Court. Isaacs J was alone in dissent concerning the validity of ss 5 and 8 of the Australian Industries Preservation Act, but upon the question of the power of the Commonwealth Parliament to provide for the creation of corporations, he was unequivocal. He said (1909) 8 CLR at 394:

> [500] The creation of corporations and their consequent investiture with powers and capacities was left entirely to the States. With these matters, as in the case of foreign corporations, the Commonwealth Parliament has nothing to do. It finds the artificial being in possession of its powers, just as it finds natural beings subject to its jurisdiction, and it has no more to do with the creation of the one class than with that of the other.

See also per Griffith CJ [at 348–9]; per Barton J [at 362]; per O'Connor J [at 371]; per Higgins J [at 412].

In *Strickland v Rocla Concrete Pipes Ltd* (1971) 124 CLR 468 this Court dealt with the validity of certain sections of the Trade Practices Act 1965 (Cth). In considering the scope of s 51(xx), it declined to follow *Huddart Parker*, recognizing that the reserved powers doctrine played no small part in the reasoning of the majority which led them to adopt a restrictive interpretation of that paragraph. But the rejection of the decision in *Huddart Parker* did not extend to the views expressed in that case concerning the power of the Commonwealth to provide for the creation of corporations. In the leading judgment (1971) 124 CLR at 488, Barwick CJ made the following observations about *Huddart Parker*:

> The Court in the course of its judgment, decided that the expression in par (xx) "formed within the Commonwealth" was apt to include only corporations formed according to the laws of the States. But in this it seems to me their Honours were clearly wrong. There are powers granted to the Commonwealth as well as those left in residue to the States to which the formation within the Commonwealth of trading corporations might be referable. There is s 122 granting legislative power with respect to the Territories. Section 51(i) for instance has been found a source of power to create a trading corporation. See *Australian National Airways Pty Ltd v The Commonwealth (No 2)* (1945) 71 CLR 115. Corporations formed under any power by the Commonwealth or under Commonwealth legislation are clearly corporations formed within the limits of the Commonwealth. Had their Honours of the majority in *Huddart, Parker & Co Pty Ltd v Moorehead* included these corporations in, rather than excluded them from, the ambit of par (xx) some of the difficulties which arise from their interpretation of par (xx) might have become apparent.

It should be said with respect that the remarks contained in that passage are not entirely accurate. Clear references were made in most of the judgments in *Huddart Parker* to the power of the [501] Commonwealth to create corporations under provisions other than s 51(xx): see per Griffith CJ (1909) 8 CLR at 349; per O'Connor J [at 371]; per Isaacs J [at 393]; per Higgins J [at 412]. But in that passage Barwick CJ casts no doubt upon the proposition that s 51(xx) does not confer power to legislate for the creation of corporations; indeed, he assumes that fact. No other member of the court in *Strickland v Rocla Concrete Pipes Ltd* questioned the proposition.

Judicial opinion after the *Engineers'* Case accepted that the Commonwealth had no power under s 51(xx) to make laws with respect to the *incorporation* of companies: *Australian National Airways Pty Ltd v Commonwealth* (1945) 71 CLR 29 at 57; *Bank of NSW v Commonwealth* (1948) 76 CLR 1 at 202, 255–6, 304; *Insurance Commissioner v Associated Dominions Assurance Society Pty Ltd* (1953) 89 CLR 78 at 86. But cf *Kathleen Investments (Aust) Ltd v Australian Atomic Energy Commission* (1977) 139 CLR 117 at 159. In *Bank of NSW v Commonwealth* (1948) 76 CLR at 202, Latham CJ said of s 51(xx):

> The one thing that is clear about it is that the provision assumes the existence of corporations either under foreign law or under some law which is in force in the Commonwealth.

Moreover, the history of s 51(xx) confirms that the language of the paragraph was not directed towards the subject of *incorporation*. That the Convention Debates may be used to establish the subject to which the paragraph was directed is made clear by *Cole v Whitfield* (1988) 165 CLR 360 at 385; see also *Port MacDonnell Professional Fishermen's Association Inc v South Australia* (1989) 168 CLR 340 at 375–7. And the draft bills prepared by the Conventions of 1891, 1897 and 1898 have long been considered a legitimate aid in the interpretation of the provisions of the Constitution: see *Tasmania v The Commonwealth and Victoria* (1904) 1 CLR 329 at 333, 350.

~~~

[10.3.36] The justices noted that the 1891 draft of the Constitution contained a power to legislate with respect to '[t]he status in the commonwealth of foreign corporations, and of corporations formed in any state or part of the commonwealth', which gave no power to make laws with respect to the *incorporation* of companies: 169 CLR at 502. The 1897 draft of the Constitution referred to '[f]oreign corporations, and trading corporations formed in any State or part of the Commonwealth', but there was no reason to suppose that, by deleting the words 'the status in the commonwealth of' and inserting the word 'trading', those who drafted the provision intended to alter the meaning of the words 'formed in': 169 CLR at 502. They noted that Quick and Garran, in their *Annotated Constitution of the Australian Commonwealth* (1901), said at p 607 that s 51(xx) apparently referred 'to companies created under State laws [which] once launched, will come within the control of Federal legislation': 169 CLR at 502–3.

Deane J dissented. He said that to deny the Commonwealth power over the formation of corporations, because s 51(xx) used the word 'formed', could be justified only if the Commonwealth's power over lighthouses, conferred by s 51(vii), did not extend to laws governing the erection of lighthouses since, until it was erected, the lighthouse did not exist as such: 169 CLR at 505–6. Rather, the word 'formed' was 'part of an adjectival phrase which is without temporal significance' and applied equally to the future as to the past: 169 CLR at 506. He said that the majority judgment in the present case had 'disinterred and selectively dissected for the occasion' *Huddart Parker & Co Pty Ltd v Moorehead* (1909) 8 CLR 330. The judgments of the majority in that case had been permeated by the doctrine of reserved powers, exploded in the *Engineers* case (1920) 28 CLR 129 at 509:

> [W]hat was said about incorporation in the majority judgments in *Huddart Parker* cannot properly be divorced from the reasoning which permeated them. The attempt to restore partial validity to those judgments must be rejected.

Turning to the judgment of Isaacs J in *Huddart Parker*, Deane J said that Isaacs J's statement that, when the Constitution intended to authorise *incorporation* it did so explicitly, was 'simply wrong', because many of the paragraphs of s 51 included power to create corporations without expressly mentioning that power; and it reflected the fallacious view that the powers in s 51 should be read down so as to avoid overlap or inconsistency between them. Deane J expressed his conclusions in the following terms at 169 CLR 512–13:

> It follows from what has been said above that I am of the view that the legislative power which the second limb of par (xx) confers upon the Parliament with respect to local trading or financial corporations extends to authorize the making of laws governing the formation or incorporation of such corporations. That is the effect of the words of the Constitution when they are construed in accordance with the principles applicable to the construction of a plenary grant of legislative power. The argument to the contrary propounds an unacceptably narrow and technical construction of those

words and attracts the criticism expressed by Dixon J in the *Australian National Airways* case (1945) 71 CLR at 81:

> It plainly ignores the fact that it is a Constitution we are interpreting, an instrument of government meant to endure and conferring powers expressed in general propositions wide enough to be capable of flexible application to changing circumstances. It confuses the unexpressed assumptions upon which the framers of the instrument supposedly proceeded with the expressed meaning of the power ... It is only by importing a limitation into the descriptive words of the power that such a law can be excluded.

Notes

[10.3.37] Following the decision in *New South Wales v Commonwealth* (the *Incorporation* case) (1990) 169 CLR 482 **[10.3.35C]**, the Commonwealth, the states and the territories negotiated the 'Alice Springs Agreement'. The Commonwealth undertook to enact a Corporations Act for the Australian Capital Territory (exercising its power under s 122 of the Constitution); each state and the Northern Territory undertook, in return for a share of the revenues generated by corporate regulation, to enact uniform legislation adopting the substantial provisions of the Australian Capital Territory Corporations Act as the Corporations Law of that state or territory. The adopting legislation is ambulatory: for example, s 7 of the Corporations (Victoria) Act 1990 (Vic) declares that the Corporations Law as set out in s 82 of the Corporations Act (Cth) as in force for the time being applies as a law of Victoria and may be referred to as the Corporations Law of Victoria. (The adopting legislation of the other states and the Northern Territory is in substantially the same terms.)

[10.3.38] The decision in *New South Wales v Commonwealth* (the *Incorporation* case) (1990) 169 CLR 482 **[10.3.35C]** did not invalidate those parts of the Corporations Act 1989 (Cth) which imposed national controls over the internal affairs and the winding-up of trading and financial corporations. Nor did the decision declare that those other aspects of the legislation were valid. However, Zines has argued that the denial to the Commonwealth of power over *incorporation* presents logical and policy arguments against Commonwealth control over the internal organisation of corporations. There would be 'an absurd division of legislative power' if the Commonwealth could not regulate formation but could regulate day-to-day internal affairs and dissolution: Zines (1997) p 106.

Nor did the decision in *New South Wales v Commonwealth* (the *Incorporation* case) (1990) 169 CLR 482 **[10.3.35C]** cast any doubt on the consistently expansive approach developed by the High Court to the scope of s 51(xx) in *Actors & Announcers Equity v Fontana Films Pty Ltd* (1982) 150 CLR 169 **[10.3.18C]** at 190–5 and *Commonwealth v Tasmania* (the *Tasmanian Dam* case) (1983) 158 CLR 1 **[10.3.26C]**. The capacity of the Commonwealth to regulate the activities of trading, financial and foreign corporations as those activities affect others remains to be fully worked out, but should not be affected by the apparent narrowing of s 51(xx) in *New South Wales v Commonwealth* (the *Incorporation* case).

Indeed, the decision may be seen as having left open the possibility of a national regulation of company law (including incorporation). It would appear consistent with *New South Wales v Commonwealth* (the *Incorporation* case) for the Commonwealth to legislate so as to restrict the activities of 'formed' trading and financial corporations unless their formation under state or territory law had complied with nationally-prescribed standards. That is, the Commonwealth might leave the formalities of incorporation to the states and territories while exerting considerable pressure to ensure that those formalities were uniform.

4   Freedom of interstate trade

Introduction

[10.4.1E]   **Commonwealth Constitution**

92 On the imposition of uniform duties of customs, trade, commerce, and intercourse among the States, whether by means of internal carriage or ocean navigation, shall be absolutely free.

But notwithstanding anything in this Constitution, goods imported before the imposition of uniform duties of customs into any State, shall, on thence passing into another State within two years after the imposition of such duties, be liable to any duty chargeable on the importation of such goods into the Commonwealth, less any duty paid in respect of the goods on their importation.

~~~

Notes

[10.4.2]   For some 87 years, s 92 posed a serious obstacle to any government which undertook to regulate commercial activity in Australia. Until the High Court's reassessment in *Cole v Whitfield* (1988) 165 CLR 360 **[10.4.27C]**, the conventional approach to that section could threaten a wide range of government programs, whether or not they were directed at regulating commerce, if those programs impinged in some way upon the freedom perceived to be guaranteed by s 92. We had seen, for example, the Privy Council declare invalid Commonwealth programmes for the collective market of dried fruit and for the nationalisation of the banking industry: *James v Commonwealth* (1936) 55 CLR 1 and *Commonwealth v Bank of New South Wales* (1948) 79 CLR 497 **[10.4.10C]**. We had also seen the High Court strike down state requirements for local pasteurisation of milk, a state registration fee on motor vehicles used for interstate transport, and a state registration system for travel agents: *North Eastern Dairy Co Ltd v Dairy Industry Authority (NSW)* (1975) 134 CLR 559 **[10.4.17]**; *Finemores Transport Pty Ltd v New South Wales* (1978) 139 CLR 338; and *Boyd v Carah Coaches Pty Ltd* (1979) 145 CLR 78.

On the other hand, the High Court had refused to invoke the section against Commonwealth controls on the import of aircraft (essential for interstate air services) and state restrictions on the manufacture of margarine intended for interstate trade: *R v Anderson; Ex parte Ipec-Air Pty Ltd* (1965) 113 CLR 117; *Grannall v Marrickville Margarine Pty Ltd* (1955) 93 CLR 55 **[10.4.15]**. The impact of the section, as applied by the High Court, was not to frustrate all government initiatives. Rather than function as an obstacle to government regulation and control of commercial activity, the section assumed the appearance of a maze, through which governments were obliged to find a way if their regulatory attempts were to survive.

[10.4.3] That maze had been built up over some 80 years of litigation, involving 140 decisions of the High Court and Privy Council. Some decisions had closed passageways, other decisions had shown openings, while yet other decisions had opened what was earlier closed, or blocked off their predecessors' openings. Until the decision in *Cole v Whitfield* (1988) 165 CLR 360 **[10.4.27C]**, the conventional view, that s 92 created a zone of freedom for traders, was confronted by political pressure for increased government intervention. These pressures, and the dilemma which they created in the context of s 92, were described by Gibbs and Wilson JJ in *Uebergang v Australian Wheat Board* (1980) 145 CLR 226 at 300:

> Absolute freedom of interstate trade commerce and intercourse requires that the citizens of this Commonwealth shall within the framework of a civilised society be free to engage in these things. The difficulty is that the trend of political theory and practice is to develop and strengthen that framework more and more and often at the cost of individual liberty; but however conservative or reactionary it may seem to some, this Court cannot write s 92 out of the Constitution. It must therefore do its best to preserve a balance between competing interests, a balance which favours freedom of the individual citizen in the absence of compelling considerations to the contrary.

[10.4.4] The reading of s 92 as endorsing 'freedom of the individual citizen' dated, as authority, only from 1949. Until the landmark decision in *Commonwealth v Bank of New South Wales* (1949) 79 CLR 49 **[10.4.10C]**, there were quite different, narrower (though hardly uniform) views as to what 'freedom' was guaranteed by the section. This reading of s 92 was unequivocally abandoned in *Cole v Whitfield* (1988) 165 CLR 360 **[10.4.27C]**, where the court declared that s 92 did not immunise interstate traders from government controls but demanded an 'equality of treatment' as between local and interstate trade. Although that decision cleared away much of the confusion generated by the earlier decisions and promised clear guidance through the maze, the more recent decision in *Bath v Alston Holdings Pty Ltd* (1988) 165 CLR 411 **[10.4.34C]** suggests that *Cole v Whitfield* defines the terms for a new inquiry rather than definitively answering an old problem.

Free trade or *laissez-faire*?

[10.4.5] That there should have been differences of and fluctuations in judicial approach to s 92 should not surprise us. The language of the section is not particularly illuminating, expressed as it is in the form of an incomplete proposition. It declares that interstate trade, commerce and intercourse are to be absolutely free but fails to identify what is the burden or restriction from which they are to be free.

The context of the section indicates that it was intended to protect interstate trade etc from taxes and other fiscal charges which placed discriminatory burdens on interstate trading and movement. It appears in Ch IV of the Constitution ('Finance and Trade') in the company of provisions establishing uniform duties of customs, depriving the states of the capacity to levy customs and excise duties and to pay bounties on the production of goods, and providing for payment of 'surplus revenue' and 'financial assistance' from the Commonwealth to the states. The presence of s 90 (prohibiting the states from levying customs and excise duties and paying bounties) might work against that limited, 'fiscal burden', reading of s 92. Why should two provisions in the Constitution be read as producing the same results?

While this is hardly a convincing refutation of the 'fiscal burden' approach to s 92 (see Sawer (1967) pp 174–5; Coper (1983) pp 297–8), there are historical reasons to suppose that s 92 was intended to confer a broader freedom, namely freedom from laws which absolutely prohibited or discriminated against the movement of goods and persons across state borders. These could be discriminatory taxes (in effect, customs duties) or more subtle forms of protectionism: preferential freight charges on the state-owned railways; quarantine requirements for out-of-state goods; or import licensing schemes. It was this view of s 92, as proscribing government controls or burdens which discriminate against interstate trade and commerce, which the High Court ultimately endorsed in *Cole v Whitfield* (1988) 165 CLR 360 **[10.4.27C]**.

[10.4.6] There is no doubt that, in the final 30 years of the 19th century, the question of protection for local industries was a great political issue which divided opinion within each colony and between the colonies. By 1877, Victoria (followed closely by South Australia and Tasmania, and at some distance by Queensland) had established a high level of protection for its industries. New South Wales, on the other hand, was firmly committed to free trade.

The dispute over this issue and the pursuit, by most of the colonies, of a protectionist policy generated considerable friction between the colonies. Its elimination provided one of the greatest incentives for the federation movement (although it also raised difficult questions over such matters as the future tariff policy of a unified Australia and compensation for the lost revenues of the protectionist colonies). La Nauze, in his authoritative study, *The Making of the Australian Constitution*, declares that all the colonial delegates to the 1891 National Australasian Convention knew (from the colonial parliamentary debates which preceded the convention):

> ... that, difficult as it might be for their existing systems of free trade or protection, a constitution must somehow impose intercolonial free trade, even if transitional arrangements might be necessary (La Nauze (1972) p 21).

The predecessor to s 92, resolution (2) proposed to the 1891 Convention by Parkes, was intended to express a 'principal object of federation ... the establishment of intercolonial free trade': La Nauze (1972) p 37. It seems that the drafting of this resolution was influenced by Samuel Griffith, later to be appointed first Chief Justice of the High Court of Australia. It was not 'a little bit of layman's language', as George Reid observed at the 1898 Convention: Convention Debates, Melbourne (1898), vol 2, p 2367. However, it was undoubtedly poorly expressed, a point made by Isaac Isaacs (a delegate from Victoria and later an influential member of the High Court) to the 1897 Convention: the clause was 'very dangerous' because it went 'much further than is intended' and contained expressions which were 'extremely large and alarming': Convention Debates, Adelaide (1897), p 1141.

At one point it seemed that these criticisms would lead to a significant drafting change. Both Edmund Barton and Richard O'Connor told the 1897 Convention that they intended to move that the clause be changed to read: 'trade and intercourse throughout the Commonwealth is not to be restricted or interfered with, by any taxes, charges or imposts'. It seems that this change was suggested by Griffith, whom Barton and O'Connor were to join as the foundation justices of the High Court. However, for some unknown reason (La Nauze suggests exhaustion) the amendment was never formally proposed: La Nauze (1972) pp 148, 169, 226–7.

[10.4.7] The open-ended nature of s 92's language made it possible to appeal to another aspect of its historical context. Nineteenth-century economic liberalism, or *laissez-faire*, asserted the freedom of the individual. That freedom was, indeed, regarded by the United States Supreme Court as constitutionally enshrined in the Fifth and Fourteenth amendments of the United States Constitution, so that neither Congress nor any state legislature could, for example, limit working hours to 60 a week because that would restrict the employer's freedom to purchase labour (*Lochner v New York* 198 US 45 (1905)), nor could they protect union members from employer victimisation because that involved an invasion of the employer's 'rights of liberty and property': *Adair v United States* 208 US 161 (1908).

The combination of s 92's broad language and the prevailing *laissez-faire* philosophy was something of an open invitation to any judge, whose values were formed in the late nineteenth or early twentieth centuries, to see the section as demanding freedom for the individual to trade without government interference. The major objection to that reading (apart from the broad contextual and historical considerations discussed above) is that s 92 confers absolute freedom only on *interstate* trade: if the provision had been intended to protect traders and commercial activity from government control, to enshrine the *laissez-faire* philosophy, surely the freedom would not have been denied to what was then the major part of Australian trade, intrastate trade?

[10.4.8] The earliest decisions on s 92 seemed to favour the free trade **[10.4.5]** rather than a *laissez-faire* **[10.4.7]** view of s 92. Differences of approach were to emerge relatively quickly but, at first, the High Court regarded s 92 as preventing the discriminatory treatment of interstate trading activities. In *Fox v Robbins* (1909) 8 CLR 115, the High Court held that Western Australia could not discriminate against trade by fixing the fee for a liquor retailer's licence at £50 where liquor from out of the state was sold, and at £2 where locally produced liquor was sold.

[10.4.9] By the 1940s, some members of the High Court had begun to develop a theory of s 92 which stressed the individual rights of interstate traders to trade free of government controls. An attempt in 1945 by the Federal Labor Government to push the view that s 92 only protected interstate trade against discriminatory controls which impeded the overall flow of interstate trade produced a strong statement of judicial commitment to the individual right view of s 92 in *Australian National Airways Pty Ltd v Commonwealth* (1945) 71 CLR 29.

The Australian National Airlines Act 1945 (Cth) established a statutory Commission to run an interstate airline (Australian, later Australian Airlines, now part of QANTAS). The Act was clearly designed to give Australian a monopoly over interstate air services for it provided that any licence issued to another airline to operate a service covered by Australian should be inoperative, and that further licences were only to be issued to other airlines where Australian could not provide a service: ss 46, 47.

The court first rejected the proposition that transport was not trade and commerce. On this point, the court (Latham CJ, Rich, Starke, Dixon and Williams JJ) was unanimous. Once the act of transport had been drawn within the protection offered by s 92, the court proceeded to reject the argument that the Commonwealth Act did not offend s 92 because it promoted and facilitated the flow of interstate transport.

Latham CJ said that the fact that the Act would secure adequate interstate air services did not save it from s 92. This was not a coordination or regulation of transport but '[t]he exclusion of competition with the Commission [which was] a violation of s 92': 71 CLR at 60, 61. Starke J said that s 92's object was 'to maintain freedom of interstate competition — the open and not the closed door', and that legislation which operated to prevent traders 'engaging their commodities in any trade, inter- or intrastate, is, in my opinion, necessarily obnoxious to s 92': 71 CLR at 78. Dixon J offered two objections to the Commonwealth legislation: the legislation denied 'freedom at the frontier', because it prohibited only those air services which crossed state boundaries; and the legislation denied the freedom 'from governmental restriction or obstruction', even if it might be said that the general business of interstate air transport would still carry on (in government hands): 71 CLR at 90–1. Williams J also referred to Isaacs J's approach; namely, to the idea that s 92 guaranteed 'a personal right attaching to the individual' which was directly negated by the Act under challenge: 71 CLR at 100; see also 71 CLR at 107.

The unequivocal assertion of the individual right theory of s 92 was to follow within a few years, prompted by the Federal Labor Government's attempt to nationalise another industry: the banking industry.

Laissez-faire endorsed: the individual right theory of s 92

[10.4.10C]   Commonwealth v Bank of New South Wales

(1949) 79 CLR 497

The Banking Act 1947 (Cth) declared (in s 3):

The several objects of this Act include —

(a) the expansion of the banking business of the Commonwealth Bank as a publicly-owned bank conducted in the interests of the people of Australia and not for private profit;

(b) the taking over by the Commonwealth Bank of the banking business in Australia of private banks and the acquisition on just terms of property used in that business;

(c) the prohibition of the carrying on of banking business in Australia by private banks.

Section 12 of the Act authorised the Commonwealth Bank to purchase all or any of the shares in a private bank. Section 13 gave the Commonwealth Treasurer power to acquire compulsorily Australian shares in an Australian private bank. Sections 17 and 18 provided for the transfer of the management of any Australian private bank to the Commonwealth Bank. Sections 22 and 24 provided for the transfer, by agreement or compulsorily, of the business of an Australian private bank or of the Australian business of a private bank. Sections 17 and 25 provided for the payment, by the Commonwealth Bank, of compensation for shares acquired under s 13 and property acquired under s 24. Sections 26 to 45 established a Court of Claims with exclusive jurisdiction to fix that compensation.

Part VII of the Act was headed 'Prohibition of the Carrying on of Banking Business by Private Banks' and contained the following section:

46(1) Notwithstanding anything contained in any other law, or in any Charter or other instrument, a private bank shall not, after the commencement of this Act, carry on banking business in Australia except as required by this section.

[Subsections (2) and (3) obliged each private bank to carry on its banking business until that business was taken over by another private bank or by the Commonwealth Bank.]

(4) The Treasurer may, by notice published in the Gazette and given in writing to a private bank, require that private bank to cease, upon a date specified in the notice, carrying on banking business in Australia.

[Subsections (5), (6) and (7) dealt with matters of procedure.]

(8) Upon and after the date specified in a notice under sub-section (4) of this section ... the private bank to which that notice was given shall not carry on banking business in Australia. Penalty: Ten thousand pounds for each day on which the contravention occurs.

The private banks and the states of Victoria, South Australia and Western Australia began proceedings in the High Court of Australia against the Commonwealth, the Commonwealth Treasurer and the Governor of the Commonwealth Bank. In these actions the plaintiffs sought declarations that the Banking Act 1947 (Cth) was invalid and injunctions to restrain the Treasurer and the Governor from using the powers granted under the Act. When the plaintiffs applied for interlocutory injunctions, the parties agreed that these applications should be treated as the trial of the actions and that the actions should be heard together.

A full bench of the High Court held that the Act did not provide 'just terms' (as demanded by s 51(xxxi) of the Constitution) for any property acquired under ss 13 and 24 of the Act and that these sections were, therefore, invalid. (This was largely because ss 26–45 of the Act, by giving the new Court of Claims exclusive jurisdiction to fix compensation, flouted s 75(iii) of the Constitution.) The court also held that s 46(4)–(8) contravened s 92 of the Constitution. This was the majority view of Rich, Starke, Dixon and Williams JJ; Latham CJ and McTiernan J dissented.

The defendants then appealed to the Privy Council against the High Court's decision on s 46(4)–(8). Other aspects of the court's decision were not challenged because the appellants assumed that s 74 of the Constitution excluded the Privy Council's jurisdiction to hear a full appeal, because those other aspects raised 'inter se questions'. In the result, the Privy Council held that it had no jurisdiction to hear the limited appeal because, although no inter se question was raised by the meaning of s 92 of the Constitution, the High Court's decision had included several matters which did raise inter se questions and there could only be a real appeal against the High Court's decision if those other matters were taken into consideration. In other words, to confine the appeal to the s 92 issue would leave the High Court's order largely undisturbed.

Despite its refusal to entertain the appeal, the Privy Council then proceeded to offer its opinion on the consistency of s 46 of the Banking Act with s 92. Two reasons for this course were offered: first, the High Court might grant a certificate under s 74 of the Constitution and the parties should not be put to the trouble of rearguing a case already fully argued; and, second, the Privy Council wished to correct some misunderstanding of two of its earlier decisions: *James v Cowan* and *James v Commonwealth*.

Lord Porter: [On behalf of Lords Porter, Simond, Norman, Morton of Henryton and McDermott] **[632]** There is upon the true construction of the section a single indivisible scheme by which the extinction of all private banking is to be brought about immediately or step by step at the will of the Treasurer. It is upon this footing that the validity of the section will be examined. As was observed by the learned Chief Justice in the course of his judgment: 'There is no doubt that the provisions mentioned are directed towards putting the plaintiff banks out of business or that, if put into operation, they will achieve that result'. From this way of stating the problem the appellants do not shrink. The question then is whether an Act which, leaving untouched the Commonwealth and State banks, authorises the total prohibition of all private banking, offends against s 92.

The Privy Council decided that the business of banking was 'included among those activities described as trade commerce and intercourse in s 92' (79 CLR at 62), and continued:

[633] The business of banking being an activity of which the freedom is protected by s 92 the next question is whether the Act offends that section, and their Lordships turn at once to the cases of *James v Cowan* [1932] AC 542; 47 CLR 386 and *James v Commonwealth* [1936] AC 578; 55 CLR 1. Of these two cases, the more important, for what it decided, is *James v Cowan*.

After summarising the decisions in *James v South Australia* (1927) 40 CLR 1, *James v Cowan* (which held that s 20 of the Dried Fruits Act (SA) was invalid) and *James v Commonwealth*, the Privy Council continued:

[634] It might well appear that these two decisions were a serious obstacle to the present appellants' case. Section 20 of the South Australian Act was invalid. It was general in its terms: it did not discriminate between interstate and intrastate trade in dried fruits. But because it authorised a determination at the will of [635] the Board the effect of which would be to interfere with the freedom of the grower to dispose of his products to a buyer in another State, it was invalid. And for the same reason the Commonwealth Act fell.

The necessary implications of these decisions are important. First may be mentioned an argument strenuously maintained on this appeal that s 92 of the Constitution does not guarantee the freedom of individuals. Yet James was an individual and James vindicated his freedom in hard-won fights. Clearly there is here a misconception. It is true, as has been said more than once in the High Court, that s 92 does not create any new juristic rights, but it does give the citizen of State or Commonwealth, as the case may be, the right to ignore, and if necessary, to call upon the judicial power to help him to resist, legislative or executive action which offends against the section. And this is just what James successfully did.

Linked with the contention last discussed was another which their Lordships do not find it easy to formulate. It was urged that, if the same volume of trade flowed from State to State before as after the interference with the individual trader, and it might be, the forcible acquisition of his goods, then the freedom of trade among the States remained unimpaired. In the first place this view seems to be in direct conflict with the decisions in the *James* case for there the section was infringed though it was not the passage of dried fruit in general, but the passage of the dried fruit of James from State to State that was impeded. Secondly the test of total volume is unreal and unpractical, for it is unpredictable whether by interference with the individual flow the total volume will be affected and it is incalculable what might have been the total volume but for the individual interference. Thirdly, whether or not it might be possible, if trade and commerce stood alone, to give some meaning to this concept of freedom, in s 92 'trade and commerce' are joined with 'intercourse' and it has not been suggested what freedom of intercourse among the States is protected except the freedom of an individual citizen of one State to cross its frontier into another State or to have such dealings with citizens of another State as his lawful occasions may require.

The bearing of those decisions with their implications upon the present appeal is manifest. Let it be admitted, let it indeed be emphatically asserted, that the impact of s 92 upon any legislative or executive action must depend upon the facts of the case. Yet it would be a strange anomaly if a grower of fruit could successfully challenge an unqualified power to interfere with his liberty to dispose [636] of his produce at his will by an interstate or intrastate transaction, but a banker could be prohibited altogether from carrying on his business both interstate and intrastate and against the prohibition would invoke s 92 in vain. In their Lordships' opinion there is no justification for such an anomaly. On the contrary the considerations which led the Board to the conclusion that s 20 of the South Australian Dried Fruits Act 1924 offended against s 92 of the Constitution led them to a similar conclusion in regard to s 46 of the Banking Act 1947. It is no answer that under the compulsion of s 11 of the Act the Commonwealth Bank will provide the banking facilities that the community may require, nor, if anyone dared so to prophesy, that the volume of banking would be the same. Nor is it relevant that the prohibition affects the intrastate transactions of a private bank as well as its interstate transactions. So also in the *James* cases there was no discrimination; his fruit, for whatever market destined, was liable to be the subject of a 'determination'.

After referring to the Commonwealth's argument that the Banking Act was not in breach of s 92 because it was not directed or aimed at interstate trade, the Privy Council responded:

[637] To this their Lordships would say that the test is clear: does the Act, not remotely or incidentally (as to which they will say something later) but directly, restrict the interstate business of banking? Beyond doubt it does, since it authorises in terms the total prohibition of private banking. If so, then in the only sense in which those words can be appropriately used in this case, it is an Act which is aimed at, directed at, and the purpose, object and intention of which is to restrict, interstate trade commerce and intercourse.

The Privy Council said that *James v Commonwealth* should not be read as deciding 'that it is only the passage of goods which is protected by s 92 or that it is only at the frontier that the stipulated freedom may be impaired': 79 CLR at 638. The Privy Council rejected an argument that the whole of Evatt J's judgment in *Vizzard* (1933) 50 CLR 30 had been approved in *James v Commonwealth* and continued:

[638] Their Lordships have thought it proper to deal at considerable length with the earlier decisions of this Board because so much [639] reliance was placed upon them by the appellants. It is, they think, clear that, far from assisting the appellants, these two decisions are, as the respondents have throughout contended, strongly against them.

In observing upon the *James* cases (1927) 40 CLR 1; [1932] AC 542; 47 CLR 386; [1936] AC 578; 55 CLR 1 and their bearing upon the present case their Lordships noted that the Act now under consideration operated to restrict the freedom of interstate trade commerce and intercourse not remotely or incidentally but directly. Upon this and upon a cognate matter, the distinction between restrictions which are regulatory and do not offend against s 92 and those which are something more than regulatory and do so offend, their Lordships think it proper to make certain further observations.

It is generally recognised that the expression 'free' in s 92, though emphasised by the accompanying 'absolutely', yet must receive some qualification. It was, indeed, common ground in the present case that the conception of freedom of trade commerce and intercourse in a community regulated by law presupposes some degree of restriction upon the individual. As long ago as 1916 in *Duncan v State of Queensland* (1916) 22 CLR 556 at 573, Sir Samuel Griffith CJ said: 'But the word 'free' does not mean *extra legem*, any more than freedom means anarchy. We boast of being an absolutely free people, but that does not mean that we are not subject to law.' And through all the subsequent cases in which s 92 has been discussed the problem has been to define the qualification of that which in the Constitution is left unqualified. In this labyrinth there is no golden thread. But it seems that two general propositions may be accepted: (1) that regulation of trade commerce and intercourse among the States is compatible with its absolute freedom and (2) that s 92 is violated only when a legislative or executive act operates to restrict such trade commerce and intercourse directly and immediately as distinct from creating some indirect or consequential impediment which may fairly be regarded as remote. In the application of these general propositions, in determining whether an enactment is regulatory or something more, or whether a restriction is direct or only remote or incidental, there cannot fail to be differences of opinion. The problem to be solved will often be not so much legal as political, social or economic. Yet it must be solved by a court of law. For where the dispute is, as here, not only between Commonwealth and citizen but between [640] Commonwealth and intervening States on the one hand and citizens and States on the other, it is only the Court that can decide the issue. It is vain to invoke the voice of Parliament.

Difficult as the application of these general propositions must be in the infinite variety of situations that in peace or in war confront a nation, it appears to their Lordships that this further guidance may be given. In the recent case of *Australian National Airways Pty Ltd v Commonwealth* (1945) 71 CLR 29 the learned Chief Justice used these words (at 61): 'I venture to repeat what I said in the former case [namely, *Milk Board (NSW) v Metropolitan Cream Pty Ltd* (1939) 62 CLR 116]: One proposition which I regard as established is that simple legislative prohibition (Federal or State), as distinct from regulation, of interstate trade and commerce is invalid. Further, a law which is directed against interstate trade and commerce is invalid. Such a law does not regulate such trade, it merely prevents it. But a law prescribing rules as to the manner in which trade (including transport) is to be conducted is not a mere prohibition and may be valid in its application to interstate trade, notwithstanding s 92'. With this statement which both repeats the general proposition and precisely states that simple prohibition is not regulation their Lordships agree. And it is, as they think, a test which must have led the Chief Justice to a different conclusion in this case had he decided that the business of banking was within the ambit of s 92. They do not doubt that it led him to a correct decision in the *Airways* case, supra. There he said: 'In the present case the Act is directed against all competition with the interstate services of the Commission. The exclusion of other services is based simply upon the fact that the competing services are themselves interstate services ... The exclusion of competition with the Commission is not a system of regulation and is, in my opinion, a violation of s 92 ...' Mutatis mutandis, these words may be applied to the Act now impugned, for it is an irrelevant factor that the prohibition prohibits interstate and intrastate activities at the same time.

Yet about this, as about every other proposition in this field, a reservation must be made. For their Lordships do not intend to lay it down that in no circumstances could the exclusion of competition so as to create a monopoly either in a State or Commonwealth agency or in some other body be justified. Every case must be [641] judged on its own facts and in its own setting of time and circumstance, and it may be that in regard to some economic activities and at some stage of social development it might be maintained that prohibition with a view to State monopoly was the only practical and reasonable manner of regulation and that interstate trade commerce and intercourse thus prohibited and thus monopolised remained absolutely free.

~~~

Notes

[10.4.11] *Commonwealth v Bank of New South Wales* (1949) 79 CLR 497 **[10.4.10C]**, through its endorsement of Dixon J's individual right theory, considerably enlarged the freedom guaranteed by s 92. This reading of the section put at risk a wide range of government controls and programmes. For instance, all states had legislation which controlled road transport, both intrastate and interstate. The legislation prohibited the road carriage of any goods or persons for reward without a licence issued by a state official. This legislation, whose purpose was to protect state railways from the rapidly expanding road transport industry, had survived constitutional challenge in *R v Vizzard* (1933) 50 CLR 30, when the High Court had described it as facilitating the flow of interstate trade; that is, when the High Court saw s 92 as guaranteeing free trade rather than any individual right. Could this legislation survive *Commonwealth v Bank of New South Wales*?

Again, some states still had price control machinery; remnants of the extensive price controls administered by the Commonwealth during the World War II. Could a state law, which fixed the wholesale price for which (say) potatoes could be sold in that state, validly apply to sales of potatoes imported from another state, or are the interstate potatoes constitutionally immune from the price controls?

And what of consumer protection laws which, for example, compel health insurance companies to maintain adequate trust funds, or prohibit any trader from offering any 'free gifts' when selling goods, or insist that only licensed persons could carry on business as travel agents? Could a health insurance company which insured people in more than one state raise s 92 and claim exemption from the trust fund requirements? Could a trader who sold goods interstate (by mail order, for example) ignore the law against offering 'free gifts'? And could a travel agent with interstate business (surely almost all travel agents fall into this group) demand the right to carry on business without a licence?

These (and many other) questions were to be litigated over the next 30 years. *Commonwealth v Bank of New South Wales* stimulated a remarkable increase in s 92 litigation. More than 90 High Court cases raised s 92 issues during 35 years after *Commonwealth v Bank of New South Wales* to 1984 compared with just over 40 cases in the 45 years before *Commonwealth v Bank of New South Wales*.

[10.4.12]　However, despite some victories for individual traders, *Commonwealth v Bank of New South Wales* (1949) 79 CLR 497 **[10.4.10C]** did not have the dramatic effect on government controls of commercial activity which the individual right theory seemed to portend. Its effect was limited through the development by the High Court of two reservations put forward by the Privy Council in *Commonwealth v Bank of New South Wales*.

The first of these was the proposition that *regulation* of interstate trade was compatible with its absolute freedom, accompanied by the suggestion that, in some circumstances, even prohibition could be reconciled with the absolute freedom: 79 CLR at 639, 641. The extent of *permissible regulation* was to remain largely unexplored for 20 years after the *Bank* case probably because the Dixon court recognised and wished to avoid the political nature of the choices involved. More recently, the High Court began to dispose of s 92 cases by applying this concept. However, cases such as *Permewan Wright Consolidated Pty Ltd v Trewhitt* (1979) 145 CLR 1 **[10.4.24]** and *Uebergang v Australian Wheat Board* (1980) 145 CLR 266 **[10.4.25]**, amply confirmed the political aspects of the concept and revealed deeply divided judicial opinion of its content.

The second reservation made by the Privy Council in *Commonwealth v Bank of New South Wales* (1949) 79 CLR 497 **[10.4.15]** raised conceptual, rather than policy-choice, problems. The problem was that s 92 struck down only direct or immediate restrictions of interstate trade; that is, an 'indirect or consequential impediment which may fairly be regarded as remote' did not violate the s 92 freedom: 79 CLR at 639. Most of the judicial development of s 92 over the succeeding 20 years concentrated on the difficult distinction between direct and indirect burdens on interstate trade. That distinction (we can now say with the wisdom of hindsight) is elusive. It raises several abstract issues: for example, what is interstate trade? When does it begin and end? By what standard do we identify a 'direct' burden? Through strict legal analysis or through practical assessment?

During the first 20 or so years after the *Bank* case, this second reservation was the major device through which the impact of decision and the 'individual right' theory was contained, even reduced. With the decision in *Cole v Whitfield* (1988) 165 CLR 360 **[10.4.27C]** and the abandonment of the individual right theory (described by the court as 'highly artificial': 165 CLR at 401), the two reservations to that theory have become obsolete. Nevertheless, they played a vital part in the evolution of the present thinking on s 92, if only by discrediting the individual right theory, and their use in almost 40 years of judicial decisions provides an important chapter in the history of constitutional adjudication in Australia.

Direct and indirect burdens

[10.4.13]　The difficulties inherent in defining interstate trade, and the problems presented by the distinction between direct burdens on interstate trade and indirect or consequential burdens on that trade were illustrated by the High Court's decision in *Wragg v New South Wales* (1953) 88 CLR 353. The decision is complex, largely because the case was brought by several plaintiffs whose positions in relation to the challenged law were not identical, and the High Court appeared non-committal on a central issue in the case.

The Prices Regulation Act 1948–49 (NSW) and the Prices Regulation Order No 322 fixed the maximum prices for which any person could sell potatoes in New

South Wales. Maximum prices were fixed for the sale of potatoes at all stages of their distribution in the state. Several individuals and companies claimed that their interstate trade in potatoes was impeded by these price controls and they sought a declaration that the controls were invalid. The plaintiffs were:

- Tasmanian potato growers who regularly sold potatoes to merchants in Tasmania, on the express understanding that the merchants would sell them to other merchants in New South Wales;

- a Tasmanian merchant who regularly bought Tasmanian potatoes and sold and shipped them to New South Wales merchants; and,

- a New South Wales merchant who regularly bought potatoes from Tasmanian merchants and, upon the arrival of those potatoes in Sydney, sold most of them at the wharf to potato wholesalers.

All the plaintiffs claimed to be involved in interstate trade which, they said, was impeded by the controls imposed by New South Wales on all sales of potatoes in that state.

It should be apparent that the plaintiffs' cases were not identical. The Tasmanian growers' and the Tasmanian merchant's activities (their sales of potatoes) were not controlled by the New South Wales laws. So far as New South Wales was concerned, they were free to sell their potatoes at any price. However, the New South Wales merchant's activities were controlled by the New South Wales laws. Its sales, because they occurred in New South Wales, were subject to price control. The court decided that the activities of none of the plaintiffs were protected by s 92. As for the Tasmanian growers and export merchant, they could only show an *indirect* impediment to their (possibly interstate) trade activities. Dixon CJ said that the New South Wales law did:

> ... not limit the legal freedom to import potatoes or to contract to buy them for shipment from Tasmania. Its operation is to create conditions of trade in potatoes within New South Wales which react on the economic, not the legal capacity of the trader desiring to import Tasmanian potatoes. The economic consequences which it may have upon interstate trade may well be serious, but that is a different thing from interference by law or government action with the freedom which s 92 confers. When it said that s 92 gives protection against restrictions upon trade, commerce and intercourse among the States which are direct as distinguished from laws or governmental acts which involve some indirect or consequential prejudice, it is this kind of thing that is contemplated (88 CLR at 387).

The New South Wales import merchant, on the other hand, lay outside the protection offered by s 92 because it had not established that any of its sales (most of which were made at the wharf to wholesalers) were part of interstate trade. Taylor J suggested that some first sales of imported goods might 'possibly, upon examination' be found to be part of interstate trade, but he indicated that the evidence before the court 'leaves this matter completely open': 88 CLR at 399.

But Dixon CJ probably committed himself to a more definite (though negative) proposition. After describing the course of business adopted by the New South Wales importer (which was to sell most of the imported potatoes at the wharf immediately upon their arrival from Tasmania), Dixon CJ said at 388:

> Does this mean that the sale by the [importer] is an inseparable part of the interstate transaction? In my opinion the facts stated are insufficient to justify that conclusion. I think that they show no more than a course of business in which it is convenient to make the first intrastate sale from the wharf.

The view, that the first sale of a commodity after its importation from another state was not part of interstate trade, was confirmed by the High Court in *Grannall v C Geo Kellaway & Sons Pty Ltd* (1955) 93 CLR 36; but was reversed in *North Eastern Dairy Co Ltd v Dairy Industry Authority (NSW)* (1975) 134 CLR 559 **[10.4.23]**.

[10.4.14] The State Transport (Co-Ordination) Act 1931–51 (NSW) prohibited the business of road transport without a licence issued by a state official, who was to take account of a wide range of factors in deciding whether to issue a licence. These included: the need for transport services; the suitability of the route; the public interest; the elimination of unnecessary services; the coordination of all forms of transport; the construction and suitability of the vehicle; and the suitability of any applicant to hold a licence.

In *Hughes and Vale Pty Ltd v New South Wales (No 1)* (1954) 93 CLR 1, the Privy Council decided that the New South Wales legislation could only survive by exploiting one of the qualifications put forward in the *Bank* case: '[I]t can only be upon the ground that the restrictions contained therein are "regulatory"': 93 CLR at 23. On this point, the Privy Council adopted Fullagar J's observations in *McCarter v Brodie* (1950) 80 CLR 432. Thus, the Board held that while safety requirements for motor vehicles and road traffic rules were permissible regulations of interstate trade, a prohibition was not. In the case before the Board, the legislation amounted to a prohibition, despite the official's discretion to exempt from the prohibition by granting a licence: 93 CLR at 23–8.

[10.4.15] In *Grannall v Marrickville Margarine Pty Ltd* (1955) 93 CLR 55 the High Court rejected a challenge to a statutory quota on the production of table margarine. Marrickville Margarine had been prosecuted for a breach of s 22A of the Dairy Industry Act 1915 (NSW), which prohibited the manufacture of table margarine without a licence, issued at the discretion of the Minister of Agriculture. Marrickville Margarine, which sold a substantial part of its product to buyers in other states, argued that s 22A was inconsistent with s 92 of the Commonwealth Constitution.

In a joint judgment, Dixon CJ, McTiernan, Webb and Kitto JJ conceded that without goods there could be no interstate trade in goods because manufacture was an essential preliminary to interstate trade in merchandise. But that did not make manufacture part of interstate trade and commerce, nor was it a reason for extending the s 92 freedom to something which preceded interstate trade and was outside the freedom conferred:

> It is a commonplace that s 92 assumes the existence of an ordered society governed by law in which commodities are bought and sold and the movement of persons and things takes place and that it undertakes in such a society to secure the freedom of no more than interstate dealing, movement, interchange, passage etc. These assumptions are made by s 92 but their fulfilment is not the subject of the constitutional guarantee of freedom which s 92 gives (95 CLR at 72).

Later, the justices identified and condemned 'two tendencies' to extend the search of s 92:

> One is to press the operation of s 92 beyond the subject matter of trade, commerce and intercourse among the States so that it denies to the legislatures of this country the power to impose any prohibition, restriction or burden if its consequences could be seen in what was done or not done in the course of interstate commerce. The other is to seek to extend the freedom which s 92 guarantees to trade, commerce and intercourse among the States to antecedent or subsequent transactions on the plea that

they are incidental, ancillary or conducive to interstate transactions or necessarily consequential upon them. There is in truth nothing to justify such notions which would go far to exclude legislative power the existence of which has never been doubted (93 CLR at 79).

[10.4.16]   The proposition, that manufacture or production was not protected by s 92, was confirmed by the High Court in *Beal v Marrickville Margarine Pty Ltd* (1966) 114 CLR 283 and *Bartter's Farms v Todd* (1978) 139 CLR 499. A parallel proposition was confirmed in *R v Anderson; Ex parte Ipec-Air Pty Ltd* (1965) 113 CLR 177 and *Ansett Transport Industries (Operations) Pty Ltd v Commonwealth* (1977) 139 CLR 54; that the importation into Australia of a product intended for interstate trade was outside s 92's protection. In *Cole v Whitfield* (1988) 165 CLR 360 **[10.4.27C]** the High Court observed that these decisions, to the effect that production and importation for the purpose of interstate trade fell outside the protection of s 92, 'scarcely seemed to make sense' when the section was seen as guaranteeing the right of the individual to engage in interstate trade, for in each case 'the legislation affected interstate trade in a substantial way': 165 CLR at 401–2.

[10.4.17]   The proposition that a substantial practical or economic effect on interstate trade rather than a direct legal burden on that trade was sufficient to invoke s 92, was persistently advanced by Sir Garfield Barwick after his appointment as Chief Justice in 1965. The first clear adoption of that proposition came in *North Eastern Dairy Co Ltd v Dairy Industry Authority (NSW)* (1975) 134 CLR 559; in a decision which effectively destroyed the fine distinctions and classifications upon which *Wragg v New South Wales* (1953) 88 CLR 353 **[10.4.13]** had been based.

The Pure Food Regulations (NSW) prohibited the supply or sale of pasteurised milk for human consumption unless the milk had been processed by a registered milk pasteuriser. Section 33(1) of the Dairy Industry Act 1970 (NSW) prohibited any person from acting as a milk vendor unless licensed under the Act. North Eastern Dairy pasteurised and processed milk in north-east Victoria. It was not registered as a milk pasteuriser under the Regulations. North Eastern Dairy regularly carried its milk from Victoria to southern New South Wales, where it sold some directly to consumers and some through retailers who were appointed and acted as its agents for the purpose of selling milk. This milk had been pasteurised in Victoria but not in New South Wales. The New South Wales retailers through whom North Eastern Dairy sold its milk held milk vendor's licences under the Act, which were subject to the condition that it should not sell milk not pasteurised in New South Wales.

In proceedings brought by North Eastern Dairy and one of the retailers, a majority of the High Court (Barwick CJ, Gibbs, Jacobs and Mason JJ; McTiernan J dissenting) held that the Dairy Industry Act was invalid. Mason J said:

> To say that consistently with s 92 it is permissible to enact laws whose practical effect is to burden interstate trade is to reduce the constitutional prohibition to a legal formulation which may be readily circumvented (134 CLR at 606–7).

He noted that, once milk was pasteurised (as North Eastern Dairy's milk was pasteurised in Victoria), it could not be pasteurised again; and concluded at 607:

> The practical effect of the regulation is therefore to put an end to the interstate trade in Victorian pasteurised milk and to discriminate against the Victorian product and the Victorian producer. In the conventional language of the cases it imposes a burden on the importer of Victorian pasteurised milk by preventing him from selling his product in the State. This results in my opinion from the direct and immediate operation of the law. It is not a mere economic or social consequence of the regulation (*SOS (Mowbray)*

Pty Ltd v Mead (at 594)). To say that the prohibition does not directly destroy the importation of pasteurised milk because it leaves the importer free to import it, though unable to sell it, seems to me to desert reality.

Jacobs J observed that it was 'necessary to examine the nature and quality of the restriction [on sale] in the light of the known and proved economic social and other circumstances of its imposition and the community in which it is imposed': 134 CLR at 624. He said that the 'clearest illustration' of legislation which directly impeded interstate trade was a law which was 'in terms discriminatory against' interstate trade, as in *Fox v Robbins* (1909) 8 CLR 115 **[10.4.8]**. However, a more common example was discrimination which resulted not from the express terms of a law but from 'its actual operation in the community': 134 CLR at 623. In the present case, Jacobs J said at 633, the Dairy Industry Act 1970 (NSW) operated directly, not indirectly, on interstate transactions between North Eastern Dairy in Victoria and consumers and resellers in New South Wales:

> There cannot practically be any such transactions. The interstate trade would for all practical purposes be brought to an end. There is nothing remote or consequential about that, especially when the impugned Act by such an operation has the effect of preferring New South Wales milk producers to those such as the plaintiff who produce milk in another State.

Permissible regulation

[10.4.18]   The Privy Council had declared in *Commonwealth v Bank of New South Wales* (1949) 79 CLR 497 **[10.4.10C]** that the freedom guaranteed by s 92 was compatible with the regulation of interstate trade. It had given little concrete guidance on how to recognise permissible regulation, as distinct from unconstitutional restriction, of interstate trade, apart from endorsing Latham CJ's example (in *Australian National Airways Pty Ltd v Commonwealth* (1945) 71 CLR 29 **[10.4.9]** at 61) of 'a law prescribing rules as to the manner in which trade ... is to be conducted' and adopting, with qualification, his distinction between regulation and prohibition.

How was this exception to the general rule in *Commonwealth v Bank of New South Wales* to be applied? Would it mean, for example, that a government could set up a scheme for the compulsory central marketing of dried fruit? Would this scheme be regulatory, even if it involved the compulsory acquisition of all dried fruit and a ban on its private sale? Could the government argue that such a scheme served the interests of all growers and processors of dried fruit by preventing intense competition and, therefore, merely regulated the manner in which those growers and processors traded? Should the question of the scheme's regulatory character be approached from the perspective of retailers and consumers? For them, a scheme which maintained high prices for dried fruit would offer few compensations for the denial of interstate trading freedom. Or is it essential, when assessing the regulatory character of such a scheme, to consider the position of the individual trader? After all, it was that trader's right to trade across state borders which, the Privy Council had said, s 92 guaranteed; perhaps only those controls which enhanced that right were consistent with s 92.

Take another example. State laws fix the maximum size, weight and speed for motor vehicles using the state's roads. When these controls are applied to interstate freight carriers, could they be described as a regulation of interstate trade? Would the answer to that question depend on judicial assessment of the interests of: the individual interstate freight carrier; of all such carriers; of all road users; or of the general public? Were all these interests to be taken into account?

[10.4.19]   The complex nature of deciding whether a law is regulatory, and therefore consistent with s 92, was recognised (though not resolved) by the Privy Council in *Commonwealth v Bank of New South Wales* (1949) 79 CLR 497 **[10.4.10C]**. In making the classification, the Privy Council said, 'there cannot fail to be differences of opinion. The problem to be solved will often be not so much legal as political, social or economic': 79 CLR at 639. Yet, the Privy Council insisted, courts had to solve the problem and they were not to defer to the opinion of parliament (as expressed in any legislation under challenge).

No doubt it was judicial recognition of the political nature of this question which prompted the High Court, over the next 20 years, to avoid the question and, as far as possible, resolve s 92 cases through the analytical development of the abstract distinction between direct and indirect burdens on interstate trade. The Privy Council and High Court did resort to the concept of regulation in a series of transport cases between 1954 and 1958 but their discussion was impressionistic (see **[10.4.20]–[10.4.22]**); it was not until the High Court began to move away from the Dixonian approach to the direct–indirect distinction that the interest-balancing choices inherent in the idea of permissible regulation began to be explored by the court, most notably in *Permewan Wright Consolidated Pty Ltd v Trewhitt* (1979) 134 CLR 1 **[10.4.24]** and *Uebergang v Australian Wheat Board* (1980) 145 CLR 266 **[10.4.25]**.

[10.4.20]   In *Hughes and Vale Pty Ltd v New South Wales (No 1)* (1954) 93 CLR 1, the Privy Council held (on appeal from the High Court) that the State Transport (Co-ordination) Act 1931–52 (NSW) infringed s 92 in its application to persons engaged in interstate road transport businesses. The Act prohibited the business of road transport without a licence issued by a state official, who was to consider a series of factors in deciding whether to issue a licence. The Act also authorised a licence fee, calculated on the capacity of the vehicle and the distance it travelled.

The Privy Council acknowledged that some government control of interstate road transport would be permissible regulation. Such controls included compulsory registration of motor vehicles, mandatory safety equipment, speed and weight limits and the observance of road rules. Further, the government could 'make a charge for the use of trading facilities, such as bridges or aerodromes', so long as the charge was reasonable. However, to prohibit interstate trading operations, as the State Transport (Co-ordination) Act did, went beyond reasonable regulation, which (according to Fullagar J) was justifiable in the interest of facilitating interstate trade. The Privy Council acknowledged that it might be necessary to limit the number or type of vehicles using public roads 'for example, on the grounds of public safety'. This could be justified as regulatory: 93 CLR at 32–3.

[10.4.21]   In *Hughes & Vale Pty Ltd v New South Wales (No 2)* (1955) 93 CLR 17, the High Court held that the State Transport (Co-ordination) Act still infringed s 92, despite its amendment following the Privy Council's decision in *Hughes and Vale (No 1)* (1954) 93 CLR 1 **[10.4.20]**, because it continued to give a government official a wide reservation to permit or prohibit interstate road transport operations.

Dixon CJ, McTiernan and Webb JJ offered at least two justifications for permitting regulation of interstate trade: first, to ensure 'the orderly and proper conduct of commercial dealings or other transactions and activities'; and, second, to ensure that the 'rights ... or interests of others' were not prejudiced and 'the just claims of the public ... to any recompense' for the use of public facilities were not disregarded: 93 CLR at 160–1. On the basis of that principle, the justices said, it would be possible for the state to make a fair and reasonable charge for the actual use made of public roads: 93 CLR at 178.

[10.4.22] Following the High Court's decision in *Hughes and Vale (No 2)* (1955) 93 CLR 17 **[10.4.21]**, the states re-drafted their systems for controlling road transport and limited their controls to imposing a charge on interstate road transport operators that would be used to pay for the maintenance of roads. The fourth schedule of the Commercial Goods Vehicle Act 1955 (Vic), for example, provided that the owner of every commercial goods vehicle should pay one-third of a penny per ton (of the total of the vehicle's unladen weight plus 40 per cent of its load capacity) per mile of public road travelled in Victoria. The Act provided that the proceeds of this tax were to be paid into a special account and applied solely for the maintenance of public roads.

In *Armstrong v Victoria (No 2)* (1957) 99 CLR 29, a majority of the High Court held that this system did not contravene s 92. Dixon CJ said that the tax did not detract from the freedom of interstate trade, even though it had to be paid if a person was to engage in that trade, because it was a contribution for maintaining a facility without which the interstate trade could not be carried out. He listed such facilities as bridges, aerodromes and wharves, and said at 43:

> However it may be stated, the ultimate ground why the exaction of the payments for using the instruments of commerce that have been mentioned is no violation of the freedom of interstate trade, lies in the relation to interstate trade which their nature and purpose give them. The reason why public authority must maintain them is in order that the commerce may use them, and so for the commerce to bear or contribute to the cost of their upkeep can involve no detraction from the freedom of commercial intercourse between States.

Dixon CJ went on to assert that contributions to maintenance of roads were consistent with s 92, but contributions to their capital cost were not. In the present case, he was satisfied that the charges imposed by the Commercial Goods Vehicle Act could 'fairly enough' be described as compensation for wear and tear caused by road transport vehicles to public roads.

[10.4.23] Disagreement over the nature of the balancing process inherent in the 'reasonable regulation' concept was articulated in *North Eastern Dairy Co Ltd v Dairy Industry Authority of New South Wales* (1975) 134 CLR 559, where a Victorian milk producer challenged New South Wales legislation which prohibited the sale in New South Wales of milk unless pasteurised in that state and unless sold by a licensed milk vendor: see **[10.4.17]**. The majority of the court decided that this legislation imposed a direct burden on interstate trade in milk (the point dealt with at **[10.4.17]**), and that the burden was not a permissible regulation. On that second issue, Barwick CJ said at 581–2:

> The freedom of the individual to engage in interstate trade and commerce is included in the freedom of interstate trade and commerce which the Constitution guarantees. Thus laws to ensure public health and honesty and fairness in commercial dealings form examples of laws which the concept of freedom of trade and commerce does not deny. Consequently, laws, for example, to secure public health, must have no impact which is reasonably unnecessary upon the activities of the individual in interstate trade and commerce. The protection of the individual is not merely incidental or peripheral to the enforcement of the constitutional guarantee. Indeed, whilst not exhausting the operation of s 92, it is central to it.

On the other hand, Mason J said that, in identifying a permissible regulation, it was helpful to recall:

> ... that s 92 has a predominant public character and that the protection which it gives to the rights of the individual is incidental to and consequential upon the protection which is given to the entire concept of interstate trade. Once the predominant public character of the provision is recognised it is more easily perceived that regulation of interstate trade, for the benefit of the community may be consistent with the freedom which is guaranteed and that it may not necessarily involve any collision with the derivative protection which that section gives to individual rights.
>
> The freedom guaranteed by s 92 is not a concept of freedom to be ascertained by reference to the doctrines of political economy which prevailed in 1900; it is a concept of freedom which should be related to a developing society and to its needs as they evolve from time to time. Section 92 finds its place in a Constitution which was intended to operate beyond the limits of then foreseeable time — it would be a serious mistake to read the guarantee or immunity which it offers as one which necessarily and rigidly reflects ideas accepted almost a century ago. Instead, the section should be seen as a provision whose operation may fluctuate as the community develops and as the need for new and different modes of regulation of trade and commerce become apparent (134 CLR at 614–5).

Despite these differences, Barwick CJ, Mason J and the other members of the court (apart from McTiernan J) agreed that the New South Wales legislation could not be described as regulatory. They did so for the same reason; namely, that it went beyond what was reasonably necessary for the preservation of health standards.

[10.4.24] In *Permewan Wright Consolidated Pty Ltd v Trewhitt* (1979) 145 CLR 1, the difference between Barwick CJ and Mason J was consolidated, obliging other members of the court to commit themselves to a position. The Marketing of Primary Products Act 1958 (Vic) prohibited the retail sale of 'any eggs which have not been graded or tested for quality and marked or stamped in accordance with this Act and the regulations': s 41D(1). Permewan Wright operated several supermarkets in Victoria where it sold eggs produced in New South Wales. These eggs had been tested and graded in New South Wales but not as required by the Victorian Act. The High Court decided that Permewan Wright's sales were part of interstate trade, and turned to the question whether the Victorian legislation was merely regulatory.

Barwick CJ said 'that the individual freedom to trade interstate is itself paramount and not required to yield to some actual or supposed public interest ... which is in its nature incompatible with that freedom', and that laws on the topic of public health would be consistent with s 92 only if their effect on the individual's interstate trade was compatible with the freedom of interstate trade: 145 CLR at 11. Aickin J adopted a similar approach. In their view, the Victorian legislation went beyond reasonable regulation in the interests of interstate trade and was, therefore, invalid.

On the other hand, Stephen J described two broad categories of law which although restrictive of interstate trade, would be classified as reasonable regulation of that trade. First, there were those laws which 'may be seen to be for the benefit of interstate trade and of those engaged in it ... [r]ules of the road are ... especially easy to recognise as conforming to this analysis': 145 CLR at 22. However, in addition the 'guaranteed freedom should also be qualified in the interests of the community at large ... Interstate trade must to that extent accommodate itself to the interests of the wider community, upon whose well-being that trade itself depends for its very existence': 145 CLR at 26. Stephen J said that there were many areas, apart from that of public health, in which interstate trade could 'lawfully be regulated in the interests of the public': 145 CLR at 27. The present legislation was no more restrictive of interstate trade than was reasonably necessary to protect consumers of eggs (which were 'not merely perishable but … enigmatic to the ordinary shopper') and did not discriminate against the interstate trade in eggs. While there might have been a less restrictive way to achieve the same protection, the legislature's choice of means should be respected unless it appeared 'clearly unreasonable': 145 CLR at 30.

Gibbs and Mason JJ adopted the same approach as Stephen J. Mason J urged the court to 'recognise that the organised society which s 92 assumes is not the society of 1900 but the Australian community as it evolves and develops from time to time': 124 CLR at 35. His Honour said that the 'predominant public character' of s 92 meant that the section should be 'understood as presupposing a society in which conduct is regulated in the interests of the community, rather than a society in which conduct is merely regulated in the interests of those engaged in trade': 145 CLR at 36.

[10.4.25] The division of judicial opinion intensified in *Uebergang v Australian Wheat Board* (1980) 145 CLR 266, where the High Court was asked to consider the validity of the wheat stabilisation scheme. The scheme, established by complementary state and Commonwealth legislation, involved the compulsory acquisition by the Australian Wheat Board of all wheat grown in Australia. The Board was given a monopoly on the sale of wheat and paid growers a standard price which was intended to 'even-out' international and national fluctuations in the market place.

In a preliminary hearing, the court was asked to answer a number of questions, including the following question:

> Does the validity of the Wheat Industry Stabilization Act 1974 (NSW), as amended, and the Wheat Industry Stabilization Act 1974 (Q), as amended, depend on the establishment to the satisfaction of the Court of any fact? If so, what is that fact?

Gibbs and Wilson JJ said that s 92 was 'concerned to protect private rights', and that, notwithstanding that 'the trend of political theory and practice' was to strengthen government controls 'at the cost of individual liberty' (at 300):

> [T]his Court cannot write s 92 out of the Constitution. It must therefore do its best to preserve a balance between competing interests, a balance which favours freedom for the individual citizen in the absence of compelling considerations to the contrary.

Gibbs and Wilson JJ said that, in order to justify the wheat stabilisation scheme, under which the Wheat Board was given a monopoly in the trade in wheat in Australia, it would have to be shown that (at 301):

> … a monopoly covering both intrastate and interstate trade is the only practical and reasonable course open in present circumstances. The test remains a most stringent one, not likely to be satisfied except in exceptional circumstances.

Stephen and Mason JJ said that no particular ultimate fact could determine the validity of the wheat stabilisation scheme. They noted that in *Commonwealth v Bank of New South Wales* (1949) 79 CLR 497 **[10.4.10C]** the Privy Council had referred to a monopoly as being permissible if it was the only practicable and reasonable way to regulate some activity:

> The formula couples two concepts, the practical and the reasonable. The quality of being practicable (that being our understanding of what is there meant by 'practical') seems to be concerned very largely, if not exclusively, with whether or not a particular statutory scheme is feasible from the viewpoint of those administering it. Reasonableness, on the other hand, we regard as concerned with the adverse effect of

the challenged law upon those whose activities in trade are affected by it, that adverse effect being weighed against the need which is felt for regulation in the interests of the public generally (145 CLR at 305–6).

Stephen and Mason JJ then offered the following guidance to the parties, at 306–7, in response to the question posed for the court:

> The evidence which we would regard as relevant in determining the validity of the present legislation would be such material as would enable the Court to determine whether or not the restrictions, which the legislation imposes upon interstate trade, are no greater than are reasonably necessary in all the circumstances. For example, it would be relevant to establish what are the goals sought to be attained by the restrictions; how these may be weighed against those restrictions and whether they can be attained by other means which do not involve such onerous restraints upon traders.
>
> It will, of course, be for the parties to determine the particular evidence to be adduced, always bearing in mind that the criterion of permissible regulation of interstate trade is that the legislation should be no more restrictive than is reasonable in all the circumstances, due regard being had to the public interest. The importance of this matter of the public interest must never be lost sight of: as Mason J has said in *Permewan Wright* (1979) 145 CLR at 36, s 92 is to be 'understood as presupposing a society in which conduct is regulated in the interests of the community'.

Aickin J disagreed with Stephen and Mason JJ. His Honour observed that it would be a rare and exceptional situation in which a government monopoly of a trade would be consistent with the freedom of those who had previously carried on that trade, and said that it was not the court's function to advise the parties on the facts which they should seek to prove.

Barwick CJ said that he could not accept that a government monopoly of interstate trade was ever consistent with the freedom guaranteed by s 92. If the other members of the court would not accept his view that the wheat stabilisation scheme offended s 92, and the validity of the scheme was regarded as depending on a question of fact, then the fact would be (at 295):

> ... whether the statutory scheme ... is the only reasonable and practicable way in which the freedom of interstate trade and commerce in wheat, including the participation therein of the individual citizen, can be secured.

Murphy J said that he would regard the wheat stabilisation scheme as valid because it contained no discriminatory financial imposts. However, if the court was not prepared to accept that view, then Murphy J would support the view expressed by Stephen and Mason JJ; that is, that the scheme would be consistent with s 92 if, as Murphy J put it at 309, it was:

> ... a reasonable way of regulating the marketing of wheat, no more restrictive than is reasonable in all the circumstances, with due regard having been given to the public interest.

[10.4.26]   In *Uebergang v Australian Wheat Board* (1980) 140 CLR 120 **[10.4.25]**, some justices emphasised the individual rights aspect of s 92 (Barwick CJ and Aickin J); for other judges it was the public character of s 92 which influenced their assessment (Stephen and Mason JJ, probably joined by Murphy J); while a third group of judges (Gibbs and Wilson JJ) searched for some compromise between these two views of the underlying theme of s 92. From this perspective, the judgments in *Uebergang v Australian Wheat Board* could be seen as part of a movement away from the 'individual right' theory of s 92 towards a 'free trade' approach. That movement culminated in the decision in *Cole v Whitfield* (1988) 165 CLR 360 **[10.4.27C]**.

Meanwhile, in *Miller v TCN Channel Nine Pty Ltd* (1986) 161 CLR 556, both Mason and Deane JJ developed a substantial criticism of the individual rights theory of s 92. Mason J said that to read s 92 as a guarantee of individual rights seemed 'to draw too heavily on the laissez-faire notions of political economy prevailing in 1900': 161 CLR at 571. He pointed to 'the divergence of views expressed by the members of the court in *Uebergang*' (1980)) 140 CLR 120 **[10.4.25]**; and observed:

> The judgments in that case demonstrate in convincing fashion that there is now no interpretation of s 92 that commands the acceptance of a majority of the court. There is much to be said for the view that in this situation the court has a responsibility to undertake a fundamental re-examination of the section (161 CLR at 571).

Deane J described the judicial decisions on s 92 as:

> ... an area where the ordinary processes of legal reasoning have had but a small part to play and where judicial exegesis has tended to confuse rather than elucidate. Indeed, it is as if many voices of authority have been speaking differently at the same time with the result that, putting to one side some basic propositions, it is all but impossible to comprehend precisely what it is that authority has said (161 CLR at 616).

After noting the court's failure in *Uebergang v Australian Wheat Board* to express an authoritative view on the constitutional validity of an important national scheme, Deane J observed that, 'somewhere along the line, things have gone wrong':

> The section was, plainly enough, intended to serve the essential function of reinforcing the economic and social unity of an emerging nation by removing the barriers to commerce, trade and intercourse which the frontiers between the federating colonies had previously represented. It has been converted into a form of constitutional guarantee of the economics of laissez-faire and the politics of 'small government'. The importance of the notion of 'freedom as at the frontier' which was recognised even in *James v Commonwealth* (1936) 55 CLR 1 at 58 as lying at the heart of s 92 has been progressively discounted and disregarded (161 CLR at 618).

The occasion for that consideration was presented to the court a few months later (in June 1987) when *Cole v Whitfield* **[10.4.27C]** was argued.

[10.4.27C]　　　　　　　　## Cole v Whitfield
(1988) 165 CLR 360

Section 9 of the Fisheries Act 1959 (Tas) authorised the Governor to make regulations 'prohibiting ... the having or possession or control of ... undersized ... fish'. The Governor accordingly made the Sea Fisheries Regulations 1962, reg 31(1)(d) of which declared that no person should 'have in his possession, or under his control' male crayfish below 11 inches in size or female crayfish below 10.5 inches in size, 'whether or not the fish was taken in State fishing waters'.

Whitfield was the manager of a business located in Tasmania, Boomer Park Crayfish Farm, which purchased and sold live crayfish. In October 1982, Whitfield purchased some live crayfish from a South Australian fishing business. The crayfish were all above the minimum size prescribed by South Australian legislation, but were below the minimum size prescribed by the Tasmanian regulations. In January 1983 a Tasmanian government inspector inspected the premises managed by Whitfield and discovered 97 crayfish below the minimum size prescribed by the Tasmanian regulations. Whitfield and Boomer Park were charged with possession of undersized crayfish.

The magistrate dismissed the charges on the basis that Whitfield's possession of the crayfish was protected by s 92 of the Commonwealth Constitution. The prosecutor applied to the Supreme Court of Tasmania for review of the magistrate's order. This application was removed to the High Court of Australia under s 40 of the Judiciary Act 1903 (Cth), where two questions were posed for the court's decision:

> (a) whether the possession in Tasmania by the respondents of 60 male and 37 female crayfish imported from South Australia is possession that is the subject of a transaction of interstate trade and commerce within the meaning of s 92 of the Commonwealth of Australia Constitution;
>
> (b) whether the provisions of reg 31(1)(d)(ix) and (x) of the Sea Fisheries Regulations 1962 made under the Fisheries Act 1959 (Tas), when applied to the possession of the aforesaid crayfish, are compatible with the freedom guaranteed by s 92 of the Constitution ...? [165 CLR at 382]

Mason CJ, Wilson, Brennan, Deane, Dawson, Toohey and Gaudron JJ: [382] If the view be taken that the guarantee of freedom contained in s 92 is one of substance rather than of legislative form, it may well be that the validity of the relevant provisions of the Sea Fisheries Regulations or their applicability to the respondents' possession of the crayfish referred to in the complaint will depend on the general circumstances in which those provisions would operate. To cover that contingency, the court has been furnished with an agreed statement of those circumstances. The statement reads:

1. The conservation of crayfish stocks in Tasmania depends upon effectively enforced legal minimum size regulations. It is common in all States of Australia and throughout the world to protect many species of fish by limiting their taking (and/or possession) according to a minimum size.

2. In Tasmania the breeding stock of crayfish is almost entirely made up of mature fish which are below the legal minimum size. Accordingly, fish may be taken above the [383] minimum legal size without endangering the future of the fishery.

3. In Tasmanian waters it takes approximately four years for a crayfish to reach maturity and be able to reproduce. The female crayfish has then a carapace length of approximately 70 mm, the male, a little greater. Measurement is made in the manner shown on the attached diagram.

4. Studies show that the mortality rate for young crayfish is such that an average of four years of breeding is necessary to maintain the current population level. After that time, the average female carapace length is approximately 105 mm and the male, 110 mm. Those sizes are thus set as the minimum permissible size at which the fish may be taken, with the object of thereby preserving stocks and ensuring the viability of the industry.

5. In South Australia the minimum size at which both male and female crayfish may be taken is 98.55 mm. Principally this reflects the fact that the reproduction of the species in South Australian waters is considered by the South Australian authorities to be protected by this minimum size of take in those waters.

6. Three hundred and thirty five fishing vessels are licensed to use a total of approximately 10,000 pots to fish for crayfish in Tasmanian waters. These vessels operate out of 22 ports around the State. Total sales realise approximately $16 m per annum at current prices in an average year.

7. At all relevant times to date, Tasmania had jurisdiction over fishing in coastal waters only to the three-mile limit. However, by virtue of a Commonwealth State agreement to become effective shortly, the jurisdiction will be extended to all waters in the 'Australian Fishing Zone' (ie approximately 200 kms offshore) south of lat 39°12'S.

8. The State does not have the personnel to police the legal minimum size regulation by any means other than random inspection and measurement, both at sea and when the catch is brought ashore. It is not possible on inspection to determine whether a particular crayfish has been caught in Tasmanian waters or elsewhere.

9. At all material times the second respondent's business involved the year-round export of live crayfish and, to maintain its market, it was necessary for the second respondent to purchase live crayfish from interstate during the month of October because the Tasmanian season is closed during that month.

10.   The subject crayfish were purchased pursuant to an oral contract by which the respondents agreed to take an entire catch of one of the vendor's fishing vessels.

It is unnecessary that we reproduce the diagram referred to in para 3 (above). The references in para 7 are, of course, to Tasmanian waters.

No provision of the Constitution has been the source of greater [384] judicial concern or the subject of greater judicial effort than s 92. That notwithstanding, judicial exegesis of the section has yielded neither clarity of meaning nor certainty of operation. Over the years the court has moved uneasily between one interpretation and another in its endeavours to solve the problems thrown up by the necessity to apply the very general language of the section to a wide variety of legislative and factual situations. Indeed, these shifts have been such as to make it difficult to speak of the section as having achieved a settled or accepted interpretation at any time since federation. The interpretation which came closest to achieving that degree of acceptance was that embodying the criterion of operation formula which we shall subsequently examine in some detail. That formula appeared to have the advantage of certainty, but that advantage proved to be illusory. Its disadvantage was that it was concerned only with the formal structure of an impugned law and ignored its real or substantive effect. It was in vogue during the 25 years that began with *Hospital Provident Fund Pty Ltd v Victoria* (1953) 87 CLR 1 and continued through to *Beal v Marrickville Margarine Pty Ltd* (1966) 114 CLR 283 and *Bartter's Farms Pty Ltd v Todd* (1978) 139 CLR 499, though the seeds of its decline were clearly visible in *Pilkington v Frank Hammond Pty Ltd* (1974) 131 CLR 124 and *North Eastern Dairy Co Ltd v Dairy Industry Authority of NSW* (1975) 134 CLR 559. In more recent years various members of the court have declined to accept and apply the criterion of operation formula. This process culminated in the two decisions on the Wheat Stabilisation Scheme — *Clark King & Co Pty Ltd v Australian Wheat Board* (1978) 140 CLR 120 and *Uebergang v Australian Wheat Board* (1980) 145 CLR 266 — in which the members of the court were unable to agree upon a common or a majority approach to the construction of the section. The divergence of opinion expressed in the judgments in *Uebergang* led Mason J in *Miller v TCN Channel Nine Pty Ltd* (1986) 161 CLR 556 at 571 to say that 'there is now no interpretation of s 92 that commands the acceptance of a majority of the court'. In the same case, Deane J observed (at 616) with reference to the decisions of the Judicial Committee of the Privy Council and of this court on s 92 that:

> ... it is as if many voices of authority have been speaking differently at the same time with the result that, putting to one side some basic propositions, it is all but impossible to comprehend precisely what it is that authority has said.

[385] His Honour, after reviewing and analysing the judgments in *Uebergang*, went on to say (at 618):

> *Clark King* and *Uebergang* demonstrated that the outcome of all the past cases was that the court was unable to give authoritative guidance or to express an authoritative view about the process of reasoning which was relevant to determine the constitutional validity of a national scheme which had been adopted by the Commonwealth and all the States for the marketing of one of the nation's most important commodities.

These comments cannot be gainsaid. They identify what we see as a quite unacceptable state of affairs.

In these circumstances, it is not surprising that the court is now pressed to reconsider the approximately 140 decisions of this court and of the Privy Council which have attempted to illuminate the meaning and operation of the section. Nor is it surprising that the section should have defied judicial attempts to define enduring criteria of its application, for its enigmatic text does not state the area of immunity which it guarantees. Though the text of the section is more than familiar, it is convenient to set out the relevant parts again in order to facilitate the examination of its history to which we shall shortly turn:

> On the imposition of uniform duties of customs, trade, commerce, and intercourse among the States, whether by means of internal carriage or ocean navigation, shall be absolutely free.

... Reference to the history of s 92 may be made, not for the purpose of substituting for the meaning of the words used the scope and effect — if such could be established — which the founding fathers subjectively intended the section to have, but for the purpose of identifying the contemporary meaning of language used, the subject to which that language was directed and the nature and objectives of the movement towards federation from which the compact of the Constitution finally emerged.

The justices referred at length to the restrictions on inter-colonial trade which were a consequence of different external tariffs established by the Australian colonies; to the push for a free trade area embracing the colonies; and to the debates at the three Federal Conventions, of 1891, 1897 and 1898, where the Commonwealth Constitution was drafted. Their Honours continued:

[391] The purpose of the section is clear enough: to create a free trade area throughout the Commonwealth and to deny to Commonwealth and States alike a power to prevent or obstruct the free movement of people, goods and communications across State boundaries. Free trade was understood to give 'equality of trade', which Mr McMillan (of the New South Wales delegation) asserted to be 'one grand principle involved in the whole of our federation': Convention Debates (Melbourne 1898), vol II, p 2345. The enemies of free trade were border taxes, discrimination, especially in railway freight rates, and preferences. Higgins pointed out: 'what will be the use of talking about free trade between the States, and diminishing the friction upon the borders, if we do not provide against a war of [392] railway rates?': ibid, p 1268. To complement the s 92 prohibition against discriminatory laws which prevented the free flow of trade, ss 99 and 102 were introduced to prohibit preferences.

The difficulties which inhere in s 92 flow from its origin as a rallying call for federationists who wanted to be rid of discriminatory burdens and benefits in trade and who would not suffer that call to be muffled by nice qualifications. By refraining from defining any limitation on the freedom guaranteed by s 92, the Conventions and the Constitution which they framed passed to the courts the task of defining what aspects of interstate trade, commerce and intercourse were excluded from legislative or executive control or regulation. Rich J in *James v Cowan* (1930) 43 CLR 386 at 422 lamented:

Some hint at least might have been dropped, some distant allusion made, from which the nature of the immunity intended could afterwards have been deduced by those whose lot it is to explain the elliptical and expound the unexpressed.

The creation of a limitation where none was expressed and where no words of limitation were acceptable was a task which, having regard to the diverse and changing nature of interstate trade, commerce and intercourse, was likely to produce a variety of propositions. And so it has. Sir Robert Garran contemplated that a student of the first 50 years of case law on s 92 might understandably 'close[] his notebook, sell his law books, and resolve[] to take up some easy study, like nuclear physics or higher mathematics': La Nauze, 'Absolutely Free', p 58 (quoting Garran, *Prosper the Commonwealth* (1958), p 415). Some 30 years on, the student who is confronted with the heightened confusion arising from the additional case law ending with *Miller v TCN Channel Nine* (1986) 161 CLR 556 would be even more encouraged to despair of identifying the effect of the constitutional guarantee.

Attention to the history which we have outlined may help to reduce the confusion that has surrounded the interpretation of s 92. That history demonstrates that the principal goals of the movement towards the federation of the Australian colonies included the elimination of intercolonial border duties and discriminatory burdens and preferences in intercolonial trade and the achievement of intercolonial free trade. As we have seen, apart from ss 99 and 102, that goal was enshrined in the various draft clauses which preceded s 92 and ultimately in the section itself.

The expression 'free trade' commonly signified in the nineteenth century, as it does today, an absence of protectionism, ie, the [393] protection of domestic industries against foreign competition. Such protection may be achieved by a variety of different measures — eg, tariffs that increase the price of foreign goods, non-tariff barriers such as quotas on imports, differential railway rates, subsidies on goods produced and discriminatory burdens on dealings with imports — which, alone or in combination, make importing and dealing with imports difficult or impossible. Sections 92, 99 and 102 were apt to eliminate these measures and thereby to ensure that the Australian States should be a free trade area in which legislative or executive discrimination against interstate trade and commerce should be prohibited. Section 92 precluded the imposition of protectionist burdens: not only interstate border customs duties but also burdens, whether fiscal or non-fiscal, which discriminated against interstate trade and commerce. That was the historical object of s 92 and the emphasis of the text of s 92 ensured that it was appropriate to attain it.

The two elements in s 92 which provide an arguable foundation for giving the section a wider operation with respect to trade and commerce than that foreshadowed by its history are the reference to 'intercourse' and the emphatic words 'absolutely free'. A constitutional guarantee of freedom of interstate intercourse, if it is to have substantial content, extends to a guarantee of personal freedom 'to pass to and fro among the States without burden, hindrance or restriction': *Gratwick v Johnson* (1945) 70 CLR 1 at 17. If s 92 were to be viewed in isolation from its history, the attachment of the guarantee to trade and commerce along with intercourse might suggest that interstate trade and commerce must also be left without any restriction or even regulatory burden or hindrance. That is not to suggest that every form of intercourse must be left without any restriction or regulation in order to satisfy the guarantee of freedom. For example, although personal movement across a border cannot, generally speaking, be impeded, it is legitimate to restrict a pedestrian's use of a highway for the purpose of his crossing or to authorise the arrest of a fugitive offender from one State at the moment of his departure into another State. It is not necessary now to consider the content of the guarantee of freedom of various forms of interstate intercourse. Much will depend on the form and circumstance of the intercourse involved. But it is clear that some forms of intercourse are so immune from legislative or executive interference that, if a like immunity were accorded to trade and commerce, anarchy would result. However, it has always been accepted that s 92 does not guarantee freedom in this sense, that is, in [394] the sense of anarchy: see eg, *Duncan v Queensland* (1916) 22 CLR 556 at 573; *Freightlines & Construction Holding Ltd v New South Wales* (1967) 116 CLR 1 at 4–5; [1968] AC 625 at 667. Once this is accepted, as it must be, there is no reason in logic or common sense for insisting on a strict correspondence between the freedom guaranteed to interstate trade and commerce and that guaranteed to interstate intercourse.

What we have just said is likewise an answer to the objection that the words 'absolutely free' are inconsistent with any interpretation of the section that concedes to interstate trade no more than a freedom from burdens of a limited kind, whether discriminatory or otherwise. Implicit in the rejection of the notion that the words 'absolutely free' are to be read in the abstract as a guarantee of anarchy is recognition of the need to identify the kinds or classes of legal burdens, restrictions, controls or standards from which the section guarantees the absolute freedom of interstate trade and commerce. As we have seen, the failure of the section to define expressly what interstate trade and commerce was to be immune from is to be explained by reference to the dictates of political expediency, not by reference to a purpose of prohibiting all legal burdens, restrictions, controls or standards. In that context, to construe s 92 as requiring that interstate trade and commerce be immune only from discriminatory burdens of a protectionist kind does not involve inconsistency with the words 'absolutely free': it is simply to identify the kinds or classes of burdens, restrictions, controls and standards from which the section guarantees absolute freedom.

The task which has confronted the court is to construe the unexpressed; to formulate in legal propositions, so far as the text of s 92 admits, the criteria for distinguishing between the burdens (including restrictions, controls and standards) to which interstate trade and commerce may be subjected by the exercise of legislative or executive power and the burdens from which interstate trade and commerce is immune. The history of s 92 points to the elimination of protection as the object of s 92 in its application to trade and commerce. The means by which that object is achieved is the prohibition of measures which burden interstate trade and commerce and which also have the effect of conferring protection on intrastate trade and commerce of the same kind. The general hallmark of measures which contravene s 92 in this way is their effect as discriminatory against interstate trade and commerce in that protectionist sense. There can be no doubt that s 92 guarantees [395] absolute freedom of interstate trade and commerce from all interstate border duties and other discriminatory fiscal charges levied on transactions of interstate trade and commerce. Indeed, the reference in each para of the section to uniform duties of Customs creates the impression that the provision is directed to fiscal charges and burdens. This impression is reinforced by the context provided by the surrounding provisions, ss 89–91 and ss 93–5. All these provisions deal with fiscal charges and burdens, appearing, as they do, in Ch IV of the Constitution which is headed 'Finance and Trade'. But the section cannot be easily confined to such matters because protection against interstate trade and commerce can be secured by non-fiscal measures.

In relation to both fiscal and non-fiscal measures, history and context alike favour the approach that the freedom guaranteed to interstate trade and commerce under s 92 is freedom from discriminatory burdens in the protectionist sense already mentioned ...

The justices referred to the Privy Council's decision in *James v Commonwealth* (1936) 55 CLR 1, which had 'provided support for the development of the doctrine of criterion of operation': 165 CLR at 397. They continued:

[398] The impact that the interpretation favoured by history and context would have on the Commonwealth's legislative power under s 51(i) was not closely explored in argument in the present case. For this reason alone we would be reluctant to attempt to express an exhaustive opinion upon that topic, even if it were possible to do so, or to identify the precise effects of the interaction between ss 51(i), 90, 92, 99 and 102, a matter that has not been examined in the decided cases. It is, however, necessary for present purposes that we make some general reference to the relationship between s 51(i) and s 92 for the reason that the guarantee of the absolute freedom of interstate trade and commerce contained in s 92 must be read in the context of the express conferral of legislative power with respect to such trade and commerce which is contained in s 51(i).

We do not accept the explanation suggested in *Grannall v Marrickville Margarine Pty Ltd* (1955) 93 CLR 55 at 77–8, that the key to the relationship between s 51(i) and s 92 is to be found in the presence of the words 'with respect to' in the opening words of s 51(i). The consequence of reconciling the two constitutional provisions in that way is to treat the legislative power conferred by s 51(i) as essentially peripheral in character. In our view, any acceptable appreciation of the interrelationship between the two sections must recognise that s 51(i) is a plenary power on a topic of fundamental importance. That being so, the express conferral of legislative power with respect to interstate trade and commerce lends some support for the view that s 92 should not be construed as precluding an exercise of legislative power which would impose any burden or restriction on interstate trade and commerce or on an essential attribute of that trade and commerce. Obviously, the provision conferring legislative power (s 51(i)) and the provision restricting the exercise of legislative power (s 92) sit more easily together if the latter is construed as being concerned with precluding particular types of burdens, such as discriminatory burdens of a protectionist kind. That is not to suggest that, if s 92 were construed in that more limited sense of being concerned with discriminatory burdens upon interstate trade and commerce, the relationship between s 51(i) and s 92 would be freed from all difficulty. Upon analysis, however, the remaining difficulty would be largely superficial. Certainly it would [399] not be any greater and it might be less than the difficulty of the relationship between s 51(i) and s 92 which is attendant upon other arguable constructions of the constitutional guarantee.

The above concept of discrimination commonly involves the notion of a departure from equality of treatment. It does not follow that every departure from equality of treatment imposes a burden or would infringe a constitutional guarantee of the freedom of interstate trade and commerce from discriminatory burdens. Nor does it follow that to construe s 92 as guaranteeing the freedom of interstate trade and commerce from discriminatory burdens would mean that interstate trade and commerce was rendered immune from any regulation which did not affect like intrastate trade. Such regulation might not constitute a burden at all. Even if it did, it might not be discriminatory in the sense to which we have referred. In that regard, experience teaches that Commonwealth legislation is often directed to the regulation of all trade within the Commonwealth's legislative reach (eg, the Trade Practices Act 1974 (Cth)) or to the regulation of a particular trade to the extent that it is within that reach. There is far less likelihood that such regulatory legislation will properly be characterised as imposing a discriminatory burden on the trade and commerce with which it deals than is the case with State legislation which singles out interstate trade and commerce for particular treatment. That is not to deny that a Commonwealth law which is regulatory on its face may operate so as to discriminate against interstate trade and commerce. Even a law which applies indiscriminately to all trade and commerce within the reach of Commonwealth legislative power might, in some circumstances, impose a discriminatory burden upon interstate trade and commerce. Plainly, however, the construction which treats s 92 as being concerned to guarantee the freedom of interstate trade and commerce from discriminatory burdens does not involve the consequence that the grant of legislative power with respect to interstate trade and commerce is deprived of its essential content.

The concept of discrimination in its application to interstate trade and commerce necessarily embraces factual discrimination as well as legal operation. A law will discriminate against interstate trade or commerce if the law on its face subjects that trade or commerce to a disability or disadvantage or if the factual operation of the law produces such a result. A majority of the court (Barwick CJ, Stephen, Mason and Jacobs JJ) so held in *North Eastern Dairy* (1975) 134 CLR at 588–9, 602, 606–7, 622–3. And the more recent decisions proceed upon that footing. The court [400] looks to the practical operation of the law in order to determine its validity. Once this is recognised, it is difficult, indeed impossible, to deny that a Commonwealth law dealing with interstate trade could operate in such a way as to work an impermissible discrimination against interstate trade, in particular the trade across State borders originating in a particular State. For reasons already given, we should not venture into this topic in any depth. However, we would add two comments. The first is that the possibility of factual discrimination by a s 51(i) law applying only in respect of interstate trade or commerce may well be eliminated in the context of a national scheme constituted by complementary Commonwealth and State law applying, by virtue of their combined operation, to all trade or commerce of the relevant kind. The second is that s 92 will obviously operate to preclude discriminatory burdens being imposed upon interstate trade or commerce by Commonwealth laws enacted pursuant to other general heads of legislative power (eg, trading corporations).

The justices said that the 'criterion of operation formula' had failed to command the acceptance of the court for several reasons:

The thrust of the criterion of operation was to make inapplicable to interstate trade, commerce and intercourse any law which 'takes a [401] fact or an event or a thing itself forming part of trade commerce or intercourse, or forming an essential attribute of that conception ... and the law proceeds, by reference thereto or in consequence thereof, to impose a restriction, a burden or a liability' which constitutes 'a real prejudice or impediment to interstate transactions ...'. The words quoted are taken from the formulation in *Hospital Provident Fund* (1953) 87 CLR at 17.

The doctrine is highly artificial. It depends on the formal and obscure distinction between the essential attributes of trade and commerce and those facts, events or things which are inessential, incidental, or, indeed, antecedent or preparatory to that trade and commerce. This distinction mirrors another distinction equally unsatisfactory, between burdens which are direct and immediate (proscribed) and those that are indirect, consequential and remote (not proscribed). What is more, the first limb of the doctrine as enunciated looks to the legal operation of the law rather than to its practical operation or its economic consequences. The emphasis on the legal operation of the law gave rise to a concern that the way was open to circumvention by means of legislative device ...

With the advantage of hindsight it is now obvious that such an artificial formula would create problems in the attempt to apply it to a variety of legislative situations. In a context in which the doctrine was seen as supporting a constitutional guarantee of the right of the individual to engage in interstate trade, it scarcely seemed to make sense to say that production for the purpose of trading interstate with the product (*Grannall v Marrickville Margarine Pty Ltd*; *Beal v Marrickville Margarine Pty Ltd*) and importation of aircraft with which to engage in interstate air transportation (*R v Anderson; Ex parte Ipec-Air Pty Ltd* (1965) 113 CLR 177; *Ansett Transport Industries (Operations) Pty Ltd v Commonwealth* (1977) 139 CLR 54) fell outside the constitutional protection on the ground that the relevant activities were not essential attributes of interstate trade ...

[402] In truth the history of the doctrine is an indication of the hazards of seeking certainty of operation of a constitutional guarantee through the medium of an artificial formula. Either the formula is consistently applied and subverts the substance of the guarantee; or an attempt is made to achieve uniformly satisfactory outcomes and the formula becomes uncertain in its application.

What we have said explains some of the reasons the criterion of operation ceased to command the acceptance of members of the court, with the consequence that we do not see ourselves as constrained by authority to accept it. There are other features of the doctrine which compel its rejection as an acceptable interpretation of s 92. First, in some respects the protection which it offers to interstate trade is too wide. Instead of placing interstate trade on an equal footing with intrastate trade, the doctrine keeps interstate trade on a privileged or preferred footing, immune from burdens to which other trade is subject ...

[403] The second major reason for rejecting the doctrine as an acceptable interpretation of s 92 is that it fails to make any accommodation for the need for laws genuinely regulating intrastate and interstate trade. The history of the movement for abolition of colonial protection and for the achievement of intercolonial free trade does not indicate that it was intended to prohibit genuine non-protective regulation of intercolonial or interstate trade. The criterion of operation makes no concession to this aspect of the section's history. In the result there has been a continuing tension between the general application of the formula and the validity of laws which are purely regulatory in character. Judged by reference to the doctrine, the validity of a regulatory law hinged on whether it imposed a burden on an essential attribute or on a mere incident of trade or commerce. To say the least of it, this was not an appropriate criterion of validity of a regulatory law divorced, as it is, from considerations of the protectionist purpose or effect of the impugned law. It is not surprising that the court found it necessary to develop a concept of a permissible 'burden' which was associated with a somewhat ill-defined notion of what is legitimate regulation in an ordered society: see *Hughes and Vale (No 2)* (1955) 93 CLR 127 at 217–19; *Samuels v* [404] *Readers' Digest Association Pty Ltd* (1969) 120 CLR 1 at 19–20; *North Eastern Dairy* (1975) 134 CLR at 614–15, 621–2; *Permewan Wright Consolidated Pty Ltd v Trewhitt* (1979) 145 CLR 1 at p 26. The problems which have arisen in this area culminating in *Clark King* (1978) 140 CLR 120 and *Uebergang* (1980) 145 CLR 266 are the inevitable consequence of any interpretation of s 92 which offers protection to interstate trade going beyond immunity from discriminatory burdens having a protectionist purpose or effect.

The justices noted that, in *Bank of New South Wales v Commonwealth* (1948) 76 CLR 1 at 386–7, Dixon J 'drew support from the opinion of Frankfurter J in *Freeman v Hewitt* 329 US 249 (1946)', which had extended the reach of the commerce clause in the United States Constitution so as to protect interstate commerce from non-discriminatory state action which had the effect of impeding the free flow of trade between states. While discounting the significance of the United States interpretation of the commerce clause (165 CLR at 405), the justices pointed out that *Freeman v Hewitt* had been unanimously overruled in *Complete Auto Transit, Inc v Brady* 430 US 274 (1977), and that the current interpretation of the negative aspect of the commerce clause gave it 'an anti-discriminatory focus': 165 CLR at 406. They referred to the view of Murphy J, that s 92 guarantees freedom from fiscal imposts only, and said: 'It would make no sense at all if the section prohibited tariff duties but allowed other forms of protection of domestic industry (eg, complete prohibition of imports) as barriers to interstate trade': 165 CLR at 407. The justices continued:

[407] Departing now from the doctrine which has failed to retain general acceptance, we adopt the interpretation which, as we have shown, is favoured by history and context. In doing so, we must say something about the resolution of cases in which no impermissible purpose appears on the face of the impugned law, but its effect is discriminatory in that it discriminates against interstate trade and commerce and thereby protects intrastate trade and commerce of the same kind. We mention first Commonwealth laws enacted under s 51(i) which govern the conduct of interstate trade and commerce. Such laws will commonly not appear to discriminate in a relevant sense if they apply to all transactions of a given kind within the reach of the Parliament. It is, however, possible for a general law enacted under s 51(i) to offend s 92 if its effect is discriminatory and the discrimination is upon protectionist grounds. Whether such a law is discriminatory in effect and whether the discrimination is of a protectionist character are questions raising issues of fact and [408] degree. The answer to those questions may, in the ultimate, depend upon judicial impression. That is, however, merely a reflection of the absence from the text of s 92 of any criterion by reference to which 'such regulations as may be necessary for the conduct of business' (to recall Parkes' original phrase) might be distinguished from laws which infringe the guarantee of free trade and the absence of protection. Indeed, the principal reason so much past judicial effort to elucidate and settle the content of the guarantee given by s 92 was foredoomed to fail was the impossibility of extracting from an intended guarantee of freedom from discriminatory protectionism a formula which was capable of automatic application by reference to the formal operation of a law.

In the case of a State law, the resolution of the case must start with a consideration of the nature of the law impugned. If it applies to all trade and commerce, interstate and intrastate alike, it is less likely to be protectionist than if there is discrimination appearing on the face of the law. But where the law in effect, if not in form, discriminates in favour of intrastate trade, it will nevertheless offend against s 92 if the discrimination is of a protectionist character. A law which has as its real object the prescription of a standard for a product or a service or a norm of commercial conduct will not ordinarily be grounded in protectionism and will not be prohibited by s 92. But if a law, which may be otherwise justified by reference to an object which is not protectionist, discriminates against interstate trade or commerce in pursuit of that object in a way or to an extent which warrants characterisation of the law as protectionist, a court will be justified in concluding that it nonetheless offends s 92.

The adoption of an interpretation prohibiting the discriminatory burdening of interstate trade will not of course resolve all problems. It does, however, permit the identification of the relevant questions and a belated acknowledgment of the implications of the long-accepted perception that 'although the decision [whether an impugned law infringes s 92] was one for a court of law the problems were likely to be largely political, social or economic': *Freightlines & Construction Holding Ltd* (1967) 116 CLR at 5. Inevitably the adoption of a new principle of law, though facilitating the resolution of old problems, brings a new array of questions in its wake. The five traditional examples of protection of domestic industry which we gave earlier are by no means exclusive or comprehensive. The means by which domestic industry or trade can be advantaged or [409] protected are legion. The consequence is that there will always be scope for difficult questions of fact in determining whether particular legislative or executive measures constitute discriminatory interference with interstate trade. And acquisition of a commodity may still involve the potential for conflict with s 92. That problem does not now arise.

The question which we must now determine is whether reg 31(1)(d) of the Sea Fisheries Regulations which reveals no discriminatory purpose on its face is impermissibly discriminatory in effect. In other words, whether the burden which the regulation imposes on interstate trade in crayfish goes beyond the prescription of a reasonable standard to be observed in all crayfish trading and, if so, whether the substantial effect of that regulation is to impose a burden which so disadvantages interstate trade in crayfish as to raise a protective barrier around Tasmanian trade in crayfish. The latter questions are questions of fact and degree on which minds might legitimately differ.

The regulation neither operates at the border or frontier nor distinguishes between local and interstate trade or produce. However, the limitation on the size of crayfish that may be sold or possessed in Tasmania is unquestionably a burden on the interstate trade and commerce in crayfish caught in South Australian waters and sold in Tasmania. But does it bear the character of being discriminatory against that interstate trade and commerce? The prohibitions against the sale and possession of undersized crayfish apply alike to crayfish caught in Tasmanian waters and to those that are imported. In that respect no discriminatory protectionist purpose appears on the face of the law. Furthermore, the object of the prohibitions, in conjunction with the prohibition against catching undersized crayfish, is to assist in the protection and conservation of an important and valuable natural resource, the stock of Tasmanian crayfish. Although the legislation operates in this way to protect the Tasmanian crayfish industry, it is not a form of protection that gives Tasmanian crayfish production or intrastate trade and commerce a competitive or market advantage over imported crayfish or the trade in such crayfish. And, even if the legislation were to give an advantage to the local trade by improving the competitive qualities of mature Tasmanian crayfish by eliminating undersized imported crayfish from the local market, the agreed facts make it clear that the extension of the prohibitions against sale and possession to imported crayfish is a necessary means of enforcing the prohibition against the catching of undersized crayfish in Tasmanian waters. The State cannot undertake inspections other than random inspections and the local crayfish are indistinguishable from those **[410]** imported from South Australia. On the materials before the court, the legislation and the burden which it imposes on interstate trade and commerce are not properly to be described as relevantly discriminatory and protectionist.

It follows that question (b) of the questions identified in the order of removal should be answered: Yes.

We would therefore set aside the order of the magistrate dismissing the complaint and remit the matter to the Supreme Court of Tasmania.

~~~

Notes

[10.4.28] The single judgment in *Cole v Whitfield* (1988) 165 CLR 360 **[10.4.27C]** was clearly conceived by the court as providing a new start for the jurisprudence of s 92. In two significant ways it cleared away the complex and confused structure developed through judicial construction and application of the section. First, the judgment unequivocally rejected the 39-year-old established criterion of reading of s 92 as offering to interstate traders a special protection against government controls. The function of the section was not to express the *laissez-faire* economic philosophy which had dominated the judicial reading of the section since *Australian National Airways Pty Ltd v Commonwealth* (1945) 71 CLR 29 **[10.4.9]** but to express the concept of free trade which had been one of the principal staples of colonial politics and which had formed the basis for the earliest decisions on s 92, such as *Fox v Robbins* (1909) 8 CLR 115 **[10.4.8]** and *Duncan v Queensland* (1916) 22 CLR 556. That rejection, in favour of a reading which prohibited differential treatment of or discrimination against interstate trade, was justified as reflecting the history and original purpose of s 92; as removing the need (reflected in the concept of 'reasonable regulation') to qualify the section's 'absolute' freedom; as eliminating the 'protectionism in reverse' which the 'criterion of operation' reading of s 92 gave to interstate trade; and as leaving more scope for necessary public interest controls of trade and commerce.

Second, the judgment endorsed the relevance of practical and economic considerations, rather than narrow legal analysis, to the resolution of s 92 problems.

The court indicated a two-stage approach to determining whether a government control discriminated against interstate trade in a protectionist fashion. The first question would be whether a 'law on its face' subjected interstate trade to a disability: Was it, in its legal operation, discriminatory? The second question would be whether 'the factual operation of the law' produced that result: 165 CLR at 399. (Embedded in this reference to a dual approach (using legal analysis and an assessment of factual operation) was an ambiguity which emerged within a few weeks in *Bath v Alston Holdings Pty Ltd* (1988) 165 CLR 411 **[10.4.34C]**: were the two approaches alternative in a negative, invalidating, sense or in a positive, validating sense? See **[10.4.35]**.)

[10.4.29]   Each of the basic propositions expressed in *Cole v Whitfield* (1988) 165 CLR 360 **[10.4.27C]** had been foreshadowed by members of the court. The return to a free trade, anti-discrimination, reading of s 92 had been suggested by Mason and Jacobs JJ in *Finemores Transport Pty Ltd v New South Wales* (1978) 139 CLR 338 at 352, 354; and by Mason and Deane JJ in *Miller v TCN Channel Nine Pty Ltd* (1986) 161 CLR 556 **[10.4.26]** at 571, 618. (A return to the free trade approach had also been urged by two of Australia's most respected academic commentators on the Commonwealth Constitution: Coper (1983) p 293; Zines (1987) pp 143–5.) Further, the proposition that the court must consider the practical operation of legislation, its real impact on commercial transactions and relationships, had been endorsed by a majority of the court in *North Eastern Dairy Co Ltd v Dairy Industry Authority of New South Wales* (1975) 134 CLR 559 **[10.4.23]**.

[10.4.30]   What effect would the court's adoption of these two basic propositions in *Cole v Whitfield* (1988) 165 CLR 360 **[10.4.27C]** have on the catalogue of decisions, accumulated over the previous 40 years? To answer that question we should need to ask of each form of government control whether it discriminated in a protectionist fashion against interstate trade either as a matter of legal form or in practical operation.

To take only a few of the entries in the catalogue, it would seem that s 46 of the Banking Act 1947 (Cth) would not be invalid, thus reversing *Commonwealth v Bank of New South Wales* (1949) 79 CLR 497 **[10.4.10C]**, although a discriminatory exercise of the Treasurer's power in s 46(4) would run foul of s 92. The State Transport (Co-ordination) Act 1931 (NSW) would not be invalid, thus reversing *Hughes and Vale Pty Ltd v New South Wales (No 1)* (1954) 93 CLR 1 **[10.4.14]**, again subject to a caveat against discriminatory exercises of the licensing power. However, the Pure Food Regulations and the Dairy Industry Act 1970 (NSW) would, because of their practical impact on interstate producers' trade in milk, still contravene s 92, thus confirming the decision in *North Eastern Dairy Co Ltd v Dairy Industry Authority of New South Wales* (1975) 134 CLR 559 **[10.4.23]**.

[10.4.31]   The revisionist impact of the decision in *Cole v Whitfield* (1988) 165 CLR 360 **[10.4.27C]** is demonstrated by the High Court's decision in *Barley Marketing Board (NSW) v Norman* (1990) 171 CLR 182. The Marketing of Primary Products Act 1983 (NSW) authorised the Governor of New South Wales to transfer ownership of any barley grown in the state to the Barley Marketing Board, to be marketed by the Board as a pool; and declared invalid every contract for the sale of barley which was not made by the Board.

In a unanimous judgment the High Court (Mason CJ, Brennan, Deane, Dawson, Toohey, Gaudron and McHugh JJ) decided that the Act did not contravene s 92, even where growers would otherwise have sold their barley interstate. The court held that, although the purpose and effect of the Act was to protect the barley industry in New South Wales, the Act did not do so by discriminating against commercial interests in other states. The legislation was not shown to restrict the supply of barley to out-of-state purchasers, nor to impose a greater burden on interstate traders than the burden on intrastate traders.

The court noted that marketing schemes had often come into conflict with s 92, and that, under the former approach to that section, the price of validity of such schemes had been to concede freedom to producers to dispose of their product interstate. However, the earlier decisions on marketing schemes had 'proceeded according to the so-called "individual rights" theory of s 92, namely, that the section guarantees the right of the individual to engage in interstate trade and commerce'. Once that theory was displaced by *Cole v Whitfield* (1988) 165 CLR 360 **[10.4.27C]**, the authority of the earlier decisions was open to question: 171 CLR at 201. The court declined to follow two earlier decisions, *Peanut Board v Rockhampton Harbour Board* (1933) 48 CLR 266 and *Australian Coarse Grains Pool Pty Ltd v Barley Marketing Board* (1985) 157 CLR 605.

[10.4.32]   If the decision and reasoning in *Cole v Whitfield* (1988) 165 CLR 360 **[10.4.27C]** have displaced the 'criterion of operation' analysis of s 92 problems, does it follow that the concept of permissible regulation is no longer relevant to that analysis? The concept had been offered by the Privy Council in *Commonwealth v Bank of New South Wales* (1949) 79 CLR 497 at 639 **[10.4.10C]** as a means of modifying the *laissez-faire* impact of the 'criterion of operation' approach and had invited judges to resolve s 92 problems in terms which would be 'not so much legal as political, social or economic'. As shown by the various judgments in, for example, *Permewan Wright Consolidated Pty Ltd v Trewhitt* (1979) 145 CLR 1 **[10.4.24]** and *Uebergang v Australian Wheat Board* (1980) 145 CLR 266 **[10.4.25]**, this form of analysis sharply divided the High Court and laid bare underlying and fundamental differences of judicial opinion over the role of law and government regulation in the Australian economy. In *Cole v Whitfield*, the court was critical of the 'somewhat ill-defined notion of what is legitimate regulation in an ordered society' (165 CLR at 403) speaking in terms which suggested that its rejection of the 'criterion of operation' approach would put an end to the need to work with that 'ill-defined notion'.

However, earlier in its judgment in *Cole v Whitfield*, the court had cautioned that some regulations directed at interstate trade might not amount to a discriminatory (that is, protectionist) burden on that trade: 165 CLR at 399. Reading this caveat in context, it seems that the court was not proposing to retain the 'permissible regulation' concept as an exception to the revived free trade, anti-protectionist view of s 92. Rather, the court was stressing that legislation which singled out interstate trade for special treatment would only offend s 92 if it placed a burden on that trade which had the effect of giving local trade an advantage; that is, if it was protectionist.

The emphasis on s 92 as a free trade, anti-protectionist mandate seems to leave little room for a reasonable regulation exception. Where government controls apply without discrimination to local and interstate trade and do not operate so as to disadvantage interstate trade, there will be no need to resort to any exception in order to validate the controls. We need expect no revival of the incomplete inquiry into the wheat stabilisation scheme, last debated in *Uebergang v Australian Wheat Board* (1980) 145 CLR 266 **[10.4.25]**. On the other hand, where government controls discriminate against interstate trade by subjecting it to a different legal regime from that imposed on local trade for the purpose of protecting that local trade, it is difficult to conceive how the differential treatment could be rationalised as reasonable regulation. Perhaps where the discrimination results from the 'factual operation' of the controls rather than different legal rules, the question could legitimately arise whether the controls are a reasonable means for protecting some public interest.

[10.4.33] The prospect of a critical reexamination of so much 'settled law' on the consistency of various government controls with s 92 is only part of the potential impact of *Cole v Whitfield* (1988) 165 CLR 360 **[10.4.27C]**. As the court pointed out, '[t]he adoption of an interpretation prohibiting the discriminatory burdening of interstate trade will not of course resolve all problems [because it] brings a new array of questions in its wake': 165 CLR at 408. By the time *Cole v Whitfield* was delivered, the justices must have been close to settling the majority and minority judgments in *Bath v Alston Holdings Pty Ltd* (1988) 165 CLR 411 **[10.4.34C]**. The observation in *Cole v Whitfield* that 'there will always be scope for difficult questions of fact' in identifying discrimination (165 CLR at 409) is, therefore, given particular point by the context in which it was made.

[10.4.34C]   **Bath v Alston Holdings Pty Ltd**
                              (1988) 165 CLR 411

The Business Franchise (Tobacco) Act 1974 (Vic) prohibited a person from selling tobacco in Victoria, whether by wholesale or retail, unless licensed. The fees for a wholesale tobacco merchant's licence and for a retail tobacconist's licence were, apart from a small flat fee, equal to 25 per cent of the value of the tobacco sold by the applicant for the licence during a period which had passed: s 10(1). In calculating the fee for a retail tobacconist's licence the value of certain tobacco was to be disregarded, namely 'tobacco purchased in Victoria from the holder of a wholesale tobacco merchant's licence': s 10(1)(c), (d).

 Alston Holdings Pty Ltd carried on business as a retail tobacconist in Victoria. It did not hold a licence under the Business Franchise (Tobacco) Act. In January 1987, Alston Holdings purchased tobacco products with a value of $26,607.48 from a tobacco wholesaler in Queensland, and arranged for the tobacco to be transported to its premises in Victoria. In January and February 1987 Alston sold this tobacco by retail to members of the public in Victoria. (This series of transactions was typical of Alston Holding's general method of business.) Bath, the Victorian Commissioner of Business Franchises, commenced proceedings in the Supreme Court of Victoria against Alston Holdings seeking an injunction to restrain Alston from selling tobacco otherwise than pursuant to a licence under the Business Franchise (Tobacco) Act. The proceedings were removed to the High Court of Australia by an order under s 40 of the Judiciary Act 1903 (Cth).

 Mason CJ, acting under s 18 of the Judiciary Act, reserved several questions for the consideration of the Full Court. The central question was whether s 10(l)(c) and (d) contravened s 92 of the Commonwealth Constitution in that the fees which they imposed discriminated against interstate trade.

Mason CJ, Brennan, Deane and Gaudron JJ: [423] Stated in summary terms, Alston's argument is that the [424] Act discriminates against interstate trade in tobacco products and against interstate wholesalers by effectively selecting as the basis of calculation of the ad valorem content of the retailer's licence fee the value of the actual or imputed sales of interstate products during the relevant earlier period. Reliance is placed upon *Fox v Robbins* (1909) 8 CLR 115.

The starting point of a consideration of Alston's argument is the plain fact that what is involved is the imposition of a tax. There is no question of mere regulation of the activities of sellers of tobacco products. Indeed, the Commissioner did not contend to the contrary. If the tax had been imposed directly on all retail sales of tobacco products in Victoria, it would not have infringed the injunction of s 92 of the Constitution. It would have been a tax which applied without differentiation or discrimination to interstate and intrastate products and transactions. Such a tax would, however, have been invalid in that it would have been an excise duty which it was beyond the constitutional competence of the Victorian parliament to impose (Constitution s 90). The tax imposed by the Act escapes invalidity as an excise duty only by reason of its character as a fee for a licence or franchise to carry on a business of selling tobacco products during a future period, calculated by reference to past actual or imputed sales (see *Dennis Hotels Pty Ltd v Victoria* (1960) 104 CLR 529; *Dickenson's Arcade Pty Ltd v Tasmania* (1974) 130 CLR 177; *Evda Nominees Pty Ltd v Victoria* (1984) 154 CLR 311). Not surprisingly, the Commissioner does not seek to argue that the tax should be seen otherwise than as what it purports to be, namely, not a tax upon goods but a fee exacted from retailers of tobacco products for a licence essential for the lawful carrying on of their respective businesses. That being so, the essential question is whether the statutory imposition upon a retailer of the obligation to pay a licence fee calculated in the manner provided by the Act is, in the circumstances, properly to be characterised as discriminatory against interstate trade and commerce in a protectionist sense (see *Cole v Whitfield* (1988) 165 CLR at 360).

The requirement of the Act that a Victorian retailer of tobacco products be licensed applies indifferently to retailers of both local and interstate products. Of itself, the requirement does not contravene s 92 of the Constitution. If the Act imposed the *ad valorem* licence fee by reference to the value of all tobacco products sold by a retailer in the relevant period, the imposition of the fee would not contravene s 92 since it would not differentiate between tobacco purchased in Victoria and tobacco purchased outside Victoria; a **[425]** fortiori it would not discriminate in a protectionist sense against the purchase of tobacco outside Victoria. The exclusion of tobacco purchased in Victoria from a licensed wholesaler from the total sale value of tobacco used as the basis of the calculation of the *ad valorem* licence fee does, however, involve an element of differentiation and at least prima facie discrimination. Since the effect of the Act is to require all Victorian wholesalers selling tobacco products in Victoria to be licensed, the tobacco products purchased by the ordinary Victorian retailer from a local wholesaler will, for practical purposes, be all purchased from the holder of a wholesaler's licence under the Act. That being so, the exclusion of tobacco purchased in Victoria from the holder of a wholesaler's licence from the value of tobacco sold in the relevant preceding period has the effect that, for practical purposes, the licence fee paid by a Victorian retailer will ordinarily consist of the flat fee of $50 (for an indefinite licence: s 10(1)(c)) or $10 (for a monthly licence: s 10(1)(d)) together with an amount equal to 25 per cent of the value of any tobacco purchased from an interstate wholesaler. In other words, the retailer who sells only tobacco products purchased by him from a Victorian wholesaler will pay the appropriate flat fee for his licence, while a retailer who sells only tobacco products purchased from an interstate wholesaler will pay that flat fee plus 25 per cent of the value of tobacco sold in the preceding relevant period. It follows that, if they be viewed in isolation, the provisions of the Act imposing the obligation to pay a retail tobacconist's licence fee of $50 or $10 plus an amount calculated by reference to the value of tobacco sold which has not been purchased in Victoria from a licensed wholesaler, discriminate against interstate purchases of tobacco in favour of purchases in Victoria. If it be viewed in isolation, that discrimination is undeniably protectionist both in form and substance. In form, the provisions of s 10(1)(c) and (d) select the fact that tobacco was 'purchased in Victoria' from a licensed wholesaler as the qualifying condition for exemption from inclusion in the products by reference to which liability to *ad valorem* tax is calculated. In substance, those provisions protect local wholesalers and the tobacco products they sell from the competition of an out of State wholesaler whose products might be cheaper in some other Australian market place for a variety of possible reasons, for example, that the laws of the State in which he carries on his business as a wholesaler either do not require that he hold a licence at all or exact a licence fee comparatively lower than the fee exacted from a Victorian wholesaler.

Even when the provisions of the Act imposing the liability to pay the retail tobacconist's licence fee are read in the context of the Act [426] as a whole, they retain their discriminatory and protectionist character. Such a reading reveals the explanation for the exclusion from the basis of calculation of the retailer's licence fee of tobacco products purchased within Victoria from a licensed wholesaler. That explanation is that the licence fee which the Act requires Victorian wholesalers to pay to the Victorian Government will not have been paid to the Victorian Government by an out of State wholesaler who does not carry on business in Victoria and therefore does not require a licence in that State. The explanation tends, however, to underline, rather than remove, the protectionist character of the discrimination at the retail level effected by the provisions imposing the tax. If wholesalers of tobacco products in another State already pay taxes and bear other costs which are reflected in wholesale prices equal to or higher than those charged by Victorian wholesalers, the practical effects of the discrimination involved in the calculation of the retailer's licence fee would be likely to be that the out of State wholesalers would be excluded from selling into Victoria and that the products which they would otherwise sell in interstate trade would be effectively excluded from the Victorian market. On the other hand, if out of State wholesalers pay less taxes and other costs than their Victorian counterparts, and in particular if they pay no (or a lower) wholesale licence fee, the effect of the discriminatory tax upon retailers will be to protect the Victorian wholesalers and the Victorian products from the competition of the wholesalers operating in the State with the lower cost structure. Either way, the operation and effect of the provisions of the Act imposing the retail tobacconist's licence fee are discriminatory against interstate trade in a protectionist sense. For practical purposes, their operation is to impose on Victorian retailers who, during the relevant earlier period, purchased tobacco products both locally and in the markets of another State, an obligation to pay to Victorian consolidated revenue an *ad valorem* tax calculated by reference to the sale value of so much of those products as came from interstate. Ignoring the flat fee of $50 or $10, the effect of s 10(1)(c) and (d) is to discriminate against tobacco products sold by wholesalers in the markets of another State and to protect both Victorian wholesalers and the products which they sell from the competition of out of State wholesalers and their products. The wholesaler's licence fee, imposed on local wholesalers by reference to all their local sales, does not infringe s 92 in that it does not discriminate against goods coming from another State. The *ad valorem* content of the retailer's licence fee does infringe s 92 in that it discriminates against interstate trade and commerce in a protectionist sense by taxing a retailer only because of, and by reference to the value of, his actual or imputed purchases of products in any State other than Victoria.

Mason CJ, Brennan, Deane and Gaudron JJ rejected an argument that the tax on retailers was 'equivalent' to the tax on wholesalers, and intended simply to ensure that the tax fell indiscriminately on all goods sold in Victoria:

[428] [I]t provides no answer to the question whether, for the purposes of s 92, a particular tax is properly to be characterised as discriminatory in a protectionist sense to say that it is but one method of collecting a 'tax on goods' which is imposed in an equal amount in respect of all local and imported goods of that kind. If a tax is challenged on the ground that it offends s 92, it is necessary first to identify what is the transaction or thing which attracts liability. If the tax is imposed, whether directly or indirectly, on a transaction in the chain of distribution of goods, the relevant inquiry is whether the tax is imposed only on transactions where the goods involved have come from or are going to another State or whether the tax is imposed on all transactions of the relevant kind without differentiation based on the source or destination of the goods involved. If the tax is imposed on transactions in a particular market — in this case, the Victorian retail tobacco market — it is the effect of the tax on transactions in that market which is material. In this case, the effect is on the supply of goods to that market. The effect [429] of an equivalent tax on transactions at another stage in the chain of distribution of the same goods or goods of the same kind is immaterial. That must be so unless

s 92 permits the protection of an entire chain of distribution of goods within a State against competition from goods which might otherwise enter the chain from interstate. That proposition has only to be stated to be rejected. If that proposition were accepted, s 92 would present no impediment to the imposition of border duties — at all events if they did not exceed the amount necessary to place on interstate goods a tax burden equivalent to the tax burden earlier placed on similar goods already in the local chain of distribution. As Barton J commented in *Fox v Robbins* (1909) 8 CLR at 123:

> By burdens of this kind and that, whether under the name of licence fees or under any other name, the operation of interstate free trade could be so hampered and restricted as to reduce the Constitution in that regard to mere futility ... There is no difference in substance or effect in its bearing on interstate commerce between a burden such as this and a duty collected at the borders or the ports of one State on the products of another. In either case that commerce is restricted which the Constitution says shall be free; and in either case the disability may be made so great as to render the product unsaleable, and therefore virtually to prohibit its introduction.

A tax upon retailers in respect of their trading in goods may burden their trade in interstate goods consistently with the guarantee of s 92 only if it applies equally to the interstate and local goods which the retailers sell; it cannot lawfully discriminate between them so as to protect the local goods. Again to quote the words of Barton J in *Fox v Robbins* (1909) 8 CLR at 124:

> When the interstate transit is over and they have become part of the mass of property within the State, any goods may be taxed, no matter whence they have come. But they must be taxed alike with all other such goods in the State. The tax must be general, and laid equally on all goods of the kind to be taxed, whether their State of origin be the taxing State or another.

It would have provided no answer in *Fox v Robbins* to have demonstrated that the price of local wine to the retailer reflected an equal or higher burden of some local tax which had been imposed on local manufacturers or wholesalers at an earlier time. Similarly, the fact that the price of local tobacco products to the retailers will reflect the burden of the licence fee imposed upon local wholesalers provides no answer to the attack upon the discriminatory *ad valorem* tax imposed upon retailers by reference to interstate purchases in the present case. Nor does the fact that s 92 invalidates the *ad valorem* content of the retailer's licence fee mean that the section has re-emerged as a source of preference for interstate trade and commerce over local trade and commerce. The source of any such preference, if it exists, lies in the fact that the imposition of the wholesaler's licence fee has placed local goods at a competitive disadvantage vis-à-vis goods which have passed through the wholesale stage of distribution in some other State.

The justices concluded that s 10(1)(c) and (d) were invalid to the extent that they calculated the fee for a retail tobacconist's licence by reference to the value of tobacco sold by the applicant.

Wilson, Dawson and Toohey JJ: **[431]** The defendant argued that the requirement that he hold a licence under the Act in order to sell tobacco brought in from outside the State necessarily burdens interstate trade in a manner prohibited by s 92. In the light of *Cole v Whitfield* (1988) 165 CLR 360, the submission in that form cannot succeed. But the argument remains that the manner in which licence fees are calculated and imposed under the Act discriminates against interstate trade in tobacco by protecting Victorian trade in that product.

That argument has a superficial plausibility in that tobacco purchased from another State is purchased from a person who is not the holder of a wholesale licence under the Act and the purchaser in Victoria, when he sells that tobacco, is therefore subject to the *ad valorem* component of the fee in relation to it. But to put the matter **[432]** thus is to present an incomplete picture of the practical operation of the Act and, as was observed in *Cole v Whitfield*, it is the practical operation of the legislation which will largely determine whether there is discrimination upon protectionist grounds. What the argument put in that way leaves out of account is the fact that an interstate wholesaler is not subject to any franchise fee under the legislation and is able to sell tobacco to the Victorian retailer at a price which will reflect the absence of this expense. This advantage which the interstate wholesaler has is, however, balanced by the fact that the Victorian retailer who imports the tobacco will bear a fee calculated by reference to its value when it is sold in Victoria and this fee will be reflected in the price of the product to the ultimate consumer. The legislation does not seek to operate to the advantage or disadvantage of the retailer according to whether he obtains his tobacco within or outside the State.

It is obvious that the reason the legislation imposes the fee at the wholesale level where it is possible to do so is because there is only a small number of wholesalers but many retailers and it is easier for that reason to collect the tax from the former rather than from the latter. But that does not suggest protectionism. The plain fact of the matter is that the object of the legislation is not to favour Victorian trade at the expense of interstate trade in the product. All trade in tobacco in Victoria is subjected to the expense of the franchise fee at one point or another and the economic effect of the tax is the same, whether the tobacco is acquired by the retailer from within or outside the State.

No doubt the form of the tax imposed by the Act was dictated by the need to avoid the imposition of an excise duty. Excise duties are denied to the States by s 90 of the Constitution. It is clear enough that in devising the franchise fee in question in this case the draftsman placed reliance upon the decisions of this court in *Dennis Hotels Pty Ltd v Victoria* (1960) 104 CLR 529 and *Dickenson's Arcade Pty Ltd v Tasmania* (1974) 130 CLR 177. The distinctions drawn in those cases between a franchise fee and an excise duty may be a matter of debate (see *Gosford Meats Pty Ltd v New South Wales* (1985) 155 CLR 368), but it is not a debate which has any relevance in the context of s 92. The difficulties in relation to s 90 arise from the duty cast upon this court by the Constitution of defining the meaning of a concept — a duty of excise — which 'has never possessed, whether in popular, political or economic usage, any certain connotation and has never received any exact application' (*Matthews v Chicory Marketing* [433] *Board (Vic)* (1938) 60 CLR 263 at 293, per Dixon J. Similar difficulties do not occur with s 92, which requires a consideration of consequences rather than concepts. The consequences which are relevant are economic consequences for it is largely the ultimate economic effect which will determine whether or not legislation has been enacted in pursuit of a protectionist object. But here, where the impost applies to all trade in tobacco in Victoria, interstate and intrastate alike, there is no basis upon which to discern any element of protectionism. It is not to be found in the alternative methods of collecting the tax which produce the same ultimate effect in economic terms.

This case may be contrasted with *Fox v Robbins* (1909) 8 CLR 115. In that case Western Australian legislation authorised the imposition of a fee for a licence to sell wine produced from fruit grown in Western Australia lower than that imposed for a licence to sell wine produced from fruit grown elsewhere in Australia. The fee prescribed for the former kind of licence was two pounds and the fee prescribed for the latter kind of licence was fifty pounds. There was thus a clear disability imposed upon the sale of the product of other States and it was of a protectionist character. The conclusion was inevitable that the legislation offended s 92. Had the imposition been the same irrespective of where the fruit was grown there would have been no distinction between that case and the present case, save that in that case there was only one point of collection of the tax whereas in the present case there are alternative points of collection. It is plain that if the imposition had been the same, the disability which the court found to have been imposed upon the sale of the product of other States would not have existed. Indeed Griffith CJ and Higgins J were prepared to read down the discriminatory provisions in that case so that they would operate in this way. Thus *Fox v Robbins* is a clear case of protectionism and the judgments in that case must be read in that light.

If the argument were to be accepted that the manner in which licence fees are calculated and imposed under the Act discriminates against interstate trade in a protectionist manner, two alternatives would exist to cure the defect. On the one hand the legislation might be amended to exclude the value of tobacco purchased in the course of interstate trade from the calculation of the *ad valorem* component of the retail tobacconist's licence fee. This would, however, result in a preference being given to interstate trade and s 92 can scarcely be read as requiring such a result. On the other hand, the collection of the fee could be restricted to the retail level and be calculated upon [434] the value of all sales of tobacco. The practical result produced by the second alternative is no different in economic terms from that produced by the Act in its present form, save that the tax would be a great deal more difficult to collect. Consideration of these alternatives serves to demonstrate the danger of restricted analysis in any attempt to ascertain whether the legislation gives rise to discrimination of a protectionist kind.

Our conclusion, therefore, is that the agreed or established facts fail to demonstrate that the Act is protectionist in character. It is wholly valid and each of the questions reserved should be answered in the negative.

~~~

Notes

[10.4.35] In *Cole v Whitfield* (1988) 165 CLR 360 **[10.4.27C]** the court had indicated that there were two ways in which a law could be found to discriminate against interstate trade in a protectionist manner. If the law so discriminated on its face, through its legal operation, 'or if the factual operation of the law produces such a result': 165 CLR at 399. The court repeated this reference to the need to consider substantial effect as well as legal form more than once in its judgment: see, for example, 165 CLR at 408, 409.

One interpretation of these references is that the substantial effect of the law will conclude the issue of its validity; that is, a law which is discriminatory in legal form but not in substantial effect would be held to be consistent with s 92. Another interpretation was suggested by the majority's decision in *Bath v Alston Holdings Pty Ltd* (1988) 165 CLR 411 **[10.4.34C]**; namely, the references to legal form and substantial effect are meant as alternatives in the sense that a law would be found to contravene s 92 if it discriminated against interstate trade either in legal form or in substantial effect.

It could be thought that the majority's reasoning in *Bath v Alston Holdings Pty Ltd* supported the second interpretation. Not only did the discriminatory form of the Business Franchise (Tobacco) Act (s 10(1)(c) and (d) in particular) correspond to the majority's characterisation of the legislation, but the majority also stressed the need in the case of a tax challenged as offending s 92, 'to identify what is the transaction or thing which attracts liability': 165 CLR at 428. However, when that statement is read in context, it does not appear that the majority treated the legal form of the Victorian legislation as determining its invalidity. Rather, the majority said that it was 'the effect of the tax on transactions in [the Victorian retail tobacco] market which is material': 165 CLR at 428. In the present case, that effect confirmed the discriminatory form of the legislation.

[10.4.36] In concluding that the Victorian legislation did operate so as to discriminate against interstate trade in tobacco by protecting Victorian wholesalers of tobacco, the majority in *Bath v Alston Holdings Pty Ltd* (1988) 165 CLR 411 **[10.4.34C]** laid some emphasis on the (hypothetical) cost structures of tobacco wholesalers in states other than Victoria, including those wholesalers' liability to pay other states' taxes. The majority said that the practical effect of the formally discriminatory tax on tobacco retailers would be to protect Victorian wholesalers against competition from interstate wholesalers by further adding to the effective cost structure within which interstate wholesalers attempted to trade in Victoria. This would be particularly so where the interstate wholesalers' cost structures included taxes or licence fees paid under the laws of other states: see 165 CLR at 426.

Is it appropriate to take into account these other elements in a trader's cost structure when calculating the discriminatory or protectionist effect of state controls?

If the Victorian tobacco tax system were recast as an exclusively *retail* licence (tax) system, could the same objection (that the system operated so as to protect local wholesalers from interstate competition) be used to challenge its validity? At an early point in their judgment, the majority had asserted that a tax 'imposed directly on all retail sales of tobacco products in Victoria ... would not have infringed the injunction of s 92 of the Constitution': 165 CLR at 424. However, that assertion is not easy to reconcile with the majority's analysis of the practical effects of s 10(1)(c) and (d). If Victorian wholesalers were not subject to any tax, but Victoria retailers were obliged to pay a licence fee calculated on the basis of all their purchases of tobacco from Victorian and interstate wholesalers, it is at least possible (indeed, likely) that the effect of this tax would be to disadvantage interstate wholesalers who may already have been obliged to pay licence fees in other states and who would, in most cases, face higher transport costs than the Victorian wholesalers. (This point was made by the minority, who said the practical result of a licence fee calculated on the value of all sales of tobacco would be 'no different in economic terms from that produced by the Act in its present form': 165 CLR at 434.) In other words, abandoning the superficially discriminatory form of s 10(l)(c) and (d) in favour of an apparently non-discriminatory tobacco retail licence fee would not preclude a judgment that the licence fee worked a protectionist effect.

[10.4.37] It may be said that, in *Bath v Alston Holdings Pty Ltd* (1988) 165 CLR 411 **[10.4.34C]**, the majority judgment's weakness was to include in their analysis of the effect of s 10(1)(c) and (d) those elements in the cost structures of interstate wholesalers which arose from causes outside the state of Victoria and beyond the influence of Victorian legislation. In assessing the validity of s 10(1)(c) and (d), the question of economic or practical effects should have concentrated more closely on the question whether the tax imposed by those paragraphs, in their legislative context, fell equally on local and interstate traders. This was the approach adopted by the minority who noted that '[a]ll trade in tobacco in Victoria is subjected to the expense of the franchise fee at one point or another', at the point of either the wholesale or the retail sale, 'and the economic effect of the tax is the same, whether the tobacco is acquired by the retailer from within or outside the State': 165 CLR at 432.

[10.4.38C]   **Castlemaine Tooheys Ltd v South Australia**
(1990) 169 CLR 436

The Beverage Container Act 1975 (SA) provided that the purchaser of any beverage must pay to the retailer of that beverage a deposit on the container in which the beverage was supplied. In the case of glass containers, the deposit was refundable by a retailer who sold beverages in containers of that type; in the case of other containers, the deposit was refundable by a collection depot. Regulations made under the 1975 Act exempted refillable beer bottles from the deposit requirement.

Several brewers of beer competed for the South Australian market in bottled beer. The South Australian Brewing Co Ltd (SAB) and Cooper and Sons Ltd (Coopers) were located in South Australia and used mostly refillable bottles; Carlton & United Breweries Ltd (CUB) was located in Victoria and used refillable bottles for its South Australian sales of beer; and the Bond Brewing Group (Bond) was located in Queensland, New South Wales and Western Australia and used non-refillable bottles for all its sales of beer. In January 1986, Bond began a marketing campaign in South Australia and, within two months, had increased its share of the market for packaged beer from less than 0.1 per cent to 4 per cent, at the expense of SAB, whose share of the South Australian market fell from 77.4 per cent to 73.5 per cent.

On 1 October 1986, the Beverage Container Act Amendment Act 1986 (SA) came into operation. The 1986 Act made substantial amendments to the 1975 Act. Under the amended 1975 Act and regulations made under that Act, the following deposits were required to be paid by purchasers of beverages:

• on non-refillable beer containers: 15c per container;
• on non-refillable soft drink containers: 5c per container;
• on non-refillable low-alcohol wine containers: 15c per container; and
• on refillable glass beer containers: 4c per container.

The amended Act and the regulations required retailers of beer in non-refillable containers to accept the return of all such containers and refund deposits on those containers. No such obligation was imposed on retailers in respect of refillable containers. The deposit paid on those containers was refundable at collection depots, which could not refund deposits paid on non-refillable containers.

Three companies owned by Bond began proceedings in the High Court of Australia against the state of South Australia, seeking a declaration that the amendments to the 1975 Act and the regulations were invalid in their application to Bond's trade and commerce by reason of s 92 of the Constitution. The parties agreed to a special case which was stated for the opinion of the Full Court.

Mason CJ, Brennan, Deane, Dawson and Toohey JJ: [462] The 1986 Act and the new regulations disadvantaged the Bond brewing companies in two respects. First, their non-refillable bottles became subject to a refund amount of 15 cents whereas the refillable bottles of their competitors, CUB and the South Australian brewers, were subject to a refund amount of 4 cents only. According to the defendant, a refund of 6 cents per non-refillable bottle for twelve months and thereafter a refund of 4 cents per non-refillable bottle would have been sufficient to ensure the return of non-refillable bottles at the same rate as refillable bottles. [463] This concession may have been prompted by the circumstance that regulations providing for refunds of that order were tabled in the South Australian Parliament in November 1986. These regulations were disallowed in the Legislative Council but their introduction was in apparent recognition of the fact that the existing regulations providing for refunds of 15 cents and 4 cents for non-refillable and refillable bottles respectively invited challenge in this court. The plaintiffs believe that a 4 cent deposit would be immediately effective to ensure the return of non-refillable bottles at the same rate as refillable bottles with a 4 cent deposit. According to the special case, a 4 cent deposit is now sufficient to ensure a reasonable and adequate rate of return of refillable bottles. The difference between the prescribed amounts of 15 cents and 4 cents resulted in a price differential which made the Bond brewing companies' product non-competitive. Before the commencement of the 1986 Act, the 'bottle cost' (excluding transport costs but including deposit and costs of return or disposal system) of the products of the Bond brewing companies was 16 cents per bottle. The 'bottle cost' in the case of SAB was 16.65 cents per bottle. Following the introduction of the 1986 Act and the regulation imposing a 15 cent deposit on non-refillable bottles, the 'bottle cost' of the products of the Bond brewing companies was 26 cents per bottle. The 'bottle cost' in the case of SAB remained at 16.65 cents per bottle.

Secondly, the Bond brewing companies' non-refillable bottles were not eligible to be exempted from the application of s 7 whereas the refillable bottles of the South Australian brewers were eligible for such exemption and were so exempted. Those retailers selling the Bond brewing companies' beer in non-refillable bottles were obliged to comply with s 7, accept delivery of such bottles and pay the refund amount of 15 cents per bottle. On the other hand, retailers selling South Australian brewed beer in refillable bottles, not being obliged to comply with s 7 in relation to such bottles, were not bound to accept delivery of them or to pay the refund of 4 cents per bottle. A customer seeking to obtain a refund for such a bottle could return it to a collection depot and obtain a refund from the depot. The natural result of the requirement that retailers pay the refund amount was that they were inclined not to stock a beer when the volume of sales of a particular brand was not high. There was no limit to the number of empty bottles of a particular brand sold by a retailer which he would be bound to accept by way of return and for which he would be liable to pay the refund amount. The fact that the customer returning the bottle may have bought the bottle elsewhere was irrelevant to the retailer's liability.

The Bond brewing companies could alleviate but not eliminate **[464]** the burden imposed upon the retailers who were willing to stock their beer by establishing their own collection depots. The establishment of such depots would not have altered the retailers' obligations under s 7. Moreover, the establishment of such depots would have increased the 'bottle cost' in the case of the Bond brewing companies by about 5 cents per bottle, making a total of 31 cents per bottle as against the 'bottle cost' in the case of SAB of 16.65 cents per bottle.

The practical effect of the 1986 Act and regulations and the notice under s 5b was to prevent the Bond brewing companies obtaining a market share in packaged beer in South Australia in excess of 1 per cent whilst their competitors used refillable beer bottles. It is uneconomic for the Bond brewing companies to convert their existing interstate plants to use refillable bottles.

It is common ground between the parties that the object and effect of the 1986 Act was to make the sale of beer in non-refillable bottles commercially disadvantageous. The plaintiffs go further and assert that the effect of the 1986 Act, the regulations and the notice under s 5b was to discriminate against the sale in South Australia of packaged beer brewed interstate and to protect the beer brewed in South Australia from interstate competition.

On the other hand the defendant claims that the 1986 Act and regulations promoted litter control and conserved energy and resources. According to the defendant, this effect was achieved by the imposition of a deposit on non-refillable containers in an amount judged sufficient to ensure their return and discourage their use and by providing a refund point — in practice any place of sale — to encourage return and to discourage manufacturers from using such containers. Thus the defendant contends that the objects of the legislation were: (1) to promote litter control by forcing non-glass containers and non-refillable bottles into a return system by encouraging return; and (2) to promote energy and resource conservation by discouraging the use of non-refillable containers by imposing a higher deposit and by requiring acceptance of returns at the point of sale (thus discouraging retailers from handling them). The special case mentions that the use, return and refilling of refillable bottles generally results in a proportionate reduction in the release into the atmosphere of carbon dioxide from the burning of natural gas in the production of glass containers. However, the defendant does not claim that this is an independent object of the legislation.

Mason CJ, Brennan, Deane, Dawson and Toohey JJ said that the present case stood on a different footing from *Cole v Whitfield* (1988) 165 CLR 360, because Bond brewing companies were disadvantaged in the two ways identified (at 462–3), 'which gave the South Australian brewers a competitive or market advantage': 169 CLR at 467. They said that the decision in *Bath v Alston Holdings Pty Ltd* (1988) 165 CLR 411 'is an example of one form of discriminatory protectionism. But it does not touch the issues which arise for decision in this case': 169 CLR at 468. After reviewing several decisions of the United States Supreme Court, the justices said:

[471] Although the American cases cannot be treated as an accurate guide to the interpretation of s 92, they identify in a useful way considerations which may be relevant in the process of characterization which an Australian court is called upon to undertake. So, the fact that a law regulates interstate and intrastate trade evenhandedly by imposing a prohibition or requirement which takes effect without regard to considerations of whether the trade affected is interstate or intrastate suggests that the law is not protectionist. Likewise, the fact that a law, whose effects include the burdening of the trade of a particular interstate trader, does not necessarily benefit local traders, as distinct from other interstate traders, suggests that the purposes of the law are not protectionist. On the other hand, where a law on its face is apt to secure a legitimate object but its effect is to impose a discriminatory burden [472] upon interstate trade as against intrastate trade, the existence of reasonable non-discriminatory alternative means of securing that legitimate object suggests that the purpose of the law is not to achieve that legitimate object but rather to effect a form of prohibited discrimination. There is also some room for a comparison, if not a balancing, of means and objects in the context of s 92. The fact that a law imposes a burden upon interstate trade and commerce that is not incidental or that is disproportionate to the attainment of the legitimate object of the law may show that the true purpose of the law is not to attain that object but to impose the impermissible burden.

The particular question in the present case is: how should the Court approach the determination of the validity of State legislation which attempts on its face to solve pressing social problems by imposing a solution which disadvantages the trade in beer brewed outside the State as against the trade in beer brewed within the State? The central problems addressed by the legislation are the litter problem and the need to conserve energy resources. If the South Australian legislation were not attempting to provide a solution to these problems, the burden on interstate trade would be discriminatory in a protectionist sense because its operation would be discriminatory and protectionist in effect, even though the legislation on its face would treat interstate and intrastate trade evenhandedly. What difference then does it make that the burden is imposed by legislation which on its face appears to be directed to the solution of social and economic problems, not being the uncompetitive quality or character of domestic trade or industry? Is the burden non-discriminatory in the relevant sense on that account? If so, how is that conclusion to be justified?

In determining what is relevantly discriminatory in the context of s 92, we must take account of the fundamental consideration that, subject to the Constitution, the legislature of a State has power to enact legislation for the well-being of the people of that State. In that context, the freedom from discriminatory burdens of a protectionist kind postulated by s 92 does not deny to the legislature of a State power to enact legislation for the well-being of the people of that State unless the legislation is relevantly discriminatory. Accordingly, interstate trade, as well as intrastate trade, must submit to such regulation as may be necessary or appropriate and adapted either to the protection of the community from a real danger or threat to its welfare or to the enhancement of its welfare.

It would extend the immunity conferred by s 92 beyond all reason if the Court were to hold that the section invalidated any [473] burden on interstate trade which disadvantaged that trade in competition with intrastate trade, notwithstanding that the imposition of the burden was necessary or appropriate and adapted to the protection of the people of the State from a real danger or threat to its well-being. And it would place the Court in an invidious position if the Court were to hold that only such regulation of interstate trade as is in fact necessary for the protection of the community is consistent with the freedom ordained by s 92. The question whether a particular legislative enactment is a necessary or even a desirable solution to a particular problem is in large measure a political question best left for resolution to the political process. The resolution of that problem by the Court would require it to sit in judgment on the legislative decision, without having access to all the political considerations that played a part in the making of that decision, thereby giving a new and unacceptable dimension to the relationship between the Court and the legislature of the State. An analogous field is the legislative implementation of treaty obligations under s 51(xxix) of the Constitution. The true object of the law in such a case is critical to its validity. The Court has upheld the validity of legislative provisions if they are appropriate and adapted to the implementation of the provisions of the treaty: *The Commonwealth v Tasmania* (the *Tasmanian Dam* Case) [(1983) 158 CLR 1, at 130–31, 172, 232–3, 259–61]; *Richardson v Foresty Commission*. [(1988) 164 CLR 261 at 292, 295–6, 303, 311–12, 326, 336, 344–6] See also *Herald and Weekly Times Ltd v The Commonwealth*. [(1966) 115 CLR 418 at 437] But if the means which the law adopts are disproportionate to the object to be achieved, the law has not been considered to be appropriate to the achievement of the object: the *Tasmanian Dam* Case [(1983) 158 CLR at 278]; *South Australia v Tanner*. [(1989) 166 CLR 161 at 165,

178] There is a compelling case for taking a similar approach to the problem now under consideration.

If we accept, as we must, that the legislature has rational and legitimate grounds for apprehending that the sale of beer in non-refillable bottles generates or contributes to the litter problem and decreases the State's finite energy resources, legislative measures which are appropriate and adapted to the resolution of those problems would be consistent with s 92 so long as any burden imposed on interstate trade was incidental and not disproportionate to their achievement. Accordingly, the validity of the 1986 legislation rests on the proposition that the legislative regime is [474] appropriate and adapted to the protection of the environment in South Australia from the litter problem and to the conservation of the State's finite energy resources and that its impact on interstate trade is incidental and not disproportionate to the achievement of those objects.

The first objection to this proposition is that the discrepancy between the 15 cents refund amount prescribed by reg 7(d) for non-refillable beer bottles and the 4 cents refund amount prescribed by reg 7(c) for refillable bottles goes beyond what is necessary to ensure the return of non-refillable bottles at the same rate as refillable bottles. The discrepancy means that the 'bottle cost' of the Bond brewing companies' product is 26 cents per bottle as against a 'bottle cost' of 16.65 cents for the SAB product. The defendant's acknowledgment that a refund amount of 6 cents per non-refillable bottle for the first twelve months, reducing to 4 cents thereafter, would have been sufficient to achieve that purpose is significant. The magnitude of the discrepancy indicates that the object of fixing the 15 cents refund amount went further than ensuring the same rate of return of non-refillable and refillable bottles and that the object was to disadvantage the sale of beer in non-refillable bottles as against the sale of beer in refillable bottles.

If, in order to protect the environment from the litter problem presented by the sale of beer in non-refillable bottles, the legislature had enacted a law whose object and effect was simply to discourage the sale of beer in such bottles, the fact that the law had a more adverse impact on interstate brewers than domestic brewers because interstate brewers sell beer in such bottles would not make the law a discriminatory or protectionist law, if that impact was incidental and not disproportionate to the resolution of the litter problem. In such a case the competitive disadvantage sustained by the interstate brewer would be merely incidental to and consequential upon a regulatory measure whose object and effect was not discriminatory in a protectionist sense.

However, this is not a case in which it is possible to characterize the legislative regime simply and comprehensively as one designed to discourage the sale of beer in non-refillable bottles. The legislative regime is one which has as its immediate purpose the return and collection of containers generally, including refillable and non-refillable bottles. The solution to the litter problem sought to be achieved by the legislature lies in the successful operation of the scheme for the return and collection of containers and it is by reference to that scheme that the validity of the law must be determined. And that is how the defendant has presented its case.

In this context, the plaintiffs assert that, in the light of the [475] difference in the refund amount, the purpose in disadvantaging the sale of beer in non-refillable bottles was to discriminate against the Bond brewing companies as interstate brewers in favour of the domestic brewers in South Australia. The defendant resists this conclusion for three reasons: first, that 15 cents is also fixed by reg 7(b) as the refund amount for a non-refillable container for a low alcohol wine-based beverage; secondly, that the fixing of the refund amount at 15 cents advantaged CUB as much as the domestic brewers so long as CUB supplied beer in refillable bottles; and, thirdly, that the need to conserve energy resources requires or justifies more severe burdens on the sale of beer in non-refillable bottles. The first reason given by the defendant is not persuasive. If the refund amount fixed for non-refillable beer bottles far exceeded what was thought necessary to ensure the success of the scheme for the return and collection of containers, the relevant provision was not appropriate and adapted to that end; the fact that a like refund amount is fixed for non-refillable containers for low alcohol wine-based beverages cannot affect that conclusion. As for the second reason, the impact of the provision on CUB might tend to suggest that the intended legislative object was not to discriminate against interstate brewers. However, it is not a conclusive consideration. It does not negate the purpose of discriminating against interstate trade consisting, in the main, of the trade of the Bond brewing companies (cf *Exxon Corporation v Governor of Maryland* [437 US 117 (1978) at 126]). After all, it was the growing market share of those companies, not CUB, that threatened the market share of the domestic brewers. Discrimination in the relevant sense against interstate trade is inconsistent with s 92, regardless of whether the discrimination is directed at, or sustained by, all, some or only one of the relevant interstate traders.

Before considering the third answer given by the defendant to the plaintiffs' objections based on the difference in the refund amounts, it is convenient to consider the second objection to the 1986 legislation, which relates to s 5b(2). That provision enables the Minister to exempt by notice refillable bottles from the operation of the retail return scheme provided for by s 7, without enabling the Minister to make a corresponding exemption for non-refillable bottles. Such an exemption disadvantages the interstate supplier of beer in refillable bottles by requiring it to make arrangements to transport its bottles back to its brewery for refilling as a condition of being eligible for an exemption from s 7. As it happens, this disadvantages CUB, without affecting the Bond brewing [476] companies as they do not sell beer in refillable bottles. What is relevant is that the Minister exempted the refillable bottles (used by the South Australian brewers and by CUB) by notice given under s 5b(2) so that retailers were relieved of the obligation to accept delivery of their bottles and refund the prescribed amount in respect of such containers. On the other hand, retailers remained under the obligation imposed by s 7 with respect to the non-refillable bottles of the Bond brewing companies. The natural effect of this discrimination was to discourage retailers from stocking the Bond brewing companies' beer in non-refillable bottles. It was a discrimination which effectively protected the domestic brewers and their intrastate trade at the expense of the Bond brewing companies because the retailers were under no similar obligation in relation to the refillable bottles of the domestic brewers.

The effect of the differential treatment resulting from the giving of the notice under s 5b(2) was that the refund amount was obtainable only from collection depots in respect of the refillable beer bottles of the domestic brewers. Yet no justification for this difference appears. If the collection depot system yielded inadequate returns, then there was no reason for exempting the bottles of the domestic producers from the operation of s 7. If the collection system generated adequate returns, then there was no reason for not exempting the non-refillable bottles of the Bond brewing companies, along with the refillable bottles of the domestic producers.

The defendant seeks to overcome this difficulty by relying on the history of the collection depot system in South Australia and pointing to its success in promoting the return of containers. Granted that this is so, neither the history of that system nor its success explains why it was necessary to subject the Bond brewing companies' products to the regime of retail return under s 7 when it was not necessary to take similar action in relation to the bottles of the domestic brewers. That regime is therefore not capable of justification as a means of achieving litter control.

It remains for us to consider the defendant's argument that any disadvantage sustained by the Bond brewing companies is merely incidental to the implementation of a legislative regime which has as its object the conservation of finite energy resources. The facts recited in the special case, so far as they relate to this issue, are extremely meagre and do little to substantiate the defendant's argument. If all beer bottles manufactured in South Australia were non-refillable bottles, the extra energy consumption in the State would be between 0.06 per cent and 0.12 per cent of the total energy consumption in the State. If all beer bottles manufactured in [477] South Australia were non-refillable bottles, then natural gas consumption in the State would increase by about 0.24 per cent. However, as the Bond brewing companies use bottles manufactured outside the State, any increase in their market share in South Australia would reduce the use of the State's resources, including natural gas, in the manufacture of bottles.

If, in the light of these facts, the legislature reasonably apprehended that the sale of beer in refillable bottles manufactured in South Australia constituted a threat to the State's reserves of natural gas, one might have expected the legislature to introduce legislation prohibiting the sale in the State of beer in non-refillable bottles produced in the State. Alternatively, and more directly, the legislature might have legislated to prohibit the manufacture in South Australia of such bottles with the use of natural gas, or at all. But none of these means was adopted. Instead a regime was introduced which subjected the Bond brewing companies' interstate trade to serious competitive disadvantages by reason of their selling beer in non-refillable bottles, even though those bottles are manufactured outside the State and do not, as far as we know, involve the use of South Australian natural gas. It may be that the result is that local trade and commerce may need to be harmed if State gas reserves are to be protected. But if that is the case, it should not be surprising, because local businesses are likely to be significant users of those reserves.

It follows that neither the need to protect the environment from the litter problem nor the need to conserve energy resources offers an acceptable explanation or justification for the differential treatment given to the products of the Bond brewing companies. Accordingly, in our view, that treatment amounted to discrimination in a protectionist sense in relation to their interstate trade.

~~~

[10.4.39] Gaudron and McHugh JJ delivered a separate judgment, in which they agreed 'that the practical effect of the [South Australian legislation] was to confer a significant competitive advantage in the South Australian market upon beer produced in that state over beer brewed by the first three plaintiffs interstate. The regime is therefore protectionist and, if also discriminatory, it infringes s 92 of the Constitution': 169 CLR at 478. They said that a law was discriminatory (at 478):

> ... if it operates by reference to a distinction which is in fact irrelevant to the object to be attained; ... if, although it operates by reference to a relevant distinction, the different treatment thereby assigned is not appropriate and adapted to the difference or differences which support the distinction [and] if, although there is a relevant difference, it proceeds as though there is no such difference, or, in other words, if it treats equally things that are unequal — unless, perhaps, there is no practical basis for differentiation.

Gaudron and McHugh JJ concluded at 480:

> [T]he essence of the legal notion of discrimination lies in the unequal treatment of equals and, conversely, in the equal treatment of unequals. Thus, if there is no inequality or relevant difference between the subject matter of interstate trade and the subject matter of intrastate trade, a law which is appropriate and adapted to an objective and burdens interstate trade only incidentally and not disproportionately to that objective will, in our view, offend against s 92 if its practical effect is protectionist — particularly if there exist alternative means involving no or a lesser burden on interstate trade.

> In the present case the questions posed in the joint judgment of Mason CJ, Brennan, Deane, Dawson and Toohey JJ reveal, for the reasons given by their Honours, that neither the objective of litter control nor the objective of energy conservation provides an acceptable explanation or justification for the different treatment assigned in the legislative regime for beverage containers.

Notes

[10.4.40] The High Court's analysis of the practical effect of the South Australian legislation in *Castlemaine Tooheys Ltd v South Australia* (1990) 169 CLR 436

[10.4.38C] emphasises the extent to which the court has abandoned the approach to testing the validity of legislation typified by such decisions as *Wragg v New South Wales* (1953) 88 CLR 353 **[10.4.13]** and *Grannall v Marrickville Margarine Pty Ltd* (1955) 93 CLR 55 **[10.4.15]**. The court's assertion of its responsibility to consider the practical operation of challenged legislation should not be viewed in isolation. The same assertion has been made by the court in the context of s 90 of the Constitution (*Philip Morris Ltd v Commissioner for Business Franchises* (1989) 167 CLR 399 **[9.4.47]**) and s 117 of the Constitution: *Street v Queensland Bar Association* (1989) 168 CLR 461 **[11.2.61C]**.

Nor should the significance of the assertion be underrated. It is not simply a matter of the justices claiming the right to look at legislation in the context of the social and economic environment, and considering the impact which the legislation has within that environment. As the reasoning in *Castlemaine Tooheys Ltd v South Australia* (1990) 169 CLR 436 **[10.4.38C]** demonstrates, the court is undertaking to weigh competing economic and social interests. In that case, the interest of South Australia in conserving natural resources and minimising environmental degradation was weighed against the interest of interstate traders in free access to the South Australian market. The point that the High Court is now engaged in an overt process of balancing competing social interests was made by several justices in *Street v Queensland Bar Association*, where the justices acknowledged that the protection against discrimination extended by s 117 could be diminished to serve legitimate state interests. Zines has written ((1997) p 152) that, in the context of s 92:

> While the court has declared that it is not its concern to determine the social benefits or otherwise of legislation that impinges on interstate trade, it is clear that a degree of balancing of social interests, in some cases at any rate, is inevitable.

[10.4.41] The reading of s 92 adopted by the High Court in *Cole v Whitfield* (1988) 165 CLR 360 **[10.4.27C]** might be regarded as substantially reducing the insulating effect which s 92 conferred on interstate traders. Their privileged immunity from governmental controls was removed and they may now be regulated and controlled in the same way as intrastate traders. However, from another perspective, the new reading of s 92 presents new dangers for public regulation of commercial activities. The High Court has shown that it will analyse the practical operation and effect of governmental regulation, taking into account the arrangements adopted by traders. The court accepted Bond brewing companies' investment in non-refillable packaging as a given, against which the practical effect of the South Australian legislation had to be tested. The intense judicial scrutiny of public regulatory controls which the new reading of s 92 entails may, in the long run, pose even more of a threat to government control of economic activity than did the 'individual right' approach, tempered as it was by the 'criterion of liability' form of analysis.

---

5   References

[10.5.1]   *Articles*

Bell, 'Section 92, Factual Discrimination and the High Court' (1992) 20 *FLR* 240.

Carney, 'Section 51(xx): No Power of Incorporation' (1990) 2 *Bond LR* 79.

Carney, 'The Re-interpretation of Section 92: The Decline of Free Enterprise and the Rise of Free Trade' (1991) 3 *Bond LR* 149.

Evans, 'The Constitutional Validity and Scope of the Trade Practices Act' (1975) 49 *ALJ* 654.

Hotop, 'The Federal Commerce Power and Labour Relations' (1974) 48 *ALJ* 169.

Kelly, 'Commonwealth Legislation Relating to Environmental Impact Statements' (1976) 50 *ALJ* 498.

Kennett, 'Constitutional interpretation in the Corporations Case' (1990) 19 *FLR* 223.

Lindell, 'The Corporations and Races Powers' (1984) 14 *FLR* 219.

Simmonds, 'The Commonwealth Cannot Incorporate Under the Corporations Power: New South Wales v Commonwealth' (1990) 20 *UWALR* 641.

Taberner and Lee, 'Section 92 and the Environment' (1991) 65 *ALJ* 266.

Wallace, 'The Constitutional Reach of the Trade Practices Act and the Liability of Corporate Officers' (1977) 51 *ALJ* 682.

[10.5.2]　*Papers and reports*

Advisory Committee on Trade and Economic Management, *Report to the Constitutional Commission,* Canberra, AGPS, 1987.

[10.5.3]　*Texts*

Coper, *Freedom of Interstate Trade,* Butterworths, Sydney, 1983.

Hanks, 'Aborigines and Government: The Developing Framework' in *Aborigines and the Law,* (eds Hanks and Keon-Cohen), George Allen & Unwin, Sydney, 1984, pp 19–49.

Howard, *Australian Federal Constitutional Law,* 3rd ed, Law Book Co, Sydney, 1985.

La Nauze, *The Making of the Australian Constitution,* Melbourne University Press, Melbourne, 1972.

Lane, *The Australian Federal System,* 2nd ed, Law Book Co, Sydney, 1979, pp 55–92 ('Trade and commerce power'); pp 153–90 ('Corporations power').

Lumb and Moens, *Constitution of the Commonwealth of Australia Annotated,* 5th ed, Butterworths, Sydney, 1995, pp 123–36 (s 51(i)); pp 189–98 (s 51(xx)); pp 453–76 (s 92).

Phillips, 'The Trade and Commerce Power' in *Essays on the Australian Constitution,* (ed Else-Mitchell), 2nd ed, Law Book Co, Sydney, 1961, pp 129–55.

Sawer, *Australian Federalism in the Courts,* Melbourne University Press, Melbourne, 1967, Ch 10 ('The Freedoms').

Zines, *The High Court and the Constitution,* 2nd ed, Butterworths, Sydney, 1987.

Zines, *The High Court and the Constitution,* 4th ed, Butterworths, Sydney, 1997.

Chapter

11

Rights and Freedoms

1   Introduction

[11.1.1]   The Commonwealth Constitution does not contain a Bill of Rights. As Dawson J observed in *Kruger v Commonwealth* (the *Stolen Generation* case) (1997) 190 CLR 1 **[11.2.54C]** at 61:

> ... the Australian Constitution, with few exceptions and in contrast with its American model, does not seek to establish personal liberty by placing restrictions upon the exercise of governmental power. Those who framed the Australian Constitution accepted the view that individual rights were on the whole best left to the protection of the common law and the supremacy of the Parliament. Thus the Constitution deals, almost without exception, with the structure and relationship of government rather than individual rights. The fetters which are placed upon legislative action are, for the most part, for the purpose of placing matters beyond the reach of any parliament. The Constitution does not contain a Bill of Rights. Indeed, the 1898 Constitutional Convention rejected a proposal to include an express guarantee of individual rights ... The framers preferred to place their faith in the democratic process for the protection of individual rights.

The High Court has, by and large, declined opportunities to develop an 'implied' Bill of Rights: see *Kruger v The Commonwealth* (1997) 190 CLR 1. The purpose of this chapter is to examine the court's construction of those few provisions in the Constitution that guarantee rights and freedoms, and its more recent jurisprudence of 'implied' rights and freedoms.

[11.1.2]   One reason for the High Court's reluctance to recognise constitutional rights can be found in the intellectual and political environment in which the Commonwealth Constitution was drafted and adopted. That environment did not encourage the development of a charter of individual rights. At the intellectual level, the fashion in political theory moved from the 18th century emphasis on natural rights (and the 'Rights of Man') to the 19th century utilitarian philosophy of Jeremy

Bentham, in which progress, science and a rational balancing of competing interests dominated. The processes of legislation and governmental action were seen, not as a threat to liberty but a mechanism through which the objectives of progress (the greatest happiness for the largest number) could be achieved: see Finn (1987) p 3; Gageler (1987) pp 171, 173. The Constitution contains an entire chapter dedicated to 'Finance and Trade' (Chapter IV) and contains more provisions dealing with railways than rights.

The political environment was also uncongenial to the notion of fundamental guarantees. Almost all of the Australian colonies had achieved responsible self-government in the middle of the 19th century (and the last, Western Australia, in 1889) through processes of evolution and negotiation with the Imperial power, the United Kingdom. The federal movement was similarly evolutionary and was not resisted by the United Kingdom. There was none of the struggle against 'oppression' and 'tyranny' which, to the drafters of the American Bill of Rights, characterised their achievement of independence: Moffatt (1965) pp 85–6.

[11.1.3] However, the drafters of the Commonwealth Constitution did include several, limited rights and freedoms in the Constitution. These include ss 51(xxxi), 80, 92, 116 and 117, which form the focus of the first part of this chapter. Provisions such as s 80 [11.2.24E] and s 116 [11.2.41E] have consistently received a narrow reading by the High Court: see Charlesworth (1986) pp 54–5 and O'Neil (1987). Other provisions, such as s 51(xxxi) [11.2.1E] and s 92 [10.4.1E], have been read more assertively by the justices and have operated as a significant constraint on the actions of governments and legislatures. Section 117 [11.2.41E], was given a cramped reading by the High Court until 1989, when the decision in *Street v Queensland Bar Association* (1989) 168 CLR 461 [11.2.57E] revived that provision. Since 1992, the court has also developed a jurisprudence of implied rights and freedoms, most dramatically in its decisions in *Australian Capital Television Pty Ltd v Commonwealth* (1992) 177 CLR 106 [11.3.7C] and *Nationwide News Pty Ltd v Wills* (1992) 177 CLR 1 [11.3.9], decisions in which the court found that the Commonwealth Constitution, particularly those provisions that describe our system of representative government, confer an implied freedom to discuss political and governmental affairs.

During the 1990s the court confirmed that the separation of judicial power effected by Ch III of the Constitution also gives rise to personal rights and freedoms. This chapter will examine the court's jurisprudence of rights and freedoms in detail.

[11.1.4] While there has been general acceptance of the court's function in drawing out implications based on federalism, there is continuing controversy, both legal and political, about the appropriate role of the court in drawing out implications that support constitutional rights. Former Chief Justice, Sir Anthony Mason, argued in 1987 for a more activist judicial role 'in enforcing and protecting fundamental rights where Parliament fails to do so': Mason (1987) p 163. In 1988, Sir Anthony suggested that the adoption of constitutional guarantees would forestall Australia's isolation from international legal developments and assert the intrinsic value of such guarantees for Australian social and legal institutions: Mason (1988).

The pursuit of that approach between 1992 and 1996 by a number of justices of the court led to widespread public criticism that the High Court was retreating from its conventional interpretative restraint and had wandered into the site of 'politics': Craven (1997). That approach was also controversial within the court itself, with the broadest cases on the implied freedom of speech, such as *Theophanous v Herald & Weekly Times Ltd* (1994) 182 CLR 104 and *Stephens v West Australian Newspapers Ltd* (1994) 182 CLR 211, decided by 4:3 majorities and characterised by divergence of reasoning within those majorities. After the retirement of Mason CJ and changes in the composition of the bench, the court returned to a more orthodox approach: see *Lange v Australian Broadcasting Corporation* (1997) 189 CLR 520 **[11.3.3C]**.

[11.1.5] More recently the debate within the court about the role and function of High Court justices in law-making has become more strident, and the positions in that debate have become more polarised. So, for example, at least one of the justices appointed since *Lange*, Callinan J, has signalled his disapproval of that decision and of the development of an implied freedom to discuss political and governmental affairs. This has provoked a response from another justice of the court, Kirby J (somewhat uncharacteristically taking the role of defender of the status quo). In *Australian Broadcasting Corporation v Lenah Game Meats Pty Ltd* (2001) 208 CLR 199 at 330–1 Callinan J said:

> With the greatest of respect to the very experienced Court (Brennan CJ, Dawson, Toohey, Gaudron, McHugh, Gummow and Kirby JJ) which unanimously put beyond doubt in *Lange* that there was an implied constitutional freedom of communication which would serve as a defence in some defamation cases, I would not myself have reached the same conclusion. In my opinion, modern conditions to which the justices referred but did not identify in *Theophanous* did not require it. Additionally, the authors of the Constitution were well aware of the First Amendment to the Constitution of the United States and most deliberately must have chosen not to incorporate such a provision in our Constitution.

Kirby J rejoined at 280 (see also at 285–6):

> *The holding in Lange*: In his reasons, Callinan J is critical of the decisions of this Court concerning the implied freedom of communication, derived from the text of the federal Constitution. No party to this appeal, including the governmental interveners, suggested that the principle stated in *Lange v Australian Broadcasting Corporation* should be reconsidered. In my view, it should not. Lange represents a recent, unanimous statement of the law by this Court ... There is ... no reason to question the correctness of *Lange*, least of all in an appeal where that correctness has not been challenged.

The debate continued in *Roberts & Case v Bass* (2002) 212 CLR 1: see at 101–2 (Callinan J), 55 (Kirby J).

More recently, shortly before his appointment to the High Court, Heydon JA (then a member of the New South Wales Court of Appeal) was caustic in his description and criticism of 'judicial activism', which he described as:

> ... using judicial power for a purpose other than that for which it is granted, namely doing justice according to law in the particular case. It means serving some function other than what is necessary for the decision of the particular dispute between the parties. Often the illegitimate function is the furthering of some political, moral or social program: the law is not seen as the touchstone by which the case in hand is to be decided, but as a possible starting point or catalyst for developing a new system to solve a range of other cases (Heydon (2003) at 5)

Heydon JA proceeded to describe the decision in *Lange v Australian Broadcasting Corporation* as:

> ... a tactical compromise of which a French politician would be proud. But it may be a compromise in the sense of an agreement by seven people to do what at different stages all seven had thought was wrong (Heydon (2003) at 7).

Heydon's extra-curial discussion of the High Court's jurisprudence has increased speculation as to whether changes in the composition of the bench are the best indicator if a change in the course of the court's jurisprudence of rights and freedoms, which is now a matter of open and public controversy.

[11.1.6] Two of the constraints expressed in the Commonwealth Constitution operate to control state parliaments and governments: s 92, which guarantees the 'absolute freedom' of interstate 'trade, commerce and intercourse' **[10.4.1E]**; and s 117, prohibiting discrimination on the basis of residence in another state **[11.2.41E]**. Apart from those constraints, state governments and parliaments were, it seems, free to develop policies which infringed on the fundamental freedoms of Australians. Although s 46 of the Constitution Act 1934 (Tas) 'guarantees' freedom of conscience and religion, the Tasmanian Parliament is free to amend or repeal the section through its normal legislative processes.

Hence, attempts to argue that state parliaments were subject to implied constraints in the interests of individual rights met with little success. In *Grace Bible Church v Reedman* (1984) 54 ALR 571, the South Australian Supreme Court held that the South Australian Parliament was not constrained in the exercise of its legislative powers by a common law right of religious freedom. White J, for example, pointed to the contrast with the Commonwealth Constitution's specific protection of religious freedom in (s 116) and observed that '[i]t takes something as powerful as a constitutional provision such as s 116 to restrict the power of the Parliament': 54 ALR at 571. He adopted a broad and unrestrained view of the state parliament's powers (at 581):

> [T]he opinion of the Parliament as to what laws are for the peace, welfare and good government of the State is paramount and conclusive as a matter of law. The Parliament's opinion, as expressed in a particular statute, cannot be impugned in a court of law as being an invalid exercise of Parliament's power.

More recently, the High Court confirmed that there is no 'deeply rooted right' to receive just compensation for property acquired under state legislation: *Durham Holdings Pty Ltd v New South Wales* (2001) 205 CLR 399 at 409–10 (Gaudron, McHugh, Gummow and Hayne JJ, at 425 per Kirby J, at 433 per Callinan J). The constitutional right to compensation under s 51(xxxi) only applies to Commonwealth law, although it may affect a state acquisition of property where that acquisition is funded by a Commonwealth appropriation (because the appropriation requires a Commonwealth law, which is subject to the s 51(xxxi) constraint): *Pye v Renshaw* (1951) 84 CLR 59 at 79–80, 83.

[11.1.7] The issue of implied constraints on state legislative power was also discussed by the New South Wales Court of Appeal in *Building Construction Employees and Builders' Labourers Federation v Minister for Industrial Relations* (NSW) (1986) 7 NSWLR 372 **[5.4.8]**. Street CJ and Priestley JA proposed that the New South Wales Parliament could not make laws which were inimical to the peace, welfare and good government of parliamentary democracy (7 NSWLR at 387, 421–2), but other members of the court disputed that there was any such constraint: 7 NSWLR at 405 per Kirby P; at 413 per Mahoney JA.

The views advanced by Street CJ and Priestley JA were described by the High Court as 'somewhat surprising' in *Union Steamship Co of Australia Pty Ltd v King* (1988) 166 CLR 1 **[5.4.9]** at 9. The courts do not, the justices said in a unanimous judgment, have the power to invalidate laws passed by state parliaments 'on the ground that they do not secure the welfare and the public interest', although they did not exclude the possibility that state legislation could be 'subject to some restraints by reference to rights deeply rooted in our democratic system of government and the common law': 166 CLR at 10.

However, in recent times it has become clear that state governments — and perhaps even territory governments — may not be able to act in total disregard of the rights protected by the Commonwealth Constitution. For example, the common law and state and territory statutory law may not infringe the implied freedom of communication (*Lange v Australian Broadcasting Corporation* (1997) 189 CLR 520 **[11.3.3C]**, **[11.3.13C]** at 566) and state courts, when exercising federal jurisdiction, must act in a manner which is compatible with the requirements of Ch III of the Commonwealth Constitution: see *Kable v Director of Public Prosecutions (NSW)* (1996) 189 CLR 51 **[11.3.34]**.

[11.1.8]   In this chapter, we shall review the work of the High Court in the reading of express and implied rights under the Constitution. We shall begin with four of the express provisions which affect the interaction between individual rights or values, and public power (ss 51(xxxi), 80, 116 and 117), and then we shall consider the court's venture into implied rights and freedoms.

The work of the court in applying other constraints on governmental power is considered in other parts of this book. The principle of separation of judicial power was discussed in Chapter 6; s 92, and its guarantee of absolute freedom for interstate trade, commerce and intercourse was reviewed in Chapter 10; while s 99 (which precludes discrimination between states or parts of states in laws of trade, commerce or revenue) and the parallel restriction in s 51(ii) were considered in Chapter 9 and Chapter 10.

---

2   Express rights

Acquisition of property

[11.2.1E]   **Commonwealth Constitution**

51 The Parliament shall, subject to this Constitution, have power to make laws for the peace, order, and good government of the Commonwealth with respect to: ...

(xxxi)   The acquisition of property on just terms from any State or person in respect of which the Parliament has power to make laws: ...

~~~

[11.2.2]   Section 51(xxxi) seems to have been placed in the Commonwealth Constitution so as to ensure that parliament would have undisputed power to legislate for the compulsory acquisition of property. However, it also seems that the provision's reference to 'just terms' was intended to provide a restraint on the power of compulsory acquisition; it was 'intended to recognise the principle of the immunity of private and provincial property from interference by the federal authority, except on fair and equitable terms': Quick and Garran (1901) p 641. The presence of the contingent right in s 51(xxxi) means that the requirement of just terms operates at any time the Commonwealth makes a compulsory acquisition of property under the section: *Johnson Fear & Kingham v Commonwealth* (1943) 67 CLR 314 at 318.

In *Bank of New South Wales v Commonwealth* (1948) 76 CLR 1 **[11.2.9C]**, Dixon J expressed the orthodox view of s 51(xxxi) (at 349–50):

> Section 51(xxxi) serves a double purpose. It provides the Commonwealth Parliament with a legislative power of acquiring property: at the same time, as a condition upon the exercise of the power, it provides the individual or the State affected with a protection against governmental interferences with his proprietary rights without just recompense ... In requiring just terms s 51(xxxi) fetters the legislative power by forbidding laws with respect to acquisition on any terms that are not just.

In *Clunies-Ross v Commonwealth* (1984) 155 CLR 193, Gibbs CJ, Mason, Wilson, Brennan, Deane and Dawson JJ referred to s 51(xxxi) as having 'assumed the status of a constitutional guarantee of just terms [which] was to be given the liberal construction appropriate to such a constitutional provision': 155 CLR at 202.

[11.2.3] The constraints which, it is now acknowledged, s 51(xxxi) imposes on Commonwealth acquisition of property are not relevant where the Commonwealth negotiates, rather than imposes, an acquisition. In other words, s 51(xxxi) is concerned with compulsory acquisition; acquisition by 'the method of requisition' and not by 'the method of agreement': *John Cooke & Co Pty Ltd v Commonwealth* (1924) 34 CLR 269 at 282. As Stephen J said in *Trade Practices Commission v Tooth & Co Ltd* (1979) 142 CLR 397 **[11.2.11C]**, where the Commonwealth acquires property through agreement, it is assumed that the terms agreed to by the owner of the property are 'just terms': 142 CLR at 417.

Section 51(xxxi) is not directed at acquisitions effected by the states under their state constitutions: *Pye v Renshaw* (1951) 84 CLR 58 at 79–80. However if the Commonwealth funds a state to effect an acquisition, then that arrangement will be subject to the 'just terms' requirement: *Pye v Renshaw* (1951) 84 CLR 58 at 83.

[11.2.4] Consistent with the fundamental character of s 51(xxxi), other Commonwealth legislative powers will not support legislation which acquires property on less than 'just terms'. Law for the acquisition of property must conform to s 51(xxxi). Dixon CJ expressed the point as follows in *Attorney-General (Cth) v Schmidt* (1961) 105 CLR 361 at 372:

> [W]hen you have, as you do in par (xxxi), an express power, subject to a safeguard, restriction or qualification, to legislate on a particular subject or to a particular effect, it is in accordance with the soundest principles of interpretation to treat that as inconsistent with any construction of other powers conferred in the context which would mean that they included the same subject or produced the same effect and so authorized the same kind of legislation but without the safeguard, restriction or qualification.

However, that proposition is not absolute. The High Court has recognised that several other heads of legislative power will, in certain circumstances, support an acquisition of property that does not provide just terms: see **[11.2.21]**.

[11.2.5C]   **Minister of State for the Army v Dalziel**
(1944) 68 CLR 261

Regulation 54 of the National Security (General) Regulations authorised the Commonwealth Government to enter into exclusive possession of privately owned land for an indefinite period. Regulation 60H authorised the Minister to make orders determining the basis for the assessment and payment of compensation to the owner of any land affected by the Commonwealth's entry into possession. The Minister made an order directing that, 'in assessing compensation loss of occupation or profits shall not be taken into account'.

Dalziel was the weekly tenant of vacant land in Sydney, used by him as a commercial car park. He had occupied and used the land for this purpose for 13 years. In May 1942, the Minister for the Army took possession of the land under reg 54 of the National Security (General) Regulations. Dalziel claimed compensation, to cover his rental payments and lost profits during the period of the Commonwealth's occupancy of the land. Acting under the Minister's order made under reg 60H, a Commonwealth official determined that Dalziel should be paid compensation limited to his rental liability, and that he should receive no compensation for his loss of profits. Dalziel applied to the Supreme Court of New South Wales for a review of the compensation (a review for which reg 60G provided). The Supreme Court held that the Commonwealth's taking of possession was an acquisition of property within s 51(xxxi) and that reg 60H did not provide for just terms. The Minister for the Army appealed to the High Court.

Rich J: [284] The placitum which is in question is concerned with the legislative power of the Commonwealth Parliament. One of the characteristic features of a fully sovereign power is its legal right to deal as it thinks fit with anything and everything within its territory. This includes what is described in the United States as eminent domain (*dominium eminens*), the right to take to itself any property within its territory, or any interest therein, on such terms and for such purposes as it thinks proper, eminent domain being thus the proprietary aspect of sovereignty. The Commonwealth of Australia is not, however, a fully sovereign power. Its legislature possesses only such powers as have been expressly conferred upon it, or as are implied in powers which have been expressly conferred. The subject of eminent domain is dealt with by the placitum now in question (s 51 (xxxi)), which is in the following terms:—'The Parliament shall, subject to this Constitution, have power to make laws for the peace, order, and good government of the Commonwealth with respect to — the acquisition of property on just terms from any State or person for any purpose in respect of which the Parliament has power to make laws.' What we are concerned with is not a private document [285] creating rights inter partes, but a Constitution containing a provision of a fundamental character designed to protect citizens from being deprived of their property by the Sovereign State except upon just terms. The meaning of property in such a connection must be determined upon general principles of jurisprudence, not by the artificial refinements of any particular legal system or by reference to *Sheppard's Touchstone*. The language used is perfectly general. It says the acquisition of property. It is not restricted to acquisition by particular methods or of particular types of interests, or to particular types of property. It extends to any acquisition of any interest in any property. It authorises such acquisition, but it expressly imposes two conditions on every such acquisition. It must be upon just terms, and it must be for a purpose in respect of which the Parliament has power to make laws. In the case now before us, the Minister has, *in adversum*, assumed possession of land of which Dalziel was weekly tenant. With all respect to the argument which has been addressed to us to the contrary, I am quite unable to understand how this can be said not to be an acquisition of property from Dalziel within the meaning of the placitum. Property, in relation to land, is a bundle of rights exercisable with respect to the land. The tenant of an unencumbered estate in fee simple in possession has the largest possible bundle. But there is nothing in the placitum to suggest that the legislature was intended to be at liberty to free itself from the restrictive provisions of the placitum by taking care to seize something short of the whole bundle owned by the person whom it was expropriating. *Possession vaut titre* in more senses than one. Not only is a right to possession a right of property, but where the object of proprietary rights is a tangible thing it is the most characteristic and essential of those rights ...

[286] It would, in my opinion, be wholly inconsistent with the language of the placitum to hold that, whilst preventing the legislature from authorizing the acquisition of a citizen's full title except upon just terms, it leaves it open to the legislature to seize possession and enjoy the full fruits of possession, indefinitely, on any terms it chooses, or upon no terms at all. In the case now before us, the Minister has seized and taken away from Dalziel everything that made his weekly tenancy worth having, and has left him with the empty husk of tenancy. In such circumstances, he may well say:

> You take my house, when you do take the prop
> That doth sustain my house; you take my life,
> When you do take the means whereby I live.

Rich J referred to the distinction drawn in United Kingdom and state legislation between the 'permanent appropriation of property' and the 'temporary assumption of the possession of adjacent property', and continued:

But, with all respect, I fail to see how the practice of such legislatures, or the language used by judges in referring to their legislation, throws any light upon the construction or operation of placitum xxxi, occurring, as it does, in a Constitution which confers powers which are both limited and conditional. I venture to repeat what I said in *Australian Apple* [287] *and Pear Marketing Board v Tonking* (1942) 66 CLR 77 at 106, 107: 'It is by the Constitution itself that the acquisition is required to be on just terms, and, since Parliament is bound by the Constitution, by no artifice or device can it withdraw from the determination by a court of justice the question whether any terms which it has provided are just, that is, terms which secure adequate compensation to those who have been expropriated ...'. If the argument which has been addressed to us on behalf of the Minister were allowed to prevail, the Commonwealth Parliament could authorize the Executive to take possession of not only all or any of the private property of citizens but also the property of the States and keep it indefinitely without paying a farthing of compensation to any one. To accede to this argument would be in effect to strike placitum xxxi out of the Constitution.

~~~

[11.2.6] Rich J held that reg 60H was invalid because it was 'intended to confer upon the Minister an arbitrary discretion even when the Minister dispossesses a citizen not only of some, but of all, his rights of property in a particular subject-matter': 68 CLR at 289. It followed that the Minister's order, limiting the amount of compensation payable, was also invalid. He held that the appeal should be dismissed.

Starke, McTiernan and Williams JJ held that reg 54 provided for an acquisition of property within s 51(xxxi). Latham CJ dissented, holding that s 51(xxxi) was concerned with ownership and that 'possession and ownership of land, though closely connected, are not identical': 68 CLR at 276. McTiernan and Williams JJ also held that reg 60H and the Minister's order were invalid and that the appeal should be dismissed. Latham CJ and Williams J held that reg 60H and the Minister's order were valid, and would have allowed the appeal.

Notes

[11.2.7] What terms must the Commonwealth provide before its acquisition can be said to be 'on just terms'? The High Court has said that a balance must be drawn between the interest of the individual whose property is acquired and the interest of the community: 'Unlike "compensation", which connotes full money equivalence, 'just terms' are concerned with fairness', Dixon J said in *Nelungaloo v*

Commonwealth (1948) 75 CLR 495 at 569. However, the underlying principle is that the terms provided should reflect the market value of the property acquired (per Williams J at 507):

> ... the price which a reasonably willing vendor would have been prepared to accept and a reasonably willing purchaser would have been prepared to pay for the property at the date of the acquisition.

On the other hand, some premium might be required to be paid where property is acquired from an owner who uses the land for non-commercial purposes (for religious or charitable purposes, for example): *Minister of State for the Army v Parbury Henty & Co Ltd* (1945) 70 CLR 459 at 491–2 per Latham CJ; at 515 per Williams J; or where the property has special significance: *Johnson Fear & Kingham v Commonwealth* (1943) 67 CLR 314 at 322–3. All the circumstances surrounding the acquisition are to be taken into account: *Andrews v Howell* (1941) 65 CLR 255 at 282.

[11.2.8] The legislation providing for acquisition may vest the assessment of the compensation to be paid in an administrative agency, so long as the agency's determination is not conclusive and is amenable to judicial review. So, in *Bank of New South Wales v Commonwealth* (1948) 76 CLR 1 **[11.2.9C]**, the Banking Act 1947 (Cth) was found not to provide just terms for the Commonwealth's compulsory acquisition of the shares in private banks because compensation for that acquisition was to be determined exclusively by a specially constituted Federal Court of Claims: see 76 CLR at 276 per Rich and Williams JJ; at 323 per Starke J; at 368 per Dixon J. For further consideration of the constitutional requirements applicable to a non-judicial tribunal vested with power to determine 'just terms', see *Commonwealth v Western Australia* (1999) 196 CLR 392 at 462–3 (Kirby J); 491 (Callinan J, contra).

[11.2.9C] Bank of New South Wales v Commonwealth
(1948) 76 CLR 1

The Banking Act 1947 (Cth) provided a comprehensive legislative scheme under which the Commonwealth was to take over the business of private banks operating in Australia. Division 2 of Pt IV of the Banking Act authorised the Commonwealth Bank to purchase shares in private banks (s 12); authorised the Commonwealth Treasurer to direct that Australian shares in a private bank be vested in the Commonwealth Bank (s 13); and directed the Commonwealth Bank to pay fair and reasonable compensation for any acquisition of shares under s 13: s 15. Division 3 of Pt IV of the Banking Act provided that, on a date to be specified, the directors of private banks should cease to hold office (s 17); that the Governor of the Commonwealth Bank with the approval of the Commonwealth Treasurer could appoint directors to fill the places of the removed directors (s 18); and that the newly-appointed directors should have full power to manage, direct and control the business and affairs of the bank of which they were directors, including a power to dispose of the business of the bank to the Commonwealth: s 19.

All the private banks and several of their shareholders began an action in the High Court, seeking a declaration that the Banking Act was invalid.

Dixon J: [Dixon J referred to the provisions of Parts 2 and 3 of Division IV and continued:] [348] It will be seen that a notice by the Treasurer under s 13(1) operates to set in motion a process which expropriates the shares localized in Australia and at the same time displaces the authority over the affairs of the company, not only of the directors chosen by the shareholders, but of the shareholders themselves. It places all the property and all the activities of the company under the supreme control of the nominees of the Treasurer and the Bank and leaves them in entire control indefinitely with complete powers of disposition and complete power to bind the company as to the recompense it will receive for its assets. The corporate entity of the company remains and in it the legal property in the assets continues to reside. Shareholders are entitled to dividends if the nominees see fit to declare any. In a winding up, if there be one, shareholders remain entitled to participate as contributories. But in all other respects the beneficial enjoyment and control of the undertaking has been placed in the hands of agents of the Commonwealth, or of the Commonwealth Bank if the distinction is insisted on and in this matter can be clearly maintained. The purpose of removing the directors appointed by the shareholders and replacing them with nominees of the Treasurer and of the Governor of the Bank is that agents of the Commonwealth may take command of the undertaking of the banking company and carry it on in the public, as opposed to private, interests pending decisions, in which they will play a part, concerning the acquisition of the assets by or their disposal to the Commonwealth Bank, the settling of the amount of compensation or the purchase price, and the transfer of the staff. The purposes of the whole operation authorized by Division 3 appear to me to be public. No doubt there is no interference with the ultimate right of the shareholders as contributories in a winding up to receive as a component of the distributable surplus so much profit as may have been earned under the regime of the nominees and as they have not chosen to distribute [349] as dividend. But that and the legal conceptions involved in the continuance of the corporate existence of the banking company as the repository of the title to the undertaking is all that is left. In other words the undertaking is taken into the hands of agents of the Commonwealth so that it may be carried on, as it is conceived, in the public interest. The company and its shareholders are in a real sense, although not formally, stripped of the possession and control of the entire undertaking. The profits which may arise from it in the hands of the Commonwealth's agents are still to be accounted for and in some form they will be represented in what the shareholders receive. But the effective deprivation of the company and its shareholders of the reality of proprietorship is the same. It must be remembered that complete dispositive power accompanies the control of the assets which passes to the nominees. It is as if an intending purchaser were enabled to put a receiver in possession of an estate and also to take a power of sale in the receiver's name, remaining however accountable, until he pays the purchase money, for the rents and profits, which nevertheless he may apply towards the upkeep of the property and, subject thereto, accumulate.

Upon consideration I have reached the conclusion that this is but a circuitous device to acquire indirectly the substance of a proprietary interest without at once providing the just terms guaranteed by s 51(xxxi) of the Constitution when that is done.

I take *Minister of State for the Army v Dalziel* [(1944) 68 CLR 261] to mean that s 51(xxxi) is not to be confined pedantically to the taking of title by the Commonwealth to some specific estate or interest in land recognized at law or in equity and to some specific form of property in a chattel or chose in action similarly recognized, but that it extends to innominate and anomalous interests and includes the assumption and indefinite continuance of exclusive possession and control for the purposes of the Commonwealth of any subject of property. Section 51(xxxi) serves a double purpose. It provides the Commonwealth Parliament with a legislative power of acquiring property: at the same time as a condition upon the exercise of the power it provides the individual or the State, affected with a protection against governmental interferences with his proprietary rights without just recompense. In both aspects consistency with the principles upon which constitutional provisions are interpreted and applied demands that the paragraph should be given as full and flexible an operation as will cover the objects it was designed to effect. Moreover, when a constitution undertakes [350] to forbid or restrain some legislative course, there can be no prohibition to which it is more proper to apply the principle embodied in the maxim *quando aliquid prohibetur, prohibetur et omne per quod devenitur ad illud*. In requiring just terms s 51(xxxi) fetters the legislative power by forbidding laws with respect to acquisition on any terms that are not just.

In my opinion the provisions of s 13(1) and ss 16, 18, 19 amount to an indirect means of doing what the paragraph does not allow.

Dixon J said that ss 13(1), 17, 18 and 19 operated to place 'agents of the Commonwealth or of the Commonwealth Bank in control of the undertaking and arming them with powers' over the private banks; and continued:

> From that point of view I think they amount to an attempt to defeat the operation of s 51(xxxi). But the powers of disposition given by s 19 are themselves open to independent attack under s 51(xxxi). They are exercisable in favour of the Commonwealth Bank. When they are so exercised the Commonwealth Bank will acquire the Australian business of the private banking company in respect of which s 13(1) has been invoked or perhaps the whole undertaking of that company. It will do so on terms agreed between the nominees whom the Governor of the Commonwealth Bank has appointed with the approval of the Treasurer. Further, if the Treasurer gives a notice under s 22(1) and, whether before or after that notice, the nominees are appointed in consequence of a notice given under s 13(1), the nominees may make an agreement under [351] s 22(5), or they may suffer an acquisition under s 24(4) and agree on the compensation under s 43(2), or fail to request a reference to the Court of Claims under s 44(3) and so accept the offer of the Commonwealth Bank. I cannot see how the powers of the nominees under s 19 can be reduced by any process of interpretation based on s 6 so as to avoid all or any of those positions.

> In my opinion each of them involves a conflict with s 51(xxxi).

> In each case the amount payable by the Commonwealth Bank for the assets of the private bank is left to the judgment of the nominees of the Commonwealth Bank. However high may be the level to which their legal duty may be raised, even if they be treated as full fiduciaries for the creditors and shareholders, it is all left to their judgment. In every case the acquisition by the Commonwealth Bank should, in my opinion, be regarded as on the side of the company an involuntary disposition. For it would, I think, be quite wrong for the purposes of s 51(xxxi) to separate out the steps by which it is accomplished and exclude from consideration the compulsory superseding of the company's directors chosen by the shareholders and the substitution of nominees of the Treasurer and the Governor. The fact that these officers may be free to act according to their own discretion in disposing of the company's assets or in binding it to an amount of purchase money as compensation, appears to me to be nothing to the point. They are not agents appointed by the company. Any relation of agency on behalf of the company is compulsory and the work of statute. Their appointment would have been against the authentic will of the company. In substance they are agents of the Commonwealth armed by statute with power to bind the company. I think that the powers conferred by s 19 involve a conflict with s 51(xxxi).

Latham CJ, Rich, Starke, McTiernan and Williams JJ also held that Division 3 of Pt IV did not comply with s 51(xxxi) and was, accordingly, invalid. The court also held that the Banking Act was invalid because it infringed the separation of judicial power required by Ch III of the Constitution and because it denied the absolute freedom of interstate trade and commerce guaranteed by s 92.

~~~

Notes

[11.2.10] The acquisition of property referred to in s 51(xxxi) need not be an acquisition by the Commonwealth Government. If a law of the Commonwealth is a law with respect to the acquisition of property for a Commonwealth purpose, then the law is subject to the 'just terms' requirement expressed in s 51(xxxi). In *P J Magennis Pty Ltd v Commonwealth* (1949) 80 CLR 382, a majority of the High Court (Latham CJ, Rich, Williams and Webb JJ; Dixon and McTiernan JJ dissenting) held that the War Service Land Settlement Agreements Act 1945 (Cth) was a law with respect to the acquisition of property and, because it did not provide for 'just terms', the Act was invalid. The Act approved an agreement made between the Commonwealth and New South Wales governments, under which the latter government was to acquire land (for distribution to discharged members of the defence forces) at 1942 values. Latham CJ said at 401:

> The constitutional provision is not limited in terms to laws providing for the acquisition of property by the Commonwealth itself ... It is obvious that the constitutional provision could readily be evaded if it did not apply to the acquisition by a corporation constituted by the Commonwealth or by an individual person authorised by a Commonwealth statute to acquire property. Further, the present case shows that the constitutional provision would be quite ineffective if by making an agreement with a State for the acquisition of property upon terms which were not just the Commonwealth Parliament could validly provide for the acquisition of property from any person to whom State legislation could be applied upon terms which paid no attention to justice.

Williams J (with whom Rich J agreed) said at 423–4:

> In my opinion the paragraph applies to all Commonwealth legislation the object of which is to acquire property for a purpose in respect of which the Commonwealth Parliament has power to make laws. It is immaterial whether the acquisition is to be made by the Commonwealth or by some body authorised to acquire the property by the Commonwealth or a State by agreement with the Commonwealth. In order to be legislation with respect to the acquisition of property within the meaning of s 51(xxxi) of the Constitution, the Commonwealth or some body authorised by the Commonwealth must no doubt have an interest in the acquisition of the property. Otherwise the acquisition could not be for a purpose in respect of which the Commonwealth Parliament has power to make laws. But the interest need not be a proprietary interest. Any legal interest including a contractual interest would be sufficient if it made the acquisition one for such a purpose.

In view of the discussion in *Trade Practices Commission v Tooth & Co Ltd* (1979) 142 CLR 397 **[11.2.11C]**, it appears that a law may be one for the acquisition of property, even though the Commonwealth takes no legal interest in the property in question.

[11.2.11C]   Trade Practices Commission v Tooth & Co Ltd

(1979) 142 CLR 397

Section 47(1) of the Trade Practices Act 1974 (Cth) prohibited a corporation from engaging in the practice of exclusive dealing. Section 76(1) of the Act provided for a 'pecuniary penalty' for breaches of s 47(1), and s 80 provided for an injunction to restrain breaches of s 47(1). Section 47(9)(a) of the Act provided that a corporation engaged in the practice of exclusive dealing if it refused to renew a lease of land for the reason that the other party to the lease was doing business with a competitor of the corporation.

Tooth & Co Ltd, a brewery and owner of many licensed hotels in New South Wales, leased those hotels to various tenants. A standard clause in the lease obliged the tenants not to purchase any alcohol or other drinks from any person other than Tooth & Co Ltd. According to evidence before the Federal Court of Australia, 'on an average several leases expire in every week'. Tooth & Co Ltd began an action in the Federal Court of Australia for a declaration that it was not obliged to comply with s 47(1) and (9)(a) of the Trade Practices Act. A majority of the Full Court of the Federal Court held that s 47(9)(a) was invalid because it amounted to an 'acquisition of property' without 'just terms'. The Trade Practices Commission appealed to the High Court of Australia.

Stephen J: [412] What the legislature has done in s 47 is to proscribe in very broad terms a particular practice in trade. In doing so it has [413] deprived all those to whom it is directed, whether they be landlords or one of the many other classes of persons capable of imposing the practice of exclusive dealing upon others, of the freedom to impose that practice ... Many, if not all, of these instances involve restraints upon the free exercise of proprietary rights. Are, then, all these to be regarded as acquisitions subject to s 51(xxxi) and hence requiring for their validity the provision of just terms? If not, is there some special feature of sub-ss (8) and (9) or of such of their provisions as relate to the renewal of leases which so requires?

I would answer 'No' to each of the questions posed above. One may, I think, approach the first question by two rather different routes, each of which has led me to the same conclusion. The first is a route not dissimilar from that followed by their Lordships in *Belfast Corporation v OD Cars Ltd* [1960] AC 490. Their Lordships were there concerned with the town planning legislation of Northern Ireland and with types of restrictions which have of recent years become familiar in legislation of that character. The impairment of the rights of owners to develop and use their land which such legislation effected was not regarded by their Lordships as a 'taking' falling within s 5(1) of the Government of Ireland Act, 1920, which forbade the local legislature from enacting any law so as to 'take any property without compensation'. Viscount Simonds [[1960] AC at 517] did not regard such restrictions upon the use of property in a particular way either as a 'taking' of 'property', as those words were commonly understood, or as within the phrase 'take property without compensation' in s 5(1). Having referred to the fact that from earliest times restraints had been imposed upon the use of property and that in modern times the very many instances of the necessary subordination of individual rights to the public interest did not encourage the giving of any enlarged meaning to that phrase, his Lordship went on to refer to American authority. He described as a clear guide in dis[414]tinguishing between mere regulation of property rights and the 'taking' of property the dissenting judgment of Brandeis J in *Pennsylvania Coal Co v Mahon* 260 US 393 (1922) [67 Law Ed 322]. His Honour had there said: [260 US at 417 (1922): [67 Law Ed at 326–7]]

Every restriction upon the use of property ... deprives the owner of some right theretofore enjoyed, and is, in that sense, an abridgment by the State of rights in property without making compensation. But restriction imposed to protect the public health, safety or morals from dangers threatened is not a taking. The restriction here in question is merely the prohibition of a noxious use.

Viscount Simonds also cited from the judgment of Holmes J, who had said [260 US at 415 (1922) [67 Law Ed at 326]] 'The general rule at least is, that, while property may be regulated to a certain extent, if regulation goes too far it will be recognised as a taking'. His Lordship recognized that the distinction between regulation and confiscation might be one of degree but was in no doubt but that the instant case was of the former kind ...

Stephen J referred to a passage from a United States encyclopaedia of law, *Corpus Juris Secundum*, on the distinction between 'regulation' and 'taking':

There is no set formula to determine where regulation ends and taking begins; so the question depends on the [415] particular facts and the necessities of each case and the court must consider the extent of the public interest to be protected and the extent of regulation essential to protect that interest.

On the one hand, many measures which in one way or another impair an owner's exercise of his proprietary rights will involve no 'acquisition' such as pl (xxxi) speaks of. On the other hand, far reaching restrictions upon the use of property may in appropriate circumstances be seen to involve such an acquisition ... In each case the particular circumstances must be ascertained and weighed and, as in all questions of degree, it will be idle to seek to draw precise lines in advance. With this in mind I turn to a statement of why it is that I do not regard the general effect of sub-ss (1) to (9) of s 47 as involving any acquisition of property.

An important consideration is that these sub-sections are clearly directed only to the prevention of a noxious use of proprietary rights. It is only to the extent that, in the exercise of those rights, the prohibited goal of exclusive dealing is sought to be attained that any restraint is imposed. So long as the supply of goods or services or the exercise of those powers which a lessor or potential lessor possesses is not made the occasion for the imposition of exclusive dealing no question of restraint occurs. In this sense the restraints imposed by s 47 are less sweeping in their impact upon proprietary rights than are those customarily imposed in, say, town planning legislation. In the latter it is common absolutely to prohibit certain uses of land, albeit in the public interest. The prohibitions contained in s 47 are never absolute but depend for their effect upon the mode of exercise: it is only when a particular mode of exercise of proprietary rights is in question, one that the legislation identifies as tending to promote exclusive dealing, that the prohibition takes effect. ...

[416] The loss of freedom of action in relation to proprietary rights which s 47 involves is narrowly confined to the suppression of what the legislature has judged to be the noxious practice of exclusive dealing. Not only is there no question of the acquisition of property for its own sake; whatever restraints the section does impose upon the free exercise of proprietary rights apply only where, and to the extent to which, but for their existence, the aim of the legislature would be defeated.

These considerations serve to confirm the initial impression gained from a reading of the section and an understanding of its operation: that s 47 effects no acquisition of property within pl (xxxi) ... In this respect the section is no more an acquisition of property within pl (xxxi) than would be a law against racial discrimination which, in its application, might operate so as to prevent a trader or lessor from refusing to sell goods to, or lease premises to, persons upon the ground of their particular race, colour or creed.

The second route which may be pursued, and which has led me to the same conclusion, employs concepts some of which differ little from those already considered. It is founded upon an analysis of the phrase 'acquisition on just terms', which is central to pl (xxxi). The reference to 'just terms' throws light upon the particular meaning of 'acquisition' in the placitum. Despite early dicta to the contrary it is now well established that pl (xxxi) contemplates acquisition by 'the method of requisition', not by 'the method of agreement' (*John Cooke & Co Pty Ltd v The Commonwealth* (1924) 34 CLR 269 at 282 and see *Poulton v The Commonwealth* (1953) 89 CLR 540 at 573, per Fullagar J) ...

[417] Section 51(xxxi) involves 'a compound conception, namely 'acquisition-on-just-terms'' (*Grace Bros Pty Ltd v The Commonwealth* (1946) 72 CLR at 290, per Dixon J). An integral part of that conception is the need for just terms. The existence of that need presupposes an inability on the part of the owner of the property to insist upon payment of whatever amount he may nominate as the price of the thing acquired. The possession by an owner of an ability to so insist goes further than to deny the need for just terms, which he will then be in a position to secure for himself. It effectively denies recourse by the would-be taker to 'the method of requisition' since the owner can, by advancing his price, deter the taker at least to the point at which the obtaining of the price becomes more attractive than retention of the property. At that point requisition necessarily ceases to have meaning and becomes, of its own accord, agreement.

Bearing in mind this feature of pl (xxxi), s 47 (references in sub-ss (8) and (9) to renewal of leases aside) can be seen nowhere to deprive the owner of property of insisting upon his own price for any property rights which he is otherwise obliged to part with. The only exception to that proposition is the case of a differential price demanded by an owner of property as a means of compelling acceptance by the buyer of some exclusive dealing arrangement.

Aickin J: [Aickin J said that it was assumed that, if s 47(9)(a) involved an acquisition of property, it would not be on just terms. He continued:] [444] The argument before us was concerned with two questions only. First whether the operation of s 47(9)(a) of the Act when read with ss 76, 77 and 80, in relation to the renewal of a lease, comprised the acquisition of property within the meaning of s 51(xxxi). In such a case the lease would be granted, not to the Commonwealth or its agent, but to some other person or corporation. The second point was whether in the circumstances the requirement of just terms was applicable to this Act, but it was not contended for the appellants that if the operation of the Act produced an 'acquisition' it was on just terms.

The cases establish that the concept of property in par (xxxi) is a wide one, see *Minister of State for the Army v Dalziel* (1944) 68 CLR 261 and that it includes interests in land which fall far short of full ownership. There can be no doubt that a leasehold interest in land is property, nor that a law requiring that the owner of land grant a lease to the Commonwealth would be an acquisition of property where that interest is by the operation of the legislation carved out of the larger interest of the landowner who holds the fee simple ...

[445] It was conceded that this court had in earlier decisions dealt with s 51(xxxi) by treating it as abstracting from other heads of power (including the incidental power) all content which would otherwise have enabled the compulsory acquisition of property, and as subjecting the power with respect to the acquisition to an obligation to provide just terms. Thus the paragraph ensured that whenever property was compulsorily acquired pursuant to a law of the Commonwealth just terms must be provided. It was acknowledged that the consequence was that no other head of power included a power to acquire property compulsorily for the purposes of that head of power because the totality of the power of compulsory acquisition was embodied in s 51(xxxi).

The view so expressed is in my opinion plainly right ...

[451] The question whether par (xxxi) applies to legislation which compulsorily acquires property ... that it vests in some person other than the Commonwealth or an agency of the Commonwealth must now be regarded as settled. It was first referred to in *Jenkins v The Commonwealth* (1947) 74 CLR 400 by Williams J sitting in the original jurisdiction. He said: [(1947) 74 CLR at 406] 'Section 51(xxxi) of the Constitution is not limited to acquisitions by the Commonwealth.' The question arose again in *McClintock v The Commonwealth* (1947) 75 CLR 1 where Rich J, Starke J and Williams J all expressed the view that s 51(xxxi) was not limited to the acquisition of property by the Commonwealth itself but extended to the acquisition of property for any purpose in respect of which the Commonwealth has power to make laws.

Aickin J quoted passages from the judgments of Starke J and Williams J, and continued:

[452] With respect this view appears to me to be soundly based. It would be a serious gap in the constitutional safeguard which is the manifest policy of par (xxxi) if the Parliament could legislate for compulsory acquisition of property without just terms by statutory bodies which were not the Commonwealth itself or its agents or by persons or bodies having no connexion with the government. Neither the words of s 51 nor the context require the adoption of so anomalous a view. Accordingly the fact that under s 47(9)(a) of the Act the lease compulsorily acquired vests in a private individual or a company provides no reason why just terms need not be provided. ...

[453] The cases dealing with bankruptcy, taxation and penalties require some examination. One general observation may however be made by way of introduction. Such subject matters may properly be said to involve, at least in some instances, the passing of the legal title and in others both the legal and the beneficial title to the Commonwealth, or its officers or to designated persons, but nonetheless the processes involved are not such as would ordinarily in 1900 or today be described as the 'acquisition of property' or as falling within its ordinary meaning.

Taxation involves the compulsory payment of money to the Commonwealth according to prescribed criteria applicable to persons who fall within the specified categories in a manner capable of testing in the courts. Its imposition creates a debt but does not compulsorily acquire property. No doubt when payment is made property in the cash or cheque passes to the [454] Commonwealth but it is not a process capable of being categorized or described as 'acquisition of property', save in a very unusual sense of that expression. It is thus not surprising to find that in *Moore v The Commonwealth* (1951) 82 CLR 547 and *Federal Commissioner of Taxation v Clyne* the Court held that legislation classified as laws with respect to taxation or imposing taxation were not laws with respect to the acquisition of property within the meaning of s 51(xxxi). In the latter case Dixon CJ said: [(1958) 100 CLR at 263]

Little need be said of the argument based upon s 51(xxxi) of the Constitution. The argument is that 'provisional tax' is paid provisionally and returned without interest in the event of no tax accruing due. That is said to be an acquisition of property on terms not just. Once it is held that provisional tax is authorised by s 51(ii) it seems absurd to say that, within the meaning of s 51(xxxi), the sums paid or payable as provisional tax constitute property acquired for a purpose in respect of which Parliament has power to make laws. The purpose of the power itself which is conferred by s 51(ii) is to acquire money for public purposes and that is no less so if the money is raised provisionally and in advance of the actual accrual of the tax as *debitum in praesenti solvendum in praesenti*.

In *Burton v Honan* (1952) 86 CLR 169 the court dealt with forfeiture of prohibited imports under the *Customs Act*. Dixon CJ said [(1952) 86 CLR at 180–1]:

> The short answer to this contention is that the whole matter lies outside the power given by s 51(xxxi). It is not an acquisition of property for any purpose in respect of which Parliament has power to make laws. It is nothing but forfeiture imposed on all persons in derogation of any rights such persons might otherwise have in relation to the goods, a forfeiture imposed as part of the incidental power for the purpose of vindicating the Customs laws. It has no more to do with the acquisition of property for a purpose in respect of which the Parliament has power to make laws within s 51(xxxi) that has the imposition of taxation itself, or the forfeiture of goods in the hands of the actual offender.

The other members of the court agreed with those reasons and did not deliver separate reasons for judgment. I take Dixon CJ in that passage and in another passage on the same page to use the expression 'the acquisition of property for a purpose in respect of which the Parliament has power to make laws within s 51(xxxi)' to indicate that in so far as the application of the Customs Act involves the passing of property to the Com[455]monwealth it is not by 'acquisition' within the meaning of that term in s 51(xxxi).

The same would be true of fines imposed by the courts for breaches of Acts of the Commonwealth Parliament and of various statutory penalties, including those referred to in s 76 of the Act. Both forfeiture under customs legislation and the imposition of fines by way of punishment for criminal offences were well known in 1900 and would not then or now ordinarily be described as the 'acquisition of property'.

Barwick CJ delivered judgment to the same effect as Aickin J. Mason J agreed that s 47(9)(a) involved an acquisition of property, but held that the acquisition was on just terms, because it left a corporation free to negotiate the terms and conditions (other than a term insisting on exclusive dealing) of any renewed lease: 142 CLR at 433. Gibbs and Murphy JJ delivered separate judgments to the same effect as Stephen J. In the result, the High Court held by a majority (Barwick CJ and Aickin J dissenting) that s 47(9)(a) was valid.

~~~

Notes

[11.2.12] In *Commonwealth v Tasmania* (the *Tasmanian Dam* case) (1983) 158 CLR 1 **[3.3.15C]**, Tasmania argued that several pieces of Commonwealth legislation effected an acquisition of the state's property because the legislation prevented the state from using land for a wide variety of purposes without the consent of the Commonwealth. Four members of the High Court considered this argument.

Mason J said that the legislation restricted the uses to which Tasmania could put its land, giving a Commonwealth Minister the power of veto; but it did not give to 'the Commonwealth nor anyone else ... a proprietary interest of any kind in the property' nor was there 'a vesting of possession in the Commonwealth' so that there was no acquisition of property: 158 CLR at 145. Murphy and Brennan JJ adopted a similar approach: 158 CLR at 181 per Murphy J; at 247–8 per Brennan J.

Deane J took a broader view of the type of legislation which could be caught by s 51(xxxi) and held that two pieces of legislation did acquire Tasmania's property in the land in question. They were s 11 of the World Heritage (Properties Conservation) Act 1983 (Cth), which prohibited interference with any site of significance to people of the Aboriginal race, and regulations made under the National Parks and Wildlife Conservation Act 1975 (Cth) which prevented any construction works on identified state land. Deane J said that the restrictions on the use of the property imposed by the two pieces of legislation were so comprehensive that they were equivalent to a restrictive covenant, even though the Commonwealth was not taking for itself any material benefit of a proprietary nature. It was enough, Deane J said, to amount to an acquisition of property within s 51(xxxi) that the Commonwealth had, through its legislation, 'brought about a position where the [state] land is effectively frozen unless the [Commonwealth] Minister consents to development of it': 158 CLR at 286.

[11.2.13]   Section 122, the territories power, once provided an exception to the proposition that s 51(xxxi) is an exhaustive statement of the Commonwealth Parliament's power to legislate for the acquisition of property. However, since *Newcrest Mining (WA) Ltd v Commonwealth* (1997) 190 CLR 513 **[11.2.14C]** this exception has been largely rendered ineffective.

In an earlier case, *Teori Tau v Commonwealth* (1969) 119 CLR 564, the entire High Court (Barwick CJ, McTiernan, Kitto, Menzies, Windeyer, Owen and Walsh JJ), decided that the power conferred by s 122, to make laws for the government of territories of the Commonwealth, was not controlled by s 51(xxxi), so that there was no constitutional requirement that laws for the acquisition of property in a territory provide just terms. The court expressed its conclusions in the following terms (at 570–1):

> Section 51 is concerned with what may be called federal legislative powers as part of the distribution of legislative power between the Commonwealth and the constituent states. Section 122 is concerned with the legislative power for the government of Commonwealth territories in respect of which there is no such division of legislative power. The grant of legislative power by s 122 is plenary in quality and unlimited and unqualified in point of subject matter. In particular, it is not limited or qualified by s 51(xxxi) or, for that matter, by any other paragraph of that section.
>
> ... Our decision applies to all territories, those on the mainland of Australia as well as those external to the continent of Australia.

The decision in *Newcrest Mining (WA) Ltd v Commonwealth* (1997) 190 CLR 513 **[11.2.14C]** effectively nullifies this exception.

[11.2.14C]   Newcrest Mining (WA) Ltd v Commonwealth
(1997) 190 CLR 513

Uranium deposits were discovered at Coronation Hill in the Northern Territory in 1953. The traditional owners of the land and environmental groups opposed mining the deposits. Newcrest Mining held a number of mining leases at Coronation Hill granted from the Commonwealth between 1947 and 1974 under the Mining Ordinance 1939 (NT), which was made under the Northern Territory (Administration) Act 1920 (Cth). Following the grant of self-government in 1978, the Northern Territory legislature passed the Mining Act 1980 (NT) repealing the 1939 Ordinance. The Northern Territory (Self-Government) Act 1978 s 50(2) provided that compulsory acquisition of property within the territory should not be made otherwise than on just terms.

In 1979, the Commonwealth Government made a proclamation under s 7(2) of the National Parks and Wildlife Conservation Act 1975 (Cth), declaring an area which included part of the Newcrest leases to be a park (Stage 1 of Kakadu National Park) for the purposes of the Act. In 1987 the Commonwealth Parliament enacted the National

Parks and Wildlife Conservation Amendment Act 1987, which inserted s 10(1A) in the principal Act. Section 10(1A) provided: 'No operations for the recovery of minerals shall be carried on in Kakadu National Park.' Section 7 of the Amendment Act provided: 'Notwithstanding any law of the Commonwealth or of the Northern Territory, the Commonwealth is not liable to pay compensation to any person by reason of the enactment of this Act.' The Commonwealth Government subsequently extended the Kakadu National Park in what became known as Stage 3 of Kakadu National Park. Further proclamations were made on 13 November 1989, and 21 June 1991. The result of the proclamations and the Amendment Act was to prevent Newcrest from exercising its mining rights under its leases and to deprive it of any compensation for the deprivation.

Newcrest commenced proceedings in the High Court in 1992 seeking a declaration that the proclamations and the provisions under which they were made were invalid. Newcrest argued that the Commonwealth had effected an acquisition of Newcrest's interests in the land and the minerals, and that the provisions in the legislation which prevented Newcrest obtaining compensation for the deprivation of its interests amounted to an acquisition of property other than on just terms contrary to s 51(xxxi) of the Constitution. The Commonwealth denied that any acquisition had occurred and contended that, if any acquisition had occurred, it was valid because it was made under the power conferred under s 122 of the Constitution, which was not subject to the requirement of just terms in s 51(xxxi).

Mason CJ reserved the constitutional question relating to the operation of s 51(xxxi) and s 122 after remitting to the Federal Court the question of the validity of the leases. In May 1996 Brennan CJ ordered that the constitutional issue be reserved for consideration by the Full Court of the High Court.

In separate judgments, a majority of the court (Toohey, Gaudron, Gummow, and Kirby JJ; Brennan CJ, Dawson and McHugh JJ dissenting) decided that the 1989 and 1991 proclamations did not apply to Newcrest's valid mining leases and the Commonwealth's acquisition was subject to a requirement to pay just terms. Three members of the majority (Gaudron, Gummow and Kirby JJ) said that *Teori Tau v Commonwealth* (1969) 119 CLR 564 **[11.2.13]** should be overruled and that the just terms guarantee applied to laws made under s 122 because they were laws 'for any purpose in respect of which the Parliament has power to make laws' within s 51(xxxi). In the alternative, the four majority judges (including Toohey J) said that the National Parks and Wildlife Conservation Act 1975 was made pursuant to s 51(xxix) as well as s 122 and so attracted the just terms guarantee in any event. The fourth member of the majority, Toohey J, declined to overrule *Teori Tau*, but said that it would rarely be an obstacle, now that the Northern Territory had gained self-government. However, he confirmed that if a law was made solely under s 122 and hence was not a law supported by any of the heads of legislative power in s 51, then no just terms were required.

In separate opinions, the minority judges (Brennan CJ, Dawson and McHugh JJ) followed *Teori Tau* and said that the requirement of just terms did not extend to the territories. In sum, four of the seven justices continued to accept the possibility that laws could be made under s 122 and not attract the just terms requirement, although in practical terms that has been largely rendered ineffective.

Toohey J agreed with the orders proposed by Gummow J. Toohey J agreed with Gaudron J's reasons except in relation to her Honour's concurrence with Gummow J that *Teori Tau v Commonwealth* should no longer be treated as authority.

Toohey J: [560] I acknowledge the force of the critical analysis to which Gummow J has subjected the judgment in *Teori Tau*. And I am not persuaded by the argument of the Commonwealth that the application of s 51(xxxi) to reduce the content of the legislative power conferred by s 122 would potentially invalidate every grant of freehold or leasehold title granted by the Commonwealth in the Northern Territory since 1911, to the extent to which any such grant may be inconsistent with the continued existence of native title as recognised at common law.

Nevertheless, it would be a serious step to overrule a decision which has stood for nearly 30 years and which reflects an approach which may have been relied on in earlier years. If, as Gaudron J has shown (and as Gummow J agrees), par (xxxi) does fetter the legislative power of the Commonwealth where property is sought to be acquired 'for any purpose in respect of which the Parliament has power to make laws' and if a purpose of the National Parks and Wildlife Conservation Act 1975 (Cth) is the performance of Australia's international obligations, *Teori Tau* is not an obstacle to giving effect to the guarantee in s 51(xxxi) in respect of that legislation. Indeed, it [561] seems almost inevitable that any acquisition of property by the Commonwealth will now attract the operation of s 51(xxxi) because it will be in pursuit of a purpose in respect of which the Parliament has power to make laws, even if that acquisition takes place within a Territory. It will only be if a law can be truly characterised as a law for the government of a territory, not in any way answering the description in par (xxxi), that *Teori Tau* will constitute such an obstacle. And that is an unlikely situation on the view I take of the operation of the paragraph. If that be right, any implications overruling *Teori Tau* would likely be for the past rather than the future.

It is particularly unlikely, since the Northern Territory (Self-Government) Act 1978 (Cth), that a law of the Parliament for the acquisition of property from any person in the Northern Territory will be a law only 'for the government of any territory' within s 122 and not a law which attracts the operation of par (xxxi) because the property is sought to be acquired for a purpose in respect of which the Parliament has power to make laws in terms of s 51(xxxi).

His Honour noted that the Australian Parliament had 'proceeded on a corresponding footing' to the United States Supreme Court's interpretation of the United States Constitution which contained a power to acquire land subject to the requirement of 'just compensation', by legislating to 'oblige territory legislatures to provide just terms': 190 CLR at 594.

Gaudron J said that the Conservation Act could be based upon the implied nationhood power; the territories power and the external affairs power: 190 CLR at 565. She said that, even if the Act was based upon s 122, it did not 'directly touch the situation where a law of the Parliament is supportable under a head of power in s 51 but the Commonwealth seeks to rely on s 122 in order to avoid a requirement of s 51': 190 CLR at 566.

Gaudron J: [566] A law, valid by reason of s 51, may operate within a territory ... As already noted, the Conservation Act is [567] one for the establishment of national parks throughout the Commonwealth and extending to the external territories. Although, as also noted, the Conservation Act makes particular reference to Kakadu, s 7 contains no geographical limitation. It is the source of the power to declare by Proclamation an area to be a park or reserve ...

[I]t is unlikely that an Act of general application throughout the Commonwealth will also be a law passed pursuant to s 122 ...

Whether or not that be so, the situation here is that the Conservation Act is supportable under s 51(xxix) as claimed by the respondents ...

[568] It is clear, as the respondents contend in this case, that a law may have more than one purpose. Even if s 51(xxxi) is construed as referring to 'any purpose in respect of which the Parliament has power to make laws [under this section]', a law which has a purpose of that kind clearly falls within its terms whether or not it is also a law 'for the government of [a] territory'.

It is one thing to read down s 51(xxxi) so that it does not apply to a law enacted pursuant to s 122 of the Constitution. It is another to treat it as not applying to a law which has two purposes, one of which falls within the terms of s 51(xxxi) and the other of which is for the government of a territory. That is to rewrite the terms of s 51(xxxi), not to read them down.

Neither course is permissible. Rather, the proper approach is to construe constitutional guarantees as liberally as their terms will allow. [See *Australian Tape Manufacturers Association Ltd v The Commonwealth* (1993) 176 CLR 480 at 509]

However, it is not necessary to take a liberal approach in this case. On the assumption that par (xxxi) is to be read down so that it applies only to laws enacted under s 51, its terms, even when strictly construed, extend to a law a purpose of which is one 'in respect of which the Parliament has power to make laws [under s 51]'. In *P J Magennis Pty Ltd v The Commonwealth* [(1949) 80 CLR 382 at 423] Williams J said of par (xxxi):

> In my opinion the paragraph applies to all Commonwealth legislation the object of which is to acquire property for a purpose in respect of which the Commonwealth Parliament has power to make laws.

A purpose of the Conservation Act is the performance of Australia's international obligations; that is a purpose in respect of which the Parliament has power to make laws under s 51(xxix); par (xxxi) operates to fetter the implementation of that purpose by means of a [569] law with respect to the acquisition of property. The Commonwealth cannot enact laws for a purpose which falls within s 51 without the condition which attaches by par (xxxi).

Gummow J: [600] I conclude (i) that, upon its proper construction, in empowering the Parliament to make laws 'for' the government of any territory, s 122 identifies a purpose, in terms of the end to be achieved, and (ii) that, within the meaning of par (xxxi), s 122 states a purpose in respect of which the Parliament has power to make laws. The question then becomes whether there is either expressed or made manifest by the words or content of the grant of power in s 122 sufficient reason to deny the operation of the constitutional guarantee in par (xxxi). There is none.

First, a construction of the Constitution which treats s 122 as disjoined from par (xxxi) produces 'absurdities and incongruities'. [*Lamshed v Lake* (1958) 99 CLR 132 at 144 per Dixon CJ] This is so particularly with respect to a territory such as the Northern Territory, the area of which, at federation, was within a State. As is made clear in covering cl 6 of the Constitution, upon federation what was then identified as 'the northern territory of South Australia' was included within an 'Original State' and thus was part [601] of the Commonwealth at its establishment. The Constitution, notably s 111, should not readily be construed as producing the result that the benefit of the constitutional guarantee with respect to the acquisition of property in what became the Northern Territory was lost ... .

Secondly, many of the powers conferred upon the Parliament by s 51 (such as par (xxix)) will be susceptible of exercise in respect of matters and things in or connected with the territories, and on its face par (xxxi) will apply to the exercise of these powers. The Conservation Act itself provides an example. One of the objects in making provision for the establishment of parks under s 7 thereof is the facilitation of the carrying out by Australia of obligations, or the exercise by Australia of rights, under agreements between Australia and other countries (s 6(1)(e)). In the present case the Commonwealth admitted on the pleadings that an object of the making of the Proclamations was to facilitate the performance by Australia of its obligations, or the exercise of rights, under the Convention for the Protection of the World Cultural and Natural Heritage. It is to give to the constitutional guarantee a capricious operation to exclude from it so much of the law which is in question in the particular case as is or might have been concurrently supported by s 122.

Thirdly, as already indicated, the criterion of validity of a law made in reliance upon s 122 is that it be for the government of a territory. A law may meet that criterion without operating solely upon property situated in that territory. As I have stated above, s 122 authorises the Parliament to make laws the operation of which extends to the States. Further, it would appear that the power of the Parliament to establish [602] territorial legislatures extends to empowering such a legislature itself to make laws with extraterritorial operation, at least within Australia. [*Traut v Rogers* (1984) 27 NTR 29] It would be a curious result if just terms were constitutionally unnecessary for the compulsory acquisition of land in a city in one of the States for the purposes of a tourist bureau for a territory. The owners of property in a State would be deprived of the constitutional guarantee where the property was acquired for the purpose of the government of a territory; the Commonwealth would be in a position to impose upon those holding property in a State a burden from which the Constitution was designed to protect them.

Fourthly, the constitutional guarantee speaks of 'property', which 'is the most comprehensive term that can be used'. [*The Commonwealth v New South Wales* (1923) 33 CLR 1 at 20–21] It includes choses in action and other incorporeal interests. [*Mutual Pools & Staff Pty Ltd v The Commonwealth* (1994) 179 CLR 155 at 172, 184–185, 194–195, 222] The situs of such interests may be neither fixed nor, at any given time, readily susceptible of identification. For example, at common law, and in the absence of statutory provision, bearer bonds and bearer stock, passing by delivery, appear to be located where the instrument of security then is to be found. Where there are two or more registers where a transfer of shares might be registered, the shares are situated where they could most effectively be dealt with having regard to business practice, or where the shareholder in question would be likely to choose a market and place of transfer when desiring to deal with the shares.

In addition, incorporeal property, such as a patent, design or registered trade mark, which exists by virtue of a grant from the Commonwealth cannot be regarded as locally situate in any particular State or territory of the Commonwealth. Rather, such property is locally situate in Australia. Fullagar J so held in *In re Usines de Melle's Patent*. [(1954) 91 CLR 42 at 49] Accordingly, the constitutional guarantee cannot be coherently construed in a universe of legal discourse which contains a dichotomy between situation of property in a State and situation of property in a territory ...

[603] The above considerations indicate that the legislative power conferred by s 122 is not immunised from the operation of the constitutional guarantee. Nevertheless, the Commonwealth referred to various matters which it submitted supported a construction which excluded from the operation of par (xxxi) any law of the Parliament which was supported, solely or concurrently with another head of power, as a law made in exercise of the power conferred by s 122 of the Constitution.

Gummow J rejected the argument that s 122's separation from the list of legislative powers in s 51 meant that s 122 was not subject to the s 51(xxxi) guarantee: 190 CLR at 605. He said that neither the 'plenary' nature of the power, nor the fact that it was not stated to be 'subject to this Constitution' excluded it from the operation of the guarantee: 190 CLR at 606.

[607] It remains to consider the obstacle to that conclusion presented by the decision in *Teori Tau v Commonwealth*. [(1969) 119 CLR 564]

Gummow J referred to 'changed circumstances since that judgment was given in 1969' including: the submission of proposed laws for alteration of the Constitution to electors in territories; territory representation in both houses of parliament; the limitation of s 122 in 'other significant decisions' of the court; and the recognition that just terms is to be construed liberally as a constitutional guarantee. Gummow J said that *Teori Tau* did not form a part of 'a consistent body of authority' and that the reasons were delivered *ex tempore* without discussion, analysis, or citation of previous authority: 190 CLR at 608–12.

[612] [T]he reasoning in *Teori Tau* at each stage is now to be seen as flawed, whether by reason of then established doctrine or by reason of later constitutional developments and decisions of this Court. A consideration sometimes given for adhering to past authority, whatever its correctness, is the inconvenience that would be caused by disturbing the reliance of governments, citizens and corporations upon the Court continuing to adhere to that authority. However, *Teori Tau* has not been the subject of more recent challenge, at least, it would appear, partly because the legislation of the Parliament and of the territorial legislatures has provided for just terms. This litigation, if the appellants are correct in their construction of the laws in question as effecting an acquisition in the constitutional sense, has arisen out of a departure from legislative practice. I referred earlier in these reasons to legislation indicative

of that practice to place those with property in a territory in no different position as regards the laws of the Commonwealth to property holders in the States ...

[613] Leave to reopen *Teori Tau* ... should be given. *Teori Tau* did not rest upon any principle carefully worked out in a succession of cases. [*See John v FCT* (1989) 166 CLR at 438–9; 83 ALR 606] Rather, it is contrary, at least as regards this tenor, to the reasoning which underlay *Lamshed v Lake* and *Spratt v Hermes*. Where the question at issue relates to an important provision of the Constitution which deals with individual rights, such as s 51(xxxi) or s 117, the 'Court has a responsibility to set the matter right'. [*Street v Queensland Bar Association* (1989) 168 CLR 461 at 489; 88 ALR 321] Ultimately, it is the Constitution itself which must provide the answer.

Gummow J said that there was an 'an additional path to the conclusion that the constitutional guarantee applies in this case'; and agreed with Gaudron J that the Conservation Act could be characterised as a law with respect to 'external affairs' within s 51(xxxix), as well as a law with respect to the territories: 190 CLR at 614. On the question whether the Conservation Act effected an acquisition of property, Gummow J said:

[633] None of the provisions relied upon by the appellants is expressed in direct language as effecting an acquisition of any property. However, the question is whether, even if not formally, the appellants effectively have been deprived of 'the reality of proprietorship' by the indirect acquisition, through the collective operation of the provisions of the Conservation Act, of 'the substance of a proprietary interest'. I have referred earlier in these reasons to the passage in the judgment of [634] Dixon J in *Bank of NSW v The Commonwealth* [(1948) 76 CLR 1 at 349] which supports these propositions.

The appellants refer to the rights enjoyed in respect of the mining tenements under the 1939 Ordinance. These included, in the terms of the grants in the prescribed forms, a grant and demise of the relevant parcel of land and all the mines, veins, seams, lodes and deposits of the relevant minerals in, on or under the land, together with:

> ... the rights, liberties, easements, advantages and appurtenances thereto belonging or appertaining, excepting and reserving out of this demise all such portions of the said piece or parcel of land as are now lawfully occupied by persons other than the lessee, or any portion thereof which is now used for any public works or buildings whatsoever.

The appellants say that, in substance, the Commonwealth and the Director acquired identifiable and measurable advantages. In the case of the Director, those advantages were the acquisition of the land freed from the rights of Newcrest to occupy and conduct mining operations thereon and, in the case of the Commonwealth, the minerals freed from the rights of Newcrest to mine them. In accordance with the authorities, that is sufficient derivation of an identifiable and measurable advantage to satisfy the constitutional requirement of an acquisition. [*Commonwealth v Tasmania* (1983) 158 CLR 1 at 246–7, 283–3; 46 ALR 625 (the *Tasmanian Dam* case)]

There is no reason why the identifiable benefit or advantage relating to the ownership or use of property, which is acquired, should correspond precisely to that which was taken. [*Georgiadis v Australian and Overseas Telecommunications Corporation* (1994) 179 CLR 279] This is not a case in the category considered in *Health Insurance Commission v Peverill* [(1994) 179 CLR 226; 119 ALR 675] where what was in issue were rights derived purely from statute and of their very nature inherently susceptible to the variation or extinguishment which had come to pass. I have referred to the proviso in the prescribed forms under the Mining Regulations made under the 1939 Ordinance. They disclose that there was an inherent but limited liability to impairment of the rights conferred by the mining tenements. But what was done was not in exercise of the rights of the Crown under that proviso and went far beyond that which could have been brought about by those means.

Further, the history of the Territory, beginning with the surrender and acceptance effected pursuant to s 111 of the Constitution, shows [635] that the Commonwealth (or the Crown in right of the Commonwealth) acquired a radical title in the sense known to the common law and thereafter the Commonwealth dealt with the subject land in exercise of its rights of dominion over it. This involved the use of statute to carve out interests from the particular species of ownership enjoyed by the Commonwealth and, after self-government, by the Territory in the manner identified earlier in these reasons. It is not correct, for the purposes of the application of s 51(xxxi), to identify the property held by Newcrest as no more than a statutory privilege under a licensing system such as that considered in such decisions as *Minister for Primary Industry and Energy v Davey* [(1993) 47 FCR 151; 119 ALR 108] and *Bienke v Minister for Primary Industries and Energy.* [(1996) 63 FCR 567; 135 ALR 128]

Nor is this a case where there was merely an impairment of the bundle of rights constituting the property of Newcrest. An example of such impairment is found in *Waterhouse v Minister for the Arts and Territories.* [(1993) 43 FCR 175; 119 ALR 89] There, the prohibition on export of the painting in question left the owner free to retain, enjoy, display or otherwise make use of the painting and left him free to sell, mortgage or otherwise turn it to advantage subject to the requirement of an export permit if the owner or any other person desired to take it out of Australia. Here, there was an effective sterilisation of the rights constituting the property in question. That this is so is only emphasised upon a consideration of the contrary submission made by the Commonwealth and the Director. It is true, as they submit, that the mining tenements were not, in terms, extinguished. It is true also that Kakadu extended only 1,000 metres beneath the surface. But, on the surface and to that depth, s 10(1A) of the Conservation Act forbade the carrying out of operations for the recovery of minerals. The vesting in the Commonwealth of the minerals to that depth and the vesting of the surface and balance of the relevant segments of the subterranean land in the Director had the effect, as a legal and practical matter, of denying to Newcrest the exercise of its rights under the mining tenements.

Kirby J: [644] Some commentators on *Teori Tau* have suggested that factors peculiar to the application of the territories power to an external territory such as Papua [as in *R v Bernasconi* (1915) 19 CLR 629] or Papua and New Guinea, [as in *Teori Tau v The Commonwealth* (1969) 119 CLR 564] with large indigenous populations and distinct cultural norms may have influenced, however unconsciously, the Court's decisions to quarantine that power from the rest of the Constitution. Whatever may be the force of that suggestion as a matter of unconscious psychology, it was expressly denied by Barwick CJ's closing words in *Teori Tau*: [(1969) 119 CLR 564 at 570–571]

> Our decision applies to all the territories, those on the mainland of Australia as well as those external to the continent of Australia.

Kirby J said that reliance on the text and earlier decisions was important (190 CLR at 646), and that constitutional judgment required 'reconciliation of the conflicting demands of loyalty to the court's past decisions and loyalty to the constitutional text, freshly examined'. His Honour continued:

[646] Each of these demands has legitimacy. The one provides the accumulated wisdom of the past in the authoritative statements of the law. The other affords recognition of the legitimate influences upon constitutional doctrine of fresh perspectives and of 'matters that might broadly be called social or political'. [Zines, *The High Court and the Constitution*, 4th ed (1997) at 429–430]

Kirby J referred to the arguments in favour of maintaining the rule in *Teori Tau v Commonwealth* (1969) 119 CLR 564 and concluded that the 'just terms' requirement applied as much in a territory as elsewhere in Australia: 190 CLR at 652. He referred to the language of s 51(xxxi) and s 122; the need to read the Constitution as one coherent instrument because the territories were connected; and the fact that an unlimited construction of s 122 would lead to 'bizarre consequences' such as the inapplicability of s 116 in the territories: 190 CLR at 655. Finally, Kirby J listed the court's recent 'gradual retreat' from a 'complete disjunction' signalled by the decision in *Capital Duplicators Pty Ltd v Australian Capital Territory (No 1)*: 'The Court read the Constitution as a unity. Doing so, it found that s 122 was subject to s 90. The same approach should be taken to the principal problem presented by this case': 190 CLR at 657. In support of his conclusion Kirby J referred to what he called 'interpretive principle': 190 CLR at 657.

[657] Where the Constitution is ambiguous, this Court should adopt that meaning which conforms to the principles of fundamental rights rather than an interpretation which would involve a departure from such rights.

Australian law, including its constitutional law, may sometimes fall short of giving effect to fundamental rights. The duty of the Court is to interpret what the Constitution says and not what individual judges may think it should have said. [See *Queensland v Commonwealth* (1977) 139 CLR 585 at 599] If the Constitution is clear, the Court must (as in the interpretation of any legislation) give effect to its terms. Nor should the Court adopt an interpretative principle as a means of introducing, by the backdoor, provisions of international treaties or other international law concerning fundamental rights not yet incorporated into Australian domestic law. [*Minister for Immigration and Ethnic Affairs v Teoh* (1995) 183 CLR 273 at 288] However, as has been recognised by this Court [*Mabo v Queensland [No 2]* (1992) 175 CLR 1 at 42] and by other courts of high authority, the inter-relationship of national and international law, including in relation to fundamental rights, is 'undergoing evolution' [*Tavita v Minister of Immigration* [1994] 2 NZLR 257 at 266]. To adapt what Brennan J said in *Mabo v Queensland [No 2]*, the common law, and constitutional law, do not necessarily conform with international law. However, international law is a legitimate and important influence on the development of the common law and constitutional law, especially when international law declares the existence of universal and fundamental rights. To the full [658] extent that its text permits, Australia's Constitution, as the fundamental law of government in this country, accommodates itself to international law, including insofar as that law expresses basic rights. The reason for this is that the Constitution not only speaks to the people of Australia who made it and accept it for their governance. It also speaks to the international community as the basic law of the Australian nation which is a member of that community.

One highly influential international statement on the understanding of universal and fundamental rights is the Universal Declaration of Human Rights. That document is not a treaty to which Australia is a party. Indeed it is not a treaty at all. It is not part of Australia's domestic law, still less of its Constitution. Nevertheless, it may in this country, as it has in other countries, influence legal development and constitutional interpretation. At least it may do so where its terms do not conflict with, but are consistent with, a provision of the Constitution. The use of international law in such a way has been specifically sanctioned by the Privy Council when giving meaning to express constitutional provisions relating to 'fundamental rights and freedoms'. Such jurisprudence has its analogies in the courts of several other countries. The growing influence of the Universal Declaration upon the jurisprudence in the International Court of Justice may also be noted.

Kirby J referred to the inclusion of a just terms guarantee in a number of international and comparative instruments including the 1947 Universal Declaration of Human Rights; the Magna Carta of 1215; the French Declaration of the Rights of Man and of the Citizen, 1789; the Fifth Amendment to the United States Constitution; the Indian Constitution; Malaysia's Constitution; the Japanese Constitution; and South Africa's 1996 Bill of Rights: 190 CLR at 658–70.

[660] In effect, the foregoing constitutional provisions do no more than reflect universal and fundamental rights by now recognised by customary international law ...

When the foregoing principles, of virtually universal application, are remembered, it becomes even more astonishing to suggest that the Australian Constitution, which in 1901 expressly and exceptionally recognised and gave effect to the applicable universal principle, should be construed today in such a way as to limit the operation of that [661] express requirement in respect of some laws made by its Federal Parliament but not others. Where there is an ambiguity in the meaning of the Constitution, as there is here, it should be resolved in favour of upholding such fundamental and universal rights. The Australian Constitution should not be interpreted so as to condone an unnecessary withdrawal of the protection of such rights. At least it should not be so interpreted unless the text is intractable and the deprivation of such rights is completely clear. Neither of these conditions applies here. Nor should arbitrary deprivation of property be lightly attributed to a constitution, such as the Australian Constitution, given the history of its origins and its purpose. That purpose is to be the basic law for the government of a free people in a nation which relates to the rest of the world in a context in which the growing influence of international law is of ever increasing importance.

... [661] The same result, as is reached by the foregoing reasoning, follows from the additional (or alternative) approach explained by Gaudron J in her reasons with which Toohey J agrees. Gummow J additionally adopts that approach. So would I.

Brennan CJ, Dawson and McHugh JJ dissented.

Brennan CJ: [Brennan CJ said that the Conservation Amendment Act was made under s 122 and it was expressed to apply only to areas of land in Kakadu National Park.]

[534] *(i) Two heads of power*

When a law is supportable by a constitutional power, it is immaterial to its validity that, if some particular requirement were met, it would also be supported by a second constitutional power. So long as the Parliament has power to enact a law, from whatever provision of the Constitution that power be derived, the law is valid ...

It follows that, unless there be some reason for denying the sufficiency of the power conferred by s 122 to support the Conservation Amendment Act, the Conservation Amendment Act is valid.

Brennan CJ referred to the structure of the Constitution and said that it indicated that s 122 stood outside of the federal division of powers. His Honour said that the power in s 122 was unqualified. Apart from the requirement that there be a nexus between the law and the territory no other condition was necessary to the law's validity. He referred to other provisions, such as s 80 and s 73, which had been held previously not to apply to s 122; and to the view that s 122 laws were not qualified by Ch III nor s 51: 190 CLR 535–9. He rejected a reopening of *Teori Tau*: 190 CLR at 544.

[544] *Teori Tau* is not only consistent with an unbroken line of authority; it is also, in my opinion, correct. If it is not adhered to, the powers of territorial legislatures with respect to the compulsory acquisition of property are denied. There is a further and powerful consideration which tells against the reopening of *Teori Tau*. Since the Common-[545]wealth first assumed the administration of territories, it has been understood that the power of compulsory acquisition of property within the territory is derived from s 122. During that time, numerous property transactions have taken place in the course of the Territories' development. If the s 122 power does not support compulsory acquisitions, any grant or transfer of property that involved a compulsory acquisition is exposed to uncertainty if not invalidity. No validation of such a transaction could be effected by a retrospective payment of compensation; the legal consequence of any invalidity would simply be that the grant or transfer must be taken never to have occurred. That would produce consequences of unforeseen and unforeseeable difficulty. *Teori Tau* ought not be reopened.

In my respectful opinion, the proposition that the Conservation Amendment Act cannot be a law for the government of the Northern Territory because those provisions are a law for the compulsory acquisition of property should be rejected as 'clearly insupportable' (to adopt the term used in *Teori Tau*).

The appeal should be dismissed and the question whether the impugned proclamations are invalid should be answered: No.

~~~

[11.2.15] Dawson J delivered a judgment to the same effect. In *obiter*, Dawson J said that s 116 and s 118 had no application to the territories: 190 CLR at 557.

McHugh J delivered reasons to the same effect on the issue of the reach of s 51(xxxi) in the territories. On the question whether the Heritage Act effected an acquisition of property, he referred to the observations of Mason J in *Commonwealth v Tasmania* (the *Tasmanian Dam* case) (1983) 158 CLR 1 at 145 **[11.2.12]**, to the effect that s 51(xxxi) did not apply merely because a pre-existing right was affected, either the Commonwealth or another must acquire an interest in property. McHugh J said at 573:

> Newcrest's right to mine was adversely affected by the proclamations. But what interest in property did the Commonwealth acquire? Newcrest's interest in the lease was not forfeited or transferred to the Commonwealth or the Director. They already owned the interests in reversion in the minerals and land. Until the leases expired, the property interests of Newcrest in the land and minerals would continue as before. The effect of the proclamations was merely to impinge on Newcrest's rights to exploit those interests. But even if there was effectively a diminution or extinguishment of all or part of Newcrest's interests, there was no gain by the Commonwealth (or the Director). Both as a matter of substance and of form, the Commonwealth obtained nothing which it did not already have. In colloquial terms, Newcrest lost but the Commonwealth did not gain.

[11.2.16] Toohey J's 'each way bet' in *Newcrest Mining (WA) Ltd v Commonwealth* (1997) 190 CLR 513 **[11.2.14C]** ensures that the status of *Teori Tau* will remain uncertain until the next opportunity arises in the High Court to test the application of s 51(xxxi) in a territory: see further Keyzer (2001). However, while Toohey J upheld *Teori Tau*, he shared the opinion of Gaudron J, with whom Gummow and Kirby JJ agreed on this point, that if another power, such as s 51(xxix), could be invoked to support the law under challenge, then that would suffice for the law to be subject to the 'just terms' requirement in s 51(xxxi). In other words, s 122 is not, as Brennan CJ said (190 CLR at 542) 'a universal legislative power' immune from the several limitations on power described in s 51 of the Constitution. It is, rather, subject to express and implied limitations on power drawn from the Constitution. The question is just which other provisions of the Constitution limit s 122? For further discussion, see **[12.5.5]–[12.5.25]**.

[11.2.17C] Health Insurance Commission v Peverill
(1994) 179 CLR 226

The Health Insurance (Pathology Services) Act 1991 (Cth), which took effect from 1 August 1986, reduced the amount of Medicare benefits payable under s 20 of the Health Insurance Act 1973 (Cth) to a pathologist for performing rubella tests. Peverill, a pathologist who had performed rubella tests and claimed from the Health Insurance Commission the amounts then payable under the 1973 Act during the period from 1986–91, sued the Commission to recover the amounts payable under the 1973 Act.

Peverill argued that the 1991 Act was invalid because it amounted to an acquisition of his property on other than just terms. In the Federal Court, Burchett J upheld Peverill's objection to the 1991 Act: *Peverill v Health Insurance Commission* (1991) 104 ALR 449. Burchett J decided that Peverill's claim to payment of Medicare benefits was 'property' within s 51(xxxi); that the 1991 Act had the effect of acquiring Peverill's property; and that acquisition did not provide Peverill with just terms. The Health Insurance Commission appealed to the Full Court of the Federal Court. The appeal was removed to the High Court under s 40 of the Judiciary Act 1903 (Cth).

Mason CJ, Deane and Gaudron JJ: [235] The assignments, pursuant to s 20A of the Principal Act, by patients to Dr Peverill of their entitlements to medical benefits vested a statutory right in Director Peverill to receive payment by the appellant Commission from consolidated revenue. But the acquisition of that statutory right by Dr Peverill was not an acquisition of property which fell within s 51(xxxi). That provision is directed, in our view, to requisition, not to voluntary acquisition. [*John Cook and Co Pty Ltd v Commonwealth* (1924) 34 CLR 269 at 282] The assignments were voluntary; there was no element of legislative compulsion about them. ...

It may be accepted that the entitlement to payment for each service is a valuable 'right' or 'interest' of a kind which constitutes 'property' for the purposes of that paragraph. [*Minister of State for the Army v Dalziel* (1944) 68 CLR 261] But it does not follow that the legislative substitution of another and less valuable statutory right to receive a payment from consolidated revenue for that previously existing brings about an 'acquisition' of the earlier right for the purposes of s 51(xxxi) ...

[**236**] There is no doubt that the derivation by the Commonwealth of a financial advantage in association with the extinguishment of a right to receive a payment from the Commonwealth may constitute an acquisition of property for the purposes of s 51(xxxi) of the Constitution [see *Mutual Pools & Staff* (1994) 179 CLR 155]. That could even be so in some cases in which extinguishment of the right takes place in the context of some genuine adjustment made in the common interests of competing claims, rights and obligations between another party and the Commonwealth. However, here, the extinguishment of the earlier right to receive payment of a larger amount has been effected not only by way of genuine adjustment of competing claims, rights and obligations in the common interests between parties who stand in a particular relationship [see *Mutual Pools & Staff* (1994) 179 CLR at 171–2] but also as an element in a regulatory scheme for the provision of welfare benefits from public funds.

The Amending Act seeks to correct a defect in the administration of the Principal Act in that, according to the decision of the Federal Court, the payments for the relevant tests carried out by Dr Peverill which it provided for were thought to be excessive ... What the Amending Act does in this situation is to bring about the position that was thought by the Commission to have existed before the Federal Court decision. By achieving that result, the Amending Act brought about a genuine legislative adjustment of the competing claims made by patients, pathologists including Dr Peverill, the Commission and taxpayers. Clearly enough, the underlying perception was that it was in the common interest that these competing interests be adjusted so as to [**237**] preserve the integrity of the health care system and ensure that the funds allocated to it are deployed to maximum advantage and not wasted in 'windfall' payments.

It is significant that the rights that have been terminated or diminished are statutory entitlements to receive payments from consolidated revenue which were not based on antecedent proprietary rights recognized by the general law. Rights of that kind are rights which, as a general rule, are inherently susceptible of variation. That is particularly so in the case of both the nature and quantum of welfare benefits, such as the provision of medicare benefits in respect of medical services. Whether a particular medicare benefit should be provided and, if so, in what amount, calls for a carefully considered assessment of what services should be covered and what is reasonable remuneration for the service provided, the nature and the amount of the medicare benefit having regard to the community's need for assistance, the capacity of government to pay and the future of health services in Australia. All these factors are susceptible of change so that it is to be expected that the level of benefits will change from time to time. Where such change is effected by a law which operates retrospectively to adjust competing claims or to overcome distortion, anomaly or unintended consequences in the working of the particular scheme, variations in outstanding entitlements to receive payments under the scheme may result. In such a case, what is involved is a variation of a right which is inherently susceptible of variation and the mere fact that a particular variation involves a reduction in entitlement and is retrospective does not convert it into an acquisition of property. More importantly, any incidental diminution in an individual's entitlement to payment in such a case does not suffice to invest the law adjusting entitlements under the relevant statutory scheme with the distinct character of a law with respect to the acquisition of property for the purposes of s 51(xxxi) of the Constitution. [See *Mutual Pools & Staff* (1994) 179 CLR 155.]

Brennan J: [243] The Principal Act confers on assignee practitioners a right to be paid medicare benefits subject to the conditions prescribed but it does not create a debt.

The right so conferred on assignee practitioners is not property: not only because the right is not assignable (though that is indicative of the incapacity of a third party to assume the right) but, more fundamentally, because a right to receive a benefit to be paid by a statutory authority in discharge of a statutory duty is not susceptible of any form of repetitive or continuing enjoyment and cannot be exchanged for or converted into any kind of property. On analysis, such a right is susceptible of enjoyment only at the moment when [244] the duty to pay is discharged. It does not have any degree of permanence or stability. That is not a right of a proprietary nature, though the money received when the medicare benefit is paid answers that description. [See *Federal Commissioner of Taxation v Official Receiver* (1956) 95 CLR 300] ...

What the assignee [245] practitioner acquires is a statutory right which, as between the practitioner and the Commonwealth (or the Commission), is a gratuity. ...

[W]here a pecuniary benefit payable out of Consolidated Revenue is gratuitously provided by the Parliament to the beneficiary, the amount of the benefit remains until payment within the unfettered control of the Parliament. The distinction between a debt and the right conferred on assignee practitioners by the Principal Act is the difference between something owned and something expected, the fulfilment of the expectation being dependent on the continued will of the Parliament.

~~~

[11.2.18] Dawson J held that no acquisition of property had occurred. He referred to the existence of a distinction between 'taking' and 'acquisition' (179 CLR at 248); the voluntary nature of the assignment (179 CLR at 249–50); the need for any acquisition to be for a Commonwealth purpose (179 CLR at 250–1); and the fact that although the Commonwealth's liability has been reduced, conferring a financial advantage upon it, 'nothing which answers the description of property' has been acquired: 179 CLR at 251.

Toohey J said that although Dr Peverill's interest was a chose in action which answered the description of property (179 CLR at 256); no 'acquisition of property' had taken place because it was 'impossible to identify any property or interest in property acquired by the Commission (179 CLR at 256). The Act was part of a 'complex regime of health insurance', and if the reduction had taken place but no assignment of benefit from patient to doctor had occurred, there would not have been any acquisition of property from the patient (179 CLR at 256).

McHugh J referred to his comments in *Mutual Pools & Staff Pty Ltd v Commonwealth* (1994) 179 CLR 155 where he had emphasised that not all acquisitions of property by the Commonwealth fall within s 51(xxxi), especially if they are 'an inevitable consequence of a power conferred by s 51' or 'a reasonably proportional consequence of a breach of a law passed under such a power': 179 CLR at 259. He said although the right to payment was property (179 CLR at 263), the amendment was in the nature of an alteration of a gratuitous statutory entitlement created by parliament (179 CLR at 260) which, consistent with the United States case law, was not in the nature of a vested right, and could be subject to change by parliament in the same way as it could alter an age pension: 179 CLR at 262–3.

Notes

[11.2.19] Several limitations to the reach or coverage of s 51(xxxi) were expressed in *Health Insurance Commission v Peverill* (1994) 179 CLR 226 **[11.2.17C]**. For example, Mason CJ, Deane and Gaudron JJ referred to the reduction in Medicare benefits as a 'genuine adjustment of competing claims, rights and obligations in the common interests between parties who stand in a particular relationship' (179 CLR at 236); and they referred to *Mutual Pools & Staff Pty Ltd v Commonwealth* (1994) 179 CLR 155.

In that case, the High Court held that the Commonwealth Parliament could legislate so as to limit the right of a manufacturer to recover from the Commonwealth moneys paid by the manufacturer by way of an unconstitutional tax. The legislation was supported by s 51(ii) of the Constitution, the High Court held, and did not contravene s 51(xxxi). Mason CJ said that, generally, s 51(xxxi) required that the other legislative powers of the Commonwealth be read so as not to authorise the making of laws for the acquisition of property on other than just terms: 179 CLR at 169. However, a contrary indication might be read in the Constitution, either because of an express indication or because such an indication was implied in the very nature of such heads of power, such as s 51(xvii) (bankruptcy and insolvency), s 51(vi) (defence) and s 51(ii) (taxation): 179 CLR at 170–1.

Mason CJ said that, if an acquisition was authorised by one of those other heads of power, they would not be restricted by the 'just terms' requirement; and that acquisitions under those heads of power commonly 'provided a means of resolving or adjusting competing claims, obligations or property rights of individuals as an incident of the regulation of their relationship': 179 CLR at 171.

In their joint judgment, Deane and Gaudron JJ listed acquisitions of property that had been held or indicated not to be subject to s 51(xxxi). These included: the imposition of a tax and provisional tax; the forfeiture of illegally imported goods in the hands of an innocent party; the imposition of a pecuniary penalty by way of civil proceedings; the seizure of property of subjects of a former enemy to be used in paying reparations; and vesting a bankrupt's estate in an Official Receiver: 179 CLR at 187–8.

[11.2.20] More recently, the justification for statutory variation of property rights reflected in the phrase 'genuine adjustment of competing rights, claims or obligations of persons in a particular relationship' has been criticised as reflecting circular reasoning, and as 'little more than a fiction intended to beautify what is disagreeable to the sufferers': *Airservices Australia v Canadian Airlines* (1999) 202 CLR 133 at 299 (Gummow J, adopting the language of a justice of the US Supreme Court in *Tyson & Brother v Banton* 273 US 418 at 446 (1927)). See also 202 CLR 133 at 312 (Callinan J).

If this criticism is right, then the question is whether it is possible to locate any unifying theme in the exceptional acquisitions referred to by the justices in the cases, such as the acquisitions identified by Deane and Gaudron JJ in *Peverill*: see **[11.2.19]**. Or is the situation that 'acquisitions', understood in their broadest sense, are effected for a variety of purposes, and the most sensible approach is to isolate which purposes are susceptible to the 'just terms' guarantee, and which ones are not, rather than to look for a unifying theme in the exceptions?

[11.2.21] An approach that emphasises the purposes for which an acquisition is effected may be preferable, given that acquisitions are effected under many different powers in many different contexts. So, in *Nintendo Co Ltd v Centronics Systems Pty Ltd* (1994) 181 CLR 134, the High Court held that the Circuit Layouts Act 1989 (Cth), which gave the designer of an electronic circuit the right to restrain other persons from using that circuit, was not a law for the acquisition of the property of those persons who were prevented from using the circuit. Mason CJ, Brennan, Deane, Toohey, Gaudron and Toohey JJ said that a law was not likely to be characterised as a law with respect to the acquisition of property within s 51(xxxi) if the law was 'concerned with the adjustment of the competing rights, claims or obligations of persons in a particular relationship or are of activity': 181 CLR at 161. They concluded that the Circuit Layouts Act was 'a law for the adjustment and regulation of the competing claims, rights and liabilities of the designers or first makers of original circuit layouts and those who take advantage of, or benefit from, their work'; and was, therefore, beyond the reach of s 51(xxxi): 181 CLR at 161. At base, the court believed that if the intellectual property power could be used to create intellectual property rights, then it could also be used to modify or extinguish those rights.

More recently, one judge has criticised this approach, at least in reference to intellectual property. In *Commonwealth v WMC Resources Ltd* (1998) 194 CLR 1 **[11.2.22]** at 70–71, Gummow J noted that intellectual property rights are defined as rights of personal property under federal laws, and it is only the modification (relevantly, the reduction in the content of such a right) by statute that might operate immune from the 'just terms' requirement of s 51(xxxi). For that reason, the proposition that a right that has no existence apart from a law of the Commonwealth is therefore inherently subject to modification or diminution by later Commonwealth statute is 'too broad': 194 CLR at 70. The true distinction is between acquisition of a right and reduction in the content of that right: the former action is subject to s 51(xxxi) and the latter is not.

[11.2.22] In *Health Insurance Commission v Peverill* (1994) 179 CLR 226 **[11.2.17C]**, it was also proposed that the status of the Medicare benefits payable to Peverill as creatures of statute was an additional reason why the parliament could legislate to reduce those benefits without acquiring any property within s 51(xxxi). That proposition was adopted by three members of the High Court to support their judgments in *Commonwealth v WMC Resources Ltd* (1998) 194 CLR 1. In that case, a majority of the High Court (Brennan CJ, Gaudron, McHugh and Gummow JJ; Toohey and Kirby JJ dissenting) held that Commonwealth legislation, which reduced the area covered by a petroleum exploration permit issued under the Petroleum (Submerged Lands) Act 1967 (Cth) and held by the respondent was not an acquisition of property that was subject to the requirement of just terms expressed in s 51(xxxi).

The permit had authorised WMC Resources Ltd to explore for petroleum in the Timor Gap (between Australia and the former Portuguese colony of East Timor) and, according to the 1967 Act, gave WMC Resources Ltd priority in the issue of a licence to recover any petroleum that might be located in the relevant area. The legislation reducing the area covered by the exploration permit was enacted in 1991 in order to give effect to an agreement between Australia and Indonesia, which established a Zone of Cooperation in the Timor Gap, in which petroleum exploration and recovery was to be jointly administered by Australia and Indonesia.

In separate judgments, Gaudron, McHugh and Gummow JJ stressed the fact that the rights formerly held by WMC Resources Ltd had been created by statute; and, because those rights depended for their creation on statute, they could be removed by statute. For example, Gaudron J noted that, in *Georgiadis v Australian and Overseas Telecommunications Corporation* (1994) 179 CLR 297, Mason CJ, Deane and Gaudron JJ pointed out that, prima facie at least, a statutory right is inherently susceptible of statutory modification or extinguishment and no acquisition of property is effected by a law which simply modifies or extinguishes a statutory right that has no basis in the general law. In Gaudron J's view, the legislation reducing the area covered by the exploration permit 'simply modified a statutory right which had no basis in the general law and which was inherently susceptible to that course and, thus, did not effect an acquisition of property': 194 CLR 1 at 38.

McHugh J expressed his conclusion in wider terms at 51:

> The power to make laws with respect to a subject described in s 51 carries with it the power to amend or repeal a law made on that subject. A property interest that is created by federal legislation, where no property interest previously existed, is necessarily of an inherently determinable character and is always liable to modification or extinguishment by a subsequent federal enactment. Section 51(xxxi) therefore does not ordinarily withdraw from the parliament the authority to use another s 51 power to revoke or amend legislation that has been passed under that power, even when the legislation has created a property right. The fact that the Commonwealth or some other person might be viewed as benefiting from that alteration or revocation is irrelevant.

[11.2.23]   A focus on the purpose for which the acquisition was made characterised the High Court's more recent decision in *Airservices Australia v Canadian Airlines* (1999) 202 CLR 133. In the case, the court considered the validity of a statutory lien imposed on aircraft to ensure payment of statutory charges under air navigation laws. The High Court concluded that the regulation, which was otherwise authorised by s 51(i) of the Constitution, did not attract the s 51(xxxi) requirement of 'just terms' because the charges were 'appropriate and adapted' to the regulation of air navigation: 202 CLR 133 at 180–1 (Gleeson CJ and Kirby J); 'part of the regulatory scheme for civil aviation safety': 202 CLR 133 at 300 (Gummow J); or 'concerned with the adjustment of competing rights, claims or obligations of persons in a particular area of activity': 202 CLR 133 at 304–5 (Hayne J). McHugh J adopted a different approach: he said that the first question was not whether the impugned law could be characterised as a law with respect to another head of power but whether the law fell within s 51(xxxi); but, '[i]f the circumstances are such that the notion of fair compensation to the transferor is irrelevant or incongruous, the law is not a law with respect to s 51(xxxi)': 202 CLR 133 at 251. Here, the common law provided the reference point against which questions of irrelevance or incongruity were judged.

Jury trial

[11.2.24E]   **Commonwealth Constitution**

80 The trial on indictment of any offence against any law of the Commonwealth shall be by jury, and every such trial shall be held in the State where the offence was committed, and if the offence was not committed within any State the trial shall be held at such place or places as the Parliament prescribes.

~~~

Notes

[11.2.25] The first draft of the Commonwealth Constitution, prepared before the 1891 Constitutional Convention, was framed to require jury trial for 'all crimes cognisable by any Court'. However, the draft was altered to confine the guarantee to indictable federal offences: see La Nauze (1972) pp 227–8. The exclusion of non-indictable offences from the guarantee of s 80 may, therefore, be regarded as deliberate: see Charlesworth (1986) p 54.

[11.2.26] In *R v Bernasconi* (1915) 19 CLR 629, the High Court held that laws made under s 122, the territories power, were not subject to s 80. The court justified this conclusion partly by drawing a distinction between the Commonwealth Parliament's power to legislate for the Commonwealth and its power to legislate for its own territories and partly by practical considerations. Griffith CJ elaborated on the first justification (at 635):

> In my judgment, Ch III is limited in its application to the exercise of the judicial power of the Commonwealth in respect of those functions of government as to which it stands in the place of the States, and has no application to territories. Section 80, therefore, relates only to offences created by the Parliament by statutes passed in execution of those functions, which are aptly described as 'laws of the Commonwealth'.

The practical considerations were developed by Isaacs J. He noted that the 'recently conquered territories' (that is, taken over from the German Empire by force of arms) might be attached to Australia. He said, to impose the British jury system on the 'German or Polynesian' population would impose 'an entirely inappropriate requirement': 19 CLR at 638 (see further **[12.5.5]**).

Evatt J was critical of this conclusion in an extra-curial comment published in the *Australian Law Journal* in 1936. The conclusion that s 80 ought not apply to the territories is by no means obvious from its text. Further, as Evatt J asked rhetorically, if the territories are not part of 'the Commonwealth' referred to in s 80, then where *are* they? For further discussion and criticism of the general proposition that the several provisions of Ch III do not apply in the territories: see **[12.5.6]–[12.5.8C]** and **[12.5.16]**ff.

Of course, s 80 is not expressed to apply to the states, and does not do so: *Byrnes v The Queen* (1999) 199 CLR 1 at 32, 39.

[11.2.27] In *Kruger v Commonwealth* (1997) 190 CLR 1 **[11.3.5]** and **[11.3.32C]** the court considered the validity of a Northern Territory Ordinance which applied from 1925 to 1949 and provided that Aboriginal and 'half-caste' children could be taken into the care, custody and control of the Chief Protector of Aborigines. One argument raised against the validity of the Ordinance was that rights such as s 116 applied to the territories. In deciding that question, some members of the High Court commented, in *obiter*, on the application of s 80 in the territories. Analogising with s 116, Dawson J said that the terms of s 80 are 'absolute' and that it did not apply to the territories: 190 CLR at 59–60. Toohey J referred to *R v Bernasconi* (1915) 19 CLR 629 **[11.2.26]**, without questioning its current status: 190 CLR at 80. Gummow J referred to the wording of s 80 which, he said, contemplated that an offence to which it applied may have been committed in a territory, and that an 'offence against a law of the Commonwealth' referred to in s 80 may be an offence against a law applicable only to a territory: 190 CLR at 172.

[11.2.28]   In *R v Bernasconi* (1915) 19 CLR 629 **[11.2.26]**, Isaacs J suggested a more significant limitation on s 80. 'If a given offence is not made triable on indictment at all,' he said, 'then s 80 does not apply': 19 CLR at 637. That limitation was endorsed by the High Court in *R v Archdall* (1928) 41 CLR 128. Section 30K of the Crimes Act 1914 (Cth) made it an offence, punishable by imprisonment for one year, for a person to hinder the provision of any public service by the Commonwealth. Section 12(1) of the Act provided that the offence could be tried summarily. On an application to quash convictions under s 30K recorded by a magistrate against two union officials, the High Court held that ss 12(1) and 30K were not inconsistent with s 80 of the Constitution. Knox CJ, Isaacs, Gavan Duffy and Powers JJ said at 136:

> The suggestion that the Parliament, by reason of s 80 of the Constitution, could not validly make the offence punishable summarily has no foundation and its rejection needs no exposition.

Higgins J observed that s 80 required that 'if there be an indictment, there must be a jury; but there is nothing to compel procedure by indictment': 41 CLR at 139–40.

[11.2.29]   This view of s 80 was criticised by Dixon and Evatt JJ in *R v Federal Court of Bankruptcy; Ex parte Lowenstein* (1938) 59 CLR 556, where the validity of s 217 of the Bankruptcy Act was challenged. The section authorised the Bankruptcy Court to charge a bankrupt with an offence, to try the bankrupt summarily and, upon conviction, to punish the bankrupt by imprisonment. After referring to the observations of Higgins J in *R v Archdall* (1928) 41 CLR 128 at 139–40 **[11.2.28]**, Dixon and Evatt JJ said:

> It is a queer intention to ascribe to a constitution; for it supposes that the concern of the framers of the provision was not to ensure that no one should be held guilty of a serious offence against the laws of the Commonwealth except by the verdict of a jury, but to prevent a procedural solecism, namely, the use of an indictment in cases where the legislature might think fit to authorise the court itself to pass upon the guilt or innocence of the prisoner. There is high authority for the proposition that 'the Constitution is not to be mocked'. A cynic might, perhaps, suggest the possibility that s 80 was drafted in mockery; that its language was carefully chosen so that the guarantee it appeared on the surface to give should be in truth illusory. No court could countenance such a suggestion and, if this explanation is rejected and an intention to produce some real operative effect is conceded to the section, then to say that its application can always be avoided by authorizing the substitution of some other form of charge for an indictment seems to mock at the provision (59 CLR at 581–2).

Dixon and Evatt JJ went on to say that s 80 should operate to compel jury trial where a prosecution had two elements:

> We think the first of them would be seen to be that some authority constituted under the law to represent the public interest for the purpose took the responsibility of the step which put the accused on his trial; the grand jury, the coroner's jury or the coroner, the law officer or the court. A second element, we think, would be found in the liability of the offender to a term of imprisonment or to some graver form of punishment. We should not have taken the view that s 80 was intended to impose no real restriction upon the legislative power to provide what kind of tribunal shall decide the guilt or innocence on a criminal charge (59 CLR at 583).

Dixon and Evatt JJ obviously were unwilling to accept the authority of the earlier decision in *R v Archdall* (1928) 41 CLR 128 **[11.2.28]**. However, they avoided the question of whether that decision should be followed by holding that s 217 of the Bankruptcy Act was invalid because it purported to vest in a federal court functions which lay outside the judicial power of the Commonwealth. (The section authorised the Bankruptcy Court to charge a bankrupt with an offence, to try the bankrupt summarily and, upon conviction, to punish the bankrupt by imprisonment.)

[11.2.30] Despite the criticisms of the narrow view of s 80 advanced in *R v Federal Court of Bankruptcy; Ex parte Lowenstein* (1938) 59 CLR 556 **[11.2.29]** by Dixon and Evatt JJ (see also Kirby J in *Cheung v The Queen* (2001) 209 CLR 1 at 38–9), that view has survived. It was endorsed by: Barwick CJ in *Spratt v Hermes* (1965) 114 CLR 226 at 244; by Barwick CJ, McTiernan, Kitto, Taylor and Owen JJ in *Zarb v Kennedy* (1968) 121 CLR 283 at 287, 296–7, 312; by Barwick CJ, Mason and Aickin JJ in *Li Chia Hsing v Rankin* (1978) 141 CLR 182 at 190; and by McHugh J in *Cheng v The Queen* (2000) 203 CLR 248: 'The words of s 80 were deliberately and carefully chosen to give the Parliament the capacity to avoid trial by jury when it wished to do so': 203 CLR 248 at 43–44.

The narrow view was also endorsed in *Kingswell v R* (1985) 159 CLR 264, where a majority of the High Court (Gibbs CJ, Mason, Wilson and Dawson JJ; Brennan and Deane JJ dissenting) held that ss 233B and 235 of the Customs Act 1901 (Cth) did not breach s 80. Section 233B made it an offence for a person to conspire with another person to import narcotic goods. As construed by the High Court, s 235 provided that, once a person was convicted under s 233B, the judge was to decide whether a commercial quantity of narcotic goods was involved, the maximum sentence varying accordingly. In their joint judgment (with which Mason J agreed on this issue), Gibbs CJ, Wilson and Dawson JJ said at 276–7:

> Section 80 requires that if there is a trial on indictment of any offence against any law of the Commonwealth it shall be by jury. The sections now in question do not provide to the contrary. If there is a trial by jury the ordinary incidents of such a trial will apply; the judge will continue to exercise his traditional functions, and, for the purpose of imposing a sentence within the limits fixed by the law, will form his own view of the facts, provided that that view is not in conflict with the verdict of the jury. Section 80 says nothing as to the manner in which an offence is to be defined. Since an offence against the law of the Commonwealth is a creature of that law, it is the law alone which defines the elements of the offence. The fact that s 80 has been given an interpretation which deprives it of much substantial effect provides a reason for refusing to import into the section restrictions on the legislative power which it does not express. It has been held that s 80 does not mean that the trial of all serious offences shall be by jury; the section applies if there is a trial on indictment, but leaves it to the Parliament to determine whether any particular offence shall be tried on indictment or summarily. This result has been criticised, but the court has consistently refused to reopen the question and the construction of the section should be regarded as settled …

In dissent, Brennan J held that, by committing certain issues to be tried by a judge, the Customs Act denied the guarantee given by s 80 of the Constitution: 159 CLR at 296.

Deane J held that the views expressed by Dixon and Evatt JJ in *R v Federal Court of Bankruptcy; Ex parte Lowenstein* (1938) 59 CLR 556 **[11.2.29]** should be accepted as a correct statement of the effect of s 80 of the Constitution, subject to the qualification that jury trial was required for a 'serious' Commonwealth offence, rather than for any Commonwealth offence punishable by imprisonment. It followed, Deane J said, that the guarantee of s 80 was available where a charge was brought by the state and the accused, if convicted, would stand convicted of a 'serious offence', a description which would ordinarily be satisfied where the offence was punishable by a maximum term of imprisonment of more than one year: 159 CLR at 319.

[11.2.31] In *Brown v R* (1986) 160 CLR 171, a majority of the High Court (Brennan, Deane and Dawson JJ; Gibbs CJ and Wilson J dissenting) held that a person charged with an indictable offence against a law of the Commonwealth (the Crimes Act 1914 s 233B), and who was to be tried in South Australia, could not invoke the Juries Act 1927 (SA) s 7(1) and elect to be tried by a judge alone. 'The mandatory requirement of s 80 of the Constitution', Deane J said, 'prevails over any contrary provision of any law of a State': 160 CLR at 205. The word 'shall' is used in s 80, importing a mandatory requirement of 'trial by jury' once the precondition of proceedings on indictment under a Commonwealth law is established.

Dawson J contrasted s 80 with art 11(f) of the Canadian Charter of Rights and Freedoms, which was couched as a personal guarantee of jury trial for certain offences and could, therefore, be waived by an accused person. On the other hand, s 80 was, Dawson J said, 'intended to be part of the structure of government rather than the grant of a privilege to individuals' (160 CLR at 214); so that the obligation imposed on the Commonwealth by s 80, to afford trial by jury, could not be waived by an accused.

[11.2.32] In *Cheatle v R* (1993) 177 CLR 541, the High Court held that a person charged with an indictable Commonwealth offence and tried in the Central District Criminal Court of South Australia could not be convicted by a majority jury verdict, notwithstanding that s 57 of the Juries Act 1927 (SA) provided for the taking of a majority verdict (of at least 10 of the 12 jurors) after the jury had deliberated for at least four hours.

In a unanimous judgment, Mason CJ, Brennan, Deane, Dawson, Toohey, Gaudron and McHugh JJ said that, at the time when the Constitution was introduced, 'it was an essential feature of the institution of jury trial that an accused person could not be convicted otherwise than by the agreement or consensus of all the jurors' (177 CLR at 552–3); that '[t]he requirement of a unanimous verdict ensures that the representative character and the collective nature of the jury are carried forward into any ultimate verdict' and reflected 'a fundamental thesis of our criminal law, namely, that a person accused of a crime should be given the benefit of any reasonable doubt' (177 CLR at 553); and that 'the clear weight of authority supports the conclusion that the requirement of unanimity is an essential feature of the institution of trial by jury adopted by s 80': 177 CLR at 554.

The court concluded that s 57 of the Juries Act could not, consistently with s 80 of the Constitution, operate to authorise the conviction by a majority verdict of a person charged with an indictable offence against a law of the Commonwealth. The trial of such an offence in South Australian courts must be conducted in accordance with s 80; that is, according to the unanimous verdict of the jury: see 177 CLR at 562, 563.

[11.2.33] In *Cheatle v R* (1993) 177 CLR 541 **[11.2.32]**, the court was urged to adopt the 'historical approach' taken by Griffith CJ in *R v Snow* (1915) 20 CLR 315, which emphasised the significance of the common law context in settling disputes over the meaning of words and phrases used in the Constitution. Snow had been charged with indictable offences under the Trading with the Enemy Act 1914 (Cth). It was alleged that Snow had committed offences before and after the Act received Royal assent. Snow was tried for the offences before Gordon J and a jury in the Supreme Court of South Australia (exercising federal jurisdiction). At the conclusion of the case, and after defence counsel's argument and an adjournment of one week, the judge decided that the Act did not operate retrospectively, and that the evidence of the offences after the date of commencement of the Act was insufficient to go to the jury. Consequently, the judge concluded that the case had to be stopped, the jury dismissed and the accused discharged. The judge then directed the jury as a matter of law that they had no function to perform except to hold that the accused was not guilty. The jury, 'in blind and dutiful obedience' (Isaacs J, 20 CLR at 328) performed this function.

The Crown appealed to the High Court on the basis that the High Court had full appellate jurisdiction under s 73 of the Constitution to hear an appeal from a jury verdict of acquittal, and grant a new trial. One of Snow's arguments was that the common law had never recognised that an appeal could be made after an acquittal by jury, and this common law right was constitutionally guaranteed by s 80. The High Court agreed. Griffith CJ said at 322–3:

> Sec 80 lays down as a fundamental law of the Commonwealth that the trial on indictment of any offence against any of the laws of the Commonwealth shall be by jury. The framers of the Constitution, the electors who accepted it, and the Parliament which enacted it, must all be taken to have been aware of the absolute protection afforded by a verdict of not guilty under the common law of all the States. With this knowledge they thought proper to enact that any indictable offence that might be created by the new legislative authority established by the Constitution should also be tried by jury. The history of the law of trial by jury as a British institution ... is, in my judgment, sufficient to show that this provision ought *prima facie* to be construed as an adoption of the institution of 'trial by jury' with all that was connoted by that phrase in constitutional law and in the common law of England.

[11.2.34] A unanimous High Court approved this approach to the application of s 80 in *Cheatle v v R* (1993) 177 CLR 541 [11.2.32]. The High Court held that the reference in s 80 of the Constitution to trial by jury was to be understood in accordance with the common law history of criminal trial by jury at the time of federation: 177 CLR at 552. The court said that unanimous jury verdicts had been a requirement at common law since the 14th century and the clear weight of judicial authority supported the unanimity requirement. The requirement could be justified on the grounds that it ensured that 'the representative character and the collective nature of the jury' was 'carried forward into any ultimate verdict'; on the basis that the requirement 'provides some insurance that the opinions of each of the jurors will be heard and discussed' thereby reducing 'the danger of hasty and unjust verdicts'; and on the basis that the requirement reinforced the rule that 'a person accused of a crime should be given the benefit of any reasonable doubt': 177 CLR at 550–5.

Although the High Court endorsed an historical approach to the application of s 80, the court said that the results of that historical inquiry could be modified to accommodate contemporary standards (at 560):

> There was, it was argued, no more justification for the perception that s 80 incorporates the requirement of unanimity than there would be for the approach that the section requires the preservation of those undesirable aspects of trial by jury in 1900 (ie the exclusion of females from juries or property qualifications for jurors). The answer to that argument is, however, clear enough. It is that to abrogate the requirement of unanimity involves an abandonment of an essential feature of the institution of trial by jury. In contrast, a liberalization of the qualifications of jurors involves no more than an adjustment of the institution to conform with contemporary standards and to bring about a situation which is more truly representative of the community.

Accordingly, when determining the scope of the constitutional guarantee of trial by jury, it is necessary to consider the content of that method of trial in 1900, and then to consider what adjustments might be contemplated by the High Court in order to 'conform with contemporary standards and to bring about a situation which is more truly representative of the community'.

[11.2.35] The principle of constitutional interpretation developed in *Cheatle v R* (1993) 177 CLR 541 **[11.2.32]** rationalises the task of the court to apply a document developed in a particular historical context with contemporary demands for justice. However, individual justices may differ in their perceptions of history, contemporary justice and the functions or purposes of the constitutional provisions to be applied. So, for example, the fact that juries were historically composed of 12 people may not lead to a conclusion that there should be 12 today.

The argument that s 80 demands 12 jurors was advanced in *Brownlee v The Queen* (2001) 207 CLR 278. Brownlee was charged with conspiracy to defraud the Commonwealth under the Crimes Act 1914 (Cth) and was tried on indictment in the District Court in Sydney. He appealed unsuccessfully to the New South Wales Court of Appeal, and then sought special leave to appeal to the High Court. He challenged provisions of the Jury Act 1977 (NSW) that had been applied at his trial on the basis that, historically, a trial by jury had to involve 12 jurors. Under the New South Wales law, if any juror died or was discharged for any other reason, the jury could still operate so long as its number did not fall below 10 persons. Brownlee also argued that the jury should not have been permitted to separate after they had retired to consider their verdict.

The court concluded that the essential features of the institution of trial by jury were independence, representativeness and randomness of selection. The court concluded that there was no constitutional requirement that a jury be made up of 12 members: 207 CLR 278 at 288 (Gleeson CJ and McHugh J), 296 (Gaudron, Gummow and Hayne JJ), 331 (Kirby J), 341 (Callinan J).

However, the court reached no concluded view regarding the minimum number of jurors needed to satisfy the essential constitutional requirements. Gleeson CJ and McHugh J approved US authority that these goals are not 'in any meaningful sense less likely to be achieved when the jury numbers six, than when it numbers 12 — particularly if the requirement of unanimity is retained': 207 CLR 278 at 289. Gaudron, Gummow and Hayne JJ remarked that 'if 12 be taken as the requisite minimum with which the trial must commence, there is much force in the contention that no reduction below 10 is permissible': 207 CLR 278 at 303–4. Callinan J said that: 'there is no reason in principle why a jury of twelve persons should necessarily be considered more representative of the community than a jury of ten persons or fourteen, although there may come a point at which a somewhat smaller number could not, in any real sense, be regarded as a jury, a matter that is unnecessary to decided in this case': 207 CLR 278 at 341.

[11.2.36] In a number of cases it has been argued that procedural defects in a criminal matter have denied a jury trial for the purposes of s 80. In *Huddart, Parker & Co Pty Ltd v Moorehead* (1909) 8 CLR 330, the High Court considered an argument that a provision authorising a Commonwealth board of inquiry to compel the giving of evidence infringed s 80, on the basis that any evidence given might prejudice a future trial by jury. This argument was rejected by the court on the basis that collateral proceedings on indictment against the witness for an offence against the Commonwealth, which might attract s 80, were not on foot, so that it was impossible to say whether the compulsion to give evidence would be damaging to a trial that may not take place: 8 CLR at 358 (Griffith CJ); 366 (Barton J); 374–5 (O'Connor J); 386 (Isaacs J); 418 (Higgins J).

[11.2.37] Murphy J criticised the decision of the court in *Huddart, Parker* in his dissenting judgment in *Hammond v The Commonwealth* (1982) 152 CLR 188 at 201, on the basis that the right of a person to a fair trial would be adversely affected if the person were required to give testimony at a Royal Commission and the evidence given could be used against the person in later proceedings. Nevertheless, the argument that compelling a witness to answer questions at a Royal Commission breached s 80 was again rejected in *Sorby v The Commonwealth* (1983) 152 CLR 281 at 308–9 (Mason, Wilson and Dawson JJ). However, Gibbs CJ provided some guidance on the relationship between the constitutional guarantee of trial by jury and the other common law incidents of a fair trial, including the right to silence. His Honour expressed the view that the argument might be given weight in circumstances where the persons giving evidence were awaiting trial for a criminal offence, although even then there might not be any 'necessary impairment' of the trial: 152 CLR at 299. The argument would only be persuasive where 'there was a real possibility that if he was required to answer incriminating questions the administration of justice would be interfered with': 152 CLR at 299. This suggests that the question is one of degree.

[11.2.38] In *Brownlee v The Queen* (2001) 207 CLR 278 **[11.2.35]**, it was argued that allowing a jury to separate after they had retired to consider their verdict infringed s 80 because it exposed jurors to the risk of improper external influence. The argument was rejected on the basis that separation of jury members does not necessarily impair the function of the jury, that jurors may be warned by the trial judge to resist external influences, and if they are affected, the trial judge can make appropriate orders: 207 CLR 278 at 290, 342–3. Furthermore, the anonymity of jurors is protected by legislation, reducing the risks of external influence: 207 CLR 278 at 290. It is possible that a trial could become so tainted that a person could be found not to have had a 'trial by jury' within s 80 of the Constitution (see 207 CLR 278 at 190) but, on the evidence available, this had not occurred in *Brownlee*.

[11.2.39] In *Katsuno v The Queen* (1999) 199 CLR 40 the court appears to have proceeded on the basis that interference with the trial of a person under s 80 is a question of degree. Under the Juries Act 1967 (Vic), the Crown had the power to make up to six peremptory challenges to members of the panel from which a jury would be selected for a trial. The Act gave the sheriff who prepared the panel the power to refer the panel list to the Chief Commissioner of Police, who carried out background checks and provided that information to the Sheriff. The Commissioner also passed the list and the information collected by the Commissioner to the state Office of Public Prosecutions, which provided the list and the information to the Commonwealth Director of Public Prosecutions (the DPP).

Katsuno was charged on indictment with importing a commercial quantity of heroin into Australia contrary to s 233B(1)(b) of the Customs Act 1901 (Cth) and was convicted by a jury convened under the Juries Act, after the DPP had challenged one potential juror on the basis of his prior convictions. Katsuno challenged his conviction on two bases. His first argument, that the Juries Act provided no statutory power to the Commissioner to pass lists of jurors to the OPP and the DPP, was accepted by a majority of the High Court. However, according to Gleeson CJ, Gaudron, Gummow and Callinan JJ, the breach of the Juries Act was not a basis for quashing Katsuno's conviction.

Katsuno's second argument was that the practice adopted by the Commissioner, the OPP and the DPP interfered with the selection of jury members to such an extent that the constitutional right to trial by jury under s 80 of the Constitution had been breached. Katsuno argued that a jury panel under s 80 must be randomly selected and be seen to be randomly selected. Impartiality, representativeness and randomness were, he argued, essential or minimum requirements of the institution of trial by jury and, to the extent that the proceedings had not conformed to these requirements, s 80 had been breached.

The argument was rejected by a majority of the court on the basis that the breaches of the Jury Act took place before the selection of the jury: 199 CLR 40 at 65 (Gaudron, Gummow and Callinan JJ, with whom Gleeson CJ agreed, at 51):

> The fact that the prosecutor made use of the information in making the peremptory challenge that he made was not such a departure from a mandatory provision relating to the authority and constitution of the jury as to deny the constitutionality of the appellant's trial (199 CLR 40 at 65).

McHugh and Kirby JJ would have set the conviction aside because the DPP's use of illegally obtained information had 'subverted the legislative scheme for selecting an impartial jury': at 67 (McHugh J). They did not base their judgments on any breach of s 80 of the Constitution.

[11.2.40] The s 80 guarantee of trial by jury has no work to do when it comes to sentencing — a matter that (despite Lewis Carroll's famous dictum) follows the verdict. 'The constitutional command in s 80 is directed to jury trial of issues joined between prosecution and accused; the process of sentencing is for the trial judge': *Cheung v The Queen* (2001) 209 CLR 1 at 24 per Gleeson CJ, Gummow and Hayne JJ, with whom Gaudron J agreed at 27; see also *Whitaker v The Queen* (1928) 41 CLR 230 at 240.

Religious freedom

[11.2.41E] **Commonwealth Constitution**

116 The Commonwealth shall not make any law for establishing any religion, or for imposing any religious observance, or for prohibiting the free exercise of any religion, and no religious test shall be required as a qualification for any office or public trust under the Commonwealth.

~~~

Notes

[11.2.42] Section 116 appears in Ch V of the Commonwealth Constitution, entitled 'The States'. The first published draft of the Commonwealth Constitution, which emerged from the 1891 Constitutional Convention, had prohibited state legislation restricting the free exercise of religion. At the 1898 Convention in Melbourne, one delegate, Henry Higgins (later to be appointed to the High Court) proposed that the prohibition be expanded to prevent either the Commonwealth or the states from restricting religious freedom, establishing any religion or imposing a religious test for public office. Higgins argued that, without the expanded version of the clause, the Commonwealth Parliament might emulate the United States Congress which, he said, had legislated for Sunday observance. The Convention first voted to remove the clause altogether and then responded to Higgins' pressure by adopting the current form of s 116. Its anomalous position in Ch V was, John La Nauze observed, '[t]he final irony', and can best be explained by the drafting committee's exhaustion: La Nauze (1972) pp 228–9; see also Pannam (1963) pp 52–54; Campbell and Whitmore (1972) pp 377–8; Constitutional Commission (1988) p 610; O'Neill (1987) p 101. This ironic position was confirmed in *Attorney-General (Vic); Ex rel Black v Commonwealth* (1981) 146 CLR 559 **[11.2.47C]** at 577, 594 and 652, where it was pointed out that s 116 has no application to the states.

[11.2.43] The language of s 116 reflects two provisions in the United States Constitution: Art VI, s 3, which declares in part that 'no religious test shall ever be required as a qualification to any office or public trust under the United States'; and the First Amendment, which includes the declaration: 'Congress shall make no law respecting any establishment of religion, or prohibiting the free exercise thereof ...'. However, the reading of s 116 adopted by the High Court of Australia has diverged sharply from the more expansive reading of its counterparts developed by the United States Supreme Court.

In Australia, the work of the court has concentrated on the free exercise and anti-establishment clauses of s 116. There has been practically no judicial discussion of the prohibitions on religious observance and religious test laws.

In *R v Winneke; Ex parte Gallagher* (1983) 152 CLR 211 at 227–9, Murphy J, dissenting, suggested that a federal law that required a person to swear an oath to tell the truth would infringe the 'religious observance' clause. However the prospect of a case arising with these facts in issue is remote because judicial and tribunal proceedings typically provide an option to 'solemnly affirm' to tell the truth rather than to swear an oath.

In *Crittenden v Anderson* (1950) 51 ALJ 171, Fullagar J, sitting as the Court of Disputed Returns, dismissed a challenge by Crittenden to Anderson's membership in the parliament on the basis that, as a Roman Catholic, Anderson had an allegiance to a 'foreign power' (that is, the Vatican State) within the meaning of s 44(i) of the Constitution. Fullagar J said:

> Effect could not be given to the petitioner's contention without the imposition of a 'religious test' [within the meaning of s 116] ... the view put forward ... is quite untenable.

[11.2.44] The court has not yet resolved the question whether s 116 applies to laws made under the territories power. In *Attorney-General (Vic); Ex rel Black v Commonwealth* (1981) 146 CLR 559 **[11.2.47C]**, four justices noted the question was open: 146 CLR at 577, 593–4, 621, 649. The question whether the section will apply to Commonwealth laws made for the territories (under the territories power, s 122) was referred to in *Teori Tau v Commonwealth* (1969) 119 CLR 564 **[11.2.13]**. In the course of deciding that laws made under s 122 were not limited by s 51(xxxi) and therefore need not provide 'just terms' for acquisition of property, Barwick CJ, McTiernan, Kitto, Menzies, Windeyer, Owen and Walsh JJ said that 'the Constitution must be read as a whole and as a consequence, s 122 may be subject to other appropriate provisions of it as, for example, s 116': 119 CLR at 570.

On the other hand, in *Attorney-General (Vic) (Ex rel Black) v Commonwealth* (1981) 146 CLR 559 **[11.2.47C]**, Gibbs J observed that the dicta which suggested that s 122 laws must conform to s 116 were very difficult to reconcile with the decision in

R v Bernasconi (1915) 19 CLR 629 **[11.2.22]**, where s 122 was held not to be restricted by s 80: 146 CLR at 593–4. Gibbs J went on to say that, if s 122 laws were subject to s 116, then 'the latter section will have a much larger operation in the territories than in the states, for although s 116 is contained in Ch V of the Constitution which is headed "The States" it is not expressed to bind the states': 146 CLR at 594.

[11.2.45]   In *Kruger v Commonwealth* (1997) 190 CLR 1 **[11.3.21C]** and **[11.3.32C]**, the court again considered whether s 116 applied to the territories. The case raised the validity of an ordinance authorising the removal of Aboriginal children from their parents in South Australia and the Northern Territory between 1925 and 1949. The plaintiffs argued that the Ordinance involved was beyond the legislative power of the Northern Territory Government, that it was contrary to a number of implied constitutional rights, and that it breached s 116 of the Constitution.

On the question whether s 116 extended to the territories, two members of the court, Dawson J, with whom on this issue McHugh J concurred, said that it did not apply. Three justices, in separate judgments, Toohey (190 CLR at 85–6), Gaudron (190 CLR at 122–3), and Gummow JJ (190 CLR at 160–1), said that it did so extend. One justice, Brennan CJ (190 CLR at 40) appeared to assume that it did, since he discussed whether the Ordinance infringed the constitutional prohibition. Gaudron J said that s 116 was unlike Ch III which was 'of critical significance' to the federal compact, and the absence of constitutional provision for self-government was 'a strong reason for reading s 122 as subject to express constitutional guarantees and freedoms unless their terms clearly indicate otherwise': 190 CLR at 122–3.

'Religion'

[11.2.46]   The leading case on the meaning of the term 'religion' is *Church of the New Faith v Commissioner for Pay-Roll Tax (Vic)* (1983) 154 CLR 120, in which the issue was whether the Church of the New Faith (which professed 'Scientology') was exempt from state pay-roll tax legislation on the basis that it was a religion. Mason ACJ and Brennan J said that any definition should be flexible enough to accommodate minority groups and new religious beliefs: 154 CLR at 123. However, it would be inappropriate to adopt a definition which allowed any group who asserted their belief to be religious to enjoy the protection of the provision. Their Honours concluded at 136 that:

> ... for the purposes of the law, the criteria of religion are twofold: first, belief in a supernatural Being, Thing or Principle; and second, the acceptance of canons of conduct in order to give effect to that belief, though canons of conduct which offend against the ordinary laws outside the area of any immunity, privilege or right conferred on the grounds of religion. Those criteria may vary in their comparative importance, and there may be a different intensity of belief or of acceptance of canons of conduct among religions or among the adherents to a religion. The tenets of a religion may give primacy to one particular belief or to one particular canon of conduct. Variations in emphasis may distinguish one religion from other religions, but they are irrelevant to the determination of an individual's or a group's freedom to profess and exercise the religion of his, or their, choice.

Mason ACJ and Brennan J concluded that Scientology was a religion, even though they found some of its canons to be 'impenetrably obscure' and they could 'readily appreciate' why the trial judge came to the conclusion that Scientology was merely 'a farrago of imitations of established religions': 154 CLR at 145.

Wilson and Deane JJ approached the task of defining the term 'religion' with caution, stating at 173–4 that:

> The most that can be done is to formulate the more important of the indicia or guidelines by reference to which that question falls to be answered. Those indicia must, in the view we take, be derived by empirical observation of accepted religions. They are liable to vary with changing social conditions and the relative importance of any particular one of them will vary from case to case. We briefly outline hereunder what we consider to be the more important of them ...
>
> One of the more important indicia of 'a religion' is that the particular collection of ideas and/or practices involves belief in the supernatural, that is to say, belief that reality extends beyond that which is capable of perception by the senses. If that be absent, it is unlikely that one has a 'religion'. Another is that the ideas relate to man's nature and place in the universe and his relation to things supernatural. A third is that the ideas are accepted by adherents as requiring or encouraging them to observe particular standards or codes of conduct or to participate in specific practices having supernatural significance. A fourth is that, however loosely knit and varying in beliefs and practices adherents may be, they constitute an identifiable group or identifiable groups. A fifth, and perhaps more controversial, indicium is that the adherents themselves see the collection of ideas and/or practices as constituting a religion.

Wilson and Deane JJ stressed that these five indicia did not form a rigid test, and that a wider test of 'religion' might need to be adopted in a case which directly dealt with s 116: 154 CLR at 173. Murphy J offered the following wider test at 151:

> The better approach is to state what is sufficient, even if not necessary, to bring a body which claims to be religious within the category. Some claims to be religious are not serious but merely a hoax, but to reach this conclusion requires an extreme case. On this approach, any body which claims to be religious, whose beliefs or practices are a revival of, or resemble, earlier cults, is religious. Any body which claims to be religious and to believe in a supernatural Being or Beings, whether physical and visible, such as the sun and the stars, or a physical invisible God or spirit, or an abstract God or entity, is religious. For example, if a few followers of astrology were to found an institution based on the belief that their destinies were influenced or controlled by the stars, and that astrologers can, by reading the stars, divine these destinies, and if it claimed to be religious, it would be a religious institution. Any body which claims to be religious, and offers a way to find meaning and purpose in life, is religious. The Aboriginal religion of Australia and other countries must be included. The list is not exhaustive; the categories of religion are not closed.

As an example of claims to be religious that would be regarded as 'not serious but merely a hoax', Murphy J cited *United States v Kuch* 288 F Supp 439 (1968), in which the claims of the Neo-American Church to be a religion were rejected. The Neo-American Church worshipped 'Chief Boo Hoo' and claimed that marijuana and LSD were sacramental foods to be used by members on religious occasions.

'Establishing any religion'

[11.2.47C]   **Attorney-General (Vic) (Ex rel Black)**
v Commonwealth

(The *DOGS* case)
(1981) 146 CLR 559

The Commonwealth Parliament enacted a series of Acts which provided for the payment of financial assistance to each state on condition that the moneys were paid to non-government schools nominated by the Commonwealth.

The Attorney-General for Victoria granted his fiat to a number of persons (loosely, the Defence of Government Schools group, or '*DOGS*'), who then commenced proceedings as relators against the Commonwealth. The relators sought a declaration that the Commonwealth Acts were, to the extent that they provided for the payment of money to church schools, invalid. They also sought an injunction restraining the Commonwealth from applying the Consolidated Revenue Fund to payments to church schools.

Stephen J: [605] At the heart of this case is the question whether Commonwealth laws offend against s 116 of the Constitution when they grant financial assistance to the States on condition that the States apply the sums granted in paying for capital projects and recurrent expenses of non-government schools. A similar question arises concerning moneys appropriated for spending on such schools in the Territories ...

Some things about the section are self-evident. It is not, in form, a constitutional guarantee of the rights of individuals; with it may be contrasted s 117 which, like s 80, at least gives promise of guaranteed rights, however illusory that promise may so far have proved in practical operation: *R v Archdall and Roskruge; Ex parte Carrigan and Brown* [(1928) 41 CLR 128] and *Henry v Boehm* [(1973) 128 CLR 482]. Section 116, like s 99, instead takes the form of express restriction upon the exercise of Commonwealth legislative power.

The section contains four quite distinct restrictions, each concerned with one aspect of the relationship between church and state and each recalling phases of that relationship as it has evolved through centuries of English history. The first three prohibit the making of laws of particular kinds, laws 'for' the doing of certain things. The fourth prohibits the imposition, whether by law or otherwise, of religious tests for the holding of Commonwealth office. It is the first of these four restrictions that is here in question. It differs in substance and form from the second and third restrictions. They are directed against the 'imposing' or the 'prohibiting' of aspects or religious practice; unlike them, the participle 'establishing' used in the first restriction does not describe a prohibited law's impact upon the citizen but its effect upon religion.

What it is which constitutes 'establishing any religion' has, of course, been central to the debate in this case. The plaintiffs say that 'establishing' in s 116 includes the provision by the Commonwealth of funds to schools associated with churches. The predominant view of the various defendants and intervenors is, I think, that 'establishing' means the constituting of a religion as an officially recognized State religion.

[606] The context provided by s 116 is enough to show that what is perhaps the most usual meaning of 'establishing', that of setting up or founding ... is inappropriate in s 116. In that section the conjunction of 'establishing' with 'law' and with 'religion' gives it its particular meaning.

It is that meaning which the *Shorter Oxford English Dictionary* alone gives to it when specifically related to religion, namely 'to place (a church or a religious body) in the position of a state church'. This I have no doubt is the meaning of the verb 'establish' and of its present participle according to common usage when used with reference to a church or religion. Only if convincing reasons can be shown will it bear a different or more particular meaning. The plaintiffs, in seeking to make good the proposition that the provision by law of funds for church schools is an establishing of religion, urge several reasons for so saying, while not conceding in the first place that 'establishing' bears the meaning which I would assign to it according to ordinary usage.

The plaintiffs' argument begins by giving to 'religion' a meaning which extends beyond a particular religious philosophy so as also to include the religious community which supports that faith and also its organization and practices. So much may readily enough be accepted: to speak of a religion being established by the laws of a country may well be to include much more than the act of according material recognition and status to a set of beliefs, a system of moral philosophy or particular doctrines of faith; it would certainly include the recognition of a particular religion or sect, with its priestly hierarchy and tenets, as that of the nation.

The plaintiffs point to the undoubted imprecision surrounding the concept of establishment as applied to the Church of England. Again, it may be accepted that there is no single characteristic of that Church which of itself constitutes the touchstone of its establishment. Over the centuries the rights enjoyed by the Church of England, as the established church, have greatly changed, as has that subjection to temporal authority which is the concomitant of establishment. Dibdin, in *Establishment in England*, traces the various phases of the Church's establishment and the disappearance, over time, of many of those characteristics which once went to make up its status as the established Church. The plaintiffs rely both upon [607] his adoption, at p 113, of Lord Selborne's statement that in different countries the particular forms and conditions of Establishment differ and upon his comment that it might be added that in England those forms and conditions have themselves 'differed greatly from time to time'. Dibdin concludes, at p 116: 'The Establishment has survived so many modifications that, whatever we may think it would be rash to assert that the irreducible minimum has now been nearly reached.'

The status of establishment which the Church of England has long enjoyed in England has no single characteristic but, rather, is the sum total of all the mutual relations for the time being existing according to law between Church and State. No single element of those relations, viewed in isolation, itself creates establishment. Because the status of establishment is, in England, the outcome of a complex of relationships does not make a law which creates one element of that complex a law 'for establishing' a religion. Still less does it mean, as the plaintiffs also contend, that any law which may represent a step in the direction of, or may be thought to have a tendency towards, producing the end result of the establishment of a religion is a law which offends against s 116.

The plaintiffs rely upon matters of colonial history as affecting the meaning of 'establishing' in s 116. First, they say that in nineteenth century Australia there was for a time a recognition of a variety of representative Christian denominations. This was accompanied by the granting of financial aid by colonial governments to those denominations and to the schools conducted under their respective auspices. By the end of the century however, under the influence of voluntaryist and separationist views of the relationship which should exist between church and state, each of the Australian colonies had by legislation ended this financial support of particular denominations and of church schools. This being the historical setting in which the terms of the federal compact were debated, it is said to colour the meaning to be given to 'establishing' in s 116 so as to include within its prohibition grants of financial support to schools affiliated with particular churches, grants which each of the federating colonies had abrogated in the three decades preceding federation.

Australia's colonial history does indeed disclose, first, something at least approaching official recognition of the Church of England; followed, however, by a general recognition of a wide variety of denominations, accompanied by impartial financial assistance to all their churches and schools; then, in [608] the latter part of the nineteenth century, there occurred a move towards complete separation of church and state, with the abolition of all financial aid to churches and to church schools. It is with this last development that the plaintiffs would seek to associate s 116, contending that it represents a continuation of the policy of colonial legislatures of the late nineteenth century.

Perhaps the first thing to be observed in examining this proposition is the marked contrast which exists between the language of the colonial Acts which abolished financial aid to churches and church schools and the words of s 116. It is in terms of 'the abolition of state aid to religion' (Victoria), of the prohibition of 'future grants of public money in aid of public worship' (New South Wales), of the discontinuance of 'grants from the revenue in aid of religion' (Queensland), of the 'termination of the parliamentary ecclesiastical grant' (Western Australia) that colonial legislatures ended their financial support of denominations. Likewise, the termination of state financial aid to church schools was also expressed in precise terms which made no reference to the concept of the establishment or disestablishment of religion.

The language of the first restriction in s 116 stands in marked contrast to the precise terms in which these colonial measures were expressed. These measures nowhere refer either to 'establishing' or 'establishment' nor, for that matter, to 'disestablishment', a phrase then much in vogue in connexion with the current disestablishment debate in the United Kingdom. The colonial Acts had no need to deal in such concepts because there existed in Australia no established church capable of being disestablished. Section 116, on the other hand, specifically speaks in terms of a prohibition against laws for 'establishing any religion'. Its language is singularly ill-adapted to ensuring that the spirit of the colonial measures should persist in the new polity which emerged from federation. It is, however, entirely apt if concerned with the quite different subject of the creation of a state church in Australia; something which had come close to occurring in the early colonial period but which s 116 would prevent for the future. So understood, it is natural that the first restriction in s 116 should speak in terms quite different from the language of the previous colonial legislation. It is significant that, writing in 1901, Quick and Garran should say of the opening words of s 116: 'by an establishment of religion is meant the erection and recognition of a State church or the concession of special favours [609] titles and advantages to one Church which is denied to others': *Annotated Constitution*, p 951. They clearly did not regard it as continuing the policy of the colonial measures. In saying what they did they were reflecting the view then prevailing in the United States as to the effect of the First Amendment, of which more hereafter.

The very form of s 116, consisting of four distinct and express restrictions upon legislative power, is also significant. It cannot readily be viewed as the repository of some broad statement of principle concerning the separation of church and state, from which may be distilled the detailed consequences of such separation. On the contrary, by fixing upon four specific restrictions of legislative power, the form of the section gives no encouragement to the undertaking of any such distillation.

The plaintiffs place much reliance upon what is said to have been the influence of the United States Constitution in the framing of s 116. The argument is that words of the First Amendment are similar to those of the first restriction in s 116; that the First Amendment was, by the time of Federation, understood in a sense which would forbid the grant by the federal government of aid to church schools; and that, by using similar language, the framers of our Constitution must have intended that the first restriction in s 116 should have a similar operation.

The argument fails on two counts. The more obvious is that the wording of the two measures differs in an important respect; the more telling is that the First Amendment had not, by the 1890s, come to bear the meaning which the plaintiffs would seek to assign to the first restriction in s 116. As to wording, the First Amendment requires that 'Congress shall make no law respecting an establishment of religion', a restriction of wider scope than s 116's prohibition of laws 'for establishing any religion'. To illustrate this wider scope one may use another of the restrictions in s 116, thus avoiding the effect of any preconception about the meaning of 'establishing': a law which did no more than require all places of entertainment to be closed on Sundays would not be a law 'for' imposing any religious observance whereas it might well be one 'respecting' the imposition of some religious observance. The difference of wording, and the effect attributed to 'respecting' in the American decisions of this century deprive those modern decisions of value in the interpretation of s 116.

Then, as to the understanding of the meaning of the First Amendment prevailing in the 1890s; despite its different and wider wording, the First Amendment was understood as [610] requiring only that no national church should be recognized or created and no one persuasion or mode of worship should be given any special privilege or particular recognition. This is made clear in the judgment of the US Court of Appeals for the District of Columbia in *Roberts v Bradfield* (1898) 12 App DC 453; the judgment of the US Supreme Court when the case went on appeal, [175 US 291 (1899) [44 Law Ed 168]] does not, on analysis, reflect any different view. That this was the then prevailing view of the First Amendment also emerges very clearly from Cooley's *Constitutional Limitations*, 6th ed (1890), pp 575 et seq and his *Principles of Constitutional Law*, 3rd ed (1898), p 224 and from Storey's *Commentaries*, 5th ed (1891), pp 631–634. As Von Holst said in his *Constitutional Law of the United States of America* (1887), p 227 'Congress is not only prohibited from making any religion whatever a state religion or any church whatever a state church, but it cannot make any laws favouring one religion or church more than any other'.

It follows that even if the framers of our Constitution had seen fit to adopt verbatim the terms of the First Amendment, they would have been doing no more than writing into our Constitution what was then believed to be a prohibition against two things, the setting up of a national church and the favouring of one church over another. They would not have been denying power to grant non-discriminatory financial aid to churches or church schools.

Section 116 is a constitutional provision of high importance. As the plaintiffs say, it does indeed provide important safeguards for religious freedom for Australians, at least so far as that freedom might otherwise be in jeopardy from laws of the Commonwealth. It does so by prohibiting three avenues of possible legislative encroachment upon that freedom — the elevation of one church above all others, the imposing of particular religious observances and the proscribing of any religious worship. It also prohibits one avenue of encroachment open to legislature and executive alike — the imposition of religious tests for office holders. These four prohibitions, the fruit of long experience of past religious intolerance in the United Kingdom, ensure that Parliament will observe that 'true distinction between what properly belongs to the Church and what to the State': *Reynolds v United States* 98 US 145 at 163 (1878) [25 Law Ed 244 at 249]. They say nothing, however, which would impugn the validity of the legislation which the plaintiffs seek to attack. Because of the meaning **[611]** which, in my view, 'establishing' bears in s 116, their attack based upon that section fails.

Barwick CJ, Gibbs, Mason, Aickin and Wilson JJ agreed that the Commonwealth legislation did not offend the first clause of s 116. Murphy J dissented, holding that s 116 prohibited Commonwealth laws which sponsored or supported religion generally, and that the Commonwealth legislation granting financial assistance to church-run schools had the effect of supporting religion. All members of the court held that, apart from the s 116 argument, the Commonwealth legislation did not exceed the Commonwealth Parliament's authority under s 96 of the Constitution.

~~~

'Prohibiting the free exercise of any religion'

[11.2.48C]   Adelaide Company of Jehovah's Witnesses v Commonwealth
(1943) 67 CLR 116

The National Security (Subversive Associations) Regulations were made under the National Security Act 1939 (Cth). The regulations authorised the Governor-General to declare that the existence of an association was prejudicial to the war effort. Such a declaration dissolved the association and allowed the Commonwealth Government to seize the association's property. On 17 January 1941, the Governor-General declared that the existence of the Adelaide Company of Jehovah's Witnesses, an association incorporated under South Australian law, was prejudicial to the war effort. On the same day, the Commonwealth Government took possession of the company's premises in Adelaide.

The Adelaide Company of Jehovah's Witnesses consisted of some 250 persons who followed the religious beliefs of the sect known as Jehovah's Witnesses. The sect claimed that all organised political bodies were agents of Satan, and that members of the sect must play no part in the political affairs of the world or in wars between nations.

The company began proceedings against the Commonwealth in the High Court, challenging the validity of the Governor-General's declaration and the seizure of the company's property. Starke J stated a case for the consideration of the Full Court.

Latham CJ: [122] 1. This proceeding raises important questions with reference to the nature and extent of the protection which is given to religion under the Constitution of the Commonwealth. Section 116 of the Constitution is as follows: 'The Commonwealth shall not make any law for establishing any region, or for imposing any religious observance, or for prohibiting the free exercise of any religion, and no religious test shall be required as a qualification for any office or public trust under the Commonwealth.'

It is plain that by this provision it is intended to place some restriction upon the power of the Commonwealth to enact legislation which favours any religion, or which interferes with any religion. The principal questions which arise in the case are:— Does s 116 prevent the Commonwealth Parliament from legislating to restrain the activities of a body, the existence of which is, in the opinion of the Governor-General, prejudicial to the defence of the Commonwealth or the efficient prosecution of the war, if that body is a religious organization? Is the answer to this question affected by the fact that the subversive activities of such a body are founded upon the religious views of its members? Can such a body be suppressed?

2. In the first place, it is important to observe that s 116 is an express prohibition of any law which falls within its terms. The section deals with laws which in some manner relate to religion. The Constitution, however, contains no provision which confers upon the Commonwealth Parliament any power to make laws with respect [123] to the subject of religion. Section 116 therefore cannot be regarded as prescribing the content of laws made with respect to religion upon the basis that the Commonwealth Parliament has some power of legislating with respect to religion. Section 116 is a general prohibition applying to all laws, under whatever power those laws may be made. It is an overriding provision. It does not compete with other provisions of the Constitution so that the Court should seek to reconcile it with other provisions. It prevails over and limits all provisions which give power to make laws.

Accordingly no law can escape the application of s 116 simply because it is a law which can be justified under ss 51 or 52, or under some other legislative power. All the legislative powers of the Commonwealth are subject to the condition which s 116 imposes.

3. Section 116 applies in express terms to 'any religion,' 'any religious observance,' the free exercise of 'any religion' and any 'religious test'. Thus the section applies in relation to all religions, and not merely in relation to some one particular religion.

It would be difficult, if not impossible, to devise a definition of religion which would satisfy the adherents of all the many and various religions which exist, or have existed, in the world. There are those who regard religion as consisting principally in a system of beliefs or statement of doctrine. So viewed religion may be either true or false. Others are more inclined to regard religion as prescribing a code of conduct. So viewed a religion may be good or bad. There are others who pay greater attention to religion as involving some prescribed form of ritual or religious observance. Many religious conflicts have been concerned with matters of ritual and observance. Section 116 must be regarded as operating in relation to all these aspects of religion, irrespective of varying opinions in the community as to the truth of particular religious doctrines, as to the goodness of conduct prescribed by a particular religion, or as to the propriety of any particular religious observance. What is religion to one is superstition to another. Some religions are regarded as morally evil by adherents of other creeds. At all times there are many who agree with the reflective comment of the Roman poet — '*Tantum religio potuit suadere malorum*'.

The prohibition in s 116 operates not only to protect the freedom of religion, but also to protect the right of a man to have no religion. No Federal law can impose any religious observance. Defaults in the performance of religious duties are not to be corrected by Federal law — *Deorum injuriae Diis curae*. Section 116 proclaims not only the principle of toleration of all religions, but also the principle of toleration of absence of religion.

[124] 4. It was suggested in argument that no system of beliefs or code of conduct or form of ritual could be protected under the section unless the general opinion of the present day regarded the belief or conduct or ritual as being really religious. It is true that in determining

what is religious and what is not religious the current application of the word 'religion' must necessarily be taken into account, but it should not be forgotten that such a provision as s 116 is not required for the protection of the religion of a majority. The religion of the majority of the people can look after itself. Section 116 is required to protect the religion (or absence of religion) of minorities, and, in particular, of unpopular minorities.

5. It is sometimes suggested in discussions on the subject of freedom of religion that, though the civil government should not interfere with religions *opinions*, it nevertheless may deal as it pleases with any *acts* which are done in pursuance of religious belief without infringing the principle of freedom of religion. It appears to me to be difficult to maintain this distinction as relevant to the interpretation of s 116. The section refers in express terms to the exercise of religion, and therefore it is intended to protect from the operation of any Commonwealth laws acts which are done in the exercise of religion. Thus the section goes far beyond protecting liberty of opinion. It protects also acts done in pursuance of religious belief as part of religion.

Latham CJ referred to the characteristics of several religious systems; observed that 'almost any matter may become an element in religious belief or religious conduct'; said that it was 'not for a court to disqualify certain beliefs as incapable of being religious in character' (67 CLR at 124); said 'that religious belief and practice cannot be absolutely separated either from politics or from ethics' (67 CLR at 125–6); and continued:

[126] Section 116, however, is based upon the principle that religion should, for political purposes, be regarded as irrelevant. It assumes that citizens of all religions can be good citizens, and that accordingly there is no justification in the interests of the community for prohibiting the free exercise of any religion.

7. The examples which have been given illustrate the difficulty of the problem with which a court is confronted when it is asked to determine whether or not a particular law infringes the constitutional provision by prohibiting 'the free exercise of ... religion.' Can any person, by describing (and honestly describing) his beliefs and practices as religious exempt himself from obedience to the law? Does s 116 protect any religious belief or any religious practice, irrespective of the political or social effect of that belief or practice?

It has already been shown that beliefs entertained by a religious body as religious beliefs may be inconsistent with the maintenance of civil government. The complete protection of all religious beliefs might result in the disappearance of organized society, because some religious beliefs, as already indicated, regard the existence of organized society as essentially evil.

8. Section 116 does not merely protect the exercise of religion, it protects the free exercise of religion. The word 'free' is vague and ambiguous, as is shown by the many decisions in this Court and in the Privy Council upon the meaning of the word 'free' in another place when it appears in the Constitution — in s 92, which provides for free trade, commerce and intercourse between the States. When a slogan is incorporated in a constitution, and the interpretation of the slogan is entrusted to a court, difficulties will inevitably arise.

The word 'free' is used in many senses, and the meaning of the word varies almost indefinitely with the context. A man is said to be free when he is not a slave, but he is also said to be free when he is not imprisoned, and is not subject to any other form of physical restraint. In another sense a man is only truly free when he has freedom of thought and expression, as well as of physical movement. But in all these cases an obligation to obey the laws which apply [127] generally to the community is not regarded as inconsistent with freedom.

Freedom of speech is a highly valued element in our society. But freedom of speech does not mean that an individual is at liberty to create a panic in a theatre by raising a false alarm of fire, as was pointed out in the United States of America in the case of *Schenck v United States* 249 US 47 at 52 (1919) [63 Law Ed 470 at 473]. In *James v The Commonwealth* (1936) AC 578; 55 CLR 1, the Privy Council dealt with the meaning of the words 'absolutely free' in s 92 of the Constitution. It was there said: "'Free' in itself is vague and indeterminate. It must take its colour from the context. Compare, for instance, its use in free speech, free love, free dinner and free trade. Free speech does not mean free speech; it means speech hedged in by all the laws against defamation, blasphemy, sedition and so forth; it means freedom governed by law, as was pointed out in *McArthur's Case* (1920) 28 CLR 530. Free love, on the contrary, means licence or libertinage, though, even so, there are limitations based on public decency and so forth. Free dinner generally means free of expense, and sometimes a meal open to anyone who comes, subject, however, to his condition or behaviour not being objectionable. Free trade means, in ordinary parlance, freedom from tariffs'. [[1936] AC at 627; 55 CLR at 56] Thus there is no dictionary meaning of the word 'free' which can be applied in all cases.

Latham CJ referred to the First Amendment to the United States Constitution and said that recent decisions of the Supreme Court of the United States had accepted that some constraints could be imposed on religious activities in the interest of other values. Latham CJ also referred to a series of United States cases decided before 1900, in which the general criminal law had been applied against persons who claimed that their actions were required by their religious beliefs — in particular, against Mormons who believed in and practised polygamy. Latham CJ continued:

[130] [T]he cases which I have cited do show that in 1900 it had been thoroughly established in the United States that the provision [131] preventing the making of any law prohibiting the free exercise of religion was not understood to mean that the criminal law dealing with the conduct of citizens generally was to be subject to exceptions in favour of persons who believed and practised a religion which was inconsistent with the provisions of the law. The result of this approach to the problem has been the development of the principle which has been applied in the later cases, to which I have already referred, according to which it is left to the court to determine whether the freedom of religion has been unduly infringed by some particular legislative provision. This view makes it possible to accord a real measure of practical protection to religion without involving the community in anarchy.

10. There is, therefore, full legal justification for adopting in Australia an interpretation of s 116 which had, before the enactment of the Commonwealth Constitution, already been given to similar words in the United States. This interpretation leaves it to the court to determine whether a particular law is an undue infringement of religious freedom. It is possible, however, in my opinion, to decide the present case upon a narrower principle which escapes the criticisms to which that interpretation may be open.

John Stuart Mill in his *Essay on Liberty* critically examines the idea of liberty, and his discussion of the subject is widely accepted as a weighty exposition of principle. The author had to make the distinction which is often made in words between liberty and licence, but which it is sometimes very difficult to apply in practice. He recognized that liberty did not mean the licence of individuals to do just what they pleased, because such liberty would mean the absence of law and of order, and ultimately the destruction of liberty. He expressed his opinion as to the limits of liberty when he said: 'The sole end for which mankind are warranted, individually or collectively, in interfering with the liberty of action of any of their number, is self-protection' (*Essay on Liberty*, sch 1, p 6 — 1871 ed). It may be going too far to say that self-protection is 'the sole end' which justifies any governmental action. But I think it must be conceded that the protection of any form of liberty as a social right within a society necessarily involves the continued existence of that society as a society. Otherwise the protection of liberty would be meaningless and ineffective. It is consistent with the maintenance of religious liberty for the State to restrain actions and courses of conduct which are inconsistent with the maintenance of civil government or prejudicial to the continued existence of the community. The Constitution protects religion within a community organized under a Constitution, so that the continuance of such protection [132] necessarily assumes the continuance of the community so organized. This view makes it possible to reconcile religious freedom with ordered government. It does not mean that the mere fact that the Commonwealth Parliament passes a law in the belief that it will promote the peace, order and good government of Australia precludes any consideration by a court of the question whether or not such a law infringes religious freedom. The final determination of that question by Parliament would remove all reality from the constitutional guarantee. That guarantee is intended to limit the sphere of action of the legislature. The interpretation and application of the guarantee cannot, under our Constitution, be left to Parliament. If the guarantee is to have any real significance it must be left to the courts of justice to determine its meaning and to give effect to it by declaring the invalidity of laws which infringe it and by declining to enforce them. The courts will therefore have the responsibility of determining whether a particular law can fairly be regarded as a law to protect the existence of the community, or whether, on the other hand, it is a law 'for prohibiting the free exercise of any religion.' The word 'for' shows that the purpose of the legislation in question may properly be taken into account in determining whether or not it is a law of the prohibited character.

11. The Commonwealth Parliament has power to make laws 'for the peace, order, and good government of the Commonwealth with respect to the naval and military defence of the Commonwealth and of the several States, and the control of the forces to execute and maintain the laws of the Commonwealth' (Constitution, s 51 (vi)). 'The executive power of the Commonwealth is vested in the Queen and is exercisable by the Governor-General as the Queen's representative, and extends to the execution and maintenance of this Constitution, and of the laws of the Commonwealth' (s 61).

In pursuance of the powers so conferred, the Commonwealth can defend the people, not only against external aggression, but also against internal attack, and in doing so can prevent aid being given to external enemies by internal agencies. No organized State can continue to exist without a law directed against treason. There are, however, subversive activities which fall short of treason (according to the legal definition of that term) but which may be equally fatal to the safety of the people. These activities, whether by way of espionage, or of what is now called fifth column work, may assume various forms. Examples are to be found in obstruction to recruiting, certainly in war-time, and, in my opinion, also in time of peace. Such obstruction may be both punished and prevented. So also [133] propaganda tending to induce members of the armed forces to refuse duty may not only be subjected to control, but may be suppressed. In *Hamilton v University of California* 293 US 245 (1934) at 262, 263 [79 Law Ed 343, at 353], it was said: 'Government, federal and state, each in its own sphere owes duty to the people within its jurisdiction to preserve itself in adequate strength to maintain peace and order and to assure the just enforcement of law. And every citizen owes the reciprocal duty, according to his capacity, to support and defend government against all enemies (*Selective Draft Law Cases (Arver v United States)* 245 US 366 (1918) at 378 [62 Law Ed 349 at 353], *Minor v Happersett* 89 US 162 (1875) at 166 [22 Law Ed 627]). *United States v Schwimmer* [279 US 644 (1929) [73 Law Ed 889]] involved a petition for naturalization by one opposed to bearing arms in defence of country. Holding the applicant not entitled to citizenship we said: 'That it is the duty of citizens by force of arms to defend our government against all enemies whenever necessity arises is a fundamental principle of the Constitution ... Whatever tends to lessen the willingness of citizens to discharge their duty to bear arms in the country's defense detracts from the strength and safety of the Government'. [279 US at 650 (1929) [73 Law Ed at 891, 892].] So also in this Court it was held in *Krygger v Williams* (1912) 15 CLR 366 that a person who is forbidden by the doctrines of his religion to bear arms is not thereby exempted or excused from undergoing the military training and rendering the personal service required by the Defence Act 1903–1910; and that the provisions of the Act imposing obligations on all male inhabitants of the Commonwealth in respect to military training do not prohibit the free exercise of any religion, and, therefore, are not an infringement of s 116 of the Constitution.

~~~

[11.2.49] Latham CJ proceeded to hold that the regulations did not offend s 116. However, the Chief Justice found that parts of the regulations were not supported by the defence power, s 51(vi), and were on that ground invalid. The other members of the court (Rich, Starke, McTiernan and Williams JJ) also dismissed the argument based on s 116, but held aspects of the regulations invalid on other grounds. Rich J said that the guarantee of freedom of religion was 'not absolute [but] subject to powers and restrictions of government essential to the preservation of the community': 67 CLR at 150. Williams J said that s 116 was part of 'a practical instrument of government', under which the Commonwealth Parliament was 'empowered to legislate in order to regulate its internal and external affairs': 67 CLR at 159. His Honour said at 160:

> The right to the free exercise of religion conferred by the Constitution postulates a continuous right to such freedom in a Commonwealth which will survive the ordeal of war. When, therefore, the safety of the nation is in jeopardy, so that the right to such free exercise can only survive if the enemy is defeated, laws which become necessary to preserve its existence would not be laws for prohibiting the free exercise of religion.

The countervailing need for 'social order' during wartime has authorised quite severe restrictions on freedom of association and movement of pacifist religious groups: see, for example, *Smith v Handcock* (1944) 46 WALR 21.

Notes

[11.2.50]   In *Krygger v Williams* (1912) 15 CLR 366, the High Court (constituted by only two justices: Griffith CJ and Barton J) rejected an argument that the compulsory military service provisions of the Defence Act 1903 (Cth) prohibited a person, with religious objections to military service, from freely exercising his religion. The Act required all male inhabitants of Australia to attend regular military training. Krygger claimed that he could not follow his religious beliefs, which were opposed to military service and fighting, if he was required to participate in military training. Griffith CJ said at 369 that s 116 prevented the Commonwealth making any law prohibiting:

> ... the doing of acts which are done in the practice of religion. To require a man to do a thing which has nothing at all to do with religion is not prohibiting him from a free exercise of religion. It may be that a law requiring a man to do an act which his religion forbids would be objectionable on moral grounds, but it does not come within the prohibition of s 116 ...

[11.2.51]   The relatively narrow view of the 'free exercise of religion' adopted in *Kryger v Williams* (1912) 15 CLR 366 **[11.2.50]** appears inconsistent with the approach suggested by Higgins J (admittedly in a minority) in *Judd v McKeon* (1926) 38 CLR 380. The question before the High Court was whether a voter could avoid the requirement to vote in an election for the Senate, imposed by s 128A(12) of the Commonwealth Electoral Act 1918 (Cth), by arguing none of the candidates appealed to the voter.

The court (Knox CJ, Isaacs, Higgins, Gavan Duffy and Starke JJ) held that s 128A(12) was a valid law, because it prescribed 'the method of choosing senators' within s 9 of the Commonwealth Constitution. The majority of the court (Higgins J dissenting) then held that the voter's objection that none of the candidates offered him a real choice because they all supported capitalism was not 'a valid and sufficient reason' for failing to vote. In his dissenting judgment, Higgins J said at 387:

> [I]f abstention from voting were part of an elector's religious duty, as it appeared to the mind of the elector, this would be a valid and sufficient reason for his failure to vote (s 116 of the Constitution).

[11.2.52]   Does the fact that no law has ever been struck down under s 116 suggest that the courts' approach to the ambit of the freedom is too narrow? Consider the fact that the free exercise of religion referred to in s 116 does not prevent the Family Court from considering religious belief as a factor in the context of a custody determination. In a series of cases the Family Court has awarded custody of a child to a non-religious parent in preference to an avidly religious parent. In the case *In the Marriage of Paisio* (1978) 26 ALR 132 at 135, the Full Court of the Family Court said at 134–5:

> An Australian court cannot commence with any premise that as a matter of public policy one religion is to be preferred to another or that a 'religious' upbringing is to be preferred to a 'non-religious' one. It is in this sense that s 116 of the Constitution has relevance … . But without even calling to aid s 116 it is clear that on general principles the courts have recognized that it is no part of the judicial function to rule that one form of religion is to be preferred to another …
>
> Nevertheless there have been cases in which courts have held that the doctrines of a particular religion, or at least those doctrines as interpreted by some of its adherents, have been so detrimental to children as to necessitate that the children should not be in the custody of the parent holding such doctrines. In these cases, while the court is necessarily showing disapproval of the practice of a particular religion, it is not doing so on any basis that religious teaching in general is harmful or suggesting that only one form of religion is permissible. The court is doing no more than saying that certain practices, albeit given a veneer of religious justification, are in fact so positively harmful to the welfare of the children that they must be removed from the influence of those who advocate such practices.

The Full Family Court concluded that the trial judge had not erred in exercising his discretion to award custody to the father on the basis that the child had a right to 'freedom of choice' — and this freedom would be more likely to be exercised in the father's home where the religion was not practised.

[11.2.53] The courts' approach to the characterisation of laws said to infringe s 116 has a narrow focus, said to be due to the fact that the text of s 116 indicates that a law must be 'for' the prohibition of the free exercise of religion to be found invalid — 'a law must have the purpose of achieving an object s 116 forbids': *Attorney-General (Vic); Ex rel Black v Commonwealth* (1981) 146 CLR 559 **[11.2.47C]** at 579, 615–16, 653; *Kruger v The Commonwealth* (1997) 190 CLR 1 **[11.2.54C]** at 40 (Brennan CJ), 86 (Toohey J); compare 190 CLR at 131 (Gaudron J).

So, for example, the freedom to exercise religion in s 116 does not prevent the Commonwealth from enacting a law which has the unintended, incidental effect of limiting the capacity to observe a religion. In *Minister for Immigration and Ethnic Affairs v Lebanese Moslem Association* (1987) 71 ALR 578, the respondents challenged the appellant's decision to deport the Imam of the Lakemba mosque, who had entered Australia on a temporary entry permit, which had since expired. It was argued that the decision was inconsistent with s 116. The Full Court of the Federal Court of Australia held that the decision was not made with an intention to prohibit the free exercise of religion, and any disruption of worship which was occasioned by the decision to deport the Imam would not involve restriction of the 'free exercise' of religion: 71 ALR at 191.

Consider the limitations of the narrow approach to characterisation in the following case.

[11.2.54C]   **Kruger v Commonwealth**

(1997) 190 CLR 1

In 1997, the Human Rights and Equal Opportunities Commission (HREOC) reported on government policy operating between 1925 and 1949 in South Australia and the

Northern Territory which authorised removal of Aboriginal children from their natural parents. HREOC found that many Aboriginal children were removed from their parents and placed in institutions, or with European Australian families. Between 1925 and 1949, the plaintiffs, who were Aboriginal Australians, were either removed from their parents or had their children removed. The removal and detention took place under the Aboriginals Ordinance 1918 (NT). The Ordinance was made by the Governor-General pursuant to power conferred by s 7(3) of the Northern Territory Acceptance Act 1920 (Cth) and by s 13 of the Northern Territory (Administration) Act 1920 (Cth). The Acts were made by the Commonwealth exercising its legislative power for the territories under s 122 of the Constitution.

Section 6 of the Ordinance provided that the Chief Protector of Aboriginals was entitled to 'undertake the care, custody, or control, of any aboriginal or half-caste, if, in his opinion it is necessary or desirable in the interests of the aboriginal or half-caste for him to do so'. Section 7 appointed the Chief Protector as the legal guardian of every Aboriginal or half-caste until he or she turned 18, regardless of whether the child had a parent or other relative living. A 1939 amendment made the Director the successor in function to the Chief Protector and appointed the Director as legal guardian of all Aboriginals. Section 16 empowered the Chief Protector to keep any Aboriginal or half-caste within any reserve or Aboriginal institution. Refusal to be removed or kept was an offence under ss16(3) subject to exceptions, including, if the person was employed, or had a permit to be absent, or was a woman married to a man of substantially European origin. Section 67 provided for the making of regulations consistent with the Ordinance.

The plaintiffs sought a declaration that the Ordinance was invalid, arguing that it was beyond the power of the Northern Territory Government, and that it breached a range of constitutional rights and immunities. Amongst the plaintiffs' arguments was a claim that the Ordinance breached s 116 of the Constitution because it prohibited the free exercise of religion.

Pursuant to s 18 of the Judiciary Act 1903 (Cth), the Chief Justice reserved a series of questions of law for the Full Court, prior to the hearing of the facts: *Kruger v Commonwealth* (1995) 69 ALJR 885. First, the court was asked to determine whether the legislative power conferred by s 122 of the Constitution or the power to enact the ordinance was restricted by any of the freedoms. Second, it was asked to decide whether a breach of any of these freedoms by an officer of the Commonwealth gave rise to a right of action (distinct from a right of action in tort or contract) against the Commonwealth for damages. The whole court rejected the existence of any right of action in damages against the Commonwealth for breach of constitutional rights: see **[11.3.5]**.

In separate judgments, a majority (Brennan CJ, Toohey, Gaudron, and Gummow JJ) confirmed that, to fall foul of s 116, a law must, on its face, demonstrate that its object or purpose is to prohibit the free exercise of religion: 190 CLR at 40 (Brennan CJ); 190 CLR at 86 (Toohey J); 190 CLR at 132 (Gaudron J); at 190 CLR at 161 (Gummow J). A majority (Brennan CJ, Dawson, McHugh and Gummow JJ) said that the Ordinance was not a law for prohibiting the free exercise of religion, because its object or purpose was not the prohibition of religious freedom: 190 CLR at 40 (Brennan CJ); 190 CLR at 60 (Dawson J); 190 CLR at 142 (McHugh J); 190 CLR at 161 (Gummow J).

Toohey J: [His Honour said that there was no evidence admissible to the court in the stage of the proceedings then before the court to show that the purpose of the ordinance was to interfere with the free exercise of religion: 190 CLR at 86. His Honour continued:]

[86] It may well be that an effect of the Ordinance was to impair, even prohibit the spiritual beliefs and practices of the Aboriginal people in the Northern Territory, though this is something that could only be demonstrated by evidence. But I am unable to discern in the language of the Ordinance such a purpose.

Gaudron J: [In asking whether the Ordinance authorised acts which prevented the free exercise of religion, Gaudron J said that this was a factual question which could not be answered at this stage of the proceedings, but she indicated that the Ordinance might be such a law.]

[132] [I]f Aboriginal people had practices and beliefs which are properly characterised as a religion for the purposes of s 116, and if, as would seem likely, those practices were carried out in association with other members of the Aboriginal community to which they belonged or at sacred sites or other places on their traditional lands, removal from their communities and their traditional lands would, necessarily, have prevented the free exercise of their religion. Whether or not that was the case remains to be decided.

Gaudron J said that, although purpose was the sole criterion of invalidity, the purpose of prohibiting the free exercise of religion did not have to be the sole purpose of the law, in order for it to infringe s 116.

In *Adelaide Company of Jehovah's Witnesses Inc*, Latham CJ observed in relation to s 116 that '[t]he word "for" shows that the purpose of the legislation in question may properly be taken into account in determining whether or not it is a law of the prohibited character.' [(1943) 67 CLR 116 at 132] In my view, that is not entirely accurate. The use of the word 'for' indicates that purpose is the criterion and the sole criterion selected by s 116 for invalidity. Thus, purpose must be taken into account. Further, it is the only matter to be taken into account in determining whether a law infringes s 116 ...

[133] In *Attorney-General (Vict); Ex rel Black*, Barwick CJ expressed the view, in relation to that part of s 116 which protects against laws 'for establishing any religion', that for '[a] law to satisfy [that] description [it] must have that objective as its express and ... single purpose.' [(1981) 146 CLR 559 at 579] If that is correct, it is because of what is involved in the notion of 'establishing [a] religion'. Certainly, that notion involves something conceptually different from 'imposing ... religious observance', 'prohibiting the free exercise of any religion' or requiring religious tests 'as a qualification for ... office or public trust under the Commonwealth', they being the other matters against which s 116 protects. Moreover, s 116 is not, in terms, directed to laws the express and single purpose of which offends one or other of its proscriptions. Rather, its terms are sufficiently wide to encompass any law which has a proscribed purpose. And the principles of construction to which reference has been made require that, save, perhaps, in its application to laws 'for establishing [a] religion', s 116 be so interpreted lest it be robbed of its efficacy.

It is convenient now to turn to the Commonwealth's plea that the purpose of the Ordinance was 'the protection and preservation of persons of the Aboriginal race' ... Clearly, a law may have more than one purpose. Similarly, a particular purpose may be subsumed in a larger or more general purpose. That latter proposition is well illustrated by the present case. It is clear from the terms of the Ordinance that one of its purposes, evident from the terms of s 16, was to remove Aboriginal and half-caste people to and keep them in Aboriginal reserves and institutions. That purpose is not necessarily inconsistent with the more general purpose which the Commonwealth asserts. And neither purpose is necessarily inconsistent with the purpose of removing Aboriginal children from their families and communities, thereby preventing them from participating in community practices. Indeed, in the absence of some overriding social or humanitarian need — and none is asserted — it might well be concluded that one purpose of the power conferred by s 16 of the Ordinance was to remove Aboriginal and half-caste children from their communities and, thus, prevent their participation in community practices. And if those practices included religious practices, that purpose necessarily extended to prohibiting the free exercise of religion.

As with the implied freedom of political communication and the implied freedoms of movement and association, a law will not be a [134] law for 'prohibiting the free exercise of any religion', notwithstanding that, in terms, it does just that or that it operates directly with that consequence, if it is necessary to attain some overriding public purpose or to satisfy some pressing social need. Nor will it have that purpose if it is a law for some specific purpose unconnected with the free exercise of religion and only incidentally affects that freedom. It is not pleaded in the present case either that the Ordinance was necessary for the protection or preservation of Aboriginal people or that its purpose was a purpose unconnected with the free exercise of religion. The plea is, thus, no answer to the plaintiffs' claim that the Ordinance was invalid by reason that it infringed s 116.

Were the Commonwealth to further amend its Defence to assert that the purpose of protecting and preserving Aboriginal people was unconnected with the purpose of prohibiting the free exercise of religion, a question might arise, if the plea were to be made good, whether the interference with religious freedom, if any, effected by the Ordinance was appropriate and adapted or, which is the same thing, proportionate to the protection and preservation of those people. And as the purpose of a law is to be determined by reference to 'the facts with which it deals', [*Arthur Yates & Co Pty Ltd v The Vegetable Seeds Committee* (1945) 72 CLR 37 at 68] that question would necessarily have to be answered by reference to the conditions of the time in which it operated. However, the answer to the question depends on an analysis of the law's operation, not on subjective views and perceptions.

Gaudron J also said that the expression 'prohibiting the free exercise of any religion' was not concerned only with laws which placed an outright ban on religious practices; it extended more broadly to 'laws which prevent the free exercise of religion': 190 CLR at 131. Gaudron J concluded that, although the legislative power conferred by s 122 was restricted by s 116, it was not possible to decide at this stage of the proceedings whether the Ordinance was invalid on this account.

Gummow J: [161] The impugned provisions of the 1918 Ordinance, and the general duties of the Chief Protector set out in s 5(1), imposed no duty upon any officer charged with the administration of the 1918 Ordinance to bring up infants in any particular religion or to educate them in schools affiliated with any particular religion. No conduct of a religious nature was proscribed or sought to be regulated in any way. The withdrawal of infants, in exercise of powers conferred by the 1918 Ordinance, from the communities in which they would otherwise have been reared, no doubt may have had the effect, as a practical matter, of denying their instruction in the religious beliefs of their community. Nevertheless, there is nothing apparent in the 1918 Ordinance which suggests that it aptly is to be characterised as a law made in order to prohibit the free exercise of any such religion, as the objective to be achieved by the implementation of the law.

~~~

Notes

[11.2.55] The need to balance religious freedom against the wider public interests served by legislation had previously been raised by Mason ACJ and Brennan J in *Church of the New Faith v Commissioner of Pay-roll Tax (Vic)* (the *Scientology* case) (1983) 154 CLR 120 **[11.2.46]**. The concept of religion could not mark out an area of legal immunity for all conduct (at 135–6):

> The freedom to act in accordance with one's religious beliefs is not as inviolate as the freedom to believe ... Conduct in which a person engages in giving effect to his faith in the supernatural is religious, but it is excluded from the area of legal immunity marked out by the concept of religion if it offends against the ordinary laws, ie if it offends against laws which do not discriminate against religion generally or against particular religions or against conduct of a kind which is characteristic only of a religion.

[11.2.56] In *Kruger v Commonwealth* (1997) 190 CLR 1 **[11.2.54C]**, Gaudron J adverted to the question whether Aboriginal beliefs constituted a religion for the purpose of s 116, and said that although there were some statements to that effect in the case law, the question remained a factual one, which could not be decided at the stage of the proceedings then before the court: 190 CLR at 130, 131. In the *Scientology* case (1983) 154 CLR 120 **[11.2.46]**, Murphy J stated: '[T]he Aboriginal religion of Australia' (sic) should be included in the religions protected by s 116 of the Constitution: 154 CLR at 151.

The Aboriginals Ordinance under challenge in *Kruger* was not *expressed* to prohibit or even to infringe the free exercise of Aboriginal religious beliefs. But had the substantial impact of the regulation, the removal of children from their mothers, interfered with the free exercise of religious beliefs?

Interstate discrimination

[11.2.57E]   **Commonwealth Constitution**

117 A subject of the Queen, resident in any State, shall not be subject in any other State to any disability or discrimination which would not be equally applicable to him if he were subject of the Queen resident in any other State.

~~~

Notes

[11.2.58] The first draft of the Commonwealth Constitution, adopted at the first Constitutional Convention of 1891, would have reflected art IV s 2 of the United States Constitution by prohibiting any state from 'abridging any privilege or immunity of the citizens of other states of the Commonwealth', and the 14th Amendment to the United States Constitution by declaring that no state should 'deny to any person, within its jurisdiction, the equal protection of the laws': see La Nauze (1972) p 68; Charlesworth (1986) p 60. However, the delegates to the 1898 Constitutional Convention saw such a clause as threatening the colonies' overtly racist laws, directed at Australian Aborigines, Pacific Islanders and Chinese. They were determined, as Charlesworth noted, 'to preserve a State's right to distinguish on racial grounds between classes of persons coming within its jurisdiction': Charlesworth (1986) p 113. The present form of s 117 was adopted so as to avoid affecting racially discriminatory laws.

[11.2.59] Until 1989, the treatment of s 117 at the hands of the High Court was as cynical as the section's origins. In *Davies and Jones v Western Australia* (1904) 2 CLR 29 the court decided that s 86 of the Administration Act 1903 (WA) did not offend s 117. Section 86 imposed a tax on property passing to a person on the death of another person, and provided that, where the property passed 'to persons bona fide residents of and domiciled in Western Australia' and standing in a specified relationship to the deceased, the rate of tax should be one-half of the tax otherwise payable. Davies, a resident of Queensland who was assessed as liable to pay the full rate of tax on inheriting property in Western Australia, challenged the validity of s 86. The court (Griffith CJ, Barton and O'Connor JJ) held that s 86 did not discriminate on the basis of residence, but on the basis of domicile. Barton J said at 47:

> [T]hough Mr Davies is discriminated against, it is not as a 'resident' of a State other than Western Australia. Mere residence in Western Australia does not give any of its inhabitants a better right to resist the higher rate of duty than Mr Davies has, residing as he does in Queensland ... It is discrimination on the sole ground of residence outside the legislating State that the Constitution aims at in the 117th section.

O'Connor J said at 49 that a Western Australian law, exempting all ratepayers resident in a municipal area in the state from the tax, would not offend s 117:

[A] resident of Queensland could not complain that he was not allowed the benefit of the exemption in respect of a beneficial interest passing to him, because in that case he would be in exactly the same position as any resident of Western Australia who was not a ratepayer residing within a municipal area. In other words the exemption in that case would arise, not from mere residence in Western Australia, but from the superadded condition of residence as a ratepayer within a municipal area.

[11.2.60] In *Henry v Boehm* (1973) 128 CLR 482, a majority of the High Court (Barwick CJ, McTiernan, Menzies and Gibbs JJ; Stephen J dissenting) dismissed a challenge to rules of the Supreme Court of South Australia brought by a legal practitioner admitted and resident in Victoria. Rule 27, for example, required that a legal practitioner admitted in another state should reside in South Australia for at least three months before becoming eligible for admission to practise in South Australia, unless the practitioner ordinarily resided in and was domiciled in South Australia.

Barwick CJ said at 489 that the rules did not make the fact of being an out-of-state resident the basis of their operation:

> [A] person resident, but not domiciled, in South Australia, temporarily absent from that State, perhaps to obtain or complete his out of State qualification, if qualified out of the State would be in precisely the same position as the plaintiff ... The rules themselves make no distinction between those who may happen already to be resident in South Australia and those who do not, where each has qualified elsewhere than in South Australia.

Gibbs J said at 497–8 that the rule applied to persons who were resident in South Australia as well as to those who were resident in any other state:

> It is obvious that 'an applicant previously admitted elsewhere' will not necessarily be a person who resides outside South Australia. He may, for example, be a South Australian resident who has obtained his legal qualifications elsewhere. Whether he is a resident of South Australia or not he is required by r 27(1) to reside for at least three calendar months in the State continuously and immediately preceding the filing of his application for admission ... This requirement applies equally to applicants who are ordinarily resident in the State and to those who are not.

Stephen J, in dissent, argued that the discrimination which s 117 proscribed was not discrimination between residents of one state and residents of another state, but between the situation of a person, not resident in the state in question, and the hypothetical situation of the same person if she or he were resident in the state: 128 CLR at 501–2. He said that the term 'resident' was not confined by concepts of permanency or of the location of the permanent home and included living in a place for a substantial and unbroken period, and concluded at 507:

> [T]hese two rules do subject the plaintiff, resident in Victoria, to a disability or discrimination which would not be equally applicable to him if he were resident, in the sense indicated above, in South Australia. They require him to leave his established home in Victoria and to live continuously in South Australia for considerable periods of time. Were he resident, in the sense indicated above, in South Australia the requirement of the rules would bear quite differently and less onerously upon him; their precise effect in such a hypothetical situation cannot be predicated but at least it is clear that were he resident in South Australia the disability involved in lengthy residence away from Victoria would either be wholly absent or be substantially mitigated.

[11.2.61C] **Street v Queensland Bar Association**

(1989) 168 CLR 461

Prior to 2 July 1987, r 38(d) of the Rules Relating to the Admission of Barristers of the Supreme Court of Queensland provided that every person, previously admitted as a barrister in another state and applying to be admitted as a barrister in Queensland should lodge an affidavit to the effect of Form 10, namely that he or she had ceased to practise as a barrister in the other state (para (6)), and had arrived in Queensland: para (7).

Street, a barrister admitted to practise in New South Wales, applied to the Supreme Court of Queensland for admission to practise as a barrister in that state. The Supreme Court refused his application in May 1987, on the ground that he had failed to comply with the requirements that he cease to practise in New South Wales and take up residence in Queensland. Street applied to the High Court of Australia for special leave to appeal.

Before the application was heard, the Supreme Court's Rules were amended, with effect from 2 July 1987, to require a person admitted to practise in another state who applied for admission as a barrister in Queensland to lodge an affidavit to the effect that he or she intended to practise principally in Queensland, and limited the admission of such a person to conditional admission for a period of one year, subject to the person having practised principally in Queensland during that year: r 15B.

Street commenced proceedings in the High Court against the Queensland Bar Association for a declaration that the amended rules were invalid, because they were contrary to ss 117 and 92 of the Constitution. Mason CJ then stated a case for the consideration of the Full Court, raising the question of the validity of the former and the current rules.

Mason CJ: [Mason CJ referred to the earlier decisions in *Davies and Jones v Western Australia* (1904) 2 CLR 29 **[11.2.45]** and *Henry v Boehm* (1973) 128 CLR 482 **[11.2.46]**; noted that, in the latter case, Stephen J had adopted the wide reading assigned to 'resident' by Griffith CJ in the former case; and continued:]

[485] There are powerful reasons for adopting this interpretation of 'resident' in s 117. The very object of federation was to bring into existence one nation and one people. This section is one of the comparatively few provisions in the Constitution which was designed to enhance national unity and a real sense of national identity by eliminating disability or discrimination on account of residence in another State. In this respect the section should be seen as a counterpart to other provisions in the Constitution which prohibit discrimination between the States in matters of taxation, trade and finance (ss 51(ii), 92 and 99). In *James v The Commonwealth* (1936) 55 CLR 1 at 43–4; [1936] AC 578 at 614 Lord Wright regarded the section as analogous to s 92 and referred to it as providing a constitutional guarantee of equal rights of all residents in all States. And, although the language of s 117 differs from that of Art IV, s 2 of the United States Constitution, there can be no doubt that the American model had an influential impact on the framers of our Constitution, at least to the extent of illustrating the need for a provision which, by guaranteeing to out-of-State residents who were British subjects an individual right to non-discriminatory treatment, would bring into existence a national unity and a national sense of identity transcending colonial and State loyalties.

These considerations, as well as the use of the expression 'resident in' rather than 'resident of' (cf ss 75(iv), 100; *Henry v Boehm* (1973) 128 CLR at 504–6), point to a liberal, rather than a narrow, interpretation of 'resident' in s 117, an interpretation which will guarantee to the individual a right to non-discriminatory treatment in relation to all aspects of residence. Accordingly, I favour the 'distributive' interpretation adopted by Griffith CJ in *Davies and Jones* and Stephen J in *Henry v Boehm* in preference to that taken by the majority in the latter case. The assimilation of 'resident' in s 117 to 'permanent resident' is arbitrary in the sense that the word is capable of a variety of shades of meaning and there is nothing in the context to support the selection of a meaning which works the greatest restriction in the operation of the section.

Section 117 is contained in Ch V of the Constitution, which is entitled 'The States'. Chapter V contains a miscellany of provisions, all of which, except s 116, relate to the States. Some of these sections (ss 114, 115, 116) expressly prohibit the States or the Commonwealth from doing certain things. Others (ss 119, 120) impose duties upon the States. Section 117 is strikingly different. It [486] is not expressed in terms similar to those of the surrounding sections. Notably, it relates not to a State or the Commonwealth but to a 'subject of the Queen'. Its form and language indicate that s 117 is directed towards individuals and their protection from disability or discrimination of the kind contemplated by the section, and that it is not, except to that extent, a restriction on State or Commonwealth legislative power. So a person not subjected to any relevant disability or discrimination by a particular law could not have that law held invalid by establishing that it subjects a third person to such a disability or discrimination; that circumstance would not lead to a striking down of the offending law. Conversely, a person who would, but for s 117, be so affected by the law is immune from its operation in so far as it subjects him to impermissible disability or discrimination, though the law itself remains valid in its application to persons who would not be so affected. Perhaps an enactment might be rendered wholly invalid by s 117 if it depended for its operation upon the imposition of a prohibited form of disability or discrimination, but that is not a question which I need to examine. Its only significance in the present case is that it may serve to explain references to the validity of the State legislation in *Davies and Jones*. These remarks are explicable on the basis that, had the Court equated domicile with residence or otherwise regarded domicile as within the province of s 117, the result would possibly have been to deny the validity of the offending enactment because it enacted a prohibited form of discrimination.

The preponderant weight of opinion denies the individual focus which Stephen J gives to s 117. With the exception of his Honour's dissenting judgment in *Henry v Boehm*, all the judgments in *Davies and Jones* and *Henry v Boehm* insist on comparing the way in which the non-resident of the legislating State is affected by the law of that State with the way in which residents of that State are affected: *Davies and Jones* (1904) 2 CLR at 39, per Griffith CJ (1904) 2 CLR at 45, Barton J and O'Connor J (1904) 2 CLR at 49; *Henry v Boehm* (1973) 128 CLR at 489, per Barwick CJ, Menzies J (1973) 128 CLR at 492–3 and Gibbs J (1973) 128 CLR at 496. This approach denies the individual focus of the section by addressing itself to the general range of circumstances in which the State law applies.

However, as Stephen J points out, the terms of the section invite a comparison of the actual situation of the out-of-State resident with what it would be if he were a resident of the legislating State. The [487] section does not invite a comparison between his actual situation and that of other residents of the legislating State. Such a comparison poses the question whether or not the law *necessarily* applies differently to residents of the legislating State. The answer to that question will almost invariably be in the negative due to the range of persons in differing situations within the legislating State and the fact that some of those persons will probably be affected by the law in the same manner as the out-of-State resident. Thus, the mode of comparison adopted in the decided cases, though not suggested by the terms of the section, has confined the operation of the constitutional guarantee. When that mode of comparison is combined with the assimilation of 'resident' to 'permanent resident', the effect has been to deprive the section of any significant utility.

Another difficulty with the existing interpretation of s 117 is that it appears to proceed according to a narrow view of what amounts to a disability or discrimination. The statement of Griffith CJ in *Davies and Jones* (1904) 2 CLR at 39 that I have already quoted, which was indorsed by Stephen J in *Henry v Boehm*, like that of Barwick CJ in *Henry v Boehm* (1973) 128 CLR at 489, suggests that, in order to bring the section into operation, the State law must make the fact of being a resident in another State the criterion of the disability or discrimination. Again, this seems to be an unduly limiting notion. In terms, the section applies when a subject of the Queen, being an out-of-State resident, is subject to a disability or discrimination under State law. The section is not concerned with the form in which that law subjects the individual to the disability or discrimination. It is enough that the individual is subject to either of the two detriments, whatever the means by which this is brought about by State law. This approach to the interpretation of the section accords with the approach generally adopted in connexion with statutes proscribing particular kinds of discrimination. They are either expressed or construed as proscribing an act or a law the effect of which is relevantly discriminatory: see, eg, *Birmingham City Council v Equal Opportunities Commission* (1989) AC 1155 at 1194–5; *Mandla v Dowell Lee* [1983] 2 AC 548; *Ontario Human Rights Commission v Simpsons-Sears Ltd* [[1985] 2 SCR 536]. It would be surprising if it were otherwise, especially since such statutes are generally intended to provide relief from discrimination rather than to punish the discriminator: see *Simpsons-Sears* [1985] 2 SCR at 547. It would make little sense to deal with laws [488] which have a discriminatory purpose and leave untouched laws which have a discriminatory effect.

Once this is recognized, it becomes all the more difficult to accept that the fact that a requirement as to residence is universal in its application is necessarily an answer to the operation of s 117. Such a requirement may have a discriminatory effect in relation to an out-of-State resident for the simple reason that it may apply unequally by subjecting him to a greater burden or disadvantage than that imposed on a resident of the legislating State. So to forbid all persons from wearing a turban is on its face a prohibition applicable to all persons without distinction, but in effect is a discrimination based upon religious grounds because its only impact will fall upon adherents of a creed or religion which requires the wearing of turbans: *Mandla v Dowell Lee; Bhinder v Canadian National Railway Co* [1985] 2 SCR 561. An examination of the effect of the relevant law is both necessary to avoid depriving s 117 of practical effect and consistent with its emphasis upon the position of the individual.

One further aspect of the section needs explanation. A disability or discrimination may still apply in theory after residence is changed, yet be so reduced in its impact as a result of the change that it is rendered illusory. Stephen J acknowledged this possibility and indeed that recognition was central to his decision. He stated: [(1973) 128 CLR at 507]

> Were he resident ... in South Australia the requirement of the rules would bear quite differently and less onerously upon him; their precise effect in such a hypothetical situation cannot be predicated but at least it is clear that were he resident in South Australia the disability involved in lengthy residence away from Victoria would either be wholly absent or be substantially mitigated.

Thus His Honour saw the phrase 'equally applicable' in s 117 as embracing the notion discussed above. It seems to me that for s 117 to apply it must appear that, were the person a resident of the legislating State, that different circumstance would of itself either effectively remove the disability or discrimination or, for practical purposes in all the circumstances, mitigate its effect to the point where it would be rendered illusory.

A disability or discrimination is rendered illusory if the fact of residence would substantially deprive it of its onerous nature. A requirement of continuous residence for a certain period would in my view be an example of a law whose onerous effect on non-[489]residents would be rendered illusory under this test. A disability or discrimination based upon grounds apart from residence is effectively removed if those grounds relate to characteristics which are in the circumstances concomitants of the individual's notionally changed residence. To this extent I would accept the argument that s 117 is not susceptible of 'colourable evasion' by State legislatures.

In the foregoing discussion I have stated why it is that I cannot accept the correctness of the interpretation placed on s 117 in *Davies and Jones* and, more importantly, *Henry v Boehm*. Moreover, the adoption of the interpretation expounded in the preceding paragraph of these reasons would be inconsistent with the actual decision in *Henry v Boehm*. Needless to say I am reluctant to depart from an earlier decision of this court. However, two of the factors relied upon by the court in *John v Commissioner of Taxation* (1989) 166 CLR 417 at 438–40, for overruling the earlier decision in *Curran v Federal Commissioner of Taxation* (1974) 131 CLR 409 are present in this case. The earlier decisions do not rest upon a principle gradually worked out in a significant succession of cases. And the decisions have not been independently acted upon in a manner or to an extent that works against reconsideration of them.

Furthermore, there is in the present case an additional factor. The question at issue relates to an important provision in the Constitution dealing with individual rights central to federation. The earlier decisions placed an incorrect interpretation upon it. The court has a responsibility to set the matter right.

Accordingly, I would apply the principle, along the lines mentioned above, that s 117 renders a disability or discrimination invalid if the notional fact of residence within the legislating State would effectively remove the disability or discrimination or substantially deprive it of its onerous nature.

Applying this test to Mr Street's appeal, it is clear that a requirement that he cease to practise outside Queensland would be less onerous were he to live in Queensland, although it would still be a significant imposition. The notional change of residence does not justify the court in assuming that, were he to live in Queensland, Mr Street would practise only or even principally in Queensland; not only is that to take the consequences of the notional change a step too far, but it is effectively to assume that, but for his residence, Mr Street would have been admitted to practice in Queensland, which is the ultimate question.

[490] But it is not necessary to take that step. If Mr Street were a resident of Queensland, a requirement that he cease practice outside Queensland would still permit him to practise in the State in which he resided. This stands in marked contrast to the actual position, which requires Mr Street to practise only in a State in which he does not reside. The disability is one imposed upon residents and non-residents alike, but in the case of a resident its effect is mitigated to a very substantial extent. Only a non-resident is prohibited from practising where he resides. The inconvenience suffered by a resident as a result of compliance with the requirement pales in significance beside the onerous and in many cases impossible burden imposed upon a non-resident. Thus par (6) of form 10 is a provision within the terms of the applicable test.

Paragraph (7) presents a certain difficulty of construction. On its face, arrival in Queensland is perhaps not indicative of the taking up of residence in Queensland. But, taken in conjunction with the requirement in par (6), it seems sufficiently clear that par (7) implicitly requires that the applicant has abandoned interstate residence and moved to Queensland. Indeed, the fact that the affidavit prescribed by the form is only to be sworn by persons previously admitted outside Queensland, coupled with the terms of par (6), compels that conclusion.

That paragraph thus requires Mr Street to reside in Queensland. That is something which, as a previously admitted barrister, he would still be required to do were he a resident of Queensland. But the notional fact of residence would effectively remove any disability or discrimination caused. Paragraph (7) therefore falls within the terms of the test I have explained.

It remains to consider whether the disability or discrimination imposed on Mr Street is of a kind contemplated as falling within the proscription in s 117. In *Davies and Jones* (1904) 2 CLR at 53, O'Connor J stated that s 117 'does not prohibit a State from conferring special privileges upon those of its own people who, in addition to residence within the State, fulfil some other substantial condition or requirement'. It is implicit in that statement that a privilege granted upon the basis of residence alone may offend s 117. Even if one were minded to draw a distinction between the imposition of a disability and the denial of a privilege, the word 'discrimination' is wide enough to cover the denial of a privilege in appropriate cases.

But this does not advance the matter very far. Clearly there must be some limit upon the ambit of s 117, especially when it is considered that it is not primarily a restriction upon legislative [491] power. The section is intended to prohibit within certain limits the imposition of a disability or discrimination based upon residence, but does not specify what limits, if any, there may be to its operation.

Mason CJ noted that, in the United States, the equivalent provision (art IV, s 2, the privileges and immunities clause) recognised that some discrimination against non-residents could be justified, and continued:

[491] In my view it is necessary to adopt a similar approach when considering whether or not a particular disability or discrimination is prohibited by s 117. To allow the section an unlimited scope would give it a reach extending beyond the object which it was designed to serve by trenching upon the autonomy of the States to a far-reaching degree. Accordingly, there may be cases where the need to preserve that autonomy leads to a recognition [492] that a particular disability or discrimination is not prohibited. The object of s 117 is very broad-ranging in its nature and it is difficult to conceive of a disability or discrimination which does not offend that object unless to prohibit the imposition of the disability or discrimination would threaten the autonomy of the relevant State.

The basis for insisting on some limitation to the operation of the privileges and immunities clause in the United States was expressed by the Supreme Court of the United States in *Baldwin* [436 US (1978) at 383] in the following terms:

> Some distinctions between residents and nonresidents merely reflect the fact that this is a Nation composed of individual States, and are permitted; other distinctions are prohibited because they hinder the formation, the purpose, or the development of a single Union of those States.

A similar basis underlies the correct approach to the interpretation of s 117. The preservation of the autonomy of the States demands that the exclusion of out-of-State residents from the enjoyment of rights naturally and exclusively associated with residence in a State must be recognised as standing outside the operation of s 117. Take, for example, the exclusion of out-of-state residents from the right to enjoy welfare benefits provided by a State under a scheme to assist the indigent, the aged or the ill. Generally speaking, I doubt that such an exclusion would amount to a disability or discrimination within the section. The exclusion would not seem to detract from the concept of Australian nationhood or national unity which it is the object of the section to ensure, because it would offend accepted notions of State autonomy and financial independence and a due sense of a State's responsibility to the people of the State to say that the Constitution required the State to extend the range of persons entitled under the scheme to out-of-State residents. The same comment might be made about a requirement that a person is not eligible to be the licensee of an hotel unless he resides on the premises.

On the other hand, the same comments could not be made about the exclusion of out-of-State residents from participation in professional activities open to residents of the legislating State or the imposition of discriminating burdens on such out-of-State residents, unless the exclusion could be justified as a proper and necessary discharge of the State's responsibility to the people of that State, which includes its responsibility to protect the interests of the public. Such an action against out-of-State residents would be inconsistent with the constitutional object of Australian nationhood [493] and national unity, unless the State were able to demonstrate that the interests of the State in maintaining its autonomy, over and above such interest it might have in giving an advantage to its residents over non-residents, required such action to be taken. Obviously, there will be circumstances in which need for regulation of activity, including professional activity, in order to protect the public in a State, requires that conditions be prescribed which may have a greater impact on out-of-State residents than residents of the legislating State. The qualifications and experience prescribed for entry into professional practice in another State may be insufficiently rigorous compared to those appropriate to the legislating State. There may even be a case for justifying the imposition of conditions on out-of-State professionals, though clearly conditions requiring any form of residence within the State would call for stronger justification.

But there is in my view no compelling justification for the disability or discrimination imposed upon Mr Street which would suffice to deny s 117 its effect. The United States Supreme Court has consistently rejected arguments invoked in support of bar residence requirements similar to those in the present case; see, eg, *Piper*; [470 US (1985) at 285–7] *Barnard v Thorstenn*. [(1989) 57 LW 4316] It was found in *Piper* that there was no evidence that non-resident attorneys would lack familiarity with local rules and procedures, would be less likely to behave in an ethical manner, would be unlikely to perform their share of voluntary work or would be unable to perform their professional duties as satisfactorily as resident attorneys. Greater difficulty in physically attending proceedings was acknowledged, but was not viewed as a sufficient ground for denying admission. These conclusions apply with equal force to the position in Queensland. I am reinforced in that view by the fact that States other than Queensland do not see the need for special treatment of residents of their home States in order to ensure that proper professional and ethical standards are maintained. No peculiar characteristic of the Queensland legal profession or of Queensland law or practice has been suggested that would call for unique treatment.

My conclusions are:

(1)   Mr Street is a subject of the Queen resident in New South Wales.

(2)   The Rules subject him to a disability or discrimination, namely giving up his practice in his State of residence, which would not be [494] equally applicable to him if he were a resident of Queensland. The Rules also subject him to a further disability or discrimination of that kind, namely giving up his residence in New South Wales.

(3)   The need to ensure proper professional and ethical standards for the legal profession in Queensland does not justify the imposition of this disability or discrimination upon practitioners resident outside Queensland.

Mason CJ proceeded to hold that the amendments made to the rules on 2 July 1987 also offended s 117, because they required an interstate barrister to abandon his or her non-Queensland practice for one year. Brennan, Deane, Dawson, Toohey, Gaudron and McHugh JJ delivered separate judgments to the same effect, holding that the relevant rules were inconsistent with s 117. Dawson J also dealt with, and rejected, a separate attack on the rules, based on the freedom of interstate intercourse guaranteed by s 92 of the Constitution.

~~~

Notes

[11.2.62]   Apart from the fact that the decision in *Street v Queensland Bar Association* (1989) 168 CLR 461 **[11.2.47C]** breathed new life into a provision which had become moribund, it appeared to signal a new enthusiasm on the part of the High Court for the active interpretation and application of constitutional limitations and guarantees; an activism which has been conspicuously absent from the High Court's former work with, for example, ss 80 and 116.

That activism can be seen in the justices' insistence that the presence of disability or discrimination was to be determined by considering the practical operation and individual effect of the challenged law: 168 CLR at 487 per Mason J; at 506–7 per Brennan J; at 527 per Deane J; at 545 per Dawson J; at 569 per Gaudron J; at 583 per McHugh J.

The operation of the section, Deane J said, depended on 'substance rather than mere form': 168 CLR at 527. The section, Brennan J said at 507–8:

... is concerned not only with legal rights and liabilities but also with the actual effect on the individual of legal rights and liabilities produced by a law or other governmental action.

The relevance of the concept of 'indirect discrimination' (the disparate impact of equal treatment on those who have unequal characteristics) was openly acknowledged by the justices. Gaudron J said that s 117's protection extended 'to indirect discrimination or different treatment which is revealed by the disparate impact of the matter in complaint': 168 CLR at 569. McHugh J said at 581 that s 117 included:

... disability or discrimination arising from the factual operation of the law ... Discrimination can arise just as readily from a law which treats as equals those who are different as it can from a law which treats differently those whose circumstances are not materially different.

[11.2.63] The justices in *Street v Queensland Bar Association* (1989) 168 CLR 461 **[11.2.61C]** were also unanimous in discarding the narrow view of 'resident' (as meaning a permanent resident) adopted in *Henry v Boehm* (1973) 128 CLR 482 **[11.2.60]**. Several justices endorsed Griffith CJ's proposition in *Davies and Jones v Western Australia* (1904) 2 CLR 29 at 39 **[11.2.59]**, that the word 'resident' in s 117 'must be construed distributively, as applying to any kind of residence which a State may attempt to make a basis of discrimination': see 168 CLR at 516–17 per Brennan J; at 543–4 per Dawson J; at 586–7 per McHugh J. Further, some justices indicated that the actual decision in that case, that s 117 did not proscribe discrimination based on residence and domicile, would not survive closer scrutiny: 168 CLR at 489 per Mason J; at 523–4 per Deane J; at 561 per Toohey J; at 568 per Gaudron J.

[11.2.64] The justices did, however, indicate limits to the immunity from discrimination granted by s 117. Some of those limits are implicit in the language of the section: only 'a subject of the Queen' can invoke s 117, and that term may not extend beyond Australian citizens (168 CLR at 525 (Deane J); 168 CLR at 541 (Dawson J); 168 CLR at 554 (Toohey J)); and may not include artificial persons (168 CLR at 505 (Brennan J)).

[11.2.65] More substantial limits to the immunity derived from s 117 may 'be found in the implications to be drawn from the Constitution' (168 CLR at 560 (Toohey J)); or in 'the preservation of the autonomy of the States' (168 CLR at 492 (Mason J)). See also 168 CLR at 512 (Brennan J); 168 CLR at 583–4 (McHugh J).

[11.2.66] Mason CJ said that s 117 would not prevent a state from limiting state-provided welfare benefits to residents of that state, because any such use of s 117 'would offend accepted notions of State autonomy and financial independence and a due sense of a State's responsibility to the people of the State': 168 CLR at 492.

McHugh J said that 's 117 was not intended as a human rights charter for interstate residents', and said at 583–4 that:

> ... the 'structural logic' of the Constitution indicates that there are some subject matters in respect of which an interstate resident is not entitled to equality of treatment with State residents in identical circumstances. The object of s 117 was to make federation fully effective by ensuring that subjects of the Queen who were residents of Australia and in comparable circumstances received equality of treatment within the boundaries of any State. But the existence of a federal system of government, composed of a union of independent States each continuing to govern its own people, necessarily requires the conclusion that some subject matters are the concern only of the people of each State. And since the residents of a State and its people are basically interchangeable concepts, it follows that laws dealing with these particular subject matters may exclude interstate residents from participation ...

> Matters which are the concern only of a State and its people and are not within the scope of s 117 would seem to include the franchise, the qualifications and conditions for holding public office in the State, and conduct which threatens the safety of the State or its people. No doubt there are other subject-matters which are also outside the reach of s 117. But since all exceptions to the terms of that section arise by necessary implication from the assumptions and structure of the Constitution, they must be confined to the extent of the need for them. The question is not whether a particular

subject-matter serves the object of s 117; it is whether, by necessary implication, the matter is so exclusively the concern of the State and its people that an interstate resident is not entitled to equality of treatment in respect of it.

Brennan J also offered the examples of electoral laws providing for a franchise based on residence in a state and residence rules for appointment to public office, as exceptions to the constraints of s 117, describing such exceptions as necessary 'to preserve the institutions of government and their ability to function': 168 CLR at 513.

3   Implied rights and freedoms

The nature of implied rights

[11.3.1]   The High Court's decisions in *Nationwide News Ltd v Wills* (1992) 177 CLR 1 **[11.3.9]** and *Australian Capital Television Pty Ltd v Commonwealth* (1992) 177 CLR 106 **[11.3.7C]** marked a dramatic turning point in Australian constitutional development. In those two cases, a majority of the High Court held that the provisions of the Constitution that created a system of representative and responsible government gave rise to an implied freedom to discuss political and governmental affairs; and that legislation which contravened those principles would be invalid. The decisions were seen at the time as opening the way for a judicially-constructed Bill of Rights for Australia.

The first two High Court decisions which recognised an implied freedom to discuss political and governmental affairs were *Nationwide News Pty Ltd v Wills* (1992) 177 CLR 1 **[11.3.9]** and *Australian Capital Television Pty Ltd v Commonwealth* (1992) 177 CLR 106 **[11.3.7C]**.

In *Nationwide News*, the court struck down legislation making it an offence to use words calculated to bring a member of the Australian Industrial Relations Commission into disrepute. In *Australian Capital Television*, the court held invalid Commonwealth legislation prohibiting certain types of political advertising during election periods. The essential basis of each decision was that the system of representative and responsible government established by the Constitution required a freedom to discuss political and governmental matters.

Following those decisions, the court handed down a series of judgments exploring the extent of, and limitations on, the implied rights and freedoms that could be derived from the Constitution. In the course of those decisions, members of the court debated the nature of the rights that were supported by constitutional implications. Were those rights personal, in the sense that they attached to and could be asserted by individuals as the basis for new legal claims; or were they limitations upon government power, so that they did no more than restrict the way in which governments could act? This question was explored in *Theophanous v Herald & Weekly Times Ltd* (1994) 182 CLR 104 **[11.3.2C]** and *Lange v Australian Broadcasting Corporation* (1997) 189 CLR 520 **[11.3.3C]**. Cases such *Kruger v Commonwealth* (1997) 190 CLR 1 **[11.3.5]** demonstrated the limits to this approach — the implications that may be drawn from the Constitution are limited by the meagre nature of the text and the historical context of its development.

[11.3.2C]   **Theophanous v Herald & Weekly Times Ltd**

(1994) 182 CLR 104

The plaintiff, a member of the House of Representatives and the chair of a joint parliamentary committee on immigration, sued the publisher of a metropolitan daily newspaper, the *Herald-Sun*, and Bruce Ruxton, a prominent and controversial commentator on public affairs, for defamation arising out of the newspaper's publication of a letter written by Ruxton. The letter, which was published under the heading 'Give Theophanous the shove', stated that Theophanous 'stands for most things Australians are against,' was biased towards Greek immigrants and conducted 'idiotic antics'.

 In its defence, the publisher (the first defendant) pleaded that the words alleged to be defamatory were published pursuant to the freedom guaranteed by the Constitution to publish material in the course of discussion of government and political matters and concerning the performance and suitability for office of members of parliament. The plaintiff moved to strike out the defence and the High Court ordered under s 40(1) of the Judiciary Act 1903 (Cth) that the matter be removed to the High Court. A series of questions was then reserved for the opinion of the Full Court pursuant to s 18 of the Judiciary Act, including the question whether the first defendant's defence was bad in law. With some important qualifications, the court affirmed the existence in the Constitution of an implied freedom of communication in relation to political matters. In the course of deciding the case, some members of the court commented upon the nature of the implied right to freedom of political communication.

Mason CJ, Toohey and Gaudron JJ: [125] The decisions in *Nationwide News* and *Australian Capital Television* establish that the implied freedom is a restriction on legislative and executive power. Whether the implied freedom could also conceivably constitute a source of positive rights was not a question which arose for decision in those cases and it is unnecessary to decide it in this case.

Brennan J: [147] Although the scope of the implication was stated in *Nationwide News* in terms of its effect on an absolute freedom, its nature was defined as a limitation on power. And so it was that, in *ACTV*, where a law of the Commonwealth was impugned on the ground that it infringed the freedom to discuss government implied by the Constitution, I said: [(1992) 177 CLR at 150]

> It is convenient in the context of Pt IIID (of the Broadcasting Act 1942) to speak of the implied limitation as a freedom of communication, for the terms are reciprocal: the extent of any relevant limitation of legislative power is the scope of the relevant freedom. But, unlike freedoms conferred by a Bill of Rights in the American model, the freedom cannot be understood as a personal right the scope of which must be ascertained in order to discover what is left for legislative [148] regulation; rather, it is a freedom of the kind for which s 92 of the Constitution provides: an immunity consequent on a limitation of legislative power.

The constitutional freedom is not the subject of an express constitutional guarantee. It is the consequence or result of an implication which, in *Nationwide News* and *ACTV*, limited the legislative power that would otherwise have been available to support the impugned laws. The nature of the implication affects the way in which its scope is ascertained.

It is one thing to be entitled, in common with others, to act freely in an area to which a law cannot or does not apply; it is another to possess a personal right or a personal immunity from the application of a general law. [*James v Cowan* (1930) 43 CLR 386 at 418; and cf *Clark King & Co Pty Ltd v Australian Wheat Board* (1978) 140 CLR 120] In either case, the individual is free to act without legal control, but the scope of a postulated freedom is differently ascertained according to its nature. If the freedom implied in the Constitution were a personal right or immunity, it would extend to what is needed to facilitate or permit its full enjoyment, subject to any qualification expressed or implied in the Constitution. The existence of such a personal right or immunity would not affect the validity of any law: the law would simply be ineffective to the extent to which it infringed the freedom. But when the freedom is the consequence of the limits on a power, the scope of the freedom is a function of the invalidity of any law which exceeds the power. A law which exceeds the power is invalid, unless it be saved from invalidity by reading it down. If the freedom to discuss government were understood to be a personal freedom, it would be open to the Court to define it in qualified or limited terms ... But if the freedom to discuss government be the consequence of a limitation on power, the issue in this case is whether the laws of defamation, in their application to the facts pleaded in the statement of claim, are valid. The issue is not the scope of the freedom but the validity of the law.

When governmental powers are conferred by the Constitution, their scope is impliedly limited to the extent necessary to maintain the structure of government prescribed by the Constitution. The limitation creates a freedom. But if a personal freedom were [**149**] conferred by the Constitution, an unexpressed restriction on its scope would probably have to be implied in order to accommodate some exercise of governmental powers. The difference is significant, since the effective scope of the freedom on the one hand and the effective scope of the governmental powers which might be exercised to restrict the freedom on the other would be ascertained first by attributing a full range of operation to what is primarily conferred — the freedom or the powers — and then diminishing that range by what is necessary to give effect to any implied restriction or limitation. If the Constitution conferred a personal freedom, its scope would be likely to be far broader than the scope of a freedom consequent on an implied limitation on power.

The freedom which flows from the implied limitation on power considered in *Nationwide News* and *ACTV* is not a personal freedom. It is not a sanctuary with defined borders from which the operation of the general law is excluded. Like s 92, the implication limits legislative and executive power. In *Nationwide News* and *ACTV*, the question in each case was whether the legislative power which prima facie supported the impugned law was limited by an implication that left the law without support. [*Nationwide News* (1992) 177 CLR at 39–40] Did the law which restricted the freedom to discuss government, governmental institutions or political matters thereby lose the constitutional support that would have been otherwise available [*ACTV* (1992) 177 CLR at 133]?

~~~

[11.3.3C] Lange v Australian Broadcasting Corporation
(1997) 189 CLR 520

David Lange, a former New Zealand Prime Minister, sued the Australian Broadcasting Corporation (ABC) for defamation in the Supreme Court of New South Wales.

In its defence, the ABC sought to rely upon *Theophanous v Herald & Weekly Times Ltd* (1994) 182 CLR 104 **[11.3.10]** and *Stephens v West Australian Newspapers Ltd* (1994) 182 CLR 211 **[11.3.12]**, by arguing that the allegedly defamatory matter was published pursuant to a freedom guaranteed by the Commonwealth Constitution to publish material in the course of discussion of government and political matters. The matter was removed to the High Court under s 40 of the Judiciary Act 1903 (Cth). Brennan CJ stated a case for the opinion of the Full Court.

The court took the opportunity to clarify a number of contentious matters left open by the earlier decisions, some of which are dealt with at **[11.3.13C]**. In a unanimous joint judgment, the court decided that the Constitution conferred no private right to publish but instead created an immunity against legislative incursion into free communication in respect of political matters. Statute and common law must conform with the constitutional limit; and so the court expanded the common law defence of qualified privilege to an extent similar to that in *Theophanous*. However, there was a significant difference. What had been achieved by an application of the Constitution in *Theophanous* was now achieved by a combination of the Constitution and the common law.

Brennan CJ, Dawson, Toohey, Gaudron, McHugh, Gummow and Kirby JJ: [560] [After referring to ss 7 and 24 of the Constitution, the justices continued:] Those sections do not confer personal rights on individuals. Rather they preclude the curtailment of the protected freedom by the exercise of legislative or executive power. As Deane J said in *Theophanous*, [(1994) 182 CLR 104 at 168] they are 'a limitation or confinement of laws and powers [which] gives rise to a pro tanto immunity on the part of the citizen from being adversely affected by those laws or by the exercise of those powers rather than to a "right" in the strict sense'. In *Cunliffe v The Commonwealth*, [(1994) 182 CLR 272 at 326] Brennan J pointed out that the freedom confers no rights on individuals and, to the extent that the freedom rests upon implication, that implication defines the nature and extent of the freedom. His Honour said: [(1994) 182 CLR 272 at 327]

> The implication is negative in nature: it invalidates laws and consequently creates an area of immunity from legal control, particularly from legislative control.

... [562] With the establishment of the Commonwealth of Australia, as with that of the United States of America, it became necessary to accommodate basic common law concepts and techniques to a federal system of government embodied in a written and rigid constitution. [563] The outcome in Australia differs from that in the United States. There is but one common law in Australia which is declared by this Court as the final court of appeal. In contrast to the position in the United States, the common law as it exists throughout the Australian States and Territories is not fragmented into different systems of jurisprudence, possessing different content and subject to different authoritative interpretations. The distinction is important for the present case and may be illustrated as follows.

The First Amendment to the United States Constitution prohibits Congress from making any law abridging 'the freedom of speech, or of the press'. This privilege or immunity of citizens of the United States may not be abridged by the making or 'the enforcement' by any State of 'any law'. That is the effect of the interpretation placed on the Fourteenth Amendment. [*New York Times Co v Sullivan* 376 US 254 at 264–265 (1964)] A civil lawsuit between private parties brought in a State court may involve the State court in the enforcement of a State rule of law which infringes the Fourteenth Amendment. If so, it is no answer that the law in question is the common law of the State, such as its defamation law. [*New York Times Co v Sullivan* 376 US 254 at 265 (1964)] The interaction in such cases between the United States Constitution and the State common laws has been said to produce 'a constitutional privilege' against the enforcement of State common law. [*Gertz v Robert Welch Inc* 418 US 323 at 327, 330, 332, 342–343 (1974)]

This constitutional classification has also been used in the United States to support the existence of a federal action for damages arising from certain executive action in violation of 'free-standing' constitutional rights, privileges or immunities. [*Bivens v Six Unknown Federal Narcotics Agents* 403 US 388 (1971)] On the other hand, in Australia, recovery of loss arising from conduct in excess of constitutional authority has been dealt with under the rubric of the common law, particularly the law of tort. [*Northern Territory v Mengel* (1995) 185 CLR 307 at 350–353, 372–373]

It makes little sense in Australia to adopt the United States doctrine so as to identify litigation between private parties over their common law rights and liabilities as involving 'State law rights'. Here, '[w]e act every day on the unexpressed assumption that the one common law surrounds us and applies where it has not been superseded by statute'. [Dixon, 'The Common Law as an Ultimate Constitutional Foundation', (1957) 31 *Australian Law Journal* 240 at 241] Moreover, that one common law operates in the federal [564] system established by the Constitution. The Constitution displaced, or rendered inapplicable, the English common law doctrine of the general competence and unqualified supremacy of the legislature. It placed upon the federal judicature the responsibility of deciding the limits of the respective powers of State and Commonwealth governments. [*R v Kirby; Ex parte Boilermakers' Society of Australia* (1956) 94 CLR 254 at 267–268] The Constitution, the federal, State and territorial laws, and the common law in Australia together constitute the law of this country and form 'one system of jurisprudence'. [*McArthur v Williams* (1936) 55 CLR

324 at 347] Covering cl 5 of the Constitution renders the Constitution 'binding on the courts, judges, and people of every State and of every part of the Commonwealth, notwithstanding anything in the laws of any State'. Within that single system of jurisprudence, the basic law of the Constitution provides the authority for the enactment of valid statute law and may have effect on the content of the common law.

Conversely, the Constitution itself is informed by the common law. This was explained extra-judicially by Sir Owen Dixon: ['Sources of Legal Authority', reprinted in *Jesting Pilate*, (1965) 198 at 199]:

> We do not of course treat the common law as a transcendental body of legal doctrine, but we do treat it as antecedent in operation to the constitutional instruments which first divided Australia into separate colonies and then united her in a federal Commonwealth. We therefore regard Australian law as a unit. Its content comprises besides legislation the general common law which it is the duty of the courts to ascertain as best they may ... The anterior operation of the common law in Australia is not just a dogma of our legal system, an abstraction of our constitutional reasoning. It is a fact of legal history.

... Under a legal system based on the common law, 'everybody is free to do anything, subject only to the provisions of the law', so that one proceeds 'upon an assumption of freedom of speech' and turns to the law 'to discover the established exceptions to it'. [*A-G v Guardian Newspapers (No 2)* [1990] 1 AC 109 at 283] The common law torts of libel and slander are such exceptions. However, these torts do not inhibit the publication of defamatory matter unless the [565] publication is unlawful — that is to say, not justified, protected or excused by any of the various defences to the publication of defamatory matter, including qualified privilege. The result is to confer upon defendants, who choose to plead and establish an appropriate defence, an immunity to action brought against them. In that way, they are protected by the law in respect of certain publications and freedom of communication is maintained.

The issue raised by the Constitution in relation to an action for defamation is whether the immunity conferred by the common law, as it has traditionally been perceived, or, where there is statute law on the subject the immunity conferred by statute, conforms with the freedom required by the Constitution. In 1901, when the Constitution of the Commonwealth took effect and when the Judicial Committee was the ultimate Court in the judicial hierarchy, the English common law defined the scope of the torts of libel and slander. At that time, the balance that was struck by the common law between freedom of communication about government and political matters and the protection of personal reputation was thought to be consistent with the freedom that was essential and incidental to the holding of the elections and referenda for which the Constitution provided. Since 1901, the common law — now the common law of Australia — has had to be developed in response to changing conditions. The expansion of the franchise, the increase in literacy, the growth of modern political structures operating at both federal and State levels and the modern development in mass communications, especially the electronic media, now demand the striking of a different balance from that which was struck in 1901. To this question we shall presently return.

The factors which affect the development of the common law equally affect the scope of the freedom which is constitutionally required. '[T]he common convenience and welfare of society' is the criterion of the protection given to communications by the common law of qualified privilege. [*Toogood v Spyring* (1834) 1 CM & R 181 at 193 [149 ER 1044 at 1050].] Similarly, the content of the freedom to discuss government and political matters must be ascertained according to what is for the common convenience and welfare of society. That requires an examination of changing circumstances [*Jumbunna Coal Mine, NL v Victorian Coal Miners' Association* (1908) 6 CLR 309 at 367–368] and the need to strike a balance in those circumstances between absolute freedom of discussion of government and politics and the [566] reasonable protection of the persons who may be involved, directly or incidentally, in the activities of government or politics.

Of necessity, the common law must conform with the Constitution. The development of the common law in Australia cannot run counter to constitutional imperatives. [*Theophanous*

(1994) 182 CLR 104 at 140] The common law and the requirements of the Constitution cannot be at odds. The common law of libel and slander could not be developed inconsistently with the Constitution, for the common law's protection of personal reputation must admit as an exception that qualified freedom to discuss government and politics which is required by the Constitution.

In any particular case, the question whether a publication of defamatory matter is protected by the Constitution or is within a common law exception to actionable defamation yields the same answer. But the answer to the common law question has a different significance from the answer to the constitutional law question. The answer to the common law question prima facie defines the existence and scope of the personal right of the person defamed against the person who published the defamatory matter; the answer to the constitutional law question defines the area of immunity which cannot be infringed by a law of the Commonwealth, a law of a State or a law of those Territories whose residents are entitled to exercise the federal franchise. That is because the requirement of freedom of communication operates as a restriction on legislative power. Statutory regimes cannot trespass upon the constitutionally required freedom.

However, a statute which diminishes the rights or remedies of persons defamed and correspondingly enlarges the freedom to discuss government and political matters is not contrary to the constitutional implication. The common law rights of persons defamed may be diminished by statute but they cannot be enlarged so as to restrict the freedom required by the Constitution. Statutes which purport to define the law of defamation are construed, if possible, conformably with the Constitution. But, if their provisions are intractably inconsistent with the Constitution, they must yield to the constitutional norm.

~~~

Notes

[11.3.4] In *Levy v Victoria* (1997) 189 CLR 579 **[11.3.14]**, three members of the High Court reconfirmed that the implied freedom of communication was not a personal right but an immunity from legislative interference: 189 CLR at 605 per Dawson J; 189 CLR at 620 per McHugh J; 189 CLR at 628 per Kirby J.

[11.3.5] In *Kruger v Commonwealth* (1997) 190 CLR 1 **[11.3.19]**, **[11.3.32C]**, the court considered whether breach of a constitutional right by an officer of the Commonwealth gave rise to a right of action for damages against the Commonwealth, as distinct from an action in tort or breach of contract. Four members of the court (Brennan CJ, Toohey, Gaudron and Gummow JJ) concluded that it did not. Brennan CJ explained the position as follows (at 46):

> The Constitution creates no private rights enforceable directly by an action for damages. It 'is concerned with the powers and functions of government and the restraints upon their exercise', as Dixon J said of s 92 in *James v The Commonwealth*. [(1939) 62 CLR 339 at 362] The Constitution reveals no intention to create a private right of action for damages for an attempt to exceed the powers it confers or to ignore the restraints it imposes. The causes of action enforceable by awards of damages are created by the common law (including for this purpose the doctrines of equity) supplemented by statutes which reveal an intention to create such a cause of action for breach of its provisions. If a government does or omits to do anything which, under the general law, would expose it or its servants or agents to a liability in damages, an attempt to deny or to escape that liability fails when justification for the act done or omission made depends on a statute or an action that is invalid for want of constitutional support. In such a case, liability is not incurred for breach of a constitutional right but by operation of the general law. But if a government does or omits to do something the doing or omission of which attracts no liability under the

general law, no liability in damages for doing or omitting to do that thing is imposed on the government by the Constitution.

It follows that no right of action distinct from a right of action in tort or for breach of contract arises by reason of any breach of the protections claimed by the plaintiffs ...

Toohey, Gaudron and Gummow JJ delivered separate opinions to similar effect. Dawson J, with whom McHugh J concurred, found it unnecessary to answer the question.

The origin of the implied freedom to discuss political and governmental affairs

[11.3.6] In *Davis v Commonwealth* (1988) 166 CLR 79 **[7.2.27C]**, the High Court said that the legislative power contained in s 51(xxxix) of the Constitution to commemorate the Australian bicentenary did not allow the Commonwealth Parliament to prohibit the use of everyday expressions such as '1988' used in conjunction with other expressions like 'Bicentenary', 'Melbourne' or 'First Settlement'.

Mason CJ, Deane and Gaudron JJ, with whom Wilson, Dawson and Toohey JJ agreed, said the legislation was 'grossly disproportionate to the need to protect the commemoration': 166 CLR at 100 per Mason, Deane and Gaudron JJ. The justices continued at 100:

Here the framework of regulation created by s 22(1)(a) with s 22(6)(d)(i) and (ii) reaches far beyond the legitimate objects sought to be achieved and impinges on freedom of expression by enabling the Authority to regulate the use of common expressions and by making unauthorised use a criminal offence. Although the statutory regime may be related to a constitutionally legitimate end, the provisions in question reach too far. This extraordinary intrusion into freedom of expression is not reasonably and appropriately adapted to achieve the ends that lie within the limits of constitutional power.

Brennan J said the incidental power in s 51(xxxix) would not extend to the particular legislation. He said at 116–17:

The limits on the legislative power to enact penal laws under s 51(xxxix) is of especial importance when the relevant activity undertaken in execution of an executive power is the commemoration of an historical event. Such a commemoration may take many forms, according to the significance placed upon it. The form of national commemorations of historical events usually reflects the significance which the majority of people place upon the event. But there may well be minority views which place a different significance on the same event, as the present case illustrates. It is of the essence of a free and mature nation that minorities are entitled to equality in the enjoyment of human rights. Minorities are thus entitled to freedom in the peaceful expression of dissident views. In this case, the plaintiffs wish to raise a voice of protest against the celebratory commemoration of the Bicentenary, and the defendants contend that ss 22 and 23 are effective to muffle the intended protest. As a matter of construction, ss 22 and 23 do muffle the intended protest. But it cannot be incidental to the organisation of the commemoration of the Bicentenary to prohibit, under criminal sanctions, the peaceful expression of opinions about the significance of the events of 1788. By prohibiting the use of the symbols and expressions apt to express such opinions, ss 22 and 23 forfeit any support which s 51(xxxix) might otherwise afford.

~~~

[11.3.7C]   **Australian Capital Television Pty Ltd**
                              v Commonwealth
                           (1992) 177 CLR 106

The Political Broadcasts and Political Disclosures Act 1991 (Cth) inserted Pt IIID into the Broadcasting Act 1942 (Cth). Division 2 of Pt IIID prohibited the radio or television broadcasting of certain material during Commonwealth, state, territory and local government election periods. An election period ran from the date when the election was announced, or from the issue of the writs, or from 33 days before polling day (whichever was the earlier) to the close of polling. The material which could not be broadcast during an election to the Commonwealth Parliament or a referendum for the alteration of the Constitution included any matter (other than certain exempt matter relating to the machinery for conducting the election or referendum) for or on behalf of the Commonwealth Government or a Commonwealth government authority, a political advertisement on behalf of a territory government or a state government or territory or state authority, and a political advertisement on behalf of any person: s 95B. A 'political advertisement' was defined to mean an advertisement that contained matter 'intended or likely to affect voting' or that contained express or implicit reference to, or comment on, the election or referendum concerned or any candidate or issue in the election.

Section 95A provided that nothing in Pt IIID prevented a broadcaster from broadcasting an item of news or current affairs, a comment on any such item or a talkback radio programme. Division 3 of Pt IIID obliged broadcasters to provide free time during an election period to a political party, in accordance with regulations to be made for that election. Section 95H required that the regulations should give effect to the principle that 90 per cent of the free time was to be allotted to the political parties already represented in the relevant parliament or legislature. Division 3 of Pt IIID enabled a broadcaster to broadcast the policy launch of a political party once only and free of charge.

Australian Capital Television Pty Ltd, a licensed television broadcaster, and other licence holders (in one action) and the state of New South Wales (in another action) sued the Commonwealth in the original jurisdiction of the High Court, claiming declarations that Pt IIID was invalid. The Commonwealth demurred to the statements of claim. The demurrers were heard together.

Mason CJ: [Mason CJ said that the effect of Part IIID was to exclude the use of radio and television during election periods as a medium of political campaigning and the dissemination of political information comment and argument. His Honour said that s 95A 'elevates news, current affairs and talkback radio programs to a position of very considerable importance during an election period': 177 CLR at 129. As a consequence, 'Part IIID severely impairs the freedoms previously enjoyed by citizens to discuss public and political affairs and to criticise federal institutions': 177 CLR at 129. He noted that the government had defended the introduction of Part IIID as a means of controlling the costs of election campaigns and that paid political advertising in the electronic media was not permitted in many other countries. The Chief Justice rejected the Commonwealth's claim that Part IIID introduced a 'level playing field' in relation to equality of access to television and radio: 177 ALR at 132. Instead it gave 'preferential treatment to political parties represented in the preceding Parliament'; it 'favour[ed] the party in government'; gave preference to incumbent senators and 'allow[ed] no scope for participation in the election campaign by persons who are not candidates': 177 CLR at 132. His Honour continued:]

[132] ... [F]reedom of speech or expression on electronic media in relation to public affairs and the political process is severely restricted by a regulatory regime which evidently favours the established political parties and their candidates without securing compensating advantages or benefits for others who wish to participate in the electoral process or in the political debate which is an integral part of that process.

Mason CJ noted that, amongst the arguments advanced by the plaintiffs, was an argument that ss 95B, 95C and 95D contravened an implied guarantee of freedom of access to, participation in and criticism of federal and state institutions amounting to a freedom of communication in relation to the political and electoral processes. His Honour continued:

[133] *Constitutional implications*

Sir Owen Dixon noted that, following the decision in *Amalgamated Society of Engineers v Adelaide Steamship Co Ltd* (the *Engineers'* case) (1920] 28 CLR 129, the notion seemed to gain currency that no implications could be made in interpreting the Constitution. [*West v Commissioner of Taxation (NSW)* (1937) 56 CLR 657, at 681] The *Engineers'* case certainly did not support such a [134] draconian and unthinking approach to constitutional interpretation. [Ibid, per Dixon J at 682.] Sir Owen expressed his own opposition to that approach when he said:

> Such a method of construction would defeat the intention of any instrument, but of all instruments a written constitution seems the last to which it could be applied [ibid, at 681].

Later, he was to say: [*Australian National Airways Pty Ltd v Commonwealth* (1945) 71 CLR 29, at 85; see also *Lamshed v Lake* (1958) 99 CLR 132, per Dixon CJ at 144] 'We should avoid pedantic and narrow constructions in dealing with an instrument of government and I do not see why we should be fearful about making implications.'

Subsequently, Windeyer J, in a passage in which he referred to that statement, remarked [*Victoria v Commonwealth* (the *Payroll Tax* case) (1971) 122 CLR 353, at 401–2] 'implications have a place in the interpretation of the Constitution' and 'our avowed task is simply the revealing or uncovering of implications that are already there'.

In conformity with this approach, the court has drawn implications from the federal structure prohibiting the Commonwealth from exercising its legislative and executive powers in such a way as to impose upon a State some special disability or burden unless the relevant power authorised that imposition or in such a way as to threaten the continued existence of a State as an independent entity or its capacity to function as such. [*Queensland Electricity Commission v Commonwealth* (1985) 159 CLR 192, at 205, 217, 226, 231, 247, 260–2; 61 ALR 1] But there is no reason to limit the process of constitutional implication to that particular source.

Of course, any implication must be securely based. Thus, it has been said that 'ordinary principles of construction are applied so as to discover *in the actual terms* of the instrument their expressed or necessarily implied meaning'. [The *Engineers'* case (1920) 28 CLR, per Knox CJ, Isaacs, Rich and Starke JJ at 155 (emphasis added).] This statement is too restrictive because, if taken literally, it would deny the very basis — the federal nature of the Constitution — from which the court has implied restrictions on Commonwealth and State legislative powers. [*West v Commissioner of Taxation (NSW)*; *Essendon Corporation v Criterion Theatres Ltd* (1947) 74 CLR 1; *Melbourne Corporation v Commonwealth* (1947) 74 CLR 31; *Queensland Electricity Commission v Commonwealth*; *State Chamber of Commerce and Industry v Commonwealth* (the *Second Fringe Benefits Tax* case) (1987) 163 CLR 329; 73 ALR 161.] That the statement is too restrictive is [135] evident from the remarks of Dixon J in *Melbourne Corporation v Commonwealth* [(1947) 74 CLR, at 83] where his Honour stated that 'the efficacy of the system logically demands' the restriction which has been implied and that 'an intention of this sort is ... to be plainly seen in the very frame of the Constitution'.

It may not be right to say that no implication will be made unless it is necessary. In cases where the implication is sought to be derived from the actual terms of the Constitution it may be sufficient that the relevant intention is manifested according to the accepted principles of interpretation. However, where the implication is structural rather than textual it is no doubt correct to say that the term sought to be implied must be logically or practically necessary for the preservation of the integrity of that structure.

It is essential to keep steadily in mind the critical difference between an implication and an unexpressed assumption upon which the framers proceeded in drafting the Constitution.

[*Australian National Airways Pty Ltd v Commonwealth* (1945) 71 CLR, per Dixon J at 81]
The former is a term or concept which inheres in the instrument and as such operates as part
of the instrument, whereas an assumption stands outside the instrument. Thus, the founders
assumed that the Senate would protect the States but in the result it did not do so. On the other
hand, the principle of responsible government — the system of government by which the
executive is responsible to the legislature — is not merely an assumption upon which the actual
provisions are based; it is an integral element in the Constitution. [The *Engineers'* case (1920)
28 CLR, per Knox CJ, Isaacs, Rich and Starke JJ at 147.] In the words of Isaacs J in
Commonwealth v Kreglinger & Fernau Ltd and Bardsley: [(1926) 37 CLR 393 at 413] 'It is
part of the fabric on which the written words of the Constitution are superimposed.'

The implication of fundamental rights

The adoption by the framers of the Constitution of the principle of responsible government
was perhaps the major reason for their disinclination to incorporate in the Constitution
comprehensive [**136**] guarantees of individual rights. They refused to adopt a counterpart to
the Fourteenth Amendment to the Constitution of the United States. Sir Owen Dixon said:

> ... [they] were not prepared to place fetters upon legislative action, except and in so far as it might
> be necessary for the purpose of distributing between the States and the central government the full
> content of legislative power. The history of their country had not taught them the need of
> provisions directed to control of the legislature itself.

The framers of the Constitution accepted, in accordance with prevailing English thinking,
that the citizen's rights were best left to the protection of the common law in association with
the doctrine of parliamentary supremacy.

So it was that Professor Harrison Moore, writing in 1901, was able to say of the
Constitution: 'The great underlying principle is, that the rights of individuals are sufficiently
secured by ensuring, as far as possible, to each a share, and an equal share, in political power.'

In the light of this well recognised background, it is difficult, if not impossible, to establish
a foundation for the implication of general guarantees of fundamental rights and freedoms.
To make such an implication would run counter to the prevailing sentiment of the framers that
there was no need to incorporate a comprehensive Bill of Rights in order to protect the rights
and freedoms of citizens. That sentiment was one of the unexpressed assumptions on which
the Constitution was drafted.

However, the existence of that sentiment when the Constitution was adopted and the
influence which it had on the shaping of the Constitution are no answer to the case which the
plaintiffs now present. Their case is that a guarantee of freedom of expression in relation to
public and political affairs must necessarily be implied from the provision which the
Constitution makes for a system of representative government. The plaintiffs say that, because
such a freedom is an essential concomitant of representative government, it is necessarily
implied in the prescription of that system.

[137] Representative government

The Constitution provided for representative government by creating the Parliament,
consisting of the Queen, a House of Representatives and a Senate, in which legislative power
is vested. The members of each House being elected by popular vote, and by vesting the
executive power in the Queen and making it exercisable by the Governor-General on the
advice of the Federal Executive Council, consisting of the Queen's Ministers of State drawn,
subject to a minor qualification, from the House of Representatives and the Senate. In the case
of the Senate, s 7 provides that it: 'shall be composed of senators for each State, directly chosen
by the people of the State, voting, until the Parliament otherwise provides, as one electorate.'

In the case of the House of Representatives, s 24 provides that it: 'shall be composed of
members directly chosen by the people of the Commonwealth.' Although s 24 contains no
reference to voting, s 25 makes it clear that 'chosen' means 'chosen by vote at an election'.

In *Attorney-General (Cth); Ex rel McKinlay v Commonwealth*, [(1975) 135 CLR, at 55–6;
7 ALR 593] Stephen J discerned in these two provisions the principles of representative

democracy (by which he meant that the legislators are directly chosen by the people) and direct popular election. The correctness of his Honour's view is incontestable, notwithstanding that the Constitution does not prescribe universal adult suffrage. Such a suffrage did not exist at that time. Although prescription of the qualifications of electors was left for the ultimate determination of the Parliament, the Constitution none the less brought into existence a system of representative government in which those who exercise legislative and executive power are directly chosen by the people. The Governor-General, though the repository of executive power, does not personally exercise that power, being bound to act with the advice of the Executive Council.

The very concept of representative government and representative democracy signifies government by the people through their representatives. Translated into constitutional terms, it denotes that the sovereign power which resides in the people is exercised on their behalf by their representatives. In the case of the Australian [138] Constitution, one obstacle to the acceptance of that view is that the Constitution owes its legal force to its character as a statute of the Imperial Parliament enacted in the exercise of its legal sovereignty; the Constitution was not a supreme law proceeding from the people's inherent authority to constitute a government, notwithstanding that it was adopted, subject to minor amendments, by the representatives of the Australian colonies at a Convention and approved by a majority of the electors in each of the colonies at the several referenda. Despite its initial character as a statute of the Imperial Parliament, the Constitution brought into existence a system of representative government for Australia in which the elected representatives exercise sovereign power on behalf of the Australian people. Hence, the prescribed procedure for amendment of the Constitution hinges upon a referendum at which the proposed amendment is approved by a majority of electors and a majority of electors in a majority of the States [s 128]. And, most recently, the Australia Act 1986 (UK) marked the end of the legal sovereignty of the Imperial Parliament and recognised that ultimate sovereignty resided in the Australian people. The point is that the representatives who are members of Parliament and Ministers of State are not only chosen by the people but exercise their legislative and executive powers as representatives of the people. And in the exercise of those powers the representatives of necessity are accountable to the people for what they do and have a responsibility to take account of the views of the people on whose behalf they act.

Freedom of communication as an indispensable element in representative government

Indispensable to that accountability and that responsibility is freedom of communication, at least in relation to public affairs and political discussion. Only by exercising that freedom can the citizen communicate his or her views on the wide range of matters that may call for, or are relevant to, political action or decision. Only by exercising that freedom can the citizen criticise government decisions and actions, seek to bring about change, call for action where none has been taken and in this way influence the elected representatives. By these means the elected representatives are equipped to discharge their role so that they may take account of [139] and respond to the will of the people. Communication in the exercise of the freedom is by no means a one-way traffic, for the elected representatives have a responsibility not only to ascertain the views of the electorate but also to explain and account for their decisions and actions in government and to inform the people so that they may make informed judgments on relevant matters. Absent such a freedom of communication, representative government would fail to achieve its purpose, namely, government by the people through their elected representatives; government would cease to be responsive to the needs and wishes of the people and, in that sense, would cease to be truly representative.

Freedom of communication in relation to public affairs and political discussion cannot be confined to communications between elected representatives and candidates for election on the one hand and the electorate on the other. The efficacy of representative government depends also upon free communication on such matters between all persons, groups and other bodies in the community. That is because individual judgment, whether that of the elector, the representative or the candidate, on so many issues turns upon free public discussion in the media of the views of all interested persons, groups and bodies and on public participation in, and access to, that discussion. [Lord Simon of Glaisdale made the point in *Attorney-General v Times Newspapers Ltd* [1974] AC 273, at 315, when he said: 'People cannot adequately influence the decisions which affect their lives unless they can be adequately informed on facts and arguments relevant to the decisions. Much of such fact-finding and argumentation necessarily has to be conducted vicariously, the public press being a principal instrument.'] In truth, in a representative democracy, public participation in political discussion is a central element of the political process.

Archibald Cox made a similar point when he said: 'Only by uninhibited publication can the flow of information be secured and the people informed concerning men, measures, and the conduct of government ... Only by freedom of speech, of the press, and of association can people build and assert political power, including the power to change the men who govern them'. [*The Court and the Constitution*, (1987), p 212.]

The last sentence in the passage just quoted is a striking comment on Professor Harrison Moore's statement that '[t]he great underlying principle' of the Constitution was that the rights of individuals were sufficiently secured by ensuring each an equal share [140] in political power. Absent freedom of communication, there would be scant prospect of the exercise of that power.

The fundamental importance, indeed the essentiality, of freedom of communication, including freedom to criticise government action, in the system of modern representative government has been recognised by courts in many jurisdictions. They include Australia, England, the United States, Canada and the European Court of Human Rights.

Implication of a guarantee of freedom of communication on matters relevant to public affairs and political discussion

Freedom of communication in the sense just discussed is so indispensable to the efficacy of the system of representative government for which the Constitution makes provision that it is necessarily implied in the making of that provision.

Mason CJ referred to a number of Canadian decisions, endorsing an implied freedom of expression, and continued:

[142] *The indivisibility of freedom of communication in relation to public affairs and political discussion*

The concept of freedom to communicate with respect to public affairs and political discussion does not lend itself to subdivision. Public affairs and political discussion are indivisible and cannot be subdivided into compartments that correspond with, or relate to, the various tiers of government in Australia. Unlike the legislative powers of the Commonwealth Parliament, there are no limits to the range of matters that may be relevant to debate in the Commonwealth Parliament or to its workings. The consequence is that the implied freedom of communication extends to all matters of public affairs and political discussion, notwithstanding that a particular matter at a given time might appear to have a primary or immediate connection with the affairs of a State, a local authority or a Territory and little or no connection with Commonwealth affairs. Furthermore, there is a continuing interrelationship between the various tiers of government. To take one example, the Parliament provides funding for the State governments, Territory governments and local governing bodies and enterprises. That continuing interrelationship makes it inevitable that matters of local concern have the potential to become matters of national concern. That potential is in turn enhanced by the predominant financial power which the Commonwealth Parliament and the Commonwealth government enjoy in the Australian federal system.

Infringement: the test to be applied

Mason CJ recognised that the freedom guaranteed by the Constitution was not absolute, and continued:

The guarantee does not postulate that the freedom must always and necessarily prevail over competing interests of the public. Thus, to take an example, Parliament may regulate the conduct of persons with regard to elections so as to prevent intimidation and undue influence, even though that regulation may fetter what otherwise would be free [143] communication. And, in the United States, despite the First Amendment, the media is subject to laws of general application.

Mason CJ distinguished between 'restrictions on communication which target ideas or information and those which restrict an activity or mode of communication by which ideas or information are transmitted'. In relation to restrictions on ideas, for legislation to be valid, the restriction must have a 'compelling justification' and it must be 'no more than is reasonably necessary to achieve the protection of the competing public interest'. Restrictions on modes of communication were 'more susceptible of justification'. Here it was necessary to balance the public interest in 'free communication against the competing public interest which the restriction is designed to serve'. The restriction need only be 'reasonably necessary to achieve the competing public interest'. It will only be invalid if it 'imposes a burden on free communication that is disproportionate to the attainment of the competing public interest': 177 CLR at 143. Mason CJ emphasised that although the 'court will give weight to the legislative judgment on these issues' ultimately 'it is for the court to determine whether the constitutional guarantee has been infringed in a given case': 177 CLR at 144.

[144] *Is Part IIID valid?*

Mason CJ said that, although the restrictions were 'expressed so as to appear to fall into the second, rather than the first, class of case' the law was 'not one of general application', but was 'specifically directed at broadcasting, in connection with the electoral process, of matters relating to public affairs and political discussion, including political advertisements' and so 'the court must scrutinise the validity of Pt IIID with scrupulous care': 177 CLR at 144.

In approaching the respective interests in this case, I am prepared to assume that the purpose of Pt IIID is to safeguard the integrity of the political process by reducing pressure on parties and candidates to raise substantial sums of money, thus lessening the risk of corruption and undue influence. I am prepared also to assume that other purposes of Pt IIID are to terminate (a) the advantage enjoyed by wealthy persons and groups in gaining access to use of the airwaves; and (b) the 'trivialising' of political debate resulting from very brief political advertisements. Moreover, I am prepared to accept that the need to raise substantial funds in order to conduct a campaign for election to political office does generate a risk of [145] corruption and undue influence, that in such a campaign the rich have an advantage over the poor and that brief political advertisements may 'trivialise' political debate.

Given the existence of these shortcomings or possible shortcomings in the political process, it may well be that some restrictions on the broadcasting of political advertisements and messages could be justified, notwithstanding that the impact of the restrictions would be to impair freedom of communication to some extent. In other words, a comparison or balancing of the public interest in freedom of communication and the public interest in the integrity of the political process might well justify some burdens on freedom of communication. But it is essential that the competition between the two interests be seen in perspective. The raison d'etre of freedom of communication in relation to public affairs and political discussion is to enhance the political process (which embraces the electoral process and the workings of Parliament), thus making representative government efficacious.

The enhancement of the political process and the integrity of that process are by no means opposing or conflicting interests and that is one reason the court should scrutinise very carefully any claim that freedom of communication must be restricted in order to protect the integrity of the political process. Experience has demonstrated on so many occasions in the past that, although freedom of communication may have some detrimental consequences for society, the manifest benefits it brings to an open society generally outweigh the detriments. All too often attempts to restrict the freedom in the name of some imagined necessity have tended to stifle public discussion and criticism of government. The court should be astute not to accept at face value claims by the legislature and the Executive that freedom of communication will, unless curtailed, bring about corruption and distortion of the political process.

As I pointed out earlier, Pt IIID severely restricts freedom of communication in relation to the political process, particularly the electoral process, in such a way as to discriminate against potential participants in that process. The sweeping prohibitions against broadcasting directly exclude potential participants in the electoral process from access to an extremely important mode of communication with the electorate. Actual and potential participants include not only the candidates and established political parties but also the electors, individuals, groups and bodies who wish to present their views to the community. In the case of referenda, or at least some of them, the States would have important interests at stake and would be participants in the process.

[146] It is said that the restrictions leave unimpaired the access of potential participants during an election period to other modes of communication with the electorate. The statement serves only to underscore the magnitude of the deprivation inflicted on those who are excluded from access to the electronic media. They must make do with other modes of communication which do not have the same striking impact in the short span of an election campaign when the electors are consciously making their judgments as to how they will vote.

It is also said that the protection given by s 95A to items of news, current affairs and comments on such items, and talkback radio programs will preserve communication on the electronic media about public and political affairs during election periods. But access on the part of those excluded is not preserved, except possibly at the invitation of the powerful interests which control and conduct the electronic media. Those who are excluded are exposed to the risk that the protection given by s 95A may result in the broadcasting of material damaging to the cause or causes they support without their being afforded an opportunity to reply.

The replacement regime, which rests substantially on the provisions relating to the grant of free time, is weighted in favour of the established political parties represented in the legislature immediately before the election and the candidates of those parties; it discriminates against new and independent candidates. By limiting their access to a maximum of 10 per cent of the free time available for allocation, Pt IIID denies them meaningful access on a non-discriminatory basis. As for persons, bodies and groups who are not candidates, they are excluded from radio and television broadcasting during election periods. The consequence is that the severe restriction of freedom of communication plainly fails to preserve or enhance fair access to the mode of communication which is the subject of the restriction. The replacement regime, though it reduces the expenses of political campaigning and the risks of trivialisation of political debate, does not introduce a 'level playing field'. It is discriminatory in the respects already mentioned. In this respect I do not accept that, because absolute equality in the sharing of free time is unattainable, the inequalities inherent in the regime introduced by Pt IIID are justified or legitimate.

On this score alone, Pt IIID is invalid, apart from the prohibitions on broadcasting matter for or on behalf of the government, or a government authority, of the Commonwealth during the various election periods. [ss 95B(1), 95C(3), 95D(1)] But it can scarcely be thought, s 95(2) notwithstanding, that those prohibitions were intended to operate alone in respect of each election period. Part [147] IIID is therefore invalid in its entirety. Moreover, I regard the presence of s 95J as an obstacle to the validity of the Part. In my view, it is impossible to justify the validity of a regime which restricts freedom of communication in relation to the electoral process when the operation of the regime depends upon the making of regulations at the discretion of the Executive government according to unspecified criteria. The existence of the discretion leaves the Executive government at any given time with the option of invoking the Pt IIID regime or discarding it; in other words, the government of the day can decide which course suits it best. It is difficult to conceive of a compelling, even of a reasonable, justification for a regime restricting freedom of communication which confers such an advantage on the Executive government.

There being no reasonable justification for the restrictions on freedom of communication imposed by Pt IIID, the Part is invalid. In the light of my conclusion as to the indivisibility of freedom of communication in relation to public affairs and political discussion, the prohibitions in connection with all forms of election and referenda must fail.

Brennan J: [Brennan J said that, for reasons given in *Nationwide News Pty Ltd v Wills* (1992) 177 CLR 1 **[11.3.9]**, the legislative powers of the Commonwealth Parliament were 'limited by implication [so] as to preclude the making of a law trenching upon that freedom of discussion of political and economic matters which is essential to sustain the system of representative government prescribed by the Constitution': 177 CLR at 149. He said that the restriction on political advertising as a means of reducing the expenditure on election campaigns had been adopted in many other liberal democracies; and noted that the attempt directly to limit expenditure by individuals and organisations on political advertising had been shown to be unworkable in Australia. His Honour continued:]

[156] If the limiting of expenditure incurred by or on behalf of candidates has proved to be unworkable in this country, the elimination of an opportunity for political parties, interest groups or individuals to engage in costly advertising on the electronic media is easily seen as an alternative means of minimising the risk of corruption or of reducing the untoward advantage of wealth on the formation of political opinion. Section 95B is appropriate and adapted to that end. The Parliament chosen by the people — not the courts, not the Executive Government — bears the chief responsibility for maintaining representative democracy in the Australian Commonwealth. Representative democracy, as a principle or institution of our Constitution, can be protected to some extent by decree of the courts and can be fostered by Executive action but, if performance of the duties of members of the Parliament were to be subverted by obligations to large benefactors or if the parties to which they belong were to trade their commitment to published policies in exchange for funds to conduct expensive campaigns, no curial decree could, and no executive action would, restore representative democracy to the Australian people.

The minimising of the risk of corruption of the Parliament and the reduction of an untoward advantage of wealth in the formation of political opinion are important objects to be advanced, if there be power to do so, by the laws of the Commonwealth. The powers available for the support of s 95B are the Parliament's powers over broadcasting and Commonwealth elections. The power conferred by s 51(v) of the Constitution extends to the control of radio and television services and of the conditions on which a licence to broadcast radio or television programs may be granted or exercised. A law prohibiting the broadcasting of some political advertisements is clearly a law falling within the power.

Brennan J said this was a law with respect to elections.

[157] Proportionality

To determine the validity of a law which purports to limit political advertising, it is necessary to consider the proportionality between the restriction which a law imposes on the freedom of communication and the legitimate interest which the law is intended to serve. If the prohibition on political advertising by means of the electronic [158] media during election periods imposed by s 95B is not disproportionate to the objects of minimising the risk of political corruption and reducing the untoward advantage of wealth in the formation of political opinion, s 95B is a valid law even though it restricts to some extent the freedom of political discussion ... [T]he implied freedom must be considered in the context of the contemporary and relevant political conditions in which the impugned law operates. If the content of the implied freedom of political discussion were ascertainable by reference solely to the constitutional text, and without reference to [159] the political conditions in which the impugned law operates, the scope of the freedom would have to be expressed as a mere matter of form, not as a matter of substance. If it were to be expressed as a mere matter of form, the court would be the only forum competent to express it definitively but the court could hardly evaluate with any pretence to accuracy the substantive effect of a freedom thus expressed on the political milieu in which the law is to operate. It follows that the court must allow the Parliament what the European Court of Human Rights calls a 'margin of appreciation'.

It is both simplistic and erroneous to regard any limitation on political advertising as offensive to the Constitution. If that were not so, there could be no blackout on advertising on polling day; indeed, even advertising in the polling booth would have to be allowed unless the demands of peace, order and decorum in the polling both qualify the limitation. Though freedom of political communication is essential to the maintenance of a representative democracy, it is not so transcendent a value as to override all interests which the law would otherwise protect. [Brennan J referred to defamation protection for public officials.]

Freedom of political discussion is essential to the democratic process, chiefly for two reasons: it is a stimulus to performance in public office and it is conducive to the flow of information needed or desired for the formation of political opinions. But the salutary effect of freedom of political discussion on performance in public office can be neutralised by covert influences, particularly by the obligations which flow from financial dependence. The financial dependence of a political party on those whose interests can be served by the favours of government could cynically turn public debate into a cloak for bartering away the public interest. If Pt IIID tangibly minimises the risk of political corruption, the restrictions it imposes on political advertising are clearly proportionate to that object of the law. Whether Pt IIID would tangibly minimise the risk [160] of corruption was a political assessment. It was for the Parliament to make that assessment; it is for the court to say whether the assessment could be reasonably made.

In reviewing the assessment made by the Parliament, it is necessary to form some estimate of the effect of the restrictions imposed by Pt IIID on the flow of information needed or desired by electors to form their political judgments. If those restrictions effectively deny electors the opportunity to form political judgments or substantially impair their ability to do so, the restrictions are invalid. There would be no proportionality between restrictions having so stifling an effect on political discussion on the one hand and the apprehended risk of corruption or the untoward advantages flowing from wealth on the other. But the restrictions do not block the flow of information. All news, current affairs and talk-back programs are unaffected by the restrictions. The print media are unaffected. The other methods of disseminating political views such as public meetings, door knocks and the distribution of handbills are unaffected.

The principal advertisements affected by Pt IIID are television advertisements. It is not necessary to determine finally the contribution made by television advertising to the mass of information needed or desired by electors to form their political judgments, but it is impossible to conclude that the Parliament could not reasonably make an adverse assessment of the information value of television advertising. Television advertising is brief; its brevity tends to trivialise the subject; it cannot deal in any depth with the complex issues of government. Its appeal is therefore directed more to the emotions than to the intellect.

Brennan J referred to the report of the Senate Select Committee on Political Broadcasts and Political Disclosures which said that the restriction on political advertising may enhance, rather than detract, from the democratic process.

[161] No doubt it is true to say that the formation of political judgment is not solely an intellectual exercise. Aspirations and ideals are the stuff of statesmanship. But the articulation of aspirations and ideals and the conveying of information can be distinguished from many forms of political advertising. It was open to the Parliament to make a low assessment of the contribution made by electronic advertising to the formation of political judgments. It was open to the Parliament to conclude, as the experience of the majority of liberal democracies has demonstrated, that representative government can survive and flourish without paid political advertising on the electronic media during election periods. The restrictions imposed by s 95B are comfortably proportionate to the important objects which it seeks to obtain. The obtaining of those objects would go far to ensuring an open and equal democracy. The openness of political discussion and the equality of the participants in the democratic process

makes governments responsive to the popular will. The restrictions on advertising do little to inhibit the democratic process. In my view, the implied limitation on the legislative powers [162] supporting s 95B is not trespassed upon by the restrictions which it imposes.

Although the restrictions imposed by s 95B preclude electronic advertising by individuals or interest groups who are unrepresented in the Parliament, individuals or interest groups are otherwise free to propose or oppose any lawful political policy. They have no personal right to advertise by the electronic media and, if the restriction on such advertising is justifiable in order to achieve the objects of Pt IIID, the incidental consequence that that avenue of advertising is closed to individuals or interest groups does not entail invalidation. Putting to one side for the moment the effect of s 95B on the States, I would hold the section to be valid.

Brennan J held that s 95C was valid in so far as it extended the effect of Pt IIID to the territories. However, that s 95D, which prohibited the broadcast of political advertisements during state and local government elections, was invalid because it 'burden[ed] the functioning of the political branches of the government of the State with statutory constraints and restrictions': 177 CLR at 164. Brennan J held that the provisions of Pt IIID which allowed for free air time during elections were not invalid because they acquired property on other than just terms.

Dawson J: [184] [T]here is no warrant in the Constitution for the implication of any guarantee of freedom of communication which operates to confer rights upon individuals or to limit the legislative power of the Commonwealth. It may be remarked in passing that even if a guarantee limiting Commonwealth legislative power were to exist by implication, it could have only a limited effect upon States in the exercise of their concurrent legislative powers. In expressing the view which I do, I do not mean to suggest that the legislative powers of the Commonwealth under s 51 may not be limited by implications drawn from other provisions of the Constitution or from the terms of the Constitution as a whole. The powers conferred by s 51 are expressed to be 'subject to this Constitution' and that expression encompasses implied limitations as well as those which are express. There is, for example, the implication drawn from the federal structure of the Constitution that prevents the Commonwealth from legislating in a way that discriminates against the States by imposing special burdens or disabilities upon them or in a way which curtails their capacity to exercise for themselves their constitutional functions.

Dawson J said that the Constitution encapsulated the principles of representative and responsible government: 177 CLR 184.

[185] But much is left to the Parliament concerning the details of the electoral system to be employed in achieving representative democracy. For example, the Constitution does not guarantee universal adult suffrage. And, subject to the Constitution, the method of electing members of Parliament and the determination of electoral divisions also rest with the Parliament.

Dawson J referred to the views of Murphy J in *Miller v TCN Channel Nine Pty Ltd* (1986) 161 CLR 556 at 581–2, to the effect that a number of fundamental freedoms were to be implied in the Commonwealth Constitution, and continued:

[186] But it is clear that Murphy J based the implication which he asserted, not upon the text of the Constitution, but upon 'the nature of our society'. In doing so, he failed, in my view, to recognise the true character of the Australian Constitution which, as I have endeavoured to explain, limits the implications which can be drawn to those which appear from the terms of the instrument itself. Indeed, those responsible for the drafting of the Constitution saw constitutional guarantees of freedoms as exhibiting a distrust of the democratic process. They preferred to place their trust in Parliament to preserve the nature of our society and regarded as undemocratic guarantees which fettered its powers. Their model in this respect was, not the United States Constitution, but the British Parliament, the supremacy of which was by then settled constitutional doctrine. Not only that, but the heresy of importing into the Constitution, by way of implication, preconceptions having their origin outside the Constitution has been exposed and decisively rejected in the *Engineers'* case. The nature of the

society or, more precisely and accurately, the nature of the federation which the Constitution established, is to be found within its four corners and not elsewhere. To say as much is not for one moment to express disagreement with the view expressed by Murphy J that freedom of movement and freedom of communication are indispensable to any free society. It is merely to differ as to the institutions in which the founding fathers placed their faith for the protection of those freedoms.

Having said that, it must nevertheless be recognised that the Constitution provides for a Parliament the members of which are to [187] be directly chosen by the people ... Thus the Constitution provides for a choice and that must mean a true choice. It may be said — at all events in the context of an election — that a choice is not a true choice when it is made without an appreciation of the available alternatives or, at least, without an opportunity to gain an appreciation of the available alternatives ... Perhaps the freedom is one which must extend beyond the election time to the period between elections, but that is something which it is unnecessary to consider in this case. It is enough to recognise, as this court did in *Evans v Crichton-Browne* (1981) 147 CLR 169, at 206; 33 ALR 609, the importance of ensuring that freedom of speech is not unduly restricted during an election period. Thus an election in which the electors are denied access to the information necessary for the exercise of a true choice is not the kind of election envisaged by the Constitution. Legislation which would have the effect of denying access to that information by the electors would therefore be incompatible with the Constitution.

Dawson J referred to the prohibitions imposed by Pt IIID, to its objective of reducing expenditure on political campaigns and to the fact that similar restrictions were to be found in a significant number of democratic countries. His Honour continued:

[189] The object of the prohibition of political advertising was, therefore, to enhance rather than impair the democratic process. In any event, it must be remembered, as is noted in the second reading speech, that television advertising (which is of far greater significance than radio advertising) leads to the packaging of information into 30 or even 15 second messages concerned with image rather than content. Of course, upon the assumption that political advertising imparts information which is capable of assisting in the making of an informed choice in an election, the prohibition clearly denies some information to electors. But the provision of information in the press and by other means is unimpeded. Even the electronic media have an undiminished capacity to present news reports, current affairs programs, editorial comment and talkback radio programs all relating to political issues. Moreover, the legislation does not prevent the broadcasting of the policy launch of a political party during an election period. And the prohibition of political advertising is, of course, only during an election period.

In these circumstances, I am unable to conclude that the prohibition of political advertising which the legislation in question effects is incompatible with the constitutional requirement that an elector be able to make an informed choice in an election. That being so, it is not for the court to express any view whether the legislation goes far enough or further than is necessary to achieve its object. These are matters for Parliament and not the court.

McHugh J: [228] *Representative government and responsible government*

His Honour referred to the purpose of the Constitution as being to furtherance of representative and responsible government.

Representative government involves the conception of a legislative chamber whose members are elected by the people. But, as Birch points out, to have a full understanding of the concept of representative government, 'we need to add that the chamber must occupy a powerful position in the political system and that the elections to it must be free, with all that this implies in the way of freedom of speech and political organisation'. Furthermore, responsible government involves the conception of a legislative chamber where the Ministers of State are answerable ultimately to the electorate for their policies ...

It is not to be supposed, therefore, that, in conferring the right to choose their representatives by voting at periodic elections, the Constitution intended to confer on the people of Australia no more than the right to mark a ballot paper with a number, a cross or a tick, as the case may be. The 'share in the government which the Constitution ensures' would be but a pious aspiration unless ss 7 **[231]** and 24 carried with them more than the right to cast a vote. The guarantees embodied in ss 7 and 24 could not be satisfied by the Parliament requiring the people to select their representatives from a list of names drawn up by government officers.

If the institutions of representative and responsible government are to operate effectively and as the Constitution intended, the business of government must be examinable and the subject of scrutiny, debate and ultimate accountability at the ballot box. The electors must be able to ascertain and examine the performances of their elected representatives and the capabilities and policies of all candidates for election. Before they can cast an effective vote at election time, they must have access to the information, ideas and arguments which are necessary to make an informed judgment as to how they have been governed and as to what policies are in the interests of themselves, their communities and the nation. As the Supreme Court of the United States pointed out in *Buckley v Valeo* 424 US 1 (1976) at 14–15, the ability of the people to make informed choices among candidates for political office is fundamental because the identity of those who are elected will shape the nation's destiny.

It follows that the electors must be able to communicate with the candidates for election concerning election issues and must be able to communicate their own arguments and opinions to other members of the community concerning those issues. Only by the spread of information, opinions and arguments can electors make an effective and responsible choice in determining whether or not they should vote for a particular candidate or the party which that person represents …

The words 'directly chosen by the people' in ss 7 and 24, interpreted against the background of the institutions of representative government and responsible government, are to be read, therefore, as referring to a process — the process which commences **[232]** when an election is called and ends with the declaration of the poll. The process includes all those steps which are directed to the people electing their representatives — nominating, campaigning, advertising, debating, criticising and voting. In respect of such steps, the people possess the right to participate, the right to associate and the right to communicate. That means that, subject to necessary exceptions, the people have a constitutional right to convey and receive opinions, arguments and information concerning matter intended or likely to affect voting in an election for the Senate or the House of Representatives. Moreover, that right must extend to the use of all forms and methods of communication which are lawfully available for general use in the community. To fail to give effect to the rights of participation, association and communication identifiable in ss 7 and 24 would be to sap and undermine the foundations of the Constitution.

~~~

[11.3.8] McHugh J held that the restrictions on political advertising imposed by s 95B could not be justified:

> [It is] for the electors and the candidates to choose which forms of otherwise lawful communication they prefer to use to disseminate political communication, ideas and argument. Their choices are a matter of private, not public, interest. Their choices are outside the zone of governmental control (177 CLR at 236).

McHugh J would have held s 95C valid, on the ground that there was no implied right of freedom of communication in a territory (177 CLR at 246), and s 95D invalid on the ground that it 'constituted an unacceptable interference with the functions of the State as an independent body politic': 177 CLR at 244.

Deane and Toohey JJ said that the doctrine of representative government embodied in the Constitution led to an implication of freedom within the Commonwealth of communication about matters relating to the government of the Commonwealth; and they referred to the reasons they had given for that conclusion in *Nationwide News Pty Ltd v Wills* (1992) 177 CLR 1 **[11.3.9]**. They held that Pt IIID of the Broadcasting Act offended that freedom, and that Pt IIID could not be justified on the ground that it served some other public interest.

Gaudron J held that the Commonwealth Constitution was constructed on a system of representative parliamentary democracy. Freedom of political discourse between the members of society generally was an essential aspect of that system: 177 CLR at 211. Part IIID was invalid because it denied that freedom and went beyond what was reasonably necessary to regulate radio and television and to regulate Commonwealth elections: 177 CLR at 220, 221. Her Honour also held that s 95C was invalid because it was not supported by s 122, as the Commonwealth Parliament had conferred a substantial measure of self-government on the Northern Territory and the Australian Capital Territory: 177 CLR at 224.

Notes

[11.3.9]   In *Nationwide News Pty Ltd v Wills* (1992) 177 CLR 1, the High Court held that s 299(1)(d)(ii) of the Industrial Relations Act 1988 (Cth) was invalid. That provision made it an offence for any person to use words calculated to bring a member of the Industrial Relations Commission, or the Commission, into disrepute. The High Court approached the validity of s 299(1)(d)(ii) on the basis that the provision did not allow for such defences as 'fair comment' or 'honest and reasonable mistake of fact'. It concluded that the provision went further than was necessary to achieve the legitimate purpose of protecting the Industrial Relations Commission and its members from unjustifiable attack.

Three members of the court, Mason CJ, Dawson and McHugh JJ, based their decisions that s 299(1)(d)(ii) was invalid on the ground that the provision could not be supported by the parliament's power to make laws with respect to conciliation and arbitration for the settlement of industrial disputes, s 51(xxxv), or by the power to make laws with respect to any matter incidental to the execution of the Commonwealth's legislative, executive or judicial powers, s 51(xxxix).

Mason CJ said there was not a sufficient connection between the law and the subject matter of s 51(xxxv), because there was not a reasonable proportionality between the designated object or purpose of protecting the authority of the Commission and the means selected by the law for achieving that object or purpose: 177 CLR at 34. Mason CJ noted that the degree of protection given to the Commission was much larger than the protection accorded to the courts by the law of contempt, and said that the need to protect the Commission's authority had to be balanced by the interest of the public in ensuring that the Commission and its activities were open to public scrutiny and criticism: 177 CLR at 38. He considered 'the adverse impact ... of the impugned law on such a fundamental freedom as freedom of expression', and concluded that s 299(1)(d)(ii) did not have a sufficient connection with s 51(xxxv) or s 51(xxxix). Since *Leask v Commonwealth* (1996) 187 CLR 579 **[1.5.23]**, it seems that the court has rejected this approach to the question of characterisation. Although purpose is still relevant when a law falls within the incidental range of a power, 'proportionality' is relevant only in two circumstances: when the power is purposive, or when the court is characterising a power which is subject to a constitutional limit. Ordinarily, proportionality has no part to play in characterising a law as being sufficiently connected to the subject matter of the power: *Leask v Commonwealth* (1996) 187 CLR 579 per Dawson J.

Four members of the court in *Nationwide*, Brennan, Deane, Toohey and Gaudron JJ, held that s 299(1)(d)(ii) was invalid because it violated the implied right to freedom of political communication. Brennan J said:

> [T]he Constitution prohibits any legislative or executive infringement of the freedom to discuss governments and governmental institutions and political matters except to the extent necessary to protect other legitimate interests and, in any event, not to an extent which substantially impairs the capacity of, or opportunity for, the Australian people to form the political judgments required for the exercise of their constitutional functions (177 CLR at 50–51).

Brennan J concluded that, although s 51(xxxv) authorised the parliament to protect the Commission's capacity to perform its functions, 'the power does not extend so far as to authorise a law prohibiting justifiable and fair and reasonable criticism of the Commission as an important instrument of government': 177 CLR at 51.

Deane and Toohey JJ said that all of the Commonwealth's legislative powers were subject to 'the fundamental implications of the doctrines of government upon which the Constitution as a whole is structured and which form part of its fabric', and the implications 'which flow from the fundamental rights and principles recognised by the common law at the time the Constitution was adopted as the compact of the Federation': 177 CLR at 69. They explained that one of those implications was derived from the doctrine of representative government enshrined in the Constitution (at 72–3):

> The doctrine presupposes an ability of represented and representatives to communicate information, needs, views, explanations and advice. It also presupposes an ability of the people of the Commonwealth as a whole to communicate, among themselves, information and opinions about matters relevant to the exercise and discharge of governmental powers and functions on their behalf.
>
> It follows from what has been said above that there is to be discerned in the doctrine of representative government which the Constitution incorporates an implication of freedom of communication of information and opinion about matters relating to the government of the Commonwealth.

Laws which restricted freedom of communication on such matters could be justified, Deane and Toohey JJ said, only if the restrictions they imposed were 'conducive to the overall availability of the effective means of such communication in a democratic society' (as with the regulation of the use of radio frequencies); or if they protected or vindicated legitimate claims of individuals to live peacefully and with dignity in such a society': 177 CLR at 77. Seen against the guaranteed freedom and the permissible qualifications to that freedom, Deane and Toohey JJ said that s 299(1)(d)(ii) was invalid (at 78–9):

> A prohibition of the communication of well-founded and relevant criticism of a governmental instrumentality or tribunal, such as the Commission or a Commonwealth court, cannot be justified as being, on balance, in the public interest merely because it is calculated to bring the instrumentality or tribunal or its members into disrepute. To the contrary, if criticism of a governmental instrumentality or tribunal or its members is well founded and relevant, its publication is an incident of the ordinary working of representative government and the fact that it will, if published, bring the relevant instrumentality or tribunal into deserved disrepute is, from the point of view of the overall public interest, a factor supporting publication rather than suppression.

Gaudron J said at 94:

> [T]he powers conferred by s 51 of the Constitution, because they are conferred 'subject to [the] Constitution', do not authorise laws which are inconsistent with a Commonwealth which is a free society governed in accordance with the principles of representative parliamentary democracy and, thus, do not authorise laws which impair or curtail freedom of political discourse, albeit that that freedom is not absolute.

The freedom might be curtailed, Gaudron J said, to secure some other end such as the protection of the authority of the Industrial Relations Commission; but only if the law in question were 'reasonably and appropriately adapted to that end': 177 CLR at 95. Section 299(1)(d)(ii) could not be so described. It was, accordingly, invalid.

[11.3.10] Both *Australian Capital Television* (1992) 177 CLR 106 **[11.3.7C]** and *Nationwide News v Wills* (1992) 177 CLR 1 **[11.3.9]** had their unacknowledged origins in the judgments of Murphy J, noted above in **[11.1.1]**. In a series of cases in the 1970s, Murphy J referred to rights that were part of the 'fabric of the Constitution': *Miller v TCN Channel Nine Pty Ltd* (1986) 161 CLR 556 at 581, citing Lord Watson in *Cooper v Stuart* (1889) 14 App Cas 286 at 293. He included amongst these:

- freedom of movement, of speech and of other communication (*Ansett Transport Industries (Operations) Pty Ltd v Commonwealth* (1977) 139 CLR 54 at 88; *Buck v Bavone* (1976) 135 CLR 110 at 137; *McGraw-Hinds (Aust) Pty Ltd v Smith* (1979) 144 CLR 633 at 670; *Uebergang v Australian Wheat Board* (1980) 145 CLR 266 at 312; *Miller v TCN Channel Nine Pty Ltd* (1986) 161 CLR 556 at 581–2);

- freedom from slavery (*R v Director-General of Social Welfare (Vic); Ex parte Henry* (1975) 133 CLR 369 at 388); and

- freedom from arbitrary discrimination on the basis of sex (*Ansett Transport Industries (Operations) Pty Ltd v Wardley* (1980) 142 CLR 237 at 267).

[11.3.11] In *Theophanous v Herald & Weekly Times Ltd* (1994) 182 CLR 104 **[11.3.2C]**, a majority of the High Court held that the implied freedom of communication could protect the publisher of a newspaper from liability for defamation based on the publication of criticism of a member of the House of Representatives.

Three of the majority justices, Mason CJ, Toohey and Gaudron JJ, said in their joint judgment that the implied freedom of communication was not limited to federal elections (182 CLR at 121) and that it extended 'to all those who participate in political discussion': 182 CLR at 122. It was not limited to matters relating to the Commonwealth, because of '[t]he interrelationship of Commonwealth and State powers and the interaction between the various tiers of government in Australia', and the underlying purpose of the implied freedom was 'to ensure the efficacious working of representative democracy': 182 CLR at 123. 'Political discussion' included discussion of the conduct, policies or fitness for office of government, political parties, public bodies, public officers and those seeking public office and it included discussion of the political views and public conduct of persons who were engaged in activities that became the subject of political debate, for example, trade union leaders, Aboriginal political leaders, political and economic commentators: 182 CLR at 214. These three justices emphasised that the freedom was a limited one and said there was a difference between 'protection of freedom of expression generally as a fundamental human right and the protection of freedom of communication in matters of political discussion as an indispensable element in ensuring the efficacious working of representative democracy and government': 182 CLR at 125. However, the implication did not protect defamatory statements which were knowingly false, or made with reckless disregard for the truth or untruth of the material published: 182 CLR 134.

Deane J (who also held that defamation laws infringed the constitutional implication) took a different position from the majority in other important respects. First, he said that the Constitution was to be interpreted as a 'living force' (182 CLR at 173): see Chapter 1. Second, he took a broader view of the ambit of the freedom, saying that it 'preclude[d] completely' the application of state defamation laws to citizens or media outlets in relation to publication of statements about the conduct or suitability of members of parliament or other high office-holders: 182 CLR 185. Accordingly Deane J did not agree with the majority's conditions upon the availability of the defence; namely, that reckless or unreasonable publication would not be protected: 182 CLR at 137. However, for the purposes of reaching an agreed conclusion, Deane J accepted those limitations: 182 CLR at 188. Therefore, until *Lange v Australian Broadcasting Corporation* (1997) 189 CLR 520 **[11.3.3C]** and **[11.3.13C]**, the case stood as authority for the propositions expounded by Mason CJ, Toohey and Gaudron JJ.

In separate judgments Brennan, Dawson and McHugh JJ dissented. Brennan J did so on the basis that, although '[t]he Constitution and the common law are bound in a symbiotic relationship ... [i]n the interpretation of the Constitution, judicial policy ha[d] no role to play': 182 CLR at 143. He applied the test of proportionality to the legislation (at 150, 151) and concluded that there was '[n]o implication from the text or structure of the Constitution' which was 'inconsistent with the availability of a cause of action in defamation to members of Parliament, candidates for election or public figures generally': 182 CLR at 153. The common law adequately balanced protection of freedom of speech and protection of individual reputation: 182 CLR at 154. He also said that the constitutional implication limited state legislative power in the same manner that it limited Commonwealth legislative power.

Dawson J said that the scope of the implication was 'minimal' (182 CLR at 189) and that freedom of communication was protected only to the extent necessary to protect representative government: 182 CLR at 190. He characterised the majority's approach as dependent upon finding implications outside the constitutional instrument in the 'nature of society' and thus as outside the principles of interpretation expounded in *Amalgamated Society of Engineers v Adelaide Steamship Co Ltd* (the *Engineers'* case) (1920) 28 CLR 129: 182 CLR at 193–4. Accordingly there was no 'free standing' implied freedom of communication (182 CLR at 190) (save that in s 92) and the implied freedom had no application to the common law rules of defamation which had co-existed quite comfortably with the notion of representative government as contained in the Constitution for over 90 years: 182 CLR at 192.

McHugh J also characterised the majority as relying on an implication which was separate from the text and structure of the Constitution: 182 CLR at 195–6. He said the majority in *Australian Capital Television Pty Ltd* (1992) 177 CLR 106 had unintentionally departed from the *Engineers'* case (1920) 28 CLR 129 in holding that representative government was part of the Constitution independent of its terms

(182 CLR at 202–3), and he distinguished the latter approach from the legitimate method of finding of implications based upon other provisions of the Constitution (separation of powers); the text (judicial review) or the federal structure of the Constitution (*Melbourne Corporation v Commonwealth* (the *State Bank* case) (1947) 74 CLR 31 **[8.2.45C]**): 182 CLR at 203–4.

[11.3.12] On the same day that the High Court decided *Theophanous v Herald & Weekly Times Ltd* (1994) 182 CLR 104 **[11.3.11]**, it published its decision in *Stephens v West Australian Newspapers Ltd* (1994) 182 CLR 211. *Stephens* raised directly the extent to which the implied freedom of communication applied to discussion of state political matters, and whether the Western Australian Constitution contained a similar implication. As in *Theophanous*, Mason CJ, Toohey and Gaudron JJ (Deane J concurring) affirmed the availability of the implication as a defence to an action for defamation.

Mason CJ, Toohey and Gaudron JJ held that the implication contained in the Commonwealth Constitution extended to discussion of state political matters for the reasons given in *Theophanous v Herald & Weekly Times Ltd* (1994) 182 CLR 104 **[11.3.11]**, *Nationwide News Pty Ltd v Wills* (1992) 177 CLR 1 **[11.3.9]** and *Australian Capital Television Pty Ltd v Commonwealth* (1992) 177 CLR 106 **[11.3.7C]** relating to the interrelationship between levels of government within the federation: 182 CLR at 232. The justices also found that entrenchment in the Constitution Act 1889 (WA) of provisions relating to members of parliament being directly chosen by the people indicated that it contained a counterpart implication with similar effect. The justices said at 233–4:

> [S]o long, at least, as the Western Australian Constitution continues to provide for a representative democracy in which the members of the legislature are 'directly chosen by the people', a freedom of communication must necessarily be implied in that Constitution, just as it is implied in the Commonwealth Constitution, in order to protect the efficacious working of representative democracy and government.

Brennan J agreed that both the Commonwealth and Western Australian Constitutions contained an implication of freedom of communication, but maintained that neither had the effect of invalidating the common law of defamation: 182 CLR at 235–6. The other members of the minority, Dawson and McHugh JJ, held that no relevant implication of freedom of communication existed at Commonwealth or state level.

[11.3.13C] Lange v Australian Broadcasting Corporation
(1997) 189 CLR 520

As noted in **[11.3.3C]**, a former New Zealand Prime Minister sued the ABC for defamation and the ABC relied on *Theophanous v Herald & Weekly Times Ltd* (1994) 182 CLR 104 **[11.3.11]** and *Stephens v West Australian Newspapers Ltd* (1994) 182 CLR 211 **[11.3.12]** in pleading its defence.

When the matter was removed to the High Court under s 40 of the Judiciary Act 1903 (Cth), the court took the opportunity to settle several of the disputed questions arising from the earlier decisions. These matters included:
* the status of the ruling in *Theophanous*;
* the relationship of representative government and responsible government to the implied freedom on communication;
* whether the implication was a personal right or a limit upon legislative competence;
* the extent of the freedom;

- the test for invalidity of a law said to infringe the implication;
- the relationship between the common law and the Constitution; and
- interpretive method.

In relation to the law of defamation the court also considered the elements of the law of qualified privilege and the compatibility of the Defamation Act (NSW) s 22 with the Constitution.

The court did not expressly overrule *Theophanous*. Rather, in a unanimous judgment, it decided that the Constitution conferred no private right of defence but instead created an immunity against legislative incursion into free communication in respect of political matters. The court expanded the common law defence of qualified privilege to provide a protection for criticism of politicians similar to that recognised in *Theophanous*. However, what was achieved in *Theophanous* by a direct application of the Constitution was achieved in *Lange* by a combination of the Constitution and the common law.

The justices said that the court was 'not bound by its previous decisions' and that it would reexamine a decision if it involved a question of 'vital constitutional importance' and was 'manifestly wrong' because '[e]rrors in constitutional interpretation are not remediable by the legislature': 189 CLR at 554. The justices said it was arguable that neither *Theophanous v Herald & Weekly Times Ltd* (1994) 182 CLR 104 **[11.3.10]** or *Stephens v West Australian Newspapers Ltd* (1994) 182 CLR 211 **[11.3.12]** 'contain[ed] a binding statement of constitutional principle' (189 CLR at 554) because, although all judges comprising the majority (Mason CJ, Toohey and Gaudron J in a joint judgment, and Deane J in a separate opinion) held the constitutional defence was good in law, Deane J did not expressly agree with the reasons of the joint judgment. The justices said that the cases decided that 'in Australia the common law rules of defamation must conform to the requirements of the Constitution': 189 CLR at 556. However, following the 'insights gained from the subsequent cases' of *McGinty v Western Australia* (1996) 186 CLR 140, *Langer v Commonwealth* (1996) 186 CLR 302, and *Muldowney v South Australia* (1996) 186 CLR 352, further consideration should be given to 'some of the expressions and reasoning in the various judgments in *Theophanous* and *Stephens*': 189 CLR at 556. The justices continued:

Brennan CJ, Dawson, Toohey, Gaudron, McHugh, Gummow and Kirby JJ: [556] Having regard to the foregoing discussion, the appropriate course is to examine the correctness of the defences pleaded in the present case as a matter of principle and not of authority. The starting point of that examination must be the terms of the Constitution illuminated by the assistance which is to be obtained from *Theophanous* and the other authorities which have dealt with the question of 'implied freedoms' under the Constitution.

The justices confirmed that the text of the Constitution expressed the principle of representative government in ss 1, 7, 8 13, 24, 25, 28, 30 and 128 and of responsible government in ss 6, 49, 83, 62, and 64, and that these provisions formed the bases of the implication of freedom of political communication: 189 CLR at 558. They reaffirmed that the implication of freedom of communication was 'an indispensable incident' of the system of representative government which the Constitution creates (189 CLR 559), and continued:

[559] At federation, representative government was understood to mean a system of government where the people in free elections elected their representatives to the legislative chamber which occupies the most powerful position in the political system. [*Theophanous* (1994) 182 CLR 104 at 200] As Birch points out, 'it is the manner of choice of members of the legislative assembly, rather than their characteristics or their behaviour, which is generally taken to be the criterion of a representative form of government.' However, to have a full understanding of the concept of representative government, Birch also states that:

> ... we need to add that the chamber must occupy a powerful position [560] in the political system and that the elections to it must be free, with all that this implies in the way of freedom of speech and political organisation.

Communications concerning political or government matters between the electors and the elected representatives, between the electors and the candidates for election and between the electors themselves were central to the system of representative government, as it was understood at federation. [*R v Smithers; Ex parte Benson* (1912) 16 CLR 99 at 108, 109–110] While the system of representative government for which the Constitution provides does not expressly mention freedom of communication, it can hardly be doubted, given the history of representative government and the holding of elections under that system in Australia prior to federation, that the elections for which the Constitution provides were intended to be free elections in the sense explained by Birch. Furthermore, because the choice given by ss 7 and 24 must be a true choice with 'an opportunity to gain an appreciation of the available alternatives', as Dawson J pointed out in *Australian Capital Television Pty Ltd v The Commonwealth*, [(1992) 177 CLR 106 at 187] legislative power cannot support an absolute denial of access by the people to relevant information about the functioning of government in Australia and about the policies of political parties and candidates for election. ...

The justices said that the implication of freedom of communication was not in the nature of a personal right but was rather a limit upon legislative power (189 CLR at 560): see **[11.3.3C]**. Their Honours said the freedom could not be confined to the election period (189 CLR at 561) and that it included 'the affairs of statutory authorities and public utilities which are obliged to report to the legislature or to a Minister who is responsible to the legislature': 189 CLR at 561. They continued:

[562] Different formulae have been used by members of this Court in other cases to express the test whether the freedom provided by the Constitution has been infringed. Some judges have expressed the test as whether the law is reasonably appropriate and adapted to the fulfilment of a legitimate purpose. Others have favoured different expressions, including proportionality. In the context of the questions raised by the case stated, there is no need to distinguish these concepts. For ease of expression, throughout these reasons we have used the formulation of reasonably appropriate and adapted. ...

A person who is defamed must find a legal remedy against those responsible for publishing defamatory matter either in the common law or in a statute which confers a right of action. The right to a remedy cannot be admitted, however, if its exercise would infringe upon the freedom to discuss government and political matters which the Constitution impliedly requires. It is necessary, therefore, to consider the relationship between the Constitution and the freedom of communication which it requires on the one hand and the common law and the statute law which govern the law of defamation on the other.

The justices said that the common law 'supplies elements of the British constitutional fabric' but that in Australia 'it became necessary to accommodate basic common law concepts and techniques to a federal system of government' (189 CLR 562), although with a different outcome from that reached in the United States. 'There is but one common law in Australia which is declared by this Court as the final court of appeal' whereas in the United States the common law is 'fragmented into different systems of jurisprudence': 189 CLR 563. Therefore, in the United States, the Constitution produces a 'constitutional privilege' against the enforcement of state common law, and a 'federal action for damages arising from certain executive action in violation of "free-standing" constitutional rights, privileges, or immunities'. By contrast in Australia 'recovery of loss arising from conduct in excess of constitutional authority has been dealt with under the rubric of the common law, particularly the law of tort' [*Northern Territory v Mengel* (1995) 185 CLR 307 at 350–353, 372–373]: 189 CLR at 563.

[563] It makes little sense in Australia to adopt the United States doctrine so as to identify litigation between private parties over their common law rights and liabilities as involving 'State law rights'. Here, '[w]e act every day on the unexpressed assumption that the one common law surrounds us and applies where it has not been superseded by statute' [Dixon, 'The Common Law as an Ultimate Constitutional Foundation', (1957) 31 *Australian Law Journal* 240 at 241]. Moreover, that one common law operates in the federal [564] system

established by the Constitution. The Constitution displaced, or rendered inapplicable, the English common law doctrine of the general competence and unqualified supremacy of the legislature. It placed upon the federal judicature the responsibility of deciding the limits of the respective powers of State and Commonwealth governments. [*R v Kirby; Ex parte Boilermakers' Society of Australia* (1956) 94 CLR 254 at 267–268] The Constitution, the federal, State and territorial laws, and the common law in Australia together constitute the law of this country and form 'one system of jurisprudence'. [*McArthur v Williams* (1936) 55 CLR 324 at 347] Covering cl 5 of the Constitution renders the Constitution 'binding on the courts, judges, and people of every State and of every part of the Commonwealth, notwithstanding anything in the laws of any State'. Within that single system of jurisprudence, the basic law of the Constitution provides the authority for the enactment of valid statute law and may have effect on the content of the common law.

Conversely, the Constitution itself is informed by the common law.

... [I]n *Cheatle v R*, [(1993) 177 CLR 541 at 552] this Court said:

> It is well settled that the interpretation of a constitution such as ours is necessarily influenced by the fact that its provisions are framed in the language of the English common law, and are to be read in the light of the common law's history.

Under a legal system based on the common law, 'everybody is free to do anything, subject only to the provisions of the law', so that one proceeds 'upon an assumption of freedom of speech' and turns to the law 'to discover the established exceptions to it'. [*A-G v Guardian Newspapers (No 2)* [1990] 1 AC 109 at 283] The common law torts of libel and slander are such exceptions. However, these torts do not inhibit the publication of defamatory matter unless the [565] publication is unlawful — that is to say, not justified, protected or excused by any of the various defences to the publication of defamatory matter, including qualified privilege. The result is to confer upon defendants, who choose to plead and establish an appropriate defence, an immunity to action brought against them. In that way, they are protected by the law in respect of certain publications and freedom of communication is maintained.

The issue raised by the Constitution in relation to an action for defamation is whether the immunity conferred by the common law, as it has traditionally been perceived, or, where there is statute law on the subject the immunity conferred by statute, conforms with the freedom required by the Constitution. In 1901, when the Constitution of the Commonwealth took effect and when the Judicial Committee was the ultimate Court in the judicial hierarchy, the English common law defined the scope of the torts of libel and slander. At that time, the balance that was struck by the common law between freedom of communication about government and political matters and the protection of personal reputation was thought to be consistent with the freedom that was essential and incidental to the holding of the elections and referenda for which the Constitution provided. Since 1901, the common law — now the common law of Australia — has had to be developed in response to changing conditions. The expansion of the franchise, the increase in literacy, the growth of modern political structures operating at both federal and State levels and the modern development in mass communications, especially the electronic media, now demand the striking of a different balance from that which was struck in 1901. To this question we shall presently return.

The factors which affect the development of the common law equally affect the scope of the freedom which is constitutionally required. '[T]he common convenience and welfare of society' is the criterion of the protection given to communications by the common law of qualified privilege. [*Toogood v Spyring* (1834) 1 CM & R 181 at 193 [149 ER 1044 at 1050]] Similarly, the content of the freedom to discuss government and political matters must be ascertained according to what is for the common convenience and welfare of society. That requires an examination of changing circumstances [*Jumbunna Coal Mine, NL v Victorian Coal Miners' Association* (1908) 6 CLR 309 at 367–368] and the need to strike a balance in those circumstances between absolute freedom of discussion of government and politics and the [566] reasonable protection of the persons who may be involved, directly or incidentally, in the activities of government or politics.

Of necessity, the common law must conform with the Constitution. The development of the common law in Australia cannot run counter to constitutional imperatives. [*Theophanous* (1994) 182 CLR 104 at 140] The common law and the requirements of the Constitution cannot be at odds. The common law of libel and slander could not be developed inconsistently with the Constitution, for the common law's protection of personal reputation must admit as an exception that qualified freedom to discuss government and politics which is required by the Constitution.

In any particular case, the question whether a publication of defamatory matter is protected by the Constitution or is within a common law exception to actionable defamation yields the same answer. But the answer to the common law question has a different significance from the answer to the constitutional law question. The answer to the common law question prima facie defines the existence and scope of the personal right of the person defamed against the person who published the defamatory matter; the answer to the constitutional law question defines the area of immunity which cannot be infringed by a law of the Commonwealth, a law of a State or a law of those Territories whose residents are entitled to exercise the federal franchise. That is because the requirement of freedom of communication operates as a restriction on legislative power. Statutory regimes cannot trespass upon the constitutionally required freedom.

However, a statute which diminishes the rights or remedies of persons defamed and correspondingly enlarges the freedom to discuss government and political matters is not contrary to the constitutional implication. The common law rights of persons defamed may be diminished by statute but they cannot be enlarged so as to restrict the freedom required by the Constitution. Statutes which purport to define the law of defamation are construed, if possible, conformably with the Constitution. But, if their provisions are intractably inconsistent with the Constitution, they must yield to the constitutional norm. ...

Since *McGinty* it has been clear, if it was not clear before, that the Constitution gives effect to the institution of 'representative govern[567]ment' only to the extent that the text and structure of the Constitution establish it. In other words, to say that the Constitution gives effect to representative government is a shorthand way of saying that the Constitution provides for that form of representative government which is to be found in the relevant sections. Under the Constitution, the relevant question is not, 'What is required by representative and responsible government?' It is, 'What do the terms and structure of the Constitution prohibit, authorise or require?'

Moreover, although it is true that the requirement of freedom of communication is a consequence of the Constitution's system of representative and responsible government, it is the requirement and not a right of communication that is to be found in the Constitution. Unlike the First Amendment to the United States Constitution, which has been interpreted to confer private rights, our Constitution contains no express right of freedom of communication or expression. Within our legal system, communications are free only to the extent that they are left unburdened by laws that comply with the Constitution.

To the extent that the requirement of freedom of communication is an implication drawn from ss 7, 24, 64, 128 and related sections of the Constitution, the implication can validly extend only so far as is necessary to give effect to these sections. Although some statements in the earlier cases might be thought to suggest otherwise, when they are properly understood, they should be seen as purporting to give effect only to what is inherent in the text and structure of the Constitution.

Their Honours reiterated the test for invalidity of the implied freedom of communication. They said:

When a law of a State or federal Parliament or a Territory legislature is alleged to infringe the requirement of freedom of communication imposed by ss 7, 24, 64 or 128 of the Constitution, two questions must be answered before the validity of the law can be determined. First, does the law effectively burden freedom of communication about government or political matters either in its terms, operation or effect? Second, if the law effectively burdens that freedom, is the law reasonably appropriate and adapted to serve a legitimate end the fulfilment of which is compatible with the maintenance of the constitutionally prescribed system of representative and responsible government and the procedure prescribed by s 128 for submitting a proposed amendment of the Constitution to the informed decision of the people [*Cunliffe* (1994) 182 CLR 272 at 300, 324, 339, 387–388] (hereafter collectively 'the system of government prescribed by the Constitution'). If the first question is [568] answered 'yes' and the second is answered 'no', the law is invalid. In *ACTV*, for example, a majority of this Court held that a law seriously impeding discussion during the course of a federal election was invalid because there were other less drastic means by which the objectives of the law could be achieved. And the common law rules, as they have traditionally been understood, must be examined by reference to the same considerations. If it is necessary, they must be developed to ensure that the protection given to personal reputation does not unnecessarily or unreasonably impair the freedom of communication about government and political matters which the Constitution requires.

The justices applied the test to the law of defamation in general and the New South Wales provision s 22 on qualified privilege in particular. They said the law of defamation effectively burdened freedom of communication concerning government or political matters relating to the Commonwealth (189 CLR at 568), but that its purpose, namely the protection of reputation, was compatible with the maintenance of constitutionally prescribed representative and responsible government (189 CLR 520 at 568); and conducive to the public good: 189 CLR 520 at 568.

Theophanous v Herald & Weekly Times Ltd (1994) 182 CLR 104 and *Stephens v West Australian Newspapers Ltd* (1994) 182 CLR 211 were, the justices said, wrong to the extent that they decided the question of whether defamation law infringed the constitutional requirement by reference to the notion of freedom of communication, and not by asking whether the law of defamation was reasonably and appropriately adapted to a legitimate end that is compatible with the system of government prescribed by the Constitution: 189 CLR at 569. Their Honours went on to consider the compatibility of the New South Wales law of defamation with such an end. They extended the scope of the defence of qualified privilege by declaring the existence of one of the essential elements of the defence (reciprocity) between members of the community in respect of the reporting of political matters.

[571] Accordingly, this Court should now declare that each member of the Australian community has an interest in disseminating and receiving information, opinions and arguments concerning government and political matters that affect the people of Australia. The duty to disseminate such information is simply the correlative of the interest in receiving it. The common convenience and welfare of Australian society are advanced by discussion — the giving and receiving of information — about government and political matters. The interest that each member of the Australian community has in such a discussion extends the categories of qualified privilege. Consequently, those categories now must be recognised as protecting a communication made to the public on a government or political matter ...

The justices also extended the common law defence of qualified privilege to include 'discussion of matters concerning the United Nations or other countries ... even if those discussions cannot illuminate the choice for electors at federal elections or in amending the Constitution or cannot throw light on the administration of federal government', as well as including 'discussion of government or politics at State or Territory level and even at local government level ... whether or not it bears on matters at the federal level': 189 CLR at 571. Finally, the justices discussed the elements of the new extended defence of qualified privilege, and concluded that s 22 of the New South Wales Act 'does not place an undue burden on communications falling within the protection of the Constitution': 189 CLR at 575.

~~~

Notes

[11.3.14] Shortly after the judgment in *Lange v Australian Broadcasting Corporation* (1997) 189 CLR 520 **[11.3.13C]** was handed down, the High Court published its decision in *Levy v Victoria* (1997) 189 CLR 579, the case which had precipitated the challenge to *Theophanous v Herald & Weekly Times Ltd* (1994) 182 CLR 104 in *Lange*.

In *Levy*, the High Court considered the validity of Victorian regulations made under the Wildlife Act 1975 (Vic) and the Conservation, Forests and Lands Act 1987 (Vic). Regulation 5(1) of the Wildlife (Game) (Hunting Season) Regulations 1994 (Vic) provided that a person must not enter into or upon any permitted hunting area at certain specified times. Regulation 5(2) exempted holders of a valid game licence. The plaintiff, Laurie Levy, was a prominent member of the anti duck-shooting lobby and regularly engaged in public protests against duck-shooting. The aim of such protests was to attract widespread media coverage by providing images of ducks injured and killed by duck-shooting and thus communicate a political message of protest. Levy entered upon land in violation of the regulations and was accordingly charged with offences under reg 5.

In his defence, Levy argued that his activities were protected by the implied freedom of communication as stated in *Australian Capital Television Pty Ltd v Commonwealth* (1992) 177 CLR 106 **[11.3.7C]** and that reg 5 was invalid. Mr Levy further argued that Regulation 5 infringed an equivalent implication in the Victorian Constitution in relation to communication on government and political matters.

The High Court was unanimous in rejecting the challenge. Although reg 5 placed a burden upon communication protected by the Commonwealth Constitution, the burden was reasonably appropriate and adapted to serve a legitimate end, which was compatible with the maintenance of the prescribed system of government contained in the Constitution, namely public safety. Five members of the court, Dawson J, Toohey and Gummow JJ, McHugh J, and Kirby J, explicitly adopted the test for invalidity articulated in *Lange v Australian Broadcasting Corporation* (1997) 189 CLR 520 **[11.3.3C]** and **[11.3.13C]**: Dawson J, 189 CLR at 609; Toohey and Gummow JJ, 189 CLR at 610; McHugh J, 189 CLR at 622; Kirby J, 189 CLR at 643. In separate judgments, the other two justices adopted tests similar to *Lange* but relied on other precedents. Brennan CJ referred to *Davis v Commonwealth* (1988) 166 CLR 75 **[11.3.6]** (189 CLR at 594); and Gaudron J referred to her formulation of principles in *Kruger v Commonwealth* (1997) 190 CLR 1 **[11.3.32C]** (189 CLR at 619).

All members of the court said it was unnecessary to decide whether the Victorian Constitution contained a similar implication in relation to freedom of communication on political matters, because, on the basis of the *Lange* test, the regulation was reasonable in any event.

Members of the court also raised the issue of whether the implied freedom of communication on political and government matters extended to non-verbal activity. The plaintiffs in the present case were not seeking to protect their verbal speech rights, but rather their physical behaviour in conducting the protest. A majority of the court said that the implication contained in the Commonwealth Constitution protected non-verbal, as well as verbal, forms of communication: 189 CLR at 594–5 per Brennan CJ; 189 CLR at 613 per Toohey and Gummow JJ; 189 CLR at 622–3 per

McHugh J; 189 CLR at 641 per Kirby J. Kirby J referred to United States authorities and said at 641:

> I have mentioned these cases from the United States, although the constitutional setting is different, to illustrate a number of points. The decisions recognise that political communication may be (and often is) expressed in non-verbal ways. Political protest as well as the more general communication of facts and opinions may occur otherwise than by words. This is as true in Australia as in the United States. Therefore, the constitutionally protected freedom of communication on political and governmental matters in Australia extends to non-verbal conduct as well as to things said and written.

McHugh J said that the implication protected not only rational speech, but extended to 'false, unreasoned and emotional communications': 189 CLR at 623.

[11.3.15] The relationship between the implied freedom and the constitutional requirement in s 24 that parliament be 'directly chosen by the people' was raised in *Langer v Commonwealth* (1996) 186 CLR 302 **[4.6.15C]**, where the plaintiff challenged the validity of s 329A of the Commonwealth Electoral Act 1918 (Cth). Section 329A prohibited publication and distribution of material which encouraged voters to indicate their preference for candidates otherwise than in accordance with the requirements of s 240 of the Act, which required voters to state a preference as between every candidate for election. Sections 268(1)(c) and 270(2) of the Act permitted certain votes to be treated as valid, even though those votes did not indicate a preference as between all the candidates.

The plaintiff, who wished to publish material encouraging voters to mark their ballot papers so as to take advantage of ss 268(1)(c) and 270(2), argued that the prohibition in s 329A upon the dissemination of material encouraging voters *not* to indicate a preference for each candidate in an election infringed the requirement in s 24 of the Constitution that members of the House of Representatives be directly chosen by the people. All members of the High Court rejected that argument, and some justices commented upon the relevance of the implied freedom of communication to the plaintiff's argument.

Brennan CJ said that, so long as a legislative measure was appropriate and adapted to a legitimate legislative purpose, it would be valid, regardless of any impairment of the implied freedom: 186 CLR 317. Here, the Act did not prohibit discussion about the method of voting, or its repeal (186 CLR 318) and the restriction on freedom of speech was imposed as 'an incident to the protection of the method of voting': 186 CLR 318. Therefore, the provision was not invalid for infringing the implied freedom. Brennan CJ said that the result may have been different if the legislation had provided for an alternative method of voting because the prohibition in s 329A would then have precluded the encouragement of voting by an alternative method: 186 CLR 318.

McHugh J said s 329A was valid because there was a 'world of difference between prohibiting advocacy that is put forward with the intention of encouraging breaches of statutory directions and prohibiting advocacy that criticises or calls for the repeal of such directions': 186 CLR at 340. Moreover, s 24 was not in the form of a personal right: 186 CLR at 341. Gummow J delivered a judgment to the same effect as McHugh J.

Toohey and Gaudron JJ largely agreed with Brennan CJ that the implied freedom was not breached because s 329A was capable of being viewed as appropriate and adapted to furthering the democratic process.

Dawson J was the sole dissentient. Consistent with his earlier views, he said that the freedom only protected speech to the extent 'necessary for the conduct of elections by direct popular vote' (186 CLR at 324), but that the voters' choice of candidates must be a 'genuine, or informed' one, involving 'access on the part of the voter to the available alternatives in the making of the choice': 186 CLR at 324. Section 329A infringed even this narrow conception of the implied freedom, because the general scheme of the legislation only established an *optional* preferential voting system. Further, s 329A prohibited voters from access to information that the voting system was optional preferential and so 'restrict the access of voters to information essential to the formation of the choice required by s 24': 186 CLR 325.

[11.3.16C]   **Roberts v Bass**

(2002) 212 CLR 1

Roberts and Case, electors in a state electorate in South Australia, authorised publication of materials intended to persuade electors not to vote for Bass, the elected member in that electorate. The materials were published during the 1997 state election campaign, and suggested that Bass had corruptly used his position to obtain a holiday and frequent flyer points for his own benefit and had neglected his constituents. Roberts was also responsible for a how-to-vote card, which contained unsubstantiated allegations regarding Bass' past and future performance as a member of parliament.

When sued for defamation by Bass, Roberts and Case raised the common law defence of 'qualified privilege', available where a person has a duty or interest in making a statement and the recipient of the statement has a corresponding duty or interest in receiving it. The trial judge found that the publications were defamatory and were not protected by the defence of qualified privilege because the conduct of Roberts and Case in publishing the defamatory material was not reasonable. The Full Court of the Supreme Court of South Australia dismissed an appeal by Roberts and Case; and the High Court granted them special leave to appeal.

Gaudron, McHugh and Gummow JJ: [The justices noted that the common law protected a defamatory statement made on an occasion where one person has a duty or interest to make the statement and the recipient of the statement has a corresponding duty or interest to receive it. 'Communications made on such occasions are privileged because their making promotes the welfare of society. But the privilege is qualified — hence the name qualified privilege — by the condition that the occasion must not be used for some purpose or motive foreign to the duty or interest that protects the making of the statement': 212 CLR at 26.]

[26] *Freedom of communication and the Constitution*

In *Lange*, the Court unanimously held that freedom of communication on matters of government and politics is an indispensable incident of the system of representative government created by the Constitution. The Court emphasised that '[c]ommunications concerning political or government matters between the electors and the elected representatives, between the electors and the candidates for election and between the electors themselves were central to the system of representative government, as it was understood at federation'. Hence, this litigation is concerned with matters at the heart of the constitutional freedom of communication respecting political or government matters.

In *Lange*, the Court pointed out that, although the constitutional freedom confers no rights on individuals, it invalidates any statutory rule that is inconsistent with the freedom. It also requires that the rules of the common law conform with the Constitution, for 'the common [27] law in Australia cannot run counter to constitutional imperatives'. It is necessary therefore to determine the extent to which, if at all, the common law rules concerning the traditional defence of qualified privilege applicable in this case are consistent with the constitutional freedom of communication.

In determining whether a rule of the common law is consistent with the constitutional freedom of communication, two questions have to be answered. First, does the rule effectively burden the freedom? Second, if so, is the rule reasonably appropriate and adapted to serve a legitimate end compatible with the constitutionally prescribed system of representative and responsible government? If the answer to the second question is 'no', the common law rule must yield to the constitutional norm, for the common law's impact on the freedom cannot be greater than that permitted by the constitutional norm.

In *Lange*, the Court held that the law of defamation effectively burdened the constitutional freedom and that the law of qualified privilege, as traditionally understood, did not qualify that burden in a way that was consistent with the freedom in respect of governmental and political matters published to the general public. The publication complained of in *Lange* concerned a television programme broadcast across Australia. Under the common law as previously understood, the law of qualified privilege did not generally recognise an interest or duty to publish defamatory matter to the general public. Hence, without that privilege, the common law imposed an unreasonable restraint upon the constitutional freedom. That necessitated the development of the common law as expounded in the balance of the judgment of the Court.

Three points in particular should be noted concerning the development of the defence of qualified privilege in *Lange*. First, in extending the law of qualified privilege to protect publications concerning governmental and political matters to mass audiences, the Court imposed as a condition of the extended privilege that the publisher's conduct be reasonable. But the Court emphasised:

> ... reasonableness of conduct is imported as an element only when the extended category of qualified privilege is invoked to protect a publication that would otherwise be held to have been made to too [28] wide an audience. For example, reasonableness of conduct is not an element of that qualified privilege which protects a member of the public who makes a complaint to a Minister concerning the administration of his or her department. Reasonableness of conduct is an element for the judge to consider only when a publication concerning a government or political matter is made in circumstances that, under the English common law, would have failed to attract a defence of qualified privilege.

Second, in *Lange*, the Court held that, having regard to the subject matters of government and politics, the motive of causing political damage to the plaintiff or his or her party is not an improper motive that would destroy a defence of qualified privilege. The Court also held that the vigour of an attack or the pungency of a defamatory statement concerning such matters cannot, without more, discharge the plaintiff's onus on the issue of malice. Third, in some respects the Court's development of the law of qualified privilege extended beyond what was required for conformity with the constitutional norm.

The present case concerns publications relating to the record and policies of a candidate for election to State Parliament for the seat of Florey. They were directed to, and generally received by, a limited class of persons — the electors in the seat of Florey. As will appear, the traditional common law defence of qualified privilege protects such publications because the reciprocity of interest required for the traditional defence is present. As will also appear, given the decision in *Lange*, that privilege will not be lost because the publisher intends to cause political damage to the candidate or his or her party. Nor will the privilege be lost merely because of the vigour of an attack on a candidate for election to Parliament that is contained in a defamatory statement concerning the record and policies of the candidate. Without more, the vigour of the attack is not evidence of improper motive ... the privilege will be lost only if it is used for a purpose other than that for which it is granted — in this case, the communicating of information, arguments, facts and opinions concerning Bass and his policies to the electors of Florey. Thus, although the common law rules of defamation make defamatory statements concerning a candidate for election actionable and impose a burden on an elector's freedom of communication, those rules also protect an elector who uses the occasion for the purpose that gives rise to the constitutional freedom. Hence the burden does not affect what is required to give effect to the constitutional freedom.

Accordingly, the second of the two questions posed in *Lange* is answered by saying that, in the present case, the common law rules governing traditional qualified privilege are reasonably appropriate and [29] adapted to serve a legitimate end compatible with the constitutionally prescribed system of representative and responsible government ...

[29] It is a serious mistake to think that *Lange* exhaustively defined the constitutional freedom's impact on the law of defamation. *Lange* dealt with publications to the general public by the general media concerning 'government and political matters'. It was not concerned with statements made by electors or candidates or those working for a candidate, during an election, to electors in a State [30] electorate, concerning the record and suitability of a candidate for election to a State Parliament. Such statements are at the heart of the freedom of communication protected by the Constitution. They are published to a comparatively small audience, most of whom have an immediate and direct interest in receiving information, arguments, facts and opinions concerning the candidates and their policies. In that context and constitutional framework, the application of traditional qualified privilege requires a holding that qualified privilege attaches to statements by electors, candidates and their helpers published to the electors of a State electorate on matters relevant to the record and suitability of candidates for the election ...

Roberts and Case, if held to their cases in the Full Court, will retain the advantage of a finding of qualified privilege. And they are entitled to rely on the impact that the constitutional freedom of communication has on the law of malice in respect of publications concerning political matters that are protected by conventional qualified privilege. As we have pointed out, intentionally causing political damage to the plaintiff or his or her party is not an improper motive where a statement on political matters is protected by conventional qualified privilege. Nor can the vigour of an attack or the pungency of a defamatory statement, without more, be evidence of improper motive in respect of such a statement (references omitted).

Gaudron, McHugh and Gummow JJ said that it was necessary for Bass to prove that Roberts and Case had acted dishonestly by not using the occasion of qualified privilege for its proper purpose (here, a proper purpose would include communicating legitimate information that would affect an elector's interest in electing Bass). The justices expressed the opinion that, even if the false frequent flyer statement contained no defamatory imputations, it supplied evidence of Roberts' intention to fabricate material that would justify defamatory statements, suggesting that he had not used the occasion of qualified privilege for a proper purpose: 212 CLR at 31–3.

As far as the other material was concerned, Roberts had jumped to the conclusion that Bass had obtained a holiday for his own benefit on the basis of inadequate material and had behaved irrationally. But his behaviour was typical in political discussions and could not be characterised as malicious. If Roberts' conduct was sufficient to destroy the privilege of communicating electoral material to voters, 'the freedom of communication protected by the Constitution would be little more than a grand idea of no practical importance': 212 CLR at 38–9.

The justices said that Case's failure to inquire into the truthfulness of the claims made in the how-to-vote card did not constitute malice.

Accordingly, the appeals were allowed and judgment was entered in favour of Case and a new trial of the action against Roberts was ordered to test whether Roberts had used the occasion of qualified privilege for an improper purpose.

Justice Kirby agreed with the order proposed in the joint reasons and said that he had 'reached a conclusion very similar to that in the joint reasons and generally on like grounds': 212 CLR at 70.

~~~

The limits of 'representative government' as a source of implied freedoms

[11.3.17C] **McGinty v Western Australia**

(1996) 186 CLR 140

The plaintiffs, who were members of the state Legislative Assembly and Council, claimed that aspects of the scheme established by Western Australian legislation for distributing seats in the two houses of the state's parliament offended the principle of representative democracy that was implicit in the Commonwealth Constitution and the constitution of the state, because that legislation denied equality of voting power.

The electoral distribution was effected under the Constitution Acts Amendment Act 1899 (WA) (the 1899 Act) and the Electoral Districts Act 1947 (WA) (the 1947 Act), as amended by the Acts Amendment (Electoral Reform) Act 1987 (WA) (the 1987 Act). The electoral distribution for the Legislative Assembly provided for the state to be divided into two areas: the metropolitan area which contained 34 electoral districts, and the remaining area containing 23 electoral districts. Boundaries were fixed by the electoral commissioner, allowing for an equal quotient of electors plus or minus 15 per cent.

In 1987, the 669,293 voters enrolled in the metropolitan area elected 34 members, and the 240,081 voters enrolled in the remainder of the state elected 23 members. Consequently, at the 1993 election the electorate of Wanneroo, the most populous electorate in the metropolitan area, had 26,580 voters, and Ashburton, the least populous electorate in the remainder of the state, had 9135 voters. Similar discrepancies existed in relation to the Legislative Council, with the number of voters in one region being 376 per cent of the number of voters in another region.

A majority of the High Court (Brennan CJ, Dawson, McHugh and Gummow JJ; Toohey and Gaudron JJ dissenting) held that the implication of representative democracy contained in the Commonwealth Constitution did not extend to any requirement of equality of voting power in state elections. Similarly, although the Western Australian Constitution contained an implication of representative democracy, it did not impose any requirement that electoral divisions contain an equal number of electors. In separate opinions, the minority justices, Toohey and Gaudron JJ, held that any election which took place under the existing Western Australian electoral legislation would infringe that state's constitutional requirement that members of the parliament be directly chosen by the people. However, while Toohey J said that any such election would fail to accord with the Western Australian Constitution's general principle of representative democracy (expressed by the words 'directly chosen by the people'), Gaudron J based her decision upon the specific words of the Western Australian Constitution which required members of parliament to be directly chosen by the people.

Brennan CJ: [Brennan CJ discussed changes to the franchise, and considered '[t]he question [of] whether differences in voting power can be justified by distinctions based on political opinion, minority interests or geographical residence', a question which did 'not admit of a definitive answer': 186 CLR at 168. The Chief Justice then considered the method by which constitutional implications should be drawn.]

[168] [I]t is unnecessary and, for reasons presently to be stated, impermissible to determine the validity of the 1987 Act by reference to its consistency with the requirements of a general principle of representative democracy ...

Implications are not devised by the judiciary; they exist in the text and structure of the Constitution and are revealed or uncovered by judicial exegesis. No implication can be drawn from the Constitution which is not based on the actual terms of the Constitution, or on its structure. [*Amalgamated Society of Engineers v Adelaide Steamship Co Ltd* ('the *Engineers Case*') (1920) 28 CLR 129 at 145, 155]. ...

[169] It is logically impermissible to treat 'representative democracy' as though it were contained in the Constitution, to attribute to the term a meaning or content derived from sources extrinsic to the Constitution and then to invalidate a law for inconsistency with the meaning or content so attributed. ...

[170] Unaffected by context, the phrase 'chosen by the people' admits of different meanings. It might connote that candidates are chosen by popular direct election as distinct from election by an electoral college; or it might connote some requirement of equality or near equality of voting power among those who hold the franchise; or it might go further and import some requirement of a franchise that is held generally by all adults or all adult citizens unless there be substantial reasons for excluding them. Equally, these meanings might be attributed to the notion of 'representative democracy'. ...

[171] A submission that equality of voting power in State as well as in Federal elections is implied in the Constitution is not advanced by an appeal to the principle of representative democracy if reference to the text and structure of the Constitution fails to reveal an implication of that kind. However, if there be such an implication, an inconsistent State law would be invalid.

Brennan CJ discussed the relationship between the Commonwealth and state constitutions. His Honour continued:

[173] The Constitutions of the several States are, by force of s 106, subject to the Commonwealth Constitution, the provisions of which may be either expressed in its text or implied in its text and structure. There is no relevant reference in the Commonwealth Constitution to the distribution of the franchise in elections for State Parliaments. ...

[175] Assuming, without deciding, that the provisions of the Commonwealth Constitution impliedly preclude electoral distributions that would produce disparities of voting power — of whatever magnitude — among those who hold the Commonwealth franchise in a State, what do those provisions have to say with respect to the Constitutions and laws of the several States governing electoral distributions for State elections? In my opinion, the Commonwealth Constitution contains no implication affecting disparities of voting power among the holders of the franchise for the election of members of a State Parliament (hereafter 'State disparities'). Far from containing an implication affecting State disparities, the text of Pts II and III of Ch I of the Commonwealth Constitution and the structure of the Constitution as a whole are inconsistent with such an implication. Sections 7, 8, 9 and 10 of the Constitution are expressed to relate only to elections for the Senate; ss 24, 25, 29 and 30 are expressed to relate only to elections for the House of Representatives; and s 41 is expressed to relate only to elections for either House of the Parliament of the Commonwealth. Not only are these sections expressly confined to elections for one or other House of the Commonwealth Parliament but they are all contained in Ch I of the Constitution which, being followed by Chs II and III, define the structure of the Commonwealth's three branches of government. Chapter V is the Chapter relating to the States and their Constitutions. The structure of the Constitution is opposed to the notion that the provisions of Ch I might affect the Constitutions of the States to which Ch V is directed.

... [A]s the principle of representative democracy applies only to the process of electing members to either House of the Parliament of the Commonwealth and as the only provisions of the Commonwealth Constitution that are advanced as capable of affecting the State Constitutions relate to [176] Federal elections, the submission fails ...

Brennan CJ then explored the issue whether the Western Australian Constitution contained any requirement of equality of voting power. He referred to provisions of the Constitution Act which entrenched the requirement that members of the parliament be 'directly chosen by the people', and quoted his own comments, in *Stephens v West Australian Newspapers Ltd* (1994) 182 CLR 211 **[11.3.12]**, that s 73(2)(c) of the Constitution Act:

... entrenches in the Constitution Act the requirement that the Legislative Council and the Legislative Assembly be composed of members chosen directly by the people. This requirement is drawn in terms similar to those found in ss 7 and 24 of the Commonwealth Constitution from which the implication that effects a constitutional freedom to discuss government, governmental institutions and political matters is substantially derived. By parity of reasoning, a similar implication can be drawn from the Constitution Act with respect to the system of government of Western Australia therein prescribed.

The 'system of government' referred to is a Legislature 'chosen directly by the people'. It is one thing to hold that that prescription [177] carries the implication in both the Commonwealth Constitution and the Constitution of Western Australia that 'the people' be free to discuss the matters that they need to discuss in order to choose their representatives; it is another thing to hold that the phrase implies that there be an equality of voting power. Whatever the phrase may prescribe in the Commonwealth Constitution in relation to the equality of voting power, its significance and effect in the Constitution of Western Australia must be ascertained from its context and the circumstances in which s 73(2)(c) was enacted.

Brennan CJ identified the context in which s 73(2)(c) was enacted; namely: the Western Australian electoral laws which 'authorised and perhaps required a disparity in voting power in respect of both elections for the Council and elections for the Assembly' (186 CLR at 177–8); the history of division of electorates with unequal voting power; and the legislative history surrounding the enactment of s 73(2). He concluded that the only requirement contained in the principle of representative democracy in the Western Australian Constitution was for election by direct popular vote, and continued:

[178] To find in s 73(2)(c) an implication that electoral power be equally distributed among the people of the State or among the people of the State possessing the franchise would be to find a legislative intention destructive of the means by which the enacting Parliament was elected.

Dawson J: [Dawson J said that the notion of representative democracy established by the Commonwealth Constitution did not extend to a requirement for equality of voting power at state level. If such a requirement existed it would only apply in respect of federal elections: 186 CLR at 189. Representative democracy had variable forms which did not demand any particular electoral system (186 CLR at 182); and the history of the colonies demonstrated that there had been no insistence upon equality of voting power: 186 CLR at 183. Dawson J referred to the Canadian authorities which held that a similar requirement in relation to representative democracy in the Canadian Charter of Rights and Freedoms was not an absolute guarantee of equality of voting power, but a requirement that representation be 'effective' (186 CLR at 186), and continued:]

[189] It is true that in *McKinlay*, McTiernan and Jacobs JJ [*McKinlay* (1975) 135 CLR 1 at 36–37] suggested that the notion of equality is to some extent present in the words 'chosen by the people' so that at some point electoral inequality might be inconsistent with a choice by the people. They rejected, however, any requirement of absolute equality or nearly as practicable equality. Similarly, Mason J said: [*McKinlay* (1975) 135 CLR 1 at 61]

> It is perhaps conceivable that variations in the numbers of electors or people in single member electorates could become so grossly disproportionate as to raise a question whether an election held on boundaries so drawn would produce a House of Representatives composed of members directly chosen by the people of the Commonwealth, but this is a matter quite removed from the proposition that s 24 insists upon a practical equality of people or electors in single member electorates.

In my view, both McTiernan and Jacobs JJ and Mason J had in mind extreme situations markedly different from that which exists under the relevant Western Australian legislation.

Dawson J concluded by expressing his agreement with the Chief Justice that the system of representative government provided for in Chapter I of the Commonwealth Constitution did not extend to the states and that the meaning of the words of the WA Constitution do not contain any implication of electoral equality: 186 CLR at 189–90.

McHugh J: [226] The scheme set up by the two Acts arbitrarily distinguishes between metropolitan and non-metropolitan voters. On no rational basis can the special needs of [227] electors in areas outside the non-metropolitan areas justify such large disparities as exist between particular electoral districts and regions. It is unnecessary, however, for me to develop these points because, contrary to the plaintiffs' submissions, I am of the opinion that neither the Constitution nor the Western Australian Constitution contains any requirement that the number of voters in electoral districts should be equal or equal so far as is reasonably practicable.

McHugh J rejected United States authorities on the meaning of s 24 (186 CLR at 229), and continued:

[231] The ordinary principles of statutory interpretation require that the text be the starting point of any interpretation of the Constitution. Part of the ordinary and natural meaning of the text is any implication which is 'manifested according to the accepted principles of interpretation'. [*Australian Capital Television Pty Ltd* (1992) 177 CLR 106 at 135, per Mason CJ] Implications derived from the structure of the Constitution are also part of the Constitution's meaning but such implications may be drawn only when they are 'logically or practically necessary for the preservation of the integrity of that structure'. [*Australian Capital Television Pty Ltd* (1992) 177 CLR 106 at 135, per Mason CJ] Thus, because the Constitution has prescribed a system for elections to the Houses of the Federal Parliament, no Australian government can pass laws which would undermine the efficacy of that system. [*Australian Capital Television Pty Ltd* (1992) 177 CLR 106] However, I cannot accept, as Deane and Toohey JJ held in *Nationwide News Pty Ltd v Wills*, [(1992) 177 CLR 1 at 70] that a constitutional implication can arise from a particular doctrine that 'underlies the Constitution'. Underlying or overarching doctrines may explain or illuminate the meaning of the text or structure of the [232] Constitution but such doctrines are not independent sources of the powers, authorities, immunities and obligations conferred by the Constitution. Top-down reasoning is not a legitimate method of interpreting the Constitution. As I pointed out in *Theophanous v Herald and Weekly Times Ltd*, [(1994) 182 CLR 104 at 198] after the decision of this court in the *Engineers'* case, [*Amalgamated Society of Engineers v Adelaide Steamship Co Ltd* (1920) 28 CLR 129] the court had consistently held, prior to *Nationwide News and Australian Capital Television Pty Ltd v The Commonwealth*, [(1992) 177 CLR 106] that it is not legitimate to construe the Constitution by reference to political principles or theories that are not anchored in the text of the Constitution or are not necessary implications from its structure. I pointed out that the *Engineers'* case had made it plain that the Constitution was not to be interpreted by using such theories to control or modify the meaning of the Constitution unless those theories could be deduced from the terms or structure of the Constitution itself. It is the text and the implications to be drawn from the text and structure that contain the meaning of the Constitution. With all due respect to the judges of this court who have held that there is a free-standing principle of representative democracy in the Constitution, their conclusion necessarily involves a rejection of the principles of interpretation laid down in the *Engineers'* case although perhaps not the philosophy that lies behind that decision. ...

[233] Prior to the series of cases which commence with *Nationwide News* in 1992, implications drawn from the Constitution were seen as either conferring power on the Commonwealth or as restraining the exercise of power by the Commonwealth or the States. ...

[T]he implication seems to have taken on another dimension, if it has not changed dramatically; for in those cases, the court has held that the implied principle is not only a restraint on federal and State legislative power but it changes common law rights and duties. That would seem to mean that the Constitution [234] directly changes the rights and duties of individuals. ...

The result seems to be that the Constitution contains by implication a principle of representative democracy that is not confined to restricting the powers of the federal or State legislatures, nor does it necessarily confer any rights on individuals. It appears to be a free-standing principle, just as if the Constitution contained a Ch IX with a s 129 which read:

Subject to this Constitution, representative democracy is the law of Australia, notwithstanding any law to the contrary.

That does not mean, of course, that the implied principle of representative democracy trumps all other rights and obligations. Because the principle arises by implication, it must be subject to the express terms of the Constitution and be weighed in appropriate cases against other implications drawn from the text and structure of the Constitution. Nevertheless, when it is seen as the equivalent of the hypothetical s 129, it is plain that it is not an implication contained in the text of the Constitution, nor is it an implication 'logically or practically necessary for the preservation of the integrity of [the] structure' of the Constitution. [*Australian Capital Television Pty Ltd* (1992) 177 CLR 106 at 135, per Mason CJ] The 'implication' has become a premise from which other implications are drawn. Thus, in *Theophanous* and *Stephens* the majority held that the preservation of representative democracy required that the common law of defamation should be restricted in its application to federal and State politicians and certain other persons. By that stage the text and structure of the Constitution have receded into the background and it is the concept of representative democracy, not the text or structure of the Constitution, that governs the application of the Constitution in such cases. ...

[235] I regard the reasoning in *Nationwide News, Australian Capital Television, Theophanous* and *Stephens* in so far as it invokes an implied principle of representative democracy as fundamentally wrong [236] and as an alteration of the Constitution without the authority of the people under s 128 of the Constitution. Moreover, as much as I admire the noble vision of the justices who have found, contrary to what the overwhelming majority of lawyers had always thought, that the Constitution contains a free-standing principle of representative democracy, the principles of constitutional interpretation compel me to reject their reasoning ... .

To decide cases by reference to what the principles of representative democracy currently require is to give this court a jurisdiction which the Constitution does not contemplate and which the Australian people have never authorised. Interpreting the Constitution is a difficult task at any time. It is not made easier by asking the justices of this court to determine what representative democracy requires. That is a political question and, unless the Constitution turns it into a constitutional question for the judiciary, it should be left to be answered by the people and their elected representatives acting within the limits of their powers as prescribed by the Constitution.

However, even if, contrary to my view, the Constitution contains a free-standing principle of representative democracy, other provisions of the Constitution show that, whatever the content of representative democracy may be in the last decade of the twentieth century, the Constitution does not require an equal number of electors in electoral divisions ...

McHugh J said that various provisions indicated that inequality, not equality, of individual voting power was one of the Constitution's 'striking features': 186 CLR at 236. Moreover, Australian referanda have not supported the principle of 'one vote-one value' and nor have the Canadian authorities: 186 CLR at 246.

[251] In my opinion, once it is held that the system of representative government set up by the Constitution does not require equal representation for equal divisions in federal elections, it must follow that the Constitution imposes no such obligation in State elections. It follows that the plaintiffs' claim based on the Constitution must be rejected.

On the question whether the Western Australian Constitution included representative democracy to the extent that it required equality of voting power, McHugh J expressed broad agreement with Brennan CJ. Referring to context, history, legislative history and the decision in *Attorney-General (Cth) (Ex rel McKinlay) v Commonwealth* (1975) 135 CLR 1, McHugh J concluded that no such implication could be made.

[254] Once that conclusion is reached, the existence of any implied principle of representative democracy in the Western Australian Constitution is irrelevant ...

Toohey J: [200] The Constitution must be construed as a living force [*Theophanous* (1994) 182 CLR 104 at 173 per Deane J] and the court must take account of political, social and economic developments since that time ...

Toohey J referred to the court's adaptation of the connotation–denotation doctrine to infer that, in order for a jury to be 'representative', it would have to include women: 186 CLR at 201.

[201] The point is that, while the essence of representative democracy remains unchanged, the method of giving expression to the concept varies over time and according to changes in society. It is the current perception which is embodied in the Australian Constitution ...

Toohey J noted that, although inequality of voting power was tolerated at federation, current state legislation indicated this was no longer the case: 186 CLR at 202.

[201] This move towards equality of electorate size reflects a change in society's perception of the appropriate expression of the concept of representative democracy ...

Toohey J distinguished *Attorney-General (Cth) (Ex rel McKinlay) v Commonwealth* (1975) 135 CLR 1 on the grounds that it decided only that s 24, rather than the principle of representative democracy, did not import a requirement of equality of voting power: 186 CLR at 205. Toohey J said that the equality of voting power implied in the Commonwealth Constitution did not extend to the state because the conduct of state elections does not 'undermine Commonwealth elections': 186 CLR at 210. However, Toohey J said, the Western Australian constitution included a principle of representative democracy similar to that contained in the Commonwealth Constitution. He concluded that the means chosen to facilitate representation in thinly populated areas were not proportionate because they arbitrarily distinguished between metropolitan and non-metropolitan areas: 186 CLR at 215.

[216] The view I take of representative democracy as found in the Constitution of Western Australia is that it is not a fixed concept but rather is responsive to the time and circumstances in which it falls for consideration. Therefore, rather than answer the questions as asked, it is appropriate to say no more than that if an election were now held for the Legislative Assembly or Legislative Council in accordance with the impugned statutory provisions, the members would not be chosen by the people in accordance with the constitutional dictates of representative democracy.

Gaudron J: [Gaudron J substantially agreed with Toohey J, except that she relied on the words 'directly chosen by the people' contained in s 73(2) of the Western Australian Constitution Act, rather than a principle of representative democracy, to support her conclusion that an election held under the existing Western Australian electoral legislation would offend the requirement of equality of voting power (186 CLR at 216); and she did not distinguish *Attorney-General (Cth) (Ex rel McKinlay) v Commonwealth* (1975) 135 CLR 1. Gaudron J agreed with Toohey J that the implication of equality of voting power derived from the Commonwealth Constitution could not affect the position in respect to state elections: 186 CLR at 216. Her Honour continued:]

[219] *McKinlay* ... is not authority for the proposition that the Constitution provides general authority for continuing significant malapportionment between electorates. Rather and save for Barwick CJ and Gibbs J, the justices who constituted the majority in that case appear to have accepted that inequalities might be of such magnitude that, at some point, members of the House of Representatives might not be 'chosen by the people' or, in the case of Stephen J, the requirements of representative democracy might not be satisfied. [*McKinlay* (1975) 135 CLR 1 at 57, 61, 69]

[220] [T]he expression 'chosen by the people' must be seen as mandating a democratic electoral system and not as requiring a particular electoral system or that it have some particular feature ...

[221] These considerations necessitate that the content and application of the words 'chosen by the people' be determined in the light of developments in democratic standards and not by reference to circumstances as they existed at federation, with the consequence, as McTiernan and Jacobs JJ acknowledged in *McKinlay*, [(1975) 135 CLR 1 at 36] that what was permitted by s 24 at one time may not be permitted at another.

Gaudron J noted changes in the meaning of the franchise, and said:

[222] Similarly, the fact that the Constitution countenanced disparity in voting value at the time of federation provides no basis for a conclusion that significant disparity in the numbers of electors in single member electorates does not now offend s 24.

It does not follow from what has been said that s 24 requires complete or even practical equality of electorate size. A distinction which is reasonably capable of being viewed as an appropriate and adapted means of taking account of geographic boundaries, community or minority interests or some other matter which bears on effective parliamentary representation, such as the dispersed nature of the population in remote areas, would not, in my view, prevent it being said that members of the House of Representatives were 'chosen by the people'. However, subject to that consideration and the requirements of the Constitution which necessitate or which may necessitate inequality by reason of population differences between the States, persons elected under a system involving significant disparity in voting value, could not, in my view, now be described as 'chosen by the people'. To so describe them would be contrary to current democratic standards reflected in the electoral laws of the Commonwealth and, putting Western Australia to one side, the electoral laws of the States referred to in the judgment of Toohey J.

Gaudron J said that the words 'chosen by the people' in the Western Australian Constitution should carry the same meaning as the same words in the Commonwealth Constitution:

[223] … In my view, the malapportionment which is detailed in the judgment of Toohey J is so great as to be distinctly at odds with democratic standards revealed in the electoral laws of the Commonwealth and the other Australian States referred to in his Honour's judgment. Moreover, the distinction between metropolitan and non-metropolitan areas is, as his Honour points out, arbitrary and inflexible and, that being so, it cannot be justified on the basis that it is reasonably capable of being seen as appropriate and adapted to the dispersed nature of the population in the remote regions of Western Australia or to any other matter or circumstance which might bear on effective parliamentary representation. …

[224] [I]f elections were now held, neither the members of the Legislative Council nor those of the Legislative Assembly would be 'chosen … by the people' within the meaning of those words in s 73(2)(c) of the 1889 Act. This is a minority view and it is, thus, unnecessary to consider what, if any, further relief is required by the answer I propose.

Gummow J delivered a judgment to the same effect as other members of the majority. In addition, he said that representative democracy existed only to the extent that it was adapted to the requirements of federalism (186 CLR at 269–4), and that the judiciary must defer to parliament's assessment of its content: 186 CLR 288. In relation to the states he said that different geographic and demographic factors applied at state and national level; and that, in any case, the states were not bound by an evolving notion of representative government: 186 CLR at 293. On the question of constitutional interpretation he labelled equality of voting power a 'secondary level implication' (186 CLR at 291), and said that the nature of deriving the implication departed from previously accepted methods of constitutional interpretation: 186 CLR at 291.

~~~

Notes

[11.3.18] The limits of the High Court's capacity to develop implied freedoms and personal rights from the system of representative government created by the Constitution were confirmed in *McGinty v Western Australia* (1996) 186 CLR 140 [11.3.16C], *Langer v Commonwealth* (1996) 186 CLR 302 [11.3.15] and *Lange v Australian Broadcasting Corporation* (1997) 189 CLR 520 [11.3.13C]. In *Lange*, the High Court said at 566–7:

Constitutional text and structure

Since *McGinty* it has been clear, if it was not clear before, that the Constitution gives effect to the institution of 'representative government' only to the extent that the text and structure of the Constitution establish it. In other words, to say that the Constitution gives effect to representative government is a shorthand way of saying that the Constitution provides for that form of representative government which is to be found in the relevant sections. Under the Constitution, the relevant question is not, 'What is required by representative and responsible government?' It is, 'What do the terms and structure of the Constitution prohibit, authorise or require?'

In *McGinty* **[11.3.16C]**, Gummow J pointed out that to draw implications from a 'doctrine of representative democracy' was to 'adopt a category of indeterminate reference': 186 CLR at 269. Critical to the conclusion, that no implication of 'one vote-one value' could be drawn from the Constitution, was the fact that ss 7, 10, 22, 24, 29, 30, 31, 34, 39, 46, 47 and 48 gave the parliament considerable legislative discretion as to the form of representative government. As Gummow J explained at 280:

> ... the recurrent phrase 'until the Parliament otherwise provides' [in those sections] has a deeper significance. Its effect is to accommodate the notion that representative government is a dynamic rather than a static institution.

In *Langer v Commonwealth* (1996) 186 CLR 302 **[11.3.15]**, a majority of the court decided that the Federal Parliament's constitutional power to regulate elections as part of the system of representative government enabled it to authorise the jailing of a person who encouraged people to vote in a way that would frustrate the two-party system.

Freedom of movement and freedom of association

[11.3.19] In *Australian Capital Television Pty Ltd v Commonwealth* (1992) 177 CLR 106 **[11.3.7C]**, Gaudron J said that representative democracy 'may entail freedom of movement, [and] freedom of association': (1992) 177 CLR 106 at 212. In the same case, McHugh J said that the process of directly choosing representatives included the right to participate and associate: 177 CLR at 232. People in Australia may enjoy a freedom of association and travel associated with the election of Federal representatives and associated activities: *Kruger v The Commonwealth* (1997) 190 CLR 1 at 115–16 (Gaudron J), 142 (McHugh J). As Gaudron J noted in *Kruger* at 115:

> ... just as communication would be impossible if 'each person was an island', so too it is substantially impeded if citizens are held in enclaves, no matter how large the enclave or congenial its composition. Freedom of political communication depends on human contact and entails at least a significant measure of freedom to associate with others. And freedom of association necessarily entails freedom of movement.

[11.3.20] Other implied freedoms may arise from the system of representative and responsible government prescribed by the Constitution. So, the people of Australia may have an implied right of access to the seat of government: *Crandall v Nevada* 73 US 35 (1867); *Cunliffe v The Commonwealth* (1994) 182 CLR 272 at 328 (Brennan CJ).

While arguments in support of the existence of these additional implied freedoms may be compelling, they have not yet been approved by the majority of the High Court in the ratio of any decision. And, as Gummow J commented in *Kruger v The Commonwealth* at 156:

The problem is in knowing what 'rights' are to be identified as constitutionally based and protected, albeit they are not stated in the text, and what methods are to be employed in discovering such 'rights'. Recognition is required of the limits imposed by the constitutional text, the importance of the democratic process and the wisdom of judicial restraint.

In *Australian Capital Television* (1992) 177 CLR 106 **[11.3.7C]**, Dawson J referred to the comments of Murphy J in *McGraw-Hinds (Aust) Pty Ltd v Smith* (1979) 144 CLR 633 at 670, and *Miller v TCN Channel Nine Pty Ltd* (1986) 161 CLR 556 at 581–2, and rejected the proposition that the Constitution, as opposed to the parliament, protected such freedoms: 177 CLR at 186. Although Dawson J's dissent in *Australian Capital Television* has been somewhat overtaken by events, and he ultimately capitulated in *Lange v Australian Broadcasting Corporation* (1997) 189 CLR 520 **[11.3.13C]**, Callinan J's contemporary criticism of the court's implied rights jurisprudence was noted at **[11.1.5]**. Should the High Court have recognised the implied freedom to discuss political and governmental affairs? What can we learn from the different opinions disclosed in these statements and what predictions can we make about the constitutional jurisprudence of Kirby J and Callinan J from reading these statements? The moral dimensions of recognising implied rights and freedoms were clearly raised by the facts of *Kruger v Commonwealth* (1997) 190 CLR 1 **[11.3.21C]**.

[11.3.21C]   **Kruger v Commonwealth**
                                       (1997) 190 CLR 1

The plaintiffs were Aboriginal Australians, who had been removed from their parents when they were children, and placed on Aboriginal reserves and institutions. The removals, which had occurred between 1929 and 1945, took place under the Aboriginals Ordinance 1918 (NT).

Section 6 of the Ordinance provided that the Chief Protector of Aborigines could take the children into 'care, custody and control' if, in the opinion of the Chief Protector, it was 'necessary or desirable in the interests of the aboriginals to do so'. Under s 7 the Chief Protector was made legal guardian of Aboriginal children until the age of 18, regardless of the existence of parents or other living relatives; and, following amendments in 1939, his successor was made legal guardian of all Aborigines. He was empowered to keep Aborigines on reserves under s 16 and regulations could be made under s 67. The plaintiffs sought a declaration that the Ordinance was invalid. They argued, inter alia, that the Ordinance and the regulations made under the Ordinance were contrary to an implied constitutional freedom of movement and association.

A majority of the court (Brennan CJ, Dawson, Toohey, McHugh and Gummow JJ; Gaudron J dissenting on this issue) declined to invalidate the Ordinance on the basis of an implied right to freedom of movement: 190 CLR at 45 per Brennan CJ; 190 CLR at 69 per Dawson J; 190 CLR at 93 per Toohey J; 190 CLR 144 per McHugh J; 190 CLR at 157 per Gummow J. However, three judges (Gaudron J, with whom Toohey J agreed on this issue, and McHugh J) reaffirmed their recognition of an implied freedom of movement associated with the implied freedom of communication; both of which were derived from the constitutional requirement of representative government: 190 CLR at 91–2 per Toohey J; 190 CLR at 115–16 per Gaudron J; 190 CLR at 142 per McHugh J. Two judges, Toohey and Gaudron JJ, also said that the implied freedom of movement applied to the territories.

Brennan CJ and Dawson J said that s 122 was not restricted by an implied right of freedom of movement and association. They did not discuss whether such a right existed in relation to the exercise of legislative power beyond s 122. Gummow J did not state whether his remarks applied to s 122 or the whole Constitution, but he expressed doubt as to whether representative government, as a matter of logical or practical necessity, included an implied restriction upon federal legislative power in relation to freedom of association: 190 CLR at 57.

Of the three justices who recognised the existence of an implication of freedom of association, two said, that for different reasons, it did not apply in this case. McHugh J said that representative government was not a requirement in the territories and, for that reason, neither was the implied freedom of movement. Toohey J said that the question of whether the Ordinance was 'reasonably adapted' or 'proportionate' to a legitimate end (following *Leask v Commonwealth* (1996) 187 CLR 579) would have to be determined according to standards prevailing at the time. According to those standards, 'at this stage of the proceedings' (190 CLR at 93), it was not possible to determine whether the law was invalid for conflicting with any implication of freedom of communication or association.

Gaudron J: [128] The various formulations in *Australian Capital Television* and in *Nationwide News* point to but one test of a law which restricts political communication; namely, whether the purpose of the law in question is to prohibit or restrict political communication. Questions directed to compelling justification, necessity and proportionality are, at base, questions directed to ascertaining the purpose of the law in question.

As earlier indicated, the purpose of a law is to be ascertained by its nature, its operation and the facts with which it deals. In ascertaining that purpose, a law which is, in terms, a prohibition or restriction on political communication or which operates directly to prevent or curtail discussion of political matters is, in my view, to be taken to have that purpose unless the prohibition or restriction is necessary for the attainment of some overriding public purpose (for example, to prevent criminal conspiracies) or, in terms used by Deane J in *Cunliffe v The Commonwealth*, to satisfy some 'pressing social need' [(1994) 182 CLR 272 at 340] referring to *Attorney-General v Guardian Newspapers (No 2)* [1990] 1 AC 109 at 283–284] (for example, to prevent sedition). Whether a law is necessary for some such purpose depends on whether it is 'no more than is proportionate to the legitimate aim pursued'. [*Cunliffe v The Commonwealth* (1994) 182 CLR 272 at 340] That in turn depends on whether less drastic measures are available. [See *Nationwide News Pty Ltd v Wills* (1992) 177 CLR 1 at 51] On the other hand, a law with respect to some subject-matter unconnected with the discussion of political matters and which only incidentally impinges on the freedom of that discussion, is not to be taken to be a law for the purpose of restricting that freedom if it is reasonably appropriate and adapted or, which is the same thing, proportionate to some legitimate purpose connected with that other subject matter.

In my view, the test applicable in the case of the implied freedom of political communication is equally applicable to the subsidiary freedoms of movement and association which support that freedom, namely, whether the purpose of the law in question is to restrict those freedoms. Although the test is the same, it may involve different considerations in the sense that the matters of public importance or pressing social need which will justify a law restricting freedom of movement or of association will ordinarily be of a different nature from those which justify a law restricting political communication. **[129]** Similarly, different considerations may be brought into play where the question is one of proportionality.

It is necessary now to turn to the terms and operation of the Ordinance. Sections 6 and 16 conferred powers on the Chief Protector and, later, the Director which, if exercised, operated directly to prevent freedom of movement and of association. Moreover, they were couched in terms directly contrary to those freedoms, s 6 conferring a power to take people into custody and s 16 conferring a power to cause Aboriginal people to be 'kept within the boundaries of … reserve[s] or aboriginal institution[s]'. Similarly, the power conferred by s 67(1)(c) to make regulations 'enabling any aboriginal or half-caste child to be sent to and detained in an Aboriginal Institution or Industrial School' permitted regulations which directly prevented freedom of movement and of association. Indeed, it only permitted regulations of that kind. Accordingly, in my view, s 6 (to the extent that it authorised the taking of people into custody), and ss 16 and 67(1)(c) were only valid if necessary for the attainment of some overriding public purpose or for the satisfaction of some pressing social need.

Because s 6 (to the extent that it authorised the taking of people into custody) and ss 16 and 67(1)(c) were only valid if necessary for the attainment of some overriding public purpose or the satisfaction of some public need, the Commonwealth's plea that the Ordinance is or is reasonably capable of being viewed as appropriate and adapted to preserving and protecting Aboriginal people provides no answer to the question whether it infringed constitutional freedoms.

If it could be said that the Ordinance was necessary for the preservation or protection of Aboriginal people, it would follow that it was valid in its entirety. However, the Commonwealth asserts no such necessity. Moreover, there is no basis on which it could be said that those provisions of the Ordinance which authorised action impairing the rights of Aboriginal people to move in society and to associate with their fellow citizens, including their fellow Aboriginal Australians, were in any way necessary for the protection or preservation of Aboriginal people or, indeed, those Aboriginal people whose rights in that regard were, in fact, curtailed. Certainly, the powers conferred on the Chief Protector and, later, the Director by ss 6 and 16 were not conditioned on any necessity to take Aboriginal people into custody or to keep and detain them in reserves and institutions for their protection or preservation. ...

[130] It follows in my view that s 6, so far as it conferred authority to take people into custody, and ss 16 and 67(1)(c) were at all times invalid.

McHugh J: [142] ... Nothing in s 122 of the Constitution gives any support for this claim. [*Australian Capital Television Pty Ltd v The Commonwealth* (1992) 177 CLR 106 at 246] Nor is there any implication in the Constitution as a whole that supports the claim.

Because ss 7, 24, 64 and 128 and related sections of the Constitution provide for a system of representative and responsible government and a procedure for amending the Constitution by referendum, the Constitution necessarily implies that 'the people' must be free from laws that prevent them from communicating with each other with respect to government and political matters. The freedom arises from the constitutional mandate 'that the members of the House of Representatives and the Senate shall be "directly chosen by the people" of the Commonwealth and the States, respectively.' It exists for the protection of 'the people of the Commonwealth' in the case of the House of Representatives and for 'the people of the State[s]' in respect of the Senate. As a matter of construction, the constitutional implication cannot protect those who are not part of 'the people' in either of those senses.

The reasons that led to the drawing of the implication of freedom of communication lead me to the conclusion that the Constitution also necessarily implies that 'the people' must be free from laws that prevent them from associating with other persons, and from travelling, inside and outside Australia for the purposes of the constitutionally prescribed system of government and referendum procedure. The implication of freedom from laws preventing association and travel must extend, at the very least, to such matters as voting for, or supporting or opposing the election of, candidates for membership of the Senate and the House of Representatives, monitoring the performance of and petitioning federal Ministers and parliamentarians and voting in referenda.

However, from the time when the 1918 Ordinance was enacted until it was repealed in 1957, the residents of the Northern Territory had no part to play in the constitutionally prescribed system of [143] government or in the procedure for amending the Constitution. The right of the Territories to elect senators or members of the House of Representatives was, as it is today, dependent on federal legislation, not constitutional entitlement. The Northern Territory had no constitutional right during the period 1918 to 1957 to elect or vote for a member of the Senate or the House of Representatives.

It was not until 1922 that the Northern Territory had any representation in the House of Representatives. Moreover, its member was not given a vote on any question arising in that House. In 1936, the member was given the right to vote on any motion for the disallowance of any Ordinance of the Northern Territory and on any amendment of such motion. In 1959, this right was extended to any question 'on or in connexion with' a proposed law that was determined to relate solely to the Northern Territory. It was not until 1968 that the member for the Northern Territory was given the same 'powers, immunities and privileges' as those enjoyed by members representing State Electoral Divisions. Furthermore, the Northern Territory had no Senate representation until the enactment of the Senate (Representation of Territories) Act 1973 (Cth), which came into force on 7 August 1974. Indeed, it was not until 1977 that the residents of the Northern Territory finally received constitutional as well as democratic recognition by being given the right to vote in a referendum to amend the Constitution. By then the 1918 Ordinance had long been repealed.

As the foregoing account shows, at no relevant time were the residents of the Northern Territory part of the constitutionally prescribed system of government. Nor, as the second paragraph of s 24 and ss 25 and 26 of the Constitution and s 15 of the Commonwealth Electoral Act 1918 (Cth) made plain, were the residents of the Territories 'people of the Commonwealth' for the purpose of s 24. Moreover, at no time during the life of the 1918 Ordinance did an 'aboriginal native of Australia', who was resident in the Northern Territory and subject to the 1918 Ordinance, have any right to vote in federal elections.

For these reasons, nothing in the Constitution implied that the [144] plaintiffs had any freedom or immunity from laws affecting their common law rights of association or travel during the life of the 1918 Ordinance.

Accordingly, I reject the plaintiffs' claim that the 1918 Ordinance is invalid because it burdened their constitutionally protected freedom of association and travel.

~~~

Notes

[11.3.22] It would be difficult to imagine a scenario that more sharply demonstrates the need for improved and increased protection of human rights in Australia than the forcible removal of children from their mothers with assimilationist intent. However, the judgments in *Kruger v Commonwealth* (1997) 190 CLR 1 demonstrate the manifest weakness of the Commonwealth Constitution to protect human rights.

Rights derived from Ch III of the Constitution

[11.3.23] While the implied freedom to discuss political and governmental affairs was being debated, a more promising path to the development of an implied Bill of Rights was opened. In a series of decisions commencing with *Polyhukovich v Commonwealth* (1991) 172 CR 501 **[11.3.28]** and *Chu Kheng Lim v Minister for Immigration* (1992) 176 CLR 1 **[11.3.29]**, the High Court has recognised that certain rights flow from the separation of judicial power effected by Ch III of the Constitution. As Zines has commented '[f]rom this seemingly simple provision, [s 71 of the Constitution], an array of entrenched rights has emerged, and is emerging with no sign of abatement': Zines (1998); Keyzer (2000).

Due process

[11.3.24] One of the major innovations in the implied rights arena has been the growing recognition of the existence of an implied right to 'due process' (or 'natural justice'). The source of the implication is the separation of power doctrine discussed in Chapter 6, but in the sphere of implied rights the doctrine takes on what Fiona Wheeler has called a new 'character'. Whereas the separation of powers doctrine was once seen as an 'institutional imperative designed to foster the supremacy of law over arbitrary power', Wheeler argues that it has now been 'subtl[y] transform[ed]' into an 'implication ... protective of individual rights': Wheeler (1996) p 96. However, the content of the implication is not settled, as the following cases demonstrate.

[11.3.25] The High Court's decision in *Leeth v Commonwealth* (1992) 174 CLR 455 provided an occasion for the development of the distinction between legislative and judicial power in the context of sentencing. The issue before the court was the validity of s 4(1) of the Commonwealth Prisoners Act 1967 (Cth), which provided that, when a court was imposing a term of imprisonment following conviction under a law of the Commonwealth, the court should approach the imposition of a non-parole period on the same basis as that required by the law of the state or territory in which the Commonwealth offender had been convicted. The laws of the several states and territories contained markedly different regimes relating to non-parole periods.

It was argued that s 4(1) was invalid on two grounds: first, it authorised unequal treatment of Commonwealth offenders, depending on the state in which they were convicted; and, second, that it infringed Ch III of the Constitution by requiring a court exercising federal jurisdiction to act in a non-judicial manner. Apart from Gaudron J, the justices rejected the second argument. However, four members of the court (Brennan, Deane, Toohey and Gaudron JJ) accepted that the Commonwealth Constitution contained an implied constitutional right to equality, although only Deane, Toohey and Gaudron JJ held that s 4(1) violated that implied right. Moreover, although Deane and Toohey JJ did not agree with Gaudron J in relation to the second argument that s 4(1) infringed Ch III, they did agree with her that the implication of equality was derived from Ch III. Brennan J, by contrast, did not rely on Ch III as a foundation for his acceptance of the implication of equality.

Three justices began by identifying the way in which judicial power was to be exercised under Ch III. Deane and Toohey JJ said at 487:

> [T]hus, in Ch III's exclusive vesting of the judicial power of the Commonwealth in the 'courts' which it designates, there is implicit a requirement that those 'courts' exhibit the essential attributes of a court and observe, in the exercise of that judicial power, the essential requirements of the curial process, including the obligation to act judicially.

Gaudron J said that it was 'an essential feature of judicial power that it should be exercised in accordance with the judicial process': 174 CLR at 502.

To this point the opinions were uncontroversial. Courts exercising judicial power under Ch III must act in a manner consistent with the essential attributes of judicial power; that is, they must act judicially, or in accordance with the judicial process. This is a requirement of *procedural* due process. However, both Deane and Toohey JJ (and, in the separate opinion, Gaudron J) went on to add that acting judicially included a right to equality under the law, a right normally associated with *substantive* due process, a right previously unrecognised in Australian constitutional law. Deane and Toohey JJ said at 487:

> At the heart of that obligation [to act judicially] is the duty of a court to extend to the parties before it equal justice, that is to say, to treat them fairly and impartially as equals before the law and to refrain from discrimination on irrelevant or irrational grounds.

Moreover, Deane and Toohey JJ suggested that the implied right to equality was based not only on Ch III but also on broader constitutional principles. They observed that the Constitution had incorporated several 'underlying doctrines or principles by implication', including a general principle protecting the continued existence and political viability of the states, and the common law doctrine of the separation of judicial power from executive and legislative powers: 174 CLR at 484–5.

Among the 'fundamental constitutional doctrines' adopted in the Commonwealth Constitution was the 'doctrine of legal equality'. The doctrine required that every person, of whatever rank, was subject to the ordinary law; and involved 'the underlying or inherent theoretical equality of all persons under the law': 174 CLR at 485. Although the common law could 'discriminate between individuals by reference to relevant differences and distinctions, such as infancy or incapacity, or by reason of conduct which it proscribes' (174 CLR at 485–6), the doctrine of equality required that such discrimination be supported 'on grounds which are reasonably capable of being seen as providing a rational and relevant basis for the discriminatory treatment': 174 CLR at 488.

Deane and Toohey JJ could not accept that there was a rational and relevant basis for the discrimination among Commonwealth offenders which s 4(1) of the Commonwealth Prisoners Act required. Accordingly, they would have held s 4(1) invalid.

Gaudron J also would have struck down s 4(1). However, her reasoning was constructed on a combination of the separation of judicial power and the principle of equality before the law. The concept of equal justice, Gaudron J said, required that 'like persons in like circumstances' were treated in the same way; and that concept was 'fundamental to the judicial process': 174 CLR at 502. Because s 4(1) required different treatment, not according to the type of offence or the circumstances of its commission but according to the place of conviction (at 502–3):

> … the exercise of that power would involve a failure to treat like offences against the laws of the Commonwealth in a like manner and also a failure to give proper account to genuine differences. That is only another way of saying that s 4(1) was discriminatory. But, stated in these terms, it is clear that a power of that kind is one that treats people unequally. As such its exercise is inconsistent with the judicial process.

Brennan J, who held that s 4(1) of the Commonwealth Prisoners Act was valid, conceded that the arguments against the provision would have 'much force' if the provision prescribed different maximum penalties for the same offence (at 475):

> It would be offensive to the constitutional unity of the Australian people 'in one indissoluble Federal Commonwealth', recited in the first preamble to the Commonwealth of Australia Constitution Act 1900, to expose offenders against the same law of the Commonwealth to different maximum penalties dependent on the locality of the court by which the offender is convicted and sentenced.

However, Brennan J held that s 4(1) was valid because there was a reasonable justification for the different treatment which it prescribed. Commonwealth offenders are imprisoned with state offenders in state prisons, in accordance with s 120 of the Constitution (at 479):

> So long as the system, contemplated by s 120 of the Constitution, of incarcerating Commonwealth prisoners in the same prisons as State prisoners continues, it will be necessary to maintain the same or substantially the same regime for fixing the minimum terms of Commonwealth prisoners and State prisoners serving their sentences in the same prison. Although s 4 of the Commonwealth Prisoners Act discriminates among Commonwealth prisoners serving sentences for the same offence, the practical ground of distinction is their incarceration in prisons shared with State and Territory prisoners. That is not only a rational ground of discrimination; it is a necessary ground.

In a joint judgment, Mason CJ, Dawson and McHugh JJ said that there was '[n]o general requirement contained in the Constitution that Commonwealth laws should have a uniform operation throughout the Commonwealth': 174 CLR at 467. They acknowledged the implication which prevented the Commonwealth Parliament legislating so as to impose special burdens on the states, and the existence of specific provisions prohibiting certain types of discrimination or preference, such as ss 51(ii), 92, 99 and 117. However, there was no question, the justices said, 'specific restrictions and implications apart, that the Commonwealth may give a varying application to its laws by reference to the laws of the States': 174 CLR at 468. And, importantly, Mason CJ, Dawson and McHugh JJ remarked at 470 that:

> It may well be that any attempt on the part of the legislature to cause a court to act in a manner contrary to natural justice would impose a non-judicial requirement inconsistent with the exercise of judicial power.

[11.3.26] In *Wilson v Minister for Aboriginal and Torres Strait Islander Affairs* (1996) 189 CLR 1 at 17, Brennan CJ, Dawson, Toohey, McHugh and Gummow JJ noted that the requirement of natural justice flows from the character of the power: Ch III judges must behave *judicially*. A critical mass of opinion flowing from majority judgments had emerged: the Federal Parliament could not require Ch III courts to act contrary to natural justice because this would require them to act non-judicially under a Constitution that contemplates that those courts exercise only judicial power and powers that are necessarily incidental to judicial power.

The *content* of any implied right of natural justice or due process is still an open question. If the separation of judicial power requires that parliaments cannot vest courts with the power to exercise their jurisdiction in a manner inconsistent with judicial power, what types of rights will be protected? Wheeler argues that the implied right to due process could demand a rethinking of a range of traditional rights such as the common law right of an accused to confront witnesses; the use of oral argument; and the use or qualification of other traditional remedies: Wheeler (1997).

The standards of constitutionally protected natural justice have not yet emerged. However, Gaudron and Gummow JJ (with whom Gleeson CJ agreed) elaborated on the ambit of the requirement of procedural fairness in the Australian constitutional context in *Re Refugee Tribunal; Ex parte Aala* (2000) 204 CLR 82. Aala applied under the Migration Act 1958 (Cth) for a protection visa on the basis that he had a well-founded fear of persecution if he returned to his country of citizenship, Iran. His claim was rejected by the minister's delegate and by the Refugee Review Tribunal. The Federal Court rejected Aala's application for judicial review of the tribunal's decision. Aala then applied to the High Court for a writ of prohibition under s 75(v) of the Constitution to prevent his deportation. Gaudron and Gummow JJ (with whom Gleeson CJ agreed) held that, if the minister's delegate had denied procedural fairness to Aala, and the Migration Act had not, on its proper construction, validly extinguished any obligation to accord procedural fairness, then the remedy of prohibition could be ordered under s 75(v): 204 CLR 82 at 97, 101:

> ... the denial of procedural fairness by an officer of the Commonwealth may result in a decision made in excess of jurisdiction in respect of which prohibition will go under s 75(v) ... if there has been a breach of the obligation to accord procedural fairness, the consequences of the breach were not gainsaid by classifying the breach as 'trivial' or non-determinative of the ultimate result — the issue is whether there has or has not been a breach of the obligation ... the practical content of the obligation, and thus the

issue of the breach, may turn upon the circumstances of the particular case; and ... the remedy of prohibition under s 75(v) does not lie as of right, but is discretionary (204 CLR 82 at 91–2).

[11.3.27] The ambit of the constitutional requirement of natural justice will depend on a number of factors, not least of which is the willingness of the judges of the High Court to assert the importance of natural justice in the exercise of judicial power. In *Aala*, Hayne J said that 's 75(v) is not a source of substantive rights': 204 CLR 82 at 139. So, it has been said that, where a statute addresses the subject of procedure with particularity, manifesting an intention to address in detail the relevant requirements of procedural fairness, then the intention of parliament will *ordinarily* be regarded to be decisive: *Re Minister for Immigration; Ex parte Miah* (2001) 206 CLR 57 at 106–7 (Gleeson CJ and Hayne J). 'Ordinarily' because, as Gaudron and Gummow JJ pointed out in *Aala*, the statute must *validly* oust procedural fairness. Again, the content of the implied right of due process or natural justice remains an open question.

[11.3.28] The idea that the Constitution contains an implied right of some form of due process, which would require that courts exercising federal judicial power act according to some minimum standard of judicial process is closely related to the proposition, said to be essential to the separation of judicial power, that the legislature cannot usurp or interfere with the judicial function by conferring judicial power on non-judicial bodies. So, for example, in *Polyukhovich v Commonwealth* (1991) 172 CLR 501 **[6.4.19]**, three justices indicated that in the case of retrospective criminal laws such laws would be invalid. Deane J said the function of determining criminal guilt was a judicial function and could only be vested in a court. Gaudron J said retrospective criminal laws breached the separation of powers doctrine. Toohey J said that the doctrine would be breached if the enactment required a court to act contrary to accepted notions of judicial power. By contrast, Mason CJ, McHugh and Dawson JJ said that the Commonwealth Parliament could enact such retrospective laws without interfering with the judicial process.

[11.3.29] In the following year, in *Chu Kheng Lim v Minister for Immigration, Local Government and Ethnic Affairs* (1992) 176 CLR 1 **[6.4.20C]**, Brennan, Deane and Dawson JJ said that the legislature could not require a court to exercise judicial power in a manner inconsistent with the essential character of a court or with the nature of judicial power.

Several Cambodian nationals arrived in Australia by boat and were detained in custody. They applied for refugee status under the Migration Act 1958. The Minister's delegate rejected their applications. The Cambodians applied to the Federal Court for orders of review of the decisions to reject their refugee applications, and orders that they be released from custody on the ground that they had been unlawfully detained. The Federal Court set aside the decisions to reject the refugee applications, referring that matter back to the minister for determination according to law, and set a hearing date to determine whether the Cambodians had been wrongfully detained.

Two days before that hearing, the Commonwealth Parliament amended the Migration Act to provide for the compulsory detention in custody of certain 'designated persons' including the Cambodians. One of the provisions (s 54R) stated that a 'court is not to order the release from custody of a designated person'. The Cambodians commenced proceedings in the High Court, challenging the validity of the amendments on the ground that the parliament had usurped the judicial power which, by virtue of s 71 of the Constitution and the separation of powers required by the Constitution, was vested exclusively in courts as defined in Ch III of the Constitution. The plaintiffs argued that, subject to exceptions which did not apply to them, the incarceration of a person was penal and could only follow a judgment of criminal guilt by a court.

The High Court upheld the validity of the provisions requiring the detention of a non-citizen who entered Australia by boat without a visa; but a majority of the court (Brennan, Deane, Dawson and Gaudron JJ) held that s 54R was invalid because it purported to undermine the jurisdiction which the Constitution vested directly in the High Court and was a direction to the courts as to the manner in which they were to exercise their jurisdiction. Brennan, Deane and Dawson JJ said at 27–8 it is:

> ... beyond the legislative power of the Parliament to invest the Executive with an arbitrary power to detain citizens in custody notwithstanding that the power was conferred in terms which sought to divorce such detention in custody from both punishment and criminal guilt. The reason why that is so is that, putting to one side the exceptional cases ... the involuntary detention of a citizen in custody by the State is penal or punitive in character and, under our system of government, exists only as an incident of the exclusively judicial function of adjudging and punishing criminal guilt. Every citizen is 'ruled by the law, and by the law alone' and 'may with us be punished for a breach of law, but he can be punished for nothing else' (Dicey, *Introduction to the Study of the Law of the Constitution*, 10th ed (1959) p 202).

Brennan, Deane and Dawson JJ considered the exceptional types of preventive detention that would be consistent with Ch III of the Constitution. They were (at 28):

> ... committal to custody awaiting trial ... involuntary detention in cases of mental illness or infectious diseases ... the traditional powers of the Parliament to punish for contempt and of military tribunals to punish for breach of military discipline ...

Otherwise, citizens of Australia enjoyed, at least in peacetime, 'constitutional immunity from being imprisoned by Commonwealth authority pursuant to an order by a court in the exercise of the judicial power of the Commonwealth': 176 CLR at 28–9. Because the doctrine of separation of powers would be infringed if the parliament conferred a judicial function on a non-judicial body (subject to certain exceptions), any attempt by the legislature to confer a power to involuntarily detain, would be an attempt to confer judicial power on a non-judicial body and would breach the separation of powers. Conversely, it could be argued, any attempt to give a court the power to order detention in the absence of a finding of guilt of an offence (and apart from the exceptional types of detention referred to above) could be an invalid conferral of non-judicial power on a judicial body.

[11.3.30] That converse proposition was applied in *Kable v Director of Public Prosecutions (NSW)* (1996) 189 CLR 51 to strike down state legislation that authorised a court to order preventive detention: see further **[6.4.48C]**.

The Community Protection Act 1994 (NSW) conferred jurisdiction on the Supreme Court of New South Wales to make 'preventive detention orders' to keep a person in prison for a specified period of time to undergo psychiatric evaluation where the court was satisfied that the person was more likely than not to commit an act of serious violence and that it was appropriate for the protection of the community that such a person continue to be held in custody. The object of the Act was declared to be 'to protect the community by providing for the preventive detention ... of Gregory Wayne Kable'.

Kable challenged the constitutional validity of the Act on a number of grounds, including that the Act was inconsistent with the requirements of Ch III of the Commonwealth Constitution. A number of key points can be drawn from the majority judgments, which concluded that the Act was invalid.

Chapter III postulates an integrated Australian court system for the exercise of the judicial power of the Commonwealth, with the High Court at its apex as a court exercising appellate jurisdiction for the nation; state courts are, by s 77 of the Constitution, part of this system, which does not permit different grades or qualities of justice to operate as between state and federal courts: 189 CLR at 101, 103 (Gaudron J).

The presence in the Constitution of covering cl 5, s 51(xxiv), 51(xxv), s 73, s 77 and s 118 indicates that a state court system, or at very least the existence of state Supreme Courts, was contemplated by the framers of the Constitution: 189 CLR at 110–11 (McHugh J).

Neither the Commonwealth nor the states could legislate to undermine the scheme set up by Ch III of the Constitution. As McHugh J put it at 115:

> Because the state courts are an integral and equal part of the judicial system set up by Ch III, it also follows that no state or federal parliament can legislate in a way that might undermine the role of those courts as repositories of federal judicial power ... neither ... parliament ... can invest functions in the Supreme Court of New South Wales that are incompatible with the exercise of federal judicial power. Neither ... can legislate in a way that permits the Supreme Court while exercising federal judicial power to disregard the rules of natural justice or to exercise legislative or executive power ...
>
> One of the basic principles which underlie Ch III and to which it gives effect is that the judges of the federal courts must be, and must be perceived to be, independent of the legislature and the executive government. Given the central role and the status that Ch III gives to state courts invested with federal jurisdiction, it necessarily follows that those courts must also be, and be perceived to be, independent of the legislature or the executive government.

Accordingly, although New South Wales had no entrenched doctrine of the separation of powers, the capacity of state courts to be invested with federal jurisdiction meant that they could not be required to exercise a power that was alien to the judicial function. Importantly, the court struck down legislation that deprived a named individual of his liberty by removing the ordinary protections inherent in the judicial process: see further 189 CLR at 107 (Gaudron J), 122 (McHugh J), 131 (Gummow J).

[11.3.31] A similar argument was unsuccessful in *Kruger v Commonwealth* (1997) 190 CLR 1 **[11.3.21C]** and **[11.3.32C]**. The plaintiffs, Aboriginal Australians, argued that a Northern Territory Ordinance authorising the removal of Aboriginal children from their natural parents was invalid. Two related grounds of attack raised by the plaintiffs were that the Ordinance interfered with an implied right of due process in the exercise of judicial power of the Commonwealth conferred in accordance with Ch III, and that it purported to confer judicial power on persons other than Ch III courts. Both grounds were rejected by the High Court. A majority characterised the Ordinance as *non-punitive* in nature and therefore not constituting an exercise of judicial power.

Dawson J said that the Ordinance did not infringe the separation of powers as an exercise of judicial power otherwise than in accordance with Ch III for two reasons.

First, it was non-punitive in nature and therefore did not involve the performance of a judicial function. Second, even if it was judicial in nature, the requirements of Ch III did not extend to the territories: 190 CLR at 62. Brennan CJ agreed that Ch III did not apply to the territories: 190 CLR at 43–4.

Toohey J said that the argument that Ch III applied to the territories was 'persuasive' (190 CLR at 84); but, in any event, this was not an exercise of judicial power other than in accordance with Ch III because it was not an exercise of a judicial function. There were many accepted categories of involuntary detention which were not exercises of judicial function, including involuntary detention for the purposes of mental illness, infectious disease, committal to custody awaiting trial, or detention of aliens for deportation. Judged by the standards at the time the Ordinance was made (1918), involuntary detention under the Ordinance had a welfare purpose, was not punitive and hence was not an exercise of judicial power: 190 CLR at 84–5.

Gaudron J said that there was 'no convincing reason' for treating Ch III as not applying to the territories: 190 CLR at 109. However, she said, the power to deprive people of their liberty was not necessarily judicial power and was therefore not, of itself, offensive to Ch III: 190 CLR at 110. There is, Gaudron J said, a broad immunity from involuntary detention, but it does not derive from Ch III; rather, it arises from the fact that the 'legislative power conferred by s 51 ... does not extend to authorise laws conferring a power of detention divorced from criminal guilt, unless they are laws with respect to the topics': 190 CLR at 111.

Gummow J implied that the Ordinance was not an attempt to confer judicial power upon a non-judicial body in contravention of Ch III. He said the categories of non-punitive, involuntary detention were not closed (190 CLR at 162); and that the ordinance was for a welfare purpose which was legitimately non-punitive. It did not involve judicial power and hence could be conferred on the Chief Protector. Gummow J also said that in his 'tentative view' Ch III protections were applicable to the territories but that 'existing authority in this court would require consideration before that conclusion could be reached and applied': 190 CLR at 162.

[11.3.32C]   Kruger v Commonwealth
(1997) 190 CLR 1

As explained in **[11.3.21C]**, the plaintiffs challenged the validity of the Aboriginals Ordinance 1918 (NT), under which they had been removed from their parents by government officials between 1929 and 1945. The plaintiffs argued, inter alia, that the Ordinance and regulations made under the Ordinance, were contrary to an implied constitutional right to legal equality under the laws of the Commonwealth.

A majority of the High Court (Brennan CJ, Dawson, Gaudron, McHugh, Gummow JJ; Toohey J dissenting) said the Constitution contained no general right of equality. Gaudron and Gummow JJ said the Constitution contained only a limited equality right based on Ch III and the manner in which Ch III courts exercise judicial power.

Dawson J: [Dawson J, with whom McHugh J concurred, said that the Commonwealth Constitution contained no general guarantee of due process of law similar to that contained in the United States Constitution: 190 CLR at 61. Dawson J explored the reasons of Toohey and Deane JJ in *Leeth v Commonwealth* (1992) 174 CLR 455 **[11.3.24]**, proceeding on the basis that any such implication must arise from Ch III.]

[63] The plaintiffs contend that by implication the Constitution guarantees legal equality before and under the law. There is reason to think that such a guarantee, if it existed, would

not prevail against the legislative power conferred by s 122, but it is convenient to proceed directly to the question whether any such implication can be made.

The separation of judicial power from the other powers of government precludes the legislature from investing a court created by or under Ch III of the Constitution with non-judicial powers that are not ancillary but are directed to some non-judicial purpose. A Ch III court cannot be made to perform a function which is of a non-judicial nature or is required to be performed in a non-judicial manner. Chapter III may, perhaps, be regarded in this way as affording a measure of due process, but it is due process of a procedural rather than substantive nature. As was pointed out in *Leeth v The Commonwealth*, [(1992) 174 CLR 455 at 469] 'to speak of judicial power in this context is to speak of the function of a court rather than the law which a court is to apply'. However, for the reasons which I have already given, the plaintiffs are unable to resort to the separation of powers so far as the territories are concerned and in any event their argument goes much further than the requirements of Ch III in asserting a guarantee of equality before and under the law.

The plaintiffs encounter difficulty at the outset by reason of the decision of this Court in *Leeth*. In that case, a majority (Mason CJ, Brennan J, McHugh J and myself) held that a law of the Commonwealth which did not operate uniformly throughout the Commonwealth was not in breach of any constitutional requirement. Deane and Toohey JJ, and Gaudron J in a separate judgment, held the law to be invalid but they were in a minority in so doing. Nevertheless, the plaintiffs base their argument upon the line of reasoning adopted by Deane and Toohey JJ in their joint judgment.

It is true that Deane and Toohey JJ found a doctrine of legal equality in the Constitution, but the reasoning which led to that conclusion did not commend itself to other members of the Court nor, with the greatest of respect, does it now commend itself to me. An analogy for the doctrine of equality was, it was said, to be discerned in the implied prohibition against Commonwealth legislation which discriminates against the States or subjects them or their instrumentalities to special burdens or disabilities. It would be surprising, it was suggested, if the Constitution 'embodied a general principle which protected the States and their instrumentalities from being singled out by Commonwealth laws for discriminatory treatment but provided no similar protection of the people who constitute the [64] Commonwealth and the States'. [(1992) 174 CLR 455 at 484] With respect, I do not find that situation surprising at all. The limitation upon the powers of the Commonwealth Parliament which prevent it from discriminating against the States is derived from different considerations entirely, which were articulated by Dixon J in *Melbourne Corporation v The Commonwealth* [(1947) 74 CLR 31 at 82] when he said:

> The foundation of the Constitution is the conception of a central government and a number of State governments separately organised. The Constitution predicates their continued existence as independent entities.

That principle does not spring from any notion of equality. Moreover the Constitution is in many respects inconsistent with a doctrine of legal equality.

Section 51 (xxvi), as Deane J recognised in *The Tasmanian Dam Case*, [(1983) 158 CLR 1 at 273] 'remains a general power to pass laws discriminating against or benefiting the people of any race'. Similarly, s 51(xix) enables the Commonwealth Parliament to make laws which discriminate in favour of or against aliens. Discrimination in relation to the qualification to vote in federal elections is clearly envisaged by the Constitution (see ss 25, 30) and equality of voting power is not guaranteed. [See *McGinty v Western Australia* (1996) 186 CLR 140] And until 1967 (which is after the last alleged act of detention ended), ss 51(xxvi) and 127 excluded Aboriginals for specified purposes. It is unnecessary to provide an exhaustive list of those respects in which the Constitution does not support the suggested doctrine of equality, for Deane and Toohey JJ recognised in *Leeth* that 'the nature of the particular grant of legislative power may be such as to rebut the assumption that such discrimination was unauthorised by the relevant provision of the Constitution' [(1992) 174 CLR 455 at 489] or may need to be 'adjusted to the extent necessary to accommodate discriminatory treatment which other provisions of the Constitution clearly contemplate'. [(1992) 174 CLR 455 at 490] To recognise as much is surely to undermine any basis for asserting that the Constitution assumes a doctrine of equality.

Not only that, but where the Constitution requires equality it does not leave it to implication. It makes provision for it by prohibiting discrimination, preference or lack of uniformity in specific instances. For example, the power of the Commonwealth Parliament to make laws with respect to taxation conferred by s 51(ii) must not be exercised so as to discriminate between States or parts of States. [65] Section 88 provides for uniform customs duties and s 51(iii) provides for uniform bounties. Section 92, in requiring trade, commerce and intercourse among the States to be absolutely free, prohibits discrimination of a protectionist kind. Section 99 forbids the Parliament to give preference to one State or any part thereof over another State or any part thereof by any law or regulation of trade, commerce or revenue. And s 117 provides that a subject of the Queen, resident in any State, shall not be subject in any other State to any disability or discrimination which would not be equally applicable to him if he were a subject of the Queen resident in such other State. In *Leeth*, Deane and Toohey JJ said that the existence of these specific provisions 'which reflect the doctrine of legal equality serves to make manifest rather than undermine the status of that doctrine as an underlying principle of the Constitution as a whole'. [*Leeth* (1992) 174 CLR 455 at 487] That statement not only denies the accepted canon of construction expressed in the maxim *expressio unius, exclusio alterius*; it turns it on its head. And as one commentator has observed: [Zines, 'A Judicially Created Bill of Rights?' (1994) 16 *Sydney Law Review* 166 at 182]

> If various provisions aimed at preventing discrimination, preference and lack of uniformity are merely reflections of a general principle of equality, it can be similarly reasoned that the specific powers given to the Commonwealth Parliament are merely examples of a general principle, mentioned from time to time by delegates, that the Commonwealth Parliament was to be given power over all subjects which could not be as effectively dealt with by the States.

The inappropriateness of the *expressio unius* maxim arose, in their Honours' view, from what was said to be the 'ordinary approach of the Constitution not to spell out the fundamental common law principles upon which it is structured' [*Leeth* (1992) 174 CLR 455 at 487] because 'the general approach of the framers of the Constitution ... was to incorporate underlying doctrines or principles by implication'. [*Leeth* (1992) 174 CLR 455 at 484] With respect, that is not the case. Guarantees of equality before the law and due process were specifically rejected, not because they were already implicit and therefore unnecessary, but because they were not wanted. Indeed, if there was a need to make specific provision for equality where that was intended, it would suggest that there is no principle of equality underlying the Constitution and that were such a doctrine intended, specific provision would have been made for it. But to be fair to Deane and Toohey JJ, they did not, I think, base a doctrine of [66] equality principally upon the existence of these specific provisions. They referred to considerations of a more fundamental kind.

The ultimate source of the doctrine was said to lie in the common law. Thus Deane and Toohey JJ said: [*Leeth* (1992) 174 CLR 455 at 485–486]

> The common law may discriminate between individuals by reference to relevant differences and distinctions, such as infancy or incapacity, or by reason of conduct which it proscribes, punishes or penalises. It may have failed adequately to acknowledge or address the fact that, in some circumstances, theoretical equality under the law sustains rather than alleviates the practical reality of social and economic inequality. Nonetheless, and putting to one side the position of the Crown and some past anomalies, notably, discriminatory treatment of women, the essential or underlying theoretical equality of all persons under the law and before the courts is and has been a fundamental and generally beneficial doctrine of the common law and a basic prescript of the administration of justice under our system of government.

However, whilst the rule of law requires the law to be applied to all without reference to rank or status, the plain matter of fact is that the common law has never required as a necessary outcome the equal, or non-discriminatory, operation of laws. It is not possible, in my view, to dismiss the discriminatory treatment of women at common law or such matters as the attainder of felons [see *Dugan v Mirror Newspapers Ltd* (1978) 142 CLR 583] as 'past anomalies'. To do so is to treat the doctrines of the common law with selectivity. Moreover, the supremacy of parliament, which is itself a principle of the common law, [*Kable v DPP (NSW)* (1996) 70 ALJR 814 at 824; 138 ALR 577 at 590] necessarily leaves the common law subject to alteration without reference to notions of equality. The common law thus provides no foundation for a doctrine of equality, at all events substantive equality as opposed to the kind of procedural equality envisaged by the rule of law.

But even if a doctrine of substantive equality were discernible in the common law, it would not appear that it was a doctrine which was adopted in the drafting of the Constitution. Apart from anything else, it is clear that the Commonwealth Parliament was intended to have the capacity, in the exercise of its legislative powers, to alter the common law. If it were not so, the scope of those powers would be less than the scope of the concurrent powers of the States. There is no reason to suppose that such a capacity would not extend to a common law doctrine of equality if such a doctrine were to exist. Nevertheless, in [67] *Leeth* Deane and Toohey JJ expressed the view that such a doctrine had been adopted in the Constitution by necessary implication by reason of its conceptual basis and because it is 'implicit in the Constitution's separation of judicial power from legislative and executive powers and the vesting of judicial power in designated "courts"'. [*Leeth* (1992) 174 CLR 455 at 486]

In referring to the conceptual basis of the Constitution, Deane and Toohey JJ had in mind the preamble and covering cl 3 of the Commonwealth of Australia Constitution Act which refer to the agreement of the people of the various colonies to unite in a Federal Commonwealth. Their Honours took the view [*Leeth* (1992) 174 CLR 455 at 486] that '[i]mplicit in that free agreement was the notion of the inherent equality of the people as the parties to the compact.' It may be observed that a degree of equality was lacking in the free agreement of which their Honours spoke, in that the referendum expressing that agreement excluded most women and many Aboriginals. But the important thing is that the Constitution to which the people agreed plainly envisages inequality in the operation of laws made under it. Moreover, those who framed the Constitution deliberately chose not to include a provision guaranteeing due process or the equal protection of the laws and it was with those omissions that the people agreed to the Constitution. It is not possible, in my view, to read into the fact of agreement any implications which do not appear from the document upon which agreement was reached. Not only does a doctrine of equality in the operation of laws made under the Constitution not appear from the Constitution, but the very basis upon which it was drafted was that matters such as that were better left to parliament and the democratic process.

The view taken of Ch III of the Constitution by Deane and Toohey JJ was as follows: [*Leeth* (1992) 174 CLR 455 at 487]

> Thus, in Ch III's exclusive vesting of the judicial power of the Commonwealth in the 'courts' which it designates, there is implicit a requirement that those 'courts' exhibit the essential attributes of a court and observe, in the exercise of that judicial power, the essential requirements of the curial process, including the obligation to act judicially. At the heart of that obligation is the duty of a court to extend to the parties before it equal justice, that is to say, to treat them fairly and impartially as equals before the law and to refrain from discrimination on irrelevant or irrational grounds.

As I read that passage, it does not draw any distinction between procedural equality and substantive equality, that is to say, between procedural equality and the equality of laws in their operation. As I have said, it is possible to regard the separation of judicial power from the other powers of government as affording a measure of due process but it is due process of an essentially procedural rather than a substantive kind. What is clear is that Ch III says nothing, either expressly or by implication, requiring equality in the operation of laws which courts created by or under that Chapter must administer. Those courts have an obligation to administer justice according to law. No doubt that duty is to do justice according to valid law, but Ch III contains no warrant for regarding a law as invalid because the substantive rights which it confers or the substantive obligations which it imposes are conferred or imposed in an unequal fashion. The passage which I have reproduced appears to me to contemplate a guarantee of what American jurisprudence calls substantive due process, but that conception is not to be found in Ch III or elsewhere in the Australian Constitution.

For these reasons, I would respectfully reject the conclusion reached by Deane and Toohey JJ that there is a doctrine of equality to be found by implication in the Constitution. For the same reasons I would reject the plaintiffs' claim based upon that doctrine. I would affirm the proposition contained in the judgment of Mason CJ, McHugh J and myself in *Leeth* [(1992) 174 CLR 455 at 467] that there is no general requirement contained in the Constitution that Commonwealth laws should have a uniform operation throughout the Commonwealth.

Toohey J: [Toohey J said that the opinions in *Leeth v Commonwealth* (1992) 174 CLR 455 **[11.3.24]** indicated that Brennan J and Gaudron J supported the recognition by Deane and Toohey JJ of some implied right to equality. To suggest otherwise 'does less than justice to the reasons of Brennan J and Gaudron J': 190 CLR at 95. His Honour continued:]

[95] Because equality is derived from the Constitution, it is no answer to refer to laws in which Aboriginals or other groups have been treated unequally. However, a particular law may not infringe the principle, for the reasons Deane J and I identified in *Leeth*. The Constitution mentioned Aboriginals only twice; one of those provisions has been amended, the other repealed. Section 51 of the Constitution empowered the Parliament to make laws with respect to:

> (xxvi)   The people of any race, other than the aboriginal race in any State, for whom it is deemed necessary to make special laws.

The words 'other than the aboriginal race in any State' were later deleted. Section 127, which was repealed by s 3 of the same Act, read:

> In reckoning the numbers of the people of the Commonwealth, or of a State or other part of the Commonwealth, aboriginal natives shall not be counted.

Referring to par (xxvi) before it was amended, Professor Sawer commented: [Sawer, 'The Australian Constitution and the Australian Aborigine' (1966) 2 *Federal Law Review* 17 at 23]

> The exclusion of the aborigines may not necessarily have been against their interests in accordance with the ideas of the time; while they might have lost the possibility of Commonwealth laws for their protection and advancement, so far as such laws had to depend on (xxvi), they were also saved from the sort of laws *against* their [96] interests which were uppermost in the minds of the delegates as likely to be passed pursuant to the placitum.

Both provisions are negative and, as Professor Sawer further observed: [(1966) 2 *Federal Law Review* 17 at 35]

> It is contrary to common sense to attribute to them any more significance than they possess considered individually and in relation to the disparate considerations with which history suggests they were intended to deal.

In particular there is nothing in the Constitution which excludes Aboriginals from citizenship. Their exclusion from citizenship rights, in particular voting rights, was the result of legislation. It is unnecessary to pursue the steps that were taken in this regard; the matter is explored in a recent article by Professors Galligan and Chesterman who conclude that nothing in the Constitution excluded Aboriginals from Australian citizenship. There is nothing that excludes Aboriginals from the principle of equality save the qualification that the principle is not infringed by a law which discriminates between people on grounds which are reasonably capable of being seen as providing a rational and relevant basis for the discriminatory treatment. Indeed, in *Leeth* [(1992) 174 CLR 455 at 489] Deane J and I spoke of the fact that:

> ... a legislative power to make special laws with respect to a particular class of persons, such as aliens (Constitution, s 51(xix)) or persons of a particular race (s 51(xxvi)), necessarily authorizes discriminatory treatment of members of that class to the extent which is reasonably capable of being seen as appropriate and adapted to the circumstance of that membership.

Of course, during the period of the Ordinance s 51(xxvi) excluded 'the aboriginal race in any State'. It is not that sub-section with which we are directly concerned. It may be noted however that the 'discriminatory treatment' referred to in *Leeth* does not stand in necessary contradistinction to laws which are beneficial to a particular class of persons; it may include such laws.

The preamble to the Constitution recites that 'the people ... have [97] agreed to unite in one indissoluble Federal Commonwealth'. These words 'proclaim that the Constitution of the Commonwealth of Australia is founded on the will of all of the people whom it is designed to unite and govern'. [Quick and Garran, *The Annotated Constitution of the Australian Commonwealth*, (1901) at 285] To repeat what Deane J and I said in *Leeth*: [(1992) 174 CLR 455 at 486]

> Implicit in that free agreement was the notion of the inherent equality of the people as the parties to the compact.

In other words, the equality derives from the very existence of a Constitution brought into existence by the will of the people, save to the extent that the Constitution itself permits discriminatory treatment in the sense discussed in these reasons.

Toohey J, who was the only judge to consider whether the Ordinance infringed the implication of equality, indicated that, taking into account standards prevailing at the time when the Ordinance was made, the Ordinance may have been valid, although it was not possible to decide at this stage of the proceedings. He said:

> When the Ordinance is analysed and placed in its historical setting, is it reasonably capable of being seen as providing a rational and relevant basis for the discriminatory treatment of persons answering the description of 'aboriginal or half-caste'? No such basis would survive analysis today. But, for the reasons advanced earlier in this judgment, the Ordinance must be assessed by reference to what was reasonably capable of being seen by the legislature at the time as a rational and relevant means of protecting Aboriginal people against the inroads of European settlement. That is a matter of evidence. It cannot be determined by reference to the pleadings. Hence the answer to this component of the question can only be a qualified one.

Brennan CJ said that the Constitution contemplated legislative inequality (for example s 51 (xix) and s 51 (xxvi)), and that there was no textual or structural requirement of substantive equality in relation to s 122: 190 CLR at 44–45. Gaudron J delivered reasons to similar effect, and added that there was no implication of equality beyond a 'limited' one in Ch III which precluded the conferral of discretionary powers on courts which could be exercised in a discriminatory manner, and this limited implication had no relevance to the Ordinance: 190 CLR at 112–13. Gummow J said there was no general doctrine of legal equality in the Constitution, or arising as a matter of logical or practical necessity from the structure of the Constitution, apart from the limited notion that the judicial power of the Commonwealth be exercised in accordance with the judicial process: 190 CLR at 153.

~~~

Notes

[11.3.33]   It appears the current court shares the view expressed by Zines that it is 'undesirable' for a guarantee of equality to be introduced as an implication from the separation of powers, rather than as a 'guarantee in its own right, resting on broader foundations': Zines (1997) 206.

[11.3.34]   The protections in Ch III extend to prohibiting the introduction of a law declaring that a named person is guilty of a crime and imposing a sanction on that person (that is, a bill of attainder), because such a law would breach the separation of judicial from legislative power: *Polyukhovich v Commonwealth* (1991) 172 CLR 501 **[6.4.19]** at 540 per Mason CJ; at 648 per Dawson J; at 721 per McHugh J.

The Community Protection Act 1994 (NSW), struck down in *Kable v Director of Public Prosecutions (NSW)* (1996) 189 CLR 51 **[11.3.30]** could be described as a bill of attainder. The Act (1) was directed to a named individual; (2) directed the punishment of that individual; (3) did not provide the procedural safeguards involved in a judicial trial. It is a necessary implication of the doctrine of the separation of powers effected by Ch III that no parliament can enact such a law. *Polyhukovich v Commonwealth* (1991) 172 CLR 501 at 536, 617, 646–8, 706, 721; *Kable v DPP (NSW)* (1996) 189 CLR 51.

The Act struck down in *Kable* deprived the Supreme Court of judicial discretion to make a determination relating to the type of facts that were relevant to the legal consequences (that is, incarceration in prison). A Ch III court was used to execute a legislative plan by means far removed from ordinary judicial process, and therefore incompatible with Ch III of the Constitution. The legislation conferred powers on a court that were incompatible 'with the proper discharge by the judiciary of its responsibilities as an institution exercising judicial power' (189 CLR at 96; 132) by requiring a court to engage in the unjudicial task of ordering the incarceration of a person, not on the basis of what the person had done, but on the basis of what the person might do. (At the time of writing, the High Court heard argument in an appeal from the Queensland Court of Appeal's judgment in *Fardon v Attorney-General (Qld)* [2003] QCA 416, upholding the validity of similar legislation applying to a class of person, rather than a single identified person.)

[11.3.35] The proposition that a basic constitutional right of due process could be implied in the Constitution was also raised in *Dietrich v R* (1992) 177 CLR 292. A majority of the court (Mason CJ, Deane, Toohey, Gaudron and McHugh JJ; Brennan and Dawson JJ dissenting) held that there would be a miscarriage of justice if an accused person, charged with a serious criminal offence and unable to afford legal representation, was refused an adjournment of the hearing of the charge until representation was available.

Deane and Gaudron JJ, in separate judgments, claimed that there was a constitutional requirement, entrenched in Ch III of the Commonwealth Constitution, that the trial of an accused person be fair: see 177 CLR at 326 (Deane J); at 362 (Gaudron J). Deane J appeared to limit the constitutional requirement to the trial of Commonwealth offences, and to base his decision that the applicant's conviction should be set aside on the general common law requirement of fairness and the court's role in supervising the administration of justice throughout Australia. Gaudron J described the constitutional requirement of a fair trial as applying to 'judicial power'. In other words, Gaudron J did not limit the requirement to 'the judicial power of the Commonwealth', as dealt with in Ch III; and she described the requirement of fairness as 'independent ... intrinsic and inherent': 177 CLR at 363.

On the other hand, Brennan J, who dissented, denied that there was a constitutional right to a fair trial (at 318):

> Rights can be declared upon a construction of the Constitution (as in *Australian Communist Party v Commonwealth* (1951) 83 CLR 1; *Street v Queensland Bar Association* (1989) 168 CLR 461; *Nationwide News Pty Ltd v Wills* (1992) 108 ALR 681), upon a construction of a statute (as in *Re Bolton; Ex parte Bean* (1987) 1162 CLR 514; and *Ainsworth v Criminal Justice Commission* (1992) 106 ALR 11) or by judicial development of the rules of the common law. In the present case, there is no constitutional or statutory provision which supports the applicant's case.

Similarly, Toohey J, who joined in the court's decision that the applicant's trial had miscarried, denied that there was a constitutional basis for the requirement of fairness in criminal trials: 177 CLR at 360.

[11.3.36] Finally, it is an open question as to whether any or all of the rights said to flow from Ch III might be extended to state courts exercising federal jurisdiction. Section 77(i) of the Constitution authorises the Commonwealth to make laws investing any state court with federal jurisdiction. In *Kable v DPP (NSW)* (1996) 189 CLR 51 **[6.4.48C]**, the High Court recognised that state courts are not bound by the separation of powers doctrine; but a majority (Toohey J, Gaudron J, McHugh J and Gummow J; Brennan CJ and Dawson J dissenting) said that, where a state court was vested with federal jurisdiction, it would be required to exercise that jurisdiction in accordance with Ch III of the Constitution: 189 CLR at 103 per Toohey J; at 189 per Gaudron J; at 116 per McHugh J; at 141, 142 per Gummow J.

Although the majority judges based their reasons upon the proposition that judges exercising federal judicial power must do so in a manner consistent with the nature of that power (the incompatibility doctrine) the consequences for implied rights still remain. The case 'opens up the possibility of constitutional implications of procedural due process etc. being applied to state courts as they have all been vested with federal jurisdiction': Zines (1998).

[11.3.37] In *North Australian Aboriginal Legal Aid Service v Bradley* [2003] HCA 31, the High Court held that courts of self-governing territories could also be invested with federal jurisdiction in a manner which attracted the *Kable* doctrine. However, in *Bradley*, the court held that the appointment of a territory judicial officer on a short-term remuneration package did not offend *Kable* because the officer was entitled, under territory law, to enforce his future remuneration entitlements: see **[12.5.22]–[12.5.23C]**.

Other implied rights

[11.3.38] In *Kruger v Commonwealth* (1997) 190 CLR 1 **[11.3.21C]** and **[11.3.32C]**, the plaintiffs argued, inter alia, that the Aboriginals Ordinance 1918 (NT), which had authorised the removal of Aboriginal children from their parents between 1922 and 1945, was invalid because the Ordinance contravened the terms of the Genocide Convention, which defined genocide as including acts which had the purpose or effect of causing serious mental harm to members of a racial group, and the Constitution should be read as impliedly prohibiting the exercise of governmental powers where the exercise amounted to genocide.

In separate opinions, all members of the court decided that the provisions of the Ordinance did not authorise intentional or purposeful infliction of mental harm. As one of the elements of the definition of genocide was not made out, it was unnecessary to consider whether the Constitution contained the freedom: 190 CLR at 39 (Brennan CJ); 190 CLR at 70 (Dawson J); 190 CLR at 87 (Toohey J); 190 CLR at 107 (Gaudron J); 190 CLR at 144 (McHugh J); 190 CLR at 159 (Gummow J).

Gaudron J said that, if the Ordinance had authorised acts intended to destroy a racial group, they would be beyond the legislative power contained in s 122. This was because under the Constitution, territory residents were ensured no share in political power, had no right to participate in elections, or to self-government, and were 'ruled as Commonwealth fiefdoms': 190 CLR at 106. The rights of territory residents were so limited that the ordinary principle of constitutional interpretation which required constitutional power to be read broadly did not apply. Accordingly 's 122 should be construed on the basis that it was not intended to extend to laws authorising gross violations of human rights and dignity contrary to established principles of the common law': 190 CLR at 107.

Dawson J and Gummow J also relied on principles relating to the incorporation of international law into municipal law (see Ch 2) and said that the Ordinance predated the Genocide Convention and that the Convention did not form part of Australian law: 190 CLR at 70 (Dawson J); 190 CLR at 159 (Gummow J). Further, Dawson J affirmed his long-standing view that there was no doctrine of fundamental rights in Australian constitutional law: 190 CLR at 73. He said also that the legislative power under s 122 was so wide that 'there is nothing which places rights of any description beyond its reach': 190 CLR at 73.

Toohey J drew a distinction between the validity of the Ordinance and the validity of any exercise of power under the Ordinance, and noted specifically that the High Court was determining only the former question: 190 CLR at 88.

Brennan CJ said that the *effect* of legislation, as a matter of fact, may have been to cause such harm. His Honour said at 40:

> It can be accepted that the detention of Aboriginal children and keeping them away from their mothers and families in Aboriginal institutions or reserves might well have caused mental harm in at least some cases but, as a matter of statutory interpretation, none of the impugned provisions can be taken to have authorised or purportedly authorised acts done for the purpose or with the intention of causing mental harm as alleged ... In retrospect, many would say that the risk of a child suffering mental harm by being kept away from its mother or family was too great to permit even a well-intentioned policy of separation to be implemented, but the existence of that risk did not deny the legislative power to make the laws which permitted the implementation of that policy.

4   References

[11.4.1] *Articles*

'Acquisition of Property: Recent Cases on Section 51(xxxi) of the Constitution', 13 *Legal Practice Briefing*, 28 July 1994, 1.

Charlesworth, 'Individual rights and the Australian High Court' (1986) *Law in Context* 53.

Cox, 'Acquiring Property On Just Terms' (1994) 19 *Melbourne Uni Law Rev* 768.

Evatt, (1936) 10 *Australian Law Journal* 49–76 (Supplement).

Hanks, 'Adjusting Medicare Benefits: Acquisition of Property?' (1992) 14 *Sydney Law Rev* 495.

Heydon, 'Judicial Activism and the Death of the Rule of Law' (2003) Jan–Feb *Quadrant* 9.

Keyzer, 'The "Federal Compact" and the Territories (and Chapter III)' (2001) 75 *Aust Law Jo* 124.

Keyzer, '*Pfeiffer, Lange,* The Common Law of the Constitution and the Constitutional Right to Natural Justice' (2000) 20 *Australian Bar Review* 87.

Mason, 'A Bill of Rights for Australia?' (1989) 5 *Aust Bar Rev* 79.

Mason, 'Future Directions in Australian Law' (1987) 13 *Monash Uni Law Rev* 149.

Moffatt, 'Philosophical Foundations of the Australian Constitutional Tradition' (1965) 5 *Sydney Law Rev* 85.

O'Neill, 'Constitutional Human Rights in Australia' (1987) 17 *Federal Law Rev* 85.

Pannam, 'Travelling Section 116 with a US Road Map' (1963) 4 *Melbourne Uni Law Rev* 41.

Wheeler, 'Original Intent and the Doctrine of the Separation of Powers in Australia' (1996) 7 *Public Law Rev* 96.

Wheeler, 'The Doctrine of Separation of Powers and Constitutionally Entrenched Due Process in Australia' (1997) 23 *Monash Uni Law Rev* 248.

[11.4.2] *Papers and reports*

Craven, 'The High Court of Australia: A Study in the Abuse of Power', 31st Alfred Deakin Lecture, Melbourne, Victoria: Alfred Deakin Lecture Trust, 1997.

Constitutional Commission, *Final Report*, AGPS, Canberra, 1988.

Gageler, 'Foundations of Australian federalism and the role of judicial review' (1987) 17 *Federal LR* 162.

Zines, 'Judicial Activism and the Rule of Law', paper delivered at Judicial Activism and Judicial Review in Australian Democracy, conference, 1998, Australian National University.

[11.4.3] *Texts*

Campbell and Whitmore, *Freedom in Australia*, 2nd ed, Sydney University Press, Sydney, 1972.

Finn, *Law and Government in Colonial Australia*, Oxford University Press, Melbourne, 1987.

La Nauze, *The Making of the Australian Constitution*, Melbourne University Press, 1972.

Quick and Garran, *Annotated Constitution of the Australian Commonwealth*, Angus & Robertson, Sydney, 1901.

Zines, *The High Court and the Constitution*, 4th ed, Butterworths, Sydney, 1997.

Chapter

12

The Territories

---

1 Introduction

[12.1.1] About 520,000 of Australia's 20 million people live in its territories, most of them in the Australian Capital Territory and the Northern Territory. The territories are politically diverse: one is technically a republic, one presses hard for statehood, many residents of a third seek to leave the Commonwealth, those of a fourth only recently voted to stay. Struggling to formulate coherent constitutional principle relating to territories, Gleeson CJ, McHugh and Callinan JJ acknowledged the impact of practical considerations in *Re the Governor, Goulburn Correctional Centre; Ex parte Eastman* (*Eastman's* case) (1999) 200 CLR 322:

> One of the reasons for the difficulty ... is the disparate nature of territories. Some (such as the ACT, the Northern Territory, and the Jervis Bay Territory) are internal. Others (such as Norfolk Island, the Coral Sea Islands, the Australian Antarctic Territory, the Ashmore and Cartier Islands, the Cocos (Keeling) Islands, Christmas Island, and the Heard and McDonald Islands) are external. The Northern Territory has already obtained a substantial measure of responsible government ... There is a view that the ACT, by reason of certain provisions of the Constitution, can never become a State ... There have been various circumstances in which external territories have come to be under the authority of the Commonwealth ... The territories have been, still are, and will probably continue to be, greatly different in size, population, and development. Yet they are all dealt with, compendiously and briefly, in s 122 [Constitution] (200 CLR at 331).

[12.1.2] In this chapter we argue that the law of territories can only be understood by reference to the territories' history and politics.

In **[12.2.1]–[12.2.16]**, we consider the geopolitics of Australia's territories in the context of a history of the law of dependencies generally. In **[12.3.1]–[12.3.17]** we consider how the history of dependencies and the themes that emerge from that history have influenced the Commonwealth's acquisition, establishment and administration of territories and their people, particularly the citizenship and representation rights of those people and the administration of territorial justice. In **[12.4.1]–[12.4.12]**, we focus on the Commonwealth's constitutional power to govern the territories, s 122 of the Constitution. In **[12.5.1]–[12.5.28C]** we consider the relationship between the territories power and other provisions '"which might qualify its scope"'; *Capital Duplicators Pty Ltd v Australian Capital Territory (No 1)* (1992) 177 CLR 248 at 272. This section includes discussion of what Gleeson CJ, McHugh and Callinan JJ described as a '"notoriously technical and difficult branch of constitutional law"' (200 CLR at 331): the relationship between Ch III of the Constitution and s 122, including the relationship between Ch III and the powers and courts of self-governing territories. Finally, we consider the self-government arrangements of two of the 'internal' or 'continental' territories, the Australian Capital Territory and the Northern Territory, and one 'external' territory, Norfolk Island. The various constitutional provisions relating to the territories are included in context.

2   The geopolitics of territories

Why do territories exist?

[12.2.1]   Why do federations like Australia, the United States, Canada and India *have* geographical areas designated 'territories' rather than 'states'? Since Australia's territories are 'greatly different in size, population and development', the traditional view that territories are under-populated does not have much explanatory power.

The *federal* spatial differentiation between Australian territories and states may be better understood partly as a legacy of *colonial* spatial differentiation: the application by European powers of different legal rules to their 'metropolitan' territories as opposed to their 'peripheral' acquisitions. In new 'settler' nations like Australia, as in the old European empires, this differentiation has produced differences in citizenship, political representation and the administration of justice. The term 'territory' is commonly used to mark these differences.

There is a racial dimension to the law of territories in much of the world: they are often places where non-'white' populations are under the (at least formal) control of 'white' nations, and whose resources have (historically) been exploited for the benefit of the controlling power. By contrast, although countries like China designate territorial units ('autonomous regions') by reference to their ethnic composition, worldwide there seems to be no majority 'white' territorial population under the control of a non-'white' power. Some of this racial dimension is present in Australia.

There is another explanation for the existence of some territories: the need for (new) federal capitals. Because federal capital territories have been carved out of existing states in federations like Australia and the United States, or built on older capitals in places like India, their populations may be more like those of neighbouring states than those of 'external' territories (although the population of the US capital, Washington DC, consists mainly of people from 'minority' racial backgrounds).

The geography, demography and resources of Australia's (former) territories

Australia in the Indian, Southern and Pacific Oceans

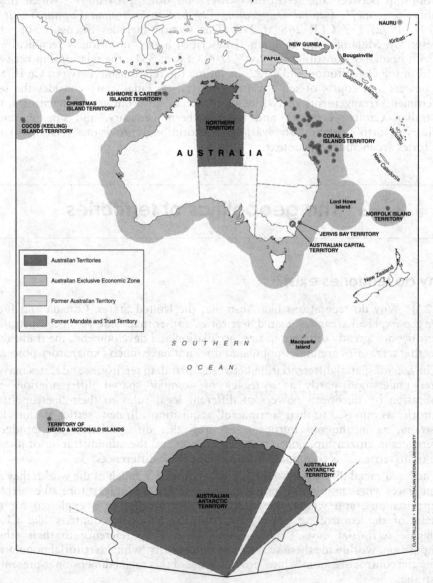

[12.2.2] This map shows Australia's past and present territories. Present territories include, in order of geographical magnitude, and by reference to the method and date of their acquisition and their present populations:

- The **Australian Antarctic Territory** (AAT) (6.1 million km², 5.9 million km² of it land, placed under Australian control by Britain in 1933, accepted by the

Commonwealth in 1936), inhabited only by residents of four permanent research stations and visitors: Australian Antarctic Territory Acceptance Act 1933 (Cth) (commenced 1936). In the early 20th century, several European and South American nations made sovereignty claims to previously unoccupied Antarctica. Britain made the earliest, and largest, claims from 1908, administering them as part of its south Atlantic Falkland Islands Territory. However, Antarctic claims are not generally recognised by non-claimant states; the Antarctic Treaty 1959 purported to freeze sovereignty claims: Crawford and Rothwell (1992), pp 54, 60, 62–5; ATS (1961), p 12.

- The **Northern Territory** (NT) (1.3 million km^2, surrendered to the Commonwealth by South Australia in 1907, accepted in 1911), north of South Australia, population almost 200,000 (about 29 per cent of them indigenous Australians — the highest proportion in any Australian jurisdiction): Northern Territory (Surrender) Act 1907 (SA), Northern Territory Acceptance Act 1910 (Cth).

- The **Australian Capital Territory** (ACT) (formerly the 'Federal Capital Territory') (2357 km^2, 'determined by Parliament' in 1908, surrendered by New South Wales in 1909, accepted 1911, contains the smaller federal 'Seat of Government', the boundaries of which are not defined), 300 km south-west of Sydney near Yass in NSW, population about 320,000: Seat of Government Act 1908 (Cth), Seat of Government Surrender Act 1909 (NSW), Seat of Government Acceptance Acts 1909 and 1922 (Cth).

- The **Territory of Heard and McDonald Islands** (400 km^2, research station established 1947, declared a territory 1953), 4100 km south of Perth, uninhabited: Heard and McDonald Islands Act 1953 (Cth).

- The **Christmas Island Territory** (135 km^2), 2600 km north north-west of Perth and 360 km south of Jakarta, Indonesia; population 1500 (mainly ethnic Chinese): Australia paid £2.9 million to acquire this phosphate-rich island from the then-colony of Singapore under the Christmas Island (Request and Consent) Act 1957 (Cth), Christmas Island Act 1958 (UK), Christmas Island Act 1958 (Cth).

- The **Coral Sea Islands Territory** (81 km^2, declared a territory 1969, enlarged 1997), east of Queensland and northern New South Wales, inhabited by only three or four meteorological staff: Coral Seas Islands Act 1969 (Cth), Environment, Sport and Territories Legislation Amendment Act 1997 (Cth).

- The **Norfolk Island Territory** (35 km^2, acquired from New South Wales in 1914), 1680 km east north-east of Sydney, closer to both Auckland, New Zealand (1100 km to the south-east) and Noumea, French New Caledonia (770 km to the north); population 1800 (about half of whom are of 'Pitcairn' descent — that is, descended from Tahitian women and the *Bounty* mutineers — including speakers of 'Norfolk', a creole of English and ancient Tahitian): Norfolk Island Act 1913 (Cth).

- The **Cocos (Keeling) Islands Territory** (14 km^2, acquired from Singapore in 1955), halfway between Australia and Sri Lanka — 2800 km north-west of Perth, 3700 km west of Darwin, 1000 km south-west of Indonesia, population 600 (mainly Moslem ethnic Malays): Cocos (Keeling) Islands (Request and Consent) Act 1954 (Cth); Cocos (Keeling) Islands Act 1955 (Cth).

- The **Jervis Bay Territory** (7.36 km², surrendered by NSW and accepted by the Commonwealth in 1915), 200 km south of Sydney near Nowra in NSW, population about 550: Seat of Government Surrender Act 1915 (NSW), Jervis Bay Acceptance Act 1915 (Cth).

- The **Ashmore and Cartier Islands Territory** (about 5 km², acquired 1931, part of the Northern Territory from 1938 until self-government in 1978), 320 km north-west of the Kimberley coast of Western Australia, 840 km west of Darwin and just 145 km from the Indonesia island of Roti; no permanent inhabitants: Ashmore and Cartier Islands Acceptance Act 1933 (Cth).

Australia's past territories have included:

- Papua and New Guinea (460,000 km²), now the independent nation of Papua New Guinea; population (mainly ethnic Melanesians) at independence from Australia about 2.5 million, now 5.3 million.

- Nauru (21 km²), now the world's smallest republic, population (ethnic Micronesians and Polynesians) at independence from Australia about 3000, now 12,500.

Remote borders and large resources claims

[12.2.3] The Australian Antarctic Territory is almost as large as continental Australia. The Northern Territory is larger than the states of South Australia, New South Wales, Victoria and Tasmania. The Australian Capital Territory is landlocked within New South Wales; Jervis Bay was acquired by the Commonwealth to provide it with a port. See generally Geoscience Australia (2004); ABS (2003); Australian Antarctic Division (2004); Administration of Norfolk Island (2001).

The greater proximity to Indonesia than Australia of Christmas, Cocos (Keeling), Ashmore and Cartier Islands partly explains their significance in recent Australian 'border protection' debates: compared with the Australian mainland, they are relatively accessible to asylum-seekers from the Middle East and south Asia, including those who stop in Indonesia. These territories are now in the odd position of being fully part of Australia yet excised from Australian territory for migration purposes: although the Migration Act 1958 (Cth) applies to these islands and there is no suggestion that Australia wants to relinquish them, people who land in them cannot lodge refugee applications under Australian law following the Migration Amendment (Excision from Migration Zone) Act 2001 (Cth). Similar problems could conceivably affect Australia's Pacific territories if the thousands of refugees from conflicts in Bougainville, the Solomon Islands or Fiji (Maclellan (2003)) used the Pacific as an escape route. If Pacific refugees fled to Norfolk Island, however, the issue might not resonate on the national stage, because Norfolk controls its own immigration law: see **[12.6.29]**. Ashmore Island has also been the subject of disputes over access to Australian waters by traditional Indonesian fishermen.

The map of Australia in the Indian, Southern and Pacific Oceans (**[12.2.2]**) also shows some remote islands which are actually parts of states, not territories. Examples include Macquarie Island between Tasmania and Antarctica, which is part of Tasmania, and Lord Howe Island, between the Australian mainland and Norfolk Island, which is part of New South Wales. There is no basis in legal principle for these islands being parts of states while others are territories: for example, at federation, it was contemplated that Lord Howe Island would become a Commonwealth territory.

[12.2.4]   Australia's territories are significant, not only because of their land mass and strategic location, but also because of their natural resources. The phosphate deposits of Nauru and Christmas Island were a mainstay of 20th century Australian agriculture, in Nauru's case at great cost to its people: see Anghie (1993); Weeramantry (1992). The Northern Territory is rich in minerals, including Commonwealth-owned uranium; and the Jabiru and Challis oil fields are adjacent to the Ashmore and Cartier Islands. A satellite launching facility is under construction on Christmas Island. Many territories — for example, the Northern Territory, Jervis Bay, Christmas Island, Coral Sea Islands, Ashmore and Cartier Islands — are the sites of important Commonwealth national parks. The Antarctic Treaty provides for Antarctica's environmental protection: see generally Department of Territories (2004).

Island territories also provide a base around which international claims to marine resources are made. Because of its Pacific, Indian and Southern Ocean holdings, Australia has been able to acquire one of the largest Exclusive Economic Zones in the world — an area larger than the Australian land mass. Under the United Nations Convention on the Law of the Sea 1982, coastal states exercise 'sovereign rights for the purpose of exploring and exploiting, conserving and managing the natural resources, whether living or non-living, of the waters superjacent to the sea-bed and of the sea-bed and its subsoil' in these zones (Art 56). Australia's claim to the Ashmore and Cartier Islands has also allowed it a strong negotiating hand in maritime boundary negotiations with Indonesia and in offshore petroleum negotiations with East Timor.

Colonial 'hand-me-downs'

The legacy of multiple administrations: multiple legal regimes and administering courts

[12.2.5]   All of Australia's (former) territories were previously under British, or other European, administration — some much more recently than the 'settler' colonies which became the Australian states. The three 'internal' or 'continental' territories — the Jervis Bay, Northern and Australian Capital Territories — were also previously parts of two 'original states' (New South Wales and South Australia) which became parts of the Commonwealth under covering cl 6 Constitution in 1901: *Capital Duplicators v Australian Capital Territory (No 1)* (1992) 177 CLR 248 at 271–2. The Northern Territory is expressly mentioned as part of one of 'the States' in covering cl 6; by contrast, Norfolk Island, which was under the jurisdiction of New South Wales at the time, is not mentioned.

A consequence of this history is that it is common for Commonwealth statutes accepting or providing for the government of these territories to direct the courts as to which body of law must be applied — inherited Imperial, colonial or state law, Commonwealth territorial law, borrowed state or territory law or (in the case of independent states) no Australian law at all. Such statutes also often set out which courts have jurisdiction over territories. While territorial appeals were once all presided over by the High Court and, after its creation, the Federal Court, there has been a recent move to assimilate the legal systems of some territories to those of neighbouring jurisdictions.

Consider these examples:

- The Seat of Government Acceptance Act 1909 (Cth) provided that NSW laws remained in force in the 'Federal Capital Territory' (the Australian Capital Territory), the Seat of Government Act 1910 (Cth) allowed these laws to be altered by Ordinances made by the Governor-General, the Supreme Court Act 1933 (Cth) established a separate court to apply ACT law, and the Australian Capital Territory (Self-Government) Act 1988 (Cth) (ACT S-G Act) converted all Imperial laws, NSW laws, ACT ordinances and some Commonwealth Acts in force in the ACT into 'enactments' which the new ACT Legislative Assembly could amend and the Supreme Court could enforce. The Australian Capital Territory Supreme Court (Transfer) Act 1992 (Cth) converted the Supreme Court to a creature of local law. In 2001, the Assembly created a new Court of Appeal (see also Jurisdiction of Courts Legislation Amendment Act 2002 (Cth), which abolished ACT appeals to the Federal Court); further appeals go to the High Court (Judiciary Act 1903 (Cth) s 35AA).

- The Northern Territory Acceptance Act 1910 (Cth) and Northern Territory (Administration) Act 1910 (Cth) converted South Australian Acts applicable to the Northern Territory into Commonwealth Ordinances, and allowed the Governor-General to amend them. The Supreme Court Ordinance 1911 (NT) created a separate court to enforce these laws, and the Northern Territory Supreme Court Act 1961 (Cth) re-established it. The Northern Territory (Administration) Act 1947 (Cth) allowed Ordinances to be made by a partly-appointed local Legislative Council, and the Northern Territory (Administration) Act 1974 (Cth) gave wider legislative powers to an elected Legislative Assembly. The Northern Territory (Self-Government) Act 1978 (Cth) (the NT S-G Act) preserved the operation of most existing territory laws as Acts which a new Legislative Assembly could amend. A new court established by the Supreme Court Act 1979 (NT) enforces them, with appeals to the Northern Territory Courts of Appeal or Criminal Appeal and then to the High Court (Judiciary Act 1903 (Cth) s 35AA).

- The Jervis Bay Acceptance Act 1915 (Cth) applied the law of the Australian Capital Territory to Jervis Bay and (after 1933) conferred jurisdiction to enforce it on the ACT Supreme Court, and the ACT Self-Government (Consequential Provisions) Act 1988 (Cth), which extended this arrangement to laws of the self-governing ACT.

- The Norfolk Island Act 1913 (Cth) continued the island's 1897 NSW laws, which had replaced earlier, more Pitcairner-friendly laws developed when the island was a separate colony: HREOC (1999) p 5. The law applicable in the territory seems to have become a political football thereafter. By proclamation on December 24, 1913, the Governor-General repealed NSW laws and applied instead Imperial law as in force in 1828 (presumably because this was the date on which Imperial statutes were received into the eastern Australian colonies). However, the Judiciary Ordinance 1936 (NI) reinstated NSW laws, and the Norfolk Island Act 1957 (Cth) preserved this position. Next, the Norfolk Island Judicature Ordinance 1960 (NI) again declared the island's legal regime subject to English statutes in force in 1828 (see ALRC (1994) Pt II Appendix 3). The Norfolk Island Act 1963 (Cth) and the Norfolk Island Act 1979 (Cth) preserved these pre-existing laws, the latter making them 'enactments' which a new Legislative Assembly could repeal or amend. A Supreme Court was established in

1960 and is dealt with under the Norfolk Island Act 1979 (Cth). Commonwealth Acts do not apply to Norfolk Island unless expressly intended to do so: see ALRC (1995), Ch 10. Appeals from the Norfolk Island Supreme Court go to the High Court: Judiciary Act 1903 (Cth), s 35AA.

- The Cocos (Keeling) Islands Act 1955 (Cth), Christmas Island Act 1958 (Cth), Territories Law Reform Act 1992 (Cth) and Territories Legislation Amendment Act 1992 (Cth) replaced these islands' prior Singaporean legal regime first with a mix of Commonwealth Ordinances, Western Australian law and a few Singaporean Ordinances, then with mainly Western Australian law (amended or suspended if necessary by Commonwealth Ordinance or Commonwealth parliamentary 'termination', supplemented by some Singaporean Ordinances). The 1992 legislation also included these territories in the definition of 'Australia' under the Acts Interpretation Act 1901 (Cth), making Commonwealth Acts generally applicable there (this has never been the position with other 'external' territories, and partly explains the 'border protection' controversy). The Supreme Courts of these territories, established by Commonwealth Ordinance soon after their acquisition, were abolished under the 1992 legislation in 2002, as were appeals from them to the Federal Court. From 1992, Western Australian courts were invested with jurisdiction to enforce territory laws: see ALRC (1995) Ch 10; Indian Ocean Territories (Administration of Laws) Act 1992 (WA). The Cocos (Keeling) Islands Act 1955 also states: 'The institutions, customs and usages of the Malay residents of the Territory shall, subject to any law in force in the Territory from time to time, be permitted to continue in existence.'

- The Australian Antarctic Territory Act 1954 (Cth) and the Heard Island and McDonald Islands Act 1953 (Cth) abolished any pre-existing laws in these territories, substituting ACT law (or the criminal law of Jervis Bay, if it be different) as if these territories formed part of the ACT or Jervis Bay, and conferring jurisdiction to enforce it on the ACT Supreme Court. An Ordinance made by the Governor-General may amend or repeal these laws. Commonwealth Acts do not apply except where expressed to do so.

- The Ashmore and Cartier Islands Acceptance Act 1933 (Cth) originally allowed the Western Australian Governor (on WA government advice) to legislate for the territory; Commonwealth Acts were not automatically applicable to it. The islands were made part of the Northern Territory in 1938. When they were separated from the Northern Territory upon self-government, laws in force at 1 July 1978 continued to apply to them, subject to amendment by Ordinance made by the Governor-General. Northern Territory courts were also given jurisdiction over the islands: Ashmore and Cartier Islands Acceptance Amendment Act 1978 (Cth). In 1978, the territory was placed in the same position as the other Indian Ocean holdings and internal territories presently occupy: it was made normally subject to Commonwealth Acts. The Ashmore and Cartier Islands Acceptance Amendment Act 1985 (Cth) reduced the role of the Governor-General by adopting Northern Territory laws in force from time to time.

- The pre-existing (Queensland) law of the Coral Sea Islands Territory was preserved by the 1969 Act declaring it a territory until 1973, when the Coral Sea Islands Territory Ordinance (No 1) 1973 changed the territory's law to that of the Australian Capital Territory. This law is now enforced by the Supreme Court of Norfolk Island.

- The Papua New Guinea Independence Act 1975 (Cth) stopped the application of earlier Commonwealth laws. However, under Pt 4 of the Constitution of the Independent State of Papua New Guinea, identified Commonwealth laws remained in force as Acts of the Papua New Guinea Parliament.

Of course, provisions of this kind have been required at the state level, but only with respect to the ongoing application of Imperial laws, or of state laws after federation (for example, s 108 of the Constitution).

An anomaly in this area is the position of Nauru. After being granted independence by Australia, Nauru adopted mainly British common law and statute as the basis of its legal system, and established its own Supreme Court: Constitution 1967, Pt V; Custom and Applied Laws Act 1971 (Nauru). However, pursuant to an agreement with the Australian Government in 1976, appeals may be made in criminal and civil matters from the Nauru Supreme Court to the High Court of Australia: see Nauru (High Court Appeals) Act 1976 (Cth). The constitutionality of these arrangements is discussed at **[12.5.19]**.

The legal categories of colonisation and decolonisation

The link between 'whiteness' and self-government

[12.2.6]   Before the era of United Nations-supervised decolonisation (see **[12.2.14]**), Britain was prepared to grant self-government only to colonies which were sufficiently 'white'. This is demonstrated by the 1842 Act allowing New South Wales and Van Diemen's Land to exercise limited self-government, which acknowledged that other new Australian colonies would first require 'a sufficient Population', ignoring their indigenous populations (Australian Constitutions Act 1842 5 & 6 Vict c 76 s 51). By the 1880s, the Imperial Parliament had borrowed an approach taken by the independent United States: it delayed Western Australian self-government for six years or until the colony's population 'exclusive of aboriginal natives, attained to 60,000 souls', an event which occurred in 1893: Constitution Act 1889 (WA) s 42; *Yougarla v Western Australia* (2001) 207 CLR 344 at 352. This racialised approach in part explains why some parts of Britain's former empire were not granted self-government, but rather attached to 'white' colonies like Australia as 'territories'.

'Crown dependencies'

[12.2.7]   Britain's colonisation of Ireland (discussed at **[2.2.3]**) was not its only local territorial expansion. In the 13th century the Channel Isles (a remnant of the Duchy of Normandy) were attached to the English Crown; the Isle of Man was attached to Britain in 1765. Both remain 'Crown dependencies' outside of the United Kingdom and the European Union, their citizens British subjects who do not vote for Westminster but for their own (ancient) parliamentary systems of government under the British Crown, not parliament. The UK Parliament rarely legislates for them, although its Acts can be applied to them by Order-in-Council; the British Crown controls their foreign affairs. In subsequent colonising endeavours, Britain extended this model of territorial government by the executive throughout the world, although elsewhere it did so with less respect for indigenous governments and laws.

'Possessions' (Crown colonies, later 'overseas territories')

[12.2.8] By the early 20th century, the British Empire covered about one-quarter of the world's land mass and a similar proportion of its people; other European powers also held significant tracts of new territory (for example, Germany and France in the Pacific). Most of these territories were not settler colonies of the kind established in Australia — rather, dominion was established over non-British peoples.

As noted in Chapter 2, the international law of the colonial period permitted European nations to acquire new territory beyond their borders by conquest, cession or (in the case of 'uninhabited' territories), settlement: see **[2.2.4]**. In colonies other than those established by settlement, the Crown enjoyed prerogative powers to legislate and to establish courts and governments — as in the Channel Isles and the Isle of Man, there was no need for Parliament to legislate, although it sometimes did so. The laws, courts and governments of these 'plantations' need not resemble those of Britain: English law and procedure were often not applied for reasons of administrative convenience or (perceived) cultural difference; their governmental structures often reflected English mercantile rather than civic interests. Thus, for example, the Act of Settlement 1701 (Eng) provided for judicial independence in England but not in those parts of India under the control of the chartered British East India Company; the institution of jury trial, guaranteed to Englishmen by Magna Carta, was often dispensed with throughout the empire. And, of course, residents of British colonies had no representation in the Imperial Parliament.

'Protectorates'

[12.2.9] The international law of this period also tolerated establishment of 'protectorates' (client states whose foreign relations, and often domestic affairs, a European power controlled). 'Protectorates' could be established by 'treaties' with local rulers, even those insufficiently 'civilised' to enjoy sovereignty under international law. Many were practically indistinguishable from colonies: Baty (1921). Protectorates were established for a range of reasons: to take advantage of indigenous resources and sometimes manpower, to 'civilise' indigenous populations or protect them from stray settler violence, to obtain strategic outposts, or to preclude similar claims by other nations — for example, British New Guinea (later Australia's Territory of Papua) was established in 1884 to fend off German colonisation. The boundaries of nations like Nauru and New Guinea originated in an 1886 Anglo-German Convention which divided the Pacific into spheres of influence, separating Nauruans and New Guineans from their neighbours in the Solomon Islands and Kiribati: Weeramantry (1992), pp 36–7. For further consideration of the practice of establishing protectorates and its implications in the Indian and Pacific Oceans, see *R v Crewe (Earl); Ex parte Sekgome* (1910) 2 KB 576; *Sobhuza II v Miller* [1926] AC 518; *Administration of Papua New Guinea v Daera Guba* (1973) 130 CLR 353 at 391–2, 415, 436, 438. Germany lost its imperial holdings in World War I, but other European powers retained theirs, in some cases until the present — for example, the French colonies in the Pacific, and the British Indian Ocean base of Diego Garcia.

Private and corporate acquisitions and 'British Settlements'

[12.2.10] Many European nations acquired territorial possessions via their settlement by private individuals or, in North America and Asia, by charter trading companies. It was a basic principle of British law that subjects could only acquire new territories if they did so for the Crown; even company acquisitions attracted overarching British sovereignty. The northern part of Australia's former Territory of New Guinea was acquired in 1884 by a German charter company and proclaimed a German colony four years later. Australia's Cocos (Keeling) Islands Territory was settled by the Englishmen Alexander Hare and John Clunies-Ross in the 1820s and claimed for Britain in 1857. In 1886, Queen Victoria granted all lands in the islands to the Clunies-Ross family, an arrangement which was only reversed in the late 20th century.

The British Settlements Act 1887 (Imp) allowed Queen Victoria to establish laws and governments in 'divers places where there is no civilized government' in which her subjects had settled but 'which [had] not been acquired by cession or conquest, and [were] not for the time being within the jurisdiction of the Legislature': in other words, it allowed British *government* to follow British *migrants* in establishing new colonies. For example, when British New Guinea was converted to a Crown colony in 1888, Queen Victoria established an all-'white' local legislature there by Letters Patent under the British Settlements Act: *Administration of Papua New Guinea v Daera Guba* (1973) 130 CLR 353 at 444. The Imperial Crown's powers under the British Settlements Act could also be delegated to local colonial authorities.

This general legislation followed Imperial enactment of similar Acts specific to particular colonies. For example, the Cocos (Keeling) Islands and Christmas Island were previously administered under the Straits Settlement Act 1866 (Imp) (repealed 1946), then as part of the colony of Singapore under the British Settlements Act 1945 (Imp).

Could Britain's independent former settler colonies annex new territory? The Australian colonies and states

[12.2.11] Britain's original Australian settler colonies enjoyed no unilateral power to acquire new territory because they could not act extra-territorially. Thus Queensland's colonising efforts in the Torres Strait in 1879 required Imperial support: see [2.3.3]. When the Queensland Governor tried to annex the area which became German New Guinea the year before Germany did so, Britain repudiated him: Quick and Garran (1901), p 110. Queensland had to press the Imperial authorities to declare the south-east of the island of New Guinea a 'protectorate' three days after Germany claimed the north, the British having already recognised earlier Dutch claims to the western half of the island.

However, the British Crown did place additional colonies under the authority of Australian Governors, sometimes with lasting consequences. British New Guinea, proclaimed a Crown colony in 1888, was placed under an Administrator advised by an appointed Executive Council, but also took instructions from the Queensland Governor advised by Queensland Ministers: *Strachan v Commonwealth* (1906) 4 CLR 455 at 461–2; Mattes, 1963. An appointed 'white' Legislative Council legislated to adopt Queensland law, including Sir Samuel Griffith's Criminal Code: Mattes, 1963, p 149; *R v Bernasconi* (1915) 19 CLR 629. The Code subsequently became the criminal law of independent Papua New Guinea.

Norfolk Island was placed under the Governor of New South Wales in 1897. Originally unoccupied, in 1825 it had become Britain's most brutal penal colony: Hughes, 1986, Ch 13. Mason J described its constitutional history in *Berwick Ltd v Gray* (1976) 133 CLR 603 at 608–9:

> It was initially part of the penal settlement established in New South Wales and was later administered by the Governor of Van Diemen's Land as part of that colony. In 1856, pursuant to the authority conferred by the Australian Waste Lands Act, 1855 (Imp.), it was separated from ... Van Diemen's Land and constituted a separate settlement administered by the Governor of New South Wales who was appointed Governor of Norfolk Island. Subsequently, on 15th January 1897, on the eve, as it were, of the establishment of the Commonwealth, by an Order in Council it was recited that it was 'expedient that other provision should be made for the government of Norfolk Island, and that, in prospect of the future annexation of that island to the colony of New South Wales, or to any federal body of which that colony may hereafter form part, in the meantime the affairs of the island should be administered by the Governor of New South Wales'. The Order in Council went on to so provide and empowered the Governor of New South Wales to make laws for the peace, order and good government of the island. The continued administration of Norfolk Island as part of, or by the governors of, the Australian colonies culminating in the Order in Council made in 1897 vesting the administration in the Governor of New South Wales makes it abundantly clear that Norfolk Island forms part of the Commonwealth of Australia.

Norfolk Island's administration by Australians remains an ongoing source of political grievance: see **[12.6.16]**.

The League of Nations mandate system

[12.2.12] Australia's participation in the 'Great War', the Treaty of Versailles and the League of Nations are often cited as crucial first steps in its emergence as an independent nation. Yet just as Australia was preparing to throw off the British Imperial yoke, it was making plans to become a greater colonial power in its own right.

After World War I, the Allies took a new approach to distributing the possessions of the former German and Ottoman empires. Under the Treaty of Versailles, these territories were to be administered by the victors on behalf of the new League of Nations. Article 22 of the Treaty provided for 'tutelage' of these territories' inhabitants by 'advanced' neighbours 'as Mandatories on behalf of the League'. '[T]he well-being and development of such peoples' formed 'a sacred trust of civilisation'.

Germany's former Pacific colonies — including the northern half of what is now Papua New Guinea, and Nauru, over which Australia and 'the British Empire' were the Mandatories — were 'C' class mandates to be 'administered under the laws of the Mandatory *as integral portions of its territory*' (emphasis added). The High Court allowed administration of mandates as ordinary territories under s 122 Constitution, despite strong dissents from Evatt J, who considered that 'federal' constitutional protections should apply to them: *Jolley v Mainka* (1933) 49 CLR 242; *Ffrost v Stevenson* (1937) 58 CLR 528.

Many mandates were exploited by their Mandatories. Examples included the British mandate over Iraq, under which Iraqis received none of the value of major oil discoveries until a revolution in 1958, and the Australian-run 'British empire' mandate over Nauru, which transferred Nauru's phosphate wealth to Australian and New Zealand farmers. This mining, conducted by a bizarre institution, the British

Phosphate Commissioners, eventually destroyed the island: see Weeramantry, 1992; Anghie, 1993.

The United Nations trust system

[12.2.13] After World War II, the new United Nations Charter established a 'trust' system, under which members undertook to administer 'territories whose peoples have not yet attained a full measure of self-government' in 'the interests of the inhabitants of these territories'. Chapter XII of the Charter established an international trusteeship system to facilitate these aims, and applied it to former mandate territories as well as other territories placed in trusteeship by members; Ch XIII established a supervisory Trusteeship Council.

In 1946 and 1947, the UN approved trusteeship agreements appointing 'Administering Authorities' to the Territories of New Guinea (Australia) and Nauru (Britain, Australia and New Zealand). The High Court ruled that trust territories could also be administered like ordinary territories: *Fishwick v Cleland* (1960) 106 CLR 186.

The UN trust system was also abused: South Africa refused to place its mineral-rich former mandate territory of South-West Africa (now Namibia) under the scheme, annexing it directly as an apartheid state. The trust system expanded (in some cases, permanently) the Pacific empire of the United States of America, providing sites for nuclear testing. The British Phosphate Commissioners' exploitation of Nauru also continued under the trust. In 1992, Nauru sued Australia in the International Court of Justice for breach of its mandate and trusteeship obligations: *Certain Phosphate Lands in Nauru* (*Nauru v Australia*) (1992) ICJ 240. The case was settled without an admission of liability for $A107 million in 1993 (ATS 1993, No 26), which partly compensated for damage to land but not for lost national wealth. See generally Anghie, 1993; Weeramantry, 1992.

Territorial decolonisation

[12.2.14] In 1960, the United Nations General Assembly adopted the Declaration on the Granting of Independence to Colonial Countries and Peoples, and began to pressure members to decolonise 'dependent' external territories. Principle VI of the General Assembly's Resolution 1541 (XV) (United Nations, 2004) states:

> A Non-Self-Governing Territory can be said to have reached a full measure of self-government by:
>
> (a) Emergence as a sovereign independent State;
>
> (b) Free association with an independent State; or
>
> (c) Integration with an independent State.

The UN maintains a list of dependent territories which require decolonisation. No Australian territories are presently on this list, despite claims by many Norfolk Islanders that that territory 'is being grotesquely, stealthily and gradually incorporated into the Australian body politic without the consent of [its] people': HREOC, 1999, p 24.

[12.2.15] Australia granted independence to three of its former territories (Papua, New Guinea and Nauru) in the 1960s and 1970s: Papua New Guinea Independence Act 1975; Nauru Independence Act 1967 (Cth). While the terrorist group Jemaah

Islamiah allegedly seeks a pan-Islamic state encompassing parts of north Australia (see AAP, 2002), the possibility that Australia's 'internal' territories might become independent nation states has not been seriously entertained by others.

In 1984, the mainly Malay population of the Cocos (Keeling) Islands voted in a United Nations-sponsored referendum for *integration* into Australia. This referendum was the culmination of a long effort to liberate that population from domination by the Clunies-Ross family, who had imported Malay labourers to work in the island's industries during their prior administration by the British colonies of Singapore and Ceylon. See *Clunies-Ross v Commonwealth* (1984) 155 CLR 193 per Murphy J at 206–7 and *Re Clunies-Ross (a bankrupt); Ex parte Totterdell* (1987) 72 ALR 241 per French J.

Many residents of Norfolk Island seek a similar referendum on that territory's future: see <http://www.pitcairners.org/government3.html>. Some Norfolk Islanders suggest that the territory should become a Crown dependency of Britain, like the Channel Isles, or be incorporated into an 'Oceanic Confederation of Polynesian Nations': see <http://nisdv.bravehost.com>; Australia, Parliament, 2003.

Unlike the United States and New Zealand, Australia does not have territories in *free association* with it, although s 122 of the Constitution would appear to allow such associations.

[12.2.16] In the remainder of this chapter we turn our attention to the Commonwealth and its territories, focussing on those which are now self-governing: the Australian Capital Territory, the Northern Territory and Norfolk Island.

3 The Commonwealth and its territories

Origins

[12.3.1] The Commonwealth of Australia began as a government in control (at least in legal theory) of an entire continent: covering cl 6 of the Constitution counted among the founding states 'South Australia, including the [then] northern territory of South Australia'. In 1901, the Commonwealth had no territories. However, the founders contemplated that Norfolk Island, Lord Howe Island (now part of NSW), British New Guinea (later Papua, now the southern part of Papua New Guinea) and Fiji would become Commonwealth territories: Quick and Garran (1901), p 376; *Capital Duplicators Pty Ltd v Australian Capital Territory (No 1)* (1992) 177 CLR 248 at 272 per Brennan, Deane and Toohey JJ. The Constitution also contemplated that the Commonwealth would acquire new territories from the states: see **[12.3.2]**.

While the preamble to the Constitution states that 'it is expedient to provide for the admission into the Commonwealth of other Australasian colonies and possessions of the Queen', no such entity has been admitted as a state since Western Australia sneaked into federation just before the Constitution was proclaimed in 1901. Besides territories surrendered by the states, the only new lands acquired by the Commonwealth have been offshore territories.

The constitutional underpinnings

[12.3.2] A number of provisions of the Constitution provide for change in the territorial boundaries of, or within, the Commonwealth, and make provision for the government of the territories. The most important is s 122, which appears in Ch VI 'New States':

> The Parliament may make laws for the government of any territory surrendered by any State to and accepted by the Commonwealth, or of any territory placed by the Queen under the authority of and accepted by the Commonwealth, or otherwise acquired by the Commonwealth, and may allow the representation of such territory in either House of Parliament to the extent and on the terms which it thinks fit.

In Chapter VII, 'Miscellaneous', s 125 *requires* that the Commonwealth acquire a particular territory:

> The seat of Government of the Commonwealth shall be determined by the Parliament, and shall be within territory which shall have been granted to or acquired by the Commonwealth, and shall be vested in and belong to the Commonwealth, and shall be in the State of New South Wales, and be distant not less than one hundred miles from Sydney.
>
>   Such territory shall contain an area of not less than one hundred square miles, and such portion thereof as shall consist of Crown lands shall be granted to the Commonwealth without any payment therefor.
>
> The Parliament shall sit at Melbourne until it meet at the seat of Government.

In Ch V, 'The States', s 111 allows states to give up territory to the Commonwealth:

> The Parliament of a State may surrender any part of the State to the Commonwealth; and upon such surrender, and the acceptance thereof by the Commonwealth, such part of the State shall become subject to the exclusive jurisdiction of the Commonwealth.

In Ch VI, ss 121, 123 and 124 deal with new states, or changes in existing states' boundaries:

> **121.** The Parliament may admit to the Commonwealth or establish new States, and may upon such admission or establishment make or impose such terms and conditions, including the extent of representation in either House of the Parliament, as it thinks fit.
>
> **123.** The Parliament of the Commonwealth may, with the consent of the Parliament of a State, and the approval of the majority of the electors of the State voting upon the question, increase, diminish, or otherwise alter the limits of the State, upon such terms and conditions as may be agreed on, and may, with the like consent, make provision respecting the effect and operation of any increase or diminution or alteration of territory in relation to any State affected.
>
> **124.** A new State may be formed by separation of territory from a State, but only with the consent of the Parliament thereof, and a new State may be formed by the union of two or more States or parts of States, but only with the consent of the Parliaments of the States affected.

And in Ch I, s 52(i) provides for the administration of 'the seat of Government':

> The Parliament shall, subject to this Constitution, have exclusive power to make laws for the peace, order and good government of the Commonwealth with respect to:
>
> (i) the seat of government of the Commonwealth, and all places acquired by the Commonwealth for public purposes;
>
> ...

'Acquisition', 'admission', 'establishment'

[12.3.3] Section 122 refers to three methods by which the Commonwealth may acquire territories: surrender from a state; action 'by the Crown acting on other than Australian advice' (*Sue v Hill* (1999) 199 CLR 462 at 497 (Gleeson CJ, Gummow and Hayne JJ)) — both of which require Commonwealth 'acceptance'; and acquisition 'otherwise'. From 1901, it was thus clearly contemplated that the Commonwealth could expand territorially on its own initiative as well as that of Britain, and that it could derive 'internal' territory from the states. Acquisition of territory is an *executive* act which lies squarely within s 61 of the Constitution (*Jolley v Mainka* (1933) 49 CLR 242; *Ffrost v Stevenson* (1937) 58 CLR 528 at 555 per Latham CJ; *Lamshed v Lake* (1958) 99 CLR 132 at 142 (Dixon CJ)), although parliament has usually *legislated* to acquire or accept territories.

The terms 'admission' and 'establishment' in s 121 of the Constitution are designed to distinguish between the situation where an existing political unit (for example, as was once contemplated, New Zealand) becomes a state of the Commonwealth on the one hand, and the situation where the Commonwealth creates a new state out of either part of an existing state (as contemplated by s 124), or a territory.

'Surrenders'

[12.3.4] Surrenders of 'internal' territory by the states have involved quite profound changes in the Australian body politic: for example, the surrenders of the NT and the ACT effectively disenfranchised their residents, who had been enfranchised at the NSW level and under the Northern Territory Representation Act 1888 (SA) as well as federally, but who initially obtained no territory-level government and no territory representation in the Commonwealth Parliament. Being constitutionally authorised, these surrenders do not require a s 128 referendum. Nor did the surrender of the 'Federal Capital Territory' require a referendum of *state* electors under s 123 of the Constitution, which requires both the consent of a state legislature and the approval of 'the majority of the electors of the State' before state limits may be altered: *Paterson v O'Brien* (1978) 138 CLR 276. However, such a referendum would be required, if, for example, as is sometimes suggested (Sanders and Arthur (2001)), the Torres Strait Islands, presently part of Queensland, were to become a self-governing territory.

Citizenship in the territories: a different and inferior class of citizens?

Territorians and citizenship

[12.3.5] In United States law, residents of some territories have been denied US citizenship; the question 'whether the constitution follows the flag' to offshore territories remains a live one, particularly in light of recent controversy over Guantanamo Bay. United States territories are either not represented in Congress, or are represented there by non-voting delegates. See generally Cleveland, 2002; Levinson, 2000; Van Dyk, 1992.

In Australian law, differences between residents of states and those of territories have been expressed through the law of citizenship only to a limited extent. Under the general rule in *Calvin's* case (1609) 7 Co Rep 2a; 77 ER 377 (see **[2.2.17]**), residents of territories colonised by Britain became British subjects upon their colonisation. This remained the position after the transfer of territories like Papua to Australia because at that time Australian law knew no concept of national citizenship. However, when Australian citizenship was invented in 1948 (Nationality and Citizenship Act 1948, later renamed as the Australian Citizenship Act 1948), its definition of 'Australia' included Papua. Thus Papuans were converted into Australian citizens. There were two important exceptions to the extension of Australian citizenship to residents of Australian territories:

- Residents of the former mandate and trust territories did not become Australian citizens, never having been British subjects.

- Residents of Christmas and Cocos Islands, who were already British subjects, did not become Australian citizens upon those territories' acquisition by Australia. Rather, people who were resident there upon their acquisition, and who had remained resident there or elsewhere in Australia, were permitted to make declarations of Australian citizenship almost 30 years later: Christmas Island Amendment Act 1980 (Cth); Cocos (Keeling) Islands Amendment Act 1979 (Cth). Presumably this late extension of citizenship reflected the fact that the migrant labour populations of these islands only became permanent under Australian administration.

Not being citizens, and residing as they did in territories outside 'Australia' for the purposes of the Migration Act 1958 (Cth), these non-'white' populations were unable to migrate to the Australian mainland without confronting the 'white Australia' policy.

Some other disadvantages visited on the people of the Indian Ocean territories flowed from their lack of citizenship: Christmas and Cocos Islanders were only admitted to the Medicare and social security systems in 1984. However, citizenship made little other practical difference for Papuans, who were never entitled to social security and lived under the same administration as the non-citizens of New Guinea from 1945.

Representation in parliament

[12.3.6] The disadvantaged position of territorians historically owes more to the fact that the Constitution gives them no right to representation in parliament, with the result that they have not always been represented there, or have been represented by non-voting delegates. At the same time, some states enjoy much higher levels of Commonwealth parliamentary representation than their populations alone justify.

Section 24 of the Constitution provides:

> The House of Representatives shall be composed of members directly chosen by the people of the Commonwealth ... chosen in the several States in proportion to the respective numbers of their people ...

Section 24 also establishes a quota for calculating the number of electorates for each state, in which the *number* of 'people of the Commonwealth' plays a role: see **[4.6.9C]**. It then continues:

> (ii.) ... But notwithstanding anything in this section, five members at least shall be chosen in each Original State.

Section 7 provides:

> The Senate shall be composed of Senators for each State, directly chosen by the people of the State...
>
> Until the Parliament otherwise provides there shall be six senators for each Original State. The Parliament may make laws increasing or diminishing the number of senators for each State, but so that equal representation of the several Original States shall be maintained and that no Original State shall have less than six senators...

As the *Territorial Senators* cases (see **[4.2.30]–[4.2.38]**) indicate, these provisions cannot be interpreted to allow representation of the *territories* in parliament. After the *Territorial Senators* cases, the High Court decided in *Attorney-General (NSW); Ex rel McKellar v Commonwealth* (1977) 139 CLR 527 **[4.6.18]** that the phrase 'the people of the Commonwealth' in s 24 did not include the people of the *territories*, only those of the *states*. (One consequence of the alternative view would have been that the people of Papua should have been counted for the purposes of allocating parliamentary seats to the states during the previous 71 years — something which had never even been contemplated.) While there are some other (sometimes rather confusing) decisions which speak of residents of some territories as part of 'the Commonwealth' for other purposes (for example, *Berwick Ltd v Gray* (1976) 133 CLR 603 at 608 (Mason J) regarding Norfolk Island; *Capital Duplicators Pty Ltd v Australian Capital Territory (No 1)* (1992) 177 CLR 248 at 275 (Brennan, Deane and Toohey JJ), and 289 (Gaudron J) regarding the internal territories' inclusion in a national 'free trade area' (see **[12.6.10C]**), the federal parliament was not designed with territorians in mind.

[12.3.7] Territorial representation has, however, been achieved by legislation under s 122 (see **[12.3.2]**). The term 'representation' in s 122 does not necessarily require the representation accorded state residents, including residents of new states. As Mason J explained in *Western Australia v Commonwealth* (the first *Territory Senators* case) (1975) 134 CLR 201 at 270–1:

> With respect to representation of a Territory in either House of the Commonwealth Parliament the Parliament has, by virtue of s 122, power to determine (a) the extent of the representation and (b) the terms of that representation. By way of contrast, upon the admission or establishment of a new State pursuant to s 121, the Parliament only has power to determine the extent of the representation to be accorded the new State. The inclusion in s 122 of a specific power to allow representation upon any terms which the Parliament thinks fit makes it plain that the Parliament may confer on representatives of a Territory rights and privileges identical or inferior to those enjoyed by a member of either House. But in the case of a new State, Parliament has power to determine only the number of representatives a new State may have; the representatives of a new State necessarily enjoy the rights and privileges of the representatives of the original States — Parliament cannot diminish their rights and privileges ...
>
> ... ss 7 and 24 make exhaustive provision for the composition of each House [of Parliament] until such time as Parliament might see fit to allow representation to a territory under s 122. This interpretation not only gives full scope to the language of that section but it supports and gives authority to the course of constitutional development by which in recent years Parliament might see fit to allow representation to a Territory in the House of Representatives, first by a member without voting rights, then by a member with qualified voting rights and finally by a member with unqualified voting rights, see the Northern Territory Representation Act 1922, the Northern Territory Representation Act 1959, the Northern Territory Representation Act 1968.

[12.3.8] Parliament did not permit the Northern Territory representation in the House of Representatives until 1922 — but even then, this was *non-voting* representation on the United States model. Only the territory's 'white' and 'coloured' population were enfranchised: 'aboriginal natives' (people of full Aboriginal descent) were disenfranchised as they were everywhere else in the Commonwealth: see Chapter 2 and Clarke (2001), pp 243–5. Nonetheless, early territory voting patterns favoured the Australian Labor Party. The Australian Capital Territory (incorporating Jervis Bay) was given similar house representation in 1948, and the members for the territories were permitted to vote on territory questions from 1959: Northern Territory Representation Act 1922 (Cth) and Australian Capital Territory Representation Act 1948 (Cth), as amended. The justification for excluding residents of the ACT from voting before 1959 seems to have been partly grounded in the desire 'to place the territory for the seat of government above the controversies of federal politics. It would be a haven of neutrality': *Re Governor, Goulburn Correctional Centre; Ex parte Eastman* (*Eastman's* case) (1999) 200 CLR 322 at 367 per Kirby J.

From 1968, the NT members, and from 1973 the ACT members, of the house had full voting rights (Northern Territory Representation Act 1968 (Cth) and Australian Capital Territory Representation (House of Representatives) Act 1973 (Cth)). Both territories were granted Senate representation in 1974: see **[4.2.32C]**.

The Northern Territory and the Australian Capital Territory presently have two senators and two members of the House each — representation which in part reflects their relatively small populations. They are not entitled to the full set of senators (now 12) guaranteed to the 'Original States' by s 7 of the Constitution. Under s 7, Tasmania has 10 more senators than the Australian Capital Territory, despite having only 150,000 more people. The push for Northern Territory statehood (discussed below at **[12.6.54]**) must be understood partly as a desire for greater Senate representation. However, as discussed at **[12.3.2]** and **[12.3.7]** above, not even new states are constitutionally entitled to the same Senate representation as 'Original States'. Similarly, although the Commonwealth Electoral Act 1918 (Cth) guarantees each territory at least one member of the House of Representatives, s 24 of the Constitution guarantees Tasmania five.

[12.3.9] Norfolk Islanders were not able to vote for parliament until 1992: Norfolk Island (Electoral and Judicial) Amendment Act 1992 (Cth). There seems to have been considerable islander opposition to their incorporation into the electoral system: more than 80 per cent voted against it in a locally sponsored referendum, although the integrity of such referenda has been questioned by Australian authorities: see Australia, Parliament, 2002, 2003, pp 20, 109–13. As a result of their small population and this opposition, islanders who are Australian citizens — a status which some argue was imposed on them in 1948 — are the only citizens for whom voting in Commonwealth elections is optional. They do not vote in a Norfolk Island electorate, but may choose an Australian electorate to which they have some connection (for example, they were recently enrolled there, their next of kin are enrolled there or they were born there), *or* the electorate of Canberra: Commonwealth Electoral Act 1918 (Cth) s 95AA. In December 2003, only 149 Norfolk Islanders had enrolled to vote in Commonwealth elections; an Australian parliamentary inquiry recently recommended that voting be made compulsory and the choice of electorates removed: Australia, Parliament, 2003, pp 142–4.

[12.3.10] Residents of Christmas and the Cocos (Keeling) Islands were first enfranchised as part of the Northern Territory in 1984: Christmas Island Administration (Miscellaneous Amendments) Act 1984 (Cth); Cocos (Keeling) Islands Self-Determination (Consequential Amendments) Act 1984 (Cth); see now s 4 of the Commonwealth Electoral Act 1918 (Cth) (as amended). That is, their parliamentary voice is not heard in a Western Australian electorate despite the fact that they are governed by Western Australian law. The residents of the Australian Antarctic Territory and Heard and McDonald Island are permitted to vote in their home electorates: Commonwealth Electoral Act 1918 (Cth) Pt VII.

[12.3.11] Australia did not provide its other non-'white' external territories with parliamentary representation. This seems to have been justified partly on the basis that Commonwealth Acts did not normally apply to Papua, New Guinea and Nauru. For the first 43 years of Australian rule, the Ordinances of Papua were made by an all-'white' Assembly, a body originally established by the British. Between 1920 and 1932, the law of New Guinea was made by the Governor-General; many Papuan Ordinances were adopted as Ordinances of New Guinea. A local legislature was established in 1932: New Guinea Act 1932 (Cth). Joint administration of the two territories led to the establishment of a joint Legislative Council under the Papua and New Guinea Act 1949 (Cth). But not all members were required to live in the territory, and only three seats were guaranteed to 'natives' out of a total of 29; 16 were reserved for Australian officials. A House of Assembly was established in 1963.

[12.3.12] Nauru was not granted an indigenous Assembly until 1965 — 45 years after it came under Australian control: Nauru Act 1965 (Cth). Before 1965, the Ordinances of Nauru were made by an administrator appointed by the Australian Government. The administrator had no authority over phosphate mining, which was the domain of the British Phosphate Commissioners: see **[12.3.17]**.

[12.3.13] The historical disenfranchisement of territorians not only left them unable to contribute meaningfully to the 'framework' laws under which their jurisdictions were administered by the Commonwealth executive before self-government, but also affected the political direction of Australia generally. For example, the Menzies Government narrowly won the 1961 election, despite having the same number of members of the House of Representatives as the opposition. This was because two opposition members representing the NT and the ACT at that time could only vote on territory issues: Lundie and Mann, 1998.

Constitutional referenda

[12.3.14] Before 1977, territory residents were unable to vote in Commonwealth constitutional referenda, even on questions that concerned them directly. However, as a result of one of the few successful referenda in Australian constitutional history, residents of territories which enjoy representation in the House of Representatives may now participate in any 'majority of electors' required for the approval of a constitutional amendment (s 128 as amended by Constitution Alteration (Referendums) 1977).

This means that not only voters of the ACT and the NT, but also Cocos and Christmas Island voters (who vote as part of the NT) and those Norfolk Islanders enrolled to vote in Canberra as well as elsewhere may influence a referendum outcome at the national level. There is, however, no requirement that a majority of electors in a majority of states *and territories* support the proposed law.

Administration of justice

[12.3.15] Because of their remote location or small populations, some territories have had trouble attracting resident judges, particularly for long periods of tenure. This is one reason why the Commonwealth adopted in some territories a practice used by some state governments of appointing judicial officers for limited terms or 'during the pleasure of the Governor-General'. Thus, for example, before 1949 even judges of the Supreme Courts of Papua and New Guinea were not appointed for life, as s 72 of the Constitution then required in the case of 'Justices of the High Court and of the other courts created by the Parliament'. The Australian Capital Territory Supreme Court still engages 'acting' judges: *Re The Governor, Goulburn Correctional Centre; Ex parte Eastman* (1999) 200 CLR 322: see further **[12.6.52]**. Another reason why the Commonwealth did not appoint territory judges consistently with s 72 was that this would have given territory judges greater security than judges appointed at the state level, yet in constituting territory courts the Commonwealth was acting in a similar capacity to a state government.

[12.3.16] The appointment of territory judges without secure remuneration has been the subject of some controversy because, on one view, at least while territorians remain unrepresented in the parliament which governed them, they were more vulnerable to abuse of their civil rights than other Australians. We return to this question in **[12.5.27]** and **[12.5.28C]**.

Public policy and 'equality with the states'

[12.3.17] The argument that the territories should be treated by the Commonwealth just as state governments treat their residents is sometimes made more generally, for example as a reason for denying the applicability to territories of the 'just terms' compensation guarantee in s 51(xxxi) Constitution (an issue discussed further in **[12.5.1]–[12.5.4]**).

However, historically at least, Commonwealth territorial administrations have allowed policy experiments in territories without political representation which state governments may have hesitated to visit on their populations or to allow within their borders. For example:

■   Australia's largest 'X-rated' pornography production industry grew up in the Australian Capital Territory before self-government. The multi-million dollar industry became concentrated in the ACT after the states refused to participate in a Commonwealth scheme establishing the 'X' classification in 1984. The ACT Legislative Assembly is prevented from legislating with respect to classification and censorship: see **[12.6.32]**. Since the High Court decisions in *Capital Duplicators (No 1)* and *(No 2)* (**[12.6.10C]**), the Assembly has been prevented from taxing this industry under s 90 of the Constitution.

■   During Australia's administration of Papua and New Guinea, the Panguna mine was established on the island of Bougainville: see further **[12.5.1]**. This mine was larger than any mine in continental Australia or Tasmania — indeed, it became the largest open-cut copper mine in the world — and involved the poorly compensated and sometimes violent takeover of surface land rights on a broad scale.

This is something which would not have happened to landowners (other than indigenous Australians, whose native title rights were not then recognised) under the Mining Acts of the Australian states. After Papua New Guinea obtained independence, these factors, the negative ecological impact of the mine, and the fact that mining profits were repatriated to the first world and royalties to the central government, fostered a violent Bougainville secessionist movement, whose armed struggle cost around 20,000 lives.

- As discussed above at [12.2.12] and [12.2.13], the British Phosphate Commissioners, rather than the Australian Administrator, controlled a large part of the economy of Nauru for the benefit of Australian and New Zealand farmers. The Commissioners also ran the Christmas Island Phosphate Company, bought by Australia and New Zealand from George Clunies-Ross and John Murray in 1948, until 1981, exercising considerable control over island life and maximising the value of island phosphate for mainland farmers.

- While the 'white Australia' policy largely excluded indentured Asian and Pacific labourers from the Australian mainland after federation, 'coolie' workforces continued to work the tax-exempt 'plantations' of the Cocos Islands until 1984 and the phosphate mine of Christmas Island until its unionisation in the 1970s.

- Some of Australia's territories (for example, Papua, New Guinea, Nauru, Christmas Island) were occupied by enemy forces during World War II; others (for example, the Northern Territory) experienced enemy attacks and were administered under National Security Act 1942 (Cth) regimes different from those applied elsewhere in Australia. Many remain extremities vulnerable to attack in traditional warfare; as discussed at [12.6.8], the Commonwealth is not constitutionally required to protect them.

- The Commonwealth has claimed for itself property in all uranium in the ground in territories: Atomic Energy Act 1953 (Cth) s 35. By contrast, the Crown in right of each state owns *in situ* uranium in the states, as it does other minerals. The powers conferred on the Commonwealth by this Act are much more amply exercisable in territories than in states: see s 34.

- The Commonwealth has established large national parks in many territories, retaining them even after granting self-government. It does not hold national parks in the states. The Commonwealth has also kept on foot in the Northern and Jervis Bay territories Aboriginal land rights regimes which it has never extended to the states, despite an original plan to do so and despite having the necessary constitutional power: see [2.4.52]. And it has kept a Commonwealth land use planning regime on foot in the Australian Capital Territory: see Australian Capital Territory (Planning and Land Management) Act 1988 (Cth).

- Some Commonwealth legislation (for example, the Workplace Relations Act 1996 (Cth)) applies differently in some territories than it does in states: see, for example, the NT S-G Act s 53.

4   The territories power

A 'plenary' power?

[12.4.1]   In an oft-quoted passage in *Berwick Ltd v Gray* (1976) 133 CLR 603 at 607, Mason J, with whom Barwick CJ, McTiernan and Murphy JJ agreed, said:

> The power conferred by s 122 is a plenary power capable of exercise in relation to Territories of varying size and importance which are at different stages of political and economic development. It is sufficiently wide enough to enable the passing of laws for the direct administration of a Territory by the Australian Government without separate fiscus; yet on the other hand it is wide enough to enable Parliament to endow a Territory with separate political, representative and administrative insitutions, having control of its own fiscus.

Unlike s 51, s 122 is not expressly made 'subject to this Constitution'. In *Kruger v Commonwealth* (1997) 190 CLR 1 at 54, Dawson J (in the majority on this issue) pointed out:

> [I]n *Capital Duplicators Pty Ltd v Australian Capital Territory* [(1992) 177 CLR 248 at 271)] Brennan, Deane and Toohey JJ described the power as 'no less than the power which would have been conferred if the "peace, order and good government" formula had been used'. The result is that 'all that need be shown to support an exercise of the power is that there should be a sufficient nexus or connection between the law and the Territory': *Berwick Ltd v Gray* (1976) 133 CLR 603 at 607.

For these reasons the power is often described as 'plenary': see *Teori Tau v Commonwealth* (1969) 199 CLR 564 at 570; *Newcrest Mining (WA) Ltd v Commonwealth* (1997) 190 CLR 513 at 539, 548. However, while it is clear that s 122 is cast in broad language and susceptible to a wide construction, it may be overstating the true position to conclude that the Commonwealth has unlimited power in the territories. We will consider now the breadth of the power and the debates about its breadth; then, in [12.5.1]–[12.5.28C], the limitations on the power.

An exclusive power

[12.4.2]   Parliament's power over its territories is an *exclusive* one. This is not expressly provided by the text of s 122, but in the case of territories surrendered by states it is established by s 111 of the Constitution, which provides that these territories 'shall become subject to the exclusive jurisdiction of the Commonwealth'. In the case of other territories, the Commonwealth's exclusive powers depend on principles derived from international law. They depend on the Commonwealth having acquired unchallenged sovereign authority by cession from Britain, for example, or having asserted sovereignty over a previously unoccupied territory. Some of these issues were explored by Isaacs J in *Buchanan v Commonwealth* (1913) 16 CLR 315 at 333–4.

The exclusive nature of s 122 led Dawson J in *Kruger v Commonwealth* (1997) 190 CLR 1 to describe the Commonwealth in territories as 'a completely sovereign legislature' (190 CLR at 55), citing Windeyer J in *Capital Applicances v Falconer* (1971) 125 CLR 591 at 611 — that is, both a *local* government and a *national* one. See also *Lamshed v Lake* (1958) 99 CLR 143–4 (Dixon CJ).

In *Spratt v Hermes* (1965) 114 CLR 226 at 242, Barwick CJ commented:

Section 122 gives to the Parliament legislative power of a different order to those given by s 51. That power is not only plenary but is unlimited by reference to subject matter. It is a complete power to make laws for the peace, order and good government of the territory — an expression condensed in s 122 to 'for the government of the Territory'. This is as large and universal a power of legislation as can be granted. It is non-federal in character in the sense that the total legislative power to make laws to operate in and for a territory is not shared in any wise with the States.

A power that may be delegated to the executive

[12.4.3] Although s 122 empowers *parliament* to legislate for territories, for most of the 20th century their laws were Ordinances made by the Governor-General on the advice of the Commonwealth Department of Territories. The executive's power to legislate for territories has gone largely unchallenged, despite its undemocratic dimensions. Unlike the Imperial Crown's *prerogative* power to legislate for conquered colonies, the Governor-General exercises s 122 power delegated by parliament under territorial Acceptance Acts or Administration Acts.

The constitutionality of these arrangements would appear to depend on the general principle in *Victorian Stevedoring & General Contracting Co v Dignan* (1931) 46 CLR 73 (see **[6.4.36C]**), that parliament may delegate legislative power to the executive in broad and unqualified terms, although such delegations are of course reversible: see *Capital Duplicators v Australian Capital Territory (No 1)* (1992) 177 CLR 248 at 264–5 per Mason CJ, Dawson and McHugh JJ; and 269–70, 280–1 per Brennan, Deane and Toohey JJ. Delegated legislation is generally treated as a 'law' for constitutional purposes (see **[8.1.11]**), although there has been some recent debate about whether territorial laws are 'laws made by the Parliament' for the purposes of Ch III Constitution: see **[12.5.21]–[12.5.22]** and Keyzer, 2001, p 132.

An extra-territorial power

[12.4.4] Covering cl 5 of the Constitution provides:

This Act, and all laws made by the Parliament of the Commonwealth under the Constitution, shall be binding on the courts, judges, and people of every State and of every part of the Commonwealth, notwithstanding anything in the laws of any State …

As noted, 'the Commonwealth' in covering cl 6 includes the internal territories formerly parts of 'Original States'; there is authority for the view that it also includes territories which were under the control of the states at federation, like Norfolk Island (*Berwick Ltd v Gray* (1976) 133 CLR 603) and perhaps even all territories: for example, *Spratt v Hermes* (1965) 114 CLR 226 at 247 per Barwick CJ, at 271 per Menzies J; compare at 250, 253 per Kitto J). If laws made under s 122 Constitution (including delegated legislation made by the Governor-General) are 'laws made by the Parliament of the Commonwealth under the Constitution', do they only apply in those 'parts of the Commonwealth' which are not states?

[12.4.5] In *Australian National Airways Pty Ltd v Commonwealth* (the *ANA* case) (1945) 71 CLR 29, Latham CJ (with whom Williams J agreed) interpreted s 122 as conferring on the Commonwealth power to make laws with territorial application only. Latham CJ described s 122 as 'the same power as a colony of Australia had before federation' or 'all the power of a State Parliament in respect of a State, but …

as if it were not limited by the co-existence of the Commonwealth with certain paramount powers' (71 CLR at 62). Dixon J disagreed:

> It is absurd to contemplate a central government with authority over a territory and yet without power to make laws, wherever its jurisdiction may run, for the establishment, maintenance and control of communications with the territory governed. The form or language of s 122 may not be particularly felicitous but, when it is read with the entire document, the conclusion that the legislative power is extensive enough to cover such a matter seems inevitable (71 CLR at 85).

[12.4.6] In *Lamshed v Lake* (1958) 99 CLR 132, Dixon CJ's view carried a majority (Webb, Kitto and Taylor JJ, McTiernan and Williams JJ dissenting). (See also *Kruger v Commonwealth* (1997) 190 CLR 1 per Dawson J at 54–8.) The High Court held (by majority) that a law under s 122 of the Constitution could operate outside of the borders of a territory — so as to operate as a 'law of the Commonwealth' capable of generating constitutional inconsistency with state law under s 109 of the Constitution. *Lamshed* concerned a statutory application of s 92 of the Constitution to the Northern Territory. Section 10 of the Northern Territory Administration Act 1910 (Cth), a version of which is still found in the NT S-G Act (see **[12.6.38]**), provided that 'trade commerce and intercourse between the Territory and the States … shall be absolutely free'. *Lamshed* was decided at a time when the High Court interpreted s 92 as prohibiting controls on interstate trade and commerce. The High Court struck down a South Australian provision, making it an offence to drive without a South Australian carrier's licence, for inconsistency with s 10 Northern Territory Administration Act.

[12.4.7C]   **Lamshed v Lake**
                                       (1958) 99 CLR 132

Dixon CJ: … [141] … [I]t is said that laws made under [s 122] cannot have a direct operation in the rest of Australia. It is just as if the Commonwealth Parliament were appointed a local legislature in and for the Territory with a power territorially restricted to the Territory.

It is an interpretation of s 122 which I wholly reject. To my mind s 122 is a power given to the national Parliament of Australia as such to make laws 'for', that is to say 'with respect to', the government of the Territory. The words 'the government of any territory' of course describe the subject matter of the power. But once the law is shown to be relevant to that subject matter it operates as a binding law of the Commonwealth wherever territorially the authority of the Commonwealth runs …

~~~

Territorial 'patches' in blanket national laws

[12.4.8] To what extent may parliament rely on s 122 when making national laws? The orthodox view was expressed by Windeyer J in *Spratt v Hermes* (1965) 114 CLR 226 at 278:

> [W]hen the Parliament makes a law intended to be of general application throughout the whole of the Commonwealth and its territories it does so in the exercise of all powers it thereunto enabling. If the law be within power under s 51 it will, by the combined effect of that section and of s 122, be law in and for the States and the territories alike. If it be invalid as beyond s 51 then, in the absence of a clear indication that it should nevertheless apply in the territories, it will I consider fail altogether of effect. Whether a particular Act is intended to extend to the territories, or to a

particular territory, as well as to the States then becomes a question of construction to be resolved either by its express provisions or by its intendment as revealed by its scope and nature.

See also *Newcrest Mining (WA) Ltd v Commonwealth* (1997) 190 CLR 513 (Brennan CJ, Dawson and McHugh JJ).

This could mean that a person in a territory who is bound by a national law experiences that law without the benefit of constitutional protections available in the states. Partly for that reason, in *Newcrest* Gaudron J argued that the validity of truly national laws (including those operating in territories) should not be assessed solely under s 122 in circumstances where it was possible to invoke powers under s 51 to support the relevant law (in this case, s 51(xxix), which is subject to a constitutional limitation (190 CLR at 568)). In *Northern Territory v GPAO* (1998) 196 CLR 553 at 598–9, Gaudron J treated national child custody legislation operating in the Northern Territory as based on *both* s 51 powers and s 122.

[12.4.9] Recent history shows that parliament is reluctant to give up territory-specific law-making, and the High Court is reluctant to give up the orthodox 'patchwork' approach to s 122. The Euthanasia Laws Act 1997 (Cth) amended territory self-government legislation to restrict the powers of the ACT, the NT and Norfolk Island to enact laws permitting voluntary euthanasia, after the Northern Territory had enacted such legislation: see **[12.6.31]**. No such Commonwealth legislation has been enacted in relation to the states. Further, the Commonwealth often seeks maximum coverage of a particular legislative field by 'patching together' all available sources of power, including if necessary s 122. There might be a particular incentive to do this where the Commonwealth's powers are limited in terms of subject matter and it has supplemented them with referrals of power from the states under s 51(xxxvii). For example, in *Northern Territory v GPAO* (1998) 196 CLR 553, the High Court considered parts of the Family Law Act 1975 (Cth) and the Evidence Act 1995 (Cth) which were unsupported by any of the Commonwealth's s 51 powers — s 51(xxi), the marriage power, s 51(xxii), the divorce power or s 51(xxxvii) powers referred by the *states* over children of unmarried parents. This legislation, which provided for the making of 'parenting orders' in relation to children of *unmarried* parents, was expressed to apply in the territories. Since the states' referrals of powers did not relate to the territories, the only possible basis on which these Acts might operate in territories was under s 122 of the Constitution.

Section 122 and s 52(i)

[12.4.10] Section 52(i) confers another *exclusive*, more specific power (see **[12.3.2]**) — one explicitly made subject to other constitutional constraints. The relationship between s 122 and s 52(i) has been considered in several cases (notably *Spratt v Hermes* (1965) 114 CLR 226, per Barwick CJ at 241, Kitto J at 258, Taylor J at 262–4, Menzies J at 271, Windeyer J at 273, Taylor J at 282) but was concisely summarised in the main judgment in *Svikart v Stewart* (1994) 181 CLR 548, by Mason CJ, Deane, Dawson and McHugh JJ.

[12.4.11C]   **Svikart v Stewart**
                                    (1994) 181 CLR 548

Per Mason CJ, Deane, Dawson and McHugh JJ: Section 52(i) provides for the exclusive power to make laws with respect to the seat of government as well as places acquired by the Commonwealth for public purposes. Under s 125, the seat of government is required to be within territory granted to or acquired by the Commonwealth. There is now a Territory, the Australian Capital Territory (see Seat of Government Act 1908 (Cth), Seat of Government Acceptance Act 1909 (Cth), Seat of Government Surrender Act 1909 (NSW)), within which the seat of government has been located, although its limits have not been precisely determined by the Parliament. The seat of government is, however, not co-extensive with the Territory in which it is located nor, under s 125, is it intended to be. The Parliament must rely upon s 122 for the power to make laws for the government of that Territory. That power is not made subject to the Constitution as is the power to make laws with respect to the seat of government under s 52(i). Moreover, the power to make laws with respect to the seat of government would seem to be concerned with its political or constitutional aspects, rather than with the government of the territory which it occupies. It is not only the presence of s 122 which indicates this to be so, but also the fact that, unlike the power under s 122, the power to make laws with respect to the seat of government is expressed to be a power to make laws for the peace, order and good government of the Commonwealth ...

~~~

[12.4.12] These comments were affirmed by Gleeson, McHugh and Callinan JJ in *Eastman's* case (1999) 200 CLR 322 at 333–4. See also Gaudron J at 336, Gummow and Hayne JJ at 353 and Kirby J's lengthy reconsideration of the topic at 365–70. This interpretation may have deprived ACT residents of the protections of constitutional limitations which constrain an exercise of the 'federal' power conferred by s 52(i) but may not limit s 122: see generally the next section of this chapter.

---

5   Limitations on the territories power

'Parliament's sense of justice and fair dealing is sufficient to protect them'

[12.5.1] In 1969, the Nasioi traditional owners of the Panguna mine site in Bougainville in the UN trust territory of New Guinea, part of Australia's (then) Territory of Papua and New Guinea, lay in front of bulldozers in an attempt to prevent Conzinc Rio Tinto Australia commencing mining under an agreement with the Australian Administration. The Nasioi did not accept the Administration's justification for the mine — that it would support the future independent state of Papua New Guinea — partly because they felt greater affinity for their neighbours in the British Solomon Islands (separated from Bougainville by the 1889 Anglo-German Convention) than they did for the 'redskins' of the New Guinea 'mainland' under Australian control. Their protest forced the Australian Administration to negotiate better compensation for loss of houses, gardens and surface rights. However, several years before, the Nasioi had been deprived of their traditional rights to sub-surface minerals (recognised by territory law) by Ordinances vesting property in those resources in the Administration. Nasioi landowners including Teori Tau challenged the validity of these Ordinances before the High Court. See generally O'Callaghan, undated; Denoon, 2000. Teori Tau argued that s 51(xxxi) of the Constitution required that the minerals acquisition be accompanied by just terms compensation. The Commonwealth demurred on the ground that s 122 supported the acquisition, unencumbered by 51(xxxi). In a contemptuously short *ex tempore* judgment delivered by Barwick CJ in *Teori Tau*, a unanimous High Court held for the Commonwealth. Barwick CJ described as 'clearly insupportable' the submission that s 122 was subject to s 51(xxxi), which was said to be the only source of power to make laws for the acquisition of property in a Commonwealth territory.

[12.5.2C]   **Teori Tau v Commonwealth**
                                (1969) 119 CLR 564

Barwick CJ: ... Section 51 is concerned with what may be called federal legislative powers as part of the distribution of legislative power between the Commonwealth and the constituent States. Section 122 is concerned with the legislative power for the government of Commonwealth territories in respect of which there is no such division of legislative power. The grant of legislative power by s 122 is plenary in quality and unlimited and unqualified in point of subject matter. In particular, it is not limited or qualified by s 51(xxxi) or, for that matter, by any other paragraph of that section ....

While the Constitution must be read as a whole and as a consequence, s 122 be subject to other appropriate provisions of it as, for example, s 116, we have no doubt whatever that the power to make laws providing for the acquisition of property in the territory of the Commonwealth is not limited to the making of laws which provide just terms of acquisition.

What we decide in this respect is not, of course, limited to the Territory of Papua and New Guinea, although it happens that the question has first arisen expressly for decision in connexion with that territory. Our decision applies to all the territories, those [571] on the mainland of Australia as well as those external to the continent of Australia.

~~~

[12.5.3] There may have been other reasons for the court's deliberate extension of its ruling to territories other than Papua and New Guinea. In the year that *Teori Tau* was decided, Yolngu Aboriginal people were launching the first of their challenges to the establishment of the Gove bauxite mine on their traditional land in the Arnhem Land Aboriginal Reserve in the Northern Territory: *Mathaman v Nabalco Pty Ltd* (1969) 14 FLR 10. The Federal Court ultimately decided these challenges against the Yolngu in *Milirrpum v Nabalco* (1971) 17 FLR 141 by holding that Australian common law did not recognise their traditional land rights, a decision reversed by *Mabo v Queensland (No 2)* (1992) 175 CLR 1 more than two decades later.

The Australian states had been depriving private mineral owners of rights for decades under Mining Acts which vested property in *in situ* resources in the Crown without compensation and opened private land to mining. However, unlike the PNG and Northern Territory Mining Ordinances, these Mining Acts were enacted by mainly democratically-elected parliaments accountable to their electorates. In PNG and the Northern Territory, the Assemblies which enacted these Ordinances were not representative: see *Kruger v Commonwealth* (1997) 190 CLR 1 at 49–50 and Altman, 1983; the Papua and New Guinea Act 1963 (Cth) established a partly appointed House of Assembly in which some of the elected representatives were also required *not* to be indigenous people: Denoon, 2000, Ch 3. The significance of this difference was highlighted in NSW in the 1980s, when the Wran Government was forced to reverse unpopular acquisitions of privately owned coal: see Coal Acquisition Act 1981 (NSW); Coal Ownership (Restitution) Act 1990 (NSW).

Note, however, that Barwick CJ's judgment did not hold s 122 immune from *all* constitutional limitations — he mentions that s 122 *is* limited by s 116. This issue is taken up at **[12.5.26]** below.

[12.5.4]   As indicated in **[12.5.12]–[12.5.14]**, the more recent decision of the court in *Newcrest Mining v Commonwealth* (1997) 190 CLR 513 has cast doubt on the correctness of *Teori Tau*. In *Newcrest*, a majority of four judges held that Commonwealth acquisitions of property in territories under national laws attract just terms compensation, but Gaudron, Gummow and Kirby JJ were prepared to overrule *Teori Tau* by holding that s 122 is limited by s 51(xxxi). *Newcrest* is one of a number of late 1990s and early 21st century decisions that have reconsidered, without re-deciding, earlier decisions on the relationship between s 122 and the Constitution. To understand these decisions, it is important to understand the peculiar history of the debate about whether s 122 is an 'integrated' part of the Constitution or, to adopt a phrase coined by the Privy Council, 'a disparate and non-federal matter' (*Attorney-General (Commonwealth) v The Queen* (the *Boilermakers'* case) (1957) 95 CLR 592 at 545) or something in between (Zines, 1966; Keyzer, 2001). That history is canvassed below in **[12.5.6]–[12.5.10C]**.

[12.5.5]   There seems little doubt that the 'disparate or integrated?' jurisprudential debate has been influenced by racism, or at least by territories' cultural difference. As Gummow J commented in *Newcrest v Commonwealth* (1997) 190 CLR 513 at 606:

> Decisions which appear to disjoin s 122 from the ... Constitution as a whole were delivered before the Papua New Guinea Independence Act 1975 (Cth). The existence of so large and comparatively populous external territory appears to have been ... of some significance.

In other words, the fact that some territories were occupied by largely non-'white' populations encouraged the court to adopt the US approach of deciding that a full application of the Constitution to them was inappropriate.

In *R v Bernasconi* (1915) 19 CLR 629, the High Court decided that Ordinances made by the 'white' Territory of Papua legislature were not 'laws of the Commonwealth' for the purposes of s 80 of the Constitution, which guarantees trial by jury where an indictment is presented: see **[11.2.28]**. *Bernasconi* was partly justified on the grounds that jury trial was an alien cultural institution to most Papuans, in a context where juries were all-'white'. Jury trial *was* available in Papuan cases in which persons of *European descent* were charged with capital offences under the adopted Queensland Criminal Code. But Bernasconi, who had perpetrated 'deliberate and cold-blooded cruelty' on an 'island labourer' (Isaacs J at 640), was charged with aggravated assault, which carried a penalty of imprisonment: see Griffith CJ at 633. He sought a jury trial, perhaps because he thought a 'white' jury would treat him more sympathetically than the Central Court judge. The High Court's reluctance to apply s 80 may well have been underpinned by a practical concern about jury composition in mainly non-'white' territories: if it became widely available, Papuans would have to sit in judgment on 'whites'. The impossibility of this occurring in the context of Papuan race relations was hinted at by Isaacs J, who noted (at 640) that Bernasconi had succeeded in having another 'island labourer' who complained against him imprisoned for deserting his employment (at 640).

In a judgment delivered just one year into World War I, prescient in its anticipation of Australia's post-war mandates over former German territories, Isaacs J's judgment emphasised the 'underdeveloped' nature of territories generally:

> ... a 'territory' is not yet in a condition to enter into the full participation of Commonwealth constitutional rights and powers. It is in a state of dependency or tutelage, and the special regulations proper for its government until, if ever, it shall be admitted as a member of the family of States, are left to the discretion of the Commonwealth Parliament. If, for instance, any of the recently conquered territories were attached to Australia by act of the King and acceptance by the Commonwealth, the population there, whether German or Polynesian [*sic*: Melanesian, Micronesian], would come within sec 122, and not within sec 80. Parliament's sense of justice and fair dealing is sufficient to protect them, without fencing them round with what would be in the vast majority of instances an entirely inappropriate requirement of the British jury system ((1915) 19 CLR at 637–8).

Although many judges have expressed reservations about this view of s 122 since (see below **[12.5.13C]**), it was only comparatively recently that the full integration of territories into the Commonwealth began to be proposed. *Newcrest v Commonwealth*, for example, came only after the Northern Territory's Aboriginal population had been reduced from almost 50 per cent to about 25 per cent and, as Gummow J pointed out, at a time when there were no longer 'populous' non-'white' territories to complicate the jurisprudence.

Genealogy of the 'disparate' approach

[12.5.6] The first case on the relationship between s 122 and constitutional limitations arose because the Commonwealth enacted a 'continuation of pre-existing laws' provision when it accepted the Northern Territory. In *Buchanan v Commonwealth* (1913) 16 CLR 315, the High Court held that the Northern Territory Administration Act 1910 (Cth)'s continuation of South Australian succession and probate taxation laws was not invalid as a result of parliament's failure, when enacting it, to observe the 'anti-tacking' requirements of s 55 Constitution ('Laws imposing taxation ... shall deal with one subject of taxation only', see **[5.2.24]–[5.2.31]**). For Barton ACJ (Gavan Duffy and Rich JJ concurring, and Isaacs J agreeing), s 55 was designed to protect the Senate's right to reject a tax bill but not amend it (s 53 Constitution), and was thus a measure concerned only with legislation operating in the states enacted under s 51 Constitution. A 'law' for s 55 purposes did not include a s 122 law.

Buchanan and *Bernasconi* speak of territories as a species of colony: outside of 'the Commonwealth proper' (19 CLR at 637), not 'fused with' it but 'annexed to' (19 CLR at 637–8) and subordinate to it, like 'dependencies': 16 CLR at 327. In *Bernasconi*, Griffith CJ held that s 122 laws were not 'laws of the Commonwealth' for any constitutional purposes (for example, under ss 41, 61, 109): 19 CLR at 635.

[12.5.7] The history of subsequent High Court decisions was set out by McHugh and Callinan JJ (then proponents of the 'disparate' theory of territories) in their dissenting judgment in *Northern Territory v GPAO* (1998) 196 CLR 553, a case about the relationship between s 122 and Ch III of the Constitution (the background to *GPAO* is discussed further at **[12.4.9]**).

In *GPAO*, the question was whether the Family Court, invested with territory-specific Family Law Act jurisdiction, was exercising jurisdiction 'arising under any laws made by the Parliament' for the purposes of s 76(ii) of the Constitution (see the discussion of this question of 'federal jurisdiction and territory courts' at **[12.5.23C]**). Where courts exercise 'federal jurisdiction', s 79 of the Judiciary Act 1903 (Cth) requires them, in the absence of Commonwealth procedural, evidentiary or 'competency of witnesses' laws, to apply the laws on these topics of the jurisdiction in which they are sitting — in this case, the Northern Territory. That would have meant that Northern Territory child protection officers were not required to answer a subpoena to provide the Family Court with information on a child custody dispute because Northern Territory law prohibited them from disclosing that information. However, if the Family Court was not exercising 'federal jurisdiction' but rather 'disparate' s 122 jurisdiction, s 79 of the Judiciary Act would not apply, and the Northern Territory child protection law would not protect the officers' files from Family Court subpoena.

[12.5.8C]   **Northern Territory v GPAO**

                              (1998) 196 CLR 553

McHugh and Callinan JJ: ... The relationship between Ch III and the s 122 'territories power' was first dealt with by this Court in *R v Bernasconi* [(1915) 19 CLR 629] where the issue was whether the Commonwealth's power under s 122 is confined by reference to s 80 of the Constitution, which contains an express guarantee of trial by jury for certain offences. Griffith CJ, with whom Gavan Duffy and Rich JJ agreed, held that 'the power conferred by s 122 is not restricted by the provisions of Chapter III of the Constitution' [at 635]. His Honour not only thought that s 80, a provision quite distinct from the remainder of Ch III, did not fetter the plenary power conferred by s 122; he appeared to have no doubt that the entirety of Ch III, including ss 73, 75, 76 and 77 which deal with jurisdiction, had no bearing on the scope of the territories power [at 635]. Isaacs J reached the same conclusion, describing the territories as 'parts annexed to the Commonwealth and subordinate to it ... not yet in a condition to enter into the full participation of Commonwealth constitutional rights and powers.' [at 637]

[167] Eleven years later, in *Porter v The King; Ex parte Yee* [(1926) 37 CLR 432] the Court again considered the relationship between Ch III and s 122... The issue in *Porter* was whether the Commonwealth Parliament had power to provide for a right of appeal from orders of the Supreme Court of the Northern Territory to this Court. A majority of the Court held that the purported right of appeal was constitutional. The majority held that, although Ch III exhaustively defined the *federal* jurisdiction of the High Court and other 'federal' courts, those courts could exercise contemporaneously such other non-federal jurisdiction, at least of an appellate variety, as the Parliament saw fit to confer [at 441 per Isaacs J, 445–6 per Higgins J, 448 per Rich J and 449 per Starke J]. The dissentients, Knox CJ and Gavan Duffy J, held that the Parliament could not confer jurisdiction on the High Court and other federal courts beyond that conferred by and under Ch III, given that they '[exist] only for the performance of the functions therein described' [at 438].

[168] The High Court's reasoning in *Bernasconi* and *Porter* was examined by the Privy Council in *Attorney-General of the Commonwealth of Australia v The Queen* [(1957) 95 CLR 529], a case concerning the circumstances in which a body not complying with s 72 of the Constitution could exercise the judicial power of the Commonwealth. Affirming this Court's decision [*R v Kirby; Ex parte Boilermakers' Society of Australia* (the *Boilermakers' Case*) (1956) 94 CLR 254], the Judicial Committee held that, in respect of matters entrusted to the Commonwealth in the Constitution's division of powers among the constituent polities of the federation, Ch III describes exhaustively the extent of the Commonwealth's judicial power. Their Lordships rejected the contention that this view was inconsistent with the decisions in

Bernasconi and *Porter.* Viscount Simonds, who delivered their Lordships' advice, noted that in terms of the Constitution's federal division of powers '[t]he legislative power in respect of the Territories is a disparate and non-federal matter.' [(1957) 95 CLR 529 at 545] Their Lordships were of the view that the power conferred by s 122 was not one held by the Colonies prior to federation and was not a subject of the 'federal' allocation of powers between Commonwealth and States on federation. Accordingly, the s 122 territories power lay outside the federal scheme of the Constitution and outside the 'federal' judicature provisions with which Ch III is concerned [at 545].

[169] *Bernasconi, Porter* and *Attorney-General (Cth) v The Queen* provide the strongest possible authority for holding that a court is not exercising federal jurisdiction in a territory when the rights and liabilities of the parties depend upon a law whose source of power is s 122 of the Constitution. Laws made under that power are not federal laws because they do not affect the relationship between the Commonwealth and the States.

[170]Although these decisions have attracted criticism in subsequent cases, the terms of Ch III, read in the light of the Convention Debates, give much support for the view that s 122 is not affected by the operation of Ch III. Considerations supporting that view include:

1. Ch III makes frequent reference to 'federal', 'Commonwealth' and 'State' but there is no mention of 'territory'.

2. The use of the term 'federal' is more consistent with Ch III being concerned with the allocation of power between the Commonwealth and the States than with the exercise of judicial power in the Commonwealth, the States *and any territory.*

3. It is settled that territory courts are not federal courts for the purpose of Ch III [*Spratt v Hermes* (1965) 114 CLR 226; *Capital TV and Appliances* (1971) 125 CLR 591]. That being so, ss 75, 76 and 77 of the Constitution — which deal with the jurisdiction of Ch III courts — are concerned with this Court, federal courts and the State courts, not territory courts. There is no reason, therefore, for thinking that Ch III generally is concerned with the territories.

4. The carefully worked out provisions of Ch III, defining the powers and securing the independence of federal courts, were necessary to ensure the maintenance of the federal structure. As the majority in *R v Kirby; Ex parte Boilermakers' Society of Australia* [(1956) 94 CLR 254 at 267–268] pointed out:

    The conception of independent governments existing in the one area and exercising powers in different fields of action carefully defined by law could not be carried into practical effect unless the ultimate responsibility of deciding upon the limits of the respective powers of the governments were placed in the federal judicature.

    Nothing in the relationship between the Commonwealth and the territories, however, requires that the jurisdiction of courts exercising jurisdiction under territorial law should be subject to the inhibitions imposed by Ch III including the appointment, removal and tenure of territory judges. Ch III imposes no obligations on the States in respect of their courts except to the extent that *Kable v Director of Public Prosecutions (NSW)* [(1996) 189 CLR 51] applies to them. There is no reason why the Commonwealth, in legislating for its territories and their courts, should be subject to constitutional burdens which do not apply to the States when they legislate for their courts.

5. If Ch III applies to the territories when the Commonwealth is creating courts or investing judicial power in the territories, then it must apply to territorial legislatures, which have been given self-government, when they do those things. The Commonwealth could no more escape the operation of Ch III by setting up self-governing legislatures than it could escape its operation by giving the Governor-General in Council power to create courts under a regulation. In contrast, s 121 permits the Parliament to admit new States into the federation upon 'such terms and conditions, including the extent of representation in either House of the Parliament, as it thinks fit.' Under s 121, the Parliament could make it a term or condition that Ch III should not apply at all or in some amended form to a new entrant. It is difficult to see why the Constitution should

require the Parliament legislating for a territory, or a self-governing territory, to comply with Ch III when the Parliament could admit the territory as a State with no obligation to comply with Ch III.

6. If 'federal jurisdiction' in Ch III includes jurisdiction over 'matters' arising under laws made under s 122, s 77(iii) of the Constitution would authorise the conscription of State courts to determine matters arising under territory laws, matters which have nothing to do with the federal nature of the Constitution.

7. At Federation, it was assumed that the Commonwealth would have a number of sparsely populated territories under its control including territories outside Australia. To require the Commonwealth to comply with such provisions of Ch III as ss 72 and 80 and to prevent it from giving non-judicial functions to a territory court would have been inconvenient to say the least.

8. One of the reasons that the Constitutional Convention rejected Sir Edward Braddon's suggestion that territorial representation in the Parliament should be 'in accordance with the ratio of representation provided in the Constitution' was that it would be 'a great mistake' to bring the territories into line with the States [Official Record of the Debates of the Australasian Federal Convention (Adelaide), 20 April 1897 at 1013–1014].

[171] Indeed, the only powerful argument in support of applying Ch III to s 122 is that s 76(ii) refers to the conferral of jurisdiction 'arising under any laws made by the Parliament'. But given the many considerations which point in the opposite direction, this seems too weak a foundation for applying Ch III as a whole to the territories or to hold that the exercise of judicial power under a law, enacted under s 122, is an exercise of 'federal jurisdiction'. However, the terms of s 76(ii) and s 77(i) seem wide enough to confer original jurisdiction [An appeal to this Court would then lie under s 73 of the Constitution] on this Court and original and appellate jurisdiction on a federal court in respect of matters arising under a s 122 law. Nevertheless, it does not follow from that conclusion that this Court or the federal court must be exercising 'federal jurisdiction' or 'the judicial power of the Commonwealth' in respect of matters arising under a s 122 law.

~~~

The temptation to partial integration

[12.5.9] While territories remained remote from the rest of Australia and their ('white') populations small, the 'disparate' approach survived. However, once the Commonwealth government moved to Canberra in 1927 and Alice Springs was linked to Adelaide by rail in 1929 and Darwin by road after World War II, this approach began to be more vulnerable. In *Northern Territory v GPAO*, McHugh and Callinan JJ continued their account of the history of s 122 decisions by examining the partial demise of the 'disparate' approach.

[12.5.10C]   **Northern Territory v GPAO**
                              (1998) 196 CLR 553

The undermining of the original view of the relationship between s 122 and Ch III

[172] Less than a year after... *Attorney-General (Cth) v The Queen*, this Court again considered the relationship between s 122 and the Constitution's 'federal' provisions. *Lamshed v Lake*, which was decided in 1958, commenced a course of decision which may eventually overthrow the confident views of the early members of this Court concerning the relationship between s 122 and Ch III of the Constitution.... The case could have been disposed of on the simple ground that a law made under s 122 was a 'law of the Commonwealth' for the purpose of s 109 of the Constitution even if s 122 conferred a non-federal power, and indeed it was

disposed of on this ground. But members of the Court used the occasion to cast doubt on the earlier line of decisions concerning the territories.

[173] A majority of the Court, led by Dixon CJ, held that s 122 authorised laws that had operation beyond the limits of the territories. ...

This was so, in his Honour's view, in spite of the fact that the territories power had earlier been construed as 'disparate and non-federal' [(1958) 99 CLR 132 at 142]. Dixon CJ also said that s 122 did not confer upon the Commonwealth a power wholly separate from that which it acquired under the federal compact, 'as if the Commonwealth Parliament were appointed a local legislature in and for the Territory' [at 141]. Though acknowledging the precedential force of cases such as *Bernasconi*, his Honour said that he had 'always found it hard to see why s 122 should be disjoined from the rest of the Constitution and ... [did] not think that [earlier cases] really meant such a disjunction' [at 145]. Indeed, Dixon CJ thought that the Commonwealth's power to legislate for the territories forms a natural and integral part of the federal design [at 143–4]. He thought it absurd that legislation made under the Commonwealth's enumerated powers, such as those concerning defence, communications, immigration and industrial relations, would not apply, or be intended to apply, in and to the territories [at 144–6]. And yet, he observed, such a restriction flows logically from an acceptance of a principle that s 122, and legislative power in respect of the territories, is somehow disjoined from the otherwise 'federal' Constitution. Because he thought that the territories power cannot be treated as entirely non-federal, Dixon CJ insisted that the decision in *Bernasconi* was only authority in respect of the relationship between s 122 and s 80. In so far as the s 109 inconsistency power was concerned, his Honour found that a law made under s 122 was a 'law of the Commonwealth' in the sense necessary for it to prevail over an inconsistent State law [at 148].

[174] The process of undermining the authority of the earlier cases continued in *Spratt v Hermes* where this Court had to determine whether a court established in a territory, under s 122, must be constituted in accordance with the requirements of Ch III in order to hear cases brought under Commonwealth legislation extending to all Australian jurisdictions. The appellant argued that a magistrate of the Court of Petty Sessions of the Australian Capital Territory was without jurisdiction to hear charges brought under the *Post and Telegraph Act* (Cth) because this amounted to an exercise of federal jurisdiction by a judicial officer not holding office on the terms specified in s 72 of the Constitution. The Court held that s 72 did not apply to territory courts.

[175] In *Spratt*, Barwick CJ refused to accept the proposition that 'Chap. III as a whole is inapplicable to or in respect of territories.' [(1965) 114 CLR 226 at 243] Although his Honour conceded that the territories power is 'non-federal in character' [at 242], he took the view that some of the restrictions contained in the federal parts of the Constitution would nevertheless operate to constrain the s 122 legislative power. Whether any given provision had that operation was, he said, a matter of construction in each instance, 'the construction being resolved upon a consideration of the text and of the purpose of the Constitution as a whole.' [at 242] Barwick CJ shared the view that Dixon CJ had expressed about *Bernasconi* in his judgment in *Lamshed*, that is, that that decision must be confined to its facts and that it is only authority in respect of the relationship between ss 80 and 122. Given that s 80 could be distinguished from other provisions within Ch III, Barwick CJ took the view that *Bernasconi* was not authority for the proposition that the whole of that Chapter has no application to s 122 and laws made under it [at 244–5]. Accordingly, in so far as the majority's reasons in *Bernasconi* were framed around the whole of Ch III, Barwick CJ thought they 'went beyond the occasion' and were obiter dicta [at 245].

[176] Other members of the Court in *Spratt* agreed that the decisions in *Bernasconi* and later cases applying its ratio were based on reasoning which would not, in the absence of widespread reliance upon those earlier decisions, justify the perpetuation of that reasoning with respect to the relationship between s 122 and Ch III [at 265–266 per Menzies J, 275 per Windeyer JJ]. Menzies J said that, while cases such as *Bernasconi* must be accepted as good law in relation to their particular facts, as a general proposition, it was untenable to regard s 122

as conferring a legislative power which stands outside 'the Federal System' [at 269–70]. His Honour said [at 270]:

> [I]t seems inescapable that territories of the Commonwealth are parts of the Commonwealth of Australia and I find myself unable to grasp how what is part of the Commonwealth is not part of 'the Federal System': see the Commonwealth of Australia Constitution Act 1903, s 5, which refers not only to every State but to 'every part of the Commonwealth'. If there be room for doubt as to this in so far as territories outside Australia are concerned, I think the terms of s 122 itself preclude doubt in the case of territories within Australia. That section contemplates that an area which is part of a State and so within 'the Federal System' will be accepted by the Commonwealth and may be represented in either House of the Parliament. I do not understand how the surrender and acceptance authorised by s 111 of the Constitution can take the area affected outside 'the Federal System. ...

Windeyer J expressed a similar view, stating that he did not think 'the conclusion that Chap. III, as a whole, can be put on one side as inapplicable to matters arising in the territories is warranted by its actual language.' [at 275] Rather, his Honour suggested, the provisions of that Chapter as well as other constitutional provisions may, as a matter of construction, operate to constrain the Commonwealth's legislative power in respect of the territories [at 277–8]. ...

[178] In *Capital TV and Appliances*, this Court unanimously held that the Supreme Court of the Australian Capital Territory was created pursuant to s 122 of the Constitution and was not a 'federal court' or a 'court exercising federal jurisdiction' within the meaning of those terms in s 73 of the Constitution. Consequently, in the absence of a statutory appeal as of right, this Court had no jurisdiction to hear the appellant's appeal. Barwick CJ said [(1971) 125 CLR 591 at 598–600] that the established doctrine of the Court was that a territorial court determining rights as the result of an exercise of s 122 power did not exercise federal jurisdiction for the purpose of s 73 of the Constitution because federal jurisdiction arose from the exercise of the powers conferred by ss 51 and 52 of the Constitution. If 'federal jurisdiction' only arises from the exercise of the powers conferred by ss 51 and 52, it means that this Court or a federal court determining a matter arising under s 122 is also not exercising federal jurisdiction. In our opinion, Barwick CJ was right so to hold ...

~~~

[12.5.11] In *GPAO*, Gleeson CJ and Gummow J (with whom Hayne J generally agreed) held that 's 76(ii), in conjunction with s 77(i) of the Constitution, operates in accordance with its terms and permits the conferral of jurisdiction on federal courts in matters arising under laws made under s 122 of the Constitution: in such cases, the constitutional source of the jurisdiction is s 76(ii) and s 77(i) and the jurisdiction is federal' (at 592). Gaudron J expressed a similar view. However, the majority judges in *GPAO* expressly limited their conclusions to the facts before them: they did not decide whether territory courts invested with jurisdiction under s 122 of the Constitution exercised federal jurisdiction (at 592). This issue, and the applicability of Ch III of the Constitution to territory courts generally, is taken up in **[12.5.15]–[12.5.25]**.

The push for full integration after territory self-government

[12.5.12] The 'full integrationist' approach to s 122 is probably best exemplified by Justice Gummow's judgment in *Newcrest Mining v Commonwealth* (1997) 190 CLR 513. This case was decided after the ACT, the NT and Norfolk Island had been granted territorial self-government (discussed in detail in **[12.6.1]–[12.6.56C]**). The invention of territory self-government increased pressure for the territories' integration into the wider constitutional framework. The question of whether some constitutional limitations constrain an exercise of s 122 by parliament has, in recent times, also translated into the question of whether those limitations constrain an exercise of power by the self-governing territories. In *Newcrest*, however, the court considered whether Newcrest was entitled to 'just terms' compensation under s 51(xxxi) Constitution for Commonwealth acquisition of its mining tenements via the proclamation of Kakadu National Park.

[12.5.13C] Newcrest Mining v Commonwealth
(1997) 190 CLR 513

Gummow J: The appellants contend that, were it not for the obstacle placed in their path by the decision in *Teori Tau v The Commonwealth*, consideration of the Constitution as a whole would indicate an answer favourable to their case. By its very terms, par (xxxi) appears to draw in all powers of the Parliament to make laws, from whatever source in the Constitution they are derived. The terms of the acquisition power refer, for example, to an acquisition associated with the exercise of the defence power in s 51(vi) as much as to an acquisition related to the exercise of legislative power under s 122 ...

Section 51(xxxi) speaks of '[t]he acquisition of property ... from any State or person' not of the acquisition of property in a State from that State. A State may own property situated outside its territory. Nor does s 51(xxxi) speak of the acquisition of property 'from any person in a State'. Further, par (xxxi) confers a power 'for *any* purpose in respect of which the Parliament has power to make laws' and one such purpose is found in s 122 (emphasis added).

There is, the appellants submit, no relevant distinction between the text of s 122 and that of s 51 in the application of par (xxxi) to other heads of power in the Constitution. These submissions should be accepted. ...

Section 51 confers power on the Parliament 'to make laws for the peace, order, and good government of the Commonwealth with respect to' the enumerated heads of power. ...Section 122 empowers the Parliament to make laws 'for the government of any territory'. The term 'for', to adapt the words of Wilson J in *Attorney-General (Vict); Ex rel Black v The Commonwealth* [(1981) 146 CLR 559 at 653] in construing s 116 of the Constitution, speaks of the purpose of the law in terms of the end to be achieved, namely the government of the territory in question. This identifies a legislative 'purpose' within the meaning of par (xxxi). Such a conclusion is consistent with the following observations of Dixon CJ in *Lamshed v Lake* ...

> To my mind s 122 is a power given to the national Parliament of Australia as such to make laws 'for', that is to say 'with respect to', the government of the Territory. The words 'the government of any territory' of course describe the subject matter of the power.

The addition of the words 'of the Commonwealth' to the phrase in s 51 'laws for the peace, order, and good government' requires further attention. Their presence does not confine the heads of power in s 51 so as to restrict the postal power to an operation with respect to the States, the borrowing of money on the public credit of the Commonwealth to borrowing in States, the census to those found in States, and the currency, coinage and legal tender to that circulating or proffered in the States.... Rather, the government referred to in the phrase 'laws for the peace, order, and good government of the Commonwealth' is that of the body politic wherein and for which the laws made by the Parliament have the binding force specified in covering cl 5. The body politic comprises 'the courts, judges, and the people of every State and of every part of the Commonwealth'. Territories are parts of the Commonwealth within the meaning of covering cl 5 [*Berwick Ltd v Gray* (1976) 133 CLR 603 at 605, 606, 608, 611; *Capital Duplicators Pty Ltd v Australian Capital Territory* (1992) 177 CLR 248 at 274–5, 286].

The basic proposition is that each provision of the Constitution, including s 122, is to be read with other provisions in the same instrument [*Bank of NSW v The Commonwealth* (1948) 76 CLR 1 at 185 per Latham CJ; *Spratt v Hermes* (1965) 114 CLR 226 at 278 per

Windeyer J]. Accordingly, and at least prima facie, par (xxxi) of s 51 and s 122 should be read together. Section 122 is not to be torn from the constitutional fabric.

In considering the operation of s 122, the starting point is the identification of '[t]he Parliament' which is to make the laws mentioned therein. That necessarily refers the reader to Ch I of the Constitution. The phrase in s 122, which is vital to the status of the Northern Territory, 'surrendered by any State to and accepted by the Commonwealth' is a reference to s 111. The reference to 'the extent' of 'the representation of [a] territory in either House of the Parliament' is to be read with the phrase in s 121 'the extent of representation in either House of the Parliament'. Section 121 does not contain the additional reference in s 122 to the terms on which representation may be allowed, a matter treated as highly significant by Mason J when upholding the validity under s 122 of the *Senate (Representation of Territories) Act 1973* (Cth) in *Western Australia v The Commonwealth* ... His Honour proceeded on the footing that the Constitution is to be treated as one coherent instrument for the government of the Federation and said [(1975) 134 CLR 201 at 269]:

> Just as s 122 requires to be read with Ch I so also account must be taken of s 122 in the interpretation of ss 7 and 24.

Moreover, this Court more recently has held in *Capital Duplicators Pty Ltd v Australian Capital Territory* [(1992) 177 CLR 248] that the power conferred by s 122 upon the Parliament to create legislative institutions for a territory is limited by a requirement beyond that in s 122 itself that the law be one for the government of the territory. The nature of the taxation power (s 51(ii)) and the bounties power (s 51(iii)) and the evident intention of other provisions of the Constitution to create a type of free trade area comprising the geographical area of the Commonwealth require some qualification to the content of s 122. The result is that the Parliament may not establish a territorial legislature with the authority to impose duties of excise within the meaning of s 90 ...

It is true in at least two respects that the legislative power conferred by s 122 may be 'of a different order' [*Capital Duplicators Pty Ltd v Australian Capital Territory* (1992) 177 CLR 248 at 288 per Gaudron J] to those concurrent heads of legislative power conferred in s 51. Nevertheless, as will be seen, this does not detract from the appellants' case. The first proposition concerning s 122 (which itself requires some qualification) is that, as Barwick CJ pointed out in *Spratt v Hermes* [at 242], the power conferred by s 122 'is non-federal in character in the sense that the total legislative power to make laws to operate in and for a territory is not shared in any wise with the States'. Nevertheless, s 122 empowers legislation which may operate inside the boundaries of the States [*Lamshed v Lake*]. The result is that out of s 122 there may arise questions as to the limits inter se of the constitutional powers of the Commonwealth and those of any State or States.... Further, as with laws made by the Parliament in the exercise of concurrent powers, by virtue of s 109 of the Constitution a law validly made under s 122 prevails over an inconsistent State law [*Lamshed v Lake*]. In *Spratt v Hermes* [(1965) 114 CLR 226 at 247, citing a passage in the judgment of Dixon CJ in *Lamshed v Lake* (1958) 99 CLR 132 at 148], Barwick CJ said of the expression 'law of the Commonwealth' (upon which s 109 turns), that it 'embraces every law made by the Parliament whatever the constitutional power under or by reference to which that law is made or supported'.

The second distinctive aspect of s 122 concerns the use of the phrase 'for the government of any territory' rather than 'for the peace, order, and good government of any territory'. In a sense, the longer expression is 'condensed' to the shorter ... Yet the phrase 'for the government of any territory' emphasises that the Parliament may prescribe the constitutional arrangements for the government of a territory ...

This latter consideration itself requires qualification as a result of the denial in *Capital Duplicators Pty Ltd v Australian Capital Territory* ... of competence of a territorial legislature, set up by a law made under s 122 of the Constitution, to impose duties of excise within the meaning of s 90. Nevertheless, the establishment of territorial political institutions is of some significance for any operation par (xxxi) may have in relation to s 122. The paragraph is directed to the acquisition of property from any State, not from any body politic constituted for a territory by a law made under s 122. However, the Parliament, by whose law the body politic in question has been created consistently with s 122, may also subject that body politic to the exercise of the power of the Parliament of the Commonwealth to acquire property from it. The provisions, if any, for compensation will be a matter for the Parliament but no requirement of just terms will flow from the Constitution ...

I conclude (i) that, upon its proper construction, in empowering the Parliament to make laws 'for' the government of any territory, s 122 identifies a purpose, in terms of the end to be achieved, and (ii) that, within the meaning of par (xxxi), s 122 states a purpose in respect of which the Parliament has power to make laws. The question then becomes whether there is either expressed or made manifest by the words or content of the grant of power in s 122 sufficient reason to deny the operation of the constitutional guarantee in par (xxxi). There is none.

First, a construction of the Constitution which treats s 122 as disjoined from par (xxxi) produces 'absurdities and incongruities' [*Lamshed v Lake* (1958) 99 CLR 132 at 144 per Dixon CJ]. This is so particularly with respect to a territory such as the Northern Territory, the area of which, at federation, was within a State. As is made clear in covering cl 6 of the Constitution, upon federation what was then identified as 'the northern territory of South Australia' was included within an 'Original State' and thus was part of the Commonwealth at its establishment ... The Constitution, notably s 111 ..., should not readily be construed as producing the result that the benefit of the constitutional guarantee with respect to the acquisition of property in what became the Northern Territory was lost...

Secondly, many of the powers conferred upon the Parliament by s 51 (such as par (xxix)) will be susceptible of exercise in respect of matters and things in or connected with the territories, and on its face par (xxxi) will apply to the exercise of these powers. The Conservation Act itself provides an example. One of the objects in making provision for the establishment of parks under s 7 thereof is the facilitation of the carrying out by Australia of obligations, or the exercise by Australia of rights, under agreements between Australia and other countries (s 6(1)(e)). In the present case the Commonwealth admitted on the pleadings that an object of the making of the Proclamations was to facilitate the performance by Australia of its obligations, or the exercise of rights, under the Convention for the Protection of the World Cultural and Natural Heritage.... It is to give to the constitutional guarantee a capricious operation to exclude from it so much of the law which is in question in the particular case as is or might have been concurrently supported by s 122.

Thirdly, as already indicated, the criterion of validity of a law made in reliance upon s 122 is that it be for the government of a territory. A law may meet that criterion without operating solely upon property situated in that territory. As I have stated above, s 122 authorises the Parliament to make laws the operation of which extends to the States. Further, it would appear that the power of the Parliament to establish territorial legislatures extends to empowering such a legislature itself to make laws with extraterritorial operation, at least within Australia [*Traut v Rogers* (1984) 27 NTR 29]. It would be a curious result if just terms were constitutionally unnecessary for the compulsory acquisition of land in a city in one of the States for the purposes of a tourist bureau for a territory. The owners of property in a State would be deprived of the constitutional guarantee where the property was acquired for the purpose of the government of a territory; the Commonwealth would be in a position to impose upon those holding property in a State a burden from which the Constitution was designed to protect them ...

Fourthly, the constitutional guarantee speaks of 'property', which 'is the most comprehensive term that can be used' [*The Commonwealth v New South Wales* (1923) 33 CLR 1 at 20–21]. It includes choses in action and other incorporeal interests [*Mutual Pools & Staff Pty Ltd v The Commonwealth* (1994) 179 CLR 155 ...]. The *situs* of such interests may be neither fixed nor, at any given time, readily susceptible of identification. For example, at common law, and in the absence of statutory provision, bearer bonds and bearer stock, passing by delivery ..., appear to be located where the instrument of security then is to be found ... Where there are two or more registers where a transfer of shares might be registered, the shares are situated where they could most effectively be dealt with having regard to business practice ..., or where the shareholder in question would be likely to choose a market and place of transfer when desiring to deal with the shares ...

In addition, incorporeal property, such as a patent, design or registered trade mark, which exists by virtue of a grant from the Commonwealth cannot be regarded as locally situate in any particular State or territory of the Commonwealth. Rather, such property is locally situate in Australia. Fullagar J so held in *In re Usines de Melle's Patent* [(1954) 91 CLR 42 at 49]. Accordingly, the constitutional guarantee cannot be coherently construed in a universe of legal discourse which contains a dichotomy between situation of property in a State and situation of property in a territory.

These considerations support a construction of the Constitution that the property referred to in par (xxxi) is that situated in Australia ...

The above considerations indicate that the legislative power conferred by s 122 is not immunised from the operation of the constitutional guarantee. Nevertheless, the Commonwealth referred to various matters which it submitted supported a construction which excluded from the operation of par (xxxi) any law of the Parliament which was supported, solely or concurrently with another head of power, ... by s 122 ...

Section 122 is placed in Ch VI of the Constitution, which is headed 'NEW STATES'. Section 51 is found in Ch I, which is headed 'THE PARLIAMENT'. However, in *Spratt v Hermes* [at 246], Barwick CJ said, with reference to s 122, that it was 'an error to compartmentalize the Constitution, merely because for drafting convenience it has been divided into chapters'. During the Third Session of the Convention Debates at Melbourne in 1898, there was an exchange between Deakin and Barton as to whether what became s 122 should be placed in what became s 52 (cl 53 of the Draft Bill), as an exclusive power of the Parliament. Their exchange concluded [*Official Record of the Debates of the Australasian Federal Convention*, (Melbourne), 28 January 1898, vol 1 at 257]:

Mr BARTON — It was thought advisable to leave that provision regarding territories where it is — under the head of 'New States' — because it refers particularly to that kind of territory which afterwards develops into a new state.

Mr DEAKIN — Yes, but it is an exclusive power, and might as well be placed in the clause relating to exclusive powers.

Mr BARTON — Is it not logically in a better place where it is?

Mr DEAKIN — It is logical where it is, and it would also be logical if included in clause 53. However that is a question for the Drafting Committee. ...

What is important is the proposition expressed by Brennan, Deane and Toohey JJ in *Capital Duplicators Pty Ltd v Australian Capital Territory*[268] that it would 'be erroneous to construe s 122 as though it stood isolated from other provisions of the Constitution which might qualify its scope' ...

That s 122 is not without limits upon the laws it authorises is further illustrated by *Davis v The Commonwealth* [(1988) 166 CLR 79]. The Australian Bicentennial Authority was a company incorporated in the Australian Capital Territory with the primary object of planning and implementing celebrations to commemorate the 1988 Bicentenary. Section 22 of the *Australian Bicentennial Authority Act* 1980 (Cth) made it an offence for a person without the consent of the Authority to use certain expressions and s 23 provided for the forfeiture to the Commonwealth of articles or goods by means of which or in relation to which there had been committed an offence against s 22. Mason CJ, Deane and Gaudron JJ said of s 122 [at 97; see also at 117 per Brennan J, 117 per Toohey J]:

That head of legislative power would extend to the incorporation of a corporation in the Australian Capital Territory and to the protection of its corporate name and symbols. But the Territories power on its own cannot sustain the regime which ss 22 and 23 attempt to create.

In this case the Commonwealth also submitted that significant consequences ... flowed from the presence in s 51 of the phrase 'subject to this Constitution' and its absence from s 122. This phrase appears in various provisions of Ch I [Sections 2, 10, 27, 31, 51, 52, 58] and Ch V

[Sections 106, 108]. The processes and procedures for the making of laws by the Parliament in pursuance of the powers conferred by ss 51 and 52 are subjected to the requirements as to manner and form and specific content imposed by provisions such as s 53 ..., s 54 ..., s 55 ... and s 57 ...

The phrase 'subject to this Constitution' also serves in s 51 to emphasise that the subject-matter with respect to which the Parliament otherwise may make laws under s 51 is restrained by provisions such as ss 92, 99, 100 and 116 ... But the same result would follow from the operation of the prohibitions in which those sections are expressed without the confirmatory warning in s 51 itself. No particular conclusion follows in this respect from the presence (in s 51) or the absence (from s 122) of the phrase 'subject to this Constitution'. It can hardly be suggested that s 122 operates other than subject to the Constitution, and, in particular, that it is not to be read with the Constitution as a whole.

It is true that, as authority presently stands, limitations imposed by s 55 do not apply to laws supported by s 122 [*Buchanan v The Commonwealth*]. Nevertheless, territory representatives are subject to the ineligibility and disqualification provisions of ss 43, 44, 45 and 46 of the Constitution [*Spratt v Hermes* at 246] and in *Spratt v Hermes* ... Barwick CJ said there seemed to be no reason why a double dissolution should not result from a disagreement between the two chambers upon a proposed law founded upon s 122 ...

~~~

[12.5.14] Justice Gummow went on to overrule *Teori Tau v Commonwealth* (1969) 119 CLR 564 as having been 'overtaken' by more recent developments, including the 1977 amendment to s 128 of the Constitution, grants of territorial representation in parliament and self-government, and the reasoning in cases like *Lamshed v Lake* (1958) 99 CLR 132.

Section 122 and Ch III

[12.5.15] While *Newcrest* concerned a constitutional limitation at the heart of the 'federal compact' expressed in s 51 of the Constitution, even *Teori Tau* indicated that the High Court might be more willing to apply to s 122 limitations derived from other parts of the Constitution. As the above extracts indicate, considerable recent debate has focussed on the relationship between s 122 and Ch III. In this section, we are mainly concerned with the impact of the 'relationship between s 122 and Ch III' controversy on the question of whether the courts of the *self-governing* territories are subject to Ch III.

An uncertain jurisprudence

[12.5.16] The following material should be approached keeping in mind that Ch III is 'a notoriously technical and difficult branch of Australian constitutional law' (Windeyer J in *Spratt v Hermes* (1965) 114 CLR 226), that the relationship between Ch III and section 122 is 'a problem of interpretation ... which has vexed judges and commentators since the earliest days of Federation' (*Re the Governor, Goulburn Correctional Centre; Ex parte Eastman* (1999) 200 CLR 322 Gleeson CJ, McHugh and Callinan JJ at 331), and that solutions devised for this problem have involved 'baroque complexities and many uncertainties' (Cowen and Zines (1978) p 172; (2002) p 192). For a more detailed discussion of the following material, see Cowen and Zines (2002) Ch 4.

The High Court has decided that:

- s 72 of the Constitution does not apply to judicial appointments to courts constituted by parliament under s 122 (*Spratt; Falconer; Eastman*) (see **[12.5.20]**);

- courts given jurisdiction by parliament under s 122 may exercise federal jurisdiction 'arising under any laws made by the Parliament' (*GPAO*) (see **[12.5.10C]**– **[12.5.11]**);

- the guarantee of trial by jury on indictment under Commonwealth laws does not apply to laws made under s 122 (*Bernasconi*) (see **[11.2.26]** and **[12.5.8C]**); and

- except where Parliament invests them with 'federal jurisdiction' (see **[12.5.21]**– **[12.5.23C]**), appeals from territory courts depend on s 122 of the Constitution, not s 73(ii) (*Porter*) (see **[12.5.8C]** and **[12.5.25]**).

While recent rulings have supported the first and second of these principles and qualified the fourth, the third and fourth are much older. Cases like *GPAO* and *North Australian Aboriginal Legal Service v Bradley* [2003] HCA 31 (see **[12.5.23C]**) demonstrate a new 'integrationist' approach to Ch III and s 122. Certainly the court has moved away from the view of Griffith CJ in *Bernasconi* that the whole of Ch III has no application to territories.

[12.5.17] Since the late 1990s the High Court has begun to emphasise features of the Australian legal system which distinguish it from, say, the legal system of the United States. Cases like *Kable v Director of Public Prosecutions for NSW* (1996) 189 CLR 51; *Lange v Australian Broadcasting Corporation* (1997) 189 CLR 520 **[11.3.13C]**; and *Lipohar v The Queen* (1999) 200 CLR 485 draw attention to:

- the 'integrated' nature of the Australian legal system;

- the position of the High Court at its apex; and

- the fact that 'there is but one common law in Australia which is declared by this Court as the final court of appeal' (*Lange* (1997) 189 CLR 520 at 563) and which must not be at odds with the Constitution, not different versions of the common law in each state and territory.

Even before the court began to emphasise the 'integrated' nature of the Australian legal system, there was considerable controversy over the relationship between s 122 and Chapter III of the Constitution, but this new emphasis adds new dimensions to that controversy: see *Kruger v Commonwealth* (1997) 190 CLR 1 at 175 per Gummow J.

[12.5.18] It may be that the High Court is willing to exempt the courts of self-governing territories from the direct application of Ch III where they exercise jurisdiction under territory laws. Such an approach would build on the older jurisprudence relating to the Supreme Courts of those territories *before* they achieved self-government, discussed in the extracts from the judgment of McHugh and Callinan JJ in *GPAO* (1998) 196 CLR 553 **[12.5.8C]**.

[12.5.19] Judicial ambivalence about the application of Ch III to self-governing territories seems to be driven by two factors:

- on the one hand, a desire (consistent with precedent) to place the courts of self-governing territories on the same footing as those of states by not requiring their judges to be appointed in accordance with the rigorous requirements of s 72 Constitution (see, for example, Gleeson CJ, McHugh and Callinan JJ in *Eastman* 200 CLR at 331);

- a countervailing anxiety about the extent to which the courts of self-governing territories are integrated into the Australian judicial hierarchy — in particular, about the extent to which the High Court's appellate jurisdiction over disputes arising under *territorial laws* is constitutionally guaranteed. There may well be legitimate judicial concern that the legislative and judicial recognition of territory self-government has proceeded without due regard to this issue.

To understand the effect of these factors on judicial opinion, it is necessary to consider several sections of Ch III, keeping in mind that Ch III has been interpreted as exhaustive on the topic of 'the judicial power of the Commonwealth', at least as it applies in the states: *Re Judiciary and Navigation Acts* (1921) 29 CLR 527. This view was recently reiterated in *Re Wakim; Ex parte McNally* (1999) 198 CLR 511, where the High Court held that federal courts cannot exercise state jurisdiction (purportedly conferred on them by 'cross-vesting' legislation). By parity of reasoning, since Ch III makes no provision for it, it is also possible that federal courts may not be invested with appellate jurisdiction from foreign courts of the kind conferred on the High Court by the Nauru (High Court Appeals) Act 1976 (Cth).

Federal judicial power, federal courts and territory courts

[12.5.20] Section 71 of the Constitution provides:

Judicial power and Courts

The judicial power of the Commonwealth shall be vested in a Federal Supreme Court, to be called the High Court of Australia, and in such other federal courts as the Parliament creates, and in such other courts as it invests with federal jurisdiction....

Section 72 provides:

Judges' appointment, tenure and remuneration

The Justices of the High Court and of the other courts created by the Parliament —

Shall be appointed by the Governor-General in Council;

Shall not be removed except by the Governor-General in Council, on an address from both Houses of the Parliament in the same session, praying for such removal on the ground of proved misbehaviour or incapacity;

Shall receive such remuneration as Parliament may fix; but the remuneration shall not be diminished during their continuance in office ...

[Provision is also made for judicial resignation and a statutory retirement age of 70.]

As Windeyer J pointed out in *Capital TV and Appliances v Falconer* (1971) 125 CLR 591 at 611, these provisions go beyond the Act of Settlement requirements for judicial security. They require more secure tenure than is provided for judges at the state level, where tenure requirements are not constitutionally entrenched. They make no mention of territories, unless territory courts are either 'federal courts' or 'such other courts as [Parliament] invests with federal jurisdiction' under s 71, or unless there is a third category of 'other courts created by the Parliament' under s 72.

In two unanimous, pre-self-government decisions relating to the Australian Capital Territory, *Spratt v Hermes* (1965) 114 CLR 226 and *Capital TV and Appliances v Falconer* (1971) 125 CLR 591, the High Court held that territory courts were not 'federal' courts 'created by the Parliament' whose judges must hold office consistently with s 72 Constitution. In *Re the Governor, Goulburn Correctional Centre; Ex parte Eastman* (1999) 200 CLR 322, the court by majority refused to overrule these decisions as they continue to apply to the self-governing

ACT. The alternative conclusion, that judges of territory courts should have been appointed in accordance with s 72, could have invalidated decades of territory judicial decisions: *Eastman* at 330 per Gleeson CJ, McHugh and Callinan JJ. *Eastman* means that territory judges may be appointed by territory authorities under territory laws without tenure or fixed remuneration, and that, at least where they make decisions under territory laws, they exercise 'territory' rather than 'federal' judicial power.

'Federal jurisdiction' and territory courts

[12.5.21] The term 'federal jurisdiction' refers to the power to adjudicate disputes involving federal judicial power: *Northern Territory v GPAO* (1998) 196 CLR 553 per Gleeson CJ and Gummow J at 589–90. The Constitution defines this jurisdiction as the 'original jurisdiction' of the High Court, but allows it to be exercised by federal courts and — under Australia's 'autochthonous expedient' (*R v Kirby; Ex parte Boilermakers' Society of Australia* (1956) 94 CLR 254 at 268) designed to avoid a proliferation of courts as occurred in the United States — by state courts as well. Even if territory courts are not 'federal courts', perhaps they are nonetheless capable of exercising 'federal jurisdiction' (for example, when applying national laws, or perhaps even when applying territory laws, which ultimately owe their existence to Commonwealth laws)?

The High Court's original jurisdiction is defined by ss 75 and 76 of the Constitution, which provide:

Section 75: Original jurisdiction of High Court

In all matters —

(i)   Arising under any treaty;

(ii) Affecting consuls or other representatives of other countries;

(iii) In which the Commonwealth, or a person suing or being sued on behalf of the Commonwealth, is a party;

(iv) Between States, or between residents of different States, or between a State and a resident of another State;

(v)   In which a writ of Mandamus or prohibition or an injunction is sought against an officer of the Commonwealth;

the High Court shall have original jurisdiction.

Section 76: Additional original jurisdiction

The Parliament may make laws conferring original jurisdiction on the High Court in any matter —

(i)   Arising under this Constitution, or involving its interpretation;

(ii) Arising under any laws made by the Parliament ...

Section 77 allows this 'federal' jurisdiction to be shared by other courts:

Section 77 Power to define jurisdiction

With respect to any of the matters mentioned in the last two sections the Parliament may make laws —

(i)   Defining the jurisdiction of any federal court other than the High Court ...

(ii) ...

(iii) Investing any court of a State with federal jurisdiction.

The original jurisdiction conferred by s 75 may be exercised in relation to disputes arising in territories — for example, a dispute between residents of Queensland and Western Australia over ownership of property located in the NT, or against 'officers of the Commonwealth' in a territory: see the comments in *Spratt v Hermes* (1965) 114 CLR 226 regarding *Waters v Commonwealth* (1951) 82 CLR 188. But there is no reference to territories in s 75.

The High Court and the Federal Court may exercise 'additional' original jurisdiction over self-governing territories where constitutional issues arise — for example, concerning the Commonwealth's ongoing power to legislate for them pursuant to s 122 — or where issues arise under a Commonwealth statute, including issues of repugnancy with territorial laws.

But what of disputes arising purely under the laws of a self-governing territory? Are such laws 'laws made by the Parliament' for the purposes of s 76(ii)? The majority reasoning in *Capital Duplicators Pty Ltd v Australian Capital Territory (No 1)* (1992) 177 CLR 248 (see **[12.6.3C]**) suggests that they are not. In *Capital TV and Appliances v Falconer* (1971) 125 CLR 591 the High Court held that the pre-self-government ACT Supreme Court did not exercise federal jurisdiction even when applying national laws; rather, it exercised only jurisdiction conferred under s 122. However, in *Northern Territory v GPAO* (1998) 196 CLR 553, Gleeson CJ, Gaudron, Gummow and Hayne JJ held that territory-specific jurisdiction vested by s 122 in a Commonwealth court (the Family Court) was 'federal jurisdiction' under s 76(ii): see below **[12.5.10C]–[12.5.11]**. The judges deliberately left open the question of whether *territory* courts applying *Commonwealth* laws were exercising federal jurisdiction, or whether *territory* courts applying *territory* laws were exercising such jurisdiction.

In *Eastman* ((1999) 200 CLR 322 at 341), Gaudron J was prepared to treat disputes under territory laws as 'arising under any law of the Parliament' because the existence of the ACT Supreme Court 'is ultimately sustained by a law under s 122 of the Constitution' (presumably, the ACT Supreme Court Transfer Act 1992 (Cth)) and decides 'rights and duties [which] ultimately depend for enforcement on the law by which that Court is sustained'.

[12.5.22] The language of s 77 does not help to answer whether disputes under territory laws are within federal jurisdiction because, as mentioned, the weight of authority tells us that territory courts are not 'federal courts'. Neither are they state courts invested with federal jurisdiction under s 77(iii).

However, in *Eastman* and *GPAO*, a number of judges began to suggest that the phrase 'such other courts as it invests with federal jurisdiction' in s 71 of the Constitution includes territory courts, and that the investment of territory courts with federal jurisdiction is authorised by s 122 without the need for a 'territory' counterpart to s 77(iii): see Gaudron J in *Northern Territory v GPAO* (1998) 196 CLR 553 and *Re the Governor, Goulburn Correctional Centre; Ex parte Eastman* (1999) at 339–40, and Gummow and Hayne JJ in *Eastman* at 347–8. This would mean that the principle established by *Kable v Director of Public Prosecutions (NSW)* (1996) 189 CLR 51 limits the constitution and powers of territory courts to ensure that they are not incompatible with those courts' exercise of federal judicial power: see **[6.4.48C]**.

The application of *Kable* to territory courts was raised in *North Australian Aboriginal Legal Aid Service v Bradley* [2003] HCA 31. Mr Hugh Bradley was appointed by the Northern Territory Government to the office of NT Chief

Magistrate until retirement age, but with remuneration prescribed for a two-year period. Section 68 of the Judiciary Act 1903 (Cth) allows territory courts to exercise jurisdiction over persons charged with offences under Commonwealth laws. The Service challenged Bradley's appointment on several grounds, including that the limited remuneration entitlement prescribed by an executive determination created a relationship of dependence on the Northern Territory executive (to provide remuneration beyond the two-year period) that was incompatible with the exercise of federal judicial power. It was argued that despite the High Court's decisions on s 72 of the Constitution and its inapplicability in the territories, the separation of judicial power effected by Ch III of the Constitution required that judicial officers exercising federal judicial power be, and be seen to be, independent of the executive government.

The Full Federal Court rejected this challenge, holding Bradley's appointment valid. The High Court unanimously dismissed the Service's appeal.

[12.5.23C]   **North Australian Aboriginal**
Legal Aid Service v Bradley
[2003] HCA 31 (17 June 2004)

McHugh, Gummow, Kirby, Hayne, Callinan and **Heydon JJ:** [16] The proper construction of the Magistrates Act is of primary and critical importance for the Legal Aid Service's case. When the statute receives its proper construction, the grounds upon which the Legal Aid Service urges invalidity cannot succeed. Accordingly, the appeal must fail.

Their honours held that the Magistrates Act allowed short-term appointments, provided an official determination of magistrates' remuneration was in force — it allowed no 'hiatus' in remuneration which 'would place the officeholder wholly at the favour of the executive government' (see [56]). Gleeson CJ agreed that the Magistrates Act (NT) allowed the Administrator to authorise short-term remuneration arrangements, but that the power to do so was coupled with a duty to exercise it. If the Administrator did not exercise the power, a magistrate could apply for mandamus to compel the administrator to do so. McHugh, Gummow, Kirby, Hayne, Callinan and Heydon JJ accepted the Service's constitutional arguments, but denied that Mr Bradley's appointment infringed the *Kable* principle.

[26] The Legal Aid Service relies upon the analysis by Spigelman CJ of *Kable* in *John Fairfax Publications Pty Ltd v Attorney-General (NSW)* (2000) 181 ALR 694 at 698, where his Honour said:

> The reasoning of the majority in *Kable* was not confined to the *character* of a function or power conferred by a State law. Some of the reasoning encompasses the *manner* in which a function or power is to be performed. Although *Kable* was concerned with the compatibility of a specific non-judicial power (to order imprisonment without any finding of criminal guilt) with the exercise by a state Supreme Court of the judicial power of the Commonwealth, the reasoning of the majority did involve principles of broader application: see *Bruce v Cole* (1998) 45 NSWLR 163 at 166.

[27] Further, in *Ebner v Official Trustee in Bankruptcy* (2000) 205 CLR 337 at 363, Gaudron J observed:

> Impartiality and the appearance of impartiality are necessary for the maintenance of public confidence in the judicial system. Because State courts are part of the Australian judicial system created by Ch III of the Constitution and may be invested with the judicial power of the Commonwealth, the Constitution also requires, in accordance with *Kable v Director of Public Prosecutions (NSW)* (1996) 189 CLR 51, that, for the maintenance of public confidence, they be constituted by persons who are impartial and who appear to be impartial even when exercising non-federal jurisdiction. And as courts created pursuant to s 122 of the Constitution may also be invested with the judicial power of the Commonwealth (see *Northern Territory v GPAO* (1999) 196 CLR 553 at 603-604 [127] per Gaudron J; *Re Governor, Goulburn Correctional Centre; Ex parte Eastman* (1999) 200 CLR 322 at 336-340 [25]-[36] per Gaudron J, 348 [63] per Gummow

and Hayne JJ; cf at 354-356 [84]-[88] per Kirby J), it should now be recognised, consistently with the decision in *Kable*, that the Constitution also requires that those courts be constituted by persons who are impartial and who appear to be impartial.

In his reasons in *Ebner* (at 373), Kirby J, by reference to *Kable*, also expressed the view that:

> ... in Australia, the ultimate foundation for the judicial requirements of independence and impartiality rests on the requirements of, and implications derived from, Ch III of the Constitution.

[29] Counsel for the Legal Aid Service put an argument in three steps. The first is that a court of the Territory may exercise the judicial power of the Commonwealth pursuant to investment by laws made by the Parliament. That proposition, to which there was no demurrer by the Territory or by the Attorney-General of the Commonwealth who intervened in this Court, is supported by the citations of authority by Gaudron J in the above passage from *Ebner*. It should be accepted.

The second step in the Legal Aid Service's argument is that it is implicit in the terms of Ch III of the Constitution, and necessary for the preservation of that structure, that a court capable of exercising the judicial power of the Commonwealth be and appear to be an independent and impartial tribunal. That proposition, which again appears in the passage from *Ebner*, also should be accepted.

[30] The difficulty arises with the third step. This requires discernment of the relevant minimum characteristic of an independent and impartial tribunal exercising the jurisdiction of the courts over which the Chief Magistrate presides. No exhaustive statement of what constitutes that minimum in all cases is possible. However, the Legal Aid Service refers in particular to the statement by McHugh J in *Kable* at 119 (see also Toohey J at 98, Gaudron J at 108 and Gummow J at 133-134) that the boundary of legislative power, in the present case that of the Territory:

> ... is crossed when the vesting of those functions or duties might lead ordinary reasonable members of the public to conclude that the [Territory] court as an institution was not free of government influence in administering the judicial functions invested in the court.

[31] Much then turns upon the permitted minimum criteria for the appearance of impartiality. In that regard, *Re Governor, Goulburn Correctional Centre; Ex parte Eastman* (1999) 200 CLR 322 established that s 72 of the Constitution had no application to the Supreme Court of the Australian Capital Territory because that Court was not a court 'created by the Parliament' within the meaning of s 72 of the Constitution. It followed that there was no objection based upon the tenure requirement of s 72 to the appointment of an acting judge in that Court. Although in *Eastman* and in earlier cases other views have been stated on this subject, for these proceedings the point should be taken as settled.

[32] Moreover, it may be added that the absence of a full commission to the trial judge in *Eastman* did not gainsay the appearance of impartiality. No question arose in *Eastman* respecting the effect upon that appearance of impartiality and the application of *Kable* to a series of acting rather than full appointments which is so extensive as to distort the character of the court concerned. No such question arises in this case.

[33] Territorial legislatures may be moved to legislate with respect to their courts by considerations extending beyond compliance with constitutional imperatives. Legislation may be designed to further the fact and the appearance of impartial judicial determinations. Provisions respecting security of remuneration assist that end, as McHugh J pointed out in *Harris v Caladine* (1991) 172 CLR 84 at 159. See also *Reference re Remuneration of Judges of the Provincial Court of Prince Edward Island; Reference re Independence and Impartiality of Judges of the Provincial Court of Prince Edward Island* [1997] 3 SCR 3 at 89–90; Johnston and Hardcastle, 'State Courts: The Limits of *Kable*', (1998) 20 *Sydney Law Review* 216 at 239–240.

[34] Accordingly, in the present case, the first step, logically anterior to the application of constitutional norms, is to ascertain whether on the proper construction of the Magistrates Act

there is evidenced a legislative purpose to advance the status of the magistracy of the Territory in the manner just indicated. When that has been done, the submissions as to invalidity will fall for consideration.

The justices concluded that the Magistrates Act was intended to provide a measure of independence to NT magistrates, but that placing a magistrate in a position in which he or she might be required to apply for mandamus to secure ongoing remuneration did not infringe Ch III principles.

[65] It is true that, however unlikely that eventuality in practice, an officeholder under the system established by the Magistrates Act may be placed in the position of seeking the aid of the Supreme Court to compel observance of the obligations of the Administrator under s 6. But that circumstance does not render the magistracy of the Territory or the office of the Chief Magistrate inappropriately dependent on the legislature or executive of the Territory in a way incompatible with requirements of independence and impartiality. It does not compromise or jeopardise the integrity of the Territory magistracy or the judicial system (*Kable v DPP (NSW)* (1996) 189 CLR 51 at 107, 117, 119, 133). Nor is it apt to lead reasonable and informed members of the public to conclude that the magistracy of the Territory was not free from the influence of the other branches of government in exercising their judicial function (*cf Ell v Alberta* [2003] 1 SCR 857 at 874–75).

~~~

Appellate jurisdiction of the High Court

[12.5.24] Sections 75 and 76 of the Constitution give the High Court the same *original* jurisdiction in the territories as it exercises in the states, which seems unobjectionable. However, on one reading at least, the High Court's power to control the legal systems of self-governing territories is more curtailed than its power to control those of the states because the Constitution guarantees it no *appellate* jurisdiction from territory courts. Section 73 of the Constitution provides:

Section 73 Appellate jurisdiction of High Court

The High Court shall have jurisdiction, with such exceptions and subject to such regulations as the Parliament prescribes, to hear and determine appeals from all judgments, decrees, orders and sentences —

(i)   Of any Justice or Justices exercising the original jurisdiction of the High Court;

(ii) Of any other federal court, or court exercising federal jurisdiction; or of the Supreme Court of any State...

(iii) ...

and the judgment of the High Court in all such cases shall be final and conclusive.

A right of appeal from the Supreme Court of a state is constitutionally guaranteed, but the Supreme Courts of the territories are not mentioned — unless of course they are 'federal courts', or 'courts exercising federal jurisdiction'.

If the right to appeal from a territory Supreme Court to the High Court is not constitutionally guaranteed, the territory courts are not constitutionally part of the integrated Australian legal system and there appears to be no constitutional guarantee that their common law will be the common law of Australia and will conform to the Constitution. Some judges have sought a way around this problem by suggesting that *all* of the law of territories, including their common law, ultimately owes its existence to Commonwealth legislation (for example, the provisions in the early territory Administration Acts, or the more recent Self-Government Acts, which preserved pre-existing laws — see **[12.2.6]**.) See, for example, the views of Dixon J in *Federal Capital Commission v Laristan Building and Investment Co Pty Ltd* (1929) 42 CLR 582 and Finn J in *O'Neil v Mann* (2000) 175 ALR 742 at 748–9, discussed in Cowen and Zines (2002) pp 183–4.

Perhaps Ch III can be supplemented by s 122?

[12.5.25] Since the High Court has heard appeals from territory courts since federation, and since '[i]t is unthinkable that they should be forbidden as outside the Constitution' (Kirby J in *Re Wakim; Ex parte McNally* (1999) 198 CLR 511 at 608), the traditional way around these problems has been to say that Ch III does not make exhaustive provision on the subject of the judicial power of the Commonwealth *in territories* or *outside of the states*. Rather, appeals from territory courts are just one aspect of the 'government' of territories on which s 122 allows parliament to legislate: for example, *Re The Governor, Goulburn Correctional Centre; Ex parte Eastman* (1999) 200 CLR 322 at 346 per Gummow and Hayne JJ at [57]. Just as s 122 allows parliament to supplement the parliamentary representation guaranteed to the states by ss 7 and 24 with parliamentary representation for the territories, s 122 allows it to supplement the jurisdiction conferred by Ch III on the High Court and other federal courts with jurisdiction in relation to the territories. (To take an even broader view, even the legislation allowing appeals to the High Court from Nauru, enacted under s 51(xxix) Constitution, might be valid because Ch III has no application at all outside of the Australian states.)

This was the effect of the High Court's decision in *Porter v The King; Ex parte Yee* (1926) 37 CLR 432 (see discussion at **[12.5.8C]**), but 'it is recognised by a number of judges that that case is inconsistent with the principle that Chapter III is exhaustive of the jurisdiction that can be possessed by the High Court or other federal courts' (Cowen and Zines, 2002) at 185, citing *Northern Territory v GPAO* (1998) 196 CLR 553 and *Gould v Brown* (1998) 193 CLR 346 at 426 per McHugh J).

This position leaves territorians with only *statutory* rights of appeal to the High Court; their access to the court's original jurisdiction under s 76(ii) may also depend on the extent to which they are governed by *Commonwealth*, rather than *territory*, legislation. The upshot is that, the more power the Commonwealth devolves to self-governing territories, the more potential there is for territory courts to escape the High Court's control.

Express constitutional limitations in the territories

[12.5.26] The language of ss 51(ii), 92, 99, 117 and even s 118 of the Constitution concerns aspects of 'states' and precludes their application in the territories or to the governments of self-governing territories. High Court decisions tell us that s 51(xxxi) applies in territories where the Commonwealth acquires property pursuant to national laws, but that territories are not entitled by s 80 to trial by jury: see **[12.5.4]**, **[12.5.12]–[12.5.13C]** and **[12.5.8C]** respectively (and **[11.2.26]**).

The question whether the religious freedoms guaranteed by s 116 apply within the territories is not yet resolved. In *Lamshed v Lake* (1958) 99 CLR 132 at 143, Dixon CJ, with whom Webb, Kitto and Taylor JJ agreed, said that there was 'no reason' why s 116 could not apply to laws made under s 122. This conclusion was consistent with their view that a law enacted by the Commonwealth pursuant to s 122 was a 'law of the Commonwealth' for the purposes of s 109, and could override an inconsistent state law: see **[12.4.7C]**. Since s 116 contains a guarantee that is territorially co-extensive with the Commonwealth (that is, it applies to laws made by the Commonwealth, which could apply throughout the Commonwealth), it ought to apply within the territories, which are part of the Commonwealth. (This position is, of course, predicated on the assumption that the territories *are* part of the Commonwealth, a view still rejected by some judges: see McHugh J in *Kruger v Commonwealth* (1997) 190 CLR 1 **[12.5.28C]**.)

Kitto J later appeared to recant the opinion he held in *Lamshed v Lake* in *Spratt v Hermes* (1965) 114 CLR 226 at 250–1, holding that:

> Whether or not one or two of the miscellaneous provisions in Ch V apply to the territories — ss 116 and 118 have been suggested, eg in *Lamshed v Lake*, though further consideration has made me more doubtful than I was about them — it seems clear enough that the limitations which Ch I puts upon legislative power in the working of the federal system, anxiously contrived as they are with the object of keeping the Parliament to the course intended for it, are thrown aside as irrelevant when the point is reached of enabling laws to be made for the government of territories which stand outside that system ...

The question was raised again in *Attorney-General (Victoria); Ex rel Black v Commonwealth* (the *DOGS* case) (1981) 146 CLR 559. Gibbs J explained the tension in the court's jurisprudence in the following terms at 593–4:

> ... There are strong dicta, in addition to those in the *Jehovah's Witnesses* case (1943) 67 CLR 116 which I have already cited, which support the view that s 116 does apply to [s 122] laws: *Lamshed v Lake* (1958) 99 CLR 132 at 143; *Teori Tau v The Commonwealth* (1969) 199 CLR 564 at 570, but those dicta are in my opinion very difficult to [593/594] reconcile with the decision in *R v Bernasconi* (1915) 19 CLR 629, where it was held that the power given by s 122 is not restricted by s 80 of the Constitution — see also *Spratt v Hermes* (1965) 114 CLR 226 at 250. If s 122 is limited by s 116, the latter section will have a much larger operation in the Territories than in the States, for although s 116 is contained in Ch V of the Constitution which is headed 'The States' it is not expressed to bind the States.

Murphy J held that s 116 applies to s 122 (146 CLR at 621); so did Wilson J (146 CLR at 649 and 660).

The question was raised again in *Kruger v Commonwealth* (1997) 190 CLR 1. Toohey, Gaudron and Gummow JJ held that s 116 applies in the territories, but because the argument was being considered in the absence of the facts of the matter having been determined, it was not possible to conclude that the appellants' case had been made out: at 85, 122 and 160. Brennan CJ did not deal with that question, and Dawson J, with whom McHugh J agreed, shared Kitto J's doubts in *Spratt v Hermes* (see 190 CLR at 57, 85).

Implied freedom of political communication and other constitutional human rights

[12.5.27] Perhaps the most interesting question about the application to s 122 of constitutional limitations is whether territorians are entitled to the benefit of the implied freedom of political communication based on representative government, discussed in Chapter 11. Once again, there are two polar positions: the 'disparate' approach, most clearly articulated by Justice McHugh (in *Newcrest Mining (WA) Pty Ltd v Commonwealth* (1997) 190 CLR 513 at 575–80), and the integrationist approach, articulated by Justice Gaudron (at 102–7 and 116–20) — both based on the same central fact: territorians' constitutional disenfranchisement.

The 'disparate' view is also premised on the idea that territorians are not part of the 'people of the Commonwealth' for electoral purposes: *Attorney-General (NSW); Ex rel McKellar v The Commonwealth* (1977) 139 CLR 527, discussed at **[12.3.6]**. These views were elaborated in *Kruger v Commonwealth*, in which both judges signalled their willingness to extend the implied freedom to include a freedom of movement and association for political purposes. Acknowledging the potential for human rights abuses against unrepresented populations, Gaudron J also held s 122 subject to an implied prohibition on the making of genocidal laws.

[12.5.28C] **Kruger v Commonwealth**

(1997) 190 CLR 1
(footnotes omitted)

Gaudron J at [104]:

Immunity from laws authorising acts of genocide: reading down of s 122

… It is settled doctrine that a constitutional grant of power is to be 'construed with all the generality which the words used admit' … Moreover because of the democratic principles enshrined in the Constitution, constitutional powers are not to be read down to prevent the possibility of abuse … At least that is so in relation to the powers conferred by s 51 of the Constitution. It was said with reference to those powers, in … *the Engineers' Case* …, that:

> If it be conceivable that the representatives of the people of Australia as a whole would ever proceed to use their national powers to injure the people of Australia considered sectionally, it is certainly within the power of the people themselves to resent and reverse what may be done.

If territories are put to one side, it may be reasonable to say, as was said by Professor Harrison Moore … that, under the Australian Constitution, 'the rights of individuals are sufficiently secured by ensuring, as far as possible, to each a share, and an equal share, in political power'. However, the Constitution ensures no share in political power to the people of a territory. They have no constitutional right to participate in elections for either House of Parliament; they have no constitutional right to self-government. Such rights as they have in these respects are purely statutory and, so far as the Northern Territory is concerned, were of a lesser order than those enjoyed by other Australians during the period with which these cases are concerned … And only since 1977 … have persons resident in a Territory had the right to vote in a referendum and, then, only if there is a law in force allowing for the Territory's representation in the House of Representatives …

At least to the extent that the Constitution makes no distinct provision for the participation of the people of a territory in any electoral processes, it may fairly be said that it allows for territories to be ruled as Commonwealth fiefdoms. That being so, the considerations which require that other grants of legislative power be construed without regard to possible abuse have no part to play in the construction of s 122. Rather, I would consider it much the better view that s 122 is to be construed in light of the fact that, unlike other Australians, persons resident in a Territory have no constitutional right to participate in the democratic processes and, thus, have no protection on that account in the event of an abuse of power. And, I would consider that that approach requires that s 122 should be construed on the basis that it was not intended to extend to laws authorising gross violations of human rights and dignity contrary to established principles of the common law …

… I am not persuaded that it is correct to say that s 122 stands wholly apart from Ch III … [or that] it is not subject to any of the express or implied constitutional limitations which confine the legislative power conferred by s 51. However, if either of those propositions is, to any extent, correct that is an additional reason for construing s 122 on the basis that it does not extend to laws authorising gross violations of human rights and dignity.

Were it necessary to decide the matter, I would hold that ... s 122 does not confer power to pass laws authorising acts of genocide as defined in Art II of the Genocide Convention ... [However, her Honour held that the Ordinance did not authorise genocide.] ...

[114] Implied freedom of movement and of association

... [T]he fundamental elements of the system of government mandated by the Constitution require that there be freedom of political communication between citizens and their elected representatives and also between citizen and citizen ... However, just as communication would be impossible if 'each person was an island' [*Nationwide News Pty Ltd v Wills* (1992) 177 CLR 1 at 72 per Deane and Toohey JJ], so too it is substantially impeded if citizens are held in enclaves [ie, Aboriginal reserves, as the plaintiffs had been held], no matter how large the enclave or congenial its composition. Freedom of political communication depends on human contact and entails at least a significant measure of freedom to associate with others ... And freedom of association necessarily entails freedom of movement [which Aboriginal people had not enjoyed under the Ordinance] ...

... [B]ecause freedom of movement and freedom of association are, at least in the respects mentioned, aspects of freedom of political communication, they, too, are implicit in the Constitution and constrain the power conferred by s 51. It is, however, another question whether the power conferred by s 122 is subject to the same freedoms ...

It does not follow that, because s 122 is not expressed to be subject to the Constitution or because it is not subject to some constitutional prohibitions or restrictions, its meaning and operation are not affected by other constitutional provisions. Indeed, *Capital Duplicators Pty Ltd v Australian Capital Territory* [*(No 1)*] establishes to the contrary ...

Nor, in my view, does it follow that, because the system of representative government for which the Constitution provides has no application to territories, s 122 is unaffected by the implied freedom of political communication ... In this regard, it is sufficient to note that the Constitution contemplates that territories will be governed by laws enacted by a Parliament comprised of persons elected by and responsible to the people; it most certainly does not contemplate that they are to be governed by an executive unanswerable either to the Parliament or to the people ...

When regard is had to the Constitution as a whole, there are two features which... necessitate the conclusion that s 122 is confined by the freedom of political communication ... and by the subsidiary freedoms of association and movement to which reference has already been made. The first is the nature and scope of the freedom of political communication ... The second is the special position of territories in our Constitutional arrangements.

Freedom of political communication is a freedom which extends to all matters which may fall for consideration in the political process. The government of the Australian territories is one such matter. Hence, the freedom extends to all matters that bear upon territory government as well as those which bear upon the actual government of the Territories ...

Moreover, the nature of the freedom is such that it extends to members of society generally ... In *Australian Capital Television*, Mason CJ pointed out that 'individual judgment, whether that of the elector, the representative or the candidate, on so many issues turns upon free public discussion in the media of the views of all interested persons, groups and bodies and on public participation in, and access to, that discussion.' [at 139] However, informed judgment does not depend simply on media discussion. At base, it depends on public discussion, that is discussion in which all are free to participate, or, as was put by Mason CJ in *Australian Capital Television*, '[t]he efficacy of representative government depends ... upon free communication ... between all persons, groups and other bodies in the community.' [*ibid*]

The nature and extent of the freedom ... assume particular significance in the context of the constitutional arrangements made with respect to territories. It may be true to say that the Territories do not form part of the federation. Even so, s 111 of the Constitution provides that the Commonwealth, which is constituted by the federating States, has 'exclusive jurisdiction' over surrendered territory, as is the case with the Northern Territory ... And given the terms of ss 111 and 122 and, so far as concerns the Australian Capital Territory, ss 52 ... and 125

..., it must be acknowledged that neither Territory is 'a *quasi* foreign country remote from and unconnected with Australia except for owing obedience to the sovereignty of the same Parliament but ... a territory of Australia about the government of which the Parliament may make every proper provision as part of its legislative power operating throughout its jurisdiction.' [*Lamshed v Lake* (1958) 99 CLR 132 at 144 per Dixon CJ]

Although it is for the Parliament to make proper provision for the government of the territories of the Commonwealth, responsibility for their government and, thus, for the welfare of those who reside in them ultimately rests with the people to whom the Constitution entrusts the responsibility of choosing the Members of Parliament ... Clearly, the proper discharge of that responsibility depends upon the free flow of information with respect to all matters bearing upon territory government and, also, those matters which bear upon the actual government of the Territories.

Moreover, the proper discharge of [that] responsibility ... depends on freedom of political communication between [voters] and persons resident in those Territories: there could hardly be informed judgment on matters relevant to their government if residents were not free to provide other members of the body politic with information as to the affairs of the Territories. And although persons resident in the Territories have no constitutional right to participate in the electoral processes for which the Constitution provides, the discharge by elected representatives and Ministers of State of their responsibilities requires that there be freedom of communication between them and persons residing in the Territories. And for discussion between persons resident in the Territories and other members of the body politic, including elected representatives and Ministers of State, to be properly informed, it is necessary that there be freedom of political communication between the persons who reside in the Territories.

It follows that, if Parliament is to remain accountable to the Australian people, the freedom of political communication... must extend to persons resident in the Territories and that, in that regard, s 122 stands in the same position as s 51. That being so ... s 122 is confined by the freedom of political communication... and... by the subsidiary freedoms of movement and association ...

[142] McHugh J: ... Because ss 7, 24, 64 and 128 and related sections of the Constitution provide for a system of representative and responsible government and a procedure for amending the Constitution by referendum, the Constitution necessarily implies that 'the people' must be free from laws that prevent them from communicating with each other with respect to government and political matters [*Lange v Australian Broadcasting Corporation* ...]. The freedom arises from the constitutional mandate 'that the members of the House of Representatives and the Senate shall be "directly chosen by the people" of the Commonwealth and the States, respectively'. [*Lange*] It exists for the protection of 'the people of the Commonwealth' in the case of the House of Representatives and for 'the people of the State[s]' in respect of the Senate. As a matter of construction, the constitutional implication cannot protect those who are not part of 'the people' in either of those senses...

... [During the time when the 1918 Ordinance was in force] ..., the residents of the Northern Territory had no part to play in the constitutionally prescribed system of government or in the procedure for amending the Constitution. The right of the Territories to elect senators or members of the House of Representatives was, as it is today, dependent on federal legislation, not constitutional entitlement. The Northern Territory had no constitutional right during the period 1918 to 1957 to elect or vote for a member of the Senate or the House of Representatives.

His Honour set out the history of Northern Territory representation, voting and non-voting, in the House of Representatives, territory Senate representation and the right of territorians to vote in constitutional referenda.

... [A]t at no relevant time were the residents of the Northern Territory part of the constitutionally prescribed system of government. Nor, as the second paragraph of s 24 and ss 25 and 26 of the Constitution and s 15 of the *Commonwealth Electoral Act* 1918 (Cth) made plain, were the residents of the Territories 'people of the Commonwealth' for the purpose of s 24 [cf *Attorney-General (NSW); Ex rel McKellar v The Commonwealth* (1977) 139 CLR 527]. Moreover, at no time during the life of the 1918 Ordinance did an 'aboriginal native of Australia', who was resident in the Northern Territory and subject to the 1918 Ordinance, have any right to vote in federal elections ...

~~~

6   Territory self-government

Self-government: a constitutional novelty

[12.6.1] Grants of self-government to the Australian Capital Territory, the Northern Territory and Norfolk Island in the late 20th century have raised novel constitutional issues. Does the Constitution even permit such grants, rather than the conversion of territories to states?

The High Court has answered this question in the affirmative, but in doing so has introduced into constitutional jurisprudence bodies politic which, in their degree of independence from the Commonwealth and similarity to states, were scarcely contemplated in 1901, and about which the Constitution is largely silent. Interesting questions remain about whether these territories should have been instead either offered statehood in their own right (for example, in the case of the Northern Territory) or incorporated into existing states (for example, in the case of Norfolk Island). Perhaps the High Court should have insisted that parliament keep territories on this approved constitutional path, instead of allowing it to forge a new one for them?

Grants of self-government have been made under ordinary legislation enacted by the Commonwealth Parliament. No attempt has been made to entrench territory self-government in the Commonwealth Constitution. These grants do not preclude the enactment of further Commonwealth legislation with respect to those territories under s 122: *Northern Land Council v Commonwealth* (1986) 161 CLR 1.

The constitutional nature of territory self-government

[12.6.2] The legal effect of the ACT S-G Act was considered in *Capital Duplicators Pty Ltd v Australian Capital Territory (No 1)* (1992) 177 CLR 248, producing a dramatically split bench. For Mason CJ, Dawson and McHugh JJ, a territory legislature established pursuant to a Commonwealth Act is 'exercising legislative power which is referable to, derived from and part of the power of the Parliament' (at 263).

Such a delegation was not improper given the broad terms of s 122 and the fact that parliament retained a power to repeal the Self-Government Acts. However, for Brennan, Deane and Toohey JJ (with whom Gaudron J agreed), territorial self-government was something very different from a delegation of legislative power to the Governor-General.

[12.6.3C]   **Capital Duplicators Pty Ltd v**
Australian Capital Territory (No 1)
(1992) 177 CLR 248

Brennan, Deane and Toohey JJ: [281] ... By contrast with the regulations whose validity was upheld in *Victorian Stevedoring*, enactments of the Legislative Assembly under s 22 of the Self-Government Act do not lack 'independent and unqualified authority'. Enactments are made under a power to make laws 'for the peace, order and good government' of the Australian Capital Territory. Such a power has been recognized as a plenary power, as this Court pointed out in *Union Steamship Co of Australia Pty Ltd v King* [(1988) 166 CLR 1 at 9], 'even in an era when emphasis was given to the character of colonial legislatures as subordinate law-making bodies'. The terms in which s 22 confers power on the Legislative Assembly show — to adapt the language of *Powell v Apollo Candle Co* [(1885) 10 App Cas at 289] — that the Parliament did not intend the Legislative Assembly to exercise its powers 'in any sense [as] an agent or delegate of the ... Parliament, but ... intended [the Legislative Assembly] to have plenary powers of legislation as large, *and of the same nature*, as those of Parliament itself' (emphasis added). In *Reg v Toohey; Ex parte Northern Land Council* [(1981) 151 CLR 170 at 279] Wilson J said of s 6 of the *Northern Territory (Self-Government) Act* 1978 (Cth), a [similar] provision ...:

> Section 6 invests the Legislative Assembly with power to make laws for the peace, order and good government of the Territory, a power which in my opinion, subject to the limits provided by the Act, is a plenary power of the same quality as, for example, that enjoyed by the legislatures of the states. The constitution of the Territory as a self-governing community is **[282]** no less efficacious because it emanates from a statute of the Parliament of the Commonwealth than was the constitution of the Australian colonies as self-governing communities in the nineteenth century by virtue of an imperial statute.

The Legislative Assembly of the Australian Capital Territory has been erected to exercise not the Parliament's powers but its own, being powers of the same nature as those vested in the Parliament ... [T]he doctrine of *Victorian Stevedoring* does not extend to legislation enacted by a legislature in exercise of its own plenary power, albeit that power was conferred by the Parliament ...

[283] ... It cannot be said that the duties imposed by the [ACT] Business Franchise Act were imposed by the will of the Parliament. Those duties were imposed solely by the 'independent and unqualified authority' of the Legislative Assembly in exercise of that 'general legislative capacity' which, as Dixon J said, distinguished an independent exercise of power by a subordinate legislature from an exercise by that legislature of a power retained in the control of a superior legislature. The question is not whether the Parliament has abdicated its legislative powers: it cannot abdicate and it has not abdicated its powers under s 122 of the Constitution. Nor is the problem whether Parliament could delegate its legislative powers: it can, but it has not done so. The question is whether the Parliament has purported to create a legislature with its own legislative powers concurrent with, and of the same nature as, the powers of the Parliament: that is what the Parliament has done, and what it has done is of a radically different constitutional character from either abdication or delegation. The Parliament has no power under the Self-Government Act to disallow any duty imposed by the Legislative Assembly; the parliament must, if it wishes to override the enactment, pass a new law to achieve that result. It cannot repeal or amend the [ACT] enactment ...

~~~

[12.6.4] However, parliament can repeal territory self-government or amend the Self-Government Acts to withdraw legislative powers as it did by enacting the Euthanasia Laws Act 1997 (Cth): *Northern Territory v GPAO* (1998) 196 CLR 553 (Gleeson CJ and Gummow J) **[12.6.31]**.

Inconsistency between Commonwealth and territory laws

[12.6.5] What happens when territory legislatures legislate inconsistently with Commonwealth laws? The power conferred by s 122 is broad enough to allow parliament to specify the outcome of such conflicts. Consider, for example:

- ACT S-G Act s 28, which states that laws made by the Legislative Assembly have no effect to the extent that they are inconsistent with Commonwealth laws, but that such a law 'shall be taken to be consistent with [a Commonwealth Act] to the extent that it is capable of operating concurrently with [it]' (a narrower basis for inconsistency than those which apply under s 109 Constitution, discussed at **[8.1.82]**, because ACT laws are not thereby rendered inoperative simply because the Commonwealth has 'covered' a particular legislative 'field');

- the Euthanasia Laws Act 1997 (Cth) which retrospectively denied legal effect to the Rights of the Terminally Ill Act 1988 (NT).

See *Northern Territory v GPAO* (1998) 196 CLR 553 at 580–1 per Gleeson CJ and Gummow J.

[12.6.6] But what approach should the courts take where parliament does not make its intentions clear? The NT S-G Act, for example, is silent on this question. Section 109 Constitution cannot be resorted to — it applies only to conflicts between Commonwealth and state laws.

In cases of conflict between Commonwealth and territory laws, the courts apply the common law's approach to 'repugnancy' between laws of the Imperial and colonial parliaments (see **[4.2.2]** and **[6.2.4]**): for example, *Federal Capital Commission v Laristan Building and Investment Co Pty Ltd* (1929) 42 CLR 582; *Webster v McIntosh* (1980) 49 FLR 317; *University of Wollongong v Metwally* (1984) 158 CLR 447 per Mason J at 464; *R v Kearney; Ex parte Japanangka* (1984) 158 CLR 395 at 418 per Brennan J; *Attorney-General (NT) v Hand* (1989) 25 FCR 345. This approach was taken most recently by Gleeson CJ, Gummow and Hayne JJ in *Northern Territory v GPAO* (1998) 196 CLR 553. It produces results almost identical to those that flow from s 109 Constitution in the case of state laws. However, the theoretical basis of 'repugnancy' differs from s 109 inconsistency: repugnancy is said to involve the territory legislature exceeding the powers conferred by the parent legislature under any Commonwealth legislation, not just under the Self-Government Act. Repugnancy is a question of powers, not just laws. In *Northern Territory v GPAO* Gleeson CJ and Gummow J explained the basis on which the Family Law Act 1975 (Cth) could be found to be repugnant to a territory law.

[12.6.7C]   **Northern Territory v GPAO**
                        (1998) 196 CLR 553

Gleeson CJ and Gummow J at [581]: There may be discerned in a law ... of general application throughout the nation ... made by the Parliament in exercise of a power conferred by s 51 of the Constitution the legislative intention to make exhaustive or exclusive provision on the subject with which it deals. Section 109 of the Constitution then will apply ... In such a case, it is to be expected also that this field will be covered with respect to the territories ...

[582] The same expectation as to legislative intention arises where the power of the Parliament to enact legislation, such as Pt VII of the Family Law Act, is drawn from several

sources, including s 122, but the scheme of the legislation is that it operates exclusively across the field it covers, whether in the States or the territories.

Different considerations may apply where the law made by the Parliament, whatever the constitutional source of authority, does not evince an intention to cover the relevant field. In such cases, one would expect greater scope for the concurrent operation of territorial laws. This would correspond with the situation respecting State laws, if narrower notions of textual collision or direct inconsistency and repugnancy be applied. Those notions apply in cases such as those where two laws may make 'contradictory provision upon the same topic, making it impossible for both laws to be obeyed', as Mason J put it in *R v Credit Tribunal; Ex parte General Motors Acceptance Corporation*, or one law, as Dixon J said in *Stock Motor Ploughs Ltd v Forsyth*, varies, detracts from or impairs the other ...

[583] In a case such as the present, the task is ... to ascertain whether it is *necessarily implied* by the enactment, in the 1995 Act, of Pt VII of the Family Law Act [1975 (Cth)] that a [territory law] has a narrower operation than would otherwise be the case ... (emphasis added)

In *GPAO*, the territory law protected territory Child Protection officials from being required to produce information (including in the Family Court) relating to their work. However, for Gleeson CJ and Gummow J, this protection did not 'vary, impair or detract from' the key principle which the Family Law Act required the Family Court to apply: that the interests of the child are paramount.

[586] It follows that there is no necessary implication in Pt VII which requires qualification to the law-making power conferred upon the Legislative Assembly of the Northern Territory by s 6 of the Self-Government Act so that it does not sustain so much of [the territory law which confers the protection]. Nor, if this be the correct method of characterising the result, does Pt VII, as a matter of necessary implication, have such an overriding effect directly upon [the territory law], rather than through the medium of a restriction on the [Legislative Assembly's] law-making power ...

Hayne J agreed: at 650–1. See also Kirby J at 630, 636–8.

~~~

The application to self-governing territories of other provisions in the Commonwealth Constitution or constitutional doctrines

[12.6.8] If the self-governing territories are not simply delegates of the Commonwealth Parliament, are they bound by constitutional limitations which bind the parliament? Alternatively, should they be bound by constitutional limitations which bind the states? Section 122 gives no guidance on this issue. As noted at [12.5.26], the text of many constitutional limitations indicates that they are entrenched in relation to *states* or their residents alone, even if some are replicated in the Self-Government Acts. Besides the examples cited at [12.5.26], it is clear that:

- the prohibitions on the raising of state military forces and inter-governmental taxation in s 114 do not apply to territories (since the language of s 114 extends only to states, the Northern Territory is not prohibited from raising an army (its Self-Government Act and earlier legislation being silent on the subject); the application of territory tax statutes to the Commonwealth or Commonwealth tax statutes to the self-governing territories depends on the general principles discussed at [12.6.12]);

- (rather disturbingly for the residents of Pacific and Indian Ocean territories), the duty of the Commonwealth to protect the states against military invasion and 'domestic violence' in s 119 of the Constitution does not extend to the territories.

Some other constitutional provisions apply *in* the territories without necessarily applying *to* the self-governing territories as political or law-making entities. Thus, for example, in *John Pfeiffer Pty Ltd v Rogerson* (2000) 203 CLR 503, the High Court treated s 118 (full faith and credit throughout the Commonwealth to state laws) as capable of requiring NSW law to be applied in the ACT, although as Kirby J pointed out, s 118 says nothing about ACT laws being applied in NSW: 203 CLR at 556.

As discussed at **[12.5.15]–[12.5.25]**, controversy continues over whether Ch III of the Constitution applies to territory courts.

Section 90

[12.6.9] Section 90 of the Constitution provides that 'the power of the Parliament to impose duties of customs and of excise, and to grant bounties on the production or export of goods' is 'exclusive'. 'Exclusive' has been interpreted to mean 'not shared with the states'. Could such a power, however, be shared with the self-governing territories? In *Capital Duplicators Pty Ltd v Australian Capital Territory (No 1)* (1992) 177 CLR 248 the High Court was divided on this issue in a manner which revealed the fundamental difference between the majority and the minority judges on the nature of territorial self-government itself: see **[12.6.2]–[12.6.3C]**. For Mason CJ, Dawson and McHugh JJ:

> What [section 90] does is to make the power of the Parliament on the topic exclusive of other powers which are not themselves part of, referable to or derived from the power of the Parliament. The section is not directed to constrain Parliament by inhibiting it from conferring upon a territory legislature or other body its power or part of its power to impose duties of customs and of excise. It would be strange indeed to constrain Parliament's freedom of action in this way; to do so would achieve nothing in securing to Parliament exclusive control over the imposition of such duties for Parliament has power at any time to repeal such statutory authority as it may have conferred on a territory legislature or other body to impose such duties and to invalidate such duties as may have been imposed in the exercise of that authority ((1992) 177 CLR 248 at 262).

However, the majority justices took a different view in **[12.6.10C]**.

[12.6.10C]   **Capital Duplicators v Australian Capital Territory (No 1)**

(1992) 177 CLR 248

Brennan, Deane and Toohey JJ at **[274]**: ...[O]ne of the objectives of the federation was the creation of a free trade area embracing the geographical territory of the uniting Colonies, that is, the Colonies which became the Original States of the Commonwealth on its establishment... The territory of the Commonwealth at that time embraced the whole of the territory of those States, including the northern territory of South Australia [covering cl 6] ... A colony or territory which was not then a part of a State did not become a part of the Commonwealth ...

[275] Except in s 128, ... the term 'territory' in the Constitution is used to describe a geographical area ... [W]hen 'territory' in s 122 is used in reference to a mainland territory, it means an area that has been surrendered by a State to, and accepted by the Commonwealth or an area acquired by the Commonwealth [as the ACT was] ... Did the [ACT], by ceasing to be part of New South Wales, cease to be part of the free trade area which the Constitution was intended to create? ... s 92 does not in terms protect trade between a State and a Territory. Nevertheless, as this Court held in *Cole v Whitfield* [(1988) 165 CLR at 391], the purpose of s 92 was 'to create a free trade area throughout the Commonwealth and to deny to Commonwealth and States alike a power to prevent or obstruct the free movement of people, goods and communications across State boundaries.' ... Treating the entirety of the Commonwealth as a free trade area, the Constitution made provision to ensure that the Parliament, and the Parliament alone, should have legislative power to impose duties of customs and excise and to grant bounties on the production or export of goods ...

... To create and maintain a [275] free trade area embracing all parts of the Commonwealth, the Constitution provided, inter alia, that uniform duties of customs should be imposed (s 88) and that, on [their] imposition ..., all State laws imposing duties of customs or excise or offering bounties on the production or export of goods should cease to have effect and the power of the [Commonwealth] Parliament ... to impose duties of customs and excise and to grant bounties on the production or export of goods should become exclusive (s 90) and, further, that trade, commerce and intercourse among the States should be absolutely free: s 92. When ss 88, 90, 92 and 99 are read, as they were read on 1 January 1901, in the context of a Constitution dealing with the distribution of the entirety of Australian legislative power ... which might be exercised over the territory of the Commonwealth, those provisions can be seen to effect the objective of creating a free trade area embracing the whole of that territory ... It would frustrate the manifest purpose of s 86 [passage of the power to collect and control customs and excise duties and bounties to the Commonwealth Executive] if, after uniform duties of customs were imposed, part of the functions of collecting and controlling duties of excise or controlling the payment of bounties were to pass *from* the Executive Government of the Commonwealth to the Executive of a territory government whose legislature might be empowered to impose its own duties of excise or to grant its own bounties on the production or export of goods.

It would be surprising if the surrender of [a territory to the Commonwealth by a state] ..., whilst leaving the territory as part of the Commonwealth, removed it from the operation of the constitutional provisions designed to create and maintain the free trade area. When the Commonwealth was established, the economic interests of all parts of the Commonwealth were protected, inter alia, by the exclusive power conferred on the Parliament by s 90 and the restrictions on any discriminatory exercise of that power imposed by ss 51(iii) and 99. The prohibition in s 99 against the Commonwealth giving legislative preference to any State or part thereof over another State or part thereof would be undermined if the Parliament, upon [277] creating subsidiary legislatures pursuant to s 122 for territories carved out of the territories of the States, were able to confer on those legislatures power to create preferences that the Parliament could not have created had those territories remained parts of the territories of the respective States ...

> ... [T]he object of s 90 was at least to prevent frustration of the tariff policy of the Parliament. It is a mistake to regard s 90 as doing no more than allocating the legislative powers to which it refers as between the Commonwealth and the States ...

[278] ... [I]t is one thing to predicate of the people of the uniting Colonies that, agreeing to live in a free trade area, they were prepared to vest exclusive power to impose duties of excise in a Parliament composed in the manner prescribed by the Constitution and required, when passing a law imposing taxation, to follow the procedures spelt out in ss 53, 55 and 57; it is another to predicate of [them]... that they were prepared to bear the burden of duties of excise imposed by a legislature purportedly created by the Parliament without responsibility to the Parliament for the laws imposing such duties and without being bound to follow any procedure which would permit the representatives of the people of the States to consider the desirability of those laws...

[279] ... Unless s 90 qualifies s 122, ... Parliament could not effectively ensure that bounties are uniform throughout the Commonwealth as s 51(iii) requires ...

It is not to the point that, if the Parliament could validly confer legislative power to impose duties of customs and excise and to grant bounties upon the Legislature of a self-governing internal Territory, it might subsequently legislate to withdraw the power or to override its exercise. The exclusivity provision of s 90 was incorporated in the Constitution not for the protection of the Parliament but for the protection of the people of the Commonwealth, including those who resided in an area of a State which was subsequently to become an internal Territory ...

~~~

[12.6.11] Note that the decision in *Capital Duplicators (No 1)* is limited to Australia's 'internal' territories. Gaudron J, who agreed with Brennan, Deane and Toohey JJ that s 90 prevented the imposition of duties of excise by the ACT Legislative Assembly, based her judgment on a more general distinction between 'Internal Territories' as parts of the geographical area of the Commonwealth on the one hand, and external territories on the other.

Intergovernmental 'immunities'

[12.6.12] The doctrine of state immunity from Commonwealth laws does not extend to self-governing territories, for two reasons. First, the territories' existence as such is not constitutionally prescribed: contrast s 106 of the Constitution, preserving the constitutions of the several states. Secondly, the Commonwealth retains plenary power to legislate for the territories, including by singling them out for discrimination (via territory-specific laws), or by destroying their existence as governments (for example, by repealing the Self-Government Acts).

To what extent do territory laws bind the Commonwealth? Again, sometimes the Self-Government Act makes a clear statement on the issue — for example, s 27 of the ACT S-G Act provides that laws of the ACT Legislative Assembly do not bind the Crown in right of the Commonwealth. But what about where there is no such statement?

This issue has been canvassed in cases relating to Commonwealth enclaves in the Northern Territory, for example, national parks, defence bases or Aboriginal land held of the Crown in right of the Commonwealth. The High Court ruled, somewhat unconvincingly, that these were not 'Commonwealth places' under exclusive Commonwealth control pursuant to s 52(i) Constitution — that s 52(i) 'places' are only places in states: *Svikart v Stewart* (1994) 181 CLR 548 and **[12.4.10]–[12.4.12]**. *Svikart* led to confusion of a kind which s 52(i) was intended to remove: are Commonwealth enclaves in territories intended to be under Commonwealth control in a proprietary sense only, or should they be subject only to Commonwealth laws? Often a Commonwealth statute regulating the land provides the answer (allowing the question to be answered as one of consistency or repugnancy of *laws*), but sometimes it does not. Where it does not, the question becomes: is the Commonwealth Executive, as a land (or uranium) owner or radical title holder, subject to territory laws?

In one such case, *Minister for Arts, Heritage and the Environment v Peko-Wallsend* (1987) 15 FCR 274 at 297, Wilcox J referred to 'a fundamental principle' that the Crown in right of a state or the Northern Territory cannot bind the Crown in right of the Commonwealth. However, in *Newcrest Mining (WA) v Commonwealth* (1993) 46 FCR 342, French J held that a lack of power on the Northern Territory's part to bind the Commonwealth must be traced to

Commonwealth statute rather than any such 'fundamental [constitutional] principle'. This approach was approved by the Full Federal Court, by Gummow J in the High Court (*Newcrest Mining (WA) Ltd v Commonwealth* (1997) 190 CLR 513) and on appeal by the Full Federal Court in *Magarula v Minister for Resources and Energy* (1998) 157 ALR 160. This approach tends to suggest that territory legislatures enjoy power to bind the Commonwealth unless Commonwealth law otherwise provides; such a view might derive support from the express inclusion of a provision to the contrary in the ACT S-G Act: see s 27. However, the recent recasting of Commonwealth immunity from *state* laws in terms of *a lack of state power* (see *Re Residential Tenancies Tribunal of NSW v Defence Housing Authority* (1997) 190 CLR 410) would seem to apply equally to territories: the territories are unable to modify the Commonwealth's 'capacities' as a government (as opposed to the 'exercise' of those capacities) simply because their legislative powers do not extend so far.

Self-government movements and early constitutional development

Northern Territory

[12.6.13] Northern Territory politics have been characterised by more robust support for 'independence' from the Commonwealth than those of the Australian Capital Territory, reflecting in part the Northern Territory's distinctive history and cultural composition. The Northern Territory is a good example of a jurisdiction that was not afforded self-government until its population became sufficiently 'white'.

At the beginning of the 20th century, the NT's tiny 'white' population was outnumbered 7–1 by Chinese. 'Asiatics' and people of 'mixed' descent made up most of its official population of 4700, with 'Aboriginals' not even counted. Early Northern Territory politics (in which 'Aboriginals' could not participate formally) was dominated by trade unions who favoured 'white Australia' labour policies: Lockwood, 1970. As early as 1919, their protests (led by the person who became the first territory Member of the House of Representatives three years later) achieved the removal of the Commonwealth Administrator and his staff. After World War II (when 17,000 troops occupied the territory and the 'white' civilian population was evacuated), Darwin's Chinatown fell victim, uncompensated, to post-war reconstruction: Multicultural Council of the Northern Territory (2002). A Commonwealth-dominated, partly-elected local Legislative Council was established in 1947. Continuing pressure from its elected members led to gradual increases in their number and steps towards representative government until the Whitlam Government made it a fully-elected Assembly in 1974.

Dawson J traced the Northern Territory's early constitutional development in *Kruger v Commonwealth* (1997) 190 CLR 1 at 49–50:

> Upon acquiring exclusive jurisdiction over the Northern Territory, the Commonwealth enacted the Northern Territory (Administration) Act 1910 (Cth). Section 13(1) of that Act empowered the Governor-General to make Ordinances having the force of law in the Northern Territory. Under s 13(2) and (3) Ordinances were required to be laid before the Houses of Parliament, either of which had the power of disallowance. Until 1947, the powers of the Governor-General remained essentially unchanged, although under the Northern Australia Act 1926 (Cth) the Northern Territory was divided into

two territories (known as North and Central Australia) which were separately administered. In 1947 the Northern Territory (Administration) Act 1947 (Cth) amended the earlier Act of the same name to create a legislative council for the Northern Territory. A new section, s 4U, provided that '[s]ubject to this Act, the Council may make Ordinances for the peace, order and good government of the Territory.' Further sections were added which provided that such Ordinances had no effect until assented to by the Administrator of the Northern Territory according to his discretion, and that the Governor-General had power to disallow any Ordinance within six months of the Administrator's assent. The Administrator was not to assent to any Ordinance relating to 'aboriginals or aboriginal labour' unless the Ordinance contained a clause suspending its operation until the signification of the Governor-General thereon.

As late as 1966, Aboriginal people constituted 46 per cent of the NT population, but this proportion halved from the early 1970s due to increased (interstate) migration, despite Darwin's 1974 destruction by Cyclone Tracy. The newly formed, territory-specific conservative Country Liberal Party (CLP) dominated the first Assembly — over which the Commonwealth retained power to veto legislation and control of finance and administration: Northern Territory (Administration) Act 1974 (Cth); *Attorney-General (NT) v Hand* (1989) 25 FCR 345 per Lockhart J at [61].

Northern Territory courts were not necessarily constituted in accordance with Ch III Constitution. The Supreme Court Ordinance 1911 (NT) allowed appointment of acting judges and did not require jury trials in criminal cases; it provided for appeals to the High Court. The Northern Territory Supreme Court Act 1961 (Cth) allowed judges from other jurisdictions to sit as the Northern Territory Supreme Court and fixed judicial salaries, but did not expressly provide secure judicial tenure.

The Northern Territory surrender agreement between South Australia and the Commonwealth was conditional on the Commonwealth constructing a north–south railway link from Darwin to the state's north. However, such inter-governmental railway agreements were held unenforceable in *South Australia v Commonwealth* (1962) 108 CLR 130 and, although Alice Springs was linked to South Australia in the 1920s, the Alice Springs–Darwin rail link was not opened until January 2004.

Australian Capital Territory

[12.6.14] In 1909, the ACT had about 1700 'white' people, an unknown number of Aborigines and 224,764 sheep: Discover Our History (2003). The seat of government was officially established in 1913, two years after Walter Burley and Marion Mahony Griffin's design was selected for Canberra. Parliament moved to Canberra from Melbourne in 1927. In the ACT, local government initiatives have been established by Ordinances rather than Acts, and much government activity has been focused on building the city of Canberra itself.

The Seat of Government (Administration) Act 1910 (Cth) allowed the Governor-General to make Ordinances for the territory (subject to parliamentary disallowance), and for New South Wales courts to apply these and adopted NSW laws. No executive institutions were established. A 1924 amendment established the Federal Capital Commission to control development and provide governmental services, an experiment abandoned in the 1930s. From 1957, a National Capital Development Commission took over planning and construction, completing key elements of the Griffins' design. This body was the predecessor to the present

National Capital Authority under the ACT (Planning and Land Management) Act 1988 (Cth).

The ACT's 1930 population of around 7000 mainly public servants grew to 13,000 after World War II. A partly elected local Advisory Council was established under the Advisory Council Ordinances 1930 and 1936 (ACT). In 1974 this body became a half-elected Legislative Assembly, advising the Department of the Capital Territory: Legislative Assembly Ordinance 1974 (ACT). In a 1978 referendum, 64 per cent of ACT voters rejected self-government in favour of continuing under Commonwealth administration; a further 6 per cent voted instead for a form of local government: Elections ACT (2002). In 1979 the Legislative Assembly became a House of Assembly, before its dissolution in 1986 in preparation for self-government. Another referendum rejected self-government shortly before it was granted: Lindell (1992).

The Seat of Government Supreme Court Act 1933 (Cth) provided for secondment of federal bankruptcy or industrial court judges to the Australian Capital Territory Supreme Court, but also allowed appointment of acting judges and trial by judge alone. It provided for limited appeals to the High Court. From 1945, Australian Capital Territory judges could hold non-judicial offices approved by the Governor-General: Seat of Government Supreme Court Amendment Act 1945 (Cth).

Norfolk Island

[12.6.15] When 194 Pitcairn Islanders were transferred to Norfolk Island and it was erected as a separate colony in 1856, they were informed they would receive land grants and that there were 'no plans at present' to open up the island to other settlers. One interpretation of this history holds that Norfolk Island was thereby 'ceded' to the Pitcairners. An Australian parliamentary committee recently described this view as a 'myth perpetuated by a minority of Pitcairn descendants and other more recent, often wealthy, arrivals motivated by self-interest to resist the imposition of [Australian] income tax': Australia, Parliament (2003), paras 2.42–2.52, especially 2.44. However, Norfolk Islanders did enjoy a period of effective self-government from 1856–1897, living under laws formulated in consultation with them by their Governor, also the Governor of New South Wales: HREOC, 1999, p 5.

Consistent with Australian practice regarding external territories, the Norfolk Island Act 1913 (Cth) stated that:

- the territory was not routinely subject to Commonwealth Acts;

- territory revenue was available to defray territory expenditure, not for general Commonwealth purposes;

- the territory was exempt from Australian customs duty for locally produced goods;

- liquor production on the island was restricted.

[12.6.16] From 1913, the Governor-General could make Ordinances subject to Parliamentary disallowance, first on the advice of a partly elected Executive Council, a body established by New South Wales, and after 1935 in response to suggestions by an elected Advisory Council. The Advisory Council also advised the Administrator, who exercised executive authority: Norfolk Island Act 1913 (Cth); Norfolk Island Act 1935 (Cth). Despite these developments, in 1955, the islanders petitioned the Queen to restore 'self-government'. In response, in 1960, Australia proposed to constitute a Norfolk Island Council with local government powers under the Norfolk Island Act 1957 (Cth), but a majority of electors rejected this proposal. See generally HREOC (1999). Opposition in part reflected the fact that this Act removed the requirement that territory revenue be spent in the territory, and placed Norfolk Island under the supervision of the Commonwealth Auditor-General.

Before 1960, Norfolk Island judges held office 'during the pleasure of the Governor-General'. Islanders were granted a statutory right to appeal to the High Court from these decisions. The Norfolk Island Act 1957 (Cth) established a Territory Supreme Court, composed of judges entitled to fixed remuneration removable by the Governor-General only for misbehaviour or incapacity — or acting judges — and provided for High Court appeals.

The Norfolk Island Act 1963 (Cth) made minor amendments to this regime, conferring powers to advise the Administrator on the Council and allowing Federal Court judges to constitute the Supreme Court. The 1975 Nimmo Royal Commission recommended establishment of a local form of government and the extension of mainland legislation to the island. However, self-government developed in a different direction: see **[12.6.18]**, **[12.6.22]**, **[12.6.31]**, **[12.6.33]**–**[12.6.34]**.

Christmas and Cocos Islands

[12.6.17] Although Christmas Island's population is similar in size to that of Norfolk Island (see **[12.2.2]**), Christmas Islanders have not been given territory self-government. Nor have the Cocos (Keeling) Islanders. Both territories now have an Australian Administrator and elected Councils under the local Government Act 1995 (WA), applied from 1992: see **[12.2.5]**.

The Self-Government Acts

Application of Commonwealth legislation to self-governing territories

[12.6.18] Self-government in the Northern Territory and the Australian Capital Territory is similar to state government: territory residents and territory institutions are normally bound by Commonwealth laws. This flows both from covering cll 5 and 6 of the Constitution, which include the 'internal' territories in 'the States' to which Commonwealth law applies and make Commonwealth laws applicable throughout the Commonwealth, but also from provisions of the Self-Government Acts which provide that 'the Crown in right of the Territory' is bound by Commonwealth laws as the states are bound: see NT S-G Act s 51; ACT S-G Act s 69A.

Norfolk Island's position is different. Its exemption from Commonwealth legislation is continued by s 18 of the Norfolk Island Act 1979 (Cth) (the NI Act). Even legislation once applicable to self-governing Norfolk Island — for example, the Medicare legislation — no longer applies there: see Health Insurance Act 1973 (Cth) s 7A, which extends this Act to the Cocos and Christmas Islands only. This position is also reflected in s 17 of the Acts Interpretation Act 1901 (Cth), which states:

> In any Act, unless the contrary intention appears:
>
> (a) *Australia* or *the Commonwealth* means the Commonwealth of Australia and, when used in a geographical sense, includes the Territory of Christmas Island and the

Territory of Cocos (Keeling) Islands, but does not include any other external Territory; ...

This means that Norfolk Island, a territory with fewer than 2000 people, must legislate for, and administer, government at both a local and effectively a national level. A recent Australian parliamentary inquiry found this was too much to ask of such a small population: 'Norfolk Island [government] is in deep and growing trouble and needs help': Australia, Parliament, 2003 at vi. The inquiry recommended that continuation of self-government be conditional on introduction of significant reforms to the island's political system, and that Commonwealth immigration legislation be extended to the island. It also suggested the extension of Commonwealth social security, Medicare and possibly other legislation: Australia, Parliament, 2003.

Legislative Assemblies

[12.6.19] The Norfolk Island Act 1979 (Cth) (the NI Act), the NT S-G Act and the ACT S-G Act, create unicameral Legislative Assemblies.

Constitution of the Assemblies

[12.6.20] The Northern Territory Legislative Assembly has 25 members, including eight Ministers. The number of members is set by Northern Territory enactment: Northern Territory (Self-Government) Act, s 13(2). A maximum term (four years) for each Assembly is prescribed: s 17. Candidates must be Australian citizens qualified to vote in House of Representatives elections who have resided for at least six months in the Commonwealth, and three months in the Northern Territory: s 20. Voting is preferential in single-member electorates of about 8000 people each. The Northern Territory is the only jurisdiction to require a candidate's photograph to appear on the ballot form. From self-government until 2001, the territory-specific Country Liberal Party held majorities in the Assembly, a remarkable 'innings'.

[12.6.21] Of the 17 members of the first ACT Legislative Assembly, a number represented parties explicitly opposed to self-government, including the Abolish Self Government Party: Australian Capital Territory Legislative Assembly (2002). Nonetheless, the newly-elected representatives quickly grew accustomed to government and representation along familiar party lines emerged, although all ACT governments have been minority governments reliant on other parties for passage of legislation: Bennett, 2002. The number of Assembly members may be varied by a combination of Assembly resolution and regulations made by the Governor-General: ACT S-G Act, ss 8(2), (3) and 74(a)(i). Anyone with a right to vote for the House of Representatives must be enfranchised: s 67C. Voting is by the (Tasmanian) Hare-Clark proportional representation method of multi-member electorates, introduced after a referendum in 1992 and entrenched after another in 1995, normally for three-year terms; from 2004, members will hold office for four-year terms. In 2001, the ACT was the first Australian jurisdiction to permit electronic voting.

[12.6.22] The Norfolk Island Legislative Assembly has nine members and three-year terms: Norfolk Island Act 1979, ss 31, 35. There are no political parties — all candidates stand as independents. Before March 2004, Norfolk Island was the only Australian jurisdiction that still allowed new voters to enrol and stand for election without being Australian citizens. (About 82 per cent of the island's residents are Australian citizens, and about 14 per cent New Zealand citizens. While the original Norfolk Island Act 1979 (Cth) required candidates to be either Australian citizens or British subjects, this requirement was removed in 1985. Other Australian jurisdictions' electoral laws allowing non-citizens to vote were reformed in the 1980s: see, for example, **[2.4.13]**.)

Before 2004, the Legislative Assembly Ordinance 1979 (NI) also required electors to have lived on the island for an incredible 900 days during the four years before enrolment. This requirement was condemned by the Commonwealth Human Rights and Equal Opportunity Commission, and a recent Australian parliamentary inquiry recommended it be reduced to six months and that Australian citizenship be a precondition of electoral participation: HREOC (1999); Australia, Parliament (2003) at para 4.95. The Norfolk Island Act 2004 (Cth) implemented these proposals. However, candidates for election to the Assembly are still required to live on Norfolk Island for five years before standing: Norfolk Island Act 2004, s 38.

Norfolk Island uses the 'Illinois' system of 'cumulative' voting under which voters cast nine votes but may allocate as many as four to one candidate. Critics claim this allows 'those with connections to large family groups or sectional interests ... "a disproportionate say in who is elected ... [and is] open to abuse and ... fraud"': Australia, Parliament (2003) at para 4.87. The parliamentary inquiry recommended the system be changed to 'the "block vote" variation of the first-past-the-post method of voting', allowing candidates to be elected on simple majorities, and that elections be supervised by the Australian Electoral Commission: Australia, Parliament, paras 4.89–4.91.

Procedures

[12.6.23] The territory Legislative Assemblies have power to declare, and provide for the manner of exercise of, their own powers (other than legislative powers), privileges and immunities, and those of their members and committees — but only to the extent that those powers do not exceed those of the House of Representatives: NT S-G Act, s 12; ACT S-G Act, s 24; NI Act s 20. The ACT Legislative Assembly has no power to imprison or fine a person: s 24(4).

[12.6.24] Questions arising in all three Assemblies are determined by a majority of votes, except when the ACT standing rules and orders require a special majority (for example, in the case of entrenching laws like those determining the electoral system): NT S-G Act, s 27(1); ACT S-G Act, s 18(2); NI Act, s 42(5).

In the Northern Territory and Norfolk Island, traditional Crown functions of issuing electoral writs or proroguing parliament are performed by the Commonwealth's representative, the Administrator: NT S-G Act, ss 15 and 22; NI Act, s 33. In the absence of an Administrator in the Australian Capital Territory (see **[12.6.30]** and **[12.6.40]**), these functions are committed to the Assembly's elected 'Presiding Officer', the Speaker: for example, ss 11, 17.

The Australia Acts (s 6) preserved the earlier requirement that state parliaments conform with any 'manner and form' requirements entrenched by them in state constitutions: see **[5.4.1]–[5.4.45]**. The ACT S-G Act also allows the ACT Assembly to make laws entrenching 'the manner and form of making particular enactments', or controlling how those 'entrenching laws' may be repealed or amended: s 27(1). However, before taking effect, 'entrenching laws' must also be approved by a majority of electors at a referendum: s 27(2). Laws entrenching 'manner and form' requirements (for example, special majorities, referenda) must themselves be passed in conformity with those requirements: s 27(5) and (6). These provisions have been used to entrench the ACT's Hare-Clark voting system: see **[12.6.21]**.

[12.6.25] Decision-making in the Norfolk Island Assembly is affected by a 'culture of direct democracy' which blurs the roles of the Assembly and the executive: see below **[12.6.41]**. Section 40 of the NI Act requires the Assembly to meet at least every two months. Although it is required to keep minutes (s 44), the Assembly is not required to meet in public. 'In practice, the Assembly meets informally and in private every week and formally each month where more controversial matters are voted on', a practice disparaged by the recent parliamentary inquiry: Australia, Parliament, 2003, para 4.8. It also makes 'steady recourse to referenda to either inform or influence government decision-making, especially in respect of controversial matters', although the results of such referenda are not legally binding and sometimes unsatisfactory in representative terms: paras 4.27–4.37. The result has been criticised as producing distorted policy outcomes: para 4.34.

Dissolution of the ACT Assembly

[12.6.26] The fact that the Australian Capital Territory is not 'Crowned' by a representative of the Commonwealth (see below **[12.6.30]** and **[12.6.40]**) is offset by a power which does not exist in relation to the Northern Territory or Norfolk Island: the power of the Governor-General to dissolve the Assembly and appoint a Commissioner to conduct executive business pending general elections '[i]f, in the opinion of the Governor-General, the Assembly: (a) is incapable of effectively performing its functions; or (b) is conducting its affairs in a grossly improper manner': ACT S-G Act, s 16. This is a less extreme form of the kind of intervention often authorised by local government legislation at the state level, and a strong reminder of the difference between ACT self-government and statehood. See Lindell (1992) pp 9–10.

Legislative power and its limitations

Legislative power and Commonwealth assent

[12.6.27] Subject to limitations outlined below, all three territories' Legislative Assemblies have broad powers to make laws for the 'peace, order and good government of the Territory', although in the Australian Capital Territory's and Norfolk Island's case legislative power is shared with the Governor-General (see below **[12.6.32]** and **[12.6.34]**): NT S-G Act, s 6(1); ACT S-G Act, s 22(1); NI Act, s 19(1). The ACT Legislative Assembly has an express power to control the executive: ACT S-G Act, s 22(2).

[12.6.28] The power of the Northern Territory Assembly is subject to 'the assent of the Administrator or the Governor-General, as provided by this Act': NT S-G Act, s 6. The Administrator's assent (on Darwin's advice) is required for laws with respect to matters 'transferred' to the territory executive under the Northern Territory (Self-Government) Regulations 1978 (Cth): s 7(2)(a). These regulations list 58 'state government type' powers (notably excluding uranium mining except pursuant to arrangements with the Commonwealth). In relation to matters other than those 'transferred', the Administrator has the option of reserving the proposed law for the Governor-General's pleasure: s 7(2)(b)(iii). The Governor-General's assent to the proposed law (on Canberra's advice) is then published locally before the law takes effect: s 8(1).

[12.6.29] A similar system operates on Norfolk Island. Norfolk Island laws are divided into those which relate to matters listed in Schedule 2 of the Act (mainly municipal or 'state government type' laws, to which the Administrator assents on Kingston's advice), those which relate to matters listed in Schedule 3 (fishing, customs, immigration, education, quarantine, industrial relations, moveable cultural heritage and social security, to which the Administrator assents on Canberra's advice), and other laws (which must be 'reserved for the Governor-General's pleasure'): NI Act, ss 19(1), 21. Reserved laws take effect when the Governor-General's assent is published in the Norfolk Island Government Gazette: s 22(5).

[12.6.30] The Australian Capital Territory is unique among Australian jurisdictions in that no assent to proposed laws of the Legislative Assembly by the Crown or its representative is required for them to be effective: there is no ACT Administrator — see below **[12.6.40]**. This 'republican' dimension of Australian Capital Territory government in part off-sets the Governor-General's draconian powers to dissolve the Assembly: see **[12.6.26]** above. However, this dimension also allows the Assembly to legislate without the support of the (typically minority) ACT government, even to spend ACT money: Lindell (1992) pp 14–15, 26–7.

Scope of legislative power

[12.6.31] The legislative powers of the Assemblies are not complete. The Self-Government Acts withhold from them power to make laws on some subjects which are denied to state parliaments, although these restraints are not imposed consistently. For example, the Australian Capital Territory and Norfolk Island Assemblies but not the Northern Territory Assembly are denied power to raise defence forces or to coin money (compare ss 114 and 115 Constitution) under the Self-Government Acts: s 23 (ACT S-G Act); s 19(2) (NI Act).

All three Assemblies are denied power to make laws authorising the acquisition of property otherwise than on just terms (s 50(1) (NT S-G Act); s 23(1)(a) (ACT S-G Act), s 19(2)(a) (NI Act)), and laws authorising euthanasia, assisted suicide or associated withdrawal of medical treatment, or to repeal pre-existing laws criminalising attempted suicide (s 23(1A) and (1B) (ACT S-G Act); s 50A (NT S-G Act); s 19(2)(d) and (2A) (NI Act), inserted by the Euthanasia Laws Act 1997 (Cth)).

[12.6.32] The Australian Capital Territory Assembly is also denied power to make laws about:

- provision of territory police services by the Australian Federal Police;

- classification of materials for the purposes of censorship;

- a number of matters on which Commonwealth laws are in force in the territory: corporations, the securities and futures industries (s 23).

The Governor-General enjoys continuing power to make Ordinances for the ACT on some of these matters under the Seat of Government (Administration) Act 1910

(Cth) s 12. This law-making power also extends to some other subject matters (for example, unlawful assembly).

The Northern Territory Assembly is denied power to make laws authorising the destruction of Aboriginal sacred sites or interfering with traditional use of Aboriginal land, waters or wildlife use: Aboriginal Land Rights (Northern Territory) Act 1978 (Cth); see Chapter 2 ([2.4.59]).

The Australian Capital Territory pornography industry (see [12.3.17]) flourishes partly because of the local legislature's lack of control over its censorship. (There is not more demand for pornography in the Australian Capital Territory than elsewhere in Australia: most of the industry's sales are in Queensland.) Aboriginal people own about 50 per cent of land in the Northern Territory, compared with much smaller holdings (in some states for numerically larger Aboriginal populations) elsewhere, largely because the Northern Territory land rights regime falls outside the Legislative Assembly's control.

[12.6.33] In 1999, the Human Rights and Equal Opportunity Commission called for removal of Norfolk Island's immigration powers, a view echoed by a recent parliamentary inquiry: HREOC, 1999; Australia, Parliament, 2003. HREOC found administration of the Immigration Act 1980 (NI) violated Australians' rights to liberty of movement and freedom of choice of residence under art 12 of the International Covenant on Civil and Political Rights by creating a large class of long-term temporary resident permit holders (mainly workers from the mainland), and that such constraints were not necessary to protect Pitcairner culture. The Commonwealth Grants Commission has also criticised the Assembly's exercise of other powers, describing the island's tax system as regressive and its health, education and social security systems as below mainland standards: Commonwealth Grants Commission (1997).

[12.6.34] The Norfolk Island Assembly shares legislative power with the Governor-General, who may both introduce a proposed law into the Assembly for its enactment, or make the law himself or herself as an Ordinance if satisfied that it does not trespass on the legislative ground notionally allocated to the Assembly by Sch 2 and Sch 3 of the Act: s 27(1) (NI Act). The Governor-General may also make an Ordinance on such matters 'on account of urgency or for any other special reason' without first introducing it into the Assembly: s 27(2). This power extends to the making of Ordinances to spend moneys out of the Norfolk Island Public Account (see below [12.6.47]) where inadequate provision has been made for their expenditure: s 27(3). These Ordinances are subject to parliamentary disallowance: s 28.

[12.6.35] The Australian Capital Territory Legislative Assembly is the only Australian parliament to have enacted a Bill of Rights: Human Rights Act 2004 (ACT).

Disallowance

[12.6.36] The Self-Government Acts also confer on the Governor-General power to disallow territory laws within six months of their enactment: s 35 (ACT S-G Act); s 9 (NT S-G Act); s 23 (NI Act). Disallowance has the effect of repealing the legislation. These powers have never been used, although the Commonwealth has taken other steps to deny effect to territory laws: see [12.6.5] and [12.6.31]. On one view, a convention is developing that the disallowance powers will not be used.

Limitations on legislative power

[12.6.37] It appears that laws passed by the Australian Capital Territory Legislative Assembly do not bind the Crown in right of the Commonwealth except as provided by the regulations made by the Governor-General in Council: ss 27 and 74(a)(i), and s 16A of the Acts Interpretation Act 1901 (Cth). In addition, either house of the Commonwealth Parliament may pass a resolution declaring that an enactment made by the Legislative Assembly does not apply to that house, its members or in the parliamentary precincts: s 29(2) (this provision essentially restates each house's power to govern its own privileges within the 'seat of Government': see Constitution, s 49).

[12.6.38] Some important constraints based on limitations in the Commonwealth Constitution have been inserted into the Self-Government Acts. As noted, these include in the case of the Australian Capital Territory and Norfolk Island parallels of ss 114 and 115 Constitution, and in the case of all three territories, parallels to s 51(xxxi) Constitution.

The constitutional guarantee of freedom of interstate trade, commerce and intercourse among the states (s 92) has been given statutory extension to the internal territories by s 49 (NT S-G Act) and s 69 (ACT S-G Act), but not to Norfolk Island. However, under s 64 (NI Act), Norfolk Island goods remain exempt from Australian customs duties.

Some of the Self-Government Acts prevent the election to the Assemblies of persons who hold offices of profit under the Crown, are bankrupt or have criminal records: for example, s 21(1) (NT S-G Act); s 39 (NI Act). However, no such provision is made by the ACT S-G Act, which leaves candidates' qualifications up to ACT law (s 67 ACT S-G Act) and only provides for an Assembly member to lose office if he or she is absent from a prescribed number (four) of Assembly meetings, or provides or agrees to provide paid services to the Assembly: s 14. Members of all three Assemblies are prohibited from participating in debates and votes concerning contracts in which they have an interest (s 15 (ACT S-G Act); s 21(3) (NT S-G Act); s 39(3) (NI Act)), although the Australian Parliamentary Committee recently recommended the strengthening of such 'conflict of interest' controls under the Norfolk Island Act: Australia, Parliament (2003), paras 3.22–3.44.

Executive government

[12.6.39] The Northern Territory and the Australian Capital Territory are established as 'bodies politic under the Crown': s 5 (NT S-G Act); s 7 (ACT S-G Act). Although, unlike many former British colonies and protectorates, these bodies are emanations of *parliament* rather than the Crown, the expression 'Crown in right of the Territory' is used elsewhere in both Acts to describe the executive: for example, s 51 (NT S-G Act); s 69A (ACT S-G Act). The Administrator of Norfolk Island is constituted as a 'body politic ... by the name of the Administration of Norfolk Island': s 5 (NI Act).

[12.6.40] In the Northern Territory and Norfolk Island, the head of government is the Administrator, appointed by the Commonwealth: s 32(1) (NT S-G Act); s 6 (NI Act). These Acts provide that the Administrator administers the government of the territory: s 32(2) (NT S-G Act); s 5 (NI Act). The High Court has held that the NT Administrator is the Crown's representative: *R v Toohey; Ex parte Northern Land Council* (1981) 151 CLR 170.

The Australian Capital Territory is unique in that no Administrator is appointed as the Crown's representative — in this limited sense, the self-governing Australian Capital Territory is sometimes described as Australia's only 'partial republic': Lindell (1992).

[12.6.41] The Self-Government Acts (NT/ACT) provide for Westminster government, but Norfolk Island governance does not always conform to this model. Only the ACT (Self-Government) Act spells out this model in detail.

In the Northern Territory and Norfolk Island the Administrator acts, in cases which involve powers transferred to the territories, on the advice of Executive Councils composed of Ministers or holders of 'executive office' appointed by the Administrator from the ranks of the Legislative Assembly: ss 33–37 (NT S-G Act); s 11–14 (NI Act). By convention in the NT, these appointments are made on the advice of the person who commands a majority in the Legislative Assembly.

However, the absence of political parties on Norfolk Island is just one factor rendering this convention ineffective, despite a practice of electing a Chief Minister. The Assembly controls the number of 'executive officers' (s 12 (NI Act)), and has limited them to four, which means the Executive and the Chief Minister (the 'executive officer' who receives the most votes) does not have a majority in the nine-member Assembly. Further, s 11(8) (NI Act) allows all Assembly members to attend Executive Council meetings. These factors, a 'culture of direct democracy' under which other Assembly members are involved in policy and expenditure decisions, the fact that the Executive Council does not observe Cabinet solidarity and the responsiveness of the public service to non-executive members make 'the operations of the Legislative Assembly resemble those of a corporate board rather than a Westminster-style parliament': Australia, Parliament (2003), para 4.23. Despite considerable islander attachment to this method of government, a recent parliamentary inquiry recommended changes to the NI Act to entrench the Westminster model (above, paras 4.48–4.52).

In the Australian Capital Territory, Westminster-style government is achieved by creation of an 'Executive' composed of the chief minister and ministers whom he or she appoints (and dismisses) from amongst the members of the Assembly to hold office during the life of his or her government: ss 36, 39, 41, 42 (ACT S-G Act). The Chief Minister is elected by the Assembly and may be removed by its no-confidence motion, at which point a general election is normally called: ss 40, 48. Ministers are required to administer their allocated portfolios: s 43. See generally Lindell (1992) pp 23–6.

Executive power and its limits

[12.6.42] The extent of executive power in each territory is spelt out in each Act.

The Northern Territory Executive Council advises the Administrator, and Ministers have executive authority, in relation to 'transferred' matters — those 'state government type' powers listed in the Northern Territory (Self-Government) Regulations: ss 33, 35 (NT S-G Act). The Administrator, the Executive Council and Ministers may exercise the prerogatives of the Crown in so far as they relate to the duties, powers, functions and authorities conferred by the Act upon them: s 31 (NT S-G Act). On matters other than those 'transferred' and the appointment of NT Ministers, the Administrator acts on Commonwealth advice: s 32(3) (NT S-G Act).

[12.6.43]   Norfolk Island's four 'executive officers' have authority over a long list of matters specified in Schedules 2 and 3 of the Act. Schedule 2 began in 1979 with a short list of mainly municipal powers and power to raise revenues, but has expanded to include 93 separate matters, including tourism, an island public service, civil defence, communications, census, public health, 'public utilities', housing, industry, mining, legal aid, corporate affairs, child welfare, law and order, prisons and private law. (Schedule 2 does not list a power to allocate land, which is conferred on the Commonwealth Minister by s 62.) Schedule 3 includes mainly 'external' matters: it began with fishing, customs (not duties), immigration and education, and has expanded to include quarantine, industrial relations and social security. These schedules could continue to expand, as they have expanded, through an exercise of Commonwealth regulation-making power. However, recent critiques of Norfolk Island governance (see **[12.6.18]–[12.6.33]**) suggest that territory's powers may instead be reduced.

[12.6.44]   On matters which, in his or her opinion, are listed in Schedule 2 or 3 of the NI Act, the Administrator acts on the advice of the Executive Council — unless the Commonwealth Territories Minister overrides these instructions with respect to Sch 3 matters. In such a case or in relation to unlisted matters, the Administrator is obliged to act in accordance with *the minister's* instructions: s 7 (NI Act).

[12.6.45]   The executive power of the Australian Capital Territory is spelt out in s 37 (ACT S-G Act). The executive has the responsibility of: (a) governing the territory with respect to matters listed in Schedule 4 of the Act (a long list of 'state government-type' powers); (b) executing and maintaining enactments and subordinate laws; (c) exercising such other powers as are vested in the executive by a law in force in the territory or arrangement between the territory and the Commonwealth, a state or another territory, and (d) exercising prerogatives of the Crown so far as they relate to the responsibilities mentioned in (a), (b) or (c) above. The list of matters in Schedule 4 includes 'Territory land as defined in the ACT (Planning and Land Management) Act 1988 (Cth)'. This Act requires the ACT Executive to manage 'Territory land' on a 99-year leasehold system consistently with the National Capital Plan for 'National Land': see ACT (Planning and Land Management) Act 1988 (Cth), ss 28 and 29.

These arrangements are consistent with the fact that the underlying fee simple or radical title in ACT land still lies with the Commonwealth: *Attorney-General (ACT) v Commonwealth* (1990) 95 ALR 739. This is not the position in the Northern Territory, where Commonwealth land was transferred to the new 'body politic' by s 69 of the NT S-G Act, although s 70 allowed reacquisition of Commonwealth enclaves. The Commonwealth also retains the power to grant land on Norfolk Island: NI Act, s 62.

Finance

[12.6.46]   All three Acts provide for territory expenditure of revenues, loans and other moneys received pursuant to territory enactment: ss 57 and 58 (NT S-G Act); ss 57 and 58 (ACT S-G Act); ss 47 and 48 (NI Act).

The NI Act establishes a Public Account of Norfolk Island in which appropriations for particular governmental purposes are segregated: s 47. As noted above

([12.6.34]), the Governor-General (as well as the Assembly) may appropriate this account by Ordinance.

[12.6.47] The Commonwealth Treasurer's permission is required for all forms of Norfolk Island revenue-raising: ss 50, 50C. With this permission, Norfolk Island can issue its own bonds or otherwise trade in securities: s 50(2).

[12.6.48] All three Acts permit territory borrowing from the Commonwealth out of funds appropriated by parliament for this purpose: s 60 (ACT S-G Act); s 46 (NT S-G Act); s 49 (NI Act). The Australian Capital Territory and the Northern Territory are not restricted in their borrowing; the NI Act permits borrowing from other sources with the permission of the Commonwealth Treasurer or his or her delegate: ss 50, 50D. The Treasurer may, on behalf of the Commonwealth, guarantee, or give security for, loans to Norfolk Island: ss 50A, 50B.

[12.6.49] Section 59 of the ACT S-G Act states that: 'The Commonwealth shall conduct its financial relations with the Territory so as to ensure that the Territory is treated on the same basis as the States and the Northern Territory, while having regard to the special circumstances arising from the existence of the national capital and the seat of government of the Commonwealth in the Territory.'

[12.6.50] The Commonwealth Auditor-General may be appointed Auditor of the Accounts of the NT and Norfolk Island: s 48 (ACT S-G Act); s 51B (NI Act). The ACT S-G Act is silent on the subject of government audit.

Norfolk Island is required to appoint an auditor registered under either the Corporations Act 2001 (Cth) or territory corporations law to conduct an annual audit and report to the Administrator and the Speaker of the Assembly for tabling in the Assembly and transmission to the Minister: ss 51C, 51D. The Norfolk Island auditor is not 'subject to the directions of the Minister, the Administrator, the Legislative Assembly or any member of the Legislative Assembly': s 51F. Where the Commonwealth Auditor-General is appointed, the auditing standards under the Auditor-General Act 1997 (Cth) apply; otherwise, the Assembly may set the standards: s 51G. The recent parliamentary inquiry recommended that Norfolk Island be required to accept audits by the Commonwealth Auditor-General: Australia, Parliament (2003), paras 3.102–3.119.

Territory courts

[12.6.51] Each self-governing territory has its own Supreme Court.

The Supreme Court of the Northern Territory is entirely a creature of NT law: the Supreme Court Act 1979 (NT) was enacted after the Northern Territory Supreme Court Act 1961 (Cth) was repealed by the Northern Territory Supreme Court (Repeal) Act 1979 (Cth).

[12.6.52] The ACT S-G Act defines the jurisdiction and powers of the ACT Supreme Court (s 48A, inserted in 1992), but does not establish it — it is constituted by the Supreme Court Act 1933 (ACT), a former Commonwealth Ordinance which became an enactment of the Legislative Assembly in 1992: see s 34; Schedule 2. The Supreme Court has 'all original and appellate jurisdiction that is necessary for the administration of justice in the Territory' and 'such further jurisdiction as is conferred on it by any [Commonwealth] Act, [territory] enactment or Ordinance' or law made thereunder. The Supreme Court is not bound to exercise its powers where it has 'concurrent jurisdiction with another court or tribunal; the ACT Legislative Assembly may confer on the Federal Court original or appellate jurisdiction in some matters: ss 48A and 48AA (ACT).

Australian Capital Territory judges may be removed from office if a judicial commission constituted by former High Court judges, or (former) judges of the Federal or another Supreme Court, finds that their behaviour 'could amount to misbehaviour or physical or mental incapacity … warranting [their] removal from office' and the Assembly agrees, passing a motion for their removal: s 48D. These conditions differ from what s 72 Constitution requires for 'federal courts'. The Supreme Court Act 1933 (ACT) also allows the appointment of acting judges. See *Re the Governor, Goulburn Correctional Centre; Ex parte Eastman* (1999) 200 CLR 322.

[12.6.53]   The Supreme Court of Norfolk Island established by the Norfolk Island Act 1957 (Cth) was continued in existence by s 52 (NI Act). It is entirely composed of Federal Court judges: s 53. Under NI Act s 59, the court's jurisdiction is defined by local enactment. The Supreme Court Act 1960 (NI Act) confers on the court 'the same jurisdiction in and in relation to the Territory as the Supreme Court of the Australian Capital Territory has in relation to the Australian Capital Territory', that is, 'all original and appellate jurisdiction that is necessary to administer justice in the Territory'.

Territories and 'advancement' towards statehood

[12.6.54]   Northern Territory governments have been lobbying for statehood since the mid-1980s but have not yet achieved it, despite a Commonwealth–NT agreement to consider its implementation by 2001. A 1998 NT referendum on whether the NT should take the steps necessary to become a state was unsuccessful — but only just: 52 per cent of territorians voted 'No' and 48 per cent voted 'Yes', with the gap being largely explained by the higher 'No' vote in remote Aboriginal communities. For further analysis, see Heatley and McNab (1998) and (1999).

[12.6.55]   Even if one of Australia's external territories pressed for statehood (there is no sign that any will), their remoteness from the mainland, small populations and limited economies make it unlikely that the Commonwealth would accede to such a request (even Norfolk Island, whose economy depends on the 35,000 mainly Australian tourists who visit each year, is vulnerable to that industry's fluctuations). There are no Australian territories with the large populations characteristic of some US territories. In *Eastman's* case, Kirby J commented that: 'It is hardly imaginable that the tiny island territories of the Commonwealth could contemplate statehood or, for that matter, that the Jervis Bay territory (now disjoined from the ACT) could be regarded as a candidate for separate statehood under the Constitution with all that that involves': 200 CLR at 368.

The High Court has suggested in *Capital Duplicators* (below) that the Australian Capital Territory is constitutionally incapable of becoming a state.

[12.6.56C] **Capital Duplicators (No 1)**
(1992) 177 CLR 248

Mason CJ, Dawson J and McHugh J: ... [266] Plainly enough, Ch VI [Constitution], in particular ss 121 and 122, contemplates that a Commonwealth territory may advance to Statehood. In the course of its evolution towards Statehood, it is natural, indeed inevitable, that a territory will be progressively endowed with institutions appropriate to self-government. That has been the history of democratic development in this country and in many parts of what was formerly the British Empire and is now the Commonwealth of Nations. Section 122 was and is the source of legislative power for the advancement of the territories along this path towards the final step of Statehood, at which point s 121 becomes the relevant source of power.

Whether the [ACT], containing as it does the seat of government, could be admitted to the Commonwealth or established as a new State is open to question ...

Brennan, Deane and Toohey JJ: ... [271]... Section 121, which provides for the admission of new States to the Commonwealth, relates not only to territories which are parts of existing States (ss 123 and 124) but also to 'such colonies or territories as may be admitted into or established by the Commonwealth as States' [Covering cl 6]. These latter colonies and territories were not part of the Original States [*ibid*]. In the Convention Debates, the forerunner of s 122 was seen primarily, though not necessarily, as designed to provide for the provisional government of territories as they moved towards Statehood. When the Commonwealth was established there were no Commonwealth territories. At that time the territories which were foreseen as possible territories of the Commonwealth included not only the northern territory of South Australia but also the Fiji Islands and British New Guinea. The possibility of territories of magnitude and importance being admitted to the Commonwealth as new States after a period of political development must have been contem-[272]plated. There is thus no reason to construe s 122 as precluding the creation of a representative legislature for a territory as a step in its political development with a view to its ultimate admission as a new State. We would respectfully agree with what Mason J said in *Berwick Ltd v Gray* [see quote in the minority judgment above]...

But the scope of s 122 may be qualified by other provisions in the Constitution ...

... [273] Section 52(i) confers on the Parliament exclusive power to make laws for the peace, order and good government of the Commonwealth with respect to the seat of government and there are some considerations of history and principle which might affect the scope of s 122 in its application to a territory containing the seat of government. Dixon J described the seat of government as 'an integral part of the Federal System', considering s 122 to be dealing 'at least primarily, with Territories which do not form part of the Federal System' [*Federal Capital Commission v Laristan Building & Investment Co Pty Ltd* (1929) 42 CLR 582 at 585]. It would be surprising if laws made by an independent legislature for the seat of government of the Commonwealth, or executive action taken pursuant to those laws, could affect the performance of any function of the government of the Commonwealth, any facility used in the performance of such a function or any otherwise lawful provision — legislative or executive — which the organs of that government wished to make for the performance of any of its functions. In our view, the Australian Capital Territory, unlike the Northern Territory, cannot become a new State. Section 52(i) precludes that possibility ...

<div align="center">~~~</div>

7   References

Australian Associated Press (AAP), 'Terror Group Targets North Australia', *The Age*, 28 October 2002, <http://www.theage.com.au/articles/2002/10/28/1035683350813.html>.

ACT Legislative Assembly, 'Fact sheet 2: Self-government: setting the scene: Australia becomes a federation in its own right', <http://www.legassembly.act.gov.au/education/factsheets/fact02/fsb02.htm> accessed 10 April 2004.

Administration of Norfolk Island, 'Census of Population and Housing, 7 August 2001' <http://www.norfolk.gov.nf/census/Main.html>, accessed March 31, 2004.

Altman, *Aborigines and Mining Royalties in the Northern Territory*, Australian Institute of Aboriginal Studies, Canberra, 1983.

Anghie, '"The heart of my home": colonialism, environmental damage, and the Nauru case' (1993) 34 *Harvard International Law Journal* 445.

Australia, Department of Territories, <http://www.dotars.gov.au>.

Australia, Human Rights and Equal Opportunity Commission, *Territorial Limits: Norfolk Island's Immigration Act and human rights*, J S McMillan Printing Group, Sydney, 1999.

Australia, Parliament, *Joint Standing Committee on National Capital and External Territories, Inquiry into Norfolk Island electoral matters* 2002 <www.aph.gov.au/house/committee/ncet/NICitizenshipRe-Referral/Norfolkindex.htm>.

Australia, Parliament, *Joint Standing Committee on National Capital and External Territories, Quis custodiet ipsos custodes?: Inquiry into Governance on Norfolk Island* 2003 <www.aph.gov.au/house/committee/ncet/NorfolkGov/report.htm>.

Australian Antarctic Division 'Poles: areas, lengths, heights, distances', <http://www.antdiv.gov.au/default.asp?casid=1845> accessed 20 March 2004.

Australian Bureau of Statistics, <www.abs.gov.au> 'Statistics' accessed on 7 January 2004.

Australian Bureau of Statistics, '3101.0 Australian Demographic Statistics', <www.abs.gov.au> accessed 31 March 2004.

Australian Law Reform Commission, *Report no 80: Legal risk in international transactions*, 1995 <http://www.austlii.edu.au/au/other/alrc/publications/reports/80/ALRC80.html>.

Baty, 'Protectorates and mandates' (1921–22) *BYIL* 109.

Bennett, Australian Capital Territory Election 2001, *Parliamentary Research Note 15/2001–02*, Australia, Department of the Parliamentary Library, 2002, <http://www.aph.gov.au/library/pubs/rn/2001–02/02rn15.htm>.

Blackshield and Dominello, 'Papua and New Guinea' in Blackshield et al, *Oxford Companion to the High Court of Australia*, Oxford University Press, 2001.

Clarke, '*Cubillo v Commonwealth*' (2001) 25 *MULR* 218.

Commonwealth Grants Commission, *Report on Norfolk Island*, 1997, available on <http://www.cgc.gov.au/>.

Cowen and Zines, *Federal jurisdiction in Australia*, 2nd ed, Oxford University Press, Melbourne, 1978; 3rd ed, 2002.

Crawford and Rothwell, 'Legal issues confronting Australia's Antarctic' (1992) Australian YBIL 53.

'Discover our history', <http://www.canberrahistory.org.au/discover.asp> accessed 20 April 2004.

Denoon, *Getting under the skin: the Bougainville Copper Agreement and the creation of the Panguna mine*, MUP, 2000.

Elections ACT, '1978 Referendum', 2002 <http://www.elections.act.gov.au/ref78.html> accessed 10 April 2004.

Geoscience Australia, 'Dimensions' and 'Maritime Zones', located on <http://www.ga.gov.au>, accessed 20 March 2004.

Heatley and McNab, 'The Northern Territory Statehood Convention 1998' (1998) 9 *Public Law Review* 155 and 'The Northern Territory Statehood Referendum 1998' (1989) 10 *Public Law Review* 3.

Horan, 'Section 122 of the Constitution: A "Disparate and Non-Federal" Power?' (1997) 25 *FLR* 97.

Hughes, *The Fatal Shore*, Vintage Books, New York, 1986.

Keyzer, 'The "Federal Compact", the Territories and Chapter III of the Constitution' (2001) 75 *Australian Law Journal* 124.

Levinson, 'Why the canon should be expanded to included the Insular Cases and the saga of American expansionism' (2000) 17 *Constitutional Commentary* 241.

Lindell, 'The arrangements for self-government for the Australian Capital Territory: a partial road to republicanism in the Seat of Government?' (1992) 3 *Public Law Review* 5.

Lockwood, *The front door: Darwin 1869–69*, Rigby, 1970.

Loveday and McNab, *Australia's Seventh State*, Law Society of the NT and North Australia Research Unit (ANU), 1988.

Lundie and Mann, *Australian Political Records*, Commonwealth of Australia Department of the Parliamentary Library, 1998, <www.aph.gov.au/library/pubs/rn/1997–98/98rn42.htm>

Maclellan, 'Australian neocolonialism in the Pacific: human rights implications', <www.law.monash.edu.au/castancentre/events/2003/maclellan-paper.pdf>, accessed 31 March 2004.

Mattes, 'Sources of law in Papua and New Guinea' (1963) 37 *Australian Law Journal* 148.

Mossop, 'The Judicial Power of the Australian Capital Territory' (1999) 27 *FLR*

Multicultural Council of the Northern Territory, *A swinging front door: MCNT's 25th anniversary history*, 2002 <http://www.mcnt.org.au/history.html> accessed 19 April 2004.

National Archives of Australia, Fact Sheet 148: Records of Papua New Guinea, 1883–1942, <www.naa.gov.au> accessed 18 December 2001.

Nicholson, 'The Concept of "One Australia" in Constitutional Law and the Place of Territories' (1997) 25 *FLR* 281.

Mary-Louise O'Callaghan, 'The origins of the conflict', undated, Conciliation Resources Accord Program, <http://www.c-r.org/accord/boug/accord12/theorigin.shtml> accessed 25 April 2004.

Quick and Garran, *The Annotated Constitution of the Australian Commonwealth*, Angus and Robertson, Sydney, 1901.

Raskin, 'Is This America? The District of Columbia and the Right to Vote' (1999) 34 *Harvard Civil Rights–Civil Liberties Law Review* 39.

Sanders and Arthur, *Autonomy Rights in the Torres Strait: From Whom, For Whom, For or Over What?*, ANU Centre for Aboriginal Economic Policy Research Discussion Paper 315, 2001.

United Nations, 'Declaration on the granting of independence', <www.un.org/Depts/dpi/decolonization/declaration.htm>.

United States, Central Intelligence Agency, *CIA World Factbook* <http://cia.gov/cia/publications/factbook/index.html> (various country entries).

Weeramantry, *Nauru: Environmental Damage under International Trusteeship*, OUP, 1992.

Zelling, 'The territories of the Commonwealth' in Else-Mitchell (ed), *Essays on the Australian Constitution*, 2nd ed, Law Book Co, 1971.

Zines, 'Nationhood and the powers of the Commonwealth' in Zines (ed), *Commentaries on the Australian Constitution*, Butterworths, 1977.

Index

References are to paragraphs

References are to paragraphs.

References are to paragraphs

Sovereignty (cont'd)
native title, 2.2.41–2.2.43
offshore, and
indigenous traditional land estates, 2.2.44
treaties with indigenous peoples, 2.2.45–2.2.48
sovereign governments, establishing, 2.2.1

Stare decisis
judicial attitudes to, 1.3.12–1.3.14

State Constitution Acts
amending, procedures for, 1.4.12–1.4.14
basic formal instruments of government, 1.4.16
form of words in, 1.4.17
Fundamental values or freedoms, 1.4.20
location of executive power, 1.4.18
repeal, 1.6.9
Supreme Courts, 1.4.19

State Courts see **Supreme Courts**

States see also **Governors of Australian states; Parliaments of states and territories; State Constitution Acts**
Australian colonies, and
establishment of the colonies, 2.3.1–2.3.3
Imperial Aboriginal protection, measures, 2.3.12–2.3.19
land policy, 2.3.4, 2.3.5C, 2.3.6–2.3.10
self government, 2.3.11
state franchises
exclusion of indigenous people, 2.3.20–2.3.21
citizens, status of, 1.2.7
collection of income tax, denial, 1.4.10
constitutions, 1.2.13
financial independence, 1.4.10
Imperial and local legislation
colonial background, 6.2.1–6.2.6
legal autonomy for states
Australia Act 1986 (Cth), 6.2.7E–6.2.11
inconsistency of laws with Commonwealth laws, 1.2.13, 1.4.6, 8.1.1, see also **Inconsistency between state and federal laws**
intergovernmental immunities, 8.2.1, see also **Intergovernmental immunities**
law-making powers, 1.2.13
parliaments, see **Parliaments of states and territories**
powers, restrictions on, 1.2.13
separation of powers
judicial power, 6.4.43–6.4.51
legislative and executive powers, 6.4.52–6.4.56

state court, see **Supreme Courts**
state parliaments legislation, territorial limits
Australia Act 1986, 6.3.17E–6.3.21
offshore settlement 1980, 6.3.27–6.3.34
Coastal Waters (State Powers) Act 1980 (Cth), 6.3.29–6.3.34
offshore waters, 6.3.13C–6.3.16
road maintenance contribution issues, 6.3.8C–6.3.12
states' extra–territorial powers, 6.3.22C–6.3.26
taxation legislation, issues, 6.3.5–6.3.7
Western Australia
Racial Discrimination Act 1975 (Cth) validation provisions, 2.4.28, 2.4.29C

Statute of Westminster
Commonwealth Parliament
legislative powers, territorial limits, 6.3.38
constitutional disabilities removed by, 1.4.23
enactment of, 1.4.22
historical significance, 1.4.21
legal autonomy for Commonwealth, 6.2.15E–6.2.23

Supreme Courts
appellate jurisdiction over decisions of High Court, by, 1.4.8
establishment, 1.4.19
federal judicial power, 1.4.19
jurisdiction, 1.4.19

Tasmania see **Parliaments of states and territories; States**

Taxation see also **Income tax; Taxing power**
Commonwealth
access to revenue, 1.4.10

Taxing power
compulsory exaction or charge, 9.2.4
Constitution, 9.2.1E
discrimination and preference
Constitution, 9.3.1E, 9.3.2
forms of words, 9.3.5
preference, 9.3.6
restrictions, 9.3.4
meaning, 9.3.7–9.3.11
customs and excise duties, 9.3.9
identification, 9.3.10
value assigned to livestock, 9.3.8
states, between, 9.3.12, 9.3.13C–9.3.18
fee for services rendered, 9.2.5–9.2.9
abalone fishing licence, 9.2.8